W9-CDL-551

GOODE'S WORLD ATLAS

Howard Veregin, Ph.D., Editor

Editorial Advisory Board

Byron Augustin, D.A., Texas State University-San Marcos

Joshua Comenetz, Ph.D., University of Florida

Francis Galgano, Ph.D., United States Military Academy

Sallie A. Marston, Ph.D., University of Arizona

Virginia Thompson, Ph.D., Towson University

21ST Edition

CONTENTS

Goode's World Atlas

Copyright ©2005 by Rand McNally & Company; 3rd Printing, Revised

Copyright ©1922, 1923, 1932, 1933, 1937, 1939, 1943, 1946, 1949, 1954, 1957, 1960, 1964, 1970, 1974, 1978, 1982, 1986, 1990, 1995, 2000 by Rand McNally & Company. All rights reserved.

Formerly *Goode's School Atlas*

Made in U.S.A.

Library of Congress Catalog Card Number 99-38535

Cover Photo: Machu Picchu, Peru

The 21st Edition of *Goode's World Atlas*

Goode's World Atlas was first published by Rand McNally in 1923 as *Goode's School Atlas*, under the editorship of J. Paul Goode, a distinguished Professor of Geography at the University of Chicago. The atlas was designed for use in schools and universities, with the choice of topics and materials reflecting Goode's thirty years of experience as a geographic educator.

Many of the features of that first atlas continue to be relevant today, including its basic organization and layout, an emphasis on map accuracy and legibility, and the admixture of maps of different types and scales to facilitate interpretation of geographic phenomena. One of the more significant innovations of the 1923 edition was the introduction of an "interrupted" map of the world, which featured large discontinuities in oceanic areas in order to reduce map distortion of continental landmasses. Goode developed this map to allow geographic phenomena to be portrayed more accurately. This map, and its descendants, have given *Goode's World Atlas* a distinctive look for more than eighty years.

The 21st Edition boasts a number of innovative features of its own:

- The world, continental, and regional population density maps have been re-created using LandScan, a digital population database developed using satellite and computer-mapping technology.

- A number of new world thematic maps have been added, including HIV Infection, Military Power, Women's Rights, and Food Aid.

- A global telecommunications map has been added, showing the submarine fiber-optic network, and worldwide internet and telephone usage.

- The world cartogram series has been redrafted to make the cartograms easier to interpret.

- The United States demographic map series has been expanded from sixteen to twenty-four maps to provide additional coverage of key census variables.

- New graphs have been added to many of the maps, showing important statistical information, trends over time, and relationships between variables.

Other maps and graphs have been updated using the most current available data in accordance with the high standards and quality that have always been a defining feature of this atlas. This edition also retains many of the "classic" maps with which longtime users of the atlas will be familiar, including Natural Vegetation (A. W. Küchler), Landforms (Richard E. Murphy), Physiography (Erwin Raisz), Climatic Regions (Glenn T. Trewartha), Agricultural Regions (Derwent Whittlesey), and Languages (Bogdan Zaborski).

Putting together a complex atlas requires the dedication of a large and diverse team. The contributions of the following individuals helped make this 21st Edition a success:

Robert Argersinger, Gregory Babiak, Julie Bastian, Karen Cuiskelly, John Davies, Dave Duncan, Marzee Eckhoff, Justin Griffin, Felix Lopez, Nina Lusterman, Chuck MacDonald, Rob Merrill, Angela Mrotek, Darren Raffel, Pat Riley, Amy Ruggles, David Simmons, Andrew Skinner, Raymond Tobiaski, Tom Vitacco, Yanyan Zhang.

The 21st Edition benefited greatly from the creative efforts of Susan Hudson, head of Rand McNally's geographical research unit.

Important contributions were also made by the members of the Editorial Advisory Board:

Byron Augustin, D.A., Texas State University-San Marcos; Joshua Comenetz, Ph.D., University of Florida; Francis Galgano, Ph.D., United States Military Academy; Sallie A. Marston, Ph.D., University of Arizona; and Virginia Thompson, Ph.D., Towson University.

With the 21st Edition, *Goode's World Atlas* is well into its ninth consecutive decade of publication. While the atlas has changed with the times, it continues to be the same accurate and reliable educational resource that J. Paul Goode originally intended. We at Rand McNally remain committed to providing the most trusted tools to help you discover, map, and navigate your world.

Howard Veregin

Howard Veregin, Ph.D., Editor
Skokie, Illinois

Introduction

Basic Earth Properties

The subject matter of **geography** includes people, landforms, climate, and all the other physical and human phenomena that make up the earth's environments and give unique character to different places. Geographers construct maps to visualize the **spatial distributions** of these phenomena: that is, how the phenomena vary over geographic space. Maps help geographers understand and explain phenomena and their interactions.

To better understand how maps portray geographic distributions, it is helpful to have an understanding of the basic properties of the earth.

The earth is essentially **spherical** in shape. Two basic reference points — the **North and South Poles** — mark the locations of the earth's axis of rotation. Equidistant between the two poles and encircling the earth is the **equator**. The equator divides the earth into two halves, called the **northern and southern hemispheres**. (See the figures to the right.)

Latitude and longitude are used to identify the locations of features on the earth's surface. They are measured in degrees, minutes and seconds. There are 60 minutes in a degree and 60 seconds in a minute. Latitude is the angle north or south of the equator. The symbols °, ', and " represent degrees, minutes and seconds, respectively. The N means north of the equator. For latitudes south of the equator, S is used. For example, the Rand McNally head office in Skokie, Illinois, is located at 42°1'51" N. The minimum latitude of 0° occurs at the equator. The maximum latitudes of 90° N and 90° S occur at the North and South Poles.

A **line of latitude** is a line connecting all points on the earth having the same latitude. Lines of latitude are also called **parallels**, as they run parallel to each other. Two parallels of special importance are the **Tropic of Cancer** and the **Tropic of Capricorn**, at approximately 23°30' N and S respectively. This angle coincides with the inclination of the earth's axis relative to its orbital plane around the sun. These tropics are the lines of latitude where the noon sun is directly overhead on the solstices. (See figure on page 66.) Two other important parallels are the **Arctic Circle** and the **Antarctic Circle**, at approximately 66°30' N and S respectively. These lines mark the most northerly and southerly points at which the sun can be seen on the solstices.

While latitude measures locations in a north-south direction, longitude measures them east-west. Longitude is the angle east or west of the **Prime Meridian**. A **meridian** is a line of longitude, a straight line extending from the North Pole to the South Pole. The Prime Meridian is the meridian passing through the Royal Observatory in Greenwich, England. For this reason the Prime Meridian is sometimes referred to as the **Greenwich Meridian**. This location for the Prime Meridian was adopted at the International Meridian Conference in Washington, D.C., in 1884.

Like latitude, longitude is measured in degrees, minutes, and seconds. For example, the Rand McNally head office is located at 87°43'6" W. The qualifiers E and W indicate whether a location is east or west of the Greenwich Meridian. Longitude ranges from 0° at Greenwich to 180° E or W. The meridian at 180° E is the same as the meridian at 180° W. This meridian, together with the Greenwich Meridian, divides the earth into **eastern and western hemispheres**.

Any circle that divides the earth into equal hemispheres is called a **great circle**. The equator is an example. The shortest distance between any two points on the earth is along a great circle. Other circles, including all other lines of latitude, are called **small circles**. Small circles divide the earth into two unequal pieces.

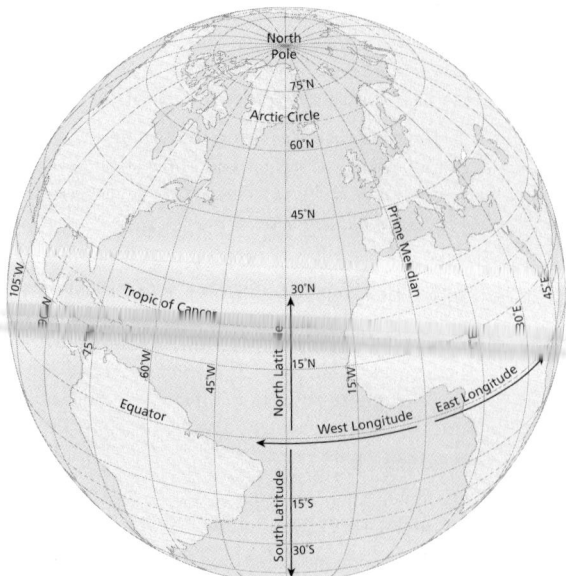

View of earth centered on 30° N, 30° W

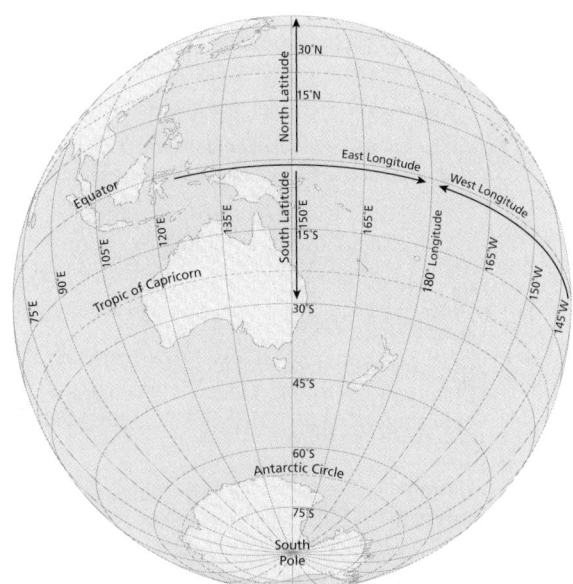

View of earth centered on 30° S, 150° E

The Geographic Grid

The grid of lines of latitude and longitude is known as the **geographic grid**. The following are some important characteristics of the grid.

All lines of longitude are equal in length and meet at the North and South Poles. These lines are called meridians.

All lines of latitude are parallel and equally spaced along meridians. These lines are called parallels.

The length of parallels increases with distance from the poles. For example, the length of the parallel at 60° latitude is one-half the length of the equator.

Meridians get closer together with increasing distance from the equator, and finally converge at the poles.

Parallels and meridians meet at right angles.

Map Scale

To use maps effectively it is important to have a basic understanding of map scale.

Map scale is defined as the ratio of distance on the map to distance on the earth's surface. For example, if a map shows two towns as separated by a distance of 1 inch, and these towns are actually 1 mile apart, then the scale of the map is 1 inch to 1 mile.

The statement "1 inch to 1 mile" is called a **verbal scale**. Verbal scales are simple and intuitive, but a drawback is that they are tied to the specific set of map and real-world units in the numerator and denominator of the ratio. This makes it difficult to compare the scales of different maps.

A more flexible way of expressing scale is as a **representative fraction**. In this case, both the numerator and denominator are converted to the same unit of measurement. For example, since there are 63,360 inches in a mile, the verbal scale "1 inch to 1 mile" can be expressed as the representative fraction 1:63,360. This means that 1 inch on the map represents 63,360 inches on the earth's surface. The advantage of the representative fraction is that it applies to any linear unit of measurement, including inches, feet, miles, meters, and kilometers.

Map scale can also be represented in graphical form. Many maps contain a **graphic scale** (or **bar scale**) showing real-world units such as miles or kilometers. The bar scale is usually subdivided to allow easy calculation of distance on the map.

Map scale has a significant effect on the amount of detail that can be portrayed on a map. This concept is illustrated here using a series of maps of the Washington, D.C., area. (See the figures to the right.) The scales of these maps range from 1:40,000,000 (top map) to 1:4,000,000 (center map) to 1:25,000 (bottom map). The top map has the **smallest scale** of the three maps, and the bottom map has the **largest scale**.

Note that as scale increases, the area of the earth's surface covered by the map decreases. The smallest-scale map covers thousands of square miles, while the largest-scale map covers only a few square miles within the city of Washington. This means that a given feature on the earth's surface will appear larger as map scale increases. On the smallest-scale map, Washington is represented by a small dot. As scale increases the dot becomes an orange shape representing the built-up area of Washington. At the largest scale Washington is so large that only a portion of it fits on the map.

Because small-scale maps cover such a large area, only the largest and most important features can be shown, such as large cities, major rivers and lakes, and international boundaries. In contrast, large-scale maps contain relatively small features, such as city streets, buildings, parks, and monuments.

Small-scale maps depict features in a more simplified manner than large-scale maps. As map scale decreases, the shapes of rivers and other features must be simplified to allow them to be depicted at a highly reduced size. This simplification process is known as **map generalization**.

Maps in *Goode's World Atlas* have a wide range of scales. The smallest scales are used for the world thematic map series, where scales range from approximately 1:200,000,000 to 1:75,000,000. Reference map scales range from a minimum of 1:100,000,000 for world maps to a maximum of 1:1,000,000 for city maps. Most reference maps are regional views with a scale of 1:4,000,000.

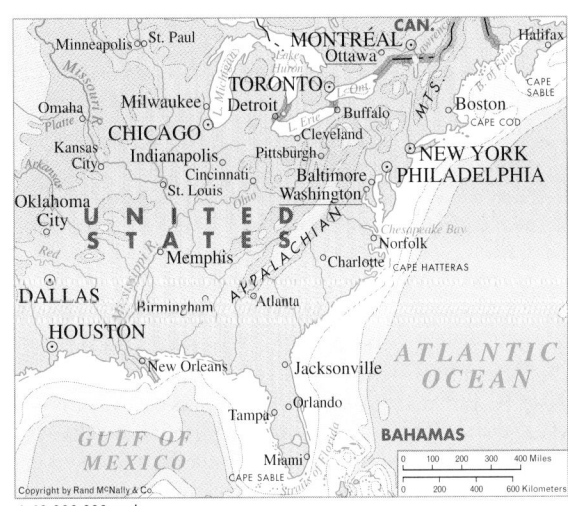

1:40,000,000 scale

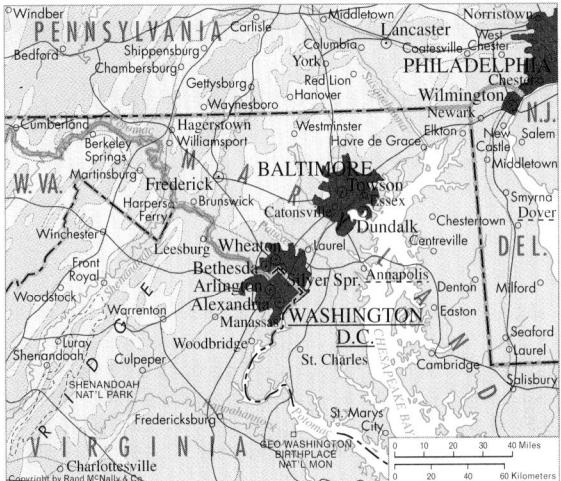

1:4,000,000 scale

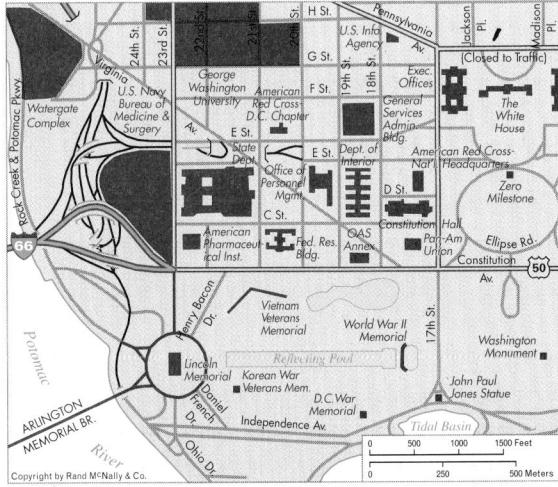

1:25,000 scale

Map Projections

Map projections influence the appearance of features on the map and the ability to interpret geographic phenomena.

A **map projection** is a geometric representation of the earth's surface on a flat or plane surface. Since the earth's surface is curved, a map projection is needed to produce any flat map, whether a page in this atlas or a computer-generated map of driving directions on www.randmcnally.com. Hundreds of projections have been developed since the dawn of mapmaking. A limitation of all projections is that they distort some geometric properties of the earth, such as shape, area, distance, or direction. However, certain properties are preserved on some projections.

If shape is preserved, the projection is called **conformal**. On conformal projections the shapes of features agree with the shapes these features have on the earth. A limitation of conformal projections is that they necessarily distort area, sometimes severely.

Equal-area projections preserve area. On equal area projections the areas of features correspond to their areas on the earth. To achieve this effect, equal-area projections distort shape.

Some projections preserve neither shape nor area, but instead balance shape and area distortion to create an aesthetically-pleasing result. These are often referred to as **compromise** projections.

Distance is preserved on **equidistant** projections, but this can only be achieved selectively, such as along specific meridians or parallels. No projection correctly preserves distance in all directions at all locations. As a result, the stated scale of a map may be accurate for only a limited set of locations. This problem is especially acute for small-scale maps covering large areas.

The projection selected for a particular map depends on the relative importance of different types of distortion, which often depends on the purpose of the map. For example, world maps showing phenomena that vary with area, such as population density or the distribution of agricultural crops, often use an equal-area projection to give an accurate depiction of the importance of each region.

Map projections are created using mathematical procedures. To illustrate the general principles of projections without using mathematics, we can view a projection as the geometric transfer of information from a globe to a flat projection surface, such as a sheet of paper. If we allow the paper to be rolled in different ways, we can derive three basic types of map projections: **cylindrical, conic,** and **azimuthal**. (See the figures to the right.)

For cylindrical projections, the sheet of paper is rolled into a tube and wrapped around the globe so that it is **tangent** (touching) along the equator. Information from the globe is transferred to the tube, and the tube is then unrolled to produce the final flat map.

Conic projections use a cone rather than a cylinder. The figure shows the cone tangent to the earth along a line of latitude with the apex of the cone over the pole. The line of tangency is called the **standard parallel** of the projection.

Azimuthal projections use a flat projection surface that is tangent to the globe at a single point, such as one of the poles.

The figures show the **normal orientation** of each type of surface relative to the globe. The **transverse orientation** is produced when the surface is rotated 90 degrees from normal. For azimuthal projections this orientation is usually called **equatorial** rather than transverse. An **oblique orientation** is created if the projection surface is oriented at an angle between normal and transverse. In general, map distortion increases with distance away from the point or line of tangency. This is why the normal orientations of the cylindrical, conic, and azimuthal projections are often used for mapping equatorial, mid-latitude, and polar regions, respectively.

The projection surface model is a visual tool useful for illustrating how information from the globe can be projected to the map. However, each of the three projection surfaces actually represents scores of individual projections. There are, for example, many projections with the term "cylindrical" in the name, each of which has the same basic rectangular shape, but different spacings of parallels and meridians. The projection surface model does not account for the numerous mathematical details that differentiate one cylindrical, conic, or azimuthal projection from another.

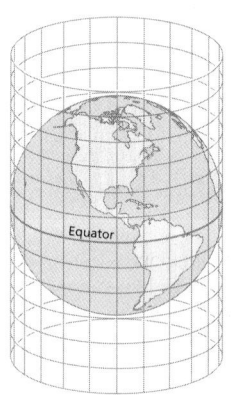
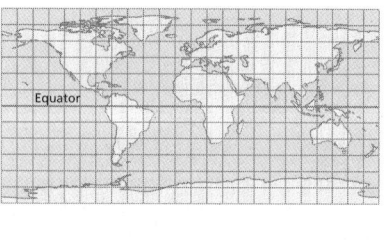

Cylindrical Projection

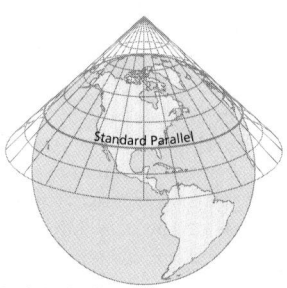
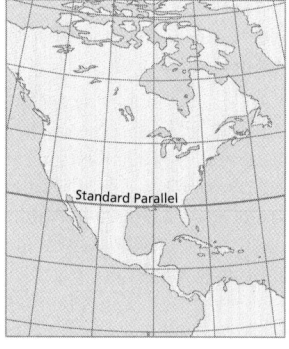

Conic Projection

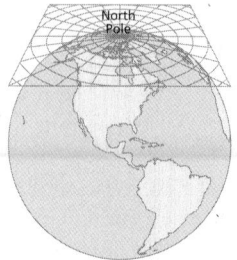

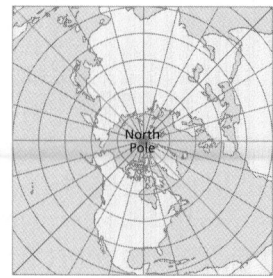

Azimuthal Projection

Map Projections Used in *Goode's World Atlas*

Of the hundreds of projections that have been developed, only a fraction are in everyday use. The main projections used in *Goode's World Atlas* are described below.

Simple Conic

Type: Conic   Conformal: No   Equal-area: No

Notes: Shape and area distortion on the Simple Conic projection are relatively low, even though the projection is neither conformal nor equal-area. The origins of the Simple Conic can be traced back nearly two thousand years, with the modern form of the projection dating to the 18th century.

Uses in *Goode's World Atlas*: Larger-scale reference maps of North America, Europe, Asia, and other regions.

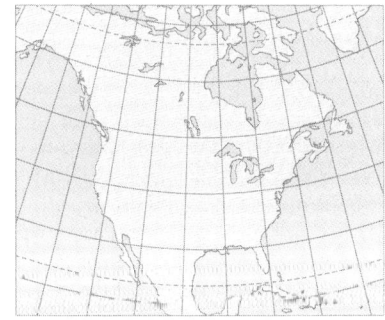
Simple Conic Projection

Lambert Conformal Conic

Type: Conic   Conformal: Yes   Equal-area: No

Notes: On the Lambert Conformal Conic projection, spacing between parallels increases with distance away from the standard parallel, which allows the property of shape to be preserved. The projection is named after Johann Lambert, an 18th century mathematician who developed some of the most important projections in use today. It became widely used in the United States in the 20th century following its adoption for many statewide mapping programs.

Uses in *Goode's World Atlas*: Thematic maps of the United States and Canada, and reference maps of parts of Asia.

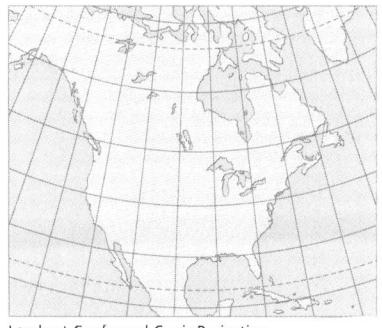
Lambert Conformal Conic Projection

Albers Equal-Area Conic

Type: Conic   Conformal: No   Equal-area: Yes

Notes: On the Albers Equal-Area Conic projection, spacing between parallels decreases with distance away from the standard parallel, which allows the property of area to be preserved. The projection is named after Heinrich Albers, who developed it in 1805. It became widely used in the 20th century, when the United States Coast and Geodetic Survey made it a standard for equal area maps of the United States.

Uses in *Goode's World Atlas*: Thematic maps of North America and Asia.

Albers Equal-Area Conic Projection

Polyconic

Type: Conic   Conformal: No   Equal-area: No

Notes: The term polyconic — literally "many-cones" — refers to the fact that this projection is an assemblage of different cones, each tangent at a different line of latitude. In contrast to many other conic projections, parallels are not concentric, and meridians are curved rather than straight. The Polyconic was first proposed by Ferdinand Hassler, who became Head of the United States Survey of the Coast (later renamed the Coast and Geodetic Survey) in 1807. The United States Geological Survey used this projection exclusively for large-scale topographic maps until the mid-20th century.

Uses in *Goode's World Atlas*: Reference maps of North America and Asia.

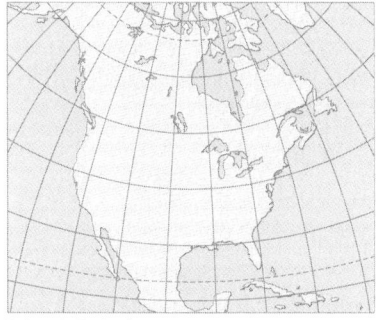
Polyconic Projection

Lambert Azimuthal Equal-Area

Type: Azimuthal   Conformal: No   Equal-area: Yes

Notes: This projection (another named after Johann Lambert) is useful for mapping large regions, as area is correctly preserved while shape distortion is relatively low. All orientations — polar, equatorial, and oblique — are common.

Uses in *Goode's World Atlas*: Thematic and reference maps of North and South America, Asia, Africa, Australia, and polar regions.

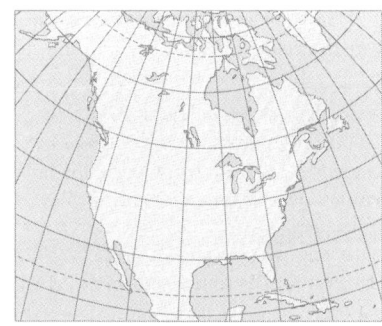
Lambert Azimuthal Equal-Area Projection

Miller Cylindrical

Type: Cylindrical   **Conformal:** No   **Equal-area:** No

Notes: This projection is useful for showing the entire earth in a simple rectangular form. However, polar areas exhibit significant exaggeration of area, a problem common to many cylindrical projections. The projection is named after Osborn Miller, Director of the American Geographical Society, who developed it in 1942 as a compromise projection that is neither conformal nor equal-area.

Uses in *Goode's World Atlas*: World climate and time zone maps.

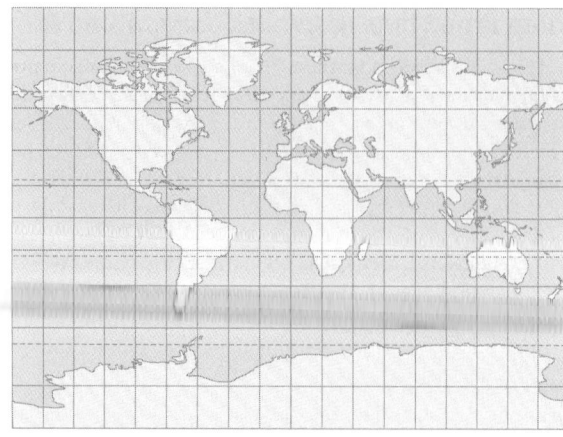
Miller Cylindrical Projection

Sinusoidal

Type: Pseudocylindrical   **Conformal:** No   **Equal-area:** Yes

Notes: The straight, evenly spaced parallels on this projection resemble the parallels on cylindrical projections. Unlike cylindrical projections, however, meridians are curved and converge at the poles. This causes significant shape distortion in polar regions. The Sinusoidal is the oldest-known pseudocylindrical projection, dating to the 16th century.

Uses in *Goode's World Atlas*: Reference maps of equatorial regions.

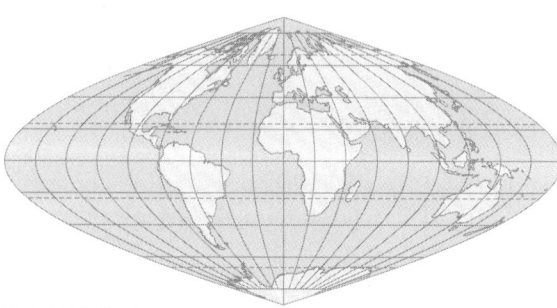
Sinusoidal Projection

Mollweide

Type: Pseudocylindrical   **Conformal:** No   **Equal-area:** Yes

Notes: The Mollweide (or Homolographic) projection resembles the Sinusoidal but has less shape distortion in polar areas due to its elliptical (or oval) form. One of several pseudocylindrical projections developed in the 19th century, it is named after Karl Mollweide, an astronomer and mathematician.

Uses in *Goode's World Atlas*: Oceanic reference maps.

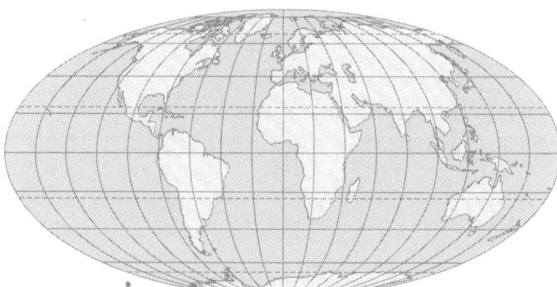
Mollweide Projection

Goode's Interrupted Homolosine

Type: Pseudocylindrical   **Conformal:** No   **Equal-area:** Yes

Notes: This projection is a fusion of the Sinusoidal between 40°44'N and S, and the Mollweide between these parallels and the poles. The unique appearance of the projection is due to the introduction of discontinuities in oceanic regions, the goal of which is to reduce distortion for continental landmasses. A condensed version of the projection also exists in which the Atlantic Ocean is compressed in an east-west direction. This modification helps maximize the scale of the map on the page. The Interrupted Homolosine projection is named after J. Paul Goode of the University of Chicago, who developed it in 1923. Goode was an advocate of interrupted projections and, as editor of *Goode's School Atlas*, promoted their use in education.

Uses in *Goode's World Atlas*: Small-scale world thematic and reference maps. Both condensed and non-condensed forms are used. An uninterrupted example is used for the Pacific Ocean map.

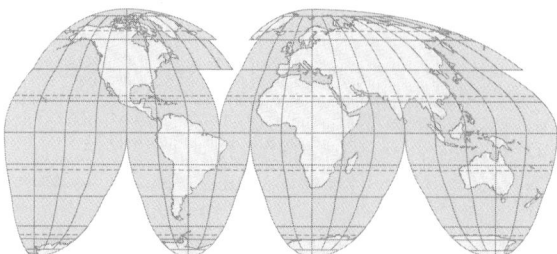
Goode's Interrupted Homolosine Projection

Robinson

Type: Pseudocylindrical   **Conformal:** No   **Equal-area:** No

Notes: This projection resembles the Mollweide except that polar regions are flattened and stretched out. While it is neither conformal nor equal-area, both shape and area distortion are relatively low. The projection was developed in 1963 by Arthur Robinson of the University of Wisconsin, at the request of Rand McNally.

Uses in *Goode's World Atlas*: World maps where the interrupted nature of Goode's Homolosine would be inappropriate, such as the World Oceanic Environments map.

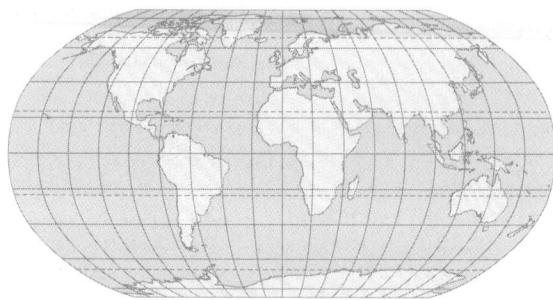
Robinson Projection

Thematic Maps in *Goode's World Atlas*

Thematic maps depict a single "theme" such as population density, agricultural productivity, or annual precipitation. The selected theme is presented on a base of locational information, such as coastlines, country boundaries, and major drainage features. The primary purpose of a thematic map is to convey an impression of the overall geographic distribution of the theme. It is usually not the intent of the map to provide exact numerical values. To obtain such information, the graphs and tables accompanying the map should be used.

Goode's World Atlas contains many different types of thematic maps. The characteristics of each are summarized below.

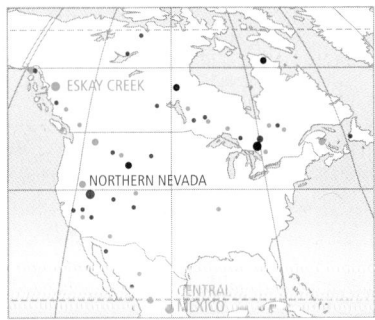

Point symbol map: Detail of Precious Metals (p. 55)

Point Symbol Maps

Point symbol maps are perhaps the simplest type of thematic map. They show features that occur at discrete locations. Examples include earthquakes, nuclear power plants, and minerals-producing areas. The Precious Metals map (p. 55) is an example of a point symbol map showing the locations of areas producing gold, silver, and platinum. A different color is used for each type of metal, while symbol size indicates relative importance.

Area Symbol Maps

Area symbol maps are useful for delineating regions of interest on the earth's surface. For example, the Tobacco and Fisheries map (p. 44) shows major tobacco-producing regions in one color and important fishing areas in another. On some area symbol maps, different shadings or colors are used to differentiate between major and minor areas.

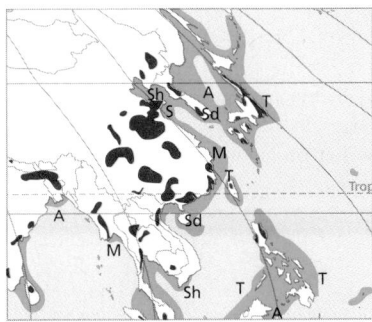

Area symbol map: Detail of Tobacco and Fisheries (p. 44)

Dot Maps

Dot maps show a distribution using a pattern of dots, where each dot represents a certain quantity or amount. For example, on the Sugar map (p. 43), each dot represents 20,000 metric tons of sugar produced. Different dot colors are used to distinguish cane sugar from beet sugar. Dot maps are an effective way of representing the variable density of geographic phenomena over the earth's surface. This type of map is used extensively in *Goode's World Atlas* to show the distribution of agricultural commodities.

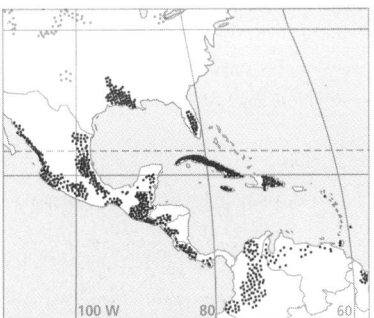

Dot map: Detail of Sugar (p. 43)

Area Class Maps

On area class maps, the earth's surface is divided into areas based on different classes or categories of a particular geographic phenomenon. For example, the Ecoregions map (pp. 28-29) differentiates natural landscape categories, such as Tundra, Savanna, and Prairie. Other examples of area class maps in *Goode's World Atlas* include Landforms (pp. 6-7), Climatic Regions (pp. 14-15), Natural Vegetation (pp. 24-25), Soils (pp. 26-27), Agricultural Areas (p. 38-39), Languages (p. 35) and Religions (p. 35).

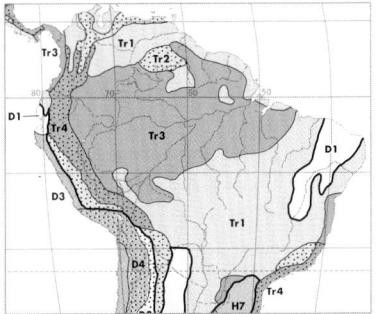

Area class map: Detail of Ecoregions (pp. 28-29)

Isoline Maps

Isoline maps are used to portray quantities that vary smoothly over the surface of the earth. These maps are frequently used for climatic variables such as precipitation and temperature, but a variety of other quantities — from crop yield to population density — can also be treated in this way.

An isoline is a line on the map that joins locations with the same value. For example, the Summer (May to October) Precipitation map (p. 19) contains isolines at 5, 10, 20, and 40 inches. On this map, any 10-inch isoline separates areas that have less than 10 inches of precipitation from areas that have more than 10 inches. Note that the areas between isolines are given different colors to assist in map interpretation.

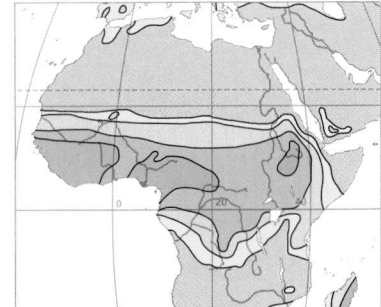

Isoline map: Detail of Precipitation (p. 19)

Proportional Symbol Maps

Proportional symbol maps portray numerical quantities, such as the total population of each state, the total value of agricultural goods produced in different regions, or the amount of hydroelectricity generated in different countries. The symbols on these maps — usually circles —- are drawn such that the size of each is proportional to the value at that location. For example the Exports map (p. 60) shows the value of goods exported by each country in the world, in millions of U.S. dollars.

Proportional symbols are frequently subdivided based on the percentage of individual components making up the total. The Exports map uses wedges of different color to show the percentages of various types of exports, such as manufactured articles and raw materials.

Flow Line Maps

Flow line maps show flows between locations. Usually, the thickness of the flow lines is proportional to flow volume. Flows may be physical commodities like petroleum, or less tangible quantities like information. The flow lines on the Mineral Fuels map (pp. 58-59) represent movement of petroleum measured in billions of U.S. dollars. Note that the locations of flow lines may not represent actual physical routes.

Choropleth Maps

Choropleth maps apply distinctive colors to predefined areas, such as counties or states, to represent different quantities in each area. The quantities shown are usually rates, percentages, or densities. For example, the Birth Rate map (p. 32) shows the annual number of births per one thousand people for each country.

Digital Images

Some maps are actually digital images, analogous to the pictures captured by digital cameras. These maps are created from a very fine grid of cells called **pixels**, each of which is assigned a color that corresponds to a specific value or range of values. The population density maps in this atlas (e.g., pp. 30-31) are examples of this type. The effect is much like an isoline map, but the isolines themselves are not shown and the resulting geographic patterns are more subtle and variable. This approach is increasingly being used to map environmental phenomena observable from remote sensing systems.

Cartograms

Cartograms deliberately distort map shapes to achieve specific effects. On **area cartograms**, the size of each area, such as a country, is made proportional to its population. Countries with large populations are therefore drawn larger than countries with smaller populations, regardless of the actual size of these countries on the earth.

The world cartogram series in this atlas depicts each country as a rectangle. This is a departure from cartograms in earlier editions of the atlas, which attempted to preserve some of the salient shape characteristics for each country. The advantage of the rectangle method is that it is easier to compare the area of countries when their shapes are consistent.

The cartogram series incorporates choropleth shading on top of the rectangular cartogram base. In this way map readers can make inferences about the relationship between population and another thematic variable, such as HIV-infection rates (p. 37).

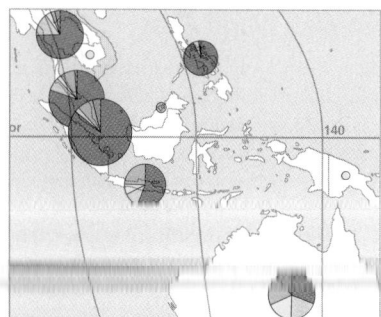
Proportional symbol map: Detail of Exports (p. 60)

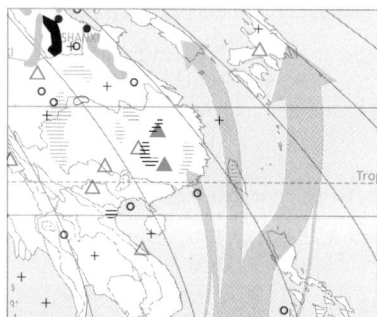
Flow line map: Detail of Mineral Fuels (pp. 58-59)

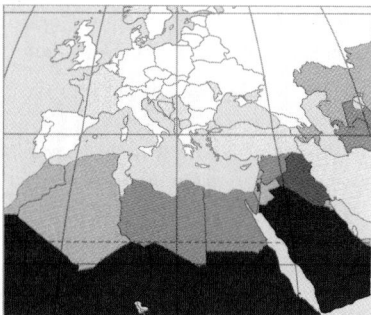
Choropleth map: Detail of Birth Rate (p. 32)

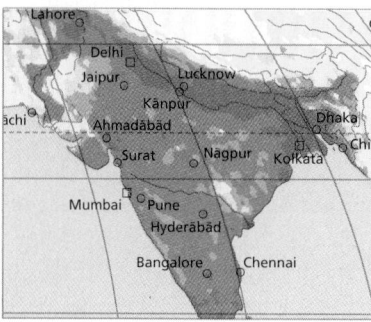
Digital image map: Detail of Population Density (pp. 30-31)

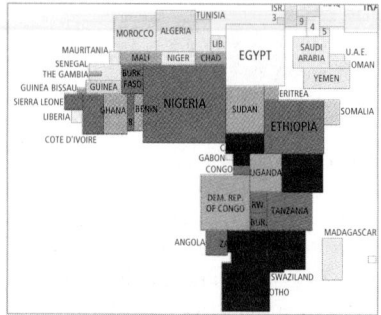
Cartogram: Detail of HIV Infection (p. 37)

Map Legend

Political Boundaries

Political maps	Physical maps	
—----	———	International (Demarcated, Undemarcated, and Administrative)
—·--	——·--	Disputed de facto
····	····	Indefinite or Undefined
—·-·	——·-■	Secondary, State, Provincial, etc.
⬚		Parks, Indian Reservations
		City Limits
🔲		Urbanized Areas

Transportation

Political maps	Physical maps	
———	———	Railroads
-------	-------	Railroad Ferries
———		Major Roads
———		Minor Roads
··········		Caravan Routes
✈		Airports

Cultural Features

⌐\⌐	Dams
···········	Pipelines
▲	Points of Interest
∴	Ruins

Populated Places

◉	1,000,000 and over
◎	250,000 to 1,000,000
⊙	100,000 to 250,000
•	25,000 to 100,000
ˌˌ	Under 25,000
▫	Neighborhoods, Sections of Cities
TŌKYŌ	National Capitals
Boise	Secondary Capitals

Note: On maps at 1:20,000,000 and smaller, symbols do not follow the population classification shown above. Some other maps use a slightly different classification, which is shown in a separate legend in the map margin. On all maps, type size indicates the relative importance of the city.

Land Features

△	Peaks, Spot Heights
≍	Passes
⠿	Sand
⬭	Contours

Elevation

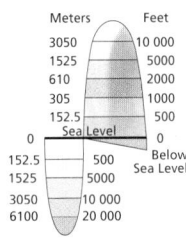

Meters	Feet
3050	10 000
1525	5000
610	2000
305	1000
152.5	500
0 Sea Level	0
152.5	500 Below Sea Level
1525	5000
3050	10 000
6100	20 000

Lakes and Reservoirs

⬭	Fresh Water
⬭	Fresh Water: Intermittent
⬭	Salt Water
⬭	Salt Water: Intermittent

Other Water Features

⬭	Salt Basins, Flats
⬭	Swamps
⬭	Ice Caps and Glaciers
⤳	Rivers
⤳	Intermittent Rivers
⌇	Aqueducts and Canals
-------	Ship Channels
⌇	Falls
⤚⤙	Rapids
♪	Springs
△	Water Depths
⠿	Sand Bars
⌇⌇⌇	Reefs
⟶	Warm Ocean Currents
⟶	Cold Ocean Currents

The legend above shows the symbols used for the political and physical reference maps in *Goode's World Atlas*.

To portray relative areas correctly, uniform map scales have been used wherever possible:

    Continents – 1:40,000,000
    Countries and regions – between 1:4,000,000 and 1:20,000,000
    World, polar areas and oceans – between 1:50,000,000
        and 1:100,000,000
    Urbanized areas – 1:1,000,000

Elevations on the maps are shown using a combination of shaded relief and hypsometric tints. Shaded relief (or hill-shading) gives a three-dimensional impression of the landscape, while hypsometric tints show elevation ranges in different colors.

The choice of names for mapped features is complicated by the fact that a variety of languages and alphabets are used throughout the world. A local-names policy is used in *Goode's World Atlas* for populated places and local physical features. For some major features, an English form of the name is used with the local name given below in parentheses. Examples include Moscow (Moskva), Vienna (Wien) and Naples (Napoli). In countries where more than one official language is used, names are given in the dominant local language. For large physical features spanning international borders, the conventional English form of the name is used. In cases where a non-Roman alphabet is used, names have been transliterated according to accepted practice.

Selected features are also listed in the Index (pp. 262-370), which includes a pronunciation guide. A list of foreign geographic terms is provided in the Glossary (p. 260).

POLITICAL

ARCTIC OCEAN

GREENLAND (Den.)

Baffin Bay

RUS. Nome
ALASKA (U.S.)
Anchorage
Juneau

Reykjavík
ICELAND

CANADA

Edmonton
Vancouver
Winnipeg
Québec
Montréal
St. John's
Portland
Ottawa
Chicago
Detroit
Toronto
Boston
Halifax

UNITED STATES

Washington

Los Angeles
Phoenix
Dallas
Houston
Atlanta
New Orleans
BERMUDA (U.K.)

MEXICO
GULF OF MEXICO
Miami
BAHAMAS

MIDWAY ISLANDS (U.S.)

ATLANTIC

Casablanca
Madeira Is. (Port.)

HAWAII (U.S.)
Honolulu
Guadalajara
Mexico City
Havana
CUBA
DOM. REP.
HAITI
PUERTO RICO (U.S.)
GUADELOUPE (Fr.)
Canary Is. (Sp.)
Tropic of Cancer
W. SAHARA
MOROCCO

JOHNSTON ATOLL (U.S.)
BELIZE
GUAT. HOND.
JAMAICA
CARIBBEAN SEA
MARTINIQUE (Fr.)
BARBADOS
MAURITANIA

EL SAL. NIC.
TRINIDAD AND TOBAGO
CAPE VERDE
THE GAMBIA
GUINEA-BISSAU
MALI

HOWLAND ISLAND (U.S.)
JARVIS ISLAND (U.S.)
COSTA RICA
PANAMA
Caracas
VENEZUELA
GUYANA
Georgetown
SURINAME
FRENCH GUIANA (Fr.)
GUINEA
SIERRA LEONE
LIBERIA
CÔTE D'IVOIRE

BAKER ISLAND (U.S.)
KIRIBATI
COLOMBIA
Bogotá
ECUADOR
Quito
Galápagos Is. (Ec.)

PACIFIC

Longitude West of Greenwich

TOKELAU (N.Z.)
PERU
Manaus
Belém
Fortaleza
Equator

SAMOA
AMERICAN SAMOA (U.S.)
Lima
BRAZIL
Recife
ST. HELENA (U.K.)

OCEAN

COOK ISLANDS (N.Z.)
FRENCH POLYNESIA (Fr.)
La Paz
BOLIVIA
Sucre
Brasília
Salvador

TONGA
PARAGUAY
Belo Horizonte

PITCAIRN ISLANDS (U.K.)
Antofagasta
Asunción
Río de Janeiro
São Paulo
OCEAN

Valparaíso
Santiago
ARGENTINA
URUGUAY
Rosario
Porto Alegre

Buenos Aires
Montevideo

SOUTHERN

ROSS SEA

OCEAN

FALKLAND ISLANDS (U.K.)
SOUTH GEORGIA AND THE SOUTH SANDWICH ISLANDS (U.K.)

Antarctic Circle

WEDDELL SEA

Scale 1 : 100 000 000 (approximate)
One inch to 1,600 miles

0 500 1000 1500 2000 miles

0 500 1000 1500 2000 2500 Kilometers

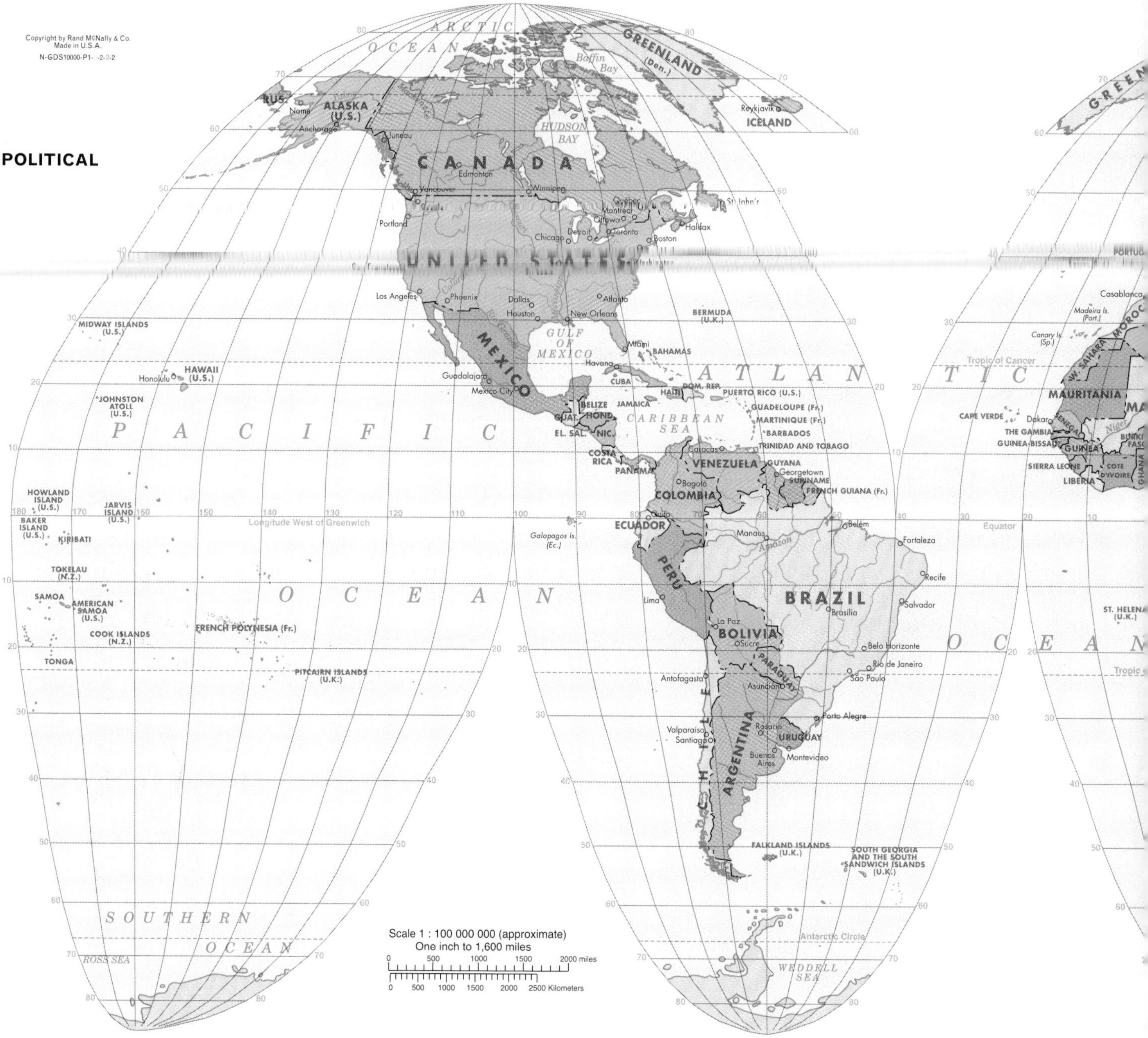

Comparative Land Areas (Land and inland water. Numbers indicate thousands of square miles.)

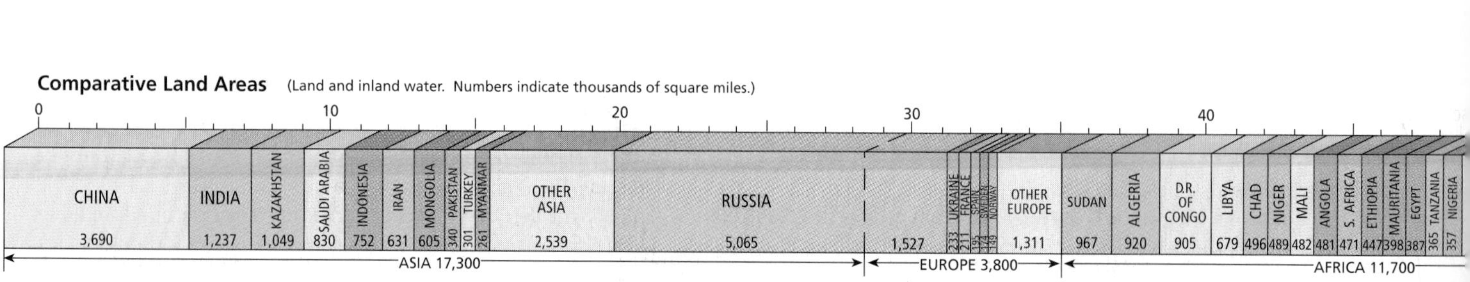

CHINA	INDIA	KAZAKHSTAN	SAUDI ARABIA	INDONESIA	IRAN	MONGOLIA	PAKISTAN	TURKEY	MYANMAR	OTHER ASIA	RUSSIA		UKRAINE	FRANCE	SPAIN	SWEDEN	NORWAY	OTHER EUROPE	SUDAN	ALGERIA	D.R. OF CONGO	LIBYA	CHAD	NIGER	MALI	ANGOLA	S. AFRICA	ETHIOPIA	MAURITANIA	EGYPT	TANZANIA	NIGERIA
3,690	1,237	1,049	830	752	631	605	340	301	261	2,539	5,065		233	211				1,311	967	920	905	679	496	489	482	481	471	447	398	387	365	357

ASIA 17,300 ← → EUROPE 3,800 ← → AFRICA 11,700

Comparative Populations (Numbers indicate millions of people.) 1/1/04 estimate

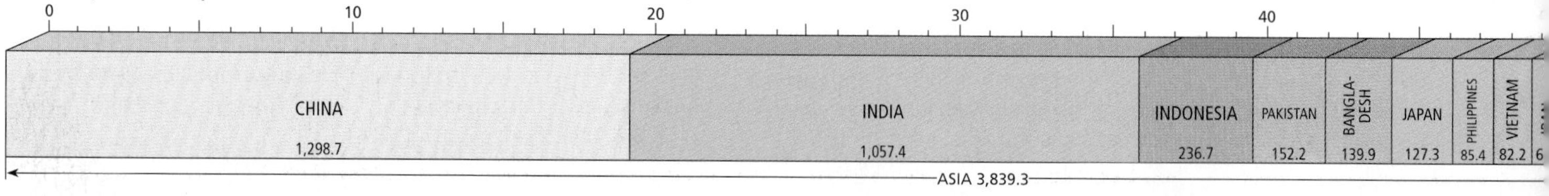

CHINA	INDIA	INDONESIA	PAKISTAN	BANGLA-DESH	JAPAN	PHILIPPINES	VIETNAM	
1,298.7	1,057.4	236.7	152.2	139.9	127.3	85.4	82.2	6

ASIA 3,839.3

ARCTIC OCEAN

SVALBARD (Nor.)

JAN MAYEN (Nor.)

ICELAND   Arctic Circle

ALASKA (U.S.)

FAROE ISLANDS (Den.)

NORWAY   SWEDEN   FINLAND

Reykjavik

UNITED KINGDOM   DENMARK   EST. LAT. LITH.

Oslo   Stockholm   St. Petersburg

Arkhangelsk

Madadan

R U S S I A

BERING SEA

SEA OF OKHOTSK

London   NETH.   POLAND   BELARUS

Moscow

Novosibirsk

Irkutsk

Paris   FRANCE   GER. CZECH SLK. HUNG. UKRAINE MOLD. ROM.

Kiev

KAZAKHSTAN

MONGOLIA

Ulan Bator

Harbin

Vladivostok

Madrid   SPAIN   ITALY   BUL.

Black Sea   GEORGIA ARM. AZER.

UZBEKISTAN KYRG.

Ürümqi

Shenyang

NORTH KOREA   SEA OF JAPAN

JAPAN

Istanbul   GREECE   TURKEY

Ankara

TURKMENISTAN TAJIK.

Beijing

SOUTH KOREA   Seoul   Tokyo   Osaka

Algiers   TUNISIA   CYPRUS SYRIA LEB.

MEDITERRANEAN SEA   ISRAEL IRAQ IRAN

JORDAN

AFGHANISTAN

C H I N A

Nanjing   Shanghai

Tripoli

KUWAIT

New Delhi   NEPAL BHU.

Chongqing

Wuhan

ALGERIA   LIBYA   EGYPT

SAUDI ARABIA   QATAR U.A.E.

Riyadh

PAKISTAN

Karachi

BANGL.

Kolkata

Guangzhou

Hong Kong   TAIWAN

WAKE ISLAND (U.S.)

NIGER   CHAD   SUDAN   YEMEN   OMAN

Mecca

ARABIAN SEA

I N D I A

Mumbai

Hyderabad

MYANMAR LAOS

Hanoi

THAILAND VIETNAM

Manila

NORTHERN MARIANA ISLANDS (U.S.)

NIGERIA   CENTRAL AFRICAN REPUBLIC   ETHIOPIA   DJIBOUTI

Addis Ababa

BAY OF BENGAL

Rangoon

Bangkok CAMBODIA

Ho Chi Minh City

PHILIPPINES

GUAM (U.S.)

MARSHALL ISLANDS

EQUATORIAL GUINEA   GABON   CONGO   DEM. REP. OF THE CONGO   KENYA   SOMALIA

Nairobi

Chennai

Colombo   SRI LANKA

MALAYSIA

BRUNEI

PALAU

FED. STATES OF MICRONESIA

Kinshasa

Brazzaville   RWANDA BURUNDI   TANZANIA

Mombasa

Dar Es Salaam

MALDIVES

Kuala Lumpur   SINGAPORE

SUMATRA

BORNEO

NAURU   KIRIBATI

Luanda

ANGOLA   ZAMBIA   MOZAMBIQUE

SEYCHELLES

COMOROS

I N D I A N   O C E A N

Jakarta

Surabaya   I N D O N E S I A

EAST TIMOR

NEW GUINEA   PAPUA NEW GUINEA

SOLOMON ISLANDS

TUVALU

Longitude East of Greenwich

CHRISTMAS ISLAND (Austl.)

COCOS ISLANDS (Austl.)

VANUATU

FIJI

ZIMBABWE   MADAGASCAR

Antananarivo

MAURITIUS

REUNION (Fr.)

Darwin

CORAL SEA

Suva

NAMIBIA   BOTSWANA

Capricorn

Johannesburg   SWAZILAND

Pretoria

LESOTHO   SOUTH AFRICA   Maputo

A U S T R A L I A

NEW CALEDONIA (Fr.)

Cape Town   Durban

Perth

Brisbane

Adelaide   Sydney   Auckland

Canberra

Melbourne   NEW ZEALAND   Wellington

S O U T H E R N

The Antarctic territorial claims of Argentina, Australia, Chile, France, New Zealand, Norway, and the United Kingdom are not recognized by other nations. Antarctica is administered under the provisions of the Antarctic Treaty of 1959.

O C E A N

A N T A R C T I C A

Goode's Homolosine Equal Area Projection

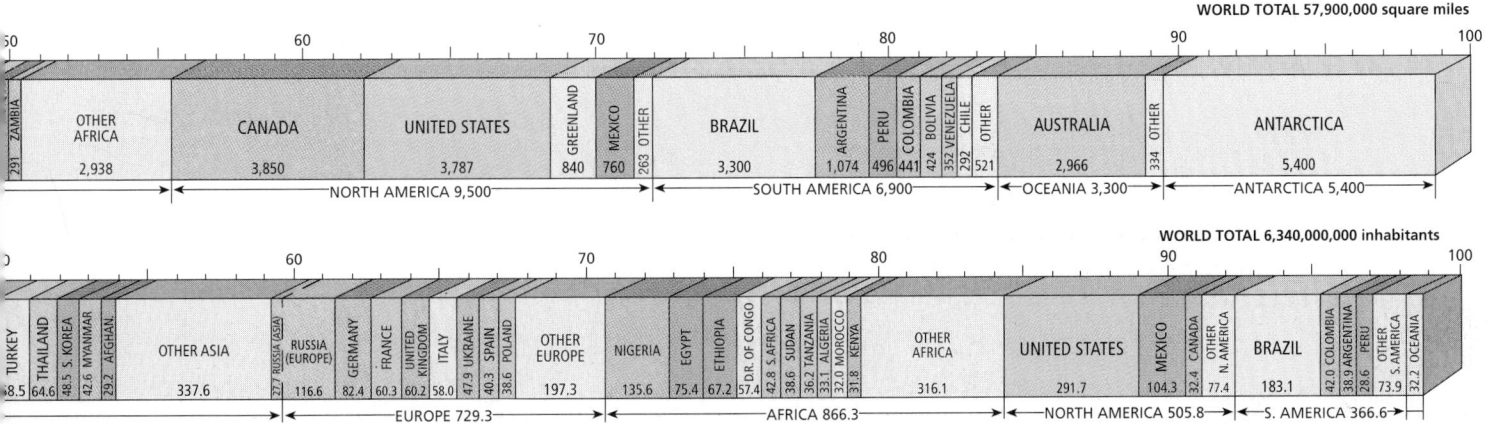

WORLD TOTAL 57,900,000 square miles

ZAMBIA 291	OTHER AFRICA 2,938	CANADA 3,850	UNITED STATES 3,787	GREENLAND 840	MEXICO 760	OTHER 263	BRAZIL 3,300	ARGENTINA 1,074	PERU 496	COLOMBIA 441	BOLIVIA 424	VENEZUELA 352	CHILE 292	OTHER 521	AUSTRALIA 2,966	OTHER 334	ANTARCTICA 5,400

NORTH AMERICA 9,500 · SOUTH AMERICA 6,900 · OCEANIA 3,300 · ANTARCTICA 5,400

WORLD TOTAL 6,340,000,000 inhabitants

| TURKEY 68.5 | THAILAND 64.6 | S. KOREA 48.5 | MYANMAR 42.6 | AFGHAN. 29.2 | OTHER ASIA 337.6 | RUSSIA (ASIA) 27.7 | RUSSIA (EUROPE) 116.6 | GERMANY 82.4 | FRANCE 60.3 | UNITED KINGDOM 60.2 | ITALY 58.0 | UKRAINE 47.9 | SPAIN 40.3 | POLAND 38.6 | OTHER EUROPE 197.3 | NIGERIA 135.6 | EGYPT 75.4 | ETHIOPIA 67.2 | D.R. OF CONGO 57.4 | S. AFRICA 42.8 | TANZANIA 38.6 | SUDAN 36.2 | ALGERIA 33.1 | MOROCCO 32.0 | KENYA 31.8 | OTHER AFRICA 316.1 | UNITED STATES 291.7 | MEXICO 104.3 | CANADA 32.4 | OTHER N. AMERICA 77.4 | BRAZIL 183.1 | COLOMBIA 42.0 | ARGENTINA 38.9 | PERU 28.6 | OTHER S. AMERICA 73.9 | OCEANIA 32.2 |

EUROPE 729.3 · AFRICA 866.3 · NORTH AMERICA 505.8 · S. AMERICA 366.6

PHYSICAL

ARCTIC OCEAN

North Pole

North Magnetic Pole

ASIA

GREENLAND

BANKS I.

PT. BARROW
Beaufort Sea

Victoria

BAFFIN ISLAND

Baffin Bay

ICELAND

KAP FARVEL

BERING SEA

Nunivak

Mt. McKinley 20 320

Mt Logan 19 551

Great Bear Lake

Great Slave Lake

HUDSON BAY

Belcher Is.

LABRADOR PENINSULA AND PLATEAU

PRIBILOF IS.

Gulf of Alaska

ROCKY

NORTHERN LOWLAND

ALEUTIAN ISLANDS

Alaska Pen.

L. Winnipeg

Great Lakes

NEWFOUNDLAND

ALEUTIAN TRENCH

N O R T H

A M E R I C A

C. MENDOCINO

Vancouver I.

Mt Rainier 14 410

CENTRAL PLAINS

St. Lawrence

C. SABLE

MIDWAY IS.

PENINSULA

Mt. Whitney 14 494

Arkansas

Red

Mt Mitchell 6684

APPALACHIAN

C. HATTERAS

BERMUDA

Guadalupe

DE BAJA CALIFORNIA

SIERRA MADRE

MEXICAN PLATEAU

GULF OF MEXICO

C. SABLE

FLORIDA PEN.

BAHAMA ISLANDS

NORTH AMERICAN BASIN

C. SAN LUCAS

Bahía de Campeche

Cuba

GREATER ANTILLES

Puerto Rico

Tropic of Cancer

MADEIRA

IS. CANARIAS

Jebel Toubkal 13 665

HAWAIIAN ISLANDS

Mauna Kea (Vol.) 13 796

REVILLAGIGEDO IS.

Pico de Orizaba 18 406

Pen. de Yucatán

G. de Honduras

Jamaica

WEST INDIES

Hispaniola

CARIBBEAN SEA

Guadeloupe

LESSER ANTILLES

Martinique

WINDWARD ISLANDS

Barbados

Trinidad

ARQUIPELAGO DE CABO VERDE

C. VERT

C. PALMAS

Johnston

Clipperton

ISTMO DE TEHUANTEPEC

ISTMO DE PANAMA

Pto. de Gallinas

Irazú (Vol.) 11 260

GUIANA HIGHLANDS

A

Palmyra

Teraina

Tabuaeran

Kiritimati

Longitude West of Greenwich

ARCH. DE COLÓN (GALAPAGOS IS.)

Chimborazo 20 702

ILHA DE MARAJO

Arch. Fernando de Noronha

Equator

ASCENSION

Howland

Baker

Jarvis

Malden

Starbuck

PTA. PARIÑAS

LLANOS

SELVAS

CABO DE SÃO ROQUE

PHOENIX ISLANDS

MANIHIKI

MARQUESAS IS.

G. de Guayaquil

S O U T H

A M E R I C A

CAMPOS

ST. HELENA

TOKELAU IS.

ÎLES

P A C I F I C   O C E A N

CENTRAL LOWLAND

BRAZILIAN HIGHLANDS

Pico da Bandeira 9 482

C. FRIO

SAMOA

Totuila

SOCIETY IS.

Tahiti

CAÑ

PLATEAU OF MATO GROSSO

FIJI IS.

TONGA IS.

COOK IS.

ÎLES AUSTRALES

TUAMOTU

Is. Gambier

I. Sala y Gómez

I. San Felix   I. San Ambrosio

ANDES MTS.

PAMPAS

Rio de la Plata

TRISTAN DA CUNHA

Tropic of

KERMADEC TRENCH

Rapa

Pitcairn

Ducie

Isla de Pascua (Easter)

PERU-CHILE TRENCH

Aconcagua (Vol.) 22 831

Rio de la Plata

GOUGH

CHATHAM IS.

IS. DE JUAN FERNANDEZ

G. San Matias

KERMADEC IS.

PATAGONIA

G. San Jorge

ARCH. DE LOS CHONOS

G. de Penas

FALKLAND IS.

SHAG ROCKS

SOUTH GEORGIA

Magallanes

TIERRA DEL FUEGO

SOUTH SANDWICH IS.

CABO DE HORNOS

Drake Passage

SOUTH SHETLAND IS.

SOUTH ORKNEY IS.

S O U T H E R N   O C E A N

ROSS SEA

Graham Coast

ANTARCTIC PENINSULA

Alexander I

WEDDELL SEA

Marie Byrd Land

Cook Land

South Pole

Scale 1 : 100 000 000 (approximate)
One inch to 1,600 miles

0   500   1000   1500   2000 miles

0   500   1000   1500   2000   2500 Kilometers

Meters		Feet
3 050		10 000
1 525		5 000
610		2 000
305		1 000
152.5		500
0	SEA L.	0
		BELOW SEA LEVEL
152.5		500
3 050		10 000
6 100		20 000

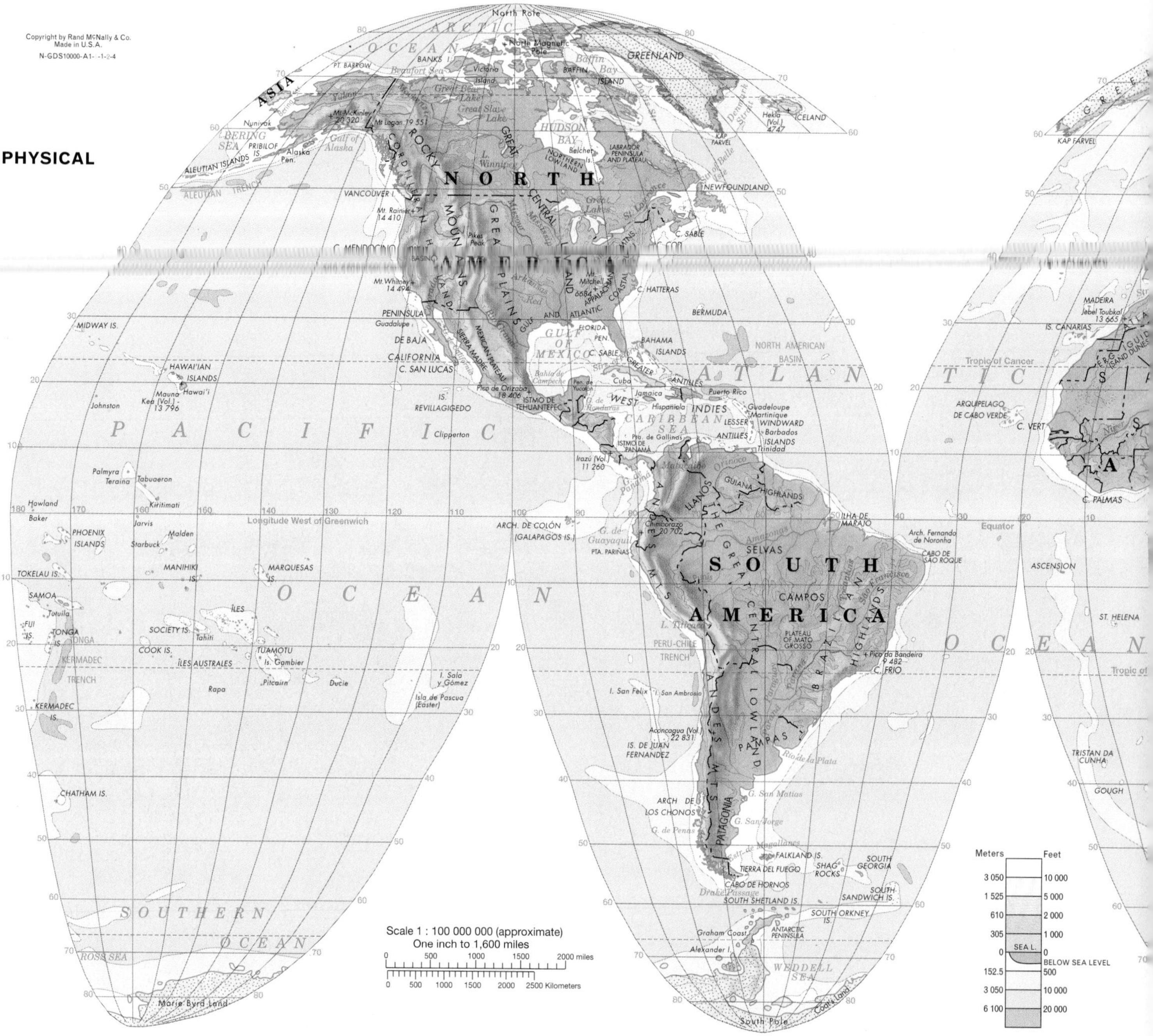

Land Elevations in Profile

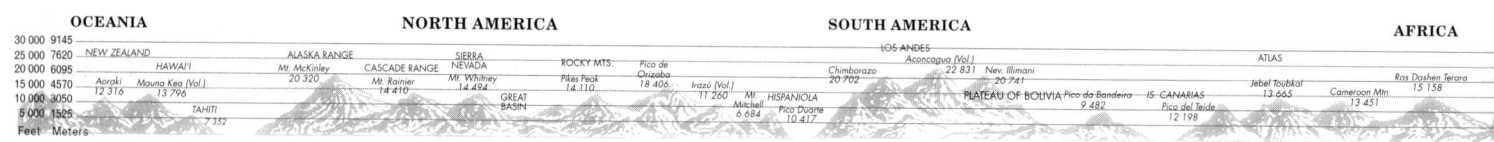

OCEANIA   NORTH AMERICA   SOUTH AMERICA   AFRICA

NEW ZEALAND   ALASKA RANGE   SIERRA NEVADA   ROCKY MTS.   Pico de Orizaba   LOS ANDES   ATLAS

HAWAI'I   Mt. McKinley 20 320   CASCADE RANGE   Aoraki 12 316   Mauna Kea (Vol.) 13 796   Mt. Rainier 14 410   Mt. Whitney 14 494   Pikes Peak 14 110   18 406   Irazú (Vol.) 11 260   Chimborazo 20 702   Aconcagua (Vol.) 22 831   Nev. Illimani 20 741   Jebel Toubkal 13 665   Cameroon Mtn. 13 451   Ras Dashen Terara 15 158

TAHITI 7 352   GREAT BASIN   Mt. Mitchell 6 684   HISPANIOLA Pico Duarte 10 417   PLATEAU OF BOLIVIA   Pico da Bandeira 9 482   IS. CANARIAS Pico del Teide 12 198

30 000 9145
25 000 7620
20 000 6095
15 000 4570
10 000 3050
5 000 1525
Feet Meters

Ocean Depths in Profile

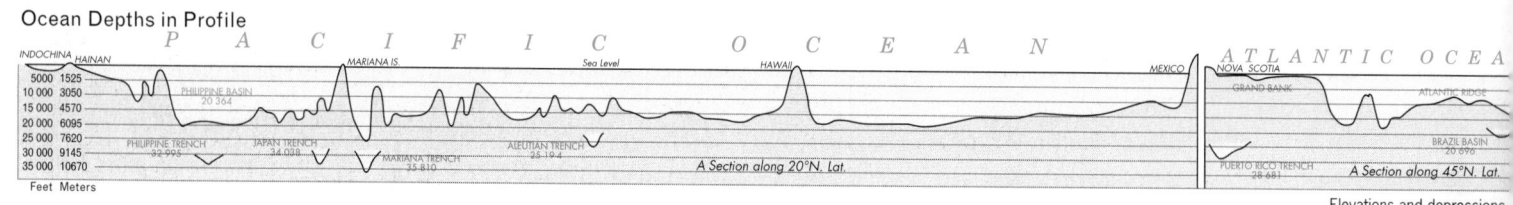

P A C I F I C   O C E A N   A T L A N T I C   O C E A N

INDOCHINA HAINAN   MARIANA IS.   Sea Level   Hawaii   MEXICO   NOVA SCOTIA   GRAND BANK   ATLANTIC RIDGE

PHILIPPINE BASIN 20 364

PHILIPPINE TRENCH 32 995   JAPAN TRENCH 34 039   MARIANA TRENCH 35 810   ALEUTIAN TRENCH 25 194   A Section along 20°N. Lat.   PUERTO RICO TRENCH 28 681   BRAZIL BASIN 20 696   A Section along 45°N. Lat.

5000 1525
10 000 3050
15 000 4570
20 000 6095
25 000 7620
30 000 9145
35 000 10670
Feet Meters

Elevations and depressions

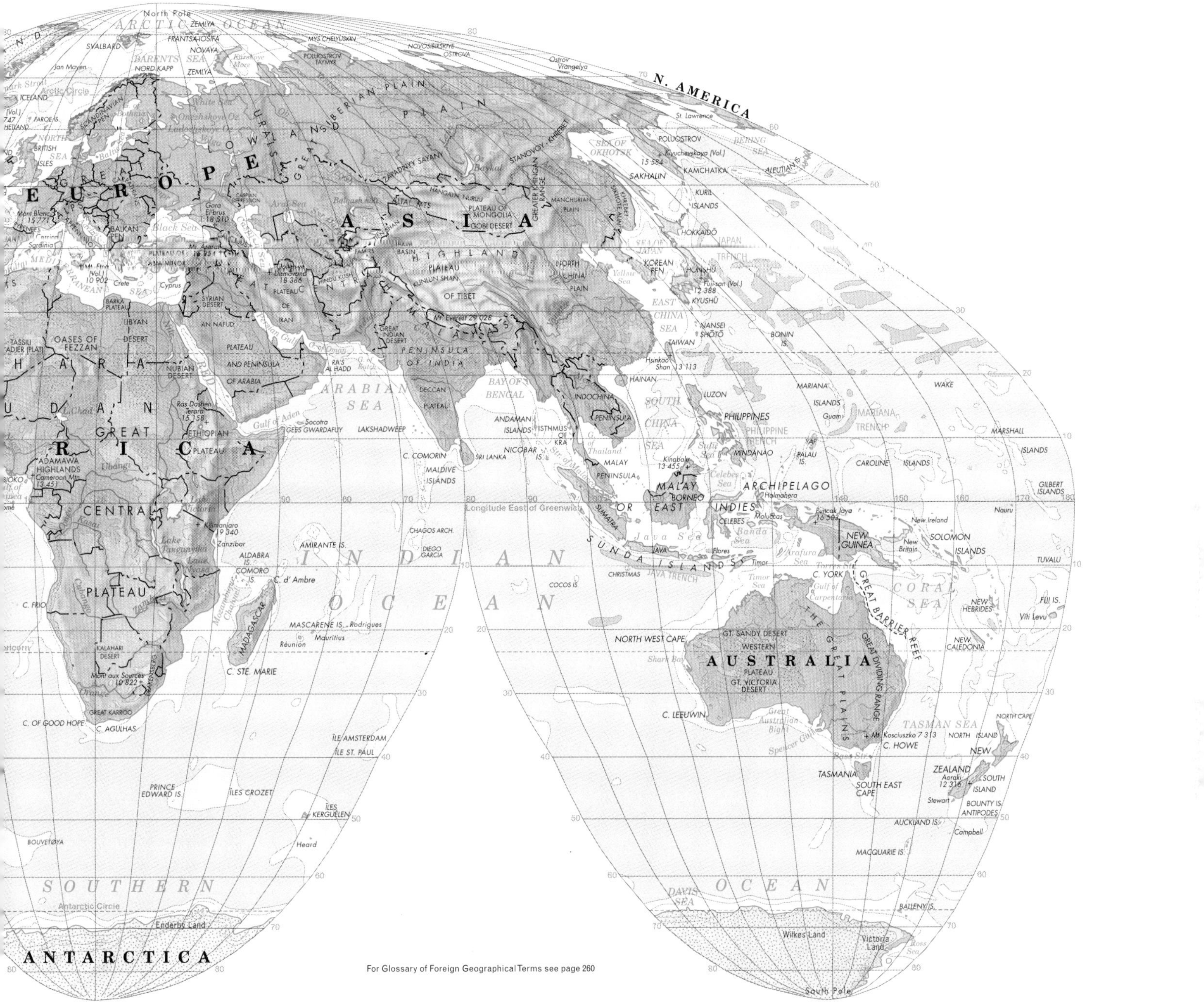

For Glossary of Foreign Geographical Terms see page 260

Goode's Homolosine Equal Area Projection

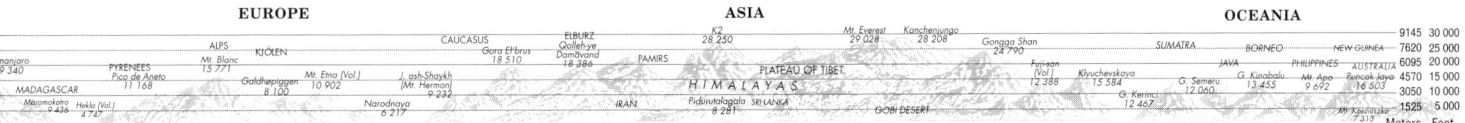

EUROPE	ASIA	OCEANIA

| | | | | | | | | | | | | | | 9145 | 30 000 |

ALPS · KJÖLEN · CAUCASUS · ELBURZ · K2 · Mt. Everest · Kanchenjunga · Gongga Shan · SUMATRA · BORNEO · NEW-GUINEA — 7620 25 000

PYRENEES · Mt. Blanc · Gora El'brus · Golleh-ye Dambavand · PAMIRS · PLATEAU OF TIBET · Fuji-san · Klyuchevskaya · JAVA · PHILIPPINES · AUSTRALIA — 6095 20 000

MADAGASCAR · Goldhøpiggen · Mt. Etna (Vol.) · J. ash-Shaykh (Mt. Hermon) · HIMALAYAS · G. Semeru · G. Kinabalu · Mt. Apo · Puncak Jaya — 4570 15 000

G. Kerinci — 3050 10 000

Hekla (Vol.) · Narodnaya · IRAN · Pidurutalagala SRI LANKA · GOBI DESERT — 1525 5 000

Mt. Kosciuszko — Meters Feet

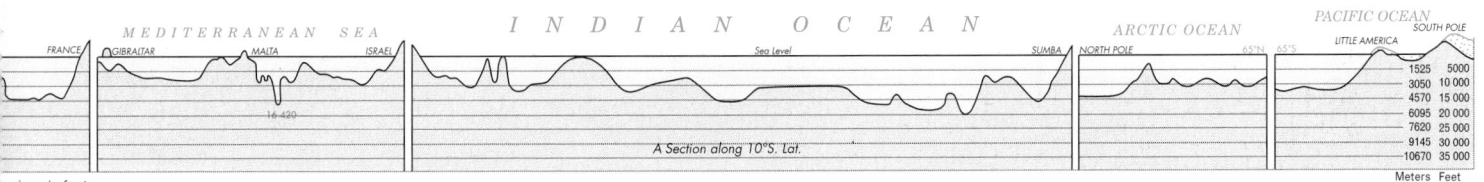

MEDITERRANEAN SEA	INDIAN OCEAN	ARCTIC OCEAN	PACIFIC OCEAN

SOUTH POLE

FRANCE · GIBRALTAR · MALTA · ISRAEL · Sea Level · SUMBA · NORTH POLE · LITTLE AMERICA

1525 5000
3050 10 000
4570 15 000
6095 20 000
7620 25 000
9145 30 000
10670 35 000

Meters Feet

A Section along 10°S. Lat.

given in feet

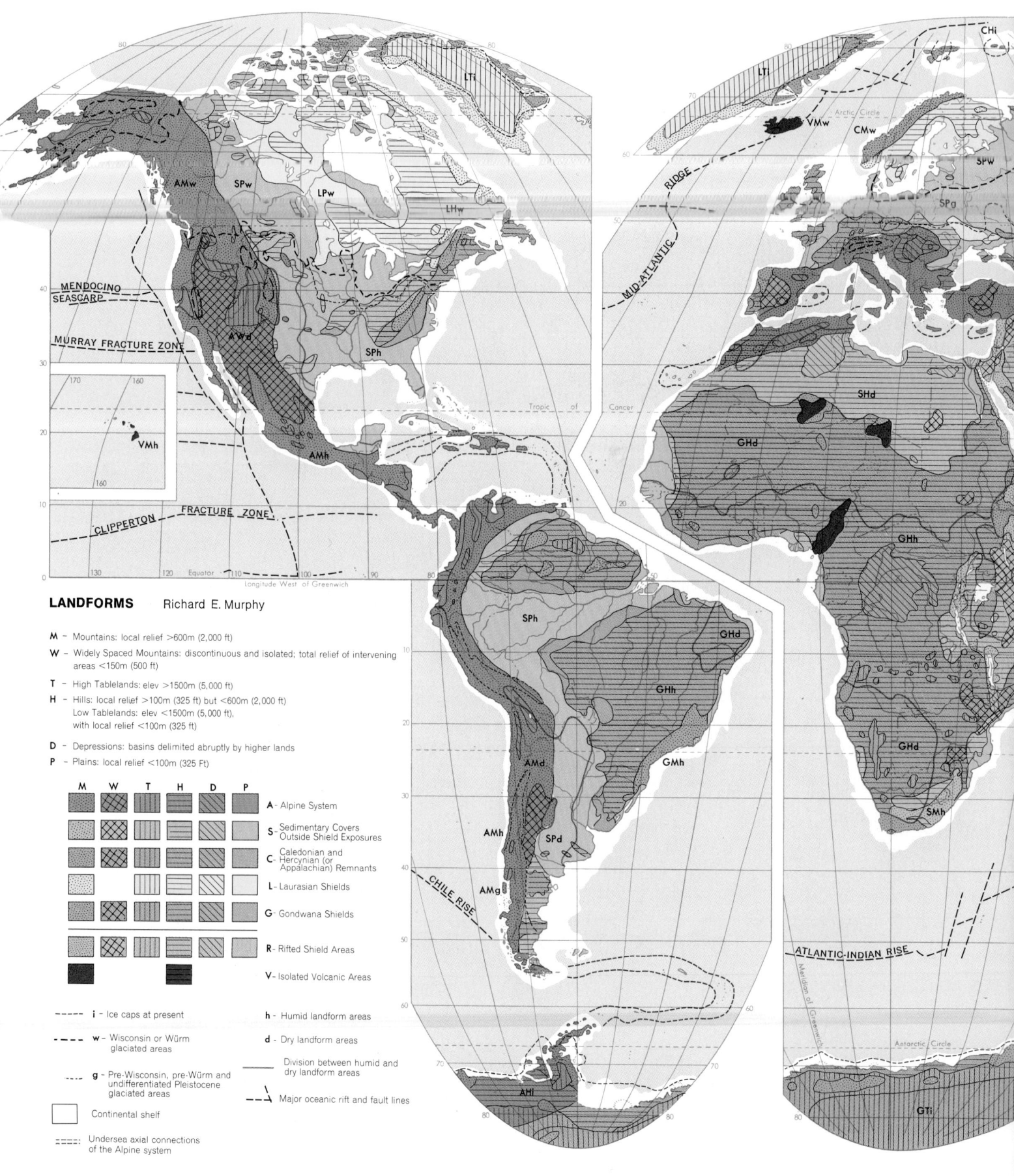

LANDFORMS   Richard E. Murphy

M – Mountains: local relief >600m (2,000 ft)

W – Widely Spaced Mountains: discontinuous and isolated; total relief of intervening areas <150m (500 ft)

T – High Tablelands: elev >1500m (5,000 ft)

H – Hills: local relief >100m (325 ft) but <600m (2,000 ft)
Low Tablelands: elev <1500m (5,000 ft), with local relief <100m (325 ft)

D – Depressions: basins delimited abruptly by higher lands

P – Plains: local relief <100m (325 Ft)

	M	W	T	H	D	P	
							A – Alpine System
							S – Sedimentary Covers Outside Shield Exposures
							C – Caledonian and Hercynian (or Appalachian) Remnants
							L – Laurasian Shields
							G – Gondwana Shields
							R – Rifted Shield Areas
							V – Isolated Volcanic Areas

----- i – Ice caps at present

- - - w – Wisconsin or Würm glaciated areas

· · · g – Pre-Wisconsin, pre-Würm and undifferentiated Pleistocene glaciated areas

Continental shelf

===== Undersea axial connections of the Alpine system

h – Humid landform areas

d – Dry landform areas

Division between humid and dry landform areas

Major oceanic rift and fault lines

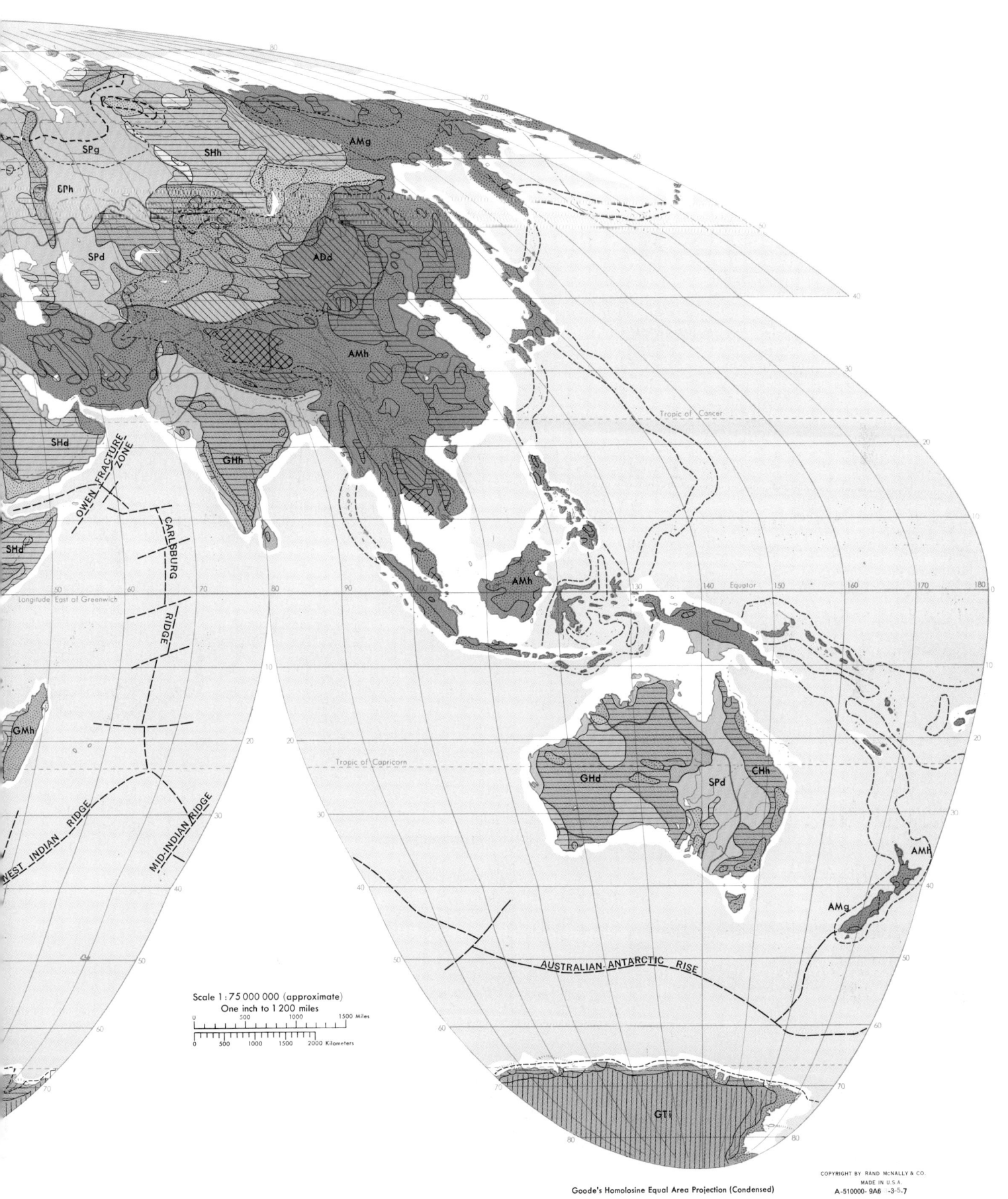

Goode's Homolosine Equal Area Projection (Condensed)

A-510000- 9A6 -3-5-7

CONTINENTAL DRIFT

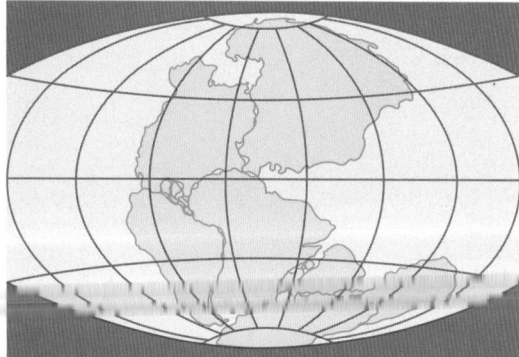

225 million years ago the supercontinent of Pangaea exists and Panthalassa forms the ancestral ocean. Tethys Sea separates Eurasia and Africa.

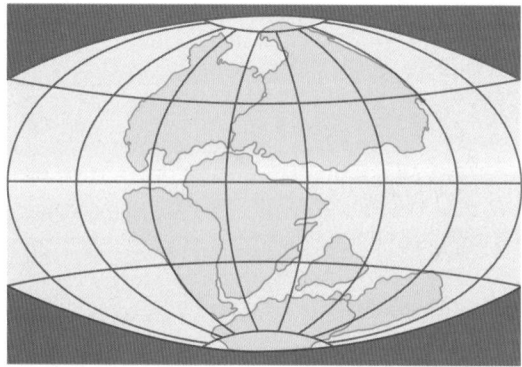

180 million years ago Pangaea splits, Laurasia drifts north. Gondwanaland breaks into South America/Africa, India, and Australia/Antarctica.

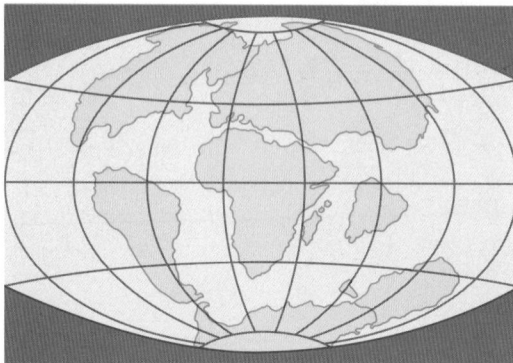

65 million years ago ocean basins take shape as South America and India move from Africa and the Tethys Sea closes to form the Mediterranean Sea.

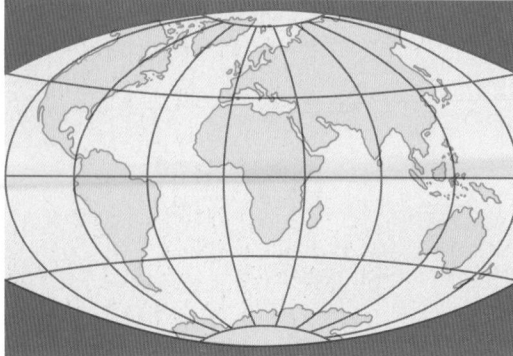

The present day: India has merged with Asia, Australia is free of Antarctica, and North America is free of Eurasia.

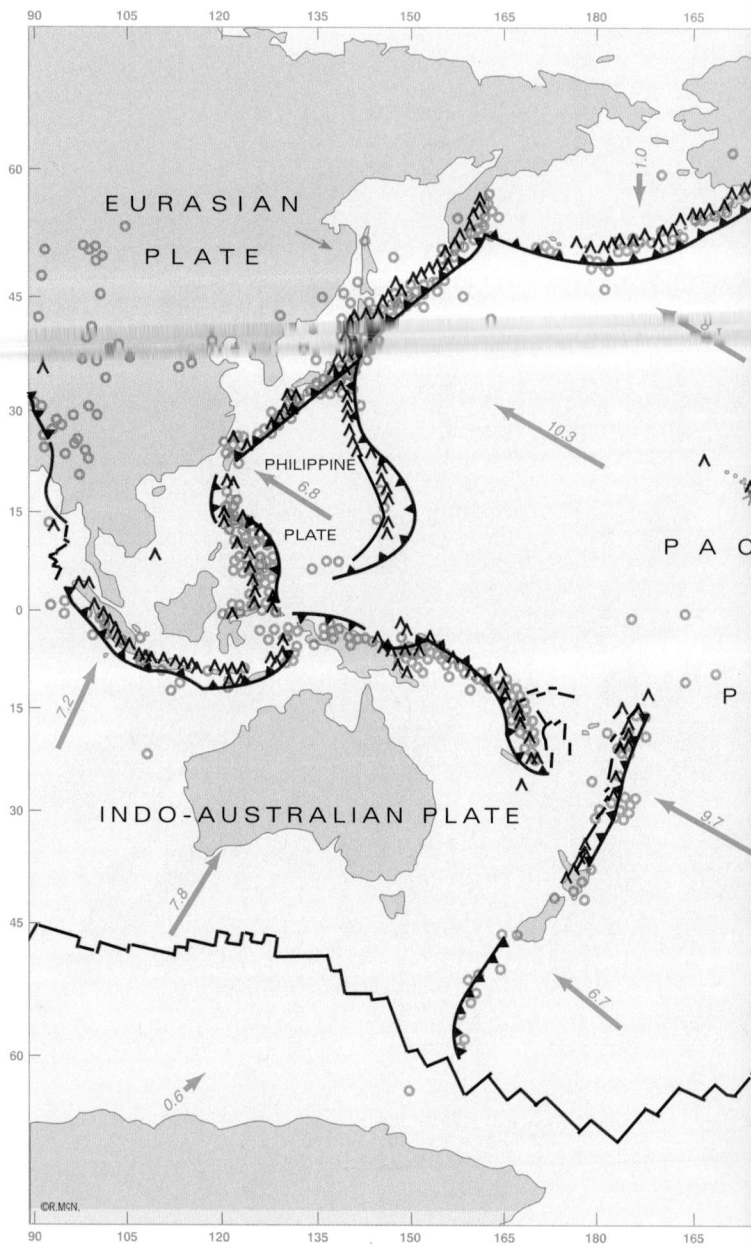

PLATE TECTONICS

Types of plate boundaries

Divergent: magma emerges from the earth's mantle at the mid-ocean ridges forming new crust and forcing the plates to spread apart at the ridges.

Convergent: plates collide at subduction zones where the denser plate is forced back into the earth's mantle forming deep ocean trenches.

Transform: plates slide past one another producing faults and fracture zones.

Other map symbols

Direction of plate movement

6.7 Length of arrow is proportional to the amount of plate movement (number indicates centimeters of movement per year)

○ Earthquake of magnitude 7.5 and above (from 10 A.D. to the present)

∧ Volcano (eruption since 1900)

✳ Selected hot spots

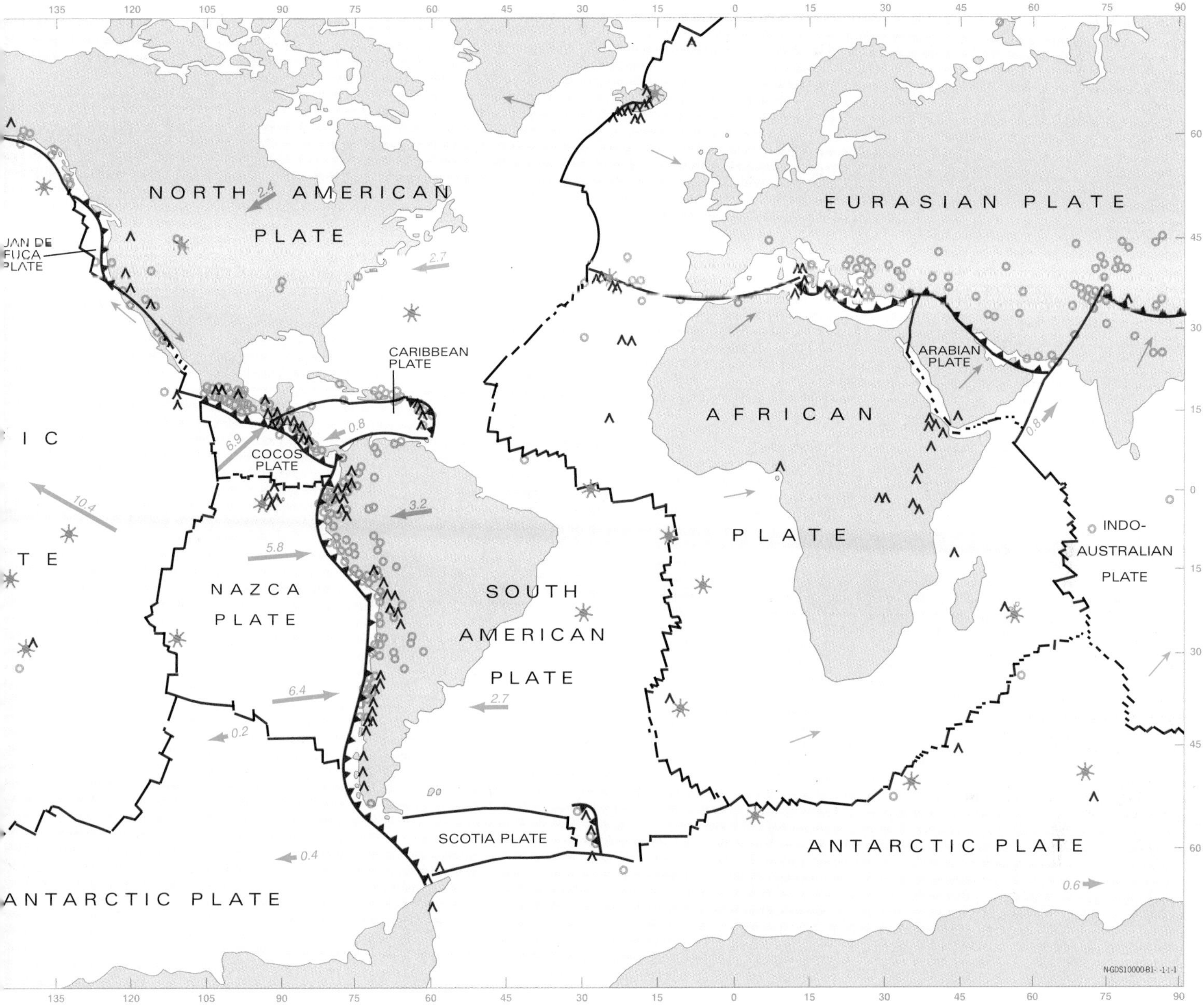

NORTH AMERICAN PLATE

JAN DE FUCA PLATE

CARIBBEAN PLATE

COCOS PLATE

NAZCA PLATE

SOUTH AMERICAN PLATE

SCOTIA PLATE

ANTARCTIC PLATE

EURASIAN PLATE

ARABIAN PLATE

AFRICAN PLATE

INDO-AUSTRALIAN PLATE

ANTARCTIC PLATE

N-GDS10000-B1- -1-1-1

The plate tectonic theory describes the movement of the earth's surface and subsurface and explains why surface features are where they are.

Stated concisely, the theory presumes the lithosphere - the outside crust and uppermost mantle of the earth - is divided into about a dozen major rigid plates and several smaller platelets that move relative to one another. The position and names of the plates are shown on the map above.

The motor that drives the plates is found deep in the mantle. The theory states that because of temperature differences in the mantle, slow convection currents circulate there. Where two molten currents converge and move upward, they separate, causing the crustal plates to bulge and move apart in mid-ocean regions. Transverse fractures disrupt these broad regions. Lava wells up at these points to cause volcanic activity and to form ridges. The plates grow larger by accretion along these mid-ocean ridges, cause vast regions of the crust to move apart, and force the plates to collide with one another. As the plates do so, they are destroyed at subduction zones, where the plates are consumed downward, back into the earth's mantle, forming deep ocean trenches. The diagrams to the right illustrate the processes.

Most of the earth's volcanic and seismic activities

occur where plates slide past each other at transform boundaries or collide along subduction zones. The friction and heat caused by the grinding motion of the subducted plates causes rock to liquify and rise to the surface as volcanoes and eventually form vast mountain ranges. Strong and deep earthquakes are common here.

Volcanoes and earthquakes also occur at random locations around the earth known as "hot spots". Hot rock from deep in the mantle rises to the surface creating some of the earth's tallest mountains. As the lithospheric plates move slowly over these stationary plumes of magma, island chains (such as the Hawaiian Islands) are formed.

The overall result of tectonic movement is that the crustal plates move slowly and inexorably as relatively rigid entitles, carrying the continents along with them. The history of this continental drifting is illustrated in the four maps to the left. It began with a single landmass called the supercontinent of Pangaea and the ancestral sea, the Panthalassa Ocean. Pangaea first split into a northern landmass called Laurasia and a southern block called Gondwanaland and subsequently into the continents we map today. The map of the future will be significantly different as the continents continue to drift.

Subduction Zone

Ocean Ridge Zone

Scale 1:72 000 000 at 40° latitude.

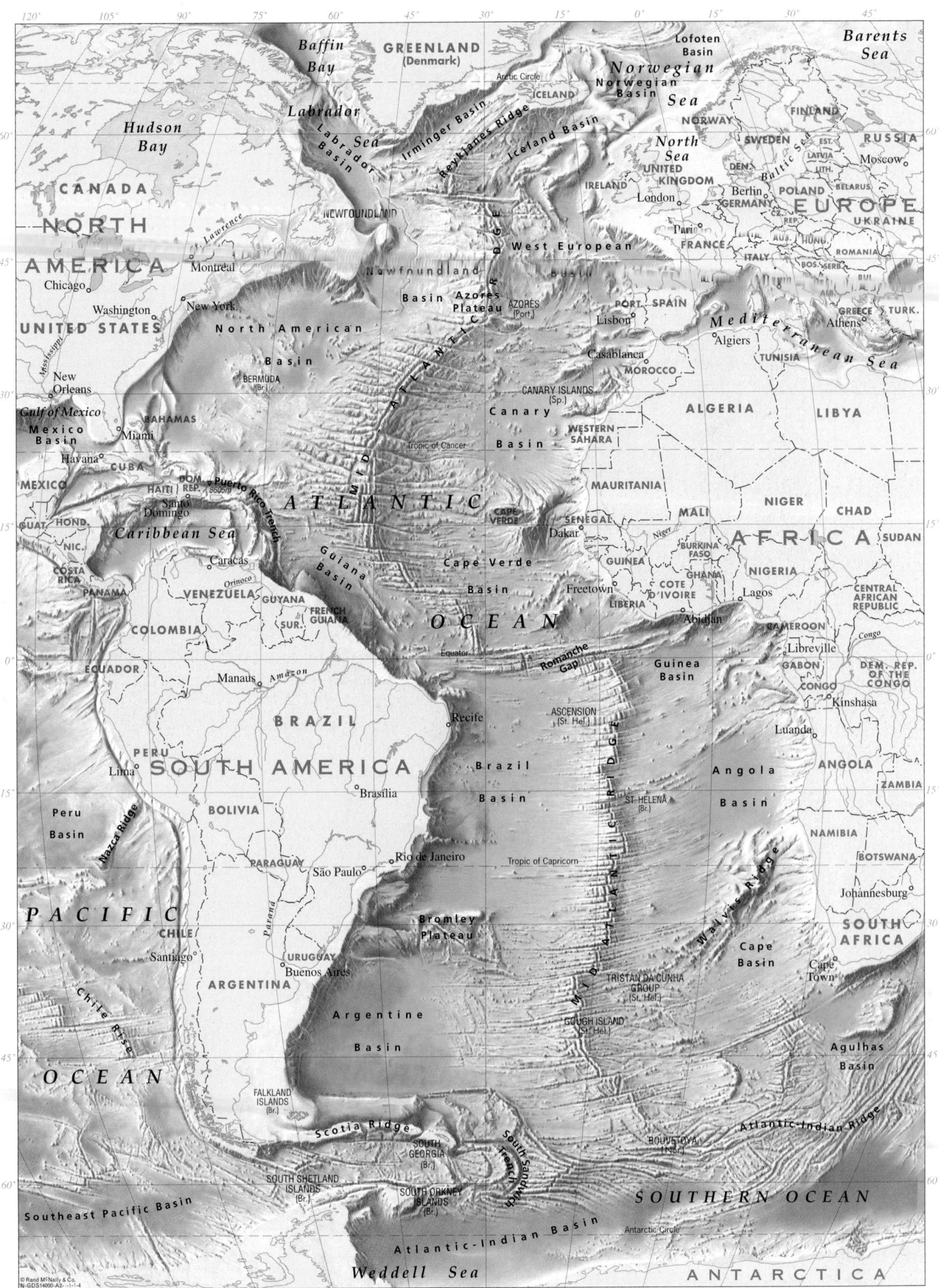

Scale 1:72 000 000 at 40° latitude. ROBINSON PROJECTION

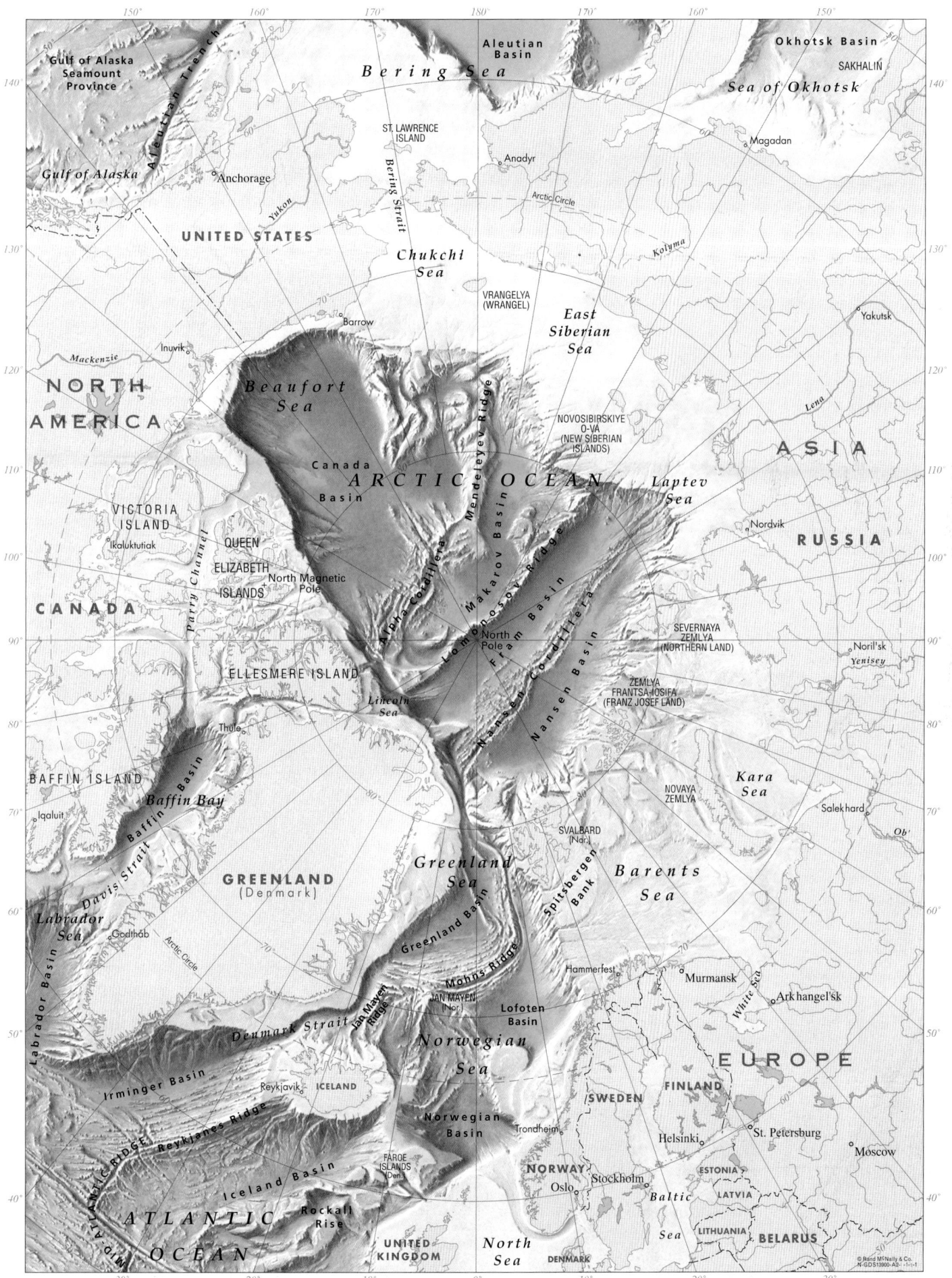

Scale 1:30 000 000. LAMBERT AZIMUTHAL EQUAL AREA PROJECTION

14

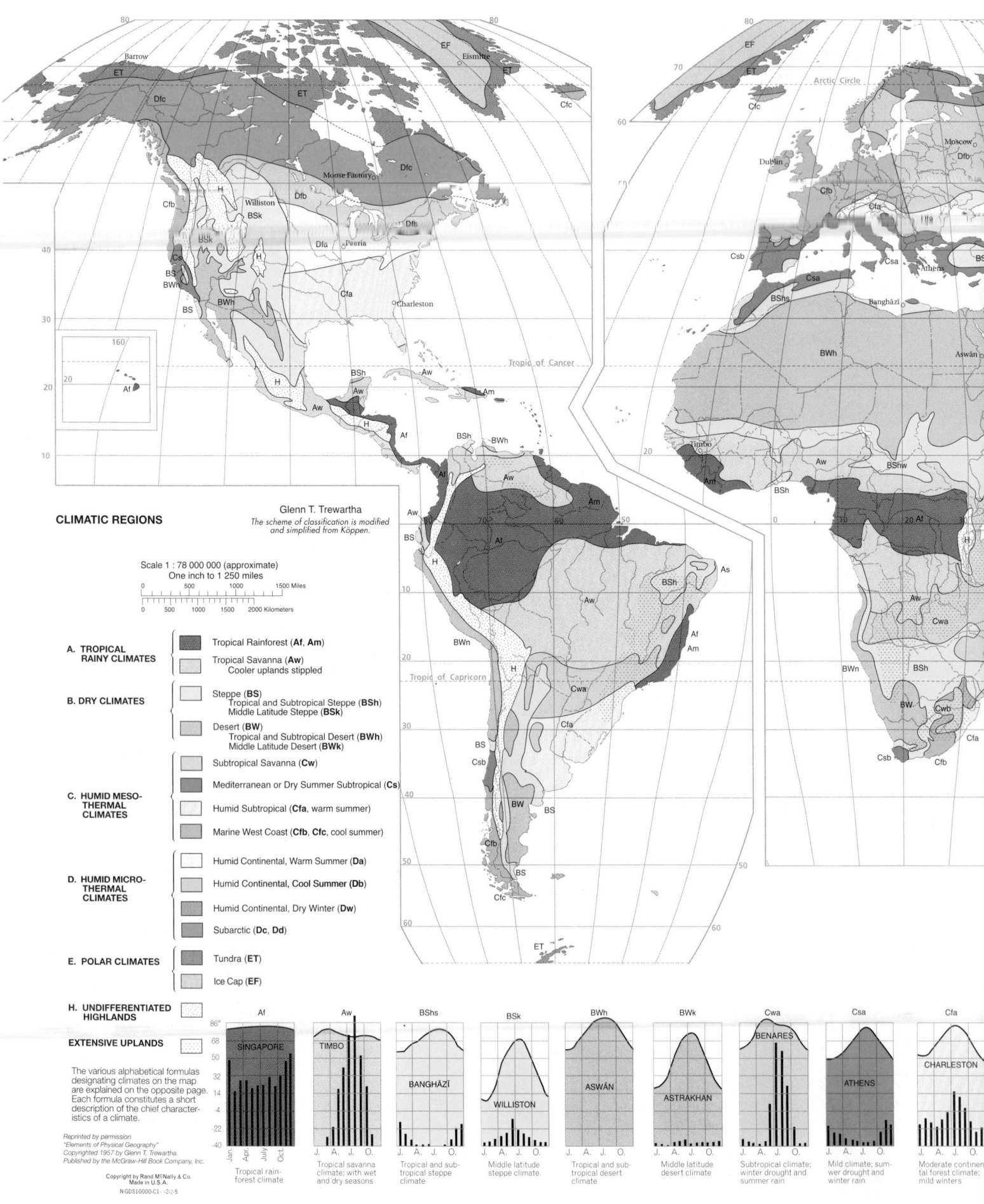

CLIMATIC REGIONS

Glenn T. Trewartha
The scheme of classification is modified and simplified from Köppen.

Scale 1 : 78 000 000 (approximate)
One inch to 1 250 miles

0   500   1000   1500 Miles

0   500   1000   1500   2000 Kilometers

A. TROPICAL RAINY CLIMATES
- Tropical Rainforest (**Af, Am**)
- Tropical Savanna (**Aw**) Cooler uplands stippled

B. DRY CLIMATES
- Steppe (**BS**) Tropical and Subtropical Steppe (**BSh**) Middle Latitude Steppe (**BSk**)
- Desert (**BW**) Tropical and Subtropical Desert (**BWh**) Middle Latitude Desert (**BWk**)

C. HUMID MESO-THERMAL CLIMATES
- Subtropical Savanna (**Cw**)
- Mediterranean or Dry Summer Subtropical (**Cs**)
- Humid Subtropical (**Cfa**, warm summer)
- Marine West Coast (**Cfb, Cfc**, cool summer)

D. HUMID MICRO-THERMAL CLIMATES
- Humid Continental, Warm Summer (**Da**)
- Humid Continental, Cool Summer (**Db**)
- Humid Continental, Dry Winter (**Dw**)
- Subarctic (**Dc, Dd**)

E. POLAR CLIMATES
- Tundra (**ET**)
- Ice Cap (**EF**)

H. UNDIFFERENTIATED HIGHLANDS

EXTENSIVE UPLANDS

The various alphabetical formulas designating climates on the map are explained on the opposite page. Each formula constitutes a short description of the chief characteristics of a climate.

Reprinted by permission
"Elements of Physical Geography"
Copyrighted 1957 by Glenn T. Trewartha.
Published by the McGraw-Hill Book Company, Inc.

Af — SINGAPORE — Tropical rain-forest climate.

Aw — TIMBO — Tropical savanna climate; with wet and dry seasons.

BShs — BANGHĀZĪ — Tropical and sub-tropical steppe climate.

BSk — WILLISTON — Middle latitude steppe climate.

BWh — ASWĀN — Tropical and sub-tropical desert climate.

BWk — ASTRAKHAN — Middle latitude desert climate.

Cwa — BENARES — Subtropical climate; winter drought and summer rain.

Csa — ATHENS — Mild climate; summer drought and winter rain.

Cfa — CHARLESTON — Moderate continental forest climate; mild winters

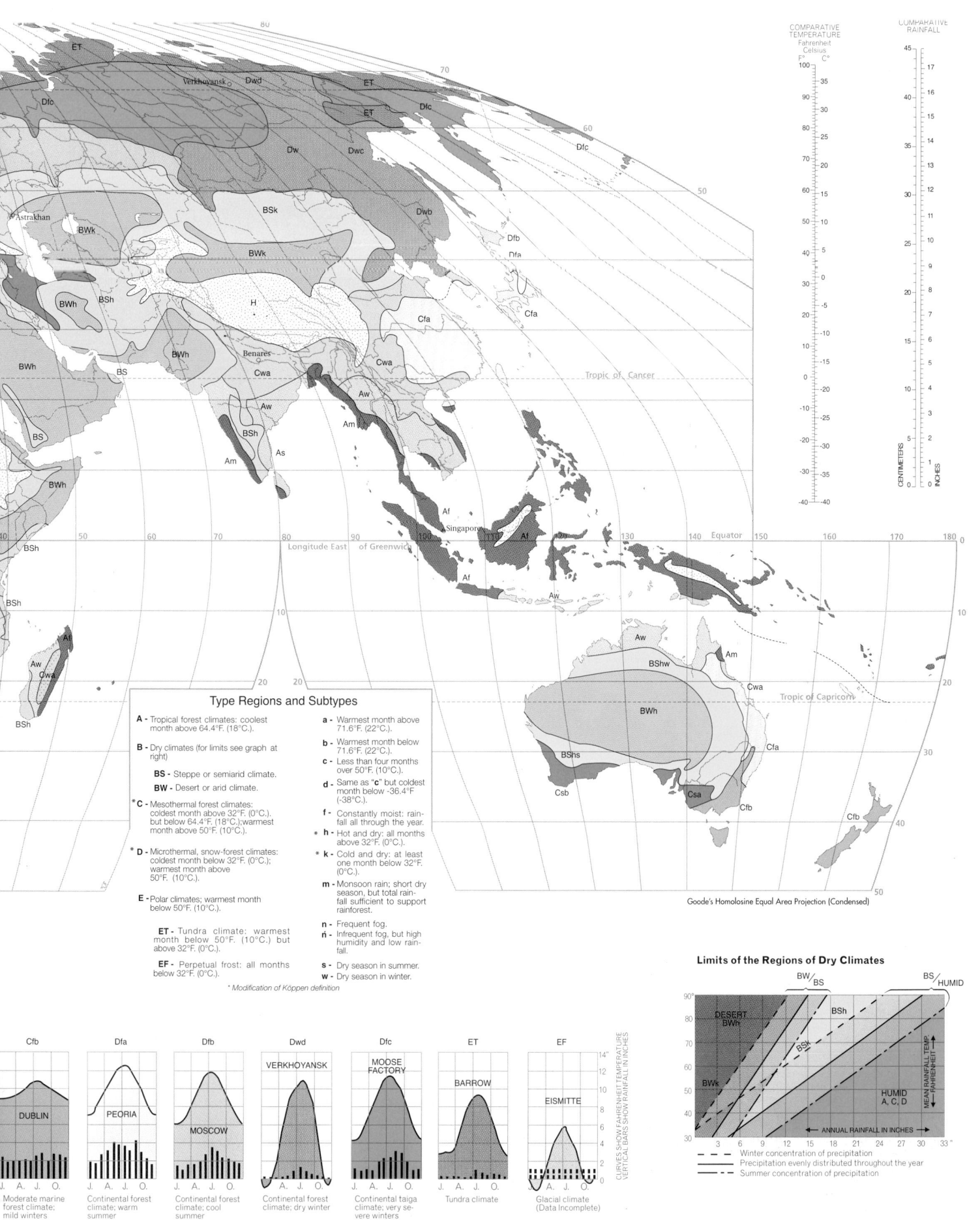

COMPARATIVE
TEMPERATURE
Fahrenheit
Celsius

COMPARATIVE
RAINFALL

Goode's Homolosine Equal Area Projection (Condensed)

Type Regions and Subtypes

A - Tropical forest climates: coolest month above 64.4°F. (18°C.).

B - Dry climates (for limits see graph at right)

    BS - Steppe or semiarid climate.

    BW - Desert or arid climate.

* **C** - Mesothermal forest climates: coldest month above 32°F. (0°C.). but below 64.4°F. (18°C.);warmest month above 50°F. (10°C.).

* **D** - Microthermal, snow-forest climates: coldest month below 32°F. (0°C.); warmest month above 50°F. (10°C.).

E - Polar climates; warmest month below 50°F. (10°C.).

    ET - Tundra climate: warmest month below 50°F. (10°C.) but above 32°F. (0°C.).

    EF - Perpetual frost: all months below 32°F. (0°C.).

* Modification of Köppen definition

a - Warmest month above 71.6°F. (22°C.).

b - Warmest month below 71.6°F. (22°C.).

c - Less than four months over 50°F. (10°C.).

d - Same as "**c**" but coldest month below -36.4°F (-38°C.).

f - Constantly moist: rainfall all through the year.

* **h** - Hot and dry: all months above 32°F. (0°C.).

* **k** - Cold and dry: at least one month below 32°F. (0°C.).

m - Monsoon rain; short dry season, but total rainfall sufficient to support rainforest.

n - Frequent fog.

ń - Infrequent fog, but high humidity and low rainfall.

s - Dry season in summer.

w - Dry season in winter.

Limits of the Regions of Dry Climates

CURVES SHOW FAHRENHEIT TEMPERATURE
VERTICAL BARS SHOW RAINFALL IN INCHES

Cfb	Dfa	Dfb	Dwd	Dfc	ET	EF
DUBLIN	PEORIA	MOSCOW	VERKHOYANSK	MOOSE FACTORY	BARROW	EISMITTE
Moderate marine forest climate; mild winters	Continental forest climate; warm summer	Continental forest climate; cool summer	Continental forest climate; dry winter	Continental taiga climate; very severe winters	Tundra climate	Glacial climate (Data Incomplete)

--- Winter concentration of precipitation
---- Precipitation evenly distributed throughout the year
—·— Summer concentration of precipitation

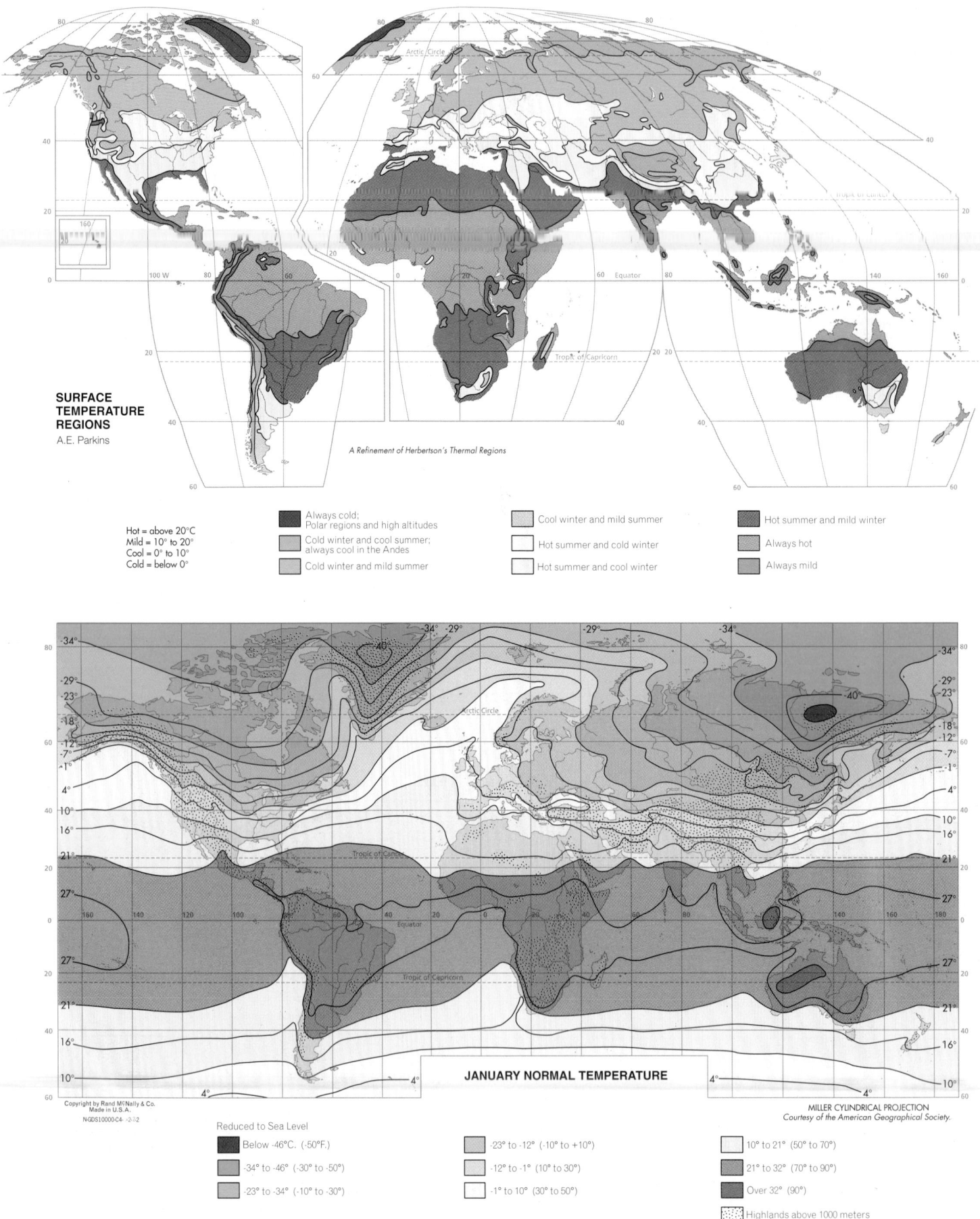

SURFACE TEMPERATURE REGIONS

A.E. Parkins

A Refinement of Herbertson's Thermal Regions

Hot = above 20°C
Mild = 10° to 20°
Cool = 0° to 10°
Cold = below 0°

- Always cold; Polar regions and high altitudes
- Cold winter and cool summer; always cool in the Andes
- Cold winter and mild summer
- Cool winter and mild summer
- Hot summer and cold winter
- Hot summer and cool winter
- Hot summer and mild winter
- Always hot
- Always mild

JANUARY NORMAL TEMPERATURE

MILLER CYLINDRICAL PROJECTION
Courtesy of the American Geographical Society.

Copyright by Rand McNally & Co.
Made in U.S.A.
NGDS10000-C4

Reduced to Sea Level

- Below -46°C. (-50°F.)
- -34° to -46° (-30° to -50°)
- -23° to -34° (-10° to -30°)
- -23° to -12° (-10° to +10°)
- -12° to -1° (10° to 30°)
- -1° to 10° (30° to 50°)
- 10° to 21° (50° to 70°)
- 21° to 32° (70° to 90°)
- Over 32° (90°)
- Highlands above 1000 meters

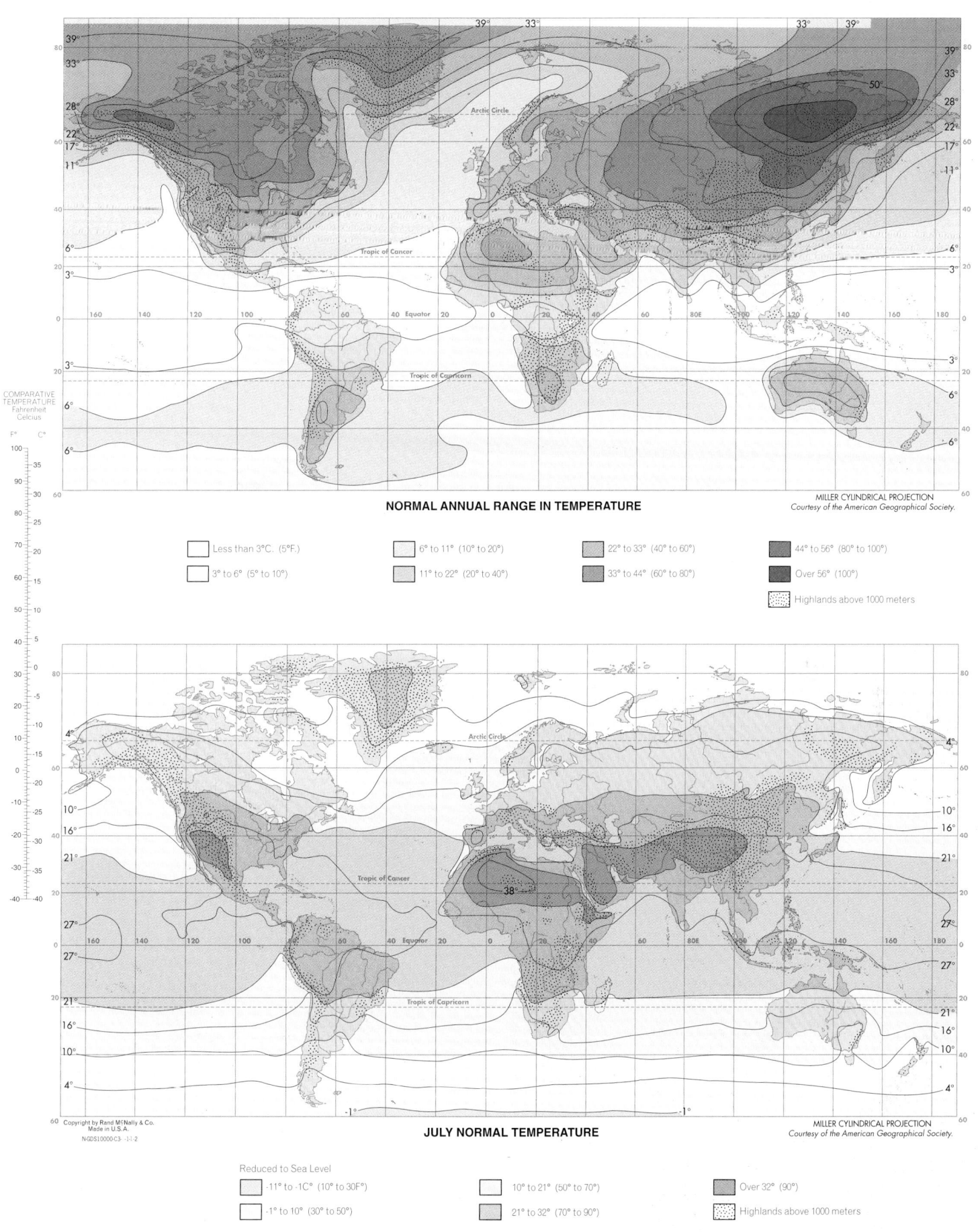

NORMAL ANNUAL RANGE IN TEMPERATURE

MILLER CYLINDRICAL PROJECTION
Courtesy of the American Geographical Society.

COMPARATIVE
TEMPERATURE
Fahrenheit
Celcius

☐ Less than 3°C. (5°F.)

☐ 3° to 6° (5° to 10°)

☐ 6° to 11° (10° to 20°)

☐ 11° to 22° (20° to 40°)

☐ 22° to 33° (40° to 60°)

☐ 33° to 44° (60° to 80°)

☐ 44° to 56° (80° to 100°)

☐ Over 56° (100°)

⫶ Highlands above 1000 meters

JULY NORMAL TEMPERATURE

MILLER CYLINDRICAL PROJECTION
Courtesy of the American Geographical Society.

Copyright by Rand McNally & Co.
Made in U.S.A.
NGDS10000C3 -14-2

Reduced to Sea Level

☐ -11° to -1C° (10° to 30F°)

☐ -1° to 10° (30° to 50°)

☐ 10° to 21° (50° to 70°)

☐ 21° to 32° (70° to 90°)

☐ Over 32° (90°)

⫶ Highlands above 1000 meters

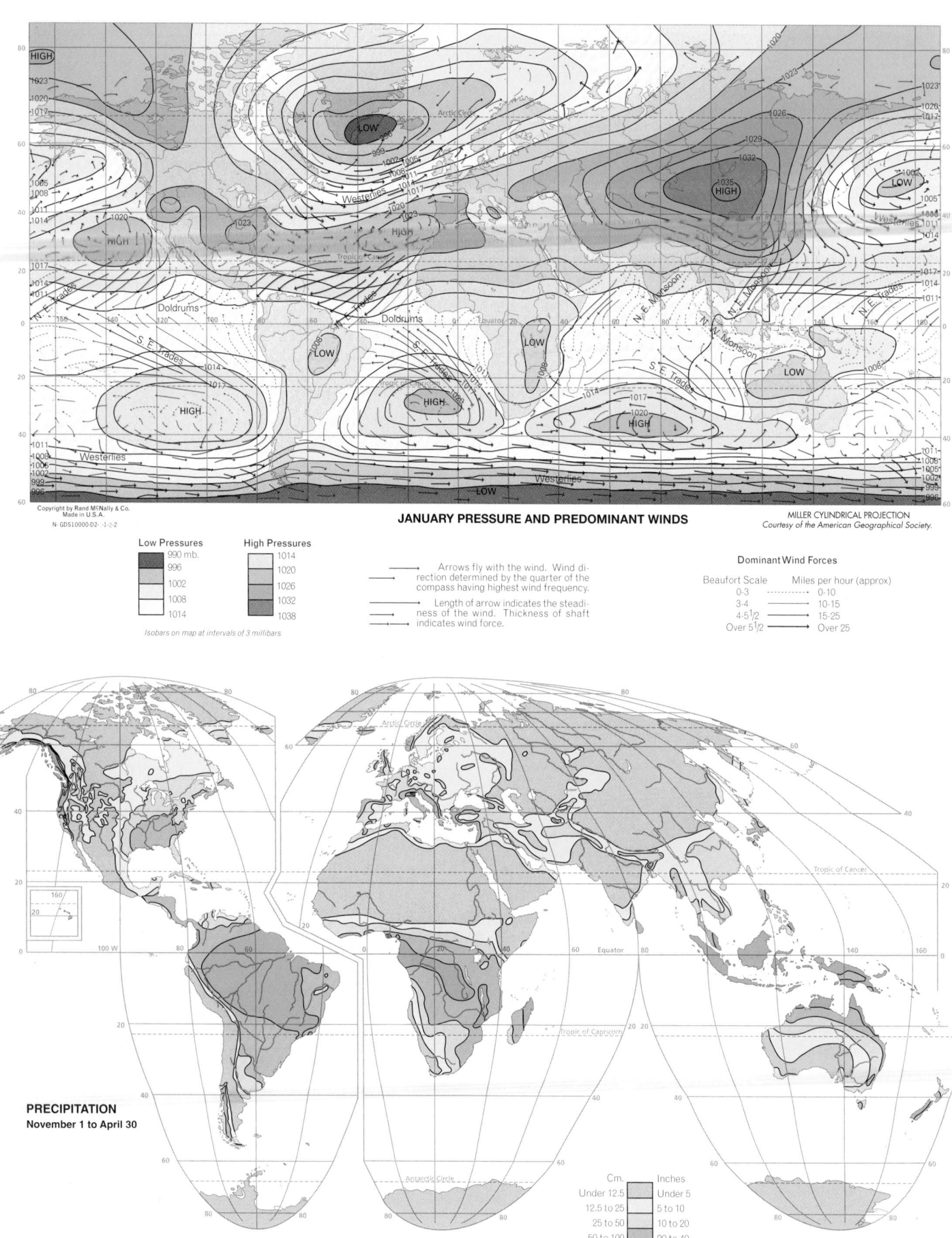

JANUARY PRESSURE AND PREDOMINANT WINDS

Copyright by Rand McNally & Co.
Made in U.S.A.
N- GDS10000-D2- -1-2-2

MILLER CYLINDRICAL PROJECTION
Courtesy of the American Geographical Society.

Low Pressures

| 990 mb. |
| 996 |
| 1002 |
| 1008 |
| 1014 |

High Pressures

| 1014 |
| 1020 |
| 1026 |
| 1032 |
| 1038 |

Isobars on map at intervals of 3 millibars

Arrows fly with the wind. Wind direction determined by the quarter of the compass having highest wind frequency.

Length of arrow indicates the steadiness of the wind. Thickness of shaft indicates wind force.

Dominant Wind Forces

Beaufort Scale	Miles per hour (approx)
0-3	0-10
3-4	10-15
4-5½	15-25
Over 5½	Over 25

PRECIPITATION
November 1 to April 30

Cm.	Inches
Under 12.5	Under 5
12.5 to 25	5 to 10
25 to 50	10 to 20
50 to 100	20 to 40
Over 100	Over 40

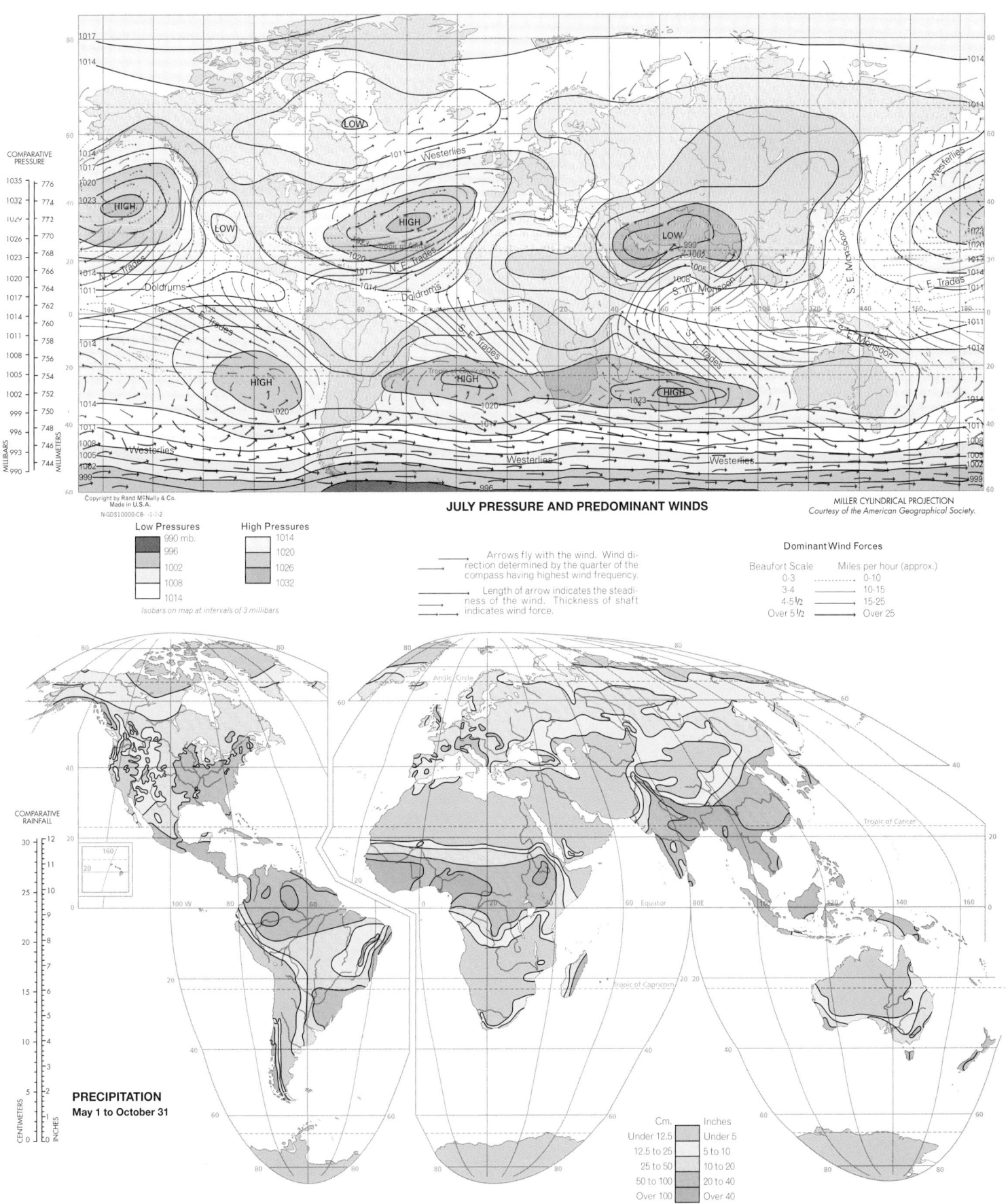

COMPARATIVE
PRESSURE

MILLIBARS	MILLIMETERS
1035	776
1032	774
1029	772
1026	770
1023	768
1020	766
1017	764
1014	762
1011	760
1008	758
1005	756
1002	754
999	752
996	750
993	748
990	746
	744

Copyright by Rand McNally & Co.
Made in U.S.A.
N-GDS10000-C8- -1-2-2

JULY PRESSURE AND PREDOMINANT WINDS

MILLER CYLINDRICAL PROJECTION
Courtesy of the American Geographical Society.

Low Pressures
- 990 mb.
- 996
- 1002
- 1008
- 1014

High Pressures
- 1014
- 1020
- 1026
- 1032

Isobars on map at intervals of 3 millibars

Arrows fly with the wind. Wind direction determined by the quarter of the compass having highest wind frequency.

Length of arrow indicates the steadiness of the wind. Thickness of shaft indicates wind force.

Dominant Wind Forces

Beaufort Scale	Miles per hour (approx.)
0-3	0-10
3-4	10-15
4-5½	15-25
Over 5½	Over 25

COMPARATIVE
RAINFALL

CENTIMETERS	INCHES
30	12
	11
25	10
	9
20	8
	7
15	6
	5
10	4
	3
5	2
	1
0	0

PRECIPITATION
May 1 to October 31

Cm.	Inches
Under 12.5	Under 5
12.5 to 25	5 to 10
25 to 50	10 to 20
50 to 100	20 to 40
Over 100	Over 40

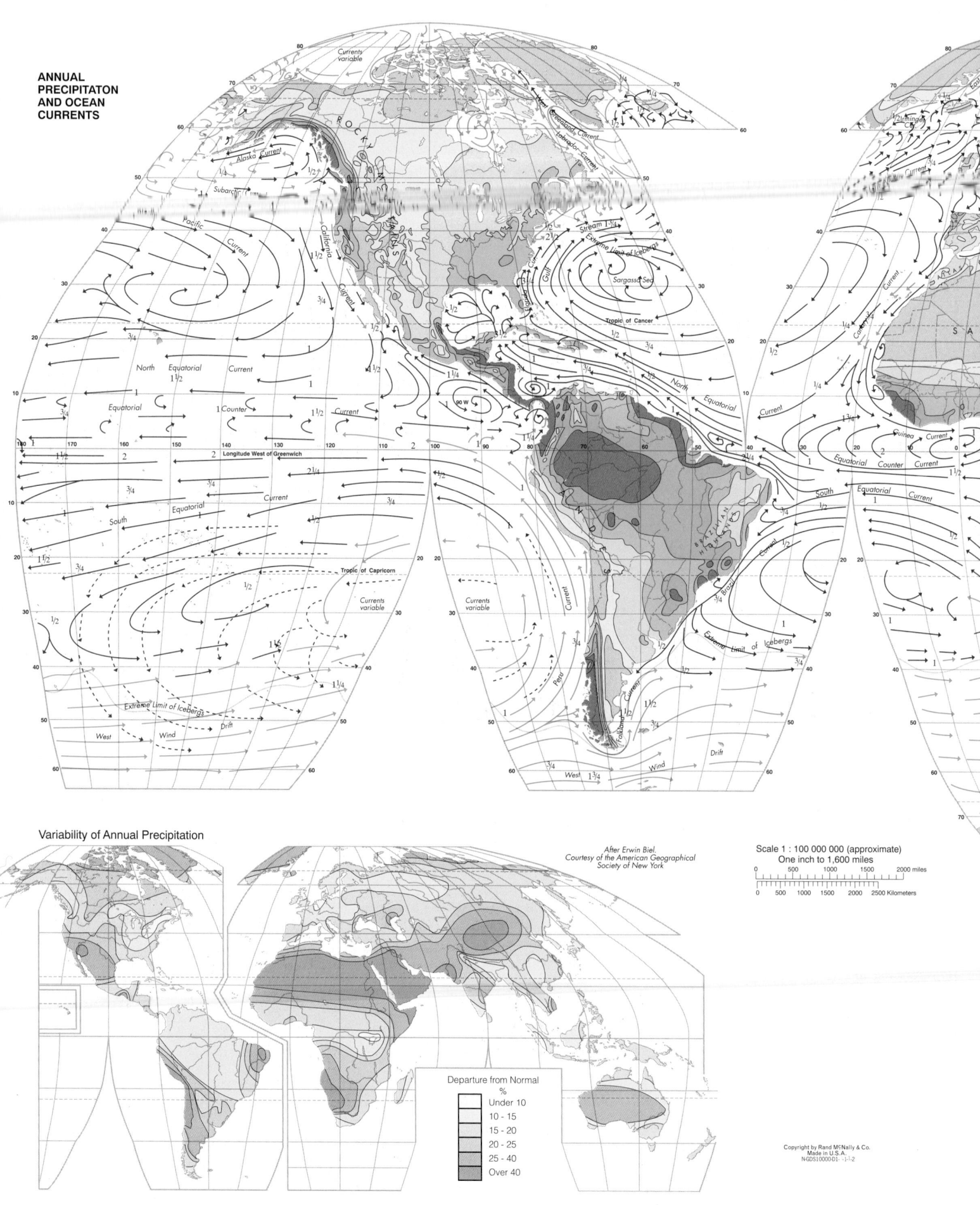

**ANNUAL
PRECIPITATON
AND OCEAN
CURRENTS**

Variability of Annual Precipitation

*After Erwin Biel.
Courtesy of the American Geographical
Society of New York*

Scale 1 : 100 000 000 (approximate)
One inch to 1,600 miles

Departure from Normal
%
Under 10
10 - 15
15 - 20
20 - 25
25 - 40
Over 40

Copyright by Rand McNally & Co.
Made in U.S.A.
N-GDS10000-D1- -\-\-2

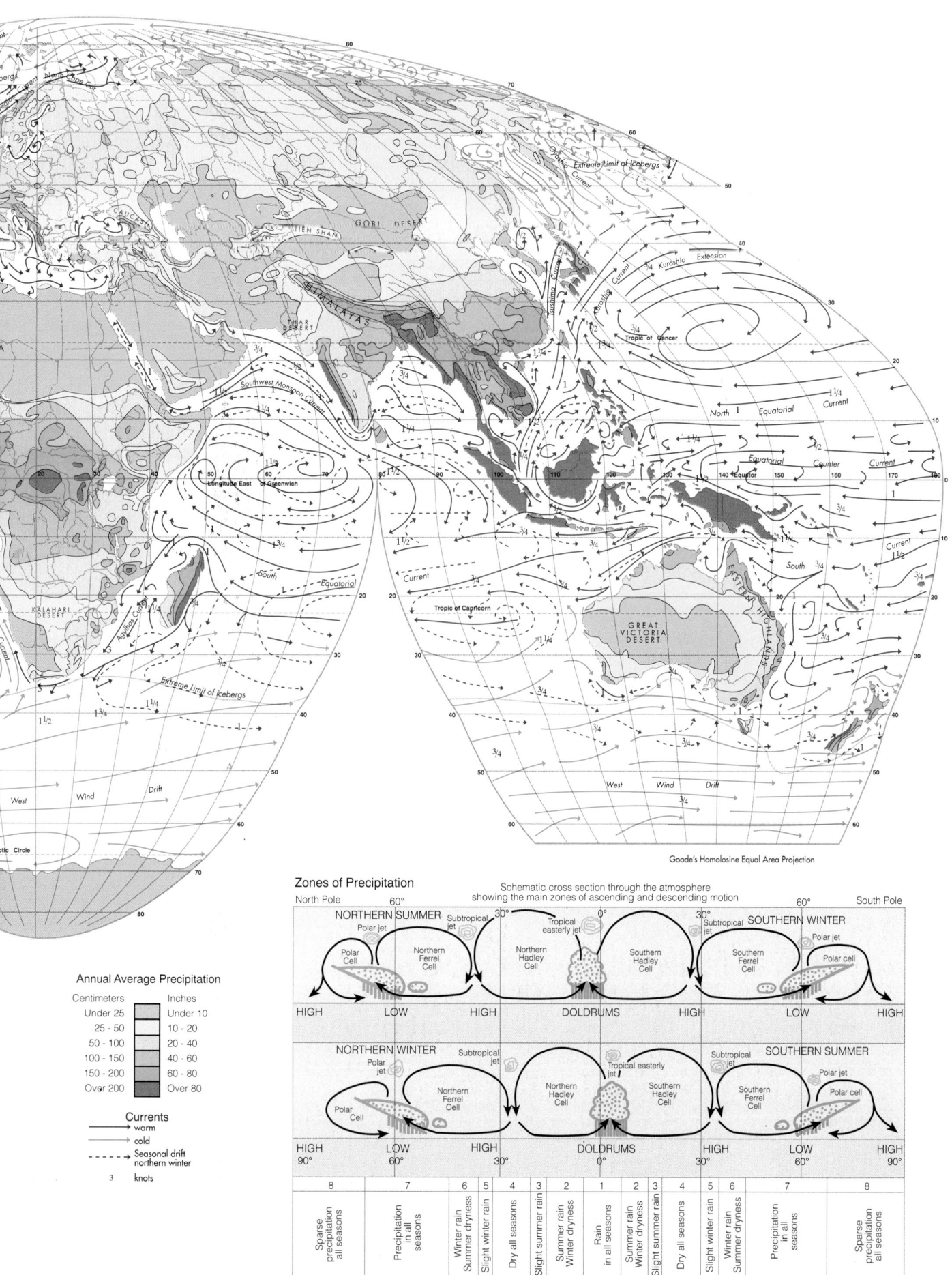

Goode's Homolosine Equal Area Projection

Zones of Precipitation

Schematic cross section through the atmosphere
showing the main zones of ascending and descending motion

North Pole   60°   30°   0°   30°   60°   South Pole

NORTHERN SUMMER   Subtropical jet   Tropical easterly jet   SOUTHERN WINTER

Polar jet   Northern Ferrel Cell   Northern Hadley Cell   Southern Hadley Cell   Southern Ferrel Cell   Polar jet

Polar Cell   Polar cell

HIGH   LOW   HIGH   DOLDRUMS   HIGH   LOW   HIGH

NORTHERN WINTER   Subtropical jet   Tropical easterly   SOUTHERN SUMMER

Polar jet   Northern Ferrel Cell   Northern Hadley Cell   Southern Hadley Cell   Southern Ferrel Cell   Polar jet

Polar Cell   Polar cell

HIGH   LOW   HIGH   DOLDRUMS   HIGH   LOW   HIGH
90°   60°   30°   0°   30°   60°   90°

8	7	6	5	4	3	2	1	2	3	4	5	6	7	8
Sparse precipitation all seasons	Precipitation in all seasons	Winter rain Summer dryness	Slight winter rain	Dry all seasons	Slight summer rain	Summer rain Winter dryness	Rain in all seasons	Summer rain Winter dryness	Slight summer rain	Dry all seasons	Slight winter rain	Winter rain Summer dryness	Precipitation in all seasons	Sparse precipitation all seasons

Annual Average Precipitation

Centimeters	Inches
Under 25	Under 10
25 - 50	10 - 20
50 - 100	20 - 40
100 - 150	40 - 60
150 - 200	60 - 80
Over 200	Over 80

Currents

→ warm
→ cold
--→ Seasonal drift
     northern winter
3   knots

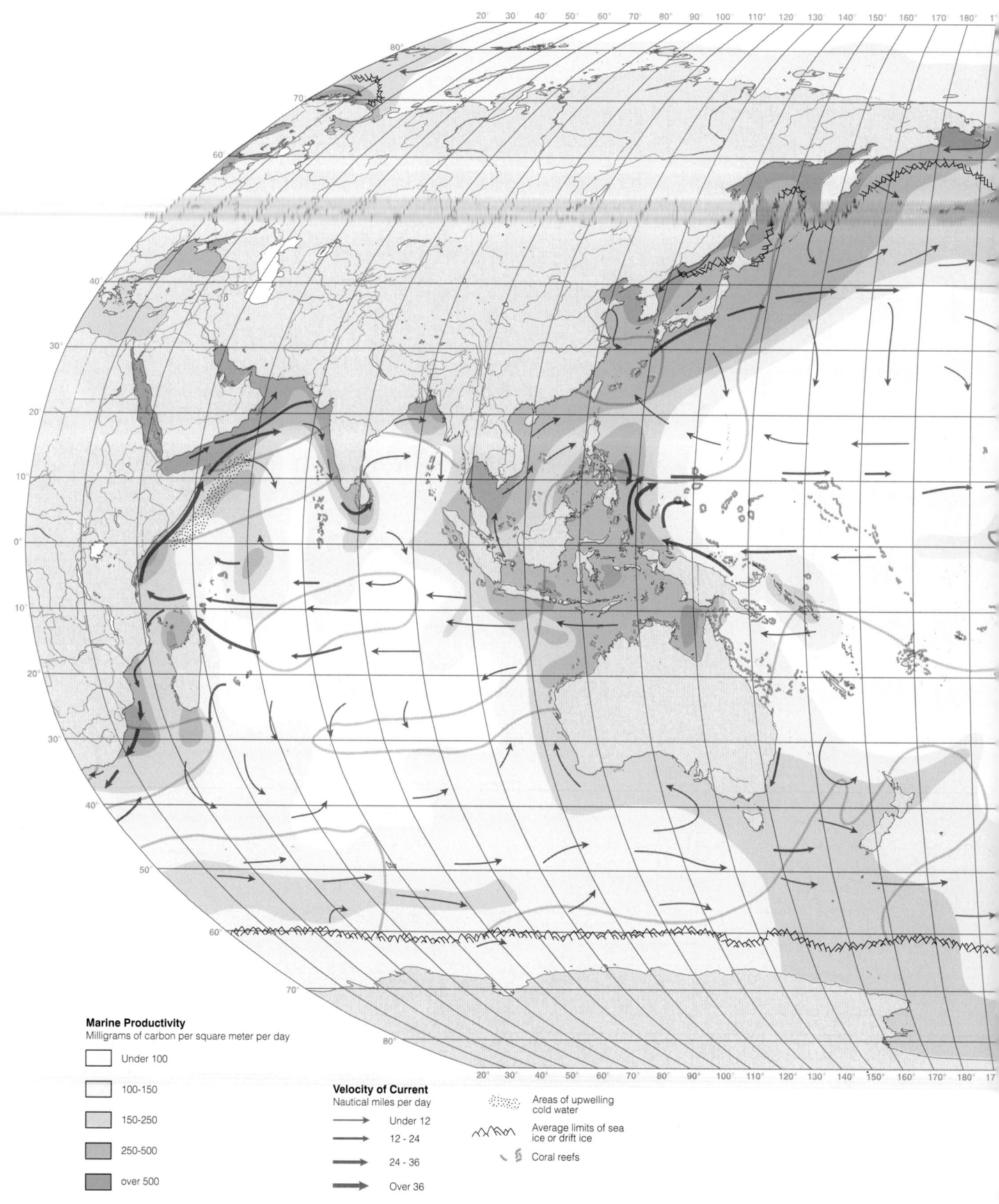

Marine Productivity
Milligrams of carbon per square meter per day

Under 100

100-150

150-250

250-500

over 500

Velocity of Current
Nautical miles per day

→ Under 12

→ 12 - 24

→ 24 - 36

→ Over 36

Areas of upwelling
cold water

Average limits of sea
ice or drift ice

Coral reefs

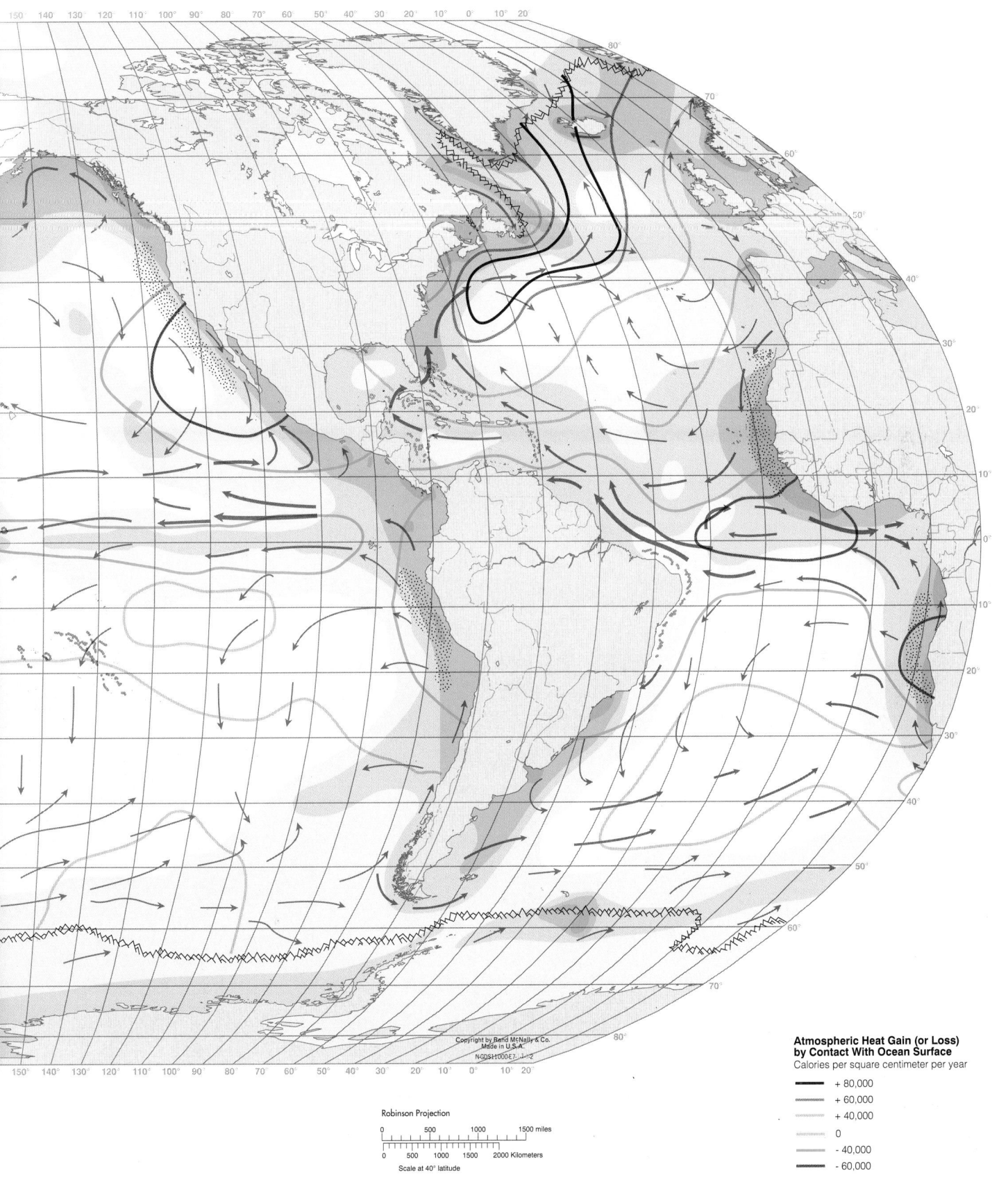

**Atmospheric Heat Gain (or Loss)
by Contact With Ocean Surface**
Calories per square centimeter per year

────	+ 80,000
────	+ 60,000
────	+ 40,000
────	0
────	- 40,000
────	- 60,000

Robinson Projection

0   500   1000   1500 miles

0   500   1000   1500   2000 Kilometers

Scale at 40° latitude

Copyright by Rand McNally & Co.
Made in U.S.A.
N0DSH1000E7.1-2

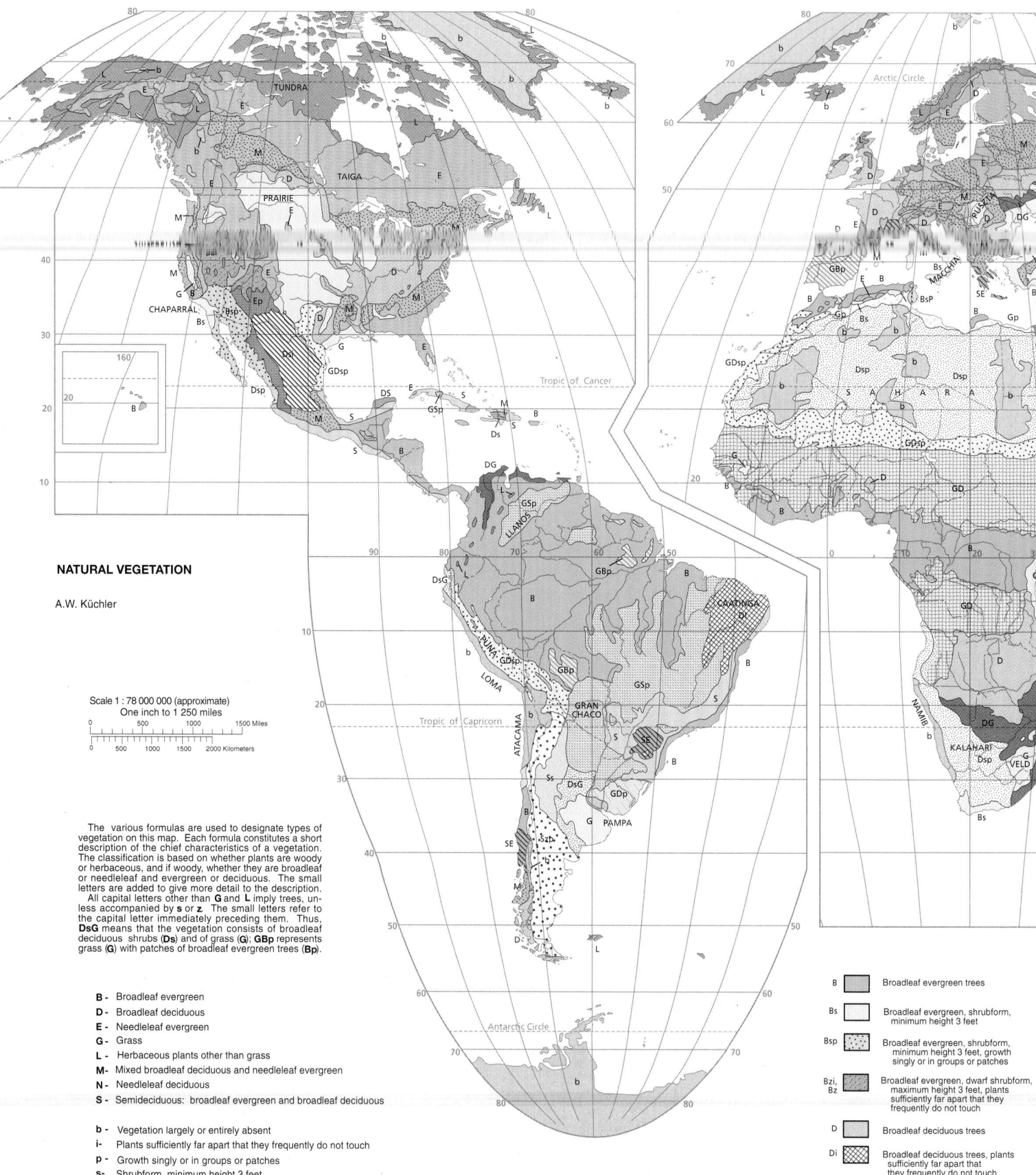

NATURAL VEGETATION

A.W. Küchler

Scale 1 : 78 000 000 (approximate)
One inch to 1 250 miles

0   500   1000   1500 Miles

0   500   1000   1500   2000 Kilometers

The various formulas are used to designate types of vegetation on this map. Each formula constitutes a short description of the chief characteristics of a vegetation. The classification is based on whether plants are woody or herbaceous, and if woody, whether they are broadleaf or needleleaf and evergreen or deciduous. The small letters are added to give more detail to the description.

All capital letters other than **G** and **L** imply trees, unless accompanied by **s** or **z**. The small letters refer to the capital letter immediately preceding them. Thus, **DsG** means that the vegetation consists of broadleaf deciduous shrubs (**Ds**) and of grass (**G**); **GBp** represents grass (**G**) with patches of broadleaf evergreen trees (**Bp**).

B - Broadleaf evergreen

D - Broadleaf deciduous

E - Needleleaf evergreen

G - Grass

L - Herbaceous plants other than grass

M - Mixed broadleaf deciduous and needleleaf evergreen

N - Needleleaf deciduous

S - Semideciduous: broadleaf evergreen and broadleaf deciduous

b - Vegetation largely or entirely absent

i - Plants sufficiently far apart that they frequently do not touch

p - Growth singly or in groups or patches

s - Shrubform, minimum height 3 feet

z - Dwarf shrubform, maximum height 3 feet

B		Broadleaf evergreen trees
Bs		Broadleaf evergreen, shrubform, minimum height 3 feet
Bsp		Broadleaf evergreen, shrubform, minimum height 3 feet, growth singly or in groups or patches
Bzi, Bz		Broadleaf evergreen, dwarf shrubform, maximum height 3 feet, plants sufficiently far apart that they frequently do not touch
D		Broadleaf deciduous trees
Di		Broadleaf deciduous trees, plants sufficiently far apart that they frequently do not touch

Goode's Homolosine Equal Area Projection (Condensed)

	Broadleaf deciduous, shrubform, minimum height 3 feet	E		Needleleaf evergreen trees	GDsp		Grass and other herbaceous plants Broadleaf deciduous, shrubform, minimum height 3 feet, growth singly or in groups or patches	S		Semideciduous: broadleaf evergreen and broadleaf deciduous trees
i	Broadleaf deciduous, shrubform, minimum height 3 feet, plants sufficiently far apart that they frequently do not touch	Ep		Needleleaf evergreen trees, growth singly or in groups or patches				Ss		Semideciduous: broadleaf evergreen and broadleaf deciduous, shrubform, minimum height 3 feet
	Broadleaf deciduous, shrubform, minimum height 3 feet, growth singly or in groups or patches	G		Grass and other herbaceous plants	GSp		Grass and other herbaceous plants Semideciduous: broadleaf evergreen and broadleaf deciduous trees, growth singly or in groups or patches	SsG		Semideciduous: broadleaf evergreen and broadleaf deciduous, shrubform, minimum height 3 feet Grass and other herbaceous plants
	Broadleaf deciduous, dwarf shrubform, maximum height 3 feet, growth singly or in groups or patches	Gp		Grass and other herbaceous plants, growth singly or in groups or patches	L		Herbaceous plants other than grass	Szp		Semideciduous: broadleaf evergeen and broadleaf deciduous, dwarf shrub-form, maximum height 3 feet, growth singly or in groups or patches
	Broadleaf deciduous, shrubform, minimum height 3 feet Grass and other herbaceous plants	GBp		Grass and other herbaceous plants Broadleaf evergreen trees, growth singly or in groups or patches	M		Mixed: broadleaf deciduous and needleleaf evergreen trees	SE		Semideciduous: broadleaf evergreen and broadleaf deciduous trees Needleleaf evergreen trees
	Broadleaf deciduous trees Grass and other herbaceous plants	GD		Grass and other herbaceous plants Broadleaf deciduous trees	N		Needleleaf deciduous trees	b		Vegetation largely or entirely absent
	Broadleaf deciduous trees Broadleaf evergreen, shrubform, minimum height 3 feet	GDp		Grass and other herbaceous plants Broadleaf deciduous trees, growth singly or in groups or patches	ND		Needleleaf deciduous trees Broadleaf deciduous trees			

26

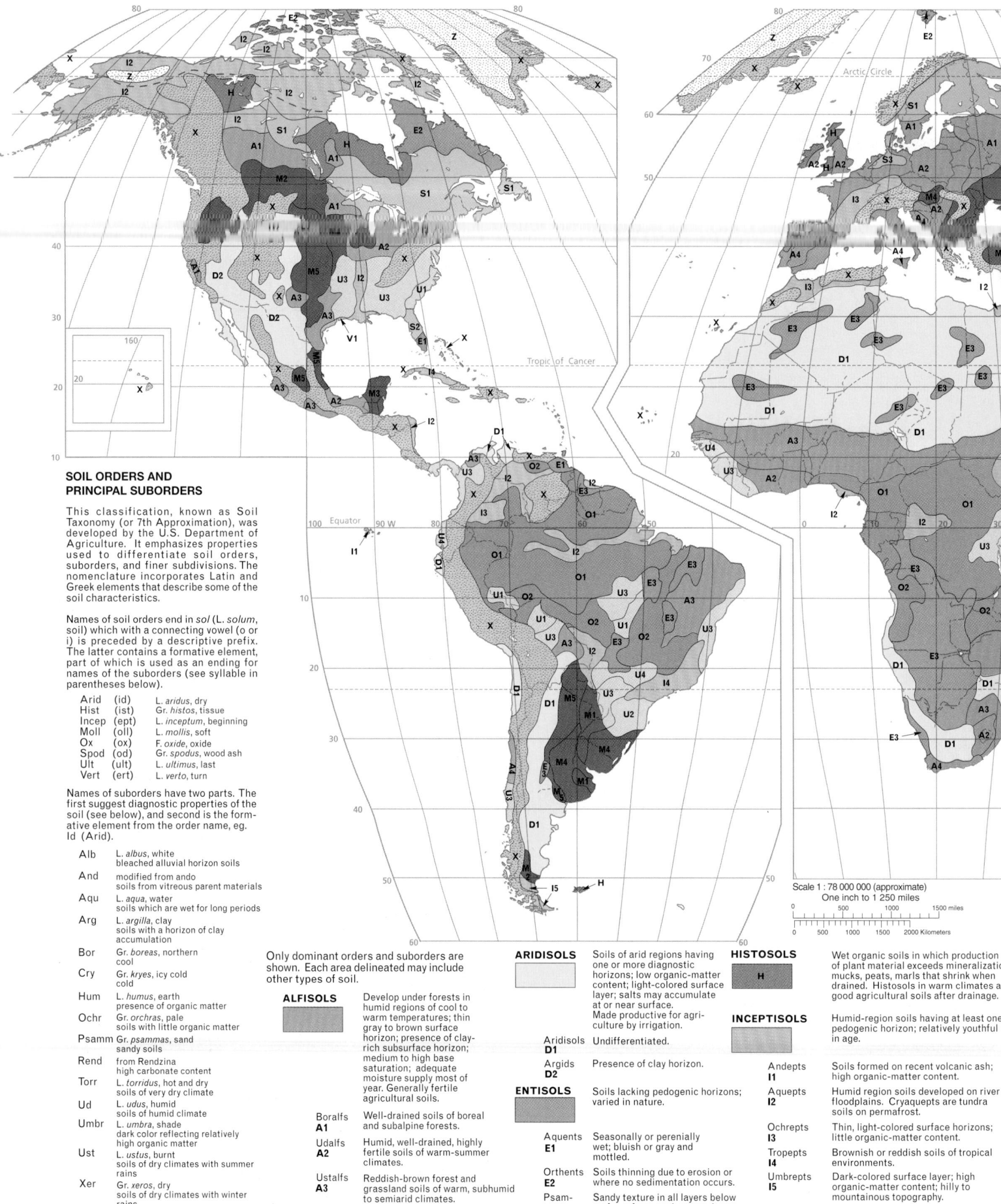

SOIL ORDERS AND PRINCIPAL SUBORDERS

This classification, known as Soil Taxonomy (or 7th Approximation), was developed by the U.S. Department of Agriculture. It emphasizes properties used to differentiate soil orders, suborders, and finer subdivisions. The nomenclature incorporates Latin and Greek elements that describe some of the soil characteristics.

Names of soil orders end in *sol* (L. *solum*, soil) which with a connecting vowel (o or i) is preceded by a descriptive prefix. The latter contains a formative element, part of which is used as an ending for names of the suborders (see syllable in parentheses below).

Arid	(id)	L. *aridus*, dry
Hist	(ist)	Gr. *histos*, tissue
Incep	(ept)	L. *inceptum*, beginning
Moll	(oll)	L. *mollis*, soft
Ox	(ox)	F. *oxide*, oxide
Spod	(od)	Gr. *spodos*, wood ash
Ult	(ult)	L. *ultimus*, last
Vert	(ert)	L. *verto*, turn

Names of suborders have two parts. The first suggest diagnostic properties of the soil (see below), and second is the formative element from the order name, eg. Id (Arid).

Alb	L. *albus*, white	bleached alluvial horizon soils
And	modified from ando	soils from vitreous parent materials
Aqu	L. *aqua*, water	soils which are wet for long periods
Arg	L. *argilla*, clay	soils with a horizon of clay accumulation
Bor	Gr. *boreas*, northern	cool
Cry	Gr. *kryes*, icy cold	cold
Hum	L. *humus*, earth	presence of organic matter
Ochr	Gr. *orchras*, pale	soils with little organic matter
Psamm	Gr. *psammas*, sand	sandy soils
Rend	from Rendzina	high carbonate content
Torr	L. *torridus*, hot and dry	soils of very dry climate
Ud	L. *udus*, humid	soils of humid climate
Umbr	L. *umbra*, shade	dark color reflecting relatively high organic matter
Ust	L. *ustus*, burnt	soils of dry climates with summer rains
Xer	Gr. *xeros*, dry	soils of dry climates with winter rains

Only dominant orders and suborders are shown. Each area delineated may include other types of soil.

ALFISOLS

Develop under forests in humid regions of cool to warm temperatures; thin gray to brown surface horizon; presence of clay-rich subsurface horizon; medium to high base saturation; adequate moisture supply most of year. Generally fertile agricultural soils.

Boralfs A1	Well-drained soils of boreal and subalpine forests.
Udalfs A2	Humid, well-drained, highly fertile soils of warm-summer climates.
Ustalfs A3	Reddish-brown forest and grassland soils of warm, subhumid to semiarid climates.
Xeralfs A4	Reddish soils lacking moisture during summer in Mediterranean climate zones.

ARIDISOLS

Soils of arid regions having one or more diagnostic horizons; low organic-matter content; light-colored surface layer; salts may accumulate at or near surface. Made productive for agriculture by irrigation.

| Aridisols D1 | Undifferentiated. |
| Argids D2 | Presence of clay horizon. |

ENTISOLS

Soils lacking pedogenic horizons; varied in nature.

Aquents E1	Seasonally or perenially wet; bluish or gray and mottled.
Orthents E2	Soils thinning due to erosion or where no sedimentation occurs.
Psamments E3	Sandy texture in all layers below surface; form on dune sands.

HISTOSOLS

Wet organic soils in which production of plant material exceeds mineralization; mucks, peats, marls that shrink when drained. Histosols in warm climates are good agricultural soils after drainage.

INCEPTISOLS

Humid-region soils having at least one pedogenic horizon; relatively youthful in age.

Andepts I1	Soils formed on recent volcanic ash; high organic-matter content.
Aquepts I2	Humid region soils developed on river floodplains. Cryaquepts are tundra soils on permafrost.
Ochrepts I3	Thin, light-colored surface horizons; little organic-matter content.
Tropepts I4	Brownish or reddish soils of tropical environments.
Umbrepts I5	Dark-colored surface layer; high organic-matter content; hilly or mountainous topography.

Scale 1 : 78 000 000 (approximate)
One inch to 1 250 miles

0   500   1000   1500 miles

0   500   1000   1500   2000 Kilometers

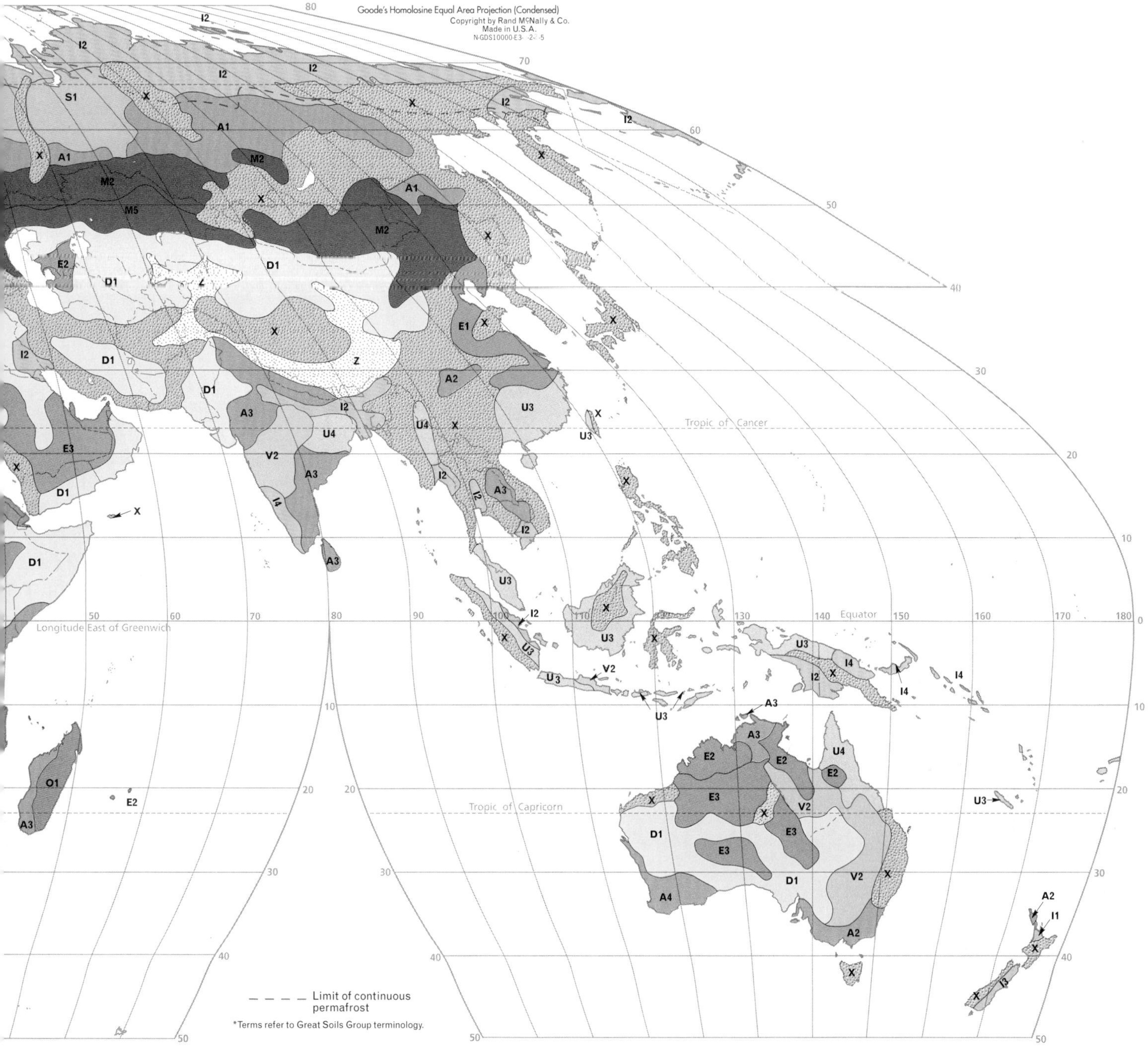

Goode's Homolosine Equal Area Projection (Condensed)
Copyright by Rand M⁰Nally & Co.
Made in U.S.A.
N-GDS10000-E3- -2- -5

Longitude East of Greenwich

Tropic of Cancer

Equator

Tropic of Capricorn

— — — Limit of continuous
permafrost

*Terms refer to Great Soils Group terminology.

▮LLISOLS	Deep-profile soils with seasonal moisture deficit associated with grasslands; dark brown to black upper layer; may have subsurface horizon of calcium accumulation; high base saturation. Very productive for grain crops.	
Albolls **M1**	Soils with a grayish subsurface horizon over clay layer and a fluctuating water table.	
Borolls **M2**	Well-drained, fertile grassland soils of cool summers and cold winters.	
Rendolls **M3**	Formed on calcareous limestones.	
Udolls **M4**	Freely drained soils of humid regions with warm summers; excellent agricultural soils.	
Ustolls **M5**	Fertile agricultural soils of subhumid climates.	
Xerolls **M6**	Pronounced soil-moisture deficit during high-sun season; associated with Mediterranean climates.	

OXISOLS

Deeply weathered tropical and subtropical soils of low natural fertility; low base saturation; limited ability to hold soil nutrients against leaching; presence of plinthite (laterite) layers. Generally unsuited to large-scale agricultural production.

Orthox **O1** — Hot and nearly always moist; associated with tropical rainforests.

Ustox **O2** — Hot to warm forest and savanna soils with a drier season of low soil-moisture availability.

SPODOSOLS

Soils of moist climates ranging from subtropical to cold conditions; include a spodic subsurface horizon incorporating active organic matter beneath a light-colored, leached, sandy horizon. Generally marginal for agriculture.

Spodo-sols **S1** — Undifferentiated, mostly in high latitudes.

Aquods **S2** — Seasonally wet developed on sandy parent material.

Humods **S3** — Considerable organic matter present in subsurface horizon.

Orthods **S4** — Subsurface accumulations of iron, aluminum, and organic matter.

ULTISOLS

Tropical and subtropical soils with a variety of soil moisture regimes; subsurface clay horizon; low base saturation; very old soils characterized by long weathering of clay minerals; low ability to hold nutrients against leaching. Often marginal for agriculture.

Aquults **U1** — Seasonally wet with mottled, gray subsurface horizon.

Humults **U2** — Dark soils with high organic-matter content, warm temperatures.

Udults **U3** — Low organic-matter content and temperate to hot conditions.

Ustults **U4** — Seasonally dry, warm to hot conditions.

VERTISOLS

Dark tropical and subtropical soils developed on heavy clays; deep shrinkage cracks appear during dry season which become filled with loose surface materials that absorb moisture and swell during wet season. Generally fertile and well suited to crop production.

Uderts **V1** — Generally moist with limited period for shrinkage cracks to develop.

Usterts **V2** — Over three months of shrinkage-crack formation.

MOUNTAIN SOILS

Soils with various moisture and temperature regimes; mainly high altitude soils forming on steep slopes; soils vary greatly within a short distance.

Areas with little or no soils.

APPROXIMATE CORRELATION WITH
OTHER SOIL CLASSIFICATION SYSTEMS

Soil Taxonomy	Great Soil Groups (former U.S. system)	Canadian system
Udalfs	Gray-brown Podzolic	Luvisolic Gray-Brown
Ustalfs	Reddish Chestnut; Red and Yellow Podzolic	
Aridisols	Desert and Reddish Desert Solonetz, Solonchak	
Entisols	Lithosols	Regosolic
Histosols	Bog	Organic
Inceptisol		Brunisolic
Orthents	Lithosols	
Aquepts	Humic Gley	Gleysolic
Cryaquept	Tundra	Cryosolic
Boralfs	Chernozem	Luvisolic Gray; Solonetzic
Borolls	Chernozem Chestnut Brown	Chernozemic, Solonetzic
Rendolls	Rendzina	
Udolls	Prairie	
Ustolls	Brown	
Oxisols	Latosols	
Humod		Humic Podzolic
Orthods	Podzols	Podzolic
Udults	Red and Yellow Podzolic Reddish Brown Lateritic	
Vertisols	Rendzina	

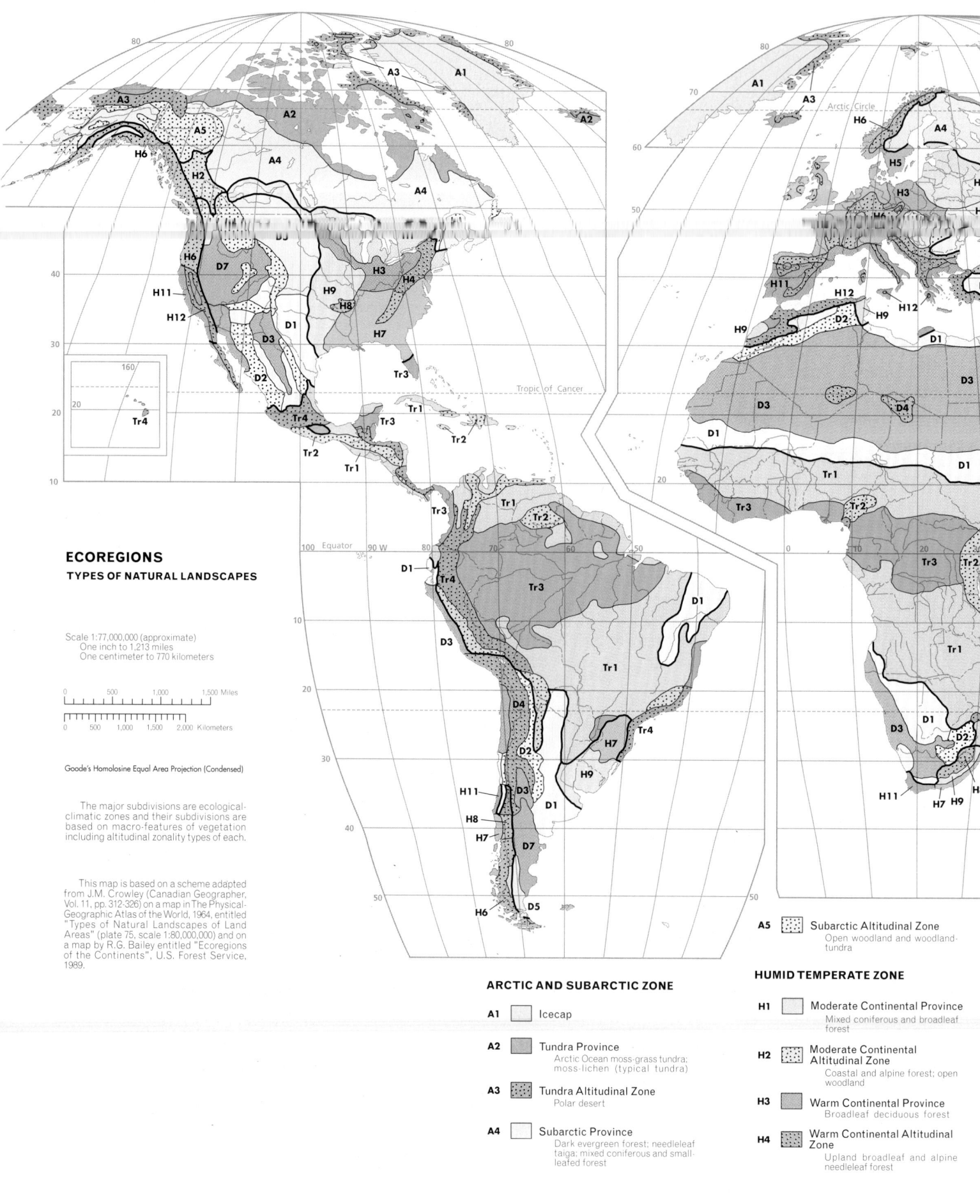

ECOREGIONS

TYPES OF NATURAL LANDSCAPES

Scale 1:77,000,000 (approximate)
One inch to 1,213 miles
One centimeter to 770 kilometers

500   1,000   1,500 Miles

500   1,000   1,500   2,000 Kilometers

Goode's Homolosine Equal Area Projection (Condensed)

The major subdivisions are ecological-climatic zones and their subdivisions are based on macro-features of vegetation including altitudinal zonality types of each.

This map is based on a scheme adapted from J.M. Crowley (Canadian Geographer, Vol. 11, pp. 312-326) on a map in The Physical-Geographic Atlas of the World, 1964, entitled "Types of Natural Landscapes of Land Areas" (plate 75, scale 1:80,000,000) and on a map by R.G. Bailey entitled "Ecoregions of the Continents", U.S. Forest Service, 1989.

ARCTIC AND SUBARCTIC ZONE

A1   Icecap

A2   Tundra Province
Arctic Ocean moss-grass tundra; moss-lichen (typical tundra)

A3   Tundra Altitudinal Zone
Polar desert

A4   Subarctic Province
Dark evergreen forest; needleleaf taiga; mixed coniferous and small-leafed forest

A5   Subarctic Altitudinal Zone
Open woodland and woodland-tundra

HUMID TEMPERATE ZONE

H1   Moderate Continental Province
Mixed coniferous and broadleaf forest

H2   Moderate Continental Altitudinal Zone
Coastal and alpine forest; open woodland

H3   Warm Continental Province
Broadleaf deciduous forest

H4   Warm Continental Altitudinal Zone
Upland broadleaf and alpine needleleaf forest

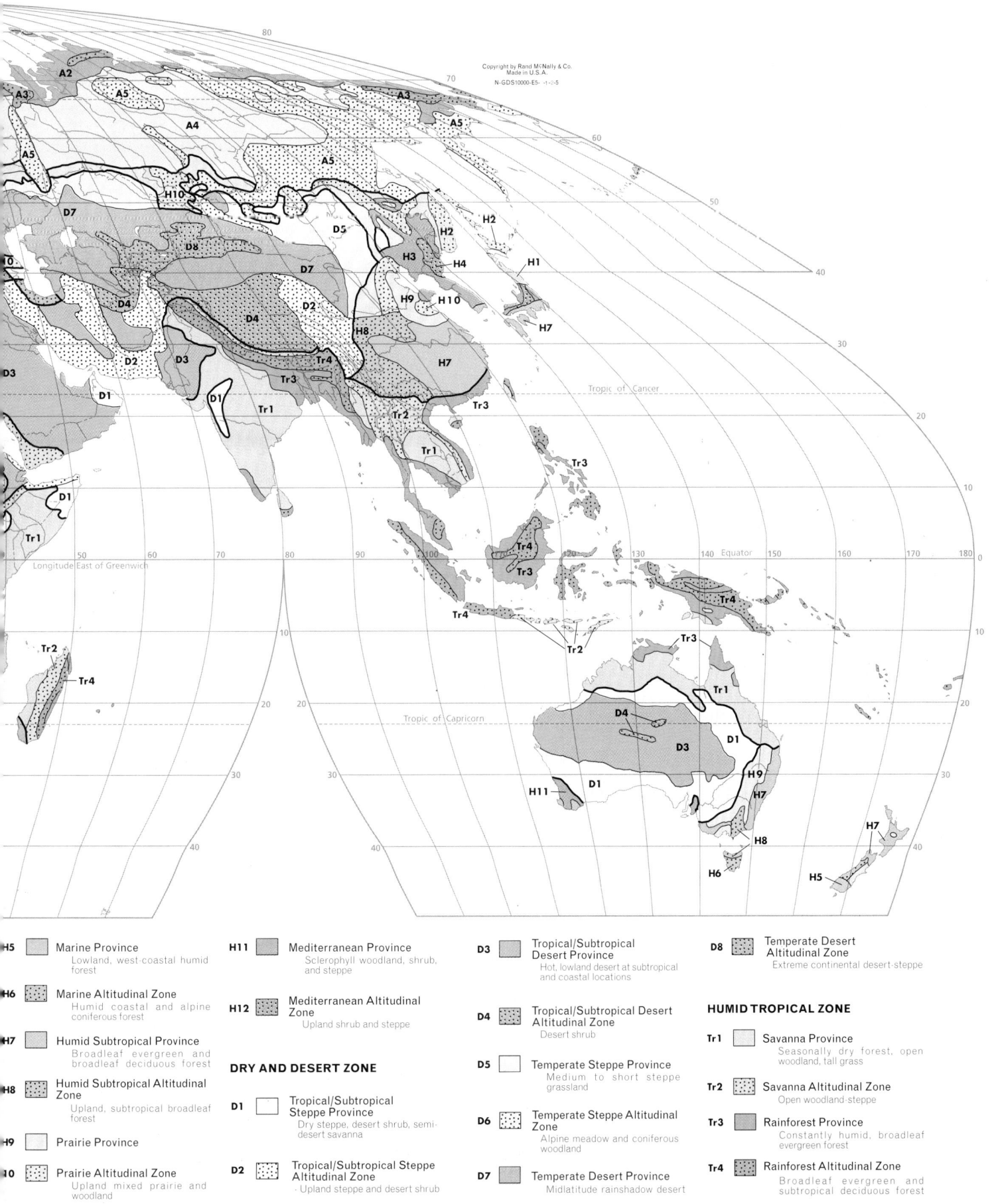

Copyright by Rand McNally & Co.
Made in U.S.A.
N-GDS10000-E5- -1-2-5

	Marine Province			Mediterranean Province			Tropical/Subtropical Desert Province			Temperate Desert Altitudinal Zone
H5	Lowland, west-coastal humid forest	H11		Sclerophyll woodland, shrub, and steppe	D3		Hot, lowland desert at subtropical and coastal locations	D8		Extreme continental desert-steppe	

H5 Marine Province
Lowland, west-coastal humid forest

H6 Marine Altitudinal Zone
Humid coastal and alpine coniferous forest

H7 Humid Subtropical Province
Broadleaf evergreen and broadleaf deciduous forest

H8 Humid Subtropical Altitudinal Zone
Upland, subtropical broadleaf forest

H9 Prairie Province

H10 Prairie Altitudinal Zone
Upland mixed prairie and woodland

H11 Mediterranean Province
Sclerophyll woodland, shrub, and steppe

H12 Mediterranean Altitudinal Zone
Upland shrub and steppe

DRY AND DESERT ZONE

D1 Tropical/Subtropical Steppe Province
Dry steppe, desert shrub, semi-desert savanna

D2 Tropical/Subtropical Steppe Altitudinal Zone
Upland steppe and desert shrub

D3 Tropical/Subtropical Desert Province
Hot, lowland desert at subtropical and coastal locations

D4 Tropical/Subtropical Desert Altitudinal Zone
Desert shrub

D5 Temperate Steppe Province
Medium to short steppe grassland

D6 Temperate Steppe Altitudinal Zone
Alpine meadow and coniferous woodland

D7 Temperate Desert Province
Midlatitude rainshadow desert

D8 Temperate Desert Altitudinal Zone
Extreme continental desert-steppe

HUMID TROPICAL ZONE

Tr1 Savanna Province
Seasonally dry forest, open woodland, tall grass

Tr2 Savanna Altitudinal Zone
Open woodland-steppe

Tr3 Rainforest Province
Constantly humid, broadleaf evergreen forest

Tr4 Rainforest Altitudinal Zone
Broadleaf evergreen and subtropical deciduous forest

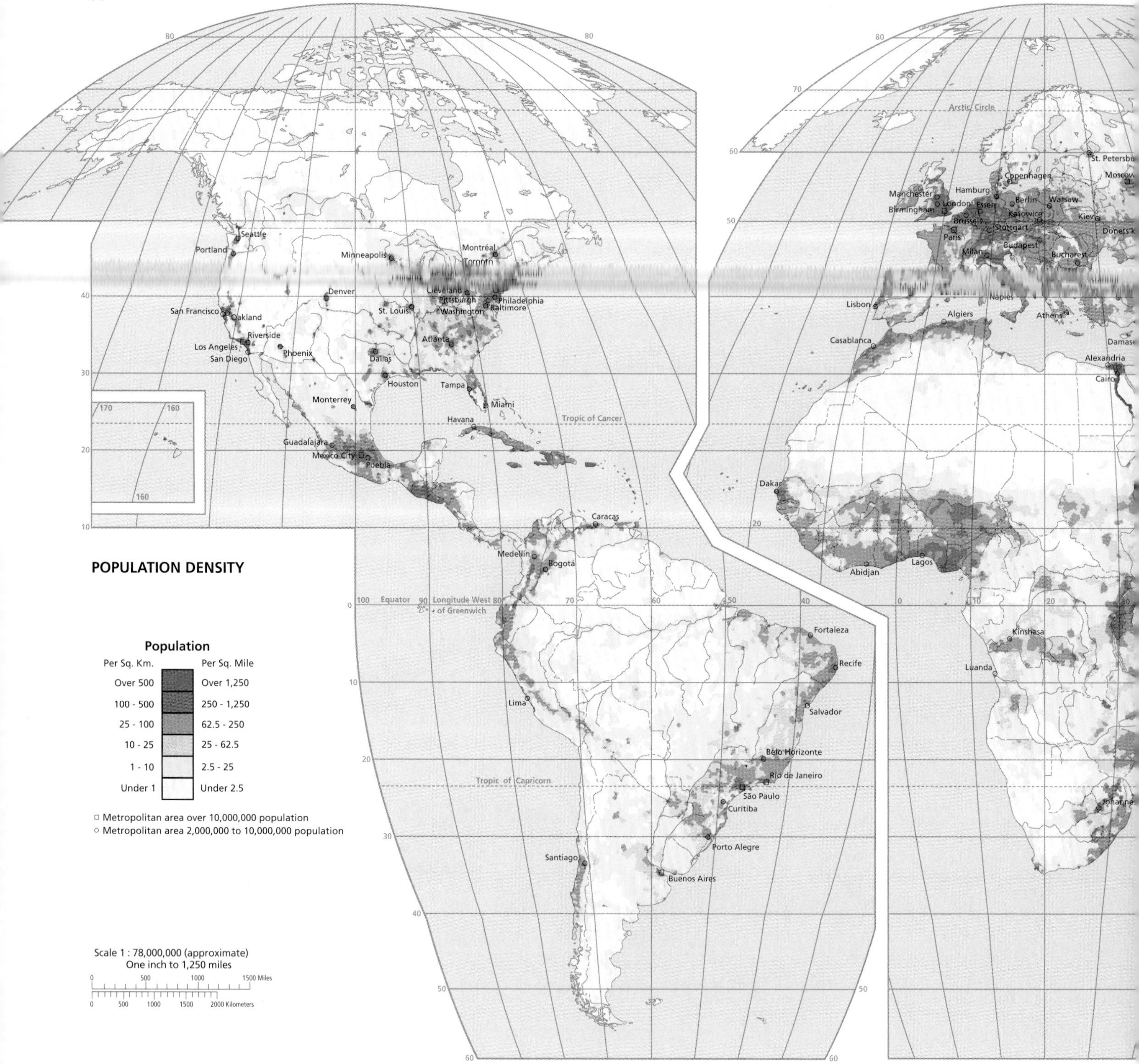

80 70 80 70

Arctic Circle

60 60

St. Petersbu

Manchester Hamburg Copenhagen Moscow
50 London Essen Berlin Warsaw
Birmingham Brussels Katowice Kiev
Paris Stuttgart Donets'k
Milan Budapest
Seattle Bucharest
Portland 50

Montréal
Minneapolis Toronto
40 Denver Lisbon Naples
Cleveland Philadelphia Algiers Athens
St. Louis Pittsburgh Baltimore Damas
San Francisco Washington Casablanca Alexandria
Oakland Atlanta Cairo
Los Angeles Riverside
San Diego Phoenix Dallas
30 Houston Tampa
Monterrey Miami
170 160 Havana Tropic of Cancer
Dakar
Guadalajara 20
Mexico City Lagos
160 Puebla Abidjan

Caracas
POPULATION DENSITY
Medellín
Bogotá KinsHasa
100 Equator 90 Longitude West 80 70 60 50 40 0 10 20
of Greenwich
Luanda
Population
Fortaleza
Per Sq. Km. Per Sq. Mile
Recife
Over 500 Over 1,250

100 - 500 250 - 1,250 Lima
Salvador
25 - 100 62.5 - 250

10 - 25 25 - 62.5 Belo Horizonte

1 - 10 2.5 - 25 Rio de Janeiro
Tropic of Capricorn Johann
Under 1 Under 2.5 São Paulo
Curitiba
□ Metropolitan area over 10,000,000 population
○ Metropolitan area 2,000,000 to 10,000,000 population Porto Alegre

Santiago
Buenos Aires

Scale 1 : 78,000,000 (approximate)
One inch to 1,250 miles
0 500 1000 1500 Miles
0 500 1000 1500 2000 Kilometers

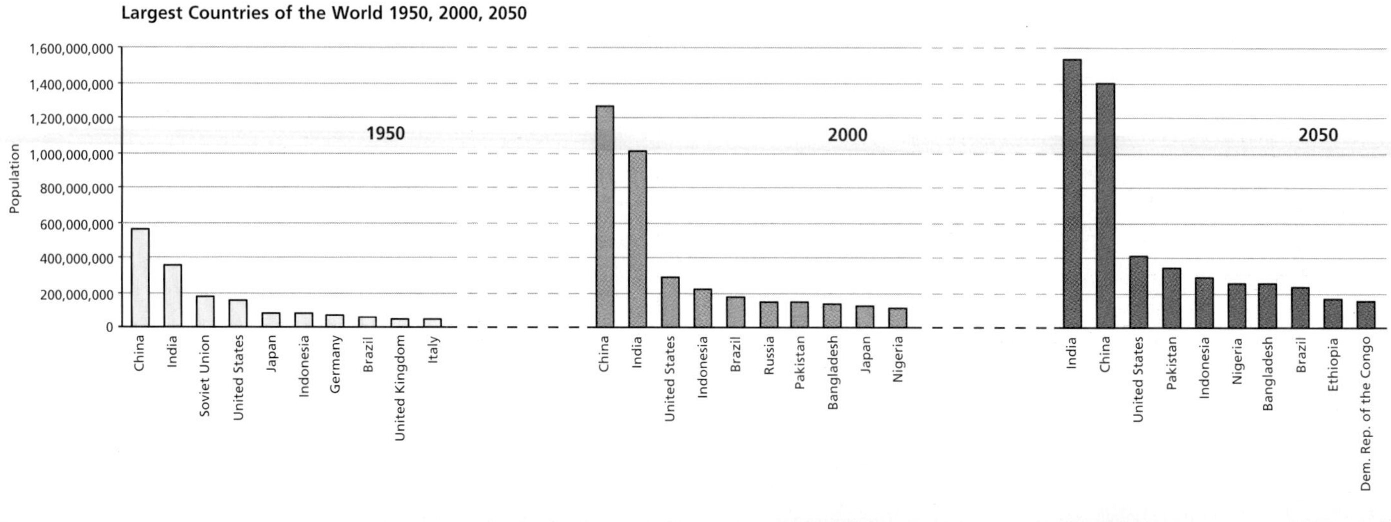

Largest Countries of the World 1950, 2000, 2050

Population

1,600,000,000
1,400,000,000
1,200,000,000
1,000,000,000 1950 2000 2050
800,000,000
600,000,000
400,000,000
200,000,000
0

1950: China, India, Soviet Union, United States, Japan, Indonesia, Germany, Brazil, United Kingdom, Italy

2000: China, India, United States, Indonesia, Brazil, Russia, Pakistan, Bangladesh, Japan, Nigeria

2050: India, China, United States, Pakistan, Indonesia, Nigeria, Bangladesh, Brazil, Ethiopia, Dem. Rep. of the Congo

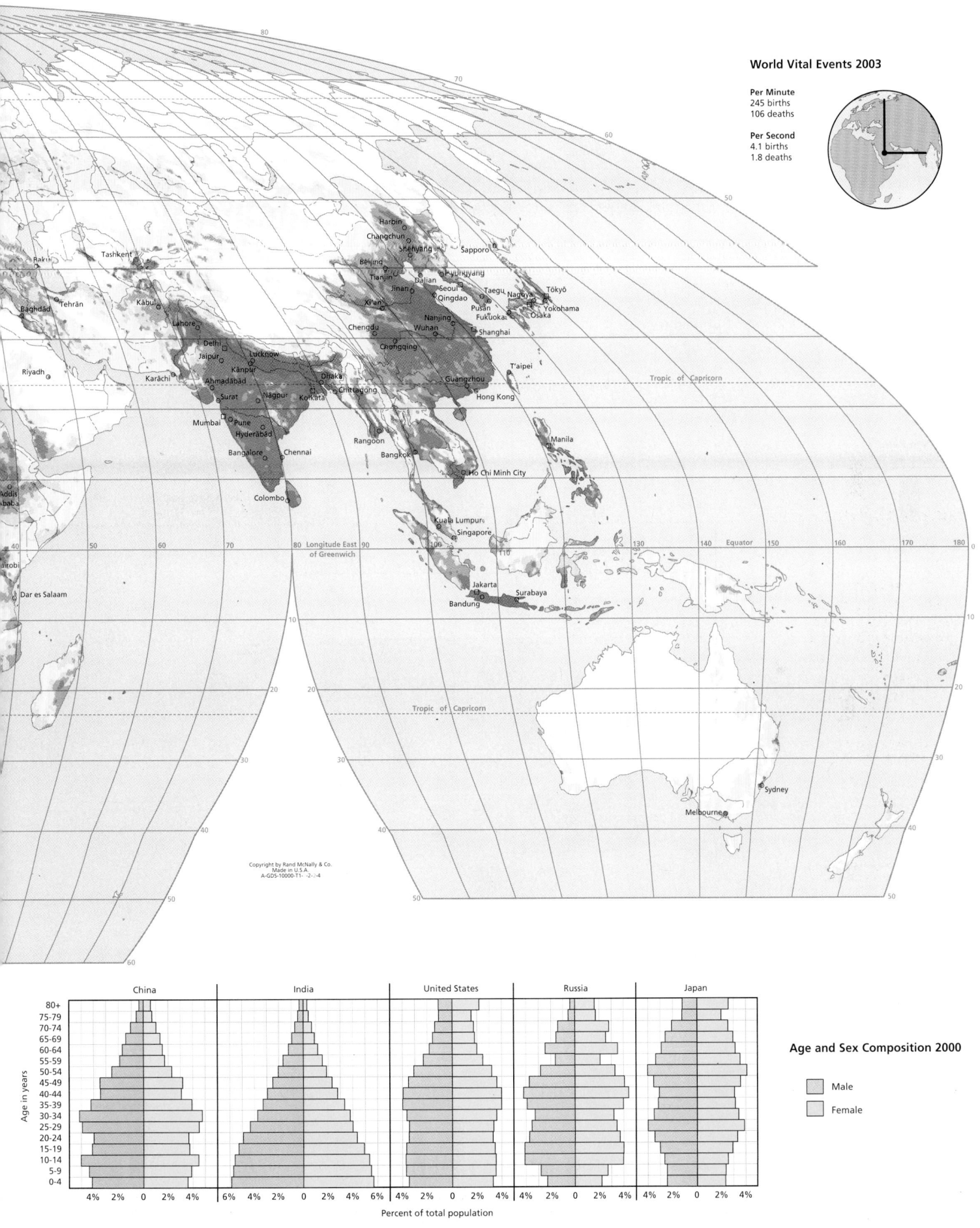

World Vital Events 2003

Per Minute
245 births
106 deaths

Per Second
4.1 births
1.8 deaths

Tropic of Capricorn

Longitude East of Greenwich

Equator

Tropic of Capricorn

Copyright by Rand McNally & Co.
Made in U.S.A.
A-GDS-10000-T1-·-2-·-4

Age and Sex Composition 2000

Male

Female

Age in years

Percent of total population

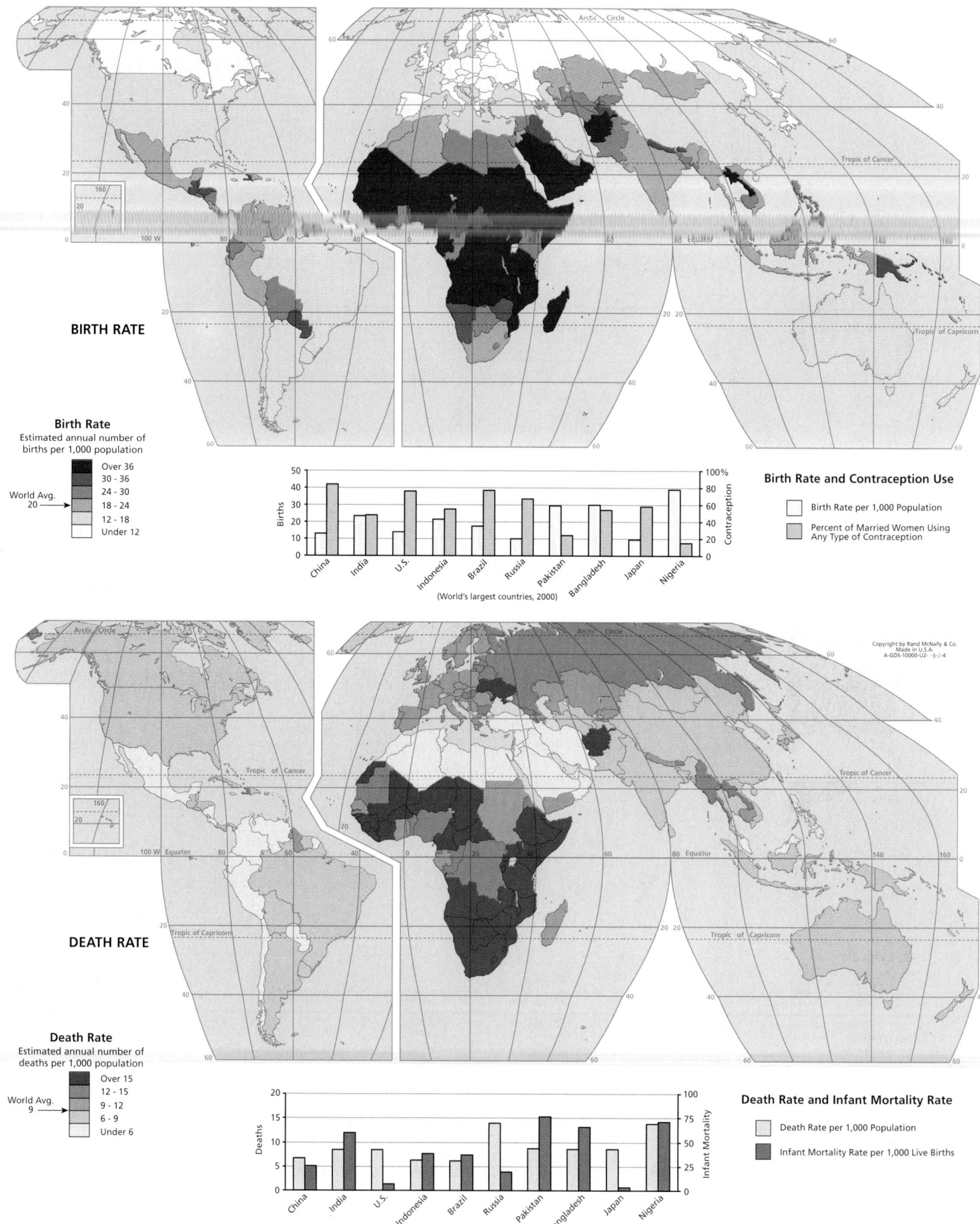

BIRTH RATE

Birth Rate
Estimated annual number of
births per 1,000 population

World Avg.
20 →

- Over 36
- 30 - 36
- 24 - 30
- 18 - 24
- 12 - 18
- Under 12

Birth Rate and Contraception Use

☐ Birth Rate per 1,000 Population

▨ Percent of Married Women Using
Any Type of Contraception

(World's largest countries, 2000)

DEATH RATE

Death Rate
Estimated annual number of
deaths per 1,000 population

World Avg.
9 →

- Over 15
- 12 - 15
- 9 - 12
- 6 - 9
- Under 6

Death Rate and Infant Mortality Rate

☐ Death Rate per 1,000 Population

▨ Infant Mortality Rate per 1,000 Live Births

(World's largest countries, 2000)

Copyright by Rand McNally & Co.
Made in U.S.A.
A-GDS-10000-U2- -3-2 4

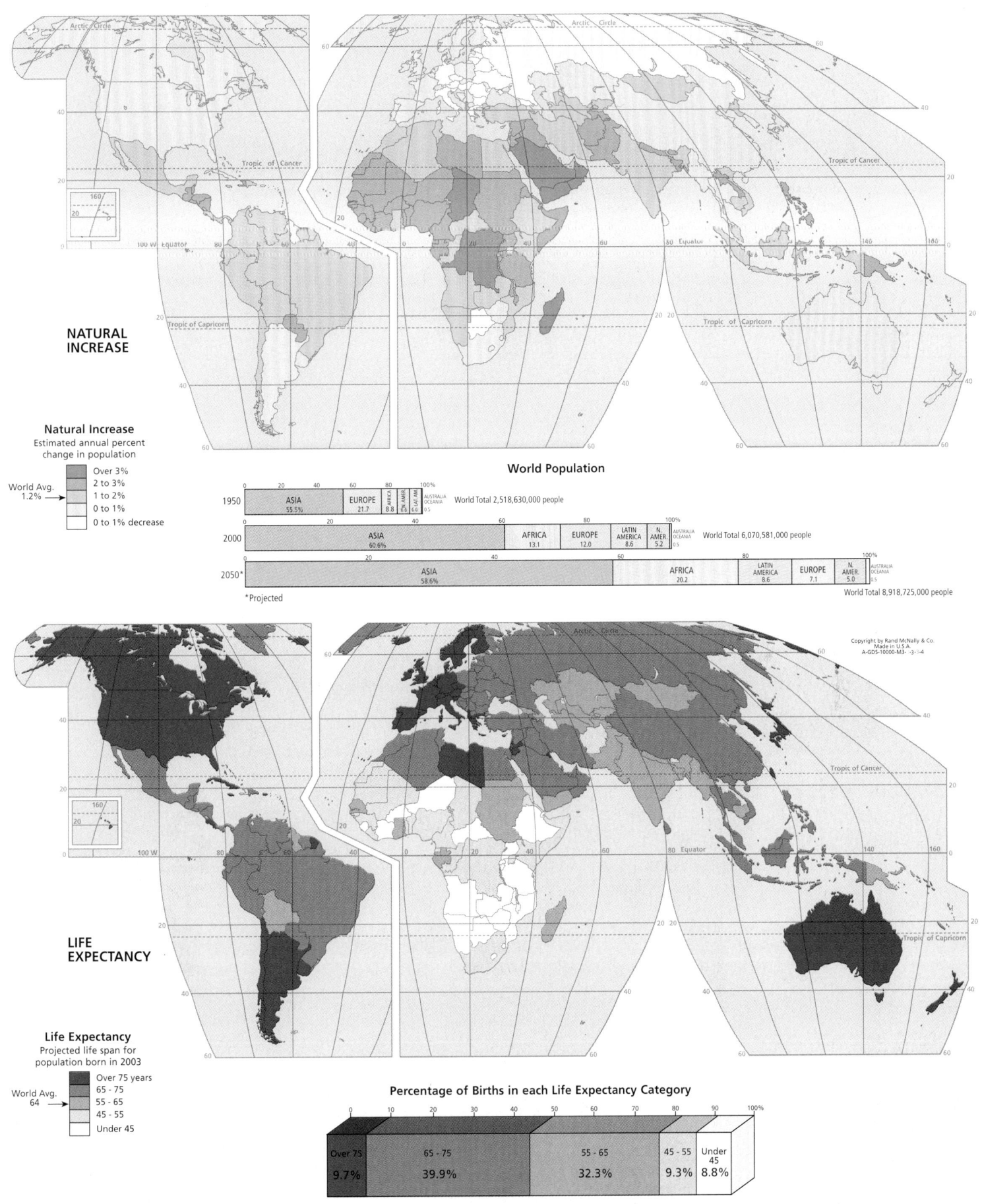

NATURAL INCREASE

Natural Increase
Estimated annual percent
change in population

World Avg.
1.2%

- Over 3%
- 2 to 3%
- 1 to 2%
- 0 to 1%
- 0 to 1% decrease

World Population

1950
ASIA 55.5% | EUROPE 21.7 | AFRICA 8.8 | N. AMER. | LAT. AM. 6.6 | AUSTRALIA OCEANIA 0.5
World Total 2,518,630,000 people

2000
ASIA 60.6% | AFRICA 13.1 | EUROPE 12.0 | LATIN AMERICA 8.6 | N. AMER. 5.2 | AUSTRALIA OCEANIA 0.5
World Total 6,070,581,000 people

2050*
ASIA 58.6% | AFRICA 20.2 | LATIN AMERICA 8.6 | EUROPE 7.1 | N. AMER. 5.0 | AUSTRALIA OCEANIA 0.5
World Total 8,918,725,000 people

*Projected

Copyright by Rand McNally & Co.
Made in U.S.A.
A-GDS-10000-M3- -3- -4

LIFE EXPECTANCY

Life Expectancy
Projected life span for
population born in 2003

World Avg.
64

- Over 75 years
- 65 - 75
- 55 - 65
- 45 - 55
- Under 45

Percentage of Births in each Life Expectancy Category

Over 75	65 - 75	55 - 65	45 - 55	Under 45
9.7%	39.9%	32.3%	9.3%	8.8%

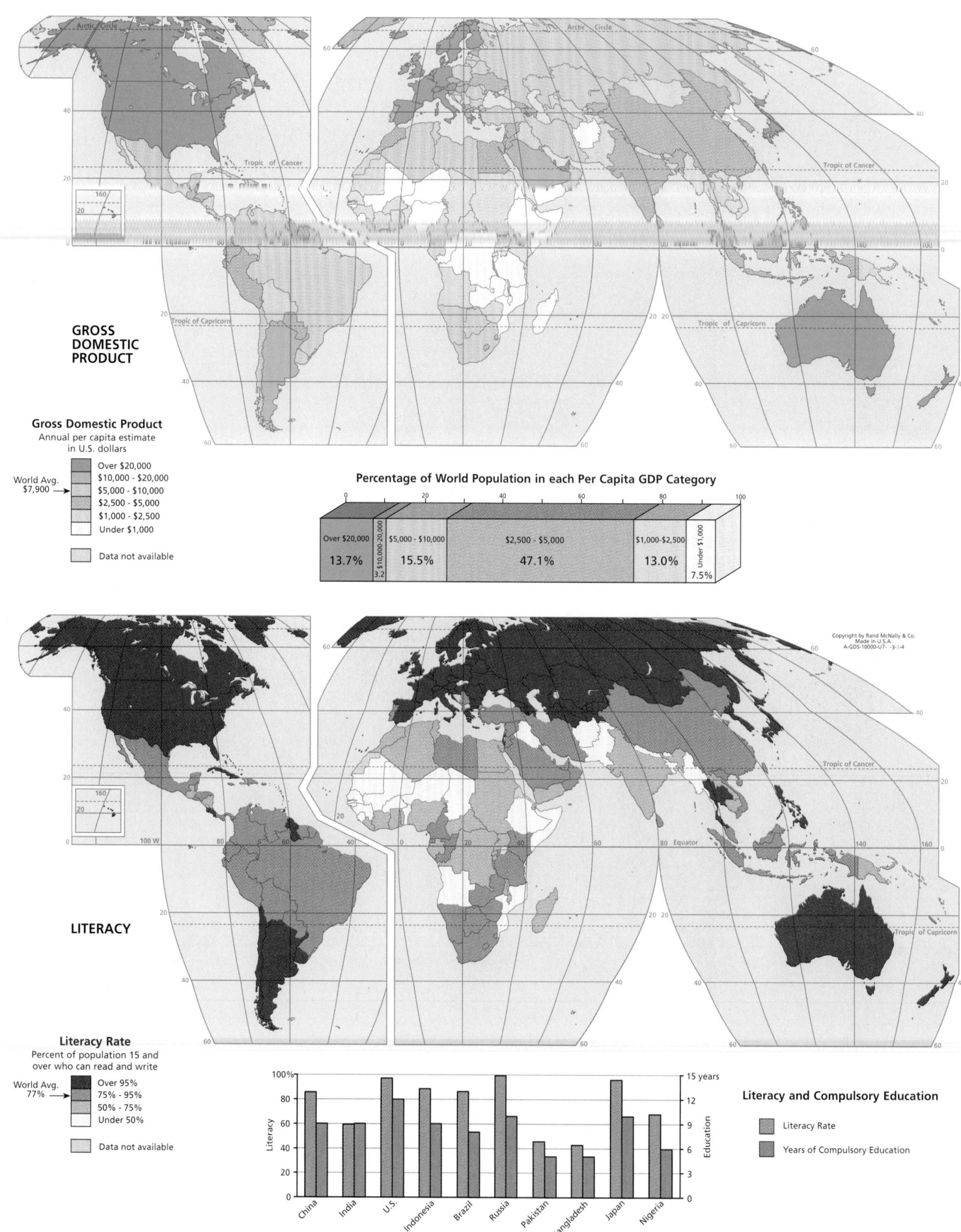

GROSS DOMESTIC PRODUCT

Gross Domestic Product
Annual per capita estimate
in U.S. dollars

Over $20,000
$10,000 - $20,000
World Avg.
$7,900 → $5,000 - $10,000
$2,500 - $5,000
$1,000 - $2,500
Under $1,000

Data not available

Percentage of World Population in each Per Capita GDP Category

Over $20,000	$10,000-20,000	$5,000 - $10,000	$2,500 - $5,000	$1,000-$2,500	Under $1,000
13.7%	3.2	15.5%	47.1%	13.0%	7.5%

Copyright by Rand McNally & Co.
Made in U.S.A.
A-GDS-10000-U7- -·3-:-4

LITERACY

Literacy Rate
Percent of population 15 and
over who can read and write

World Avg.
77% →   Over 95%
75% - 95%
50% - 75%
Under 50%

Data not available

Literacy and Compulsory Education

Literacy Rate

Years of Compulsory Education

(World's largest countries, 2000)

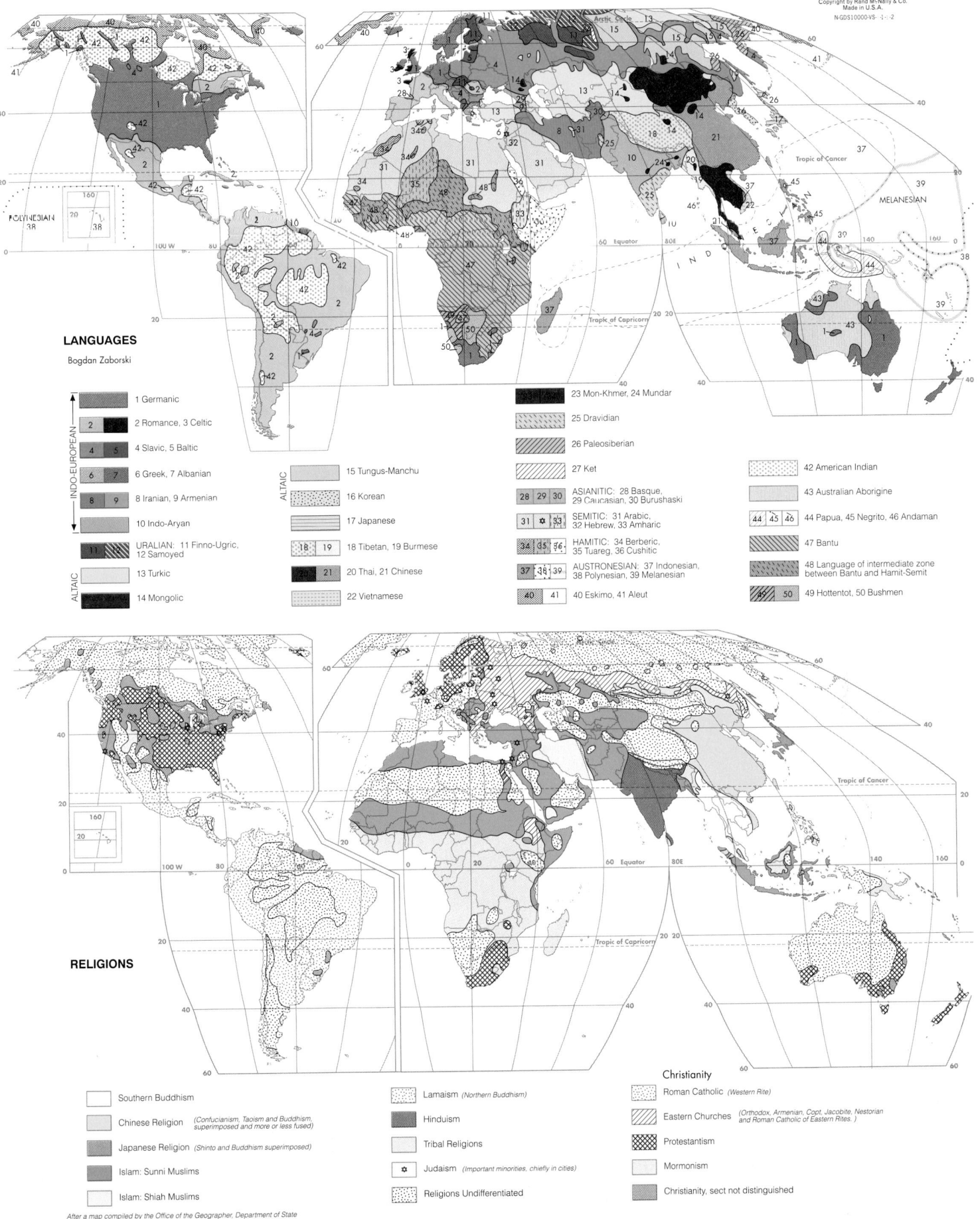

LANGUAGES

Bogdan Zaborski

INDO-EUROPEAN
- 1 Germanic
- 2 Romance, 3 Celtic
- 4 Slavic, 5 Baltic
- 6 Greek, 7 Albanian
- 8 Iranian, 9 Armenian
- 10 Indo-Aryan

URALIAN: 11 Finno-Ugric, 12 Samoyed

ALTAIC
- 13 Turkic
- 14 Mongolic
- 15 Tungus-Manchu
- 16 Korean
- 17 Japanese
- 18 Tibetan, 19 Burmese
- 20 Thai, 21 Chinese
- 22 Vietnamese

- 23 Mon-Khmer, 24 Mundar
- 25 Dravidian
- 26 Paleosiberian
- 27 Ket
- ASIANITIC: 28 Basque, 29 Caucasian, 30 Burushaski
- SEMITIC: 31 Arabic, 32 Hebrew, 33 Amharic
- HAMITIC: 34 Berberic, 35 Tuareg, 36 Cushitic
- AUSTRONESIAN: 37 Indonesian, 38 Polynesian, 39 Melanesian
- 40 Eskimo, 41 Aleut

- 42 American Indian
- 43 Australian Aborigine
- 44 Papua, 45 Negrito, 46 Andaman
- 47 Bantu
- 48 Language of intermediate zone between Bantu and Hamit-Semit
- 49 Hottentot, 50 Bushmen

RELIGIONS

- Southern Buddhism
- Chinese Religion (Confucianism, Taoism and Buddhism, superimposed and more or less fused)
- Japanese Religion (Shinto and Buddhism superimposed)
- Islam: Sunni Muslims
- Islam: Shiah Muslims

- Lamaism (Northern Buddhism)
- Hinduism
- Tribal Religions
- Judaism (Important minorities, chiefly in cities)
- Religions Undifferentiated

Christianity
- Roman Catholic (Western Rite)
- Eastern Churches (Orthodox, Armenian, Copt, Jacobite, Nestorian and Roman Catholic of Eastern Rites.)
- Protestantism
- Mormonism
- Christianity, sect not distinguished

After a map compiled by the Office of the Geographer, Department of State

URBANIZED POPULATION

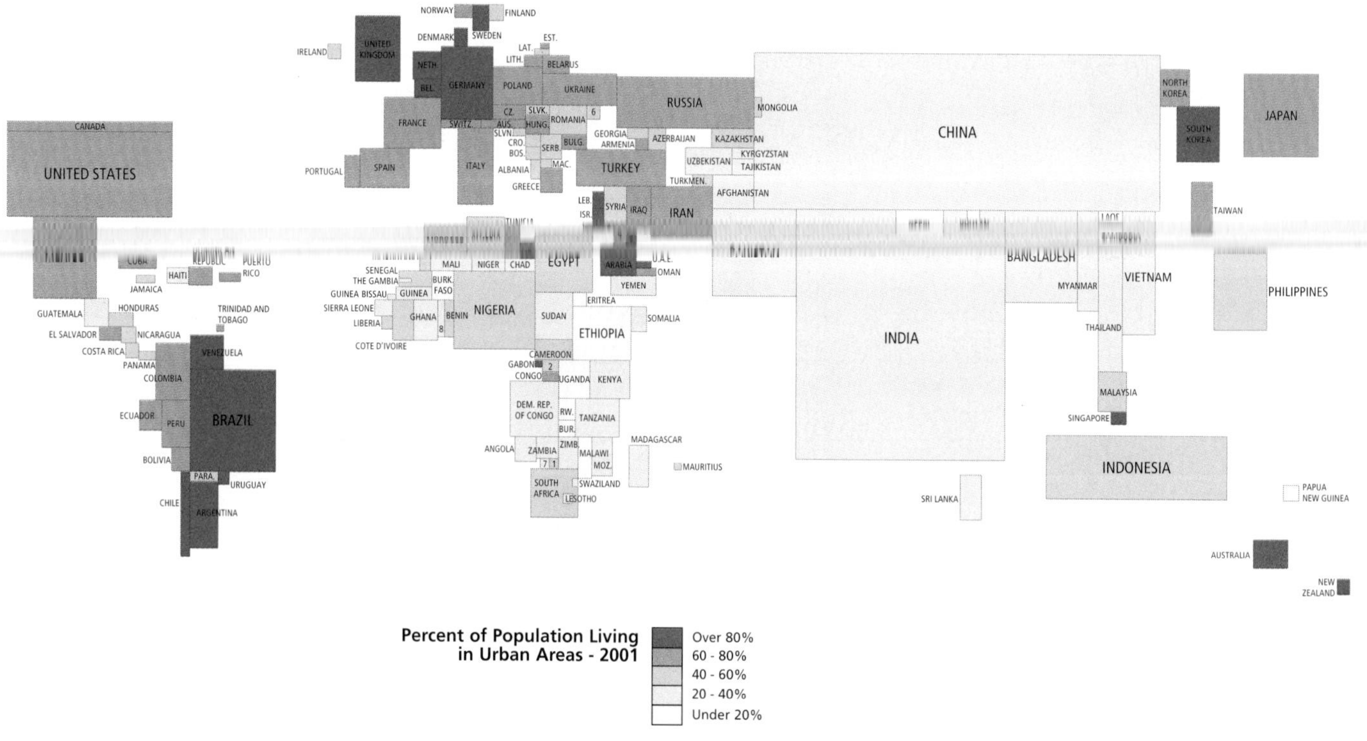

NORWAY FINLAND
IRELAND UNITED KINGDOM DENMARK SWEDEN EST. LAT. LITH. BELARUS
NETH. GERMANY POLAND UKRAINE
BEL. CZ. SLVK. ROMANIA 6
FRANCE SWITZ. AUS. HUNG. GEORGIA ARMENIA AZERBAIJAN KAZAKHSTAN
PORTUGAL SPAIN ITALY SLVN. CRO. BOS. SERB. BULG. MAC. TURKEY UZBEKISTAN KYRGYZSTAN TAJIKISTAN
ALBANIA GREECE TURKMEN. AFGHANISTAN
LEB. SYRIA IRAQ IRAN
ISR.
TUNISIA
SENEGAL MALI NIGER CHAD EGYPT ARABIA U.A.E. OMAN
THE GAMBIA BURK. YEMEN
GUINEA BISSAU GUINEA FASO
SIERRA LEONE GHANA BENIN NIGERIA SUDAN ERITREA SOMALIA
LIBERIA 8
COTE D'IVOIRE ETHIOPIA
CAMEROON
GABON 2 UGANDA KENYA
CONGO
DEM. REP. RW. TANZANIA
OF CONGO BUR.
ANGOLA ZAMBIA ZIMB. MALAWI MADAGASCAR
7 1 MOZ.
SOUTH SWAZILAND
AFRICA LESOTHO

RUSSIA MONGOLIA CHINA NORTH KOREA JAPAN SOUTH KOREA TAIWAN
PAKISTAN NEPAL BHUTAN BANGLADESH LAOS
MYANMAR VIETNAM PHILIPPINES
INDIA THAILAND
MALAYSIA
SINGAPORE
SRI LANKA INDONESIA PAPUA NEW GUINEA
MAURITIUS
AUSTRALIA
NEW ZEALAND

CANADA
UNITED STATES
CUBA DOMINICAN PUERTO
REPUBLIC RICO
JAMAICA HAITI
GUATEMALA HONDURAS TRINIDAD AND
EL SALVADOR NICARAGUA TOBAGO
COSTA RICA VENEZUELA
PANAMA COLOMBIA
ECUADOR PERU BRAZIL
BOLIVIA
PARA.
CHILE URUGUAY
ARGENTINA

**Percent of Population Living
in Urban Areas - 2001**

- Over 80%
- 60 - 80%
- 40 - 60%
- 20 - 40%
- Under 20%

Copyright by Rand McNally & Co.
Made in U.S.A.

Size of each country is proportional to its population.

= 25,000,000 people

Countries with populations under
1,000,000 are not shown.

1 Botswana	6 Moldova
2 Central African Republic	7 Namibia
3 Gaza Strip	8 Togo
4 Jordan	9 West Bank
5 Kuwait	

NUTRITION

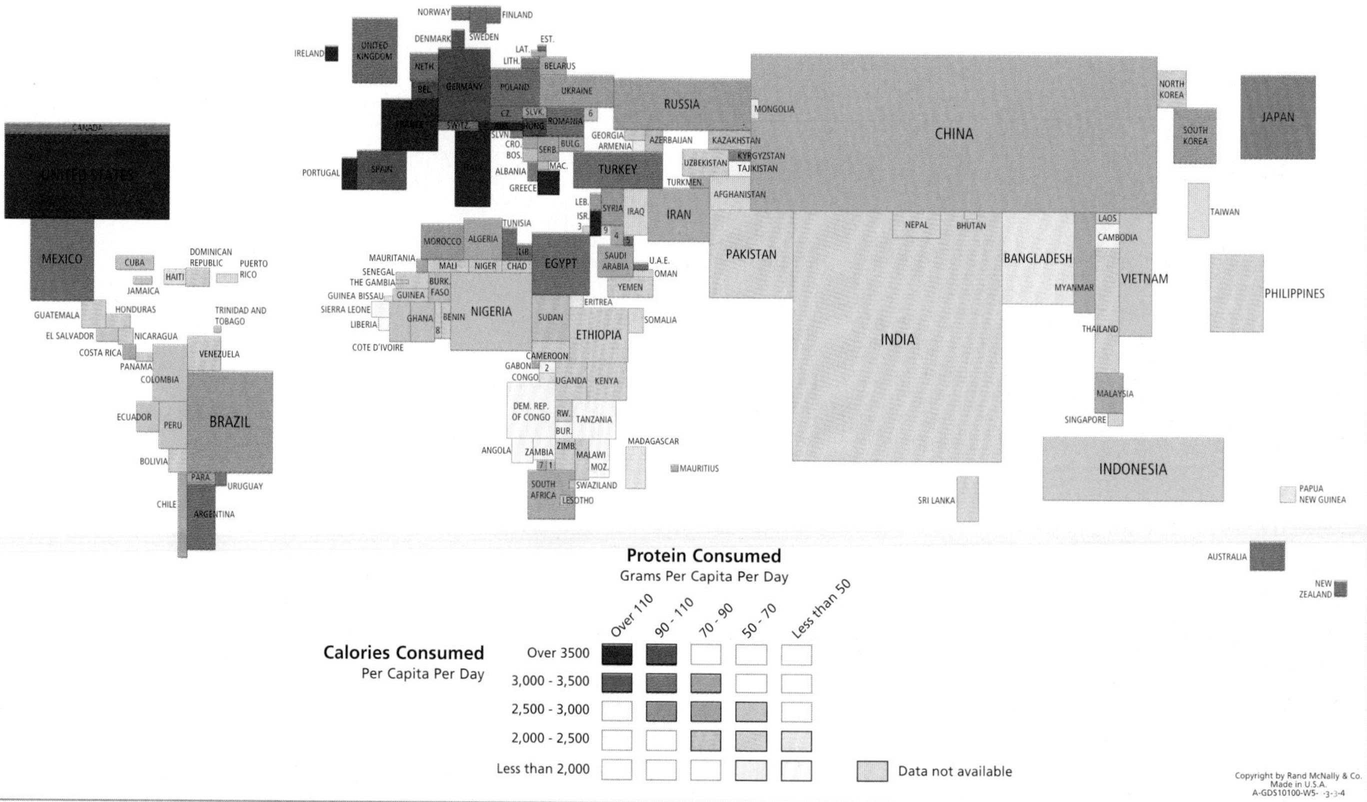

NORWAY FINLAND
IRELAND UNITED DENMARK SWEDEN EST.
KINGDOM LAT.
NETH. LITH. BELARUS
BEL. GERMANY POLAND
FRANCE CZ. SLVK. UKRAINE
SWITZ. HUNG. ROMANIA 6
SLVN. GEORGIA AZERBAIJAN KAZAKHSTAN
PORTUGAL SPAIN CRO. BOS. SERB. BULG. ARMENIA
MAC. TURKEY UZBEKISTAN
ALBANIA TAJIKISTAN
GREECE TURKMEN.
LEB. SYRIA IRAQ AFGHANISTAN
ISR. IRAN
3
MOROCCO ALGERIA 4 SAUDI U.A.E.
MAURITANIA TUNISIA ARABIA OMAN
SENEGAL MALI NIGER CHAD EGYPT YEMEN
THE GAMBIA BURK.
GUINEA BISSAU GUINEA FASO
SIERRA LEONE GHANA BENIN NIGERIA SUDAN ERITREA
LIBERIA SOMALIA
COTE D'IVOIRE ETHIOPIA
CAMEROON
GABON 2 UGANDA KENYA
CONGO
DEM. REP. RW. TANZANIA
OF CONGO BUR.
ANGOLA ZAMBIA ZIMB. MALAWI MADAGASCAR
MOZ.
SOUTH SWAZILAND MAURITIUS
AFRICA LESOTHO

RUSSIA MONGOLIA CHINA NORTH KOREA JAPAN
SOUTH KOREA TAIWAN
NEPAL BHUTAN LAOS
PAKISTAN CAMBODIA
BANGLADESH
MYANMAR VIETNAM PHILIPPINES
INDIA THAILAND
MALAYSIA
SINGAPORE
SRI LANKA INDONESIA PAPUA NEW GUINEA
AUSTRALIA
NEW ZEALAND

CANADA
UNITED STATES
MEXICO CUBA DOMINICAN PUERTO
REPUBLIC RICO
JAMAICA HAITI
GUATEMALA HONDURAS TRINIDAD AND
EL SALVADOR NICARAGUA TOBAGO
COSTA RICA VENEZUELA
PANAMA COLOMBIA
ECUADOR PERU BRAZIL
BOLIVIA
PARA. URUGUAY
CHILE ARGENTINA

Protein Consumed
Grams Per Capita Per Day

Over 110 / 90 - 110 / 70 - 90 / 50 - 70 / Less than 50

Calories Consumed
Per Capita Per Day

- Over 3500
- 3,000 - 3,500
- 2,500 - 3,000
- 2,000 - 2,500
- Less than 2,000

Data not available

Copyright by Rand McNally & Co.
Made in U.S.A.
A-GDS10100-W5- -3-3-4

PHYSICIANS

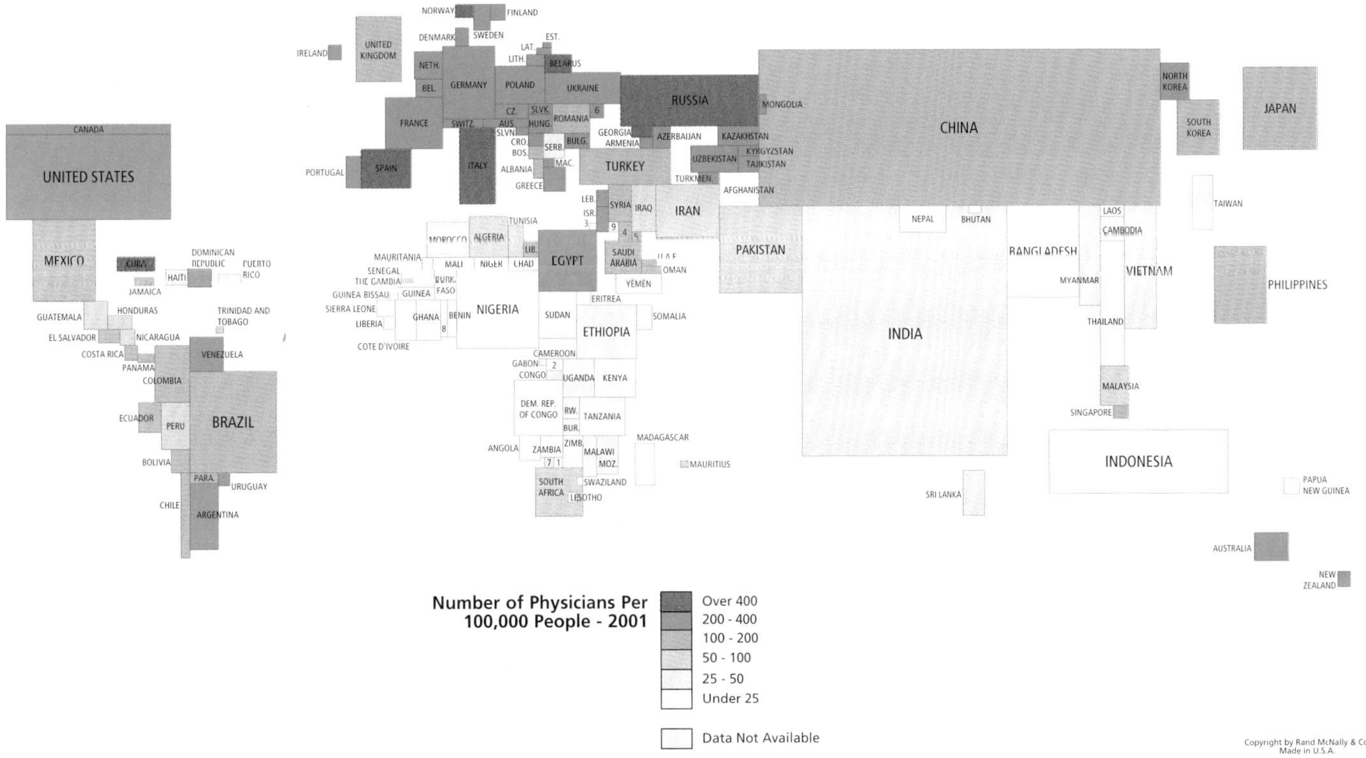

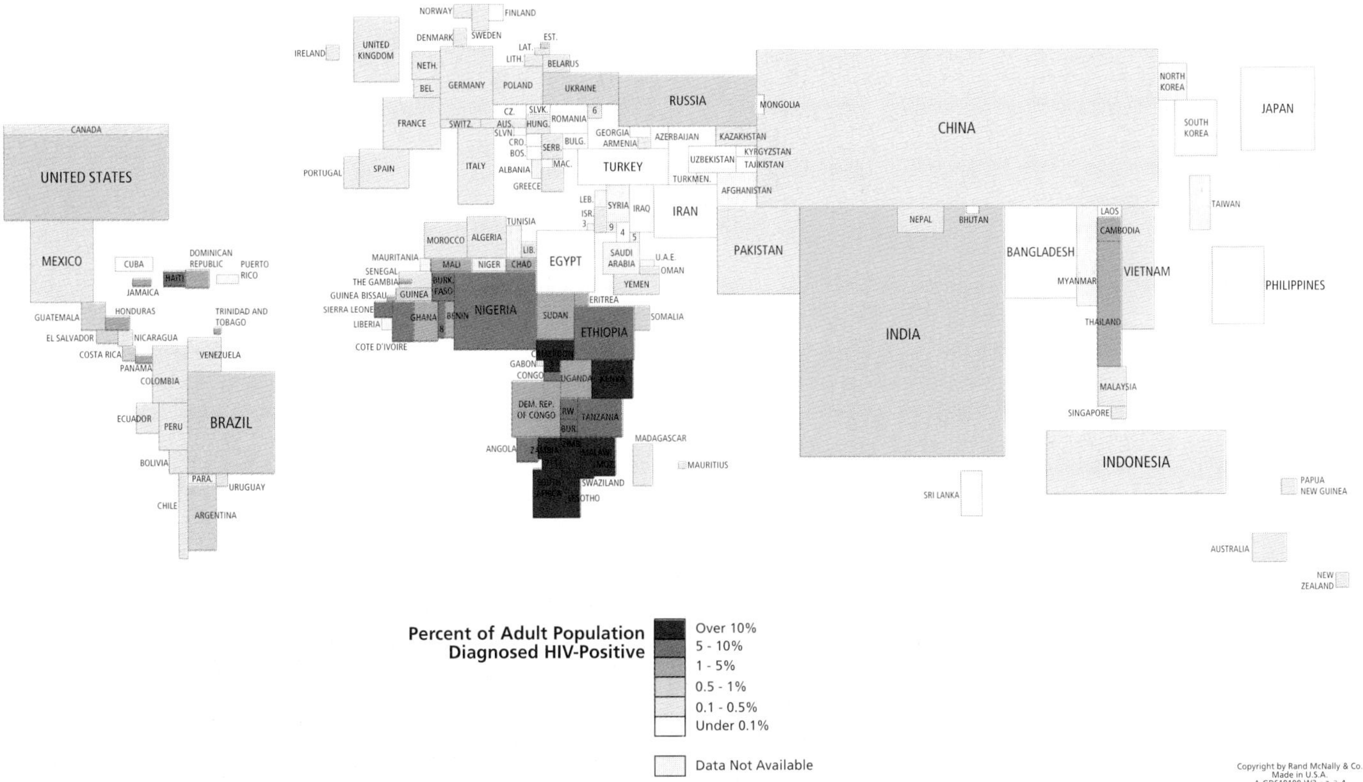

NORWAY FINLAND
SWEDEN
DENMARK EST.
IRELAND UNITED LAT.
KINGDOM LITH.
NETH. BELARUS
BEL. GERMANY POLAND UKRAINE RUSSIA MONGOLIA NORTH
KOREA JAPAN
FRANCE SWITZ. CZ. SLVK. ROMANIA 6 SOUTH
AUS. HUNG. KOREA
SLVNI. GEORGIA AZERBAIJAN KAZAKHSTAN CHINA
PORTUGAL CRO. SERB. BULG. ARMENIA UZBEKISTAN KYRGYZSTAN
SPAIN ITALY BOS. MAC. TURKEY TAJIKISTAN
ALBANIA TURKMEN. TAIWAN
GREECE AFGHANISTAN
LEB. SYRIA IRAQ
ISR. 3 IRAN LAOS
CANADA 9 4 PAKISTAN NEPAL BHUTAN CAMBODIA
TUNISIA VIETNAM
UNITED STATES MAURITANIA MOROCCO NIGERIA SAUDI BANGLADESH PHILIPPINES
MALI NIGER LIB. EGYPT ARABIA U.A.E. MYANMAR
SENEGAL CHAD YEMEN OMAN THAILAND
MEXICO DOMINICAN THE GAMBIA BURK.
REPUBLIC PUERTO GUINEA BISSAU FASO ERITREA INDIA
HAITI RICO SIERRA LEONE GUINEA GHANA BENIN SUDAN SOMALIA MALAYSIA
CUBA LIBERIA 8 NIGERIA
JAMAICA ETHIOPIA SINGAPORE
GUATEMALA HONDURAS COTE D'IVOIRE
EL SALVADOR NICARAGUA CAMEROON
COSTA RICA GABON 2 UGANDA KENYA INDONESIA PAPUA
PANAMA CONGO NEW GUINEA
VENEZUELA DEM. REP. RW. TANZANIA
COLOMBIA OF CONGO BUR.
ANGOLA ZAMBIA ZIMB. MADAGASCAR
ECUADOR PERU BRAZIL MALAWI MAURITIUS
7 1 MOZ. SRI LANKA
BOLIVIA SOUTH SWAZILAND AUSTRALIA
PARA. AFRICA LESOTHO
URUGUAY NEW
CHILE ZEALAND
ARGENTINA

Number of Physicians Per 100,000 People - 2001

- Over 400
- 200 - 400
- 100 - 200
- 50 - 100
- 25 - 50
- Under 25
- Data Not Available

Copyright by Rand McNally & Co.
Made in U.S.A.

Size of each country is proportional to its population.

☐ = 25,000,000 people

Countries with populations under 1,000,000 are not shown.

1 Botswana	6 Moldova
2 Central African Republic	7 Namibia
3 Gaza Strip	8 Togo
4 Jordan	9 West Bank
5 Kuwait	

HIV INFECTION

Percent of Adult Population Diagnosed HIV-Positive

- Over 10%
- 5 - 10%
- 1 - 5%
- 0.5 - 1%
- 0.1 - 0.5%
- Under 0.1%
- Data Not Available

Copyright by Rand McNally & Co.
Made in U.S.A.
A-GDS10100-W3- -g- -4

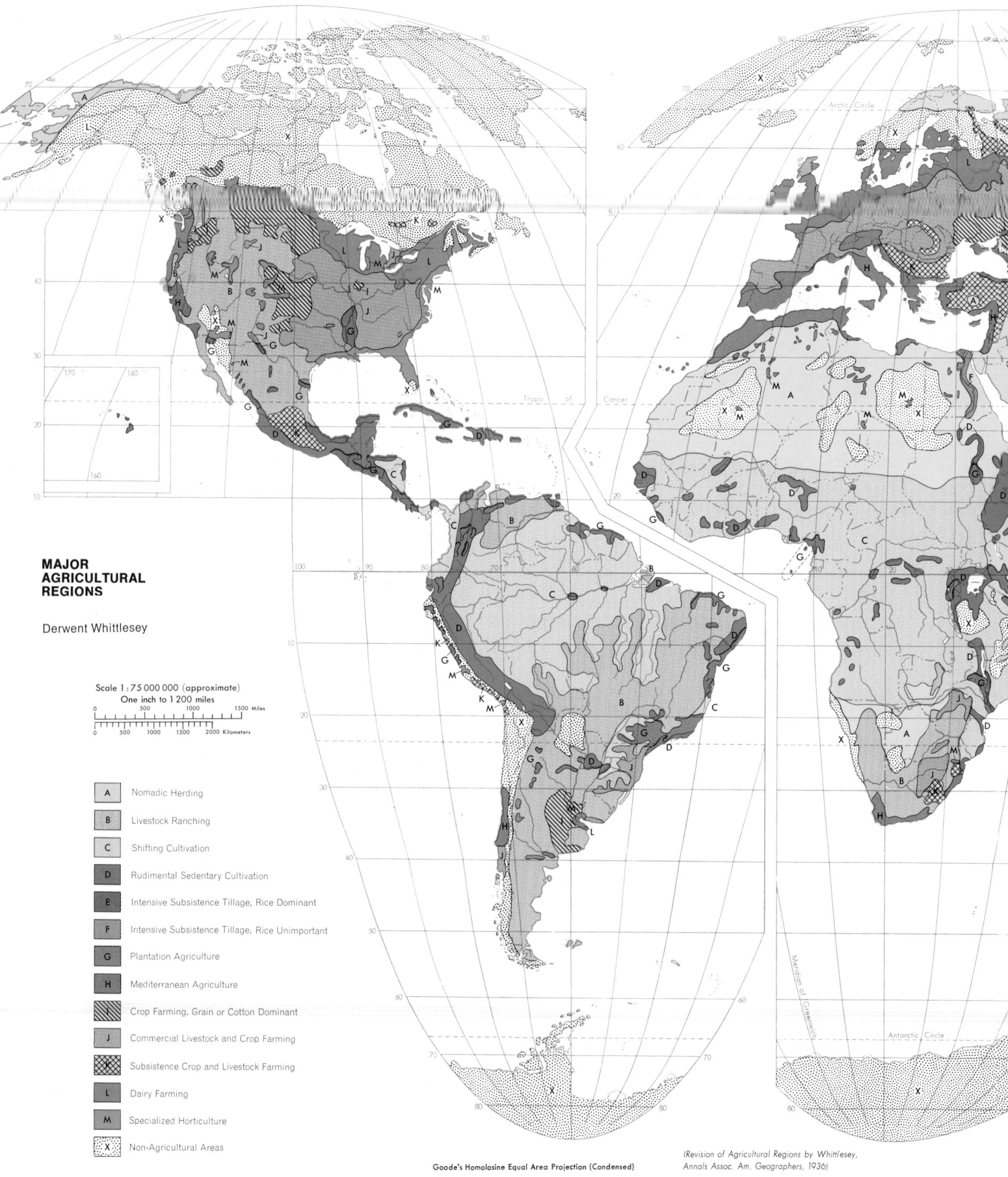

**MAJOR
AGRICULTURAL
REGIONS**

Derwent Whittlesey

Scale 1 : 75 000 000 (approximate)
One inch to 1 200 miles

0	500	1000	1500 Miles

0	500	1000	1500	2000 Kilometers

A	Nomadic Herding
B	Livestock Ranching
C	Shifting Cultivation
D	Rudimental Sedentary Cultivation
E	Intensive Subsistence Tillage, Rice Dominant
F	Intensive Subsistence Tillage, Rice Unimportant
G	Plantation Agriculture
H	Mediterranean Agriculture
I	Crop Farming, Grain or Cotton Dominant
J	Commercial Livestock and Crop Farming
K	Subsistence Crop and Livestock Farming
L	Dairy Farming
M	Specialized Horticulture
X	Non-Agricultural Areas

Goode's Homolosine Equal Area Projection (Condensed)

(Revision of Agricultural Regions by Whittlesey,
Annals Assoc. Am. Geographers, 1936)

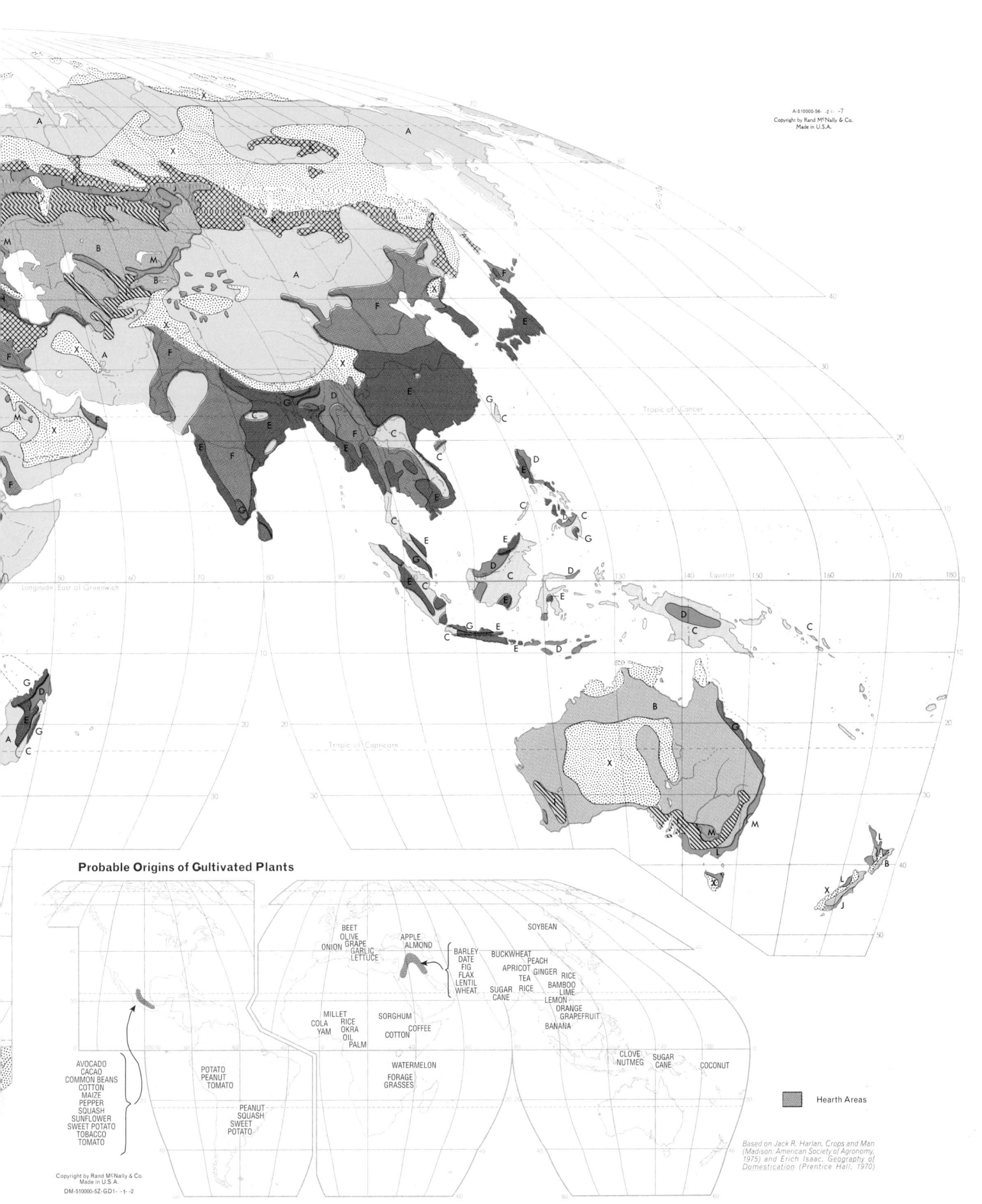

Tropic of Cancer

Equator

Tropic of Capricorn

Longitude East of Greenwich

Probable Origins of Cultivated Plants

SOYBEAN

BEET
OLIVE
GRAPE
ONION GARLIC
LETTUCE

APPLE
ALMOND

BARLEY
DATE
FIG
FLAX
LENTIL
WHEAT

BUCKWHEAT
PEACH
APRICOT
TEA GINGER
RICE
SUGAR BAMBOO
RICE LIME
CANE
LEMON
ORANGE
GRAPEFRUIT
BANANA

MILLET
COLA RICE
YAM OKRA
OIL
PALM

SORGHUM

COTTON COFFEE

CLOVE SUGAR
NUTMEG CANE COCONUT

AVOCADO
CACAO
COMMON BEANS
COTTON
MAIZE
PEPPER
SQUASH
SUNFLOWER
SWEET POTATO
TOBACCO
TOMATO

POTATO
PEANUT
TOMATO

WATERMELON

FORAGE
GRASSES

PEANUT
SQUASH
SWEET
POTATO

Hearth Areas

*Based on Jack R. Harlan, Crops and Man
(Madison: American Society of Agronomy,
1975) and Erich Isaac, Geography of
Domestication (Prentice Hall, 1970)*

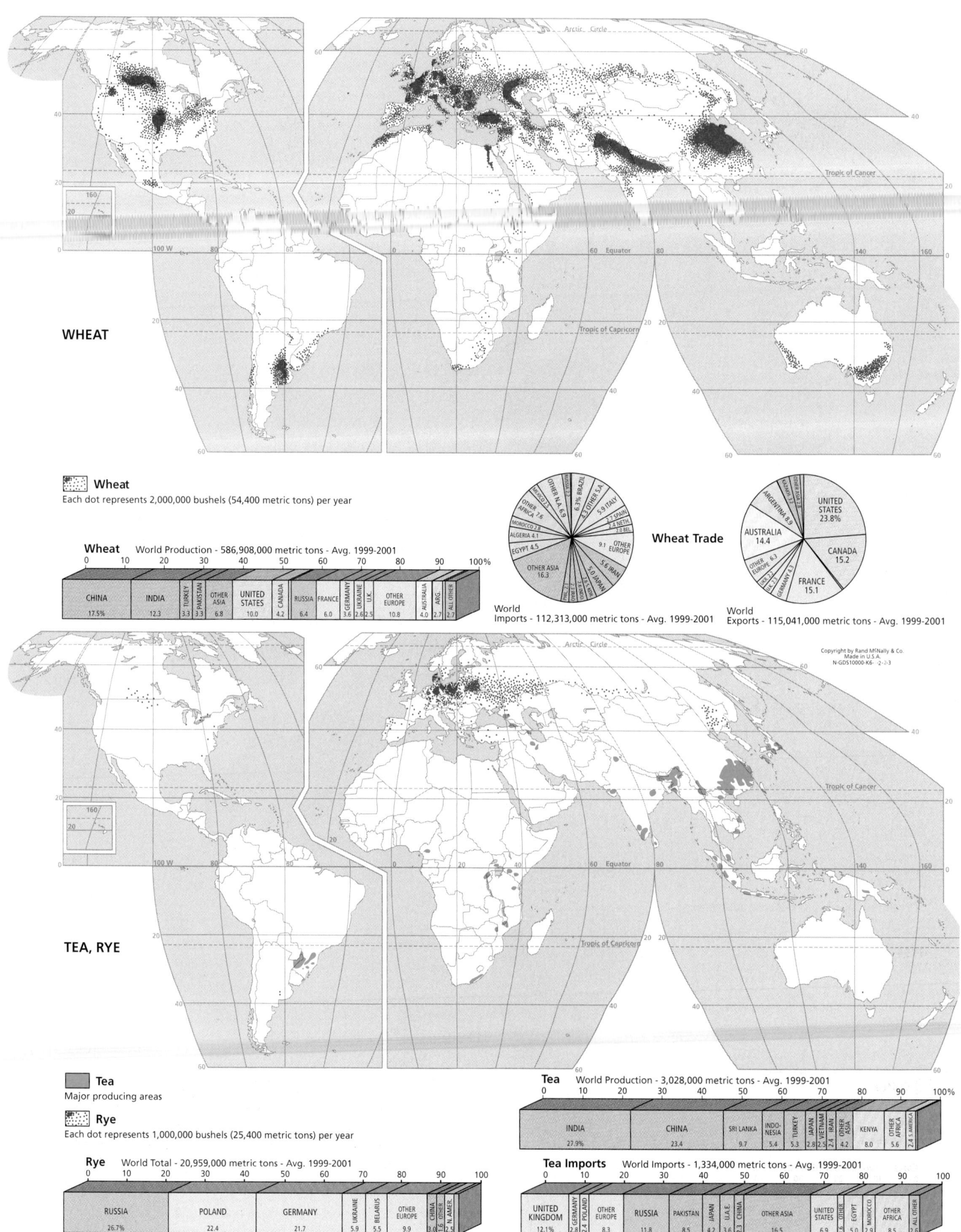

WHEAT

Wheat
Each dot represents 2,000,000 bushels (54,400 metric tons) per year

Wheat Trade

World Imports - 112,313,000 metric tons - Avg. 1999-2001

World Exports - 115,041,000 metric tons - Avg. 1999-2001

Wheat World Production - 586,908,000 metric tons - Avg. 1999-2001

0	10	20	30	40	50	60	70	80	90	100%
CHINA 17.5%	INDIA 12.3	TURKEY 3.3	PAKISTAN 3.3	OTHER ASIA 6.8	UNITED STATES 10.0	CANADA 4.2	RUSSIA 6.4	FRANCE 6.0	GERMANY 3.6	UKRAINE 2.6	U.K. 2.5	OTHER EUROPE 10.8	AUSTRALIA 4.0	ARG. 2.7	ALL OTHER 2.7

TEA, RYE

Tea
Major producing areas

Rye
Each dot represents 1,000,000 bushels (25,400 metric tons) per year

Tea World Production - 3,028,000 metric tons - Avg. 1999-2001

0	10	20	30	40	50	60	70	80	90	100%
INDIA 27.9%	CHINA 23.4	SRI LANKA 9.7	INDO-NESIA 5.4	TURKEY 2.8	JAPAN	VIETNAM	IRAN	OTHER ASIA 4.2	KENYA 8.0	OTHER AFRICA 5.6	S. AMERICA 2.4

Rye World Total - 20,959,000 metric tons - Avg. 1999-2001

0	10	20	30	40	50	60	70	80	90	100
RUSSIA 26.7%	POLAND 22.4	GERMANY 21.7	UKRAINE 5.9	BELARUS 5.5	OTHER EUROPE 9.9	CHINA 3.0	OTHER 1.6	N. AMER. 2.5

Tea Imports World Imports - 1,334,000 metric tons - Avg. 1999-2001

0	10	20	30	40	50	60	70	80	90	100
UNITED KINGDOM 12.1%	GERMANY 2.8	POLAND 2.4	OTHER EUROPE 8.3	RUSSIA 11.8	PAKISTAN 8.5	JAPAN 4.2	U.A.E. 3.6	CHINA 2.3	OTHER ASIA 16.5	UNITED STATES 6.9	OTHER 1.6	EGYPT 5.0	MOROCCO 2.9	OTHER AFRICA 8.5	ALL OTHER 2.6

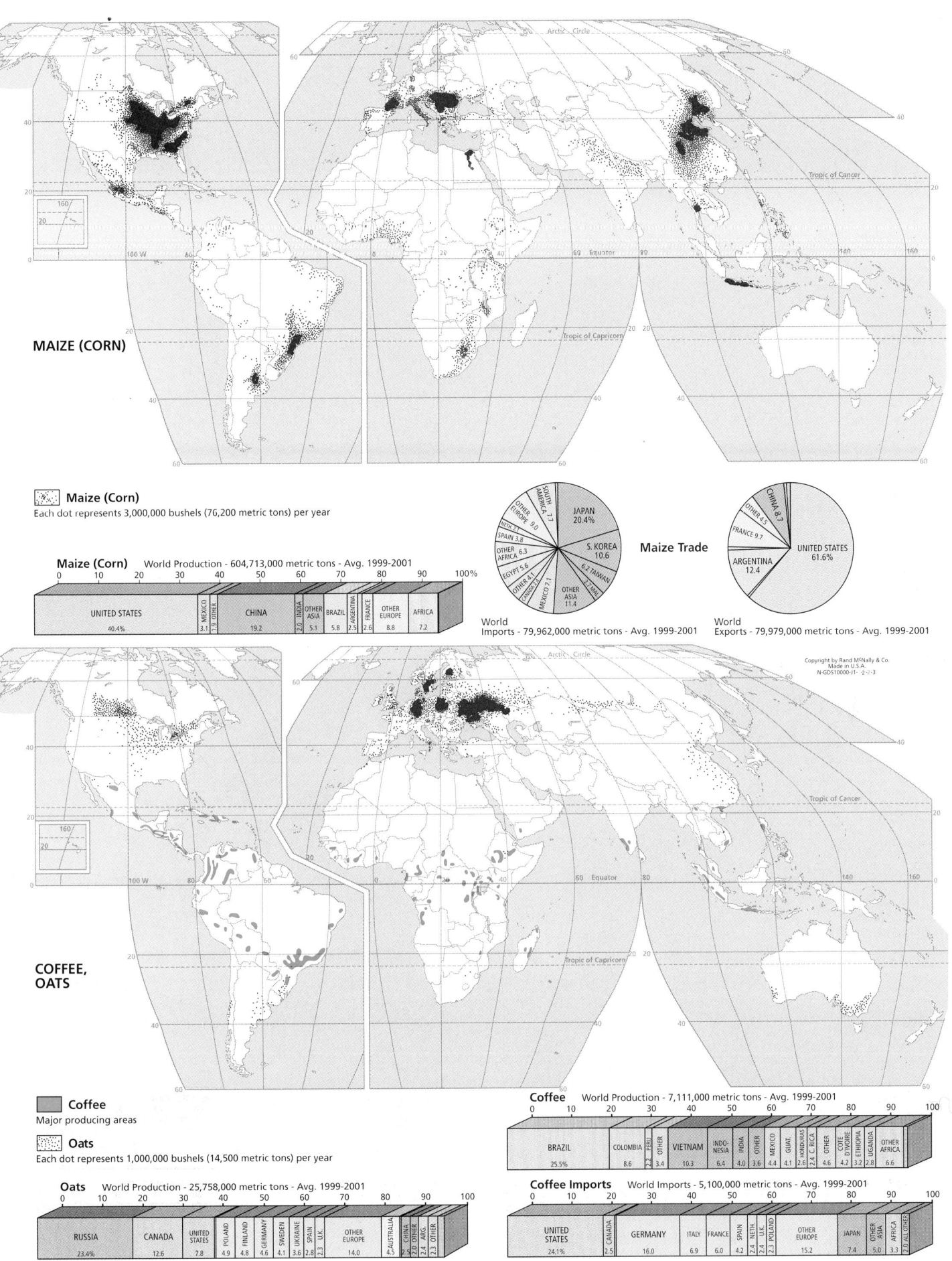

MAIZE (CORN)

⠿ Maize (Corn)
Each dot represents 3,000,000 bushels (76,200 metric tons) per year

Maize (Corn) World Production - 604,713,000 metric tons - Avg. 1999-2001

UNITED STATES 40.4%	MEXICO 3.1	OTHER 1.9	CHINA 19.2	INDIA 2.0	OTHER ASIA 5.1	BRAZIL 5.8	ARGENTINA 2.5	FRANCE 2.6	OTHER EUROPE 8.8	AFRICA 7.2

Maize Trade

World Imports - 79,962,000 metric tons - Avg. 1999-2001
- JAPAN 20.4%
- S. KOREA 10.6
- TAIWAN 6.2
- MALI 2.7
- OTHER ASIA 11.4
- MEXICO 7.1
- CANADA 4.1
- EGYPT 5.6
- OTHER 4.1
- OTHER AFRICA 6.3
- SPAIN 3.8
- NETH. 2.1
- OTHER EUROPE 9.0
- SOUTH AMERICA 7.7

World Exports - 79,979,000 metric tons - Avg. 1999-2001
- UNITED STATES 61.6%
- ARGENTINA 12.4
- FRANCE 9.7
- OTHER 4.5
- CHINA 8.7

Copyright by Rand McNally & Co.
Made in U.S.A.
N-GDS10000-J1- -2-/-3

COFFEE, OATS

▨ Coffee
Major producing areas

⠿ Oats
Each dot represents 1,000,000 bushels (14,500 metric tons) per year

Coffee World Production - 7,111,000 metric tons - Avg. 1999-2001

BRAZIL 25.5%	COLOMBIA 8.6	PERU 2.2	OTHER 3.4	VIETNAM 10.3	INDO-NESIA 6.4	INDIA 4.0	OTHER 3.6	MEXICO 4.4	GUAT. 4.1	HONDURAS 2.6	C. RICA 2.4	OTHER 4.6	COTE D'IVOIRE 4.2	ETHIOPIA 3.2	UGANDA 2.8	OTHER AFRICA 6.6

Oats World Production - 25,758,000 metric tons - Avg. 1999-2001

RUSSIA 23.4%	CANADA 12.6	UNITED STATES 7.8	POLAND 4.9	FINLAND 4.8	GERMANY 4.6	SWEDEN 4.1	UKRAINE 3.6	SPAIN 2.8	U.K. 2.3	OTHER EUROPE 14.0	AUSTRALIA 4.5	CHINA 2.9	OTHER 2.0	ARG. 2.4	OTHER 2.3

Coffee Imports World Imports - 5,100,000 metric tons - Avg. 1999-2001

UNITED STATES 24.1%	CANADA 2.5	GERMANY 16.0	ITALY 6.9	FRANCE 6.0	SPAIN 4.2	NETH. 2.4	U.K. 2.3	POLAND	OTHER EUROPE 15.2	JAPAN 7.4	OTHER ASIA 5.0	AFRICA 3.3	ALL OTHER 2.0

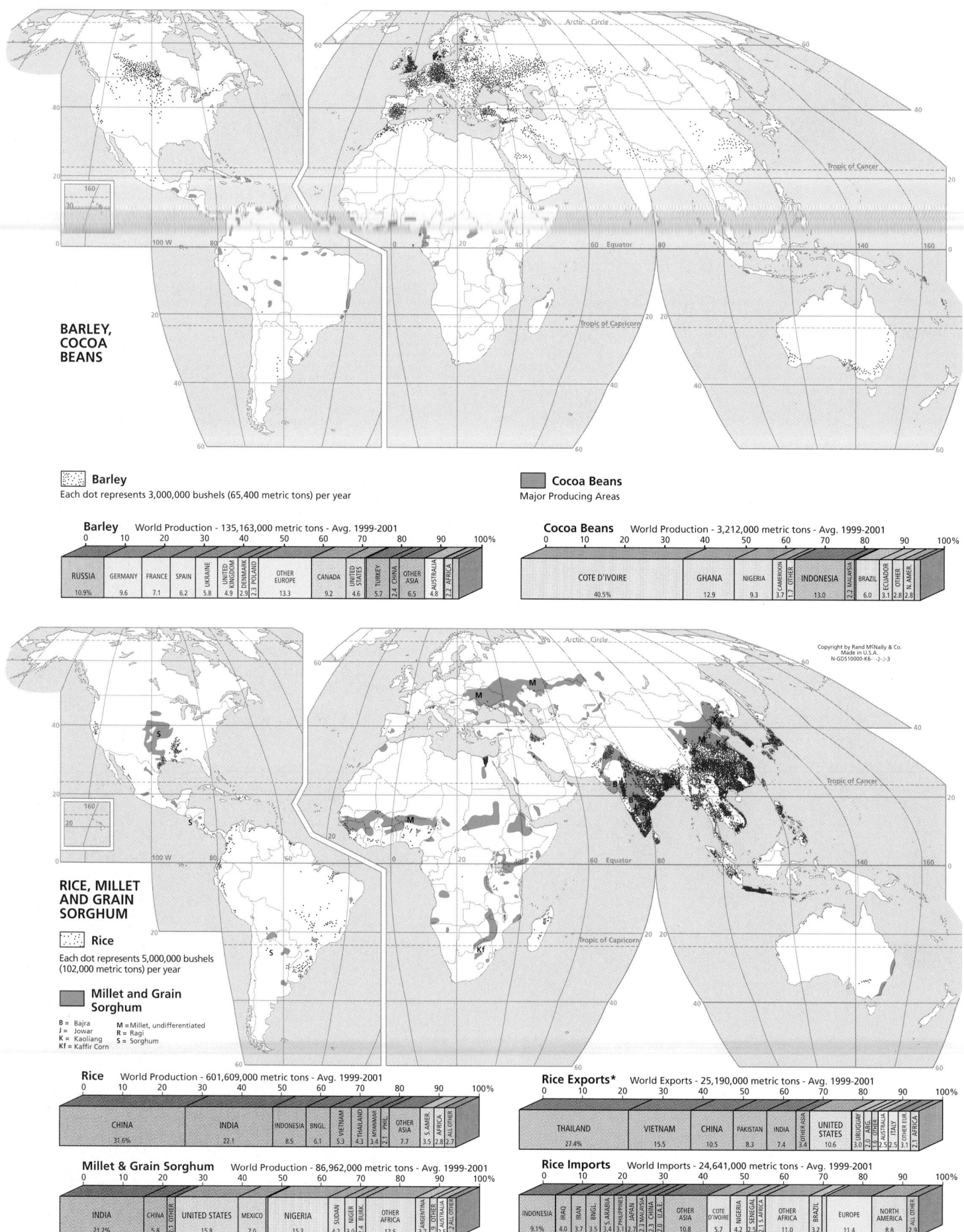

Barley
Each dot represents 3,000,000 bushels (65,400 metric tons) per year

Cocoa Beans
Major Producing Areas

BARLEY, COCOA BEANS

Barley   World Production - 135,163,000 metric tons - Avg. 1999-2001

	0	10	20	30	40	50	60	70	80	90	100%

RUSSIA	GERMANY	FRANCE	SPAIN	UKRAINE	UNITED KINGDOM	DENMARK	POLAND	OTHER EUROPE	CANADA	UNITED STATES	TURKEY	CHINA	OTHER ASIA	AUSTRALIA	AFRICA
10.9%	9.6	7.1	6.2	5.8	4.9	2.9	2.3	13.3	9.2	4.6	5.7	2.4	6.5	4.8	2.2

Cocoa Beans   World Production - 3,212,000 metric tons - Avg. 1999-2001

	0	10	20	30	40	50	60	70	80	90	100%

COTE D'IVOIRE	GHANA	NIGERIA	CAMEROON	OTHER	INDONESIA	MALAYSIA	BRAZIL	ECUADOR	OTHER	N. AMER.
40.5%	12.9	9.3	3.7	1.7	13.0	2.2	6.0	3.1	2.8	2.8

Copyright by Rand McNally & Co.
Made in U.S.A.
N-GDS10000-K6--2-2-3

RICE, MILLET AND GRAIN SORGHUM

Rice
Each dot represents 5,000,000 bushels (102,000 metric tons) per year

Millet and Grain Sorghum

B = Bajra
J = Jowar
K = Kaoliang
Kf = Kaffir Corn
M = Millet, undifferentiated
R = Ragi
S = Sorghum

Rice   World Production - 601,609,000 metric tons - Avg. 1999-2001

	0	10	20	30	40	50	60	70	80	90	100%

CHINA	INDIA	INDONESIA	BNGL.	VIETNAM	THAILAND	MYANMAR	PHIL.	OTHER ASIA	S. AMER.	AFRICA	ALL OTHER
31.6%	22.1	8.5	6.1	5.3	4.3	3.4	2.1	7.7	3.5	2.8	2.7

Rice Exports*   World Exports - 25,190,000 metric tons - Avg. 1999-2001

	0	10	20	30	40	50	60	70	80	90	100%

THAILAND	VIETNAM	CHINA	PAKISTAN	INDIA	OTHER ASIA	UNITED STATES	URUGUAY	ARG.	OTHER	ITALY	OTHER EUR.	AFRICA
27.4%	15.5	10.5	8.3	7.4	3.4	10.6	2.0	1.6	2.5	2.5	3.1	2.1

Millet & Grain Sorghum   World Production - 86,962,000 metric tons - Avg. 1999-2001

	0	10	20	30	40	50	60	70	80	90	100%

INDIA	CHINA	OTHER	UNITED STATES	MEXICO	NIGERIA	SUDAN	NIGER	BURK.	OTHER AFRICA	ARGENTINA	OTHER	AUSTRALIA	ALL OTHER
21.2%	5.8	2.1	15.8	7.0	15.3	4.2	3.0	2.4	12.5	3.7	1.9	2.8	2.2

Rice Imports   World Imports - 24,641,000 metric tons - Avg. 1999-2001

	0	10	20	30	40	50	60	70	80	90	100%

INDONESIA	IRAQ	IRAN	BNGL.	S. ARABIA	PHILIPPINES	JAPAN	MALAYSIA	CHINA	U.A.E.	OTHER ASIA	COTE D'IVOIRE	NIGERIA	SENEGAL	OTHER AFRICA	BRAZIL	EUROPE	NORTH AMERICA	ALL OTHER
9.1%	4.0	3.7	3.5	3.4	3.1	2.9	2.3	2.3	2.0	10.8	5.7	4.2	2.5	11.0	3.2	11.4	8.8	2.9

*including reexports

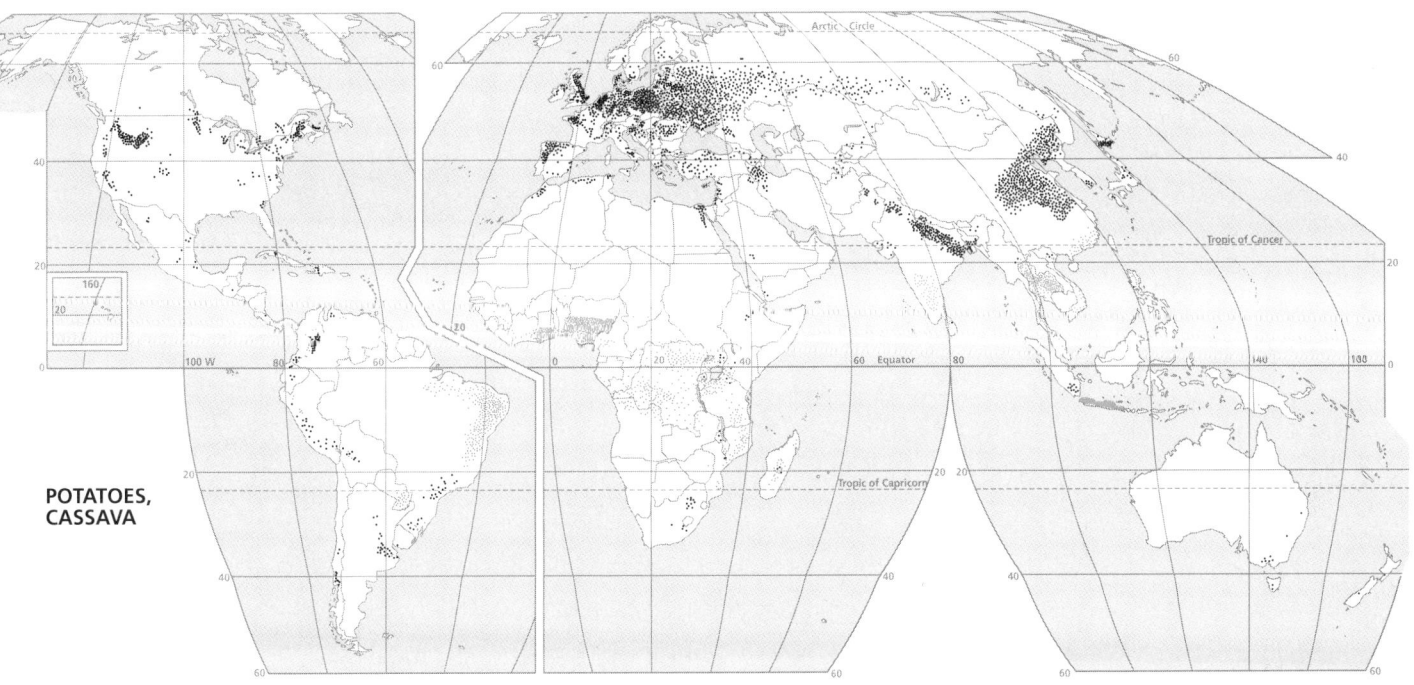

POTATOES, CASSAVA

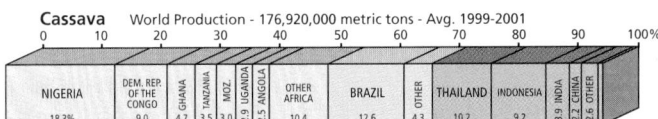

Copyright by Rand McNally & Co.
Made in U.S.A.
N-GDS10000-J8- -2-?-3

Potatoes

Each dot represents 100,000 metric tons average annual production

Potatoes   World Total - 312,408,000 metric tons - Avg. 1999-2001

CHINA	INDIA	OTHER ASIA	RUSSIA	UNITED STATES	POLAND	UKRAINE	GERMANY	BELARUS	NETH.	U.K.	FRANCE	OTHER EUROPE	SOUTH AMERICA	AFRICA
19.9%	7.5	9.5	10.7	6.9	6.8	5.3	4.0	2.6	2.5	2.1	2.1	8.9	4.4	3.9

Cassava

Each dot represents 100,000 metric tons average annual production

Cassava   World Production - 176,920,000 metric tons - Avg. 1999-2001

NIGERIA	DEM. REP. OF THE CONGO	GHANA	TANZANIA	MOZ.	UGANDA	ANGOLA	OTHER AFRICA	BRAZIL	OTHER	THAILAND	INDONESIA	INDIA	CHINA	OTHER
18.3%	9.0	4.7	3.5	3.0	2.9	2.5	10.4	12.6	4.3	10.2	9.2	3.9	2.2	2.6

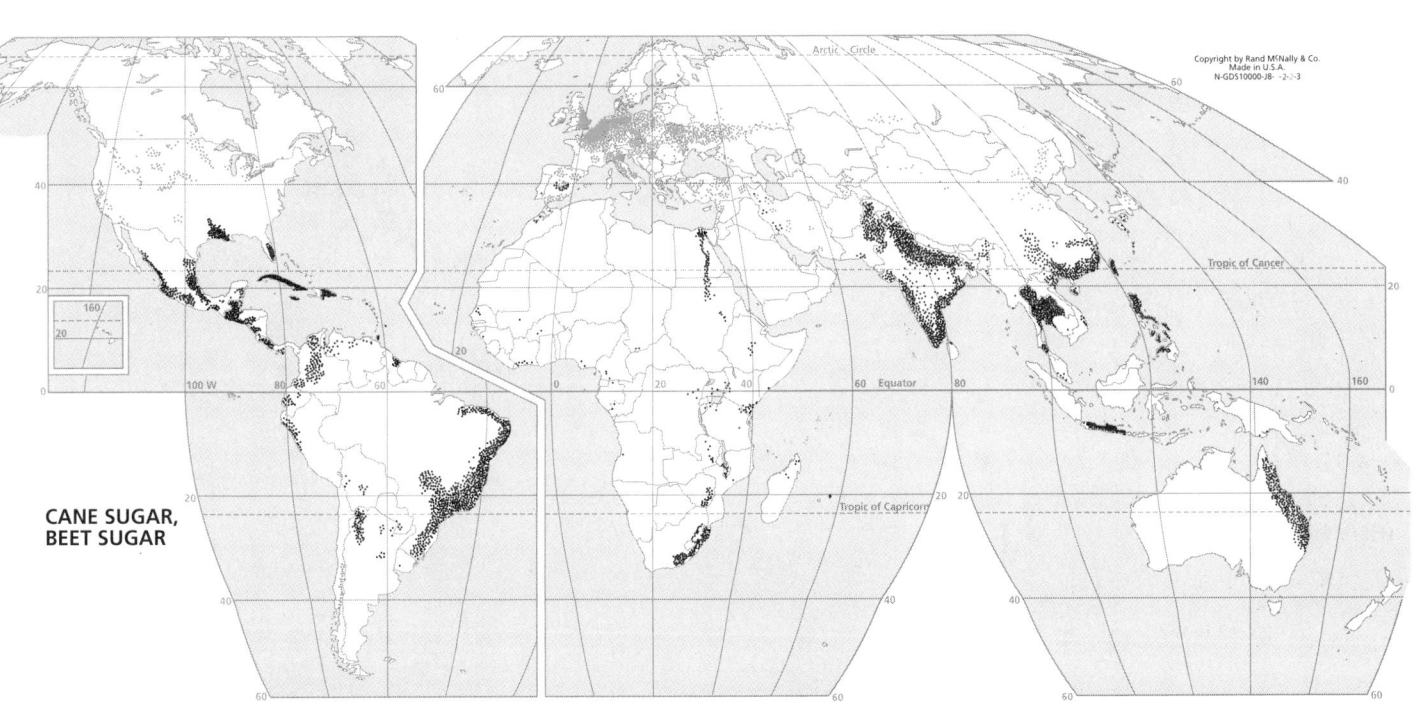

CANE SUGAR, BEET SUGAR

Cane Sugar

Each dot represents 20,000 metric tons average annual production

Cane Sugar   World Production - 98,587,000 metric tons - Avg. 1999-2001

INDIA	CHINA	THAILAND	PAKISTAN	OTHER ASIA	BRAZIL	COL.	OTHER S.A.	MEXICO	CUBA	UNITED STATES	OTHER N.A.	AUSTRALIA	S. AFRICA	OTHER AFRICA
20.3%	7.0	6.0	2.9	5.8	19.5	2.4	4.3	5.2	3.9	3.7	4.6	5.0	2.5	6.4

Beet Sugar

Each dot represents 20,000 metric tons average annual production

Beet Sugar   World Production - 35,732,000 metric tons - Avg. 1999-2001

GERMANY	FRANCE	POLAND	UKRAINE	ITALY	UNITED KINGDOM	SPAIN	NETH.	BELGIUM	OTHER EUROPE	UNITED STATES	TURKEY	CHINA	OTHER ASIA	RUSSIA	AFRICA & ALL OTHER
12.7%	12.6	5.4	4.9	4.6	4.2	3.2	3.2	2.9	12.7	11.6	6.3	2.6	4.4	4.8	2.2

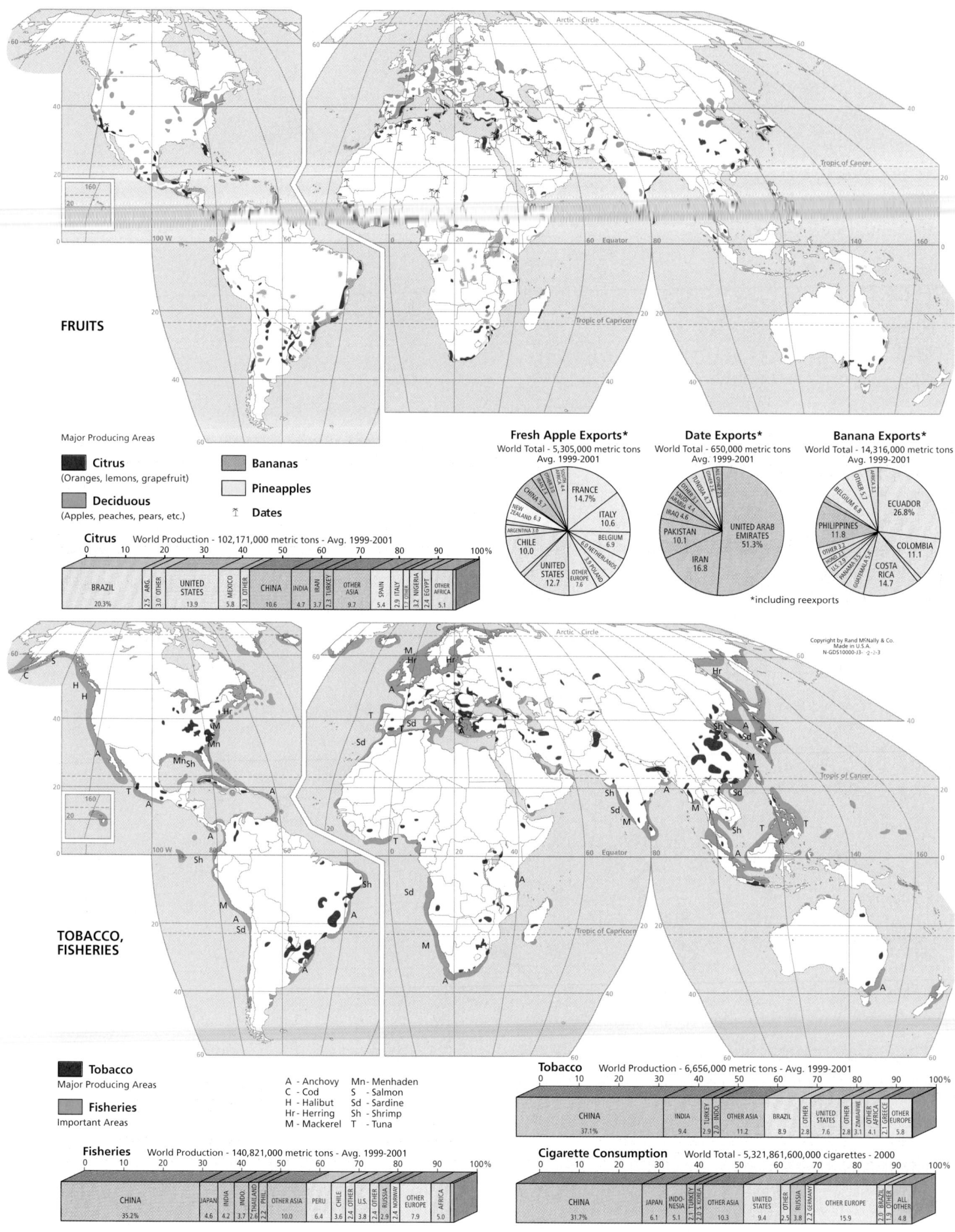

FRUITS

Major Producing Areas

Citrus
(Oranges, lemons, grapefruit)

Deciduous
(Apples, peaches, pears, etc.)

Bananas

Pineapples

⌘ **Dates**

Citrus • World Production - 102,171,000 metric tons - Avg. 1999-2001

| 0 | 10 | 20 | 30 | 40 | 50 | 60 | 70 | 80 | 90 | 100% |

| BRAZIL 20.3% | ARG. 2.5 | OTHER 3.0 | UNITED STATES 13.9 | MEXICO 5.8 | OTHER 2.3 | CHINA 10.6 | INDIA 4.7 | IRAN 3.7 | TURKEY 2.3 | OTHER ASIA 9.7 | SPAIN 5.4 | ITALY 2.9 | OTHER 1.7 | NIGERIA 3.2 | EGYPT 2.1 | OTHER AFRICA 5.1 |

Fresh Apple Exports*
World Total - 5,305,000 metric tons
Avg. 1999-2001

FRANCE 14.7%
ITALY 10.6
BELGIUM 6.9
NETHERLANDS 6.0
POLAND 3.3
OTHER EUROPE 7.6
UNITED STATES 12.7
CHILE 10.0
ARGENTINA 3.0
NEW ZEALAND 6.3
CHINA 5.7
OTHER ASIA 3.3
SOUTH AFRICA 4.4

Date Exports*
World Total - 650,000 metric tons
Avg. 1999-2001

UNITED ARAB EMIRATES 51.3%
IRAN 16.8
PAKISTAN 10.1
IRAQ 4.6
SAUDI ARABIA 4.4
TUNISIA 4.7
OTHER 4.7
ALL OTHERS 3.3

Banana Exports*
World Total - 14,316,000 metric tons
Avg. 1999-2001

ECUADOR 26.8%
COLOMBIA 11.1
COSTA RICA 14.7
GUATEMALA 5.4
PANAMA 3.2
HOND. 2.9
U.S. 2.1
PHILIPPINES 11.8
BELGIUM 6.8
OTHER 5.7
AFRICA 3.3

*including reexports

TOBACCO, FISHERIES

Tobacco
Major Producing Areas

Fisheries
Important Areas

A - Anchovy   Mn- Menhaden
C - Cod   S - Salmon
H - Halibut   Sd - Sardine
Hr - Herring   Sh - Shrimp
M - Mackerel   T - Tuna

Tobacco World Production - 6,656,000 metric tons - Avg. 1999-2001

| 0 | 10 | 20 | 30 | 40 | 50 | 60 | 70 | 80 | 90 | 100% |

| CHINA 37.1% | INDIA 9.4 | TURKEY 2.9 | INDO. 2.0 | OTHER ASIA 11.2 | BRAZIL 8.9 | OTHER 2.8 | UNITED STATES 7.6 | OTHER 2.8 | ZIMBABWE 4.1 | OTHER AFRICA 3.1 | OTHER EUROPE 5.8 |

Fisheries World Production - 140,821,000 metric tons - Avg. 1999-2001

| 0 | 10 | 20 | 30 | 40 | 50 | 60 | 70 | 80 | 90 | 100% |

| CHINA 35.2% | JAPAN 4.6 | INDIA 4.2 | INDO. 3.7 | THAILAND 2.6 | PHIL 2.2 | OTHER ASIA 10.0 | PERU 6.4 | CHILE 3.6 | U.S. 2.4 | OTHER RUSSIA 2.9 | NORWAY 2.4 | OTHER EUROPE 7.9 | AFRICA 5.0 |

Cigarette Consumption World Total - 5,321,861,600,000 cigarettes - 2000

| 0 | 10 | 20 | 30 | 40 | 50 | 60 | 70 | 80 | 90 | 100% |

| CHINA 31.7% | JAPAN 6.1 | INDO-NESIA 5.1 | TURKEY 2.1 | S. KOREA 2.0 | OTHER ASIA 10.3 | UNITED STATES 9.4 | OTHER 2.5 | RUSSIA 3.8 | GERMANY 2.2 | OTHER EUROPE 15.9 | BRAZIL 2.0 | OTHER 1.9 | ALL OTHER 4.8 |

Copyright by Rand McNally & Co.
Made in U.S.A.
N-GDS10000-J3- 2-2-3

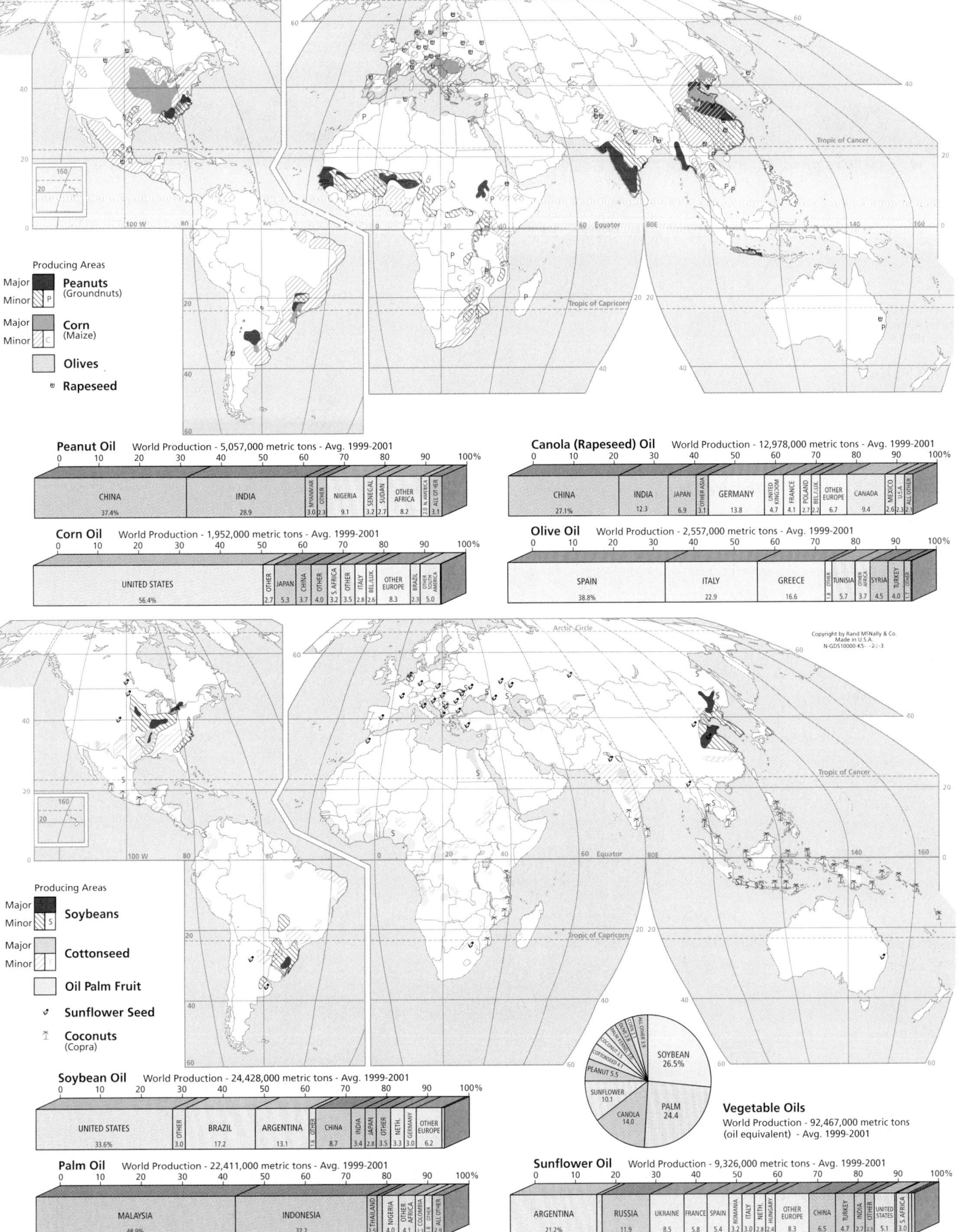

Producing Areas
Major / Minor — Peanuts (Groundnuts)
Major / Minor — Corn (Maize)
Olives
Rapeseed

Producing Areas
Major / Minor — Soybeans
Major / Minor — Cottonseed
Oil Palm Fruit
Sunflower Seed
Coconuts (Copra)

Peanut Oil World Production - 5,057,000 metric tons - Avg. 1999-2001
CHINA 37.4% | INDIA 28.9 | MYANMAR 3.0 | OTHER 2.3 | NIGERIA 9.1 | SENEGAL 3.2 | SUDAN 2.7 | OTHER AFRICA 8.2 | S. AMERICA 7.0 | ALL OTHER 3.1

Corn Oil World Production - 1,952,000 metric tons - Avg. 1999-2001
UNITED STATES 56.4% | OTHER 2.7 | JAPAN 5.3 | CHINA 3.7 | S. AFRICA 4.0 | OTHER 3.2 | ITALY 3.5 | BEL./LUX. 2.6 | OTHER EUROPE 8.3 | BRAZIL 2.3 | OTHER SOUTH AMERICA 5.0

Canola (Rapeseed) Oil World Production - 12,978,000 metric tons - Avg. 1999-2001
CHINA 27.1% | INDIA 12.3 | JAPAN 6.9 | OTHER ASIA 3.1 | GERMANY 13.8 | UNITED KINGDOM 4.7 | FRANCE 4.1 | POLAND 2.7 | BEL./LUX. 2.2 | OTHER EUROPE 6.7 | CANADA 9.4 | MEXICO 2.6 | U.S.A. 2.3 | ALL OTHER 2.1

Olive Oil World Production - 2,557,000 metric tons - Avg. 1999-2001
SPAIN 38.8% | ITALY 22.9 | GREECE 16.6 | OTHER 1.8 | TUNISIA 5.7 | OTHER AFRICA 3.7 | SYRIA 4.5 | TURKEY 4.0 | OTHER

Soybean Oil World Production - 24,428,000 metric tons - Avg. 1999-2001
UNITED STATES 33.6% | OTHER 3.0 | BRAZIL 17.2 | ARGENTINA 13.1 | OTHER 1.6 | CHINA 8.7 | INDIA 3.4 | JAPAN 2.8 | OTHER 3.5 | NETH. 3.3 | OTHER EUROPE 6.2

Palm Oil World Production - 22,411,000 metric tons - Avg. 1999-2001
MALAYSIA 48.9% | INDONESIA 32.2 | THAILAND 2.5 | NIGERIA 4.0 | OTHER AFRICA 4.1 | COLOMBIA 3.0 | OTHER 1.8 | ALL OTHER 2.9

Sunflower Oil World Production - 9,326,000 metric tons - Avg. 1999-2001
ARGENTINA 21.2% | RUSSIA 11.9 | UKRAINE 8.5 | FRANCE 5.8 | SPAIN 5.4 | ROMANIA 3.2 | ITALY 3.0 | NETH. 2.8 | HUNGARY 2.4 | OTHER EUROPE 8.3 | CHINA 6.5 | TURKEY 4.7 | INDIA 2.7 | OTHER 5.1 | UNITED STATES | S. AFRICA 3.0

Vegetable Oils World Production - 92,467,000 metric tons (oil equivalent) - Avg. 1999-2001
SOYBEAN 26.5% | PALM 24.4 | CANOLA 14.0 | SUNFLOWER 10.1 | PEANUT 5.5 | COTTONSEED 4.7 | COCONUT 3.5 | PALM KERNEL 3.1 | OLIVE 2.7 | ALL OTHER 5.5

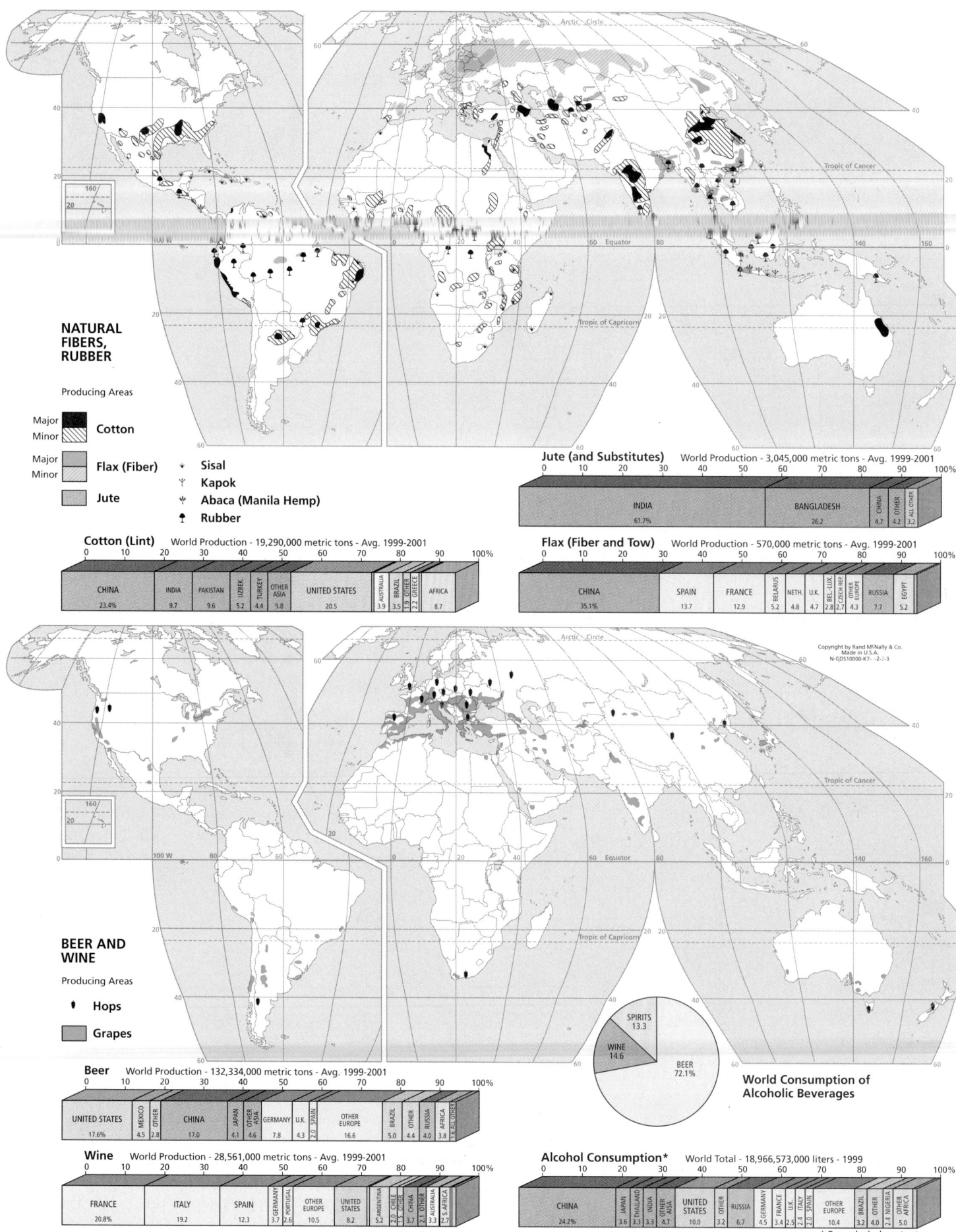

NATURAL FIBERS, RUBBER

Producing Areas

Major / Minor — Cotton

Major / Minor — Flax (Fiber)

Jute

- ↓ Sisal
- ⍦ Kapok
- ⍦ Abaca (Manila Hemp)
- ♣ Rubber

Cotton (Lint)
World Production - 19,290,000 metric tons - Avg. 1999-2001

CHINA 23.4%	INDIA 9.7	PAKISTAN 9.6	UZBEK 5.2	TURKEY 4.4	OTHER ASIA 5.8	UNITED STATES 20.5	AUSTRALIA 3.9	BRAZIL 3.5	OTHER 1.9	GREECE 2.2	AFRICA 8.7	

Jute (and Substitutes)
World Production - 3,045,000 metric tons - Avg. 1999-2001

INDIA 61.7%	BANGLADESH 26.2	CHINA 4.7	OTHER 4.2	ALL OTHER 3.2

Flax (Fiber and Tow)
World Production - 570,000 metric tons - Avg. 1999-2001

CHINA 35.1%	SPAIN 13.7	FRANCE 12.9	BELARUS 5.2	NETH. 4.8	U.K. 4.7	BEL.-LUX. 2.8	CZECH REP. 2.7	OTHER EUROPE 4.3	RUSSIA 7.7	EGYPT 5.2

BEER AND WINE

Producing Areas

- ♦ Hops
- Grapes

Beer
World Production - 132,334,000 metric tons - Avg. 1999-2001

UNITED STATES 17.6%	MEXICO 4.5	OTHER 2.8	CHINA 17.0	JAPAN 4.1	OTHER ASIA 4.6	GERMANY 7.8	U.K. 4.3	OTHER 2.0	OTHER EUROPE 16.6	BRAZIL 5.2	OTHER 4.4	RUSSIA 4.0	AFRICA 3.8	ALL OTHER 1.6

Wine
World Production - 28,561,000 metric tons - Avg. 1999-2001

FRANCE 20.8%	ITALY 19.2	SPAIN 12.3	GERMANY 3.7	PORTUGAL 2.6	OTHER EUROPE 10.5	UNITED STATES 8.2	ARGENTINA 5.2	CHILE 2.0	OTHER 1.3	CHINA 3.7	OTHER 2.1	AUSTRALIA 3.3	S. AFRICA 2.7

World Consumption of Alcoholic Beverages

- SPIRITS 13.3
- WINE 14.6
- BEER 72.1%

Alcohol Consumption*
World Total - 18,966,573,000 liters - 1999

CHINA 24.2%	JAPAN 3.6	THAILAND 3.3	INDIA 3.3	OTHER ASIA 4.7	UNITED STATES 10.0	OTHER 3.2	RUSSIA 6.7	GERMANY 4.5	FRANCE 3.4	U.K. 2.5	ITALY 2.4	SPAIN 2.3	OTHER EUROPE 10.4	BRAZIL 3.2	NIGERIA 4.0	OTHER AFRICA 5.0

* Pure alcohol content

Copyright by Rand McNally & Co.
Made in U.S.A.
N-GDS10000-K7- -2-2-3

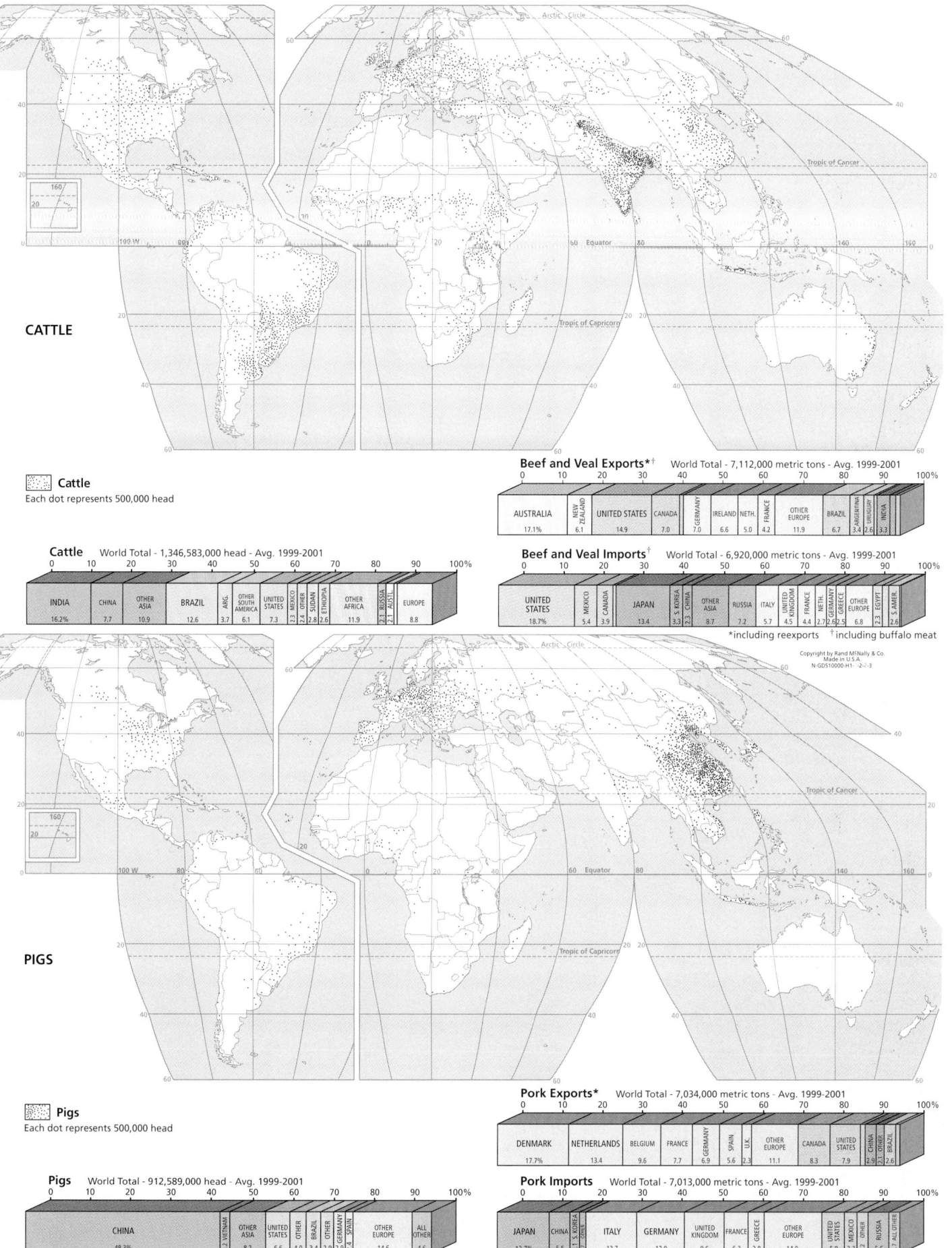

CATTLE

Cattle
Each dot represents 500,000 head

Cattle   World Total - 1,346,583,000 head - Avg. 1999-2001

0	10	20	30	40	50	60	70	80	90	100%

INDIA	CHINA	OTHER ASIA	BRAZIL	ARG.	OTHER SOUTH AMERICA	UNITED STATES	MEXICO	OTHER	SUDAN	ETHIOPIA	OTHER AFRICA	RUSSIA	AUSTL	EUROPE
16.2%	7.7	10.9	12.6	3.7	6.1	7.3	2.3	2.4	2.8	2.6	11.9	2.2	2.1	8.8

Beef and Veal Exports*[†]   World Total - 7,112,000 metric tons - Avg. 1999-2001

0	10	20	30	40	50	60	70	80	90	100%

AUSTRALIA	NEW ZEALAND	UNITED STATES	CANADA	GERMANY	IRELAND	NETH.	FRANCE	OTHER EUROPE	BRAZIL	ARGENTINA	URUGUAY	INDIA
17.1%	6.1	14.9	7.0	7.0	6.6	5.0	4.2	11.9	6.7	3.4	2.6	3.3

Beef and Veal Imports[†]   World Total - 6,920,000 metric tons - Avg. 1999-2001

0	10	20	30	40	50	60	70	80	90	100%

UNITED STATES	MEXICO	CANADA	JAPAN	S. KOREA	CHINA	OTHER ASIA	RUSSIA	ITALY	UNITED KINGDOM	FRANCE	NETH.	GERMANY	GREECE	OTHER EUROPE	EGYPT	S. AMER.
18.7%	5.4	3.9	13.4	3.3	2.3	8.7	7.2	5.7	4.5	4.4	2.7	2.6	2.5	6.8	2.1	2.6

*including reexports †including buffalo meat

Copyright by Rand McNally & Co.
Made in U.S.A.
N-GDS10000-H1- -2-2-3

PIGS

Pigs
Each dot represents 500,000 head

Pigs   World Total - 912,589,000 head - Avg. 1999-2001

0	10	20	30	40	50	60	70	80	90	100%

CHINA	VIETNAM	OTHER ASIA	UNITED STATES	OTHER	BRAZIL	OTHER	GERMANY	SPAIN	OTHER EUROPE	ALL OTHER
48.3%	2.2	8.2	6.6	4.0	3.4	2.9	2.4		14.6	4.6

Pork Exports*   World Total - 7,034,000 metric tons - Avg. 1999-2001

0	10	20	30	40	50	60	70	80	90	100%

DENMARK	NETHERLANDS	BELGIUM	FRANCE	GERMANY	SPAIN	U.K.	OTHER EUROPE	CANADA	UNITED STATES	CHINA	OTHER	BRAZIL
17.7%	13.4	9.6	7.7	6.9	5.6	2.3	11.1	8.3	7.9	2.9	2.1	2.6

Pork Imports   World Total - 7,013,000 metric tons - Avg. 1999-2001

0	10	20	30	40	50	60	70	80	90	100%

JAPAN	CHINA	S. KOREA	OTHER	ITALY	GERMANY	UNITED KINGDOM	FRANCE	GREECE	OTHER EUROPE	UNITED STATES	MEXICO	OTHER	RUSSIA	ALL OTHER
12.7%	5.5	2.1	1.7	12.7	12.0	9.6	6.3	3.8	14.0	5.9	3.2	2.1	5.6	2.7

*including reexports

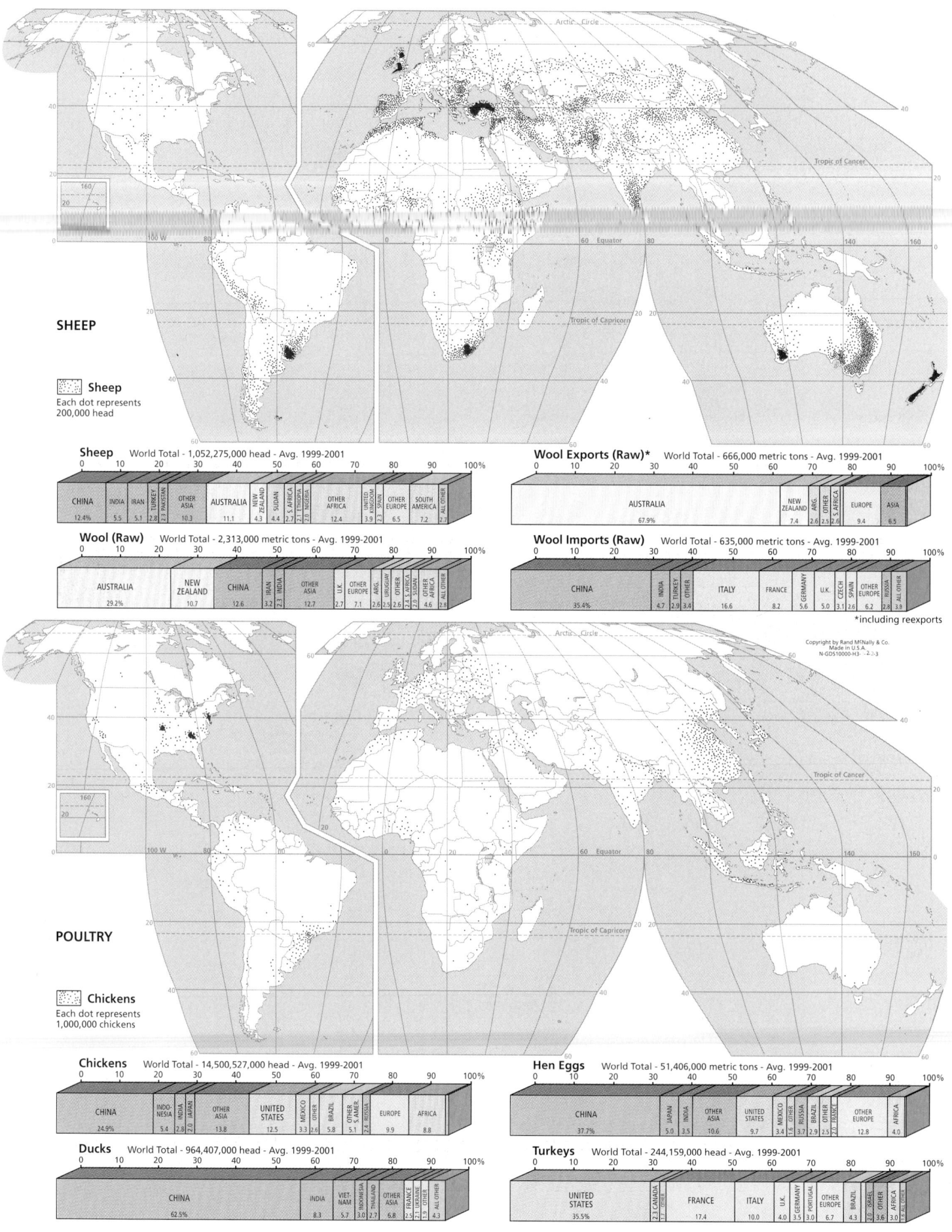

SHEEP

Sheep
Each dot represents
200,000 head

POULTRY

Chickens
Each dot represents
1,000,000 chickens

Sheep World Total - 1,052,275,000 head - Avg. 1999-2001

| CHINA 12.4% | INDIA 5.5 | IRAN 5.1 | TURKEY 2.8 | PAKISTAN 2.3 | OTHER ASIA 10.3 | AUSTRALIA 11.1 | NEW ZEALAND 4.3 | SUDAN 4.4 | S. AFRICA 2.7 | ETHIOPIA 2.0 | NIGERIA 2.0 | OTHER AFRICA 12.4 | UNITED KINGDOM 3.9 | OTHER EUROPE 6.5 | SOUTH AMERICA 7.2 | ALL OTHER 2.7 |

Wool (Raw) World Total - 2,313,000 metric tons - Avg. 1999-2001

| AUSTRALIA 29.2% | NEW ZEALAND 10.7 | CHINA 12.6 | IRAN 3.2 | INDIA 2.3 | OTHER ASIA 12.7 | U.K. 2.7 | OTHER EUROPE 7.1 | ARG. 2.6 | URUGUAY 2.5 | OTHER 2.6 | S. AFRICA 2.4 | SUDAN 2.0 | OTHER AFRICA 4.6 | ALL OTHER 2.8 |

Wool Exports (Raw)* World Total - 666,000 metric tons - Avg. 1999-2001

| AUSTRALIA 67.9% | NEW ZEALAND 7.4 | ARG. 2.6 | OTHER 2.5 | S. AFRICA 2.6 | EUROPE 9.4 | ASIA 6.5 |

Wool Imports (Raw) World Total - 635,000 metric tons - Avg. 1999-2001

| CHINA 35.4% | INDIA 4.7 | TURKEY 2.9 | OTHER 3.4 | ITALY 16.6 | FRANCE 8.2 | GERMANY 5.6 | U.K. 5.0 | CZECH 3.1 | SPAIN 2.6 | OTHER EUROPE 6.2 | RUSSIA 2.8 | ALL OTHER 3.8 |

*including reexports

Copyright by Rand McNally & Co.
Made in U.S.A.
N-GDS10000-H3---2/2-3

Chickens World Total - 14,500,527,000 head - Avg. 1999-2001

| CHINA 24.9% | INDO-NESIA 5.4 | INDIA 2.8 | JAPAN 2.0 | OTHER ASIA 13.8 | UNITED STATES 12.5 | MEXICO 3.3 | OTHER 2.6 | BRAZIL 5.8 | OTHER S. AMER. 5.1 | RUSSIA 2.4 | EUROPE 9.9 | AFRICA 8.8 |

Hen Eggs World Total - 51,406,000 metric tons - Avg. 1999-2001

| CHINA 37.7% | JAPAN 5.0 | INDIA 3.5 | OTHER ASIA 10.6 | UNITED STATES 9.7 | MEXICO 3.4 | OTHER 1.6 | RUSSIA 3.7 | BRAZIL 2.9 | OTHER 2.5 | FRANCE 2.0 | OTHER EUROPE 12.8 | AFRICA 4.0 |

Ducks World Total - 964,407,000 head - Avg. 1999-2001

| CHINA 62.5% | INDIA 8.3 | VIET-NAM 5.7 | INDONESIA 3.0 | THAILAND 2.7 | OTHER ASIA 6.8 | FRANCE 2.5 | UKRAINE 2.1 | OTHER 1.9 | ALL OTHER 4.3 |

Turkeys World Total - 244,159,000 head - Avg. 1999-2001

| UNITED STATES 35.5% | CANADA 2.3 | OTHER 1.7 | FRANCE 17.4 | ITALY 10.0 | U.K. 4.0 | GERMANY 3.5 | PORTUGAL 3.0 | OTHER EUROPE 6.7 | BRAZIL 4.3 | ISRAEL 2.0 | OTHER 3.6 | AFRICA 1.5 | ALL OTHER |

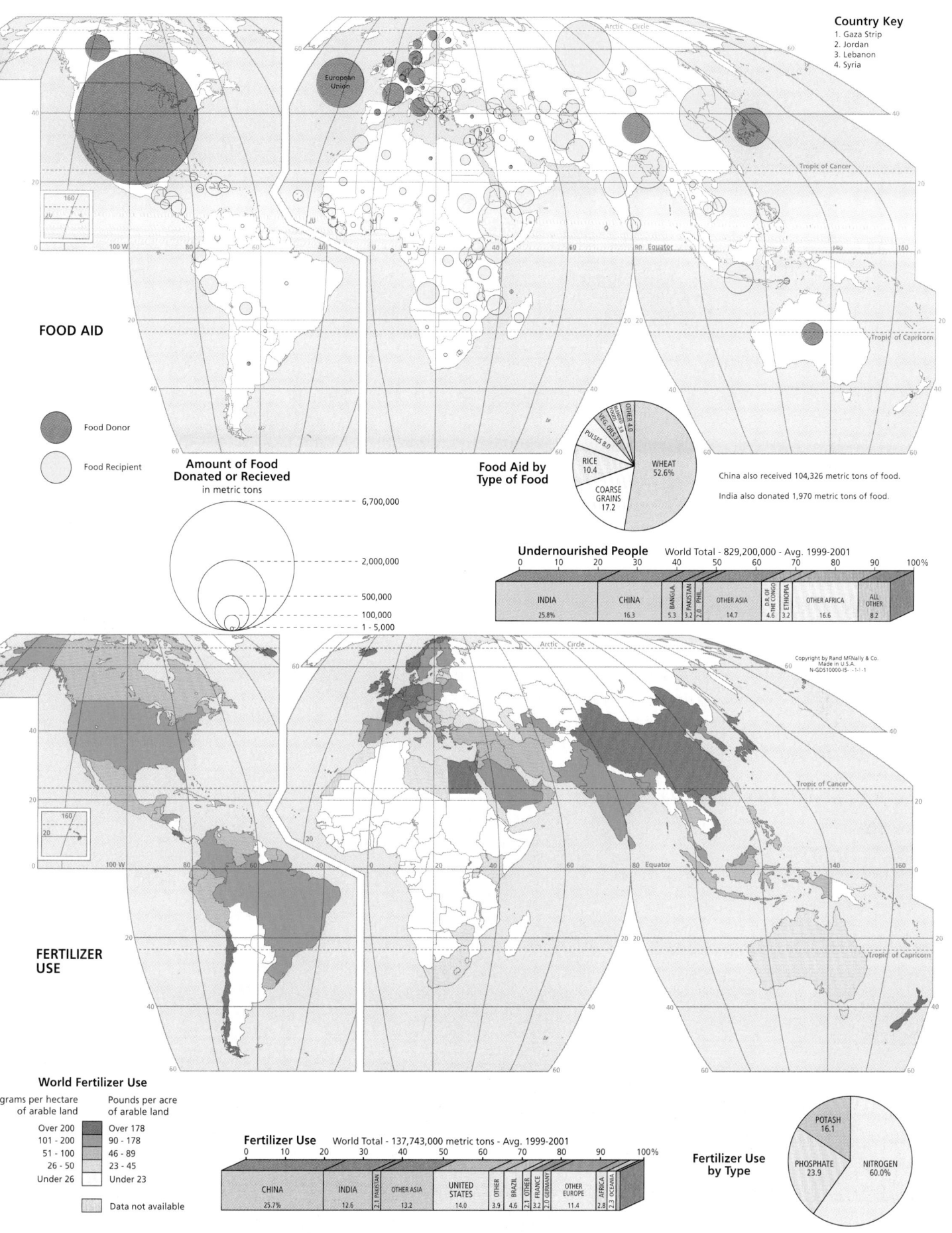

Country Key
1. Gaza Strip
2. Jordan
3. Lebanon
4. Syria

FOOD AID

European Union

Food Donor

Food Recipient

Amount of Food Donated or Recieved
in metric tons

6,700,000

2,000,000

500,000

100,000

1 - 5,000

Food Aid by Type of Food

OTHER 4.0
MISCELL. 4.0
VEG. OILS 3.7
PULSES 8.0
RICE 10.4
COARSE GRAINS 17.2
WHEAT 52.6%

China also received 104,326 metric tons of food.

India also donated 1,970 metric tons of food.

Undernourished People   World Total - 829,200,000 - Avg. 1999-2001

INDIA	CHINA	BANGLA.	PAKISTAN	PHIL.	OTHER ASIA	D.R. OF THE CONGO	ETHIOPIA	OTHER AFRICA	ALL OTHER
25.8%	16.3	5.3	3.2	2.0	14.7	4.6	3.2	16.6	8.2

Copyright by Rand McNally & Co.
Made in U.S.A.
N-GDS10000-I5- -1-1-1

FERTILIZER USE

World Fertilizer Use

Kilograms per hectare of arable land	Pounds per acre of arable land
Over 200	Over 178
101 - 200	90 - 178
51 - 100	46 - 89
26 - 50	23 - 45
Under 26	Under 23

Data not available

Fertilizer Use   World Total - 137,743,000 metric tons - Avg. 1999-2001

CHINA	INDIA	PAKISTAN	OTHER ASIA	UNITED STATES	OTHER	BRAZIL	OTHER	FRANCE	GERMANY	OTHER EUROPE	AFRICA	OCEANIA
25.7%	12.6	2.1	13.2	14.0	3.9	4.6	2.1	3.2	2.0	11.4	2.8	2.3

Fertilizer Use by Type

POTASH 16.1
PHOSPHATE 23.9
NITROGEN 60.0%

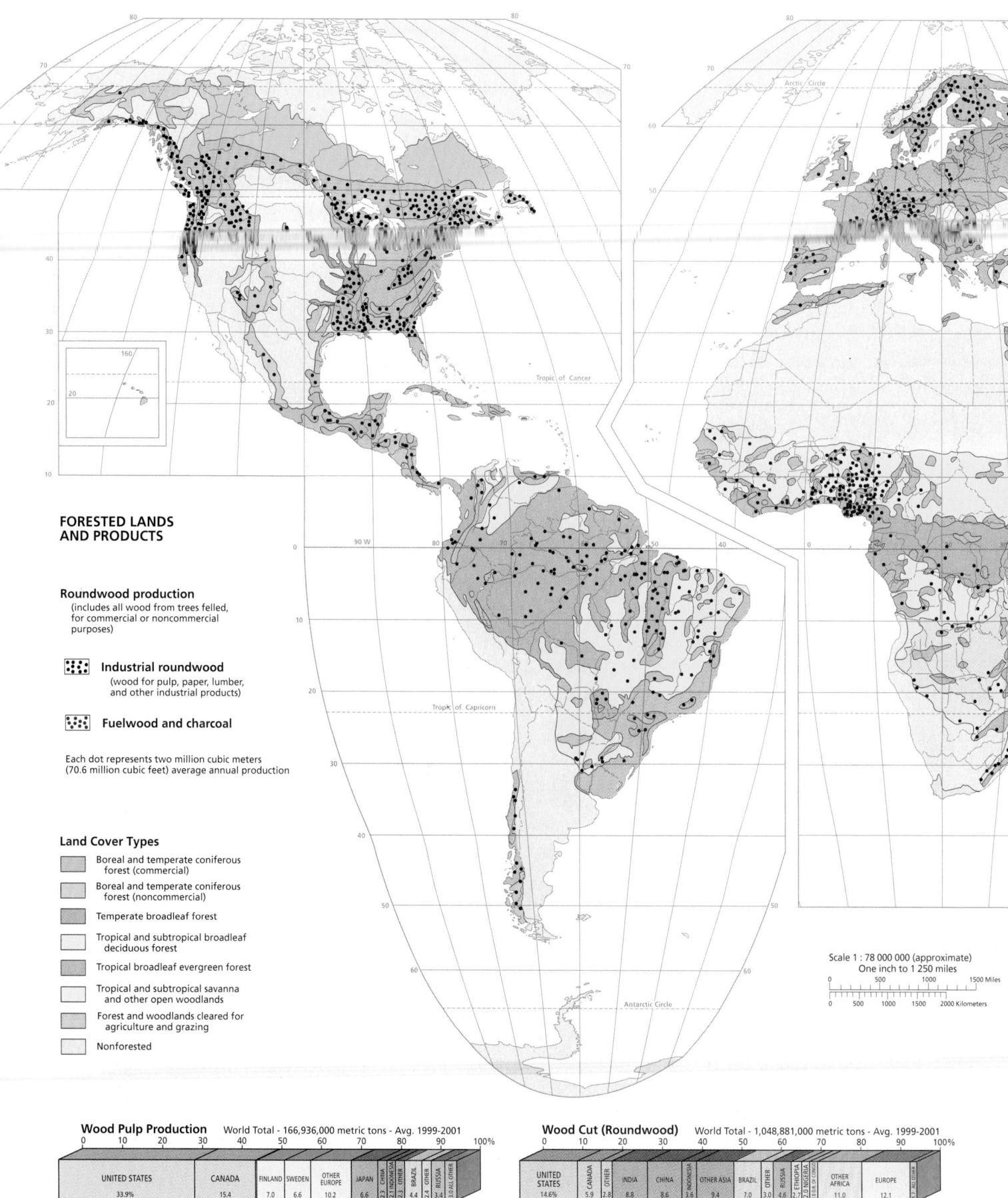

FORESTED LANDS AND PRODUCTS

Roundwood production
(includes all wood from trees felled, for commercial or noncommercial purposes)

Industrial roundwood
(wood for pulp, paper, lumber, and other industrial products)

Fuelwood and charcoal

Each dot represents two million cubic meters (70.6 million cubic feet) average annual production

Land Cover Types

- Boreal and temperate coniferous forest (commercial)
- Boreal and temperate coniferous forest (noncommercial)
- Temperate broadleaf forest
- Tropical and subtropical broadleaf deciduous forest
- Tropical broadleaf evergreen forest
- Tropical and subtropical savanna and other open woodlands
- Forest and woodlands cleared for agriculture and grazing
- Nonforested

Scale 1 : 78 000 000 (approximate)
One inch to 1 250 miles

| 0 | 500 | 1000 | 1500 Miles |
| 0 | 500 | 1000 | 1500 | 2000 Kilometers |

Wood Pulp Production
World Total - 166,936,000 metric tons - Avg. 1999-2001

| 0 | 10 | 20 | 30 | 40 | 50 | 60 | 70 | 80 | 90 | 100% |

UNITED STATES	CANADA	FINLAND	SWEDEN	OTHER EUROPE	JAPAN	CHINA	OTHER	BRAZIL	RUSSIA	ALL OTHER
33.9%	15.4	7.0	6.6	10.2	6.6	2.3	2.3	4.4	3.4	3.0

Wood Cut (Roundwood)
World Total - 1,048,881,000 metric tons - Avg. 1999-2001

| 0 | 10 | 20 | 30 | 40 | 50 | 60 | 70 | 80 | 90 | 100% |

UNITED STATES	CANADA	OTHER	INDIA	CHINA	INDONESIA	OTHER ASIA	BRAZIL	OTHER	RUSSIA	ETHIOPIA	NIGERIA	OTHER AFRICA	EUROPE	ALL OTHER
14.6%	5.9	2.8	8.8	8.6	3.6	9.4	7.0	3.0	4.6	2.7	2.0	11.0	12.1	

Tropic of Cancer

Longitude East of Greenwich

Equator

Tropic of Capricorn

Goode's Homolosine Equal Area Projection (Condensed)

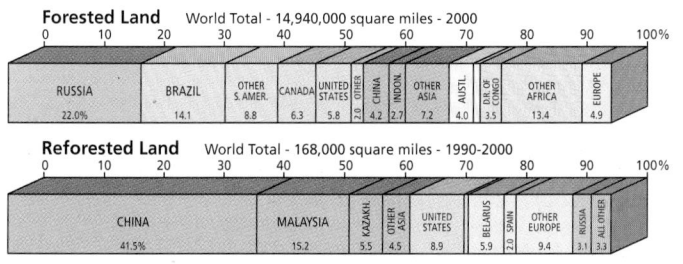

Forested Land World Total - 14,940,000 square miles - 2000

0	10	20	30	40	50	60	70	80	90	100%

| RUSSIA 22.0% | BRAZIL 14.1 | OTHER S. AMER. 8.8 | CANADA 6.3 | UNITED STATES 5.8 | OTHER 2.0 | CHINA 4.2 | INDON. 2.7 | OTHER ASIA 7.2 | AUSTL. 4.0 | D.R. OF CONGO 3.5 | OTHER AFRICA 13.4 | EUROPE 4.9 |

Reforested Land World Total - 168,000 square miles - 1990-2000

0	10	20	30	40	50	60	70	80	90	100%

| CHINA 41.5% | MALAYSIA 15.2 | KAZAKH. 5.5 | OTHER ASIA 4.5 | UNITED STATES 8.9 | BELARUS 5.9 | SPAIN 2.0 | OTHER EUROPE 9.4 | RUSSIA 3.1 | ALL OTHER 3.3 |

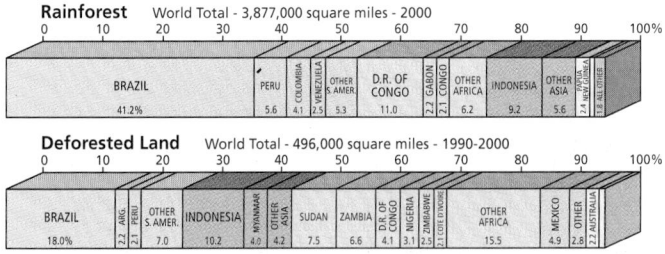

Rainforest World Total - 3,877,000 square miles - 2000

0	10	20	30	40	50	60	70	80	90	100%

| BRAZIL 41.2% | PERU 5.6 | COLOMBIA 4.1 | VENEZUELA 2.5 | OTHER S. AMER. 5.3 | D.R. OF CONGO 11.0 | GABON 2.2 | CONGO 2.1 | OTHER AFRICA 6.2 | INDONESIA 9.2 | OTHER ASIA 5.6 | PAPUA NEW GUINEA 2.4 | ALL OTHER 1.8 |

Deforested Land World Total - 496,000 square miles - 1990-2000

0	10	20	30	40	50	60	70	80	90	100%

| BRAZIL 18.0% | ARG. 2.2 | PERU 2.1 | OTHER S. AMER. 7.0 | INDONESIA 10.2 | MYANMAR 4.0 | OTHER ASIA 4.2 | SUDAN 7.5 | ZAMBIA 6.6 | D.R. OF CONGO 4.1 | NIGERIA 3.4 | ZIMBABWE 2.5 | CÔTE D'IVOIRE 2.1 | OTHER AFRICA 15.5 | MEXICO 4.9 | OTHER 2.8 | AUSTRALIA 2.2 |

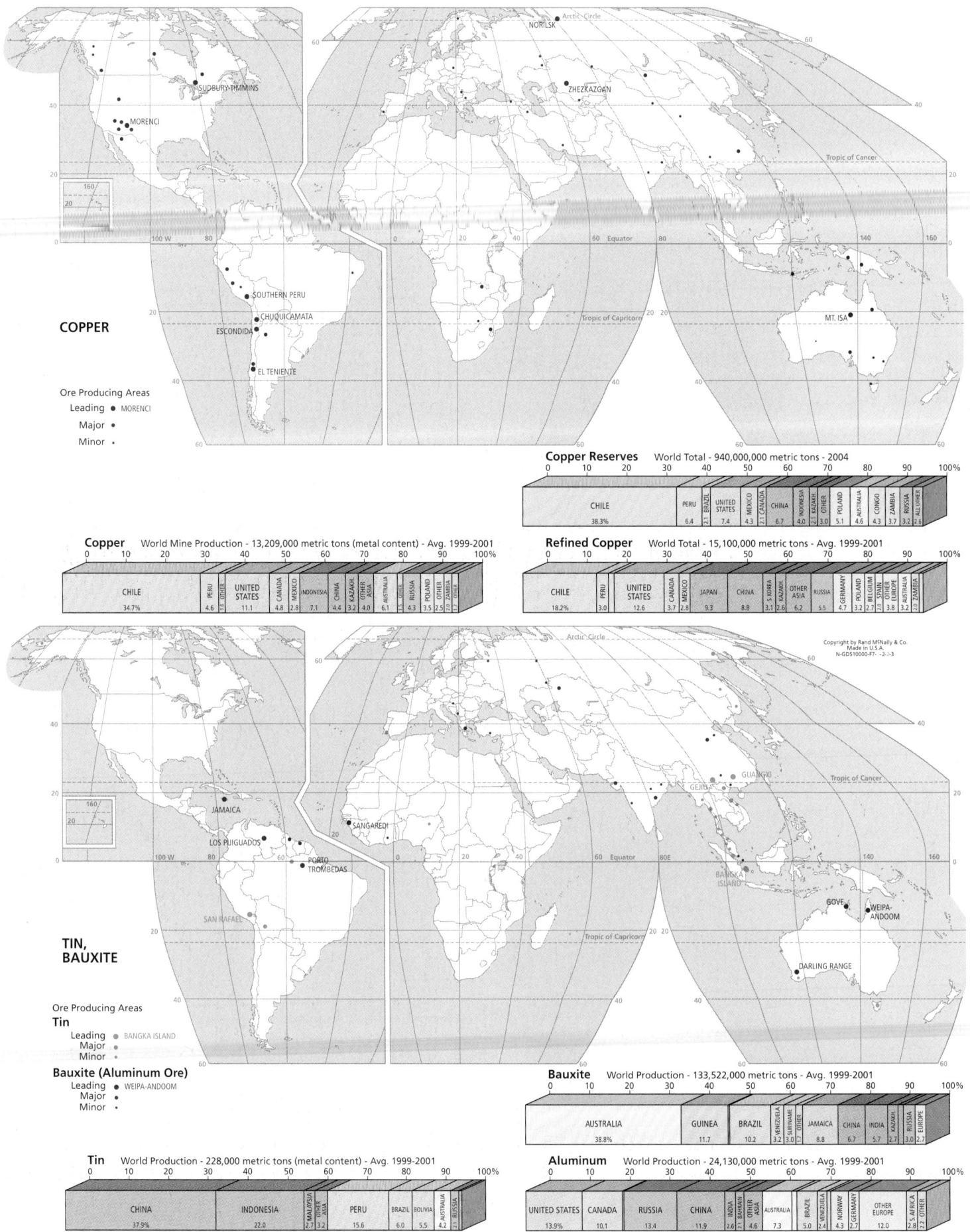

COPPER

Ore Producing Areas

Leading ● MORENCI

Major •

Minor ·

Copper Reserves World Total - 940,000,000 metric tons - 2004

CHILE	PERU	BRAZIL	UNITED STATES	MEXICO	CANADA	CHINA	INDONESIA	KAZAKH.	OTHER	POLAND	AUSTRALIA	CONGO	ZAMBIA	RUSSIA	ALL OTHER
38.3%	6.4	2.1	7.4	4.3	2.1	6.7	4.0	2.1	3.0	5.1	4.6	4.3	3.7	3.2	2.6

Copper World Mine Production - 13,209,000 metric tons (metal content) - Avg. 1999-2001

CHILE	PERU	OTHER	UNITED STATES	CANADA	MEXICO	INDONESIA	CHINA	KAZAKH.	OTHER ASIA	AUSTRALIA	OTHER	RUSSIA	POLAND	ZAMBIA	OTHER
34.7%	4.6	1.8	11.1	4.8	2.8	7.1	4.4	3.2	4.0	6.1	1.5	4.3	3.5	2.0	1.7

Refined Copper World Total - 15,100,000 metric tons - Avg. 1999-2001

CHILE	PERU	UNITED STATES	CANADA	MEXICO	JAPAN	CHINA	S. KOREA	KAZAKH.	OTHER ASIA	RUSSIA	GERMANY	POLAND	BELGIUM	SPAIN	OTHER EUROPE	AUSTRALIA	ZAMBIA
18.2%	3.0	12.6	3.7	2.8	9.3	8.8	3.1	2.6	6.2	5.5	4.7	3.2	2.7	3.8	2.7

Copyright by Rand McNally & Co.
Made in U.S.A.
N-GDS10000-F7- -2-?-3

TIN, BAUXITE

Ore Producing Areas

Tin

Leading ● BANGKA ISLAND

Major •

Minor ·

Bauxite (Aluminum Ore)

Leading ● WEIPA-ANDOOM

Major •

Minor ·

Tin World Production - 228,000 metric tons (metal content) - Avg. 1999-2001

CHINA	INDONESIA	MALAYSIA	OTHER ASIA	PERU	BRAZIL	BOLIVIA	AUSTRALIA	RUSSIA
37.9%	22.0	2.7	3.2	15.6	6.0	5.5	4.2	2.1

Bauxite World Production - 133,522,000 metric tons - Avg. 1999-2001

AUSTRALIA	GUINEA	BRAZIL	VENEZUELA	SURINAME	OTHER	JAMAICA	CHINA	INDIA	KAZAKH	RUSSIA	EUROPE
38.8%	11.7	10.2	3.2	3.0	1.7	8.8	6.7	5.7	2.7	3.0	2.7

Aluminum World Production - 24,130,000 metric tons - Avg. 1999-2001

UNITED STATES	CANADA	RUSSIA	CHINA	INDIA	BAHRAIN	OTHER ASIA	AUSTRALIA	BRAZIL	VENEZUELA	NORWAY	GERMANY	OTHER EUROPE	S. AFRICA	OTHER
13.9%	10.1	13.4	11.9	2.6	2.1	4.6	7.3	5.0	2.4	4.3	2.7	12.0	2.8	2.2

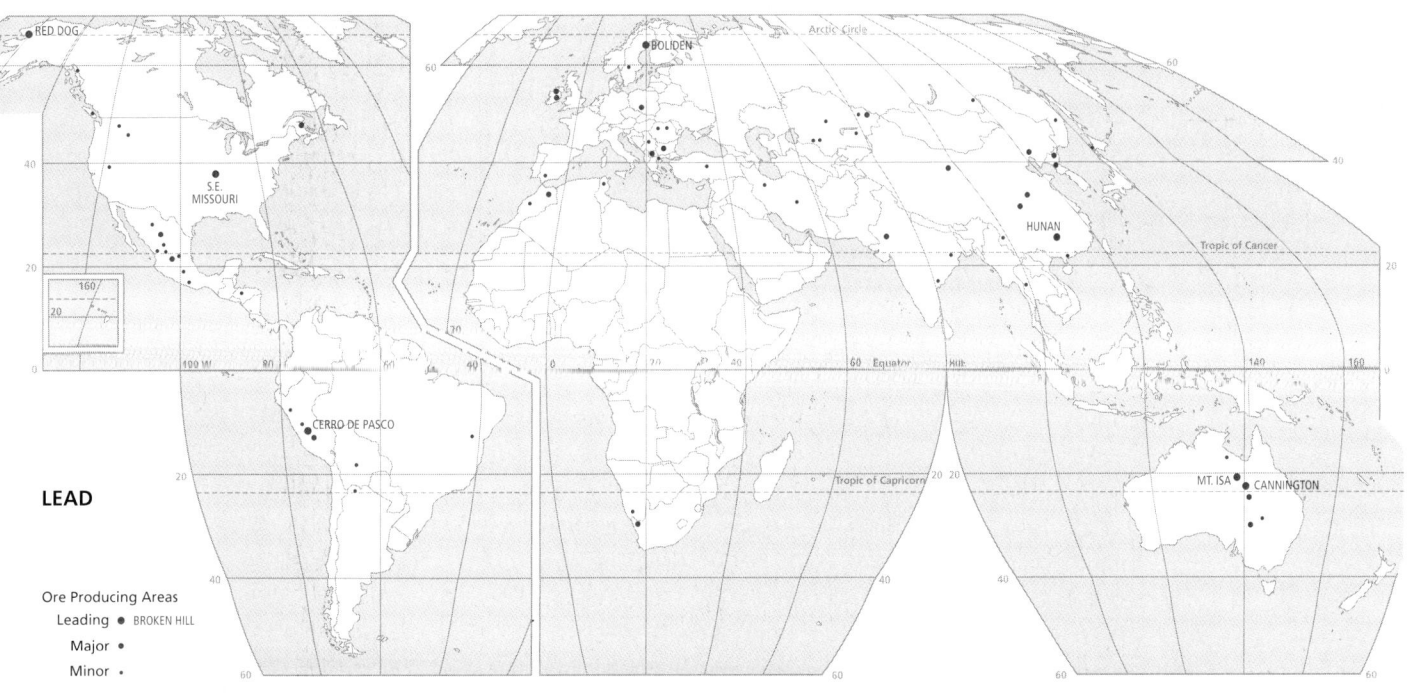

LEAD

Ore Producing Areas

Leading ● BROKEN HILL

Major ●

Minor ·

The percentage of lead smelted by each country is not necessarily identical to its percentage of lead ore production. Some countries, such as Australia, export large amounts of ore to other countries for smelting.

Lead World Mine Production - 3,124,000 metric tons (metal content) - Avg. 1999-2001

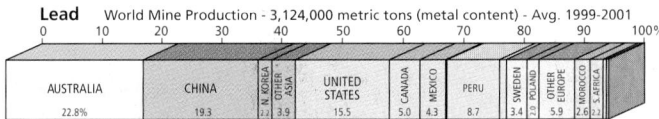

AUSTRALIA	CHINA	N. KOREA	OTHER ASIA	UNITED STATES	CANADA	MEXICO	PERU	SWEDEN	POLAND	OTHER EUROPE	MOROCCO	S. AFRICA
22.8%	19.3	2.2	3.9	15.5	5.0	4.3	8.7	3.4	2.0	5.9	2.6	2.2

Lead Smelted* World Production - 6,417,000 metric tons - Avg. 1999-2001

UNITED STATES	CANADA	ARUBA	MEXICO	CHINA	JAPAN	S. KOREA	KAZAKH.	OTHER ASIA	GERMANY	U.K.	FRANCE	ITALY	BELGIUM	SPAIN	OTHER EUROPE	PERU	ALL OTHER
22.4%	4.3	4.3	2.2	16.5	4.7	2.7	2.6	6.0	6.0	5.5	3.4	1.6	1.6	2.6	5.0	1.8	4.0

*includes recycled materials

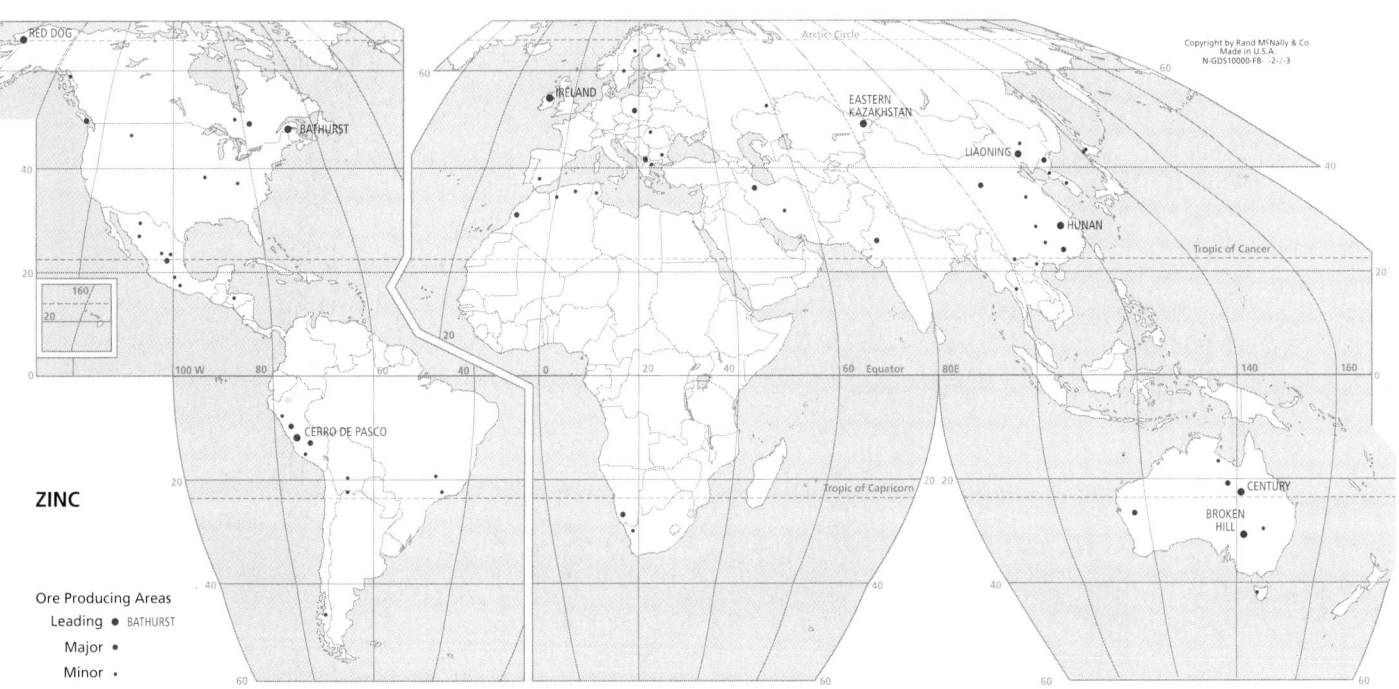

Copyright by Rand McNally & Co.
Made in U.S.A.
N-GDS10000-FB · -2-/-3

ZINC

Ore Producing Areas

Leading ● BATHURST

Major ●

Minor ·

The percentage of zinc smelted by each country is not necessarily identical to its percentage of zinc ore production. Some countries, such as Australia, export large amounts of ore to other countries for smelting.

Zinc World Mine Production - 8,559,000 metric tons (metal content) - Avg. 1999-2001

CHINA	KAZAKHSTAN	N. KOREA	OTHER ASIA	AUSTRALIA	CANADA	UNITED STATES	MEXICO	PERU	OTHER S. AMERICA	IRELAND	OTHER EUROPE	ALL OTHER
18.9%	3.7	2.2	4.1	16.0	11.3	9.9	4.5	11.2	3.3	2.8	6.6	5.1

Zinc Smelted* World Production - 9,011,000, metric tons - Avg. 1999-2001

CHINA	JAPAN	SOUTH KOREA	KAZAKHSTAN	INDIA	N. KOREA	CANADA	UNITED STATES	MEXICO	AUSTL.	SPAIN	GERMANY	FRANCE	BELGIUM	FINLAND	NETH.	OTHER EUROPE	RUSSIA	PERU	BRAZIL	ALL OTHER
21.2%	7.7	5.1	2.9	2.3	2.1	8.7	3.9	2.6	5.2	4.1	3.9	3.8	2.7	2.6	2.4	8.5	2.5	2.2	2.2	1.3

*includes recycled materials

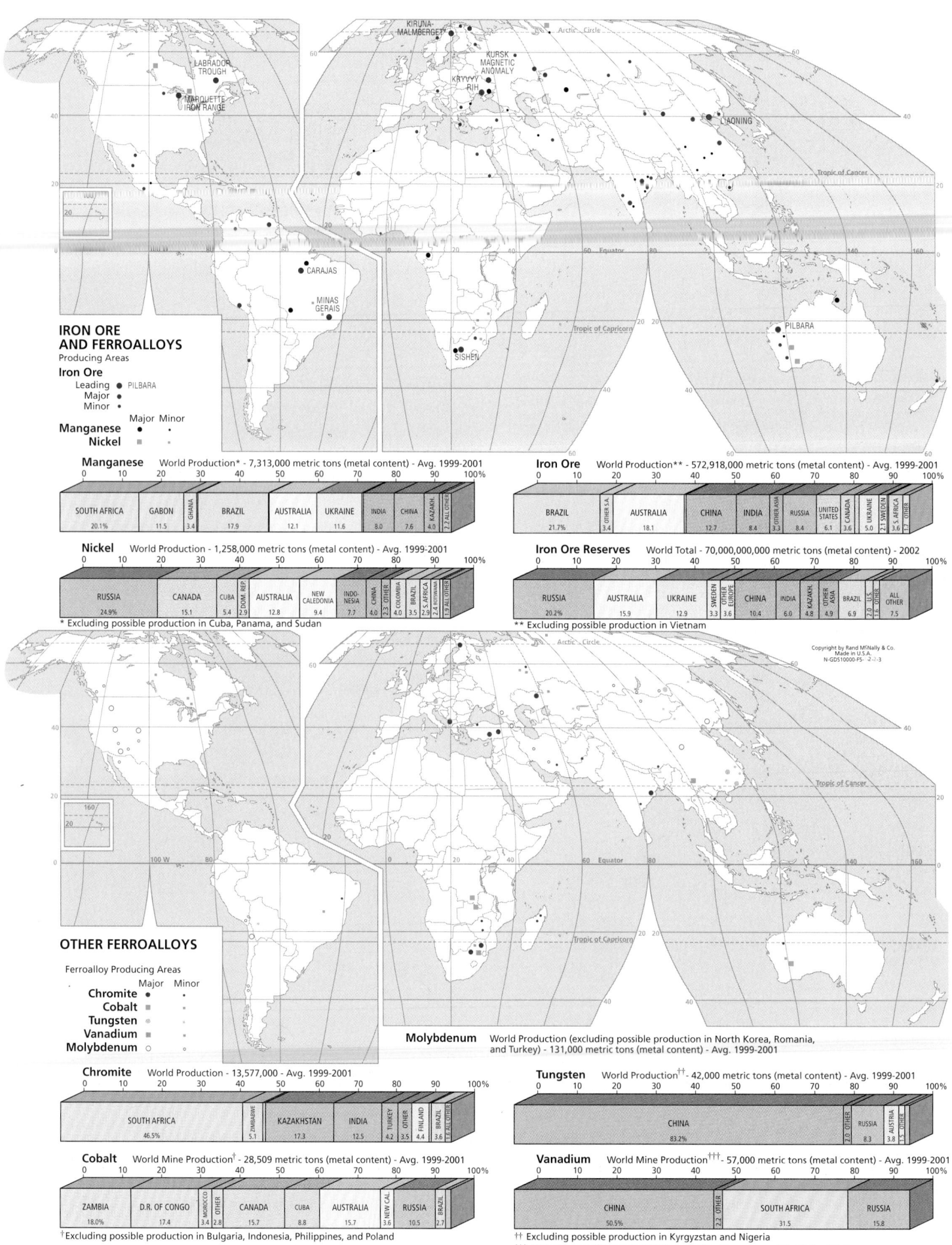

IRON ORE AND FERROALLOYS
Producing Areas

Iron Ore
- Leading ● PILBARA
- Major ●
- Minor ·

	Major	Minor
Manganese	●	·
Nickel	■	▪

Manganese
World Production* - 7,313,000 metric tons (metal content) - Avg. 1999-2001

0	10	20	30	40	50	60	70	80	90	100%

SOUTH AFRICA	GABON	GHANA	BRAZIL	AUSTRALIA	UKRAINE	INDIA	CHINA	KAZAKH.	ALL OTHER
20.1%	11.5	3.4	17.9	12.1	11.6	8.0	7.6	4.0	2.2 1.7

Nickel
World Production - 1,258,000 metric tons (metal content) - Avg. 1999-2001

0	10	20	30	40	50	60	70	80	90	100%

RUSSIA	CANADA	CUBA	DOM. REP.	AUSTRALIA	NEW CALEDONIA	INDO-NESIA	CHINA	OTHER	BRAZIL	S. AFRICA	ALL OTHER
24.9%	15.1	5.4	2.9	12.8	9.4	7.7	4.0	2.3	4.0	3.5	2.4 BOTSWANA 1.9

*Excluding possible production in Cuba, Panama, and Sudan

Iron Ore
World Production** - 572,918,000 metric tons (metal content) - Avg. 1999-2001

0	10	20	30	40	50	60	70	80	90	100%

BRAZIL	OTHER S.A.	AUSTRALIA	CHINA	INDIA	OTHER ASIA	RUSSIA	UNITED STATES	CANADA	UKRAINE	SWEDEN	OTHER
21.7%	3.4	18.1	12.7	8.4	3.3	8.4	6.1	3.6	5.0	2.1	3.6 1.7

Iron Ore Reserves
World Total - 70,000,000,000 metric tons (metal content) - 2002

0	10	20	30	40	50	60	70	80	90	100%

RUSSIA	AUSTRALIA	UKRAINE	SWEDEN	OTHER EUROPE	CHINA	INDIA	KAZAKH.	OTHER ASIA	BRAZIL	U.S.	ALL OTHER
20.2%	15.9	12.9	3.3		10.4	6.0	4.8	4.9	6.9	2.0 1.6	7.5

** Excluding possible production in Vietnam

Copyright by Rand McNally & Co.
Made in U.S.A.
N-GDS10000-FS- -2-2-3

OTHER FERROALLOYS

Ferroalloy Producing Areas

	Major	Minor
Chromite	●	·
Cobalt	■	▪
Tungsten	◉	∘
Vanadium	■	▪
Molybdenum	○	∘

Molybdenum
World Production (excluding possible production in North Korea, Romania, and Turkey) - 131,000 metric tons (metal content) - Avg. 1999-2001

Chromite
World Production - 13,577,000 - Avg. 1999-2001

0	10	20	30	40	50	60	70	80	90	100%

SOUTH AFRICA	ZIMBABWE	KAZAKHSTAN	INDIA	TURKEY	OTHER	FINLAND	BRAZIL	ALL OTHER
46.5%	5.1	17.3	12.5	4.2	3.5	4.4	3.6 2.8

Cobalt
World Mine Production† - 28,509 metric tons (metal content) - Avg. 1999-2001

0	10	20	30	40	50	60	70	80	90	100%

ZAMBIA	D.R. OF CONGO	MOROCCO	OTHER	CANADA	CUBA	AUSTRALIA	NEW CAL.	RUSSIA	BRAZIL
18.0%	17.4	3.4	2.8	15.7	8.8	15.7		10.5	2.7

† Excluding possible production in Bulgaria, Indonesia, Philippines, and Poland

Tungsten
World Production†† - 42,000 metric tons (metal content) - Avg. 1999-2001

0	10	20	30	40	50	60	70	80	90	100%

CHINA	OTHER	RUSSIA	AUSTRIA	OTHER
83.2%	2.0	8.3	3.8	1.5

Vanadium
World Mine Production††† - 57,000 metric tons (metal content) - Avg. 1999-2001

0	10	20	30	40	50	60	70	80	90	100%

CHINA	OTHER	SOUTH AFRICA	RUSSIA
50.5%	2.2	31.5	15.8

†† Excluding possible production in Kyrgyzstan and Nigeria
††† Excluding possible production in Australia, Germany, and the United States

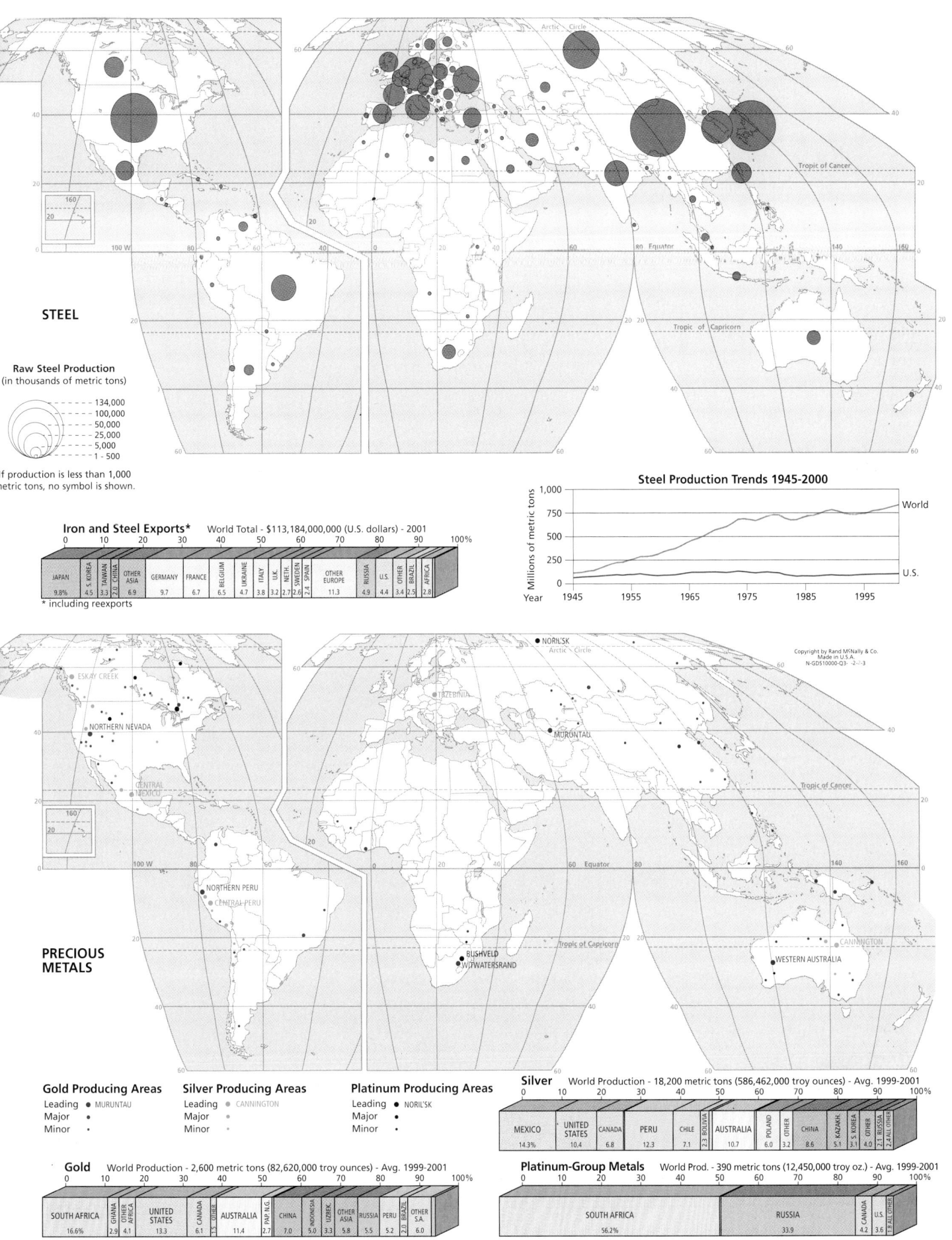

STEEL

Raw Steel Production
(in thousands of metric tons)

- - - - - - - 134,000
- - - - - - - 100,000
- - - - - - - 50,000
- - - - - - - 25,000
- - - - - - - 5,000
- - - - - - - 1 - 500

If production is less than 1,000 metric tons, no symbol is shown.

Iron and Steel Exports* World Total - $113,184,000,000 (U.S. dollars) - 2001

0	10	20	30	40	50	60	70	80	90	100%

JAPAN	S. KOREA	TAIWAN	CHINA	OTHER ASIA	GERMANY	FRANCE	BELGIUM	UKRAINE	ITALY	U.K.	SWEDEN	NETH.	SPAIN	OTHER EUROPE	RUSSIA	U.S.	OTHER	BRAZIL	AFRICA
9.8%	4.5	3.3	2.0	6.9	9.7	6.7	6.5	4.7	3.8	3.2	2.7	2.6	2.4	11.3	4.9	4.4	3.4	2.5	2.8

* including reexports

Steel Production Trends 1945-2000

Millions of metric tons / Year

1,000 / 750 / 500 / 250 / World / U.S.

1945 1955 1965 1975 1985 1995

PRECIOUS METALS

NORIL'SK
ESKAY CREEK
NORTHERN NEVADA
CENTRAL MEXICO
TREBINJA
MURUNTAU
NORTHERN PERU
CENTRAL PERU
BUSHVELD
WITWATERSRAND
WESTERN AUSTRALIA
CANNINGTON

Gold Producing Areas
- Leading ● MURUNTAU
- Major ●
- Minor ·

Silver Producing Areas
- Leading ● CANNINGTON
- Major ●
- Minor ·

Platinum Producing Areas
- Leading ● NORIL'SK
- Major ●
- Minor ·

Silver World Production - 18,200 metric tons (586,462,000 troy ounces) - Avg. 1999-2001

0	10	20	30	40	50	60	70	80	90	100%

MEXICO	UNITED STATES	CANADA	PERU	CHILE	BOLIVIA	AUSTRALIA	POLAND	OTHER	CHINA	KAZAKH.	S. KOREA	OTHER	RUSSIA	ALL OTHER
14.3%	10.4	6.8	12.3	7.1	2.3	10.7	6.0	3.2	8.6	5.1	3.1	4.0	2.1	2.4

Gold World Production - 2,600 metric tons (82,620,000 troy ounces) - Avg. 1999-2001

0	10	20	30	40	50	60	70	80	90	100%

SOUTH AFRICA	GHANA	OTHER AFRICA	UNITED STATES	CANADA	OTHER	AUSTRALIA	PAP N.G.	CHINA	INDONESIA	UZBEK.	OTHER ASIA	RUSSIA	PERU	BRAZIL	OTHER S.A.
16.6%	2.9	4.1	13.3	6.1	1.5	11.4	2.7	7.0	5.0	3.3	5.8	5.5	5.2	2.0	6.0

Platinum-Group Metals World Prod. - 390 metric tons (12,450,000 troy oz.) - Avg. 1999-2001

0	10	20	30	40	50	60	70	80	90	100%

SOUTH AFRICA	RUSSIA	CANADA	U.S.	RUSSIA	ALL OTHER
56.2%	33.9	4.2	3.6	2.1	1.8

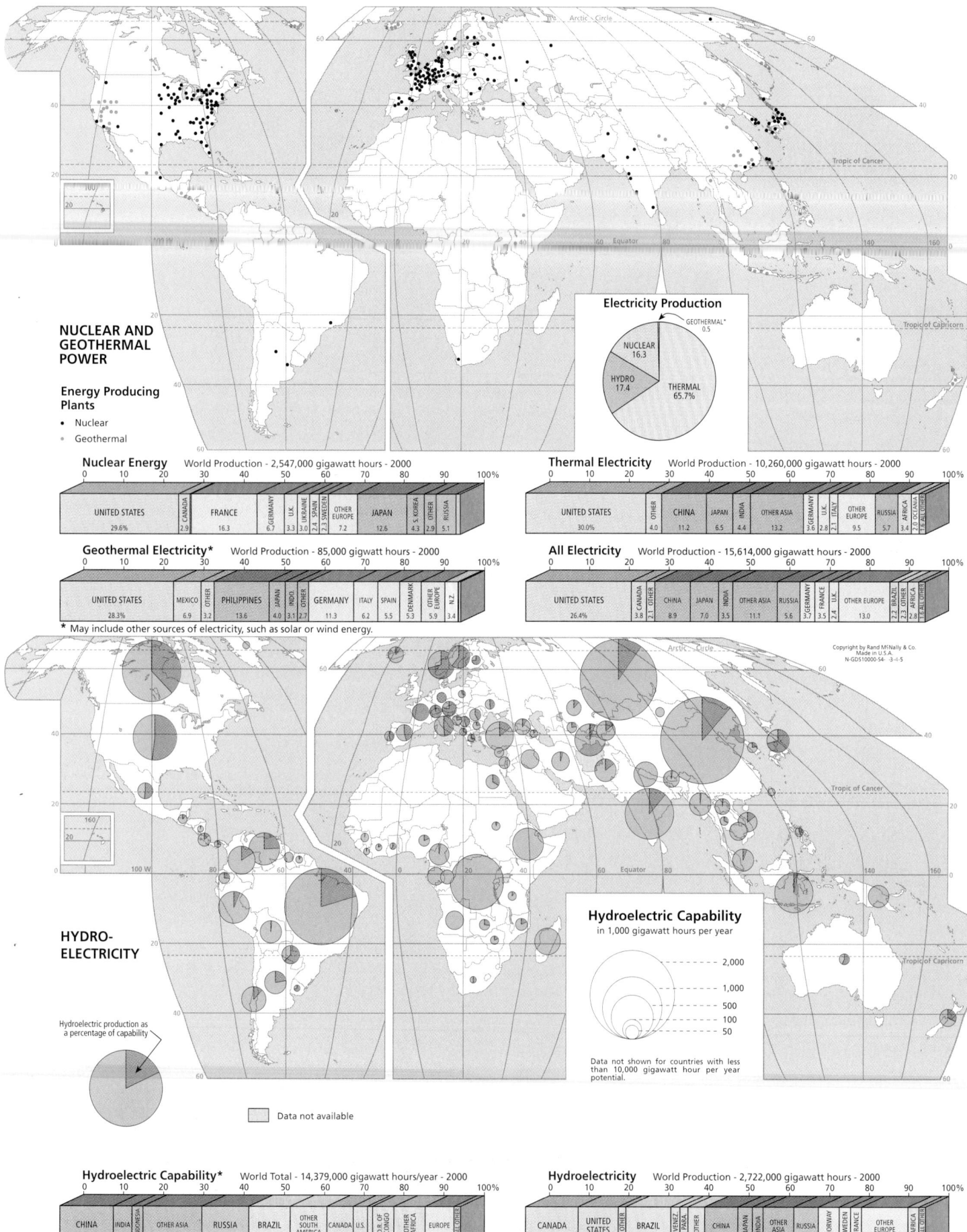

NUCLEAR AND GEOTHERMAL POWER

Energy Producing Plants

- Nuclear
- Geothermal

Electricity Production

GEOTHERMAL* 0.5
NUCLEAR 16.3
HYDRO 17.4
THERMAL 65.7%

Nuclear Energy World Production - 2,547,000 gigawatt hours - 2000

| UNITED STATES 29.6% | CANADA 2.9 | FRANCE 16.3 | GERMANY 6.7 | U.K. 3.3 | UKRAINE 2.4 | SPAIN 2.3 | SWEDEN | OTHER EUROPE 7.2 | JAPAN 12.6 | S. KOREA 4.3 | OTHER 2.9 | RUSSIA 5.1 |

Thermal Electricity World Production - 10,260,000 gigawatt hours - 2000

| UNITED STATES 30.0% | OTHER 4.0 | CHINA 11.2 | JAPAN 6.5 | INDIA 4.4 | OTHER ASIA 13.2 | GERMANY 3.6 | U.K. 2.8 | ITALY 2.1 | OTHER EUROPE 9.5 | RUSSIA 5.7 | AFRICA 3.4 | OCEANIA 2.0 | ALL OTHER 1.6 |

Geothermal Electricity* World Production - 85,000 gigawatt hours - 2000

| UNITED STATES 28.3% | MEXICO 6.9 | OTHER 3.2 | PHILIPPINES 13.6 | JAPAN 4.0 | INDO. 3.1 | OTHER 2.7 | GERMANY 11.3 | ITALY 6.2 | SPAIN 5.5 | DENMARK 5.3 | OTHER EUROPE 5.9 | N.Z. 3.4 |

All Electricity World Production - 15,614,000 gigawatt hours - 2000

| UNITED STATES 26.4% | CANADA 3.8 | OTHER 2.1 | CHINA 8.9 | JAPAN 7.0 | INDIA 3.5 | OTHER ASIA 11.1 | RUSSIA 5.6 | GERMANY 3.7 | FRANCE 3.5 | U.K. 2.4 | OTHER EUROPE 13.0 | BRAZIL 2.2 | OTHER 2.3 | AFRICA 2.8 | ALL OTHER 1.6 |

*May include other sources of electricity, such as solar or wind energy.

Copyright by Rand McNally & Co.
Made in U.S.A.
N-GDS10000-S4- -3-I-S

HYDRO-ELECTRICITY

Hydroelectric production as a percentage of capability

Data not available

Hydroelectric Capability
in 1,000 gigawatt hours per year

2,000
1,000
500
100
50

Data not shown for countries with less than 10,000 gigawatt hour per year potential.

Hydroelectric Capability* World Total - 14,379,000 gigawatt hours/year - 2000

| CHINA 13.4% | INDIA 4.6 | INDONESIA 2.8 | OTHER ASIA 14.7 | RUSSIA 11.6 | BRAZIL 10.3 | OTHER SOUTH AMERICA 9.1 | CANADA 6.6 | U.S. 3.7 | D.R. OF CONGO 5.4 | OTHER AFRICA 7.7 | EUROPE 7.2 | ALL OTHER 1.4 |

*Technically exploitable capability

Hydroelectricity World Production - 2,722,000 gigawatt hours - 2000

| CANADA 13.2% | UNITED STATES 10.1 | OTHER 1.9 | BRAZIL 11.2 | VENEZ. 2.3 | PARA. 2.0 | OTHER 4.2 | CHINA 8.2 | JAPAN 3.6 | INDIA 2.7 | OTHER ASIA 7.6 | RUSSIA 6.1 | NORWAY 5.2 | SWEDEN 2.9 | FRANCE 2.7 | OTHER EUROPE 11.8 | AFRICA 2.8 | ALL OTHER 1.4 |

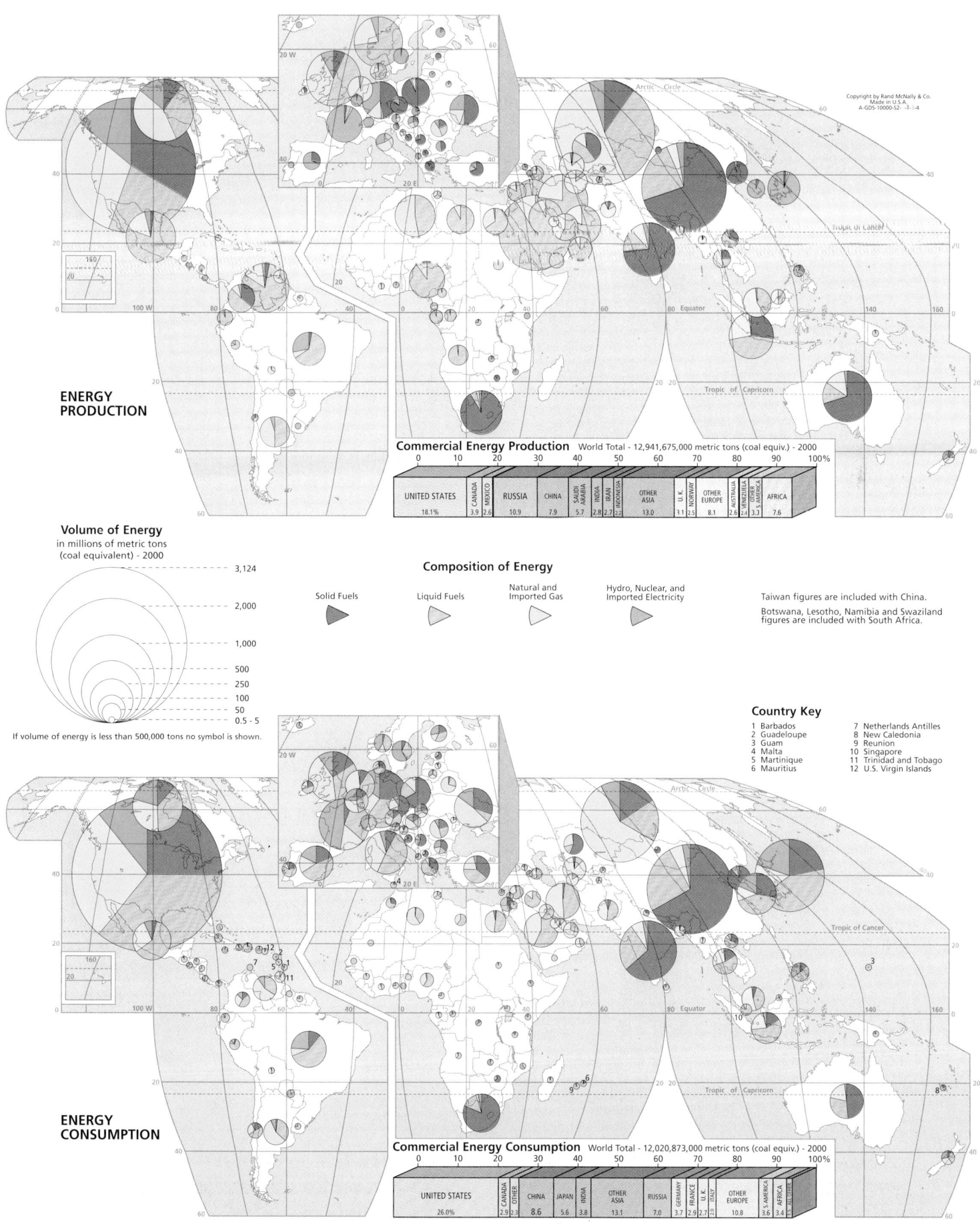

ENERGY
PRODUCTION

Copyright by Rand McNally & Co.
Made in U.S.A.
A-GDS-10000-52- -3-)-4

Commercial Energy Production World Total - 12,941,675,000 metric tons (coal equiv.) - 2000

0	10	20	30	40	50	60	70	80	90	100%						
UNITED STATES	CANADA	MEXICO	RUSSIA	CHINA	SAUDI ARABIA	INDIA	IRAN	INDONESIA	OTHER ASIA	U.K.	NORWAY	OTHER EUROPE	AUSTRALIA	VENEZUELA	OTHER S. AMERICA	AFRICA
18.1%	3.9	2.6	10.9	7.9	5.7	2.8	2.7	2.2	13.0	3.1	2.5	8.1	2.6	2.4	3.3	7.6

Volume of Energy
in millions of metric tons
(coal equivalent) - 2000

3,124
2,000
1,000
500
250
100
50
0.5 - 5

If volume of energy is less than 500,000 tons no symbol is shown.

Composition of Energy

Solid Fuels   Liquid Fuels   Natural and Imported Gas   Hydro, Nuclear, and Imported Electricity

Taiwan figures are included with China.

Botswana, Lesotho, Namibia and Swaziland figures are included with South Africa.

Country Key

1	Barbados	7	Netherlands Antilles
2	Guadeloupe	8	New Caledonia
3	Guam	9	Reunion
4	Malta	10	Singapore
5	Martinique	11	Trinidad and Tobago
6	Mauritius	12	U.S. Virgin Islands

ENERGY
CONSUMPTION

Commercial Energy Consumption World Total - 12,020,873,000 metric tons (coal equiv.) - 2000

0	10	20	30	40	50	60	70	80	90	100%					
UNITED STATES	CANADA	OTHER	CHINA	JAPAN	INDIA	OTHER ASIA	RUSSIA	GERMANY	FRANCE	U.K.	ITALY	OTHER EUROPE	S. AMERICA	AFRICA	S./ALL OTHER
26.0%	2.9	2.3	8.6	5.6	3.8	13.1	7.0	3.7	2.9	2.7	2.0	10.8	3.6	3.4	

MINERAL FUELS

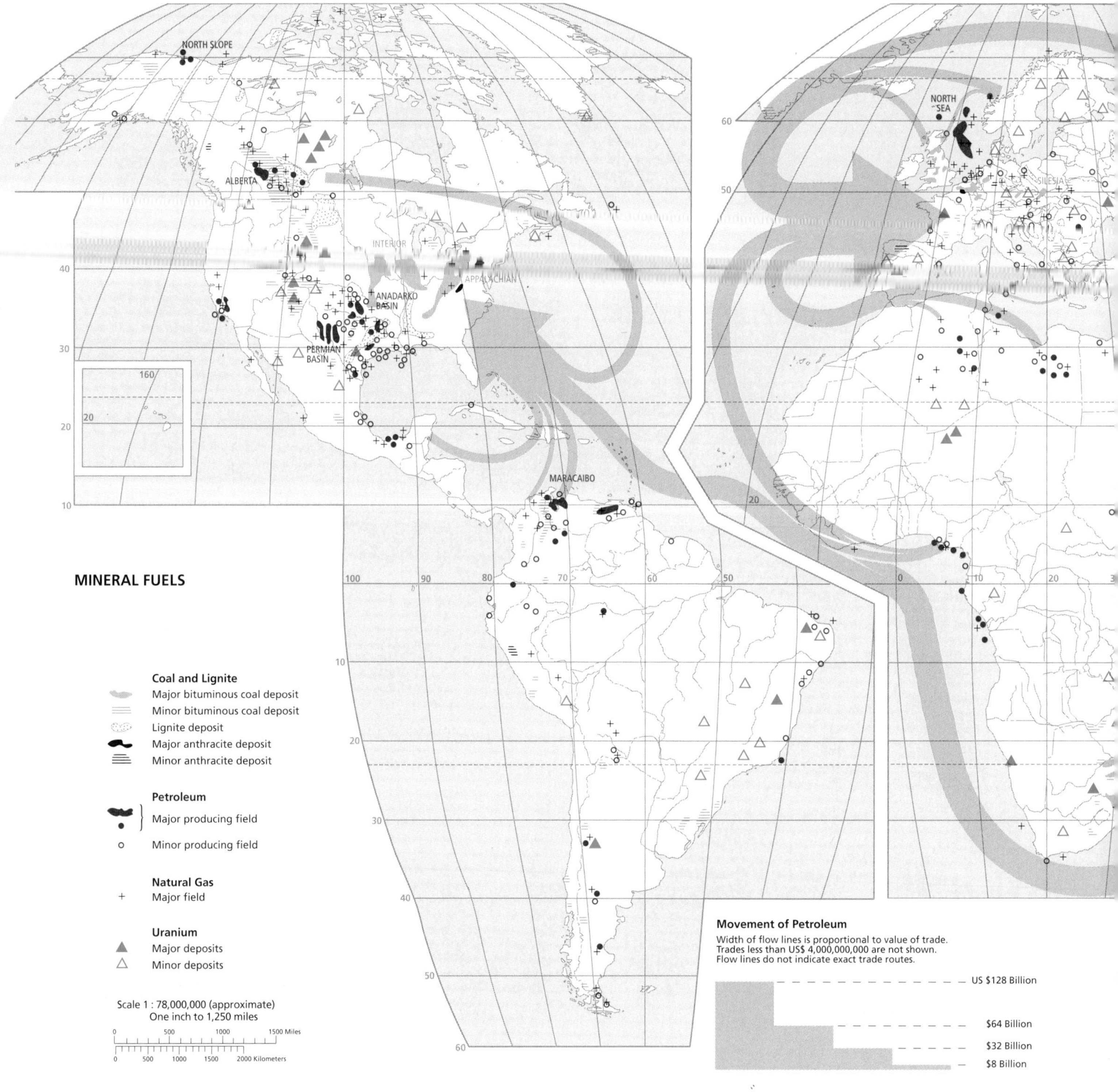

NORTH SLOPE

ALBERTA

INTERIOR

APPALACHIAN

ANADARKO BASIN

PERMIAN BASIN

MARACAIBO

NORTH SEA

SILESIA

Coal and Lignite

Major bituminous coal deposit

Minor bituminous coal deposit

Lignite deposit

Major anthracite deposit

Minor anthracite deposit

Petroleum

Major producing field

○ Minor producing field

Natural Gas

+ Major field

Uranium

▲ Major deposits

△ Minor deposits

Scale 1 : 78,000,000 (approximate)
One inch to 1,250 miles

0 500 1000 1500 Miles

0 500 1000 1500 2000 Kilometers

Movement of Petroleum

Width of flow lines is proportional to value of trade.
Trades less than US$ 4,000,000,000 are not shown.
Flow lines do not indicate exact trade routes.

US $128 Billion

$64 Billion

$32 Billion

$8 Billion

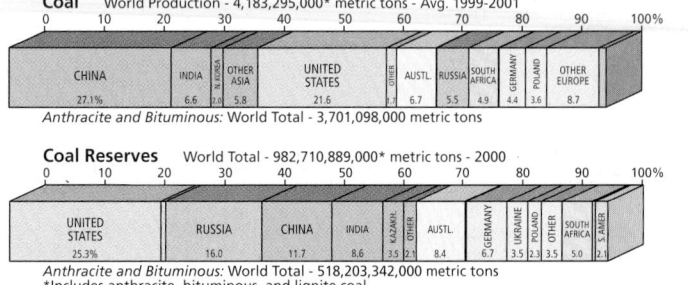

Coal World Production - 4,183,295,000* metric tons - Avg. 1999-2001

0	10	20	30	40	50	60	70	80	90	100%

CHINA	INDIA	OTHER ASIA	UNITED STATES	OTHER	AUSTL.	RUSSIA	SOUTH AFRICA	GERMANY	POLAND	OTHER EUROPE
27.1%	6.6	5.8	21.6	2.6	6.7	5.5	4.9	4.4	3.6	8.7

Anthracite and Bituminous: World Total - 3,701,098,000 metric tons

Coal Reserves World Total - 982,710,889,000* metric tons - 2000

0	10	20	30	40	50	60	70	80	90	100%

UNITED STATES	RUSSIA	CHINA	INDIA	KAZAKH.	AUSTL.	GERMANY	UKRAINE	POLAND	OTHER	SOUTH AFRICA	S. AMER.
25.3%	16.0	11.7	8.6	3.5	8.4	6.7	3.5	2.3	3.5	5.0	2.1

Anthracite and Bituminous: World Total - 518,203,342,000 metric tons
*Includes anthracite, bituminous, and lignite coal

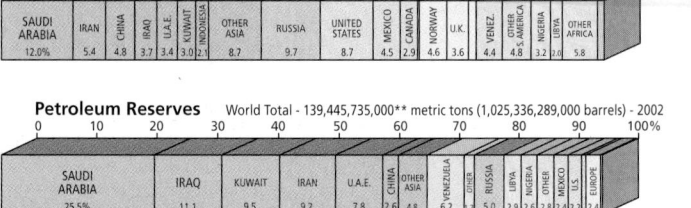

Petroleum World Production - 3,346,515,000** metric tons (24,606,731,000 barrels) - Avg. 1999-2001

0	10	20	30	40	50	60	70	80	90	100%

SAUDI ARABIA	IRAN	CHINA	IRAQ	U.A.E.	KUWAIT	INDONESIA	OTHER ASIA	RUSSIA	UNITED STATES	MEXICO	CANADA	NORWAY	U.K.	VENEZ.	OTHER S. AMERICA	NIGERIA	LIBYA	OTHER AFRICA
12.0%	5.4	4.8	3.7	3.4	3.0	2.1	8.7	9.7	8.7	4.5	2.9	4.6	3.6	4.4	4.8	3.2	2.0	5.8

Petroleum Reserves World Total - 139,445,735,000** metric tons (1,025,336,289,000 barrels) - 2002

0	10	20	30	40	50	60	70	80	90	100%

SAUDI ARABIA	IRAQ	KUWAIT	IRAN	U.A.E.	CHINA	OTHER ASIA	VENEZUELA	RUSSIA	LIBYA	NIGERIA	OTHER	MEXICO	U.S.	EUROPE
25.5%	11.1	9.5	9.2	7.8	2.6	2.9	6.2	4.8	5.0	2.9	2.6	2.8	2.4	2.4

**Crude Petroleum

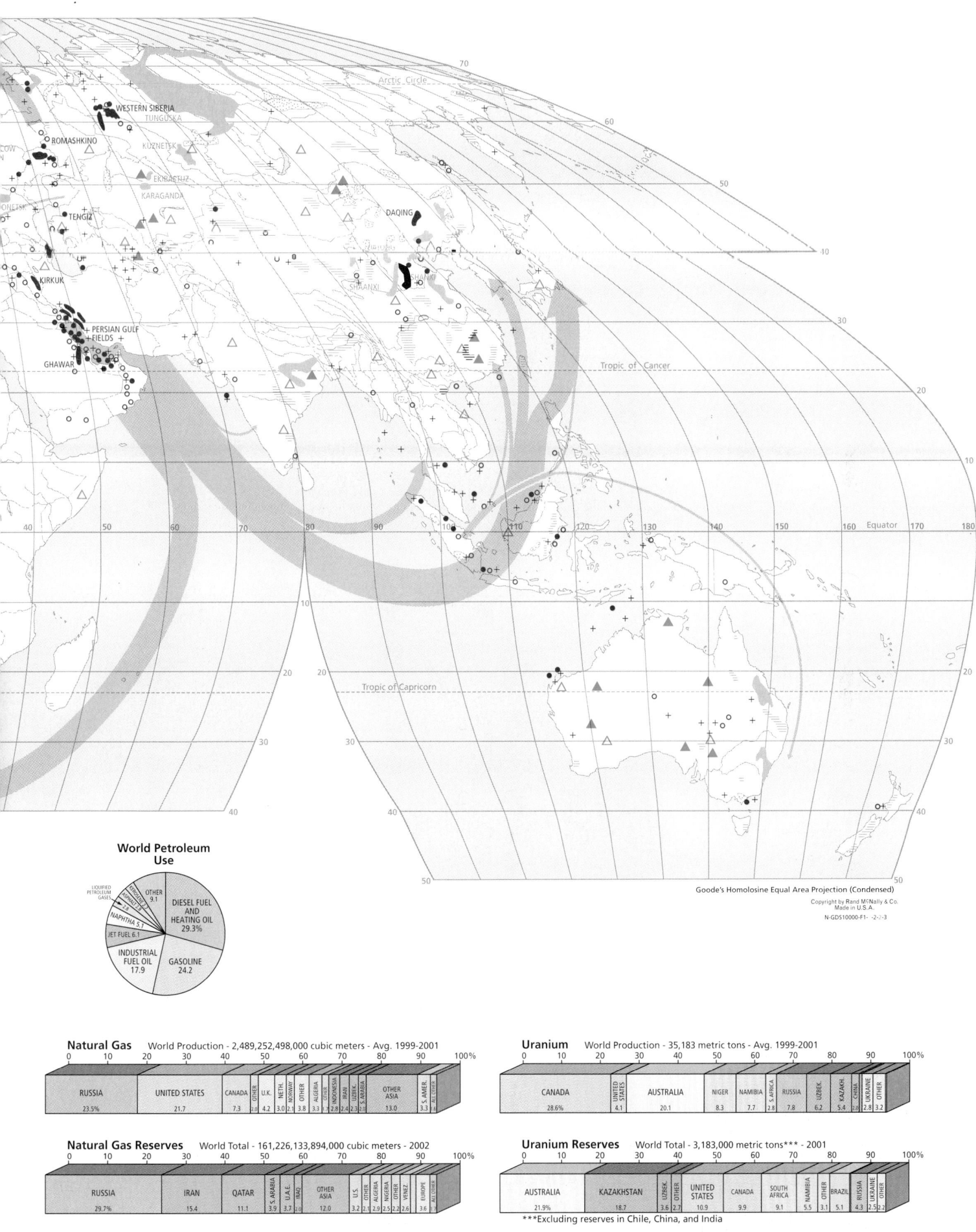

WESTERN SIBERIA
TUNGUSKA
ROMASHKINO
KUZNETSK
EKIBASTUZ
KARAGANDA
TENGIZ
DAQING
KIRKUK
SHAANXI
PERSIAN GULF
FIELDS
GHAWAR

Arctic Circle

Tropic of Cancer

Equator

Tropic of Capricorn

Goode's Homolosine Equal Area Projection (Condensed)

Copyright by Rand McNally & Co.
Made in U.S.A.

N-GDS10000-F1- -2-/-3

**World Petroleum
Use**

LIQUIFIED
PETROLEUM
GASES
OTHER 9.1
NAPHTHA 5.1
JET FUEL 6.1
INDUSTRIAL
FUEL OIL
17.9
GASOLINE
24.2
DIESEL FUEL
AND
HEATING OIL
29.3%

Natural Gas World Production - 2,489,252,498,000 cubic meters - Avg. 1999-2001

0	10	20	30	40	50	60	70	80	90	100%

RUSSIA	UNITED STATES	CANADA	OTHER	U.K.	NETH.	NORWAY	OTHER	ALGERIA	Other	INDONESIA	IRAN	UZBEK.	S. ARABIA	OTHER ASIA	S. AMER.	ALL OTHER
23.5%	21.7	7.3	2.0	4.2	2.1	3.0	3.8	3.3	1.7	2.8	2.4	2.3	2.0	13.0	3.3	1.4

Natural Gas Reserves World Total - 161,226,133,894,000 cubic meters - 2002

0	10	20	30	40	50	60	70	80	90	100%

RUSSIA	IRAN	QATAR	S. ARABIA	U.A.E.	IRAQ	OTHER ASIA	U.S.	OTHER	ALGERIA	NIGERIA	VENEZ.	OTHER	EUROPE	ALL OTHER
29.7%	15.4	11.1	3.9	3.7	2.0	12.0	3.2	2.1	2.9	2.5	2.2	2.6	3.6	

Uranium World Production - 35,183 metric tons - Avg. 1999-2001

0	10	20	30	40	50	60	70	80	90	100%

CANADA	UNITED STATES	AUSTRALIA	NIGER	NAMIBIA	S. AFRICA	RUSSIA	UZBEK.	KAZAKH.	CHINA	UKRAINE	OTHER
28.6%	4.1	20.1	8.3	7.7	2.8	7.8	6.2	5.4	2.8	2.6	3.2

Uranium Reserves World Total - 3,183,000 metric tons*** - 2001

0	10	20	30	40	50	60	70	80	90	100%

AUSTRALIA	KAZAKHSTAN	UZBEK.	OTHER	UNITED STATES	CANADA	SOUTH AFRICA	NAMIBIA	OTHER	BRAZIL	RUSSIA	UKRAINE	OTHER
21.9%	18.7	3.6	2.7	10.9	9.9	9.1	5.5	3.1	5.1	4.3	2.5	2.2

***Excluding reserves in Chile, China, and India

EXPORTS

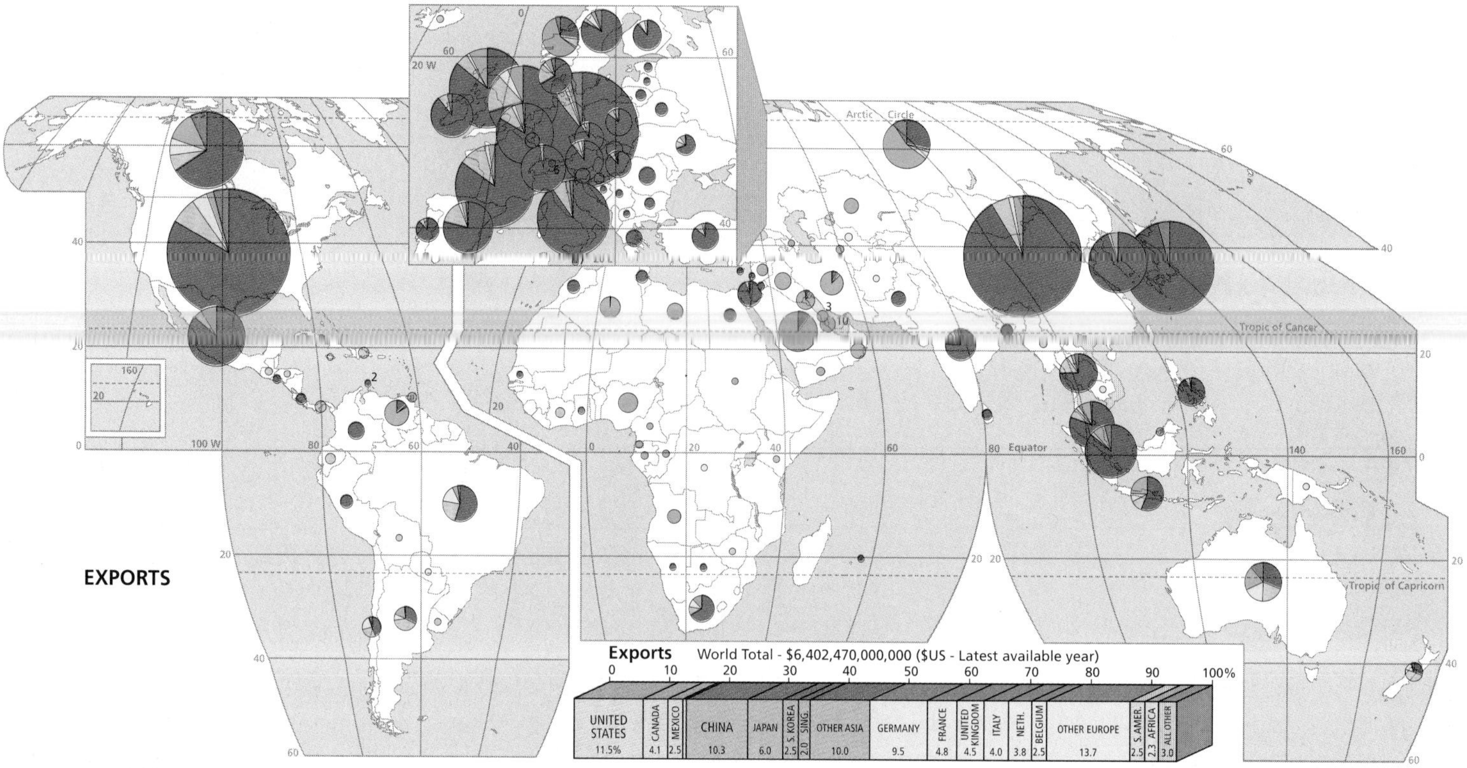

Exports   World Total - $6,402,470,000,000 ($US - Latest available year)

0	10	20	30	40	50	60	70	80	90	100%

UNITED STATES	CANADA	MEXICO	CHINA	JAPAN	S. KOREA	SING.	OTHER ASIA	GERMANY	FRANCE	UNITED KINGDOM	ITALY	NETH.	BELGIUM	OTHER EUROPE	S. AMER.	AFRICA	ALL OTHER
11.5%	4.1	2.5	10.3	6.0	2.5	2.0	10.0	9.5	4.8	4.5	4.0	3.8	2.5	13.7	2.5	2.3	3.0

Volume of Trade
in billions of U.S. dollars - latest available year

1,200
500
200
100
50
20
10
1 - 2

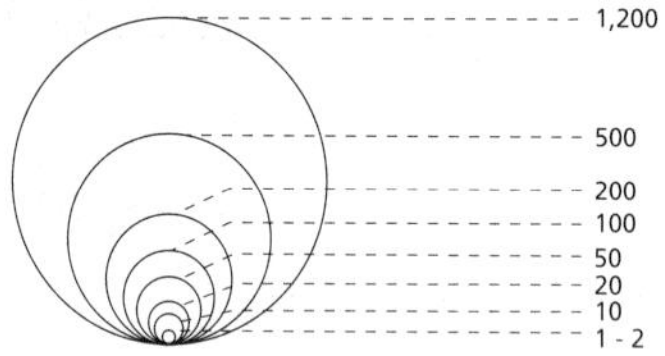

If volume of trade is less than 15 billion dollars, color indicates major class only. If no symbol is shown, volume of trade is less than 1 billion dollars.

Composition of Trade

Manufactured Articles	Food, Beverage & Tobacco	Raw Materials	Fuel & Related Products	All Other or Undifferentiated

Taiwan figures are included with China.
Puerto Rico figures are included with the United States.

Data not available

Country Key

1	Andorra	6	Liechtenstein
2	Aruba	7	Malta
3	Bahrain	8	Martinique
4	Gaza Strip and West Bank	9	Netherlands Antilles
5	Guadeloupe	10	Qatar

IMPORTS

Imports   World Total - $6,388,329,000,000 ($US - Latest available year)

0	10	20	30	40	50	60	70	80	90	100%

UNITED STATES	CANADA	MEXICO	CHINA	JAPAN	S. KOREA	OTHER ASIA	GERMANY	UNITED KINGDOM	FRANCE	ITALY	NETH.	SPAIN	BELGIUM	OTHER EUROPE	AFRICA	ALL OTHER
18.7%	3.6	2.6	9.7	4.6	2.3	10.4	7.6	5.2	4.8	3.7	3.1	2.5	2.4	11.4	2.2	4.2

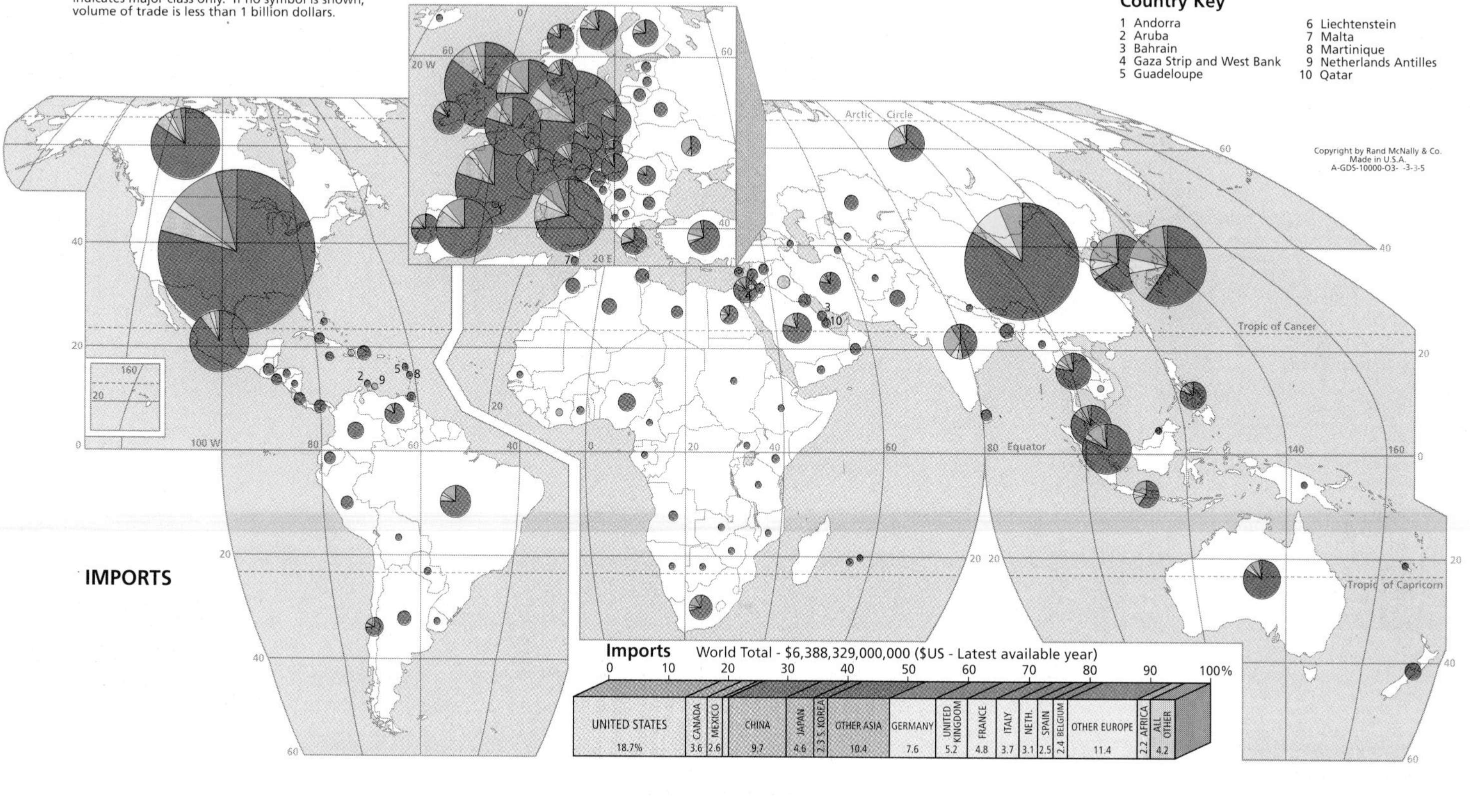

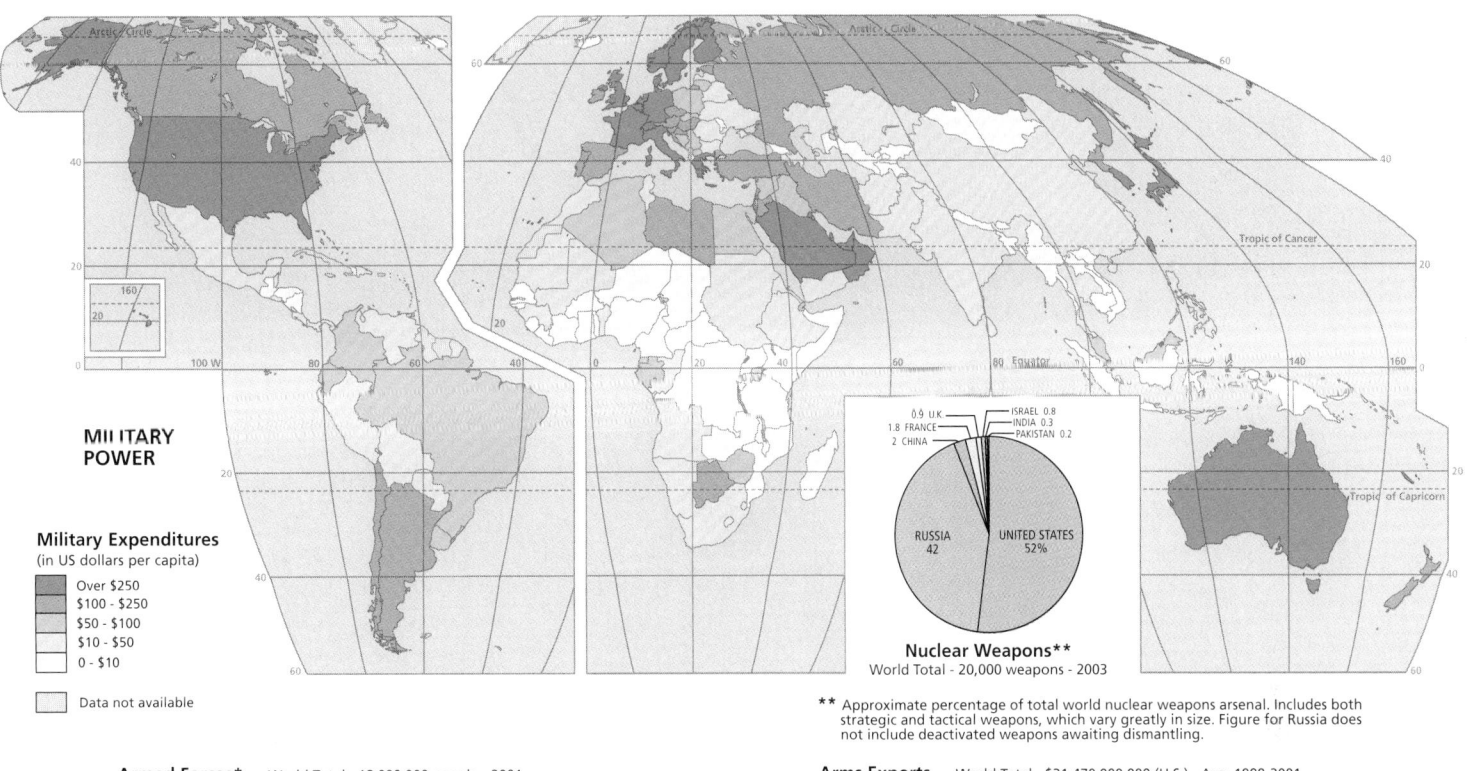

MILITARY POWER

Military Expenditures
(in US dollars per capita)

- Over $250
- $100 - $250
- $50 - $100
- $10 - $50
- 0 - $10

- Data not available

Nuclear Weapons**
World Total - 20,000 weapons - 2003

0.9 U.K.
1.8 FRANCE
2 CHINA
ISRAEL 0.8
INDIA 0.3
PAKISTAN 0.2
RUSSIA 42
UNITED STATES 52%

** Approximate percentage of total world nuclear weapons arsenal. Includes both strategic and tactical weapons, which vary greatly in size. Figure for Russia does not include deactivated weapons awaiting dismantling.

Armed Forces* World Total - 18,000,000 people - 2001

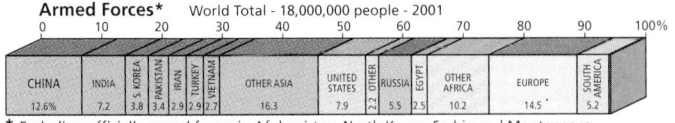

CHINA	INDIA	S. KOREA	PAKISTAN	IRAN	TURKEY	VIETNAM	OTHER ASIA	UNITED STATES	OTHER	RUSSIA	EGYPT	OTHER AFRICA	EUROPE	SOUTH AMERICA
12.6%	7.2	3.8	3.4	2.9	2.9	2.7	16.3	7.9	2.2	5.5	2.5	10.2	14.5	5.2

* Excluding officially armed forces in Afghanistan, North Korea, Serbia and Montenegro, Somalia, and Taiwan.

Arms Exports World Total - $31,470,000,000 (U.S.) - Avg. 1999-2001

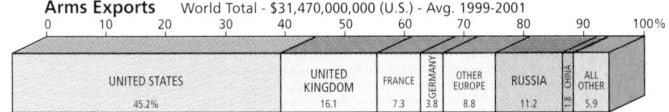

UNITED STATES	UNITED KINGDOM	FRANCE	GERMANY	OTHER EUROPE	RUSSIA	CHINA	ALL OTHER
45.2%	16.1	7.3	3.8	8.8	11.2	1.8	5.9

Copyright by Rand McNally & Co.
Made in U.S.A.
A-GDS-10000-Y6- -:1-1

WOMEN'S RIGHTS

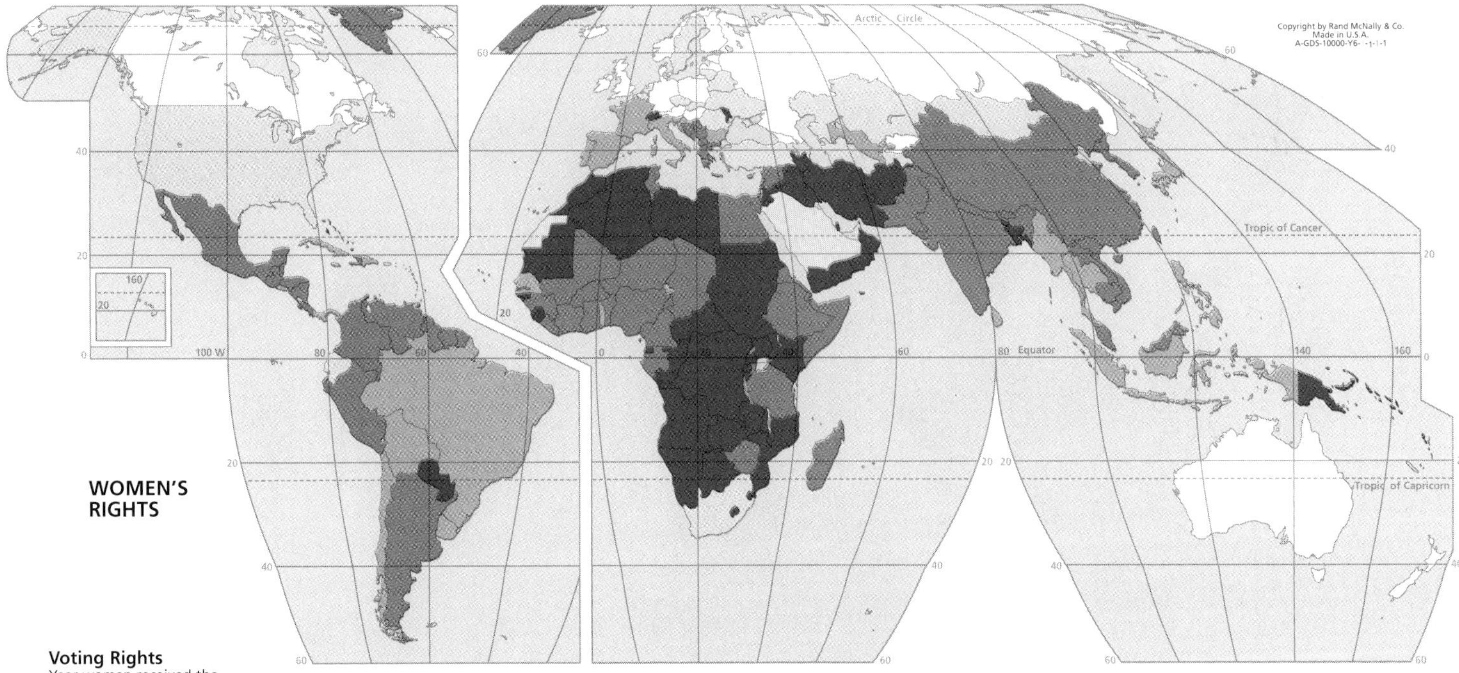

Voting Rights
Year women received the right to vote

- After 1960
- 1946 - 1960
- 1931 - 1945
- 1919 - 1930
- Before 1919

- Not Applicable*

*Women are not allowed to vote in Kuwait. Neither women nor men are allowed to vote in Brunei, Saudi Arabia, United Arab Emirates, or Western Sahara.

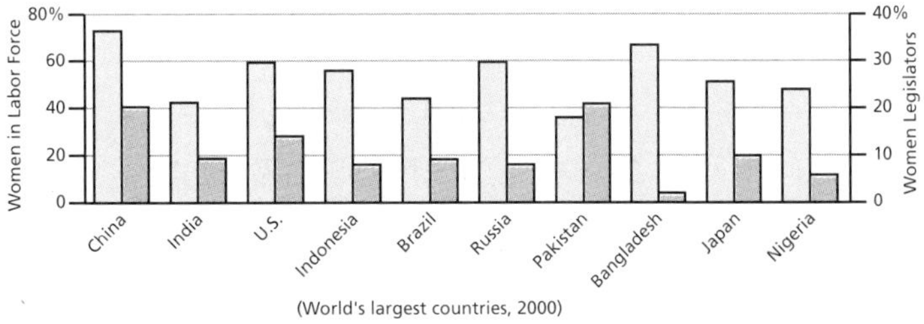

Women's Economic Activity and Legislative Participation Rates

- Percentage of women aged 15 and above in the economically active labor force
- Percentage of seats in national legislature held by women

(World's largest countries, 2000)

China, India, U.S., Indonesia, Brazil, Russia, Pakistan, Bangladesh, Japan, Nigeria

Women in Labor Force / Women Legislators

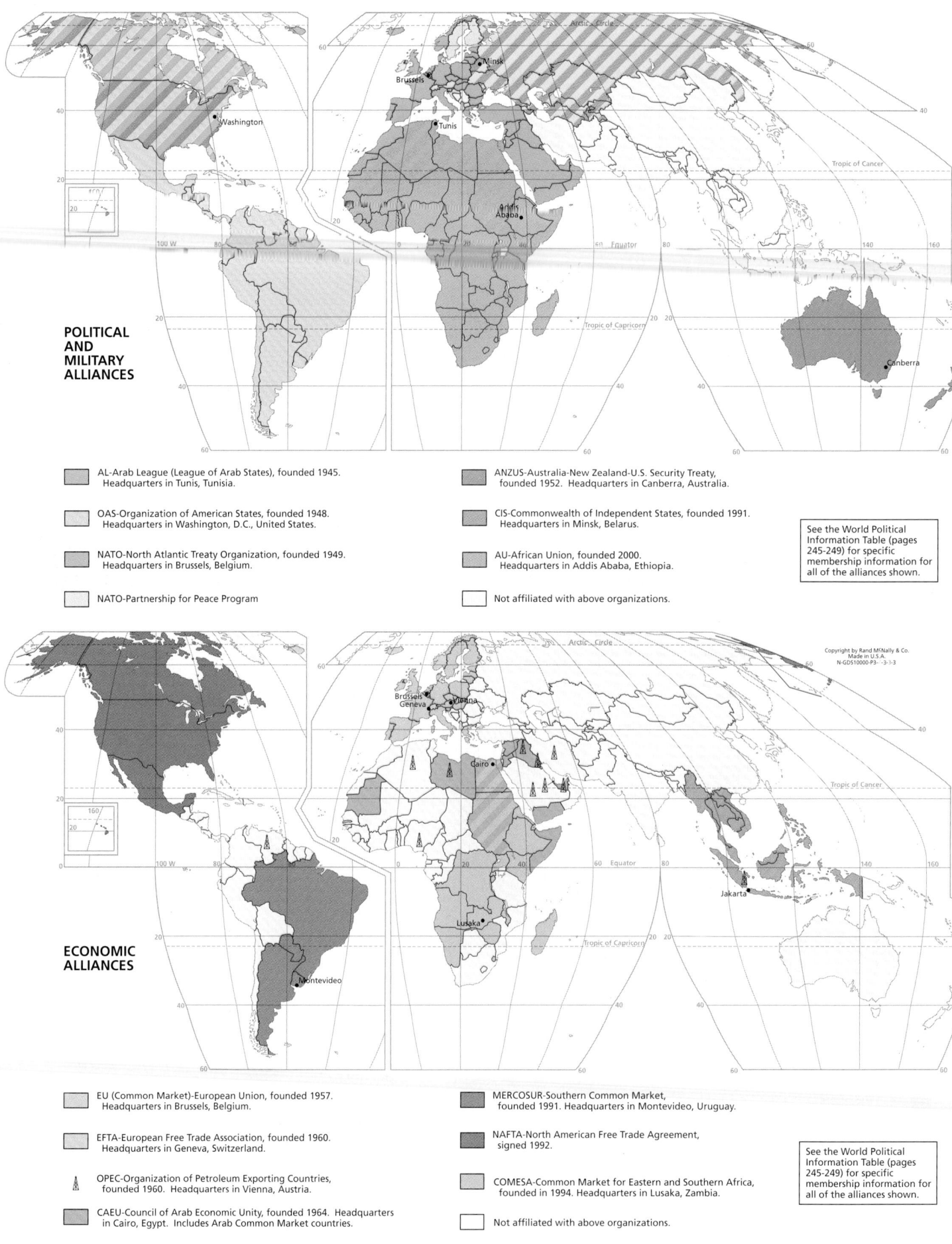

POLITICAL AND MILITARY ALLIANCES

AL-Arab League (League of Arab States), founded 1945. Headquarters in Tunis, Tunisia.

OAS-Organization of American States, founded 1948. Headquarters in Washington, D.C., United States.

NATO-North Atlantic Treaty Organization, founded 1949. Headquarters in Brussels, Belgium.

NATO-Partnership for Peace Program

ANZUS-Australia-New Zealand-U.S. Security Treaty, founded 1952. Headquarters in Canberra, Australia.

CIS-Commonwealth of Independent States, founded 1991. Headquarters in Minsk, Belarus.

AU-African Union, founded 2000. Headquarters in Addis Ababa, Ethiopia.

Not affiliated with above organizations.

See the World Political Information Table (pages 245-249) for specific membership information for all of the alliances shown.

ECONOMIC ALLIANCES

EU (Common Market)-European Union, founded 1957. Headquarters in Brussels, Belgium.

EFTA-European Free Trade Association, founded 1960. Headquarters in Geneva, Switzerland.

OPEC-Organization of Petroleum Exporting Countries, founded 1960. Headquarters in Vienna, Austria.

CAEU-Council of Arab Economic Unity, founded 1964. Headquarters in Cairo, Egypt. Includes Arab Common Market countries.

ASEAN-Association of Southeast Asian Nations, founded 1967. Headquarters in Jakarta, Indonesia.

MERCOSUR-Southern Common Market, founded 1991. Headquarters in Montevideo, Uruguay.

NAFTA-North American Free Trade Agreement, signed 1992.

COMESA-Common Market for Eastern and Southern Africa, founded in 1994. Headquarters in Lusaka, Zambia.

Not affiliated with above organizations.

See the World Political Information Table (pages 245-249) for specific membership information for all of the alliances shown.

Copyright by Rand McNally & Co.
Made in U.S.A.
N-GD510000-P3- -3-1-3

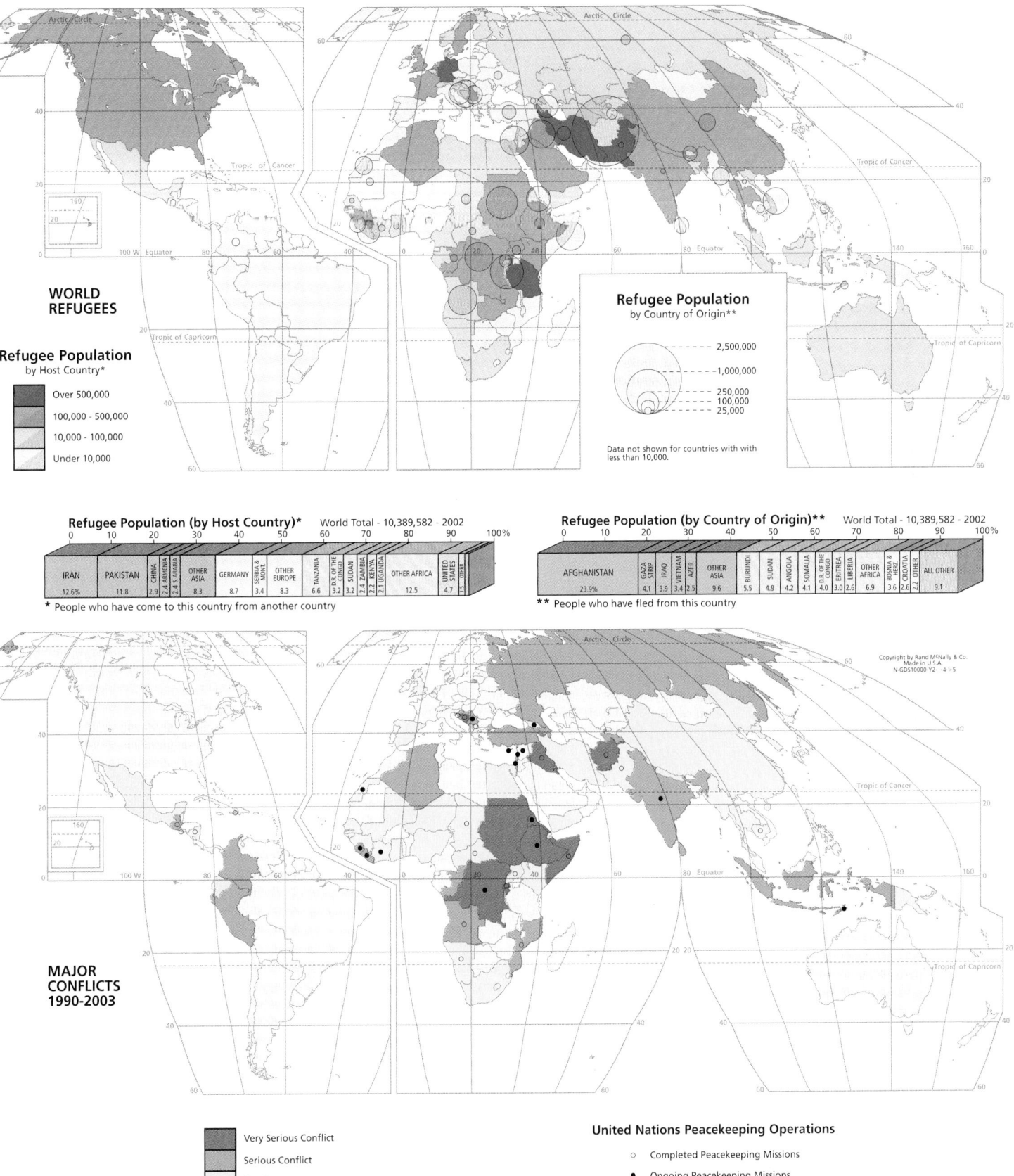

WORLD REFUGEES

Refugee Population
by Host Country*

- Over 500,000
- 100,000 – 500,000
- 10,000 – 100,000
- Under 10,000

Refugee Population
by Country of Origin**

- 2,500,000
- 1,000,000
- 250,000
- 100,000
- 25,000

Data not shown for countries with less than 10,000.

Refugee Population (by Host Country)*   World Total - 10,389,582 - 2002

	0	10	20	30	40	50	60	70	80	90	100%

IRAN	PAKISTAN	CHINA	ARMENIA	S. ARABIA	OTHER ASIA	GERMANY	SERBIA & MONT.	OTHER EUROPE	TANZANIA	D.R. OF THE CONGO	SUDAN	ZAMBIA	KENYA	UGANDA	OTHER AFRICA	UNITED STATES	OTHER
12.6%	11.8	2.9	2.4	2.4	8.3	8.7	3.4	8.3	6.6	3.2	3.2	2.4	2.2	2.1	12.5	4.7	1%

* People who have come to this country from another country

Refugee Population (by Country of Origin)**   World Total - 10,389,582 - 2002

	0	10	20	30	40	50	60	70	80	90	100%

AFGHANISTAN	GAZA STRIP	IRAQ	VIETNAM	AZER.	OTHER ASIA	BURUNDI	SUDAN	ANGOLA	SOMALIA	D.R. OF THE CONGO	ERITREA	LIBERIA	OTHER AFRICA	BOSNIA & HERZ.	CROATIA	OTHER	ALL OTHER
23.9%	4.1	3.9	3.4	2.5	9.6	5.5	4.9	4.2	4.1	4.0	3.0	2.6	6.9	3.6	2.6	2.2	9.1

** People who have fled from this country

MAJOR CONFLICTS 1990-2003

- Very Serious Conflict
- Serious Conflict
- Hot Spot

United Nations Peacekeeping Operations

- ○ Completed Peacekeeping Missions
- ● Ongoing Peacekeeping Missions

64

TELECOMMUNICATIONS

Teledensity
Number of fixed telephone lines and
mobile phones per 100 people - 2007

- Over 120
- 60 - 120
- 30 - 60
- 15 - 30
- Under 15

No data available

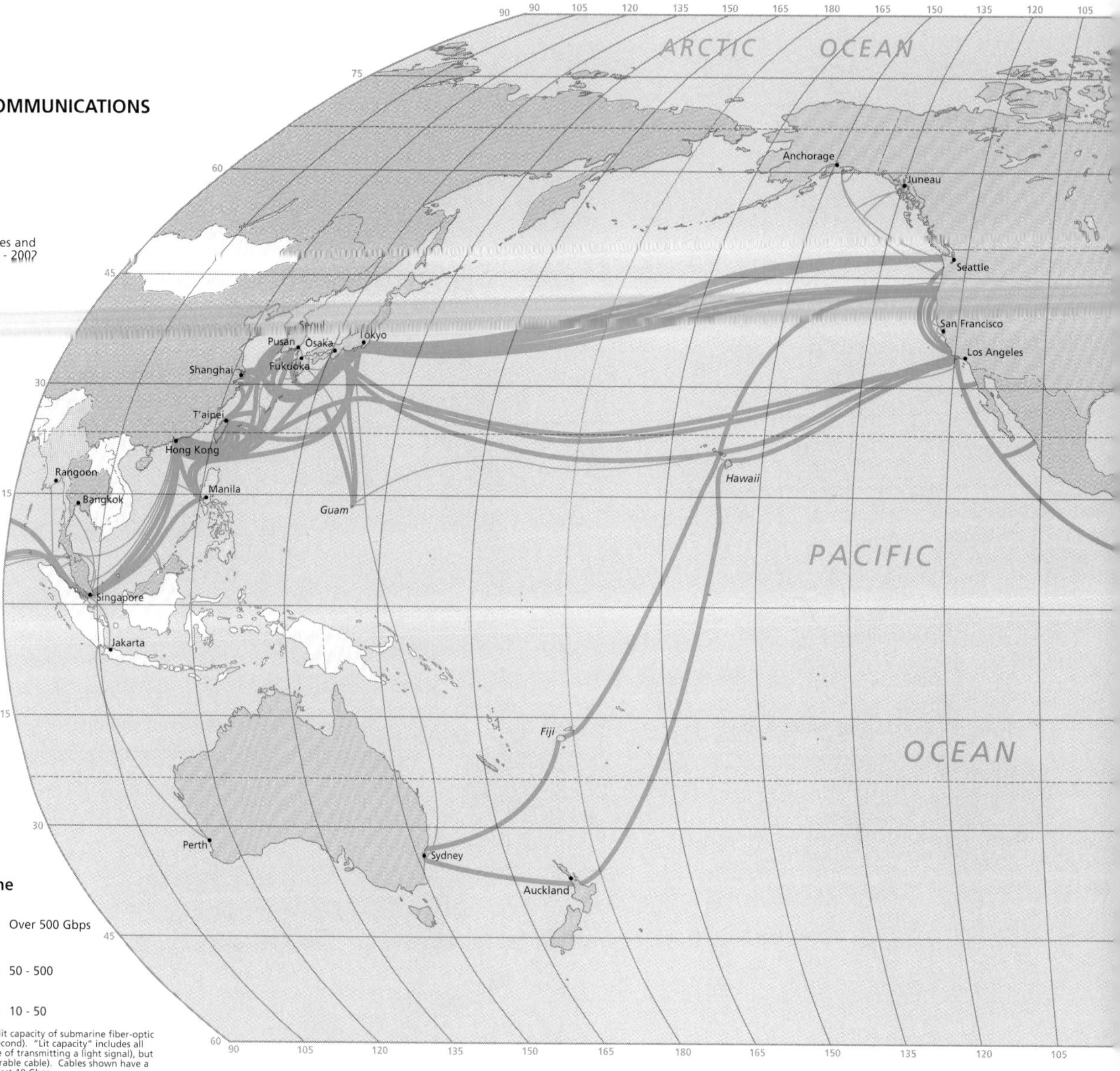

**International Submarine
Cable Capacity - 2004**

Over 500 Gbps

50 - 500

10 - 50

Note: Line thickness is proportional to lit capacity of submarine fiber-optic
cable measured in Gbps (Gigabits per second). "Lit capacity" includes all
cable that is "lit" (operable and capable of transmitting a light signal), but
excludes "dark fiber" (inactive or inoperable cable). Cables shown have a
maximum upgradeable capacity of at least 10 Gbps.

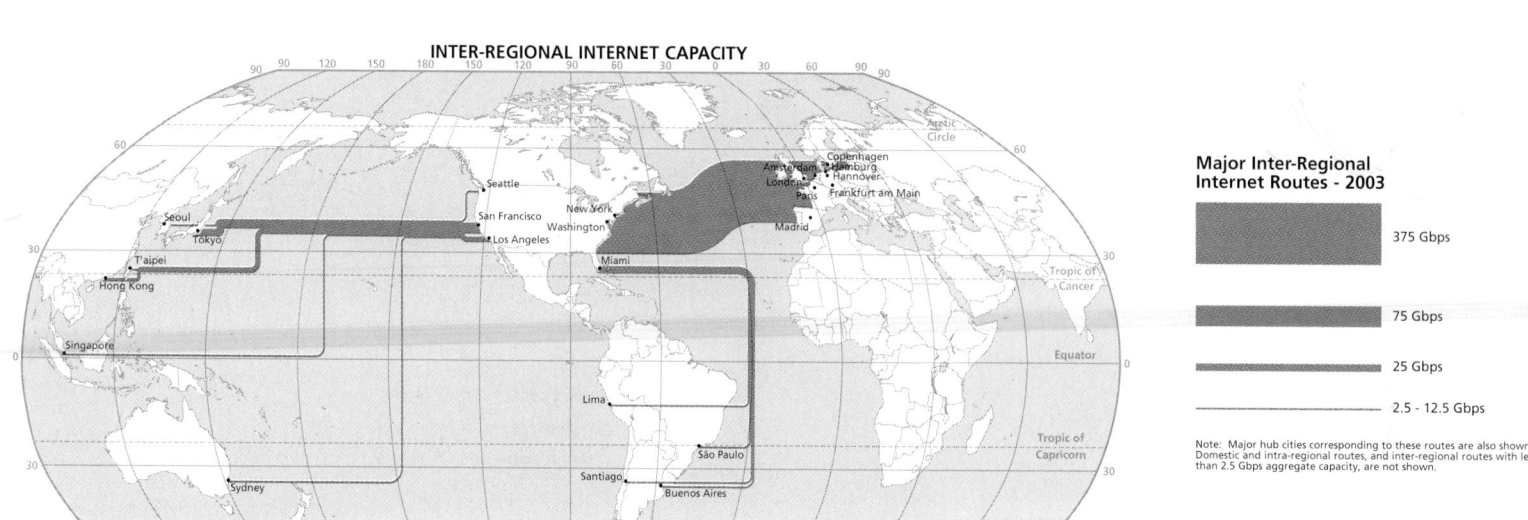

INTER-REGIONAL INTERNET CAPACITY

**Major Inter-Regional
Internet Routes - 2003**

375 Gbps

75 Gbps

25 Gbps

2.5 - 12.5 Gbps

Note: Major hub cities corresponding to these routes are also shown.
Domestic and intra-regional routes, and inter-regional routes with less
than 2.5 Gbps aggregate capacity, are not shown.

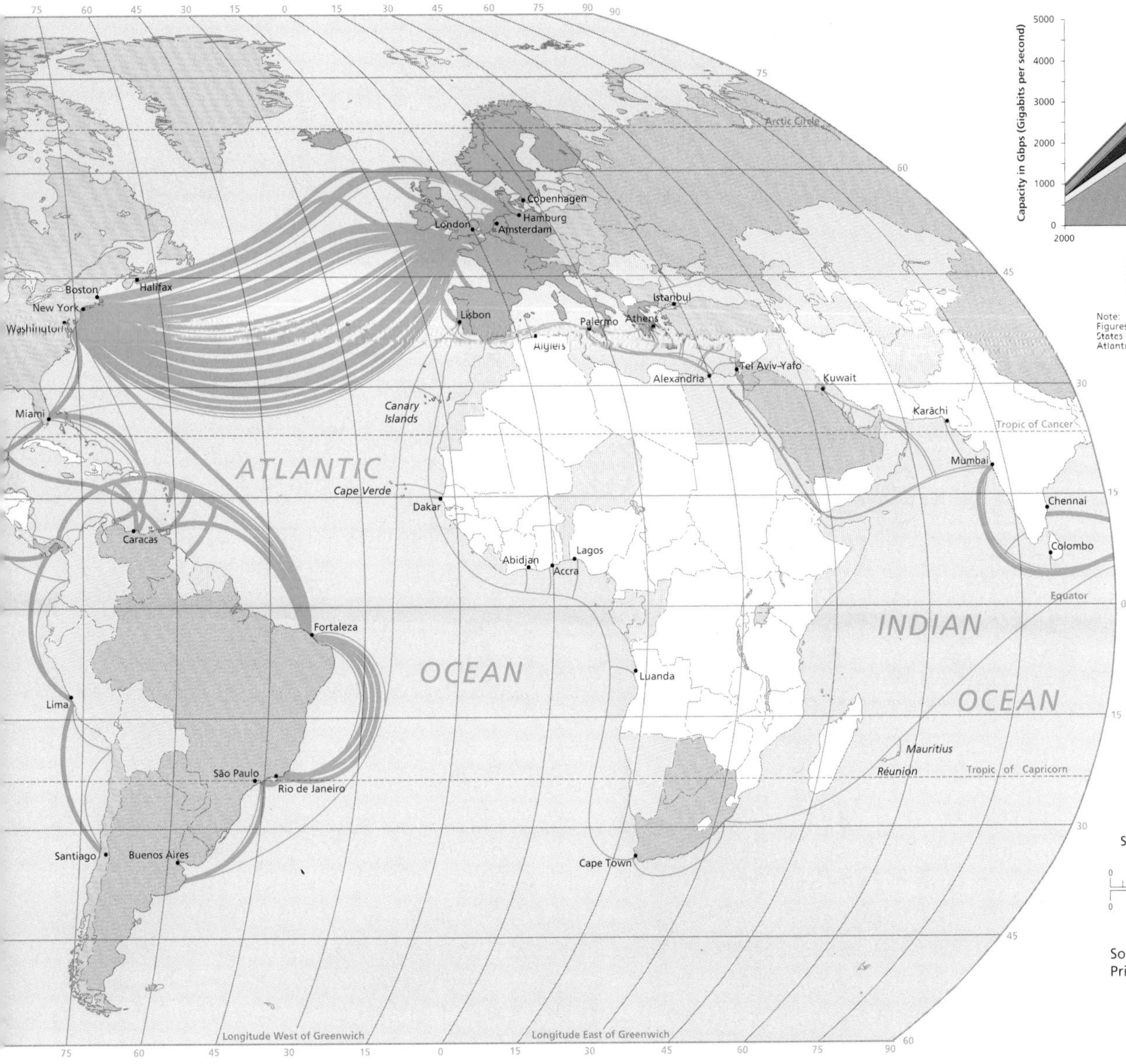

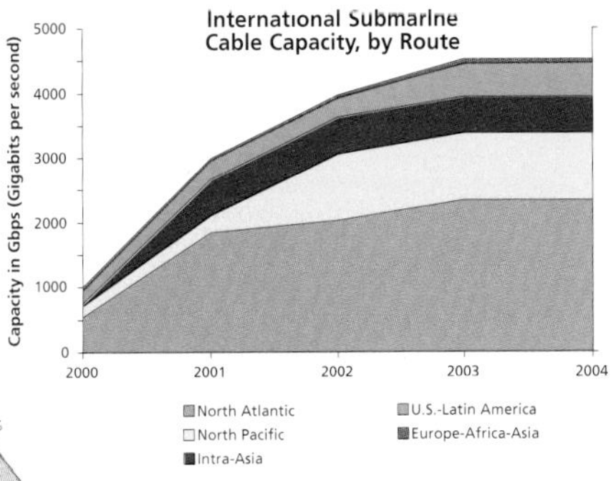

International Submarine Cable Capacity, by Route

Capacity in Gbps (Gigabits per second)

5000
4000
3000
2000
1000

2000 2001 2002 2003 2004

☐ North Atlantic ▨ U.S.-Latin America
☐ North Pacific ▨ Europe-Africa-Asia
■ Intra-Asia

Note: Figures denote lit capacity of submarine fiber-optic cable. Figures for the North Pacific exclude cables linking the United States to Australia and New Zealand. Figures for the North Atlantic exclude cables linking South America to Europe.

Robinson Projection
Scale 1 : 100,000,000 (approximate)
One inch to 1,600 miles

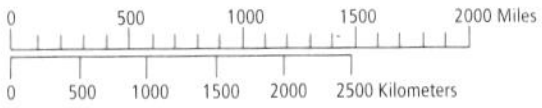

0   500   1000   1500   2000 Miles
0   500   1000   1500   2000   2500 Kilometers

Source: TeleGeography research,
PriMetrica, Inc. (www.primetrica.com)

INTER-REGIONAL INTERNET HUBS

Fifty Largest Inter-Regional Internet Hubs - 2003

Circle size is proportional to each metropolitan area's aggregate capacity connected across international borders.

270 Gbps
100
50
25
10
1

Note: Hubs for domestic and intra-regional routes are not shown. Internet bandwidth for domestic and intra-regional routes is excluded.

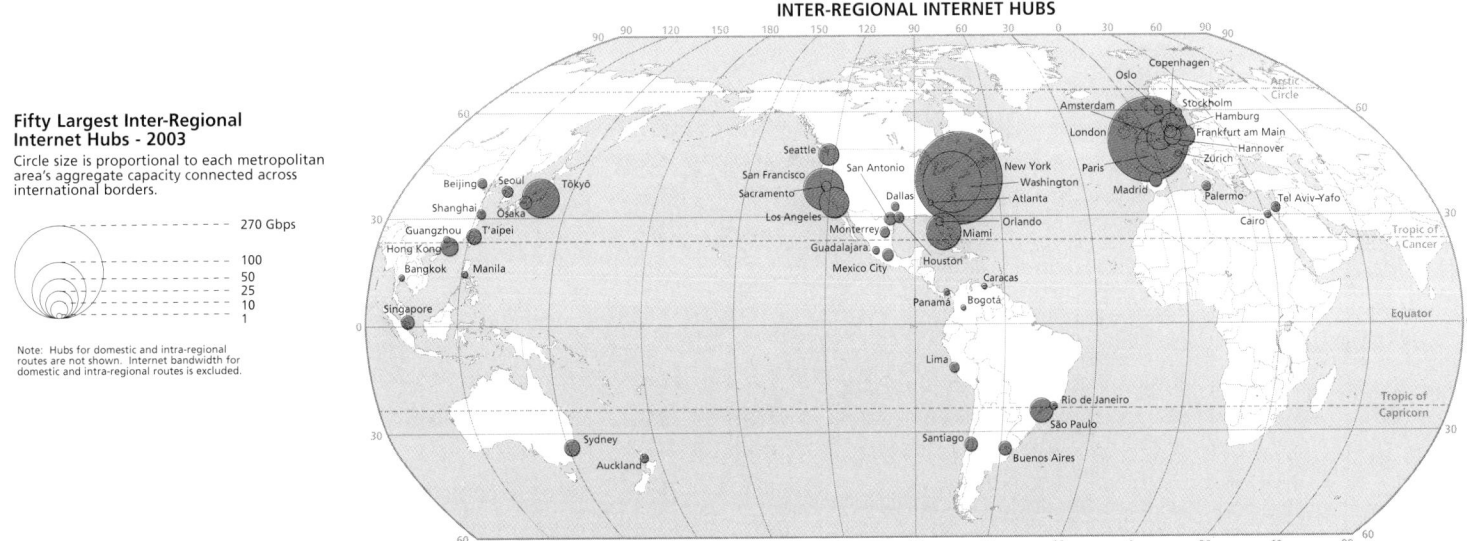

THE SEASONS (NORTHERN HEMISPHERE)

SUMMER SOLSTICE (JUNE SOLSTICE)
Noon sun is directly overhead at 23½° N. Longest day of year in the northern hemisphere.

VERNAL EQUINOX
Noon sun is directly overhead at the equator, on its apparent migration North. Day and night are equal in length.

AUTUMNAL EQUINOX
Noon sun is directly overhead at the equator, on its apparent migration South. Day and night are equal in length.

WINTER SOLSTICE (DECEMBER SOLSTICE)
Noon sun is directly overhead at 23½° S. Shortest day of year in the northern hemisphere.

The Earth, sun, and moon are not shown in correct relative sizes.

PATHS OF EARTH AND MOON DURING ONE LUNAR MONTH

Time Zones

The surface of the earth is divided into 24 time zones. Each zone represents 15° of longitude or one hour of time. The time of the initial, or zero, zone is based on the Greenwich Meridian and extends eastward and westward for a distance of 7½° of longitude. Each of the zones is designated by a number representing the hours (+ or -) by which its standard time differs from Greenwich mean time. These standard time zones are indicated by bands of orange and yellow. Areas which have a fractional deviation from standard time are shown in an intermediate color. The irregularities in the zones and the fractional deviations are due to political and economic factors.

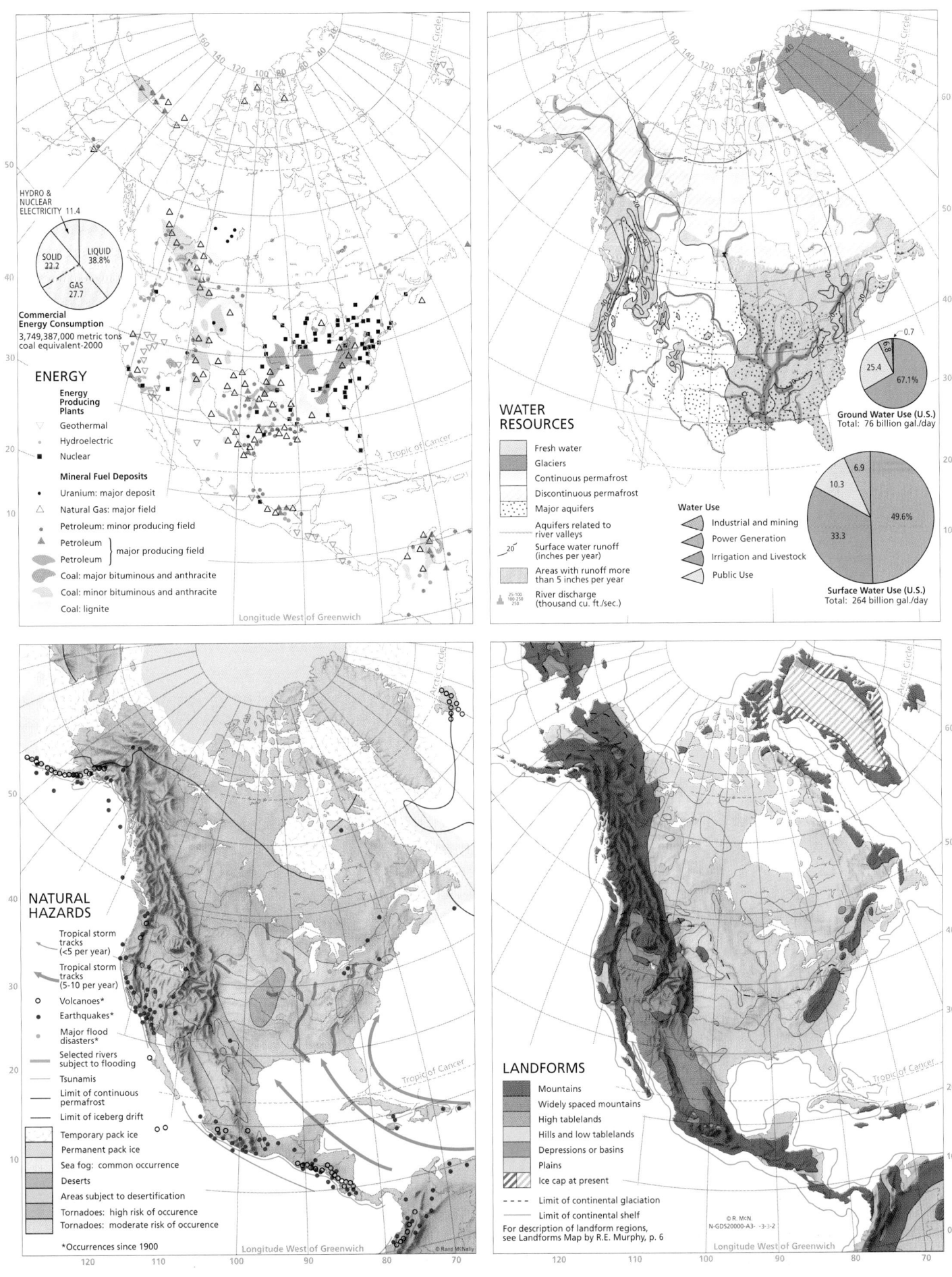

ENERGY

HYDRO & NUCLEAR ELECTRICITY 11.4

SOLID 22.2
LIQUID 38.8%
GAS 27.7

Commercial Energy Consumption
3,749,387,000 metric tons coal equivalent-2000

Energy Producing Plants
△ Geothermal
• Hydroelectric
■ Nuclear

Mineral Fuel Deposits
• Uranium: major deposit
△ Natural Gas: major field
• Petroleum: minor producing field
▲ Petroleum } major producing field
▼ Petroleum
Coal: major bituminous and anthracite
Coal: minor bituminous and anthracite
Coal: lignite

WATER RESOURCES

Fresh water
Glaciers
Continuous permafrost
Discontinuous permafrost
Major aquifers
Aquifers related to river valleys
20″ Surface water runoff (inches per year)
Areas with runoff more than 5 inches per year
River discharge (thousand cu. ft./sec.)
25-100
100-250
250

Ground Water Use (U.S.)
Total: 76 billion gal./day
67.1%
25.4
6.9
0.7

Water Use
Industrial and mining
Power Generation
Irrigation and Livestock
Public Use

Surface Water Use (U.S.)
Total: 264 billion gal./day
49.6%
33.3
10.3
6.9

NATURAL HAZARDS

Tropical storm tracks (<5 per year)
Tropical storm tracks (5-10 per year)
○ Volcanoes*
● Earthquakes*
• Major flood disasters*
Selected rivers subject to flooding
Tsunamis
Limit of continuous permafrost
Limit of iceberg drift
Temporary pack ice
Permanent pack ice
Sea fog: common occurrence
Deserts
Areas subject to desertification
Tornadoes: high risk of occurence
Tornadoes: moderate risk of occurence

*Occurrences since 1900

LANDFORMS

Mountains
Widely spaced mountains
High tablelands
Hills and low tablelands
Depressions or basins
Plains
Ice cap at present

Limit of continental glaciation
Limit of continental shelf

For description of landform regions, see Landforms Map by R.E. Murphy, p. 6

© R. McN.
N-GDS20000-A3- -3-3-2

Longitude West of Greenwich

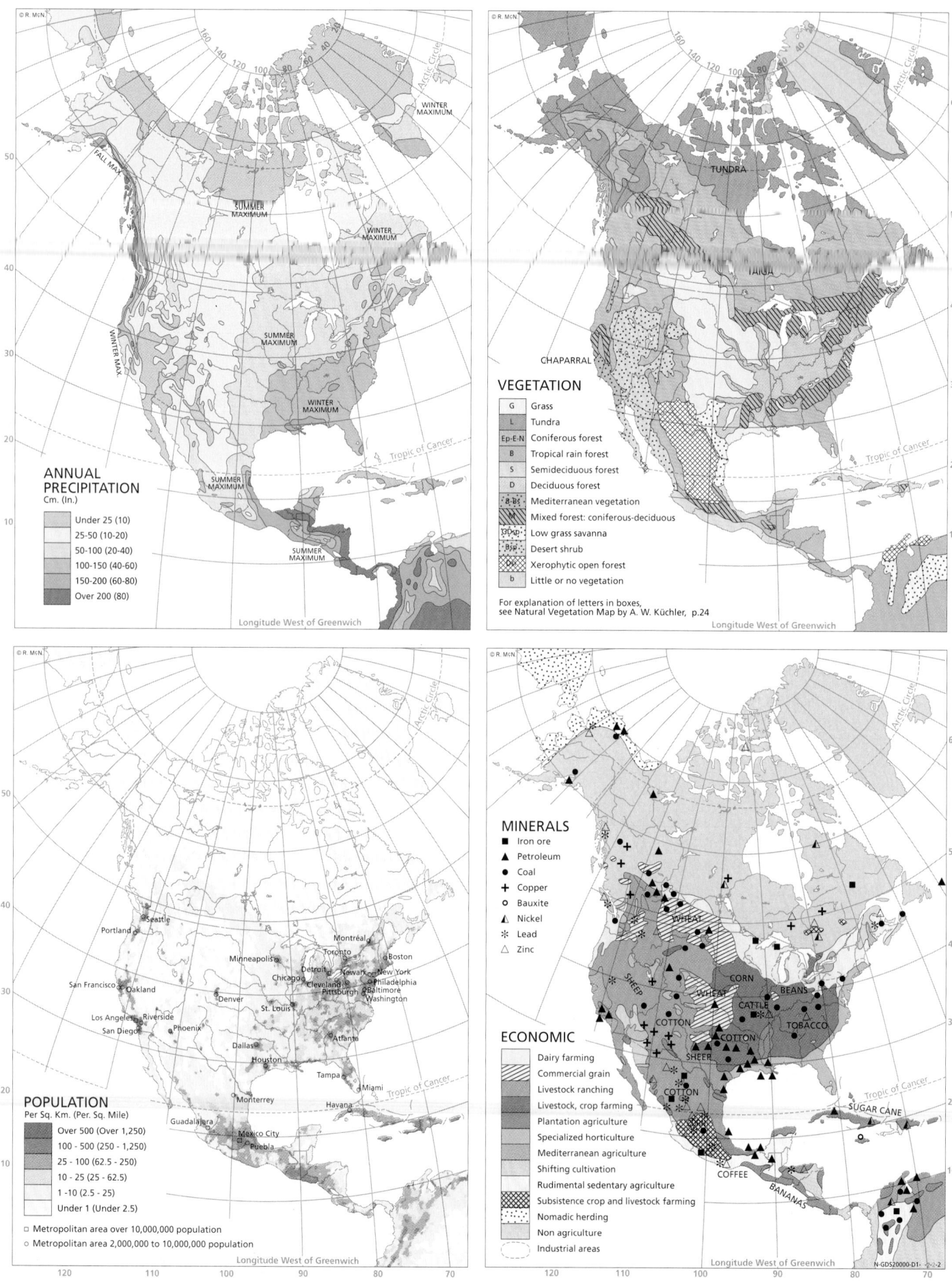

© R. McN.

ANNUAL PRECIPITATION
Cm. (In.)

- Under 25 (10)
- 25-50 (10-20)
- 50-100 (20-40)
- 100-150 (40-60)
- 150-200 (60-80)
- Over 200 (80)

WINTER MAXIMUM
FALL MAX.
SUMMER MAXIMUM
WINTER MAXIMUM
WINTER MAX.
SUMMER MAXIMUM
WINTER MAXIMUM
SUMMER MAXIMUM
SUMMER MAXIMUM
SUMMER MAXIMUM

Longitude West of Greenwich

© R. McN.

TUNDRA
TAIGA
CHAPARRAL

VEGETATION

G	Grass
L	Tundra
Ep-E-N	Coniferous forest
B	Tropical rain forest
S	Semideciduous forest
D	Deciduous forest
a-B	Mediterranean vegetation
M	Mixed forest: coniferous-deciduous
G-sp	Low grass savanna
Bsp	Desert shrub
	Xerophytic open forest
b	Little or no vegetation

For explanation of letters in boxes,
see Natural Vegetation Map by A. W. Küchler, p.24

Longitude West of Greenwich

© R. McN.

Seattle
Portland
San Francisco Oakland
Los Angeles Riverside
San Diego Phoenix
Denver
Minneapolis
Chicago
St. Louis
Dallas
Houston
Montréal
Toronto
Detroit
Cleveland Pittsburgh
Newark New York
Philadelphia
Baltimore
Washington
Boston
Atlanta
Tampa
Miami
Monterrey
Havana
Guadalajara
Mexico City
Puebla

POPULATION
Per Sq. Km. (Per. Sq. Mile)

- Over 500 (Over 1,250)
- 100 - 500 (250 - 1,250)
- 25 - 100 (62.5 - 250)
- 10 - 25 (25 - 62.5)
- 1 -10 (2.5 - 25)
- Under 1 (Under 2.5)

□ Metropolitan area over 10,000,000 population
○ Metropolitan area 2,000,000 to 10,000,000 population

Longitude West of Greenwich

© R. McN.

MINERALS

- ■ Iron ore
- ▲ Petroleum
- ● Coal
- + Copper
- ○ Bauxite
- ◭ Nickel
- ✳ Lead
- △ Zinc

WHEAT
WHEAT
SHEEP
CORN
CATTLE
BEANS
COTTON
COTTON
TOBACCO
SHEEP
COTTON
SUGAR CANE
COFFEE
BANANAS

ECONOMIC

- Dairy farming
- Commercial grain
- Livestock ranching
- Livestock, crop farming
- Plantation agriculture
- Specialized horticulture
- Mediterranean agriculture
- Shifting cultivation
- Rudimental sedentary agriculture
- Subsistence crop and livestock farming
- Nomadic herding
- Non agriculture
- Industrial areas

Longitude West of Greenwich

N-GDS20000-D1- 2-2-2

Tropic of Cancer

120 110 100 90 80 70

ARCTIC OCEAN

Bering Strait
Nome
ALEUTIAN ISLANDS
Bering Sea
BROOKS RANGE
Yukon
ALASKA RANGE
Fairbanks
Anchorage
Gulf of Alaska
Juneau
Prince Rupert
PACIFIC OCEAN

ELLESMERE ISLAND
BANKS ISLAND
MELVILLE ISLAND
DEVON ISLAND
VICTORIA ISLAND
Great Slave Lake
Peace
GREENLAND
Baffin Bay
BAFFIN ISLAND
Godthåb
Arctic Circle

Vancouver
Seattle
Portland
ROCKY
Edmonton
Calgary
Churchill
Hudson Bay
UNGAVA PENINSULA
Labrador Sea

SAN FRANCISCO
SIERRA NEVADA
Salt Lake City
GREAT BASIN
Regina
Winnipeg
Billings
Bismarck
MOUNTAINS
Minneapolis
Lake Superior
St. Lawrence
St. John's
Halifax

LOS ANGELES
Colorado
Phoenix
Albuquerque
Denver
Rapid City
Omaha
Missouri
Mississippi
Lake Michigan
CHICAGO
L. Huron
DETROIT
L. Erie
MONTRÉAL
TORONTO
Ont.
BOSTON
Pittsburgh
Cincinnati
NEW YORK
PHILADELPHIA
WASHINGTON
APPALACHIAN
MOUNTAINS

Kansas City
ST LOUIS
Ohio
Nashville
Dallas
Chihuahua
Rio Grande
Houston
Mississippi
Atlanta

La Paz
Golfo de California
SIERRA MADRE OCCIDENTAL
Mazatlán
Monterrey
SIERRA MADRE ORIENTAL
New Orleans
Jacksonville
Gulf of Mexico

Guadalajara
MEXICO CITY
SIERRA MADRE DEL SUR
Mérida
Havana
CUBA
Miami
Nassau
BAHAMA ISLANDS
Tropic of Cancer

ATLANTIC OCEAN

San Salvador
Managua
San Jose
PACIFIC OCEAN
Panamá
San Salvador
Port-au-Prince
JAMAICA Kingston
HISPANIOLA
San Juan
PUERTO RICO
Caribbean Sea
Maracaibo CARACAS
TRINIDAD

Legend:
- Urban
- Cropland
- Cropland & Woodland
- Cropland & Grazing Land
- Grassland, Grazing Land
- Forest, Woodland
- Swamp, Marshland
- Tundra
- Shrub, Sparse Grass, Wasteland
- Barren Land

COPYRIGHT BY RAND MCNALLY & COMPANY MADE IN U.S.A.
A-520000-36   -2-6

Scale 1:36,000,000; one inch to 570 miles. Lambert Azimuthal Equal-Area Projection

0 100 200 400 600 800 Miles
0 150 300 600 900 1200 Kilometers

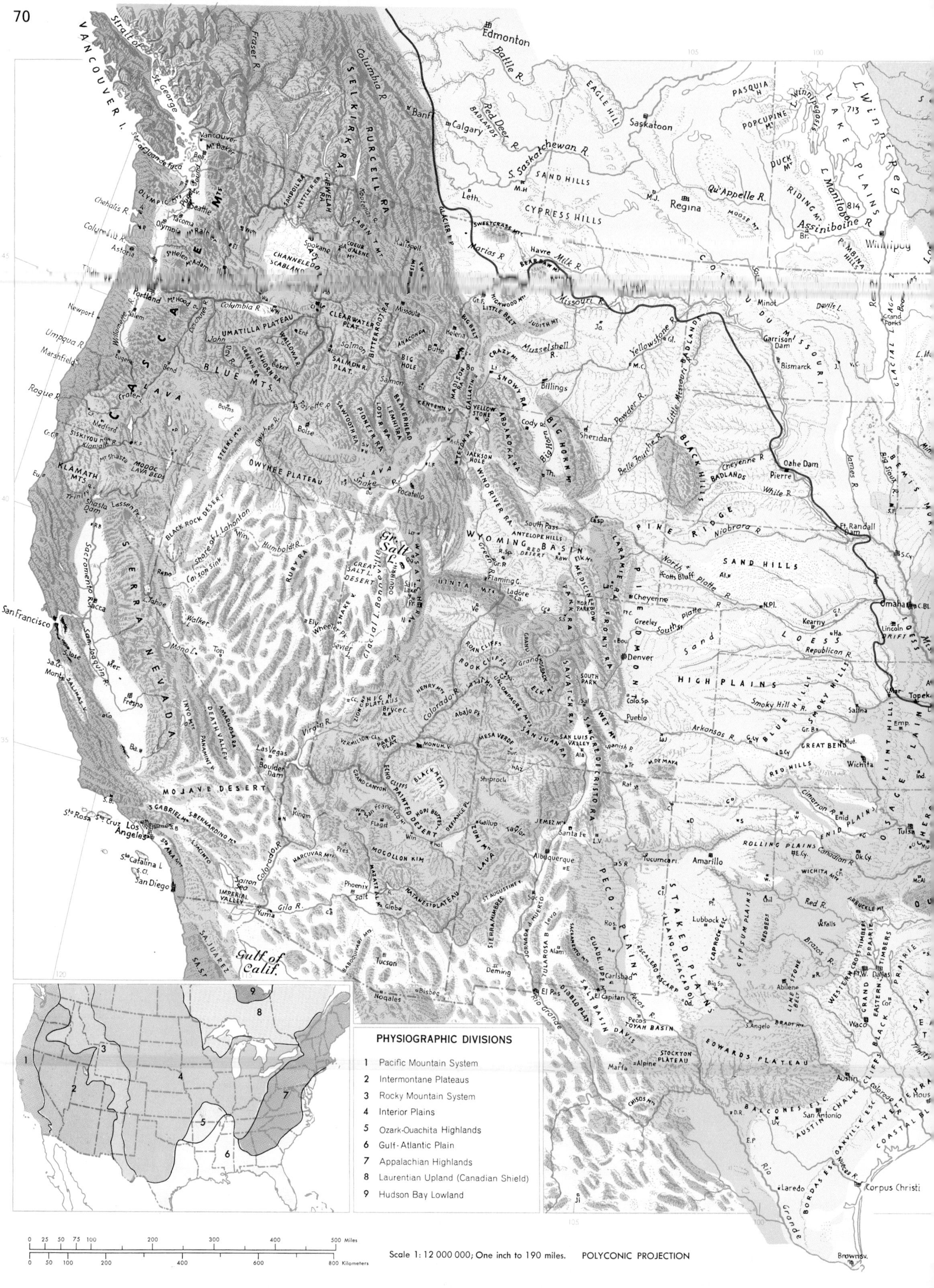

PHYSIOGRAPHIC DIVISIONS
1 Pacific Mountain System
2 Intermontane Plateaus
3 Rocky Mountain System
4 Interior Plains
5 Ozark-Ouachita Highlands
6 Gulf-Atlantic Plain
7 Appalachian Highlands
8 Laurentian Upland (Canadian Shield)
9 Hudson Bay Lowland
Scale 1: 12 000 000; One inch to 190 miles. POLYCONIC PROJECTION
0 25 50 75 100 200 300 400 500 Miles
0 50 100 200 400 600 800 Kilometers
Strait of St. George
VANCOUVER I.
Str. of Juan de Fuca
Vancouver
Mt. Baker
Edmonton
Battle R.
Calgary
Banff
Red Deer R.
S. Saskatchewan R.
SAND HILLS
Saskatoon
EAGLE HILL
PASQUIA H
PORCUPINE Mt.
L. Winnipegosis
L. Winnipeg
LAKE PLAINS
L. Manitoba
DUCK Mt.
RIDING Mt.
Assiniboine R.
Winnipeg
Regina
Qu'Appelle R.
MOOSE Mt.
CYPRESS HILLS
Leth.
SWEETGRASS MTS.
Marias R.
Havre
Milk R.
Missouri R.
Minot
Devils L.
Grand Forks
Garrison Dam
Bismarck
MISSOURI
Fraser R.
Columbia R.
SELKIRK RA.
PURCELL RA.
OLYMPIC MTS.
Seattle
Tacoma
Olympia
Mt. Rainier
Chehalis R.
Columbia R.
Astoria
St. Helens
Mt. Adam
Spokane
COEUR d'ALENE Mt.
CHANNELED SCABLANDS
Kalispell
Portland
Mt. Hood
Newport
Salem
Umpqua R.
Marshfield
Willamette R.
Eugene
Bend
CASCADE MTS.
UMATILLA PLATEAU
CLEARWATER PLAT.
Missoula
BITTERROOT RA.
BLUE MTS.
WALLOWA R.
ELKHORN RA.
Baker
SALMON R. PLAT.
Salmon
BIG HOLE
ANACONDA
Helena
Butte
BIG BELT
LITTLE BELT
JUDITH Mt.
CRAZY Mt.
Musselshell R.
Yellowstone R.
Billings
SNOWY RA.
MADISON RA.
GALLATIN
Rogue R.
Crater L.
LAVA
Burns
Payette R.
Boise
SAWTOOTH RA.
PIONEER RA.
LOST R. RA.
LEMHI RA.
BEAVERHEAD
CENTENNIAL V.
YELLOWSTONE
ABSAROKA RA.
Cody
BIG HORN Mt.
Sheridan
Powder R.
Little Missouri R.
BADLANDS
BLACK HILLS
Belle Fourche R.
Cheyenne R.
Oahe Dam
Pierre
White R.
James R.
Big Sioux R.
Medford
SISKIYOU Mts.
Klamath
Mt. Shasta
MODOC LAVA BEDS
KLAMATH MTS.
Trinity
Shasta Dam
Lassen Pk.
STEENS MTS.
OWYHEE PLATEAU
Owyhee R.
LAVA
Snake R.
Pocatello
TETON RA.
JACKSON HOLE
WIND RIVER RA.
South Pass
ANTELOPE HILLS
WYOMING BASIN
RED DESERT
Casper
LARAMIE RA.
PINE RIDGE
Niobrara R.
Ft. Randall Dam
SAND HILLS
North Platte R.
Scotts Bluff
Cheyenne
MEDICINE BOW
NORTH PARK
Greeley
South Platte
N. Pl.
Kearny
Omaha
Lincoln
LOESS
Republican R.
BLACK ROCK DESERT
Shore of L. Lahontan
Humboldt R.
RUBY RA.
GREAT SALT L. DESERT
Gr. Salt L.
WASATCH RA.
Salt Lake
UINTA MTS.
Flaming G.
Ladore Ca.
Sacramento R.
SIERRA NEVADA
Carson Sink
L. Tahoe
Sacra.
San Francisco
S. Jose
San Joaquin R.
Walker L.
Mono L.
Ely
Wheeler Pk.
SNAKE V.
Sevier L.
Glacial L. Bonneville
ROAN CLIFFS
BOOK CLIFFS
Grand
UNCOMPAGRE
SAVATCH RA.
SOUTH PARK
Denver
HIGH PLAINS
Colo. Sp.
Pueblo
Smoky Hill R.
SMOKY HILLS
Salina
Topeka
FLINT HILLS
Fresno
SALINAS V.
INYO Mts.
DEATH VALLEY
PANAMINT V.
AMARGOSA RA.
HIGH PLATEAUS
HENRY MTS.
Bryce C.
Colorado R.
Abajo Pk.
SAN JUAN RA.
SAN LUIS VALLEY
SANGRE DE CRISTO RA.
WET Mt.
Arkansas R.
GREAT BEND
Wichita
Virgin R.
Las Vegas
Boulder Dam
VERMILION CL.
PARIA PLAT.
MONUM. V.
MESA VERDE
Shiprock
MESA DE MAYA
RED HILLS
Cimarron R.
Enid
OSAGE PLAINS
Tulsa
MOJAVE DESERT
GRAND CANYON
ECHO CLIFFS
BLACK MESA
PAINTED DESERT
HOPI BUTTES
Flagst.
Kingm.
Gallup
ZUNI Mt.
JEMEZ Mt.
Santa Fe
S. GABRIEL Mt.
S. BERNARDINO Mt.
Los Angeles
S. JACINTO
Sta. Catalina I.
San Diego
HARCUVAR Mts.
MOGOLLON RIM
LAVA
Albuquerque
Tucumcari
Amarillo
ROLLING PLAINS
Canadian R.
WICHITA Mts.
Salton Sea
IMPERIAL VALLEY
Phoenix
Salt
NATANES PLATEAU
Gila R.
Yuma
Globe
PECOS PLAINS
STAKED PLAINS (LLANO ESTACADO)
Lubbock
CAPROCK ESC.
GYPSUM PLAINS
RED BEDS
Red R.
ARBUCKLE Mt.
Gulf of Calif.
Tucson
Nogales
Bisbee
Deming
JORNADA del MUERTO
TULAROSA B.
SACRAMENTO Mts.
GUADALUPE Mts.
Carlsbad
El Capitan
El Paso
Rio Grande
DIABLO PLAT.
SALT BASIN
Pecos R.
TOYAH BASIN
DAVIS
Marfa
Alpine
STOCKTON PLATEAU
EDWARDS PLATEAU
CHISOS MTS.
S. Angelo
Abilene
Brazos R.
WESTERN CROSS TIMBERS
GRAND PRAIRIE
EASTERN CROSS TIMBERS
BLACK PRAIRIE
Dallas
Waco
Austin
Colorado R.
BALCONES ESC.
San Antonio
AUSTIN CHALK CLIFFS
OAKVILLE ESC.
FAYETTE
COASTAL PLAIN
BORDAS ESC.
Nueces R.
Laredo
Corpus Christi
Rio Grande
Brownsv.

PHYSIOGRAPHY
BY
ERWIN RAISZ

LITHOLOGY AND STRUCTURE

Unconsolidated deposits: alluvium, sands, playa deposits, etc.

Essentially horizontal sedimentary rocks; many partially unconsolidated.

Slightly to moderately tilted, older sedimentary rocks.

Steeply folded or faulted, sedimentary rocks

Volcanics; largely lava flows.

Metamorphic and intrusive igneous rocks; structure complex.

Limits of continental glaciation.

LANDFORMS

PLATEAUS   BASIN RANGES

HILLS   VOLCANO AND
                         LAVA

MOUNTAINS   SAND

MESAS   SINKS

CUESTAS   MORAINES

FOLDED   DRUMLINS
MOUNTAINS

A-520500-9A6   -3- 7
Copyright by Rand McNally & Co.
Made in U.S.A.

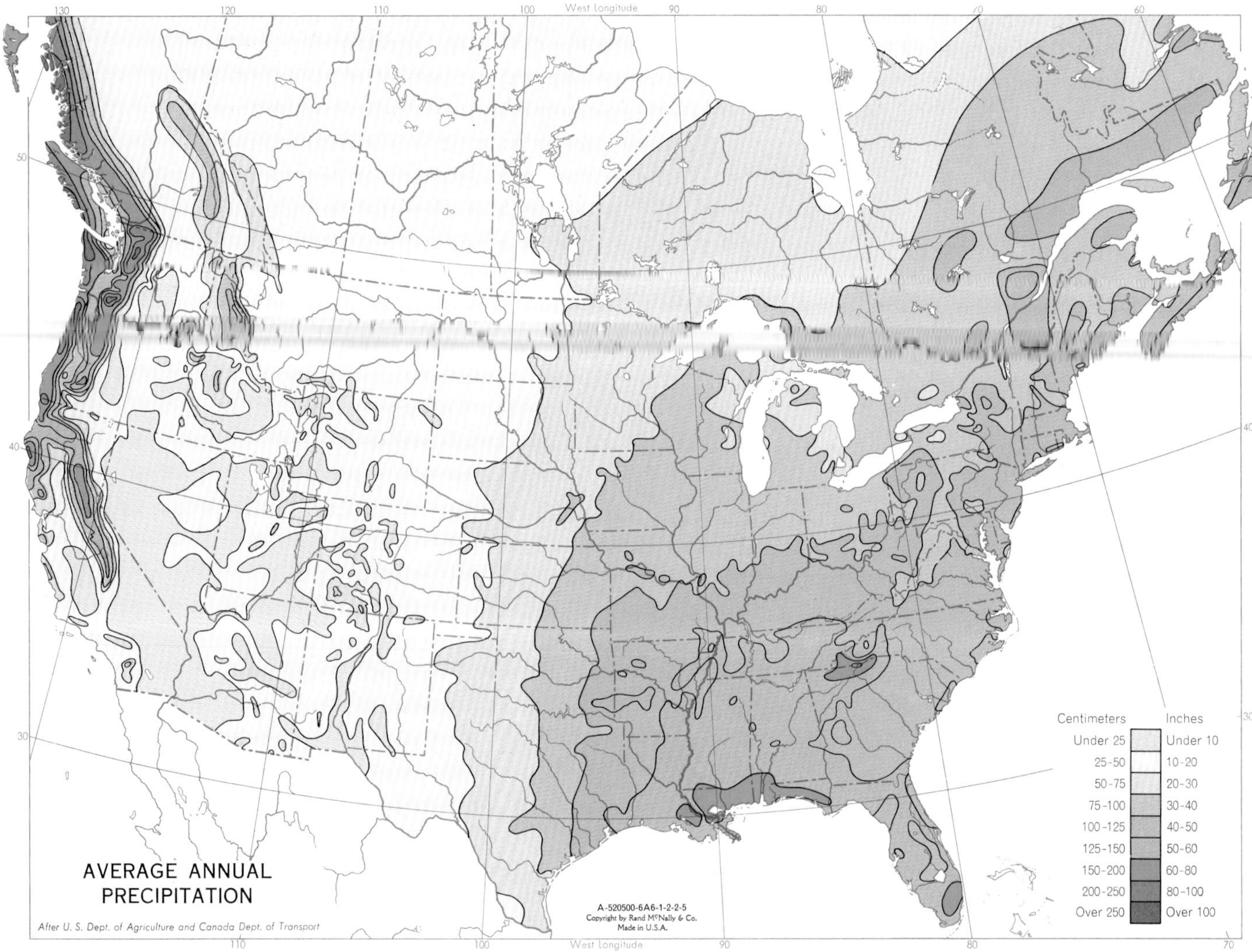
AVERAGE ANNUAL
PRECIPITATION
After U. S. Dept. of Agriculture and Canada Dept. of Transport
West Longitude
Centimeters Inches
Under 25 Under 10
25-50 10-20
50-75 20-30
75-100 30-40
100-125 40-50
125-150 50-60
150-200 60-80
200-250 80-100
Over 250 Over 100
A-520500-6A6-1-2-2-5
Copyright by Rand McNally & Co.
Made in U.S.A.

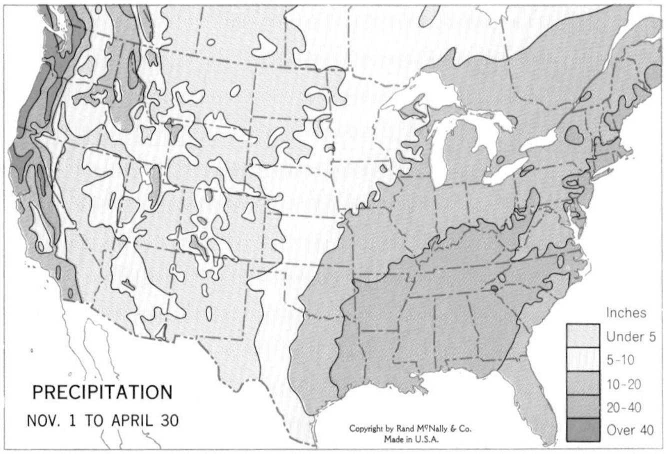
PRECIPITATION
NOV. 1 TO APRIL 30
Inches
Under 5
5-10
10-20
20-40
Over 40
Copyright by Rand McNally & Co.
Made in U.S.A.

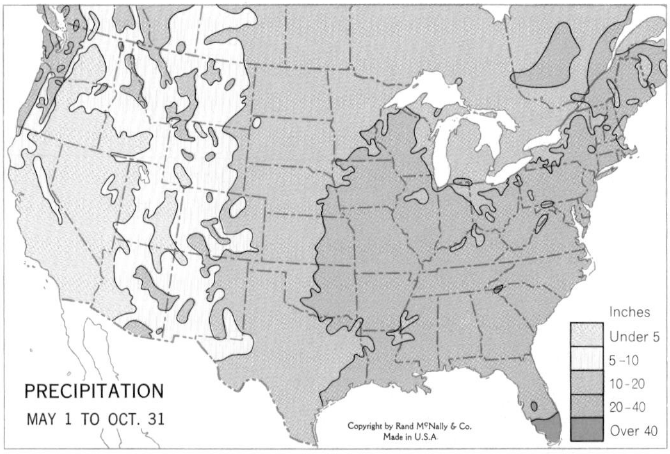
PRECIPITATION
MAY 1 TO OCT. 31
Inches
Under 5
5-10
10-20
20-40
Over 40
Copyright by Rand McNally & Co.
Made in U.S.A.

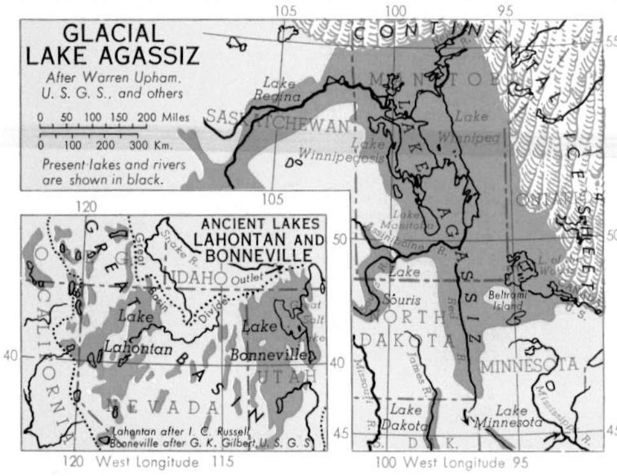
GLACIAL
LAKE AGASSIZ
After Warren Upham, U. S. G. S., and others
0 50 100 150 200 Miles
0 100 200 300 Km.
Present lakes and rivers are shown in black.
LAKE AGASSIZ
Lake Winnipeg
MINNESOTA
NORTH DAKOTA
Lake Dakota
Lake Minnesota
100 West Longitude 95
ANCIENT LAKES
LAHONTAN AND
BONNEVILLE
Lake Lahontan
Lake Bonneville
NEVADA
UTAH
IDAHO
Lahontan after I. C. Russell
Bonneville after G. K. Gilbert, U. S. G. S.
120 West Longitude 115

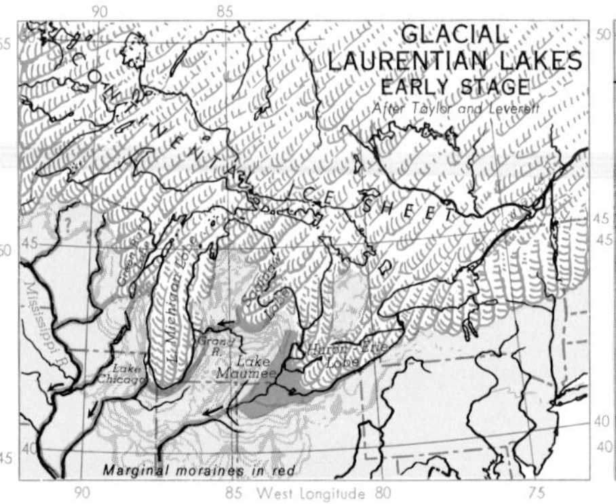
GLACIAL
LAURENTIAN LAKES
EARLY STAGE
After Taylor and Leverett
Lake Chicago
Lake Maumee
Marginal moraines in red
85 West Longitude 80

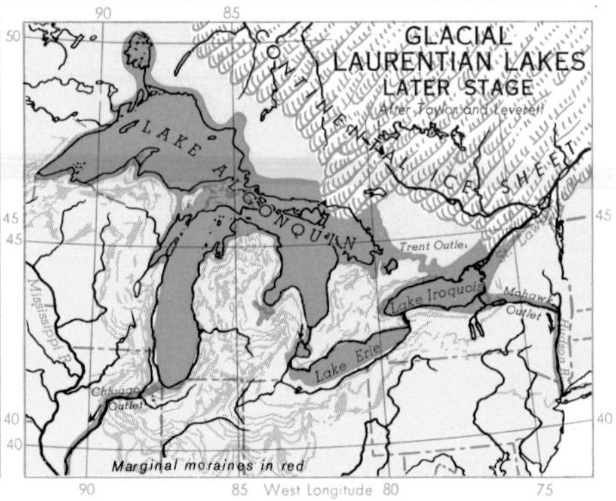
GLACIAL
LAURENTIAN LAKES
LATER STAGE
After Taylor and Leverett
LAKE ALGONQUIN
Trent Outlet
Lake Iroquois
Mohawk Outlet
Lake Erie
Chicago Outlet
Marginal moraines in red
85 West Longitude 80

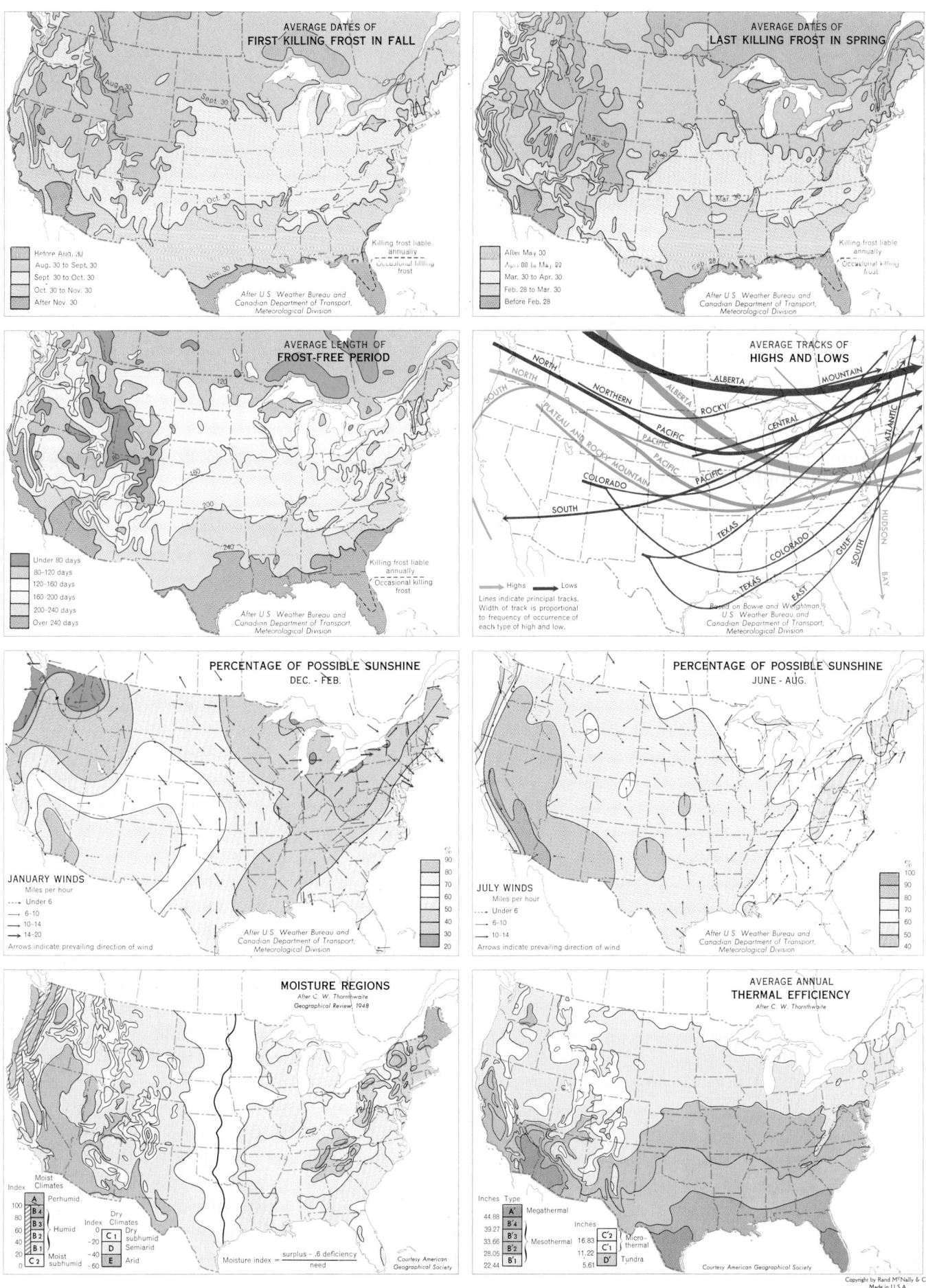

AVERAGE DATES OF
FIRST KILLING FROST IN FALL

Before Aug. 30
Aug. 30 to Sept. 30
Sept. 30 to Oct. 30
Oct. 30 to Nov. 30
After Nov. 30

Killing frost liable
annually
Occasional killing
frost

After U.S. Weather Bureau and
Canadian Department of Transport,
Meteorological Division

AVERAGE DATES OF
LAST KILLING FROST IN SPRING

After May 30
Apr. 30 to May 30
Mar. 30 to Apr. 30
Feb. 28 to Mar. 30
Before Feb. 28

Killing frost liable
annually
Occasional killing
frost

After U.S. Weather Bureau and
Canadian Department of Transport,
Meteorological Division

AVERAGE LENGTH OF
FROST-FREE PERIOD

Under 80 days
80-120 days
120-160 days
160-200 days
200-240 days
Over 240 days

Killing frost liable
annually
Occasional killing
frost

After U.S. Weather Bureau and
Canadian Department of Transport,
Meteorological Division

AVERAGE TRACKS OF
HIGHS AND LOWS

Highs   Lows

Lines indicate principal tracks.
Width of track is proportional
to frequency of occurrence of
each type of high and low.

Based on Bowie and Weightman,
U.S. Weather Bureau and
Canadian Department of Transport,
Meteorological Division

PERCENTAGE OF POSSIBLE SUNSHINE
DEC. - FEB.

JANUARY WINDS
Miles per hour
Under 6
6-10
10-14
14-20
Arrows indicate prevailing direction of wind

%
90
80
70
60
50
40
30
20

After U.S. Weather Bureau and
Canadian Department of Transport,
Meteorological Division

PERCENTAGE OF POSSIBLE SUNSHINE
JUNE - AUG.

JULY WINDS
Miles per hour
Under 6
6-10
10-14
Arrows indicate prevailing direction of wind

%
100
90
80
70
60
50
40

After U.S. Weather Bureau and
Canadian Department of Transport,
Meteorological Division

MOISTURE REGIONS
After C. W. Thornthwaite
Geographical Review, 1948

Moist
Climates
Index
100 A   Perhumid
80   B4
60   B3 Humid
40   B2
20   B1 Moist
0   C2 subhumid

Dry Climates
Index
0   C1 Dry
-20 D   subhumid
-40   Semiarid
-60 E   Arid

Moisture index = surplus − .6 deficiency / need

Courtesy American
Geographical Society

AVERAGE ANNUAL
THERMAL EFFICIENCY
After C. W. Thornthwaite

Inches Type
44.88 A'   Megathermal
39.27 B'4
33.66 B'3 Mesothermal
28.05 B'2
22.44 B'1

Inches
16.83 C'2 Micro-
11.22 C'1 thermal
5.61   D'   Tundra

Courtesy American Geographical Society

Copyright by Rand M⊆Nally & Co.
Made in U.S.A.
A-520500-66   -5

74

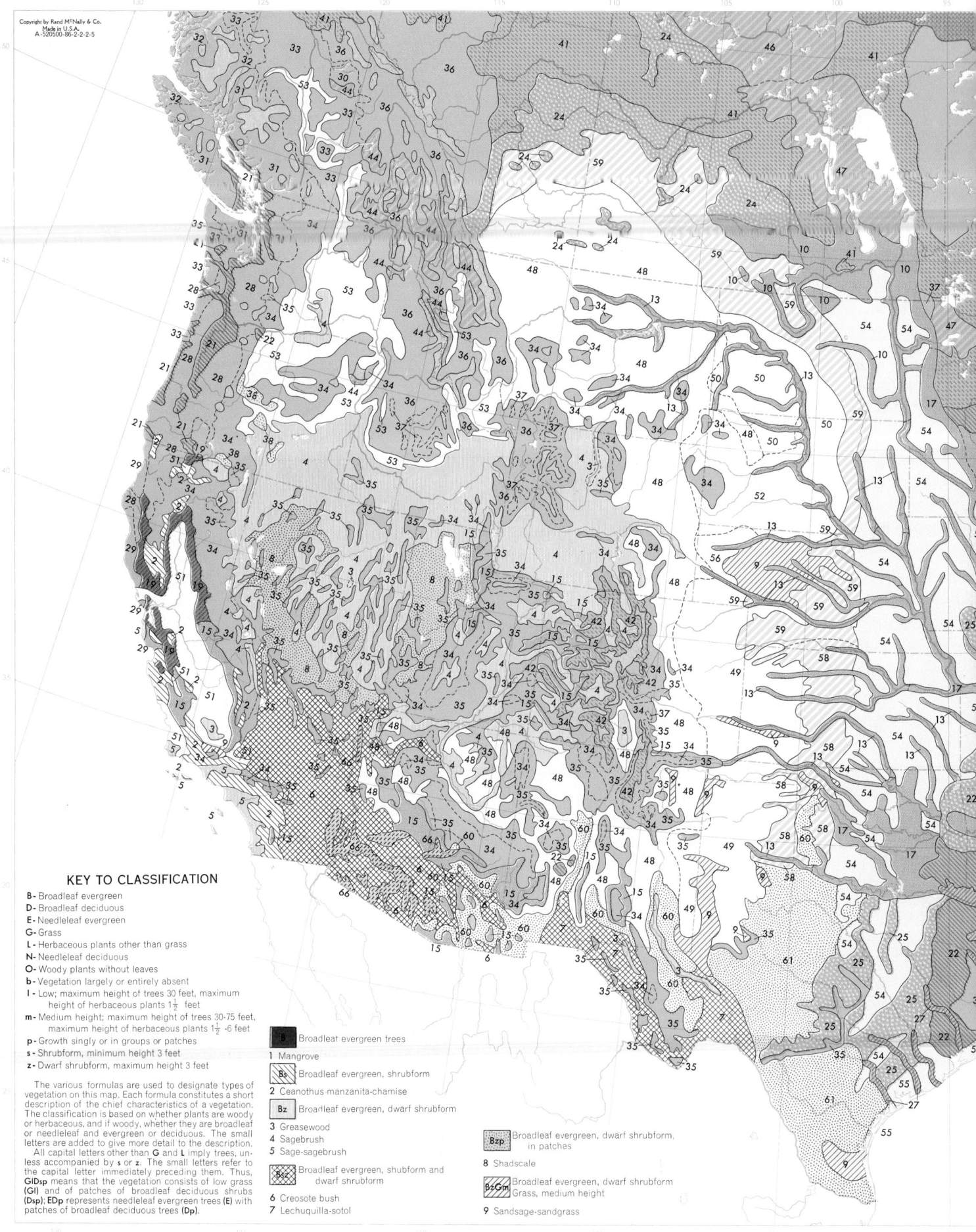

KEY TO CLASSIFICATION

B- Broadleaf evergreen
D- Broadleaf deciduous
E- Needleleaf evergreen
G- Grass
L- Herbaceous plants other than grass
N- Needleleaf deciduous
O- Woody plants without leaves
b- Vegetation largely or entirely absent
l- Low; maximum height of trees 30 feet, maximum
    height of herbaceous plants 1½ feet
m- Medium height; maximum height of trees 30-75 feet,
    maximum height of herbaceous plants 1½ -6 feet
p- Growth singly or in groups or patches
s- Shrubform, minimum height 3 feet
z- Dwarf shrubform, maximum height 3 feet

The various formulas are used to designate types of
vegetation on this map. Each formula constitutes a short
description of the chief characteristics of a vegetation.
The classification is based on whether plants are woody
or herbaceous, and if woody, whether they are broadleaf
or needleleaf and evergreen or deciduous. The small
letters are added to give more detail to the description.
All capital letters other than G and L imply trees, unless accompanied by s or z. The small letters refer to
the capital letter immediately preceding them. Thus,
GlDsp means that the vegetation consists of low grass
(Gl) and of patches of broadleaf deciduous shrubs
(Dsp); EDp represents needleleaf evergreen trees (E) with
patches of broadleaf deciduous trees (Dp).

B Broadleaf evergreen trees

1 Mangrove

Bs Broadleaf evergreen, shrubform

2 Ceanothus-manzanita-chamise

Bz Broadleaf evergreen, dwarf shrubform

3 Greasewood
4 Sagebrush
5 Sage-sagebrush

Bsz Broadleaf evergreen, shubform and
    dwarf shrubform

6 Creosote bush
7 Lechuquilla-sotol

Bzp Broadleaf evergreen, dwarf shrubform,
    in patches

8 Shadscale

BzGm Broadleaf evergreen, dwarf shrubform
    Grass, medium height

9 Sandsage-sandgrass

Copyright by Rand McNally & Co.
Made in U.S.A.
A-520500-86-2-2-2-5

0 25 50 75 100   200   300   400   500 Miles

0 50 100   200   400   600   800 Kilometers

Scale 1:14 000 000;   One inch to 220 mile

NATURAL VEGETATION

BY A. W. KÜCHLER

Based on "A Physiognomic Classification of Vegetation"
Annals of the Assoc. of American Geographers, Vol. 39, September, 1949

D Broadleaf deciduous trees

10 Aspen-oak
11 Beech-maple
12 Beech-tulip tree-maple-basswood
13 Cottonwood-willow
14 Maple-basswood
15 Oak
16 Oak-ash-maple
17 Oak-hickory
18 Oak-tulip tree

DB Broadleaf deciduous trees
Broadleaf evergreen trees

19 Oak-madrone

DE Broadleaf deciduous trees
Needleleaf evergreen trees

20 Maple-yellow birch-hemlock-pine
21 Oak-Douglas fir
22 Oak-pine
23 Maple-beech-hemlock

D Broadleaf deciduous trees
Gmp Grass, medium height, in patches

24 Aspen-needle grass-wheat grass
25 Oak-hickory-bluestem

DN Broadleaf deciduous trees
Needleleaf deciduous trees

26 Bay trees-bald cypress
27 Tupelo-gum-bald cypress

E Needleleaf evergreen trees

28 Douglas fir
29 Douglas fir-redwood
30 Hemlock-arbor vitae
31 Hemlock-arbor vitae-Douglas fir
32 Hemlock-arbor vitae-fir
33 Hemlock-spruce
34 Pine
35 Pine-juniper
36 Pine-spruce
37 Spruce-fir

Esp Needleleaf evergreen, shrubform,
in patches

38 Juniper

EDp Needleleaf evergreen trees
Broadleaf deciduous trees, in patches

39 Douglas fir-pine-aspen
40 Pine-spruce-birch
41 Spruce-aspen
42 Spruce-fir-aspen
43 Spruce-poplar-birch

EN Needleleaf evergreen trees
Needleleaf deciduous trees

44 Hemlock-arbor vitae-Douglas fir-larch
45 Pine-bald cypress
46 Pine-spruce-larch
47 Spruce-larch

Gl Grass, low

48 Grama grass
49 Grama grass-buffalo grass
50 Grama grass-needle grass
51 Needle grass-blue grass
52 Wheat grass
53 Wheat grass-blue grass

Gm Grass, medium height

54 Bluestem
55 Broom grass-water grass
56 Marsh grass
57 Saw grass

Gml Grass, medium and low height

58 Bluestem-bunch grass
59 Needle grass-wheat grass

Gl Grass, low
Dsp Broadleaf deciduous, shrubform, in patches

60 Bunch grass-oak

Gm Grass, medium height
Dsp Broadleaf deciduous, shrubform, in patches

61 Mesquite grass-mesquite

L Herbaceous plants other than grass

62 Lichens, etc.

LEp Herbaceous plants other than grass
Needleleaf evergreen trees, in patches

63 Lichens-spruce

LEp Herbaceous plants other than grass
Np Needleleaf evergreen trees, in patches
Needleleaf deciduous trees, in patches

64 Lichens-spruce-larch

N Needleleaf deciduous trees

65 Bald cypress

Op Woody plants without leaves, in patches

66 Palo verde-cacti-ocotillo

b Vegetation largely or entirely absent

LAMBERT CONFORMAL CONIC PROJECTION

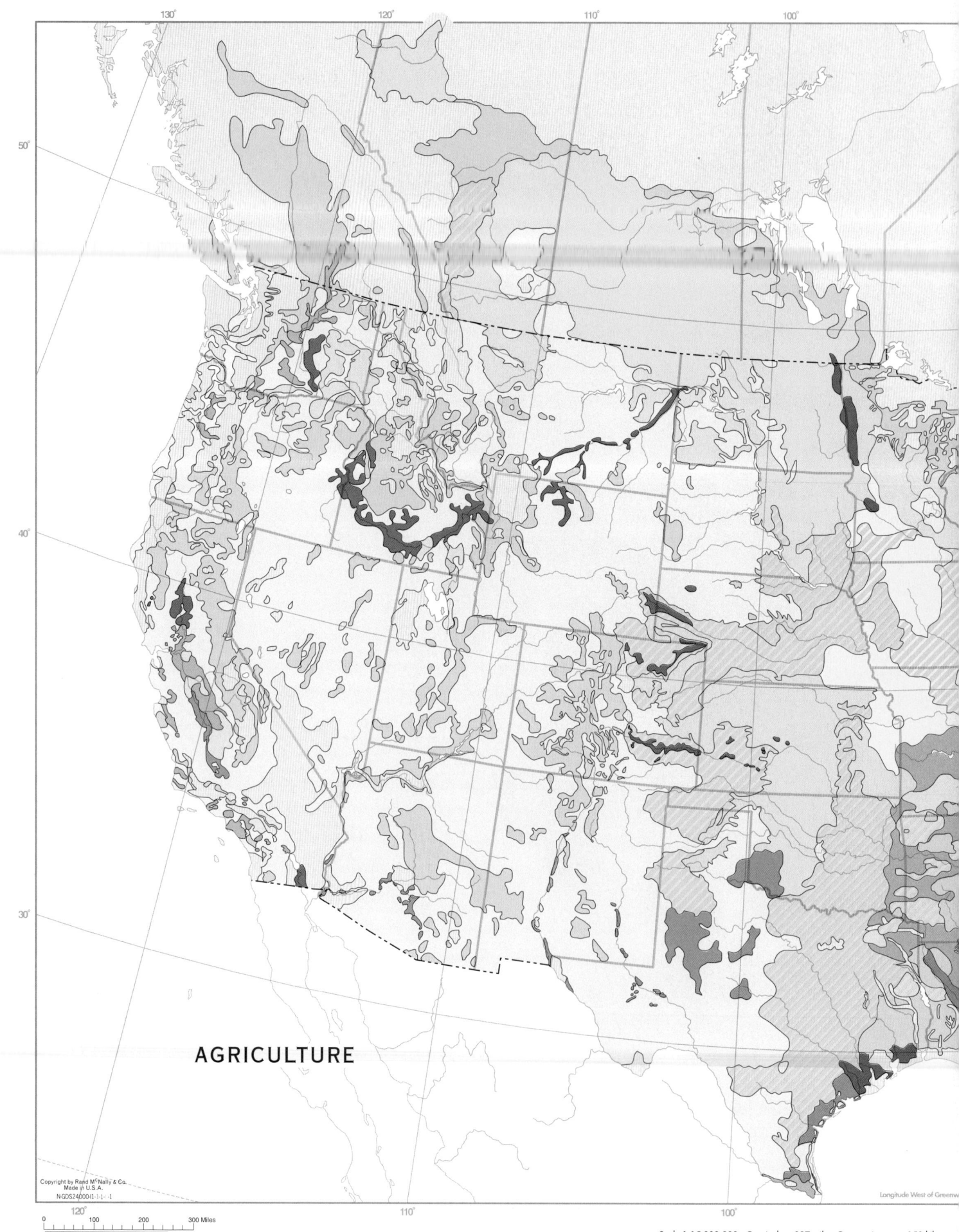

AGRICULTURE

Longitude West of Greenwi

Scale 1:15,000,000; One inch to 237 miles. One centimeter to 150 kilometer

120°

| 0 | 100 | 200 | 300 Miles |

| 0 | 100 | 200 | 300 | 400 Kilometers |

Dairying

Fruits and Vegetables

Wheat, Barley, and Oilseeds

Cash Corn and Soybeans

Tobacco

Cotton

Livestock and Feed Grains: Beef

Livestock and Feed Grains: Hogs

Livestock and Feed Grains: Poultry

Livestock and Feed Grains: Mixed

Specialty Crops (Peanuts, Potatoes, Rice, Sugar)

Western Livestock Ranching

Western Feedlots

Agriculture and Forestry

Non-Agricultural Areas

Tropic of Cancer

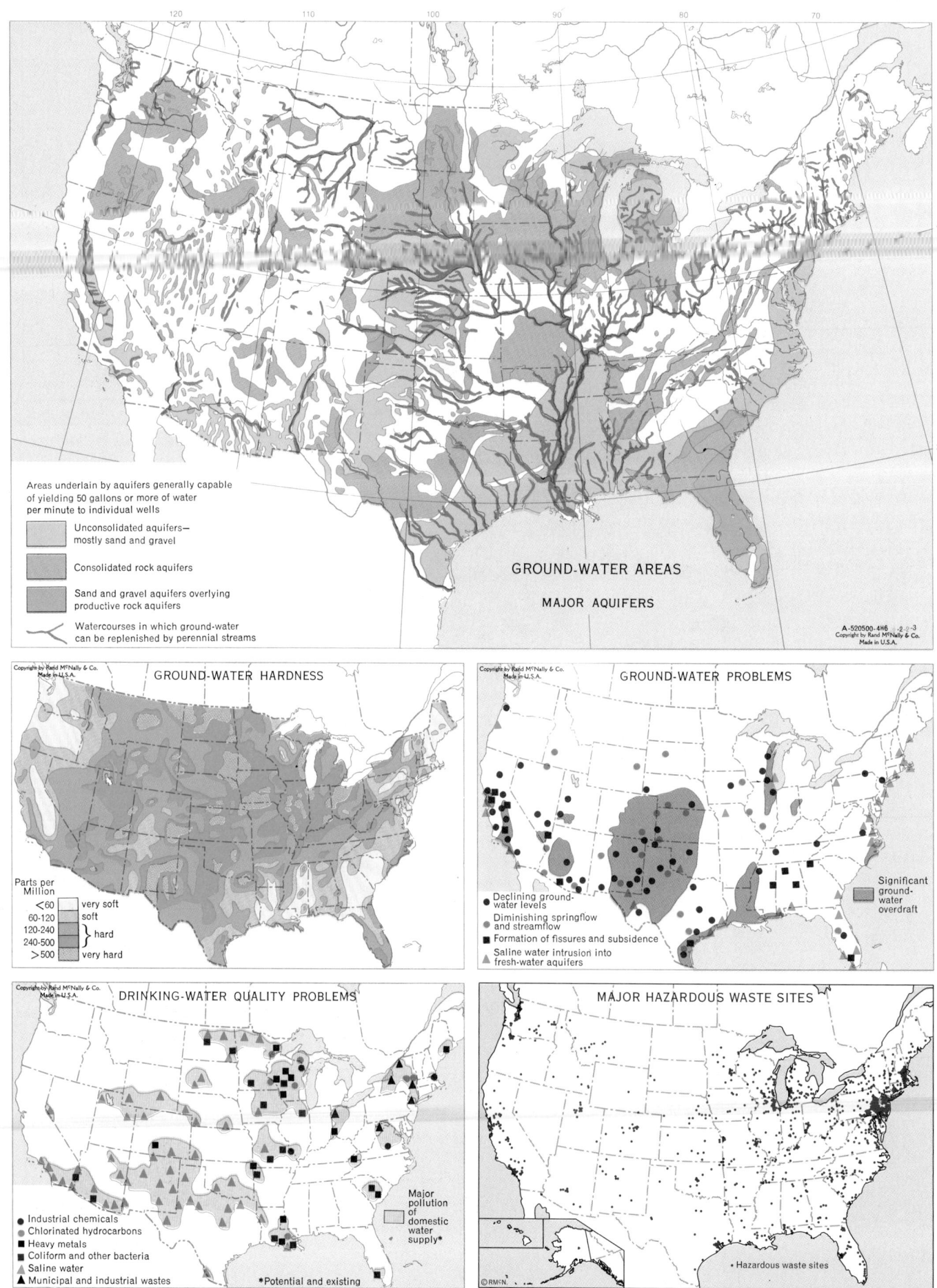

Areas underlain by aquifers generally capable
of yielding 50 gallons or more of water
per minute to individual wells

Unconsolidated aquifers—
mostly sand and gravel

Consolidated rock aquifers

Sand and gravel aquifers overlying
productive rock aquifers

Watercourses in which ground-water
can be replenished by perennial streams

GROUND-WATER AREAS

MAJOR AQUIFERS

A-520500-4H6
Copyright by Rand McNally & Co.
Made in U.S.A.

GROUND-WATER HARDNESS

Parts per
Million
<60   very soft
60-120 soft
120-240 } hard
240-500
>500   very hard

GROUND-WATER PROBLEMS

● Declining ground-
  water levels
● Diminishing springflow
  and streamflow
■ Formation of fissures and subsidence
▲ Saline water intrusion into
  fresh-water aquifers

Significant
ground-
water
overdraft

DRINKING-WATER QUALITY PROBLEMS

● Industrial chemicals
● Chlorinated hydrocarbons
■ Heavy metals
■ Coliform and other bacteria
▲ Saline water
▲ Municipal and industrial wastes

Major
pollution
of
domestic
water
supply*

*Potential and existing

MAJOR HAZARDOUS WASTE SITES

• Hazardous waste sites

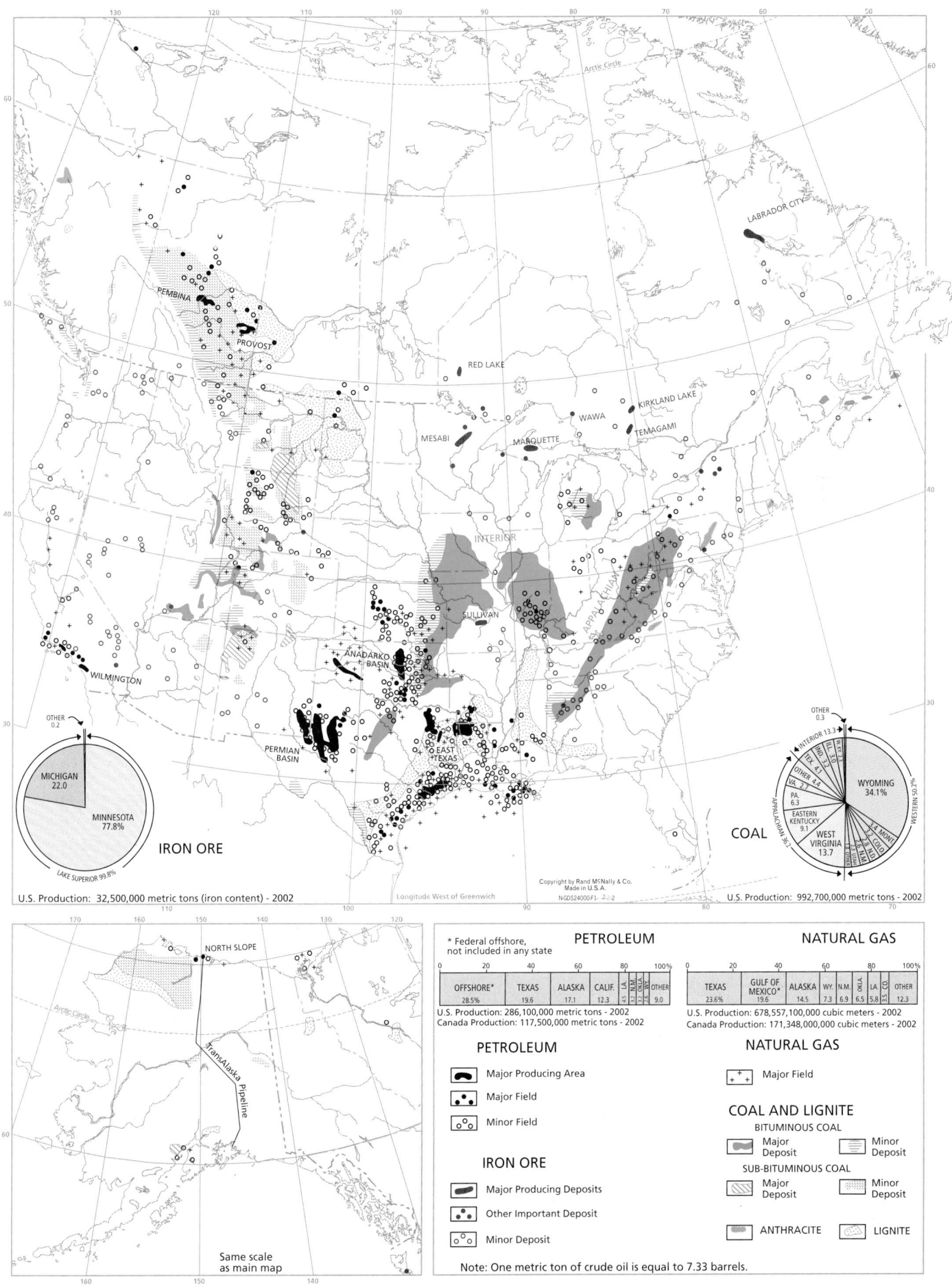

IRON ORE

OTHER
0.2

MICHIGAN
22.0

MINNESOTA
77.8%

LAKE SUPERIOR 99.8%

U.S. Production: 32,500,000 metric tons (iron content) - 2002

COAL

OTHER
0.3

INTERIOR 13.3

ILL. 5.9

IND. 5.2

OTHER 4.4

VA. 2.7

PA.
6.3

EASTERN
KENTUCKY
9.1

APPALACHIAN 36.2

WEST
VIRGINIA
13.7

N.D. 4.4 MONT.

N. COLO.

TEXAS

OHIO

N.M.

WESTERN 50.2%

WYOMING
34.1%

U.S. Production: 992,700,000 metric tons - 2002

PEMBINA

PROVOST

RED LAKE

KIRKLAND LAKE

WAWA

TEMAGAMI

LABRADOR CITY

MESABI

MARQUETTE

SULLIVAN

INTERIOR

APPALACHIAN

ANADARKO
BASIN

WILMINGTON

PERMIAN
BASIN

EAST
TEXAS

Copyright by Rand McNally & Co.
Made in U.S.A.

Longitude West of Greenwich

NGDS24000-F1-2-2

Arctic Circle

NORTH SLOPE

TransAlaska Pipeline

Arctic Circle

Same scale
as main map

* Federal offshore,
not included in any state

PETROLEUM

	OFFSHORE*	TEXAS	ALASKA	CALIF.	N.M.	OKLA.	WY.	OTHER
0 20 40 60 80 100%	28.5%	19.6	17.1	12.3	4.5	3.7	1.9	9.0

U.S. Production: 286,100,000 metric tons - 2002
Canada Production: 117,500,000 metric tons - 2002

NATURAL GAS

	TEXAS	GULF OF MEXICO*	ALASKA	WY.	N.M.	OKLA.	LA.	CO.	OTHER
0 20 40 60 80 100%	23.6%	19.6	14.5	7.3	6.9	6.5	5.8	3.5	12.3

U.S. Production: 678,557,100,000 cubic meters - 2002
Canada Production: 171,348,000,000 cubic meters - 2002

PETROLEUM

Major Producing Area

Major Field

Minor Field

IRON ORE

Major Producing Deposits

Other Important Deposit

Minor Deposit

NATURAL GAS

Major Field

COAL AND LIGNITE

BITUMINOUS COAL

Major
Deposit

Minor
Deposit

SUB-BITUMINOUS COAL

Major
Deposit

Minor
Deposit

ANTHRACITE   LIGNITE

Note: One metric ton of crude oil is equal to 7.33 barrels.

Scale 1:29,000,000; One inch to 457 miles.   ALBERS CONIC PROJECTION

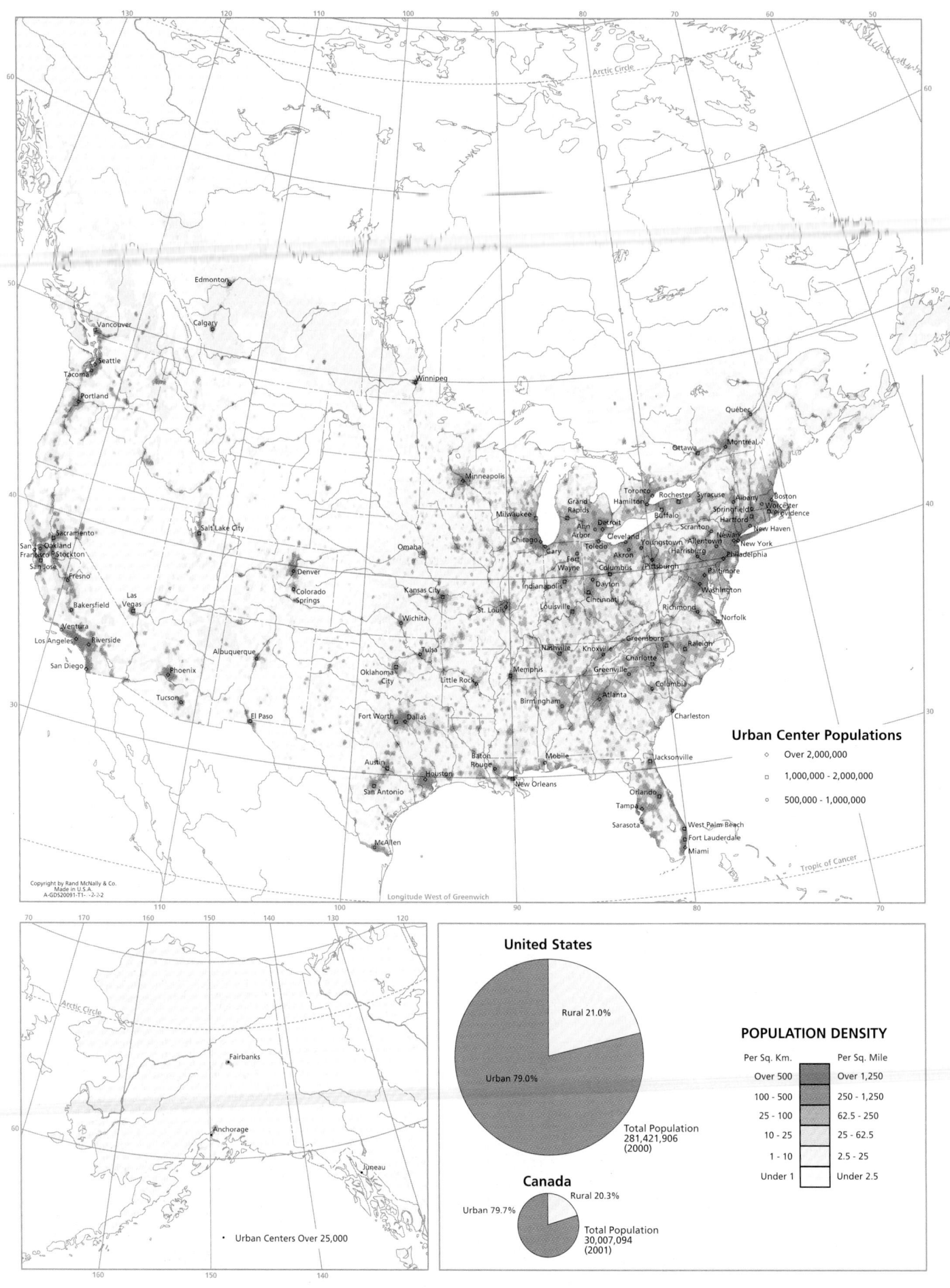

Urban Center Populations

◇   Over 2,000,000

□   1,000,000 - 2,000,000

○   500,000 - 1,000,000

•   Urban Centers Over 25,000

United States

Rural 21.0%

Urban 79.0%

Total Population
281,421,906
(2000)

Canada

Rural 20.3%

Urban 79.7%

Total Population
30,007,094
(2001)

POPULATION DENSITY

Per Sq. Km.	Per Sq. Mile
Over 500	Over 1,250
100 - 500	250 - 1,250
25 - 100	62.5 - 250
10 - 25	25 - 62.5
1 - 10	2.5 - 25
Under 1	Under 2.5

Copyright by Rand McNally & Co.
Made in U.S.A.
A-GDS20091-T1--2-2-2

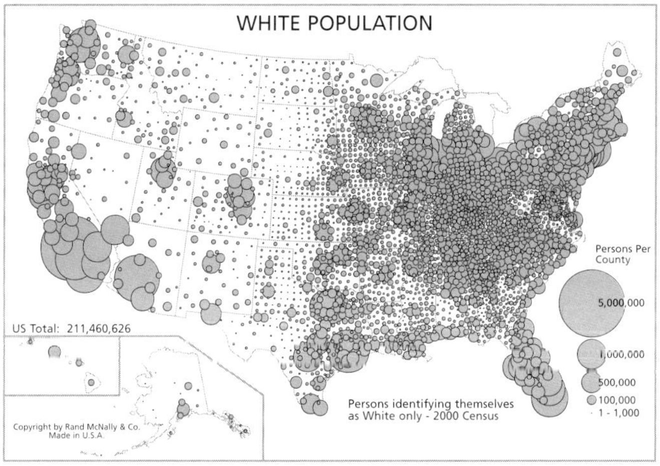

WHITE POPULATION

US Total: 211,460,626

Persons Per County

5,000,000
1,000,000
500,000
100,000
1 - 1,000

Persons identifying themselves as White only - 2000 Census

Copyright by Rand McNally & Co.
Made in U.S.A.

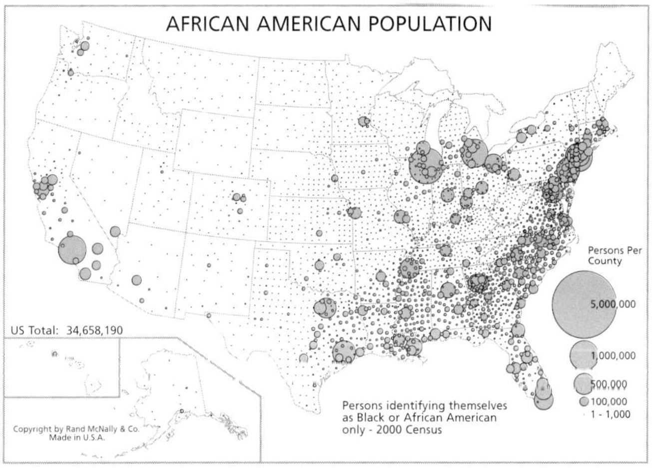

AFRICAN AMERICAN POPULATION

US Total: 34,658,190

Persons Per County

5,000,000
1,000,000
500,000
100,000
1 - 1,000

Persons identifying themselves as Black or African American only - 2000 Census

Copyright by Rand McNally & Co.
Made in U.S.A.

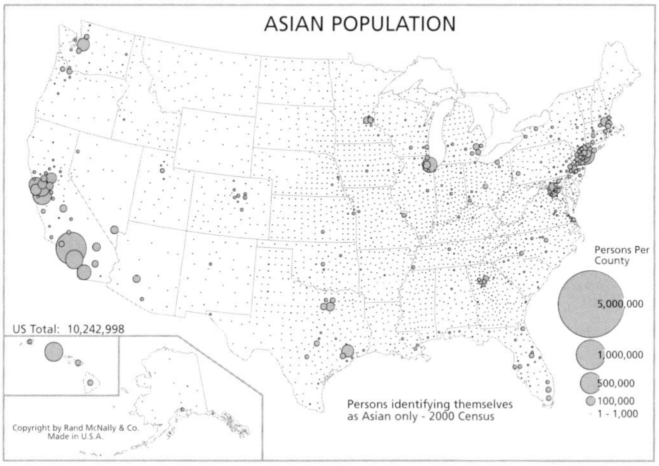

ASIAN POPULATION

US Total: 10,242,998

Persons Per County

5,000,000
1,000,000
500,000
100,000
1 - 1,000

Persons identifying themselves as Asian only - 2000 Census

Copyright by Rand McNally & Co.
Made in U.S.A.

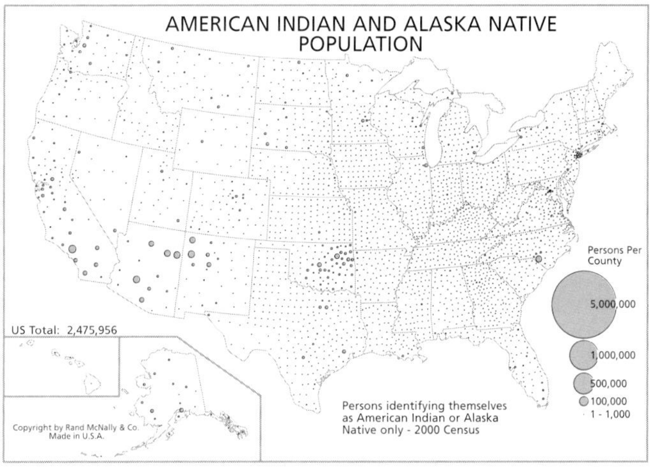

AMERICAN INDIAN AND ALASKA NATIVE POPULATION

US Total: 2,475,956

Persons Per County

5,000,000
1,000,000
500,000
100,000
1 - 1,000

Persons identifying themselves as American Indian or Alaska Native only - 2000 Census

Copyright by Rand McNally & Co.
Made in U.S.A.

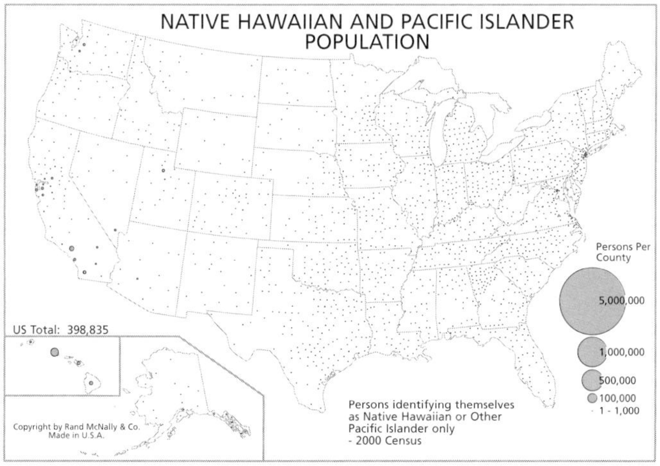

NATIVE HAWAIIAN AND PACIFIC ISLANDER POPULATION

US Total: 398,835

Persons Per County

5,000,000
1,000,000
500,000
100,000
1 - 1,000

Persons identifying themselves as Native Hawaiian or Other Pacific Islander only - 2000 Census

Copyright by Rand McNally & Co.
Made in U.S.A.

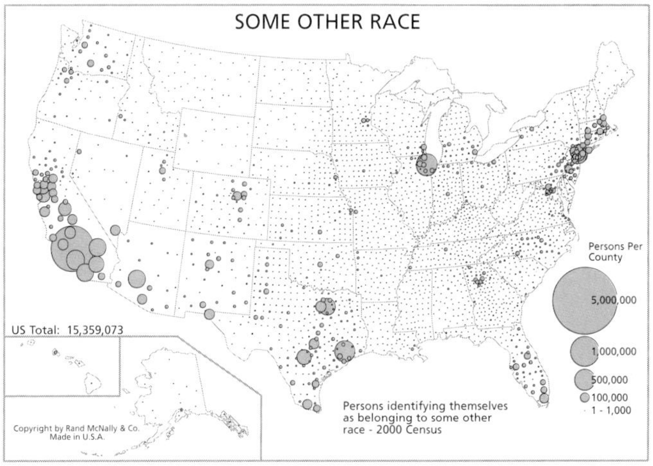

SOME OTHER RACE

US Total: 15,359,073

Persons Per County

5,000,000
1,000,000
500,000
100,000
1 - 1,000

Persons identifying themselves as belonging to some other race - 2000 Census

Copyright by Rand McNally & Co.
Made in U.S.A.

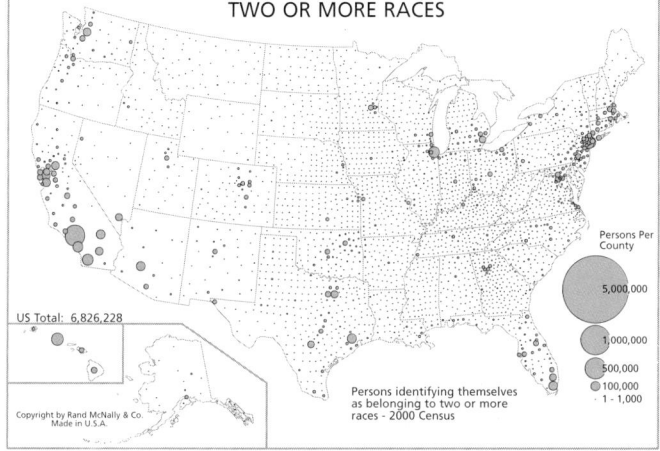

TWO OR MORE RACES

US Total: 6,826,228

Persons Per County

5,000,000
1,000,000
500,000
100,000
1 - 1,000

Persons identifying themselves as belonging to two or more races - 2000 Census

Copyright by Rand McNally & Co.
Made in U.S.A.

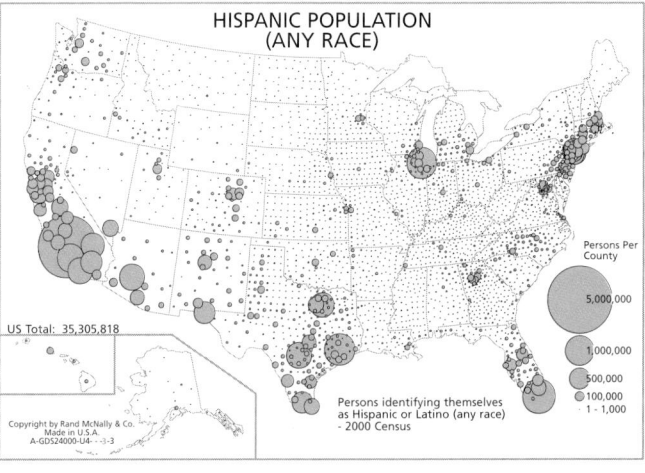

HISPANIC POPULATION (ANY RACE)

US Total: 35,305,818

Persons Per County

5,000,000
1,000,000
500,000
100,000
1 - 1,000

Persons identifying themselves as Hispanic or Latino (any race) - 2000 Census

Copyright by Rand McNally & Co.
Made in U.S.A.
A-GD524000-U4- --3-3

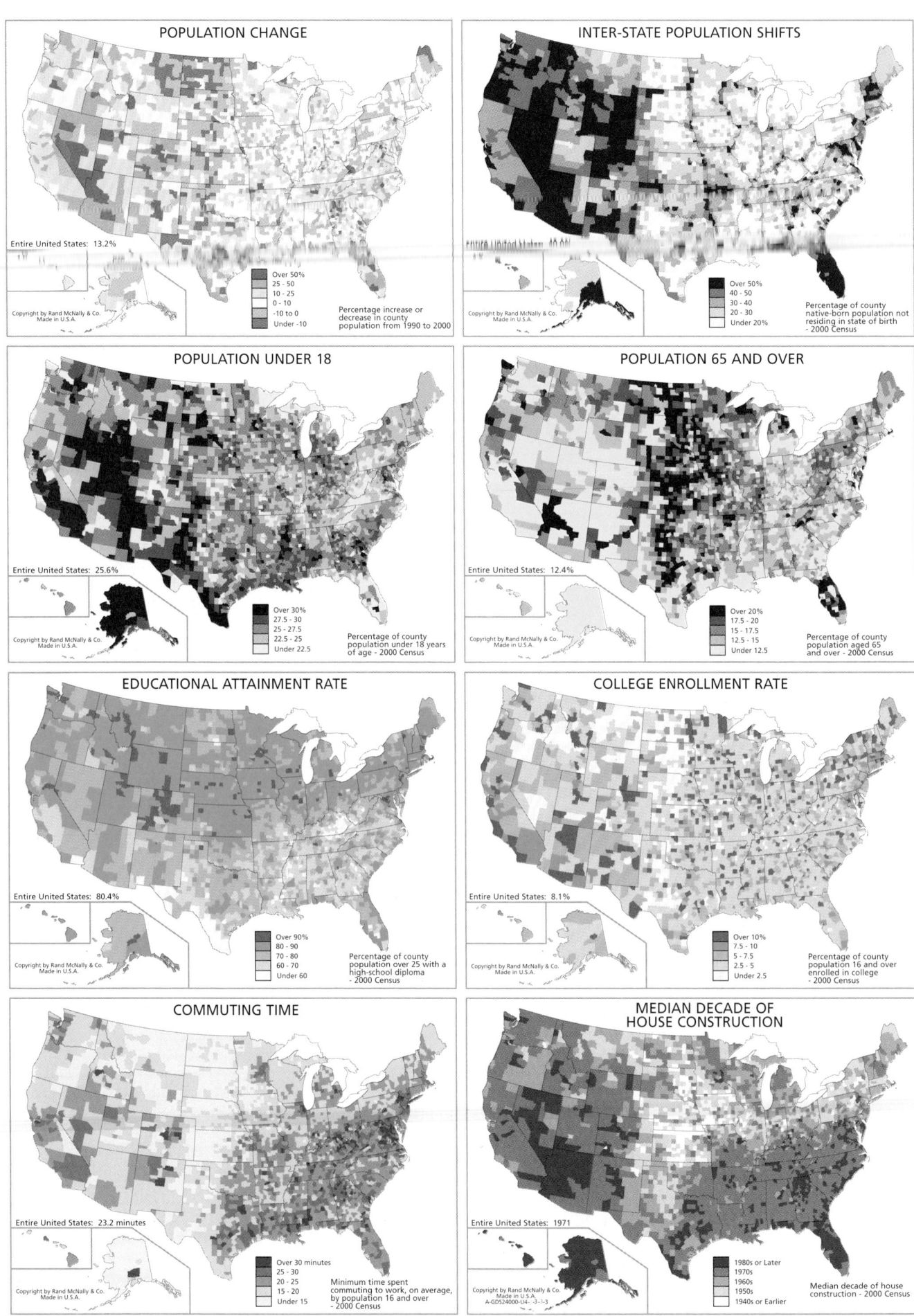

POPULATION CHANGE

Entire United States: 13.2%

Copyright by Rand McNally & Co.
Made in U.S.A.

Over 50%
25 - 50
10 - 25
0 - 10
-10 to 0
Under -10

Percentage increase or
decrease in county
population from 1990 to 2000

INTER-STATE POPULATION SHIFTS

Entire United States: 40.6%

Copyright by Rand McNally & Co.
Made in U.S.A.

Over 50%
40 - 50
30 - 40
20 - 30
Under 20%

Percentage of county
native-born population not
residing in state of birth
- 2000 Census

POPULATION UNDER 18

Entire United States: 25.6%

Copyright by Rand McNally & Co.
Made in U.S.A.

Over 30%
27.5 - 30
25 - 27.5
22.5 - 25
Under 22.5

Percentage of county
population under 18 years
of age - 2000 Census

POPULATION 65 AND OVER

Entire United States: 12.4%

Copyright by Rand McNally & Co.
Made in U.S.A.

Over 20%
17.5 - 20
15 - 17.5
12.5 - 15
Under 12.5

Percentage of county
population aged 65
and over - 2000 Census

EDUCATIONAL ATTAINMENT RATE

Entire United States: 80.4%

Copyright by Rand McNally & Co.
Made in U.S.A.

Over 90%
80 - 90
70 - 80
60 - 70
Under 60

Percentage of county
population over 25 with a
high-school diploma
- 2000 Census

COLLEGE ENROLLMENT RATE

Entire United States: 8.1%

Copyright by Rand McNally & Co.
Made in U.S.A.

Over 10%
7.5 - 10
5 - 7.5
2.5 - 5
Under 2.5

Percentage of county
population 16 and over
enrolled in college
- 2000 Census

COMMUTING TIME

Entire United States: 23.2 minutes

Copyright by Rand McNally & Co.
Made in U.S.A.

Over 30 minutes
25 - 30
20 - 25
15 - 20
Under 15

Minimum time spent
commuting to work, on average,
by population 16 and over
- 2000 Census

**MEDIAN DECADE OF
HOUSE CONSTRUCTION**

Entire United States: 1971

Copyright by Rand McNally & Co.
Made in U.S.A.
A-GDS24000-U4--3-3-3

1980s or Later
1970s
1960s
1950s
1940s or Earlier

Median decade of house
construction - 2000 Census

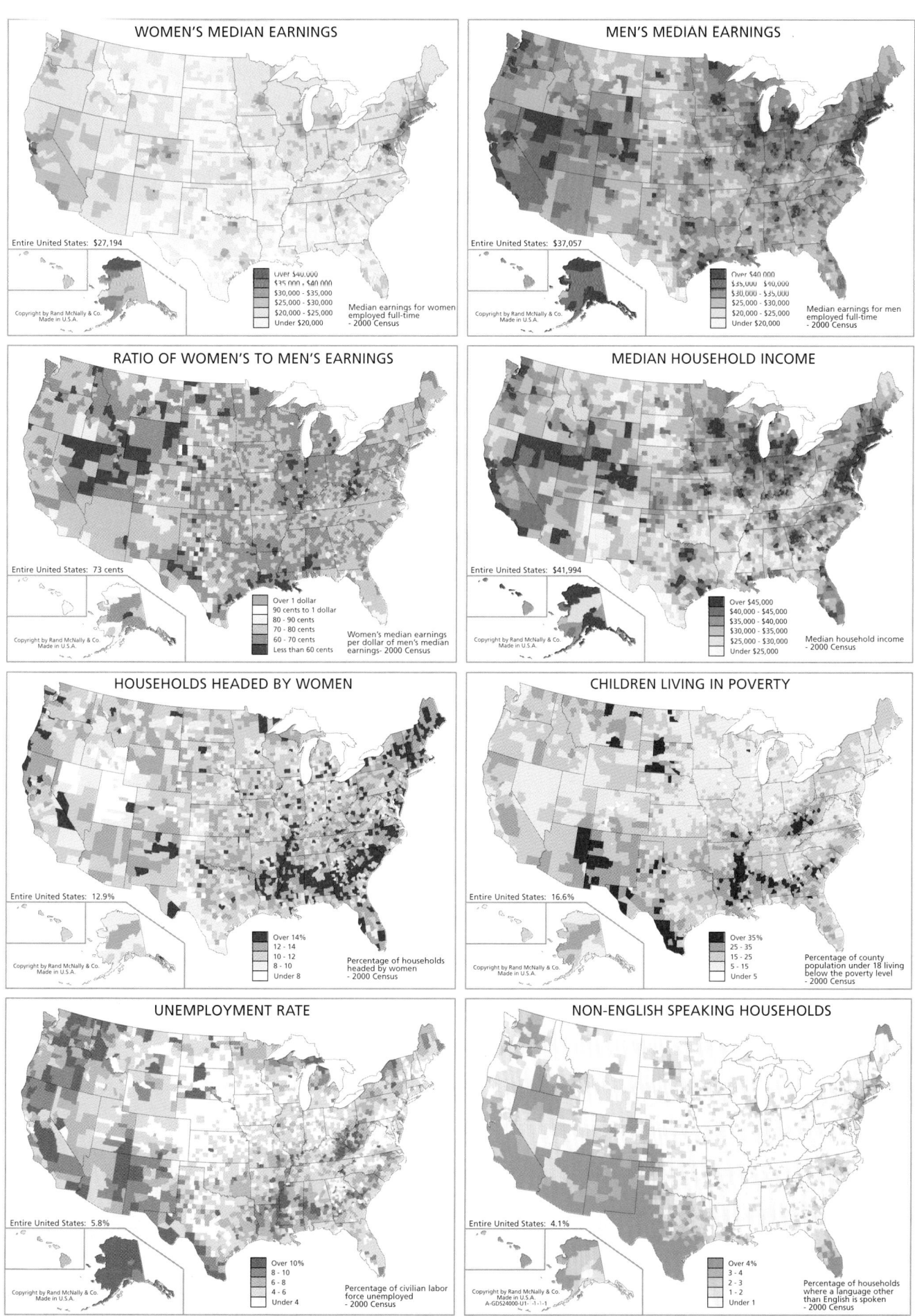

WOMEN'S MEDIAN EARNINGS

Entire United States: $27,194

Over $40,000
$35,000 - $40,000
$30,000 - $35,000
$25,000 - $30,000
$20,000 - $25,000
Under $20,000

Median earnings for women employed full-time - 2000 Census

Copyright by Rand McNally & Co.
Made in U.S.A.

MEN'S MEDIAN EARNINGS

Entire United States: $37,057

Over $40,000
$35,000 - $40,000
$30,000 - $35,000
$25,000 - $30,000
$20,000 - $25,000
Under $20,000

Median earnings for men employed full-time - 2000 Census

Copyright by Rand McNally & Co.
Made in U.S.A.

RATIO OF WOMEN'S TO MEN'S EARNINGS

Entire United States: 73 cents

Over 1 dollar
90 cents to 1 dollar
80 - 90 cents
70 - 80 cents
60 - 70 cents
Less than 60 cents

Women's median earnings per dollar of men's median earnings- 2000 Census

Copyright by Rand McNally & Co.
Made in U.S.A.

MEDIAN HOUSEHOLD INCOME

Entire United States: $41,994

Over $45,000
$40,000 - $45,000
$35,000 - $40,000
$30,000 - $35,000
$25,000 - $30,000
Under $25,000

Median household income - 2000 Census

Copyright by Rand McNally & Co.
Made in U.S.A.

HOUSEHOLDS HEADED BY WOMEN

Entire United States: 12.9%

Over 14%
12 - 14
10 - 12
8 - 10
Under 8

Percentage of households headed by women - 2000 Census

Copyright by Rand McNally & Co.
Made in U.S.A.

CHILDREN LIVING IN POVERTY

Entire United States: 16.6%

Over 35%
25 - 35
15 - 25
5 - 15
Under 5

Percentage of county population under 18 living below the poverty level - 2000 Census

Copyright by Rand McNally & Co.
Made in U.S.A.

UNEMPLOYMENT RATE

Entire United States: 5.8%

Over 10%
8 - 10
6 - 8
4 - 6
Under 4

Percentage of civilian labor force unemployed - 2000 Census

Copyright by Rand McNally & Co.
Made in U.S.A.

NON-ENGLISH SPEAKING HOUSEHOLDS

Entire United States: 4.1%

Over 4%
3 - 4
2 - 3
1 - 2
Under 1

Percentage of households where a language other than English is spoken - 2000 Census

Copyright by Rand McNally & Co.
Made in U.S.A.
A-GDS24000-U1- -1 -1- 1

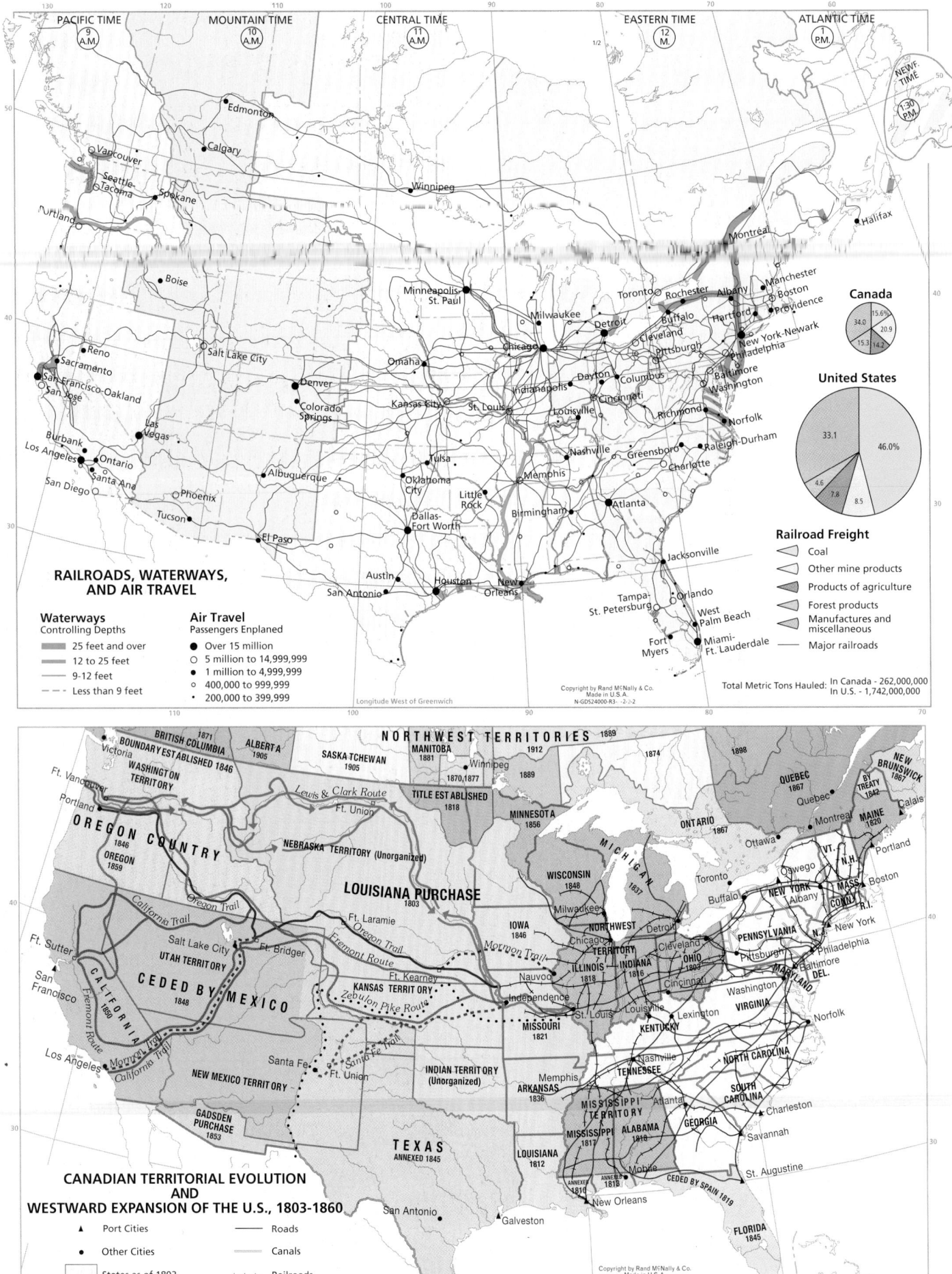

RAILROADS, WATERWAYS, AND AIR TRAVEL

Waterways
Controlling Depths

▬▬ 25 feet and over
▬ 12 to 25 feet
— 9-12 feet
- - - Less than 9 feet

Air Travel
Passengers Enplaned

● Over 15 million
○ 5 million to 14,999,999
● 1 million to 4,999,999
○ 400,000 to 999,999
• 200,000 to 399,999

Canada

34.0 / 15.6% / 20.9 / 15.3 / 14.2

United States

46.0% / 33.1 / 4.6 / 7.8 / 8.5

Railroad Freight

◁ Coal
◁ Other mine products
◤ Products of agriculture
◁ Forest products
◁ Manufactures and miscellaneous
— Major railroads

Total Metric Tons Hauled: In Canada - 262,000,000
In U.S. - 1,742,000,000

Copyright by Rand McNally & Co.
Made in U.S.A.
N-GD524000-R3- -2-2-2

Longitude West of Greenwich

CANADIAN TERRITORIAL EVOLUTION AND WESTWARD EXPANSION OF THE U.S., 1803-1860

▲ Port Cities
● Other Cities
▭ States as of 1803
— Roads
— Canals
┼┼┼┼ Railroads

Copyright by Rand McNally & Co.
Made in U.S.A.
H-GD524000-B6- -1-1-2

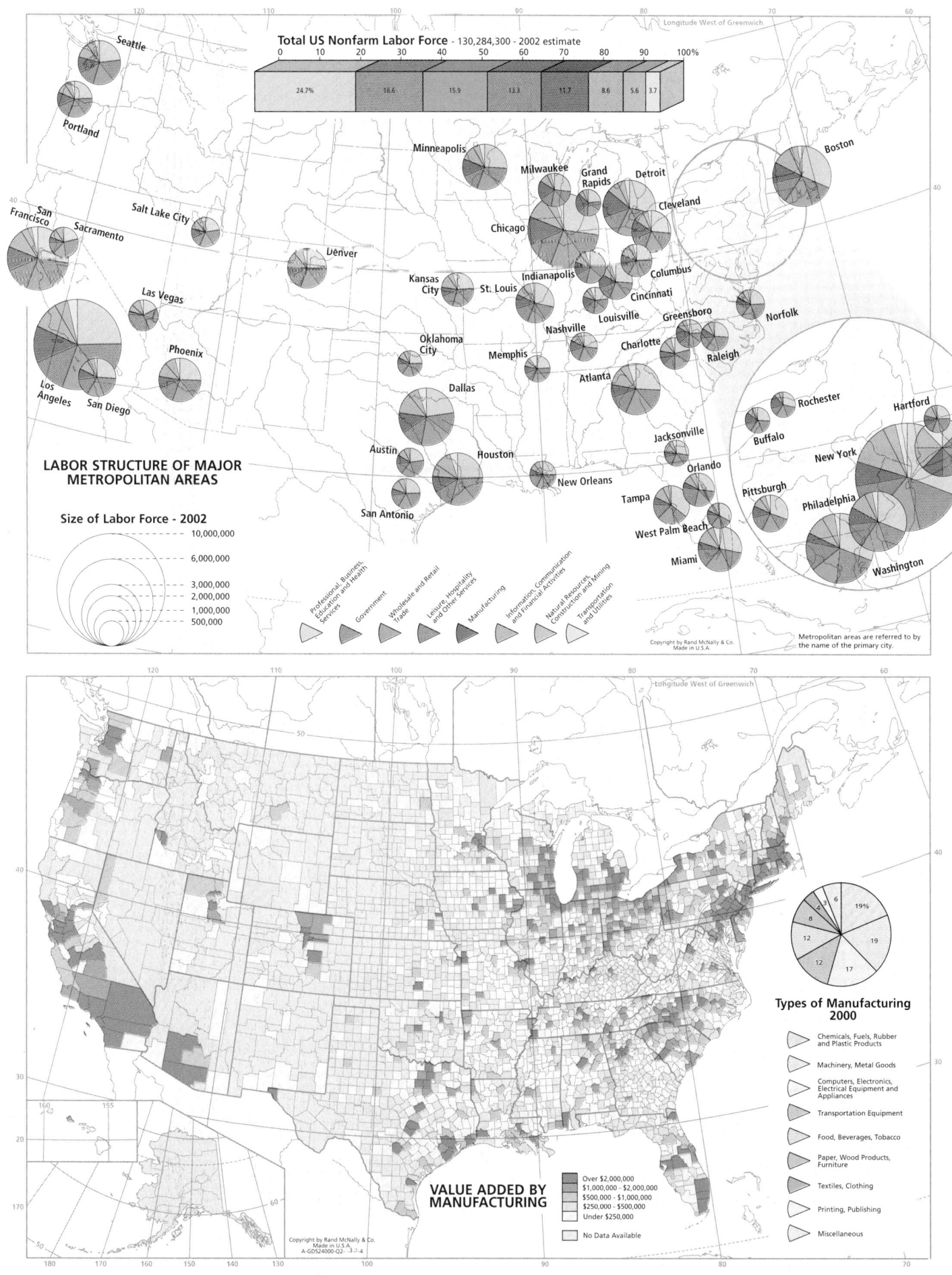

Total US Nonfarm Labor Force - 130,284,300 - 2002 estimate

| 24.7% | 16.6 | 15.9 | 13.3 | 11.7 | 8.6 | 5.6 | 3.7 |

LABOR STRUCTURE OF MAJOR METROPOLITAN AREAS

Size of Labor Force - 2002

10,000,000
6,000,000
3,000,000
2,000,000
1,000,000
500,000

Professional, Business, Education and Health Services
Government
Wholesale and Retail Trade
Leisure, Hospitality and Other Services
Manufacturing
Information Communication and Financial Activities
Natural Resources, Construction and Mining
Transportation and Utilities

Seattle
Portland
San Francisco
Sacramento
Salt Lake City
Los Angeles
San Diego
Las Vegas
Phoenix
Denver
Minneapolis
Milwaukee
Grand Rapids
Detroit
Cleveland
Chicago
Kansas City
St. Louis
Indianapolis
Columbus
Cincinnati
Oklahoma City
Memphis
Nashville
Louisville
Greensboro
Charlotte
Raleigh
Norfolk
Dallas
Austin
San Antonio
Houston
Atlanta
New Orleans
Jacksonville
Orlando
Tampa
West Palm Beach
Miami
Boston
Buffalo
Rochester
Hartford
New York
New Haven
Pittsburgh
Philadelphia
Washington

Copyright by Rand McNally & Co.
Made in U.S.A.

Metropolitan areas are referred to by the name of the primary city.

VALUE ADDED BY MANUFACTURING

| Over $2,000,000 |
| $1,000,000 - $2,000,000 |
| $500,000 - $1,000,000 |
| $250,000 - $500,000 |
| Under $250,000 |
| No Data Available |

Types of Manufacturing 2000

19%
19
17
12
12
8
7
6
3

Chemicals, Fuels, Rubber and Plastic Products
Machinery, Metal Goods
Computers, Electronics, Electrical Equipment and Appliances
Transportation Equipment
Food, Beverages, Tobacco
Paper, Wood Products, Furniture
Textiles, Clothing
Printing, Publishing
Miscellaneous

Copyright by Rand McNally & Co.
Made in U.S.A.
A-GDS24000-Q2--3-3-4

Scale 1:12,000,000.   One inch to 190 miles.
One centimeter to 120 kilometers.   Albers Conic Projection

0 50 100   200   300   400 Miles

0 50 100 150 200   300   400   500   600 Kilometers

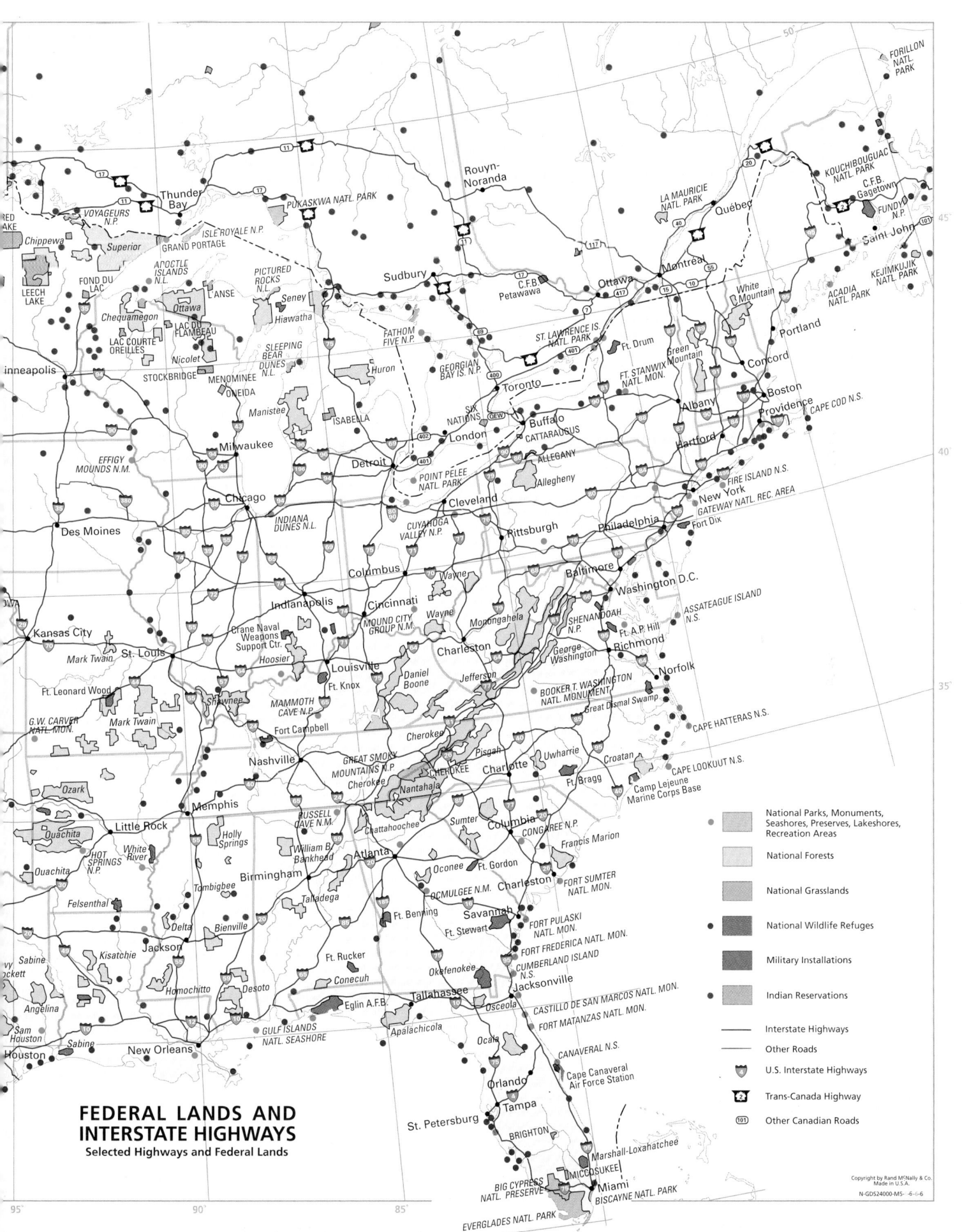

FEDERAL LANDS AND INTERSTATE HIGHWAYS
Selected Highways and Federal Lands

National Parks, Monuments, Seashores, Preserves, Lakeshores, Recreation Areas	
National Forests	
National Grasslands	
National Wildlife Refuges	
Military Installations	
Indian Reservations	
Interstate Highways	
Other Roads	
U.S. Interstate Highways	
Trans-Canada Highway	
Other Canadian Roads	

Copyright by Rand McNally & Co.
Made in U.S.A.

N-GD524000-M5- -6-6-6

Scale 1:40 000 000; one inch to 630 miles. Lambert's Azimuthal Equal Area Projection
Elevations and depressions are given in feet

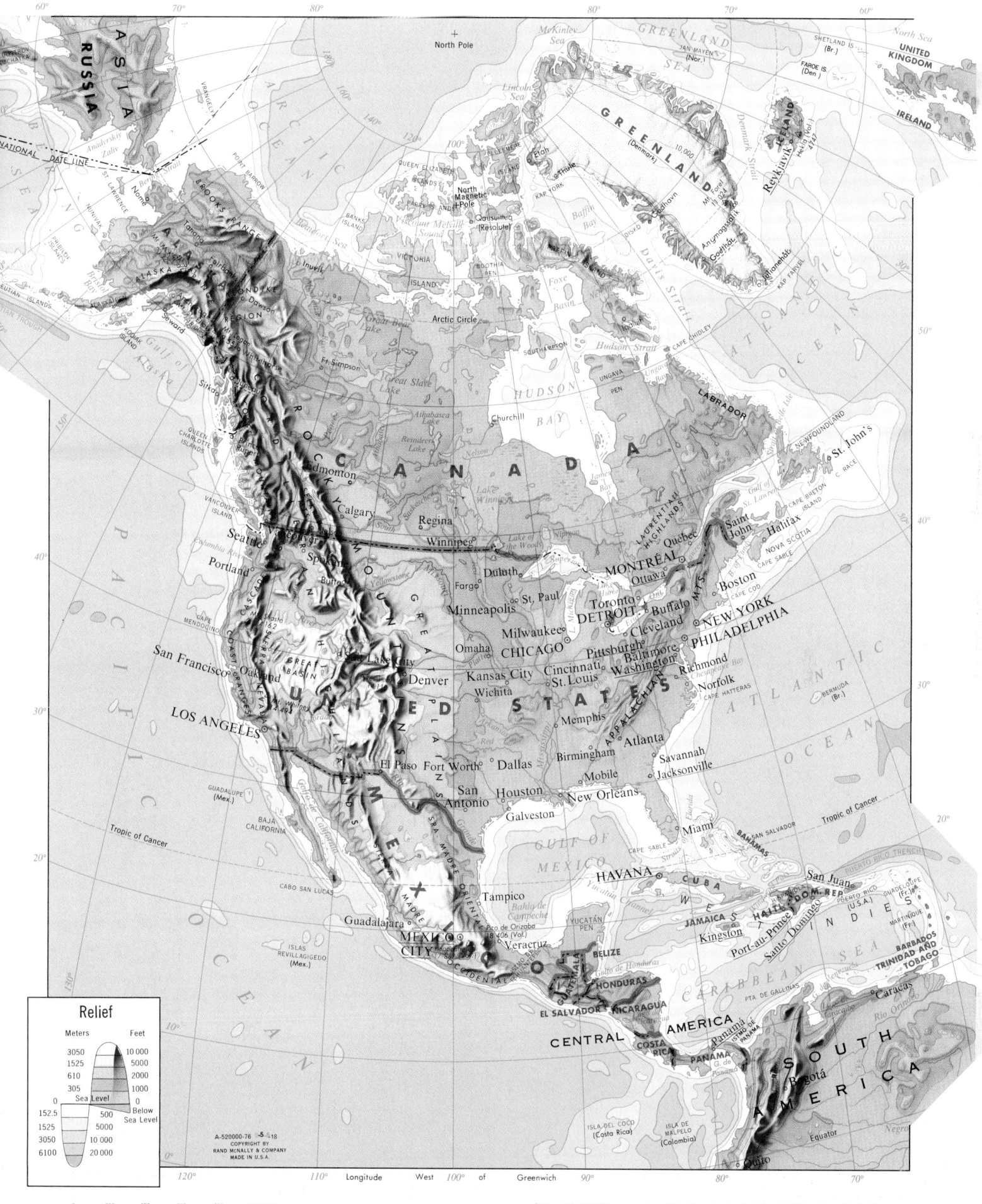

Relief

Meters	Feet
3050	10 000
1525	5000
610	2000
305	1000
0 Sea Level	0
	Below Sea Level
152.5	500
1525	5000
3050	10 000
6100	20 000

A-520000-76 -5 -18
COPYRIGHT BY
RAND McNALLY & COMPANY
MADE IN U.S.A.

Scale 1:40 000 000; one inch to 630 miles. Lambert's Azimuthal Equal Area Projection
Elevations and depressions are given in feet

145°

CAPE BATHURST

130°

70°

135°

125°

120°

115°

110°

105°

100°

95°

90°

ALASKA

KLONDIKE REGION

OGILVIE MTS.

Dawson

USA
CANADA

Stewart

YUKON

Mayo

Whitehorse

Carcross

White Pass

Skagway

Atlin

Teslin

Watson Lake

RICHARDSON MTS.

Old Crow

Porcupine

Inuvik

Aklavik

Ft. McPherson

Ft. Good Hope

Norman Wells

FRANKLIN

Arctic Circle

Great
Bear Lake

Tuktoyaktuk

Amundsen Gulf

C. BARING

Prince Albert Sound

Dolphin and Union Str.

Coronation Gulf

VICTORIA
ISLAND

Dease Strait

Queen Maud
Gulf

BOOTHIA
PENINSULA

KING
WILLIAM I.

MELVILLE
HILLS

TUKTUT NOGAIT
NAT'L PARK

Kugluktuk
(Coppermine)

Kent Pen

MACKENZIE MTS.

NAHANNI
NAT'L
PARK

Frances

HORN PLATEAU

Ft. Simpson

Yellowknife

Ft. Providence

NORTHWEST

TERRITORIES

Great Slave
Lake

MacKay

Clinton-Colden

PEACOCK

Dubawnt

NUNAVUT

Baker Lake

Rankin Inlet

PELLY MTS.

STIKINE RANGES

Telegraph Creek

Ft. Nelson

Ft. Liard

CAMERON HILLS

Hay River

Ft. Resolution

Ft. Smith

WOOD BUFFALO
NAT'L PARK

Ft. Fitzgerald

CARIBOU
MTS.

Ft. Chipewyan

Uranium City

Selwyn

ROCKY

COAST
MOUNTAINS

BRITISH

COLUMBIA

Williston
Lake

Ft. St. John

Dawson Creek

CLEAR
HILLS

BUFFALO
HEAD HILLS

Peace River

BIRCH
MTS.

Fort McMurray

CHEECHAM
HILLS

Athabasca

Wollaston

Cree

SASKATCHEWAN

MANITOBA

Thompson

MOUNTAINS

ALBERTA

SWAN HILLS

Edmonton

Calgary

Lake Winnipeg

Winnipeg

Regina

Saskatoon

Prince Albert

WASHINGTON

SEATTLE

Tacoma

Spokane

MONTANA

NORTH DAKOTA

SOUTH DAKOTA

OREGON

IDAHO

WYO.

CANADA
U.S.A.

Portland

PACIFIC

OCEAN

VANCOUVER
ISLAND

Vancouver

Victoria

Continued on pages 104-105

125°

120°

115°

110°

105°

Longitude West of Greenwich

100°

Scale 1: 12 000 000; one inch to 190 miles. Conic Projection
Elevations and depressions are given in feet

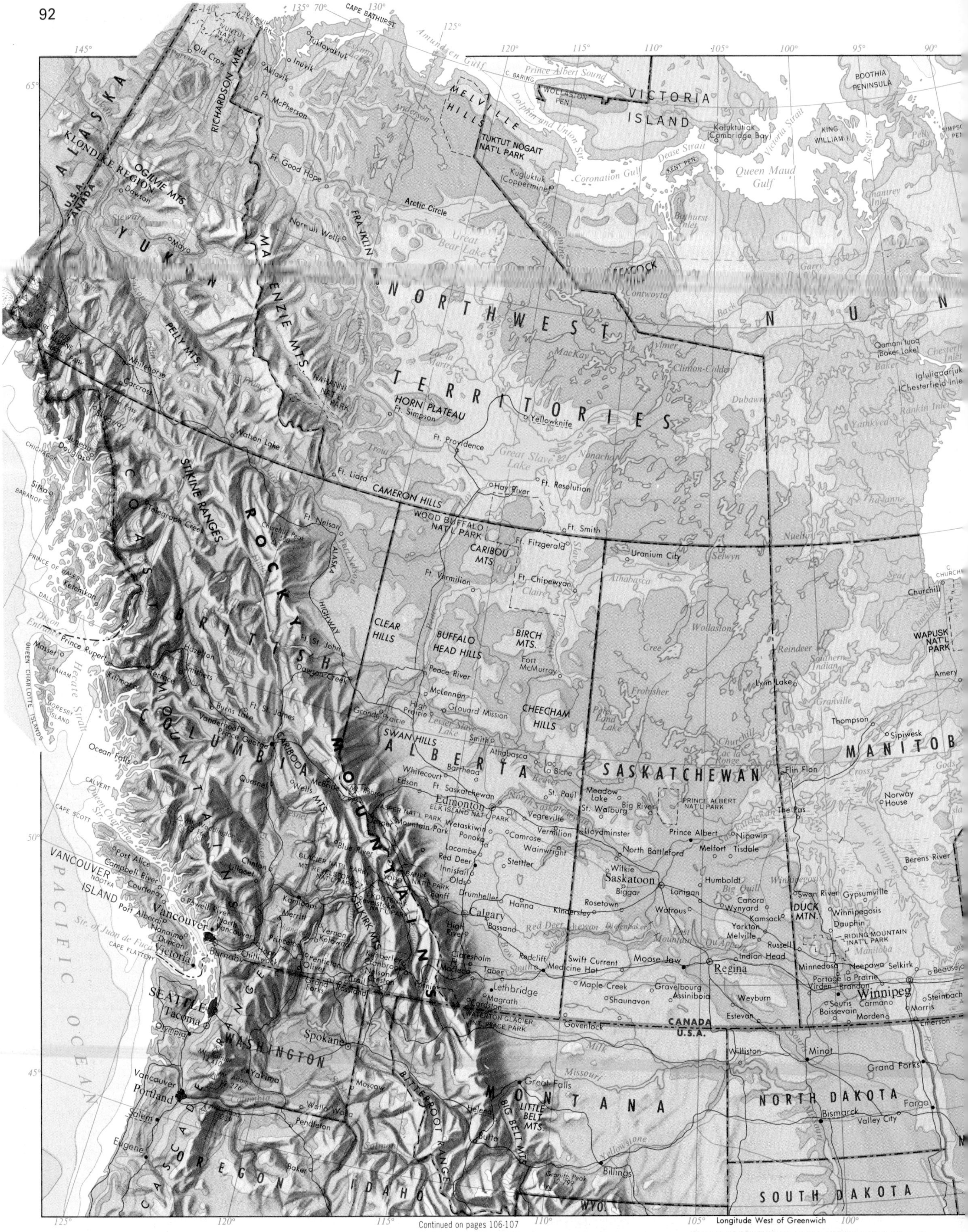

ALASKA
KLONDIKE REGION
U.S.A. CANADA
OGILVIE MTS.
RICHARDSON MTS.
Old Crow
Aklavik
Inuvik
Tuktoyaktuk
CAPE BATHURST
Amundsen Gulf
C. BARING
Prince Albert Sound
WOLLASTON PEN.
VICTORIA ISLAND
BOOTHIA PENINSULA
Kugluktuk (Coppermine)
Kaluktutiak (Cambridge Bay)
KING WILLIAM I.
Pelly Bay
Dolphin and Union Str.
Coronation Gulf
Dease Strait
Queen Maud Gulf
Victoria Strait
Chantrey Inlet

Ft. McPherson
IVVAVIK NAT'L PARK
MELVILLE HILLS
TUKTUT NOGAIT NAT'L PARK
Ft. Good Hope
Arctic Circle
Anderson

YUKON
Dawson
Mayo
Stewart
Norman Wells
MACKENZIE MTS.
FRANKLIN MTS.
Great Bear Lake

PELLY MTS.
Whitehorse
Carcross
White Pass
Skagway
Haines
Juneau
Atlin
NAHANNI NAT'L PARK
Watson Lake
Ft. Simpson
HORN PLATEAU
Ft. Providence
Yellowknife
NORTHWEST TERRITORIES
Lac la Martre
MacKay
Contwoyto
Back
Clinton-Colden
Aylmer
Tyrrell
PEACOCK
Dubawnt
Bathurst Inlet

NUNAVUT
Qamani'tuaq (Baker Lake)
Iglulligaarjuk (Chesterfield Inlet)
Chesterfield Inlet
Rankin Inlet
Yathkyed
Kazan

SITKA
BARANOF
Sitka
PRINCE OF WALES
Ketchikan
DIXON ENTRANCE
Prince Rupert
Masset
QUEEN CHARLOTTE ISLANDS
GRAHAM ISLAND
MORESBY ISLAND
Hecate Strait

STIKINE RANGES
Telegraph Creek
COAST MOUNTAINS
Kitimat
Ocean Falls
Bella Coola
CALVERT
CAPE SCOTT
Port Alice
Campbell River
Courtenay
Powell River
Port Alberni
Nanaimo
VANCOUVER ISLAND
Victoria
CAPE FLATTERY
Str. of Juan de Fuca
PACIFIC OCEAN

ROCKY MOUNTAINS
Ft. Nelson
ALASKA HIGHWAY
Ft. St. John
Dawson Creek
CAMERON HILLS
Ft. Liard
WOOD BUFFALO NAT'L PARK
CARIBOU MTS.
Ft. Vermilion
Ft. Smith
Ft. Fitzgerald
Ft. Chipewyan
Claire
Uranium City
CLEAR HILLS
BUFFALO HEAD HILLS
BIRCH MTS.
Fort McMurray
Peace River
High Prairie
McLennan
Grande Prairie
Girouard Mission
Lesser Slave Lake
SWAN HILLS
Smith
Athabasca
Lac La Biche
BRITISH COLUMBIA
Burns Lake
Vanderhoof
Prince George
Ft. St. James
McBride
Quesnel
Wells
CARIBOO MTS.
COLUMBIA MTS.
Hazelton
Smithers
Houston

Hay River
Ft. Resolution
Great Slave Lake
Nonacho
Athabasca
Lake
Wollaston
Cree
CHEECHAM HILLS
Pete Pond Lake
Lac la Ronge
Reindeer
Southern Indian
Churchill
Thompson
Sipiwesk
Granville
WAPUSK NAT'L PARK
Amery
CHURCHILL
Churchill

MANITOBA
Flin Flon
Lynn Lake
The Pas
Norway House
Nipawin
Melfort Tisdale
PRINCE ALBERT NAT'L PARK
Prince Albert
Meadow Lake
St. Walburg
Big River
North Battleford
Wilkie
Biggar
Saskatoon
Humboldt
Lanigan
Big Quill
Wynyard
Kamsack
Canora
Yorkton
Melville
Russell
Indian Head
Regina
Swan River
Gypsumville
DUCK MTN.
Dauphin
Winnipegosis
RIDING MOUNTAIN NAT'L PARK
Minnedosa
Neepawa
Selkirk
Portage la Prairie
Virden Brandon
Souris
Boissevain
Morden
Winnipeg
Steinbach
Morris
Emerson

SASKATCHEWAN
ALBERTA
Whitecourt
Edson
Ft. Saskatchewan
Edmonton
ELK ISLAND NAT'L PARK
Wetaskiwin
Ponoka
Lacombe
Red Deer
Innisfail
Olds
Vegreville
Vermilion
Lloydminster
St. Paul
Camrose
Wainwright
Stettler
Rosthern
Watrous
Moose Jaw
Weyburn
Estevan
CANADA
U.S.A.

JASPER NAT'L PARK
Mt. Robson
MT. REVELSTOKE NAT'L PARK
GLACIER NAT'L PARK
Blue River
Clearwater
Kamloops
Revelstoke
YOHO NAT'L PARK
Golden
BANFF NAT'L PARK
Banff
Canmore
Calgary
Drumheller
Hanna
Kindersley
Rosetown
Gravelbourg
Assiniboia
Shaunavon
Maple Creek
Swift Current
Gull Lake
Medicine Hat
Bassano
Brooks
Lethbridge
Magrath
Taber
WATERTON GLACIER INT'L PEACE PARK
Govenlock
Milk
Williston
Minot

MONTANA
NORTH DAKOTA
Bismarck
Valley City
Fargo
Grand Forks

Merritt
Vernon
Kelowna
Penticton
Princeton
Hope
Chilliwack
Abbotsford
Vancouver
North Vancouver
Burnaby
New Westminster
Nanaimo
Duncan
SEATTLE
Tacoma
Olympia
WASHINGTON
Spokane
Yakima
Vancouver
Portland
Salem
Eugene
OREGON
CASCADE RANGE
Mt. Rainier
Columbia
Moscow
Pendleton
Walla Walla
Baker
IDAHO
BITTERROOT RANGE
BIG BELT MTS.
LITTLE BELT MTS.
Helena
Butte
Great Falls
Missouri
Yellowstone
Granite Peak 799
Billings
WYO.
SOUTH DAKOTA

Grand Forks
Cranbrook
Creston
Nelson
Trail
Rossland
Grand Forks
Castlegar
Fernie
Pincher Creek
Cardston
Raymond
Claresholm
High River
Okotoks
Nanton
Vulcan
Macleod
Cardston

Continued on pages 106-107

Longitude West of Greenwich

Scale 1: 12 000 000; one inch to 190 miles. Conic Projection

Elevations and depressions are given in feet

NEWFOUNDLAND AND LABRADOR

Relief

Meters		Feet
3050		10 000
1525		5000
610		2000
305		1000
152.5		500
0	Sea Level	0
152.5		500
1525		5000
3050		10 000

A-520200-76 • 10-9-23
COPYRIGHT BY
RAND MCNALLY & COMPANY
MADE IN U.S.A.

0 25 50 75 100   200   300   400   500 Miles

0   100   200   400   600   800 Kilometers

94

Continued on pages 114-115

Longitude West of Greenwich

Scale 1:4 000 000; one inch to 64 miles. Conic Projection

Elevations and depressions are given in feet.

Relief

Meters		Feet
3050		10 000
1525		5000
610		2000
305		1000
152.5		500
0	Sea Level	0
152.5		500
1525		5000

A-520220-76 6-9
COPYRIGHT BY
RAND McNALLY & COMPANY
MADE IN U.S.A.

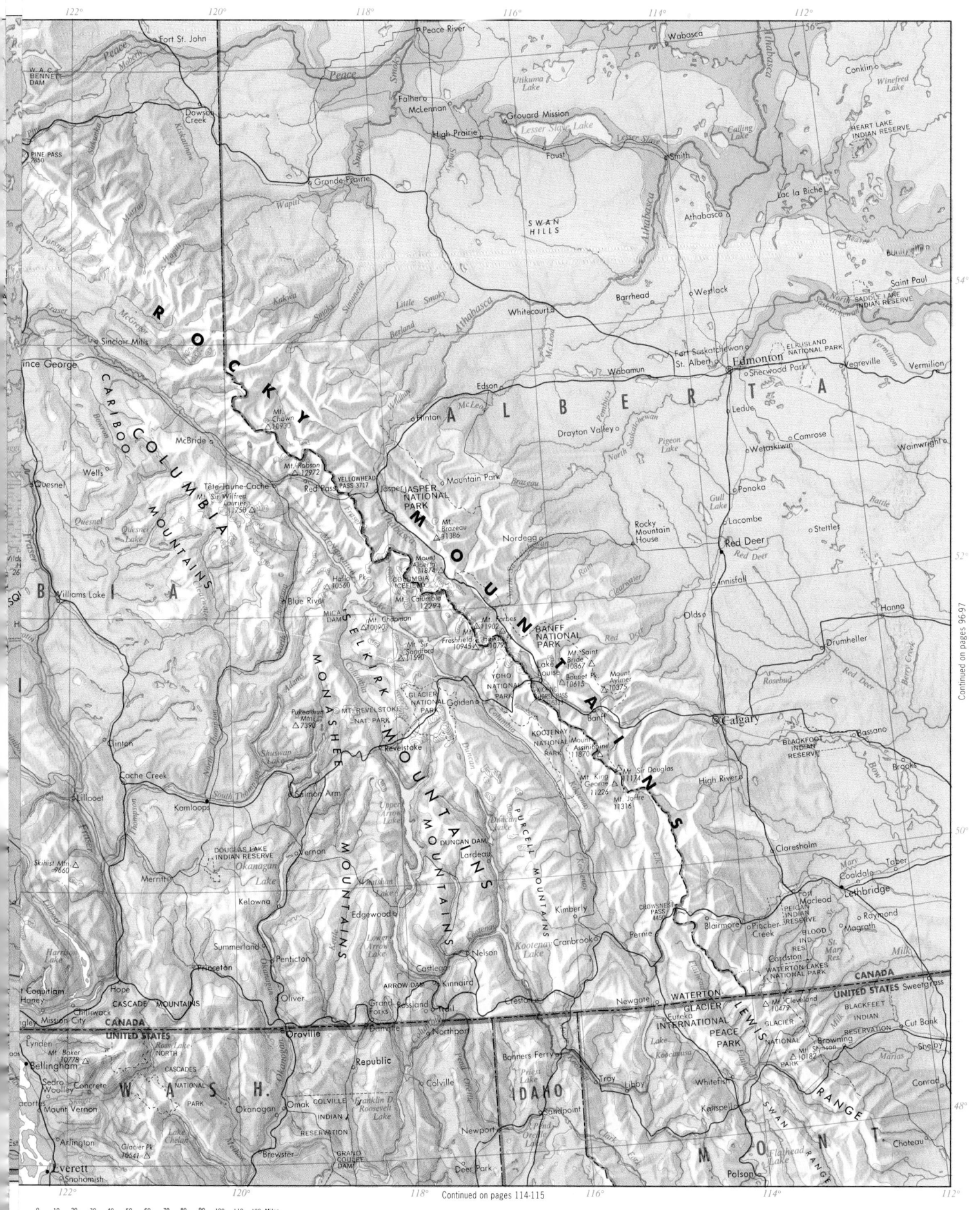

Continued on pages 96-97

Continued on pages 114-115

0 10 20 30 40 50 60 70 80 90 100 110 120 Miles

0 20 40 60 80 100 120 140 160 180 200 Kilometers

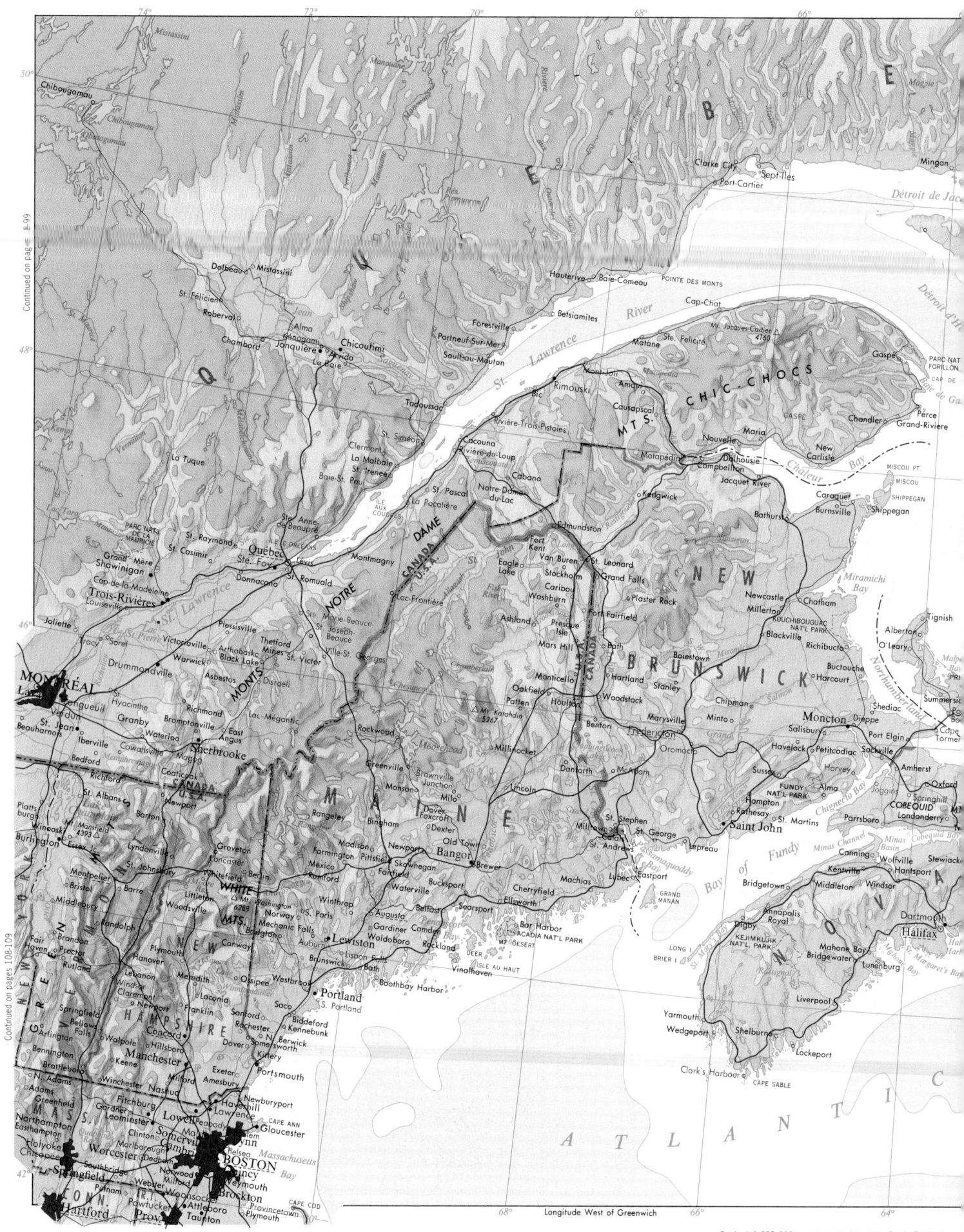

Scale 1:4 000 000; one inch to 64 miles. Conic Projection
Elevations and depressions are given in feet

Longitude West of Greenwich

Continued on page 99

Continued on pages 108-109

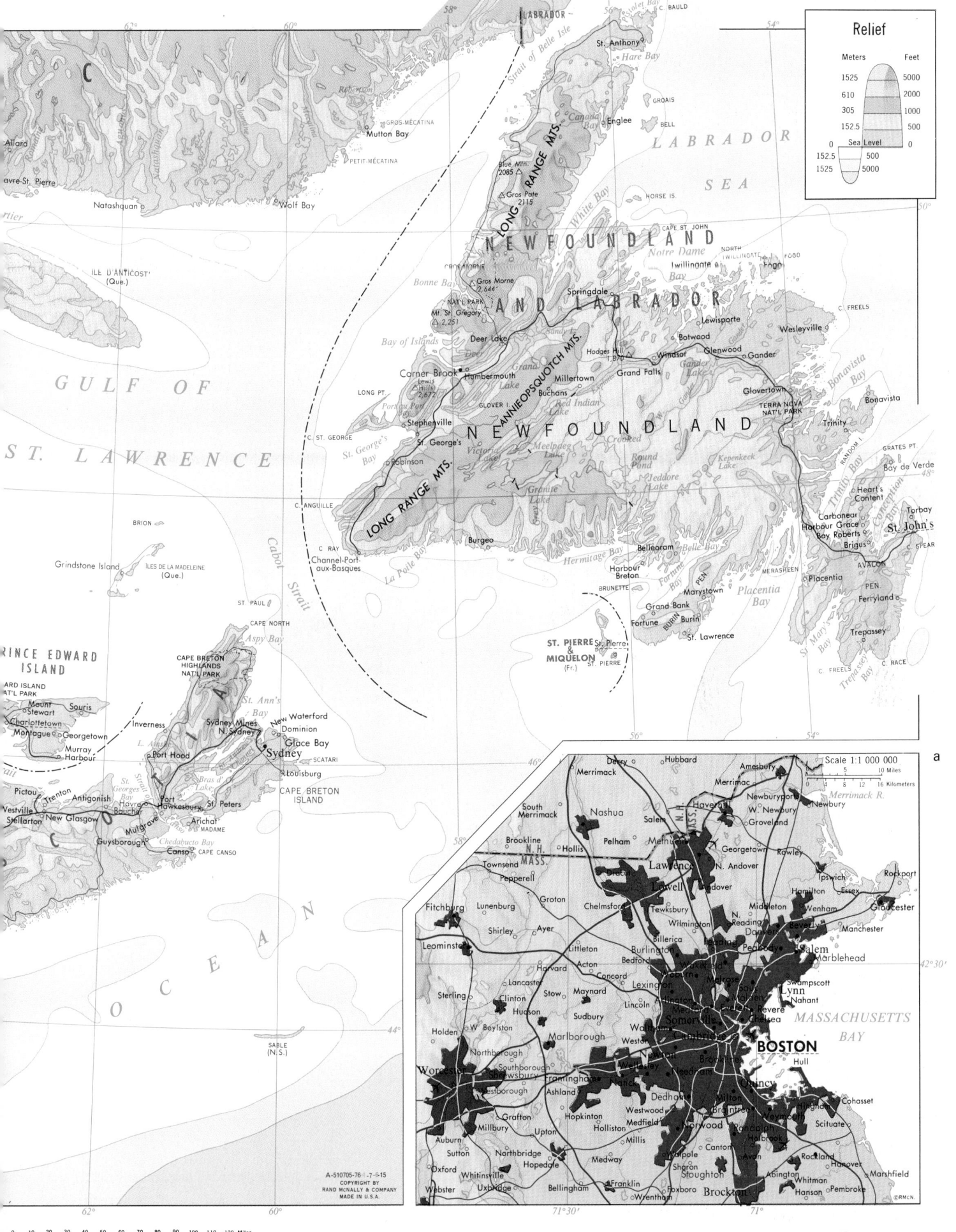

Relief

Meters	Feet
1525	5000
610	2000
305	1000
152.5	500
0 Sea Level	0
152.5	500
1525	5000

LABRADOR SEA

NEWFOUNDLAND AND LABRADOR

NEWFOUNDLAND

GULF OF ST. LAWRENCE

PRINCE EDWARD ISLAND

CAPE BRETON ISLAND

Scale 1:1 000 000

BOSTON

MASSACHUSETTS BAY

O C E A N

A-510705-76-7-6-15
COPYRIGHT BY
RAND McNALLY & COMPANY
MADE IN U.S.A.

0 10 20 30 40 50 60 70 80 90 100 110 120 Miles
0 20 40 60 80 100 120 140 160 180 200 Kilometers

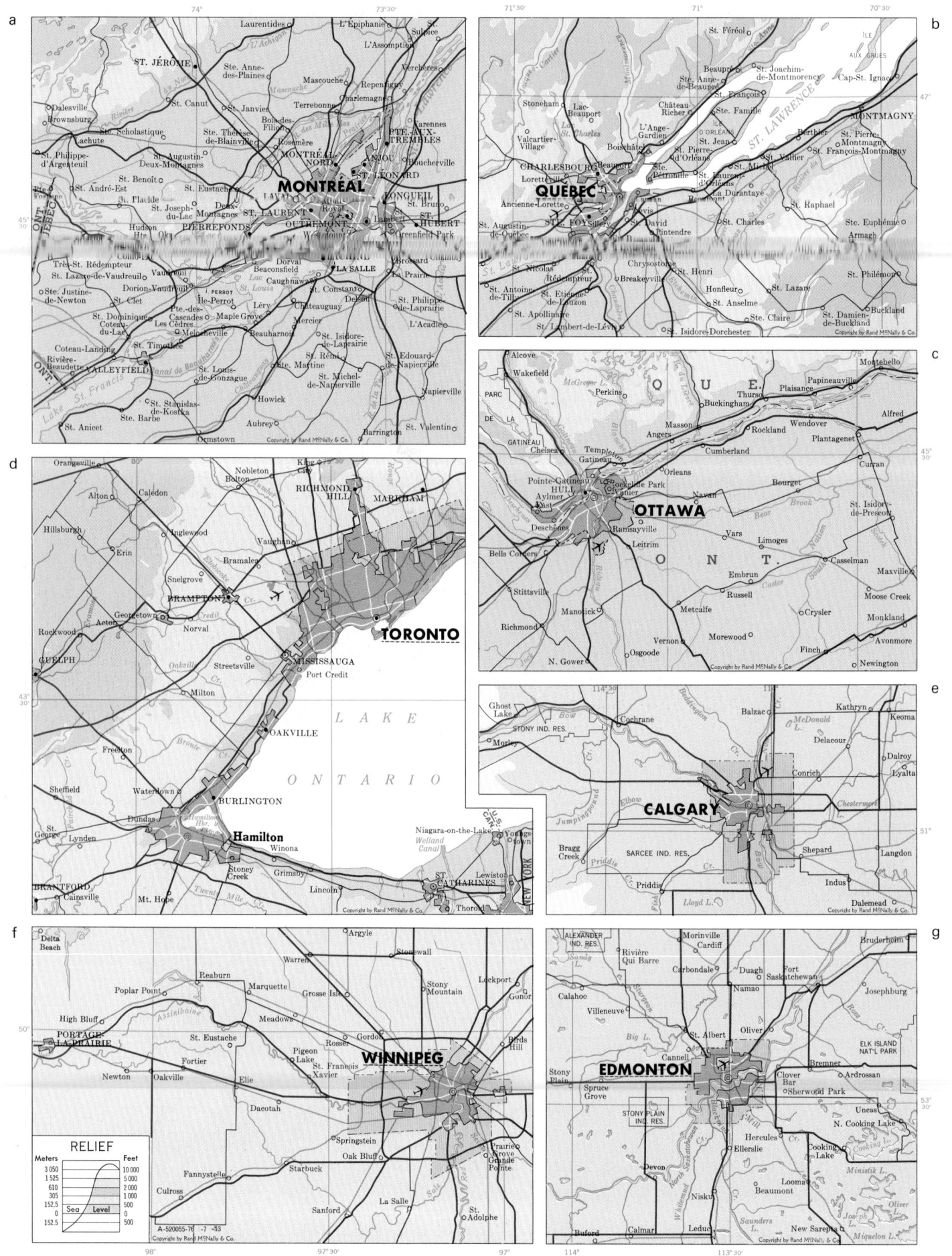

RELIEF

Meters		Feet
3 050		10 000
1 525		5 000
610		2 000
305		1 000
152.5		500
0	Sea Level	0
152.5		500

A-520055-76 -7 -13

Scale 1:1 000 000; One inch to 16 miles.
Elevations and depressions are given in feet.

Miles
Kilometers

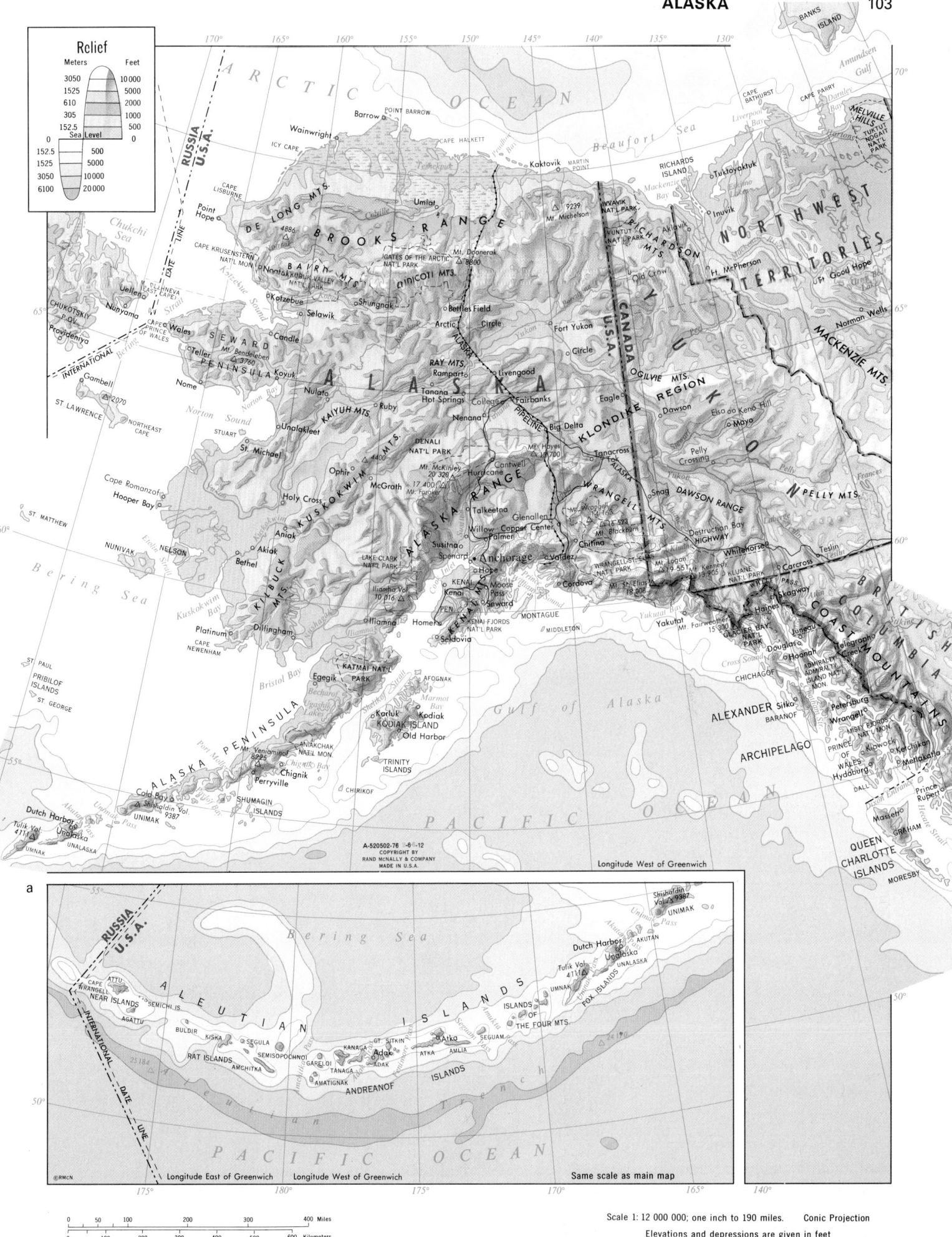

Scale 1: 12 000 000; one inch to 190 miles.   Conic Projection

Elevations and depressions are given in feet

Continued on pages 90-91

CANADA

BRITISH COLUMBIA
ALBERTA
SASKATCHEWAN
MANIT

WASHINGTON
Seattle
Tacoma
Olympia
Everett
Bellingham
Vancouver
Victoria
Port Angeles
Aberdeen
Hoquiam
Astoria
OLYMPIC NAT'L PARK
Mt. Baker 10 778
Mt. Adams 12 276
Mt. Rainier 14 410
GRAND COULEE DAM
Spokane
Coeur d'Alene
Moscow
Walla Walla
Pendleton
Lewiston
Kalispell
Cardston
Lethbridge
Medicine Hat
Havre
Great Falls
WATERTON GLACIER INT. PEACE PARK

OREGON
Portland
Salem
Corvallis
Albany
Roseburg
Medford
Eugene
The Dalles
Hood River
La Grande
CRATER LAKE NAT'L PARK
Klamath Falls
Mt. Hood
Mt. Jefferson

MONTANA
ROCKY
Helena
Missoula
Anaconda
Butte
Billings
Bozeman
Lewistown
Glendive
Miles City
LITTLE BELT MTS.
SALMON RIVER MTS.
Granite Peak 12 799
ABSAROKA RANGE
YELLOWSTONE NAT'L PARK

NORTH DAKOTA
Williston
Minot
Devils Lake
Grand Forks
Bismarck

IDAHO
Boise
Nampa
Twin Falls
Pocatello
Idaho Falls
SAWTOOTH RANGE

WYOMING
WIND RIVER RA.
BIG HORN MTS.
Sheridan
Cloud Peak 13 167
Casper
Grand Teton 13 770
Gannett Peak
Rock Springs
Rawlins
Laramie
Cheyenne
FLAMING GORGE

SOUTH DAKOTA
Deadwood
Lead
Rapid City
BLACK HILLS
WIND CAVE NAT'L PARK
Harney Pk. 7242
Pierre
Mitchell
Sioux Falls
Yankton
Aberdeen
Lake Oahe

NEBRASKA
North Platte
Grand Island
Valentine
Norfolk
Chadron
Lincoln
Hastings

NEVADA
Reno
Carson City
Winnemucca
Elko
Tonopah
Ely
Las Vegas
GREAT BASIN
Wheeler Peak 13 061
Boulder City
HOOVER DAM
LAKE TAHOE

UTAH
Salt Lake City
Ogden
Logan
Provo
GREAT SALT LAKE
GREAT SALT LAKE DESERT
UINTA MTS.
Kings Peak
Mt. Emmons 13 428
BRYCE CANYON NAT'L PARK
ZION NAT'L PARK
Lake Powell
GLEN CANYON DAM
HENRY MTS.
Delano Peak 12 173

COLORADO
DENVER
Colorado Springs
Pueblo
Grand Junction
Fort Collins
Boulder
Sterling
Greeley
Trinidad
Mt. Massive 14 421
Mt. Elbert 14 433
Pikes Pk. 14 110
Longs Peak 14 255
Blanca Peak 14 345
ROCKY MT.
MESA VERDE NAT'L PARK
SANGRE DE CRISTO RANGE
COLORADO

KANSAS
Dodge City
Hutchinson
Wichita

CALIFORNIA
SAN FRANCISCO
Berkeley
Oakland
San Jose
Sacramento
Stockton
Santa Rosa
Napa
Vallejo
Santa Cruz
Monterey
Fresno
Bakersfield
Santa Barbara
Santa Monica
LOS ANGELES
Glendale
Pasadena
Pomona
San Bernardino
Riverside
Long Beach
Santa Ana
SAN DIEGO
San Luis Obispo
Mt. Whitney 14 494
Mt. Shasta 14 162
Lassen Peak 10 457
Telescope Peak 11 045
DEATH VALLEY
MOJAVE DESERT
POINT CONCEPTION
Santa Catalina
San Clemente
Salton Sea
Brawley
Calexico
Mexicali
YOSEMITE NAT'L PARK
SEQUOIA NAT'L PARK
KINGS CANYON NAT'L PARK
LASSEN VOLCANIC NAT'L PARK
Eureka
C. MENDOCINO
Tijuana
Ensenada

PACIFIC OCEAN

ARIZONA
Phoenix
Flagstaff
Prescott
Globe
Yuma
Miami
Humphreys Peak 12 633
GRAND CANYON NAT'L PARK
PARKER DAM
MOGOLLON PLATEAU
Baldy Peak 11 590
Nogales
Bisbee
Douglas

NEW MEXICO
Santa Fe
Albuquerque
Las Vegas
Roswell
Gallup
Clovis
Las Cruces
Deming
Truchas Pk. 13 110
Mt. Taylor 11 301
Sierra Blanca Pk. 11 973
SAN ANDRES MTS.
BLACK RANGE
LLANO ESTACADO
Elephant Butte Res.
El Paso

TEXAS
Amarillo
Lubbock
Wichita Falls
Fort Worth
DALLAS
Abilene
San Angelo
Waco
Austin
San Antonio
Del Rio
Laredo
Brownwood
Ranger
Cleburne
Corsicana
STOCKTON PLATEAU
EDWARDS PLATEAU
BIG BEND NAT'L PARK
Piedras Negras
Eagle Pass

OKLAHOMA
Oklahoma City
Lawton
Enid
Chickasha
Ardmore
WICHITA MTS.

BAJA CALIFORNIA

MEXICO
SONORA
CHIHUAHUA
COAHUILA
NUEVO LEON
DURANGO
TAMAULIPAS
Ciudad Juárez
Nogales
Cananea
Magdalena
Nuevo Laredo
Nueva Rosita
Monterrey
Saltillo
Torreón
Gómez Palacio
Matamoros
Reynosa
Harlingen
Brownsville
SANTIAGO MTS.

A-520500-26 -921
COPYRIGHT BY
RAND McNALLY & COMPANY
MADE IN U.S.A.

---

a

ARCTIC OCEAN
Barrow
C. LISBURNE
RUSSIA
Kotzebue
Nome
ST. LAWRENCE
NUNIVAK
Bethel
Dillingham
ALASKA
BROOKS RANGE
Umiat
Ft. Yukon
Arctic Circle
Circle
Ruby
Fairbanks
McGrath
Anchorage
Cordova
Seward
Kodiak
DENALI NAT'L PARK
Mt. McKinley 20 320
KATMAI NAT'L PARK
Dutch Harbor
NORTHWEST TERR.
Inuvik
Dawson
CANADA
YUKON
Watson Lake
Whitehorse
Burwash Landing
Skagway
Juneau
GLACIER BAY NAT'L PARK
BRITISH COLUMBIA
Wrangell
Sitka
Ketchikan
Prince Rupert
QUEEN CHARLOTTE IS.

b
Scale 1: 36 000 000
Dutch Harbor
ALEUTIAN IS.
ATTU
KISKA
ANDREANOF IS.
ATKA
UNALASKA
UMNAK

Scale 1: 36 000 000
One inch to 570 miles

c
Longitude West of Greenwich
HAWAIIAN ISLANDS
KAUA'I
NI'IHAU
Lihue
O'AHU
Honolulu
Kailua
MOLOKA'I
Wailuku
Kahului
MAUI
LĀNA'I
KAHO'OLAWE
HAWAI'I
Hilo
Mauna Kea 13 796
Mauna Loa 13 680
HAWAI'I VOLCANOES NAT'L PARK
PACIFIC OCEAN

d
Scale 1: 3 400 000
O'AHU
KAHUKU
Wahiawā
Waipahu
Kailua
Honolulu
Pearl Harbor

Same scale as main map

Scale 1:12 000 000; one inch to 190 miles. Polyconic Projection
Elevations and depressions are given in feet
Longitude West of Greenwich

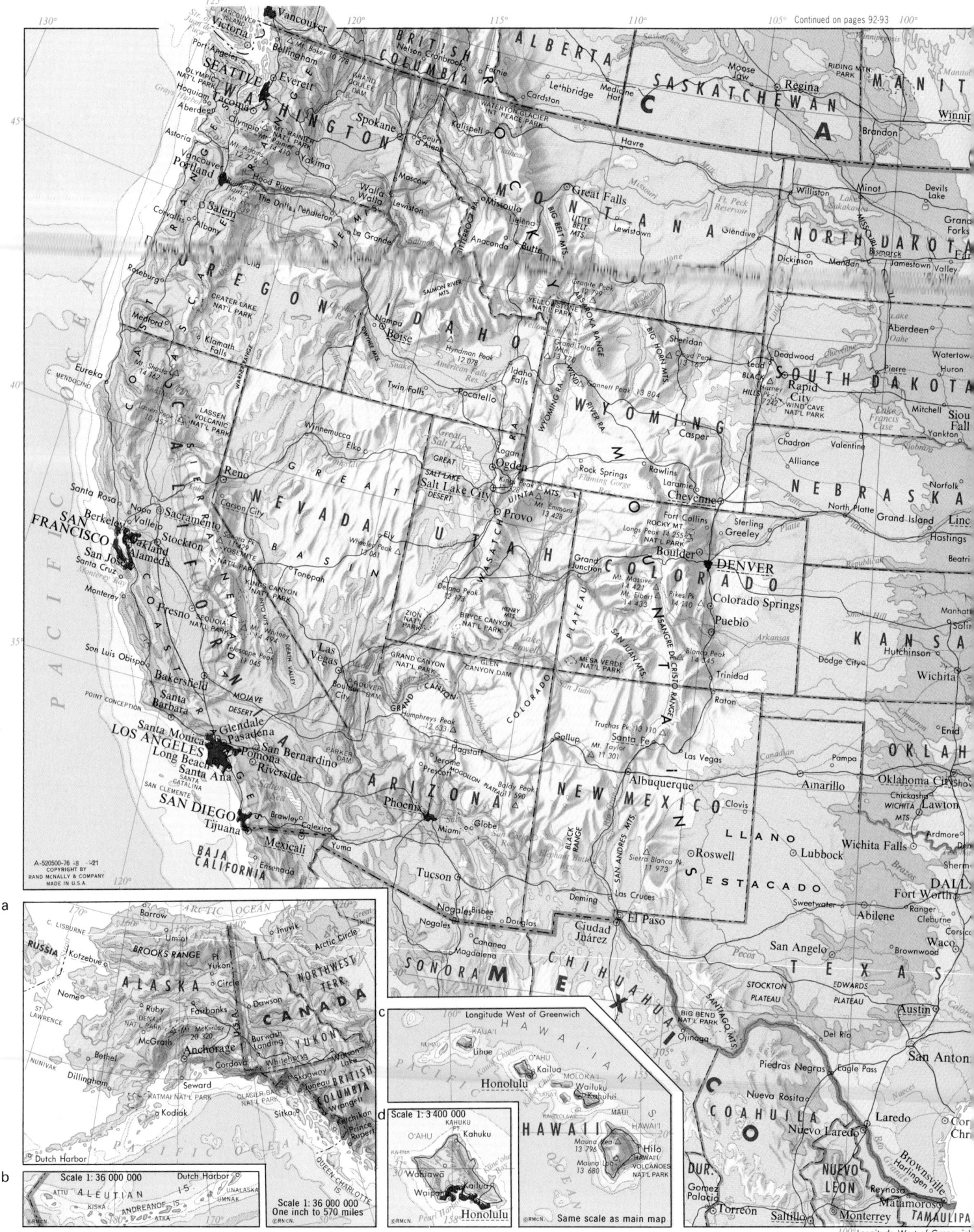

Continued on pages 92-93

Scale 1:12 000 000; one inch to 190 miles. Polyconic Projection
Elevations and depressions are given in feet

Longitude West of Greenwich

a

c

d

b

Scale 1:36 000 000
Dutch Harbor

Scale 1:36 000 000
One inch to 570 miles

Scale 1:3 400 000

Same scale as main map

A-520500-76 -8 -21
COPYRIGHT BY
RAND McNALLY & COMPANY
MADE IN U.S.A.

Scale 1:1 000 000; One inch to 16 miles.
Elevations and depressions are given in feet.

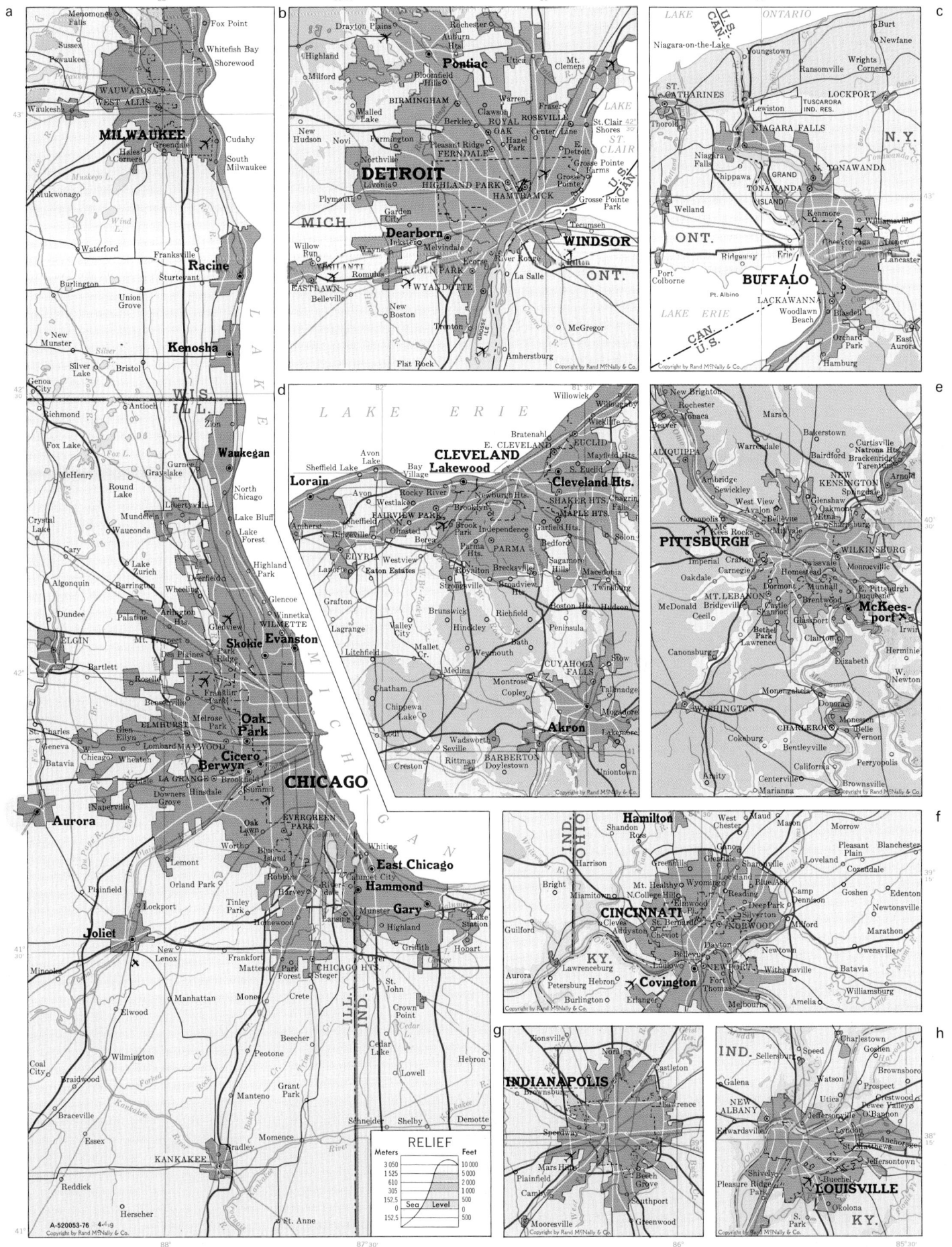

a — Milwaukee area

Menomonee Falls, Sussex, Pewaukee, Fox Point, Whitefish Bay, Shorewood, Waukesha, WAUWATOSA, WEST ALLIS, **MILWAUKEE**, Hales Corners, Greendale, Cudahy, South Milwaukee, Mukwonago, Waterford, Franksville, **Racine**, Sturtevant, Burlington, Union Grove, New Munster, Silver Lake, Bristol, **Kenosha**, Genoa City

b — Detroit area

Drayton Plains, Rochester, Auburn Hts., Utica, Mt. Clemens, Highland, Milford, Bloomfield Hills, **Pontiac**, Warren, Fraser, ROSEVILLE, St. Clair Shores, BIRMINGHAM, Clawson, ROYAL OAK, Berkley, Center Line, LAKE ST. CLAIR, New Hudson, Novi, Walled Lake, Farmington, Pleasant Ridge, Hazel Park, E. Detroit, Northville, FERNDALE, Grosse Pointe Farms, **DETROIT**, HIGHLAND PARK, HAMTRAMCK, Grosse Pointe, Grosse Pointe Park, Plymouth, Garden City, **Dearborn**, Livonia, Wayne, Inkster, Melvindale, Ecorse, River Rouge, WINDSOR, Willow Run, YPSILANTI, Romulus, LINCOLN PARK, La Salle, ONT., EASTLAWN, Belleville, WYANDOTTE, New Boston, Trenton, McGregor, Flat Rock, Amherstburg, MICH.

c — Buffalo area

LAKE ONTARIO, U.S. CAN., Niagara-on-the-Lake, Youngstown, Burt, Newfane, ST. CATHARINES, Lewiston, Ransomville, Wrights Corners, LOCKPORT, Thorold, NIAGARA FALLS, TUSCARORA IND. RES., Niagara Falls, Chippawa, GRAND ISLAND, N. TONAWANDA, N.Y., Welland, Kenmore, Williamsville, Depew, Ridgeway, Erie, Lancaster, Port Colborne, **BUFFALO**, Pt. Albino, LACKAWANNA, CAN. U.S., Woodlawn Beach, Blasdell, LAKE ERIE, Orchard Park, East Aurora, Hamburg

d — Chicago area

Waukegan, Zion, North Chicago, Lake Bluff, Lake Forest, Highland Park, Antioch, Richmond, Fox Lake, McHenry, Gurnee, Grayslake, Libertyville, Crystal Lake, Round Lake, Mundelein, Wauconda, Deerfield, Glencoe, Winnetka, WILMETTE, Cary, Lake Zurich, Barrington, Wheeling, Algonquin, Dundee, Palatine, Arlington Hts., Glenview, **Evanston**, Skokie, ELGIN, Mt. Prospect, Park Ridge, Des Plaines, Bartlett, Roselle, Franklin Park, Bensenville, St. Charles, Glen Ellyn, ELMHURST, Melrose Park, MAYWOOD, **Oak Park**, Geneva, Lombard, Wheaton, LA GRANGE, Brookfield, **Cicero**, **Berwyn**, Batavia, Chicago, Summit, **CHICAGO**, Naperville, Downers Grove, Hinsdale, **Aurora**, EVERGREEN PARK, Oak Lawn, Worth, Blue Island, Whiting, **East Chicago**, **Hammond**, Lemont, Robbins, Calumet City, Riverdale, Harvey, Homewood, Lansing, Munster, **Gary**, Lake Station, Plainfield, Lockport, Tinley Park, Highland, Griffith, Hobart, **Joliet**, New Lenox, Frankfort, Matteson, CHICAGO HTS., Dyer, Minooka, Park Forest, Steger, St. John, Crown Point, Cedar Lake, Manhattan, Mokena, Crete, Beecher, Elwood, Wilmington, Peotone, Grant Park, Schneider, Shelby, Demotte, Coal City, Braidwood, Manteno, Momence, Hebron, Lowell, Essex, Reddick, KANKAKEE, Bradley, Herscher, St. Anne, WIS. ILL., IND.

e — Cleveland / Pittsburgh area

LAKE ERIE, Willowick, Willoughby, New Brighton, Rochester, Monaca, Mars, Bakerstown, Curtisville, Avon Lake, Bratenahl, Wickliffe, Beaver, Warrendale, Natrona Hts., Brackenridge, Tarentum, Sheffield Lake, Bay Village, E. CLEVELAND, EUCLID, Mayfield Hts., ALIQUIPPA, Bairdford, NEW KENSINGTON, Arnold, **Lorain**, **CLEVELAND**, **Lakewood**, S. Euclid, Ambridge, Sewickley, West View, Glenshaw, Springdale, Avon, Westlake, Rocky River, **Cleveland Hts.**, SHAKER HTS., MAPLE HTS., Chagrin Falls, Coraopolis, McKees Rocks, Avalon, Etna, Sharpsburg, Amherst, Sheffield, FAIRVIEW PARK, Brooklyn, Newburgh Hts., Garfield Hts., Solon, Imperial, Crafton, **PITTSBURGH**, Swissvale, Monroeville, Ripleyville, Olmsted, Brook Park, Independence, Bedford, Oakdale, Carnegie, Homestead, Wilkinsburg, ELYRIA, Westview, Berea, PARMA, Sagamore Hills, Macedonia, McDonald, Dormont, Munhall, E. Pittsburgh, Laporte, Eaton Estates, Royalton, Parma Hts., Brecksville, Boston Hts., Hudson, MT. LEBANON, Brentwood, **McKees-port**, Brunswick, Strongsville, Broadview Hts., Twinsburg, Cecil, Bridgeville, Castle Shannon, Glassport, Clairton, Duquesne, Irwin, Valley City, Hinckley, Richfield, Bath, Peninsula, Stow, Bethel Park, Lawrence, Elizabeth, Herminie, Litchfield, Mallet Cr., Weymouth, CUYAHOGA FALLS, Canonsburg, W. Newton, Chatham, Copley, Montrose, Talmadge, Chippewa Lake, Medina, **Akron**, Monongahela, Donora, WASHINGTON, Seville, Wadsworth, Mogadore, Lakemore, CHARLEROI, Belle Vernon, Creston, Rittman, BARBERTON, Doylestown, Uniontown, Cokeburg, Bentleyville, Amity, Centerville, California, Perryopolis, Marianna, Brownsville

f — Cincinnati area

IND. OHIO, Hamilton, Shandon, Ross, West Chester, Maud, Mason, Morrow, Harrison, Greenhills, Glendale, Sharonville, Loveland, Pleasant Plain, Blanchester, Bright, Miamitown, Mt. Healthy, Wyoming, Lockland, Blue Ash, Cozaddale, N. College Hill, Reading, Deer Park, Camp Dennison, Goshen, Edenton, Guilford, Cleves, St. Bernard, NORWOOD, Silverton, Milford, Newtonsville, Aurora, Addyston, Cheviot, **CINCINNATI**, Dayton, Newtown, Marathon, Lawrenceburg, Belleview, Ludlow, NEWPORT, Withamsville, Batavia, Petersburg, Hebron, **Covington**, Fort Thomas, Amelia, Williamsburg, Burlington, Erlanger, Melbourne, KY.

g — Indianapolis area

Zionsville, Nora, Castleton, **INDIANAPOLIS**, Brownsburg, Lawrence, Speedway, Mars Hill, Beech Grove, Plainfield, Camby, Southport, Mooresville, Greenwood

h — Louisville area

IND., Sellersburg, Speed, Charlestown, Goshen, Brownsboro, Galena, Watson, Prospect, Crestwood, Utica, Pewee Valley, O'Bannon, NEW ALBANY, Jeffersonville, Lyndon, **LOUISVILLE**, Edwardsville, St. Matthews, Jeffersontown, Shively, Buechel, Pleasure Ridge Park, Okolona, S. Park, KY.

RELIEF

Meters	Feet
3 050	10 000
1 525	5 000
610	2 000
305	1 000
152.5	500
Sea Level	0
152.5	500

Scale 1:1 000 000; One inch to 16 miles.
Elevations and depressions are given in feet.

0 2 4 6 8 10 12 14 16 18 20 22 24 Miles
0 4 8 12 16 20 24 28 32 36 40 Kilometers

A-520053-76

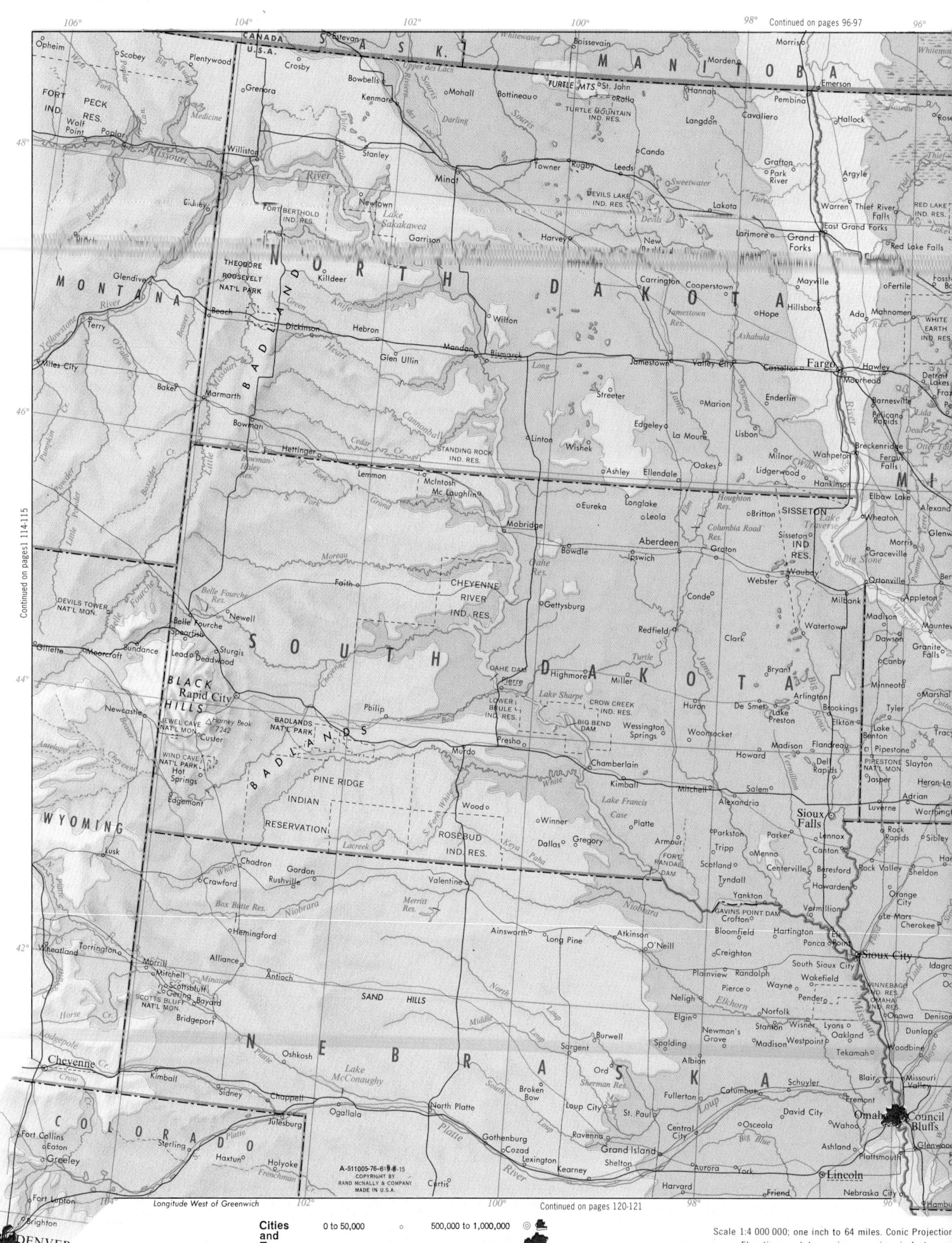

Continued on pages 96-97

Continued on pages 114-115

CANADA
U.S.A.
SASK. MANITOBA

MONTANA

NORTH DAKOTA

SOUTH DAKOTA

WYOMING

NEBRASKA

COLORADO

DENVER

Cities and Towns

| | 0 to 50,000 | o | 500,000 to 1,000,000 | ◎ |
| | 50,000 to 500,000 | ⊙ | 1,000,000 and over | |

Scale 1:4 000 000; one inch to 64 miles. Conic Projection
Elevations and depressions are given in feet

A-511005-76-6-9-8-15
COPYRIGHT BY
RAND McNALLY & COMPANY
MADE IN U.S.A.

Longitude West of Greenwich

Continued on pages 120-121

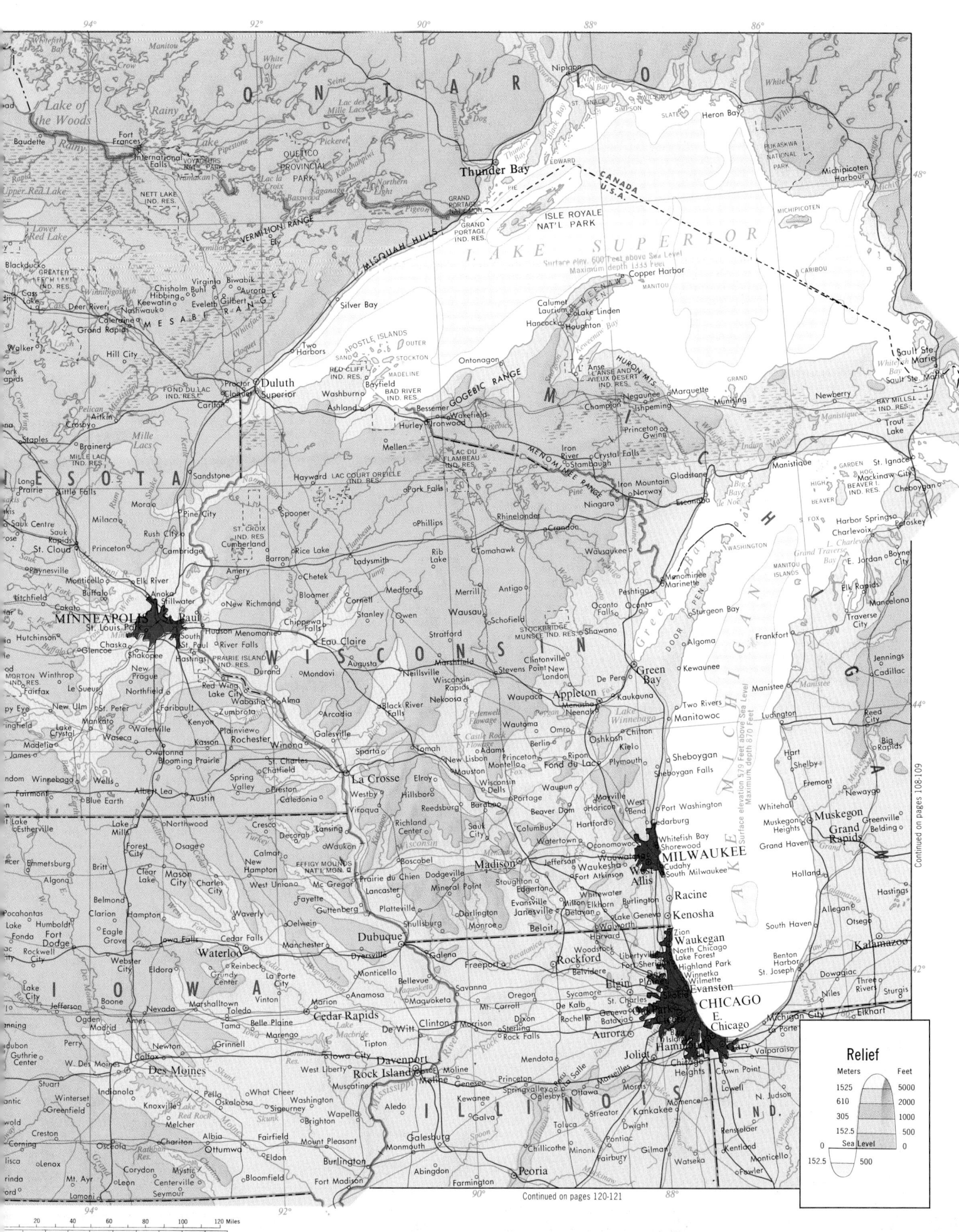

Continued on pages 108-109

Continued on pages 120-121

ONTARIO

Lake of the Woods

Thunder Bay

CANADA
U.S.A.

LAKE SUPERIOR
Surface elev. 600 Feet above Sea Level
Maximum depth 1333 Feet

ISLE ROYALE NAT'L PARK

PUKASKWA NATIONAL PARK

Michipicoten Harbour

Sault Ste. Marie

MICHIGAN

MESABI RANGE

VERMILION RANGE

MISQUAH HILLS

GOGEBIC RANGE

MENOMINEE RANGE

Duluth
Superior

MINNESOTA

WISCONSIN

MINNEAPOLIS
St. Paul

La Crosse

Madison

MILWAUKEE
West Allis

Green Bay

Appleton

Lake Winnebago

LAKE MICHIGAN
Surface elevation 579 Feet above Sea Level
Maximum depth 870 Feet

Muskegon
Grand Rapids

Kalamazoo

IOWA

Dubuque

Waterloo

Cedar Rapids

Des Moines

Davenport
Rock Island
Moline

ILLINOIS

Rockford

Elgin

CHICAGO
E. Chicago
Hammond
Gary

Aurora

Joliet

Peoria

IND.

Relief

Meters	Feet
1525	5000
610	2000
305	1000
152.5	500
Sea Level	0
152.5	500

0   20   40   60   80   100   120 Miles
0 20 40 60 80 100 120 140 160 180 200 Kilometers

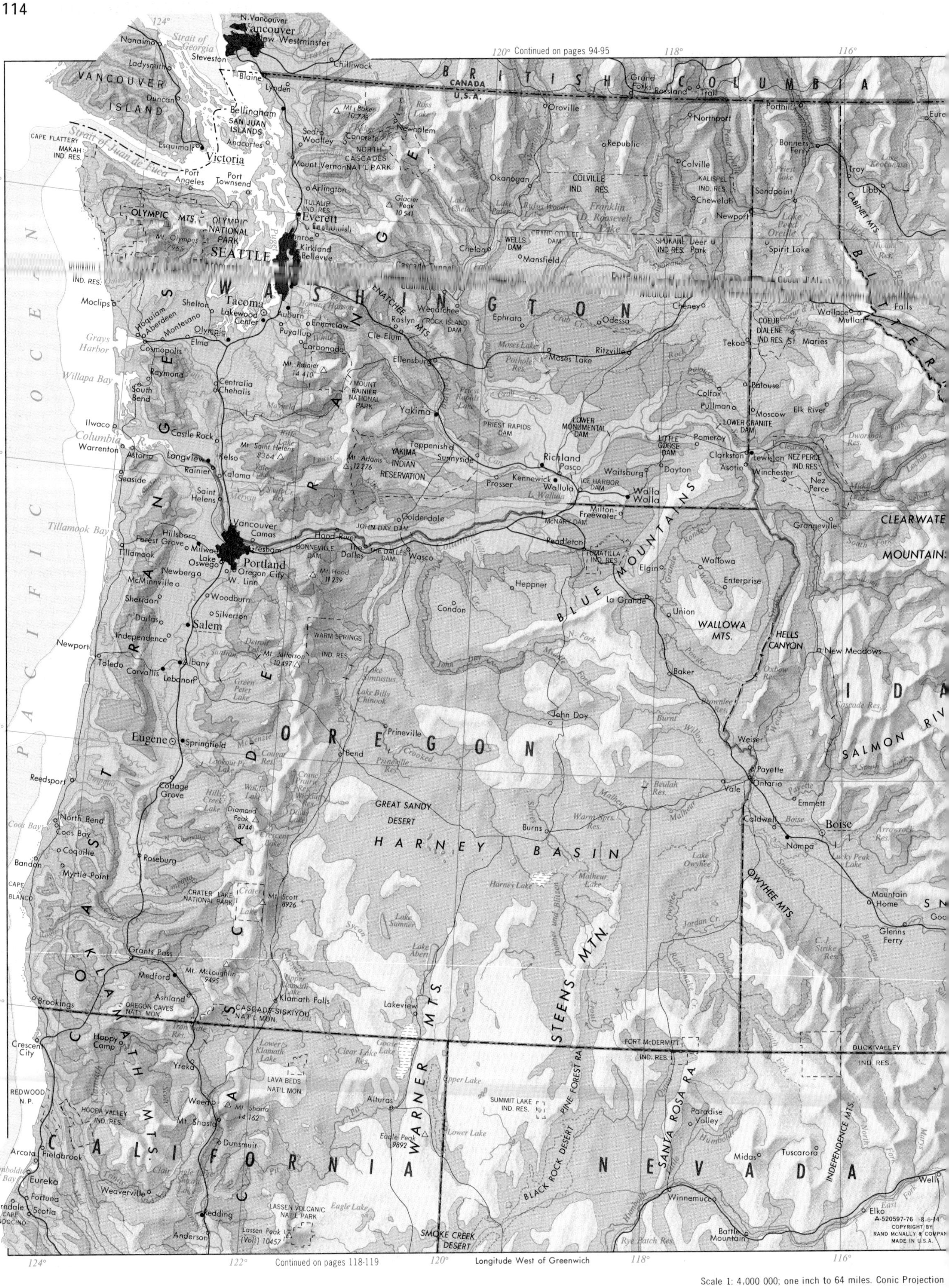

BRITISH COLUMBIA

Continued on pages 94-95

CANADA
U.S.A.

VANCOUVER ISLAND

Strait of Georgia

Nanaimo
Ladysmith
Duncan
Esquimalt
Victoria
Port Angeles
Port Townsend
CAPE FLATTERY
MAKAH IND. RES.
Strait of Juan de Fuca

N. Vancouver
Vancouver
New Westminster
Steveston
Blaine
Lynden
Chilliwack
Grand Forks
Rossland
Trail
Northport
Porthill
Bonners Ferry
Troy
Libby
Lake Koocanusa

SAN JUAN ISLANDS
Bellingham
Sedro Woolley
Anacortes
Mount Vernon
Arlington
Concrete
Newhalem
Mt. Baker 10,778
Ross Dam
NORTH CASCADES NAT'L PARK
Oroville
Republic
Colville
COLVILLE IND. RES.
Chewelah
Sandpoint
KALISPEL IND. RES.
Priest Lake
CABINET MTS.
Wallace
Mullan
BITTERROOT

OLYMPIC MTS.
Mt. Olympus 7965
OLYMPIC NATIONAL PARK
IND. RES.
Everett
Monroe
Kirkland
Bellevue
SEATTLE
Tacoma
Lakewood Center
Auburn
Enumclaw
Glacier Peak 10,541
Lake Chelan
Chelan
Mansfield
WELLS DAM
GRAND COULEE DAM
Franklin D. Roosevelt Lake
SPOKANE IND. RES.
Deer Park
Newport
Lake Pend Oreille
Spirit Lake

WASHINGTON

Moclips
Hoquiam
Aberdeen
Montesano
Elma
Olympia
Shelton
Puyallup
Carbonado
Roslyn
Cle Elum
ENATCHEE MTS.
Wenatchee
ROCK ISLAND DAM
Ephrata
Cheney
COEUR D'ALENE IND. RES.
St. Maries
Tekoa

Grays Harbor
Cosmopolis
Raymond
South Bend
Centralia
Chehalis
Mt. Rainier 14,410
MOUNT RAINIER NATIONAL PARK
Ellensburg
Yakima
Moses Lake
Ritzville
Colfax
Palouse
Moscow
Elk River

Willapa Bay
Castle Rock
Mt. Saint Helens 8364
Toppenish
YAKIMA INDIAN RESERVATION
PRIEST RAPIDS DAM
LOWER MONUMENTAL DAM
Pomeroy
LOWER GRANITE DAM
Pullman

Ilwaco
Astoria
Warrenton
Longview
Kelso
Kalama
Rainier
Saint Helens
Mt. Adams 12,276
Sunnyside
Richland
Pasco
Kennewick
Prosser
Wallula
Waitsburg
Dayton
Clarkston
Lewiston
Asotin
NEZ PERCE IND. RES.
Winchester
Nez Perce
Dworshak Res.

Columbia R.
Seaside
Vancouver
Camas
Portland
Gresham
Oregon City
W. Linn
Goldendale
JOHN DAY DAM
Hood River
The Dalles
Wasco
ICE HARBOR DAM
Walla Walla
Milton-Freewater
McNARY DAM
UMATILLA IND. RES.
Pendleton
Elgin
Wallowa
Enterprise
Grangeville
CLEARWATER MOUNTAINS

Tillamook Bay
Hillsboro
Forest Grove
Tillamook
Lake Oswego
Milwaukie
Newberg
McMinnville
Sheridan
Dallas
Woodburn
Silverton
Mt. Hood 11,239
BONNEVILLE DAM
THE DALLES DAM
Heppner
Condon
La Grande
Union
WALLOWA MTS.
HELLS CANYON
New Meadows

Newport
Independence
Salem
Albany
Corvallis
Lebanon
Mt. Jefferson 10,497
WARM SPRINGS IND. RES.
Detroit Lake
Green Peter Lake
John Day
Baker
Oxbow Res.
Brownlee Res.

Toledo
Eugene
Springfield
Prineville
Bend
Prineville Res.
Crooked R.
OREGON
John Day
Burnt R.
Weiser
Payette
Ontario
SALMON RIVER

Reedsport
Cottage Grove
Lookout Pt. Lake
Hills Creek Lake
Diamond Peak 8744
Crescent Lake
Crane Prairie Res.
Wickiup Res.
GREAT SANDY DESERT
HARNEY BASIN
Burns
Beulah Res.
Warm Sprs.
Malheur R.
Vale
Emmett
Caldwell
Boise
Nampa
Lucky Peak Lake
Arrowrock Res.

Coos Bay
North Bend
Coquille
Myrtle Point
Roseburg
CAPE BLANCO
Lake Sumner
Malheur Lake
Harney Lake
Lake Owyhee
OWYHEE MTS.
Mountain Home
Glenns Ferry

CRATER LAKE NATIONAL PARK
Mt. Scott 8926
Lake Sumner
Lake Abert
Jordan Cr.
C. J. Strike Res.

Grants Pass
Medford
Mt. McLoughlin 9495
Ashland
OREGON CAVES NAT'L MON.
Klamath Falls
Lakeview
STEENS MTN.
FORT McDERMITT IND. RES.
DUCK VALLEY IND. RES.

Brookings
CASCADE-SISKIYOU NAT'L MON.
Upper Klamath Lake
WARNER MTS.
PINE FOREST RANGE
SANTA ROSA RANGE
INDEPENDENCE MTS.

Crescent City
Happy Camp
Yreka
Weed
Lower Klamath Lake
LAVA BEDS NAT'L MON.
Clear Lake Res.
Alturas
Upper Lake
SUMMIT LAKE IND. RES.
Paradise Valley
Midas
Tuscarora
Wells

REDWOOD N.P.
KLAMATH
HOOPA VALLEY IND. RES.
Mt. Shasta 14,162
Mt. Shasta
Dunsmuir
Lower Lake
Eagle Peak 9892
BLACK ROCK DESERT
Winnemucca
Elko

PACIFIC OCEAN

COAST RANGE

CASCADE RANGE

KLAMATH MTS.

CALIFORNIA

NEVADA

Arcata
Fieldbrook
Eureka
Fortuna
Ferndale
Scotia
CAPE MENDOCINO
Humboldt Bay
Weaverville
LASSEN VOLCANIC NAT'L PARK
Lassen Peak (Vol.) 10,457
Redding
Anderson
Eagle Lake
SMOKE CREEK DESERT
Battle Mountain
Rye Patch Res.

Longitude West of Greenwich

Continued on pages 118-119

Scale 1: 4,000,000; one inch to 64 miles. Conic Projection
Elevations and depressions are given in feet

A-520597-76 8-6-74
COPYRIGHT BY
RAND McNALLY & COMPANY
MADE IN U.S.A.

Continued on pages 96-97

Continued on pages 112-113

Continued on pages 118-119

Relief

Meters		Feet
3050		10000
1525		5000
610		2000
305		1000
152.5		500
0	Sea Level	0
1525		500

ALBERTA CANADA U.S.A. SASKATCHEWAN

MONTANA

WYOMING

UTAH

COLO.

N. DAK.

20 40 60 80 100 120 Miles
20 40 60 80 100 120 140 160 180 200 Kilometers

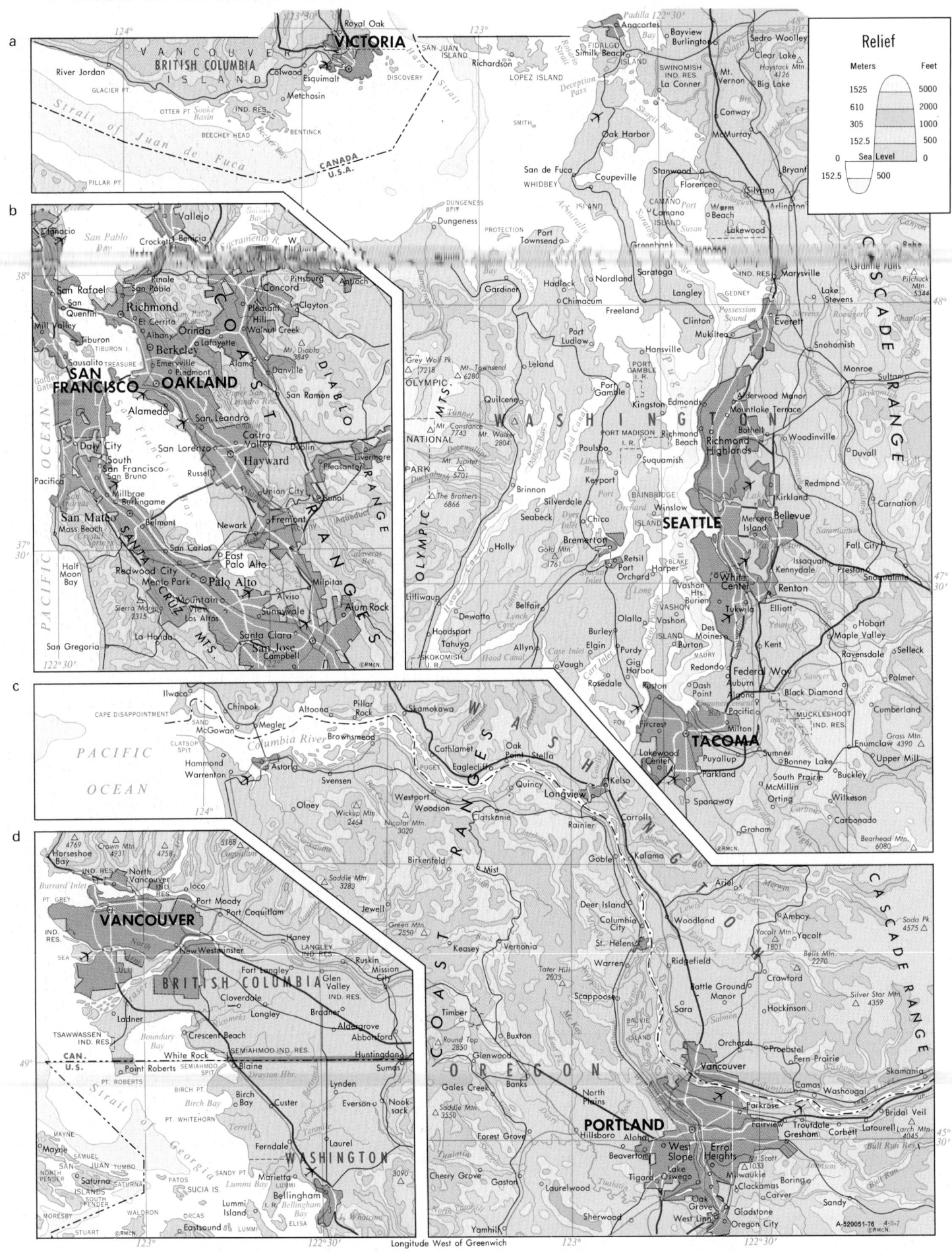

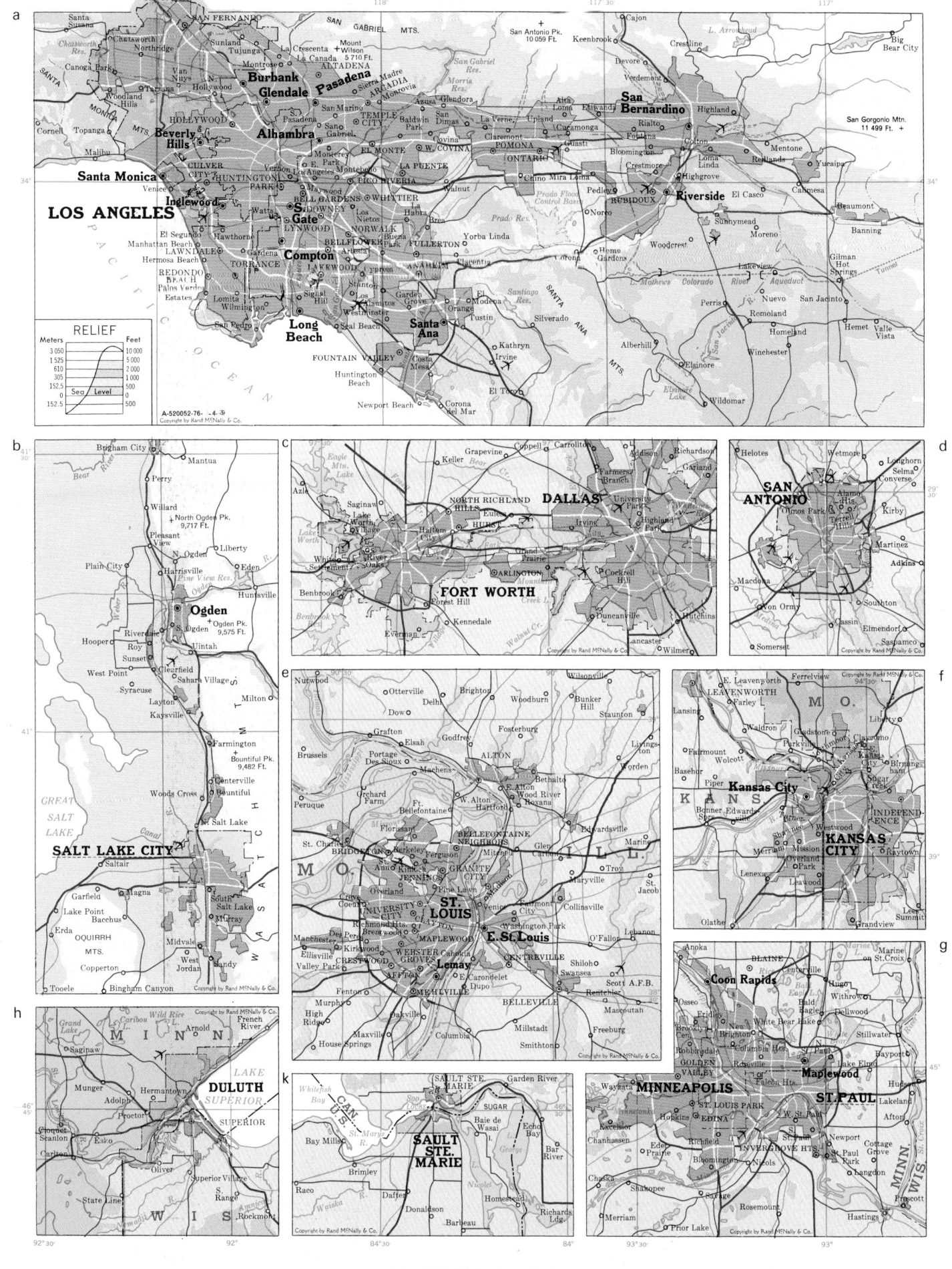

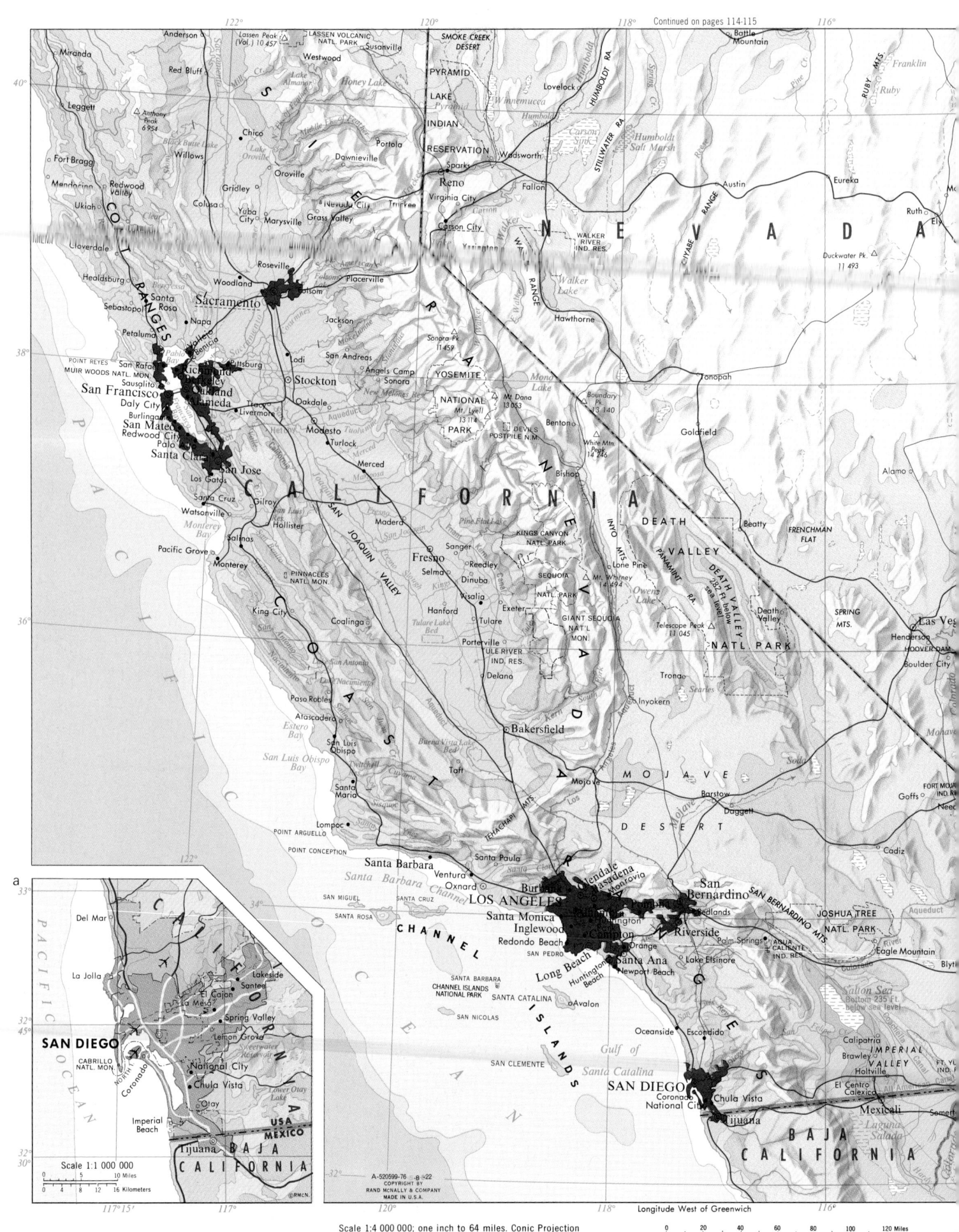

Continued on pages 114-115

Scale 1:4 000 000; one inch to 64 miles. Conic Projection
Elevations and depressions are given in feet

Longitude West of Greenwich

A-520599-76   B 22
COPYRIGHT BY
RAND McNALLY & COMPANY
MADE IN U.S.A.

Relief

Meters		Feet
3050		10000
1525		5000
610		2000
305		1000
152.5		500
0	Sea Level	0
152.5		500 Below
1525		5000 Sea Level
3050		10000

GREAT SALT LAKE DESERT

Great Salt Lake

Salt Lake City
Murray Park City
Midvale Heber City
West Jordan Lehi
American Fork TIMPANOGOS CAVE N.M.
Orem Provo Springville
Spanish Fork
Eureka Payson
Nephi
Fairview Mount Pleasant
Moroni
Ephraim Manti
Delta Gunnison
Fillmore Salina
Richfield
Monroe
Milford
Beaver

GOSHUTE IND. RES.

GREAT BASIN NATL PARK
Wheeler Peak 13,061

Sevier Lake

Little Salt Lake

Parowan
Panguitch
Cedar City
CEDAR BREAKS NATL. MON.
BRYCE CANYON NATL. PARK
Escalante
GRAND STAIRCASE-ESCALANTE NATL. MON.
ZION NATL. PARK
Hurricane
Saint George
Kanab
PIPE SPRING NATL. MON.
KAIBAB IND. RES.

WASATCH PLATEAU
Castle Dale

UINTA PLATEAU
Helper Price Sunnyside
Hiawatha
WEST TAVAPUTS PLATEAU
EAST TAVAPUTS PLATEAU
Green River

Vernal
Roosevelt Duchesne
UINTAH AND OURAY IND. RES.
UINTAH AND OURAY IND. RES.

Oak Creek
Meeker
Rifle Glenwood Springs
ROCKY
Bond
Leadville
Mt. Massive 14,421
Aspen Mt. Elbert 14,433
Mt. Harvard 14,420 Buena Vista
Castle Pk. 14,265 La Plata Pk. 14,361
Crested Butte
Cripple Creek

Fruita Grand Junction
COLORADO NATL. MON.
Delta
UNCOMPAHGRE PLATEAU
Montrose
BLACK CANYON OF THE GUNNISON NATL. PARK
Gunnison
Salida
SANGRE DE CRISTO MTS.

CAPITOL REEF NATL. PARK
Mt. Ellen 11,522
HENRY MTS.
Abajo Pk. 11,360

Moab
Mt. Peale 12,721
CANYONLANDS NATL. PARK
La Sal
Monticello
Blanding

COLORADO PLATEAUS

Mt. Sneffels 14,150
Ouray Uncompahgre Pk. 14,309
Telluride Silverton
SAN JUAN MTS.
Summit Peak 13,300
Durango Pagosa Springs

GREAT SAND DUNES N.M.
Saguache
Del Norte
Monte Vista
Alamosa
Blanca Pk. 14,345

Lake Powell
NATURAL BRIDGES NATL. MON.
GLEN CANYON NATL. RECR. AREA
CANYONS OF THE ANCIENTS NATL. MON.
HOVENWEEP NAT'L MON.
Cortez MESA VERDE NATL. PARK
Bluff
Mexican Hat

RAINBOW BRIDGE NATL. MON.
GLEN CANYON DAM
Page
INSCRIPTION HOUSE RUIN
KEET SEEL RUIN
BETATAKIN RUIN
NAVAJO NATL. MON.

SOUTHERN UTE INDIAN RES.
UTE MTN. IND. RES.
AZTEC RUINS NATL. MON.
Aztec Farmington
JICARILLA APACHE
Wheeler Peak 13,161
Taos

Mt. Bangs 8,012
GRAND CANYON-PARASHANT NATL. MON.
KANAB PLATEAU
KAIBAB PLATEAU
SHIVWITS PLATEAU
Lake Mead
MEAD RECR. AREA
HUALAPAI IND. RES.
GRAND CANYON NATIONAL PARK
MARBLE CANYON
PAINTED DESERT
NAVAJO INDIAN RES.
BLACK MESA
NAVAJO HOPI JOINT USE AREA
CANYON DE CHELLY NATL. MON.
CHUSKA MTS.
NAVAJO INDIAN RESERVATION
CHACO CANYON NATL. MON.
INDIAN
CHACO CULTURE NATL. HIST. PARK
SANTA CLARA IND. RES.
Truchas 13,101
Los Alamos
JEMEZ IND. RES.
BANDELIER NATL. MON.
ZIA IND. RES.
Santa Fe
SANTO DOMINGO IND. RES.
SAN PECOS
SAN FELIPE IND. RES.
Galisteo

Chloride
Kingman
HUALAPAI MTS.
Tapock
Lake Havasu City
PARKER DAM
COLORADO RIVER IND. RES.
Quartzite
Ajo

Moenkopi HOPI
INDIAN RESERVATION
HAVASUPAI IND. RES.
Grand Canyon
COCONINO PLATEAU
WUPATKI NATL. MON.
Humphreys Pk. 12,633
SUNSET CRATER N.M.
Ash Fork Williams Flagstaff
WALNUT CANYON NATL. MON.
Winslow Holbrook
Clarkdale
Jerome TUZIGOOT N.M.
MONTEZUMA CASTLE NATL. MON.
Prescott
MOGOLLON RIM
AGUA FRIA NATL. MON.
Wickenburg

COLORADO DESERT
Sanders
PETRIFIED FOREST NATL. PARK
Saint Johns
Mt. Taylor 11,301
Gallup CANONCITO IND. RES.
ZUNI ZUNI MTS.
EL MORRO NATL. MON.
ACOMA IND. RES.
LAGUNA IND. RES.
ISLETA IND. RES.
Albuquerque
SANDIA IND. RES.
Bernalillo
Belen

NEW MEXICO

McNary Springerville
FORT APACHE INDIAN RESERVATION
Mt. Ord 11,357 Baldy Peak 11,403
Maverick
Theodore Roosevelt Lake
THEODORE ROOSEVELT DAM
SALT RIVER IND. RES.
TONTO NATL. MON.
Glendale Mesa
Phoenix Tempe
Miami Globe
Superior
SAN CARLOS INDIAN RESERVATION
San Carlos Lake
Morenci Clifton
GILA CLIFF DWELLINGS NATL. MON.
Glenwood
BLACK RANGE
Truth or Consequences
Magdalena Socorro
SALINAS NATL. MON.
San Marcial
Carrizozo
Sierra Blanca Peak 11,973
Elephant Butte
Reservoir
MESCALERO APACHE IND. RES.
Tularosa
Alamogordo
WHITE SANDS NATL. MON.
SAN ANDRES MTS.
Caballo Res.

GILA RIVER IND. RES.
Florence Hayden
CASA GRANDE RUINS NATL. MON.
Casa Grande
Gila Bend
Painted Rock Res.
IRONWOOD FOREST NATL. MON.
San Manuel
TOHONO O'ODHAM INDIAN RESERVATION
ORGAN PIPE CACTUS N.M.
Tucson
SAN XAVIER IND. RES.
SAGUARO NATL. PARK
Nogales
TUMACACORI NATL. MON.
Fort Huachuca

Safford
PELONCILLO MTS.
Silver City
Bayard
Lordsburg
Deming
FLORIDA MTS.
Las Cruces
Mesilla
 Yeleta
N. Franklin Mtn. 7,192
El Paso
Ciudad Juárez

Willcox
CHIRICAHUA NATL. MON.
Willcox Playa Lake
Benson
Tombstone
Bisbee Lowell
Pirtleville
Douglas
Columbus
Playas Lake

SONORA

USA MEXICO

CHIHUAHUA

Continued on pages 120-121
Continued on pages 122-123

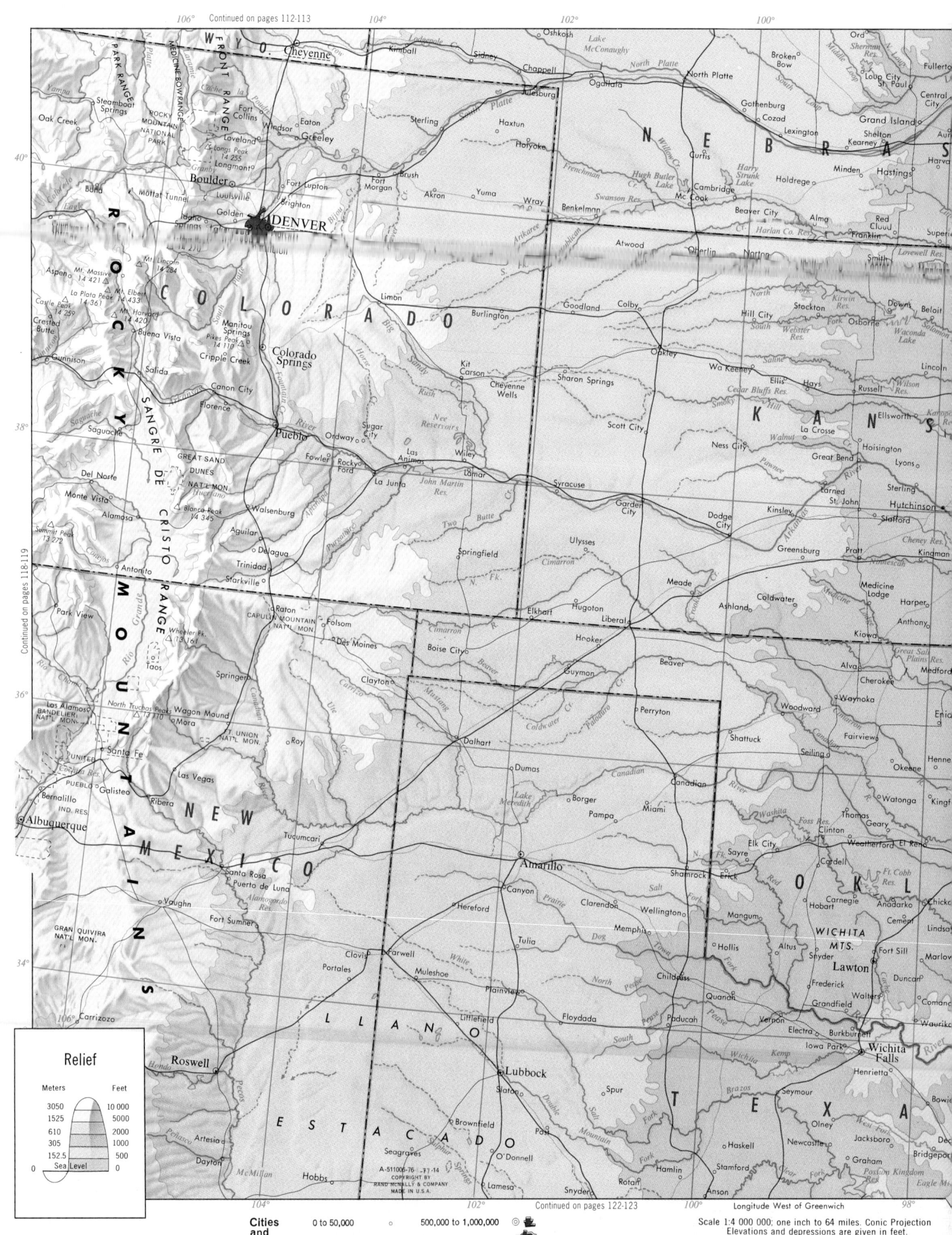

120

Continued on pages 112-113

106°   104°   102°   100°

Continued on pages 118-119

WYO.   Cheyenne   Kimball   Sidney   Oshkosh   Lake McConaughy   Ord   Sherman   Fullerton

PARK RANGE   Chappell   North Platte   North Platte   Broken Bow   Loup City   St. Paul   Loup   Central City   Aur

FRONT RANGE   Steamboat Springs   Ogallala   Gothenburg   Cozad   Grand Island

MEDICINE BOW RANGE   Oak Creek   Fort Collins   Sterling   Haxtun   Holyoke   Curtis   Willow Cr.   Lexington   Shelton   Kearney

ROCKY MOUNTAIN NATIONAL PARK   Loveland   Eaton   Greeley   Hugh Butler Lake   Cambridge   Mc Cook   Minden   Hastings   Harva

Longs Peak 14 255   Longmont   Brush   Akron   Yuma   Wray   Benkelman   Beaver City   Alma   Red Cloud   Superi

40°   Boulder   Fort Lupton   Fort Morgan   Holdrege   Franklin

Moffat Tunnel   Louisville   Brighton   Harlan Co. Res.   Lovewell Res.   Smith   Smith

Golden   DENVER   Atwood   Oberlin   Norton

COLORADO   Aspen   Mt. Massive 14 421   Mt. Lincoln 14 284   Limon   Goodland   Colby   Hill City   Stockton   Downs   Beloit

La Plata Peak 14 361   Mt. Elbert 14 433   Burlington   North Fork   Osborne   Solomon   Waconda Lake

Castle Peak 14 259   Mt. Harvard 14 420   Manitou Springs   Pikes Peak 14 110   Colorado Springs   Oakley   Wa Keeney   Ellis   Hays   Russell   Wilson Res.   Lincoln

Crested Butte   Buena Vista   Cripple Creek   Kit Carson   Cheyenne Wells   Sharon Springs   Scott City   K A N S   Ellsworth

Gunnison   Salida   Canon City   Nee Reservoirs   Ness City   La Crosse   Hoisington

38°   Florence   Pueblo   Ordway   Sugar City   Wiley   Great Bend   Lyons   Sterling

GREAT SAND DUNES NAT'L MON.   Saguache   Fowler   Rocky Ford   Las Animas   Lamar   Garden City   Dodge City   Kinsley   Larned   St. John   Hutchinson

Del Norte   Walsenburg   La Junta   John Martin Res.   Syracuse   Stafford

Monte Vista   Blanca Peak 14 345   Aguilar   Springfield   Ulysses   Greensburg   Pratt   Kingman

Summit Peak 13 272   Alamosa   Delagua   Two Butte Cr.   Cimarron   Meade   Coldwater   Medicine Lodge

Antonito   Trinidad   N. Fk.   Elkhart   Hugoton   Liberal   Ashland   Harper   Anthony

36°   Park View   Starkville   Cimarron   Hooker   Kiowa

CAPULIN MOUNTAIN NAT'L MON.   Raton   Folsom   Boise City   Guymon   Beaver   Alva   Cherokee   Medford

Wheeler Pk. 13 161   Taos   Des Moines   Clayton   Perryton   Woodward   Waynoka   Enid

Los Alamos   North Truchas Peaks 13 110   Wagon Mound   Dalhart   Shattuck   Fairview   Okeene   Henne

BANDELIER NAT'L MON.   Mora   Roy   Dumas   Borger   Canadian   Thomas   Watonga   Kingf

UNITED   Santa Fe   T. UNION NAT'L MON.   Lake Meredith   Pampa   Miami   Foss Res.   Clinton   Geary

PUEBLO IND. RES.   Galisteo   Las Vegas   Elk City   Weatherford   El Reno

Albuquerque   Ribera   Tucumcari   Sayre   Erick   Cordell

NEW   Santa Rosa   Amarillo   Shamrock   Ft. Cobb Res.   Anadarko   Chick

Bernalillo   Puerto de Luna   Canyon   Clarendon   Wellington   Mangum   Hobart   Lindsa

MEXICO   Vaughn   Hereford   Prairie Dog   Memphis   Hollis   Altus   Snyder   Frederick   Walters   Duncan   Coman

34°   GRAN QUIVIRA NAT'L MON.   Fort Sumner   Tulia   WICHITA MTS.   Fort Sill   Lawton

Clovis   Farwell   Childress   Quanah   Grandfield   Marlow

Carrizozo   Portales   Muleshoe   Plainview   Paducah   Vernon   Electra   Burkburnett   Iowa Park   Wichita Falls

Roswell   Littlefield   Floydada   Henrietta

Lubbock   Spur   Double   Seymour   Bowie

RELIEF   Slaton   O L   T E X A   Graham   Eagle

106°   Brownfield   Post   Newcastle   Bridgepor

L L A N O   E S T A C A D O   Seagraves   O'Donnell   Haskell   Stamford   Jacksboro

McMillan   Hobbs   Lamesa   Rotan   Anson

Artesia   Dayton   Snyder   Hamlin

Continued on pages 122-123   Longitude West of Greenwich

Relief

Meters		Feet
3050		10 000
1525		5000
610		2000
305		1000
152.5		500
0	Sea Level	0

A-511006-76   77-14   COPYRIGHT BY   RAND McNALLY & COMPANY   MADE IN U.S.A.

Cities and Towns

| | 0 to 50,000 | ○ | 500,000 to 1,000,000 | ◉ |
| | 50,000 to 500,000 | ⊙ | 1,000,000 and over | |

Scale 1:4 000 000; one inch to 64 miles. Conic Projection
Elevations and depressions are given in feet.

Aurora

CHICAGO

Joliet

Continued on pages 112-113

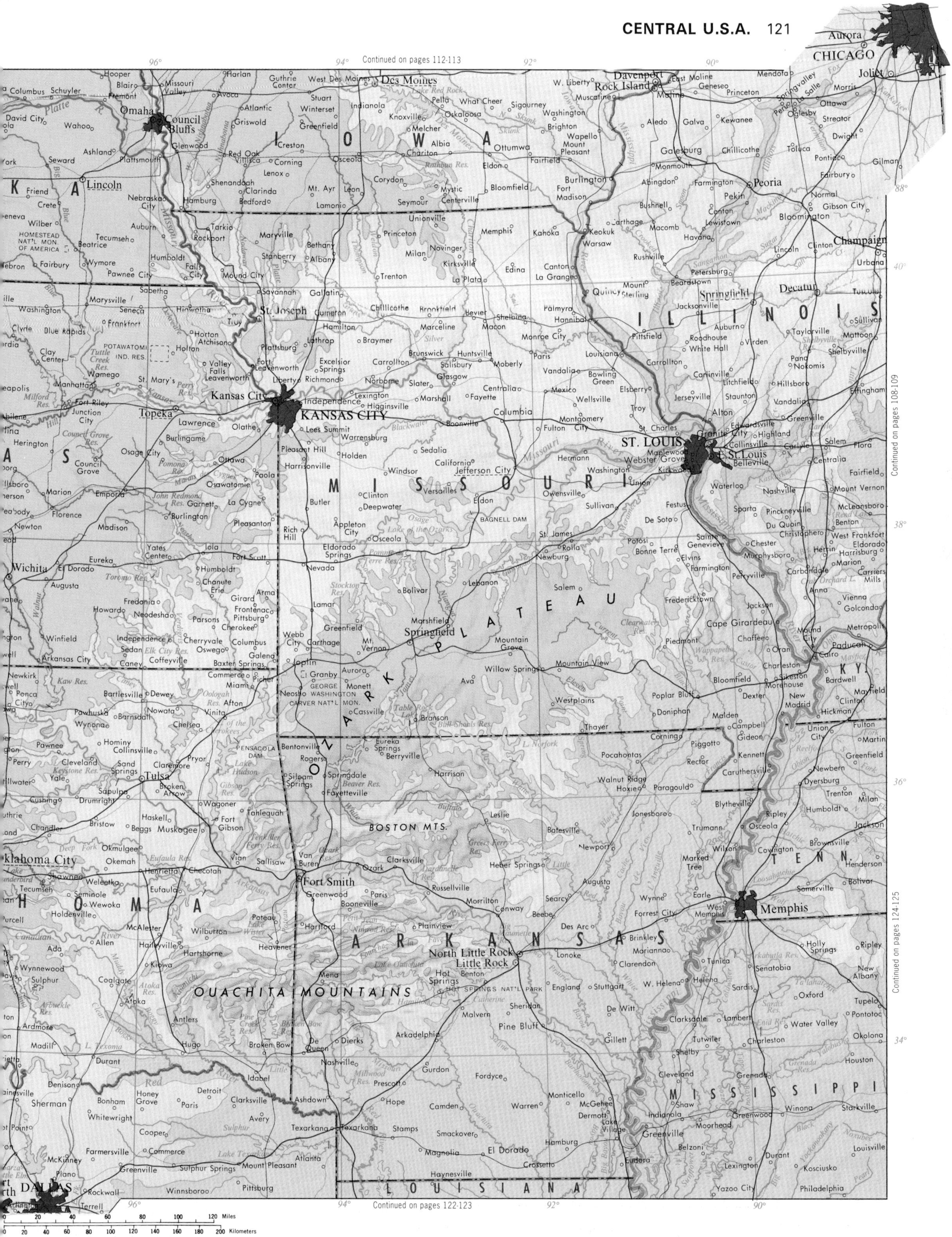

Continued on pages 108-109

Continued on pages 124-125

Continued on pages 122-123

96° 94° 92° 90° 88°

40° 38° 36° 34°

IOWA

Hooper Harlan Guthrie West Des Moines Des Moines W. Liberty Davenport Mendota Morris
Columbus Schuyler Blair Missouri Valley Contar Rock Island East Moline Geneseo Princeton Springvalley La Salle Ottawa
David City Fremont Avoca Stuart Indianola Pella What Cheer Sigourney Washington Muscatine Aledo Galva Kewanee Oglesby Streator Dwight Gilman
Omaha Council Bluffs Atlantic Griswold Winterset Knoxville Melcher Oskaloosa Brighton Wapello Galesburg Monmouth Chillicothe Toluca Pontiac
Wahoo Glenwood Red Oak Creston Albia Ottumwa Mount Pleasant Burlington Abingdon Farmington Peoria Pekin Normal Fairbury

KANSAS Lincoln Nebraska City Tarkio Maryville Bethany Memphis Kahoka Keokuk Warsaw Carthage Macomb Lewistown Bloomington Champaign
Friend Crete Wilber Beatrice Wymore Pawnee City Falls City Rockport Albany Milan Kirksville Edina Canton La Grange Hannibal Quincy Rushville Havana Lincoln Clinton
Fairbury Washington Marysville Seneca Frankfort Horton Atchison St. Joseph Chillicothe Brookfield Bevier Shelbina Macon Monroe City Palmyra Louisiana Pittsfield Jacksonville Springfield Auburn Taylorville Mattoon Sullivan

ILLINOIS

MISSOURI

Topeka Lawrence Kansas City Independence Lees Summit Warrensburg Sedalia Columbia Fulton City Jefferson City St. Charles ST. LOUIS St. Louis Belleville
Emporia Osage City Ottawa Paola Harrisonville Holden Windsor California Versailles Eldon Hermann Washington Union Waterloo Nashville

Wichita El Dorado Augusta Winfield Arkansas City
Independence Coffeyville Bartlesville Tulsa

OKLAHOMA **ARKANSAS**

Oklahoma City Okmulgee Muskogee Fort Smith Russellville Conway Searcy

Little Rock North Little Rock Hot Springs HOT SPRINGS NAT'L PARK

OUACHITA MOUNTAINS

BOSTON MTS.

OZARK PLATEAU

Springfield Joplin Neosho Monett Aurora Branson

GEORGE WASHINGTON CARVER NAT'L MON.

Memphis

TENN. **KY.** **MISSISSIPPI** **LOUISIANA**

Cape Girardeau Cairo Paducah

Poplar Bluff Jonesboro West Memphis

Texarkana El Dorado

DALLAS

0 20 40 60 80 100 120 Miles
0 20 40 60 80 100 120 140 160 180 200 Kilometers

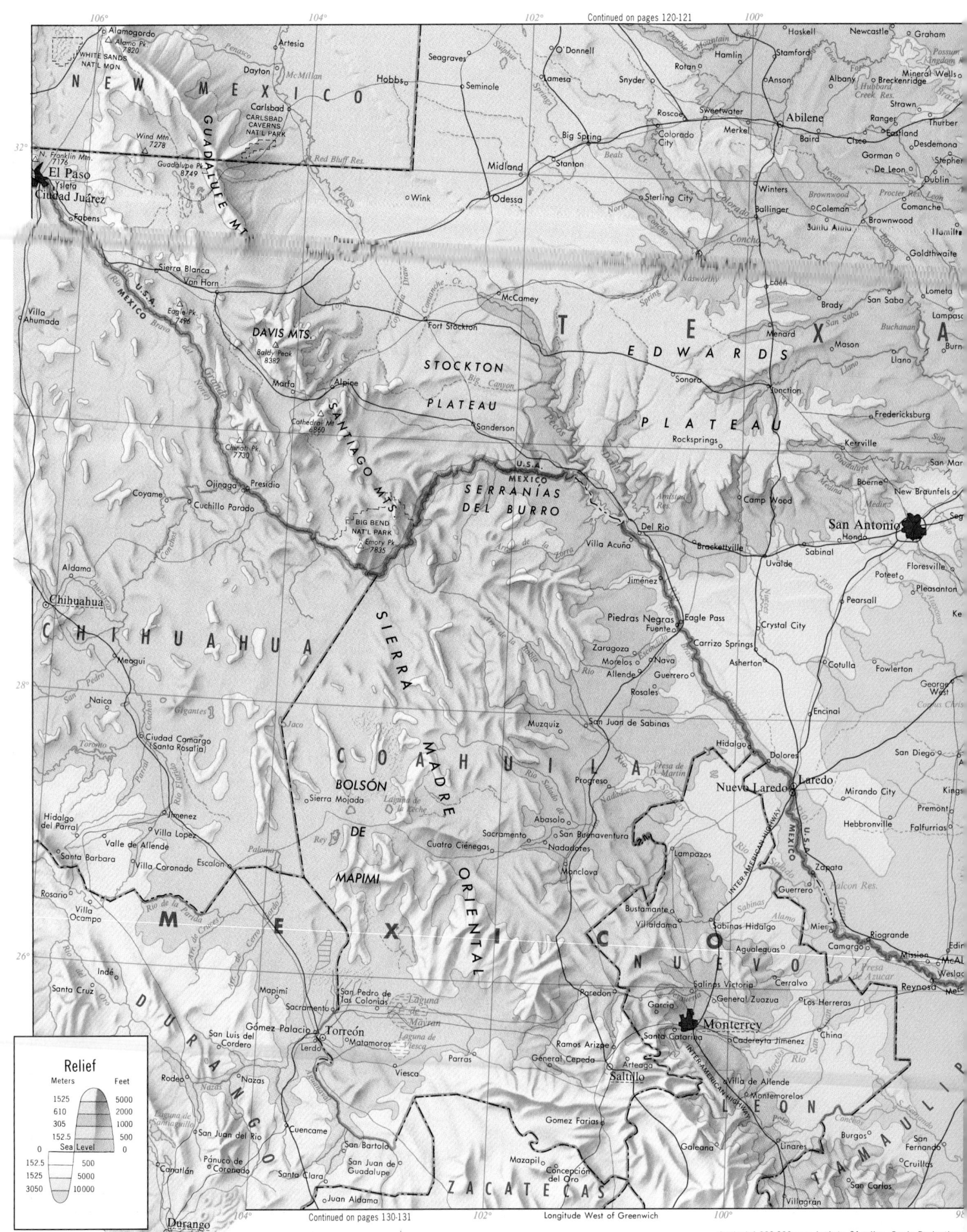

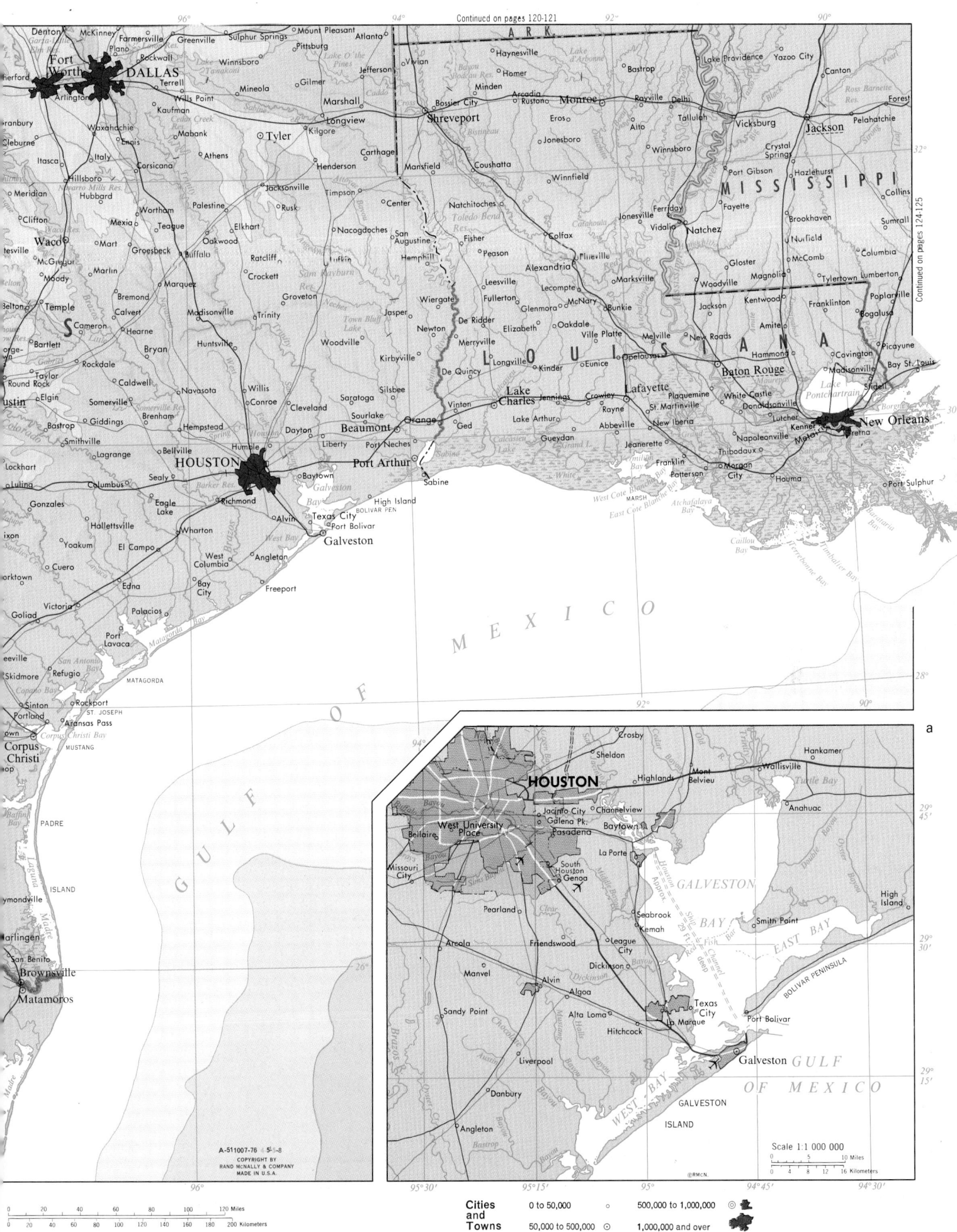

Continued on pages 120-121

Continued on pages 124-125

ARK.

MISSISSIPPI

LOUISIANA

GULF OF MEXICO

a

HOUSTON

GALVESTON BAY

EAST BAY

BOLIVAR PENINSULA

GALVESTON ISLAND

Scale 1:1 000 000

0   5   10 Miles
0 4 8 12 16 Kilometers

©RMcN.

Cities and Towns

0 to 50,000	500,000 to 1,000,000
50,000 to 500,000	1,000,000 and over

A-511007-76 5-5-8
COPYRIGHT BY
RAND McNALLY & COMPANY
MADE IN U.S.A.

0 20 40 60 80 100 120 Miles
0 20 40 60 80 100 120 140 160 180 200 Kilometers

Continued on pages 108-109

Continued on pages 120-121

Continued on pages 122-123

GULF OF MEXICO

A-520598-76 -7-7-14
COPYRIGHT BY
RAND McNALLY & COMPANY
MADE IN U.S.A

Longitude West of Greenwich

Scale 1:4 000 000; one inch to 64 miles. Conic Projection
Elevations and depressions are given in feet

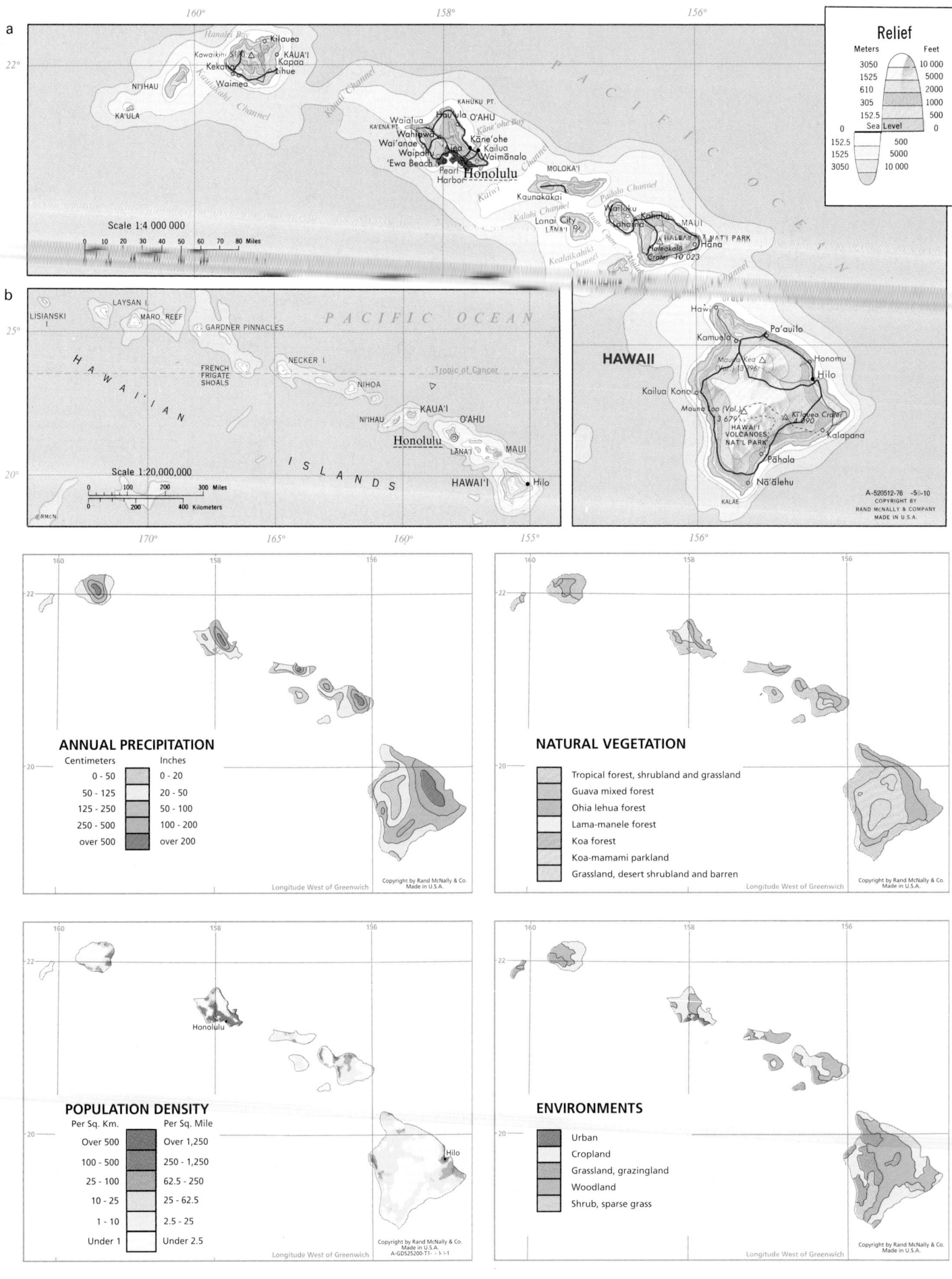

a

Relief

Meters		Feet
3050		10 000
1525		5000
610		2000
305		1000
152.5		500
0	Sea Level	0
152.5		500
1525		5000
3050		10 000

Scale 1:4 000 000

0 10 20 30 40 50 60 70 80 Miles

b

PACIFIC OCEAN

Tropic of Cancer

HAWAIIAN ISLANDS

Honolulu

Scale 1:20,000,000

0 100 200 300 Miles
0 200 400 Kilometers

HAWAII

A-520512-76 -5-1-10
COPYRIGHT BY
RAND McNALLY & COMPANY
MADE IN U.S.A.

ANNUAL PRECIPITATION

Centimeters	Inches
0 - 50	0 - 20
50 - 125	20 - 50
125 - 250	50 - 100
250 - 500	100 - 200
over 500	over 200

Longitude West of Greenwich

Copyright by Rand McNally & Co.
Made in U.S.A.

NATURAL VEGETATION

- Tropical forest, shrubland and grassland
- Guava mixed forest
- Ohia lehua forest
- Lama-manele forest
- Koa forest
- Koa-mamami parkland
- Grassland, desert shrubland and barren

Longitude West of Greenwich

Copyright by Rand McNally & Co.
Made in U.S.A.

POPULATION DENSITY

Per Sq. Km.	Per Sq. Mile
Over 500	Over 1,250
100 - 500	250 - 1,250
25 - 100	62.5 - 250
10 - 25	25 - 62.5
1 - 10	2.5 - 25
Under 1	Under 2.5

Longitude West of Greenwich

Copyright by Rand McNally & Co.
Made in U.S.A.
A-GDS25200-T1- - 1-1-1

ENVIRONMENTS

- Urban
- Cropland
- Grassland, grazingland
- Woodland
- Shrub, sparse grass

Longitude West of Greenwich

Copyright by Rand McNally & Co.
Made in U.S.A.

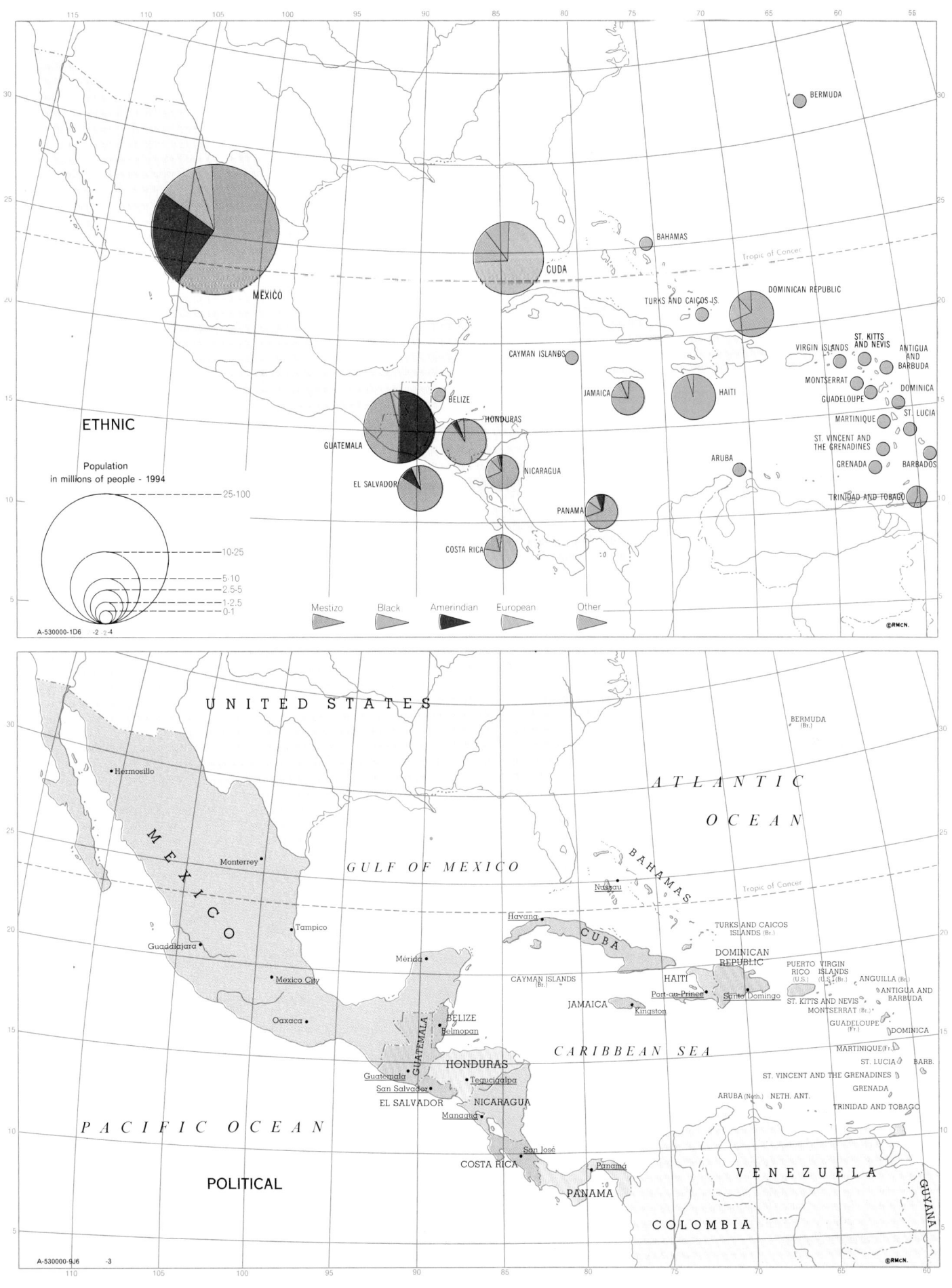

ETHNIC

Population
in millions of people - 1994

25-100

10-25

5-10
2.5-5
1-2.5
0-1

A-530000-1D6   -2 -2 -4

Mestizo   Black   Amerindian   European   Other

MEXICO

BERMUDA

BAHAMAS

CUBA

TURKS AND CAICOS IS.

DOMINICAN REPUBLIC

CAYMAN ISLANDS

ST. KITTS
AND NEVIS

VIRGIN ISLANDS   ANTIGUA
AND
BARBUDA

MONTSERRAT

JAMAICA   HAITI   GUADELOUPE   DOMINICA

MARTINIQUE   ST. LUCIA

BELIZE

HONDURAS

ST. VINCENT AND
THE GRENADINES

GUATEMALA

ARUBA   GRENADA   BARBADOS

NICARAGUA

EL SALVADOR   TRINIDAD AND TOBAGO

PANAMA

COSTA RICA

©RMCN.

POLITICAL

UNITED STATES

• Hermosillo

ATLANTIC

OCEAN

BERMUDA
(Br.)

M
E
X
I
C
O

• Monterrey

GULF OF MEXICO

BAHAMAS

Tropic of Cancer

• Tampico

• Guadalajara

Nassau

Havana   CUBA

TURKS AND CAICOS
ISLANDS (Br.)

• Mérida

CAYMAN ISLANDS
(Br.)

DOMINICAN
REPUBLIC

PUERTO   VIRGIN
RICO   ISLANDS
(U.S.)   (U.S.)   ANGUILLA (Br.)

• Mexico City

HAITI

• Oaxaca

JAMAICA   Kingston   Port-au-Prince   Santo Domingo

ANTIGUA AND
BARBUDA
ST. KITTS AND NEVIS   MONTSERRAT (Br.)

GUADELOUPE
(Fr.)

BELIZE
Belmopan

CARIBBEAN SEA

DOMINICA

MARTINIQUE(Fr.)

GUATEMALA

HONDURAS

ST. LUCIA   BARB.

Guatemala   • Tegucigalpa

ST. VINCENT AND THE GRENADINES

San Salvador

ARUBA (Neth.)   NETH. ANT.

GRENADA

EL SALVADOR   NICARAGUA

PACIFIC OCEAN

Managua

TRINIDAD AND TOBAGO

San José

COSTA RICA   Panamá

VENEZUELA

GUYANA

PANAMA

COLOMBIA

A-530000-9J6   -3   ©RMCN.

Scale 1:16 000 000; one inch to 250 miles. Polyconic Projection
Elevations and depressions are given in feet

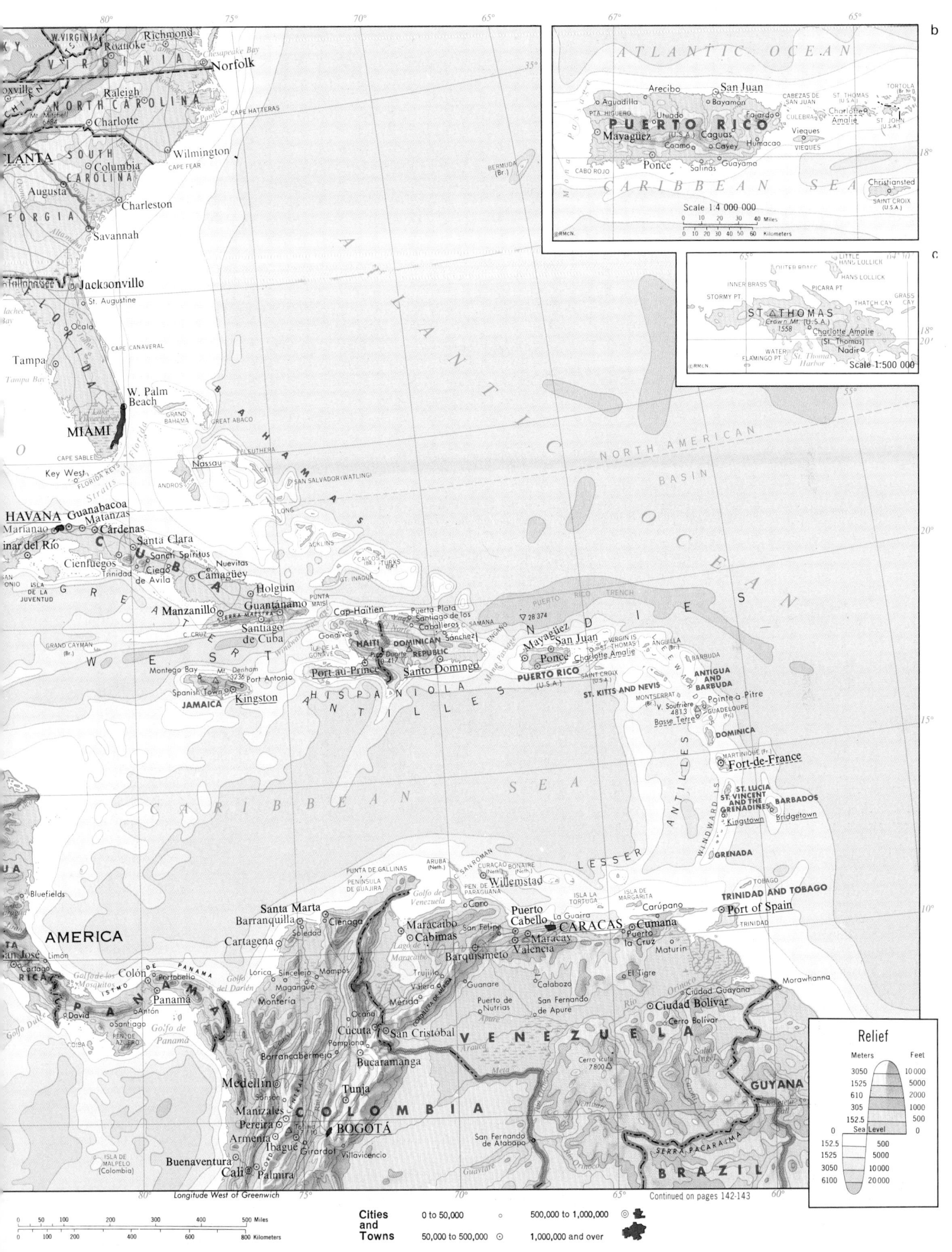

b

ATLANTIC OCEAN

Arecibo · San Juan
○ Aguadilla ○ Bayamón   CABEZAS DE   ST. THOMAS   TORTOLA
PTA. HIGUERO   Utuado   SAN JUAN   (U.S.A.)   (Br. Is.)
Mayagüez ○   Caguas ○ Fajardo   CULEBRA   Charlotte
                                           Amalie
CABO ROJO   Coamo ○ Cayey ○ Humacao   Vieques   St. JOHN (U.S.A.)
PUERTO RICO   VIEQUES
(U.S.A.)
          ○ Ponce   Salinas ○ Guayama   Christiansted

CARIBBEAN   SEA   SAINT CROIX
                                            (U.S.A.)

Scale 1:4 000 000
0   10   20   30   40 Miles
0 10 20 30 40 50 60 Kilometers

©RMCN

c

LITTLE
HANS LOLLICK
OUTER BRASS   HANS LOLLICK
INNER BRASS   PICARA PT
STORMY PT   THATCH CAY   GRASS
                                                  CAY
         ST △ THOMAS
         Crown Mt. (U.S.A.)
              1558   Charlotte Amalie
                    (St. Thomas)
                       Nadir ○
         WATER
FLAMINGO PT   St. Thomas
              Harbor   Scale 1:500 000

©RMCN

Relief

Meters	Feet
3050	10 000
1525	5000
610	2000
305	1000
152.5	500
Sea Level	0
152.5	500
1525	5000
3050	10 000
6100	20 000

Continued on pages 142-143

0   50   100   200   300   500 Miles
0   100   200   400   600   800 Kilometers

Cities	0 to 50,000 ○	500,000 to 1,000,000 ◎
and		
Towns	50,000 to 500,000 ⊙	1,000,000 and over

Longitude West of Greenwich

Continued on pages 122-123

PACIFIC OCEAN

Relief

Meters		Feet
3050		10 000
1525		5000
610		2000
305		1000
152.5		500
0	Sea Level	0
152.5		500
1525		5000
3050		10 000

A-531695-76 · 6 · 15
COPYRIGHT BY
RAND McNALLY & COMPANY
MADE IN U.S.A.

Cities and Towns

0 to 50,000   o   500,000 to 1,000,000 ◎

50,000 to 500,000 ⊙   1,000,000 and over

Scale 1:4 000 000; one inch to 64 miles. Conic Projection
Elevations and depressions are given in feet

Longitude West of Greenwich

Inset map (Mexico City area):

Morelos
Nicolás Romero
Cahuacán
Cuautitlán
Tutitlán
Tecamac
Teotihuacán
Acolman
Chiconautla
Tepexpan
Otumba
Pyramids of Teotihuacán
HIDALGO
Calpulalpan
TLAXCALA

San Bartolo
Ixtlahuaca
Jiquilpico
Cerro La Catedral 13 000
Mazatla
Tlalnepantla
Atizapán
Coacalco
Tulpetlac
Tepetlaoxtoc
San Jerónimo
Nanacamilpa

MÉXICO
Atzcapotzalco
Naucalpan de Juárez
Mimiapan
Chimalpa
Gustavo A. Madero
Texcoco (Dry Lake)
Lago de Texcoco
Texcoco
Coatlinchán
Chicoloapan

Temoaya
Cuajimalpa
Huixquilucan
MEXICO CITY
Nezahualcóyotl
Los Reyes
Río Frío
HY
Texmelucan

Toluca
Lerma
Villa Obregón Contreras
Ixtacalco
Ixtapalapa
Ayotla INTER-AMERICAN
Ixtapaluca
PUEBLA

Capultitlán
Metepec
Mexicalcingo
Ajusco
Coyoacán
Tláhuac
Chalco
Tlalpan
Xochimilco
Tecómitl
Tlalmanalco

Almoloya
Cerro Muneca 12 655
Cerro Ajusco 12 850
Topilejo
Oxtotepec
Milpa Alta
Tenango
Iztaccíhuatl 17 343

Coatepec
DISTRITO FEDERAL
Amecameca

Nevado de Toluca 14 409
Tenango
Tres Cumbres
Ozumba
Volcán Popocatépetl 17 887

Scale 1:1 000 000
0   5   10 Miles
0 4 8 12 16 Kilometers
©RMcN.
Huitzilac
Tepoztlán
Tlalnepantla
Tlayacapan
MORELOS
Cuernavaca

Main map:

Laguna Almagre
Tropic of Cancer
PTA JEREZ
Laguna de San Andrés
Itamira
Ciudad Madero
Tampico
Villa Cuauhtémoc
Tampico Alto
Laguna Tamiahua
CABO ROJO
BARRECIFE BLANQUILLA
ISLA DE LOBOS
euluama
Tancoco
Tamiahua
Alamo
Túxpan
ARRECIFE TANQUIJO
ARRECIFE TÚXPAN
Tihuatlán
capalapa
Poza Rica
Tecolutla
Gutiérrez Zamora
Furbero
Nautla
Coyutla
Coxquihui
ytlalpan
Cuetzalan del Progreso
Tlapacoyan
Vega de Alatorre
catlán
apoaxtla
Atempan
Misantla
Teziutlán
Jalacingo
Altotonga
Naolinco
Las Vigas
Perote
14 048 Nauhcampatépetl
Xalapa
Libres
Coatepec
amantla
Teocelo
PUNTA ZEMPOALA
San Juan Ixtenco
Antigua Veracruz
eaca
Ciudad Serdán
18 406 Pico de Orizaba (Vol.)
Huatusco
Coscomatepec
Veracruz
ARRECIFE CABEZA
Acatzingo de Hidalgo
atoyatempan
Orizaba
Córdoba
Heroica Nogales
Medellín
Tlacotepec
Maltrata
Omeatea
Cotaxtla
Tlalixcoyan
Alvarado
Tehuacan
Ajalpan
Zoquitlán
San Martín (Vol.) 6000
PTA. ZAPOTITLÁN
San Gabriel Chilac
Zinacatepec
Tlacotálpan
Santiago Tuxtla
San Andrés Tuxtla
Chazumba
Huatla de Jiménez
Ojitlán (S. Lucas)
Tierra Blanca
Cosamaloápan
Catemaco
Pájapan
Coatzacoalcos (Puerto México)
ISLA DEL CARMEN
Sabancuy
Chicbul
Mamantel
San Pedro
Ciudad del Carmen
Laguna de Términos
CAMPECHE
PUNTA FONTERA
Paraíso
Allende
Frontera
Palizada
Pétlalcingo
San Miguel
Teotitlán del Camino
Jalapa de Díaz (San Felipe)
Tuxtepec
Chacaltianguis
Soteapan
Cosoleacaque
Comalcalco
Jálpa
Januta
mazulapan
el Progreso
Tejupan (Santiago)
Cuicatlán
Acayucan
Minatitlán
Texistepec
Cárdenas
Cunduacán
TABASCO
Balancán
Huajuapan de León
Coixtlahuaca
San Juan Evangelista
Sayula
Villahermosa
San Carlos
Emiliano Zapata
Teposcolula
Nochixtlán (Asunción)
n Pedro y San Pablo
Talea de Castro (San Miguel)
Villa Alta (San Ildefonso)
Jesús Carranza
Puebla Viejo
Laguna Rosario
Huimanguillo
Tacotalpa
Teapa
Palenque
Tenosique
Tlaxiaco
Sta. María Asunción
Ixtlán de Juárez
Hidalgo Yalalag
11 142 Zempoaltépetl
ISTMO
DE
Presa de Malpaso
Pichucalco
Chapultenango
Yajalón
MESETA DE AGUA ESCONDIDA
tla de uerrero
Chalcatongo
San Mateo (Etlatongo)
Zacatepec (Santiago)
TEHUANTEPEC
Tecpatán
Pantepec
Simojovel
Bachajón
Ocosingo
Yosonotu (Sta. Catarina)
Oaxaca
Tlacolula de Matamoros
Mazatlán (San Juan)
Guichicovi (San Juan)
Compainalá
Jitotol
Yosonotu
Zaachila
Zimatlán de Alvarez
DE
Berriozabal
Tuxtla Gutiérrez
9400 Bohom
Cancuc
Oxchuc
San Cristóbal de las Casas
azulolotitlán (Sta. María)
Sola de Vega (S. Miguel)
Ocotlán de Morelos
Táviche (S. Miguel)
INTER AMERICAN
Cintalapa
Cozozoautla
Chiapa de Corzo
Acala
Teopisca
Amatenango
pomilitepe
Jalapa del Marqués
Ixtepec
Ixtaltepec (Asunción)
Zanatepec (Sto. Domingo)
Las Cruces
Suchiapa
Las Rosas
Comitán
SIERRA DE OAXACA
Ejutla de Crespo
Ixhuatán (San Francisco)
8202
Venustiano Carranza
Socaltenango
Las Vacas
Tehuantepec Sta. Domingo
Juchitán de Zaragoza
Tapanatepec
Villa Flores
La Concordia
Trinitaria
SA. CUCHUMATANES
Loxicha (Sta. Catarina)
Miahuatlán
Laguna Superior
Arriaga
Tonalá
GUATEMALA
Pluma Hidalgo
Salina Cruz
Laguna Inferior
Mar Muerto
La Concordia
Pochutla (San Pedro)
Puerto Ángel
SIERRA MADRE
CORD. DE CHIAPAS
San Miguel
Cuauhtémoc
Jacatenango
Golfo de Tehuantepec
Mapastepec

GULF OF MEXICO
BAHÍA DE CAMPECHE
YUCATÁN
Sisal
Hunucmá
Maxcanú
Halachó
Calkiní
Dzitbalché
Hecelchakán
Lerma
Campeche
Seybaplaya
Champotón
Pustunich
CAMPECHE

Continued on pages 132-133

MÉXICO
GUATEMALA

0   20   40   60   80   100   120 Miles
0 20 40 60 80 100 120 140 160 180 200 Kilometers

96°   99°30'   99°   98°30'
94°   92°   90°
24°   22°   20°   18°   16°
19° 30'   19°

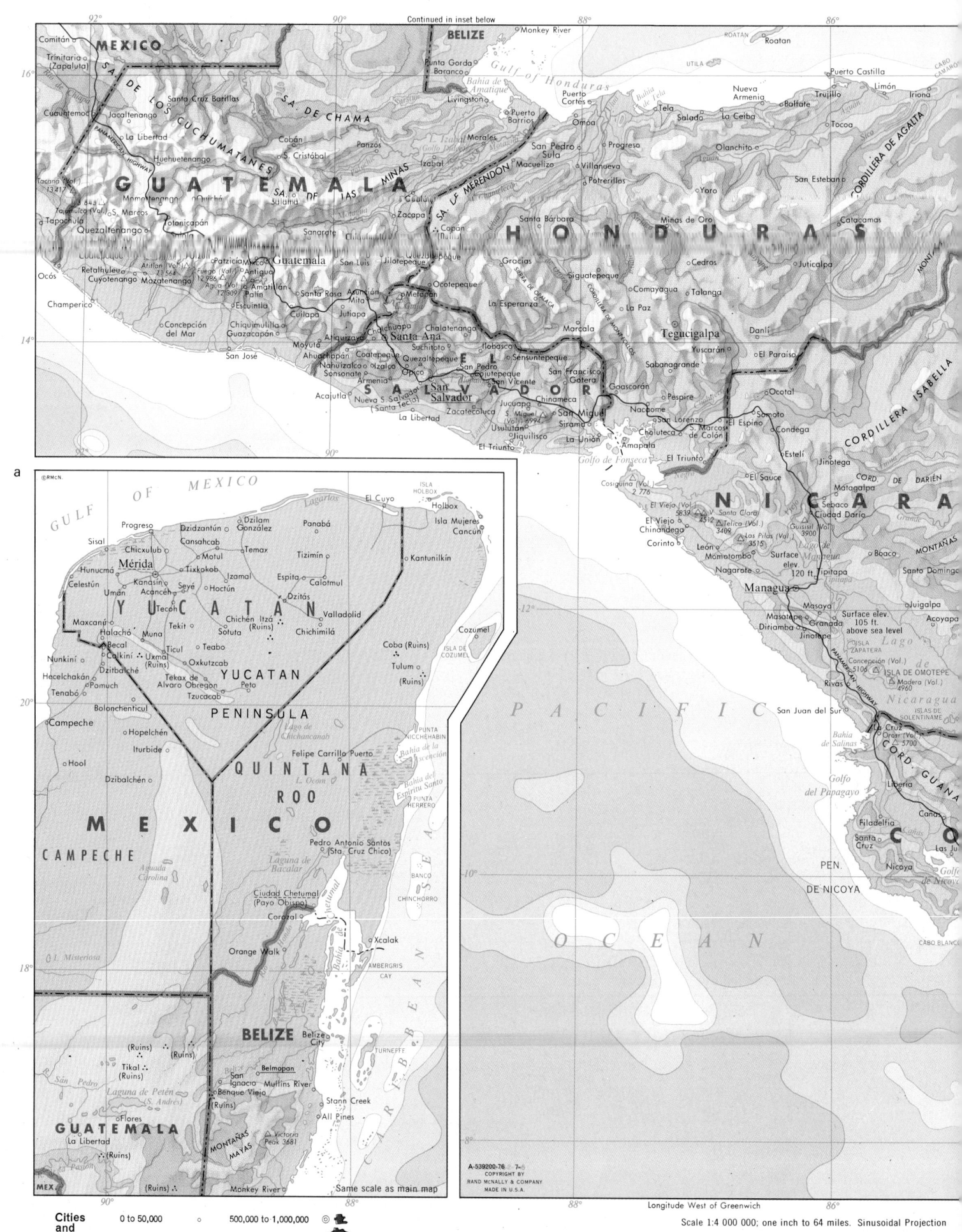

Cities
and
Towns

Scale 1:4 000 000; one inch to 64 miles. Sinusoidal Projection

Elevations and depressions are given in feet

ANGUILLA (Br.)
ST. MARTIN (Neth. and Fr.)
ST. BARTHÉLEMY (Fr.)

Longitude West of Greenwich

SABA (Neth.)

ST. EUSTATIUS (Neth.)
Mt. Misery 3792
Basseterre
ST. KITTS
Charlestown △ Nevis Peak 3596
NEVIS
ST. KITTS AND NEVIS

Codrington BARBUDA

St. Johns
Boggy Peak 1319 △
ANTIGUA AND BARBUDA

REDONDA

MONTSERRAT (Br.)
Plymouth △ Chauces Pk. 3000

Relief

Meters	Feet
3050	10 000
1525	5000
610	2000
305	1000
152.5	500
Sea Level	
152.5	500
1525	5000
3050	10 000

b

POINTE DE LA GRANDE VIGIE

L E E W A R D

Guadeloupe Passage

GRANDE TERRE
Ste. Rose Le Moule
Pointe à Pitre Ste. Anne GRANDE TERRE (Fr.)
BASSE TERRE PETITE TERRE
Soufrière 4813 △ **GUADELOUPE**
Basse Terre Capesterre (Fr.)
MARIE GALANTE (Fr.)
Grand Bourg
LES SAINTES IS.

Portsmouth Morne Diablotins 4747
St. Joseph **DOMINICA**
Roseau

Dominica Channel

Mt. Pelée (Vol.) 4583 △ Trinité
St. Pierre Pitons du Carbet 3960 △
Fort-de-France Le François
Le Marin **MARTINIQUE** (Fr.)
POINTE D'ENFER

St. Lucia Channel

Castries
Morne Gimie 3117 △ **ST. LUCIA**
Soufrière

St. Vincent Passage

Soufrière 4048 △
ST. VINCENT AND THE GRENADINES
Kingstown
BEQUIA
MUSTIQUE
CANOUAN
THE GRENADINES
CARRIACOU
Mt. St. Catherine 2757 △ Grenville
St. George's **GRENADA**

W I N D W A R D   I S.

C A R I B B E A N   S E A

A T L A N T I C   O C E A N

NORTH POINT
BARBADOS
Mt. Hillaby 1115 △ Bathsheba
Bridgetown
SOUTH POINT

© RMCN.

Same scale as main map

PUNTA PATUCA

Laguna Caratasca

COLÓN ○ Cabo Gracias a Dios
(Segovia)

CAYOS MISKITO

M O S Q U I T O S

Lone Star
Laguna Caratasca
○ Puerto Cabezas

U A
Huaunta ○ Huaunta
○ Prinzapolca
Prinzapolca

C A R I B B E A N

ISLA DE PROVIDENCIA (Colombia)

D E

Laguna las Perlas

○ Rama

SAN ANDRÉS (Colombia)
CAYOS DE ESE

LITTLE CORN
GREAT CORN (Nicaragua)

CAYOS DE ALBUQUERQUE (Colombia)

Bluefields
ISLA DE LA CIERVO

PUNTA MICO

ORD DE YOLAINA
API
Río Punta Gorda
Grande

S E A

C O S T A   D E

Bahía de San Juan del Norte

Carlos
San Juan del Norte (Greytown)

Carlos

S T A

San Ramón
parita Alajuela Heredia Guapiles ○ Caira
itacenas **San José** △ 11 260 Matina ○
Cartago ○ Irazú Vol. △ Turrialba Limón
Paraíso Turrialba

R I C A
CORDILLERA

PUNTA CAHUITA

Parrita
Quepos DE

PUNTA QUEPOS
San Isidro Cerro Chirripó 12 530
Cerro Kámuk △ 11 696
Buenos Aires
Bahía Cerro Echandi △ 10 394
de Coronada TALAMANCA
Puerto Cortés
ISLA DE CAÑO PENÍNSULA ○ Boquete
Puerto Jiménez DE OSA Volcán Barú △ 11 401
CABO MATAPALO Golfito
Concepción
La Cuesta David
Puerto Armuelles Horconcitos
PUNTA BURICA Remedios

Bahía Charco de Azul

Golfo PENÍNSULA
DE AZUERO

ISLA COIBA

Bahía Bahía Honda
de Chiriquí

PUNTA MANZANILLO Nombre de Dios El Porvenir PUNTA SAN BLAS
Portobelo Mandinga Golfo de San Blas
Colón C. Brewster 3018
Silver City CORD. DE SAN BLAS
Gatun North Gamboa Chepo
Lago Gatún Balboa Heights
Balboa **Panamá**
Chorrera Bahía de Panamá

ISTMO DE PANAMÁ

P A N A M Á

C. de Santa C. Negro 4429
Catalina 5249
SERRANÍA DE TABASARÁ
Bejuco
Penonomé
Antón
Natá ○ Río Hato
Aguadulce ○
Las Palmas Santiago
Chitré ○ Los Santos
Río de Jesús Las Tablas
Soná

ARCHIPIÉLAGO DE LAS PERLAS
San Miguel ○ ISLA DEL REY
ISLA DE SAN JOSE La Palma
ISLA SAN JOSE
PUNTA CHAME
PUNTA GARACHINE

Golfo de Parita

Golfo de Panamá

Garachiné
El Real

CABO TIBURON

S E R R A N Í A   D E L   D A R I E N

PUNTA MARIATO

ISLA JICARON

COLOMBIA

Golfo de los Mosquitos

Bocas del Toro
Bahía de Almirante
Almirante
PUNTA CHIRIQUI
Chiriquí Grande
Guabito

ESCUDO DE VERAGUAS

Laguna de Chiriquí

84° 82° 62° 18° 16° 60° 16° 14° 14° 12° 12° 10° 80° 78°

0 20 40 60 80 100 120 Miles
0 20 40 60 80 100 120 140 160 180 200 Kilometers

FLORIDA

Sanibel
Naples
Big Cypress Swamp
SEMINOLE IND. RES.
THE EVERGLADES
Delray Beach
Fort Lauderdale
Dania
GREAT ISAAC
MIAMI
Miami Beach
EVERGLADES
Cape Romano
TEN THOUSAND ISLANDS
Everglades
EVERGLADES NATIONAL PARK
Homestead
Biscayne Bay
Whitewater Bay
KEY LARGO
CAPE SABLE
Florida Bay
KEYS
FLORIDA KEYS

LITTLE BAHAMA BANK
GREAT SALE CAY
SETTLEMENT PT.
West End
GRAND BAHAMA
Freeport
Carrion Crow Harbor
PINDER POINT
GORDA CAY
LITTLE ABACO
Whale Cay
Marsh Harbour
The Marls
ELBOW
GREAT ABACO
MORES
Pelican Harbor
Cherokee Sound
Cornwall

Northwest Providence Channel

GREAT ISAAC
BROTHERS
LITTLE ISAAC
NORTH BIMINI
SOUTH BIMINI
Barnett Harbor
N. CAT CAY
GREAT STIRRUP CAY
GREAT HARBOR CAY
BERRY ISLANDS
BONDS CAY
FRAZIERS HOG CAY
WHALE CAY
SOUTHWEST PT.
ROYAL
Northeast Providence Cha

Dollar Harbor
RIDING ROCKS
ORANGE CAY
JOULTER'S CAYS
Nicolls Town
Nassau
NEW PROVIDENCE
PARADISE
SIMMS PT.
Staniard Creek
SHIP CHANNEL CAY

GULF OF MEXICO

DRY TORTUGAS
MARQUESAS KEYS
Key West
Straits of Florida

Santaren Channel
NORTH ELBOW CAYS
DOG ROCKS
CAY SAL BANK
DAMAS CAYS
CAY SAL
ANGUILLA CAYS
HURRICANE FLATS

Nicholas Channel

Old Bahama Channel

ANDROS ISLAND
Turner Sound
North Bight
Middle Bight
South Bight
GREEN CAY
BOOBY ROC
SNAP PT.
CURLY CUT CAYS
TONGUE OF THE OCEAN

Tropic of Cancer

HAVANA
CIUDAD DE LA HABANA
Marianao
Guanabacoa
Regla
Bahía Honda
Bahía de Matanzas
CAYO BLANCOS
Bahía de Cárdenas
Bahía de Santa Clara
ARCHIPIÉLAGO DE SABANA
CAYO SANTA MARÍA
CAYO COCO
CAYO GUILLERMO

Matanzas
Cárdenas
Corralillo
HABANA
San Antonio de los Baños
Bejucal
Güines
Jovellanos
Martí
MATANZAS
Colón
Sagua la Grande
CAYO FRAGOSO
VILLA CLARA
Caibarién
CAYO LOBOS

Pan de Guajaibón 2532
Candelaria
Güira de Melena
Batabanó
Unión de Reyes
Pedro Betancourt
Santo Domingo
Esperanza
Remedios
Zulueta
Bahía Buena Vista
CAYO ROMANO

PINAR DEL RÍO
Consolación del Sur
Los Palacios
VUELTA
Pinar del Río
Bondrón
Navajas
Jagüey Grande
Santa Clara
Cruces
Lajas
Camajuaní
Yaguajay
Morón
SANCTI SPIRITUS
CIEGO DE ÁVILA
Laguna de Leche

ARCHIPIÉLAGO DE LOS COLORADOS
SIERRA
Mantua
Guane
San Diego Martínez
PUNTA GORDA
GOLFO DE BATABANÓ
PENÍNSULA DE ZAPATA
Aguada
Rodas
Palmira
CIENFUEGOS
Florida
Placetas
Jatibonico
Ciego de Ávila
Júcaro
Fomento
B
CAMAGÜEY

Bahía de Guadiana
PEN. DE GUANAHACABIBES
CABO CORRIENTES
Ensenada de Cortés
CAYO DE DIOS
ISLAS DE MANGLES
CAYOS LAGUNA
CAYOS DE JUAN LUIS
Ensenada de la Broa
Bahía Cochinos
Cienfuegos
Palmira
Pico San Juan
SIERRA DE TRINIDAD
Trinidad
Sancti Spíritus
Minas
Santa Lucía
Camagüey
Nuevitas
Bahía de Nuevi
PTA. FRANCES
Nueva Gerona
CAYOS INGLES
CAYOS CANARREOS
Santa Fé
ISLA DE LA JUVENTUD
BANCO JARDINES
CAYO LARGO
BANCO XAGUA
Bahía Cienfuegos
Casilda
Tunas de Zaza
CAYOS ANA MARÍA
CAYO GUAJABA
CAYO SABINAL
LAS TUNAS

CABO PEPE
CAYO ROSARIO
CAYO CANTILES
CAYOS CINCO BALAS
CAYOS DE LAS DOCE LEGUAS
Canal de Caballones
Santa Cruz del Sur
GOLFO DE GUACANAYABO
Guayabal
Manzanillo
Bay
Campechuela
GRAN
Victoria de las Tunas
Guayabal

C A R I B B E A N

Niquero
SIERRA
Pico Ojo del Toro 1748
Pico Turquino 64
CABO CRUZ

LITTLE CAYMAN
CAYMAN BRAC (Br.)
CAYMAN ISLANDS
George Town
GRAND CAYMAN

S E A

Montego Bay
Lucea
Falmouth
St. Ann's Bay
GALINA
Annotto Bay
SOUTH NEGRIL PT.
Savanna la Mar
JAMAICA
Mt. Denham 3236
Black River
May Pen
Kingst
Spanish T
Portland Bight
GT. PEDRO BLUFF
PORTLAND PT.

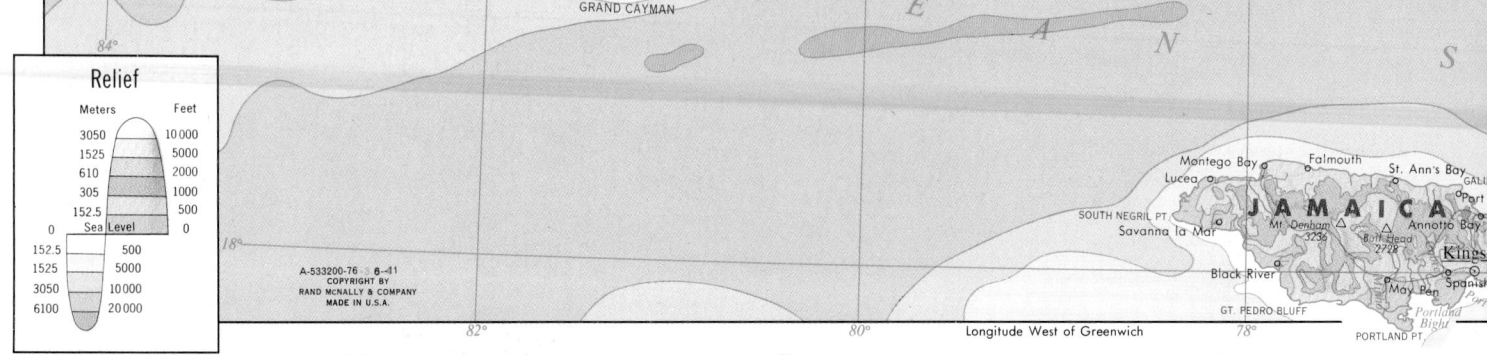

Relief		
Meters		Feet
3050		10 000
1525		5000
610		2000
305		1000
152.5		500
0	Sea Level	0
152.5		500
1525		5000
3050		10 000
6100		20 000

A-533200-76   6-41
COPYRIGHT BY
RAND MCNALLY & COMPANY
MADE IN U.S.A.

Longitude West of Greenwich

Cities and Towns
0 to 50,000
50,000 to 500,000
500,000 to 1,000,000
1,000,000 and over

Scale 1:4 000 000; one inch to 64 miles. Conic Projection
Elevations and depressions are given in feet.

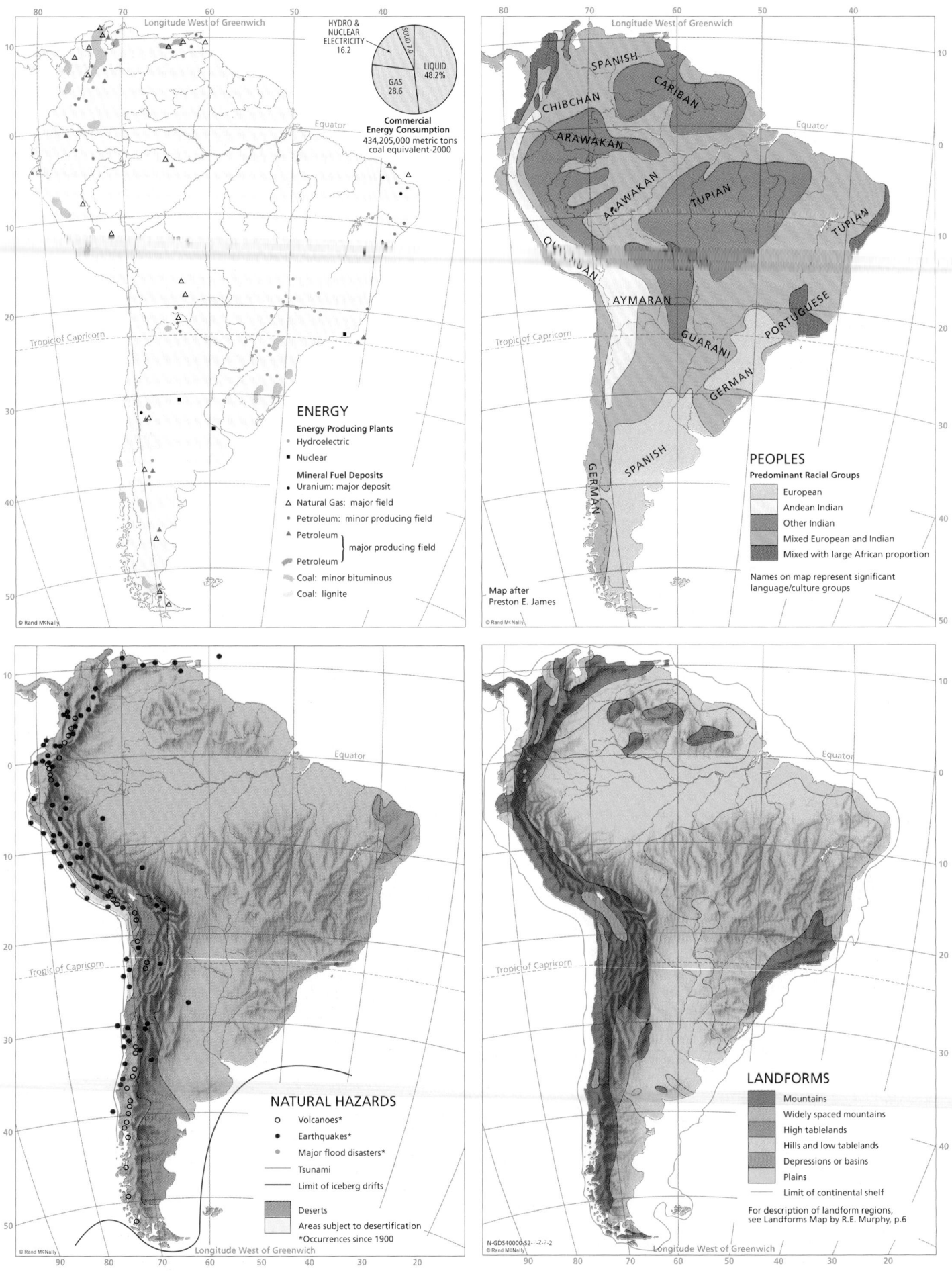

ENERGY

Energy Producing Plants

- Hydroelectric
- Nuclear

Mineral Fuel Deposits

- Uranium: major deposit
- △ Natural Gas: major field
- Petroleum: minor producing field
- ▲ Petroleum
- Petroleum } major producing field
- Coal: minor bituminous
- Coal: lignite

HYDRO & NUCLEAR ELECTRICITY 16.2

SOLID 7.0

LIQUID 48.2%

GAS 28.6

Commercial Energy Consumption
434,205,000 metric tons coal equivalent-2000

PEOPLES

Predominant Racial Groups

- European
- Andean Indian
- Other Indian
- Mixed European and Indian
- Mixed with large African proportion

Names on map represent significant language/culture groups

Map after Preston E. James

SPANISH
CHIBCHAN
CARIBAN
ARAWAKAN
ARAWAKAN
TUPIAN
TUPIAN
QUECHUAN
AYMARAN
GUARANI
PORTUGUESE
GERMAN
GERMAN
SPANISH

NATURAL HAZARDS

- ○ Volcanoes*
- ● Earthquakes*
- Major flood disasters*
- Tsunami
- Limit of iceberg drifts
- Deserts
- Areas subject to desertification

*Occurrences since 1900

LANDFORMS

- Mountains
- Widely spaced mountains
- High tablelands
- Hills and low tablelands
- Depressions or basins
- Plains
- Limit of continental shelf

For description of landform regions, see Landforms Map by R.E. Murphy, p.6

N-GDS40000-S2- -2-2-2

© Rand McNally

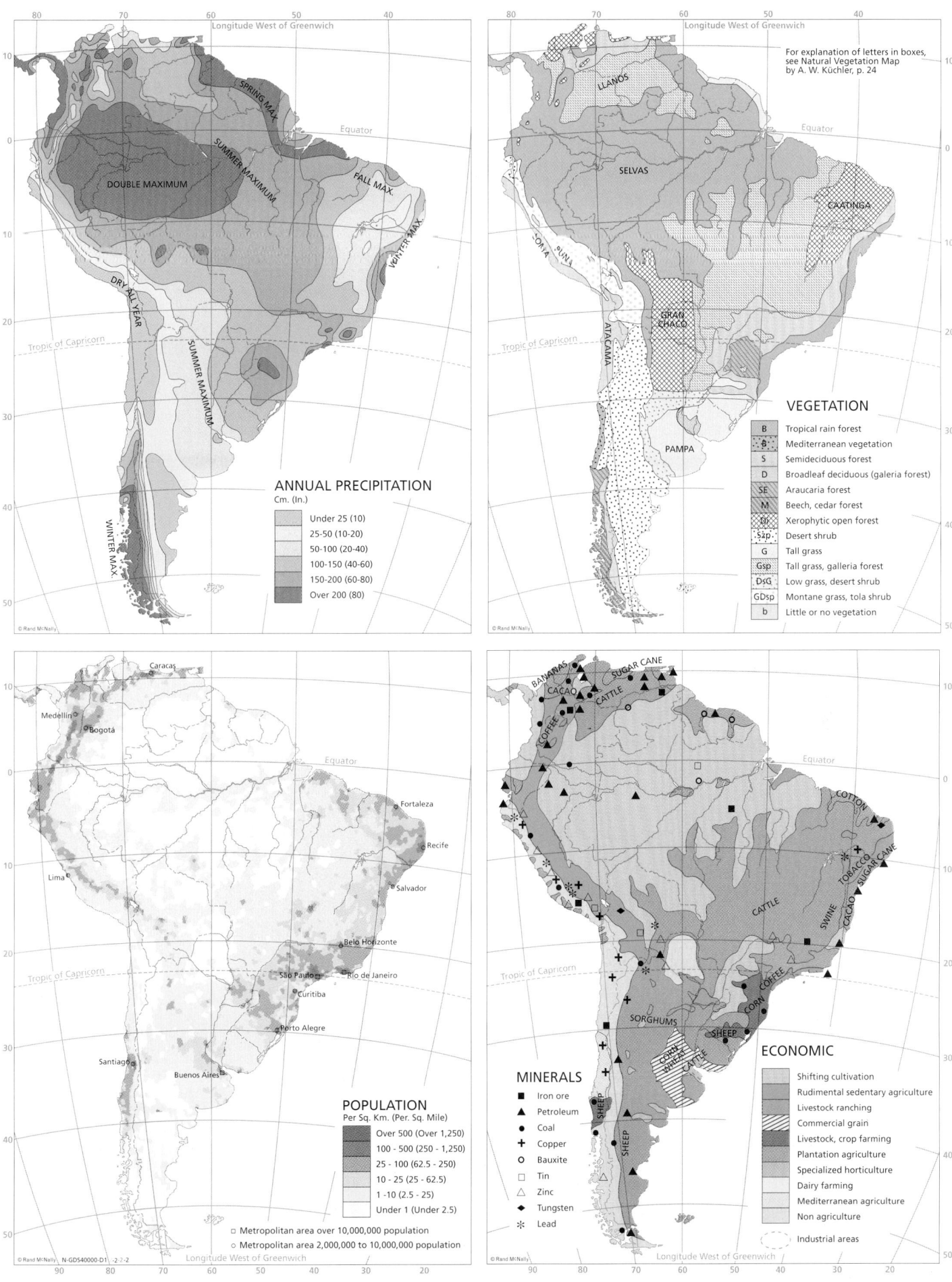

ANNUAL PRECIPITATION
Cm. (In.)

- Under 25 (10)
- 25-50 (10-20)
- 50-100 (20-40)
- 100-150 (40-60)
- 150-200 (60-80)
- Over 200 (80)

VEGETATION

B	Tropical rain forest
B	Mediterranean vegetation
S	Semideciduous forest
D	Broadleaf deciduous (galeria forest)
SE	Araucaria forest
M	Beech, cedar forest
Df	Xerophytic open forest
Szp	Desert shrub
G	Tall grass
Gsp	Tall grass, galleria forest
DsG	Low grass, desert shrub
GDsp	Montane grass, tola shrub
b	Little or no vegetation

For explanation of letters in boxes, see Natural Vegetation Map by A. W. Küchler, p. 24

POPULATION
Per Sq. Km. (Per. Sq. Mile)

- Over 500 (Over 1,250)
- 100 - 500 (250 - 1,250)
- 25 - 100 (62.5 - 250)
- 10 - 25 (25 - 62.5)
- 1 - 10 (2.5 - 25)
- Under 1 (Under 2.5)

□ Metropolitan area over 10,000,000 population
○ Metropolitan area 2,000,000 to 10,000,000 population

MINERALS

- ■ Iron ore
- ▲ Petroleum
- ● Coal
- ✛ Copper
- ○ Bauxite
- □ Tin
- △ Zinc
- ◆ Tungsten
- ✳ Lead

ECONOMIC

- Shifting cultivation
- Rudimental sedentary agriculture
- Livestock ranching
- Commercial grain
- Livestock, crop farming
- Plantation agriculture
- Specialized horticulture
- Dairy farming
- Mediterranean agriculture
- Non agriculture
- Industrial areas

Scale 1:40 000 000; one inch to 630 miles. Lambert's Azimuthal, Equal Area Projection
Elevations and depressions are given in feet

40,000 SQ MI
AREA

0   300   600
Miles

0   200   400   600   800   1000 Miles
0   400   800   1200   1600 Kilometers

A-540000-26 1-4-7-16
COPYRIGHT BY
RAND McNALLY & COMPANY
MADE IN U.S.A.

TROPIC OF CANCER

HAVANA
CUBA
PEN DE YUCATÁN
Bahía de Campeche
HISPANIOLA
JAMAICA
Gulf of Honduras
PUERTO RICO (U.S.A.)
San Juan
PUERTO RICO
GUADELOUPE (Fr.)
MARTINIQUE (Fr.)
BARBADOS
NORTH AMERICAN BASIN

CARIBBEAN SEA
WEST INDIES

ATLANTIC OCEAN

CENTRAL
AMERICA
Lago de Nicaragua
Panama
IST. DE PAN.
ISLA DEL COCO (Costa Rica)
ISLA DE MALPELO (Colombia)

PUNTA DE GALLINAS
Barranquilla
Cartagena
Maracaibo
Valencia
CARACAS
La Guaira
Port of Spain
TRINIDAD AND TOBAGO
Mérida
VENEZUELA
Ciudad Bolívar
Orinoco
Cerro Icutú 7800
Georgetown
Paramaribo
GUYANA
SURINAME
FR. GUIANA
Cayenne
LLANOS
Medellín
BOGOTÁ
Boa Vista do Rio Branco
GUIANA HIGHLANDS

COLOMBIA
Guaviare
Quito
Cotopaxi 19,347
ECUADOR
Chimborazo 20,702
Guayaquil
ARCHIPIÉLAGO DE COLÓN (GALÁPAGOS ISLANDS) (Ec.)
Golfo de Guayaquil
Iquitos
Leticia
Napo
Putumayo
Japurá
Negro (Solimões)
Manaus (Manáos)
Amazon (Amazonas)
ILHA DE MARAJÓ
Belém (Pará)
São Luís (Maranhão)
Equator
ROCEDOS SÃO PEDRO E SÃO PAULO (Brazil)

Chiclayo
Trujillo
Nevs. Huascarán 22,133
PERU
LIMA
Callao
Cusco
Volcán Misti 19,101
Arequipa
Mollendo
Pacaya
Juruá
Purus
Madeira
Tapajós
Xingu
Tocantins
Fortaleza (Ceará)
ARQUIPÉLAGO FERNANDO DE NORONHA (Brazil)
Teresina
CABO DE SÃO ROQUE
Natal
João Pessoa (Paraíba)
RECIFE (Pernambuco)
Maceió

BRAZIL
CHAPADA DE MATO GROSSO
Cuiabá
Brasília
Diamantina
BRAZILIAN HIGHLANDS
SERRA DO ESPINHAÇO
Salvador (Bahia)

La Paz
Nev. Illimani 20,741
BOLIVIA
Sucre
Potosí
Lago de Poopó
Iquique
Antofagasta
DESIERTO DE ATACAMA
GRAN CHACO
PARAGUAY
Asunción
Belo Horizonte
Pico da Bandeira 9482
Vitória
SÃO PAULO
Diamantina

Tropic of Capricorn
ISLA DE SAN FÉLIX (Chile)
ISLA DE SAN AMBROSIO (Chile)
Cerro Azufre (Copiapó) 19,947
Cerro Aconcagua 22,835
Salta
Tucumán
Corrientes
Iguassú Falls
Santos
RIO DE JANEIRO
CABO FRIO
Florianópolis

Copiapó
Coquimbo
ISLAS JUAN FERNÁNDEZ (Chile)
Santa Fe
Salto
URUGUAY
Rio Grande
Porto Alegre

Valparaíso
SANTIAGO
Mendoza
Córdoba
Rosario
BUENOS AIRES
MONTEVIDEO
La Plata
PAMPAS
Río de la Plata

Concepción
ARGENTINA
Colorado
Bahía Blanca

Valdivia
Viedma
Golfo San Matías

Puerto Montt
ISLA DE CHILOÉ
ARCHIPIÉLAGO DE LOS CHONOS
Chubut
Monte San Valentín 13,314
Comodoro Rivadavia
Golfo San Jorge

WELLINGTON
HANOVER
DESOLACIÓN
Punta Arenas
Mt. Sarmiento 8100
Estrecho de Magallanes
FALKLAND IS. (ISLAS MALVINAS) (Br.)
Río Gallegos
Stanley
TIERRA DEL FUEGO
ISLA DE LOS ESTADOS
CABO DE HORNOS (CAPE HORN)

PACIFIC OCEAN

ATLANTIC OCEAN

Drake Passage

SOUTH GEORGIA (Br.)
SOUTH SANDWICH ISLANDS
SOUTH ORKNEY IS. (Br.)
SOUTH SHETLAND IS. (Br.)
JOINVILLE
JAMES ROSS
Antarctic Circle

A-540000-76-3-16
COPYRIGHT BY
RAND MCNALLY & COMPANY
MADE IN U.S.A.

Longitude West of Greenwich

Relief	
Meters	Feet
3050	10 000
1525	5000
610	2000
305	1000
0	Sea Level	0
152.5	500
1525	5000
3050	10 000
6100	20 000

0 200 400 600 800 1000 Miles
0 400 800 1200 1600 Kilometers

Scale 1:40 000 000, one inch to 630 miles. Lambert's Azimuthal. Equal Area Projection
Elevations and depressions are given in feet

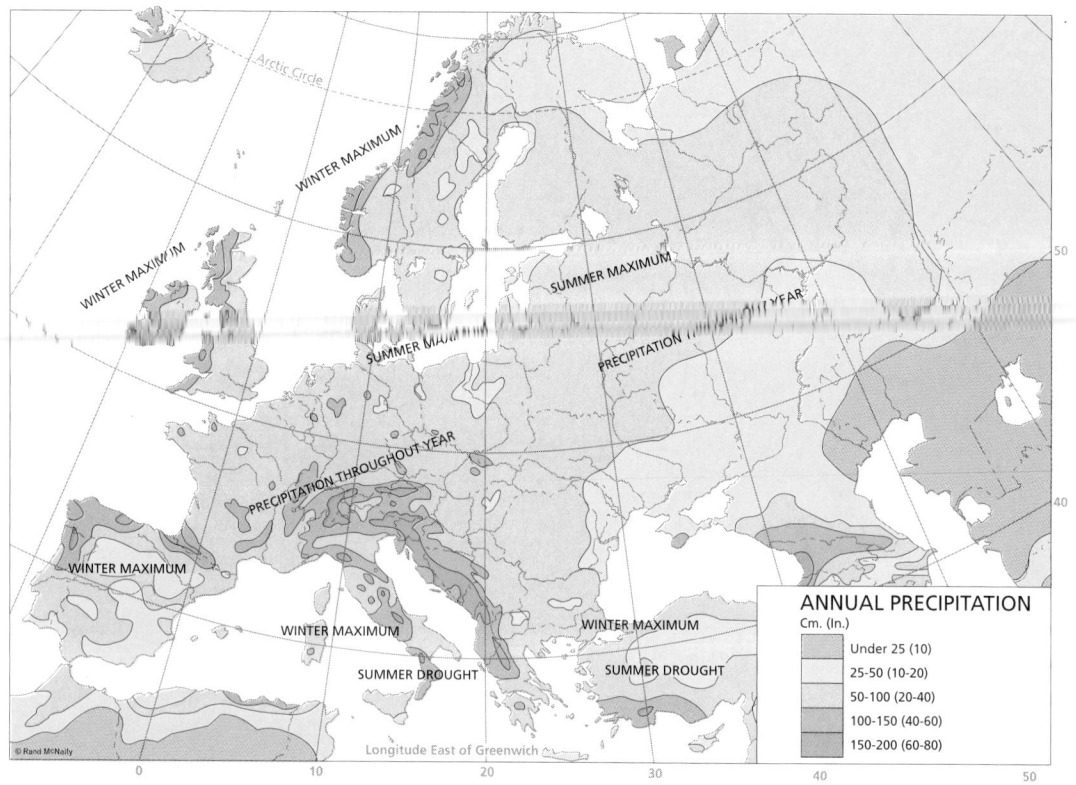

WINTER MAXIMUM

WINTER MAXIMUM

SUMMER MAXIMUM

SUMMER MAXIMUM

PRECIPITATION THROUGHOUT YEAR

PRECIPITATION THROUGHOUT YEAR

WINTER MAXIMUM

WINTER MAXIMUM

WINTER MAXIMUM

SUMMER DROUGHT

SUMMER DROUGHT

Longitude East of Greenwich

© Rand McNally

ANNUAL PRECIPITATION

Cm. (In.)

	Under 25 (10)
	25-50 (10-20)
	50-100 (20-40)
	100-150 (40-60)
	150-200 (60-80)

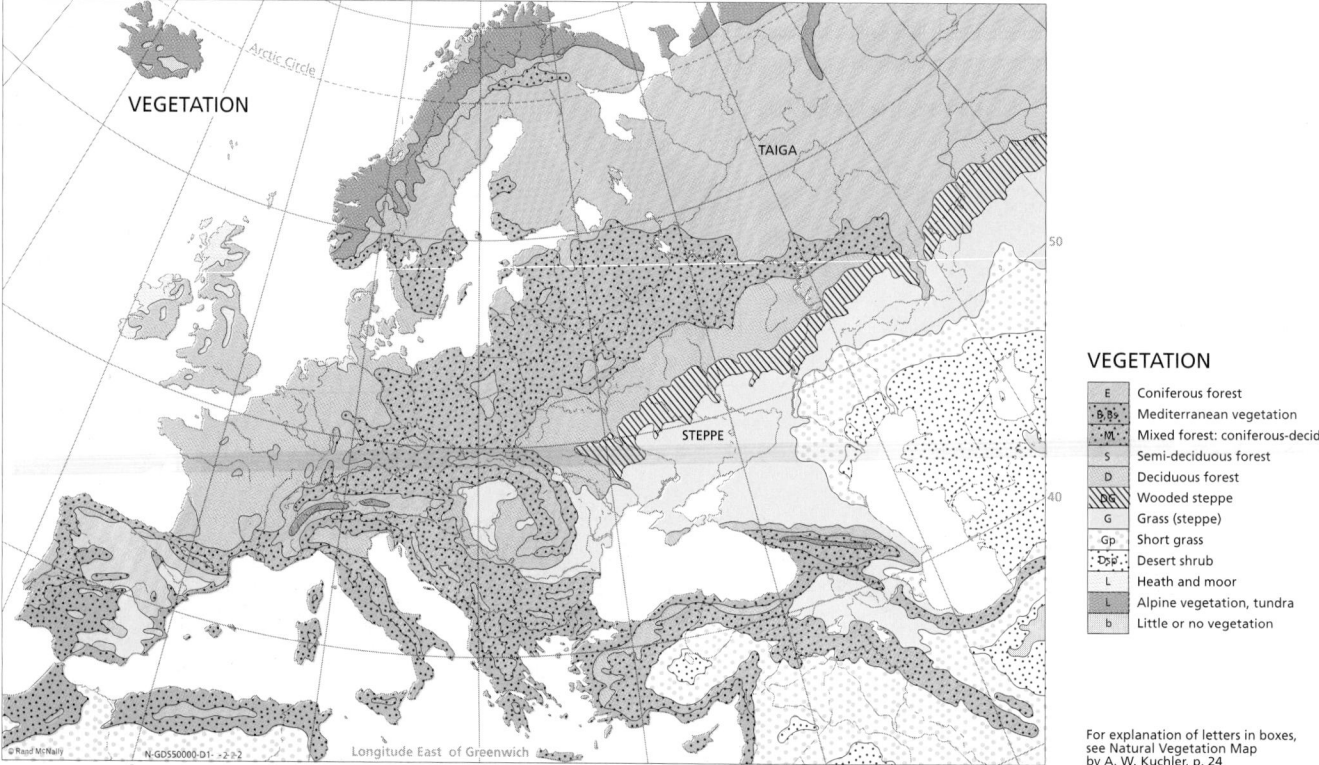

VEGETATION

Arctic Circle

TAIGA

STEPPE

Longitude East of Greenwich

© Rand McNally

N-GDS50000-D1 -2-2²

VEGETATION

E	Coniferous forest
B,Bs	Mediterranean vegetation
M	Mixed forest: coniferous-deciduous
S	Semi-deciduous forest
D	Deciduous forest
DG	Wooded steppe
G	Grass (steppe)
Gp	Short grass
Dsh	Desert shrub
L	Heath and moor
L	Alpine vegetation, tundra
b	Little or no vegetation

For explanation of letters in boxes,
see Natural Vegetation Map
by A. W. Kuchler, p. 24

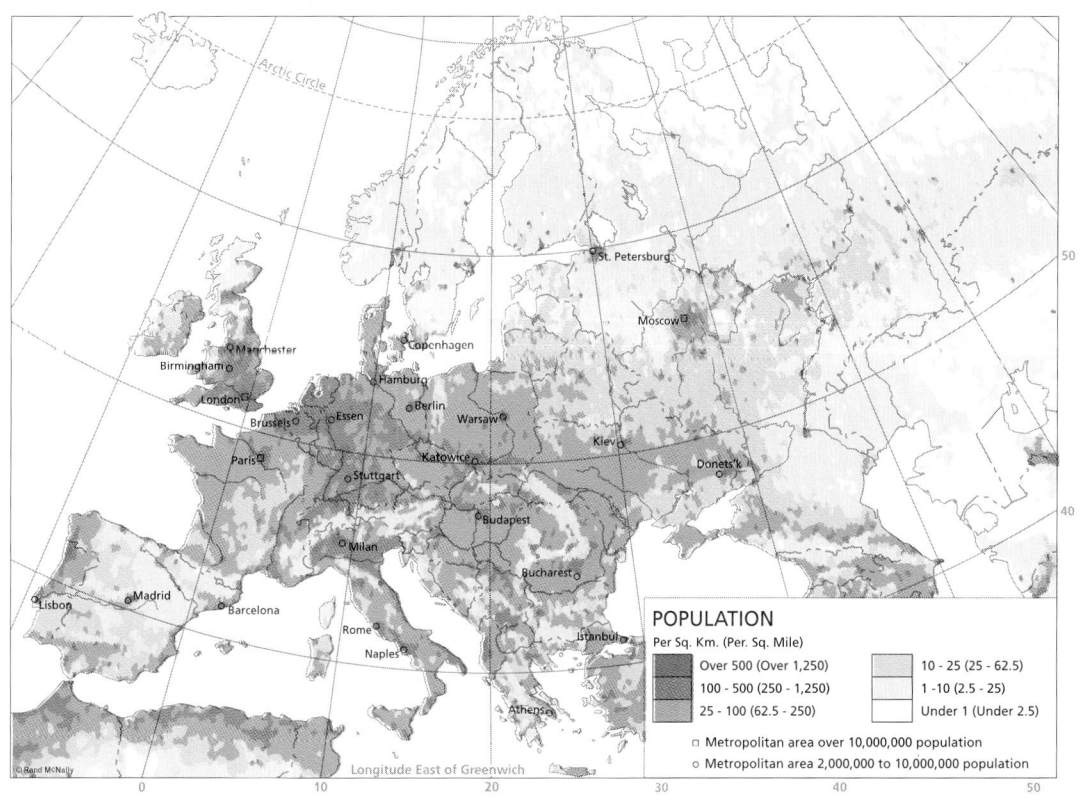

POPULATION

Per Sq. Km. (Per. Sq. Mile)

Over 500 (Over 1,250)	10 - 25 (25 - 62.5)
100 - 500 (250 - 1,250)	1 -10 (2.5 - 25)
25 - 100 (62.5 - 250)	Under 1 (Under 2.5)

□ Metropolitan area over 10,000,000 population
o Metropolitan area 2,000,000 to 10,000,000 population

© Rand McNally

Longitude East of Greenwich

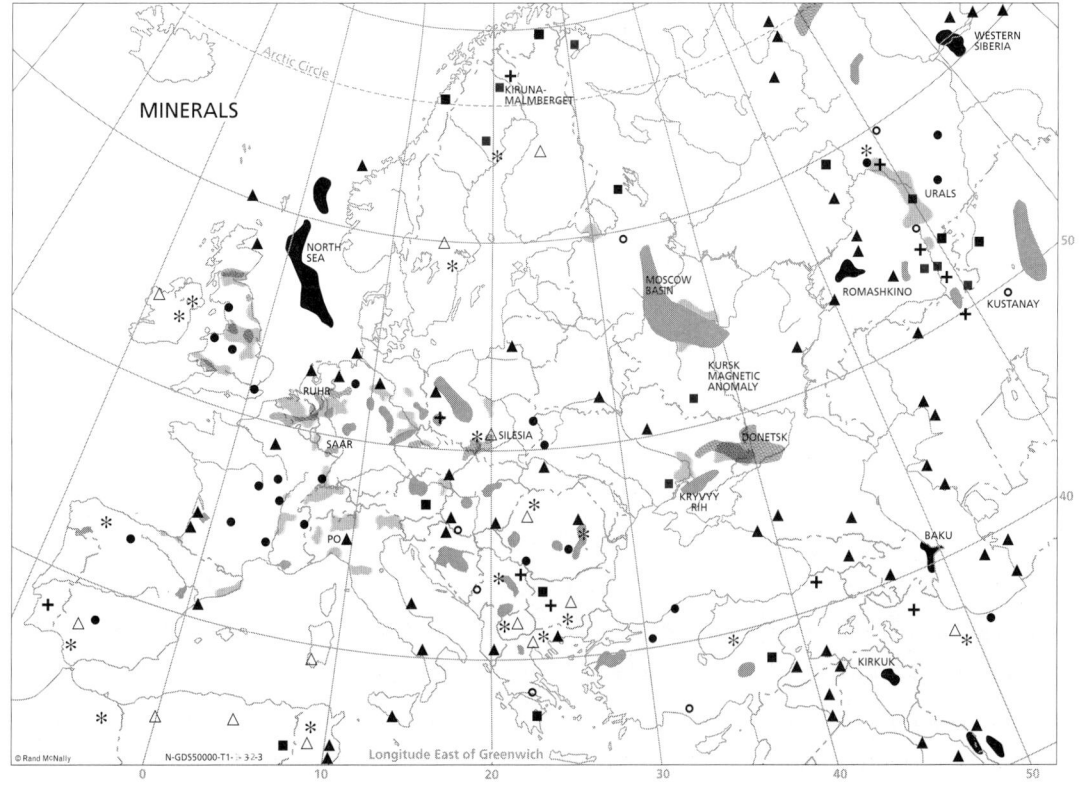

MINERALS

- ▨ Industrial areas
- ▨ Major coal deposits
- ⬤ Major petroleum deposits
- ▬ Lignite deposits
- ▲ Minor petroleum deposits
- ● Minor coal deposits
- ■ Major iron ore
- ▪ Minor iron ore
- ✳ Lead
- ○ Bauxite
- △ Zinc
- ✚ Copper

© Rand McNally   N-GD550000-T1- 3 2-3   Longitude East of Greenwich

Urban

Cropland

Cropland & Woodland

Cropland & Grazing Land

Grassland, Grazing Land

Forest, Woodland

Swamp, Marshland

Tundra

Shrub, Sparse Grass,
Wasteland (pattern)

Barren Land

Oasis

20° 10° 0° 10° 20° 30°

Reykjavik

ATLANTIC

OCEAN

60°

50°

40°

Longitude West of Greenwich 0° Longitude East of Greenwich 10° 20°

Scale 1: 16,000,000; one inch to 250 miles. Conic Projection

0 50 100 200 300 400 500 Miles
0 100 200 400 600 800 Kilometers

Narvik
Murma
Trondheim
Bergen
Oslo
Helsinki ST. PETERSBURG
Stockholm Tallinn
Göteborg
Riga
Copenhagen Kaliningrad Baltic Sea Vilnius
Minsk
Glasgow
Belfast
MANCHESTER
Dublin
Hamburg Elbe BERLIN Oder Warsaw Pripet
Amsterdam
LONDON
Antwerp Essen Leipzig Kraków L'viv
Brest
PARIS Seine Strasbourg Prague CARPATHIANS
Loire Rhine Danube VIENNA BUDAPEST
Munich Tisza
A Coruña Zürich A L P S
Bordeaux Lyon MILAN Zagreb Belgrade
Bilbao Garonne Venice Sava Bucharest
Duero Rhône Genoa Danube
MADRID PYRENEES Marseille CORSICA ROME Sofia
Lisbon Ebro BARCELONA Tiranë
Sevilla SARDINIA Naples Athens
ISLAS BALEARES Tyrrhenian Sea Aegean Sea
Tanger Palermo
Casablanca Oran Algiers Tunis SICILY
ATLAS MOUNTAINS M e d i t e r r a n e a n S e a
MALTA CRETE

North Sea
Bay of Biscay
Gulf of Bothnia
Adriatic Sea
Frankfurt
Sofia

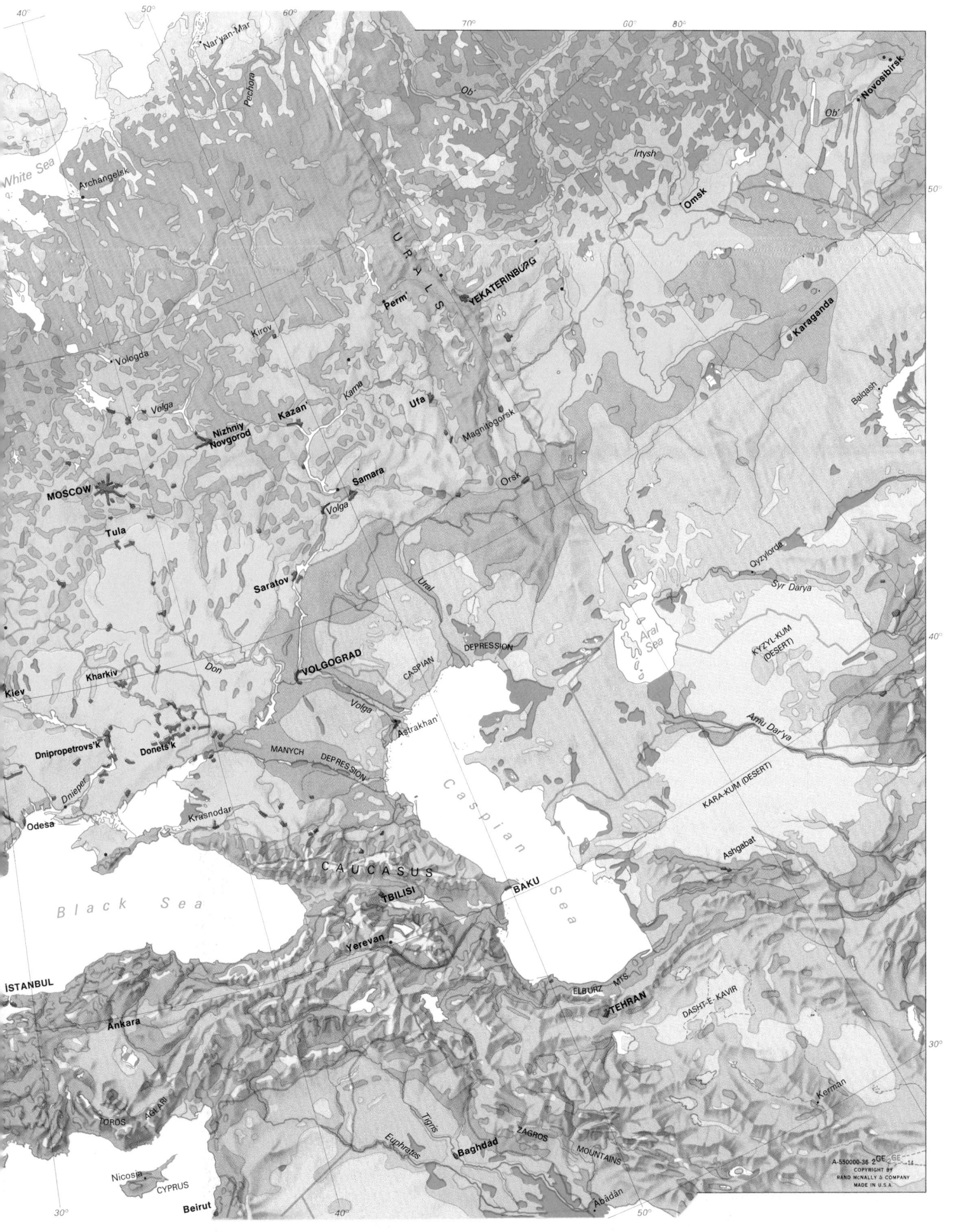

White Sea

Nar'yan-Mar

Pechora

Ob'

Ob'

Novosibirsk

Archangelsk

Irtysh

Omsk

U R A L S

Vologda

Kirov

Perm'

YEKATERINBURG

Karaganda

Volga

Kama

Ufa

Balqash

Nizhniy Novgorod

Kazan'

Magnitogorsk

Orsk

Samara

Volga

Qyzylorda

Syr Darya

MOSCOW

Saratov

Ural

Aral Sea

KYZYL-KUM (DESERT)

Tula

DEPRESSION

CASPIAN

VOLGOGRAD

Kharkiv

Don

Volga

Amu Dar'ya

Kiev

Astrakhan'

Dnipropetrovs'k

Donets'k

MANYCH   DEPRESSION

KARA-KUM (DESERT)

Dnieper

C a s p i a n

Odesa

Krasnodar

Ashgabat

C A U C A S U S

BAKU

S e a

Black   Sea

TBILISI

İSTANBUL

Yerevan

Ankara

ELBURZ   MTS.

DASHT-E KAVIR

TEHRAN

Kerman

TOROS

AĞLARI

Tigris

ZAGROS

Nicosia

Euphrates

Baghdad

MOUNTAINS

CYPRUS

Beirut

Ābādān

Scale 1:16 000 000; one inch to 250 miles. Conic Projection
Elevations and depressions are given in feet.

PHYSIOGRAPHIC PROVINCES

Western Uplands (Mostly old rocks) | Great European Plain | Central Uplands | Alpine System

EUROPE DURING THE ICE AGE

Tundra | Forest | Steppe

PHYSIOGRAPHY
BY
ERWIN RAISZ

LITHOLOGY AND STRUCTURE

Unconsolidated deposits: alluvium, sands, bottom lands.

Strongly folded and faulted rocks. The "Younger Series" in Norway.

Essentially horizontal sediments, also uplands and terraces in the plains.

Metamorphic and intrusive igneous rocks.

Moderately folded sedimentary rocks.

volcanics, lava flows, basalts, etc.

LANDFORMS

PLATEAUS | CUESTAS | SAND

HILLS | FOLDED MOUNTAINS | SINKS

MOUNTAINS | BASIN RANGES | MORAINES

MESAS | VOLCANO AND LAVA | DRUMLINS

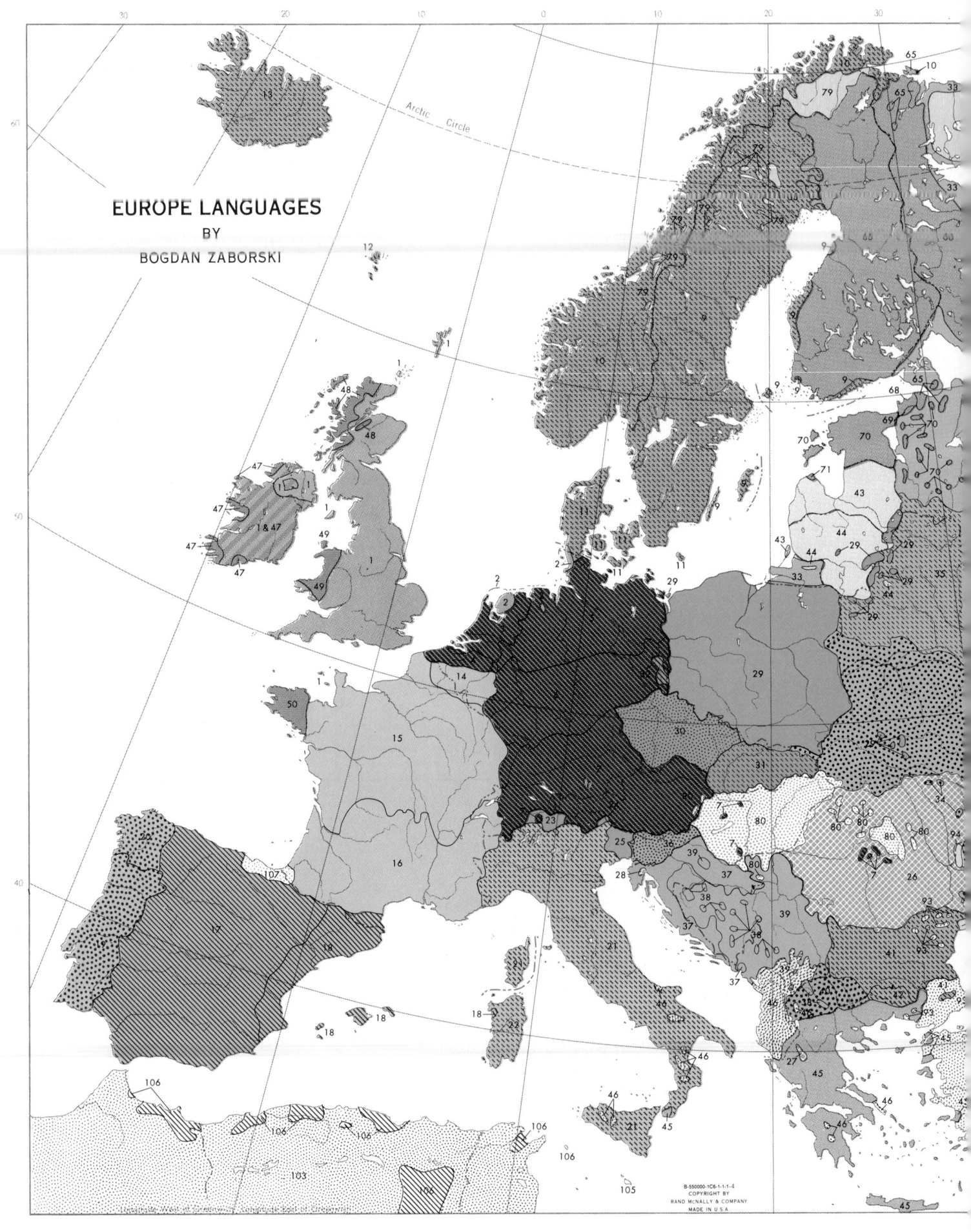

EUROPE LANGUAGES
BY
BOGDAN ZABORSKI

Scale 1:16,500,000; one inch to 260 miles Conic Projection

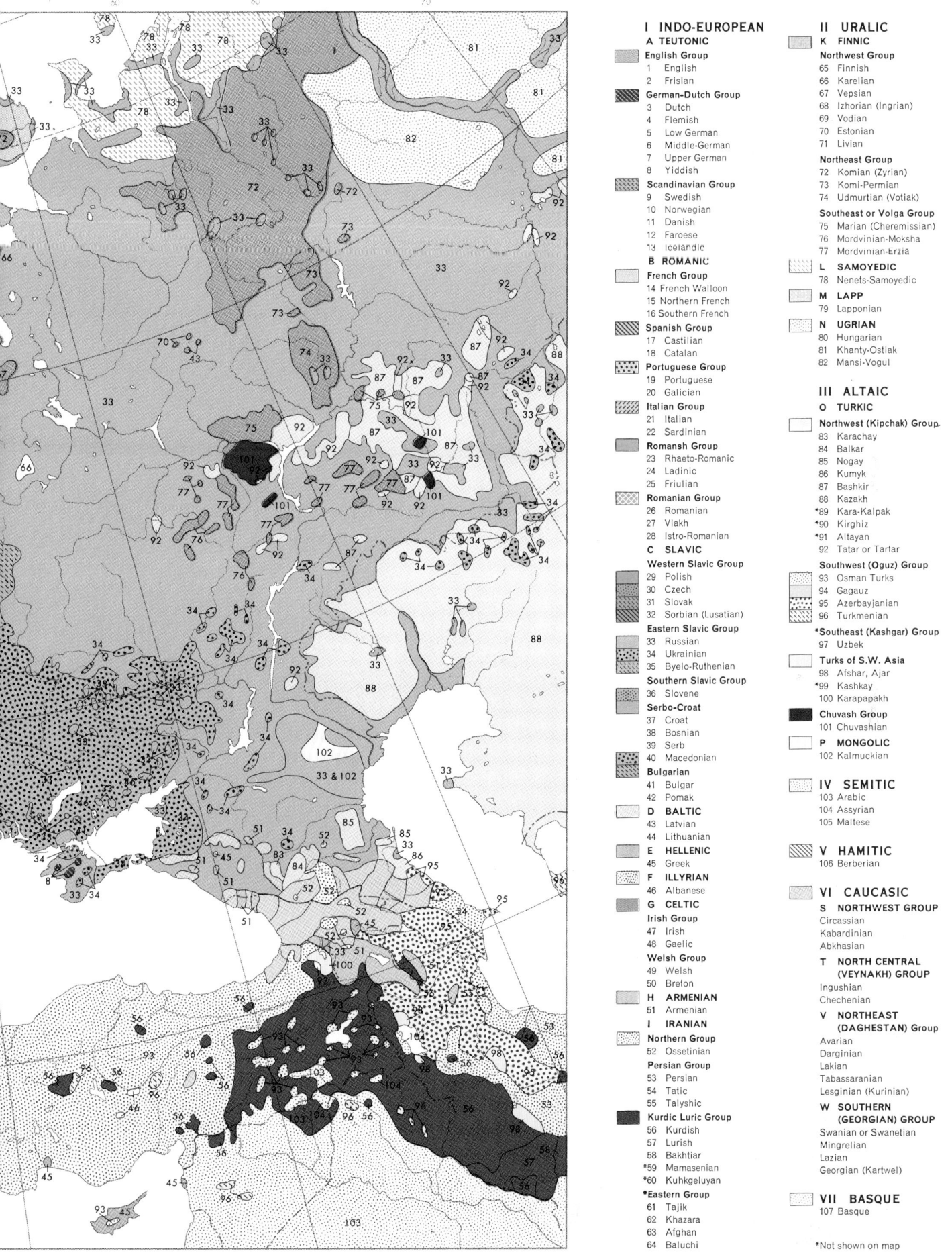

I INDO-EUROPEAN

A TEUTONIC

English Group
1. English
2. Frisian

German-Dutch Group
3. Dutch
4. Flemish
5. Low German
6. Middle-German
7. Upper German
8. Yiddish

Scandinavian Group
9. Swedish
10. Norwegian
11. Danish
12. Faroese
13. Icelandic

B ROMANIC

French Group
14. French Walloon
15. Northern French
16. Southern French

Spanish Group
17. Castilian
18. Catalan

Portuguese Group
19. Portuguese
20. Galician

Italian Group
21. Italian
22. Sardinian

Romansh Group
23. Rhaeto-Romanic
24. Ladinic
25. Friulian

Romanian Group
26. Romanian
27. Vlakh
28. Istro-Romanian

C SLAVIC

Western Slavic Group
29. Polish
30. Czech
31. Slovak
32. Sorbian (Lusatian)

Eastern Slavic Group
33. Russian
34. Ukrainian
35. Byelo-Ruthenian

Southern Slavic Group
36. Slovene
Serbo-Croat
37. Croat
38. Bosnian
39. Serb
40. Macedonian
Bulgarian
41. Bulgar
42. Pomak

D BALTIC
43. Latvian
44. Lithuanian

E HELLENIC
45. Greek

F ILLYRIAN
46. Albanese

G CELTIC

Irish Group
47. Irish
48. Gaelic

Welsh Group
49. Welsh
50. Breton

H ARMENIAN
51. Armenian

I IRANIAN

Northern Group
52. Ossetinian

Persian Group
53. Persian
54. Tatic
55. Talyshic

Kurdic Luric Group
56. Kurdish
57. Lurish
58. Bakhtiar
*59. Mamasenian
*60. Kuhkgeluyan

***Eastern Group**
61. Tajik
62. Khazara
63. Afghan
64. Baluchi

II URALIC

K FINNIC

Northwest Group
65. Finnish
66. Karelian
67. Vepsian
68. Izhorian (Ingrian)
69. Vodian
70. Estonian
71. Livian

Northeast Group
72. Komian (Zyrian)
73. Komi-Permian
74. Udmurtian (Votiak)

Southeast or Volga Group
75. Marian (Cheremissian)
76. Mordvinian-Moksha
77. Mordvinian-Erzia

L SAMOYEDIC
78. Nenets-Samoyedic

M LAPP
79. Lapponian

N UGRIAN
80. Hungarian
81. Khanty-Ostiak
82. Mansi-Vogul

III ALTAIC

O TURKIC

Northwest (Kipchak) Group
83. Karachay
84. Balkar
85. Nogay
86. Kumyk
87. Bashkir
88. Kazakh
*89. Kara-Kalpak
*90. Kirghiz
*91. Altayan
92. Tatar or Tartar

Southwest (Oguz) Group
93. Osman Turks
94. Gagauz
95. Azerbayjanian
96. Turkmenian

***Southeast (Kashgar) Group**
97. Uzbek

Turks of S.W. Asia
98. Afshar, Ajar
*99. Kashkay
100. Karapapakh

Chuvash Group
101. Chuvashian

P MONGOLIC
102. Kalmuckian

IV SEMITIC
103. Arabic
104. Assyrian
105. Maltese

V HAMITIC
106. Berberian

VI CAUCASIC

S NORTHWEST GROUP
Circassian
Kabardinian
Abkhasian

T NORTH CENTRAL (VEYNAKH) GROUP
Ingushian
Chechenian

V NORTHEAST (DAGHESTAN) Group
Avarian
Darginian
Lakian
Tabassaranian
Lesginian (Kurinian)

W SOUTHERN (GEORGIAN) GROUP
Swanian or Swanetian
Mingrelian
Lazian
Georgian (Kartwel)

VII BASQUE
107. Basque

*Not shown on map

Scale 1: 16 000 000; one inch to 250 miles. Conic Projection
Elevations and depressions are given in feet

Continued on pages 194-195

Relief

Meters		Feet
3050		10 000
1525		5000
610		2000
305		1000
152.5		500
0	Sea Level	0
152.5		Below Sea Level
152.5		500
1525		5000
3050		10 000

Scale 1: 16 000 000; one inch to 250 miles. Conic Projection
Elevations and depressions are given in feet

Longitude West of Greenwich   Longitude East of Greenwich

Continued on pages 230-231

| 0 | 50 | 100 | 200 | 300 | 400 | 500 Miles |

| 0 | 100 | 200 | 400 | 600 | 800 Kilometers |

Continued on pages 184–185

Continued on pages 198–199

a

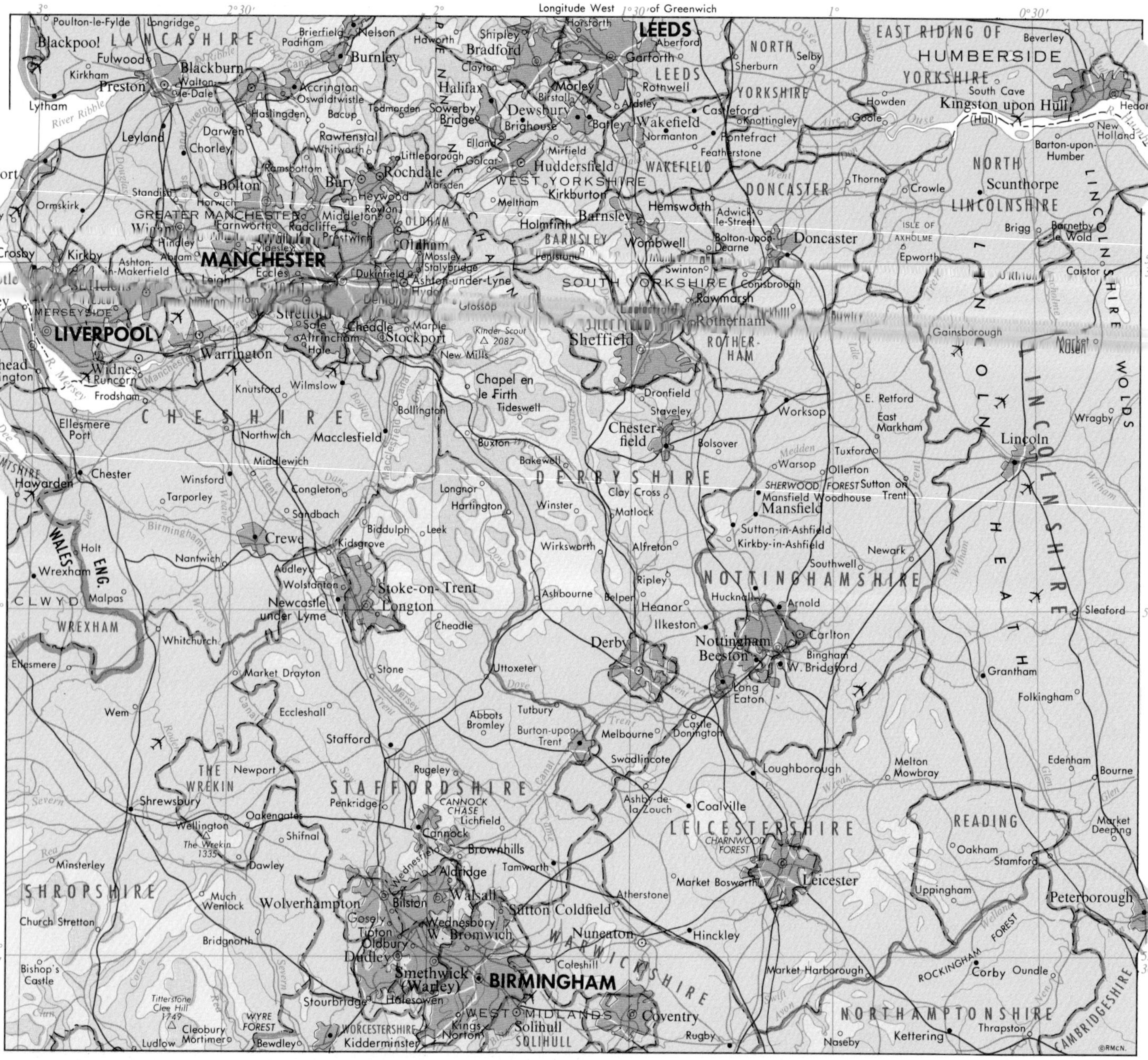

Longitude West of Greenwich

Blackpool LANCASHIRE
Poulton-le-Fylde Longridge Brierfield Nelson Haworth Shipley EAST RIDING OF HUMBERSIDE
Fulwood Kirkham Padiham Burnley Clayton Bradford LEEDS Aberford Sherburn Selby Beverley
Blackburn Accrington Oswaldtwistle Halifax Morley Aldsley LEEDS NORTH South Cave
Preston Walton-le-Dale Haslingden Bacup Todmorden Sowerby Bridge Brighouse Dewsbury Batley Wakefield Rothwell YORKSHIRE Howden Goole New Holland Hedon
Lytham Darwen Chorley Rawtenstall Whitworth Littleborough Elland Mirfield Normanton WAKEFIELD Knottingley Kingston upon Hull Hull Barton-upon-Humber
Southport Leyland Ramsbottom Rochdale Huddersfield Kirkburton WEST YORKSHIRE Castleford Pontefract Featherstone Thorne Crowle Scunthorpe NORTH LINCOLNSHIRE
Formby Ormskirk Standish Bury Heywood Middleton Meltham Holmfirth Barnsley Hemsworth Adwick-le-Street Bolton-upon-Dearne Doncaster ISLE OF AXHOLME Brigg Barnetby le Wold Caistor
Crosby Kirkby GREATER MANCHESTER Horwich Farnworth Radcliffe Prestwich OLDHAM Penistone BARNSLEY Wombwell Swinton DONCASTER Epworth
Bootle Wigan Leigh Eccles Ashton-in-Makerfield MANCHESTER Oldham Mossley SOUTH YORKSHIRE Consbrough Rawmarsh Gainsborough
Wallasey MERSEYSIDE St Helens Irlam Stretton Sale Dukinfield Stalybridge Ashton-under-Lyne Glossop Rotherham ROTHER-HAM E. Retford Lincoln Wragby
Hoylake Widnes Warrington Cheadle Altrincham Hale Marple Kinder Scout 2087 Sheffield Worksop East Markham LINCOLNSHIRE WOLDS
West Kirby Bebington Runcorn Frodsham Knutsford Wilmslow New Mills Dronfield Staveley Bolsover Ollerton Mansfield Woodhouse Tuxford Warsop
Birkenhead Flint Ellesmere Port Northwich Bollington Chapel en le Frith Tideswell Chesterfield Clay Cross SHERWOOD FOREST Sutton-on-Trent Newark
CHESHIRE Macclesfield Buxton Bakewell DERBYSHIRE Matlock Mansfield Sutton-in-Ashfield Kirkby-in-Ashfield Southwell
FLINTSHIRE Hawarden Chester Winsford Congleton Sandbach Middlewich Wirksworth Winster Alfreton Hucknall Arnold Carlton Sleaford
WALES ENG. Tarporley Crewe Biddulph Leek Ashbourne Belper Ripley Heanor NOTTINGHAMSHIRE Nottingham Bingham Grantham
Wrexham Holt Audley Kidsgrove Ilkeston Beeston W. Bridgford Folkingham
CLWYD Malpas Nantwich Wolstanton Newcastle under Lyme Stoke-on-Trent Longton Cheadle Derby Long Eaton
WREXHAM Whitchurch Market Drayton Stone Uttoxeter Tutbury Castle Donington Melton Mowbray Edenham Bourne
Ellesmere Wem Eccleshall Abbots Bromley Burton-upon-Trent Melbourne Swadlincote Loughborough Market Deeping
THE WREKIN Newport Stafford Rugeley Ashby-de-la-Zouch Coalville LEICESTERSHIRE Oakham Stamford Uppingham Peterborough
Shrewsbury Wellington Oakengates Shifnal Penkridge Lichfield CANNOCK CHASE Atherstone CHARNWOOD FOREST Market Bosworth Leicester READING
The Wrekin 1335 Dawley Cannock Brownhills Tamworth Nuneaton Hinckley Market Harborough Corby Oundle
SHROPSHIRE Minsterley Much Wenlock Wolverhampton Aldridge Walsall Sutton Coldfield WARWICKSHIRE Coleshill ROCKINGHAM FOREST
Church Stretton Bridgnorth Goseley Bilston Wednesbury Tipton Oldbury W. Bromwich Dudley NORTHAMPTONSHIRE
Bishop's Castle Titterstone Clee Hill 1749 WYRE FOREST Smethwick (Warley) Halesowen BIRMINGHAM Rugby Naseby Kettering Thrapston
Ludlow Cleobury Mortimer Bewdley Stourbridge WORCESTERSHIRE Kings Norton Solihull SOLIHULL WEST MIDLANDS Coventry Kidderminster

b

Woodstock Harpenden Hatfield Broad Oak Witham Brightlingsea
Burford Witney Oxford Aylesbury Tring Hertford HERTFORDSHIRE Great Waltham Tollesbury
Thame Wendover Welwyn Garden City Harlow Chelmsford Maldon
Bampton OXFORDSHIRE Headington Cowley Princes Risborough Berkhamsted Hemel Hempstead St Albans Cheshunt High Ongar Danbury ESSEX
Faringdon Abingdon Chalgrove BUCKINGHAMSHIRE Chesham Potters Bar Epping Brentwood Billericay Burnham on Crouch
Didcot Watlington High Wycombe Watford Enfield Chigwell Basildon Rayleigh Southend-on-Sea
Wantage Wallingford Marlow Gerrards Cross Harrow Tottenham Walthamstow Romford Bulphan
Goring Maidenhead Hendon Ilford Dagenham THURROCK
East Isley Henley on Thames Slough Ealing LONDON W. Ham Grays Thurrock Tilbury Gravesend Sheerness
Hampstead Norris Reading Windsor Egham Willesden Woolwich Greenwich MEDWAY TOWNS
Bradfield Sunninghill Staines Twickenham Wandsworth Bromley Bexley Dartford Rochester Whitstable
BERKSHIRE Bracknell Chertsey Esher Sutton Croydon Farningham Gillingham Chatham Sittingbourne
NEWBURY Wokingham Weybridge Epsom Banstead Wrotham Faversham Canterbury
HAMPSHIRE Tadley Swallowfield Sandhurst Camberley Woking Leatherhead Caterham Sevenoaks Maidstone Doddington
Kingsclere Fleet Farnborough Aldershot Guildford Dorking Reigate Westerham KENT Charing
Basingstoke Odiham Farnham Woking Edenbridge Mereworth Wye
Tonbridge

Relief

Meters	Feet
610	2000
305	1000
152.5	500
0 Sea Level	0

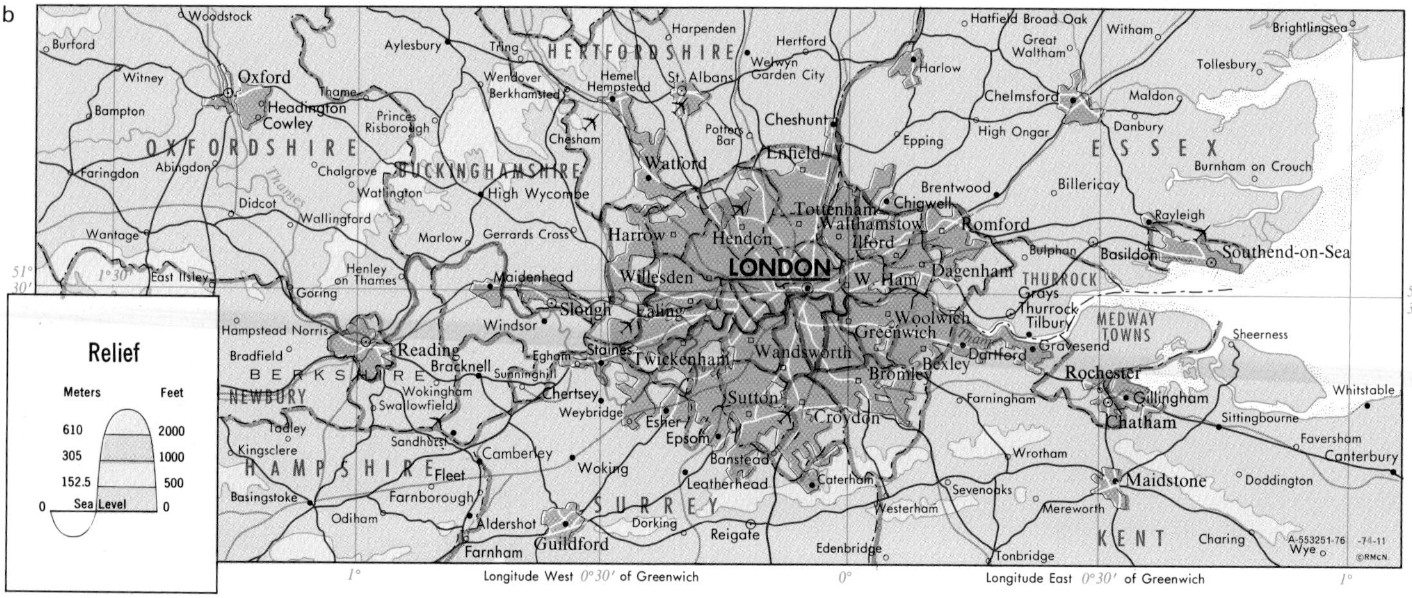

Scale 1:1 000 000; one inch to 16 miles.
Elevations and depressions are given in feet.

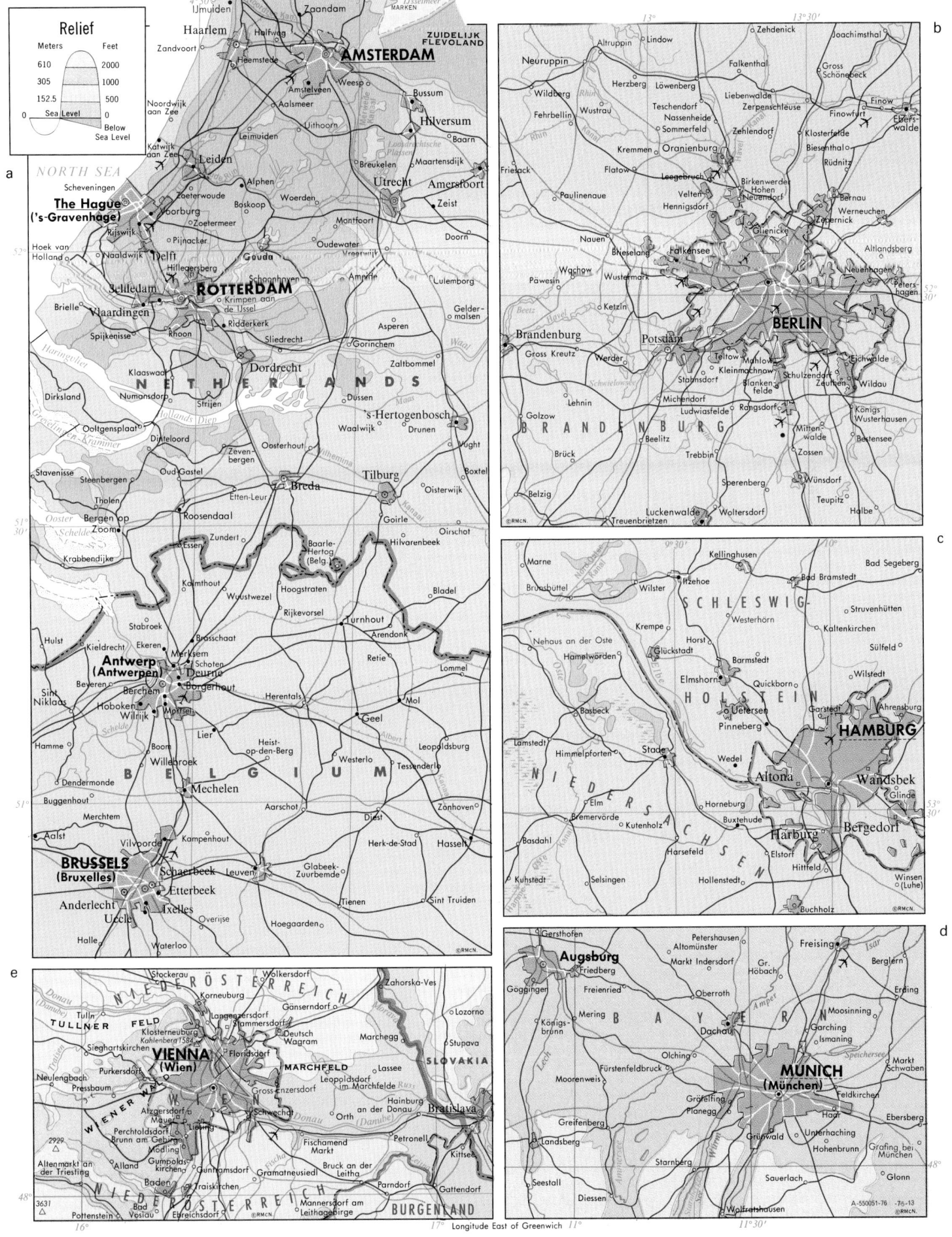

Scale 1:1 000 000; one inch to 16 miles.

Elevations and depressions are given in feet.

Continued on pages 180-181

BELARUS

RUSSIA

LAPLAND

FINLAND

Murmansk

Kola

Kuopio

Lahti

Helsinki

Gulf of Finland

ESTONIA

Tallinn

Tartu

Pärnu

HIIUMAA

SAAREMAA

Gulf of Riga

Riga

LATVIA

LITHUANIA

Šiauliai

Kaunas

RUSSIA

Kaliningrad

Klaipėda

Liepāja

Oulu

GULF OF BOTHNIA

Tornio

Vaasa

Pori

Rauma

Turku

Tampere

STOCKHOLM

Uppsala

GOTLAND

ÖLAND

BORNHOLM

Gdynia

Gdańsk

S W E D E N

N O R W A Y

Östersund

Sundsvall

Gävle

Västerås

Falun

Örebro

Norrköping

Linköping

Jönköping

Göteborg

Halmstad

Helsingborg

Kalmar

Karlstad

Trondheim

Namsos

Bodø

Narvik

VESTERÅLEN

LOFOTEN

ANDØYA

SENJA

Hammerfest

Tromsø

Alta

Oslo

Drammen

Bergen

Stavanger

Haugesund

Egersund

Kristiansand

Kristiansund

Molde

Ålesund

LINDESNES

Frederikshavn

Aalborg

Århus

Esbjerg

Odense

DENMARK

COPENHAGEN

(København)

Flensburg

JUTLAND

Skagerrak

Kattegat

SKANE

N O R T H   S E A

DOGGER BANK

UNITED KINGDOM

Aberdeen

Dundee

Edinburgh

GLASGOW

Greenock

Paisley

Newcastle-upon-Tyne

South Shields

Sunderland

Hartlepool

Middlesbrough

MANCHESTER

Barrow-in-Furness

Carlisle

Belfast

NORTHERN IRELAND

Londonderry

Sligo

Dublin

IRELAND

SCOTLAND

Wick

Stornoway

HEBRIDES

ISLAY

SKYE

TIREE

ORKNEY IS. (Br.)

Kirkwall

SHETLAND IS. (Br.)

Lerwick

MAINLAND

KINNAIRDS HEAD

BRITISH ISLES

FAROE IS. (Den.)

Tórshavn

Arctic Circle

N O R W E G I A N   S E A

A R C T I C   O C E A N

JAN MAYEN (Nor.)

ICELAND

Reykjavík

Siglufjörður

Akureyri

Seyðisfjörður

Eskifjörður

Vopnafjörður

GRÍMSEY

Vestmannaeyjar

Vatnajökull

Scale 1: 10 000 000; one inch to 160 miles. Conic Projection

Elevations and depressions are given in feet

Relief

Meters	Feet
3050	10 000
1525	5000
610	2000
305	1000
152.5	500
0	Sea Level
	Below Sea Level

Sea Level	0
152.5	500
1525	5000
3050	10 000

POLAND

UKRAINE

ROMANIA

SERBIA

MONTENEGRO

ALBANIA

BOSNIA AND HERZEGOVINA

CROATIA

HUNGARY

SLOVAKIA

CZECH REP.

AUSTRIA

SLOVENIA

SWITZERLAND

LIECHTENSTEIN

GERMANY

NETHERLANDS

BELGIUM

LUX.

FRANCE

ENGLAND

WALES

MONACO

ANDORRA

SPAIN

PORTUGAL

ITALY

VATICAN CITY

CORSICA (Fr.)

SARDINIA (It.)

SICILY

MALTA

TUNISIA

ALGERIA

MOROCCO

BERLIN · BUDAPEST · PRAGUE · WIEN · MUNICH · STUTTGART · FRANKFURT · COLOGNE · DÜSSELDORF · ESSEN · BRUSSELS · AMSTERDAM · THE HAGUE · Rotterdam · LONDON · BIRMINGHAM · PARIS · Versailles · LYON · MILAN · TURIN · GENOA · Venice · Bologna · Florence · ROME · NAPLES · Palermo · Catania · BARCELONA · VALÈNCIA · MADRID · LISBON · Sevilla · Algiers

ATLAS MOUNTAINS

ADRIATIC SEA

LIGURIAN SEA

TYRRHENIAN SEA

IONIAN SEA

MEDITERRANEAN SEA

BAY OF BISCAY

ENGLISH CHANNEL

ATLANTIC OCEAN

ISLES OF SCILLY

LAND'S END

BALEARS (Sp.)

MALLORCA · MENORCA · EIVISSA · FORMENTERA

Longitude West of Greenwich · Longitude East of Greenwich

| 0 | 50 | 100 | 150 | 200 | 250 | 300 Miles |
| 0 | 100 | 200 | 300 | 400 | 500 Kilometers |

164

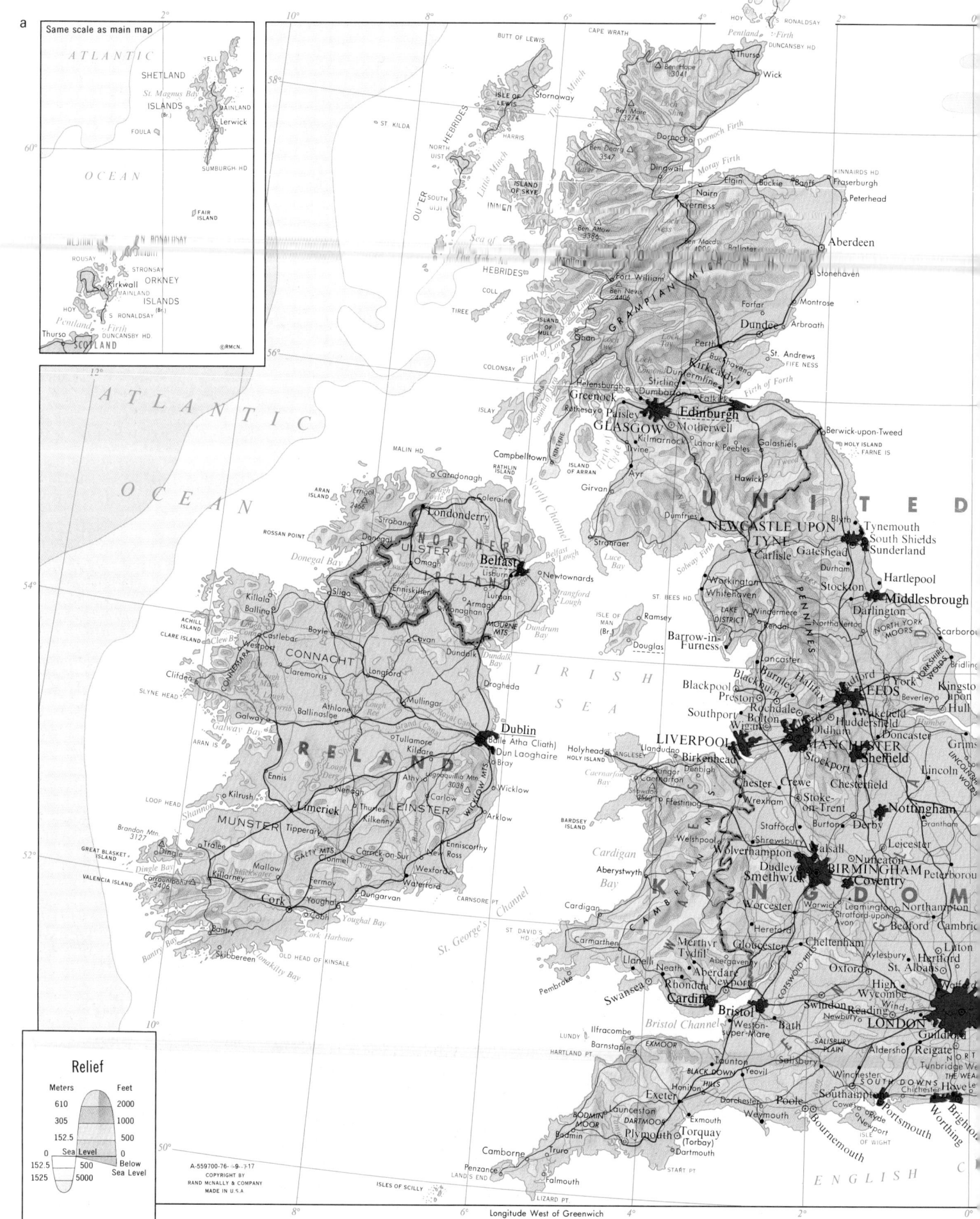

Scale 1: 4 000 000; one inch to 64 miles. Conic Projection
Elevations and depressions are given in feet

Longitude West of Greenwich

a

Same scale as main map

Relief

Meters		Feet
610		2000
305		1000
152.5		500
0	Sea Level	0
152.5	500	Below
1525	5000	Sea Level

Continued on pages 166-167

Continued on pages 168-169

Continued on pages 170-171

Longitude East of Greenwich

0 10 20 30 40 50 60 70 80 90 100 110 120 Miles
0 20 40 60 80 100 120 140 160 180 200 Kilometers

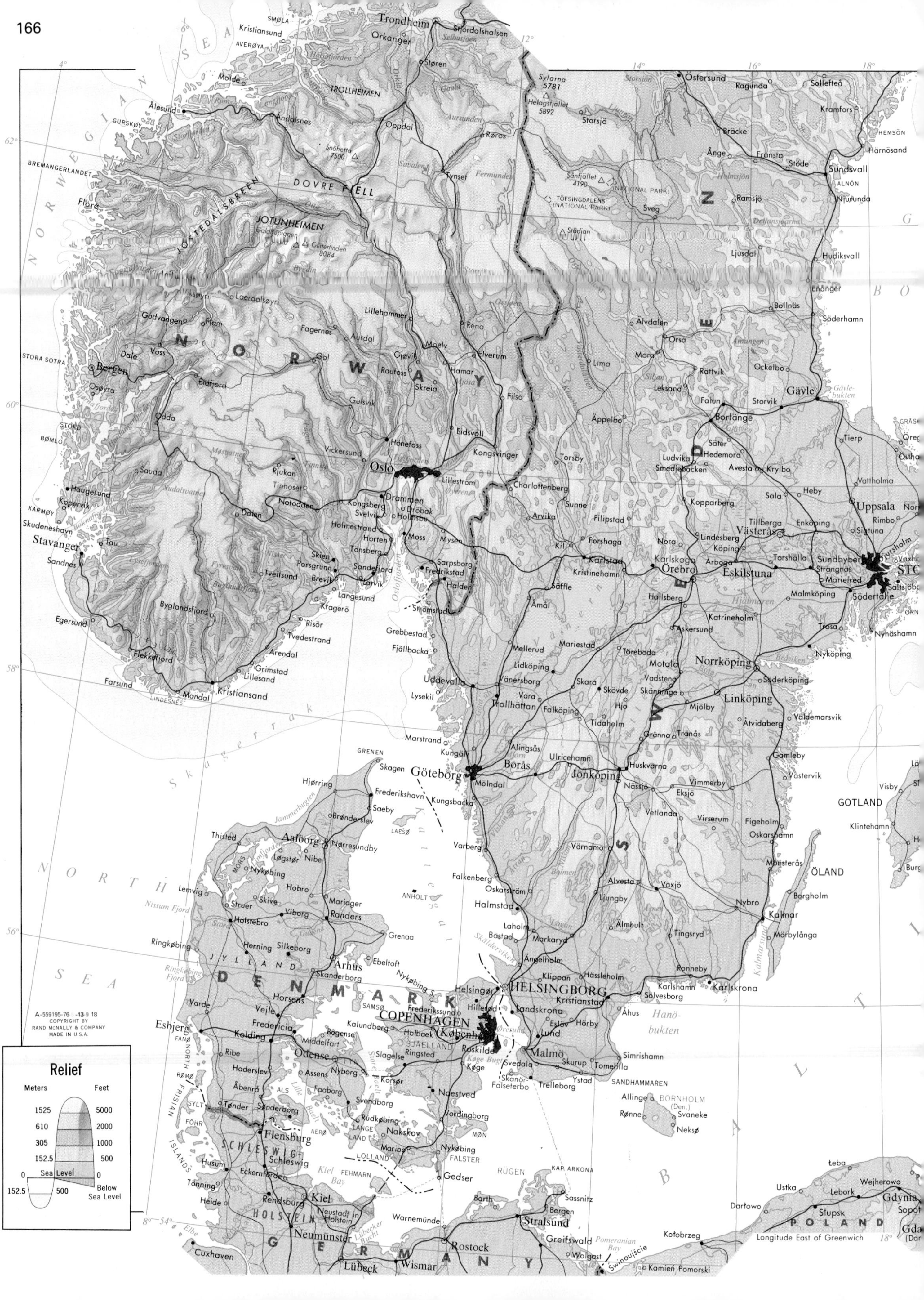

NORWEGIAN SEA

NORWAY

SWEDEN

DENMARK

GERMANY

POLAND

GOTLAND

ÖLAND

BORNHOLM (Den.)

NORTH SEA

BALTIC SEA

Skagerrak

Kattegat

Trondheim · Kristiansund · Molde · Ålesund · Åndalsnes · Oppdal · Røros · Østersund · Sundsvall

Bergen · Oslo · Stavanger · Kristiansand · Göteborg · Stockholm · Uppsala · Gävle

Copenhagen · København · Malmö · Helsingborg · Aalborg · Århus · Odense

Lübeck · Kiel · Rostock · Stralsund · Gdynia · Gdańsk

TROLLHEIMEN · DOVRE FJELL · JOTUNHEIMEN

Snøhetta 7500

Galdhøpiggen · Glittertinden 8084

Relief

Meters		Feet
1525		5000
610		2000
305		1000
152.5		500
0	Sea Level	0
152.5		500
	Below Sea Level	

Longitude East of Greenwich

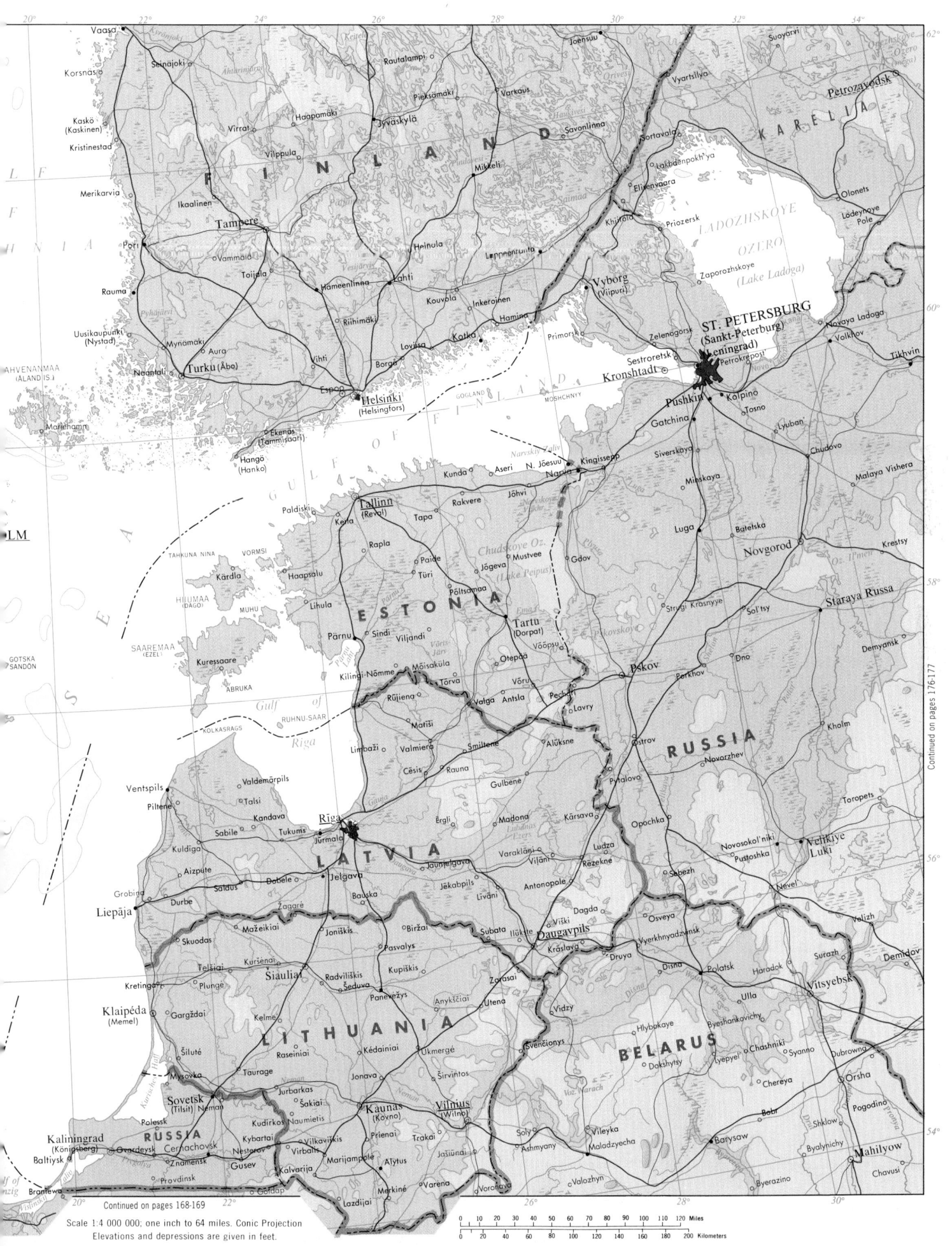

Continued on pages 176-177

Continued on pages 168-169

Scale 1:4 000 000; one inch to 64 miles. Conic Projection
Elevations and depressions are given in feet.

0 10 20 30 40 50 60 70 80 90 100 110 120 Miles
0   20   40   60   80   100   120   140   160   180   200 Kilometers

Continued on pages 166-167

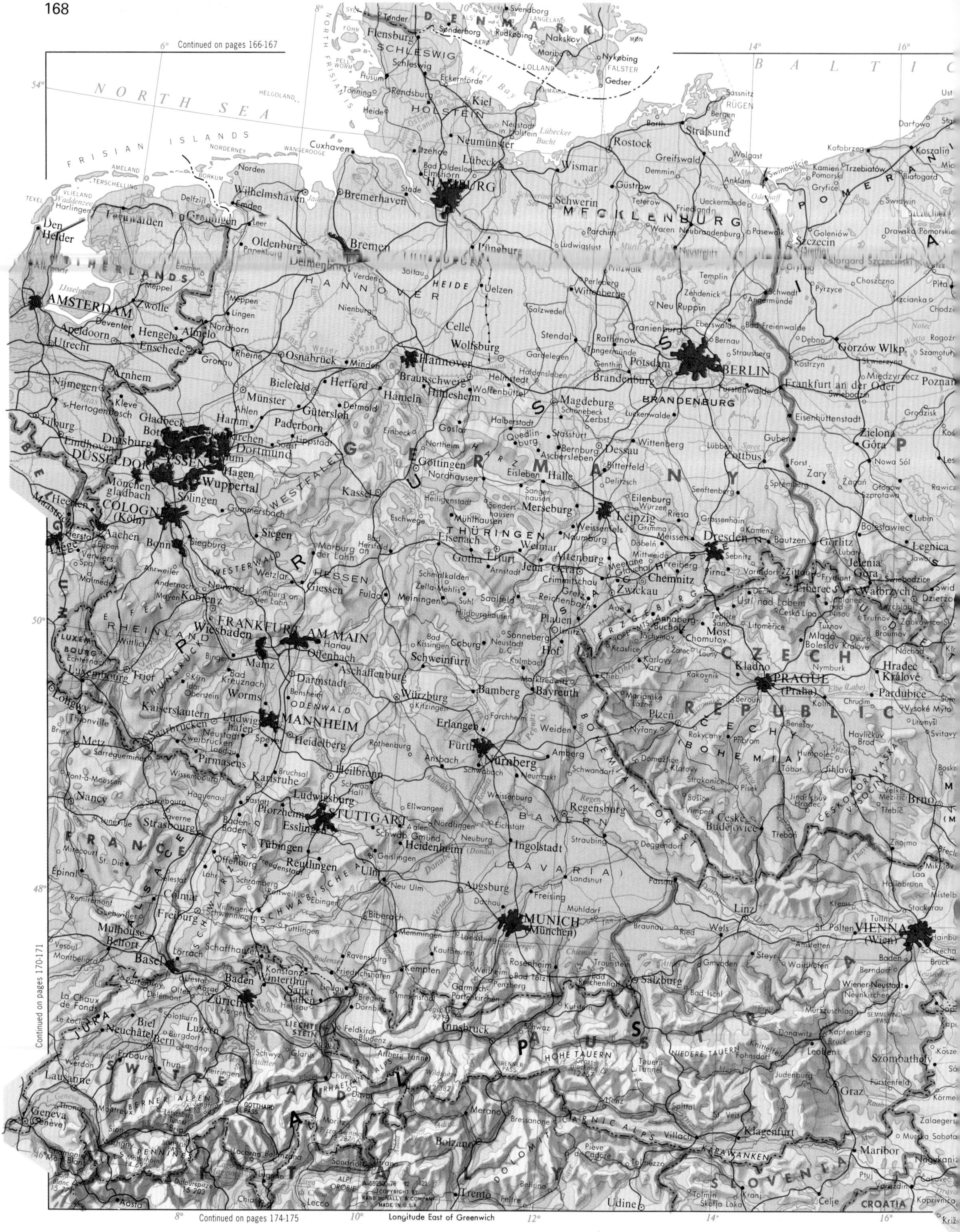

Continued on pages 170-171

Continued on pages 174-175

NORTH SEA

DENMARK

BALTIC

FRISIAN ISLANDS

SCHLESWIG

HOLSTEIN

MECKLENBURG

POMERANIA

Flensburg
Schleswig
Husum
Heide
Rendsburg
Kiel
Neumünster
Itzehoe
Lübeck
HAMBURG
Stade
Cuxhaven
Bremerhaven
Wilhelmshaven
Emden
Norden
Leer
Oldenburg
Delmenhorst
Bremen
Lüneburg
Rostock
Wismar
Schwerin
Güstrow
Teterow
Parchim
Ludwigslust
Neubrandenburg
Waren
Demmin
Greifswald
Stralsund
Sassnitz
Bergen
RÜGEN
Barth
Anklam
Ueckermünde
Swinoujscie
Szczecin
Koszalin

Den Helder
AMSTERDam
Utrecht
Apeldoorn
Deventer
Zwolle
Almelo
Hengelo
Enschede
Nordhorn
Lingen
Meppen
Nienburg
Celle
Wolfsburg
Stendal
Tangermünde
Rathenow
Brandenburg
Potsdam
BERLIN
Oranienburg
Eberswalde
Angermünde
Schwedt
Gorzów Wlkp.
Poznan

NETHERLANDS

HANNOVER

HEIDE

Nijmegen
Arnhem
Kleve
's-Hertogenbosch
Eindhoven
Tilburg
Gladbeck
Duisburg
DÜSSELDORF
ESSEN
Mönchengladbach
Wuppertal
COLOGNE (Köln)
Aachen
Bonn
Osnabrück
Minden
Bielefeld
Herford
Gütersloh
Münster
Ahlen
Hamm
Dortmund
Hagen
Soest
Lippstadt
Paderborn
Detmold
Hameln
Hildesheim
Braunschweig
Hannover
Wolfenbüttel
Helmstedt
Magdeburg
Schönebeck
Zerbst
Stassfurt
Bernburg
Aschersleben
Dessau
Wittenberg
Lübben
Cottbus
Guben
Zielona Góra
Nowa Sól

WESTFALEN

GERMANY

HARZ

THÜRINGEN

HESSEN

Kassel
Göttingen
Northeim
Nordhausen
Heiligenstadt
Mühlhausen
Sangerhausen
Eisleben
Halle
Merseburg
Leipzig
Riesa
Meissen
Dresden
Bautzen
Görlitz
Jelenia Góra
Legnica

Siegen
Gummersbach
Marburg an der Lahn
Bad Hersfeld
Fulda
Eisenach
Gotha
Erfurt
Weimar
Jena
Gera
Zwickau
Chemnitz
Freiberg
Pirna
Zittau
Liberec

Koblenz
Wetzlar
Giessen
Meiningen
Suhl
Saalfeld
Plauen
Hof
ERZGEBIRGE
Most
Chomutov
Teplice
Ústí nad Labem
Ceská Lípa
Mladá Boleslav

FRANKFURT AM MAIN
Wiesbaden
Mainz
Offenbach
Hanau
Aschaffenburg
Würzburg
Schweinfurt
Bamberg
Bayreuth
Coburg
Sonneberg
Neustadt
Kulmbach
Marktredwitz
Weiden
Karlovy Vary
Kladno
PRAGUE (Praha)
Hradec Králové
Pardubice

RHEINLAND
PFALZ
LUXEMBOURG
Trier
Bad Kreuznach
Worms
Darmstadt
Bensheim
ODENWALD
MANNHEIM
Heidelberg
Ludwigshafen
Speyer
Kaiserslautern
Pirmasens
Neustadt
Saarbrücken
Zweibrücken

CZECH REPUBLIC
CECHY
BOHEMIA

Metz
Nancy
Strasbourg
Colmar
Mulhouse
Belfort
Freiburg

FRANCE

Karlsruhe
Baden-Baden
Pforzheim
STUTTGART
Esslingen
Tübingen
Reutlingen
Heilbronn
Ludwigsburg
Schwäbisch Hall
Aalen
Heidenheim
Ulm
Neu Ulm
Augsburg
Ingolstadt
Regensburg
Nürnberg
Fürth
Schwabach
Erlangen
Ansbach
Amberg
Schwandorf
Straubing
Passau
Deggendorf
Ceské Budejovice
Trebon
Tábor
Pisek
Strakonice
Brno
Znojmo

BAYERN (BAVARIA)

BOHEMIAN FOREST

SCHWARZWALD

Basel
Zürich
Winterthur
Sankt Gallen
Konstanz
Bregenz
Friedrichshafen
Kempten
Memmingen
Kaufbeuren
Landsberg
MUNICH (München)
Dachau
Freising
Landshut
Mühldorf
Rosenheim
Bad Tölz
Bad Reichenhall
Salzburg
Traunstein
Wels
Linz
St. Pölten
VIENNA (Wien)
Wiener Neustadt

SWITZERLAND

Bern
Luzern
Innsbruck
HOHE TAUERN
NIEDERE TAUERN
Leoben
Graz

AUSTRIA

ALPS

Geneva (Genève)
Lausanne
BERNER ALPEN
GOTTHARD PASS
BRENNER PASS
Bolzano
Merano
Bressanone
DOLOMITI
CARNIC ALPS
KARAWANKEN
Villach
Klagenfurt
Maribor

SLOVENIA
CROATIA

Udine
Trento

Scale 1:4 000 000; one inch to 64 miles. Conic Projection
Elevations and depressions are given in feet

Longitude East of Greenwich

RAND M¢NALLY & COMPANY

SEA

Relief

Meters	Feet
3050	10 000
1525	5000
610	2000
305	1000
152.5	500
0 Sea Level	0
	Below Sea Level

Continued on pages 166-167

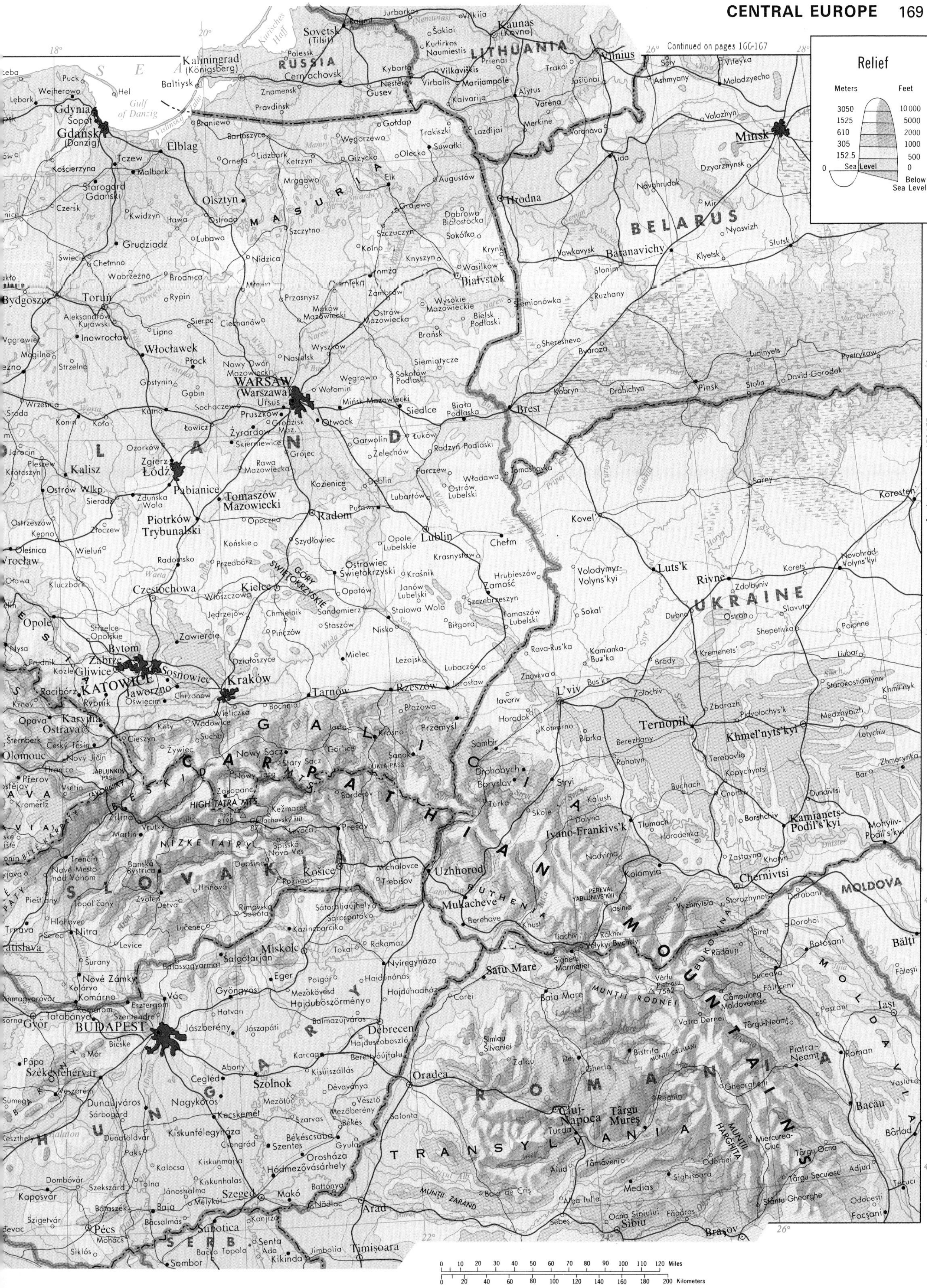

Continued on pages 176-177

RUSSIA

LITHUANIA

BELARUS

Kaliningrad (Königsberg)

Minsk

Kaunas (Kovno)

Vilnius

Sovetsk (Tilsit)

Cernachovsk

Gusev

Gulf of Danzig

Gdynia
Sopot
Gdańsk (Danzig)

Baltiysk

Elblag

Hel

Puck
Wejherowo

Lębork

Tczew
Malbork

Kościerzyna
Starogard Gdański
Czersk

Grudziadz

Olsztyn

MASURIA

Hrodna

Białystok

Toruń
Bydgoszcz

WARSAW (Warszawa)

Brest

P O L A N D

Łódź

Radom

Lublin

Kielce

Częstochowa

Kraków

KATOWICE

UKRAINE

Luts'k
Rivne

L'viv

Ternopil'

Khmel'nyts'kyi

Chernivtsi

MOLDOVA

SLOVAKIA

CARPATHIAN

GALICIA

Uzhhorod
Mukacheve

RUTHENIA

MOUNTAINS

BUDAPEST

H U N G A R Y

Miskolc

Debrecen

Satu Mare

Baia Mare

Oradea

R O M A N I A

TRANSYLVANIA

Cluj-Napoca
Târgu Mureş

Sibiu

Braşov

Bacău

Iaşi

MOLDAVIA

SERB

Timişoara

Arad

0 10 20 30 40 50 60 70 80 90 100 110 120 Miles

0 20 40 60 80 100 120 140 160 180 200 Kilometers

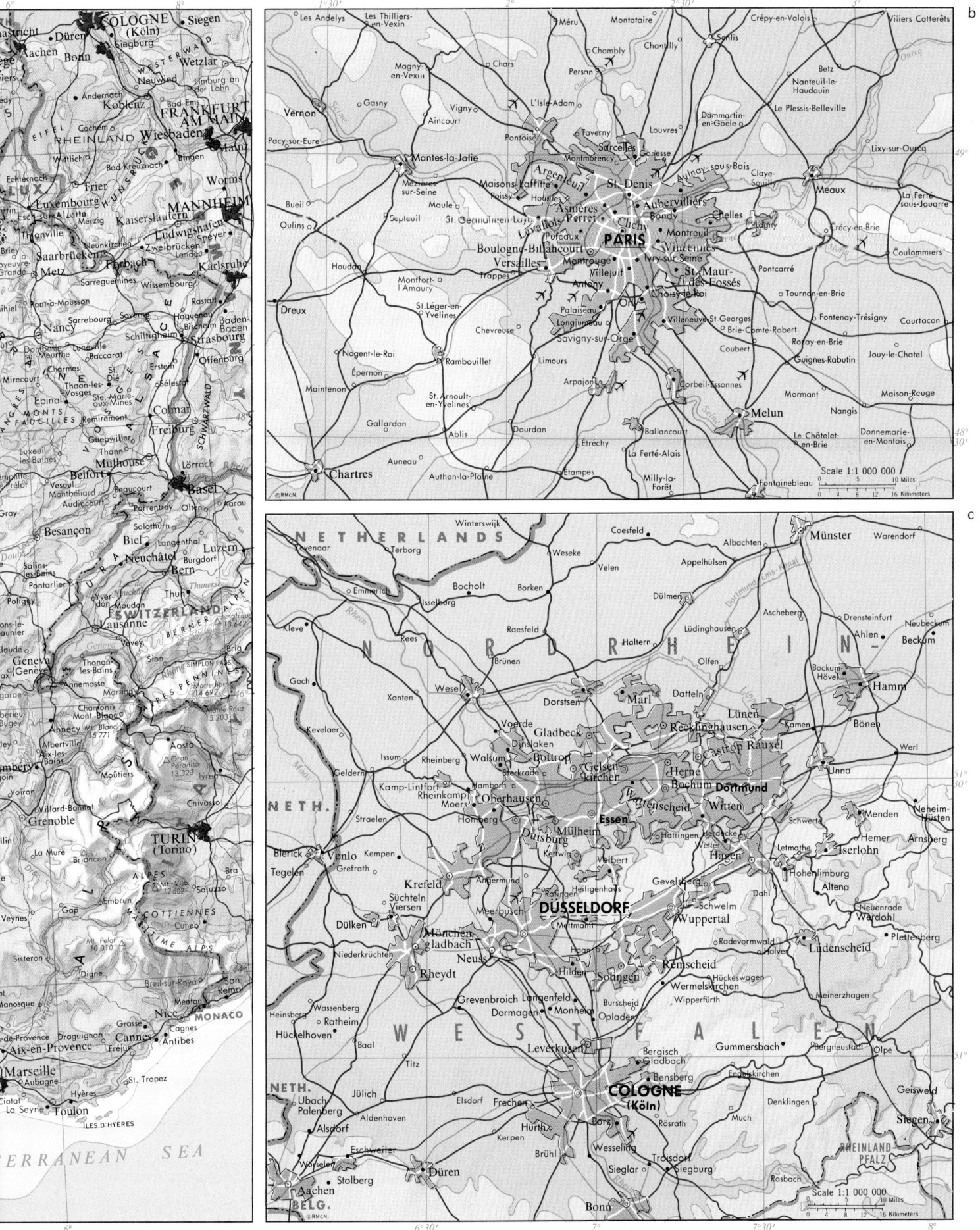

Relief

Meters		Feet
3050		10000
1525		5000
610		2000
305		1000
152.5		500
0	Sea Level	0
152.5		500
1525		5000
3050		10000

A-552900-76 -6-12
COPYRIGHT BY
RAND McNALLY & COMPANY
MADE IN U.S.A.

Scale 1:4 000 000, one inch to 64 miles. Conic Projection
Elevations and depressions are given in feet

Longitude West of Greenwich

Continued on pages 170 171

a

MADRID

Scale 1:1 000 000

b

LISBON
(Lisboa)

ATLANTIC

OCEAN

Scale 1:1 000 000

c

NAPLES
(Napoli)

TYRRHENIAN   SEA

Scale 1:1 000 000

d

ROME
(Roma)

VATICAN CITY

TYRRHENIAN

SEA

Scale 1:1 000 000

Longitude East of Greenwich

Continued on pages 168-169

Continued on pages 170-171

Scale 1:4 000 000; one inch to 64 miles. Conic Projection
Elevations and depressions are given in feet

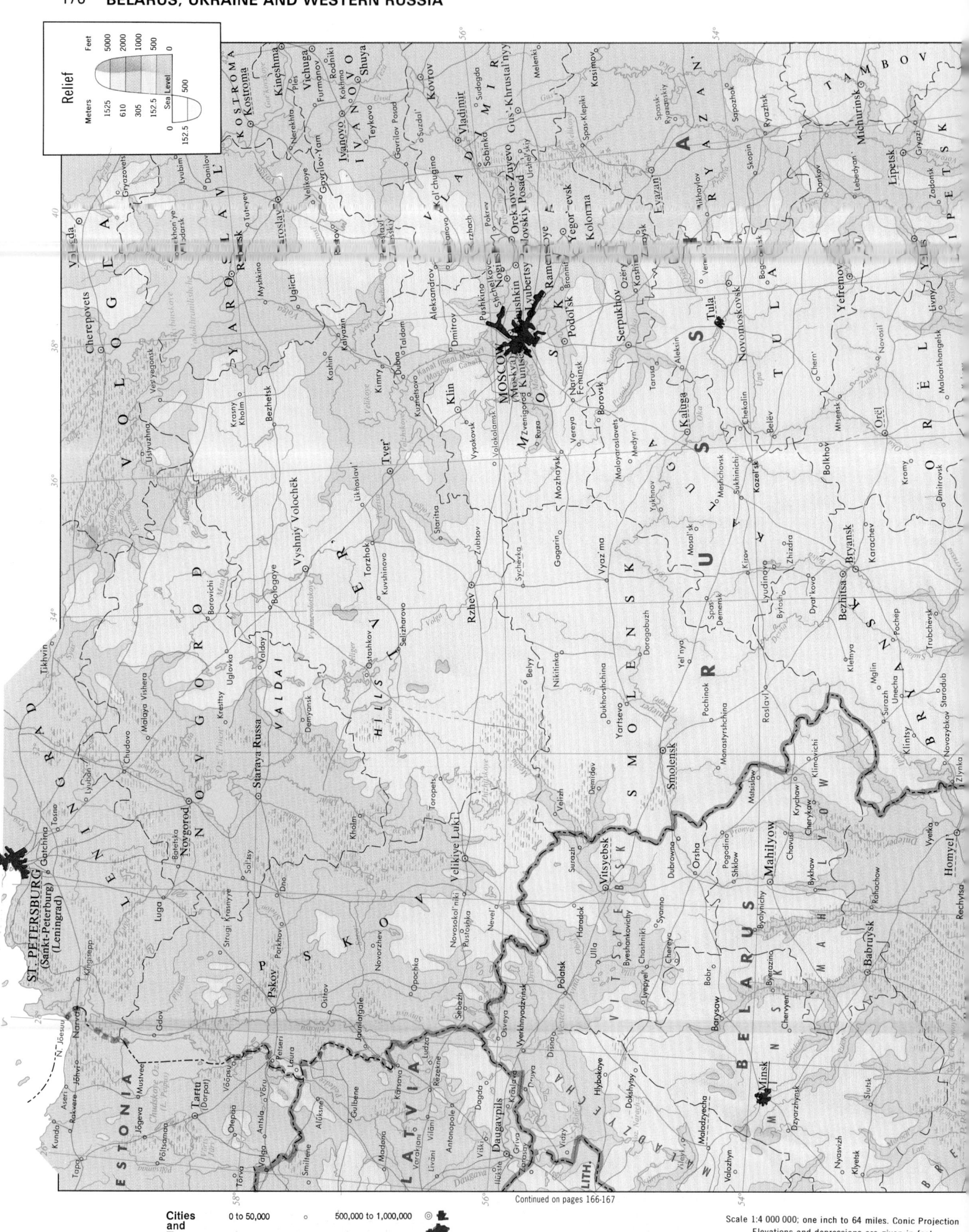

Relief

Feet				
5000	2000	1000	500	0
1525	610	305	152.5	Sea Level

Meters

0 · 152.5

Sea Level · 500

Continued on pages 166-167

Cities and Towns

0 to 50,000 ○   500,000 to 1,000,000 ◉

50,000 to 500,000 ⊙   1,000,000 and over

Scale 1:4 000 000; one inch to 64 miles. Conic Projection
Elevations and depressions are given in feet

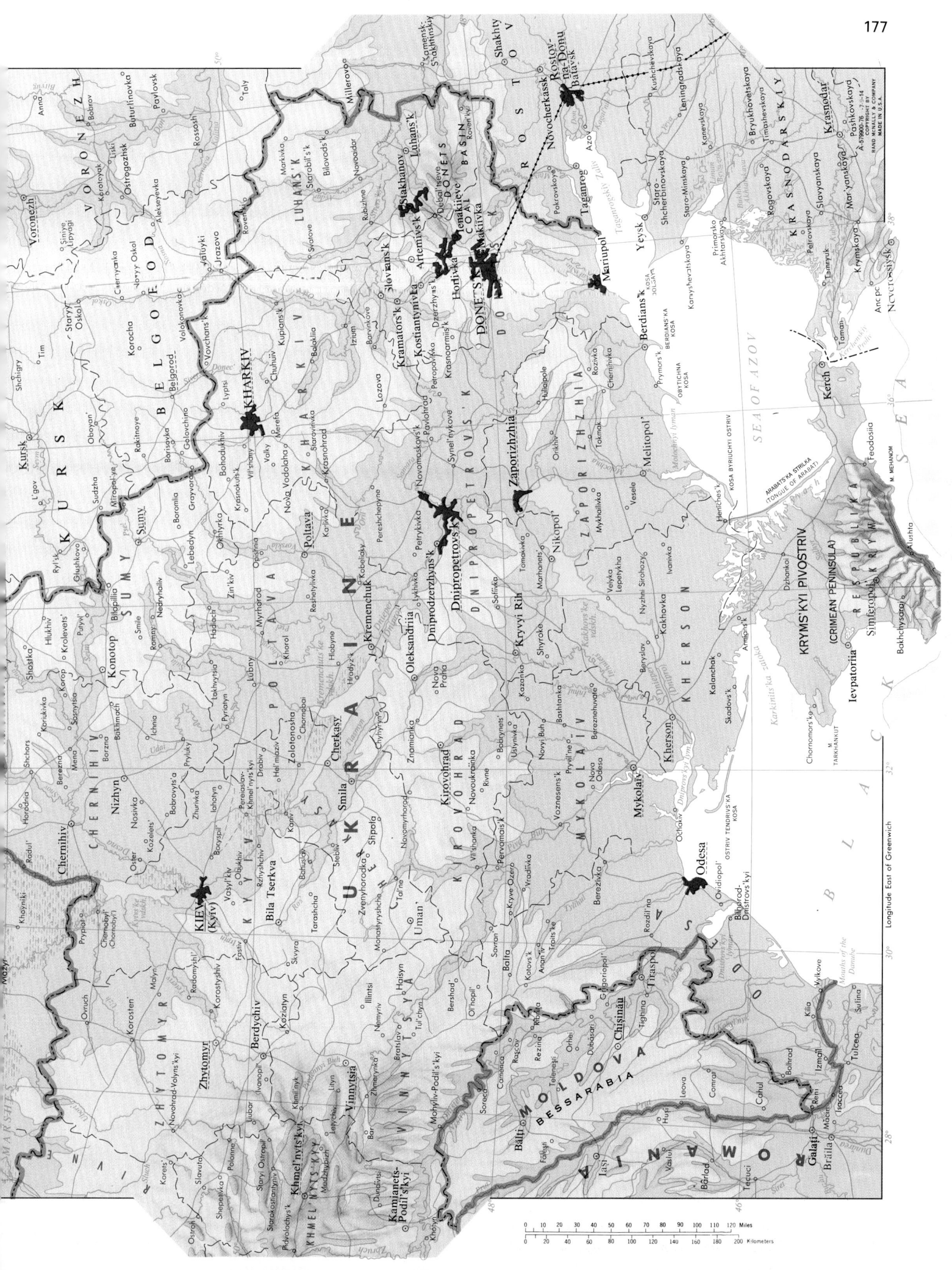

Scale 1:20 000 000; one inch to 315 miles.
Lambert's Azimuthal, Equal Area Projection.
Elevations and depressions are given in feet.

Cities and Towns

0 to 50,000   ○   500,000 to 1,000,000   ◎

50,000 to 500,000   ⊙   1,000,000 and over

Relief

Feet	Meters
10000	3050
5000	1525
2000	610
1000	305
500	152.5
0 Sea Level	Sea Level
Below Sea Level	
500	152.5
5000	1525
10000	3050

ARCTIC OCEAN

KARA SEA

BARENTS SEA

Obskaya Guba

WESTERN SIBERIAN LOWLAND

NOVAYA ZEMLYA

PECHORA BASIN

MALOZEMEL'SKAYA TUNDRA

KHREBET PAYKHOY

KOLGUYEV

P-OV KANIN

M. KANIN NOS

Cheshskaya Guba

MORZHOVETS

SOLOVETSKIYE OSTROVA

KARELIA

LAPLAND

NORWAY

SWEDEN

FINLAND

ESTONIA

LATVIA

LITHUANIA

BELARUS

R U S S I A

U R A L

BASHKORTOSTAN

TATARSTAN

UDMURTIA

MARI EL

CHUVASHIA

MORDVINIA

VALDAI HILLS

CENTRAL

Gulf of Finland

BALTIC SEA

Gulf of Riga

Arctic Circle

Cities:

Murmansk, Monchegorsk, Kandalakša, Kirovsk, Arkhangelsk (Arhangel), Severodvinsk, Onega, Petrozavodsk, Medvezhegorsk, Belomorsk, Kem, ST. PETERSBURG (Sankt-Peterburg) (Leningrad), Vyborg, Pushkin, Kronshtadt, Kolpino, Gatchina, Novgorod, Pskov, Staraya Russa, Velikiye Luki, Rzhev, Tver, Torzhok, Vyshniy Volochek, Bologoye, Cherepovets, Rybinsk, Yaroslavl, Kostroma, Ivanovo, Vladimir, MOSCOW (Moskva), Podol'sk, Serpukhov, Kaluga, Tula, Ryazan, Kolomna, Murom, NIZHNIY NOVGOROD, DZERZHINSK, Arzamas, Cheboksary, Yoshkar-Ola, Kazan, Volzhsk, Nolinsk, Kirov, Slobodskoy, Glazov, Izhevsk, Sarapul, Perm', EKATERINBURG, Chelyabinsk, Magnitogorsk, Ufa, Sterlitamak, Birsk, Nizhniy Tagil, Krasnoufimsk, Krasnouralsk, Kushva, Lys'va, Solikamsk, Vorkuta, Pechora, Ukhta, Syktyvkar, Kotlas, Vel'sk, Velikiy Ustyug, Vologda, Shenkursk, Mezen, Pinega, Yemetsk, Helsinki, Tampere, Turku, Oulu, Tallinn, Tartu, Pärnu, Riga, Daugavpils, Šiauliai, Kaunas, Klaipeda, Vilnius, Minsk, Smolensk, Vitsyebsk, Mahilyow

Continued on pages 160-161

Continued on pages 160-161

0   50   100   150   200   250   300 Miles

0   100   200   300   400   500 Kilometers

Scale 1:10 000 000; one inch to 160 miles. Conic Projection
Elevations and depressions are given in feet.

Continued on pages 162-163

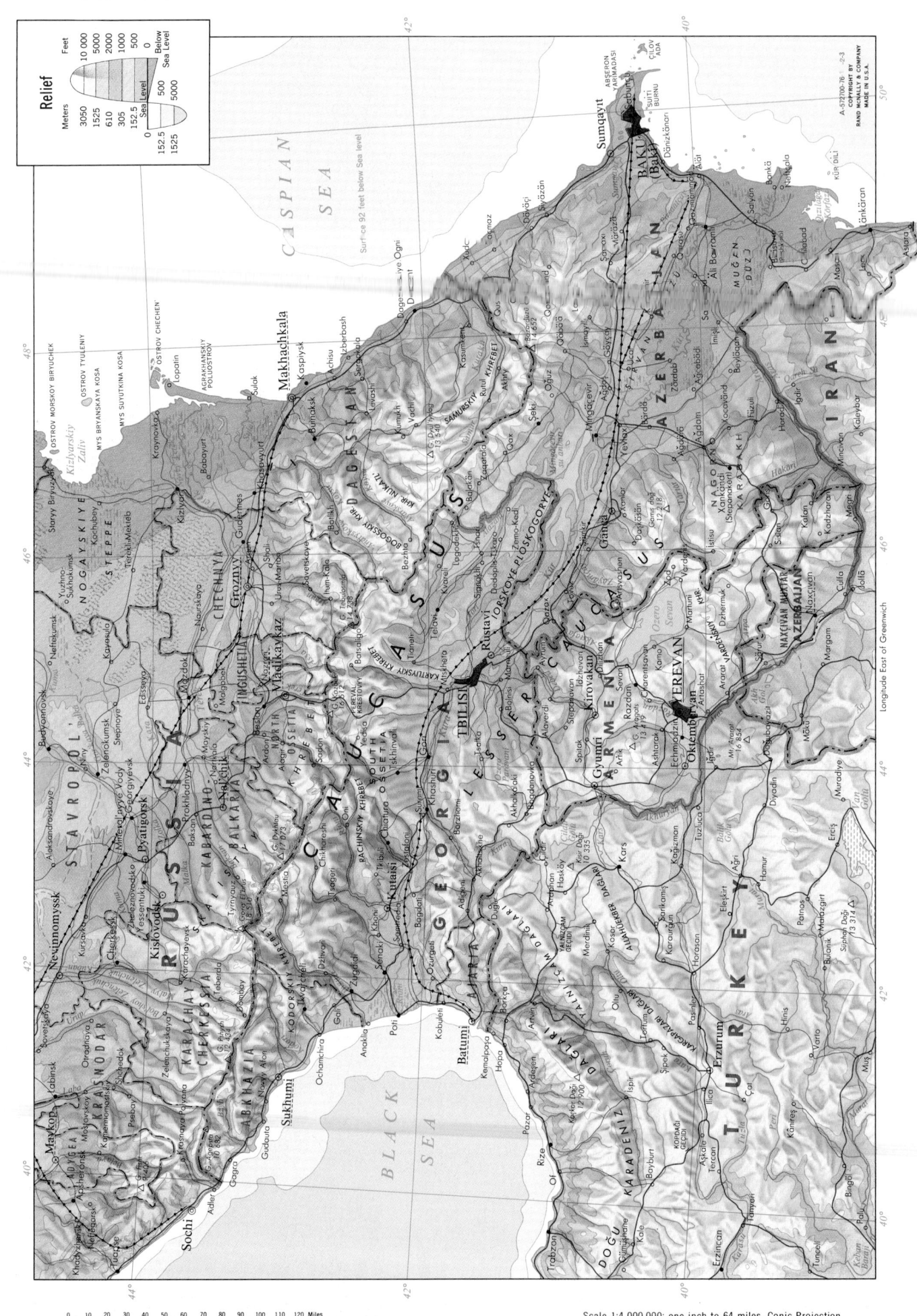

Scale 1:4 000 000; one inch to 64 miles. Conic Projection
Elevations and depressions are given in feet

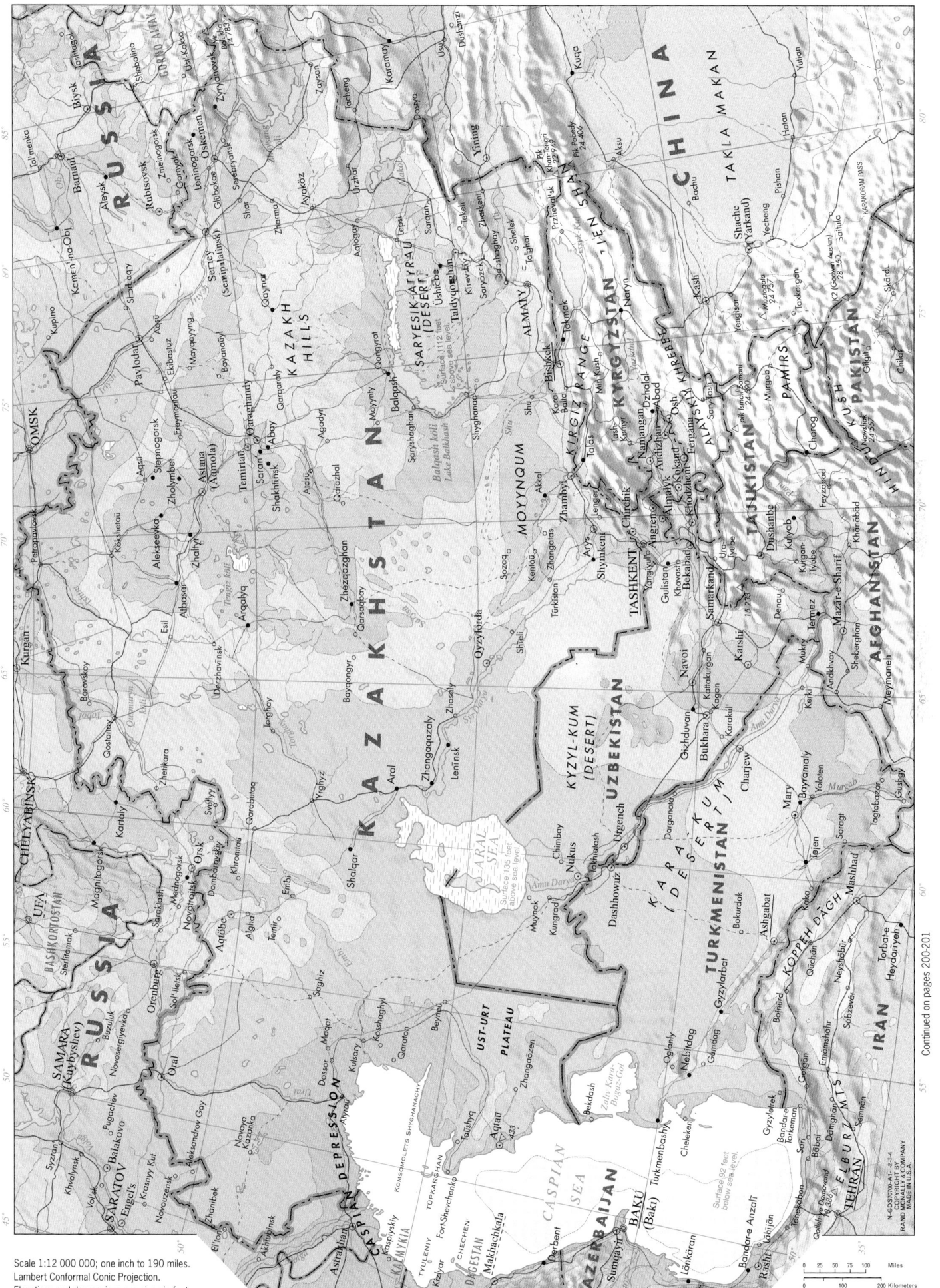

Continued on pages 200-201

Scale 1:12 000 000; one inch to 190 miles.
Lambert Conformal Conic Projection.
Elevations and depressions are given in feet.

| 0 | 25 | 50 | 75 | 100 | Miles |
| 0 | | 100 | | 200 | Kilometers |

N-SDS0000-A1-4-2-4
COPYRIGHT BY
RAND M?NALLY & COMPANY
MADE IN U.S.A.

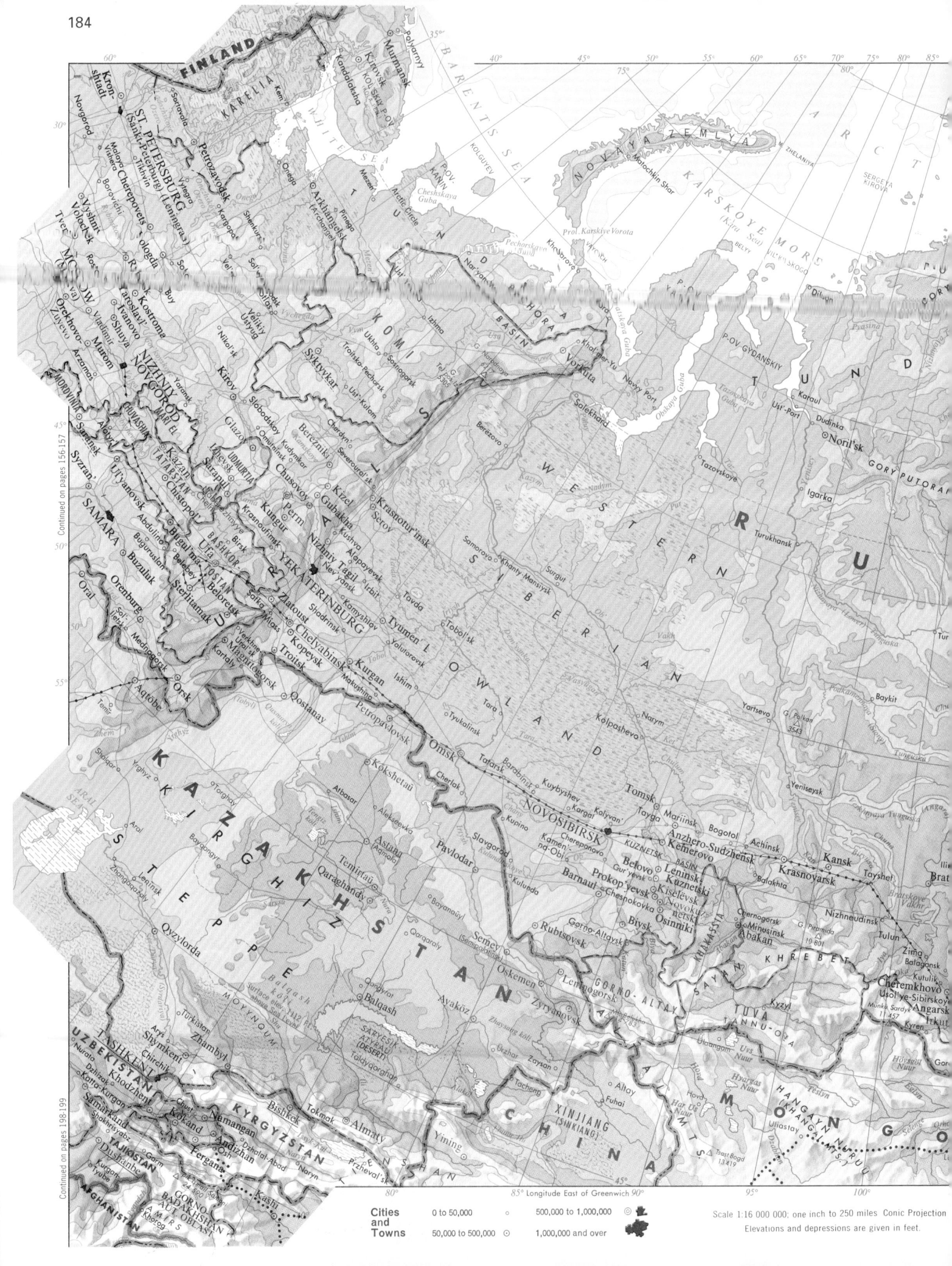

184

Continued on pages 156-157

Continued on pages 198-199

FINLAND

BARENTS SEA

NOVAYA ZEMLYA

KARSKOYE MORE
(Kara Sea)

KOMI

WESTERN SIBERIAN LOWLAND

R U S S I A

MURMANSK
Kronshtadt
Novgorod
ST. PETERSBURG
(Sankt-Peterburg) (Leningrad)
Petrozavodsk
Cherepovets
MOSCOW
Tver
NIZHNIY NOVGOROD
Kazan
TATARSTAN
BASHKOR-TOSTAN
YEKATERINBURG
Perm
Tyumen'
Tobol'sk
Chelyabinsk
Kurgan
Omsk
Tomsk
NOVOSIBIRSK
Krasnoyarsk
Noril'sk

Arkhangel'sk

SAMARA
MORDVINIA
Orenburg
Oral

K A Z A K H S T A N

KIRGIZ STEPPE

ARAL SEA

UZBEKISTAN
TASHKENT
Samarkand
Dushanbe
TAJIKISTAN

KYRGYZSTAN
Bishkek
Almaty

Astana (Aqmola)

Pavlodar

Semey
(Semipalatinsk)

Oskemen

GORNO-ALTAY

TUVA
TANNU-OLA

Kyzyl

C H I N A

XINJIANG
(SINKIANG)

M O N G O L I A

AFGHANISTAN

85° Longitude East of Greenwich 90°

Cities and Towns

| 0 to 50,000 | ○ | 500,000 to 1,000,000 | ◉ |
| 50,000 to 500,000 | ◉ | 1,000,000 and over | ● |

Scale 1:16 000 000; one inch to 250 miles Conic Projection
Elevations and depressions are given in feet.

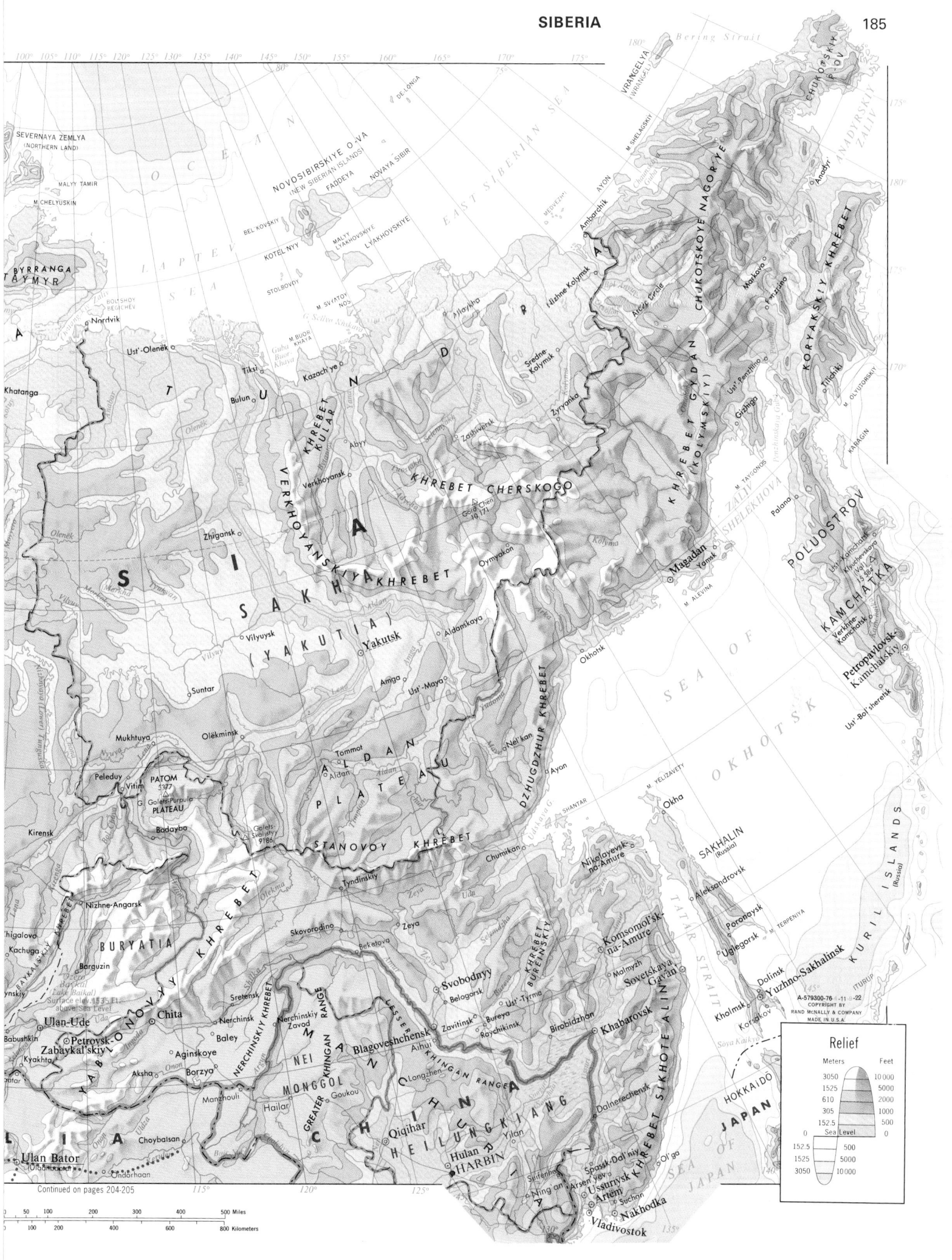

Continued on pages 204-205

SEVERNAYA ZEMLYA
(NORTHERN LAND)

MALYY TAIMYR

M. CHELYUSKIN

NOVOSIBIRSKIYE O-VA
(NEW SIBERIAN ISLANDS)

FADDEYA

NOVAYA SIBIR

DE LONGA

BEL'KOVSKIY

KOTEL NYY

MALYY
LYAKHOVSKIY

STOLBOVOY

BOL'SHOY
LYAKHOVSKIY

M SVYATOY
NOS

G Sellya Khskoto

M BUOR
KHAYA

Guba
Buor
Khaya

BOL'SHOY
BEGICHEV

Nordvik

Ust'-Olenek

Tiksi

Kazach'ye

Aloykha

MEDVEZH'I

Nizhne Kolymsk

AYON

M SHELAGSKIY

Ambarchik

Srednee Kolymsk

Zyryanka

Zashiversk

VRANGELYA I.
(WRANGEL I.)

Bering Strait

CHUKOTSKIY
P-OV

Anadyr'

ANADYRSKIY
ZALIV

Arey Grele

Markovo

KORYAKSKIY KHREBET

M. OLYUTORSKIY

Tilichiki

KARAGIN

POLUOSTROV

KAMCHATKA

M TAYGONOS

ZALIV
SHELEKHOVA

Palana

Gizhiga

Ust' Penzhino

Verkhne-Kamchatsk

Klyuchevskaya
Vulkan
15 584

SEA
OF
OKHOTSK

SIBERIA

BYRRANGA
TAYMYR

Khatanga

Olenek

Bulun

Zhigansk

SAKHA
(YAKUTIA)

Vilyuysk

Suntar

Mukhtuya

Peleduy

Vitim

Kirensk

Badaybo

KHREBET KULAR

VERKHOYANSKIY KHREBET

Verkhoyansk

Abyy

Oymyakon

KHREBET CHERSKOGO

Gora Chen
10,171

Kolyma

Magadan

Yagsk

M ALEVINA

PATOM
1377

Golets Purpula
PLATEAU

Golets-
Skalistyy
9186

STANOVOY KHREBET

ALDAN

Tommot

Aldan

PLATEAU

Amga

Ust'-Maya

Nel'kan

Ayon

DZHUGDZHUR KHREBET

Okhotsk

M YELIZAVETY

M TERPENIYA

Petropavlovsk-
Kamchatskiy

Ust'-Bol'sheretsk

SEA OF
OKHOTSK

Olekminsk

Yakutsk

Aldanskaya

Vilyuy

Lena

Vilyuy

Chumikan

Uda

Tyndinskiy

Zeya

KURIL ISLANDS

Okha

Aleksandrovsk

SAKHALIN
(Russia)

Poronaysk

Uglegorsk

Dolinsk

Yuzhno-Sakhalinsk

Kholmsk

Korsakov

TATAR
STRAIT

Nizhne-Angarsk

BURYATIA

YABLONOVYY KHREBET

Nikolayevsk-
na-Amure

Komsomol'sk-
na-Amure

Sovetskaya
Gavan'

SIKHOTE ALIN'

Ozero
Baykal
(Lake Baikal)
Surface elev 1535 Ft.
above Sea Level

Chigalovo

Kachuga

Barguzin

Ulan-Ude

Petrovsk-
Zabaykal'skiy

Kyakhta

Babushkin

Chita

Nerchinsk

Aginskoye

Borzya

Sretensk

Baley

Nerchinskiy
Zavod

Skovorodino

Beketova

Zeya

Svobodnyy

Belogorsk

Zavitinsk

Bureya

Raychikinsk

KHREBET
BUREINSKIY

Khabarovsk

Birobidzhan

Spassk-Dal'niy

Ussuriysk

Artëm

Nakhodka

Vladivostok

Malmyzh

Dal'nerechensk

SEA
OF
JAPAN

MONGOLIA

Ulan Bator

Ulaanbaatar

Ondorhaan

Choybalsan

Kyakhta

Aksha

Manzhouli

Hailar

Qiqihar

Yilan

Ning'an

NEI
MONGGOL

GREATER KHINGAN RANGE

LESSER KHINGAN RANGE

Longzhen

Goukou

HEILUNGKIANG

Hulan

HARBIN

Shifenhe

Suchon

Ol'ga

HOKKAIDŌ

JAPAN

CHINA

NERCHINSKIY KHREBET

Soya Kaikyō

HamanN

Onon

Argun

Relief

Meters		Feet
3050		10 000
1525		5000
610		2000
305		1000
152.5		500
0	Sea Level	0
152.5		500
1525		5000
3050		10000

0 50 100 200 300 400 500 Miles

0 100 200 400 600 800 Kilometers

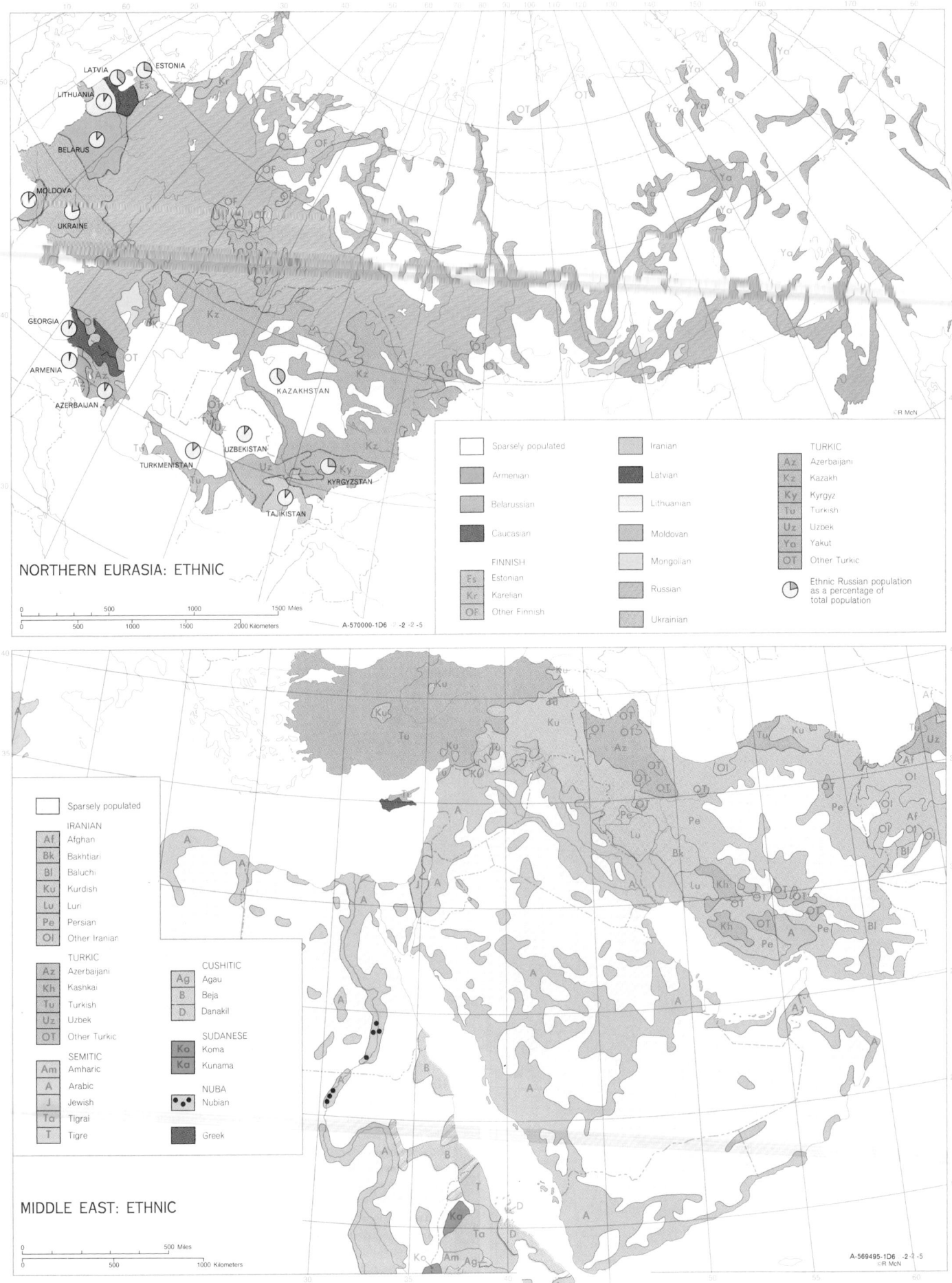

NORTHERN EURASIA: ETHNIC

0   500   1000   1500 Miles
0   500   1000   1500   2000 Kilometers

A-570000-1D6

☐	Sparsely populated
	Armenian
	Belarussian
	Caucasian
	FINNISH
Es	Estonian
Kr	Karelian
OF	Other Finnish

	Iranian
	Latvian
	Lithuanian
	Moldovan
	Mongolian
	Russian
	Ukrainian

TURKIC

Az	Azerbaijani
Kz	Kazakh
Ky	Kyrgyz
Tu	Turkish
Uz	Uzbek
Ya	Yakut
OT	Other Turkic

◔ Ethnic Russian population as a percentage of total population

MIDDLE EAST: ETHNIC

0   500 Miles
0   500   1000 Kilometers

A-569495-1D6

☐	Sparsely populated
	IRANIAN
Af	Afghan
Bk	Bakhtiari
Bl	Baluchi
Ku	Kurdish
Lu	Luri
Pe	Persian
OI	Other Iranian
	TURKIC
Az	Azerbaijani
Kh	Kashkai
Tu	Turkish
Uz	Uzbek
OT	Other Turkic
	SEMITIC
Am	Amharic
A	Arabic
J	Jewish
Ta	Tigrai
T	Tigre

	CUSHITIC
Ag	Agau
B	Beja
D	Danakil
	SUDANESE
Ko	Koma
Ka	Kunama
	NUBA
●●●	Nubian
	Greek

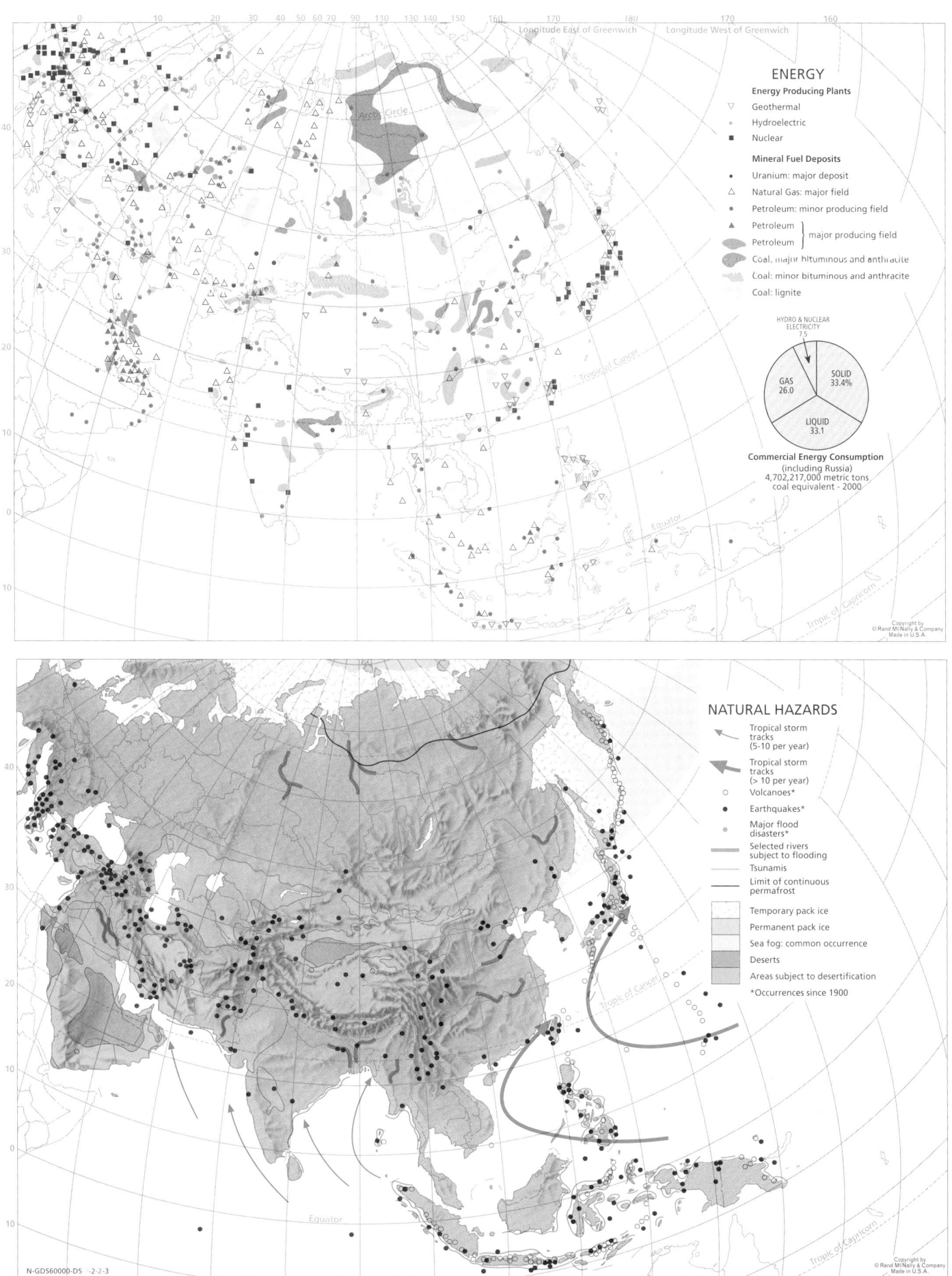

ENERGY

Energy Producing Plants
▽ Geothermal
• Hydroelectric
■ Nuclear

Mineral Fuel Deposits
• Uranium: major deposit
△ Natural Gas: major field
• Petroleum: minor producing field
▲ Petroleum } major producing field
Petroleum }
Coal, major bituminous and anthracite
Coal: minor bituminous and anthracite
Coal: lignite

HYDRO & NUCLEAR
ELECTRICITY
7.5

GAS 26.0
SOLID 33.4%
LIQUID 33.1

Commercial Energy Consumption
(including Russia)
4,702,217,000 metric tons
coal equivalent - 2000

NATURAL HAZARDS

→ Tropical storm tracks (5-10 per year)
→ Tropical storm tracks (> 10 per year)
○ Volcanoes*
● Earthquakes*
• Major flood disasters*
— Selected rivers subject to flooding
— Tsunamis
— Limit of continuous permafrost
Temporary pack ice
Permanent pack ice
Sea fog: common occurrence
Deserts
Areas subject to desertification
*Occurrences since 1900

N-GDS60000-D5 -2-2-3

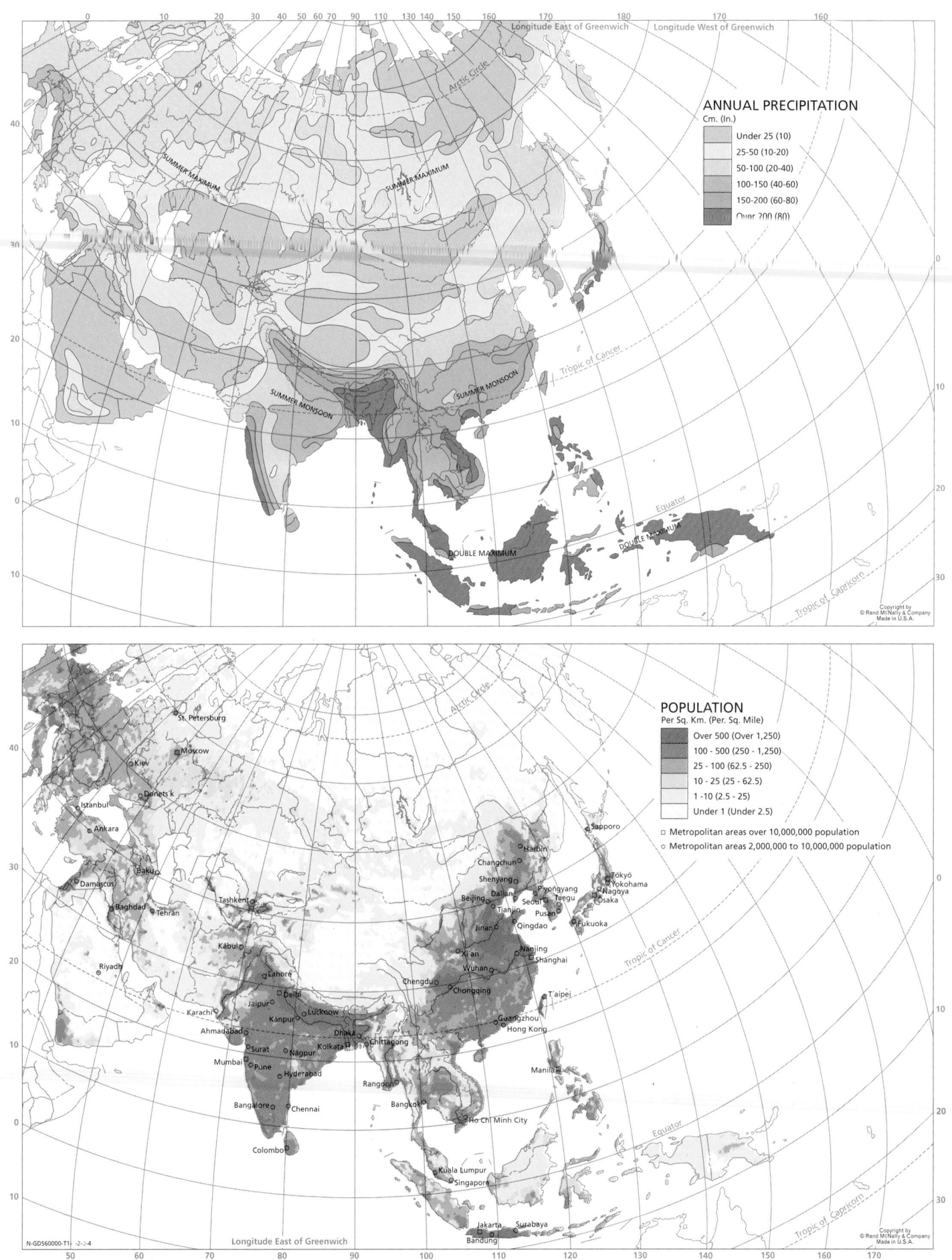

ANNUAL PRECIPITATION
Cm. (In.)

- Under 25 (10)
- 25-50 (10-20)
- 50-100 (20-40)
- 100-150 (40-60)
- 150-200 (60-80)
- Over 200 (80)

SUMMER MAXIMUM

SUMMER MAXIMUM

SUMMER MONSOON

SUMMER MONSOON

DOUBLE MAXIMUM

DOUBLE MAXIMUM

Tropic of Cancer

Equator

Tropic of Capricorn

Longitude East of Greenwich   Longitude West of Greenwich

Copyright by
© Rand McNally & Company
Made in U.S.A.

POPULATION
Per Sq. Km. (Per. Sq. Mile)

- Over 500 (Over 1,250)
- 100 - 500 (250 - 1,250)
- 25 - 100 (62.5 - 250)
- 10 - 25 (25 - 62.5)
- 1 -10 (2.5 - 25)
- Under 1 (Under 2.5)

□ Metropolitan areas over 10,000,000 population
○ Metropolitan areas 2,000,000 to 10,000,000 population

St. Petersburg
Moscow
Kiev
Donets k
Istanbul
Ankara
Baku
Damascus
Baghdad
Tehran
Tashkent
Riyadh
Kābul
Lahore
Delhi
Jaipur
Karachi
Kanpur
Lucknow
Ahmadabad
Surat
Nagpur
Kolkata
Dhaka
Chittagong
Mumbai
Pune
Hyderabad
Rangoon
Bangalore
Chennai
Bangkok
Colombo
Ho Chi Minh City
Kuala Lumpur
Singapore
Jakarta   Surabaya
Bandung

Sapporo
Harbin
Changchun
Shenyang
Tōkyō
Yokohama
Beijing   Dallan   Pyongyang   Nagoya
Tianjin   Seoul   Taegu   Osaka
Jinan   Pusan
Qingdao   Fukuoka
Xi'an   Nanjing
Wuhan   Shanghai
Chengdu   Chongqing
T'aipei
Guangzhou
Hong Kong
Manila

Arctic Circle

Tropic of Cancer

Equator

Tropic of Capricorn

Longitude East of Greenwich

Copyright by
© Rand McNally & Company
Made in U.S.A.

N-GD560000-T1 -2-2-4

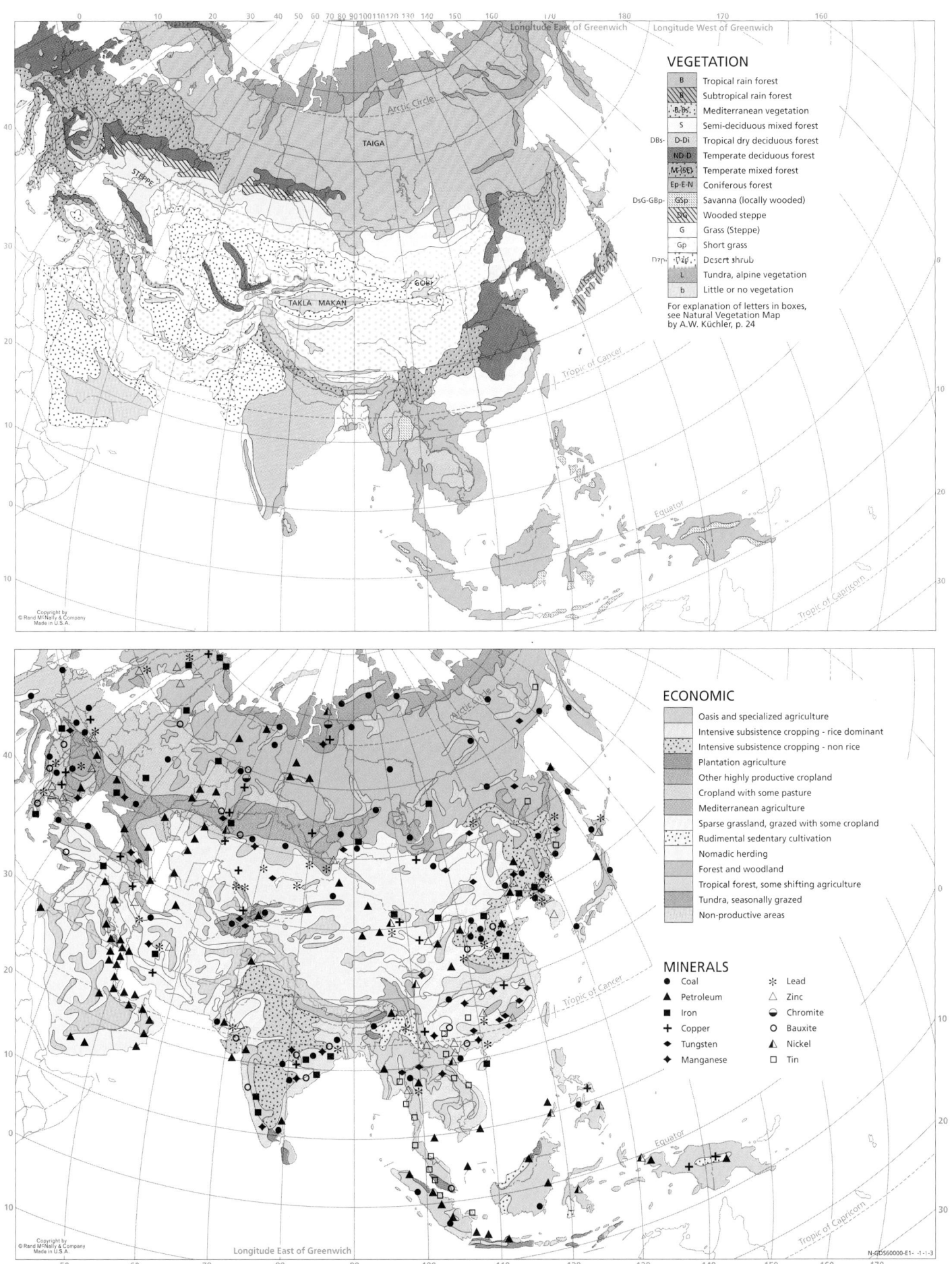

VEGETATION

B	Tropical rain forest
R	Subtropical rain forest
B-Bs	Mediterranean vegetation
S	Semi-deciduous mixed forest
DBs- D-Di	Tropical dry deciduous forest
ND-D	Temperate deciduous forest
M-(6E)	Temperate mixed forest
Ep-E-N	Coniferous forest
DsG-GBp- GSp	Savanna (locally wooded)
BG	Wooded steppe
G	Grass (Steppe)
Gp	Short grass
Dzp- Did	Desert shrub
L	Tundra, alpine vegetation
b	Little or no vegetation

For explanation of letters in boxes,
see Natural Vegetation Map
by A.W. Küchler, p. 24

ECONOMIC

- Oasis and specialized agriculture
- Intensive subsistence cropping - rice dominant
- Intensive subsistence cropping - non rice
- Plantation agriculture
- Other highly productive cropland
- Cropland with some pasture
- Mediterranean agriculture
- Sparse grassland, grazed with some cropland
- Rudimental sedentary cultivation
- Nomadic herding
- Forest and woodland
- Tropical forest, some shifting agriculture
- Tundra, seasonally grazed
- Non-productive areas

MINERALS

●	Coal	✳	Lead
▲	Petroleum	△	Zinc
■	Iron	◐	Chromite
✚	Copper	○	Bauxite
◆	Tungsten	◮	Nickel
◆	Manganese	□	Tin

Longitude East of Greenwich

N-GDS60000-E1- -1-1-3

Urban
Cropland
Cropland & Woodland
Cropland & Grazing Land
Grassland, Grazing Land
Forest, Woodland
Swamp, Marshland
Tundra
Shrub, Sparse Grass, Wasteland
Barren Land
Oasis

Scale 1:36,000,000; one inch to 570 miles. Lambert Azimuthal Equal-Area Projection

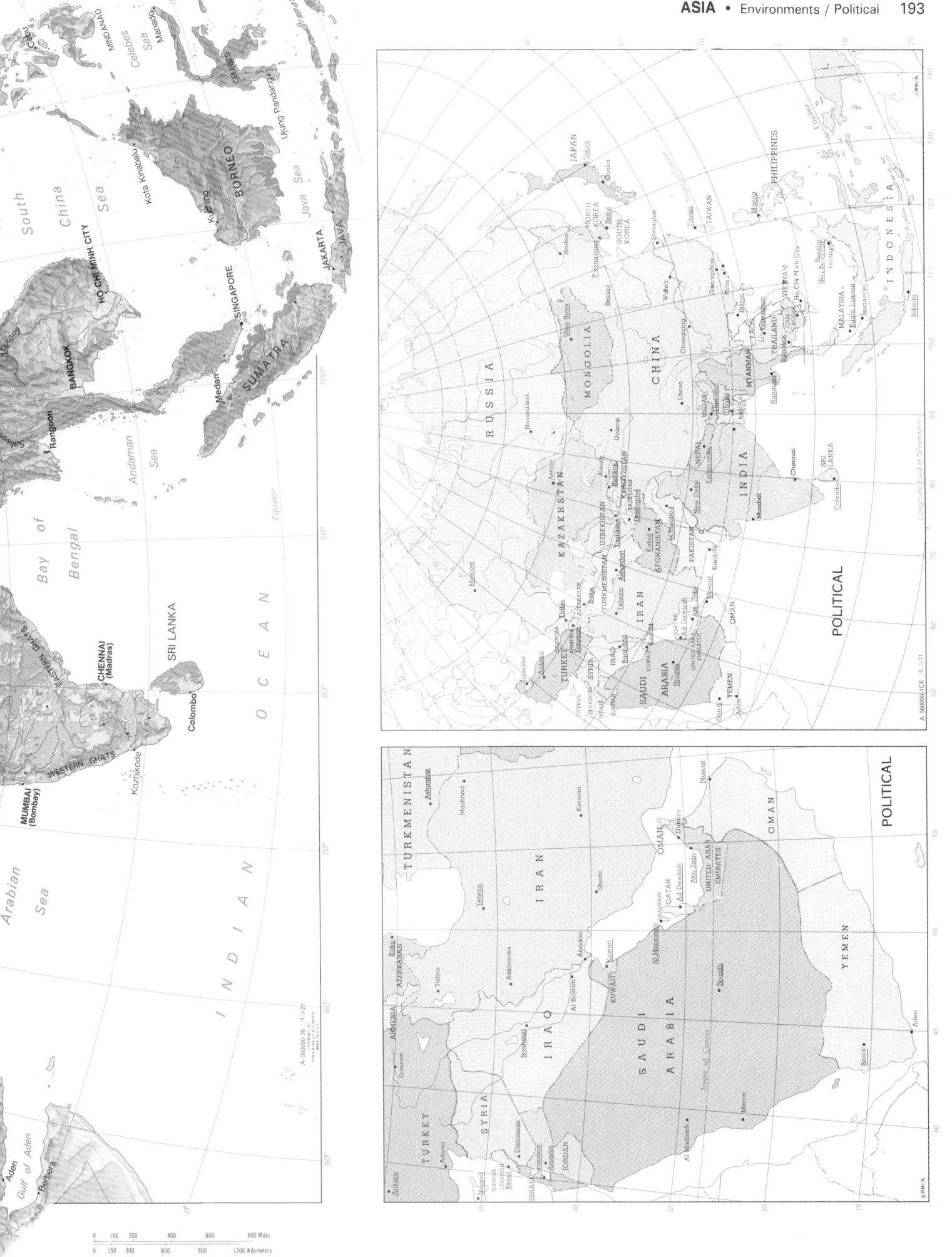

Continued on page 228

40,000 SQ MI
AREA

A-519695-26 — -24-23-46
COPYRIGHT BY
RAND McNALLY & COMPANY
MADE IN U.S.A.

0   300   600
Miles

Scale 1:40 000 000; one inch to 630 miles. Lambert's Azimuthal, Equal Area Projection
Elevations and depressions are given in feet

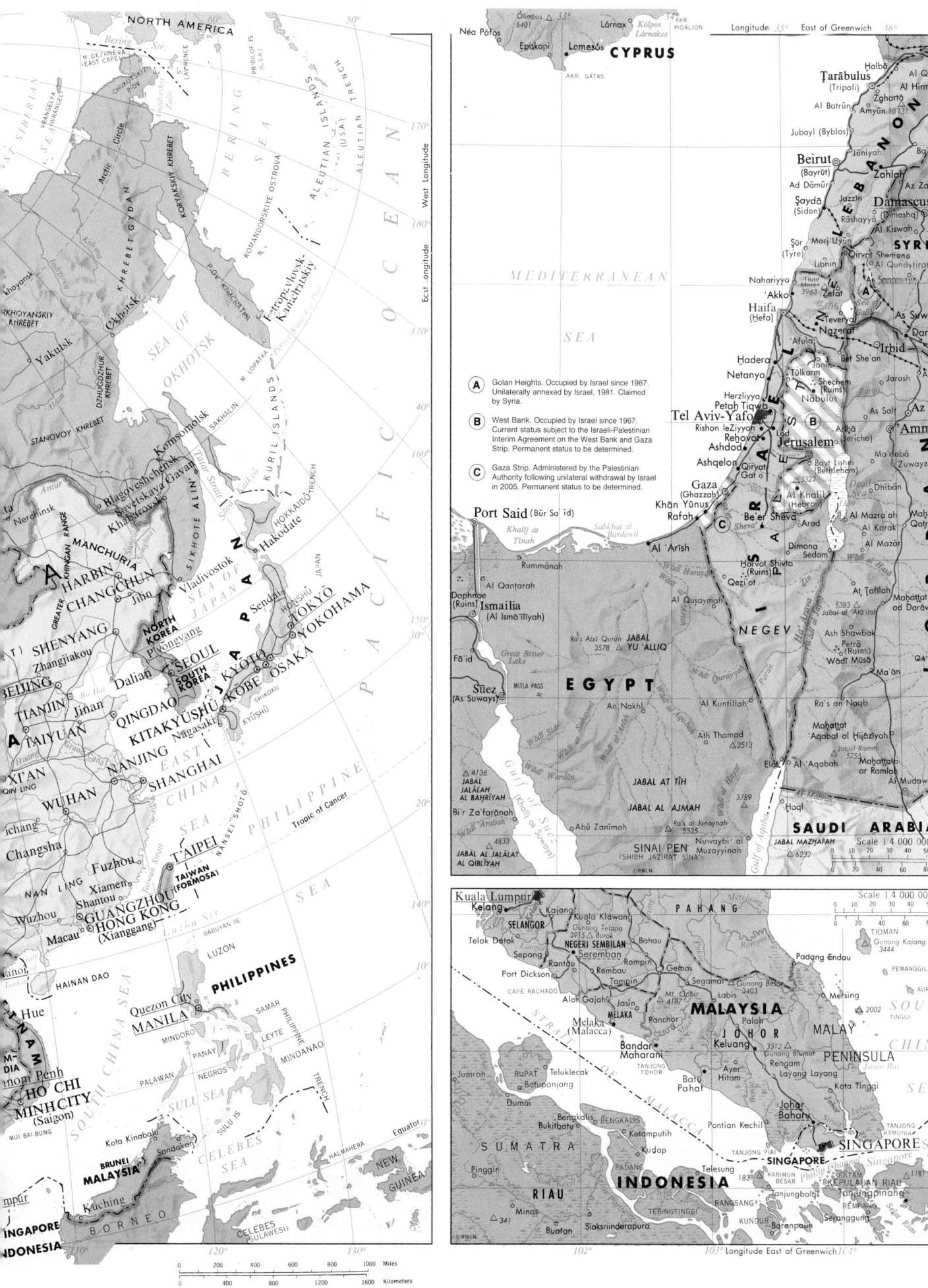

CYPRUS

LEBANON

Beirut
(Bayrūt)

Damascus
(Dimashq)

SYRIA

MEDITERRANEAN

SEA

Ṭarābulus
(Tripoli)

Al Quṣayt
Al Hirmil
Zgharta
Amyūn 10131
Al Batrūn
Jubayl (Byblos)
Jūniyah
Baʻlabakk
Zaḥlah
Az Zabdānī
Ad Dāmūr
Jazzīn
Rāshayyā
Dūmā
Ṣaydā
(Sidon)
Marj ʻUyūn
Al Kiswah
Ṣūr
(Tyre)
Qiryat Shemona
Al Qunayṭirah
Libnin
As Sanamayn
Nahariyya
As Suwaydā
ʻAkko
Zefat
Haifa
(Ḥefa)
Teverya
Dar ʻā
Nazeret
Irbid
Al Mafraq
Hadera
Jenin
Netanya
Ṭūlkarm
Jarash
Herzliyya
Shechem
(Ruins)
Nabulus
Petaḥ Tiqwa
As Salt
Az Zarqaʻ
Tel Aviv-Yafo
Ariha
(Jericho)
Ammān
Rishon leẕiyyon
Madabā
Rehovot
Lod
Jerusalem
Ashdod
Zuwayza
Ashqelon
Qiryat
Gat
Bayt Laḥm
(Bethlehem)
Dhībān
Gaza
(Ghazzah)
Al Khalīl
(Hebron)
Al Mazraʻah
Khān Yūnus
Beʻer Sheva
Al Karak
Rafah
Arad
Al Mazār
Maḥaṭṭat al
Qaṭrānah
Port Said (Būr Saʻīd)
Dimona
Sedom

Golan Heights. Occupied by Israel since 1967.
Unilaterally annexed by Israel, 1981. Claimed
by Syria.

West Bank. Occupied by Israel since 1967.
Current status subject to the Israeli-Palestinian
Interim Agreement on the West Bank and Gaza
Strip. Permanent status to be determined.

Gaza Strip. Administered by the Palestinian
Authority following unilateral withdrawal by Israel
in 2005. Permanent status to be determined.

Sabkhat al
Bardawīl
Al ʻArīsh
Rummānah
Al Qanṭarah
Al Quṣaymah
At Ṭafīlah
Maḥaṭṭat Jurf
ad Darāwīsh
Ismailia
(Al Ismāʻīlīyah)
Horvot Shivta
(Ruins)
Qeziʻot
NEGEV
Ash Shawbak
Petra
(Ruins)
Wādī Mūsā
Fāʻid
Maʻān
EGYPT
An Nakhl
Al Kuntillah
Raʻs an Naqb
Suez
(As Suways)
Athī Thamad
Maḥattat
ʻAqabat al Hijāziyah
Elāt
Al ʻAqabah
Mahaṭṭah
ar Ramlah
Al Mudawwarah
JABAL AT TĪH
JABAL AL AJMAH
Haql
JABAL MAZHAFAH
SAUDI ARABIA
Scale 1:4 000 000
JABAL
JALĀLAH
AL BAHRĪYAH
Biʻr Zaʻfarānah
Abū Zanīmah
Nuwaybiʻ al
Muzayyinah
SINAI PEN
(SHIBH JAZĪRAT SĪNĀ)
JABĀL AL JALĀLAT
AL QIBLĪYAH

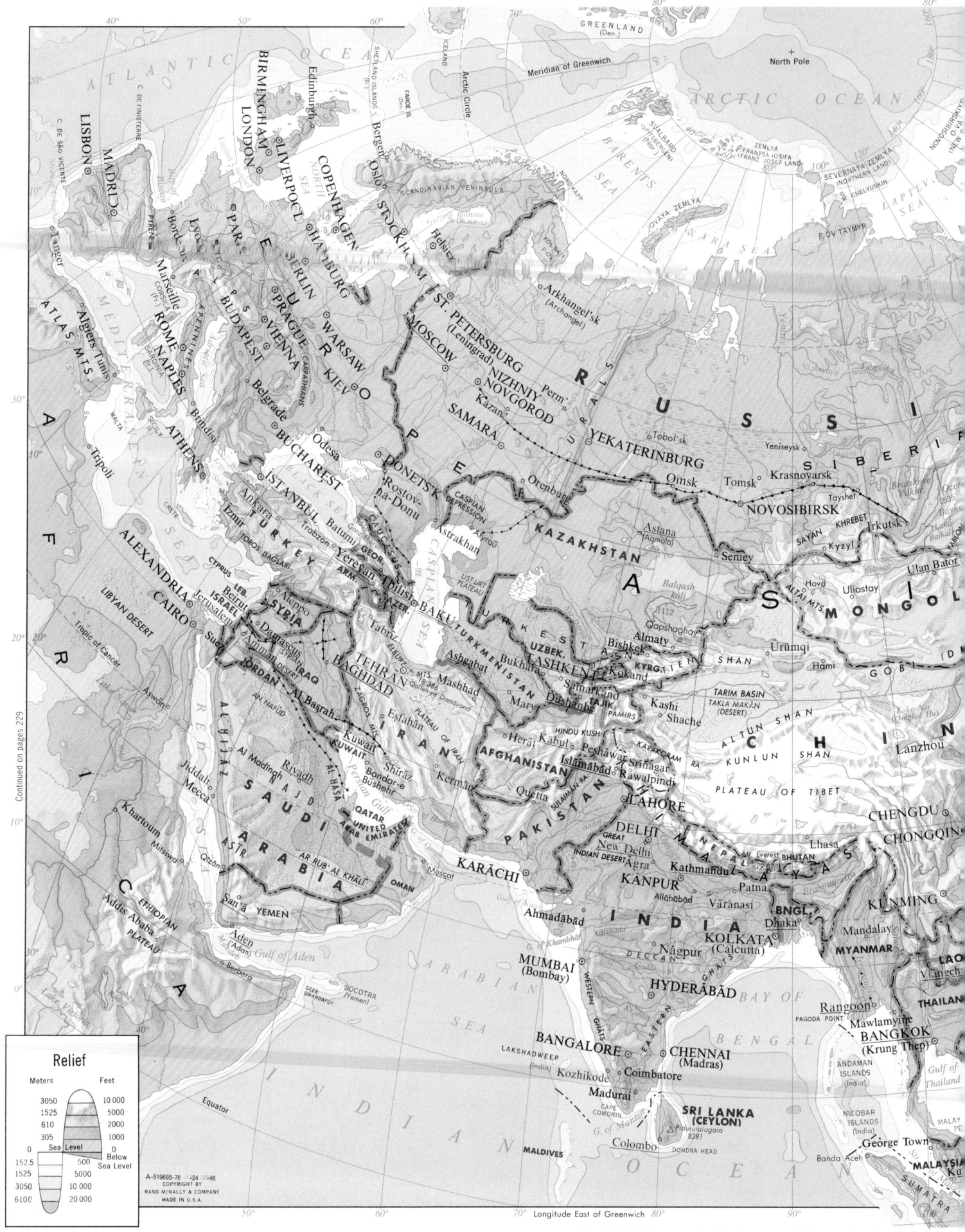

Continued on pages 229

Relief

Meters		Feet
3050		10 000
1525		5000
610		2000
305		1000
0	Sea Level	0
		Below
152.5		500 Sea Level
1525		5000
3050		10 000
6100		20 000

A-519695-76 1:24-2646
COPYRIGHT BY
RAND McNALLY & COMPANY
MADE IN U.S.A.

Scale 1:40 000 000; one inch to 630 miles. Lambert's Azimuthal, Equal Area Projection
Elevations and depressions are given in feet

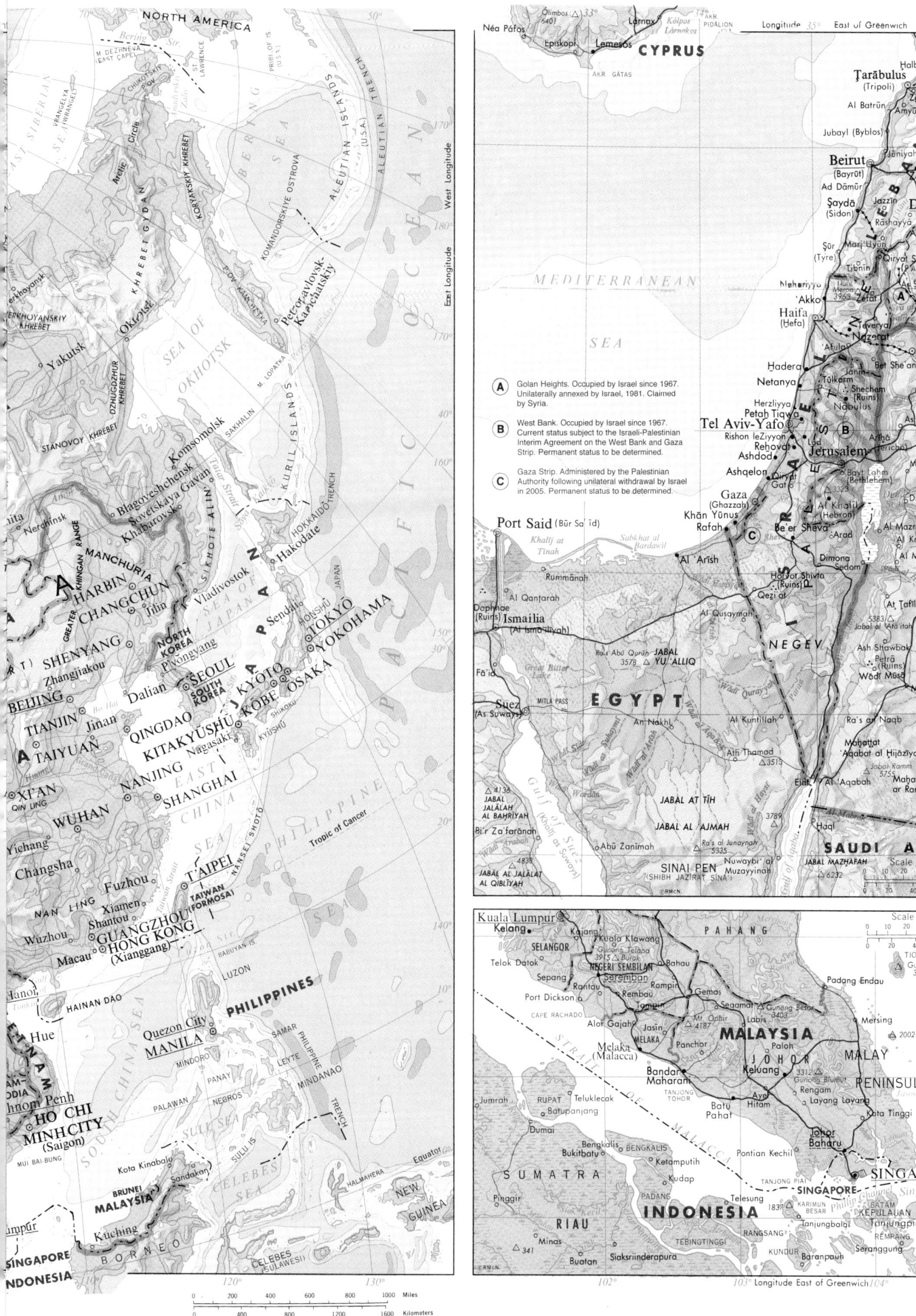

a

CYPRUS

Néa Páfos
Epískopi
Lemesós
AKR. GÁTAS
Ólimbos △33°
6401
Lárnax
Kólpos
Lárnakos
AKR.
PIDÁLION

Longitude 35° East of Greenwich 36°

MEDITERRANEAN

SEA

Ṭarābulus
(Tripoli)
Halba
Al Qubayt
Al Hirmil
Az Zaharta
Amyūn △10131
Jubayl (Byblos)
Ba'labakk
Beirut
(Bayrūt)
Jūniya
Ad Dāmūr
Aḥzahle
Az Zabdāni
Ṣaydā
(Sidon)
Jazzin
Damascus
(Dimashq)
Dūmā
Ṣūr
(Tyre)
Marj 'Uyūn
Rāshayyā
Kiswah
Nahariyya
Qiryat Shemona
('Ayn Junayyirah)
Tibnin
Meron △
Zefat
3962
As Suwaydā'
Dar'ā
'Akko
Haifa
(Hefa)
Tayeriya
Nazerat
Afula
Bet She'an
Irbid
Al Maţraq
Hadera
Netanya
Jenin
Tülkarm
Shechem
(Ruins)
Nablus
Jarash
Herzliyya
Petaħ Tiqwa
As Salt
Az Zarqā'
Tel Aviv-Yafo
Rishon leZiyyon
Reħovot
Lod
Ashdod
Jerusalem
Arīħa
(Jericho)
'Ammān
Madaba
Zuwayza'
Ashqelon
Qiryat
Gat
△3323
Bayt Laḥm
(Bethlehem)
Dhībān
Gaza
(Ghazzah)
Al Khalīl
(Hebron)
Khān Yūnis
Rafaħ
Be'er Sheva'
Al Mazra'ah
Al Karak
Maħaṭṭat al
Qaṭrānah
Port Said (Būr Sa'īd)
Khalīj at
Tīnah
Sabkhat al
Bardawīl
Arad
Sedom
Al Maz
Dimona
Al 'Arīsh
Rummānah
Mahaṭṭat Jurt
ad Darwīsh
Hor'at Shivta
(Ruins)
Qezi'ot
At Tafīlah
5383 △
Al Qanṭarah
Al Qusaymah
Ḥamam al
'Ata'ițah
Ash Shawbak
Petra
(Ruins)
Wādī Mūsā
Daphnae
(Ruins)
Ismailia
(Al Ismā'iliyah)
Ra's Abū Qurūn
JABAL
3578 △ YU 'ALLIQ
NEGEV
QA' AL JAFR
Fā'id
Great Bitter
Lake
Ma'ān
Suez
(As Suways)
MITLA PASS
EGYPT
An Nakhl
Wādī Qurayy
Ra's an Naqb
Mahaṭṭat Ramm
5755 △
Wādī al Ḥayy
Mahaṭṭat
'Aqabat al Hijāzīyah
Mahaṭṭat
ar Ramlah
Ejat
Al 'Aqabah
Al Mudawwarah
Ath Thamad
△3513
3789
△
Ḥaql
JABAL AT TĪH
JABAL AL AJMAH
SAUDI ARABIA
JABAL MAZHAFAH
Scale 1:4 000 000
△4138
JABAL
JALĀLAH
AL BAHRIYAH
Bi'r Za'farānah
Abū Zanīmah
Ra's al Junaynah
5335
Nuwaybi' al
Muzayyinah
0 10 20 30 40 50 Miles
SINAI PEN.
(SHIBH JAZIRAT SINA')
△6232
JABAL AL JALĀLAT
AL QIBLĪYAH
4838
△
0 20 40 60 80 Kilometers
©RMCN.

Golan Heights. Occupied by Israel since 1967.
Unilaterally annexed by Israel, 1981. Claimed
by Syria.

West Bank. Occupied by Israel since 1967.
Current status subject to the Israeli-Palestinian
Interim Agreement on the West Bank and Gaza
Strip. Permanent status to be determined.

Gaza Strip. Administered by the Palestinian
Authority following unilateral withdrawal by Israel
in 2005. Permanent status to be determined.

NORTH AMERICA

Bering
Str.
M. DEZHNEVA
(EAST CAPE)
ST. LAWRENCE
I.
PRIBILOF IS.
(U.S.A.)
M. OLYUTORSKIY
VRANGELYA
(WRANGEL)
CHUKOTSKIY
ALEUTIAN ISLANDS (U.S.A.)
ALEUTIAN TRENCH

East Longitude
West Longitude

ARCTIC Circle

SEVERNYY
KHREBET GYDA
KORYAKSKIY KHREBET
KOMANDORSKIYE OSTROVA

Verkhoyansk
KHREBET
Yakutsk
Petropavlovsk-
Kamchatskiy
SEA OF
OKHOTSK
M. LOPATKA
KURIL ISLANDS
STANOVOY KHREBET
Komsomolsk
Blagoveshchensk
Sovetskaya Gavan'
Khabarovsk
SAKHALIN
Nerchinsk
Tatar Strait
Vladivostok
SEA OF
JAPAN
MANCHURIA
HARBIN
CHANGCHUN
Jilin
North Korea
Pyongyang
Hokkaido
Hakodate
HONSHŪ
Sendai
TOKYO
YOKOHAMA
Chita
Amur
GREATER KHINGAN RANGE
SHENYANG
Zhangjiakou
BEIJING
Dalian
Bo Hai
SEOUL
South Korea
Kyoto
Kobe Osaka
Shikoku
Kyushu
Tianjin
Jinan
Qingdao
Taiyuan
Nanjing
Shanghai
Xi'an
Qin Ling
Wuhan
Yichang
Changsha
Nan Ling
Fuzhou
Xiamen
Shantou
Guangzhou
Hong Kong
(Xianggang)
Macau
Wuzhou
T'AIPEI
TAIWAN
(FORMOSA)
Nansei Shoto
Tropic of Cancer
EAST
CHINA
SEA
PHILIPPINE
SEA
PACIFIC
OCEAN
JAPAN
HAINAN DAO
Hue
Hanoi
VIETNAM
ODIA
hnom Penh
HO CHI
MINHCITY
(Saigon)
MUI BAI BUNG
SOUTH CHINA SEA
BABUYAN IS.
LUZON
Quezon City
MANILA
MINDORO
PHILIPPINES
SAMAR
PANAY
LEYTE
PHILIPPINE TRENCH
PALAWAN
NEGROS
MINDANAO
SULU SEA
SULU IS.
Kota Kinabalu
Sandakan
CELEBES SEA
(SULAWESI)
BRUNEI
MALAYSIA
Kuching
BORNEO
SINGAPORE
INDONESIA
NEW
GUINEA
HALMAHERA
Equator

0 200 400 600 800 1000 Miles
0 400 800 1200 1600 Kilometers

b

Scale 1:4 000 000
0 10 20 30 40 50 Miles
0 20 40 60 80 Kilometers

Kuala Lumpur
Kelang
Kajang
PAHANG
Kuala Klawang
SELANGOR
Gunong Telapa
Buruk
3915 △
Bahau
TIOMAN
Gunong Kajang
3444
Telok Datok
NEGERI SEMBILAN
Seremban
Rantau
Rembau
Rompin
Padang Endau
PEMANGGIL
Sepang
Gemas
Port Dickson
Segamat
Gunong Besar
3403 △
Mersing
AUR
CAPE RACHADO
Jasin
Labis
Alor Gajah
Mt. Ophir
4187 △
MALAYSIA
SOUTH
TINGGI
MELAKA
Panchor
2002 △
Melaka
(Malacca)
JOHOR
MALAY
Kluang
Bandar
Maharani
Gunong Blumut
3312 △
PENINSULA
CHINA
Jumrah
Teluklecak
Paloh
Rengam
Ayer
Hitam
Layang Layang
Kota Tinggi
SEA
RUPAT
Batu
Pahat
TANJONG
TOHOR
Dumai
Batupanjang
Pontian Kechil
Johor
Baharu
TANJONG
RAMUNIA
SUMATRA
Bengkalis
BENGKALIS
Ketamputih
SINGAPORE
SINGAPORE
TANJUNG
BERAKIT
Pinggir
Kudap
TANJONG PIAI
Singapore Strait
Pingir
Telesung
1837 △
KARIMUN
BESAR
BATAM
KEPULAUAN RIAU
BINTAN
RIAU
INDONESIA
Minas
△341
Buatan
Siaksriinderapura
RANGSANG
Baranpan
Tanjungbalai
Tanjungpinang
KUNDUR
TEBINGTINGGI
SERANGGUNG
Singkep Str.

102°
103° Longitude East of Greenwich 104°
©RMCN.

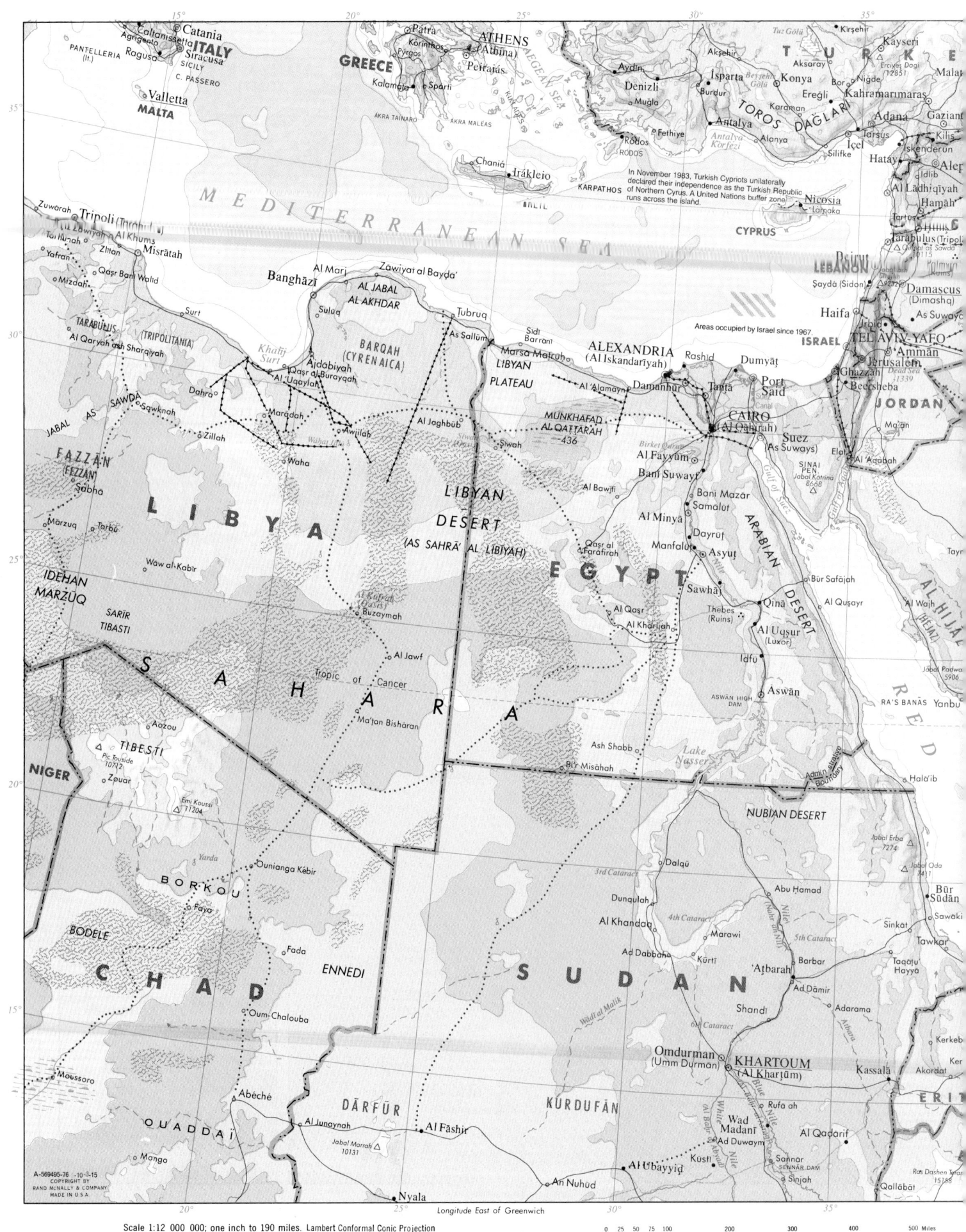

Scale 1:12 000 000; one inch to 190 miles. Lambert Conformal Conic Projection
Elevations and depressions are given in feet

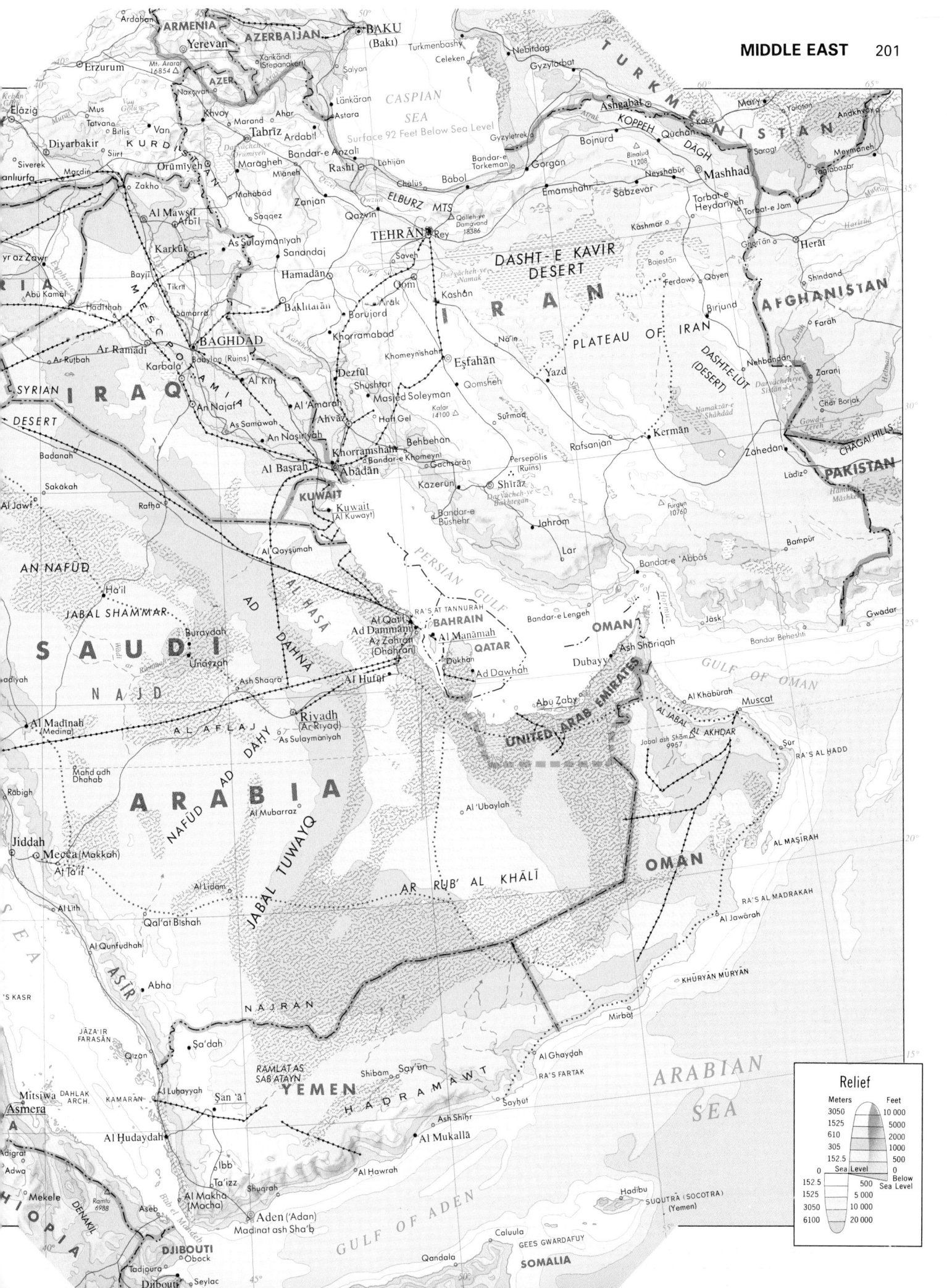

Relief

Meters		Feet
3050		10 000
1525		5000
610		2000
305		1000
152.5		500
0	Sea Level	0
		Below
		Sea Level
152.5		500
1525		5 000
3050		10 000
6100		20 000

a

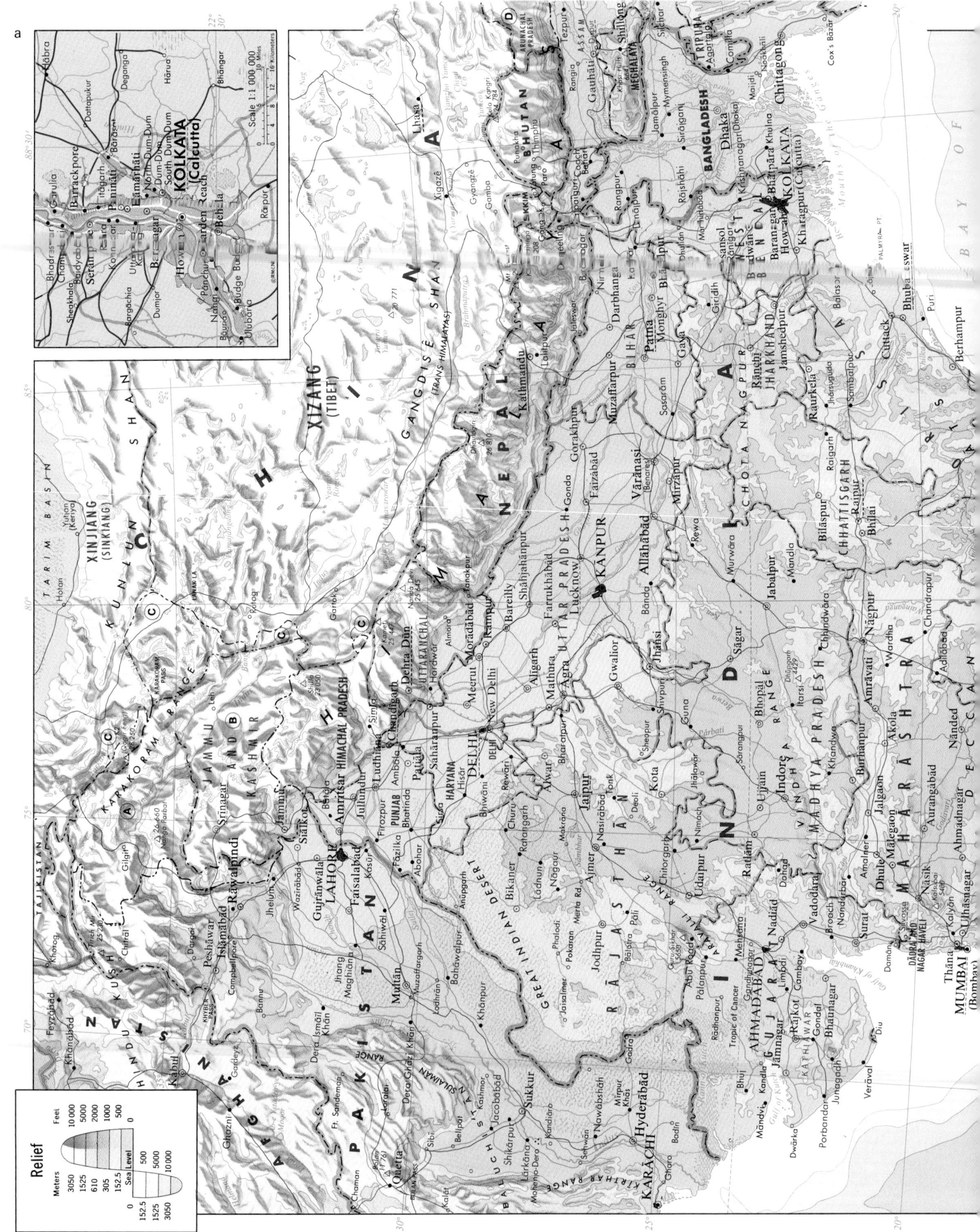

Scale 1:10 000 000; one inch to 160 miles. Lambert Conformal Conic Projection
Elevations and depressions are given in feet

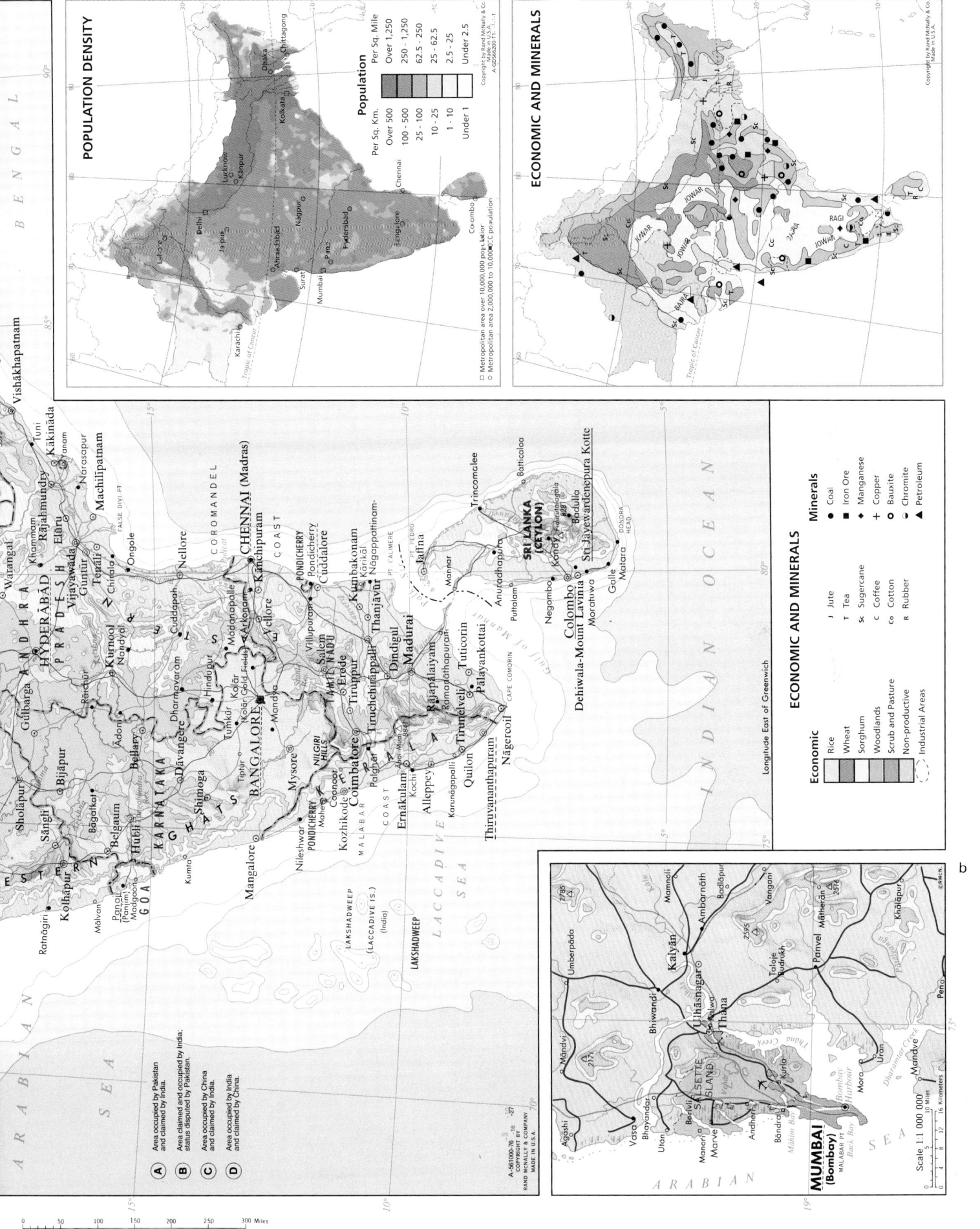

Continued on pages 184-185

Continued on pages 198-199

Scale 1:16 000 000; one inch to 250 miles. Polyconic Projection
Elevations and depressions are given in feet

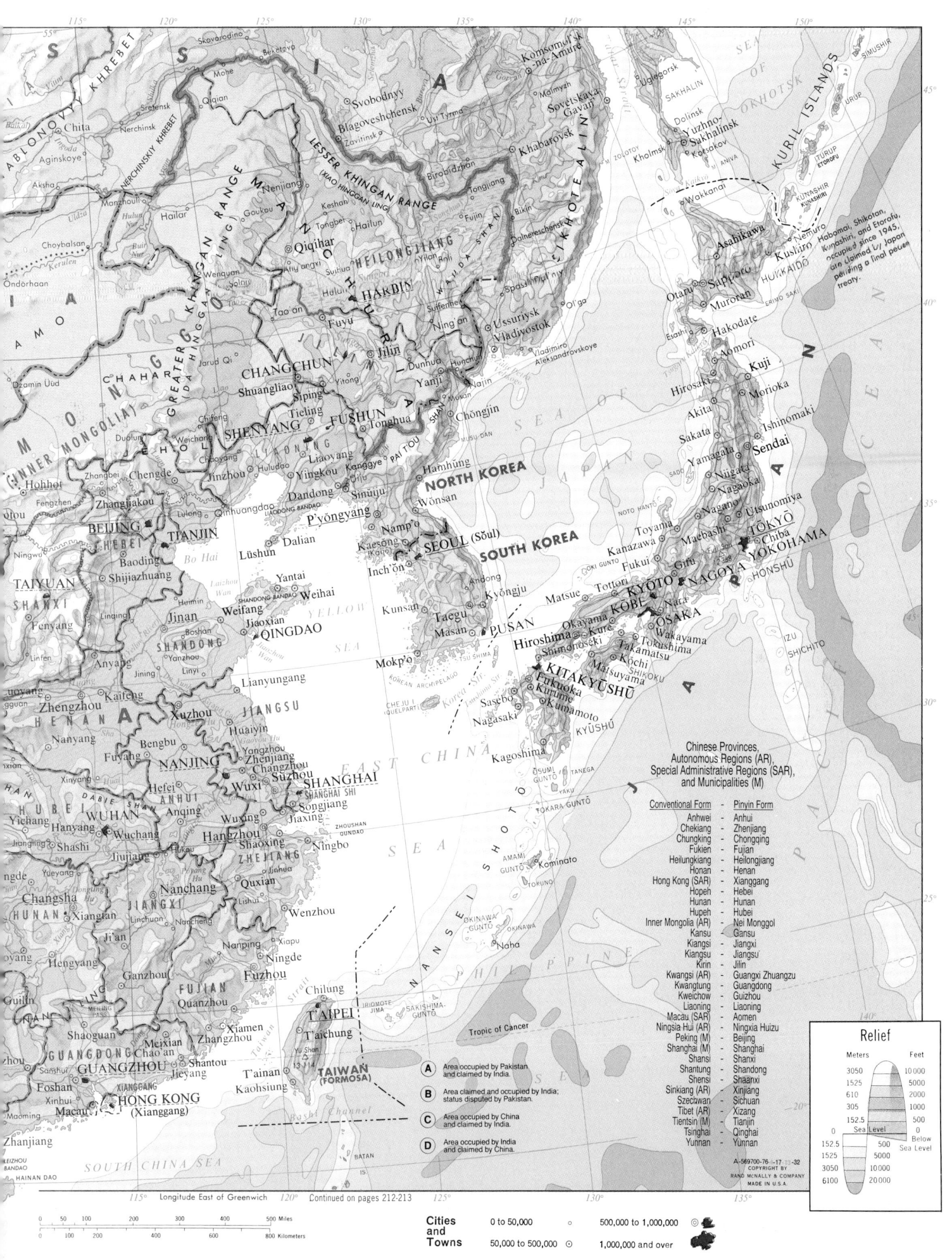

Chinese Provinces,
Autonomous Regions (AR),
Special Administrative Regions (SAR),
and Municipalities (M)

Conventional Form	Pinyin Form
Anhwei	Anhui
Chekiang	Zhejiang
Chungking	Chongqing
Fukien	Fujian
Heilungkiang	Heilongjiang
Honan	Henan
Hong Kong (SAR)	Xianggang
Hopeh	Hebei
Hunan	Hunan
Hupeh	Hubei
Inner Mongolia (AR)	Nei Monggol
Kansu	Gansu
Kiangsi	Jiangxi
Kiangsu	Jiangsu
Kirin	Jilin
Kwangsi (AR)	Guangxi Zhuangzu
Kwangtung	Guangdong
Kweichow	Guizhou
Liaoning	Liaoning
Macau (SAR)	Aomen
Ningsia Hui (AR)	Ningxia Huizu
Peking (M)	Beijing
Shanghai (M)	Shanghai
Shansi	Shanxi
Shantung	Shandong
Shensi	Shaanxi
Sinkiang (AR)	Xinjiang
Szechwan	Sichuan
Tibet (AR)	Xizang
Tientsin (M)	Tianjin
Tsinghai	Qinghai
Yunnan	Yunnan

Ⓐ Area occupied by Pakistan
and claimed by India.

Ⓑ Area claimed and occupied by India;
status disputed by Pakistan.

Ⓒ Area occupied by China
and claimed by India.

Ⓓ Area occupied by India
and claimed by China.

A-569700-76—17-73-32
COPYRIGHT BY
RAND McNALLY & COMPANY
MADE IN U.S.A.

Relief

Meters	Feet
3050	10000
1525	5000
610	2000
305	1000
152.5	500
Sea Level	0
	Below
152.5	Sea Level
1525	500
3050	5000
6100	10000
	20000

Longitude East of Greenwich   Continued on pages 212-213

0 50 100 200 300 400 500 Miles
0 100 200 400 600 800 Kilometers

Cities and Towns

0 to 50,000 ○   500,000 to 1,000,000 ◎

50,000 to 500,000 ⊙   1,000,000 and over ▉

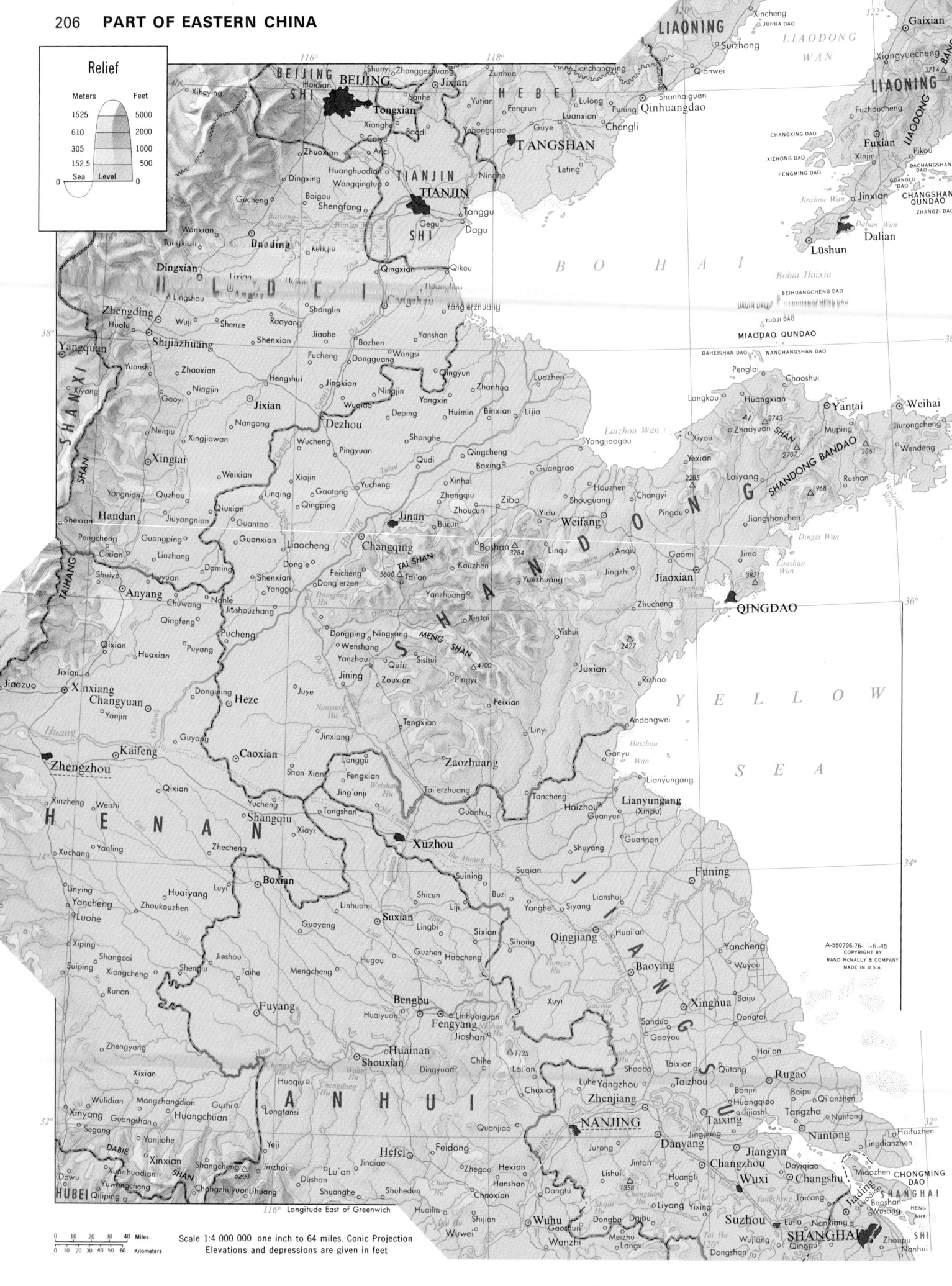

Relief

Meters	Feet
1525	5000
610	2000
305	1000
152.5	500
Sea Level	0
0	0

LIAONING

LIAODONG WAN

Gaixian

Xincheng
JUHUA DAO
Suizhong

Xiongyuecheng

LIAONING

3714

LIAODONG BANDAO

Fuxian

Fuzhoucheng

Pikou

DACHANGSHAN DAO

CHANGXING DAO

XIZHONG DAO

FENGMING DAO

Xinjin

GUANGLU DAO

CHANGSHAN QUNDAO

ZHANGZI DAO

Jinxian

Jinzhou Wan

Dalian Wan

Dalian

Lüshun

BEIJING SHI

BEIJING

Shunyi Zhanggezhuang

Xiheying Haidian Jixian

Tongxian

Xianghe Baodi

Zhuoxian Anci

Dingxing Wangqingtu

Gucheng Baigou Shengfang

Wanxian Baiyang Dian

Tongxulu Kehui

Dading

HEBEI

Zunhua Jianchangying

Yutian Fengrun Lulong

Sanhe Fengrun

TANGSHAN

Leting

Guye Changli

Qinhuangdao

Shanhaiguan Funing

Luanxian

Yahongqiao

TIANJIN SHI

TIANJIN

Gegu Tanggu

Dagu

Ninghe

Qingxian Qikou

BOHAI

Bohai Haixia

DADN DADN BEIHUANGCHENG DAO

TUOJI DAO

MIAODAO QUNDAO

DAHEISHAN DAO NANCHANGSHAN DAO

Penglai Chaoshui

Longkou Huangxian

SHANDONG BANDAO

Yantai Weihai

Muping Jiurongcheng

Wendeng

Rushan

2861

SHANXI

Yangquan

Yuanshi

Xiyang

Shexian

Handan

Pengcheng Guangping

Cixian Linzhang

Shuiye Liyuan

TAIHANG SHAN

Anyang Chuwang

Nanle

Qingfeng

Huaxian Puyang

Xinxiang

Jiaozuo

Changyuan

Zhengzhou Kaifeng

Qixian

HENAN

Xuchang

Xinzheng Weishi

Linying Yanling

Yancheng

Luohe

Xiping Shangcai

Suiping Xiangcheng

Runan

HUBEI

DABIE SHAN

Dawu Xuanhuadian

Qiliping

Yuwangcheng

Zhengding

Huolu Wuji

Shijiazhuang

Zhaoxian

Ningjin Gaoyi

Yongnian Quzhou

Jiuyongnian

Guantao

Daming

Zhengyang

Xixian

Wulidian Mangzhangdian

Gushi Longtansi

Huangchuan

Segang

Yanjiahe

Dabu

Xinyang Guangshan

Yeji

Shenze Jiaohe

Raoyang

Hengshui Jingxian

Wuqiao

Fucheng Dongguang

Nangong

Neiqiu Xingjiawan

Xiajin Gaotang

Linqing Qingping

Qiuxian

Dong'e

Shenxian

Yanggu

Jushouzhang

Pucheng

Dongming

Guyang

Heze

Juye

Caoxian

Shan Xian Fengxian

Jinxiang

Yucheng

Shangqiu

Xiayi

Zhecheng

Luyi

Boxian

Huaiyang Guoyang

Zhoukouzhen

Shangcheng

Jinzhai

Shenqiu Taihe

Jieshou

Fuyang

Mengcheng

Shuanghe

L'an

Dushan

Huoqiu

Huaiyuan

Shouxian

Huainan

Dingyuan

ANHUI

HEFEI

Feidong

Feixian

Hexian Zhegao

Chaoxian

Hanshan

Dangtu

Wuwei

Jizhou

Dezhou

Wucheng

Pingyuan Shanghe

Yucheng

Qingping

Liaocheng

Changqing

Feicheng

Dong'erzen

Tai'an

TAI SHAN 5000

Yanzhuang

Xintai

Ningyang

Wenshang

Yanzhou

Qufu

Sishui

Zouxian Pingyi

Jining

Tengxian

Linyi

Feixian

Shanghe

Shanglin

Wangsi

Yanshan

Bozhen

Qingyun

Deping

Huimin Binxian Lijia

Yangxin Zhanhua

Qingcheng Boxing

Qudi

Xinhai

Zhangqiu Zibo Yidu

Zhoucun

JINAN

Bucun

Boshan 3284

Kouzhen

MENG SHAN 4100

Luozhen

Houzhen Shouguang

Guangrao

Yangjiaogou

Laizhou Wan

Xiyou

Zhaoyuan Shan 2743

2707

Yexian

AI SHAN

Laiyang

2285

1968

Pingdu

Changyi

Weifang

Anqiu Linqu

Yuezhuang

Jingzhi

Gaomi

Jiaoxian

Jimo

3871

Laoshan Wan

QINGDAO

SHANDONG

Juxian

Rizhao

2427

Yishui

Andongwei

Haizhou Wan

Linyi

Tancheng

Ganyu

Lianyungang (Xinpu)

YELLOW SEA

Zaozhuang

Tai'erzhuang

Guanhu

Longgu

Xuzhou

Tongshan

Suining

Shicun Buzi

Suxian Lingbi

Guzhen

Haocheng

Sixian

Sihong

Shuyang

Guannan

Haizhou

Guanyun

Lianshui

Siyang

Yanghe

Qingjiang

Huai'an

Funing

Sanduo

Baying

Xinghua

Wuyou

Yancheng

Dongtai

Hai'an

Rugao

Baipu Qi'anzhen

Banjin

Tangzha

Nantong

Haifuzhen

Lingdaizhen

CHONGMING DAO

Miaozhen

Dayiqiao

Jiading

SHANGHAI SHI

HENG

Baoshan

Wusong

Nanxiang

SHANGHAI

Zhoupu

Qingpu

Dongshan

A-560796-76- -6-40

COPYRIGHT BY

RAND MCNALLY & COMPANY

MADE IN U.S.A.

Suqian

Qingjiang

Lianshui

JIANGSU

Sihong

Xuyi

Gaoyou Hu

Luhe Yangzhou

Lai'an Chuxian

Zhenjiang

Taixian Qutang

Taizhou

Jurong

Jintan

Lishui

Danyang

Taixing

Jiangyin

Changzhou

Wuxi

Yixing

Suzhou

Wujiang

NANJING

Quanjiao

Feidong

Chihe

1735

Shaobo Hu

Hongze Hu

Gaoyou

Xinghua

Sanduo

Shaoyang

Taizhou

Huangqiao

Jijiashi

Jinjiang

Changshu

1358

Tai Hu

Dongdong Hu

Liyang

Wuhu

Gaoshun

Dongba

Meizhou

Langxi

Wanzhi

Nanhui

Shijian

Huailin

Dongba

Lujia

Nanxiang

Chengdong Hu

Nushan Hu

Jiashan

Fengyang Linhuaiguan

Wabu Hu

Chengdong Hu

0 10 20 30 40 Miles

0 10 20 30 40 50 60 Kilometers

Scale 1:4 000 000 one inch to 64 miles. Conic Projection

Elevations and depressions are given in feet

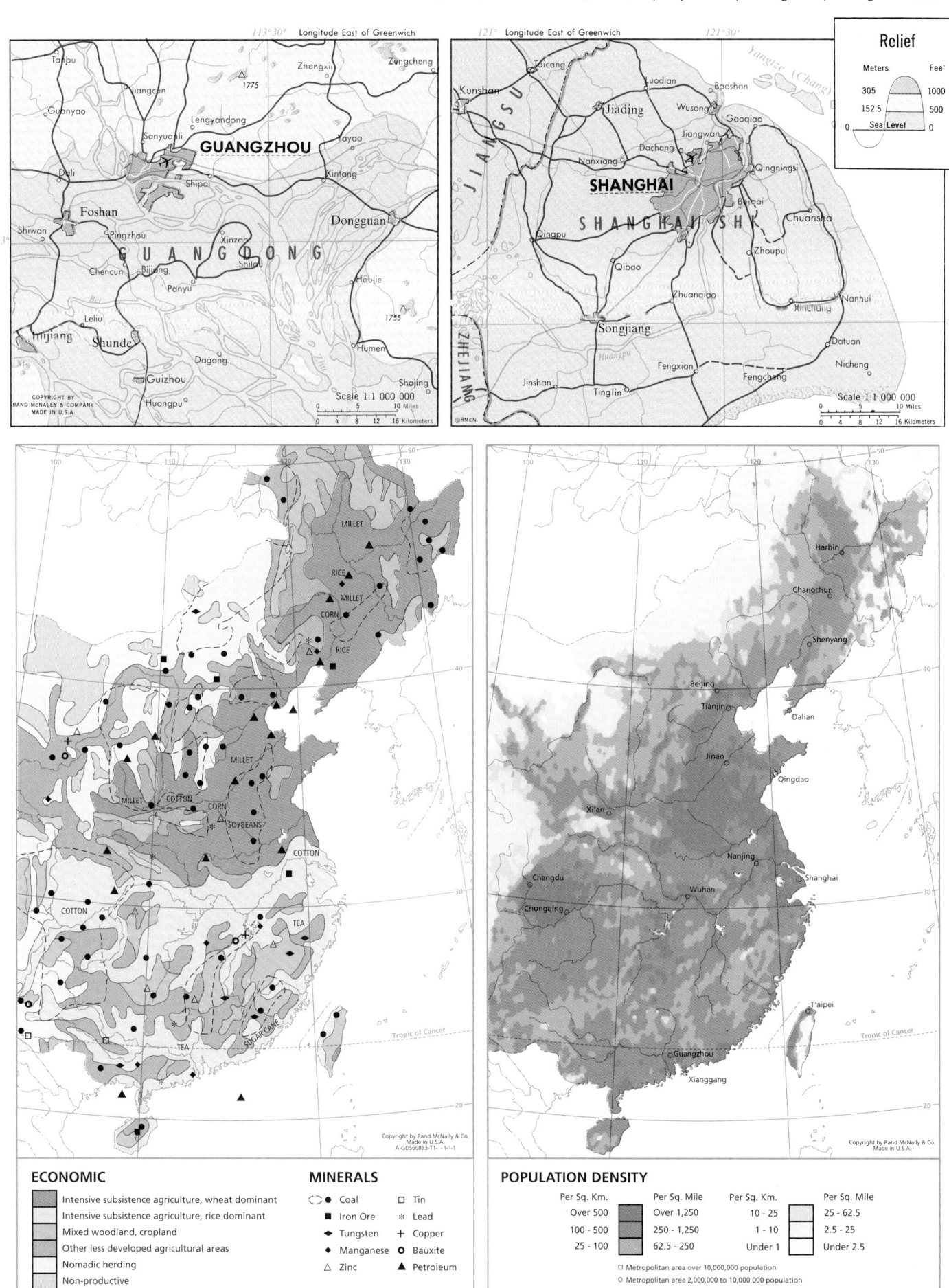

GUANGZHOU

Longitude East of Greenwich 113°30'

Tanbu
Zhongxin
Zengcheng
1775
Jiangcun
Guanyao
Lengyandong
Yayao
Sanyuanli
GUANGZHOU
Xintang
Duli
Shipai
Foshan
Dongguan
Pingzhou
Xinzao
G U A N G D O N G
Shiwan
Chencun Bijiang Shilou
Panyu
Houjie
23°
1755
Leliu
Humen
Injiang Shunde
Dagang
Guizhou
Shajing
COPYRIGHT BY
RAND McNALLY & COMPANY
MADE IN U.S.A.
Huangpu
Scale 1:1 000 000
0   5   10 Miles
0 4 8 12 16 Kilometers

SHANGHAI

Longitude East of Greenwich 121° 121°30'

Taicang
Luodian
Baoshan
Kunshan
J I A N G S U
Wusong
Jiading
Gaoqiao
Jiangwan
Nanxiang Dachang
Qingningsi
SHANGHAI
Qingpu
S H A N G H A I   SH.
Beicai
Chuansha
Qibao
Zhoupu
Zhuangqiao
Xinchang
31°
Nanhui
Z H E J I A N G
Songjiang
Datuan
Jinshan
Fengxian Fengcheng
Nicheng
Tinglin
©RMcN.
Scale 1:1 000 000
0   5   10 Miles
0 4 8 12 16 Kilometers

Relief

Meters		Fee'
305		1000
152.5		500
0	Sea Level	0

Copyright by Rand McNally & Co.
Made in U.S.A.
A-GDS60893-T1- - 1- : 1

Copyright by Rand McNally & Co.
Made in U.S.A.

ECONOMIC

- Intensive subsistence agriculture, wheat dominant
- Intensive subsistence agriculture, rice dominant
- Mixed woodland, cropland
- Other less developed agricultural areas
- Nomadic herding
- Non-productive

MINERALS

- ● Coal
- ■ Iron Ore
- ◆ Tungsten
- ◆ Manganese
- △ Zinc
- □ Tin
- ∗ Lead
- + Copper
- ○ Bauxite
- ▲ Petroleum

POPULATION DENSITY

Per Sq. Km.	Per Sq. Mile	Per Sq. Km.	Per Sq. Mile
Over 500	Over 1,250	10 - 25	25 - 62.5
100 - 500	250 - 1,250	1 - 10	2.5 - 25
25 - 100	62.5 - 250	Under 1	Under 2.5

□ Metropolitan area over 10,000,000 population
○ Metropolitan area 2,000,000 to 10,000,000 population

Continued on page 210

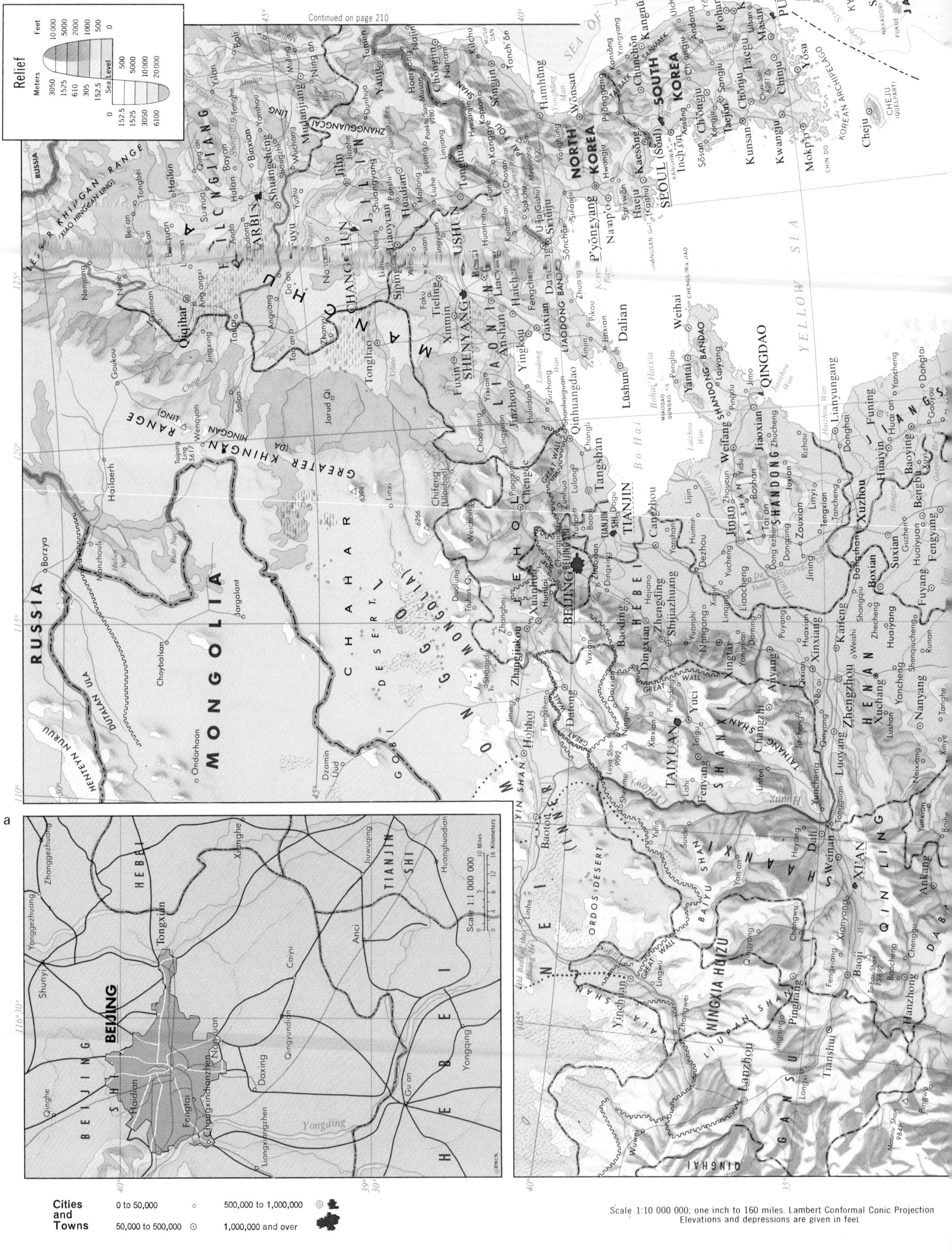

Relief

Feet	Meters
10 000	3050
5000	1525
2000	610
1000	305
500	152.5
0	Sea Level
500	152.5
5000	1525
10 000	3050
20 000	6100

RUSSIA

MONGOLIA

LESSER KHINGAN RANGE (XIAO HINGGAN LING)

GREATER KHINGAN RANGE (DA HINGGAN LING)

HEILONGJIANG

JILIN

CHANGBAI SHAN

MANCHURIA

LIAONING

HEBEI

SHANDONG

SHANXI

SHAANXI

HENAN

NINGXIA HUIZU

GANSU

QINGHAI

INNER MONGOLIA (NEI MONGOL)

ORDOS DESERT

GOBI DESERT

CHAHAR

REHO

NORTH KOREA

SOUTH KOREA

JAPAN

KYUSHU

SEOUL (Soul)

P'yŏngyang

BEIJING

TIANJIN

TAIYUAN

XIAN

QINGDAO

SHENYANG

HARBIN

Qiqihar

Dalian

GREAT WALL

YIN SHAN

TAIHANG SHAN

QIN LING

DABA SHAN

YELLOW SEA

Bo Hai

SEA OF JAPAN

a

BEIJING SHI

HEBEI

TIANJIN SHI

BEIJING

Scale 1:1 000 000

0 to 50 000
50 000 to 500 000
500 000 to 1 000 000
1 000 000 and over

Cities and Towns

Scale 1:10 000 000; one inch to 160 miles. Lambert Conformal Conic Projection
Elevations and depressions are given in feet

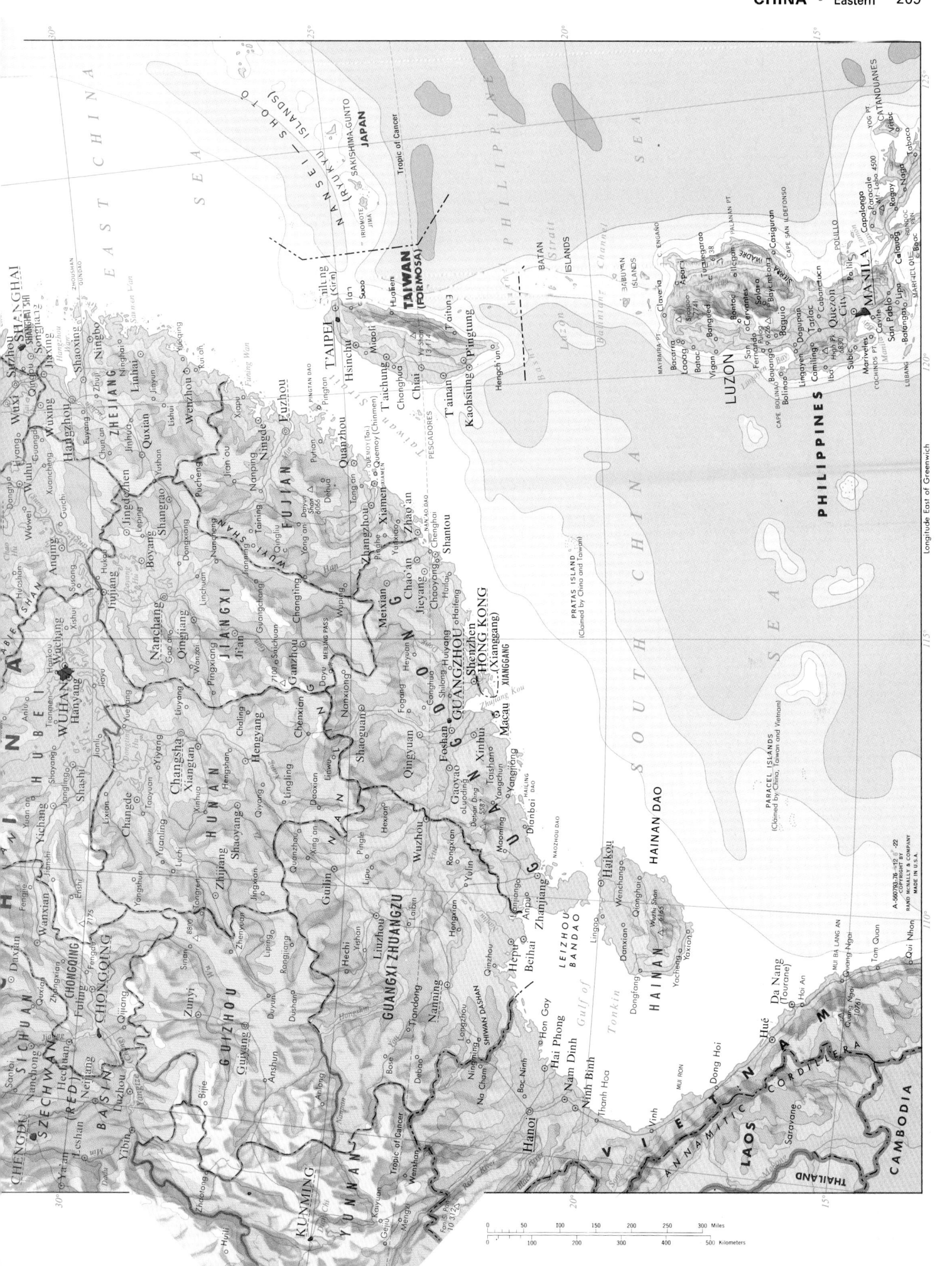

CHINA • Eastern

SHANGHAI
Suzhou
Wuxi
Yiyang
Wuhu
Wuwei
ANHUI

EAST CHINA SEA

NANSEI-SHOTO (RYUKYU ISLANDS)
SAKISHIMA-GUNTO
IRIOMOTE-JIMA
JAPAN

ZHEJIANG
Hangzhou
Ningbo
Shaoxing
Wenzhou

Tropic of Cancer

PHILIPPINE SEA

CATANDUANES

TAIPEI
TAIWAN (FORMOSA)
Hsinchu
Taichung
Chiai
Tainan
Kaohsiung
Pingtung

Fuzhou
FUJIAN
WU SHAN
Quanzhou
Xiamen (Amoy)
Zhangzhou
Shantou

BATAN ISLANDS
BABUYAN ISLANDS

LUZON
MANILA
PHILIPPINES

Longitude East of Greenwich

JIANGXI
Nanchang
Ganzhou

G U A N G D O N G
Meixian
Chaozhou
Shantou

PRATAS ISLAND
(Claimed by China and Taiwan)

SOUTH CHINA SEA

WUHAN
Hanyang
HUBEI

Changsha
Xiangtan
HUNAN
Hengyang
Shaoyang

Shaoguan
GUANGZHOU
Foshan
Shenzhen
HONG KONG (Xianggang)
Macau
Zhujiang Kou

HAINAN DAO

PARACEL ISLANDS
(Claimed by China, Taiwan and Vietnam)

GUIZHOU
Guiyang
Zunyi
Anshun

GUANGXI ZHUANGZU
Nanning
Guilin
Liuzhou

Zhanjiang
LEIZHOU BANDAO

Haikou
HAINAN
Sanya

Gulf of Tonkin

CHONGQING
SICHUAN
SZECHWAN
RED BASIN
Chengdu

YUNNAN
KUNMING

Tropic of Cancer

Hanoi
Haiphong
V I E T N A M
ANNAMITIC CORDILLERA

LAOS
THAILAND
CAMBODIA

Da Nang (Tourane)
Hué

A-560793,06 -12 -22
COPYRIGHT BY
RAND McNALLY & COMPANY
MADE IN U.S.A.

0   50   100 150 200 250 300 Miles
0   100   200   300   400   500 Kilometers

Continued on pages 208-209

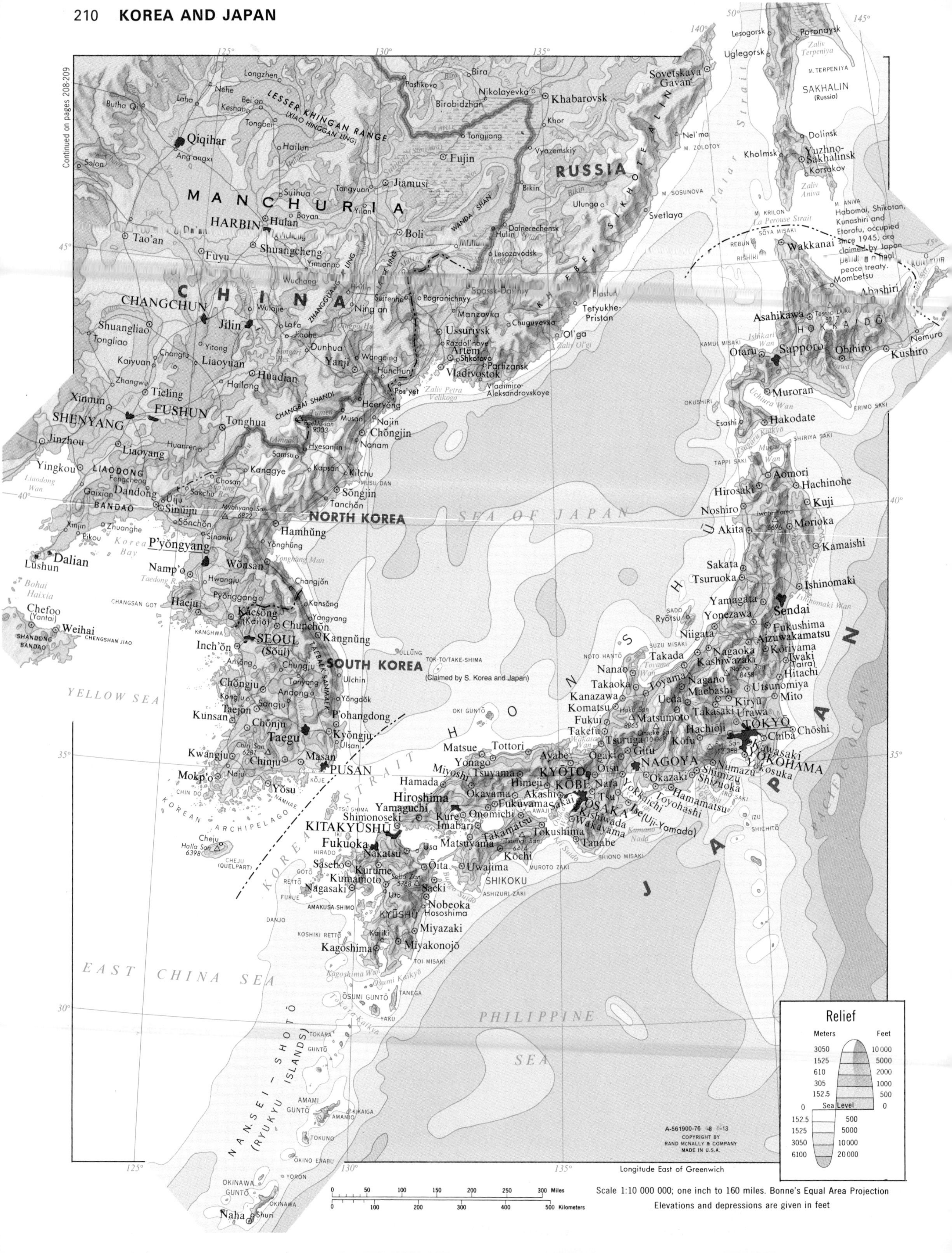

50°

140° 145°

Lesogorsk
Poronaysk
Uglegorsk
Zaliv Terpeniya

125° 130° 135°

Longzhen
Nehe
Butha Qi
Laha
Bei'an
Keshan
Tongbei

LESSER KHINGAN RANGE (XIAO HINGGAN LING)

Pashkovo
Bira
Birobidzhan
Nikolayevka
Khabarovsk

Sovetskaya Gavan'

M. TERPENIYA

SAKHALIN (Russia)

Dolinsk

Qiqihar
Ang'angxi
Hailun
Fujin

Kholmsk
Yuzhno-Sakhalinsk
Korsakov

Solon
Tongjiang

RUSSIA

Zaliv Aniva

MANCHURIA
Tao'an
HARBIN
Hulan
Fuyu
Shuangcheng
Suihua
Boyan
Jiamusi
Yilan
Boli
Khor
Vyazemskiy
Bikin
Ulunga
Svetlaya

M. ZOLOTOY
M. SOSNUOVA
'Nel'ma

M. KRILON
SOYA MISAKI
La Perouse Strait

REBUN
RISHIRI

Wakkanai

45°

M. ANIVA
Habomai, Shikotan, Kunashiri and Etorofu, occupied since 1945, are claimed by Japan but held under no peace treaty.
Mombetsu

CHINA
CHANGCHUN
Jilin
Shuangliao
Tongliao
Yitong
Changtu
Liaoyuan
Kaiyuan
Huadian
Hailong
Zhangwu
Xinmin
Tieling
FUSHUN
SHENYANG
Jinzhou
Liaoyang
Huanren
Tonghua

Wuchang
Shulan
Jiaohe
Lafa
Dunhua
Yanji
Wangqing
Hunchun

CHANGBAI SHANDI
Tumen
Yanbian

Suifenhe
Pogranichnyy
Spassk-Dal'niy
Manzovka
Ussuriysk
Chuguyevka
Razdol'noye
Shkotovo
Artem
Partizansk
Pos'yet
Vladivostok
Vladimiro-Aleksandrovskoye

Tetyukhe-Pristan
Plastun

Zaliv Ol'gi

Zaliv Petra Velikogo

OKUSHIRI

Abashiri

Asahikawa

HOKKAIDO

Ishikari Wan
KAMUI MISAKI
Otaru
Sapporo
Obihiro
Kushiro
Muroran
Uchiura Wan
ERIMO SAKI
Nemuro

Liaodong
LIAODONG BANDAO
Fengcheng
Dandong
Uiju
Sinuiju
Sonchon

Hoeryong
Musan
Najin
Chongjin
Nanam
Kilchu
Songjin

Esashi
Hakodate

TSUGARU KAIKYO
TAPPI SAKI
SHIRIYA SAKI
MUTSU WAN
Aomori
Hachinohe
Hirosaki
Noshiro
Akita
Morioka
Kuji

Jinzhou
Yingkou
Gaixian
Zhuanghe
Xinjin
Pikou

Korea Bay

P'yongyang
NORTH KOREA
Hamhung
Yonghung

Kanggye
Hyesanjin
Kapsan
Samsu
Paektu-san 9003
Myohyang-san 6322

SEA OF JAPAN

White Rock

Sakata
Tsuruoka
Yamagata
Yonezawa
Niigata
Nagaoka
Kashiwazaki
Fukushima
Aizuwakamatsu
Koriyama
Iwaki (Taira)
Hitachi
Sendai
Ishinomaki Wan
Ishinomaki
Kamaishi

Lüshun
Dalian
Bohai Haixia
SHANDONG BANDAO
Chefoo (Yantai)
Weihai
CHENGSHAN JIAO

Namp'o
Hwangju
Pyonggang
Changjon
CHANGSAN GOT
Taedong R.

Wonsan
Changjon
Kumhwa

SADO
Ryotsu
Nanao
Takada
NOTO HANTO
Toyama
Toyama Wan

40°

Haeju
Kaesong (Kaijo)
KANGHWA
Chunchon
Kangnung
TAEBAEK RANGE
ULLUNG
TOK-TO/TAKE-SHIMA
(Claimed by S. Korea and Japan)

SUZU MISAKI
Takaoka
Kanazawa
Komatsu
Fukui
Takefu

Nagano
Ueda
Maebashi
Takasaki
Kiryu
Mito
Utsunomiya
Matsumoto
8865
Nagoya

INCH'ON
SEOUL (Soul)
Ansong
Chongju
Kongju
Chunju
Tanyang
Yongju
Yongdok
Ulchin

OKI GUNTO

S
H
O

HONSHU

Takada

N
S

J
A
P
A
N

Omaezaki
Hachioji
Urawa
Kawasaki
Yokohama
TOKYO
Chiba
Choshi

35°

Kunsan
Taejon
Sangju
Andong
Chonju
Kyongju
Taegu
Masan
Chinju
Naju
PUSAN
Mokp'o

Matsue
Tottori
Yonago
Miyoshi
Tsuyama
Hamada
Yamaguchi
Hiroshima
Shimonoseki
Kure
Onomichi
Imabari
Usa
Matsuyama

Ayabe
Otsu
KYOTO
Gifu
Ogaki
Himeji
Akashi
Nara
OSAKA
Sakai
KOBE
Wakayama
Kishiwada
Tsu
Yokkaichi
Okazaki
Toyohashi
Hamamatsu
Shizuoka
Shimizu
Yokosuka
Mt. Fuji 12,388
Numazu
Suruga Wan
IZU
SHICHITO

PACIFIC OCEAN

KOREA STRAIT
NAMHAE
KOJE
CHIN DO
TSUSHIMA
IKI
KITAKYUSHU
Fukuoka
Nakatsu
Sasebo
Kurume
Kumamoto
Saeki
Nagasaki

Hamada

Kwangju
Chiri San 6283
Ulsan
Pohangdong

Takamatsu
Tokushima
AWAJI
Kii Suido
Tanabe
Kumano Nada
SHIONO MISAKI

Oita
SHIKOKU
Kochi
MUROTO ZAKI
ASHIZURI ZAKI
Uwajima

Nobeoka
Hososhima
Miyazaki
Miyakonojo
Kagoshima
Kagoshima Wan
OSUMI GUNTO
TANEGA
YAKU
OSUMI KAIKYO

YELLOW SEA

Cheju
Halla San 6398
CHEJU (QUELPART)

KOREAN ARCHIPELAGO

GOTO RETTO
AMAKUSA-SHIMO
KOSHIKI RETTO
KYUSHU

EAST CHINA SEA

DANJO

NANSEI - SHOTO (RYUKYU ISLANDS)

30°

TOKARA KAIKYO
TOKARA GUNTO
OSUMI GUNTO
TOKARAYAKU

AMAMI GUNTO
AMAMI
KIKAIGA
TOKUNO

OKINAWA GUNTO
OKINAWA
YORON
OKINO ERABU
NAHA Shuri

125° 130° 135°

PHILIPPINE SEA

Longitude East of Greenwich

A-561900-76 -8 6-13
COPYRIGHT BY
RAND McNALLY & COMPANY
MADE IN U.S.A.

Scale 1:10 000 000; one inch to 160 miles. Bonne's Equal Area Projection
Elevations and depressions are given in feet

Relief		
Meters		Feet
3050		10 000
1525		5000
610		2000
305		1000
152.5		500
0	Sea Level	0
152.5		500
1525		5000
3050		10 000
6100		20 000

0 50 100 150 200 250 300 Miles
0 100 200 300 400 500 Kilometers

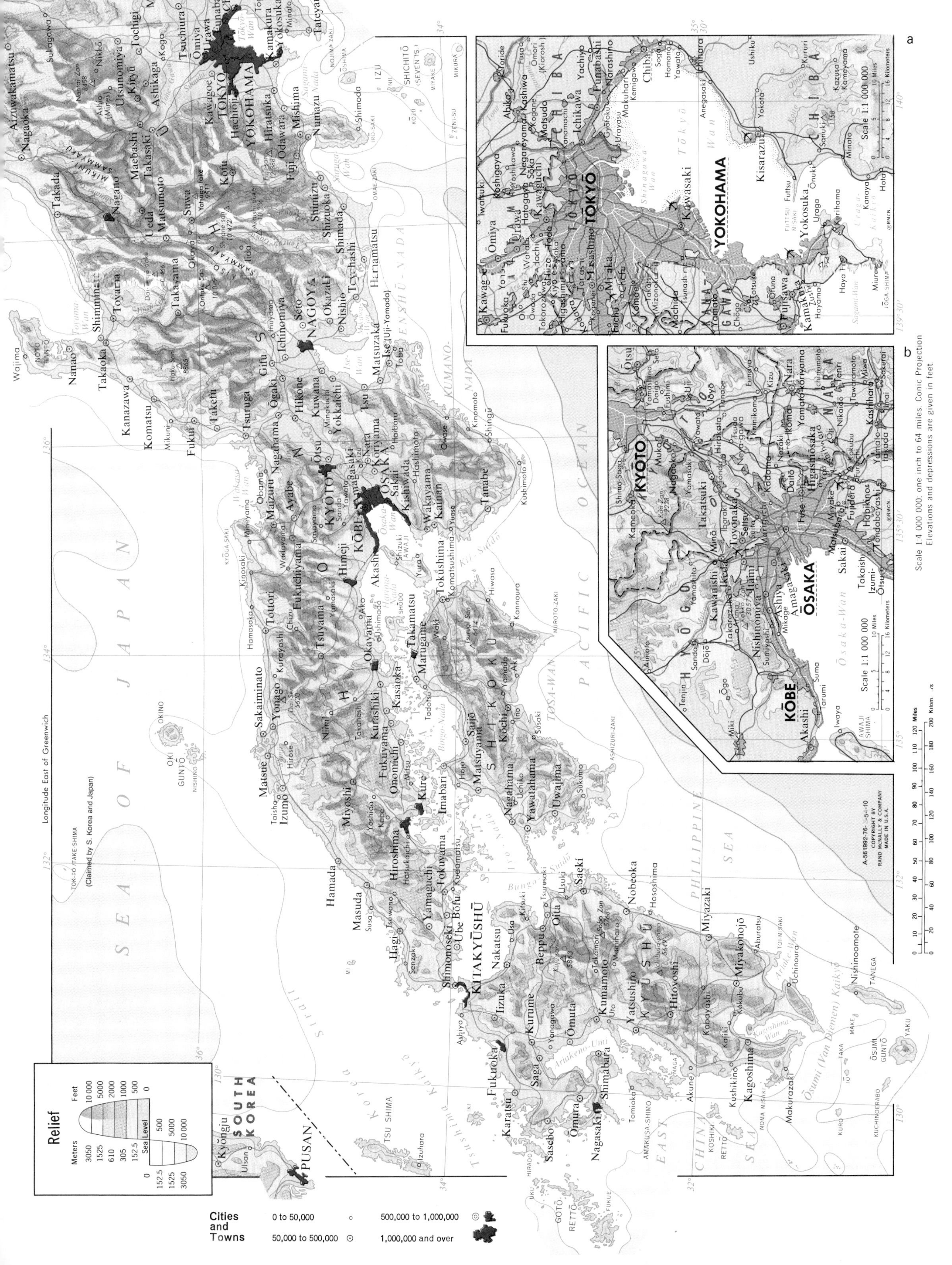

a

Scale 1:1 000 000

b

Scale 1:4 000 000, one inch to 64 miles. Conic Projection
Elevations and depressions are given in feet.

Scale 1:1 000 000

TŌKYŌ
YOKOHAMA
KAWASAKI

CHIBA

KYŌTŌ
ŌSAKA
KŌBE
NARA

Relief

Meters	Feet
3050	10 000
1525	5000
610	2000
305	1000
152.5	500
0	Sea Level
152.5	500
1525	5000
3050	10 000

SEA OF JAPAN

Longitude East of Greenwich

TOK-TO /TAKE-SHIMA
(Claimed by S. Korea and Japan)

SOUTH KOREA

Kyŏngju
Ulsan
PUSAN

OKI GUNTŌ
OKINO
NISHINO

PACIFIC OCEAN

PHILIPPINE SEA

EAST CHINA SEA

TOKYO
YOKOHAMA
NAGOYA
KYŌTŌ
OSAKA
KŌBE
Himeji
Okayama
Hiroshima
Matsuyama
SHIKOKU
KITAKYŪSHŪ
Fukuoka
Nagasaki
Kumamoto
Kagoshima
KYŪSHŪ
Miyazaki
Ōita
Beppu

A-561992-76—5i-10
COPYRIGHT BY
RAND McNALLY & COMPANY
MADE IN U.S.A.

Cities and Towns

0 to 50,000	○
50,000 to 500,000	⊙
500,000 to 1,000,000	◎
1,000,000 and over	●

212

Scale 1:16 000 000; one inch to 250 miles. Polyconic Projection
Elevations and depressions are given in feet

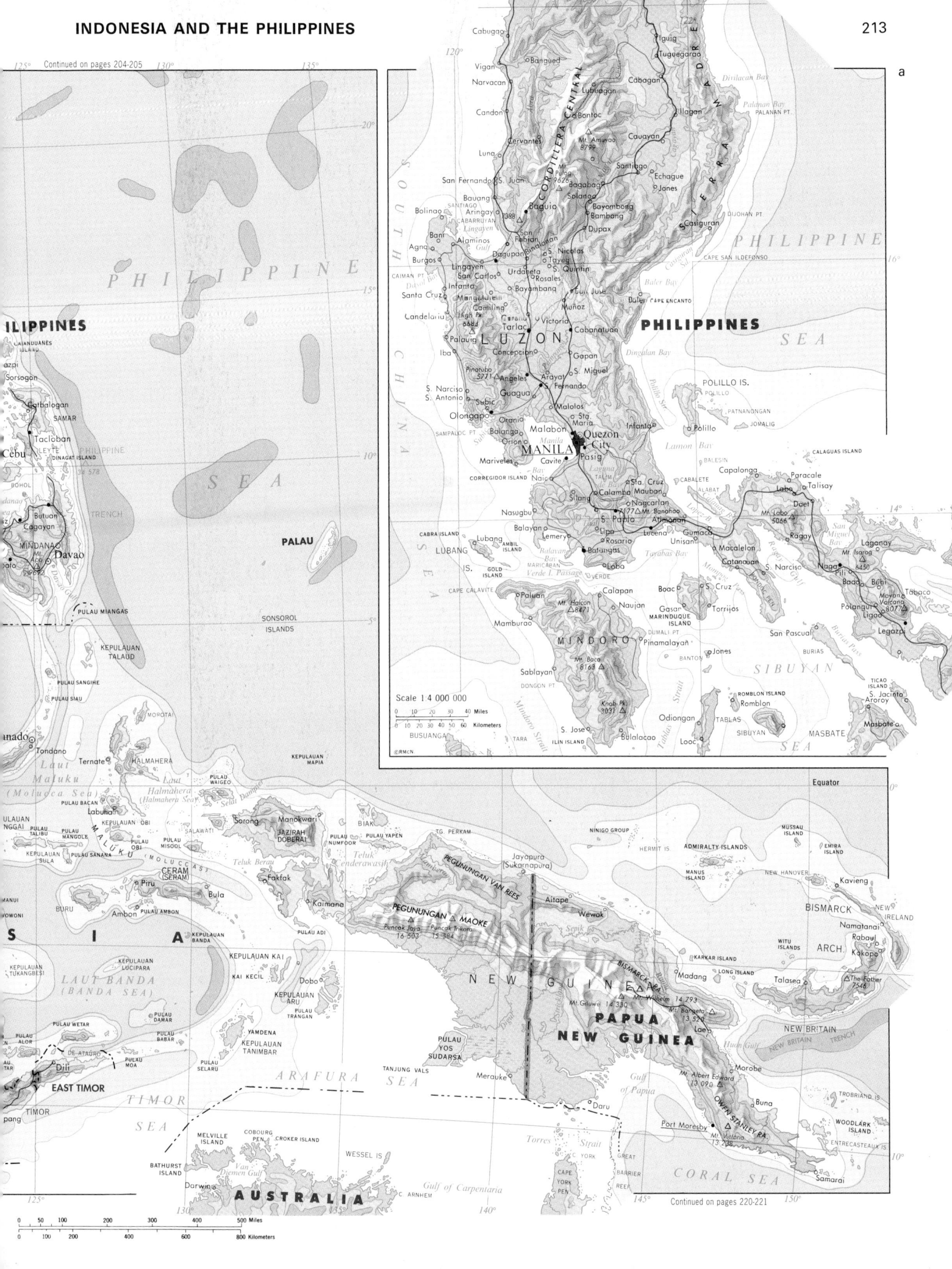

Continued on pages 204-205

a

PHILIPPINE

SEA

ILIPPINES

CALANDUANES ISLAND

azpi

Sorsogon

Catbalogan

SAMAR

Tacloban

Cebu

LEYTE

BOHOL

dana

Butuan

MINDANAO

Cagayan

Davao

Mt. Apo 9692

to

PULAU MIANGAS

KEPULAUAN TALAUD

PHILIPPINE TRENCH

10 578

PALAU

SONSOROL ISLANDS

PULAU SANGIHE

PULAU SIAU

nado

Tondano

Ternate

HALMAHERA

KEPULAUAN MAPIA

Laut Maluku (Molucca Sea)

Laut Halmahera (Halmahera Sea)

PULAU WAIGEO

Selat Dampier

ULAUAN NGGAI

PULAU BACAN

Labuha

PULAU OBI

KEPULAUAN OBI

Sorong

JAZIRAH DOBERAI

BIAK

PULAU YAPEN

Manokwari

PULAU NUMFOOR

TG. PERKAM

NINIGO GROUP

Equator

0°

HERMIT IS.

ADMIRALTY ISLANDS

MUSSAU ISLAND

EMIRA ISLAND

PULAU TALIBU

PULAU MANGOLE

KEPULAUAN SULA

PULAU MISOOL

SALAWATI

Teluk Berau

Teluk Cenderawasih

Jayapura (Sukarnapura)

Aitape

Wewak

MANUS ISLAND

NEW HANOVER

Kavieng

PULAU SANANA

(MOLUCCAS)

CERAM (SERAM)

Piru

Fakfak

Kaimana

Senik

BISMARCK

NEW IRELAND

MANUI

OWONI

BURU

Ambon

PULAU AMBON

Bula

PEGUNUNGAN VAN REES

PEGUNUNGAN MAOKE

Namatanai

Rabaul

Kokopo

S I A

KEPULAUAN BANDA

PULAU ADI

Puncak Jaya 16 503

Puncak Trikora 15 584

KARKAR ISLAND

WITU ISLANDS

ARCH.

KEPULAUAN TUKANGBESI

KEPULAUAN LUCIPARA

KEPULAUAN KAI

KAI KECIL

Dobo

Madang

LONG ISLAND

NEW GUINEA

BISMARCK RA.

Talasea

The Father 7546

Laut Banda (Banda Sea)

KEPULAUAN ARU

KEPULAUAN TRANGAN

Mt. Gluwe 14 330

Mt. Wilhelm 14 293

Mt. Bangeta 13 529

NEW BRITAIN

PULAU WETAR

PULAU DAMAR

YAMDENA

KEPULAUAN TANIMBAR

PAPUA NEW GUINEA

Lae

NEW BRITAIN TRENCH

PULAU ALOR

DE ATAURO

PULAU BABAR

PULAU MOA

PULAU SELARU

PULAU YOS SUDARSA

Mt. Albert Edward 13 090

Morobe

Huon Gulf

AU TAR

Dili

EAST TIMOR

TANJUNG VALS

Merauke

Gulf of Papua

Buna

TROBRIAND IS.

pang

TIMOR SEA

ARAFURA SEA

Daru

Port Moresby

OWEN STANLEY RA.

WOODLARK ISLAND

TIMOR

Van Diemen Gulf

MELVILLE ISLAND

COBOURG PEN.

CROKER ISLAND

WESSEL IS.

CAPE YORK PEN.

Torres Strait

Mt. Victoria 13 208

ENTRECASTEAUX IS.

BATHURST ISLAND

Darwin

AUSTRALIA

Gulf of Carpentaria

C. ARNHEM

CAPE YORK

GREAT BARRIER REEF

CORAL SEA

Samarai

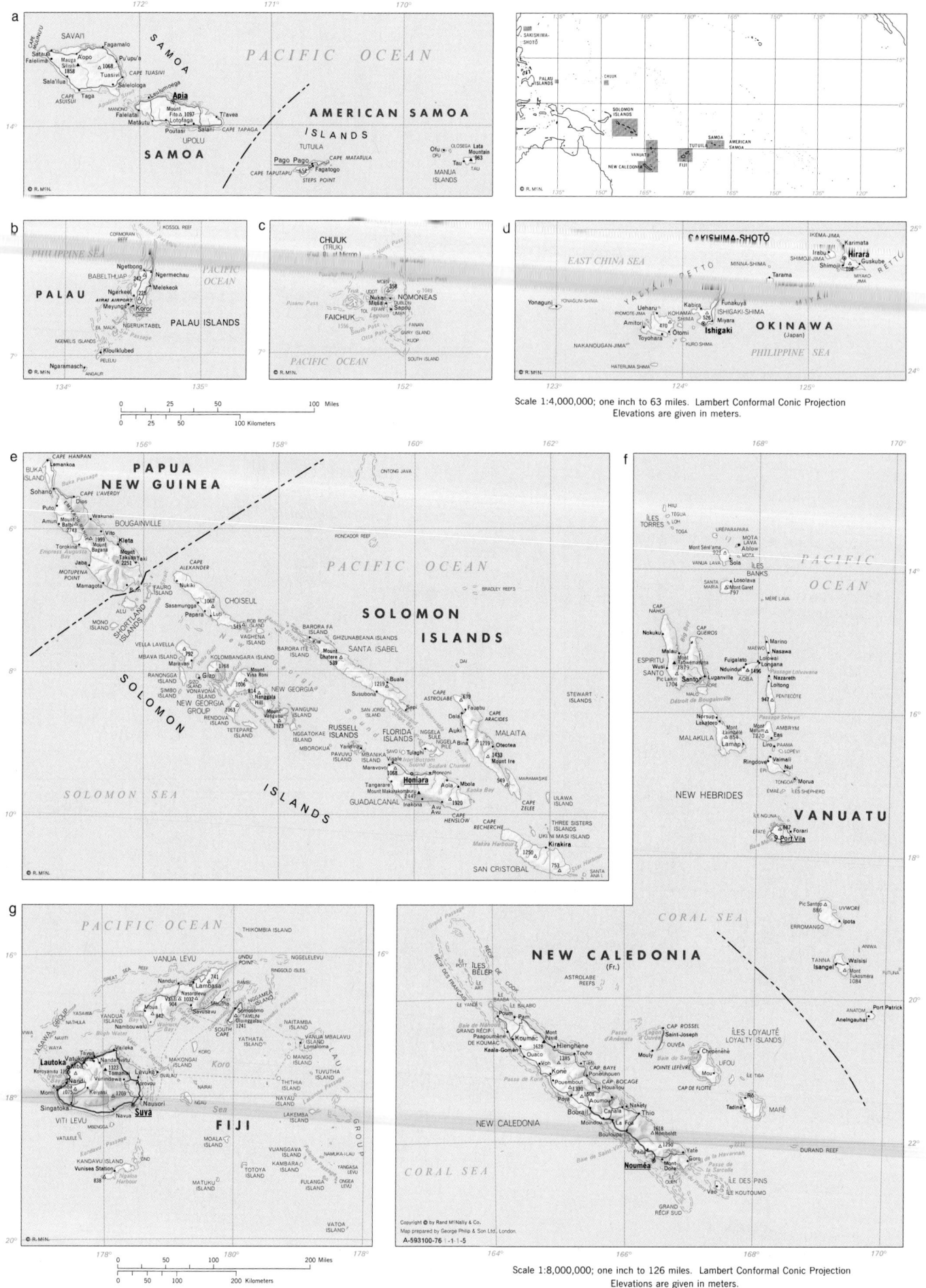

a

PACIFIC OCEAN

SAMOA

SAVAI'I

Fagamalo

CAPE OGENUU

Satapuu
Falelima

Aopo
Mauga △1068
Silisili
1858

Pu'upu'a

Sala'ilua

Taga

Manono
Falelatai

Leulumoega

Matautu
Poutasi
Salani

Mount
Fito △1097
Lotofaga

CAPE TUASIVI

SAMOA

UPOLU

CAPE TAPAGA

Ti'avea

AMERICAN SAMOA

ISLANDS

TUTUILA

Pago Pago

CAPE MATATULA

Fagatogo

CAPE TAPUTAPU

STEPS POINT

Ofu
OFU

OLOSEGA
Lata
Mountain
963
TAU
Tau

MANUA
ISLANDS

© R. MtN.

b

PHILIPPINE SEA

CORMORAN
REEF

KOSSOL REEF

PALAU

Ngetbong

BABELTHUAP

242

Ngermechau

Ngerkeuil
325

Melekeok

PACIFIC
OCEAN

AIRAI AIRPORT
Meyungs

Koror
KOROR

EIL MALK

NGERUKTABEL

PALAU ISLANDS

NGEMELIS ISLANDS

Kloulklubed

PELELIU

Ngaramasch

ANGAUR

© R. MtN.

134°   135°

c

CHUUK
(TRUK)
(Incl. Is. of Micron.)

North Pass

Fanuang Pass

MOEN
358

UDOT

Nukan
Mela
TOL
UMAN
SUBLOI
Sapou

Piaanu Pass

FAICHUK
1556

South Pass

Otta Pass

NOMONEAS

FANAN

GIVRY REEF
KUOP

SOUTH ISLAND

PACIFIC OCEAN

© R. MtN.

152°

d

SAKISHIMA-SHOTŌ

EAST CHINA SEA

IKEMA-JIMA
Karimata

Irabu
SHIMOJI-JIMA
Shimoji
198

Hirara

Guskube

RETTO

MINNA-SHIMA

Tarama

MIYAKO
JIMA

Yonaguni

YONAGUNI-SHIMA

Funakuyā

PROMOTE-JIMA

Ueharu
KOHAMA
SHIMA

Kabira
ISHIGAKI-SHIMA

Amitori
470

Miyara
526

Otomi

Ishigaki

OKINAWA
(Japan)

NAKANOUGAN-JIMA

Toyohara

PHILIPPINE SEA

HATERUMA SHIMA

KURO-SHIMA

© R. MtN.

123°   124°   125°

Scale 1:4,000,000; one inch to 63 miles. Lambert Conformal Conic Projection
Elevations are given in meters.

Scale bar:
0   25   50   100 Miles
0   25   50   100 Kilometers

e

CAPE HANPAN

PAPUA

Lemankoa

BUKA
ISLAND

NEW GUINEA

Sohano

CAPE L'AVERDY

Puto
Amun

Wakunai

BOUGAINVILLE

Mount
Balbi △
2743

Vito

Kieta

Mount
Bagana
1999

Torokina

Mount
Takuan △
2251

Empress Augusta Bay

Jaba

Buin

MOTUPENA
POINT

Mamagota

FAURO
ISLAND

ALU

Nukiki

SHORTLAND ISLANDS

MONO
ISLAND

CHOISEUL

Sasamungga

Papara

Luti

1067

549

PACIFIC OCEAN

ONTONG JAVA

RONCADOR REEF

BRADLEY REEFS

SOLOMON

ISLANDS

CAPE
ALEXANDER

BARORA FA
ISLAND

GHIZUNABEANA ISLANDS

SANTA ISABEL

DAI

VELLA LAVELLA

792

BARORA ITE
ISLAND

Kia

Ghatere
539

MBAVA ISLAND

Marovaka

1768

RANONGGA
SIMBO
ISLAND

Gizo
GIZO

Mount
Vina Roni

KOLOMBANGARA
ISLAND

1006

814

Buala

1219

STEWART
ISLANDS

NEW GEORGIA

Susubona

Sepi

CAPE
ASTROLABE

679

CAPE
ARACIDES

NEW GEORGIA
GROUP

Nanggala
Hill

Mount
Vangunu
1123

VANGUNU
ISLAND

SAN JORGE
ISLAND

Dala

Fauabu

Auki

CAPE

RENDOVA
ISLAND

1063

NGGATOKAE
ISLAND

RUSSELL
ISLANDS

NGELLA
SULE

1219

MALAITA

Oteotea

TETEPARE
ISLAND

MBOROKUA

PAVUVU
ISLAND

FLORIDA
ISLANDS

NGELLA
PILE

549

MARAMASIKE

Maravovo

Yandina

MBANIKA
ISLAND

Tulaghi
Vigale

Roroni

2433
Mount Ire

SOLOMON

Tangarare

Mount
Makarakomburu △
2447

Honiara

Aola

Mbola

ULAWA
ISLAND

Inakona

Avu
Avu
1920

Kaoka Bay

CAPE
ZELEE

GUADALCANAL

CAPE
HENSLOW

THREE SISTERS
ISLANDS

UKI NI MASI ISLAND

Kirakira

SOLOMON SEA

ISLANDS

1250

Makira Harbour

753

SAN CRISTOBAL

Star Harbour

SANTA
ANA I.

© R. MtN.

156°   158°   160°   162°

6°

8°

10°

f

MIU
TEGUA

ÎLES
TORRES

UREPARAPARA

TOGA

MOTA
LAVA

VANUA LAVA

Mont Sére'ama
92

Ablow
MOTA

Sola

ÎLES
BANKS

SANTA
MARIA

MERE LAVA

Losolava
Mont Garet
797

PACIFIC

OCEAN

CAP
NAHOI

Nokuku

Malali

CAP
QUEIROS

Marino

Nasawa

ESPIRITU
SANTO

Wusi

Mont
Tabwemasana △
1879

Santo

MAEWO

Fuigalato

Nduindui

1496

Luganville

AOBA

Nazareth

Loitong

Pic Latiri
1704

MALO

PENTECÔTE

Détroit de Bougainville

947

Nórsup
Lakatoro

Mont
Lambele △
854

AMBRYM

Eas

MALAKULA

Lamap

Lini

Tiro
PAAMA

C. LOPEVI

EPI

Ringdove

Vaimali

Nul

TONGOA
Morua

ÉMAÉ
ÎLES SHEPHERD

NEW HEBRIDES

ÎLE NGUNA

847
Forari

ÉFATÉ

Port Vila

VANUATU

168°   170°

14°

16°

18°

g

PACIFIC OCEAN

THIKOMBIA ISLAND

VANUA LEVU

UNDU
POINT

NGGELELEVU

Nandarivatu

741

Nasorolevu
904

Lambasa

Mbua
RAMBI

NGGAMEA

RINGGOLD ISLES

YASAWA GROUP

FANUA LEVU

NATHULA

Nasavusavu
1241

TAVEUNI

SOUTH
CAPE

NAITAMBA
ISLAND

VANUA MBALAVU
Lomaloma

Nambouwalu

Bligh Water

KORO

MANGO
ISLAND

YATHATA
ISLAND

VIWA

WAYA

NAVITI

Tavua

Mba

Vatukoula

Ndama
Vaileka

Tavua

Nandi

Tamavua
1323

Viti △
1195

KORO
SEA

MAKONGAI
ISLAND

OVALAU

THITHIA
ISLAND

TUVUTHA
ISLAND

NAYAU
ISLAND

LAKEMBA
ISLAND

Nausori

Lautoka
Koroyantu △ 1195

Nandarivatu
1323

Namosi
1073

Keiyasi
Viti Levu 1208

Singatoka

Navua

Suva

NAIRAI

MBENGGA

MOALA
ISLAND

NAMUKA-I-LAU

VANGGAVA
ISLAND

KAMBARA
ISLAND

YANGASA
GROUP

FULANGA
ISLAND

ONGEA
LEVU

VITI LEVU

FIJI

VATULELE

KANDAVU PASSAGE

KANDAVU ISLAND

Vunisea Station

838

Ngaloa Harbour

TOTOYA
ISLAND

MATUKU
ISLAND

VATOA
ISLAND

© R. MtN.

178°   180°   178°

16°

18°

20°

Scale bar:
0   50   100   200 Miles
0   50   100   200 Kilometers

CORAL SEA

Pic Santop △
846

UVWORÉ
Ipota

ERROMANGO

ANIWA

TANNA

Waisisi

Isangel

Mont
Tukosméra △
1084

FUTUNA

Port Patrick

ANATOM

Anelgauhat

NEW CALEDONIA
(Fr.)

Grand Passage

RÉCIF DES FRANÇAIS

ÎLES
BÉLEP

RÉCIF
COOK

ASTROLABE
REEFS

ÎLE
POTT

ÎLE
ART

ÎLE
BAABA

ÎLE YANDÉ

ÎLE BALABIO

Poum
Pam

CAP ROSSEL

Saint-Joseph

ANATOM

ÎLES LOYAUTÉ
LOYALTY ISLANDS

Koumac
Paagoumène

Baie du Santal

OUVÉA

GRAND RÉCIF
DE KOUMAC

Keala-Gomen

1628

Hienghène
Touho

Chépénéhé

LIFOU

Baie d'Anémata

Mouly

Koné

CAP BAYE

1385

Pass
d'Amos

Pouembout

CAP BOCAGE

Bopope
1390

Houailou

Poya

ÎLE TIGA

Bourail

Nakéty
Thio

MARÉ

Moindou

La Foa

Tadine

1618
Mont Humboldt

NEW CALEDONIA

Boulouparis

Pouembout

1250

Yaté

POINTE LEFÈVRE

CAP DE FLOTTE

Passe de la Sarcelle

Nouméa

Mont
Dore

DURAND REEF

CORAL SEA

Baie de Saint-Vincent

QUEN

Yaté

Passe de la Havannah

Goro

ÎLE DES PINS

GRAND
RÉCIF SUD

Vao

ÎLE KOUTOUMO

Copyright © by Rand McNally & Co.
Map prepared by George Philip & Son Ltd., London.

A-593100-76 -1-1-5

Scale 1:8,000,000; one inch to 126 miles. Lambert Conformal Conic Projection
Elevations are given in meters.

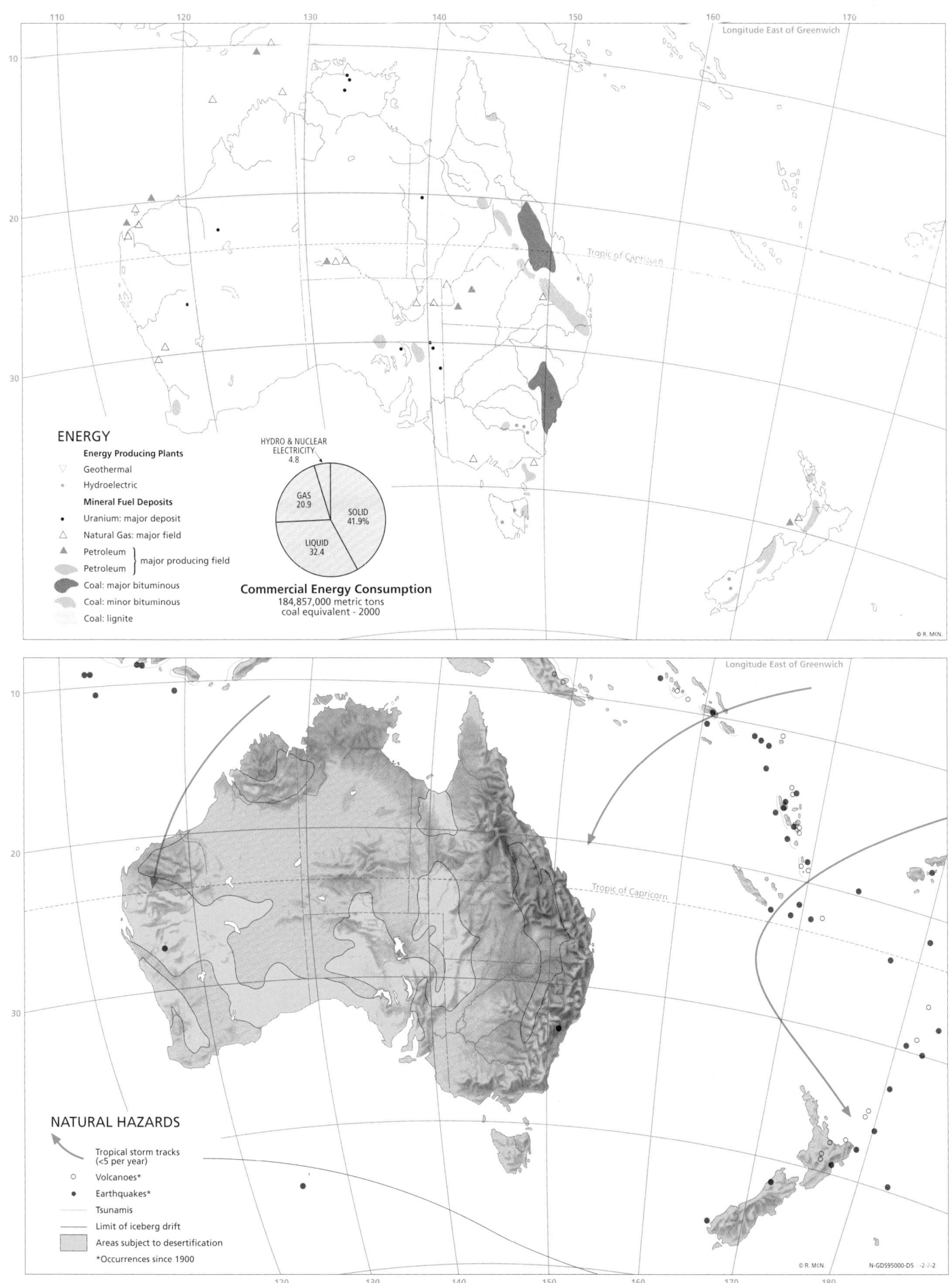

ENERGY

Energy Producing Plants

▽ Geothermal

• Hydroelectric

Mineral Fuel Deposits

• Uranium: major deposit

△ Natural Gas: major field

▲ Petroleum } major producing field

⬭ Petroleum }

⬛ Coal: major bituminous

⬛ Coal: minor bituminous

⬛ Coal: lignite

HYDRO & NUCLEAR
ELECTRICITY
4.8

GAS
20.9

SOLID
41.9%

LIQUID
32.4

Commercial Energy Consumption
184,857,000 metric tons
coal equivalent - 2000

© R. McN.

NATURAL HAZARDS

⬏ Tropical storm tracks
(<5 per year)

○ Volcanoes*

• Earthquakes*

〜 Tsunamis

— Limit of iceberg drift

⬛ Areas subject to desertification

*Occurrences since 1900

© R. McN.   N-GDS95000-D5 -2-2-2

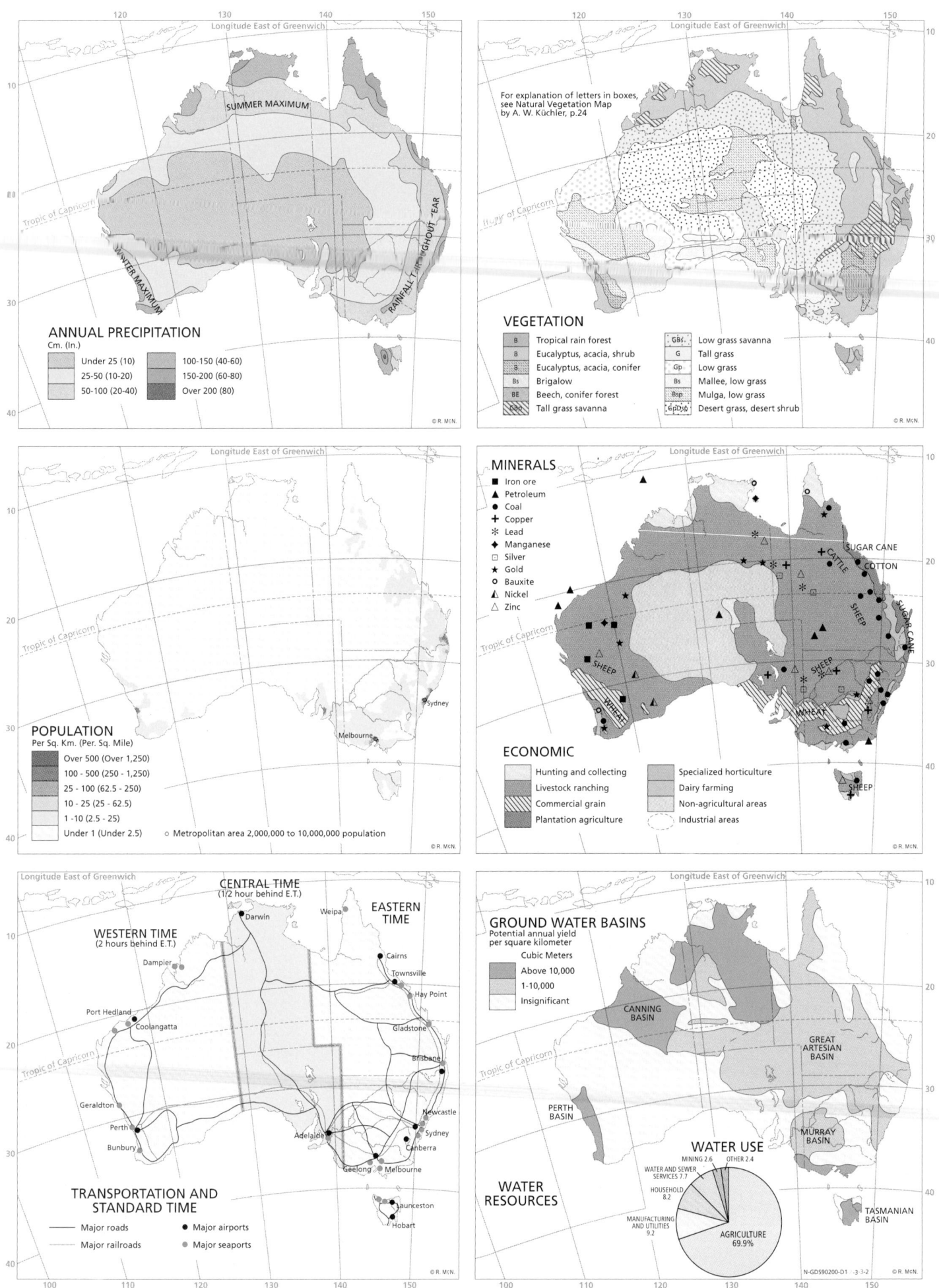

ANNUAL PRECIPITATION

Cm. (In.)

- Under 25 (10)
- 25-50 (10-20)
- 50-100 (20-40)
- 100-150 (40-60)
- 150-200 (60-80)
- Over 200 (80)

SUMMER MAXIMUM

WINTER MAXIMUM

RAINFALL THROUGHOUT YEAR

Tropic of Capricorn

Longitude East of Greenwich

© R. McN.

VEGETATION

For explanation of letters in boxes, see Natural Vegetation Map by A. W. Küchler, p.24

- B — Tropical rain forest
- B — Eucalyptus, acacia, shrub
- B — Eucalyptus, acacia, conifer
- Bs — Brigalow
- BE — Beech, conifer forest
- GBr — Tall grass savanna
- GBs — Low grass savanna
- G — Tall grass
- Gp — Low grass
- Bs — Mallee, low grass
- Bsp — Mulga, low grass
- GpDsp — Desert grass, desert shrub

© R. McN.

POPULATION

Per Sq. Km. (Per. Sq. Mile)

- Over 500 (Over 1,250)
- 100 - 500 (250 - 1,250)
- 25 - 100 (62.5 - 250)
- 10 - 25 (25 - 62.5)
- 1 - 10 (2.5 - 25)
- Under 1 (Under 2.5)

○ Metropolitan area 2,000,000 to 10,000,000 population

Sydney
Melbourne

Tropic of Capricorn

Longitude East of Greenwich

© R. McN.

MINERALS

- ■ Iron ore
- ▲ Petroleum
- ● Coal
- + Copper
- ✳ Lead
- ◆ Manganese
- ☐ Silver
- ★ Gold
- ○ Bauxite
- ▲ Nickel
- △ Zinc

SUGAR CANE
COTTON
CATTLE
SHEEP
SUGAR CANE
SHEEP
WHEAT
WHEAT
SHEEP

Tropic of Capricorn

Longitude East of Greenwich

ECONOMIC

- Hunting and collecting
- Livestock ranching
- Commercial grain
- Plantation agriculture
- Specialized horticulture
- Dairy farming
- Non-agricultural areas
- Industrial areas

© R. McN.

TRANSPORTATION AND STANDARD TIME

CENTRAL TIME (1/2 hour behind E.T.)
EASTERN TIME
WESTERN TIME (2 hours behind E.T.)

Darwin
Weipa
Dampier
Cairns
Townsville
Hay Point
Port Hedland
Coolangatta
Gladstone
Brisbane
Geraldton
Newcastle
Perth
Sydney
Bunbury
Adelaide
Canberra
Geelong
Melbourne
Launceston
Hobart

Tropic of Capricorn

Longitude East of Greenwich

- —— Major roads
- —— Major railroads
- ● Major airports
- ● Major seaports

© R. McN.

GROUND WATER BASINS

Potential annual yield per square kilometer

Cubic Meters

- Above 10,000
- 1-10,000
- Insignificant

CANNING BASIN
GREAT ARTESIAN BASIN
PERTH BASIN
MURRAY BASIN
TASMANIAN BASIN

Tropic of Capricorn

Longitude East of Greenwich

WATER RESOURCES

WATER USE

- MINING 2.6
- OTHER 2.4
- WATER AND SEWER SERVICES 7.7
- HOUSEHOLD 8.2
- MANUFACTURING AND UTILITIES 9.2
- AGRICULTURE 69.9%

N-GDS90200-D1 -3-3-2

© R. McN.

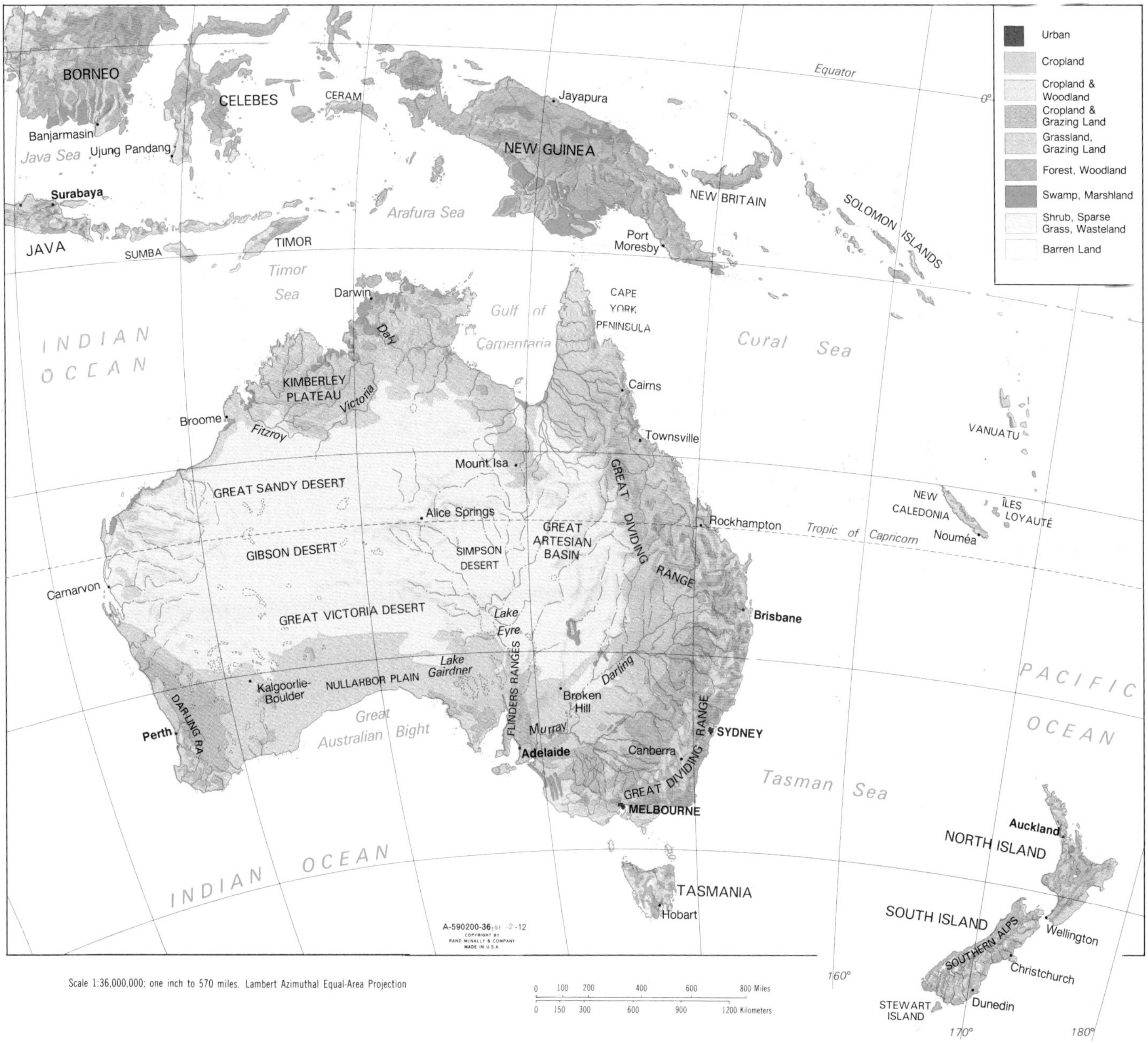

Urban
Cropland
Cropland & Woodland
Cropland & Grazing Land
Grassland, Grazing Land
Forest, Woodland
Swamp, Marshland
Shrub, Sparse Grass, Wasteland
Barren Land
Equator
BORNEO
CELEBES
CERAM
Jayapura
Banjarmasin
Java Sea
Ujung Pandang
NEW GUINEA
Surabaya
Arafura Sea
NEW BRITAIN
SOLOMON ISLANDS
JAVA
SUMBA
TIMOR
Port Moresby
Timor Sea
Darwin
Gulf of Carpentaria
CAPE YORK PENINSULA
INDIAN OCEAN
Coral Sea
Daly
KIMBERLEY PLATEAU
Victoria
Cairns
Broome
Fitzroy
Townsville
VANUATU
Mount Isa
GREAT SANDY DESERT
GREAT DIVIDING RANGE
NEW CALEDONIA
ÎLES LOYAUTÉ
Alice Springs
Rockhampton
Tropic of Capricorn
Nouméa
GIBSON DESERT
SIMPSON DESERT
GREAT ARTESIAN BASIN
Carnarvon
GREAT VICTORIA DESERT
Lake Eyre
Brisbane
Lake Gairdner
Darling
FLINDERS RANGES
PACIFIC OCEAN
Kalgoorlie-Boulder
NULLARBOR PLAIN
Broken Hill
DARLING RA.
Great Australian Bight
Murray
SYDNEY
Perth
Adelaide
Canberra
Tasman Sea
GREAT DIVIDING RANGE
MELBOURNE
Auckland
NORTH ISLAND
INDIAN OCEAN
TASMANIA
Hobart
SOUTH ISLAND
SOUTHERN ALPS
Wellington
Christchurch
Dunedin
STEWART ISLAND
A-590200-36
COPYRIGHT BY RAND McNALLY & COMPANY MADE IN U.S.A.
160°
170°
180°
0 100 200 400 600 800 Miles
0 150 300 600 900 1200 Kilometers

Scale 1:36,000,000; one inch to 570 miles. Lambert Azimuthal Equal-Area Projection

a

Relief
Meters Feet
305 1000
152.5 500
0 Sea Level 0
152.5 500
Scale 1:1 000 000
0 5 10 Miles
0 4 8 12 16 Kilometers
Broadmeadows
Melton
VICTORIA
Rockbank
Keilor
Coburg
Preston
Eltham
St. Albans
Heidelberg
Essendon
Yarra
Doncaster
Croydon
Werribee
Sunshine
Kew
Box Hill
Ringwood
Footscray
Truganina
Camberwell
Nunawading
Williamstown
MELBOURNE
Altona
Hobson's Bay
Caulfield
Saint Kilda
Oakleigh
Ferntree Gully
Little
Werribee
Brighton
Moorabbin
Springvale
Sandringham
Dandenong
38°
Lara
Mordialloc
Bannockburn
PORT PHILLIP BAY
Lyndhurst
Chelsea
Corio
Carrum
PT. WILSON
Portarlington
Cranbourne
Corio Bay
West Geelong
Geelong
Frankston
Barwon
Moolap
Drysdale
Belmont
Mt. Eliza
Baxter
Mt. Moriac
Mornington
Mt. Duneed
SWAN I
Moriac
Sommerville
Barwon Heads
Ocean Grove
Mt. Martha
Tyabb
Queenscliff
©RMCN.
144°30′
Longitude East of Greenwich
145°

b

Kurrajong
Broken Bay
Richmond
Berowra
Windsor
Newport
Nepean
Riverstone
South Cr.
Springwood
Hornsby
NEW SOUTH WALES
Narrabeen
LONG REEF
Blacktown
Penrith
Manly
Parramatta
Ryde
Port Jackson
Parramatta
Wallacia
Fairfield
SYDNEY
Warragamba
Liverpool
Randwick
Bankstown
Rockdale
Nepean
Georges
Botany Bay
TASMAN SEA
La Perouse
CAPE BANKS
34°
Sutherland
Camden
C. SOLANDER
Cronulla
The Oaks
Campbelltown
Menangle
Woronora Res.
Scale 1:1 000 000
0 5 10 Miles
0 4 8 12 16 Kilometers
Picton
Helensburgh
©RMCN.
151°
Longitude East of Greenwich

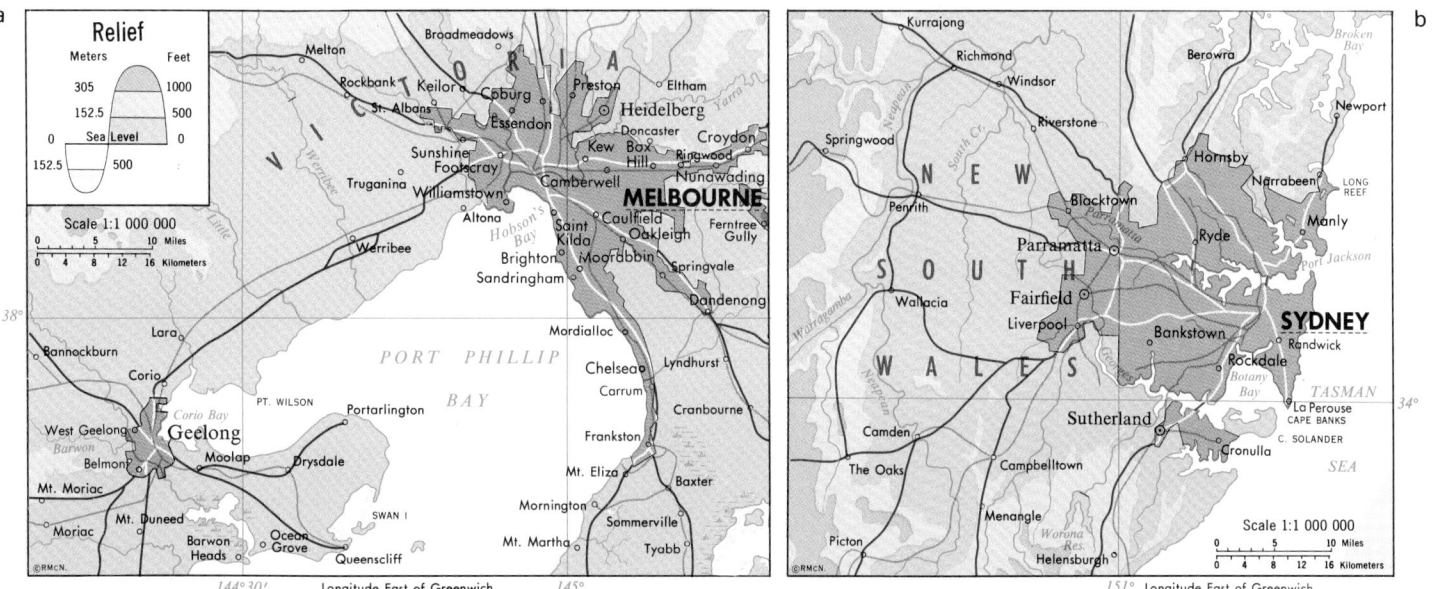

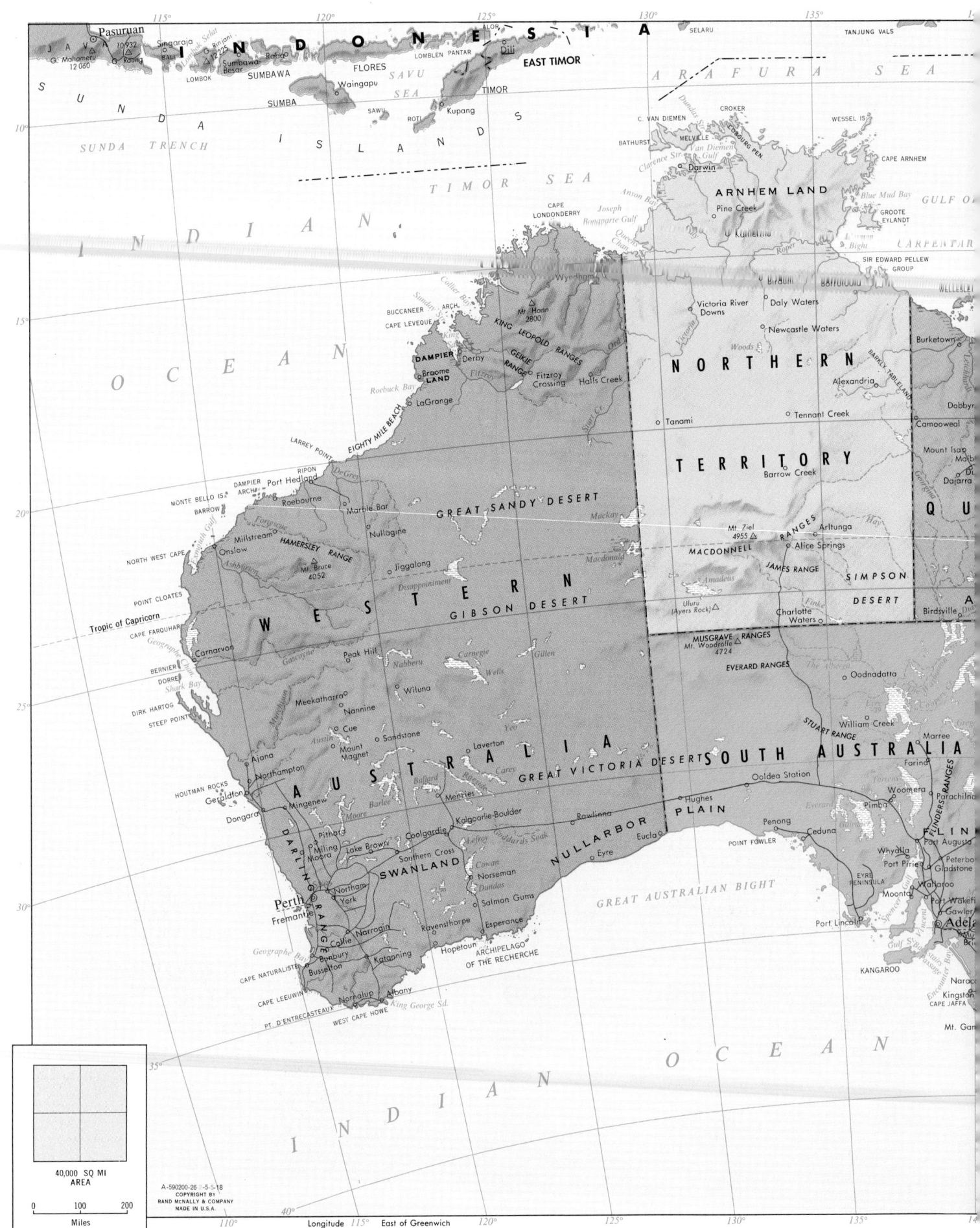

Scale 1:16 000 000; one inch to 250 miles. Lambert's Azimuthal, Equal Area Projection
Elevations and depressions are given in feet

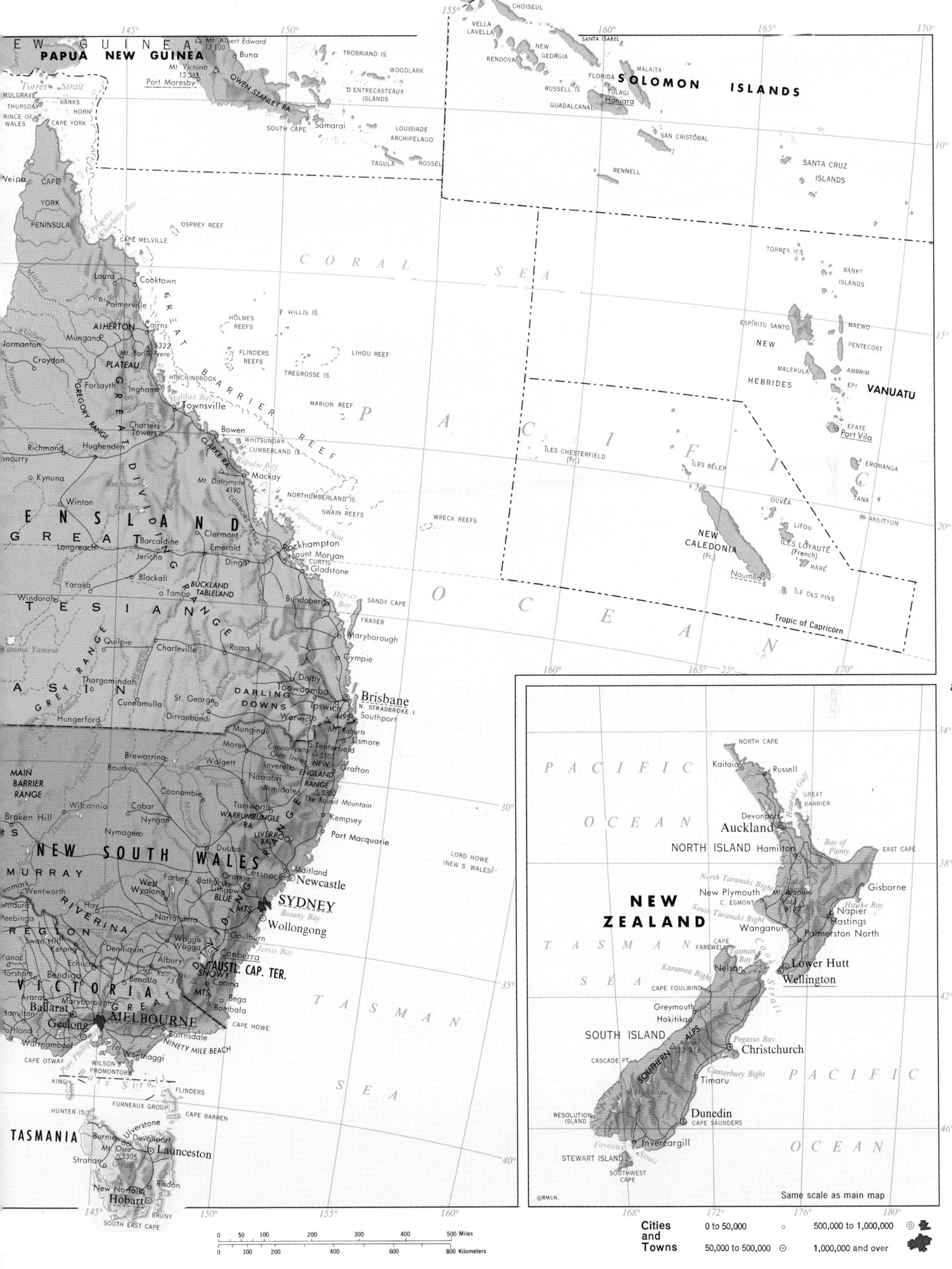

PAPUA NEW GUINEA

NEW GUINEA

Mt. Albert Edward 13 100
Mt. Victoria 13 363
Port Moresby
Buna
OWEN STANLEY RA.
TROBRIAND IS.
WOODLARK
D'ENTRECASTEAUX ISLANDS
SOUTH CAPE
Samarai
LOUISIADE ARCHIPELAGO
TAGULA ROSSEL

Torres Strait
MULGRAVE
BANKS
THURSDAY
HORN
RINCE OF WALES
CAPE YORK

CHOISEUL
VELLA LAVELLA
RENDOVA
NEW GEORGIA
SANTA ISABEL
FLORIDA
MALAITA
RUSSELL IS.
TULAGI
Honiara
GUADALCANAL
SOLOMON ISLANDS
SAN CRISTÓBAL
RENNELL
SANTA CRUZ ISLANDS

CAPE YORK PENINSULA
Veipa
CAPE YORK

CORAL SEA

TORRES IS.
BANKS ISLANDS
ESPÍRITU SANTO
MAEWO
NEW
PENTECOST
MALEKULA
AMBRIM
EPI
HEBRIDES
VANUATU
EFATE
Port Vila
EROMANGA
TANA
ANEITYUM

OSPREY REEF
CAPE MELVILLE
HÖLMES REEFS
WILLIS IS.
FLINDERS REEFS
TREGROSSE IS.
LIHOU REEF
MARION REEF

ÎLES CHESTERFIELD (Fr.)
ÎLES BÉLEP
OUVÉA
LIFOU
NEW CALEDONIA (Fr.)
ÎLES LOYAUTÉ (French)
MARÉ
Nouméa
ÎLE DES PINS

P A C I F I C   O C E A N

Tropic of Capricorn

Cooktown
Laura
Palmerville
Mungana
ATHERTON
Cairns
PLATEAU
Mt. Bartle Frere 5322
HINCHINBROOK
Ingham
Townsville
Halifax Bay
Charters Towers
Bowen
WHITSUNDAY
CUMBERLAND IS.
Repulse Bay
Mackay
Mt. Dalrymple 4190
NORTHUMBERLAND IS.
SWAIN REEFS
WRECK REEFS

GREAT BARRIER REEF
GREAT DIVIDING RANGE

QUEENSLAND
Barcaldine
Longreach
Jericho
Clermont
Emerald
Dingo
Rockhampton
Mount Morgan
CURTIS
Gladstone
BUCKLAND TABLELAND
Blackall
Tambo
Windorah
Quilpie
Charleville
Roma
Bundaberg
Hervey Bay
SANDY CAPE
FRASER
Maryborough
Gympie
MARY BOROUGH

NEW SOUTH WALES

Brisbane
N. STRADBROKE I.
Ipswich
Southport
Warwick
Moree
Inverell
Glen Innes
Grafton
Tenterfield
NEW ENGLAND RANGE
The Round Mountain
Armidale
Tamworth
Kempsey
Port Macquarie

MAIN BARRIER RANGE
Broken Hill
Wilcannia
Cobar
Nyngan
Dubbo
WARRUMBUNGLE RA.
LIVERPOOL RA.
Maitland
Cessnock
Newcastle

SYDNEY
Botany Bay
Wollongong
BLUE MTS.
Bathurst
Orange
Goulburn
Canberra
AUSTL. CAP. TER.
Jervis Bay
Cooma
SNOWY MTS.
Bega
Bombala
CAPE HOWE

VICTORIA
MELBOURNE
Ballarat
Geelong
Bendigo
Benalla
Albury
Wangaratta
Warrnambool
CAPE OTWAY
Port Phillip
WILSON'S PROMONTORY
NINETY MILE BEACH
Bairnsdale

LORD HOWE (NEW S. WALES)

TASMAN SEA

KING
FLINDERS
FURNEAUX GROUP
CAPE BARREN
HUNTER IS.

TASMANIA
Burnie
Ulverstone
Devonport
Launceston
Mt. Ossa 5305
Strahan
New Norfolk
Hobart
SOUTH EAST CAPE
BRUNY

NEW ZEALAND

PACIFIC OCEAN
NORTH CAPE
Kaitaia
Russell
HAURAKI GULF
Devonport
Auckland
NORTH ISLAND
Hamilton
GREAT BARRIER
Bay of Plenty
EAST CAPE
New Plymouth
C. EGMONT
North Taranaki Bight
South Taranaki Bight
Gisborne
Hawke Bay
Napier
Hastings
Wanganui
Palmerston North
CAPE FAREWELL
Nelson
Lower Hutt
Wellington
Cook Strait
Karamea Bight
CAPE FOULWIND
Greymouth
Hokitika
SOUTH ISLAND
SOUTHERN ALPS
Pegasus Bay
Christchurch
CASCADE PT.
Canterbury Bight
Timaru
RESOLUTION ISLAND
Dunedin
CAPE SAUNDERS
Invercargill
STEWART ISLAND
SOUTHWEST CAPE
Foveaux Strait
PACIFIC OCEAN

TASMAN SEA

Scale:
0 50 100 200 300 400 500 Miles
0 100 200 400 600 800 Kilometers

Cities and Towns
0 to 50,000
50,000 to 500,000
500,000 to 1,000,000
1,000,000 and over

©RMcN.
Same scale as main map

Continued on pages 212-213

Relief

Meters	Feet
3050	10 000
1525	5000
610	2000
305	1000
152.5	500
0	Sea Level
152.5	Below Sea Level
	500
1525	5000
3050	10 000
6100	20 000

Scale 1:16 000 000; one inch to 250 miles. Lambert's Azimuthal, Equal Area Projection
Elevations and depressions are given in feet

Longitude 115° East of Greenwich

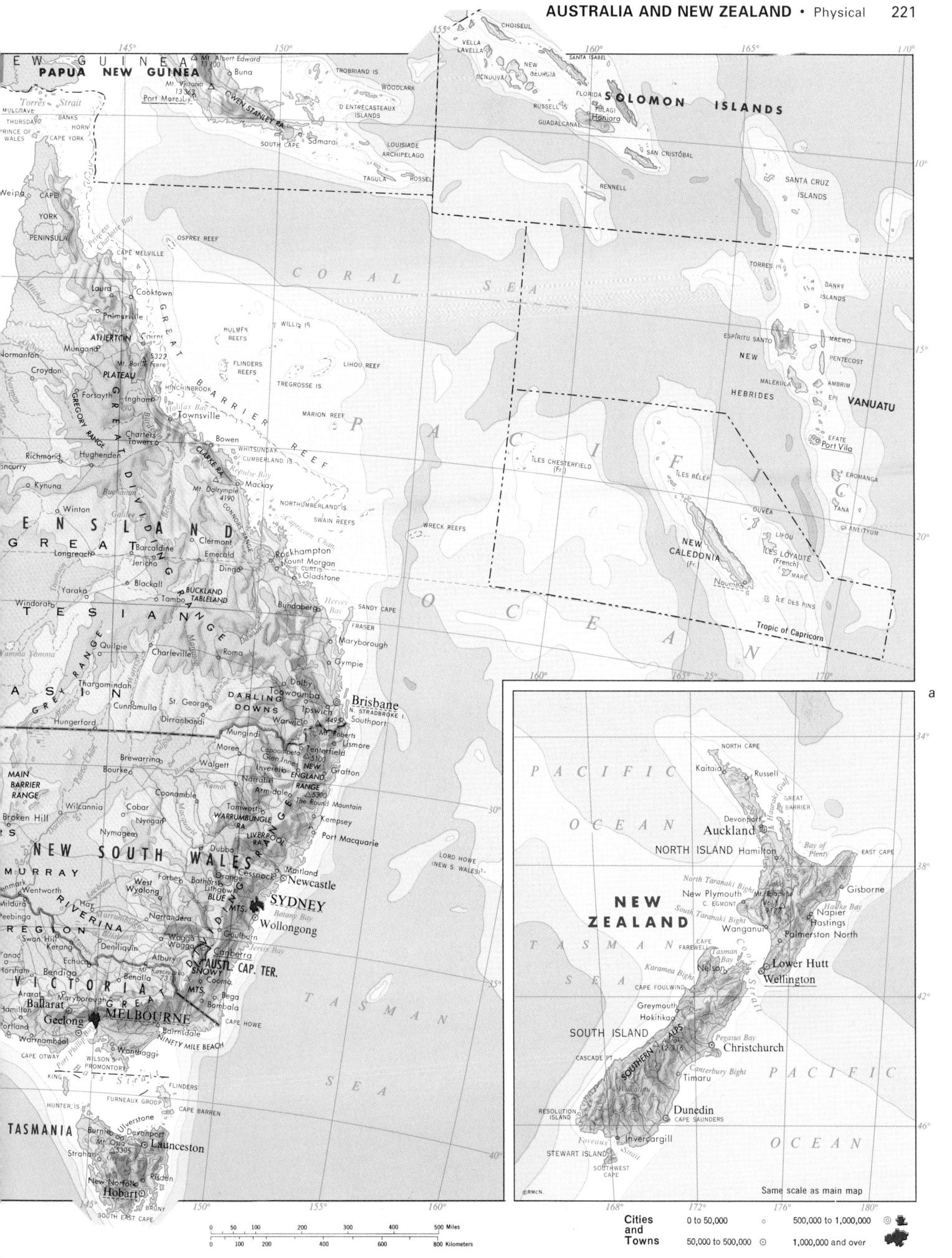

NEW GUINEA

PAPUA NEW GUINEA

Torres Strait

SOLOMON ISLANDS

CORAL SEA

VANUATU

NEW HEBRIDES

NEW CALEDONIA (Fr.)

ÎLES LOYAUTÉ (French)

Tropic of Capricorn

CAPE YORK PENINSULA

GREAT BARRIER REEF

ATHERTON PLATEAU

QUEENSLAND

GREAT DIVIDING RANGE

NEW ENGLAND RANGE

NEW SOUTH WALES

RIVERINA REGION

GREAT DIVIDING RANGE

Brisbane

SYDNEY

Wollongong

Canberra
AUSTL. CAP. TER.

SNOWY MTS.

VICTORIA

MELBOURNE

Ballarat
Geelong

NINETY MILE BEACH

BASS STRAIT

TASMANIA

Hobart
Launceston

TASMAN SEA

PACIFIC OCEAN

NEW ZEALAND

NORTH CAPE

Auckland
NORTH ISLAND Hamilton

New Plymouth

Napier
Hastings
Wanganui Palmerston North

Gisborne

TASMAN SEA

Nelson
Lower Hutt
Wellington

SOUTH ISLAND

SOUTHERN ALPS

Greymouth
Hokitika

Christchurch
Timaru

Dunedin

Invercargill
STEWART ISLAND

PACIFIC OCEAN

New Zealand inset: Same scale as main map

Cities and Towns	0 to 50,000	500,000 to 1,000,000
	50,000 to 500,000	1,000,000 and over

0   50 100   200   300   400   500 Miles
0   100 200   400   600   800 Kilometers

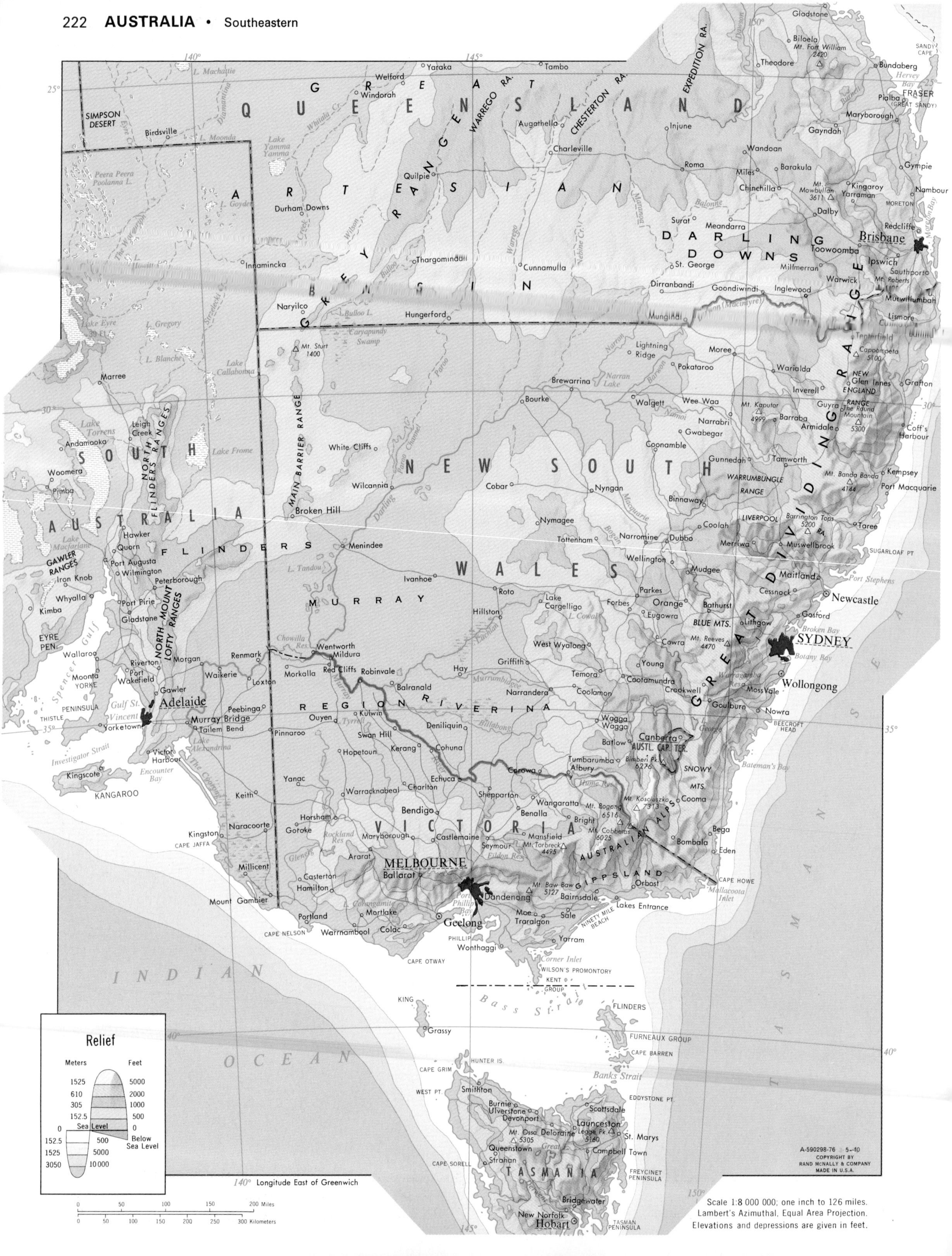

QUEENSLAND

SIMPSON DESERT

GREAT DIVIDING RANGE

WARREGO RA.
CHESTERTON RA.
EXPEDITION RA.

Yaraka
Welford
Windorah
Yaraka
Tambo
Theodore
Mt. Fort William 2420
Biloela
Gladstone

Birdsville
Durham Downs
Quilpie
Charleville
Augathella
Injune
Roma
Wandoan
Barakula
Gayndah
Maryborough
Bundaberg
Hervey Bay
FRASER (GREAT SANDY) I.
SANDY CAPE

Innamincka
Thargomindah
Cunnamulla
St. George
Surat
Meandarra
Dalby
Toowoomba
Kingaroy
Yarraman
Nambour
MORETON I.

Naryilco
Hungerford
Dirranbandi
Goondiwindi
Inglewood
Warwick
Mt. Roberts
Lismore
Redcliffe
Ipswich
Southport
Murwillumbah
Brisbane

GREAT ARTESIAN BASIN

Mt. Sturt 1400
Lightning Ridge
Moree
Tenterfield
Capoompeta 5100
NEW ENGLAND
Grafton
Coff's Harbour

Brewarrina
Pokataroo
Walgett
Warialda
Inverell
Glen Innes
Guyra
The Round Mountain 5300
Armidale
Barraba
Mt. Banda Banda 4144
Kempsey
Port Macquarie

SOUTH AUSTRALIA

Lake Eyre
Marree
L. Gregory
L. Blanche
Lake Callabonna
FLINDERS RANGES
NORTH FLINDERS RANGES

Andamooka
Woomera
Pimba
Leigh Creek
Hawker
Quorn

NEW SOUTH WALES

Bourke
Wee Waa
Narrabri
Gwabegar
Coonamble
Gunnedah
Tamworth
WARRUMBUNGLE RANGE
Mt. Kaputar 4999
Coonabarabran

White Cliffs
Wilcannia
Cobar
Nyngan
Coolah
Merriwa
Muswellbrook
Taree
Barrington Tops 5200
LIVERPOOL RA.
Sugarloaf Pt.

MAIN BARRIER RANGE
Broken Hill
Menindee
Nymagee
Tottenham
Narromine
Dubbo
Wellington
Mudgee
Maitland
Port Stephens

FLINDERS
Port Augusta
Wilmington
Peterborough
Iron Knob
Whyalla
Kimba
NORTH MOUNT LOFTY RANGES
Port Pirie
Gladstone
Crystal Brook

GAWLER RANGES
EYRE PEN.
Wallaroo
Moonta
YORKE PENINSULA
Kadina
Riverton
Morgan
Waikerie
Loxton
Renmark
Wentworth
Mildura
Red Cliffs
Morkalla

MURRAY
L. Tandou
Ivanhoe
Roto
Hillston
Hay
Griffith
West Wyalong
Lake Cargelligo
L. Cowal
Forbes
Parkes
Orange
Eugowra
Cowra
BLUE MTS.
Mt. Reeves 4470
Lithgow
Gosford
Broken Bay

SYDNEY
Botany Bay
Wollongong

Adelaide
Gawler
Murray Bridge
Tailem Bend
Pinnaroo
Peebinga
Ouyen
Kulwin
Swan Hill
REGION RIVERINA
Deniliquin
Narrandera
Coolamon
Wagga Wagga
Temora
Young
Cootamundra
Crookwell
Goulburn
Moss Vale
Nowra
BEECROFT HEAD

Yorketown
Victor Harbour
Encounter Bay
Kingscote
KANGAROO I.

Pinnaroo
Hopetoun
Kerang
Cohuna
Echuca
Shepparton
Carowa
Albury
Tumbarumba
Bimberi Pk. 6276
Canberra
AUSTL. CAP. TER.
SNOWY MTS.
Cooma
Batemans Bay

VICTORIA
Yanac
Warracknabeal
Charlton
Bendigo
Benalla
Wangaratta
Mt. Bogong 6516
Mt. Kosciuszko 7313
AUSTRALIAN ALPS
Bombala
Bega
Eden

Kingston
Naracoorte
Gorbke
Horsham
Maryborough
Castlemaine
Seymour
Mansfield
Mt. Torbreck 4495
Mt. Cobberas 6025
Bright
GIPPSLAND
Orbost
CAPE HOWE
Mallacoota Inlet

Millicent
Ararat
Ballarat
MELBOURNE
Mt. Baw Baw 5127
Bairnsdale
Lakes Entrance

Mount Gambier
Hamilton
Casterton
Colac
Geelong
Dandenong
Moe
Traralgon
Sale
Yarram
NINETY MILE BEACH

Portland
Warrnambool
Mortlake
CAPE NELSON
CAPE OTWAY
Wonthaggi
PHILLIP I.
Corner Inlet
WILSON'S PROMONTORY
KENT GROUP

INDIAN OCEAN

Bass Strait
KING I.
Grassy
FLINDERS I.
FURNEAUX GROUP
CAPE BARREN
Banks Strait
EDDYSTONE PT.

TASMANIA
HUNTER IS.
CAPE GRIM
WEST PT.
Smithton
Burnie
Ulverstone
Devonport
Scottsdale
Launceston
St. Marys
Deloraine
Mt. Ossa 5305
Legge Pk. 5160
Campbell Town
Queenstown
Strahan
Bridgewater
New Norfolk
Hobart
CAPE SOREL
FREYCINET PENINSULA
TASMAN PENINSULA

TASMAN SEA

Relief

Meters		Feet
1525		5000
610		2000
305		1000
152.5		500
0	Sea Level	0
152.5		500 Below Sea Level
1525		5000
3050		10 000

140° Longitude East of Greenwich

0   50   100   150   200 Miles
0   50   100   150   200   250   300 Kilometers

A-590298-76   5-40
COPYRIGHT BY
RAND McNALLY & COMPANY
MADE IN U.S.A.

Scale 1:8 000 000; one inch to 126 miles.
Lambert's Azimuthal, Equal Area Projection.
Elevations and depressions are given in feet.

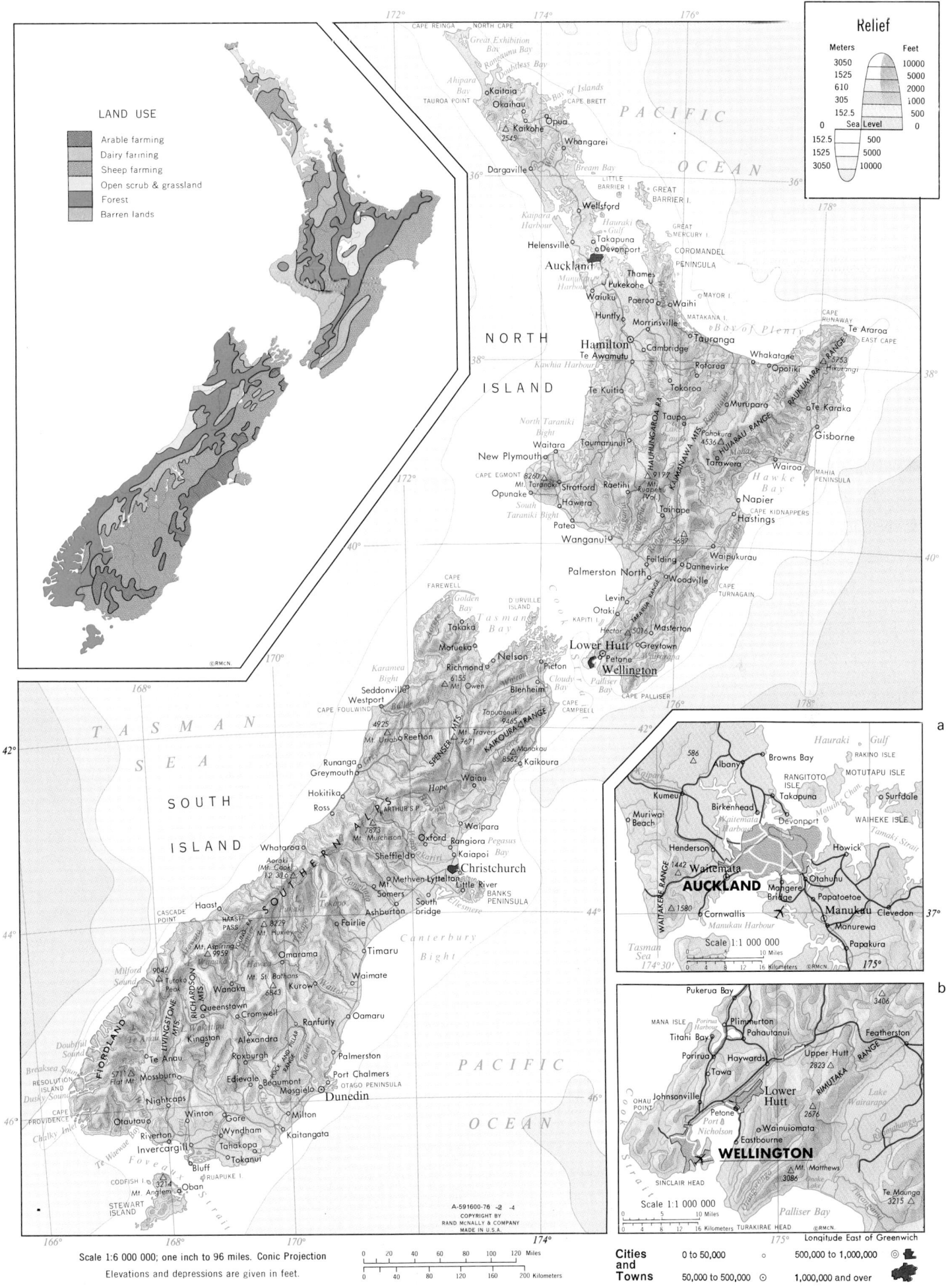

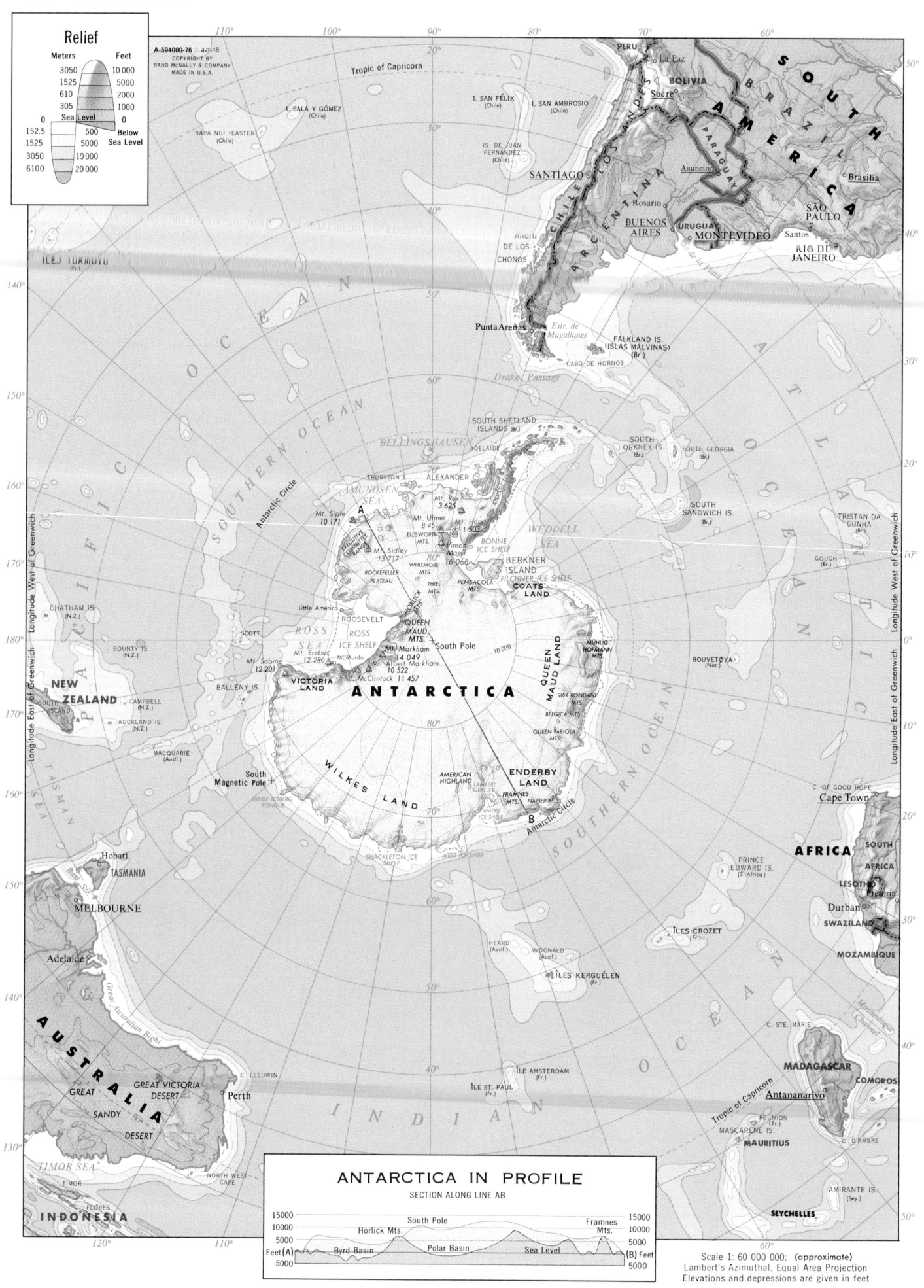

Relief

Meters	Feet
3050	10 000
1525	5000
610	2000
305	1000
Sea Level	0
0	
152.5	500
	Below Sea Level
1525	5000
3050	10 000
6100	20 000

A-594000-76 4-7-18
COPYRIGHT BY
RAND MᶜNALLY & COMPANY
MADE IN U.S.A.

ANTARCTICA IN PROFILE

SECTION ALONG LINE AB

15000	South Pole		15000
10000	Horlick Mts.	Framnes Mts.	10000
5000			5000
Feet (A)	Byrd Basin	Polar Basin	Sea Level	(B) Feet
5000			5000

Scale 1: 60 000 000; (approximate)
Lambert's Azimuthal, Equal Area Projection
Elevations and depressions are given in feet

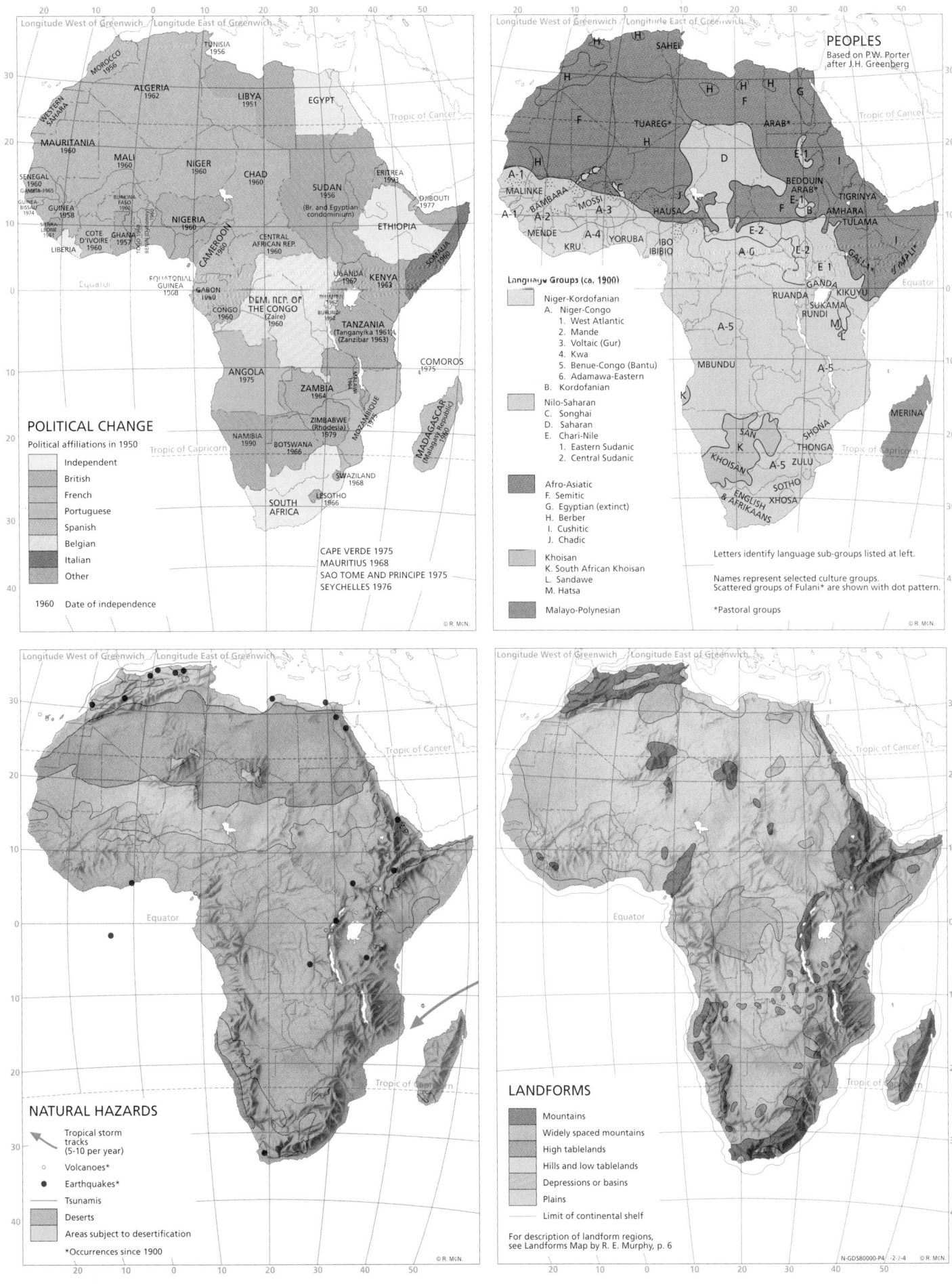

POLITICAL CHANGE

Longitude West of Greenwich / Longitude East of Greenwich

TUNISIA 1956
MOROCCO 1956
ALGERIA 1962
LIBYA 1951
EGYPT
WESTERN SAHARA
MAURITANIA 1960
MALI 1960
NIGER 1960
CHAD 1960
SUDAN 1956 (Br. and Egyptian condominium)
ERITREA 1993
DJIBOUTI 1977
SENEGAL 1960
GAMBIA 1965
GUINEA BISSAU 1974
GUINEA 1958
SIERRA LEONE 1961
LIBERIA
COTE D'IVOIRE 1960
GHANA 1957
BURKINA FASO 1960
BENIN 1960
TOGO 1960
NIGERIA 1960
CAMEROON 1960
CENTRAL AFRICAN REP. 1960
ETHIOPIA
SOMALIA 1960
EQUATORIAL GUINEA 1968
GABON 1960
CONGO 1960
DEM. REP. OF THE CONGO (Zaire) 1960
UGANDA 1962
KENYA 1963
RWANDA 1962
BURUNDI 1962
TANZANIA (Tanganyika 1961) (Zanzibar 1963)
COMOROS 1975
ANGOLA 1975
ZAMBIA 1964
MALAWI
ZIMBABWE (Rhodesia) 1979
MOZAMBIQUE 1975
MADAGASCAR (Malagasy Republic) 1960
NAMIBIA 1990
BOTSWANA 1966
SWAZILAND 1968
LESOTHO 1966
SOUTH AFRICA

Tropic of Cancer
Equator
Tropic of Capricorn

POLITICAL CHANGE
Political affiliations in 1950

- Independent
- British
- French
- Portuguese
- Spanish
- Belgian
- Italian
- Other

1960 Date of independence

CAPE VERDE 1975
MAURITIUS 1968
SAO TOME AND PRINCIPE 1975
SEYCHELLES 1976

© R. McN.

PEOPLES
Based on P.W. Porter after J.H. Greenberg

Longitude West of Greenwich / Longitude East of Greenwich

SAHEL
H TUAREG* ARAB* BEDOUIN ARAB*
F D
A-1 MALINKE
BAMBARA
MOSSI
HAUSA
TIGRINYA
AMHARA
TULAMA
A-2 MENDE
A-3
A-4 YORUBA
KRU
IBO IBIBIO
GALLA
SOMALI
GANDA
RUANDA SUKAMA KIKUYU
RUNDI
A-5
MBUNDU
K
SAN
KHOISAN
SHONA
THONGA
ZULU
SOTHO
XHOSA
ENGLISH & AFRIKAANS
MERINA

Tropic of Cancer
Equator
Tropic of Capricorn

Language Groups (ca. 1900)

Niger-Kordofanian
A. Niger-Congo
 1. West Atlantic
 2. Mande
 3. Voltaic (Gur)
 4. Kwa
 5. Benue-Congo (Bantu)
 6. Adamawa-Eastern
B. Kordofanian

Nilo-Saharan
C. Songhai
D. Saharan
E. Chari-Nile
 1. Eastern Sudanic
 2. Central Sudanic

Afro-Asiatic
F. Semitic
G. Egyptian (extinct)
H. Berber
I. Cushitic
J. Chadic

Khoisan
K. South African Khoisan
L. Sandawe
M. Hatsa

Malayo-Polynesian

Letters identify language sub-groups listed at left.

Names represent selected culture groups.
Scattered groups of Fulani* are shown with dot pattern.

*Pastoral groups

© R. McN.

NATURAL HAZARDS

Longitude West of Greenwich / Longitude East of Greenwich

Tropic of Cancer
Equator
Tropic of Capricorn

NATURAL HAZARDS

→ Tropical storm tracks (5-10 per year)
○ Volcanoes*
● Earthquakes*
— Tsunamis
 Deserts
 Areas subject to desertification

*Occurrences since 1900

LANDFORMS

Longitude West of Greenwich / Longitude East of Greenwich

Tropic of Cancer
Equator
Tropic of Capricorn

LANDFORMS

- Mountains
- Widely spaced mountains
- High tablelands
- Hills and low tablelands
- Depressions or basins
- Plains
- Limit of continental shelf

For description of landform regions, see Landforms Map by R. E. Murphy, p. 6

N-GDS80000-P4 -2-2-4 © R. McN.

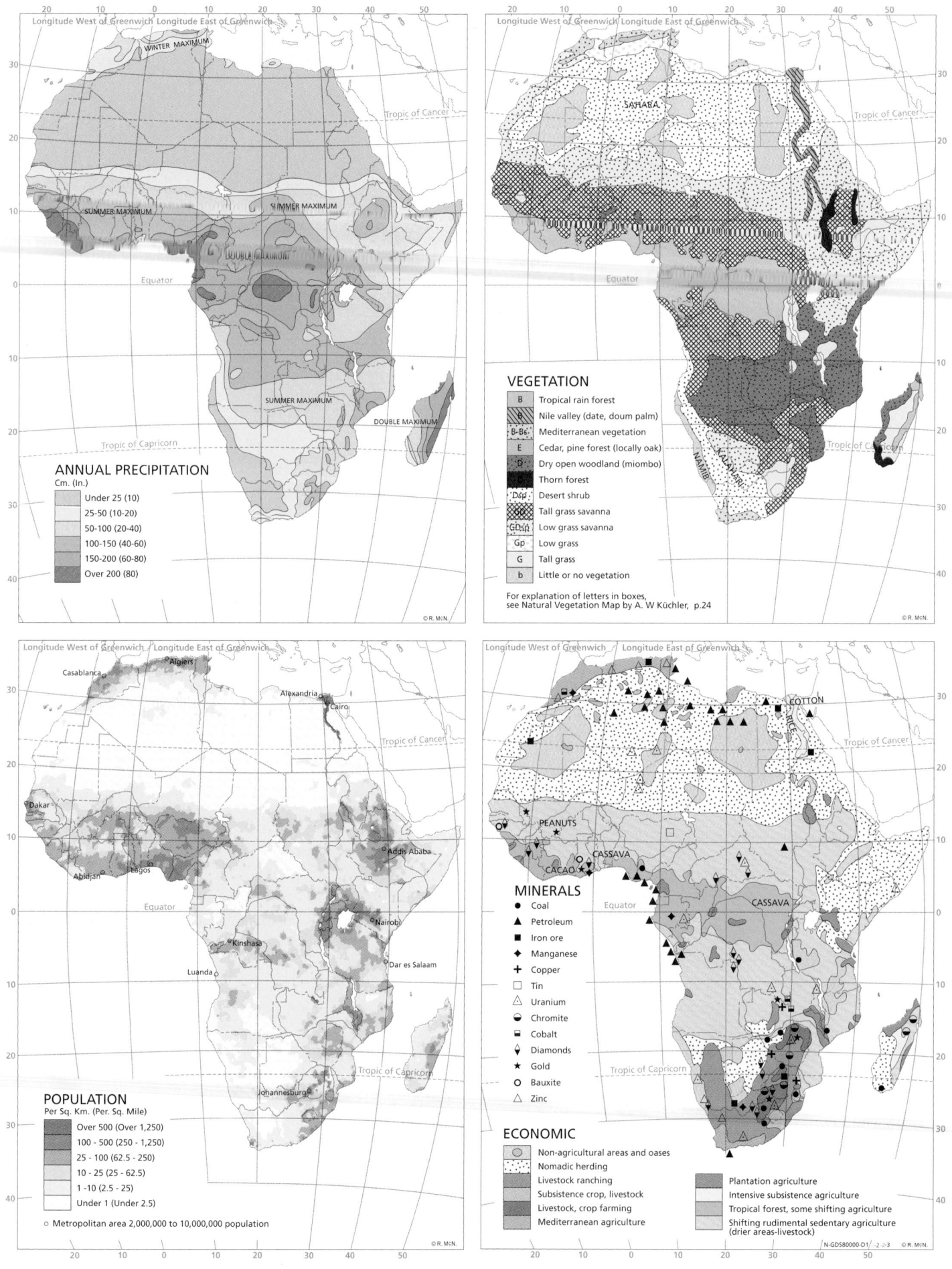

ANNUAL PRECIPITATION
Cm. (In.)

- Under 25 (10)
- 25-50 (10-20)
- 50-100 (20-40)
- 100-150 (40-60)
- 150-200 (60-80)
- Over 200 (80)

WINTER MAXIMUM

SUMMER MAXIMUM

SUMMER MAXIMUM

DOUBLE MAXIMUM

SUMMER MAXIMUM

DOUBLE MAXIMUM

© R. McN.

VEGETATION

B	Tropical rain forest
B	Nile valley (date, doum palm)
B-Bs	Mediterranean vegetation
E	Cedar, pine forest (locally oak)
D	Dry open woodland (miombo)
	Thorn forest
Dsp	Desert shrub
	Tall grass savanna
GDsa	Low grass savanna
Gp	Low grass
G	Tall grass
b	Little or no vegetation

SAHARA

NAMIB

KALAHARI

For explanation of letters in boxes,
see Natural Vegetation Map by A. W Küchler, p.24

© R. McN.

POPULATION
Per Sq. Km. (Per. Sq. Mile)

- Over 500 (Over 1,250)
- 100 - 500 (250 - 1,250)
- 25 - 100 (62.5 - 250)
- 10 - 25 (25 - 62.5)
- 1 - 10 (2.5 - 25)
- Under 1 (Under 2.5)

○ Metropolitan area 2,000,000 to 10,000,000 population

Casablanca
Algiers
Alexandria
Cairo
Dakar
Abidjan
Lagos
Addis Ababa
Kinshasa
Nairobi
Luanda
Dar es Salaam
Johannesburg

© R. McN.

MINERALS

- ● Coal
- ▲ Petroleum
- ■ Iron ore
- ◆ Manganese
- ✛ Copper
- ☐ Tin
- △ Uranium
- ◗ Chromite
- ⊟ Cobalt
- ⬦ Diamonds
- ★ Gold
- ○ Bauxite
- △ Zinc

COTTON
PEANUTS
CASSAVA
CACAO
CASSAVA

ECONOMIC

	Non-agricultural areas and oases
	Nomadic herding
	Livestock ranching
	Subsistence crop, livestock
	Livestock, crop farming
	Mediterranean agriculture
	Plantation agriculture
	Intensive subsistence agriculture
	Tropical forest, some shifting agriculture
	Shifting rudimental sedentary agriculture (drier areas-livestock)

N-GDS80000-D1/ -2-2-3   © R. McN.

ATLANTIC OCEAN

MADRID

CORSICA
ROME

SARDINIA

İSTANBUL

BAKU

Black Sea

Caspian Sea

Algiers

Tunis

SICILY

Athens

Mediterranean Sea

MALTA

CRETE

CYPRUS

TEHRAN

Casablanca

ATLAS MOUNTAINS

Tripoli

Banghāzī

Beirut

Baghdad

Tigris

Euphrates

CANARY ISLANDS

GRAND ERG OCCIDENTAL

GRAND ERG ORIENTAL

Alexandria

CAIRO

SYRIAN DESERT

El Aaiun

Tropic of Cancer

AHAGGAR

LIBYAN DESERT

ARABIAN DESERT

Nile

Red Sea

AN NAFŪD

Riyadh

Tamenghest

S   A   H   A   R   A

TIBESTI

NUBIAN DESERT

Mecca

ADRAR DES·IFÔGHAS

Lake Nasser

Tombouctou

S   U   D   A   N

ENNEDI

Nile

Khartoum

Asmera

Dakar

Niger

Lake Chad

Al-Fāshir

White Nile

DANAKIL

Aden

Gulf of Aden

Bamako

Kano

N'Djamena

Berbera

Freetown

Niger

Blue Nile

Addis Ababa

Lake Volta

Abidjan

Lagos

Gulf of Guinea

Yaoundé

Bangui

Congo

Ubangi

Uele

Mogadishu

Equator

Kisangani

Mountain Nile

Lake Victoria

Nairobi

INDIAN OCEAN

Congo

Kasai

Kinshasa

Lake Tanganyika

Dar es Salaam

Luanda

ATLANTIC OCEAN

Lubumbashi

Lake Nyasa

COMORO ISLANDS

Moçambique

Lusaka

Zambezi

Blantyre

Antananarivo

Harare

MADAGASCAR

Mozambique Channel

NAMIB DESERT

Windhoek

KALAHARI DESERT

Limpopo

Tropic of Capricorn

Johannesburg

Durban

Orange

Orange

INDIAN OCEAN

Cape Town

Legend:
- Urban
- Cropland
- Cropland & Woodland
- Cropland & Grazing Land
- Grassland, Grazing Land
- Forest, Woodland
- Swamp, Marshland
- Shrub, Sparse Grass, Wasteland
- Barren Land
- Oasis

A-580000-36   -2 3-13

COPYRIGHT BY
RAND McNALLY & COMPANY
MADE IN U.S.A.

Scale 1:36,000,000; one inch to 570 miles.   Lambert Azimuthal Equal-Area Projection

0   100   200   400   600   800 Miles

0   150   300   600   900   1200 Kilometers

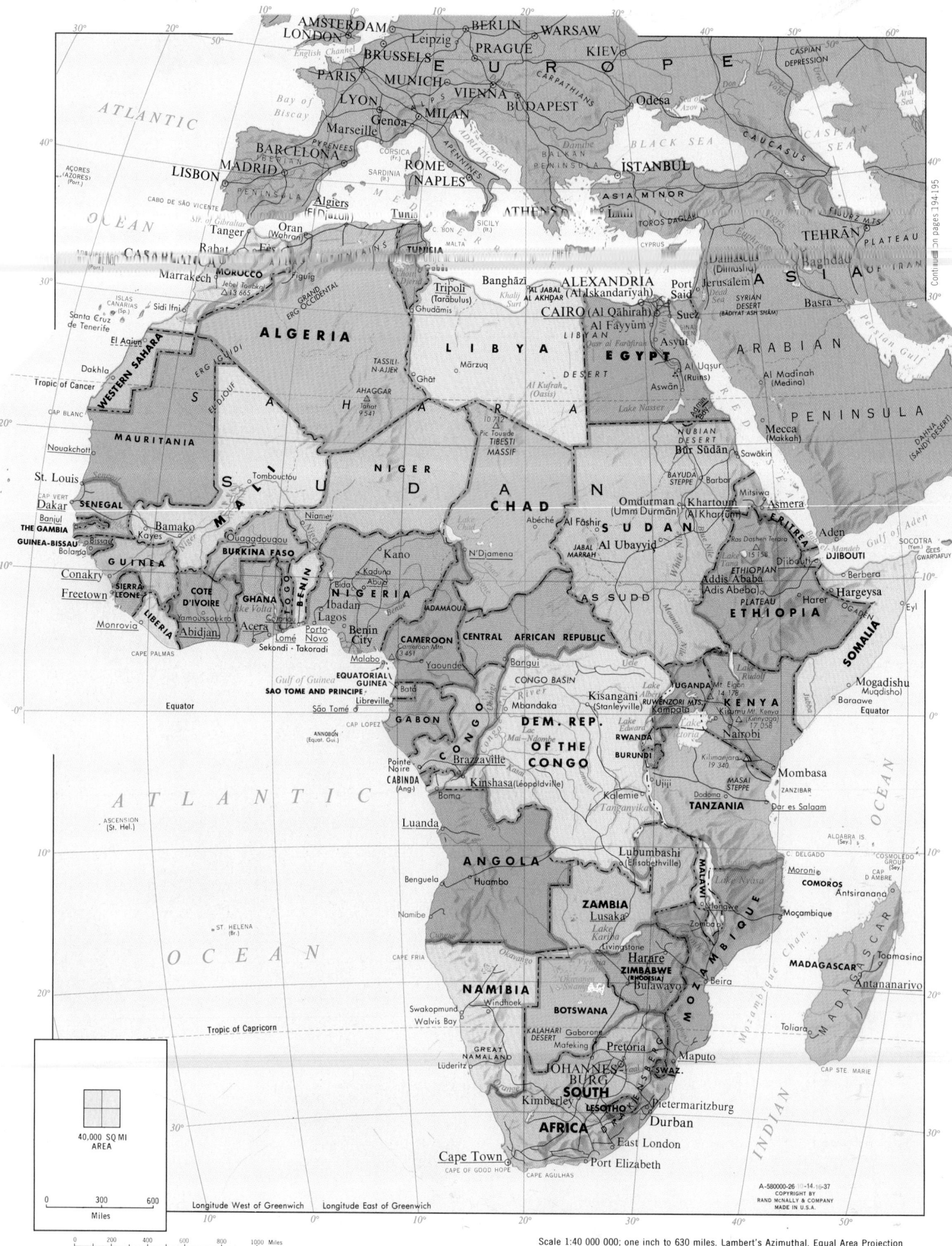

Continued on pages 194-195

40,000 SQ MI AREA

0   300   600
Miles

Longitude West of Greenwich   Longitude East of Greenwich

0   200   400   600   800   1000 Miles
0   400   800   1200   1600 Kilometers

Scale 1:40 000 000; one inch to 630 miles. Lambert's Azimuthal, Equal Area Projection
Elevations and depressions are given in feet.

A-580000-26 10-14-16-37
COPYRIGHT BY
RAND MCNALLY & COMPANY
MADE IN U.S.A.

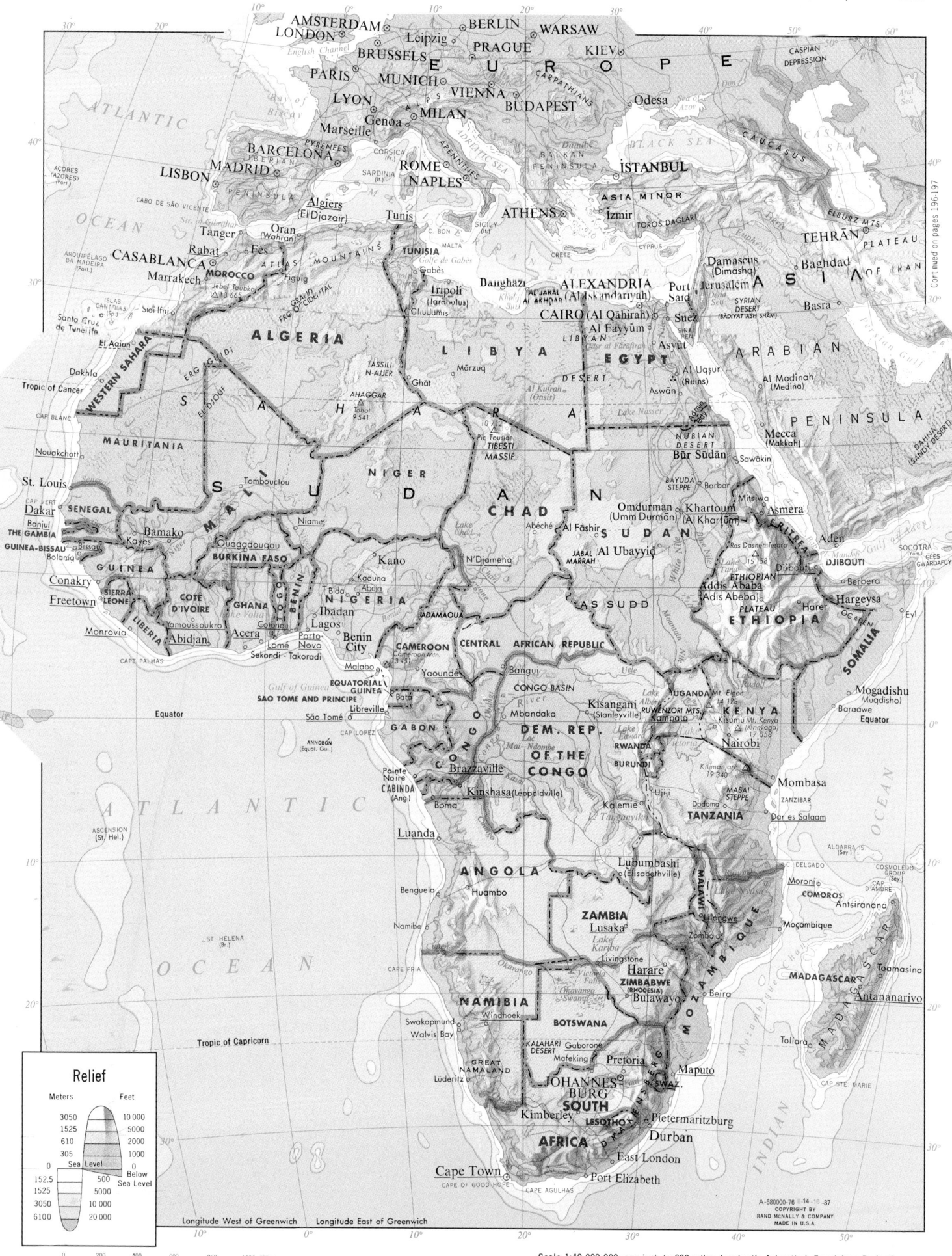

Continued on pages 196-197

Relief

Meters		Feet
3050		10 000
1525		5000
610		2000
305		1000
	Sea Level	
152.5		500
1525		5000 Below
		Sea Level
3050		10 000
6100		20 000

Longitude West of Greenwich   Longitude East of Greenwich

A-580000-76 8-14-16 -37
COPYRIGHT BY
RAND MCNALLY & COMPANY
MADE IN U.S.A.

0   200   400   600   800   1000 Miles
0   400   800   1200   1600 Kilometers

Scale 1:40 000 000; one inch to 630 miles. Lambert's Azimuthal, Equal Area Projection
Elevations and depressions are given in feet.

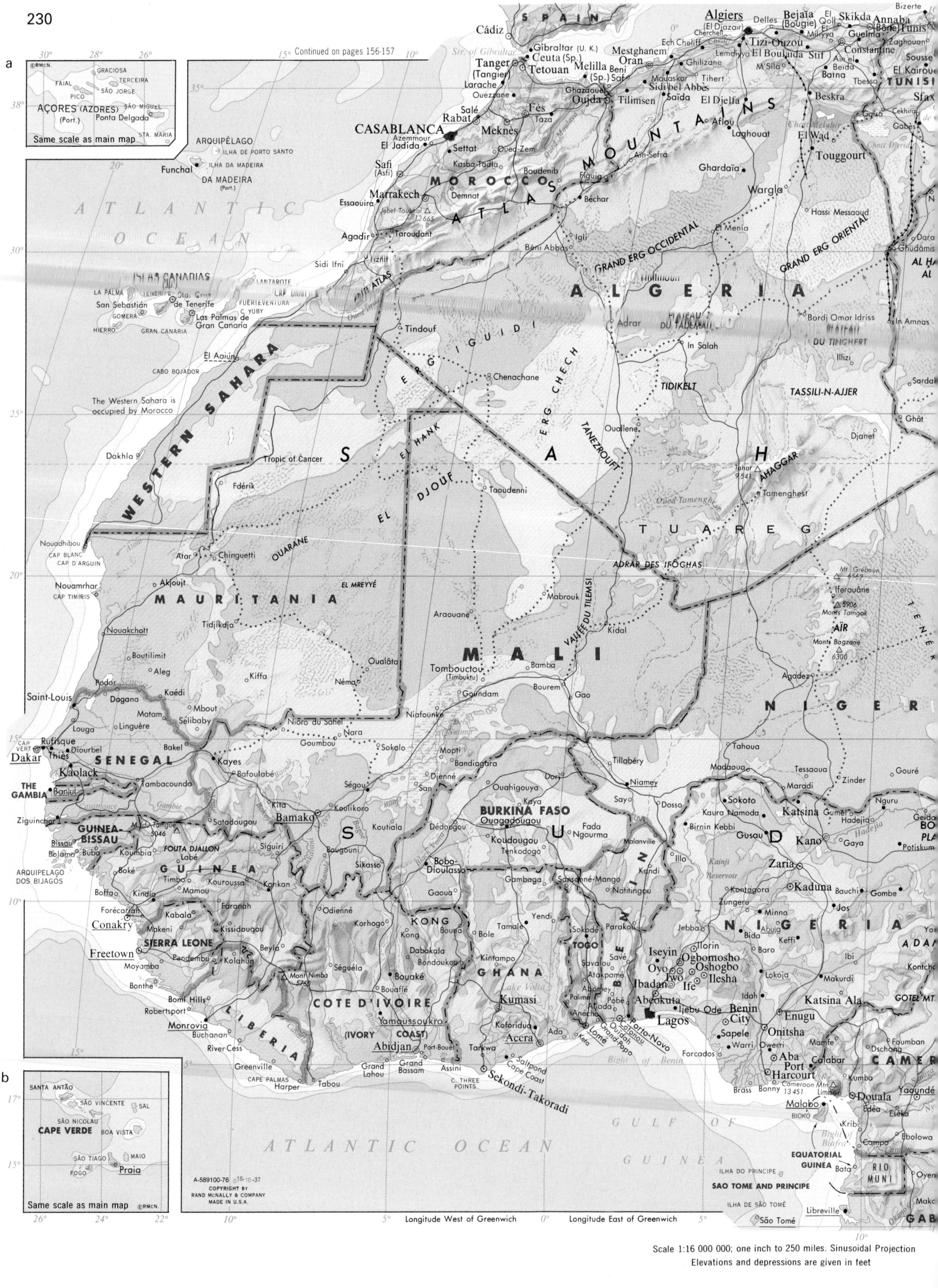

a

©RMCN.

GRACIOSA
FAIAL PICO TERCEIRA SÃO JORGE
AÇORES (AZORES) SÃO MIGUEL
(Port.) Ponta Delgada
STA. MARIA
Same scale as main map

ARQUIPÉLAGO ILHA DE PORTO SANTO
DA MADEIRA
Funchal ILHA DA MADEIRA
(Port.)

Continued on pages 156-157

SPAIN
Cádiz Gibraltar (U.K.)
Ceuta (Sp.) Algiers (El Djazair) Delles Bejaïa (Bougie) El Qoll Skikda Annaba Bizerte
Tanger (Tangier) Melilla Mestghanem Tizi-Ouzou Lemchiya El Boulaïda Stif Bône Tunis
Tetouan Beni Saf Oran Ghilizane Constantine Sousse
Larache Ghazaouet Sidi bel Abbès Mascara Tihert M'Sila Aïn el Beida Zaghouan El Kairouan
Salé Oujda Tilimsen Saïda El Djelfa Biskra Sfax
Rabat Fès Taza Aflou Laghouat El Wad Gabès
CASABLANCA Meknès Touggourt
El Jadida Azemmour Oued-Zem Aïn-Sefra Ghardaïa Wargla
Safi (Asfi) Kasba-Tadla Boudenib Figuig Béchar Hassi Messaoud
MOROCCO Demnat ALGERIA
Marrakech ATLAS MOUNTAINS El Menia Bordj Omar Idriss In Amnas AL HA AI
Essaouira Jebel Toubkal 13665
Agadir Taroudant GRAND ERG OCCIDENTAL GRAND ERG ORIENTAL
Sidi Ifni Tiznit Igli Tindouf Adrar In Salah Ghudâmis
ANTI ATLAS Béni Abbès Chenachane PLATEAU DU TADEMAÏT Illizi PLATEAU DU TINGHERT
ISLAS CANARIAS CAP DRAA ERG IGUIDI ERG CHECH TIDIKELT TASSILI-N-AJJER
LA PALMA LANZAROTE El Aaiún Ouallene Sardai
San Sebastián TENERIFE GRAN CANARIA FUERTEVENTURA CAP JUBY TANEZROUFT Ghât
GOMERA Las Palmas de Gran Canaria El Hank Taoudenni Djanet
HIERRO CABO BOJADOR WESTERN SAHARA EL DJOUF TUAREG AHAGGAR Tamenghest
Dakhla Tropic of Cancer SAHARA Tahat 9541
The Western Sahara is occupied by Morocco Fdérik EL MREYYÉ ADRAR DES IFOGHAS Mt Gréboun 4562
Nouadhibou CAP BLANC CAP D'ARGUIN Atar Chinguetti OUARÂNE VALLÉE DU TILEMSI Iferouâne Monts Tamgak 5906
Nouâmrhâr CAP TIMIRIS Akjoujt Mabrouk AÏR Monts Bagzane 6300
Nouakchott MAURITANIA Araouane Kidal Agadez
Tidjikdja Tombouctou (Timbuktu) Bamba
Boutilimit Kiffa Oualâta Néma Bourem NIGER
Saint-Louis Aleg Goundam Gao MALI
Podor Kaédi Nioro du Sahel Niafounké Tahoua
Dagana Mbout Nara Mopti Tillabéry Madaoua Tessaoua Gouré
Louga Sélibaby Goumbou Bandiagara Dori Niamey Zinder
Matam Bakel Sokolo San Dosso Sokoto Maradi Nguru
Linguère Kayes Djenné Ouahigouya Say Kaura Namoda Katsina Gumel
CAP VERT Thiès Bafoulabé Ségou Dédougou Kaya BURKINA FASO Ouagadougou Birnin Kebbi Gusau Kano Hadejia Potiskum
Rufisque SENEGAL Kita Koulikoro Koutiala Fada N'gourma Malanville Gaya
Dakar Diourbel Tambacounda BAMAKO Sikasso Koudougou Tenkodogo Illo Zaria
Kaolack Satadougou Bougouni Bobo-Dioulasso Gambaga Kandi Zungeru Kontagora Kaduna Bauchi Gombe
THE GAMBIA Banjul FOUTA DJALLON Siguiri Odienné Gaoua Sansanné-Mango Natitingou Minna Jos
Ziguinchor GUINEA-BISSAU Labé Kankan Korhogo Kong Yendi Parakou Jebba NIGERIA Abuja
Bissau Koumbia Timbo Kouroussa Bouna Tamale Sokodé Bida Baro Keffi Ibi
Bolama Buba GUINEA Mamou Beyla Dabakala Bole Kintampo Savalou Iseyin Ilorin Lokoja Makurdi Katsina Ala
ARQUIPÉLAGO DOS BIJAGÓS Boffa Kindia Mont Nimba 5750 Séguéla Bondoukou TOGO Atakpamé Oyo Ogbomosho Idah GOTEL MT
Boké Forécariah Kabala Faranah Bouaké GHANA Palime Oshogbo Ilesha Enugu Foumban
Conakry Mpkeni Kissidougou SIERRA LEONE Bouaflé Kumasi Ibadan Ife Benin City Onitsha CAMEROON
Freetown Moyamba Kolahun COTE D'IVOIRE (IVORY COAST) Koforidua Abeokuta Ijebu Ode Sapele Aba Mamfe Calabar Dschang
Bonthe Pandembu Yamoussoukro Accra Ada Porto-Novo Lagos Warri Port Harcourt Kumba Yagoundé Yaoundé
Bomi Hills Séguéla Abidjan Port-Bouet Tarkwa Ouidah Cotonou Forcados Douala Edéa
Robertsport LIBERIA Grand Lahou Sassandra Sekondi-Takoradi Bight of Benin Brass Bonny Cameroon Mtn 13451 Kribi GAB
Monrovia Buchanan Grand Bassam Assini C. Three Points Malabo BIOKO Bata Eseka
River Cess Greenville CAPE PALMAS Tabou Harper ATLANTIC OCEAN GULF OF GUINEA EQUATORIAL GUINEA RIO MUNI Ebolowa
ILHA DO PRINCIPE SÃO TOMÉ AND PRINCIPE Campo
ILHA DE SÃO TOMÉ Libreville Oyem

ATLANTIC OCEAN

b
SANTA ANTÃO
SÃO VICENTE SAL
SÃO NICOLAU BOA VISTA
CAPE VERDE
SÃO TIAGO MAIO
FOGO Praia
Same scale as main map
©RMCN.

A-589100-76
COPYRIGHT BY
RAND MCNALLY & COMPANY
MADE IN U.S.A.

Longitude West of Greenwich Longitude East of Greenwich

Scale 1:16 000 000; one inch to 250 miles. Sinusoidal Projection
Elevations and depressions are given in feet

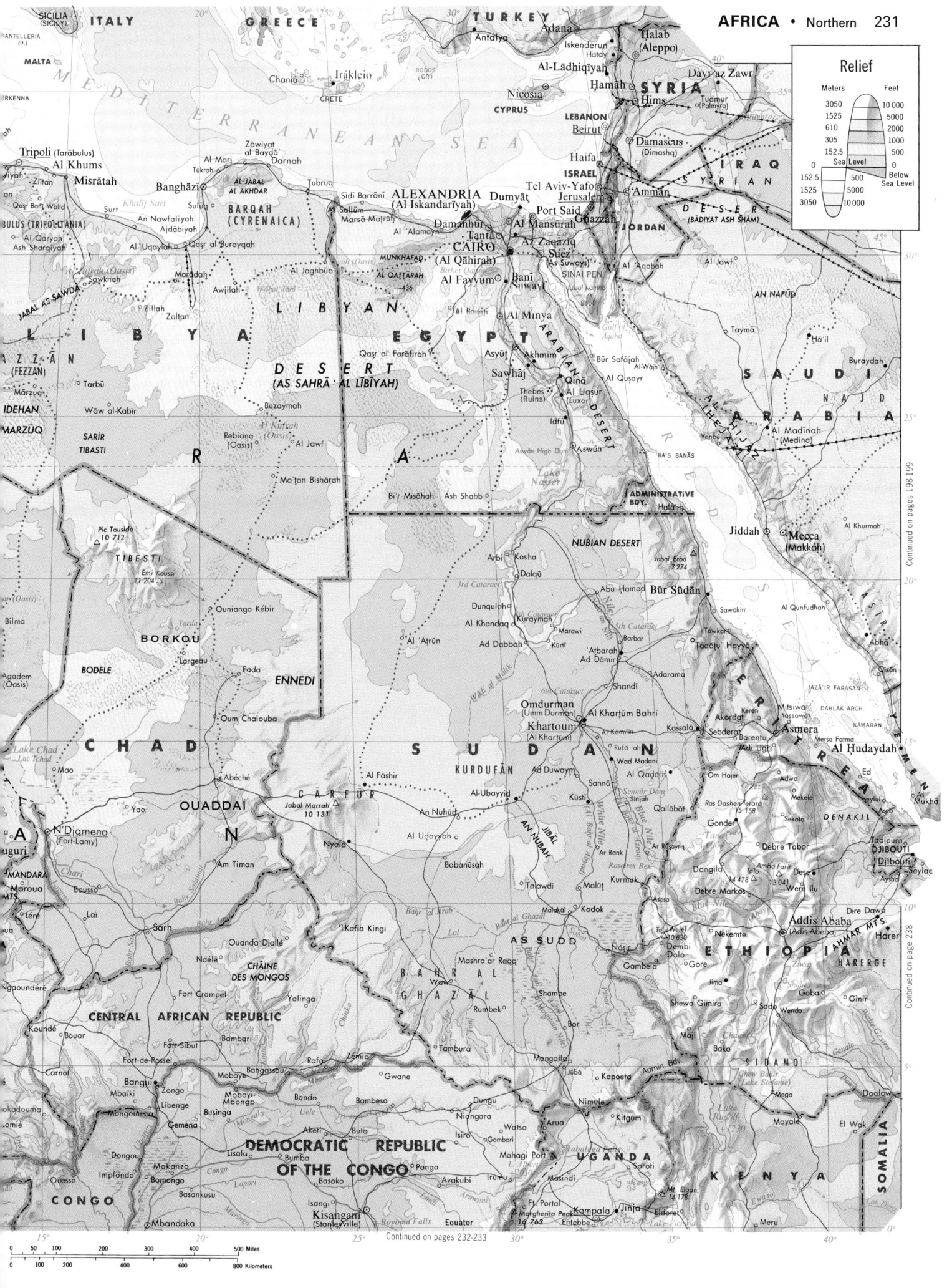

Relief

Meters	Feet
3050	10 000
1525	5000
610	2000
305	1000
152.5	500
0 Sea Level	0
	Below
152.5	Sea Level
1525	500
3050	5000
	10 000

SICILY (ITALY)
PANTELLERIA (It.)
MALTA
ITALY
GREECE
TURKEY
Antalya
Adana
Iskenderun
Hatay
Halab (Aleppo)
Al-Lādhiqīyah
Hamāh
SYRIA
Dayr az Zawr
Tudmur (Palmyra)
Chania
Irákleio
RODOS
CRETE
Nicosia
CYPRUS
LEBANON
Beirut
Damascus (Dimashq)
Hims
IRAQ
SYRIAN DESERT (BADIYAT ASH SHAM)
Haifa
Tel Aviv-Yafo
Jerusalem
Amman
JORDAN
Al 'Aqabah
Al Jawf
Tripoli (Tarābulus)
Al Khums
Misrātah
Zliten
Qaşr Aḥmad
Banghāzī
Zāwiyat al Baydā'
Darnah
Tūkrah
Al Marj
AL JABAL AL AKHDAR
Sūluq
Tubruq
Sīdī Barrānī
Marsá Matrūh
As Sallūm
ALEXANDRIA (Al Iskandarīyah)
Dumyāţ
Damanhūr
Tanţā
Al Manşūrah
Port Said
Ghazzah
Az Zaqāzīq
Suez (As Suways)
SINAI PEN.
Al 'Aqabah
SAUDI ARABIA
Buraydah
Ḥā'il
Taymā'
NAJD
AL HIJAZ
BARQAH (CYRENAICA)
An Nawfalīyah
Ajdābiyah
Qaşr al Burayqah
Al 'Uqaylah
Surt
Khalīj Surt
LIBYA
TRIPOLITANIA
Al Qaryah Ash Sharqīyah
Qaşr Bū Hādī
Banī Walīd
FEZZAN
Marzūq
Tarbū
Wāw al-Kabīr
JABAL AS SAWDA
Sawknah
Marādah
Awjilah
Zīllah
Zaltan
Buzaymah
LIBYAN DESERT (AS SAHRĀ' AL LĪBĪYAH)
Al Jaghbūb
Sīwah (Oasis)
MUNKHAFAD AL QATTARAH
-436
Birket Qārūn
CAIRO (Al Qāhirah)
Al Fayyūm
Banī Suwayf
Al Minyā
Al Bawīţī
Al Farāfirah
Qaşr al Farāfirah
Asyūţ
Akhmīm
Sawhāj
Thebes (Ruins)
Al Uqşur (Luxor)
Qinā
Idfū
Aswān
Aswan High Dam
Lake Nasser
EGYPT
ARABIAN DESERT
Gulf of Aqaba
Būr Safājah
Al-Wajh
Al Qusayr
RA'S BANĀS
Yanbu'
Al Madīnah (Medina)
Jiddah
Mecca (Makkāh)
Al Khurmah
AN NAFŪD
IDEHAN MARZŪQ
SARIR TIBASTI
Rebiana (Oasis)
Al Kufrah (Oasis)
Al Jawf
Ma'tan Bishārah
Bi'r Misāhah
Ash Shabb
S A H A R A
Halā'ib
ADMINISTRATIVE BDY.
Jiddah
Pic Touside 10 712
TIBESTI
Emi Koussi 11 204
Ounianga Kébir
BORKOU
Largeau
Fada
ENNEDI
Oum Chalouba
NUBIAN DESERT
Jabal Erba 7 274
'Arbi
Kosha
Dalqū
3rd Cataract
Dungulah
Kuraymah
Marawi
Kūrtī
Barbar
Abu Hamad
Būr Sūdān
Sawākin
Al Qunfudhah
Abha
ERITREA
Qīzān
JAZĀ'IR FARASAN
BODELE
Agadem (Oasis)
Bilma
Yarda
Al 'Atrūn
Al Khandaq
Ad Dabbah
'Atbarah
Ad Dāmir
Shandī
6th Cataract
Kassalā
Akordat
Keren
Mitsiwa (Massawa)
DAHLAK ARCH.
Asmera
KAMARAN
Lake Chad (Lac Tchad)
Mao
CHAD
Abéché
OUADDAĪ
Yao
DARFUR
Jabal Marrah 10 131
Al Fāshir
An Nuhūd
Al Ubayyid
KURDUFAN
Ad Duwaym
Sannār
Al Qadārif
Om Hajer
Adwa
Mekele
DENAKIL
Ed
Al Mukhā
N'Djamena (Fort-Lamy)
MANDARA MTS
Maroua
Bousso
Laï
Chari
Am Timan
Nyala
Al Udayyah
Babanūsah
Talawdī
Malūt
JIBAL AN NUBAH
Kurmuk
Asosa
Dangila
Debre Markos
Debre Tabor
Gonder
Ras Dashen Terara 15 158
Lake Tana
Amba Farit 14 478
Dese
Were Ilu
Dire Dawa
Harer
DJIBOUTI
Tadjoura
Seylac
Aysha
Léré
Sarh
Kafia Kingi
Lol
BAHR AL GHAZAL
AS SUDD
Bahr al Arab
Malakāl
Kodok
Nāşir
Gambela
Shewa Gimira
Jima
Goba
Ginir
SIDAMO
HARERGE
Addis Ababa (Adis Abeba)
ETHIOPIA
Dembi Dolo
Gore
Talī Welel 10 830
Nekemte
Koundé
Bouar
Bambari
Fort-Sibut
Fort Crampel
CENTRAL AFRICAN REPUBLIC
CHAÎNE DES MONGOS
Ndélé
Ouanda Djallé
Yalinga
Zémio
Rafaï
Bangassou
Mobaye
Bondo
Gwane
Tambura
Wāw
Rumbek
Shambe
Bor
Mongalla
Jūbā
Kapoeta
Admin. Bdy.
Mega
Lake Stefanie (Chew Bahir)
Moyale
El Wak
SOMALIA
KENYA
Bangui
Zongo
Mbaïki
Libenge
Gemena
Businga
Bambesa
Aketi
Buta
Dungu
Niangara
Watsa
Gombari
Isiro
Arua
Kitgum
Soroti
Mt. Elgon 14 178
UGANDA
DEMOCRATIC REPUBLIC OF THE CONGO
Lisala
Bumba
Panga
Avakubi
Trumu
Masindi
Mahagi Port
Kampala
Jinja
Eldoret
Meru
Kisangani (Stanleyville)
Margherita Peak 16 763
Ft. Portal
Entebbe
Lake Victoria
Equator
CONGO
Ouésso
Impfondo
Bomongo
Makanza
Basoko
Basankusu
Mbandaka
Boyoma Falls
RWAMAR MTS
Genale

Continued on pages 198-199
Continued on page 238
Continued on pages 232-233

0 50 100   200   300   400   500 Miles
0   100 200   400   600   800 Kilometers

232

Continued on pages 230-231

GABON

CONGO

Libreville
Kango
Equator
Ndjolé
Port Gentil
Lambaréné
Lastoursville
Mbigou
Moanda
Franceville
Sette Cama
Tchibanga
Mayumba
Sibiti
Brazzaville
Pointe-Noire
Tshela
Kinshasa (Léopoldville)
CABINDA (Angola)
Cabinda
Boma
Matadi
Nóqui
Maquela do Zombo
Cuango

DEMOCRATIC REPUBLIC OF THE CONGO (ZAIRE)

Owando
Mbandaka
Mondombe
Ubundu
Lukolela
Bikoro
Boende
Itoko
Inongo
Lac Mai-Ndombe (Lake Leopold II) +1076
Monkoto
Kindu
Mushie
Fimi
Lomela
Bandundu
Ilebo
Bena Dibele
Lusanga
Kikwit
Bulungu
Kasongo
Kabambare
Popokabaka
Djokupunda
Tshikapa
Lusambo
Kananga (Luluabourg)
Kabinda
Kabalo
Kalemie
Mutombo Mukulu
Kabongo
Kamina
Bukama

KATANGA

Sandoa
Dilolo
Kolwezi
Tenke
Kambove
Likasi
Lubumbashi (Elisabethville)
Sakania

RWANDA
BURUNDI

Rutshuru
Giseyi
Kigali
Astrida
Bukavu
Uvira
Bujumbura
Kigoma
Ujiji
Tabora

UGANDA

Bukoba
Entebbe
Kampala
Lake Victoria +3720
Mwanza
Shinyanga

TANZA...

ANGOLA

Luanda
Catete
Dondo
Golungo Alto
Kalandula
Malanje
Porto Amboim
Sumbe
Waku Kungo
Saurimo
Cassai
Lobito
Benguela
Chinguar
Kuito
Huambo
Munhango
Cazombo
Caconda
Cangumbe
Lungué-Bungo
Lubango
Donga
Cuchi
Namibe
SERRA DA CHELA
Cassinga
Tombua
Cahama
Dima
PENINSULA DOS TIGRES
Humbe
Xangongo
CAPE FRIA

ZAMBIA

Kongolo
Mbata
Moliro
Lake Mweru +3035
Pweto
Mporokoso
Kasenga
Kasama
Lake Bangweulu +3764
Mansa
Chingola
Ndola
Serenje
Kasempa
Kafue
Mumbwa
Mongu
Lusaka
Kafue
Mazabuka
Pemba
Kalomo
Livingstone
Zumbo
Cabora Bassa Res.
Chipata
Lilongwe

BAROTSELAND

CAPRIVI STRIP

Rundu
Okavango
Victoria Falls
Hwange
Kadoma
Chegutu
Harare (Salisbury)
Chitungwiza
Chinhoyi
Shamva
Tete

ZIMBABWE (RHODESIA)

Kwekwe
Gweru
Shurugwi
Chivhu
Mutare (Umtali)
Masvingo
Zvishavane
Bulawayo
Mandidzudzure
Beira
Vila de Manica
Dondo

OWAMBO

Namutoni
Tsumeb
Otavi
Grootfontein
Ondjiva
Etosha Pan
Outjo
Ojjiwarongo
Brandberg 8550
Omaruru
Karibib
Usakos
Okahandja

NAMIBIA

DAMARALAND

Swakopmund
Walvis Bay
Windhoek
Gobabis
Rehoboth

BOTSWANA

Maun
Nxai Pan
Ntwetwe Pan
Ngami
Lake Xau
Makgadikgadi Pans
Ghanzi
Francistown
Old Tate
Serowe
Palapye
Tuli
Messina
Thohoyandou

KALAHARI DESERT

Maltahöhe
Gibeon
Mochudi
Molepolole
Gaborone
Nylstroom
Pietersburg
Potgietersrus

GREAT NAMALAND

Bethanien
Keetmanshoop
Aroab
Tshabong
Lobatse
Mafeking
Mmabatho
Zeerust
Krugersdorp
Pretoria
Barberton
Komatipoort
Carolina
Mbabane

MAPUTO (Lourenço Marques)

SWAZILAND

Lüderitz

Tropic of Capricorn

A-589200-76 -14-12-33
COPYRIGHT BY
RAND McNALLY & COMPANY
MADE IN U.S.A.

SOUTH AFRICA

Oranjemund
Port Nolloth
BUSHMANLAND
Warmbad
Upington
Kuruman
Vryburg
Taung
Johannesburg
Benoni
Germiston
Potchefstroom
Kroonstad
Welkom
Bethlehem
Vryheid
Nongoma
KWAZULU
Ladysmith
Springbok
Calvinia
Prieska
Hopetown
Kimberley
Bloemfontein
Maseru
Wepener
Springfontein
Pietermaritzburg
Durban
LESOTHO
DRAKENSBERG
Mt. aux Sources 10 822
Cathkin Peak 10 438
Harding
Scottburgh
Port Shepstone
De Aar
Britstown
Colesberg
Middelburg
Cradock
Umtata
Port St. Johns
Carnarvon
Victoria West
Beaufort West
GREAT KARROO
Graaff Reinet
Bisho
East London
Sutherland
Willowmore
Oudtshoorn
Uitenhage
Port Alfred (Kowie)
Saldanha
St. Helenabaai
Malmesbury
Worcester
Paarl
LITTLE KARROO
Mosselbaai
Humansdorp
Port Elizabeth
CAPE OF GOOD HOPE
Bredasdorp
Cape Agulhas
Cape Town

15° Longitude East of Greenwich 20°
Scale 1:16 000 000; one inch to 250 miles. Sinusoidal Projection
Elevations and depressions are given in feet

a

CAPE TOWN
MOUILLE PT.
Scale 1:1 000 000

ROBBENEILAND
Bloubergstrand
Kanonkop 1502
Durbanville
Milnerton
Parow
Bellville
Table Bay
Camps Bay
Table Mt. 3567
Goodwood
Kuilsrivier
Pinelands
Nuweland
Wynberg
Ottery
CAPE FLATS
Houtbaai
3048
Muizenberg
Vishoek
SEAL ISLAND
Kommetjie
Grootkop 1286
Simonstad
Swartkop 2229
Valsbaai (False Bay)
Chapman's Bay
SMITSWINKEL VLAKTE
KLAASPUNT
CAPE OF GOOD HOPE

0 4 8 12 16 Kilometers
0 10 Miles

18°30'

0 50 100 200 300 400 500 Miles
0 100 200 400 600 800 Kilometers

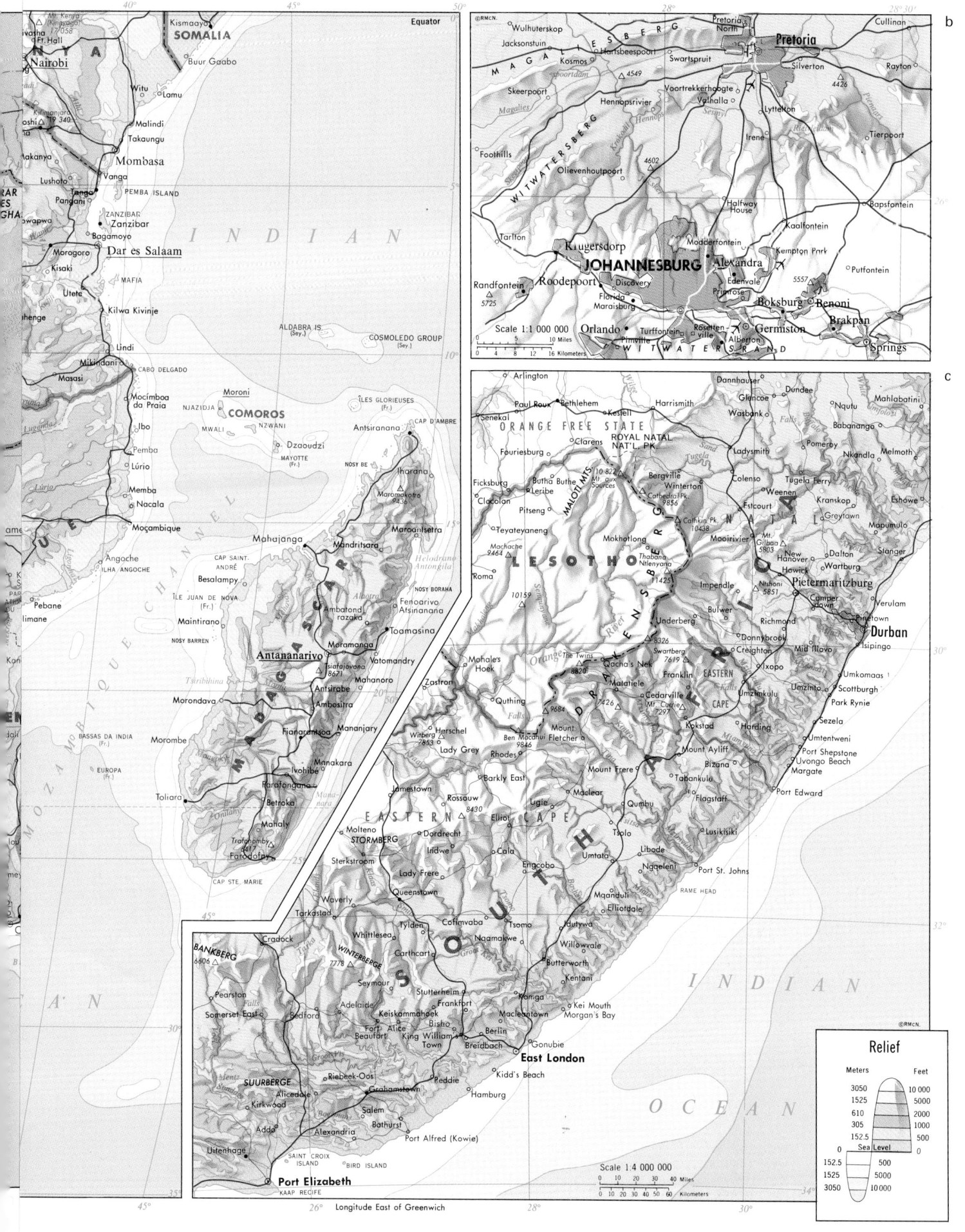

SOMALIA

Mt. Kenya (Kirinyaga) 17,058
Nairobi
Kismaayo
Equator
40°   45°   50°

Buur Gaabo

Mombasa
Witu
Lamu
Takaungu
Kilimanjaro 19,340
Vanga
Lushoto
Tanga
PEMBA ISLAND
Pangani
ZANZIBAR
Zanzibar
Bagamoyo
Dar es Salaam
Morogoro
Kisaki
MAFIA
Utete

INDIAN

Kilwa Kivinje
Lindi

Mikindani
CABO DELGADO
Masasi
ALDABRA IS. (Sey.)
COSMOLEDO GROUP (Sey.)

Mocímboa da Praia
Ibo
COMOROS
Moroni
NJAZIDJA NZWANI
MWALI
ÎLES GLORIEUSES (Fr.)
CAP D'AMBRE
Pemba
Dzaoudzi
MAYOTTE (Fr.)
Antsiranana

Lúrio
Memba
NOSY BE
Iharana
Nacala
Maromokotro 9436
Moçambique
Antalaha
Maroantsetra

Angoche
ILHA ANGOCHE
CAP SAINT ANDRÉ
Mahajanga
Mandritsara
Helodrano Antongila
NOSY BORAHA
Besalampy
Alaotra
Fenoarivo Atsinanana

Pebane
ÎLE JUAN DE NOVA (Fr.)
Ambatondrazaka
Moramanga
Toamasina
NOSY BARREN
Maintirano
Antananarivo
Tsiafajavona 8671
Vatomandry
Tsiribihina

Morondava
Mahanoro
Antsirabe
Ambositra

BASSAS DA INDIA (Fr.)
EUROPA (Fr.)
Morombe
Fianarantsoa
Mananjary
Manakara

Mandrare
Betroka
Ivohibe
Ihosy

Toliara
MADAGASCAR
Farafangana

Tropic of Capricorn
Trafonomby 4417
Fandofotra
Mahaly

CAP STE. MARIE

MOZAMBIQUE CHANNEL

b

Wolhuterskop
Pretoria North
Cullinan
Jacksonstuin
MAGALIESBERG
Kosmos
Hartbeespoort
Swartspruit
Pretoria
Silverton
Rayton
Skeerpoort
4549
Voortrekkerhoogte
Valhalla
Lyttelton
4426
Magalies
Hennopsrivier
Tierpoort
Foothills
WITWATERSBERG
Olievenhoutpoort
4602
Halfway House
Bapsfontein
Tarlton
Kaalfontein
Krugersdorp
Modderfontein
Kempton Park
Randfontein
5725
Roodepoort
Discovery
Florida
JOHANNESBURG
Alexandra
5557
Putfontein
Maraisburg
Edenvale
Boksburg
Benoni
Scale 1:1 000 000
Orlando
Primrose
Brakpan
0 5 10 Miles
Turffontein
Rosettenville
Germiston
Springs
0 4 8 12 16 Kilometers
Pimville
Alberton
WITWATERSRAND

c

Arlington
Dannhauser
Glencoe
Dundee
Mahlabatini
Paul Roux
Bethlehem
Kestell
Harrismith
Wasbank
Nqutu
Senekal
ORANGE FREE STATE
ROYAL NATAL NAT'L PK.
Babanango
Fouriesburg
Clarens
Ladysmith
Pomeroy
Nkandla
Melmoth
Ficksburg
Butha Buthe
10,822 Mt. aux Sources
Bergville
Winterton
Colenso
Weenen
Tugela Ferry
Clocolan
Leribe
Cathedral Pk. 9856
Kranskop
Eshowe
Pitseng
MALOTI MTS.
Cathkin Pk. 10438
Estcourt
Greytown
Teyateyaneng
Mapumulo
Machache 9464
Mokhotlong
Mooirivier
Mt. Gilboa 5803
New Hanover
Dalton
Stanger
Roma
LESOTHO
Thabana Ntlenyana 11425
Impendle
Nhloni 5851
Howick
Wartburg
Pietermaritzburg
10159
Underberg
8326
Bulwer
Camperdown
Verulam
Mohale's Hoek
The Twins 8820
Qacha's Nek
Richmond
Pinetown
Durban
Zastron
Orange
Swartberg 7619
Matatiele
Franklin
EASTERN CAPE
Creighton
Donnybrook
Mid Illovo
Isipingo
Quthing
Falls
9684
Cedarville
Mt. Currie 7297
Kokstad
Harding
Umzinto
Scottburgh
Witberg 7853
Herschel
Ben Macdhui 9846
Mount Fletcher
Bizana
Umtentweni
Port Shepstone
Lady Grey
Rhodes
Mount Ayliff
Tabankulu
Uvongo Beach
Margate
Jamestown
Barkly East
Maclear
Mount Frere
Flagstaff
Port Edward
Rossouw
8430
Elliot
Ugie
Qumbu
Tsolo
Libode
Lusikisiki
Molteno
STORMBERG
Dordrecht
Indwe
Cala
Engcobo
Umtata
Ngqeleni
Port St. Johns
Sterkstroom
Lady Frere
RAME HEAD
Waverly
Queenstown
Tsomo
Mqanduli
Elliotdale
Tarkastad
Tylden
Cofimvaba
Idutywa
Cradock
Whittlesea
Carthcart
Ngamakwe
Willowvale
BANKBERG
6606
WINTERBERGE
7778
Seymour
Stutterheim
Frankfort
Tsomo
Butterworth
Kentani
Pearston
Adelaide
Keiskammahoek
Komga
Kei Mouth
Somerset East
Bedford
Fort Beaufort
Bisho
Berlin
Morgan's Bay
Alice
King William Town
Breidbach
Gonubie
SUURBERGE
Riebeek-Oos
Peddie
East London
Mentz
Alicedale
Kidd's Beach
Kirkwood
Grahamstown
Hamburg
Addo
Salem
Bathurst
Uitenhage
Alexandria
Port Alfred (Kowie)
SAINT CROIX ISLAND
BIRD ISLAND
Port Elizabeth
KAAP RECIFE

SOUTH AFRICA
DRAKENSBERG
NATAL

Scale 1:4 000 000
0 10 20 30 40 Miles
0 10 20 30 40 50 60 Kilometers

26°   Longitude East of Greenwich   28°   30°   34°

Relief

Meters	Feet
3050	10 000
1525	5000
610	2000
305	1000
152.5	500
0 Sea Level	0
152.5	500
1525	5000
3050	10 000

INDIAN OCEAN

Continued on pages 234-235

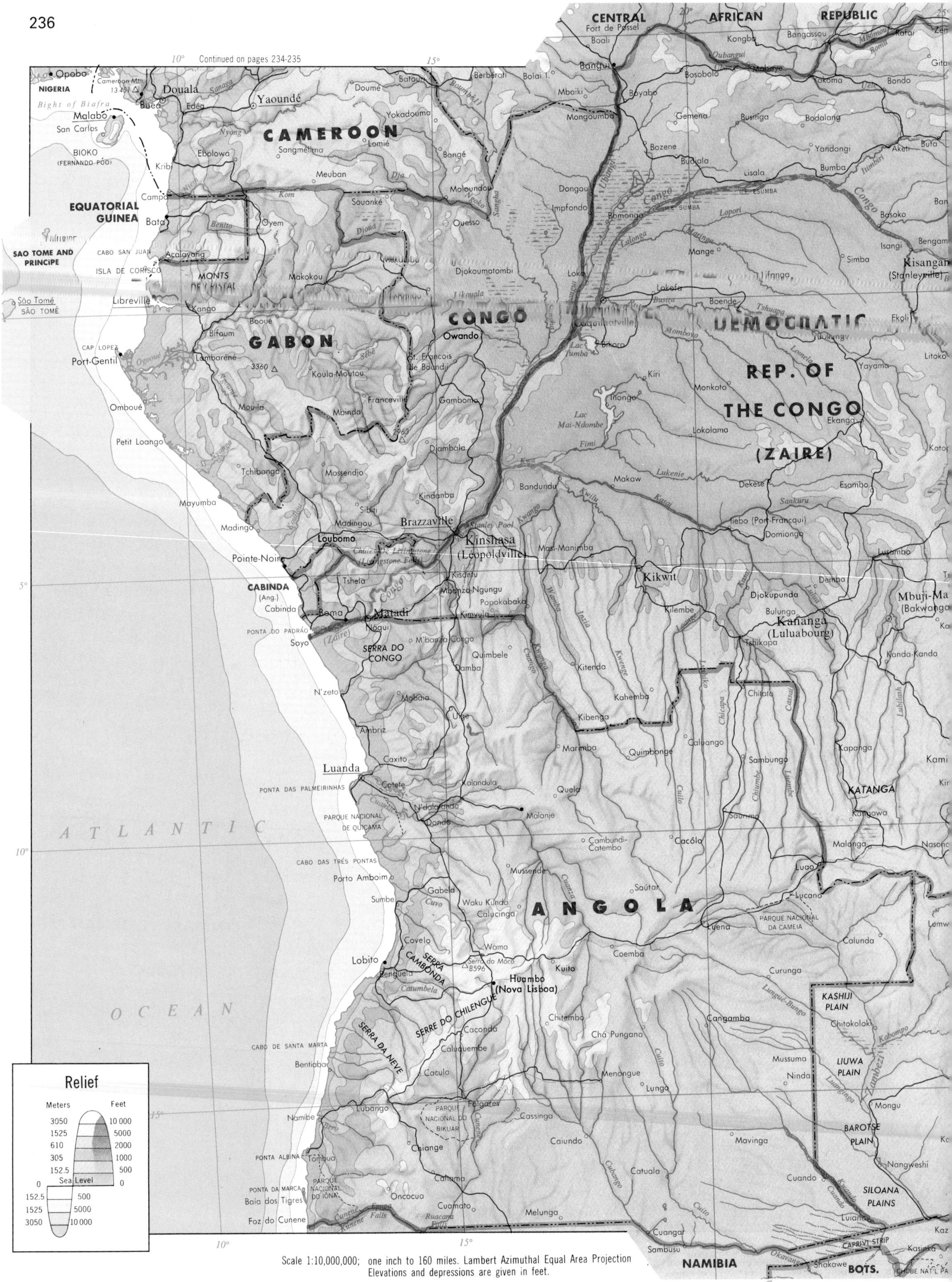

10°   15°

CENTRAL   **AFRICAN**   **REPUBLIC**
Fort de Passel
Boali   Kongba   Bangassou
Bangui   Bosobolo   Kongbo
Opobo   Cameroon Mtn.   Batouri   Berberati   Bolai I.   Mbaiki   Boyabu   Gemena   Businga   Bodalang
13 451   Douala   Doume   Batonga   Mongoumba   Bozene   Budala   Lisala   Bumba   Yandongi
NIGERIA   Buea   Edéa   Yokadouma   Mongoumba   Dongou   Le-Esumba   Basoko
Bight of Biafra   Yaoundé   Impfondo   Bomonga   Isangi   Kisangani
Malabo   CAMEROON   Sangmélima   Lomié   Bangé   Mange   Simba   (Stanleyville)
San Carlos   Ebolowa   Meuban   Ouesso   Loko   Boende   Litoko
BIOKO   Nyong   Moloundou   Basoko   Tshuapa   Ekoli
(FERNANDO PÓO)   Kribi   Dja   Souanké   Coquilhatville   Mombeya   Litoko
EQUATORIAL   Campo   Oyem   Makoua   DEMOCRATIC   Yayama
GUINEA   Bata   Acalayong   Owando   CONGO   Basica   Boende   Litoko
SAO TOME AND   MONTS   Makokou   Djoumatombi   Lac   REP. OF   Monkoto   Ekanga
PRINCIPE   DE CRISTAL   Kango   Booué   Tumba   Inongo   THE CONGO   Lokolama   Esambo
CABO SAN JUAN   Libreville   Bifoum   St. François   Kiri   (ZAIRE)   Dekese   Sankuru
São Tomé   ISLA DE CORISCO   3360   de Baundji   Lac   Fimi   Makaw   Lusambo
SÃO TOMÉ   Lambaréné   Koula-Moutou   Mai-Ndombe   Lukenie   Tiebo (Port-Francqui)   Domionga
0°   GABON   Mossendjo   Franceville   Gambona   Bandundu   Kwilu   Dekese   Katok
CAP LOPEZ   Movila   Mbinda   Djambala   Bundundu   Kwango   Lomela
Port-Gentil   Sibiti   Kindanba   Kikwit   Damba   Mbuji-Ma
Omboué   Madingou   Brazzaville   Masi-Manimba   Djokupunda   (Bakwanga)
Petit Loango   Madingo   Stanley Pool   Kinshasa   Kikwit   Bulunga   Kanda-Kanda
Tchibanga   Loubomo   (Léopoldville)   Kilembe   Kananga
Mayumba   Chutes de   Kisantu   Kitenda   Tshikapa   (Luluabourg)
5°   Pointe-Noire   Livingstone Falls   Mbanza-Ngungu   Kahemba   Chitato
CABINDA   Tshela   Popokabaka   Kimvula   Kibenga   KATANGA
(Ang.)   Cabinda   Boma   Matadi   Kenge   Quimbele   Xapanga
PONTA DO PADRÃO   Nóqui   M'banza Congo   Damba   Caluango   Kami
Soyo   (Zaire)   SERRA DO   Quimbele   Marimba   Quimbonge   Sambungo
CONGO   N'zeto   Mobaia   Uíge   Quela   Cacola   Malanga
Ambriz   Caxito   Kalandula   Cambundi-   Nason
Luanda   Cuanza   N'dalatando   Catembo   Luao   Lucano
PONTA DAS PALMEIRINHAS   Dondo   Malanje   Saútar   Cuilo   Curunga   Lungué-Bungo
10°   CABO DAS TRÊS PONTAS   Parque Nacional   Coemba   Calunda   KASHIJI
de Quiçama   Mussende   Cangamba   PLAIN
Porto Amboim   Gabela   Waku Kungu   Gabela   Chitokoloki
Sumbe   Cuvo   Calucinga   Wama   ANGOLA   Chá Pungana   LIUWA
Lobito   Covelo   SERRA   Serra do Môco   Kuito   Coemba   Mussuma   PLAIN
Benguela   CAMBONDA   8596   Huambo   Chitembo   Ninda   Mongu
Catumbela   (Nova Lisboa)   Cassinga   Lunga   BAROTSE
OCEAN   SERRE DO CHILENGUE   Caconda   Menongue   Cangamba   PLAIN
SERRA DA NEVE   Caluquembe   Caiundo   Mavinga   Nangweshi
CABO DE SANTA MARTA   Cacula   SILOANA
Bentiaba   Lubango   Folgares   PLAINS
15°   Namibe   Parque   Chiange   Cassinga   Cuando   Luanginga
Nacional do   Caiundo   Luiana
BIKUAR   Cubango   Catuala   Cuangar   Luiana
PONTA ALBINA   Tômbua   Oncocua   Cahama   Melunga   Mavinga   Cuando   CAPRIVI STRIP
PONTA DA MARCA   Parque   Cuamato   NAMIBIA   Shakawe   BOTS.
Baía dos Tigres   Nacional do Iona   Foz do Cunene   Ruacana Falls   Okavango   Chobe Natl. Par.   Kasinka
10°   15°   20°

Scale 1:10,000,000; one inch to 160 miles. Lambert Azimuthal Equal Area Projection
Elevations and depressions are given in feet.

Relief

Meters		Feet
3050		10 000
1525		5000
610		2000
305		1000
152.5		500
0	Sea Level	0
152.5		500
1525		5000
3050		10 000

ATLANTIC

OCEAN

SUDAN
ETHIOPIA

Maridi
Jubá
Admin Bay
Kapoeta
Didinga Hills
ETHIOPIA
Imero Stefanie

ane
Yambio
Gobur
Keyala
LOTIKIPI PLAIN
Lokitaung
Lake Rudolf
CHALBI
Damisa Hills
Baidoa

Bwindi
Niangara
Bagbele
Abo
Nimule
Kitgeti 10 450
Muruasigar △ 7 050
Lodwar
DESERT
Moyale

Isiro (Paulis)
Watsa
Padibe
Kaabong
Moroto
Lokichar
Marsabit
Wajir
Baardheere

Panga
Mungbere
Arua
PANGA MOUNTAINS
Gulu
Moroto
11 118
NDOTO MOUNTAINS
Laisamis
BUN PLAINS
SOMALIA

Kondolole
Avakubi
Nduye
Bunia
Lira
Soroti
Maralal
Mado Gashi
Solola
Jamaame

Mambasa
Nabiswera
Mount Elgon 14 178
CHERANGANY HILLS
Kitale
Mt Kenya 17 058
Alanga Arba
Garissa

UGANDA
Butsha
Fort Portal
Mubende
Mbale
Mumias
Eldoret
Nanyuki
Kolbio
Kismaayo

Balobe
Margherita Peak 16 763
Kasese
Kampala
Jinja
Kisumu
Thomson's Falls
Nakuru
Nyeri
Embu
NGANGERBELI PLAIN
Kiunga

ndu
Lake Albert
Masaka
SESE ISLANDS
Kericho
MAU ESCARPMENT
Thika
Mwingi
Kaningo
Bura
LAMU ISLAND

rville)
Lake George
Mbarara
Lake Victoria
Bukoba
Musoma
Subugo 8 668
Nairobi
Machakos
Magadi
Makindu
Garsen
Lamu

yumbi
Rutshuru
Volcan Karisimbi 14 787
Kabale
BUMBIRE ISLAND
UKEREWE ISLAND
RUBONDO ISLAND
Loliondo
SERENGETI NATIONAL PARK
Longido
Kilimanjaro 19 340
TSAVO NATIONAL PARK
Malindi

Walikale
Giseni
Kigali
RWANDA
Biharamulo
Mwanza
Geita
SERENGETI PLAIN
Loolmalassin 11 969
Mount Meru 14 978
Moshi
Kilifi
Formosa Bay

Kasese
Bukavu
Butare
BURUNDI
Bujumbura
Nyakanazi
Salawe
Shinyanga
Lake Eyasi
Arusha
Mackinnon Road
Mombasa

Kamituga
Mwenga
Kibondo
Nzega
Ipala
Sekenke
Bereku
Hanang 11 215
MASAI STEPPE
Kisiwani
USAMBARA MTS
Shimoni
Chake Chake

Kampene
Kigoma
Uvinza
Masangwe △ 5 372
Tabora
Igalula
Itigi
Ngoywa
Dodoma
Mziha
Tanga
PEMBA ISLAND

Lusangi
Kongolo
Kalima
Lake Tanganyika
Kalema (Albertville)
Mpanda
Kitunda
TANZANIA
Bahi Swamp
Ugalla
Mpwapwa
Kimamba
INGURU MOUNTAINS
Mkwaja
ZANZIBAR
Zanzibar

Kabalo
Kahia
MAHALI MTS
Karema
MLALA HILLS
Mboga
RUAHA NATIONAL PARK
Morogoro
Bagamoyo
Zanzibar Channel

mpi
Ankoro
Kiambi
Kipili
Lake Rukwa
Kipembawe
Mikumi
Kibiti
Dar es Salaam
INDIAN

Mariono
Kamudilo
Sumbawanga
USANGU FLATS
Great Ruaha
Iringa
Mahenge
Kwangwazi
MAFIA ISLAND

omeshia
Dubie
MONTS MULUMBE
Mollie
Kasongo
Mbeya
Chunya
Sao Hill
Mahenge
Ngarimbi
Somanga
OCEAN

PARC NATIONAL DE L'UPEMBA
Kialwe
MONTS MITUMBA
Mbala
Mbeya
KIPENGERE RANGE
Njombe
Lifoo
Lindi
Kilwa Kisiwani

uena
Luubu
Kasenga
Mparoto
Kasama
Livingstonia
Songea
Masasi
Mikindani
Mtwara
Quionga

Kishi
Tenke
Johnston Falls
Luwingu
Chambeshi
NYIKA PLATEAU
Liuli
Tunduru
Newalo
CABO DELGADO

Likasi (Jadotville)
Kalwe
Kasama
Chinsali
Mzuzu
Mbamba Bay
Mocimboa da Praia
COMOROS

wezi
Lubumbashi (Elisabethville)
Mansa
BANGWEULU SWAMP
Lake Bangweulu
Mpika
Mzimba
Côbue
Diaco
Ibo
Moroni
Karthala 7 746 NZWANI

Kipushi
Chililabombwe (Bancroft)
Sonqwe
MUCHINGA MOUNTAINS
Chitambo
Chamama
Lichinga
Marrupa
Montepuez
Pemba

Chingola
Mufulira
Sakania
Kabunda
Kipushia
Chifambo
MALAWI
Lake Nyasa
Mucata

Kitwe
Ndola
Luanshya
Mkushi
Chipata
MALAWI
Salima
Monkey Bay
MOZAMBIQUE
Nampuecha

Kasempa
Kapiri Mposhi
Katete
Mchinji
Lilongwe
Mandimba
Cuamba
Malema
Ribauè
Nacala

ZAMBIA
Busanga Swamp
Kabwe (Broken Hill)
Mtakataka
SERRA NAMULI △ 7 936
Nampula
Mogincual

Luktinga Swamp
Mumbwa
Rutunsa
Furancungo
Mpimbe
Lake Chilwa
Zomba
Alto Molócuè
Errego
António Enes

Lusaka
Chilanga
CABORA BASSA RES.
Fingoe
Zumbo
Casula
Blantyre
MLANJE MTS
Saptwa
ILHA ANGOCHE

Mazapuka
Ibwe Munyama
CABORA BASSA
Tete
Caldas Xavier
Mucuba
Namiti
Moma

Gwembe
Kariba
Changara
Chemba
Nsanje
Pebane

ZIMBABWE
Chinhoyi
Bindura
Mtoko
Mucubela

Victoria Falls
Tundazi △ 4 702
Harare (Salisbury)
Chitungwiza
Chegutu
Marondera

Hwange
Lake Kariba
(RHODESIA)

INDIAN OCEAN

Baia de Fernão Veloso

ZAMBEZI

0°
5°
10°
15°

30°
35°
40°

0 50 100 150 200 250 300 Miles
0 100 200 300 400 500 Kilometers

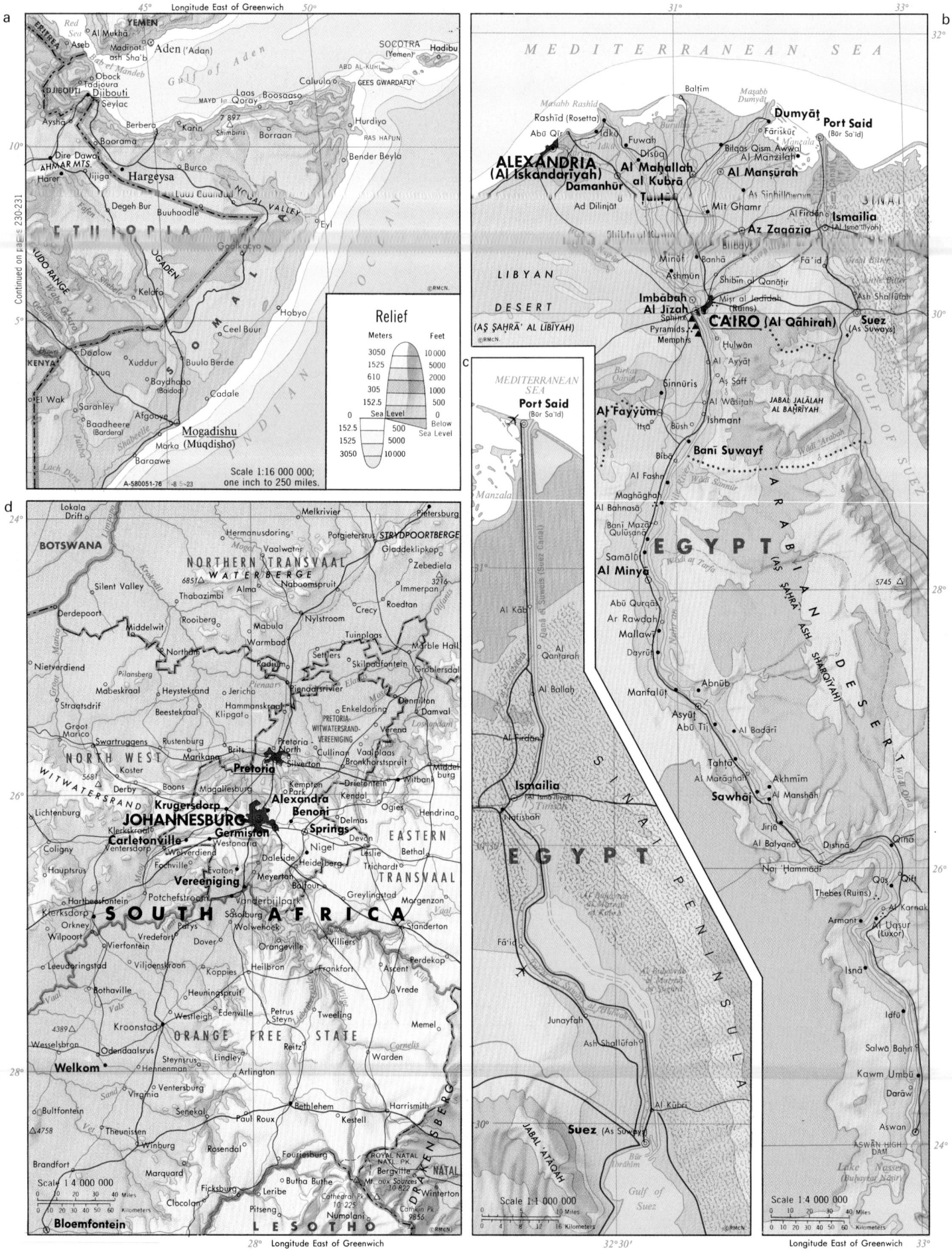

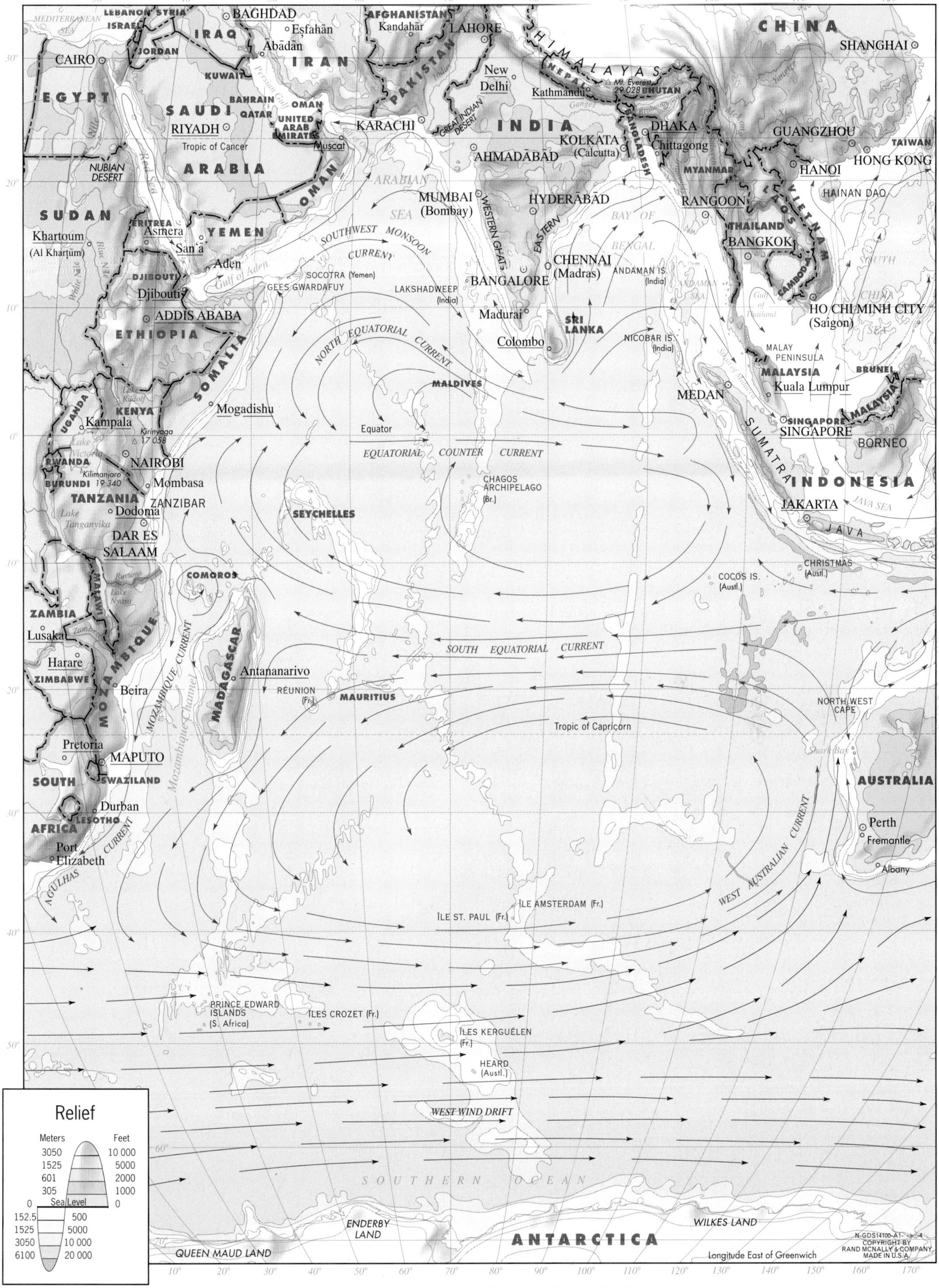

MEDITERRANEAN SEA
LEBANON SYRIA
ISRAEL
JORDAN
IRAQ
BAGHDAD
Esfahān
Abādān
KUWAIT
IRAN
AFGHANISTAN
Kandahār
LAHORE
HIMALAYAS
CHINA
SHANGHAI
CAIRO
EGYPT
BAHRAIN QATAR
OMAN
UNITED ARAB EMIRATES
RIYADH
SAUDI ARABIA
Tropic of Cancer
Muscat
ARABIA
PAKISTAN
New Delhi
Kathmandu
NEPAL
Mt. Everest 29,028
BHUTAN
Ganges
BANGLADESH
DHAKA
GUANGZHOU
TAIWAN
HONG KONG
HANOI
HAINAN DAO
KARACHI
INDIA
KOLKATA (Calcutta)
Chittagong
MYANMAR
AHMADĀBAD
NUBIAN DESERT
SUDAN
ERITREA
Asmera
San'ā
YEMEN
Aden
Gulf of Aden
SOCOTRA (Yemen)
GEES GWARDAFUY
ARABIAN SEA
SOUTHWEST MONSOON CURRENT
MUMBAI (Bombay)
WESTERN GHATS
HYDERĀBAD
EASTERN
BAY OF BENGAL
RANGOON
THAILAND
BANGKOK
Khartoum (Al Kharṭūm)
Blue Nile
Red Sea
OMAN
Djibouti
DJIBOUTI
ADDIS ABABA
ETHIOPIA
SOMALIA
LAKSHADWEEP (India)
CHENNAI (Madras)
BANGALORE
Madurai
ANDAMAN IS. (India)
ANDAMAN SEA
HO CHI MINH CITY (Saigon)
VIETNAM
CAMBODIA
Gulf of Thailand
SOUTH CHINA SEA
UGANDA
Kampala
Kirinyaga 17,058
KENYA
NAIROBI
NORTH EQUATORIAL CURRENT
MALDIVES
SRI LANKA
Colombo
NICOBAR IS. (India)
MALAY PENINSULA
MALAYSIA
BRUNEI
RWANDA
BURUNDI
Lake Victoria
Kilimanjaro 19,340
Mombasa
ZANZIBAR
Equator
EQUATORIAL COUNTER CURRENT
Strait of Malacca
MEDAN
Kuala Lumpur
MALAYSIA
BORNEO
TANZANIA
Dodoma
Lake Tanganyika
DAR ES SALAAM
Mogadishu
SEYCHELLES
CHAGOS ARCHIPELAGO (Br.)
SUMATRA
SINGAPORE
SINGAPORE
INDONESIA
ZAMBIA
Lusaka
Lake Nyasa
COMOROS
MALAWI
MOZAMBIQUE CURRENT
JAKARTA
JAVA SEA
JAVA
Harare
ZIMBABWE
Beira
MOZAMBIQUE
MOZAMBIQUE CHANNEL
MADAGASCAR
Antananarivo
RÉUNION (Fr.)
MAURITIUS
SOUTH EQUATORIAL CURRENT
COCOS IS. (Austl.)
CHRISTMAS (Austl.)
Pretoria
MAPUTO
SWAZILAND
LESOTHO
SOUTH AFRICA
Durban
Port Elizabeth
AGULHAS CURRENT
Tropic of Capricorn
NORTH WEST CAPE
Shark Bay
AUSTRALIA
Perth
Fremantle
Albany
WEST AUSTRALIAN CURRENT
ÎLE AMSTERDAM (Fr.)
ÎLE ST. PAUL (Fr.)
PRINCE EDWARD ISLANDS (S. Africa)
ÎLES CROZET (Fr.)
ÎLES KERGUÉLEN (Fr.)
HEARD (Austl.)
WEST WIND DRIFT
SOUTHERN OCEAN
ENDERBY LAND
WILKES LAND
QUEEN MAUD LAND
ANTARCTICA
Longitude East of Greenwich

N-GDS14100-A1
COPYRIGHT BY
RAND MCNALLY & COMPANY
MADE IN U.S.A.

Relief

Meters	Feet
3050	10 000
1525	5000
601	2000
305	1000
0	Sea Level 0
152.5	500
1525	5000
3050	10 000
6100	20 000

Warm ocean currents
Cold ocean currents

Scale 1:50 000 000; one inch to 790 miles. Mollweide Projection
Elevations and depressions are given in feet

0 200 400 600 800 1000 Miles
0 400 800 1200 1600 Kilometers

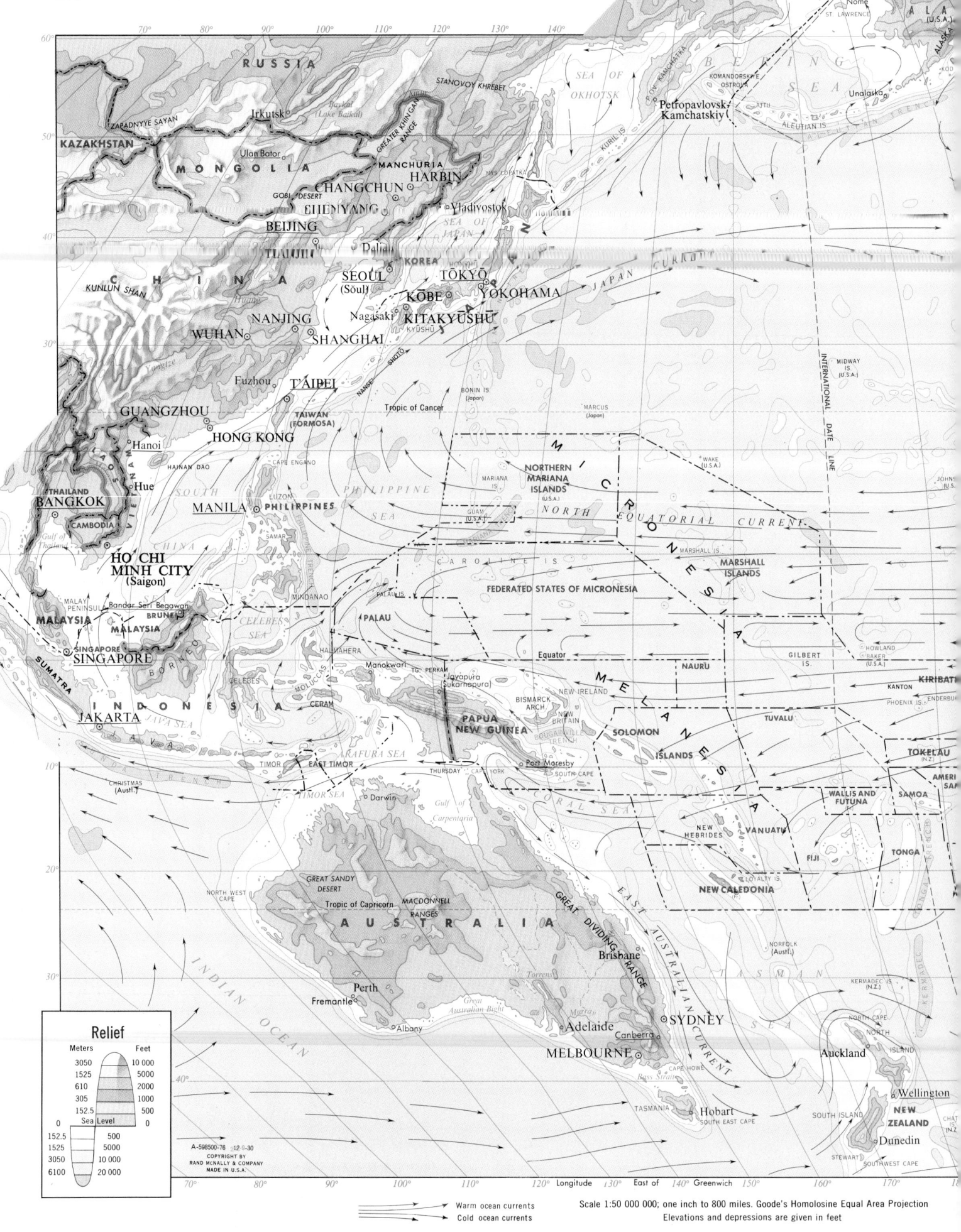

Relief

Meters		Feet
3050		10 000
1525		5000
610		2000
305		1000
152.5		500
0	Sea Level	0
152.5		500
1525		5000
3050		10 000
6100		20 000

A-598500-76   12-8-30

COPYRIGHT BY
RAND McNALLY & COMPANY
MADE IN U.S.A.

→————→ Warm ocean currents
→————→ Cold ocean currents

Scale 1:50 000 000; one inch to 800 miles. Goode's Homolosine Equal Area Projection
Elevations and depressions are given in feet

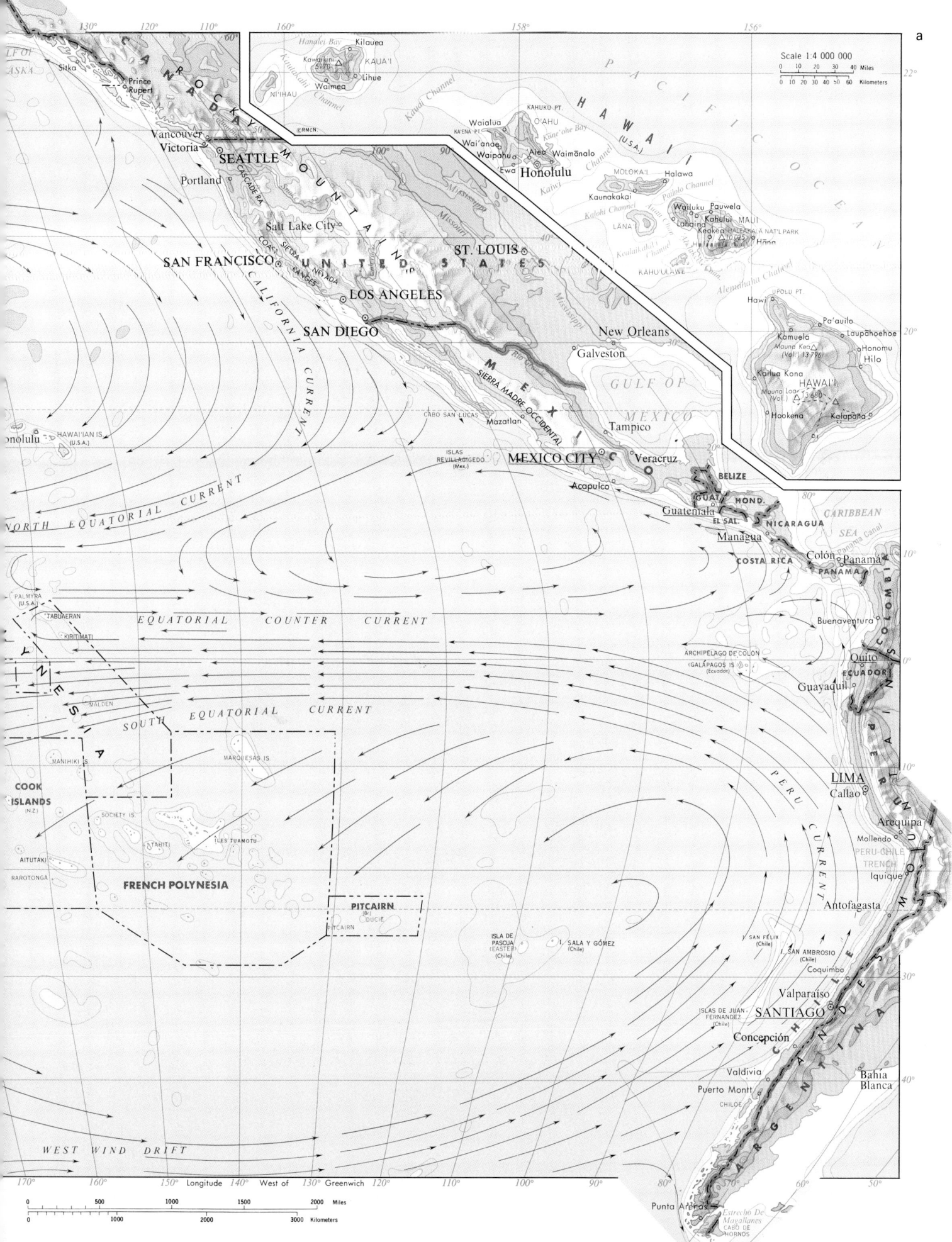

242

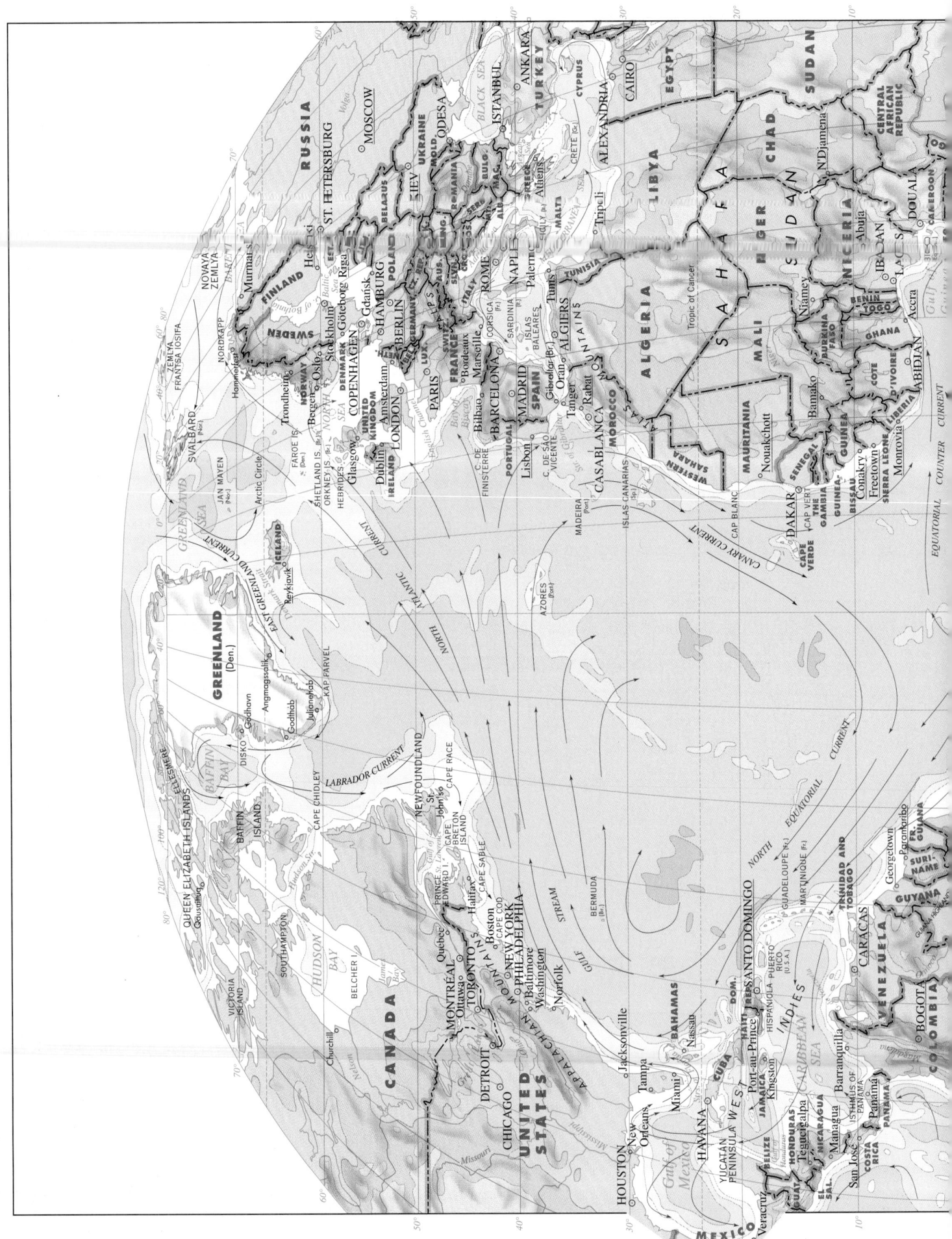

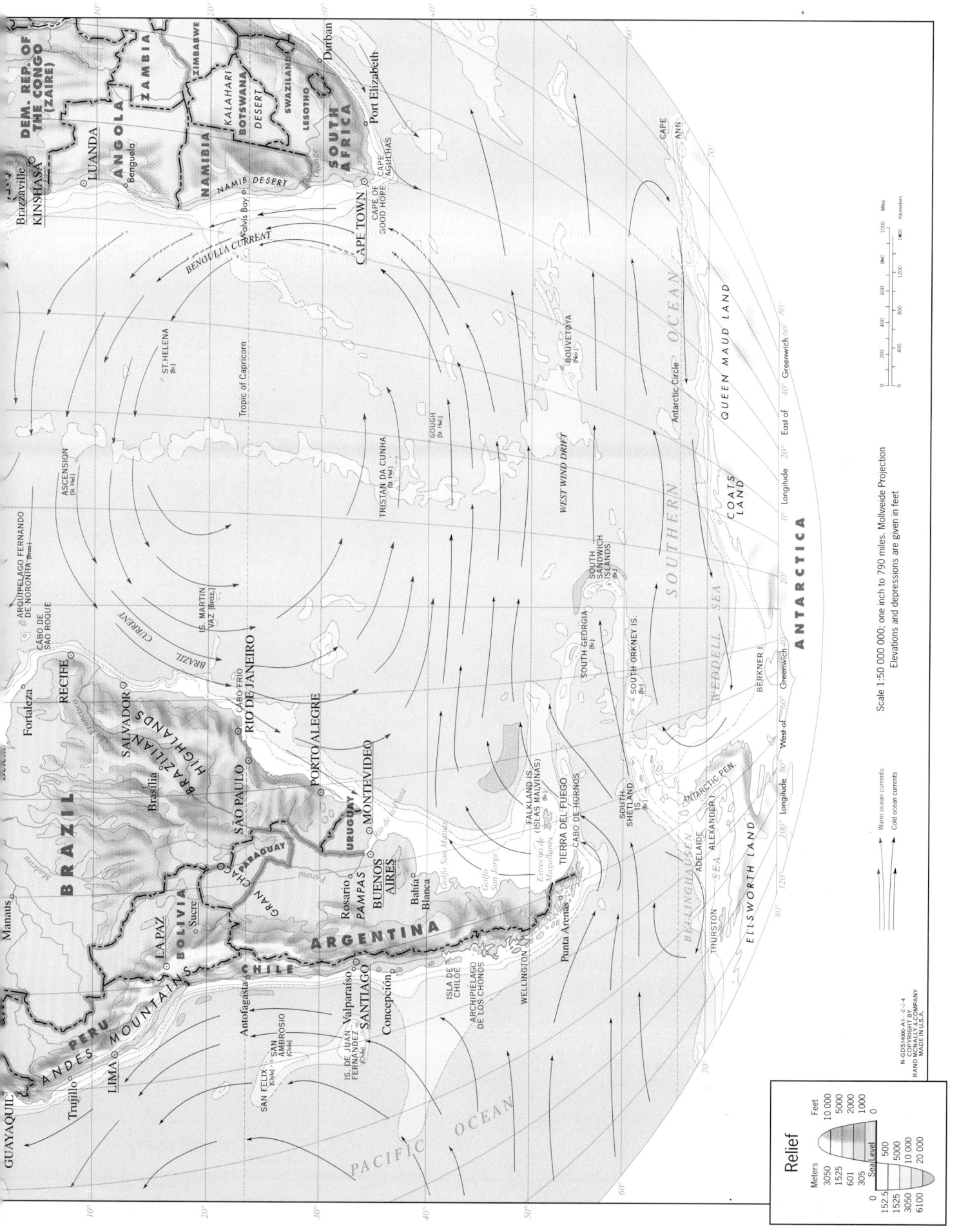

SOUTHERN OCEAN

ANTARCTICA

QUEEN MAUD LAND

COATS LAND

WEDDELL SEA

WEST WIND DRIFT

CAPE ANN

Antarctic Circle

East of Greenwich
Longitude
West of Greenwich

BERKNER I.

SOUTH ORKNEY IS. (Br.)

SOUTH GEORGIA (Br.)

SOUTH SANDWICH ISLANDS (Br.)

BOUVETØYA (Nor.)

GOUGH (St. Hel.)

TRISTAN DA CUNHA (St. Hel.)

ST. HELENA (Br.)

ASCENSION (St. Hel.)

Tropic of Capricorn

IS. MARTIN VAZ (Braz.)

ARQUIPÉLAGO FERNANDO DE NORONHA (Braz.)

CABO DE SÃO ROQUE

BENGUELA CURRENT

BRAZIL CURRENT

Walvis Bay

NAMIB DESERT

DEM. REP. OF THE CONGO (ZAIRE)

Brazzaville
KINSHASA

LUANDA

ANGOLA

Benguela

NAMIBIA

ZAMBIA

ZIMBABWE

BOTSWANA

KALAHARI DESERT

SWAZILAND

LESOTHO

SOUTH AFRICA

Durban

Port Elizabeth

CAPE TOWN

CAPE OF GOOD HOPE

CAPE AGULHAS

BELLINGHAUSEN SEA

ELLSWORTH LAND

THURSTON

ALEXANDER I.

ANTARCTIC PEN.

ADELAIDE

SOUTH SHETLAND (Br.)

CABO DE HORNOS

TIERRA DEL FUEGO

Estrecho de Magallanes

Punta Arenas

WELLINGTON

ARCHIPIÉLAGO DE LOS CHONOS

ISLA DE CHILOÉ

Concepción

Valparaíso
SANTIAGO

IS. DE JUAN FERNÁNDEZ (Chile)

SAN AMBROSIO (Chile)

SAN FÉLIX (Chile)

Antofagasta

CHILE

ANDES MOUNTAINS

LA PAZ

Sucre

BOLIVIA

PERU

LIMA

Trujillo

GUAYAQUIL

Manaus

Madeira

BRAZIL

Fortaleza

RECIFE

SALVADOR

BRAZILIAN HIGHLANDS

Brasília

SÃO PAULO

RIO DE JANEIRO

CABO FRIO

PORTO ALEGRE

MONTEVIDEO

URUGUAY

Rio de la Plata

BUENOS AIRES

Rosario

PAMPAS

Bahía Blanca

ARGENTINA

PARAGUAY

GRAN CHACO

Paraná

Golfo San Matías

Golfo San Jorge

FALKLAND IS. (ISLAS MALVINAS) (Br.)

São Francisco

PACIFIC OCEAN

Scale 1:50 000 000; one inch to 790 miles. Mollweide Projection

Elevations and depressions are given in feet

→ Warm ocean currents

→ Cold ocean currents

N-GD54000-A1—2—4
COPYRIGHT BY
RAND MCNALLY & COMPANY
MADE IN U.S.A.

Relief

Meters	Feet
3050	10 000
1525	5000
601	2000
305	1000
0	Sea Level
152.5	500
1525	5000
3050	10 000
6100	20 000

Miles
Kilometers
0 200 400 600 800 1000
0 400 800 1200 1600

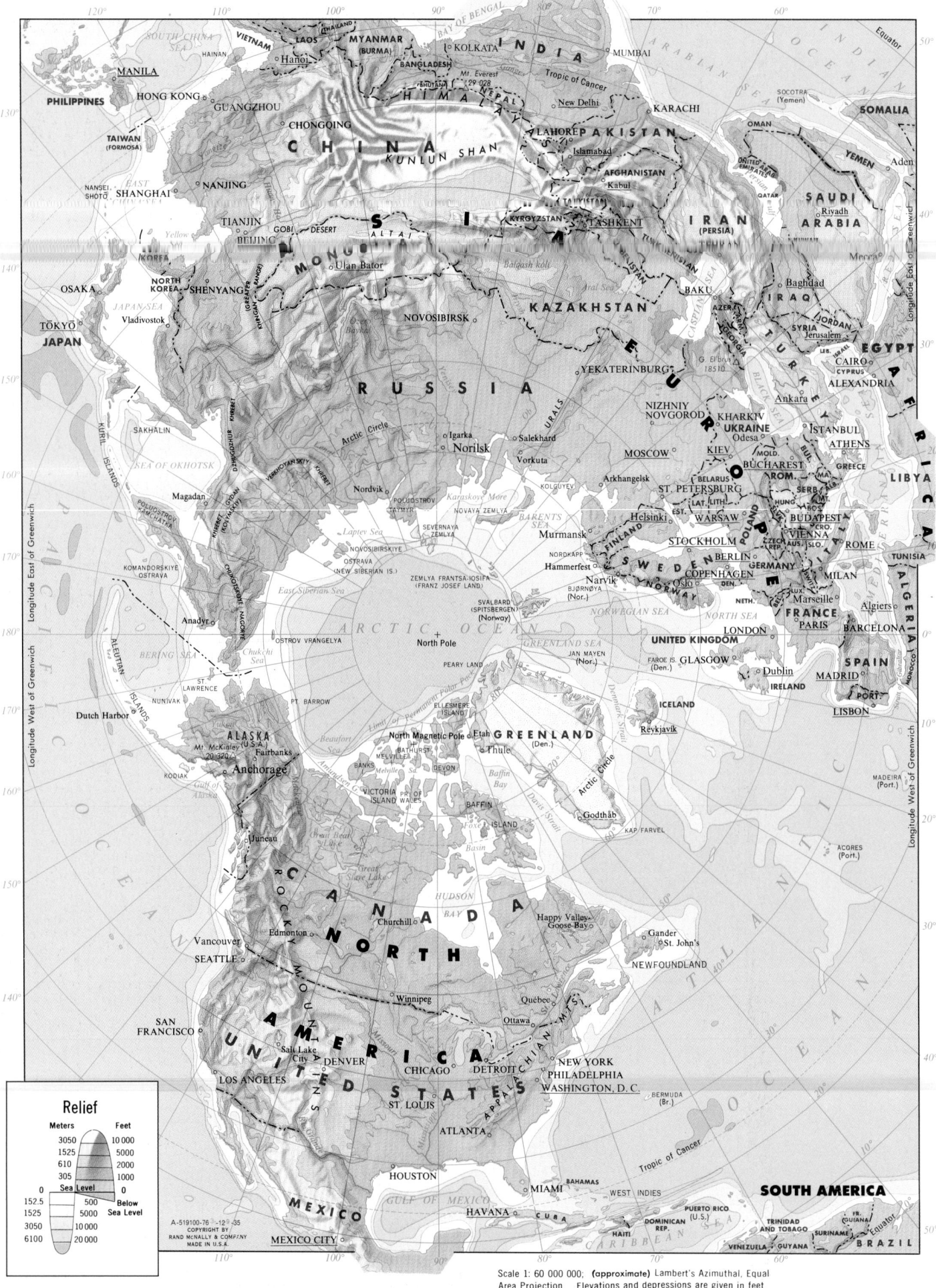

Scale 1: 60 000 000; (approximate) Lambert's Azimuthal, Equal
Area Projection   Elevations and depressions are given in feet

WORLD POLITICAL INFORMATION TABLE

This table gives the area, population, population density, political status, capital, and predominant languages for every country in the world. The political units listed are categorized by political status in the form of government column of the table, as follows: A—independent countries; B—internally independent political entities which are under the protection of another country in matters of defense and foreign affairs; C—colonies and other dependent political units; and D—the major administrative subdivisions of Australia, Canada, China, the United Kingdom, and the United States. For comparison, the table also includes the continents and the world. All footnotes appear at the end of the table.

The populations are estimates for January 1, 2004, made by Rand McNally on the basis of official data, United States Census Bureau estimates, and other available information. Area figures include inland water.

REGION OR POLITICAL DIVISION	Area Sq. Mi.	Est. Pop. 1/1/04	Pop. Per Sq. Mi.	Form of Government and Ruling Power	Capital	Predominant Languages	International Organizations
Afars and Issas see Djibouti							
Afghanistan	251,773	29,205,000	116	Transitional A	Kabul	Dari, Pashto, Uzbek, Turkmen	UN
Africa	11,700,000	866,305,000	74				
Alabama	52,419	4,515,000	86	State (U.S.) D	Montgomery	English	
Alaska	663,267	650,000	1.0	State (U.S.) D	Juneau	English, indigenous	
Albania	11,100	3,535,000	318	Republic A	Tiranë	Albanian, Greek	NATO/PP, UN
Alberta	255,541	3,215,000	13	Province (Canada) D	Edmonton	English	
Algeria	919,595	33,090,000	36	Republic A	Algiers (El Djazaïr)	Arabic, Berber dialects, French	AL, AU, OPEC, UN
American Samoa	77	58,000	753	Unincorporated territory (U.S.) C	Pago Pago	Samoan, English	
Andorra	181	70,000	387	Parliamentary co-principality (Spanish and French) B	Andorra	Catalan, Spanish (Castilian), French, Portuguese	UN
Angola	481,354	10,875,000	23	Republic A	Luanda	Portuguese, indigenous	AU, COMESA, UN
Anguilla	37	13,000	351	Overseas territory (U.K.) C	The Valley	English	
Anhui	53,668	61,215,000	1,141	Province (China) D	Hefei	Chinese (Mandarin)	
Antarctica	5,400,000	([1])					
Antigua and Barbuda	171	68,000	398	Parliamentary state A	St. John's	English, local dialects	OAS, UN
Aomen (Macau)	6.9	445,000	64,493	Special administrative region (China) D	Macau (Aomen)	Chinese (Cantonese), Portuguese	
Argentina	1,073,519	38,945,000	36	Republic A	Buenos Aires	Spanish, English, Italian, German, French	MERCOSUR, OAS, UN
Arizona	113,998	5,600,000	49	State (U.S.) D	Phoenix	English	
Arkansas	53,179	2,735,000	51	State (U.S.) D	Little Rock	English	
Armenia	11,506	3,325,000	289	Republic A	Yerevan	Armenian, Russian	CIS, NATO/PP, UN
Aruba	75	71,000	947	Self-governing territory (Netherlands protection) B	Oranjestad	Dutch, Papiamento, English, Spanish	
Ascension	34	1,000	29	Dependency (St. Helena) C	Georgetown	English	
Asia	17,300,000	3,839,320,000	222				
Australia	2,969,910	19,825,000	6.7	Federal parliamentary state A	Canberra	English, indigenous	ANZUS, UN
Australian Capital Territory	911	325,000	357	Territory (Australia) D	Canberra	English	
Austria	32,378	8,170,000	252	Federal republic A	Vienna (Wien)	German	EU, NATO/PP, UN
Azerbaijan	33,437	7,850,000	235	Republic A	Baku (Bakı)	Azeri, Russian, Armenian	CIS, NATO/PP, UN
Bahamas	5,382	300,000	56	Parliamentary state A	Nassau	English, Creole	OAS, UN
Bahrain	267	675,000	2,528	Monarchy A	Al Manāmah	Arabic, English, Persian, Urdu	AL, UN
Bangladesh	55,598	139,875,000	2,516	Republic A	Dkaha (Dacca)	Bangla, English	UN
Barbados	166	280,000	1,687	Parliamentary state A	Bridgetown	English	OAS, UN
Beijing (Peking)	6,487	14,135,000	2,179	Autonomous city (China) D	Beijing (Peking)	Chinese (Mandarin)	
Belarus	80,155	10,315,000	129	Republic A	Minsk	Belarussian, Russian	CIS, NATO/PP, UN
Belau see Palau							
Belgium	11,787	10,340,000	877	Constitutional monarchy A	Brussels (Bruxelles)	Dutch (Flemish), French, German	EU, NATO, UN
Belize	8,867	270,000	30	Parliamentary state A	Belmopan	English, Spanish, Mayan, Garifuna, Creole	OAS, UN
Benin	43,484	7,145,000	164	Republic A	Porto-Novo and Cotonou	French, Fon, Yoruba, indigenous	AU, UN
Bermuda	21	65,000	3,095	Overseas territory (U.K. protection) B	Hamilton	English, Portuguese	
Bhutan	17,954	2,160,000	120	Monarchy (Indian protection) B	Thimphu	Dzongkha, Tibetan and Nepalese dialects	UN
Bolivia	424,165	8,655,000	20	Republic A	La Paz and Sucre	Aymara, Quechua, Spanish	OAS, UN
Bosnia and Herzegovina	19,767	4,000,000	202	Republic A	Sarajevo	Bosnian, Serbian, Croatian	UN
Botswana	224,607	1,570,000	7.0	Republic A	Gaborone	English, Tswana	AU, UN
Brazil	3,300,172	183,080,000	55	Federal republic A	Brasília	Portuguese, Spanish, English, French	MERCOSUR, OAS, UN
British Columbia	364,764	4,245,000	12	Province (Canada) D	Victoria	English	
British Indian Ocean Territory	23	([1])		Overseas territory (U.K.) C		English	
British Virgin Islands	58	22,000	379	Overseas territory (U.K.) C	Road Town	English	
Brunei	2,226	360,000	162	Monarchy A	Bandar Seri Begawan	Malay, English, Chinese	ASEAN, UN
Bulgaria	42,855	7,550,000	176	Republic A	Sofia (Sofiya)	Bulgarian, Turkish	NATO, UN
Burkina Faso	105,869	13,400,000	127	Republic A	Ouagadougou	French, indigenous	AU, UN
Burma see Myanmar							
Burundi	10,745	6,165,000	574	Republic A	Bujumbura	French, Kirundi, Swahili	AU, COMESA, UN
California	163,696	35,590,000	217	State (U.S.) D	Sacramento	English	
Cambodia	69,898	13,245,000	189	Constitutional monarchy A	Phnom Penh (Phnum Pénh)	Khmer, French, English	ASEAN, UN
Cameroon	183,568	15,905,000	87	Republic A	Yaoundé	English, French, indigenous	AU, UN
Canada	3,855,103	32,360,000	8.4	Federal parliamentary state A	Ottawa	English, French, other	NAFTA, NATO, OAS, UN
Cape Verde	1,557	415,000	267	Republic A	Praia	Portuguese, Crioulo	AU, UN
Cayman Islands	102	43,000	422	Overseas territory (U.K.) C	George Town	English	
Central African Republic	240,536	3,715,000	15	Republic A	Bangui	French, Sango, indigenous	AU, UN
Ceylon see Sri Lanka							
Chad	495,755	9,395,000	19	Republic A	N'Djamena	Arabic, French, indigenous	AU, UN
Channel Islands	75	155,000	2,067	Two crown dependencies (U.K. protection)		English, French	
Chile	291,930	15,745,000	54	Republic A	Santiago	Spanish	OAS, UN
China (excl. Taiwan)	3,690,045	1,298,720,000	352	Socialist republic A	Beijing (Peking)	Chinese dialects	UN
Chongqing	31,815	31,600,000	993	Autonomous city (China) D	Chongqing (Chungking)	Chinese (Mandarin)	
Christmas Island	52	400	7.7	External territory (Australia) C	Settlement	English, Chinese, Malay	
Cocos (Keeling) Islands	5.4	600	111	External territory (Australia) C	West Island	English, Cocos-Malay	
Colombia	439,737	41,985,000	95	Republic A	Bogotá	Spanish	OAS, UN
Colorado	104,094	4,565,000	44	State (U.S.) D	Denver	English	
Comoros (excl. Mayotte)	863	640,000	742	Republic A	Moroni	Arabic, French, Shikomoro	AL, AU, COMESA, UN
Congo	132,047	2,975,000	23	Republic A	Brazzaville	French, Lingala, Monokutuba, indigenous	AU, UN
Congo, Democratic Republic of the (Zaire)	905,446	57,445,000	63	Republic A	Kinshasa	French, Lingala, indigenous	AU, COMESA, UN
Connecticut	5,543	3,495,000	631	State (U.S.) D	Hartford	English	

REGION OR POLITICAL DIVISION	Area Sq. Mi.	Est. Pop. 1/1/04	Pop. Per Sq. Mi.	Form of Government and Ruling Power		Capital	Predominant Languages	International Organizations
Cook Islands	91	21,000	231	Self-governing territory (New Zealand protection)	B	Avarua	English, Maori	
Costa Rica	19,730	3,925,000	199	Republic	A	San José	Spanish, English	OAS, UN
Cote d'Ivoire (Ivory Coast)	124,504	17,145,000	138	Republic	A	Abidjan and Yamoussoukro	French, Dioula and other indigenous	AU, UN
Croatia	21,829	4,430,000	203	Republic	A	Zagreb	Croatian	NATO/PP, UN
Cuba	42,804	11,290,000	264	Socialist republic	A	Havana (La Habana)	Spanish	OAS, UN
Cyprus	3,572	775,000	217	Republic	A	Nicosia	Greek, Turkish, English	EU, UN
Czech Republic	30,450	10,250,000	337	Republic	A	Prague (Praha)	Czech	EU, NATO, UN
Delaware	2,489	820,000	329	State (U.S.)	D	Dover	English	
Denmark	16,640	5,405,000	325	Constitutional monarchy	A	Copenhagen (København)	Danish	EU, NATO, UN
District of Columbia	68	580,000	8,309	Federal district (U.S.)	D	Washington	English	
Djibouti	8,958	460,000	51	Republic	A	Djibouti	French, Arabic, Somali, Afar	AL, AU, COMESA, UN
Dominica	290	69,000	238	Republic	A	Roseau	English, French	OAS, UN
Dominican Republic	18,730	8,775,000	400	Republic	A	Santo Domingo	Spanish	OAS, UN
East Timor	5,743	1,010,000	176	Republic	A	Dili	Portuguese, Tetum, Bahasa Indonesia (Malay), English	UN
Ecuador	109,484	13,840,000	126	Republic	A	Quito	Spanish, Quechua, indigenous	OAS, UN
Egypt	386,662	75,420,000	195	Republic	A	Cairo (Al Qāhirah)	Arabic	AL, AU, CAEU, COMESA, UN
Ellice Islands see Tuvalu								
El Salvador	8,124	6,530,000	804	Republic	A	San Salvador	Spanish, Nahua	OAS, UN
England	50,356	50,360,000	1,000	Administrative division (U.K.)	D	London	English	
Equatorial Guinea	10,831	515,000	48	Republic	A	Malabo	French, Spanish, indigenous, English	AU, UN
Eritrea	45,406	4,390,000	97	Republic	A	Asmera	Afar, Arabic, Tigre, Kunama, Tigrinya, other	AU, COMESA, UN
Estonia	17,462	1,405,000	80	Republic	A	Tallinn	Estonian, Russian, Ukrainian, Finnish, other	EU, NATO, UN
Ethiopia	426,373	67,210,000	158	Federal republic	A	Addis Ababa (Adis Abeba)	Amharic, Tigrinya, Orominga, Guaraginga, Somali, Arabic	AU, COMESA, UN
Europe	3,800,000	729,330,000	192					
Falkland Islands (¹)	4,700	3,000	0.6	Overseas territory (U.K.)	C	Stanley	English	
Faroe Islands	540	47,000	87	Self-governing territory (Danish protection)	B	Tórshavn	Danish, Faroese	
Fiji	7,056	875,000	124	Republic	A	Suva	English, Fijian, Hindustani	UN
Finland	130,559	5,210,000	40	Republic	A	Helsinki (Helsingfors)	Finnish, Swedish, Sami, Russian	EU, NATO/PP, UN
Florida	65,755	17,070,000	260	State (U.S.)	D	Tallahassee	English	
France (excl. Overseas Departments)	208,482	60,305,000	289	Republic	A	Paris	French	EU, NATO, UN
French Guiana	32,253	190,000	5.9	Overseas department (France)	C	Cayenne	French	
French Polynesia	1,544	265,000	172	Overseas territory (France)	C	Papeete	French, Tahitian	
Fujian	46,332	35,495,000	766	Province (China)	D	Fuzhou	Chinese dialects	
Gabon	103,347	1,340,000	13	Republic	A	Libreville	French, Fang, indigenous	AU, UN
Gambia, The	4,127	1,525,000	370	Republic	A	Banjul	English, Malinke, Wolof, Fula, indigenous	AU, UN
Gansu	173,746	26,200,000	151	Province (China)	D	Lanzhou	Chinese (Mandarin), Mongolian, Tibetan dialects	
Gaza Strip	139	1,300,000	9,353	Israeli territory with limited self-government			Arabic, Hebrew	(²)
Georgia	59,425	8,710,000	147	State (U.S.)	D	Atlanta	English	
Georgia	26,911	4,920,000	183	Republic	A	Tbilisi	Georgian, Russian, Armenian, Azeri, other	NATO/PP, UN
Germany	137,847	82,415,000	598	Federal republic	A	Berlin	German	EU, NATO, UN
Ghana	92,098	20,615,000	224	Republic	A	Accra	English, Akan and other indigenous	AU, UN
Gibraltar (¹)	2.3	28,000	12,174	Overseas territory (U.K.)	C	Gibraltar	English, Spanish, Italian, Portuguese	
Gilbert Islands see Kiribati								
Golan Heights	454	37,000	81	Occupied by Israel			Arabic, Hebrew	
Great Britain see United Kingdom								
Greece	50,949	10,635,000	209	Republic	A	Athens (Athína)	Greek, English, French	EU, NATO, UN
Greenland	836,331	56,000	0.07	Self-governing territory (Danish protection)	B	Godthåb (Nuuk)	Danish, Greenlandic, English	
Grenada	133	89,000	669	Parliamentary state	A	St. George's	English, French	OAS, UN
Guadeloupe (incl. Dependencies)	687	440,000	640	Overseas department (France)	C	Basse-Terre	French, Creole	
Guam	212	165,000	778	Unincorporated territory (U.S.)	C	Hagåtña (Agana)	English, Chamorro, Japanese	
Guangdong	68,649	88,375,000	1,287	Province (China)	D	Guangzhou (Canton)	Chinese dialects, Miao-Yao	
Guangxi Zhuangzu	91,236	45,905,000	503	Autonomous region (China)	D	Nanning	Chinese dialects, Thai, Miao-Yao	
Guatemala	42,042	14,095,000	335	Republic	A	Guatemala	Spanish, indigenous	OAS, UN
Guernsey (incl. Dependencies)	30	65,000	2,167	Crown dependency (U.K. protection)	B	St. Peter Port	English, French	
Guinea	94,926	9,135,000	96	Republic	A	Conakry	French, indigenous	AU, UN
Guinea-Bissau	13,948	1,375,000	99	Republic	A	Bissau	Portuguese, Crioulo, indigenous	AU, UN
Guizhou	65,637	36,045,000	549	Province (China)	D	Guiyang	Chinese (Mandarin), Thai, Miao-Yao	
Guyana	83,000	705,000	8.5	Republic	A	Georgetown	English, indigenous, Creole, Hindi, Urdu	OAS, UN
Hainan	13,205	8,050,000	610	Province (China)	D	Haikou	Chinese, Min, Tai	
Haiti	10,714	7,590,000	708	Republic	A	Port-au-Prince	Creole, French	OAS, UN
Hawaii	10,931	1,260,000	115	State (U.S.)	D	Honolulu	English, Hawaiian, Japanese	
Hebei	73,359	68,965,000	940	Province (China)	D	Shijiazhuang	Chinese (Mandarin)	
Heilongjiang	181,082	37,725,000	208	Province (China)	D	Harbin	Chinese dialects, Mongolian, Tungus	
Henan	64,479	94,655,000	1,468	Province (China)	D	Zhengzhou	Chinese (Mandarin)	
Holland see Netherlands								
Honduras	43,277	6,745,000	156	Republic	A	Tegucigalpa	Spanish, indigenous	OAS, UN
Hubei	72,356	61,645,000	852	Province (China)	D	Wuhan	Chinese dialects	
Hunan	81,082	65,855,000	812	Province (China)	D	Changsha	Chinese dialects, Miao-Yao	
Hungary	35,919	10,045,000	280	Republic	A	Budapest	Hungarian	EU, NATO, UN
Iceland	39,769	280,000	7.0	Republic	A	Reykjavík	Icelandic, English, other	EFTA, NATO, UN
Idaho	83,570	1,370,000	16	State (U.S.)	D	Boise	English	
Illinois	57,914	12,690,000	219	State (U.S.)	D	Springfield	English	
India (incl. part of Jammu and Kashmir)	1,222,510	1,057,415,000	865	Federal republic	A	New Delhi	English, Hindi, Telugu, Bengali, indigenous	UN
Indiana	36,418	6,215,000	171	State (U.S.)	D	Indianapolis	English	
Indonesia	735,310	236,680,000	322	Republic	A	Jakarta	Bahasa Indonesia (Malay), English, Dutch, indigenous	ASEAN, OPEC, UN
Iowa	56,272	2,955,000	53	State (U.S.)	D	Des Moines	English	
Iran	636,372	68,650,000	108	Islamic republic	A	Tehrān	Persian, Turkish dialects, Kurdish, other	OPEC, UN
Iraq	169,235	25,025,000	148	Republic	A	Baghdād	Arabic, Kurdish, Assyrian, Armenian	AL, CAEU, OPEC, UN
Ireland	27,133	3,945,000	145	Republic	A	Dublin (Baile Átha Cliath)	English, Irish Gaelic	EU, NATO/PP, UN
Isle of Man	221	74,000	335	Crown dependency (U.K. protection)	B	Douglas	English, Manx Gaelic	

REGION OR POLITICAL DIVISION	Area Sq. Mi.	Est. Pop. 1/1/04	Pop. Per Sq. Mi.	Form of Government and Ruling Power	Capital	Predominant Languages	International Organizations
Israel (excl. Occupied Areas)	8,019	6,160,000	768	Republic A	Jerusalem (Yerushalayim)	Hebrew, Arabic	UN
Italy	116,342	58,030,000	499	Republic A	Rome (Roma)	Italian, German, French, Slovene	EU, NATO, UN
Ivory Coast see Cote d'Ivoire							
Jamaica	4,244	2,705,000	637	Parliamentary state A	Kingston	English, Creole	OAS, UN
Japan	145,850	127,285,000	873	Constitutional monarchy A	Tōkyō	Japanese	UN
Jersey	45	90,000	2,000	Crown dependency (U.K. protection) B	St. Helier	English, French	
Jiangsu	39,614	76,065,000	1,920	Province (China) D	Nanjing (Nanking)	Chinese dialects	
Jiangxi	64,325	42,335,000	658	Province (China) D	Nanchang	Chinese dialects	
Jilin	72,201	27,895,000	386	Province (China) D	Changchun	Chinese (Mandarin), Mongolian, Korean	
Jordan	34,495	5,535,000	160	Constitutional monarchy A	'Ammān	Arabic	AL, CAEU, UN
Kansas	82,277	2,730,000	33	State (U.S.) D	Topeka	English	
Kazakhstan	1,049,156	16,780,000	16	Republic A	Astana (Aqmola)	Kazakh, Russian	CIS, NATO/PP, UN
Kentucky	40,409	4,130,000	102	State (U.S.) D	Frankfort	English	
Kenya	224,961	31,840,000	142	Republic A	Nairobi	English, Swahili, indigenous	AU, COMESA, UN
Kiribati	313	100,000	319	Republic A	Bairiki	English, I-Kiribati	UN
Korea, North	46,540	22,585,000	485	Socialist republic A	P'yŏngyang	Korean	UN
Korea, South	38,328	48,450,000	1,264	Republic A	Seoul (Sŏul)	Korean	UN
Kuwait	6,880	2,220,000	323	Constitutional monarchy A	Kuwait (Al Kuwayt)	Arabic, English	AL, CAEU, OPEC, UN
Kyrgyzstan	77,182	4,930,000	64	Republic A	Bishkek	Kirghiz, Russian	CIS, NATO/PP, UN
Laos	91,429	5,995,000	66	Socialist republic A	Viangchan (Vientiane)	Lao, French, English	ASEAN, UN
Latvia	24,942	2,340,000	94	Republic A	Rīga	Latvian, Lithuanian, Russian, other	EU, NATO, UN
Lebanon	4,016	3,755,000	935	Republic A	Beirut (Bayrūt)	Arabic, French, Armenian, English	AL, UN
Lesotho	11,720	1,865,000	159	Constitutional monarchy A	Maseru	English, Sesotho, Zulu, Xhosa	AU, UN
Liaoning	56,255	43,340,000	770	Province (China) D	Shenyang (Mukden)	Chinese (Mandarin), Mongolian	
Liberia	43,000	3,345,000	78	Republic A	Monrovia	English, indigenous	AU, UN
Libya	679,362	5,565,000	8.2	Socialist republic A	Tripoli (Ţarābulus)	Arabic	AL, AU, CAEU, OPEC, UN
Liechtenstein	62	33,000	532	Constitutional monarchy A	Vaduz	German	EFTA, UN
Lithuania	25,213	3,590,000	142	Republic A	Vilnius	Lithuanian, Polish, Russian	EU, NATO, UN
Louisiana	51,840	4,510,000	87	State (U.S.) D	Baton Rouge	English	
Luxembourg	999	460,000	460	Constitutional monarchy A	Luxembourg	French, Luxembourgish, German	EU, NATO, UN
Macedonia	9,928	2,065,000	208	Republic A	Skopje	Macedonian, Albanian, other	NATO/PP, UN
Madagascar	226,658	17,235,000	76	Republic A	Antananarivo	French, Malagasy	AU, COMESA, UN
Maine	35,385	1,310,000	37	State (U.S.) D	Augusta	English	
Malawi	45,747	11,780,000	258	Republic A	Lilongwe	Chichewa, English, indigenous	AU, COMESA, UN
Malaysia	127,320	23,310,000	183	Federal constitutional monarchy A	Kuala Lumpur and Putrajaya [5]	Bahasa Melayu, Chinese dialects, English, other	ASEAN, UN
Maldives	115	335,000	2,913	Republic A	Male'	Dhivehi	UN
Mali	478,841	11,790,000	25	Republic A	Bamako	French, Bambara, indigenous	AU, UN
Malta	122	400,000	3,279	Republic A	Valletta	English, Maltese	EU, UN
Manitoba	250,116	1,190,000	4.8	Province (Canada) D	Winnipeg	English	
Marshall Islands	70	57,000	814	Republic (U.S. protection) B	Majuro (island)	English, indigenous, Japanese	UN
Martinique	425	430,000	1,012	Overseas department (France) C	Fort-de-France	French, Creole	
Maryland	12,407	5,525,000	445	State (U.S.) D	Annapolis	English	
Massachusetts	10,555	6,455,000	612	State (U.S.) D	Boston	English	
Mauritania	397,956	2,955,000	7.4	Republic A	Nouakchott	Arabic, Wolof, Pular, Soninke, French	AL, AU, CAEU, UN
Mauritius (incl. Dependencies)	788	1,215,000	1,542	Republic A	Port Louis	English, French, Creole, other	AU, COMESA, UN
Mayotte [4]	144	180,000	1,250	Departmental collectivity (France) C	Mamoutzou	French, Swahili (Mahorian)	
Mexico	758,452	104,340,000	138	Federal republic A	Mexico City (Ciudad de México)	Spanish, indigenous	NAFTA, OAS, UN
Michigan	96,716	10,110,000	105	State (U.S.) D	Lansing	English	
Micronesia, Federated States of	271	110,000	406	Republic (U.S. protection) B	Palikir	English, indigenous	UN
Midway Islands	2.0	[1]		Unincorporated territory (U.S.) C		English	
Minnesota	86,939	5,075,000	58	State (U.S.) D	St. Paul	English	
Mississippi	48,430	2,890,000	60	State (U.S.) D	Jackson	English	
Missouri	69,704	5,720,000	82	State (U.S.) D	Jefferson City	English	
Moldova	13,070	4,440,000	340	Republic A	Chişinău (Kishinev)	Romanian (Moldovan), Russian, Gagauz	CIS, NATO/PP, UN
Monaco	0.8	32,000	40,000	Constitutional monarchy A	Monaco	French, English, Italian, Monegasque	UN
Mongolia	604,829	2,730,000	4.5	Republic A	Ulan Bator (Ulaanbaatar)	Khalkha Mongol, Turkish dialects, Russian	UN
Montana	147,042	920,000	6.3	State (U.S.) D	Helena	English	
Montenegro	5,333	660,000	124	Republic A	Podgorica	Serbian, Albanian	UN
Montserrat	39	9,000	231	Overseas territory (U.K.) C	Plymouth	English	
Morocco (excl. Western Sahara)	172,414	31,950,000	185	Constitutional monarchy A	Rabat	Arabic, Berber dialects, French	AL, UN
Mozambique	309,496	18,695,000	60	Republic A	Maputo	Portuguese, indigenous	AU, UN
Myanmar (Burma)	261,228	42,620,000	163	Provisional military government A	Rangoon (Yangon)	Burmese, indigenous	ASEAN, UN
Namibia	317,818	1,940,000	6.1	Republic A	Windhoek	English, Afrikaans, German, indigenous	AU, COMESA, UN
Nauru	8.1	13,000	1,605	Republic A	Yaren District	Nauruan, English	UN
Nebraska	77,354	1,745,000	23	State (U.S.) D	Lincoln	English	
Nei Mongol (Inner Mongolia)	456,759	24,295,000	53	Autonomous region (China) D	Hohhot	Mongolian	
Nepal	56,827	26,770,000	471	Constitutional monarchy A	Kathmandu	Nepali, indigenous	UN
Netherlands	16,164	16,270,000	1,007	Constitutional monarchy A	Amsterdam and The Hague ('s-Gravenhage)	Dutch, Frisian	EU, NATO, UN
Netherlands Antilles	309	215,000	696	Self-governing territory (Netherlands protection) B	Willemstad	Dutch, Papiamento, English, Spanish	
Nevada	110,561	2,250,000	20	State (U.S.) D	Carson City	English	
New Brunswick	28,150	770,000	27	Province (Canada) D	Fredericton	English, French	
New Caledonia	7,172	210,000	29	Territorial collectivity (France) C	Nouméa	French, indigenous	
Newfoundland and Labrador	156,453	535,000	3.4	Province (Canada) D	St. John's	English	
New Hampshire	9,350	1,290,000	138	State (U.S.) D	Concord	English	
New Hebrides see Vanuatu							
New Jersey	8,721	8,665,000	994	State (U.S.) D	Trenton	English	
New Mexico	121,590	1,880,000	15	State (U.S.) D	Santa Fe	English, Spanish	
New South Wales	309,129	6,665,000	22	State (Australia) D	Sydney	English	
New York	54,556	19,245,000	353	State (U.S.) D	Albany	English	
New Zealand	104,454	3,975,000	38	Parliamentary state A	Wellington	English, Maori	ANZUS, UN
Nicaragua	50,054	5,180,000	103	Republic A	Managua	Spanish, English, indigenous	OAS, UN
Niger	489,192	11,210,000	23	Repubic A	Niamey	French, Hausa, Djerma, indigenous	AU, UN
Nigeria	356,669	135,570,000	380	Transitional military government A	Abuja	English, Hausa, Fulani, Yorbua, Ibo, indigenous	AU, OPEC, UN
Ningxia Huizu	25,637	5,745,000	224	Autonomous region (China) D	Yinchuan	Chinese (Mandarin)	
Niue	100	2,000	20	Self-governing territory (New Zealand protection) B	Alofi	Niuean, English	
Norfolk Island	14	2,000	143	External territory (Australia) C	Kingston	English, Norfolk	

REGION OR POLITICAL DIVISION	Area Sq. Mi.	Est. Pop. 1/1/04	Pop. Per Sq. Mi.	Form of Government and Ruling Power	Capital	Predominant Languages	International Organizations
North America	9,500,000	505,780,000	53				
North Carolina	53,819	8,430,000	157	State (U.S.) D	Raleigh	English	
North Dakota	70,700	635,000	9.0	State (U.S.) D	Bismarck	English	
Northern Ireland	5,242	1,725,000	329	Administrative division (U.K.) D	Belfast	English	
Northern Mariana Islands	179	77,000	430	Commonwealth (U.S. protection) B	Saipan (island)	English, Chamorro, Carolinian	
Northern Territory	520,902	200,000	0.4	Territory (Australia) D	Darwin	English, indigenous	
Northwest Territories	519,735	43,000	0.08	Territory (Canada) D	Yellowknife	English, indigenous	
Norway (incl. Svalbard and Jan Mayen)	125,050	4,565,000	37	Constitutional monarchy A	Oslo	Norwegian, Sami, Finnish	EFTA, NATO, UN
Nova Scotia	21,345	965,000	45	Province (Canada) D	Halifax	English	
Nunavut	808,185	30,000	0.04	Territory (Canada) D	Iqaluit	English, indigenous	
Oceania (incl. Australia)	3,300,000	32,170,000	9.7				
Ohio	44,825	11,470,000	256	State (U.S.) B	Columbus	English	
Oklahoma	69,898	3,520,000	50	State (U.S.) D	Oklahoma City	English	
Oman	119,499	2,855,000	24	Monarchy A	Muscat (Masqat)	Arabic, English, Baluchi, Urdu, Indian dialects	AL, UN
Ontario	415,599	12,495,000	30	Province (Canada) D	Toronto	English	
Oregon	98,381	3,570,000	36	State (U.S.) D	Salem	English	
Pakistan (incl. part of Jammu and Kashmir)	339,732	152,210,000	448	Federal Islamic republic A	Islāmābād	English, Urdu, Punjabi, Sindhi, Pashto, other	UN
Palau (Belau)	188	20,000	106	Republic (U.S. protection) B	Koror and Melekeok (')	Angaur, English, Japanese, Palauan, Sonsorolese, Tobi	UN
Panama	29,157	2,980,000	102	Republic A	Panamá	Spanish, English	OAS, UN
Papua New Guinea	178,704	5,360,000	30	Parliamentary state A	Port Moresby	English, Motu, Pidgin, indigenous	UN
Paraguay	157,048	6,115,000	39	Republic A	Asunción	Guarani, Spanish	MERCOSUR, OAS, UN
Pennsylvania	46,055	12,400,000	269	State (U.S.) D	Harrisburg	English	
Peru	496,225	28,640,000	58	Republic A	Lima	Quechua, Spanish, Aymara	OAS, UN
Philippines	115,831	85,430,000	738	Republic A	Manila	English, Filipino, indigenous	ASEAN, UN
Pitcairn Islands (incl. Dependencies)	19	100	5.3	Overseas territory (U.K.) C	Adamstown	English, Pitcairnese	
Poland	120,728	38,625,000	320	Republic A	Warsaw (Warszawa)	Polish	EU, NATO, UN
Portugal	35,516	10,110,000	285	Republic A	Lisbon (Lisboa)	Portuguese, Mirandese	EU, NATO, UN
Prince Edward Island	2,185	140,000	64	Province (Canada) D	Charlottetown	English	
Puerto Rico	3,515	3,890,000	1,107	Commonwealth (U.S. protection) B	San Juan	Spanish, English	
Qatar	4,412	830,000	188	Monarchy A	Ad Dawḩah (Doha)	Arabic	AL, OPEC, UN
Qinghai	277,994	5,295,000	19	Province (China) D	Xining	Tibetan dialects, Mongolian, Turkish dialects, Chinese (Mandarin)	
Quebec	595,391	7,675,000	13	Province (Canada) D	Québec	French, English	
Queensland	668,208	3,785,000	5.7	State (Australia) D	Brisbane	English	
Reunion	969	760,000	784	Overseas department (France) C	Saint-Denis	French, Creole	
Rhode Island	1,545	1,080,000	699	State (U.S.) D	Providence	English	
Rhodesia see Zimbabwe							
Romania	91,699	22,370,000	244	Republic A	Bucharest (Bucureşti)	Romanian, Hungarian, German	NATO, UN
Russia	6,592,849	144,310,000	22	Federal republic A	Moscow (Moskva)	Russian, other	CIS, NATO/PP, UN
Rwanda	10,169	7,880,000	775	Republic A	Kigali	English, French, Kinyarwanda, Kiswahili	AU, COMESA, UN
St. Helena (incl. Dependencies)	121	7,500	62	Overseas territory (U.K.) C	Jamestown	English	
St. Kitts and Nevis	101	39,000	386	Parliamentary state A	Basseterre	English	OAS, UN
St. Lucia	238	165,000	693	Parliamentary state A	Castries	English, French	OAS, UN
St. Pierre and Miquelon	93	7,000	75	Territorial collectivity (France) C	Saint-Pierre	French	
St. Vincent and the Grenadines	150	115,000	767	Parliamentary state A	Kingstown	English, French	OAS, UN
Samoa	1,093	180,000	165	Constitutional monarchy A	Apia	English, Samoan	UN
San Marino	24	28,000	1,167	Republic A	San Marino	Italian	UN
Sao Tome and Principe	372	180,000	484	Republic A	São Tomé	Portuguese	AU, UN
Saskatchewan	251,366	1,025,000	4.1	Province (Canada) D	Regina	English	
Saudi Arabia	830,000	24,690,000	30	Monarchy A	Riyadh (Ar Riyāḑ)	Arabic	AL, OPEC, UN
Scotland	30,167	5,135,000	170	Administrative division (U.K.) D	Edinburgh	English, Scots Gaelic	
Senegal	75,951	10,715,000	141	Republic A	Dakar	French, Wolof and other indigenous	AU, UN
Serbia	34,116	10,000,000	293	Republic A	Belgrade (Beograd)	Serbian, Albanian	UN
Seychelles	176	81,000	460	Republic A	Victoria	English, French, Creole	AU, COMESA, UN
Shaanxi	79,151	36,865,000	466	Province (China) D	Xi'an (Sian)	Chinese (Mandarin)	
Shandong	59,074	92,845,000	1,572	Province (China) D	Jinan	Chinese (Mandarin)	
Shanghai	2,394	17,120,000	7,151	Autonomous city (China) D	Shanghai	Chinese (Wu)	
Shanxi	60,232	33,715,000	560	Province (China) D	Taiyuan	Chinese (Mandarin)	
Sichuan	188,263	85,175,000	452	Province (China) D	Chengdu	Chinese (Mandarin), Tibetan dialects, Miao-Yao	
Sierra Leone	27,699	5,815,000	210	Republic A	Freetown	English, Krio, Mende, Temne, indigenous	AU, UN
Singapore	264	4,685,000	17,746	Republic A	Singapore	Chinese (Mandarin), English, Malay, Tamil	ASEAN, UN
Slovakia	18,924	5,420,000	286	Republic A	Bratislava	Slovak, Hungarian	EU, NATO, UN
Slovenia	7,821	1,935,000	247	Republic B	Ljubljana	Slovenian, Croatian, Serbian	EU, NATO, UN
Solomon Islands	10,954	515,000	47	Parliamentary state A	Honiara	English, indigenous	UN
Somalia	246,201	8,165,000	33	Transitional A	Mogadishu (Muqdisho)	Arabic, Somali, English, Italian	AL, AU, CAEU, UN
South Africa	470,693	42,770,000	91	Republic A	Pretoria, Cape Town, and Bloemfontein	Afrikaans, English, Xhosa, Zulu, other indigenous	AU, UN
South America	6,900,000	366,600,000	53				
South Australia	379,724	1,525,000	4.0	State (Australia) D	Adelaide	English	
South Carolina	32,020	4,160,000	130	State (U.S.) D	Columbia	English	
South Dakota	77,117	765,000	9.9	State (U.S.) D	Pierre	English	
South Georgia and the South Sandwich Islands (')	1,450	(')		Overseas territory (U.K.) C		English	
South West Africa see Namibia							
Spain	194,885	40,250,000	207	Constitutional monarchy A	Madrid	Spanish (Castilian), Catalan, Galician, Basque	EU, NATO, UN
Spanish North Africa (')	12	140,000	11,667	Five possessions (Spain) C		Spanish, Arabic, Berber dialects	
Spanish Sahara see Western Sahara							
Sri Lanka	25,332	19,825,000	783	Socialist republic A	Colombo and Sri Jayewardenepura Kotte	English, Sinhala, Tamil	UN
Sudan	967,500	38,630,000	40	Provisional military government A	Khartoum (Al Kharţūm)	Arabic, Nubian, and other indigenous, English	AL, AU, CAEU, COMESA, UN
Suriname	63,037	435,000	6.9	Republic A	Paramaribo	Dutch, Sranan Tongo, English, Hindustani, Javanese	OAS, UN

REGION OR POLITICAL DIVISION	Area Sq. Mi.	Est. Pop. 1/1/04	Pop. Per Sq. Mi.	Form of Government and Ruling Power		Capital	Predominant Languages	International Organizations
Swaziland	6,704	1,165,000	174	Monarchy	A	Mbabane and Lobamba	English, siSwati	AU, COMESA, UN
Sweden	173,732	8,980,000	52	Constitutional monarchy	A	Stockholm	Swedish, Sami, Finnish	EU, NATO/PP, UN
Switzerland	15,943	7,430,000	466	Federal republic	A	Bern (Berne)	German, French, Italian, Romansch	EFTA, NATO/PP, UN
Syria	71,498	17,800,000	249	Republic	A	Damascus (Dimashq)	Arabic, Kurdish, Armenian, Aramaic, Circassian	AL, CAEU, UN
Taiwan	13,901	22,675,000	1,631	Republic	A	T'aipei	Chinese (Mandarin), Taiwanese (Min), Hakka	....
Tajikistan	55,251	6,935,000	126	Republic	A	Dushanbe	Tajik, Russian	CIS, NATO/PP, UN
Tanzania	364,900	36,230,000	99	Republic	A	Dar es Salaam and Dodoma	English, Swahili, indigenous	AU, UN
Tasmania	26,409	475,000	18	State (Australia)	D	Hobart	English	....
Tennessee	42,143	5,860,000	139	State (U.S.)	D	Nashville	English	....
Texas	268,581	22,185,000	83	State (U.S.)	D	Austin	English, Spanish	....
Thailand	198,115	64,570,000	326	Constitutional monarchy	A	Bangkok (Krung Thep)	Thai, indigenous	ASEAN, UN
Tianjin (Tientsin)	4,363	10,235,000	2,346	Autonomous city (China)	D	Tianjin (Tientsin)	Chinese (Mandarin)	....
Togo	21,925	5,495,000	251	Republic	A	Lomé	French, Ewe, Mina, Kabye, Dagomba	AU, UN
Tokelau	4.6	1,500	326	Island territory (New Zealand)	C		English, Tokelauan	....
Tonga	251	110,000	438	Constitutional monarchy	A	Nuku'alofa	Tongan, English	UN
Trinidad and Tobago	1,980	1,100,000	556	Republic	A	Port of Spain	English, Hindi, French, Spanish, Chinese	OAS, UN
Tristan da Cunha	40	300	7.5	Dependency (St. Helena)	C	Edinburgh	English	....
Tunisia	63,170	9,980,000	158	Republic	A	Tunis	Arabic, French	AL, AU, UN
Turkey	302,541	68,505,000	226	Republic	A	Ankara	Turkish, Kurdish, Arabic, Armenian, Greek	NATO, UN
Turkmenistan	188,457	4,820,000	26	Republic	A	Ashgabat (Ashkhabad)	Turkmen, Russian, Uzbek	CIS, NATO/PP, UN
Turks and Caicos Islands	166	20,000	120	Overseas territory (U.K.)	C	Grand Turk	English	....
Tuvalu	10	11,000	1,100	Parliamentary state	A	Funafuti	Tuvaluan, English, Samoan, I-Kiribati	UN
Uganda	93,065	26,010,000	279	Republic	A	Kampala	English, Luganda, Swahili, indigenous, Arabic	AU, COMESA, UN
Ukraine	233,090	47,890,000	205	Republic	A	Kiev (Kyïv)	Ukrainian, Russian, Romanian, Polish, Hungarian	CIS, NATO/PP, UN
United Arab Emirates	32,278	2,505,000	78	Federation of monarchs	A	Abū Ẓaby (Abu Dhabi)	Arabic, Persian, English, Hindi, Urdu	AL, CAEU, OPEC, UN
United Kingdom	93,788	60,185,000	642	Constitutional monarchy	A	London	English, Welsh, Scots Gaelic	EU, NATO, UN
United States	3,794,083	291,680,000	77	Federal republic	A	Washington	English, Spanish	ANZUS, NAFTA, NATO, OAS, UN
Upper Volta see Burkina Faso	....	....	....					....
Uruguay	67,574	3,425,000	51	Republic	A	Montevideo	Spanish	MERCOSUR, OAS, UN
Utah	84,899	2,360,000	28	State (U.S.)	D	Salt Lake City	English	....
Uzbekistan	172,742	26,195,000	152	Republic	A	Tashkent (Toshkent)	Uzbek, Russian, Tajik	CIS, NATO/PP, UN
Vanuatu	4,707	200,000	42	Republic	A	Port Vila	Bislama, English, French	UN
Vatican City	0.2	900	4,500	Ecclesiastical state	A	Vatican City	Italian, Latin, French, other	....
Venezuela	352,145	24,835,000	71	Federal republic	A	Caracas	Spanish, indigenous	OAS, OPEC, UN
Vermont	9,614	620,000	64	State (U.S.)	D	Montpelier	English	....
Victoria	87,807	4,905,000	56	State (Australia)	D	Melbourne	English	....
Vietnam	128,066	82,150,000	641	Socialist republic	A	Hanoi	Vietnamese, English, French, Chinese, Khmer, indigenous	ASEAN, UN
Virginia	42,774	7,410,000	173	State (U.S.)	D	Richmond	English	....
Virgin Islands (U.S.)	134	110,000	821	Unincorporated territory (U.S.)	C	Charlotte Amalie	English, Spanish, Creole	....
Wake Island	3.0	(¹)	....	Unincorporated territory (U.S.)	C		English	....
Wales	8,023	2,965,000	370	Administrative division (U.K.)	D	Cardiff	English, Welsh Gaelic	....
Wallis and Futuna	99	16,000	162	Overseas territory (France)	C	Mata-Utu	French, Wallisian	....
Washington	71,300	6,150,000	86	State (U.S.)	D	Olympia	English	....
West Bank (incl. Jericho and East Jerusalem)	2,263	2,275,000	1,005	Israeli territory with limited self-government			Arabic, Hebrew	(⁴)
Western Australia	976,792	1,945,000	2.0	State (Australia)	D	Perth	English	....
Western Sahara	102,703	265,000	2.6	Occupied by Morocco	C		Arabic	....
West Virginia	24,230	1,815,000	75	State (U.S.)	D	Charleston	English	....
Wisconsin	65,498	5,490,000	84	State (U.S.)	D	Madison	English	....
Wyoming	97,814	505,000	5.2	State (U.S.)	D	Cheyenne	English	....
Xianggang (Hong Kong)	425	7,440,000	17,506	Special administrative region (China)	D	Hong Kong (Xianggang)	Chinese (Cantonese), English	....
Xinjiang Uygur (Sinkiang)	617,764	19,685,000	32	Autonomous region (China)	D	Ürümqi	Turkish dialects, Mongolian, Tungus, English	....
Xizang (Tibet)	471,045	2,680,000	5.7	Autonomous region (China)	D	Lhasa	Tibetan dialects	....
Yemen	203,850	19,680,000	97	Republic	A	Ṣan'ā' (Sanaa)	Arabic	AL, CAEU, UN
Yukon Territory	186,272	32,000	0.2	Territory (Canada)	D	Whitehorse	English, Inuktitut, indigenous	....
Yunnan	152,124	43,850,000	288	Province (China)	D	Kunming	Chinese (Mandarin), Tibetan dialects, Khmer, Miao-Yao	....
Zaire see Congo, Democratic Republic of the	....	....	....					....
Zambia	290,586	10,385,000	36	Republic	A	Lusaka	English, indigenous	AU, COMESA, UN
Zhejiang	39,305	47,830,000	1,217	Province (China)	D	Hangzhou	Chinese dialects	....
Zimbabwe	150,873	12,630,000	84	Republic	A	Harare (Salisbury)	English, indigenous	AU, COMESA, UN
WORLD	57,900,000	6,339,505,000	109					....

... None, or not applicable
(1) No permanent population
(2) Claimed by Argentina
(3) Claimed by Spain
(4) The Palestinian Liberation Organization (PLO) is a member of AL and CAEU
(5) Future capital
(6) Claimed by Comoros
(7) Comprises Ceuta, Melilla, and several small islands

AL	Arab League (League of Arab States)
ANZUS	Australia-New Zealand-U.S. Security Treaty
ASEAN	Association of Southeast Asian Nations
AU	African Union
CAEU	Council of Arab Unity
CIS	Commonwealth of Independent States
COMESA	Common Market for Eastern and Southern Africa
EFTA	European Free Trade Association
EU	European Union
MERCOSUR	Southern Common Market
NAFTA	North American Free Trade Agreement
NATO	North Atlantic Treaty Organization
NATO/PP	NATO-Partnership for Peace Program
OAS	Organization of American States
OPEC	Organization of Petroleum Exporting Countries

WORLD DEMOGRAPHIC TABLE

CONTINENT/Country	Population Estimate 2004	Pop. Per Sq. Mile 2004	Percent Urban[1] 2001	Crude Birth Rate per 1,000[2] 2003	Crude Death Rate per 1,000[2] 2003	Natural Increase Percent[2] 2003	Fertility Rate (Children born/Woman)[3] 2003	Infant Mortality Rate per 1,000[3] 2003	Median Age[2] 2002	Life Expectancy Male[2] 2003	Life Expectancy Female[2] 2003
NORTH AMERICA											
Bahamas	300,000	56	64.7	19	9	1.0%	2	26	27	62	69
Belize	270,000	30	48.1	30	6	2.4%	4	27	19	65	70
Canada	32,360,000	8	78.9	11	8	0.3%	2	5	38	76	83
Costa Rica	3,925,000	199	59.5	19	4	1.5%	2	11	25	74	79
Cuba	11,290,000	264	75.5	12	7	0.5%	2	7	35	75	79
Dominica	69,000	238	71.4	17	7	1.0%	2	15	28	71	77
Dominican Republic	8,775,000	469	66.0	24	7	1.7%	3	34	24	66	70
El Salvador	6,530,000	804	61.5	28	6	2.2%	3	27	21	67	74
Guatemala	14,095,000	335	39.9	35	7	2.8%	5	38	18	64	66
Haiti	7,590,000	708	36.3	34	13	2.1%	5	76	18	50	53
Honduras	6,743,000	156	53.7	30	6	2.6%	4	40	19	65	68
Jamaica	2,705,000	637	56.6	17	5	1.2%	2	13	27	74	78
Mexico	104,340,000	138	74.6	22	5	1.7%	3	22	24	72	78
Nicaragua	5,180,000	103	56.5	26	5	2.2%	3	31	20	68	72
Panama	2,980,000	102	56.5	21	6	1.5%	3	21	26	70	75
St. Lucia	165,000	693	38.0	21	5	1.6%	2	14	24	70	77
Trinidad and Tobago	1,100,000	556	74.5	13	9	0.4%	2	25	30	67	72
United States	291,680,000	77	77.4	14	8	0.6%	2	7	36	74	80
SOUTH AMERICA											
Argentina	38,945,000	36	88.3	17	8	1.0%	2	16	29	72	79
Bolivia	8,655,000	20	62.9	26	8	1.8%	3	56	21	62	67
Brazil	183,080,000	55	81.7	18	6	1.2%	2	32	27	67	75
Chile	15,745,000	54	86.1	16	6	1.0%	2	9	30	73	80
Colombia	41,985,000	95	75.5	22	6	1.6%	3	22	26	67	75
Ecuador	13,840,000	126	63.4	25	5	2.0%	3	32	23	69	75
Guyana	705,000	9	36.7	18	9	0.9%	2	38	26	61	66
Paraguay	6,115,000	39	56.7	30	5	2.6%	4	28	21	72	77
Peru	28,640,000	58	73.1	23	6	1.7%	3	37	24	68	73
Suriname	435,000	7	74.8	19	7	1.3%	2	25	26	67	72
Uruguay	3,425,000	51	92.1	17	9	0.8%	2	14	32	73	79
Venezuela	24,835,000	71	87.2	20	5	1.5%	2	24	25	71	77
EUROPE											
Albania	3,535,000	318	42.9	15	5	1.0%	2	23	27	74	80
Austria	8,170,000	252	67.4	9	9	0%	1	5	39	76	82
Belarus	10,315,000	129	69.6	10	14	-0.4%	1	14	37	63	75
Belgium	10,340,000	877	97.4	11	10	0.1%	2	5	40	75	82
Bosnia and Herzegovina	4,000,000	202	43.4	13	8	0.4%	2	23	36	70	75
Bulgaria	7,550,000	176	67.4	10	14	-0.5%	1	22	41	68	75
Croatia	4,430,000	203	58.1	13	11	0.2%	2	7	39	71	78
Czech Republic	10,250,000	337	74.5	9	11	-0.1%	1	4	38	72	79
Denmark	5,405,000	325	85.1	12	11	0.1%	2	5	39	75	80
Estonia	1,405,000	80	69.4	9	13	-0.4%	1	12	38	64	77
Finland	5,210,000	40	58.5	11	10	0.1%	2	4	40	75	82
France	60,305,000	289	75.5	13	9	0.3%	2	4	38	76	83
Germany	82,415,000	598	87.7	9	10	-0.2%	1	4	41	75	82
Greece	10,635,000	209	60.3	10	10	0%	1	6	40	76	81
Hungary	10,045,000	280	64.8	10	13	-0.3%	1	9	38	68	77
Iceland	280,000	7	92.7	14	7	0.7%	2	4	34	78	82
Ireland	3,945,000	145	59.3	14	8	0.6%	2	6	33	75	80
Italy	58,030,000	499	67.1	9	10	-0.1%	1	6	41	76	83
Latvia	2,340,000	94	59.8	9	15	-0.6%	1	15	39	63	75
Lithuania	3,590,000	142	68.6	10	13	-0.2%	1	14	37	64	76
Luxembourg	460,000	460	91.9	12	8	0.4%	2	5	38	75	82
Macedonia	2,065,000	208	59.4	13	8	0.5%	2	12	33	72	77
Moldova	4,440,000	340	41.4	14	13	0.2%	2	42	32	61	69
Netherlands	16,270,000	1,007	89.6	12	9	0.3%	2	5	39	76	81
Norway	4,565,000	37	75.0	12	10	0.3%	2	4	38	77	82
Poland	38,625,000	320	62.5	10	10	0.1%	1	9	36	70	78
Portugal	10,110,000	285	65.8	11	10	0.1%	1	6	38	73	80
Romania	22,370,000	244	55.2	11	12	-0.1%	1	28	35	67	75
Serbia and Montenegro	10,660,000	270	51.7	13	11	0.2%	2	17	36	71	77
Slovakia	5,420,000	286	57.6	10	10	0.1%	1	8	35	70	78
Slovenia	1,935,000	247	49.1	9	10	-0.1%	1	4	39	72	80
Spain	40,250,000	207	77.8	10	9	0.1%	1	5	39	76	83
Sweden	8,980,000	52	83.3	11	10	0%	2	3	40	78	83
Switzerland	7,430,000	466	67.3	10	8	0.1%	1	4	40	77	83
Ukraine	47,890,000	205	68.0	10	16	-0.7%	1	21	38	61	72
United Kingdom	60,185,000	642	89.5	11	10	0.1%	2	5	38	76	81
Russia	144,310,000	22	72.9	10	14	-0.4%	1	20	38	62	73
ASIA											
Afghanistan	29,205,000	116	22.3	41	17	2.3%	6	142	19	48	46
Armenia	3,325,000	289	67.2	13	10	0.2%	2	41	32	62	71
Azerbaijan	7,850,000	235	51.8	19	10	1.0%	2	82	27	59	68
Bahrain	675,000	2,528	92.5	19	4	1.5%	3	19	29	71	76
Bangladesh	139,875,000	2,516	25.6	30	9	2.1%	3	66	21	61	61
Brunei	360,000	162	72.8	20	3	1.6%	2	14	26	72	77
Cambodia	13,245,000	189	17.5	27	9	1.8%	4	76	19	55	60
China	1,298,720,000	352	37.1	13	7	0.6%	2	25	32	70	74
Cyprus	775,000	217	70.2	13	8	0.5%	2	8	34	75	80
East Timor	1,010,000	176	7.5	28	6	2.1%	4	50	20	63	68
Georgia	4,920,000	183	56.5	12	15	-0.3%	2	51	35	61	68
India	1,057,415,000	865	27.9	23	8	1.5%	3	60	24	63	64
Indonesia	236,680,000	322	42.1	21	6	1.5%	3	38	26	67	71
Iran	68,650,000	108	64.7	17	6	1.2%	2	44	23	68	71
Iraq	25,025,000	148	67.4	34	6	2.8%	5	55	19	67	69
Israel	6,160,000	768	91.8	19	6	1.2%	3	7	29	77	81
Japan	127,285,000	873	78.9	10	9	0.1%	1	3	42	78	84
Jordan	5,535,000	160	78.7	24	3	2.1%	3	19	22	75	81
Kazakhstan	16,780,000	16	55.8	18	11	0.8%	2	59	28	58	69
Korea, North	22,585,000	485	60.5	18	7	1.1%	2	26	31	68	74
Korea, South	48,450,000	1,264	82.5	13	6	0.7%	2	7	33	72	79
Kuwait	2,220,000	323	96.1	22	2	1.9%	3	11	26	76	78

CONTINENT/Country	Population Estimate 2004	Pop. Per Sq. Mile 2004	Percent Urban[1] 2001	Crude Birth Rate per 1,000[2] 2003	Crude Death Rate per 1,000[2] 2003	Natural Increase Percent[2] 2003	Fertility Rate (Children born/Woman)[3] 2003	Infant Mortality Rate per 1,000[3] 2003	Median Age[2] 2002	Life Expectancy Male[2] 2003	Life Expectancy Female[2] 2003
Kyrgyzstan	4,930,000	64	34.3	26	9	1.7%	3	75	23	59	68
Laos	5,995,000	66	19.7	37	12	2.5%	5	89	19	52	56
Lebanon	3,755,000	935	90.1	20	6	1.3%	2	26	26	70	75
Malaysia	23,310,000	183	58.1	24	5	1.9%	3	19	24	69	75
Mongolia	2,730,000	5	56.6	21	7	1.4%	2	57	24	62	66
Myanmar	42,620,000	163	28.1	19	12	0.7%	2	70	25	54	58
Nepal	26,770,000	471	12.2	32	10	2.3%	4	71	20	59	59
Oman	2,855,000	24	76.5	37	4	3.4%	6	21	19	70	75
Pakistan	152,210,000	448	33.4	30	9	2.1%	4	77	20	61	63
Philippines	85,430,000	738	59.4	26	6	2.1%	3	25	22	66	72
Qatar	830,000	188	92.9	16	4	1.1%	3	20	31	71	76
Saudi Arabia	24,690,000	30	86.7	37	6	3.1%	6	48	19	67	71
Singapore	4,685,000	17,746	100.0	13	4	0.8%	1	4	35	77	84
Sri Lanka	19,825,000	783	23.1	16	6	1.0%	2	15	29	70	75
Syria	17,900,000	249	51.8	30	5	2.5%	4	32	20	68	71
Taiwan	22,675,000	1,631	[5]	13	6	0.7%	2	7	33	74	80
Tajikistan	6,935,000	126	27.7	33	8	2.4%	4	113	19	61	68
Thailand	64,570,000	326	20.0	16	7	1.0%	2	22	30	69	74
Turkey	68,505,000	226	66.2	18	6	1.2%	2	44	27	69	74
Turkmenistan	4,820,000	26	44.9	28	9	1.9%	4	73	21	58	65
United Arab Emirates	2,505,000	78	87.2	18	4	1.4%	3	16	28	72	77
Uzbekistan	26,195,000	152	36.6	26	8	1.8%	3	72	22	61	68
Vietnam	82,150,000	641	24.5	20	6	1.3%	2	31	25	68	73
Yemen	19,680,000	97	25.0	43	9	3.4%	7	65	16	59	63
AFRICA											
Algeria	33,090,000	36	57.7	22	5	1.7%	3	38	23	69	72
Angola	10,875,000	23	34.9	46	26	2.0%	6	194	18	36	38
Benin	7,145,000	164	43.0	43	14	3.0%	6	87	16	50	52
Botswana	1,570,000	7	49.4	26	31	-0.6%	3	67	19	32	32
Burkina Faso	13,400,000	127	16.9	45	19	2.6%	6	100	17	43	46
Burundi	6,165,000	574	9.3	40	18	2.2%	6	72	16	43	44
Cameroon	15,905,000	87	49.7	35	15	2.0%	5	70	18	47	49
Cape Verde	415,000	267	63.5	27	7	2.0%	4	51	19	67	73
Central African Republic	3,715,000	15	41.7	36	20	1.6%	5	93	18	40	43
Chad	9,395,000	19	24.1	47	16	3.1%	6	96	16	47	50
Comoros	640,000	742	33.8	39	9	3.0%	5	80	19	59	64
Congo	2,975,000	23	66.1	29	14	1.5%	4	95	20	49	51
Congo, Democratic Republic of the	57,445,000	63	30.7	45	15	3.0%	7	97	16	47	51
Cote d'Ivoire	17,145,000	138	44.0	40	18	2.2%	6	98	17	40	45
Djibouti	460,000	51	84.2	41	19	2.1%	6	107	18	42	44
Egypt	75,420,000	195	42.7	24	5	1.9%	3	35	23	68	73
Equatorial Guinea	515,000	48	49.3	37	13	2.4%	5	89	19	53	57
Eritrea	4,390,000	97	19.1	39	13	2.6%	6	76	18	51	55
Ethiopia	67,210,000	158	15.9	40	20	2.0%	6	103	17	40	42
Gabon	1,340,000	13	82.3	37	11	2.5%	5	55	19	55	59
Gambia, The	1,525,000	370	31.3	41	12	2.8%	6	75	17	52	56
Ghana	20,615,000	224	36.4	26	11	1.5%	3	53	20	56	57
Guinea	9,135,000	96	27.9	43	16	2.7%	6	93	18	48	51
Guinea-Bissau	1,375,000	99	32.3	38	17	2.2%	5	110	19	45	49
Kenya	31,840,000	142	34.4	29	16	1.3%	3	63	18	45	45
Lesotho	1,865,000	159	28.8	27	25	0.3%	4	86	20	37	37
Liberia	3,345,000	78	45.5	45	18	2.7%	6	132	18	47	49
Libya	5,565,000	8	88.0	27	3	2.4%	3	27	22	74	78
Madagascar	17,235,000	76	30.1	42	12	3.0%	6	80	17	54	59
Malawi	11,780,000	258	15.1	45	23	2.2%	6	105	16	38	38
Mali	11,790,000	25	30.9	48	19	2.9%	7	119	16	45	46
Mauritania	2,955,000	7	59.1	42	13	2.9%	6	74	17	50	54
Mauritius	1,215,000	1,542	41.6	16	7	0.9%	2	16	30	68	76
Morocco	31,950,000	185	56.1	23	6	1.7%	3	45	23	68	72
Mozambique	18,695,000	60	33.3	37	23	1.4%	5	138	19	39	37
Namibia	1,940,000	6	31.4	34	19	1.5%	5	68	18	44	41
Niger	11,210,000	23	21.1	50	22	2.8%	7	124	16	42	42
Nigeria	135,570,000	380	44.9	39	14	2.5%	5	71	18	51	51
Rwanda	7,880,000	775	6.3	40	22	1.8%	6	103	18	39	40
Sao Tome and Principe	180,000	484	47.7	42	7	3.5%	6	46	16	65	68
Senegal	10,715,000	141	48.2	36	11	2.5%	5	58	18	55	58
Sierra Leone	5,815,000	210	37.3	44	21	2.3%	6	147	18	40	45
Somalia	8,165,000	33	27.9	46	18	2.9%	7	120	18	46	49
South Africa	42,770,000	91	57.7	19	18	0%	2	61	25	47	47
Sudan	38,630,000	40	37.1	36	10	2.7%	5	66	18	57	59
Swaziland	1,165,000	174	26.7	29	21	0.8%	4	67	19	41	38
Tanzania	36,230,000	99	33.3	40	17	2.2%	5	104	18	43	46
Togo	5,495,000	251	33.9	35	12	2.4%	5	69	17	51	55
Tunisia	9,980,000	158	66.2	17	5	1.2%	2	27	26	73	76
Uganda	26,010,000	279	14.5	47	17	3.0%	7	88	15	43	46
Zambia	10,385,000	36	39.8	40	24	1.5%	5	99	17	35	35
Zimbabwe	12,630,000	84	36.0	30	22	0.8%	4	66	19	40	38
OCEANIA											
Australia	19,825,000	7	91.2	13	7	0.5%	2	5	36	77	83
Fiji	875,000	124	50.2	23	6	1.7%	3	13	24	66	71
Kiribati	100,000	319	38.6	31	9	2.3%	4	51	20	58	64
Micronesia, Federated States of	110,000	406	28.6	26	5	2.1%	4	32	19[4]	67	71
New Zealand	3,975,000	38	85.9	14	8	0.7%	2	6	33	75	81
Papua New Guinea	5,360,000	30	17.6	31	8	2.3%	4	55	21	62	66
Samoa	180,000	165	22.3	15	6	0.9%	3	30	24	67	73
Solomon Islands	515,000	47	20.2	32	4	2.8%	4	23	18	70	75
Tonga	110,000	438	33.0	25	6	1.9%	3	13	20	66	71
Vanuatu	200,000	42	22.1	24	8	1.6%	3	58	22	60	63

This table presents data for most independent nations having an area greater than 200 square miles
(1) Source: United Nations World Urbanization Prospects
(2) Source: United States Census Bureau International Database
(3) Source: United States Central Intelligence Agency World Factbook
(4) 2000 Census preliminary count from www.fsmgov.org/info/people.html
(5) Data for Taiwan is included with China

WORLD AGRICULTURE TABLE

	Agricultural Area 2001					Average Production 1999-2001			Average 1999-2001		
CONTINENT/Country	Total Area Sq. Miles	Cropland Area[1] Sq. Miles	Cropland Area[1] %	Pasture Area[1] Sq. Miles	Pasture Area[1] %	Wheat[1] 1,000 metric tons	Rice[1] 1,000 metric tons	Corn[1] 1,000 metric tons	Cattle[1] 1,000	Pigs[1] 1,000	Sheep[1] 1,000
NORTH AMERICA											
Bahamas	5,382	46	0.9%	8	0.1%	-	-	-	1	5	6
Belize	8,867	402	4.5%	193	2.2%	-	12	36	52	25	4
Canada	3,855,103	177,144	4.6%	111,970	2.9%	24,676	-	8,168	13,340	12,970	819
Costa Rica	19,730	2,027	10.3%	9,035	45.8%	-	267	20	1,358	438	3
Cuba	42,804	17,239	40.3%	8,494	19.8%	-	342	207	4,305	2,600	310
Dominica	290	77	26.6%	8	2.7%	-	-	-	13	5	8
Dominican Republic	18,730	6,162	32.9%	8,108	43.3%	-	615	30	2,026	548	106
El Salvador	8,124	3,314	45.2%	3,066	37.7%	-	47	605	1,190	195	5
Guatemala	42,042	7,355	17.5%	10,046	23.9%	9	46	1,057	2,500	1,417	170
Haiti	10,714	4,247	39.6%	1,892	17.7%	-	111	211	1,390	934	147
Honduras	43,277	7,707	12.7%	5,822	13.5%	1	9	509	1,737	474	14
Jamaica	4,244	1,097	25.8%	884	20.0%	-	-	7	400	180	1
Mexico	758,452	105,406	13.9%	308,882	40.7%	3,263	324	18,466	30,428	16,112	6,048
Nicaragua	50,054	8,382	16.7%	18,591	37.1%	-	234	374	2,008	402	4
Panama	29,157	2,683	9.2%	5,927	20.3%	-	237	71	1,348	279	-
St. Lucia	238	69	29.2%	8	3.2%	-	-	-	12	15	13
Trinidad and Tobago	1,980	471	23.8%	42	2.1%	-	13	5	36	41	12
United States	3,794,083	684,401	18.0%	903,479	23.8%	58,862	9,222	244,296	98,197	60,229	7,071
SOUTH AMERICA											
Argentina	1,073,519	135,136	12.6%	548,265	51.1%	15,642	1,140	15,217	49,299	4,200	13,588
Bolivia	424,165	11,973	2.8%	130,618	30.8%	121	281	607	6,715	2,786	8,743
Brazil	3,300,172	256,623	7.8%	760,621	23.0%	2,461	10,998	35,119	170,295	30,608	14,728
Chile	291,930	8,880	3.0%	49,942	17.1%	1,490	113	685	4,117	2,395	4,153
Colombia	439,737	16,405	3.7%	161,391	36.7%	37	2,262	1,128	25,274	2,726	2,247
Ecuador	109,484	11,525	10.5%	19,653	18.0%	19	1,340	483	5,261	2,654	2,214
Guyana	83,000	1,969	2.4%	4,749	5.7%	-	560	3	220	20	130
Paraguay	157,048	12,008	7.6%	83,784	53.3%	256	112	804	9,758	2,633	402
Peru	496,225	16,255	3.3%	104,634	21.1%	180	1,963	1,205	4,936	2,795	14,414
Suriname	63,037	259	0.4%	81	0.1%	-	178	-	128	22	8
Uruguay	67,574	5,174	7.7%	52,290	77.4%	284	1,189	190	10,446	375	13,257
Venezuela	352,145	13,158	3.7%	70,425	20.0%	1	696	1,547	14,620	5,555	780
EUROPE											
Albania	11,100	2,699	24.3%	1,699	15.3%	298	-	203	719	96	1,929
Austria	32,378	5,676	17.5%	7,413	22.9%	1,412	-	1,774	2,166	3,556	357
Belarus	80,155	24,151	30.1%	11,564	14.4%	903	-	13	4,411	3,565	96
Belgium	11,787	3,344[2]	26.2%[2]	2,618[2]	20.5%[2]	1,535	-	420	3,165	7,462	150
Bosnia and Herzegovina	19,767	3,243	16.4%	4,633	23.4%	289	-	656	448	345	645
Bulgaria	42,855	17,900	41.8%	6,236	14.6%	3,071	8	1,137	664	1,459	2,536
Croatia	21,829	6,124	28.1%	6,035	27.6%	852	-	1,958	435	1,276	519
Czech Republic	30,450	12,788	42.0%	3,730	12.2%	4,196	-	324	1,604	3,761	87
Denmark	16,640	8,880	53.4%	1,452	8.7%	4,683	-	-	1,887	12,052	147
Estonia	17,462	2,691	15.4%	745	4.3%	123	-	-	276	304	29
Finland	130,559	8,490	6.5%	77	0.1%	427	-	-	1,060	1,303	101
France	208,482	75,618	36.3%	38,788	18.6%	35,327	110	15,928	20,377	14,693	9,754
Germany	137,847	46,409	33.7%	19,355	14.0%	21,358	-	3,362	14,723	26,021	2,746
Greece	50,949	14,873	29.2%	17,954	35.2%	2,111	153	2,007	584	925	8,977
Hungary	35,919	18,548	51.6%	4,097	11.4%	3,843	9	6,664	845	5,216	991
Iceland	39,769	27	0.1%	8,780	22.1%	-	-	-	72	44	477
Ireland	27,133	4,050	14.9%	12,934	47.7%	688	-	-	6,613	1,765	5,311
Italy	116,342	42,379	36.4%	16,907	14.5%	7,239	1,310	10,222	7,167	8,356	11,000
Latvia	24,942	7,220	28.9%	2,355	9.4%	410	-	-	393	407	28
Lithuania	25,213	11,541	45.8%	1,923	7.6%	1,062	-	-	856	984	14
Luxembourg	999	[3]	[3]	[3]	[3]	-	-	2	134	-	-
Macedonia	9,928	2,363	23.8%	2,432	24.5%	308	20	135	267	209	1,285
Moldova	13,070	8,398	64.3%	1,483	11.3%	902	-	1,096	423	646	929
Netherlands	16,164	3,622	22.4%	3,834	23.7%	995	-	148	4,108	13,253	1,335
Norway	125,050	3,398	2.7%	625	0.5%	265	-	-	1,017	414	2,342
Poland	120,728	55,267	45.8%	15,745	13.0%	8,946	-	962	6,124	17,588	366
Portugal	35,516	10,444	29.4%	5,548	15.6%	295	146	907	1,415	2,346	4,337
Romania	91,699	38,305	41.8%	19,039	20.8%	5,610	3	8,317	3,021	5,946	8,062
Serbia and Montenegro	39,449	14,394	36.5%	7,197	18.2%	2,207	-	5,013	1,550	4,012	1,853
Slovakia	18,924	6,085	32.2%	3,375	17.8%	1,445	-	612	671	1,548	344
Slovenia	7,821	784	10.0%	1,185	15.2%	153	-	283	473	585	80
Spain	194,885	69,298	35.6%	44,209	22.7%	5,785	844	4,208	6,140	22,079	24,185
Sweden	173,732	10,413	6.0%	1,726	1.0%	2,135	-	-	1,683	1,975	440
Switzerland	15,943	1,683	10.6%	4,417	27.7%	535	-	214	1,603	1,499	421
Ukraine	233,090	129,321	55.5%	30,541	13.1%	15,043	74	3,075	10,591	9,270	1,074
United Kingdom	93,788	22,019	23.5%	43,440	46.3%	14,380	-	-	11,052	6,537	41,205
Russia	6,592,849	485,400	7.4%	351,905	5.3%	37,455	509	1,133	27,936	17,076	12,954
ASIA											
Afghanistan	251,773	31,097	12.4%	115,831	46.0%	1,821	205	172	2,600	-	12,762
Armenia	11,506	2,162	18.8%	3,089	26.8%	211	-	9	478	75	515
Azerbaijan	33,437	7,471	22.3%	10,039	30.0%	1,172	19	107	1,965	21	5,321
Bahrain	267	23	8.7%	15	5.8%	-	-	-	12	-	17
Bangladesh	55,598	32,761	58.9%	2,317	4.2%	1,807	36,909	8	23,817	-	1,128
Brunei	2,226	27	1.2%	23	1.0%	-	-	-	2	6	2
Cambodia	69,898	14,699	21.0%	5,792	8.3%	-	4,035	146	2,896	2,079	-
China	3,690,045	599,520[4]	16.2%[4]	1,544,412[4]	41.9%[4]	102,463[4]	189,840[4]	116,240[4]	104,179[4]	440,384[4]	130,536[4]
Cyprus	3,572	436	12.2%	15	0.4%	12	-	-	55	419	240
East Timor	5,743	309	5.4%	579	10.1%	-	33	93	173	300	36
Georgia	26,911	4,104	15.3%	7,490	27.8%	207	-	358	1,117	433	541
India	1,222,510	655,987	53.7%	42,124	3.4%	72,140	132,818	12,285	217,773	17,000	57,900
Indonesia	735,310	129,730	17.6%	43,155	5.9%	-	50,953	9,409	11,370	6,098	7,316
Iran	636,372	63,892	10.0%	169,885	26.7%	8,740	2,103	1,113	8,273	-	53,900
Iraq	169,235	23,514	13.9%	15,444	9.1%	667	110	73	1,342	-	6,770
Israel	8,019	1,637	20.4%	548	6.8%	94	-	73	393	138	373
Japan	145,850	18,510	12.7%	1,564	1.1%	657	11,551	-	4,592	9,823	11
Jordan	34,495	1,544	4.5%	2,865	8.3%	18	-	13	66	-	1,900
Kazakhstan	1,049,156	83,672	8.0%	714,667	68.1%	10,938	225	256	4,021	984	8,785
Korea, North	46,540	10,811	23.2%	193	0.4%	98	2,031	1,253	575	3,076	186
Korea, South	38,328	7,293	19.0%	208	0.5%	4	7,204	67	2,191	8,266	1
Kuwait	6,880	58	0.8%	525	7.6%	-	-	-	19	-	543

CONTINENT/Country	Agricultural Area 2001 Total Area Sq. Miles	Cropland Area(1) Sq. Miles	Cropland Area(1) %	Pasture Area(1) Sq. Miles	Pasture Area(1) %	Average Production 1999-2001 Wheat(1) 1,000 metric tons	Rice(1) 1,000 metric tons	Corn(1) 1,000 metric tons	Average 1999-2001 Cattle(1) 1,000	Pigs(1) 1,000	Sheep(1) 1,000
Kyrgyzstan	77,182	5,664	7.3%	35,873	46.5%	1,113	17	363	942	98	3,101
Laos	91,429	3,699	4.0%	3,390	3.7%	-	2,213	108	1,106	1,390	-
Lebanon	4,016	1,208	30.1%	62	1.5%	60	-	4	76	63	354
Malaysia	127,320	29,286	23.0%	1,100	0.9%	-	2,170	63	744	1,943	167
Mongolia	604,829	4,633	0.8%	499,230	82.5%	148	-	-	2,997	17	14,587
Myanmar	261,228	41,023	15.7%	1,212	0.5%	105	20,683	413	10,974	3,923	390
Nepal	56,827	12,324	21.7%	6,784	11.9%	1,143	4,137	1,528	7,012	872	852
Oman	119,499	313	0.3%	3,861	3.2%	1	-	-	299	-	342
Pakistan	339,732	85,560	25.2%	19,305	5.7%	19,319	6,920	1,653	22,007	-	24,067
Philippines	115,831	41,120	35.5%	4,942	4.3%	-	12,377	4,540	2,467	10,724	30
Qatar	4,412	81	1.8%	193	4.4%	-	-	1	15	-	214
Saudi Arabia	830,000	14,649	1.8%	656,373	79.1%	1,871	-	5	304	-	7,848
Singapore	264	4	1.5%	-	0.0%	*	-	-	-	190	-
Sri Lanka	25,332	7,378	29.1%	1,699	6.7%	-	2,804	30	1,580	71	12
Syria	71,498	21,043	29.4%	31,942	44.7%	3,514	-	106	955	*	13,288
Taiwan	13,901	(5)	(5)	(5)	(5)	(5)	(5)	(5)	(5)	(5)	(5)
Tajikistan	55,251	4,093	7.4%	13,514	24.5%	375	67	38	1,045	1	1,481
Thailand	198,115	70,657	35.7%	3,089	1.6%	1	25,578	4,405	4,973	6,539	40
Turkey	302,541	101,757	33.6%	47,792	15.8%	19,341	350	2,266	10,949	4	29,394
Turkmenistan	188,457	7,008	3.7%	118,533	62.9%	1,472	33	9	863	46	5,750
United Arab Emirates	32,278	919	2.8%	1,178	3.6%	-	-	-	94	-	504
Uzbekistan	172,742	18,649	10.8%	88,031	51.0%	3,637	219	133	5,279	83	7,980
Vietnam	128,066	32,579	25.4%	2,479	1.9%	-	31,964	1,961	4,029	20,273	-
Yemen	203,850	6,158	3.0%	62,027	30.4%	145	-	48	1,320	-	4,758
AFRICA											
Algeria	919,595	31,861	3.5%	122,780	13.4%	1,414	-	1	1,667	6	19,000
Angola	481,354	12,741	2.6%	208,495	43.3%	4	16	417	3,995	800	345
Benin	43,484	8,745	20.1%	2,124	4.9%	-	46	740	1,486	463	650
Botswana	224,607	1,440	0.6%	98,842	44.0%	1	-	8	2,035	6	347
Burkina Faso	105,869	15,444	14.6%	23,166	21.9%	-	102	500	4,767	621	6,722
Burundi	10,745	4,865	45.3%	3,610	33.6%	7	57	124	321	67	215
Cameroon	183,568	27,645	15.1%	7,722	4.2%	-	69	759	5,761	1,232	3,734
Cape Verde	1,557	158	10.2%	97	6.2%	-	-	27	22	195	9
Central African Republic	240,536	7,799	3.2%	12,066	5.0%	-	23	101	3,096	669	218
Chad	495,755	14,016	2.8%	173,746	35.0%	3	114	88	5,852	22	2,374
Comoros	863	510	59.1%	58	6.7%	-	17	4	51	-	21
Congo	132,047	849	0.6%	38,610	29.2%	-	1	5	87	46	102
Congo, Democratic Republic of the	905,446	30,425	3.4%	57,915	6.4%	9	338	1,184	823	1,050	925
Cote d'Ivoire	124,504	28,958	23.3%	50,193	40.3%	-	1,217	693	1,398	333	1,439
Djibouti	8,958	4	0.0%	5,019	56.0%	-	-	-	269	-	465
Egypt	386,662	12,888	3.3%	-	0.0%	6,388	5,681	6,487	3,583	29	4,510
Equatorial Guinea	10,831	888	8.2%	402	3.7%	-	-	-	5	6	37
Eritrea	45,406	1,942	4.3%	26,900	59.2%	32	-	13	2,150	-	1,570
Ethiopia	426,373	44,255	10.4%	77,220	18.1%	1,340	-	2,938	35,025	25	22,333
Gabon	103,347	1,911	1.8%	18,012	17.4%	-	1	26	36	213	197
Gambia, The	4,127	985	23.9%	1,772	42.9%	-	28	24	350	12	115
Ghana	92,098	22,780	24.7%	32,240	35.0%	-	244	988	1,297	327	2,715
Guinea	94,926	5,888	6.2%	41,313	43.5%	-	830	96	2,576	93	824
Guinea-Bissau	13,948	2,116	15.2%	4,170	29.9%	-	95	26	509	347	283
Kenya	224,961	19,923	8.9%	82,240	36.6%	184	58	2,419	13,229	311	7,000
Lesotho	11,720	1,290	11.0%	7,722	65.9%	39	-	128	547	63	839
Liberia	43,000	2,317	5.4%	7,722	18.0%	-	188	-	36	127	210
Libya	679,362	8,301	1.2%	51,352	7.6%	128	-	-	207	-	5,100
Madagascar	226,658	13,707	6.0%	92,664	40.9%	9	2,412	175	10,339	1,267	793
Malawi	45,747	9,035	19.7%	7,143	15.6%	2	86	2,190	741	450	110
Mali	478,841	18,147	3.8%	115,831	24.2%	8	801	378	6,594	72	6,282
Mauritania	397,956	1,931	0.5%	151,545	38.1%	-	65	7	1,470	-	7,437
Mauritius	788	409	51.9%	27	3.4%	-	-	-	27	12	10
Morocco	172,414	37,529	21.8%	81,081	47.0%	2,284	33	95	2,629	8	17,059
Mozambique	309,496	16,351	5.3%	169,885	54.9%	1	168	1,136	1,317	179	125
Namibia	317,818	3,166	1.0%	146,719	46.2%	4	-	26	2,436	21	2,330
Niger	489,192	17,375	3.6%	46,332	9.5%	10	66	5	2,217	39	4,386
Nigeria	356,669	120,464	33.8%	151,352	42.4%	75	3,109	4,734	19,677	5,000	20,833
Rwanda	10,169	5,019	49.4%	2,124	20.9%	6	13	66	766	172	264
Sao Tome and Principe	372	205	55.0%	4	1.0%	-	-	-	4	2	3
Senegal	75,951	9,653	12.7%	21,815	28.7%	-	229	84	3,076	263	4,619
Sierra Leone	27,699	2,178	7.9%	8,494	30.7%	-	215	9	413	52	365
Somalia	246,201	4,135	1.7%	166,024	67.4%	1	2	188	5,133	4	13,100
South Africa	470,693	60,664	12.9%	324,048	68.8%	2,200	3	9,147	13,594	1,542	28,677
Sudan	967,500	64,298	6.6%	452,434	46.8%	230	8	48	37,081	-	45,980
Swaziland	6,704	734	10.9%	4,633	69.1%	-	-	94	613	32	27
Tanzania	364,900	19,112	5.2%	135,136	37.0%	87	509	2,567	17,350	449	3,513
Togo	21,925	10,154	46.3%	3,861	17.6%	-	69	480	277	287	1,528
Tunisia	63,170	18,954	30.0%	15,792	25.0%	1,111	-	-	760	6	6,862
Uganda	93,065	27,799	29.9%	19,738	21.2%	12	106	1,108	5,977	1,540	1,065
Zambia	290,586	20,386	7.0%	115,831	39.9%	80	11	768	2,709	324	137
Zimbabwe	150,873	12,934	8.6%	66,410	44.0%	282	-	1,698	5,840	494	602
OCEANIA											
Australia	2,969,910	195,368	6.6%	1,563,327	52.6%	23,654	1,417	363	27,645	2,607	116,736
Fiji	7,056	1,100	15.6%	676	9.6%	-	16	1	335	139	7
Kiribati	313	151	48.1%	-	0.0%	-	-	-	-	10	-
Micronesia, Federated States of	271	139	51.3%	42	15.7%	-	-	-	14	32	-
New Zealand	104,454	13,019	12.5%	53,525	51.2%	337	-	185	9,025	364	45,114
Papua New Guinea	178,704	3,320	1.9%	676	0.4%	-	1	7	87	1,583	6
Samoa	1,093	498	45.6%	8	0.7%	-	-	-	28	179	-
Solomon Islands	10,954	286	2.6%	154	1.4%	-	5	-	11	63	-
Tonga	251	185	73.8%	15	6.2%	-	-	-	11	81	-
Vanuatu	4,707	463	9.8%	162	3.4%	-	-	1	151	62	-

This table presents data for most independent nations having an area greater than 200 square miles
- Zero, insignificant, or not available
(1) Source: United Nations Food and Agriculture Organization
(2) Includes data for Luxembourg
(3) Data for Luxembourg is included with Belgium
(4) Includes data for Taiwan
(5) Data for Taiwan is included with China

WORLD ECONOMIC TABLE

CONTINENT/Country	GDP 2002		Trade		Commercial Energy Production Avg. 2000[2]					Average Production 1999-2001 in Metric Tons			
	Total GDP[1]	GDP Per Capita[1]	Value of Exports[1]	Value of Imports[1]	Total (1,000 Metric Tons of Coal Equiv.)	Solid %	Liquid %	Gas %	Hydro & Nuclear %	Coal[3]	Petroleum[3]	Iron Ore[4]	Bauxite[4]
NORTH AMERICA													
Bahamas	$4,590,000,000	$17,000	$560,700,000	$1,860,000,000	-	-	-	-	-	-	-	-	-
Belize	$1,280,000,000	$4,900	$290,000,000	$430,000,000	12	-	-	-	100%	-	-	-	-
Canada	$934,100,000,000	$29,400	$260,500,000,000	$229,000,000,000	507,218	10%	33%	43%	14%	70,711,084	97,834,913	20,527,000	-
Costa Rica	$32,000,000,000	$8,500	$5,100,000,000	$6,400,000,000	1,937	-	-	-	100%	-	-	-	-
Cuba	$30,690,000,000	$2,300	$1,800,000,000	$4,800,000,000	4,626	-	83%	17%	-	-	2,134,520	-	-
Dominica	$380,000,000	$5,400	$50,000,000	$135,000,000	4	-	-	-	100%	-	-	-	-
Dominican Republic	$53,780,000,000	$6,100	$5,300,000,000	$8,700,000,000	115	-	-	-	100%	-	-	-	-
El Salvador	$29,110,000,000	$4,700	$3,000,000,000	$4,900,000,000	1,110	-	-	-	100%	-	-	-	-
Guatemala	$53,200,000,000	$3,700	$2,700,000,000	$5,600,000,000	1,822	-	81%	1%	18%	-	1,076,320	5,000	
Haiti	$10,600,000,000	$1,700	$298,000,000	$1,140,000,000	33	-	-	-	100%	-	-	-	-
Honduras	$16,290,000,000	$2,600	$1,300,000,000	$2,700,000,000	347	-	-	-	100%	-	-	-	-
Jamaica	$10,080,000,000	$3,900	$1,400,000,000	[illegible]	18	-	-	-	100%	-	-	-	11,728,000
Mexico	$924,400,000,000	$9,000	$158,400,000,000	$160,400,000,000	340,594	1%	79%	16%	4%	11,097,943	150,165,451	6,860,000	-
Nicaragua	$11,160,000,000	$2,500	$637,000,000	$1,700,000,000	706	-	-	-	100%	-	-	-	-
Panama	$18,060,000,000	$6,000	$5,800,000,000	$6,700,000,000	418	-	-	-	100%	-	-	-	-
St. Lucia	$866,000,000	$5,400	$68,300,000	$319,400,000	-	-	-	-	-	-	-	-	-
Trinidad and Tobago	$11,070,000,000	$9,500	$4,200,000,000	$3,800,000,000	22,768	-	39%	61%	-	-	5,964,991	-	-
United States	$10,450,000,000,000	$37,600	$733,900,000,000	$1,194,100,000,000	2,342,228	33%	22%	30%	14%	996,498,186	289,640,487	35,178,000	-
SOUTH AMERICA													
Argentina	$403,800,000,000	$10,200	$25,300,000,000	$9,000,000,000	118,739	-	50%	45%	5%	260,299	38,783,798	-	-
Bolivia	$21,150,000,000	$2,500	$1,300,000,000	$1,600,000,000	7,732	-	33%	64%	3%	-	1,599,401	-	-
Brazil	$1,376,000,000,000	$7,600	$59,400,000,000	$46,200,000,000	143,640	3%	63%	6%	28%	4,446,477	61,155,586	124,667,000	13,654,000
Chile	$156,100,000,000	$10,000	$17,800,000,000	$15,600,000,000	6,180	6%	11%	45%	38%	475,484	349,201	5,523,000	-
Colombia	$251,600,000,000	$6,500	$12,900,000,000	$12,500,000,000	99,513	36%	52%	9%	4%	38,112,136	34,896,672	348,000	-
Ecuador	$42,650,000,000	$3,100	$4,900,000,000	$6,000,000,000	32,171	-	94%	3%	3%	-	19,520,185	-	-
Guyana	$2,628,000,000	$4,000	$500,000,000	$575,000,000	1	-	-	-	100%	-	-	-	2,272,000
Paraguay	$25,190,000,000	$4,200	$2,000,000,000	$2,400,000,000	6,577	-	-	-	100%	-	-	-	-
Peru	$138,800,000,000	$4,800	$7,600,000,000	$7,300,000,000	10,933	-	73%	9%	18%	52,297	4,932,561	2,701,000	-
Suriname	$1,469,000,000	$3,500	$445,000,000	$300,000,000	1,022	-	84%	-	16%	-	496,400	-	3,946,000
Uruguay	$26,820,000,000	$7,800	$2,100,000,000	$1,870,000,000	867	-	-	-	100%	-	-	-	-
Venezuela	$131,700,000,000	$5,500	$28,600,000,000	$18,800,000,000	311,899	3%	81%	14%	2%	7,482,998	146,621,238	10,497,000	4,309,000
EUROPE													
Albania	$15,690,000,000	$4,500	$340,000,000	$1,500,000,000	1,089	1%	42%	2%	55%	32,666	284,321	-	-
Austria	$227,700,000,000	$27,700	$70,000,000,000	$74,000,000,000	9,611	5%	15%	24%	56%	1,197,660	921,120	525,000	-
Belarus	$90,190,000,000	$8,200	$7,700,000,000	$8,800,000,000	3,644	18%	73%	9%	-	-	1,830,872	-	-
Belgium	$299,700,000,000	$29,000	$162,000,000,000	$152,000,000,000	18,451	2%	-	-	98%	318,998	-	-	-
Bosnia and Herzegovina	$7,300,000,000	$1,900	$1,150,000,000	$2,800,000,000	6,553	90%	-	-	10%	8,414,623	-	50,000	75,000
Bulgaria	$49,230,000,000	$6,600	$5,300,000,000	$6,900,000,000	13,500	46%	-	-	53%	28,841,963	37,048	310,000	-
Croatia	$43,120,000,000	$8,800	$4,900,000,000	$10,700,000,000	4,962	-	42%	43%	15%	5,104	1,191,360	-	-
Czech Republic	$157,100,000,000	$15,300	$40,800,000,000	$43,200,000,000	39,843	85%	1%	1%	14%	63,466,671	283,097	-	-
Denmark	$155,300,000,000	$29,000	$56,300,000,000	$47,900,000,000	36,502	-	70%	29%	2%	-	16,701,163	-	-
Estonia	$15,520,000,000	$10,900	$3,400,000,000	$4,400,000,000	3,892	100%	-	-	-	-	-	-	-
Finland	$133,800,000,000	$26,200	$40,100,000,000	$31,800,000,000	11,933	15%	-	-	85%	-	-	-	-
France	$1,558,000,000,000	$25,700	$307,800,000,000	$303,700,000,000	175,306	2%	4%	1%	93%	3,616,981	1,446,228	12,000	-
Germany	$2,160,000,000,000	$26,600	$608,000,000,000	$487,300,000,000	181,697	47%	2%	13%	38%	204,685,080	3,044,206	5,000	-
Greece	$203,300,000,000	$19,000	$12,600,000,000	$31,400,000,000	12,988	92%	3%	1%	4%	64,503,999	166,807	583,000	1,975,000
Hungary	$134,000,000,000	$13,300	$31,400,000,000	$33,900,000,000	16,319	25%	19%	24%	32%	14,796,257	1,301,710	-	994,000
Iceland	$8,444,000,000	$25,000	$2,300,000,000	$2,100,000,000	1,638	-	-	-	100%	-	-	-	-
Ireland	$113,700,000,000	$30,500	$86,600,000,000	$48,600,000,000	3,232	47%	-	47%	6%	-	-	-	-
Italy	$1,455,000,000,000	$25,000	$259,200,000,000	$238,200,000,000	40,332	-	16%	54%	30%	47,666	4,144,278	-	-
Latvia	$20,990,000,000	$8,300	$2,300,000,000	$3,900,000,000	369	6%	-	-	94%	-	-	-	-
Lithuania	$30,080,000,000	$8,400	$5,400,000,000	$6,800,000,000	3,677	-	12%	-	87%	-	251,824	-	-
Luxembourg	$21,940,000,000	$44,000	$10,100,000,000	$13,250,000,000	113	-	-	-	100%	-	-	-	-
Macedonia	$10,570,000,000	$5,000	$1,100,000,000	$1,900,000,000	3,038	95%	-	-	5%	7,463,628	-	9,000	-
Moldova	$11,510,000,000	$2,500	$590,000,000	$980,000,000	7	-	-	-	100%	-	-	-	-
Netherlands	$437,800,000,000	$26,900	$243,300,000,000	$201,100,000,000	87,974	-	4%	94%	2%	-	1,437,293	-	-
Norway	$149,100,000,000	$31,800	$68,200,000,000	$37,300,000,000	324,396	-	72%	22%	5%	847,996	154,419,533	355,000	-
Poland	$373,200,000,000	$9,500	$32,400,000,000	$43,400,000,000	108,277	94%	1%	5%	-	164,737,813	645,072	-	-
Portugal	$195,200,000,000	$18,000	$25,900,000,000	$39,000,000,000	1,560	-	-	-	100%	-	-	6,000	-
Romania	$169,300,000,000	$7,400	$13,700,000,000	$16,700,000,000	37,598	19%	24%	46%	10%	27,392,191	6,038,110	24,000	-
Serbia and Montenegro	$23,150,000,000	$2,370	$2,400,000,000	$6,300,000,000	14,188	74%	8%	8%	10%	34,480,488	810,787	10,000	580,000
Slovakia	$67,340,000,000	$12,200	$12,900,000,000	$15,400,000,000	8,813	17%	1%	2%	79%	3,606,648	48,134	200,000	-
Slovenia	$37,060,000,000	$18,000	$10,300,000,000	$11,100,000,000	3,644	38%	-	-	62%	4,391,644	991	-	-
Spain	$850,700,000,000	$20,700	$122,200,000,000	$156,600,000,000	40,444	28%	2%	1%	68%	23,479,212	296,665	-	-
Sweden	$230,700,000,000	$25,400	$80,600,000,000	$68,600,000,000	31,413	1%	-	-	99%	-	-	12,114,000	-
Switzerland	$233,400,000,000	$31,700	$100,300,000,000	$94,400,000,000	14,710	-	-	-	100%	-	-	-	-
Ukraine	$218,000,000,000	$4,500	$18,100,000,000	$18,000,000,000	118,973	50%	5%	20%	25%	81,998,575	3,747,936	28,933,000	-
United Kingdom	$1,528,000,000,000	$25,300	$286,300,000,000	$330,100,000,000	397,906	7%	47%	38%	8%	32,758,497	119,820,635	1,000	-
Russia	$1,409,000,000,000	$9,300	$104,600,000,000	$60,700,000,000	1,412,286	10%	33%	52%	5%	253,376,954	324,436,632	48,300,000	3,983,000
ASIA													
Afghanistan	$19,000,000,000	$700	$1,200,000,000	$1,300,000,000	195	1%	-	79%	20%	1,000	-	-	-
Armenia	$12,130,000,000	$3,800	$525,000,000	$991,000,000	901	-	-	-	100%	-	-	-	-
Azerbaijan	$28,610,000,000	$3,500	$2,000,000,000	$1,800,000,000	27,748	-	72%	27%	1%	-	14,183,985	-	-
Bahrain	$9,910,000,000	$14,000	$5,800,000,000	$4,200,000,000	14,442	-	22%	78%	-	-	1,827,397	-	-
Bangladesh	$238,200,000,000	$1,700	$6,200,000,000	$8,500,000,000	11,713	-	-	99%	1%	-	120,476	-	-
Brunei	$6,500,000,000	$18,600	$3,000,000,000	$1,400,000,000	27,922	-	49%	51%	-	-	9,435,323	-	-
Cambodia	$20,420,000,000	$1,500	$1,380,000,000	$1,730,000,000	10	-	-	-	100%	-	-	-	-
China	$5,989,000,000,000	$4,400	$658,260,000,000	$618,930,000,000	1,023,314[5]	70%[5]	23%[5]	4%[5]	3%[5]	1,251,423,183	161,226,848	72,967,000	9,000,000
Cyprus	$9,400,000,000	$15,000	$1,030,000,000	$3,900,000,000	-	-	-	-	-	-	-	-	-
East Timor	$440,000,000	$500	$8,000,000	$237,000,000	-	-	-	-	-	-	-	-	-
Georgia	$16,050,000,000	$3,100	$515,000,000	$750,000,000	963	1%	16%	8%	75%	10,000	102,258	-	-
India	$2,664,000,000,000	$2,540	$44,500,000,000	$53,800,000,000	367,807	73%	14%	8%	4%	304,842,421	32,123,682	48,080,000	7,554,000
Indonesia	$714,200,000,000	$3,100	$52,300,000,000	$32,100,000,000	279,695	27%	45%	26%	2%	79,664,587	70,565,213	282,000	1,168,000
Iran	$458,300,000,000	$7,000	$24,800,000,000	$21,800,000,000	350,729	-	77%	23%	-	1,376,993	181,632,777	5,367,000	136,000
Iraq	$58,000,000,000	$2,400	$13,000,000,000	$7,800,000,000	186,519	-	97%	3%	-	-	124,281,583	-	-
Israel	$117,400,000,000	$19,000	$28,100,000,000	$30,800,000,000	334	94%	2%	4%	1%	-	5,957	-	-
Japan	$3,651,000,000,000	$28,000	$383,800,000,000	$292,100,000,000	142,731	2%	1%	2%	95%	3,286,983	351,650	1,000	-
Jordan	$22,630,000,000	$4,300	$2,500,000,000	$4,400,000,000	316	-	1%	97%	2%	-	1,986	-	-
Kazakhstan	$120,000,000,000	$6,300	$10,300,000,000	$9,600,000,000	113,390	40%	45%	14%	1%	70,311,969	30,508,827	7,467,000	3,668,000
Korea, North	$22,260,000,000	$1,000	$842,000,000	$1,314,000,000	65,932	96%	-	-	4%	94,174,845	-	3,000,000	-
Korea, South	$941,500,000,000	$19,400	$162,600,000,000	$148,400,000,000	43,892	6%	-	-	94%	4,054,646	-	175,000	-
Kuwait	$36,850,000,000	$15,000	$16,000,000,000	$7,300,000,000	161,322	-	92%	8%	-	-	98,844,823	-	-

CONTINENT/Country	Total GDP[1]	GDP Per Capita[1]	Value of Exports[1]	Value of Imports[1]	Total (1,000 Metric Tons of Coal Equiv.)	Solid %	Liquid %	Gas %	Hydro & Nuclear %	Coal[3]	Petroleum[3]	Iron Ore[4]	Bauxite[4]
Kyrgyzstan	$13,880,000,000	$2,800	$488,000,000	$587,000,000	2,026	9%	5%	2%	83%	423,664	91,503	-	-
Laos	$10,400,000,000	$1,700	$345,000,000	$555,000,000	146	1%	-	-	99%	1,000		-	-
Lebanon	$17,610,000,000	$5,400	$1,000,000,000	$6,000,000,000	55	-	-	-	100%			-	-
Malaysia	$198,400,000,000	$9,300	$95,200,000,000	$76,800,000,000	110,069	-	41%	58%	1%	314,332	33,792,132	208,000	137,000
Mongolia	$5,060,000,000	$1,840	$501,000,000	$659,000,000	2,212	100%	-	-	-	5,099,640		-	-
Myanmar	$73,690,000,000	$1,660	$2,700,000,000	$2,500,000,000	9,297	3%	6%	88%	2%	358,331	587,374	-	-
Nepal	$37,320,000,000	$1,400	$720,000,000	$1,600,000,000	172	10%	-	-	90%	9,667		-	-
Oman	$22,400,000,000	$8,300	$10,600,000,000	$5,500,000,000	74,376	-	92%	8%	-		46,989,489	-	-
Pakistan	$295,300,000,000	$2,100	$9,800,000,000	$11,100,000,000	33,773	6%	12%	74%	7%	3,247,391	2,768,108	-	10,000
Philippines	$379,700,000,000	$4,200	$35,100,000,000	$33,500,000,000	16,244	6%	-	-	94%	1,306,993	173,128	-	-
Qatar	$15,910,000,000	$21,500	$10,900,000,000	$3,900,000,000	92,237	-	57%	43%	-		35,018,538	-	-
Saudi Arabia	$268,900,000,000	$10,500	$71,000,000,000	$39,500,000,000	736,996	-	91%	9%	-	-	401,559,222	-	-
Singapore	$112,400,000,000	$24,000	$127,000,000,000	$113,000,000,000		-	-	-	-	-	-	-	-
Sri Lanka	$73,700,000,000	$3,700	$4,600,000,000	$5,400,000,000	394	-	-	-	100%	-	-	-	-
Syria	$63,480,000,000	$3,500	$6,200,000,000	$4,900,000,000	47,898	-	83%	15%	2%	-	26,119,029	-	-
Taiwan	$406,000,000,000	$18,000	$130,000,000,000	$113,000,000,000	[6]	[6]	[6]	[7]	[8]	58,284	38,686	-	-
Tajikistan	$8,476,000,000	$1,250	$710,000,000	$830,000,000	1,790	-	1%	3%	95%	20,667	16,613	-	-
Thailand	$445,800,000,000	$6,900	$67,700,000,000	$58,100,000,000	44,127	25%	24%	50%	2%	18,551,756	5,080,720	20,000	-
Turkey	$489,700,000,000	$7,000	$35,100,000,000	$50,800,000,000	28,167	69%	14%	3%	14%	65,334,995	2,642,106	2,300,000	303,000
Turkmenistan	$31,340,000,000	$5,500	$2,970,000,000	$2,250,000,000	71,764	-	15%	85%	-		7,139,688	-	-
United Arab Emirates	$53,970,000,000	$22,000	$44,900,000,000	$30,800,000,000	199,656	-	83%	17%	-		112,737,023	-	-
Uzbekistan	$66,060,000,000	$2,500	$2,800,000,000	$2,500,000,000	85,806	1%	13%	85%	1%	2,736,319	4,419,300	-	-
Vietnam	$183,800,000,000	$2,250	$16,500,000,000	$16,800,000,000	39,300	30%	59%	5%	7%	9,688,950	15,926,911	-	-
Yemen	$15,070,000,000	$840	$3,400,000,000	$2,900,000,000	30,622	-	100%	-	-	-	21,304,264	-	-
AFRICA													
Algeria	$173,800,000,000	$5,300	$19,500,000,000	$10,600,000,000	222,648	-	47%	53%	-	24,000	61,651,110	757,000	-
Angola	$18,360,000,000	$1,600	$8,600,000,000	$4,100,000,000	53,315	-	98%	1%	-	-	36,961,745	-	-
Benin	$7,380,000,000	$1,070	$207,000,000	$479,000,000	69	-	100%	-	-	-	39,547	-	-
Botswana	$13,480,000,000	$9,500	$2,400,000,000	$1,900,000,000	[7]	[7]	[7]	[7]	[7]	956,767	-	-	-
Burkina Faso	$14,510,000,000	$1,080	$250,000,000	$525,000,000	15	-	-	-	100%	-	-	-	-
Burundi	$3,146,000,000	$600	$26,000,000	$135,000,000	21	29%	-	-	71%	-	-	-	-
Cameroon	$26,840,000,000	$1,700	$1,900,000,000	$1,700,000,000	10,722	-	96%	-	4%	1,000	4,326,440	-	-
Cape Verde	$600,000,000	$1,400	$30,000,000	$220,000,000		-	-	-	-	-	-	-	-
Central African Republic	$4,296,000,000	$1,300	$134,000,000	$102,000,000	10	-	-	-	100%	-	-	-	-
Chad	$9,297,000,000	$1,100	$197,000,000	$570,000,000		-	-	-	-	-	-	-	-
Comoros	$441,000,000	$720	$16,300,000	$39,800,000		-	-	-	-	-	-	-	-
Congo	$2,500,000,000	$900	$2,400,000,000	$73,000,000	19,097	-	99%	1%	-	-	13,651,000	-	-
Congo, Democratic Republic of the	$34,000,000,000	$610	$1,200,000,000	$890,000,000	2,630	4%	71%	-	25%	96,000	1,194,669	-	-
Cote d'Ivoire	$24,030,000,000	$1,500	$4,400,000,000	$2,500,000,000	4,439	-	50%	45%	5%	-	620,450	-	-
Djibouti	$619,000,000	$1,300	$70,000,000	$255,000,000		-	-	-	-	-	-	-	-
Egypt	$289,800,000,000	$3,900	$7,000,000,000	$15,200,000,000	86,315	-	65%	32%	2%	-	38,024,058	1,283,000	-
Equatorial Guinea	$1,270,000,000	$2,700	$2,500,000,000	$562,000,000	7,531	-	100%	-	-	-	7,461,521	-	-
Eritrea	$3,300,000,000	$740	$20,000,000	$500,000,000		-	-	-	-	-	-	-	-
Ethiopia	$48,530,000,000	$750	$433,000,000	$1,630,000,000	211	-	-	-	100%	-	-	-	-
Gabon	$8,354,000,000	$5,700	$2,600,000,000	$1,100,000,000	23,273	-	95%	5%	-	-	15,674,359	-	-
Gambia, The	$2,582,000,000	$1,800	$138,000,000	$225,000,000		-	-	-	-	-	-	-	-
Ghana	$41,250,000,000	$2,100	$2,200,000,000	$2,800,000,000	830	-	2%	-	98%	-	330,933	-	525,000
Guinea	$18,690,000,000	$2,000	$835,000,000	$670,000,000	25	-	-	-	100%	-	-	-	15,663,000
Guinea-Bissau	$901,400,000	$800	$71,000,000	$59,000,000		-	-	-	-	-	-	-	-
Kenya	$32,890,000,000	$1,020	$2,100,000,000	$3,000,000,000	642	-	-	-	100%	-	-	-	-
Lesotho	$5,106,000,000	$2,700	$422,000,000	$738,000,000	[7]	[7]	[7]	[7]	[7]	-	-	-	-
Liberia	$3,116,000,000	$1,100	$110,000,000	$165,000,000	24	-	-	-	100%	-	-	-	-
Libya	$33,360,000,000	$7,600	$11,800,000,000	$6,300,000,000	103,205	-	92%	8%	-	-	67,767,436	-	-
Madagascar	$12,590,000,000	$760	$700,000,000	$985,000,000	64	-	-	-	100%	-	-	-	-
Malawi	$6,811,000,000	$670	$435,000,000	$505,000,000	107	-	-	-	100%	-	-	-	-
Mali	$9,775,000,000	$860	$680,000,000	$630,000,000	29	-	-	-	100%	-	-	-	-
Mauritania	$4,891,000,000	$1,900	$355,000,000	$360,000,000	4	-	-	-	100%	-	-	7,492,000	-
Mauritius	$12,150,000,000	$11,000	$1,600,000,000	$1,800,000,000	12	-	-	-	100%	-	-	-	-
Morocco	$121,800,000,000	$3,900	$7,500,000,000	$10,400,000,000	201	14%	9%	33%	43%	61,000	15,223	4,000	-
Mozambique	$19,520,000,000	$1,000	$680,000,000	$1,180,000,000	874	2%	-	-	98%	18,667	-	-	8,000
Namibia	$13,150,000,000	$6,900	$1,210,000,000	$1,380,000,000	[7]	[7]	[7]	[7]	[7]	-	-	-	-
Niger	$8,713,000,000	$830	$293,000,000	$368,000,000	175	100%	-	-	-	151,666	-	-	-
Nigeria	$112,500,000,000	$875	$17,300,000,000	$13,600,000,000	172,641	-	90%	10%	-	61,000	108,397,478	-	-
Rwanda	$8,920,000,000	$1,200	$68,000,000	$253,000,000	20	-	-	-	100%	-	-	-	-
Sao Tome and Principe	$200,000,000	$1,200	$5,500,000	$24,800,000	1	-	-	100%	-	-	-	-	-
Senegal	$15,640,000,000	$1,500	$1,150,000,000	$1,460,000,000	1	-	-	-	100%	-	-	-	-
Sierra Leone	$2,826,000,000	$580	$35,000,000	$190,000,000	[7]	[7]	[7]	[7]	[7]	-	-	-	-
Somalia	$4,270,000,000	$550	$126,000,000	$343,000,000		-	-	-	-	-	-	-	-
South Africa	$427,700,000,000	$10,000	$31,800,000,000	$26,600,000,000	245,195[8]	92%[8]	5%[8]	1%[8]	2%[8]	224,286,505	1,277,485	20,751,000	-
Sudan	$52,900,000,000	$1,420	$1,800,000,000	$1,500,000,000	13,436	-	99%	-	1%	-	7,679,837	-	-
Swaziland	$5,542,000,000	$4,400	$820,000,000	$938,000,000	[7]	[7]	[7]	[7]	[7]	288,665	-	-	-
Tanzania	$20,420,000,000	$630	$863,000,000	$1,670,000,000	343	23%	-	-	77%	5,000	-	-	-
Togo	$7,594,000,000	$1,500	$449,000,000	$561,000,000		-	-	-	-	-	-	-	-
Tunisia	$67,130,000,000	$6,500	$6,800,000,000	$8,700,000,000	8,065	-	66%	34%	-	-	3,826,400	105,000	-
Uganda	$30,490,000,000	$1,260	$476,000,000	$1,140,000,000	193	-	-	-	100%	-	-	3,000	-
Zambia	$8,240,000,000	$890	$709,000,000	$1,123,000,000	1,117	15%	-	-	85%	192,358	-	-	-
Zimbabwe	$26,070,000,000	$2,400	$1,570,000,000	$1,739,000,000	4,801	92%	-	-	8%	4,508,643	-	237,000	-
OCEANIA													
Australia	$525,500,000,000	$27,000	$66,300,000,000	$68,000,000,000	331,923	71%	14%	14%	1%	307,176,075	31,728,994	104,014,000	51,834,000
Fiji	$4,822,000,000	$5,500	$442,000,000	$642,000,000	53	-	-	-	100%	-	-	-	-
Kiribati	$79,000,000	$840	$6,000,000	$44,000,000		-	-	-	-	-	-	-	-
Micronesia, Federated States of	$277,000,000	$2,000	$22,000,000	$149,000,000		-	-	-	-	-	-	-	-
New Zealand	$78,400,000,000	$20,200	$15,000,000,000	$12,500,000,000	19,812	14%	13%	40%	33%	3,452,315	1,839,394	660,000	-
Papua New Guinea	$10,860,000,000	$2,300	$1,800,000,000	$1,100,000,000	5,864	-	96%	2%	2%	-	3,874,601	-	-
Samoa	$1,000,000,000	$5,600	$15,500,000	$130,100,000	3	-	-	-	100%	-	-	-	-
Solomon Islands	$800,000,000	$1,700	$47,000,000	$82,000,000		-	-	-	-	-	-	-	-
Tonga	$236,000,000	$2,200	$8,900,000	$70,000,000		-	-	-	-	-	-	-	-
Vanuatu	$563,000,000	$2,900	$22,000,000	$93,000,000		-	-	-	-	-	-	-	-

This table presents data for most independent nations having an area greater than 200 square miles
- Zero, insignificant, or not available
(1) Source: United States Central Intelligence Agency World Factbook
(2) Source: United Nations Energy Statistics Yearbook
(3) Source: United States Energy Information Administration International Energy Annual
(4) Source: United States Geological Survey Minerals Yearbook
(5) Includes data for Taiwan
(6) Data for Taiwan is included with China
(7) Data for countries in the South Africa Customs Union are included with South Africa
(8) Includes data for countries in the South Africa Customs Union

WORLD ENVIRONMENT TABLE

CONTINENT/Country	Total Area Sq. Miles	Protected Area 2002[1,2] Sq. Miles	Protected Area 2002[1,2] %	Endangered Species 2003[3] Mammal	Bird	Reptile	Amphib.	Fish	Invrt.	Forest Cover[4] Sq. Miles 2000	Forest Cover[4] Percent Change 1990-2000
NORTH AMERICA											
Bahamas	5,382	-	-	5	4	6	0	15	1	3,251	-
Belize	8,867	3,999	45.1%	5	2	4	0	17	1	5,205	-20.9%
Canada	3,855,103	427,916	11.1%	16	8	2	1	25	11	944,294	-
Costa Rica	19,730	4,538	23.0%	13	13	7	1	13	9	7,598	-7.4%
Cuba	42,804	29,578	69.1%	11	18	7	0	23	3	9,066	13.4%
Dominica	290	-	-	1	3	4	0	11	0	178	-8.0%
Dominican Republic	18,730	9,721	51.9%	5	15	10	1	10	2	5,313	-
El Salvador	8,124	33	0.4%	2	0	4	0	5	1	467	-37.3%
Guatemala	42,042	8,408	20.0%	7	6	8	0	14	0	11,004	15.9%
Haiti	10,714	43	0.4%	4	14	8	1	12	2	340	-44.3%
Honduras	43,277	2,770	6.4%	10	5	6	0	14	2	20,784	-9.9%
Jamaica	4,244	1,111	24.6%	5	12	8	4	12	5	1,255	-14.2%
Mexico	758,452	77,302	10.2%	72	40	18	4	106	41	215,148	-10.5%
Nicaragua	50,054	8,910	17.8%	6	5	7	0	17	2	12,656	-26.3%
Panama	29,157	6,327	21.7%	17	16	7	0	17	2	11,104	-15.3%
St. Lucia	238	-	-	2	5	6	0	10	0	35	-35.7%
Trinidad and Tobago	1,980	119	6.0%	1	1	5	0	15	0	1,000	-7.8%
United States	3,794,083	982,668	25.9%	39	56	27	25	155	557	872,563	1.7%
SOUTH AMERICA											
Argentina	1,073,519	70,852	6.6%	32	39	5	5	9	10	133,777	-7.6%
Bolivia	424,165	56,838	13.4%	25	28	2	1	0	1	204,897	-2.9%
Brazil	3,300,172	221,112	6.7%	74	113	22	6	33	34	2,100,028	-4.1%
Chile	291,930	55,175	18.9%	21	22	0	3	9	0	59,985	-1.3%
Colombia	439,737	44,853	10.2%	39	78	14	0	23	0	191,510	-3.7%
Ecuador	109,484	20,036	18.3%	34	62	10	0	11	48	40,761	-11.5%
Guyana	83,000	249	0.3%	13	2	6	0	13	1	65,170	-2.8%
Paraguay	157,048	5,497	3.5%	10	26	2	0	0	0	90,240	-5.0%
Peru	496,225	30,270	6.1%	46	76	6	1	8	2	251,796	-4.0%
Suriname	63,037	3,089	4.9%	12	1	6	0	12	0	54,491	-
Uruguay	67,574	203	0.3%	6	11	3	0	8	1	4,988	63.3%
Venezuela	352,145	224,669	63.8%	26	24	13	0	19	1	191,144	-4.2%
EUROPE											
Albania	11,100	422	3.8%	3	3	4	0	16	4	3,826	-7.3%
Austria	32,378	10,685	33.0%	7	3	0	0	7	44	15,004	2.0%
Belarus	80,155	5,050	6.3%	7	3	0	0	0	5	36,301	37.5%
Belgium	11,787	-	-	11	2	0	0	7	11	2,811	-1.8%
Bosnia and Herzegovina	19,767	99	0.5%	10	3	1	1	10	10	8,776	-
Bulgaria	42,855	1,928	4.5%	14	10	2	0	10	9	14,247	5.9%
Croatia	21,829	1,637	7.5%	9	4	1	1	26	11	6,884	1.1%
Czech Republic	30,450	4,902	16.1%	8	2	0	0	7	19	10,162	0.2%
Denmark	16,640	5,658	34.0%	5	1	0	0	7	11	1,757	2.2%
Estonia	17,462	2,061	11.8%	5	3	0	0	1	4	7,954	6.5%
Finland	130,559	12,142	9.3%	4	3	0	0	1	10	84,691	0.4%
France	208,482	27,728	13.3%	18	5	3	2	15	65	59,232	4.2%
Germany	137,847	43,973	31.9%	11	5	0	0	12	31	41,467	-
Greece	50,949	1,834	3.6%	13	7	6	1	26	11	13,896	9.1%
Hungary	35,919	2,514	7.0%	9	8	1	0	8	25	7,104	4.1%
Iceland	39,769	3,897	9.8%	7	0	0	0	8	0	120	24.0%
Ireland	27,133	461	1.7%	6	1	0	0	6	3	2,544	34.8%
Italy	116,342	9,191	7.9%	14	5	4	4	16	58	38,622	3.0%
Latvia	24,942	3,342	13.4%	5	3	0	0	3	8	11,286	4.5%
Lithuania	25,213	2,597	10.3%	6	4	0	0	3	5	7,699	2.5%
Luxembourg	999	-	-	3	1	0	0	0	4	-	-
Macedonia	9,928	705	7.1%	11	3	2	0	4	5	3,498	-
Moldova	13,070	183	1.4%	6	5	1	0	9	5	1,255	2.2%
Netherlands	16,164	2,295	14.2%	10	4	0	0	7	7	1,448	2.7%
Norway	125,050	8,503	6.8%	10	2	0	0	7	9	34,240	3.6%
Poland	120,728	14,970	12.4%	14	4	0	0	3	15	34,931	2.0%
Portugal	35,516	2,344	6.6%	17	7	0	1	19	82	14,154	18.4%
Romania	91,699	4,310	4.7%	17	8	2	0	10	22	24,896	2.3%
Serbia and Montenegro	39,449	1,302	3.3%	12	5	1	0	19	19	11,147	-0.5%
Slovakia	18,924	4,315	22.8%	9	4	1	0	8	19	8,405	9.0%
Slovenia	7,821	469	6.0%	9	1	0	1	15	42	4,274	2.0%
Spain	194,885	16,565	8.5%	24	7	7	3	23	63	55,483	6.4%
Sweden	173,732	15,810	9.1%	6	2	0	0	6	13	104,765	-
Switzerland	15,943	4,783	30.0%	5	2	0	0	4	30	4,629	3.7%
Ukraine	233,090	9,091	3.9%	16	8	2	0	11	14	37,004	3.3%
United Kingdom	93,788	19,602	20.9%	12	2	0	0	11	10	10,788	6.5%
Russia	6,592,849	514,242	7.8%	45	38	6	0	18	30	3,287,242	0.2%
ASIA											
Afghanistan	251,773	755	0.3%	13	11	1	1	0	1	5,216	-
Armenia	11,506	874	7.6%	11	4	5	0	1	7	1,355	13.6%
Azerbaijan	33,437	2,040	6.1%	13	8	5	0	5	6	4,224	13.5%
Bahrain	267	-	-	1	6	0	0	6	0	-	-
Bangladesh	55,598	445	0.8%	22	23	20	0	8	0	5,151	14.1%
Brunei	2,226	-	-	11	14	4	0	6	0	1,707	-2.2%
Cambodia	69,898	12,931	18.5%	24	19	10	0	11	0	36,043	-5.7%
China	3,690,045	287,824	7.8%	81	75	31	1	46	4	631,200	12.4%
Cyprus	3,572	-	-	3	3	3	0	6	0	664	44.5%
East Timor	5,743	-	-	0	6	0	0	2	0	1,958	-6.3%
Georgia	26,911	619	2.3%	13	3	7	1	6	10	11,537	-
India	1,222,510	63,571	5.2%	86	72	25	3	27	23	247,542	0.6%
Indonesia	735,310	151,474	20.6%	147	114	28	0	91	31	405,353	-11.1%
Iran	636,372	30,546	4.8%	22	13	8	2	14	3	28,182	-
Iraq	169,235	-	-	11	11	2	0	3	2	3,085	-
Israel	8,019	1,267	15.8%	15	12	4	0	10	10	510	61.0%
Japan	145,850	9,918	6.8%	37	35	11	10	27	45	92,977	0.1%
Jordan	34,495	1,173	3.4%	9	8	1	0	5	3	332	-
Kazakhstan	1,049,156	28,327	2.7%	17	15	2	1	7	4	46,904	24.5%
Korea, North	46,540	1,210	2.6%	13	19	0	0	5	1	31,699	-
Korea, South	38,328	2,645	6.9%	13	25	0	0	7	1	24,124	-0.8%

CONTINENT/Country	Total Area Sq. Miles	Protected Area 2002[1,2] Sq. Miles	%	Mammal	Bird	Endangered Species 2003[3] Reptile	Amphib.	Fish	Invrt.	Forest Cover[4] Sq. Miles 2000	Percent Change 1990-2000
Kuwait	6,880	103	1.5%	1	7	1	0	6	0	19	66.7%
Kyrgyzstan	77,182	2,779	3.6%	7	4	2	0	0	3	3,873	29.4%
Laos	91,429	11,429	12.5%	31	20	11	0	6	0	48,498	-4.0%
Lebanon	4,016	20	0.5%	6	7	1	0	8	1	139	-2.7%
Malaysia	127,320	7,257	5.7%	50	37	21	0	34	3	74,487	52.4%
Mongolia	604,829	69,555	11.5%	14	16	0	0	1	3	41,101	-5.3%
Myanmar	261,228	784	0.3%	39	35	20	0	7	2	132,892	-13.1%
Nepal	56,827	5,058	8.9%	29	25	6	0	0	1	15,058	-16.7%
Oman	119,499	16,730	14.0%	11	10	4	0	17	1	4	-
Pakistan	339,732	16,647	4.9%	17	17	9	0	14	0	9,116	-14.3%
Philippines	115,831	6,602	5.7%	50	67	8	23	48	19	22,351	-13.3%
Qatar	4,412	-	-	0	6	1	0	4	0	-	-
Saudi Arabia	830,000	317,890	38.3%	9	15	2	0	8	1	5,807	
Singapore	264	13	4.9%	3	7	3	0	12	1	8	
Sri Lanka	25,332	3,420	13.5%	22	14	8	0	22	7	7,490	15.3%
Syria	71,400	-	-	4	8	3	0	8	3	1,780	-
Taiwan	13,901	-	-	12	21	8	0	23	0	-	-
Tajikistan	55,251	2,321	4.2%	9	7	1	0	3	2	1,544	5.3%
Thailand	198,115	27,538	13.9%	37	37	19	0	35	1	56,996	-7.1%
Turkey	302,541	4,841	1.6%	17	11	12	3	29	13	39,479	2.2%
Turkmenistan	188,457	7,915	4.2%	13	6	2	0	8	5	14,498	-
United Arab Emirates	32,278	-	-	4	8	1	0	6	0	1,239	32.1%
Uzbekistan	172,742	3,455	2.0%	9	9	2	0	4	1	7,602	2.4%
Vietnam	128,066	4,738	3.7%	42	37	24	1	22	0	37,911	5.5%
Yemen	203,850	-	-	6	12	2	0	10	2	1,734	-17.0%
AFRICA											
Algeria	919,595	45,980	5.0%	13	6	2	0	9	12	8,282	14.2%
Angola	481,354	31,769	6.6%	19	15	4	0	8	6	269,329	-1.7%
Benin	43,484	4,957	11.4%	9	2	1	0	7	0	10,232	-20.9%
Botswana	224,607	41,552	18.5%	7	7	0	0	0	0	47,981	-8.7%
Burkina Faso	105,869	12,175	11.5%	7	2	1	0	0	0	27,371	-2.1%
Burundi	10,745	612	5.7%	6	7	0	0	0	3	363	-61.0%
Cameroon	183,568	8,261	4.5%	38	15	1	1	34	4	92,116	-8.5%
Cape Verde	1,557	-	-	3	2	0	0	13	0	328	142.9%
Central African Republic	240,536	20,927	8.7%	14	3	1	0	0	0	88,444	-1.3%
Chad	495,755	45,114	9.1%	15	5	1	0	0	1	49,004	-6.0%
Comoros	863	-	-	2	9	2	0	3	4	31	-33.3%
Congo	132,047	6,602	5.0%	15	3	1	0	9	1	85,174	-0.8%
Congo, Democratic Republic of the	905,446	58,854	6.5%	40	28	2	0	9	45	522,037	-3.8%
Cote d'Ivoire	124,504	7,470	6.0%	19	12	2	1	10	1	27,479	-27.1%
Djibouti	8,958	-	-	5	5	0	0	9	0	23	-
Egypt	386,662	37,506	9.7%	13	7	6	0	13	1	278	38.5%
Equatorial Guinea	10,831	-	-	16	5	2	1	7	2	6,765	-5.7%
Eritrea	45,406	1,952	4.3%	12	7	6	0	8	0	6,120	-3.3%
Ethiopia	426,373	72,057	16.9%	35	16	1	0	0	4	17,734	-8.1%
Gabon	103,347	723	0.7%	14	5	1	0	11	1	84,271	-0.5%
Gambia, The	4,127	95	2.3%	3	2	1	0	10	0	1,857	10.3%
Ghana	92,098	5,157	5.6%	14	8	2	0	7	0	24,460	-15.9%
Guinea	94,926	664	0.7%	12	10	1	1	7	3	26,753	-4.8%
Guinea-Bissau	13,948	-	-	3	0	1	0	9	1	8,444	-9.0%
Kenya	224,961	17,997	8.0%	50	24	5	0	27	15	66,008	-5.2%
Lesotho	11,720	23	0.2%	6	7	0	0	1	1	54	-
Liberia	43,000	731	1.7%	16	11	2	0	7	2	13,440	-17.9%
Libya	679,362	679	0.1%	8	1	3	0	8	0	1,382	15.1%
Madagascar	226,658	9,746	4.3%	50	27	18	2	25	32	45,278	-9.1%
Malawi	45,747	5,124	11.2%	8	11	0	0	0	8	9,892	-21.6%
Mali	478,841	17,717	3.7%	13	4	1	0	1	0	50,911	-7.0%
Mauritania	397,956	6,765	1.7%	10	2	2	0	10	1	1,224	-23.6%
Mauritius	788	-	-	3	9	4	0	7	32	62	-5.9%
Morocco	172,414	1,207	0.7%	16	9	2	0	10	8	11,680	-0.4%
Mozambique	309,496	25,998	8.4%	15	16	5	0	19	7	118,151	-2.0%
Namibia	317,818	43,223	13.6%	14	11	3	1	11	1	31,043	-8.4%
Niger	489,192	37,668	7.7%	11	3	0	0	0	1	5,127	-31.7%
Nigeria	356,669	11,770	3.3%	27	9	2	0	11	1	52,189	-22.8%
Rwanda	10,169	630	6.2%	8	9	0	0	0	2	1,185	-32.8%
Sao Tome and Principe	372	-	-	3	9	1	0	6	2	104	-
Senegal	75,951	8,810	11.6%	12	4	6	0	17	0	23,958	-6.8%
Sierra Leone	27,699	582	2.1%	12	10	3	0	7	4	4,073	-25.5%
Somalia	246,201	1,970	0.8%	19	10	2	0	16	1	29,016	-9.3%
South Africa	470,693	25,888	5.5%	36	28	19	9	47	113	34,429	-0.9%
Sudan	967,500	50,310	5.2%	22	6	2	0	7	1	237,943	-13.5%
Swaziland	6,704	-	-	5	5	0	0	0	0	2,015	12.5%
Tanzania	364,900	108,740	29.8%	41	33	5	0	26	47	149,850	-2.3%
Togo	21,925	1,732	7.9%	9	0	2	0	7	0	1,969	-29.1%
Tunisia	63,170	190	0.3%	11	5	3	0	8	5	1,969	2.2%
Uganda	93,065	22,894	24.6%	20	13	0	0	27	10	16,178	-17.9%
Zambia	290,586	92,697	31.9%	11	11	0	0	0	6	120,641	-21.4%
Zimbabwe	150,873	18,256	12.1%	11	10	0	0	0	2	73,514	-14.4%
OCEANIA											
Australia	2,969,910	397,968	13.4%	63	35	38	35	74	282	596,678	-1.8%
Fiji	7,056	78	1.1%	5	13	6	1	8	2	3,147	-2.0%
Kiribati	313	-	-	0	4	1	0	4	1	108	-
Micronesia, Federated States of	271	-	-	6	5	2	0	6	4	58	-37.5%
New Zealand	104,454	30,918	29.6%	8	63	11	1	16	13	30,680	5.2%
Papua New Guinea	178,704	4,110	2.3%	58	32	9	0	31	12	118,151	-3.6%
Samoa	1,093	-	-	3	8	1	0	4	1	405	-19.2%
Solomon Islands	10,954	33	0.3%	20	23	4	0	4	6	9,792	-1.7%
Tonga	251	-	-	2	3	2	0	3	2	15	-
Vanuatu	4,707	-	-	5	8	2	0	4	0	1,726	1.4%

This table presents data for most independent nations having an area greater than 200 square miles
- Zero, insignificant, or not available
(1) Source: World Resources Institute, 2003. Earth Trends: The Environmental Information Portal. Available at http://earthtrends.wri.org. Washington D. C. World Resources Institute
(2) Source: United Nations Environment Programme - World Conservation Monitoring Centre (UNEP-WCMC); World Database on Protected Areas
(3) Source: International Union of Conservation of Nature and Natural Resources; IUCN 2003 Red List of Threatened Species <www.redlist.org>
(4) Source: United Nations Food and Agriculture Organization; Global Forest Resources Assessment 2000

WORLD COMPARISONS

General Information

Equatorial diameter of the earth, 7,926.38 miles.
Polar diameter of the earth, 7,899.80 miles.
Mean diameter of the earth, 7,917.52 miles.
Equatorial circumference of the earth, 24,901.46 miles.
Polar circumference of the earth, 24,855.34 miles.
Mean distance from the earth to the sun, 93,020,000 miles.
Mean distance from the earth to the moon, 238,857 miles.
Total area of the earth, 197,000,000 sq. miles.

Highest elevation on the earth's surface, Mt. Everest, Asia, 29,028 ft.
Lowest elevation on the earth's land surface, shores of the Dead Sea, Asia, 1,339 ft. below sea level.
Greatest known depth of the ocean, southwest of Guam, Pacific Ocean, 35,810 ft.
Total land area of the earth (incl. inland water and Antarctica), 57,900,000 sq. miles.

Area of Africa, 11,700,000 sq. miles.
Area of Antarctica, 5,400,000 sq. miles.
Area of Asia, 17,300,000 sq. miles.
Area of Europe, 3,800,000 sq. miles.
Area of North America, 9,500,000 sq. miles.
Area of Oceania (incl. Australia) 3,300,000 sq. miles.
Area of South America, 6,900,000 sq. miles.
Population of the earth (est. 1/1/04), 6,339,505,000.

Principal Islands and Their Areas

ISLAND	Area (Sq. Mi.)
Baffin I., Canada	195,928
Banks I., Canada	27,038
Borneo (Kalimantan), Asia	287,300
Bougainville, Papua New Guinea	3,591
Cape Breton I., Canada	3,981
Celebes (Sulawesi), Indonesia	73,057
Ceram (Seram), Indonesia	7,191
Corsica, France	3,367
Crete, Greece	3,189
Cuba, N. America	42,780
Cyprus, Asia	3,572
Devon I., Canada	21,331
Ellesmere I., Canada	75,767
Flores, Indonesia	5,502
Great Britain, U.K.	88,795
Greenland, N. America	840,000
Guadalcanal, Solomon Is.	2,000
Hainan Dao, China	13,127
Hawaii, U.S.	4,028
Hispaniola, N. America	29,300
Hokkaidō, Japan	32,245
Honshū, Japan	89,176
Iceland, Europe	39,769
Ireland, Europe	32,587
Jamaica, N. America	4,247
Java (Jawa), Indonesia	51,038
Kodiak I., U.S.	3,670
Kyūshū, Japan	17,129
Leyte, Philippines	2,785
Long Island, U.S.	1,377
Luzon, Philippines	40,420
Madagascar, Africa	226,642
Melville I., Canada	16,274
Mindanao, Philippines	36,537
Mindoro, Philippines	3,759
Negros, Philippines	4,907
New Britain, Papua New Guinea	14,093
New Caledonia, Oceania	6,252
Newfoundland, Canada	42,031
New Guinea, Asia-Oceania	308,882
New Ireland, Papua New Guinea	3,475
North East Land, Norway	6,350
North I., New Zealand	44,111
Novaya Zemlya, Russia	31,892
Palawan, Philippines	4,550
Panay, Philippines	4,446
Prince of Wales I., Canada	12,872
Puerto Rico, N. America	3,514
Sakhalin, Russia	29,498
Samar, Philippines	5,050
Sardinia, Italy	9,301
Shikoku, Japan	7,258
Sicily, Italy	9,926
Somerset I., Canada	9,570
Southampton I., Canada	15,913
South I., New Zealand	57,708
Spitsbergen, Norway	15,260
Sri Lanka, Asia	24,942
Sumatra (Sumatera), Indonesia	182,860
Taiwan, Asia	13,900
Tasmania, Australia	26,178
Tierra del Fuego, S. America	18,600
Timor, Asia	5,743
Vancouver I., Canada	12,079
Victoria I., Canada	83,897
Vrangelya (Wrangel), Russia	2,819

Principal Lakes, Oceans, Seas, and Their Areas

LAKE Country	Area (Sq. Mi.)
Arabian Sea	1,492,000
Aral Sea, Kazakhstan-Uzbekistan	13,000
Arctic Ocean	5,400,000
Athabasca, L., Canada	3,064
Atlantic Ocean	29,600,000
Balqash köli (L. Balkhash), Kazakhstan	7,027
Baltic Sea, Europe	163,000
Baykal, Ozero (L. Baikal), Russia	12,162
Bering Sea, Asia-N.A.	876,000
Black Sea, Europe-Asia	178,000
Caribbean Sea, N.A.-S.A.	1,063,000
Caspian Sea, Asia-Europe	144,402
Chad, L., Cameroon-Chad-Nigeria	595
Erie, L., Canada-U.S.	9,910
Eyre, L., Australia	3,668
Gairdner, L., Australia	1,076
Great Bear Lake, Canada	12,096
Great Salt Lake, U.S.	1,700
Great Slave Lake, Canada	11,030
Hudson Bay, Canada	475,000
Huron, L., Canada-U.S.	23,000
Indian Ocean	26,500,000
Japan, Sea of, Asia	389,000
Koko Nor (Qinghai Hu), China	1,722
Ladozhskoye Ozero (L. Ladoga), Russia	7,002
Manitoba, L., Canada	1,785
Mediterranean Sea, Europe-Africa-Asia	967,000
Mexico, Gulf of, N. America	596,000
Michigan, L., U.S.	22,300
Nicaragua, Lago de, Nicaragua	3,147
North Sea, Europe	222,000
Nyasa, L., Malawi-Mozambique-Tanzania	11,120
Onezhskoye Ozero (L. Onega), Russia	3,819
Ontario, L., Canada-U.S.	7,340
Pacific Ocean	60,100,000
Red Sea, Africa-Asia	169,000
Rudolf, L., Ethiopia-Kenya	2,471
Southern Ocean	7,800,000
Superior, L., Canada-U.S.	31,700
Tanganyika. L., Africa	12,355
Titicaca, Lago, Bolivia-Peru	3,232
Torrens, L., Australia	1,076
Vänern (L.), Sweden	2,181
Van Gölü (L.), Turkey	1,434
Victoria, L., Kenya-Tanzania-Uganda	26,564
Winnipeg, L., Canada	9,416
Winnipegosis, L., Canada	2,075
Yellow Sea, China-Korea	480,000

Principal Mountains and Their Heights

MOUNTAIN Country	Elev. (Ft.)
Aconcagua, Cerro, Argentina	22,831
Annapurna, Nepal	26,504
Aoraki, New Zealand	12,316
Api, Nepal	23,399
Apo, Philippines	9,692
Ararat, Mt., Turkey	16,854
Barú, Volcán, Panama	11,401
Bangueta, Mt., Papua New Guinea	13,520
Belukha, Mt., Kazakhstan-Russia	14,783
Bia, Phou, Laos	9,249
Blanc, Mont (Monte Bianco), France-Italy	15,771
Blanca Pk., Colorado, U.S.	14,345
Bolívar, Pico, Venezuela	16,427
Bonete, Cerro, Argentina	22,546
Borah Pk., Idaho, U.S.	12,662
Boundary Pk., Nevada, U.S.	13,140
Cameroon Mtn., Cameroon	13,451
Carrauntoohil, Ireland	3,406
Chaltel, Cerro (Monte Fitzroy), Argentina-Chile	10,958
Chimborazo, Ecuador	20,702
Chirripó, Cerro, Costa Rica	12,530
Colima, Nevado de, Mexico	13,911
Cotopaxi, Ecuador	19,347
Cristóbal Colón, Pico, Colombia	19,029
Damāvand, Qolleh-ye, Iran	18,386
Dhawalāgiri, Nepal	26,810
Duarte, Pico, Dominican Rep.	10,417
Dufourspitze (Monte Rosa), Italy-Switzerland	15,203
Elbert, Mt., Colorado, U.S.	14,433
El'brus, Gora, Russia	18,510
Elgon, Mt., Kenya-Uganda	14,178
Erciyeş, Dağı, Turkey	12,848
Etna, Mt., Italy	10,902
Everest, Mt., China-Nepal	29,028
Fairweather, Mt., Alaska-Canada	15,300
Folādī, Koh-e, Afghanistan	16,847
Foraker, Mt., Alaska, U.S.	17,400
Fuji San, Japan	12,388
Galdhøpiggen, Norway	8,100
Gannett Pk., Wyoming, U.S.	13,804
Gasherbrum, China-Pakistan	26,470
Gerlachovský štit, Slovakia	8,711
Giluwe, Mt., Papua New Guinea	14,331
Gongga Shan, China	24,790
Grand Teton, Wyoming, U.S.	13,770
Grossglockner, Austria	12,457
Hadūr Shu'ayb, Yemen	12,008
Haleakalā Crater, Hawaii, U.S.	10,023
Hekla, Iceland	4,892
Hood, Mt., Oregon, U.S.	11,239
Huascarán, Nevado, Peru	22,133
Huila, Nevado de, Colombia	18,865
Hvannadalshnúkur, Iceland	6,952
Illampu, Nevado, Bolivia	21,066
Illimani, Nevado, Bolivia	20,741
Ismail Samani, pik, Tajikistan	24,590
Iztaccíhuatl, Mexico	17,159
Jaya, Puncak, Indonesia	16,503
Jungfrau, Switzerland	13,642
K2 (Qogir Feng), China-Pakistan	28,250
Kāmet, China-India	25,447
Kānchenjunga, India-Nepal	28,208
Kātrīna, Jabal, Egypt	8,668
Kebnekaise, Sweden	6,926
Kenya, Mt. (Kirinyaga), Kenya	17,058
Kerinci, Gunung, Indonesia	12,467
Kilimanjaro, Tanzania	19,340
Kinabalu, Gunong, Malaysia	13,455
Klyuchevskaya, Russia	15,584
Kosciuszko, Mt., Australia	7,313
Koussi, Emi, Chad	11,204
Kula Kangri, Bhutan	24,784
La Selle, Massif de, Haiti	8,793
Lassen Pk., California, U.S.	10,457
Llullaillaco, Volcán, Argentina-Chile	22,110
Logan, Mt., Canada	19,551
Longs Pk., Colorado, U.S.	14,255
Makalu, China-Nepal	27,825
Margherita Peak, Dem. Rep. of the Congo-Uganda	16,763
Markham, Mt., Antarctica	14,049
Maromokotro, Madagascar	9,436
Massive, Mt., Colorado, U.S.	14,421
Matterhorn, Italy-Switzerland	14,692
Mauna Kea, Hawaii, U.S.	13,796
Mauna Loa, Hawaii, U.S.	13,679
Mayon Volcano, Philippines	8,077
McKinley, Mt., Alaska, U.S.	20,320
Meron, Hare, Israel	3,963
Meru, Mt., Tanzania	14,978
Misti, Volcán, Peru	19,101
Mitchell, Mt., North Carolina, U.S.	6,684
Môco, Serra do, Angola	8,596
Moldoveanu, Romania	8,346
Mulhacén, Spain	11,424
Musala, Bulgaria	9,596
Muztag, China	25,338
Muztagata, China	24,757
Namjagbarwa Feng, China	25,446
Nanda Devi, India	25,645
Nanga Parbat, Pakistan	26,660
Narodnaya, Gora, Russia	6,217
Nevis, Ben, United Kingdom	4,406
Ojos del Salado, Nevado, Argentina-Chile	22,615
Ólimbos, Cyprus	6,401
Ólympos, Greece	9,570
Olympus, Mt., Washington, U.S.	7,965
Orizaba, Pico de, Mexico	18,406
Paektu San, North Korea-China	9,003
Parícutin, Mexico	9,186
Parnassós, Greece	8,061
Pelée, Montagne, Martinique	4,583
Pidurutalagala, Sri Lanka	8,281
Pikes Pk., Colorado, U.S.	14,110
Pobedy, pik, China-Kyrgyzstan	24,406
Popocatépetl, Volcán, Mexico	17,930
Pulog, Mt., Philippines	9,626
Rainier, Mt., Washington, U.S.	14,410
Ramm, Jabal, Jordan	5,755
Ras Dashen Terara, Ethiopia	15,158
Rinjani, Gunung, Indonesia	12,224
Robson, Mt., Canada	12,972
Roraima, Mt., Brazil-Guyana-Venezuela	9,432
Ruapehu, Mt., New Zealand	9,177
St. Elias, Mt., Alaska, U.S.-Canada	18,008
Sajama, Nevado, Bolivia	21,391
Semeru, Gunung, Indonesia	12,060
Shām, Jabal ash, Oman	9,957
Shasta, Mt., California, U.S.	14,162
Snowdon, United Kingdom	3,560
Tahat, Algeria	9,541
Tajumulco, Guatemala	13,845
Taranaki, Mt., New Zealand	8,260
Tirich Mīr, Pakistan	25,230
Tomanivi (Victoria), Fiji	4,341
Toubkal, Jebel, Morocco	13,665
Triglav, Slovenia	9,396
Trikora, Puncak, Indonesia	15,584
Tupungato, Cerro, Argentina-Chile	21,555
Turquino, Pico, Cuba	6,470
Uluru (Ayers Rock), Australia	2,844
Uncompahgre Pk, Colorado, U.S.	14,309
Vesuvio (Vesuvius), Italy	4,190
Victoria, Mt., Papua New Guinea	13,238
Vinson Massif, Antarctica	16,066
Waddington, Mt., Canada	13,163
Washington, Mt., New Hampshire, U.S.	6,288
Whitney, Mt., California, U.S.	14,494
Wilhelm, Mt., Papua New Guinea	14,793
Wrangell, Mt., Alaska, U.S.	14,163
Xixabangma Feng (Gosainthan), China	26,286
Yü Shan, Taiwan	13,114
Zugspitze, Austria-Germany	9,718

Principal Rivers and Their Lengths

RIVER Continent	Length (Mi.)
Albany, N. America	610
Aldan, Asia	1,412
Amazonas-Ucayali, S. America	4,000
Amu Darya, Asia	1,578
Amur, Asia	1,752
Araguaia, S. America	1,367
Arkansas, N. America	1,460
Atchafalaya, N. America	1,420
Athabasca, N. America	765
Brahmaputra, Asia	1,770
Brazos, N. America	1,280
Canadian, N. America	906
Churchill, N. America	1,000
Colorado, N. America (U.S.-Mexico)	1,450
Colorado, N. America (Texas)	862
Columbia, N. America	1,243
Congo (Zaïre), Africa	2,715
Danube, Europe	1,777
Darling, Australia	864
Dnieper (Dnipro), Europe	1,367
Don, Europe	1,162
Elbe, Europe	690
Essequibo, S. America	603
Euphrates, Asia	1,510
Fraser, N. America	851
Ganges, Asia	1,864
Gila, N. America	649
Godāvari, Asia	932
Huang (Yellow), Asia	2,902
Indigirka, Asia	1,072
Indus, Asia	1,118
Irrawaddy, Asia	1,300
Juruá, S. America	1,250
Kama, Europe	1,122
Kasai, Africa	1,338
Kolyma, Asia	1,323
Lena, Asia	2,734
Limpopo, Africa	1,100
Loire, Europe	690
Mackenzie, N. America	2,635
Madeira, S. America	2,013
Magdalena, S. America	951
Marañón, S. America	1,000
Mekong, Asia	2,796
Meuse, Europe	575
Mississippi, N. America	2,340
Mississippi-Missouri, N. America	3,710
Missouri, N. America	2,540
Murray-Darling, Australia	2,169
Negro, S. America	1,305
Nelson, N. America	1,600
Niger, Africa	2,585
Nile, Africa	4,132
Ob', Asia	2,268
Oder, Europe	565
Ohio, N. America	1,310
Oka, Europe	932
Orange, Africa	1,300
Orinoco, S. America	1,703
Ottawa, N. America	790
Paraguay, S. America	1,610
Paraná, S. America	901
Peace, N. America	1,195
Pechora, Europe	1,125
Pecos, N. America	926
Pilcomayo, S. America	1,550
Plata-Paraná, S. America	2,920
Platte, N. America	990
Purús, S. America	1,860
Red, N. America	1,290
Rhine, Europe	820
Rhône, Europe	503
Rio Grande, N. America	1,900
Roosevelt, S. America	950
St. Lawrence, N. America	1,900
Salado, S. America	870
Salween (Nu), Asia	1,750
São Francisco, S. America	1,740
Saskatchewan-Bow, N. America	1,205
Severnaya Dvina (Northern Dvina), Europe	462
Snake, N. America	1,040
Sungari (Songhua), Asia	1,140
Syr Darya, Asia	1,370
Tagus, Europe	625
Tarim, Asia	1,328
Tennessee, N. America	886
Tigris, Asia	1,180
Tisa, Europe	607
Tocantins, S. America	1,640
Ucayali, S. America	1,220
Ural, Asia	1,509
Uruguay, S. America	1,025
Verkhnyaya Tunguska (Angara), Asia	1,105
Vilyuy, Asia	1,647
Volga, Europe	2,082
Volta, Africa	994
Wisła (Vistula), Europe	630
Xiang, Asia	930
Xingú, S. America	1,230
Yangtze (Chang), Asia	3,915
Yellowstone, N. America	692
Yenisey, Asia	2,169
Yukon, N. America	1,980
Zambezi, Africa	1,653

PRINCIPAL CITIES OF THE WORLD

Abidjan, Cote d'Ivoire 1,929,079
Abū Ẓaby (Abu Dhabi), United Arab Emirates 242,975
Accra, Ghana (1,390,000) 949,113
Addis Ababa, Ethiopia 2,424,000
Ahmadābād, India (4,519,278) 3,515,361
Aleppo (Ḥalab), Syria (1,640,000) 1,591,400
Alexandria (Al Iskandarīyah), Egypt (3,350,000) 3,339,076
Algiers (El Djazaïr), Algeria (2,547,983) 1,507,241
Al Jīzah (Giza), Egypt (*Al Qāhirah) 2,221,817
Almaty, Kazakhstan (1,190,000) 1,129,356
'Ammān, Jordan (1,500,000) 1,147,447
Amsterdam, Netherlands (1,121,303) 727,053
Ankara, Turkey (3,294,220) 2,984,099
Antananarivo, Madagascar 1,250,000
Antwerp (Antwerpen), Belgium (1,135,000) 453,030
Ashgabat (Ashkhabad), Turkmenistan 557,600
Asmera, Eritrea 358,100
Astana (Aqmola), Kazakhstan (319,324) 312,965
Asunción, Paraguay (700,000) 546,637
Athens (Athína), Greece (3,150,000) 772,072
Atlanta, Georgia, U.S. (4,112,198) 416,474
Auckland, New Zealand (1,074,510) 367,737
Baghdād, Iraq 3,841,268
Baku (Bakı), Azerbaijan (2,020,000) 1,792,300
Bamako, Mali 658,275
Bandung, Indonesia 5,919,400
Bangalore, India (5,686,844) 4,292,223
Banghāzī, Libya 800,000
Bangkok (Krung Thep), Thailand (7,060,000) 5,620,591
Bangui, Central African Republic 451,690
Barcelona, Spain (4,000,000) 1,496,266
Beijing, China (7,320,000) 6,690,000
Beirut (Bayrūt), Lebanon (1,675,000) 509,000
Belfast, N. Ireland, U.K. (730,000) 297,300
Belgrade (Beograd), Serbia 1,594,483
Belo Horizonte, Brazil (4,055,000) 1,366,301
Berlin, Germany (4,220,000) 3,386,667
Birmingham, England, U.K. (2,705,000) 1,020,589
Bishkek, Kyrgyzstan 753,400
Bogotá, Colombia 6,422,198
Bonn, Germany (600,000) 301,048
Boston, Massachusetts, U.S. (5,819,100) 589,141
Brasília, Brazil 1,947,133
Bratislava, Slovakia 451,395
Brazzaville, Congo 693,712
Brisbane, Australia (1,627,535) 888,449
Brussels (Bruxelles), Belgium (2,390,000) 133,845
Bucharest (București), Romania (2,300,000) 2,016,131
Budapest, Hungary (2,450,000) 1,825,153
Buenos Aires, Argentina (11,000,000) 2,960,976
Cairo (Al Qāhirah), Egypt (9,300,000) 6,800,992
Calgary, Alberta, Canada (951,395) 878,866
Cali, Colombia 2,128,920
Canberra, Australia (342,798) 311,518
Cape Town, South Africa (1,900,000) 854,616
Caracas, Venezuela (4,000,000) 1,822,465
Cardiff, Wales, U.K. (645,000) 315,040
Casablanca, Morocco (3,400,000) 3,022,000
Changchun, China 2,470,000
Chelyabinsk, Russia (1,320,000) 1,086,300
Chengdu, China 2,760,000
Chennai (Madras), India (6,424,624) 4,216,268
Chicago, Illinois, U.S. (9,157,540) 2,896,016
Chișinău (Kishinev), Moldova (746,500) 658,300
Chittagong, Bangladesh (2,342,662) 1,566,070
Chongqing, China 3,870,000
Cincinnati, Ohio, U.S. (1,979,202) 331,285
Cleveland, Ohio, U.S. (2,945,831) 478,403
Cologne (Köln), Germany (1,830,000) 962,507
Colombo, Sri Lanka (2,050,000) 615,000
Conakry, Guinea 950,000
Copenhagen (København), Denmark (2,030,000) 499,148
Córdoba, Argentina (1,260,000) 1,179,067
Cotonou, Benin 650,660
Curitiba, Brazil (2,595,000) 1,586,848
Dakar, Senegal (1,976,533) 879,703
Dalian, China 2,400,000
Dallas, Texas, U.S. (5,221,801) 1,188,580
Damascus (Dimashq), Syria (2,230,000) 1,549,932
Dar es Salaam, Tanzania 1,360,850
Delhi, India (12,791,458) 9,817,439
Denver, Colorado, U.S. (2,581,506) 554,636
Detroit, Michigan, U.S. (5,456,428) 951,270
Dhaka (Dacca), Bangladesh (6,537,308) 3,637,892
Djibouti, Djibouti 329,337
Dnipropetrovs'k, Ukraine (1,590,000) 1,108,682
Donets'k, Ukraine (2,090,000) 1,050,369
Douala, Cameroon 712,251
Dublin (Baile Átha Cliath), Ireland (1,175,000) 481,854
Durban, South Africa (1,740,000) 669,242
Dushanbe, Tajikistan (700,000) 528,600
Düsseldorf, Germany (1,200,000) 568,855
Edinburgh, Scotland, U.K. (640,000) 448,850
Edmonton, Alberta, Canada (937,845) 666,104
Eşfahān, Iran (1,525,000) 1,266,072
Essen, Germany (5,040,000) 599,515
Fortaleza, Brazil (2,780,000) 788,956
Frankfurt am Main, Germany (1,960,000) 643,821
Fukuoka, Japan (2,000,000) 1,341,489
Geneva (Génève), Switzerland (450,592) 172,598
Glasgow, Scotland, U.K. (1,870,000) 616,430
Goiânia, Brazil 1,075,761
Guadalajara, Mexico (3,669,021) 1,646,183
Guangzhou (Canton), China 3,750,000
Guatemala, Guatemala (1,500,000) 1,006,954
Guayaquil, Ecuador 2,117,553
Halifax, Nova Scotia, Canada (359,183) 119,300
Hamburg, Germany (2,460,000) 1,704,735
Hannover, Germany (1,015,000) 514,718
Hanoi, Vietnam (1,275,000) 1,073,760
Harare, Zimbabwe (1,470,000) 1,189,103
Harbin, China 3,120,000
Havana (La Habana), Cuba (2,285,000) 2,189,716
Helsinki, Finland (939,697) 548,720
Hiroshima, Japan (1,600,000) 1,126,282
Ho Chi Minh City (Saigon), Vietnam (3,300,000) 3,015,743
Hong Kong (Xianggang), China (4,770,000) 1,250,993
Honolulu, Hawaii, U.S. (876,156) 371,657
Houston, Texas, U.S. (4,669,571) 1,953,631
Hyderābād, India (5,533,640) 3,449,878
Ibadan, Nigeria 1,144,000
Islāmābād, Pakistan (*Rāwalpindi) 529,180
İstanbul, Turkey (8,506,026) 8,260,438
İzmir, Turkey (2,554,363) 2,081,556
Jaipur, India 2,324,319
Jakarta, Indonesia (10,200,000) 9,373,900
Jerusalem (Yerushalayim), Israel (685,000) 633,700
Jiddah, Saudi Arabia 1,450,000
Jinan, China 2,150,000
Johannesburg, South Africa (4,000,000) 752,349
Kābul, Afghanistan 1,424,400
Kampala, Uganda 773,463
Kānpur, India (2,690,486) 2,540,069
Kaohsiung, Taiwan (1,845,000) 1,468,586
Karāchi, Pakistan 9,339,023
Katowice, Poland (2,755,000) 343,158
Kharkiv, Ukraine (1,950,000) 1,494,235
Khartoum (Al Kharṭūm), Sudan (1,450,000) 947,483
Kiev (Kyïv), Ukraine (3,250,000) 2,589,541
Kingston, Jamaica (830,000) 516,500
Kinshasa, Dem. Rep. of the Congo 3,000,000
Kitakyūshū, Japan (1,550,000) 1,011,491
Kolkata (Calcutta), India (13,216,546) 4,580,544
Kuala Lumpur, Malaysia (2,500,000) 1,297,526
Kuwait (Al Kuwayt), Kuwait (1,126,000) 28,859
Lagos, Nigeria (3,800,000) 1,213,000
Lahore, Pakistan 5,143,495
La Paz, Bolivia (1,487,854) 792,611
Libreville, Gabon (418,616) 362,386
Lilongwe, Malawi 435,964
Lima, Peru (6,321,173) 340,422
Lisbon (Lisboa), Portugal (2,350,000) 563,210
Liverpool, England, U.K. (1,515,000) 467,995
Ljubljana, Slovenia 263,832
Lomé, Togo 450,000
London, England, U.K. (12,000,000) 7,074,265
Los Angeles, California, U.S. (16,373,645) 3,694,820
Luanda, Angola 1,459,900
Lucknow, India (2,266,933) 2,207,340
Lusaka, Zambia 1,269,848
Lyon, France (1,648,216) 445,452
Madrid, Spain (4,690,000) 2,882,860
Managua, Nicaragua 864,201
Manaus, Brazil 1,394,724
Manchester, England, U.K. (2,760,000) 430,818
Manila, Philippines (11,200,000) 1,654,761
Mannheim, Germany (1,525,000) 307,730
Maputo, Mozambique 966,837
Maracaibo, Venezuela 1,249,670
Marseille, France (1,516,340) 798,430
Mashhad, Iran 1,887,405
Mecca (Makkah), Saudi Arabia 630,000
Medan, Indonesia 1,988,200
Medellín, Colombia (2,290,000) 1,885,001
Melbourne, Australia (3,366,542) 67,784
Mexico City (Ciudad de México), Mexico (17,786,983) 8,605,239
Miami, Florida, U.S. (3,876,380) 362,470
Milan (Milano), Italy (3,790,000) 1,305,591
Milwaukee, Wisconsin, U.S. (1,689,572) 596,974
Minneapolis, Minnesota, U.S. (2,968,806) 382,618
Minsk, Belarus (1,680,567) 1,677,137
Mogadishu (Muqdisho), Somalia 600,000
Monrovia, Liberia 465,000
Monterrey, Mexico (3,236,604) 1,110,909
Montevideo, Uruguay (1,650,000) 1,303,182
Montréal, Quebec, Canada (3,426,350) 1,039,534
Moscow (Moskva), Russia (12,850,000) 8,389,700
Mumbai (Bombay), India (16,368,084) 11,914,398
Munich (München), Germany (1,930,000) 1,194,560
Nagoya, Japan (5,250,000) 2,171,378
Nāgpur, India (2,122,965) 2,051,320
Nairobi, Kenya 2,143,254
Nanjing, China 2,490,000
Naples (Napoli), Italy (3,150,000) 1,046,987
N'Djamena, Chad 546,572
Newcastle upon Tyne, England, U.K. (1,350,000) 282,338
New Delhi, India (*Delhi) 294,783
New York, New York, U.S. (21,199,865) 8,008,278
Niamey, Niger 392,165
Nizhniy Novgorod, Russia (1,950,000) 1,364,900
Nouakchott, Mauritania 393,325
Novosibirsk, Russia (1,505,000) 1,402,400
Nürnberg, Germany (1,065,000) 486,628
Odesa, Ukraine (1,150,000) 1,002,246
Omsk, Russia (1,190,000) 1,157,600
Ōsaka, Japan (17,050,000) 2,598,589
Oslo, Norway (773,498) 504,040
Ottawa, Ontario, Canada (1,063,664) 774,072
Ouagadougou, Burkina Faso 634,479
Palembang, Indonesia 1,415,500
Panamá, Panama (995,000) 415,964
Paris, France (11,174,743) 2,125,246
Patna, India (1,707,429) 1,376,950
Perm', Russia (1,110,000) 1,017,100
Perth, Australia (1,244,320) 10,195
Philadelphia, Pennsylvania, U.S. (6,188,463) 1,517,550
Phnom Penh (Phnum Pénh), Cambodia 570,155
Phoenix, Arizona, U.S. (3,251,876) 1,321,045
Podgorica, Montenegro 163,493
Port Moresby, Papua New Guinea 246,664
Port-au-Prince, Haiti (1,425,594) 990,558
Portland, Oregon, U.S. (2,265,223) 529,121
Porto, Portugal (1,230,000) 273,060
Porto Alegre, Brazil (3,375,000) 1,304,998
Prague (Praha), Czech Republic (1,328,000) 1,193,270
Pretoria, South Africa (1,100,000) 692,348
Pune, India (3,755,525) 2,540,069
Pusan, South Korea 3,814,325
P'yŏngyang, North Korea 2,741,260
Qingdao, China 2,300,000
Québec, Quebec, Canada (682,757) 169,076
Quezon City, Philippines (*Manila) 1,989,419
Quito, Ecuador 1,615,809
Rabat, Morocco (1,200,000) 717,000
Rangoon (Yangon), Myanmar (2,800,000) 2,705,039
Recife, Brazil (3,160,000) 1,421,993
Regina, Saskatchewan, Canada (192,800) 178,225
Reykjavík, Iceland (166,015) 107,684
Rīga, Latvia (1,000,000) 792,508
Rio de Janeiro, Brazil (10,465,000) 5,851,914
Riyadh (Ar Riyāḍ), Saudi Arabia 1,800,000
Rome (Roma), Italy (3,235,000) 2,649,765
Rosario, Argentina (1,190,000) 894,645
Rostov-na-Donu, Russia (1,160,000) 1,017,300
Rotterdam, Netherlands (1,089,979) 539,000
Sacramento, California, U.S. (1,796,857) 407,018
St. Louis, Missouri, U.S. (2,603,607) 348,189
St. Petersburg (Leningrad), Russia (6,000,000) 4,728,200
Salvador, Brazil (2,855,000) 2,439,823
Samara, Russia (1,450,000) 1,168,000
San Diego, California, U.S. (2,813,833) 1,223,400
San Francisco, California, U.S. (7,039,362) 776,733
San José, Costa Rica (996,194) 309,672
San Juan, Puerto Rico (1,967,627) 421,958
San Salvador, El Salvador (1,908,921) 473,372
Santiago, Chile 4,788,543
Santo Domingo, Dominican Republic 2,677,056
São Paulo, Brazil (17,380,000) 9,713,692
Sapporo, Japan (2,000,000) 1,822,300
Sarajevo, Bosnia and Herzegovina 367,703
Saratov, Russia (1,135,000) 881,000
Seattle, Washington, U.S. (3,554,760) 563,374
Seoul (Sŏul), South Korea (15,850,000) 10,231,217
Shanghai, China (11,010,000) 8,930,000
Shenyang (Mukden), China 4,050,000
Singapore, Singapore (4,400,000) 4,017,700
Skopje, Macedonia 440,577
Sofia (Sofiya), Bulgaria (1,189,794) 1,138,629
Stockholm, Sweden (1,643,366) 743,703
Stuttgart, Germany (2,020,000) 582,443
Surabaya, Indonesia 2,801,300
Sūrat, India (2,811,466) 2,433,787
Sydney, Australia (3,741,290) 11,115
T'aipei, Taiwan (6,200,000) 2,640,322
Tallinn, Estonia 403,981
Tashkent (Toshkent), Uzbekistan (2,325,000) 2,142,700
Tbilisi, Georgia (1,460,000) 1,279,000
Tegucigalpa, Honduras 576,661
Tehrān, Iran (8,800,000) 6,758,845
Tel Aviv-Yafo, Israel (1,890,000) 348,100
Tianjin (Tientsin), China 5,000,000
Tiranë, Albania 244,153
Tōkyō, Japan (30,300,000) 8,130,408
Toronto, Ontario, Canada (4,682,897) 2,481,494
Tripoli (Ṭarābulus), Libya 1,500,000
Tunis, Tunisia (1,300,000) 702,330
Turin (Torino), Italy (1,550,000) 921,485
Ufa, Russia (1,110,000) 1,088,900
Ulan Bator (Ulaanbaatar), Mongolia 672,882
Ürümqi, China 1,130,000
València, Spain (1,340,000) 739,014
Vancouver, British Columbia, Canada (1,986,965) 545,671
Viangchan (Vientiane), Laos 464,000
Vienna (Wien), Austria (1,950,000) 1,609,631
Vilnius, Lithuania 578,334
Volgograd (Stalingrad), Russia (1,358,000) 1,000,000
Warsaw (Warszawa), Poland (2,300,000) 1,615,369
Washington, D.C., U.S. (7,608,070) 572,059
Wellington, New Zealand (346,500) 167,400
Winnipeg, Manitoba, Canada (671,274) 619,544
Wuhan, China 3,870,000
Xi'an, China 2,410,000
Yekaterinburg, Russia (1,530,000) 1,272,900
Yerevan, Armenia (1,315,000) 1,249,202
Yokohama, Japan (*Tōkyō) 3,426,506
Zagreb, Croatia 867,865
Zürich, Switzerland (932,681) 337,553

Metropolitan area populations are shown in parentheses.
* City is located within the metropolitan area of another city; for example, Yokohama, Japan is located in the Tōkyō metropolitan area.

GLOSSARY OF FOREIGN GEOGRAPHICAL TERMS

Annam . . . Annamese
Arab . . . Arabic
Bantu . . . Bantu
Bur . . . Burmese
Camb . . . Cambodian
Celt . . . Celtic
Chn . . . Chinese
Czech . . . Czech
Dan . . . Danish
Du . . . Dutch
Fin . . . Finnish
Fr . . . French
Ger . . . German
Gr . . . Greek
Hung . . . Hungarian
Ice . . . Icelandic
India . . . India
Indian . . . American Indian
Indon . . . Indonesian
It . . . Italian
Jap . . . Japanese
Kor . . . Korean
Mal . . . Malayan
Mong . . . Mongolian
Nor . . . Norwegian
Per . . . Persian
Pol . . . Polish
Port . . . Portuguese
Rom . . . Romanian
Rus . . . Russian
Siam . . . Siamese
So. Slav . . . Southern Slavonic
Sp . . . Spanish
Swe . . . Swedish
Tib . . . Tibetan
Tur . . . Turkish
Yugo . . . Yugoslav

å, Nor., Swe . . . brook, river
aa, Dan., Nor . . . brook
aas, Dan., Nor . . . ridge
âb, Per . . . water, river
abad, India, Per . . . town, city
ada, Tur . . . island
adrar, Berber . . . mountain
air, Indon . . . stream
akrotírion, Gr . . . cape
älf, Swe . . . river
alp, Ger . . . mountain
altipiano, It . . . plateau
alto, Sp . . . height
archipel, Fr . . . archipelago
archipiélago, Sp . . . archipelago
arquipélago, Port . . . archipelago
arroyo, Sp . . . brook, stream
ås, Nor., Swe . . . ridge
austral, Sp . . . southern
baai, Du . . . bay
bab, Arab . . . gate, port
bach, Ger . . . brook, stream
backe, Swe . . . hill
bad, Ger . . . bath, spa
bahía, Sp . . . bay, gulf
bahr, Arab . . . river, sea, lake
baia, It . . . bay, gulf
baía, Port . . . bay
baie, Fr . . . bay, gulf
bajo, Sp . . . depression
bak, Indon . . . stream
bakke, Dan., Nor . . . hill
balkan, Tur . . . mountain range
bana, Jap . . . point, cape
banco, Sp . . . bank
bandar, Mal., Per. . . . town, port, harbor
bang, Siam . . . village
bassin, Fr . . . basin
batang, Indon., Mal . . . river
ben, Celt . . . mountain, summit
bender, Arab . . . harbor, port
bereg, Rus . . . coast, shore
berg, Du., Ger., Nor., Swe. . . . mountain, hill
bir, Arab . . . well
birkat, Arab . . . lake, pond, pool
bit, Arab . . . house
bjaerg, Dan., Nor . . . mountain
bocche, It . . . mouth
boğazı, Tur . . . strait
bois, Fr . . . forest, wood
boloto, Rus . . . marsh
bolsón, Sp. . . . flat-floored desert valley
boreal, Sp . . . northern
borg, Dan., Nor., Swe . . . castle, town
borgo, It . . . town, suburb
bosch, Du . . . forest, wood
bouche, Fr . . . river mouth
bourg, Fr . . . town, borough
bro, Dan., Nor., Swe . . . bridge
brücke, Ger . . . bridge
bucht, Ger . . . bay, bight
bugt, Dan., Nor., Swe . . . bay, gulf
bulu, Indon . . . mountain
burg, Du., Ger . . . castle, town
buri, Siam . . . town
burun, burnu, Tur . . . cape
by, Dan., Nor., Swe . . . village
caatinga, Port. (Brazil) . . . open brushland
cabezo, Sp . . . summit
cabo, Port., Sp . . . cape
campo, It., Port., Sp . . . plain, field
campos, Port. (Brazil) . . . plains
cañón, Sp . . . canyon
cap, Fr . . . cape
capo, It . . . cape
casa, It., Port., Sp . . . house
castello, It., Port . . . castle, fort
castillo, Sp . . . castle
càte, Fr . . . hill
çay, Tur . . . stream, river
cayo, Sp . . . rock, shoal, islet
cerro, Sp . . . mountain, hill
champ, Fr . . . field
chang, Chn . . . village, middle
château, Fr . . . castle
chen, Chn . . . market town
chiang, Chn . . . river
chott, Arab . . . salt lake
chou, Chn. capital of district; island
chu, Tib . . . water, stream
cidade, Port . . . town, city
cima, Sp . . . summit, peak
città, It . . . town, city
ciudad, Sp . . . town, city
coxilha, Port . . . ridge
col, Fr . . . pass
colina, Sp . . . hill
cordillera, Sp . . . mountain chain
costa, It., Port., Sp . . . coast
côte, Fr . . . coast
cuchilla, Sp . . . mountain ridge
dağ, Tur . . . mountain(s)
dake, Jap . . . peak, summit
dal, Dan., Du., Nor., Swe . . . valley
dan, Kor . . . point, cape
danau, Indon . . . lake
dar, Arab . . . house, abode, country
darya, Per . . . river, sea
dasht, Per . . . plain, desert
deniz, Tur . . . sea
désert, Fr . . . desert
deserto, It . . . desert
desierto, Sp . . . desert
détroit, Fr . . . strait
dijk, Du . . . dam, dike
djebel, Arab . . . mountain
do, Kor . . . island
dorf, Ger . . . village
dorp, Du . . . village
duin, Du . . . dune
dzong, Tib. . . . fort, administrative capital
eau, Fr . . . water
ecuador, Sp . . . equator
eiland, Du . . . island
elv, Dan., Nor . . . river, stream
embalse, Sp . . . reservoir
erg, Arab . . . dune, sandy desert
est, Fr., It . . . east
estado, Sp . . . state
este, Port., Sp . . . east
estrecho, Sp . . . strait
étang, Fr . . . pond, lake
état, Fr . . . state
eyjar, Ice . . . islands
feld, Ger . . . field, plain
festung, Ger . . . fortress
fiume, It . . . river
fjäll, Swe . . . mountain
fjärd, Swe . . . bay, inlet
fjeld, Nor . . . mountain, hill
fjord, Dan., Nor . . . fiord, inlet
fjördur, Ice . . . fiord, inlet
fleuve, Fr . . . river
flod, Dan., Swe . . . river
flói, Ice . . . bay, marshland
fluss, Ger . . . river
foce, It . . . river mouth
fontein, Du . . . a spring
forêt, Fr . . . forest
fors, Swe . . . waterfall
forst, Ger . . . forest
fos, Dan., Nor . . . waterfall
fu, Chn . . . town, residence
fuente, Sp . . . spring, fountain
fuerte, Sp . . . fort
furt, Ger . . . ford
gang, Kor . . . stream, river
gangri, Tib . . . mountain
gat, Dan., Nor . . . channel
gâve, Fr . . . stream
gawa, Jap . . . river
gebergte, Du . . . mountain range
gebiet, Ger . . . district, territory
gebirge, Ger . . . mountains
ghat, India . . . pass, mountain range
gobi, Mong . . . desert
gol, Mong . . . river
göl, gölü, Tur . . . lake
golf, Du., Ger . . . gulf, bay
golfe, Fr . . . gulf, bay
golfo, It., Port., Sp . . . gulf, bay
gomba, gompa, Tib . . . monastery
gora, Rus., So. Slav . . . mountain
góra, Pol . . . mountain
gorod, Rus . . . town
grad, Rus., So. Slav . . . town
guba, Rus . . . bay, gulf
gundung, Indon . . . mountain
guntō, Jap . . . archipelago
gunung, Mal . . . mountain
haf, Swe . . . sea, ocean
hafen, Ger . . . port, harbor
haff, Ger . . . gulf, inland sea
hai, Chn . . . sea, lake
hama, Jap . . . beach, shore
hamada, Arab . . . rocky plateau
hamn, Swe . . . harbor
hāmūn, Per . . . swampy lake, plain
hantō, Jap . . . peninsula
hassi, Arab . . . well, spring
haus, Ger . . . house
haut, Fr . . . summit, top
hav, Dan., Nor . . . sea, ocean
havn, Dan., Nor . . . harbor, port
havre, Fr . . . harbor, port
háza, Hung . . . house, dwelling of
heim, Ger . . . hamlet, home
hem, Swe . . . hamlet, home
higashi, Jap . . . east
hisar, Tur . . . fortress
hissar, Arab . . . fort
ho, Chn . . . river
hoek, Du . . . cape
hof, Ger . . . court, farmhouse
höfn, Ice . . . harbor
hoku, Jap . . . north
holm, Dan., Nor., Swe . . . island
hora, Czech . . . mountain
horn, Ger . . . peak
hoved, Dan., Nor . . . cape
hsien, Chn . . . district, district capital
hu, Chn . . . lake
hügel, Ger . . . hill
huk, Dan., Swe . . . point
hus, Dan., Nor., Swe . . . house
île, Fr . . . island
ilha, Port . . . island
indsö, Dan., Nor . . . lake
insel, Ger . . . island
insjö, Swe . . . lake
irmak, irmagi, Tur . . . river
isla, Sp . . . island
isola, It . . . island
istmo, It., Sp . . . isthmus
järvi, jaur, Fin . . . lake
jebel, Arab . . . mountain
jima, Jap . . . island
jökel, Nor . . . glacier
joki, Fin . . . river
jökull, Ice . . . glacier
kaap, Du . . . cape
kai, Jap . . . bay, gulf, sea
kaikyō, Jap . . . channel, strait
kalat, Per . . . castle, fortress
kale, Tur . . . fort
kali, Mal . . . creek, river
kand, Per . . . village
kang, Chn . mountain ridge; village
kap, Dan., Ger . . . cape
kapp, Nor., Swe . . . cape
kasr, Arab . . . fort, castle
kawa, Jap . . . river
kefr, Arab . . . village
kei, Jap . . . creek, river
ken, Jap . . . prefecture
khor, Arab . . . bay, inlet
khrebet, Rus . . . mountain range
kiang, Chn . . . large river
king, Chn . . . capital city, town
kita, Jap . . . north
ko, Jap . . . lake
köbstad, Dan . . . market-town
kol, Mong . . . lake
kólpos, Gr . . . gulf
kong, Chn . . . river
kopf, Ger . . . head, summit, peak
köpstad, Swe . . . market-town
körfezi, Tur . . . gulf
kosa, Rus . . . spit
kou, Chn . . . river mouth
köy, Tur . . . village
kraal, Du. (Africa) . . . native village
ksar, Arab . . . fortified village
kuala, Mal . . . bay, river mouth
kuh, Per . . . mountain
kum, Tur . . . sand
kuppe, Ger . . . summit
küste, Ger . . . coast
kyo, Jap . . . town, capital
la, Tib . . . mountain pass
labuan, Mal . . . anchorage, port
lac, Fr . . . lake
lago, It., Port., Sp . . . lake
lagoa, Port . . . lake, marsh
laguna, It., Port., Sp . . . lagoon, lake
lahti, Fin . . . bay, gulf
län, Swe . . . county
landsby, Dan., Nor . . . village
liehtao, Chn . . . archipelago
liman, Tur . . . bay, port
ling, Chn . . . pass, ridge, mountain
llanos, Sp . . . plains
loch, Celt. (Scotland) . . . lake, bay
loma, Sp . . . long, low hill
lough, Celt. (Ireland) . . . lake, bay
machi, Jap . . . town
man, Kor . . . bay
mar, Port., Sp . . . sea
mare, It., Rom . . . sea
marisma, Sp . . . marsh, swamp
mark, Ger . . . boundary, limit
massif, Fr . . . block of mountains
mato, Port . . . forest, thicket
me, Siam . . . river
meer, Du., Ger . . . lake, sea
mer, Fr . . . sea
mesa, Sp . . . flat-topped mountain
meseta, Sp . . . plateau
mina, Port., Sp . . . mine
minami, Jap . . . south
minato, Jap . . . harbor, haven
misaki, Jap . . . cape, headland
mont, Fr . . . mount, mountain
montagna, It . . . mountain
montagne, Fr . . . mountain
montaña, Sp . . . mountain
monte, It., Port., Sp. . . . mount, mountain
more, Rus., So. Slav . . . sea
morro, Port., Sp . . . hill, bluff
mühle, Ger . . . mill
mund, Ger . . . mouth, opening
mündung, Ger . . . river mouth
mura, Jap . . . township
myit, Bur . . . river
mys, Rus . . . cape
nada, Jap . . . sea
nadi, India . . . river, creek
naes, Dan., Nor . . . cape
nafud, Arab . . desert of sand dunes
nagar, India . . . town, city
nahr, Arab . . . river
nam, Siam . . . river, water
nan, Chn., Jap . . . south
näs, Nor., Swe . . . cape
nez, Fr . . . point, cape
nishi, nisi, Jap . . . west
njarga, Fin . . . peninsula
nong, Siam . . . marsh
noord, Du . . . north
nor, Mong . . . lake
nord, Dan., Fr., Ger., It., Nor., Swe . . . north
norte, Port., Sp . . . north
nos, Rus . . . cape
nyasa, Bantu . . . lake
ö, Dan., Nor., Swe . . . island
occidental, Sp . . . western
ocna, Rom . . . salt mine
odde, Dan., Nor . . . point, cape
oeste, Port., Sp . . . west
oka, Jap . . . hill
oost, Du . . . east
oriental, Sp . . . eastern
óros, Gr . . . mountain
ost, Ger., Swe . . . east
öster, Dan., Nor., Swe . . . eastern
ostrov, Rus . . . island
oued, Arab . . . river, stream
ouest, Fr . . . west
ozero, Rus . . . lake
pää, Fin . . . mountain
padang, Mal . . . plain, field
pampas, Sp. (Argentina) . . . grassy plains
pará, Indian (Brazil) . . . river
pas, Fr . . . channel, passage
paso, Sp . mountain pass, passage
passo, It., Port. mountain pass, passage, strait
patam, India . . . city, town
pei, Chn . . . north
pélagos, Gr . . . open sea
pegunungan, Indon . . . mountains
peña, Sp . . . rock
peresheyek, Rus . . . isthmus
pertuis, Fr . . . strait
peski, Rus . . . desert
pic, Fr . . . mountain peak
pico, Port., Sp . . . mountain peak
piedra, Sp . . . stone, rock
ping, Chn . . . plain, flat
planalto, Port . . . plateau
planina, Yugo . . . mountains
playa, Sp . . . shore, beach
pnom, Camb . . . mountain
pointe, Fr . . . point
polder, Du., Ger . . reclaimed marsh
polje, So. Slav . . . plain, field
poluostrov, Rus . . . peninsula
pont, Fr . . . bridge
ponta, Port . . . point, headland
ponte, It., Port . . . bridge
pore, India . . . city, town
porthmós, Gr . . . strait
porto, It., Port . . . port, harbor
potamós, Gr . . . river
p'ov, Rus . . . peninsula
prado, Sp . . . field, meadow
presqu'île, Fr . . . peninsula
proliv, Rus . . . strait
pu, Chn . . . commercial village
pueblo, Sp . . . town, village
puerto, Sp . . . port, harbor
pulau, Indon . . . island
punkt, Ger . . . point
punt, Du . . . point
punta, It., Sp . . . point
pur, India . . . city, town
puy, Fr . . . peak
qal'a, qal'at, Arab . . . fort, village
qasr, Arab . . . fort, castle
rann, India . . . wasteland
ra's, Arab . . . cape, head
reka, Rus., So. Slav . . . river
represa, Port . . . reservoir
rettō, Jap . . . island chain
ría, Sp . . . estuary
ribeira, Port . . . stream
riberão, Port . . . river
rio, It., Port . . . stream, river
río, Sp . . . river
rivière, Fr . . . river
roca, Sp . . . rock
rt, Yugo . . . cape
rūd, Per . . . river
saari, Fin . . . island
sable, Fr . . . sand
sahara, Arab . . . desert, plain
saki, Jap . . . cape
sal, Sp . . . salt
salar, Sp . . . salt flat, salt lake
salto, Sp . . . waterfall
san, Jap., Kor . . . mountain, hill
sat, satul, Rom . . . village
schloss, Ger . . . castle
sebkha, Arab . . . salt marsh
see, Ger . . . lake, sea
şehir, Tur . . . town, city
selat, Indon . . . stream
selvas, Port. (Brazil) . . . tropical rain forests
seno, Sp . . . bay
serra, Port . . . mountain chain
serranía, Sp . . . mountain ridge
seto, Jap . . . strait
severnaya, Rus . . . northern
shahr, Per . . . town, city
shan, Chn . . . mountain, hill, island
shatt, Arab . . . river
shi, Jap . . . city
shima, Jap . . . island
shotō, Jap . . . archipelago
si, Chn . . . west, western
sierra, Sp . . . mountain range
sjö, Nor., Swe . . . lake, sea
sö, Dan., Nor . . . lake, sea
söder, södra, Swe . . . south
song, Annam . . . river
sopka, Rus . . . peak, volcano
source, Fr . . . a spring
spitze, Ger . . . summit, point
staat, Ger . . . state
stad, Dan., Du., Nor., Swe. . . . city, town
stadt, Ger . . . city, town
stato, It . . . state
step', Rus . . . treeless plain, steppe
straat, Du . . . strait
strand, Dan., Du., Ger., Nor., Swe . . . shore, beach
stretto, It . . . strait
strom, Ger . . . river, stream
ström, Dan., Nor., Swe. . . . stream, river
stroom, Du . . . stream, river
su, suyu, Tur . . . water, river
sud, Fr., Sp . . . south
süd, Ger . . . south
suidō, Jap . . . channel
sul, Port . . . south
sund, Dan., Nor., Swe . . . sound
sungai, sungei, Indon., Mal . . . river
sur, Sp . . . south
syd, Dan., Nor., Swe . . . south
tafelland, Ger . . . plateau
take, Jap . . . peak, summit
tal, Ger . . . valley
tanjung, tanjong, Mal . . . cape
tao, Chn . . . island
târg, târgul, Rom . . . market, town
tell, Arab . . . hill
teluk, Indon . . . bay, gulf
terra, It . . . land
terre, Fr . . . earth, land
thal, Ger . . . valley
tierra, Sp . . . earth, land
tō, Jap . . . east; island
tonle, Camb . . . river, lake
top, Du . . . peak
torp, Swe . . . hamlet, cottage
tsangpo, Tib . . . river
tsi, Chn . . . village, borough
tso, Tib . . . lake
tsu, Jap . . . harbor, port
tundra, Rus . . treeless arctic plains
tung, Chn . . . east
tuz, Tur . . . salt
udde, Swe . . . cape
ufer, Ger . . . shore, riverbank
ujung, Indon . . . point, cape
umi, Jap . . . sea, gulf
ura, Jap . . . bay, coast, creek
ust'ye, Rus . . . river mouth
valle, It., Port., Sp . . . valley
vallée, Fr . . . valley
valli, It . . . lake
vár, Hung . . . fortress
város, Hung . . . town
varoš, So. Slav . . . town
veld, Du . . . open plain, field
verkh, Rus . . . top, summit
ves, Czech . . . village
vest, Dan., Nor., Swe . . . west
vik, Swe . . . cove, bay
vila, Port . . . town
villa, Sp . . . town
villar, Sp . . . village, hamlet
ville, Fr . . . town, city
vostok, Rus . . . east
wad, wādī, Arab. . . . intermittent stream
wald, Ger . . . forest, woodland
wan, Chn., Jap . . . bay, gulf
weiler, Ger . . . hamlet, village
westersch, Du . . . western
wüste, Ger . . . desert
yama, Jap . . . mountain
yarimada, Tur . . . peninsula
yug, Rus . . . south
zaki, Jap . . . cape
zaliv, Rus . . . bay, gulf
zapad, Rus . . . west
zee, Du . . . sea
zemlya, Rus . . . land
zuid, Du . . . south

ABBREVIATIONS OF GEOGRAPHICAL NAMES AND TERMS

Afg.	Afghanistan
Afr.	Africa
Ak., U.S.	Alaska, U.S.
Al., U.S.	Alabama, U.S.
Alb.	Albania
Alg.	Algeria
Am. Sam.	American Samoa
And.	Andorra
Ang.	Angola
Ant.	Antarctica
Antig.	Antigua and Barbuda
aq.	Aqueduct
Ar., U.S.	Arkansas, U.S.
Arg.	Argentina
Arm.	Armenia
arpt.	Airport
Aus.	Austria
Austl.	Australia
Az., U.S.	Arizona, U.S.
Azer.	Azerbaijan
b.	Bay, Gulf, Inlet, Lagoon
Bah.	Bahamas
Bahr.	Bahrain
Barb.	Barbados
Bdi.	Burundi
Bel.	Belgium
Bela.	Belarus
Ber.	Bermuda
Bhu.	Bhutan
bk.	Undersea Bank
bldg.	Building
Blg.	Bulgaria
Bngl.	Bangladesh
Bol.	Bolivia
Bos.	Bosnia and Herzegovina
Bots.	Botswana
Braz.	Brazil
Bru.	Brunei
Br. Vir. Is.	British Virgin Islands
bt.	Bight
Burkina	Burkina Faso
c.	Cape, Point
Ca., U.S.	California, U.S.
Cam.	Cameroon
Camb.	Cambodia
can.	Canal
Can.	Canada
C.A.R.	Central African Republic
Cay. Is.	Cayman Islands
C. Iv.	Cote d'Ivoire
clf.	Cliff, Escarpment
co.	County, Parish
Co., U.S.	Colorado, U.S.
Col.	Colombia
Com.	Comoros
cont.	Continent
Cook Is.	Cook Islands
C.R.	Costa Rica
Cro.	Croatia
cst.	Coast, Beach
Ct., U.S.	Connecticut, U.S.
C.V.	Cape Verde
Cyp.	Cyprus
Czech Rep.	Czech Republic
d.	Delta
D.C., U.S.	District of Columbia, U.S.
De., U.S.	Delaware, U.S.
Den.	Denmark
dep.	Dependency, Colony
depr.	Depression
dept.	Department, District
des.	Desert
Dji.	Djibouti
Dom.	Dominica
Dom. Rep.	Dominican Republic
D.R.C.	Democratic Republic of the Congo
Ec.	Ecuador
educ.	Educational Facility
El Sal.	El Salvador
Eng., U.K.	England, U.K.
Eq. Gui.	Equatorial Guinea
Erit.	Eritrea
Est.	Estonia
est.	Estuary
Eth.	Ethiopia
E. Timor	East Timor
Eur.	Europe
Falk. Is.	Falkland Islands
Far. Is.	Faroe Islands
Fin.	Finland
fj.	Fjord
Fl., U.S.	Florida, U.S.
for.	Forest, Moor
Fr.	France
Fr. Gu.	French Guiana
Fr. Poly.	French Polynesia
Ga., U.S.	Georgia, U.S.
Gam.	The Gambia
Gaza	Gaza Strip
Geor.	Georgia
Ger.	Germany

Grc.	Greece
Gren.	Grenada
Grnld.	Greenland
Guad.	Guadeloupe
Guat.	Guatemala
Guern.	Guernsey
Gui.	Guinea
Gui.-B.	Guinea-Bissau
Guy.	Guyana
Hi., U.S.	Hawaii, U.S.
hist.	Historic Site, Ruins
hist. reg.	Historic Region
Hond.	Honduras
Hung.	Hungary
i.	Island
Ia., U.S.	Iowa, U.S.
ice	Ice Feature, Glacier
Ice.	Iceland
Id., U.S.	Idaho, U.S.
Il., U.S.	Illinois, U.S.
In., U.S.	Indiana, U.S.
Indon.	Indonesia
I. of Man	Isle of Man
I.R.	Indian Reservation
Ire.	Ireland
is.	Islands
Isr.	Israel
isth.	Isthmus
Jam.	Jamaica
Jord.	Jordan
Kaz.	Kazakhstan
Kir.	Kiribati
Kor., N.	Korea, North
Kor., S.	Korea, South
Ks., U.S.	Kansas, U.S.
Kuw.	Kuwait
Ky., U.S.	Kentucky, U.S.
Kyrg.	Kyrgyzstan
l.	Lake, Pond
La., U.S.	Louisiana, U.S.
Lat.	Latvia
Leb.	Lebanon
Leso.	Lesotho
Lib.	Liberia
Liech.	Liechtenstein
Lith.	Lithuania
Lux.	Luxembourg
Ma., U.S.	Massachusetts, U.S.
Mac.	Macedonia
Madag.	Madagascar
Malay.	Malaysia
Mald.	Maldives
Marsh. Is.	Marshall Islands
Mart.	Martinique
Maur.	Mauritania
May.	Mayotte
Md., U.S.	Maryland, U.S.
Me., U.S.	Maine, U.S.
Mex.	Mexico
Mi., U.S.	Michigan, U.S.
Micron.	Micronesia, Federated States of
Mn., U.S.	Minnesota, U.S.
Mo., U.S.	Missouri, U.S.
Mol.	Moldova
Mong.	Mongolia
Mont.	Montenegro
Monts.	Montserrat
Mor.	Morocco
Moz.	Mozambique
Ms., U.S.	Mississippi, U.S.
Mt., U.S.	Montana, U.S.
mth.	River Mouth or Channel
mtn.	Mountain
mts.	Mountains
Mwi.	Malawi
Mya.	Myanmar
N.A.	North America
N.C., U.S.	North Carolina, U.S.
N. Cal.	New Caledonia
N.D., U.S.	North Dakota, U.S.
Ne., U.S.	Nebraska, U.S.
neigh.	Neighborhood
Neth.	Netherlands
Neth. Ant.	Netherlands Antilles
N.H., U.S.	New Hampshire, U.S.
Nic.	Nicaragua
Nig.	Nigeria
N. Ire., U.K.	Northern Ireland, U.K.
N.J., U.S.	New Jersey, U.S.
N.M., U.S.	New Mexico, U.S.
N. Mar. Is.	Northern Mariana Islands
Nmb.	Namibia
Nor.	Norway
Nv., U.S.	Nevada, U.S.
N.Y., U.S.	New York, U.S.
N.Z.	New Zealand
o.	Ocean
Oc.	Oceania

Oh., U.S.	Ohio, U.S.
Ok., U.S.	Oklahoma, U.S.
Or., U.S.	Oregon, U.S.
p.	Pass
Pa., U.S.	Pennsylvania, U.S.
Pak.	Pakistan
Pan.	Panama
Pap. N. Gui.	Papua New Guinea
Para.	Paraguay
pen.	Peninsula
Phil.	Philippines
Pit.	Pitcairn
pl.	Plain, Flat
plat.	Plateau, Highland
Pol.	Poland
Port.	Portugal
P.R.	Puerto Rico
prov.	Province, Region
pt. of i.	Point of Interest
r.	River, Creek
Reu.	Reunion
rec.	Recreational Site, Park
reg.	Physical Region
rel.	Religious Institution
res.	Reservoir
rf.	Reef, Shoal
R.I., U.S.	Rhode Island, U.S.
Rom.	Romania
Rw.	Rwanda
S.A.	South America
S. Afr.	South Africa
Sau. Ar.	Saudi Arabia
S.C., U.S.	South Carolina, U.S.
sci.	Scientific Station
Scot., U.K.	Scotland, U.K.
S.D., U.S.	South Dakota, U.S.
sea feat.	Undersea Feature
Sen.	Senegal
Serb.	Serbia
Sey.	Seychelles
S. Geor.	South Georgia
Sing.	Singapore
S.L.	Sierra Leone
Slvk.	Slovakia
Slvn.	Slovenia
S. Mar.	San Marino
Sol. Is.	Solomon Islands
Som.	Somalia
Sp. N. Afr.	Spanish North Africa
Sri L.	Sri Lanka
St. Hel.	St. Helena
St. K./N.	St. Kitts and Nevis
St. Luc.	St. Lucia
St. P./M.	St. Pierre and Miquelon
strt.	Strait, Channel, Sound
S. Tom./P.	Sao Tome and Principe
St. Vin.	St. Vincent and the Grenadines
Sur.	Suriname
Sval.	Svalbard
sw.	Swamp, Marsh
Swaz.	Swaziland
Swe.	Sweden
Switz.	Switzerland
Tai.	Taiwan
Taj.	Tajikistan
Tan.	Tanzania
T./C. Is.	Turks and Caicos Islands
ter.	Territory
Thai.	Thailand
Tn., U.S.	Tennessee, U.S.
trans.	Transportation Facility
Trin.	Trinidad and Tobago
Tun.	Tunisia
Tur.	Turkey
Turkmen.	Turkmenistan
Tx., U.S.	Texas, U.S.
U.A.E.	United Arab Emirates
Ug.	Uganda
U.K.	United Kingdom
Ukr.	Ukraine
Ur.	Uruguay
U.S.	United States
Ut., U.S.	Utah, U.S.
Uzb.	Uzbekistan
Va., U.S.	Virginia, U.S.
val.	Valley, Watercourse
Ven.	Venezuela
Viet.	Vietnam
V.I.U.S.	Virgin Islands (U.S.)
vol.	Volcano
Vt., U.S.	Vermont, U.S.
Wa., U.S.	Washington, U.S.
W.B.	West Bank
Wi., U.S.	Wisconsin, U.S.
W. Sah.	Western Sahara
wtfl.	Waterfall
W.V., U.S.	West Virginia, U.S.
Wy., U.S.	Wyoming, U.S.
Zam.	Zambia
Zimb.	Zimbabwe

PRONUNCIATION OF GEOGRAPHICAL NAMES

Key to the Sound Values of Letters and Symbols Used in the Index to Indicate Pronunciation

ă-ăt; băttle
ă-finăl; appeăl
ā-rāte; elāte
å-senåte; inanimåte
ä-ärm; cälm
à-àsk; båth
a-sofa; marine (short neutral or indeterminate sound)
â-fâre; prepâre
ch-choose; church
dh-as th in other; either
ē-bē, ēve
ĕ-ĕvent; crĕate
ĕ-bĕt; ĕnd
ĕ-recĕnt (short neutral or indeterminate sound)
ẽ-cratẽr; cindẽr
g-gō; gāme
gh-guttural g
ĭ-bĭt; wĭll
i-(short neutral or indeterminate sound)
ī-rīde; bīte
κ-gutteral k as ch in German ich
ng-sing
ŋ-baŋk; liŋger
N-indicates nasalized
ŏ-nŏd; ŏdd
ŏ-cŏmmit; cŏnnect
ō-ōld; bōld
ô-ôbey; hôtel
ô-ôrder; nôrth
oi-boil
ōō-fōōd; rōōt
ȯ-as oo in foot; wood
ou-out; thou
s-soft; so; sane
sh-dish; finish
th-thin; thick
ū-pūre; cūre
ů-ůnite; ůsůrp
û-ûrn; fûr
ŭ-stŭd; ŭp
ŭ-circŭs; sŭbmit
ü-as in French tu
zh-as z in azure
'-indeterminate vowel sound

In many cases the spelling of foreign geographical names does not even remotely indicate the pronunciation to an American, i.e., Słupsk in Poland is pronounced swȯpsk; Jujuy in Argentina is pronounced hōōhwē', La Spezia in Italy is lä-spē'zyä.

This condition is hardly surprising, however, when we consider that in our own language Worcester, Massachusetts, is pronounced wȯs'tẽr; Sioux City, Iowa, sōō sĭ'tĭ; Schuylkill Haven, Pennsylvania, skōōl'kĭl hā-vĕn; Poughkeepsie, New York, pŏ-kĭp'sĕ.

The indication of pronunciation of geographic names presents several peculiar problems:

1. Many foreign tongues use sounds that are not present in the English language and which an American cannot normally articulate. Thus, though the nearest English equivalent sound has been indicated, only approximate results are possible.

2. There are several dialects in each foreign tongue which cause variation in the local pronunciation of names. This also occurs in identical names in the various divisions of a great language group, as the Slavic or the Latin.

3. Within the United States there are marked differences in pronunciation, not only of local geographic names, but also of common words, indicating that the sound and tone values for letters as well as the placing of the emphasis vary considerably from one part of the country to another.

4. A number of different letters and diacritical combinations could be used to indicate essentially the same or approximate pronunciations.

Some variation in pronunciation other than that indicated in this index may be encountered, but such a difference does not necessarily indicate that either is in error, and in many cases it is a matter of individual choice as to which is preferred. In fact, an exact indication of pronunciation of many foreign names using English letters and diacritical marks is extremely difficult and sometimes impossible.

PRONOUNCING INDEX

This universal index includes in a single alphabetical list approximately 30,000 names of features that appear on the reference maps. Each name is followed by a page reference and geographical coordinates.

Abbreviation and Capitalization Abbreviations of names on the maps have been standardized as much as possible. Names that are abbreviated on the maps are generally spelled out in full in the index. Periods are used after all abbreviations regardless of local practice. The abbreviation "St." is used only for "Saint". "Sankt" and other forms of this term are spelled out.

Most initial letters of names are capitalized, except for a few Dutch names, such as "s-Gravenhage". Capitalization of noninitial words in a name generally follows local practice.

Alphabetization Names are alphabetized in the order of the letters of the English alphabet. Spanish *ll* and *ch*, for example, are not treated as direct letters. Furthermore, diacritical marks are disregarded in alphabetization — German or Scandinavian *ä* or *ö* are treated as *a* or *o*.

The names of physical features may appear inverted, since they are always alphabetized under the proper, not the generic, part of the name, thus: "Gibraltar, Strait of". Otherwise every entry, whether consisting of one word or more, is alphabetized as a single continuous entity. "Lakeland", for example, appears after "La Crosse" and before "La Salle". Names beginning with articles (Le Harve, Den Helder, Al Manāmah, Ad Dawhah) are not inverted.

In the case of identical names, towns are listed first, then political divisions, then physical features.

Generic Terms Except for cities, the names of all features are followed by terms that represent broad classes of features, for example, Mississippi, r. or Alabama, state. A list of all abbreviations used in the index is on page 261.

Country names and the names of features that extend beyond the boundaries of one county are followed by the name of the continent in which each is located. Country designations follow the names of all other places in the index. The locations of places in the United States and the United Kingdom are further defined by abbreviations that include the state or political division in which each is located.

Pronunciations Pronunciations are included for most names listed. An explanation of the pronunciation system used appears on page 261.

Page References and Geographical Coordinates The geographical coordinates and page references are found in the last columns of each entry.

If a page contains several maps or insets, a lowercase letter identifies the specific map or inset.

Latitude and longitude coordinates for point features, such as cities and mountain peaks, indicate the location of the symbols. For extensive areal features, such as countries or mountain ranges, or linear features, such as canals and rivers, locations are given for the position of the type as it appears on the map.

PLACE (Pronunciation)	PAGE	LAT.	LONG.
A			
Aachen, Ger. (ä′kĕn)	161	50°46′N	6°07′E
Aalborg, Den. (ôl′bôr)	154	57°02′N	9°55′E
Aalen, Ger. (ä′lĕn)	168	48°49′N	10°08′E
Aalsmeer, Neth.	159a	52°16′N	4°44′E
Aalst, Bel.	165	50°58′N	4°00′E
Aarau, Switz. (ärôu)	161	47°22′N	8°03′E
Aarschot, Bel.	159a	50°59′N	4°51′E
Aba, D.R.C.	237	3°52′N	30°14′E
Aba, Nig.	230	5°06′N	7°21′E
Ābādān, Iran (ä-bŭ-dän′)	198	30°15′N	48°30′E
Abaetetuba, Braz. (ä′bä-tĕ-tōō′bá)	143	1°44′S	48°45′W
Abajo Peak, mtn., Ut., U.S. (ä-bá′hō)	119	37°51′N	109°28′W
Abakaliki, Nig.	235	6°21′N	8°06′E
Abakan, Russia (ŭ-bá-kän′)	179	53°43′N	91°28′E
Abakan, r., Russia (u-bá-kän′)	184	53°00′N	91°06′E
Abancay, Peru (ä-bän-kä′ē)	142	13°44′S	72°46′W
Abashiri, Japan (ä-bä-shē′rē)	210	44°00′N	144°13′E
Abasolo, Mex. (ä-bä-sō′lō)	130	24°05′N	98°24′W
Abasolo, Mex. (ä-bä-sō′lō)	122	27°13′N	101°25′W
Abaya, Lake, l., Eth. (ä-bä′yà)	231	6°24′N	38°22′E
'Abbāsah, Tur'at al, can., Egypt	238d	30°45′N	32°15′E
Abbeville, Fr. (áb-vēl′)	161	50°08′N	1°49′E
Abbeville, Al., U.S.	124	31°35′N	85°15′W
Abbeville, Ga., U.S. (áb′ē-vïl)	124	31°53′N	83°23′W
Abbeville, La., U.S.	123	29°59′N	92°07′W
Abbeville, S.C., U.S.	125	34°09′N	82°25′W
Abbiategrasso, Italy (äb-byä′tä-gräs′sō)	174	45°23′N	8°52′E
Abbots Bromley, Eng., U.K. (áb′ŭts brŭm′lē)	158a	52°49′N	1°52′W
Abbotsford, Can. (áb′ŭts-fêrd)	116d	49°03′N	122°17′W
'Abd al Kūri, i., Yemen (ábd-ĕl-kŏ′rē)	238a	12°12′N	51°00′E
Abdulino, Russia (äb-dó-lē′nō)	180	53°42′N	53°40′E
Abengourou, C. Iv.	234	6°44′N	3°29′W
Abeokuta, Nig. (ä-bā-ô-kōō′tä)	230	7°10′N	3°26′E
Abercorn *see* Mbala, Zam.	232	8°50′S	31°22′E
Aberdare, Wales, U.K. (áb-ĕr-dâr′)	164	51°45′N	3°35′W
Aberdeen, Scot., U.K. (áb-ĕr-dēn′)	154	57°10′N	2°05′W
Aberdeen, Ms., U.S.	124	33°49′N	88°33′W
Aberdeen, S.D., U.S. (áb-ĕr-dēn′)	104	45°28′N	98°29′W
Aberdeen, Wa., U.S. (áb-ĕr-dēn′)	104	47°00′N	123°48′W
Aberford, Eng., U.K. (áb′ĕr-fêrd)	158a	53°49′N	1°21′W
Abergavenny, Wales, U.K. (áb′ĕr-gá-vĕn′ĭ)	164	51°45′N	3°05′W
Abert, Lake, l., Or., U.S. (ā′bĕrt)	114	42°39′N	120°24′W
Aberystwyth, Wales, U.K. (á-bĕr-ĭst′wĭth)	164	52°25′N	4°04′W
Abidjan, C. Iv. (ä-bĕd-zhäɴ′)	230	5°19′N	4°02′W
Abiko, Japan (ä-bē-kō)	211a	35°53′N	140°01′E
Abilene, Ks., U.S. (áb′ĭ-lēn)	121	38°54′N	97°12′W
Abilene, Tx., U.S.	104	32°25′N	99°45′W
Abingdon, Eng., U.K.	158b	51°38′N	1°17′W
Abingdon, Il., U.S. (áb′ĭng-dŭn)	113	40°48′N	90°21′W
Abingdon, Va., U.S.	125	36°42′N	81°57′W
Abington, Ma., U.S.	101a	42°07′N	70°57′W
Abiquiu Reservoir, res., N.M., U.S.	119	36°26′N	106°42′W
Abitibi, l., Can. (áb-ĭ-tĭb′ĭ)	93	48°27′N	80°20′W
Abitibi, r., Can.	93	49°30′N	81°10′W
Abkhazia, state, Geor.	181	43°10′N	40°45′E
Ablis, Fr. (ä-blē′)	171b	48°31′N	1°50′E
Abnūb, Egypt (áb-nōōb′)	238b	27°18′N	31°11′E
Åbo *see* Turku, Fin.	154	60°28′N	22°12′E
Abohar, India	202	30°12′N	74°13′E
Aboisso, C. Iv.	234	5°28′N	3°12′W
Abomey, Benin (äb-ô-mā′)	230	7°11′N	1°59′E
Abony, Hung. (ŏ′bô-ny′)	169	47°12′N	20°00′E
Abou Deïa, Chad	235	11°27′N	19°17′E
Abra, r., Phil. (ä′brä)	213a	17°16′N	120°38′E
Abraão, Braz. (äbrä-ouɴ′)	141a	23°10′S	44°10′W
Abraham's Bay, b., Bah.	135	22°20′N	73°50′W
Abram, Eng., U.K. (ä′brăm)	158a	53°31′N	2°36′W
Abrantes, Port. (á-brän′tēs)	172	39°28′N	8°13′W
Abrolhos, Arquipélago dos, is., Braz.	143	17°58′S	38°40′W
Abruka, i., Est. (ä-brô′kä)	167	58°09′N	22°30′E
Abruzzi e Molise, hist. reg., Italy	174	42°10′N	13°55′E
Absaroka Range, mts., U.S. (áb-sä-rō-ká)	106	44°50′N	109°47′W
Abşeron Yarımadası, pen., Azer.	181	40°20′N	50°30′E
Abū Arīsh, Sau. Ar. (ä-bōō á-rēsh′)	198	16°48′N	43°00′E
Abu Dhabi *see* Abū Ẓaby, U.A.E.	198	24°15′N	54°28′E
Abū Ḥamad, Sudan (ä′bōō hä′-mĕd)	231	19°37′N	33°21′E
Abuja, Nig.	230	9°12′N	7°11′E
Abū Kamāl, Syria	198	34°45′N	40°46′E
Abunā, r., S.A. (ä-bōō-nä′)	142	10°25′S	67°00′W
Abū Qīr, Egypt (ä′bōō kêr′)	238b	31°18′N	30°06′E
Abū Qurūn, Ra's, mtn., Egypt	197a	30°22′N	33°32′E
Aburatsu, Japan (ä′bô-rät′sōō)	211	31°33′N	131°20′E
Abu Road, India (ä′bōō)	199	24°38′N	72°45′E
Abū Tīj, Egypt	238b	27°03′N	31°19′E
Abū Ẓaby, U.A.E.	198	24°15′N	54°28′E
Abū Zanimah, Egypt	197a	29°03′N	33°08′E
Abyy, Russia	179	68°24′N	134°00′E
Acacias, Col. (ä-kä′sēäs)	142a	3°59′N	73°44′W
Acadia National Park, rec., Me., U.S. (á-kā′dǐ-á)	107	44°19′N	68°01′W
Acajutla, El Sal. (ä-kä-hōōt′lä)	132	13°37′N	89°50′W
Acala, Mex. (ä-kä′lä)	131	16°38′N	92°49′W
Acalayong, Eq. Gui.	236	1°05′N	9°40′E
Acámbaro, Mex. (ä-käm′bä-rō)	130	20°03′N	100°42′W
Acanceh, Mex. (ä-kän-sĕ′)	132a	20°50′N	89°27′W
Acapetlahuaya, Mex. (ä-kä-pĕt′lä-hwä′yä)	130	18°24′N	100°04′W
Acaponeta, Mex. (ä-kä-pô-nā′tä)	130	22°31′N	105°25′W
Acaponeta, r., Mex. (ä-kä-pô-nā′tä)	130	22°47′N	105°23′W
Acapulco, Mex. (ä-kä-pōōl′kō)	128	16°49′N	99°57′W
Acaraí Mountains, mts., S.A.	143	1°30′N	57°40′W
Acarigua, Ven. (äkä-rē′gwä)	142	9°29′N	69°11′W
Acatlán de Osorio, Mex. (ä-kät-län′dä ô-sō′rē-ō)	130	18°11′N	98°04′W
Acatzingo de Hidalgo, Mex.	131	18°58′N	97°47′W
Acayucan, Mex. (ä-kä-yōō′kän)	131	17°56′N	94°55′W
Accoville, W.V., U.S. (ák′kô-vïl)	108	37°45′N	81°50′W
Accra, Ghana (ä′krá)	230	5°33′N	0°13′W
Accrington, Eng., U.K. (ák′rĭng-tŭn)	158a	53°45′N	2°22′W
Acerra, Italy (ä-chĕ′r-rä)	173c	40°42′N	14°22′E
Achacachi, Bol. (ä-chä-kä′chē)	142	16°11′S	68°32′W
Achelóos, r., Grc.	175	38°45′N	21°26′E
Achill Island, i., Ire. (ä-chǐl′)	160	53°55′N	10°05′W
Achinsk, Russia (ä-chēnsk′)	184	56°13′N	90°32′E
Acireale, Italy (ä-chē-rä-ä′lä)	174	37°37′N	15°12′E
Acklins, i., Bah. (ák′lĭns)	129	22°30′N	73°55′W
Acklins, The Bight of, b., Bah. (ák′lĭns)	135	22°35′N	74°20′W
Acolman, Mex. (ä-kôl-má′n)	131a	19°38′N	98°56′W
Acoma Indian Reservation, I.R., N.M., U.S.	119	34°52′N	107°40′W
Aconcagua, prov., Chile (ä-kôn-kä′gwä)	141b	32°20′S	71°00′W
Aconcagua, r., Chile (ä-kôn-kä′gwä)	141b	32°43′S	70°53′W
Aconcagua, Cerro, mtn., Arg. (ä-kôn-kä′gwä)	144	32°38′S	70°00′W
Açores (Azores), is., Port.	229	37°44′N	29°25′W
A Coruña, Spain	154	43°20′N	8°22′W
Acoyapa, Nic. (ä-kô-yä′pä)	132	11°54′N	85°11′W
Acqui, Italy (äk′kwē)	174	44°41′N	8°22′E
Acre, state, Braz. (ä′krä)	142	8°50′S	70°45′W
Acre, r., S.A.	142	10°33′S	68°34′W
Acton, Can. (ák′tŭn)	102d	43°38′N	80°02′W
Acton, Al., U.S. (ák′tŭn)	110h	33°21′N	86°49′W
Acton, Ma., U.S. (ák′tŭn)	101a	42°29′N	71°26′W
Actopan, Mex. (äk-tô-pän′)	130	20°16′N	98°57′W
Actópan, r., Mex. (äk-tô′pän)	131	19°25′N	96°31′W
Acuitzio del Canje, Mex. (ä-kwēt′zĕ-ō dĕl kän′hä)	130	19°28′N	101°21′W
Acul, Baie de l′, b., Haiti (ä-kōōl′)	135	19°55′N	72°20′W
Ada, Mn., U.S. (ā′dü)	112	47°17′N	96°32′W
Ada, Oh., U.S. (ā′dü)	108	40°45′N	83°45′W
Ada, Ok., U.S. (ā′dü)	121	34°45′N	96°43′W

āt; fināl; rāte; senåte; ärm; àsk; sofà; fâre; ch-choose; dh-as th in other; bē; ĕvent; bĕt; recĕnt; cratēr; g-gō; gh-guttural g; bĭt; ĭ-short neutral; rīde; ᴋ-guttural k as ch in German ich;

PLACE (Pronunciation)	PAGE	LAT.	LONG.
Ada, Serb. (ä'dä)	175	45°48'N	20°06'E
Adachi, Japan	211a	35°50'N	39°36'E
Adak, Ak., U.S. (ă-dăk')	103a	56°50'N	176°48'W
Adak, i., Ak., U.S. (ă-dăk')	103a	51°40'N	176°28'W
Adak Strait, strt., Ak., U.S. (ă-dăk')	103a	51°42'N	177°16'W
Adamaoua, mts., Afr.	230	6°30'N	11°50'E
Adams, Ma., U.S. (ăd'ămz)	109	42°35'N	73°10'W
Adams, Wi., U.S. (ăd'ămz)	113	43°55'N	89°48'W
Adams, r., Can. (ăd'ămz)	95	51°30'N	119°20'W
Adams, Mount, mtn., Wa., U.S. (ăd'ămz)	106	46°15'N	121°19'W
Adamsville, Al., U.S. (ăd'ămz-vĭl)	110h	33°36'N	86°57'W
Adana, Tur. (ä'dä-nä)	198	37°05'N	35°20'E
Adapazarı, Tur. (ä-dä-pä-zä'rė)	163	40°45'N	30°20'E
Adarama, Sudan (ä-dä-rä'mä)	231	17°11'N	34°56'E
Adda, r., Italy (äd'dä)	174	45°43'N	9°31'E
Ad Dabbah, Sudan	231	18°04'N	30°58'E
Ad Dahnā, des., Sau. Ar.	198	26°05'N	47°15'E
Ad-Dāmir, Sudan (ad-dä'mēr)	231	17°38'N	33°57'E
Ad Dammām, Sau. Ar.	198	26°27'N	49°59'E
Ad Damur, Leb.	197a	33°44'N	35°27'E
Ad Dawhah, Qatar	198	25°02'N	51°28'E
Ad Dilam, Sau. Ar.	198	23°47'N	47°03'E
Ad Dilinjāt, Egypt	238b	30°48'N	30°32'E
Addis Ababa, Eth.	231	9°00'N	38°44'E
Addison, Tx., U.S. (ă'dĭ-sŭn)	117c	32°58'N	96°50'W
Addo, S. Afr. (ădō)	233c	33°33'S	25°43'E
Ad Duwaym, Sudan (ad-dò-ām')	231	13°56'N	32°22'E
Addyston, Oh., U.S. (ăd'ē-stŭn)	111f	39°09'N	84°42'W
Adel, Ga., U.S. (ā-dĕl')	124	31°08'N	83°55'W
Adelaide, Austl. (ăd'ē-lād)	218	34°46'S	139°08'E
Adelaide, S. Afr. (ăd-ĕl'ăd)	233c	32°41'S	26°07'E
Adelaide Island, i., Ant. (ăd'ē-lād)	224	67°15'S	68°40'W
Aden ('Adan), Yemen (ä'dĕn)	198	12°48'N	45°00'E
Aden, Gulf of, b.	198	11°45'N	45°45'E
Adi, Pulau, i., Indon. (ä'dē)	213	4°25'S	133°52'E
Adige, r., Italy (ä'dē-jā)	162	46°38'N	10°43'E
Adigrat, Eth.	201	14°17'N	39°28'E
Adilābād, India (ŭ-dĭl-ä-băd')	202	19°47'N	78°30'E
Adirondack Mountains, mts., N.Y., U.S. (ăd-ĭ-rŏn'dăk)	107	43°45'N	74°40'W
Adis Abeba *see* Addis Ababa, Eth.	231	9°00'N	38°44'E
Adi Ugri, Erit. (ä-dē o͞o'grē)	231	14°54'N	38°52'E
Adjud, Rom. (äd'zhōd)	169	46°05'N	27°12'E
Adkins, Tx., U.S.	117d	29°22'N	98°18'W
Admiralty, i., Ak., U.S. (ăd'mĭ-răl-tė)	103	57°50'N	133°50'W
Admiralty Inlet, Wa., U.S. (ăd'mĭ-răl-tė)	116a	48°10'N	122°45'W
Admiralty Island National Monument, rec., Ak., U.S. (ăd'mĭ-răl-tė)	103	57°50'N	137°30'W
Admiralty Islands, is., Pap. N. Gui. (ăd'mĭ-răl-tė)	213	1°40'S	146°45'E
Ado-Ekiti, Nig.	235	7°38'N	5°12'E
Adolph, Mn., U.S. (ā'dolf)	117h	46°47'N	92°17'W
Ādoni, India	203	15°42'N	77°18'E
Adour, r., Fr. (à-do͞or')	161	43°43'N	0°38'W
Adra, Spain (ä'drä)	172	36°45'N	3°02'W
Adrano, Italy (ä-drä'nō)	174	37°42'N	14°52'E
Adrar, Alg.	230	27°53'N	0°15'W
Adria, Italy (ä'drė-ä)	174	45°03'N	12°01'E
Adrian, Mi., U.S. (ā'drĭ-ăn)	108	41°55'N	84°00'W
Adrian, Mn., U.S. (ā'drĭ-ăn)	112	43°39'N	95°56'W
Adrianople *see* Edirne, Tur.	154	41°41'N	26°35'E
Adriatic Sea, sea, Eur.	156	43°30'N	14°27'E
Adwa, Eth.	231	14°02'N	38°58'E
Adwick-le-Street, Eng., U.K. (ăd'wĭk-lė-strēt')	158a	53°35'N	1°11'W
Adycha, r., Russia (ä'dĭ-chà)	185	66°11'N	136°45'E
Adygea, prov., Russia	180	45°00'N	40°00'E
Adz'va, r., Russia (ädz'vá)	180	67°00'N	59°20'E
Aegean Sea, sea (ė-jē'ăn)	156	39°04'N	24°56'E
A Estrada, Spain	172	42°42'N	8°29'W
Affton, Mo., U.S.	117e	38°33'N	90°20'W
Afghanistan, nation, Asia (ăf-găn-ĭ-stăn')	198	33°00'N	63°00'E
Afgooye, Som. (äf-gô'ĭ)	238a	2°08'N	45°08'E
Afikpo, Nig.	235	5°53'N	7°56'E
Aflou, Alg. (ä-flo͞o')	230	33°59'N	2°04'E
Afognak, i., Ak., U.S. (ä-fŏg-nák')	103	58°28'N	151°35'W
A Fonsagrada, Spain	172	43°08'N	7°07'W
Afonso Claudio, Braz. (äl-fōn'sō-klou'dēō)	141a	20°05'S	41°05'W
Afragola, Italy (ä-frá'gō-lä)	173c	40°40'N	14°19'E
Africa, cont.	229	10°00'N	22°00'E
Afton, Mn., U.S. (ăf'tŭn)	117g	44°54'N	92°47'W
Afton, Ok., U.S. (ăf'tŭn)	121	36°42'N	94°56'W
Afton, Wy., U.S. (ăf'tŭn)	115	42°42'N	110°52'W
'Afula, Isr. (ä-fò'là)	197a	32°36'N	35°17'E
Afyon, Tur. (ä-fē-ōn)	198	38°45'N	30°20'E
Agadem, Niger (ä'gá-dĕm)	231	16°50'N	13°17'E
Agadez, Niger (ä'gá-dĕs)	230	16°58'N	7°59'E
Agadir, Mor. (ä-gá-dēr)	230	30°30'N	9°37'W
Agalta, Cordillera de, mts., Hond. (kôr-dēl-yĕ'rä-dĕ-ä-gä'l-tä)	132	15°15'N	85°42'W
Agapovka, Russia (ä-gä-pôv'kä)	186a	53°18'N	59°10'E
Agartala, India	202	23°53'N	91°22'E
Agāshi, India	203b	19°28'N	72°46'E
Agashkino, Russia (á-gäsh'kĭ-nô)	186b	55°18'N	38°13'E
Agattu, i., Ak., U.S. (á'gä-to͞o)	103a	52°14'N	173°40'E
Agboville, C. Iv.	234	5°56'N	4°13'W
Ağdam, Azer. (äg'dām)	181	40°00'N	47°00'E
Agde, Fr. (ägd)	170	43°19'N	3°30'E
Agen, Fr. (à-zhäN')	161	44°13'N	0°31'E
Agiásos, Grc.	175	39°06'N	26°25'E
Aginskoye, Russia (ä-hĭn'skô-yĕ)	179	51°15'N	113°15'E

PLACE (Pronunciation)	PAGE	LAT.	LONG.
Ágios Efstrátios, i., Grc.	163	39°30'N	24°58'E
Agíou Órous, Kólpos, b., Grc.	175	40°15'N	24°00'E
Agno, Phil. (äg'nō)	213a	16°07'N	119°49'E
Agno, r., Phil.	213a	15°42'N	120°28'E
Agnone, Italy (än-yō'nā)	174	41°49'N	14°23'E
Agogo, Ghana	234	6°47'N	1°04'W
Agra, India (ä'grä)	199	27°18'N	78°00'E
Ağrı, Tur.	181	39°50'N	43°10'E
Agri, r., Italy (ä'grē)	174	40°15'N	16°21'E
Agrínio, Grc.	163	38°38'N	21°06'E
Agua, vol., Guat. (ä'gwä)	132	14°28'N	90°43'W
Agua Blanca, Río, r., Mex. (rē'ō-ä-gwä-blä'n-kä)	130	21°46'N	102°54'W
Agua Brava, Laguna de, l., Mex.	130	22°04'N	105°40'W
Agua Caliente Indian Reservation, I.R., Ca., U.S. (ä'gwä kal-yĕn'tä)	118	33°50'N	116°24'W
Aguada, Cuba (ä-gwä'dä)	134	22°25'N	80°50'W
Aguada, l., Mex. (ä-gwä'dä)	132a	18°46'N	89°40'W
Aguadas, Col. (ä-gwä'däs)	142	5°37'N	75°27'W
Aguadilla, P.R. (ä-gwä-dēl'yä)	129b	18°27'N	67°10'W
Aguadulce, Pan. (ä-gwä-do͞ol'sä)	133	8°15'N	80°33'W
Agua Escondida, Meseta de, plat., Mex.	131	16°54'N	91°35'W
Agua Fria, r., Az., U.S. (ä'gwä frē-ä)	119	33°43'N	112°22'W
Agua Fria National Monument, rec., Az., U.S.	119	34°13'N	112°03'W
Aguai, Braz. (ägwä-ē')	141a	22°04'S	46°57'W
Agualeguas, Mex. (ä-gwä-lä'gwäs)	122	26°19'N	99°33'W
Aguán, r., Hond. (ä-gwà'n)	132	15°22'N	87°00'W
Aguanaval, r., Mex. (á-guä-nä-väl')	122	25°12'N	103°28'W
Aguanus, r., Can. (á-gwä'nŭs)	101	50°45'N	62°03'W
Aguascalientes, Mex. (ä'gwäs-käl-yĕn'tās)	128	21°52'N	102°17'W
Aguascalientes, state, Mex. (ä'gwäs-käl-yĕn'tās)	130	22°00'N	102°18'W
Águeda, Port. (ä-gwä'dä)	172	40°36'N	8°26'W
Agueda, r., Eur. (ä-gĕ-dä)	172	40°50'N	6°44'W
Aguelhok, Mali	234	19°28'N	0°52'E
Aguilar, Spain	172	37°32'N	4°39'W
Aguilar, Co., U.S. (ä-gē-lär')	120	37°24'N	104°38'W
Aguilas, Spain (ä-gē-läs)	162	37°26'N	1°35'W
Aguililla, Mex. (ä-gē-lēl-yä)	130	18°44'N	102°44'W
Aguililla, r., Mex. (ä-gē-lēl-yä)	130	18°30'N	102°48'W
Aguja, Punta, c., Peru (pŭn'tá á-go͞o' hä)	142	6°00'S	81°15'W
Agulhas, Cape, c., S. Afr. (ä-go͞ol'yäs)	232	34°47'S	20°00'E
Agusan, r., Phil. (ä-go͞o'sän)	213	8°12'N	126°07'E
Ahaggar, mts., Alg. (á-há-gär')	230	23°14'N	6°00'E
Ahar, Iran	201	38°28'N	47°04'E
Ahlen, Ger. (ä'lĕn)	168	51°45'N	7°52'E
Ahmadābād, India (ŭ-mĕd-ä-băd')	199	23°04'N	72°38'E
Ahmadnagar, India (ä'mŭd-nŭ-gŭr)	199	19°09'N	74°45'E
Ahmar Mountains, mts., Eth.	231	9°22'N	42°00'E
Ahoskie, N.C., U.S. (ä-hŏs'kē)	125	36°15'N	77°00'W
Ahrensburg, Ger. (ä'rĕns-bòrg)	159c	53°40'N	10°14'E
Ahrweiler, Ger. (är'vī-lĕr)	168	50°34'N	7°05'E
Ähtärinjärvi, l., Fin.	167	62°46'N	24°25'E
Ahuacatlán, Mex. (ä-wä-kät-län')	130	21°05'N	104°28'W
Ahuachapán, El Sal. (ä-wä-chä-pän')	132	13°57'N	89°53'W
Ahualulco, Mex. (ä-wä-lo͞ol'kō)	130	20°43'N	103°57'W
Ahuatempan, Mex. (ä-wä-tĕm-pän)	130	18°11'N	98°02'W
Åhus, Swe. (ô'hōs)	166	55°56'N	14°19'E
Ahvāz, Iran	198	31°15'N	48°54'E
Ahvenanmaa (Åland), is., Fin. (ä'vĕ-nàn-mô) (ô'lănd)	160	60°36'N	19°55'E
'Aiea, Hi., U.S.	126a	21°18'N	157°52'W
Aígina, Grc.	175	37°43'N	23°35'E
Aígina, i., Grc.	175	37°43'N	23°35'E
Aígio, Grc.	175	38°13'N	22°04'E
Aiken, S.C., U.S. (ā'kĕn)	125	33°32'N	81°43'W
Aimorès, Serra dos, mts., Braz. (sĕ'r-rä-dôs-ī-mō-rĕ's)	143	17°40'S	42°38'W
Aimoto, Japan (ī-mô-tō)	211b	34°59'N	135°09'E
Aincourt, Fr. (ăN-ko͞o'r)	171b	49°04'N	1°47'E
Aïn el Beïda, Alg.	230	35°57'N	7°25'E
Ainsworth, Ne., U.S. (ānz'wûrth)	112	42°32'N	99°51'W
Aïn Témouchent, Alg. (ä'ēntĕ-mo͞o-shaN')	162	35°20'N	1°23'W
Aïn Wessara, Alg. (ĕn o͞o-sā-rà)	173	35°25'N	2°50'E
Aipe, Col. (ī'pĕ)	142a	3°13'N	75°15'W
Aïr, mts., Niger	230	18°00'N	8°30'E
Aire, r., Eng., U.K.	158a	53°42'N	1°00'W
Aire-sur-l'Adour, Fr. (âr)	170	43°42'N	0°17'W
Airhitam, Selat, strt., Indon.	197b	0°58'N	102°38'E
Ai Shan, mts., China (äī'shän)	206	37°27'N	120°35'E
Aisne, r., Fr. (ĕn)	161	49°28'N	3°32'E
Aitape, Pap. N. Gui. (ä-ē-tä'pä)	213	3°00'S	142°10'E
Aitkin, Mn., U.S. (āt'kĭn)	113	46°32'N	93°43'W
Aitolikó, Grc.	175	38°27'N	21°21'E
Aitos, Blg. (ä-ē'tōs)	175	42°42'N	27°17'E
Aitutaki, i., Cook Is. (ī-to͞o-tä'kē)	241	19°00'S	162°00'W
Aiud, Rom. (ä'ē-òd)	163	46°19'N	23°40'E
Aiuruoca, Braz. (äē'o͞o-ro͞oō'-kà)	141a	21°57'S	44°36'W
Aiuruoca, r., Braz.	141a	22°11'S	44°35'W
Aix-en-Provence, Fr. (ĕks-prô-väNs)	161	43°32'N	5°27'E
Aix-les-Bains, Fr. (ĕks'-lā-băN')	171	45°42'N	5°56'E
Aizpute, Lat. (ä'ēz-po͞o-tĕ)	167	56°44'N	21°37'E
Aizuwakamatsu, Japan	210	37°27'N	139°51'E
Ajaccio, Fr. (ä-yät'chō)	154	41°55'N	8°42'E
Ajalpan, Mex. (ä-häl'pän)	131	18°21'N	97°14'W
Ajana, Austl. (ăj-ăn'ĕr)	218	28°00'S	114°45'E
Ajaria, state, Geor.	182	41°40'N	42°00'E
Ajdābiyah, Libya	231	30°56'N	20°16'E
Ajjer, Tassili-n-, plat., Alg.	230	25°40'N	6°57'E

PLACE (Pronunciation)	PAGE	LAT.	LONG.
Ajmah, Jabal al, mts., Egypt	197a	29°12'N	34°03'E
Ajman, U.A.E.	198	25°15'N	54°30'E
Ajmer, India (ŭj-mēr')	199	26°26'N	74°42'E
Ajo, Az., U.S. (ä'hō)	119	32°20'N	112°55'W
Ajuchitlán del Progreso, Mex. (ä-ho͞o-chet-lån)	130	18°11'N	100°32'W
Ajusco, Mex. (ä-ho͞o's-kō)	131a	19°13'N	99°12'W
Ajusco, Cerro, mtn., Mex. (sĕ'r-rô-ä-ho͞o's-kō)	131a	19°12'N	99°16'W
Akaishi-dake, mtn., Japan (ä-kī-shē dä'kä)	211	35°30'N	138°00'E
Akashi, Japan (ä'kä-shē)	210	34°38'N	134°59'E
Aketi, D.R.C. (ä-kå-tē)	231	2°44'N	23°46'E
Akhaltsikhe, Geor. (äkä'l-tsĭ-kĕ)	181	41°40'N	42°50'E
Akhdar, Al Jabal al, mts., Libya	231	32°00'N	22°00'E
Akhdar, Al Jabal al, mts., Oman	198	23°30'N	56°43'W
Akhisar, Tur. (äk-hĭs-sär')	163	38°58'N	27°58'E
Akhtarskaya, Bukhta, b., Russia (bo͞ok'tä äk-tär'skä-yä)	177	45°53'N	38°22'E
Akhtopol, Blg. (äx'tô-pôl)	175	42°06'N	27°54'E
Akhunovo, Russia (ä-kŭ'nô-vô)	186a	54°13'N	59°36'E
Aki, Japan (ä'kē)	211	33°31'N	133°51'E
Akiak, Ak., U.S. (äk'yák)	103	61°00'N	161°02'W
Akimiski, i., Can. (ä-kĭ-mĭ'skĭ)	93	52°54'N	80°22'W
Akita, Japan (ä'kē-tä)	205	39°40'N	140°12'E
Akjoujt, Maur.	230	19°45'N	14°23'W
'Akko, Isr.	197a	32°56'N	35°05'E
Aklavik, Can. (äk'lä-vĭk)	90	68°28'N	135°26'W
'Aklé'Âouâna, dunes, Afr.	234	18°07'N	6°00'W
Ako, Japan (ä'kō)	211	34°44'N	134°22'E
Akola, India (á-kō'lä)	199	20°47'N	77°00'E
Akordat, Erit.	231	15°34'N	37°54'E
Akpatok, i., Can. (ăk'pá-tŏk)	93	60°30'N	67°10'W
Akranes, Ice.	160	64°18'N	21°40'W
Akron, Co., U.S. (ăk'rŭn)	120	40°09'N	103°14'W
Akron, Oh., U.S. (ăk'rŭn)	105	41°05'N	81°30'W
Aksaray, Tur. (äk-sà-rī')	163	38°30'N	34°05'E
Akşehir, Tur. (äk'shå-hēr)	163	38°20'N	31°20'E
Akşehir Gölü, l., Tur. (äk'shå-hēr)	198	38°40'N	31°30'E
Aksha, Russia (äk'shà)	179	50°28'N	113°00'E
Aksu, China (ä-kŭ-so͞o)	204	41°29'N	80°15'E
Akune, Japan (ä'kò-nå)	211	32°03'N	130°16'E
Akureyri, Ice. (ä-kò-rå'rē)	160	65°39'N	18°01'W
Akutan, i., Ak., U.S. (ä-ko͞o-tän')	103a	53°58'N	169°54'W
Akwatia, Ghana	234	6°04'N	0°49'W
Alabama, state, U.S. (ăl-á-băm'á)	105	32°50'N	87°30'W
Alabama, r., Al., U.S. (ăl-á-băm'á)	107	31°20'N	87°39'W
Alabat, i., Phil. (ä-lä-bät')	213a	14°14'N	122°05'E
Alacam, Tur. (ä-lä-chäm')	181	41°30'N	35°40'E
Alacant, Spain	162	38°20'N	0°30'W
Alacranes, Cuba (ä-lä-krä'nås)	134	22°45'N	81°35'W
Al Aflaj, des., Sau. Ar.	198	24°00'N	44°47'E
Alagôas, state, Braz. (ä-lä-gō'äzh)	143	9°50'S	36°33'W
Alagoinhas, Braz. (ä-lä-gō-ēn'yäzh)	143	12°13'S	38°12'W
Alagón, Spain (ä-lä-gōn')	172	41°46'N	1°07'W
Alagón, r., Spain (ä-lä-gōn')	172	39°53'N	6°42'W
Alahuatán, r., Mex. (ä-lä-wä-tá'n)	130	18°30'N	100°00'W
Alajuela, C.R. (ä-lä-hwa'lä)	133	10°01'N	84°14'W
Alajuela, Lago, l., Pan. (ä-lä-hwa'lä)	128a	9°15'N	79°34'W
Alaköl, l., Kaz.	183	45°45'N	81°13'E
'Alalakeiki Channel, strt., Hi., U.S. (ä-lä-lä-kä'kē)	126a	20°40'N	156°30'W
Al 'Alamayn, Egypt	231	30°53'N	28°52'E
Al 'Amārah, Iraq	201	31°50'N	47°09'E
Alameda, Ca., U.S. (ăl-á-mā'dá)	104	37°46'N	122°15'W
Alameda, r., Ca., U.S. (ăl-á-mā'dá)	116b	37°36'N	122°02'W
Alaminos, Phil. (ä-lä-mē'nōs)	213a	16°09'N	119°58'E
Al 'Amirīyah, Egypt	163	31°01'N	29°52'E
Alamo, Mex. (ä'lä-mō)	131	20°55'N	97°41'W
Alamo, Ca., U.S. (ă'lá-mō)	116b	37°51'N	122°02'W
Alamo, Nv., U.S. (ă'lá-mō)	118	37°22'N	115°10'W
Alamo, r., Mex. (ä'lä-mō)	122	26°33'N	99°35'W
Alamogordo, N.M., U.S. (ăl-á-mō-gôr'dō)	119	32°55'N	106°00'W
Alamo Heights, Tx., U.S. (ă'lá-mō)	117d	29°28'N	98°27'W
Alamo Indian Reservation, I.R., N.M., U.S.	119	34°30'N	107°30'W
Alamo Peak, mtn., N.M., U.S. (ă'lá-mō pēk)	122	32°50'N	105°55'W
Alamosa, Co., U.S. (ăl-á-mō'sá)	119	37°25'N	105°50'W
Åland *see* Ahvenanmaa, is., Fin.	160	60°36'N	19°55'E
Alandskiy, Russia (ä-länt'skĭ)	186a	52°14'N	59°48'E
Alanga Arba, Kenya	237	0°07'N	40°25'E
Alanya, Tur.	163	36°40'N	32°10'E
Alaotra, l., Madag. (ä-lä-ō'trá)	233	17°15'S	48°17'E
Alapayevsk, Russia (ä-lä-pä'yĕfsk)	178	57°50'N	61°35'E
Al 'Aqabah, Jord.	198	29°32'N	35°00'E
Alaquines, Mex. (ä-lá-kē'nås)	130	22°07'N	99°35'W
Al 'Arīsh, Egypt (ä-rēsh')	197a	31°08'N	33°48'E
Alaska, state, U.S. (á-lăs'ká)	106a	64°00'N	150°00'W
Alaska, Gulf of, b., Ak., U.S. (á-lăs'ká)	103	57°42'N	147°40'W
Alaska Highway, Ak., U.S. (á-lăs'ká)	103	63°00'N	142°00'W
Alaska Peninsula, pen., Ak., U.S. (á-lăs'ká)	103	55°50'N	162°10'W
Alaska Range, mts., Ak., U.S. (á-lăs'ká)	103	62°00'N	152°18'W
Al 'Atrūn, Sudan	231	18°13'N	26°44'E
Alatyr', Russia (ä'lä-tür)	178	54°55'N	46°30'E
Alazani, r., Asia	182	41°05'N	46°40'E
Alba, Italy (äl'bä)	174	44°41'N	8°02'E
Albacete, Spain (äl-bä-thā'tā)	162	39°00'N	1°49'W
Albachten, Ger. (äl-bá'ĸ-tĕn)	171c	51°55'N	7°31'E
Alba de Tormes, Spain (äl-bà dā tôr'mās)	172	40°48'N	5°28'W
Alba Iulia, Rom. (äl-bä yo͞o'lyà)	163	46°05'N	23°32'E

ng-sing; ŋ-baŋk; N-nasalized n; nŏd; cŏmmit; ōld; ôbey; ôrder; oi-boil; fo͞od; ò-as oo in foot; ou-out; s-soft; sh-dish; th-thin; pūre; ûnite; ûrn; stŭd; circŭs; ü-as in French tu; '-indeterminate vowel.

PLACE (Pronunciation)	PAGE	LAT.	LONG.
Albani, Colli, hills, Italy	173d	41°46'N	12°45'E
Albania, nation, Eur. (äl-bā'nĭ-ȧ)	154	41°45'N	20°00'E
Albano, Lago, l., Italy (lä'-gō äl-bä'nō)	173d	41°45'N	12°44'E
Albano Laziale, Italy (äl-bä'nō lät-zē-ä'lā)	174	41°44'N	12°43'E
Albany, Austl. (ôl'bȧ-nĭ)	218	35°00'S	118°00'E
Albany, Ca., U.S. (ôl'bȧ-nĭ)	116b	37°54'N	122°18'W
Albany, Ga., U.S. (ôl'bȧ-nĭ)	105	31°35'N	84°10'W
Albany, Mo., U.S. (ôl'bȧ-nĭ)	121	40°14'N	94°18'W
Albany, N.Y., U.S. (ôl'bȧ-nĭ)	105	42°40'N	73°50'W
Albany, Or., U.S. (ôl'bȧ-nĭ)	104	44°38'N	123°06'W
Albany, r., Can. (ôl'bȧ-nĭ)	93	51°45'N	83°30'W
Al Başrah, Iraq	198	30°35'N	47°59'E
Al Batrūn, Leb. (äl-bä-troon')	197a	34°16'N	35°39'E
Albemarle, N.C., U.S. (ăl'bē-märl)	125	35°24'N	80°36'W
Albemarle Sound, strt., N.C., U.S. (ăl'bē märl)	107	36°00'N	76°17'W
Albenga, Italy (äl-bĕŋ'gä)	174	44°04'N	8°13'E
Alberche, r., Spain (äl-bĕr'chå)	172	40°08'N	4°19'W
Alberga, The, r., Austl. (ăl-bŭr'gȧ)	220	27°15'S	135°00'E
Albergaria-a-Velha, Port.	172	40°47'N	8°31'W
Alberhill, Ca., U.S. (ăl'bẽr-hĭl)	117a	33°43'N	117°23'W
Albert, Fr. (ȧl-bâr')	170	50°00'N	2°49'E
Albert, l., Afr. (ăl'bẽrt) (ȧl-bâr')	231	1°50'N	30°40'E
Albert, Parc National, rec., D.R.C.	237	0°05'N	29°30'E
Alberta, prov., Can. (ăl-bûr'tȧ)	90	54°33'N	117°10'W
Alberta, Mount, mtn., Can. (ăl-bûr'tȧ)	95	52°18'N	117°28'W
Albert Edward, Mount, mtn., Pap. N. Gui. (ăl'bẽrt ĕd'wẽrd)	213	8°25'S	147°25'E
Alberti, Arg. (äl-bĕ'r-tē)	141c	35°01'S	60°16'W
Albert Kanaal, can., Bel.	159a	51°07'N	5°07'E
Albert Lea, Mn., U.S. (ăl'bẽrt lē')	113	43°38'N	93°24'W
Albert Nile, r., Ug.	237	3°25'N	31°35'E
Alberton, Can. (ăl'bẽr-tŭn)	100	46°49'N	64°04'W
Alberton, S. Afr.	233b	26°16'S	28°08'E
Albertville see Kalemie, D.R.C.	232	5°56'S	29°12'E
Albertville, Fr. (ȧl-bêr-vēl')	171	45°42'N	6°25'E
Albertville, Al., U.S. (ăl'bẽrt-vĭl)	124	34°15'N	86°10'W
Albi, Fr. (äl-bē')	161	43°54'N	2°07'E
Albia, Ia., U.S. (ăl-bĭ-ȧ)	113	41°01'N	92°44'W
Albina, Sur. (äl-bē'nä)	143	5°30'N	54°33'W
Albina, Ponta, c., Ang.	236	15°51'S	11°44'E
Albino, Point, c., Can. (äl-bē'nō)	111c	42°50'N	79°05'W
Albion, Mi., U.S. (ăl'bĭ-ŭn)	108	42°15'N	84°50'W
Albion, Ne., U.S. (ăl'bĭ-ŭn)	112	41°42'N	98°00'W
Albion, N.Y., U.S. (ăl'bĭ-ŭn)	109	43°15'N	78°10'W
Alboran, Isla del, i., Spain (ē's-lä-dĕl-äl-bō-rä'n)	156	35°58'N	3°02'W
Albuquerque, N.M., U.S. (ăl-bů-kûr'kē)	104	35°05'N	106°40'W
Albuquerque, Cayos de, is., Col.	133	12°12'N	81°24'W
Alburquerque, Spain (äl-boor-kĕr'kā)	172	39°13'N	6°58'W
Albury, Austl. (ôl'bẽr-ē)	219	36°00'S	147°00'E
Alcabideche, Port. (äl-kȧ-bē-dā'chå)	173b	38°43'N	9°24'W
Alcácer do Sal, Port. (äb'ĭ-lēn)	172	38°24'N	8°33'W
Alcalá de Henares, Spain (äl-kä-lä' dā ā-na'räs)	173a	40°29'N	3°22'W
Alcalá la Real, Spain (äl-kä-lä'lä rā-äl')	172	37°27'N	3°57'W
Alcamo, Italy (äl'kȧ-mō)	174	37°58'N	13°03'E
Alcanadre, r., Spain (äl-kä-nä'drå)	173	41°41'N	0°18'W
Alcanar, Spain (äl-kä-när')	173	40°35'N	0°27'E
Alcañiz, Spain (äl-kän-yēth')	162	41°03'N	0°08'W
Alcântara, Braz. (äl-kän'tȧ-rȧ)	143	2°17'S	44°29'W
Alcaraz, Spain (äl-kä-räth')	172	38°39'N	2°28'W
Alcaudete, Spain (äb'ĭng-dŭn)	172	37°38'N	4°05'W
Alcázar de San Juan, Spain (äl-kä'thär dā sän hwän')	162	39°22'N	3°12'W
Alcira, Spain (ä-thē'rä)	173	39°09'N	0°26'W
Alcoa, Tn., U.S. (ăl-kō'ȧ)	124	35°45'N	84°00'W
Alcobendas, Spain (äl-kō-bĕn'dås)	173a	40°32'N	3°39'W
Alcochete, Port. (äl-kō-chā'ta)	173b	38°45'N	8°58'W
Alcoi, Spain	162	38°42'N	0°30'W
Alcorcón, Spain	173a	40°22'N	3°50'W
Alcorta, Arg. (ȧl-kôr'tä)	141c	33°32'S	61°08'W
Alcova Reservoir, res., Wy., U.S. (ăl-kō'vȧ)	115	42°31'N	106°33'W
Alcove, Can. (ăl-kōv')	102c	45°41'N	75°55'W
Alcúdia, Badia d', b., Spain	173	39°48'N	3°20'E
Aldabra Islands, is., Sey. (äl-dä'brä)	233	9°16'S	46°17'E
Aldama, Mex. (äl-dä'mä)	130	22°54'N	98°04'W
Aldama, Mex. (äl-dä'mä)	122	28°50'N	105°54'W
Aldan, Russia	179	58°46'N	125°19'E
Aldan, r., Russia	179	63°00'N	134°00'E
Aldan Plateau, plat., Russia	185	57°42'N	130°28'E
Aldanskaya, Russia	179	61°52'N	135°29'E
Aldenhoven, Ger. (äl'dĕn-hō'vĕn)	171c	50°54'N	6°18'E
Aldergrove, Can. (ôl'dẽr-grōv)	116d	49°03'N	122°28'W
Alderney, i., Guern. (ôl'dẽr-nĭ)	170	49°43'N	2°11'W
Aldershot, Eng., U.K. (ôl'dẽr-shŏt)	164	51°14'N	0°46'W
Alderson, W.V., U.S. (ôl-dẽr-sŭn)	108	37°40'N	80°40'W
Alderwood Manor, Wa., U.S. (ôl'dẽr-wŏŏd măn'ŏr)	116a	47°49'N	122°18'W
Aldridge-Brownhills, Eng., U.K.	158a	52°38'N	1°55'W
Aledo, Il., U.S. (ȧ-le'dō)	121	41°12'N	90°47'W
Aleg, Maur.	230	17°03'N	13°55'W
Alegre, Braz. (ȧlĕ'grĕ)	141a	20°41'S	41°32'W
Alegre, r., Braz. (ȧlĕ'grĕ)	144b	22°22'S	43°34'W
Alegrete, Braz. (ä-lå-grā'tä)	144	29°46'S	55°44'W
Aleksandrov, Russia (ä-lyĕk-sän' drôf)	180	56°24'N	38°45'E
Aleksandrovsk, Russia (ä-lyĕk-sän'drôfsk)	186a	59°11'N	57°36'E
Aleksandrovsk, Russia (ä-lyĕk-sän'drôfsk)	179	51°02'N	142°21'E
Aleksandrów Kujawski, Pol. (ä-lĕk-säh'droov koo-yav'skē)	169	52°54'N	18°45'E
Alekseyevka, Russia (ä-lyĕk-sā-yĕf'kȧ)	177	50°39'N	38°40'E
Aleksin, Russia (äb'ĭng-tŭn)	176	54°31'N	37°07'E
Aleksinac, Serb. (ȧ-lyĕk-sē-nȧk')	175	43°33'N	21°42'E
Alemán, Presa, res., Mex. (prā'sä-lĕ-mȧ'n)	131	18°20'N	96°35'W
Alem Paraíba, Braz. (ä-lĕ'm-pȧ-räē'bȧ)	141a	21°54'S	42°40'W
Alençon, Fr. (ȧ-läɴ-sôɴ')	161	48°26'N	0°08'E
Alenquer, Braz. (ä-lĕŋ-kĕr')	143	1°58'S	54°44'W
Alenquer, Port. (ä-lĕŋ-kĕr')	172	39°04'N	9°01'W
Alentejo, hist. reg., Port. (ä-lĕŋ-tā'zhō)	172	38°05'N	7°45'W
Alenuihaha Channel, strt., Hi., U.S. (ä'lå-noo-ē-hä'hä)	126a	20°20'N	156°05'W
Aleppo, Syria (ȧ-lĕp-ō)	198	36°10'N	37°18'E
Alès, Fr. (ä-lĕs')	161	44°07'N	4°06'E
Alessandria, Italy (ä-lĕs-sän'drē-ä)	162	[illegible]	[illegible]
Ålesund, Nor. (ô'le-soon')	100	62°28'N	6°14'E
Aleutian Islands, is., Ak., U.S. (ȧ-lu'shăn)	106b	52°40'N	177°30'W
Aleutian Trench, deep	103a	50°40'N	177°10'E
Alevina, Mys, c., Russia	179	58°49'N	151°44'E
Alexander Archipelago, is., Ak., U.S. (ăl-ĕg-zăn'dẽr)	103	57°05'N	138°10'W
Alexander City, Al., U.S.	124	32°55'N	85°55'W
Alexander Indian Reserve, I.R., Can.	102g	53°47'N	114°00'W
Alexander Island, i., Ant.	224	71°00'S	71°00'W
Alexandra, S. Afr. (ȧl-ex-än'drȧ)	238c	26°07'S	28°07'E
Alexandria, Austl. (ăl-ĕg-zăn'drĭ-ȧ)	218	19°00'S	136°56'E
Alexandria, Can. (ăl-ĕg-zăn'drĭ-ȧ)	99	45°50'N	74°35'W
Alexandria, Egypt (ăl-ĕg-zăn'drĭ-ȧ)	231	31°12'N	29°58'E
Alexandria, Rom. (ăl-ĕg-zăn'drĭ-ȧ)	175	43°55'N	25°21'E
Alexandria, S. Afr. (äl-ĕx-än-drĭ-ȧ)	233c	33°40'S	26°26'E
Alexandria, In., U.S. (ăl-ĕg-zăn'drĭ-ȧ)	108	40°20'N	85°20'W
Alexandria, La., U.S. (ăl-ĕg-zăn'drĭ-ȧ)	105	31°18'N	92°28'W
Alexandria, Mn., U.S. (ăl-ĕg-zăn'drĭ-ȧ)	112	45°53'N	95°23'W
Alexandria, S.D., U.S. (ăl-ĕg-zăn'drĭ-ȧ)	112	43°39'N	97°45'W
Alexandria, Va., U.S. (ăl-ĕg-zăn'drĭ-ȧ)	105	38°50'N	77°05'W
Alexandria Bay, N.Y., U.S. (ăl-ĕg-zăn'drĭ-ȧ)	109	44°20'N	75°55'W
Alexandroúpoli, Grc.	163	40°41'N	25°51'E
Alfaro, Spain (äl-färō)	172	42°08'N	1°43'W
Al-Fāshir, Sudan (äl-fä'shēr)	231	13°38'N	25°21'E
Al Fashn, Egypt	238b	28°47'N	30°53'E
Al Fayyūm, Egypt	231	29°14'N	30°48'E
Alfeiós, r., Grc.	175	37°33'N	21°50'E
Alfenas, Braz. (äl-fĕ'nås)	141a	21°26'S	45°55'W
Al Firdān, Egypt (äl-fer-dän')	238b	30°43'N	32°20'E
Alfred, Can. (ăl'frĕd)	102c	45°34'N	74°52'W
Alfreton, Eng., U.K. (ăl'fẽr-tŭn)	158a	53°06'N	1°23'W
Algarve, hist. reg., Port. (äl-gär'vĕ)	172	37°15'N	8°12'W
Algeciras, Spain (äl-hā-thē'räs)	172	36°08'N	5°25'W
Algeria, nation, Afr. (äl-gē'rĭ-ȧ)	230	28°45'N	1°00'E
Algete, Spain (äl-hā'tä)	173a	40°36'N	3°30'W
Al Ghayḑah, Yemen	201	16°12'N	52°15'E
Alghero, Italy (äl-gâ'rō)	162	40°32'N	8°22'E
Algiers, Alg. (äl-jērs)	230	36°51'N	2°56'E
Algoa, Tx., U.S. (ăl-gō'ȧ)	123a	29°24'N	95°11'W
Algoma, Wa., U.S.	116a	47°17'N	122°15'W
Algoma, Wi., U.S.	113	44°38'N	87°29'W
Algona, Ia., U.S.	113	43°04'N	94°11'W
Algonac, Mi., U.S. (ăl'gō-năk)	108	42°35'N	82°30'W
Algonquin, Il., U.S. (ăl-gŏŋ'kwĭn)	111a	42°10'N	88°17'W
Algonquin Provincial Park, rec., Can.	107	45°50'N	78°20'W
Alhama de Granada, Spain (äl-hä'mä-dĕ-grä-nä'dä)	172	37°00'N	3°59'W
Alhama de Murcia, Spain	172	37°50'N	1°24'W
Alhambra, Ca., U.S. (ăl-hăm'brȧ)	117a	34°05'N	118°08'W
Al Ḩammān, Egypt	163	30°46'N	29°42'E
Alhandra, Port. (äl-yän'drȧ)	173b	38°55'N	9°01'W
Alhaurín, Spain (äl-lou-rēn')	172	36°40'N	4°40'W
Al Ḩawrah, Yemen	201	13°49'N	47°37'E
Al Ḩawţah, Yemen	198	15°58'N	48°26'E
Al Ḩijāz, reg., Sau. Ar.	198	23°45'N	39°08'E
Al Hirmil, Leb.	197a	34°23'N	36°22'E
Alhos Vedros, Port. (äl'yōs'vā'drōs)	173b	38°39'N	9°02'W
Alhucemas, Baie d', b., Afr.	172	35°18'N	3°50'W
Al Ḩudaydah, Yemen	198	14°43'N	43°03'E
Al Hufūf, Sau. Ar.	198	25°15'N	49°43'E
Al Ḩulwān, Egypt (äl-hĕl'wän)	238b	29°51'N	31°20'E
Aliákmonas, r., Grc.	163	40°26'N	22°17'E
Äli Bayramlı, Azer.	182	39°56'N	48°56'E
Alibori, r., Benin	235	11°40'N	2°55'E
Alice, S. Afr. (ăl-ĭs)	233c	32°47'S	26°51'E
Alice, Tx., U.S. (ăl'ĭs)	122	27°45'N	98°04'W
Alice, Punta, c., Italy (ä-lē'chĕ)	175	39°23'N	17°10'E
Alice Arm, Can.	94	55°29'N	129°29'W
Alicedale, S. Afr. (ăl'ĭs-dāl)	233c	33°18'S	26°04'E
Alice Springs, Austl. (ăl'ĭs)	218	23°38'S	133°56'E
Alicudi, i., Italy (ä-lē-koo'dē)	174	38°34'N	14°21'E
Alifkulovo, Russia (ä-lĭf-kû'lô-vô)	186a	55°57'N	62°06'E
Alīgarh, India (ä-lē-gŭr')	199	27°58'N	78°08'E
Alingsås, Swe. (ȧ'lĭŋ-sôs)	166	57°57'N	12°30'E
Aliquippa, Pa., U.S. (ăl-ĭ-kwĭp'ȧ)	111e	40°37'N	80°15'W
Al Iskandarīyah see Alexandria, Egypt	238b	31°12'N	29°58'E
Aliwal North, S. Afr. (ä-lē-wäl')	232	31°09'S	28°26'E
Al Jafr, Qa'al, pl., Jord.	197a	30°15'N	36°24'E
Al Jaghbūb, Libya	231	29°46'N	24°32'E
Al Jawārah, Oman	201	18°55'N	57°17'E
Al Jawf, Libya	231	24°14'N	23°15'E
Al Jawf, Sau. Ar.	198	29°45'N	39°30'E
Aljezur, Port. (äl-zhä-zoor')	172	37°18'N	8°52'W
Al Jīzah, Egypt	238b	30°01'N	31°12'E
Al Jubayl, Sau. Ar.	198	27°01'N	49°40'E
Al Jufrah, oasis, Libya	231	29°30'N	15°16'E
Al Junaynah, Sudan	200	13°27'N	22°27'E
Aljustrel, Port. (äl-zhoo-strĕl')	172	37°44'N	8°23'W
Al Kāb, Egypt	238d	30°56'N	32°19'E
Al Kāmilīn, Sudan (käm-lēn')	231	15°09'N	33°06'E
Al Karak, Jord. (kĕ-räk')	197a	31°11'N	35°42'E
Al Karnak, Egypt (kär'nak)	238b	25°42'N	32°43'E
Al Khābūrah, Oman	198	23°45'N	57°30'E
Al Khalīl, W.B.	197a	31°31'N	35°07'E
Al Khandaq, Sudan (kän-däk')	231	18°38'N	30°29'E
Al Khārijah, Egypt	200	25°26'N	30°33'E
Al Khums, Libya	231	32°35'N	14°10'E
Al Khurmah, Sau. Ar.	198	21°37'N	41°44'E
Al Kiswah, Syria	197a	33°31'N	36°13'E
Alkmaar, Neth. (älk-mär')	165	52°39'N	4°42'E
Al Kufrah, oasis, Libya	231	24°45'N	22°45'E
Al Kuntillah, Egypt	197a	29°59'N	34°42'E
Al Kūt, Iraq	201	32°30'N	45°49'E
Al Kuwayt, Kuw. (äl-koo-wit)	198	29°04'N	47°59'E
Al Lādhiqīyah, Syria	198	35°32'N	35°51'E
Allagash, r., Me., U.S. (ăl'ȧ-găsh)	100	46°50'N	69°24'W
Allāhābād, India (ŭl-ŭ-hä-bäd')	199	25°32'N	81°53'E
All American Canal, can., Ca., U.S. (ôl ȧ-mĕr'ĭ-kăn)	118	32°43'N	115°12'W
Alland, Aus.	159e	48°04'N	16°05'E
Allariz, Spain (äl-yä-rēth')	162	42°10'N	7°48'W
Allatoona Lake, res., Ga., U.S. (ăl'ȧ-toon'ȧ)	124	34°05'N	84°57'W
Allauch, Fr. (ä-lĕ'ō)	170a	43°21'N	5°30'E
Allaykha, Russia (ä-lī'ᴋȧ)	179	70°32'N	148°53'E
Allegan, Mi., U.S. (ăl'ē-găn)	108	42°30'N	85°55'W
Allegany Indian Reservation, I.R., N.Y., U.S. (ăl-ē-gā'nĭ)	109	42°05'N	78°55'W
Allegheny, r., Pa., U.S. (ăl-ē-gā'nĭ)	109	41°10'N	79°20'W
Allegheny Front, mtn., U.S. (ăl-ē-gā'nĭ)	108	38°12'N	80°03'W
Allegheny Mountains, mts., U.S. (ăl-ē-gā'nĭ)	107	37°35'N	81°55'W
Allegheny Plateau, plat., U.S. (ăl-ē-gā'nĭ)	108	39°00'N	81°15'W
Allegheny Reservoir, res., U.S. (ăl-ē-gā'nĭ)	109	41°50'N	78°55'W
Allen, Ok., U.S. (ăl'ĕn)	121	34°51'N	96°26'W
Allen, Lough, l., Ire. (lŏk ăl'ĕn)	164	54°07'N	8°09'W
Allendale, N.J., U.S. (ăl'ĕn-dāl)	110a	41°02'N	74°08'W
Allendale, S.C., U.S. (ăl'ĕn-dāl)	125	33°00'N	81°19'W
Allende, Mex. (äl-yĕn'då)	131	18°23'N	92°49'W
Allende, Mex.	122	28°20'N	100°50'W
Allentown, Pa., U.S. (ălĕn-toun)	105	40°35'N	75°30'W
Alleppey, India (ȧ-lĕp'ē)	203	9°33'N	76°22'E
Aller, r., Ger. (äl'ĕr)	168	52°43'N	9°50'E
Alliance, Ne., U.S. (ȧ-lī'ăns)	104	42°06'N	102°53'W
Alliance, Oh., U.S. (ȧ-lī'ăns)	108	40°55'N	81°10'W
Al Lidām, Sau. Ar.	198	20°45'N	44°12'E
Allier, r., Fr. (ȧ-lyā')	170	46°43'N	3°03'E
Alligator Point, c., La., U.S. (al'ĭ-gā-tẽr)	110d	30°57'N	89°41'W
Allinge, Den. (äl'ĭŋ-ĕ)	166	55°16'N	14°48'E
Al Līth, Sau. Ar.	201	20°09'N	40°16'E
All Pines, Belize (ôl pīnz)	132a	16°55'N	88°15'W
Al Luḩayyah, Yemen	198	15°58'N	42°48'E
Alluvial City, La., U.S.	110d	29°51'N	89°42'W
Allyn, Wa., U.S. (ăl'ĭn)	116a	47°23'N	122°51'W
Alma, Can. (ăl'mȧ)	100	45°36'N	64°59'W
Alma, Can.	91	48°29'N	71°42'W
Alma, S. Afr.	238c	24°30'S	28°05'E
Alma, Ga., U.S.	125	31°33'N	82°31'W
Alma, Mi., U.S.	108	43°25'N	84°40'W
Alma, Ne., U.S.	120	40°08'N	99°21'W
Alma, Wi., U.S.	113	44°21'N	91°57'W
Alma-Ata see Almaty, Kaz.	183	43°19'N	77°08'E
Almada, Port. (äl-mä'dä)	173b	38°40'N	9°09'W
Almadén, Spain (äl-mȧ-dhān)	172	38°47'N	4°50'W
Al Madīnah, Sau. Ar.	198	24°26'N	39°42'E
Al Mafraq, Jord.	197a	32°21'N	36°13'E
Almagre, Laguna, l., Mex. (lä-goo'nä-äl-mä'grĕ)	131	23°48'N	97°45'W
Almagro, Spain (äl-mä'grō)	172	38°52'N	3°41'W
Al Maḩallah al Kubrā, Egypt	238b	30°58'N	31°10'E
Al Manāmah, Bahr.	198	26°01'N	50°33'E
Almanor, Lake, l., Ca., U.S. (ăl-măn'ôr)	118	40°11'N	121°20'W
Almansa, Spain (äl-män'sä)	172	38°52'N	1°09'W
Al Manshāh, Egypt	238b	26°31'N	31°46'E
Almansor, r., Port. (äl-män-sôr)	172	38°41'N	8°27'W
Al Manşūrah, Egypt	231	31°02'N	31°25'E
Al Manzilah, Egypt (män'za-la)	238b	31°09'N	32°05'E
Almanzora, r., Spain (äl-män-thō'rä)	172	37°20'N	2°25'W
Al Marāghah, Egypt	238b	26°41'N	31°35'E
Almargem do Bispo, Port. (äl-mär-zhĕn)	173b	38°51'N	9°16'W
Al-Marj, Libya	231	32°44'N	21°08'E
Al Maşīrah, i., Oman	198	20°43'N	58°58'E
Almaty (Alma-Ata), Kaz.	183	43°19'N	77°08'E
Almaty, val., Sau. Ar.	197a	29°16'N	35°12'E
Al Mawşil, Iraq	198	36°00'N	42°53'E
Almazán, Spain (äl-mä-thän')	172	41°30'N	2°33'W
Al Mazār, Jord.	197a	31°04'N	35°41'E
Al Mazra'ah, Jord.	197a	31°17'N	35°33'E
Almeirim, Port. (äl-māī-rēn')	172	39°13'N	8°31'W
Almelo, Neth. (äl'mĕ-lō)	165	52°20'N	6°42'E

ăt; finăl; rāte; senāte; ärm; ȧsk; sofȧ; fâre; ch-choose; dh-as th in other; bē; ēvent; bĕt; recĕnt; cratẽr; g-gō; gh-guttural g; bĭt; ĭ-short neutral; rīde; ᴋ-guttural k as ch in German ich;

PRONOUNCING INDEX Almendra – Andrelândia 265

PLACE (Pronunciation)	PAGE	LAT.	LONG.
Almendra, Embalse de, res., Spain	172	41°15'N	6°10'W
Almendralejo, Spain (äl-män-drä-lā'hō)	172	38°43'N	6°24'W
Almería, Spain (äl-mā-rē'ä)	154	36°52'N	2°28'W
Almería, Golfo de, b., Spain (gål-fô-dĕ-äl-māĭ-reɴ')	172	36°45'N	2°26'W
Älmhult, Swe. (älm'hōōlt)	166	56°35'N	14°08'E
Almina, Punta, c., Mor. (äl-mē'nä)	172	35°58'N	5°17'W
Al Minyā, Egypt	231	28°06'N	30°45'E
Almirante, Pan. (äl-mē-rän'tā)	133	9°18'N	82°24'W
Almirante, Bahía de, b., Pan.	133	9°22'N	82°07'W
Almodóvar del Campo, Spain (äl-mō-dhō'vär)	172	38°43'N	4°10'W
Almoloya, Mex. (äl-mō-lō'yä)	130	19°32'N	99°44'W
Almoloya, Mex. (äl-mō-lō'yä)	131a	19°11'N	99°28'W
Almonte, Can. (ăl-mŏn'tē)	99	45°15'N	76°15'W
Almonte, Spain (äl-mōn'tā)	172	37°16'N	6°32'W
Almonte, r., Spain (äl-mōn'tā)	172	39°35'N	5°50'W
Almora, India	100	29°20'N	79°40'E
Al Mubarraz, Sau. Ar.	198	22°31'N	46°27'E
Al Mudawwarah, Jord.	197a	29°20'N	36°01'E
Al Mukhā (Mocha), Yemen	198	13°11'N	43°20'E
Almuñécar, Spain (äl-mōōn-yā'kär)	172	36°44'N	3°43'W
Almyrós, Grc.	175	39°13'N	22°47'E
Alnön, i., Swe.	166	62°20'N	17°39'E
Aloha, Or., U.S. (ä'lō-hā)	116c	45°29'N	122°52'W
Alor, Pulau, i., Indon. (ä'lōr)	213	8°07'S	125°00'E
Álora, Spain (ä'lō-rä)	172	36°49'N	4°42'W
Alor Gajah, Malay.	197b	2°23'N	102°13'E
Alor Setar, Malay. (ä'lōr stär)	212	6°10'N	100°16'E
Alouette, r., Can. (ä-lōō-ĕt')	116d	49°16'N	122°32'W
Alpena, Mi., U.S. (ăl-pē'nȧ)	105	45°05'N	83°30'W
Alpes Cotiennes, mts., Eur.	171	44°46'N	7°02'E
Alphen, Neth.	159a	52°07'N	4°38'E
Alpiarça, Port. (äl-pyär'sȧ)	172	39°38'N	8°37'W
Alpine, Tx., U.S. (ăl'pīn)	122	30°21'N	103°41'W
Alps, mts., Eur. (ălps)	156	46°18'N	8°42'E
Alpujarra, Col. (ȧl-pōō-κȧ'rȧ)	142a	3°23'N	74°56'W
Al Qaḑārif, Sudan	231	14°03'N	35°11'E
Al Qāhirah *see* Cairo, Egypt	231	30°00'N	31°17'E
Al Qanţarah, Egypt	238d	30°51'N	32°20'E
Al Qaryah Ash Sharqīyah, Libya	231	30°36'N	13°13'E
Al Qaşr, Egypt	200	25°42'N	28°53'E
Al Qaţīf, Sau. Ar.	198	26°30'N	50°00'E
Al Qayşūmah, Sau. Ar.	198	28°15'N	46°20'E
Al Qunaytirah, Syria	197a	33°09'N	35°49'E
Al Qunfudhah, Sau. Ar.	198	19°08'N	41°05'E
Al Quşaymah, Egypt	197a	30°40'N	34°23'E
Al Quşayr, Egypt	231	26°14'N	34°11'E
Al Qusayr, Syria	197a	34°32'N	36°33'E
Als, i., Den. (äls)	166	55°06'N	9°40'E
Alsace, hist. reg., Fr. (äl-sȧ's)	171	48°25'N	7°24'E
Altadena, Ca., U.S. (ăl-tä-dē'nä)	117a	34°12'N	118°08'W
Alta Gracia, Arg. (äl'tä grä'sē-a)	144	31°41'S	64°19'W
Altagracia, Ven.	142	10°42'N	71°34'W
Altagracia de Orituco, Ven.	143b	9°53'N	66°22'W
Altai Mountains, mts., Asia (äl'tī')	204	49°11'N	87°15'E
Alta Loma, Ca., U.S. (ăl'tă lō'mä)	117a	34°07'N	117°35'W
Alta Loma, Tx., U.S. (ăl'tȧ lō-mȧ)	123a	29°22'N	95°05'W
Altamaha, r., Ga., U.S. (ôl-tȧ-mȧ-hô')	125	31°50'N	82°00'W
Altamira, Braz. (äl-tä-mē'rä)	143	3°13'S	52°14'W
Altamira, Mex.	131	22°25'N	97°55'W
Altamirano, Arg. (äl-tä-mē-rā'nō)	144	35°26'S	58°12'W
Altamura, Italy (äl-tä-mōō'rä)	163	40°40'N	16°35'E
Altavista, Va., U.S. (äl-tä-vĭs'tȧ)	125	37°08'N	79°14'W
Altay, China (äl-tā)	204	47°52'N	86°50'E
Altenburg, Ger. (äl-tĕn-bōōrgh)	168	50°59'N	12°27'E
Altenmarkt an der Triesting, Aus.	159e	48°02'N	16°00'E
Alter do Chão, Port. (äl-tĕr'dō shäɴ'ōɴ)	172	39°13'N	7°38'W
Altiplano, pl., Bol. (äl-tē-plȧ'nō)	142	18°38'S	68°20'W
Altlandsberg, Ger. (ält länts'bĕrgh)	159b	52°34'N	13°44'E
Alto, La., U.S. (ăl'tō)	123	32°21'N	91°52'W
Alto Marañón, r., Peru (ȧl'tô-mä-rän-yŏ'n)	142	8°18'S	77°13'W
Altomünster, Ger. (äl'tō-mün'stĕr)	159d	48°24'N	11°16'E
Alton, Can. (ôl'tŭn)	102d	43°52'N	80°05'W
Alton, Il., U.S. (ôl'tŭn)	105	38°53'N	90°11'W
Altona, Austl.	217a	37°52'S	144°50'E
Altona, Can.	97	49°06'N	97°33'W
Altona, Ger. (äl'tō-nȧ)	159c	53°33'N	9°54'E
Altoona, Al., U.S. (ăl-tōō'nȧ)	124	34°01'N	86°15'W
Altoona, Pa., U.S. (ăl-tōō'nȧ)	105	40°25'N	78°25'W
Altoona, Wa., U.S. (ăl-tōō'nȧ)	116c	46°16'N	123°39'W
Alto Rio Doce, Braz. (äl'tō-rē'ō-dō'sĕ)	141a	21°02'S	43°23'W
Alto Songo, Cuba (äl-fō-sôŋ'gō)	135	20°10'N	75°45'W
Altotonga, Mex. (ȧl-tō-tôŋ'gä)	131	19°44'N	97°13'W
Alto Velo, i., Dom. Rep. (äl-tō-vĕ'lō)	135	17°30'N	71°35'W
Altrincham, Eng., U.K. (ôl'trĭng-ăm)	158a	53°18'N	2°21'W
Altruppin, Ger. (ält rōō'ppēn)	159b	52°56'N	12°50'E
Altun Shan, mts., China (äl-tōn shän)	204	36°58'N	85°09'E
Alturas, Ca., U.S. (ăl-tōō'rȧs)	114	41°29'N	120°33'W
Altus, Ok., U.S. (ăl'tŭs)	120	34°38'N	99°20'W
Al 'Ubaylah, Sau. Ar.	201	21°59'N	50°57'E
Al-Uḑayyah, Sudan	231	12°06'N	28°16'E
Alūksne, Lat. (ä'lōks-nĕ)	180	57°24'N	27°04'E
Alumette Island, i., Can. (ȧ-lü-mĕt')	99	45°50'N	77°00'W
Alum Rock, Ca., U.S.	116b	37°23'N	121°50'W
Al 'Uqaylah, Libya	231	30°15'N	19°07'E
Al Uqşur, Egypt	231	25°38'N	32°59'E
Alushta, Ukr. (ä'lshō-tȧ)	177	44°39'N	34°23'E
Alva, Ok., U.S. (ăl'vȧ)	120	36°46'N	98°41'W

PLACE (Pronunciation)	PAGE	LAT.	LONG.
Alvarado, Mex. (äl-vä-rä'dhō)	131	18°48'N	95°45'W
Alvarado, Luguna de, l., Mex. (lä-gō'nä-dĕ-äl-vä-rȧ'dō)	131	18°44'N	95°45'W
Älvdalen, Swe. (ĕlv'dä-lĕn)	166	61°14'N	14°04'E
Alverca, Port. (al-vĕr'kȧ)	173b	38°53'N	9°02'W
Alvesta, Swe. (äl-vĕs'tä)	166	56°55'N	14°29'E
Alvin, Tx., U.S. (ăl'vĭn)	123a	29°25'N	95°14'W
Alvinópolis, Braz. (äl-vēnō'pō-lēs)	141a	20°07'S	43°03'W
Alviso, Ca., U.S. (ăl-vī'sō)	116b	37°26'N	121°59'W
Al Wajh, Sau. Ar.	198	26°15'N	36°32'E
Alwar, India (ŭl'wŭr)	199	27°39'N	76°39'E
Al Wāsiţah, Egypt	238b	29°21'N	31°15'E
Alytus, Lith. (ä'lē-tōs)	167	54°25'N	24°05'E
Amacuzac, r., Mex. (ä-mä-kōō-zȧk)	130	18°00'N	99°03'W
Amadeus, l., Austl. (ăm-ȧ-dē'ŭs)	220	24°30'S	131°25'E
Amadjuak, l., Can. (ä-mädj'wäk)	93	64°50'N	69°20'W
Amadora, Port.	173b	38°45'N	9°14'W
Amagasaki, Japan (ä'mä-gä-sä'kē)	211	34°43'N	135°25'E
Amakusa-Shimo, i., Japan (ämä-kōō'sä shē-mō)	210	32°24'N	129°35'E
Åmål, Swe. (ō'mōl)	166	59°05'N	12°40'E
Amalfi, Col. (ä'mȧ'l-fē)	142a	6°55'N	75°04'W
Amalfi, Italy (ä-mä'l-fē)	173c	40°23'N	14°36'E
Amaliáda, Grc.	175	37°48'N	21°23'E
Amalner, India	202	21°07'N	75°06'E
Amambai, Serra de, mts., S.A.	143	20°06'S	57°08'W
Amami, i., Japan	205	28°10'N	129°55'E
Amapala, Hond. (ä-mä-pä'lä)	132	13°16'N	87°39'W
Amarante, Braz. (ä-mä-rän'tā)	143	6°17'S	42°43'W
Amargosa, r., Ca., U.S. (ȧ'mär-gō'sȧ)	118	35°55'N	116°45'W
Amarillo, Tx., U.S. (ăm-ȧ-rĭl'ō)	104	35°14'N	101°49'W
Amaro, Mount, mtn., Italy (ä-mä'rō)	162	42°07'N	14°07'E
Amasya, Tur. (ä-mä'sē-ȧ)	163	40°40'N	35°50'E
Amatenango, Mex. (ä-mä-tā-naŋ'gō)	131	16°30'N	92°29'W
Amatignak, i., Ak., U.S. (ä-mȧ'tē-näk)	103a	51°12'N	178°30'W
Amatique, Bahía de, b., N.A. (bä-ē'ä-dĕ-ä-mä-tē'kā)	132	15°58'N	88°50'W
Amatitlán, Guat. (ä-mä-tē-tlän')	132	14°27'N	90°39'W
Amatlán de Cañas, Mex. (ä-mät-län'dā kän-yäs)	130	20°50'N	104°22'W
Amazon (Amazonas) (Solimões), r., S.A.	143	2°03'S	53°18'W
Amazonas, state, Braz. (ä-mä-thō'näs)	142	4°15'S	64°30'W
Ambāla, India (ŭm-bä'lŭ)	199	30°31'N	76°48'E
Ambalema, Col. (äm-bä-lā'mä)	142	4°47'N	74°45'W
Ambarchik, Russia (ŭm-bär'chĭk)	179	69°39'N	162°18'E
Ambarnāth, India	203b	19°12'N	73°10'E
Ambato, Ec. (äm-bä'tō)	142	1°15'S	78°30'W
Ambatondrazaka, Madag.	233	17°58'S	48°43'E
Amberg, Ger. (äm'bĕrgh)	168	49°26'N	11°51'E
Ambergris Cay, i., Belize (ăm'bẽr-grēs kāz)	132a	18°04'N	87°43'W
Ambergris Cays, is., T./C. Is.	135	21°20'N	71°40'W
Ambérieu-en-Bugey, Fr. (äɴ-bā-rē-u')	171	45°57'N	5°21'E
Ambert, Fr. (äɴ-bĕr')	170	45°32'N	3°41'E
Ambil Island, i., Phil. (äm'bēl)	213a	13°51'N	120°25'E
Ambler, Pa., U.S. (ăm'blĕr)	110f	40°09'N	75°13'W
Amboise, Fr. (äɴ-bwăz')	170	47°25'N	0°56'E
Ambon, Indon.	213	3°45'S	128°17'E
Ambon, Pulau, i., Indon.	213	4°50'S	128°45'E
Ambositra, Madag. (äɴ-bō-sē'trä)	233	20°31'S	47°28'E
Amboy, Il., U.S. (ăm'boi)	108	41°41'N	89°15'W
Amboy, Wa., U.S. (ăm'boi)	116c	45°55'N	122°27'W
Ambre, Cap d', c., Madag.	233	12°06'S	49°15'E
Ambridge, Pa., U.S. (ăm'brĭdj)	111e	40°36'N	80°13'W
Ambrim, i., Vanuatu	221	16°25'S	168°15'E
Ambriz, Ang.	232	7°50'S	13°06'E
Amchitka, i., Ak., U.S. (ăm-chĭt'kȧ)	103a	51°25'N	178°10'E
Amchitka Passage, strt., Ak., U.S. (ăm-chĭt'kȧ)	103a	51°30'N	179°36'W
Amealco, Mex. (ä-mā-äl'kō)	130	20°12'N	100°08'W
Ameca, Mex. (ä-mĕ'kä)	128	20°34'N	104°02'W
Amecameca, Mex. (ä-mȧ-kä-mā'kä)	130	19°06'N	98°46'W
Ameide, Neth.	159a	51°57'N	4°57'E
Ameland, i., Neth.	165	53°29'N	5°54'E
Amelia, Oh., U.S. (ȧ-mēl'yā)	111f	39°01'N	84°12'W
American, South Fork, r., Ca., U.S. (ȧ-mĕr'ĭ-kăn)	118	38°43'N	120°45'W
Americana, Braz. (ä-mĕ-rē-kȧ'nȧ)	141a	22°46'S	47°19'W
American Falls, Id., U.S. (ȧ-mĕr'ĭ-kăn-fäls')	115	42°45'N	112°53'W
American Falls Reservoir, res., Id., U.S. (ȧ-mĕr'ĭ-kăn-fäls')	106	42°56'N	113°18'W
American Fork, Ut., U.S.	119	40°20'N	111°50'W
American Highland, plat., Ant.	224	72°00'S	79°00'E
American Samoa, dep., Oc.	2	14°20'S	170°00'W
Americus, Ga., U.S. (ȧ-mĕr'ĭ-kŭs)	105	32°04'N	84°15'W
Amersfoort, Neth. (ä'mĕrz-fōrt)	159a	52°08'N	5°23'E
Amery, Can. (ā'mẽr-ē)	91	56°34'N	94°03'W
Amery, Wi., U.S.	113	45°19'N	92°24'W
Ames, Ia., U.S. (āmz)	113	42°00'N	93°36'W
Amesbury, Ma., U.S. (āmz'bẽr-ē)	101a	42°51'N	70°56'W
Amfissa, Grc. (ȧm-fĭ'sȧ)	175	38°32'N	22°26'E
Amga, Russia (ŭm-gä')	179	61°08'N	132°09'E
Amga, r., Russia	185	61°41'N	133°11'E
Amgun', r., Russia	185	52°30'N	138°00'E
Amherst, Can. (ăm'hẽrst)	91	45°49'N	64°14'W
Amherst, Oh., U.S.	111d	41°24'N	82°13'W
Amherst, i., Can. (ăm'hẽrst)	99	44°08'N	76°45'W
Amiens, Fr. (ä-myäɴ')	161	49°54'N	2°18'E
Amirante Islands, is., Sey.	5	6°02'S	52°30'E
Amisk Lake, l., Can.	97	54°35'N	102°13'W
Amistad Reservoir, res., N.A.	122	29°20'N	101°00'W
Amite, La., U.S. (ä-mēt')	123	30°43'N	90°32'W

PLACE (Pronunciation)	PAGE	LAT.	LONG.
Amite, r., La., U.S.	123	30°45'N	90°48'W
Amity, Pa., U.S. (ăm'ĭ-tĭ)	111e	40°02'N	80°11'W
Amityville, N.Y., U.S. (ăm'ĭ-tĭ-vĭl)	110a	40°41'N	73°24'W
Amlia, i., Ak., U.S. (ȧ'mlēä)	103a	52°00'N	173°28'W
'Ammān, Jord. (äm'mȧn)	198	31°57'N	35°57'E
Ammersee, l., Ger. (äm'mĕr)	159d	48°00'N	11°08'E
Amnicon, r., Wi., U.S. (ăm'nē-kŏn)	117h	46°35'N	91°56'W
Amorgós, i., Grc. (ä-môr'gōs)	163	36°47'N	25°47'E
Amory, Ms., U.S. (āmō-rē)	124	33°58'N	88°27'W
Amos, Can. (ā'mŭs)	91	48°31'N	78°04'W
Amoy *see* Xiamen, China	205	24°30'N	118°10'E
Amparo, Braz. (äm-pȧ'-rô)	141a	22°43'S	46°44'W
Amper, r., Ger. (äm'pĕr)	159d	48°18'N	11°32'E
Amposta, Spain (äm-pōs'tä)	173	40°42'N	0°34'E
Amqui, Can.	100	48°28'N	67°28'W
Amrāvati, India	199	20°58'N	77°47'E
Amritsar, India (ŭm-rĭt'sŭr)	199	31°43'N	74°52'E
Amstelveen, Neth.	159a	52°18'N	4°51'E
Amsterdam, Neth. (äm-stĕr-däm')	154	52°21'N	4°52'E
Amsterdam, N.Y., U.S. (ăm'stĕr-dăm)	109	42°55'N	74°10'W
Amsterdam, Île, i., Afr.	224	37°52'S	77°32'E
Amstetten, Aus. (äm'stĕt-ĕn)	168	48°09'N	14°53'E
Am Timan, Chad (äm'tē-män')	231	11°18'N	20°30'E
Amu Darya, r., Asia (ä-mō-dä'rēä)	178	38°30'N	64°00'E
Amukta Passage, strt., Ak., U.S. (ä-mōōk'tȧ)	103a	52°30'N	172°00'W
Amundsen Gulf, b., Can. (ä'mŭn-sĕn-gŭlf')	92	70°17'N	123°28'W
Amundsen Sea, sea, Ant. (ä'mŭn-sĕn-sē')	224	72°00'S	110°00'W
Amungen, l., Swe.	166	61°07'N	16°00'E
Amur, r., Asia	179	49°00'N	136°00'E
Amurskiy, Russia (ä-mûr'skĭ)	186a	52°35'N	59°36'E
Amurskiy, Zaliv, b., Russia (zä'lĭf ä-mōr'skĭ)	210	43°20'N	131°40'E
Amusgos, Mex.	130	16°39'N	98°09'W
Amuyao, Mount, mtn., Phil. (ä-mōō-yä'ō)	213a	17°04'N	121°09'E
Amvrakikos Kólpos, b., Grc.	175	39°00'N	21°00'E
Amyun, Leb.	197a	34°18'N	35°48'E
Anabar, r., Russia (ăn-ȧ-bär')	185	71°15'N	113°00'E
Anaco, Ven. (ä-nȧ'kô)	143b	9°29'N	64°27'W
Anaconda, Mt., U.S. (ăn-ȧ-kŏn'dȧ)	104	46°07'N	112°55'W
Anacortes, Wa., U.S. (ăn-ȧ-kôr'tĕz)	116a	48°30'N	122°37'W
Anadarko, Ok., U.S. (ăn-ȧ-där'kō)	120	35°05'N	98°14'W
Anadyr', Russia (ŭ-nȧ-dĭr')	179	64°47'N	177°01'E
Anadyr, r., Russia	185	65°30'N	172°45'E
Anadyrskiy Zaliv, b., Russia	178	64°10'N	178°00'W
Anaheim, Ca., U.S. (ăn'ȧ-hīm)	117a	33°50'N	117°55'W
Anahuac, Tx., U.S. (ä-nä'wäk)	123a	29°46'N	94°41'W
Ānai Mudi, mtn., India	203	10°10'N	77°00'E
Anama Bay, Can.	97	51°56'N	98°05'W
Ana María, Cayos, is., Cuba	134	21°25'N	78°50'W
Anambas, Kepulauan, is., Indon. (ä-näm-bäs)	212	2°41'N	106°38'E
Anamosa, Ia., U.S. (ăn-ȧ-mō'sȧ)	113	42°06'N	91°18'W
Anan'ïv, Ukr.	181	47°43'N	29°59'E
Anapa, Russia (ȧ-nä'pä)	181	44°54'N	37°19'E
Anápolis, Braz. (ä-nȧ'pō-lēs)	143	16°17'S	48°47'W
Añatuya, Arg. (ȧ-nyä-tōō'yȧ)	144	28°22'S	62°45'W
Anchieta, Braz. (ȧn-chyĕ'tä)	144b	22°49'S	43°24'W
Ancholme, r., Eng., U.K. (ăn'chŭm)	158a	53°28'N	0°27'W
Anchorage, Ak., U.S. (ăŋ'kẽr-ȧj)	106a	61°12'N	149°48'W
Anchorage, Ky., U.S.	111h	38°16'N	85°32'W
Anci, China (än-tsŭ)	206	39°31'N	116°41'E
Ancienne-Lorette, Can. (äɴ-syĕn' lō-rĕt')	102b	46°48'N	71°21'W
Ancon, Pan. (ăŋ-kōn')	128a	8°55'N	79°32'W
Ancona, Italy (än-kō'nä)	154	43°37'N	13°32'E
Ancud, Chile (äŋ-kōōdh')	144	41°52'S	73°45'W
Ancud, Golfo de, b., Chile (gål-fô-dĕ-äŋ-kōōdh')	144	41°15'S	73°00'W
Anda, China	208	46°20'N	125°20'E
Åndalsnes, Nor.	166	62°33'N	7°46'E
Andalucia, hist. reg., Spain (än-dä-lōō-sē'ä)	172	37°35'N	5°40'W
Andalusia, Al., U.S. (ăn-dȧ-lōō'zhĭȧ)	124	31°19'N	86°19'W
Andaman Islands, is., India (ăn-dȧ-măn')	212	11°38'N	92°17'E
Andaman Sea, sea, Asia	212	12°44'N	95°45'E
Andarax, r., Spain	172	37°00'N	2°40'W
Anderlecht, Bel. (än'dẽr-lĕkt)	159a	50°49'N	4°16'E
Andernach, Ger. (än'dẽr-näk)	168	50°25'N	7°23'E
Anderson, Arg. (ȧ'n-dĕr-sōn)	141c	35°15'S	60°15'W
Anderson, Ca., U.S. (ăn'dẽr-sŭn)	114	40°28'N	122°19'W
Anderson, In., U.S. (ăn'dẽr-sŭn)	108	40°05'N	85°50'W
Anderson, S.C., U.S. (ăn'dẽr-sŭn)	105	34°30'N	82°40'W
Anderson, r., Can. (ăn'dẽr-sŭn)	92	68°32'N	125°12'W
Andes Mountains, mts., S.A. (ăn'dēz) (än'dās)	139	13°00'S	75°00'W
Andheri, neigh., India	203b	19°08'N	72°50'E
Andhra Pradesh, state, India	199	16°00'N	79°00'E
Andikýthira, i., Grc.	163	35°50'N	23°20'E
Andizhan, Uzb. (än-dē-zhän')	183	40°45'N	72°22'E
Andong, Kor., S. (än'dŭng')	205	36°31'N	128°42'E
Andongwei, China (än-dōŋ-wā)	206	35°08'N	119°19'E
Andorra, And. (än-dōr'rä)	173	42°38'N	1°30'E
Andorra, nation, Eur. (än-dōr'rä)	154	42°30'N	2°00'E
Andover, Ma., U.S. (ăn'dō-vẽr)	101a	42°39'N	71°08'W
Andover, N.J., U.S. (ăn'dō-vẽr)	110a	40°59'N	74°45'W
Andøya, i., Nor. (änd-ûē)	160	69°12'N	14°58'E
Andreanof Islands, is., Ak., U.S. (än-drā-ä'nōf-ĭ'ăndz)	106b	51°10'N	177°00'W
Andrelândia, Braz. (än-drĕ-lá'n-dyá)	141a	21°45'S	44°18'W

ng-sing; ŋ-baŋk; ɴ-nasalized n; nŏd; cŏmmit; ōld; ôbey; ôrder; oi-boil; fōōd; ō-as oo in foot; ou-out; s-soft; sh-dish; th-thin; pūre; ûnite; ûrn; stŭd; circŭs; ü-as in French tu; '-indeterminate vowel.

266 Andrew Johnson National Historic Site – Archidona PRONOUNCING INDEX

PLACE (Pronunciation)	PAGE	LAT.	LONG.
Andrew Johnson National Historic Site, rec., Tn., U.S. (ăn'drōō jŏn'sŭn)	125	36°15'N	82°55'W
Andrews, N.C., U.S. (ăn'drōōz)	124	35°12'N	83°48'W
Andrews, S.C., U.S. (ăn'drōōz)	125	33°25'N	79°32'W
Andria, Italy (än'drê-ä)	163	41°17'N	15°55'E
Andros, Grc. (ȧn'dhrôs)	175	37°50'N	24°54'E
Ándros, i., Grc. (ȧn'drôs)	163	37°59'N	24°55'E
Androscoggin, r., Me., U.S. (ăn-drŭs-kŏg'ĭn)	100	44°25'N	70°45'W
Andros Island, i., Bah. (ăn'drŏs)	129	24°30'N	78°00'W
Anefis i-n-Darane, Mali	234	18°03'N	0°36'E
Anegasaki, Japan (ä'nå-gä-sä'kê)	211a	35°29'N	140°02'E
Aneityum, i., Vanuatu (ä-nå-ē'tê-ŭm)	221	20°15'S	169°49'E
Aneta, N.D., U.S. (ă-nē'tȧ)	112	47°41'N	97°57'W
Aneto, Pico de, mtn., Spain (pê'kō-dĕ-ä-nĕ'tô)	156	42°35'N	0°38'E
Angamacutiro, Mex. (än'gä mä-kōō-tē'rô)	130	20°08'N	101°44'W
Angangueo, Mex. (än-gäŋ'gwå-ō)	130	19°36'N	100°18'W
Ang'angxi, China (äŋ-äŋ-shyē)	205	47°05'N	123°58'E
Angarsk, Russia	179	52°48'N	104°15'E
Ånge, Swe. (ông'ā)	166	62°31'N	15°39'E
Angel, Salto, wtfl., Ven. (säl'tō-á'n-hĕl)	142	5°44'N	62°27'W
Ángel de la Guarda, i., Mex. (á'n-hĕl-dĕ-lä-gwä'r-dä)	128	29°30'N	113°00'W
Angeles, Phil. (än'hâ-lās)	213a	15°09'N	120°35'E
Ängelholm, Swe. (ĕng'ĕl-hôlm)	166	56°14'N	12°50'E
Angelina, r., Tx., U.S. (ăn-jê lē'nȧ)	123	31°30'N	94°53'W
Angels Camp, Ca., U.S. (ān'jĕls kămp')	118	38°03'N	120°33'W
Ångermanälven, r., Swe.	160	64°10'N	17°30'E
Angermund, Ger. (än'ngĕr-mūnd)	171c	51°20'N	6°47'E
Angermünde, Ger. (äng'ĕr-mûn-dĕ)	168	53°02'N	14°00'E
Angers, Can. (äN-zhā')	102c	45°31'N	75°29'W
Angers, Fr.	170	47°29'N	0°36'W
Angkor, hist., Camb. (äng'kôr)	212	13°52'N	103°50'E
Anglesey, i., Wales, U.K. (ăŋ'g'l-sê)	164	53°35'N	4°28'W
Angleton, Tx., U.S. (aŋ'g'l-tŭn)	123a	29°10'N	95°25'W
Angmagssalik, Grnld. (äŋ-mȧ'sȧ-lĭk)	89	65°40'N	37°40'W
Angoche, Ilha, i., Moz. (ê'lä-ăn-gō'chå)	233	16°20'S	40°00'E
Angol, Chile (aŋ-gōl')	144	37°47'S	72°43'W
Angola, In., U.S. (ăŋ-gō'lȧ)	108	41°35'S	85°00'W
Angola, nation, Afr. (ăŋ-gō'lȧ)	232	14°15'S	16°00'E
Angora *see* Ankara, Tur.	198	39°55'N	32°50'E
Angoulême, Fr. (äŋ-gōō-lâm')	170	45°40'N	0°09'E
Angra dos Reis, Braz. (aŋ'grä dōs rā'ēs)	141a	23°01'S	44°17'W
Angri, Italy (ä'n-grê)	173c	40°30'N	14°35'E
Anguang, China (än-gůäŋ)	208	45°28'N	123°42'E
Anguilla, dep., N.A.	129	18°15'N	62°54'W
Anguilla Cays, is., Bah. (ăŋ-gwĭl'ȧ)	134	23°30'N	79°35'W
Anguille, Cape, c., Can. (kăp'-äŋ-gē'yĕ)	101	47°55'N	59°25'W
Anguo, China (än-gwô)	206	38°27'N	115°19'E
Anholt, i., Den. (än'hôlt)	166	56°43'N	11°34'E
Anhui, prov., China (än-hwā)	205	31°30'N	117°15'E
Aniak, Ak., U.S. (ă-nyà'k)	103	61°32'N	159°35'W
Aniakchak National Monument, rec., Ak., U.S.	104	56°50'N	157°50'W
Animas, r., Co., U.S. (ä'nê-mäs)	119	37°03'N	107°50'W
Anina, Rom. (ä-nē'nä)	175	45°03'N	21°50'E
Anita, Pa., U.S. (ȧ-nē'ȧ)	109	41°05'N	79°00'W
Aniva, Mys, c., Russia (mĭs ȧ-nē'vȧ)	210	46°08'N	143°13'E
Aniva, Zaliv, b., Russia (zä'lĭf ȧ-nē'vȧ)	210	46°30'N	143°00'E
Anjou, Can.	102a	45°37'N	73°33'W
Ankang, China (än-käŋ)	204	32°38'N	109°10'E
Ankara, Tur. (äŋ'kȧ-rȧ)	198	39°55'N	32°50'E
Anklam, Ger. (än'kläm)	168	53°52'N	13°43'E
Ankoro, D.R.C. (ăŋ-kō'rō)	232	6°45'S	26°57'E
Anloga, Ghana	234	5°47'N	0°50'E
Anlong, China (än-loŋ)	209	25°01'N	105°32'E
Anlu, China (än'lōō)	209	31°18'N	113°40'E
Ann, Cape, c., Ma., U.S. (kăp ăn')	109	42°40'N	70°40'W
Anna, Russia (än'ä)	177	51°31'N	40°27'E
Anna, Il., U.S. (ăn'ȧ)	121	37°28'N	89°15'W
Annaba, Alg.	230	36°57'N	7°39'E
Annaberg-Bucholz, Ger. (än'ä-bĕrgh)	168	50°35'N	13°02'E
An Nafūd, des., Sau. Ar.	198	28°30'N	40°30'E
An Najaf, Iraq (än nä-jäf')	198	32°00'N	44°25'E
An Nakhl, Egypt	197a	29°55'N	33°45'E
Annamese Cordillera, mts., Asia	212	17°34'N	105°38'E
Annapolis, Md., U.S. (ă-năp'ô-lĭs)	105	39°00'N	76°25'W
Annapolis Royal, Can.	100	44°45'N	65°31'W
Ann Arbor, Mi., U.S. (ăn är'bẽr)	105	42°15'N	83°45'W
An Nāṣirīyah, Iraq	198	31°08'N	46°15'E
An Nawfalīyah, Libya	231	30°57'N	17°38'E
Annecy, Fr. (ȧn sē')	171	45°54'N	6°07'E
Annemasse, Fr. (ȧn'mäs')	171	46°09'N	6°13'E
Annette Island, i., Ak., U.S.	94	55°13'N	131°30'W
An Nhon, Viet.	212	13°55'N	109°00'E
Annieopsquotch Mountains, mts., Can.	101	48°37'N	57°17'W
Anniston, Al., U.S. (ăn'ĭs-tŭn)	105	33°39'N	85°47'W
Annobón, i., Eq. Gui.	229	2°00'S	3°30'E
Annonay, Fr. (ȧn'ô-nĕ)	170	45°16'N	4°36'E
Annotto Bay, Jam. (än-nō'tō)	134	18°15'N	76°45'W
An Nuhūd, Sudan	231	12°39'N	28°18'E
Anoka, Mn., U.S. (ȧ-nō'kȧ)	117g	45°12'N	93°24'W
Anori, Col. (ȧ-nō'rê)	142a	7°01'N	75°09'W
Áno Viánnos, Grc.	174a	35°02'N	25°26'E
Anpu, China (än-pōō)	204	21°28'N	110°00'E
Anqiu, China (än-chyô)	206	36°26'N	119°12'E
Ansbach, Ger. (äns'bäk)	168	49°18'N	10°35'E
Anse à Veau, Haiti (äNs' ä-vō')	135	18°30'N	73°25'W
Anse d'Hainault, Haiti (äNs'dĕnō)	135	18°30'N	74°25'W
Anserma, Col. (á'n-sĕ'r-mȧ)	142a	5°13'N	75°47'W
Ansermanuevo, Col. (á'n-sĕ'r-mȧ-nwĕ'vō)	142a	4°47'N	75°59'W
Anshan, China	208	41°00'N	123°00'E
Anshun, China (än-shōōn')	204	26°12'N	105°50'E
Anson, Tx., U.S. (ăn'sŭn)	122	32°45'N	99°52'W
Anson Bay, b., Austl.	220	13°10'S	130°00'E
Ansŏng, Kor., S. (än'sŭng')	210	37°00'N	127°12'E
Ansongo, Mali	234	15°40'N	0°30'E
Ansonia, Ct., U.S. (ăn-sōnĭ-ȧ)	109	41°20'N	73°05'W
Antalya, Tur. (än-tä'lê-ä) (ä-dä'lê-ä)	163	37°00'N	30°50'E
Antalya Körfezi, b., Tur.	163	36°40'N	31°20'E
Antananarivo, Madag.	233	18°51'S	47°40'E
Antarctica, cont.	224	80°15'S	127°00'E
Antarctic Peninsula, pen., Ant.	224	70°00'S	65°00'W
Antelope Creek, r., Wy., U.S. (ăn'tē-lōp)	116	43°29'N	105°42'W
Antequera, Spain (än-tĕ-kĕ'rä)	162	37°01'N	4°34'W
Anthony, Ks., U.S. (ăn'thô-nê)	120	37°08'N	98°01'W
Anthony Peak, mtn., Ca., U.S.	118	39°51'N	122°58'W
Anti Atlas, mts., Mor.	230	28°45'N	9°30'W
Antibes, Fr. (äN-tēb')	171	43°36'N	7°12'E
Anticosti, Île d', i., Can. (ăn-tĭ-kôs'tê)	93	49°30'N	62°00'W
Antigo, Wi., U.S. (ăn'tĭ-gō)	113	45°09'N	89°11'W
Antigonish, Can. (ăn-tĭ-gô-nêsh')	101	45°35'N	61°55'W
Antigua, Guat. (än-tē'gwä)	128	14°32'N	90°43'W
Antigua, r., Mex.	131	19°16'N	96°36'W
Antigua and Barbuda, nation, N.A.	129	17°15'N	61°15'W
Antigua Veracruz, Mex. (än-tē'gwä vā-rä-krōōz')	131	19°18'N	96°17'W
Antilla, Cuba (än-tē'lyä)	135	20°50'N	75°50'W
Antioch, Ca., U.S. (ăn'tĭ-ŏk)	116b	38°00'N	121°48'W
Antioch, Il., U.S.	111a	42°29'N	88°06'W
Antioch, Ne., U.S.	112	42°05'N	102°36'W
Antioquia, Col. (än-tê-ō'kêä)	142	6°34'N	75°49'W
Antioquia, dept., Col.	142a	6°48'N	75°42'W
Antlers, Ok., U.S. (ănt'lẽrz)	121	34°14'N	95°38'W
Antofagasta, Chile (än-tô-fä-gäs'tä)	144	23°32'S	70°21'W
Antofalla, Salar de, pl., Arg. (sȧ-lär'de än'tō-fä'lä)	144	26°00'S	67°52'W
Antón, Pan. (än-tōn')	129	8°24'N	80°15'W
Antongila, Helodrano, b., Madag.	233	16°15'S	50°15'E
Antônio Carlos, Braz. (än-tō'nēō-ka'r-lôs)	141a	21°19'S	43°45'W
António Enes, Moz. (än-to'nyō ĕn'ĕs)	233	16°14'S	39°58'E
Antonito, Co., U.S. (ăn-tô-nē'tō)	120	37°04'N	106°01'W
Antonopole, Lat. (än'tô-nô-pō lyĕ)	167	56°19'N	27°11'E
Antony, Fr.	171b	48°45'N	2°18'E
Antsirabe, Madag. (änt-sê-rä'bä)	233	19°49'S	47°16'E
Antsiranana, Madag.	233	12°18'S	49°16'E
Antsla, Est. (änt'slȧ)	167	57°49'N	26°29'E
Antuco, vol., S.A. (än-tōō'kō)	144	37°30'S	72°30'W
Antwerp, Bel.	154	51°13'N	4°24'E
Antwerpen *see* Antwerp, Bel.	154	51°13'N	4°24'E
Anūpgarh, India (ŭ-nōp'gŭr)	202	29°22'N	73°20'E
Anuradhapura, Sri L. (ŭ-nōō'rä-dŭ-pōō'rŭ)	203	8°24'N	80°25'E
Anxi, China (än-shyē)	204	40°36'N	95°49'E
Anyang, China (än'yäng)	205	36°05'N	114°22'E
Anykščiai, Lith. (anīksh-chä'ē)	167	55°34'N	25°04'E
Anzhero-Sudzhensk, Russia (än'zhâ-rô-sōd'zhĕnsk)	178	56°08'N	86°08'E
Anzio, Italy (änt'zê-ō)	174	41°28'N	12°39'E
Anzoátegui, dept., Ven. (än-zôä'tĕ-gê)	143b	9°38'N	64°45'W
Aoba, i., Vanuatu	214f	15°25'S	167°50'E
Aomori, Japan (äô-mō'rê)	205	40°45'N	140°52'E
Aoraki (Cook, Mount), mtn., N.Z.	221a	43°27'S	170°13'E
Aosta, Italy (ä-ôs'tä)	174	45°45'N	7°20'E
Aouk, Bahr, r., Afr. (ä-ōk')	231	9°30'N	20°45'E
Aoukâr, reg., Maur.	234	18°00'N	9°40'W
Apalachicola, Fl., U.S. (ăp-ȧ-lăch-ĭ-kō'lȧ)	124	29°43'N	84°59'W
Apan, Mex. (ä-pä'n)	130	19°43'N	98°27'W
Apango, Mex. (ä-päŋ'gō)	130	17°41'N	99°22'W
Apaporis, r., S.A. (ä-pä-pô'rĭs)	142	0°48'N	72°32'W
Aparri, Phil. (ä-pär'rē)	212	18°15'N	121°40'E
Apasco, Mex. (ä-pä's-kō)	130	20°33'N	100°43'W
Apatin, Serb. (ŏ'pŏ-tĭn)	175	45°40'N	19°00'E
Apatzingán de la Constitución, Mex.	130	19°07'N	102°21'W
Apeldoorn, Neth. (ä'pĕl-dōōrn)	161	52°14'N	5°55'E
Apennines *see* Appennino, mts., Italy	156	43°48'N	11°06'E
Apía, Col. (ä-pē'ä)	142a	5°07'N	75°58'W
Apia, Samoa	214a	13°50'S	171°44'W
Apipilulco, Mex. (ä-pĭ-pĭ-lōōl'kō)	130	18°09'N	99°40'W
Apishapa, r., Co., U.S. (ăp-ĭ-shä'pȧ)	120	37°40'N	104°08'W
Apizaco, Mex. (ä-pê-zä'kō)	130	19°18'N	98°11'W
Apo, Mount, mtn., Phil. (ä'pō)	213	6°56'N	125°05'E
Apopka, Fl., U.S. (ä-pŏp'kȧ)	125a	28°37'N	81°30'W
Apopka, Lake, l., Fl., U.S.	125a	28°38'N	81°50'W
Apostle Islands, is., Wi., U.S. (ȧ-pŏs'l)	113	47°05'N	90°55'W
Appalachia, Va., U.S. (ăpȧ-lăch'ĭ-ȧ)	125	36°54'N	82°49'W
Appalachian Mountains, mts., N.A. (ăp-ȧ-lăch'ĭ-ăn)	107	37°20'N	82°00'W
Appalachicola, r., Fl., U.S. (ăpȧ-lăch'ĭ-cōlȧ)	107	30°11'N	85°00'W
Äppelbo, Swe. (ĕp-ĕl-bōō)	166	60°30'N	14°02'E
Appelhülsen, Ger. (ä'pĕl-hül'sĕn)	171c	51°55'N	7°26'E
Appennino, mts., Italy (äp-pĕn-nê'nô)	156	43°48'N	11°06'E
Appleton, Mn., U.S. (ăp'l-tŭn)	112	45°10'N	96°01'W
Appleton, Wi., U.S.	105	44°14'N	88°27'W
Appleton City, Mo., U.S.	121	38°10'N	94°02'W
Appomattox, r., Va., U.S. (ăp-ô-măt'ŭks)	125	37°22'N	78°09'W
Aprília, Italy (ȧ-prē'lyȧ)	174	41°36'N	12°40'E
Apsheronsk, Russia	182	44°28'N	39°44'E
Apt, Fr. (äpt)	171	43°54'N	5°19'E
Apure, r., Ven. (ä-pōō'rā)	142	8°08'N	68°46'W
Apurimac, r., Peru (ä-pōō-rê-mäk')	142	11°39'S	73°48'W
Aqaba, Gulf of, b. (ä'kȧ-bȧ)	198	28°30'N	34°40'E
Aqabah, Wādī al, r., Egypt	197a	29°48'N	34°05'E
Aqmola *see* Astana, Kaz.	183	51°10'N	71°43'E
Aqtaū, Kaz.	183	43°35'N	51°05'E
Aqtöbe, Kaz.	183	50°20'N	57°00'E
Aquasco, Md., U.S. (ȧ'gwȧ'scô)	110e	38°35'N	76°44'W
Aquidauana, Braz. (ä-kē-däwä'nä)	143	20°24'S	55°46'W
Aquin, Haiti (ä-kăN')	135	18°20'N	73°25'W
Ara, r., Japan (ä-rä)	211a	35°40'N	139°52'E
Arab, Baḩr al, r., Sudan	231	9°46'N	26°52'E
'Arabah, Wādī, val., Egypt	238b	29°02'N	32°10'E
Arabats'ka Strilka (Tongue of Arabat), spit, Ukr.	177	[illegible]	[illegible]
Arabi, La., U.S.	110d	29°58'N	90°01'W
Arabian Desert, des., Egypt (ȧ-rā'bĭ-ăn)	231	27°06'N	32°49'E
Arabian Sea, sea (ȧ-rā'bĭ-ăn)	196	16°00'N	65°15'E
Aracaju, Braz. (ä-rä'kä-zhōō')	143	11°00'S	37°01'W
Aracati, Braz. (ä-rä'kä-tē')	143	4°31'S	37°41'W
Araçatuba, Braz. (ä-rä-sȧ-tōō'bä)	143	21°14'S	50°19'W
Aracena, Spain (ä-rä-thā'nä)	172	37°53'N	6°34'W
Arachthos, r., Grc. (är'äk-thôs)	175	39°10'N	21°05'E
Aracruz, Braz. (ä-rä-krōō's)	143	19°58'S	40°11'W
'Arad, Isr.	197a	31°20'N	35°15'E
Arad, Rom. (ŏ'rŏd)	163	46°10'N	21°18'E
Arafura Sea, sea (ä-rä-fōō'rä)	213	8°40'S	130°00'E
Aragats, Gora, mtn., Arm.	182	40°32'N	44°14'E
Aragon, hist. reg., Spain (ä-rä-gōn')	173	40°55'N	0°45'W
Aragón, r., Spain	172	42°35'N	1°10'W
Aragua, dept., Ven. (ä-rä'gwä)	143b	10°00'N	67°05'W
Aragua de Barcelona, Ven.	142	9°29'N	64°48'W
Araguaia, r., Braz. (ä-rä-gwä'yä)	143	8°37'S	49°43'W
Araguari, Braz. (ä-rä-gwä'rê)	143	18°43'S	48°03'W
Araguatins, Braz. (ä-rä-gwä-tēns)	143	5°41'S	48°04'W
Aragüita, Ven. (ärä-gwê'tä)	143b	10°13'N	66°28'W
Araj, oasis, Egypt (ä-räj')	163	29°05'N	26°51'E
Arāk, Iran	198	34°08'N	49°57'E
Arakan Yoma, mts., Mya. (ŭ-rŭ-kŭn'yō'mȧ)	199	19°51'N	94°13'E
Aral, Kaz.	183	46°47'N	62°00'E
Aral Sea, sea, Asia	178	45°17'N	60°02'E
Aralsor köli, l., Kaz. (ȧ-räl'sôr')	181	49°00'N	48°20'E
Aramberri, Mex. (ä-räm-bĕr-rē')	130	24°05'N	99°47'W
Arana, Sierra, mts., Spain	172	37°17'N	3°28'W
Aranda de Duero, Spain (ä-rän'dä dā dwā'rō)	172	41°43'N	3°45'W
Arandas, Mex. (ä-rän'däs)	130	20°43'N	102°18'W
Aran Island, i., Ire. (ăr'ăn)	164	54°58'N	8°33'W
Aran Islands, is., Ire.	160	53°04'N	9°59'W
Aranjuez, Spain (ä-rän-hwāth')	162	40°02'N	3°24'W
Aransas Pass, Tx., U.S. (ȧ-răn'sȧs pȧs)	123	27°55'N	97°09'W
Araouane, Mali	230	18°54'N	3°33'W
Arapkir, Tur. (ä-räp-kēr')	163	39°00'N	38°10'E
Araraquara, Braz. (ä-rä-rä-kwä'rä)	143	21°47'S	48°08'W
Araras, Braz. (ä-rä'räs)	141a	22°21'S	47°22'W
Araras, Serra das, mts., Braz. (sĕ'r-rä-däs-ä-rä'räs)	143	18°03'S	53°23'W
Araras, Serra das, mts., Braz.	144b	22°24'S	43°15'W
Araras, Serra das, mts., Braz. (sĕ'r-rä-däs-ä-rä'räs)	144	23°30'S	53°00'W
Ararat, Austl. (ăr'ărăt)	219	37°17'S	142°56'E
Ararat, Mount, mtn., Tur.	198	39°50'N	44°20'E
Arari, l., Braz. (ä-rä'rē)	143	0°30'S	48°50'W
Araripe, Chapada do, hills, Braz. (shä-pä'dä-dô-ä-rä-rē'pĕ)	143	5°55'S	40°42'W
Araruama, Braz. (ä-rä-rōō-ä'mä)	141a	22°53'S	42°19'W
Araruama, Lagoa de, l., Braz.	141a	23°00'S	42°15'W
Aras, r., Asia (ȧ-räs)	198	39°15'N	47°10'E
Aratuípe, Braz. (ä-rä-tōō-ē'pĕ)	143	13°12'S	38°58'W
Arauca, Col. (ä-rou'kä)	142	6°56'N	70°45'W
Arauca, r., S.A.	142	7°13'N	68°43'W
Aravalli Range, mts., India (ä-rä'vŭ-lê)	199	24°15'N	72°40'E
Araya, Punta de, c., Ven. (pŭn'tä-dĕ-ä-rä'yä)	143b	10°40'N	64°15'W
Arayat, Phil. (ä-rä'yät)	213a	15°10'N	120°44'E
'Arbi, Sudan	231	20°36'N	29°57'E
Arbīl, Iraq	198	36°10'N	44°00'E
Arboga, Swe. (är-bō'gä)	166	59°26'N	15°50'E
Arborea, Italy (är-bō-rĕ'ä)	174	39°50'N	8°36'E
Arbroath, Scot., U.K. (är-brōth')	164	56°36'N	2°25'W
Arcachon, Fr. (är-kä-shôN')	161	44°39'N	1°12'W
Arcachon, Bassin d', Fr. (bä-sĕn' där-kä-shôn')	170	44°42'N	1°50'W
Arcadia, Ca., U.S. (är-kā'dĭ-ȧ)	117a	34°08'N	118°02'W
Arcadia, Fl., U.S.	125a	27°12'N	81°51'W
Arcadia, La., U.S.	123	32°33'N	92°56'W
Arcadia, Wi., U.S.	113	44°15'N	91°30'W
Arcata, Ca., U.S. (är-kȧ'tȧ)	114	40°54'N	124°05'W
Arc Dome Mountain, mtn., Nv., U.S. (ärk dōm)	118	38°51'N	117°21'W
Arcelia, Mex. (är-sā'lê-ä)	130	18°19'N	100°14'W
Archbald, Pa., U.S. (ärch'bôld)	109	41°30'N	75°35'W
Arches National Park, rec., Ut., U.S. (är'ches)	119	38°45'N	109°35'W
Archidona, Ec. (är-chê-do'nä)	142	1°01'S	77°49'W
Archidona, Spain (är-chē-dô'nä)	172	37°08'N	4°24'W

PRONOUNCING INDEX Arcis-sur-Aube – Atacama 267

PLACE (Pronunciation)	PAGE	LAT.	LONG.
Arcis-sur-Aube, Fr. (är-sēs'sûr-ōb')	170	48°31'N	4°04'E
Arco, Id., U.S. (är'kô)	115	43°39'N	113°15'W
Arcola, Tx., U.S.	123a	29°30'N	95°28'W
Arcola, Va., U.S. (ăr'cōlă)	110e	38°57'N	77°32'W
Arcos de la Frontera, Spain (är'kōs-dĕ-lä-frôn-tĕ'rä)	172	36°44'N	5°48'W
Arctic Ocean, o.	244	85°00'N	170°00'E
Arda, r., Blg. (är'dä)	175	41°36'N	25°18'E
Ardabīl, Iran	198	38°15'N	48°00'E
Ardahan, Tur. (är-dá-hän')	181	41°10'N	42°40'E
Ardatov, Russia (är-dá-tôf')	180	54°58'N	46°10'E
Ardennes, mts., Eur. (år-dĕn')	161	50°01'N	5°12'E
Ardila, r., Eur. (är-dē'lå)	172	38°10'N	7°15'W
Ardmore, Ok., U.S. (ärd'mōr)	104	34°10'N	97°08'W
Ardmore, Pa., U.S.	110f	40°01'N	75°18'W
Ardrossan, Can. (är-dros'ăn)	102g	53°33'N	113°08'W
Ardsley, Eng., U.K. (ärdz'lē)	158a	53°43'N	1°33'W
Åre, Swe.	160	63°12'N	13°12'E
Arecibo, P.R. (ä-rå-sē'bō)	129b	18°28'N	66°45'W
Areia Branca, Braz. (ä-rĕ'yä-brä'n-kä)	143	4°58'S	37°02'W
Arena, Point, c., Ca., U.S. (ä-rā'nȧ)	118	38°57'N	123°40'W
Arenas, Punta, c., Ven. (pōn'tä-rĕ'näs)	143b	10°57'N	64°24'W
Arenas de San Pedro, Spain	172	40°12'N	5°04'W
Arendal, Nor. (ä'rĕn-däl)	166	58°29'N	8°44'E
Arendonk, Bel.	159a	51°19'N	5°07'E
Arequipa, Peru (ä-rå-kē'pä)	142	16°27'S	71°30'W
Arezzo, Italy (ä-rĕt'sō)	162	43°28'N	11°54'E
Arga, r., Spain (är'gä)	172	42°35'N	1°55'W
Arganda, Spain (är-gän'dä)	173a	40°18'N	3°27'W
Argazi, l., Russia (är'gä-zĭ)	186a	55°24'N	60°37'E
Argazi, r., Russia	186a	55°33'N	57°30'E
Argentan, Fr. (år-zhäɴ-täɴ')	170	48°45'N	0°01'W
Argentat, Fr. (år-zhäɴ-tä')	170	45°07'N	1°57'E
Argenteuil, Fr. (år-zhäɴ-tû'y')	170	48°56'N	2°15'E
Argentina, nation, S.A. (är-jĕn-tē'nȧ)	144	35°30'S	67°00'W
Argentino, l., Arg. (är-ĸĕn-tē'nō)	144	50°15'S	72°45'W
Argenton-sur-Creuse, Fr. (är-zhäɴ'tôɴ-sür-krôs)	170	46°34'N	1°28'E
Argolikos Kólpos, b., Grc.	175	37°20'N	23°00'E
Argonne, mts., Fr. (ä'r-gôn)	171	49°21'N	5°54'E
Argos, Grc. (är'gŏs)	175	37°38'N	22°45'E
Argostóli, Grc.	175	38°10'N	20°30'E
Arguello, Point, c., Ca., U.S. (är-gwĕl'yō)	118	34°35'N	120°40'W
Arguin, Cap d', c., Maur.	230	20°28'N	17°46'W
Argun', r., Asia (år-gōōn')	179	50°00'N	119°00'E
Argungu, Nig.	235	12°45'N	4°31'E
Argyle, Can. (är'gīl)	102f	50°11'N	97°27'W
Argyle, Mn., U.S.	112	48°21'N	96°48'W
Århus, Den. (ôr'hōōs)	160	56°09'N	10°10'E
Ariakeno-Umi, b., Japan (ä-rē'ä-kä'nō ōō'nē)	211	33°03'N	130°18'E
Ariake-Wan, b., Japan (ä'rē-ä'kå wän)	211	31°19'N	131°15'E
Ariano, Italy (ä-rē-ä'nō)	174	41°09'N	15°11'E
Ariari, r., Col. (ä-ryá'rē)	142a	3°34'N	73°42'W
Aribinda, Burkina	234	14°14'N	0°52'W
Arica, Chile (ä-rē'kä)	142	18°34'S	70°14'W
Arichat, Can. (ä-rĭ-shät')	101	45°31'N	61°01'W
Ariège, r., Fr. (å-rê-ĕzh')	170	43°26'N	1°29'E
Ariel, Wa., U.S. (ā'rĭ-ĕl)	116c	45°57'N	122°34'W
Arieș, r., Rom.	169	46°25'N	23°15'E
Ariguanabo, Lago de, l., Cuba (lä'gô-dĕ-ä-rē-gwä-nä'bô)	135a	22°52'N	82°33'W
Arikaree, r., Co., U.S. (ă-rĭ-kȧ-rē')	120	39°51'N	102°18'W
Arima, Japan (ä'rē-mä')	211b	34°48'N	135°16'E
Aringay, Phil. (ä-rĭŋ-gä'ē)	213a	16°25'N	120°20'E
Arinos, r., Braz. (ä-rē'nōzsh)	143	12°09'S	56°49'W
Aripuanã, r., Braz. (å-rē-pwän'yȧ)	143	7°06'S	60°29'W
'Arīsh, Wādī al, r., Egypt (å-rēsh')	197a	30°36'N	34°07'E
Aristazabal Island, i., Can.	94	52°30'N	129°20'W
Arizona, state, U.S. (ăr-ĭ-zō'nȧ)	104	34°00'N	113°00'W
Arjona, Spain (är-hō'nä)	172	37°58'N	4°03'W
Arka, r., Russia	185	60°45'N	142°30'E
Arkabutla Lake, res., Ms., U.S. (är-kȧ-bŭt'lă)	124	34°48'N	90°00'W
Arkadelphia, Ar., U.S. (är-kȧ-dĕl'fĭ-ȧ)	121	34°06'N	93°05'W
Arkansas, state, U.S. (är'kăn-sô) (är-kăn'sȧs)	105	34°50'N	93°40'W
Arkansas, r., U.S.	106	37°30'N	97°00'W
Arkansas City, Ks., U.S.	121	37°04'N	97°02'W
Arkhangelsk (Archangel), Russia (år-kän'gĕlsk)	178	64°30'N	40°25'E
Arkhangel'skoye, Russia (är-kän-gĕl'skô-yĕ)	186a	54°25'N	56°48'E
Arklow, Ire. (ärk'lō)	164	52°47'N	6°10'W
Arkonam, India (ăr-kō-năm')	203	13°05'N	79°43'E
Arlanza, r., Spain (är-län-thä')	172	42°08'N	3°45'W
Arlanzón, r., Spain (är-län-thōn')	172	42°12'N	3°58'W
Arlberg Tunnel, trans., Aus. (ärl'bĕrgh)	168	47°05'N	10°15'E
Arles, Fr. (ärl)	170	43°42'N	4°38'E
Arlington, S. Afr.	238c	28°02'S	27°52'E
Arlington, Ga., U.S. (är'lĭng-tun')	124	31°25'N	84°42'W
Arlington, Ma., U.S.	101a	42°26'N	71°13'W
Arlington, S.D., U.S. (är'lĕng-tŭn)	112	44°23'N	97°09'W
Arlington, Tx., U.S. (är'lĭng-tŭn)	117c	32°44'N	97°07'W
Arlington, Va., U.S.	110e	38°55'N	77°10'W
Arlington, Vt., U.S.	109	43°05'N	73°05'W
Arlington, Wa., U.S.	116a	48°11'N	122°08'W
Arlington Heights, Il., U.S. (är'lĕng-tŭn-hī'ts)	111a	42°05'N	87°59'W
Arltunga, Austl. (ärl-tòŋ'gȧ)	218	23°19'S	134°45'E
Arma, Ks., U.S. (är'mȧ)	121	37°34'N	94°43'W
Armagh, Can. (är-mä') (är-mäĸ')	102b	46°45'N	70°36'W
Armagh, N. Ire., U.K.	160	54°21'N	6°25'W
Armant, Egypt (är-mänt')	238b	25°37'N	32°32'E
Armaro, Col. (är-mà'rō)	142a	4°58'N	74°54'W
Armavir, Russia (år-mȧ-vĭr')	178	45°00'N	41°00'E
Armenia, Col. (år-mĕ'nē-ȧ)	142	4°33'N	75°40'W
Armenia, El Sal. (är-mā'nē-ä)	132	13°44'N	89°31'W
Armenia, nation, Asia	178	41°00'N	44°39'E
Armentières, Fr. (år-mäɴ-tyâr')	170	50°43'N	2°53'E
Armeria, Río de, r., Mex. (rē'ō-dĕ-är-må-rē'ä)	130	19°36'N	104°10'W
Armherstburg, Can. (ärm'hĕrst-bōōrgh)	98	42°06'N	83°06'W
Armians'k, Ukr.	177	46°06'N	33°42'E
Armidale, Austl. (är'mĭ-dāl)	219	30°27'S	151°50'E
Armour, S.D., U.S. (är'mēr)	112	43°18'N	98°21'W
Armstrong Station, Can. (ärm'strŏng)	91	50°21'N	89°00'W
Arnedo, Spain (är-nā'dō)	172	42°12'N	2°03'W
Arnhem, Neth. (ärn'hĕm)	161	51°58'N	5°56'E
Arnhem, Cape, c., Austl.	220	12°15'S	137°00'E
Arnhem Land, reg., Austl. (ärn'hĕm-lănd)	220	13°15'S	133°00'E
Arno, r., Italy (ä'r-nô)	162	43°30'N	11°00'E
Arnold, Eng., U.K. (är'nŭld)	158a	53°00'N	1°08'W
Arnold, Mn., U.S. (år'nŭld)	117h	46°53'N	92°06'W
Arnold, Pa., U.S.	111e	40°35'N	79°45'W
Arnprior, Can. (ärn-prī'ẽr)	99	45°25'N	76°20'W
Arnsberg, Ger. (ärns'bĕrgh)	171c	51°25'N	8°02'E
Arnstadt, Ger. (ärn'shtät)	168	50°51'N	10°57'E
Aroab, Nmb. (är'ō-åb)	232	25°40'S	19°45'E
Aroostook, r., Me., U.S. (å-rōs'tòk)	100	46°44'N	68°15'W
Aroroy, Phil. (ä-rō-rō'ē)	213a	12°30'N	123°24'E
Arpajon, Fr. (är-pä-jō'n)	171b	48°35'N	2°15'E
Arpoador, Ponta do, c., Braz. (pō'n-tä-dō-är'pōä-dō'r)	144b	22°59'S	43°11'W
Arraiolos, Port. (är-rī-ō'lōzh)	172	38°47'N	7°59'W
Ar Ramādī, Iraq	198	33°26'N	43°19'E
Arran, Island of, Scot., U.K. (ă'răn)	164	55°25'N	5°25'W
Ar Rank, Sudan	231	11°45'N	32°53'E
Arras, Fr. (å-räs')	161	50°21'N	2°40'E
Ar Rawḍah, Egypt	238b	27°47'N	30°52'E
Arrecifes, Arg. (är-rå-sē'fås)	141c	34°03'S	60°05'W
Arrecifes, r., Arg.	141c	34°07'S	59°50'W
Arrée, Monts d', mts., Fr. (är-rā')	170	48°27'N	4°00'W
Arriaga, Mex. (är-rēä'gä)	131	16°15'N	93°54'W
Arrone, r., Italy	173d	41°57'N	12°17'E
Arrow Creek, r., Mt., U.S. (ăr'ō)	115	47°29'N	109°53'W
Arrowhead, Lake, l., Ca., U.S. (lăk ăr'ōhĕd)	117a	34°17'N	117°13'W
Arrowrock Reservoir, res., Id., U.S. (ăr'ō-rŏk)	114	43°40'N	115°30'W
Arroya Arena, Cuba (är-rō'yä-rĕ'nä)	135a	23°01'N	82°30'W
Arroyo de la Luz, Spain (är-rō'yō-dĕ-lä-lōō'z)	172	39°39'N	6°46'W
Arroyo Seco, Mex. (är-rō'yō sä'kō)	130	21°31'N	99°44'W
Ar Rub' al Khālī, des., Asia	198	20°00'N	51°00'E
Ar Ruṭbah, Iraq	201	33°02'N	40°17'E
Arsen'yev, Russia	179	44°13'N	133°32'E
Arsinskiy, Russia (är-sĭn'skĭ)	186a	53°46'N	59°54'E
Árta, Grc. (är'tä)	163	39°08'N	21°02'E
Arteaga, Mex. (är-tä-ä'gä)	122	25°28'N	100°50'W
Artëm, Russia (ár-tyôm')	179	43°28'N	132°29'E
Artemisa, Cuba (är-tå-mē'sä)	134	22°50'N	82°45'W
Artemivs'k, Ukr.	181	48°37'N	38°00'E
Artesia, N.M., U.S. (är-tē'sĭ-ȧ)	120	32°44'N	104°23'W
Arthabaska, Can.	99	46°03'N	71°54'W
Arthur's Town, Bah.	135	24°40'N	75°40'W
Arti, Russia (är'tĭ)	186a	56°20'N	58°38'E
Artibonite, r., N.A. (är-tē-bô-nē'tā)	135	19°00'N	72°25'W
Aru, Kepulauan, is., Indon.	213	6°20'S	133°00'E
Arua, Ug. (ä'rōō-ä)	231	3°01'N	30°55'E
Aruba, i., Aruba (ä-rōō'bå)	129	12°29'N	70°00'W
Arunachal Pradesh, state, India	199	27°35'N	92°56'E
Arusha, Tan. (å-rōō'shä)	232	3°22'S	36°41'E
Arvida, Can.	91	48°26'N	71°11'W
Arvika, Swe. (är-vē'kå)	166	59°41'N	12°35'E
Arzamas, Russia (är-zä-mäs')	180	55°20'N	43°52'E
Arziw, Alg.	162	35°50'N	0°20'W
Arzúa, Spain	172	42°54'N	8°19'W
Aš, Czech Rep. (äsh')	168	50°12'N	12°13'E
Asahi-Gawa, r., Japan (ä-sä'hē-gä'wä)	211	35°01'N	133°40'E
Asahikawa, Japan	205	43°50'N	142°09'E
Asaka, Japan (ä-sä'kä)	211a	35°47'N	139°36'E
Asansol, India	199	23°45'N	86°58'E
Asbest, Russia (äs-bĕst')	180	57°02'N	61°28'E
Asbestos, Can. (ăs-bĕs'tōs)	99	45°49'N	71°52'W
Asbestovskiy, Russia	186a	57°46'N	61°23'E
Asbury Park, N.J., U.S. (ăz'bĕr-ĭ)	110a	40°13'N	74°01'W
Ascención, Bahía de la, b., Mex.	132a	19°39'N	87°30'W
Ascensión, Mex. (äs-sĕn-sē-ōn')	130	24°21'N	99°54'W
Ascension, i., St. Hel. (å-sĕn'shŭn)	229	8°00'S	13°00'W
Ascent, S. Afr. (ăs-ĕnt')	238c	27°14'S	29°06'E
Aschaffenburg, Ger. (ä-shäf'ĕn-bòrgh)	168	49°58'N	9°12'E
Ascheberg, Ger. (ä'shĕ-bĕrg)	171c	51°47'N	7°38'E
Aschersleben, Ger. (äsh'ĕrs-lā-bĕn)	168	51°46'N	11°28'E
Ascoli Piceno, Italy (äs'kô-lēpē-chā'nō)	174	42°50'N	13°55'E
Aseb, Erit.	231	12°52'N	43°39'E
Asenovgrad, Blg.	175	42°00'N	24°49'E
Aseri, Est. (á'sĕ-rĭ)	167	59°26'N	26°58'E
Asha, Russia (ä'shä)	186a	55°01'N	57°17'E
Ashabula, l., N.D., U.S. (ăsh'á-bū-lă)	112	47°07'N	97°51'W
Ashan, Russia (ä'shän)	186a	57°08'N	56°25'E
Ashbourne, Eng., U.K. (ăsh'bŭrn)	158a	53°01'N	1°44'W
Ashburn, Ga., U.S. (ăsh'bŭrn)	124	31°42'N	83°42'W
Ashburn, Va., U.S.	110e	39°02'N	77°30'W
Ashburton, r., Austl. (ăsh'bûr-tŭn)	220	22°30'S	115°30'E
Ashby-de-la-Zouch, Eng., U.K. (ăsh'bĭ-dē-lȧ zōōsh')	158a	52°44'N	1°23'W
Ashdod, Isr.	197a	31°46'N	34°39'E
Ashdown, Ar., U.S. (ăsh'doun)	121	33°41'N	94°07'W
Asheboro, N.C., U.S. (ăsh'bŭr-ô)	125	35°41'N	79°50'W
Asherton, Tx., U.S. (ăsh'ẽr-tŭn)	122	28°26'N	99°45'W
Asheville, N.C., U.S. (ăsh'vĭl)	105	35°35'N	82°35'W
Ash Fork, Az., U.S.	119	35°13'N	112°29'W
Ashgabat, Turkmen.	183	37°57'N	58°23'E
Ashikaga, Japan (ä'shē-kä'gȧ)	211	36°22'N	139°26'E
Ashiya, Japan (a'shē-yä')	211	33°54'N	130°40'E
Ashiya, Japan	211b	34°44'N	135°18'E
Ashizuri-Zaki, c., Japan (ä-shē-zò-rē zä-kē)	210	32°43'N	133°04'E
Ashland, Al., U.S. (ăsh'lȧnd)	124	33°15'N	85°50'W
Ashland, Ks., U.S.	120	37°11'N	99°46'W
Ashland, Ky., U.S.	108	38°25'N	82°40'W
Ashland, Ma., U.S.	101a	42°16'N	71°28'W
Ashland, Me., U.S.	100	46°37'N	68°26'W
Ashland, Ne., U.S.	112	41°02'N	96°23'W
Ashland, Oh., U.S.	108	40°50'N	82°15'W
Ashland, Or., U.S.	114	42°12'N	122°42'W
Ashland, Pa., U.S.	109	40°45'N	76°20'W
Ashland, Wi., U.S.	105	46°34'N	90°55'W
Ashley, N.D., U.S. (ăsh'lē)	112	46°03'N	99°23'W
Ashley, Pa., U.S.	109	41°15'N	75°55'W
Ashmūn, Egypt (ash-mōōn')	238b	30°19'N	30°57'E
Ashmyany, Bela.	167	54°27'N	25°55'E
Ashqelon, Isr. (äsh'kĕ-lōn)	197a	31°40'N	34°36'E
Ash Shabb, Egypt (shĕb)	231	22°34'N	29°52'E
Ash Shallūfah, Egypt (shäl'lò-fȧ)	238b	30°09'N	32°33'E
Ash Shaqrā', Sau. Ar.	198	25°10'N	45°08'E
Ash Shāriqah, U.A.E.	201	25°22'N	55°23'E
Ash Shawbak, Jord.	197a	30°31'N	35°35'E
Ash Shiḥr, Yemen	198	14°45'N	49°32'E
Ashtabula, Oh., U.S. (ăsh-tȧ-bū'lȧ)	105	41°55'N	80°50'W
Ashton, Id., U.S. (ăsh'tŭn)	115	44°04'N	111°28'W
Ashton-in-Makerfield, Eng., U.K. (ăsh'tŭn-ĭn-măk'ẽr-fēld)	158a	53°29'N	2°39'W
Ashton-under-Lyne, Eng., U.K. (ăsh'tŭn-ŭn-dẽr-līn')	158a	53°29'N	2°04'W
Ashuanipi, l., Can. (ăsh-wȧ-nĭp'ĭ)	93	52°40'N	67°42'W
Ashukino, Russia (á-shōō'kinô)	186b	56°10'N	37°57'E
Asia, cont.	196	50°00'N	100°00'E
Asia Minor, reg., Tur. (ā'zhȧ)	157	38°18'N	31°18'E
Asientos, Mex. (ä-sē-ĕn'tōs)	130	22°13'N	102°05'W
Asilah, Mor.	172	35°30'N	6°05'W
Asinara, i., Italy	174	41°02'N	8°22'E
Asinara, Golfo dell', b., Italy (gôl'fō-dĕl-ä-sē-nä'rä)	174	40°58'N	8°28'E
Asīr, reg., Sau. Ar. (ä-sēr')	198	19°30'N	42°00'E
Askarovo, Russia (äs-kä-rō'vô)	186a	53°21'N	58°32'E
Askersund, Swe. (äs'kĕr-sònd)	166	58°43'N	14°53'E
Askino, Russia (äs'kĭ-nô)	186a	56°06'N	56°29'E
Asmara see Asmera, Erit.	230	15°17'N	38°56'E
Asmera, Erit. (äs-mä'rä)	231	15°17'N	38°56'E
Asnieres, Fr. (ä-nyâr')	171b	48°55'N	2°18'E
Asosa, Eth.	231	10°13'N	34°28'E
Asotin, Wa., U.S. (ȧ-sō'tĭn)	114	46°19'N	117°01'W
Aspen, Co., U.S. (ăs'pĕn)	119	39°15'N	106°55'W
Asperen, Neth.	159a	51°52'N	5°07'E
Aspy Bay, b., Can. (ăs'pē)	101	46°55'N	60°25'W
Aş Şaff, Egypt	238b	29°33'N	31°23'E
As Sallūm, Egypt	231	31°35'N	25°05'E
As Salt, Jord.	197a	32°02'N	35°44'E
Assam, state, India (ăs-săm')	199	26°00'N	91°00'E
As Samāwah, Iraq	201	31°18'N	45°17'E
Assens, Den. (äs'sĕns)	166	55°16'N	9°54'E
As Sinbillāwayn, Egypt	238b	30°53'N	31°37'E
Assini, C. Iv. (ä-sē-nē')	230	4°52'N	3°16'W
Assiniboia, Can.	90	49°38'N	105°59'W
Assiniboine, r., Can. (ă-sĭn'ĭ-boin)	97	50°03'N	97°57'W
Assiniboine, Mount, mtn., Can.	95	50°52'N	115°39'W
Assis, Braz. (ä-sē's)	143	22°39'S	50°21'W
Assisi, Italy	162	43°04'N	12°37'E
As-Sudd, reg., Sudan	231	8°45'N	30°45'E
As Sulaymānīyah, Iraq	198	35°47'N	45°23'E
As Sulaymānīyah, Sau. Ar.	201	24°09'N	46°19'E
As Suwaydā', Syria	198	32°41'N	36°41'E
Astakós, Grc. (äs'tä-kôs)	175	38°42'N	21°00'E
Astana (Aqmola), Kaz.	183	51°10'N	71°43'E
Astara, Azer.	181	38°30'N	48°50'E
Asti, Italy (äs'tē)	162	44°54'N	8°12'E
Astorga, Spain (äs-tôr'gä)	172	42°28'N	6°03'W
Astoria, Or., U.S. (ăs-tō'rĭ-ȧ)	104	46°11'N	123°51'W
Astrakhan', Russia (äs-trá-kän')	178	46°15'N	48°00'E
Astrida, Rw. (äs-trē'dȧ)	232	2°37'S	29°48'E
Asturias, hist. reg., Spain (äs-tōō'ryäs)	172	43°21'N	6°00'W
Astypalaia, i., Grc.	163	36°31'N	26°19'E
Asunción see Ixtaltepec, Mex.	131	16°33'N	95°04'W
Asunción see Nochistlán, Mex.	130	21°23'N	102°52'W
Asunción, Para. (ä-sōōn-syōn')	144	25°25'S	57°30'W
Asunción Mita, Guat. (ä-sōōn-syō'n-mē'tä)	132	14°19'N	89°43'W
Aswān, Egypt (ä-swän')	231	24°05'N	32°57'E
Aswān High Dam, dam, Egypt	231	23°58'N	32°53'E
Atacama, Desierto de, des., Chile (dĕ-syĕ'r-tô-dĕ-ä-tä-kä'mä)	139	23°50'S	69°00'W

ng-sing; ŋ-baŋk; ɴ-nasalized n; nŏd; cŏmmit; ōld; ôbey; ôrder; oi-boil; fōōd; ò-as oo in foot; ou-out; s-soft; sh-dish; th-thin; pūre; ůnite; ûrn; stŭd; circŭs; ü-as in French tu; '-indeterminate vowel.

268 Atacama – Babylon PRONOUNCING INDEX

PLACE (Pronunciation)	PAGE	LAT.	LONG.
Atacama, Puna de, plat., Bol. (pōō´nä-dĕ-ä-tä-kȧ´mä)	142	21°35'S	66°58'W
Atacama, Puna de, reg., Chile (pōō´nä-dĕ-ȧtä-kȧ´mä)	144	23°15'S	68°45'W
Atacama, Salar de, l., Chile (sȧ-lȧr´dĕ-ȧtä-kȧ´mä)	144	23°38'S	68°15'W
Ataco, Col. (ä-tȧ´kŏ)	142a	3°36'N	75°22'W
Atacora, Chaîne de l', mts., Benin	234	10°15'N	1°15'E
Atā 'itah, Jabal al, mtn., Jord.	197a	30°48'N	35°19'E
Atamanovskiy, Russia (ä-tä-mä´nôv-skĭ)	186a	52°15'N	60°47'E
'Atāqah, Jabal, mts., Egypt	238d	29°59'N	32°20'E
Atar, Maur. (ä-tär´)	230	20°45'N	13°16'W
Atascadero, Ca., U.S. (ăt-ăs-kȧ-dâ´rō)	118	35°29'N	120°40'W
Atascosa, r., Tx., U.S. (ăt-ăs-kō´sȧ)	122	28°50'N	98°17'W
Atauro, Ilha de, i., E. Timor (ä-tä´ōō-rō)	213	8°20'S	126°15'E
Atbara, r., Afr.	231	17°14'N	34°27'E
'Aṭbarah, Sudan (ät´bȧ-rȧ)	231	17°45'N	33°15'E
Atbasar, Kaz. (ät´bä-sär´)	183	51°42'N	68°28'E
Atchafalaya, r., La., U.S.	123	30°53'N	91°51'W
Atchafalaya Bay, b., La., U.S. (ăch-ȧ-fȧ-lī´ȧ)	123	29°25'N	91°30'W
Atchison, Ks., U.S. (ăch´ĭ-sŭn)	105	39°33'N	95°08'W
Atco, N.J., U.S. (ăt´kō)	110f	39°46'N	74°53'W
Atempan, Mex. (ä-tĕm-pȧ´n)	131	19°49'N	97°25'W
Atenguillo, r., Mex. (ä-tĕn-gē´l-yô)	130	20°18'N	104°35'W
Athabasca, Can. (ăth-ȧ-băs´kȧ)	90	54°43'N	113°17'W
Athabasca, l., Can.	92	59°04'N	109°10'W
Athabasca, r., Can.	92	57°30'N	112°00'W
Athens (Athína), Grc.	175	38°00'N	23°38'E
Athens, Al., U.S. (ăth´ĕnz)	124	34°47'N	86°58'W
Athens, Ga., U.S.	105	33°55'N	83°24'W
Athens, Oh., U.S.	108	39°20'N	82°10'W
Athens, Pa., U.S.	109	42°00'N	76°30'W
Athens, Tn., U.S.	124	35°26'N	84°36'W
Athens, Tx., U.S.	123	32°13'N	95°51'W
Atherstone, Eng., U.K. (ăth´ẽr-stŭn)	158a	52°34'N	1°33'W
Atherton, Eng., U.K. (ăth´ẽr-tŭn)	158a	53°32'N	2°29'W
Atherton Plateau, plat., Austl. (ădh-ẽr-tŏn)	221	17°00'S	144°30'E
Athi, r., Kenya (ä´tē)	233	2°43'S	38°30'E
Athína see Athens, Grc.	154	38°00'N	23°38'E
Athlone, Ire. (ăth-lōn´)	160	53°24'N	7°30'W
Áthos, mtn., Grc. (ăth´ŏs)	175	40°10'N	24°15'E
Ath Thamad, Egypt	197a	29°41'N	34°17'E
Athy, Ire. (ȧ-thī)	164	52°59'N	7°08'W
Ati, Chad	235	13°13'N	18°20'E
Atibaia, Braz. (ä-tē-bȧ´yȧ)	141a	23°08'S	46°32'W
Atikonak, l., Can.	93	52°34'N	63°49'W
Atimonan, Phil. (ä-tē-mō´nän)	213a	13°59'N	121°56'E
Atiquizaya, El Sal. (ä´tē-kē-zä´yä)	132	14°00'N	89°42'W
Atitlan, vol., Guat. (ä-tē-tlän´)	132	14°35'N	91°11'W
Atitlan, Lago, l., Guat. (ä-tē-tlän´)	132	14°38'N	91°23'W
Atizapán, Mex. (ä´tē-zȧ-pän´)	131a	19°33'N	99°16'W
Atka, Ak., U.S. (ăt´kȧ)	103a	52°18'N	174°18'W
Atka, i., Ak., U.S.	106b	51°58'N	174°30'W
Atkarsk, Russia (ȧt-kärsk´)	181	51°50'N	45°00'E
Atkinson, Ne., U.S. (ăt´kĭn-sŭn)	112	42°32'N	98°58'W
Atlanta, Ga., U.S. (ăt-lăn´tȧ)	105	33°45'N	84°23'W
Atlanta, Tx., U.S.	121	33°09'N	94°09'W
Atlantic, Ia., U.S. (ăt-lăn´tĭk)	113	41°23'N	94°58'W
Atlantic, N.C., U.S.	125	34°54'N	76°20'W
Atlantic City, N.J., U.S.	105	39°20'N	74°30'W
Atlantic Highlands, N.J., U.S.	110a	40°25'N	74°04'W
Atlantic Ocean, o.	4	5°00'S	25°00'W
Atlas Mountains, mts., Afr. (ăt´lăs)	230	31°22'N	4°57'W
Atliaca, Mex. (ät-lē-ȧ´kä)	130	17°38'N	99°24'W
Atlin, l., Can. (ăt´lĭn)	92	59°34'N	133°20'W
Atlixco, Mex. (ät-lēz´kō)	130	18°52'N	98°27'W
Atmore, Al., U.S. (ăt´mōr)	124	31°01'N	87°31'W
Atoka, Ok., U.S. (ȧ-tō´kȧ)	121	34°23'N	96°07'W
Atoka Reservoir, res., Ok., U.S.	121	34°30'N	96°05'W
Atotonilco el Alto, Mex.	130	20°35'N	102°32'W
Atotonilco el Grande, Mex.	130	20°17'N	98°41'W
Atoui, r., Afr. (ȧ-tōō-ē´)	230	21°00'N	15°32'W
Atoyac, Mex. (ä-tô-yäk´)	130	20°01'N	103°28'W
Atoyac, r., Mex.	130	18°35'N	98°16'W
Atoyac, r., Mex.	131	16°27'N	97°28'W
Atoyac de Alvarez, Mex. (ä-tô-yäk´dā äl´vä-rāz)	130	17°13'N	100°29'W
Atoyatempan, Mex. (ä-tō´yȧ-tĕm-pän´)	131	18°47'N	97°54'W
Atrak, r., Asia	198	37°45'N	56°30'E
Ätran, r., Swe.	166	57°02'N	12°43'E
Atrato, Río, r., Col. (rē´ō-ä-trä´tō)	142	7°15'N	77°18'W
Aṭ Ṭafilah, Jord. (tä-fē´la)	197a	30°50'N	35°36'E
Aṭ Ṭā'if, Sau. Ar.	198	21°03'N	41°00'E
Attalla, Al., U.S. (ă-tăl´yȧ)	124	34°01'N	86°05'W
Attawapiskat, r., Can. (ăt´ȧ-wȧ-pĭs´kăt)	93	52°31'N	86°22'W
Attersee, l., Aus.	168	47°57'N	13°25'E
Attica, N.Y., U.S. (ăt´ĭ-kȧ)	109	42°55'N	78°15'W
Attleboro, Ma., U.S. (ăt´'l-bŭr-ô)	110b	41°56'N	71°15'W
Attow, Ben, mtn., Scot., U.K. (bĕn ăt´tô)	164	57°15'N	5°25'W
Attoyac Bay, Tx., U.S. (ă-toi´yăk)	123	31°45'N	94°23'W
Attu, i., Ak., U.S. (ät-tōō´)	106b	53°08'N	173°18'E
Aṭ Ṭūr, Egypt	163	28°09'N	33°47'E
Aṭ Ṭurayf, Sau. Ar.	198	31°32'N	38°30'E
Åtvidaberg, Swe. (ôt-vē´dȧ-bĕrgh)	166	58°12'N	15°55'E
Atwood, Ks., U.S. (ăt´wŏŏd)	120	39°48'N	101°06'W
Atyraū, Kaz.	183	47°10'N	51°50'E
Atzcapotzalco, Mex. (ät´zkä-pô-tzäl´kō)	130	19°29'N	99°11'W
Atzgersdorf, Aus.	159e	48°10'N	16°17'E
Auau Channel, strt., Hi., U.S. (ä´ô-ä´ôo)	126a	20°55'N	156°50'W
Aubagne, Fr. (ō-bän´y´)	171	43°18'N	5°34'E
Aube, r., Fr. (ōb)	170	48°42'N	3°49'E
Aubenas, Fr. (ōb-nä´)	170	44°37'N	4°22'E
Aubervilliers, Fr. (ō-bĕr-vē-yā')	171b	48°54'N	2°23'E
Aubin, Fr. (ō-băɴ´)	170	44°29'N	2°12'E
Aubrey, Can. (ô-brē´)	102a	45°08'N	73°47'W
Auburn, Al., U.S. (ô´bŭrn)	124	32°35'N	85°26'W
Auburn, Ca., U.S.	118	38°52'N	121°05'W
Auburn, Il., U.S.	121	39°36'N	89°46'W
Auburn, In., U.S.	108	41°20'N	85°05'W
Auburn, Ma., U.S.	101a	42°11'N	71°51'W
Auburn, Me., U.S.	105	44°04'N	70°24'W
Auburn, Ne., U.S.	121	40°23'N	95°50'W
Auburn, N.Y., U.S.	109	42°55'N	76°35'W
Auburn, Wa., U.S.	116a	47°18'N	122°14'W
Auburn Heights, Mi., U.S.	111b	42°37'N	83°13'W
Aubusson, Fr. (ō-bü-sôɴ´)	170	45°57'N	2°10'E
Auch, Fr. (ōsh)	161	43°38'N	0°35'E
Aucilla, r., Fl., U.S. (ô-sĭl´ȧ)	124	30°15'N	83°55'W
Auckland, N.Z. (ôk´lănd)	221a	36°53'S	174°45'E
Auckland Islands, is., N.Z.	3	50°30'S	166°30'E
Aude, r., Fr. (ōd)	170	42°55'N	2°08'E
Audierne, Fr. (ō-dyĕrn´)	170	48°02'N	4°31'W
Audincourt, Fr. (ō-dăn-kōōr´)	171	47°30'N	6°49'E
Audley, Eng., U.K. (ôd´lĭ)	158a	53°03'N	2°18'W
Audo Range, mts., Eth.	238a	6°58'N	41°18'E
Audubon, Ia., U.S. (ô´dŏ-bŏn)	113	41°43'N	94°57'W
Audubon, N.J., U.S.	110f	39°54'N	75°04'W
Aue, Ger. (ou´ē)	168	50°35'N	12°44'E
Augathella, Austl. (ôr´gȧ´thĕ-lȧ)	222	25°49'S	146°40'E
Augrabiesvalle, wtfl., S. Afr.	232	28°30'S	20°00'E
Augsburg, Ger. (ouks´bŏŏrgh)	161	48°23'N	10°55'E
Augusta, Ar., U.S. (ô-gŭs´tȧ)	121	35°16'N	91°21'W
Augusta, Ga., U.S.	105	33°26'N	82°00'W
Augusta, Ks., U.S.	121	37°41'N	96°58'W
Augusta, Ky., U.S.	108	38°45'N	84°00'W
Augusta, Me., U.S.	105	44°19'N	69°42'W
Augusta, N.J., U.S.	110a	41°07'N	74°44'W
Augusta, Wi., U.S.	113	44°40'N	91°09'W
Augustow, Pol. (ou-gŏs´tŏf)	169	53°52'N	23°00'E
Auki, Sol. Is.	214e	8°46'S	160°42'E
Aulnay-sous-Bois, Fr. (ō-nĕ´sōō-bwä´)	171b	48°56'N	2°30'E
Aulne, r., Fr. (ōn)	170	48°08'N	3°53'W
Auneau, Fr. (ō-nĕü)	171b	48°28'N	1°45'E
Auob, r., Afr. (ä´wŏb)	232	25°00'S	19°00'E
Aur, i., Malay.	197b	2°27'N	104°51'E
Aura, Fin.	167	60°38'N	22°32'E
Aurangābād, India (ou-rŭŋ-gä-bäd´)	199	19°56'N	75°19'E
Aurdal, Nor. (äûr-däl)	160	60°54'N	9°24'E
Aurès, Massif de l', mts., Alg.	162	35°16'N	5°53'E
Aurillac, Fr. (ō-rē-yȧk´)	161	44°57'N	2°27'E
Aurora, Can.	99	43°59'N	79°25'W
Aurora, Co., U.S.	120	39°44'N	104°50'W
Aurora, Il., U.S. (ô-rō´rȧ)	105	41°45'N	88°18'W
Aurora, In., U.S.	111f	39°04'N	84°55'W
Aurora, Mn., U.S.	113	47°31'N	92°17'W
Aurora, Mo., U.S.	121	36°58'N	93°42'W
Aurora, Ne., U.S.	120	40°54'N	98°01'W
Aursunden, l., Nor. (äûr-sûnděn)	166	62°42'N	11°10'E
Au Sable, r., Mi., U.S. (ô-sā´b'l)	108	44°40'N	84°25'W
Ausable, r., N.Y., U.S.	109	44°25'N	73°50'W
Austin, Mn., U.S. (ôs´tĭn)	113	43°40'N	92°58'W
Austin, Nv., U.S.	118	39°30'N	117°05'W
Austin, Tx., U.S.	104	30°15'N	97°42'W
Austin, l., Austl.	220	27°45'S	117°30'E
Austin Bayou, Tx., U.S. (ôs´tĭn bī-ōō´)	123a	29°17'N	95°21'W
Australia, nation, Oc.	218	25°00'S	135°00'E
Australian Alps, mts., Austl.	222	37°10'S	147°55'E
Australian Capital Territory, ter., Austl. (ôs-trā´lĭ-ăn)	219	35°30'S	148°40'E
Austria, nation, Eur. (ôs´trĭ-ȧ)	154	47°15'N	11°53'E
Authon-la-Plaine, Fr. (ō-tôɴ´-lä-plĕ´n)	171b	48°27'N	1°58'E
Autlán, Mex. (ä-ōōt-län´)	128	19°47'N	104°24'W
Autun, Fr. (ō-tŭɴ´)	170	46°58'N	4°14'E
Auvergne, mts., Fr. (ō-vĕrn´y´)	170	45°12'N	2°31'E
Auxerre, Fr. (ō-sâr´)	161	47°48'N	3°32'E
Ava, Mo., U.S. (ā´vȧ)	121	36°56'N	92°40'W
Avakubi, D.R.C. (ä-vȧ-kōō´bē)	231	1°20'N	27°34'E
Avallon, Fr. (ȧ-vȧ-lôɴ´)	170	47°30'N	3°58'E
Avalon, Ca., U.S.	118	33°21'N	118°22'W
Avalon, Pa., U.S. (ăv´ȧ-lŏn)	111e	40°31'N	80°05'W
Aveiro, Port. (ä-vā´rō)	162	40°38'N	8°38'W
Avelar, Braz. (ä´vĕ-lä´r)	144b	22°20'S	43°25'W
Avellaneda, Arg. (ä-vĕl-yä-nā´dhä)	144	34°40'S	58°23'W
Avellino, Italy (ä-vĕl-lē´nō)	174	40°40'N	14°46'E
Averøya, i., Nor. (ävĕr-ûê)	166	63°40'N	7°16'E
Aversa, Italy (ä-vĕr´sä)	174	40°58'N	14°13'E
Avery, Tx., U.S. (ā´vẽr-ĭ)	121	33°34'N	94°46'W
Avesta, Swe. (ä-vĕs´tä)	166	60°16'N	16°09'E
Aveyron, r., Fr. (ä-vā-rôɴ)	170	44°07'N	1°45'E
Avezzano, Italy (ä-vāt-sä´nō)	174	42°03'N	13°27'E
Avigliano, Italy (ä-vēl-yä´nō)	174	40°45'N	15°44'E
Avignon, Fr. (ȧ-vē-nyôɴ´)	161	43°55'N	4°50'E
Ávila, Spain (ä-vē-lä)	172	40°39'N	4°42'W
Avilés, Spain (ä-vē-lās´)	162	43°33'N	5°55'W
Aviño, Spain	172	43°36'N	8°05'W
Avoca, Ia., U.S. (ȧ-vō´kȧ)	121	41°29'N	95°16'W
Avon, Ct., U.S. (ā´vŏn)	109	41°40'N	72°50'W
Avon, Ma., U.S. (ā´vŏn)	101a	42°08'N	71°03'W
Avon, Oh., U.S.	111d	41°27'N	82°02'W
Avon, r., Eng., U.K. (ā´vŭn)	164	52°05'N	1°55'W
Avondale, Ga., U.S.	110c	33°47'N	84°16'W
Avon Lake, Oh., U.S.	111d	41°31'N	82°01'W
Avonmore, Can. (ä´vōɴ-mōr)	102c	45°11'N	74°58'W
Avon Park, Fl., U.S. (ā´vŏn pärk´)	125a	27°35'N	81°29'W
Avranches, Fr. (ȧ-vränsh´)	170	48°43'N	1°34'W
Awaji-Shima, i., Japan	210	34°32'N	135°02'E
Awe, Loch, l., Scot., U.K. (lŏk ôr)	164	56°22'N	5°04'W
Awjilah, Libya	231	29°07'N	21°21'E
Ax-les-Thermes, Fr. (äks´lā tĕrm´)	170	42°43'N	1°50'E
Axochiapan, Mex. (äks-ō-chyä´pän)	130	18°29'N	98°49'W
Ay, r., Russia	180	55°55'N	57°55'E
Ayabe, Japan (ä´yä-bĕ)	210	35°16'N	135°17'E
Ayachi, Arin', mtn., Mor.	162	32°29'N	4°57'W
Ayacucho, Arg. (ä-yä-kōō´chō)	144	37°05'S	58°30'W
Ayacucho, Peru	142	13°12'S	74°03'W
Ayaköz, Kaz.	183	48°00'N	80°12'E
Ayamonte, Spain (ä-yä-mō´n-tĕ)	162	37°14'N	7°28'W
Ayan, Russia (ȧ-yän´)	179	56°26'N	138°18'E
Ayata, Bol. (ä-yä´tä)	142	15°17'S	68°43'W
Ayaviri, Peru (ä-yä-vē´rē)	142	14°46'S	70°38'W
Aydar, r., Eur. (ī-där´)	177	49°15'N	38°48'E
Ayden, N.C., U.S. (ā´dĕn)	125	35°27'N	77°25'W
Aydın, Tur. (āĭy-dĕn)	198	37°40'N	27°40'E
Ayer, Ma., U.S. (âr)	101a	42°33'N	71°36'W
Ayer Hitam, Malay.	197b	1°55'N	103°11'E
Ayers Rock see Uluru, mtn., Austl.	220	25°23'S	131°05'E
Aylesbury, Eng., U.K. (ālz´bẽr-ĭ)	164	51°47'N	0°49'W
Aylmer, l., Can. (āl´mẽr)	92	64°27'N	108°22'W
Aylmer, Mount, mtn., Can.	95	51°19'N	115°26'W
Aylmer East, Can. (āl´mẽr)	99	45°24'N	75°50'W
Ayo el Chico, Mex. (ä´yō el chē´kō)	130	20°31'N	102°21'W
Ayon, i., Russia (ī-ôn´)	179	69°50'N	168°40'E
Ayorou, Niger	234	14°44'N	0°55'E
Ayotla, Mex. (ä-yōt´lä)	131a	19°18'N	98°55'W
Ayoun el Atrous, Maur.	234	16°40'N	9°37'W
Ayr, Scot., U.K. (âr)	164	55°27'N	4°40'W
Aysha, Eth.	231	10°48'N	42°32'E
Ayutla, Guat. (ȧ-yōōt´lä)	132	14°44'N	92°11'W
Ayutla, Mex.	130	16°50'N	99°16'W
Ayutla, Mex.	130	20°09'N	104°20'W
Ayvalık, Tur. (āīy-wă-lĭk)	163	39°19'N	26°40'E
Azaouad, reg., Mali	234	18°00'N	3°20'W
Azaouak, Vallée de l', val., Afr.	235	15°50'N	3°10'E
Azare, Nig.	235	11°40'N	10°11'E
Azemmour, Mor. (ȧ-zē-mōōr´)	230	33°20'N	8°21'W
Azerbaijan, nation, Asia	178	40°30'N	47°30'E
Azle, Tx., U.S. (ăz´lē)	117c	35°54'N	97°33'W
Azogues, Ec. (ä-sō´gās)	142	2°47'S	78°45'W
Azores see Açores, is., Port.	229	37°44'N	29°25'W
Azov, Russia (ȧ-zôf´) (ä-zôf)	181	47°07'N	39°19'E
Azov, Sea of, sea, Eur.	178	46°00'N	36°20'E
Aztec, N.M., U.S. (ăz´tĕk)	119	36°40'N	108°00'W
Aztec Ruins National Monument, rec., N.M., U.S.	119	36°50'N	108°00'W
Azua, Dom. Rep. (ä´swä)	135	18°30'N	70°45'W
Azuaga, Spain (ä-thwä´gä)	172	38°15'N	5°42'W
Azucar, Presa de, res., Mex.	122	26°06'N	98°44'W
Azuero, Península de, pen., Pan.	129	7°30'N	80°34'W
Azufre, Cerro (Copiapó), mtn., Chile	144	27°10'S	69°00'W
Azul, Arg. (ä-sōōl´)	144	36°46'S	59°51'W
Azul, Cordillera, mts., Peru	142	7°15'S	75°30'W
Azul, Sierra, mts., Mex.	130	23°20'N	98°28'W
Azusa, Ca., U.S. (ȧ-zōō´sȧ)	117a	34°08'N	117°55'W
Aẓ Ẓahrān (Dhahran), Sau. Ar.	198	26°13'N	50°00'E
Az Zaqāzīq, Egypt	231	30°36'N	31°36'E
Az Zarqā', Jord.	197a	32°03'N	36°07'E
Az Zāwiyah, Libya	230	32°28'N	11°55'E

B

PLACE (Pronunciation)	PAGE	LAT.	LONG.
Baadheere (Bardera), Som.	238a	2°13'N	42°24'E
Baal, Ger. (bäl)	171c	51°02'N	6°17'E
Baao, Phil. (bä´ō)	213a	13°27'N	123°22'E
Baarle-Hertog, Bel.	159a	51°26'N	4°57'E
Baarn, Neth.	159a	52°12'N	5°18'E
Babaeski, Tur. (bä´bä-ĕs´kĭ)	175	41°25'N	27°05'E
Babahoyo, Ec. (bä-bä-ō´yō)	142	1°56'S	79°24'W
Babana, Nig.	235	10°36'N	3°50'E
Babanango, S. Afr.	233c	28°24'S	31°11'E
Babanūsah, Sudan	231	11°30'N	27°55'E
Babar, Pulau, i., Indon. (bä´bȧr)	213	7°50'S	129°15'E
Bab-el-Mandeb see Mandeb, Bab-el-, strt.	198	13°17'N	42°49'E
Babelthuap, i., Palau	214b	7°30'N	134°36'E
Babia, Arroyo de la, r., Mex.	122	28°26'N	101°50'W
Babine, r., Can.	94	55°10'N	127°00'W
Babine Lake, l., Can. (băb´ēn)	92	54°45'N	126°00'W
Bābol, Iran	198	36°30'N	52°48'E
Babruysk, Bela.	180	53°07'N	29°13'E
Babushkin, Russia (bä´bŏsh-kĭn)	184	51°47'N	106°08'W
Babushkin, Russia	176	55°52'N	37°42'E
Babuyan Islands, is., Phil. (bä-bōō-yän´)	212	19°30'N	122°38'E
Babyak, Blg. (bäb´zhák)	175	41°59'N	23°42'E
Babylon, N.Y., U.S. (băb´ĭ-lŏn)	110a	40°42'N	73°19'W
Babylon, hist., Iraq	198	32°15'N	45°23'E

ăt; finȧl; rāte; senāte; ärm; ȧsk; sofȧ; fâre; ch-choose; dh-as th in other; bē; ėvent; bĕt; recĕnt; cratẽr; g-gō; gh-guttural g; bĭt; ĭ-short neutral; rīde; ĸ-guttural k as ch in German ich;

PRONOUNCING INDEX

Bacalar – Bangor 269

PLACE (Pronunciation)	PAGE	LAT.	LONG.
Bacalar, Laguna de, l., Mex.			
(lä-gōō-nä-dĕ-bä-kä-lär′)	132a	18°50′N	88°31′W
Bacan, Pulau, i., Indon.	213	0°30′S	127°00′E
Bacarra, Phil. (bä-kär′rä)	209	18°22′N	120°40′E
Bacău, Rom.	163	46°34′N	27°00′E
Baccarat, Fr. (bȧ-kȧ-rȧ′)	171	48°29′N	6°42′E
Bacchus, Ut., U.S. (băk′ŭs)	117b	40°40′N	112°06′W
Bachajón, Mex. (bä-chä-hōn′)	131	17°08′N	92°18′W
Bachu, China (bä-chōō)	204	39°50′N	78°23′E
Back, r., Can.	92	65°30′N	104°15′W
Bačka Palanka, Serb.			
(bäch′kä pälän-kä)	175	45°14′N	19°24′E
Bačka Topola, Serb.			
(bäch′kä tô′pô-lä′)	175	45°48′N	19°38′E
Back Bay, India (băk)	203b	18°55′N	72°45′E
Backstairs Passage, strt., Austl.			
(băk-stârs′)	220	35°50′S	138°15′E
Bac Lieu, Viet.	212	9°45′N	105°50′E
Bac Ninh, Viet. (bäk′nēn′)	209	21°10′N	106°02′E
Baco, Mount, mtn., Phil. (bä′kô)	213a	12°50′N	121°11′E
Bacoli, Italy (bä-kō-lē′)	173c	40°33′N	14°05′E
Bacolod, Phil. (bä-kō′lôd)	213	10°42′N	123°03′E
Bácsalmás, Hung. (bäch′ôl-mäs)	169	46°07′N	19°18′E
Bacup, Eng., U.K. (băk′ŭp)	158a	53°42′N	2°12′W
Bad, r., S.D., U.S. (băd)	112	44°04′N	100°58′W
Badajoz, Spain (bȧ-dhä-hōth′)	162	38°52′N	6°56′W
Badalona, Spain (bä-dhä-lō′nä)	173	41°27′N	2°15′E
Badanah, Sau. Ar.	198	30°49′N	40°45′E
Bad Axe, Mi., U.S. (băd′ ăks)	108	43°50′N	82°55′W
Bad Bramstedt, Ger. (bät bräm′shtĕt)	159c	53°55′N	9°53′E
Baden, Aus. (bä′dĕn)	168	48°00′N	16°14′E
Baden, Switz.	168	47°28′N	8°17′E
Baden-Baden, Ger. (bä′dĕn-bä′dĕn)	161	48°46′N	8°11′E
Bad Freienwalde, Ger.			
(bät frī′ĕn-väl′dĕ)	168	52°47′N	14°00′E
Bad Hersfeld, Ger. (bät hĕrsh′fĕlt)	168	50°53′N	9°43′E
Badīn, Pak.	202	24°47′N	69°51′E
Bad Ischl, Aus. (bät ĭsh′′l)	168	47°46′N	13°37′E
Bad Kissingen, Ger. (bät kĭs′ĭng-ĕn)	168	50°12′N	10°05′E
Bad Kreuznach, Ger. (bät kroits′näk)	168	49°52′N	7°53′E
Badlands, reg., N.D., U.S.			
(băd′ lănds)	112	46°43′N	103°22′W
Badlands, reg., S.D., U.S.	112	43°43′N	102°36′W
Badlands National Park, rec., S.D.,			
U.S.	112	43°56′N	102°37′W
Badlāpur, India	203b	19°12′N	73°12′E
Badogo, Mali	234	11°02′N	8°13′W
Bad Oldesloe, Ger. (bät ōl′dĕs-lōē)	168	53°48′N	10°21′E
Bad Reichenhall, Ger.			
(bät rī′κĕn-häl)	168	47°43′N	12°53′E
Bad River Indian Reservation, I.R.,			
Wi., U.S. (băd)	113	46°41′N	90°36′W
Bad Segeberg, Ger.			
(bät sĕ′gĕ-bōōrgh)	159c	53°56′N	10°18′E
Bad Tölz, Ger. (bät tûltz)	168	47°46′N	11°35′E
Badulla, Sri L.	203	6°55′N	81°07′E
Bad Vöslau, Aus.	159e	47°58′N	16°13′E
Badwater Creek, r., Wy., U.S.			
(băd′wô-tēr)	115	43°13′N	107°55′W
Baena, Spain (bä-ā′nä)	162	37°38′N	4°20′W
Baependi, Braz. (bä-å-pĕn′dĭ)	141a	21°57′S	44°51′W
Baffin Bay, b., N.A. (băf′ĭn)	89	72°00′N	65°00′W
Baffin Bay, b., Tx., U.S.	123	27°11′N	97°35′W
Baffin Island, i., Can.	89	67°20′N	71°00′W
Bāfq, Iran (bäfk)	198	31°48′N	55°23′E
Bafra, Tur. (bäf′rä)	163	41°30′N	35°50′E
Bagabag, Phil. (bä-gä-bäg′)	213a	16°38′N	121°16′E
Bāgalkot, India	203	16°14′N	75°40′E
Bagamoyo, Tan. (bä-gä-mō′yō)	233	6°26′S	38°54′E
Bagaryak, Russia (bȧ-gȧr-yăk′)	186a	56°13′N	61°32′E
Bagbele, D.R.C.	237	4°21′N	29°17′E
Bagdad see Baghdād, Iraq	198	33°14′N	44°22′E
Baghdād, Iraq (bagh-dad′)(băg′dăd)	198	33°14′N	44°22′E
Bagheria, Italy (bä-gå-rē′ä)	174	38°03′N	13°32′E
Bagley, Mn., U.S. (băg′lē)	112	47°31′N	95°24′W
Bagnara, Italy (bän-yä′rä)	174	38°17′N	15°52′E
Bagnell Dam, Mo., U.S. (băg′nĕl)	121	38°13′N	92°40′W
Bagnères-de-Bigorre, Fr.			
(bän-yâr′dē-bē-gor′)	170	43°04′N	0°09′E
Bagnères-de-Luchon, Fr.			
(bän-yâr′ dē-lu chôN′)	170	42°46′N	0°36′E
Bagnols-sur-Ceze, Fr. (bä-nyôl′)	170	44°09′N	4°37′E
Bago, Mya.	212	17°17′N	96°29′E
Bagoé, r., Mali (bȧ-gō′ȧ)	230	12°22′N	6°34′W
Baguio, Phil. (bä-gē-ō′)	212	16°24′N	120°36′E
Bagzane, Monts, mtn., Niger	230	18°40′N	8°40′E
Bahamas, nation, N.A. (bȧ-hā′mȧs)	129	26°15′N	76°00′W
Bahau, Malay.	197b	2°48′N	102°25′E
Bahāwalpur, Pak. (bŭ-hä′wŭl-pōōr)	199	29°29′N	71°41′E
Bahia, state, Braz.	143	11°05′S	43°00′W
Bahía, Islas de la, i., Hond.			
(ē′s-läs-dĕ-lä-bä-ē′ä)	128	16°15′N	86°30′W
Bahía Blanca, Arg. (bä-ē′ä bläŋ′kä)	144	38°45′S	62°07′W
Bahía de Caráquez, Ec.			
(bä-ē′ä dä kä-rä′kĕz)	142	0°45′S	80°29′W
Bahía Negra, Para. (bä-ē′ä nā′grä)	143	20°11′S	58°05′W
Bahi Swamp, sw., Tan.	237	6°05′S	35°10′E
Bahoruco, Sierra de, mts., Dom. Rep.			
(sē-ĕ′r-rä-dĕ-bä-ō-rōō′kô)	135	18°10′N	71°25′W
Bahrain, nation, Asia (bä-rān′)	198	26°15′N	51°17′E
Baḥr al Ghazāl, hist. reg., Sudan			
(bär ĕl ghä-zäl′)	231	7°56′N	27°15′E
Baḥrīyah, oasis, Egypt (bȧ-hȧ-rē′yä)	163	28°34′N	29°01′E
Baía dos Tigres, Ang.	236	16°36′S	11°43′E
Baia Mare, Rom. (bä′yä mä′rä)	163	47°40′N	23°35′E
Baidyabātī, India	202a	22°47′N	88°21′E
Baie-Comeau, Can.	100	49°13′N	68°10′W
Baie de Wasai, Mi., U.S.			
(bā dē wä-sā′ē)	117k	46°27′N	84°15′W
Baie-Saint Paul, Can. (bā′sănt-pôl′)	91	47°27′N	70°30′W
Baigou, China (bī-gō)	206	39°08′N	116°02′E
Baihe, China (bī-hŭ)	208	32°30′N	110°15′E
Bai Hu, l., China (bī-hōō)	206	31°22′N	117°38′E
Baiju, China (bī-jyōō)	206	33°04′N	120°17′E
Baikal, Lake see Baykal, Ozero, l.,			
Russia	179	53°00′N	109°28′E
Bailén, Spain (bā-ĕ-lān′)	172	38°05′N	3°48′W
Băileşti, Rom. (bă-ĭ-lĕsh′tĕ)	175	44°01′N	23°21′E
Bainbridge, Ga., U.S. (bān′brĭj)	124	30°52′N	84°35′W
Bainbridge Island, i., Wa., U.S.	116a	47°39′N	122°32′W
Baipu, China (bī-pōō)	206	32°15′N	120°47′E
Baiquan, China (bī-chyuäŋ)	208	47°22′N	126°00′E
Baird, Tx., U.S. (bârd)	122	32°22′N	99°28′W
Bairdford, Pa., U.S. (bârd′fŏrd)	111e	40°37′N	79°53′W
Baird Mountains, mts., Ak., U.S.	100	67°35′N	160°10′W
Bairnsdale, Austl. (bârnz′dāl)	219	37°50′S	147°39′E
Baïse, r., Fr. (bä-ēz′)	170	43°52′N	0°23′E
Baiyang Dian, l., China (bī-yäŋ-dĭĕn)	206	39°00′N	115°45′E
Baiyu Shan, mts., China (bī-yōō shän)	208	37°02′N	108°30′E
Baja, Hung. (bŏ′yŏ)	169	46°11′N	18°55′E
Baja California, state, Mex. (bä-hä)	128	30°15′N	117°25′W
Baja California, pen., Mex.	89	28°00′N	113°30′W
Baja California Sur, state, Mex.	128	26°00′N	113°30′W
Bajo, Canal, can., Spain	173a	40°36′N	3°41′W
Bakal, Russia (bä′kăl)	186a	54°57′N	58°50′E
Baker, Mt., U.S. (bā′kēr)	115	46°21′N	104°12′W
Baker, Or., U.S.	104	44°46′N	117°52′W
Baker, i., Oc.	2	1°00′N	176°00′W
Baker, l., Can.	92	63°51′N	96°10′W
Baker, Mount, mtn., Wa., U.S.	106	48°46′N	121°52′W
Baker Creek, r., Il., U.S.	111a	41°13′N	87°47′W
Bakersfield, Ca., U.S. (bā′kērz-fēld)	104	35°23′N	119°00′W
Bakerstown, Pa., U.S. (bā′kerz-toun)	111e	40°39′N	79°56′W
Bakewell, Eng., U.K. (bāk′wĕl)	158a	53°12′N	1°40′W
Bakhchysarai, Ukr.	177	44°46′N	33°54′E
Bakhmach, Ukr. (bȧκ-mäch′)	177	51°09′N	32°47′E
Bakhtarān, Iran	198	34°01′N	47°00′E
Bakhtegan, Daryācheh-ye, l., Iran	198	29°29′N	54°31′E
Bakhteyevo, Russia	186b	55°35′N	38°32′E
Bako, Eth. (bä′kō)	231	5°47′N	36°39′E
Bakony, mts., Hung. (bȧ-kōn′y′)	169	46°57′N	17°30′E
Bakoye, r., Afr. (bȧ-kō′ē)	230	12°47′N	9°35′W
Bakr Uzyak, Russia (bȧkr ōōz′yȧk)	186a	52°59′N	58°43′E
Baku (Bakı), Azer. (bȧ-kōō′)	178	40°28′N	49°45′E
Bakwanga see Mbuji-Mayi, D.R.C.	236	6°09′S	23°28′E
Balabac Island, i., Phil. (bä′lä-bäk)	212	8°00′N	116°28′E
Balabac Strait, strt., Asia	212	7°23′N	116°30′E
Ba′labakk, Leb.	197a	34°00′N	36°13′E
Balabanovo, Russia (bä-lä-bä′nô-vô)	186b	56°10′N	37°44′E
Balagansk, Russia (bä-lä-gänsk′)	184	53°58′N	103°09′E
Balaguer, Spain (bä-lä-gĕr′)	173	41°48′N	0°50′E
Balakhta, Russia (bȧ′lák-tȧ′)	179	55°22′N	91°43′E
Balakliia, Ukr.	177	49°28′N	36°51′E
Balakovo, Russia (bȧ′lȧ-kô′vô)	181	52°00′N	47°40′E
Balancán, Mex. (bä-läŋ-kän′)	131	17°47′N	91°32′W
Balanga, Phil. (bä-läŋ′gä)	213a	14°41′N	120°31′E
Ba Lang An, Mui, c., Viet.	209	15°18′N	109°10′E
Balashikha, Russia (bȧ-lä′shĭ-kȧ)	186b	55°48′N	37°58′E
Balashov, Russia (bȧ′lȧ-shôf)	181	51°30′N	43°00′E
Balasore, India (bä-lȧ-sōr′)	199	21°38′N	86°59′E
Balassagyarmat, Hung.			
(bô′lôsh-shô-dyôr′môt)	169	48°04′N	19°19′E
Balaton Lake, l., Hung. (bô′lô-tôn)	163	46°47′N	17°55′E
Balayan, Phil. (bä-lä-yän′)	213a	13°56′N	120°44′E
Balayan Bay, b., Phil.	213a	13°46′N	120°46′E
Balboa Heights, Pan. (bäl-bô′ä)	133	8°59′N	79°33′W
Balboa Mountain, mtn., Pan.	128a	9°05′N	79°44′W
Balcarce, Arg. (bäl-kär′sā)	144	37°49′S	58°17′W
Balchik, Blg.	175	43°24′N	28°13′E
Bald Eagle, Mn., U.S. (bôld ē′g′l)	117g	45°06′N	93°01′W
Bald Eagle Lake, l., Mn., U.S.	117g	45°08′N	93°03′W
Baldock Lake, l., Can.	97	56°33′N	97°57′W
Baldwin Park, Ca., U.S. (bôld′wĭn)	117a	34°05′N	117°58′W
Baldwinsville, N.Y., U.S.			
(bôld′wĭns-vĭl)	109	43°10′N	76°20′W
Baldy Mountain, mtn., Can.	97	51°28′N	100°44′W
Baldy Peak, mtn., Az., U.S. (bôl′dē)	106	33°55′N	109°35′W
Baldy Peak, mtn., Tx., U.S. (bôl′dē pĕk)	122	30°38′N	104°11′W
Balearic Islands see Balears, Illes,			
is., Spain	156	39°25′N	1°28′E
Balearic Sea, sea, Spain (băl-ē-ăr′ĭk)	173	39°40′N	1°05′E
Balears, Illes, is., Spain	156	39°25′N	1°28′E
Baleine, Grande Rivière de la,			
r., Can.	93	55°00′N	75°30′W
Baler, Phil. (bä-lar′)	213a	15°46′N	121°33′E
Baler Bay, b., Phil.	213a	15°51′N	121°40′E
Balesin, i., Phil.	213a	14°28′N	122°10′E
Baley, Russia (bȧl-yā′)	185	51°29′N	116°12′E
Balfate, Hond. (bäl-fä′tē)	132	15°48′N	86°24′W
Balfour, S. Afr. (băl′fōr)	238c	26°41′S	28°37′E
Bali, i., Indon. (bä′lē)	212	8°00′S	115°22′E
Balıkeşir, Tur. (balĭk′ĭysĭr)	181	39°40′N	27°50′E
Balikpapan, Indon. (bä′lēk-pä′pän)	212	1°13′S	116°52′E
Balintang Channel, strt., Phil.			
(bä-lĭn-täng′)	212	19°50′N	121°08′E
Balkan Mountains see Stara Planina,			
mts., Blg.	156	42°50′N	24°45′E
Balkh, Afg. (bälk)	199	36°48′N	66°50′E
Balkhash, Lake see Balqash			
köli, l., Kaz.	183	45°58′N	72°15′E
Ballancourt, Fr. (bä-läN-kōōr′)	171b	48°31′N	2°23′E
Ballarat, Austl. (băl′ȧ-răt)	219	37°37′S	144°00′E
Ballard, l., Austl. (băl′ȧrd)	220	29°15′S	120°45′E
Ballater, Scot., U.K. (bȧl′ȧ-tēr)	164	57°05′N	3°06′W
Balleny Islands, is., Ant. (băl′ĕ nē)	224	67°00′S	164°00′E
Ballina, Austl. (băl-ĭ-nä′)	222	28°50′S	153°35′E
Ballina, Ire.	164	54°06′N	9°05′W
Ballinasloe, Ire. (băl′ĭ-nȧ-slō′)	164	53°20′N	8°09′W
Ballinger, Tx., U.S. (băl′ĭn-jēr)	122	31°45′N	99°58′W
Ballston Spa, N.Y., U.S. (bôls′tŭn spä′)	109	43°05′N	73°50′W
Balmazújváros, Hung.			
(bŏl′mŏz-ōō′y′vä′rôsh)	169	47°35′N	21°23′E
Balobe, D.R.C.	237	0°05′N	28°00′E
Balonne, r., Austl. (băl-ōn′)	221	27°00′S	149°10′E
Bālotra, India	202	25°56′N	72°12′E
Balqash, Kaz.	183	46°58′N	75°00′E
Balqash köli, l., Kaz.	183	45°58′N	72°15′E
Balranald, Austl. (băl′-rȧn-ăld)	222	34°42′S	143°30′E
Balsam, l., Can. (bôl′sȧm)	90	44°30′N	78°50′W
Balsas, Braz. (bäl′säs)	143	7°09′S	46°04′W
Balsas, r., Mex.	128	18°00′N	101°00′W
Balta, Ukr. (bȧl′tȧ)	181	47°57′N	29°38′E
Bălţi, Mol.	181	47°47′N	27°57′E
Baltic Sea, sea, Eur. (bôl′tĭk)	156	55°20′N	16°50′E
Baltīm, Egypt (bȧl-tēm′)	238b	31°33′N	31°04′E
Baltimore, Md., U.S. (bôl′tĭ-mŏr)	105	39°20′N	76°38′W
Baltiysk, Russia (bäl-tēysk′)	167	54°40′N	19°55′E
Baluarte, Río del, Mex.			
(rē′ō-dĕl-bä-lōō′r-tē)	130	23°09′N	105°42′W
Baluchistān, hist. reg., Asia			
(bȧ-lō-chĭ-stän′)	199	27°30′N	65°30′E
Balzac, Can. (bôl′zăk)	102e	51°10′N	114°01′W
Bama, Nig.	235	11°30′N	13°41′E
Bamako, Mali (bä-mä-kō′)	230	12°39′N	8°00′W
Bambang, Phil. (bäm-bäng′)	213a	16°24′N	121°08′E
Bambari, C.A.R. (bäm-bȧ-rē)	231	5°44′N	20°40′E
Bamberg, Ger. (bäm′bĕrgh)	161	49°53′N	10°52′E
Bamberg, S.C., U.S. (băm′bûrg)	125	33°17′N	81°04′W
Bamenda, Cam.	235	5°56′N	10°10′E
Bamingui, r., C.A.R.	235	7°35′N	19°45′E
Bampton, Eng., U.K. (băm′tŭn)	158b	51°42′N	1°33′W
Bampūr, Iran (bŭm-pōōr′)	198	27°15′N	60°22′E
Bam Yanga, Ngao, mts., Cam.	235	8°20′N	14°40′E
Banahao, Mount, mtn., Phil.			
(bä-nä-hä′ô)	213a	14°04′N	121°45′E
Banalia, D.R.C.	237	1°33′N	25°20′E
Banamba, Mali	234	13°33′N	7°27′W
Bananal, Braz. (bä-nä-näl′)	141a	22°42′S	44°17′W
Bananal, Ilha do, i., Braz.			
(ē′lä-dô-bä-nä-näl′)	143	12°09′S	50°27′W
Banās, r., India (bän-äs′)	199	25°20′N	75°20′E
Banās, Ra′s, c., Egypt	231	23°48′N	36°39′E
Banat, reg., Eur. (bä-nät′)	175	45°35′N	21°05′E
Bancroft, Can. (băn′krŏft)	91	45°05′N	77°55′W
Bancroft see Chililabombwe, Zam.	237	12°18′S	27°43′E
Bānda, India (bän′dä)	199	25°36′N	80°21′E
Banda, Kepulauan, is., Indon.	213	4°40′S	129°56′E
Banda, Laut (Banda Sea), sea, Indon.	213	6°05′S	127°28′E
Banda Aceh, Indon.	212	5°10′N	95°10′E
Banda Banda, Mount, mtn., Austl.			
(băn′dȧ băn′dȧ)	222	31°09′S	152°15′E
Bandama Blanc, r., C. Iv.			
(bän-dä′mä)	234	6°15′N	5°00′W
Bandar Beheshtī, Iran	198	25°18′N	60°45′E
Bandar-e ′Abbās, Iran			
(bän-där′ ȧb-bäs′)	198	27°04′N	56°22′E
Bandar-e Būshehr, Iran	198	28°48′N	50°53′E
Bandar-e Lengeh, Iran	198	26°44′N	54°47′E
Bandar-e Torkeman, Iran	198	37°05′N	54°08′E
Bandar Lampung, Indon.	212	5°16′S	105°06′E
Bandar Maharani, Malay.			
(bän-där′ mä-hä-rä′nē)	197b	2°02′N	102°34′E
Bandar Seri Begawan, Bru.	212	5°00′N	114°59′E
Bande, Spain (bän′dā)	172	42°02′N	7°58′W
Bandeira, Pico da, mtn., Braz.			
(pē′kō dä bän-dā′rä)	143	20°27′S	41°47′W
Bandelier National Monument, rec.,			
N.M., U.S. (băn-dĕ-lēr′)	119	35°50′N	106°45′W
Banderas, Bahía de, b., Mex.			
(bä-ē′ä dĕ bän-dĕ′räs)	130	20°38′N	105°35′W
Bandirma, Tur. (bän-dĭr′mȧ)	163	40°25′N	27°50′E
Bandon, Or., U.S. (băn′dŭn)	114	43°06′N	124°25′W
Bāndra, India	203b	19°04′N	72°49′E
Bandundu, D.R.C.	232	3°18′S	17°20′E
Bandung, Indon.	212	7°00′S	107°22′E
Banes, Cuba (bä′näs)	135	21°00′N	75°45′W
Banff, Can. (bănf)	90	51°10′N	115°34′W
Banff, Scot., U.K.	164	57°39′N	2°37′W
Banff National Park, rec., Can.	92	51°38′N	116°22′W
Bānfield, Arg. (bȧ′n-fyĕ′ld)	144a	34°44′S	58°24′W
Banfora, Burkina	234	10°38′N	4°46′W
Bangalore, India (băŋ′gȧ′lôr)	199	13°03′N	77°39′E
Bangassou, C.A.R. (bän-gȧ-sōō′)	231	4°47′N	22°49′E
Bangeta, Mount, mtn., Pap. N. Gui.	213	6°20′S	147°00′E
Banggai, Kepulauan, is., Indon.			
(bäng-gī′)	213	1°05′S	123°45′E
Banggi, Pulau, i., Malay.	212	7°12′N	117°10′E
Banghāzī, Libya	231	32°07′N	20°04′E
Bangka, i., Indon. (bäŋ′kȧ)	212	2°24′S	106°55′E
Bangkalan, Indon. (bäng-kȧ-län′)	212	6°07′S	112°50′E
Bangkok, Thai.	212	13°50′N	100°29′E
Bangladesh, nation, Asia	199	24°15′N	90°00′E
Bangong Co, l., Asia (bäŋ-gôŋ tswo)	202	33°40′N	79°30′E
Bangor, Wales, U.K. (băŋ′ŏr)	164	53°13′N	4°05′W
Bangor, Me., U.S. (băn′gēr)	105	44°47′N	68°47′W

ng-sing; ŋ-baŋk; N-nasalized n; nŏd; cŏmmit; ōld; ôbey; ôrder; oi-boil; fōōd; ŏŏ-as oo in foot; ou-out; s-soft; sh-dish; th-thin; pūre; ûnite; ûrn; stŭd; circŭs; ü-as in French tu; ′-indeterminate vowel.

ăt; finăl; rāte; senâte; ärm; àsk; sofá; fâre; ch-choose; dh-as th in other; bē; ĕvent; bĕt; recĕnt; cratēr; g-gō; gh-guttural g; bĭt; ĭ-short neutral; rīde; ĸ-guttural k as ch in German ich;

PRONOUNCING INDEX Bayard – Bengamisa 271

PLACE (Pronunciation)	PAGE	LAT.	LONG.
Bayard, N.M., U.S.	119	32°45'N	108°07'W
Bayard, W.V., U.S.	109	39°15'N	79°20'W
Bayburt, Tur. (bä'ī-bŏort)	181	40°15'N	40°10'E
Bay City, Mi., U.S. (bā)	105	43°35'N	83°55'W
Bay City, Tx., U.S.	123	28°59'N	95°58'W
Baydaratskaya Guba, b., Russia	180	69°20'N	66°10'E
Bay de Verde, Can.	101	48°05'N	52°54'W
Baydhabo (Baidoa), Som.	238a	3°19'N	44°20'E
Baydrag, r., Mong.	204	46°09'N	98°52'E
Bayern, state, Ger.	159d	48°05'N	11°30'E
Bayern (Bavaria), hist. reg., Ger. (bī'ĕrn) (bȧ-vâ-rĭ-ȧ)	168	49°00'N	11°16'E
Bayeux, Fr. (bȧ-yû')	161	49°19'N	0°41'W
Bayfield, Wi., U.S. (bā'fēld)	113	46°48'N	90°51'W
Baykal, Ozero (Lake Baikal), l., Russia	179	53°00'N	109°28'E
Baykal'skiy Khrebet, mts., Russia	179	53°30'N	107°30'E
Baykit, Russia (bī-kēt')	179	61°43'N	96°39'E
Baymak, Russia (bȧy'mäk)	186a	52°35'N	58°21'E
Bay Mills, Mi., U.S. (bā mĭlz)	117k	46°27'N	84°36'W
Bay Mills Indian Reservation, I.R., Mi., U.S.	113	46°19'N	85°03'W
Bay Minette, Al., U.S. (bā'mĭn-ĕt')	124	30°52'N	87°44'W
Bayombong, Phil. (bä-yŏm-bŏng')	213a	16°28'N	121°09'E
Bayonne, Fr. (bȧ-yŏn')	154	43°28'N	1°30'W
Bayonne, N.J., U.S. (bā-yōn')	110a	40°40'N	74°07'W
Bayou Bodcau Reservoir, res., La., U.S. (bī'yōō bŏd'kō)	107	32°49'N	93°22'W
Bayport, Mn., U.S. (bā'pōrt)	117g	45°02'N	92°46'W
Bayqongyr, Kaz.	183	47°46'N	66°11'E
Bayramiç, Tur.	175	39°48'N	26°35'E
Bayreuth, Ger. (bī-roit')	168	49°56'N	11°35'E
Bay Roberts, Can. (bā rŏb'ērts)	101	47°36'N	53°16'W
Bays, Lake of, l., Can. (bās)	99	45°15'N	79°00'W
Bay Saint Louis, Ms., U.S. (bā' sânt lōō'ĭs)	124	30°19'N	89°20'W
Bay Shore, N.Y., U.S. (bā' shôr)	110a	40°44'N	73°15'W
Bayt Lahm, W.B. (bĕth'lē-hĕm)	197a	31°42'N	35°13'E
Baytown, Tx., U.S. (bā'town)	123a	29°44'N	95°01'W
Bayview, Al., U.S. (bā'vū)	110h	33°34'N	86°59'W
Bayview, Wa., U.S.	116a	48°29'N	122°28'W
Bay Village, Oh., U.S. (bā)	111d	41°29'N	81°56'W
Baza, Spain (bä'thä)	162	37°29'N	2°46'W
Baza, Sierra de, mts., Spain	172	37°19'N	2°48'W
Bazar-Dyuzi, mtn., Azer. (bä'zȧr-dyōō'zĕ)	181	41°20'N	47°40'E
Bazaruto, Ilha do, i., Moz. (bȧ-zȧ-rōō'tō)	232	21°42'S	36°10'E
Bazièges, Fr.	170	43°25'N	1°41'E
Be, Nosy, i., Madag.	233	13°14'S	47°28'E
Beach, N.D., U.S. (bēch)	112	46°55'N	104°00'W
Beachy Head, c., Eng., U.K. (bēchē hĕd)	165	50°40'N	0°25'E
Beacon, N.Y., U.S. (bē'kŭn)	109	41°30'N	73°55'W
Beaconsfield, Can. (bē'kŭnz-fēld)	102a	45°26'N	73°51'W
Beals Creek, r., Tx., U.S. (bēls)	122	32°10'N	101°14'W
Bear, r., Ut., U.S.	117b	41°28'N	112°10'W
Bear, r., U.S.	115	42°17'N	111°42'W
Bear Brook, r., Can.	102c	45°24'N	75°15'W
Bear Creek, Mt., U.S. (bâr krēk)	115	45°11'N	109°07'W
Bear Creek, r., Al., U.S. (bâr)	124	34°27'N	88°00'W
Bear Creek, r., Tx., U.S.	117c	32°56'N	97°09'W
Beardstown, Il., U.S. (bērds'toun)	121	40°01'N	90°26'W
Bearfort Mountain, mtn., N.J., U.S. (bē'fōrt)	110a	41°08'N	74°23'W
Bearhead Mountain, mtn., Wa., U.S. (bâr'hĕd)	116a	47°01'N	121°49'W
Bear Lake, l., Can.	97	55°08'N	96°00'W
Bear Lake, l., Id., U.S.	115	41°56'N	111°10'W
Bear River Range, mts., U.S.	115	41°50'N	111°30'W
Beas de Segura, Spain (bā'äs dā sä-gōō'rä)	172	38°16'N	2°53'W
Beata, i., Dom. Rep. (bĕ-ä'tä)	135	17°40'N	71°40'W
Beata, Cabo, c., Dom. Rep. (kȧ'bō-bĕ-ä'tä)	135	17°40'N	71°20'W
Beatrice, Ne., U.S. (bē'ȧ-trĭs)	104	40°16'N	96°45'W
Beatty, Nv., U.S. (bēt'ē)	118	36°58'N	116°48'W
Beattyville, Ky., U.S. (bēt'ē-vĭl)	108	37°35'N	83°40'W
Beaucaire, Fr. (bō-kâr')	170	43°49'N	4°37'E
Beaucourt, Fr. (bō-kōōr')	171	47°30'N	6°54'E
Beaufort, N.C., U.S. (bō'frt)	125	34°43'N	76°40'W
Beaufort, S.C., U.S.	125	32°25'N	80°40'W
Beaufort Sea, sea, N.A.	103	70°30'N	138°40'W
Beaufort West, S. Afr.	232	32°20'S	22°45'E
Beauharnois, Can. (bō-är-nwä')	99	45°23'N	73°52'W
Beaumont, Can.	102b	46°50'N	71°01'W
Beaumont, Can.	102g	53°22'N	113°18'W
Beaumont, Ca., U.S. (bō'mŏnt)	117a	33°57'N	116°57'W
Beaumont, Tx., U.S.	105	30°05'N	94°06'W
Beaune, Fr. (bōn)	170	47°02'N	4°49'E
Beauport, Can. (bō-pôr')	102b	46°52'N	71°11'W
Beauséjour, Can.	90	50°04'N	96°33'W
Beauvais, Fr. (bō-vĕ')	170	49°25'N	2°05'E
Beaver, Ok., U.S. (bē'vēr)	120	36°46'N	100°31'W
Beaver, Pa., U.S.	111e	40°42'N	80°18'W
Beaver, Ut., U.S.	119	38°15'N	112°40'W
Beaver, i., Mi., U.S.	108	45°40'N	85°30'W
Beaver, r., Can.	92	54°20'N	111°10'W
Beaver City, Ne., U.S.	120	40°08'N	99°52'W
Beaver Creek, r., Co., U.S.	120	39°42'N	103°37'W
Beaver Creek, r., Ks., U.S.	120	39°44'N	101°05'W
Beaver Creek, r., Mt., U.S.	112	46°45'N	104°18'W
Beaver Creek, r., Wy., U.S.	112	43°46'N	104°25'W
Beaver Dam, Wi., U.S.	113	43°29'N	88°50'W
Beaverhead, r., Mt., U.S.	115	45°25'N	112°35'W
Beaverhead Mountains, mts., Mt., U.S. (bē'vēr-hĕd)	115	44°33'N	112°59'W
Beaver Indian Reservation, I.R., Mi., U.S.	108	45°40'N	85°30'W
Beaverton, Or., U.S. (bē'vēr-tŭn)	116c	45°29'N	122°49'W
Bebington, Eng., U.K. (bē'bĭng-tŭn)	158a	53°20'N	2°59'W
Bečej, Serb. (bĕ'chā)	175	45°36'N	20°03'E
Béchar, Alg.	230	31°39'N	2°14'W
Becharof, l., Ak., U.S. (bĕk-ȧ-rôf)	103	57°58'N	156°58'W
Becher Bay, b., Can. (bēch'ēr)	116a	48°18'N	123°37'W
Beckley, W.V., U.S. (bĕk'lĭ)	108	37°40'N	81°15'W
Bédarieux, Fr. (bā-dȧ-ryû')	170	43°36'N	3°11'E
Beddington Creek, r., Can. (bĕd'ĕng tŭn)	102e	51°14'N	114°13'W
Bedford, Can. (bĕd'fērd)	99	45°10'N	73°00'W
Bedford, S. Afr.	233c	32°43'S	26°19'E
Bedford, Eng., U.K.	161	52°10'N	0°25'W
Bedford, Ia., U.S.	113	40°40'N	94°41'W
Bedford, In., U.S.	108	38°50'N	86°30'W
Bedford, Ma., U.S.	101a	42°30'N	71°17'W
Bedford, N.Y., U.S.	110a	41°12'N	73°38'W
Bedford, Oh., U.S.	111d	41°23'N	81°32'W
Bedford, Pa., U.S.	109	40°05'N	78°20'W
Bedford, Va., U.S.	125	37°19'N	79°27'W
Bedford Hills, N.Y., U.S.	110a	41°14'N	73°41'W
Beebe, Ar., U.S. (bē'bē)	121	35°04'N	91°54'W
Beecher, Il., U.S. (bē'chŭr)	111a	41°20'N	87°38'W
Beechey Head, c., Can. (bē'chĭ hĕd)	116a	48°19'N	123°40'W
Beech Grove, In., U.S. (bēch grōv)	111g	39°43'N	86°05'W
Beecroft Head, c., Austl. (bē'krŭft)	222	35°03'S	151°15'E
Beelitz, Ger. (bĕ'lētz)	159b	52°14'N	12°59'E
Be'er Sheva', Isr. (bēr-shē'bȧ)	197a	31°15'N	34°48'E
Be'er Sheva', r., Isr.	197a	31°23'N	34°30'E
Beestekraal, S. Afr.	238c	25°22'S	27°34'E
Beeston, Eng., U.K. (bēs't'n)	158a	52°55'N	1°11'W
Beetz, r., Ger. (bĕtz)	159b	52°28'N	12°37'E
Beeville, Tx., U.S. (bē'vĭl)	123	28°24'N	97°44'W
Bega, Austl. (bā'gȧ)	219	36°50'S	149°49'E
Beggs, Ok., U.S. (bĕgz)	121	35°46'N	96°06'W
Bégles, Fr. (bĕ'gl')	170	44°47'N	0°34'W
Begoro, Ghana	234	6°23'N	0°23'W
Behala, India	202a	22°31'N	88°19'E
Behbehān, Iran	201	30°35'N	50°14'E
Behm Canal, can., Ak., U.S.	94	55°41'N	131°35'W
Bei, r., China (bā)	207a	22°54'N	113°08'E
Bei'an, China (bā-än)	208	48°05'N	126°26'E
Beicai, China (bā-tsī)	207b	31°12'N	121°33'E
Beifei, r., China (bā-fā)	206	33°14'N	117°03'E
Beihai, China (bā-hī)	204	21°30'N	109°10'E
Beihuangcheng Dao, i., China (bā-hūäŋ-chŭŋ dou)	206	38°23'N	120°55'E
Beijing, China	205	39°55'N	116°23'E
Beijing Shi, prov., China (bā-jyĭŋ shr)	208	40°07'N	116°00'E
Beira, Moz. (bā'rȧ)	232	19°45'N	34°58'E
Beira, hist. reg., Port. (bĕ'y-rä)	172	40°38'N	8°00'W
Beirut, Leb. (bā-rōōt')	198	33°53'N	35°30'E
Beja, Port. (bä'zhä)	162	38°03'N	7°53'W
Béja, Tun.	162	36°52'N	9°20'E
Bejaïa (Bougie), Alg.	230	36°46'N	5°00'E
Bejar, Spain	172	40°25'N	5°43'W
Bejestān, Iran	198	34°30'N	58°22'E
Bejucal, Cuba (bā-hōō-käl')	134	22°56'N	82°23'W
Bejuco, Pan. (bĕ-kōō'kō)	133	8°37'N	79°54'W
Békés, Hung. (bā'kāsh)	169	46°45'N	21°08'E
Békéscsaba, Hung. (bā'kāsh-chô'bô)	163	46°39'N	21°06'E
Beketova, Russia (bĕkĕ-to'vȧ)	185	53°23'N	125°21'E
Bela Crkva, Serb. (bĕ'lä tsĕrk'vä)	175	44°53'N	21°25'E
Belalcázar, Spain (bāl-ȧ-kä'thär)	172	38°35'N	5°12'W
Belarus, nation, Eur.	178	53°30'N	25°33'E
Belau see Palau, nation, Oc.	3	7°15'N	134°30'E
Bela Vista de Goiás, Braz.	143	16°57'S	48°47'W
Belawan, Indon. (bȧ-lä'wän)	212	3°43'N	98°43'E
Belaya, r., Russia (byĕ'lī-yȧ)	181	52°30'N	56°15'E
Belcher Islands, is., Can. (bĕl'chēr)	93	56°20'N	80°40'W
Belding, Mi., U.S. (bĕl'dĭng)	108	43°05'N	85°25'W
Belebey, Russia (byĕ'lĕ-bā'ĭ)	180	54°00'N	54°10'E
Belém, Braz. (bȧ-lĕN')	143	1°18'S	48°27'W
Belén, Para. (bā-lān')	144	23°30'S	57°09'W
Belen, N.M., U.S. (bĕ-lȧn')	119	34°40'N	106°45'W
Bélep, Îles, is., N. Cal.	221	19°30'S	164°00'E
Belëv, Russia (byĕl'yĕf)	180	53°49'N	36°06'E
Belfair, Wa., U.S. (bĕl'far)	116a	47°27'N	122°50'W
Belfast, N. Ire., U.K.	154	54°36'N	5°45'W
Belfast, Me., U.S. (bĕl'fast)	100	44°25'N	69°01'W
Belfast, Lough, b., N. Ire., U.K. (lŏk bĕl'fast)	164	54°45'N	6°00'W
Belford Roxo, Braz.	144b	22°46'S	43°24'W
Belfort, Fr. (bā-fōr')	161	47°40'N	7°50'E
Belgaum, India	199	15°57'N	74°32'E
Belgium, nation, Eur. (bĕl'jĭ-ŭm)	154	51°00'N	2°52'E
Belgorod, Russia (byĕl'gŭ-rŭt)	181	50°36'N	36°32'E
Belgorod, prov., Russia	177	50°40'N	36°42'E
Belgrade (Beograd), Serb.	154	44°48'N	20°32'E
Belhaven, N.C., U.S. (bĕl'hā-vĕn)	125	35°33'N	76°37'W
Belington, W.V., U.S. (bĕl'ĭng-tŭn)	109	39°00'N	79°55'W
Belitung, i., Indon.	212	3°30'S	107°30'E
Belize, nation, N.A.	128	17°00'N	88°40'W
Belize, r., Belize	132a	17°16'N	88°56'W
Belize City, Belize (bĕ-lēz')	128	17°31'N	88°10'W
Bel'kovo, Russia (byĕl'kô-vô)	186b	56°15'N	38°49'E
Bel'kovskiy, i., Russia (byĕl-kôf'skĭ)	185	75°45'N	137°00'E
Bell, i., Can. (bĕl)	101	50°45'N	55°35'W
Bell, r., Can.	99	49°25'N	77°15'W
Bella Bella, Can.	94	52°10'N	128°07'W
Bella Coola, Can.	94	52°22'N	126°46'W
Bellaire, Oh., U.S. (bĕl-âr')	108	40°00'N	80°45'W
Bellaire, Tx., U.S.	123a	29°43'N	95°28'W
Bellary, India (bĕl-lä'rē)	199	15°15'N	76°56'E
Bella Union, Ur. (bĕ'l-yȧ-ōō-nyô'n)	144	30°18'S	57°26'W
Bella Vista, Arg. (bä'lyȧ vēs'tȧ)	144	27°07'S	65°14'W
Bella Vista, Arg.	144	28°35'S	58°53'W
Bella Vista, Arg.	144a	34°35'S	58°41'W
Bella Vista, Para.	143	22°16'S	56°14'W
Belle-Anse, Haiti	135	18°15'N	72°00'W
Belle Bay, b., Can. (bĕl)	101	47°35'N	55°15'W
Belle Chasse, La., U.S. (bĕl shäs')	110d	29°52'N	90°00'W
Bellefontaine, Oh., U.S. (bel-fŏn'tān)	108	40°25'N	83°50'W
Bellefontaine Neighbors, Mo., U.S.	117e	38°46'N	90°13'W
Belle Fourche, S.D., U.S. (bĕl' fōōrsh')	112	44°28'N	103°50'W
Belle Fourche, r., Wy., U.S.	112	44°29'N	104°40'W
Belle Fourche Reservoir, res., S.D., U.S.	112	44°51'N	103°44'W
Bellegarde, Fr. (bĕl-gärd')	171	46°06'N	5°50'E
Belle Glade, Fl., U.S. (bĕl glād)	125a	26°39'N	80°37'W
Belle Île, i., Fr. (bĕ-lēl')	161	47°15'N	3°30'W
Belle Isle, Strait of, strt., Can.	93	51°35'N	56°30'W
Belle Mead, N.J., U.S. (bĕl mēd)	110a	40°28'N	74°40'W
Belleoram, Can.	101	47°31'N	55°25'W
Belle Plaine, Ia., U.S. (bĕl plān')	113	41°52'N	92°19'W
Belle Vernon, Pa., U.S. (bĕl vŭr'nŭn)	111e	40°08'N	79°52'W
Belleville, Can. (bĕl'vĭl)	99	44°15'N	77°25'W
Belleville, Il., U.S.	117e	38°31'N	89°59'W
Belleville, Ks., U.S.	121	39°49'N	97°37'W
Belleville, Mi., U.S.	111b	42°12'N	83°29'W
Belleville, N.J., U.S.	110a	40°47'N	74°09'W
Bellevue, Ia., U.S. (bĕl'vū)	113	42°14'N	90°26'W
Bellevue, Ky., U.S.	111f	39°06'N	84°29'W
Bellevue, Mi., U.S.	108	42°30'N	85°00'W
Bellevue, Oh., U.S.	108	41°15'N	82°45'W
Bellevue, Pa., U.S.	111e	40°30'N	80°04'W
Bellevue, Wa., U.S.	116a	47°37'N	122°12'W
Belley, Fr. (bĕ-lē')	171	45°46'N	5°41'E
Bellflower, Ca., U.S. (bĕl-flou'ēr)	117a	33°53'N	118°08'W
Bell Gardens, Ca., U.S.	117a	33°59'N	118°11'W
Bellingham, Ma., U.S. (bĕl'ĭng-hăm)	101a	42°05'N	71°28'W
Bellingham, Wa., U.S.	104	48°46'N	122°29'W
Bellingham Bay, b., Wa., U.S.	116d	48°44'N	122°34'W
Bellingshausen Sea, sea, Ant. (bĕl'ĭngz hou'n)	224	72°00'S	80°30'W
Bellinzona, Switz. (bĕl-ĭn-tsō'nä)	168	46°10'N	9°09'E
Bellmore, N.Y., U.S. (bĕl-mōr)	110a	40°40'N	73°31'W
Bello, Col. (bĕ'l-yō)	142	6°20'N	75°33'W
Bellow Falls, Vt., U.S. (bĕl'ōz fôls)	109	43°10'N	72°30'W
Bellpat, Pak.	202	29°08'N	68°00'E
Bell Peninsula, pen., Can.	93	63°50'N	81°16'W
Bells Corners, Can.	102c	45°20'N	75°49'W
Bells Mountain, mtn., Wa., U.S. (bĕls)	116c	45°50'N	122°21'W
Belluno, Italy (bĕl-lōō'nō)	174	46°08'N	12°14'E
Bell Ville, Arg. (bĕl vēl')	144	32°33'S	62°36'W
Bellville, S. Afr.	232a	33°54'S	18°38'E
Bellville, Tx., U.S. (bĕl'vĭl)	123	29°57'N	96°15'W
Bélmez, Spain (bĕl'mĕth)	172	38°17'N	5°17'W
Belmond, Ia., U.S. (bĕl'mŏnd)	113	42°49'N	93°37'W
Belmont, Ca., U.S.	116b	37°34'N	122°18'W
Belmonte, Braz. (bĕl-mōn'tȧ)	143	15°58'S	38°47'W
Belmopan, Belize	128	17°15'N	88°47'W
Belogorsk, Russia	179	51°09'N	128°32'E
Belo Horizonte, Braz. (bĕ'lôre-sô'n-tĕ)	143	19°54'S	43°56'W
Beloit, Ks., U.S. (bē-loit')	120	39°26'N	98°06'W
Beloit, Wi., U.S.	105	42°31'N	89°04'W
Belomorsk, Russia (byĕl-ô-môrsk')	180	64°30'N	34°42'E
Beloretsk, Russia (byĕ'lō-rĕtsk)	180	53°58'N	58°25'E
Belosarayskaya, Kosa, c., Ukr.	177	46°43'N	37°18'E
Belovo, Russia (byĕ'lŭ-vû)	184	54°25'N	86°18'E
Beloye, l., Russia	180	60°10'N	38°05'E
Belozersk, Russia (byĕ-lŭ-zyôrsk')	180	60°00'N	38°00'E
Belper, Eng., U.K. (bĕl'pēr)	158a	53°01'N	1°28'W
Belt, Mt., U.S. (bĕlt)	115	47°11'N	110°58'W
Belt Creek, r., Mt., U.S.	115	47°19'N	110°58'W
Belton, Tx., U.S. (bĕl'tŭn)	123	31°04'N	97°27'W
Belton Lake, l., Tx., U.S.	123	31°15'N	97°35'W
Beltsville, Md., U.S. (belts-vĭl)	110e	39°03'N	76°56'W
Belukha, Mount, mtn., Asia	178	49°47'N	86°23'E
Belvidere, Il., U.S. (bĕl-vē-dēr')	113	42°14'N	88°52'W
Belvidere, N.J., U.S.	109	40°50'N	75°05'W
Belyando, r., Austl. (bĕl-yän'dō)	221	22°09'S	146°48'E
Belyanka, Russia (byĕl'yȧn-kȧ)	186a	56°04'N	59°16'E
Belyy, Russia (byĕ'lē)	180	55°52'N	32°58'E
Belyy, i., Russia	178	73°19'N	72°00'E
Belyye Stolby, Russia (byĕ'lĭ-ye stôl'bĭ)	186b	55°20'N	37°52'E
Belzig, Ger. (bĕl'tsēg)	159b	52°08'N	12°35'E
Belzoni, Ms., U.S. (bĕl-zō'nē)	124	33°09'N	90°30'W
Bembe, Ang. (bĕN'bĕ)	232	7°00'S	14°20'E
Bembézar, r., Spain (bĕm-bā-thär')	172	38°00'N	5°18'W
Bemidji, Mn., U.S. (bē-mĭj'ĭ)	113	47°28'N	94°54'W
Bena Dibele, D.R.C. (bĕn'ȧ dē-bĕ'lē)	232	4°00'S	22°49'E
Benalla, Austl. (bĕn-ăl'ȧ)	219	36°30'S	146°00'E
Benares see Vārānasi, India	199	25°25'N	83°00'E
Benavente, Spain (bā-nä-vĕn'tä)	162	42°01'N	5°43'W
Benbrook, Tx., U.S. (bĕn'brōōk)	117c	32°41'N	97°27'W
Benbrook Reservoir, res., Tx., U.S.	117c	32°35'N	97°30'W
Bend, Or., U.S. (bĕnd)	104	44°04'N	121°17'W
Bendeleben, Mount, mtn., Ak., U.S. (bĕn-dĕl-bĕn)	103	65°18'N	163°45'W
Bender Beyla, Som.	238a	9°40'N	50°45'E
Bendigo, Austl. (bĕn'dĭ-gō)	219	36°39'S	144°20'E
Benedict, Md., U.S. (bĕnĕ'dĭct)	110e	38°31'N	76°41'W
Benešov, Czech Rep. (bĕn'ĕ-shôf)	168	49°48'N	14°40'E
Benevento, Italy (bā-nā-vĕn'tō)	162	41°08'N	14°46'E
Bengal, Bay of, b., Asia (bĕn-gôl')	196	17°30'N	87°00'E
Bengamisa, D.R.C.	237	0°57'N	25°10'E

ng-sing; ŋ-baŋk; N-nasalized n; nŏd; cŏmmit; ōld; ôbey; ôrder; oi-boil; fōōd; ŏŏ-as oo in foot; ou-out; s-soft; sh-dish; th-thin; pūre; ûnite; ûrn; stŭd; circŭs; ü-as in French tu; '-indeterminate vowel.

PLACE (Pronunciation)	PAGE	LAT.	LONG.
Bengbu, China (bŭn-bōō)	205	32°52'N	117°22'E
Benghazi see Banghāzī, Libya	230	32°07'N	20°04'E
Bengkalis, Indon. (bĕng-kä'lĭs)	212	1°29'N	102°06'E
Bengkulu, Indon.	212	3°46's	102°18'E
Benguela, Ang. (bĕn-gĕl'ä)	232	12°35's	13°25'E
Beni, r., Bol. (bā'nĕ)	142	13°41's	67°30'W
Béni-Abbas, Alg. (bā'nĕ ä-bĕs')	230	30°11'N	2°13'W
Benicia, Ca., U.S. (bĕ-nĭsh'ĭ-á)	116b	38°03'N	122°09'W
Benin, nation, Afr.	230	8°00'N	2°00'E
Benin, r., Nig. (bĕn-ēn')	235	5°55'N	5°15'E
Benin, Bight of, b., Afr.	230	5°30'N	3°00'E
Benin City, Nig.	230	6°19'N	5°41'E
Beni Sof, Alg. (bā'nĕ sŏf')	230	35°23'N	1°20'W
Benkelman, Ne., U.S. (bĕn-kĕl-mán)	120	40°03'N	101°35'W
Benkovac, Cro. (bĕn'kô-váts)	174	44°02'N	15°41'E
Bennington, Vt., U.S. (bĕn'ĭng-tŭn)	109	42°55'N	73°15'W
Benns Church, Va., U.S. (bĕnz' chûrch')	110g	36°47'N	76°35'W
Benoni, S. Afr. (bĕ-nō'nĭ)	232	26°11's	28°19'E
Benoy, Chad	235	8°59'N	16°19'E
Benque Viejo, Belize (bĕn-kĕ bĭĕ'hō)	132a	17°07'N	89°07'W
Bensberg, Ger.	171c	50°58'N	7°09'E
Bensenville, Il., U.S. (bĕn'sĕn-vĭl)	111a	41°57'N	87°56'W
Bensheim, Ger. (bĕns-hīm)	168	49°42'N	8°38'E
Benson, Az., U.S. (bĕn-sŭn)	119	32°00'N	110°20'W
Benson, Mn., U.S.	112	45°18'N	95°36'W
Bentiaba, Ang.	236	14°15's	12°21'E
Bentleyville, Pa., U.S. (bent'lē vĭl)	111e	40°07'N	80°01'W
Benton, Can.	100	45°59'N	67°36'W
Benton, Ar., U.S. (bĕn'tŭn)	121	34°34'N	92°34'W
Benton, Ca., U.S.	118	37°44'N	118°22'W
Benton, Il., U.S.	108	38°00'N	88°55'W
Benton Harbor, Mi., U.S. (bĕn'tŭn här'bĕr)	108	42°05'N	86°30'W
Bentonville, Ar., U.S. (bĕn'tŭn-vĭl)	121	36°22'N	94°11'W
Benue, r., Afr. (bā'nōō-å)	230	8°00'N	8°00'E
Benut, r., Malay.	197b	1°43'N	103°20'E
Benwood, W.V., U.S. (bĕn-wŏd)	108	39°55'N	80°45'W
Benxi, China	208	41°25'N	123°50'E
Beograd see Belgrade, Serb.	154	44°48'N	20°32'E
Beppu, Japan (bĕp'pōō)	211	33°16'N	131°30'E
Bequia Island, i., St. Vin. (bĕk-ē'ä)	133b	13°00'N	61°08'W
Berakit, Tanjung, c., Indon.	197b	1°16'N	104°44'E
Berat, Alb. (bĕ-rät')	175	40°43'N	19°59'E
Berau, Teluk, b., Indon.	213	2°22's	131°40'E
Berazategui, Arg. (bĕ-rä-zä'tĕ-gē)	144a	34°46's	58°14'W
Berbera, Som. (bûr'bûr-á)	238a	10°25'N	45°05'E
Berbérati, C.A.R.	235	4°16'N	15°47'E
Berck, Fr. (bĕrk)	170	50°26'N	1°36'E
Berdians'k, Ukr.	181	46°45'N	36°47'E
Berdians'ka kosa, c., Ukr.	177	46°38'N	36°42'E
Berdyaush, Russia (bĕr'dyáush)	186a	55°10'N	59°12'E
Berdychiv, Ukr.	178	49°53'N	28°32'E
Berea, Ky., U.S. (bĕ-rē'á)	124	37°30'N	84°19'W
Berea, Oh., U.S.	111d	41°22'N	81°51'W
Berehove, Ukr.	178	48°13'N	22°40'E
Bereku, Tan.	237	4°27's	35°44'E
Berens, r., Can. (bĕ'rĕnz)	97	52°15'N	96°30'W
Berens Island, i., Can.	97	52°18'N	97°40'W
Berens River, Can.	90	52°22'N	97°02'W
Beresford, S.D., U.S. (bĕr'ĕs-fĕrd)	112	43°05'N	96°46'W
Berettyóújfalu, Hung. (bĕ'rĕt-tyō-ōō'y'fō-lōō)	169	47°14'N	21°33'E
Berezhany, Ukr. (bĕr-yĕ'zhá-nĕ)	169	49°25'N	24°58'E
Berezivka, Ukr.	177	47°12'N	30°56'E
Berezna, Ukr. (bĕr-yŏz'ná)	177	51°32'N	31°47'E
Bereznehuvate, Ukr.	177	47°19'N	32°58'E
Berezniki, Russia (bĕr-yôz'nyĕ-kĕ)	180	59°25'N	56°46'E
Berëzovka, Russia	186a	57°35'N	57°19'E
Berëzovo, Russia (bĭr-yô'zĕ-vû)	178	64°10'N	65°10'E
Berëzovskiy, Russia (bĕr-yô'zôf-skī')	186a	56°54'N	60°47'E
Berga, Spain (bĕr'gä)	173	42°05'N	1°52'E
Bergama, Tur. (bĕr'gä-mä)	198	39°08'N	27°09'E
Bergamo, Italy (bĕr'gä-mō)	172	45°43'N	9°41'E
Bergantin, Ven. (bĕr-gän-tē'n)	143b	10°04'N	64°23'W
Bergara, Spain	172	43°08'N	2°23'W
Bergedorf, Ger. (bĕr'gĕ-dôrf)	159c	53°29'N	10°12'E
Bergen, Ger. (bĕr'gĕn)	168	54°26'N	13°26'E
Bergen, Nor.	154	60°24'N	5°20'E
Bergenfield, N.J., U.S.	110a	40°55'N	73°59'W
Bergen op Zoom, Neth.	165	51°29'N	4°16'E
Bergerac, Fr. (bĕr-zhĕ-rä')	161	44°49'N	0°28'E
Bergisch Gladbach, Ger. (bĕrg'ĭsh-glät'bäk)	171c	50°59'N	7°08'E
Berglern, Ger. (bĕrgh'lĕrn)	159d	48°24'N	11°55'E
Bergneustadt, Ger.	171c	51°01'N	7°39'E
Bergville, S. Afr. (bĕrg'vĭl)	233c	28°44's	29°22'E
Berhampur, India	199	19°19'N	84°48'E
Bering Sea, sea	240	58°00'N	175°00'W
Bering Strait, strt.	106a	64°50'N	169°50'W
Berja, Spain (bĕr'hä)	172	36°50'N	2°56'W
Berkeley, Ca., U.S. (bûrk'lĭ)	114	37°52'N	122°17'W
Berkeley, Mo., U.S.	117e	38°45'N	90°20'W
Berkeley Springs, W.V., U.S. (bûrk'lĭ springz)	109	39°40'N	78°10'W
Berkhamsted, Eng., U.K. (bĕk'hám'stĕd)	158b	51°44'N	0°34'W
Berkley, Mi., U.S. (bûrk'lĭ)	111b	42°30'N	83°10'W
Berkovitsa, Blg. (bĕr-kō've-tsá)	173	43°14'N	23°08'E
Berkshire, hist. reg., Eng., U.K.	158b	51°23'N	1°07'W
Berland, r., Can.	95	54°00'N	117°10'W
Berlenga, is., Port. (bĕr-lĕn'gäzh)	172	39°25'N	9°33'W
Berlin, Ger. (bĕr-lēn')	154	52°31'N	13°28'E
Berlin, S. Afr. (bĕr-lĭn)	233c	32°53's	27°36'E
Berlin, N.H., U.S. (bûr-lĭn)	109	44°25'N	71°10'W
Berlin, N.J., U.S.	110f	39°47'N	74°56'W
Berlin, Wi., U.S. (bûr-lĭn')	113	43°58'N	88°58'W
Bermejo, r., S.A. (bĕr-mā'hō)	144	25°05's	61°00'W
Bermeo, Spain (bĕr-mā'yō)	172	43°23'N	2°43'W
Bermuda, dep., N.A.	129	32°20'N	65°45'W
Bern, Switz. (bĕrn)	154	46°55'N	7°25'E
Bernal, Arg. (bĕr-näl')	144a	34°43's	58°17'W
Bernalillo, N.M., U.S. (bĕr-nä-lē'yō)	119	35°20'N	106°30'W
Bernard, I., Can. (bĕr-närd')	109	45°45'N	79°25'W
Bernardsville, N.J., U.S. (bûr nårds'vĭl)	110a	40°43'N	74°34'W
Bernau, Ger. (bĕr nóu)	168	52°40'N	13°35'E
Bernburg, Ger. (bĕrn'bôrgh)	168	51°48'N	11°43'E
Berndorf, Aus. (bĕrn'dôrf)	168	47°57'N	16°05'E
Berne, Wi., U.S. (bûrn)	108	40°40'N	84°55'W
Berner Alpen, mts., Switz.	168	46°29'N	7°30'E
Bernier, i., Austl. (bĕr-ner')	220	24°58's	113°15'E
Bernina, Pizzo, mtn., Eur.	168	46°23'N	9°58'E
Bero, r., Ang.	236	15°10's	12°20'E
Beroun, Czech Rep. (bā'rŏn)	168	49°57'N	14°03'E
Berounka, r., Czech Rep. (bĕ-rŏn'ká)	168	49°53'N	13°40'E
Berowra, Austl.	217b	33°36's	151°10'E
Berre, Étang de, l., Fr. (ã-tôn' dĕ bär')	170a	43°27'N	5°07'E
Berre-l'Étang, Fr. (bär'lä-tôn')	170a	43°28'N	5°11'E
Berriozabal, Mex. (bä'rēô-zä-bäl')	131	16°47'N	93°16'W
Berriyyane, Alg.	162	32°50'N	3°49'E
Berry Creek, r., Can.	96	51°15'N	111°40'W
Berryessa, r., Ca., U.S. (bĕ'rĭ ĕs'á)	118	38°35'N	122°33'W
Berry Islands, is., Bah.	134	25°40'N	77°50'W
Berryville, Ar., U.S.	121	36°21'N	93°34'W
Berryville, Va., U.S. (bĕr'ĕ-vĭl)	121	39°09'N	77°59'W
Bershad', Ukr. (byĕr'shät)	177	48°22'N	29°31'E
Berthier, Can.	102b	46°56'N	70°44'W
Bertrand, r., Wa., U.S. (bûr'tränd)	116d	48°58'N	122°31'W
Berwick, Pa., U.S. (bûr'wĭk)	109	41°05'N	76°10'W
Berwick-upon-Tweed, Eng., U.K. (bûr'ĭk)	160	55°45'N	2°01'W
Berwyn, Il., U.S. (bûr'wĭn)	111a	41°49'N	87°47'W
Beryslav, Ukr.	177	46°49'N	33°24'E
Besalampy, Madag. (bĕz-ä-läm-pē')	233	16°48's	44°40'E
Besançon, Fr. (bĕ-sän-sôn)	161	47°14'N	6°02'E
Besar, Gunong, mtn., Malay.	197b	2°31'N	103°09'E
Besed', r., Eur. (byĕ'syĕt)	176	52°58'N	31°36'E
Beskid Mountains, mts., Eur.	169	49°23'N	19°00'E
Beskra, Alg.	230	34°52'N	5°39'E
Beslan, Russia	182	43°12'N	44°33'E
Bessarabia, hist. reg., Mol.	177	47°00'N	28°30'E
Bességes, Fr. (bĕ-sĕzh')	170	44°20'N	4°07'E
Bessemer, Al., U.S. (bĕs'ĕ-mĕr)	110h	33°24'N	86°58'W
Bessemer, Mi., U.S.	113	46°29'N	90°04'W
Bessemer City, N.C., U.S.	125	35°16'N	81°17'W
Bestensee, Ger. (bĕs'tĕn-zā)	159b	52°15'N	13°39'E
Betanzos, Spain (bĕr-tän'thôs)	172	43°18'N	8°14'W
Betatakin Ruin, Az., U.S. (bĕt-á-tāk'ĭn)	119	36°40'N	110°29'W
Bethal, S. Afr. (bĕth'äl)	238c	26°27's	29°28'E
Bethalto, Il., U.S. (bá-thäl'tō)	117e	38°54'N	90°03'W
Bethanien, Nmb.	232	26°20's	16°10'E
Bethany, Mo., U.S.	121	40°15'N	94°04'W
Bethel, Ak., U.S. (bĕth'ĕl)	106a	60°50'N	161°50'W
Bethel, Ct., U.S.	110a	41°22'N	73°24'W
Bethel, Vt., U.S.	109	43°50'N	72°40'W
Bethel Park, Pa., U.S.	111e	40°19'N	80°02'W
Bethesda, Md., U.S. (bĕ-thĕs'dá)	110e	39°00'N	77°10'W
Bethlehem, S. Afr.	232	28°14's	28°18'E
Bethlehem, Pa., U.S. (bĕth'lĕ-hĕm)	109	40°40'N	75°25'W
Bethlehem see Bayt Lahm, W.B.	197a	31°42'N	35°13'E
Béthune, Fr. (bā-tün')	170	50°32'N	2°07'E
Betroka, Madag. (bĕ-trōk'á)	233	23°13's	46°17'E
Bet She'an, Isr.	197a	32°30'N	35°30'E
Betsiamites, Can.	91	48°57'N	68°36'W
Betsiamites, r., Can.	100	49°11'N	69°20'W
Betsiboka, r., Madag. (bĕt-sĭ-bō'ká)	233	16°47's	46°40'E
Bettles Field, Ak., U.S. (bĕt'tŭls)	103	66°58'N	151°48'W
Betwa, r., India (bĕt'wá)	199	25°00'N	78°00'E
Betz, Fr.	171b	49°09'N	2°58'E
Beveren, Bel.	159a	51°13'N	4°14'E
B. Everett Jordan Lake, res., N.C., U.S.	125	35°45'N	79°00'W
Beverly, Ma., U.S.	101a	42°34'N	70°53'W
Beverly, W.V., U.S.	110f	38°50'N	79°56'W
Beverly Hills, Ca., U.S.	117a	34°05'N	118°24'W
Bevier, Mo., U.S. (bĕ-vēr')	121	39°44'N	92°36'W
Bewdley, Eng., U.K. (būd'lĭ)	158a	52°22'N	2°19'W
Bexhill, Eng., U.K. (bĕks'hĭl)	165	50°49'N	0°25'E
Bexley, Eng., U.K. (bĕks'ly)	158b	51°26'N	0°09'E
Beyla, Gui. (bā'lä)	230	8°41'N	8°37'W
Beylul, Erit.	231	13°15'N	42°20'E
Beypazari, Tur. (bā-pá-zä'rĭ)	163	40°10'N	31°40'E
Beyşehir, Tur.	181	38°00'N	31°45'E
Beysugskiy, Liman, b., Russia (lĭ-män' bĕy-sōōg'skĭ)	177	46°07'N	38°35'E
Bezhetsk, Russia (byĕ-zhĕtsk')	180	57°46'N	36°40'E
Bezhitsa, Russia (byĕ-zhĭ'tsá)	180	53°19'N	34°18'E
Béziers, Fr. (bā-zyā')	161	43°21'N	3°12'E
Bhadreswar, India	202a	22°49'N	88°21'E
Bhagalpur, India (bä'gŭl-pór)	199	25°15'N	86°59'E
Bhamo, Mya. (bŭ-mō')	193	24°16'N	97°11'E
Bhangar, India	202a	22°30'N	88°36'E
Bharatpur, India (bĕrt'pór)	199	27°21'N	77°33'E
Bhatinda, India (bŭ-tĭn-dä)	199	30°19'N	74°56'E
Bhatpara, India	199	22°52'N	88°24'E
Bhaunagar, India (bäv-nŭg'ŭr)	199	21°45'N	72°58'E
Bhayandar, India	203b	19°20'N	72°50'E
Bhilai, India	202	21°14'N	81°23'E
Bhīma, r., India (bē'má)	199	18°00'N	74°45'E
Bhiwandi, India	203b	19°18'N	73°03'E
Bhiwāni, India	202	28°53'N	76°08'E
Bhopāl, India (bô-päl)	199	23°20'N	77°25'E
Bhubaneswar, India (bô-bû-nāsh'vûr)	199	20°21'N	85°53'E
Bhuj, India (bōōj)	199	23°22'N	69°39'E
Bhutan, nation, Asia (bōō-tän')	199	27°15'N	90°30'E
Biafra, Bight of, b., Afr.	230	4°05'N	7°10'E
Biak, i., Indon. (bē'äk)	213	1°00's	136°00'E
Biała Podlaska, Pol. (byä'wä pôd läs'kä)	169	52°01'N	23°08'E
Białogard, Pol.	168	54°00'N	16°01'E
Białystok, Pol. (byä-wĭs'tŏk)	154	53°08'N	23°12'E
Biankouma, C. Iv.	234	7°44'N	7°37'W
Biarritz, Fr. (byä-rēts')	161	43°29'N	1°39'W
Bibb City, Ga., U.S. (bĭb' sĭ'tē)	124	32°31'N	84°56'W
Biberach, Ger. (bē'bĕräk)	168	48°06'N	9°49'E
Bibiani, Ghana	234	6°28'N	2°20'W
Bic, Can. (bĭk)	100	48°22'N	68°42'W
Bicknell, In., U.S. (bĭk'nĕl)	108	38°45'N	87°20'W
Bicske, Hung. (bĭsh'kĕ)	169	47°29'N	18°38'E
Bida, Nig. (bē'dä)	230	9°05'N	6°01'E
Biddeford, Me., U.S. (bĭd'ê-fĕrd)	100	43°29'N	70°29'W
Biddulph, Eng., U.K. (bĭd'ŭlf)	158a	53°07'N	2°10'W
Biebrza, r., Pol. (byĕb'zhä)	169	53°18'N	22°25'E
Biel, Switz. (bēl)	168	47°09'N	7°12'E
Bielefeld, Ger. (bē'lĕ-fĕlt)	161	52°01'N	8°35'E
Biella, Italy (byĕl'lä)	174	45°34'N	8°05'E
Bielsk Podlaski, Pol. (byĕlsk pŭd-lä'skĭ)	161	52°47'N	23°14'E
Bien Hoa, Viet.	212	10°59'N	106°49'E
Bienville, Lac, l., Can.	93	55°32'N	72°45'W
Biesenthal, Ger. (bē'sĕn-täl)	159b	52°46'N	13°38'E
Biferno, r., Italy (bē-fĕr'nō)	174	41°49'N	14°46'E
Bifoum, Gabon	236	0°22's	10°23'E
Biga, Tur. (bē'ghá)	175	40°13'N	27°14'E
Big Bay de Noc, Mi., U.S. (bĭg bā dĕ nok')	113	45°48'N	86°41'W
Big Bayou, Ar., U.S. (bĭg'bĭ'yōō)	121	33°04'N	91°28'W
Big Bear City, Ca., U.S. (bĭg bär)	117a	34°16'N	116°51'W
Big Belt Mountains, mts., Mt., U.S. (bĭg bĕlt)	106	46°53'N	111°43'W
Big Bend Dam, S.D., U.S. (bĭg bĕnd)	112	44°11'N	99°33'W
Big Bend National Park, rec., Tx., U.S.	106	29°15'N	103°15'W
Big Black, r., Ms., U.S. (bĭg bläk)	124	32°05'N	90°49'W
Big Blue, r., Ne., U.S. (bĭg blōō)	121	40°53'N	97°00'W
Big Canyon, Tx., U.S. (bĭg kän'yŭn)	122	30°27'N	102°19'W
Big Cypress Indian Reservation, I.R., Fl., U.S.	125a	26°19'N	81°11'W
Big Cypress Swamp, sw., Fl., U.S. (bĭg sī'prĕs)	125a	26°02'N	81°20'W
Big Delta, Ak., U.S. (bĭg dĕl'tá)	103	64°08'N	145°48'W
Big Fork, r., Mn., U.S. (bĭg fôrk)	113	48°08'N	93°47'W
Biggar, Can.	90	52°04'N	108°00'W
Big Hole, r., Mt., U.S. (bĭg hŏl)	115	45°53'N	113°15'W
Big Hole National Battlefield, Mt., U.S. (bĭg hŏl bät'l-fēld)	115	45°44'N	113°35'W
Bighorn, r., Mt., U.S.	106	45°30'N	108°00'W
Bighorn Lake, res., Mt., U.S.	115	45°00'N	108°10'W
Bighorn Mountains, mts., U.S. (bĭg hôrn)	106	44°47'N	107°40'W
Big Island, i., Can.	97	49°10'N	94°40'W
Big Lake, Wa., U.S. (bĭg lāk)	116a	48°24'N	122°14'W
Big Lake, l., Can.	102g	53°35'N	113°47'W
Big Lake, l., Wa., U.S.	116a	48°24'N	122°14'W
Big Lost, r., Id., U.S. (lôst)	115	43°56'N	113°38'W
Big Mossy Point, c., Can.	97	53°55'N	97°50'W
Big Muddy, r., Il., U.S.	108	37°50'N	89°00'W
Big Muddy Creek, r., Mt., U.S. (bĭg mud'ĭ)	115	48°53'N	105°02'W
Bignona, Sen.	234	12°49'N	16°14'W
Big Porcupine Creek, r., Mt., U.S. (pôr'kŭ-pīn)	115	46°38'N	107°04'W
Big Quill Lake, l., Can.	92	51°55'N	104°22'W
Big Rapids, Mi., U.S. (bĭg răp'ĭdz)	108	43°40'N	85°30'W
Big River, Can.	90	53°50'N	107°01'W
Big Sandy, r., Az., U.S. (bĭg sänd'ê)	119	34°59'N	113°36'W
Big Sandy, r., Ky., U.S.	108	38°15'N	82°35'W
Big Sandy, r., Wy., U.S.	115	42°00'N	109°35'W
Big Sandy Creek, r., Co., U.S.	120	39°08'N	103°36'W
Big Sandy Creek, r., Mt., U.S.	115	48°20'N	110°08'W
Bigsby Island, i., Can.	97	49°04'N	94°35'W
Big Sioux, r., U.S. (bĭg sōō)	112	44°34'N	97°00'W
Big Spring, Tx., U.S. (bĭg spring)	122	32°15'N	101°28'W
Big Stone, I., Mn., U.S. (bĭg stōn)	112	45°25'N	96°40'W
Big Stone Gap, Va., U.S.	125	36°50'N	82°50'W
Big Sunflower, r., Ms., U.S. (sŭn-flou'ĕr)	124	32°57'N	90°40'W
Big Timber, Mt., U.S. (bĭg tĭm'bĕr)	115	45°50'N	109°57'W
Big Wood, r., Id., U.S. (bĭg wŏd)	115	43°02'N	114°30'W
Bihār, state, India (bē-här)	199	25°30'N	87°00'E
Biharamulo, Tan. (bē-hä-rä-mōō'lō)	232	2°38's	31°20'E
Bihorului, Munţii, mts., Rom.	169	46°37'N	22°37'E
Bijagós, Arquipélago dos, is., Gui.-B.	230	11°20'N	17°10'W
Bijāpur, India	203	16°53'N	75°42'E
Bijeljina, Bos.	175	44°44'N	19°15'E
Bijelo Polje, Mont. (bē'yĕ-lô pô'lyĕ)	175	43°02'N	19°48'E
Bijiang, China (bē-jyän)	207a	22°57'N	113°15'E
Bijie, China (bē-jyĕ)	209	27°20'N	105°18'E
Bijou Creek, r., Co., U.S. (bē'zhōō)	120	39°41'N	104°13'W

ăt; fināl; rāte; senåte; ärm; åsk; sofá; fâre; ch-choose; dh-as th in other; bē; ĕvent; bĕt; recĕnt; cratĕr; g-gō; gh-guttural g; bĭt; ĭ-short neutral; rīde; κ-guttural k as ch in German ich;

PLACE (Pronunciation)	PAGE	LAT.	LONG.
Bīkaner, India (bĭ-kă'nûr)	199	28°07'N	73°19'E
Bikin, Russia (bê-kēn')	210	46°41'N	134°29'E
Bikin, r., Russia	210	46°37'N	135°55'E
Bikoro, D.R.C. (bê-kō'rō)	232	0°45'S	18°07'E
Bikuar, Parque Nacional do, rec., Ang.	236	15°07'S	14°40'E
Bilāspur, India (bê-läs'pōōr)	199	22°08'N	82°12'E
Bila Tserkva, Ukr.	181	49°48'N	30°09'E
Bilauktaung, mts., Asia	212	14°40'N	98°50'E
Bilbao, Spain (bĭl-bä'ō)	154	43°12'N	2°48'W
Bilbays, Egypt	238b	30°26'N	31°37'E
Bileća, Bos. (bē'lĕ-chä)	175	42°52'N	18°26'E
Bilecik, Tur. (bē-lĕd-zhēk')	163	40°10'N	29°58'E
Bilé Karpaty, mts., Eur.	169	48°53'N	17°35'E
Biłgoraj, Pol. (bēw-gō'rī)	169	50°31'N	22°43'E
Bilhorod-Dnistrovs'kyi, Ukr.	181	46°09'N	30°19'E
Bilimbay, Russia (bē'lĭm-bȧy)	186a	56°59'N	59°53'E
Billabong, r., Austl. (bĭl'ă-bŏng)	221	35°15'S	145°20'E
Billerica, Ma., U.S. (bĭl'rĭk-ȧ)	101a	42°33'N	71°16'W
Billericay, Eng., U.K.	158b	51°38'N	0°25'E
Billings, Mt., U.S. (bĭl'ĭngz)	104	45°47'N	108°20'W
Bill Williams, r., Az., U.S. (bĭl-wĭl'yumz)	119	34°10'N	113°50'W
Bilma, Niger (bēl'mä)	231	18°41'N	13°20'E
Bilopillia, Ukr.	181	51°10'N	34°19'E
Bilovods'k, Ukr.	177	49°12'N	39°36'E
Biloxi, Ms., U.S. (bĭ-lŏk'sĭ)	105	30°24'N	88°50'W
Bilqās Qism Awwal, Egypt	238b	31°14'N	31°25'E
Bimberi Peak, mtn., Austl. (bĭm'bĕrĭ)	222	35°45'S	148°50'E
Binalonan, Phil. (bē-nä-lô'nän)	213a	16°03'N	120°35'E
Bingen, Ger. (bĭn'gĕn)	168	49°57'N	7°54'E
Bingham, Eng., U.K. (bĭng'ăm)	158a	52°57'N	0°57'W
Bingham, Me., U.S.	100	45°03'N	69°51'W
Bingham Canyon, Ut., U.S.	117b	40°33'N	112°09'W
Binghamton, N.Y., U.S. (bĭng'ăm-tŭn)	105	42°05'N	75°55'W
Bingo-Nada, b., Japan (bĭn'gō nä-dä)	211	34°06'N	133°14'E
Binjai, Indon.	212	3°59'N	108°00'E
Binnaway, Austl. (bĭn'ă-wă)	222	31°42'S	149°22'E
Bintan, i., Indon. (bĭn'tän)	197b	1°09'N	104°43'E
Bintimani, mtn., S.L.	234	9°13'N	11°07'W
Bintulu, Malay. (bēn'tōō-lōō)	212	3°07'N	113°06'E
Binxian, China	208	45°40'N	127°20'E
Binxian, China (bĭn-shyän)	206	37°27'N	117°58'E
Bio Gorge, val., Ghana	234	8°30'N	2°05'W
Bioko (Fernando Póo), i., Eq. Gui.	230	3°35'N	7°45'E
Bira, Russia (bē'rȧ)	210	49°00'N	133°18'E
Bira, r., Russia	210	48°55'N	132°25'E
Birātnagar, Nepal (bĭ-rät'nŭ-gŭr)	202	26°35'N	87°18'E
Birbka, Ukr.	169	49°36'N	24°18'E
Birch Bay, Wa., U.S. (bûrch)	116d	48°55'N	122°45'W
Birch Bay, b., Wa., U.S.	116d	48°55'N	122°52'W
Birch Island, i., Can.	97	52°25'N	99°55'W
Birch Mountains, mts., Can.	92	57°36'N	113°10'W
Birch Point, c., Wa., U.S.	116d	48°57'N	122°50'W
Bird Island, i., S. Afr. (bĕrd)	233c	33°51'S	26°21'E
Bird Rock, i., Bah. (bûrd)	135	22°50'N	74°20'W
Birds Hill, Can. (bûrds)	102f	49°58'N	97°00'W
Birdsville, Austl. (bûrdz'vĭl)	218	25°50'S	139°31'E
Birdum, Austl. (bûrd'ŭm)	218	15°45'S	133°25'E
Birecik, Tur. (bē-rĕd-zhĕk')	163	37°10'N	37°50'E
Bir Gara, Chad	235	13°11'N	15°58'E
Bīrjand, Iran (bēr'jänd)	198	33°07'N	59°16'E
Birkenfeld, Or., U.S.	116c	45°59'N	123°20'W
Birkenhead, Eng., U.K. (bûr'kĕn-hĕd)	164	53°23'N	3°02'W
Birkenwerder, Ger. (bēr'kĕn-vĕr-dĕr)	159b	52°41'N	13°22'E
Birmingham, Eng., U.K.	154	52°29'N	1°53'W
Birmingham, Al., U.S. (bûr'mĭng-häm)	105	33°31'N	86°49'W
Birmingham, Mi., U.S.	111b	42°32'N	83°13'W
Birmingham, Mo., U.S.	117f	39°10'N	94°22'W
Birmingham Canal, can., Eng., U.K.	158a	53°07'N	2°40'W
Bi'r Misāhah, Egypt	231	22°16'N	28°04'E
Birnin Kebbi, Nig.	230	12°32'N	4°12'E
Birobidzhan, Russia (bē'rô-bê-jän')	179	48°42'N	133°28'E
Birsk, Russia (bĭrsk)	178	55°25'N	55°30'E
Birstall, Eng., U.K. (bûr'stôl)	158a	53°44'N	1°39'W
Biryulëvo, Russia (bēr-yōōl'yô-vô)	186b	55°35'N	37°39'E
Biryusa, r., Russia (bēr-yōō'sä)	184	56°43'N	97°30'E
Bi'r Za'farānah, Egypt	197a	29°07'N	32°38'E
Biržai, Lith. (bēr-zhä'ē)	167	56°11'N	24°45'E
Bisbee, Az., U.S. (bĭz'bē)	104	31°30'N	109°55'W
Biscay, Bay of, b., Eur. (bĭs'kā')	156	45°19'N	3°51'W
Biscayne Bay, b., Fl., U.S. (bĭs-kān')	125a	25°22'N	80°15'W
Bischeim, Fr. (bĭsh'hĭm)	171	48°40'N	7°48'E
Biscotasi Lake, l., Can.	98	47°20'N	81°55'W
Biser, Russia (bē'sĕr)	186a	58°24'N	58°54'E
Biševo, is., Cro. (bē'shĕ-vō)	174	42°58'N	15°50'E
Bishkek, Kyrg.	183	42°49'N	74°42'E
Bisho, S. Afr.	232	32°50'S	27°20'E
Bishop, Ca., U.S. (bĭsh'ŭp)	118	37°22'N	118°25'W
Bishop, Tx., U.S.	123	27°35'N	97°46'W
Bishop's Castle, Eng., U.K. (bĭsh'ŏps käs'l)	158a	52°29'N	2°57'W
Bishopville, S.C., U.S. (bĭsh'ŭp-vĭl)	125	34°11'N	80°13'W
Bismarck, N.D., U.S. (bĭz'märk)	104	46°48'N	100°46'W
Bismarck Archipelago, is., Pap. N. Gui.	213	3°15'S	150°45'E
Bismarck Range, mts., Pap. N. Gui.	213	5°15'S	144°15'E
Bissau, Gui.-B. (bê-sa'ōō)	234	11°51'N	15°35'W
Bissett, Can.	97	51°01'N	95°45'W
Bistineau, l., La., U.S. (bĭs-tĭ-nō')	123	32°19'N	93°45'W
Bistrita, Rom. (bĭs-trĭt-sȧ)	163	47°09'N	24°29'E
Bistrita, r., Rom.	169	47°08'N	25°47'E
Bitlis, Tur. (bĭt-lēs')	198	38°30'N	42°00'E
Bitola, Mac. (bē'tô-lä) (mô'nä-stēr)	174	41°02'N	21°22'E
Bitonto, Italy (bê-tôn'tō)	174	41°08'N	16°42'E

PLACE (Pronunciation)	PAGE	LAT.	LONG.
Bitter Creek, r., Wy., U.S. (bĭt'ẽr)	115	41°36'N	108°29'W
Bitterfeld, Ger. (bĭt'ẽr-fĕlt)	168	51°39'N	12°19'E
Bitterroot, r., Mt., U.S.	115	46°28'N	114°10'W
Bitterroot Range, mts., U.S. (bĭt'ẽr-ōōt)	106	47°15'N	115°13'W
Bityug, r., Russia (bĭt'yōōg)	177	51°23'N	40°33'E
Biu, Nig.	235	10°35'N	12°13'E
Biwabik, Mn., U.S. (bê-wä'bĭk)	113	47°32'N	92°24'W
Biwa-ko, l., Japan (bê-wä'kō)	211	35°03'N	135°51'E
Biya, r., Russia (bĭ'yȧ)	184	52°22'N	87°28'E
Biysk, Russia (bēsk)	178	52°32'N	85°28'E
Bizana, S. Afr. (bĭz-änä)	233c	30°51'S	29°54'E
Bizerte, Tun. (bê-zĕrt')	230	37°23'N	9°52'E
Bjelovar, Cro. (byĕ-lō'vär)	174	45°54'N	16°53'E
Bjørnafjorden, b., Nor.	166	60°11'N	5°26'E
Bla, Mali	234	12°57'N	5°46'W
Black, l., Mi., U.S. (blăk)	108	45°25'N	84°15'W
Black, l., N.Y., U.S.	109	44°30'N	75°35'W
Black, r., Asia	212	21°00'N	103°30'E
Black, r., Can.	98	49°20'N	81°15'W
Black, r., Az., U.S.	119	33°35'N	109°35'W
Black, r., N.Y., U.S.	109	43°45'N	75°20'W
Black, r., S.C., U.S.	125	33°55'N	80°10'W
Black, r., Wi., U.S.	113	44°07'N	90°56'W
Black, r., U.S.	121	35°47'N	91°22'W
Blackall, Austl. (blăk'ŭl)	219	24°23'S	145°37'E
Black Bay, b., Can. (blăk)	98	48°36'N	88°32'W
Blackburn, Eng., U.K. (blăk'bûrn)	164	53°45'N	2°28'W
Blackburn Mount, mtn., Ak., U.S.	103	61°50'N	143°12'W
Black Butte Lake, res., Ca., U.S.	118	39°45'N	122°20'W
Black Canyon of the Gunnison National Park, rec., Co., U.S.	119	38°34'N	107°43'W
Black Diamond, Wa., U.S. (dī'mŭnd)	116a	47°19'N	122°00'W
Black Down Hills, hills, Eng., U.K. (blăk'doun)	164	50°58'N	3°19'W
Blackduck, Mn., U.S. (blăk'dŭk)	113	47°41'N	94°33'W
Blackfeet Indian Reservation, I.R., Mt., U.S.	115	48°40'N	113°00'W
Blackfoot, Id., U.S. (blăk'fŏt)	115	43°11'N	112°23'W
Blackfoot, r., Mt., U.S.	115	46°53'N	113°33'W
Blackfoot Indian Reservation, I.R., Mt., U.S.	115	48°49'N	112°53'W
Blackfoot Indian Reserve, I.R., Can.	95	50°45'N	113°00'W
Blackfoot Reservoir, res., Id., U.S.	115	42°53'N	111°23'W
Black Forest *see* Schwarzwald, for., Ger.	168	47°54'N	7°57'E
Black Hills, mts., U.S.	106	44°08'N	103°47'W
Black Island, i., Can.	97	51°10'N	96°30'W
Black Lake, Can.	99	46°02'N	71°24'W
Black Mesa, Az., U.S. (blăk māsȧ)	119	36°33'N	110°40'W
Blackmud Creek, r., Can. (blăk'mŭd)	102g	53°28'N	113°34'W
Blackpool, Eng., U.K. (blăk'pōōl)	164	53°49'N	3°02'W
Black Range, mts., N.M., U.S.	106	33°15'N	107°55'W
Black River, Jam. (blăk')	134	18°00'N	77°50'W
Black River Falls, Wi., U.S.	113	44°18'N	90°51'W
Black Rock Desert, des., Nv., U.S. (rŏk)	114	40°55'N	119°00'W
Blacksburg, S.C., U.S. (blăks'bûrg)	125	35°09'N	81°30'W
Black Sea, sea	157	43°01'N	32°16'E
Blackshear, Ga., U.S. (blăk'shĭr)	125	31°20'N	82°15'W
Blackstone, Va., U.S. (blăk'stôn)	125	37°04'N	78°00'W
Black Sturgeon, r., Can. (stû'jŭn)	98	49°12'N	88°41'W
Blacktown, Austl. (blăk'toun)	217b	33°47'S	150°55'E
Blackville, Can. (blăk'vĭl)	100	46°44'N	65°50'W
Blackville, S.C., U.S.	125	33°21'N	81°19'W
Black Volta (Volta Noire), r., Afr.	230	11°30'N	4°00'W
Black Warrior, r., Al., U.S. (blăk wŏr'ĭ-ẽr)	124	32°37'N	87°42'W
Blackwater, r., Ire. (blăk-wô'tẽr)	164	52°05'N	9°02'W
Blackwater, r., Mo., U.S.	121	38°53'N	93°22'W
Blackwater, r., Va., U.S.	125	37°07'N	77°10'W
Blackwell, Ok., U.S. (blăk'wĕl)	121	36°47'N	97°19'W
Bladel, Neth.	159a	51°22'N	5°15'E
Blagodarnoye, Russia (blä'gô-där-nō'yĕ)	181	45°00'N	43°30'E
Blagoevgrad, Blg.	175	42°01'N	23°06'E
Blagoveshchensk, Russia (blä'gŏ-vyĕsh'chĕnsk)	179	50°16'N	127°47'E
Blagoveshchensk, Russia	186a	55°03'N	56°00'E
Blaine, Mn., U.S. (blān)	117g	45°11'N	93°14'W
Blaine, Wa., U.S.	116d	48°59'N	122°49'W
Blaine, W.V., U.S.	109	39°25'N	79°10'W
Blair, Ne., U.S. (blâr)	112	41°33'N	96°09'W
Blairmore, Can.	95	49°38'N	114°25'W
Blairsville, Pa., U.S. (blârs'vĭl)	109	40°30'N	79°40'W
Blake, i., Wa., U.S. (blāk)	116a	47°37'N	122°28'W
Blakely, Ga., U.S. (blāk'lē)	124	31°22'N	84°55'W
Blanc, Cap, c., Afr.	230	20°39'N	18°08'W
Blanc, Mont, mtn., Eur. (môn blän)	156	45°50'N	6°53'E
Blanca, Bahía, b., Arg. (bä-ē'ä-blàn'kä)	144	39°30'S	61°00'W
Blanca Peak, mtn., Co., U.S. (blăŋ'kȧ)	106	37°36'N	105°22'W
Blanche, r., Can.	102c	45°34'N	75°38'W
Blanche, Lake, l., Austl. (blănch)	222	29°20'S	139°12'E
Blanchester, Oh., U.S. (blăn'chĕs-tẽr)	111f	39°18'N	83°58'W
Blanco, r., Mex.	130	24°05'N	99°21'W
Blanco, r., Mex.	131	18°42'N	96°03'W
Blanco, Cabo, c., Arg. (blăŋ'kô)	144	47°08'S	65°47'W
Blanco, Cabo, c., C.R. (kȧ'bô-blăŋ'kō)	132	9°29'N	85°15'W
Blanco, Cape, c., Or., U.S. (blăn'kō)	114	42°53'N	124°38'W
Blancos, Cayo, i., Cuba (kä'yō-blăŋ'kōs)	134	23°15'N	80°55'W

PLACE (Pronunciation)	PAGE	LAT.	LONG.
Blanding, Ut., U.S.	119	37°40'N	109°31'W
Blankenfelde, Ger. (blän'kĕn-fĕl-dĕ)	159b	52°20'N	13°24'E
Blanquefort, Fr.	170	44°53'N	0°38'W
Blanquilla, Arrecife, i., Mex. (är-rĕ-sē'fĕ-blän-kē'l-yä)	131	21°32'N	97°14'W
Blantyre, Mwi. (blăn-tīyr)	232	15°47'S	35°00'E
Blasdell, N.Y., U.S. (blăz'dĕl)	111c	42°48'N	78°51'W
Blato, Cro. (blä'tō)	174	42°55'N	16°47'E
Blaye-et-Sainte Luce, Fr. (blā'ā-sănt-lüs')	170	45°08'N	0°40'W
Błażowa, Pol. (bwä-zhō'vȧ)	169	49°51'N	22°05'E
Bleus, Monts, mts., D.R.C.	237	1°10'N	30°10'E
Blind River, Can. (blīnd)	91	46°10'N	83°09'W
Blissfield, Mi., U.S. (blĭs-fēld)	108	41°50'N	83°50'W
Blithe, r., Eng., U.K. (blĭth)	158a	52°22'N	1°49'W
Blitta, Togo	234	8°19'N	0°59'E
Block, i., R.I., U.S. (blŏk)	109	41°05'N	71°35'W
Bloedel, Can.	94	50°07'N	125°23'W
Bloomfontein, S. Afr. (blōōm'fon-tan)	232	29°09'S	26°16'E
Blois, Fr. (blwä)	161	47°36'N	1°21'E
Blood Indian Reserve, I.R., Can.	95	49°30'N	113°10'W
Bloomer, Wi., U.S. (blōōm'ẽr)	113	45°07'N	91°30'W
Bloomfield, Ia., U.S.	113	40°44'N	92°21'W
Bloomfield, In., U.S. (blōōm'fēld)	108	39°00'N	86°55'W
Bloomfield, Mo., U.S.	121	36°54'N	89°55'W
Bloomfield, Ne., U.S.	112	42°36'N	97°40'W
Bloomfield, N.J., U.S.	110a	40°48'N	74°12'W
Bloomfield Hills, Mi., U.S.	111b	42°35'N	83°15'W
Blooming Prairie, Mn., U.S. (blōōm'ĭng prā'rĭ)	113	43°52'N	93°04'W
Bloomington, Ca., U.S. (blōōm'ĭng-tŭn)	117a	34°04'N	117°24'W
Bloomington, Il., U.S.	105	40°30'N	89°00'W
Bloomington, In., U.S.	108	39°10'N	86°35'W
Bloomington, Mn., U.S.	117g	44°50'N	93°18'W
Bloomsburg, Pa., U.S. (blōōmz'bûrg)	109	41°00'N	76°25'W
Blossburg, Al., U.S. (blŏs'bûrg)	110h	33°38'N	86°57'W
Blossburg, Pa., U.S.	109	41°45'N	77°00'W
Bloubergstrand, S. Afr.	232a	33°48'S	18°28'E
Blountstown, Fl., U.S. (blŭnts'tun)	124	30°24'N	85°02'W
Bludenz, Aus. (blōō-dĕnts')	168	47°09'N	9°50'E
Blue Ash, Oh., U.S. (blōō ăsh)	111f	39°14'N	84°23'W
Blue Earth, Mn., U.S. (blōō ûrth)	113	43°38'N	94°05'W
Blue Earth, r., Mn., U.S.	113	43°55'N	94°16'W
Bluefield, W.V., U.S. (blōō'fēld)	125	37°15'N	81°11'W
Bluefields, Nic. (blōō'fēldz)	129	12°03'N	83°45'W
Blue Island, Il., U.S.	111a	41°39'N	87°41'W
Blue Mesa Reservoir, res., Co., U.S.	119	38°25'N	107°00'W
Blue Mountain, mtn., Can.	101	50°28'N	57°11'W
Blue Mountains, mts., Austl.	221	33°35'S	149°00'E
Blue Mountains, mts., Jam.	134	18°05'N	76°35'W
Blue Mountains, mts., U.S.	106	45°15'N	118°50'W
Blue Mud Bay, b., Austl. (bōō mŭd)	220	13°20'S	136°45'E
Blue Nile, r., Afr.	231	12°30'N	34°00'E
Blue Rapids, Ks., U.S. (blōō răp'ĭdz)	121	39°40'N	96°41'W
Blue Ridge, mtn., U.S. (blōō rĭj)	107	35°30'N	82°50'W
Blue River, Can.	90	52°05'N	119°17'W
Blue River, r., Mo., U.S.	117f	38°55'N	94°33'W
Bluff, Ut., U.S.	119	37°18'N	109°34'W
Bluff Park, Al., U.S.	110h	33°24'N	86°52'W
Bluffton, In., U.S. (blŭf-tŭn)	108	40°40'N	85°15'W
Bluffton, Oh., U.S.	108	40°50'N	83°55'W
Blumenau, Braz. (blōō'mĕn-ou)	144	26°53'S	48°58'W
Blumut, Gunong, mtn., Malay.	197b	2°03'N	103°34'E
Blyth, Eng., U.K. (blĭth)	164	55°03'N	1°34'W
Blythe, Ca., U.S.	119	33°37'N	114°37'W
Blytheville, Ar., U.S. (blĭth'vĭl)	121	35°55'N	89°51'W
Bo, S.L.	234	7°56'N	11°21'W
Boac, Phil.	213a	13°26'N	121°50'E
Boaco, Nic. (bô-ä'kō)	132	12°24'N	85°41'W
Bo'ai, China (bwo-ī)	208	35°10'N	113°08'E
Boa Vista, i., C.V. (bō-ä-vēsh'tȧ)	230b	16°01'N	23°52'W
Boa Vista do Rio Branco, Braz.	143	2°46'N	60°45'W
Bobo Dioulasso, Burkina (bō'bô-dyōō-lȧs-sō')	230	11°12'N	4°18'W
Bobr, Bela. (bô'b'r)	176	54°19'N	29°11'E
Bóbr, r., Pol. (bŭ'br)	168	51°44'N	15°13'E
Bobrov, Russia (bŭb-rôf')	181	51°07'N	40°01'E
Bobrovyts'a, Ukr.	177	50°43'N	31°27'E
Bobrynets', Ukr.	177	48°04'N	32°10'E
Boca del Pozo, Ven. (bô-kä-dĕl-pô'zō)	143b	11°00'N	64°21'W
Boca de Uchire, Ven. (bô-kä-dĕ-ōō-chē'rĕ)	143b	10°09'N	65°27'W
Bocaina, Serra da, mtn., Braz. (sĕ'r-rä-dȧ-bô-kä'ē-nä)	141a	22°47'S	44°39'W
Bocas, Mex. (bō'käs)	130	22°29'N	101°03'W
Bocas del Toro, Pan. (bō'käs dĕl tō'rō)	133	9°24'N	82°15'W
Bochnia, Pol. (bōk'nyä)	169	49°58'N	20°28'E
Bocholt, Ger. (bō'kōlt)	171c	51°50'N	6°37'E
Bochum, Ger.	168	51°29'N	7°13'E
Bockum-Hövel, Ger. (bō'kōm-hû'fĕl)	171c	51°41'N	7°45'E
Bodalang, D.R.C.	236	3°14'N	22°14'E
Bodaybo, Russia (bō-dī'bō)	179	57°12'N	114°46'E
Bodele, depr., Chad (bō-dȧ-lā')	231	16°45'N	17°05'E
Boden, Swe.	160	65°51'N	21°29'E
Bodensee, l., Eur. (bō'dĕn zā)	156	47°48'N	9°22'E
Bodmin, Eng., U.K. (bŏd'mĭn)	164	50°29'N	4°45'W
Bodmin Moor, Eng., U.K. (bŏd'mĭn mòr)	164	50°36'N	4°43'W
Bodrum, Tur.	181	37°10'N	27°07'E
Boende, D.R.C. (bô-ĕn'dȧ)	232	0°13'S	20°52'E
Boerne, Tx., U.S. (bō'ẽrn)	122	29°49'N	98°44'W
Boesmans, r., S. Afr.	233c	33°29'S	26°09'E
Boeuf, r., U.S. (bĕf)	123	32°23'N	91°57'W

ng-sing; ŋ-baŋk; ɴ-nasalized n; nŏd; cŏmmit; ōld; ôbey; ôrder; oi-boil; fōōd; ŏ-as oo in foot; ou-out; s-soft; sh-dish; th-thin; pūre; ûnite; ûrn; stŭd; circŭs; ü-as in French tu; '-indeterminate vowel.

274 Boffa – Bowie PRONOUNCING INDEX

PLACE (Pronunciation)	PAGE	LAT.	LONG.
Boffa, Gui. (bôf´ä)	230	10°10'N	14°02'W
Bôfu, Japan (bō´fōō)	211	34°03'N	131°35'E
Bogalusa, La., U.S. (bō-gá-lōō´sá)	123	30°48'N	89°52'W
Bogan, r., Austl. (bô´gĕn)	222	32°10'S	147°40'E
Bogense, Den. (bô´gĕn-sĕ)	166	55°34'N	10°09'E
Boggy Peak, mtn., Antig. (bŏg´ĭ-pēk)	133b	17°03'N	61°50'W
Bogong, Mount, mtn., Austl.	222	36°50'S	147°15'E
Bogor, Indon.	212	6°45'S	106°45'E
Bogoroditsk, Russia (bŏ-gŏ´rô-dĭtsk)	176	53°48'N	38°06'E
Bogorodsk, Russia	180	56°02'N	43°40'E
Bogorodskoye, Russia (bô-gô-rôd´skô-yĕ)	186a	56°43'N	56°53'E
Bogotá, Col.	142	4°36'N	74°05'W
Bogotol, Russia (bŏ gŏ-tôl)	170	56°15'N	89°45'E
Boguchar, Russia (bō´gô-chär)	181	49°40'N	41°00'E
Bogue Chitto, Ms., U.S. (nôr´fēld)	124	31°26'N	90°25'W
Boquete, Pan. (bô gĕ´tă)	133	8°54'N	82°29'W
Bo Hai, b., China	[illegible]	[illegible]	[illegible]
Bohai Haixia, strt., China (bwo-hī hī-shyä)	208	38°05'N	121°40'E
Bohain-en-Vermandois, Fr. (bô-ăn-ŏn-vâr-män-dwä´)	170	49°58'N	3°22'E
Bohemia *see* Čechy, hist. reg., Czech Rep.	168	49°51'N	13°55'E
Bohemian Forest, mts., Eur. (bô-hē´mĭ-ăn)	156	49°35'N	12°27'E
Bohodukhiv, Ukr.	181	50°10'N	35°31'E
Bohol, i., Phil. (bô-hôl´)	213	9°28'N	124°35'E
Bohom, Mex. (bō-ō´m)	131	16°47'N	92°42'W
Bohuslav, Ukr.	177	49°34'N	30°51'W
Boiestown, Can. (boiz´toun)	100	46°27'N	66°25'W
Bois Blanc, i., Mi., U.S. (boi´ blăŋk)	108	45°45'N	84°30'W
Boischâtel, Can. (bwä-shä-tĕl´)	102b	46°54'N	71°08'W
Bois-des-Filion, Can. (bōō-ä´dĕ-fē-yōn´)	102a	45°40'N	73°46'W
Boise, Id., U.S. (boi´zē)	104	43°38'N	116°12'W
Boise, r., Id., U.S.	114	43°43'N	116°30'W
Boise City, Ok., U.S.	120	36°42'N	102°30'W
Boissevain, Can. (bois´vān)	90	49°14'N	100°03'W
Bojador, Cabo, c., W. Sah.	230	26°21'N	16°08'W
Bojnūrd, Iran	198	37°29'N	57°13'E
Bokani, Nig.	235	9°26'N	5°13'E
Boknafjorden, b., Nor.	160	59°12'N	5°37'E
Boksburg, S. Afr. (bŏks´bûrgh)	233b	26°13'S	28°15'E
Bokungu, D.R.C.	236	0°41'S	22°19'E
Bol, Chad	235	13°28'N	14°43'E
Bolai I, C.A.R.	235	4°20'N	17°21'E
Bolama, Gui.-B. (bô-lä´mä)	230	11°34'S	15°41'W
Bolan, mtn., Pak. (bô-län´)	202	30°13'N	67°09'E
Bolaños, Mex. (bō-län´yôs)	130	21°40'N	103°48'W
Bolaños, r., Mex.	130	21°26'N	103°54'W
Bolan Pass, p., Pak.	199	29°50'N	67°10'E
Bolbec, Fr. (bôl-bĕk´)	170	49°37'N	0°26'E
Bole, Ghana (bō´lå)	230	9°02'N	2°29'W
Bolesławiec, Pol. (bō-lĕ-slä´vyĕts)	168	51°15'N	15°35'E
Bolgatanga, Ghana	234	10°46'N	0°52'W
Bolhrad, Ukr.	181	45°41'N	28°38'E
Boli, China (bwo-lē)	205	45°40'N	130°38'E
Bolinao, Phil. (bō-lē-nä´ō)	213a	16°24'N	119°53'E
Bolívar, Arg. (bô-lē´vär)	144	36°15'S	61°05'W
Bolívar, Col.	142	1°46'N	76°58'W
Bolivar, Mo., U.S. (bŏl´ĭ-vȧr)	121	37°37'N	93°22'W
Bolivar, Tn., U.S.	124	35°14'N	88°56'W
Bolívar, Pico, mtn., Ven.	142	8°44'N	70°54'W
Bolivar Peninsula, pen., Tx., U.S. (bŏl´ĭ-vȧr)	123a	29°25'N	94°40'W
Bolivia, nation, S.A. (bô-lĭv´ĭ-ä)	142	17°00'S	64°00'W
Bolkhov, Russia (bŏl-kôf´)	180	53°27'N	35°59'E
Bollin, r., Eng., U.K. (bŏl´ĭn)	158a	53°18'N	2°11'W
Bollington, Eng., U.K. (bôl´ĭng-tŭn)	158a	53°18'N	2°06'W
Bollnäs, Swe. (bôl´nĕs)	166	61°22'N	16°20'E
Bolmen, l., Swe. (bôl´mĕn)	166	56°58'N	13°25'E
Bolobo, D.R.C. (bō´lô-bô)	232	2°14'S	16°18'E
Bologna, Italy (bô-lōn´yä)	154	44°30'N	11°18'E
Bologoye, Russia (bô-lô-gô´yĕ)	180	57°52'N	34°02'E
Bolonchenticul, Mex. (bô-lôn-chĕn-tē-kōō´l)	132a	20°03'N	89°47'W
Bolondrón, Cuba (bô-lôn-drōn´)	134	22°45'N	81°25'W
Bolseno, Lago di, l., Italy (lä´gō-dē-bôl-sā´nō)	174	42°35'N	11°40'E
Bol'shaya Anyuy, r., Russia	185	67°58'N	161°15'E
Bol'shaya Chuya, r., Russia	185	58°15'N	111°40'E
Bol'shaya Kinel', r., Russia	180	53°20'N	52°40'E
Bol'she Ust'ikinskoye, Russia (bôl´she ôs-tyĭ-kĕn´skô-yĕ)	186a	55°58'N	58°18'E
Bol'shoy Begichëv, i., Russia	179	74°30'N	114°40'E
Bol'shoye Ivonino, Russia (ĭ-vô´nĭ-nô)	186a	59°41'N	61°12'E
Bol'shoy Kuyash, Russia (bôl´-shôy kōō´yásh)	186a	55°52'N	61°07'E
Bolsover, Eng., U.K. (bōl´zō-vẽr)	158a	53°14'N	1°17'W
Boltaña, Spain (bôl-tä´nä)	173	42°28'N	0°03'E
Bolton, Can. (bōl´tŭn)	102d	43°53'N	79°44'W
Bolton, Eng., U.K.	164	53°35'N	2°26'W
Bolton-upon-Dearne, Eng., U.K. (bōl´tŭn-ŭp´ŏn-dûrn)	158a	53°31'N	1°19'W
Bolu, Tur. (bō´lŏ)	163	40°45'N	31°45'E
Bolva, r., Russia (bôl´vä)	176	53°30'N	34°30'E
Bolvadin, Tur. (bôl-vä-dēn´)	163	38°50'N	30°50'E
Bolzano, Italy (bôl-tsä´nō)	163	46°31'N	11°22'E
Boma, D.R.C. (bō´mä)	232	5°51'S	13°03'E
Bombala, Austl. (bŭm-bă´lă)	219	36°55'S	149°07'E
Bombay *see* Mumbai, India	199	18°58'N	72°50'E
Bombay Harbour, b., India	203b	18°55'N	72°52'E
Bomi Hills, Lib.	230	7°00'N	11°00'W

PLACE (Pronunciation)	PAGE	LAT.	LONG.
Bom Jardim, Braz. (bôn zhär-dēn´)	141a	22°10'S	42°25'W
Bom Jesus do Itabapoana, Braz.	141a	21°08'S	41°51'W
Bømlo, i., Nor. (bûmlô)	166	59°47'N	4°57'E
Bomongo, D.R.C.	231	1°22'N	18°21'E
Bom Sucesso, Braz. (bôn-sōō-sĕ´sō)	141a	21°02'S	44°44'W
Bomu *see* Mbomou, r., Afr.	231	4°50'N	24°00'E
Bon, Cap, c., Tun. (bôn)	162	37°04'N	11°13'E
Bonaire, i., Neth. Ant. (bô-nâr´)	142	12°10'N	68°15'W
Bonavista, Can. (bŏ-nȧ-vĭs´tȧ)	93a	48°39'N	53°07'W
Bonavista Bay, b., Can.	93a	48°45'N	53°20'W
Bond, Co., U.S. (bŏnd)	120	39°53'N	106°40'W
Bondo, D.R.C. (bôn´dô)	184	3°49'N	23°40'E
Bondoc Peninsula, pen., Phil. (bôn dŏk´)	213a	13°24'N	122°30'E
Bondoukou, C. Iv. (bŏn-dōō´kōō)	230	8°02'N	2°48'W
Bonds Cay, i., Bah. (bŏnds kē)	134	25°30'N	77°45'W
Bondy, Fr.	171b	48°54'N	2°28'E
Bône *see* Annaba, Alg.	230	[illegible]	7°30'E
Bone, Teluk, b., Indon.	212	4°09'S	121°00'E
Bonete, Cerro, mtn., Arg. (bô´nĕtĕh çĕrrô)	144	27°50'S	68°35'W
Bonfim, Braz. (bôn-fē´n)	141a	20°20'S	44°15'W
Bongor, Chad	235	10°17'N	15°22'E
Bonham, Tx., U.S. (bŏn´ăm)	121	33°35'N	96°09'W
Bonhomme, Pic, mtn., Haiti	135	19°10'N	72°20'W
Bonifacio, Fr. (bō-nē-fä´chō)	174	41°23'N	9°10'E
Bonifacio, Strait of, strt., Eur.	162	41°14'N	9°02'E
Bonifay, Fl., U.S. (bŏn-ĭ-fā´)	124	30°46'N	85°40'W
Bonin Islands, is., Japan (bō´nĭn)	241	26°30'N	141°00'E
Bonn, Ger. (bôn)	154	50°44'N	7°06'E
Bonne Bay, b., Can. (bŏn)	101	49°33'N	57°55'W
Bonners Ferry, Id., U.S. (bonĕrz fĕr´ĭ)	114	48°41'N	116°19'W
Bonner Springs, Ks., U.S. (bŏn´ẽr sprĭngz)	117f	39°04'N	94°52'W
Bonne Terre, Mo., U.S. (bŏn târ´)	121	37°55'N	90°32'W
Bonnet Peak, mtn., Can. (bŏn´ĭt)	95	51°26'N	115°53'W
Bonneville Dam, dam, U.S. (bŏn´ē-vĭl)	114	45°37'N	121°57'W
Bonny, Nig. (bŏn´ē)	230	4°29'N	7°13'E
Bonny Lake, Wa., U.S. (bŏn´ē lăk)	116a	47°11'N	122°11'W
Bonnyville, Can. (bŏnē-vĭl)	95	54°16'N	110°44'W
Bonorva, Italy (bō-nôr´vä)	174	40°26'N	8°46'E
Bonthain, Indon. (bŏn-tīn´)	212	5°30'S	119°52'E
Bonthe, S.L.	230	7°32'N	12°30'W
Bontoc, Phil. (bŏn-tŏk´)	213a	17°10'N	121°01'E
Booby Rocks, is., Bah. (bōō´bĭ rŏks)	134	23°55'N	77°00'W
Booker T. Washington National Monument, rec., Va., U.S. (bŏŏk´ẽr tē wŏsh´ĭng-tŭn)	125	37°07'N	79°45'W
Boom, Bel.	159a	51°05'N	4°22'E
Boone, Ia., U.S. (bōōn)	113	42°04'N	93°51'W
Booneville, Ar., U.S. (bōōn´vĭl)	121	35°09'N	93°54'W
Booneville, Ky., U.S.	108	37°25'N	83°40'W
Booneville, Ms., U.S.	124	34°37'N	88°35'W
Boons, S. Afr.	238c	25°59'S	27°15'E
Boonton, N.J., U.S. (bōōn´tŭn)	110a	40°54'N	74°24'W
Boonville, In., U.S.	108	38°00'N	87°15'W
Boonville, Mo., U.S.	121	38°57'N	92°44'W
Boorama, Som.	238a	10°05'N	43°08'E
Boosaaso, Som.	238a	11°19'N	49°10'E
Boothbay Harbor, Me., U.S. (bōōth´bā här´bẽr)	100	43°51'N	69°39'W
Boothia, Gulf of, b., Can. (bōō´thĭ-ȧ)	93	69°04'N	86°04'W
Boothia Peninsula, pen., Can.	89	73°30'N	95°00'W
Bootle, Eng., U.K. (bōōt´l)	158a	53°29'N	3°02'W
Bor, Sudan (bôr)	231	6°13'N	31°35'E
Bor, Tur. (bōr)	181	37°50'N	34°40'E
Boraha, Nosy, i., Madag.	233	16°58'S	50°15'E
Borah Peak, mtn., Id., U.S. (bō´rä)	115	44°12'N	113°47'W
Borås, Swe. (bŏ´rōs)	160	57°43'N	12°55'E
Borāzjān, Iran (bō-räz-jän´)	198	29°13'N	51°13'E
Borba, Braz. (bôr´bä)	143	4°23'S	59°31'W
Borborema, Planalto da, plat., Braz. (plä-nál´tō-dä-bôr-bō-rĕ´mä)	143	7°35'S	36°40'W
Bordeaux, Fr. (bôr-dō´)	154	44°50'N	0°37'W
Bordentown, N.J., U.S. (bôr´dĕn-toun)	109	40°05'N	74°40'W
Bordj-bou-Arréridj, Alg. (bôrj-bōō-ȧ-rā-rēj´)	162	36°03'N	4°48'E
Bordj Omar Idriss, Alg.	230	28°06'N	6°34'E
Borgarnes, Ice.	160	64°31'N	21°40'W
Borger, Tx., U.S. (bôr´gẽr)	120	35°40'N	101°23'W
Borgholm, Swe. (bôrg-hŏlm´)	166	56°52'N	16°40'E
Borgne, l., La., U.S. (bôrn´y´)	123	30°03'N	89°36'W
Borgomanero, Italy (bôr´gō-mä-nâ´rō)	174	45°40'N	8°28'E
Borgo Val di Taro, Italy (bô´r-zhō-väl-dē-tá´rō)	174	44°29'N	9°44'E
Börili, Kaz.	186a	53°36'N	61°55'E
Boring, Or., U.S. (bōring)	116c	45°26'N	122°22'W
Borisoglebsk, Russia (bŏ-rē sō-glyĕpsk´)	178	51°20'N	42°00'E
Borisovka, Russia (bō-rē-sôf´kȧ)	181	50°38'N	36°00'E
Borivli, India	203b	19°15'N	72°48'E
Borja, Spain (bôr´hä)	172	41°50'N	1°33'W
Borken, Ger. (bōr´kĕn)	171c	51°50'N	6°51'E
Borkou, reg., Chad (bôr-kōō´)	231	18°11'N	18°28'E
Borkum, i., Ger. (bōr´kōōm)	168	53°31'N	6°50'E
Borlänge, Swe. (bôr-lĕŋ´gĕ)	166	60°30'N	15°24'E
Borneo, i., Asia	212	0°25'N	112°39'E
Bornholm, i., Den. (bôrn-hôlm)	156	55°16'N	15°15'E
Boromlia, Ukr.	177	50°36'N	34°58'E
Boromo, Burkina	234	11°45'N	2°56'W
Borovan, Blg. (bō-rō-vän´)	175	43°24'N	23°47'E
Borovichi, Russia (bō-rô-vē´chē)	178	58°22'N	33°56'E
Borovsk, Russia (bô´rŏvsk)	176	55°13'N	36°26'E
Borraan, Som.	238a	10°38'N	48°30'E

PLACE (Pronunciation)	PAGE	LAT.	LONG.
Borracha, Isla la, i., Ven. (ē´s-lä-lȧ-bôr-rȧ´chä)	143b	10°18'N	64°44'W
Borriana, Spain	162	39°53'N	0°05'W
Borroloola, Austl. (bŏr-rô-lōō´lȧ)	218	16°15'S	136°19'E
Borshchiv, Ukr.	169	48°47'N	26°04'E
Bort-les-Orgues, Fr. (bôr-lā-zôrg)	170	45°26'N	2°26'E
Borūjerd, Iran	198	33°45'N	48°53'E
Boryslav, Ukr.	169	49°17'N	23°24'E
Boryspil', Ukr.	177	50°17'N	30°54'E
Borzna, Ukr. (bôrz´nȧ)	181	51°15'N	32°26'E
Borzya, Russia (bôrz´yȧ)	179	50°37'N	116°53'E
Bosa, Italy (bō´sä)	174	40°18'N	8°34'E
Bosanska Dubica, Bos. (bō´sän-skä dōō´bĭt-sä)	174	45°10'N	16°49'E
Bosanska Gradiška, Bos. (bō´sän-skä grä-dĭsh´kä)	175	45°08'N	17°15'E
Bosanski Novi, Bos. (bō´s sän-skĭ nō´vē)	174	45°00'N	16°22'E
Bosanski Petrovac, Bos. (bō´sän-skĭ pĕt´rō-väts)	174	44°33'N	16°23'E
Bosanski Šamac, Bos. (bō´sän-skĭ shä´mȧts)	175	45°03'N	18°30'E
Boscobel, Wi., U.S. (bŏs´kô-bĕl)	113	43°08'N	90°44'W
Bose, China (bwo-sŭ)	209	24°00'N	106°38'E
Boshan, China (bwo-shan)	205	36°32'N	117°51'E
Boskoop, Neth.	159a	52°04'N	4°39'E
Boskovice, Czech Rep. (bŏs´kō-vē-tsĕ)	168	49°26'N	16°37'E
Bosna, r., Bos.	175	44°19'N	17°54'E
Bosnia and Herzegovina, nation, Eur.	175	44°15'N	17°30'E
Bosobolo, D.R.C.	236	4°11'N	19°54'E
Bosporus *see* İstanbul Boğazı, strt., Tur.	198	41°10'N	29°10'E
Bossangoa, C.A.R.	235	6°29'N	17°27'E
Bossier City, La., U.S. (bŏsh´ẽr)	123	32°31'N	93°42'W
Bosten Hu, l., China (bwo-stŭn hōō)	204	42°06'N	88°01'E
Boston, Ga., U.S. (bôs´tŭn)	124	30°47'N	83°47'W
Boston, Ma., U.S.	105	42°15'N	71°07'W
Boston Heights, Oh., U.S.	111d	41°15'N	81°30'W
Boston Mountains, mts., Ar., U.S.	107	35°46'N	93°32'W
Botany Bay, b., Austl. (bŏt´ȧ-nĭ)	221	33°58'S	151°11'E
Botevgrad, Blg.	175	42°54'N	23°41'E
Bothaville, S. Afr. (bō´tȧ-vĭl)	238c	27°24'S	26°38'E
Bothell, Wa., U.S. (bŏth´ĕl)	116a	47°46'N	122°12'W
Bothnia, Gulf of, b., Eur. (bŏth´nĭ-ȧ)	156	63°40'N	21°30'E
Botoşani, Rom. (bō-tô-shän´ĭ)	169	47°46'N	26°40'E
Botswana, nation, Afr. (bŏtswănă)	232	22°10'S	23°13'E
Bottineau, N.D., U.S. (bŏt-ĭ-nō´)	112	48°48'N	100°28'W
Bottrop, Ger. (bōt´trōp)	168	51°31'N	6°56'E
Botwood, Can. (bŏt´wŏŏd)	93a	49°08'N	55°21'W
Bouafle, C. Iv. (bō-á-flā´)	230	6°59'N	5°45'W
Bouar, C.A.R. (bōō-är)	231	5°57'N	15°36'E
Bou Areg, Sebkha, Mor.	172	35°09'N	3°02'W
Boubandjidah, Parc National de, rec., Cam.	235	8°20'N	14°40'E
Boucherville, Can. (bōō-shȧ-vēl´)	102a	45°37'N	73°27'W
Boudenib, Mor. (bōō-dĕ-nēb´)	230	32°14'N	3°04'W
Boudette, Mn., U.S. (bōō-dĕt)	113	48°42'N	94°34'W
Boudouaou, Alg.	173	36°44'N	3°25'E
Boufarik, Alg. (bōō-fȧ-rēk´)	173	36°35'N	2°55'E
Bougainville, i., Pap. N. Gui.	214e	6°00'S	155°00'E
Bougainville Trench, deep (bōō-găn-vēl´)	241	7°00'S	152°00'E
Bougie *see* Bejaïa, Alg.	230	36°46'N	5°00'E
Bougouni, Mali (bōō-gōō-nē´)	230	11°27'N	7°30'W
Bouïra, Alg. (boo-ē´rȧ)	162	36°25'N	3°55'E
Bouïra-Sahary, Alg. (bwē-rȧ sȧ´ȧ-rē)	173	35°16'N	3°23'E
Bouka, r., Gui.	234	11°05'N	10°40'W
Boulder, Co., U.S.	104	40°02'N	105°19'W
Boulder, r., Mt., U.S.	115	46°10'N	112°07'W
Boulder City, Nv., U.S.	104	35°57'N	114°50'W
Boulder Peak, mtn., Id., U.S.	115	43°53'N	114°33'W
Boulogne-Billancourt, Fr. (bōō-lôn´y´-bē-yän-kōōr´)	170	48°50'N	2°14'E
Boulogne-sur-Mer, Fr. (bōō-lôn´y-sür-mâr´)	161	50°44'N	1°37'E
Boumba, r., Cam.	235	3°20'N	14°40'E
Bouna, C. Iv. (bōō-nä´)	230	9°16'N	3°00'W
Bouna, Parc National de, rec., C. Iv.	234	9°20'N	3°35'W
Boundary Bay, b., N.A. (boun´dȧ-rĭ)	116d	49°03'N	122°59'W
Boundary Peak, mtn., Nv., U.S.	118	37°52'N	118°20'W
Bound Brook, N.J., U.S. (bound brŏŏk)	110a	40°34'N	74°32'W
Bountiful, Ut., U.S. (boun´tĭ-fŏŏl)	117b	40°55'N	111°53'W
Bountiful Peak, mtn., Ut., U.S. (boun´tĭ-fŏŏl)	117b	40°58'N	111°49'W
Bounty Islands, is., N.Z.	5	47°42'S	179°05'E
Bourail, N. Cal.	214f	21°34'S	165°30'E
Bourem, Mali (bōō-rĕm´)	230	16°43'N	0°15'W
Bourg-en-Bresse, Fr. (bōōr-gĕn-brĕs´)	161	46°12'N	5°13'E
Bourges, Fr. (bōōrzh)	161	47°06'N	2°22'E
Bourget, Can. (bōōr-zhĕ´)	102c	45°26'N	75°09'W
Bourgoin, Fr. (bōōr-gwăn´)	171	45°46'N	5°17'E
Bourke, Austl. (bŭrk)	219	30°10'S	146°00'E
Bourne, Eng., U.K. (bôrn)	158a	52°46'N	0°22'W
Bournemouth, Eng., U.K. (bôrn´mŭth)	164	50°44'N	1°55'W
Bou Saâda, Alg. (bōō-sä´dä)	162	35°13'N	4°17'E
Bousso, Chad (bōō-sô´)	231	10°33'N	16°45'E
Boutilimit, Maur.	230	17°30'N	14°54'W
Bouvetøya, i., Ant.	3	55°00'S	3°00'E
Bow, r., Can. (bō)	92	50°35'N	112°15'W
Bowbells, N.D., U.S. (bō´bĕls)	112	48°50'N	102°16'W
Bowdle, S.D., U.S. (bōd´'l)	112	45°28'N	99°42'W
Bowen, Austl. (bō´ĕn)	219	20°02'S	148°14'E
Bowie, Md., U.S. (bōō´ĭ) (bō´ē)	110e	38°59'N	76°47'W
Bowie, Tx., U.S.	121	33°34'N	97°50'W

PRONOUNCING INDEX

Bowling Green – Brownsville 275

PLACE (Pronunciation)	PAGE	LAT.	LONG.
Bowling Green, Ky., U.S. (bōlĭng grēn)	105	37°00'N	86°26'W
Bowling Green, Mo., U.S.	121	39°19'N	91°09'W
Bowling Green, Oh., U.S.	108	41°25'N	83°40'W
Bowman, N.D., U.S. (bō′măn)	112	46°11'N	103°23'W
Bowron, r., Can. (bō′rŭn)	95	53°20'N	121°10'W
Boxelder Creek, r., Mt., U.S. (bŏks′ĕl-dẽr)	112	45°35'N	104°28'W
Box Elder Creek, r., Mt., U.S.	115	47°17'N	108°37'W
Box Hill, Austl.	217a	37°49'S	145°08'E
Boxian, China (bwo shyĕn)	208	33°52'N	115°47'E
Boxing, China (bwo-shyĭŋ)	206	37°09'N	118°08'E
Boxtel, Neth.	159a	51°40'N	5°21'E
Boyabo, D.R.C.	236	3°43'N	18°46'E
Boyang, China (bwo-yäŋ)	209	29°00'N	116°42'E
Boyer, r., Can. (boi′ẽr)	102b	46°45'N	70°56'W
Boyer, r., Ia., U.S.	112	41°45'N	95°36'W
Boyle, Ire. (boil)	164	53°59'N	8°15'W
Boyne, r., Ire. (boin)	164	53°40'N	6°40'W
Boyne City, Mi., U.S.	108	45°15'N	85°05'W
Boyoma Falls, wtfl., D.R.C.	231	0°30'N	25°12'E
Boysen Reservoir, res., Wy., U.S.	115	43°19'N	108°11'W
Bozcaada, Tur. (bōz-cä′dä)	175	39°50'N	26°05'E
Bozca Ada, i., Tur.	175	39°50'N	26°00'E
Bozeman, Mt., U.S. (bōz′măn)	104	45°41'N	111°00'W
Bozene, D.R.C.	236	2°56'N	19°12'E
Bozhen, China (bwo-jŭn)	206	38°05'N	116°35'E
Bozoum, C.A.R.	235	6°19'N	16°23'E
Bra, Italy (brä)	174	44°41'N	7°52'E
Bracciano, Lago di, l., Italy (lä′gō-dē-brä-chä′nō)	174	42°05'N	12°00'E
Bracebridge, Can. (brās′brĭj)	99	45°05'N	79°20'W
Braceville, Il., U.S. (brās′vĭl)	111a	41°13'N	88°16'W
Bräcke, Swe. (brĕk′kĕ)	160	62°44'N	15°28'E
Brackenridge, Pa., U.S. (brăk′ĕn-rĭj)	111e	40°37'N	79°44'W
Brackettville, Tx., U.S. (brăk′ĕt-vĭl)	122	29°19'N	100°24'W
Braço Maior, mth., Braz.	143	11°00'S	51°00'W
Braço Menor, mth., Braz. (brä′zō-mĕ-nō′r)	143	11°38'S	50°00'W
Bradano, r., Italy (brä-dä′nō)	174	40°43'N	16°22'E
Bradenton, Fl., U.S. (brā′dĕn-tŭn)	125a	27°28'N	82°35'W
Bradfield, Eng., U.K. (brăd′fēld)	158b	51°25'N	1°08'W
Bradford, Eng., U.K. (brăd′fẽrd)	160	53°47'N	1°44'W
Bradford, Oh., U.S.	108	40°10'N	84°30'W
Bradford, Pa., U.S.	109	42°00'N	78°40'W
Bradley, Il., U.S. (brăd′lĭ)	111a	41°09'N	87°52'W
Bradner, Can. (brăd′nẽr)	116d	49°05'N	122°26'W
Brady, Tx., U.S. (brā′dĭ)	122	31°09'N	99°21'W
Braga, Port. (brä′gä)	162	41°20'N	8°25'W
Bragado, Arg. (brä-gä′dō)	144	35°07'S	60°28'W
Bragança, Braz. (brä-gän′sä)	143	1°02'S	46°50'W
Bragança, Port.	172	41°48'N	6°46'W
Bragança Paulista, Braz. (brä-gän′sä-pä′o͞o-lē′s-tà)	144	22°58'S	46°31'W
Bragg Creek, Can. (brăg)	102e	50°57'N	114°35'W
Brahmaputra, r., Asia (brä′mȧ-po͞o′trȧ)	199	26°45'N	92°45'E
Brāhui, mts., Pak.	199	28°32'N	66°15'E
Braidwood, Il., U.S. (brād′wo͝od)	111a	41°16'N	88°13'W
Brăila, Rom. (brē′ēlȧ)	154	45°15'N	27°58'E
Brainerd, Mn., U.S. (brān′ẽrd)	113	46°20'N	94°09'W
Braintree, Ma., U.S. (brān′trē)	101a	42°14'N	71°00'W
Braithwaite, La., U.S. (brīth′wīt)	110d	29°52'N	89°57'W
Brakpan, S. Afr. (brăk′păn)	233b	26°15'S	28°22'E
Bralorne, Can. (brā′lôrn)	95	50°47'N	122°49'W
Bramalea, Can.	102d	43°48'N	79°41'W
Brampton, Can. (brămp′tŭn)	99	43°41'N	79°46'W
Branca, Pedra, mtn., Braz. (pĕ′drä-brà′n-kä)	144b	22°55'S	43°28'W
Branchville, N.J., U.S. (branch′vĭl)	110a	41°09'S	74°44'W
Branchville, S.C., U.S.	125	33°17'N	80°48'W
Branco, r., Braz. (bräŋ′kō)	143	2°21'N	60°38'W
Brandberg, mtn., Nmb.	232	21°15'S	14°15'E
Brandenburg, Ger. (brän′dĕn-bo͝orgh)	161	52°25'N	12°33'E
Brandenburg, state, Ger.	159b	52°15'N	13°00'E
Brandenburg, hist. reg., Ger.	168	52°12'N	13°31'E
Brandfort, S. Afr. (brăn′d-fôrt)	238c	28°42'S	26°29'E
Brandon, Can. (brăn′dŭn)	90	49°50'N	99°57'W
Brandon, Vt., U.S.	109	43°45'N	73°05'W
Brandon Mountain, mtn., Ire. (brăn-dŏn)	164	52°15'N	10°12'W
Brandywine, Md., U.S. (brăndĭ′wīn)	110e	38°42'N	76°51'W
Branford, Ct., U.S. (brăn′fẽrd)	109	41°15'N	72°50'W
Braniewo, Pol. (brä-nyĕ′vô)	169	54°23'N	19°50'E
Brańsk, Pol. (brän′ sk)	169	52°44'N	22°51'E
Branson, Mo., U.S.	121	36°39'N	93°13'W
Brantford, Can. (brănt′fẽrd)	99	43°09'N	80°17'W
Bras d'Or Lake, l., Can. (brä-dôr′)	101	45°52'N	60°50'W
Brasília, Braz. (brä-sē′lvä)	143	15°49'S	47°39'W
Brasília Legal, Braz.	143	3°45'S	55°46'W
Brasópolis, Braz. (brä-sô′pō-lēs)	141a	22°30'S	45°36'W
Braşov, Rom.	163	45°39'N	25°35'E
Brass, Nig. (brăs)	230	4°28'N	6°28'E
Brasschaat, Bel. (bräs′kät)	159a	51°19'N	4°30'E
Bratenahl, Oh., U.S. (bră′tĕn-ôl)	111d	41°34'N	81°36'W
Bratislava, Slvk. (brä′tĭs-lä-vä)	154	48°09'N	17°07'E
Bratsk, Russia (brätsk)	179	56°10'N	102°04'E
Bratskoye Vodokhranilishche, res., Russia	179	56°10'N	102°05'E
Bratslav, Ukr. (brät′slâf)	177	48°48'N	28°59'E
Brattleboro, Vt., U.S. (brăt′'l-bŭr-ô)	109	42°50'N	72°35'W
Braunau, Aus. (brou′nou)	168	48°15'N	13°05'E
Braunschweig, Ger. (broun′shvīgh)	161	52°16'N	10°32'E

PLACE (Pronunciation)	PAGE	LAT.	LONG.
Bråviken, r., Swe.	166	58°40'N	16°40'E
Brawley, Ca., U.S. (brô′lĭ)	104	32°59'N	115°32'W
Bray, Ire. (brā)	164	53°10'N	6°05'W
Braymer, Mo., U.S. (brā′mẽr)	121	39°34'N	93°47'W
Brays Bay, Tx., U.S. (brās′bī′yo͞o)	123a	29°41'N	95°33'W
Brazeau, r., Can.	95	52°55'N	116°10'W
Brazeau, Mount, mtn., Can. (brä-zō′)	95	52°33'N	117°21'W
Brazil, In., U.S. (brȧ-zĭl′)	108	39°30'N	87°00'W
Brazil, nation, S.A.	143	9°00'S	53°00'W
Brazilian Highlands, mts., Braz. (brȧ zĭl yȧn hī-lȧndz)	139	14°00'S	48°00'W
Brazos, r., Tx., U.S. (brä′zōs)	106	33°10'N	98°50'W
Brazos, Clear Fork, r., Tx., U.S.	122	32°56'N	99°14'W
Brazos, Double Mountain Fork, r., Tx., U.S.	120	33°23'N	101°21'W
Brazos, Salt Fork, r., Tx., U.S. (sôlt fôrk)	120	33°20'N	101°57'W
Brazzaville, Congo (brá-zá-vēl′)	232	4°16'S	15°17'E
Brčko, Bos. (bẽrch′kô)	175	44°54'N	18°49'E
Brda, r., Pol. (bẽr-da)	169	53°18'N	17°55'E
Brea, Ca., U.S. (brē′ȧ)	117a	33°55'N	117°54'W
Breakeyville, Can.	102b	46°40'N	71°13'W
Breckenridge, Mn., U.S. (brĕk′ĕn-rĭj)	112	46°17'N	96°35'W
Breckenridge, Tx., U.S.	122	32°46'N	98°53'W
Brecksville, Oh., U.S. (brĕks′vĭl)	111d	41°19'N	81°38'W
Břeclav, Czech Rep. (brzhĕl′láf)	168	48°46'N	16°54'E
Breda, Neth. (brā-dä′)	165	51°35'N	4°47'E
Bredasdorp, S. Afr. (brā′das-dôrp)	232	34°15'S	20°00'E
Bredy, Russia (brĕ′dĭ)	186a	52°25'N	60°23'E
Bregenz, Aus. (brā′gĕnts)	168	47°30'N	9°46'E
Bregovo, Blg. (brĕ′gô-vô)	175	44°07'N	22°45'E
Breidafjördur, b., Ice.	160	65°15'N	22°50'W
Breidbach, S. Afr. (brĕd′băk)	233c	32°54'S	27°26'E
Breil-sur-Roya, Fr. (brĕ′y′)	171	43°57'N	7°36'E
Brejo, Braz. (brå′zhô)	143	3°33'S	42°46'W
Bremangerlandet, i., Nor.	166	61°51'N	4°25'E
Bremen, Ger. (brā-mĕn)	154	53°05'N	8°50'E
Bremen, In., U.S. (brē′mĕn)	108	41°25'N	86°05'W
Bremerhaven, Ger. (brām-ẽr-hä′fĕn)	160	53°33'N	8°38'E
Bremerton, Wa., U.S. (brĕm′ẽr-tŭn)	114	47°34'N	122°38'W
Bremervörde, Ger. (brĕ′mẽr-fûr-dĕ)	159c	53°29'N	9°09'E
Bremner, Can. (brĕm′nẽr)	102g	53°34'N	113°14'W
Bremond, Tx., U.S. (brĕm′ŭnd)	123	31°11'N	96°40'W
Brenham, Tx., U.S. (brĕn′ăm)	123	30°10'N	96°24'W
Brenner Pass, p., Eur. (brĕn′ẽr)	161	47°00'N	11°30'E
Brentwood, Eng., U.K. (brĕnt′wo͝od)	165	51°37'N	0°18'E
Brentwood, Md., U.S.	109	39°00'N	76°55'W
Brentwood, Mo., U.S.	117e	38°37'N	90°21'W
Brentwood, Pa., U.S.	111e	40°22'N	79°59'W
Brescia, Italy (brā′shä)	162	45°33'N	10°15'E
Bressanone, Italy (brĕs-sä-nō′nā)	174	46°42'N	11°40'E
Bressuire, Fr. (grĕ-swēr′)	170	46°49'N	0°14'W
Brest, Bela.	178	52°06'N	23°43'E
Brest, Fr. (brĕst)	154	48°24'N	4°30'W
Brest, prov., Bela.	176	52°30'N	26°50'E
Bretagne, hist. reg., Fr. (brĕ-täN′yĕ)	170	48°00'N	3°00'W
Breton, Pertuis, strt., Fr. (pâr-twē′brĕ-tôN′)	170	46°18'N	1°43'W
Breton Sound, strt., La., U.S. (brĕt′ŭn)	124	29°38'N	89°15'W
Breukelen, Neth.	159a	52°09'N	5°00'E
Brevard, N.C., U.S. (brē-värd′)	125	35°14'N	82°45'W
Breves, Braz. (brā′vĕzh)	143	1°32'S	50°13'W
Brevik, Nor. (brĕ′vĕk)	166	59°04'N	9°39'E
Brewarrina, Austl. (bro͞o-ẽr-rē′nȧ)	219	29°54'S	146°50'E
Brewer, Me., U.S. (bro͞o′ẽr)	100	44°46'N	68°46'W
Brewerville, Lib.	234	6°26'N	10°47'W
Brewster, N.Y., U.S. (bro͞o′stẽr)	110a	41°23'N	73°38'W
Brewster, Cerro, mtn., Pan. (sĕ′r-rô-bro͞o′stẽr)	133	9°19'N	79°15'W
Brewton, Al., U.S. (bro͞o′tŭn)	124	31°06'N	87°04'W
Brežice, Slvn. (brĕ′zhē-tsĕ)	174	45°55'N	15°37'E
Breznik, Blg. (brĕs′nĕk)	175	42°44'N	22°55'E
Briancon, Fr. (brē-äN-sôN′)	171	44°54'N	6°39'E
Briare, Fr. (brē-är′)	170	47°40'N	2°46'E
Bridal Veil, Or., U.S. (brīd′ȧl vāl)	116c	45°33'N	122°10'W
Bridge Point, c., Bah. (brĭj)	134	25°35'N	76°40'W
Bridgeport, Al., U.S. (brĭj′pôrt)	124	34°55'N	85°42'W
Bridgeport, Ct., U.S.	105	41°12'N	73°12'W
Bridgeport, Il., U.S.	108	38°40'N	87°45'W
Bridgeport, Ne., U.S.	112	41°40'N	103°06'W
Bridgeport, Oh., U.S.	108	40°00'N	80°45'W
Bridgeport, Pa., U.S.	110f	40°06'N	75°21'W
Bridgeport, Tx., U.S.	121	33°13'N	97°46'W
Bridgeton, Al., U.S. (brĭj′tŭn)	110h	33°27'N	86°39'W
Bridgeton, Mo., U.S.	117e	38°45'N	90°23'W
Bridgeton, N.J., U.S.	109	39°30'N	75°15'W
Bridgetown, Barb. (brĭj′ toun)	129	13°08'N	59°37'W
Bridgetown, Can.	100	44°51'N	65°18'W
Bridgeville, Pa., U.S. (brĭj′vĭl)	111e	40°22'N	80°07'W
Bridgewater, Austl. (brĭj′wô-tẽr)	222	42°50'S	147°28'E
Bridgewater, Can.	91	44°23'N	64°31'W
Bridgnorth, Eng., U.K. (brĭj′nôrth)	158a	52°32'N	2°25'W
Bridgton, Me., U.S. (brĭj′tŭn)	100	44°04'N	70°45'W
Bridlington, Eng., U.K. (brĭd′lĭng-tŭn)	164	54°06'N	0°10'W
Brie-Comte-Robert, Fr. (brē-kôNt-ĕ-rō-bâr′)	171b	48°42'N	2°37'E
Brielle, Neth.	159a	51°54'N	4°08'E
Brierfield, Eng., U.K. (brī′ẽr fēld)	158a	53°49'N	2°14'W
Brierfield, Al., U.S. (brī′ẽr-fēld)	124	33°01'N	86°55'W
Brier Island, i., Can. (brī′ẽr)	100	44°16'N	66°24'W
Brieselang, Ger. (brē′zĕ-läng)	159b	52°36'N	12°59'E
Briey, Fr. (brē-ĕ′)	171	49°15'N	5°57'E
Brig, Switz. (brēg)	161	46°17'N	7°59'E
Brigg, Eng., U.K. (brĭg)	158a	53°33'N	0°29'W

PLACE (Pronunciation)	PAGE	LAT.	LONG.
Brigham City, Ut., U.S. (brĭg′ăm)	117b	41°31'N	112°01'W
Brighouse, Eng., U.K. (brĭg′hous)	158a	53°42'N	1°47'W
Bright, Austl. (brīt)	222	36°43'S	147°00'E
Bright, In., U.S. (brīt)	111f	39°13'N	84°51'W
Brightlingsea, Eng., U.K. (brī′t-lĭng-sē)	158b	51°50'N	1°00'E
Brighton, Austl.	217a	37°55'S	145°00'E
Brighton, Eng., U.K.	161	50°47'N	0°07'W
Brighton, Al., U.S. (brīt′ŭn)	110h	33°27'N	86°56'W
Brighton, Co., U.S.	120	39°58'N	104°49'W
Brighton, Ia., U.S.	113	41°11'N	91°47'W
Brighton, Il., U.S.	117e	39°03'N	90°08'W
Brighton Indian Reservation, I.R., Fl., U.S.	125a	27°05'N	81°25'W
Brihuega, Spain (brē-wā′gä)	172	40°32'N	2°52'W
Brimley, Mi., U.S. (brĭm′lē)	117k	46°24'N	84°34'W
Brindisi, Italy (brēn′dē-zē)	154	40°38'N	17°57'E
Brinje, Cro. (brēn′yĕ)	174	45°00'N	15°08'E
Brinkley, Ar., U.S. (brĭŋk′lĭ)	121	34°52'N	91°12'W
Brinnon, Wa., U.S. (brĭn′ŭn)	116a	47°41'N	122°54'W
Brion, i., Can. (brē-ôN′)	101	47°47'N	61°29'W
Brioude, Fr. (brē-o͞od′)	170	45°18'N	3°22'E
Brisbane, Austl. (brĭz′bȧn)	222	27°30'S	153°10'E
Bristol, Eng., U.K.	161	51°29'N	2°39'W
Bristol, Ct., U.S. (brĭs′tŭl)	109	41°40'N	72°55'W
Bristol, Pa., U.S.	110f	40°06'N	74°51'W
Bristol, R.I., U.S.	110b	41°41'N	71°14'W
Bristol, Tn., U.S.	105	36°35'N	82°10'W
Bristol, Va., U.S.	105	36°36'N	82°00'W
Bristol, Vt., U.S.	109	44°10'N	73°00'W
Bristol, Wi., U.S.	111a	42°32'N	88°04'W
Bristol Bay, b., Ak., U.S.	103	58°05'N	158°54'W
Bristol Channel, strt., Eng., U.K.	161	51°20'N	3°47'W
Bristow, Ok., U.S. (brĭs′tō)	121	35°50'N	96°25'W
British Columbia, prov., Can. (brĭt′ĭsh kŏl′ŭm-bĭ-ȧ)	90	56°00'N	124°53'W
British Indian Ocean Territory, dep., Afr.	2	7°00'S	72°00'E
British Isles, is., Eur.	156	54°00'N	4°00'W
Brits, S. Afr.	238c	25°39'S	27°47'E
Britstown, S. Afr. (brĭts′toun)	232	30°30'S	23°40'E
Britt, Ia., U.S. (brĭt)	113	43°05'N	93°47'W
Brittany *see* Bretagne, hist. reg., Fr.	170	48°00'N	3°00'W
Britton, S.D., U.S. (brĭt′ŭn)	112	45°47'N	97°44'W
Brive-la-Gaillarde, Fr. (brēv-lä-gī-yärd′ĕ)	161	45°10'N	1°31'E
Briviesca, Spain (brē-vyās′kȧ)	172	42°34'N	3°21'W
Brno, Czech Rep. (b′r′nô)	154	49°18'N	16°37'E
Broa, Ensenada de la, b., Cuba	134	22°30'N	82°00'W
Broach, India	202	21°47'N	72°58'E
Broad, r., Ga., U.S. (brôd)	124	34°15'N	83°14'W
Broad, r., N.C., U.S.	125	35°38'N	82°40'W
Broadmeadows, Austl. (brôd′mĕd-ōz)	217a	37°40'S	144°53'E
Broadview Heights, Oh., U.S. (brôd′vū)	111d	41°18'N	81°41'W
Brockport, N.Y., U.S. (brŏk′pōrt)	109	43°15'N	77°55'W
Brockton, Ma., U.S. (brŏk′tŭn)	101a	42°04'N	71°01'W
Brockville, Can. (brŏk′vĭl)	91	44°35'N	75°40'W
Brockway, Mt., U.S. (brŏk′wā)	115	47°24'N	105°41'W
Brodnica, Pol. (brôd′nĭt-sȧ)	169	53°16'N	19°26'E
Brody, Ukr. (brô′dĭ)	181	50°05'N	25°10'E
Broken Arrow, Ok., U.S. (brō′kĕn ăr′ō)	121	36°03'N	95°48'W
Broken Bay, b., Austl.	222	33°34'S	151°20'E
Broken Bow, Ne., U.S. (brō′kĕn bō)	112	41°24'N	99°37'W
Broken Bow, Ok., U.S.	121	34°02'N	94°43'W
Broken Hill, Austl. (brōk′ĕn)	219	31°55'S	141°35'E
Broken Hill *see* Kabwe, Zam.	232	14°27'S	28°27'E
Bromley, Eng., U.K. (brŭm′lĭ)	158b	51°23'N	0°01'E
Bromptonville, Can. (brŭmp′tŭn-vĭl)	99	45°30'N	72°00'W
Brønderslev, Den. (brûn′dẽr-slĕv)	166	57°15'N	9°56'E
Bronkhorstspruit, S. Afr.	238c	25°50'S	28°48'E
Bronnitsy, Russia (brô-nyĭ′tsĭ)	176	55°26'N	38°16'E
Bronson, Mi., U.S. (brŏn′sŭn)	108	41°55'N	85°15'W
Bronte Creek, r., Can.	102d	43°25'N	79°53'W
Brood, r., S.C., U.S. (bro͞od)	125	34°46'N	81°25'W
Brookfield, Il., U.S. (bro͝ok′fēld)	111a	41°49'N	87°51'W
Brookfield, Mo., U.S.	121	39°45'N	93°04'W
Brookhaven, Ga., U.S. (bro͝ok′hāv′n)	110c	33°52'N	84°21'W
Brookhaven, Ms., U.S.	124	31°35'N	90°26'W
Brookings, Or., U.S. (bro͝ok′ĭngs)	114	42°04'N	124°16'W
Brookings, S.D., U.S.	112	44°18'N	96°47'W
Brookline, Ma., U.S. (bro͝ok′līn)	101a	42°20'N	71°08'W
Brookline, N.H., U.S.	101a	42°44'N	71°37'W
Brooklyn, Oh., U.S. (bro͝ok′lĭn)	111d	41°26'N	81°44'W
Brooklyn Center, Mn., U.S.	117g	45°05'N	93°21'W
Brook Park, Oh., U.S. (bro͝ok)	111d	41°24'N	81°50'W
Brooks, Can.	95	50°35'N	111°53'W
Brooks Range, mts., Ak., U.S. (bro͝oks)	106a	68°20'N	159°00'W
Brooksville, Fl., U.S. (bro͝oks′vĭl)	125a	28°32'N	82°28'W
Brookville, In., U.S. (bro͝ok′vĭl)	108	39°20'N	85°00'W
Brookville, Pa., U.S.	109	41°10'N	79°00'W
Brookwood, Al., U.S. (bro͝ok′wo͝od)	124	33°15'N	87°17'W
Broome, Austl. (bro͞om)	218	18°00'S	122°15'E
Brossard, Can.	102a	45°26'N	73°28'W
Brothers, is., Bah. (brŭd′hẽrs)	134	26°05'N	79°00'W
Broumov, Czech Rep. (bro͞o′môf)	168	50°33'N	15°55'E
Brown Bank, bk.	135	21°30'N	74°35'W
Brownfield, Tx., U.S. (broun′fēld)	120	33°11'N	102°16'W
Browning, Mt., U.S. (broun′ĭng)	115	48°37'N	113°05'W
Brownsboro, Ky., U.S. (brounz′bō-rô)	111h	38°22'N	85°30'W
Brownsburg, Can. (brouns′bûrg)	102a	45°40'N	74°24'W
Brownsburg, In., U.S.	111g	39°51'N	86°23'W
Brownsmead, Or., U.S. (brounz′-mēd)	116c	46°13'N	123°33'W
Brownstown, In., U.S. (brounz′toun)	108	38°50'N	86°00'W
Brownsville, Pa., U.S. (brounz′vĭl)	111e	40°01'N	79°53'W
Brownsville, Tn., U.S.	124	35°35'N	89°15'W

ng-sing; ŋ-baŋk; N-nasalized n; nŏd; cŏmmit; ōld; ôbey; ôrder; oi-boil; fo͞od; o͝o-as oo in foot; ou-out; s-soft; sh-dish; th-thin; pūre; ûnite; ûrn; stŭd; circŭs; ü-as in French tu; ′-indeterminate vowel.

276 Brownsville – Byeshankovichy PRONOUNCING INDEX

PLACE (Pronunciation)	PAGE	LAT.	LONG.
Brownsville, Tx., U.S.	104	25°55'N	97°30'W
Brownville Junction, Me., U.S. (broun'vĭl)	100	45°20'N	69°04'W
Brownwood, Tx., U.S. (broun'wo͝od)	104	31°44'N	98°58'W
Brownwood, l., Tx., U.S.	122	31°55'N	99°15'W
Brozas, Spain (brō'thäs)	172	39°37'N	6°44'W
Bruce, Mount, mtn., Austl. (bro͞os)	220	22°35'S	118°15'E
Bruce Peninsula, pen., Can.	98	44°50'N	81°20'W
Bruceton, Tn., U.S. (bro͞os'tŭn)	124	36°02'N	88°14'W
Bruchsal, Ger. (bro͝ok'zäl)	168	49°08'N	8°34'E
Bruck, Aus. (bro͝ok)	168	47°25'N	15°14'E
Bruck, Aus.	168	48°01'N	16°47'E
Brück, Ger. (brük)	159b	52°12'N	12°45'E
Bruderheim, Can. (bro͞o'dĕr-hīm)	102g	53°47'N	112°56'W
Brugge, Bel.	161	51°13'N	3°05'E
Brühl, Ger. (brül)	171c	50°49'N	6°54'E
Bruneau, r., Id., U.S. (bro͞o-nō')	114	42°47'N	115°43'W
Brunei, nation, Asia (bro͝o-nī')	212	4°52'N	113°38'E
Brünen, Ger. (brü'nĕn)	171c	51°43'N	6°41'E
Brunete, Spain (bro͞o-nā'tå)	173a	40°24'N	4°00'W
Brunette, i., Can. (bro͝o-nĕt')	101	47°16'N	55°54'W
Brunn am Gebirge, Aus. (bro͞on'äm gĕ-bĭr'gĕ)	159e	48°07'N	16°18'E
Brunsbüttel, Ger. (bro͝ons'büt-tĕl)	159c	53°58'N	9°10'E
Brunswick, Ga., U.S. (brŭnz'wĭk)	105	31°08'N	81°30'W
Brunswick, Md., U.S.	109	39°20'N	77°35'W
Brunswick, Me., U.S.	100	43°54'N	69°57'W
Brunswick, Mo., U.S.	121	39°25'N	93°07'W
Brunswick, Oh., U.S.	111d	41°14'N	81°50'W
Brunswick, Península de, pen., Chile	144	53°25'S	71°15'W
Bruny, i., Austl. (bro͞o'nē)	221	43°30'S	147°50'E
Brush, Co., U.S. (brŭsh)	120	40°14'N	103°40'W
Brusque, Braz. (bro͞o's-ko͞o'ĕ)	144	27°15'S	48°45'W
Brussels, Bel.	154	50°51'N	4°21'E
Brussels, Il., U.S. (brŭs'ĕls)	117e	38°57'N	90°36'W
Bruxelles *see* Brussels, Bel.	154	50°51'N	4°21'E
Bryan, Oh., U.S. (brī'ăn)	108	41°25'N	84°30'W
Bryan, Tx., U.S.	123	30°40'N	96°22'W
Bryansk, Russia	178	53°15'N	34°22'E
Bryansk, prov., Russia	176	52°43'N	32°25'E
Bryant, S.D., U.S. (brī'ănt)	112	44°35'N	97°29'W
Bryant, Wa., U.S.	116a	48°14'N	122°10'W
Bryce Canyon National Park, rec., Ut., U.S. (brīs)	106	37°35'N	112°15'W
Bryn Mawr, Pa., U.S. (brĭn mär')	110f	40°02'N	75°20'W
Bryson City, N.C., U.S. (brĭs'ŭn)	124	35°25'N	83°25'W
Bryukhovetskaya, Russia (b'ryŭk'ô-vyĕt-skä'yä)	177	45°56'N	38°58'E
Buala, Sol. Is.	214e	8°08'S	159°35'E
Buatan, Indon.	197b	0°45'N	101°49'E
Buba, Gui.-B. (bo͞o'bȧ)	230	11°39'N	14°58'W
Bucaramanga, Col. (bo͞o-kä'rä-mäŋ'gä)	142	7°12'N	73°14'W
Buccaneer Archipelago, is., Austl. (bŭk-ȧ-nēr')	220	16°05'S	122°00'E
Buchach, Ukr. (bo͝o'chách)	169	49°04'N	25°25'E
Buchanan, Lib. (bů-kăn'ăn)	230	5°57'N	10°02'W
Buchanan, Mi., U.S.	108	41°50'N	86°25'W
Buchanan, l., Austl. (bû-kân'nŏn)	221	21°40'S	145°00'E
Buchanan, l., Tx., U.S. (bû-kăn'ăn)	122	30°55'N	98°40'W
Buchans, Can.	101	48°49'N	56°52'W
Bucharest, Rom.	154	44°23'N	26°10'E
Buchholz, Ger. (bo͞ok'hōltz)	159c	53°19'N	9°53'E
Buck Creek, r., In., U.S. (bŭk)	111g	39°43'N	85°58'W
Buckhannon, W.V., U.S. (bŭk-hăn'ŭn)	108	39°00'N	80°10'W
Buckhaven, Scot., U.K. (bŭk-hā'v'n)	164	56°10'N	3°10'W
Buckie, Scot., U.K. (bŭk'ĭ)	164	57°40'N	2°50'W
Buckingham, Can. (bŭk'ĭng-ăm)	102c	45°35'N	75°25'W
Buckingham, can., India (bŭk'ĭng-ăm)	203	15°18'N	79°50'E
Buckinghamshire, co., Eng., U.K.	158b	51°45'N	0°48'W
Buckland, Can. (bŭk'lănd)	102b	46°37'N	70°33'W
Buckland Tableland, reg., Austl.	221	24°31'S	148°00'E
Buckley, Wa., U.S. (bŭk'lē)	116a	47°10'N	122°02'W
Bucksport, Me., U.S. (bŭks'pôrt)	100	44°35'N	68°47'W
Buctouche, Can. (bük-to͞osh')	100	46°28'N	64°43'W
Bucun, China (bo͞o-tso͝on)	206	36°38'N	117°26'E
București *see* Bucharest, Rom.	154	44°23'N	26°10'E
Bucyrus, Oh., U.S. (bů-sī'rŭs)	108	40°50'N	82°55'W
Budapest, Hung. (bo͞o'dȧ-pĕsht')	154	47°30'N	19°05'E
Budge Budge, India	202a	22°28'N	88°08'E
Budjala, D.R.C.	236	2°39'N	19°42'E
Budyonnovsk, Russia	182	44°46'N	44°09'E
Buea, Cam.	235	4°09'N	9°14'E
Buechel, Ky., U.S. (bĕ-chûl')	111h	38°12'N	85°38'W
Bueil, Fr. (bwā')	171b	48°55'N	1°27'E
Buena Park, Ca., U.S. (bwā'nȧ pärk)	117a	33°52'N	118°00'W
Buenaventura, Col. (bwā'nä-vĕn-to͞o'rá)	142	3°46'N	77°09'W
Buenaventura, Cuba	135a	22°53'N	82°22'W
Buenaventura, Bahía de, b., Col.	142	3°45'N	79°23'W
Buena Vista, Co., U.S. (bū'nȧ vĭs'tȧ)	120	38°51'N	106°07'W
Buena Vista, Ga., U.S.	124	32°15'N	84°30'W
Buena Vista, Va., U.S.	109	37°45'N	79°20'W
Buena Vista, Bahía, b., Cuba (bä-ē'ä-bwĕ-nä-vē's-tä)	134	22°30'N	79°10'W
Buena Vista Lake Bed, l., Ca., U.S. (bū'nȧ vĭs'tȧ)	118	35°14'N	119°17'W
Buendia, Embalse de, res., Spain	172	40°30'N	2°45'W
Buenos Aires, Arg. (bwā'nōs ī'rās)	144	34°20'S	58°30'W
Buenos Aires, Col.	142a	3°01'N	76°34'W
Buenos Aires, C.R.	133	9°10'N	83°21'W
Buenos Aires, prov., Arg.	144	36°15'S	61°45'W
Buenos Aires, l., S.A.	144	46°30'S	72°15'W
Buffalo, Mn., U.S. (bŭf'ȧ lō)	113	45°10'N	93°50'W
Buffalo, N.Y., U.S.	105	42°54'N	78°51'W
Buffalo, Tx., U.S.	123	31°28'N	96°04'W
Buffalo, Wy., U.S.	115	44°19'N	106°42'W
Buffalo, r., S. Afr.	233c	28°35'S	30°27'E
Buffalo, r., Ar., U.S.	121	35°56'N	92°58'W
Buffalo, r., Tn., U.S.	124	35°24'N	87°10'W
Buffalo Bayou, Tx., U.S.	123a	29°46'N	95°32'W
Buffalo Creek, r., Mn., U.S.	113	44°46'N	94°28'W
Buffalo Head Hills, hills, Can.	92	57°16'N	116°18'W
Buford, Can. (bū'fûrd)	102g	53°15'N	113°55'W
Buford, Ga., U.S. (bū'fĕrd)	124	34°05'N	84°00'W
Bug (Zakhidnyy Buh), r., Eur.	169	52°29'N	21°20'E
Buga, Col. (bo͞o'gä)	142	3°54'N	76°17'W
Buggenhout, Bel.	159a	51°01'N	4°10'E
Bygglandsfjorden, l., Nor.	166	58°53'N	7°55'E
Bugojno, Bos. (bo͝o-gō ĭ nō)	175	44°03'N	17°28'E
Bugul'ma, Russia (bo͝o-go͝ol'mȧ)	178	54°40'N	52°40'E
Buguruslan, Russia (bo͝o go͝o ro͝os lán')	178	53°30'N	52°32'E
Buhi, Phil. (bo͞o'ē)	213a	13°26'N	123°31'E
Buhl, Id., U.S. (būl)	115	42°30'N	114°45'W
Buhl, Mn., U.S.	113	47°28'N	92°49'W
Buin, Chile (bo͝o-ēn')	141b	33°44'S	70°44'W
Buinaksk, Russia (bo͝o'ĕ-näksk)	181	42°40'N	47°20'E
Buir Nur, l., Asia (bo͞o-ēr no͞or)	205	47°50'N	117°00'E
Bujalance, Spain (bo͞o-hä-län'thā)	172	37°54'N	4°22'W
Bujumbura, Bdi.	237	3°23'S	29°22'E
Buka Island, i., Pap. N. Gui.	214e	5°15'S	154°35'E
Bukama, D.R.C. (bo͞o-kä'mä)	232	9°08'S	26°00'E
Bukavu, D.R.C.	232	2°30'S	28°52'E
Bukhara, Uzb. (bo͝o-kä'rä)	183	39°31'N	64°22'E
Bukitbatu, Indon.	197b	1°25'N	101°58'E
Bukittinggi, Indon.	212	0°25'S	100°28'E
Bukoba, Tan.	232	1°20'S	31°49'E
Bukovina, hist. reg., Eur. (bo͝o-kō'vĭ-nȧ)	169	48°06'N	25°20'E
Bula, Indon. (bo͞o'lä)	213	3°00'S	130°30'E
Bulalacao, Phil. (bo͞o-lä-lä'kä-ō)	213a	12°30'N	121°20'E
Bulawayo, Zimb. (bo͞o-lȧ-wā'yō)	232	20°12'S	28°43'E
Buldir, i., Ak., U.S. (bŭl dĭr)	103a	52°22'N	175°50'E
Bulgaria, nation, Eur. (bo͝ol-gā'rĭ-ă)	154	42°12'N	24°13'E
Bulkley Ranges, mts., Can. (bŭlk'lē)	94	54°30'N	127°30'W
Bullaque, r., Spain (bo͝o-lä'kå)	172	39°15'N	4°13'W
Bullas, Spain (bo͞ol'yäs)	172	38°07'N	1°48'W
Bullfrog Creek, r., Ut., U.S.	119	37°45'N	110°55'W
Bull Harbour, Can. (hăr'bĕr)	94	50°45'N	127°55'W
Bull Head, mtn., Jam.	134	18°10'N	77°15'W
Bull Run, r., Or., U.S. (bo͝ol)	116c	45°26'N	122°11'W
Bull Run Reservoir, res., Or., U.S.	116c	45°29'N	122°11'W
Bull Shoals Reservoir, res., U.S. (bo͝ol shōlz)	107	36°35'N	92°57'W
Bulpham, Eng., U.K. (bo͝ol'făn)	158b	51°33'N	0°21'E
Bultfontein, S. Afr. (bo͝olt'fŏn-tān')	238c	28°18'S	26°10'E
Bulun, Russia (bo͞o-lo͝on')	179	70°48'N	127°27'E
Bulungu, D.R.C. (bo͞o-lo͝oŋ'go͞o)	236	6°04'S	21°54'E
Bulwer, S. Afr. (bo͝ol-wĕr)	233c	29°49'S	29°48'E
Bumba, D.R.C. (bo͝om'bȧ)	231	2°11'N	22°28'E
Bumbire Island, i., Tan.	237	1°40'S	32°05'E
Buna, Pap. N. Gui. (bo͞o'nȧ)	213	8°58'S	148°38'E
Bunbury, Austl. (bŭn'bŭrĭ)	218	33°25'S	115°45'E
Bundaberg, Austl. (bŭn'dȧ-bûrg)	219	24°45'S	152°18'E
Bunguran Utara, Kepulauan, is., Indon.	212	3°22'N	108°00'E
Bunia, D.R.C.	237	1°34'N	30°15'E
Bunker Hill, Il., U.S. (bŭnk'ĕr hĭl)	117e	39°03'N	89°57'W
Bunkie, La., U.S. (bŭŋ'kĭ)	123	30°55'N	92°10'W
Bun Plains, pl., Kenya	237	0°55'N	40°35'E
Bununu Dass, Nig.	235	10°00'N	9°31'E
Buor-Khaya, Guba, b., Russia	185	71°45'N	131°00'E
Buor Khaya, Mys, c., Russia	179	71°47'N	133°22'E
Bura, Kenya	237	1°06'S	39°57'E
Buraydah, Sau. Ar.	198	26°23'N	44°14'E
Burbank, Ca., U.S. (bûr'bănk)	117a	34°11'N	118°19'W
Burco, Som.	238a	9°20'N	45°45'E
Burdekin, r., Austl. (bûr'dē-kĭn)	221	19°22'S	145°07'E
Burdur, Tur. (bo͞or-do͞or')	163	37°50'N	30°15'E
Burdwān, India (bo͝od-wän')	199	23°29'N	87°53'E
Bureinskiy, Khrebet, mts., Russia	179	51°15'N	133°30'E
Bureya, Russia (bo͝orā'ȧ)	179	49°55'N	130°00'E
Bureya, r., Russia (bo͝o-rā'yä)	185	51°00'N	131°15'E
Burford, Eng., U.K. (bûr-fĕrd)	158b	51°46'N	1°38'W
Burgas, Blg. (bo͝or-gäs')	163	42°29'N	27°30'E
Burgas, Gulf of, b., Blg.	163	42°30'N	27°40'E
Burgaw, N.C., U.S. (bûr'gô)	125	34°31'N	77°56'W
Burgdorf, Switz. (bo͝org'dôrf)	168	47°04'N	7°37'E
Burgenland, state, Aus.	159e	47°58'N	16°57'E
Burgeo, Can.	101	47°36'N	57°34'W
Burgess, Va., U.S.	109	37°53'N	76°21'W
Burgo de Osma, Spain	172	41°35'N	3°02'W
Burgos, Mex. (bo͝or'gōs)	122	24°57'N	98°47'W
Burgos, Phil.	213a	16°03'N	119°52'E
Burgos, Spain (bo͞o'r-gōs)	162	42°20'N	3°44'W
Burgsvik, Swe. (bo͝orgs'vĭk)	166	57°04'N	18°18'E
Burhānpur, India (bo͝or'hán-po͞or)	199	21°26'N	76°08'E
Burias Island, i., Phil. (bo͞o'rē-äs)	213a	12°56'N	122°56'E
Burias Pass, strt., Phil. (bo͞o'rē-äs)	213a	13°04'N	123°11'E
Burica, Punta, c., N.A. (po͞o'n-tä-bo͞o'rē-kä)	133	8°02'N	83°12'W
Burien, Wa., U.S. (bū'rĭ-ĕn)	116a	47°28'N	122°20'W
Burin, Can. (bûr'ĭn)	93a	47°02'N	55°10'W
Burin Peninsula, pen., Can.	101	47°00'N	55°40'W
Burkburnett, Tx., U.S. (bûrk-bûr'nĕt)	120	34°04'N	98°35'W
Burke, Vt., U.S. (bûrk)	109	44°40'N	72°00'W
Burke Channel, strt., Can.	94	52°07'N	127°38'W
Burketown, Austl. (bûrk'toun)	218	17°50'S	139°30'E
Burkina Faso, nation, Afr.	230	13°00'N	2°00'W
Burley, Id., U.S. (bûr'lĭ)	115	42°31'N	113°48'W
Burley, Wa., U.S.	116a	47°25'N	122°38'W
Burlingame, Ca., U.S. (bûr'lĭn-gām)	116b	37°35'N	122°22'W
Burlingame, Ks., U.S.	121	38°45'N	95°49'W
Burlington, Can. (bûr'lĭng-tŭn)	99	43°19'N	79°48'W
Burlington, Co., U.S.	120	39°17'N	102°26'W
Burlington, Ia., U.S.	105	40°48'N	91°05'W
Burlington, Ks., U.S.	121	38°10'N	95°46'W
Burlington, Ky., U.S.	111f	39°01'N	84°44'W
Burlington, Ma., U.S.	101a	42°31'N	71°13'W
Burlington, N.C., U.S.	125	36°05'N	79°26'W
Burlington, N.J., U.S.	110f	40°04'N	74°52'W
Burlington, Vt., U.S.	105	44°30'N	73°15'W
Burlington, Wa., U.S.	116a	48°28'N	122°20'W
Burlington, Wi., U.S.	111a	42°41'N	88°16'W
Burma *see* Myanmar, nation, Asia	194	21°00'N	95°15'E
Burnaby, Can.	90	49°14'N	122°58'W
Burnet, Tx., U.S. (bûrn'ĕt)	122	30°46'N	98°14'W
Burnham on Crouch, Eng., U.K. (bûrn'ăm ŏn krouch)	156b	51°38'N	0°48'E
Burnie, Austl. (bûr'nē)	219	41°15'S	146°05'E
Burnley, Eng., U.K. (bûrn'lē)	164	53°47'N	2°19'W
Burns, Or., U.S. (bûrnz)	114	43°35'N	119°05'W
Burnside, Ky., U.S. (bûrn'sīd)	124	36°57'N	84°33'W
Burns Lake, Can. (bûrnz lăk)	90	54°14'N	125°46'W
Burnsville, Can. (bûrnz'vĭl)	100	47°44'N	65°07'W
Burnt, r., Or., U.S. (bûrnt)	114	44°26'N	117°53'W
Burntwood, r., Can.	97	55°53'N	97°30'W
Burrard Inlet, b., Can. (bûr'ȧrd)	116d	49°19'N	123°15'W
Burr Gaabo, Som.	233	1°14'N	51°47'E
Burro, Serranías del, mts., Mex. (sĕr-rä-nē'äs dĕl bo͞o'r-rō)	122	29°39'N	102°07'W
Bursa, Tur. (bo͞or'sȧ)	198	40°10'N	28°10'E
Būr Safājah, Egypt	231	26°57'N	33°56'E
Burscheid, Ger. (bo͞or'shīd)	171c	51°05'N	7°07'E
Būr Sūdān, Sudan (so͞o-dán')	231	19°30'N	37°10'E
Burt, N.Y., U.S. (bŭrt)	111c	43°19'N	78°45'W
Burt, l., Mi., U.S. (bŭrt)	108	45°25'N	84°45'W
Burton, Wa., U.S. (bûr'tŭn)	116a	47°24'N	122°28'W
Burton, Lake, res., Ga., U.S.	124	34°46'N	83°40'W
Burtonsville, Md., U.S. (bûrtōns-vil)	110e	39°07'N	76°57'W
Burton-upon-Trent, Eng., U.K. (bŭr'tŭn-ŭp'-ŏn-trĕnt)	164	52°48'N	1°37'W
Buru, i., Indon.	213	3°30'S	126°30'E
Burullus, l., Egypt	238b	31°20'N	30°58'E
Burundi, nation, Afr.	232	3°00'S	29°30'E
Burwell, Ne., U.S. (bûr'wĕl)	112	41°46'N	99°08'W
Bury, Eng., U.K. (bĕr'ĭ)	158a	53°36'N	2°17'W
Buryatia, prov., Russia	185	55°15'N	112°00'E
Bury Saint Edmunds, Eng., U.K. (bĕr'ĭ-sānt ĕd'mŭndz)	165	52°14'N	0°44'E
Burzaco, Arg. (bo͞or-zá'kō)	144a	34°50'S	58°23'W
Busanga Swamp, sw., Zam.	237	14°10'S	25°50'E
Būsh, Egypt (bo͞osh)	238b	29°13'N	31°08'E
Bushmanland, hist. reg., S. Afr. (bo͝osh-măn lănd)	232	29°15'S	18°45'E
Bushnell, Il., U.S. (bo͝osh'nĕl)	121	40°33'N	90°28'W
Businga, D.R.C. (bo͝o-sĭŋ'gȧ)	231	3°20'N	20°53'E
Busira, r., D.R.C.	236	0°05'S	19°20'E
Bus'k, Ukr.	169	49°58'N	24°39'E
Busselton, Austl. (bŭs'l-tŭn)	218	33°40'S	115°30'E
Bussum, Neth.	159a	52°16'N	5°10'E
Bustamante, Mex. (bo͞os-tȧ-män'tå)	122	26°34'N	100°30'W
Busto Arsizio, Italy (bo͞os'tō är-sēd'zē-ō)	174	45°47'N	8°51'E
Busuanga, i., Phil. (bo͞o-swäŋ'gä)	213a	12°20'N	119°43'E
Buta, D.R.C. (bo͞o'tȧ)	231	2°48'N	24°44'E
Butha Buthe, Leso. (bo͞o-thȧ-bo͞o'thȧ)	233c	28°49'S	28°16'E
Butler, Al., U.S. (bŭt'lĕr)	124	32°05'N	88°10'W
Butler, In., U.S.	108	41°25'N	84°50'W
Butler, Md., U.S.	110e	39°32'N	76°46'W
Butler, N.J., U.S.	110a	41°00'N	74°20'W
Butler, Pa., U.S.	109	40°50'N	79°55'W
Butovo, Russia (bo͝o-tô'vô)	186b	55°33'N	37°36'E
Butsha, D.R.C.	237	0°57'N	29°13'E
Buttahatchee, r., Al., U.S. (bŭt-ȧ-hăch'ē)	124	34°02'N	88°05'W
Butte, Mt., U.S. (būt)	104	46°00'N	112°31'W
Butterworth, S. Afr. (bŭ tĕr'wûrth)	233c	32°20'S	28°09'E
Butt of Lewis, c., Scot., U.K. (bŭt ŏv lū'ĭs)	164	58°34'N	6°15'W
Butuan, Phil. (bo͞o-to͞o'än)	213	8°40'N	125°33'E
Buturlinovka, Russia (bo͞o-to͞o'lē-nôf'ka)	181	50°47'N	40°35'E
Buuhoodle, Som.	238a	8°15'N	46°20'E
Buulo Berde, Som.	238a	3°53'N	45°30'E
Buxtehude, Ger.	159c	53°29'N	9°42'E
Buxton, Eng., U.K. (bŭks't'n)	158a	53°15'N	1°55'W
Buxton, Or., U.S.	116c	45°41'N	123°11'W
Buy, Russia (bwē)	178	58°30'N	41°48'E
Büyükmenderes, r., Tur.	198	37°50'N	28°20'E
Buzău, Rom. (bo͞o-zĕ'ō)	175	45°09'N	26°51'E
Buzău, r., Rom.	177	45°17'N	27°22'E
Buzaymah, Libya	231	25°14'N	22°13'E
Buzi, China (bo͞o-dz)	206	33°48'N	118°13'E
Buzuluk, Russia (bo͝o-zo͝o-lo͝ok')	178	52°50'N	52°10'E
Bwendi, D.R.C.	237	4°01'N	26°41'E
Byala, Blg.	175	43°26'N	25°44'E
Byala Slatina, Blg. (byä'la slä'tēnä)	175	43°26'N	23°56'E
Byalynichy, Bela. (byĕl-ĭ-nĭ'chĭ)	176	54°02'N	29°42'E
Byarezina, r., Bela. (bĕr-yĕ'zē-ná)	176	53°20'N	29°05'E
Byaroza, Bela.	169	52°29'N	24°59'E
Byblos *see* Jubayl, Leb.	197a	34°07'N	35°38'E
Bydgoszcz, Pol. (bĭd'gôshch)	160	53°07'N	18°00'E
Byelorussia *see* Belarus, nation, Eur.	178	53°30'N	25°33'E
Byerazino, Bela. (bĕr-yä'zē-nô)	176	53°51'N	28°54'E
Byeshankovichy, Bela.	176	55°04'N	29°29'E

ăt; finăl; rāte; senåte; ärm; ásk; sofȧ; fâre; ch-choose; dh-as th in other; bē; ēvent; bĕt; recĕnt; cratẽr; g-gō; gh-guttural g; bĭt; ĭ-short neutral; rīde; ĸ-guttural k as ch in German ich;

PRONOUNCING INDEX   Byesville – Camp Indian Reservation 277

PLACE (Pronunciation)	PAGE	LAT.	LONG.
Byesville, Oh., U.S. (bīz-vĭl)	108	39°55'N	81°35'W
Bygdin, l., Nor. (bügh-dên′)	166	61°24'N	8°31'E
Byglandsfjord, Nor. (bügh′länds-fyôr)	166	58°40'N	7°49'E
Bykhaw, Bela.	176	53°32'N	30°15'E
Bykovo, Russia (bĭ-kô′vô)	186b	55°38'N	38°05'E
Byrranga, Gory, mts., Russia	184	74°15'N	94°28'E
Bytantay, r., Russia (byän′täy)	185	68°15'N	132°15'E
Bytom, Pol. (bĭ′tŭm)	161	50°21'N	18°55'E
Bytosh′, Russia (bĭ-tôsh′)	176	53°48'N	34°06'E
Bytow, Pol. (bĭ′tŭf)	169	54°10'N	17°30'E

C

PLACE (Pronunciation)	PAGE	LAT.	LONG.
Cabagan, Phil. (kä-bä-gän′)	213a	17°27'N	121°50'E
Cabalete, i., Phil. (kä-bä-lā′tå)	213a	14°19'N	122°00'E
Caballones, Canal de, strt., Cuba (kä-näl-dĕ-kä-bäl-yô′nĕs)	134	20°45'N	79°20'W
Caballo Reservoir, res., N.M., U.S. (kä-bä-lyō′)	119	33°00'N	107°20'W
Cabanatuan, Phil. (kä-bä-nä-twän′)	213a	15°30'N	120°56'E
Cabano, Can. (kä-bä-nō′)	100	47°41'N	68°54'W
Cabarruyan, i., Phil. (kä-bä-rōō′yän)	213a	16°21'N	120°10'E
Cabedelo, Braz. (kä-bē-dā′lō)	143	6°58'S	34°49'W
Cabeza, Arrecife, i., Mex.	131	19°07'N	95°52'W
Cabeza del Buey, Spain (kä-bā′thä dĕl bwā′)	172	38°43'N	5°18'W
Cabimas, Ven. (kä-bē′mäs)	142	10°21'N	71°27'W
Cabinda, Ang.	232	5°33'S	12°12'E
Cabinda, hist. reg., Ang. (kä-bĭn′då)	232	5°10'S	10°00'E
Cabinet Mountains, mts., Mt., U.S. (kăb′ĭ-nĕt)	114	48°13'N	115°52'W
Cabo Frio, Braz. (kä′bô-frē′ô)	141a	22°53'S	42°02'W
Cabo Frio, Ilha do, Braz. (ē′lä-dô-kä′bô frē′ô)	141a	23°01'S	42°00'W
Cabo Gracias a Dios, Hond. (kä′bô-grä-syäs-ä-dyô′s)	133	15°00'N	83°13'W
Cabonga, Réservoir, res., Can.	99	47°25'N	76°35'W
Cabora Bassa Reservoir, res., Moz.	232	15°45'S	32°00'E
Cabot Head, c., Can. (kăb′ŭt)	98	45°15'N	81°20'W
Cabot Strait, strt., Can. (kăb′ŭt)	93a	47°35'N	60°00'W
Cabra, Spain (käb′rä)	172	37°28'N	4°29'W
Cabra, i., Phil.	213a	13°55'N	119°55'E
Cabrera, Illa de, i., Spain	173	39°08'N	2°57'E
Cabrera, Sierra de la, mts., Spain	172	42°15'N	6°45'W
Cabriel, r., Spain (kä-brē-ĕl′)	172	39°25'N	1°20'W
Cabrillo National Monument, rec., Ca., U.S. (kä-brēl′yō)	118a	32°41'N	117°03'W
Cabuçu, r., Braz. (kä-bōō′-sōō)	144b	22°57'S	43°36'W
Cabugao, Phil. (kä-bōō′gä-ô)	213a	17°48'N	120°28'E
Čačak, Serb. (chä′chåk)	175	43°51'N	20°22'E
Caçapava, Braz. (kä′sä-pá′vä)	141a	23°05'S	45°52'W
Cáceres, Braz. (ká′sĕ-rĕs)	143	16°11'S	57°32'W
Cáceres, Spain (ká′thå-räs)	162	39°28'N	6°20'W
Cachapoal, r., Chile (kä-chä-pô-á′l)	141b	34°23'S	70°19'W
Cache, r., Ar., U.S. (kåsh)	121	35°24'N	91°12'W
Cache Creek, Can.	95	50°48'N	121°19'W
Cache Creek, r., Ca., U.S. (kăsh)	118	38°53'N	122°24'W
Cache la Poudre, r., Co., U.S. (kàsh lá pōōd′r′)	120	40°43'N	105°39'W
Cachi, Nevados de, mtn., Arg. (nĕ-vá′dôs-dĕ-ká′chē)	144	25°05'S	66°40'W
Cachinal, Chile (kä-chē-näl′)	144	24°57'S	69°33'W
Cachoeira, Braz. (kä-shō-ā′rä)	143	12°32'S	38°47'W
Cachoeirá do Sul, Braz. (kä-shō-ā′rä-dō-sōō′l)	144	30°02'S	52°49'W
Cachoeiras de Macacu, Braz. (kä-shô-ā′räs-dē-mä-kä′kōō)	141a	22°28'S	42°39'W
Cachoeiro de Itapemirim, Braz.	143	20°51'S	41°06'W
Cacólo, Ang.	236	10°07'S	19°17'E
Caconda, Ang. (kä-kōn′dä)	232	13°43'S	15°06'E
Cacouna, Can.	100	47°54'N	69°31'W
Cacula, Ang.	236	14°29'S	14°10'E
Cadale, Som.	238a	2°45'N	46°15'E
Caddo, l., La., U.S. (kăd′ō)	123	32°37'N	94°15'W
Cadereyta, Mex. (kä-då-rā′tä)	130	20°42'N	99°47'W
Cadereyta Jimenez, Mex. (kä-dā-rā′tä hē-mā′nāz)	122	25°36'N	99°59'W
Cadi, Sierra de, mts., Spain (sē-ĕ′r-rä-dĕ-kä′dē)	173	42°17'N	1°34'E
Cadillac, Mi., U.S. (kăd′ĭ-lăk)	108	44°15'N	85°25'W
Cádiz, Spain (ká′dēz)	154	36°34'N	6°20'W
Cadiz, Ca., U.S. (kā′dĭz)	118	34°33'N	115°30'W
Cadiz, Oh., U.S.	108	40°15'N	81°00'W
Cádiz, Golfo de, b., Spain (gôl-fô-dĕ-ká′dēz)	162	36°50'N	7°00'W
Caen, Fr. (kän)	161	49°13'N	0°22'W
Caernarfon, Wales, U.K.	160	53°08'N	4°17'W
Caernarfon Bay, b., Wales, U.K.	164	53°09'N	4°56'W
Cagayan, Phil. (kä-gä-yän′)	213	8°13'N	124°30'E
Cagayan, r., Phil.	212	16°45'N	121°55'E
Cagayan Islands, is., Phil.	212	9°40'N	120°30'E
Cagayan Sulu, i., Phil. (kä-gä-yän sōō′lōō)	212	7°00'N	118°30'E
Cagli, Italy (käl′yē)	174	43°35'N	12°40'E
Cagliari, Italy (käl′yä-rē)	154	39°16'N	9°08'E
Cagliari, Golfo di, b., Italy (gôl-fô-dē-käl′yä-rē)	162	39°08'N	9°12'E
Cagnes, Fr. (kän′y′)	171	43°40'N	7°14'E
Cagua, Ven. (kä′gwä)	143b	10°12'N	67°27'W
Caguas, P.R. (kä′gwäs)	129b	18°12'N	66°01'W
Cahaba, r., Al., U.S. (kȧ hä-bä)	124	32°50'N	87°15'W
Cahama, Ang. (kä-á′mä)	232	16°17'S	14°19'E
Cahokia, Il., U.S. (kȧ-hō′kĭ-ȧ)	117e	38°34'N	90°11'W
Cahora-Bassa, wtfl., Moz.	237	15°40'S	32°50'E
Cahors, Fr. (kȧ-ôr′)	161	44°27'N	1°27'E
Cahuacán, Mex. (kä-wä-kä′n)	131a	19°38'N	99°25'W
Cahuita, Punta, c., C.R. (pōō′n-tä-kä-wē′tȧ)	133	9°47'N	82°41'W
Cahul, Mol.	177	45°49'N	28°17'E
Caibarién, Cuba (kī-bä-rē-ĕn′)	134	22°35'N	79°30'W
Caicedonia, Col. (kī-sĕ-dô-nĕä)	142a	4°21'N	75°48'W
Caicos Bank, bk. (kī′kōs)	135	21°35'N	72°00'W
Caicos Islands, is., T./C. Is.	129	21°45'N	71°50'W
Caicos Passage, strt., N.A.	135	21°55'N	72°45'W
Caillou Bay, b., La., U.S. (kȧ-yōō′)	123	29°07'N	91°00'W
Caimanera, Cuba (kī-mä-nā′rä)	135	20°00'N	75°10'W
Caiman Point, c., Phil. (kī′mȧn)	213a	15°56'N	119°33'E
Caimito, r., Pan. (kä-ē-mē′tô)	128a	8°50'N	79°45'W
Caimito del Guayabal, Cuba (kä-ē-mē′tō-dĕl-gwä-yä-bä′l)	135a	22°57'N	82°36'W
Cairns, Austl. (kârnz)	219	17°02'S	145°49'E
Cairo, C.R. (kī′rô)	133	10°06'N	83°47'W
Cairo, Egypt	231	30°00'N	31°17'E
Cairo, Ga., U.S. (kā′rō)	124	30°48'N	84°12'W
Cairo, Il., U.S.	105	36°59'N	89°11'W
Caistor, Eng., U.K. (kâs′tēr)	158a	53°30'N	0°20'W
Caiundo, Ang.	236	15°46'S	17°28'E
Caiyu, China (tsī-yōō)	206	39°39'N	116°36'E
Cajamarca, Col. (kä-kä-má′r-kä)	142a	4°25'N	75°25'W
Cajamarca, Peru (kä-hä-mär′kä)	142	7°16'S	78°30'W
Čajniče, Bos. (chī′nĭ-chĕ)	175	43°32'N	19°04'E
Cajon, Ca., U.S. (kȧ-hōn′)	117a	34°18'N	117°28'W
Cajuru, Braz. (kȧ-zhōō′rōō)	141a	21°17'S	47°17'W
Čakovec, Cro. (chä′kō-vĕts)	174	46°23'N	16°27'E
Cala, S. Afr. (cä-lȧ)	233c	31°33'S	27°41'E
Calabar, Nig. (kăl-ȧ-bär′)	230	4°57'N	8°19'E
Calabazar, Cuba (kä-lä-bä-zä′r)	135a	23°02'N	82°25'W
Calabozo, Ven. (kä-lä-bō′zō)	142	8°48'N	67°27'W
Calabria, hist. reg., Italy (kä-lä′brē-ä)	174	39°26'N	16°23'E
Calafat, Rom. (kȧ-lȧ-fát′)	175	43°59'N	22°56'E
Calaguas Islands, is., Phil. (kä-läg′wäs)	213a	14°30'N	123°06'E
Calahoo, Can. (kă-lȧ-hōō′)	102g	53°42'N	113°58'W
Calahorra, Spain (kä-lä-ôr′rä)	162	42°18'N	1°58'W
Calais, Fr. (kȧ-lĕ′)	154	50°56'N	1°51'E
Calais, Me., U.S.	105	45°11'N	67°15'W
Calama, Chile (kä-lä′mä)	144	22°17'S	68°58'W
Calamar, Col. (kä-lä-mär′)	142	10°24'N	75°00'W
Calamar, Col.	142	1°55'N	72°33'W
Calamba, Phil. (kä-läm′bä)	213a	14°12'N	121°10'E
Calamian Group, is., Phil. (kä-lä-myän′)	212	12°14'N	118°38'E
Calañas, Spain (kä-län′yäs)	172	37°41'N	6°52'W
Calanda, Spain	173	40°53'N	0°20'W
Calapan, Phil. (kä-lä-pän′)	213a	13°25'N	121°11'E
Călăraşi, Rom. (kŭ-lŭ-rash′ĭ)	163	44°09'N	27°20'E
Calatayud, Spain (kä-lä-tä-yōōdh′)	162	41°23'N	1°37'W
Calauag Bay, b., Phil.	213a	14°07'N	122°10'E
Calaveras Reservoir, res., Ca., U.S. (kăl-ȧ-vēr′ăs)	116b	37°29'N	121°47'W
Calavite, Cape, c., Phil. (kä-lä-vē′tä)	213a	13°29'N	120°00'E
Calcasieu, r., La., U.S. (kăl′kȧ-shū)	123	30°22'N	93°08'W
Calcasieu Lake, l., La., U.S.	123	29°58'N	93°08'W
Calcutta *see* Kolkata, India (kăl-kŭt′ȧ)	199	22°32'N	88°22'E
Caldas, Col. (kä′l-däs)	142a	6°06'N	75°38'W
Caldas, dept., Col.	142a	5°20'N	75°38'W
Caldas da Rainha, Port. (käl′däs dä rīn′yȧ)	172	39°25'N	9°08'W
Calder, r., Eng., U.K. (kôl′dēr)	158a	53°39'N	1°30'W
Caldera, Chile (käl-dā′rä)	144	27°02'S	70°53'W
Calder Canal, can., Eng., U.K.	158a	53°48'N	2°25'W
Caldwell, Id., U.S. (kôld′wĕl)	114	43°40'N	116°43'W
Caldwell, Ks., U.S.	121	37°04'N	97°36'W
Caldwell, Oh., U.S.	108	39°40'N	81°30'W
Caldwell, Tx., U.S.	123	30°30'N	96°40'W
Caledon, Can. (kăl′ē-dŏn)	102d	43°52'N	79°59'W
Caledonia, Mn., U.S. (kăl-ē-dō′nĭ-ȧ)	113	43°38'N	91°31'W
Calella, Spain (kä-lĕl′yä)	173	41°37'N	2°39'E
Calera Victor Rosales, Mex. (kä-lā′rä-vē′k-tôr-rô-sá′lĕs)	130	22°57'N	102°42'W
Calexico, Ca., U.S. (kȧ-lĕk′sĭ-kō)	104	32°41'N	115°30'W
Calgary, Can. (kăl′gȧ-rĭ)	90	51°03'N	114°05'W
Calhoun, Ga., U.S. (kăl-hōōn′)	124	34°30'N	84°56'W
Cali, Col. (kä′lē)	142	3°26'N	76°30'W
Caliente, Nv., U.S. (käl-yĕn′tā)	119	37°38'N	114°30'W
California, Mo., U.S. (kăl-ĭ-fôr′nĭ-ȧ)	121	38°38'N	92°38'W
California, Pa., U.S.	111e	40°03'N	79°53'W
California, state, U.S.	104	38°10'N	121°20'W
California, Golfo de, b., Mex. (gôl-fô-dĕ-kä-lē-fôr-nyä)	128	30°30'N	113°45'W
California Aqueduct, aq., Ca., U.S.	118	37°10'N	121°10'W
Călimani, Munţii, mts., Rom.	169	47°05'N	24°47'E
Calimere, Point, c., India	203	10°20'N	80°20'E
Calimesa, Ca., U.S. (kă-lĭ-mă′sȧ)	117a	34°00'N	117°04'W
Calipatria, Ca., U.S. (kăl-ĭ-pát′rĭ-ȧ)	118	33°03'N	115°30'W
Calkini, Mex. (käl-kē-nē′)	131	20°21'N	90°06'W
Callabonna, Lake, l., Austl. (călă′bŏnȧ)	222	29°35'S	140°28'E
Callao, Peru (käl-yä′ô)	142	12°02'S	77°07'W
Calling, l., Can. (kôl′ĭng)	95	55°15'N	113°12'W
Calmar, Can. (kăl′mär)	102g	53°16'N	113°49'W
Calmar, Ia., U.S.	113	43°12'N	91°54'W
Caloosahatchee, r., Fl., U.S. (kȧ-loo-sȧ-hăch′ē)	125a	26°45'N	81°41'W
Calotmul, Mex. (kä-lôt-mōōl)	132a	20°58'N	88°11'W
Calpulalpan, Mex. (käl-pōō-läl′pän)	130	19°35'N	98°33'W
Caltagirone, Italy (käl-tä-jē-rō′nâ)	162	37°14'N	14°32'E
Caltanissetta, Italy (käl-tä-nê-sĕt′tä)	162	37°30'N	14°02'E
Caluango, Ang.	236	8°21'S	19°40'E
Calucinga, Ang.	236	11°18'S	16°12'E
Calumet, Mi., U.S. (kă-lū-mĕt′)	113	47°15'N	88°29'W
Calumet, Lake, l., Il., U.S.	111a	41°43'N	87°36'W
Calumet City, Il., U.S.	111a	41°37'N	87°33'W
Calunda, Ang.	236	12°06'S	23°23'E
Caluquembe, Ang.	236	13°47'S	14°44'E
Caluula, Som.	238a	11°53'N	50°40'E
Calvert, Tx., U.S. (kăl′vērt)	123	30°59'N	96°41'W
Calvert Island, i., Can.	92	51°35'N	128°00'W
Calvi, Fr. (käl′vē)	174	42°33'N	8°35'E
Calvillo, Mex. (käl vēl′yō)	131	21°51'N	102°44'W
Calvinia, S. Afr. (kăl-vĭn′ĭ-ȧ)	232	31°20'S	19°50'E
Cam, r., Eng., U.K. (kăm)	165	52°15'N	0°05'E
Camagüey, Cuba (kä-mä-gwā′)	129	21°25'N	78°00'W
Camagüey, prov., Cuba	134	21°30'N	78°10'W
Camajuani, Cuba (kä-mä-hwä′nê)	134	22°25'N	79°50'W
Camano, Wa., U.S. (kä-mä′no)	116a	48°10'N	122°32'W
Camano Island, i., Wa., U.S.	116a	48°11'N	122°29'W
Camargo, Mex. (kä-mär gō)	122	26°19'N	98°49'W
Camarón, Cabo, c., Hond. (ká′bô-kä-mä-rōn′)	132	16°06'N	85°05'W
Camas, Wa., U.S. (kăm′ȧs)	116c	45°36'N	122°24'W
Camas Creek, r., Id., U.S.	115	44°10'N	112°09'W
Camatagua, Ven. (kä-mä-tá′gwä)	143b	9°49'N	66°55'W
Ca Mau, Mui, c., Viet.	212	8°36'N	104°43'E
Cambay, India (kăm-bā′)	202	22°22'N	72°39'E
Cambodia, nation, Asia	212	12°15'N	104°00'E
Cambonda, Serra, mts., Ang.	236	12°10'S	14°15'E
Camborne, Eng., U.K. (kăm′bôrn)	164	50°15'N	5°28'W
Cambrai, Fr. (käɴ-brĕ′)	161	50°10'N	3°15'E
Cambrian Mountains, mts., Wales, U.K. (kăm′brĭ-ăn)	164	52°05'N	4°05'W
Cambridge, Can.	99	43°22'N	80°19'W
Cambridge, Eng., U.K. (kăm′brĭj)	161	52°12'N	0°11'E
Cambridge, Ma., U.S.	101a	42°23'N	71°07'W
Cambridge, Md., U.S.	109	38°35'N	76°10'W
Cambridge, Mn., U.S.	113	45°35'N	93°14'W
Cambridge, Ne., U.S.	120	40°17'N	100°10'W
Cambridge, Oh., U.S.	108	40°00'N	81°35'W
Cambridge Bay *see* Kaluktutiak, Can.	92	69°15'N	105°00'W
Cambridge City, In., U.S.	108	39°45'N	85°15'W
Cambridgeshire, co., Eng., U.K.	158a	52°26'N	0°19'W
Cambuci, Braz. (käm-bōō′sē)	141a	21°35'S	41°54'W
Cambundi-Catembo, Ang.	236	10°09'S	17°31'E
Camby, In., U.S. (kăm′bē)	111g	39°40'N	86°19'W
Camden, Austl.	217b	34°03'S	150°42'E
Camden, Al., U.S. (kăm′dĕn)	124	31°58'N	87°15'W
Camden, Ar., U.S.	121	33°36'N	92°49'W
Camden, Me., U.S.	100	44°11'N	69°05'W
Camden, N.J., U.S.	105	39°56'N	75°06'W
Camden, S.C., U.S.	125	34°14'N	80°37'W
Cameia, Parque Nacional da, rec., Ang.	236	11°40'S	21°20'E
Camenca, Mol.	177	48°02'N	28°43'E
Cameron, Mo., U.S. (kăm′ēr-ŭn)	121	39°44'N	94°14'W
Cameron, Tx., U.S.	123	30°52'N	96°57'W
Cameron, W.V., U.S.	108	39°40'N	80°35'W
Cameron Hills, hills, Can.	92	60°13'N	120°20'W
Cameroon, nation, Afr.	230	5°48'N	11°00'E
Cameroon Mountain, mtn., Cam.	230	4°12'N	9°11'E
Camiling, Phil. (kä-mê-lĭng′)	213a	15°42'N	120°24'E
Camilla, Ga., U.S. (kȧ-mĭl′ȧ)	124	31°13'N	84°12'W
Caminha, Port. (kä-mĭn′yȧ)	172	41°52'N	8°44'W
Camoçim, Braz. (kä-mô-sēɴ′)	143	2°56'S	40°55'W
Camooweal, Austl.	218	20°00'S	138°13'E
Campana, Arg. (käm-pä′nä)	141c	34°10'S	58°58'W
Campana, i., Chile (käm-pän′yä)	144	48°20'S	75°15'W
Campanario, Spain (kä-pä-nä′rē-ō)	172	38°51'N	5°36'W
Campanella, Punta, c., Italy (pô′n-tä-käm-pä-nĕ′lä)	173c	40°20'N	14°21'E
Campanha, Braz. (käm-pän-yäɴ′)	141a	21°51'S	45°24'W
Campania, hist. reg., Italy (käm-pän′yä)	174	41°00'N	14°40'E
Campbell, Ca., U.S. (kăm′bĕl)	116b	37°17'N	121°57'W
Campbell, Mo., U.S.	121	36°29'N	90°04'W
Campbell, is., N.Z.	3	52°30'S	169°00'E
Campbellpore, Pak.	202	33°49'N	72°24'E
Campbell River, Can.	90	50°01'N	125°15'W
Campbellsville, Ky., U.S. (kăm′bĕlz-vĭl)	124	37°19'N	85°20'W
Campbellton, Can. (kăm′bĕl-tŭn)	91	48°00'N	66°40'W
Campbelltown, Austl. (kăm′bĕl-toun)	217b	34°04'S	150°49'E
Campbelltown, Scot., U.K. (kăm′b′l-toun)	164	55°25'N	5°50'W
Camp Dennison, Oh., U.S. (dĕ′nĭ-sŏn)	111f	39°12'N	84°17'W
Campeche, Mex. (käm-pā′chå)	128	19°51'N	90°32'W
Campeche, state, Mex.	128	18°55'N	90°20'W
Campeche, Bahía de, b., Mex. (bä-ē′ä-dĕ-käm-pā′chā)	128	19°30'N	93°40'W
Campechuela, Cuba (käm-på-chwā′lä)	134	20°15'N	77°15'W
Camperdown, S. Afr. (kăm′pēr-doun)	233c	29°44'S	30°33'E
Câmpina, Rom.	175	45°08'N	25°47'E
Campina Grande, Braz. (käm-pē′nä grän′dĕ)	143	7°15'S	35°49'W
Campinas, Braz. (käm-pē′näzh)	143	22°53'S	47°03'W
Camp Indian Reservation, I.R., Ca., U.S. (kămp)	118	32°39'N	116°26'W

ng-sing; ŋ-baŋk; ɴ-nasalized n; nŏd; cŏmmit; ōld; ôbey; ôrder; oi-boil; fōōd; ȯ-as oo in foot; ou-out; s-soft; sh-dish; th-thin; pūre; ûnite; ûrn; stŭd; circŭs; ü-as in French tu; ′-indeterminate vowel.

PLACE (Pronunciation)	PAGE	LAT.	LONG.
Campo, Cam. (käm´pō)	230	2°22'N	9°49'E
Campoalegre, Col. (kä´m-pô-ä-lĕ´grĕ)	142	2°34'N	75°20'W
Campobasso, Italy (käm´pô-bäs´sō)	174	41°35'N	14°39'E
Campo Belo, Braz.	141a	20°52'S	45°15'W
Campo de Criptana, Spain (käm´pō dä krĕp-tä´nä)	172	39°24'N	3°09'W
Campo Florido, Cuba (kä´m-pō flô-rĕ´dō)	135a	23°07'N	82°07'W
Campo Grande, Braz. (käm-pô grän´dĕ)	143	20°28'S	54°32'W
Campo Grande, Braz.	144b	22°54'S	43°33'W
Campo Maior, Braz. (käm-pô mä-yôr´)	143	4°48'S	42°12'W
Campo Maior, Port.	170	[illegible]	[illegible]
Campo Real, Spain (käm´pô rå-äl´)	173a	40°21'N	3°23'W
Campos, Braz. (kä´m-pôs)	143	21°46'S	41°19'W
Campos do Jordão, Braz. ([illegible])	[illegible]	[illegible]	[illegible]
Campos Gerais, Braz. (kä´m-pôs-zhĕ-rȧēs)	141a	21°17'S	45°43'W
Camps Bay, S. Afr. (kămps)	232a	33°57'S	18°22'E
Camp Springs, Md., U.S. (cămp sprĭngz)	110e	38°48'N	76°55'W
Câmpulung, Rom.	163	45°15'N	25°03'E
Câmpulung Moldovenesc, Rom.	169	47°31'N	25°36'E
Camp Wood, Tx., U.S. (kămp wood)	122	29°39'N	100°02'W
Camrose, Can. (kăm-rōz)	90	53°01'N	112°50'W
Camu, r., Dom. Rep. (kä´mōō)	135	19°05'N	70°15'W
Canada, nation, N.A. (kăn´à-dà)	90	50°00'N	100°00'W
Canada Bay, b., Can.	101	50°43'N	56°10'W
Cañada de Gómez, Arg. (kä-nyä´dä-dĕ-gô´mĕz)	144	32°49'S	61°24'W
Canadian, Tx., U.S. (kȧ-nā´dĭ-ăn)	120	35°54'N	100°24'W
Canadian, r., U.S.	106	35°30'N	102°30'W
Canajoharie, N.Y., U.S. (kăn-à-jō-hăr´ē)	109	42°55'N	74°35'W
Çanakkale, Tur. (chä-näk-kä´lĕ)	163	40°10'N	26°26'E
Çanakkale Boğazi (Dardanelles), strt., Tur.	163	40°05'N	25°50'E
Canandaigua, N.Y., U.S. (kăn-ăn-dā´gwȧ)	109	42°55'N	77°20'W
Canandaigua, l., N.Y., U.S.	109	42°45'N	77°20'W
Cananea, Mex. (kä-nä-nĕ´ä)	128	31°00'N	110°20'W
Canarias, Islas (Canary Is.), is., Spain (ē´s-läs-kä-nä´ryäs)	229	29°15'N	16°30'W
Canarreos, Archipiélago de los, is., Cuba	134	21°35'N	82°20'W
Canary Islands *see* Canarias, Islas, is., Spain	229	29°15'N	16°30'W
Cañas, C.R. (kä´-nyäs)	132	10°26'N	85°06'W
Cañas, r., C.R.	132	10°20'N	85°21'W
Cañasgordas, Col. (kä´nyäs-gô´r-däs)	142a	6°44'N	76°01'W
Canastota, N.Y., U.S. (kăn-ȧs-tō´tȧ)	109	43°05'N	75°45'W
Canastra, Serra de, mts., Braz. (sĕ´r-rä-dĕ-kä-nä´s-trä)	143	19°53'S	46°57'W
Canatlán, Mex. (kä-nät-län´)	122	24°30'N	104°45'W
Canaveral, Cape, c., Fl., U.S.	107	28°30'N	80°23'W
Canavieiras, Braz. (kä-nà-vē-ā´räs)	143	15°40'S	38°49'W
Canberra, Austl. (kăn´bĕr-ȧ)	219	35°21'S	149°10'E
Canby, Mn., U.S. (kăn´bĭ)	112	44°43'N	96°15'W
Canchyuaya, Cerros de, mts., Peru (sĕ´r-rôs-dĕ-kän-chōō-ȧ´īä)	142	7°30'S	74°30'W
Cancuc, Mex. (kän-kōōk)	131	16°58'N	92°17'W
Cancún, Mex.	132a	21°25'N	86°50'W
Candelaria, Cuba (kän-dĕ-lä´ryä)	134	22°45'N	82°55'W
Candelaria, Phil. (kän-dȧ-lä´rē-ä)	213a	15°39'N	119°55'E
Candelaria, r., Mex. (kän-dĕ-lä-ryä)	131	18°25'N	91°21'W
Candeleda, Spain (kän-dhå-lā´dhä)	172	40°09'N	5°18'W
Candia *see* Iráklion, Grc.	154	35°20'N	25°10'E
Candle, Ak., U.S. (kăn´d'l)	103	65°00'N	162°04'W
Cando, N.D., U.S. (kăn´dō)	112	48°27'N	99°13'W
Candon, Phil. (kän-dōn´)	213a	17°13'N	120°26'E
Canelones, Ur. (kä-nĕ-lô-nĕs)	141c	34°32'S	56°19'W
Canelones, dept., Ur.	141c	34°34'S	56°15'W
Cañete, Peru (kän-yā´tå)	142	13°06'S	76°17'W
Caney, Cuba (kä-nā´) (kā´nĭ)	135	20°05'N	75°45'W
Caney, Ks., U.S. (kā´nĭ)	121	37°00'N	95°57'W
Caney Fork, r., Tn., U.S.	124	36°10'N	85°50'W
Cangamba, Ang.	232	13°40'S	19°54'E
Cangas, Spain (kän´gäs)	172	42°15'N	8°43'W
Cangas de Narcea, Spain (kä´n-gäs-dĕ-när-sĕ-ä)	172	43°08'N	6°36'W
Cangzhou, China (tsäŋ-jō)	208	38°21'N	116°53'E
Caniapiscau, l., Can.	93	54°10'N	71°13'E
Caniapiscau, r., Can.	93	57°00'N	68°45'W
Canicatti, Italy (kä-nė-kät´tē)	174	37°18'N	13°58'E
Cañitas, Mex. (kän-yē´täs)	130	23°38'N	102°44'W
Cannell, Can.	102g	53°35'N	113°38'W
Cannelton, In., U.S. (kăn´ĕl-tŭn)	108	37°55'N	86°45'W
Cannes, Fr. (kȧn)	161	43°34'N	7°05'E
Canning, Can. (kăn´ĭng)	100	45°09'N	64°25'W
Cannock, Eng., U.K. (kăn´ŭk)	158a	52°41'N	2°02'W
Cannock Chase, reg., Eng., U.K. (kăn´ŭk chās)	158a	52°43'N	1°54'W
Cannon, r., Mn., U.S. (kăn´ŭn)	113	44°18'N	93°24'W
Cannonball, r., N.D., U.S. (kăn´ŭn-bäl)	112	46°17'N	101°35'W
Caño, Isla de, i., C.R. (ē´s-lä-dĕ-kä´nō)	133	8°38'N	84°00'W
Canoga Park, Ca., U.S. (kä-nō´gȧ)	117a	34°07'N	118°36'W
Canoncito Indian Reservation, I.R., N.M., U.S.	119	35°00'N	107°05'W
Canon City, Co., U.S. (kăn´yŭn)	120	38°27'N	105°16'W
Canonsburg, Pa., U.S. (kăn´ŭnz-bûrg)	111e	40°16'N	80°11'W
Canoochee, r., Ga., U.S. (kȧ-nōō´chē)	125	32°25'N	82°11'W
Canora, Can. (kȧ-nōrȧ)	90	51°37'N	102°26'W
Canosa, Italy (kä-nō´sä)	174	41°14'N	16°03'E
Canouan, i., St. Vin.	133b	12°44'N	61°10'W
Cansahcab, Mex.	132a	21°11'N	89°05'W
Canso, Can. (kăn´sō)	101	45°20'N	61°00'W
Canso, Cape, c., Can.	101	45°21'N	60°46'W
Canso, Strait of, strt., Can.	101	45°37'N	61°25'W
Cantabrica, Cordillera, mts., Spain	156	43°05'N	6°05'W
Cantagalo, Braz. (kän-tä-gȧ´lo)	141a	21°59'S	42°22'W
Cantanhede, Port. (kän-täɴ-yā´då)	172	40°22'N	8°35'W
Canterbury, Eng., U.K. (kăn´tĕr-bĕr-ė)	165	51°17'N	1°06'E
Canterbury Bight, b., N.Z.	221a	44°15'S	172°08'E
Cantiles, Cayo, i., Cuba (ky-ō-kän-tē´lås)	134	21°40'N	82°00'W
Canton *see* Guangzhou, China	205	23°07'N	113°15'E
Canton, Ga., U.S.	124	34°13'N	[illegible]
Canton, Il., U.S.	121	40°34'N	90°02'W
Canton, Ma., U.S.	101a	42°09'N	71°09'W
Canton, Mo., U.S.	121	40°08'N	91°33'W
Canton, Ms., U.S.	124	32°36'N	90°01'W
Canton, N.C., U.S.	125	35°32'N	82°50'W
Canton, Oh., U.S.	105	40°50'N	81°25'W
Canton, Pa., U.S.	109	41°50'N	76°45'W
Canton, S.D., U.S.	112	43°17'N	96°37'W
Cantu, Italy (kän-tōō´)	174	45°43'N	9°09'E
Cañuelas, Arg. (kä-nyōĕ´-läs)	141c	35°03'S	58°45'W
Canyon, Tx., U.S. (kăn´yŭn)	120	34°59'N	101°57'W
Canyon, r., Wa., U.S.	116a	48°09'N	121°48'W
Canyon de Chelly National Monument, rec., Az., U.S.	119	36°14'N	110°00'W
Canyon Ferry Lake, res., Mt., U.S.	115	46°33'N	111°37'W
Canyonlands National Park, rec., Ut., U.S.	119	38°10'N	110°00'W
Canyons of the Ancients National Monument, rec., Co., U.S.	119	37°30'N	108°50'W
Caoxian, China (tsou shyĕn)	206	34°48'N	115°33'E
Capalonga, Phil. (kä-pä-lôn´gä)	213a	14°20'N	122°30'E
Capannori, Italy (kä-pän´nô-rē)	174	43°50'N	10°30'E
Capaya, r., Ven. (kä-pä-īä)	143b	10°28'N	66°15'W
Cap-Chat, Can. (kȧp-shä´)	91	48°02'N	65°20'W
Cap-de-la-Madeleine, Can. (kȧp dē lȧ mȧ-d'lĕn´)	99	46°23'N	72°30'W
Cape Breton, i., Can. (kāp brĕt´ŭn)	101	45°48'N	59°50'W
Cape Breton Highlands National Park, rec., Can.	91	46°45'N	60°45'W
Cape Charles, Va., U.S. (kāp chärlz)	125	37°13'N	76°02'W
Cape Coast, Ghana	230	5°05'N	1°15'W
Cape Fear, r., N.C., U.S. (kāp fēr)	107	35°00'N	79°00'W
Cape Flats, pl., S. Afr. (kāp flăts)	232a	34°01'S	18°37'E
Cape Girardeau, Mo., U.S. (jē-rär-dō´)	105	37°17'N	89°32'W
Cape Krusenstern National Monument, rec., Ak., U.S.	103	67°30'N	163°40'W
Cape May, N.J., U.S. (kāp mā)	109	38°55'N	74°50'W
Cape May Court House, N.J., U.S.	109	39°05'N	75°00'W
Cape Romanzof, Ak., U.S. (rō´ măn zôf)	103	61°50'N	165°45'W
Capesterre, Guad.	133b	16°02'N	61°37'W
Cape Tormentine, Can.	100	46°08'N	63°47'W
Cape Town, S. Afr. (kāp toun)	232	33°48'S	18°28'E
Cape Verde, nation, Afr.	230b	15°48'N	26°02'W
Cape York Peninsula, pen., Austl. (kāp yôrk)	221	12°30'S	142°35'E
Cap-Haïtien, Haiti (kȧp ȧ-ē-syăn´)	129	19°45'N	72°15'W
Capilla de Señor, Arg. (kä-pēl´yä dā sān-yôr´)	141c	34°18'S	59°07'W
Capitachouane, r., Can.	99	47°50'N	76°45'W
Capitol Reef National Park, rec., Ut., U.S. (kăp´ĭ-tŏl)	119	38°15'N	111°10'W
Capivari, Braz. (kä-pē-vä´rė)	141a	22°59'S	47°29'W
Capivari, r., Braz.	144b	22°39'S	43°19'W
Capoompeta, mtn., Austl. (kȧ-pōōm-pē´tȧ)	221	29°15'S	152°12'E
Capraia, i., Italy (kä-prä´yä)	162	43°02'N	9°51'E
Caprara Point, c., Italy (kä-prä´rä)	174	41°08'N	8°20'E
Capreol, Can.	99	46°43'N	80°56'W
Caprera, i., Italy (kä-prā´rä)	174	41°12'N	9°28'E
Capri, Italy	173c	40°18'N	14°16'E
Capri, Isola di, i., Italy (ē´-sō-lä-dē-kä´prē)	173c	40°19'N	14°10'E
Capricorn Channel, strt., Austl. (kăp´rĭ-kôrn)	221	22°27'S	151°24'E
Caprivi Strip, hist. reg., Nmb.	232	18°00'S	22°00'E
Cap-Rouge, Can. (kȧp rōōzh´)	102b	46°45'N	71°21'W
Cap-Saint Ignace, Can. (kĭp săɴ-tē-nyás´)	102b	47°02'N	70°27'W
Capua, Italy (kä´pwä)	162	41°07'N	14°14'E
Capulhuac, Mex. (kä-pōl-hwäk´)	130	19°33'N	99°43'W
Capulin Mountain National Monument, rec., N.M., U.S. (kȧ-pū´lĭn)	120	36°15'N	103°58'W
Capultitlán, Mex. (kä-pō´l-tē-tlä´n)	131a	19°15'N	99°40'W
Caquetá (Japurá), r., S.A.	142	0°20'S	73°00'W
Carabaña, Spain (kä-rä-bän´yä)	173a	40°16'N	3°15'W
Carabelle, Fl., U.S. (kăr´á-bĕl)	124	29°50'N	84°40'W
Carabobo, dept., Ven. (kä-rä-bô´-bô)	143b	10°07'N	68°06'W
Caracal, Rom. (kȧ-rȧ-kȧl´)	175	44°06'N	24°22'E
Caracas, Ven. (kä-rä´käs)	142	10°30'N	66°58'W
Carácuaro de Morelos, Mex. (kä-rä´kwä-rō-dĕ-mô-rĕ-lôs)	130	18°44'N	101°04'W
Caraguatatuba, Braz. (kä-rä-gwä-tä-tōō´bä)	141a	23°37'S	45°26'W
Carajás, Serra dos, mts., Braz. (sĕ´r-rä-dôs-kä-rä-zhà´s)	143	5°58'S	51°45'W
Caramanta, Cerro, mtn., Col. (sĕ´r-rô-kä-rä-mä´n-tä)	142a	5°29'N	76°01'W
Carangola, Braz. (kä-rȧn´gō´lä)	141a	20°46'S	42°02'W
Caraquet, Can. (kă-rȧ-kĕt´)	91	47°48'N	64°57'W
Carata, Laguna, l., Nic. (lä-gō´nä-kä-rä´tä)	133	13°59'N	83°41'W
Caratasca, Laguna, l., Hond. (lä-gȯ´nä-kä-rä-täs´kä)	133	15°20'N	83°45'W
Caravaca, Spain (kä-rä-vä´kä)	172	38°05'N	1°51'W
Caravelas, Braz. (kȧ-rä-vĕl´äzh)	143	17°46'S	39°06'W
Carayaca, Ven. (kȧ-rä-īȧ´kä)	143b	10°32'N	67°07'W
Caràzinho, Braz. (kä-rȧ´zē-nyŏ)	144	28°22'S	52°33'W
Carballiño, Spain	162	42°26'N	8°04'W
Carballo, Spain (kär-bäl´yō)	172	43°13'N	8°40'W
Carbet, Pitons du, mtn., Mart.	133b	14°40'N	61°05'W
Carbon, r., Wa., U.S. (kär´bŏn)	116a	47°06'N	122°08'W
Carbonado, Wa., U.S. (kȧr-bō-nā´dō)	116a	47°05'N	122°03'W
Carbonara, Capo, c., Italy (kär-bō-nä´rä)	162	39°08'N	9°33'E
Carbondale, Can. (kär´bŏn-dāl)	102g	53°45'N	113°32'W
Carbondale, Il., U.S.	108	37°42'N	89°12'W
Carbondale, Pa., U.S.	109	41°35'N	75°30'W
Carbonear, Can. (kär-bô-nēr´)	101	47°45'N	53°14'W
Carbon Hill, Al., U.S. (kär´bŏn hĭl)	124	33°53'N	87°34'W
Carcaixent, Spain	173	39°09'N	0°29'W
Carcans, Étang de, l., Fr. (ā-taɴ-dĕ-kär-kăɴ)	170	45°12'N	1°00'W
Carcassonne, Fr. (kȧr-kȧ-sôn´)	161	43°12'N	2°23'E
Carcross, Can. (kär´krôs)	90	60°18'N	134°54'W
Cárdenas, Cuba (kär´då-näs)	129	23°00'N	81°10'W
Cárdenas, Mex. (kà´r-dĕ-näs)	131	17°59'N	93°23'W
Cárdenas, Mex.	130	22°01'N	99°38'W
Cárdenas, Bahía de, b., Cuba (bä-ē´ä-dĕ-kär´då-näs)	134	23°10'N	81°10'W
Cardiff, Can. (kär´dĭf)	102g	53°46'N	113°36'W
Cardiff, Wales, U.K.	161	51°30'N	3°18'W
Cardigan, Wales, U.K. (kär´dĭ-găn)	161	52°05'N	4°40'W
Cardigan Bay, b., Wales, U.K.	161	52°35'N	4°40'W
Cardston, Can. (kärds´tŭn)	90	49°12'N	113°18'W
Carei, Rom. (kä-rĕ´)	169	47°42'N	22°28'E
Carentan, Fr. (kä-rôɴ-täɴ´)	170	49°19'N	1°14'W
Carey, Oh., U.S. (kā´rē)	108	40°55'N	83°25'W
Carey, l., Austl. (kâr´ē)	220	29°20'S	123°35'E
Carhaix-Plouguer, Fr. (kär-ĕ´)	170	48°17'N	3°37'W
Caribbean Sea, sea (kăr-ĭ-bē´ăn)	129	14°30'N	75°30'W
Caribe, Arroyo, r., Mex. (är-ro´i-kä-rē´bĕ)	131	18°18'N	90°38'W
Cariboo Mountains, mts., Can. (kă´rĭ-bōō)	92	53°00'N	121°00'W
Caribou, Me., U.S.	100	46°51'N	68°01'W
Caribou, i., Can.	98	47°22'N	85°42'W
Caribou Lake, l., Mn., U.S.	117h	46°54'N	92°16'W
Caribou Mountains, mts., Can.	92	59°20'N	115°30'W
Carinhanha, Braz. (kä-rĭ-nyän´yä)	143	14°14'S	43°44'W
Carini, Italy (kä-rē´nē)	174	38°09'N	13°10'E
Carleton Place, Can. (kärl´tŭn)	99	45°15'N	76°10'W
Carletonville, S. Afr.	238c	26°20'S	27°23'E
Carlinville, Il., U.S. (kär´lĭn-vĭl)	121	39°16'N	89°52'W
Carlisle, Eng., U.K. (kär-lĭl´)	154	54°54'N	3°03'W
Carlisle, Ky., U.S.	108	38°20'N	84°00'W
Carlisle, Pa., U.S.	109	40°10'N	77°15'W
Carloforte, Italy (kär´lō-fôr-tå)	174	39°11'N	8°28'E
Carlos Casares, Arg. (kär-lôs-kä-sá´rĕs)	144	35°38'S	61°17'W
Carlow, Ire. (kär´lō)	164	52°50'N	7°00'W
Carlsbad, N.M., U.S. (kärlz´băd)	122	32°24'N	104°12'W
Carlsbad Caverns National Park, rec., N.M., U.S.	122	32°08'N	104°30'W
Carlton, Eng., U.K. (kärl´tŭn)	158a	52°58'N	1°05'W
Carlton, Mn., U.S.	117h	46°40'N	92°26'W
Carlton Center, Mi., U.S. (kärl´tŭn sĕn´tēr)	108	42°45'N	85°20'W
Carlyle, Il., U.S. (kärlīl´)	121	38°37'N	89°23'W
Carmagnola, Italy (kär-mä-nyô´lä)	174	44°52'N	7°48'E
Carman, Can. (kär´mȧn)	90	49°32'N	98°00'W
Carmarthen, Wales, U.K. (kär-mär´thĕn)	164	51°50'N	4°20'W
Carmaux, Fr. (kȧr-mō´)	170	44°05'N	2°09'E
Carmel, N.Y., U.S. (kär´mĕl)	110a	41°25'N	73°42'W
Carmelo, Ur. (kär-mĕ´lô)	141c	33°59'S	58°15'W
Carmen, Isla del, i., Mex. (ē´s-lä-dĕl-kȧ´r-mĕn)	131	18°43'N	91°40'W
Carmen, Laguna del, l., Mex. (lä-gô´nä-dĕl-kȧ´r-mĕn)	131	18°15'N	93°26'W
Carmen de Areco, Arg. (kär´mĕn´ dā ä-rā´kô)	141c	34°21'S	59°50'W
Carmen de Patagones, Arg. (kȧ´r-mĕn-dĕ-pä-tä-gô´nĕs)	144	41°00'S	63°00'W
Carmi, Il., U.S. (kär´mī)	108	38°05'N	88°10'W
Carmo, Braz. (kȧ´r-mô)	141a	21°57'S	42°45'W
Carmo do Rio Clara, Braz. (kȧ´r-mô-dô-rē´ô-klä´rä)	141a	20°57'S	46°04'W
Carmona, Spain	172	37°28'N	5°38'W
Carnarvon, Austl. (kär-när´vŭn)	218	24°45'S	113°45'E
Carnarvon, S. Afr.	232	31°00'S	22°15'E
Carnation, Wa., U.S. (kär-nā´shŭn)	116a	47°39'N	121°55'W
Carnaxide, Port. (kär-nä-shē´dĕ)	173b	38°44'N	9°15'W
Carndonagh, Ire. (kärn-dō-nä´)	164	55°15'N	7°15'W
Carnegie, Ok., U.S. (kär-nĕg´ĭ)	120	35°06'N	98°38'W
Carnegie, Pa., U.S.	111e	40°24'N	80°06'W
Carneys Point, N.J., U.S. (kär´nĕs)	109	39°45'N	75°25'W
Carnic Alps, mts., Eur.	161	46°43'N	12°38'E
Carnot, Alg. (kär nō´)	173	36°15'N	1°40'E
Carnot, C.A.R.	231	5°00'N	15°52'E
Carnsore Point, c., Ire. (kärn´sôr)	164	52°10'N	6°16'W
Caro, Mi., U.S. (kā´rō)	108	43°30'N	83°25'W
Carolina, Braz. (kä-rô-lē´nä)	143	7°26'S	47°16'W

PRONOUNCING INDEX

Carolina – Celestún 279

PLACE (Pronunciation)	PAGE	LAT.	LONG.
Carolina, S. Afr. (kăr-ô-lī′nȧ)	232	26°07′S	30°09′E
Carolina, I., Mex. (kä-rŏ-lē′nä)	132a	18°41′N	89°40′W
Caroline Islands, is., Oc.	5	8°00′N	140°00′E
Caroni, r., Ven. (kä-rō′nē)	142	5°49′N	62°57′W
Carora, Ven. (kä-rô′rä)	142	10°09′N	70°12′W
Carpathians, mts., Eur. (kär-pā′thĭ-ăn)	156	49°23′N	20°14′E
Carpaţii Meridionali (Transylvanian Alps), mts., Rom.	156	45°30′N	23°30′E
Carpentaria, Gulf of, b., Austl. (kär-pĕn-târ′ĭȧ)	220	14°45′S	138°50′E
Carpentras, Fr. (kär-päɴ-träs′)	171	44°04′N	5°01′E
Carpi, Italy	174	44°48′N	10°54′E
Carrara, Italy (kä-rä′rä)	162	44°05′N	10°05′E
Carrauntoohil, Ire. (kă-răn-to͞o′ĭl)	164	52°01′N	9°48′W
Carretas, Punta, c., Peru (po͞o′n tä kär rĕ′tĕ′räs)	142	14°15′S	76°25′W
Carriacou, i., Gren.	133b	12°28′N	61°20′W
Carrick-on-Sur, Ire. (kăr′-ĭk)	164	52°20′N	7°35′W
Carrier, Can. (kăr′ĭ-ẽr)	102b	46°43′N	71°05′W
Carriere, Ms., U.S. (kȧ-rēr′)	124	30°37′N	89°37′W
Carriers Mills, Il., U.S. (kăr′ĭ-ẽrs)	108	37°40′N	88°40′W
Carrington, N.D., U.S. (kăr′ĭng-tŭn)	112	47°26′N	99°06′W
Carr Inlet, Wa., U.S. (kăr ĭn′lĕt)	116a	47°20′N	122°42′W
Carrion Crow Harbor, b., Bah. (kăr′ĭŭn krō)	134	26°35′N	77°55′W
Carrión de los Condes, Spain (kär-rē̊-ōn′ dā los kōn′dås)	172	42°20′N	4°35′W
Carrizo Creek, r., N.M., U.S. (kär-rē′zō)	120	36°22′N	103°39′W
Carrizo Springs, Tx., U.S.	122	28°32′N	99°51′W
Carrizozo, N.M., U.S. (kär-rē̊-zō′zō)	119	33°40′N	105°55′W
Carroll, Ia., U.S. (kăr′ŭl)	113	42°03′N	94°51′W
Carrollton, Ga., U.S. (kăr-ŭl-tŭn)	124	33°35′N	85°05′W
Carrollton, Il., U.S.	121	39°18′N	90°22′W
Carrollton, Ky., U.S.	108	38°45′N	85°15′W
Carrollton, Mi., U.S.	108	43°30′N	83°55′W
Carrollton, Mo., U.S.	121	39°21′N	93°29′W
Carrollton, Oh., U.S.	108	40°35′N	81°10′W
Carrollton, Tx., U.S.	117c	32°58′N	96°53′W
Carrols, Wa., U.S. (kăr′ŭlz)	116c	46°05′N	122°51′W
Carrot, r., Can.	96	53°12′N	103°50′W
Carry-le-Rouet, Fr. (kä-rē′lĕ-rȯ-ā′)	170a	43°20′N	5°10′E
Carsamba, Tur. (chär-shäm′bä)	163	41°05′N	36°40′E
Carson, r., Nv., U.S. (kär′sŭn)	118	39°15′N	119°25′W
Carson City, Nv., U.S.	104	39°10′N	119°45′W
Carson Sink, Nv., U.S.	118	39°51′N	118°25′W
Cartagena, Col. (kär-tä-hā′nä)	142	10°30′N	75°40′W
Cartagena, Spain (kär-tä-ĸĕ′nä)	154	37°46′N	1°00′W
Cartago, Col. (kär-tä′gō)	142a	4°44′N	75°54′W
Cartago, C.R.	129	9°52′N	83°56′W
Cartaxo, Port. (kär-tä′shō)	172	39°10′N	8°48′W
Carteret, N.J., U.S. (kär′tē-ret)	110a	40°35′N	74°13′W
Cartersville, Ga., U.S. (kär′tẽrs-vĭl)	124	34°09′N	84°47′W
Carthage, Tun.	230	37°04′N	10°18′E
Carthage, Il., U.S. (kär′thåj)	121	40°27′N	91°09′W
Carthage, Mo., U.S.	121	37°10′N	94°18′W
Carthage, N.C., U.S.	125	35°22′N	79°25′W
Carthage, N.Y., U.S.	109	44°00′N	75°45′W
Carthage, Tx., U.S.	123	32°09′N	94°20′W
Carthcart, S. Afr. (cärth-că′t)	233c	32°18′S	27°11′E
Cartwright, Can. (kärt′rít)	91	53°36′N	57°00′W
Caruaru, Braz. (kä-rȯ-ȧ-ro͞o′)	143	8°19′S	35°52′W
Carúpano, Ven. (kä-ro͞o′pä-nō)	142	10°45′N	63°21′W
Caruthersville, Mo., U.S. (kȧ-rŭdh′ẽrz-vĭl)	121	36°09′N	89°41′W
Carver, Or., U.S. (kärv′ẽr)	116c	45°24′N	122°30′W
Carvoeiro, Cabo, c., Port. (kȧ′bō-kär-vô-ĕ′y-rō)	172	39°22′N	9°24′W
Cary, Il., U.S. (kă′rē̊)	111a	42°13′N	88°14′W
Casablanca, Chile (kä-sä-bläŋ′kä)	141b	33°19′S	71°24′W
Casablanca, Mor.	230	33°32′N	7°41′W
Casa Branca, Braz. (kȧ′sä-brȧ′ɴ-kä)	141a	21°47′S	47°04′W
Casa Grande, Az., U.S. (kä′sä grän′dā)	119	32°50′N	111°45′W
Casa Grande Ruins National Monument, rec., Az., U.S.	119	33°00′N	111°33′W
Casale Monferrato, Italy (kä-sä′lā)	174	45°08′N	8°26′E
Casalmaggiore, Italy (kä-säl-mäd-jō′rā)	174	45°00′N	10°24′E
Casamance, r., Sen. (kä-sä-mäɴs′)	230	12°30′N	15°00′W
Cascade Mountains, mts., N.A.	95	49°10′N	121°00′W
Cascade Point, c., N.Z. (kăs-kād′)	221a	43°59′S	168°23′E
Cascade Range, mts., N.A.	106	42°50′N	122°20′W
Cascade-Siskiyou National Monument, rec., Or., U.S.	114	42°05′N	122°30′W
Cascade Tunnel, trans., Wa., U.S.	114	47°41′N	120°53′W
Cascais, Port. (käs-kȧ-ēzh)	172	38°42′N	9°25′W
Case Inlet, Wa., U.S. (kās)	116a	47°22′N	122°47′W
Caseros, Arg. (kä-sā′rôs)	144a	34°35′S	58°34′W
Caserta, Italy (kä-zĕr′tä)	174	41°04′N	14°21′E
Casey, Il., U.S. (kā′sĭ)	108	39°20′N	88°00′W
Cashmere, Wa., U.S. (kăsh′mĭr)	114	47°30′N	120°28′W
Casiguran, Phil. (käs-sē-go͞o′rän)	213a	16°15′N	122°10′E
Casiguran Sound, strt., Phil.	213a	16°02′N	121°51′E
Casilda, Arg. (kä-sē′l-dä)	144	33°02′S	61°11′W
Casilda, Cuba	134	21°50′N	80°00′W
Casimiro de Abreu, Braz. (kä′sē̊-mē′ro-dĕ-ȧ-brĕ′o͞oo)	141a	22°30′S	42°11′W
Casino, Austl. (kȧ-sē′nō)	222	28°35′S	153°10′E
Casiquiare, r., Ven. (kä-sē̊-kyä′rā)	142	2°11′N	66°15′W
Caspe, Spain (käs′på)	173	41°18′N	0°02′W
Casper, Wy., U.S. (kăs′pẽr)	104	42°51′N	106°18′W
Caspian Depression, depr. (kăs′pĭ-ȧn)	178	47°40′N	52°35′E

PLACE (Pronunciation)	PAGE	LAT.	LONG.
Caspian Sea, sea	178	40°00′N	52°00′E
Cass, W.V., U.S. (kăs)	109	38°25′N	79°55′W
Cass, I., Mn., U.S.	113	47°23′N	94°28′W
Cassai (Kasai), r., Afr. (kä-sä′ē)	232	11°30′S	21°00′E
Cass City, Mi., U.S. (kăs)	108	43°35′N	83°10′W
Casselman, Can. (kăs′′l-mȧn)	102c	45°18′N	75°05′W
Casselton, N.D., U.S. (kăs′′l-tŭn)	112	46°53′N	97°14′W
Cássia, Braz. (kȧ′syä)	141a	20°36′S	46°53′W
Cassin, Tx., U.S. (kăs′ĭn)	117d	29°16′N	98°29′W
Cassinga, Ang.	232	15°05′S	16°15′E
Cassino, Italy (käs-sē′nō)	162	41°30′N	13°50′E
Cass Lake, Mn., U.S. (kăs)	113	47°23′N	94°37′W
Cassopolis, Mi., U.S. (kăs-ŏ′pô-lĭs)	108	41°55′N	86°00′W
Cassville, Mo., U.S. (kăs′vĭl)	121	36°41′N	93°52′W
Castanheira de Pêra, Port. (käs-tän-yā′rä-dĕ-pĕ′rä)	172	40°00′N	8°07′W
Castellammare di Stabia, Italy	173c	40°26′N	14°29′E
Castelli, Arg. (kas-tĕ′zhē)	141c	36°07′S	57°48′W
Castelló de la Plana, Spain	162	39°59′N	0°05′W
Castelnaudary, Fr. (kȧs′tĕl-nō-dȧ-rē′)	170	43°20′N	1°57′E
Castelo, Braz. (käs-tĕ′lô)	141a	20°37′S	41°13′W
Castelo Branco, Port. (käs-tā′lȯ bräŋ′kȯ)	162	39°48′N	7°37′W
Castelo de Vide, Port. (käs-tā′lȯ dĭ vē′dĭ)	172	39°25′N	7°25′W
Castelsarrasin, Fr. (kȧs′tĕl-sȧ-rȧ-zăɴ′)	170	44°03′N	1°05′E
Castelvetrano, Italy (käs′tĕl-vē̊-trä′nō)	174	37°43′N	12°50′E
Castilla, Peru (kȧs-tē′l-yä)	142	5°18′S	80°40′W
Castilla La Nueva, hist. reg., Spain (käs-tē′lyä lä nwā′vȧ)	172	39°15′N	3°55′W
Castilla La Vieja, hist. reg., Spain (käs-tēl′yä lä vyā′hä)	172	40°48′N	4°24′W
Castillo de San Marcos National Monument, rec., Fl., U.S. (käs-tē′lyā de-sän măr-kŏs)	125	29°55′N	81°25′W
Castle, i., Bah. (kȧs′′l)	135	22°05′N	74°20′W
Castlebar, Ire. (kȧs′′l-bär)	164	53°55′N	9°15′W
Castle Dale, Ut., U.S. (kȧs′l dāl)	119	39°15′N	111°00′W
Castle Donington, Eng., U.K. (dŏn′ĭng-tŭn)	158a	52°50′N	1°21′W
Castleford, Eng., U.K. (kȧs′l-fẽrd)	158a	53°43′N	1°21′W
Castlegar, Can. (kȧs′′l-gär)	95	49°19′N	117°40′W
Castlemaine, Austl. (käs′′l-mān)	222	37°05′S	144°10′E
Castle Peak, mtn., Co., U.S.	119	39°00′N	106°50′W
Castle Rock, Wa., U.S. (kȧs′′l-rŏk)	114	46°17′N	122°53′W
Castle Rock Flowage, res., Wi., U.S.	113	44°03′N	89°48′W
Castle Shannon, Pa., U.S. (shăn′ŭn)	111e	40°22′N	80°02′W
Castleton, In., U.S. (kȧs′′l-tŏn)	111g	39°54′N	86°03′W
Castor, r., Can. (kăs′tôr)	102c	45°16′N	75°14′W
Castor, r., Mo., U.S.	121	36°59′N	89°53′W
Castres, Fr. (kȧs′tr′)	170	43°36′N	2°13′E
Castries, St. Luc. (kȧs-trē′)	133b	14°01′N	61°00′W
Castro, Braz. (käs′trȯ)	143	24°56′S	50°00′W
Castro, Chile (käs′tro)	144	42°27′S	73°48′W
Castro Daire, Port. (käs′trȯ dīr′ĭ)	172	40°56′N	7°57′W
Castro del Río, Spain (käs-trô-dĕl rē̊′ō)	172	37°42′N	4°28′W
Castrop Rauxel, Ger. (käs′trōp rou′ksĕl)	171c	51°33′N	7°19′E
Castro-Urdiales, Spain	162	43°23′N	3°11′W
Castro Valley, Ca., U.S.	116b	37°42′N	122°05′W
Castro Verde, Port. (käs-trō vĕr′dĕ)	172	37°43′N	8°05′W
Castrovillari, Italy (käs′trō-vēl-lyä′rē)	174	39°48′N	16°11′E
Castuera, Spain (käs-tȯ-ā′rä)	172	38°43′N	5°33′W
Casula, Moz.	237	15°25′S	33°40′E
Cat, i., Bah.	135	24°30′N	75°30′W
Catacamas, Hond. (kä-tä-kȧ′mäs)	132	14°52′N	85°55′W
Cataguases, Braz. (kä-tä-gwȧ′sĕs)	141a	21°23′S	42°42′W
Catahoula, I., La., U.S. (kăt-ȧ-hȯ′lȧ)	123	31°35′N	92°20′W
Catalão, Braz. (kä-tä-louɴ′)	143	18°09′S	47°42′W
Catalina, i., Dom. Rep. (kä-tä-lē̊′nä)	135	18°20′N	69°00′W
Catalunya, hist. reg., Spain	173	41°23′N	0°50′E
Catamarca, Arg. (kä-rä-mȧ′r-kä)	144	28°29′S	65°45′W
Catamarca, prov., Arg. (kä-tä-mär′kä)	144	27°15′S	67°15′W
Catanaun, Phil. (kä-tä-nä′wän)	213a	13°36′N	122°20′E
Catanduanes Island, i., Phil. (kä-tän-dwä′nĕs)	213	13°55′N	125°00′E
Catanduva, Braz. (kä-tȧn-do͞o′vä)	143	21°12′S	48°47′W
Catania, Italy (kä-tä′nyä)	154	37°30′N	15°09′E
Catania, Golfo di, b., Italy (gôl-fô-dē-kȧ-tä′nyä)	174	37°24′N	15°28′E
Catanzaro, Italy (kä-tän-dzä′rō)	163	38°53′N	16°34′E
Catarroja, Spain (kä-tär-rō′hä)	173	39°24′N	0°25′W
Catawba, r., N.C., U.S. (kȧ-tô′bȧ)	125	35°25′N	80°55′W
Catbalogan, Phil. (kät-bä-lō′gän)	213	11°45′N	124°52′E
Catemaco, Mex. (kä-tā-mä′kō)	131	18°26′N	95°06′W
Catemaco, Lago, I., Mex. (lä′gô-kä-tā-mä′kō)	131	18°23′N	95°04′W
Caterham, Eng., U.K. (kā′tẽr-ŭm)	158b	51°16′N	0°04′W
Catete, Ang. (kä-tĕ′tĕ)	232	9°06′S	13°43′E
Cathedral Mountain, mtn., Tx., U.S. (kȧ-thē′drăl)	122	30°09′N	103°46′W
Cathedral Peak, mtn., Afr. (kă-thē̊′drȧl)	233c	28°53′S	29°04′E
Catherine, Lake, I., Ar., U.S. (kă-thẽr-ĭn)	121	34°26′N	92°47′W
Cathkin Peak, mtn., Afr. (kăth′kĭn)	232	29°08′S	29°22′E
Cathlamet, Wa., U.S. (kăth-lăm′ĕt)	116c	46°12′N	123°22′W
Catlettsburg, Ky., U.S. (kăt′lĕts-bŭrg)	108	38°20′N	82°35′W
Catoche, Cabo, c., Mex. (kä-tô′chĕ)	128	21°30′N	87°15′W
Catonsville, Md., U.S. (kā′tŭnz-vĭl)	110e	39°16′N	76°45′W
Catorce, Mex. (kä-tôr′sȧ)	130	23°41′N	100°51′W
Catskill, N.Y., U.S. (kăts′kĭl)	109	42°15′N	73°50′W

PLACE (Pronunciation)	PAGE	LAT.	LONG.
Catskill Mountains, mts., N.Y., U.S.	107	42°20′N	74°35′W
Cattaraugus Indian Reservation, I.R., N.Y., U.S. (kăt′tā-ră-gŭs)	109	42°30′N	79°05′W
Catu, Braz. (kȧ-to͞o)	143	12°26′S	38°12′W
Catuala, Ang.	236	16°29′S	19°03′E
Catumbela, r., Ang. (kä′tŏm-bĕl′ȧ)	236	12°40′S	14°10′E
Cauayan, Phil. (kou-ä′yän)	213a	16°56′N	121°46′E
Cauca, r., Col. (kou′kä)	142	7°30′N	75°26′W
Caucagua, Ven. (käȯ-kȧ′gwä)	143b	10°17′N	66°22′W
Caucasus, mts.	178	43°20′N	42°00′E
Cauchon Lake, I., Can. (kô-shŏn′)	97	55°25′N	96°30′W
Caughnawaga, Can.	102a	45°24′N	73°41′W
Caulfield, Austl.	217a	37°53′S	145°03′E
Caulonia, Italy (kou-lō′nyä)	174	38°24′N	16°22′E
Cauquenes, Chile (kou-kā′nās)	144	35°54′S	72°14′W
Caura, r., Ven. (kou′rä)	142	6°48′N	64°40′W
Causapscal, Can.	100	48°22′N	67°14′W
Caution, Cape, c., Can. (kô′shŭn)	94	51°10′N	127°47′W
Cauto, r., Cuba (kou tô)	134	20°33′N	70°20′W
Cauvery, r., India	199	12°00′N	77°00′E
Cava, Braz. (kȧ′vä)	144b	22°41′S	43°26′W
Cava de′ Tirreni, Italy (kä′vä-dĕ-tēr-rĕ′nē)	173c	40°27′N	14°43′E
Cávado, r., Port. (kä-vä′dō)	172	41°43′N	8°08′W
Cavalcante, Braz. (kä-väl-kän′tā)	143	13°45′S	47°33′W
Cavalier, N.D., U.S. (kăv-ȧ-lēr′)	112	48°45′N	97°39′W
Cavally, r., Afr.	234	4°40′N	7°30′W
Cavan, Ire. (kăv′ȧn)	164	54°01′N	7°00′W
Cavarzere, Italy (kä-vär′dzå-rā)	174	45°08′N	12°06′E
Cavendish, Vt., U.S. (kăv′ĕn-dĭsh)	109	43°25′N	72°35′W
Caviana, Ilha, i., Braz. (kä-vyä′nä)	143	0°45′N	49°33′W
Cavite, Phil. (kä-vē′tā)	213a	14°30′N	120°54′E
Caxambu, Braz. (kä-shȧ′m-bo͞o)	143	22°00′S	44°45′W
Caxias, Braz. (kä′shē̊-äzh)	143	4°48′S	43°16′W
Caxias do Sul, Braz. (kä′shē̊-äzh-dô-so͞o′l)	144	29°13′S	51°03′W
Caxito, Ang. (kä-shē′tȯ)	232	8°33′S	13°36′E
Cayambe, Ec. (kȧ-īä′m-bĕ)	142	0°03′N	79°09′W
Cayenne, Fr. Gu. (kā-ĕn′)	143	4°56′N	52°18′W
Cayetano Rubio, Mex. (kä-yĕ-tȧ-nô-ro͞o′byô)	130	20°37′N	100°21′W
Cayey, P.R.	129b	18°05′N	66°12′W
Cayman Brac, i., Cay. Is. (kī-män′ brȧk)	134	19°45′N	79°50′W
Cayman Islands, dep., N.A.	134	19°30′N	80°30′W
Cay Sal Bank, bk. (kē-săl)	134	23°55′N	80°20′W
Cayuga, I., N.Y., U.S. (kā-yo͞o′gȧ)	109	42°35′N	76°35′W
Cazalla de la Sierra, Spain	172	37°55′N	5°48′W
Cazaux, Étang de, I., Fr. (ā-täɴ′ dĕ kä-zō′)	170	44°32′N	0°59′W
Cazenovia, N.Y., U.S. (kăz-ē̊-nō′vĭ-ă)	109	42°55′N	75°50′W
Cazenovia Creek, r., N.Y., U.S.	111c	42°49′N	78°45′W
Čazma, Cro. (chäz′mä)	174	45°44′N	16°39′E
Cazombo, Ang. (kä-zô′m-bŏ)	232	11°54′S	22°52′E
Cazones, r., Mex. (kä-zô′nĕs)	131	20°37′N	97°28′W
Cazones, Ensenada de, b., Cuba (ĕn-sĕ-nä-dä-dĕ-kä-zō′nås)	134	22°05′N	81°30′W
Cazones, Golfo de, b., Cuba (gôl-fô-dĕ-kä-zō′nås)	134	21°55′N	81°15′W
Cazorla, Spain (kä-thôr′lå)	172	37°55′N	2°58′W
Cea, r., Spain (thā′ä)	172	42°18′N	5°10′W
Ceará-Mirim, Braz. (sā-ä-rä′mē-rē̊′ɴ)	143	6°00′S	35°13′W
Cebaco, Isla, i., Pan. (ē̊′s-lä-så-bä′kō)	133	7°27′N	81°08′W
Cebolla Creek, r., Co., U.S. (sē-bōl′yä)	119	38°15′N	107°10′W
Cebreros, Spain (sĕ-brĕ′rôs)	172	40°28′N	4°28′W
Cebu, Phil. (sā-bo͞o′)	213	10°22′N	123°49′E
Čechy (Bohemia), hist. reg., Czech Rep.	168	49°51′N	13°55′E
Cecil, Pa., U.S. (sē′sĭl)	111e	40°20′N	80°10′W
Cedar, r., Ia., U.S.	113	42°23′N	92°07′W
Cedar, r., Wa., U.S.	116c	45°56′N	122°32′W
Cedar, West Fork, r., Ia., U.S.	113	42°49′N	93°10′W
Cedar Bayou, Tx., U.S.	123a	29°54′N	94°58′W
Cedar Breaks National Monument, rec., Ut., U.S.	119	37°35′N	112°55′W
Cedarburg, Wi., U.S. (sē′dẽr bûrg)	113	43°23′N	88°00′W
Cedar City, Ut., U.S.	119	37°40′N	113°10′W
Cedar Creek, r., N.D., U.S.	112	46°05′N	102°10′W
Cedar Falls, Ia., U.S.	113	42°31′N	92°29′W
Cedar Keys, Fl., U.S.	124	29°06′N	83°03′W
Cedar Lake, In., U.S.	111a	41°22′N	87°27′W
Cedar Lake, I., In., U.S.	111a	41°23′N	87°25′W
Cedar Lake, res., Can.	92	53°10′N	100°00′W
Cedar Rapids, Ia., U.S.	105	42°00′N	91°43′W
Cedar Springs, Mi., U.S.	108	43°15′N	85°40′W
Cedartown, Ga., U.S. (sē′dẽr-toun)	124	34°00′N	85°15′W
Cedarville, S. Afr. (cē̊dȧr′vĭl)	233c	30°23′S	29°04′E
Cedral, Mex. (sā-dräl′)	130	23°47′N	100°42′W
Cedros, Hond. (sā′drōs)	132	14°36′N	87°07′W
Cedros, i., Mex.	128	28°10′N	115°10′W
Ceduna, Austl. (sē̊-dȯ′nȧ)	218	32°15′S	133°55′E
Ceel Buur, Som.	238a	4°35′N	46°40′E
Cega, r., Spain (thā′gä)	172	41°25′N	4°27′W
Cegléd, Hung. (tsă′glād)	169	47°10′N	19°49′E
Ceglie, Italy (chĕ′lyĕ)	175	40°39′N	17°32′E
Cehegín, Spain (thā-å-hēn′)	172	38°05′N	1°48′W
Ceiba del Agua, Cuba (sā′bä-dĕl-ȧ′gwä)	135a	22°53′N	82°38′W
Cekhira, Tun.	230	34°17′N	10°00′E
Celaya, Mex. (sā-lä′yä)	128	20°33′N	100°49′W
Celebes (Sulawesi), i., Indon.	212	2°15′S	120°30′E
Celebes Sea, sea, Asia	212	3°45′N	121°52′E
Celestún, Mex. (sĕ-lĕs-to͞o′n)	132a	20°57′N	90°18′W

ng-sing; ŋ-baŋk; ɴ-nasalized n; nŏd; cŏmmit; ōld; ôbey; ôrder; oi-boil; fo͞od; ȯ-as oo in foot; ou-out; s-soft; sh-dish; th-thin; pūre; ůnite; ûrn; stŭd; circŭs; ü-as in French tu; ′-indeterminate vowel.

PLACE (Pronunciation)	PAGE	LAT.	LONG.
Celina, Oh., U.S. (sĕlī′na)	108	40°30′N	84°35′W
Celje, Slvn. (tsĕl′yĕ)	174	46°13′N	15°17′E
Celle, Ger. (tsĕl′ē)	161	52°37′N	10°05′E
Cement, Ok., U.S. (sē-mĕnt′)	120	34°56′N	98°07′W
Cenderawasih, Teluk, b., Indon.	213	2°20′S	135°30′E
Ceniza, Pico, mtn., Ven. (pē′kŏ-sĕ-nē′zä)	143b	10°24′N	67°26′W
Center, Tx., U.S. (sĕn′tẽr)	123	31°50′N	94°10′W
Center Hill Lake, res., Tn., U.S. (sĕn′tẽr-hĭl)	124	36°02′N	86°00′W
Center Line, Mi., U.S. (sĕn′tẽr līn)	111b	42°29′N	83°01′W
Centerville, Ia., U.S. (sĕn′tẽr-vĭl)	113	40°44′N	92°48′W
Centerville, Mn., U.S.	117g	45°10′N	[illegible]
Centerville, Pa., U.S.	111e	40°02′N	79°58′W
Centerville, S.D., U.S.	112	43°07′N	96°56′W
Centerville, Ut., U.S.	117b	40°55′N	111°53′W
[illegible] (kôr dēl yĕ′rä sĕn trä′l)	142	[illegible]	[illegible]
Central, Cordillera, mts., Col.	142a	3°58′N	75°55′W
Central, Cordillera, mts., Dom. Rep.	135	19°05′N	71°30′W
Central, Cordillera, mts., Phil. (kôr-dēl-yĕ′rä-sĕn′träl)	213a	17°05′N	120°55′E
Central African Republic, nation, Afr.	231	7°50′N	21°00′E
Central America, reg., N.A. (ä-mĕr′ĭ-kȧ)	128	10°45′N	87°15′W
Central City, Ky., U.S. (sĕn′trȧl)	124	37°15′N	87°09′W
Central City, Ne., U.S. (sĕn′trȧl sĭ′tĭ)	112	41°07′N	98°00′W
Central Falls, R.I., U.S. (sĕn′trȧl fôlz)	110b	41°54′N	71°23′W
Centralia, Il., U.S. (sĕn-trā′lĭ-ȧ)	108	38°35′N	89°05′W
Centralia, Mo., U.S.	121	39°11′N	92°07′W
Centralia, Wa., U.S.	114	46°42′N	122°58′W
Central Plateau, plat., Russia	180	55°00′N	33°30′E
Central Valley, N.Y., U.S.	110a	41°19′N	74°07′W
Centreville, Il., U.S. (sĕn′tẽr-vĭl)	117e	38°33′N	90°06′W
Centreville, Md., U.S.	109	39°05′N	76°05′W
Century, Fl., U.S. (sĕn′tů-rĭ)	124	30°57′N	87°15′W
Ceram (Seram), i., Indon.	213	2°45′S	129°30′E
Céret, Fr.	170	42°29′N	2°47′E
Cerignola, Italy (chā-rē-nyô′lä)	174	41°16′N	15°55′E
Cerknica, Slvn. (tsĕr′knē-tsȧ)	174	45°48′N	14°21′E
Cern′achovsk, Russia (chĕr-nyä′kôfsk)	180	54°38′N	21°49′E
Cerralvo, Mex. (sĕr-räl′vō)	122	26°05′N	99°37′W
Cerralvo, i., Mex.	128	24°00′N	109°59′W
Cerrito, Col. (sĕr-rē′-tô)	142a	3°41′N	76°17′W
Cerritos, Mex. (sĕr-rē′tôs)	130	22°26′N	100°16′W
Cerro de Pasco, Peru (sĕr′rō dā päs′kō)	142	10°45′S	76°14′W
Cerro Gordo, Arroyo de, r., Mex. (är-rô-yō-dĕ-sĕ′r-rō-gôr-dō)	122	26°12′N	104°06′W
Certegui, Col. (sĕr-tĕ′gē)	142a	5°21′N	76°35′W
Cervantes, Phil. (sĕr-vän′tās)	213a	16°59′N	120°42′E
Cervera del Río Alhama, Spain	172	42°02′N	1°55′W
Cerveteri, Italy (chĕr-vĕ′tĕ-rē)	173d	42°00′N	12°06′E
Cesena, Italy (chĕ′sĕ-nä)	174	44°08′N	12°16′E
Cēsis, Lat. (sā′sĭs)	167	57°19′N	25°17′E
Česká Lípa, Czech Rep. (chĕs′kä lē′pa)	168	50°41′N	14°31′E
České Budějovice, Czech Rep. (chĕs′kā bōō′dyĕ-yô-vēt-sĕ)	161	49°00′N	14°30′E
Českomoravská Vysočina, hills, Czech Rep.	168	49°21′N	15°40′E
Český Těšín, Czech Rep.	169	49°43′N	18°22′E
Çeşme, Tur. (chĕsh′mĕ)	175	38°20′N	26°20′E
Cessnock, Austl.	219	32°58′S	151°15′E
Cestos, r., Lib.	234	5°40′N	9°25′W
Cetinje, Mont. (tsĕt′in-yĕ)	175	42°23′N	18°55′E
Ceuta, Sp. N. Afr. (thā-ōō′tä)	230	36°04′N	5°36′W
Cévennes, reg., Fr. (sā-vĕn′)	161	44°20′N	3°48′E
Ceylon *see* Sri Lanka, nation, Asia	203	8°45′N	82°30′E
Chabot, Lake, l., Ca., U.S. (sha′bŏt)	116b	37°44′N	122°06′W
Chacabuco, Arg. (chä-kä-bōō′kō)	141c	34°37′S	60°27′W
Chacaltianguis, Mex. (chä-käl-tē-äŋ′gwēs)	131	18°18′N	95°50′W
Chachapoyas, Peru (chä-chä-poi′yäs)	142	6°16′S	77°48′W
Chaco, prov., Arg. (chä′kō)	144	26°00′S	60°45′W
Chaco Culture National Historic Park, rec., N.M., U.S. (chä′kŏ)	119	36°05′N	108°00′W
Chad, Russia (chăd)	186a	56°33′N	57°11′E
Chad, nation, Afr.	231	17°48′N	19°00′E
Chad, Lake, l., Afr.	231	13°55′N	13°40′E
Chadbourn, N.C., U.S. (chăd′bŭn)	125	34°19′N	78°55′W
Chadron, Ne., U.S. (chăd′rŭn)	104	42°50′N	103°10′W
Chafarinas, Islas, is., Sp. N. Afr.	172	35°08′N	2°20′W
Chaffee, Mo., U.S. (chăf′ē)	121	37°10′N	89°39′W
Chāgal Hills, hills, Afg.	198	29°15′N	63°28′E
Chagodoshcha, r., Russia (chä-gō-dôsh-chä)	176	59°08′N	35°13′E
Chagres, r., Pan. (chä′grĕs)	133	9°18′N	79°22′W
Chagrin, r., Oh., U.S. (shȧ′grĭn)	111d	41°34′N	81°24′W
Chagrin Falls, Oh., U.S. (shȧ′grĭn fôls)	111d	41°26′N	81°23′W
Chahar, hist. reg., China (chä-här)	205	44°25′N	115°00′E
Chake Chake, Tan.	237	5°15′S	39°46′E
Chalatenango, El Sal. (chäl-ä-tĕ-näŋ′gō)	132	14°04′N	88°54′W
Chalbi Desert, des., Kenya	237	3°40′N	36°50′E
Chalcatongo, Mex. (chäl-kä-tôŋ′gō)	131	17°04′N	97°41′W
Chalchihuites, Mex. (chäl-chē-wē′tās)	130	23°28′N	103°57′W
Chalchuapa, El Sal. (chäl-chwä′pä)	132	14°01′N	89°39′W
Chalco, Mex. (chäl-kō)	131a	19°15′N	98°54′W
Chaleur Bay, b., Can. (shȧ-lûr′)	93	47°58′N	65°33′W
Chalgrove, Eng., U.K. (chăl′grôv)	158b	51°38′N	1°05′W
Chaling, China (chä′lĭng)	209	27°00′N	113°31′E
Chalkída, Grc.	163	38°28′N	23°38′E
Chalmette, La., U.S. (shăl-mĕt′)	110d	29°57′N	89°57′W
Châlons-sur-Marne, Fr. (shȧ-lôn′sür-märn)	161	48°57′N	4°23′E
Chalon-sur-Saône, Fr.	161	46°47′N	4°54′E
Chaltel, Cerro (Monte Fitzroy), mtn., S.A. (sĕ′r-rô-chäl′tĕl)	144	48°10′S	73°18′W
Chālūs, Iran	201	36°38′N	51°26′E
Chama, Rio, r., N.M., U.S. (chä′mä)	119	36°19′N	106°31′W
Chama, Sierra de, mts., Guat. (sē-ĕ′r-rä-dĕ-chä-mä)	132	15°48′N	90°20′W
Chamama, Mwi.	237	12°55′S	33°43′E
Chaman, Pak. (chŭm-än′)	199	30°58′N	66°21′E
Chambal, r., India (chŭm-bäl′)	199	24°30′N	75°30′E
Chamberlain, S.D., U.S. (chām′bẽr-lĭn)	[illegible]	[illegible]	[illegible]
Chamberlain, l., Me., U.S.	100	46°15′N	69°10′W
Chambersburg, Pa., U.S. (chām′bẽrz-bûrg)	109	40°00′N	77°40′W
Chambéry, Fr. (shäm-bā-rē′)	161	45°35′N	5°54′E
Chambeshi, r., Zam.	237	10°35′S	31°20′E
Chamblee, Ga., U.S. (chăm-blē′)	110c	33°55′N	84°18′W
Chambly, Can. (shäɴ-blē′)	102a	45°27′N	73°17′W
Chambly, Fr.	171b	49°11′N	2°14′E
Chambord, Can.	91	48°22′N	72°01′W
Chame, Punta, c., Pan. (pŏ′n-tä-chä′mȧ)	133	8°41′N	79°27′W
Chamelecón, r., Hond. (chä-mĕ-lĕ-kŏ′n)	132	15°09′N	88°42′W
Chamo, l., Eth.	231	5°58′N	37°00′E
Chamonix-Mont-Blanc, Fr. (shȧ-mô-nē′)	171	45°55′N	6°50′E
Champagne, reg., Fr. (shäm-păn′yĕ)	170	48°53′N	4°48′E
Champaign, Il., U.S. (shăm-pān′)	105	40°10′N	88°15′W
Champdāni, India	202a	22°48′N	88°21′E
Champerico, Guat. (chăm-pā-rē′kō)	132	14°18′N	91°55′W
Champion, Mi., U.S. (chăm′pĭ-ŭn)	113	46°30′N	87°59′W
Champlain, Lake, l., N.A. (shăm-plān′)	107	44°45′N	73°20′W
Champlitte-et-le-Prálot, Fr. (shäɴ-plēt′)	171	47°38′N	5°28′E
Champotón, Mex. (chäm-pō-tōn′)	131	19°21′N	90°43′W
Champotón, r., Mex.	131	19°19′N	90°15′W
Chañaral, Chile (chän-yä-räl′)	144	26°20′S	70°46′W
Chances Peak, vol., Monts.	133b	16°43′N	62°10′W
Chandeleur Islands, is., La., U.S. (shăn-dē-lōōr′)	124	29°53′N	88°35′W
Chandeleur Sound, strt., La., U.S.	124	29°47′N	89°08′W
Chandīgarh, India	199	30°51′N	77°13′E
Chandler, Can. (chăn′dlẽr)	91	48°21′N	64°41′W
Chandler, Ok., U.S.	121	35°42′N	96°52′W
Chandrapur, India	199	19°58′N	79°21′E
Chang *see* Yangtze, r., China	205	30°30′N	117°25′E
Changane, r., Moz.	232	22°42′S	32°46′E
Changara, Moz.	237	16°54′S	33°14′E
Changchun, China (chäŋ-chòn)	205	43°55′N	125°25′E
Changdang Hu, l., China (chäŋ-däŋ hōō)	206	31°37′N	119°29′E
Changde, China (chäŋ-dŭ)	205	29°00′N	111°38′E
Changhua, Tai. (chäng′hwä′)	209	24°02′N	120°32′E
Changjŏn, Kor., N. (chäng′jŭn′)	210	38°40′N	128°05′E
Changli, China (chäŋ-lē)	208	39°46′N	119°10′E
Changning, China (chäŋ-nĭŋ)	204	24°34′N	99°49′E
Changping, China (chäŋ-pĭŋ)	208	40°12′N	116°10′E
Changqing, China (chäŋ-chyĭŋ)	206	36°33′N	116°42′E
Changsan Got, c., Kor., N.	210	38°06′N	124°50′E
Changsha, China (chäŋ-shä)	205	28°20′N	113°00′E
Changshan Qundao, is., China (chäŋ-shän chyòn-dou)	206	39°08′N	122°26′E
Changshu, China (chäŋ-shōō)	206	31°40′N	120°45′E
Changting, China	209	25°50′N	116°18′E
Changwu, China (chäng′wōō′)	208	35°12′N	107°45′E
Changxindianzhen, China (chäŋ-shyĭn-dĭĕn-jŭn)	208a	39°49′N	116°12′E
Changxing Dao, i., China (chäŋ-shyĭŋ dou)	206	39°38′N	121°10′E
Changyi, China (chäŋ-yē)	206	36°51′N	119°23′E
Changyuan, China (chyäŋ-yuän)	206	35°10′N	114°41′E
Changzhi, China (chäŋ-jr)	208	35°58′N	112°58′E
Changzhou, China (chäŋ-jō)	205	31°47′N	119°56′E
Changzhuyuan, China (chäŋ-jōō-yuän)	206	31°33′N	115°17′E
Chanhassen, Mn., U.S. (shăn′hăs-sĕn)	117g	44°52′N	93°32′W
Chaniá, Grc.	162	35°31′N	24°01′E
Channel Islands, is., Eur. (chăn′ĕl)	156	49°15′N	3°30′W
Channel Islands, is., Ca., U.S.	118	33°30′N	119°15′W
Channel-Port-aux-Basques, Can.	91	47°35′N	59°11′W
Channelview, Tx., U.S. (chănĕlvū)	123a	29°46′N	95°07′W
Chantada, Spain (chän-tä′dä)	172	42°38′N	7°36′W
Chanthaburi, Thai.	212	12°37′N	102°04′E
Chantilly, Fr. (shäɴ-tē-yē′)	171b	49°12′N	2°30′E
Chantilly, Va., U.S. (shăn′tĭlē)	110e	38°53′N	77°26′W
Chantrey Inlet, b., Can. (chăn-trē)	92	67°49′N	95°00′W
Chanute, Ks., U.S. (shȧ-nōōt′)	105	37°41′N	95°27′W
Chany, l., Russia (chä′nē)	178	54°15′N	77°31′E
Chao′an, China (chou-än)	205	23°48′N	116°35′E
Chao Hu, l., China	209	31°45′N	116°59′E
Chao Phraya, r., Thai.	212	16°13′N	99°33′E
Chaor, r., China (chou-r)	208	47°20′N	121°40′E
Chaoshui, China (chou-shwā)	206	37°43′N	120°56′E
Chaoxian, China (chou shyĕn)	206	31°37′N	117°50′E
Chaoyang, China	205	41°32′N	120°20′E
Chaoyang, China (chou-yäŋ)	209	23°18′N	116°32′E
Chapada, Serra da, mts., Braz. (sĕ′r-rä-dä-shä-pä′dä)	143	14°57′S	54°34′W
Chapadão, Serra do, mtn., Braz. (sĕ′r-rä-dô-shä-pä-dou′ɴ)	141a	20°31′S	46°20′W
Chapala, Mex. (chä-pä′lä)	130	20°18′N	103°10′W
Chapala, Lago de, l., Mex. (lä′gô-dĕ-chä-pä′lä)	128	20°14′N	103°02′W
Chapalagana, r., Mex. (chä-pä-lä-gȧ′nä)	130	22°11′N	104°09′W
Chaparral, Col. (chä-pär-rȧ′l)	142	3°44′N	75°28′W
Chapayevsk, Russia (châ-pī′ĕfsk)	180	53°00′N	49°30′E
Chapel Hill, N.C., U.S. (chăp′′l hĭl)	125	35°55′N	79°05′W
Chaplain, l., Wa., U.S. (chăp′lĭn)	116a	47°58′N	121°50′W
Chapleau, Can. (chăp-lō′)	91	47°43′N	83°28′W
Chapman, Mount, mtn., Can. (chăp′mȧn)	95	51°50′N	118°20′W
Chapman′s Bay, b., S. Afr. [illegible]	[illegible]	[illegible]	[illegible]
Chappell, Ne., U.S. (chȧ-pĕl′)	112	41°06′N	102°29′W
Chapultenango, Mex. (chä-pòl-tē-näŋ′gō)	131	17°19′N	93°08′W
Chá Pungana, Ang.	236	13°44′S	18°39′E
Chār Borjak, Afg.	201	30°17′N	62°03′E
Charcas, Mex. (chär′käs)	130	23°09′N	101°09′W
Charco de Azul, Bahía, b., Pan.	133	8°14′N	82°45′W
Charente, r., Fr. (shȧ-räɴt′)	170	45°48′N	0°28′W
Chari, r., Afr. (shä-rē′)	235	12°45′N	14°55′E
Charing, Eng., U.K. (chă′rĭng)	158b	51°13′N	0°49′E
Chariton, Ia., U.S. (châr′ĭ-tŭn)	113	41°02′N	93°16′W
Chariton, r., Mo., U.S.	121	40°24′N	92°38′W
Charjew, Turkmen.	183	38°52′N	63°37′E
Charlemagne, Can. (shärl-mäny′)	102a	45°43′N	73°29′W
Charleroi, Bel. (shȧr-lē-rwä′)	161	50°25′N	4°35′E
Charleroi, Pa., U.S. (shär′lē-roi)	111e	40°08′N	79°54′W
Charles, Cape, c., Va., U.S. (chärlz)	109	37°05′N	75°48′W
Charlesbourg, Can. (shȧrl-bōōr′)	102b	46°51′N	71°16′W
Charles City, Ia., U.S. (chärlz)	113	43°03′N	92°40′W
Charleston, Il., U.S. (chärlz′tŭn)	108	39°30′N	88°10′W
Charleston, Mo., U.S.	121	36°53′N	89°20′W
Charleston, Ms., U.S.	124	34°00′N	90°02′W
Charleston, S.C., U.S.	105	32°47′N	79°56′W
Charleston, W.V., U.S.	105	38°20′N	81°35′W
Charlestown, St. K./N.	133b	17°10′N	62°32′W
Charlestown, In., U.S. (chärlz′toun)	111h	38°46′N	85°39′W
Charleville, Austl. (chär′lē-vĭl)	219	26°16′S	146°28′E
Charleville Mézières, Fr. (shärl-vĕl′)	170	49°48′N	4°41′E
Charlevoix, Mi., U.S. (shär′lē-voi)	108	45°20′N	85°15′W
Charlevoix, Lake, l., Mi., U.S.	113	45°17′N	85°43′W
Charlotte, Mi., U.S. (shär′lŏt)	108	42°35′N	84°50′W
Charlotte, N.C., U.S.	105	35°15′N	80°50′W
Charlotte Amalie, V.I.U.S. (shär-lŏt′ĕ ä-mä′lĭ-ȧ)	129	18°21′N	64°54′W
Charlotte Harbor, b., Fl., U.S.	125a	26°49′N	82°00′W
Charlotte Lake, l., Can.	94	52°07′N	125°30′W
Charlottenberg, Swe. (shär-lŭt′ĕn-bĕrg)	166	59°53′N	12°17′E
Charlottesville, Va., U.S. (shär′lŏtz-vĭl)	105	38°00′N	78°25′W
Charlottetown, Can. (shär′lŏt-toun)	91	46°14′N	63°08′W
Charlotte Waters, Austl. (shär′lŏt)	218	26°00′S	134°50′E
Charmes, Fr. (shärm)	171	48°23′N	6°19′E
Charnwood Forest, for., Eng., U.K. (chärn′wŏd)	158a	52°42′N	1°15′W
Charny, Can. (shär-nē′)	102b	46°43′N	71°16′W
Chars, Fr. (shär)	171b	49°09′N	1°57′E
Chārsadda, Pak. (chŭr-sä′dä)	199a	34°17′N	71°43′E
Charters Towers, Austl. (chär′tẽrz)	219	20°03′S	146°20′E
Chartres, Fr. (shärt′r′)	161	48°26′N	1°29′E
Chascomús, Arg. (chäs-kō-mōōs′)	144	35°32′S	58°01′W
Chase City, Va., U.S. (chās)	125	36°45′N	78°27′W
Chashniki, Bela. (chäsh′nyē-kē)	176	54°51′N	29°08′E
Chaska, Mn., U.S. (chăs′kȧ)	117g	44°48′N	93°36′W
Châteaudun, Fr. (shä-tō-däɴ′)	170	48°04′N	1°23′E
Château-Gontier, Fr. (chȧ-tō′gôɴ′tyā′)	170	47°48′N	0°43′W
Châteauguay, Can. (chȧ-tō-gā)	102a	45°22′N	73°45′W
Châteauguay, r., N.A.	102a	45°13′N	73°51′W
Châteauneuf, Fr.	170a	43°23′N	5°11′E
Château-Renault, Fr. (shȧ-tō-rē-nō′)	170	47°36′N	0°57′E
Château-Richer, Can. (shȧ-tō′rē-shā′)	102b	47°00′N	71°01′W
Châteauroux, Fr. (shȧ-tō-rōō′)	161	46°47′N	1°39′E
Château-Thierry, Fr. (shȧ-tō′ty-ĕr-rē′)	170	49°03′N	3°22′E
Châtellerault, Fr. (shä-tĕl-rō′)	161	46°48′N	0°31′E
Chatfield, Mn., U.S. (chăt′fēld)	113	43°50′N	92°10′W
Chatham, Can. (chăt′ȧm)	91	42°25′N	82°10′W
Chatham, Can.	91	47°02′N	65°28′W
Chatham, Eng., U.K. (chăt′ŭm)	165	51°23′N	0°32′E
Chatham, N.J., U.S. (chăt′ȧm)	110a	40°44′N	74°23′W
Chatham, Oh., U.S.	111d	41°06′N	82°01′W
Chatham Islands, is., N.Z.	2	44°00′S	178°00′W
Chatham Sound, strt., Can.	94	54°32′N	130°35′W
Chatham Strait, strt., Ak., U.S.	103	57°00′N	134°40′W
Chatsworth, Ca., U.S. (chătz′wûrth)	117a	34°16′N	118°36′W
Chatsworth Reservoir, res., Ca., U.S.	117a	34°15′N	118°41′W
Chattahoochee, Fl., U.S. (chăt-tȧ-hōō′chē)	124	30°42′N	84°47′W
Chattahoochee, r., U.S.	107	32°00′N	85°10′W
Chattanooga, Tn., U.S. (chăt-ȧ-nōō′gȧ)	105	35°01′N	85°15′W
Chattooga, r., Ga., U.S. (chȧ-tōō′gȧ)	124	34°47′N	83°13′W
Chaudière, r., Can. (shō-dyĕr′)	99	46°26′N	71°10′W
Chaumont, Fr. (shō-mōɴ′)	161	48°08′N	5°07′E
Chaunskaya Guba, b., Russia	185	69°15′N	170°00′E
Chauny, Fr. (shō-nē′)	170	49°40′N	3°09′E
Chau-phu, Viet.	212	10°49′N	104°57′E

ăt; finȧl; rāte; senȧte; ärm; ȧsk; sofȧ; fâre; ch-choose; dh-as th in other; bē; ĕvent; bĕt; recĕnt; cratẽr; g-gō; gh-guttural g; bĭt; ĭ-short neutral; rīde; ĸ-guttural k as ch in German ich;

PRONOUNCING INDEX Chautauqua – Chippewa Lake 281

PLACE (Pronunciation)	PAGE	LAT.	LONG.
Chautauqua, l., N.Y., U.S. (shȧ-tô'kwȧ)	109	42°10′N	79°25′W
Chavaniga, Russia	180	66°02′N	37°50′E
Chaves, Port. (chä'vězh)	172	41°44′N	7°30′W
Chavinda, Mex. (chä-vē'n-dä)	130	20°01′N	102°27′W
Chavusi, Bela.	176	53°57′N	30°58′E
Chazumba, Mex. (chä-zòm'bä)	131	18°11′N	97°41′W
Cheadle, Eng., U.K. (chē'd'l)	158a	52°59′N	1°59′W
Cheat, W.V., U.S. (chēt)	109	39°35′N	79°40′W
Cheb, Czech Rep. (κěb)	168	50°05′N	12°23′E
Chebarkul', Russia (chě-bȧr-kûl')	186a	54°59′N	60°22′E
Cheboksary, Russia (chyě-bôk-sä'rě)	180	56°00′N	47°20′E
Cheboygan, Mi., U.S. (shė-boi'găn)	108	45°40′N	84°30′W
Chech, Erg, des., Alg.	230	24°45′N	2°07′W
Chechen', i., Russia (chyěch'ěn)	181	44°00′N	48°10′E
Chechnya, prov., Russia	182	43°30′N	45°50′E
Checotah, Ok., U.S. (chė-kō'tȧ)	121	35°27′N	95°32′W
Chedabucto Bay, b., Can. (chěd-ȧ-bŭk-tō)	101	45°23′N	61°10′W
Cheduba Island, i., Mya.	212	18°45′N	93°01′E
Cheecham Hills, hills, Can. (chēē'hăm)	96	56°20′N	111°10′W
Cheektowaga, N.Y., U.S. (chēk-tŏ-wä'gȧ)	111c	42°54′N	78°46′W
Chefoo *see* Yantai, China	205	37°32′N	121°22′E
Chegutu, Zimb.	232	18°18′S	30°10′E
Chehalis, Wa., U.S. (chė-hā'lĭs)	114	46°39′N	122°58′W
Chehalis, r., Wa., U.S.	114	46°47′N	123°17′W
Cheju, Kor., S. (chě'jōō')	210	33°29′N	126°40′E
Cheju (Quelpart), i., Kor., S.	210	33°20′N	126°25′E
Chekalin, Russia (chě-kä'lĭn)	176	54°05′N	36°13′E
Chela, Serra da, mts., Ang. (sěr'rȧ dā shā'lȧ)	232	15°30′S	13°30′E
Chelan, Wa., U.S. (chė-lăn')	114	47°51′N	119°59′W
Chelan, Lake, l., Wa., U.S.	114	48°09′N	120°20′W
Cheleiros, Port. (shě-la'rōzh)	173b	38°54′N	9°19′W
Chéliff, r., Alg. (shā-lēf)	230	36°00′N	2°00′E
Chelles, Fr.	171b	48°53′N	2°36′E
Chełm, Pol. (κělm)	161	51°08′N	23°30′E
Chełmno, Pol. (κělm'nō)	169	53°20′N	18°25′E
Chelmsford, Can.	98	46°35′N	81°12′W
Chelmsford, Eng., U.K. (chělm's-fērd)	165	51°44′N	0°28′E
Chelmsford, Ma., U.S.	101a	42°36′N	71°21′W
Chelsea, Austl.	217a	38°05′S	145°08′E
Chelsea, Can.	102c	45°30′N	75°46′W
Chelsea, Al., U.S. (chěl'sė)	110h	33°20′N	86°38′W
Chelsea, Ma., U.S.	101a	42°23′N	71°02′W
Chelsea, Mi., U.S.	108	42°20′N	84°00′W
Chelsea, Ok., U.S.	121	36°32′N	95°23′W
Cheltenham, Eng., U.K. (chělt'nŭm)	164	51°57′N	2°06′W
Cheltenham, Md., U.S. (chěltěn-hăm)	110e	38°45′N	76°50′W
Chelyabinsk, Russia (chěl-yä-bėnsk')	178	55°10′N	61°25′E
Chelyuskin, Mys, c., Russia (chěl-yòs'-kĭn)	179	77°45′N	104°45′E
Chemba, Moz.	237	17°08′S	34°52′E
Chemnitz, Ger.	161	50°48′N	12°53′E
Chemung, r., N.Y., U.S. (shė-mŭng)	109	42°20′N	77°25′W
Chĕn, Gora, mtn., Russia	179	65°13′N	142°12′E
Chenāb, r., Asia (chė-näb)	199	30°30′N	71°30′E
Chenachane, Alg. (shě-nȧ-shän')	230	26°14′N	4°14′W
Chencun, China (chŭn-tsòn)	207a	22°58′N	113°14′E
Cheney, Wa., U.S. (chē'nȧ)	114	47°29′N	117°34′W
Chengde, China (chŭŋ-dŭ)	205	40°50′N	117°50′E
Chengdong Hu, l., China (chŭŋ-dôŋ hōō)	206	32°22′N	116°32′E
Chengdu, China (chŭŋ-dōō)	204	30°30′N	104°10′E
Chenggu, China (chŭŋ-gōō)	208	33°05′N	107°25′E
Chenghai, China (chŭŋ-hī)	209	23°22′N	116°40′E
Chengshan Jiao, c., China (jyou chŭŋ-shän)	208	37°28′N	122°40′E
Chengxi Hu, l., China (chŭŋ-shyē hōō)	206	32°31′N	116°04′E
Chennai (Madras), India	199	13°08′N	80°15′E
Chenxian, China (chŭn-shyěn)	209	25°40′N	113°00′E
Chepén, Peru (chě-pě'n)	142	7°17′S	79°24′W
Chepo, Pan. (chā'pō)	133	9°12′N	79°06′W
Chepo, r., Pan.	133	9°10′N	78°36′W
Cher, r., Fr. (shâr)	161	47°14′N	1°34′E
Cherán, Mex. (chā-rän')	130	19°41′N	101°54′W
Cherangany Hills, hills, Kenya	237	1°25′N	35°20′E
Cheraw, S.C., U.S. (chē'rô)	125	34°40′N	79°52′W
Cherbourg, Fr. (shär-bōōr')	154	49°39′N	1°43′W
Cherdyn', Russia (chěr-dyěn')	178	60°25′N	56°32′E
Cheremkhovo, Russia (chěr'yěm-kô-vō)	179	52°58′N	103°18′E
Cherëmukhovo, Russia (chěr-yě-mû-kô-vô)	186a	60°20′N	60°00′E
Cherepanovo, Russia (chěr'yě pä-nô'vō)	178	54°13′N	83°22′E
Cherepovets, Russia (chěr-yě-pô'vyětz)	178	59°08′N	37°59′E
Chereya, Bela. (chěr-ā'yȧ)	176	54°38′N	29°16′E
Chergui, i., Tun.	162	34°50′N	11°40′E
Chergui, Chott ech, l., Alg. (chěr gē)	162	34°12′N	0°10′W
Cherkasy, Ukr.	177	49°26′N	32°03′E
Cherkasy, prov., Ukr.	177	48°58′N	30°55′E
Cherkessk, Russia	182	44°14′N	42°04′E
Cherlak, Russia (chĭr-läk')	178	54°04′N	74°28′E
Chermoz, Russia (chěr-môz')	180	58°47′N	56°08′E
Chern', Russia (chěrn)	176	53°28′N	36°49′E
Chërnaya Kalitva, r., Russia (chôr'nȧ yȧ kȧ-lēt'vȧ)	177	50°15′N	39°16′E
Chernihiv, Ukr.	181	51°23′N	31°15′E
Chernihiv, prov., Ukr.	177	51°28′N	31°18′E
Chernihivka, Ukr.	177	47°08′N	36°20′E
Chernivtsi, Ukr.	178	48°18′N	25°56′E
Chernobyl' *see* Chornobai, Ukr.	176	51°17′N	30°14′E
Chernogorsk, Russia (chěr-nŏ-gôrsk')	184	54°01′N	91°07′E
Chernoistochinsk, Russia (chěr-nôy-stô'chĭnsk)	186a	57°44′N	59°55′E
Chernyanka, Russia (chěrn-yäŋ'kä)	177	50°56′N	37°48′E
Cherokee, Ia., U.S. (chěr-ô-kē')	112	42°43′N	95°33′W
Cherokee, Ks., U.S.	121	37°21′N	94°50′W
Cherokee, Ok., U.S.	120	36°44′N	98°22′W
Cherokee Lake, res., Tn., U.S.	124	36°22′N	83°22′W
Cherokees, Lake of the, res., Ok., U.S. (chěr-ô-kēz')	107	36°32′N	95°14′W
Cherokee Sound, Bah.	134	26°15′N	76°55′W
Cherryfield, Me., U.S. (chěr'ĭ-fēld)	100	44°37′N	67°56′W
Cherry Grove, Or., U.S.	116c	45°27′N	123°15′W
Cherryvale, Ks., U.S.	121	37°16′N	95°33′W
Cherryville, N.C., U.S. (chěr'ĭ-vĭl)	125	35°32′N	81°22′W
Cherskogo, Khrebet, mts., Russia	179	67°15′N	140°00′E
Chertsey, Eng., U.K.	158b	51°24′N	0°30′W
Chervonoye, Vozyera, l., Bela. (chěr-vô'nô-yě)	176	52°24′N	28°00′E
Chervyen', Bela. (chěr'vyěn)	176	53°43′N	28°26′E
Cherykaw, Bela.	176	53°34′N	31°22′E
Chesaning, Mi., U.S. (chěs'ȧ-nĭng)	108	43°10′N	84°10′W
Chesapeake, Va., U.S. (chěs'ȧ-pēk)	110g	36°48′N	76°16′W
Chesapeake Bay, b., U.S.	107	38°20′N	76°15′W
Chesapeake Beach, Md., U.S.	110e	38°42′N	76°33′W
Chesham, Eng., U.K. (chěsh'ŭm)	158b	51°41′N	0°37′W
Cheshire, Mi., U.S. (chěsh'ĭr)	108	42°25′N	86°00′W
Cheshire, co., Eng., U.K.	158a	53°16′N	2°30′W
Chëshskaya Guba, b., Russia	178	67°25′N	46°00′E
Cheshunt, Eng., U.K.	158b	51°43′N	0°02′W
Chesma, Russia (chěs'mȧ)	186a	53°50′N	60°42′E
Chesnokovka, Russia (chěs-nŏ-kôf'kȧ)	178	53°28′N	83°41′E
Chester, Eng., U.K. (chěs'tēr)	164	53°12′N	2°53′W
Chester, Il., U.S.	121	37°54′N	89°48′W
Chester, Pa., U.S.	110f	39°51′N	75°22′W
Chester, S.C., U.S.	125	34°42′N	81°11′W
Chester, Va., U.S.	125	37°20′N	77°24′W
Chester, W.V., U.S.	108	40°35′N	80°30′W
Chesterfield, Eng., U.K. (chěs'tēr-fēld)	164	53°14′N	1°26′W
Chesterfield, Îles, is., N. Cal.	221	19°38′S	160°08′E
Chesterfield Inlet *see* Igluligaarjuk, Can.	92	63°19′N	91°11′W
Chesterfield Inlet, b., Can.	93	63°59′N	92°09′W
Chestermere Lake, l., Can. (chěs'tě-mēr)	102e	51°03′N	113°45′W
Chesterton, In., U.S. (chěs'tēr-tŭn)	108	41°35′N	87°05′W
Chestertown, Md., U.S. (chěs'tēr-toun)	109	39°15′N	76°05′W
Chesuncook, l., Me., U.S. (chěs'ŭn-kòk)	100	46°03′N	69°40′W
Chetek, Wi., U.S. (chě'těk)	113	45°18′N	91°41′W
Chetumal, Bahía de, b., N.A. (bä-ē-ä dě chět-ōō-mäl')	128	18°07′N	88°05′W
Chevelon Creek, r., Az., U.S. (shěv'ȧ-lŏn)	119	34°35′N	111°00′W
Cheviot, Oh., U.S. (shěv'ĭ-ŭt)	111f	39°10′N	84°37′W
Chevreuse, Fr. (shě-vrûz')	171b	48°42′N	2°02′E
Chevy Chase, Md., U.S. (shěvĭ chās)	110e	38°58′N	77°06′W
Chew Bahir, Afr. (stĕf-a-nē)	231	4°46′N	37°31′E
Chewelah, Wa., U.S. (chē-wē'lä)	114	48°17′N	117°42′W
Cheyenne, Wy., U.S. (shī-ěn')	104	41°10′N	104°49′W
Cheyenne, r., U.S.	106	44°20′N	102°15′W
Cheyenne River Indian Reservation, I.R., S.D., U.S.	112	45°07′N	100°46′W
Cheyenne Wells, Co., U.S.	120	38°46′N	102°21′W
Chhattisgarh, state, India	199	23°00′N	83°00′E
Chhindwāra, India	202	22°08′N	78°57′E
Chiai, Tai. (chī'ī')	209	23°28′N	120°28′E
Chiange, Ang.	236	15°45′S	13°48′E
Chiang Mai, Thai.	212	18°38′N	98°44′E
Chiang Rai, Thai.	212	19°53′N	99°48′E
Chiapa, Río de, r., Mex.	132	16°00′N	92°20′W
Chiapa de Corzo, Mex. (chė-ä'pä dā kôr'zō)	131	16°44′N	93°01′W
Chiapas, state, Mex. (chė-ä'päs)	128	17°10′N	93°00′W
Chiapas, Cordilla de, mts., Mex. (kôr-děl-yě'rä-dě-chyȧ'räs)	131	15°55′N	93°15′W
Chiari, Italy (kyä'rē)	174	45°31′N	9°57′E
Chiasso, Switz.	168	45°50′N	8°57′E
Chiatura, Geor.	182	42°17′N	43°17′E
Chiautla, Mex. (chyä-ōōt'lȧ)	130	18°16′N	98°37′W
Chiavari, Italy (kyä-vä'rē)	174	44°18′N	9°21′E
Chiba, Japan (chē'bȧ)	205	35°37′N	140°08′E
Chiba, dept., Japan	211a	35°47′N	140°02′E
Chibougamau, Can. (chē-bōō'gä-mou)	91	49°57′N	74°23′W
Chibougamau, l., Can.	99	49°53′N	74°21′W
Chicago, Il., U.S. (shĭ-kô-gō) (chĭ-kä'gō)	105	41°49′N	87°37′W
Chicago Heights, Il., U.S.	111a	41°30′N	87°38′W
Chicapa, r., Afr. (chē-kä'pä)	232	7°45′S	20°25′E
Chicbul, Mex. (chēk-bōō'l)	131	18°45′N	90°56′W
Chic-Chocs, Monts, mts., Can.	93	48°38′N	66°37′W
Chichagof, i., Ak., U.S. (chė-chä'gôf)	103	57°50′N	137°00′W
Chichancanab, Lago de, l., Mex. (lä'gô-dě-chē-chän-kä-nä'b)	132a	19°50′N	88°28′W
Chichén Itzá, hist., Mex.	132a	20°40′N	88°35′W
Chichester, Eng., U.K. (chĭch'ěs-tēr)	164	50°50′N	0°55′W
Chichimilá, Mex. (chē-chē-mē'lä)	132a	20°36′N	88°14′W
Chichiriviche, Ven. (chē-chē-rē-vē-chě)	143b	10°56′N	68°17′W
Chickamauga, Ga., U.S. (chĭk-ȧ-mô'gȧ)	124	34°50′N	85°15′W
Chickamauga Lake, res., Tn., U.S.	124	35°18′N	85°22′W
Chickasawhay, r., Ms., U.S. (chĭk-ȧ-sô'wā)	124	31°45′N	88°45′W
Chickasha, Ok., U.S. (chĭk'ȧ-shā)	104	35°04′N	97°56′W
Chiclana de la Frontera, Spain (chė-klä'nä)	172	36°25′N	6°09′W
Chiclayo, Peru (chė-klä'yō)	142	6°46′S	79°50′W
Chico, Ca., U.S. (chē'kō)	118	39°43′N	121°51′W
Chico, Wa., U.S.	116a	47°37′N	122°43′W
Chico, r., Arg.	144	44°30′S	66°00′W
Chico, r., Arg.	144	49°15′S	69°30′W
Chico, r., Phil.	213a	17°33′N	121°24′E
Chicoloapan, Mex. (chė-kō-lwä'pän)	131a	19°24′N	98°54′W
Chiconautla, Mex.	131a	19°39′N	99°01′W
Chicontepec, Mex. (chė-kōn'tě-pěk')	130	20°58′N	98°08′W
Chicopee, Ma., U.S. (chĭk'ô-pē)	109	42°10′N	72°35′W
Chicoutimi, Can. (shē-kōō'tē-mē')	91	48°26′N	71°04′W
Chicxulub, Mex. (chēk-sōō-lōō'b)	132a	21°10′N	89°30′W
Chiefland, Fl., U.S. (chēf'lănd)	125	29°30′N	82°50′W
Chiemsee, l., Ger. (κēm zā)	168	47°58′N	12°20′E
Chieri, Italy (kyâ'rē)	174	45°03′N	7°48′E
Chieti, Italy (kyě'tē)	162	42°22′N	14°22′E
Chifeng, China (chr-fŭŋ)	205	42°18′N	118°52′E
Chignanuapan, Mex. (chē'g-ŋä-nwä-pȧ'n)	130	19°49′N	98°02′W
Chignecto Bay, b., Can. (shĭg-něk'tō)	100	45°33′N	64°50′W
Chignik, Ak., U.S. (chĭg'nĭk)	103	56°14′N	158°12′W
Chignik Bay, b., Ak., U.S.	103	56°18′N	157°22′W
Chigu Co, l., China (chr-gōō tswo)	202	28°55′N	91°47′E
Chigwell, Eng., U.K.	158b	51°38′N	0°05′E
Chihe, China (chr-hŭ)	206	32°32′N	117°57′E
Chihuahua, Mex. (chė-wä'wä)	128	28°37′N	106°06′W
Chihuahua, state, Mex.	128	29°00′N	107°30′W
Chikishlyar, Turkmen. (chė-kėsh-lyär')	183	37°40′N	53°50′E
Chilanga, Zam.	237	15°34′S	28°17′E
Chilapa, Mex. (chė-lä'pä)	130	17°34′N	99°14′W
Chilchota, Mex. (chěl-chō'tä)	130	19°40′N	102°04′W
Chilcotin, r., Can. (chĭl-kō'tĭn)	94	52°20′N	124°15′W
Childress, Tx., U.S. (chīld'rěs)	120	34°26′N	100°11′W
Chile, nation, S.A. (chē'lā)	144	35°00′S	72°00′W
Chilecito, Arg. (chē-lȧ-sē'tō)	144	29°06′S	67°25′W
Chilengue, Serra do, mts., Ang.	236	13°20′S	15°00′E
Chilibre, Pan. (chē-lē'brě)	128a	9°09′N	79°37′W
Chililabombwe, Zam.	237	12°18′S	27°43′E
Chilka, l., India	202	19°26′N	85°42′E
Chilko, r., Can. (chĭl'kō)	94	51°53′N	123°53′W
Chilko Lake, l., Can.	94	51°20′N	124°05′W
Chillán, Chile (chēl-yän')	144	36°44′S	72°06′W
Chillicothe, Il., U.S. (chĭl-ĭ-kŏth'ė)	108	41°55′N	89°30′W
Chillicothe, Mo., U.S.	121	39°46′N	93°32′W
Chillicothe, Oh., U.S.	108	39°20′N	83°00′W
Chilliwack, Can. (chĭl'ĭ-wăk)	90	49°10′N	121°57′W
Chiloé, Isla de, i., Chile	144	42°30′S	73°55′W
Chilpancingo de los Bravo, Mex.	128	17°32′N	99°30′W
Chilton, Wi., U.S. (chĭl'tŭn)	113	44°00′N	88°12′W
Chilung, Tai. (chī'lung)	205	25°02′N	121°48′E
Chilwa, Lake, l., Afr.	232	15°12′S	36°30′E
Chimacum, Wa., U.S. (chĭm'ȧ-kŭm)	116a	48°01′N	122°47′W
Chimalpa, Mex. (chē-mäl'pä)	131a	19°26′N	99°22′W
Chimaltenango, Guat. (chė-mäl-tā-näŋ'gō)	132	14°39′N	90°48′W
Chimaltitan, Mex. (chėmäl-tē-tän')	130	21°36′N	103°50′W
Chimbay, Uzb. (chĭm-bī')	183	43°00′N	59°44′E
Chimborazo, mtn., Ec. (chēm-bô-rä'zō)	142	1°35′S	78°45′W
Chimbote, Peru (chėm-bō'tȧ)	142	9°02′S	78°33′W
China, Mex. (chē'nä)	122	25°43′N	99°13′W
China, nation, Asia (chī'nȧ)	204	36°45′N	93°00′E
Chinameca, El Sal. (Chē-nä-mā'kä)	132	13°31′N	88°18′W
Chinandega, Nic. (chē-nän-dā'gä)	132	12°38′N	87°08′W
Chinati Peak, mtn., Tx., U.S. (chĭ-nä'tē)	122	29°56′N	104°29′W
Chincha Alta, Peru (chĭn'chä äl'tä)	142	13°24′S	76°04′W
Chinchas, Islas, is., Peru (ē's-läs-chē'n-chäs)	142	11°27′S	79°05′W
Chinchilla, Austl. (chĭn-chĭl'ȧ)	222	26°44′S	150°36′E
Chinchorro, Banco, bk., Mex. (bä'n-kô-chěn-chô'r-rō)	132a	18°43′N	87°25′W
Chincilla de Monte Aragon, Spain	172	38°54′N	1°43′W
Chinde, Moz. (shēn'dě)	232	17°39′S	36°34′E
Chin Do, i., Kor., S.	210	34°30′N	125°43′E
Chindwin, r., Mya. (chĭn-dwĭn)	199	23°30′N	94°34′E
Chingola, Zam. (chĭng-gōlä)	232	12°32′S	27°52′E
Chinguar, Ang. (chĭng-gär)	232	12°35′S	16°15′E
Chinguetti, Maur. (chėŋ-gět'ė)	230	20°34′N	12°34′W
Chinhoyi, Zimb.	232	17°22′S	30°12′E
Chinju, Kor., S. (chĭn'jōō)	210	35°13′N	128°10′E
Chinko, r., C.A.R. (shĭn'kō)	231	6°37′N	24°31′E
Chinmen *see* Quemoy, Tai.	209	24°30′N	118°20′E
Chino, Ca., U.S. (chē'nō)	117a	34°01′N	117°42′W
Chinon, Fr. (shē-nôn')	170	47°09′N	0°13′E
Chinook, Mt., U.S. (shĭn-ók')	115	48°35′N	109°15′W
Chinsali, Zam.	237	10°34′S	32°03′E
Chinteche, Mwi. (chĭn-tě'chě)	232	11°48′S	34°14′E
Chioggia, Italy (kyôd'jä)	174	45°12′N	12°17′E
Chíos, Grc. (kē'ŏs)	163	38°23′N	26°09′E
Chíos, i., Grc.	163	38°20′N	25°45′E
Chipata, Zam.	232	13°39′S	32°40′E
Chipera, Moz. (zhė-pě'rä)	232	15°16′S	32°30′E
Chipley, Fl., U.S. (chĭp'lĭ)	124	30°45′N	85°33′W
Chipman, Can. (chĭp'mȧn)	100	46°11′N	65°53′W
Chipola, r., Fl., U.S. (chĭ-pō'lȧ)	124	30°40′N	85°14′W
Chippawa, Can. (chĭp'ė-wä)	111c	43°03′N	79°03′W
Chippewa, r., Mn., U.S. (chĭp'ė-wä)	112	45°07′N	95°41′W
Chippewa, r., Wi., U.S.	113	45°07′N	91°19′W
Chippewa Falls, Wi., U.S.	113	44°55′N	91°26′W
Chippewa Lake, Oh., U.S.	111d	41°04′N	81°54′W

ng-sing; ŋ-baŋk; ɴ-nasalized n; nŏd; cŏmmit; ōld; ôbey; ôrder; oi-boil; fōōd; ŏ-as oo in foot; ou-out; s-soft; sh-dish; th-thin; pūre; ûnite; ûrn; stŭd; circŭs; ü-as in French tu; ′-indeterminate vowel.

ăt; finǎl; rāte; senǎte; ärm; ásk; sofá; fâre; ch-choose; dh-as th in other; bē; ėvent; bĕt; recĕnt; cratēr; g-gō; gh-guttural g; bĭt; ī-short neutral; rīde; к-guttural k as ch in German ich;

PRONOUNCING INDEX Clearwater – Comacchio 283

PLACE (Pronunciation)	PAGE	LAT.	LONG.
Clearwater, Middle Fork, r., Id., U.S.	114	46°10'N	115°48'W
Clearwater, North Fork, r., Id., U.S.	114	46°34'N	116°08'W
Clearwater, South Fork, r., Id., U.S.	114	45°46'N	115°53'W
Clearwater Mountains, mts., Id., U.S.	114	45°56'N	115°15'W
Cleburne, Tx., U.S. (klē'bŭrn)	104	32°21'N	97°23'W
Cle Elum, Wa., U.S. (klē ĕl'ŭm)	114	47°12'N	120°55'W
Clementon, N.J., U.S. (klē'mĕn-tŭn)	110f	39°49'N	75°00'W
Cleobury Mortimer, Eng., U.K. (klēŏ-bĕr'ĭ môr'tĭ-mĕr)	158a	52°22'N	2°29'W
Clermont, Austl. (klĕr'mŏnt)	219	23°02'S	147°46'E
Clermont, Can.	99	47°45'N	70°20'W
Clermont-Ferrand, Fr. (klĕr-môn'fĕr-rän')	154	45°47'N	3°03'E
Cleveland, Ms., U.S. (klēv'lănd)	124	33°45'N	90°42'W
Cleveland, Oh., U.S.	105	41°30'N	81°42'W
Cleveland, Ok., U.S.	121	36°18'N	96°28'W
Cleveland, Tn., U.S.	124	35°09'N	84°52'W
Cleveland, Tx., U.S.	123	30°18'N	95°05'W
Cleveland Heights, Oh., U.S.	111d	41°30'N	81°35'W
Cleveland Peninsula, pen., Ak., U.S.	94	55°45'N	132°00'W
Cleves, Oh., U.S. (klē'vĕs)	111f	39°10'N	84°45'W
Clew Bay, b., Ire. (klo͞o)	164	53°47'N	9°45'W
Clewiston, Fl., U.S. (klē'wis-tŭn)	125a	26°44'N	80°55'W
Clichy, Fr. (klē-shē)	170	48°54'N	2°18'E
Clifden, Ire. (klĭf'dĕn)	164	53°31'N	10°04'W
Clifton, Az., U.S. (klĭf'tŭn)	119	33°05'N	109°20'W
Clifton, N.J., U.S.	110a	40°52'N	74°09'W
Clifton, S.C., U.S.	125	35°00'N	81°47'W
Clifton, Tx., U.S.	123	31°45'N	97°31'W
Clifton Forge, Va., U.S.	109	37°50'N	79°50'W
Clinch, r., Tn., U.S. (klĭnch)	124	36°30'N	83°19'W
Clingmans Dome, mtn., U.S. (klĭng'măns dōm)	124	35°37'N	83°26'W
Clinton, Can. (klĭn-'tŭn)	90	51°05'N	121°35'W
Clinton, Ia., U.S.	113	41°50'N	90°13'W
Clinton, Il., U.S.	108	40°10'N	88°55'W
Clinton, In., U.S.	108	39°40'N	87°25'W
Clinton, Ky., U.S.	124	36°39'N	88°56'W
Clinton, Ma., U.S.	101a	42°25'N	71°41'W
Clinton, Md., U.S.	110e	38°46'N	76°54'W
Clinton, Mo., U.S.	121	38°23'N	93°46'W
Clinton, N.C., U.S.	125	34°58'N	78°20'W
Clinton, Ok., U.S.	120	35°31'N	98°56'W
Clinton, S.C., U.S.	125	34°27'N	81°53'W
Clinton, Tn., U.S.	124	36°05'N	84°08'W
Clinton, Wa., U.S.	116a	47°59'N	122°22'W
Clinton, r., Mi., U.S.	111b	42°36'N	83°00'W
Clinton-Colden, l., Can.	92	63°58'N	106°34'W
Clintonville, Wi., U.S. (klĭn'tŭn-vĭl)	113	44°37'N	88°46'W
Clio, Mi., U.S. (klē'ō)	108	43°10'N	83°45'W
Cloates, Point, c., Austl. (klōts)	220	22°47'S	113°45'E
Clocolan, S. Afr.	238c	28°56'S	27°35'E
Clonakilty Bay, b., Ire. (klŏn-á-kĭltē)	164	51°30'N	8°50'W
Cloncurry, Austl. (klŏn-kŭr'ē)	218	20°58'S	140°42'E
Clonmel, Ire. (klŏn-mĕl)	164	52°21'N	7°45'W
Cloquet, Mn., U.S. (klô-kā')	117h	46°42'N	92°28'W
Closter, N.J., U.S. (klōs'tēr)	110a	40°58'N	73°57'W
Cloud Peak, mtn., Wy., U.S. (kloud)	106	44°23'N	107°11'W
Clover, S.C., U.S. (klō'vēr)	125	35°08'N	81°08'W
Clover Bar, Can. (klō'vēr bär)	102g	53°34'N	113°20'W
Cloverdale, Can.	116d	49°06'N	122°44'W
Cloverdale, Ca., U.S. (klō'vēr-dāl)	118	38°47'N	123°03'W
Cloverport, Ky., U.S. (klō'vēr pōrt)	108	37°50'N	86°35'W
Clovis, N.M., U.S. (klō'vĭs)	104	34°24'N	103°11'W
Cluj-Napoca, Rom.	154	46°46'N	23°34'E
Clun, r., Eng., U.K. (klŭn)	158a	52°25'N	2°56'W
Cluny, Fr. (klü-nē')	170	46°27'N	4°40'E
Clutha, r., N.Z. (klo͞o'thȧ)	221a	45°52'S	169°30'E
Clwyd, hist. reg., Wales, U.K.	158a	53°01'N	2°59'W
Clyde, Ks., U.S.	121	39°34'N	97°23'W
Clyde, Oh., U.S.	108	41°15'N	83°00'W
Clyde, r., Scot., U.K.	164	55°35'N	3°50'W
Clyde, Firth of, b., Scot., U.K. (fûrth ŏv klīd)	164	55°28'N	5°01'W
Côa, r., Port. (kô'ä)	172	40°28'N	6°55'W
Coacalco, Mex. (kō-ä-käl'kō)	131a	19°37'N	99°06'W
Coachella, Canal, can., Ca., U.S. (kō'chĕl-lȧ)	118	33°15'N	115°25'W
Coahuayana, Río de, r., Mex. (rē'ō-dĕ-kō-ä-wä-yä'nä)	130	19°00'N	103°33'W
Coahuayutla, Mex. (kō'ä-wī-yo͞ot'lä)	130	18°19'N	101°44'W
Coahuila, state, Mex. (kō-ä-wē'lä)	128	27°30'N	103°00'W
Coal City, Il., U.S. (kōl sĭ'tĭ)	111a	41°17'N	88°17'W
Coalcomán, Río de, r., Mex. (rē'ō-dĕ-kō-äl-kō-män')	130	18°45'N	103°15'W
Coalcomán, Sierra de, mts., Mex.	130	18°30'N	102°45'W
Coalcomán de Matamoros, Mex.	130	18°46'N	103°10'W
Coaldale, Can. (kōl'dāl)	95	49°43'N	112°37'W
Coalgate, Ok., U.S. (kōl'gāt)	121	34°44'N	96°13'W
Coal Grove, Oh., U.S. (kōl grōv)	108	38°20'N	82°40'W
Coalinga, Ca., U.S. (kō-ȧ-lĭŋ'gȧ)	118	36°09'N	120°23'W
Coalville, Eng., U.K. (kōl'vĭl)	158a	52°43'N	1°21'W
Coamo, P.R. (kō-ä'mō)	129b	18°05'N	66°21'W
Coari, Braz. (kō-är'ē)	142	4°06'S	63°10'W
Coast Mountains, mts., N.A. (kōst)	92	54°10'N	128°00'W
Coast Ranges, mts., U.S.	106	41°28'N	123°30'W
Coatepec, Mex. (kō-ä-tā-pĕk)	130	19°23'N	98°44'W
Coatepec, Mex.	131a	19°08'N	99°25'W
Coatepec, Mex.	131	19°26'N	96°56'W
Coatepeque, El Sal.	132	13°56'N	89°30'W
Coatepeque, Guat. (kō-ä-tā-pā'kā)	132	14°40'N	91°52'W
Coatesville, Pa., U.S. (kōts'vĭl)	109	40°00'N	75°50'W

PLACE (Pronunciation)	PAGE	LAT.	LONG.
Coatetelco, Mex. (kō-ä-tå-tĕl'kō)	130	18°43'N	99°17'W
Coaticook, Can. (kō'tĭ-ko͝ok)	99	45°10'N	71°55'W
Coatlinchán, Mex. (kô-ä-tlē'n-chä'n)	131a	19°26'N	98°52'W
Coats, i., Can. (kōts)	93	62°23'N	82°11'W
Coats Land, reg., Ant.	224	74°00'S	30°00'W
Coatzacoalcos, Mex.	128	18°09'N	94°26'W
Coatzacoalcos, r., Mex.	131	17°40'N	94°41'W
Coba, hist., Mex. (kô'bä)	132a	20°23'N	87°23'W
Cobalt, Can. (kō'bôlt)	91	47°21'N	79°40'W
Cobán, Guat. (kō-bän')	128	15°28'N	90°19'W
Cobar, Austl.	219	31°28'S	145°50'E
Cobberas, Mount, mtn., Austl. (cŏ-bẽr-ăs)	222	36°45'S	148°15'E
Cobequid Mountains, mts., Can.	100	45°35'N	64°10'W
Cobh, Ire. (kôv)	154	51°52'N	8°09'W
Cobija, Bol. (kô-bē'hä)	142	11°12'S	68°49'W
Cobourg, Can. (kō'bôrgh)	91	43°55'N	78°05'W
Cobre, r., Jam. (kō'brā)	134	18°05'N	77°00'W
Coburg, Austl.	217a	37°45'S	144°58'E
Coburg, Ger. (kō'bo͞org)	168	50°16'N	10°57'E
Cocentaina, Spain (kō-thån-tä-ē'nȧ)	173	38°44'N	0°27'W
Cochabamba, Bol.	142	17°24'S	66°09'W
Cochinos, Bahía, b., Cuba (bä-ē'ä-kô-chê'nōs)	134	22°05'N	81°10'W
Cochinos Banks, bk.	134	22°20'N	76°15'W
Cochiti Indian Reservation, I.R., N.M., U.S.	119	35°37'N	106°20'W
Cochran, Ga., U.S. (kŏk'răn)	124	32°23'N	83°23'W
Cochrane, Can. (kŏk'răn)	91	49°01'N	81°06'W
Cochrane, Can.	102e	51°11'N	114°28'W
Cockburn, i., Can. (kŏk-bûrn)	98	45°55'N	83°25'W
Cockeysville, Md., U.S. (kŏk'ĭz-vĭl)	110e	39°30'N	76°40'W
Cockrell Hill, Tx., U.S. (kŏk'rĕl)	117c	32°44'N	96°53'W
Coco, r., N.A.	129	14°55'N	83°45'W
Coco, Cayo, i., Cuba (kä'-yō-kô'kô)	134	22°30'N	78°30'W
Coco, Isla del, i., C.R. (ē's-lä-dĕl-kô-kô)	128	5°33'N	87°02'W
Cocoa, Fl., U.S. (kō'kō)	125a	28°21'N	80°44'W
Cocoa Beach, Fl., U.S.	125a	28°20'N	80°35'W
Cocoli, Pan. (kŏ-kŏ'lē)	128a	8°58'N	79°36'W
Coconino, Plateau, plat., Az., U.S. (kō kō nē'nō)	119	35°45'N	112°28'W
Cocos (Keeling) Islands, is., Oc. (kō'kôs) (kē'lĭng)	3	11°50'S	90°50'E
Coco Solito, Pan. (kô-kô-sŏ-lē'tŏ)	128a	9°21'N	79°53'W
Cocula, Mex. (kō-ko͞o'lä)	130	20°23'N	103°47'W
Cocula, r., Mex.	130	18°17'N	99°45'W
Cod, Cape, pen., Ma., U.S.	107	41°42'N	70°15'W
Codajás, Braz. (kō-dä-häzh')	142	3°44'S	62°09'W
Codera, Cabo, c., Ven. (kä'bô-kô-dĕ'rä)	143b	10°35'N	66°06'W
Codogno, Italy (kô-dō'nyō)	174	45°08'N	9°43'E
Codrington, Antig. (kŏd'rĭng-tŭn)	133b	17°39'N	61°49'W
Cody, Wy., U.S. (kō'dĭ)	115	44°31'N	109°02'W
Coelho da Rocha, Braz.	144b	22°47'S	43°23'W
Coemba, Ang.	236	12°08'S	18°05'E
Coesfeld, Ger. (kûs'fĕld)	171c	51°56'N	7°10'E
Coeur d'Alene, Id., U.S. (kûr dȧ-lān')	104	47°43'N	116°35'W
Coeur d'Alene, r., Id., U.S.	114	47°26'N	116°35'W
Coeur d'Alene Indian Reservation, I.R., Id., U.S.	114	47°18'N	116°45'W
Coeur d'Alene Lake, l., Id., U.S.	114	47°32'N	116°39'W
Coffeyville, Ks., U.S. (kŏf'ĭ-vĭl)	105	37°01'N	95°38'W
Coff's Harbour, Austl.	222	30°20'S	153°10'E
Cofimvaba, S. Afr. (căfĭm'vä-bȧ)	233c	32°01'S	27°37'E
Coghinas, r., Italy (kō'gē-nås)	174	40°31'N	9°00'E
Cognac, Fr. (kôn-yak')	161	45°41'N	0°22'W
Cohasset, Ma., U.S. (kô-hăs'ĕt)	101a	42°14'N	70°48'W
Cohoes, N.Y., U.S. (kô-hōz')	109	42°50'N	73°40'W
Coig, r., Arg. (kô'ĕk)	144	51°15'S	71°00'W
Coimbatore, India (kō-ēm-bȧ-tôr')	199	11°03'N	76°56'E
Coimbra, Port. (kô-ēm'brä)	154	40°14'N	8°23'W
Coín, Spain (kô-ēn')	172	36°40'N	4°45'W
Coina, Port. (kô-ē'nȧ)	173b	38°35'N	9°03'W
Coina, r., Port. (kô'y-nä)	173b	38°35'N	9°02'W
Coipasa, Salar de, pl., Bol. (sä-lä'r-dĕ-koi-pä'-sä)	142	19°12'S	69°13'W
Coixtlahuaca, Mex. (kō-ēks'tlä-wä'kä)	131	17°42'N	97°17'W
Cojedes, dept., Ven. (kô-kĕ'dĕs)	143b	9°50'N	68°21'W
Cojimar, Cuba (kō-hē-mär')	135a	23°10'N	82°19'W
Cojutepeque, El Sal. (kô-hô-tĕ-pā'kå)	132	13°45'N	88°50'W
Cokato, Mn., U.S. (kô-kā'tō)	113	45°03'N	94°11'W
Cokeburg, Pa., U.S. (kōk bûgh)	111e	40°06'N	80°03'W
Colac, Austl. (kŏ'lác)	221	38°25'S	143°40'E
Colares, Port. (kō-lä'rĕs)	173b	38°47'N	9°27'W
Colatina, Braz. (kō-lä-tē'nä)	143	19°33'S	40°42'W
Colby, Ks., U.S. (kōl'bĭ)	120	39°23'N	101°04'W
Colchagua, prov., Chile (kôl-chá'gwä)	141b	34°42'S	71°24'W
Colchester, Eng., U.K. (kōl'chĕs-tēr)	165	51°52'N	0°50'E
Cold Lake, l., Can. (kōld)	96	54°33'N	110°05'W
Coldwater, Ks., U.S. (kōld'wô-tēr)	120	37°14'N	99°21'W
Coldwater, Mi., U.S.	108	41°55'N	85°00'W
Coldwater, r., Ms., U.S.	124	34°25'N	90°12'W
Coldwater Creek, r., Tx., U.S.	120	36°10'N	101°45'W
Coleman, Tx., U.S. (kōl'măn)	122	31°50'N	99°25'W
Colenso, S. Afr. (kō-lĕnz'ō)	233c	28°48'S	29°49'E
Coleraine, N. Ire., U.K.	164	55°08'N	6°40'W
Coleraine, Mn., U.S. (kōl-rān')	113	47°16'N	93°29'W
Coleshill, Eng., U.K. (kōlz'hĭl)	158a	52°30'N	1°42'W
Colfax, Ia., U.S. (kōl'făks)	113	41°40'N	93°13'W
Colfax, La., U.S.	123	31°31'N	92°42'W
Colfax, Wa., U.S.	114	46°53'N	117°21'W
Colhué Huapi, l., Arg. (kôl-wā'ōä'pē)	144	45°30'S	68°45'W
Coligny, S. Afr.	238c	26°20'S	26°18'E

PLACE (Pronunciation)	PAGE	LAT.	LONG.
Colima, Mex. (kōlē'mä)	128	19°13'N	103°45'W
Colima, state, Mex.	130	19°10'N	104°00'W
Colima, Nevado de, mtn., Mex. (nĕ-vä'dô-dĕ-kô-lē'mä)	128	19°30'N	103°38'W
Coll, i., Scot., U.K. (kŏl)	164	56°42'N	6°23'W
College, Ak., U.S.	103	64°43'N	147°50'W
College Park, Ga., U.S. (kŏl'ĕj)	110c	33°39'N	84°27'W
College Park, Md., U.S.	110e	38°59'N	76°58'W
Collegeville, Pa., U.S. (kŏl'ĕj-vĭl)	110f	40°11'N	75°27'W
Collie, Austl. (kŏl'ē)	218	33°20'S	116°20'E
Collier Bay, b., Austl. (kŏl-yēr)	220	15°30'S	123°30'E
Collingswood, N.J., U.S. (kŏl'ĭngz-wŏŏd)	110f	39°54'N	75°04'W
Collingwood, Can.	99	44°30'N	80°20'W
Collins, Ms., U.S. (kŏl'ĭns)	124	31°40'N	89°34'W
Collinsville, Il., U.S. (kŏl'ĭnz-vĭl)	117e	38°41'N	89°59'W
Collinsville, Ok., U.S.	121	36°21'N	95°50'W
Colmar, Fr. (kôl'mär)	161	48°03'N	7°25'E
Colmenar de Oreja, Spain (kôl-mā-när'dāōrā'hä)	172	40°06'N	3°25'W
Colmenar Viejo, Spain (kôl-mā-när'vyā'hō)	172	40°40'N	3°46'W
Cologne, Ger.	154	50°56'N	6°57'E
Colombia, Col. (kô-lôm'bē-ä)	142a	3°23'N	74°48'W
Colombia, nation, S.A.	142	3°30'N	72°30'W
Colombo, Sri L. (kô-lôm'bō)	203	6°58'N	79°52'E
Colón, Arg. (kō-lōn')	141c	33°55'S	61°08'W
Colón, Cuba (kô-lô'n)	134	22°45'N	80°55'W
Colón, Mex. (kō-lōn')	130	20°46'N	100°02'W
Colón, Pan. (kō-lô'n)	129	9°22'N	79°54'W
Colón, Archipiélago de, is., Ec.	142	0°10'S	87°45'W
Colón, Montañas de, mts., Hond. (môn-tä'n-yäs-dĕ-kŏ-lô'n)	133	14°58'N	84°39'W
Colonia, Ur. (kō-lō'nē-ä)	144	34°27'S	57°50'W
Colonia, dept., Ur.	141c	34°08'S	57°50'W
Colonia Suiza, Ur. (kô-lô'nēä-sōē'zä)	141c	34°17'S	57°15'W
Colonna, Capo, c., Italy	175	39°02'N	17°15'E
Colonsay, i., Scot., U.K. (kŏl-ŏn-sā')	165	56°08'N	6°08'E
Coloradas, Lomas, Arg. (lô'mäs-kô-lō-rä'däs)	144	43°30'S	68°00'W
Colorado, state, U.S.	104	39°30'N	106°55'W
Colorado, r., Arg.	144	38°30'S	66°00'W
Colorado, r., N.A.	106	36°00'N	113°30'W
Colorado, r., Tx., U.S.	106	30°08'N	97°33'W
Colorado City, Tx., U.S. (kŏl-ô-rä'dō sĭ'tĭ)	122	32°24'N	100°50'W
Colorado National Monument, rec., Co., U.S.	119	39°00'N	108°40'W
Colorado Plateau, plat., U.S.	106	36°20'N	109°25'W
Colorado River Aqueduct, aq., Ca., U.S.	118	33°38'N	115°43'W
Colorado River Indian Reservation, I.R., Az., U.S.	119	34°03'N	114°02'W
Colorados, Archipiélago de los, is., Cuba	134	22°25'N	84°25'W
Colorado Springs, Co., U.S. (kŏl-ô-rä'dō)	104	38°49'N	104°48'W
Colotepec, r., Mex. (kô-lô'tĕ-pĕk)	131	15°56'N	96°57'W
Colotlán, Mex. (kô-lô-tlän')	130	22°06'N	103°14'W
Colotlán, r., Mex.	130	22°09'N	103°17'W
Colquechaca, Bol. (kôl-kā-chä'kä)	142	18°47'S	66°02'W
Colstrip, Mt., U.S. (kōl'strip)	115	45°54'N	106°38'W
Colton, Ca., U.S. (kōl'tŭn)	117a	34°04'N	117°20'W
Columbia, Il., U.S. (kô-lŭm'bĭ-ȧ)	117e	38°26'N	90°12'W
Columbia, Ky., U.S.	124	37°06'N	85°15'W
Columbia, Md., U.S.	110e	39°15'N	76°51'W
Columbia, Mo., U.S.	105	38°55'N	92°19'W
Columbia, Ms., U.S.	124	31°15'N	89°49'W
Columbia, Pa., U.S.	109	40°00'N	76°25'W
Columbia, S.C., U.S.	105	34°00'N	81°00'W
Columbia, Tn., U.S.	124	35°36'N	87°02'W
Columbia, r., N.A.	92	46°00'N	120°00'W
Columbia, Mount, mtn., Can.	95	52°09'N	117°25'W
Columbia City, In., U.S.	108	41°10'N	85°30'W
Columbia City, Or., U.S.	116c	45°53'N	112°49'W
Columbia Heights, Mn., U.S.	117g	45°03'N	93°15'W
Columbia Icefield, ice, Can.	95	52°08'N	117°26'W
Columbia Mountains, mts., N.A.	95	51°30'N	118°30'W
Columbiana, Al., U.S. (kô-ŭm-bĭ-ă'nȧ)	124	33°10'N	86°35'W
Columbretes, is., Spain (kô-lo͞om-brĕ'tĕs)	173	39°54'N	0°54'E
Columbus, Ga., U.S. (kô-lŭm'bŭs)	105	32°29'N	84°56'W
Columbus, In., U.S.	108	39°15'N	85°55'W
Columbus, Ks., U.S.	121	37°10'N	94°50'W
Columbus, Ms., U.S.	124	33°30'N	88°25'W
Columbus, Mt., U.S.	115	45°39'N	109°15'W
Columbus, Ne., U.S.	112	41°25'N	97°25'W
Columbus, N.M., U.S.	119	31°50'N	107°40'W
Columbus, Oh., U.S.	105	40°00'N	83°00'W
Columbus, Tx., U.S.	123	29°44'N	96°34'W
Columbus, Wi., U.S.	113	43°20'N	89°01'W
Columbus Bank, bk. (kô-lŭm'bŭs)	135	22°05'N	75°30'W
Columbus Grove, Oh., U.S.	108	40°55'N	84°05'W
Columbus Point, c., Bah.	135	24°10'N	75°15'W
Colusa, Ca., U.S. (kô-lū'sȧ)	118	39°12'N	122°01'W
Colville, Wa., U.S. (kŏl'vĭl)	114	48°33'N	117°53'W
Colville, r., Ak., U.S.	103	69°00'N	156°25'W
Colville Indian Reservation, I.R., Wa., U.S.	114	48°15'N	119°00'W
Colville R, Wa., U.S.	114	48°25'N	117°58'W
Colvos Passage, strt., Wa., U.S. (kŏl'vōs)	116a	47°24'N	122°32'W
Colwood, Can. (kŏl'wo͝od)	116a	48°26'N	123°30'W
Comacchio, Italy (kô-mäk'kyō)	174	44°42'N	12°12'E

ng-sing; ŋ-baŋk; ɴ-nasalized n; nŏd; cŏmmit; ōld; ŏbey; ôrder; oi-boil; fo͞od; ŏŏ-as oo in foot; ou-out; s-soft; sh-dish; th-thin; pūre; ûnite; ûrn; stŭd; circŭs; ü-as in French tu; '-indeterminate vowel.

284 Comala – Cosamaloápan PRONOUNCING INDEX

PLACE (Pronunciation)	PAGE	LAT.	LONG.
Comala, Mex. (kō-mä-lä′)	130	19°22′N	103°47′W
Comalapa, Guat. (kō-mä-lä′-pä)	132	14°43′N	90°56′W
Comalcalco, Mex. (kō-mäl-käl′kō)	131	18°16′N	93°13′W
Comanche, Ok., U.S. (kō-măn′chē)	121	34°20′N	97°58′W
Comanche, Tx., U.S.	122	31°54′N	98°37′W
Comanche Creek, r., Tx., U.S.	122	31°02′N	102°47′W
Comayagua, Hond. (kō-mä-yä′gwä)	128	14°24′N	87°36′W
Combahee, r., S.C., U.S. (kŏm-bȧ-hē′)	125	32°42′N	80°40′W
Comer, Ga., U.S. (kŭm′ẽr)	124	34°02′N	83°07′W
Comete, Cape, c., T./C. Is. (kō-mā′tå)	135	21°45′N	71°25′W
Comilla, Bngl. (kō-mĭl′ä)	199	23°33′N	91°17′E
Comino, Cape, c., Italy (kō-mē′nō)	174	40°30′N	9°48′E
Comitán, Mex. (kō-mē-tän′)	128	16°16′N	92°09′W
Commencement Bay, b., Wa., U.S. (kŏ-mĕns′mĕnt bā)	116a	47°17′N	122°21′W
Commentry, Fr. (kō-mäN-trē′)	170	46°16′N	2°44′E
Commerce, Ga., U.S. (kŏm′ẽrs)	124	34°10′N	83°27′W
Commerce, Ok., U.S.	121	36°57′N	94°54′W
Commerce, Tx., U.S.	121	33°15′N	95°52′W
Como, Italy (kō′mō)	162	45°48′N	9°03′E
Como, Lago di, l., Italy (lä′gō-dē-kō′mō)	162	46°00′N	9°30′E
Comodoro Rivadavia, Arg.	144	45°47′S	67°31′W
Como-Est, Can.	102a	45°27′N	74°08′W
Comonfort, Mex. (kō-mōn-fō′rt)	130	20°43′N	100°47′W
Comorin, Cape, c., India (kŏ′mō-rĭn)	203	8°05′N	78°05′E
Comoros, nation, Afr.	233	12°30′S	42°45′E
Comox, Can. (kō′mŏks)	94	49°40′N	124°55′W
Companario, Cerro, mtn., S.A. (sĕ′r-rō-kôm-pä-nä′ryō)	141b	35°54′S	70°23′W
Compiègne, Fr. (kôN-pyĕn′y′)	161	49°25′N	2°49′E
Comporta, Port. (kôm-pôr′tȧ)	173b	38°24′N	8°48′W
Compostela, Mex. (kōm-pō-stā′lä)	130	21°14′N	104°54′W
Compton, Ca., U.S. (kŏmpt′tŭn)	117a	33°54′N	118°14′W
Comrat, Mol. (kôm-rät′)	181	46°17′N	28°38′E
Conakry, Gui. (kō-nȧ-krē′)	230	9°31′N	13°43′W
Conanicut, i., R.I., U.S. (kŏn′ȧ-nĭ-kŭt)	110b	41°34′N	71°20′W
Conasauga, r., Ga., U.S. (kō-nȧ)	124	34°40′N	84°51′W
Concarneau, Fr. (kôN-kär-nō′)	170	47°54′N	3°52′W
Concepción, Bol. (kôn-sĕp′syōn′)	143	15°47′S	61°08′W
Concepción, Chile	144	36°51′S	72°59′W
Concepción, Pan.	133	8°31′N	82°38′W
Concepción, Para.	144	23°29′S	57°18′W
Concepcion, Phil.	213a	15°19′N	120°40′E
Concepción, vol., Nic.	132	11°36′N	85°43′W
Concepción, r., Mex.	128	30°25′N	112°20′W
Concepción del Mar, Guat. (kôn-sĕp-syōn′dĕl mär′)	132	14°07′N	91°23′W
Concepción del Oro, Mex. (kôn-sĕp-syōn′ dĕl ō′rō)	128	24°39′N	101°24′W
Concepción del Uruguay, Arg. (kôn-sĕp-syô′n-dĕl-ōō-rōō-gwī′)	144	32°31′S	58°10′W
Conception, i., Bah.	135	23°50′N	75°05′W
Conception, Point, c., Ca., U.S.	106	34°27′N	120°28′W
Conception Bay, b., Can. (kŏn-sĕp′shŭn)	101	47°50′N	52°50′W
Concho, r., Tx., U.S. (kŏn′chō)	122	31°34′N	100°00′W
Conchos, r., Mex.	128	29°30′N	105°00′W
Conchos, r., Mex. (kōn′chōs)	122	25°03′N	99°00′W
Concord, Ca., U.S. (kŏŋ′kŏrd)	116b	37°58′N	122°02′W
Concord, Ma., U.S.	101a	42°28′N	71°21′W
Concord, N.C., U.S.	125	35°23′N	80°11′W
Concord, N.H., U.S.	105	43°10′N	71°30′W
Concordia, Arg. (kŏn-kôr′dĭ-ȧ)	144	31°18′S	57°59′W
Concordia, Col.	142a	6°04′N	75°54′W
Concordia, Mex. (kôn-kô′r-dyä)	130	23°17′N	106°06′W
Concordia, Ks., U.S.	121	39°32′N	97°39′W
Concrete, Wa., U.S. (kŏn-′krēt)	114	48°33′N	121°44′W
Conde, Fr.	170	48°50′N	0°36′W
Conde, S.D., U.S. (kŏn-dē′)	112	45°10′N	98°06′W
Condega, Nic. (kŏn-dĕ′gä)	132	13°20′N	86°27′W
Condeúba, Braz. (kōn-dā-ōō′bä)	143	14°47′S	41°44′W
Condom, Fr.	170	43°58′N	0°22′E
Condon, Or., U.S. (kŏn′dŭn)	114	45°14′N	120°10′W
Conecun, r., Al., U.S. (kō-nē′kŭ)	124	31°05′N	86°52′W
Conegliano, Italy (kō-nål-yä′nō)	174	45°59′N	12°17′E
Conejos, r., Co., U.S. (kō-nā′hōs)	119	37°07′N	106°19′W
Conemaugh, Pa., U.S. (kŏn′ē-mô)	109	40°25′N	78°50′W
Coney Island, i., N.Y., U.S. (kō′nĭ)	110a	40°34′N	73°27′W
Confolens, Fr. (kôN-fä-läN′)	170	46°01′N	0°41′E
Congaree, r., S.C., U.S. (kŏŋ-gȧ-rē′)	125	33°53′N	80°55′W
Conghua, China (tsōŋ-hwä)	209	23°30′N	113°40′E
Congleton, Eng., U.K. (kŏŋ′g′l-tŭn)	158a	53°10′N	2°13′W
Congo, nation, Afr. (kŏn′gō)	232	3°00′S	13°48′E
Congo (Zaire), r., Afr. (kŏn′gō)	229	2°00′S	17°00′E
Congo, Democratic Republic of the (Zaire), nation, Afr.	232	1°00′S	22°15′E
Congo, Serra do, mts., Ang.	236	6°25′S	13°30′E
Congo Basin, basin, D.R.C.	229	2°47′N	20°58′E
Conisbrough, Eng., U.K. (kŏn′ĭs-bŭr-ō)	158a	53°29′N	1°13′W
Coniston, Can.	99	46°29′N	80°51′W
Conklin, Can. (kŏŋk′lĭn)	95	55°38′N	111°05′W
Conley, Ga., U.S. (kŏn′lĭ)	110c	33°38′N	84°19′W
Conn, Lough, l., Ire. (lŏk kŏn)	164	53°56′N	9°25′W
Connacht, hist. reg., Ire. (cŏn′ât)	164	53°50′N	8°45′W
Conneaut, Oh., U.S. (kŏn-ē-ôt′)	108	41°55′N	80°35′W
Connecticut, state, U.S. (kŏ-nĕt′ĭ-kŭt)	105	41°40′N	73°10′W
Connecticut, r., U.S.	107	43°55′N	72°15′W
Connellsville, Pa., U.S. (kŏn′nĕlz-vĭl)	109	40°00′N	79°40′W
Connemara, mts., Ire. (kŏn-nē-mȧ′rȧ)	164	53°30′N	9°54′W
Connersville, In., U.S. (kŏn′ẽrz-vĭl)	108	39°35′N	85°10′W
Connors Range, mts., Austl. (kŏn′nŏrs)	221	22°15′S	149°00′E
Conrad, Mt., U.S. (kŏn′răd)	115	48°11′N	111°56′W
Conrich, Can. (kŏn′rĭch)	102e	51°06′N	113°51′W
Conroe, Tx., U.S. (kŏn′rō)	123	30°18′N	95°23′W
Conselheiro Lafaiete, Braz.	143	20°40′S	43°46′W
Conshohocken, Pa., U.S. (kŏn-shō-hŏk′ĕn)	110f	40°04′N	75°18′W
Consolación del Sur, Cuba (kōn-sō-lä-syōn′)	134	22°30′N	83°55′W
Con Son, is., Viet.	212	8°30′N	106°28′E
Constance, Mount, mtn., Wa., U.S. (kŏn′stăns)	116a	47°46′N	123°08′W
Constanţa, Rom. (kōn-stan′tsȧ)	154	44°12′N	28°36′E
Constantina, Spain (kŏn-stän-tē′nä)	172	37°52′N	5°39′W
Constantine, Alg. (kôN-stäN′tēn′)	[illegible]	[illegible]	[illegible]
Constantine, Mi., U.S. (kŏn′stăn-tēn)	108	41°50′N	85°40′W
Constitución, Chile (kōn′stĭ-tōō-syōn′)	144	35°24′S	72°25′W
Constitution, Ga., U.S. (kŏn-stĭ-tū′shŭn)	110c	33°41′N	84°20′W
Contagem, Braz. (kōn-tá′zhĕm)	141a	19°54′S	44°05′W
Contepec, Mex. (kōn-tĕ-pĕk′)	130	20°04′N	100°07′W
Contreras, Mex. (kôn-trĕ′räs)	131a	19°18′N	99°14′W
Contwoyto, l., Can.	92	65°42′N	110°50′W
Converse, Tx., U.S. (kŏn′vẽrs)	117d	29°31′N	98°17′W
Conway, Ar., U.S. (kŏn′wā)	121	35°06′N	92°27′W
Conway, N.H., U.S.	109	44°00′N	71°10′W
Conway, S.C., U.S.	125	33°49′N	79°01′W
Conway, Wa., U.S.	116a	48°20′N	122°20′W
Conyers, Ga., U.S. (kŏn′yẽrz)	124	33°41′N	84°01′W
Cooch Behār, India (kōōch bē-här′)	199	26°25′N	89°34′E
Cook, Cape, c., Can. (kŏŏk)	94	50°08′N	127°55′W
Cook, Mount see Aoraki, mtn., N.Z.	221a	43°27′S	170°13′E
Cookeville, Tn., U.S. (kŏŏk′vĭl)	124	36°07′N	85°30′W
Cooking Lake, Can. (kŏŏk′ĭng)	102g	53°25′N	113°08′W
Cooking Lake, l., Can.	102g	53°25′N	113°02′W
Cook Inlet, b., Ak., U.S.	103	60°50′N	151°38′W
Cook Islands, dep., Oc.	2	20°00′S	158°00′W
Cook Strait, strt., N.Z.	221a	40°37′S	174°15′E
Cooktown, Austl. (kŏŏk′toun)	219	15°40′S	145°20′E
Cooleemee, N.C., U.S. (kōō-lē′mē)	125	35°50′N	80°32′W
Coolgardie, Austl. (kōōl-gär′dē)	218	31°00′S	121°25′E
Cooma, Austl. (kōō′mȧ)	219	36°22′S	149°10′E
Coonamble, Austl. (kōō-năm′b′l)	219	31°00′S	148°30′E
Coonoor, India	203	10°22′N	76°15′E
Coon Rapids, Mn., U.S. (kōn)	117g	45°09′N	93°17′W
Cooper, Tx., U.S. (kōōp′ẽr)	121	33°23′N	95°40′W
Cooper Center, Ak., U.S.	103	61°54′N	15°30′W
Coopers Creek, r., Austl. (kōō′pẽrz)	221	27°32′N	141°19′E
Cooperstown, N.D., U.S.	112	47°26′N	98°07′W
Cooperstown, N.Y., U.S. (kōōp′ẽrs-toun)	109	42°45′N	74°55′W
Coosa, Al., U.S. (kōō′sȧ)	124	32°43′N	86°25′W
Coosa, r., U.S.	107	34°00′N	86°00′W
Coosawattee, r., Ga., U.S.	124	34°37′N	84°45′W
Coos Bay, Or., U.S. (kōōs)	114	43°21′N	124°12′W
Coos Bay, b., Or., U.S.	114	43°19′N	124°40′W
Cootamundra, Austl. (kŏŏtȧ-mŭnd′rȧ)	222	34°25′S	148°00′E
Copacabana, Braz. (kô′pä-kȧ-bá′nä)	144b	22°57′S	43°11′W
Copalita, r., Mex. (kō-pä-lē′tä)	131	15°55′N	96°06′W
Copán, hist., Hond. (kō-pän′)	132	14°50′N	89°10′W
Copano Bay, b., Tx., U.S. (kō-pän′ō)	123	28°08′N	97°25′W
Copenhagen (København), Den.	154	55°43′N	12°27′E
Copiapó, Chile (kō-pyä-pō′)	144	27°16′S	70°28′W
Copley, Oh., U.S. (kŏp′lē)	111d	41°06′N	81°38′W
Copparo, Italy (kōp-pä′rō)	174	44°53′N	11°50′E
Coppell, Tx., U.S. (kŏp′pĕl)	117c	32°57′N	97°00′W
Copper, r., Ak., U.S. (kŏp′ẽr)	103	62°38′N	145°00′W
Copper Cliff, Can.	98	46°28′N	81°04′W
Copper Harbor, Mi., U.S.	113	47°27′N	87°53′W
Copperhill, Tn., U.S. (kŏp′ẽr hĭl)	124	35°00′N	84°22′W
Coppermine see Kugluktuk, Can.	92	67°46′N	115°19′W
Coppermine, r., Can.	92	66°48′N	114°59′W
Copper Mountain, mtn., Ak., U.S.	94	55°14′N	132°36′W
Copperton, Ut., U.S. (kŏp′ẽr-tŭn)	117b	40°34′N	112°06′W
Coquilee, Or., U.S. (kô-kēl′)	114	43°11′N	124°11′W
Coquilhatville see Mbandaka, D.R.C.	232	0°04′N	18°16′E
Coquimbo, Chile (kō-kēm′bō)	144	29°58′S	71°31′W
Coquimbo, prov., Chile	141b	31°50′S	71°05′W
Coquitlam Lake, l., Can. (kō-kwĭt-lȧm)	116d	49°23′N	122°44′W
Corabia, Rom. (kō-rä′bĭ-ȧ)	163	43°45′N	24°29′E
Coracora, Peru (kō′rä-kō′rä)	142	15°12′S	73°42′W
Coral Gables, Fl., U.S.	125a	25°43′N	80°14′W
Coral Rapids, Can. (kŏr′ăl)	91	50°18′N	81°49′W
Coral Sea, sea, Oc. (kŏr′ăl)	221	13°30′S	150°00′E
Coralville Reservoir, res., Ia., U.S.	113	41°45′N	91°50′W
Corangamite, Lake, l., Austl. (cŏr-ăŋg′á-mīt)	222	38°05′S	142°55′E
Coraopolis, Pa., U.S. (kō-rä-ŏp′ō-lĭs)	111e	40°30′N	80°09′W
Corato, Italy (kō′rä-tō)	174	41°08′N	16°28′E
Corbeil-Essonnes, Fr. (kôr-bā′yĕ-sŏn′)	170	48°31′N	2°29′E
Corbett, Or., U.S. (kôr′bĕt)	116c	45°31′N	122°17′W
Corbie, Fr. (kôr-bē′)	170	49°55′N	2°27′E
Corbin, Ky., U.S. (kôr′bĭn)	124	36°55′N	84°06′W
Corby, Eng., U.K. (kôr′bĭ)	158a	52°29′N	0°38′W
Corcovado, mtn., Braz. (kôr-kō-vä′dō)	144b	22°57′S	43°13′W
Corcovado, Golfo, b., Chile (kôr-kō-vä′dhō)	144	43°40′S	75°00′W
Cordeiro, Braz. (kôr-dā′rō)	141a	22°03′S	42°22′W
Cordele, Ga., U.S. (kôr-dēl′)	124	31°55′N	83°50′W
Cordell, Ok., U.S. (kôr-dĕl′)	120	35°19′N	98°58′W
Córdoba, Arg. (kôr′dō-vä)	144	30°20′S	64°03′W
Córdoba, Mex. (kô′r-dō-bä)	128	18°53′N	96°54′W
Córdoba, Spain (kô′r-dô-bä)	172	37°55′N	4°45′W
Córdoba, prov., Arg. (kôr′dō-vä)	144	32°00′S	64°00′W
Córdoba, Sierra de, mts., Arg.	144	31°15′S	64°30′W
Cordova, Ak., U.S. (kôr′dō-vä)	106a	60°34′N	145°38′W
Cordova, Al., U.S. (kôr′dō-ȧ)	124	33°45′N	86°22′W
Cordova Bay, b., Ak., U.S.	94	54°55′N	132°35′W
Corfu see Kérkira, i., Grc.	156	39°33′N	19°36′E
Corigliano, Italy (kō-rē-lyä′nō)	174	39°35′N	16°30′E
Corinth see Kórinthos, Grc.	154	37°56′N	22°54′E
Corinth, Ms., U.S. (kŏr′ĭnth)	124	34°55′N	88°30′W
Corinto, Braz. (kô-rē′n-tō)	143	18°20′S	44°16′W
Corinto, Col.	142a	3°09′N	76°12′W
Corinto, Nic. (kōr ĭn′to)	132	12°30′N	87°12′W
Corio, Austl.	217a	38°05′S	144°22′E
Corio Bay, b., Austl.	217a	38°07′S	144°25′E
Corisco, Isla de, i., Eq. Gui.	236	0°50′N	8°40′E
Cork, Ire. (kôrk)	154	51°54′N	8°25′W
Cork Harbour, b., Ire.	164	51°44′N	8°15′W
Corleone, Italy (kôr-lå-ō′nā)	174	37°48′N	13°18′E
Cormorant Lake, l., Can.	97	54°13′N	100°47′W
Cornelia, Ga., U.S. (kôr-nē′lyȧ)	124	34°31′N	83°30′W
Cornelis, r., S. Afr. (kôr-nē′lĭs)	238c	27°48′S	29°15′E
Cornell, Ca., U.S. (kôr-nĕl′)	117a	34°06′N	118°46′W
Cornell, Wi., U.S.	113	45°10′N	91°10′W
Corner Brook, Can. (kôr′nẽr)	91	48°57′N	57°57′W
Corner Inlet, b., Austl.	222	38°55′S	146°45′E
Corning, Ar., U.S. (kôr′nĭng)	121	36°26′N	90°35′W
Corning, Ia., U.S.	113	40°58′N	94°40′W
Corning, N.Y., U.S.	109	42°10′N	77°05′W
Corno, Monte, mtn., Italy (kôr′nō)	162	42°28′N	13°37′E
Cornwall, Bah.	134	25°55′N	77°15′W
Cornwall, Can. (kôrn′wôl)	99	45°05′N	74°35′W
Coro, Ven. (kō′rō)	142	11°22′N	69°43′W
Corocoro, Bol. (kō-rō-kō′rō)	142	17°15′S	68°21′W
Coromandel Coast, cst., India (kŏr-ō-man′dĕl)	199	13°30′N	80°30′E
Coromandel Peninsula, pen., N.Z.	223	36°50′S	176°00′E
Corona, Al., U.S. (kō-rō′nȧ)	124	33°42′N	87°28′W
Corona, Ca., U.S.	117a	33°52′N	117°34′W
Coronada, Bahía de, b., C.R. (bä-ē′ä-dĕ-kō-rō-nä′dō)	133	8°47′N	84°04′W
Corona del Mar, Ca., U.S. (kō-rō′nȧ dĕl mär)	117a	33°36′N	117°53′W
Coronado, Ca., U.S. (kŏr-ō-nä′dō)	118a	32°42′N	117°12′W
Coronation Gulf, b., Can. (kŏr-ō-nā′shŭn)	92	68°07′N	112°50′W
Coronel, Chile (kō-rō-nĕl′)	144	37°00′S	73°10′W
Coronel Brandsen, Arg. (kŏ-rō-nĕl-brá′nd-sĕn)	141c	35°09′S	58°15′W
Coronel Dorrego, Arg. (kŏ-rō-nĕl-dôr-rĕ′gō)	144	38°43′S	61°16′W
Coronel Oviedo, Para. (kŏ-rō-nĕl-ō-vē′dō)	144	25°28′S	56°22′W
Coronel Pringles, Arg. (kŏ-rō-nĕl-prēn′glĕs)	144	37°54′S	61°22′W
Coronel Suárez, Arg. (kŏ-rō-nĕl-swä′rās)	144	37°27′S	61°49′W
Corowa, Austl. (cŏr-ōwȧ)	222	36°02′S	146°23′E
Corozal, Belize (cŏr-ŏth-äl′)	132a	18°25′N	88°23′W
Corpus Christi, Tx., U.S. (kôr′pŭs krĭstē)	104	27°48′N	97°24′W
Corpus Christi Bay, b., Tx., U.S.	123	27°47′N	97°14′W
Corpus Christi Lake, l., Tx., U.S.	122	28°08′N	98°20′W
Corral, Chile (kō-räl′)	144	39°57′S	73°15′W
Corral de Almaguer, Spain (kō-räl′dā äl-mä-gâr′)	172	39°45′N	3°10′W
Corralillo, Cuba (kō-rä-lē-yō)	134	23°00′N	80°40′W
Corregidor Island, i., Phil. (kō-rā-hē-dōr′)	213a	14°21′N	120°25′E
Correntina, Braz. (kō-rĕn-tē-nȧ)	143	13°18′S	44°33′W
Corrib, Lough, l., Ire. (lŏk kŏr′ĭb)	164	53°25′N	9°19′W
Corrientes, Arg. (kō-ryĕn′tās)	144	27°25′S	58°39′W
Corrientes, prov., Arg.	144	28°45′S	58°00′W
Corrientes, Cabo, c., Col. (kȧ′bō-kō-ryĕn′tās)	142	5°34′N	77°35′W
Corrientes, Cabo, c., Cuba (kȧ′bō-kōr-rē-ĕn′tĕs)	134	21°50′N	84°25′W
Corrientes, Cabo, c., Mex.	128	20°25′N	105°41′W
Corry, Pa., U.S. (kŏr′ĭ)	109	41°55′N	79°40′W
Corse, Cap, c., Fr. (kôrs)	161	42°59′N	9°19′E
Corsica, i., Fr. (kô′r-sē-kä)	156	42°10′N	8°55′E
Corsicana, Tx., U.S. (kôr-sĭ-kăn′ȧ)	104	32°06′N	96°28′W
Cortazar, Mex. (kôr-tä-zär)	130	20°30′N	100°57′W
Corte, Fr. (kôr′tå)	174	42°18′N	9°10′E
Cortegana, Spain (kôr-tå-gä′nä)	172	37°54′N	6°48′W
Cortés, Ensendada de, b., Cuba (ĕn-sĕ-nä-dä-dĕ-kōr-tās′)	134	22°05′N	83°45′W
Cortez, Co., U.S.	119	37°21′N	108°35′W
Cortland, N.Y., U.S. (kôrt′lănd)	109	42°35′N	76°10′W
Cortona, Italy (kōr-tō′nä)	174	43°16′N	12°00′E
Corubal, r., Gui.-B.	234	11°43′N	14°40′W
Coruche, Port. (kō-rōō′she)	172	38°58′N	8°34′W
Çoruh, r., Asia (chō-rōōk′)	181	40°30′N	41°10′E
Çorum, Tur. (chō-rōōm′)	198	40°34′N	34°45′E
Corunna, Mi., U.S. (kō-rŭn′ȧ)	108	43°00′N	84°05′W
Coruripe, Braz. (kō-rō-rē′pĭ)	143	10°09′S	36°13′W
Corvallis, Or., U.S. (kŏr-văl′ĭs)	104	44°34′N	123°17′W
Corve, r., Eng., U.K. (kôr′vē)	158a	52°28′N	2°43′W
Corydon, Ia., U.S.	113	40°45′N	93°20′W
Corydon, In., U.S. (kŏr′ĭ-dŭn)	108	38°10′N	86°05′W
Corydon, Ky., U.S.	108	37°45′N	87°40′W
Cosamaloápan, Mex. (kō-sä-mä-lwä′pän)	131	18°21′N	95°48′W

ăt; finăl; rāte; senâte; ärm; åsk; sofȧ; fâre; ch-choose; dh-as th in other; bē; ēvent; bĕt; recĕnt; cratẽr; g-gō; gh-guttural g; bĭt; ĭ-short neutral; rīde; κ-guttural k as ch in German ich;

PRONOUNCING INDEX
Coscomatepec – Cuilo 285

PLACE (Pronunciation)	PAGE	LAT.	LONG.
Coscomatepec, Mex. (kôs'kōmä-tĕ-pĕk')	131	19°04'N	97°03'W
Cosenza, Italy (kô-zĕnt'sä)	163	39°18'N	16°15'E
Coshocton, Oh., U.S. (kô-shŏk'tŭn)	108	40°15'N	81°55'W
Cosigüina, vol., Nic.	132	12°59'N	87°35'W
Cosmoledo Group, is., Sey. (kŏs-mô-lā'dō)	233	9°42'S	47°45'E
Cosmopolis, Wa., U.S. (kŏz-mŏp'ō-lĭs)	114	46°58'N	123°47'W
Cosne-sur-Loire, Fr. (kōn-sür-lwär')	170	47°25'N	2°57'E
Cosoleacaque, Mex. (kō sō lā-ä-kä'kē)	131	18°01'N	94°38'W
Costa de Caparica, Port.	173b	38°40'N	9°12'W
Costa Mesa, Ca., U.S. (kŏs'tȧ mā'sȧ)	117a	33°39'N	118°54'W
Costa Rica, nation, N.A. (kŏs'tȧ rē'kȧ)	129	10°30'N	84°30'W
Cosumnes, r., Ca., U.S. (kŏ-sŭm'nĕz)	118	38°21'N	121°17'W
Cotabambas, Peru (kô-tä-bȧm'bäs)	142	13°49'S	72°17'W
Cotabato, Phil. (kō-tä-bä'tō)	213	7°06'N	124°13'E
Cotaxtla, Mex. (kō-täs'tlä)	131	18°49'N	96°22'W
Cotaxtla, r., Mex.	131	18°54'N	96°21'W
Coteau-du-Lac, Can. (cō-tō'dü-läk)	102a	45°17'N	74°11'W
Coteau-Landing, Can.	102a	45°15'N	74°13'W
Coteaux, Haiti	135	18°15'N	74°05'W
Cote d'Ivoire (Ivory Coast), nation, Afr.	230	7°43'N	6°30'W
Côte d'Or, reg., Fr.	170	47°02'N	4°35'E
Cotija de la Paz, Mex. (kô-tē'-кä-dĕ-lä-pá'z)	130	19°46'N	102°43'W
Cotonou, Benin (kô-tô-nōō')	230	6°21'N	2°26'E
Cotopaxi, mtn., Ec. (kō-tô-păk'sê)	142	0°40'S	78°26'W
Cotorro, Cuba (kô-tôr-rō)	135a	23°03'N	82°17'W
Cotswold Hills, hills, Eng., U.K. (kŭtz'wōld)	164	51°35'N	2°16'W
Cottage Grove, Mn., U.S. (kŏt'áj grōv)	117g	44°50'N	92°52'W
Cottage Grove, Or., U.S.	114	43°48'N	123°04'W
Cottbus, Ger. (kōt'bōōs)	161	51°47'N	14°20'E
Cottonwood, r., Mn., U.S. (kŏt'ŭn-wŏod)	112	44°25'N	95°35'W
Cotulla, Tx., U.S. (kŏ-tŭl'lȧ)	122	28°26'N	99°14'W
Coubert, Fr. (kōō-bâr')	171b	48°40'N	2°43'E
Coudersport, Pa., U.S. (kou'dẽrz-pōrt)	109	41°45'N	78°00'W
Coudres, Île aux, i., Can.	100	47°17'N	70°12'W
Coulommiers, Fr. (kōō-lô-myā')	171b	48°49'N	3°05'E
Coulto, Serra do, mts., Braz. (sĕ'r-rä-dô-kô-ó'tô)	144b	22°33'S	43°27'W
Council Bluffs, Ia., U.S. (koun'sĭl blŭf)	105	41°16'N	95°53'W
Council Grove, Ks., U.S. (koun'sĭl grōv)	121	38°39'N	96°30'W
Coupeville, Wa., U.S. (kōōp'vĭl)	116a	48°13'N	122°41'W
Courantyne, r., S.A. (kôr'ántĭn)	143	4°28'N	57°42'W
Courtenay, Can. (cōōrt-nā')	90	49°41'N	125°00'W
Coushatta, La., U.S. (kou-shăt'ȧ)	123	32°02'N	93°21'W
Coutras, Fr. (kōō-trá')	170	45°02'N	0°07'W
Covelo, Ang.	236	12°06'S	13°55'E
Coventry, Eng., U.K. (kŭv'ĕn-trĭ)	164	52°25'N	1°29'W
Covina, Ca., U.S. (kô-vē'nȧ)	117a	34°06'N	117°54'W
Covington, Ga., U.S. (kŭv'ĭng-tŭn)	124	33°36'N	83°50'W
Covington, In., U.S.	108	40°10'N	87°15'W
Covington, Ky., U.S.	105	39°05'N	84°31'W
Covington, La., U.S.	123	30°30'N	90°06'W
Covington, Oh., U.S.	108	40°10'N	84°20'W
Covington, Ok., U.S.	121	36°18'N	97°32'W
Covington, Tn., U.S.	124	35°33'N	89°40'W
Covington, Va., U.S.	108	37°50'N	80°00'W
Cowal, Lake, l., Austl. (kou'ăl)	222	33°30'S	147°10'E
Cowan, l., Austl. (kou'ȧn)	220	32°00'S	122°30'E
Cowansville, Can.	99	45°13'N	72°47'W
Cow Creek, r., Or., U.S. (kou)	114	42°45'N	123°35'W
Cowes, Eng., U.K. (kouz)	164	50°43'N	1°25'W
Cowichan Lake, l., Can.	94	48°54'N	124°20'W
Cowlitz, r., Wa., U.S. (kou'lĭts)	114	46°30'N	122°45'W
Cowra, Austl. (kou'rȧ)	222	33°50'S	148°33'E
Coxim, Braz. (kō-shēɴ')	143	18°32'S	54°43'W
Coxquihui, Mex. (kōz-kē-wē')	131	20°10'N	97°34'W
Cox's Bāzār, Bngl.	202	21°32'N	92°00'E
Coyaima, Col. (kô-yäē'mä)	142a	3°48'N	75°11'W
Coyame, Mex. (kō-yä'mä)	122	29°26'N	105°05'W
Coyanosa Draw, Tx., U.S. (kō yá-nō'sä)	122	30°55'N	103°07'W
Coyoacán, Mex. (kô-yô-á-kän')	130	19°21'N	99°10'W
Coyote, r., Ca., U.S. (kī'ōt)	116b	37°37'N	121°57'W
Coyuca de Benítez, Mex. (kō-yōō'kä dā bā-nē'tāz)	130	17°04'N	100°06'W
Coyuca de Catalán, Mex. (kō-yōō'kä dā kä-tä-län')	130	18°19'N	100°41'W
Coyutla, Mex. (kō-yōō'tlä)	131	20°13'N	97°40'W
Cozad, Ne., U.S. (kō'zăd)	120	40°53'N	99°59'W
Cozaddale, Oh., U.S. (kō-zăd-dāl)	111f	39°16'N	84°09'W
Cozoyoapan, Mex. (kô-zō-yô-ä-pá'n)	130	16°45'N	98°17'W
Cozumel, Mex. (kŏ-zōō-mĕ'l)	132a	20°31'N	86°55'W
Cozumel, Isla de, i., Mex. (ē's-lä-dĕ-kŏ-zōō-mĕ'l)	128	20°26'N	87°10'W
Crab Creek, r., Wa., U.S. (krăb)	114	46°47'N	119°43'W
Crab Creek, r., Wa., U.S.	114	47°21'N	119°09'W
Cradock, S. Afr. (kră'dŭk)	232	32°12'S	25°38'E
Crafton, Pa., U.S. (krăf'tŭn)	111e	40°26'N	80°04'W
Craig, Co., U.S. (krāg)	115	40°32'N	107°31'W
Craiova, Rom. (krá-yō'vá)	163	44°18'N	23°50'E
Cranberry, l., N.Y., U.S. (krăn'bĕr-ĭ)	109	44°10'N	74°50'W
Cranbourne, Austl.	217a	38°07'S	145°16'E
Cranbrook, Can. (krăn'brŏok)	90	49°31'N	115°46'W
Cranbury, N.J., U.S. (krăn'bē-rĭ)	110a	40°19'N	74°31'W
Crandon, Wi., U.S. (krăn'dŭn)	113	45°35'N	88°55'W

PLACE (Pronunciation)	PAGE	LAT.	LONG.
Crane Prairie Reservoir, res., Or., U.S.	114	43°50'N	121°55'W
Cranston, R.I., U.S. (krăns'tŭn)	110b	41°46'N	71°25'W
Crater Lake, l., Or., U.S. (krā'tẽr)	114	43°00'N	122°08'W
Crater Lake National Park, rec., Or., U.S.	114	42°58'N	122°40'W
Craters of the Moon National Monument, rec., Id., U.S. (krā'tẽr)	115	43°28'N	113°15'W
Crateús, Braz. (krä-tå-ōōzh')	143	5°09'S	40°35'W
Crato, Braz. (krä'tò)	143	7°19'S	39°13'W
Crawford, Ne., U.S. (krô'fẽrd)	112	42°41'N	103°25'W
Crawford, Wa., U.S.	116c	45°49'N	122°24'W
Crawfordsville, In., U.S. (krô'fẽrdz-vĭl)	108	40°00'N	86°55'W
Crazy Mountains, mts., Mt., U.S. (krā'zĭ)	115	46°11'N	110°25'W
Crazy Woman Creek, r., Wy., U.S.	115	44°08'N	106°40'W
Crecy, S. Afr. (krĕ-sē)	230c	24°38'S	28°52'E
Crécy-en-Brie, Fr. (krā-sē'-ĕɴ-brē')	171b	48°52'N	2°55'E
Crécy-en-Ponthieu, Fr.	170	50°13'N	1°48'E
Credit, r., Can.	102d	43°41'N	79°55'W
Cree, l., Can. (krē)	92	57°35'N	107°52'W
Creighton, S. Afr. (cre-tŏn)	233c	30°02'S	29°52'E
Creighton, Ne., U.S. (krā'tŭn)	112	42°27'N	97°54'W
Creil, Fr. (krĕ'y')	170	49°18'N	2°28'E
Crema, Italy (krā'mä)	174	45°21'N	9°53'E
Cremona, Italy (krā-mō'nä)	162	45°09'N	10°02'E
Crépy-en-Valois, Fr. (krā-pē'ĕɴ-vä-lwä')	171b	49°14'N	2°53'E
Cres, Cro. (tsrĕs)	174	44°58'N	14°21'E
Crescent Beach, Can.	116d	49°03'N	122°58'W
Crescent City, Ca., U.S. (krĕs'ĕnt)	114	41°46'N	124°13'W
Crescent City, Fl., U.S.	125	29°26'N	81°35'W
Crescent Lake, l., Fl., U.S. (krĕs'ĕnt)	125	29°33'N	81°30'W
Crescent Lake, l., Or., U.S.	114	43°25'N	121°58'W
Cresco, Ia., U.S. (krĕs'kō)	113	43°23'N	92°07'W
Crested Butte, Co., U.S. (krĕst'ĕd būt)	119	38°50'N	107°00'W
Crestline, Ca., U.S. (krĕst-līn)	117a	34°15'N	117°17'W
Crestline, Oh., U.S.	108	40°50'N	82°40'W
Crestmore, Ca., U.S. (krĕst'môr)	117a	34°02'N	117°23'W
Creston, Can. (krĕs'tŭn)	90	49°06'N	116°31'W
Creston, Ia., U.S.	113	41°04'N	94°22'W
Creston, Oh., U.S.	111d	40°59'N	81°54'W
Crestview, Fl., U.S. (krĕst'vū)	124	30°44'N	86°35'W
Crestwood, Ky., U.S. (krĕst'wŏod)	111h	38°20'N	85°28'W
Crestwood, Mo., U.S.	117e	38°33'N	90°23'W
Crete, Il., U.S. (krēt)	111a	41°26'N	87°38'W
Crete, Ne., U.S.	121	40°38'N	96°56'W
Crete, i., Grc.	156	35°15'N	24°30'E
Creus, Cap de, c., Spain	173	42°16'N	3°18'E
Creuse, r., Fr. (krûz)	170	46°51'N	0°49'E
Creve Coeur, Mo., U.S. (krēv kôr)	117e	38°40'N	90°27'W
Crevillent, Spain	173	38°12'N	0°48'W
Crewe, Eng., U.K. (krōō)	164	53°06'N	2°27'W
Crewe, Va., U.S.	125	37°09'N	78°08'W
Crimean Peninsula *see* Kryms'kyi Pivostriv, pen., Ukr.	181	45°18'N	33°30'E
Crimmitschau, Ger. (krĭm'ĭt-shou)	168	50°49'N	12°22'E
Cripple Creek, Co., U.S. (krĭp''l)	120	38°44'N	105°12'W
Crisfield, Md., U.S. (krĭs-fēld)	109	38°00'N	75°50'W
Cristal, Monts de, mts., Gabon	236	0°50'N	10°30'E
Cristina, Braz. (krēs-tē'-nä)	141a	22°13'S	45°15'W
Cristóbal Colón, Pico, mtn., Col. (pē'kô-krēs-tô'bäl-kō-lôn')	142	11°00'N	74°00'W
Crişul Alb, r., Rom. (krē'shōōl älb)	169	46°20'N	22°15'E
Črna, r., Mac. (ts'r'nä)	175	41°03'N	21°46'E
Črnomelj, Slvn. (ch'r'nō-māl')	174	45°35'N	15°11'E
Croatia, nation, Eur.	174	45°24'N	15°18'E
Crockett, Ca., U.S. (krŏk'ĕt)	116b	38°03'N	122°14'W
Crockett, Tx., U.S.	123	31°19'N	95°28'W
Crofton, Md., U.S.	110e	39°01'N	76°43'W
Crofton, Ne., U.S.	112	42°44'N	97°32'W
Croix, Lac la, l., N.A. (läk lä krōō-ä')	113	48°19'N	91°53'W
Croker, i., Austl. (krō'kȧ)	220	10°45'S	132°25'E
Cronulla, Austl. (krō-nŭl'ȧ)	217b	34°03'S	151°09'E
Crooked, i., Bah.	135	22°45'N	74°10'W
Crooked, l., Can.	101	48°25'N	56°05'W
Crooked, r., Can.	95	54°30'N	122°55'W
Crooked, r., Or., U.S.	114	44°07'N	120°30'W
Crooked Creek, r., Il., U.S. (krŏŏk'ĕd)	121	40°21'N	90°49'W
Crooked Island Passage, strt., Bah.	135	22°40'N	74°50'W
Crookston, Mn., U.S. (krŏŏks'tŭn)	112	47°44'N	96°35'W
Crooksville, Oh., U.S. (krŏŏks'vĭl)	108	39°45'N	82°05'W
Crosby, Eng., U.K.	158a	53°30'N	3°02'W
Crosby, Mn., U.S. (krôz'bĭ)	113	46°29'N	93°58'W
Crosby, N.D., U.S.	112	48°55'N	103°18'W
Crosby, Tx., U.S.	123a	29°55'N	95°04'W
Cross, l., La., U.S.	123	32°33'N	93°58'W
Cross, r., Nig.	235	5°35'N	8°05'E
Cross City, Fl., U.S.	124	29°55'N	83°25'W
Crossett, Ar., U.S. (krôs'ĕt)	121	33°08'N	92°00'W
Cross Lake, l., Can.	92	54°45'N	97°30'W
Cross River Reservoir, res., N.Y., U.S. (krôs)	110a	41°14'N	73°34'W
Cross Sound, strt., Ak., U.S. (krŏs)	103	58°12'N	137°20'W
Crosswell, Mi., U.S. (krŏz'wĕl)	108	43°15'N	82°35'W
Croswell, i., Serb.	174	44°50'N	14°31'E
Crotch, l., Can.	99	44°55'N	76°55'W
Crotone, Italy (krō-tô'nĕ)	175	39°05'N	17°08'E
Croton Falls Reservoir, res., N.Y., U.S. (krōtŭn)	110a	41°22'N	73°44'W

PLACE (Pronunciation)	PAGE	LAT.	LONG.
Croton-on-Hudson, N.Y., U.S. (krō'tŭn-ŏn hŭd'sŭn)	110a	41°12'N	73°53'W
Crow, l., Can.	113	49°13'N	93°29'W
Crow Agency, Mt., U.S.	115	45°36'N	107°27'W
Crow Creek, r., Co., U.S.	120	41°08'N	104°25'W
Crow Creek Indian Reservation, I.R., S.D., U.S.	112	44°17'N	99°17'W
Crow Indian Reservation, I.R., Mt., U.S. (krō)	115	45°26'N	108°12'W
Crowle, Eng., U.K. (kroul)	158a	53°36'N	0°49'W
Crowley, La., U.S. (krou'lē)	123	30°13'N	92°22'W
Crown Mountain, mtn., Can. (kroun)	116d	49°24'N	123°05'W
Crown Mountain, mtn., V.I.U.S.	129c	18°22'N	64°58'W
Crown Point, In., U.S. (kroun point')	111a	41°25'N	87°22'W
Crown Point, N.Y., U.S.	109	44°00'N	73°25'W
Crowsnest Pass, p., Can.	95	49°39'N	114°45'W
Crow Wing, r., Mn., U.S. (krō)	113	44°50'N	94°01'W
Crow Wing, r., Mn., U.S.	113	46°42'N	94°48'W
Crow Wing, North Fork, r., Mn., U.S.	113	45°16'N	94°28'W
Crow Wing, South Fork, r., Mn., U.S.	113	44°59'N	94°42'W
Croydon, Austl. (kroi'dŭn)	219	18°15'S	142°15'E
Croydon, Austl.	217a	37°48'S	145°17'E
Croydon, Eng., U.K.	161	51°22'N	0°06'W
Croydon, Pa., U.S.	110f	40°05'N	74°55'W
Crozet, Îles, is., Afr. (krô-zĕ')	3	46°20'S	51°30'E
Cruces, Cuba (krōō'sås)	134	22°20'N	80°20'W
Cruces, Arroyo de, r., Mex. (är-rŏ'yô-dĕ-krōō'sĕs)	122	26°17'N	104°32'W
Cruillas, Mex. (krōō-ēl'yäs)	122	24°45'N	98°31'W
Cruz, Cabo, c., Cuba (ká'-bô-krōōz)	129	19°50'N	77°45'W
Cruz, Cayo, i., Cuba (kä'yō-krōōz)	134	22°15'N	77°50'W
Cruz Alta, Braz. (krōōz äl'tä)	144	28°41'S	54°02'W
Cruz del Eje, Arg. (krōō's-dĕl-ĕ-kĕ)	144	30°46'S	64°45'W
Cruzeiro, Braz. (krōō-zā'rò)	141a	22°36'S	44°57'W
Cruzeiro do Sul, Braz. (krōō-zā'rò dò sōōl)	142	7°34'S	72°40'W
Crysler, Can.	102c	45°13'N	75°09'W
Crystal City, Tx., U.S. (krĭs'tăl sĭ'tĭ)	122	28°40'N	99°50'W
Crystal Falls, Mi., U.S. (krĭs'tăl fôls)	113	46°06'N	88°21'W
Crystal Lake, Il., U.S. (krĭs'tăl lăk)	111a	42°15'N	88°18'W
Crystal Springs, Ms., U.S. (krĭs'tăl sprĭngz)	124	31°58'N	90°20'W
Crystal Springs, oasis, Ca., U.S.	116b	37°31'N	122°26'W
Csongrád, Hung. (chôn'gräd)	169	46°42'N	20°09'E
Csorna, Hung. (chôr'nä)	169	47°39'N	17°11'E
Cúa, Ven. (kōō'ä)	143b	10°10'N	66°54'W
Cuajimalpa, Mex. (kwä-hē-mäl'pä)	131a	19°21'N	99°18'W
Cuale, Sierra del, mts., Mex. (sē-ĕ'r-rä-dĕl-kwä'lĕ)	130	20°20'N	104°58'W
Cuamato, Ang. (kwä-mä'tō)	236	17°05'S	15°09'E
Cuamba, Moz.	237	14°49'S	36°33'E
Cuando, Ang. (kwän'dō)	236	16°32'S	22°07'E
Cuando, r., Afr.	232	14°30'S	20°00'E
Cuangar, Ang.	236	17°36'S	18°39'E
Cuango, r., Afr.	232	9°00'S	18°00'E
Cuanza, r., Ang. (kwän'zä)	232	9°45'S	15°00'E
Cuarto, r., Arg.	144	33°00'S	63°25'W
Cuatro Caminos, Cuba (kwä'trô-kä-mē'nôs)	135a	23°01'N	82°13'W
Cuatro Ciénegas, Mex. (kwä'trō syā'nā-gäs)	122	26°59'N	102°03'W
Cuauhtemoc, Mex. (kwä-ōō-tē-mōk')	131	15°43'N	91°57'W
Cuautepec, Mex. (kwä-ōō-tĕ-pĕk)	130	16°41'N	99°04'W
Cuautepec, Mex.	130	20°01'N	98°19'W
Cuautitlán, Mex. (kwä-ōō-tēt-län')	131a	19°40'N	99°12'W
Cuautla, Mex. (kwä-ōō'tlá)	130	18°47'N	98°57'W
Cuba, Port. (kōō'bá)	172	38°10'N	7°55'W
Cuba, nation, N.A. (kū'bȧ)	129	22°00'N	79°00'W
Cubagua, Isla, i., Ven. (ē's-lä-kōō-bä'gwä)	143b	10°48'N	64°10'W
Cubango (Okavango), r., Afr. (kōō-bäŋ'gō)	232	17°10'S	18°20'E
Cub Hills, hills, Can. (kŭb)	96	54°20'N	104°30'W
Cucamonga, Ca., U.S. (kōō-kȧ-mŏn'gȧ)	117a	34°05'N	117°35'W
Cuchi, Ang.	232	14°40'S	16°50'E
Cuchillo Parado, Mex. (kōō-chē'lyô pä-rä'dô)	122	29°26'N	104°52'W
Cuchumatanes, Sierra de los, mts., Guat.	132	15°35'N	91°10'W
Cúcuta, Col. (kōō'kōō-tä)	142	7°56'N	72°30'W
Cudahy, Wi., U.S. (kŭd'ȧ-hĭ)	111a	42°57'N	87°52'W
Cuddalore, India (kŭd ȧ-lōr')	199	11°49'N	79°46'E
Cuddapah, India (kŭd'ȧ-pä)	199	14°31'N	78°52'E
Cue, Austl. (kū)	218	27°30'S	118°10'E
Cuéllar, Spain (kwā'lyär')	172	41°24'N	4°15'W
Cuenca, Ec. (kwĕn'kä)	142	2°52'S	78°54'W
Cuenca, Spain	162	40°05'N	2°07'W
Cuenca, Sierra de, mts., Spain (sē-ĕ'r-rä-dĕ-kwĕ'n-kä)	172	40°02'N	1°50'W
Cuencame, Mex. (kwĕn-kä-mā')	122	24°52'N	103°42'W
Cuerámaro, Mex. (kwā-rä'mä-rô)	130	20°39'N	101°44'W
Cuernavaca, Mex. (kwĕr-nä-vä'kä)	128	18°55'N	99°15'W
Cuero, Tx., U.S. (kwā'rō)	123	29°05'N	97°16'W
Cuetzalá del Progreso, Mex. (kwĕt-zä-lä dĕl prō-grā'sō)	130	18°07'N	99°51'W
Cuetzalan del Almanzora, Mex.	131	20°02'N	97°33'W
Cuevas del Almanzora, Spain (kwĕ'väs-dĕl-äl-män-zō-rä)	162	37°19'N	1°54'W
Cuglieri, Italy (kōō-lyā'rē)	174	40°11'N	8°37'E
Cuicatlán, Mex. (kwē-kä-tlän')	131	17°46'N	96°57'W
Cuilapa, Guat. (kò-ē-lä'pä)	132	14°16'N	90°20'W
Cuilo (Kwilu), r., Afr.	236	9°15'S	19°30'E

ng-sing; ŋ-baŋk; ɴ-nasalized n; nŏd; cŏmmit; ōld; ôbey; ôrder; oi-boil; fōōd; ŏŏ-as oo in foot; ou-out; s-soft; sh-dish; th-thin; pūre; ûnite; ûrn; stŭd; circŭs; ü-as in French tu; '-indeterminate vowel.

286 Cuito – Davenport PRONOUNCING INDEX

PLACE (Pronunciation)	PAGE	LAT.	LONG.
Cuito, r., Ang. (kōō-ē′-tō)	232	14°45′S	19°00′E
Cuitzeo, Mex. (kwēt′zā-ō)	130	19°57′N	101°11′W
Cuitzeo, Laguna de, l., Mex. (lä-ó′nä-dĕ-kwēt′zā-ō)	130	19°58′N	101°05′W
Cul de Sac, pl., Haiti (kōō′l-dĕ-sä′k)	135	18°35′N	72°05′W
Culebra, i., P.R. (kōō-lā′brä)	129b	18°19′N	65°32′W
Culebra, Sierra de la, mts., Spain (sē-ĕ′r-rä-dĕ-lä-kōō-lĕ-brä)	172	41°52′N	6°21′W
Culemborg, Neth.	159a	51°57′N	5°14′E
Culfa, Azer.	182	38°58′N	45°38′E
Culgoa, r., Austl. (kŭl-gō′ȧ)	221	29°21′S	147°00′E
Culiacán, Mex. (kōō-lyä-kȧ′n)	128	24°45′N	107°30′W
Culion, Phil. (kōō-lē-ōn′)	[illegible]	[illegible]	[illegible]
Cúllar de Baza, Spain (kōō′l-yär-dĕ-bä′zä)	172	37°36′N	2°35′W
Cullera, Spain (kōō-lyā′rä)	162	39°12′N	0°15′W
[illegible]	[illegible]	[illegible]	[illegible]
Cullman, Al., U.S. (kŭl′măn)	124	34°10′N	86°50′W
Culpeper, Va., U.S. (kŭl′pĕp-ẽr)	109	38°30′N	77°55′W
Culross, Can. (kŭl′rôs)	102f	49°43′N	97°54′W
Culver, In., U.S. (kŭl′vẽr)	108	41°15′N	86°25′W
Culver City, Ca., U.S.	117a	34°00′N	118°23′W
Cumaná, Ven.	142	10°28′N	64°10′W
Cumberland, Can. (kŭm′bẽr-lănd)	102c	45°31′N	75°25′W
Cumberland, Md., U.S.	105	39°40′N	78°40′W
Cumberland, Wa., U.S.	116a	47°17′N	121°55′W
Cumberland, Wi., U.S.	113	45°31′N	92°01′W
Cumberland, r., U.S.	124	36°45′N	85°33′W
Cumberland, Lake, res., Ky., U.S.	107	36°55′N	85°20′W
Cumberland Islands, is., Austl.	221	20°20′S	149°46′E
Cumberland Peninsula, pen., Can.	93	65°59′N	64°05′W
Cumberland Plateau, plat., U.S.	124	35°25′N	85°30′W
Cumberland Sound, strt., Can.	93	65°27′N	65°44′W
Cundinamarca, dept., Col. (kōōn-dē-nä-mä′r-kȧ)	142a	4°57′N	74°27′W
Cunduacán, Mex. (kōn-dōō-ȧ-kän′)	131	18°04′N	93°23′W
Cunene (Kunene), r., Afr.	232	17°05′S	12°35′E
Cuneo, Italy (kōō′nā-ō)	174	44°24′N	7°31′E
Cunha, Braz. (kōō′nyȧ)	141a	23°05′S	44°56′W
Cunnamulla, Austl. (kŭn-ȧ-mŭl-ȧ)	219	28°00′S	145°55′E
Cupula, Pico, mtn., Mex. (pē′kō-kōō′pōō-lä)	128	24°45′N	111°10′W
Cuquío, Mex. (kōō-kē′ō)	130	20°55′N	103°03′W
Curaçao, i., Neth. Ant. (kōō-rä-sä′ō)	142	12°12′N	68°58′W
Curacautín, Chile (kä-rä-käōō-tē′n)	144	38°25′S	71°53′W
Curaumilla, Punta, c., Chile (kōō-rou-mē′lyä)	141b	33°05′S	71°44′W
Curepto, Chile (kōō-rĕp-tô)	141b	35°06′S	72°02′W
Curitiba, Braz. (kōō-rē-tē′bȧ)	143	25°20′S	49°15′W
Curly Cut Cays, is., Bah.	134	23°40′N	77°40′W
Currais Novos, Braz. (kōōr-rä′ēs nō-vōs)	143	6°02′S	36°39′W
Curran, Can. (kü-răn′)	102c	45°30′N	74°59′W
Current, i., Bah. (kŭ-rĕnt)	134	25°20′N	76°50′W
Current, r., Mo., U.S. (kûr′ĕnt)	121	37°18′N	91°21′W
Currie, Mount, mtn., S. Afr. (kŭ-rē)	233c	30°28′S	29°23′E
Currituck Sound, strt., N.C., U.S. (kûr′ĭ-tŭk)	125	36°27′N	75°42′W
Curtis, Ne., U.S. (kûr′tĭs)	120	40°36′N	100°29′W
Curtis, i., Austl.	221	23°38′S	151°43′E
Curtisville, Pa., U.S. (kûr′tĭs-vĭl)	111e	40°38′N	79°50′W
Ćurug, Serb. (chōō′rôg)	175	45°27′N	20°03′E
Curunga, Ang.	236	12°51′S	21°12′E
Curupira, Serra, mts., S.A. (sĕr′rȧ kōō-rōō-pē′rȧ)	142	1°00′N	65°30′W
Cururupu, Braz. (kōō-rō-rō-pōō′)	143	1°40′S	44°56′W
Curvelo, Braz. (kôr-vĕl′ō)	143	18°47′S	44°14′W
Cusco, Peru	142	13°36′S	71°52′W
Cushing, Ok., U.S. (kŭsh′ĭng)	121	35°58′N	96°46′W
Custer, S.D., U.S. (kŭs′tẽr)	112	43°46′N	103°36′W
Custer, Wa., U.S.	116d	48°55′N	122°39′W
Cut Bank, Mt., U.S. (kŭt bănk)	115	48°38′N	112°19′W
Cuthbert, Ga., U.S. (kŭth′bẽrt)	124	31°47′N	84°48′W
Cuttack, India (kŭ-tăk′)	199	20°38′N	85°53′E
Cutzamala, r., Mex. (kōō-tzä-mä-lä′)	130	18°57′N	100°41′W
Cutzamalá de Pinzón, Mex. (kōō-tzä-mä-lä′dĕ-pēn-zō′n)	130	18°28′N	100°36′W
Cuvo, r., Ang. (kōō′vō)	232	11°00′S	14°30′E
Cuxhaven, Ger. (kōks′hä-fĕn)	160	53°51′N	8°43′E
Cuyahoga, r., Oh., U.S. (kī-ȧ-hō′gȧ)	111d	41°22′N	81°38′W
Cuyahoga Falls, Oh., U.S.	111d	41°08′N	81°29′W
Cuyapaire Indian Reservation, I.R., Ca., U.S. (kū-yȧ-pâr)	118	32°46′N	116°20′W
Cuyo Islands, is., Phil. (kōō′yō)	212	10°54′N	120°08′E
Cuyotenango, Guat. (kōō-yō-tĕ-näŋ′gō)	132	14°30′N	91°35′W
Cuyuni, r., S.A. (kōō-yōō′nē)	143	6°40′N	60°44′W
Cuyutlán, Mex. (kōō-yōō-tlän′)	130	18°54′N	104°04′W
Cyclades *see* Kikládhes, is., Grc.	156	37°30′N	24°45′E
Cynthiana, Ky., U.S. (sĭn-thĭ-ăn′ȧ)	108	38°20′N	84°20′W
Cypress, Ca., U.S. (sī′prĕs)	117a	33°50′N	118°03′W
Cypress Hills, hills, Can.	96	49°40′N	110°20′W
Cypress Lake, l., Can.	96	49°28′N	109°43′W
Cyprus, nation, Asia (sī′prŭs)	198	35°00′N	31°00′E
Cyrenaica *see* Barqah, hist. reg., Libya	231	31°09′N	21°45′E
Czech Republic, nation, Eur.	154	50°00′N	15°00′E
Czersk, Pol. (chĕrsk)	169	53°47′N	17°58′E
Częstochowa, Pol. (chăn-stô kô′vȧ)	161	50°49′N	19°10′E
D			
Da'an, China (dä-än)	208	45°25′N	124°22′E
Dabakala, C. Iv. (dä-bä-kä′lä)	230	8°16′N	4°36′W
Daba Shan, mts., China (dä-bä shän)	204	32°25′N	108°20′E
Dabeiba, Col. (dȧ-bā′bä)	142a	7°01′N	76°16′W
Dabie Shan, mts., China (dä-bĭĕ shän)	205	31°40′N	114°50′E
Dabnou, Niger	235	14°09′N	5°22′E
Dabob Bay, b., Wa., U.S. (dā′bŏb)	116a	47°50′N	122°50′W
Dabola, Gui.	234	10°45′N	11°07′W
Dąbrowa Białostocka, Pol.	169	53°37′N	23°18′E
Dacca *see* Dhaka, Bngl.	[illegible]	[illegible]	[illegible]
Dachang, China (dä-chäŋ)	207b	31°18′N	121°25′E
Dachangshan Dao, i., China (dä-chäŋ-shän dou)	206	39°21′N	122°31′E
[illegible]	[illegible]	[illegible]	[illegible]
Dacotah, Can. (dȧ-kō′tȧ)	102f	[illegible]	[illegible]
Dade City, Fl., U.S. (dād)	125a	28°22′N	82°09′W
Dadeville, Al., U.S. (dād′vĭl)	124	32°48′N	85°44′W
Dādra & Nagar Haveli, India	199	20°00′N	73°00′E
Dadu, r., China (dä-dōō)	209	29°20′N	103°03′E
Daet, mtn., Phil. (dä′āt)	213a	14°07′N	122°59′E
Dafoe, r., Can.	97	55°50′N	95°50′W
Dafter, Mi., U.S. (dăf′tẽr)	117k	46°21′N	84°26′W
Dagana, Sen. (dä-gä′nä)	230	16°31′N	15°30′W
Dagana, reg., Chad	235	12°20′N	15°15′E
Dagang, China (dä-gäŋ)	207a	22°48′N	113°24′E
Dagda, Lat. (dȧg′dȧ)	167	56°04′N	27°30′E
Dagenham, Eng., U.K. (dăg′ĕn-ăm)	158b	51°32′N	0°09′E
Dagestan, prov., Russia (dä-gĕs-tän′)	181	43°40′N	46°10′E
Daggett, Ca., U.S. (dăg′ĕt)	118	34°50′N	116°52′W
Dagu, China (dä-gōō)	208	39°00′N	117°42′E
Dagu, r., China	206	36°29′N	120°06′W
Dagupan, Phil. (dä-gōō′pän)	213a	16°02′N	120°20′E
Daheishan Dao, i., China (dä-hā-shän dou)	206	37°57′N	120°37′E
Dahl, Ger. (däl)	171c	51°18′N	7°33′E
Dahlak Archipelago, is., Erit.	231	15°45′N	40°30′E
Dahomey *see* Benin, nation, Afr.	230	8°00′N	2°00′E
Dahra, Libya	200	29°34′N	17°50′E
Daibu, China (dī-bōō)	206	31°22′N	119°29′E
Daigo, Japan (dī-gō)	211b	34°57′N	135°49′E
Daimiel Manzanares, Spain (dī-myĕl′män-zä-nä′rĕs)	172	39°05′N	3°36′W
Dairen *see* Dalian, China	204	38°54′N	121°35′E
Dairy, r., Or., U.S. (dâr′ĭ)	116c	45°33′N	123°04′W
Dai-Sen, mtn., Japan (dī′sĕn′)	211	35°22′N	133°35′E
Dai-Tenjo-dake, mtn., Japan (dī-tĕn′jō dä-kā)	211	36°21′N	137°38′E
Daiyun Shan, mtn., China (dī-yòn shän)	209	25°40′N	118°08′E
Dajabón, Dom. Rep. (dä-κä-bô′n)	135	19°35′N	71°40′W
Dajarra, Austl. (dȧ-jăr′ȧ)	218	21°45′S	139°30′E
Dakar, Sen. (dȧ-kär′)	230	14°40′N	17°26′W
Dakhla, W. Sah.	230	23°45′N	16°04′W
Dakouraoua, Niger	235	13°58′N	6°15′E
Dakovica, Serb.	175	42°33′N	20°28′E
Dalälven, r., Swe.	156	60°26′N	15°50′E
Dalby, Austl. (dôl′bē)	219	27°10′S	151°15′E
Dalcour, La., U.S. (dăl-kour)	110d	29°49′N	89°59′W
Dale, Nor. (dä′lĕ)	166	60°35′N	5°55′E
Dale Hollow Lake, res., Tn., U.S. (dāl hŏl′ō)	107	36°33′N	85°03′W
Dalemead, Can. (dä′lĕ-mēd)	102e	50°53′N	113°38′W
Dalen, Nor. (dä′lĕn)	166	59°28′N	8°01′E
Daleside, S. Afr. (dāl′sīd)	238c	26°30′S	28°03′E
Dalesville, Can. (dālz′vĭl)	102a	45°42′N	74°23′W
Daley Waters, Austl. (dā lē)	218	16°15′S	133°30′E
Dalhart, Tx., U.S. (dăl härt)	120	36°04′N	102°32′W
Dalhousie, Can. (dăl-hōō′zē)	100	48°04′N	66°23′W
Dali, China (dä-lē)	207a	23°07′N	113°06′E
Dali, China	204	26°00′N	100°08′E
Dali, China	204	35°00′N	109°38′E
Dalian, China (lü-dä)	205	38°54′N	121°35′E
Dalian Wan, b., China (dä-lĭĕn wän)	206	38°55′N	121°50′E
Dalías, Spain (dä-lē′ȧs)	172	36°49′N	2°50′W
Dall, i., Ak., U.S. (dăl)	103	54°50′N	133°10′W
Dallas, Or., U.S. (dăl′lȧs)	114	44°55′N	123°20′W
Dallas, S.D., U.S.	112	43°13′N	99°34′W
Dallas, Tx., U.S.	104	32°45′N	96°48′W
Dalles Dam, Or., U.S.	114	45°36′N	121°08′W
Dall Island, i., Ak., U.S.	94	54°50′N	132°55′W
Dalmacija, hist. reg., Eur. (däl-mä′tsē-yä)	174	43°25′N	16°37′E
Dalnerechensk, Russia	179	46°07′N	133°21′E
Daloa, C. Iv.	234	6°53′N	6°27′W
Dalroy, Can. (dăl′roi)	102e	51°07′N	113°39′W
Dalrymple, Mount, mtn., Austl. (dăl′rĭm-p′l)	221	21°14′S	148°46′E
Dalton, S. Afr. (dôl′tŏn)	233c	29°21′S	30°41′E
Dalton, Ga., U.S. (dôl′tŭn)	124	34°46′N	84°58′W
Daly, r., Austl. (dā′lĭ)	220	14°15′S	131°15′E
Daly City, Ca., U.S. (dā′lē)	116b	37°42′N	122°27′W
Damān, India	199	20°32′N	72°53′E
Damanhûr, Egypt (dä-män-hōōr′)	231	30°59′N	30°31′E
Damar, Pulau, i., Indon.	213	7°15′S	129°15′E
Damara, C.A.R.	235	4°58′N	18°42′E
Damaraland, hist. reg., Nmb. (dă′nȧ-rȧ-lănd)	232	22°15′S	16°15′E
Damas Cays, is., Bah. (dä′mäs)	134	23°50′N	79°50′W
Damascus, Syria	198	33°30′N	36°18′E
Damāvand, Qolleh-ye, mtn., Iran	198	36°05′N	52°05′E
Damba, Ang. (däm′bä)	232	6°41′S	15°08′E
Dâmbovița, r., Rom.	175	44°43′N	25°41′E
Dame Marie, Cap, c., Haiti (dăm mȧrē′)	135	18°35′N	74°50′W
Dāmghān, Iran (dām-gän′)	198	35°50′N	54°15′E
Daming, China (dä-mĭŋ)	208	36°15′N	115°09′E
Dammartin-en-Goële, Fr. (däɴ-mär-tăɴ-äɴ-gō-ĕl′)	171b	49°03′N	2°40′E
Dampier, Selat, strt., Indon. (dăm′pēr)	213	0°40′S	131°15′E
Dampier Archipielago, is., Austl.	220	20°15′S	116°25′E
Dampier Land, reg., Austl.	220	17°30′S	122°25′E
Dan, r., N.C., U.S. (dȧn)	125	36°26′N	79°40′W
Dana, Mount, mtn., Ca., U.S.	118	37°54′N	119°13′W
Da Nang, Viet.	212	16°08′N	108°22′E
Danbury, Eng., U.K.	158b	51°42′N	0°34′E
Danbury, Ct., U.S. (dăn′bẽr-ĭ)	110a	41°23′N	73°27′W
Danbury, Tx., U.S.	123a	29°14′N	95°22′W
[illegible] (dăn′dē-nông)	[illegible]	[illegible]	[illegible]
Dandong, China (dän-dôŋ)	205	40°10′N	124°30′E
Dane, r., Eng., U.K. (dān)	158a	53°11′N	2°14′W
Danea, Gui.	234	11°27′N	13°12′W
Danforth, Me., U.S.	100	45°38′N	67°53′W
Dan Gora, Nig.	235	11°30′N	8°09′E
Dangtu, China (däŋ-tōō)	209	31°35′N	118°28′E
Dani, Burkina	230	13°43′N	0°10′W
Dania, Fl., U.S. (dā′nĭ-ȧ)	125a	26°01′N	80°10′W
Danilov, Russia (dä′nē-lôf)	180	58°12′N	40°08′E
Danissa Hills, hills, Kenya	237	3°20′N	40°55′E
Dänizkänarı, Azer.	182	40°13′N	49°33′E
Dankov, Russia (däŋ′kôf)	180	53°17′N	39°09′E
Dannemora, N.Y., U.S. (dăn-ē-mō′rȧ)	109	44°45′N	73°45′W
Dannhauser, S. Afr. (dän′hou-zẽr)	233c	28°07′S	30°04′E
Dansville, N.Y., U.S. (dănz′vĭl)	109	42°30′N	77°40′W
Danube, r., Eur.	156	43°00′N	24°00′E
Danube, Mouths of the, mth., Rom. (dăn′ūb)	177	45°13′N	29°37′E
Danvers, Ma., U.S. (dăn′vẽrz)	101a	42°34′N	70°57′W
Danville, Ca., U.S. (dăn′vĭl)	116b	37°49′N	122°00′W
Danville, Il., U.S.	108	40°10′N	87°35′W
Danville, In., U.S.	108	39°45′N	86°30′W
Danville, Ky., U.S.	108	37°35′N	84°50′W
Danville, Pa., U.S.	109	41°00′N	76°35′W
Danville, Va., U.S.	105	36°35′N	79°24′W
Danxian, China (dän shyĕn)	209	19°30′N	109°38′E
Danyang, China (dän-yäŋ)	206	32°01′N	119°32′E
Danzig *see* Gdańsk, Pol.	154	54°20′N	18°40′E
Danzig, Gulf of, b., Eur. (dȧn′tsĭk)	160	54°41′N	19°01′E
Daoxian, China (dou shyĕn)	209	25°35′N	111°27′E
Dapango, Togo	234	10°52′N	0°12′E
Daphnae, hist., Egypt	197a	30°43′N	32°12′E
Daqin Dao, i., China (dä-chyĭn dou)	206	38°18′N	120°50′E
Darabani, Rom. (dă-rä-băn′ĭ)	169	48°13′N	26°38′E
Daraj, Libya	230	30°12′N	10°14′E
Darāw, Egypt (dȧ-rä′ōō)	238b	24°24′N	32°56′E
Darbhanga, India (dŭr-bŭŋ′gä)	199	26°03′N	85°09′E
Darby, Pa., U.S. (där′bĭ)	110f	39°55′N	75°16′W
Darby, i., Bah.	134	23°50′N	76°20′W
Dardanelles *see* Çanakkale Boğazi, strt., Tur.	163	40°05′N	25°50′E
Dar es Salaam, Tan. (där ĕs sȧ-läm′)	233	6°48′S	39°17′E
Dārfūr, hist. reg., Sudan (där-fōōr′)	231	13°21′N	23°46′E
Dargai, Pak. (dŭr-gä′ē)	202	34°35′N	72°00′E
Darien, Col. (dä-rĭ-ĕn′)	142a	3°56′N	76°30′W
Darien, Ct., U.S. (dâ-rē-ĕn′)	110a	41°04′N	73°28′W
Darién, Cordillera de, mts., Nic.	132	13°00′N	85°42′W
Darien, Serranía del, mts.	133	8°13′N	77°28′W
Darjeeling, India (dŭr-jē′lĭng)	199	27°05′N	88°16′E
Darling, r., Austl.	221	31°50′S	143°20′E
Darling Downs, reg., Austl.	221	27°22′S	150°00′E
Darling Range, mts., Austl.	220	30°30′S	115°45′E
Darlington, Eng., U.K. (där′lĭng-tŭn)	164	54°32′N	1°35′W
Darlington, S.C., U.S.	125	34°15′N	79°52′W
Darlington, Wi., U.S.	113	42°41′N	90°06′W
Darłowo, Pol. (där-lô′vô)	168	54°26′N	16°23′E
Darmstadt, Ger. (därm′shtät)	161	49°53′N	8°40′E
Darnah, Libya	231	32°44′N	22°41′E
Darnley Bay, b., Ak., U.S. (därn′lē)	103	70°00′N	124°00′W
Daroca, Spain (dä-rō-kä)	172	41°08′N	1°24′W
Dartford, Eng., U.K.	158b	51°27′N	0°14′E
Dartmoor, for., Eng., U.K. (därt′mōōr)	164	50°35′N	4°05′W
Dartmouth, Can. (därt′mŭth)	91	44°40′N	63°34′W
Dartmouth, Eng., U.K.	164	50°33′N	3°28′W
Daru, Pap. N. Gui. (dä′rōō)	213	9°04′S	143°21′E
Daruvar, Cro. (där′rōō-vär)	175	45°37′N	17°16′E
Darwen, Eng., U.K. (där′wĕn)	158a	53°42′N	2°28′W
Darwin, Austl. (där′wĭn)	218	12°25′S	131°00′E
Darwin, Cordillera, mts., Chile (kôr-dēl-yĕ′rä-där′wĕn)	144	54°40′S	69°30′W
Dashhowuz, Turkmen.	183	41°50′N	59°45′E
Dash Point, Wa., U.S. (dăsh)	116a	47°19′N	122°25′W
Dasht, r., Pak. (dŭsht)	198	25°30′N	62°30′E
Dasol Bay, b., Phil. (dä-sōl′)	213a	15°53′N	119°40′E
Datian Ding, mtn., China (dä-tĭĕn dĭŋ)	209	22°25′N	111°20′E
Datong, China (dä-tôŋ)	208	40°00′N	113°30′E
Dattapukur, India	202a	22°45′N	88°32′E
Datteln, Ger. (dät′tĕln)	171c	51°39′N	7°20′E
Datu, Tandjung, c., Asia	212	2°08′N	110°15′E
Datuan, China (dä-tůän)	207b	30°57′N	121°43′E
Daugava (Zapadnaya Dvina), r., Eur.	167	56°40′N	24°40′E
Daugavpils, Lat. (dä′ŏ-gäv-pĕls)	180	55°52′N	26°32′E
Dauphin, Can. (dô′fĭn)	90	51°09′N	100°00′W
Dauphin Lake, l., Can.	97	51°17′N	99°48′W
Dāvangere, India	203	14°30′N	75°55′E
Davao, Phil. (dä′vä-ô)	213	7°05′N	125°30′E
Davao Gulf, b., Phil.	213	6°30′N	125°45′E
Davenport, Ia., U.S. (dăv′ĕn-pōrt)	105	41°34′N	90°38′W

ăt; finăl; rāte; senȧte; ärm; ȧsk; sofȧ; fâre; ch-choose; dh-as th in other; bē; ēvent; bĕt; recĕnt; cratẽr; g-gō; gh-guttural g; bĭt; ĭ-short neutral; rīde; κ-guttural k as ch in German ich;

ng-sing;   ŋ-baŋk;   ɴ-nasalized n;   nŏd;   cŏmmit;   ōld;   ŏbey;   ôrder;   oi-boil;   fōōd;   ȯ-as oo in foot;   ou-out;   s-soft;   sh-dish;   th-thin;   pūre;   ûnite;   ûrn;   stŭd;   circŭs;   ü-as in French tu;   ′-indeterminate vowel.

PLACE (Pronunciation)	PAGE	LAT.	LONG.
Diaca, Moz.	237	11°30′S	39°59′E
Diaka, r., Mali	235	14°40′N	5°00′E
Diamantina, Braz.	143	18°14′S	43°32′W
Diamantina, r., Austl. (dī′man-tē′nȧ)	220	25°38′S	139°53′E
Diamantino, Braz. (dê-ȧ-män-tē′no)	143	14°22′S	56°23′W
Diamond Peak, mtn., Or., U.S.	114	43°32′N	122°08′W
Diana Bank, bk. (dī′ăn′ȧ)	135	22°30′N	74°45′W
Dianbai, China (dĭĕn-bī)	209	21°30′N	111°20′E
Dian Chi, l., China (dĭĕn chē)	204	24°58′N	103°18′E
Dickinson, N.D., U.S. (dĭk′ĭn-sŭn)	104	46°52′N	102°49′W
Dickinson, Tx., U.S. (dĭk′ĭn-sŭn)	123a	29°28′N	95°02′W
Dickinson Bayou, Tx., U.S.	123a	29°26′N	95°08′W
Dickson, Tn., U.S. (dĭk′sŭn)	124	36°03′N	87°24′W
Dickson City, Pa., U.S.	109	41°25′N	75°40′W
Didcot, Eng., U.K. (dĭd′cŏt)	158b	51°35′N	1°15′W
Didiéni, Mali	234	13°50′N	8°00′W
Die, Fr. (dē)	171	44°45′N	5°22′E
Diefenbaker, res., Can.	92	51°20′N	108°10′W
Diego de Ocampo, Pico, mtn., Dom. Rep. (pē′-kô-dyĕ′gô-dĕ-ō-kä′m-pô)	135	19°40′N	70°45′W
Diego Ramirez, Islas, is., Chile (dê ā′gō rä-mē′rāz)	144	56°15′S	70°15′W
Diéma, Mali	234	14°32′N	9°12′W
Dien Bien Phu, Viet.	204	21°38′N	102°49′E
Dieppe, Can. (dê-ĕp′)	100	46°06′N	64°45′W
Dieppe, Fr.	161	49°54′N	1°05′E
Dierks, Ar., U.S. (dērks)	121	34°06′N	94°02′W
Diessen, Ger. (dēs′sĕn)	159d	47°57′N	11°06′E
Diest, Bel.	159a	50°59′N	5°05′E
Digby, Can. (dĭg′bĭ)	91	44°37′N	65°46′W
Dighton, Ma., U.S. (dī-tŭn)	110b	41°49′N	71°05′W
Digne, Fr. (dēn′y′)	171	44°07′N	6°16′E
Digoin, Fr. (dē-gwăn′)	170	46°28′N	4°06′E
Digul, r., Indon.	213	7°00′S	140°27′E
Dijohan Point, c., Phil. (dē-kô-än)	213a	16°24′N	122°25′E
Dijon, Fr. (dē-zhôn′)	154	47°21′N	5°02′E
Dikson, Russia (dĭk′sŏn)	178	73°30′N	80°35′E
Dikwa, Nig. (dē′kwȧ)	231	12°06′N	13°53′E
Dili, E. Timor (dĭl′ê)	213	8°35′S	125°35′E
Di Linosa Island, i., Italy (dê-lê-nô′sä)	162	36°01′N	12°43′E
Dilizhan, Arm.	181	40°45′N	45°00′E
Dillingham, Ak., U.S. (dĭl′ĕng-hăm)	106a	59°10′N	158°38′W
Dillon, Mt., U.S. (dĭl′ŭn)	115	45°12′N	112°40′W
Dillon, S.C., U.S.	125	34°24′N	79°28′W
Dillon Reservoir, res., Oh., U.S.	108	40°05′N	82°05′W
Dilolo, D.R.C. (dê-lō′lō)	232	10°19′S	22°23′E
Dimashq *see* Damascus, Syria	198	33°31′N	36°18′E
Dimbokro, C. Iv.	234	6°39′N	4°42′W
Dimitrovo *see* Pernik, Blg.	163	42°36′N	23°04′E
Dimlang, mtn., Nig.	235	8°24′N	11°47′E
Dimona, Isr.	197a	31°03′N	35°01′E
Dinagat Island, i., Phil.	213	10°15′N	126°15′E
Dinājpur, Bngl.	202	25°38′N	87°39′E
Dinan, Fr. (dē-nän′)	170	48°27′N	2°03′W
Dinant, Bel. (dē-nän′)	165	50°17′N	4°50′E
Dinara, mts., Cro. (dē′nä-rä)	163	43°50′N	16°15′E
Dinard, Fr.	170	48°38′N	2°04′W
Dindigul, India	203	10°25′N	78°03′E
Dingalan Bay, b., Phil. (dĭŋ-gä′län)	213a	15°19′N	121°33′E
Dingle, Ire. (dĭng′′l)	164	52°10′N	10°13′W
Dingle Bay, b., Ire.	161	52°02′N	10°15′W
Dingo, Austl. (dĭŋ′gō)	219	23°45′S	149°26′E
Dinguiraye, Gui.	234	11°18′N	10°43′W
Dingwall, Scot., U.K. (dĭng′wôl)	164	57°37′N	4°23′W
Dingxian, China (dĭŋ shyĕn)	208	38°30′N	115°00′E
Dingxing, China (dĭŋ-shyĭŋ)	208	39°18′N	115°50′E
Dingyuan, China (dĭŋ-yůän)	206	32°32′N	117°40′E
Dingzi Wan, b., China	206	36°33′N	121°06′E
Dinosaur National Monument, rec., Co., U.S. (dī′nô-sôr)	115	40°45′N	109°17′W
Dinslaken, Ger. (dēns′lä-kĕn)	171c	51°33′N	6°44′E
Dinteloord, Neth.	159a	51°38′N	4°21′E
Dinuba, Ca., U.S. (dĭ-nū′bȧ)	118	36°33′N	119°29′W
Dios, Cayo de, i., Cuba (kä′yō-dĕ-dē-ōs′)	134	22°05′N	83°05′W
Diourbel, Sen. (dê-ōōr-bĕl′)	230	14°40′N	16°15′W
Diphu Pass, p., Asia (dĭ-pōō)	204	28°15′N	96°45′E
Diquis, r., C.R. (dê-kēs′)	133	8°59′N	83°24′W
Dire Dawa, Eth.	231	9°40′N	41°47′E
Diriamba, Nic. (dēr-yäm′bä)	132	11°52′N	86°15′W
Dirk Hartog, i., Austl.	220	26°25′S	113°15′E
Dirksland, Neth.	159a	51°45′N	4°04′E
Dirranbandi, Austl. (dĭ-rȧ-băn′dê)	219	28°24′S	148°29′E
Dirty Devil, r., Ut., U.S. (dûr′tĭ dĕv′′l)	119	38°20′N	110°30′W
Disappointment, l., Austl.	220	23°20′S	123°00′E
Disappointment, Cape, c., Wa., U.S. (dĭs′ȧ-point′ment)	116c	46°16′N	124°11′W
Discovery, S. Afr. (dĭs-kŭv′ēr-ĭ)	233b	26°10′S	27°53′E
Discovery, is., Can. (dĭs-kŭv′ēr-ê)	116a	48°25′N	123°13′W
Disko, i., Grnld. (dĭs′kō)	89	70°00′N	54°00′W
Disna, Bela. (dēs′nȧ)	180	55°34′N	28°15′E
Dispur, India	202	26°00′N	91°50′E
Disraëli, Can. (dĭs-rā′lĭ)	99	45°53′N	71°23′W
District of Columbia, dept., U.S.	105	38°50′N	77°00′W
Distrito Federal, dept., Braz. (dēs-trē′tô-fĕ-dĕ-rä′l)	143	15°49′S	47°39′W
Distrito Federal, dept., Mex.	130	19°14′N	99°08′W
Disūq, Egypt (dê-sōōk′)	238b	31°07′N	30°41′E
Diu, India (dē′ōō)	199	20°48′N	70°58′E
Divilacan Bay, b., Phil. (dê-vê-lä′kän)	213a	17°26′N	122°25′E
Divinópolis, Braz. (dē-vē-nô′pō-lēs)	143	20°10′S	44°53′W
Divo, C. Iv.	234	5°50′N	5°22′W
Dixon, Il., U.S. (dĭks′ŭn)	113	41°50′N	89°30′W
Dixon Entrance, strt., N.A.	92	54°25′N	132°00′W
Diyarbakir, Tur. (dê-yär-bĕk′ĭr)	198	38°00′N	40°10′E
Dja, r., Afr.	231	2°30′N	14°00′E
Djambala, Congo	236	2°33′S	14°45′E
Djanet, Alg.	230	24°29′N	9°26′E
Djebobo, mtn., Ghana	234	8°20′N	0°37′E
Djedi, Oued, r., Alg.	162	34°18′N	4°39′E
Djember, Chad	235	10°25′N	17°50′E
Djerba, Île de, i., Tun.	162	33°53′N	11°26′E
Djerid, Chott, l., Tun. (jĕr′ĭd)	230	33°15′N	8°29′E
Djibasso, Burkina	234	13°07′N	4°10′W
Djibo, Burkina	234	14°06′N	1°38′W
Djibouti, Dji. (jē-bōō-tē′)	238a	11°34′N	43°00′E
Djibouti, nation, Afr.	238a	11°35′N	48°08′E
Djokoumatombi, Congo	236	0°47′N	15°22′E
Djokupunda, D.R.C.	232	5°27′S	20°58′E
Djoua, r., Afr.	236	[illegible]	[illegible]
Djursholm, Swe. (djōōrs′hōlm)	166	59°26′N	18°01′E
Dmitriyev-L′govskiy, Russia (d′mē′trĭ-yĕf l′gôf′skĭ)	176	52°07′N	35°05′E
Dmitrov, Russia (d′mē′trôf)	176	56°21′N	37°32′E
Dmitrovsk, Russia (d′mē′trôfsk)	176	52°30′N	35°10′E
Dmytrivka, Ukr.	177	47°57′N	38°56′E
Dnepropetrovsk *see* Dnipropetrovs′k, Ukr.	178	48°15′N	34°08′E
Dnieper (Dnipro), r., Eur.	181	46°45′N	33°40′E
Dniester, r., Eur.	181	48°21′N	28°10′E
Dniprodzerzhyns′k, Ukr.	181	48°32′N	34°38′E
Dniprodzerzhyns′ke vodoskhovyshche, res., Ukr.	178	49°00′N	34°10′E
Dnipropetrovs′k, Ukr.	178	48°15′N	34°08′E
Dnipropetrovs′k, prov., Ukr.	177	48°15′N	34°10′E
Dniprovs′kyi lyman, b., Ukr.	177	46°33′N	31°45′E
Dnistrovs′kyi lyman, l., Ukr.	177	46°13′N	29°50′E
Dno, Russia (d′nô′)	176	57°49′N	29°59′E
Do, Lac, l., Mali	234	15°50′N	2°20′W
Doba, Chad	235	8°39′N	16°51′E
Dobbs Ferry, N.Y., U.S. (dŏbz′fĕ′rē)	110a	41°01′N	73°53′W
Dobbyn, Austl. (dŏb′ĭn)	218	19°45′S	140°02′E
Dobele, Lat. (dô′bĕ-lĕ)	167	56°37′N	23°18′E
Doberai, Jazirah, pen., Indon.	213	1°25′S	133°15′E
Dobo, Indon.	213	6°00′S	134°18′E
Doboj, Bos. (dō′boi)	175	44°42′N	18°04′E
Dobrich, Blg.	163	43°33′N	27°52′E
Dobryanka, Russia (dôb-ryän′kȧ)	186a	58°27′N	56°26′E
Dobšina, Slvk. (dôp′shê-nä)	169	48°48′N	20°25′E
Doce, r., Braz. (dō′så)	143	19°01′S	42°14′W
Doce, Canal Numero, can., Arg.	141c	36°47′S	59°00′W
Doce Leguas, Cayos de las, is., Cuba	134	20°55′N	79°05′W
Doctor Arroyo, Mex. (dŏk-tōr′ är-rō′yō)	130	23°41′N	100°10′W
Doddington, Eng., U.K. (dŏd′dĭng-tŏn)	158b	51°17′N	0°47′E
Dodecanese *see* Dodekanisoy, is., Grc.	175	38°00′N	26°10′E
Dodekanisoy (Dodecanese), is., Grc.	175	38°00′N	26°10′E
Dodge City, Ks., U.S. (dŏj)	104	37°44′N	100°01′W
Dodgeville, Wi., U.S. (dŏj′vĭl)	113	42°58′N	90°07′W
Dodoma, Tan. (dō′dō-mȧ)	232	6°11′S	35°45′E
Dog, l., Can. (dŏg)	98	48°42′N	89°24′W
Dogger Bank, bk. (dŏg′gẽr)	165	55°07′N	2°25′E
Dogubayazit, Tur.	181	39°35′N	44°00′E
Doha *see* Ad Dawhah, Qatar	198	25°02′N	51°28′E
Dohad, India	202	22°52′N	74°18′E
Dokshytsy, Bela. (dôk-shētsĕ)	176	54°53′N	27°49′E
Dolbeau, Can.	91	48°52′N	72°16′W
Dole, Fr. (dōl)	161	47°07′N	5°28′E
Dolgaya, Kosa, c., Russia (kô-sa′ dôl-gä′yä)	177	46°42′N	37°42′E
Dolgeville, N.Y., U.S.	109	43°10′N	74°45′W
Dolgiy, i., Russia	180	69°20′N	59°20′E
Dolgoprudnyy, Russia	186b	55°57′N	37°33′E
Dolinsk, Russia (dȧ-lēnsk′)	185	47°29′N	142°31′E
Dollar Harbor, b., Bah.	134	25°30′N	79°15′W
Dolomite, Al., U.S. (dŏl′ô-mīt)	110h	33°28′N	86°57′W
Dolomiti, mts., Italy	174	46°16′N	11°43′E
Dolores, Arg. (dô-lō′rĕs)	144	36°20′S	57°42′W
Dolores, Col.	142a	3°33′N	74°54′W
Dolores, Ur.	141c	33°32′S	58°15′W
Dolores, Tx., U.S. (dô-lō′rĕs)	122	27°42′N	99°47′W
Dolores, r., Co., U.S.	119	38°35′N	108°50′W
Dolores Hidalgo, Mex. (dô-lô′rĕs-ē-däl′gō)	130	21°09′N	100°56′W
Dolphin and Union Strait, strt., Can. (dŏl′fĭn ūn′yŭn)	92	69°22′N	117°10′W
Dolyna, Ukr.	169	48°57′N	24°01′E
Domažlice, Czech Rep. (dō′mäzh-lê-tsĕ)	168	49°27′N	12°55′E
Dombasle-sur-Meurthe, Fr. (dôn-bäl′)	171	48°38′N	6°18′E
Dombóvár, Hung. (dŏm′bō-vär)	169	46°22′N	18°08′E
Domeyko, Cordillera, mts., Chile (kôr-dēl-yĕ′rä-dô-mā′kô)	142	20°50′S	69°02′W
Dominica, nation, N.A. (dŏ-mĭ-nē′kȧ)	129	15°30′N	60°45′W
Dominica Channel, strt., N.A.	133b	15°00′N	61°30′W
Dominican Republic, nation, N.A. (dô-mĭn′ĭ-kăn)	129	19°00′N	70°45′W
Dominion, Can. (dô-mĭn′yŭn)	101	46°13′N	60°01′W
Domiongo, D.R.C.	236	4°37′S	21°15′E
Domodedovo, Russia (dô-mô-dyĕ′do-vô)	186b	55°27′N	37°45′E
Dom Silvério, Braz. (don-sĕl-vĕ′ryō)	141a	20°09′S	42°57′W
Don, r., Russia	178	49°50′N	41°30′E
Don, r., Eng., U.K.	158a	53°39′N	0°58′W
Don, r., Scot., U.K.	164	57°19′N	2°39′W
Donaldson, Mi., U.S. (dŏn′ăl-sŭn)	117k	46°19′N	84°22′W
Donaldsonville, La., U.S. (dŏn′ăld-sŭn-vĭl)	123	30°05′N	90°58′W
Donalsonville, Ga., U.S.	124	31°02′N	84°50′W
Donawitz, Aus. (dō′nȧ-vĭts)	168	47°23′N	15°05′E
Don Benito, Spain (dōn′bå-nē′tō)	172	38°55′N	5°52′W
Doncaster, Austl. (doŋ′kăs-tẽr)	217a	37°47′S	145°08′E
Doncaster, Eng., U.K. (doŋ′kăs-tẽr)	164	53°32′N	1°07′W
Doncaster, co., Eng., U.K.	158a	53°35′N	1°10′W
Dondo, Ang. (dōn′dō)	232	9°38′S	14°25′E
Dondo, Moz.	232	19°33′S	34°47′E
Dondra Head, c., Sri L.	203	5°52′N	80°52′E
Donegal, Ire. (dŏn-ê-gôl′)	164	54°44′N	8°05′W
Donegal Bay, Ire. (dŏn-ê-gôl′)	160	54°35′N	8°36′W
Donets Coal Basin, reg., Ukr. (dō-nyĕts′)	177	48°15′N	38°50′E
Donets′k, Ukr.	178	48°00′N	37°35′E
Donets′k, prov., Ukr.	177	47°55′N	37°40′E
Dong, r., China (dôŋ)	205	24°13′N	115°08′E
Dongara, Austl. (dôn-gă′rȧ)	218	29°15′S	115°00′E
Dongba, China (dôŋ-bä)	206	31°40′N	119°02′E
Dong′e, China (dôŋ-ŭ)	206	36°21′N	116°14′E
Dong′ezhen, China	208	36°11′N	116°16′E
Dongfang, China (dôŋ-fäŋ)	209	19°08′N	108°42′E
Donggala, Indon. (dôn-gä′lä)	212	0°45′S	119°32′E
Dongguan, China (dôŋ-gůän)	207a	23°03′N	113°46′E
Dongguang, China (dôŋ-gůäŋ)	206	37°54′N	116°33′E
Donghai, China (dôŋ-hī)	208	34°35′N	119°05′E
Dong Hoi, Viet. (dông-hô-ē′)	212	17°25′N	106°42′E
Dongila, Eth.	231	11°17′N	37°00′E
Dongming, China (dôŋ-mĭŋ)	206	35°16′N	115°06′E
Dongo, Ang. (dôŋ′gō)	232	14°45′S	15°30′E
Dongon Point, c., Phil. (dŏng-ŏn′)	213a	12°43′N	120°35′E
Dongou, Congo (dôŋ-gōō′)	231	2°02′N	18°04′E
Dongping, China (dôŋ-pĭŋ)	208	35°50′N	116°24′E
Dongping Hu, l., China (dôŋ-pĭŋ hōō)	206	36°06′N	116°24′E
Dongshan, China (doŋ-shän)	206	31°05′N	120°24′E
Dongtai, China	206	32°51′N	120°20′E
Dongting Hu, l., China (dôŋ-tĭŋ hōō)	205	29°10′N	112°30′E
Dongxiang, China (dôŋ-shyän)	209	28°18′N	116°38′E
Doniphan, Mo., U.S. (dŏn′ĭ-făn)	121	36°37′N	90°50′W
Donji Vakuf, Bos. (dōn′yĭ väk′ōof)	175	44°08′N	17°25′E
Don Martin, Presa de, res., Mex. (prĕ′sä-dĕ-dôn-mär-tē′n)	122	27°35′N	100°38′W
Donnacona, Can.	99	46°40′N	71°46′W
Donnemarie-en-Montois, Fr. (dôn-mä-rē′ĕn-môn-twä′)	171b	48°29′N	3°09′E
Donner und Blitzen, r., Or., U.S. (dŏn′ẽr ont′blĭ′tsĕn)	114	42°45′N	118°57′W
Donnybrook, S. Afr. (dŏ-nĭ-brók)	233c	29°56′S	29°54′E
Donora, Pa., U.S. (dŏ-nō′rȧ)	111e	40°10′N	79°51′W
Donostia-San Sebastián, Spain	154	43°19′N	1°59′W
Donoússa, i., Grc.	175	37°09′N	25°53′E
Doolow, Som.	238a	4°10′N	42°05′E
Doonerak, Mount, mtn., Ak., U.S. (dōō′nē-răk)	103	68°00′N	150°34′W
Doorn, Neth.	159a	52°02′N	5°21′E
Door Peninsula, pen., Wi., U.S. (dōr)	113	44°40′N	87°36′W
Dora Baltea, r., Italy (dō′rä bäl′tā-ä)	174	45°40′N	7°34′E
Doraville, Ga., U.S. (dō′rȧ-vĭl)	110c	33°54′N	84°17′W
Dorchester, Eng., U.K. (dôr′chĕs-tẽr)	164	50°45′N	2°34′W
Dordogne, r., Fr. (dôr-dôn′yĕ)	156	44°53′N	0°16′E
Dordrecht, Neth. (dôr′drĕkt)	165	51°48′N	4°39′E
Dordrecht, S. Afr. (dô′drĕkt)	233c	31°24′S	27°06′E
Doré Lake, l., Can.	96	54°31′N	107°06′W
Dorgali, Italy (dôr′gä-lē)	174	40°18′N	9°37′E
Dörgön Nuur, l., Mong.	204	47°47′N	94°01′E
Dorion-Vaudreuil, Can. (dôr-yō)	102a	45°23′N	74°01′W
Dorking, Eng., U.K. (dôr′kĭng)	158b	51°12′N	0°20′W
Dormont, Pa., U.S. (dôr′mŏnt)	111e	40°24′N	80°02′W
Dornbirn, Aus. (dōrn′bĕrn)	168	47°24′N	9°45′E
Dornoch, Scot., U.K. (dôr′nŏk)	160	57°55′N	4°01′W
Dornoch Firth, b., Scot., U.K. (dôr′nŏk fûrth)	164	57°55′N	3°55′W
Dorogobuzh, Russia (dôrôgô′-bōō′zh)	176	54°57′N	33°18′E
Dorohoi, Rom. (dō-rô-hoi′)	169	47°57′N	26°28′E
Dorre Island, i., Austl. (dôr)	220	25°19′S	113°10′E
Dorstsen, Ger.	171c	51°40′N	6°58′E
Dortmund, Ger. (dôrt′mònt)	161	51°31′N	7°28′E
Dortmund-Ems-Kanal, can., Ger. (dôrt′mōōnd-ĕms′kä-näl′)	171c	51°50′N	7°25′E
Dörtyol, Tur. (dûrt′yôl)	163	36°50′N	36°20′E
Dorval, Can. (dôr-vȧl′)	102a	45°26′N	73°44′W
Dos Bahías, Cabo, c., Arg. (kȧ′bô-dôs-bä-ē′äs)	144	44°55′S	65°35′W
Dos Caminos, Ven. (dôs-kä-mē′nôs)	143b	9°38′N	67°17′W
Dosewallips, r., Wa., U.S. (dō′sē-wäl′lĭps)	116a	47°45′N	123°04′W
Dos Hermanas, Spain (dōsĕr-mä′näs)	172	37°17′N	5°56′W
Dosso, Niger (dôs-ō′)	230	13°03′N	3°12′E
Dothan, Al., U.S. (dō′thăn)	105	31°13′N	85°23′W
Douai, Fr. (dōō-å′)	161	50°23′N	3°04′E
Douala, Cam. (dōō-ä′lä)	230	4°03′N	9°42′E
Douarnenez, Fr. (dōō-ár-nē-nĕs′)	170	48°06′N	4°18′W
Double Bayou, Tx., U.S. (dŭb′′l bī′yōō)	123a	29°40′N	94°38′W
Doubs, r., Eur.	171	46°15′N	5°50′E
Douentza, Mali	234	15°00′N	2°57′W
Douglas, I. of Man (dŭg′lȧs)	164	54°10′N	4°24′W
Douglas, Ak., U.S. (dŭg′lȧs)	103	58°18′N	134°35′W
Douglas, Az., U.S.	104	31°20′N	109°30′W
Douglas, Ga., U.S.	125	31°30′N	82°53′W
Douglas, Wy., U.S. (dŭg′lȧs)	115	42°45′N	105°21′W
Douglas, r., Eng., U.K. (dŭg′lȧs)	158a	53°38′N	2°48′W

ăt; finȧl; rāte; senåte; ärm; åsk; sofȧ; fâre; ch-choose; dh-as th in other; bē; ėvent; bĕt; recĕnt; cratẽr; g-gō; gh-guttural g; bĭt; ĭ-short neutral; rīde; ĸ-guttural k as ch in German ich;

PRONOUNCING INDEX
Douglas Channel – East Cleveland 289

PLACE (Pronunciation)	PAGE	LAT.	LONG.
Douglas Channel, strt., Can.	94	53°30'N	129°12'W
Douglas Lake, res., Tn., U.S. (dŭg'lăs)	124	36°00'N	83°35'W
Douglas Lake Indian Reserve, I.R., Can.	95	50°10'N	120°49'W
Douglasville, Ga., U.S. (dŭg'lăs-vĭl)	124	33°45'N	84°47'W
Dourada, Serra, mts., Braz. (sĕ'r-rä-dôōō-rá'dă)	143	15°11'S	49°57'W
Dourdan, Fr. (dōōr-däN')	171b	48°32'N	2°01'E
Douro, r., Port. (dô'ō-rô)	172	41°03'N	8°12'W
Dove, r., Eng., U.K. (dŭv)	158a	52°53'N	1°47'W
Dover, S. Afr.	238c	27°05'S	27°44'E
Dover, Eng., U.K.	154	51°08'N	1°19'E
Dover, De., U.S. (dō vēr)	105	39°10'N	75°30'W
Dover, N.H., U.S.	109	43°15'N	71°00'W
Dover, N.J., U.S.	110a	40°53'N	74°33'W
Dover, Oh., U.S.	108	40°35'N	81°30'W
Dover, Strait of, strt., Eur.	156	50°50'N	1°15'W
Dover-Foxcroft, Me., U.S. (dō'vẽr fŏks'krôft)	100	45°10'N	69°15'W
Dovre Fjell, mts., Nor. (dŏv'rĕ fyĕl')	156	62°03'N	8°36'E
Dow, Il., U.S. (dou)	117e	39°01'N	90°20'W
Dowagiac, Mi., U.S. (dō-wô'jăk)	108	42°00'N	86°05'W
Downers Grove, Il., U.S. (dou'nẽrz grōv)	111a	41°48'N	88°00'W
Downey, Ca., U.S. (dou'nĭ)	117a	33°56'N	118°08'W
Downieville, Ca., U.S. (dou'nĭ-nĭl)	118	39°35'N	120°48'W
Downs, Ks., U.S. (dounz)	120	39°29'N	98°32'W
Doylestown, Oh., U.S. (doilz'toun)	111d	40°58'N	81°43'W
Drâa, Cap, c., Mor. (drá)	230	28°39'N	12°15'W
Drâa, Oued, r., Afr.	230	28°00'N	9°31'W
Drabiv, Ukr.	177	49°57'N	32°14'E
Drac, r., Fr. (dräk)	171	44°50'N	5°47'E
Dracut, Ma., U.S. (drā'kŭt)	101a	42°40'N	71°19'W
Draganovo, Blg. (drä-gä-nō'vō)	175	43°13'N	25°45'E
Drăgăşani, Rom. (drä-gá-shän'ĭ)	175	44°39'N	24°18'E
Draguignan, Fr. (drä-gēn-yäN')	171	43°35'N	6°28'E
Drahichyn, Bela.	169	52°10'N	25°11'E
Drakensberg, mts., Afr. (drä'kĕnz-bĕrgh)	232	29°15'S	29°07'E
Drake Passage, strt. (drāk păs'ĭj)	139	57°00'S	65°00'W
Dráma, Grc. (drä'mä)	163	41°09'N	24°10'E
Drammen, Nor. (dräm'ĕn)	160	59°45'N	10°15'E
Drau (Drava), r., Eur. (drou)	168	46°44'N	13°45'E
Drava, r., Eur. (drä'vä)	156	45°45'N	17°30'E
Dravograd, Slvn. (drä'vō-gräd')	174	46°37'N	15°01'E
Drawsko Pomorskie, Pol. (dräv'skō pō-mōr'skyĕ)	168	53°31'N	15°50'E
Drayton Harbor, b., Wa., U.S. (drā'tŭn)	116d	48°58'N	122°40'W
Drayton Plains, Mi., U.S.	111b	42°41'N	83°23'W
Drayton Valley, Can.	95	53°13'N	114°59'W
Drensteinfurt, Ger. (drĕn'shtīn-fōōrt)	171c	51°47'N	7°44'E
Dresden, Ger. (drās'dĕn)	154	51°05'N	13°45'E
Dreux, Fr. (drû)	170	48°44'N	1°24'E
Driefontein, S. Afr.	238c	25°53'S	29°10'E
Drin, r., Alb. (drēn)	175	42°13'N	20°13'E
Drina, r., Eur. (drē'nä)	163	44°09'N	19°30'E
Drinit, Pellg i, b., Alb.	175	41°42'N	19°17'E
Dr. Ir. W. J. van Blommestein Meer, res., Sur.	143	4°45'N	55°05'W
Drissa, r., Eur.	176	55°44'N	28°58'E
Driver, Va., U.S.	110g	36°50'N	76°30'W
Dröbak, Nor. (drû'bäk)	166	59°40'N	10°35'E
Drobeta-Turnu Severin, Rom.	163	43°54'N	24°49'E
Drogheda, Ire. (drŏ'hĕ-dȧ)	160	53°43'N	6°15'W
Drohobych, Ukr.	169	49°21'N	23°31'E
Drôme, r., Fr. (drōm)	170	44°42'N	4°53'E
Dronfield, Eng., U.K. (drŏn'fēld)	158a	53°18'N	1°28'W
Drumheller, Can. (drŭm-hĕl-ẽr)	90	51°28'N	112°42'W
Drummond, i., Mi., U.S. (drŭm'ŭnd)	108	46°00'N	83°50'W
Drummondville, Can. (drŭm'ŭnd-vĭl)	91	45°53'N	72°33'W
Drumright, Ok., U.S. (drŭm'rīt)	121	35°59'N	96°37'W
Drunen, Neth.	159a	51°41'N	5°10'E
Drut', r., Bela. (drōōt)	176	53°40'N	29°45'E
Druya, Bela. (drò'yȧ)	176	55°45'N	27°26'E
Drwęca, r., Pol. (d'r-vän'tsȧ)	169	53°06'N	19°13'E
Dryden, Can. (drī-dĕn)	91	49°47'N	92°50'W
Drysdale, Austl.	217a	38°11'S	144°34'E
Dry Tortugas, is., Fl., U.S. (tôr-tōō'gäz)	125a	24°37'N	82°45'W
Dry Tortugas National Park, rec., Fl., U.S.	125a	24°42'N	83°02'W
Dschang, Cam. (dshäng)	230	5°34'N	10°09'E
Duabo, Lib.	234	5°40'N	8°05'W
Duagh, Can.	102g	53°43'N	113°24'W
Duarte, Pico, mtn., Dom. Rep. (dŭĭ'ărtĕh pēcô)	129	19°00'N	71°00'W
Duas Barras, Braz. (dōō'äs-bá'r-räs)	141a	22°03'S	42°30'W
Dubai *see* Dubayy, U.A.E.	198	25°18'N	55°26'E
Dubăsari, Mol.	177	47°16'N	29°11'E
Dubawnt, l., Can. (dōō-bônt')	92	63°27'N	103°30'W
Dubawnt, r., Can.	92	61°30'N	103°49'W
Dubayy, U.A.E.	198	25°18'N	55°26'E
Dubbo, Austl. (dŭb'ō)	219	32°20'S	148°42'E
Dubie, D.R.C.	237	8°33'S	28°32'E
Dublin, Ire.	154	53°20'N	6°15'W
Dublin, Ca., U.S. (dŭb'lĭn)	116b	37°42'N	121°56'W
Dublin, Ga., U.S.	125	32°33'N	82°55'W
Dublin, Tx., U.S.	122	32°05'N	98°20'W
Dubna, Russia	176	56°44'N	37°10'E
Dubno, Ukr. (dōō'b-nō)	169	50°24'N	25°44'E
Du Bois, Pa., U.S. (dò-bois')	109	41°10'N	78°45'W
Dubovka, Russia (dò-bôf'kȧ)	181	49°00'N	44°50'E
Dubrovka, Russia (dōō-brôf'kȧ)	186c	59°51'N	30°56'E
Dubrovnik, Cro. (dō'brôv-nĕk) (rä-gōō'sä)	154	42°40'N	18°10'E
Dubrowna, Bela.	176	54°39'N	30°54'E
Dubuque, Ia., U.S. (dò-būk')	105	42°30'N	90°43'W
Duchesne, Ut., U.S. (dò-shān')	119	40°12'N	110°23'W
Duchesne, r., Ut., U.S.	119	40°20'N	110°50'W
Duchess, Austl. (dŭch'ĕs)	218	21°30'S	139°55'E
Ducie Island, i., Pit. (dü-sē')	2	25°30'S	126°20'W
Duck, r., Tn., U.S.	124	35°55'N	87°40'W
Duckabush, r., Wa., U.S. (dŭk'ȧ-bòsh)	116a	47°41'N	123°09'W
Duck Lake, Can.	96	52°47'N	106°13'W
Duck Mountain, mtn., Can.	97	51°35'N	101°00'W
Ducktown, Tn., U.S. (dŭk'toun)	124	35°03'N	84°20'W
Duck Valley Indian Reservation, I.R., Id., U.S.	114	42°02'N	115°49'W
Duckwater Peak, mtn., Nv., U.S. (dŭk-wô-tẽr)	118	39°00'N	115°31'W
Duda, r., Col. (dōō'dä)	142a	3°25'N	74°23'W
Dudinka, Russia (dōō-dĭn'kȧ)	178	69°15'N	85°42'E
Dudley, Eng., U.K. (dŭd'lĭ)	161	52°28'N	2°07'E
Duero, r., Eur.	156	41°30'N	4°30'W
Dufourspitze, mtn., Eur.	168	45°55'N	7°52'E
Dugger, In., U.S. (dŭg'ẽr)	108	39°00'N	87°10'W
Dugi Otok, i., Cro. (dōō'gē o'tôk)	174	44°03'N	14°40'E
Duisburg, Ger. (dōō'ĭs-bòrgh)	161	51°26'N	6°46'E
Dukhān, Qatar	201	25°25'N	50°48'E
Dukhovshchina, Russia (dōō-kôfsh-'chēnȧ)	176	55°13'N	32°26'E
Dukinfield, Eng., U.K. (dŭk'ĭn-fēld)	158a	53°28'N	2°05'W
Dukla Pass, p., Eur. (dò'klä)	161	49°25'N	21°44'E
Dulce, Golfo, b., C.R. (gōl'fō dōōl'sä)	129	8°25'N	83°13'W
Dülken, Ger. (dül'kĕn)	171c	51°15'N	6°21'E
Dülmen, Ger. (dül'mĕn)	171c	51°50'N	7°17'E
Duluth, Mn., U.S. (dò-lōōth')	105	46°50'N	92°07'W
Dumai, Indon.	197b	1°39'N	101°30'E
Dumali Point, c., Phil. (dōō-mä'lē)	213a	13°07'N	121°42'E
Dumas, Tx., U.S.	120	35°52'N	101°58'W
Dumbarton, Scot., U.K. (dŭm'bȧr-tŭn)	164	56°00'N	4°35'W
Dum-Dum, India	202a	22°37'N	88°25'E
Dumfries, Scot., U.K. (dŭm-frēs')	164	55°05'N	3°40'W
Dumjor, India	202a	22°37'N	88°14'E
Dumont, N.J., U.S. (dōō'mŏnt)	110a	40°56'N	74°00'W
Dumyāt, Egypt	231	31°22'N	31°50'E
Dunaföldvár, Hung. (dò'nô-füld'vär)	169	46°48'N	18°55'E
Dunaïvtsi, Ukr.	177	48°52'N	26°51'E
Dunajec, r., Pol. (dò-nä'yĕts)	169	49°52'N	20°53'E
Dunaújváros, Hung.	169	46°57'N	18°55'E
Dunay, Russia (dōō'nĭ)	186c	59°59'N	30°57'E
Dunbar, W.V., U.S.	108	38°20'N	81°45'W
Duncan, Can. (dŭŋ'kȧn)	90	48°47'N	123°42'W
Duncan, Ok., U.S.	121	34°29'N	97°56'W
Duncan, r., Can.	95	50°30'N	116°45'W
Duncan Dam, dam, Can.	95	50°15'N	116°55'W
Duncan Lake, l., Can.	95	50°20'N	117°00'W
Duncansby Head, c., Scot., U.K. (dŭn'kănz-bĭ)	164	58°40'N	3°01'W
Duncanville, Tx., U.S. (dŭn'kȧn-vĭl)	117c	32°39'N	96°55'W
Dundalk, Ire. (dŭn'kôk)	160	54°00'N	6°18'W
Dundalk, Md., U.S.	110e	39°16'N	76°31'W
Dundalk Bay, b., Ire. (dŭn'dôk)	164	53°55'N	6°15'W
Dundas, Can. (dŭn-dăs')	99	43°16'N	79°58'W
Dundas, l., Austl. (dŭn-dȧs)	220	32°15'S	122°00'E
Dundas Island, i., Can.	94	54°33'N	130°55'W
Dundas Strait, strt., Austl.	220	10°35'S	131°15'E
Dundedin, Fl., U.S. (dŭn-ē'dĭn)	125a	28°00'N	82°43'W
Dundee, S. Afr.	233c	28°14'S	30°16'E
Dundee, Scot., U.K.	154	56°30'N	2°55'W
Dundee, Il., U.S. (dŭn-dē)	111a	42°06'N	88°17'W
Dundrum Bay, b., N. Ire., U.K. (dŭn-drŭm')	164	54°13'N	5°47'W
Dunedin, N.Z.	221a	45°48'S	170°32'E
Dunellen, N.J., U.S. (dŭn-ĕl'l'n)	110a	40°36'N	74°28'W
Dunfermline, Scot., U.K. (dŭn-fĕrm'lĭn)	164	56°05'N	3°30'W
Dungarvan, Ire. (dŭn-gȧr'vȧn)	164	52°06'N	7°50'W
Dungeness, Wa., U.S. (dŭnj-nĕs')	116a	48°09'N	123°07'W
Dungeness, r., Wa., U.S.	116a	48°03'N	123°10'W
Dungeness Spit, Wa., U.S.	116a	48°11'N	123°03'W
Dunhua, China (dòn-hwä)	205	43°18'N	128°10'E
Dunkerque, Fr. (dŭN-kĕrk')	161	51°02'N	2°37'E
Dunkirk, In., U.S. (dŭn'kûrk)	108	40°20'N	85°25'W
Dunkwa, Ghana	234	5°22'N	1°12'W
Dun Laoghaire, Ire. (dŭn-lā'rĕ)	160	53°16'N	6°09'W
Dunlap, Ia., U.S. (dŭn'lăp)	112	41°53'N	95°33'W
Dunlap, Tn., U.S.	124	35°23'N	85°23'W
Dunmore, Pa., U.S. (dŭn'mōr)	109	41°25'N	75°30'W
Dunn, N.C., U.S. (dŭn)	125	35°18'N	78°37'W
Dunnellon, Fl., U.S. (dŭn-ĕl'ŏn)	125	29°02'N	82°28'W
Dunnville, Can. (dŭn'vĭl)	99	42°55'N	79°40'W
Dunqulah, Sudan	231	19°21'N	30°19'E
Dunsmuir, Ca., U.S. (dŭnz'mūr)	114	41°08'N	122°17'W
Dunwoody, Ga., U.S. (dŭn-wòd'ĭ)	110c	33°57'N	84°20'W
Duolun, China (dwô-lōōn)	205	42°12'N	116°15'E
Du Page, r., Il., U.S. (dōō pāj)	111a	41°41'N	88°11'W
Du Page, East Branch, r., Il., U.S.	111a	41°42'N	88°09'W
Du Page, West Branch, r., Il., U.S.	111a	41°42'N	88°09'W
Dupax, Phil. (dōō'päks)	213a	16°16'N	121°06'E
Dupo, Il., U.S. (dū'pō)	117e	38°31'N	90°12'W
Duque de Caxias, Braz. (dōō'kĕ-dĕ-kä'shyás)	141a	22°46'S	43°18'W
Duquesne, Pa., U.S. (dò-kān')	111e	40°22'N	79°51'W
Du Quoin, Il., U.S. (dò-kwoin')	121	38°01'N	89°14'W
Durance, r., Fr. (dü-räNs')	161	43°46'N	5°52'E
Durand, Mi., U.S. (dŭ-rănd')	108	42°50'N	84°00'W
Durand, Wi., U.S.	113	44°37'N	91°58'W
Durango, Mex. (dōō-rä'n-gō)	128	24°02'N	104°42'W
Durango, Co., U.S. (dò-răŋ'gō)	119	37°15'N	107°55'W
Durango, state, Mex.	128	25°00'N	106°00'W
Durant, Ms., U.S. (dŭ-rănt')	124	33°05'N	89°50'W
Durant, Ok., U.S.	121	33°59'N	96°23'W
Duratón, r., Spain (dōō-rä-tōn')	172	41°30'N	3°55'W
Durazno, Ur. (dōō-räz'nō)	144	33°21'S	56°31'W
Durazno, dept., Ur.	141c	33°00'S	56°35'W
Durban, S. Afr. (dûr'bȧn)	232	29°48'S	31°00'E
Durbanville, S. Afr. (dûr-bȧn'vĭl)	232a	33°50'S	18°39'E
Durbe, Lat. (dōōr'bĕ)	167	56°36'N	21°24'E
Đurđevac, Cro.	163	46°03'N	17°03'E
Düren, Ger. (dü'rĕn)	171c	50°48'N	6°30'E
Durham, Eng., U.K. (dûr'ăm)	164	54°47'N	1°46'W
Durham, N.C., U.S.	105	36°00'N	78°55'W
Durham Downs, Austl.	222	27°30'S	141°55'E
Durrës, Alb. (dòr'ĕs)	154	41°19'N	19°27'E
Duryea, Pa., U.S. (dòòr-yā')	109	41°20'N	75°50'W
Dushan, China	206	31°38'N	116°16'E
Dushan, China (dōō-shän)	209	25°50'N	107°42'E
Dushanbe, Taj.	183	38°30'N	68°45'E
Düsseldorf, Ger. (düs'ĕl-dôrf)	161	51°14'N	6°47'E
Dussen, Neth.	159a	51°43'N	4°58'E
Dutalan Ula, mts., Mong.	208	49°25'N	112°40'E
Dutch Harbor, Ak., U.S. (dŭch här'bẽr)	106a	53°58'N	166°30'W
Duvall, Wa., U.S. (dōō'vâl)	116a	47°44'N	121°59'W
Duwamish, r., Wa., U.S. (dōō-wăm'ĭsh)	116a	47°24'N	122°18'W
Duyun, China (dōō-yòn)	204	26°18'N	107°40'E
Dvinskaya Guba, b., Russia	180	65°10'N	38°40'E
Dwārka, India	202	22°18'N	68°59'E
Dwight, Il., U.S. (dwīt)	108	41°00'N	88°20'W
Dworshak Res, Id., U.S.	114	46°45'N	115°50'W
Dyat'kovo, Russia (dyăt'kō-vō)	176	53°36'N	34°19'E
Dyer, In., U.S. (dī'ẽr)	111a	41°30'N	87°31'W
Dyersburg, Tn., U.S. (dī'ẽrz-bûrg)	124	36°02'N	89°23'W
Dyersville, Ia., U.S. (dī'ẽrz-vĭl)	113	42°28'N	91°09'W
Dyes Inlet, Wa., U.S. (dīz)	116a	47°37'N	122°45'W
Dykhtau, Gora, mtn., Russia	182	43°03'N	43°08'E
Dyment, Can. (dī'mĕnt)	97	49°37'N	92°19'W
Dzamïn Üüd, Mong.	205	44°38'N	111°32'E
Dzaoudzi, May. (dzou'dzĭ)	233	12°44'S	45°15'E
Dzavhan, r., Mong.	204	48°19'N	94°08'E
Dzerzhinsk, Russia	180	56°20'N	43°50'E
Dzerzhyns'k, Ukr.	177	48°26'N	37°50'E
Dzhalal-Abad, Kyrg. (jȧ-läl'ȧ-bät')	183	40°56'N	73°00'E
Dzhambul *see* Zhambyl, Kaz.	183	42°51'N	71°29'E
Dzhankoi, Ukr.	181	45°43'N	34°22'E
Dzhizak, Uzb. (dzhĕ'zäk)	183	40°13'N	67°58'E
Dzhugdzhur Khrebet, mts., Russia (jòg-jōōr')	179	56°15'N	137°00'E
Działoszyce, Pol. (jyä-wō-shē'tsĕ)	169	50°21'N	20°22'E
Dzibalchén, Mex. (zē-bäl-chĕ'n)	132a	19°25'N	89°39'W
Dzidzantún, Mex. (zēd-zän-tōō'n)	132a	21°18'N	89°00'W
Dzierżoniów, Pol. (dzyĕr-zhôn'yŭf)	168	50°44'N	16°38'E
Dzilam González, Mex. (zē-lä'm-gôn-zä'lĕz)	132a	21°21'N	88°53'W
Dzitás, Mex. (zē-tá's)	132a	20°47'N	88°32'W
Dzungaria, reg., China (dzòŋ-gä'rĭ-ȧ)	204	44°39'N	86°13'E
Dzungarian Gate, p., Asia	204	45°00'N	88°00'E
Dzyarzhynsk, Bela.	176	53°41'N	27°14'E

E

PLACE (Pronunciation)	PAGE	LAT.	LONG.
Eagle, W.V., U.S.	108	38°10'N	81°20'W
Eagle, r., Co., U.S. (ē'g'l)	119	39°32'N	106°28'W
Eaglecliff, Wa., U.S. (ē'gl-klĭf)	116c	46°10'N	123°13'W
Eagle Creek, r., In., U.S.	111g	39°54'N	86°17'W
Eagle Grove, Ia., U.S.	113	42°39'N	93°55'W
Eagle Lake, Me., U.S.	100	47°03'N	68°38'W
Eagle Lake, Tx., U.S.	123	29°37'N	96°20'W
Eagle Lake, l., Ca., U.S.	114	40°45'N	120°52'W
Eagle Mountain, Ca., U.S.	118	33°49'N	115°27'W
Eagle Mountain L, Tx., U.S.	117c	32°56'N	97°27'W
Eagle Pass, Tx., U.S.	104	28°49'N	100°30'W
Eagle Pk, Ca., U.S.	114	41°18'N	120°11'W
Ealing, Eng., U.K. (ē'lĭng)	158b	51°29'N	0°19'W
Earle, Ar., U.S. (ûrl)	121	35°14'N	90°28'W
Earlington, Ky., U.S. (ûr'lĭng-tŭn)	124	37°15'N	87°31'W
Easley, S.C., U.S. (ēz'lĭ)	125	34°48'N	82°37'W
East, Mount, mtn., Pan.	128a	9°09'N	79°46'W
East Alton, Il., U.S. (ôl'tŭn)	117e	38°53'N	90°08'W
East Angus, Can. (ăŋ'gŭs)	99	45°35'N	71°40'W
East Aurora, N.Y., U.S. (ô-rō'rȧ)	111c	42°46'N	78°38'W
East Bay, b., Tx., U.S.	123a	29°30'N	94°41'W
East Bernstadt, Ky., U.S. (bûrn'stăt)	124	37°09'N	84°08'W
Eastbourne, Eng., U.K. (ēst'bôrn)	165	50°48'N	0°16'E
East Caicos, i., T./C. Is. (kī'kōs)	135	21°40'N	71°35'W
East Cape, c., N.Z.	221a	37°37'S	178°33'E
East Cape *see* Dezhnëva, Mys, c., Russia	196	68°00'N	172°00'W
East Carondelet, Il., U.S. (kȧ-rŏn'dĕ-lĕt)	117e	38°33'N	90°14'W
East Cherokee Indian Reservation, I.R., N.C., U.S.	124	35°33'N	83°12'W
East Chicago, In., U.S. (shĭ-kô'gō)	111a	41°39'N	87°29'W
East China Sea, sea, Asia	205	30°28'N	125°52'E
East Cleveland, Oh., U.S. (klēv'lănd)	111d	41°33'N	81°35'W

ng-sing; ŋ-baŋk; N-nasalized n; nŏd; cŏmmit; ōld; ôbey; ôrder; oi-boil; fōōd; ò-as oo in foot; ou-out; s-soft; sh-dish; th-thin; pūre; ûnite; ûrn; stŭd; circŭs; ü-as in French tu; '-indeterminate vowel.

290 East Cote Blanche Bay – Ellice Islands PRONOUNCING INDEX

PLACE (Pronunciation)	PAGE	LAT.	LONG.
East Cote Blanche Bay, b., La., U.S. (kōt blänsh′)	123	29°30'N	92°07'W
East Des Moines, r., Ia., U.S. (dē moin′)	113	42°57'N	94°17'W
East Detroit, Mi., U.S. (dē-troit′)	111b	42°28'N	82°57'W
Easter Island *see* Pascua, Isla de, i., Chile	241	26°50'S	109°00'W
Eastern Ghāts, mts., India	199	13°50'N	78°45'E
Eastern Turkestan, hist. reg., China (tȯr-kĕ-stän′)(tûr-kĕ-stăn′)	204	39°40'N	78°20'E
East Grand Forks, Mn., U.S. (grănd fôrks)	112	47°56'N	97°02'W
East Greenwich, R.I., U.S. (grĭn′ĭj)	110b	41°40'N	71°27'W
Easthampton, Ma., U.S. (ēst-hămp′tŭn)	109	42°15'N	72°45'W
East Hartford, Ct., U.S. (härt′fẽrd)	109	41°45'N	72°35'W
East Helena, Mt., U.S. (hĕ-hē′nȧ)	115	46°31'N	111°50'W
East [illegible], Eng., U.K. ([illegible])	[illegible]	[illegible]	[illegible]
East Jordan, Mi., U.S. (jôr′dăn)	100	45°05'N	85°05'W
East Kansas City, Mo., U.S. (kăn′zȧs)	117f	39°09'N	94°30'W
Eastland, Tx., U.S. (ēst′lănd)	122	32°24'N	98°47'W
East Lansing, Mi., U.S. (lăn′sĭng)	108	42°45'N	84°30'W
Eastlawn, Mi., U.S.	111b	42°15'N	83°35'W
East Leavenworth, Mo., U.S. (lĕv′ĕn-wûrth)	117f	39°18'N	94°50'W
East Liverpool, Oh., U.S. (lĭv′ẽr-pōōl)	108	40°40'N	80°35'W
East London, S. Afr. (lŭn′dŭn)	232	33°02'S	27°54'E
East Los Angeles, Ca., U.S. (lōs ăn′hȧ-lās)	117a	34°01'N	118°09'W
Eastmain, r., Can. (ēst′mān)	93	52°12'N	73°19'W
Eastman, Ga., U.S. (ēst′măn)	124	32°10'N	83°11'W
East Millstone, N.J., U.S. (mĭl′stōn)	110a	40°30'N	74°35'W
East Moline, Il., U.S. (mȯ-lēn′)	113	41°31'N	90°28'W
East Nishnabotna, r., Ia., U.S. (nĭsh-nȧ-bŏt′nȧ)	112	40°53'N	95°23'W
Easton, Md., U.S. (ēs′tŭn)	109	38°45'N	76°05'W
Easton, Pa., U.S.	109	40°45'N	75°15'W
Easton L, Ct., U.S.	110a	41°18'N	73°17'W
East Orange, N.J., U.S. (ŏr′ĕnj)	110a	40°46'N	74°12'W
East Pakistan *see* Bangladesh, nation, Asia	199	24°15'N	90°00'E
East Palo Alto, Ca., U.S.	116b	37°27'N	122°07'W
East Peoria, Il., U.S. (pē-ō′rĭ-ȧ)	108	40°40'N	89°30'W
East Pittsburgh, Pa., U.S. (pĭts′bûrg)	111e	40°24'N	79°50'W
East Point, Ga., U.S.	110c	33°41'N	84°27'W
Eastport, Me., U.S. (ēst′pōrt)	100	44°53'N	67°01'W
East Providence, R.I., U.S. (prŏv′ĭ-dĕns)	110b	41°49'N	71°22'W
East Retford, Eng., U.K. (rĕt′fẽrd)	158a	53°19'N	0°56'W
East Riding of Yorkshire, co., Eng., U.K.	158a	53°45'N	0°40'W
East Rochester, N.Y., U.S. (rŏch′ĕs-tẽr)	109	43°10'N	77°30'W
East Saint Louis, Il., U.S.	105	38°38'N	90°10'W
East Siberian Sea, sea, Russia (sī-bĭr′y′n)	179	73°00'N	153°28'E
Eastsound, Wa., U.S. (ēst-sound)	116d	48°42'N	122°42'W
East Stroudsburg, Pa., U.S. (stroudz′bûrg)	109	41°00'N	75°10'W
East Syracuse, N.Y., U.S. (sĭr′ȧ-kūs)	109	43°05'N	76°00'W
East Tavaputs Plateau, plat., Ut., U.S. (tă-vă′-pŭts)	119	39°25'N	109°45'W
East Tawas, Mi., U.S. (tô′wȧs)	108	44°15'N	83°30'W
East Timor, nation, Asia	213	9°00'S	125°30'E
East Walker, r., U.S. (wôk′ẽr)	118	38°36'N	119°02'W
Eaton, Co., U.S. (ē′tŭn)	120	40°31'N	104°42'W
Eaton, Oh., U.S.	108	39°45'N	84°40'W
Eaton Estates, Oh., U.S.	111d	41°19'N	82°01'W
Eaton Rapids, Mi., U.S. (răp′ĭdz)	108	42°30'N	84°40'W
Eatonton, Ga., U.S. (ē′tŭn-tŭn)	124	33°20'N	83°24'W
Eatontown, N.J., U.S. (ē′tŭn-toun)	110a	40°18'N	74°04'W
Eau Claire, Wi., U.S. (ō klâr′)	105	44°47'N	91°32'W
Ebeltoft, Den. (ĕ′bĕl-tŭft)	166	56°11'N	10°39'E
Ebensburg, Pa., U.S.	109	40°29'N	78°44'W
Ebersberg, Ger. (ĕ′bĕrs-bĕrgh)	159d	48°05'N	11°58'E
Ebingen, Ger. (ā′bĭng-ĕn)	168	48°13'N	9°04'E
Eboli, Italy (ĕb′ō-lē)	174	40°38'N	15°04'E
Ebolowa, Cam.	230	2°54'N	11°09'E
Ebreichsdorf, Aus.	159e	47°58'N	16°24'E
Ebrié, Lagune, b., C. Iv.	234	5°20'N	4°50'W
Ebro, r., Spain (ā′brō)	156	42°00'N	2°00'W
Eccles, Eng., U.K. (ĕk′'lz)	158a	53°29'N	2°20'W
Eccles, W.V., U.S.	108	37°45'N	81°10'W
Eccleshall, Eng., U.K.	158a	52°51'N	2°15'W
Eceabat, Tur.	175	40°10'N	26°21'E
Echague, Phil. (ā-chä′gwä)	213a	16°43'N	121°40'E
Echandi, Cerro, mtn., N.A. (sĕ′r-rō-ĕ-chä′nd)	133	9°05'N	82°51'W
Ech Cheliff, Alg.	230	36°14'N	1°32'E
Echimamish, r., Can.	97	54°15'N	97°30'W
Echmiadzin, Arm.	182	40°10'N	44°18'E
Echo Bay, Can. (ĕk′ō)	117k	46°29'N	84°04'W
Echoing, r., Can. (ĕk′ō-ĭng)	97	55°15'N	91°30'W
Echternach, Lux. (ĕk′tẽr-näk)	171	49°48'N	6°25'E
Echuca, Austl. (ē-chō′kȧ)	219	36°10'S	144°47'E
Écija, Spain (ā′thē-hä)	162	37°20'N	5°07'W
Eckernförde, Ger.	168	54°27'N	9°51'E
Eclipse, Va., U.S. (ē-klĭps′)	110g	36°55'N	76°29'W
Ecorse, Mi., U.S. (ē-kôrs′)	111b	42°15'N	83°09'W
Ecuador, nation, S.A. (ĕk′wȧ-dôr)	142	0°00'N	78°30'W
Ed, Erit.	231	13°57'N	41°37'E
Eddyville, Ky., U.S. (ĕd′ĭ-vĭl)	124	37°03'N	88°03'W
Ede, Nig.	235	7°44'N	4°27'E
Edéa, Cam. (ĕ-dā′ä)	230	3°48'N	10°08'E

PLACE (Pronunciation)	PAGE	LAT.	LONG.
Eden, Tx., U.S.	122	31°13'N	99°51'W
Eden, Ut., U.S.	117b	41°18'N	111°49'W
Eden, r., Eng., U.K. (ē′dĕn)	164	54°40'N	2°35'W
Edenbridge, Eng., U.K. (ē′dĕn-brĭj)	158b	51°11'N	0°05'E
Edenham, Eng., U.K. (ē′d'n-ăm)	158a	52°46'N	0°25'W
Eden Prairie, Mn., U.S. (prâr′ĭ)	117g	44°51'N	93°29'W
Edenton, N.C., U.S. (ē′dĕn-tŭn)	125	36°02'N	76°37'W
Edenton, Oh., U.S.	111f	39°14'N	84°02'W
Edenvale, S. Afr. (ēd′ĕn-vāl)	233b	26°09'S	28°10'E
Edenville, S. Afr. (ē′d'n-vĭl)	238c	27°33'S	27°42'E
Eder, r., Ger. (ā′dẽr)	168	51°05'N	8°52'E
Édessa, Grc.	163	40°48'N	22°04'E
Edgefield, S.C., U.S. (ĕj′fēld)	125	33°52'N	81°55'W
Edgeley, N.D., U.S. (ĕj′lĭ)	112	46°24'N	98°43'W
Edgemont, S.D., U.S. (ĕj′mŏnt)	112	43°19'N	103°50'W
Edgerton, Wi., U.S. (ĕj′ẽr-tŭn)	113	42°49'N	89°06'W
Edgewater, Al., U.S. ([illegible])	110h	[illegible]	[illegible]
Edgewater, Md., U.S.	110e	38°58'N	76°35'W
Edgewood, Can. (ĕj′wo̊d)	95	49°47'N	118°08'W
Edina, Mn., U.S. (ē-dī′nȧ)	117g	44°55'N	93°20'W
Edina, Mo., U.S.	121	40°10'N	92°11'W
Edinburg, In., U.S. (ĕd′'n-bûrg)	108	39°20'N	85°55'W
Edinburg, Tx., U.S.	122	26°18'N	98°08'W
Edinburgh, Scot., U.K. (ĕd′'n-bŭr-ō)	154	55°57'N	3°10'W
Edirne, Tur.	175	41°41'N	26°35'E
Edisto, r., S.C., U.S. (ĕd′ĭs-tō)	125	33°10'N	80°50'W
Edisto, North Fork, r., S.C., U.S.	125	33°42'N	81°24'W
Edisto, South Fork, r., S.C., U.S.	125	33°43'N	81°35'W
Edisto Island, S.C., U.S.	125	32°32'N	80°20'W
Edmond, Ok., U.S. (ĕd′mŭnd)	121	35°39'N	97°29'W
Edmonds, Wa., U.S. (ĕd′mŭndz)	116a	47°49'N	122°23'W
Edmonton, Can.	90	53°33'N	113°28'W
Edmundston, Can. (ĕd′mŭn-stŭn)	91	47°22'N	68°20'W
Edna, Tx., U.S. (ĕd′nȧ)	123	28°59'N	96°39'W
Edremit, Tur. (ĕd-rĕ-mĕt′)	163	39°35'N	27°00'E
Edremit Körfezi, b., Tur.	175	39°28'N	26°35'E
Edson, Can. (ĕd′sŭn)	90	53°35'N	116°26'W
Edward, i., Can. (ĕd′wẽrd)	98	48°21'N	88°29'W
Edward, l., Afr.	232	0°25'S	29°40'E
Edwardsville, Il., U.S. (ĕd′wẽrdz-vĭl)	117e	38°49'N	89°58'W
Edwardsville, In., U.S.	111h	38°17'N	85°53'W
Edwardsville, Ks., U.S.	117f	39°04'N	94°49'W
Eel, r., Ca., U.S. (ēl)	114	40°39'N	124°15'W
Eel, r., In., U.S.	108	40°50'N	85°55'W
Efate, i., Vanuatu (ā-fä′tä)	221	18°02'S	168°29'E
Effigy Mounds National Monument, rec., Ia., U.S. (ĕf′ĭ-jŭ mounds)	113	43°04'N	91°15'W
Effingham, Il., U.S. (ĕf′ĭng-hăm)	108	39°05'N	88°30'W
Ega, r., Spain (ā′gä)	172	42°40'N	2°20'W
Egadi, Isole, is., Italy (ĕ′sō-lĕ-ĕ′gä-dē)	162	38°01'N	12°00'E
Egegik, Ak., U.S. (ĕg′ĕ-jĭt)	103	58°10'N	157°22'W
Eger, Hung. (ĕ gĕr)	169	47°53'N	20°24'E
Egersund, Nor. (ĕ′ghĕr-sōn′)	160	58°29'N	6°01'E
Egg Harbor, N.J., U.S. (ĕg här′bẽr)	109	39°30'N	74°35'W
Egham, Eng., U.K. (ĕg′ŭm)	158b	51°24'N	0°33'W
Egiyn, r., Mong.	204	49°41'N	100°40'E
Egmont, Cape, c., N.Z. (ĕg′mŏnt)	221a	39°18'S	173°49'E
Egypt, nation, Afr. (ē′jĭpt)	231	26°58'N	27°01'E
Eha-Amufu, Nig.	235	6°40'N	7°46'E
Eibar, Spain (ā′ē-bär)	172	43°12'N	2°20'W
Eichstätt, Ger. (īk′shtät)	168	48°54'N	11°14'E
Eichwalde, Ger. (īk′väl-dĕ)	159b	52°22'N	13°37'E
Eidfjord, Nor. (ĕĭd′fyŏr)	166	60°28'N	7°04'E
Eidsvoll, Nor. (ĭdhs′vŏl)	160	60°19'N	11°15'E
Eifel, mts., Ger. (ī′fĕl)	168	50°08'N	6°30'E
Eighty Mile Beach, cst., Austl.	220	19°00'S	121°00'E
Eilenburg, Ger. (ī′lĕn-bo̅o̅rgh)	168	51°27'N	12°38'E
Einbeck, Ger. (īn′bĕk)	168	51°49'N	9°52'E
Eindhoven, Neth. (īnd′hō-vĕn)	165	51°29'N	5°20'E
Eisenach, Ger. (ī′zĕn-äk)	161	50°58'N	10°18'E
Eisenhüttenstadt, Ger.	168	52°08'N	14°40'E
Eivissa, Spain	173	38°55'N	1°24'E
Eivissa, i., Spain	156	38°55'N	1°24'E
Ejea de los Caballeros, Spain	172	42°07'N	1°05'W
Ejura, Ghana	234	7°23'N	1°22'W
Ejutla de Crespo, Mex. (ā-hōt′lä dā krās′pō)	131	16°34'N	96°44'W
Ekanga, D.R.C.	236	2°23'S	23°14'E
Ekenäs, Fin. (ĕ′kĕ-nâs)	167	59°59'N	23°25'E
Ekeren, Bel.	159a	51°17'N	4°27'E
Ekoli, D.R.C.	236	0°23'S	24°16'E
El Aaiún, W. Sah.	230	26°45'N	13°15'W
El Affroun, Alg. (ĕl ȧf-froun′)	173	36°28'N	2°38'E
Elands, r., S. Afr. (ēlȧnds)	233c	31°48'S	26°09'E
Elands, r., S. Afr.	238c	25°11'S	28°52'E
El Arahal, Spain (ĕl ä-rä-äl′)	172	37°17'N	5°32'W
El Arba, Alg.	173	36°35'N	3°10'E
Elat, Isr.	198	29°34'N	34°57'E
Elazığ, Tur. (ĕl-ä′zēz)	198	38°40'N	39°00'E
Elba, Al., U.S. (ĕl′bȧ)	124	31°25'N	86°01'W
Elba, Isola d', i., Italy (ē-sō lä-d-ĕl′bȧ)	162	42°42'N	10°25'E
El Banco, Col. (ĕl băn′cō)	142	8°58'N	74°01'W
Elbansan, Alb. (ĕl-bä-sän′)	163	41°08'N	20°05'E
Elbe (Labe), r., Eur. (ĕl′bĕ)(lä′bĕ)	156	52°30'N	11°30'E
Elbert, Mount, mtn., Co., U.S. (ĕl′bẽrt)	106	39°05'N	106°25'W
Elberton, Ga., U.S. (ĕl′bẽr-tŭn)	125	34°05'N	82°53'W
Elbeuf, Fr. (ĕl-bûf′)	161	49°16'N	0°59'E
El Beyadh, Alg.	162	33°42'N	1°06'E
Elbistan, Tur. (ĕl-bē-stän′)	163	38°20'N	37°10'E
Elblag, Pol. (ĕl′blăng)	160	54°11'N	19°25'E
El Bonillo, Spain (ĕl bō-nēl′yō)	172	38°56'N	2°31'W
El Boulaïda, Alg.	230	36°33'N	2°45'E
Elbow, r., Can. (ĕl′bō)	102e	51°03'N	114°24'W

PLACE (Pronunciation)	PAGE	LAT.	LONG.
Elbow Cay, i., Bah.	134	26°25'N	76°55'W
Elbow Lake, Mn., U.S.	112	46°00'N	95°59'W
El'brus, Gora, mtn., Russia (ĕl′brȯs′)	178	43°20'N	42°25'E
Elbrus, Mount *see* El'brus, Gora, mtn., Russia	178	43°20'N	42°25'E
Elburz Mountains, mts., Iran (ĕl′bo̅o̅rz′)	198	36°30'N	51°00'E
El Cajon, Col. (ĕl-kä-kô′n)	142a	4°50'N	76°35'W
El Cajon, Ca., U.S.	118a	32°48'N	116°58'W
El Cambur, Ven. (käm-bo̅o̅r′)	143b	10°24'N	68°06'W
El Campo, Tx., U.S. (kăm′pō)	123	29°13'N	96°17'W
El Carmen, Chile (kȧ′r-mĕn)	141b	34°14'S	71°23'W
El Carmen, Col. (kȧ′r-mĕn)	142	9°54'N	75°12'W
El [illegible], Ca., U.S. ([illegible])	117a	33°59'N	117°08'W
El Centro, Ca., U.S. (sĕn′trō)	118	32°47'N	115°33'W
El Cerrito, Ca., U.S. (sĕr-rē′tō)	116b	37°55'N	122°19'W
El Cuyo, Mex.	132a	[illegible]	[illegible]
El[illegible], [illegible] ([illegible])	173	38°28'N	0°44'W
El Djelfa, Alg.	230	34°40'N	3°17'E
El Djouf, des., Afr. (ĕl djo̅o̅f)	230	21°45'N	7°05'W
Eldon, Ia., U.S. (ĕl-dŭn)	113	40°55'N	92°15'W
Eldon, Mo., U.S.	121	38°21'N	92°36'W
Eldora, Ia., U.S. (ĕl-dō′rȧ)	113	42°21'N	93°08'W
El Dorado, Ar., U.S. (ĕl dō-rä′dō)	105	33°13'N	92°39'W
Eldorado, Il., U.S.	108	37°50'N	88°30'W
El Dorado, Ks., U.S.	121	37°49'N	96°51'W
Eldorado Springs, Mo., U.S. (sprĭngz)	121	37°51'N	94°02'W
Eldoret, Kenya (ĕl-dō-rĕt′)	237	0°31'N	35°17'E
El Ebano, Mex. (ā-bä′nō)	130	22°13'N	98°26'W
Electra, Tx., U.S. (ē-lĕk′trȧ)	120	34°02'N	98°54'W
Electric Peak, mtn., Mt., U.S. (ē-lĕk′trĭk)	115	45°03'N	110°52'W
Elek, r.	181	51°20'N	53°10'E
Elektrogorsk, Russia (ĕl-yĕk′trō-gôrsk)	186b	55°53'N	38°48'E
Elektrostal', Russia (ĕl-yĕk′trō-stál)	186b	55°47'N	38°27'E
Elektrougli, Russia	186b	55°43'N	38°13'E
Elephant Butte Reservoir, res., N.M., U.S. (ĕl′ē-fănt būt)	106	33°25'N	107°10'W
El Escorial, Spain (ĕl-ĕs-kō-ryä′l)	173a	40°38'N	4°08'W
El Espino, Nic. (ĕl-ĕs-pē′nō)	132	13°26'N	86°48'W
Eleuthera, i., Bah. (ē-lū′thẽr-ȧ)	129	25°05'N	76°10'W
Eleuthera Point, c., Bah.	134	24°35'N	76°05'W
Eleven Point, r., Mo., U.S. (ē-lĕv′ĕn)	121	36°53'N	91°39'W
Elgin, Scot., U.K.	164	57°40'N	3°30'W
Elgin, Il., U.S. (ĕl′jĭn)	111a	42°03'N	88°16'W
Elgin, Ne., U.S.	112	41°58'N	98°04'W
Elgin, Or., U.S.	114	45°34'N	117°58'W
Elgin, Tx., U.S.	123	30°21'N	97°22'W
Elgin, Wa., U.S.	116a	47°23'N	122°42'W
Elgon, Mount, mtn., Afr. (ĕl′gŏn)	231	1°00'N	34°25'E
El Grara, Alg.	162	32°50'N	4°26'E
El Grullo, Mex. (gro̅o̅l-yō)	130	19°46'N	104°10'W
El Guapo, Ven. (gwȧ′pō)	143b	10°07'N	66°00'W
El Hank, reg., Afr.	230	23°44'N	6°45'W
El Hatillo, Ven. (ä-tē′l-yō)	143b	10°08'N	65°13'W
Elie, Can. (ē′lē)	102f	49°55'N	97°45'W
Elila, r., D.R.C. (ĕ-lē′lȧ)	232	3°30'S	28°00'E
Elisa, i., Wa., U.S. (ē-lī′sȧ)	116d	48°43'N	122°37'W
Élisabethville *see* Lubumbashi, D.R.C.	232	11°40'S	27°28'E
Elisenvaara, Russia (ā-lē′sĕn-vä′rȧ)	167	61°25'N	29°46'E
Elizabeth, La., U.S. (ē-lĭz′ȧ-bĕth)	123	30°50'N	92°47'W
Elizabeth, N.J., U.S.	110a	40°40'N	74°13'W
Elizabeth, Pa., U.S.	111e	40°16'N	79°53'W
Elizabeth City, N.C., U.S.	125	36°15'N	76°15'W
Elizabethton, Tn., U.S. (ē-lĭz-ȧ-bĕth′tŭn)	125	36°19'N	82°12'W
Elizabethtown, Ky., U.S. (ē-lĭz′ȧ-bĕth-toun)	108	37°40'N	85°55'W
El Jadida, Mor.	230	33°14'N	8°34'W
Elk, Pol.	160	53°53'N	22°23'E
Elk, r., Can.	95	50°00'N	115°00'W
Elk, r., Tn., U.S.	124	35°05'N	86°36'W
Elk, r., W.V., U.S.	108	38°30'N	81°05'W
El Kairouan, Tun. (kĕr-ō-än)	230	35°46'N	10°04'E
Elk City, Ok., U.S. (ĕlk)	120	35°23'N	99°23'W
El Kef, Tun. (xĕf′)	162	36°14'N	8°42'E
Elkhart, In., U.S. (ĕlk′härt)	108	41°40'N	86°00'W
Elkhart, Ks., U.S.	120	37°00'N	101°54'W
Elkhart, Tx., U.S.	123	31°38'N	95°35'W
Elkhorn, Wi., U.S. (ĕlk′hôrn)	113	42°39'N	88°32'W
Elkhorn, r., Ne., U.S.	112	42°06'N	97°46'W
Elkin, N.C., U.S. (ĕl′kĭn)	125	36°15'N	80°50'W
Elk Island, i., Can.	97	50°45'N	96°32'W
Elk Island National Park, rec., Can. (ĕlk ī′lănd)	92	53°37'N	112°45'W
Elko, Nv., U.S. (ĕl′kō)	104	40°51'N	115°46'W
Elk Point, S.D., U.S.	112	42°41'N	96°41'W
Elk Rapids, Mi., U.S. (răp′ĭdz)	108	44°55'N	85°25'W
Elk River, Id., U.S. (rĭv′ẽr)	114	46°47'N	116°11'W
Elk River, Mn., U.S.	113	45°17'N	93°33'W
Elkton, Ky., U.S. (ĕlk′tŭn)	124	36°47'N	87°08'W
Elkton, Md., U.S.	109	39°35'N	75°50'W
Elkton, S.D., U.S.	112	44°15'N	96°28'W
Elland, Eng., U.K. (ĕl′ănd)	158a	53°41'N	1°50'W
Ellen, Mount, mtn., Ut., U.S. (ĕl′ĕn)	119	38°05'N	110°50'W
Ellendale, N.D., U.S. (ĕl′ĕn-dāl)	112	46°01'N	98°33'W
Ellensburg, Wa., U.S. (ĕl′ĕnz-bûrg)	114	47°00'N	120°31'W
Ellenville, N.Y., U.S. (ĕl′ĕn-vĭl)	109	41°40'N	74°25'W
Ellerslie, Can. (ĕl′ẽrz-lē)	102g	53°25'N	113°30'W
Ellesmere, Eng., U.K. (ĕlz′mẽr)	158a	52°55'N	2°54'W
Ellesmere Island, i., Can.	89	81°00'N	80°00'W
Ellesmere Port, Eng., U.K.	158a	53°17'N	2°54'W
Ellice Islands *see* Tuvalu, nation, Oc.	3	5°20'S	174°00'E

ăt; finăl; rāte; senȧte; ärm; ȧsk; sofȧ; fâre; ch-choose; dh-as th in other; bē; ėvent; bĕt; recĕnt; cratẽr; g-gō; gh-guttural g; bĭt; ĭ-short neutral; rīde; ĸ-guttural k as ch in German ich;

PRONOUNCING INDEX

Ellicott City – Estarreja 291

PLACE (Pronunciation)	PAGE	LAT.	LONG.
Ellicott City, is., Md., U.S. (ĕl'ĭ-kŏt sĭ'tē)	110e	39°16'N	76°48'W
Ellicott Creek, r., N.Y., U.S.	111c	43°00'N	78°46'W
Elliot, S. Afr.	233c	31°19'S	27°52'E
Elliot, Wa., U.S. (el'ĭ-ŭt)	116a	47°28'N	122°08'W
Elliotdale, S. Afr. (ĕl-ĭ-ŏt'dāl)	233c	31°58'S	28°42'E
Elliot Lake, Can.	98	46°23'N	82°39'W
Ellis, Ks., U.S. (ĕl'ĭs)	120	38°56'N	99°34'W
Ellisville, Mo., U.S.	117e	38°35'N	90°35'W
Ellisville, Ms., U.S. (ĕl'ĭs-vĭl)	124	31°37'N	89°10'W
Ellsworth, Ks., U.S. (ĕlz'wûrth)	120	38°43'N	98°14'W
Ellsworth, Me., U.S.	100	44°33'N	68°26'W
Ellsworth Mountains, mts., Ant.	224	77°00'S	90°00'W
Ellwangen, Ger. (ĕl'väŋ-gĕn)	168	48°47'N	10°08'E
Elm, Ger. (ĕlm)	159c	53°31'N	9°13'E
Elm, r., S.D., U.S.	112	45°47'N	98°28'W
Elm, r., W.V., U.S.	108	38°30'N	81°05'W
Elma, Wa., U.S. (ĕl'mȧ)	114	47°02'N	123°20'W
El Mahdia, Tun. (mä-dē'ä)(mä'dē-ȧ)	102	35°30'N	11°09'E
Elmendorf, Tx., U.S. (ĕl'mĕn-dôrf)	117d	29°16'N	98°20'W
El Menia, Alg.	230	30°39'N	2°52'E
Elm Fork, Tx., U.S. (ĕlm fôrk)	117c	32°55'N	96°56'W
Elmhurst, Il., U.S. (ĕlm'hûrst)	111a	41°54'N	87°56'W
El Miliyya, Alg. (mē'ä)	230	36°30'N	6°16'E
Elmira, N.Y., U.S. (ĕl-mī'rȧ)	109	42°05'N	76°50'W
Elmira Heights, N.Y., U.S.	109	42°10'N	76°50'W
El Modena, Ca., U.S. (mȯ-dē'nȯ)	117a	33°47'N	117°48'W
El Mohammadia, Alg.	173	35°35'N	0°05'E
El Monte, Ca., U.S. (mōn'tȧ)	117a	34°04'N	118°02'W
El Morro National Monument, rec., N.M., U.S.	119	35°05'N	108°20'W
Elmshorn, Ger. (ĕlms'hôrn)	168	53°45'N	9°39'E
Elmwood Place, Oh., U.S. (ĕlm'wȯd plās)	111f	39°11'N	84°30'W
Elokomin, r., Wa., U.S. (ė-lō'kō-mĭn)	116c	46°16'N	123°16'W
El Oro, Mex. (ô-rȯ)	130	19°49'N	100°04'W
El Pao, Ven. (ĕl pá'ō)	142	8°08'N	62°37'W
El Paraíso, Hond. (pä-rä-ē'sō)	132	13°55'N	86°35'W
El Pardo, Spain (pä'r-dȯ)	173a	40°31'N	3°47'W
El Paso, Tx., U.S. (pas'ō)	104	31°47'N	106°27'W
El Pilar, Ven. (pē-lä'r)	143b	9°56'N	64°48'W
El Porvenir, Pan. (pôr-vä-nēr')	133	9°34'N	78°55'W
El Puerto de Santa María, Spain	172	36°36'N	6°18'W
El Qala, Alg.	162	36°52'N	8°23'E
El Qoll, Alg.	230	37°02'N	6°29'E
El Real, Pan. (rā-äl)	133	8°07'N	77°43'W
El Reno, Ok., U.S. (rē'nō)	121	35°31'N	97°57'W
Elroy, Wi., U.S. (ĕl'roi)	113	43°44'N	90°17'W
Elsa, Can.	103	63°55'N	135°25'W
Elsah, Il., U.S. (ĕl'zȧ)	117e	38°57'N	90°22'W
El Salto, Mex. (säl'tō)	130	23°48'N	105°22'W
El Salvador, nation, N.A.	128	14°00'N	89°30'W
El Sauce, Nic. (ĕl-sà'ō-sē)	132	13°00'N	86°40'W
Elsberry, Mo., U.S. (ĕlz'bĕr-ĭ)	121	39°09'N	90°44'W
Elsdorf, Ger. (ĕls'dōrf)	171c	50°56'N	6°35'E
El Segundo, Ca., U.S. (sĕgŭn'dō)	117a	33°55'N	118°24'W
Elsinore, Ca., U.S. (ĕl'sĭ-nôr)	117a	33°40'N	117°19'W
Elsinore Lake, l., Ca., U.S.	117a	33°38'N	117°21'W
Elstorf, Ger. (ĕls'tōrf)	159c	53°25'N	9°48'E
Eltham, Austl. (ĕl'thăm)	217a	37°43'S	145°08'E
El Tigre, Ven. (tē'grĕ)	142	8°49'N	64°15'W
El'ton, l., Russia	181	49°10'N	47°00'E
El Toro, Ca., U.S. (tō'rō)	117a	33°37'N	117°42'W
El Triunfo, El Sal.	132	13°17'N	88°32'W
El Triunfo, Hond. (ĕl-trē-ōō'n-fō)	132	13°06'N	87°00'W
Elūru, India	199	16°44'N	80°09'E
El Vado Res, N.M., U.S.	119	36°37'N	106°30'W
Elvas, Port. (ĕl'väzh)	162	38°53'N	7°11'W
Elverum, Nor. (ĕl'vĕ-rȯm)	166	60°53'N	11°33'E
El Viejo, Nic. (ĕl-vyĕ'κô)	132	12°10'N	87°10'W
El Viejo, vol., Nic.	132	12°44'N	87°03'W
Elvins, Mo., U.S. (ĕl'vĭnz)	121	37°49'N	90°31'W
El Wad, Alg.	230	33°23'N	6°49'E
El Wak, Kenya (wäk')	231	3°00'N	41°00'E
Elwell, Lake, res., Mt., U.S.	115	48°22'N	111°17'W
Elwood, Il., U.S. (ĕ'wȯd)	111a	41°24'N	88°07'W
Elwood, In., U.S.	108	40°15'N	85°50'W
Elx, Spain	173	38°15'N	0°42'W
Ely, Eng., U.K. (ē'lĭ)	165	52°25'N	0°17'E
Ely, Mn., U.S.	113	47°54'N	91°53'W
Ely, Nv., U.S.	104	39°16'N	114°53'W
Elyria, Oh., U.S. (ė-lĭr'ĭ-ȧ)	111d	41°22'N	82°07'W
Ema, r., Est. (ā'mȧ)	167	58°25'N	27°00'E
Emāmshahr, Iran	198	36°25'N	55°01'E
Emån, r., Swe.	166	57°15'N	15°46'E
Embarrass, r., Il., U.S. (ĕm-băr'ăs)	108	39°15'N	88°05'W
Embrun, Can. (ĕm'brŭn)	102c	45°16'N	75°17'W
Embrun, Fr. (äɴ-brûɴ')	171	44°35'N	6°32'E
Embu, Kenya	237	0°32'S	37°27'E
Emden, Ger. (ĕm'dĕn)	168	53°21'N	7°15'E
Emerson, Can. (ĕm'ẽr-sŭn)	90	49°00'N	97°12'W
Emeryville, Ca., U.S. (ĕm'ẽr-ĭ-vĭl)	116b	37°50'N	122°17'W
Emi Koussi, mtn., Chad (ā'mē kōō-sē')	231	19°50'N	18°30'E
Emiliano Zapata, Mex. (ĕ-mē-lyä'nō-zä-pä'tä)	131	17°45'N	91°46'W
Emilia-Romagna, hist. reg., Italy (ē-mēl'yä rô-mä'n-yä)	174	44°35'N	10°48'E
Eminence, Ky., U.S. (ĕm'ĭ-nĕns)	108	38°25'N	85°15'W
Emira Island, i., Pap. N. Gui. (ā-mē-rä')	213	1°40'S	150°28'E
Emmen, Neth. (ĕm'ĕn)	165	52°48'N	6°55'E
Emmerich, Ger. (ĕm'ẽr-ĭk)	171c	51°51'N	6°16'E
Emmetsburg, Ia., U.S. (ĕm'ĕts-bûrg)	113	43°07'N	94°41'W
Emmett, Id., U.S. (ĕm'ĕt)	114	43°53'N	116°30'W
Emmons, Mount, mtn., Ut., U.S. (ĕm'ŭnz)	106	40°43'N	110°20'W
Emory Peak, mtn., Tx., U.S. (ĕ'mŏ-rē pēk)	122	29°13'N	103°20'W
Empoli, Italy (ām'pô-lē)	174	43°43'N	10°55'E
Emporia, Ks., U.S. (ĕm-pō'rĭ-ȧ)	104	38°24'N	96°11'W
Emporia, Va., U.S.	125	37°40'N	77°34'W
Emporium, Pa., U.S. (ĕm-pō'rĭ-ŭm)	109	41°30'N	78°15'W
Empty Quarter *see* Ar Rub' al Khālī, des., Asia	198	20°00'N	51°00'E
Ems, r., Ger. (ĕms)	168	52°52'N	7°16'E
Ems-Weser Kanal, can., Ger.	168	52°23'N	8°11'E
Enånger, Swe. (ĕn-ôŋ'gĕr)	166	61°36'N	16°55'E
Encantada, Cerro de la, mtn., Mex. (sĕ'r-rô-dĕ-lä-ĕn-kän-tä'dä)	128	31°58'N	115°15'W
Encanto, Cape, c., Phil. (ĕn-kän'tō)	213a	15°44'N	121°46'E
Encarnación, Para. (ĕn-kär-nä-syōn')	144	27°26'S	55°52'W
Encarnación de Díaz, Mex. (ĕn-kär-nä-syōn dà dē'àz)	130	21°34'N	102°15'W
Encinal, Tx., U.S. (ĕn'sĭ-nŏl)	122	28°02'N	99°22'W
Encontrados, Ven. (ĕn-kōn-trä'dōs)	142	9°01'N	72°10'W
Encounter Bay, b., Austl. (ĕn-koun'tẽr)	220	35°50'S	138°45'E
Endako, r., Can.	94	54°05'N	125°30'W
Endau, r., Malay.	197b	2°29'N	103°40'E
Enderbury, i., Kir. (ĕn'dẽr-bûrĭ)	240	2°00'S	171°00'W
Enderby Land, reg., Ant. (ĕn'dĕr bĭī)	224	72°00'S	52°00'E
Enderlin, N.D., U.S. (ĕn'dẽr-lĭn)	112	46°38'N	97°37'W
Endicott, N.Y., U.S. (ĕn'dĭ-kŏt)	109	42°05'N	76°00'W
Endicott Mountains, mts., Ak., U.S.	103	67°30'N	153°45'W
Enez, Tur.	175	40°42'N	26°05'E
Enfer, Pointe d', c., Mart.	133b	14°21'N	60°48'W
Enfield, Eng., U.K.	158b	51°38'N	0°06'W
Enfield, Ct., U.S. (ĕn'fēld)	109	41°55'N	72°35'W
Enfield, N.C., U.S.	125	36°10'N	77°41'W
Engaño, Cabo, c., Dom. Rep. (kà'-bô- ĕn-gä-nô)	129	18°40'N	68°30'W
Engcobo, S. Afr. (ĕng-cô-bô)	233c	31°41'S	27°59'E
Engel's, Russia (ĕn'gĕls)	181	51°20'N	45°40'E
Engelskirchen, Ger. (ĕn'gĕls-kĕr'κĕn)	171c	50°59'N	7°25'E
Enggano, Pulau, i., Indon. (ĕng-gä'nō)	212	5°22'S	102°18'E
England, Ar., U.S. (ĭŋ'glănd)	121	34°33'N	91°58'W
England, state, U.K. (ĭŋ'glănd)	154	51°35'N	1°40'W
Englewood, Co., U.S. (ĕn'g'l-wȯd)	120	39°39'N	105°00'W
Englewood, N.J., U.S.	110a	40°54'N	73°59'W
English, In., U.S. (ĭn'glĭsh)	108	38°15'N	86°25'W
English, r., Can.	93	50°31'N	94°12'W
English Channel, strt., Eur.	156	49°45'N	3°06'W
Énguera, Spain (ān'gärä)	173	38°58'N	0°42'W
Enid, Ok., U.S. (ē'nĭd)	104	36°25'N	97°52'W
Enid Lake, res., Ms., U.S.	124	34°13'N	89°47'W
Enkeldoring, S. Afr. (ĕŋ'k'l-dôr-ĭng)	238c	25°24'S	28°43'E
Enköping, Swe. (ĕn'kû-pĭng)	166	59°39'N	17°05'E
Ennedi, mts., Chad (ĕn-nĕd'ē)	231	16°45'N	22°45'E
Ennis, Ire. (ĕn'ĭs)	164	52°54'N	9°05'W
Ennis, Tx., U.S.	123	32°20'N	96°38'W
Enniscorthy, Ire. (ĕn-ĭs-kôr'thĭ)	164	52°33'N	6°27'W
Enniskillen, N. Ire., U.K. (ĕn-ĭs-kĭl'ĕn)	164	54°20'N	7°25'W
Ennis Lake, res., Mt., U.S.	115	45°15'N	111°30'W
Enns, r., Aus. (ĕns)	161	47°37'N	14°35'E
Enoree, S.C., U.S. (ė-nō'rē)	125	34°43'N	81°58'W
Enoree, r., S.C., U.S.	125	34°35'N	81°55'W
Enriquillo, Dom. Rep. (ĕn-rē-kĕ'l-yō)	135	17°55'N	71°15'W
Enriquillo, Lago, l., Dom. Rep. (lä'gô-ĕn-rē-kĕ'l-yō)	135	18°35'N	71°35'W
Enschede, Neth. (ĕns'κä-dĕ)	161	52°10'N	6°50'E
Ensenada, Arg.	141c	34°50'S	57°55'W
Ensenada, Mex. (ĕn-sĕ-nä'dä)	128	32°00'N	116°30'W
Enshi, China (ŭn-shr)	204	30°18'N	109°25'E
Enshū-Nada, b., Japan (ĕn'shōō nä-dä)	211	34°25'N	137°14'E
Entebbe, Ug.	231	0°04'N	32°28'E
Enterprise, Al., U.S. (ĕn'tẽr-prīz)	124	31°20'N	85°50'W
Enterprise, Or., U.S.	114	45°25'N	117°16'W
Entiat, L, Wa., U.S.	114	45°43'N	120°11'W
Entraygues, Fr. (ĕɴ-trĕg')	170	44°39'N	2°33'E
Entre Rios, prov., Arg.	144	31°30'S	59°00'W
Enugu, Nig. (ĕ-nōō'gōō)	230	6°27'N	7°27'E
Enumclaw, Wa., U.S. (ĕn'ŭm-klô)	116a	47°12'N	121°59'W
Envigado, Col. (ĕn-vē-gá'dō)	142a	6°10'N	75°34'W
Eolie, Isole, is., Italy (ĕ'sō-lĕ-ĕ-ô'lyĕ)	162	38°43'N	14°43'E
Epe, Nig.	235	6°37'N	3°59'E
Épernay, Fr. (ā-pĕr-nĕ')	161	49°02'N	3°54'E
Épernon, Fr. (ā-pĕr-nôɴ')	171b	48°36'N	1°41'E
Ephraim, Ut., U.S. (ē'frā-ĭm)	119	39°20'N	111°40'W
Ephrata, Wa., U.S. (ēfrā'tȧ)	114	47°18'N	119°35'W
Epi, Vanuatu (ā'pē)	219	16°59'S	168°29'E
Épila, Spain (ā'pē-lä)	172	41°38'N	1°15'W
Épinal, Fr. (ā-pē-nàl')	161	48°11'N	6°27'E
Episkopi, Cyp.	197a	34°38'N	32°55'E
Epping, Eng., U.K. (ĕp'ĭng)	158b	51°41'N	0°06'E
Epsom, Eng., U.K.	158b	51°20'N	0°16'W
Epupa Falls, wtfl., Afr.	236	17°00'S	13°05'E
Epworth, Eng., U.K. (ĕp'wûrth)	158a	53°31'N	0°50'W
Equatorial Guinea, nation, Afr.	230	2°00'N	7°15'E
Équilles, Fr.	170a	43°34'N	5°21'E
Eramosa, r., Can. (ĕr-ȧ-mō'sȧ)	102d	43°39'N	80°08'W
Erba, Jabal, mtn., Sudan (ĕr-bȧ)	231	20°53'N	36°45'E
Erciyeş Daği, mtn., Tur.	163	38°30'N	35°36'E
Erding, Ger. (ĕr'dēng)	159d	48°19'N	11°54'E
Erechim, Braz. (ĕ-rĕ-shē'ɴ)	144	27°43'S	52°11'W
Ereğli, Tur. (ĕ-rā'ĭ-le)	163	37°40'N	34°00'E
Ereğli, Tur.	163	41°15'N	31°25'E
Erfurt, Ger. (ĕr'fŏort)	161	50°59'N	11°04'E
Ergene, r., Tur. (ĕr'gĕ-nĕ)	175	41°17'N	26°50'E
Erges, r., Eur. (ĕr'-zhĕs)	172	39°45'N	7°01'W
Ērgļi, Lat.	167	56°54'N	25°38'E
Eria, r., Spain (ā-rē'ä)	172	42°10'N	6°08'W
Erick, Ok., U.S. (âr'ĭk)	120	35°14'N	99°51'W
Erie, Ks., U.S. (ē'rĭ)	121	37°35'N	95°17'W
Erie, Pa., U.S.	105	42°05'N	80°05'W
Erie, Lake, l., N.A.	107	42°15'N	81°25'W
Erimo Saki, c., Japan (ā'rē-mō sä-kē)	205	41°53'N	143°20'E
Erin, Can. (ĕ'rĭn)	102d	43°46'N	80°04'W
Eritrea, nation, Afr. (ā-rē-trā'ȧ)	231	16°15'N	38°30'E
Erlangen, Ger. (ĕr'läng-ĕn)	168	49°36'N	11°03'E
Erlanger, Ky., U.S. (ẽr'lăng-ẽr)	111f	39°01'N	84°36'W
Ermoúpoli, Grc.	175	37°30'N	24°56'E
Ernākulam, India	199	9°58'N	76°23'E
Erne, Lower Lough, l., N. Ire., U.K.	164	54°30'N	7°40'W
Erne, Upper Lough, l., N. Ire., U.K. (lŏk ûrn)	164	54°20'N	7°24'W
Erode, India	203	11°20'N	77°45'E
Erromanga, i., Vanuatu	221	18°58'S	169°18'E
Eros, La., U.S. (ē'rōs)	123	32°23'N	92°22'W
Errego, Moz.	237	16°02'S	37°14'E
Errigal, mtn., Ire. (ĕr-ĭ-gôl')	164	55°02'N	8°07'W
Errol Heights, Or., U.S.	116c	45°29'N	122°38'W
Erstein, Fr. (ĕr'shtīn)	171	48°27'N	7°40'E
Erwin, N.C., U.S. (ûr'wĭn)	125	35°16'N	78°40'W
Erwin, Tn., U.S.	125	36°07'N	82°25'W
Erzgebirge, mts., Eur. (ĕrts'gĕ-bē'gĕ)	156	50°29'N	12°40'E
Erzincan, Tur. (ĕr-zĭn-jän')	198	39°50'N	39°30'E
Erzurum, Tur. (ĕrz'rōōm')	198	39°55'N	41°10'E
Esambo, D.R.C.	236	3°40'S	23°24'E
Esashi, Japan (ĕs'ä-shē)	205	41°50'N	140°10'E
Esbjerg, Den. (ĕs'byĕrgh)	160	55°29'N	8°25'E
Escalante, Ut., U.S. (ĕs-kȧ-lăn'tē)	119	37°50'N	111°40'W
Escalante, r., Ut., U.S.	119	37°40'N	111°20'W
Escalón, Mex.	122	26°45'N	104°20'W
Escambia, r., Fl., U.S. (ĕs-kăm'bĭ-ȧ)	124	30°38'N	87°20'W
Escanaba, Mi., U.S. (ĕs-kȧ-nô'bȧ)	105	45°44'N	87°05'W
Escanaba, r., Mi., U.S.	113	46°10'N	87°22'W
Escarpada Point, Phil.	212	18°40'N	122°45'E
Esch-sur-Alzette, Lux.	171	49°32'N	6°21'E
Eschwege, Ger. (ĕsh'vä-gĕ)	168	51°11'N	10°02'E
Eschweiler, Ger. (ĕsh'vī-lẽr)	171c	50°49'N	6°15'E
Escondido, Ca., U.S. (ĕs-kŏn-dē'dō)	118	33°07'N	117°00'W
Escondido, r., Nic.	133	12°04'N	84°09'W
Escondido, Río, r., Mex. (rē'ō-ĕs-kōn-dĕ'dô)	122	28°30'N	100°45'W
Escudo de Veraguas, i., Pan. (ĕs-kōō'dä dā vā-rä'gwäs)	133	9°07'N	81°25'W
Escuinapa, Mex. (ĕs-kwē-nä'pä)	128	22°49'N	105°44'W
Escuintla, Guat. (ĕs-kwēn'tlä)	132	14°16'N	90°47'W
Ese, Cayos de, i., Col.	133	12°24'N	81°07'W
Eşfahān, Iran	198	32°38'N	51°30'E
Esgueva, r., Spain (ĕs-gĕ'vä)	172	41°48'N	4°10'W
Esher, Eng., U.K.	158b	51°23'N	0°22'W
Eshowe, S. Afr. (ĕsh'ō-wê)	233c	28°54'S	31°28'E
Esiama, Ghana	234	4°56'N	2°21'W
Eskdale, W.V., U.S. (ĕsk'dāl)	108	38°05'N	81°25'W
Eskifjördur, Ice. (ĕs'kē-fyûr'dōōr)	154	65°04'N	14°01'W
Eskilstuna, Swe. (ā'shĕl-stü-na)	160	59°23'N	16°28'E
Eskimo Lakes, l., Can. (ĕs'kĭ-mō)	92	69°40'N	130°10'W
Eskişehir, Tur. (ĕs-kē-shĕ'h'r)	198	39°40'N	30°20'E
Esko, Mn., U.S. (ĕs'kō)	117h	46°27'N	92°22'W
Esla, r., Spain (ĕs-lä)	172	41°50'N	5°48'W
Eslöv, Swe. (ĕs'lûv)	166	55°50'N	13°17'E
Esmeraldas, Ec. (ĕs-mä-räl'däs)	142	0°58'N	79°45'W
Espanola, Can. (ĕs-pȧ-nō'lȧ)	91	46°11'N	81°59'W
Esparta, C.R. (ĕs-pär'tä)	133	9°59'N	84°40'W
Esperance, Austl. (ĕs'pē-răns)	218	33°45'S	122°07'E
Esperanza, Cuba (ĕs-pĕ-rä'n-zä)	134	22°30'N	80°10'W
Espichel, Cabo, c., Port. (kä'bō-ĕs-pē-shĕl')	172	38°25'N	9°13'W
Espinal, Col. (ĕs-pē-näl')	142	4°10'N	74°53'W
Espinhaço, Serra do, mts., Braz. (sĕ'r-rä-dô-ĕs-pē-nä-sô)	143	16°00'S	44°00'W
Espinillo, Punta, c., Ur. (pōō'n-tä-ĕs-pē-nē'l-yô)	141c	34°49'S	56°27'W
Espírito Santo, Braz. (ĕs-pē'rē-tô-sän'tô)	143	20°27'S	40°18'W
Espírito Santo, state, Braz.	143	19°57'S	40°58'W
Espiritu Santo, i., Vanuatu (ĕs-pē'rē-tōō sän'tō)	221	15°45'S	166°50'E
Espíritu Santo, Bahía del, b., Mex.	132a	19°25'N	87°28'W
Espita, Mex. (ĕs-pē'tä)	132a	20°57'N	88°22'W
Espoo, Fin.	167	60°13'N	24°41'E
Es Port de Pollença, Spain	173	39°50'N	3°00'E
Esposende, Port. (ĕs-pō-zĕn'dā)	172	41°33'N	8°45'W
Esquel, Arg. (ĕs-kĕ'l)	144	42°47'S	71°22'W
Esquimalt, Can. (ĕs-kwī'mŏlt)	94	48°26'N	123°24'W
Essaouira, Mor.	230	31°34'N	9°44'W
Essen, Bel.	159a	51°28'N	4°27'E
Essen, Ger. (ĕs'sĕn)	154	51°26'N	6°59'E
Essendon, Austl.	217a	37°46'S	144°55'E
Essequibo, r., Guy. (ĕs-ā-kē'bō)	143	4°26'N	58°17'W
Essex, Il., U.S.	111a	41°11'N	88°11'W
Essex, Ma., U.S.	101a	42°38'N	70°47'W
Essex, Md., U.S.	110e	39°19'N	76°29'W
Essex, Vt., U.S.	109	44°30'N	73°05'W
Essex Fells, N.J., U.S. (ĕs'ĕks fĕlz)	110a	40°50'N	74°16'W
Essexville, Mi., U.S. (ĕs'ĕks-vĭl)	108	43°35'N	83°50'W
Esslingen, Ger. (ĕs'slēn-gĕn)	168	48°45'N	9°19'E
Estacado, Llano, pl., U.S. (yä-nō ĕs-tȧcȧ-dō')	106	33°50'N	103°20'W
Estância, Braz. (ĕs-tän'sĭ-ä)	143	11°17'S	37°18'W
Estarreja, Port. (ĕ-tär-rä'zhä)	172	40°44'N	8°39'W

ng-sing; ŋ-baŋk; ɴ-nasalized n; nŏd; cŏmmit; ōld; ôbey; ôrder; oi-boil; fōōd; ȯ-as oo in foot; ou-out; s-soft; sh-dish; th-thin; pūre; ûnite; ûrn; stŭd; circŭs; ü-as in French tu; '-indeterminate vowel.

292 Estats – Felipe Carrillo Puerto

PRONOUNCING INDEX

PLACE (Pronunciation)	PAGE	LAT.	LONG.
Estats, Pique d', mtn., Eur.	173	42°43'N	1°30'E
Estcourt, S. Afr. (ĕst-coort)	233c	29°04'S	29°53'E
Este, Italy (ĕs'tā)	174	45°13'N	11°40'E
Estella, Spain (ĕs-tāl'yä)	172	42°40'N	2°01'W
Estepa, Spain (ĕs-tā'pä)	172	37°18'N	4°54'W
Estepona, Spain (ĕs-tå-pō'nä)	172	36°26'N	5°08'W
Esterhazy, Can. (ĕs'tēr-hā-zē)	97	50°40'N	102°08'W
Estero Bay, b., Ca., U.S. (ĕs-tā'rōs)	118	35°22'N	121°04'W
Estevan, Can. (ĕ-stē'văn)	90	49°07'N	103°05'W
Estevan Group, is., Can.	94	53°05'N	129°40'W
Estherville, Ia., U.S. (ĕs'tẽr-vĭl)	113	43°24'N	94°49'W
Estill, S.C., U.S. (ĕs'tĭl)	125	32°46'N	81°15'W
Eston, Can.	96	51°10'N	108°45'W
Estonia, nation, Eur.	179	59°10'N	[illegible]
Estoril, Port. (ĕs-tô-rēl')	173b	38°45'N	9°24'W
Estrêla, mtn., Port.			
(mäl-you'ɴ-dä-ĕs-trĕ'lä)	172	40°20'N	7°38'W
Estrêla, r., Braz. (ĕs-trĕ'lä)	[illegible]	[illegible]	[illegible]
Estrela, Serra da, mts., Port.			
(sĕr'rȧ dä ĕs-trā'lȧ)	172	40°25'N	7°45'W
Estremadura, hist. reg., Port.			
(ĕs-trā-mä-dōō'rȧ)	172	39°00'N	8°36'W
Estremoz, Port. (ĕs-trā-mōzh')	172	38°50'N	7°35'W
Estrondo, Serra do, mts., Braz.			
(sĕr'-rȧ dȯ ĕs-trôn'-dȯ)	143	9°52'S	48°56'W
Esumba, Île, i., D.R.C.	236	2°00'N	21°12'E
Esztergom, Hung. (ĕs'tẽr-gōm)	169	47°46'N	18°45'E
Etah, Grnld. (ē'tȧ)	89	78°20'N	72°42'W
Étampes, Fr. (ā-täɴp')	170	48°26'N	2°09'E
Étaples, Fr. (ā-täp'l')	170	50°32'N	1°38'E
Etchemin, r., Can. (ĕch'ĕ-mĭn)	102b	46°39'N	71°03'W
Ethiopia, nation, Afr. (ē-thē-ō'pē-ȧ)	231	7°53'N	37°55'E
Eticoga, Gui.-B.	234	11°09'N	16°08'W
Etiwanda, Ca., U.S. (ĕ-tĭ-wän'dȧ)	117a	34°07'N	117°31'W
Etna, Pa., U.S. (ĕt'nȧ)	111e	40°30'N	79°55'W
Etna, Mount, vol., Italy	156	37°48'N	15°00'E
Etobicoke Creek, r., Can.	102d	43°44'N	79°48'W
Etolin Strait, strt., Ak., U.S. (ĕt ō lĭn)	103	60°35'S	165°40'W
Etoshapan, pl., Nmb. (ĕtō'shä)	232	19°07'S	15°30'E
Etowah, Tn., U.S. (ĕt'ō-wä)	124	35°18'N	84°31'W
Etowah, r., Ga., U.S.	124	34°23'N	84°19'W
Étréchy, Fr. (ā-trā-shē')	171b	48°29'N	2°12'E
Etten-Leur, Neth.	159a	51°34'N	4°38'E
Etterbeek, Bel. (ĕt'ẽr-bāk)	159a	50°51'N	4°24'E
Etzatlán, Mex. (ĕt-zä-tlän')	130	20°44'N	104°04'W
Eucla, Austl. (ū'klȧ)	218	31°45'S	128°50'E
Euclid, Oh., U.S. (ū'klĭd)	111d	41°34'N	81°32'W
Eudora, Ar., U.S. (u-dō'rȧ)	121	33°07'N	91°16'W
Eufaula, Al., U.S. (ů-fô'lȧ)	124	31°53'N	85°09'W
Eufaula, Ok., U.S.	121	35°16'N	95°35'W
Eufaula Reservoir, res., Ok., U.S.	121	35°00'N	94°45'W
Eugene, Or., U.S. (ů-jēn')	104	44°02'N	123°06'W
Euless, Tx., U.S. (ū'lĕs)	117c	32°50'N	97°05'W
Eunice, La., U.S. (ū'nĭs)	123	30°30'N	92°25'W
Eupen, Bel. (oi'pĕn)	165	50°39'N	6°05'E
Euphrates, r., Asia (ů-frā'tēz)	198	36°00'N	40°00'E
Eure, r., Fr. (ûr)	170	49°03'N	1°22'E
Eureka, Ca., U.S. (ů-rē'kȧ)	104	40°45'N	124°10'W
Eureka, Ks., U.S.	121	37°48'N	96°17'W
Eureka, Mt., U.S.	114	48°53'N	115°07'W
Eureka, Nv., U.S.	118	39°33'N	115°58'W
Eureka, S.D., U.S.	112	45°46'N	99°38'W
Eureka, Ut., U.S.	119	39°55'N	112°10'W
Eureka Springs, Ar., U.S.	121	36°24'N	93°43'W
Europe, cont. (ū'rŭp)	156	50°00'N	15°00'E
Eustis, Fl., U.S. (ūs'tĭs)	125	28°50'N	81°41'W
Eutaw, Al., U.S. (ū-tå)	124	32°48'N	87°50'W
Eutsuk Lake, l., Can. (ōōt'sŭk)	94	53°20'N	126°44'W
Evanston, Il., U.S. (ĕv'ăn-stŭn)	105	42°03'N	87°41'W
Evanston, Wy., U.S.	115	41°17'N	111°02'W
Evansville, In., U.S. (ĕv'ănz-vĭl)	105	38°00'N	87°30'W
Evansville, Wi., U.S.	113	42°46'N	89°19'W
Evart, Mi., U.S. (ĕv'ẽrt)	108	43°55'N	85°10'W
Evaton, S. Afr. (ĕv'ȧ-tŏn)	238c	26°32'S	27°53'E
Eveleth, Mn., U.S. (ĕv'ē-lĕth)	113	47°27'N	92°35'W
Everard, l., Austl. (ĕv'ẽr-ȧrd)	220	31°20'S	134°10'E
Everard Ranges, mts., Austl.	220	27°15'S	132°00'E
Everest, Mount, mtn., Asia (ĕv'ẽr-ĕst)	199	28°00'N	86°57'E
Everett, Ma., U.S. (ĕv'ẽr-ĕt)	101a	42°24'N	71°03'W
Everett, Wa., U.S. (ĕv'ẽr-ĕt)	104	47°59'N	122°11'W
Everett Mountains, mts., Can.	93	62°34'N	68°00'W
Everglades, The, sw., Fl., U.S.	125a	25°35'N	80°55'W
Everglades City, Fl., U.S. (ĕv'ẽr-glādz)	125a	25°50'N	81°25'W
Everglades National Park, rec.,			
Fl., U.S.	107	25°39'N	80°57'W
Evergreen, Al., U.S. (ĕv'ẽr-grēn)	124	31°25'N	87°56'W
Evergreen Park, Il., U.S.	111a	41°44'N	87°42'W
Everman, Tx., U.S. (ĕv'ẽr-măn)	117c	32°38'N	97°17'W
Everson, Wa., U.S. (ĕv'ẽr-sŭn)	116d	48°55'N	122°21'W
Évora, Port. (ĕv'ō-rä)	162	38°35'N	7°54'W
Évreux, Fr. (ā-vrû')	161	49°02'N	1°11'E
Evrótas, r., Grc. (ĕv-rō'täs)	175	37°15'N	22°17'E
Évvoia, i., Grc.	163	38°38'N	23°45'E
'Ewa Beach, Hi., U.S. (ē'wä)	126a	21°17'N	158°03'W
Ewaso Ng'iro, r., Kenya	231	0°59'N	37°47'E
Excelsior, Mn., U.S. (ĕk-sel'sĭ-ŏr)	117g	44°54'N	93°35'W
Excelsior Springs, Mo., U.S.	121	39°20'N	94°13'W
Exe, r., Eng., U.K. (ĕks)	164	50°57'N	3°37'W
Exeter, Eng., U.K.	161	50°45'N	3°33'W
Exeter, Ca., U.S. (ĕk'sē-tẽr)	118	36°18'N	119°09'W
Exeter, N.H., U.S.	109	43°00'N	71°00'W
Exmoor, for., Eng., U.K. (ĕks'mȯr)	164	51°10'N	3°55'W
Exmouth, Eng., U.K. (ĕks'mŭth)	164	50°40'N	3°20'W
Exmouth Gulf, b., Austl.	220	21°45'S	114°30'E
Exploits, r., Can. (ĕks-ploits')	101	48°50'N	56°15'W
Extórrax, r., Mex. (ĕx-tó'ràx)	130	21°04'N	99°39'W
Extrema, Braz. (ĕsh-trĕ'mä)	141a	22°52'S	46°19'W
Extremadura, hist. reg., Spain			
(ĕks-trā-mä-doo'rä)	172	38°43'N	6°30'W
Exuma Sound, strt., Bah. (ĕk-sōō'mä)	134	24°20'N	76°20'W
Eyasi, Lake, l., Tan. (å-yä'sẻ)	232	3°25'S	34°55'E
Eyjafjördur, b., Ice.	160	66°21'N	18°20'W
Eyl, Som.	238a	7°53'N	49°45'E
Eyrarbakki, Ice.	160	63°51'N	20°52'W
Eyre, Austl. (âr)	218	32°15'S	126°20'E
Eyre, l., Austl.	220	28°43'S	137°50'E
Eyre Peninsula, pen., Austl.	220	33°30'S	136°00'E
Ezeiza, Arg. (ĕ-zā'zä)	144a	34°52'S	58°31'W
Ezine, Tur. (ā'zĭ-nā)	175	39°47'N	26°18'E

F

PLACE (Pronunciation)	PAGE	LAT.	LONG.
Faaborg, Den. (fô'bȯrg)	166	55°06'N	10°19'E
Fabens, Tx., U.S. (fā'bĕnz)	122	31°30'N	106°07'W
Fabriano, Italy (fä-brē-ä'nȯ)	174	43°20'N	12°55'E
Fada, Chad (fä'dä)	231	17°06'N	21°18'E
Fada Ngourma, Burkina			
(fä'dä''n gōōr'mä)	230	12°04'N	0°21'E
Faddeya, i., Russia (fȧd-yä')	179	76°12'N	145°00'E
Faenza, Italy (fä-ĕnd'zä)	174	44°16'N	11°53'E
Fafe, Port. (fä'fā)	172	41°30'N	8°10'W
Fafen, r., Eth.	238a	8°15'N	42°40'E
Făgăras, Rom. (fȧ-gä'rāsh)	175	45°50'N	24°55'E
Fagerness, Nor. (fä'ghēr-nĕs)	160	61°00'N	9°10'E
Fagnano, l., S.A. (fäk-nä'nȯ)	144	54°35'S	68°20'W
Faguibine, Lac, l., Mali	234	16°50'N	4°20'W
Faial, i., Port. (fä-yä'l)	230a	38°40'N	29°19'W
Fā'id, Egypt (fä-yēd')	238d	30°19'N	32°18'E
Fairbanks, Ak., U.S. (fâr'bănks)	106a	64°50'N	147°48'W
Fairbury, Il., U.S. (fâr'bĕr-ĭ)	108	40°45'N	88°25'W
Fairbury, Ne., U.S.	121	40°09'N	97°11'W
Fairchild Creek, r., Can. (fâr'chīld)	102d	43°18'N	80°10'W
Fairfax, Mn., U.S. (fâr'făks)	113	44°29'N	94°44'W
Fairfax, S.C., U.S.	125	32°29'N	81°13'W
Fairfax, Va., U.S.	110e	38°51'N	77°20'W
Fairfield, Austl.	217b	33°52'S	150°57'E
Fairfield, Al., U.S. (fâr'fēld)	110h	33°30'N	86°50'W
Fairfield, Ct., U.S.	110a	41°08'N	73°22'W
Fairfield, Ia., U.S.	113	41°00'N	91°59'W
Fairfield, Il., U.S.	108	38°25'N	88°20'W
Fairfield, Me., U.S.	100	44°35'N	69°38'W
Fairhaven, Ma., U.S. (fâr-hā'vĕn)	109	41°35'N	70°55'W
Fair Haven, Vt., U.S.	109	43°35'N	73°15'W
Fair Island, i., Scot., U.K. (fâr)	164a	59°34'N	1°41'W
Fairmont, Mn., U.S. (fâr'mŏnt)	113	43°39'N	94°26'W
Fairmont, W.V., U.S.	108	39°30'N	80°10'W
Fairmont City, Il., U.S.	117e	38°39'N	90°05'W
Fairmount, In., U.S.	108	40°25'N	85°45'W
Fairmount, Ks., U.S.	117f	39°12'N	95°55'W
Fair Oaks, Ga., U.S. (fâr ōks)	110c	33°56'N	84°33'W
Fairport, N.Y., U.S. (fâr'pōrt)	109	43°05'N	77°30'W
Fairport Harbor, Oh., U.S.	108	41°45'N	81°15'W
Fairview, Ok., U.S. (fâr'vū)	120	36°16'N	98°28'W
Fairview, Or., U.S.	116c	45°32'N	112°26'W
Fairview, Ut., U.S.	119	39°35'N	111°30'W
Fairview Park, Oh., U.S.	111d	41°27'N	81°52'W
Fairweather, Mount, mtn., N.A.			
(fâr-wĕdh'ẽr)	103	59°12'N	137°22'W
Faisalabad, Pak.	199	31°29'N	73°06'E
Faith, S.D., U.S. (fāth)	112	45°02'N	120°02'W
Faizābād, India	199	26°50'N	82°17'E
Fajardo, P.R.	129b	18°20'N	65°40'W
Fakfak, Indon.	213	2°56'S	132°25'E
Faku, China (fä-kōō)	208	42°28'N	123°20'E
Falcón, dept., Ven. (fäl-kô'n)	143b	11°00'N	68°28'W
Falconer, N.Y., U.S. (fô'k'n-ẽr)	109	42°10'N	79°10'W
Falcon Heights, Mn., U.S. (fô'k'n)	117g	44°59'N	93°10'W
Falcon Reservoir, res., N.A. (fôk'n)	122	26°47'N	99°03'W
Fălești, Mol.	177	47°33'N	27°46'E
Falfurrias, Tx., U.S. (fäl'fōō-rē'ȧs)	122	27°15'N	98°08'W
Falher, Can. (făl'ẽr)	95	55°44'N	117°12'W
Falkenberg, Swe. (fäl'kĕn-bĕrgh)	166	56°54'N	12°25'E
Falkensee, Ger. (fäl'kĕn-zā)	159b	52°34'N	13°05'E
Falkenthal, Ger. (fäl'kĕn-täl)	159b	52°54'N	13°18'E
Falkirk, Scot., U.K. (fôl'kûrk)	164	55°59'N	3°55'W
Falkland Islands, dep., S.A. (fôk'lănd)	144	50°45'S	61°00'W
Falköping, Swe. (fäl'chûp-ĭng)	166	58°09'N	13°30'E
Fall City, Wa., U.S.	116a	47°34'N	121°53'W
Fall Creek, r., In., U.S. (fôl)	111g	39°52'N	86°04'W
Fallon, Nv., U.S. (făl'ŭn)	118	39°30'N	118°48'W
Fall River, Ma., U.S.	105	41°42'N	71°07'W
Falls Church, Va., U.S. (fălz chûrch)	110e	38°53'N	77°10'W
Falls City, Ne., U.S.	121	40°04'N	95°37'W
Fallston, Md., U.S. (făls'ton)	110e	39°32'N	76°26'W
Falmouth, Jam.	134	18°30'N	77°40'W
Falmouth, Eng., U.K. (făl'mŭth)	164	50°08'N	5°04'W
Falmouth, Ky., U.S.	108	38°40'N	84°20'W
False Divi Point, c., India	203	15°45'N	80°50'E
Falster, i., Den. (fäls'tẽr)	166	54°48'N	11°58'E
Fălticeni, Rom. (fŭl-tē-chān'y')	169	47°27'N	26°17'E
Falun, Swe. (fä-lōōn')	160	60°38'N	15°35'E
Famagusta, Cyp. (fä-mä-gōōs'tä)	163	35°08'N	33°59'E
Famatina, Sierra de, mts., Arg.	144	29°00'S	67°50'W
Fangxian, China (fäŋ-shyĕn)	208	32°05'N	110°45'E
Fanning, i., Can.	102f	49°45'N	97°46'W
Fano, Italy (fä'nō)	174	43°49'N	13°01'E
Fanø, i., Den. (fän'û)	166	55°24'N	8°10'E
Fan Si Pan, mtn., Viet.	209	22°25'N	103°50'E
Farafangana, Madag.			
(fä-rä-fäŋ-gä'nä)	233	23°18'S	47°59'E
Farāh, Afg. (fä-rä')	198	32°15'N	62°13'E
Farallón, Punta, c., Mex.			
(pȯ'n-tä-fä-rä-lōn)	130	19°21'N	105°03'W
Faranah, Gui. (fä-rä'nä)	230	10°02'N	10°44'W
Farasān, Jaza'ir, is., Sau. Ar.	198	16°45'N	41°08'E
Faregh, Wadi al, r., Libya			
(wädẻ ĕl fä-rĕg')	163	30°10'N	19°34'E
Farewell, Cape, c., N.Z. (fâr-wĕl')	221a	40°37'S	172°40'E
Fargo, N.D., U.S. (fär'gō)	104	46°53'N	96°48'W
Far Hills, N.J., U.S. (fär hĭlz)	110a	40°41'N	74°38'W
Faribault, Mn., U.S. (fâ'rĭ-bō)	113	44°19'N	93°10'W
[illegible]	172	39°28'N	9°32'W
Faringdon, Eng., U.K. (fă'rĭng-dŏn)	158b	51°38'N	1°35'W
Fāriskūr, Egypt (fä-rẻs-kōōr')	238b	31°19'N	31°46'E
Farit, Amba, mtn., Eth.	231	10°51'N	37°52'E
Farley, Mo., U.S. (făr'lē)	117f	39°16'N	94°49'W
Farmers Branch, Tx., U.S.	117c	32°56'N	96°53'W
Farmersburg, In., U.S. (fär'mẽrz-bûrg)	108	39°15'N	87°25'W
Farmersville, Tx., U.S. (fär'mẽrz-vĭl)	121	33°11'N	96°22'W
Farmingdale, N.J., U.S.			
(färm'ĕng-dāl)	110a	40°11'N	74°10'W
Farmingdale, N.Y., U.S.	110a	40°44'N	73°26'W
Farmingham, Ma., U.S.			
(färm-ĭng-hăm)	101a	42°17'N	71°25'W
Farmington, Il., U.S. (färm-ĭng-tŭn)	121	40°42'N	90°01'W
Farmington, Me., U.S.	100	44°40'N	70°10'W
Farmington, Mi., U.S.	111b	42°28'N	83°23'W
Farmington, Mo., U.S.	121	37°46'N	90°26'W
Farmington, N.M., U.S.	119	36°40'N	108°10'W
Farmington, Ut., U.S.	117b	40°59'N	111°53'W
Farmville, N.C., U.S. (färm-vĭl)	125	35°35'N	77°35'W
Farmville, Va., U.S.	125	37°15'N	78°23'W
Farnborough, Eng., U.K. (färn'bŭr-ô)	158b	51°15'N	0°45'W
Farne Islands, is., Eng., U.K. (färn)	164	55°40'N	1°32'W
Farnham, Can. (fär'năm)	109	45°15'N	72°55'W
Farningham, Eng., U.K. (fär'nĭng-ŭm)	158b	51°22'N	0°14'E
Farnworth, Eng., U.K. (färn'wŭrth)	158a	53°34'N	2°24'W
Faro, Braz. (fä'rō)	143	2°05'S	56°32'W
Faro, Port.	162	37°01'N	7°57'W
Farodofay, Madag.	233	24°59'S	46°58'E
Faroe Islands, is., Eur.	156	62°00'N	5°45'W
Fårön, i., Swe.	167	57°57'N	19°10'E
Farquhar, Cape, c., Austl. (fär'kwȧr)	220	23°50'S	112°55'E
Farrell, Pa., U.S. (făr'ĕl)	108	41°10'N	80°30'W
Farrukhābād, India (fŭ-rȯk-hä-bäd')	199	27°29'N	79°35'E
Fársala, Grc.	175	39°18'N	22°25'E
Farsund, Nor. (fär'sȯn)	166	58°05'N	6°47'E
Fartak, Ra's, c., Yemen	198	15°43'N	52°17'E
Fartura, Serra da, mts., Braz.			
(sĕ'r-rä-dȧ-fär-tōō'rä)	144	26°40'S	53°15'W
Farvel, Kap, c., Grnld.	89	60°00'N	44°00'W
Farwell, Tx., U.S. (fär'wĕl)	120	34°24'N	103°03'W
Fasano, Italy (fä-zä'nō)	175	40°50'N	17°22'E
Fastiv, Ukr.	177	50°04'N	29°57'E
Fatëzh, Russia	176	52°06'N	35°51'E
Fatima, Port.	173	39°36'N	9°36'E
Fatsa, Tur. (fät'sä)	163	40°50'N	37°30'E
Faucilles, Monts, mts., Fr.			
(môn' fō-sēl')	171	48°07'N	6°13'E
Fauske, Nor.	160	67°15'N	15°24'E
Faust, Can. (foust)	95	55°19'N	115°38'W
Faustovo, Russia	186b	55°27'N	38°29'E
Faversham, Eng., U.K. (fă'vẽr-sh'm)	158b	51°19'N	0°54'E
Faxaflói, b., Ice.	160	64°33'N	22°40'W
Fayette, Al., U.S. (fā-yĕt')	124	33°40'N	87°54'W
Fayette, Ia., U.S.	113	42°49'N	91°49'W
Fayette, Mo., U.S.	121	39°09'N	92°41'W
Fayette, Ms., U.S.	124	31°43'N	91°00'W
Fayetteville, Ar., U.S. (fā-yĕt'vĭl)	121	36°03'N	94°08'W
Fayetteville, N.C., U.S.	125	35°02'N	78°54'W
Fayetteville, Tn., U.S.	124	35°10'N	86°33'W
Fazao, Forêt Classée du, for., Togo	234	8°50'N	0°40'E
Fazilka, India	202	30°30'N	74°02'E
Fazzān (Fezzan), hist. reg., Libya	231	26°45'N	13°01'E
Fdérik, Maur.	230	22°45'N	12°38'W
Fear, Cape, c., N.C., U.S. (fēr)	125	33°52'N	77°48'W
Feather, r., Ca., U.S. (fĕth'ẽr)	118	38°56'N	121°41'W
Feather, Middle Fork of, r.,			
Ca., U.S.	118	39°49'N	121°10'W
Feather, North Fork of, r.,			
Ca., U.S.	118	40°00'N	121°20'W
Featherstone, Eng., U.K.			
(fĕdh'ẽr stŭn)	158a	53°39'N	1°21'W
Fécamp, Fr. (fā-käɴ')	161	49°45'N	0°20'E
Federal, Distrito, dept., Ven.			
(dės-trē'tô-fĕ-dĕ-rä'l)	143b	10°34'N	66°55'W
Federal Way, Wa., U.S.	116a	47°20'N	122°20'W
Fëdorovka, Russia (fyô'dô-rôf-kȧ)	186b	56°15'N	37°14'E
Fehmarn, i., Ger. (fā'märn)	168	54°28'N	11°15'E
Fehrbellin, Ger. (fĕr'bĕl-lēn)	159b	52°49'N	12°46'E
Feia, Logoa, l., Braz. (lô-gôä-fĕ'yä)	141a	21°54'S	41°15'W
Feicheng, China (fā-chŭŋ)	206	36°18'N	116°45'E
Feidong, China (fā-dôŋ)	206	31°53'N	117°28'E
Feira de Santana, Braz.			
(fĕ'ē-rä dä sänt-än'ä)	143	12°16'S	38°46'W
Feixian, China (fā-shyĕn)	206	35°17'N	117°59'E
Felanitx, Spain (fā-lä-nēch')	162	39°29'N	3°09'E
Feldkirch, Aus. (fĕlt'kĭrk)	168	47°15'N	9°36'E
Feldkirchen, Ger. (fĕld'kĕr-kĕn)	159d	48°09'N	11°44'E
Felipe Carrillo Puerto, Mex.	132a	19°36'N	88°04'W

ăt; finăl; rāte; senåte; ärm; åsk; sofȧ; fâre; ch-choose; dh-as th in other; bē; ėvent; bĕt; recĕnt; cratẽr; g-gō; gh-guttural g; bĭt; ĭ-short neutral; rīde; ᴋ-guttural k as ch in German ich;

PRONOUNCING INDEX Feltre – Fort Bellefontaine 293

PLACE (Pronunciation)	PAGE	LAT.	LONG.
Feltre, Italy (fĕl'trā)	174	46°02'N	11°56'E
Femunden, l., Nor.	160	62°17'N	11°40'E
Fengcheng, China (fŭŋ-chŭŋ)	208	40°28'N	124°03'E
Fengcheng, China	207b	30°55'N	121°38'E
Fengdu, China (fŭŋ-dōō)	204	29°58'N	107°50'E
Fengjie, China (fŭŋ-jyĕ)	204	31°02'N	109°30'E
Fengming Dao, i., China (fŭŋ-mĭŋ dou)	206	39°19'N	121°15'E
Fengrun, China (fŭŋ-rôn)	206	39°51'N	118°06'E
Fengtai, China (fŭŋ-tī)	208a	39°51'N	116°19'E
Fengxian, China (fŭŋ-shyĕn)	207b	30°55'N	121°26'E
Fengxian, China	206	34°41'N	116°36'E
Fengxiang, China (fŭŋ-shyäŋ)	204	34°25'N	107°20'E
Fengyang, China (fŭng'yäng')	208	32°55'N	117°32'E
Fengzhen, China (fŭŋ-jŭn)	205	40°28'N	113°20'E
Fennimore Pass, strt., Ak., U.S. (fĕn-ĭ-mōr)	103a	51°40'N	175°38'W
Fenoarivo Atsinanana, Madag.	233	17°30'S	49°31'E
Fenton, Mi., U.S. (fĕn-tŭn)	108	42°50'N	83°40'W
Fenton, Mo., U.S.	117e	38°31'N	90°27'W
Fenyang, China	205	37°20'N	111°48'E
Feodosiia, Ukr.	181	45°02'N	35°21'E
Ferdows, Iran	198	34°00'N	58°13'E
Ferentino, Italy (fā-rĕn-tē'nō)	174	41°42'N	13°18'E
Fergana, Uzb.	183	40°23'N	71°46'E
Fergus Falls, Mn., U.S. (fûr'gŭs)	104	46°17'N	96°03'W
Ferguson, Mo., U.S. (fûr-gŭ-sŭn)	117e	38°45'N	90°18'W
Ferkéssédougou, C. Iv.	234	9°36'N	5°12'W
Fermo, Italy (fĕr'mō)	174	43°10'N	13°43'E
Fermoselle, Spain (fĕr-mō-säl'yå)	172	41°20'N	6°23'W
Fermoy, Ire. (fûr-moi')	164	52°05'N	8°06'W
Fernandina Beach, Fl., U.S. (fûr-năn-dē'nȧ)	125	30°38'N	81°29'W
Fernando de Noronha, Arquipélago, is., Braz.	143	3°51'S	32°25'W
Fernando Póo *see* Bioko, i., Eq. Gui.	230	3°35'N	7°45'E
Fernán-Núñez, Spain (fĕr-nän'nōōn'yåth)	172	37°42'N	4°43'W
Fernão Veloso, Baia de, b., Moz.	237	14°20'S	40°55'E
Ferndale, Ca., U.S. (fûrn'dāl)	114	40°34'N	124°18'W
Ferndale, Mi., U.S.	111b	42°27'N	83°08'W
Ferndale, Wa., U.S.	116d	48°51'N	122°36'W
Fernie, Can. (fûr'nĭ)	90	49°30'N	115°03'W
Fern Prairie, Wa., U.S. (fûrn prâr'ĭ)	116c	45°38'N	122°25'W
Ferrara, Italy (fĕr-rä'rä)	162	44°50'N	11°37'E
Ferrat, Cap, c., Alg. (kăp fĕr-rät)	173	35°49'N	0°29'W
Ferreira do Alentejo, Port.	172	38°03'N	8°06'W
Ferreira do Zezere, Port. (fĕr-rĕ'ê-rä dò zå-zā'rĕ)	172	39°49'N	8°17'W
Ferrelview, Mo., U.S. (fĕr'rĕl-vū)	117f	39°18'N	94°40'W
Ferreñafe, Peru (fĕr-rĕn-yä'fĕ)	142	6°38'S	79°48'W
Ferriday, La., U.S. (fĕr'ĭ-dā)	123	31°38'N	91°33'W
Ferrol, Spain	154	43°30'N	8°12'W
Fershampenuaz, Russia (fĕr-shäm'pĕn-wäz)	186a	53°32'N	59°50'E
Fertile, Mn., U.S. (fur'tĭl)	112	47°33'N	96°18'W
Fès, Mor. (fĕs)	230	34°08'N	5°00'W
Fessenden, N.D., U.S. (fĕs'ĕn-dĕn)	112	47°39'N	99°40'W
Festus, Mo., U.S. (fĕst'ŭs)	121	38°12'N	90°22'W
Fethiye, Tur. (fĕt-hē'yĕ)	163	36°40'N	29°05'E
Feuilles, Rivière aux, r., Can.	93	58°30'N	70°50'W
Ffestiniog, Wales, U.K.	164	52°59'N	3°58'W
Fianarantsoa, Madag. (fyȧ-nä'rȧn-tsō'ȧ)	233	21°21'S	47°15'E
Ficksburg, S. Afr. (fĭks'bûrg)	238c	28°53'S	27°53'E
Fidalgo Island, i., Wa., U.S. (fĭ-dăl'gō)	116a	48°28'N	122°39'W
Fieldbrook, Ca., U.S. (fēld'brŏk)	114	40°59'N	124°02'W
Fier, Alb. (fyĕr)	175	40°43'N	19°34'E
Fife Ness, c., Scot., U.K. (fīf'nes')	164	56°15'N	2°19'W
Fifth Cataract, wtfl., Sudan	231	18°27'N	33°38'E
Figeac, Fr. (fē-zhåk')	170	44°37'N	2°02'E
Figeholm, Swe. (fē-ghĕ-hōlm)	166	57°24'N	16°33'E
Figueira da Foz, Port. (fē-gwĕy-rä-dȧ-fō'z)	172	40°10'N	8°50'W
Figuig, Mor.	230	32°20'N	1°30'W
Fiji, nation, Oc. (fē'jē)	3	18°40'S	175°00'E
Filadelfia, C.R. (fīl-ȧ-dĕl'fĭ-ȧ)	132	10°26'N	85°37'W
Filatovskoye, Russia (fĭ-lä'tôf-skô-yĕ)	186a	56°49'N	62°20'E
Filchner Ice Shelf, ice, Ant. (fĭlk'nĕr)	224	80°00'S	35°00'W
Filicudi, i., Italy (fē'le-kōō'dē)	174	38°34'N	14°39'E
Filippovskoye, Russia (fĭ-lĭ-pôf'skô-yĕ)	186b	56°06'N	38°38'E
Filipstad, Swe. (fĭl'ĭps-städh)	166	59°44'N	14°09'E
Fillmore, Ut., U.S. (fĭl'môr)	119	39°00'N	112°20'W
Filsa, Nor.	166	60°35'N	12°03'E
Fimi, r., D.R.C.	232	2°43'S	17°50'E
Finch, Can. (fĭnch)	102c	45°09'N	75°06'W
Findlay, Oh., U.S. (fĭnd'lå)	108	41°05'N	83°40'W
Fingoe, Moz.	237	15°12'S	31°50'E
Finke, r., Austl. (fĭŋ'kē)	220	25°25'S	134°30'E
Finland, nation, Eur. (fĭn'lănd)	154	62°45'N	26°13'E
Finland, Gulf of, b., Eur. (fĭn'lănd)	156	59°35'N	23°35'E
Finlandia, Col. (fēn-lä'n-dêä)	142a	4°38'N	75°39'W
Finlay, r., Can. (fĭn'lå)	92	57°45'N	125°30'W
Finow, Ger. (fē'nōv)	159b	52°50'N	13°44'E
Finowfurt, Ger. (fē'nō-fōōrt)	159b	52°50'N	13°41'E
Fircrest, Wa., U.S. (fûr'krĕst)	116a	47°14'N	122°31'W
Firenze *see* Florence, Italy	154	43°47'N	11°15'E
Firenzuola, Italy (fē-rĕnt-swô'lä)	174	44°08'N	11°21'E
Firozpur, India	199	30°58'N	74°39'E
Fischa, r., Aus.	159e	48°04'N	16°33'E
Fischamend Markt, Aus.	159e	48°07'N	16°37'E
Fish, r., Nmb. (fĭsh)	232	28°00'S	17°30'E
Fish Cay, i., Bah.	135	22°30'N	74°20'W
Fish Creek, r., Can. (fĭsh)	102e	50°52'N	114°21'W
Fisher, La., U.S. (fĭsh'ẽr)	123	31°28'N	93°30'W
Fisher Bay, b., Can.	97	51°30'N	97°16'W
Fisher Channel, strt., Can.	94	52°10'N	127°42'W
Fisher Strait, strt., Can.	93	62°43'N	84°28'W
Fisterra, Cabo de, c., Spain	156	42°52'N	9°48'W
Fitchburg, Ma., U.S. (fĭch'bûrg)	109	42°35'N	71°48'W
Fitri, Lac, l., Chad	235	12°50'N	17°28'E
Fitzgerald, Ga., U.S. (fĭts-jĕr'ăld)	124	31°42'N	83°17'W
Fitz Hugh Sound, strt., Can. (fĭts hū)	94	51°40'N	127°57'W
Fitzroy, r., Austl. (fĭts-roi')	220	18°00'S	124°05'E
Fitzroy, r., Austl.	221	23°45'S	150°02'E
Fitzroy, Monte (Cerro Chaltel), mtn., S.A.	144	48°10'S	73°18'W
Fitzroy Crossing, Austl.	218	18°08'S	126°00'E
Fitzwilliam, i., Can. (fĭts-wĭl'yŭm)	98	45°30'N	81°45'W
Fiume *see* Rijeka, Cro.	162	45°22'N	14°24'E
Fiumicino, Italy (fyōō-mē-chē'nō)	173d	41°47'N	12°19'E
Fjällbacka, Swe. (fyĕl'bäk-ȧ)	166	58°37'N	11°17'E
Flagstaff, S. Afr. (flăg'stäf)	233c	31°06'S	29°31'E
Flagstaff, Az., U.S. (flăg-ståf)	104	35°15'N	111°40'W
Flagstaff, l., Me., U.S. (flăg-ståf)	109	45°05'N	70°30'W
Flåm, Nor. (flôm)	166	60°50'N	7°00'E
Flambeau, r., Wi., U.S. (flăm-bō')	113	45°32'N	91°05'W
Flaming Gorge Reservoir, res., U.S.	106	41°13'N	109°30'W
Flamingo, Fl., U.S. (flȧ-mĭŋ'gō)	125	25°10'N	80°55'W
Flamingo Cay, i., Bah. (flȧ-mĭŋ'gō)	135	22°50'N	75°50'W
Flamingo Point, c., V.I.U.S.	129c	18°19'N	65°00'W
Flanders, hist. reg., Fr. (flăn'dẽrz)	165	50°53'N	2°29'E
Flandreau, S.D., U.S. (flăn'drō)	112	44°02'N	96°35'W
Flathead, r., N.A.	95	49°30'N	114°30'W
Flathead, Middle Fork, r., Mt., U.S.	115	48°30'N	113°47'W
Flathead, North Fork, r., N.A.	115	48°45'N	114°20'W
Flathead, South Fork, r., Mt., U.S.	115	48°05'N	113°45'W
Flathead Indian Reservation, I.R., Mt., U.S.	115	47°30'N	114°25'W
Flathead Lake, l., Mt., U.S. (flăt'hĕd)	106	47°57'N	114°20'W
Flatow, Ger.	159b	52°44'N	12°58'E
Flat Rock, Mi., U.S. (flăt rŏk)	111b	42°06'N	83°17'W
Flattery, Cape, c., Wa., U.S. (flăt'ẽr-ĭ)	114	48°22'N	124°45'W
Flatwillow Creek, r., Mt., U.S. (flat wĭl'ō)	115	46°45'N	108°47'W
Flekkefjord, Nor. (fläk'kĕ-fyôr)	166	58°19'N	6°38'E
Flemingsburg, Ky., U.S. (flĕm'ĭngz-bûrg)	108	38°25'N	83°45'W
Flensburg, Ger. (flĕns'bòrgh)	160	54°48'N	9°27'E
Flers, Fr. (flĕr)	161	48°43'N	0°37'W
Fletcher, N.C., U.S.	125	35°26'N	82°30'W
Flinders, i., Austl.	221	39°35'S	148°10'E
Flinders, r., Austl.	221	18°48'S	141°07'E
Flinders, reg., Austl. (flĭn'dẽrz)	220	32°15'S	138°45'E
Flinders Reefs, rf., Austl.	221	17°30'S	149°02'E
Flin Flon, Can. (flĭn flŏn)	90	54°46'N	101°53'W
Flint, Wales, U.K.	158a	53°15'N	3°07'W
Flint, Mi., U.S.	105	43°00'N	83°45'W
Flint, r., Ga., U.S. (flĭnt)	107	31°25'N	84°15'W
Flintshire, co., Wales, U.K.	158a	53°13'N	3°00'W
Flora, Il., U.S. (flō'rȧ)	108	38°40'N	88°25'W
Flora, In., U.S.	108	40°25'N	86°30'W
Florala, Al., U.S. (flŏr-ăl'ȧ)	124	31°01'N	86°19'W
Floral Park, N.Y., U.S. (flôr'ăl pärk)	110a	40°42'N	73°42'W
Florence, Italy	154	43°47'N	11°15'E
Florence, Al., U.S. (flŏr'ĕns)	105	34°46'N	87°40'W
Florence, Az., U.S.	119	33°00'N	111°25'W
Florence, Co., U.S.	120	38°23'N	105°08'W
Florence, Ks., U.S.	121	38°14'N	96°56'W
Florence, S.C., U.S.	125	34°10'N	79°45'W
Florence, Wa., U.S.	116a	48°13'N	122°21'W
Florencia, Col. (flō-rĕn'sê-ȧ)	142	1°31'N	75°13'W
Florencio Sánchez, Ur. (flō-rĕn-sêō-sá'n-chĕz)	141c	33°52'S	57°24'W
Florencio Varela, Arg. (flō-rĕn'sê-o vä-rā'lä)	144a	34°50'S	58°16'W
Flores, Braz. (flō'rĕzh)	143	7°57'S	37°48'W
Flores, Guat.	132a	16°53'N	89°54'W
Flores, dept., Ur.	141c	33°33'S	57°00'W
Flores, i., Indon.	212	8°14'S	121°08'E
Flores, r., Arg.	141c	36°13'S	60°28'W
Flores, Laut (Flores Sea), sea, Indon.	212	7°09'S	120°30'E
Floresville, Tx., U.S. (flō'rĕs-vĭl)	122	29°10'N	98°08'W
Floriano, Braz. (flō-rä-ä'nò)	143	6°17'S	42°58'W
Florianópolis, Braz. (flō-rē-ä-nō'pò-lēs)	144	27°30'S	48°30'W
Florida, Col. (flō-rē'dä)	142a	3°20'N	76°12'W
Florida, Cuba	134	22°10'N	79°50'W
Florida, S. Afr.	233b	26°11'S	27°56'E
Florida, Ur. (flò-rê-dhä)	144	34°06'S	56°14'W
Florida, N.Y., U.S. (flŏr'ĭ-dȧ)	110a	41°20'N	74°21'W
Florida, state, U.S. (flŏr'ĭ-dȧ)	105	30°30'N	84°40'W
Florida, dept., Ur. (flô-rē'dhä)	141c	33°48'S	56°15'W
Florida, i., Sol. Is.	221	8°56'S	159°45'E
Florida, Straits of, strt., N.A.	129	24°10'N	81°00'W
Florida Bay, b., Fl., U.S. (flŏr'ĭ-dȧ)	125a	24°55'N	80°55'W
Florida Keys, is., Fl., U.S.	107	24°33'N	81°20'W
Florida Mountains, mts., N.M., U.S.	119	32°10'N	107°35'W
Florido, Río, r., Mex. (flò-rē'dō)	122	27°21'N	104°48'W
Floridsdorf, Aus. (flō'rĭds-dôrf)	159e	48°16'N	16°25'E
Florina, Grc. (flò-rē'nä)	163	40°48'N	21°24'E
Florissant, Mo., U.S. (flŏr'ĭ-sănt)	117e	38°47'N	90°20'W
Floyd, r., Ia., U.S. (floid)	112	42°38'N	96°15'W
Floydada, Tx., U.S. (floi-dā'dȧ)	120	33°59'N	101°19'W
Floyds Fork, r., Ky., U.S. (floi-dz)	111h	38°08'N	85°30'W
Flumendosa, r., Italy	174	39°45'N	9°18'E
Flushing, Mi., U.S. (flŭsh'ĭng)	108	43°05'N	83°50'W
Fly, r. (flī)	213	8°00'S	141°45'E
Foča, Bos. (fō'chä)	175	43°29'N	18°48'E
Fochville, S. Afr. (fŏk'vĭl)	238c	26°29'S	27°29'E
Focşani, Rom. (fōk-shä'nē)	169	45°41'N	27°17'E
Fogang, China (fwo-gäŋ)	209	23°50'N	113°35'E
Foggia, Italy (fôd'jä)	163	41°30'N	15°34'E
Fogo, Can. (fō'gō)	101	49°43'N	54°17'W
Fogo, i., Can.	99	49°40'N	54°13'W
Fogo, i., C.V.	230b	14°46'N	24°51'W
Fohnsdorf, Aus. (fōns'dôrf)	168	47°13'N	14°40'E
Föhr, i., Ger. (fûr)	168	54°47'N	8°30'E
Foix, Fr. (fwä)	170	42°58'N	1°34'E
Fokku, Nig.	235	11°40'N	4°31'E
Folādī, Koh-e, mtn., Afg.	199	34°38'N	67°32'E
Folgares, Ang.	236	14°54'S	15°08'E
Foligno, Italy (fō-lēn'yō)	174	42°58'N	12°41'E
Folkeston, Eng., U.K.	165	51°05'N	1°18'E
Folkingham, Eng., U.K. (fō'kĭng-ăm)	158a	52°53'N	0°24'W
Folkston, Ga., U.S.	125	30°50'N	82°01'W
Folsom, Ca., U.S.	118	38°40'N	121°10'W
Folsom, N.M., U.S. (fōl'sŭm)	120	36°47'N	103°56'W
Fomento, Cuba (fō-mĕ'n-tō)	134	21°35'N	78°20'W
Fómeque, Col. (fō'mĕ-kĕ)	142a	4°29'N	73°52'W
Fonda, Ia., U.S. (fŏn'dȧ)	113	42°33'N	94°51'W
Fond du Lac, Wi., U.S. (fŏn dū lăk')	105	43°47'N	88°29'W
Fond du Lac Indian Reservation, I.R., Mn., U.S.	113	46°44'N	93°04'W
Fondi, Italy (fŏn'dē)	174	41°23'N	13°25'E
Fonseca, Golfo de, b., N.A. (gôl-fô-dĕ-fōn-sä'kä)	128	13°09'N	87°55'W
Fontainebleau, Fr. (fôn-tĕn-blō')	161	48°24'N	2°42'E
Fontana, Ca., U.S. (fŏn-tă'nȧ)	117a	34°06'N	117°27'W
Fonte Boa, Braz. (fōn'tå bō'ȧ)	142	2°32'S	66°05'W
Fontenay-le-Comte, Fr. (fônt-nĕ'lē-kônt')	170	46°28'N	0°53'W
Fontenay-Trésigny, Fr. (fôn-te-nā' tra-sēn-yē')	171b	48°43'N	2°53'E
Fontenelle Reservoir, res., Wy., U.S.	115	42°05'N	110°05'W
Fontera, Punta, c., Mex. (pōō'n-tä-fōn-tĕ'rä)	131	18°36'N	92°43'W
Fontibón, Col. (fōn-tē-bôn')	142a	4°42'N	74°09'W
Fontur, c., Ice.	156	66°21'N	14°02'W
Foothills, S. Afr. (fòt-hĭls)	233b	25°55'S	27°36'E
Footscray, Austl.	217a	37°48'S	144°54'E
Foraker, Mount, mtn., Ak., U.S. (fôr'ȧ-kẽr)	103	62°40'N	152°40'W
Forbach, Fr. (fôr'bäk)	171	49°12'N	6°54'E
Forbes, Austl. (fôrbz)	219	33°24'S	148°05'E
Forbes, Mount, mtn., Can.	95	51°52'N	116°56'W
Forchheim, Ger. (fôrk'hīm)	168	49°43'N	11°05'E
Fordyce, Ar., U.S. (fôr'dīs)	121	33°48'N	92°24'W
Forécariah, Gui. (fōr-kȧ-rē'ȧ')	230	9°26'N	13°06'W
Forel, Mont, mtn., Grnld.	89	65°50'N	37°41'W
Forest, Ms., U.S. (fŏr'ĕst)	124	32°22'N	89°29'W
Forest, r., N.D., U.S.	112	48°08'N	97°45'W
Forest City, Ia., U.S.	113	43°14'N	93°40'W
Forest City, N.C., U.S.	125	35°20'N	81°52'W
Forest City, Pa., U.S.	109	41°35'N	75°30'W
Forest Grove, Or., U.S. (grōv)	116c	45°31'N	123°07'W
Forest Hill, Md., U.S.	110e	39°35'N	76°26'W
Forest Hill, Tx., U.S.	117c	32°40'N	97°16'W
Forestville, Can. (fŏr'ĕst-vĭl)	100	48°45'N	69°06'W
Forestville, Md., U.S.	110e	38°51'N	76°55'W
Forez, Monts du, mts., Fr. (môn dü fō-rā')	170	44°55'N	3°43'E
Forfar, Scot., U.K. (fôr'fȧr)	164	57°10'N	2°55'W
Forillon, Parc National, rec., Can.	100	48°50'N	64°05'W
Forio, mtn., Italy (fô'ryō)	173c	40°29'N	13°55'E
Forked Creek, r., Il., U.S. (fôrk'd)	111a	41°16'N	88°01'W
Forked Deer, r., Tn., U.S.	124	35°53'N	89°29'W
Forli, Italy (fôr-lē')	162	44°13'N	12°03'E
Formby, Eng., U.K. (fôrm'bē)	158a	53°34'N	3°04'W
Formby Point, c., Eng., U.K.	158a	53°33'N	3°06'W
Formentera, Isla de, i., Spain (ē's-lä-dĕ-fôr-mĕn-tā'rä)	162	38°43'N	1°25'E
Formiga, Braz. (fôr-mē'gȧ)	143	20°27'S	45°25'W
Formigas Bank, bk. (fôr-mē'gäs)	135	18°30'N	75°40'W
Formosa, Arg. (fôr-mō'sä)	144	27°25'S	58°12'W
Formosa, Braz.	143	15°32'S	47°10'W
Formosa, prov., Arg.	144	24°30'S	60°45'W
Formosa, Serra, mts., Braz. (sĕ'r-rä)	143	12°59'S	55°11'W
Formosa Bay, b., Kenya	237	2°45'S	40°30'E
Formosa Strait *see* Taiwan Strait, strt., Asia	205	24°30'N	120°00'E
Fornosovo, Russia (fôr-nô'sô vô)	186c	59°35'N	30°34'E
Forrest City, Ar., U.S. (for'ĕst sĭ'tĭ)	121	35°00'N	90°46'W
Forsayth, Austl. (fôr-sīth')	219	18°33'S	143°42'E
Forshaga, Swe. (fôrs'hä'gä)	166	59°34'N	13°25'E
Forst, Ger. (fôrst)	161	51°45'N	14°38'E
Forsyth, Ga., U.S. (fôr-sīth')	124	33°02'N	83°56'W
Forsyth, Mt., U.S.	115	46°15'N	106°41'W
Fort Albany, Can. (fôrt ôl'bȧ nĭ)	91	52°20'N	81°30'W
Fort Alexander Indian Reserve, I.R., Can.	97	50°27'N	96°15'W
Fortaleza, Braz. (fôr'tä-lā'zȧ)	143	3°35'S	38°31'W
Fort Apache Indian Reservation, I.R., Az., U.S. (ȧ-păch'ē)	119	34°02'N	110°27'W
Fort Atkinson, Wi., U.S. (ăt'kĭn-sŭn)	113	42°55'N	88°46'W
Fort Beaufort, S. Afr. (bō'fôrt)	233c	32°47'S	26°39'E
Fort Belknap Indian Reservation, I.R., Mt., U.S.	115	48°16'N	108°38'W
Fort Bellefontaine, Mo., U.S. (bĕl-fōn-tān')	117f	38°50'N	90°15'W

294 Fort Benton – Fryazino PRONOUNCING INDEX

PLACE (Pronunciation)	PAGE	LAT.	LONG.
Fort Benton, Mt., U.S. (bĕn'tŭn)	115	47°51'N	110°40'W
Fort Berthold Indian Reservation, I.R., N.D., U.S. (bĕrth'ôld)	112	47°47'N	103°28'W
Fort Bragg, Ca., U.S.	118	39°26'N	123°48'W
Fort Branch, In., U.S. (brănch)	108	38°15'N	87°35'W
Fort Chipewyan, Can.	90	58°46'N	111°15'W
Fort Cobb Reservoir, res., Ok., U.S.	120	35°12'N	98°28'W
Fort Collins, Co., U.S. (kŏl'ĭns)	104	40°36'N	105°04'W
Fort Crampel, C.A.R. (krȧm-pĕl')	231	6°59'N	19°11'E
Fort-de-France, Mart. (dē fräns)	129	14°37'N	61°06'W
Fort Deposit, Al., U.S. (dė-pŏz'ĭt)	124	31°58'N	86°35'W
Fort-de-Possel, C.A.R. (dē pō-sĕl')	231	5°03'N	19°11'E
Fort Dodge, Ia., U.S. (dŏj)	105	42°31'N	94°10'W
Fort Edward, N.Y., U.S. (wĕrd)	109	43°15'N	73°30'W
Fort Erie, Can. (ē'rĭ)	111c	42°55'N	78°56'W
Fortescue, r., Austl. (fôr'tĕs-kū)	220	21°25'S	116°50'E
Fort Fairfield, Me., U.S. (fâr'fēld)	100	46°46'N	[illegible]
Fort Fitzgerald, Can. (fĭts-jĕr'ăld)	90	59°48'N	111°50'W
Fort Frances, Can. (frăn'sĕs)	91	48°36'N	93°24'W
Fort Frederica National Monument, rec., Ga., U.S. (frĕd'ĕ-rĭ-kȧ)	124	31°13'N	85°25'W
Fort Gaines, Ga., U.S. (gānz)	124	31°35'N	85°03'W
Fort Gibson, Ok., U.S. (gĭb'sŭn)	121	35°50'N	95°13'W
Fort Good Hope, Can. (go͝od hōp)	90	66°19'N	128°52'W
Forth, Firth of, b., Scot., U.K. (fûrth ôv fôrth)	156	56°04'N	3°03'W
Fort Hall, Kenya (hôl)	233	0°47'S	37°13'E
Fort Hall Indian Reservation, I.R., Id., U.S.	115	43°02'N	112°21'W
Fort Huachuca, Az., U.S. (wä-cho͞o'kä)	119	31°30'N	110°25'W
Fortier, Can. (fôr'tyā')	102f	49°56'N	97°55'W
Fort Kent, Me., U.S. (kĕnt)	100	47°14'N	68°37'W
Fort Langley, Can. (lăng'lĭ)	116d	49°10'N	122°35'W
Fort Lauderdale, Fl., U.S. (lô'dēr-dāl)	125a	26°07'N	80°09'W
Fort Lee, N.J., U.S.	110a	40°50'N	73°58'W
Fort Liard, Can.	90	60°16'N	123°34'W
Fort Loudoun Lake, res., Tn., U.S. (fôrt lou'dĕn)	124	35°52'N	84°10'W
Fort Lupton, Co., U.S. (lŭp'tŭn)	120	40°04'N	104°54'W
Fort Macleod, Can. (mȧ-kloud')	90	49°43'N	113°25'W
Fort Madison, Ia., U.S. (măd'ĭ-sŭn)	113	40°40'N	91°17'W
Fort Matanzas, Fl., U.S. (mä-tän'zäs)	125	29°39'N	81°17'W
Fort McDermitt Indian Reservation, I.R., Or., U.S. (mȧk dēr'mĭt)	114	42°04'N	118°07'W
Fort McMurray, Can. (mȧk-mŭr'ĭ)	90	56°44'N	111°23'W
Fort McPherson, Can. (mȧk-fŭr's'n)	90	67°37'N	134°59'W
Fort Meade, Fl., U.S. (mēd)	125a	27°45'N	81°48'W
Fort Mill, S.C., U.S. (mĭl)	125	35°03'N	80°57'W
Fort Mojave Indian Reservation, I.R., Ca., U.S. (mō-hä'vâ)	118	34°59'N	115°02'W
Fort Morgan, Co., U.S. (môr'gȧn)	120	40°14'N	103°49'W
Fort Myers, Fl., U.S. (mī'ērz)	125a	26°36'N	81°45'W
Fort Nelson, Can. (nĕl'sŭn)	90	58°57'N	122°30'W
Fort Nelson, r., Can. (nĕl'sŭn)	92	58°44'N	122°20'W
Fort Payne, Al., U.S. (pān)	124	34°26'N	85°41'W
Fort Peck, Mt., U.S. (pĕk)	115	47°58'N	106°30'W
Fort Peck Indian Reservation, I.R., Mt., U.S.	112	48°22'N	105°40'W
Fort Peck Lake, res., Mt., U.S.	106	47°52'N	106°59'W
Fort Pierce, Fl., U.S. (pērs)	125a	27°25'N	80°20'W
Fort Portal, Ug. (pōr'tȧl)	231	0°40'N	30°16'E
Fort Providence, Can. (prŏv'ĭ-dĕns)	90	61°27'N	117°59'W
Fort Pulaski National Monument, rec., Ga., U.S. (pu-lăs'kĭ)	125	31°59'N	80°56'W
Fort Qu'Appelle, Can.	96	50°46'N	103°55'W
Fort Randall Dam, dam, S.D., U.S.	112	42°48'N	98°35'W
Fort Resolution, Can. (rĕz'ō-lū'shŭn)	90	61°08'N	113°42'W
Fort Riley, Ks., U.S. (rī'lĭ)	121	39°05'N	96°46'W
Fort Saint James, Can. (fôrt sānt jāmz)	90	54°26'N	124°15'W
Fort Saint John, Can. (sānt jŏn)	90	56°15'N	120°51'W
Fort Sandeman, Pak. (săn'da-mȧn)	199	31°28'N	69°29'E
Fort Saskatchewan, Can. (săs-kăt'cho͞o-ån)	102g	53°43'N	113°13'W
Fort Scott, Ks., U.S. (skŏt)	105	37°50'N	94°43'W
Fort Severn, Can. (sĕv'ērn)	91	55°58'N	87°50'W
Fort-Shevchenko, Kaz. (shĕv-chĕn'kô)	183	44°30'N	50°18'E
Fort Sibut, C.A.R. (fôr sē-bü')	231	5°44'N	19°05'E
Fort Sill, Ok., U.S. (fōrt sĭl)	120	34°41'N	98°25'W
Fort Simpson, Can. (sĭmp'sŭn)	90	61°52'N	121°48'W
Fort Smith, Can.	90	60°09'N	112°08'W
Fort Smith, Ar., U.S. (smĭth)	105	35°23'N	94°24'W
Fort Stockton, Tx., U.S. (stŏk'tŭn)	122	30°54'N	102°51'W
Fort Sumner, N.M., U.S. (sŭm'nēr)	120	34°30'N	104°17'W
Fort Sumter National Monument, rec., S.C., U.S. (sŭm'tēr)	125	32°43'N	79°54'W
Fort Thomas, Ky., U.S. (tŏm'ăs)	111f	39°05'N	84°27'W
Fortuna, Ca., U.S. (fôr-tū'nȧ)	114	40°36'N	124°10'W
Fortune, Can. (fôr'tŭn)	101	47°04'N	55°51'W
Fortune, i., Bah.	135	22°35'N	74°20'W
Fortune Bay, b., Can.	93a	47°25'N	55°25'W
Fort Union National Monument, rec., N.M., U.S. (ūn'yŭn)	120	35°51'N	104°57'W
Fort Valley, Ga., U.S. (văl'ĭ)	124	32°33'N	83°53'W
Fort Vermilion, Can. (vēr-mĭl'yŭn)	90	58°23'N	115°50'W
Fort Victoria *see* Masvingo, Zimb.	232	20°07'S	30°47'E
Fort Wayne, In., U.S. (wān)	105	41°00'N	85°10'W
Fort William, Scot., U.K. (wĭl'yŭm)	164	56°50'N	3°00'W
Fort William, Mount, mtn., Austl. (wĭ'ĭ-ăm)	222	24°45'S	151°15'E
Fort Worth, Tx., U.S. (wûrth)	104	32°45'N	97°20'W
Fort Yukon, Ak., U.S. (yo͞o'kŏn)	106a	66°30'N	145°00'W
Fort Yuma Indian Reservation, I.R., Ca., U.S. (yo͞o'mä)	119	32°54'N	114°47'W
Foshan, China	205	23°02'N	113°07'E
Fossano, Italy (fŏs-sä'nō)	174	44°34'N	7°42'E
Fossil Creek, r., Tx., U.S. (fŏs-ĭl)	117c	32°53'N	97°19'W
Fossombrone, Italy (fŏs-sôm-brō'nā)	174	43°41'N	12°48'E
Foss Res, Ok., U.S.	120	35°38'N	99°11'W
Fosston, Mn., U.S. (fŏs'tŭn)	112	47°34'N	95°44'W
Fosterburg, Il., U.S. (fŏs'tēr-bûrg)	117e	38°58'N	90°04'W
Fostoria, Oh., U.S. (fŏs-tō'rĭ-ȧ)	108	41°10'N	83°20'W
Fougéres, Fr. (fo͞o-zhâr')	161	48°23'N	1°14'W
Foula, i., Scot., U.K. (fou'lȧ)	164a	60°08'N	2°04'W
Foulwind, Cape, c., N.Z. (foul'wĭnd)	221a	41°45'S	171°00'E
Foumban, Cam. (fo͞om-bän')	230	5°43'N	10°55'E
Fountain Creek, r., Co., U.S. (foun'tĭn)	120	38°36'N	104°37'W
Fountain Valley, Ca., U.S.	117a	33°42'N	117°57'W
Fourche la Fave, r., Ar., U.S. (fo͞orsh lȧ fāv')	111	[illegible]	[illegible]
Fouriesburg, S. Afr. (fō'rēz-bûrg)	238c	28°38'S	28°13'E
Fourmies, Fr. (fo͞or-mē')	170	50°01'N	4°01'E
Four Mountains, Islands of the, is., Ak., U.S.	103a	52°58'N	170°40'W
Fourth Cataract, wtfl., Sudan	231	18°52'N	32°07'E
Fouta Djallon, mts., Gui. (fo͞o'tä jä-lôn)	230	11°37'N	12°29'W
Foveaux Strait, strt., N.Z. (fō-vō')	221a	46°30'S	167°43'E
Fowler, Co., U.S. (foul'ēr)	120	38°04'N	104°02'W
Fowler, In., U.S.	108	40°35'N	87°20'W
Fowler, Point, c., Austl.	220	32°05'S	132°30'E
Fowlerton, Tx., U.S. (foul'ēr-tŭn)	122	28°26'N	98°48'W
Fox, i., Wa., U.S. (fŏks)	116a	47°15'N	122°08'W
Fox, r., Il., U.S.	113	41°35'N	88°43'W
Fox, r., Wi., U.S.	113	44°18'N	88°23'W
Foxboro, Ma., U.S. (fŏks'bŭrō)	101a	42°04'N	71°15'W
Foxe Basin, b., Can. (fŏks)	93	67°35'N	79°21'W
Foxe Channel, strt., Can.	93	64°30'N	79°23'W
Foxe Peninsula, pen., Can.	93	64°57'N	77°26'W
Fox Islands, is., Ak., U.S. (fŏks)	103a	53°04'N	167°30'W
Fox Lake, Il., U.S. (lăk)	111a	42°24'N	88°11'W
Fox Lake, l., Il., U.S.	111a	42°24'N	88°07'W
Fox Point, Wi., U.S.	111a	43°10'N	87°54'W
Foyle, Lough, b., Eur. (lŏk foil')	164	55°07'N	7°08'W
Foz do Cunene, Ang.	236	17°16'S	11°50'E
Fraga, Spain (frä'gä)	173	41°31'N	0°20'E
Fragoso, Cayo, i., Cuba (kä'yō-frä-gō'sō)	134	22°45'N	79°30'W
Framnes Mountains, mts., Ant.	224	67°50'S	62°35'E
Franca, Braz. (frä'n-kä)	143	20°28'S	47°20'W
Francavilla, Italy (fräŋ-kä-vēl'lä)	175	40°32'N	17°37'E
France, nation, Eur. (fråns)	154	46°39'N	0°47'E
Frances, l., Can. (frăn'sĭs)	92	61°27'N	128°28'W
Frances, Cabo, c., Cuba (kä'bō-frän-sĕ's)	134	21°55'N	84°05'W
Frances, Punta, c., Cuba (po͞o'n-tä-frän-sĕ's)	134	21°45'N	83°10'W
Francés Viejo, Cabo, c., Dom. Rep. (kȧ'bô-frän'sås vyā'hô)	135	19°40'N	69°35'W
Franceville, Gabon (fräns-vēl')	232	1°38'S	13°35'E
Francis Case, Lake, res., S.D., U.S. (frăn'sĭs)	106	43°15'N	99°00'W
Francisco Sales, Braz. (frän-sē's-kô-sá'lĕs)	141a	21°42'S	44°26'W
Francistown, Bots. (från'sĭs-toun)	232	21°17'S	27°28'E
Frankfort, S. Afr. (frănk'fŏrt)	233c	32°43'S	27°28'E
Frankfort, S. Afr.	238c	27°17'S	28°30'E
Frankfort, Il., U.S. (fräŋk'fŭrt)	111a	41°30'N	87°51'W
Frankfort, In., U.S.	108	40°15'N	86°30'W
Frankfort, Ks., U.S.	121	39°42'N	96°27'W
Frankfort, Ky., U.S.	105	38°10'N	84°55'W
Frankfort, Mi., U.S.	108	44°40'N	86°15'W
Frankfort, N.Y., U.S.	109	43°05'N	75°05'W
Frankfurt am Main, Ger.	154	50°07'N	8°40'E
Frankfurt an der Oder, Ger.	161	52°20'N	14°31'E
Franklin, S. Afr.	233c	30°19'S	29°28'E
Franklin, In., U.S. (frănk'lĭn)	108	39°25'N	86°00'W
Franklin, Ky., U.S.	124	36°42'N	86°34'W
Franklin, La., U.S.	123	29°47'N	91°31'W
Franklin, Ma., U.S.	101a	42°05'N	71°24'W
Franklin, Ne., U.S.	120	40°06'N	99°01'W
Franklin, N.H., U.S.	109	43°25'N	71°40'W
Franklin, N.J., U.S.	110a	41°08'N	74°35'W
Franklin, Oh., U.S.	108	39°30'N	84°20'W
Franklin, Pa., U.S.	109	41°25'N	79°50'W
Franklin, Tn., U.S.	124	35°54'N	86°54'W
Franklin, Va., U.S.	125	36°41'N	76°57'W
Franklin, l., Nv., U.S.	118	40°23'N	115°10'W
Franklin D. Roosevelt Lake, res., Wa., U.S.	114	48°12'N	118°43'W
Franklin Mountains, mts., Can.	92	65°36'N	125°55'W
Franklin Park, Il., U.S.	111a	41°56'N	87°53'W
Franklin Square, N.Y., U.S.	110a	40°43'N	73°40'W
Franklinton, La., U.S. (fräŋk'lĭn-tŭn)	123	30°49'N	90°09'W
Frankston, Austl.	217a	38°09'S	145°08'E
Franksville, Wi., U.S. (frănkz'vĭl)	111a	42°46'N	87°55'W
Fransta, Swe.	166	62°30'N	16°04'E
Franz Josef Land *see* Zemlya Frantsa-Iosifa, is., Russia	178	81°32'N	40°00'E
Frascati, Italy (fräs-kä'tē)	174	41°49'N	12°45'E
Fraser, Mi., U.S. (frā'zēr)	111b	42°32'N	82°57'W
Fraser, i., Austl.	221	25°12'S	153°00'E
Fraser, r., Can.	92	51°30'N	122°00'W
Fraserburgh, Scot., U.K. (frā'zēr-bûrg)	164	57°40'N	2°01'W
Fraser Plateau, plat., Can.	95	51°30'N	122°00'W
Frattamaggiore, Italy (frät-tä-mäg-zhyō'rē)	173c	40°41'N	14°16'E
Fray Bentos, Ur. (frī bĕn'tōs)	144	33°10'S	58°19'W
Frazee, Mn., U.S. (frȧ-zē')	112	46°42'N	95°43'W
Fraziers Hog Cay, i., Bah.	134	25°25'N	77°55'W
Frechen, Ger. (frĕ'κĕn)	171c	50°54'N	6°49'E
Fredericia, Den. (frĕdh-ĕ-rē'tsē-ȧ)	166	55°35'N	9°45'E
Frederick, Md., U.S. (frĕd'ēr-ĭk)	105	39°25'N	77°25'W
Frederick, Ok., U.S.	120	34°23'N	99°01'W
Frederick House, r., Can.	98	49°05'N	81°20'W
Fredericksburg, Tx., U.S. (frĕd'ēr-ĭkz-bûrg)	122	30°16'N	98°52'W
Fredericksburg, Va., U.S.	109	38°20'N	77°30'W
Fredericktown, Mo., U.S. (frĕd'ēr-ĭk-toun)	121	37°32'N	90°16'W
Fredericton, Can. (frĕd'ēr-ĭk-tŭn)	91	45°48'N	66°39'W
Frederikshavn, Den. (frĕdh'ĕ-rēks-houn)	160	57°27'N	10°31'E
Frederikssund, Den. (frĕdh'ĕ-rēks-so͝on)	166	55°51'N	12°04'E
Fredonia, Col. (frĕ-dō'nyä)	142a	5°55'N	75°40'W
Fredonia, Ks., U.S. (frė-dō'nĭ-ȧ)	121	36°31'N	95°50'W
Fredonia, N.Y., U.S.	109	42°25'N	79°20'W
Fredrikstad, Nor. (frådh'rēks-ståd)	160	59°14'N	10°58'E
Freeburg, Il., U.S. (frē'bûrg)	117e	38°26'N	89°59'W
Freehold, N.J., U.S. (frē'hōld)	110a	40°15'N	74°16'W
Freeland, Pa., U.S. (frē'lȧnd)	109	41°00'N	75°50'W
Freeland, Wa., U.S.	116a	48°01'N	122°32'W
Freels, Cape, c., Can. (frēlz)	101	46°37'N	53°45'W
Freelton, Can. (frēl'tŭn)	102d	43°24'N	80°02'W
Freeport, Bah.	134	26°30'N	78°45'W
Freeport, Il., U.S. (frē'pōrt)	105	42°19'N	89°30'W
Freeport, N.Y., U.S.	110a	40°39'N	73°35'W
Freeport, Tx., U.S.	123	28°56'N	95°21'W
Freetown, S.L. (frē'toun)	230	8°30'N	13°15'W
Fregenal de la Sierra, Spain (frā-hå-näl' dā lä syĕr'rä)	172	38°09'N	6°40'W
Fregene, Italy (frĕ-zhĕ'-nĕ)	173d	41°52'N	12°12'E
Freiberg, Ger. (frī'bĕrgh)	161	50°54'N	13°18'E
Freiburg, Ger.	161	48°00'N	7°50'E
Freienried, Ger. (frī'ĕn-rēd)	159d	48°20'N	11°08'E
Freirina, Chile (frå-ĭ-rē'nä)	144	28°35'S	71°26'W
Freising, Ger. (frī'zĭng)	168	48°25'N	11°45'E
Fréjus, Fr. (frā-zhüs')	171	43°28'N	6°46'E
Fremantle, Austl. (frē'măn-t'l)	218	32°03'S	116°05'E
Fremont, Ca., U.S. (frė-mŏnt')	116b	37°33'N	122°00'W
Fremont, Mi., U.S.	108	43°25'N	85°55'W
Fremont, Ne., U.S.	112	41°26'N	96°30'W
Fremont, Oh., U.S.	108	41°20'N	83°05'W
Fremont, r., Ut., U.S.	119	38°20'N	111°30'W
Fremont Peak, mtn., Wy., U.S.	115	43°05'N	109°35'W
French Broad, r., Tn., U.S. (frĕnch brôd)	124	35°59'N	83°01'W
French Frigate Shoals, Hi., U.S.	126b	23°30'N	167°10'W
French Guiana, dep., S.A. (gē-ä'nä)	143	4°20'N	53°00'W
French Lick, In., U.S. (frĕnch lĭk)	108	38°35'N	86°35'W
Frenchman, r., N.A.	96	49°25'N	108°30'W
Frenchman Creek, r., Mt., U.S. (frĕnch-măn)	115	48°51'N	107°20'W
Frenchman Creek, r., Ne., U.S.	120	40°24'N	101°50'W
Frenchman Flat, Nv., U.S.	118	36°55'N	116°11'W
French Polynesia, dep., Oc.	2	15°00'S	140°00'W
French River, Mn., U.S.	117h	46°54'N	91°54'W
Freshfield, Mount, mtn., Can. (frĕsh'fēld)	95	51°44'N	116°57'W
Fresnillo, Mex. (frås-nēl'yō)	128	23°10'N	102°52'W
Fresno, Col. (frĕs'nō)	142a	5°10'N	75°01'W
Fresno, Ca., U.S.	104	36°44'N	119°46'W
Fresno, r., Ca., U.S. (frĕz'nō)	118	37°00'N	120°24'W
Fresno Slough, Ca., U.S.	118	36°39'N	120°12'W
Freudenstadt, Ger. (froi'dĕn-shtät)	168	48°28'N	8°26'E
Freycinet Peninsula, pen., Austl. (frā-sē-nĕ')	222	42°13'S	148°56'E
Fria, Gui.	234	10°05'N	13°32'W
Fria, r., Az., U.S. (frē-ä)	119	34°03'N	112°12'W
Fria, Cape, c., Nmb. (frīȧ)	232	18°15'S	12°10'E
Friant-Kern Canal, can., Ca., U.S. (kûrn)	118	36°57'N	119°37'W
Frias, Arg. (frē-äs)	144	28°43'S	65°03'W
Fribourg, Switz. (frē-bo͞or')	161	46°48'N	7°07'E
Fridley, Mn., U.S. (frĭd'lĭ)	117g	45°05'N	93°16'W
Friedberg, Ger. (frēd'bĕrgh)	159d	48°22'N	11°00'E
Friedland, Ger. (frēt'länt)	168	53°39'N	13°34'E
Friedrichshafen, Ger. (frē-drēks-häf'ĕn)	168	47°39'N	9°28'E
Friend, Ne., U.S. (frĕnd)	121	40°40'N	97°16'W
Friendswood, Tx., U.S. (frĕnds'wo͝od)	123a	29°31'N	95°11'W
Fries, Va., U.S. (frēz)	125	36°42'N	80°59'W
Friesack, Ger. (frē'säk)	159b	52°44'N	12°35'E
Frio, Cabo, c., Braz. (kä'bō-frē'ō)	143	22°58'S	42°08'W
Frio R, Tx., U.S.	122	29°00'N	99°15'W
Frisian Islands, is., Neth. (frē'zhăn)	160	53°30'N	5°20'E
Friuli-Venezia Giulia, hist. reg., Italy	174	46°20'N	13°20'E
Frobisher Bay, b., Can.	93	62°49'N	66°41'W
Frobisher Lake, l., Can. (frŏb'ĭsh'ēr)	92	56°25'N	108°20'W
Frodsham, Eng., U.K. (frŏdz'ăm)	158a	53°18'N	2°48'W
Frohavet, b., Nor.	160	63°49'N	9°12'E
Frome, Lake, l., Austl. (fro͞om)	220	30°40'S	140°13'E
Frontenac, Ks., U.S. (frŏn'tē-năk)	121	37°27'N	94°41'W
Frontera, Mex. (frôn-tā'rä)	131	18°34'N	92°38'W
Front Range, mts., Co., U.S. (frŭnt)	120	40°59'N	105°29'W
Front Royal, Va., U.S. (frŭnt)	109	38°55'N	78°10'W
Frosinone, Italy (frō-zē-nō'nā)	174	41°38'N	13°22'E
Frostburg, Md., U.S. (frŏst'bûrg)	109	39°40'N	78°55'W
Fruita, Co., U.S. (fro͞ot-ȧ)	119	39°10'N	108°45'W
Frunze *see* Bishkek, Kyrg.	183	42°49'N	74°42'E
Fryanovo, Russia (f'ryä'nô-vô)	186b	56°08'N	38°28'E
Fryazino, Russia (f'ryä'zĭ-nô)	186b	55°58'N	38°05'E

ăt; finăl; rāte; senåte; ärm; åsk; sofȧ; fâre; ch-choose; dh-as th in other; bē; ėvent; bĕt; recĕnt; cratẽr; g-gō; gh-guttural g; bĭt; ĭ-short neutral; rīde; κ-guttural k as ch in German ich;

PRONOUNCING INDEX
Frydlant – Gattendorf 295

PLACE (Pronunciation)	PAGE	LAT.	LONG.
Frydlant, Czech Rep. (frēd´länt)	168	50°56'N	15°05'E
Fucheng, China (fōō-chŭŋ)	206	37°53'N	116°08'E
Fuchu, Japan (fōō´chōō)	211a	35°41'N	139°29'E
Fuchun, r., China (fōō-chọ̄n)	209	29°50'N	120°00'E
Fuego, vol., Guat. (fwā´gō)	132	14°29'N	90°52'W
Fuencarral, Spain (fuān-kär-räl´)	173a	40°29'N	3°42'W
Fuensalida, Spain (fwān-sä-lē´dä)	172	40°04'N	4°15'W
Fuente, Mex. (fwĕ´n-tĕ´)	122	28°39'N	100°34'W
Fuente de Cantos, Spain (fwĕn´tå dā kän´tōs)	172	38°15'N	6°18'W
Fuente el Saz, Spain (fwĕn´tå ĕl säth´)	173a	40°39'N	3°30'W
Fuenteobejuna, Spain	172	38°15'N	5°30'W
Fuentesaúco, Spain (fwĕn-tå-sä-ōō´kō)	172	41°18'N	5°25'W
Fuerte, Río del, r., Mex. (rē´ō-dĕl-fōō-ĕ´r-tĕ)	128	26°15'N	108°50'W
Fuerte Olimpo, Para. (fwĕr´tå ō-lēm-pō)	144	21°10'S	57°49'W
Fuerteventura Island, I., Spain (fwĕr´tå-vĕn-tōō´rä)	230	28°24'N	13°21'W
Fuhai, China	204	47°01'N	87°07'E
Fuji, Japan (jōō´jē)	211	35°11'N	138°44'E
Fuji, r., Japan	211	35°20'N	138°23'E
Fujian, prov., China (fōō-jyĕn)	205	25°40'N	117°30'E
Fujidera, Japan	211b	34°34'N	135°37'E
Fujin, China (fōō-jyĭn)	205	47°13'N	132°11'E
Fuji San, mtn., Japan (fōō´jē sän)	205	35°23'N	138°44'E
Fujisawa, Japan (fōō´jē-sä´wa)	211a	35°20'N	139°29'E
Fujiyama *see* Fuji San, mtn., Japan	205	35°23'N	138°44'E
Fukuchiyama, Japan (fō´kō-chē-yä´ma)	211	35°18'N	135°07'E
Fukue, i., Japan (fō-kōō´ā)	210	32°40'N	129°02'E
Fukui, Japan (fōō´kōō-ē)	205	36°05'N	136°14'E
Fukuoka, Japan (fōō´kō-ō´kä)	205	33°35'N	130°23'E
Fukuoka, Japan	211a	35°52'N	139°31'E
Fukushima, Japan (fōō´kō-shē´mä)	210	37°45'N	140°29'E
Fukuyama, Japan (fōō´kō-yä´mä)	210	34°31'N	133°21'E
Fulda, Ger.	161	50°33'N	9°41'E
Fulda, r., Ger. (fōl´dä)	168	51°05'N	9°40'E
Fuling, China (fōō-lĭŋ)	204	29°40'N	107°30'E
Fullerton, Ca., U.S. (fōl´ẽr-tŭn)	117a	33°53'N	117°56'W
Fullerton, La., U.S.	123	31°00'N	93°00'W
Fullerton, Ne., U.S.	112	41°21'N	97°59'W
Fulton, Ky., U.S. (fŭl´tŭn)	124	36°30'N	88°53'W
Fulton, Mo., U.S.	121	38°51'N	91°56'W
Fulton, N.Y., U.S.	109	43°20'N	76°25'W
Fultondale, Al., U.S. (fŭl´tŭn-dāl)	110h	33°37'N	86°48'W
Funabashi, Japan (fōō´nä-bä´shē)	211	35°43'N	139°59'E
Funaya, Japan (fōō-nä´yä)	211b	34°45'N	135°52'E
Funchal, Port. (fōn-shäl´)	230	32°41'N	16°15'W
Fundación, Col. (fōōn-dä-syō´n)	142	10°43'N	74°13'W
Fundão, Port. (fōn-douN´)	172	40°08'N	7°32'W
Fundy, Bay of, b., Can. (fŭn´dĭ)	93	45°00'N	66°00'W
Fundy National Park, rec., Can.	93	45°38'N	65°00'W
Funing, China (fōō-nĭŋ)	208	33°55'N	119°54'E
Funing, China	206	39°55'N	119°16'E
Funing Wan, b., China	209	26°48'N	120°35'E
Funtua, Nig.	235	11°31'N	7°17'E
Furancungo, Moz.	237	14°55'S	33°35'E
Furbero, Mex. (fōōr-bĕ´rō)	131	20°21'N	97°32'W
Furgun, mtn., Iran	198	28°47'N	57°00'E
Furmanov, Russia (fûr-mä´nôf)	180	57°14'N	41°11'E
Furnas, Represa de, res., Braz.	143	21°00'S	46°00'W
Furneaux Group, is., Austl. (fûr´nō)	221	40°15'S	146°27'E
Fürstenfeld, Aus. (für´stĕn-fĕlt)	168	47°02'N	16°03'E
Fürstenfeldbruck, Ger. (fur´stĕn-fĕld´brōōk)	159d	48°11'N	11°16'E
Fürstenwalde, Ger. (für´stĕn-väl-dĕ)	168	52°21'N	14°04'E
Fürth, Ger. (fürt)	161	49°28'N	11°03'E
Furuichi, Japan (fōō´rō-ē´chē)	211b	34°33'N	135°37'E
Fusa, Japan (fōō´sä)	211a	35°52'N	140°08'E
Fuse, Japan	211b	34°40'N	135°33'E
Fushimi, Japan (fōō´shē-mē)	211b	34°57'N	135°47'E
Fushun, China (fōō´shōōn´)	205	41°50'N	124°00'E
Fusong, China (fōō-sọŋ)	208	42°12'N	127°12'E
Futtsu, Japan (fōō´tsōō´)	211a	35°19'N	139°49'E
Futtsu Misaki, c., Japan (fōōt´tsōō´ mē-sä´kē)	211a	35°19'N	139°46'E
Fuwah, Egypt (fōō´wå)	238b	31°13'N	30°35'E
Fuxian, China (fōō shyĕn)	206	39°36'N	121°59'E
Fuxin, China (fōō-shyĭn)	208	42°05'N	121°40'E
Fuyang, China (fōō-yäŋ)	205	32°53'N	115°48'E
Fuyang, China	209	30°10'N	119°58'E
Fuyang, r., China (fōō-yäŋ)	206	36°59'N	114°48'E
Fuyu, China (fōō-yōō)	205	45°20'N	125°00'E
Fuzhou, China (fōō-jō)	205	26°02'N	119°18'E
Fuzhou, r., China	206	39°38'N	121°43'E
Fuzhoucheng, China (fōō-jō-chŭŋ)	206	39°46'N	121°44'E
Fyn, i., Den. (fü´'n)	166	55°24'N	10°33'E
Fyne, Loch, I., Scot., U.K. (fīn)	164	56°14'N	5°10'W
Fyresvatn, I., Nor.	166	59°04'N	7°55'E

G

PLACE (Pronunciation)	PAGE	LAT.	LONG.
Gaalkacyo, Som.	238a	7°00'N	47°30'E
Gabela, Ang.	236	10°48'S	14°20'E
Gabès, Tun. (gä´bĕs)	230	33°51'N	10°04'E
Gabés, Golfe de, b., Tun.	230	32°22'N	10°59'E
Gabil, Chad	235	11°09'N	18°12'E
Gąbin, Pol. (gôN´bĕn)	169	52°23'N	19°47'E
Gabon, nation, Afr. (gå-bôN´)	232	0°30'S	10°45'E
Gaborone, Bots.	232	24°28'S	25°59'E
Gabriel, r., U.S. (gā´brĭ-ĕl)	123	30°38'N	97°15'W
Gabrovo, Blg. (gäb´rō-vō)	175	42°52'N	25°19'E
Gachsārān, Iran	201	30°12'N	50°47'E
Gacko, Bos. (gäts´kō)	175	43°10'N	18°34'E
Gadsden, Al., U.S. (gădz´dĕn)	105	34°00'N	86°00'W
Găeşti, Rom. (gă-yĕsh´tē)	175	44°43'N	25°21'E
Gaeta, Italy (gä-å´tä)	174	41°18'N	13°34'E
Gaffney, S.C., U.S. (găf´nĭ)	125	35°04'N	81°47'W
Gafsa, Tun. (gäf´sä)	230	34°16'N	8°37'E
Gagarin, Russia	176	55°32'N	34°58'E
Gagnoa, C. Iv.	234	6°08'N	5°56'W
Gagra, Geor.	182	43°20'N	40°15'E
Gaillac-sur-Tarn, Fr. (gå-yäk´sür-tärn´)	170	43°54'N	1°52'E
Gaillard Cut, reg., Pan. (gä-ēl-yä´rd)	128a	9°03'N	79°42'W
Gainesville, Fl., U.S. (gānz´vĭl)	105	29°40'N	82°20'W
Gainesville, Ga., U.S.	124	34°16'N	83°48'W
Gainesville, Tx., U.S.	121	33°38'N	97°08'W
Gainsborough, Eng., U.K. (gānz´bŭr-ô)	158a	53°23'N	0°46'W
Gairdner, Lake, I., Austl. (gård´nẽr)	220	32°20'S	136°30'E
Gaithersburg, Md., U.S. (gā´thẽrs´bûrg)	110e	39°08'N	77°13'W
Gaixian, China (gī-shyĕn)	208	40°25'N	122°20'E
Galana, r., Kenya	237	3°00'S	39°30'E
Galapagar, Spain (gä-lä-pä-gär´)	173a	40°36'N	4°00'W
Galapagos Islands *see* Colón, Archipiélago de, is., Ec.	142	0°10'S	87°45'W
Galaria, r., Italy	173d	41°58'N	12°21'E
Galashiels, Scot., U.K. (găl-*ȧ*-shēlz)	164	55°40'N	2°57'W
Galați, Rom.	154	45°25'N	28°05'E
Galatina, Italy (gä-lä-tē´nä)	175	40°10'N	18°12'E
Galaxídi, Grc.	175	38°26'N	22°22'E
Galdhøpiggen, mtn., Nor.	166	61°37'N	8°17'E
Galeana, Mex. (gä-lå-ä´nä)	122	24°50'N	100°04'W
Galena, Il., U.S. (*gȧ*-lē´*nȧ*)	113	42°26'N	90°27'W
Galena, In., U.S.	111h	38°21'N	85°55'W
Galena Peak, mtn., Tx., U.S.	123a	29°44'N	95°14'W
Galera, Cerro, mtn., Pan. (sĕ´r-rô-gä-lĕ´rä)	128a	8°55'N	79°38'W
Galeras, vol., Col. (gä-lĕ´räs)	142	0°57'N	77°27'W
Gales, r., Or., U.S. (gālz)	116c	45°33'N	123°11'W
Galesburg, Il., U.S. (gālz´bûrg)	105	40°56'N	90°21'W
Galesville, Wi., U.S. (gālz´vĭl)	113	44°04'N	91°22'W
Galeton, Pa., U.S. (gāl´t*ŭ*n)	109	41°45'N	77°40'W
Galich, Russia (gäl´ĭch)	180	58°20'N	42°38'E
Galicia, hist. reg., Pol. (gȧ-lĭsh´ĭ-ȧ)	169	49°48'N	21°05'E
Galicia, hist. reg., Spain (gä-lē´thyä)	172	43°35'N	8°03'W
Galilee, I., Austl. (găl´ĭ-lē)	221	22°23'S	145°09'E
Galilee, Sea of, I., Isr.	197a	32°53'N	35°45'E
Galina Point, c., Jam. (gä-lē´nä)	134	18°25'N	76°50'W
Galion, Oh., U.S. (găl´ĭ-*ŭ*n)	108	40°45'N	82°50'W
Galisteo, N.M., U.S. (gä-lĭs-tå´ō)	120	35°20'N	106°00'W
Gallarate, Italy (gäl-lä-rä´tä)	174	45°37'N	8°48'E
Gallardon, Fr. (gä-lär-dôN´)	171b	48°31'N	1°40'E
Gallatin, Mo., U.S. (găl´*ȧ*-tĭn)	121	39°55'N	93°58'W
Gallatin, Tn., U.S.	124	36°23'N	86°28'W
Gallatin, r., Mt., U.S.	115	45°12'N	111°10'W
Galle, Sri L. (gäl)	203	6°13'N	80°10'E
Gállego, r., Spain (gäl-yā´gō)	173	42°27'N	0°37'W
Gallinas, Punta de, c., Col. (gä-lyē´näs)	142	12°10'N	72°10'W
Gallipoli, Italy (gäl-lē´pô-lē)	175	40°03'N	17°58'E
Gallipoli *see* Gelibolu, Tur. (gäl-lē´pô-lē)	163	40°25'N	26°40'E
Gallipoli Peninsula, pen., Tur.	175	40°23'N	25°10'E
Gallipolis, Oh., U.S. (găl-ĭ-pô-lēs)	108	38°50'N	82°10'W
Gällivare, Swe. (yĕl-ĭ-vär´*ĕ*)	160	68°06'N	20°29'E
Gallo, r., Spain (gäl´yō)	172	40°43'N	1°42'W
Gallup, N.M., U.S. (găl´*ŭ*p)	104	35°30'N	108°45'W
Galty Mountains, mts., Ire.	164	52°19'N	8°20'W
Galva, Il., U.S. (găl´vȧ)	121	41°11'N	90°02'W
Galveston, Tx., U.S. (găl´vĕs-t*ŭ*n)	105	29°18'N	94°48'W
Galveston Bay, b., Tx., U.S.	107	29°39'N	94°45'W
Galveston I, Tx., U.S.	123a	29°12'N	94°53'W
Galway, Ire.	154	53°16'N	9°05'W
Galway Bay, b., Ire. (gôl´wā)	164	53°10'N	9°47'W
Gamba, China (gäm-bä)	202	28°23'N	89°42'E
Gambaga, Ghana (gäm-bä´gä)	230	10°32'N	0°26'W
Gambela, Eth. (gäm-bā´*lȧ*)	231	8°15'N	34°33'E
Gambia (Gambie), r., Afr.	234	13°20'N	15°55'W
Gambia, The, nation, Afr.	230	13°38'N	19°38'W
Gambie, r., Afr.	230	12°30'N	13°00'W
Gamboma, Congo (gäm-bō´mä)	232	1°53'S	15°51'E
Gamleby, Swe. (gäm´lĕ-bü)	166	57°54'N	16°20'E
Gan, r., China (gän)	209	26°50'N	115°00'E
Gäncä, Azer.	180	40°40'N	46°22'E
Gandak, r., India	202	26°37'N	84°22'E
Gander, Can. (găn´dẽr)	91	48°57'N	54°34'W
Gander, r., Can.	101	49°10'N	54°35'W
Gander Lake, I., Can.	101	48°55'N	55°40'W
Gandhinagar, India	202	23°30'N	72°47'E
Gandi, Nig.	235	12°55'N	5°49'E
Gandía, Spain (gän-dē´ä)	173	38°56'N	0°10'W
Gangdisê Shan (Trans Himalayas), mts., China	204	30°25'N	83°43'E
Ganges, r., Asia (găn´jēz)	199	24°00'N	89°30'E
Ganges, Mouths of the, mth., Asia (găn´jēz)	199	21°18'N	88°40'E
Gangi, Italy (gän´jē)	174	37°48'N	14°15'E
Gangtok, India	199	27°15'N	88°30'E
Gannan, China (gän-nän)	208	47°50'N	123°30'E
Gannett Peak, mtn., Wy., U.S. (găn´ĕt)	106	43°10'N	109°38'W
Gano, Oh., U.S. (ă´nô)	111f	39°18'N	84°24'W
Gänserndorf, Aus.	159e	48°21'N	16°43'E
Gansu, prov., China (gän-sōō)	204	38°50'N	101°10'E
Ganwo, Nig.	235	11°13'N	4°42'E
Ganyu, China (gän-yōō)	206	34°52'N	119°07'E
Ganzhou, China (gän-jō)	205	25°50'N	114°30'E
Gao, Mali (gä´ō)	230	16°16'N	0°03'W
Gao'an, China (gou-än)	209	28°30'N	115°02'E
Gaomi, China (gou-mē)	206	36°23'N	119°46'E
Gaoqiao, China (gou-chyou)	207b	31°21'N	121°35'E
Gaoshun, China (gou-shọ̄n)	206	31°22'N	118°50'E
Gaotang, China (gou-täŋ)	206	36°52'N	116°12'E
Gaoyao, China (gou-you)	209	23°08'N	112°25'E
Gaoyi, China (gou-yē)	206	37°37'N	114°39'E
Gaoyou, China (gou-yō)	208	32°46'N	119°26'E
Gaoyou Hu, I., China (kä´ō-yōō´hōō)	205	32°42'N	118°40'E
Gap, Fr. (gȧp)	161	44°34'N	6°08'E
Gapan, Phil. (gä-pän)	213a	15°18'N	120°56'E
Gar, China	204	31°11'N	80°35'E
Garanhuns, Braz. (gä-rän-yọ̄Nsh´)	143	8°49'S	36°28'W
Garber, Ok., U.S. (gär´bēr)	121	36°28'N	97°35'W
Garching, Ger. (gär´κeng)	159d	48°15'N	11°39'E
García, Mex. (gär-sē´ä)	122	25°50'N	100°37'W
García de la Cadena, Mex.	130	21°14'N	103°26'W
Garda, Lago di, I., Italy (lä-gō-dē-gär´dä)	162	45°43'N	10°26'E
Gardanne, Fr. (gȧr-dȧn´)	170a	43°28'N	5°29'E
Gardelegen, Ger. (gär-dĕ-lå´ghĕn)	168	52°32'N	11°22'E
Garden, i., Mi., U.S. (gär´d'n)	108	45°50'N	85°50'W
Gardena, Ca., U.S. (gär-dē´nȧ)	117a	33°53'N	118°19'W
Garden City, Ks., U.S.	120	37°58'N	100°52'W
Garden City, Mi., U.S.	111b	42°20'N	83°21'W
Garden Grove, Ca., U.S. (gär´d'n grōv)	117a	33°47'N	117°56'W
Garden Reach, India	202a	22°33'N	88°17'E
Garden River, Can.	117k	46°33'N	84°10'W
Gardeyz, Afg.	202	33°43'N	69°09'E
Gardiner, Me., U.S. (gärd´nẽr)	100	44°12'N	69°46'W
Gardiner, Mt., U.S.	115	45°03'N	110°43'W
Gardiner, Wa., U.S.	116a	48°03'N	122°55'W
Gardiner Dam, dam, Can.	96	51°17'N	106°51'W
Gardner, Ma., U.S.	109	42°35'N	72°00'W
Gardner Canal, strt., Can.	94	53°28'N	128°15'W
Gardner Pinnacles, Hi., U.S.	126b	25°10'N	167°00'W
Gareloi, i., Ak., U.S. (gär-lōō-ä´)	103a	51°40'N	178°48'W
Garfield, N.J., U.S. (gär´fēld)	110a	40°53'N	74°06'W
Garfield, Ut., U.S.	117b	40°45'N	112°10'W
Garfield Heights, Oh., U.S.	111d	41°25'N	81°36'W
Gargaliánoi, Grc. (gär-gä-lyä´nē)	175	37°07'N	21°50'E
Gargždai, Lith. (gärgzh´dī)	167	55°43'N	20°09'E
Garibaldi, Mount, mtn., Can. (gâr-ĭ-băl´dē)	94	49°51'N	123°01'W
Garin, Arg. (gä-rē´n)	144a	34°25'S	58°44'W
Garissa, Kenya	237	0°28'S	39°38'E
Garland, Tx., U.S. (gär´lănd)	117c	32°55'N	96°39'W
Garland, Ut., U.S.	115	41°45'N	112°10'W
Garm, Taj.	183	39°12'N	70°28'E
Garmisch-Partenkirchen, Ger. (gär´mēsh pär´tĕn-kēr´κĕn)	168	47°38'N	11°10'E
Garnett, Ks., U.S. (gär´nĕt)	121	38°16'N	95°15'W
Garonne, r., Fr. (gȧ-rọ̄n)	156	44°00'N	1°00'E
Garoua, Cam. (gär´wä)	231	9°18'N	13°24'E
Garrett, In., U.S. (găr´ĕt)	108	41°20'N	85°10'W
Garrison, N.D., U.S.	112	47°38'N	101°24'W
Garrison, N.Y., U.S. (găr´ĭ-s*ŭ*n)	110a	41°23'N	73°57'W
Garrovillas, Spain (gä-rō-vēl´yäs)	172	39°42'N	6°30'W
Garry, I., Can. (găr´ĭ)	92	66°16'N	99°23'W
Garsen, Kenya	237	2°16'S	40°07'E
Garson, Can.	99	46°34'N	80°52'W
Garstedt, Ger. (gär´shtĕt)	159c	53°40'N	9°58'E
Garulia, India	202a	22°48'N	88°23'E
Garwolin, Pol. (gär-vō´lĕn)	169	51°54'N	21°40'E
Gary, In., U.S. (gā´rĭ)	105	41°35'N	87°21'W
Gary, W.V., U.S. (fĭl´bĕrt)	125	37°21'N	81°33'W
Garzón, Col. (gär-thōn´)	142	2°13'N	75°44'W
Gasan, Phil. (gä-sän´)	213a	13°19'N	121°52'E
Gasan-Kuli, Turkmen.	183	37°25'N	53°55'E
Gas City, In., U.S. (găs)	108	40°30'N	85°40'W
Gascogne, reg., Fr. (gäs-kôn´y*ĕ*)	170	43°45'N	1°49'W
Gasconade, r., Mo., U.S. (găs-kô-nād´)	121	37°46'N	92°15'W
Gascoyne, r., Austl. (găs-koin´)	220	25°15'S	117°00'E
Gashland, Mo., U.S. (găsh´-lănd)	117f	39°15'N	94°35'W
Gashua, Nig.	235	12°54'N	11°00'E
Gasny, Fr. (gäs-nē´)	171b	49°05'N	1°36'E
Gaspé, Can.	91	48°50'N	64°29'W
Gaspé, Péninsule de, pen., Can.	93	48°30'N	65°00'W
Gasper Hernández, Dom. Rep. (gäs-pär´ ĕr-nän´dāth)	135	19°40'N	70°15'W
Gassaway, W.V., U.S. (găs´*ȧ*-wā)	108	38°40'N	80°45'W
Gaston, Or., U.S. (găs´tŭn)	116c	45°26'N	123°08'W
Gastonia, N.C., U.S. (găs-tô´nĭ-ȧ)	125	35°15'N	81°14'W
Gastre, Arg. (gäs-trĕ)	144	42°12'S	68°50'W
Gata, Cabo de, c., Spain (kå´bô-dĕ-gä´tä)	162	36°42'N	2°00'W
Gata, Sierra de, mts., Spain (syĕr´*rä* dä gä´tä)	162	40°12'N	6°39'W
Gatchina, Russia (gä-chē´nȧ)	180	59°33'N	30°08'E
Gátes, Akrotírion, c., Cyp.	197a	34°30'N	33°15'E
Gateshead, Eng., U.K. (gāts´hĕd)	164	54°56'N	1°38'W
Gates of the Arctic National Park, rec., Ak., U.S.	103	67°45'N	153°30'W
Gatesville, Tx., U.S. (gāts´vĭl)	123	31°26'N	97°34'W
Gâtine, Hauteurs de, hills, Fr.	170	46°40'N	0°50'W
Gatineau, Can. (gá´tē-nō)	102c	45°29'N	75°38'W
Gatineau, r., Can.	99	45°45'N	75°50'W
Gatineau, Parc de la, rec., Can.	99	45°32'N	75°53'W
Gattendorf, Aus.	159e	48°01'N	17°00'E

PLACE (Pronunciation)	PAGE	LAT.	LONG.
Gatun, Pan. (gä-tōōn')	133	9°16'N	79°25'W
Gatun, r., Pan.	128a	9°21'N	79°40'W
Gatún, Lago, l., Pan.	133	9°13'N	79°24'W
Gatun Locks, trans., Pan.	128a	9°16'N	79°57'W
Gauhāti, India	199	26°09'N	91°51'E
Gauja, r., Lat. (gå'ò-yå)	167	57°10'N	24°30'E
Gaula, r., Nor.	166	62°55'N	10°45'E
Gávdos, i., Grc. (gäv'dôs)	163	34°48'N	24°08'E
Gavins Point Dam, Ne., U.S. (gă'-vĭns)	112	42°47'N	97°47'W
Gāvkhūnī, Bātlāq-e, l., Iran	198	31°40'N	52°48'E
Gävle, Swe. (yĕv'lĕ)	154	60°40'N	17°07'E
Gävlebukten, b., Swe.	166	60°45'N	17°30'E
Gavrilov Posad, Russia (gå'vrê-lôf'ka po-såt)	176	56°34'N	40°09'E
Gavrilov-Yam, Russia (gå'vrê-lôf yäm')	176	57°17'N	39°49'E
Gawler, Austl. ([illegible])	[illegible]	[illegible]	[illegible]
Gawler Ranges, mts., Austl.	222	32°35'S	136°30'E
Gaya, India (gŭ'yä)(gī'å)	199	24°53'N	85°00'E
Gaya, Nig. (gä'yä)	230	11°58'N	9°05'E
Gaylord, Mi., U.S. (gā'lôrd)	108	45°00'N	84°35'W
Gayndah, Austl. (gān'däh)	222	25°43'S	151°33'E
Gaza, Gaza	198	31°30'N	34°29'E
Gaziantep, Tur. (gä-zē-än'tĕp)	198	37°10'N	37°30'E
Gbarnga, Lib.	234	7°00'N	9°29'W
Gdańsk, Pol. (g'dänsk)	154	54°20'N	18°40'E
Gdov, Russia (g'dôf')	180	58°44'N	27°51'E
Gdynia, Pol. (g'dēn'yä)	160	54°29'N	18°30'E
Geary, Ok., U.S. (gē'rĭ)	120	35°36'N	98°19'W
Géba, r., Gui.-B.	234	12°25'N	14°35'W
Gebo, Wy., U.S. (gĕb'ō)	115	43°49'N	108°13'W
Ged, La., U.S. (gĕd)	123	30°07'N	93°36'W
Gediz, r., Tur.	163	38°44'N	28°45'E
Gedney, i., Wa., U.S. (gĕd-nê)	116a	48°01'N	122°18'W
Gedser, Den.	166	54°35'N	12°08'E
Geel, Bel.	159a	51°09'N	5°01'E
Geelong, Austl. (jē-lông')	219	38°06'S	144°13'E
Gegu, China (gŭ-gōō)	206	39°00'N	117°30'E
Ge Hu, l., China (gŭ hōō)	206	31°37'N	119°57'E
Geidam, Nig.	230	12°57'N	11°57'E
Geikie Range, mts., Austl. (gē'kê)	220	17°35'S	125°32'E
Geislingen, Ger. (gīs'lĭng-ĕn)	168	48°37'N	9°52'E
Geist Reservoir, res., In., U.S. (gēst)	111g	39°57'N	85°59'W
Geita, Tan.	237	2°52'S	32°10'E
Gejiu, China (gŭ-jĭo)	209	23°32'N	102°50'E
Geldermalsen, Neth.	159a	51°53'N	5°18'E
Geldern, Ger. (gĕl'dĕrn)	171c	51°31'N	6°20'E
Gelibolu, Tur. (gĕ-lĭb'ô-lò)	163	40°25'N	26°40'E
Gelsenkirchen, Ger. (gĕl-zĕn-kĭrk-ĕn)	168	51°31'N	7°05'E
Gemas, Malay. (jĕm'ás)	197b	2°35'N	102°37'E
Gemena, D.R.C.	231	3°15'N	19°46'E
Gemlik, Tur. (gĕm'lĭk)	163	40°30'N	29°10'E
Genale (Jubba), r., Afr.	238a	5°15'N	41°00'E
General Alvear, Arg. (gĕ-nĕ-räl'ál-vĕ-å'r)	141c	36°04'S	60°02'W
General Arenales, Arg. (ä-rĕ-nä'lĕs)	141c	34°19'S	61°16'W
General Belgrano, Arg. (bĕl-grå'nô)	141c	35°45'S	58°32'W
General Cepeda, Mex. (sĕ-pĕ'dä)	122	25°24'N	101°29'W
General Conesa, Arg. (kô-nĕ'sä)	141c	36°30'S	57°19'W
General Guido, Arg. (gē'dô)	141c	36°41'S	57°48'W
General Lavalle, Arg. (lå-vå'l-yĕ)	141c	36°25'S	56°55'W
General Madariaga, Arg. (män-då-rêä'gä)	144	36°59'S	57°14'W
General Paz, Arg. (på'z)	141c	35°30'S	58°20'W
General Pedro Antonio Santos, Mex.	130	21°37'N	98°58'W
General Pico, Arg. (pē'kô)	144	36°46'S	63°44'W
General Roca, Arg. (rô-kä)	144	39°01'S	67°31'W
General San Martín, Arg. (sän-mår-tē'n)	144a	34°35'S	58°32'W
General Sarmiento (San Miguel), Arg.	144a	34°33'S	58°43'W
General Viamonte, Arg. (vēå'môn-tĕ)	141c	35°01'S	60°59'W
General Zuazua, Mex. (zwä'zwä)	122	25°54'N	100°07'W
Genesee, r., N.Y., U.S. (jĕn-ē-sē')	109	42°25'N	78°10'W
Geneseo, Il., U.S. (jē-nĕsēō)	108	41°28'N	90°11'W
Geneva (Genève), Switz.	154	46°14'N	6°04'E
Geneva, Al., U.S. (jê-nē'vå)	124	31°03'N	85°50'W
Geneva, Il., U.S.	111a	41°53'N	88°18'W
Geneva, Ne., U.S.	121	40°32'N	97°37'W
Geneva, N.Y., U.S.	109	42°50'N	77°00'W
Geneva, Oh., U.S.	108	41°45'N	80°55'W
Geneva, Lake, l., Switz.	161	46°28'N	6°30'E
Genève *see* Geneva, Switz.	154	46°14'N	6°04'E
Genil, r., Spain (hå-nēl')	172	37°15'N	4°05'W
Genoa, Italy	154	44°23'N	9°52'E
Genoa, Ne., U.S. (jen'ô-å)	121	41°26'N	97°43'W
Genoa City, Wi., U.S.	111a	42°31'N	88°19'W
Genova, Golfo di, b., Italy (gôl-fô-dē-jĕn'ō-vä)	156	44°10'N	8°45'E
Genovesa, i., Ec. (ĕ's-lä-gĕ-nō-vĕ-sä)	142	0°08'N	90°15'W
Gent, Bel.	161	51°05'N	3°40'E
Genthin, Ger. (gĕn-tēn')	168	52°24'N	12°10'E
Genzano di Roma, Italy (gzhĕnt-zä'-nô-dē-rô'mä)	173d	41°43'N	12°49'E
Geographe Bay, b., Austl. (jē-ô-grăf')	220	33°00'S	114°00'E
Geographe Channel, strt., Austl. (jēô'grä-fĭk)	220	24°15'S	112°50'E
George, l., N.Y., U.S. (jôrj)	109	43°40'N	73°30'W
George, Lake, l., N.A. (jôrg)	117k	46°26'N	84°09'W
George, Lake, l., Ug.	237	0°02'N	30°25'E
George, Lake, l., Fl., U.S. (jôr-ĭj)	125	29°10'N	81°50'W
George, Lake, l., In., U.S.	111a	41°31'N	87°17'W
Georges, r., Austl.	217b	33°57'S	151°00'E
George Town, Bah.	135	23°30'N	75°50'W
Georgetown, Can. (jôrg-toun)	102d	43°39'N	79°56'W
Georgetown, Can. (jôr-ĭj-toun)	101	46°11'N	62°32'W
George Town, Cay. Is.	134	19°20'N	81°20'W
Georgetown, Guy. (jôrj'toun)	143	7°45'N	58°04'W
George Town, Malay.	212	5°21'N	100°09'E
Georgetown, Ct., U.S.	110a	41°15'N	73°25'W
Georgetown, De., U.S.	109	38°40'N	75°20'W
Georgetown, Il., U.S.	108	40°00'N	87°40'W
Georgetown, Ky., U.S.	108	38°10'N	84°35'W
Georgetown, Ma., U.S. (jôrg-toun)	101a	42°43'N	71°00'W
Georgetown, Md., U.S.	109	39°25'N	75°55'W
Georgetown, S.C., U.S. (jôr-ĭj-toun)	125	33°22'N	79°17'W
Georgetown, Tx., U.S. (jôrg-toun)	123	30°37'N	97°40'W
George Washington Birthplace National Monument, rec., Va., U.S. (jôrj wŏsh'ĭng-tŭn)	109	38°10'N	77°00'W
George Washington Carver National Monument, rec., Mo., U.S. (jörg wåsh-ĭng-tŭn kär'vēr)	121	36°58'N	94°21'W
George West, Tx., U.S.	122	28°20'N	98°07'W
Georgia, nation, Asia	178	42°17'N	43°00'E
Georgia, state, U.S. (jôr'ji-ă)	105	32°40'N	83°50'W
Georgia, Strait of, strt., N.A.	94	49°20'N	124°00'W
Georgiana, Al., U.S. (jôr-jē-än'å)	124	31°39'N	86°44'W
Georgian Bay, b., Can.	93	45°15'N	80°50'W
Georgian Bay Islands National Park, rec., Can.	98	45°20'N	81°40'W
Georgina, r., Austl. (jôr-jē'nå)	220	22°00'S	138°15'E
Georgiyevsk, Russia (gyôr-gyĕfsk')	181	44°05'N	43°30'E
Gera, Ger. (gā'rä)	161	50°52'N	12°06'E
Geral, Serra, mts., Braz. (sĕr'rå zhå-räl')	144	28°30'S	51°00'W
Geral de Goiás, Serra, mts., Braz. (zhå-räl'-dĕ-gô-yá's)	143	14°22'S	45°40'W
Geraldton, Austl. (jĕr'ăld-tŭn)	218	28°40'S	114°35'E
Geraldton, Can.	91	49°43'N	87°00'W
Gérgal, Spain (gĕr'gäl)	172	37°08'N	2°29'W
Gering, Ne., U.S. (gē'rĭng)	112	41°49'N	103°41'W
Gerlachovský štít, mtn., Slvk.	169	49°12'N	20°08'E
Germantown, Oh., U.S. (jûr'mán-toun)	108	39°35'N	84°25'W
Germany, nation, Eur. (jûr'må-nĭ)	154	51°00'N	10°00'E
Germiston, S. Afr. (jûr'mĭs-tŭn)	232	26°19'S	28°11'E
Gerona, Phil. (hā-rō'nä)	213a	15°36'N	120°36'E
Gerrards Cross, Eng., U.K. (jĕrårds krōs)	158b	51°34'N	0°33'W
Gers, r., Fr. (zhĕr)	173	43°25'N	0°30'E
Gersthofen, Ger. (gĕrst-hō'fĕn)	159d	48°26'N	10°54'E
Getafe, Spain (hā-tä'få)	172	40°19'N	3°44'W
Gettysburg, Pa., U.S. (gĕt'ĭs-bûrg)	109	39°50'N	77°15'W
Gettysburg, S.D., U.S.	112	45°01'N	99°59'W
Gevelsberg, Ger. (gĕ-fĕls'bĕrgh)	171c	51°18'N	7°20'E
Ghāghra, r., India	199	26°00'N	83°00'E
Ghana, nation, Afr. (gän'ä)	230	8°00'N	2°00'W
Ghanzi, Bots. (gän'zē)	232	21°30'S	22°00'E
Ghardaïa, Alg. (gär-dä'ē-ä)	230	32°29'N	3°38'E
Gharo, Pak.	202	24°50'N	68°35'E
Ghāt, Libya	230	24°52'N	10°16'E
Ghazāl, Bahr al-, r., Sudan	231	9°30'N	30°00'E
Ghazal, Bahr el, r., Chad (bär ĕl ghä-zäl')	235	14°30'N	17°00'E
Ghazzah *see* Gaza, Gaza	198	31°30'N	34°29'E
Gheorgheni, Rom.	163	46°48'N	25°30'E
Gherla, Rom. (gĕr'lä)	169	47°01'N	23°55'E
Ghilizane, Alg.	230	35°43'N	0°43'E
Ghorīān, Afg.	201	34°21'N	61°30'E
Ghost Lake, Can.	102e	51°15'N	114°46'W
Ghudāmis, Libya	230	30°07'N	9°26'E
Giannitsá, Grc.	175	40°47'N	22°26'E
Giannutri, Isola di, i., Italy (jän-nōō'trē)	174	42°15'N	11°06'E
Giant Sequoia National Monument, rec., Ca., U.S.	118	36°10'N	118°35'W
Gibara, Cuba (hē-bä'rä)	134	21°05'N	76°10'W
Gibeon, Nmb. (gĭb'ē-ŭn)	232	25°15'S	17°30'E
Gibraleón, Spain (hē-brä-lå-ōn')	172	37°24'N	7°00'W
Gibraltar, dep., Eur. (gĭ-bräl-tă'r)	154	36°08'N	5°22'W
Gibraltar, Strait of, strt.	156	35°55'N	5°45'W
Gibson City, Il., U.S. (gĭb'sŭn)	108	40°25'N	88°20'W
Gibson Desert, des., Austl.	220	24°45'S	123°15'E
Gibson Island, Md., U.S.	110e	39°05'N	76°26'W
Gibson Reservoir, res., Ok., U.S.	121	36°07'N	95°08'W
Giddings, Tx., U.S. (gĭd'ĭngz)	123	30°11'N	96°55'W
Gideon, Mo., U.S. (gĭd'ē-ŭn)	121	36°27'N	89°56'W
Gien, Fr. (zhē-äɴ')	161	47°43'N	2°37'E
Giessen, Ger. (gēs'sĕn)	168	50°35'N	8°40'E
Gifu, Japan (gē'fōō)	205	35°25'N	136°45'E
Gig Harbor, Wa., U.S. (gĭg)	116a	47°20'N	122°36'W
Giglio, Isola del, i., Italy (jēl'yō)	174	42°23'N	10°55'E
Gijón, Spain (hē-hōn')	154	43°33'N	5°37'W
Gila, r., U.S. (hē'lå)	106	33°00'N	110°00'W
Gila Bend, Az., U.S.	119	32°59'N	112°41'W
Gila Cliff Dwellings National Monument, rec., N.M., U.S.	119	33°15'N	108°20'W
Gila River Indian Reservation, I.R., Az., U.S.	119	33°11'N	112°38'W
Gilbert, Mn., U.S. (gĭl'bērt)	113	47°27'N	92°29'W
Gilbert, r., Austl. (gĭl-bĕrt)	221	17°15'S	142°09'E
Gilbert, Mount, mtn., Can.	94	50°51'N	124°20'W
Gilbert Islands, is., Kir.	241	0°30'S	174°00'E
Gilboa, Mount, mtn., S. Afr. (gĭl-bōå)	233c	29°13'N	30°17'W
Gilford Island, i., Can. (gĭl'fērd)	94	50°45'N	126°25'W
Gilgit, Pak. (gĭl'gĭt)	199	35°58'N	73°48'E
Gil Island, i., Can. (gĭl)	94	53°13'N	129°15'W
Gillen, l., Austl. (jĭl'ĕn)	220	26°15'S	125°15'E
Gillett, Ar., U.S. (jĭ-lĕt')	121	34°07'N	91°22'W
Gillette, Wy., U.S.	115	44°17'N	105°30'W
Gillingham, Eng., U.K. (gĭl'ĭng ăm)	165	51°23'N	0°33'E
Gilman, Il., U.S. (gĭl'măn)	108	40°45'N	87°55'W
Gilman Hot Springs, Ca., U.S.	117a	33°49'N	116°57'W
Gilmer, Tx., U.S. (gĭl'mēr)	123	32°43'N	94°57'W
Gilmore, Ga., U.S. (gĭl'môr)	110c	33°51'N	84°29'W
Gilo, r., Eth.	231	7°40'N	34°17'E
Gilroy, Ca., U.S. (gĭl-roi')	118	37°00'N	121°34'W
Giluwe, Mount, mtn., Pap. N. Gui.	213	6°04'S	144°00'E
Gimli, Can. (gĭm'lē)	97	50°39'N	97°00'W
Gimone, r., Fr. (zhē-mōn')	170	43°26'N	0°36'E
Ginir, Eth.	231	7°13'N	40°44'E
Ginosa, Italy (jê-nō'zä)	174	40°35'N	16°48'E
Gioia del Colle, Italy (jô'yä dĕl kôl'lā)	174	40°40'N	[illegible]
Girard, Ks., U.S. ([illegible])	121	37°30'N	94°50'W
Girardot, Col. (hē-rär-dōt')	142	4°19'N	74°47'W
Giresun, Tur. (ghēr'ĕ-sòn')	198	40°55'N	38°20'E
Giridih, India (jē-rê-dê)	199	24°12'N	86°18'E
Girona, Spain	162	41°55'N	2°48'E
Gironde, r., Fr. (zhē-rôɴd')	156	45°31'N	1°00'W
Girvan, Scot., U.K. (gûr'văn)	164	55°15'N	5°01'W
Gisborne, N.Z. (gĭz'bŭrn)	221a	38°40'S	178°08'E
Gisenyi, Rw.	232	1°43'S	29°15'E
Gisors, Fr. (zhē-zôr')	170	49°19'N	1°47'E
Gitambo, D.R.C.	236	4°21'N	24°45'E
Gitega, Bdi.	232	3°39'S	30°05'E
Giurgiu, Rom. (jòr'jò)	175	43°53'N	25°58'E
Givet, Fr. (zhē-vĕ')	170	50°08'N	4°47'E
Givors, Fr. (zhē-vôr')	170	45°35'N	4°46'E
Giza *see* Al Jīzah, Egypt	238b	30°01'N	31°12'E
Gizhiga, Russia (gē'zhi-gå)	179	61°59'N	160°46'E
Gizo, Sol. Is.	214e	8°06'S	156°51'E
Gizycko, Pol. (gĭ'zhĭ-ko)	160	54°03'N	21°48'E
Gjirokastër, Alb.	163	40°04'N	20°10'E
Gjøvik, Nor. (gyû'vêk)	160	60°47'N	10°36'E
Glabeek-Zuurbemde, Bel.	159a	50°52'N	4°59'E
Glace Bay, Can. (glās bā)	101	46°12'N	59°57'W
Glacier Bay National Park, rec., Ak., U.S. (glā'shēr)	106a	58°40'N	136°50'W
Glacier National Park, rec., Can.	92	51°45'N	117°35'W
Glacier Peak, mtn., Wa., U.S.	114	48°07'N	121°10'W
Glacier Point, c., Can.	116a	48°24'N	123°59'W
Gladbeck, Ger. (gläd'bĕk)	168	51°35'N	6°59'E
Gladdeklipkop, S. Afr.	238c	24°17'S	29°36'E
Gladstone, Austl. (glăd'stōn)	219	23°45'S	152°00'E
Gladstone, Austl.	218	33°15'S	138°20'E
Gladstone, Mi., U.S.	113	45°50'N	87°04'W
Gladstone, N.J., U.S.	110a	40°43'N	74°39'W
Gladstone, Or., U.S.	116c	45°23'N	122°36'W
Gladwin, Mi., U.S. (glăd'wĭn)	108	44°00'N	84°25'W
Glåma, r., Nor.	156	61°30'N	10°30'E
Glarus, Switz. (glä'ròs)	168	47°02'N	9°03'E
Glasgow, Scot., U.K. (glås'gō)	154	55°54'N	4°25'W
Glasgow, Ky., U.S.	124	37°00'N	85°55'W
Glasgow, Mo., U.S.	121	39°14'N	92°48'W
Glasgow, Mt., U.S.	115	48°14'N	106°39'W
Glassport, Pa., U.S. (glås'pōrt)	111e	40°19'N	79°53'W
Glauchau, Ger. (glou'kou)	168	50°51'N	12°28'E
Glazov, Russia (glä'zôf)	178	58°05'N	52°52'E
Glen, r., Eng., U.K. (glĕn)	158a	52°44'N	0°18'W
Glénan, Îles de, is., Fr. (ēl-dĕ-glā-näɴ')	170	47°43'N	4°42'W
Glen Burnie, Md., U.S. (bûr'nê)	110e	39°10'N	76°38'W
Glen Canyon, p., Ut., U.S.	119	37°10'N	110°50'W
Glen Canyon Dam, dam, Az., U.S. (glĕn kăn'yŭn)	106	36°57'N	111°25'W
Glen Canyon National Recreation Area, rec., U.S.	119	37°00'N	111°20'W
Glen Carbon, Il., U.S. (kär'bŏn)	117e	38°45'N	89°59'W
Glencoe, S. Afr. (glĕn-cō)	233c	28°14'S	30°09'E
Glencoe, Il., U.S.	111a	42°08'N	87°45'W
Glencoe, Mn., U.S. (glĕn'kō)	113	44°44'N	94°07'W
Glen Cove, N.Y., U.S. (kōv)	110a	40°51'N	73°38'W
Glendale, Az., U.S. (glĕn'dāl)	119	33°30'N	112°15'W
Glendale, Ca., U.S.	104	34°09'N	118°15'W
Glendale, Oh., U.S.	111f	31°16'N	84°22'W
Glendive, Mt., U.S. (glĕn'dīv)	104	47°08'N	104°41'W
Glendo, Wy., U.S.	115	42°32'N	104°54'W
Glendora, Ca., U.S. (glĕn-dō'rå)	117a	34°08'N	117°52'W
Glenelg, r., Austl.	222	37°20'S	141°30'E
Glen Ellyn, Il., U.S. (glĕn ĕl'-lĕn)	111a	41°53'N	88°04'W
Glen Innes, Austl. (ĭn'ĕs)	219	29°45'S	152°02'E
Glenns Ferry, Id., U.S. (fĕr'ĭ)	114	42°58'N	115°21'W
Glen Olden, Pa., U.S. (ōl'd'n)	110f	39°54'N	75°17'W
Glenomra, La., U.S. (glĕn-mō'rå)	123	30°58'N	92°36'W
Glenrock, Wy., U.S. (glĕn'rŏk)	115	42°50'N	105°53'W
Glens Falls, N.Y., U.S. (glĕnz fôlz)	109	43°20'N	73°40'W
Glenshaw, Pa., U.S. (glĕn'shô)	111e	40°33'N	79°57'W
Glen Valley, Can.	116d	49°09'N	122°30'W
Glenview, Il., U.S. (glĕn'vū)	111a	42°04'N	87°48'W
Glenville, Ga., U.S. (glĕn'vĭl)	125	31°55'N	81°56'W
Glenwood, Ia., U.S.	112	41°03'N	95°44'W
Glenwood, Mn., U.S.	112	45°39'N	95°23'W
Glenwood, N.M., U.S.	119	33°19'N	108°52'W
Glenwood Springs, Co., U.S.	119	39°35'N	107°20'W
Glienicke, Ger. (glē'nē-kĕ)	159b	52°38'N	13°19'E
Glinde, Ger. (glĕn'dĕ)	159c	53°32'N	10°13'E
Glittertinden, mtn., Nor.	166	61°39'N	8°33'E
Gliwice, Pol. (gwĭ-wĭt'sĕ)	161	50°18'N	18°40'E
Globe, Az., U.S. (glōb)	104	33°20'N	110°50'W
Głogów, Pol. (gwō'gōōv)	161	51°40'N	16°04'E
Glommen, r., Nor. (glôm'ĕn)	166	60°03'N	11°15'E
Glonn, Ger. (glônn)	159d	47°59'N	11°52'E

ăt; finăl; rāte; senâte; ärm; åsk; sofå; fâre; ch-choose; dh-as th in other; bē; êvent; bĕt; recĕnt; cratēr; g-gō; gh-guttural g; bĭt; ĭ-short neutral; rīde; ĸ-guttural k as ch in German ich;

PRONOUNCING INDEX

Glorieuses – Grand Rapids 297

PLACE (Pronunciation)	PAGE	LAT.	LONG.
Glorieuses, Îles, is., Reu.	233	11°28′S	47°50′E
Glossop, Eng., U.K. (glŏs′ŭp)	158a	53°26′N	1°57′W
Gloster, Ms., U.S. (glŏs′tẽr)	124	31°10′N	91°00′W
Gloucester, Eng., U.K. (glŏs′tẽr)	161	51°54′N	2°11′W
Gloucester, Ma., U.S.	101a	42°37′N	70°40′W
Gloucester City, N.J., U.S.	110f	39°53′N	75°08′W
Glouster, Oh., U.S. (glŏs′tẽr)	108	39°35′N	82°05′W
Glover Island, i., Can. (glŭv′ẽr)	101	48°44′N	57°45′W
Gloversville, N.Y., U.S. (glŭv′ẽrz-vĭl)	109	43°05′N	74°20′W
Glovertown, Can. (glŭv′ẽr-toun)	101	48°41′N	54°02′W
Glückstadt, Ger. (glük-shtät)	159c	53°47′N	9°25′E
Glushkovo, Russia (glòsh′kô-vō)	177	51°21′N	34°43′E
Gmünden, Aus. (g′mòn′dĕn)	168	47°57′N	13°47′E
Gniezno, Pol. (g′nyåz′nô)	161	52°32′N	17°34′E
Gnjilane, Serb. (gnyē′là-nĕ)	175	42°28′N	21°27′E
Goa, state, India (gō′á)	199	15°45′N	74°00′E
Goascorán, Hond. (gō-ás′kō-rän′)	132	13°37′N	87°43′W
Goba, Eth. (gō′bä)	231	7°17′N	39°58′E
Gobabis, Nmb. (gō-bä′bĭs)	232	22°25′S	18°50′E
Gobi, des., Asia (gō′be)	204	43°29′N	103°15′E
Goble, Or., U.S. (gō′b′l)	116c	46°01′N	122°53′W
Goch, Ger. (gôk)	171c	51°35′N	6°10′E
Godāvari, r., India (gô-dä′vŭ-rê)	199	19°00′N	78°30′E
Goddards Soak, sw., Austl. (gŏd′árdz)	220	31°20′S	123°30′E
Goderich, Can. (gōd′rĭch)	98	43°45′N	81°45′W
Godfrey, Il., U.S. (gŏd′frê)	117e	38°57′N	90°12′W
Godhavn, Grnld. (gōdh′håvn)	89	69°15′N	53°30′W
Gods, r., Can. (ŏodz)	97	55°17′N	93°35′W
Gods Lake, Can.	91	54°40′N	94°09′W
Godthåb, Grnld. (gŏt′hòb)	89	64°10′N	51°32′W
Goéland, Lac au, l., Can.	99	49°47′N	76°41′W
Goffs, Ca., U.S. (gôfs)	118	34°57′N	115°06′W
Gogebic, l., Mi., U.S. (gô-gē′bĭk)	113	46°24′N	89°25′W
Gogebic Range, mts., Mi., U.S.	113	46°37′N	89°48′W
Göggingen, Ger. (gûg′gĕn-gĕn)	159d	48°21′N	10°53′E
Gogland, i., Russia	167	60°04′N	26°55′E
Gogonou, Benin	235	10°50′N	2°50′E
Gogorrón, Mex. (gō-gô-rōn′)	130	21°51′N	100°54′W
Goiânia, Braz. (gô-yá′nyä)	143	16°41′S	48°57′W
Goiás, Braz. (gô-yá′s)	143	15°57′S	50°10′W
Goiás, state, Braz.	143	16°00′S	48°00′W
Goirle, Neth.	159a	51°31′N	5°06′E
Gökçeada, i., Tur.	175	40°10′N	25°27′E
Göksu, r., Tur. (gûk′sōō′)	181	36°40′N	33°30′E
Gol, Nor. (gûl)	166	60°58′N	8°54′E
Golax, Va., U.S. (gō′lăks)	125	36°41′N	80°56′W
Golcar, Eng., U.K. (gŏl′kár)	158a	53°38′N	1°52′W
Golconda, Il., U.S. (gŏl-kŏn′dá)	121	37°21′N	88°32′W
Gołdap, Pol. (gôl′dăp)	169	54°17′N	22°17′E
Golden, Can.	95	51°18′N	116°58′W
Golden, Co., U.S.	120	39°44′N	105°15′W
Goldendale, Wa., U.S. (gōl′dĕn-dāl)	114	45°49′N	120°48′W
Golden Gate, strt., Ca., U.S. (gōl′dĕn gāt)	116b	37°48′N	122°32′W
Golden Hinde, mtn., Can. (hīnd)	94	49°40′N	125°45′W
Golden's Bridge, N.Y., U.S.	110a	41°17′N	73°41′W
Golden Valley, Mn., U.S.	117g	44°58′N	93°23′W
Goldfield, Nv., U.S. (gōld′fēld)	118	37°42′N	117°15′W
Gold Hill, mtn., Pan.	128a	9°03′N	79°08′W
Gold Mountain, mtn., Wa., U.S. (gōld)	116a	47°33′N	122°48′W
Goldsboro, N.C., U.S. (gōldz-bûr′ô)	125	35°23′N	77°59′W
Goldthwaite, Tx., U.S. (gōld′thwāt)	122	31°27′N	98°34′W
Goleniów, Pol. (gô-lĕ-nyŭf′)	168	53°33′N	14°51′E
Golets-Purpula, Gora, mtn., Russia	179	59°08′N	115°22′E
Golfito, C.R. (gôl-fē′tō)	133	8°40′N	83°12′W
Goliad, Tx., U.S. (gō-lĭ-ăd′)	123	28°40′N	97°12′W
Golo, r., Fr.	174	42°28′N	9°18′E
Golo Island, i., Phil. (gō′lō)	213a	13°38′N	120°17′E
Golovchino, Russia (gō-lôf′chĕ-nō)	177	50°34′N	35°52′E
Golyamo Konare, Blg. (gō′lå-mō-kō′nä-rĕ)	175	42°16′N	24°33′E
Golzow, Ger. (gōl′tsōv)	159b	52°17′N	12°36′E
Gombe, Nig.	230	10°19′N	11°02′E
Gomera Island, i., Spain (gô-mā′rä)	230	28°00′N	18°01′W
Gomez Farias, Mex. (gō′măz fä-rē′ás)	122	24°59′N	101°02′W
Gómez Palacio, Mex. (pä-lä′syō)	128	25°35′N	103°30′W
Gonaïves, Haiti (gō-nå-ēv′)	129	19°25′N	72°45′W
Gonaïves, Golfe des, b., Haiti (gō-nå-ēv′)	135	19°20′N	73°20′W
Gonâve, Île de la, i., Haiti (gô-näv′)	129	18°50′N	73°30′W
Gonda, India	202	27°13′N	82°00′E
Gondal, India	202	22°02′N	70°47′E
Gonder, Eth.	231	12°39′N	37°30′E
Gonesse, Fr. (gô-nĕs′)	171b	48°59′N	2°28′E
Gongga Shan, mtn., China (gôŋ-gä shän)	204	29°16′N	101°46′E
Goniri, Nig.	235	11°30′N	12°20′E
Gonō, r., Japan (gô′nō)	211	35°00′N	132°25′E
Gonor, Can. (gō′nŏr)	102f	50°04′N	96°57′W
Gonubie, S. Afr. (gŏn′ōō-bē)	233c	32°56′S	28°02′E
Gonzales, Mex. (gôn-zá′lĕs)	130	22°47′N	98°26′W
Gonzales, Tx., U.S. (gŏn-zä′lĕz)	123	29°31′N	97°25′W
González Catán, Arg. (gōn-zá′lĕz-kä-tá′n)	144a	34°47′S	58°39′W
Good Hope, Cape of, c., S. Afr. (kāp ov gŏŏd hōp)	232	34°21′S	18°29′E
Good Hope Mountain, mtn., Can.	94	51°09′N	124°10′W
Gooding, Id., U.S. (gòd′ĭng)	115	42°55′N	114°43′W
Goodland, In., U.S. (gòd′lănd)	108	40°50′N	87°15′W
Goodland, Ks., U.S.	120	39°19′N	101°43′W
Goodwood, S. Afr. (gòd′wòd)	232a	33°54′S	18°33′E
Goole, Eng., U.K. (gōōl)	158a	53°42′N	0°52′W
Goose, r., N.D., U.S.	112	47°40′N	97°41′W

PLACE (Pronunciation)	PAGE	LAT.	LONG.
Gooseberry Creek, r., Wy., U.S. (gōōs-bĕr′ĭ)	115	44°04′N	108°35′W
Goose Creek, r., Id., U.S. (gōōs)	115	42°07′N	113°53′W
Goose Lake, l., Ca., U.S.	114	41°56′N	120°35′W
Gorakhpur, India (gō′rŭk-pōōr)	199	26°45′N	82°39′E
Gorda, Punta, c., Cuba (pōō′n-tä-gôr-dä)	134	22°25′N	82°10′W
Gorda Cay, i., Bah. (gôr′dä)	134	26°05′N	77°30′W
Gordon, Can. (gôr′dŭn)	102f	50°00′N	97°20′W
Gordon, Ne., U.S.	112	42°47′N	102°14′W
Gore, Eth. (gō′rĕ)	231	8°12′N	35°34′E
Gorgān, Iran	198	36°44′N	54°30′E
Gorgona, Isola di, Italy (gôr-gō′nä)	162	43°27′N	9°55′E
Gori, Geor. (gō′rê)	181	42°00′N	44°08′E
Gorinchem, Neth. (gō′rĭn-κĕm)	159a	51°50′N	4°59′E
Goring, Eng., U.K. (gôr′ĭng)	158b	51°30′N	1°08′W
Gorizia, Italy (gô-rê′tsê-yä)	174	45°56′N	13°40′E
Gor'kiy *see* Nizhniy Novgorod, Russia	178	56°15′N	44°05′E
Gor'kovskoye, res., Russia	178	56°38′N	43°40′E
Gorlice, Pol. (gôr-lē′tsĕ)	169	49°38′N	21°11′E
Görlitz, Ger. (gŭr′lĭts)	161	51°10′N	15°01′E
Gorman, Tx., U.S. (gôr′măn)	122	32°13′N	98°40′W
Gorna Oryakhovitsa, Blg. (gôr′nä-ôr-yĕk′ô-vē-tsá)	175	43°08′N	25°40′E
Gornji Milanovac, Serb. (gôrn′yē-mē′la-nô-väts)	175	44°02′N	20°29′E
Gorno-Altay, prov., Russia	184	51°00′N	86°00′E
Gorno-Altaysk, Russia (gôr′nŭ′ŭl-tīsk′)	178	51°58′N	85°58′E
Gorodishche, Russia (gô-rô′dĭsh-chĕ)	186a	57°57′N	57°03′E
Gorodok, Russia	179	50°30′N	103°58′E
Gorontalo, Indon. (gō-rōn-tä′lo)	213	0°40′N	123°04′E
Gorzów Wielkopolski, Pol. (gō-zhōōv′vyĕl-ko-pōl′skē)	160	53°44′N	15°15′E
Gosely, Eng., U.K.	158a	52°33′N	2°10′W
Goshen, In., U.S. (gō′shĕn)	108	41°35′N	85°50′W
Goshen, Ky., U.S.	111h	38°24′N	85°34′W
Goshen, N.Y., U.S.	110a	41°24′N	74°19′W
Goshen, Oh., U.S.	111f	39°14′N	84°09′W
Goshute Indian Reservation, I.R., Ut., U.S. (gō-shōōt′)	119	39°50′N	114°00′W
Goslar, Ger. (gôs′lär)	168	51°55′N	10°25′E
Gospa, r., Ven. (gôs-pä)	143b	9°43′N	64°23′W
Gostivar, Mac. (gos′tê-vär)	175	41°46′N	20°58′E
Gostynin, Pol. (gôs-tē′nĭn)	169	52°24′N	19°30′E
Göta, r., Swe. (gōĕtä)	166	58°11′N	12°03′E
Göta Kanal, can., Swe. (yŭ′tá)	166	58°35′N	15°24′E
Göteborg, Swe. (yû′tĕ-bôrgh)	154	57°39′N	11°56′E
Gotel Mountains, mts., Afr.	235	7°05′N	11°20′E
Gotera, El Sal. (gō-tā′rä)	132	13°41′N	88°06′W
Gotha, Ger. (gō′tá)	161	50°47′N	10°43′E
Gothenburg *see* Göteborg, Swe.	154	57°39′N	11°56′E
Gothenburg, Ne., U.S. (gŏth′ĕn-bûrg)	120	40°57′N	100°08′W
Gotland, i., Swe.	156	57°35′N	17°35′E
Gotska Sandön, i., Swe.	167	58°24′N	19°15′E
Göttingen, Ger. (gŭt′ĭng-ĕn)	168	51°32′N	9°57′E
Gouda, Neth. (gou′dä)	159a	52°00′N	4°42′E
Gough, i., St. Hel. (gŏf)	2	40°00′S	10°00′W
Gouin, Réservoir, res., Can.	93	48°15′N	74°15′W
Goukou, China (gō-kō)	205	48°45′N	121°42′E
Goulais, r., Can.	98	46°45′N	84°10′W
Goulburn, Austl. (gōl′bŭrn)	219	34°47′S	149°40′E
Goumbati, mtn., Sen.	234	13°08′N	12°06′W
Goumbou, Mali (gōōm-bōō′)	230	14°59′N	7°27′W
Gouna, Cam.	235	8°32′N	13°34′E
Goundam, Mali (gōōn-däṅ′)	230	16°29′N	3°37′W
Gouverneur, N.Y., U.S. (gŭv-ẽr-nōōr′)	109	44°20′N	75°25′W
Govenlock, Can. (gŭvĕn-lŏk)	90	49°15′N	109°48′W
Governador, Ilha do, i., Braz. (gô-vĕr-nä-dō-ī-ē-lä′dō)	144b	22°48′S	43°13′W
Governador Portela, Braz. (pōr-tĕ′là)	144b	22°28′S	43°30′W
Governador Valadares, Braz. (vä-lä-dä′rĕs)	143	18°47′S	41°45′W
Governor's Harbour, Bah.	134	25°15′N	76°15′W
Gowanda, N.Y., U.S. (gô-wŏn′dá)	109	42°30′N	78°55′W
Goya, Arg. (gō′yä)	144	29°06′S	59°12′W
Göyçay, Azer. (gē-ôk′chī)	181	40°40′N	47°40′E
Goyt, r., Eng., U.K. (goit)	158a	53°19′N	2°03′W
Graaff-Reinet, S. Afr. (gräf′rī′nĕt)	232	32°10′S	24°40′E
Gračac, Cro. (grä′chäts)	174	44°16′N	15°50′E
Gračanica, Bos.	175	44°42′N	18°18′E
Graceville, Fl., U.S. (grās′vĭl)	124	30°57′N	85°30′W
Graceville, Mn., U.S.	112	45°33′N	96°25′W
Gracias, Hond. (grä′sê-äs)	132	14°35′N	88°37′W
Graciosa Island, i., Port. (grä-syō′sä)	230a	39°07′N	27°30′W
Gradačac, Bos. (gra-dä′chats)	163	44°50′N	18°28′E
Grado, Spain (grä′dō)	172	43°24′N	6°04′W
Gräfelfing, Ger. (grä′fĕl-fĕng)	159d	48°07′N	11°27′E
Grafing bei München, Ger. (grä′fĕng)	159d	48°03′N	11°58′E
Grafton, Austl. (graf′tŭn)	219	29°38′S	153°05′E
Grafton, Il., U.S.	117e	38°58′N	90°26′W
Grafton, Ma., U.S.	101a	42°13′N	71°41′W
Grafton, N.D., U.S.	112	48°24′N	97°25′W
Grafton, Oh., U.S.	111d	41°16′N	82°04′W
Grafton, W.V., U.S.	108	39°20′N	80°00′W
Gragnano, Italy (grän-yä′nô)	173c	40°27′N	14°32′E
Graham, N.C., U.S. (grā′ăm)	125	36°03′N	79°23′W
Graham, Tx., U.S.	120	33°07′N	98°34′W
Graham, Wa., U.S.	116a	47°03′N	122°18′W
Graham, i., Can.	92	53°50′N	132°40′W
Grahamstown, S. Afr. (grā′ăms′toun)	233c	33°19′S	26°33′E
Grajewo, Pol. (grä-yā′vo)	169	53°38′N	22°28′E

PLACE (Pronunciation)	PAGE	LAT.	LONG.
Grama, Serra de, mtn., Braz. (sĕ′r-rä-dĕ-grá′mà)	141a	20°42′S	42°28′W
Gramada, Blg. (grä′mä-dä)	175	43°46′N	22°41′E
Gramatneusiedl, Aus.	159e	48°02′N	16°29′E
Grampian Mountains, mts., Scot., U.K. (grăm′pĭ-ăn)	156	56°30′N	4°55′W
Granada, Nic. (grä-nä′dhä)	128	11°55′N	85°58′W
Granada, Spain (grä-nä′dä)	162	37°13′N	3°37′W
Gran Bajo, reg., Arg. (grán′bä′kô)	144	47°35′S	68°45′W
Granbury, Tx., U.S. (grăn′bĕr-ĭ)	123	32°26′N	97°45′W
Granby, Can. (grăn′bĭ)	91	45°30′N	72°40′W
Granby, Mo., U.S.	121	36°54′N	94°15′W
Granby, l., Co., U.S.	120	40°07′N	105°40′W
Gran Canaria Island, i., Spain (grän′kä-nä′rê-ä)	230	27°39′N	15°39′W
Gran Chaco, reg., S.A. (grán′chá′kō)	144	25°30′S	62°15′W
Grand, i., Mi., U.S.	113	46°37′N	86°38′W
Grand, l., Can.	100	45°59′N	66°15′W
Grand, l., Me., U.S.	100	45°17′N	67°42′W
Grand, r., Can.	99	43°45′N	80°20′W
Grand, r., Mi., U.S.	108	42°58′N	85°13′W
Grand, r., Mo., U.S.	121	39°50′N	93°52′W
Grand, r., S.D., U.S.	112	45°40′N	101°55′W
Grand, North Fork, r., U.S.	112	45°52′N	102°49′W
Grand, South Fork, r., S.D., U.S.	112	45°38′N	102°56′W
Grand Bahama, i., Bah.	129	26°35′N	78°30′W
Grand Bank, Can. (grănd băngk)	93a	47°06′N	55°47′W
Grand Bassam, C. Iv. (gräN bà-säN′)	230	5°12′N	3°44′W
Grand Bourg, Guad. (gräN bōōr′)	133b	15°54′N	61°20′W
Grand Caicos, i., T./C. Is. (grănd kä-ē′kōs)	135	21°45′N	71°50′W
Grand Canal *see* Da Yunhe, can., China	205	35°00′N	117°00′E
Grand Canal, can., Ire.	164	53°21′N	7°15′W
Grand Canyon, Az., U.S.	119	36°05′N	112°10′W
Grand Canyon, p., Az., U.S.	106	35°50′N	113°16′W
Grand Canyon National Park, rec., Az., U.S.	106	36°15′N	112°20′W
Grand Canyon-Parashant National Monument, rec., Az., U.S.	119	36°25′N	113°45′W
Grand Cayman, i., Cay. Is. (kā′măn)	129	19°15′N	81°15′W
Grand Coulee Dam, dam, Wa., U.S. (kōō′lē)	106	47°58′N	119°28′W
Grande, r., Arg.	141b	35°25′S	70°14′W
Grande, r., Bol.	142	16°49′S	63°19′W
Grande, r., Braz.	143	19°48′S	49°54′W
Grande, r., Mex.	131	17°37′N	96°41′W
Grande, r., Nic. (grän′dĕ)	133	13°01′N	84°21′W
Grande, r., Ur.	141c	33°19′S	57°15′W
Grande, Arroyo, r., Mex. (är-rō′yō-grä′n-dĕ)	130	23°30′N	98°45′W
Grande, Bahía, b., Arg. (bä-ē′ä-grán′dĕ)	144	50°45′S	68°00′W
Grande, Boca, mth., Ven. (bō′kä-grä′n-dĕ)	143	8°46′N	60°17′W
Grande, Cuchilla, mts., Ur. (kōō-chē′l-yä)	144	33°00′S	55°15′W
Grande, Ilha, i., Braz. (grän′dĕ)	141a	23°11′S	44°14′W
Grande, Rio, r., N.A. (grän′dā)	106	26°50′N	99°10′W
Grande, Salinas, l., Arg. (sä-lē′nás)	144	29°45′S	65°00′W
Grande, Salto, wtfl., Braz. (säl-tô)	143	16°18′S	39°38′W
Grande Cayemite, Île, i., Haiti	135	18°45′N	73°45′W
Grande de Otoro, r., Hond. (grä′dą dā ô-tō′rô)	132	14°42′N	88°21′W
Grande de Santiago, Río, r., Mex. (rêô-grä′n-dĕ-dĕ-săn-tyá′gô)	128	20°30′N	104°00′W
Grande Pointe, Can. (grănd point′)	102f	49°47′N	97°03′W
Grande Prairie, Can. (prâr′ĭ)	90	55°10′N	118°48′W
Grand Erg Occidental, des., Alg.	230	30°00′N	1°00′E
Grand Erg Oriental, des., Alg.	230	30°00′N	7°00′E
Grande Rivière du Nord, Haiti (rē-vyâr′ dü nôr′)	135	19°35′N	72°10′W
Grande Ronde, r., Or., U.S. (rŏnd′)	114	45°32′N	117°52′W
Gran Desierto, des., Mex. (grän-dĕ-syĕ′r-tô)	119	32°14′N	114°28′W
Grande Terre, i., Guad.	133b	16°28′N	61°13′W
Grande Vigie, Pointe de la, c., Guad. (grănd vē-gē′)	133b	16°32′N	61°25′W
Grand Falls, Can. (fôlz)	93a	48°56′N	55°40′W
Grandfather Mountain, mtn., N.C., U.S. (grănd-fä-thẽr)	125	36°07′N	81°48′W
Grandfield, Ok., U.S. (grănd′fēld)	120	34°13′N	98°39′W
Grand Forks, Can. (fôrks)	90	49°02′N	118°27′W
Grand Forks, N.D., U.S.	104	47°55′N	97°05′W
Grand Haven, Mi., U.S. (hā′v′n)	108	43°05′N	86°15′W
Grand Island, Ne., U.S. (ī′lánd)	104	40°56′N	98°20′W
Grand Island, i., N.Y., U.S.	111c	43°03′N	78°58′W
Grand Junction, Co., U.S. (jŭngk′shŭn)	104	39°05′N	108°35′W
Grand Lake, l., Can. (lāk)	93a	49°00′N	57°10′W
Grand Lake, l., La., U.S.	123	29°57′N	91°25′W
Grand Lake, l., Mn., U.S.	117h	46°54′N	92°26′W
Grand Ledge, Mi., U.S. (lĕj)	108	42°45′N	84°50′W
Grand Lieu, Lac de, l., Fr. (grăN′-lyû)	170	47°00′N	1°45′W
Grand Manan, i., Can. (má-năn)	100	44°40′N	66°50′W
Grand Mère, Can. (gräN mâr′)	91	46°36′N	72°43′W
Grândola, Port. (grăN′dô-lá)	172	38°10′N	8°36′W
Grand Portage Indian Reservation, I.R., Mn., U.S. (pōr′tĭj)	113	47°54′N	89°34′W
Grand Portage National Monument, rec., Mi., U.S.	113	47°59′N	89°47′W
Grand Prairie, Tx., U.S. (prĕ′rê)	117c	32°45′N	97°00′W
Grand Rapids, Can.	97	53°08′N	99°20′W
Grand Rapids, Mi., U.S. (răp′ĭdz)	105	43°00′N	85°45′W
Grand Rapids, Mn., U.S.	113	47°16′N	93°33′W

ng-sing; ŋ-baŋk; N-nasalized n; nŏd; cŏmmit; ōld; ôbey; ôrder; oi-boil; fōōd; ò-as oo in foot; ou-out; s-soft; sh-dish; th-thin; pūre; ûnite; ûrn; stŭd; circŭs; ü-as in French tu; ′-indeterminate vowel.

298 Grand-Riviere – Guadalajara PRONOUNCING INDEX

PLACE (Pronunciation)	PAGE	LAT.	LONG.
Grand-Riviere, Can.	100	48°26'N	64°30'W
Grand Staircase-Escalante National Monument, rec., Ut., U.S.	119	37°25'N	111°30'W
Grand Teton, mtn., Wy., U.S.	106	43°46'N	110°50'W
Grand Teton National Park, rec., Wy., U.S. (tē'tŏn)	115	43°54'N	110°15'W
Grand Traverse Bay, b., Mi., U.S. (trăv'ērs)	108	45°00'N	85°30'W
Grand Turk, T./C. Is. (tûrk)	135	21°30'N	71°10'W
Grand Turk, i., T./C. Is.	135	21°30'N	71°10'W
Grandview, Mo., U.S. (grănd'vyōō)	117f	38°53'N	94°32'W
Granger, Wy., U.S. (grān'jēr)	115	41°37'N	109°58'W
Grangeville, Id., U.S. (grānj'vĭl)	114	45°56'N	116°08'W
Granite City, Il., U.S. (grăn'ĭt sĭt'ĭ)	117e	38°42'N	90°09'W
Granite Falls, Mn., U.S. (fôlz)	112	44°46'N	95°34'W
Granite Falls, N.C., U.S.	125	35°49'N	81°25'W
Granite Falls, Wy., U.S.	[illegible]	[illegible]	[illegible]
Granite Lake, l., Can.	101	48°01'N	57°00'W
Granite Peak, mtn., Mt., U.S.	106	45°13'N	109°48'W
Graniteville, S.C., U.S. (grăn'ĭt-vĭl)	125	33°35'N	81°50'W
Granito, Braz. (grä-nē'tō)	143	7°39'S	39°34'W
Granma, prov., Cuba	134	20°10'N	76°50'W
Gränna, Swe. (grĕn'å)	166	58°02'N	14°38'E
Granollers, Spain (grä-nôl-yĕrs')	173	41°36'N	2°19'E
Gran Pajonal, reg., Peru (grä'n-pä-κô-näl')	142	11°14'S	71°45'W
Gran Paradiso, mtn., Italy	174	45°32'N	7°16'E
Gran Piedra, mtn., Cuba (grän-pyĕ'drä)	135	20°00'N	75°40'W
Grantham, Eng., U.K. (grăn'tăm)	164	52°54'N	0°38'W
Grant Park, Il., U.S. (grănt pärk)	111a	41°14'N	87°39'W
Grants Pass, Or., U.S. (grănts pås)	114	42°26'N	123°20'W
Granville, Fr. (gräɴ-vēl')	161	48°52'N	1°35'W
Granville, N.Y., U.S. (grăn'vĭl)	109	43°25'N	73°15'W
Granville, l., Can.	92	56°18'N	100°30'W
Grão Mogol, Braz. (grouɴ' mō-gôl')	143	16°34'S	42°35'W
Grapevine, Tx., U.S. (grāp'vīn)	117c	32°56'N	97°05'W
Gräso, i., Swe.	166	60°30'N	18°35'E
Grass, r., N.Y., U.S.	109	44°45'N	75°10'W
Grass Cay, i., V.I.U.S.	129c	18°22'N	64°50'W
Grasse, Fr. (gräs)	171	43°39'N	6°57'E
Grass Mountain, mtn., Wa., U.S. (grås)	116a	47°13'N	121°48'W
Grates Point, c., Can. (grāts)	101	48°09'N	52°57'W
Gravelbourg, Can. (grăv'ĕl-bôrg)	90	49°53'N	106°34'W
Gravesend, Eng., U.K. (grāvz'ĕnd')	158b	51°26'N	0°22'E
Gravina, Italy (grä-vē'nä)	174	40°48'N	16°27'E
Gravois, Pointe à, c., Haiti (grà-vwä')	135	18°00'N	74°20'W
Gray, Fr. (grå)	171	47°26'N	5°35'E
Grayling, Mi., U.S. (grā'lĭng)	108	44°40'N	84°40'W
Grays Harbor, b., Wa., U.S. (grās)	106	46°55'N	124°23'W
Grayslake, Il., U.S. (grāz'lāk)	111a	42°20'N	88°20'W
Grays Peak, mtn., Co., U.S. (grāz)	120	39°29'N	105°52'W
Grays Thurrock, Eng., U.K. (thŭ'rŏk)	158b	51°28'N	0°19'E
Grayvoron, Russia (grá-ē'vô-rôn)	177	50°28'N	35°41'E
Graz, Aus. (gräts)	154	47°05'N	15°26'E
Great Abaco, i., Bah. (ä'bä-kō)	129	26°30'N	77°05'W
Great Artesian Basin, basin, Austl. (är-tēzh-ăn bā-sĭn)	221	23°16'S	143°37'E
Great Australian Bight, b., Austl. (ôs-trā'lĭ-ăn bĭt)	220	33°30'S	127°00'E
Great Bahama Bank, bk. (bá-hā'má)	134	25°00'N	78°50'W
Great Barrier, i., N.Z. (băr'ĭ-ēr)	221a	36°10'S	175°30'E
Great Barrier Reef, rf., Austl. (bă-rĭ-ēr rēf)	221	16°43'S	146°34'E
Great Basin, basin, U.S. (grāt bā's'n)	106	40°08'N	117°10'W
Great Bear Lake, l., Can. (bâr)	92	66°10'N	119°53'W
Great Bend, Ks., U.S. (bĕnd)	120	38°41'N	98°46'W
Great Bitter Lake, l., Egypt	238b	30°24'N	32°27'E
Great Blasket Island, i., Ire. (blăs'kĕt)	164	52°05'N	10°55'W
Great Corn Island, i., Nic.	133	12°10'N	82°54'W
Great Dismal Swamp, sw., U.S. (dĭz'măl)	125	36°35'N	76°34'W
Great Divide Basin, basin, Wy., U.S. (dĭ-vīd' bā's'n)	115	42°10'N	108°10'W
Great Dividing Range, mts., Austl. (dĭ-vī-dĭng rānj)	221	35°16'S	146°38'E
Great Duck, i., Can. (dŭk)	98	45°40'N	83°22'W
Greater Antilles, is., N.A.	129	20°30'N	79°15'W
Greater Khingan Range, mts., China (dä hĭŋ-gän lĭŋ)	205	46°30'N	120°00'E
Greater Leech Indian Reservation, I.R., Mn., U.S. (grāt'ēr lēch)	113	47°39'N	94°27'W
Greater Manchester, hist. reg., Eng., U.K.	158a	53°34'N	2°41'W
Greater Sunda Islands, is., Asia	212	4°00'S	108°00'E
Great Exuma, i., Bah. (ĕk-sōō'mä)	134	23°35'N	76°00'W
Great Falls, Mt., U.S. (fôlz)	104	47°30'N	111°15'W
Great Falls, S.C., U.S.	125	34°32'N	80°53'W
Great Guana Cay, i., Bah. (gwä'nä)	134	24°00'N	76°20'W
Great Harbor Cay, i., Bah. (kē)	134	25°45'N	77°50'W
Great Inagua, i., Bah. (ē-nä'gwä)	129	21°00'N	73°15'W
Great Indian Desert, des., Asia	199	27°35'N	71°37'E
Great Isaac, i., Bah. (ī'zăk)	134	26°05'N	79°05'W
Great Karroo, plat., S. Afr. (grāt kă'rōō)	232	32°45'S	22°00'E
Great Limpopo Transfrontier Park, rec., Afr.	232	22°00'S	31°30'E
Great Namaland, hist. reg., Nmb.	232	25°45'S	16°15'E
Great Neck, N.Y., U.S. (nĕk)	110a	40°48'N	73°44'W
Great Nicobar Island, i., India (nĭk-ō-bär')	212	7°00'N	94°18'E
Great Pedro Bluff, c., Jam.	134	17°50'N	78°05'W
Great Pee Dee, r., S.C., U.S. (pē-dē')	107	34°01'N	79°26'W
Great Plains, pl., N.A. (plāns)	89	45°00'N	104°00'W
Great Ragged, i., Bah.	135	22°10'N	75°45'W
Great Ruaha, r., Tan.	232	7°30'S	37°00'E
Great Salt Lake, l., Ut., U.S. (sôlt lāk)	106	41°19'N	112°48'W
Great Salt Lake Desert, des., Ut., U.S.	106	41°00'N	113°30'W
Great Salt Plains Reservoir, res., Ok., U.S.	120	36°56'N	98°14'W
Great Sand Dunes National Monument, rec., Co., U.S.	120	37°56'N	105°25'W
Great Sand Hills, hills, Can. (sănd)	96	50°35'N	109°05'W
Great Sandy Desert, des., Austl. (săn'dē)	220	21°50'S	123°10'E
Great Sandy Desert, des., Or., U.S. (săn'dĭ)	114	43°43'N	120°44'W
Great Sitkin, i., Ak., U.S. (sĭt-kĭn)	103a	52°18'N	176°22'W
Great Slave Lake, l., Can. (slāv)	92	61°37'N	114°58'W
Great Smoky Mountains National Park, rec., U.S. (smōk-ē)	107	35°43'N	83°20'W
Great Stirrup Cay, i., Bah. (stĭr-ŭp)	134	25°50'N	77°55'W
Great Victoria Desert, des., Austl. (vĭk-tō'rĭ-à)	220	29°45'S	124°30'E
Great Wall, hist., China	204	38°00'N	109°00'E
Great Waltham, Eng., U.K. (wôl'thŭm)	158b	51°47'N	0°27'E
Great Yarmouth, Eng., U.K. (yär-mŭth)	161	52°35'N	1°45'E
Grebbestad, Swe. (grĕb-bĕ-städh)	166	58°42'N	11°15'E
Gréboun, Mont, mtn., Niger	230	20°00'N	8°35'E
Gredos, Sierra de, mts., Spain (syĕr'rä dā grā'dōs)	172	40°13'N	5°30'W
Greece, nation, Eur. (grēs)	154	39°00'N	21°30'E
Greeley, Co., U.S. (grē'lĭ)	104	40°25'N	104°41'W
Green, r., Ky., U.S. (grēn)	124	37°13'N	86°30'W
Green, r., N.D., U.S.	112	47°05'N	103°05'W
Green, r., Ut., U.S.	119	38°30'N	110°05'W
Green, r., Wa., U.S.	116a	47°17'N	121°57'W
Green, r., Wy., U.S.	115	41°08'N	110°27'W
Green, r., U.S.	106	38°30'N	110°10'W
Greenbank, Wa., U.S. (grēn'bănk)	116a	48°06'N	122°35'W
Green Bay, Wi., U.S.	105	44°30'N	88°04'W
Green Bay, b., U.S.	107	44°55'N	87°40'W
Green Bayou, Tx., U.S.	123a	29°53'N	95°13'W
Greenbelt, Md., U.S. (grēn'bĕlt)	110e	38°59'N	76°53'W
Greencastle, In., U.S. (grēn-kás''l)	108	39°40'N	86°50'W
Green Cay, i., Bah.	134	24°05'N	77°10'W
Green Cove Springs, Fl., U.S. (kōv)	125	29°56'N	81°42'W
Greendale, Wi., U.S. (grēn'dāl)	111a	42°56'N	87°59'W
Greenfield, Ia., U.S.	113	41°16'N	94°30'W
Greenfield, In., U.S. (grēn'fēld)	108	39°45'N	85°40'W
Greenfield, Ma., U.S.	109	42°35'N	72°35'W
Greenfield, Mo., U.S.	121	37°23'N	93°48'W
Greenfield, Oh., U.S.	108	39°15'N	83°25'W
Greenfield, Tn., U.S.	124	36°08'N	88°45'W
Greenfield Park, Can.	102a	45°29'N	73°29'W
Greenhills, Oh., U.S. (grēn-hĭls)	111f	39°16'N	84°31'W
Greenland, dep., N.A. (grēn'lănd)	89	74°00'N	40°00'W
Greenland Sea, sea	244	77°00'N	1°00'W
Green Mountain, mtn., Or., U.S.	116c	45°52'N	123°24'W
Green Mountain Reservoir, res., Co., U.S.	119	39°50'N	106°20'W
Green Mountains, mts., N.A.	107	43°10'N	73°05'W
Greenock, Scot., U.K. (grēn'ŭk)	160	55°55'N	4°45'W
Green Peter Lake, res., Or., U.S.	114	44°28'N	122°30'W
Green Pond Mountain, mtn., N.J., U.S. (pŏnd)	110a	41°00'N	74°32'W
Greenport, N.Y., U.S.	109	41°06'N	72°22'W
Green River, Ut., U.S. (grēn rĭv'ēr)	119	39°00'N	110°05'W
Green River, Wy., U.S.	115	41°32'N	109°26'W
Green River Lake, res., Ky., U.S.	124	37°15'N	85°15'W
Greensboro, Al., U.S. (grēnz'bŭro)	124	32°42'N	87°36'W
Greensboro, Ga., U.S. (grēns-bûr'ô)	124	33°34'N	83°11'W
Greensboro, N.C., U.S.	105	36°04'N	79°45'W
Greensburg, In., U.S. (grēnz'bûrg)	108	39°20'N	85°30'W
Greensburg, Ks., U.S. (grēns-bûrg)	120	37°36'N	99°17'W
Greensburg, Pa., U.S.	109	40°20'N	79°30'W
Greenville, Lib.	230	5°01'N	9°03'W
Greenville, Al., U.S. (grēn'vĭl)	124	31°49'N	86°39'W
Greenville, Il., U.S.	121	38°52'N	89°22'W
Greenville, Ky., U.S.	124	37°11'N	87°11'W
Greenville, Me., U.S.	100	45°26'N	69°35'W
Greenville, Mi., U.S.	108	43°10'N	85°25'W
Greenville, Ms., U.S.	105	33°25'N	91°00'W
Greenville, N.C., U.S.	125	35°35'N	77°22'W
Greenville, Oh., U.S.	108	40°05'N	84°35'W
Greenville, Pa., U.S.	108	41°20'N	80°25'W
Greenville, S.C., U.S.	105	34°50'N	82°25'W
Greenville, Tn., U.S.	125	36°08'N	82°50'W
Greenville, Tx., U.S.	123	33°09'N	96°07'W
Greenwich, Eng., U.K.	158b	51°28'N	0°00'
Greenwich, Ct., U.S.	110a	41°01'N	73°37'W
Greenwood, Ar., U.S. (grēn-wŏŏd)	121	35°13'N	94°15'W
Greenwood, In., U.S.	111g	39°37'N	86°07'W
Greenwood, Ms., U.S.	124	33°30'N	90°09'W
Greenwood, S.C., U.S.	125	34°10'N	82°10'W
Greenwood, Lake, res., S.C., U.S.	125	34°17'N	81°55'W
Greenwood Lake, l., N.Y., U.S.	110a	41°13'N	74°20'W
Greer, S.C., U.S. (grēr)	125	34°55'N	81°56'W
Grefrath, Ger. (grĕf'rät)	171c	51°20'N	6°21'E
Gregory, S.D., U.S. (grĕg'ō-rĭ)	112	43°12'N	99°27'W
Gregory, Lake, l., Austl. (grĕg'ō-rē)	220	28°47'S	139°15'E
Gregory Range, mts., Austl.	221	19°23'S	143°45'E
Greifenberg, Ger. (grī'fĕn-bĕrgh)	159d	48°04'N	11°06'E
Greifswald, Ger. (grīfs'vält)	168	54°05'N	13°24'E
Greiz, Ger. (grīts)	168	50°39'N	12°14'E
Gremyachinsk, Russia (grâ'myá-chĭnsk)	186a	58°35'N	57°53'E
Grenada, Ms., U.S. (grē-nā'da)	124	33°45'N	89°47'W
Grenada, nation, N.A.	129	12°02'N	61°15'W
Grenada Lake, res., Ms., U.S.	124	33°52'N	89°30'W
Grenadines, The, is., N.A. (grĕn'à-dēnz)	133b	12°37'N	61°35'W
Grenen, c., Den.	160	57°43'N	10°31'E
Grenoble, Fr. (grē-nô'bl')	161	45°14'N	5°45'E
Grenora, N.D., U.S. (grė-nō'rȧ)	112	48°38'N	103°55'W
Grenville, Can. (grĕn'vĭl)	109	45°40'N	74°35'W
Grenville, Gren.	133b	12°07'N	61°38'W
Gresham, Or., U.S. (grĕsh'ăm)	116c	45°30'N	122°25'W
Gretna, La., U.S. (grĕt'nȧ)	110d	29°56'N	90°03'W
Grevelingen Krammer, r., Neth.	159a	51°42'N	4°03'E
[illegible]	[illegible]	[illegible]	[illegible]
Grey, r., Can. (grā)	101	47°53'N	57°00'W
Grey, Point, c., Can.	116d	49°22'N	123°16'W
Greybull, Wy., U.S. (grā'bŏŏl)	115	44°28'N	108°05'W
Greybull, r., Wy., U.S.	115	44°13'N	108°43'W
Greylingstad, S. Afr. (grā-lĭng'shtát)	238c	26°40'S	29°13'E
Greymouth, N.Z. (grā'mouth)	221a	42°27'S	171°17'E
Grey Range, mts., Austl.	221	28°40'S	142°05'E
Greytown, S. Afr. (grā'toun)	233c	29°07'S	30°38'E
Grey Wolf Peak, mtn., Wa., U.S. (grā wŏŏlf)	116a	48°53'N	123°12'W
Gridley, Ca., U.S. (grĭd'lĭ)	118	39°22'N	121°43'W
Griffin, Ga., U.S. (grĭf'ĭn)	124	33°15'N	84°16'W
Griffith, Austl. (grĭf-ĭth)	222	34°16'S	146°10'E
Griffith, In., U.S.	111a	41°31'N	87°26'W
Grigoriopol', Mol. (grĭ'gor-i-ō'pôl)	177	47°09'N	29°18'E
Grijalva, r., Mex. (grē-häl'vä)	131	17°25'N	93°23'W
Grim, Cape, c., Austl. (grĭm)	222	40°43'S	144°30'E
Grimma, Ger. (grĭm'á)	168	51°14'N	12°43'E
Grimsby, Can. (grĭmz'bĭ)	102d	43°11'N	79°33'W
Grimsby, Eng., U.K.	160	53°35'N	0°05'W
Grímsey, i., Ice. (grĭms'å)	160	66°30'N	17°50'W
Grimstad, Nor. (grĭm-städh)	160	58°21'N	8°30'E
Grindstone Island, Can.	101	47°25'N	61°51'W
Grinnel, Ia., U.S. (grĭ-nĕl')	113	41°44'N	92°44'W
Griswold, Ia., U.S. (grĭz'wŭld)	112	41°11'N	95°05'W
Groais Island, i., Can.	101	50°57'N	55°35'W
Grobina, Lat. (grō'bĭŋĭa)	167	56°35'N	21°10'E
Groblersdal, S. Afr.	238c	25°11'S	29°25'E
Grodzisk, Pol. (grō'jēsk)	168	52°14'N	16°22'E
Grodzisk Masowiecki, Pol. (grō'jēsk mä-zō-vyĕts'ke)	169	52°06'N	20°40'E
Groesbeck, Tx., U.S. (grōs'bĕk)	123	31°32'N	96°31'W
Groix, Île de, i., Fr. (ēl dē grwä')	170	47°39'N	3°28'W
Grójec, Pol. (grō'yĕts)	169	51°53'N	20°52'E
Gronau, Ger. (grō'nou)	168	52°12'N	7°05'E
Groningen, Neth. (grō'nĭng-ĕn)	160	53°13'N	6°30'E
Groote Eylandt, i., Austl. (grō'tē ī'länt)	220	13°50'S	137°30'E
Grootfontein, Nmb. (grōt'fōn-tān')	232	19°30'S	18°15'E
Groot-Kei, r., Afr. (kē)	233c	32°17'S	27°30'E
Grootkop, mtn., S. Afr.	232a	34°11'S	18°23'E
Groot Marico, S. Afr.	238c	25°36'S	26°23'E
Groot Marico, r., Afr.	238c	25°13'S	26°20'E
Groot-Vis, r., S. Afr.	233c	33°04'S	26°08'E
Groot Vloer, pl., S. Afr. (grōt' vlôr')	232	30°00'S	21°00'E
Gros-Mécatina, i., Can.	101	50°50'N	58°33'W
Gros Morne, mtn., Can. (grō môrn')	101	49°36'N	57°48'W
Gros Morne National Park, rec., Can.	93a	49°45'N	59°15'W
Gros Pate, mtn., Can.	101	50°16'N	57°25'W
Grosse Island, i., Mi., U.S. (grōs)	111b	42°08'N	83°09'W
Grosse Isle, Can. (īl')	102f	50°04'N	97°27'W
Grossenhain, Ger. (grōs'ĕn-hīn)	168	51°17'N	13°33'E
Gross-Enzersdorf, Aus.	159e	48°13'N	16°33'E
Grosse Pointe, Mi., U.S. (point')	111b	42°23'N	82°54'W
Grosse Pointe Farms, Mi., U.S. (färm)	111b	42°25'N	82°53'W
Grosse Pointe Park, Mi., U.S. (pärk)	111b	42°23'N	82°55'W
Grosseto, Italy (grôs-sā'tō)	174	42°46'N	11°09'E
Grossglockner, mtn., Aus.	161	47°06'N	12°45'E
Gross Höbach, Ger. (hû'bäk)	159d	48°21'N	11°36'E
Gross Kreutz, Ger. (kroitz)	159b	52°24'N	12°47'E
Gross Schönebeck, Ger. (shō'nĕ-bĕk)	159b	52°54'N	13°32'E
Gros Ventre, r., Wy., U.S. (grōvĕn't'r)	115	43°38'N	110°34'W
Groton, Ct., U.S. (grŏt'ŭn)	109	41°20'N	72°00'W
Groton, Ma., U.S.	101a	42°37'N	71°34'W
Groton, S.D., U.S.	112	45°25'N	98°04'W
Grottaglie, Italy (grôt-täl'yā)	175	40°32'N	17°26'E
Grouard Mission, Can.	90	55°31'N	116°09'W
Groveland, Ma., U.S. (grōv'lănd)	101a	42°25'N	71°02'W
Groveton, N.H., U.S. (grōv'tŭn)	109	44°35'N	71°30'W
Groveton, Tx., U.S.	123	31°04'N	95°07'W
Groznyy, Russia (grôz'nĭ)	178	43°20'N	45°40'E
Grudziądz, Pol. (grō'jyôɴts)	160	53°30'N	18°48'E
Grues, Île aux, i., Can. (ō grü)	102b	47°05'N	70°32'W
Grundy Center, Ia., U.S. (grŭn'dĭ sĕn'tēr)	113	42°22'N	92°45'W
Gruñidora, Mex. (grōō-nyē-dō'rō)	130	24°10'N	101°49'W
Grünwald, Ger. (grōōn'väld)	159d	48°04'N	11°34'E
Gryazi, Russia (gryä'zĭ)	176	52°31'N	39°59'E
Gryazovets, Russia (gryä'zō-vĕts)	180	58°52'N	40°14'E
Gryfice, Pol. (grĭ'fĭ-tsĕ)	168	53°55'N	15°11'E
Gryfino, Pol. (grĭ'fē-nō)	168	53°16'N	14°30'E
Guabito, Pan. (gwä-bē'tō)	133	9°30'N	82°33'W
Guacanayabo, Golfo de, b., Cuba (gôl-fô-dĕ-gwä-kä-nä-yä'bō)	134	20°30'N	77°40'W
Guacara, Ven. (gwá'kä-rä)	143b	10°16'N	67°48'W
Guadalajara, Mex. (gwä-dhä-lä-hä'rä)	128	20°41'N	103°21'W

ăt; finăl; rāte; senåte; ärm; åsk; sofá; fâre; ch-choose; dh-as th in other; bē; ėvent; bĕt; recĕnt; cratēr; g-gō; gh-guttural g; bĭt; ĭ-short neutral; rīde; κ-guttural k as ch in German ich;

PRONOUNCING INDEX

Guadalajara – Haines City 299

PLACE (Pronunciation)	PAGE	LAT.	LONG.
Guadalajara, Spain (gwä-dä-lä-kä´rä)	162	40°37′N	3°10′W
Guadalcanal, Spain (gwä-dhäl-kä-näl´)	172	38°05′N	5°48′W
Guadalcanal, i., Sol. Is.	221	9°48′S	158°43′E
Guadalcázar, Mex. (gwä-dhäl-kä´zär)	130	22°38′N	100°24′W
Guadalete, r., Spain (gwä-dhä-lā´tå)	172	36°53′N	5°38′W
Guadalhorce, r., Spain (gwä-dhäl-ôr´thā)	172	37°05′N	4°50′W
Guadalimar, r., Spain (gwä-dhä-lē-mär´)	172	38°29′N	2°53′W
Guadalope, r., Spain (gwä-dä-lȯ-pě)	173	40°48′N	0°10′W
Guadalquivir, Río, r., Spain (rē´ō-gwä-dhäl-kē-vēr´)	156	37°30′N	5°00′W
Guadalupe, Mex.	122	31°23′N	106°06′W
Guadalupe, i., Mex.	128	29°00′N	118°45′W
Guadalupe, r., Tx., U.S. (gwä-dhä-lōō´på)	122	29°54′N	99°03′W
Guadalupe, Sierra de, mts., Spain (syĕr´rä dā gwä-dhä-lōō´pā)	162	39°30′N	5°25′W
Guadalupe Mountains, mts., N.M., U.S.	122	32°00′N	104°55′W
Guadalupe Peak, mtn., Tx., U.S.	122	31°55′N	104°55′W
Guadarrama, r., Spain (gwä-dhär-rä´mä)	173a	40°34′N	3°58′W
Guadarrama, Sierra de, mts., Spain (gwä-dhär-rä´mä)	156	41°00′N	3°40′W
Guadatentin, r., Spain	172	37°43′N	1°58′W
Guadeloupe, dep., N.A. (gwä-dē-lōōp)	129	16°40′N	61°10′W
Guadeloupe Passage, strt., N.A.	133b	16°26′N	62°00′W
Guadiana, r., Eur. (gwä-dvä´nä)	156	39°00′N	6°00′W
Guadiana, Bahía de, b., Cuba (bä-ē´ä-dĕ-gwä-dhē-ä´nä)	134	22°10′N	84°35′W
Guadiana Alto, r., Spain (äl´tō)	172	39°02′N	2°52′W
Guadiana Menor, r., Spain (mā´nôr)	172	37°43′N	2°45′W
Guadiaro, r., Spain (gwä-dhē-ä´rō)	172	36°38′N	5°25′W
Guadiela, r., Spain (gwä-dhē-ā´lä)	172	40°27′N	2°05′W
Guadix, Spain (gwä-dēsh´)	172	37°18′N	3°09′W
Guaira, Braz. (gwä-ē-rä)	143	24°03′S	54°02′W
Guaire, r., Ven. (gwī´rĕ)	143b	10°25′N	66°43′W
Guajaba, Cayo, i., Cuba (kä´yō-gwä-hä´bä)	134	21°50′N	77°35′W
Guajará Mirim, Braz. (gwä-zhä-rä´mē-rēN´)	142	10°58′S	65°12′W
Guajira, Península de, pen., S.A.	142	12°35′N	73°00′W
Gualán, Guat. (gwä-län´)	132	15°08′N	89°21′W
Gualeguay, Arg. (gwä-lĕ-gwä´y)	144	33°10′S	59°20′W
Gualeguay, r., Arg.	144	32°49′S	59°05′W
Gualicho, Salina, l., Arg. (sä-lē´nä-gwä-lē´chō)	144	40°20′S	65°15′W
Guam, i., Oc. (gwäm)	3	14°00′N	143°20′E
Guamo, Col. (gwá´mō)	142a	4°02′N	74°58′W
Gu'an, China (gōō-än)	208a	39°25′N	116°18′E
Guan, r., China (gůän)	206	31°56′N	115°19′E
Guanabacoa, Cuba (gwä-nä-bä-kō´ä)	129	23°08′N	82°19′W
Guanabara, Baía de, b., Braz.	141a	22°44′S	43°09′W
Guanacaste, Cordillera, mts., C.R.	132	10°54′N	85°27′W
Guanacevi, Mex. (gwä-nä-sĕ-vē´)	128	25°30′N	105°45′W
Guanahacabibes, Península de, pen., Cuba	134	21°55′N	84°35′W
Guanajay, Cuba (gwänä-hī´)	134	22°55′N	82°40′W
Guanajuato, Mex. (gwä-nä-hwä´tō)	128	21°01′N	101°16′W
Guanajuato, state, Mex.	128	21°00′N	101°00′W
Guanape, Ven. (gwä-nä´pĕ)	143b	9°55′N	65°32′W
Guanape, r., Ven.	143b	9°52′N	65°20′W
Guanare, Ven. (gwä-nä´rä)	142	8°57′N	69°47′W
Guanduçu, r., Braz. (gwä´n-dōō´sōō)	144b	22°50′S	43°40′W
Guane, Cuba (gwä´nå)	134	22°10′N	84°05′W
Guangchang, China (gůäŋ-chäŋ)	209	26°50′N	116°18′E
Guangde, China (gůäŋ-dŭ)	209	30°40′N	119°20′E
Guangdong, prov., China (gůäŋ-dôŋ)	205	23°45′N	113°15′E
Guanglu Dao, i., China (gůäŋ-lōō dou)	206	39°13′N	122°21′E
Guangping, China (gůäŋ-pĭŋ)	206	36°30′N	114°57′E
Guangrao, China (gůäŋ-rou)	206	37°04′N	118°24′E
Guangshan, China (gůäŋ-shän)	206	32°02′N	114°53′E
Guangxi Zhuangzu, prov., China (gůäŋ-shyē)	204	24°00′N	108°30′E
Guangzhou, China	204	23°07′N	113°15′W
Guanhu, China (gůän-hōō)	206	34°26′N	117°59′E
Guannan, China (gůän-nän)	206	34°17′N	119°17′E
Guanta, Ven. (gwän´tä)	143b	10°15′N	64°35′W
Guantánamo, Cuba (gwän-tä´nä-mȯ)	135	20°10′N	75°10′W
Guantánamo, prov., Cuba	135	20°10′N	75°05′W
Guantánamo, Bahía de, b., Cuba	135	19°35′N	75°35′W
Guantao, China (gůän-tou)	206	36°39′N	115°25′E
Guanxian, China (gůän-shyĕn)	206	36°30′N	115°28′E
Guanyao, China (gůän-you)	207a	23°13′N	113°04′E
Guanyun, China (gůän-yòn)	206	34°28′N	119°16′E
Guapiles, C.R. (gwä-pē-lĕs)	133	10°05′N	83°54′W
Guapimirim, Braz. (gwä-pē-mē-rē´N)	144b	22°31′S	42°59′W
Guaporé, r., S.A. (gwä-pȯ-rā´)	142	12°11′S	63°47′W
Guaqui, Bol. (guä´kē)	142	16°42′S	68°47′W
Guara, Sierra de, mts., Spain (sē-ĕ´r-rä-dĕ-gwä´rä)	173	42°24′N	0°15′W
Guarabira, Braz. (gwä-rä-bē´rá)	143	6°49′S	35°27′W
Guaranda, Ec. (gwä-rán´dä)	142	1°39′S	78°57′W
Guarapari, Braz. (gwä-rä-pä´rē)	143	20°34′S	40°31′W
Guarapiranga, Represa do, res., Braz.	141a	23°45′S	46°44′W
Guarapuava, Braz. (gwä-rä-pwä´vá)	144	25°29′S	51°26′W
Guarda, Port. (gwär´dä)	172	40°32′N	7°17′W
Guardiato, r., Spain	172	38°10′N	5°05′W
Guarena, Spain (gwä-rā´nyä)	172	38°52′N	6°08′W
Guaribe, r., Ven. (gwä-rē´bĕ)	143b	9°48′N	65°17′W
Guárico, dept., Ven.	143b	9°42′N	67°25′W
Guarulhos, Braz. (gwá-rò´l-yôs)	141a	23°28′S	46°30′W
Guarus, Braz. (gwá´rōōs)	141a	21°44′S	41°19′W
Guasca, Col. (gwäs´kä)	142a	4°52′N	73°52′W
Guasipati, Ven. (gwä-sē-pä´tē)	143	7°26′N	61°57′W
Guastalla, Italy (gwäs-täl´lä)	174	44°53′N	10°39′E
Guasti, Ca., U.S. (gwäs´tĭ)	117a	34°04′N	117°35′W
Guatemala, Guat. (guä-tå-mä´lä)	128	14°37′N	90°32′W
Guatemala, nation, N.A.	128	15°45′N	91°45′W
Guatire, Ven. (gwä-tē´rĕ)	143b	10°28′N	66°34′W
Guaviare, r., Col.	142	3°35′N	69°28′W
Guayabal, Cuba (gwä-yä-bä´l)	134	20°40′N	77°40′W
Guayalejo, r., Mex. (gwä-yä-lĕ´hȯ)	130	23°24′N	99°09′W
Guayama, P.R. (gwä-yä´mä)	129b	18°00′N	66°08′W
Guayamouc, r., Haiti	135	19°05′N	72°00′W
Guayaquil, Ec. (gwī-ä-kēl´)	142	2°16′S	79°53′W
Guayaquil, Golfo de, b., Ec. (gȯl-fô-dĕ)	142	3°03′S	82°12′W
Guaymas, Mex. (gwá´y-mäs)	128	27°49′N	110°58′W
Guayubin, Dom. Rep. (gwá-yōō-bĕ´n)	135	19°40′N	71°25′W
Guazacapán, Guat. (gwä-zä-kä pan´)	132	14°04′N	90°20′W
Gubakha, Russia (gōō-bä´kä)	170	58°50′N	57°36′E
Gubbio, Italy (gōōb´byô)	174	43°23′N	12°36′E
Guben, Ger.	168	51°57′N	14°43′E
Gucheng, China (gōō-chŭŋ)	206	39°09′N	115°43′E
Gúdar, Sierra de, mts., Spain	173	40°28′N	0°47′W
Gudena, r., Den.	166	56°20′N	9°47′E
Gudermes, Russia	182	43°20′N	46°08′E
Gudvangen, Nor. (gōōdh´väŋ-gĕn)	166	60°52′N	6°45′E
Guebwiller, Fr. (gĕb-vē-lâr´)	171	47°53′N	7°10′E
Guédi, Mont, mtn., Chad	235	12°14′N	18°58′E
Guelma, Alg. (gwĕl´mä)	230	36°32′N	7°17′E
Guelph, Can. (gwĕlf)	99	43°33′N	80°15′W
Güere, r., Ven. (gwĕ´rĕ)	143b	9°39′N	65°00′W
Guéret, Fr. (gā-rĕ´)	170	46°09′N	1°52′E
Guernsey, dep., Eur.	170	49°28′N	2°35′W
Guernsey, i., Guern. (gûrn´zĭ)	161	49°27′N	2°36′W
Guerrero, Mex. (gĕr-rā´rō)	122	26°47′N	99°20′W
Guerrero, Mex.	122	28°20′N	100°24′W
Guerrero, state, Mex.	128	17°45′N	100°15′W
Gueydan, La., U.S. (gā´dăn)	123	30°01′N	92°31′W
Guia de Pacobaíba, Braz. (gwē´ä-dĕ-pä´kō-bī´bä)	144b	22°42′S	43°10′W
Guiana Highlands, mts., S.A.	139	3°20′N	60°00′W
Guichi, China (gwā-chr)	209	30°35′N	117°28′E
Guichicovi, Mex. (gwē-chē-kō´vē)	131	16°58′N	95°10′W
Guidonia, Italy (gwē-dō´nyä)	174	42°00′N	12°45′E
Guiglo, C. Iv.	234	6°33′N	7°29′W
Guignes-Rabutin, Fr. (gēN´yĕ)	171b	48°38′N	2°48′E
Güigüe, Ven. (gwĕ´gwĕ)	143b	10°05′N	67°48′W
Guija, Lago, l., N.A. (gē´hä)	132	14°16′N	89°21′W
Guildford, Eng., U.K. (gĭl´fērd)	164	51°13′N	0°34′W
Guilford, In., U.S. (gĭl´fērd)	111f	39°10′N	84°55′W
Guilin, China (gwā-lĭn)	205	25°18′N	110°22′E
Guimarães, Port. (gē-mä-rănsh´)	172	41°27′N	8°22′W
Guinea, nation, Afr. (gĭn´ē)	230	10°48′N	12°28′W
Guinea, Gulf of, b., Afr.	230	2°00′N	1°00′E
Guinea-Bissau, nation, Afr. (gĭn´ē)	230	12°00′N	20°00′W
Guingamp, Fr. (găN-găN´)	170	48°35′N	3°10′W
Guir, r., Mor.	162	31°55′N	2°48′W
Güira de Melena, Cuba (gwē´rä dā må-lā´nä)	134	22°45′N	82°30′W
Güiria, Ven. (gwē-rē´ä)	142	10°43′N	62°16′W
Guise, Fr. (guēz)	170	49°54′N	3°37′E
Guisisil, vol., Nic. (gē-sē-sēl´)	132	12°40′N	86°11′W
Guiyang, China (gwā-yäŋ)	204	26°45′N	107°00′E
Guizhou, China (gwā-jō)	207a	22°46′N	113°15′E
Guizhou, prov., China	204	27°00′N	106°10′E
Gujānwāla, Pak. (gòj-rän´va-lá)	199	32°08′N	74°14′E
Gujarat, India	199	22°54′N	72°00′E
Gulbarga, India (gòl-bŭr´gá)	199	17°25′N	76°52′E
Gulbene, Lat. (gòl-bā´nĕ)	167	57°09′N	26°49′E
Gulfport, Ms., U.S. (gŭlf´pōrt)	124	30°24′N	89°05′W
Gulja *see* Yining, China	204	43°58′N	80°40′E
Gull Lake, Can.	96	50°10′N	108°25′W
Gull Lake, l., Can.	95	52°35′N	114°00′W
Gulu, Ug.	237	2°47′N	32°18′E
Gumaca, Phil. (gōō-mä-kä´)	213a	13°55′N	122°06′E
Gumbeyka, r., Russia (gòm-bĕy´ká)	186a	53°20′N	59°42′E
Gumel, Nig.	230	12°39′N	9°22′E
Gummersbach, Ger. (gòm´ĕrs-bäk)	168	51°02′N	7°34′E
Gummi, Nig.	235	12°09′N	5°09′E
Gumpoldskirchen, Aus.	159e	48°04′N	16°15′E
Guna, India	202	24°44′N	77°17′E
Gunisao, r., Can. (gŭn-*i*-sä´ō)	97	53°40′N	97°35′W
Gunisao Lake, l., Can.	97	53°35′N	96°10′W
Gunnedah, Austl. (gŭ´nē-dä)	222	31°00′S	150°10′E
Gunnison, Co., U.S. (gŭn´ĭ-sŭn)	119	38°33′N	106°56′W
Gunnison, Ut., U.S.	119	39°10′N	111°50′W
Gunnison, r., Co., U.S.	119	38°45′N	108°20′W
Guntersville, Al., U.S. (gŭn´tērz-vĭl)	124	34°20′N	86°19′W
Guntersville Lake, res., Al., U.S.	124	34°30′N	86°20′W
Guntramsdorf, Aus.	159e	48°04′N	16°19′E
Guntūr, India (gòn´tōōr)	199	16°22′N	80°29′E
Guoyang, China (gwô-yäŋ)	206	33°32′N	116°10′E
Gurdon, Ar., U.S. (gûr´dŭn)	121	33°56′N	93°10′W
Gurgueia, r., Braz.	143	8°12′S	43°49′W
Guri, Embalse, res., Ven.	142	7°30′N	63°00′W
Gurnee, Il., U.S. (gûr´nē)	111a	42°22′N	87°55′W
Gurskøy, i., Nor. (gōōrskûē)	166	62°18′N	5°20′E
Gurupi, Serra do, mts., Braz. (sĕ´r-rä-dò-gōō-rōō-pē´)	143	5°32′S	47°02′W
Guru Sikhar, mtn., India	202	29°42′N	72°50′E
Gur'yevsk, Russia (gōōr-yĭfsk´)	178	54°17′N	85°56′E
Gusau, Nig. (gōō-zä´ōō)	230	12°12′N	6°40′E
Gusev, Russia (gōō´sĕf)	167	54°35′N	22°15′E
Gushi, China (gōō-shr)	206	32°11′N	115°39′E
Gushiago, Ghana	234	9°55′N	0°12′W
Gusinje, Mont. (gōō-sēn´yĕ)	175	42°34′N	19°54′E
Gus'-Khrustal'nyy, Russia (gōōs-krōō-stäl´ny´)	180	55°39′N	40°41′E
Gustavo A. Madero, Mex. (gōōs-tä´vô-á-mä-dĕ´rȯ)	130	19°29′N	99°07′W
Güstrow, Ger. (güs´trō)	168	53°48′N	12°12′E
Gütersloh, Ger. (gü´tērs-lo)	168	51°54′N	8°22′E
Guthrie, Ok., U.S. (gŭth´rĭ)	121	35°52′N	97°26′W
Guthrie Center, Ia., U.S.	113	41°41′N	94°33′W
Gutiérrez Zamora, Mex. (gōō-tĭ-âr´rāz zä-mō´rä)	131	20°27′N	97°17′W
Guttenberg, Ia., U.S. (gŭt´ĕn-bûrg)	113	42°48′N	91°09′W
Guyana, nation, S.A. (gŭy´ănă)	143	7°45′N	59°00′W
Guyang, China (gōō-yäŋ)	206	34°56′N	114°57′E
Guye, China (gōō-yŭ)	206	39°46′N	118°23′E
Guymon, Ok., U.S. (gī´mŏn)	120	36°41′N	101°29′W
Guysborough, Can. (gīz´bŭr ȯ)	101	45°23′N	61°30′W
Guzhon, China (gōō-jŭn)	208	33°20′N	117°18′E
Gvardeysk, Russia (gvår-dĕysk´)	167	54°39′N	21°11′E
Gwadabawa, Nig.	235	13°20′N	5°15′E
Gwādar, Pak. (gwä´dŭr)	198	25°15′N	62°29′E
Gwalior, India	199	26°13′N	78°10′E
Gwane, D.R.C. (gwän)	231	4°43′N	25°50′E
Gwardafuy, Gees, c., Som.	238a	11°55′N	51°30′E
Gwda, r., Pol.	168	53°27′N	16°52′E
Gwembe, Zam.	237	16°30′S	27°35′E
Gweru, Zimb.	232	19°15′S	29°48′E
Gwinn, Mi., U.S. (gwĭn)	113	46°15′N	87°30′W
Gyaring Co, l., China	202	30°37′N	88°33′E
Gydan, Khrebet (Kolymskiy), mts., Russia	179	61°45′N	155°00′E
Gydanskiy Poluostrov, pen., Russia	178	70°42′N	76°03′E
Gympie, Austl. (gĭm´pē)	219	26°20′S	152°50′E
Gyöngyös, Hung. (dyûn´dyûsh)	163	47°47′N	19°55′E
Györ, Hung. (dyûr)	163	47°40′N	17°37′E
Gyōtoku, Japan (gyō´tō-kōō´)	211a	35°42′N	139°56′E
Gypsumville, Can. (jĭp´s*ŭ*m-vĭl)	90	51°45′N	98°35′W
Gýtheio, Grc.	175	36°50′N	22°37′E
Gyula, Hung. (dyò´lä)	169	46°38′N	21°18′E
Gyumri, Arm.	181	40°40′N	43°50′E
Gyzylarbat, Turkmen.	183	38°55′N	56°33′E

H

PLACE (Pronunciation)	PAGE	LAT.	LONG.
Haan, Ger. (hän)	171c	51°12′N	7°00′E
Haapamäki, Fin. (häp´ä-mĕ-kē)	167	62°16′N	24°20′E
Haapsalu, Est. (häp´sä-lò)	167	58°56′N	23°33′E
Haar, Ger. (här)	159d	48°06′N	11°44′E
Ha'Arava (Wādī al Jayb), val., Asia	197a	30°33′N	35°10′E
Haarlem, Neth. (här´lĕm)	165	52°22′N	4°37′E
Habana, prov., Cuba (hä-vä´nä)	134	22°45′N	82°25′W
Hābra, India	202a	22°49′N	88°38′E
Hachinohe, Japan (hä´chē-nō´hå)	210	40°29′N	141°40′E
Hachiōji, Japan (hä´chē-ō´jē)	210	35°39′N	139°18′E
Hackensack, N.J., U.S. (hăk´ĕn-săk)	110a	40°54′N	74°03′W
Ḩadd, Ra's al, c., Oman	198	22°29′N	59°46′E
Haddonfield, N.J., U.S. (hăd´ŭn-fēld)	110f	39°53′N	75°02′W
Haddon Heights, N.J., U.S. (hăd´ŭn hīts)	110f	39°53′N	75°03′W
Hadejia, Nig. (hä-dā´jä)	230	12°30′N	9°59′E
Hadejia, r., Nig.	230	12°15′N	10°00′E
Ḩadera, Isr. (kå-dĕ´rá)	197a	32°26′N	34°55′E
Haderslev, Den. (hä´dhĕrs-lĕv)	166	55°17′N	9°28′E
Hadiach, Ukr.	181	50°22′N	33°59′E
Ḩadīdū, Yemen	198	12°40′N	53°50′E
Hadlock, Wa., U.S. (hăd´lŏk)	116a	48°02′N	122°46′W
Ḩaḑramawt, reg., Yemen	198	15°22′N	48°40′E
Hadūr Shu'ayb, mtn., Yemen	198	15°45′N	43°45′E
Haeju, Kor., N. (hä´ĕ-jŭ)	210	38°03′N	125°42′E
Hafnarfjördur, Ice.	160	64°02′N	21°32′W
Haft Gel, Iran	201	31°27′N	49°27′E
Hafun, Ras, c., Som. (hä-fōōn´)	238a	10°15′N	51°35′E
Hageland, Mt., U.S. (hăge´lănd)	115	48°53′N	108°43′W
Hagen, Ger. (hä´gĕn)	168	51°21′N	7°29′E
Hagerstown, In., U.S. (hā´gērz-toun)	108	39°55′N	85°10′W
Hagerstown, Md., U.S.	105	39°40′N	77°45′W
Hagi, Japan (hä´gĭ)	211	34°25′N	131°25′E
Hague, Cap de la, c., Fr. (dē lå åg´)	170	49°44′N	1°55′W
Haguenau, Fr. (åg´nō´)	171	48°47′N	7°48′E
Hai'an, China (hī-än)	206	32°35′N	120°25′E
Haibara, Japan (hä´ē-bä´rä)	211	34°29′N	135°57′E
Haicheng, China (hī-chŭŋ)	208	40°58′N	122°45′E
Haidian, China (hī-dĭĕn)	206	39°59′N	116°17′E
Haifa, Isr. (hä´ē-fä)	198	32°48′N	35°00′E
Haifeng, China (hä´ē-fĕng´)	209	23°00′N	115°20′E
Haifuzhen, China (hī-fōō-jŭn)	206	31°57′N	121°48′E
Haikou, China (hī-kō)	209	20°00′N	110°20′E
Ḩā'il, Sau. Ar.	198	27°30′N	41°47′E
Hailar, China	205	49°10′N	118°40′E
Hailey, Id., U.S. (hā´lĭ)	115	43°31′N	114°19′W
Haileybury, Can.	99	47°27′N	79°38′W
Haileyville, Ok., U.S. (hā´lĭ-vĭl)	121	34°51′N	95°34′W
Hailing Dao, i., China (hī-lĭŋ dou)	209	21°30′N	112°15′E
Hailong, China (hī-loŋ)	208	42°32′N	125°52′E
Hailun, China (hä´ē-lōōn´)	205	47°18′N	126°50′E
Hainan, prov., China	204	19°00′N	109°30′E
Hainan Dao, i., China (hī-nän dou)	205	19°00′N	111°10′E
Hainburg, Aus.	168	48°09′N	16°57′E
Haines, Ak., U.S. (hānz)	103	59°10′N	135°38′W
Haines City, Fl., U.S.	125a	28°05′N	81°38′W

ng-sing; ŋ-baŋk; N-nasalized n; nŏd; cŏmmit; ōld; ôbey; ôrder; oi-boil; fōōd; ŏ-as oo in foot; ou-out; s-soft; sh-dish; th-thin; pūre; ûnite; ûrn; stŭd; circŭs; ü-as in French tu; ´-indeterminate vowel.

PLACE (Pronunciation)	PAGE	LAT.	LONG.
Hai Phong, Viet. (hī'fŏng')(hä'ēp-hŏng)	212	20°52'N	106°40'E
Haisyn, Ukr.	181	48°46'N	29°22'E
Haiti, nation, N.A. (hā'tĭ)	129	19°00'N	72°15'W
Haizhou, China	206	34°34'N	119°11'E
Haizhou Wan, b., China	208	34°49'N	120°35'E
Hajduböszormény, Hung. (hôl'dȯ-bû'sûr-mān')	169	47°41'N	21°30'E
Hajdúhadház, Hung. (hô'ĭ-dȯ-hôd'häz)	169	47°32'N	21°32'E
Hajdúnánás, Hung. (hô'ĭ-dȯ-nä'näsh)	169	47°52'N	21°27'E
Hakodate, Japan (hä-kō-dä't å)	205	41°46'N	140°42'E
Haku-San, mtn., Japan (hä'kōō-sän')	210	36°11'N	136°45'E
Halā'ib, Egypt (hä-lä'ēb)	231	22°10'N	36°40'E
Halbe, Ger. (häl'bĕ)	159b	52°07'N	13°43'E
Halberstadt, Ger. (häl'bĕr-shtät)	168	51°54'N	11°07'E
Halcon, Mount, mtn., Phil. (häl-kōn')	213a	13°19'N	120°55'E
Halden, Nor. (häl'dĕn)	160	59°10'N	11°01'E
Haldensleben, Ger.	168	52°18'N	11°23'E
Hale, Eng., U.K. (hāl)	158a	53°22'N	2°20'W
Haleakalā Crater, depr., Hi., U.S. (hä'lå-ä'kä-lä)	126a	20°44'N	156°15'W
Haleakalā National Park, rec., Hi., U.S.	126a	20°46'N	156°00'W
Hales Corners, Wi., U.S. (hālz kŏr'nĕrz)	111a	42°56'N	88°03'W
Halesowen, Eng., U.K. (hālz'ō-wĕn)	158a	52°26'N	2°03'W
Halethorpe, Md., U.S. (hāl-thôrp)	110e	39°15'N	76°40'W
Haleyville, Al., U.S. (hā'lĭ-vĭl)	124	34°11'N	87°36'W
Half Moon Bay, Ca., U.S. (häf'mōōn)	116b	37°28'N	122°26'W
Halfway House, S. Afr. (häf-wā hous)	233b	26°00'S	28°08'E
Halfweg, Neth.	159a	52°23'N	4°45'E
Halifax, Can. (hăl'ĭ-făks)	91	44°39'N	63°36'W
Halifax, Eng., U.K.	164	53°44'N	1°52'W
Halifax Bay, b., Austl. (hăl'ĭ-făx)	221	18°56'S	147°07'E
Halifax Harbour, b., Can.	100	44°35'N	63°31'W
Halkett, Cape, c., Ak., U.S.	103	70°50'N	151°15'W
Hallam Peak, mtn., Can.	95	52°11'N	118°46'E
Halla San, mtn., Kor., S. (häl'lä-sän)	210	33°20'N	126°37'E
Halle, Bel. (häl'lĕ)	159a	50°45'N	4°13'E
Halle, Ger.	161	51°30'N	11°59'E
Hallettsville, Tx., U.S. (hăl'ĕts-vĭl)	123	29°26'N	96°55'W
Hallock, Mn., U.S. (hăl'ŭk)	112	48°46'N	96°57'W
Hall Peninsula, pen., Can. (hôl)	93	63°14'N	65°40'W
Halls Bayou, Tx., U.S.	123a	29°55'N	95°23'W
Hallsberg, Swe. (häls'bĕrgh)	166	59°04'N	15°04'E
Halls Creek, Austl. (hôlz)	218	18°15'S	127°45'E
Halmahera, i., Indon. (häl-mä-hā'rä)	213	0°45'N	128°45'E
Halmahera, Laut, Indon.	213	1°00'S	129°00'E
Halmstad, Swe. (hälm'städ)	160	56°40'N	12°46'E
Halsafjorden, b., Nor. (häl'sĕ fyôrd)	166	63°03'N	8°23'E
Halstead, Ks., U.S. (hôl'stĕd)	121	38°02'N	97°36'W
Haltern, Ger. (häl'tĕrn)	171c	51°45'N	7°10'E
Haltom City, Tx., U.S. (hôl'tŏm)	117c	32°48'N	97°13'W
Halver, Ger.	171c	51°11'N	7°30'E
Hamada, Japan	210	34°53'N	132°05'E
Hamadān, Iran (hŭ-mŭ-dän')	198	34°45'N	48°07'E
Ḩamāh, Syria (hä'mä)	198	35°08'N	36°53'E
Hamamatsu, Japan (hä'mä-mät'sȯ)	210	34°41'N	137°43'E
Hamar, Nor. (hä'mär)	160	60°49'N	11°05'E
Hamasaka, Japan (hä'mȧ-sä'kȧ)	211	35°57'N	134°27'E
Hamborn, Ger. (häm'bōrn)	171c	51°30'N	6°43'E
Hamburg, Ger. (häm'bŏŏrgh)	154	53°34'N	10°02'E
Hamburg, S. Afr. (hăm'bûrg)	233c	33°18'S	27°28'E
Hamburg, Ar., U.S. (hăm'bûrg)	121	33°15'N	91°49'W
Hamburg, N.J., U.S.	110a	41°09'N	74°35'W
Hamburg, N.Y., U.S.	111c	42°44'N	78°51'W
Hamden, Ct., U.S. (hăm'dĕn)	109	41°20'N	72°55'W
Hämeenlinna, Fin. (hĕ'mân-lĭn-nȧ)	160	61°00'N	24°29'E
Hameln, Ger. (hä'mĕln)	168	52°06'N	9°23'E
Hamelwörden, Ger. (hä'mĕl-vûr-dĕn)	159c	53°47'N	9°19'E
Hamersley Range, mts., Austl. (hăm'ẽrz-lē)	220	22°15'S	117°50'E
Hamhŭng, Kor., N. (häm'hŏng')	205	39°57'N	127°35'E
Hami, China (hä-mē)	204	42°58'N	93°14'E
Hamilton, Austl. (hăm'ĭl-tŭn)	219	37°50'S	142°10'E
Hamilton, Can.	91	43°15'N	79°52'W
Hamilton, N.Z.	221a	37°45'S	175°28'E
Hamilton, Al., U.S.	124	34°09'N	88°01'W
Hamilton, Ma., U.S.	101a	42°37'N	70°52'W
Hamilton, Mo., U.S.	121	39°43'N	93°59'W
Hamilton, Mt., U.S.	115	46°15'N	114°09'W
Hamilton, Oh., U.S.	105	39°22'N	84°33'W
Hamilton, Tx., U.S.	122	31°42'N	98°07'W
Hamilton, Lake, l., Ar., U.S.	121	34°25'N	93°32'W
Hamilton Harbour, b., Can.	102d	43°17'N	79°50'W
Hamilton Inlet, b., Can.	93	54°20'N	56°57'W
Hamina, Fin. (hȧ'mē-nȧ)	167	60°34'N	27°15'E
Hamlet, N.C., U.S. (hăm'lĕt)	125	34°53'N	79°42'W
Hamlin, Tx., U.S. (hăm'lĭn)	120	32°54'N	100°08'W
Hamm, Ger. (häm)	168	51°40'N	7°48'E
Hammanskraal, S. Afr. (hä-mȧns-kräl')	238c	25°24'S	28°17'E
Hamme, Bel.	159a	51°06'N	4°07'E
Hamme-Oste Kanal, can., Ger. (hä'mĕ-ōs'tĕ kä-näl)	159c	53°20'N	8°59'E
Hammerfest, Nor. (hä'mĕr-fĕst)	154	70°38'N	23°59'E
Hammond, In., U.S. (hăm'ŭnd)	105	41°37'N	87°31'W
Hammond, La., U.S.	123	30°30'N	90°28'W
Hammond, Or., U.S.	116c	46°12'N	123°57'W
Hammonton, N.J., U.S. (hăm'ŭn-tŭn)	109	39°40'N	74°45'W
Hampden, Me., U.S. (hăm'dĕn)	100	44°44'N	68°51'W
Hampstead, Md., U.S.	110e	39°36'N	76°54'W
Hampstead Norris, Eng., U.K. (hămp-stĕd nō'rĭs)	158b	51°27'N	1°14'W
Hampton, Can. (hămp'tŭn)	100	45°32'N	65°51'W
Hampton, Ia., U.S.	113	42°43'N	93°15'W
Hampton, Va., U.S.	109	37°02'N	76°21'W
Hampton Roads, b., Va., U.S.	110g	36°56'N	76°23'W
Hams Fork, r., Wy., U.S.	115	41°55'N	110°40'W
Hamtramck, Mi., U.S. (hăm-trăm'ĭk)	111b	42°24'N	83°03'W
Han, r., China (hän)	209	25°00'N	116°35'E
Han, r., China	205	31°40'N	112°04'E
Han, r., Kor., S.	210	37°10'N	127°40'E
Hāna, Hi., U.S. (hä'nä)	126a	20°43'N	155°59'W
Hanábana, r., Cuba (hä-nä-bä'nä)	134	22°30'N	80°55'W
Hanalei Bay, b., Hi., U.S. (hä-nä-lā'ē)	126a	22°15'N	159°40'W
Hanang, mtn., Tan.	237	4°26'S	35°24'E
Hanau, Ger. (hä'nou)	168	50°08'N	8°56'E
Hancock, Mi., U.S. (hăn'kŏk)	105	47°08'N	88°37'W
Handan, China (hän dän)	209	36°37'N	114°30'E
Haney, Can. (hā'nē)	95	49°13'N	122°36'W
Hanford, Ca., U.S. (hăn'fērd)	118	36°20'N	119°38'W
Hangayn Nuruu, mts., Mong.	204	48°03'N	99°45'E
Hango, Fin. (häŋ'gû)	154	59°49'N	22°56'E
Hangzhou, China (hăng'chō')	205	30°17'N	120°12'E
Hangzhou Wan, b., China (häŋ-jō wän)	209	30°20'N	121°25'E
Hankamer, Tx., U.S. (hăn'kȧ-mẽr)	123a	29°52'N	94°42'W
Hankinson, N.D., U.S. (hăŋ'kĭn-sŭn)	112	46°04'N	96°54'W
Hankou, China (hän-kō)	209	30°42'N	114°22'E
Hann, Mount, mtn., Austl. (hän)	220	16°05'S	126°07'E
Hanna, Can. (hăn'ȧ)	90	51°38'N	111°54'W
Hanna, Wy., U.S.	115	41°51'N	106°34'W
Hannah, N.D., U.S.	112	48°58'N	98°42'W
Hannibal, Mo., U.S. (hăn'ĭ bȧl)	105	39°42'N	91°22'W
Hannover, Ger. (hän-ō'vẽr)	154	52°22'N	9°45'E
Hannover, hist. reg., Ger.	168	52°52'N	8°27'E
Hanöbukten, b., Swe.	166	55°54'N	14°55'E
Hanoi, Viet. (hä-noi')	212	21°04'N	105°50'E
Hanover, Can. (hăn'ō-vẽr)	98	44°10'N	81°05'W
Hanover, Ma., U.S.	101a	42°07'N	70°49'W
Hanover, N.H., U.S.	109	43°45'N	72°15'W
Hanover, Pa., U.S.	109	39°50'N	77°00'W
Hanover, i., Chile	144	51°00'S	74°45'W
Hanshan, China (hän'shän')	206	31°43'N	118°06'E
Hans Lollick, i., V.I.U.S. (häns'lŏl'ĭk)	129c	18°24'N	64°55'W
Hanson, Ma., U.S. (hăn'sŭn)	101a	42°04'N	70°53'W
Hansville, Wa., U.S. (hăns'-vĭl)	116a	47°55'N	122°33'W
Hantengri Feng, mtn., Asia (hän-tŭŋ-rē fŭŋ)	204	42°10'N	80°20'E
Hantsport, Can. (hănts'pōrt)	100	45°04'N	64°11'W
Hanyang, China (han'yäng')	205	30°30'N	114°10'E
Hanzhong, China (hän-jôŋ)	208	33°02'N	107°00'E
Haocheng, China (hou-chŭŋ)	206	33°19'N	117°33'E
Haparanda, Swe. (hä-pa-rän'dä)	160	65°54'N	23°57'E
Hapeville, Ga., U.S. (hāp'vĭl)	110c	33°39'N	84°25'W
Happy Camp, Ca., U.S.	114	41°47'N	123°22'W
Happy Valley-Goose Bay, Can.	91	53°19'N	60°33'W
Ḩaql, Sau. Ar.	197a	29°15'N	34°57'E
Har, Laga, r., Kenya	237	2°15'N	39°30'E
Haradok, Bela.	176	55°27'N	29°58'E
Harare, Zimb.	232	17°50'S	31°03'E
Harbin, China	205	45°40'N	126°30'E
Harbor Beach, Mi., U.S. (här'bẽr bēch)	108	43°50'N	82°40'W
Harbor Springs, Mi., U.S.	108	45°25'N	85°05'W
Harbour Breton, Can. (brĕt'ŭn) (brē-tôn')	101	47°29'N	55°48'W
Harbour Grace, Can. (grās)	101	47°32'N	53°13'W
Harburg, Ger. (här-bȯrgh)	159c	53°28'N	9°58'E
Hardangerfjorden, Nor. (här-däng'ẽr fyôrd)	160	59°58'N	6°30'E
Hardin, Mt., U.S. (här'dĭn)	115	45°44'N	107°36'W
Harding, S. Afr. (här'dĭng)	232	30°34'S	29°54'E
Harding, Lake, res., U.S.	124	32°43'N	85°00'W
Hardwār, India (hŭr'dvär)	199	29°56'N	78°06'E
Hardy, r., Mex. (här'dĭ)	118	32°04'N	115°10'W
Hare Bay, b., Can. (hâr)	101	51°18'N	55°50'W
Harer, Eth.	231	9°43'N	42°10'E
Harerge, hist. reg., Eth.	231	8°15'N	41°00'E
Hargeysa, Som. (här-gā'ē-sȧ)	238a	9°20'N	43°57'E
Harghita, Munţii, mts., Rom.	169	46°25'N	25°40'E
Harima-Nada, b., Japan (hä'rē-mä nä-dä)	211	34°34'N	134°37'E
Haringvliet, r., Neth.	159a	51°49'N	4°03'E
Harīrūd, r., Asia	198	34°29'N	61°16'E
Harlan, Ia., U.S. (här'lăn)	121	41°40'N	95°10'W
Harlan, Ky., U.S.	124	36°50'N	83°19'W
Harlan County Reservoir, res., Ne., U.S.	120	40°03'N	99°51'W
Harlem, Mt., U.S. (här'lĕm)	115	48°33'N	108°50'W
Harlingen, Neth. (här'lĭng-ĕn)	165	53°10'N	5°24'E
Harlingen, Tx., U.S.	104	26°12'N	97°42'W
Harlow, Eng., U.K. (här'lō)	158b	51°46'N	0°08'E
Harlowton, Mt., U.S. (här'lō-tun)	115	46°26'N	109°50'W
Harmony, In., U.S. (här'mȯ-nĭ)	108	39°35'N	87°00'W
Harney Basin, Or., U.S. (här'nĭ)	114	43°26'N	120°19'W
Harney Lake, l., Or., U.S.	114	43°11'N	119°23'W
Harney Peak, mtn., S.D., U.S.	106	43°52'N	103°32'W
Härnosand, Swe. (hĕr-nû-sänd)	160	62°37'N	17°54'E
Haro, Spain (ä'rō)	172	42°35'N	2°49'W
Haro Strait, strt., N.A. (hä'rō)	116a	48°27'N	123°11'W
Harpenden, Eng., U.K. (här'pĕn-d'n)	158b	51°48'N	0°22'W
Harper, Lib.	230	4°25'N	7°43'W
Harper, Ks., U.S. (här'pẽr)	120	37°17'N	98°02'W
Harper, Wa., U.S.	116a	47°31'N	122°32'W
Harpers Ferry, W.V., U.S. (här'pẽrz)	109	39°20'N	77°45'W
Harricana, r., Can.	99	50°10'N	78°50'W
Harriman, Tn., U.S. (hă'ĭ-mȧn)	124	35°55'N	84°34'W
Harrington, De., U.S. (hăr'ĭng-tŭn)	109	38°55'N	75°35'W
Harris, i., Scot., U.K. (hăr'ĭs)	164	57°55'N	6°40'W
Harris, Lake, l., Fl., U.S.	125a	28°43'N	81°40'W
Harrisburg, Il., U.S. (hăr'ĭs-bûrg)	108	37°45'N	88°35'W
Harrisburg, Pa., U.S.	105	40°15'N	76°50'W
Harrismith, S. Afr. (hă-rĭs'mĭth)	238c	28°17'S	29°08'E
Harrison, Ar., U.S. (hăr'ĭ-sŭn)	121	36°13'N	93°06'W
Harrison, Oh., U.S.	111f	39°16'N	84°45'W
Harrisonburg, Va., U.S. (hăr'ĭ-sŭn-bûrg)	109	38°30'N	78°50'W
Harrison Lake, l., Can.	95	49°31'N	121°59'W
Harrisonville, Mo., U.S. (hăr-ĭ-sŭn-vĭl)	121	38°39'N	94°21'W
Harrisville, Ut., U.S. (hăr'ĭs-vĭl)	117b	41°17'N	112°00'W
Harrisville, W.V., U.S.	109	39°10'N	81°05'W
Harrodsburg, Ky., U.S. (hăr'ŭdz-bûrg)	108	37°45'N	84°50'W
Harrods Creek, r., Ky., U.S. (hăr'ŭdz)	111h	38°24'N	35°33'W
Harrow, Eng., U.K. (hăr'ō)	158b	51°34'N	0°21'W
Harsefeld, Ger. (här'zĕ-fĕld')	[illegible]	[illegible]	[illegible]
Harstad, Nor. (här'städh)	160	60°40'N	10°10'E
Hart, Mi., U.S. (härt)	108	43°40'N	86°25'W
Hartbeesfontein, S. Afr.	238c	26°46'S	26°25'E
Hartbeespoortdam, res., S. Afr.	233b	25°47'S	27°43'E
Hartford, Al., U.S. (härt'fẽrd)	124	31°05'N	85°42'W
Hartford, Ar., U.S.	121	35°01'N	94°21'W
Hartford, Ct., U.S.	105	41°45'N	72°40'W
Hartford, Il., U.S.	117e	38°50'N	90°06'W
Hartford, Ky., U.S.	124	37°25'N	86°50'W
Hartford, Mi., U.S.	108	42°15'N	86°15'W
Hartford, Wi., U.S.	113	43°19'N	88°25'W
Hartford City, In., U.S.	108	40°35'N	85°25'W
Hartington, Eng., U.K. (här'tĭng-tŭn)	158a	53°08'N	1°48'W
Hartington, Ne., U.S.	112	42°37'N	97°18'W
Hartland Point, c., Eng., U.K.	164	51°03'N	4°40'W
Hartlepool, Eng., U.K. (här't'l-pōōl)	160	54°40'N	1°12'W
Hartley, Ia., U.S. (härt'lĭ)	112	43°12'N	95°29'W
Hartley Bay, Can.	94	53°25'N	129°15'W
Hart Mountain, mtn., Can. (härt)	97	52°25'N	101°30'W
Hartsbeespoort, S. Afr.	233b	25°44'S	27°51'E
Hartselle, Al., U.S. (härt'sĕl)	124	34°24'N	86°55'W
Hartshorne, Ok., U.S. (härts'hôrn)	121	34°49'N	95°34'W
Hartsville, S.C., U.S. (härts'vĭl)	125	34°20'N	80°04'W
Hartwell, Ga., U.S. (härt'wĕl)	125	34°21'N	82°56'W
Hartwell Lake, res., U.S.	107	34°30'N	83°00'W
Hārua, India	202a	22°36'N	88°40'E
Harvard, Il., U.S. (här'vȧrd)	113	42°25'N	88°39'W
Harvard, Ma., U.S.	101a	42°30'N	71°35'W
Harvard, Ne., U.S.	120	40°36'N	98°08'W
Harvard, Mount, mtn., Co., U.S.	119	38°55'N	106°20'W
Harvey, Can.	100	45°44'N	64°46'W
Harvey, Il., U.S.	111a	41°37'N	87°39'W
Harvey, La., U.S.	110d	29°54'N	90°05'W
Harvey, N.D., U.S.	112	47°46'N	99°55'W
Harwich, Eng., U.K. (här'wĭch)	165	51°53'N	1°13'E
Haryana, state, India	199	29°00'N	75°45'E
Harz Mountains, mts., Ger. (härts)	168	51°42'N	10°50'E
Hashimoto, Japan (hä'shē-mō'tō)	211	34°19'N	135°37'E
Haskell, Ok., U.S. (hăs'kĕl)	121	35°49'N	95°41'W
Haskell, Tx., U.S.	120	33°09'N	99°43'W
Haslingden, Eng., U.K. (hăz'lĭng dĕn)	158a	53°43'N	2°19'W
Hassi Messaoud, Alg.	230	31°17'N	6°13'E
Hässleholm, Swe. (hĕs'lĕ-hōlm)	166	56°10'N	13°44'E
Hastings, N.Z.	221a	39°33'S	176°53'E
Hastings, Eng., U.K. (hās'tĭngz)	161	50°52'N	0°28'E
Hastings, Mi., U.S.	108	42°40'N	85°20'W
Hastings, Mn., U.S.	117g	44°44'N	92°51'W
Hastings, Ne., U.S.	104	40°34'N	98°42'W
Hastings-on-Hudson, N.Y., U.S. (ŏn-hŭd'sŭn)	110a	40°59'N	75°53'W
Hatay, Tur.	198	36°20'N	36°10'E
Hatchie, r., Tn., U.S. (hăch'ē)	124	35°28'N	89°14'W
Haţeg, Rom. (kät-säg')	175	45°35'N	22°57'E
Hatfield Broad Oak, Eng., U.K. (hăt-fēld brôd ōk)	158b	51°50'N	0°14'E
Hatogaya, Japan (hä'tō-gä-yä)	211a	35°50'N	139°45'E
Hatsukaichi, Japan (hät'sōō-kȧ'ē-chē)	211	34°22'N	132°19'E
Hatteras, Cape, c., N.C., U.S. (hăt'ẽr-ȧs)	107	35°15'N	75°24'W
Hattiesburg, Ms., U.S. (hăt'ĭz-bûrg)	105	31°20'N	89°18'W
Hattingen, Ger. (hä'tĕn-gĕn)	171c	51°24'N	7°11'E
Hatvan, Hung. (hôt'vôn)	169	47°39'N	19°44'E
Hat Yai, Thai.	212	7°01'N	100°29'E
Haugesund, Nor. (hou'gĕ-soon')	160	59°26'N	5°20'E
Haukivesi, l., Fin. (hou'kē-vĕ'sē)	167	62°02'N	29°02'E
Haultain, r., Can.	96	56°15'N	106°35'W
Hauptsrus, S. Afr.	238c	26°35'S	26°16'E
Hauraki Gulf, b., N.Z. (hä-ōō-rä'kē)	221a	36°30'S	175°00'E
Haut, Isle au, Me., U.S. (hō)	100	44°03'N	68°13'W
Haut Atlas, mts., Mor.	162	32°10'N	5°49'W
Hauterive, Can.	101	49°11'N	68°16'W
Hau'ula, Hi., U.S.	126a	21°37'N	157°45'W
Havana, Cuba	129	23°08'N	82°23'W
Havana, Il., U.S. (hȧ-vă'nȧ)	121	40°17'N	90°02'W
Havasu, Lake, res., U.S. (hăv'ȧ-sōō)	119	34°26'N	114°09'W
Havel, r., Ger. (hä'fĕl)	168	53°09'N	13°10'E
Havel-Kanal, can., Ger.	159b	52°36'N	13°12'E
Haverhill, Ma., U.S. (hā'vẽr-hĭl)	101a	42°46'N	71°05'W
Haverhill, N.H., U.S.	109	44°00'N	72°05'W
Haverstraw, N.Y., U.S. (hā'vẽr-strô)	110a	41°11'N	73°58'W
Havlíčkův Brod, Czech Rep.	161	49°38'N	15°34'E
Havre, Mt., U.S. (hăv'ẽr)	104	48°34'N	109°42'W
Havre-Boucher, Can. (häv'rȧ-bōō-shā')	101	45°42'N	61°30'W
Havre de Grace, Md., U.S. (hăv'ẽr dē grȧs')	109	39°35'N	76°05'W
Havre-Saint Pierre, Can.	100	50°15'N	63°36'W
Haw, r., N.C., U.S. (hô)	125	36°17'N	79°46'W

ăt; finȧl; rāte; senāte; ärm; ȧsk; sofȧ; fâre; ch-choose; dh-as th in other; bē; ēvent; bĕt; recĕnt; cratẽr; g-gō; gh-guttural g; bĭt; ĭ-short neutral; rīde; κ-guttural k as ch in German ich;

PRONOUNCING INDEX Hawaii – Hindupur 301

PLACE (Pronunciation)	PAGE	LAT.	LONG.
Hawaii, state, U.S.	106c	20°00'N	157°40'W
Hawai'i, i., Hi., U.S. (häw wī'ē)	106c	19°30'N	155°30'W
Hawai'ian Islands, is., Hi., U.S. (hä-wī'ăn)	106c	22°00'N	158°00'W
Hawai'i Volcanoes National Park, rec., Hi., U.S.	106c	19°30'N	155°25'W
Hawarden, Ia., U.S. (hā'wàr-dĕn)	112	43°00'N	96°28'W
Hawi, Hi., U.S. (hä'wē)	126a	20°16'N	155°48'W
Hawick, Scot., U.K. (hô'ĭk)	164	55°25'N	2°55'W
Hawke Bay, b., N.Z. (hôk)	221a	39°17'S	177°20'E
Hawker, Austl. (hô'kēr)	222	31°58'S	138°12'E
Hawkesbury, Can. (hôks'bĕr-ĭ)	99	45°35'N	74°35'W
Hawkinsville, Ga., U.S. (hô'kĭnz-vĭl)	124	32°15'N	83°30'W
Hawks Nest Point, c., Bah.	135	24°05'N	75°30'W
Hawley, Mn., U.S. (hô'lĭ)	112	46°52'N	96°18'W
Haworth, Eng., U.K. (hā'wûrth)	158a	53°50'N	1°57'W
Hawthorne, Ca., U.S. (hô'thôrn)	117a	33°55'N	118°22'W
Hawthorne, Nv., U.S.	118	38°33'N	118°39'W
Haxtun, Co., U.S. (hăks'tŭn)	120	40°39'N	102°38'W
Hay, r., Austl. (hā)	220	23°00'S	136°45'E
Hay, r., Can.	92	60°21'N	117°14'W
Hayama, Japan (hä-yä'mä)	211a	35°16'N	139°35'E
Hayashi, Japan (hä-yä'shē)	211a	35°13'N	139°38'E
Hayden, Az., U.S. (hā'dĕn)	119	33°00'N	110°50'W
Hayes, r., Can.	93	55°25'N	93°55'W
Hayes, Mount, mtn., Ak., U.S. (hāz)	103	63°32'N	146°40'W
Haynesville, La., U.S. (hānz'vĭl)	123	32°55'N	93°08'W
Hayrabolu, Tur.	175	41°14'N	27°05'E
Hay River, Can.	90	60°50'N	115°53'W
Hays, Ks., U.S. (hāz)	120	38°51'N	99°20'W
Haystack Mountain, mtn., Wa., U.S. (hā-stăk')	116a	48°26'N	122°07'W
Hayward, Ca., U.S. (hā'wērd)	116b	37°40'N	122°06'W
Hayward, Wi., U.S.	113	46°01'N	91°31'W
Hazard, Ky., U.S. (hăz'ard)	124	37°13'N	83°10'W
Hazelhurst, Ga., U.S. (hā'z'l-hûrst)	125	31°50'N	82°36'W
Hazelhurst, Ms., U.S.	124	31°52'N	90°23'W
Hazel Park, Mi., U.S.	111b	42°28'N	83°06'W
Hazelton, Can. (hā'z'l-tŭn)	90	55°15'N	127°40'W
Hazelton Mountains, mts., Can.	94	55°00'N	128°00'W
Hazleton, Pa., U.S.	109	41°00'N	76°00'W
Headland, Al., U.S. (hĕd'lănd)	124	31°22'N	85°20'W
Healdsburg, Ca., U.S. (hēldz'bûrg)	118	38°37'N	122°52'W
Healdton, Ok., U.S. (hēld'tŭn)	121	34°13'N	97°28'W
Heanor, Eng., U.K. (hēn'ŏr)	158a	53°01'N	1°22'W
Heard Island, i., Austl. (hûrd)	3	53°10'S	74°35'E
Hearne, Tx., U.S. (hûrn)	123	30°53'N	96°35'W
Hearst, Can. (hûrst)	91	49°36'N	83°40'W
Heart, r., N.D., U.S. (härt)	112	46°46'N	102°34'W
Heart Lake Indian Reserve, I.R., Can.	95	55°02'N	111°30'W
Heart's Content, Can. (härts kŏn'tĕnt)	101	47°52'N	53°22'W
Heavener, Ok., U.S. (hēv'nēr)	121	34°52'N	94°36'W
Hebbronville, Tx., U.S. (hē'brŭn-vĭl)	122	27°18'N	98°40'W
Hebei, prov., China (hŭ-bā)	205	39°15'N	115°40'E
Heber City, Ut., U.S. (hē'bēr)	119	40°30'N	111°25'W
Heber Springs, Ar., U.S.	121	35°28'N	91°59'W
Hebgen Lake, res., Mt., U.S. (hĕb'gĕn)	115	44°47'N	111°38'W
Hebrides, is., Scot., U.K.	156	57°00'N	6°30'W
Hebrides, Sea of the, sea, Scot., U.K.	164	57°00'N	7°00'W
Hebron, Can. (hēb'rŭn)	91	58°11'N	62°56'W
Hebron, In., U.S.	111a	41°19'N	87°13'W
Hebron, Ky., U.S.	111f	39°04'N	84°43'W
Hebron, N.D., U.S.	112	46°54'N	102°04'W
Hebron, Ne., U.S.	121	40°11'N	97°36'W
Hebron *see* Al Khalīl, W.B.	197a	31°31'N	35°07'E
Heby, Swe. (hĭ'bü)	166	59°56'N	16°48'E
Hecate Strait, strt., Can. (hĕk'ā-tē)	92	53°00'N	131°00'W
Hecelchakán, Mex. (ā-sĕl-chä-kän')	131	20°10'N	90°09'W
Hechi, China (hŭ-chr)	209	24°50'N	108°18'E
Hechuan, China (hŭ-chyuän)	204	30°00'N	106°20'E
Hecla Island, i., Can.	97	51°08'N	96°45'W
Hedemora, Swe. (hĭ-dĕ-mō'rä)	166	60°16'N	15°55'E
Hedon, Eng., U.K. (hĕ-dŭn)	158a	53°44'N	0°12'W
Heemstede, Neth.	159a	52°20'N	4°36'E
Heerlen, Neth.	165	50°55'N	5°58'E
Hefei, China (hŭ-fā)	205	31°51'N	117°15'E
Heflin, Al., U.S. (hĕf'lĭn)	124	33°40'N	85°33'W
Heide, Ger. (hī'dē)	168	54°13'N	9°06'E
Heidelberg, Austl. (hī'dĕl-bûrg)	217a	37°45'S	145°04'E
Heidelberg, Ger. (hīdĕl-bĕrgh)	161	49°24'N	8°43'E
Heidelberg, S. Afr.	238c	26°32'S	28°22'E
Heidenheim, Ger. (hī'dĕn-hīm)	168	48°41'N	10°09'E
Heilbron, S. Afr. (hĭl'brōn)	238c	27°17'S	27°58'E
Heilbronn, Ger. (hīl'brōn)	161	49°09'N	9°16'E
Heiligenhaus, Ger. (hī'lē-gĕn-houz)	171c	51°19'N	6°58'E
Heiligenstadt, Ger. (hī'lē-gĕn-shtät)	168	51°21'N	10°10'E
Heilongjiang, prov., China (hā-lôŋ-jyäŋ)	205	46°36'N	128°07'E
Heinola, Fin. (hå-nō'lå)	167	61°13'N	26°03'E
Heinsberg, Ger. (hīnz'bĕrgh)	171c	51°04'N	6°07'E
Heist-op-den-Berg, Bel.	159a	51°05'N	4°14'E
Hejaz *see* Al Ḩijāz, reg., Sau. Ar.	198	23°45'N	39°08'E
Hejian, China (hŭ-jyĕn)	208	38°28'N	116°05'E
Hekla, vol., Ice.	156	63°53'N	19°37'W
Hel, Pol. (hāl)	169	54°37'N	18°53'E
Helagsfjället, mtn., Swe.	160	62°54'N	12°24'E
Helan Shan, mts., China (hŭ-län shän)	204	38°02'N	105°20'E
Helena, Ar., U.S. (hē-lē'nà)	105	34°33'N	90°35'W
Helena, Mt., U.S. (hĕ-lē'nȧ)	104	46°35'N	112°01'W
Helensburgh, Austl. (hĕl'ĕnz-bŭr-ŏ)	217b	34°11'S	150°59'E
Helensburgh, Scot., U.K.	164	56°01'N	4°53'W
Helgoland, i., Ger. (hĕl'gô-länd)	168	54°13'N	7°30'E
Hellier, Ky., U.S. (hĕl'yēr)	125	37°16'N	82°27'W

PLACE (Pronunciation)	PAGE	LAT.	LONG.
Hellín, Spain (ĕl-yēn')	162	38°30'N	1°40'W
Hells Canyon, p., U.S.	114	45°20'N	116°45'W
Helmand, r., Afg. (hĕl'mŭnd)	198	31°00'N	63°48'E
Hel'miaziv, Ukr.	177	49°49'N	31°54'E
Helmond, Neth. (hĕl'mŏnt) (ĕl'môN')	165	51°35'N	5°04'E
Helmstedt, Ger. (hĕlm'shtĕt)	168	52°14'N	11°03'E
Helotes, Tx., U.S. (hē'lōts)	117d	29°35'N	98°41'W
Helper, Ut., U.S. (hĕlp'ēr)	119	39°40'N	110°55'W
Helsingborg, Swe. (hĕl'sĭng-bôrgh)	160	56°04'N	12°40'E
Helsingfors *see* Helsinki, Fin.	154	60°10'N	24°53'E
Helsingør, Den. (hĕl-sĭng-ŭr')	160	56°03'N	12°33'E
Helsinki, Fin. (hĕl'sēn-kē)	154	60°10'N	24°53'E
Hemel Hempstead, Eng., U.K. (hĕm'ĕl hĕmp'stĕd)	158b	51°43'N	0°29'W
Hemer, Ger.	171c	51°22'N	7°46'E
Hemet, Ca., U.S. (hĕm'ĕt)	117a	33°45'N	116°57'W
Hemingford, Ne., U.S. (hĕm'ĭng fērd)	112	42°21'N	103°30'W
Hemphill, Tx., U.S. (hĕmp'hĭl)	123	31°20'N	93°48'W
Hempstead, N.Y., U.S. (hĕmp'stĕd)	110a	40°42'N	73°37'W
Hempstead, Tx., U.S.	123	30°07'N	96°05'W
Hemse, Swe. (hĕm'sē)	166	57°15'N	18°25'E
Hemsön, i., Swe.	166	62°43'N	18°22'E
Henan, prov., China (hŭ-nän)	205	33°58'N	112°33'E
Henares, r., Spain (å-nä'rås)	172	40°50'N	2°55'W
Henderson, Ky., U.S. (hĕn'dēr-sŭn)	108	37°50'N	87°30'W
Henderson, N.C., U.S.	125	36°18'N	78°24'W
Henderson, Nv., U.S.	118	36°09'N	115°04'W
Henderson, Tn., U.S.	124	35°25'N	88°40'W
Henderson, Tx., U.S.	123	32°09'N	94°48'W
Hendersonville, N.C., U.S. (hĕn'dēr-sŭn-vĭl)	125	35°17'N	82°28'W
Hendersonville, Tn., U.S.	124	36°18'N	86°37'W
Hendon, Eng., U.K. (hĕn'dŭn)	158b	51°34'N	0°13'W
Hendrina, S. Afr. (hĕn-drē'nȧ)	238c	26°10'S	29°44'E
Hengch'un, Tai. (hĕng'chŭn')	209	22°00'N	120°42'E
Hengelo, Neth. (hĕngĕ-lō)	165	52°20'N	6°45'E
Hengshan, China (hĕng'shän')	209	27°20'N	112°40'E
Hengshui, China (hĕng'shōō-ē')	206	37°43'N	115°42'E
Hengxian, China (hŭŋ shyĕn)	209	22°40'N	109°20'E
Hengyang, China	205	26°58'N	112°30'E
Heniches'k, Ukr.	181	46°11'N	34°47'E
Henley on Thames, Eng., U.K. (hĕn'lē ŏn tĕmz)	158b	51°31'N	0°54'W
Henlopen, Cape, c., De., U.S. (hĕn-lō'pĕn)	109	38°45'N	75°05'W
Hennebont, Fr. (ĕn-bôN')	170	47°47'N	3°16'W
Hennenman, S. Afr.	238c	27°59'S	27°03'E
Hennessey, Ok., U.S. (hĕn'ĕ-sĭ)	121	36°04'N	97°53'W
Hennigsdorf, Ger. (hĕ'nēngz-dōrf))	159b	52°39'N	13°12'E
Hennops, r., S. Afr. (hĕn'ŏps)	233b	25°51'S	27°57'E
Hennopsrivier, S. Afr.	233b	25°50'S	27°59'E
Henrietta, Ok., U.S. (hĕn-rĭ-ĕt'ȧ)	121	35°25'N	95°58'W
Henrietta, Tx., U.S. (hen-rĭ-ĕ'tȧ)	120	33°47'N	98°11'W
Henrietta Maria, Cape, c., Can. (hĕn-rĭ-ĕt'ȧ)	93	55°10'N	82°20'W
Henry Mountains, mts., Ut., U.S. (hĕn'rĭ)	106	37°55'N	110°45'W
Henrys Fork, r., Id., U.S.	115	43°52'N	111°55'W
Henteyn Nuruu, mtn., Russia	208	49°40'N	111°00'E
Hentiyn Nuruu, mts., Mong.	204	49°25'N	107°51'E
Henzada, Mya.	199	17°38'N	95°28'E
Heppner, Or., U.S. (hĕp'nēr)	114	45°21'N	119°33'W
Hepu, China (hŭ-pōō)	209	21°28'N	109°10'E
Herāt, Afg. (hĕ-rät')	198	34°28'N	62°13'E
Hercules, Can.	102g	53°27'N	113°20'W
Herdecke, Ger. (hĕr'dĕ-kĕ)	171c	51°24'N	7°26'E
Heredia, C.R. (ā-rā'dhē-ä)	133	10°04'N	84°06'W
Hereford, Eng., U.K. (hĕrĕ'fērd)	164	52°05'N	2°44'W
Hereford, Md., U.S.	110e	39°35'N	76°42'W
Hereford, Tx., U.S. (hĕr'ĕ-fērd)	120	34°47'N	102°25'W
Hereford and Worcester, co., Eng., U.K.	158a	52°24'N	2°15'W
Herencia, Spain (å-rān'thē-ä)	172	39°23'N	3°22'W
Herentals, Bel.	159a	51°10'N	4°51'E
Herford, Ger. (hĕr'fōrt)	168	52°06'N	8°42'E
Herington, Ks., U.S. (hĕr'ĭng-tŭn)	121	38°41'N	96°57'W
Herisau, Switz. (hā'rē-zou)	168	47°23'N	9°18'E
Herk-de-Stad, Bel.	159a	50°56'N	5°13'E
Herkimer, N.Y., U.S. (hûr'kĭ-mēr)	109	43°05'N	75°00'W
Hermansville, Mi., U.S. (hûr'mȧns-vĭl)	108	45°40'N	87°35'W
Hermantown, Mn., U.S. (hĕr'mȧn-toun)	117h	46°46'N	92°12'W
Hermanusdoringś, S. Afr.	238c	24°08'S	27°46'E
Herminie, Pa., U.S. (hûr-mĭ'nē)	111e	40°16'N	79°45'W
Hermitage Bay, b., Can. (hûr'mĭ-tĕj)	101	47°35'N	56°05'W
Hermit Islands, is., Pap. N. Gui. (hûr'mĭt)	213	1°48'S	144°55'E
Hermosa Beach, Ca., U.S. (hēr-mō'sȧ)	117a	33°51'N	118°24'W
Hermosillo, Mex. (ĕr-mō-sē'l-yŏ)	128	29°00'N	110°57'W
Herndon, Va., U.S. (hĕrn'don)	110e	38°58'N	77°22'W
Herne, Ger. (hĕr'nĕ)	171c	51°32'N	7°13'E
Herning, Den. (hĕr'nĭng)	160	56°08'N	8°55'E
Heron, l., Mn., U.S. (hĕr'ŭn)	112	43°42'N	95°23'W
Heron Lake, Mn., U.S.	112	43°48'N	95°20'W
Herrero, Punta, Mex. (pô'n-tä-ĕr-rĕ'rô)	132a	19°18'N	87°24'W
Herrin, Il., U.S. (hĕr'ĭn)	108	37°50'N	89°00'W
Herschel, S. Afr. (hĕr'-shĕl)	233c	30°37'S	27°12'E
Herscher, Il., U.S. (hĕr'shēr)	111a	41°03'N	88°06'W
Herstal, Bel. (hĕr'stäl)	165	50°42'N	5°32'E
Hertford, Eng., U.K.	164	51°48'N	0°05'W
Hertford, N.C., U.S. (hûrt'fērd)	125	36°10'N	76°30'W
Hertfordshire, co., Eng., U.K.	158b	51°46'N	0°05'W
Hertzberg, Ger. (hĕrtz'bĕrgh)	159b	52°54'N	12°58'E

PLACE (Pronunciation)	PAGE	LAT.	LONG.
Hervás, Spain	172	40°16'N	5°51'W
Herzliyya, Isr.	197a	32°10'N	34°49'E
Hessen, hist. reg., Ger. (hĕs'ĕn)	168	50°42'N	9°00'E
Hetch Hetchy Aqueduct, Ca., U.S. (hĕtch hĕt'chĭ ăk'wē-dŭkt)	118	37°27'N	120°54'W
Hettinger, N.D., U.S. (hĕt'ĭn-jēr)	112	45°58'N	102°36'W
Heuningspruit, S. Afr.	238c	27°28'S	27°26'E
Hexian, China (hŭ shyĕn)	209	24°20'N	111°28'E
Hexian, China	206	31°44'N	118°20'E
Heyang, China (hŭ-yäŋ)	208	35°18'N	110°18'E
Heystekrand, S. Afr.	238c	25°16'S	27°14'E
Heyuan, China (hŭ-yůän)	209	23°48'N	114°45'E
Heywood, Eng., U.K. (hā'wŏd)	158a	53°36'N	2°12'W
Heze, China (hŭ-dzŭ)	206	35°13'N	115°28'E
Hialeah, Fl., U.S. (hī-ȧ-lē'ăh)	125a	25°49'N	80°18'W
Hiawatha, Ks., U.S. (hī-ȧ-wô'thȧ)	121	39°50'N	95°33'W
Hiawatha, Ut., U.S.	119	39°25'N	111°05'W
Hibbing, Mn., U.S. (hĭb'ĭng)	105	47°26'N	92°58'W
Hickman, Ky., U.S. (hĭk'mȧn)	124	34°33'N	89°10'W
Hickory, N.C., U.S. (hĭk'ō-rĭ)	125	35°43'N	81°21'W
Hicksville, N.Y., U.S.	108	41°15'N	84°45'W
Hicksville, N.Y., U.S. (hĭks'vĭl)	110a	40°47'N	73°25'W
Hico, Tx., U.S. (hī'kō)	122	32°00'N	98°02'W
Hidalgo, Mex. (ē-dhäl'gō)	130	24°14'N	99°25'W
Hidalgo, Mex.	122	27°49'N	99°53'W
Hidalgo, state, Mex.	128	20°45'N	99°30'W
Hidalgo del Parral, Mex. (ē-dä'l-gō-dĕl-pär-rä'l)	128	26°55'N	105°40'W
Hidalgo Yalalag, Mex. (ē-dhäl'gō-yä-lä-läg)	131	17°12'N	96°11'W
Hierro Island, i., Spain (yĕ'r-rô)	230	27°37'N	18°29'W
Higashimurayama, Japan	211a	35°46'N	139°28'E
Higashiōsaka, Japan	211b	34°40'N	135°44'E
Higgins, l., Mi., U.S. (hĭg'ĭnz)	108	44°20'N	84°45'W
Higginsville, Mo., U.S. (hĭg'ĭnz-vĭl)	121	39°05'N	93°44'W
High, i., Mi., U.S.	108	45°45'N	85°45'W
High Bluff, Can.	102f	50°01'N	98°08'W
Highborne Cay, i., Bah. (hībôrn kē)	134	24°45'N	76°50'W
Highgrove, Ca., U.S. (hī'grōv)	117a	34°01'N	117°20'W
High Island, Tx., U.S.	123a	29°34'N	94°24'W
Highland, Ca., U.S. (hī'lănd)	117a	34°08'N	117°13'W
Highland, Il., U.S.	121	38°44'N	89°41'W
Highland, In., U.S.	111a	41°33'N	87°28'W
Highland, Mi., U.S.	111b	42°38'N	83°37'W
Highland Park, Il., U.S.	111a	42°11'N	87°47'W
Highland Park, Mi., U.S.	111b	42°24'N	83°06'W
Highland Park, N.J., U.S.	110a	40°30'N	74°25'W
Highland Park, Tx., U.S.	117c	32°49'N	96°48'W
Highlands, N.J., U.S. (hī-lăndz)	110a	40°24'N	73°59'W
Highlands, Tx., U.S.	123a	29°49'N	95°01'W
Highmore, S.D., U.S. (hī'mōr)	112	44°30'N	99°26'W
High Ongar, Eng., U.K. (on'gēr)	158b	51°43'N	0°15'E
High Peak, mtn., Phil.	213a	15°38'N	120°05'E
High Point, N.C., U.S.	125	35°55'N	80°00'W
High Prairie, Can.	90	55°26'N	116°29'W
High Ridge, Mo., U.S.	117e	38°27'N	90°32'W
High River, Can.	90	50°35'N	113°52'W
High Rock Lake, res., N.C., U.S. (hī'-rŏk)	125	35°40'N	80°15'W
High Springs, Fl., U.S.	125	29°48'N	82°38'W
High Tatra Mountains, mts., Eur.	169	49°15'N	19°40'E
Hightstown, N.J., U.S. (hīts-toun)	110a	40°16'N	74°32'W
High Wycombe, Eng., U.K. (wĭ-kŭm)	164	51°36'N	0°45'W
Higuero, Punta, c., P.R.	129b	18°21'N	67°11'W
Higuerote, Ven. (ē-gĕ-rô'tĕ)	143b	10°29'N	66°06'W
Higüey, Dom. Rep. (ē-gwĕ'y)	135	18°40'N	68°45'W
Hiiumaa, i., Est. (hē'ōm-ô)	180	58°47'N	22°05'E
Hikone, Japan (hē'kō-nĕ)	211	35°15'N	136°15'E
Hildburghausen, Ger. (hĭld'bŏrg hou-zĕn)	168	50°26'N	10°45'E
Hilden, Ger. (hĕl'dĕn)	171c	51°10'N	6°56'E
Hildesheim, Ger. (hĭl'dĕs-hīm)	161	52°08'N	9°56'E
Hillaby, Mount, mtn., Barb. (hĭl'ȧ-bĭ)	133b	13°15'N	59°35'W
Hill City, Ks., U.S. (hĭl)	120	39°22'N	99°54'W
Hill City, Mn., U.S.	113	46°58'N	93°38'W
Hillegersberg, Neth.	159a	51°57'N	4°29'E
Hillerød, Den. (hē'lĕ-rûdh)	166	55°56'N	12°17'E
Hillsboro, Il., U.S. (hĭlz'bŭr-ō)	121	39°09'N	89°28'W
Hillsboro, Ks., U.S.	121	38°22'N	97°11'W
Hillsboro, N.D., U.S.	112	47°23'N	97°05'W
Hillsboro, N.H., U.S.	109	43°05'N	71°55'W
Hillsboro, Oh., U.S.	108	39°10'N	83°40'W
Hillsboro, Or., U.S.	116c	45°31'N	122°59'W
Hillsboro, Tx., U.S.	123	32°01'N	97°06'W
Hillsboro, Wi., U.S.	113	43°39'N	90°20'W
Hillsburgh, Can. (hĭlz'bûrg)	102d	43°48'N	80°09'W
Hills Creek Lake, res., Or., U.S.	114	43°41'N	122°26'W
Hillsdale, Mi., U.S. (hĭls-dāl)	119	41°55'N	84°35'W
Hilo, Hi., U.S. (hē'lō)	106c	19°44'N	155°01'W
Hilvarenbeek, Neth.	159a	51°29'N	5°10'E
Hilversum, Neth. (hĭl'vēr-sŭm)	159a	52°13'N	5°10'E
Himachal Pradesh, India	199	32°00'N	77°30'E
Himalayas, mts., Asia	199	29°30'N	85°02'E
Himeji, Japan (hē'mȧ-jē)	210	34°50'N	134°42'E
Himmelpforten, Ger. (hē'mĕl-pfōr-tĕn)	159c	53°37'N	9°19'E
Ḩimş, Syria	198	34°44'N	36°43'E
Hinche, Haiti (hēn'chȧ) (äNsh)	135	19°10'N	72°05'W
Hinchinbrook, i., Austl. (hĭn-chĭn-brŏŏk)	220	18°23'S	146°57'W
Hinckley, Eng., U.K. (hĭnk'lĭ)	158a	52°32'N	1°21'W
Hindley, Eng., U.K. (hĭnd'lĭ)	158a	53°32'N	2°35'W
Hindu Kush, mts., Asia (hĭn'dōō kōōsh')	199	35°15'N	68°44'E
Hindupur, India (hĭn'dōō-pōōr)	203	13°52'N	77°34'E

ng-sing; ŋ-baŋk; N-nasalized n; nŏd; cŏmmit; ōld; ôbey; ôrder; oi-boil; fōōd; ŏ-as oo in foot; ou-out; s-soft; sh-dish; th-thin; pūre; ûnite; ûrn; stŭd; circŭs; ü-as in French tu; '-indeterminate vowel.

302 Hingham – Hualapai Mountains PRONOUNCING INDEX

PLACE (Pronunciation)	PAGE	LAT.	LONG.
Hingham, Ma., U.S. (hĭng'ăm)	101a	42°14'N	70°53'W
Hinkley, Oh., U.S. (hĭnk'-lĭ)	111d	41°14'N	81°45'W
Hinojosa del Duque, Spain (ē-nŏ-kō'sä)	172	38°30'N	5°09'W
Hinsdale, Il., U.S. (hĭnz'dāl)	111a	41°48'N	87°56'W
Hinton, Can. (hĭn'tŭn)	95	53°25'N	117°34'W
Hinton, W.V., U.S. (hĭn'tŭn)	108	37°40'N	80°55'W
Hirado, i., Japan (hē'rä-dō)	210	33°19'N	129°18'E
Hirakata, Japan (hē'rä-kä'tä)	211b	34°49'N	135°40'E
Hirara, Japan	214d	24°48'N	125°17'E
Hiratsuka, Japan (hē-rät-sōō'kå)	211	35°20'N	139°19'E
Hirosaki, Japan (hē'rŏ-sä'kė)	205	40°31'N	140°38'E
Hirose, Japan (hē'rŏ-sä)	211	35°20'N	133°11'E
Hiroshima, Japan (hē-rŏ-shē'mȧ)	205	34°22'N	132°25'E
Hirson, Fr. (ēr-sôN')	170	49°54'N	4°00'E
Hisar, India	207	29°15'N	75°47'E
Hispaniola, i., N.A. (hĭ'spăn-ĭ-ō-lȧ)	129	17°30'N	73°15'W
Hitachi, Japan (hē-tä'chē)	210	36°42'N	140°47'E
Hitchcock, Tx., U.S. (hĭch'kŏk)	123a	29°21'N	95°01'W
Hitoyoshi, Japan (hē'tŏ-yō'shė)	211	32°13'N	130°45'E
Hitra, i., Nor. (hĭträ)	160	63°34'N	7°37'E
Hittefeld, Ger. (hē'tĕ-fĕld)	159c	53°23'N	9°59'E
Hiwasa, Japan (hē'wȧ-sä)	211	33°44'N	134°31'E
Hiwassee, r., Tn., U.S. (hī-wôs'sē)	124	35°10'N	84°35'W
Hjälmaren, l., Swe.	160	59°07'N	16°05'E
Hjo, Swe. (yō)	166	58°19'N	14°11'E
Hjørring, Den. (jûr'ĭng)	160	57°27'N	9°59'E
Hlobyne, Ukr.	177	49°22'N	33°17'E
Hlohovec, Slvk. (hlō'ho-vĕts)	169	48°24'N	17°49'E
Hlukhiv, Ukr.	181	51°42'N	33°52'E
Hlybokaye, Bela.	180	55°08'N	27°44'E
Hobart, Austl. (hō'bȧrt)	219	43°00'S	147°30'E
Hobart, In., U.S.	111a	41°31'N	87°15'W
Hobart, Ok., U.S.	120	35°02'N	99°06'W
Hobart, Wa., U.S.	116a	47°25'N	121°58'W
Hobbs, N.M., U.S. (hŏbs)	120	32°41'N	103°15'W
Hoboken, Bel. (hō'bō-kĕn)	159a	51°11'N	4°20'E
Hoboken, N.J., U.S.	110a	40°43'N	74°03'W
Hobro, Den. (hŏ-brō')	166	56°38'N	9°47'E
Hobson, Va., U.S. (hŏb'sŭn)	110g	36°54'N	76°31'W
Hobson's Bay, b., Austl. (hŏb'sŭnz)	217a	37°54'S	144°45'E
Hobyo, Som.	238a	5°24'N	48°28'E
Ho Chi Minh City, Viet.	212	10°46'N	106°34'E
Hockinson, Wa., U.S. (hŏk'ĭn-sŭn)	116c	45°44'N	122°29'W
Hoctún, Mex. (ôk-tōō'n)	132a	20°52'N	89°10'W
Hodgenville, Ky., U.S. (hŏj'ĕn-vĭl)	108	37°35'N	85°45'W
Hodges Hill, mtn., Can. (hŏj'ĕz)	101	49°04'N	55°53'W
Hódmezővásárhely, Hung. (hōd'mĕ-zû-vô'shôr-hĕl-y')	169	46°24'N	20°21'E
Hodna, Chott el, l., Alg.	162	35°20'N	3°27'E
Hodonin, Czech Rep. (hē'dō-nén)	169	48°50'N	17°06'E
Hoegaarden, Bel.	159a	50°46'N	4°55'E
Hoek van Holland, Neth.	159a	51°59'N	4°05'E
Hoeryŏng, Kor., N. (hwĕr'yŭng)	210	42°28'N	129°39'E
Hof, Ger. (hōf)	168	50°19'N	11°55'E
Hofsjökull, ice, Ice. (hôfs'yü'kōōl)	160	64°55'N	18°40'W
Hog, i., Mi., U.S.	108	45°50'N	85°20'W
Hogansville, Ga., U.S. (hō'gănz-vĭl)	124	33°10'N	84°54'W
Hog Cay, i., Bah.	135	23°35'N	75°30'W
Hogsty Reef, rf., Bah.	135	21°45'N	73°50'W
Hohenbrunn, Ger. (hō'hĕn-brōōn)	159d	48°03'N	11°42'E
Hohenlimburg, Ger. (hō'hĕn lĕm'bōōrg)	171c	51°20'N	7°35'E
Hohen Neuendorf, Ger. (hō'hĕn noi'ĕn-dōrf)	159b	52°40'N	13°22'E
Hohe Tauern, mts., Aus. (hō'ĕ tou'ĕrn)	168	47°11'N	12°12'E
Hohhot, China (hŭ-hōō-tŭ)	205	41°05'N	111°50'E
Hohoe, Ghana	234	7°09'N	0°28'E
Hohokus, N.J., U.S. (hō-hō-kŭs)	110a	41°01'N	74°08'W
Hoi An, Viet.	209	15°48'N	108°30'E
Hoisington, Ks., U.S. (hoi'zĭng-tŭn)	120	38°30'N	98°46'W
Hojo, Japan (hō'jō)	211	33°58'N	132°50'E
Hokitika, N.Z. (hō-kĭ-tē'kä)	221a	42°43'S	170°59'E
Hokkaidō, i., Japan (hŏk'kī-dō)	210	43°30'N	142°45'E
Holbaek, Den. (hôl'bĕk)	166	55°42'N	11°40'E
Holbox, Mex. (ôl-bŏ'x)	132a	21°33'N	87°19'W
Holbox, Isla, i., Mex. (ē's-lä-ôl-bŏ'x)	132a	21°40'N	87°21'W
Holbrook, Az., U.S. (hōl'brŏk)	119	34°55'N	110°15'W
Holbrook, Ma., U.S.	101a	42°10'N	71°01'W
Holden, Ma., U.S. (hōl'dĕn)	101a	42°21'N	71°51'W
Holden, Mo., U.S.	121	38°42'N	94°00'W
Holden, W.V., U.S.	108	37°45'N	82°05'W
Holdenville, Ok., U.S. (hōl'dĕn-vĭl)	121	35°05'N	96°25'W
Holdrege, Ne., U.S. (hōl'drĕj)	120	40°25'N	99°28'W
Holguín, Cuba (ôl-gēn')	129	20°55'N	76°15'W
Holguín, prov., Cuba	134	20°40'N	76°15'W
Holidaysburg, Pa., U.S. (hŏl'ĭ-dāz-bûrg)	109	40°30'N	78°30'W
Hollabrunn, Aus.	168	48°33'N	16°04'E
Holland, Mi., U.S. (hŏl'ănd)	108	42°45'N	86°10'W
Hollands Diep, strt., Neth.	159a	51°43'N	4°25'E
Hollenstedt, Ger. (hō'lĕn-shtĕt)	159c	53°22'N	9°43'E
Hollis, N.H., U.S. (hŏl'ĭs)	101a	42°30'N	71°29'W
Hollis, Ok., U.S.	120	34°39'N	99°56'W
Hollister, Ca., U.S. (hŏl'ĭs-tēr)	118	36°50'N	121°25'W
Holliston, Ma., U.S. (hŏl'ĭs-tŭn)	101a	42°12'N	71°25'W
Holly, Mi., U.S. (hŏl'ĭ)	108	42°45'N	83°30'W
Holly, Wa., U.S.	116a	47°34'N	122°58'W
Holly Springs, Ms., U.S. (hŏl'ĭ sprĭngz)	124	34°45'N	89°28'W
Hollywood, Ca., U.S. (hŏl'ė-wŏd)	117a	34°06'N	118°20'W
Hollywood, Fl., U.S.	125a	26°00'N	80°11'W
Holmes Reefs, rf., Austl. (hōmz)	221	16°33'S	148°43'E
Holmestrand, Nor. (hôl'mĕ-strän)	166	59°29'N	10°17'E
Holmsbu, Nor. (hôlms'bōō)	166	59°36'N	10°26'E
Holmsjön, l., Swe.	166	62°23'N	15°43'E
Holstebro, Den. (hôl'stĕ-brŏ)	160	56°22'N	8°39'E
Holstein, hist. reg., Ger.	168	54°10'N	9°40'E
Holston, r., Tn., U.S. (hōl'stŭn)	124	36°02'N	83°42'W
Holt, Eng., U.K. (hōlt)	158a	53°05'N	2°53'W
Holton, Ks., U.S. (hōl'tŭn)	121	39°27'N	95°43'W
Holy Cross, Ak., U.S. (hō'lĭ krôs)	103	62°10'N	159°40'W
Holyhead, Wales, U.K. (hŏl'ė-hĕd)	164	53°18'N	4°45'W
Holy Island, i., Eng., U.K.	164	55°43'N	1°48'W
Holy Island, i., Wales, U.K. (hō'lĭ)	164	53°15'N	4°45'W
Holyoke, Co., U.S. (hōl'yōk)	120	40°36'N	102°18'W
Holyoke, Ma., U.S.	109	42°10'N	72°40'W
Homano, Japan (hō-mä'nō)	211a	35°33'N	140°08'E
Homberg, Ger. (hōm'bĕrgh)	171c	51°27'N	6°42'E
Hombori, Mali	234	15°17'N	1°42'W
Home Gardens, Ca., U.S. (hōm gär'd'nz)	117a	33°53'N	117°32'W
Homeland, Ca., U.S. (hōm'lănd)	117a	33°44'N	117°07'W
Homer, Ak., U.S. (hō'mēr)	103	59°42'N	151°30'W
Homer, La., U.S.	123	32°46'N	93°05'W
Homer Youngs Peak, mtn., Mt., U.S.	115	45°19'N	113°41'W
Homestead, Fl., U.S. (hōm'stĕd)	125a	25°27'N	80°28'W
Homestead, Mi., U.S.	117k	46°20'N	84°07'W
Homestead, Pa., U.S.	111e	40°29'N	79°55'W
Homestead National Monument of America, rec., Ne., U.S.	121	40°16'N	96°51'W
Homewood, Al., U.S. (hōm'wŏd)	110h	33°28'N	86°48'W
Homewood, Il., U.S.	111a	41°34'N	87°40'W
Hominy, Ok., U.S. (hŏm'ĭ-nĭ)	121	36°25'N	96°24'W
Homochitto, r., Ms., U.S. (hō-mō-chĭt'ō)	124	31°23'N	91°15'W
Homyel', Bela.	180	52°20'N	31°03'E
Homyel', prov., Bela.	176	52°18'N	29°00'E
Honda, Col. (hōn'dȧ)	142	5°13'N	74°45'W
Honda, Bahía, b., Cuba (bä-ē'ä-ō'n-dä)	134	23°10'N	83°20'W
Hondo, Tx., U.S. (hŏn'dō)	122	29°20'N	99°08'W
Hondo, r., N.M., U.S.	120	33°22'N	105°06'W
Hondo, Río, r., N.A. (hon-dō')	132a	18°16'N	88°32'W
Honduras, nation, N.A. (hŏn-dōō'rȧs)	128	14°30'N	88°00'W
Honduras, Gulf of, b., N.A.	128	16°30'N	87°30'W
Honea Path, S.C., U.S. (hŭn'ĭ păth)	125	34°25'N	82°16'W
Hönefoss, Nor. (hē'nĕ-fŏs)	160	60°10'N	10°15'E
Honesdale, Pa., U.S. (hōnz'dāl)	109	41°30'N	75°15'W
Honey Grove, Tx., U.S. (hŭn'ĭ grōv)	121	33°35'N	95°54'W
Honey Lake, l., Ca., U.S. (hŭn'ĭ)	118	40°11'N	120°34'W
Honfleur, Can. (ôN-flûr')	102b	46°39'N	70°53'W
Honfleur, Fr. (ôN-flûr')	170	49°26'N	0°13'E
Hon Gay, Viet.	209	20°58'N	107°10'E
Hong Kong (Xianggang), China	205	21°45'N	115°00'E
Hongshui, r., China (hôŋ-shwā)	204	24°30'N	105°00'E
Honguedo, Détroit d', strt., Can.	100	49°08'N	63°45'W
Hongze Hu, l., China	205	33°17'N	118°37'E
Honiara, Sol. Is.	219	9°26'S	159°57'E
Honiton, Eng., U.K. (hŏn'ĭ-tŏn)	164	50°49'N	3°10'W
Honolulu, Hi., U.S. (hŏn-ō-lōō'lōō)	106c	21°18'N	157°50'W
Honomu, Hi., U.S. (hŏn'ō-mōō)	126a	19°50'N	155°04'W
Honshū, i., Japan	205	36°00'N	138°00'E
Hood, Mount, mtn., Or., U.S.	106	45°20'N	121°43'W
Hood Canal, b., Wa., U.S. (hŏd)	116a	47°45'N	122°45'W
Hood River, Or., U.S.	104	45°42'N	121°30'W
Hoodsport, Wa., U.S. (hŏdz'pōrt)	116a	47°25'N	123°09'W
Hoogly, r., India (hōōg'lĭ)	199	21°35'N	87°50'E
Hoogstraten, Bel.	159a	51°24'N	4°46'E
Hooker, Ok., U.S. (hŏk'ēr)	120	36°49'N	101°13'W
Hool, Mex. (ōō'l)	132a	19°32'N	90°22'W
Hoonah, Ak., U.S. (hōō'nä)	103	58°05'N	135°25'W
Hoopa Valley Indian Reservation, I.R., Ca., U.S.	114	41°18'N	123°35'W
Hooper, Ne., U.S. (hŏp'ēr)	121	41°37'N	96°31'W
Hooper, Ut., U.S.	117b	41°10'N	112°08'W
Hooper Bay, Ak., U.S.	103	61°32'N	166°02'W
Hoopeston, Il., U.S. (hōōps'tŭn)	108	40°35'N	87°40'W
Hoosick Falls, N.Y., U.S. (hōō'sĭk)	109	42°55'N	73°15'W
Hoover Dam, Nv., U.S. (hōō'vēr)	118	36°00'N	115°06'W
Hoover Dam, dam, U.S.	106	36°00'N	114°27'W
Hopatcong, Lake, l., N.J., U.S. (hō-păt'kong)	110a	40°57'N	74°38'W
Hope, Ak., U.S. (hōp)	103	60°54'N	149°48'W
Hope, Ar., U.S.	121	33°41'N	93°35'W
Hope, N.D., U.S.	112	47°17'N	97°45'W
Hope, Ben, mtn., Scot., U.K. (bĕn hōp)	164	58°25'N	4°25'W
Hopedale, Can. (hōp'dāl)	91	55°26'N	60°11'W
Hopedale, Ma., U.S. (hōp'dāl)	101a	42°08'N	71°33'W
Hopelchén, Mex. (o-pĕl-chĕ'n)	132a	19°47'N	89°51'W
Hopes Advance, Cap, c., Can. (hōps ăd-vans')	93	61°05'N	69°35'W
Hopetoun, Austl. (hōp'toun)	218	33°50'S	120°15'E
Hopetown, S. Afr. (hōp'toun)	232	29°35'S	24°10'E
Hopewell, Va., U.S. (hōp'wĕl)	125	37°14'N	77°15'W
Hopewell Culture National Historical Park, rec., Oh., U.S.	108	39°25'N	83°00'W
Hopi Indian Reservation, I.R., Az., U.S. (hō'pē)	119	36°20'N	110°30'W
Hopkins, Mn., U.S. (hŏp'kĭns)	117g	44°55'N	93°24'W
Hopkinsville, Ky., U.S. (hŏp'kĭns-vĭl)	105	36°50'N	87°28'W
Hopkinton, Ma., U.S. (hŏp'kĭn-tŭn)	101a	42°14'N	71°31'W
Hoquiam, Wa., U.S. (hō'kwĭ-ăm)	104	47°00'N	123°53'W
Horconcitos, Pan. (ŏr-kôn-sē'-tŏs)	133	8°18'N	82°11'W
Horgen, Switz. (hôr'gĕn)	166	47°16'N	8°35'E
Horicon, Wi., U.S. (hŏr'ĭ-kŏn)	113	43°26'N	88°40'W
Horlivka, Ukr.	181	48°17'N	38°03'E
Hormuz, Strait of, strt., Asia (hôr'mŭz')	198	26°30'N	56°30'E
Horn, i., Austl. (hôrn)	221	10°30'S	143°30'E
Horn, Cape see Hornos, Cabo de, c., Chile	144	56°00'S	67°00'W
Hornavan, l., Swe.	160	65°54'N	16°17'E
Horneburg, Ger. (hŏr'nĕ-bŏrgh)	159c	53°30'N	9°35'E
Hornell, N.Y., U.S. (hŏr-nĕl')	109	42°20'N	77°40'W
Hornos, Cabo de, c., Chile	144	56°00'S	67°00'W
Horn Plateau, plat., Can.	92	62°12'N	120°29'W
Hornsby, Austl. (hôrnz'bĭ)	217b	33°43'S	151°06'E
Horodenka, Ukr.	169	48°40'N	25°30'E
Horodnia, Ukr.	177	51°54'N	31°31'E
Horodok, Ukr.	169	49°47'N	23°39'E
Horqueta, Para. (ŏr-kĕ'tä)	144	23°20'S	57°00'W
Horse Creek, r., Co., U.S. (hôrs)	120	38°49'N	103°48'W
Horse Creek, r., Wy., U.S.	[illegible]	[illegible]	104°39'W
Horse Islands, is., Can.	101	50°11'N	55°45'W
Horsens, Den. (hôrs'ĕns)	166	55°50'N	9°49'E
Horseshoe Bay, Can. (hôrs-shōō)	116d	49°23'N	123°16'W
Horsforth, Eng., U.K. (hôrs'fŭrth)	158a	53°50'N	1°38'W
Horsham, Austl. (hôr'shăm) (hôrs'ăm)	219	36°42'S	142°17'E
Horst, Ger. (hôrst)	159c	53°49'N	9°37'E
Horten, Nor. (hŏr'tĕn)	166	59°26'N	10°27'E
Horton, Ks., U.S. (hôr'tŭn)	121	39°38'N	95°32'W
Horton, r., Ak., U.S. (hôr'tŭn)	103	68°38'N	122°00'W
Horwich, Eng., U.K. (hŏr'ĭch)	158a	53°36'N	2°33'W
Horyn', r., Eur. (gō'rĕn')	169	50°55'N	26°07'E
Hososhima, Japan (hō'sō-shē'mä)	210	32°25'N	131°40'E
Hoste, i., Chile (ŏs'tā)	144	55°20'S	70°45'W
Hostotipaquillo, Mex. (ŏs-tō'tĭ-pä-kēl'yō)	130	21°09'N	104°05'W
Hota, Japan (hō'tä)	211a	35°08'N	139°50'E
Hotan, China (hwŏ-tän)	204	37°11'N	79°50'E
Hotan, r., China	204	39°09'N	81°08'E
Hoto Mayor, Dom. Rep. (ô-tô-mä-yō'r)	135	18°45'N	69°10'W
Hot Springs, Ak., U.S. (hŏt sprĭngs)	103	65°00'N	150°20'W
Hot Springs, Ar., U.S.	105	34°29'N	93°02'W
Hot Springs, S.D., U.S.	112	43°28'N	103°32'W
Hot Springs, Va., U.S.	109	38°00'N	79°55'W
Hot Springs National Park, rec., Ar., U.S.	107	34°30'N	93°00'W
Hotte, Massif de la, mts., Haiti	135	18°25'N	74°00'W
Hotville, Ca., U.S. (hŏt'vĭl)	118	32°50'N	115°24'W
Houdan, Fr. (ōō-dän')	171b	48°47'N	1°36'E
Houghton, Mi., U.S. (hō'tŭn)	113	47°06'N	88°36'W
Houghton, l., Mi., U.S.	108	44°20'N	84°45'W
Houilles, Fr. (ōō-yēs')	171b	48°55'N	2°11'E
Houjie, China (hwŏ-jyĕ)	207a	22°58'N	113°39'E
Houlton, Me., U.S. (hōl'tŭn)	100	46°07'N	67°50'W
Houma, La., U.S. (hōō'mȧ)	123	29°36'N	90°43'W
Housatonic, r., U.S. (hōō-sȧ-tŏn'ĭk)	109	41°50'N	73°25'W
House Springs, Mo., U.S. (hous sprĭngs)	117e	38°24'N	90°34'W
Houston, Ms., U.S. (hūs'tŭn)	124	33°53'N	89°00'W
Houston, Tx., U.S.	105	29°46'N	95°21'W
Houston Ship Channel, strt., Tx., U.S.	123a	29°38'N	94°57'W
Houtbaai, S. Afr.	232a	34°03'S	18°22'E
Houtman Rocks, is., Austl. (hout'män)	220	28°15'S	112°45'E
Houzhen, China (hwŏ-jŭn)	206	36°59'N	118°59'E
Hovd, Mong.	204	48°08'N	91°40'E
Hovd Gol, r., Mong.	204	49°06'N	91°16'E
Hove, Eng., U.K. (hōv)	164	50°50'N	0°09'W
Hövsgöl Nuur, l., Mong.	204	51°11'N	99°11'E
Howard, Ks., U.S. (hou'ȧrd)	121	37°27'N	96°10'W
Howard, S.D., U.S.	112	44°01'N	97°31'W
Howden, Eng., U.K. (hou'dĕn)	158a	53°44'N	0°52'W
Howe, Cape, c., Austl. (hou)	221	37°30'S	150°40'E
Howell, Mi., U.S. (hou'ĕl)	108	42°40'N	84°00'W
Howe Sound, strt., Can.	94	49°22'N	123°18'W
Howick, Can. (hou'ĭk)	102a	45°11'N	73°51'W
Howick, S. Afr.	233c	29°29'S	30°16'E
Howland, i., Oc. (hou'lănd)	2	1°00'N	176°00'W
Howrah, India (hou'rä)	199	22°33'N	88°20'E
Howse Peak, mtn., Can.	95	51°30'N	116°40'W
Howson Peak, mtn., Can.	94	54°25'N	127°45'W
Hoxie, Ar., U.S. (kŏh'sĭ)	121	36°03'N	91°00'W
Hoy, i., Scot., U.K. (hoi)	164a	58°53'N	3°10'W
Hōya, Japan	211a	35°45'N	139°35'E
Hoylake, Eng., U.K. (hoi-lāk')	158a	53°23'N	3°11'W
Hoyo, Sierra del, mts., Spain (sē-ĕ'r-rä-dĕl-ō'yō)	173a	40°39'N	3°56'W
Hradec Králové, Czech Rep.	161	50°12'N	15°50'E
Hradyz'k, Ukr.	177	49°12'N	33°06'E
Hranice, Czech Rep. (hrän'yĕ-tsĕ)	169	49°33'N	17°45'E
Hröby, Swe. (hûr'bü)	166	55°50'N	13°41'E
Hrodna, Bela.	180	53°40'N	23°49'E
Hron, r., Slvk.	169	48°22'N	18°42'E
Hrubieszów, Pol. (hrōō-byā'shōōf)	169	50°48'N	23°54'E
Hsawnhsup, Mya.	204	24°29'N	94°45'E
Hsinchu, Tai. (hsĭn'chōō')	209	24°48'N	121°00'E
Huadian, China (hwä-dĭĕn)	208	42°38'N	126°45'E
Huai, r., China (hwī)	205	32°07'N	114°38'E
Huai'an, China (hwī-än)	208	33°31'N	119°11'E
Huailai, China	208	40°20'N	115°45'E
Huailin, China (hwī-lĭn)	206	31°27'N	117°36'E
Huainan, China	206	32°38'N	117°02'E
Huaiyang, China (hōōāī'yang)	208	33°45'N	114°54'E
Huaiyuan, China (hwī-yüän)	208	32°53'N	117°13'E
Huajicori, Mex. (wä-jė-kō'rė)	130	22°41'N	105°24'W
Huajuapan de León, Mex. (wäj-wä'päm dā lā-ōn')	131	17°46'N	97°45'W
Hualapai Indian Reservation, I.R., Az., U.S. (wälåpī)	119	35°41'N	113°38'W
Hualapai Mountains, mts., Az., U.S.	119	34°53'N	113°54'W

ăt; fināl; rāte; senāte; ärm; ȧsk; sofȧ; fâre; ch-choose; dh-as th in other; bē; ėvent; bĕt; recĕnt; cratēr; g-gō; gh-guttural g; bĭt; ĭ-short neutral; rīde; K-guttural k as ch in German ich;

PLACE (Pronunciation)	PAGE	LAT.	LONG.
Hualien, Tai. (hwä'lyĕn')	209	23°58'N	121°58'E
Huallaga, r., Peru (wäl-yä'gä)	142	8°12'S	76°34'W
Huamachuco, Peru (wä-mä-chōō'kō)	142	7°52'S	78°11'W
Huamantla, Mex. (wä-män'tlä)	131	19°18'N	97°54'W
Huambo, Ang.	232	12°44'S	15°47'E
Huamuxtitlán, Mex. (wä-mōōs-tē-tlän')	130	17°49'N	98°38'W
Huancavelica, Peru (wän'kä-vä-lē'kä)	142	12°47'S	75°02'W
Huancayo, Peru (wän-kä'yȯ)	142	12°09'S	75°04'W
Huanchaca, Bol. (wän-chä'kä)	142	20°09'S	66°40'W
Huang (Yellow), r., China (hůäŋ)	205	35°06'N	113°39'E
Huang, Old Beds of the, mth., China	204	40°28'N	106°34'E
Huang, Old Course of the, r., China	206	34°28'N	116°59'E
Huangchuan, China (hůäŋ-chůän)	208	32°07'N	115°01'E
Huanghua, China (hůäŋ-hwä)	206	38°28'N	117°18'E
Huanghuadian, China (hůäŋ-hwä dĭĕn)	206	39°22'N	116°53'E
Huangli, China (hōōäng'lē)	206	31°39'N	119°42'E
Huangpu, China (hůäŋ-pōō)	207a	22°44'N	113°20'E
Huangpu, r., China	207b	30°56'N	121°16'E
Huangqiao, China (hůän-chyou)	206	32°15'N	120°13'E
Huangxian, China (hůäŋ shyĕn)	206	37°39'N	120°32'E
Huangyuan, China (hůäŋ-yůän)	204	37°00'N	101°01'E
Huanren, China (hůän-rŭn)	208	41°10'N	125°30'E
Huánuco, Peru (wä-nōō'kȯ)	142	9°50'S	76°17'W
Huánuni, Bol. (wä-nōō'nē)	142	18°11'S	66°43'W
Huaquechula, Mex. (wä-kē-chōō'lä)	130	18°44'N	98°37'W
Huaral, Peru (wä-rä'l)	142	11°28'S	77°11'W
Huarás, Peru (ōä'rä's)	142	9°32'S	77°29'W
Huascarán, Nevados, mts., Peru (wäs-kä-rän')	142	9°05'S	77°50'W
Huasco, Chile (wäs'kō)	144	28°32'S	71°16'W
Huatla de Jiménez, Mex. (wä'tlä-dĕ-kē-mĕ'nĕz)	131	18°08'N	96°49'W
Huatlatlauch, Mex. (wä'tlä-tlä-ōō'ch)	130	18°40'N	98°04'W
Huatusco, Mex. (wä-tōōs'kȯ)	131	19°09'N	96°57'W
Huauchinango, Mex. (wä-ōō-chē-näŋ'gō)	130	20°09'N	98°03'W
Huaunta, Nic. (wä-ö'n-tä)	133	13°30'N	83°32'W
Huaunta, Laguna, l., Nic. (lä-gö'nä-wä-ö'n-tä)	133	13°35'N	83°46'W
Huautla, Mex. (wä-ōō'tlä)	130	21°04'N	98°13'W
Huaxian, China (hwä shyĕn)	208	35°34'N	114°32'E
Huaynamota, Río de, r., Mex. (rē'ō-dĕ-wäy-nä-mō'tä)	130	22°10'N	104°36'W
Huazolotitlán, Mex. (wäzȯ-lȯ-tlē-tlän')	131	16°18'N	97°55'W
Hubbard, N.H., U.S. (hŭb'ērd)	101a	42°53'N	71°12'W
Hubbard, Tx., U.S.	123	31°53'N	96°46'W
Hubbard, l., Mi., U.S.	108	44°45'N	83°30'W
Hubbard Creek Reservoir, res., Tx., U.S.	122	32°50'N	98°55'W
Hubei, prov., China (hōō-bā)	205	31°20'N	111°58'E
Hubli, India (hȯ'blē)	199	15°25'N	75°09'E
Hückeswagen, Ger. (hü'kĕs-vä'gĕn)	171c	51°09'N	7°20'E
Hucknall, Eng., U.K. (hŭk'năl)	158a	53°02'N	1°12'W
Huddersfield, Eng., U.K. (hŭd'ērz-fēld)	164	53°39'N	1°47'W
Hudiksvall, Swe. (hōō'dĭks-väl)	160	61°44'N	17°05'E
Hudson, Can. (hŭd'sŭn)	102a	45°26'N	74°08'W
Hudson, Ma., U.S.	101a	42°24'N	71°34'W
Hudson, Mi., U.S.	108	41°50'N	84°15'W
Hudson, N.Y., U.S.	109	42°15'N	73°45'W
Hudson, Oh., U.S.	111d	41°15'N	81°27'W
Hudson, Wi., U.S.	117g	44°59'N	92°45'W
Hudson, r., U.S.	107	42°30'N	73°55'W
Hudson Bay, Can.	97	52°52'N	102°25'W
Hudson Bay, b., Can.	93	60°15'N	85°30'W
Hudson Falls, N.Y., U.S.	109	43°20'N	73°30'W
Hudson Heights, Can.	102a	45°28'N	74°09'W
Hudson Strait, strt., Can.	93	63°25'N	74°05'W
Hue, Viet. (ü-ā')	212	16°28'N	107°42'E
Huebra, r., Spain (wĕ'brä)	172	40°44'N	6°17'W
Huehuetenango, Guat. (wā-wå-tå-näŋ'gȯ)	132	15°19'N	91°26'W
Huejotzingo, Mex. (wā-hȯ-tzĭŋ'gō)	130	19°09'N	98°24'W
Huejúcar, Mex. (wā-hōō'kär)	130	22°26'N	103°12'W
Huejuquilla el Alto, Mex. (wā-hōō-kēl'yä ĕl äl'tō)	130	22°42'N	103°54'W
Huejutla, Mex. (wā-hōō'tlä)	130	21°08'N	98°26'W
Huelma, Spain (wĕl'mä)	172	37°39'N	3°36'W
Huelva, Spain (wĕl'vä)	162	37°16'N	6°58'W
Huércal-Overa, Spain (wĕr-käl' ō-vä'rä)	172	37°12'N	1°58'W
Huerfano, r., Co., U.S. (wâr'fā-nō)	120	37°41'N	105°13'W
Huésca, Spain (wĕs-kä)	162	42°07'N	0°25'W
Huéscar, Spain (wās'kär)	172	37°50'N	2°34'W
Huetamo de Núñez, Mex.	130	18°34'N	100°53'W
Huete, Spain (wā'tå)	172	40°09'N	2°42'W
Hueycatenango, Mex. (wĕy-kä-tĕ-nä'n-gȯ)	130	17°31'N	99°10'W
Hueytlalpan, Mex. (wā'ī-tläl'păn)	131	20°03'N	97°41'W
Hueytown, Al., U.S.	110h	33°28'N	86°59'W
Huffman, Al., U.S. (hŭf'măn)	110h	33°36'N	86°42'W
Hugh Butler, l., Ne., U.S.	120	40°21'N	100°40'W
Hughenden, Austl. (hū'ĕn-dĕn)	219	20°58'S	144°13'E
Hughes, Austl. (hūz)	218	30°45'S	129°30'E
Hughesville, Md., U.S.	110e	38°32'N	76°48'W
Hugo, Mn., U.S. (hū'gō)	117g	45°10'N	93°00'W
Hugo, Ok., U.S.	121	34°01'N	95°32'W
Hugoton, Ks., U.S. (hū'gō-tŭn)	120	37°10'N	101°28'W
Hugou, China (hōō-gō)	206	33°22'N	117°07'E
Huichapan, Mex. (wē-chä-pän')	130	20°22'N	99°39'W
Huila, dept., Col. (wē'lä)	142a	3°10'N	75°20'W
Huila, Nevado de, mtn., Col. (nĕ-vä-dȯ-de-wē'lä)	142a	2°59'N	76°01'W

PLACE (Pronunciation)	PAGE	LAT.	LONG.
Huilai, China	209	23°02'N	116°18'E
Huili, China	204	26°48'N	102°20'E
Huimanguillo, Mex. (wē-män-gēl'yō)	131	17°50'N	93°16'W
Huimin, China (hōōĭ mĭn)	205	37°29'N	117°32'E
Huitzilac, Mex. (ōē't-zē-lä'k)	131a	19°01'N	99°16'W
Huitzitzilingo, Mex. (wē-tzē-tzē-lē'n-go)	130	21°11'N	98°42'W
Huitzuco, Mex. (wė-tzōō'kō)	130	18°16'N	99°20'W
Huixquilucan, Mex. (ȯē'x-kē-lōō-kä'n)	131a	19°21'N	99°22'W
Huiyang, China	209	23°05'N	114°25'E
Hukou, China (hōō-kō)	205	29°58'N	116°20'E
Hulan, China (hōō'län')	205	45°58'N	126°32'E
Hulan, r., China	208	47°20'N	126°30'E
Huliaipole, Ukr.	177	47°39'N	36°12'E
Hulin, China (hōō'lĭn')	210	45°45'N	133°25'E
Hull, Can. (hŭl)	91	45°26'N	75°43'W
Hull, Ma., U.S.	101a	42°18'N	70°54'W
Hull, r., Eng., U.K.	158a	53°47'N	0°20'W
Hulst, Neth. (hȯlst)	159a	51°17'N	4°01'E
Huludao, China (hōō-lōō-dou)	205	40°40'N	120°55'E
Hulun Nur, l., China (hōō-lȯn nȯr)	205	48°50'N	116°45'E
Humacao, P.R. (ōō-mä-kä'ō)	129b	18°09'N	65°49'W
Humansdorp, S. Afr. (hōō'mäns-dȯrp)	232	33°57'S	24°45'E
Humbe, Ang. (hȯm'bå)	232	16°50'S	14°55'E
Humber, r., Can.	102d	43°53'N	79°40'W
Humber, r., Eng., U.K. (hŭm'bēr)	160	53°30'N	0°30'E
Humbermouth, Can. (hŭm'bēr-mŭth)	101	48°58'N	57°55'W
Humberside, hist. reg., Eng., U.K.	158a	53°47'N	0°36'W
Humble, Tx., U.S. (hŭm'b'l)	123	29°58'N	95°15'W
Humboldt, Can. (hŭm'bōlt)	90	52°12'N	105°07'W
Humboldt, Ia., U.S.	113	42°43'N	94°11'W
Humboldt, Ks., U.S.	121	37°48'N	95°26'W
Humboldt, Ne., U.S.	121	40°10'N	95°57'W
Humboldt, r., Nv., U.S.	106	40°30'N	116°50'W
Humboldt, East Fork, r., Nv., U.S.	114	40°59'N	115°21'W
Humboldt, North Fork, r., Nv., U.S.	114	41°25'N	115°45'W
Humboldt Bay, b., Ca., U.S.	114	40°48'N	124°25'W
Humboldt Range, mts., Nv., U.S.	118	40°12'N	118°16'W
Humbolt, Tn., U.S.	124	35°47'N	88°55'W
Humbolt Salt Marsh, Nv., U.S.	118	39°49'N	117°41'W
Humbolt Sink, Nv., U.S.	118	39°58'N	118°54'W
Humen, China (hōō-mŭn)	207a	22°49'N	113°39'E
Humphreys Peak, mtn., Az., U.S. (hŭm'frĭs)	106	35°20'N	111°40'W
Humpolec, Czech Rep. (hȯm'pō-lĕts)	168	49°33'N	15°21'E
Humuya, r., Hond. (ōō-mōō'yä)	132	14°38'N	87°36'W
Húnaflói, b., Ice. (hōō'nä-flō'ī)	160	65°41'N	20°44'W
Hunan, prov., China (hōō'nän')	205	28°08'N	111°25'E
Hunchun, China (hȯn-chůn)	205	42°53'N	130°34'E
Hunedoara, Rom. (κōō'nĕd-wä'rä)	175	45°45'N	22°54'E
Hungary, nation, Eur. (hŭŋ'gå-rĭ)	154	46°44'N	17°55'E
Hungerford, Austl. (hŭn'gēr-fērd)	219	28°50'S	144°32'E
Hungry Horse Reservoir, res., Mt., U.S. (hŭŋ'gå-rĭ hôrs)	115	48°11'N	113°30'W
Hunsrück, mts., Ger. (hōōns'rûk)	168	49°43'N	7°12'E
Hunte, r., Ger. (hȯn'tē)	168	52°45'N	8°26'E
Hunter Islands, is., Austl. (hŭn-tēr)	221	40°33'S	143°36'E
Huntingburg, In., U.S. (hŭnt'ĭng-bûrg)	108	38°15'N	86°55'W
Huntingdon, Can. (hŭnt'ĭng-dŭn)	99	45°10'N	74°05'W
Huntingdon, Can.	116d	49°00'N	122°16'W
Huntingdon, Tn., U.S.	124	36°00'N	88°23'W
Huntington, In., U.S.	108	40°55'N	85°30'W
Huntington, Pa., U.S.	109	40°30'N	78°00'W
Huntington, W.V., U.S.	105	38°25'N	82°25'W
Huntington Beach, Ca., U.S.	117a	33°39'N	118°00'W
Huntington Park, Ca., U.S.	117a	33°59'N	118°14'W
Huntington Station, N.Y., U.S.	110a	40°51'N	73°25'W
Huntley, Mt., U.S.	115	45°54'N	108°01'W
Huntsville, Can.	91	45°20'N	79°15'W
Huntsville, Al., U.S. (hŭnts'vĭl)	124	34°44'N	86°36'W
Huntsville, Mo., U.S.	121	39°24'N	92°32'W
Huntsville, Tx., U.S.	123	30°44'N	95°34'W
Huntsville, Ut., Ut., U.S.	117b	41°16'N	111°46'W
Huolu, China (hȯŭ lōō)	206	38°05'N	114°20'E
Huon Gulf, b., Pap. N. Gui.	213	7°15'S	147°45'E
Huoqiu, China (hwȯ-chyō)	206	32°19'N	116°17'E
Huoshan, China (hwȯ-shän)	209	31°30'N	116°25'E
Ḩuraydin, Wādī, r., Egypt	197a	30°55'N	34°12'E
Hurd, Cape, c., Can. (hûrd)	98	45°15'N	81°45'W
Hurdiyo, Som.	238a	10°43'N	51°05'E
Hurley, Wi., U.S. (hûr'lĭ)	113	46°26'N	90°11'W
Hurlingham, Arg. (ōō'r-lēn-gäm)	144a	34°36'S	58°38'W
Huron, Oh., U.S. (hū'rŏn)	108	41°20'N	82°35'W
Huron, S.D., U.S.	104	44°22'N	98°15'W
Huron, r., Mi., U.S.	111b	42°12'N	83°26'W
Huron, Lake, l., N.A. (hū'rŏn)	107	45°15'N	82°40'W
Huron Mountains, mts., Mi., U.S. (hū'rŏn)	113	46°47'N	87°52'W
Hurricane, Ak., U.S. (hŭr'ĭ-kān)	103	63°00'N	149°30'W
Hurricane, Ut., U.S.	119	37°10'N	113°20'W
Hurricane Flats, bk. (hŭ-rĭ-kăn flăts)	134	23°35'N	78°30'W
Hurst, Tx., U.S.	117c	32°48'N	97°12'W
Húsavik, Ice.	160	66°00'N	17°10'W
Huşi, Rom. (kȯsh')	177	46°52'N	28°04'E
Huskvarna, Swe. (hȯsk-vär'nä)	166	57°48'N	14°16'E
Husum, Ger. (hōō'zȯm)	168	54°29'N	9°04'E
Hutchins, Tx., U.S. (hŭch'ĭnz)	117c	32°38'N	96°43'W
Hutchinson, Ks., U.S. (hŭch'ĭn-sŭn)	104	38°02'N	97°56'W
Hutchinson, Mn., U.S.	113	44°53'N	94°23'W
Hutuo, r., China (hōō-tô)	208	38°10'N	114°00'E
Huy, Bel. (û-ē') (hū'ē)	165	50°33'N	5°14'E
Hvannadalshnúkur, mtn., Ice.	160	64°09'N	16°46'W

PLACE (Pronunciation)	PAGE	LAT.	LONG.
Hvar, i., Cro. (кhvär)	174	43°08'N	16°28'E
Hwange, Zimb.	232	18°22'S	26°29'E
Hwangju, Kor., N. (hwäng'jōō')	210	38°39'N	125°49'E
Hyargas Nuur, l., Mong.	204	48°00'N	92°32'E
Hyattsville, Md., U.S. (hī'ăt's-vĭl)	110e	38°57'N	76°58'W
Hyco Lake, res., N.C., U.S. (rōks' bŭr-ō)	125	36°22'N	78°58'W
Hydaburg, Ak., U.S. (hī-dă'bûrg)	103	55°12'N	132°49'W
Hyde, Eng., U.K. (hīd)	158a	53°27'N	2°05'W
Hyderābād, India (hī-dēr-å-băd')	199	17°29'N	78°28'E
Hyderabad, India	199	18°30'N	76°50'E
Hyderābād, Pak.	199	25°29'N	68°28'E
Hyéres, Fr. (ē-år')	161	43°09'N	6°08'E
Hyéres, Îles d', is., Fr. (ēl'dyâr')	161	42°57'N	6°17'E
Hyesanjin, Kor., N. (hyĕ'sän-jĭn')	210	41°11'N	128°12'E
Hymera, In., U.S. (hī-mē'rȧ)	108	39°10'N	87°20'W
Hyndman Peak, mtn., Id., U.S. (hīnd'măn)	106	43°30'N	114°04'W
Hyōgo, dept., Japan (hĭyō'gō)	211b	34°54'N	135°15'E

I

PLACE (Pronunciation)	PAGE	LAT.	LONG.
Ia, r., Japan (ē'ä)	211b	34°54'N	135°34'E
Iahotyn, Ukr.	177	50°18'N	31°46'E
Ialomiţa, r., Rom.	175	44°37'N	26°42'E
Iaşi, Rom. (yä'shē)	154	47°10'N	27°40'E
Iasinia, Ukr.	169	48°17'N	24°21'E
Iavoriv, Ukr.	169	49°56'N	23°24'E
Iba, Phil. (ē'bä)	213a	15°20'N	119°59'E
Ibadan, Nig. (ē-bä'dän)	230	7°17'N	3°30'E
Ibagué, Col.	142	4°27'N	75°14'W
Ibar, r., Serb. (ē'bär)	175	43°22'N	20°35'E
Ibaraki, Japan (ē-bä'rä-gē)	211b	34°49'N	135°35'E
Ibarra, Ec. (ē-bär'rä)	142	0°19'N	78°08'W
Ibb, Yemen	201	14°01'N	44°10'E
Iberville, Can. (ē-bâr-vēl')(ī'bēr-vĭl)	99	45°14'N	73°01'W
Ibi, Nig. (ē'bē)	230	8°12'N	9°45'E
Ibiapaba, Serra da, mts., Braz. (sĕ'r-rä-dä-ē-byä-pä'bä)	143	3°30'S	40°55'W
Ibiza *see* Eivissa, i., Spain	156	38°55'N	1°24'E
Ibo, Moz. (ē'bō)	233	12°20'S	40°35'E
Ibrāhīm, Būr, b., Egypt	238d	29°57'N	32°33'E
Ibrahim, Jabal, mtn., Sau. Ar.	198	20°31'N	41°17'E
Ibwe Munyama, Zam.	237	16°09'S	28°34'E
Ica, Peru (ē'kä)	142	14°09'S	75°42'W
Icá (Putumayo), r., S.A.	142	3°00'S	69°00'W
Içana, Braz. (ē-sä'nä)	142	0°15'N	67°19'W
Ice Harbor Dam, Wa., U.S.	114	46°15'N	118°54'W
İçel, Tur.	198	37°00'N	34°40'E
Iceland, nation, Eur. (īs'lănd)	154	65°12'N	19°45'W
Ichibusayama, mtn., Japan (ē'chē-bōō'sá-yä'mä)	211	32°19'N	131°08'E
Ichihara, Japan	211a	35°31'N	140°05'E
Ichikawa, Japan (ē'chē-kä'wä)	211a	35°44'N	139°54'E
Ichinomiya, Japan (ē'chē-nō-mē'yȧ)	211	35°19'N	136°49'E
Ichinomoto, Japan (ē-chē'nō-mō-tō)	211b	34°37'N	135°50'E
Ichnia, Ukr.	181	50°47'N	32°23'E
Icy Cape, c., Ak., U.S. (ī'sĭ)	103	70°20'N	161°40'W
Idabel, Ok., U.S. (ī'dȧ-bĕl)	121	33°52'N	94°47'W
Idagrove, Ia., U.S. (ī'dȧ-grōv)	112	42°22'N	95°29'W
Idah, Nig. (ē'dä)	230	7°07'N	6°43'E
Idaho, state, U.S. (ī'dȧ-hō)	104	44°00'N	115°10'W
Idaho Falls, Id., U.S.	104	43°30'N	112°01'W
Idaho Springs, Co., U.S.	120	39°43'N	105°32'W
Idanha-a-Nova, Port. (ē-dän'yȧ-ä-nō'vȧ)	172	39°58'N	7°13'W
Ider, r., Mong.	204	48°58'N	98°38'E
Idi, Indon. (ē'dē)	212	4°58'N	97°47'E
Idkū Lake, l., Egypt	238b	31°13'N	30°22'E
Idle, r., Eng., U.K. (īd''l)	158a	53°22'N	0°56'W
Idlib, Syria	200	35°55'N	36°38'E
Idriaj, Slvn. (ē'drē-ȧ)	174	46°01'N	14°01'E
Idutywa, S. Afr. (ē-dō-tī'wȧ)	233c	32°06'S	28°18'E
Ienakiieve, Ukr.	177	48°14'N	38°12'E
Ieper, Bel.	165	50°50'N	2°53'E
Ierápetra, Grc.	174a	35°01'N	25°48'E
Iesi, Italy (yā'sê)	174	43°37'N	13°20'E
Ievpatoriia, Ukr.	181	45°13'N	33°22'E
Ife, Nig.	230	7°30'N	4°30'E
Iferouâne, Niger (ēf'rōō-än')	230	19°04'N	8°24'E
Ifôghas, Adrar des, plat., Afr.	230	19°55'N	2°00'E
Igalula, Tan.	237	5°14'S	33°00'E
Igarka, Russia (ē-gär'kȧ)	178	67°22'N	86°16'E
Iglesias, Italy (ē-lĕ'syōs)	162	39°20'N	8°34'E
Igli, Alg. (ē-glē')	230	30°32'N	2°15'W
Igluligaarjuk (Chesterfield Inlet), Can.	91	63°19'N	91°11'W
Iglulik, Can.	91	69°33'N	81°18'W
Ignacio, Ca., U.S. (ĭg-nā'cĭ-ō)	116b	38°05'N	122°32'W
Iguaçu, r., Braz. (ē-gwä-sōō')	144b	22°42'S	43°19'W
Iguala, Mex. (ē-gwä'lä)	130	18°18'N	99°34'W
Igualada, Spain (ē-gwä-lä'dä)	173	41°35'N	1°38'E
Iguassu, r., S.A. (ē-gwä-sōō')	144	25°45'S	52°30'W
Iguassu Falls, wtfl., S.A.	143	25°40'S	54°16'W
Iguatama, Braz. (ē-gwä-tá'mä)	141a	20°13'S	45°40'W
Iguatu, Braz. (ē-gwä-tōō')	143	6°22'S	39°17'W
Iguidi, Erg, Afr.	230	26°22'N	6°53'W
Iguig, Phil. (ē-gēg')	213a	17°46'N	121°44'E
Iharana, Madag.	233	13°35'S	50°05'E
Ihiala, Nig.	235	5°51'N	6°51'E
Iida, Japan (ē'ē-dȧ)	211	35°39'N	137°53'E

ng-sing; ŋ-baŋk; ɴ-nasalized n; nŏd; cŏmmit; ōld; ôbey; ôrder; oi-boil; fōōd; ȯ-as oo in foot; ou-out; s-soft; sh-dish; th-thin; pūre; ûnite; ûrn; stŭd; circŭs; ü-as in French tu; '-indeterminate vowel.

304 Iijoki – Isla-Cristina PRONOUNCING INDEX

PLACE (Pronunciation)	PAGE	LAT.	LONG.
Iijoki, r., Fin. (ē′yō′kĭ)	180	65°28′N	27°00′E
Iizuka, Japan (ē′ē-zō-kȧ)	211	33°39′N	130°39′E
Ijebu-Ode, Nig. (ē-jĕ′bōō ōdȧ)	230	6°50′N	3°56′E
IJmuiden, Neth.	159a	52°27′N	4°36′E
IJsselmeer, l., Neth. (ī′sĕl-mār)	165	52°46′N	5°14′E
Ikaalinen, Fin. (ē′kä-lĭ-nĕn)	167	61°47′N	22°55′E
Ikaría, i., Grc. (ē-kä′ryȧ)	175	37°43′N	26°07′E
Ikeda, Japan (ē′kȧ-dä)	211b	34°49′N	135°26′E
Ikerre, Nig.	235	7°31′N	5°14′E
Ikhtiman, Blg. (ēk′tē-män)	175	42°26′N	23°49′E
Iki, i., Japan (ē′kē)	210	33°46′N	129°44′E
Ikoma, Japan	211b	34°41′N	135°43′E
Ikoma, Tan. (ē-kō′mä)	232	2°08′S	34°47′E
Iksha, Russia (ĭk′shȧ)	186b	56°10′N	37°30′E
Ila, Nig.	235	8°01′N	4°55′E
Ilagan, Phil.	[illegible]	[illegible]	[illegible]
Ilan, Tai. (ē′län′)	209	24°50′N	121°42′E
Iława, Pol. (ē-lä′vä)	169	53°35′N	19°36′E
Île-á-la-Crosse, Can.	96	55°34′N	108°00′W
Ilebo, D.R.C.	232	4°19′S	20°35′E
Ilek, Russia (ē′lyĕk)	181	51°30′N	53°10′E
Île-Perrot, Can. (yl-pĕ-rōt′)	102a	45°21′N	73°54′W
Ilesha, Nig.	230	7°38′N	4°45′E
Ilford, Eng., U.K. (ĭl′fērd)	158b	51°33′N	0°06′E
Ilfracombe, Eng., U.K. (ĭl-frȧ-kōōm′)	164	51°13′N	4°08′W
Ilhabela, Braz. (ē′lä-bĕ′lä)	141a	23°47′S	45°21′W
Ilha Grande, Baía de, b., Braz. (ēl′yȧ grän′dĕ)	141a	23°17′S	44°25′W
Ílhavo, Port. (ēl′yȧ-vō)	162	40°36′N	8°41′W
Ilhéus, Braz. (ē-lĕ′ōōs)	143	14°52′S	39°00′W
Ili, r., Asia	184	44°30′N	76°45′E
Iliamna, Ak., U.S. (ē-lē-ăm′nȧ)	103	59°45′N	155°05′W
Iliamna, Ak., U.S.	103	60°18′N	153°25′W
Iliamna, l., Ak., U.S.	103	59°25′N	155°30′W
Ilim, r., Russia (ē-lyĕm′)	184	57°28′N	103°00′E
Ilimsk, Russia (ē-lyĕmsk′)	179	56°47′N	103°43′E
Ilin Island, i., Phil. (ē-lyēn′)	213a	12°16′N	120°57′E
Ilion, N.Y., U.S. (ĭl′ĭ-ŭn)	109	43°00′N	75°05′W
Ilkeston, Eng., U.K. (ĭl′kĕs-tŭn)	158a	52°58′N	1°19′W
Illampu, Nevado, mtn., Bol. (nĕ-vä′dō-ēl-yäm-pōō′)	142	15°50′S	68°15′W
Illapel, Chile (ē-zhä-pĕ′l)	144	31°37′S	71°10′W
Iller, r., Ger. (ĭlĕr)	168	47°52′N	10°06′E
Illimani, Nevado, mtn., Bol. (nĕ-vä′dō-ēl-yē-mä′nē)	142	16°50′S	67°38′W
Illinois, state, U.S. (ĭl-ĭ-noi′) (ĭl-ĭ-noiz′)	105	40°25′N	90°40′W
Illinois, r., Il., U.S.	107	39°00′N	90°30′W
Illintsi, Ukr.	177	49°07′N	29°13′E
Illizi, Alg.	230	26°35′N	8°24′E
Il′men, l., Russia (ô′zē-rō ēl′mĕn′) (ĭl′mĕn)	180	58°18′N	32°00′E
Ilo, Peru	142	17°46′S	71°13′W
Ilobasco, El Sal. (ē-lō-bäs′kō)	132	13°57′N	88°46′W
Iloilo, Phil. (ē-lō-ē′lō)	212	10°49′N	122°33′E
Ilopango, Lago, l., El Sal. (ē-lō-päŋ′gō)	132	13°48′N	88°50′W
Ilorin, Nig. (ē-lō-rēn′)	230	8°30′N	4°32′E
Ilūkste, Lat.	167	55°59′N	26°20′E
Ilwaco, Wa., U.S. (ĭl-wä′kō)	116c	46°19′N	124°02′W
Ilych, r., Russia (ē′lĭch)	180	62°30′N	57°30′E
Imabari, Japan (ē′mä-bä′rē)	210	34°05′N	132°58′E
Imai, Japan (ē-mī′)	211b	34°30′N	135°47′E
Iman, r., Russia (ē-män′)	210	45°40′N	134°31′E
Imandra, l., Russia (ē-män′drȧ)	180	67°40′N	32°30′E
Imbābah, Egypt (ēm-bä′bȧ)	238b	30°06′N	31°09′E
Imeni Morozova, Russia (ĭm-yĕ′nyĭ mô rô′zô vȧ)	186c	59°58′N	31°02′E
Imeni Moskvy, Kanal (Moscow Canal), can., Russia (kȧ-näl′ĭm-yȧ′nĭ mōs-kvĭ)	176	56°33′N	37°15′E
Imeni Tsyurupy, Russia	186b	55°30′N	38°39′E
Imeni Vorovskogo, Russia	186b	55°43′N	38°21′E
Imlay City, Mi., U.S. (ĭm′lā)	108	43°00′N	83°15′W
Immenstadt, Ger. (ĭm′ĕn-shtät)	168	47°34′N	10°12′E
Immerpan, S. Afr. (ĭmĕr-pän)	238c	24°29′S	29°14′E
Imola, Italy (ē′mō-lä)	174	44°19′N	11°43′E
Imotski, Cro. (ē-mōts′kē)	175	43°25′N	17°15′E
Impameri, Braz.	143	17°44′S	48°03′W
Impendle, S. Afr. (ĭm-pĕnd′lȧ)	233c	29°38′S	29°54′E
Imperia, Italy (ēm-pā′rē-ä)	162	43°52′N	8°00′E
Imperial, Pa., U.S. (ĭm-pē′rĭ-ăl)	111e	40°27′N	80°15′W
Imperial Beach, Ca., U.S.	118a	32°34′N	117°08′W
Imperial Valley, Ca., U.S.	118	33°00′N	115°22′W
Impfondo, Congo (ĭmp-fōn′dō)	231	1°37′N	18°04′E
Imphāl, India (ĭmp′hŭl)	199	24°42′N	94°00′E
Ina, r., Japan (ē-nä′)	211b	34°56′N	135°21′E
Inaja Indian Reservation, I.R., Ca., U.S. (ē-nä′hä)	118	32°56′N	116°37′W
Inari, l., Fin.	160	69°02′N	26°22′E
Inca, Spain (ēŋ′kä)	173	39°43′N	2°53′E
Ince Burun, c., Tur. (ĭn′jȧ)	163	42°00′N	35°00′E
Inch′ŏn, Kor., S. (ĭn′chŭn)	205	37°26′N	126°46′E
Incudine, Monte, mtn., Fr. (ēn-kōō-dē′nȧ) (ăɴ-kü-dēn′)	174	41°53′N	9°17′E
Indalsälven, r., Swe.	160	62°50′N	16°50′E
Independence, Ks., U.S. (ĭn-dē-pĕn′dĕns)	121	37°14′N	95°42′W
Independence, Mo., U.S.	117f	39°06′N	94°26′W
Independence, Oh., U.S.	111d	41°23′N	81°39′W
Independence, Or., U.S.	114	44°49′N	123°13′W
Independence Mountains, mts., Nv., U.S.	114	41°15′N	116°02′W
Inder köli, l., Kaz.	181	48°20′N	52°10′E
India, nation, Asia (ĭn′dĭ-ȧ)	199	23°00′N	77°30′E
Indian, l., Mi., U.S. (ĭn′dĭ-ăn)	113	46°04′N	86°34′W
Indian, r., N.Y., U.S.	109	44°05′N	75°45′W
Indiana, Pa., U.S. (ĭn-dĭ-ăn′ȧ)	109	40°40′N	79°10′W
Indiana, state, U.S.	105	39°50′N	86°45′W
Indianapolis, In., U.S. (ĭn-dĭ-ăn-ăp′ō-lĭs)	105	39°45′N	86°08′W
Indian Arm, b., Can. (ĭn′dĭ-ăn ärm)	116d	49°21′N	122°55′W
Indian Head, Can.	90	50°29′N	103°44′W
Indian Lake, l., Can.	98	47°00′N	82°00′W
Indian Ocean, o.	5	10°00′S	70°00′E
Indianola, Ia., U.S. (ĭn-dĭ-ăn-ō′lȧ)	113	41°22′N	93°33′W
Indianola, Ms., U.S.	124	33°29′N	90°35′W
Indigirka, r., Russia (ēn-dē-gēr′kȧ)	185	67°45′N	145°45′E
Indio, r., Pan. (ē′n-dyô)	128a	9°13′N	79°28′W
Indochina, reg., Asia (ĭn-dō-chī′nȧ)	212	17°22′N	105°18′E
Indonesia, nation, Asia [illegible]	212	4°00′S	118°45′E
Indore, India (ĭn-dōr′)	199	22°48′N	76°51′E
Indragiri, r., Indon. (ĭn-drȧ-jē′rē)	212	0°27′S	102°05′E
Indrāvati, r., India (ĭn-drŭ-vä′tē)	199	19°00′N	82°00′E
Indre, r., Fr. (ăɴ′dr′)	170	47°13′N	0°29′E
Indus, Can. (ĭn′dŭs)	102e	50°55′N	113°45′W
Indus, r., Asia	199	26°43′N	67°41′E
Indwe, S. Afr. (ĭnd′wȧ)	233c	31°30′S	27°21′E
Inebolu, Tur. (ē-nȧ-bō′lōō)	163	41°50′N	33°40′E
Inego, Tur. (ē′nȧ-gŭ)	181	40°05′N	29°20′E
Infanta, Phil. (ēn-făn′tä)	213a	14°44′N	121°39′E
Infanta, Phil.	213a	15°50′N	119°53′E
Inferror, Laguna, l., Mex. (lä-gō′nä-ēn-fĕr-rôr)	131	16°18′N	94°40′W
Infiernillo, Presa de, res., Mex.	130	18°50′N	101°50′W
Infiesto, Spain (ēn-fyĕ′s-tō)	172	43°21′N	5°24′W
I-n-Gall, Niger	235	16°47′N	6°56′E
Ingersoll, Can. (ĭn′gēr-sŏl)	98	43°05′N	81°00′W
Ingham, Austl. (ĭng′ăm)	219	18°45′S	146°14′E
Ingles, Cayos, is., Cuba (kä-yōs-ē′n-glĕ′s)	134	21°55′N	82°35′W
Inglewood, Can.	102d	43°48′N	79°56′W
Inglewood, Ca., U.S. (ĭn′g′l-wŏd)	117a	33°57′N	118°22′W
Ingoda, r., Russia (ēn-gō′dȧ)	185	51°29′N	112°32′E
Ingolstadt, Ger. (ĭŋ′gōl-shtät)	168	48°46′N	11°27′E
Ingur, r., Geor. (ēn-gōr′)	181	42°30′N	42°00′E
Ingushetia, prov., Russia	182	43°15′N	45°00′E
Inhambane, Moz. (ēn-äm-bä′-nĕ)	232	23°47′S	35°28′E
Inhambupe, Braz. (ēn-yäm-bōō′pä)	143	11°47′S	38°13′W
Inharrime, Moz. (ēn-yär-rē′mä)	232	24°17′S	35°07′E
Inhomirim, Braz. (ē-nô-mē-rē′ɴ)	144b	22°34′S	43°11′W
Inhul, r., Ukr.	177	47°22′N	32°52′E
Inhulets′, r., Ukr.	177	47°12′N	33°12′E
Inírida, r., Col. (ē-nē-rē′dä)	142	2°25′N	70°38′W
Injune, Austl. (ĭn′jōn)	222	25°52′S	148°30′E
Inkeroinem, Fin. (ĭn′kĕr-oi-nĕn)	167	60°42′N	26°50′E
Inkster, Mi., U.S. (ĭngk′stēr)	111b	42°18′N	83°19′W
Inn, r., Eur. (ĭn)	161	48°00′N	12°00′E
Innamincka, Austl. (ĭnn-ă′mĭn-kă)	222	27°50′S	140°48′E
Inner Brass, i., V.I.U.S. (bräs)	129c	18°23′N	64°58′W
Inner Hebrides, is., Scot., U.K.	164	57°20′N	6°20′W
Inner Mongolia *see* Nei Monggol, prov., China	204	40°15′N	105°00′E
Innisfail, Can.	90	52°02′N	113°57′W
Innsbruck, Aus. (ĭns′brŏk)	161	47°15′N	11°25′E
Ino, Japan (ē′nō)	211	33°34′N	133°23′E
Inongo, D.R.C. (ē-nôŋ′gō)	232	1°57′S	18°16′E
Inowrocław, Pol. (ē-nô-vrōts′läf)	169	52°48′N	18°16′E
In Salah, Alg.	230	27°13′N	2°22′E
Inscription House Ruin, Az., U.S. (ĭn′skrĭp-shŭn hous rōō′ĭn)	119	36°45′N	110°47′W
International Falls, Mn., U.S. (ĭn′tēr-năsh′ŭn-ăl fôlz)	105	48°34′N	93°26′W
Inuvik, Can.	90	68°40′N	134°10′W
Inuyama, Japan (ē′nōō-yä′mä)	211	35°24′N	137°01′E
Invercargil, N.Z. (ĭn-vēr-kär′gĭl)	223	46°25′S	168°27′E
Inverel, Austl. (ĭn-vēr-el′)	219	29°50′S	151°32′E
Invergrove Heights, Mn., U.S. (ĭn′vēr-grōv)	117g	44°51′N	93°01′W
Inverness, Can. (ĭn-vēr-nĕs′)	101	46°14′N	61°18′W
Inverness, Scot., U.K.	160	57°30′N	4°07′W
Inverness, Fl., U.S.	125	28°48′N	82°22′W
Investigator Strait, strt., Austl. (ĭn-vĕst′ĭ′gā-tôr)	222	35°33′S	137°00′E
Inyangani, mtn., Zimb. (ēn-yän-gä′nē)	232	18°06′S	32°37′E
Inyokern, Ca., U.S.	118	35°39′N	117°51′W
Inyo Mountains, mts., Ca., U.S. (ĭn′yō)	106	36°55′N	118°04′W
Inzer, r., Russia (ĭn′zĕr)	186a	54°24′N	57°17′E
Inzia, r., D.R.C.	236	5°55′S	17°50′E
Ioánnina, Grc. (yō-ä′nē-nȧ)	163	39°39′N	20°52′E
Ioco, Can.	116d	49°18′N	122°53′W
Iola, Ks., U.S. (ī-ō′lȧ)	121	37°55′N	95°23′W
Iôna, Parque Nacional do, rec., Ang.	236	16°35′S	12°00′E
Ionia, Mi., U.S. (ī-ō′nĭ-ȧ)	108	43°00′N	85°10′W
Ionian Islands, is., Grc. (ī-ō′nĭ-ăn)	163	39°10′N	20°05′E
Ionian Sea, sea, Eur.	156	38°59′N	18°48′E
Iori, r., Asia	182	41°03′N	46°17′E
Íos, i., Grc. (ī′ŏs)	175	36°48′N	25°25′E
Iowa, state, U.S. (ī′ō-wȧ)	105	42°05′N	94°20′W
Iowa, r., Ia., U.S.	113	41°55′N	92°20′W
Iowa City, Ia., U.S.	105	41°39′N	91°31′W
Iowa Falls, Ia., U.S.	113	42°32′N	93°16′W
Iowa Park, Tx., U.S.	120	33°57′N	98°39′W
Ipala, Tan.	237	4°30′S	32°53′E
Ipeirus, hist. reg., Grc.	175	39°35′N	20°45′E
Ipel′, r., Eur. (ē′pĕl)	169	48°08′N	19°00′E
Ipiales, Col. (ē-pē-ä′lås)	142	0°48′N	77°45′W
Ipoh, Malay.	212	4°45′N	101°05′E
Ipswich, Austl. (ĭps′wĭch)	219	27°40′S	152°50′E
Ipswich, Eng., U.K.	161	52°05′N	1°05′E
Ipswich, Ma., U.S.	101a	42°41′N	70°50′W
Ipswich, S.D., U.S.	112	45°26′N	99°01′W
Ipu, Braz. (ē-pōō)	143	4°11′S	40°45′W
Iput′, r., Eur. (ē-pōt′)	181	52°53′N	31°57′E
Iqaluit, Can.	91	63°48′N	68°31′W
Iquique, Chile (ē-kē′kĕ)	142	20°16′S	70°07′W
Iquitos, Peru (ē-kē′tōs)	142	3°39′S	73°18′W
Irákleio, Grc.	154	35°20′N	25°10′E
Iran, nation, Asia (ē-rän′)	198	31°15′N	53°30′E
Iran, Plateau of, plat., Iran	198	32°28′N	58°00′E
Iran Mountains, mts., Asia	212	2°30′N	114°30′E
Irapuato, Mex. (ē-rä-pwä′tō)	130	20°41′N	101°24′W
Iraq, nation, Asia (ē-räk′)	198	[illegible]	[illegible]
Irazú, Vol., C.R. (ē-rä-zōō′)	133	9°58′N	83°54′W
Irbid, Jord. (ēr-bēd′)	200	32°33′N	35°51′E
Irbit, Russia (ēr-bēt′)	178	57°40′N	63°10′E
Irébou, D.R.C. (ē-rā′bōō)	232	0°40′S	17°48′E
Ireland, nation, Eur. (īr-lănd)	154	53°33′N	8°00′W
Iremel′, Gora, mtn., Russia (gȧ-rä′ĭ-rĕ′mĕl)	186a	54°32′N	58°52′E
Irene, S. Afr. (ĭ-rē-nē)	233b	25°53′S	28°13′E
Irîgui, reg., Mali	234	16°45′N	5°35′W
Iriklinskoye Vodokhranilishche, res., Russia	181	52°20′N	58°50′E
Iringa, Tan. (ē-rĭŋ′gä)	232	7°46′S	35°42′E
Iriomote Jima, i., Japan (ērē′-ō-mō-tä)	205	24°20′N	123°30′E
Iriona, Hond. (ē-rē-ō′nä)	132	15°53′N	85°12′W
Irish Sea, sea, Eur. (ī′rĭsh)	156	53°55′N	5°25′W
Irkutsk, Russia (ĭr-kōtsk′)	179	52°16′N	104°00′E
Irlam, Eng., U.K. (ûr′lăm)	158a	53°26′N	2°26′W
Irois, Cap des, c., Haiti	135	18°25′N	74°50′W
Iron Bottom Sound, strt., Sol. Is.	214e	9°15′S	160°00′E
Irondale, Al., U.S. (ī′ērn-dăl)	110h	33°32′N	86°43′W
Iron Gate, val., Eur.	175	44°43′N	22°32′E
Iron Knob, Austl. (ī-ăn nŏb)	222	32°47′S	137°10′E
Iron Mountain, Mi., U.S. (ī′ērn)	113	45°49′N	88°04′W
Iron River, Mi., U.S.	113	46°09′N	88°39′W
Ironton, Oh., U.S. (ī′ērn-tŭn)	108	38°30′N	82°45′W
Ironwood, Mi., U.S. (ī′ērn-wŏd)	113	46°28′N	90°10′W
Ironwood Forest National Monument, rec., Az., U.S.	119	32°30′N	111°25′W
Iroquois, r., Il., U.S. (ĭr′ō-kwoi)	108	40°55′N	87°20′W
Iroquois Falls, Can.	91	48°41′N	80°39′W
Irō-Saki, c., Japan (ē′rō sä′kē)	210	34°35′N	138°54′E
Irpin, r., Ukr.	177	50°13′N	29°55′E
Irrawaddy, r., Mya. (ĭr-ȧ-wäd′ē)	199	23°27′N	96°25′E
Irtysh, r., Asia (ĭr-tĭsh′)	178	59°00′N	69°00′E
Irumu, D.R.C. (ē-rō′mōō)	231	1°30′N	29°52′E
Irun, Spain (ē-rōōn′)	172	43°20′N	1°47′W
Irvine, Scot., U.K.	164	55°39′N	4°40′W
Irvine, Ca., U.S. (ûr′vĭn)	117a	33°40′N	117°45′W
Irvine, Ky., U.S.	108	37°40′N	84°00′W
Irving, Tx., U.S. (ûr′vēng)	117c	32°49′N	96°57′W
Irvington, N.J., U.S. (ûr′vēng-tŭn)	110a	40°43′N	74°15′W
Irwin, Pa., U.S. (ûr′wĭn)	111e	40°19′N	79°42′W
Is, Russia (ēs)	186a	58°48′N	59°44′E
Isa, Nig.	235	13°14′N	6°24′E
Isaacs, Mount, mtn., Pan. (ē-sä-ä′ks)	128a	9°22′N	79°31′W
Isabela, i., Ec. (ē-sä-bā′lä)	142	0°47′S	91°35′W
Isabela, Cabo, c., Dom. Rep. (kä′bō-ē-sä-bĕ′lä)	135	20°00′N	71°00′W
Isabella, Cordillera, mts., Nic. (kôr-dēl-yĕ′rä-ē-sä-bĕlä)	132	13°20′N	85°37′W
Isabella Indian Reservation, I.R., Mi., U.S. (ĭs-ȧ-bĕl′-lȧ)	108	43°35′N	84°55′W
Isaccea, Rom. (ē-säk′chä)	177	45°16′N	28°26′E
Ísafjördur, Ice. (ēs′ȧ-fyr-dōr)	160	66°09′N	22°39′W
Isangi, D.R.C. (ē-säŋ′gē)	204	0°46′N	24°15′E
Isar, r., Ger. (ē′zär)	161	48°30′N	12°30′E
Isarco, r., Italy (ē-sär′kō)	174	46°37′N	11°25′E
Isarog, Mount, mtn., Phil. (ē-sä-rō-g)	213a	13°40′N	123°23′E
Ischia, Italy (ēs′kyä)	173c	40°29′N	13°58′E
Ischia, Isola d′, i., Italy (dĕ′sh-kyä)	162	40°26′N	13°55′E
Ise, Japan (ĭs′hē) (ū′gē-yă′mä′dȧ)	210	34°30′N	136°43′E
Iseo, Lago d′, l., Italy (lä-′gō-dĕ-ē-zĕ′ō)	174	45°50′N	9°55′E
Isére, r., Fr. (ē-zâr′)	161	45°15′N	5°15′E
Iserlohn, Ger. (ē′zĕr-lōn)	171c	51°22′N	7°42′E
Isernia, Italy (ē-zĕr′nyä)	174	41°35′N	14°14′E
Ise-Wan, b., Japan (ē′sĕ wän)	210	34°49′N	136°44′E
Iseyin, Nig.	230	7°58′N	3°36′E
Ishigaki, Japan	214d	24°20′N	124°09′E
Ishikari Wan, b., Japan (ē′shē-kä-rē wän)	210	43°30′N	141°05′E
Ishim, Russia (ĭsh-ēm′)	178	56°07′N	69°13′E
Ishim, r., Asia	178	53°17′N	67°45′E
Ishimbay, Russia (ē-shēm-bī′)	186a	53°28′N	56°02′E
Ishinomaki, Japan (ĭsh-nō-mä′kē)	205	38°22′N	141°22′E
Ishinomaki Wan, b., Japan (ē-shē-nō-mä′kē wän)	210	38°10′N	141°40′E
Ishly, Russia (ĭsh′lĭ)	186a	54°13′N	55°55′E
Ishlya, Russia (ĭsh′lyȧ)	186a	53°54′N	57°48′E
Ishmant, Egypt	238b	29°17′N	31°15′E
Ishpeming, Mi., U.S. (ĭsh′pē-mĭng)	113	46°28′N	87°42′W
Isipingo, S. Afr. (ĭs-ĭ-pĭng-gō)	233c	29°59′S	30°58′E
Isiro, D.R.C.	231	2°47′N	27°37′E
İskenderun, Tur. (ĭs-kĕn′dĕr-ōōn)	198	36°45′N	36°15′E
İskenderun Körfezi, b., Tur.	163	36°22′N	35°25′E
İskilip, Tur. (ēs′kĭ-lēp′)	163	40°40′N	34°30′E
Iskŭr, r., Blg. (ĭs′k′r)	175	43°05′N	23°37′E
Isla-Cristina, Spain (ī′lä-krē-stē′nä)	172	37°13′N	7°20′W

ăt; finăl; rāte; senåte; ärm; åsk; sofȧ; fâre; ch-choose; dh-as th in other; bē; ēvent; bĕt; recĕnt; cratēr; g-gō; gh-guttural g; bĭt; ĭ-short neutral; rīde; ĸ-guttural k as ch in German ich;

PLACE (Pronunciation)	PAGE	LAT.	LONG.
Islāmābād, Pak.	199	33°55′N	73°05′E
Isla Mujeres, Mex. (ē′s-lä-mōō-kĕ′rĕs)	132a	21°25′N	86°53′W
Island Lake, l., Can.	93	53°47′N	94°25′W
Islands, Bay of, b., Can. (ī′lăndz)	101	49°10′N	58°15′W
Islay, i., Scot., U.K. (ī′lā)	160	55°55′N	6°35′W
Isle, r., Fr. (ēl)	170	45°02′N	0°29′E
Isle of Axholme, reg., Eng., U.K. (ăks′-hôm)	158a	53°33′N	0°48′W
Isle of Man, dep., Eur. (măn)	164	54°26′N	4°21′W
Isle Royale National Park, rec., Mi., U.S. (īl′roi-ăl′)	107	47°57′N	88°37′W
Isleta, N.M., U.S. (ės-lā′tȧ) (ī-lē′tȧ)	119	34°55′N	106°45′W
Isleta Indian Reservation, I.R., N.M., U.S.	119	34°55′N	106°45′W
Ismailia, Egypt (ēs-mä-ēl′ēȧ)	238b	30°35′N	32°17′E
Ismā′īlīyah Canal, can., Egypt	238b	30°25′N	31°45′E
Ismail Samani, pik, mtn., Taj.	183	38°57′N	72°01′E
Ismaning, Ger. (ēz′mä-nēng)	159d	48°14′N	11°41′E
Isparta, Tur. (ė-spär′tȧ)	198	37°50′N	30°40′E
Israel, nation, Asia	198	32°40′N	34°00′E
Issaquah, Wa., U.S. (ĭz′să-kwăh)	116a	47°32′N	122°02′W
Isselburg, Ger. (ē′sĕl-bōōrg)	171c	51°50′N	6°28′E
Issoire, Fr. (ē-swȧr′)	170	45°32′N	3°13′E
Issoudun, Fr. (ē-sōō-dăN′)	170	46°56′N	2°00′E
Issum, Ger. (ē′sōōm)	171c	51°32′N	6°24′E
Issyk-Kul, Ozero, l., Kyrg.	183	42°13′N	76°12′E
İstanbul, Tur. (ė-stän-bōōl′)	198	41°02′N	29°00′E
İstanbul Boğazı (Bosporus), strt., Tur.	198	41°10′N	29°10′E
Istiaía, Grc. (ĭs-tyī′yä)	175	38°58′N	23°11′E
Istmina, Col. (ēst-mē′nä)	142a	5°10′N	76°40′W
Istokpoga, Lake, l., Fl., U.S. (ĭs-tŏk-pō′gȧ)	125a	27°20′N	81°33′W
Istra, pen., Eur. (ė-strä)	174	45°18′N	13°48′E
Istranca Dağlari, mts., Eur. (ĭ-strän′jȧ)	175	41°50′N	27°25′E
Istres, Fr. (ēs′tr′)	170a	43°30′N	5°00′E
Itabaiana, Braz. (ē-tä-bä-yä-nä)	143	10°42′S	37°17′W
Itabapoana, Braz. (ē-tä′-bä-pōä′nä)	141a	21°19′S	40°58′W
Itabapoana, r., Braz.	141a	21°11′S	41°18′W
Itabirito, Braz. (ē-tä-bē-rē′tō)	141a	20°15′S	43°46′W
Itabuna, Braz. (ē-tä-bōō′nȧ)	143	14°47′S	39°17′W
Itacoara, Braz. (ē-tä-kô′ä-rä)	141a	21°41′S	42°04′W
Itacoatiara, Braz. (ē-tȧ-kwȧ-tyä′rȧ)	143	3°03′S	58°18′W
Itagüí, Col. (ē-tä′gwê)	142a	6°11′N	75°36′W
Itagui, r., Braz.	144b	22°53′S	43°43′W
Itaipava, Braz. (ē-tī-pȧ′-vä)	144b	22°23′S	43°09′W
Itaipu, Braz. (ē-tī′pōō)	144b	22°58′S	43°02′W
Itaituba, Braz. (ē-tä′ī-tōō′bȧ)	143	4°12′S	56°00′W
Itajái, Braz. (ē-tä-zhī′)	144	26°52′S	48°39′W
Italy, Tx., U.S.	123	32°11′N	96°51′W
Italy, nation, Eur. (ĭt′ȧ-lē)	154	43°58′N	11°14′E
Itambi, Braz. (ē-tä′m-bē)	144b	22°44′S	42°57′W
Itami, Japan (ē′tä′mē′)	211b	34°47′N	135°25′E
Itapecerica, Braz. (ē-tä-pĕ-sĕ-rē′kȧ)	141a	20°29′S	45°08′W
Itapecuru-Mirim, Braz. (ē-tä-pĕ′kōō-rōō-mē-rēN′)	143	3°17′S	44°15′W
Itaperuna, Braz. (ē-tȧ′pâ-rōō′nä)	143	21°12′S	41°53′W
Itapetininga, Braz. (ē-tä-pĕ-tē-nē′N-gä)	143	23°37′S	48°03′W
Itapira, Braz. (ē-tȧ-pē′rȧ)	143	20°42′S	51°19′W
Itapira, Braz.	141a	22°27′S	46°47′W
Itarsi, India	202	22°43′N	77°45′E
Itasca, Tx., U.S. (ī-tăs′kȧ)	123	32°09′N	97°08′W
Itasca, l., Mn., U.S.	112	47°13′N	95°14′W
Itatiaia, Pico da, mtn., Braz. (pē′-kô-dä-ē-tä-tyá′ēä)	143	22°18′S	44°41′W
Itatiba, Braz. (ē-tä-tē′bä)	141a	23°01′S	46°48′W
Itaúna, Braz. (ē-tä-ōō′nä)	141a	20°05′S	44°35′W
Ithaca, Mi., U.S. (ĭth′ȧ-kȧ)	108	43°20′N	84°35′W
Ithaca, N.Y., U.S.	105	42°25′N	76°30′W
Itháka, i., Grc. (ē′thä-kĕ)	175	38°27′N	20°48′E
Itigi, Tan.	237	5°42′S	34°29′E
Itimbiri, r., D.R.C.	236	2°40′N	23°30′E
Itoko, D.R.C. (ē-tō′kō)	232	1°13′S	22°07′E
Itu, Braz. (ē-tōō′)	141a	23°16′S	47°16′W
Ituango, Col. (ē-twäŋ′gō)	142	7°07′N	75°44′W
Ituiutaba, Braz. (ē-tōō-ēōō-tä′bä)	143	18°56′S	49°17′W
Itumirim, Braz. (ē-tōō-mē-rē′N)	141a	21°20′S	44°51′W
Itundujia Santa Cruz, Mex. (ē-tōōn-dōō-hē′ä sä′n-tä krōō′z)	131	16°50′N	97°43′W
Iturbide, Mex. (ē′tōōr-bē′dhä)	132a	19°38′N	89°31′W
Iturup, i., Russia (ē-tōō-rōōp′)	185	45°35′N	147°15′E
Ituzaingo, Arg. (ē-tōō-zä-ē′n-gô)	144a	34°40′S	58°40′W
Itzehoe, Ger. (ē′tzĕ-hō)	168	53°55′N	9°31′E
Iuka, Ms., U.S. (ī-ū′kȧ)	124	34°47′N	88°10′W
Iúna, Braz. (ē-ōō′-nä)	141a	20°22′S	41°32′W
Ivanhoe, Austl. (ĭv′ăn-hô)	222	32°53′S	144°10′E
Ivanivka, Ukr.	176	46°43′N	34°33′E
Ivano-Frankivs'k, Ukr.	181	48°53′N	24°46′E
Ivanopil', Ukr.	177	49°51′N	28°11′E
Ivanovo, Russia (ė-vä′nô-vō)	178	57°02′N	41°54′E
Ivanovo, prov., Russia	176	56°55′N	40°30′E
Ivanteyevka, Russia (ė-vän-tyĕ′yĕf-kȧ)	186b	55°58′N	37°56′E
Ivdel', Russia (ĭv′dyĕl)	186a	60°42′N	60°27′E
Iviza see Eivissa, i., Spain	156	38°55′N	1°24′E
Ivohibé, Madag. (ė-vō-hē-bā′)	233	22°28′S	46°59′E
Ivory Coast see Cote d'Ivoire, nation, Afr.	230	7°43′N	6°30′W
Ivrea, Italy (ė-vrĕ′ä)	162	45°25′N	7°54′E
Ivry-sur-Seine, Fr.	171b	48°49′N	2°23′E
Ivujivik, Can.	91	62°17′N	77°52′W
Ivvavik National Park, rec., Can.	103	69°10′N	139°30′W
Iwaki, Japan	210	37°03′N	140°57′E

PLACE (Pronunciation)	PAGE	LAT.	LONG.
Iwate Yama, mtn., Japan (ē-wä-tĕ-yä′mä)	210	39°50′N	140°56′E
Iwatsuki, Japan	211a	35°48′N	139°43′E
Iwaya, Japan (ē′wȧ-yȧ)	211b	34°35′N	135°01′E
Iwo, Nig.	230	7°38′N	4°11′E
Ixcateopán, Mex. (ēs-kä-tä-ō-pän′)	130	18°29′N	99°49′W
Ixelles, Bel.	159a	50°49′N	4°23′E
Ixhautlán, Mex. (ēs-wȧt-län′)	130	20°41′N	98°01′W
Ixhuatán, Mex. (ēs-hwä-tän′)	131	16°19′N	94°30′W
Ixmiquilpan, Mex. (ēs-mē-kēl′pän)	130	20°30′N	99°12′W
Ixopo, S. Afr.	233c	30°10′S	30°04′E
Ixtacalco, Mex. (ēs-tȧ-käl′kō)	131a	19°23′N	99°07′W
Ixtaltepec, Mex. (ēs-täl-tĕ-pĕk′)	131	16°33′N	95°04′W
Ixtapalapa, Mex. (ēs′tä-pä-lä′pä)	131a	19°21′N	99°06′W
Ixtapaluca, Mex. (ēs′tä-pä-lōō′kä)	131a	19°18′N	98°53′W
Ixtepec, Mex. (ĕks-tĕ′pĕk)	131	16°37′N	95°09′W
Ixtlahuaca, Mex. (ēs-tlä-wä′kä)	130	19°34′N	99°46′W
Ixtlán de Juárez, Mex. (ēs-tlän′ dā hwä′râz)	131	17°20′N	96°29′W
Ixtlán del Río, Mex. (ēs-tlän′dĕl rē′ō)	130	21°05′N	104°22′W
Iya, r., Russia	184	53°45′N	99°30′E
Iyo-Nada, b., Japan (ē′yō nä-dä)	211	33°33′N	132°07′E
Izabal, Guat. (ē′zä-bäl′)	132	15°23′N	89°10′W
Izabal, Lago, l., Guat.	132	15°30′N	89°04′W
Izalco, El Sal. (ē-zäl′kō)	132	13°50′N	89°40′W
Izamal, Mex. (ē-zä-mä′l)	132a	20°55′N	89°00′W
Izberbash, Russia	182	42°33′N	47°52′E
Izhevsk, Russia (ē-zhyĕfsk′)	178	56°50′N	53°15′E
Izhma, Russia (ĭzh′mȧ)	180	65°00′N	54°05′E
Izhma, r., Russia	180	64°00′N	53°00′E
Izhora, r., Russia (ēz′hô-rȧ)	186c	59°36′N	30°20′E
Izmaïl, Ukr.	181	45°00′N	28°49′E
İzmir, Tur. (ĭz-mēr′)	198	38°25′N	27°05′E
İzmit, Tur. (ĭz-mēt′)	163	40°45′N	29°45′E
Iznajar, Embalse de, res., Spain	172	37°15′N	4°30′W
Iztaccíhuatl, mtn., Mex.	130	19°10′N	98°38′W
Izuhara, Japan (ē′zōō-hä′rä)	211	34°11′N	129°18′E
Izumi-Ōtsu, Japan (ē′zōō-mōō ō′tsōō)	211b	34°30′N	135°24′E
Izumo, Japan (ē′zōō-mō)	211	35°22′N	132°45′E
Izu Shichitō, is., Japan	205	34°32′N	139°25′E

J

PLACE (Pronunciation)	PAGE	LAT.	LONG.
Jabal, Bahr al, r., Sudan	231	7°30′N	31°00′E
Jabalpur, India	199	23°18′N	79°59′E
Jablonec nad Nisou, Czech Rep. (yäb′lō-nyĕts)	168	50°43′N	15°12′E
Jablunkov Pass, p., Eur. (yäb′lōn-kôf)	169	49°31′N	18°35′E
Jaboatão, Braz. (zhä-bô-ȧ-touN)	143	8°14′S	35°08′W
Jaca, Spain (hä′kä)	173	42°35′N	0°30′W
Jacala, Mex. (hä-kȧ′lä)	130	21°01′N	99°11′W
Jacaltenango, Guat. (hä-kàl-tĕ-näŋ′gō)	132	15°39′N	91°41′W
Jacarézinho, Braz. (zhä-kä-rĕ′zē-nyô)	143	23°13′S	49°58′W
Jachymov, Czech Rep. (yä′chĭ-môf)	168	50°22′N	12°51′E
Jacinto City, Tx., U.S. (hä-sēn′tō) (jȧ-sĭn′tō)	123a	29°45′N	95°14′W
Jacksboro, Tx., U.S. (jăks′bŭr-ô)	120	33°13′N	98°11′W
Jackson, Al., U.S. (jăk′sŭn)	124	31°31′N	87°52′W
Jackson, Ca., U.S.	118	38°22′N	120°47′W
Jackson, Ga., U.S.	124	33°19′N	83°55′W
Jackson, Ky., U.S.	124	37°32′N	83°17′W
Jackson, La., U.S.	123	30°50′N	91°13′W
Jackson, Mi., U.S.	105	42°15′N	84°25′W
Jackson, Mn., U.S.	112	43°37′N	95°00′W
Jackson, Mo., U.S.	121	37°23′N	89°40′W
Jackson, Ms., U.S.	105	32°17′N	90°10′W
Jackson, Oh., U.S.	108	39°00′N	82°40′W
Jackson, Tn., U.S.	105	35°37′N	88°49′W
Jackson, Port, b., Austl.	217b	33°50′S	151°18′E
Jackson Lake, l., Wy., U.S.	115	43°57′N	110°28′W
Jacksonville, Al., U.S. (jăk′sŭn-vĭl)	124	33°52′N	85°45′W
Jacksonville, Fl., U.S.	105	30°20′N	81°40′W
Jacksonville, Il., U.S.	105	39°43′N	90°12′W
Jacksonville, Tx., U.S.	123	31°58′N	95°18′W
Jacksonville Beach, Fl., U.S.	125	31°18′N	81°25′W
Jacmel, Haiti (zhák-mĕl′)	135	18°15′N	72°30′W
Jaco, l., Mex. (hä′kō)	122	27°51′N	103°50′W
Jacobābad, Pak.	202	28°22′N	68°30′E
Jacobina, Braz. (zhä-kô-bē′nȧ)	143	11°13′S	40°30′W
Jacques-Cartier, r., Can.	102b	47°04′N	71°28′W
Jacques Cartier, Détroit de, strt., Can.	100	50°07′S	63°58′W
Jacques-Cartier, Mont, mtn., Can.	100	48°59′N	66°00′W
Jacquet River, Can. (zhȧ-kĕ′) (jăk′ĕt)	100	47°55′N	66°00′W
Jacutinga, Braz. (zhȧ-kōō-tēn′gä)	141a	22°17′S	46°36′W
Jadebusen, b., Ger.	168	53°28′N	8°17′E
Jadotville see Likasi, D.R.C.	232	10°59′S	26°44′E
Jaén, Peru (kä-ĕ′n)	142	5°38′S	78°49′W
Jaen, Spain	162	37°45′N	3°48′W
Jaffa, Cape, c., Austl. (jăf′ȧ)	220	36°58′S	139°29′E
Jaffna, Sri L. (jäf′nȧ)	203	9°44′N	80°09′E
Jagüey Grande, Cuba (hä′gwā grän′dā)	134	22°35′N	81°05′W
Jahore Strait, strt., Asia	197b	1°22′N	103°37′E
Jahrom, Iran	198	28°30′N	53°28′E
Jaibo, r., Cuba (hä-ē′bō)	135	20°10′N	75°20′W
Jaipur, India	199	27°00′N	75°50′E
Jaisalmer, India	202	27°00′N	70°54′E

PLACE (Pronunciation)	PAGE	LAT.	LONG.
Jajce, Bos. (yī′tsĕ)	175	44°20′N	17°19′E
Jajpur, India	199	20°49′N	86°37′E
Jakarta, Indon. (yä-kär′tä)	212	6°17′S	106°45′E
Jakobstad, Fin. (yá′kôb-stádh)	160	63°33′N	22°31′E
Jalacingo, Mex. (hä-lä-sĭŋ′gō)	131	19°47′N	97°16′W
Jalālābād, Afg. (jŭ-lä-lȧ-bäd)	199a	34°25′N	70°27′E
Jalālah al Baḩrīyah, Jabal, mts., Egypt	238b	29°20′N	32°00′E
Jalapa, Guat. (hä-lä′pȧ)	132	14°38′N	89°58′W
Jalapa de Díaz, Mex.	131	18°06′N	96°33′W
Jalapa del Marqués, Mex. (dĕl mär-kās′)	131	16°30′N	95°29′W
Jaleswar, Nepal	202	26°50′N	85°55′E
Jalgaon, India	202	21°08′N	75°33′E
Jalisco, Mex. (hä-lēs′kō)	130	21°27′N	104°54′W
Jalisco, state, Mex.	128	20°07′N	104°45′W
Jalón, r., Spain (hä-lōn′)	172	41°22′N	1°46′W
Jalostotitlán, Mex. (hä-lōs-tē-tlän′)	130	21°09′N	102°30′W
Jalpa, Mex. (häl′pä)	131	18°12′N	93°06′W
Jalpa, Mex. (häl′pä)	130	21°40′N	103°04′W
Jalpan, Mex. (häl′pän)	130	21°13′N	99°31′W
Jaltepec, Mex. (häl-tå-pĕk′)	131	17°20′N	95°15′W
Jaltipan, Mex. (häl-tå-pän′)	131	17°59′N	94°42′W
Jaltocan, Mex. (häl-tō-kän′)	130	21°08′N	98°32′W
Jamaare, r., Nig.	235	11°50′N	10°10′E
Jamaica, nation, N.A.	129	17°45′N	78°00′W
Jamaica Cay, i., Bah.	135	22°45′N	75°55′W
Jamālpur, Bngl.	202	24°56′N	89°58′E
Jamay, Mex. (hä-mī′)	130	20°16′N	102°43′W
Jambi, Indon. (mäm′bē)	212	1°45′S	103°28′E
James, r., Mo., U.S.	121	36°51′N	93°22′W
James, r., Va., U.S.	107	37°35′N	77°50′W
James, r., U.S.	106	46°25′N	98°55′W
James, Lake, res., N.C., U.S.	125	36°07′N	81°48′W
James Bay, b., Can. (jāmz)	93	53°53′N	80°40′W
Jamesburg, N.J., U.S. (jāmz′bûrg)	110a	40°21′N	74°26′W
James Point, c., Bah.	134	25°20′N	76°30′W
James Range, mts., Austl.	220	24°15′S	133°30′E
James Ross, i., Ant.	139	64°20′S	58°20′W
Jamestown, S. Afr.	233c	31°07′S	26°49′E
Jamestown, N.D., U.S.	104	46°54′N	98°42′W
Jamestown, N.Y., U.S. (jāmz′toun)	105	42°05′N	79°15′W
Jamestown, R.I., U.S.	110b	41°30′N	71°21′W
Jamestown Reservoir, res., N.D., U.S.	112	47°16′N	98°40′W
Jamiltepec, Mex. (hä-mēl-tȧ-pĕk)	131	16°16′N	97°54′W
Jammerbugten, b., Den.	166	57°20′N	9°28′E
Jammu, India	199	32°50′N	74°52′E
Jammu and Kashmir, state, India (kȧsh-mēr′)	199	34°30′N	76°00′E
Jammu and Kashmīr, hist. reg., Asia (kȧsh-mēr′)	199	39°10′N	75°05′E
Jāmnagar, India (jäm-nŭ′gŭr)	199	22°33′N	70°03′E
Jamshedpur, India (jăm′shĕd-pōōr)	199	22°52′N	86°11′E
Jándula, r., Spain (hän′dōō-lȧ)	172	38°28′N	3°52′W
Janesville, Wi., U.S. (jānz′vĭl)	113	42°41′N	89°03′W
Janin, W.B.	197a	32°27′N	35°19′E
Jan Mayen, i., Nor. (yän mī′ĕn)	160	70°59′N	8°05′W
Jánoshalma, Hung. (yä′nôsh-hôl-mô)	169	46°17′N	19°18′E
Janów Lubelski, Pol. (yä′nōōf lŭ-bĕl′skĭ)	169	50°40′N	22°25′E
Januária, Braz. (zhä-nwä′rē-ä)	143	15°31′S	44°17′W
Japan, nation, Asia (jȧ-păn′)	205	36°30′N	133°30′E
Japan, Sea of, sea, Asia (jȧ-păn′)	205	40°08′N	132°55′E
Japeri, Braz. (zhä-pĕ′rē)	144b	22°38′S	43°40′W
Japurá (Caquetá), r., S.A.	142	2°00′S	68°00′W
Jarabacoa, Dom. Rep. (kä-rä-bä-kô′ä)	135	19°05′N	70°40′W
Jaral del Progreso, Mex. (hä-räl dĕl prō-grā′sō)	130	20°21′N	101°05′W
Jarama, r., Spain (hä-rä′mä)	172	40°33′N	3°30′W
Jarash, Jord.	197a	32°17′N	35°53′E
Jardines, Banco, bk., Cuba (bä′n-kō-här-dē′nås)	134	21°45′N	81°40′W
Jargalant, Mong.	208	46°28′N	115°10′E
Jari, r., Braz. (zhä-rē)	143	0°28′N	53°00′W
Jarocin, Pol. (yȧ-rō′tsyēn)	169	51°58′N	17°31′E
Jarosław, Pol. (yȧ-rôs-wáf)	161	50°01′N	22°41′E
Jarud Qi, China (jya-lōō-tŭ shyē)	205	44°35′N	120°40′E
Jasin, Malay.	197b	2°19′N	102°26′E
Jašiūnai, Lith. (dzȧ-shōō-nä′yĕ)	167	54°27′N	25°25′E
Jāsk, Iran (jäsk)	198	25°46′N	57°48′E
Jasło, Pol. (yäs′wō)	169	49°44′N	21°28′E
Jason Bay, b., Malay.	197b	1°53′N	104°14′E
Jasonville, In., U.S. (jā′sŭn-vĭl)	108	39°10′N	87°15′W
Jasper, Can.	90	52°53′N	118°05′W
Jasper, Al., U.S. (jăs′pēr)	124	33°50′N	87°17′W
Jasper, Fl., U.S.	125	30°30′N	82°56′W
Jasper, In., U.S.	108	38°20′N	86°55′W
Jasper, Mn., U.S.	112	43°51′N	96°22′W
Jasper, Tx., U.S.	123	30°55′N	93°59′W
Jasper National Park, rec., Can.	92	53°09′N	117°45′W
Jászapáti, Hung. (yäs′ô-pä-tē)	169	47°29′N	20°10′E
Jászberény, Hung.	169	47°30′N	19°56′E
Jatibonico, Cuba (hä-tē-bō-nē′kō)	134	22°00′N	79°15′W
Jauja, Peru (kä-ō′κ)	142	11°43′S	75°32′W
Jaumave, Mex. (hou-mä′vä)	130	23°23′N	99°24′W
Jaunjelgava, Lat. (youn′yĕl′gȧ-vȧ)	180	56°37′N	25°06′E
Java (Jawa), i., Indon.	212	8°35′S	111°11′E
Javari, r., S.A. (kä-vä-rē)	142	4°25′S	72°07′W
Java Trench, deep	212	9°45′S	107°30′E
Jawa, Laut (Java Sea), sea, Indon.	212	5°10′S	110°30′E
Jawor, Pol. (yä′vôr)	168	51°04′N	16°12′E
Jaworzno, Pol. (yä-vôzh′nô)	169	50°11′N	19°18′E
Jaya, Puncak, mtn., Indon.	213	4°00′S	137°00′E
Jayapura, Indon.	212	2°30′S	140°45′E
Jayb, Wādī al (Ha'Arava), val., Asia	197a	30°33′N	35°10′E

ng-sing; ŋ-baŋk; N-nasalized n; nŏd; cŏmmit; ōld; ôbey; ôrder; oi-boil; fōōd; ŏŏ-as oo in foot; ou-out; s-soft; sh-dish; th-thin; pūre; ûnite; ûrn; stŭd; circŭs; ü-as in French tu; ′-indeterminate vowel.

PLACE (Pronunciation)	PAGE	LAT.	LONG.
Jazzīn, Leb.	197a	33°34'N	35°37'E
Jeanerette, La., U.S. (jĕn-ẽr-et') (zhän-rĕt')	123	29°54'N	91°41'W
Jebba, Nig. (jĕb'ȧ)	230	9°07'N	4°46'E
Jeddore Lake, l., Can.	101	48°07'N	55°35'W
Jędrzejów, Pol. (yăN-dzhā'yòf)	169	50°38'N	20°18'E
Jefferson, Ga., U.S. (jĕf'ẽr-sŭn)	124	34°05'N	83°35'W
Jefferson, Ia., U.S.	113	42°10'N	94°22'W
Jefferson, La., U.S.	110d	29°57'N	90°04'W
Jefferson, Tx., U.S.	123	32°47'N	94°21'W
Jefferson, Wi., U.S.	113	42°59'N	88°45'W
Jefferson, r., Mt., U.S.	115	45°37'N	112°22'W
Jefferson, Mount, mtn., Or., U.S.	114	44°41'N	121°50'W
Jefferson City, Mo., U.S.	105	38°34'N	92°10'W
Jeffersontown, Ky., U.S. (jĕf'ẽr-sŭn-toun)	111h	38°11'N	85°34'W
Jeffersonville, In., U.S. (jĕf'ẽr-sŭn-vĭl)	111h	38°17'N	85°44'W
Jega, Nig.	235	12°15'N	4°23'E
Jehol, hist. reg., China (jĕ-hŏl)	205	42°31'N	118°12'E
Jēkabpils, Lat. (yĕk'ȧb-pĭls)	180	56°29'N	25°50'E
Jelenia Góra, Pol. (yĕ-lĕn'yȧ gò'rȧ)	168	50°53'N	15°43'E
Jelgava, Lat.	167	56°39'N	23°42'E
Jellico, Tn., U.S. (jĕl'ĭ-kō)	124	36°34'N	84°06'W
Jemez Indian Reservation, I.R., N.M., U.S.	119	35°35'N	106°45'W
Jena, Ger. (yā'nä)	161	50°55'N	11°37'E
Jenkins, Ky., U.S. (jĕŋ'kĭnz)	125	37°09'N	82°38'W
Jenkintown, Pa., U.S. (jĕŋ'kĭn-toun)	110f	40°06'N	75°08'W
Jennings, La., U.S. (jĕn'ĭngz)	123	30°14'N	92°40'W
Jennings, Mi., U.S.	108	44°20'N	85°20'W
Jennings, Mo., U.S.	117e	38°43'N	90°16'W
Jequitinhonha, r., Braz. (zhĕ-kē-tĕŋ-ŏ'n-yä)	143	16°47'S	41°19'W
Jérémie, Haiti (zhā-rȧ-mē')	135	18°40'N	74°10'W
Jeremoabo, Braz. (zhĕ-rā-mō-ȧ'bō)	143	10°03'S	38°13'W
Jerez, Punta, c., Mex. (pōō'n-tä-κĕ-räz')	131	23°04'N	97°44'W
Jerez de la Frontera, Spain	162	36°42'N	6°09'W
Jerez de los Caballeros, Spain	172	38°20'N	6°45'W
Jericho, Austl. (jĕr'ĭ-kō)	219	23°38'S	146°24'E
Jericho, S. Afr. (jĕr-ĭkô)	238c	25°16'N	27°47'E
Jericho *see* Arīḥā, W.B.	197a	31°51'N	35°28'E
Jerome, Az., U.S. (jė-rōm')	104	34°45'N	112°10'W
Jerome, Id., U.S.	115	42°44'N	114°31'W
Jersey, dep., Eur.	170	49°15'N	2°10'W
Jersey, i., Jersey (jûr'zĭ)	161	49°13'N	2°07'W
Jersey City, N.J., U.S.	105	40°43'N	74°05'W
Jersey Shore, Pa., U.S.	109	41°10'N	77°15'W
Jerseyville, Il., U.S. (jẽr'zē-vĭl)	121	39°07'N	90°18'W
Jerusalem, Isr. (jė-rōō'sȧ-lĕm)	198	31°46'N	35°14'E
Jesup, Ga., U.S. (jĕs'ŭp)	125	31°36'N	81°53'W
Jesús Carranza, Mex. (hĕ-sōō's-kär-rȧ'n-zä)	131	17°26'N	95°01'W
Jewel, Or., U.S. (jū'ĕl)	116c	45°56'N	123°30'W
Jewel Cave National Monument, rec., S.D., U.S.	112	43°44'N	103°52'W
Jhālawār, India	199	24°30'N	76°00'E
Jhang Maghiāna, Pak.	202	31°21'N	72°19'E
Jhānsi, India (jän'sē)	199	25°29'N	78°32'E
Jharkhand, state, India	199	23°30'N	85°00'E
Jhārsuguda, India	202	22°51'N	84°13'E
Jhelum, Pak.	199	32°59'N	73°43'E
Jhelum, r., Asia (jā'lŭm)	199	31°40'N	71°51'E
Jiading, China (jyä-dĭŋ)	206	31°23'N	121°15'E
Jialing, r., China (jyä-lĭŋ)	204	32°30'N	105°30'E
Jiamusi, China	210	46°50'N	130°21'E
Ji'an, China (jyē-än)	205	27°15'N	115°10'E
Ji'an, China	208	41°00'N	126°04'E
Jianchangying, China (jyĕn-chäŋ-yĭŋ)	206	40°09'N	118°47'E
Jiangcun, China (jyän-tsòn)	207a	23°16'N	113°14'E
Jiangling, China (jyäŋ-lĭŋ)	205	30°30'N	112°10'E
Jiangshanzhen, China (jyäŋ-shän-jŭn)	206	36°39'N	120°31'E
Jiangsu, prov., China (jyäŋ-sōō)	205	33°45'N	120°30'E
Jiangwan, China (jyäŋ-wän)	207b	31°18'N	121°29'E
Jiangxi, prov., China (jyäŋ-shyē)	205	28°15'N	116°00'E
Jiangyin, China (jyäŋ-yĭn)	209	31°54'N	120°15'E
Jianli, China (jyĕn-lē)	209	29°50'N	112°52'E
Jianning, China (jyĕn-nĭŋ)	209	26°50'N	116°55'E
Jian'ou, China (jyĕn-ō)	209	27°10'N	118°18'E
Jianshi, China (jyĕn-shr)	209	30°40'N	109°45'E
Jiaohe, China	206	38°03'N	116°18'E
Jiaohe, China (jyou-hŭ)	208	43°40'N	127°20'E
Jiaoxian, China (jyou shyĕn)	205	36°18'N	120°01'E
Jiaozuo, China (jyou-dzwô)	205	35°15'N	113°18'E
Jiashan, China (jyä-shän)	206	32°41'N	118°00'E
Jiaxing, China (jyä-shyĭŋ)	205	30°45'N	120°50'E
Jiayu, China (jyä-yōō)	209	30°00'N	114°00'E
Jiazhou Wan, b., China (jyä-jō wän)	205	36°10'N	119°55'E
Jicarilla Apache Indian Reservation, I.R., N.M., U.S. (κē-kȧ-rēl'yȧ)	119	36°45'N	107°00'W
Jicarón, Isla, i., Pan. (κē-kä-rōn')	133	7°14'N	81°41'W
Jiddah, Sau. Ar.	198	21°30'N	39°15'E
Jieshou, China	206	33°17'N	115°20'E
Jieyang, China (jyĕ-yäŋ)	205	23°38'N	116°20'E
Jiggalong, Austl. (jĭg'ȧ-lông)	218	23°20'S	120°45'E
Jiguani, Cuba (κē-gwä-nē')	134	20°20'N	76°30'W
Jigüey, Bahía, b., Cuba (bä-ē'ä-κĕ'gwā)	134	22°15'N	78°10'W
Jihlava, Czech Rep. (yē'hlȧ-vȧ)	161	49°23'N	15°33'E
Jijel, Alg.	161	36°49'N	5°47'E
Jijia, r., Rom.	169	47°35'N	27°02'E
Jijiashi, China (jyē-jyä-shr)	206	32°10'N	120°17'E
Jijiga, Eth.	238a	9°15'N	42°48'E
Jilin, China (jyē-lĭn)	205	43°58'N	126°40'E

PLACE (Pronunciation)	PAGE	LAT.	LONG.
Jilin, prov., China	205	44°20'N	124°50'E
Jiloca, r., Spain (κē-lō'kȧ)	172	41°13'N	1°30'W
Jilotepeque, Guat. (κē-lô-tĕ-pĕ'kĕ)	132	14°39'N	89°36'W
Jima, Eth.	231	7°41'N	36°52'E
Jimbolia, Rom. (zhĭm-bô'lyä)	175	45°45'N	20°44'E
Jiménez, Mex. (κē-mā'nāz)	130	24°12'N	98°29'W
Jiménez, Mex.	122	27°09'N	104°55'W
Jiménez, Mex.	122	29°03'N	100°42'W
Jiménez del Téul, Mex. (tĕ-ōō'l)	130	21°28'N	103°51'W
Jimo, China (jyē-mwo)	208	36°22'N	120°28'E
Jim Thorpe, Pa., U.S. (jĭm' thôrp')	109	40°50'N	75°45'W
Jinan, China (jyē-nän)	205	36°40'N	117°01'E
Jincheng, China (jyĭn-chŭŋ)	208	35°30'N	112°50'E
Jindřichův Hradec, Czech Rep. (yēn'd'r zhĭ kōōf hrä'dĕts)	168	49°09'N	15°00'E
Jing, r., China (jyĭŋ)	208	34°40'N	108°20'E
Jing'anji, China (jyiŋ-än-jē)	206	34°30'N	116°55'E
Jingdezhen, China (jyĭn-dŭ-jŭn)	209	29°18'N	117°18'E
Jingjiang, China (jyĭŋ-jyäŋ)	206	32°02'N	120°15'E
Jingning, China (jyĭŋ-nĭŋ)	208	35°28'N	105°50'E
Jingpo Hu, l., China (jyĭŋ-pwo hōō)	208	44°10'N	129°00'E
Jingxian, China (jyĭŋ shyĕn)	209	26°32'N	109°45'E
Jingxian, China	206	37°43'N	116°17'E
Jingxing, China (jyĭŋ-shyĭŋ)	208	47°00'N	123°00'E
Jingzhi, China (jyĭŋ-jr)	206	36°19'N	119°23'E
Jinhua, China (jyĭn-hwä)	205	29°10'N	119°42'E
Jining, China (jyē-nĭŋ)	205	35°26'N	116°34'E
Jining, China	208	41°00'N	113°10'E
Jinja, Ug. (jĭn'jä)	231	0°26'N	33°12'E
Jinotega, Nic. (κē-nô-tā'gä)	132	13°07'N	86°00'W
Jinotepe, Nic. (κē-nô-tā'pā)	132	11°52'N	86°12'W
Jinqiao, China (jyĭn-chyou)	206	31°46'N	116°46'E
Jinshan, China (jyĭn-shän)	207b	30°53'N	121°09'E
Jinta, China (jyĭn-tä)	204	40°11'N	98°45'E
Jintan, China (jyĭn-tän)	206	31°47'N	119°34'E
Jin Xian, China (jyĭn shyĕn)	208	39°04'N	121°40'E
Jinxiang, China (jyĭn-shyäŋ)	206	35°03'N	116°20'E
Jinyun, China (jyĭn-yòn)	209	28°40'N	120°08'E
Jinzhai, China (jyĭn-jī)	206	31°41'N	115°51'E
Jinzhou, China (jyĭn-jō)	205	41°00'N	121°00'E
Jinzhou Wan, b., China (jyĭn-jō wän)	206	39°07'N	121°17'E
Jinzū-Gawa, r., Japan (jĕn'zōō gä'wä)	211	36°26'N	137°18'E
Jipijapa, Ec. (κē-pė-hä'pä)	142	1°36'S	80°52'W
Jiquilisco, El Sal. (κē-kē-lē's-kô)	132	13°18'N	88°32'W
Jiquilpan de Juárez, Mex. (κē-kēl'pän dā hwä'rāz)	130	20°00'N	102°43'W
Jiquipilco, Mex. (κē-kē-pē'l-kô)	131a	19°32'N	99°37'W
Jitotol, Mex. (κē-tô-tōl')	131	17°03'N	92°54'W
Jiu, r., Rom.	175	44°45'N	23°17'E
Jiujiang, China (jyô-jyän)	207a	22°50'N	113°02'E
Jiujiang, China	205	29°43'N	116°00'E
Jiuquan, China (jyô-chyän)	204	39°46'N	98°26'E
Jiurongcheng, China (jyô-rôŋ-chŭŋ)	206	37°23'N	122°31'E
Jiushouzhang, China (jyô-shō-jäŋ)	206	35°59'N	115°52'E
Jiuwuqing, China (jyô-wōō-chyĭŋ)	208a	39°31'N	116°51'E
Jiuyongnian, China (jyô-yôŋ-nĭĕn)	206	36°41'N	114°46'E
Jixian, China (jyē shyĕn)	206	35°25'N	114°03'E
Jixian, China	206	37°37'N	115°33'E
Jixian, China	206	40°03'N	117°25'E
Jiyun, r., China (jyē-yōōm)	206	39°35'N	117°34'E
Joachimsthal, Ger.	159b	52°58'N	13°45'E
João Pessoa, Braz.	143	7°09'S	34°45'W
João Ribeiro, Braz. (zhô-uN-rē-bā'rō)	141a	20°42'S	44°03'W
Jobabo, r., Cuba (hō-bä'bä)	134	20°50'N	77°15'W
Jock, r., Can. (jŏk)	102c	45°08'N	75°51'W
Jocotepec, Mex. (jô-kō-tȧ-pĕk')	130	20°17'N	103°26'W
Jodar, Spain (hō'där)	172	37°54'N	3°20'W
Jodhpur, India (hŏd'pōōr)	199	26°23'N	73°00'E
Joensuu, Fin. (yô-ĕn'sōō)	167	62°35'N	29°46'E
Joffre, Mount, mtn., Can. (jŏ'f'r)	95	50°32'N	115°13'W
Jōgeva, Est. (yû'gĕ-vȧ)	167	58°45'N	26°23'E
Joggins, Can. (jŏ'gĭnz)	100	45°42'N	64°27'W
Johannesburg, S. Afr. (yô-hän'ĕs-bôrgh)	232	26°08'S	27°54'E
John Day, r., Or., U.S. (jŏn'dā)	114	44°46'N	120°15'W
John Day, Middle Fork, r., Or., U.S.	114	44°53'N	119°04'W
John Day, North Fork, r., Or., U.S.	114	45°03'N	118°50'W
John Day Dam, Or., U.S.	114	45°40'N	120°15'W
John H. Kerr Reservoir, res., U.S.	107	36°30'N	78°38'W
John Martin Reservoir, res., Co., U.S. (jŏn mär'tĭn)	120	37°57'N	103°04'W
Johnson, r., Or., U.S. (jŏn'sŭn)	116c	45°27'N	122°20'W
Johnsonburg, Pa., U.S. (jŏn'sŭn-bûrg)	109	41°30'N	78°40'W
Johnson City, Il., U.S. (jŏn'sŭn)	108	37°50'N	88°55'W
Johnson City, N.Y., U.S.	109	42°10'N	76°00'W
Johnson City, Tn., U.S.	105	36°17'N	82°23'W
Johnston, i., Oc. (jŏn'stŭn)	2	17°00'N	168°00'W
Johnstone Strait, strt., Can.	94	50°25'N	126°00'W
Johnston Falls, wtfl., Afr.	237	10°35'S	28°50'E
Johnstown, N.Y., U.S. (jonz'toun)	109	43°00'N	74°20'W
Johnstown, Pa., U.S.	105	40°20'N	78°50'W
Johor, r., Malay. (jŭ-hōr')	197b	1°39'N	103°52'E
Johor Baharu, Malay.	212	1°28'N	103°46'E
Jōhvi, Est. (yû'vĭ)	167	59°21'N	27°21'E
Joigny, Fr. (zhwȧn-yē')	170	47°58'N	3°26'E
Joinville, Braz. (zhwăn-vēl')	144	26°18'S	48°47'W
Joinville, Fr.	171	48°28'N	5°05'E
Joinville, i., Ant.	139	63°00'S	53°30'W
Jojutla, Mex. (hô-hōō'tlȧ)	130	18°39'N	99°11'W
Jola, Mex. (kô'lä)	130	21°08'N	104°26'W
Joliet, Il., U.S. (jō-lĭ-ĕt')	111a	41°32'N	88°05'W
Joliette, Can. (zhô-lyĕt')	91	46°01'N	73°30'W
Jolo, Phil. (hō-lō)	212	5°59'N	121°05'E
Jolo Island, i., Phil.	212	5°55'N	121°15'E

PLACE (Pronunciation)	PAGE	LAT.	LONG.
Jomalig, i., Phil. (hô-mä'lĕg)	213a	14°44'N	122°34'E
Jomulco, Mex. (hô-mōōl'kō)	130	21°08'N	104°24'W
Jonacatepec, Mex.	130	18°39'N	98°46'W
Jonava, Lith. (yō-nä'vȧ)	167	55°05'N	24°15'E
Jones, Phil. (jōnz)	213a	12°56'N	122°05'E
Jones, Phil.	213a	16°35'N	121°39'E
Jonesboro, Ar., U.S. (jōnz'bûro)	105	35°49'N	90°42'W
Jonesboro, La., U.S.	123	32°14'N	92°43'W
Jonesville, La., U.S. (jōnz'vĭl)	123	31°35'N	91°50'W
Jonesville, Mi., U.S.	108	42°00'N	84°45'W
Jong, r., S.L.	234	8°10'N	12°10'W
Joniškis, Lith. (yô'nĭsh-kĭs)	167	56°14'N	23°36'E
Jönköping, Swe. (yûn'chû-pĭng)	160	57°47'N	14°10'E
Jonquiere, Can. (zhôN-kyâr')	91	48°25'N	71°15'W
Jonuta, Mex. (hō-nōō'tä)	131	18°07'N	92°09'W
Jonzac, Fr. (zhôN-zȧk')	170	45°27'N	0°27'W
Joplin, Mo., U.S. (jŏp'lĭn)	105	37°05'N	94°31'W
Jordan, nation, Asia (jôr'dăn)	198	30°15'N	38°00'E
Jordan, r., Asia	197a	32°05'N	35°35'E
Jordan, r., Ut., U.S.	117b	40°42'N	111°56'W
Jorhāt, India (jȯr-hät')	199	26°43'N	94°16'E
Jorullo, Volcán de, vol., Mex. (vȯl-kȧ'n-dĕ-hȯ-rōōl'yō)	130	18°54'N	101°38'W
José C. Paz, Arg.	144a	34°32'S	58°44'W
Joseph Bonaparte Gulf, b., Austl. (jō'sĕf bō'nȧ-pärt)	220	13°30'S	128°40'E
Josephburg, Can.	102g	53°45'N	113°06'W
Joseph Lake, l., Can. (jō'sĕf lăk)	102g	53°18'N	113°06'W
Joshua Tree National Park, rec., Ca., U.S. (jō'shū-ȧ trē)	118	34°02'N	115°53'W
Jos Plateau, plat., Nig. (jŏs)	235	9°53'N	9°05'E
Jostedalsbreen, ice, Nor. (yôstĕ-däls-brĕĕn)	160	61°40'N	6°55'E
Jotunheimen, mts., Nor.	160	61°44'N	8°11'E
Joulter's Cays, is., Bah. (jōl'tẽrz)	134	25°20'N	78°10'W
Jouy-le-Chatel, Fr. (zhwē-lĕ-shä-tĕl')	171b	48°40'N	3°07'E
Jovellanos, Cuba (hō-vĕl-yä'nōs)	134	22°50'N	81°10'W
J. Percy Priest Lake, res., Tn., U.S.	124	36°00'N	86°45'W
Juan Aldama, Mex. (kȯä'n-äl-dȧ'mä)	130	24°16'N	103°21'W
Juan de Fuca, Strait of, strt., N.A. (hwän' dā fōō'kä)	92	48°25'N	124°37'W
Juan de Nova, Île, i., Reu.	233	17°18'S	43°07'E
Juan Diaz, r., Pan. (κōōä'n-dē'äz)	128a	9°05'N	79°30'W
Juan Fernández, Islas de, is., Chile	139	33°30'S	79°00'W
Juan L. Lacaze, Ur. (hōōȧ'n-ĕ'lĕ-lä-kȧ'zĕ)	141c	34°25'S	57°28'W
Juan Luis, Cayos de, is., Cuba (kȧ-yōs-dĕ-hwän lōō-ēs')	134	22°15'N	82°00'W
Juárez, Arg. (hōōȧ'rĕz)	144	37°42'S	59°46'W
Juázeiro, Braz. (zhōōȧ'zā'rō)	143	9°27'S	40°28'W
Juazeiro do Norte, Braz. (zhōōȧ'zā'rō-dō-nôr-tĕ)	143	7°16'S	38°57'W
Jubayl, Leb. (jōō-bĭl')	197a	34°07'N	35°38'E
Jubba (Genale), r., Afr.	238a	1°30'N	42°25'E
Juby, Cap, c., Mor. (yōō'bĕ)	230	28°01'N	13°21'W
Júcar, r., Spain (hōō'kär)	162	39°10'N	1°22'W
Júcaro, Cuba (hōō'kȧ-rô)	134	21°40'N	78°50'W
Juchipila, Mex. (hōō-chē-pē'lȧ)	130	21°26'N	103°09'W
Juchitán, Mex. (hōō-chē-tän')	128	16°15'N	95°00'W
Juchitlán, Mex. (hōō-chē-tlän)	130	20°05'N	104°07'W
Jucuapa, El Sal. (κōō-kwä'pä)	132	13°30'N	88°24'W
Judenburg, Aus. (jōō'dĕn-bûrg)	168	47°10'N	14°40'E
Judith, r., Mt., U.S. (jōō'dĭth)	115	47°20'N	109°36'W
Juhua Dao, i., China (jyōō-hwä dou)	206	40°30'N	120°47'E
Juigalpa, Nic. (hwē-gäl'pä)	132	12°02'N	85°24'W
Juiz de Fora, Braz. (zhò-ēzh' dā fō'rä)	143	21°47'S	43°20'W
Jujuy, Arg. (hōō-hwē')	144	24°14'S	65°15'W
Jujuy, prov., Arg. (hōō-hwē')	144	23°00'S	65°45'W
Jukskei, r., S. Afr.	233b	25°58'S	27°58'E
Julesburg, Co., U.S. (jōōlz'bûrg)	120	40°59'N	102°16'W
Juliaca, Peru (hōō-lē-ä'kä)	142	15°26'S	70°12'W
Julian Alps, mts., Eur.	162	46°05'N	14°05'E
Julianehåb, Grnld.	89	60°07'N	46°20'W
Jülich, Ger. (yü'lĕk)	171c	50°55'N	6°22'E
Jullundur, India	199	31°29'N	75°39'E
Julpaiguri, India	202	26°35'N	88°48'E
Jumento Cays, is., Bah. (hōō-mĕn'tō)	135	23°05'N	75°40'W
Jumilla, Spain (hōō-mēl'yä)	172	38°28'N	1°20'W
Jump, r., Wi., U.S. (jŭmp)	113	45°18'N	90°53'W
Jumpingpound Creek, r., Can. (jŭmp-ĭng-pound)	102e	51°01'N	114°34'W
Jumrah, Indon.	197b	1°48'N	101°04'E
Junagādh, India (jȯ-nä'gŭd)	199	21°33'N	70°25'E
Junayfah, Egypt	238d	30°11'N	32°26'E
Junaynah, Ra's al, mtn., Egypt	197a	29°02'N	33°58'E
Junction, Tx., U.S. (jŭŋk'shŭn)	122	30°29'N	99°48'W
Junction City, Ks., U.S.	121	39°01'N	96°49'W
Jundiaí, Braz.	143	23°11'S	46°52'W
Juneau, Ak., U.S. (jōō'nō)	106a	58°25'N	134°30'W
Jungfrau, mtn., Switz. (yòng'frou)	168	46°30'N	7°59'E
Junín, Arg. (hōō-nē'n)	144	34°35'S	60°56'W
Junín, Col.	142a	4°47'N	73°39'W
Juniyah, Leb. (jōō-nē'ĕ)	197a	33°59'N	35°38'E
Jupiter, r., Can.	100	49°40'N	63°20'W
Jupiter, Mount, mtn., Wa., U.S.	116a	47°42'N	123°04'W
Jur, r., Sudan (jòr)	231	6°38'N	27°52'E
Jura, mts., Eur. (zhü-rȧ')	161	46°55'N	6°49'E
Jura, i., Scot., U.K. (jōō'rȧ)	164	56°09'N	6°45'W
Jura, Sound of, strt., Scot., U.K. (jōō'rȧ)	164	55°45'N	5°55'W
Jurbarkas, Lith. (yōōr-bär'käs)	167	55°06'N	22°50'E
Jūrmala, Lat.	167	56°57'N	23°37'E
Jurong, China (jyōō-roŋ)	206	31°58'N	119°12'E
Juruá, r., S.A.	142	5°30'S	67°30'W
Juruena, r., Braz. (zhōō-rōōĕ'nä)	143	12°22'S	58°34'W

ăt; fĭnăl; rāte; senåte; ärm; åsk; sofȧ; fâre; ch-choose; dh-as th in other; bē; ēvent; bĕt; recĕnt; cratẽr; g-gō; gh-guttural g; bĭt; ĭ-short neutral; rīde; κ-guttural k as ch in German ich;

PRONOUNCING INDEX Jutiapa – Kara-Kum 307

PLACE (Pronunciation)	PAGE	LAT.	LONG.
Jutiapa, Guat. (hōō-tē-ä′pä)	132	14°16′N	89°55′W
Juticalpa, Hond. (hōō-tē-käl′pä)	128	14°35′N	86°17′W
Jutland *see* Jylland, reg., Den.	160	56°04′N	9°00′E
Juventino Rosas, Mex.	130	20°38′N	101°02′W
Juventud, Isla de la, i., Cuba	129	21°40′N	82°45′W
Juxian, China (jyōō shyĕn)	208	35°35′N	118°50′E
Juxtlahuaca, Mex. (hōōs-tlȧ-hwä′kä)	130	17°20′N	98°02′W
Juye, China (jyōō-yü)	206	35°25′N	116°05′E
Južna Morava, r., Serb. (ū′zhnȧ mô′rä-vä)	175	42°30′N	22°00′E
Jylland, reg., Den.	160	56°04′N	9°00′E

K

PLACE (Pronunciation)	PAGE	LAT.	LONG.
K2(Qogir Feng), mtn., Asia	199	36°06′N	76°38′E
Kaabong, Ug.	237	3°31′N	34°08′E
Kaalfontein, S. Afr. (kärl-fōn-tān)	233b	26°02′S	28°16′E
Kaappunt, c., S. Afr.	232a	34°21′S	18°30′E
Kabaena, Pulau, i., Indon. (kä-bȧ-ā′nȧ)	212	5°35′S	121°07′E
Kabala, S.L. (kȧ-bȧ′lȧ)	230	9°43′N	11°39′W
Kabale, Ug.	237	1°15′S	29°59′E
Kabalega Falls, wtfl., Ug.	231	2°15′N	31°41′E
Kabalo, D.R.C. (kä-bä′lō)	232	6°03′S	26°55′E
Kabambare, D.R.C. (kä-bäm-bä′rȧ)	232	4°47′S	27°45′E
Kabardino-Balkaria, prov., Russia	180	43°30′N	43°30′E
Kabba, Nig.	235	7°50′N	6°03′E
Kabe, Japan (kä′bā)	211	34°32′N	132°30′E
Kabinakagami, r., Can.	98	49°00′N	84°15′W
Kabinda, D.R.C. (kä-bĕn′dä)	232	6°08′S	24°29′E
Kabompo, r., Zam. (kȧ-bôm′pō)	232	14°00′S	23°40′E
Kabongo, D.R.C. (kȧ-bông′ō)	232	7°58′S	25°10′E
Kabot, Gui.	234	10°48′N	14°57′W
Kaboudia, Ra's, c., Tun.	162	35°17′N	11°28′E
Kābul, Afg. (kä′bōōl)	199	34°39′N	69°14′E
Kabul, r., Asia (kä′bōōl)	199	34°44′N	69°43′E
Kabunda, D.R.C.	237	12°25′S	29°22′E
Kabwe, Zam.	232	14°27′S	28°27′E
Kachuga, Russia (kȧ-chōō-gȧ)	179	54°09′N	105°43′E
Kadei, r., Afr.	235	4°00′N	15°10′E
Kadnikov, Russia (käd′nē-kôf)	180	59°30′N	40°10′E
Kadoma, Japan	211b	34°43′N	135°36′E
Kadoma, Zimb.	232	18°21′S	29°55′E
Kaduna, Nig. (kä-dōō′nä)	230	10°33′N	7°27′E
Kaduna, r., Nig.	235	9°30′N	6°00′E
Kaédi, Maur. (kä-ā-dē′)	230	16°09′N	13°30′W
Ka′ena Point, c., Hi., U.S. (kä′ȧ-nä)	106d	21°33′N	158°19′W
Kaesŏng, Kor., N. (kä′ĕ-sŭng) (kī′jō)	205	38°00′N	126°35′E
Kafanchan, Nig.	235	9°36′N	8°17′E
Kafia Kingi, Sudan (kä′fē-ȧ kĭŋ′gē)	231	9°17′N	24°28′E
Kafue, Zam. (kä′fōō)	232	15°45′S	28°17′E
Kafue, r., Zam.	232	15°45′S	26°30′E
Kafue Flats, sw., Zam.	237	16°15′S	26°30′E
Kafue National Park, rec., Zam.	237	15°00′S	25°35′E
Kafwira, D.R.C.	237	12°10′S	27°33′E
Kagal′nik, r., Russia (kä-gäl′′nēk)	177	46°58′N	39°25′E
Kagera, r., Afr. (kä-gā′rȧ)	232	1°10′S	31°10′E
Kagoshima, Japan (kä′gô-shē′mȧ)	205	31°35′N	130°31′E
Kagoshima-Wan, b., Japan (kä′gô-shē′mä wän)	210	31°24′N	130°39′E
Kahayan, r., Indon.	212	1°45′S	113°40′E
Kahemba, D.R.C.	236	7°17′S	19°00′E
Kahia, D.R.C.	237	6°21′S	28°24′E
Kahoka, Mo., U.S. (kȧ-hō′kȧ)	121	40°26′N	91°42′W
Kaho′olawe, i., Hi., U.S. (kä-hōō-lä′wē)	106c	20°28′N	156°48′W
Kahramanmaraş, Tur.	198	37°40′N	36°50′W
Kahshahpiwi, r., Can.	113	48°24′N	90°56′W
Kahuku Point, c., Hi., U.S. (kä-hōō′kōō)	106d	21°50′N	157°50′W
Kahului, Hi., U.S.	106c	20°53′N	156°28′W
Kai, Kepulauan, is., Indon.	213	5°35′S	132°45′E
Kaiang, Malay.	197b	3°00′N	101°47′E
Kaiashk, r., Can.	98	49°40′N	89°30′W
Kaibab Indian Reservation, I.R., Az., U.S. (kä′ē-bȧb)	119	36°55′N	112°45′W
Kaibab Plat, Az., U.S.	119	36°30′N	112°10′W
Kaidu, r., China (kī-dōō)	204	42°35′N	84°04′E
Kaieteur Fall, wtfl., Guy. (kī-ĕ-tōōr′)	143	4°48′N	59°24′W
Kaifeng, China (kī-fŭŋ)	205	34°48′N	114°22′E
Kai Kecil, i., Indon.	213	5°45′S	132°40′E
Kailua, Hi., U.S. (kä′ē-lōō′ä)	106c	21°18′N	157°43′W
Kailua Kona, Hi., U.S.	126a	19°49′N	155°59′W
Kaimana, Indon.	213	3°32′S	133°47′E
Kaimanawa Mountains, mts., N.Z.	223	39°10′S	176°00′E
Kainan, Japan (kä′ē-nän′)	211	34°09′N	135°14′E
Kainji Lake, res., Nig.	230	10°25′N	4°50′E
Kaiserslautern, Ger. (kī-zĕrs-lou′tĕrn)	161	49°26′N	7°46′E
Kaitaia, N.Z. (kä-ē-tä′ē-ȧ)	221a	35°30′S	173°28′E
Kaiwi Channel, strt., Hi., U.S. (käē-wē)	106c	21°10′N	157°38′W
Kaiyuan, China (kī-yuän)	209	23°42′N	103°20′E
Kaiyuan, China	208	42°30′N	124°00′E
Kaiyuh Mountains, mts., Ak., U.S. (kī-yōō′)	103	64°25′N	157°38′W
Kajaani, Fin. (kä′yȧ-nē)	160	64°15′N	27°16′E
Kajang, Gunong, mtn., Malay.	197b	2°47′N	104°05′E
Kajiki, Japan (kä′jē-kē)	210	31°44′N	130°41′E
Kakhovka, Ukr. (kä-kôf′kȧ)	177	46°46′N	33°32′E
Kakhovs′ke vodoskhovyshche, res., Ukr.	178	47°21′N	33°33′E
Kākināda, India	199	16°58′N	82°18′E
Kaktovik, Ak., U.S. (käk-tō′vĭk)	103	70°08′N	143°51′W
Kakwa, r., Can. (käk′wȧ)	95	54°00′N	118°55′W
Kalach, Russia (kȧ-lȧch′)	181	50°15′N	40°55′E
Kaladan, r., Asia	204	21°07′N	93°04′E
Kalae, c., Hi., U.S.	126a	18°55′N	155°41′W
Kalahari Desert, des., Afr. (kä-lä-hä′rē)	232	23°00′S	22°03′E
Kalama, Wa., U.S. (kȧ-lăm′ȧ)	116c	46°01′N	122°50′W
Kalama, r., Wa., U.S.	116c	46°03′N	122°47′W
Kalamáta, Grc.	154	37°04′N	22°08′E
Kalamazoo, Mi., U.S. (kăl-ȧ-mȧ-zōō′)	105	42°20′N	85°40′W
Kalamazoo, r., Mi., U.S.	108	42°35′N	86°00′W
Kalanchak, Ukr. (kä-län-chäk′)	177	46°17′N	33°14′E
Kalandula, Ang. (dōō′kȧ dȧ brä-gäN′sä)	232	9°06′S	15°57′E
Kalaotoa, Pulau, i., Indon.	212	7°22′S	122°30′E
Kalapana, Hi., U.S. (kä-lä-pä′nä)	126a	19°25′N	155°00′W
Kalar, mtn., Iran	198	31°43′N	51°41′E
Kalāt, Pak. (kŭ-lät′)	199	29°05′N	66°36′E
Kalemie, D.R.C.	232	5°56′S	29°12′E
Kalgan *see* Zhangjiakou, China	205	40°45′N	114°58′E
Kalgoorlie-Boulder, Austl. (kăl-gōōr′lē)	218	30°45′S	121°35′E
Kaliakra, Nos, c., Blg.	163	43°25′N	28°42′E
Kalima, D.R.C.	237	2°34′S	26°37′E
Kaliningrad, Russia	178	54°42′N	20°32′E
Kaliningrad, Russia (kä-lē-nēn′grät)	186b	55°55′N	37°49′E
Kalinkavichy, Bela.	176	52°07′N	29°19′E
Kalispel Indian Reservation, I.R., Wa., U.S. (kăl-ĭ-spĕl′)	114	48°25′N	117°30′W
Kalispell, Mt., U.S. (kăl′ĭ-spĕl)	104	48°12′N	114°18′W
Kalisz, Pol. (kä′lēsh)	161	51°45′N	18°05′E
Kaliua, Tan.	237	5°04′S	31°48′E
Kalixälven, r., Swe.	160	67°12′N	22°00′E
Kalmar, Swe. (käl′mär)	160	56°40′N	16°19′E
Kalmarsund, strt., Swe. (käl′mär)	166	56°30′N	16°17′E
Kal′mius, r., Ukr. (käl′′myōōs)	177	47°15′N	37°38′E
Kalmykia, prov., Russia	181	46°56′N	46°00′E
Kalocsa, Hung. (kä′lō-chä)	169	46°32′N	19°00′E
Kalohi Channel, strt., Hi., U.S. (kä-lō′hĭ)	126a	20°55′N	157°15′W
Kaloko, D.R.C.	232	6°47′S	25°48′E
Kalomo, Zam. (kä-lō′mō)	237	17°02′S	26°30′E
Kalsubai Mount, mtn., India	202	19°43′N	73°47′E
Kaltenkirchen, Ger. (käl′tĕn-kēr-kĕn)	159c	53°50′N	9°57′E
Kālu, r., India	203b	19°18′N	73°14′E
Kaluga, Russia (kȧ-lō′gä)	178	54°29′N	36°12′E
Kaluga, prov., Russia	176	54°10′N	35°00′E
Kaluktutiak (Cambridge Bay), Can.	90	69°15′N	105°00′W
Kalundborg, Den. (kȧ-lòn′′bôr′)	166	55°42′N	11°07′E
Kalush, Ukr. (kä′lòsh)	169	49°02′N	24°24′E
Kalvarija, Lith. (käl-vä-rē′yȧ)	167	54°24′N	23°17′E
Kalwa, India	203b	19°12′N	72°59′E
Kal′ya, Russia (käl′yȧ)	186a	60°17′N	59°58′E
Kalyān, India	202	19°16′N	73°07′E
Kalyazin, Russia (käl-yȧ′zĭn)	176	57°13′N	37°55′E
Kama, r., Russia (kä′mä)	178	56°10′N	53°50′E
Kamaishi, Japan (kä′mä-ē′shē)	210	39°16′N	142°03′E
Kamakura, Japan (kä′mä-kōō′rä)	211	35°19′N	139°33′E
Kamarān, i., Yemen	198	15°19′N	41°47′E
Kāmārhāti, India	202a	22°41′N	88°23′E
Kambove, D.R.C. (käm-bō′vĕ)	232	10°58′S	26°43′E
Kamchatka, r., Russia	185	54°15′N	158°38′E
Kamchatka, Poluostrov, pen., Russia	185	55°19′N	157°45′E
Kamen, Ger. (kä′mĕn)	171c	51°35′N	7°40′E
Kamenjak, Rt, c., Cro. (kä′mĕ-nyäk)	174	44°45′N	13°57′E
Kamen′-na-Obi, Russia (kä-mĭny′nŭ ô′bĕ)	178	53°43′N	81°28′E
Kamensk-Shakhtinskiy, Russia (kä′mĕnsk shäk′tĭn-skĭ)	177	48°17′N	40°16′E
Kamensk-Ural′skiy, Russia (kä′mĕnsk ōō-räl′skĭ)	180	56°27′N	61°55′E
Kamenz, Ger. (kä′mĕnts)	168	51°16′N	14°05′E
Kameoka, Japan (kä′mā-ōkä)	211b	35°01′N	135°35′E
Kāmet, mtn., Asia	202	30°50′N	79°42′E
Kamianets′-Podil′s′kyi, Ukr.	181	48°41′N	26°34′E
Kamianka-Buz′ka, Ukr.	169	50°06′N	24°20′E
Kamień Pomorski, Pol.	168	53°57′N	14°48′E
Kamikoma, Japan (kä′mē-kō′mä)	211b	34°45′N	135°50′E
Kamina, D.R.C.	232	8°44′S	25°00′E
Kaministikwia, r., Can. (kȧ-mĭ-nĭ-stĭk′wĭ-ȧ)	113	48°40′N	89°41′W
Kamituga, D.R.C.	237	3°04′S	28°11′E
Kamloops, Can. (kăm′lōōps)	90	50°40′N	120°20′W
Kamp, r., Aus. (kämp)	168	48°30′N	15°45′E
Kampala, Ug. (käm-pä′lä)	231	0°19′N	32°25′E
Kampar, r., Indon. (käm′pär)	212	0°30′N	101°30′E
Kampene, D.R.C.	237	3°36′S	26°40′E
Kampenhout, Bel.	159a	50°56′N	4°33′E
Kamp-Lintfort, Ger. (kämp-lĕnt′fōrt)	171c	51°30′N	6°34′E
Kâmpóng Saôm, Camb.	212	10°40′N	103°50′E
Kâmpóng Thum, Camb. (kŏm′pŏng-tŏm)	212	12°41′N	104°29′E
Kâmpôt, Camb. (käm′pōt)	212	10°41′N	104°07′E
Kampuchea *see* Cambodia, nation, Asia	212	12°15′N	104°00′E
Kamsack, Can. (kăm′săk)	90	51°34′N	101°54′W
Kamskoye, res., Russia	178	59°08′N	56°30′E
Kamudilo, D.R.C.	237	7°42′S	27°18′E
Kamuela, Hi., U.S.	126a	20°01′N	155°40′W
Kamui Misaki, c., Japan	210	43°25′N	139°35′E
Kámuk, Cerro, mtn., C.R. (sĕ′r-rô-kä-mōō′k)	133	9°18′N	83°02′W
Kamyshevatskaya, Russia	177	46°24′N	37°58′E
Kamyshin, Russia (kä-mwēsh′ĭn)	178	50°08′N	45°20′E
Kamyshlov, Russia (kä-mēsh′lôf)	178	56°50′N	62°32′E
Kan, r., Russia (kän)	184	56°30′N	94°17′E
Kanab, Ut., U.S. (kăn′ăb)	119	37°00′N	112°30′W
Kanabeki, Russia (kȧ-nä′byĕ-kĭ)	186a	57°48′N	57°16′E
Kanab Plateau, plat., Az., U.S.	119	36°31′N	112°55′W
Kanaga, i., Ak., U.S. (kă-nă′gă)	103a	52°02′N	177°38′W
Kanagawa, dept., Japan (kä′nä-gä′wä)	211a	35°29′N	139°32′E
Kanā′is, Ra′s al, c., Egypt	163	31°14′N	28°08′E
Kanamachi, Japan (kä-nä-mä′chē)	211a	35°46′N	139°52′E
Kananga, D.R.C.	232	6°14′S	22°17′E
Kananikol′skoye, Russia	186a	52°48′N	57°29′E
Kanasín, Mex. (kä-nä-sē′n)	132a	20°54′N	89°31′W
Kanatak, Ak., U.S. (kă-nă′tŏk)	103	57°35′N	155°48′W
Kanawha, r., W.V., U.S. (kȧ-nô′wȧ)	107	37°55′N	81°50′W
Kanaya, Japan (kä-nä′yä)	211a	35°10′N	139°49′E
Kanazawa, Japan (kä′nȧ-zä′wȧ)	205	36°34′N	136°38′E
Kānchenjunga, mtn., Asia (kĭn-chĭn-jŏŋ′gȧ)	199	27°30′N	88°18′E
Kānchipuram, India	199	12°55′N	79°43′E
Kandahār, Afg.	199	31°43′N	65°58′E
Kanda Kanda, D.R.C. (kän′dȧ kän′dȧ)	232	6°56′S	23°36′E
Kandalaksha, Russia (kȧn-dȧ-lȧk′shȧ)	178	67°10′N	33°05′E
Kandalakshskiy Zaliv, b., Russia	180	66°20′N	35°00′E
Kandava, Lat. (kän′dȧ-vȧ)	167	57°03′N	22°45′E
Kandi, Benin (kän-dē′)	230	11°08′N	2°56′E
Kandiāro, Pak.	202	27°09′N	68°12′E
Kandla, India (kŭnd′lŭ)	202	23°00′N	70°20′E
Kandy, Sri L. (kän′dē)	203	7°18′N	80°42′E
Kane, Pa., U.S. (kān)	109	41°40′N	78°50′W
Kāne′ohe, Hi., U.S. (kä-nā-ō′hā)	126a	21°25′N	157°47′W
Kāne′ohe Bay, b., Hi., U.S.	106d	21°32′N	157°40′W
Kanevskaya, Russia (kȧ-nyĕf′skȧ)	177	46°07′N	38°58′E
Kangaroo, i., Austl. (kăŋ-gȧ-rōō′)	220	36°05′S	137°05′E
Kangāvar, Iran (kŭŋ′gä-vär)	198	34°37′N	46°45′E
Kangean, Kepulauan, is., Indon. (käŋ′gē-än)	212	6°50′S	116°22′E
Kanggye, Kor., N. (käng′gyĕ)	205	40°55′N	126°40′E
Kanghwa, i., Kor., S. (käng′hwä)	210	37°38′N	126°00′E
Kangnŭng, Kor., S. (käng′nō ng)	210	37°42′N	128°50′E
Kango, Gabon (käN-gō)	232	0°09′N	10°08′E
Kangowa, D.R.C.	236	9°55′S	22°48′E
Kanin, Poluostrov, pen., Russia	178	68°00′N	45°00′E
Kaningo, Kenya	237	0°49′S	38°32′E
Kanin Nos, Mys, c., Russia	180	68°40′N	44°00′E
Kaniv, Ukr.	177	49°46′N	31°27′E
Kanivs′ke vodoskhovyshche, res., Ukr.	178	50°10′N	30°40′E
Kanjiža, Serb. (kä′nyē-zhä)	175	46°05′N	20°02′E
Kankakee, Il., U.S. (kăŋ-kȧ-kē′)	108	41°07′N	87°53′W
Kankakee, r., Il., U.S.	108	41°15′N	88°15′W
Kankan, Gui. (kän-kän) (kän-kän′)	230	10°23′N	9°18′W
Kannapolis, N.C., U.S. (kăn-ăp′ô-lĭs)	125	35°30′N	80°38′W
Kannoura, Japan (kä′nō-ō′rä)	211	33°34′N	134°18′E
Kano, Nig. (kä′nō)	230	12°00′N	8°30′E
Kanonkop, mtn., S. Afr.	232a	33°49′S	18°37′E
Kanopolis Reservoir, res., Ks., U.S. (kăn-ŏp′ō-lĭs)	120	38°44′N	98°01′W
Kānpur, India (kän′pûr)	202	26°30′N	80°10′E
Kansas, state, U.S. (kăn′zȧs)	104	38°30′N	99°40′W
Kansas, r., Ks., U.S.	121	39°08′N	95°52′W
Kansas City, Ks., U.S.	105	39°06′N	94°39′W
Kansas City, Mo., U.S.	105	39°05′N	94°35′W
Kansk, Russia	179	56°14′N	95°43′E
Kansŏng, Kor., S.	210	38°09′N	128°29′E
Kantang, Thai. (kän′täng′)	212	7°26′N	99°28′E
Kantchari, Burkina	234	12°29′N	1°31′E
Kanton, i., Kir.	240	3°50′S	174°00′W
Kantunilkin, Mex. (kän-tōō-nēl-kē′n)	132a	21°07′N	87°30′W
Kanzhakovskiy Kamen, Gora, mtn., Russia (kȧn-zhä′kôvs-kēē kämĭen)	186a	59°38′N	59°12′E
Kaohsiung, Tai. (kä-ô-syông′)	205	22°35′N	120°25′E
Kaolack, Sen.	230	14°09′N	16°04′W
Kaouar, oasis, Niger	231	19°16′N	13°09′E
Kapaa, Hi., U.S.	126a	22°06′N	159°20′W
Kapanga, D.R.C.	236	8°21′S	22°35′E
Kapfenberg, Aus. (käp′fĕn-bĕrgh)	168	47°27′N	15°16′E
Kapiri Mposhi, Zam.	237	13°58′S	28°41′E
Kapoeta, Sudan	231	4°45′N	33°35′E
Kaposvár, Hung. (kô′pōsh-vär)	169	46°21′N	17°45′E
Kapsan, Kor., N. (käp′sän′)	210	40°59′N	128°22′E
Kapuskasing, Can.	91	49°28′N	82°22′W
Kapuskasing, r., Can.	98	48°55′N	82°55′W
Kapustin Yar, Russia (kä′pōōs-tĕn yär′)	181	48°30′N	45°40′E
Kaputar, Mount, mtn., Austl. (kă-pû-tăr)	222	30°11′S	150°11′E
Kapuvár, Hung. (kô′pōō-vär)	169	47°35′N	17°02′E
Kara, Russia (kärȧ)	178	68°42′N	65°30′E
Kara, r., Russia	180	68°30′N	65°20′E
Karabalā′, Iraq (kŭr′bȧ-lä)	198	32°31′N	43°58′E
Karabanovo, Russia (kä′rȧ-bȧ-nō-vō)	176	56°19′N	38°43′E
Karabash, Russia (kō-rȧ-bäsh′)	186a	55°27′N	60°14′E
Kara-Bogaz-Gol, Zaliv, b., Turkmen. (kȧ-rä′ bŭ-gäs′)	183	41°30′N	53°40′E
Karachay-Cherkessia, prov., Russia	182	44°00′N	42°00′E
Karachev, Russia (kȧ-rȧ-chôf′)	180	53°08′N	34°54′E
Karāchi, Pak.	199	24°59′N	68°56′E
Karaganda *see* Qaraghandy, Kaz.	183	49°42′N	73°18′E
Karaidel′, Russia (kä′rī-dĕl)	186a	55°52′N	56°54′E
Karakoram Pass, p., Asia	199	35°35′N	77°45′E
Karakoram Range, mts., India (kä′rä kō′rôm)	199	35°24′N	76°38′E
Karakorum, hist., Mong.	204	47°25′N	102°22′E
Kara-Kum, des., Turkmen.	183	40°00′N	57°00′E

308 Kara Kum Canal – Keshan PRONOUNCING INDEX

PLACE (Pronunciation)	PAGE	LAT.	LONG.
Kara Kum Canal, can., Turkmen.	183	37°35'N	61°50'E
Karaman, Tur. (kä-rä-män´)	163	37°10'N	33°00'E
Karamay, China (kär-äm-ā)	204	45°37'N	84°53'E
Karamea Bight, b., N.Z. (kå-rå-mē´å bīt)	221a	41°20'S	171°30'E
Kara Sea *see* Karskoye More, sea, Russia	178	74°00'N	68°00'E
Karashahr (Yanqui), China (kä-rä-shä-är) (yän-chyē)	204	42°14'N	86°28'E
Karatsu, Japan (kä´rå-tso͞o)	211	33°28'N	129°59'E
Karaul, Russia (kä-rä-ôl´)	184	70°13'N	83°46'E
Karawanken, mts., Eur.	168	46°32'N	14°07'E
Karcag, Hung. (kär´tsäg)	169	47°18'N	20°58'E
Kárditsa, Grc.	175	39°23'N	21°57'E
Kärdla, Est. (kĕrd´lå)	167	58°59'N	22°44'E
Karelia, prov., Russia	184	62°30'N	[illegible]
Karema, Tan.	232	6°49'S	30°26'E
Kargat, Russia (kär-gät´)	178	55°17'N	80°07'E
Karghalik *see* Yecheng, China	204	37°54'N	77°25'E
Kargopol', Russia (kär-gō-pōl´´)	178	61°30'N	38°50'E
Kariba, Lake, res., Afr.	232	17°15'S	27°55'E
Karibib, Nmb. (kår´å-bĭb)	232	21°55'S	15°50'E
Kārikāl, India (kä-rē-käl´)	203	10°58'N	79°49'E
Karimata, Kepulauan, is., Indon. (kä-rē-mä´tå)	212	1°08'S	108°10'E
Karimata, Selat, strt., Indon.	212	1°00'S	107°10'E
Karimun Besar, i., Indon.	197b	1°10'N	103°28'E
Karimunjawa, Kepulauan, is., Indon. (kä´rē-mo͞on-yä´vä)	212	5°36'S	110°15'E
Karin, Som. (kår´ĭn)	238a	10°43'N	45°50'E
Karkar Island, i., Pap. N. Gui. (kär´kär)	213	4°50'S	146°45'E
Karkheh, r., Iran	198	32°45'N	47°50'E
Karkinits'ka zatoka, b., Ukr.	177	45°50'N	32°45'E
Karkūk, Iraq	198	35°28'N	44°22'E
Karlivka, Ukr.	177	49°26'N	35°08'E
Karlobag, Cro. (kär-lō-bäg´)	174	44°30'N	15°03'E
Karlovac, Cro. (kär´lō-våts)	163	45°29'N	15°16'E
Karlovo, Blg. (kär´lō-vō)	175	42°39'N	24°48'E
Karlovy Vary, Czech Rep. (kär´lô-vē vä´rē)	161	50°13'N	12°53'E
Karlshamn, Swe. (kärls´häm)	166	56°11'N	14°50'E
Karlskrona, Swe. (kärls´krô-nä)	160	56°10'N	15°33'E
Karlsruhe, Ger. (kärls´ro͞o-ē)	161	49°00'N	8°23'E
Karlstad, Swe. (kärl´städ)	154	59°25'N	13°28'E
Karluk, Ak., U.S. (kär´lŭk)	103	57°30'N	154°22'W
Karmøy, i., Nor. (kärm-ûe)	166	59°14'N	5°00'E
Karnataka, state, India	199	14°55'N	75°00'E
Karnobat, Blg. (kär-nō´bät)	175	42°39'N	26°59'E
Karonga, Mwi. (kå-rōŋ´gå)	232	9°52'S	33°57'E
Kárpathos, i., Grc.	163	35°34'N	27°26'E
Karpinsk, Russia (kär´pĭnsk)	186a	59°46'N	60°00'E
Kars, Tur. (kärs)	198	40°35'N	43°00'E
Kārsava, Lat. (kär´sä-vä)	167	56°46'N	27°39'E
Karshi, Uzb. (kär´shē)	183	38°30'N	66°08'E
Karskiye Vorota, Proliv, strt., Russia	178	70°30'N	58°07'E
Karskoye More (Kara Sea), sea, Russia	178	74°00'N	68°00'E
Kartaly, Russia (kår´tå lē)	178	53°05'N	60°40'E
Karunagapalli, India	203	9°09'N	76°34'E
Karvina, Czech Rep.	169	49°50'N	18°30'E
Kasai (Cassai), r., Afr.	232	3°45'S	19°10'E
Kasama, Zam. (kå-sä´må)	232	10°13'S	31°12'E
Kasanga, Tan. (kå-säŋ´gå)	232	8°28'S	31°09'E
Kasaoka, Japan (kä´så-ō´kå)	211	34°33'N	133°29'E
Kasba-Tadla, Mor. (käs´bå-täd´lå)	230	32°37'N	5°57'W
Kasempa, Zam. (kå-sĕm´på)	232	13°27'S	25°50'E
Kasenga, D.R.C. (kå-seŋ´gå)	232	10°22'S	28°38'E
Kasese, D.R.C.	237	1°38'S	27°07'E
Kasese, Ug.	237	0°10'N	30°05'E
Kāshān, Iran (kä-shän´)	198	33°52'N	51°15'E
Kashgar *see* Kashi, China	204	39°29'N	76°00'E
Kashi (Kashgar), China (kä-shr) (käsh-gär)	204	39°29'N	76°00'E
Kashihara, Japan (kä´shē-hä´rä)	211b	34°31'N	135°48'E
Kashiji Plain, pl., Zam.	236	13°25'S	22°30'E
Kashin, Russia (kä-shēn´)	176	57°20'N	37°38'E
Kashira, Russia (kä-shē´rå)	176	54°49'N	38°11'E
Kashiwa, Japan (kä´shē-wä)	211a	35°51'N	139°58'E
Kashiwara, Japan	211b	34°35'N	135°38'E
Kashiwazaki, Japan (kä´shē-wä-zä´kē)	210	37°06'N	138°17'E
Kāshmar, Iran	201	35°12'N	58°27'E
Kashmir *see* Jammu and Kashmir, state, India	199	34°30'N	76°00'E
Kashmor, Pak.	202	28°33'N	69°34'E
Kashtak, Russia (käsh´tåk)	186a	55°18'N	61°25'E
Kasimov, Russia (kå-sē´môf)	180	54°56'N	41°23'E
Kaskanak, Ak., U.S. (kăs-kă´năk)	103	60°00'N	158°00'W
Kaskaskia, r., Il., U.S. (kăs-kăs´kĭ-å)	108	39°10'N	88°50'W
Kaskattama, r., Can. (kăs-kă-tä´må)	97	56°28'N	90°55'W
Kaskö (Kaskinen), Fin. (käs´kû) (käs´kē-nĕn)	167	62°24'N	21°18'E
Kasli, Russia (käs´lĭ)	180	55°53'N	60°46'E
Kasongo, D.R.C. (kä-sôŋ´gō)	232	4°31'S	26°42'E
Kásos, i., Grc.	163	35°20'N	26°55'E
Kaspiysk, Russia	182	42°52'N	47°38'E
Kassándras, Kólpos, b., Grc.	175	40°10'N	23°35'E
Kassel, Ger. (käs´ĕl)	161	51°19'N	9°30'E
Kasson, Mn., U.S. (kăs´ŭn)	113	44°01'N	92°45'W
Kastamonu, Tur. (kå-stå-mō´no͞o)	198	41°20'N	33°50'E
Kastoría, Grc. (kås-tō´rĭ-å)	163	40°28'N	21°17'E
Kasūr, Pak.	202	31°10'N	74°29'E
Kataba, Zam.	237	16°05'S	25°10'E
Katahdin, Mount, mtn., Me., U.S. (kå-tä´dĭn)	100	45°56'N	68°57'W
Katanga, hist. reg., D.R.C. (kå-täŋ´gå)	232	8°30'S	25°00'E
Katanning, Austl. (kå-tăn´ĭng)	218	33°45'S	117°45'E
Katav-Ivanovsk, Russia (kä´tåf ĭ-vä´nôfsk)	186a	54°46'N	58°13'E
Kateninskiy, Russia (kåtyĕ´nĭs-kĭ)	186a	53°12'N	61°05'E
Kateríni, Grc.	175	40°18'N	22°36'E
Katete, Zam.	237	14°05'S	32°07'E
Katherine, Austl. (kăth´ẽr-ĭn)	218	14°15'S	132°20'E
Kāthiāwār, pen., India (kä´tyå-wär´)	199	22°10'N	70°20'E
Kathmandu, Nepal (kāt-mān-do͞o´)	199	27°49'N	85°21'E
Kathryn, Can. (kăth´rĭn)	102e	51°13'N	113°42'W
Kathryn, Ca., U.S.	117a	33°42'N	117°45'W
Katihār, India	202	25°39'N	87°39'E
Katiola, C. Iv.	234	8°08'N	5°06'W
Katmai National Park, rec., Ak., U.S. (kăt´mī)	106a	58°30'N	155°00'W
Katompi, D.R.C.	237	6°11'S	26°20'E
Katopa, D.R.C.	237	2°45'S	25°06'E
Katowice, Pol.	154	50°15'N	19°00'E
Katrineholm, Swe. (kå-trē´nĕ-hōlm)	166	59°01'N	16°10'E
Katsbakhskiy, Russia (kåts-bäk´skĭ)	186a	52°57'N	59°37'E
Katsina, Nig. (kät´sē-nå)	230	13°00'N	7°32'E
Katsina Ala, Nig.	230	7°10'N	9°17'E
Katsura, r., Japan (kä´tsö-rä)	211b	34°55'N	135°43'E
Katta-Kurgan, Uzb. (kå-tå-kör-gän´)	183	39°45'N	66°42'E
Kattegat, strt., Eur. (kăt´ĕ-gät)	156	56°57'N	11°25'E
Katumba, D.R.C.	237	7°45'S	25°18'E
Katun', r., Russia (kå-tōn´)	184	51°30'N	86°18'E
Katwijk aan Zee, Neth.	159a	52°12'N	4°23'E
Kaua'i, i., Hi., U.S.	106c	22°09'N	159°15'W
Kauai Channel, strt., Hi., U.S. (kä-o͞o-ä´ē)	106c	21°35'N	158°52'W
Kaufbeuren, Ger. (kouf´boi-rĕn)	168	47°52'N	10°38'E
Kaufman, Tx., U.S. (kôf´măn)	123	32°36'N	96°18'W
Kaukauna, Wi., U.S. (kô-kô´nå)	113	44°17'N	88°15'W
Kaulakahi Channel, strt., Hi., U.S. (kä´o͞o-lå-kä´hē)	126a	22°00'N	159°55'W
Kaunakakai, Hi., U.S. (kä´o͞o-nå-kä´kī)	126a	21°06'N	156°59'W
Kaunas, Lith. (kou´nås) (kôv´nō)	178	54°42'N	23°54'E
Kaura Namoda, Nig.	230	12°35'N	6°35'E
Kavála, Grc. (kä-vä´lä)	163	40°55'N	24°24'E
Kavieng, Pap. N. Gui. (kä-vē-ĕng´)	213	2°44'S	151°02'E
Kavīr, Dasht-e, des., Iran (dŭsht-ē-ka-vēr´)	198	34°41'N	53°30'E
Kawagoe, Japan (kä-wä-gō´å)	211	35°55'N	139°29'E
Kawaguchi, Japan (kä-wä-go͞o-chē)	211a	35°48'N	139°44'E
Kawaikini, mtn., Hi., U.S. (kä-wä´ē-kĭ-nĭ)	126a	22°05'N	159°33'W
Kawanishi, Japan (kä-wä´nē-shē)	211b	34°49'N	135°26'E
Kawasaki, Japan (kä-wä-sä´kē)	210	35°32'N	139°43'E
Kaxgar, r., China	204	39°30'N	75°00'E
Kaya, Burkina (kä´yä)	230	13°05'N	1°05'W
Kayan, r., Indon.	212	1°45'N	115°38'E
Kaycee, Wy., U.S. (kā-sē´)	115	43°43'N	106°38'W
Kayes, Mali (kāz)	230	14°27'N	11°26'W
Kayseri, Tur. (kī´sĕ-rē)	198	38°45'N	35°20'E
Kazach'ye, Russia	179	70°46'N	135°47'E
Kazakhstan, nation, Asia	178	48°45'N	59°00'E
Kazan', Russia (kå-zän´)	178	55°50'N	49°18'E
Kazanka, Ukr. (kå-zän´kå)	177	47°49'N	32°50'E
Kazanlŭk, Blg. (kå´zån-lĕk)	175	42°47'N	25°23'E
Kazbek, Gora, mtn. (kåz-bĕk´)	181	42°42'N	44°31'E
Kāzerūn, Iran	198	29°37'N	51°44'E
Kazincbarcika, Hung. (kô´zĭnts-bôr-tsĭ-ko)	169	48°15'N	20°39'E
Kazungula, Zam.	237	17°45'S	25°20'E
Kazusa Kameyama, Japan (kä-zo͞o-sä kä-mä´yä-mä)	211a	35°14'N	140°06'E
Kazym, r., Russia (kä-zĕm´)	184	63°30'N	67°41'E
Kéa, i., Grc.	175	37°36'N	24°13'E
Kealaikahiki Channel, strt., Hi., U.S. (kā-ä´lä-ē-kä-hē´kē)	126a	20°38'N	157°00'W
Keansburg, N.J., U.S. (kēnz´bûrg)	110a	40°26'N	74°08'W
Kearney, Ne., U.S. (kär´nĭ)	112	40°42'N	99°05'W
Kearny, N.J., U.S.	110a	40°46'N	74°09'W
Keasey, Or., U.S. (kēz´ĭ)	116c	45°51'N	123°20'W
Kebnekaise, mtn., Swe. (kĕp´nĕ-kå-ēs´ĕ)	156	67°53'N	18°10'E
Kecskemét, Hung. (kĕch´kĕ-māt)	163	46°52'N	19°42'E
Kedah, hist. reg., Malay. (kä´dä)	212	6°00'N	100°31'E
Kédainiai, Lith. (kē-dī´nĭ-ī)	167	55°16'N	23°58'E
Kedgwick, Can. (kĕdj´wĭk)	100	47°39'N	67°21'W
Keenbrook, Ca., U.S. (kēn´bro͝ok)	117a	34°16'N	117°29'W
Keene, N.H., U.S. (kēn)	109	42°55'N	72°15'W
Keetmanshoop, Nmb. (kāt´måns-hōp)	232	26°30'S	18°05'E
Keet Seel Ruin, Az., U.S. (kēt sēl)	119	36°46'N	110°32'W
Keewatin, Mn., U.S. (kē-wā´tĭn)	113	47°24'N	93°03'W
Kefallinía, i., Grc.	163	38°08'N	20°58'E
Keffi, Nig. (kĕf´ē)	230	8°51'N	7°52'E
Ke Ga, Mui, c., Viet.	212	12°58'N	109°50'E
Kei, r., Afr. (kā)	233c	32°57'S	26°50'E
Keila, Est. (kā´lå)	167	59°19'N	24°25'E
Keilor, Austl.	217a	37°43'S	144°50'E
Kei Mouth, S. Afr.	233c	32°40'S	28°23'E
Keiskammahoek, S. Afr. (kās´kämä-ho͞ok´)	233c	32°42'S	27°11'E
Kéita, Bahr, r., Chad	235	9°30'N	19°17'E
Keitele, l., Fin. (kā´tĕ-lĕ)	167	62°50'N	25°40'E
Kekaha, Hi., U.S.	126a	21°57'N	159°42'W
Kelafo, Eth.	238a	5°40'N	44°00'E
Kelang, Malay.	212	3°20'N	101°27'E
Kelang, r., Malay.	197b	3°00'N	101°40'E
Kelkit, r., Tur.	163	40°38'N	37°03'E
Keller, Tx., U.S. (kĕl´ẽr)	117c	32°56'N	97°15'W
Kellinghusen, Ger. (kĕ´lĕng-ho͞o-zĕn)	159c	53°57'N	9°43'E
Kellogg, Id., U.S. (kĕl´ŏg)	114	47°32'N	116°07'W
Kelme', Lith. (kĕl-må)	167	55°36'N	22°53'E
Kélo, Chad	235	9°19'N	15°48'E
Kelowna, Can.	90	49°53'N	119°29'W
Kelsey Bay, Can. (kĕl´sē)	94	50°24'N	125°57'W
Kelso, Wa., U.S.	116c	46°09'N	122°54'W
Keluang, Malay.	197b	2°01'N	103°19'E
Kem', Russia (kĕm)	178	65°00'N	34°48'E
Kemah, Tx., U.S. (kē´må)	123a	29°32'N	95°01'W
Kemerovo, Russia	178	55°31'N	86°05'E
Kemi, Fin. (kā´mē)	160	65°48'N	24°38'E
Kemi, r., Fin.	160	67°02'N	27°50'E
Kemigawa, Japan (kĕ´mē-gä´wä)	211a	35°38'N	140°07'E
Kemijarvi, Fin. (kā´mē-yĕr-vē)	160	66°48'N	27°21'E
Kemijärvi, l., Fin.	160	66°37'N	28°13'E
Kemmerer, Wy., U.S. (kĕm´ẽr-ẽr)	115	41°48'N	110°36'W
Kemp, l., Tx., U.S. (kĕmp)	120	33°55'N	99°22'W
Kempen, Ger. (kĕm´pĕn)	171c	51°22'N	6°25'E
Kempsey, Austl. (kĕmp´sē)	219	30°59'S	152°50'E
Kempt, l., Can. (kĕmpt)	99	47°28'N	74°00'W
Kempten, Ger. (kĕmp´tĕn)	161	47°44'N	10°17'E
Kempton Park, S. Afr. (kĕmp´tŏn pärk)	238c	26°07'S	28°29'E
Ken, r., India	202	25°00'N	79°55'E
Kenai, Ak., U.S. (kĕ-nī´)	103	60°38'N	151°18'W
Kenai Fjords National Park, rec., Ak., U.S.	103	59°45'N	150°00'W
Kenai Mountains, mts., Ak., U.S.	103	60°00'N	150°00'W
Kenai Pen, Ak., U.S.	103	64°40'N	150°18'W
Kendal, S. Afr.	238c	26°03'S	28°58'E
Kendal, Eng., U.K. (kĕn´dål)	164	54°20'N	1°48'W
Kendallville, In., U.S. (kĕn´dăl-vĭl)	108	41°25'N	85°20'W
Kenedy, Tx., U.S. (kĕn´ĕ-dĭ)	123	28°49'N	97°50'W
Kenema, S.L.	234	7°52'N	11°12'W
Kenitra, Mor. (kĕ-nē´trå)	162	34°21'N	6°34'W
Kenmare, N.D., U.S. (kĕn-mâr´)	112	48°41'N	102°05'W
Kenmore, N.Y., U.S. (kĕn´mōr)	111c	42°58'N	78°53'W
Kennebec, r., Me., U.S. (kĕn-ē-bĕk´)	100	44°23'N	69°48'W
Kennebunk, Me., U.S. (kĕn-ē-buŋk´)	100	43°24'N	70°33'W
Kennedale, Tx., U.S. (kĕn´-ē-dāl)	117c	32°38'N	97°13'W
Kennedy, Cape *see* Canaveral, Cape, c., Fl., U.S.	107	28°30'N	80°23'W
Kennedy, Mount, mtn., Can.	103	60°25'N	138°50'W
Kenner, La., U.S. (kĕn´ẽr)	123	29°58'N	90°15'W
Kennett, Mo., U.S. (kĕn´ĕt)	121	36°14'N	90°01'W
Kennewick, Wa., U.S. (kĕn´ē-wĭk)	114	46°12'N	119°06'W
Kenney Dam, dam, Can.	94	53°37'N	124°58'W
Kennydale, Wa., U.S. (kĕn-nē´dāl)	116a	47°31'N	122°12'W
Kénogami, Can. (kĕn-ō´gä-mē)	91	48°26'N	71°14'W
Kenogamissi Lake, l., Can.	98	48°15'N	81°31'W
Keno Hill, Can.	103	63°58'N	135°18'W
Kenora, Can. (kē-nō´rå)	91	49°47'N	94°29'W
Kenosha, Wi., U.S. (kē-nō´shå)	105	42°34'N	87°50'W
Kenova, W.V., U.S. (kē-nō´vå)	108	38°20'N	82°35'W
Kensico Reservoir, res., N.Y., U.S. (kĕn´sĭ-kō)	110a	41°08'N	73°45'W
Kent, Oh., U.S. (kĕnt)	108	41°05'N	81°20'W
Kent, Wa., U.S.	116a	47°23'N	122°14'W
Kentani, S. Afr. (kĕnt-änĭ´)	233c	32°31'S	28°19'E
Kentland, In., U.S. (kĕnt´lånd)	108	40°50'N	87°25'W
Kenton, Oh., U.S. (kĕn´tŭn)	108	40°40'N	83°35'W
Kent Peninsula, pen., Can.	92	68°28'N	108°10'W
Kentucky, state, U.S. (kĕn-tŭk´ĭ)	105	37°30'N	87°35'W
Kentucky, res., U.S.	107	36°20'N	88°50'W
Kentucky, r., Ky., U.S.	107	38°15'N	85°01'W
Kentwood, La., U.S. (kĕnt´wo͝od)	123	30°56'N	90°31'W
Kenya, nation, Afr. (kĕn´yå)	232	1°00'N	36°53'E
Kenya, Mount (Kirinyaga), mtn., Kenya	233	0°10'S	37°20'E
Kenyon, Mn., U.S. (kĕn´yŭn)	113	44°15'N	92°58'W
Keokuk, Ia., U.S. (kē´ō-kŭk)	105	40°24'N	91°34'W
Keoma, Can. (kē-ō´må)	102e	51°13'N	113°39'W
Kepenkeck Lake, l., Can.	101	48°13'N	54°45'W
Kępno, Pol. (kăŋ´pnō)	169	51°17'N	17°59'E
Kerala, state, India	199	16°38'N	76°00'E
Kerang, Austl. (kē-răng´)	219	35°32'S	143°58'E
Kerch, Ukr.	178	45°20'N	36°26'E
Kerchenskiy Proliv, strt., Eur. (kĕr-chĕn´skĭ prô´lĭf)	177	45°08'N	36°35'E
Kerempe Burun, c., Tur.	163	42°00'N	33°20'E
Keren, Erit.	231	15°46'N	38°28'E
Kerguélen, Îles, is., Afr. (kĕr´gå-lĕn)	3	49°50'S	69°30'E
Kericho, Kenya	237	0°22'S	35°17'E
Kerinci, Gunung, mtn., Indon.	212	1°45'S	101°18'E
Keriya *see* Yutian, China	204	36°55'N	81°39'E
Keriya, r., China (kē´rē-yä)	204	37°13'N	81°59'E
Kerkebet, Erit.	200	16°18'N	37°24'E
Kerkenna, Îles, i., Tun. (kĕr´kĕn-nä)	230	34°49'N	11°37'E
Kerki, Turkmen. (kĕr´kē)	183	37°52'N	65°15'E
Kérkyra, Grc.	163	39°36'N	19°56'E
Kérkyra, i., Grc.	162	39°33'N	19°36'E
Kermadec Islands, is., N.Z. (kẽr-mad´ĕk)	3	30°30'S	177°00'E
Kermān, Iran (kĕr-män´)	198	30°23'N	57°08'E
Kermānshāh *see* Bakhtarān, Iran	198	34°01'N	47°00'E
Kern, r., Ca., U.S.	118	35°31'N	118°37'W
Kern, South Fork, r., Ca., U.S.	118	35°40'N	118°15'W
Kerpen, Ger. (kĕr´pĕn)	171c	50°52'N	6°42'E
Kerrobert, Can.	96	51°53'N	109°13'W
Kerrville, Tx., U.S. (kûr´vĭl)	122	30°02'N	99°07'W
Kerulen, r., Asia (kĕr´o͞o-lĕn)	205	47°52'N	113°22'E
Kesagami Lake, l., Can.	99	50°23'N	80°15'W
Keşan, Tur. (kĕ´shån)	175	40°50'N	26°37'E
Keshan, China (kŭ-shän)	205	48°00'N	126°30'E

ăt; finăl; rāte; senåte; ärm; åsk; sofå; fâre; ch-choose; dh-as th in other; bē; ēvent; bĕt; recĕnt; cratẽr; g-gō; gh-guttural g; bĭt; ĭ-short neutral; rīde; κ-guttural k as ch in German ich;

PRONOUNCING INDEX Kesour – Kitgum 309

PLACE (Pronunciation)	PAGE	LAT.	LONG.
Kesour, Monts des, mts., Alg.	162	32°51'N	0°30'W
Kestell, S. Afr. (kĕs'tĕl)	238c	28°19'N	28°43'E
Keszthely, Hung. (kĕst'hĕl-lĭ)	169	46°46'N	17°12'E
Ket', r., Russia (kyĕt)	184	58°30'N	84°15'E
Keta, Ghana	230	6°00'N	1°00'E
Ketamputih, Indon.	197b	1°25'N	102°19'E
Ketapang, Indon. (kĕ-tȧ-päng')	212	2°00'S	109°57'E
Ketchikan, Ak., U.S. (kĕch-ĭ-kăn')	106a	55°21'N	131°35'W
Kętrzyn, Pol. (kaŋ't'r-zĭn)	169	54°04'N	21°24'E
Kettering, Eng., U.K. (kĕt'ẽr-ĭng)	158a	52°23'N	0°43'W
Kettering, Oh., U.S.	108	39°40'N	84°15'W
Kettle, r., Can.	95	49°40'N	119°00'W
Kettle, r., Mn., U.S. (kĕt''l)	113	46°20'N	92°57'W
Kettwig, Ger. (kĕt'vēg)	171c	51°22'N	6°56'E
Kęty, Pol. (kȧŋ tĭ)	169	49°54'N	19°16'E
Ketzin, Ger. (kĕ'tzēn)	159b	52°29'N	12°51'E
Keuka, l., N.Y., U.S. (kė-ū'kȧ)	109	42°30'N	77°10'W
Kevelaer, Ger. (kĕ'fĕ-lăr)	171c	51°35'N	6°15'E
Kew, Austl.	217a	37°49'S	145°02'E
Kewanee, Il., U.S. (kē-wä'nē)	113	41°15'N	89°55'W
Kewaunee, Wi., U.S. (kė-wô'nė)	113	44°27'N	87°33'W
Keweenaw Bay, b., Mi., U.S. (kē'wė-nô)	113	46°59'N	88°15'W
Keweenaw Peninsula, pen., Mi., U.S.	113	47°28'N	88°12'W
Keya Paha, r., S.D., U.S. (kē-yȧ pä'hä)	112	43°11'N	100°10'W
Key Largo, i., Fl., U.S.	125a	25°11'N	80°15'W
Keyport, N.J., U.S. (kē'pōrt)	110a	40°26'N	74°12'W
Keyport, Wa., U.S.	116a	47°42'N	122°38'W
Keyser, W.V., U.S. (kī'sẽr)	109	39°25'N	79°00'W
Key West, Fl., U.S. (kē wĕst')	105	24°31'N	81°47'W
Kežmarok, Slvk. (kĕzh'mȧ-rôk)	169	49°10'N	20°27'E
Khabarovo, Russia (kŭ-bár-ôvŏ)	178	69°31'N	60°41'E
Khabarovsk, Russia (kä-bä'rôfsk)	179	48°35'N	135°12'E
Khakassia, prov., Russia	184	52°32'N	89°33'E
Khālāpur, India	203b	18°48'N	73°17'E
Khalkidhiki, pen., Grc.	175	40°30'N	23°18'E
Khal'mer-Yu, Russia (kŭl-myĕr'-yōō')	178	67°52'N	64°25'E
Khalturin, Russia (кäl'tōō-rēn)	180	58°28'N	49°00'E
Khambhāt, Gulf of, b., India	199	21°20'N	72°27'E
Khammam, India	203	17°09'N	80°13'E
Khānābād, Afg.	202	36°43'N	69°11'E
Khandwa, India	202	21°53'N	76°22'E
Khaníon, Kólpos, b., Grc.	174a	35°35'N	23°55'E
Khanka, l., Asia (kän'kȧ)	179	45°09'N	133°28'E
Khānpur, Pak.	202	28°42'N	70°42'E
Khanty-Mansiysk, Russia (kŭn-te'mŭn-sēsk')	178	61°02'N	69°01'E
Khān Yūnus, Gaza	197a	31°21'N	34°19'E
Kharagpur, India (kŭ-rŭg'pòr)	199	22°26'N	87°21'E
Kharkiv, Ukr.	178	50°00'N	36°10'E
Kharkiv, prov., Ukr.	177	49°33'N	35°55'E
Kharkov *see* Kharkiv, Ukr.	178	50°00'N	36°10'E
Kharlovka, Russia	180	68°47'N	37°20'E
Kharmanli, Blg. (кár-män'lė)	175	41°54'N	25°55'E
Khartoum, Sudan	231	15°34'N	32°36'E
Khasavyurt, Russia	182	43°15'N	46°37'E
Khāsh, Iran	198	28°08'N	61°08'E
Khāsh, r., Afg.	198	32°30'N	64°27'E
Khasi Hills, hills, India	199	25°38'N	91°55'E
Khaskovo, Blg. (кás'kô-vô)	163	41°56'N	25°32'E
Khatanga, Russia (kȧ-tän'gȧ)	179	71°48'N	101°47'E
Khatangskiy Zaliv, b., Russia (kä-tän'g-skē)	179	73°45'N	108°30'E
Khaybār, Sau. Ar.	198	25°45'N	39°28'E
Kherson, Ukr. (kĕr-sôn')	181	46°38'N	32°34'E
Kherson, prov., Ukr.	177	46°32'N	32°55'E
Khiitola, Russia (khē'tō-lȧ)	167	61°14'N	29°40'E
Khimki, Russia (кēm'kĭ)	186b	55°54'N	37°27'E
Khmel'nyts'kyi, Ukr.	181	49°29'N	26°54'E
Khmel'nyts'kyy, prov., Ukr.	177	49°27'N	26°30'E
Khmil'nyk, Ukr.	177	49°34'N	27°58'E
Kholm, Russia (kôlm)	176	57°09'N	31°07'E
Kholmsk, Russia (кŭlmsk)	179	47°09'N	142°33'E
Khomeynīshahr, Iran	201	32°41'N	51°31'E
Khon Kaen, Thai.	212	16°37'N	102°41'E
Khopër, r., Russia (кô'pĕr)	181	52°00'N	43°00'E
Khor, Russia (kôr')	210	47°50'N	134°52'E
Khor, r., Russia	210	47°23'N	135°20'E
Khóra Sfakíon, Grc.	174a	35°12'N	24°10'E
Khorog, Taj.	183	37°30'N	71°36'E
Khorol, Ukr. (kô'rôl)	177	49°48'N	33°17'E
Khorol, r., Ukr.	177	49°50'N	33°21'E
Khorramābād, Iran	201	33°30'N	48°20'E
Khorramshahr, Iran (kô-ram'shär)	198	30°36'N	48°15'E
Khot'kovo, Russia	186b	56°15'N	38°00'E
Khotyn, Ukr.	181	48°29'N	26°32'E
Khoyniki, Bela.	177	51°54'N	30°00'E
Khudzhand, Taj.	183	40°17'N	69°37'E
Khulna, Bngl.	199	22°50'N	89°38'E
Khūryān Mūryān, is., Oman	198	17°27'N	56°02'E
Khust, Ukr. (кōōst)	169	48°10'N	23°18'E
Khvalynsk, Russia (кvá-lĭnsk')	181	52°30'N	48°00'E
Khvoy, Iran	198	38°32'N	45°01'E
Khyber Pass, p., Asia (kī'bẽr)	199	34°28'N	71°18'E
Kialwe, D.R.C.	237	9°22'S	27°08'E
Kiambi, D.R.C. (kyäm'bē)	232	7°20'S	28°01'E
Kiamichi, r., Ok., U.S. (kyȧ-mē'chē)	121	34°31'N	95°34'W
Kianta, l., Fin. (kyȧn'tȧ)	180	65°00'N	28°15'E
Kibenga, D.R.C.	236	7°55'S	17°35'E
Kibiti, Tan.	237	7°44'S	38°57'E
Kibombo, D.R.C.	237	3°54'S	25°55'E
Kibondo, Tan.	237	3°35'S	30°42'E
Kičevo, Mac. (kē'chĕ-vô)	175	41°30'N	20°59'E
Kickapoo, r., Wi., U.S. (kĭk'ȧ-pōō)	113	43°20'N	90°55'W
Kicking Horse Pass, p., Can.	95	51°25'N	116°10'W
Kidal, Mali (kē-dȧl')	230	18°33'N	1°00'E
Kidderminster, Eng., U.K. (kĭd'ẽr-mĭn-stẽr)	158a	52°23'N	2°14'W
Kidd's Beach, S. Afr. (kĭdz)	233c	33°09'S	27°43'E
Kidsgrove, Eng., U.K. (kĭdz'grōv)	158a	53°05'N	2°15'W
Kiel, Ger. (kēl)	154	54°19'N	10°08'E
Kiel, Wi., U.S.	113	43°52'N	88°04'W
Kiel Bay, b., Ger.	168	54°33'N	10°19'E
Kiel Canal *see* Nord-Ostsee Kanal, can., Ger.	168	54°03'N	9°23'E
Kielce, Pol. (kyĕl'tsĕ)	169	50°50'N	20°41'E
Kieldrecht, Bel. (kēl'drĕκt)	159a	51°17'N	4°09'E
Kiev (Kyïv), Ukr.	178	50°27'N	30°30'E
Kiffa, Maur. (kēf'ȧ)	230	16°37'N	11°24'W
Kigali, Rw. (kė-gä'lė)	232	1°59'S	30°05'E
Kigoma, Tan. (kė-gō'mä)	232	4°57'S	29°38'E
Kii-Suido, strt., Japan (kē sōō-ė'dō)	210	33°53'N	134°55'E
Kikaiga, i., Japan	210	28°25'N	130°10'E
Kikinda, Serb. (kē'kēn-dä)	175	45°49'N	20°30'E
Kikládes, is., Grc.	162	37°30'N	24°45'E
Kikwit, D.R.C. (kē'kwėt)	232	5°02'S	18°49'E
Kil, Swe. (kėl)	166	59°30'N	13°15'E
Kilauea, Hi., U.S. (kē-lä-ōō-ā'ä)	126a	22°12'N	159°25'W
Kīlauea Crater, depr., Hi., U.S.	126a	19°28'N	155°18'W
Kilbuck Mountains, mts., Ak., U.S. (kĭl-bŭk)	103	60°05'N	160°00'W
Kilchu, Kor., N. (kĭl'chò)	210	40°59'N	129°23'E
Kildare, Ire. (kĭl-dār')	164	53°09'N	7°05'W
Kilembe, D.R.C.	236	5°42'S	19°55'E
Kilgore, Tx., U.S.	123	32°23'N	94°53'W
Kilia, Ukr.	177	45°28'N	29°17'E
Kilifi, Kenya	237	3°38'S	39°51'E
Kilimanjaro, mtn., Tan. (kyl-ē-măn-jä'rō)	233	3°09'S	37°19'E
Kilimatinde, Tan. (kĭl-ē-mä-tĭn'dā)	232	5°48'S	34°58'E
Kilindoni, Tan.	237	7°55'S	39°39'E
Kilingi-Nõmme, Est. (kē'lĭn-gė-nôm'mĕ)	167	58°08'N	25°03'E
Kilis, Tur. (kē'lės)	163	36°50'N	37°20'E
Kilkenny, Ire. (kĭl-kĕn-ĭ)	161	52°40'N	7°30'W
Kilkis, Grc. (kĭl'kĭs)	175	40°59'N	22°51'E
Killala, Ire. (kĭ-lă'lȧ)	164	54°11'N	9°10'W
Killarney, Ire.	164	52°03'N	9°05'W
Killdeer, N.D., U.S. (kĭl'dēr)	112	47°22'N	102°45'W
Killiniq Island, i., Can.	93	60°32'N	63°56'W
Kilmarnock, Scot., U.K. (kĭl-mär'nŭk)	164	55°38'N	4°25'W
Kilrush, Ire. (kĭl'rŭsh)	164	52°40'N	9°16'W
Kilwa Kisiwani, Tan.	237	8°58'S	39°30'E
Kilwa Kivinje, Tan.	233	8°43'S	39°18'E
Kim, r., Cam.	235	5°40'N	11°17'E
Kimamba, Tan.	237	6°47'S	37°08'E
Kimba, Austl. (kĭm'bȧ)	222	33°08'S	136°25'E
Kimball, Ne., U.S. (kĭm-bȧl)	112	41°14'N	103°41'W
Kimball, S.D., U.S.	112	43°44'N	98°58'W
Kimberley, Can. (kĭm'bẽr-lĭ)	90	49°41'N	115°59'W
Kimberley, S. Afr.	232	28°40'S	24°50'E
Kimi, Cam.	235	6°05'N	11°30'E
Kimmirut (Lake Harbour), Can.	91	62°43'N	69°40'W
Kímolos, i., Grc. (kē'mô-lôs)	175	36°52'N	24°20'E
Kimry, Russia (kĭm'rė)	180	56°53'N	37°24'E
Kimvula, D.R.C.	236	5°44'S	15°58'E
Kinabalu, Gunong, mtn., Malay.	212	5°45'N	115°26'E
Kincardine, Can. (kĭn-kär'dĭn)	91	44°10'N	81°15'W
Kinda, D.R.C.	237	9°18'S	25°04'E
Kindanba, Congo	236	3°44'S	14°31'E
Kinder, La., U.S. (kĭn'dẽr)	123	30°30'N	92°50'W
Kindersley, Can. (kĭn'dẽrz-lė)	90	51°27'N	109°10'W
Kindia, Gui. (kĭn'dė-ȧ)	230	10°04'N	12°51'W
Kindu, D.R.C.	232	2°57'S	25°56'E
Kinel'-Cherkassy, Russia	180	53°32'N	51°32'E
Kineshma, Russia (kė-nĕsh'mȧ)	180	57°27'N	41°02'E
King, i., Austl. (kĭng)	221	39°35'S	143°40'E
Kingaroy, Austl. (kĭŋ'gȧ-roi)	222	26°37'S	151°50'E
King City, Can.	102d	43°56'N	79°32'W
King City, Ca., U.S. (kĭng sĭ'tĭ)	118	36°12'N	121°08'W
Kingcome Inlet, b., Can. (kĭng'kŭm)	94	50°50'N	126°10'W
Kingfisher, Ok., U.S. (kĭng'fĭsh-ẽr)	121	35°51'N	97°55'W
King George Sound, strt., Austl. (jôrj)	220	35°17'S	118°30'E
Kingisepp, Russia (kĭŋ-gė-sep')	180	59°22'N	28°38'E
King Leopold Ranges, mts., Austl. (lē'ô-pōld)	220	16°25'S	125°00'E
Kingman, Az., U.S. (kĭng'măn)	119	35°10'N	114°05'W
Kingman, Ks., U.S. (kĭng'măn)	120	37°38'N	98°07'W
Kings, r., Ca., U.S.	118	36°28'N	119°43'W
Kings Canyon National Park, rec., Ca., U.S. (kăn'yŭn)	106	36°52'N	118°53'W
Kingsclere, Eng., U.K. (kĭngs-clēr)	158b	51°18'N	1°15'W
Kingscote, Austl. (kĭngz'kŭt)	222	35°45'S	137°32'E
King's Lynn, Eng., U.K. (kĭngz lĭn')	165	52°45'N	0°20'E
Kings Mountain, N.C., U.S.	125	35°13'N	81°30'W
Kings Norton, Eng., U.K. (nôr'tŭn)	158a	52°25'N	1°54'W
King Sound, strt., Austl.	220	16°50'S	123°35'E
Kings Park, N.Y., U.S. (kĭngz pärk)	110a	40°53'N	73°16'W
Kings Peak, mtn., Ut., U.S.	106	40°46'N	110°20'W
Kingsport, Tn., U.S. (kĭngz'pōrt)	125	36°33'N	82°36'W
Kingston, Austl. (kĭngz'tŭn)	218	37°52'S	139°52'E
Kingston, Can.	91	44°15'N	76°30'W
Kingston, Jam.	129	18°00'N	76°45'W
Kingston, N.Y., U.S.	105	42°00'N	74°00'W
Kingston, Pa., U.S.	109	41°15'N	75°50'W
Kingston, Wa., U.S.	116a	47°04'N	122°29'W
Kingston upon Hull, Eng., U.K.	154	53°45'N	0°25'W
Kingstown, St. Vin. (kĭngz'toun)	129	13°10'N	61°14'W
Kingstree, S.C., U.S. (kĭngz'trē)	125	33°30'N	79°50'W
Kingsville, Tx., U.S. (kĭngz'vĭl)	123	27°32'N	97°52'W
King William Island, i., Can. (kĭng wĭl'yăm)	92	69°25'N	97°00'W
King William's Town, S. Afr. (kĭng-wĭl'-yŭmz-toun)	233c	32°53'S	27°24'E
Kinira, r., S. Afr.	233c	30°37'S	28°52'E
Kinloch, Mo., U.S. (kĭn-lŏk)	117e	38°44'N	90°19'W
Kinnaird, Can. (kĭn-ärd')	95	49°17'N	117°39'W
Kinnairds Head, c., Scot., U.K. (kĭn-ârds'hĕd)	160	57°42'N	3°55'W
Kinomoto, Japan (kē'nō-mōtō)	211	33°53'N	136°07'E
Kinosaki, Japan (kē'nō-sä'kė)	211	35°38'N	134°47'E
Kinshasa, D.R.C.	232	4°18'S	15°18'E
Kinsley, Ks., U.S. (kĭnz'lĭ)	120	37°55'N	99°24'W
Kinston, N.C., U.S. (kĭnz'tŭn)	125	35°15'N	77°35'W
Kintampo, Ghana (kēn-täm'pō)	230	8°03'N	1°43'W
Kintyre, pen., Scot., U.K.	164	55°50'N	5°40'W
Kiowa, Ks., U.S. (kī'ô wȧ)	120	37°01'N	98°30'W
Kiowa, Ok., U.S.	121	34°42'N	95°53'W
Kipawa, Lac, l., Can.	99	46°55'N	79°00'W
Kipembawe, Tan. (kē-pĕm-bä'wå)	232	7°39'S	33°24'E
Kipengere Range, mts., Tan.	237	9°10'S	34°00'E
Kipili, Tan.	237	7°26'S	30°36'E
Kipushi, D.R.C.	237	11°46'S	27°14'E
Kirakira, Sol. Is.	214e	10°27'S	161°55'E
Kirby, Tx., U.S. (kŭr'bĭ)	117d	29°29'N	98°23'W
Kirbyville, Tx., U.S. (kŭr'bĭ-vĭl)	123	30°39'N	93°54'W
Kirenga, r., Russia (kė-rĕŋ'gȧ)	185	56°30'N	108°18'E
Kirensk, Russia (kė-rĕnsk')	179	57°47'N	108°22'E
Kirgiz Range, mts., Asia	183	42°30'N	74°00'E
Kiri, D.R.C.	236	1°27'S	19°00'E
Kiribati, nation, Oc.	3	1°30'S	173°00'E
Kirin *see* Chilung, Tai.	205	25°02'N	121°48'E
Kiritimati, i., Kir.	2	2°20'N	157°40'W
Kirkby, Eng., U.K.	158a	53°29'N	2°54'W
Kirkby-in-Ashfield, Eng., U.K. (kûrk'bē-ĭn-ăsh'fēld)	158a	53°06'N	1°16'W
Kirkcaldy, Scot., U.K. (kẽr-kô'dĭ)	164	56°06'N	3°15'W
Kirkenes, Nor.	160	69°40'N	30°03'E
Kirkham, Eng., U.K. (kûrk'ăm)	158a	53°47'N	2°53'W
Kirkland, Wa., U.S. (kûrk'lănd)	116a	47°41'N	122°12'W
Kirklareli, Tur. (kĕrk'lär-ĕ'lė)	163	41°44'N	27°15'E
Kirksville, Mo., U.S. (kûrks'vĭl)	105	40°12'N	92°35'W
Kirkwall, Scot., U.K. (kûrk'wôl)	160	58°58'N	2°59'W
Kirkwood, S. Afr.	233c	33°26'S	25°24'E
Kirkwood, Mo., U.S. (kûrk'wŏd)	117e	38°35'N	90°24'W
Kirn, Ger. (kērn)	168	49°47'N	7°23'E
Kirov, Russia	176	54°04'N	34°19'E
Kirov, Russia	178	58°35'N	49°35'E
Kirovakan, Arm.	182	40°48'N	44°30'E
Kirovgrad, Russia (kē'rŭ-vŭ-grad)	186a	57°26'N	60°03'E
Kirovohrad, Ukr.	181	48°33'N	32°17'E
Kirovohrad, prov., Ukr.	177	48°23'N	31°10'E
Kirovsk, Russia (kė-rôfsk')	186c	59°52'N	30°59'E
Kirovsk, Russia	178	67°40'N	33°58'E
Kirsanov, Russia (kẽr-sá'nôf)	181	52°40'N	42°40'E
Kırşehir, Tur. (kẽr-shĕ'hẽr)	198	39°10'N	34°00'E
Kirtachi Seybou, Niger	235	12°48'N	2°29'E
Kirthar Range, mts., Pak. (kĭr-tŭr)	199	27°00'N	67°10'E
Kirton, Eng., U.K. (kûr'tŭn)	158a	53°29'N	0°35'W
Kiruna, Swe. (kē-rōō'nä)	160	67°49'N	20°08'E
Kirundu, D.R.C.	237	0°44'S	25°32'E
Kirwin Reservoir, res., Ks., U.S. (kûr'wĭn)	120	39°34'N	99°04'W
Kiryū, Japan	210	36°24'N	139°20'E
Kirzhach, Russia (kĭr-zhák')	176	56°08'N	38°53'E
Kisaki, Tan. (kē-sä'kē)	233	7°37'S	37°43'E
Kisangani, D.R.C.	231	0°30'N	25°12'E
Kisarazu, Japan (kē'sȧ-rá'zōō)	211a	35°23'N	139°55'E
Kiselëvsk, Russia (kē-sĭ-lyôfsk')	178	54°00'N	86°39'E
Kishinev *see* Chişinău, Mol.	178	47°02'N	28°52'E
Kishiwada, Japan (kē'shė-wä'dä)	210	34°25'N	135°18'E
Kishkino, Russia (kēsh'kĭ-nô)	186b	55°15'N	38°04'E
Kisiwani, Tan.	237	4°08'S	37°57'E
Kiska, i., Ak., U.S. (kĭs'kä)	106b	52°08'N	177°10'E
Kiskatinaw, r., Can.	95	55°10'N	120°20'W
Kiskittogisu Lake, l., Can.	97	54°05'N	99°00'W
Kiskitto Lake, l., Can. (kĭs-kĭ'tō)	97	54°16'N	98°34'W
Kiskunfélegyháza, Hung. (kĭsh'kòn-fā'lĕd-y'hä'zô)	169	46°42'N	19°52'E
Kiskunhalas, Hung. (kĭsh'kòn-hô'lôsh)	169	46°24'N	19°26'E
Kiskunmajsa, Hung. (kĭsh'kòn-mĭ'shô)	169	46°29'N	19°42'E
Kislovodsk, Russia	182	43°55'N	42°44'E
Kismaayo, Som.	233	0°18'S	42°30'E
Kiso-Gawa, r., Japan (kē'sō-gä'wä)	211	35°29'N	137°12'E
Kiso-Sammyaku, mts., Japan (kė'sō säm'myá-kōō)	211	35°47'N	137°39'E
Kissamos, Grc.	174a	35°13'N	23°35'E
Kissidougou, Gui. (kē'sė-dōō'gōō)	230	9°11'N	10°06'W
Kissimmee, Fl., U.S. (kĭ-sĭm'ė)	125a	28°17'N	81°25'W
Kissimmee, r., Fl., U.S.	125a	27°45'N	81°07'W
Kissimmee, Lake, l., Fl., U.S.	125a	27°58'N	81°17'W
Kisujszallás, Hung.	169	47°12'N	20°47'E
Kisumu, Kenya (kē'sōō-mōō)	232	0°06'S	34°45'E
Kita, Mali (kē'tá)	230	13°03'N	9°29'W
Kitakami Gawa, r., Japan	210	39°20'N	141°10'E
Kitakyūshū, Japan	205	33°53'N	130°50'E
Kitale, Kenya	237	1°01'N	35°00'E
Kit Carson, Co., U.S.	120	38°46'N	102°48'W
Kitchener, Can. (kĭch'ĕ-nẽr)	91	43°25'N	80°35'W
Kitenda, D.R.C.	236	6°53'S	17°21'E
Kitgum, Ug. (kĭt'gòm)	231	3°29'N	33°04'E

ng-sing; ŋ-baŋk; ɴ-nasalized n; nŏd; cŏmmit; ōld; ôbey; ôrder; oi-boil; fōōd; ŏŏ-as oo in foot; ou-out; s-soft; sh-dish; th-thin; pūre; ûnite; ûrn; stŭd; circŭs; ü-as in French tu; '-indeterminate vowel.

310 Kitimat – Kozhikode PRONOUNCING INDEX

PLACE (Pronunciation)	PAGE	LAT.	LONG.
Kitimat, Can. (kĭ'tĭ-măt)	90	54°03'N	128°33'W
Kitimat, r., Can.	94	53°50'N	129°00'W
Kitimat Ranges, mts., Can.	94	53°30'N	128°50'W
Kitlope, r., Can. (kĭt'lōp)	94	53°00'N	128°00'W
Kitsuki, Japan (kēt'sò-kė)	211	33°24'N	131°35'E
Kittanning, Pa., U.S. (kĭ-tăn'ĭng)	109	40°50'N	79°30'W
Kittatinny Mountains, mts., N.J., U.S. (kĭ-tŭ-tĭ'nė)	110a	41°16'N	74°44'W
Kittery, Me., U.S. (kĭt'ẽr-ĭ)	100	43°07'N	70°45'W
Kittsee, Aus.	159e	48°05'N	17°05'E
Kitty Hawk, N.C., U.S. (kĭt'tė hôk)	125	36°04'N	75°42'W
Kitunda, Tan.	237	6°48'S	33°13'E
Kitwe, Zam.	237	12°49'S	28°13'E
Kitzingen, Ger. (kĭt'zĭng-ĕn)	168	49°44'N	10°08'E
Kiunga, Kenya	237	1°45'S	41°29'E
Kivu, Lac, l., Afr.	232	1°45'S	28°55'E
Kiyose, Japan	[illegible]	[illegible]	[illegible]
Kızel, Russia (kē'zĕl)	180	59°05'N	57°42'E
Kızıl, r., Tur.	198	40°00'N	34°00'E
Kizil'skoye, Russia (kĭz'ĭl-skô-yĕ)	186a	52°43'N	58°53'E
Kizlyar, Russia (kĭz-lyär')	181	44°00'N	46°50'E
Kizlyarskiy Zaliv, b., Russia	182	44°33'N	46°55'E
Kizu, Japan (kē'zōō)	211	34°43'N	135°49'E
Klaas Smits, r., S. Afr.	233c	31°45'S	26°33'E
Klaaswaal, Neth.	159a	51°46'N	4°25'E
Kladno, Czech Rep. (kläd'nō)	168	50°10'N	14°05'E
Klagenfurt, Aus. (klä'gĕn-fòrt)	161	46°38'N	14°19'E
Klaipėda, Lith. (klī'pā-dȧ)	180	55°43'N	21°10'E
Klamath, r., U.S.	114	41°40'N	123°25'W
Klamath Falls, Or., U.S.	104	42°13'N	121°49'W
Klamath Mountains, mts., Ca., U.S.	114	42°00'N	123°25'W
Klarälven, r., Swe.	160	60°40'N	13°00'E
Klaskanine, r., Or., U.S. (klăs'kȧ-nīn)	116c	46°02'N	123°43'W
Klatovy, Czech Rep. (klä'tō-vė)	161	49°23'N	13°18'E
Klawock, Ak., U.S. (klă'wăk)	103	55°32'N	133°10'W
Kleinmachnow, Ger. (klīn-mäк'nō)	159b	52°22'N	13°12'E
Klerksdorp, S. Afr. (klĕrks'dôrp)	238c	26°52'S	26°40'E
Klerksraal, S. Afr. (klĕrks'kräl)	238c	26°15'S	27°10'E
Kletnya, Russia (klyĕt'nyȧ)	176	53°19'N	33°14'E
Kleve, Ger. (klĕ'fĕ)	168	51°47'N	6°09'E
Klickitat, r., Wa., U.S.	114	46°01'N	121°07'W
Klimovichi, Bela. (klē-mô-vē'chė)	176	53°37'N	31°21'E
Klimovsk, Russia (klĭ'môfsk)	186b	55°21'N	37°32'E
Klin, Russia (klĕn)	176	56°18'N	36°43'E
Klintehamn, Swe. (klĕn'tĕ-häm)	166	57°24'N	18°14'E
Klintsy, Russia (klĭn'tsĭ)	181	52°46'N	32°14'E
Klip, r., S. Afr. (klĭp)	238c	27°18'N	29°25'E
Klipgat, S. Afr.	238c	25°26'S	27°57'E
Klippan, Swe. (klyp'pán)	166	56°08'N	13°09'E
Kłodzko, Pol. (klôd'skō)	168	50°26'N	16°38'E
Klondike Region, hist. reg., N.A. (klŏn'dīk)	90	64°12'N	142°38'W
Klosterfelde, Ger. (klōs'tĕr-fĕl-dĕ)	159b	52°47'N	13°29'E
Klosterneuburg, Aus. (klōs-tĕr-noi'bōōrgh)	159e	48°19'N	16°20'E
Kluane, l., Can.	92	61°15'N	138°40'W
Kluane National Park, rec., Can.	92	60°25'N	137°53'W
Kluczbork, Pol. (klōōch'bŏrk)	169	50°59'N	18°15'E
Klyaz'ma, r., Russia (klyäz'mȧ)	176	55°49'N	39°19'E
Klyetsk, Bela. (klĕtsk)	176	53°04'N	26°43'E
Klyuchevskaya, vol., Russia (klyōō-chĕfskä'yä)	179	56°13'N	160°00'E
Klyuchi, Russia (klyōō'chĭ)	186a	57°03'N	57°20'E
Knezha, Blg. (knyä'zhȧ)	163	43°27'N	24°03'E
Knife, r., N.D., U.S. (nīf)	112	47°06'N	102°33'W
Knight Inlet, b., Can. (nīt)	94	50°41'N	125°40'W
Knightstown, In., U.S. (nīts'toun)	108	39°45'N	85°30'W
Knin, Cro. (knēn)	174	44°02'N	16°14'E
Knittelfeld, Aus.	161	47°13'N	14°50'E
Knob Peak, mtn., Phil. (nŏb)	213a	12°30'N	121°20'E
Knottingley, Eng., U.K. (nŏt'ĭng-lĭ)	158a	53°42'N	1°14'W
Knox, In., U.S. (nŏks)	108	41°15'N	86°40'W
Knox, Cape, c., Can.	94	54°12'N	133°20'W
Knoxville, Ia., U.S. (nŏks'vĭl)	113	41°19'N	93°05'W
Knoxville, Tn., U.S.	105	35°58'N	83°55'W
Knutsford, Eng., U.K. (nŭts'fẽrd)	158a	53°18'N	2°22'W
Knyszyn, Pol. (knĭ'shĭn)	169	53°16'N	22°59'E
Kobayashi, Japan (kō'bá-yä'shė)	211	31°58'N	130°59'E
Kōbe, Japan (kō'bĕ)	205	34°30'N	135°10'E
Kobeliaky, Ukr.	181	49°11'N	34°12'E
København *see* Copenhagen, Den.	154	55°43'N	12°27'E
Koblenz, Ger. (kō'blĕntz)	161	50°18'N	7°36'E
Kobozha, r., Russia (kô-bō'zhȧ)	176	58°55'N	35°18'E
Kobrinskoye, Russia (kô-brĭn'skô-yĕ)	186c	59°25'N	30°07'E
Kobryn, Bela. (kō'brĕn')	181	52°13'N	24°23'E
Kobuk, r., Ak., U.S. (kō'bŭk)	103	66°58'N	158°48'W
Kobuk Valley National Park, rec., Ak., U.S.	103	67°20'N	159°00'W
Kobuleti, Geor. (kô-bò-lyā'tė)	181	41°50'N	41°40'E
Kočani, Mac. (kô'chä-nĕ)	175	41°54'N	22°25'E
Kočevje, Slvn. (kô'chäv-ye)	174	45°38'N	14°51'E
Kocher, r., Ger. (kôк'ẽr)	168	49°00'N	9°52'E
Kochi, India	203	9°58'N	76°19'E
Kōchi, Japan (kō'chė)	205	33°35'N	133°32'E
Kodaira, Japan	211a	35°43'N	139°29'E
Kodiak, Ak., U.S. (kō'dyăk)	106a	57°50'N	152°30'W
Kodiak Island, i., Ak., U.S.	103	57°24'N	153°32'W
Kodok, Sudan (ko'dŏk)	231	9°57'N	32°08'E
Koforidua, Ghana (kō fō-rĭ-dōō'ȧ)	230	6°03'N	0°17'W
Kōfu, Japan (kō'fōō')	210	35°41'N	138°34'E
Koga, Japan (kō'gȧ)	211	36°13'N	139°40'E
Kogan, r., Gui.	234	11°30'N	14°05'W
Kogane, Japan (kō'gä-nȧ)	211a	35°50'N	139°56'E
Koganei, Japan (kō'gä-nā)	211a	35°42'N	139°31'E
Køge, Den. (kû'gĕ)	166	55°27'N	12°09'E
Køge Bugt, b., Den.	166	55°30'N	12°25'E
Kogoni, Mali	234	14°44'N	6°02'W
Kohīma, India (kô-ē'mȧ)	199	25°45'N	94°41'E
Kohyl'nyk, r., Eur.	177	46°08'N	29°10'E
Koito, r., Japan (kô'ê-tō)	211a	35°19'N	139°58'E
Kŏje, i., Kor., S. (kû'jĕ)	210	34°53'N	129°00'E
Kokand, Uzb. (kô-känt')	183	40°27'N	71°07'E
Kokemäenjoki, r., Fin.	167	61°23'N	22°03'E
Kokhma, Russia (kôк'mȧ)	176	56°57'N	41°08'E
Kokkola, Fin. (kô'kô-lȧ)	160	63°47'N	22°58'E
Kokomo, In., U.S. (kō'kô-mô)	108	40°30'N	86°20'W
Koko Nor (Qinghai Hu), l., China (kō'kô nor) (chyĭŋ-hī hōō)	204	37°20'N	90°00'E
Kokopo, Pap. N. Gui. (kô-kô'pō)	213	4°25'S	152°27'E
Kökshetaū, Kaz.	183	53°15'N	69°13'E
Koksoak, r., Can. (kŏk'sō-ăk)	93	57°42'N	69°50'W
Kokstad, S. Afr. (kŏk'shtát)	233c	[illegible]	[illegible]
Kokubu, Japan (kō'kōō-bōō)	211	31°42'N	130°40'E
Kokuou, Japan (kô'kōō-ô'ōōo)	211b	34°34'N	135°39'E
Kola Peninsula *see* Kol'skiy Poluostrov, pen., Russia	178	67°15'N	37°40'E
Kolār (Kolār Gold Fields), India (kôl-är')	199	13°39'N	78°33'E
Kolárvo, Slvk. (kŏl-árōvō)	169	47°54'N	17°59'E
Kolbio, Kenya	237	1°10'S	41°15'E
Kol'chugino, Russia (kôl-chò'gē-nô)	176	56°19'N	39°29'E
Kolda, Sen.	234	12°53'N	14°57'W
Kolding, Den. (kŭl'dĭng)	166	55°29'N	9°24'E
Kole, D.R.C. (kō'lȧ)	232	3°19'S	22°46'E
Kolguyev, i., Russia (kôl-gò'yĕf)	178	69°00'N	49°00'E
Kolhāpur, India	203	16°48'N	74°15'E
Kolín, Czech Rep. (kō'lēn)	168	50°01'N	15°11'E
Kolkasrags, c., Lat. (kôl-käs'rágz)	167	57°46'N	22°39'E
Kolkata (Calcutta), India	199	22°32'N	88°22'E
Köln *see* Cologne, Ger.	171c	50°56'N	6°57'E
Kolno, Pol. (kôw'nô)	169	53°23'N	21°56'E
Koło, Pol. (kô'wô)	169	52°11'N	18°37'E
Kołobrzeg, Pol. (kô-lô'bzhĕk)	160	54°10'N	15°35'E
Kolomna, Russia (kál-ôm'nȧ)	180	55°06'N	38°47'E
Kolomyia, Ukr.	169	48°32'N	25°04'E
Kolp', r., Russia (kôlp)	176	59°18'N	35°32'E
Kolpashevo, Russia (kŭl pȧ shô'vȧ)	178	58°16'N	82°43'E
Kolpino, Russia (kôl'pē-nô)	180	59°45'N	30°37'E
Kolpny, Russia (kôlp'nyė)	176	52°14'N	36°54'E
Kol'skiy Poluostrov, pen., Russia	178	67°15'N	37°40'E
Kolva, r., Russia	180	61°00'N	57°00'E
Kolwezi, D.R.C. (kōl-wĕ'zē)	232	10°43'S	25°28'E
Kolyberovo, Russia (kô-lĭ-byâ'rô-vô)	186b	55°16'N	38°45'E
Kolyma, r., Russia	179	66°30'N	151°45'E
Kolymskiy Mountains *see* Gydan, Khrebet, mts., Russia	179	61°45'N	155°00'E
Kom, r., Afr.	236	2°15'N	12°05'E
Komadugu Gana, r., Nig.	235	12°15'N	11°10'E
Komae, Japan	211a	35°37'N	139°35'E
Komandorskiye Ostrova, is., Russia	197	55°40'N	167°13'E
Komárno, Slvk. (kô'mär-nô)	169	47°46'N	18°08'E
Komarno, Ukr.	169	49°38'N	23°42'E
Komárom, Hung. (kô'mä-rôm)	169	47°45'N	18°06'E
Komatipoort, S. Afr. (kō-mä'tē-pōrt)	232	25°21'S	32°00'E
Komatsu, Japan (kō-mät'sōō)	210	36°23'N	136°26'E
Komatsushima, Japan (kō-mät'sōō-shē'mä)	211	34°04'N	134°32'E
Komeshia, D.R.C.	237	8°01'S	27°07'E
Komga, S. Afr. (kōm'gȧ)	233c	32°36'S	27°54'E
Komi, prov., Russia (kômė)	184	63°00'N	55°00'E
Kommetjie, S. Afr.	232a	34°09'S	18°19'E
Komoé, r., C. Iv.	234	5°40'N	3°40'W
Komsomolets, Kaz.	186a	53°45'N	62°04'E
Komsomol'sk-na-Amure, Russia	179	50°46'N	137°14'E
Kona, Mali	234	14°57'N	3°53'W
Konda, r., Russia (kôn'dȧ)	180	60°50'N	64°00'E
Kondas, r., Russia (kôn'dȧs)	186a	59°30'N	56°28'E
Kondoa, Tan. (kôn-dō'ȧ)	232	4°52'S	36°00'E
Kondolole, D.R.C.	237	1°20'N	25°58'E
Koné, N. Cal.	214f	21°04'S	164°52'E
Kong, C. Iv. (kông)	230	9°05'N	4°41'W
Kongbo, C.A.R.	236	4°44'N	21°23'E
Kongolo, D.R.C. (kôŋ'gō'lō)	232	5°23'S	27°00'E
Kongsberg, Nor. (kŭngs'bĕrg)	166	59°40'N	9°36'E
Kongsvinger, Nor. (kŭngs'vĭŋ-gẽr)	166	60°12'N	12°00'E
Koni, D.R.C. (kō'nē)	232	10°32'S	27°27'E
Königsberg *see* Kaliningrad, Russia	178	54°42'N	20°32'E
Königsbrunn, Ger. (kû'nēgs-brōōn)	159d	48°16'N	10°53'E
Königs Wusterhausen, Ger. (kû'nēgs vōōs'tĕr-hou-zĕn)	159b	52°18'N	13°38'E
Konin, Pol. (kô'nyĕn)	161	52°11'N	18°17'E
Kónitsa, Grc. (kô'nyē'tsȧ)	175	40°03'N	20°46'E
Konjic, Bos. (kôn'yēts)	175	43°38'N	17°59'E
Konju, Kor., S.	210	36°21'N	127°05'E
Konnagar, India	202a	22°41'N	88°22'E
Konotop, Ukr. (kô-nô-tôp')	181	51°13'N	33°14'E
Konpienga, r., Burkina	234	11°15'N	0°35'E
Konqi, r., China (kôn-chyē)	204	41°09'N	87°46'E
Końskie, Pol. (koin''skyĕ)	169	51°12'N	20°26'E
Konstanz, Ger. (kôn'shtänts)	168	47°39'N	9°10'E
Kontagora, Nig. (kôn-tȧ-gō'rä)	230	10°24'N	5°28'E
Konya, Tur. (kōn'yȧ)	198	36°55'N	32°25'E
Koocanusa, Lake, res., N.A.	114	49°00'N	115°10'W
Kootenay (Kootenai), r., N.A.	95	49°45'N	117°05'W
Kootenay Lake, l., Can.	95	49°35'N	116°50'W
Kootenay National Park, rec., Can. (kōō'tē-nā)	90	51°06'N	117°02'W
Kōō-zan, mtn., Japan (kōō'zän)	211b	34°53'N	135°32'E
Kopervik, Nor. (kô'pĕr-vêk)	166	59°18'N	5°20'E
Kopeysk, Russia (kô-pāsk')	184	55°07'N	61°37'E
Köping, Swe. (chû'pĭng)	166	59°32'N	15°58'E
Kopparberg, Swe. (kŏp'pár-bĕrgh)	166	59°53'N	15°00'E
Koppeh Dāgh, mts., Asia	198	37°28'N	58°29'E
Koppies, S. Afr.	238c	27°15'S	27°35'E
Koprivnica, Cro. (kô'prēv-nē'tsȧ)	174	46°10'N	16°48'E
Kopychyntsi, Ukr.	169	49°06'N	25°55'E
Korčula, i., Cro. (kôr'chōō-lȧ)	175	42°50'N	17°05'E
Korea, North, nation, Asia	205	40°00'N	127°00'E
Korea, South, nation, Asia	205	36°30'N	128°00'E
Korea Bay, b., Asia	208	39°18'N	123°50'E
Korean Archipelago, is., Kor., S.	205	34°05'N	125°35'E
Korea Strait, strt., Asia	205	33°30'N	128°30'E
Korets', Ukr.	169	50°35'N	27°13'E
Korhogo, C. Iv. (kôr-hō'gō)	230	9°27'N	5°38'W
Korinthiakós Kólpos, b., Grc.	163	38°15'N	22°33'E
Kórinthos, Grc. (kô-rĕn'thôs) (kŏr'ĭnth)	154	37°56'N	22°54'E
[illegible], Ukr.	177	51°44'N	32°24'E
Kōriyama, Japan (kō'rė-yä'mä)	210	37°18'N	140°25'E
Korkino, Russia (kôr'kē-nŭ)	186a	54°53'N	61°25'E
Korla, China (kōr-lä)	204	41°37'N	86°03'E
Körmend, Hung. (kûr'mĕnt)	168	47°02'N	16°36'E
Kornat, i., Cro. (kôr-nät')	174	43°46'N	15°10'E
Korneuburg, Aus. (kôr'noi-bòrgh)	159e	48°22'N	16°21'E
Koro, Mali	234	14°04'N	3°05'W
Korocha, Russia (kô-rō'chȧ)	177	50°50'N	37°13'E
Korop, Ukr. (kō'rôp)	177	51°33'N	32°54'E
Koro Sea, sea, Fiji	214g	18°00'S	179°50'E
Korosten', Ukr. (kô'rôs-tĕn)	181	50°51'N	28°39'E
Korostyshiv, Ukr.	177	50°19'N	29°05'E
Koro Toro, Chad	235	16°05'N	18°30'E
Korotoyak, Russia (kô'rô-tô-yák')	177	51°00'N	39°06'E
Korsakov, Russia (kôr'sȧ-kôf')	179	46°42'N	143°16'E
Korsnäs, Fin. (kôrs'nĕs)	167	62°51'N	21°17'E
Korsør, Den. (kôrs'ûr')	166	55°19'N	11°08'E
Kortrijk, Bel.	165	50°49'N	3°10'E
Koryakskiy Khrebet, mts., Russia	179	62°00'N	168°45'E
Kosa Byriuchyi ostriv, i., Ukr.	177	46°07'N	35°12'E
Kościan, Pol. (kŭsh'tsyán)	168	52°05'N	16°38'E
Kościerzyna, Pol. (kŭsh-tsyĕ-zhē'nȧ)	169	54°08'N	17°59'E
Kosciusko, Ms., U.S. (kŏs-ĭ-ŭs'kō)	124	33°04'N	89°35'W
Kosciuszko, Mount, mtn., Austl.	221	36°26'S	148°20'E
Kosha, Sudan	231	20°49'N	30°27'E
Koshigaya, Japan (kō'shê-gä'yä)	211a	35°53'N	139°48'E
Köshim, r., Kaz.	181	50°30'N	50°40'E
Kosi, r., India (kō'sē)	202	26°00'N	86°20'E
Košice, Slvk. (kō'shē-tsĕ')	161	48°43'N	21°17'E
Kosmos, S. Afr. (kŏz'mŏs)	233b	25°45'S	27°51'E
Kosobrodskiy, Russia (kä-sô'brôd-skĭ)	186a	54°14'N	60°53'E
Kosovo, hist. reg., Serb.	175	42°35'N	21°00'E
Kosovska Mitrovica, Serb. (kô'sôv-skä' mē'trô-vē-tsä')	175	42°51'N	20°50'E
Kostajnica, Cro. (kôs'tä-ē-nē'tsȧ)	174	45°14'N	16°32'E
Koster, S. Afr.	238c	25°52'S	26°52'E
Kostiantynivka, Ukr.	177	48°33'N	37°42'E
Kostino, Russia (kôs'tĭ-nô)	186b	55°54'N	37°51'E
Kostroma, Russia (kôs-trô-mȧ')	178	57°46'N	40°55'E
Kostroma, prov., Russia	176	57°50'N	41°10'E
Kostrzyn, Pol. (kôst'chĕn)	161	52°35'N	14°38'E
Kos'va, r., Russia (kôs'vȧ)	186a	58°44'N	57°08'E
Koszalin, Pol. (kô-shä'lĭn)	160	54°12'N	16°10'E
Kőszeg, Hung. (kû'sĕg)	168	47°21'N	16°32'E
Kota, India	199	25°17'N	75°49'E
Kota Baharu, Malay. (kō'tä bä'rōō)	212	6°15'N	102°23'E
Kotabaru, Indon.	212	3°22'S	116°15'E
Kota Kinabalu, Malay.	212	5°55'N	116°05'E
Kota Tinggi, Malay.	197b	1°43'N	103°54'E
Kotel, Blg. (kô-tĕl')	175	42°54'N	26°28'E
Kotel'nich, Russia (kô-tyĕl'nĕch)	180	58°15'N	48°20'E
Kotel'nyy, i., Russia (kô-tyĕl'nė)	179	74°51'N	134°09'E
Kotka, Fin. (kŏt'kȧ)	160	60°28'N	26°56'E
Kotlas, Russia (kōt'läs)	180	61°10'N	46°50'E
Kotlin, Ostrov, i., Russia (ôs-trôf' kôt'lĭn)	186c	60°02'N	29°49'E
Kotor, Mont.	175	42°25'N	18°46'E
Kotorosl', r., Russia (kô-tô'rôsl)	176	57°18'N	39°08'E
Kotovs'k, Ukr.	177	47°49'N	29°31'E
Kotto, r., C.A.R.	231	5°17'N	22°04'E
Kotuy, r., Russia (kô-tōō')	184	71°00'N	103°15'E
Kotzebue, Ak., U.S. (kŏt'sē-bōō)	106a	66°48'N	162°42'W
Kotzebue Sound, strt., Ak., U.S.	103	67°00'N	164°28'W
Kouchibouguac National Park, rec., Can.	100	46°53'N	65°35'W
Koudougou, Burkina (kōō-dōō'gōō)	230	12°15'N	2°22'W
Kouilou, r., Congo	232	4°30'S	12°00'E
Koula-Moutou, Gabon	236	1°08'S	12°29'E
Koulikoro, Mali (kōō-lê-kō'rō)	230	12°53'N	7°33'W
Koulouguidi, Mali	235	13°27'N	17°33'E
Koumac, N. Cal.	214f	20°33'S	164°17'E
Koumra, Chad	235	8°55'N	17°33'E
Koundara, Gui.	234	12°29'N	13°18'W
Kouroussa, Gui. (kōō-rōō'sä)	230	10°39'N	9°53'W
Koutiala, Mali (kōō-tē-ä'lä)	230	12°29'N	5°29'W
Kouvola, Fin. (kō'ŏ-vô-lä)	167	60°51'N	26°40'E
Kouzhen, China (kō-jŭn)	206	36°19'N	117°37'E
Kovda, l., Russia (kôv'dȧ)	180	66°45'N	32°00'E
Kovel', Ukr. (kō'vĕl)	181	51°13'N	24°45'E
Kovno *see* Kaunas, Lith.	178	54°42'N	23°54'E
Kovrov, Russia (kôv-rôf')	180	56°23'N	41°21'E
Koyuk, Ak., U.S. (kō-yōōk')	103	65°00'N	161°18'W
Koyukuk, r., Ak., U.S. (kō-yōō'kòk)	103	66°25'N	153°50'W
Kozáni, Grc.	163	40°16'N	21°51'E
Kozelets', Ukr. (kôzĕ-lyĕts)	177	50°53'N	31°07'E
Kozel'sk, Russia (kô-zĕlsk')	176	54°01'N	35°49'E
Kozhikode, India	199	11°19'N	75°49'E

ăt; finăl; rāte; senåte; ärm; ȧsk; sofȧ; fâre; ch-choose; dh-as th in other; bē; ėvent; bĕt; recĕnt; cratẽr; g-gō; gh-guttural g; bĭt; ĭ-short neutral; rīde; κ-guttural k as ch in German ich;

L

ăt; finȧl; rāte; senȧte; ärm; ȧsk; sofȧ; fâre; ch-choose; dh-as th in other; bē; ĕvent; bĕt; recĕnt; crætĕr; g-gō; gh-guttural g; bĭt; ī-short neutral; rīde; ᴋ-guttural k as ch in German ich;

PRONOUNCING INDEX
L'Anse and Vieux Desert – Leivádia 313

PLACE (Pronunciation)	PAGE	LAT.	LONG.
L'Anse and Vieux Desert Indian Reservation, I.R., Mi., U.S.	113	46°41'N	88°12'W
Lansford, Pa., U.S. (lănz´fērd)	109	40°50'N	75°50'W
Lansing, Ia., U.S.	113	43°22'N	91°16'W
Lansing, Il., U.S.	111a	41°34'N	87°33'W
Lansing, Ks., U.S.	117f	39°15'N	94°53'W
Lansing, Mi., U.S.	105	42°45'N	84°35'W
Lanús, Arg. (lä-nōōs´)	144a	34°42'S	58°24'W
Lanusei, Italy (lä-nōō-sĕ´y)	174	39°51'N	9°34'E
Lanúvio, Italy (lä-nōō´vyô)	173d	41°41'N	12°42'E
Lanzarote Island, i., Spain (län-zȧ-rō´tā)	230	29°04'N	13°03'W
Lanzhou, China (län-jō)	204	35°55'N	103°55'E
Laoag, Phil. (lä-wäg´)	212	18°13'N	120°38'E
Laon, Fr. (län)	170	49°36'N	3°35'E
La Oroya, Peru (lä-ô-rŏ´yă)	142	11°30'S	76°00'W
Laos, nation, Asia (lā-ōs) (lȧ-ōs´)	212	20°15'N	102°00'E
Laoshan Wan, b., China (lou-shän wän)	206	36°21'N	120°48'E
La Palma, Pan. (lä-päl´mä)	133	8°25'N	78°07'W
La Palma, Spain	172	37°24'N	6°36'W
La Palma Island, i., Spain	230	28°42'N	19°03'W
La Pampa, prov., Arg.	144	37°25'S	67°00'W
Lapa Rio Negro, Braz. (lä-pä-rē´ō-nĕ´grô)	144	26°12'S	49°56'W
La Paz, Arg. (lä päz´)	144	30°48'S	59°47'W
La Paz, Bol.	142	16°31'S	68°03'W
La Paz, Hond.	132	14°15'N	87°40'W
La Paz, Mex. (lä-pá´z)	130	23°39'N	100°44'W
La Paz, Mex.	128	24°00'N	110°15'W
Lapeer, Mi., U.S. (lȧ-pēr´)	108	43°05'N	83°15'W
La-Penne-sur-Huveaune, Fr. (la-pĕn´sür-ü-vōn´)	170a	43°18'N	5°33'E
La Perouse, Austl.	217b	33°59'S	151°14'E
La Piedad Cabadas, Mex. (lä pyā-dhädh´ kä-bä´dhäs)	130	20°20'N	102°04'W
Lapland, hist. reg., Eur. (lăp´lȧnd)	154	68°20'N	22°00'E
La Plata, Arg. (lä plä´tä)	144	34°54'S	57°57'W
La Plata, Mo., U.S. (lȧ plā´tȧ)	121	40°03'N	92°28'W
La Plata Peak, mtn., Co., U.S.	119	39°00'N	106°25'W
La Pocatière, Can. (lá pô-ká-tyår´)	99	47°24'N	70°01'W
La Poile Bay, b., Can. (lá pwäl´)	101	47°38'N	58°20'W
La Porte, In., U.S. (lȧ pōrt´)	108	41°35'N	86°45'W
Laporte, Oh., U.S.	111d	41°19'N	82°05'W
La Porte, Tx., U.S.	123a	29°40'N	95°01'W
La Porte City, Ia., U.S.	113	42°20'N	92°10'W
Lappeenranta, Fin. (lä´pēn-rän´tä)	167	61°04'N	28°08'E
La Prairie, Can. (lá-prå-rē´)	102a	45°24'N	73°30'W
Lâpseki, Tur. (läp´sá-kē)	175	40°20'N	26°41'E
Laptev Sea, sea, Russia (läp´tyĭf)	179	75°39'N	120°00'E
La Puebla de Montalbán, Spain	172	39°54'N	4°21'W
La Puente, Ca., U.S. (pwĕn´tē)	117a	34°01'N	117°57'W
Lapușul, r., Rom. (lä´pōō-shōōl)	169	47°29'N	23°46'E
La Quiaca, Arg. (lä kē-ä´kä)	144	22°15'S	65°44'W
L'Aquila, Italy (lä´kē-lä)	162	42°22'N	13°24'E
Lār, Iran (lär)	198	27°31'N	54°12'E
Lara, Austl.	217a	38°02'S	144°24'E
Larache, Mor. (lä-räsh´)	230	35°15'N	6°09'W
Laramie, Wy., U.S. (lăr´ȧ-mĭ)	104	41°20'N	105°40'W
Laramie, r., Co., U.S.	120	40°56'N	105°55'W
Larchmont, N.Y., U.S. (lärch´mŏnt)	110a	40°56'N	73°46'W
Larch Mountain, mtn., Or., U.S. (lärch)	116c	45°32'N	122°06'W
Laredo, Spain (lä-rā´dhō)	172	43°24'N	3°24'W
Laredo, Tx., U.S.	104	27°31'N	99°29'W
La Réole, Fr. (lá rå-ōl´)	170	44°37'N	0°03'W
Largeau, Chad (lär-zhō´)	231	17°55'N	19°07'E
Largo, Cayo, Cuba (kä´yō-lär´gō)	134	21°40'N	81°30'W
Larimore, N.D., U.S. (lăr´ĭ-môr)	112	47°53'N	97°38'W
Larino, Italy (lä-rē´nô)	174	41°48'N	14°54'E
La Rioja, Arg. (lä rê-ōhä)	144	29°18'S	67°42'W
La Rioja, prov., Arg. (lä-rê-ō´kä)	144	28°45'S	68°00'W
Lárisa, Grc. (lä´rê-sá)	163	39°38'N	22°25'E
Lārkāna, Pak.	202	27°40'N	68°12'E
Larnaka, Cyp.	163	34°55'N	33°37'E
Lárnakos, Kólpos, b., Cyp.	197a	36°50'N	33°45'E
Larned, Ks., U.S. (lär´nĕd)	120	38°09'N	99°07'W
La Robla, Spain (lä rōb´lä)	172	42°48'N	5°36'W
La Rochelle, Fr. (lá rô-shĕl´)	154	46°10'N	1°09'W
La Roche-sur-Yon, Fr. (lá rôsh´sûr-yôn´)	161	46°39'N	1°27'W
La Roda, Spain (lä rō´dä)	172	39°13'N	2°08'W
La Romona, Dom. Rep. (lä-rä-mô´nä)	135	18°25'N	69°00'W
Larrey Point, c., Austl. (lăr´ē)	220	19°15'S	118°15'E
Laruns, Fr. (lá-răns´)	170	42°58'N	0°28'W
Larvik, Nor. (lär´vĕk)	160	59°06'N	10°03'E
La Sabana, Ven. (lä-sä-bá´nä)	143b	10°38'N	66°24'W
La Sabina, Cuba (lä-sä-bē´nä)	135a	22°51'N	82°05'W
La Sagra, mtn., Spain (lä sä´grä)	162	37°56'N	2°35'W
La Sal, Ut., U.S. (lá sál´)	119	38°10'N	109°20'W
La Salle, Can. (lȧ sál´)	111b	42°14'N	83°06'W
La Salle, Can.	102a	45°26'N	73°39'W
La Salle, Can.	102f	49°41'N	97°16'W
La Salle, Il., U.S.	108	41°20'N	89°05'W
Las Animas, Co., U.S. (lás ä´nĭ-más)	120	38°03'N	103°16'W
La Sarre, Can.	91	48°43'N	79°12'W
Lascahobas, Haiti (läs-kä-ō´bás)	135	19°00'N	71°55'W
Las Cruces, Mex. (läs-krōō´sĕs)	131	16°37'N	93°54'W
Las Cruces, N.M., U.S.	104	32°20'N	106°50'W
La Selle, Massif de, mtn., Haiti (lä´sĕl´)	135	18°25'N	72°05'W
La Serena, Chile (lä-sĕ-rē´nä)	144	29°55'S	71°24'W
La Seyne, Fr. (lä-sån´)	161	43°07'N	5°52'E
Las Flores, Arg. (läs flo´rĕs)	144	36°01'S	59°07'W
Lashio, Mya. (lăsh´ē-ō)	204	22°58'N	98°03'E
Las Juntas, C.R. (läs-kōō´n-täs)	132	10°15'N	85°00'W
Las Maismas, sw., Spain (läs-mī´s-mäs)	172	37°05'N	6°25'W
La Solana, Spain (lä-sô-lä-nä)	172	38°56'N	3°13'W
Las Palmas, Pan.	133	8°08'N	81°30'W
Las Palmas de Gran Canaria, Spain (läs päl´mäs)	230	28°07'N	15°28'W
La Spezia, Italy (lä-spĕ´zyä)	154	44°07'N	9°48'E
Las Piedras, Ur. (läs-pyĕ´dräs)	141c	34°42'S	56°08'W
Las Pilas, vol., Nic. (läs-pē´läs)	132	12°32'N	86°43'W
Las Rosas, Mex. (läs rō thäs)	131	16°24'N	92°23'W
Las Rozas de Madrid, Spain (läs rō´thas dā mä-dhrēd´)	173a	40°29'N	3°53'W
Lassee, Aus.	159e	48°14'N	16°50'E
Lassen Peak, mtn., Ca., U.S. (lăs´ĕn)	106	40°30'N	121°32'W
Lassen Volcanic National Park, rec., Ca., U.S.	106	40°43'N	121°35'W
L'Assomption, Can. (lás-sôm-syôn)	102a	45°50'N	73°25'W
Lass Qoray, Som.	230a	11°13'N	48°19'E
Las Tablas, Pan. (läs tä´bläs)	133	7°48'N	80°16'W
Last Mountain, l., Can. (lást moun´tĭn)	92	51°05'N	105°10'W
Lastoursville, Gabon (lás-tōōr-vēl´)	232	1°00'S	12°49'E
Las Tres Vírgenes, Volcán, vol., Mex. (vē´r-hĕ-nĕs)	128	26°00'N	111°45'W
Las Tunas, prov., Cuba	134	21°05'N	77°00'W
Las Vacas, Mex. (läs-vá´käs)	131	16°24'N	95°48'W
Las Vegas, Chile (läs-vĕ´gäs)	141b	32°50'S	70°59'W
Las Vegas, N.M., U.S.	104	35°36'N	105°13'W
Las Vegas, Nv., U.S. (läs vā´gäs)	104	36°12'N	115°10'W
Las Vegas, Ven. (läs-vĕ´gäs)	143b	10°26'N	64°08'W
Las Vigas, Mex.	131	19°38'N	97°03'W
Las Vizcachas, Meseta de, plat., Arg.	144	49°35'S	71°00'W
Latacunga, Ec. (lä-tä-kōŋ´gä)	142	1°02'S	78°33'W
Latakia see Al Lādhiqīyah, Syria	198	35°32'N	35°51'E
La Teste-de-Buch, Fr. (lä-tĕst-dĕ-büsh)	170	44°38'N	1°11'W
Lathrop, Mo., U.S. (lā´thrŭp)	121	39°32'N	94°21'W
La Tortuga, Isla, i., Ven. (ĕ´s-lä-lä-tôr-tōō´gä)	142	10°55'N	65°18'W
Latorytsia, r., Eur.	169	48°27'N	22°30'E
Latourell, Or., U.S. (lá-tou´rĕl)	116c	45°32'N	122°13'W
La Tremblade, Fr. (lä-trĕn-bläd´)	170	45°45'N	1°12'W
Latrobe, Pa., U.S. (lá-trōb´)	109	40°25'N	79°15'W
La Tuque, Can. (lá´tük´)	91	47°27'N	72°49'W
Lātūr, India (lä-tōōr´)	202	18°20'N	76°35'E
Latvia, nation, Eur.	178	57°28'N	24°29'E
Lau Group, is., Fiji	214g	18°20'S	178°30'W
Launceston, Austl. (lôn´sĕs-tŭn)	219	41°35'S	147°22'E
Launceston, Eng., U.K. (lôrn´stŏn)	164	50°38'N	4°26'W
La Unión, Chile (lä-ōō-nyô´n)	144	40°15'S	73°04'W
La Unión, El Sal.	132	13°18'N	87°51'W
La Unión, Mex. (lä ōōn-nyōn´)	130	17°59'N	101°48'W
La Unión, Spain	162	37°38'N	0°50'W
Laura, Austl. (lôrá)	219	15°40'S	144°45'E
Laurel, De., U.S. (lô´rĕl)	109	38°30'N	75°40'W
Laurel, Md., U.S.	110e	39°06'N	76°51'W
Laurel, Ms., U.S.	105	31°42'N	89°07'W
Laurel, Mt., U.S.	115	45°41'N	108°45'W
Laurel, Wa., U.S.	116d	48°52'N	122°29'W
Laurelwood, Or., U.S. (lô´rĕl-wŏd)	116c	45°25'N	123°05'W
Laurens, S.C., U.S. (lô´rĕnz)	125	34°29'N	82°03'W
Laurentian Highlands, hills, Can. (lô´rĕn-tĭ-ăn)	89	49°00'N	74°50'W
Laurentides, Can. (lô´rĕn-tīdz)	102a	45°51'N	73°46'W
Lauria, Italy (lou´rē-ä)	163	40°03'N	15°02'E
Laurinburg, N.C., U.S. (lô´rĭn-bûrg)	125	34°45'N	79°27'W
Laurium, Mi., U.S. (lô´rĭ-ŭm)	113	47°13'N	88°28'W
Lausanne, Switz. (lō-zán´)	154	46°32'N	6°35'E
Laut, Pulau, i., Indon.	212	3°39'S	116°07'E
Lautaro, Chile (lou-tä´rô)	144	38°40'S	72°24'W
Laut Kecil, Kepulauan, is., Indon.	212	4°44'S	115°43'E
Lautoka, Fiji	214g	17°37'S	177°27'E
Lauzon, Can. (lō-zōn´)	102b	46°50'N	71°10'W
Lava Beds National Monument, rec., Ca., U.S. (lä´vá bĕds)	114	41°38'N	121°44'W
Lavaca, r., Tx., U.S. (lá-vák´á)	123	29°05'N	96°50'W
Lava Hot Springs, Id., U.S.	115	42°37'N	111°58'W
Laval, Can.	91	45°31'N	73°44'W
Laval, Fr. (lä-väl´)	161	48°05'N	0°47'W
La Vecilla de Curueño, Spain	172	42°53'N	5°18'W
La Vega, Dom. Rep. (lä-vĕ´gä)	135	19°15'N	70°35'W
Lavello, Italy (lä-vĕl´lô)	174	41°05'N	15°50'E
La Verne, Ca., U.S. (lá vûrn´)	117a	34°06'N	117°46'W
Laverton, Austl. (lā´vĕr-tŭn)	218	28°45'S	122°30'E
La Victoria, Ven. (lä vêk-tō´rē-ä)	142	10°14'N	67°20'W
La Vila Joiosa, Spain	173	38°30'N	0°14'W
Lavonia, Ga., U.S. (lá-vō´nĭ-á)	124	34°26'N	83°05'W
Lavon Reservoir, res., Tx., U.S.	123	33°06'N	96°20'W
Lavras, Braz. (lä´vräzh)	141a	21°15'S	44°59'W
Lávrio, Grc.	175	37°44'N	24°05'E
Lavry, Russia (lou´rá)	176	57°35'N	27°28'E
Lawndale, Ca., U.S. (lôn´dāl)	117a	33°54'N	118°22'W
Lawra, Ghana	234	10°39'N	2°52'W
Lawrence, In., U.S. (lô´rĕns)	111g	39°59'N	86°01'W
Lawrence, Ks., U.S.	105	38°57'N	95°13'W
Lawrence, Ma., U.S.	101a	42°42'N	71°09'W
Lawrence, Pa., U.S.	111e	40°18'N	80°07'W
Lawrenceburg, In., U.S. (lô´rĕns-bûrg)	111f	39°06'N	84°47'W
Lawrenceburg, Ky., U.S.	108	38°00'N	85°00'W
Lawrenceburg, Tn., U.S.	124	35°13'N	87°20'W
Lawrenceville, Ga., U.S. (lô-rĕns-vĭl)	124	33°56'N	83°57'W
Lawrenceville, Il., U.S.	108	38°45'N	87°45'W
Lawrenceville, N.J., U.S.	110a	40°17'N	74°44'W
Lawrenceville, Va., U.S.	125	36°43'N	77°52'W
Lawsonia, Md., U.S. (lô-sō´nĭ-á)	109	38°00'N	75°50'W
Lawton, Ok., U.S. (lô´tŭn)	104	34°36'N	98°25'W
Lawz, Jabal al, mtn., Sau. Ar.	198	28°46'N	35°37'E
Layang Layang, Malay. (lä-yäng´ lä-yäng´)	197b	1°49'N	103°28'E
Laysan, i., Hi., U.S.	126b	26°00'N	171°00'W
Layton, Ut., U.S. (lā´tŭn)	117b	41°04'N	111°58'W
Lazdijai, Lith. (läzh´dē-yī´)	167	54°12'N	23°35'E
Lazio (Latium), hist. reg., Italy	174	42°05'N	12°25'E
Lead, S.D., U.S. (lēd)	104	44°22'N	103°47'W
Leader, Can.	96	50°55'N	109°32'W
Leadville, Co., U.S. (lĕd´vĭl)	120	39°14'N	106°18'W
Leaf, r., Ms., U.S. (lēf)	124	31°43'N	89°20'W
League City, Tx., U.S. (lēg)	123a	29°31'N	95°05'W
Leamington, Can. (lĕm´ĭng-tŭn)	98	42°05'N	82°35'W
Leamington, Eng., U.K. (lĕ´mĭng-tŭn)	164	52°17'N	1°25'W
Leatherhead, Eng., U.K. (lĕth´ēr-hĕd´)	158b	51°17'N	0°20'W
Leavenworth, Ks., U.S. (lĕv´ĕn-wûrth)	105	39°19'N	94°54'W
Leavenworth, Wa., U.S.	114	47°35'N	120°39'W
Leawood, Ks., U.S. (lē´wŏd)	117f	38°58'N	94°37'W
Łeba, Pol. (lā´bä)	169	54°45'N	17°34'E
Lebam, r., Malay.	197b	1°35'N	104°09'E
Lebango, Congo	236	0°22'N	14°49'E
Lebanon, Il., U.S. (lĕb´á-nŭn)	117e	38°36'N	89°49'W
Lebanon, In., U.S.	108	40°00'N	86°30'W
Lebanon, Ky., U.S.	124	37°32'N	85°15'W
Lebanon, Mo., U.S.	121	37°40'N	92°43'W
Lebanon, N.H., U.S.	109	43°40'N	72°15'W
Lebanon, Oh., U.S.	108	39°25'N	84°10'W
Lebanon, Or., U.S.	114	44°31'N	122°53'W
Lebanon, Pa., U.S.	109	40°20'N	76°20'W
Lebanon, Tn., U.S.	124	36°10'N	86°16'W
Lebanon, nation, Asia	198	34°00'N	34°00'E
Lebedyan', Russia (lyĕ´bĕ-dyän´)	180	53°03'N	39°08'E
Lebedyn, Ukr.	181	50°34'N	34°27'E
Le Blanc, Fr. (lĕ-blän´)	170	46°38'N	0°59'E
Le Borgne, Haiti (lē bōrn´y´)	135	19°50'N	72°30'W
Lębork, Pol. (lăn-bòrk´)	169	54°33'N	17°46'E
Lebrija, Spain (lå-brē´hä)	172	36°55'N	6°06'W
Lecce, Italy (lĕt´chā)	163	40°22'N	18°11'E
Lecco, Italy (lĕk´kō)	174	45°52'N	9°28'E
Lech, r., Ger. (lĕk)	168	47°41'N	10°52'E
Le Châtelet-en-Brie, Fr. (lĕ-shä-tĕ-lā´ĕn-brē´)	171b	48°29'N	2°50'E
Leche, Laguna de, l., Cuba (lä-gō´nä-dĕ-lĕ´chĕ)	134	22°10'N	78°30'W
Leche, Laguna de la, l., Mex.	122	27°16'N	102°45'W
Lecompte, La., U.S.	123	31°06'N	92°25'W
Le Creusot, Fr. (lĕkrû-zō)	161	46°48'N	4°23'E
Ledesma, Spain (lå-dĕs´mä)	172	41°05'N	5°59'W
Leduc, Can. (lĕ-dōōk´)	95	53°16'N	113°33'W
Leech, l., Mn., U.S. (lēch)	113	47°06'N	94°16'W
Leeds, Eng., U.K.	154	53°48'N	1°33'W
Leeds, Al., U.S. (lēdz)	110h	33°33'N	86°33'W
Leeds, N.D., U.S.	112	48°18'N	99°24'W
Leeds, co., Eng., U.K.	158a	53°50'N	1°30'W
Leeds and Liverpool Canal, can., Eng., U.K. (lĭv´ēr-pōōl)	158a	53°36'N	2°38'W
Leegebruch, Ger. (lĕh´gĕn-brōōk)	159b	52°43'N	13°12'E
Leek, Eng., U.K. (lēk)	158a	53°06'N	2°01'W
Leer, Ger. (lār)	168	53°14'N	7°27'E
Leesburg, Fl., U.S. (lēz´bûrg)	125	28°49'N	81°53'W
Leesburg, Va., U.S.	109	39°10'N	77°30'W
Lees Summit, Mo., U.S.	117f	38°55'N	94°23'W
Lee Stocking, i., Bah.	134	23°45'N	76°05'W
Leesville, La., U.S. (lēz´vĭl)	123	31°09'N	93°17'W
Leetonia, Oh., U.S. (lē-tō´nĭ-á)	108	40°50'N	80°45'W
Leeuwarden, Neth. (lā´wär-dĕn)	161	52°12'N	5°50'E
Leeuwin, Cape, c., Austl. (lōō´wĭn)	220	34°15'S	114°30'E
Leeward Islands, is., N.A. (lē´wērd)	123	17°00'N	62°15'W
Lefkáda, Grc.	175	38°49'N	20°43'E
Lefkáda, i., Grc.	163	38°42'N	20°22'E
Le François, Mart.	133b	14°37'N	60°55'W
Lefroy, l., Austl. (lē-froi´)	220	31°30'S	122°00'E
Leganés, Spain (lå-gä´nås)	173a	40°20'N	3°46'W
Legazpi, Phil. (lå-gäs´pē)	213	13°09'N	123°44'E
Legge Peak, mtn., Austl. (lĕg)	222	41°33'S	148°10'E
Leggett, Ca., U.S.	118	39°51'N	123°42'W
Leghorn see Livorno, Italy	154	43°32'N	11°18'E
Legnano, Italy (lå-nyä´nō)	174	45°35'N	8°53'E
Legnica, Pol. (lĕk-nĭt´sá)	161	51°13'N	16°10'E
Leh, India (lā)	202	34°10'N	77°40'E
Le Havre, Fr. (lē äv´r´)	154	49°31'N	0°07'E
Lehi, Ut., U.S. (lē´hī)	119	40°25'N	111°55'W
Lehman Caves National Monument, rec., Nv., U.S. (lē´mán)	119	38°54'N	114°08'W
Lehnin, Ger. (lĕh´nēn)	159b	52°19'N	12°45'E
Leicester, Eng., U.K. (lĕs´tēr)	154	52°37'N	1°08'W
Leicestershire, co., Eng., U.K.	158a	52°40'N	1°12'W
Leichhardt, r., Austl. (līk´härt)	220	18°30'S	139°45'E
Leiden, Neth. (lī´dĕn)	165	52°09'N	4°29'E
Leigh Creek, Austl. (lē krēk)	222	30°33'S	138°30'E
Leikanger, Nor. (lī´käŋ´gēr)	166	61°11'N	6°51'E
Leimuiden, Neth.	159a	52°13'N	4°40'E
Leine, r., Ger. (lī´nĕ)	168	51°58'N	9°56'E
Leinster, hist. reg., Ire. (lĕn-stēr)	164	52°45'N	7°19'W
Leipsic, Oh., U.S. (līp´sĭk)	108	41°05'N	84°00'W
Leipzig, Ger. (līp´tsĭk)	154	51°20'N	12°24'E
Leiria, Port. (lā-rē´ä)	172	39°45'N	8°50'W
Leitchfield, Ky., U.S. (lēch´fēld)	124	37°28'N	86°20'W
Leitha, r., Aus.	159e	48°04'N	16°57'E
Leitrim, Can.	102c	45°20'N	75°36'W
Leivádia, Grc.	175	38°25'N	22°51'E

ng-sing; ŋ-baŋk; ɴ-nasalized n; nŏd; cŏmmit; ōld; ŏbey; ôrder; oi-boil; fōōd; ŏ-as oo in foot; ou-out; s-soft; sh-dish; th-thin; pūre; ûnite; ûrn; stŭd; circŭs; ü-as in French tu; ´-indeterminate vowel.

ăt; fīnăl; rāte; senâte; ärm; ȧsk; sofȧ; fâre; ch-choose; dh-as th in other; bē; ĕvent; bĕt; recĕnt; cratẽr; g-gō; gh-guttural g; bĭt; ī-short neutral; rīde; ᴋ-guttural k as ch in German ich;

PLACE (Pronunciation)	PAGE	LAT.	LONG.
Lincolnshire, co., Eng., U.K.	158a	53°12'N	0°29'W
Lincolnshire Wolds, Eng., U.K. (woldz')	164	53°25'N	0°23'W
Lincolnton, N.C., U.S. (lĭŋ'kŭn-tŭn)	125	35°27'N	81°15'W
Lindale, Ga., U.S. (lĭn'dāl)	124	34°10'N	85°10'W
Lindau, Ger. (lĭn'dou)	168	47°33'N	9°40'E
Linden, Al., U.S. (lĭn'dĕn)	124	32°16'N	87°47'W
Linden, Mo., U.S.	117f	39°13'N	94°35'W
Linden, N.J., U.S.	110a	40°39'N	74°14'W
Lindenhurst, N.Y., U.S. (lĭn'dĕn-hûrst)	110a	40°41'N	73°23'W
Lindenwold, N.J., U.S. (lĭn'dĕn-wôld)	110f	39°50'N	75°00'W
Lindesberg, Swe. (lĭn'dĕs-bĕrgh)	166	59°37'N	15°14'E
Lindesnes, c., Nor. (lĭn'ĕs-nĕs)	156	58°00'N	7°05'E
Lindi, Tan. (lĭn'dē)	233	10°00'S	39°43'E
Lindi, r., D.R.C.	231	1°00'N	27°13'E
Lindian, China (lĭn-dĭĕn)	208	47°08'N	124°59'E
Lindley, S. Afr. (lĭnd'lē)	238c	27°52'S	27°55'E
Lindow, Ger. (lēn'dōv)	159b	52°50'N	12°59'E
Lindsay, Can. (lĭn'zē)	99	44°20'N	78°45'W
Lindsay, Ok., U.S.	121	34°50'N	97°38'W
Lindsborg, Ks., U.S. (lĭnz'bôrg)	121	38°34'N	97°42'W
Lineville, Al., U.S. (līn'vĭl)	124	33°18'N	85°45'W
Linfen, China	205	36°00'N	111°38'E
Linga, Kepulauan, is., Indon.	212	0°35'S	105°05'E
Lingao, China (lĭn-gou)	209	19°58'N	109°40'E
Lingayen, Phil. (lĭŋ'gä-yān')	212	16°01'N	120°13'E
Lingayen Gulf, b., Phil.	213a	16°18'N	120°11'E
Lingdianzhen, China	206	31°52'N	121°28'E
Lingen, Ger. (lĭŋ'gĕn)	168	52°32'N	7°20'E
Lingling, China (lĭŋ-lĭŋ)	209	26°10'N	111°40'E
Lingshou, China (lĭŋ-shō)	206	38°21'N	114°41'E
Linguère, Sen. (lĭŋ-gĕr')	230	15°24'N	15°07'W
Lingwu, China	208	38°05'N	106°18'E
Lingyuan, China (lĭŋ-yůän)	208	41°12'N	119°20'E
Linhai, China	209	28°52'N	121°08'E
Linhe, China (lĭn-hŭ)	208	40°49'N	107°45'E
Linhuaiguan, China (lĭn-hwī-gůän)	206	32°55'N	117°38'E
Linhuanji, China	206	33°42'N	116°33'E
Linjiang, China (lĭn-jyäŋ)	208	41°45'N	127°00'E
Linköping, Swe. (lĭn'chû-pĭng)	160	58°25'N	15°35'E
Linnhe, Loch, b., Scot., U.K. (lĭn'ē)	164	56°35'N	4°30'W
Linqing, China (lĭn-chyĭŋ)	205	36°49'N	115°42'E
Linqu, China (lĭn-chyōō)	206	36°31'N	118°33'E
Lins, Braz. (lē'ns)	143	21°42'S	49°41'W
Linthicum Heights, Md., U.S. (lĭn'thĭ-kŭm)	110e	39°12'N	76°39'W
Linton, In., U.S. (lĭn'tŭn)	108	39°05'N	87°15'W
Linton, N.D., U.S.	112	46°16'N	100°15'W
Linwu, China (lĭn'wōō')	209	25°20'N	112°30'E
Linxi, China (lĭn-shyē)	208	43°30'N	118°02'E
Linyi, China (lĭn-yē)	205	35°04'N	118°21'E
Linying, China (lĭn'yĭng')	206	33°48'N	113°56'E
Linz, Aus. (lĭnts)	161	48°18'N	14°18'E
Linzhang, China (lĭn-jäŋ)	206	36°19'N	114°40'E
Lion, Golfe du, b., Fin.	156	43°00'N	4°00'E
Lipa, Phil. (lē-pä')	212	13°55'N	121°10'E
Lipari, Italy (lē'pä-rē)	174	38°29'N	15°00'E
Lipari, i., Italy	174	38°32'N	15°04'E
Lipetsk, Russia (lyē'pĕtsk)	178	52°26'N	39°34'E
Lipetsk, prov., Russia	176	52°18'N	38°30'E
Liping, China (lē-pĭŋ)	204	26°18'N	109°00'E
Lipno, Pol. (lēp'nō)	169	52°50'N	19°12'E
Lippe, r., Ger. (lĭp'ĕ)	171b	51°36'N	6°45'E
Lippstadt, Ger. (lĭp'shtät)	168	51°39'N	8°20'E
Lipscomb, Al., U.S. (lĭp'skŭm)	110h	33°26'N	86°56'W
Lipu, China (lē-pōō)	209	24°38'N	110°35'E
Lira, Ug.	237	2°15'N	32°54'E
Liri, r., Italy (lē'rē)	174	41°49'N	13°30'E
Lisala, D.R.C. (lē-sä'lä)	231	2°09'N	21°31'E
Lisboa *see* Lisbon, Port.	154	38°42'N	9°05'W
Lisbon (Lisboa), Port.	154	38°42'N	9°05'W
Lisbon, N.D., U.S.	112	46°21'N	97°43'W
Lisbon, Oh., U.S.	108	40°45'N	80°50'W
Lisbon Falls, Me., U.S.	100	43°59'N	70°03'W
Lisburn, N. Ire., U.K. (lĭs'bŭrn)	164	54°35'N	6°05'W
Lisburne, Cape, c., Ak., U.S.	106a	68°20'N	165°40'W
Lishi, China (lē-shr)	208	37°32'N	111°12'E
Lishu, China	208	43°12'N	124°18'E
Lishui, China (lĭ'shwĭ')	206	31°41'N	119°01'E
Lishui, China	205	28°28'N	120°00'E
Lisianski Island, i., Hi., U.S.	126b	25°30'N	174°00'W
Lisieux, Fr. (lē-zyû')	170	49°10'N	0°13'E
Lisiy Nos, Russia (lĭ'sĭy-nôs)	186c	60°01'N	30°00'E
Liski, Russia (lyēs'kē)	177	50°56'N	39°28'E
Lisle, Il., U.S. (lĭl)	111a	41°48'N	88°04'W
L'Isle-Adam, Fr. (lēl-ädän')	171b	49°05'N	2°13'E
Lismore, Austl. (lĭz'môr)	219	28°48'S	153°18'E
Litani, r., Leb.	197a	33°28'N	35°42'E
Litchfield, Il., U.S. (lĭch'fēld)	121	39°10'N	89°38'W
Litchfield, Mn., U.S.	113	45°08'N	94°34'W
Litchfield, Oh., U.S.	111d	41°10'N	82°01'W
Lithgow, Austl. (lĭth'gō)	219	33°23'S	149°31'E
Lithinon, Akra, c., Grc.	174a	34°59'N	24°35'E
Lithonia, Ga., U.S. (lĭ-thō'nĭ-å)	110c	33°43'N	84°07'W
Lithuania, nation, Eur. (lĭth-ů-ā'-nĭ-å)	178	55°42'N	23°30'E
Litóchoro, Grc.	175	40°05'N	22°29'E
Litoko, D.R.C.	236	1°13'S	24°47'E
Litoměřice, Czech Rep. (lē'tô-myĕr'zhĭ-tsĕ)	168	50°33'N	14°10'E
Litomyšl, Czech Rep. (lē'tô-mêsh'l)	168	49°52'N	16°14'E
Litoo, Tan.	237	9°45'S	38°24'E
Little, r., Austl.	217a	37°54'S	144°27'E
Little, r., Tn., U.S.	124	36°28'N	89°39'W
Little, r., Tx., U.S.	123	30°48'N	96°50'W
Little Abaco, i., Bah. (ä'bä-kō)	134	26°55'N	77°45'W
Little Abitibi, r., Can.	98	50°15'N	81°30'W
Little America, sci., Ant.	224	78°30'S	161°30'W
Little Andaman, i., India (ăn-då-măn')	212	10°39'N	93°08'E
Little Bahama Bank, bk. (bå-hā'må)	134	26°55'N	78°40'W
Little Belt Mountains, mts., Mt., U.S. (bĕlt)	106	47°00'N	110°50'W
Little Bighorn, r., Mt., U.S. (bĭg-hôrn)	115	45°08'N	107°30'W
Little Bighorn Battlefield National Monument, rec., Mt., U.S. (bĭg-hôrn băt''l-fēld)	115	45°44'N	107°15'W
Little Bitter Lake, l., Egypt	238b	30°10'N	32°36'E
Little Bitterroot, r., Mt., U.S. (bĭt'ẽr-ōōt)	115	47°45'N	114°45'W
Little Blue, r., Ia., U.S. (blōō)	117f	38°52'N	94°25'W
Little Blue, r., Ne., U.S.	120	40°15'N	98°01'W
Littleborough, Eng., U.K. (lĭt''l-bŭr-ō)	158a	53°39'N	2°06'W
Little Calumet, r., Il., U.S. (kăl-ů-mĕt')	111a	41°38'N	87°38'W
Little Cayman, i., Cay. Is. (kā'mån)	134	19°40'N	80°05'W
Little Colorado, r., Az., U.S. (kŏl-ō-rā'dō)	106	36°05'N	111°35'W
Little Compton, R.I., U.S. (kŏmp'tŏn)	110b	41°31'N	71°07'W
Little Corn Island, i., Nic.	133	12°19'N	82°50'W
Little Exuma, i., Bah. (ĕk-sōō'mä)	135	23°25'N	75°40'W
Little Falls, Mn., U.S. (fôlz)	113	45°58'N	94°23'W
Little Falls, N.Y., U.S.	109	43°05'N	74°55'W
Littlefield, Tx., U.S. (lĭt''l-fēld)	120	33°55'N	102°17'W
Little Fork, r., Mn., U.S. (fôrk)	113	48°24'N	93°30'W
Little Goose Dam, dam, Wa., U.S.	114	46°35'N	118°02'W
Little Hans Lollick, i., V.I.U.S. (häns lŏl'lĭk)	129c	18°25'N	64°54'W
Little Humboldt, r., Nv., U.S. (hŭm'bōlt)	114	41°10'N	117°40'W
Little Inagua, i., Bah. (ē-nä'gwä)	135	21°30'N	73°00'W
Little Isaac, i., Bah. (ĭ'zåk)	134	25°55'N	79°00'W
Little Kanawha, r., W.V., U.S. (kå-nô'wå)	108	39°05'N	81°30'W
Little Karroo, plat., S. Afr. (kä-rōō)	232	33°50'S	21°02'E
Little Mecatina, r., Can. (mĕ cå tĭ nå)	93	52°40'N	62°21'W
Little Miami, r., Oh., U.S. (mī-ăm'ĭ)	111f	39°19'N	84°15'W
Little Minch, strt., Scot., U.K.	164	57°35'N	6°45'W
Little Missouri, r., Ar., U.S. (mĭ-sōō'rĭ)	121	34°15'N	93°54'W
Little Missouri, r., U.S.	106	46°00'N	104°00'W
Little Pee Dee, r., S.C., U.S. (pē-dē')	125	34°35'N	79°21'W
Little Powder, r., Wy., U.S. (pou'dẽr)	115	44°51'N	105°20'W
Little Red, r., Ar., U.S. (rĕd)	121	35°25'N	91°55'W
Little Red, r., Ok., U.S.	121	33°53'N	94°38'W
Little Rock, Ar., U.S. (rôk)	105	34°42'N	92°16'W
Little Sachigo Lake, l., Can. (să'chĭ-gō)	97	54°09'N	92°11'W
Little Salt Lake, l., Ut., U.S.	119	37°55'N	112°53'W
Little San Salvador, i., Bah. (săn săl'vå-dôr)	135	24°35'N	75°55'W
Little Satilla, r., Ga., U.S. (så-tĭl'å)	125	31°43'N	82°47'W
Little Sioux, r., Ia., U.S. (sōō)	112	42°22'N	95°47'W
Little Smoky, r., Can. (smōk'ĭ)	95	55°10'N	116°55'W
Little Snake, r., Co., U.S. (snāk)	115	40°40'N	108°21'W
Little Tallapoosa, r., Al., U.S. (tăl-å-pōō'så)	124	32°25'N	85°28'W
Little Tennessee, r., Tn., U.S. (tĕn-ĕ-sē')	124	35°36'N	84°05'W
Littleton, Co., U.S. (lĭt''l-tŭn)	120	39°34'N	105°01'W
Littleton, Ma., U.S.	101a	42°32'N	71°29'W
Littleton, N.H., U.S.	109	44°15'N	71°45'W
Little Wabash, r., Il., U.S. (wô'băsh)	108	38°50'N	88°30'W
Little Wood, r., Id., U.S. (wŏŏd)	115	43°00'N	114°08'W
Lityn, Ukr.	177	49°16'N	28°11'E
Liubar, Ukr.	177	49°56'N	27°44'E
Liuhe, China	208	42°10'N	125°38'E
Liuli, Tan.	237	11°05'S	34°38'E
Liupan Shan, mts., China	208	36°20'N	105°30'E
Liuwa Plain, pl., Zam.	236	14°30'S	22°40'E
Liuyang, China (lyōō'yäng')	209	28°10'N	113°35'E
Liuyuan, China (liō-yůän)	206	36°09'N	114°37'E
Liuzhou, China (liō-jō)	204	24°25'N	109°30'E
Līvāni, Lat. (lē'vå-nē)	167	56°24'N	26°12'E
Lively, Can.	98	46°26'N	81°09'W
Livengood, Ak., U.S. (lĭv'ĕn-gŏŏd)	103	65°30'N	148°35'W
Live Oak, Fl., U.S. (lĭv'ōk)	124	30°15'N	83°00'W
Livermore, Ca., U.S. (lĭv'ẽr-mōr)	116b	37°41'N	121°46'W
Livermore, Ky., U.S.	108	37°30'N	87°05'W
Liverpool, Austl. (lĭv'ẽr-pōōl)	217b	33°55'S	150°56'E
Liverpool, Can.	91	44°02'N	64°41'W
Liverpool, Eng., U.K.	154	53°25'N	2°52'W
Liverpool, Tx., U.S.	123a	29°18'N	95°17'W
Liverpool Bay, b., Can.	103	69°45'N	130°00'W
Liverpool Range, mts., Austl.	221	31°47'S	151°00'E
Livindo, r., Afr.	231	1°09'N	13°30'E
Livingston, Guat.	132	15°50'N	88°45'W
Livingston, Al., U.S. (lĭv'ĭng-stŭn)	124	32°35'N	88°09'W
Livingston, Il., U.S.	117e	38°58'N	89°51'W
Livingston, Mt., U.S.	104	45°40'N	110°35'W
Livingston, N.J., U.S.	110a	40°47'N	74°20'W
Livingston, Tn., U.S.	124	36°23'N	85°20'W
Livingstone, Zam. (lĭv-ĭng-stôn)	232	17°50'S	25°53'E
Livingstone, Chutes de, wtfl., Afr.	236	4°50'S	14°30'E
Livingstonia, Mwi. (lĭv-ĭng-stō'nĭ-å)	232	10°36'S	34°07'E
Livno, Bos. (lēv'nō)	163	43°50'N	17°03'E
Livny, Russia (lĕv'nē)	181	52°28'N	37°36'E
Livonia, Mi., U.S. (lĭ-vō-nĭ-å)	111b	42°25'N	83°23'W
Livorno, Italy (lē-vôr'nō) (lĕg'hôrn)	154	43°32'N	11°18'E
Livramento, Braz. (lē-vrå-mĕ'n-tô)	144	30°46'S	55°21'W
Lixian, China (lē shyĕn)	209	29°42'N	111°40'E
Lixian, China	206	38°30'N	115°38'E
Liyang, China (lē'yäng')	209	31°30'N	119°29'E
Lizard Point, c., Eng., U.K. (lĭz'ård)	161	49°55'N	5°09'W
Lizy-sur-Ourcq, Fr. (lēk-sē'sür-ōōrk')	171b	49°01'N	3°02'E
Ljubljana, Slvn. (lyōō'blyä'na)	154	46°04'N	14°29'E
Ljubuški, Bos. (lyōō'bōsh-kē)	175	43°11'N	17°29'E
Ljungan, r., Swe.	166	62°50'N	13°45'E
Ljungby, Swe. (lyông'bü)	166	56°49'N	13°56'E
Ljusdal, Swe. (lyōōs'däl)	166	61°50'N	16°11'E
Ljusnan, r., Swe.	160	61°55'N	15°33'E
Llandudno, Wales, U.K. (lăn-düd'nō)	164	53°20'N	3°46'W
Llanelli, Wales, U.K. (lå-nĕl'ĭ)	161	51°44'N	4°09'W
Llanes, Spain (lyä'nås)	162	43°25'N	4°41'W
Llano, Tx., U.S. (lă'nō) (lyä'nō)	122	30°45'N	98°41'W
Llano, r., Tx., U.S.	122	30°38'N	99°04'W
Llanos, reg., S.A. (lyå'nōs)	142	4°00'N	71°15'W
Lleida, Spain	162	41°38'N	0°37'E
Llera, Mex. (lyā'rä)	130	23°16'N	99°03'W
Llerena, Spain (lyā-rā'nä)	172	38°14'N	6°02'W
Lliria, Spain	173	39°35'N	0°34'W
Llobregat, r., Spain (lyō-brĕ-gät')	173	41°55'N	1°55'E
Lloyd Lake, l., Can. (loid)	102e	50°52'N	114°13'W
Lloydminster, Can.	90	53°17'N	110°00'W
Llucena, Spain	173	40°08'N	0°18'W
Llucmajor, Spain	173	39°28'N	2°53'E
Llullaillaco, Volcán, vol., S.A. (lyōō-lyī-lyä'kō)	144	24°50'S	68°30'W
Loange, r., Afr. (lō-äŋ'gā)	232	5°00'S	20°15'E
Lobamba, Swaz.	232	26°27'S	31°12'E
Lobatse, Bots. (lō-bä'tsē)	232	25°13'S	25°35'E
Lobería, Arg. (lō-bĕ'rē'ä)	144	38°13'S	58°48'W
Lobito, Ang. (lō-bē'tō)	232	12°30'S	13°34'E
Lobnya, Russia (lôb'nyå)	186b	56°01'N	37°29'E
Lobo, Phil.	213a	13°39'N	121°14'E
Lobos, Arg. (lō'bôs)	141c	35°10'S	59°08'W
Lobos, Cayo, i., Bah. (lō'bôs)	134	22°25'N	77°40'W
Lobos, Isla de, i., Mex. (ē's-lä-dĕ-lō'bōs)	131	21°24'N	97°11'W
Lobos de Tierra, i., Peru (lō'bō-dĕ-tyĕ'r-rä)	142	6°29'S	80°55'W
Lobva, Russia (lôb'vå)	186a	59°12'N	60°28'E
Lobva, r., Russia	186a	59°14'N	60°17'E
Locarno, Switz. (lô-kär'nō)	168	46°10'N	8°43'E
Loches, Fr. (lôsh)	170	47°08'N	0°56'E
Loch Raven Reservoir, res., Md., U.S.	110e	39°28'N	76°38'W
Lockeport, Can.	100	43°42'N	65°07'W
Lockhart, S.C., U.S. (lŏk'härt)	125	34°47'N	81°30'W
Lockhart, Tx., U.S.	123	29°54'N	97°40'W
Lock Haven, Pa., U.S. (lŏk'hā-vĕn)	109	41°05'N	77°30'W
Lockland, Oh., U.S. (lŏk'lănd)	111f	39°14'N	84°27'W
Lockport, Il., U.S.	111a	41°35'N	88°04'W
Lockport, N.Y., U.S.	109	43°11'N	78°43'W
Loc Ninh, Viet. (lōk'nĭng')	212	12°00'N	106°30'E
Lod, Isr. (lōd)	197a	31°57'N	34°55'E
Lodève, Fr. (lō-dĕv')	170	43°43'N	3°18'E
Lodeynoye Pole, Russia (lō-dĕy-nô'yĕ)	180	60°43'N	33°24'E
Lodge Creek, r., N.A. (lŏj)	115	49°20'N	110°20'W
Lodge Creek, r., Mt., U.S.	115	48°51'N	109°30'W
Lodgepole Creek, r., Wy., U.S. (lŏj'pōl)	112	41°22'N	104°48'W
Lodhran, Pak.	202	29°40'N	71°39'E
Lodi, Italy (lô'dē)	174	45°18'N	9°30'E
Lodi, Ca., U.S. (lō'dī)	118	38°07'N	121°17'W
Lodi, Oh., U.S. (lō'dī)	111d	41°02'N	82°01'W
Lodosa, Spain (lō-dō'sä)	172	42°27'N	2°04'W
Lodwar, Kenya	237	3°07'N	35°36'E
Łódź, Pol.	154	51°46'N	19°30'E
Loeches, Spain (lō-āch'ĕs)	173a	40°22'N	3°25'W
Loffa, r., Afr.	234	7°10'N	10°35'W
Lofoten, is., Nor. (lō'fō-tĕn)	156	68°26'N	13°42'E
Logăn, Oh., U.S. (lō'gån)	108	39°35'N	82°25'W
Logan, Ut., U.S.	104	41°46'N	111°51'W
Logan, W.V., U.S.	108	37°50'N	82°00'W
Logan, Mount, mtn., Can.	92	60°54'N	140°33'W
Logansport, In., U.S. (lō'gănz-pōrt)	105	40°45'N	86°25'W
Logone, r., Afr. (lō-gō'nä) (lō-gôn')	231	10°20'N	15°30'E
Logroño, Spain (lō-grō-nyō)	162	42°28'N	2°25'W
Logrosán, Spain (lō-grō-sän')	172	39°22'N	5°29'W
Løgstør, Den. (lügh-stûr')	166	56°56'N	9°15'E
Loir, r., Fr. (lwår)	170	47°40'N	0°07'E
Loire, r., Fr.	156	47°30'N	2°00'E
Loja, Ec. (lō'hä)	142	3°49'S	79°13'W
Loja, Spain (lō'-kä)	172	37°10'N	4°11'W
Loka, D.R.C.	236	0°20'N	17°57'E
Lokala Drift, Bots. (lō'kä-lå drĭft)	238c	24°00'S	26°38'E
Lokandu, D.R.C.	237	2°31'S	25°47'E
Lokhvytsia, Ukr.	181	50°21'N	33°16'E
Lokichar, Kenya	237	2°23'N	35°39'E
Lokitaung, Kenya	237	4°16'N	35°45'E
Lokofa-Bokolongo, D.R.C.	236	0°12'N	19°22'E
Lokoja, Nig. (lō-kō'yä)	230	7°47'N	6°45'E
Lokolama, D.R.C.	236	2°34'S	19°53'E
Lokosso, Burkina	234	10°19'N	3°40'W
Lol, r., Sudan (lōl)	231	9°06'N	28°09'E
Loliondo, Tan.	237	2°03'S	35°37'E
Lolland, i., Den. (lôl'än')	166	54°41'N	11°00'E
Lolo, Mt., U.S.	115	46°45'N	114°05'W
Lom, Blg. (lōm)	163	43°48'N	23°15'E

ng-sing; ŋ-baŋk; N-nasalized n; nŏd; cŏmmit; ōld; ŏbey; ôrder; oi-boil; fōōd; ō-as oo in foot; ou-out; s-soft; sh-dish; th-thin; pūre; ûnite; ûrn; stŭd; circŭs; ü-as in French tu; '-indeterminate vowel.

ăt; finăl; rāte; senăte; ărm; ásk; sofá; fâre; ch-choose; dh-as th in other; bē; ĕvent; bĕt; recĕnt; cratēr; g-gō; gh-guttural g; bĭt; ī-short neutral; rīde; κ-guttural k as ch in German ich;

PRONOUNCING INDEX

Lukuga – Maḩaţţat Jurf ad Darāwīsh 317

PLACE (Pronunciation)	PAGE	LAT.	LONG.
Lukuga, r., D.R.C. (lo͞o-ko͞o′gȧ)	232	5°50′S	27°35′E
Lüleburgaz, Tur. (lü′lĕ-bȯr-gäs′)	175	41°25′N	27°23′E
Luling, Tx., U.S. (lū′lĭng)	123	29°41′N	97°38′W
Lulong, China (lo͞o-lôŋ)	205	39°54′N	118°53′E
Lulonga, r., D.R.C.	236	1°00′N	18°37′E
Luluabourg *see* Kananga, D.R.C.	232	6°14′S	22°17′E
Lulu Island, i., Can.	116d	49°09′N	123°05′W
Lulu Island, i., Ak., U.S.	94	55°28′N	133°30′W
Lumajangdong Co, l., China	202	34°00′N	81°47′E
Lumber, r., N.C., U.S. (lŭm′bẽr)	125	34°45′N	79°10′W
Lumberton, Ms., U.S. (lŭm′bẽr-tŭn)	124	31°00′N	89°25′W
Lumberton, N.C., U.S.	125	34°47′N	79°00′W
Luminárias, Braz. (lo͞o-mē-nȧ′ryäs)	141a	21°32′S	44°53′W
Lummi, i., Wa., U.S.	116d	48°42′N	122°43′W
Lummi Bay, b., Wa., U.S. (lūm′ĭ)	116d	48°47′N	122°44′W
Lummi Island, Wa., U.S.	116d	48°44′N	122°42′W
Lumwana, Zam.	237	11°50′S	25°10′E
Lün, Mong.	204	47°58′N	104°52′E
Luna, Phil. (lo͞o′nȧ)	213a	16°51′N	120°22′E
Lund, Swe. (lŭnd)	100	55°42′N	13°10′E
Lundy, i., Eng., U.K. (lŭn′dē)	164	51°12′N	4°50′W
Lüneburg, Ger. (lü′nē-bòrgh)	168	53°16′N	10°25′E
Lunel, Fr. (lü-nĕl′)	170	43°41′N	4°07′E
Lünen, Ger. (lü′nĕn)	171c	51°36′N	7°30′E
Lunenburg, Can. (lo͞o′nĕn-bûrg)	91	44°23′N	64°19′W
Lunenburg, Ma., U.S.	101a	42°36′N	71°44′W
Lunéville, Fr. (lü-nå-vel′)	171	48°37′N	6°29′E
Lunga, Ang.	236	14°42′S	18°32′E
Lungué-Bungo, r., Afr.	232	13°00′S	20°30′E
Lunsar, S.L.	234	8°41′N	12°32′W
Luodian, China (lwỏ-dĭĕn)	206	31°25′N	121°20′E
Luoding, China (lwỏ-dĭŋ)	209	23°42′N	111°35′E
Luohe, China (lwỏ-hŭ)	206	33°35′N	114°02′E
Luoyang, China (lwỏ-yäŋ)	205	34°45′N	112°32′E
Luozhen, China (lwỏ-jŭn)	206	37°45′N	118°29′E
Luque, Para. (loo′kā)	144	25°18′S	57°17′W
Luray, Va., U.S. (lū-rā′)	109	38°40′N	78°25′W
Lurgan, N. Ire., U.K. (lûr′găn)	160	54°27′N	6°28′W
Lúrio, Moz. (lo͞o′rẻ-ỏ)	233	13°17′S	40°29′E
Lúrio, Moz.	233	14°00′S	38°45′E
Lusaka, D.R.C.	237	7°10′S	29°27′E
Lusaka, Zam. (lò-sä′kȧ)	232	15°25′S	28°17′E
Lusambo, D.R.C. (lo͞o-säm′bō)	232	4°58′S	23°27′E
Lusanga, D.R.C.	232	5°13′S	18°43′E
Lusangi, D.R.C.	237	4°37′S	27°08′E
Lushan, China	208	33°45′N	113°00′E
Lushiko, r., Afr.	236	6°35′S	19°45′E
Lushoto, Tan. (lo͞o-shō′tō)	233	4°47′S	38°17′E
Lüshun, China (lü-shŭn)	205	38°49′N	121°15′E
Lusikisiki, S. Afr. (lo͞o-sẻ-kẻ-sē′kẻ)	233c	31°22′S	29°37′E
Lusk, Wy., U.S. (lŭsk)	112	42°46′N	104°27′W
Lūt, Dasht-e, des., Iran (dă′sht-ē-lo͞ot)	198	31°47′N	58°38′E
Lutcher, La., U.S. (lŭch′ẽr)	123	30°03′N	90°43′W
Luton, Eng., U.K. (lū′tŭn)	164	51°55′N	0°28′W
Luts′k, Ukr.	181	50°45′N	25°20′E
Luuq, Som.	238a	3°38′N	42°35′E
Luverne, Al., U.S. (lū-vûn′)	124	31°42′N	86°15′W
Luverne, Mn., U.S.	112	43°40′N	96°13′W
Luwingu, Zam.	237	10°15′S	29°55′E
Luxapallila Creek, r., U.S. (lŭk-sȧ-pôl′ĭ-lȧ)	124	33°36′N	88°08′W
Luxembourg, Lux.	154	49°38′N	6°30′E
Luxembourg, nation, Eur.	154	49°30′N	6°22′E
Luxeuil-les-Baines, Fr.	171	47°49′N	6°19′E
Luxomni, Ga., U.S. (lŭx′ỏm-nī)	110c	33°54′N	84°07′W
Luxor *see* Al Uqşur, Egypt	231	25°38′N	32°59′E
Luya Shan, mtn., China	208	38°50′N	111°40′E
Luyi, China (lo͞o-yē)	206	33°52′N	115°32′E
Luzern, Switz. (lò-tsĕrn)	161	47°03′N	8°18′E
Luzhou, China (lo͞o-jō)	204	28°58′N	105°25′E
Luziânia, Braz. (lo͞o-zyȧ′nēȧ)	143	16°17′S	47°44′W
Luzon, i., Phil. (lo͞o-zŏn′)	212	17°10′N	119°45′E
Luzon Strait, strt., Asia	209	20°40′N	121°00′E
L′viv, Ukr.	178	49°50′N	24°00′E
L′vov *see* L′viv, Ukr.	178	49°50′N	24°00′E
Lyalta, Can.	102e	51°07′N	113°36′W
Lyalya, r., Russia (lyȧ′lyȧ)	186a	58°58′N	60°17′E
Lyaskovets, Blg.	175	43°07′N	25°41′E
Lydenburg, S. Afr. (lī′dĕn-bûrg)	232	25°06′S	30°21′E
Lyell, Mount, mtn., Ca., U.S. (lī′ĕl)	118	37°44′N	119°22′W
Lyepye′, Bela. (lyĕ-pĕl′)	176	54°52′N	28°41′E
Lykens, Pa., U.S. (lī′kĕnz)	109	40°35′N	76°45′W
Lykhivka, Ukr.	177	48°52′N	33°57′E
Lyna, r., Eur. (lĭn′ȧ)	169	53°56′N	20°30′E
Lynch, Ky., U.S. (lĭnch)	125	36°56′N	82°55′W
Lynchburg, Va., U.S. (lĭnch′bûrg)	105	37°23′N	79°08′W
Lynch Cove, Wa., U.S. (lĭnch)	116a	47°26′N	122°54′W
Lynden, Can. (lĭn′dĕn)	102d	43°14′N	80°08′W
Lynden, Wa., U.S.	116d	48°56′N	122°27′W
Lyndhurst, Austl.	217a	38°03′S	145°14′E
Lyndon, Ky., U.S. (lĭn′dŭn)	111h	38°15′N	85°36′W
Lyndonville, Vt., U.S. (lĭn′dŭn-vĭl)	109	44°35′N	72°00′W
Lynn, Ma., U.S. (lĭn)	105	42°28′N	70°57′W
Lynn Lake, Can. (lāk)	90	56°51′N	101°05′W
Lynwood, Ca., U.S. (lĭn′wȯd)	117a	33°56′N	118°13′W
Lyon, Fr. (lē-ôɴ′)	154	45°44′N	4°52′E
Lyons, Ga., U.S. (lī′ŭnz)	125	32°08′N	82°19′W
Lyons, Ks., U.S.	120	38°20′N	98°11′W
Lyons, Ne., U.S.	112	41°57′N	96°28′W
Lyons, N.J., U.S.	110a	40°41′N	74°33′W
Lyons, N.Y., U.S.	109	43°05′N	77°00′W
Lyptsi, Ukr.	177	50°11′N	36°25′E
Lysefjorden, b., Nor.	166	58°59′N	6°35′E
Lysekil, Swe. (lü′sĕ-kẻl)	166	58°17′N	11°22′E
Lys′va, Russia (lĭs′vȧ)	180	58°07′N	57°47′E
Lytham, Eng., U.K. (lĭth′ăm)	158a	53°44′N	2°58′W
Lytkarino, Russia	186b	55°35′N	37°55′E
Lyttelton, S. Afr. (lĭt′l′ton)	233b	25°51′S	28°13′E
Lyuban′, Russia (lyo͞o′bȧn)	176	59°21′N	31°15′E
Lyubertsy, Russia (lyo͞o′bĕr-tsẻ)	176	55°40′N	37°55′E
Lyubim, Russia (lyo͞o-bẻm′)	176	58°24′N	40°39′E
Lyublino, Russia (lyo͞ob′lĭ-nỏ)	186b	55°41′N	37°45′E
Lyudinovo, Russia (lū-dē′novō)	176	53°52′N	34°28′E

M

PLACE (Pronunciation)	PAGE	LAT.	LONG.
Ma′an, Jord. (mä-än′)	198	30°12′N	35°45′E
Maartensdijk, Neth.	159a	52°09′N	5°10′E
Maas (Meuse), r., Eur.	165	51°50′N	5°40′E
Maastricht, Neth. (mäs′trĭкt)	165	50°51′N	5°35′E
Mabaia, Ang.	236	7°13′S	14°03′E
Mabana, Wa., U.S. (mä-bä-nä)	116a	48°06′N	122°25′W
Mabank, Tx., U.S. (mā′bănk)	123	32°21′N	96°05′W
Mabeskraal, S. Afr.	238c	25°12′S	26°47′E
Mableton, Ga., U.S. (mā′b′l-tŭn)	110c	33°49′N	84°34′W
Mabrouk, Mali	230	19°27′N	1°16′W
Mabula, S. Afr. (mă′bo͞o-la)	238c	24°49′S	27°59′E
Macalelon, Phil. (mä-kä-lā-lōn′)	213a	13°46′N	122°09′E
Macau, Braz. (mä-kȧ′ò)	143	5°12′S	36°34′W
Macau, China	205	22°00′N	113°00′E
Macaya, Pico de, mtn., Haiti	135	18°25′N	74°00′W
Macclesfield, Eng., U.K. (măk′′lz-fēld)	158a	53°15′N	2°07′W
Macclesfield Canal, can., Eng., U.K. (măk′′lz-fēld)	158a	53°14′N	2°07′W
Macdona, Tx., U.S. (măk-dō′nā)	117d	29°20′N	98°42′W
Macdonald, l., Austl. (măk-dŏn′ăld)	220	23°40′S	127°40′E
Macdonnell Ranges, mts., Austl. (măk-dŏn′ĕl)	220	23°40′S	131°30′E
MacDowell Lake, l., Can. (măk-dou ĕl)	97	52°15′N	92°45′W
Macdui, Ben, mtn., Scot., U.K. (bĕn măk-do͞o′ẻ)	160	57°06′N	3°45′W
Macedonia, Oh., U.S. (măs-ẻ-dō′nĭ-ȧ)	111d	41°19′N	81°30′E
Macedonia, nation, Eur.	175	41°50′N	22°00′E
Macedonia, hist. reg., Eur. (măs-ẻ-dō′nĭ-ȧ)	163	41°05′N	22°15′E
Maceió, Braz.	143	9°40′S	35°43′W
Macerata, Italy (mä-chå-rä′tä)	174	43°18′N	13°28′E
Macfarlane, Lake, l., Austl. (måc′fär-lān)	222	32°10′S	137°00′E
Machache, mtn., Leso.	233c	29°22′S	27°53′E
Machado, Braz. (mä-shȧ-dô)	141a	21°42′S	45°55′W
Machakos, Kenya	237	1°31′S	37°16′E
Machala, Ec. (mä-chȧ′lä)	142	3°18′S	78°54′W
Machens, Mo., U.S. (măk′ĕns)	117e	38°54′N	90°20′W
Machias, Me., U.S. (mȧ-chī′ȧs)	100	44°22′N	67°29′W
Machida, Japan (mä-chẻ′dä)	211a	35°32′N	139°28′E
Machilīpatnam, India	199	16°22′N	81°10′E
Machu Picchu, Peru (mȧ′chò-pẻ′k-chò)	142	13°07′S	72°34′W
Măcin, Rom. (mȧ-chēn′)	177	45°15′N	28°09′E
Macina, reg., Mali	234	14°50′N	4°40′W
Mackay, Austl. (mă-kī′)	219	21°15′S	149°08′E
Mackay, Id., U.S. (măk-kā′)	115	43°55′N	113°38′W
Mackay, l., Austl. (mă-kī′)	220	22°30′S	127°45′E
MacKay, l., Can. (măk-kā′)	92	64°10′N	112°35′W
Mackenzie, r., Can.	92	63°38′N	124°23′W
Mackenzie Bay, b., Can.	103	69°20′N	137°10′W
Mackenzie Mountains, mts., Can. (mȧ-kĕn′zĭ)	92	63°41′N	129°27′W
Mackinaw, r., Il., U.S.	108	40°35′N	89°25′W
Mackinaw City, Mi., U.S. (măk′ĭ-nô)	108	45°45′N	84°45′W
Mackinnon Road, Kenya	237	3°44′S	39°03′E
Macleantown, S. Afr. (măk-lăn′toun)	233c	32°48′S	27°48′E
Maclear, S. Afr. (mȧ-klēr′)	232	31°06′S	28°23′E
Macomb, Il., U.S. (mȧ-ko͞om′)	121	40°27′N	90°40′W
Mâcon, Fr. (mä-kôɴ)	161	46°19′N	4°51′E
Macon, Ga., U.S. (mā′kŏn)	105	32°49′N	83°39′W
Macon, Mo., U.S.	121	39°42′N	92°29′W
Macon, Ms., U.S.	124	32°07′N	88°31′W
Macquarie, r., Austl.	221	31°43′S	148°04′E
Macquarie Islands, is., Austl. (mȧ-kwŏr′ẻ)	3	54°36′S	158°45′E
Macuelizo, Hond. (mä-kwĕ-lē′zô)	132	15°22′N	88°32′W
Mad, r., Ca., U.S. (măd)	114	40°38′N	123°37′W
Madagascar, nation, Afr. (măd-ȧ-găs′kȧr)	233	18°05′S	43°12′E
Madame, i., Can. (mȧ-dȧm′)	101	45°33′N	61°02′W
Madanapalle, India	203	13°06′N	78°09′E
Madang, Pap. N. Gui. (mä-däng′)	213	5°15′S	145°45′E
Madaoua, Niger (mȧ-dou′ȧ)	230	14°04′N	6°03′E
Madawaska, r., Can. (mäd-ȧ-wôs′kȧ)	99	45°20′N	77°25′W
Madeira, r., S.A.	142	6°48′S	62°43′W
Madeira, Arquipélago da, is., Port.	229	33°26′N	16°44′W
Madeira, Ilha da, i., Port. (mä-dā′rä)	230	32°41′N	16°15′W
Madeleine, Îles de la, is., Can.	93	47°30′N	61°45′W
Madelia, Mn., U.S. (mȧ-dē′lĭ-ȧ)	113	44°03′N	94°23′W
Madeline, i., Wi., U.S. (măd′ĕ-lĭn)	113	46°47′N	91°30′W
Madera, Ca., U.S. (mȧ-dā′rȧ)	118	36°57′N	120°04′W
Madera, vol., Nic.	132	11°27′N	85°30′W
Madgaon, India	203	15°09′N	73°58′E
Madhya Pradesh, state, India (mŭd′vŭ prŭ-dāsh′)	199	22°04′N	77°48′E
Madill, Ok., U.S. (mȧ-dĭl′)	121	34°04′N	96°45′W
Madīnat ash Sha′b, Yemen	198	12°45′N	44°00′E
Madingo, Congo	236	4°07′S	11°22′E
Madingou, Congo	236	4°09′S	13°34′E
Madison, Fl., U.S. (măd′ĭ-sŭn)	124	30°28′N	83°25′W
Madison, Ga., U.S.	124	33°34′N	83°29′W
Madison, Il., U.S.	117e	38°40′N	90°09′W
Madison, In., U.S.	108	38°45′N	85°25′W
Madison, Ks., U.S.	121	38°08′N	96°07′W
Madison, Me., U.S.	100	44°47′N	69°52′W
Madison, Mn., U.S.	112	44°59′N	96°13′W
Madison, N.C., U.S.	125	36°22′N	79°59′W
Madison, Ne., U.S.	112	41°49′N	97°27′W
Madison, N.J., U.S.	110a	40°46′N	74°25′W
Madison, S.D., U.S.	112	44°01′N	97°08′W
Madison, Wi., U.S.	105	43°05′N	89°23′W
Madison Res, Mt., U.S.	115	45°25′N	111°28′W
Madisonville, Ky., U.S. (măd′ĭ-sŭn-vĭl)	108	37°20′N	87°30′W
Madisonville, La., U.S.	123	30°22′N	90°10′W
Madisonville, Tx., U.S.	123	30°57′N	95°55′W
Madjori, Burkina	234	11°26′N	1°15′E
Mado Gashi, Kenya	237	0°44′N	39°10′E
Madona, Lat. (mȧ′dō′nȧ)	167	56°50′N	26°14′E
Madrakah, Ra′s al, c., Oman	198	18°53′N	57°48′E
Madras *see* Chennai, India	199	13°08′N	80°15′E
Madre, Laguna, l., Mex. (lă-go͞o′nă mă′drå)	123	25°08′N	97°41′W
Madre, Sierra, mts., N.A. (sē-ĕ′r-rä-mȧ′drĕ)	131	15°55′N	92°40′W
Madre, Sierra, mts., Phil.	213a	16°40′N	122°10′E
Madre de Dios, r., S.A. (mä′drå dā dẻ-ōs′)	142	12°07′S	68°02′W
Madre de Dios, Archipiélago, is., Chile (mȧ′drå dā dẻ-ōs′)	144	50°40′S	76°30′W
Madre del Sur, Sierra, mts., Mex. (sē-ĕ′r-rä-mä′drå dĕlso͞or′)	128	17°35′N	100°35′W
Madre Occidental, Sierra, mts., Mex.	128	29°30′N	107°30′W
Madre Oriental, Sierra, mts., Mex.	128	25°30′N	100°45′W
Madrid, Spain (mä-drẻ′d)	154	40°26′N	3°42′W
Madrid, Ia., U.S. (măd′rĭd)	113	41°51′N	93°48′W
Madridejos, Spain (mä-dhrẻ-dhā′hōs)	172	39°29′N	3°32′W
Madura, i., Indon. (mȧ-do͞o′rä)	212	6°45′S	113°30′E
Madurai, India (mä-do͞o′rä)	199	9°57′N	78°04′E
Madureira, Serra do, mtn., Braz. (sĕ′r-rä-dỏ-mä-do͞o-rā′rȧ)	144b	22°49′S	43°30′W
Maebashi, Japan (mä-ĕ-bä′shẻ)	205	36°26′N	139°04′E
Maestra, Sierra, mts., Cuba (sē-ĕ′r-rȧ-mä-ās′trä)	129	20°05′N	77°05′W
Maewo, i., Vanuatu	221	15°17′S	168°16′E
Mafeking, S. Afr. (mȧf′ê′kĭng)	232	25°46′S	24°45′E
Mafra, Braz. (mä′frä)	144	26°21′N	49°59′W
Mafra, Port. (mäf′rȧ)	173b	38°56′N	9°20′W
Magadan, Russia (mȧ-gȧ-dän′)	179	59°39′N	150°43′E
Magadan Oblast, Russia	185	65°00′N	160°00′E
Magadi, Kenya	237	1°54′S	36°17′E
Magalies, r., S. Afr. (mä-gä′lyĕs)	233b	25°51′S	27°42′E
Magaliesberg, mts., S. Afr.	233b	25°45′S	27°43′E
Magaliesburg, S. Afr.	238c	26°01′S	27°32′E
Magallanes, Estrecho de, strt., S.A.	144	52°30′S	68°45′W
Magat, r., Phil. (mä-gät′)	213a	16°45′N	121°16′E
Magdalena, Arg. (mäg-dä-lā′nä)	141c	35°05′S	57°32′W
Magdalena, Bol.	142	13°17′S	63°57′W
Magdalena, Mex.	104	30°34′N	110°50′W
Magdalena, N.M., U.S.	119	34°10′N	107°45′W
Magdalena, i., Chile	144	44°45′S	73°15′W
Magdalena, r., Col.	142	7°45′N	74°04′W
Magdalena, Bahía, b., Mex. (bä-ē′ä-mäg-dä-lā′nä)	128	24°30′N	114°00′W
Magdeburg, Ger. (mäg′dĕ-bòrgh)	154	52°07′N	11°39′E
Magellan, Strait of *see* Magallanes, Estrecho de, strt., S.A.	144	52°30′S	68°45′W
Magenta, Italy (mȧ-jĕn′tȧ)	174	45°26′N	8°53′E
Magerøya, i., Nor.	160	71°10′N	24°11′E
Maggiore, Lago, l., Italy	162	46°03′N	8°25′E
Maghāghah, Egypt	238b	28°38′N	30°50′W
Maghniyya, Alg.	162	34°52′N	1°40′W
Magiscatzin, Mex. (mä-kẻs-kät-zēn′)	130	22°48′N	98°42′W
Maglaj, Bos. (mȧ′glä-ẻ)	175	44°34′N	18°12′E
Maglie, Italy (mäl′yā)	175	40°06′N	18°20′E
Magna, Ut., U.S. (măg′nȧ)	117b	40°43′N	112°06′W
Magnitogorsk, Russia (mȧg-nyē′tỏ-gỏrsk)	178	53°26′N	59°05′E
Magnolia, Ar., U.S. (măg-nō′lĭ-ȧ)	121	33°16′N	93°13′W
Magnolia, Ms., U.S.	124	31°08′N	90°27′W
Magny-en-Vexin, Fr. (mä-nyē′ĕɴ-vĕ-sȧɴ′)	171b	49°09′N	1°45′E
Magog, Can. (mȧ-gŏg′)	99	45°15′N	72°10′W
Magpie, r., Can.	100	50°40′N	64°30′W
Magpie, r., Can.	98	48°13′N	84°50′W
Magpie, Lac, l., Can.	100	50°55′N	64°39′W
Magrath, Can.	90	49°25′N	112°52′W
Magude, Moz. (mä-go͞o′då)	232	24°58′S	32°39′E
Magwe, Mya. (mŭg-wā′)	199	20°19′N	94°57′E
Mahābād, Iran	201	36°55′N	45°50′E
Mahahi Port, D.R.C. (mä-hä′gẻ)	231	2°14′N	31°12′E
Mahajanga, Madag.	233	15°12′S	46°26′E
Mahakam, r., Indon.	212	0°30′S	116°15′E
Mahali Mountains, mts., Tan.	237	6°20′S	30°00′E
Mahaly, Madag. (mȧ-hȧl-ē′)	233	24°09′S	46°20′E
Mahanoro, Madag. (mȧ-hȧ-nỏ′rō)	233	19°57′S	48°47′E
Mahanoy City, Pa., U.S. (mä-hȧ-noi′)	109	40°50′N	76°10′W
Maḩaţţat al Qaţrānah, Jord.	197a	31°15′N	36°04′E
Maḩaţţat ′Aqabat al Ḩijāzīyah, Jord.	197a	29°45′N	35°55′E
Maḩaţţat ar Ramlah, Jord.	197a	29°31′N	35°57′E
Maḩaţţat Jurf ad Darāwīsh, Jord.	197a	30°41′N	35°51′E

318 Mahd adh-Dhahab – Mansfield PRONOUNCING INDEX

PLACE (Pronunciation)	PAGE	LAT.	LONG.
Mahd adh-Dhahab, Sau. Ar.	201	23°30′N	40°52′E
Mahe, India (mä-ā′)	199	11°42′N	75°39′E
Mahenge, Tan. (mä-hĕŋ′gȧ)	232	7°38′S	36°16′E
Mahi, r., India	202	23°16′N	73°20′E
Mahilyow, Bela.	180	53°53′N	30°22′E
Mahilyow, prov., Bela.	176	53°28′N	30°15′E
Māhīm Bay, b., India	203b	19°03′N	72°45′E
Mahlabatini, S. Afr. (mä′lȧ-bȧ-tē′nė)	233c	28°15′S	31°29′E
Mahlow, Ger. (mä′lōv)	159b	52°23′N	13°24′E
Mahnomen, Mn., U.S. (mô-nō′mĕn)	112	47°18′N	95°58′W
Mahone Bay, Can. (mȧ-hōn′)	100	44°27′N	64°23′W
Mahone Bay, b., Can.	100	44°30′N	64°15′W
Mahopac, Lake, l., N.Y., U.S. (mā-hō′păk)	110a	41°24′N	73°45′W
Mahwah, N.J., U.S. (mȧ-wă′)	110a	41°05′N	74°09′W
Maidenhead, Eng., U.K. (mād′ĕn-hĕd)	158b	51°30′N	0°44′W
[illegible], Eng., U.K.	[illegible]	[illegible]	[illegible]
Maiduguri, Nig. (mä′ē-dȧ-gōō′rė)	231	11°51′N	13°10′E
Maigualida, Sierra, mts., Ven. (sē-ĕ′r-rȧ-mī-gwä′lē-dĕ)	142	6°30′N	65°50′W
Maijdi, Bngl.	202	22°59′N	91°08′E
Maikop *see* Maykop, Russia	178	44°35′N	40°07′E
Main, r., Ger. (mīn)	168	49°49′N	9°20′E
Main Barrier Range, mts., Austl. (băr′′ēr)	221	31°25′S	141°40′E
Mai-Ndombe, Lac, l., D.R.C.	232	2°16′S	19°00′E
Maine, state, U.S. (mān)	105	45°25′N	69°50′W
Mainland, i., Scot., U.K. (măn-lănd)	160	60°19′N	2°40′W
Maintenon, Fr. (măn-tē-nôn′)	171b	48°35′N	1°35′E
Maintirano, Madag. (mä′ēn-tē-rä′nō)	233	18°05′S	44°08′E
Mainz, Ger. (mīnts)	154	49°59′N	8°16′E
Maio, i., C.V. (mä′yo)	230b	15°15′N	22°50′W
Maipo, S.A.	144	34°08′S	69°51′W
Maipo, r., Chile (mī′pō)	141b	33°45′S	71°08′W
Maiquetía, Ven. (mī-kĕ-tē′ä)	142	10°37′N	66°56′W
Maison-Rouge, Fr. (mā-zôn-rōōzh′)	171b	48°34′N	3°09′E
Maisons-Laffitte, Fr.	171b	48°57′N	2°09′E
Maitland, Austl. (māt′lănd)	219	32°45′S	151°40′E
Maizuru, Japan (mä-ī′zōō-rōō)	211	35°26′N	135°15′E
Majene, Indon.	212	3°34′S	119°00′E
Maji, Eth.	231	6°14′N	35°34′E
Majorca *see* Mallorca, i., Spain	156	39°18′N	2°22′E
Makah Indian Reservation, I.R., Wa., U.S.	114	48°17′N	124°52′W
Makanya, Tan. (mä-kän′yä)	233	4°15′S	37°49′E
Makanza, D.R.C.	231	1°42′N	19°08′E
Makarakomburu, Mount, mtn., Sol. Is.	214e	9°43′S	160°02′E
Makarska, Cro. (mȧ′kär-skȧ)	175	43°17′N	17°05′E
Makar′yev, Russia	180	57°50′N	43°48′E
Makasar *see* Ujung Pandang, Indon.	212	5°08′S	119°28′E
Makasar, Selat (Makassar Strait), strt., Indon.	212	2°00′S	118°07′E
Makaw, D.R.C.	236	3°29′S	18°19′E
Make, i., Japan (mä′kå)	211	30°43′N	130°49′E
Makeni, S.L.	230	8°53′N	12°03′W
Makgadikgadi Pans, pl., Bots.	232	20°38′S	21°31′E
Makhachkala, Russia (mäk′äch-kä′lä)	181	43°00′N	47°40′E
Makhaleng, r., Leso.	233c	29°53′S	27°33′E
Makiïvka, Ukr.	181	48°03′N	38°00′E
Makindu, Kenya	237	2°17′S	37°49′E
Makkah *see* Mecca, Sau. Ar.	198	21°27′N	39°45′E
Makkovik, Can.	91	55°01′N	59°10′W
Makokou, Gabon (mȧ-kô-kōō′)	230	0°34′N	12°52′E
Maków Mazowiecki, Pol. (mä′kōov mä-zō-vyĕts′kē)	169	52°51′N	21°07′E
Makuhari, Japan (mä-kōō-hä′rē)	211a	35°39′N	140°04′E
Makurazaki, Japan (mä′kô-rä-zä′kė)	211	31°16′N	130°18′E
Makurdi, Nig.	230	7°45′N	8°32′E
Makushin, Ak., U.S. (mȧ-kô′shĭn)	103	53°57′N	166°28′W
Makushino, Russia (mȧ-kô-shēn′ô)	178	55°03′N	67°43′E
Mala, Punta, c., Pan. (pōō′n-tä-mä′lä)	133	7°32′N	79°44′W
Malabar Coast, cst., India (măl′ȧ-bär)	203	11°19′N	75°33′E
Malabar Point, c., India	203b	18°57′N	72°47′E
Malabo, Eq. Gui.	230	3°45′N	8°47′E
Malabon, Phil.	213a	14°39′N	120°57′E
Malacca, Strait of, strt., Asia (mȧ-lăk′ȧ)	212	4°15′N	99°44′E
Malad City, Id., U.S. (mȧ-lăd′)	115	42°11′N	112°15′W
Maladzyecha, Bela.	180	54°18′N	26°57′E
Málaga, Col. (mȧ′lä-gȧ)	142	6°41′N	72°46′W
Málaga, Spain	154	36°45′N	4°25′W
Malagón, Spain (mä-lä-gōn′)	172	39°12′N	3°52′W
Malaita, i., Sol. Is. (mȧ-lä′ē-tȧ)	221	8°38′S	161°15′E
Malakāl, Sudan (mȧ-lȧ-käl′)	231	9°46′N	31°54′E
Malakhovka, Russia (mȧ-läk′ôf-kȧ)	186b	55°38′N	38°01′E
Malang, Indon.	212	8°06′S	112°50′E
Malanje, Ang. (mȧ-läŋ-gȧ)	232	9°32′S	16°20′E
Malanville, Benin	230	12°04′N	3°09′E
Mälaren, l., Swe.	160	59°38′N	16°55′E
Malartic, Can.	91	48°07′N	78°11′W
Malatya, Tur. (mȧ-lä′tyȧ)	198	38°30′N	38°15′E
Malawi, nation, Afr.	232	11°15′S	33°45′E
Malawi, Lake *see* Nyasa, Lake, l., Afr.	232	10°45′S	34°30′E
Malaya Vishera, Russia (vē-shä′rä)	178	58°51′N	32°13′E
Malay Peninsula, pen., Asia (mȧ-lā′) (mā′lā)	212	6°00′N	101°00′E
Malaysia, nation, Asia (mȧ-lā′zhȧ)	212	4°10′N	101°22′E
Malbon, Austl. (măl′bŭn)	218	21°15′S	140°30′E
Malbork, Pol. (mäl′bôrk)	160	54°02′N	19°04′E
Malcabran, r., Port. (mäl-kä-brän′)	173b	38°47′N	8°46′W
Malden, Ma., U.S. (môl′dĕn)	101a	42°26′N	71°04′W
Malden, Mo., U.S.	121	36°32′N	89°56′W
Malden, i., Kir.	2	4°20′S	154°30′W
Maldives, nation, Asia	194	4°30′N	71°30′E
Maldon, Eng., U.K. (môrl′dŏn)	158b	51°44′N	0°39′E
Maldonado, Ur. (mäl-dŏ-nȧ′dô)	144	34°54′S	54°57′W
Maldonado, Punta, c., Mex. (pōō′n-tä)	130	16°18′N	98°34′W
Maléas, Ákra, c., Grc.	163	36°31′N	23°13′E
Mālegaon, India	202	20°35′N	74°30′E
Malé Karpaty, mts., Slvk.	169	48°31′N	17°15′E
Malekula, i., Vanuatu (mä-lā-kōō′lä)	221	16°44′S	167°45′E
Malema, Moz.	237	14°57′S	37°20′E
Malheur, r., Or., U.S. (mȧ-lōōr′)	114	43°45′N	117°41′W
Malheur Lake, l., Or., U.S. (mȧ-lōōr′)	114	43°16′N	118°37′W
Mali, nation, Afr.	230	15°45′N	0°15′W
Malibu, Ca., U.S. (mă′lĭ-bōō)	117a	34°03′N	118°38′W
Malik, Wādī al, r., Sudan	231	16°48′N	29°30′E
Malimba, Monts, mts., D.R.C.	237	7°45′S	29°15′E
Malinalco, Mex. (mä-lė-näl′kō)	130	18°54′N	99°31′W
Malinaltepec, Mex. (mä-lē-näl-tȧ-pĕk′)	130	17°01′N	98°41′W
Malindi, Kenya (mä-lēn′dē)	233	[illegible]	[illegible]
Malin Head, c., Ire.	160	55°23′N	7°24′W
Malino, Russia (mä′lĭ-nô)	186b	55°07′N	38°12′E
Malkara, Tur. (mäl′kȧ-rȧ)	175	40°51′N	26°52′E
Malko Tŭrnovo, Blg. (mäl′kō-t′r′nô-vȧ)	175	41°59′N	27°28′E
Mallaig, Scot., U.K.	164	56°59′N	5°55′W
Mallet Creek, Oh., U.S. (măl′ĕt)	111d	41°10′N	81°55′W
Mallorca, i., Spain	156	39°30′N	3°00′E
Mallow, Ire. (măl′ō)	164	52°07′N	9°04′W
Malmédy, Bel. (mȧl-mā-dē′)	165	50°25′N	6°01′E
Malmesbury, S. Afr. (mämz′bēr-ĭ)	232	33°30′S	18°35′E
Malmköping, Swe. (mälm′chû′pĭng)	166	59°09′N	16°39′E
Malmö, Swe.	154	55°36′N	13°00′E
Malmyzh, Russia (mȧl-mēzh′)	179	49°58′N	137°07′E
Malmyzh, Russia	180	56°30′N	50°48′E
Maloarkhangelsk, Russia (mä′lô-ȧr-kän′gĕlsk)	176	52°26′N	36°29′E
Malolos, Phil. (mä-lō′lôs)	213a	14°51′N	120°49′E
Malomal′sk, Russia (mȧ-lô-mälsk′′)	186a	58°47′N	59°55′E
Malone, N.Y., U.S. (mȧ-lōn′)	109	44°50′N	74°20′W
Malonga, D.R.C.	236	10°24′S	23°10′E
Maloti Mountains, mts., Leso.	233c	29°00′S	28°29′E
Maloyaroslavets, Russia (mä′lô-yä-rô-slä-vyĕts)	176	55°01′N	36°25′E
Malozemel′skaya Tundra, reg., Russia	180	67°30′N	50°00′E
Malpas, Eng., U.K. (măl′pȧz)	158a	53°01′N	2°46′W
Malpelo, Isla de, i., Col. (mäl-pā′lō)	142	3°55′N	81°30′W
Malpeque Bay, b., Can. (môl-pĕk′)	100	46°30′N	63°47′W
Malta, Mt., U.S. (môl′tȧ)	115	48°20′N	107°50′W
Malta, nation, Eur.	154	35°52′N	13°30′E
Maltahöhe, Nmb. (mäl′tä-hō′ē)	232	24°45′S	16°45′E
Maltrata, Mex. (mäl-trä′tä)	131	18°48′N	97°16′W
Maluku (Moluccas), is., Indon.	213	2°22′S	128°25′E
Maluku, Laut (Molucca Sea), sea, Indon.	213	0°15′N	125°41′E
Malūţ, Sudan	231	10°30′N	32°17′E
Mālvan, India	203	16°08′N	73°32′E
Malvern, Ar., U.S. (măl′vērn)	121	34°21′N	92°47′W
Malyn, Ukr.	177	50°44′N	29°15′E
Malynivka, Ukr.	177	49°50′N	36°43′E
Malyy Anyuy, r., Russia	185	67°52′N	164°30′E
Malyy Tamir, i., Russia	185	78°10′N	107°30′E
Mamantel, Mex. (mä-mȧn-tĕl′)	131	18°36′N	91°06′W
Mamaroneck, N.Y., U.S. (măm′ȧ-rō-nĕk)	110a	40°57′N	73°44′W
Mambasa, D.R.C.	237	1°21′N	29°03′E
Mamburao, Phil. (mäm-bōō′rä-ō)	213a	13°14′N	120°35′E
Mamfe, Cam. (mäm′fĕ)	230	5°46′N	9°17′E
Mamihara, Japan (mä′mė-hä-rä)	211	32°41′N	131°12′E
Mammoth Cave, Ky., U.S. (măm′ŏth)	124	37°10′N	86°04′W
Mammoth Cave National Park, rec., Ky., U.S.	107	37°20′N	86°21′W
Mammoth Hot Springs, Wy., U.S. (măm′ŭth hôt sprĭngz)	115	44°55′N	110°50′W
Mamnoli, India	203b	19°17′N	73°15′E
Mamoré, r., S.A.	142	13°00′S	65°20′W
Mamou, Gui.	230	10°26′N	12°07′W
Mampong, Ghana	234	7°04′N	1°24′W
Mamry, Jezioro, l., Pol. (mäm′rĭ)	169	54°10′N	21°28′E
Man, C. Iv.	234	7°24′N	7°33′W
Manacor, Spain (mä-nä-kôr′)	173	39°35′N	3°15′E
Manado, Indon.	213	1°29′N	124°50′E
Managua, Cuba (mä-nä′gwä)	135a	22°58′N	82°17′W
Managua, Nic.	128	12°10′N	86°16′W
Managua, Lago de, l., Nic. (lá′gô-dĕ)	132	12°28′N	86°10′W
Manakara, Madag. (mä-nä-kä′rŭ)	233	22°17′S	48°06′E
Manama *see* Al Manāmah, Bahr.	198	26°01′N	50°33′E
Mananara, r., Madag. (mä-nä-nä′rŭ)	233	23°15′S	48°15′E
Mananjary, Madag. (mä-nän-zhä′rė)	233	20°16′S	48°13′E
Manas, China	204	44°30′N	86°00′E
Manassas, Va., U.S. (mȧ-năs′ȧs)	109	38°45′N	77°30′W
Manaus, Braz. (mä-nä′ōōzh)	143	3°01′S	60°00′W
Mancelona, Mi., U.S. (măn-sē-lō′nȧ)	108	44°50′N	85°05′W
Mancha Real, Spain (män′chä rā-äl′)	172	37°48′N	3°37′W
Manchazh, Russia (män′chȧsh)	186a	56°30′N	58°10′E
Manchester, Eng., U.K.	154	53°28′N	2°14′W
Manchester, Ct., U.S. (măn′chĕs-tēr)	109	41°45′N	72°30′W
Manchester, Ga., U.S.	124	32°50′N	84°37′W
Manchester, Ia., U.S.	113	42°30′N	91°30′W
Manchester, Ma., U.S.	101a	42°35′N	70°47′W
Manchester, Mo., U.S.	117e	38°36′N	90°31′W
Manchester, N.H., U.S.	105	43°00′N	71°30′W
Manchester, Oh., U.S.	108	38°40′N	83°35′W
Manchester Ship Canal, Eng., U.K.	158a	53°20′N	2°40′W
Manchuria, hist. reg., China (măn-chōō′rē-ȧ)	205	48°00′N	124°58′E
Mandal, Nor. (män′däl)	166	58°03′N	7°28′E
Mandalay, Mya. (măn′dȧ-lā)	199	22°00′N	96°08′E
Mandalselva, r., Nor.	166	58°25′N	7°30′E
Mandan, N.D., U.S. (măn′dăn)	104	46°49′N	100°54′W
Mandara Mountains, mts., Afr. (män-dä′rä)	231	10°15′N	13°23′E
Mandau Siak, r., Indon.	197b	1°03′N	101°25′E
Mandeb, Bab-el-, strt. (bäb′ĕl män-dĕb′)	198	13°17′N	42°49′E
Mandimba, Moz.	237	14°21′S	35°39′E
Mandinga, Pan. (män-dĭŋ′gä)	133	9°32′N	79°04′W
Mandla, India	202	22°43′N	80°23′E
Mándra, Grc. (män′drä)	175	38°06′N	23°32′E
Mandritsara, Madag. (mȧn-drēt-sä′rȧ)	233	15°49′S	48°47′E
Manduria, Italy (män-dōō′rė-ä)	175	40°23′N	17°41′E
[illegible], India	203b	[illegible]	[illegible]
Māndvi, India (mŭnd′vē)	203b	19°29′N	72°53′E
Māndvi, India (mŭnd′vē)	199	22°54′N	69°23′E
Mandya, India	203	12°40′N	77°00′E
Manfredonia, Italy (män-frå-dô′nyä)	174	41°39′N	15°55′E
Manfredónia, Golfo di, b., Italy (gôl-fō-dē)	174	41°34′N	16°05′E
Mangabeiras, Chapada das, pl., Braz.	143	8°05′S	47°32′W
Mangalore, India (mŭŋ-gŭ-lōr′)	199	12°53′N	74°52′E
Mangaratiba, Braz. (män-gä-rä-tē′bȧ)	141a	22°56′S	44°03′W
Mangatarem, Phil. (män′gȧ-tä′rĕm)	213a	15°48′N	120°18′E
Mange, D.R.C.	236	0°54′N	20°30′E
Mangkalihat, Tanjung, c., Indon.	212	1°25′N	119°55′E
Mangles, Islas de, Cuba (ē′s-läs-dĕ-mäŋ′gläs) (măn′g′lz)	134	22°05′N	82°50′W
Mangoche, Mwi.	232	14°16′S	35°14′E
Mangoky, r., Madag. (män-gō′kē)	233	22°02′S	44°11′E
Mangole, Pulau, i., Indon.	213	1°35′S	126°22′E
Mangualde, Port. (män-gwäl′dĕ)	172	40°38′N	7°44′W
Mangueira, Lagoa da, l., Braz.	144	33°15′S	52°45′W
Mangum, Ok., U.S. (măŋ′gŭm)	120	34°52′N	99°31′W
Mangzhangdian, China (mäŋ-jäŋ-dĭĕn)	206	32°07′N	114°44′E
Manhattan, Il., U.S.	111a	41°25′N	87°29′W
Manhattan, Ks., U.S. (măn-hăt′ăn)	104	39°11′N	96°34′W
Manhattan Beach, Ca., U.S.	117a	33°53′N	118°24′W
Manhuaçu, Braz. (män-ōȧ′sōō)	141a	20°17′S	42°01′W
Manhumirim, Braz. (män-ōō-mē-rē′n)	141a	22°30′S	41°57′W
Manicouagane, r., Can.	93	50°00′N	68°35′W
Manicouagane, Lac, res., Can.	93	51°30′N	68°19′W
Manicuare, Ven. (mä-nē-kwä′rē)	143b	10°35′N	64°10′W
Manihiki Islands, is., Cook Is. (mä′nē-hē′kė)	241	9°40′S	158°00′W
Manila, Phil.	212	14°37′N	121°00′E
Manila Bay, b., Phil. (mȧ-nĭl′ȧ)	213a	14°38′N	120°46′E
Manisa, Tur. (mä′nē-sȧ)	163	38°40′N	27°30′E
Manistee, Mi., U.S. (măn-ĭs-tē′)	108	44°15′N	86°20′W
Manistee, r., Mi., U.S.	108	44°25′N	85°45′W
Manistique, Mi., U.S. (măn-ĭs-tēk′)	113	45°58′N	86°16′W
Manistique, l., Mi., U.S.	113	46°14′N	85°30′W
Manistique, r., Mi., U.S.	113	46°05′N	86°09′W
Manitoba, prov., Can. (măn-ĭ-tō′bȧ)	90	55°12′N	97°29′W
Manitoba, Lake, l., Can.	92	51°00′N	98°45′W
Manito Lake, l., Can. (măn′ĭ-tō)	96	52°45′N	109°45′W
Manitou, i., Mi., U.S. (măn′ĭ-tōō)	113	47°21′N	87°33′W
Manitou, l., Can.	113	49°21′N	93°01′W
Manitou Islands, is., Mi., U.S.	108	45°05′N	86°00′W
Manitoulin Island, i., Can. (măn-ĭ-tōō′lĭn)	93	45°45′N	81°30′W
Manitou Springs, Co., U.S.	120	38°51′N	104°58′W
Manitowoc, Wi., U.S. (măn-ĭ-tô-wŏk′)	113	44°05′N	87°42′W
Manitqueira, Serra da, mts., Braz.	141a	22°40′S	45°12′W
Maniwaki, Can.	99	46°23′N	76°00′W
Manizales, Col. (mä-nē-zä′lås)	142	5°05′N	75°31′W
Manjacaze, Moz. (man′yä-kä′zĕ)	232	24°37′S	33°49′E
Mankato, Ks., U.S. (măn-kā′tō)	120	39°45′N	98°12′W
Mankato, Mn., U.S.	105	44°10′N	93°59′W
Mankim, Cam.	235	5°01′N	12°00′E
Manlléu, Spain (män-lyā′ōō)	173	42°00′N	2°16′E
Mannar, Sri L. (mȧ-när′)	203	9°48′N	80°03′E
Mannar, Gulf of, b., Asia	199	8°47′N	78°33′E
Mannheim, Ger. (män′hīm)	161	49°30′N	8°31′E
Manning, Ia., U.S. (măn′ĭng)	112	41°53′N	95°04′W
Manning, S.C., U.S.	125	33°41′N	80°12′W
Mannington, W.V., U.S. (măn′ĭng-tŭn)	108	39°30′N	80°55′W
Mano, r., Afr.	234	7°00′N	11°25′W
Man of War Bay, b., Bah.	135	21°05′N	74°05′W
Man of War Channel, strt., Bah.	134	22°45′N	76°10′W
Manokwari, Indon. (mȧ-nŏk-wä′rė)	213	0°56′S	134°10′E
Manono, D.R.C.	237	7°18′S	27°25′E
Manor, Can. (măn′ēr)	97	49°36′N	102°05′W
Manor, Wa., U.S.	116c	45°45′N	122°36′W
Manori, neigh., India	203b	19°13′N	72°43′E
Manosque, Fr. (mȧ-nôsh′)	171	43°51′N	5°48′E
Manotick, Can.	102c	45°13′N	75°41′W
Manouane, r., Can.	99	50°15′N	70°30′W
Manouane, Lac, l., Can. (mä-nōō′ån)	100	50°36′N	70°50′W
Manresa, Spain (män-rā′sä)	162	41°44′N	1°52′E
Mansa, Zam.	232	11°12′S	28°53′E
Mansel, i., Can. (măn′sĕl)	93	61°56′N	81°10′W
Manseriche, Pongo de, reg., Peru (pô′n-gô-dĕ-män-sĕ-rē′chĕ)	142	4°15′S	77°45′W
Mansfield, Eng., U.K. (mănz′fēld)	158a	53°08′N	1°12′W
Mansfield, La., U.S.	123	32°02′N	93°43′W
Mansfield, Oh., U.S.	108	40°45′N	82°30′W
Mansfield, Wa., U.S.	114	47°48′N	119°39′W
Mansfield, Mount, mtn., Vt., U.S.	109	44°30′N	72°45′W

ăt; finăl; rāte; senåte; ärm; åsk; sofȧ; fâre; ch-choose; dh-as th in other; bē; ēvent; bĕt; recĕnt; cratēr; g-gō; gh-guttural g; bĭt; ĭ-short neutral; rīde; ĸ-guttural k as ch in German ich;

PRONOUNCING INDEX
Mansfield Woodhouse – Marystown 319

PLACE (Pronunciation)	PAGE	LAT.	LONG.
Mansfield Woodhouse, Eng., U.K. (wo̤d-hous)	158a	53°08′N	1°12′W
Manta, Ec. (män′tä)	142	1°03′S	80°16′W
Manteno, Il., U.S. (măn-tē-nō)	111a	41°15′N	87°50′W
Manteo, N.C., U.S.	125	35°55′N	75°40′W
Mantes-la-Jolie, Fr. (mäɴt-ĕ-lä-zhō-lē′)	170	48°59′N	1°42′E
Manti, Ut., U.S. (măn′tī)	119	39°15′N	11°40′W
Mantova, Italy (män′tô-vä) (măn′tů-ȧ)	162	45°09′N	10°47′E
Mantua, Cuba (män-to͞o′ä)	134	22°20′N	84°15′W
Mantua *see* Mantova, Italy	162	45°09′N	10°47′E
Mantua, Ut., U.S. (măn′tů-ȧ)	117b	41°30′N	111°57′W
Manua Islands, is., Am. Sam.	214a	14°13′S	169°35′W
Manui, Pulau, i., Indon. (mä-no͞o′ē)	213	3°35′S	123°38′E
Manus Island, i., Pap. N. Gui. (mä′no͞os)	213	2°22′S	146°22′E
Manvel, Tx., U.S. (măn′vel)	123a	29°28′N	95°22′W
Manville, N.J., U.S. (măn′vĭl)	110a	40°33′N	74°36′W
Manville, R.I., U.S.	110b	41°57′N	71°27′W
Manzala Lake, l., Egypt	238b	31°14′N	32°04′E
Manzanares, Col. (män-sä-nä′rĕs)	142a	5°15′N	75°09′W
Manzanares, r., Spain (mänz-nä′rĕs)	173a	40°36′N	3°48′W
Manzanares, Canal del, Spain (kä-nä′l-dĕl-män-thä-nä′rĕs)	173a	40°20′N	3°38′W
Manzanillo, Cuba (män′zä-nēl′yō)	129	20°20′N	77°05′W
Manzanillo, Mex.	128	19°02′N	104°21′W
Manzanillo, Bahía de, b., Mex. (bä-ē′ä-dĕ-män-zä-nē′l-yō)	130	19°00′N	104°38′W
Manzanillo, Bahía de, b., N.A.	135	19°55′N	71°50′W
Manzanillo, Punta, c., Pan.	133	9°40′N	79°33′W
Manzhouli, China (män-jō-lē)	205	49°25′N	117°15′E
Manzovka, Russia (mȧn-zhô′f-kȧ)	210	44°16′N	132°13′E
Mao, Chad (mä′ō)	231	14°07′N	15°19′E
Mao, Dom. Rep.	135	19°35′N	71°10′W
Maó, Spain	162	39°52′N	4°15′E
Maoke, Pegunungan, mts., Indon.	213	4°00′S	138°00′E
Maoming, China	205	21°55′N	110°40′E
Maoniu Shan, mtn., China (mou-nĭō shän)	208	32°45′N	104°09′E
Mapastepec, Mex. (ma-päs-tā-pĕk′)	131	15°24′N	92°52′W
Mapia, Kepulauan, i., Indon.	213	0°57′N	134°22′E
Mapimí, Mex. (mä-pē-mē′)	122	25°50′N	103°50′W
Mapimí, Bolsón de, des., Mex. (bôl-sŏ′n-dĕ-mä-pē′mē)	122	27°27′N	103°20′W
Maple Creek, Can. (mā′p′l) (crēk)	90	49°55′N	109°27′W
Maple Grove, Can. (grōv)	102a	45°19′N	73°51′W
Maple Heights, Oh., U.S.	111d	41°25′N	81°34′W
Maple Shade, N.J., U.S. (shād)	110f	39°57′N	75°01′W
Maple Valley, Wa., U.S. (văl′ē)	116a	47°24′N	122°02′W
Maplewood, Mn., U.S. (wo̤d)	117g	45°00′N	93°03′W
Maplewood, Mo., U.S.	117e	38°37′N	90°20′W
Mapumulo, S. Afr. (mä-pä-mo͞o′lō)	233c	29°12′S	31°05′E
Maputo, Moz.	232	26°50′S	32°30′E
Maquela do Zombo, Ang. (mȧ-kā′lȧ dò zôm′bò)	232	6°08′S	15°15′E
Maquoketa, Ia., U.S. (mȧ-kō-kê-tȧ)	113	42°04′N	90°42′W
Maquoketa, r., Ia., U.S.	113	42°08′N	90°40′W
Mar, Serra do, mts., Braz. (sĕr′rȧ dò mär′)	144	26°30′S	49°15′W
Maracaibo, Ven. (mä-rä-kī′bō)	142	10°38′N	71°45′W
Maracaibo, Lago de, l., Ven. (lä′gô-dĕ-mä-rä-kī′bō)	142	9°55′N	72°13′W
Maracay, Ven. (mä-rä-käy′)	142	10°15′N	67°35′W
Marādah, Libya	231	29°10′N	19°07′E
Maradi, Niger (mȧ-rä-dē′)	230	13°29′N	7°06′E
Marāgheh, Iran	201	37°20′N	46°10′E
Maraisburg, S. Afr.	233b	26°12′S	27°57′E
Marais des Cygnes, r., Ks., U.S.	121	38°30′N	95°30′W
Marajó, Ilha de, i., Braz.	143	1°00′S	49°30′W
Maralal, Kenya	237	1°06′N	36°42′E
Marali, C.A.R.	235	6°01′N	18°24′E
Marand, Iran	201	38°26′N	45°46′E
Maranguape, Braz. (mä-räŋ-gwä′pĕ)	143	3°48′S	38°38′W
Maranhão, state, Braz. (mä-rän-youɴ)	143	5°15′S	45°52′W
Maranoa, r., Austl. (mä-rä-nō′ä)	221	27°01′S	148°03′E
Marano di Napoli, Italy (mä-rä′nô-dē-nä′pô-lē)	173c	40°39′N	14°12′E
Marañón, r., Peru (mä-rä-nyōn′)	142	4°26′S	75°08′W
Marapanim, Braz. (mä-rä-pä-nē′ɴ)	143	0°45′S	47°42′W
Marathon, Can.	91	48°50′N	86°10′W
Marathon, Fl., U.S. (măr′ȧ-thŏn)	125a	24°41′N	81°06′W
Marathon, Oh., U.S.	111f	39°09′N	83°59′W
Maravatio, Mex. (mä-rȧ-vä′tē-ō)	130	19°54′N	100°25′W
Marawi, Sudan	231	18°07′N	31°57′E
Marble Bar, Austl. (märb′′l bär)	218	21°15′S	119°15′E
Marble Canal, can., Az., U.S. (mär′b′l)	119	36°21′N	111°48′W
Marblehead, Ma., U.S. (mär′b′l-hĕd)	101a	42°30′N	70°51′W
Marburg an der Lahn, Ger.	168	50°49′N	8°46′E
Marca, Ponta da, c., Ang.	236	16°31′S	11°42′E
Marcala, Hond. (mär-kä-lä)	132	14°08′N	88°01′W
Marceline, Mo., U.S. (mär-sê-lēn′)	121	39°42′N	92°56′W
Marche, hist. reg., Italy (mär′kā)	174	43°35′N	12°33′E
Marchegg, Aus.	159e	48°18′N	16°55′E
Marchena, Spain (mär-chā′nä)	162	37°20′N	5°25′W
Marchena, i., Ec. (ê′s-lä-mär-chĕ′nä)	142	0°29′N	90°31′W
Marchfeld, reg., Aus.	159e	48°14′N	16°37′E
Mar Chiquita, Laguna, l., Arg. (lä-go͞o′nä-mär-chê-kĕ′tä)	141c	34°25′S	61°10′W
Marcos Paz, Arg. (mär-kōs′ päz)	141c	34°49′S	58°51′W
Marcus, i., Japan (mär′kŭs)	241	24°00′N	155°00′E
Marcus Hook, Pa., U.S. (mär′kŭs ho̤k)	110f	39°49′N	75°25′W
Marcy, Mount, mtn., N.Y., U.S. (mär′sê)	109	44°10′N	73°55′W
Mar de Espanha, Braz. (mär-dĕ-ĕs-pá′nyä)	141a	21°53′S	43°00′W
Mar del Plata, Arg. (mär dĕl- plä′ta)	144	37°59′S	57°35′W
Mardin, Tur. (mär-dēn′)	198	37°25′N	40°40′E
Maré, i., N. Cal. (mȧ-rā′)	221	21°53′S	168°30′E
Maree, Loch, b., Scot., U.K. (mä-rē′)	164	57°40′N	5°44′W
Marengo, Ia., U.S. (mȧ-rĕŋ′gō)	113	41°47′N	92°04′W
Marennes, Fr. (mȧ-rĕn′)	170	45°49′N	1°08′W
Marfa, Tx., U.S. (mär′fȧ)	122	30°19′N	104°01′W
Margarita, Pan. (mär-go͞o-rē′tä)	128a	9°20′N	79°55′W
Margarita, Isla de, i., Ven. (mä-gȧ-rē′tȧ)	142	11°00′N	64°15′W
Margate, S. Afr. (mä-gāt′)	233c	30°52′S	30°21′E
Margate, Eng., U.K. (mär′gāt)	165	51°21′N	1°17′E
Margherita Peak, mtn., Afr.	231	0°22′N	29°51′E
Marguerite, r., Can.	100	50°39′N	66°42′W
Marhanets′, Ukr.	177	47°41′N	34°33′E
Maria, Can. (mȧ-rē′ȧ)	100	48°10′N	66°04′W
Mariager, Den. (mä-rê-āgh′ĕr)	166	56°38′N	10°00′E
Mariana, Braz. (ma-rya′na)	141a	20°23′S	43°24′W
Mariana Islands, is., Oc.	5	16°00′N	145°30′E
Marianao, Cuba (mä-rê-ä-nä′ō)	129	23°05′N	82°26′W
Mariana Trench, deep	241	12°00′N	144°00′E
Marianna, Ar., U.S. (mā-rĭ-ăn′ȧ)	121	34°45′N	90°45′W
Marianna, Fl., U.S.	124	30°46′N	85°14′W
Marianna, Pa., U.S.	111e	40°01′N	80°05′W
Mariano Acosta, Arg. (mä-rēȧ′nô-á-kŏs′tä)	144a	34°28′S	58°48′W
Mariánské Lázně, Czech Rep. (mär′yán-skĕ′läz′nyĕ)	168	49°58′N	12°42′E
Marias, r., Mt., U.S. (mȧ-rī′ȧz)	115	48°15′N	110°50′W
Marías, Islas, is., Mex. (mä-rē′äs)	128	21°30′N	106°40′W
Mariato, Punta, c., Pan.	133	7°17′N	81°09′W
Maribo, Den. (mä′rê-bō)	166	54°46′N	11°29′E
Maribor, Slvn. (mä′re-bôr)	154	46°33′N	15°37′E
Maricaban, i., Phil. (mä-rê-kä-bän′)	213a	13°40′N	120°44′E
Mariefred, Swe. (mä-rē′ĕ-frĭd)	166	59°17′N	17°09′E
Marie Galante, i., Guad. (mȧ-rē′ gȧ-länt′)	133b	15°58′N	61°05′W
Mariehamn, Fin. (mȧ-rē′ê-häm′′n)	167	60°07′N	19°57′E
Mari El, prov., Russia	180	56°30′N	48°00′E
Mariestad, Swe. (mä-rē′ĕ-städ′)	166	58°43′N	13°45′E
Marietta, Ga., U.S. (mā-rĭ-′ĕt′ȧ)	110c	33°57′N	84°33′W
Marietta, Oh., U.S.	108	39°25′N	81°30′W
Marietta, Ok., U.S.	121	33°53′N	97°07′W
Marietta, Wa., U.S.	116d	48°48′N	122°35′W
Mariinsk, Russia (mȧ-rē′ĭnsk)	184	56°15′N	87°28′E
Marijampole, Lith. (mä-rê-yäm-pô′lĕ)	167	54°33′N	23°26′E
Marikana, S. Afr. (mă′-rĭ-kä-nȧ)	238c	25°40′S	27°28′E
Marília, Braz. (mä-rē′lyȧ)	143	22°02′S	49°48′W
Marimba, Ang.	236	8°28′S	17°08′E
Marín, Spain	172	42°24′N	8°40′W
Marinduque Island, i., Phil. (mä-rên-do͞o′kä)	213a	13°14′N	121°45′E
Marine, Il., U.S. (mȧ-rēn′)	117e	38°48′N	89°47′W
Marine City, Mi., U.S.	108	42°45′N	82°30′W
Marine Lake, l., Mn., U.S.	117g	45°13′N	92°55′W
Marine on Saint Croix, Mn., U.S.	117g	45°11′N	92°47′W
Marinette, Wi., U.S. (mär-ĭ-nĕt′)	105	45°04′N	87°40′W
Maringa, r., D.R.C. (mä-riŋ′gä)	231	0°30′N	21°00′E
Marinha Grande, Port. (mä-rēn′yȧ grän′dĕ)	172	39°49′N	8°53′W
Marion, Al., U.S. (măr′ĭ-ŭn)	124	32°36′N	87°19′W
Marion, Ia., U.S.	113	42°01′N	91°39′W
Marion, Il., U.S.	108	37°40′N	88°55′W
Marion, In., U.S.	105	40°35′N	85°45′W
Marion, Ks., U.S.	121	38°21′N	97°02′W
Marion, Ky., U.S.	124	37°19′N	88°05′W
Marion, N.C., U.S.	125	35°40′N	82°00′W
Marion, N.D., U.S.	112	46°37′N	98°20′W
Marion, Oh., U.S.	108	40°35′N	83°10′W
Marion, S.C., U.S.	125	34°08′N	79°23′W
Marion, Va., U.S.	125	36°48′N	81°33′W
Marion, Lake, res., S.C., U.S.	125	33°25′N	80°35′W
Marion Reef, rf., Austl.	221	18°57′S	151°31′E
Mariposa, Chile (mä-rê-pô′sä)	141b	35°33′S	71°21′W
Mariposa Creek, r., Ca., U.S.	118	37°14′N	120°30′W
Mariquita, Col. (mä-rê-kē′tä)	142a	5°13′N	74°52′W
Mariscal Estigarribia, Para.	144	22°03′S	60°28′W
Marisco, Ponta do, c., Braz. (pô′n-tä-dô-mä-rē′s-kö)	144b	23°01′S	43°17′W
Maritime Alps, mts., Eur. (mă′rĭ-tīm ălps)	161	44°20′N	7°02′E
Mariupol′, Ukr.	178	47°07′N	37°32′E
Mariveles, Phil.	213a	14°27′N	120°29′E
Marj Uyan, Leb.	197a	33°21′N	35°36′E
Marka, Som.	238a	1°45′N	44°47′E
Markaryd, Swe. (mär′kä-rüd)	166	56°30′N	13°34′E
Marked Tree, Ar., U.S. (märkt trē)	121	35°31′N	90°26′W
Marken, i., Neth.	159a	52°26′N	5°08′E
Market Bosworth, Eng., U.K. (bŏz′wûrth)	158a	52°37′N	1°23′W
Market Deeping, Eng., U.K. (dēp′ĭng)	158a	52°40′N	0°19′W
Market Drayton, Eng., U.K. (drā′tŭn)	158a	52°54′N	2°29′W
Market Harborough, Eng., U.K. (här′bŭr-ô)	158a	52°28′N	0°55′W
Market Rasen, Eng., U.K. (rā′zĕn)	158a	53°23′N	0°21′W
Markham, Can. (märk′ăm)	99	43°53′N	79°15′W
Markham, Mount, mtn., Ant.	224	82°59′S	159°30′E
Markivka, Ukr.	177	49°32′N	39°34′E
Markovo, Russia (mär′kô-vô)	179	64°46′N	170°48′E
Markrāna, India	202	27°08′N	74°43′E
Marks, Russia	181	51°42′N	46°46′E
Marksville, La., U.S. (märks′vĭl)	123	31°09′N	92°05′W
Markt Indersdorf, Ger. (märkt ĕn′dĕrs-dōrf)	159d	48°22′N	11°23′E
Marktredwitz, Ger. (märk-rĕd′vēts)	168	50°02′N	12°05′E
Markt Schwaben, Ger. (märkt shvä′bĕn)	159d	48°12′N	11°52′E
Marl, Ger. (märl)	171c	51°40′N	7°05′E
Marlboro, N.J., U.S.	110a	40°18′N	74°15′W
Marlborough, Ma., U.S.	101a	42°21′N	71°33′W
Marlette, Mi., U.S. (mär-lĕt′)	108	43°25′N	83°05′W
Marlin, Tx., U.S. (mär′lĭn)	123	31°18′N	96°52′W
Marlinton, W.V., U.S. (mär′lĭn-tŭn)	108	38°15′N	80°10′W
Marlow, Eng., U.K. (mär′lō)	158b	51°33′N	0°46′W
Marlow, Ok., U.S.	121	34°38′N	97°56′W
Marls, The, b., Bah. (märls)	134	26°30′N	77°15′W
Marmande, Fr. (mȧr-mäɴd′)	170	44°30′N	0°10′E
Marmara Denizi, sea, Tur.	198	40°40′N	28°00′E
Marmarth, N.D., U.S. (mär′mȧrth)	112	46°19′N	103°57′W
Mar Muerto, l., Mex. (mär-mòĕ′r-tô)	131	16°13′N	94°22′W
Marne, Ger. (mär′nĕ)	159c	53°57′N	9°01′E
Marne, r., Fr. (märn)	161	49°00′N	4°30′E
Maroa, Ven. (mä-rō′ä)	142	2°43′N	67°37′W
Maroantsetra, Madag. (mȧ-rō-äŋ-tsā′trȧ)	233	15°18′S	49°48′E
Maro Jarapeto, mtn., Col. (mä-rô-hä-rä-pĕ′tô)	142a	6°29′N	76°39′W
Maromokotro, mtn., Madag.	233	14°00′S	49°11′E
Marondera, Zimb.	232	18°10′S	31°36′E
Maroni, r., S.A. (mȧ-rō′nê)	143	3°02′N	53°54′W
Maro Reef, rf., Hi., U.S.	126b	25°15′N	170°00′W
Maroua, Cam. (mär′wä)	231	10°36′N	14°20′E
Marple, Eng., U.K. (mär′p′l)	158a	53°24′N	2°04′W
Marquard, S. Afr.	238c	28°41′S	27°26′E
Marquesas Islands, is., Fr. Poly. (mär-kĕ′säs)	2	8°50′S	141°00′W
Marquesas Keys, is., Fl., U.S. (mȧr-kē′zȧs)	125a	24°37′N	82°15′W
Marquês de Valença, Braz. (mȧr-kĕ′s-dĕ-vä-lĕ′n-sȧ)	141a	22°16′S	43°42′W
Marquette, Can. (mȧr-kĕt′)	102f	50°04′N	97°43′W
Marquette, Mi., U.S.	105	46°32′N	87°25′W
Marquez, Tx., U.S. (mär-kāz′)	123	31°14′N	96°15′W
Marra, Jabal, mtn., Sudan (jĕb′ĕl mär′ä)	231	13°00′N	23°47′E
Marrakech, Mor. (mȧr-rä′kĕsh)	230	31°38′N	8°00′W
Marree, Austl. (măr′rē)	218	29°38′S	137°55′E
Marrero, La., U.S.	110d	29°55′N	90°06′W
Marrupa, Moz.	237	13°08′S	37°30′E
Mars, Pa., U.S. (märz)	111e	40°42′N	80°01′W
Marsabit, Kenya	237	2°20′N	37°59′E
Marsala, Italy (mär-sä′lä)	162	37°48′N	12°28′E
Marsden, Eng., U.K. (märz′dĕn)	158a	53°36′N	1°55′W
Marseille, Fr. (mȧr-sâ′y′)	154	43°18′N	5°25′E
Marseilles, Il., U.S. (mär-sĕlz′)	108	41°20′N	88°40′W
Marshall, Il., U.S. (mär′shăl)	108	39°20′N	87°40′W
Marshall, Mi., U.S.	108	42°20′N	84°55′W
Marshall, Mn., U.S.	112	44°28′N	95°49′W
Marshall, Mo., U.S.	121	39°07′N	93°12′W
Marshall, Tx., U.S.	105	32°33′N	94°22′W
Marshall Islands, nation, Oc.	3	10°00′N	165°00′E
Marshalltown, Ia., U.S. (mär′shăl-toun)	113	42°02′N	92°55′W
Marshallville, Ga., U.S. (mär′shăl-vĭl)	124	32°29′N	83°55′W
Marshfield, Ma., U.S. (märsh′fēld)	101a	42°06′N	70°43′W
Marshfield, Mo., U.S.	121	37°20′N	92°53′W
Marshfield, Wi., U.S.	113	44°40′N	90°10′W
Marsh Harbour, Bah.	134	26°30′N	77°00′W
Mars Hill, In., U.S. (märz′hĭl′)	111g	39°43′N	86°15′W
Mars Hill, Me., U.S.	100	46°34′N	67°54′W
Marstrand, Swe. (mär′stränd)	166	57°54′N	11°33′E
Marsyaty, Russia (märs′yȧ-tĭ)	186a	60°03′N	60°28′E
Mart, Tx., U.S. (märt)	123	31°32′N	96°49′W
Martaban, Gulf of, b., Mya. (mär-tŭ-bän′)	212	16°34′N	96°58′E
Martapura, Indon.	212	3°19′S	114°45′E
Martha's Vineyard, i., Ma., U.S. (mär′thȧz vĭn′yȧrd)	109	41°25′N	70°35′W
Martigny, Switz. (mȧr-tē-nyē′)	168	46°06′N	7°00′E
Martigues, Fr.	171	43°24′N	5°05′E
Martin, Tn., U.S. (mär′tĭn)	124	36°20′N	88°45′W
Martina Franca, Italy (mär-tē′nä fräŋ′kä)	175	40°43′N	17°21′E
Martinez, Ca., U.S. (mär-tē′nĕz)	116b	38°01′N	122°08′W
Martinez, Tx., U.S.	117d	29°25′N	98°20′W
Martinique, dep., N.A. (mȧr-tê-nēk′)	129	14°50′N	60°40′W
Martin Lake, res., Al., U.S.	124	32°40′N	86°05′W
Martin Point, c., Ak., U.S.	103	70°10′N	142°00′W
Martinsburg, W.V., U.S. (mär′tĭnz-bûrg)	109	39°30′N	78°00′W
Martins Ferry, Oh., U.S. (mär′tĭnz)	108	40°05′N	80°45′W
Martinsville, In., U.S. (mär′tĭnz-vĭl)	108	39°25′N	86°25′W
Martinsville, Va., U.S.	125	36°40′N	79°53′W
Martos, Spain (mär′tōs)	172	37°43′N	3°58′W
Martre, Lac la, l., Can. (läk la märtr)	92	63°24′N	119°58′W
Marugame, Japan (mä′ro͞o-gä′mä)	211	34°19′N	133°48′E
Marungu, mts., D.R.C.	237	7°50′S	29°50′E
Marve, neigh., India	203b	19°12′N	72°43′E
Mary, Turkmen. (mä′rê)	183	37°45′N	61°47′E
Mar′yanskaya, Russia (mȧr-yän′skȧ-yȧ)	177	45°04′N	38°39′E
Maryborough, Austl. (mā′rĭ-bŭr-ô)	219	25°35′S	152°40′E
Maryborough, Austl.	219	37°00′S	143°50′E
Maryland, state, U.S. (mĕr′ĭ-lănd)	105	39°10′N	76°25′W
Marys, r., Nv., U.S. (mā′rĭz)	114	41°25′N	115°10′W
Marystown, Can. (mâr′ĭz-toun)	101	47°11′N	55°10′W

320 Marysville – Medan PRONOUNCING INDEX

PLACE (Pronunciation)	PAGE	LAT.	LONG.
Marysville, Can.	100	45°59'N	66°35'W
Marysville, Ca., U.S.	118	39°09'N	121°37'W
Marysville, Oh., U.S.	108	40°15'N	83°25'W
Marysville, Wa., U.S.	116a	48°03'N	122°11'W
Maryville, Il., U.S. (mâ´rĭ-vĭl)	117e	38°44'N	89°57'W
Maryville, Mo., U.S.	121	40°21'N	94°51'W
Maryville, Tn., U.S.	124	35°44'N	83°59'W
Mārzuq, Libya	231	26°00'N	14°09'E
Marzūq, Idehan, des., Libya	230	24°30'N	13°00'E
Masai Steppe, plat., Tan.	237	4°30'S	36°40'E
Masaka, Ug.	237	0°20'S	31°44'E
Masalasef, Chad	235	11°43'N	17°08'E
Masalembo-Besar, i., Indon.	212	5°40'S	114°28'E
Masan, Kor., S. (mä-sän´)	205	35°10'N	128°31'E
Masangwe, Tan.	237	5°28'S	30°05'E
Masasi, Tan. (mä-sä´sē)	233	10°43'S	38°48'E
Masatepe, Nic. [illegible]	[illegible]	[illegible]	[illegible]
Masaya, Nic. (mä-sä´yä)	132	11°58'N	86°05'W
Masbate, Phil. (mäs-bä´tā)	213a	12°21'N	123°38'E
Masbate, i., Phil.	213	12°19'N	123°03'E
Mascarene Islands, is., Afr.	5	20°20'S	56°40'E
Mascot, Tn., U.S. (măs´kŏt)	124	36°04'N	83°45'W
Mascota, Mex. (mäs-kō´tä)	130	20°33'N	104°45'W
Mascota, r., Mex.	130	20°33'N	104°52'W
Mascouche, Can. (mȧs-kōōsh´)	102a	45°45'N	73°36'W
Mascouche, r., Can.	102a	45°44'N	73°45'W
Mascoutah, Il., U.S. (măs-kū´tā)	117e	38°29'N	89°48'W
Maseru, Leso. (măz´ẽr-ōō)	232	29°09'S	27°11'E
Mashhad, Iran	198	36°17'N	59°30'E
Māshkel, Hāmūn-i-, l., Asia (hā-mōōn´ē māsh-kĕl´)	198	28°28'N	64°13'E
Mashra'ar Raqq, Sudan	231	8°28'N	29°15'E
Masi-Manimba, D.R.C.	236	4°46'S	17°55'E
Masindi, Ug. (mä-sēn´dē)	231	1°44'N	31°43'E
Masjed Soleymān, Iran	198	31°45'N	49°17'E
Mask, Lough, b., Ire. (lŏk mȧsk)	164	53°35'N	9°23'W
Maslovo, Russia (mäs´lô-vô)	186a	60°08'N	60°28'E
Mason, Mi., U.S. (mā´sŭn)	108	42°35'N	84°25'W
Mason, Oh., U.S.	111f	39°22'N	84°18'W
Mason, Tx., U.S.	122	30°46'N	99°14'W
Mason City, Ia., U.S.	105	43°08'N	93°14'W
Massa, Italy (mäs´sä)	174	44°02'N	10°08'E
Massachusetts, state, U.S. (măs-ȧ-chōō´sĕts)	105	42°20'N	72°30'W
Massachusetts Bay, b., Ma., U.S.	100	42°26'N	70°20'W
Massafra, Italy (mäs-sä´frä)	175	40°35'N	17°05'E
Massa Marittima, Italy	174	43°03'N	10°55'E
Massapequa, N.Y., U.S.	110a	40°41'N	73°28'W
Massaua *see* Mitsiwa, Erit.	231	15°40'N	39°19'E
Massena, N.Y., U.S. (mă-sē´nȧ)	109	44°55'N	74°55'W
Masset, Can. (măs´ĕt)	90	54°02'N	132°09'W
Masset Inlet, b., Can.	95	53°42'N	132°20'E
Massif Central, Fr. (mȧ-sēf´ säɴ-trȧl´)	154	45°12'N	3°02'E
Massillon, Oh., U.S. (măs´ĭ-lŏn)	108	40°50'N	81°35'W
Massinga, Moz. (mä-sĭn´gä)	232	23°18'S	35°18'E
Massive, Mount, mtn., Co., U.S. (măs´ĭv)	106	39°05'N	106°30'W
Masson, Can. (mäs-sŭn)	102c	45°33'N	75°25'W
Masuda, Japan (mä-sōō´dȧ)	211	34°42'N	131°53'E
Masuria, reg., Pol.	169	53°40'N	21°10'E
Masvingo, Zimb.	232	20°07'S	30°47'E
Matadi, D.R.C. (mȧ-tä´dē)	232	5°49'S	13°27'E
Matagalpa, Nic. (mä-tä-gäl´pä)	128	12°52'N	85°57'W
Matagami, l., Can. (mȧ-tä-gä´mē)	93	50°10'N	78°28'W
Matagorda Bay, b., Tx., U.S. (măt-ȧ-gôr´dȧ)	123	28°32'N	96°13'W
Matagorda Island, i., Tx., U.S.	123	28°13'N	96°27'W
Matam, Sen. (mä-täm´)	230	15°40'N	13°15'W
Matamoros, Mex. (mä-tä-mō´rôs)	122	25°32'N	103°13'W
Matamoros, Mex.	128	25°52'N	97°30'W
Matane, Can. (mȧ-tȧn´)	91	48°51'N	67°32'W
Matanzas, Cuba (mä-tän´zäs)	129	23°05'N	81°35'W
Matanzas, prov., Cuba	134	22°45'N	81°20'W
Matanzas, Bahía, b., Cuba (bä-ē´ä)	134	23°10'N	81°30'W
Matapalo, Cabo, c., C.R. (kȧ´bō-mä-tä-pä´lō)	133	8°22'N	83°25'W
Matapédia, Can. (mă-tȧ-pā´dē-ȧ)	100	47°58'N	66°56'W
Matapédia, l., Can.	100	48°33'N	67°32'W
Matapédia, r., Can.	100	48°10'N	67°10'W
Mataquito, r., Chile (mä-tä-kē´tô)	141b	35°08'S	71°35'W
Matara, Sri L. (mä-tä´rä)	203	5°59'N	80°35'E
Mataram, Indon.	212	8°45'S	116°15'E
Matatiele, S. Afr. (mä-tä-tyā´lā)	233c	30°21'S	28°49'E
Matawan, N.J., U.S.	110a	40°24'N	74°13'W
Matehuala, Mex. (mä-tȧ-wä´lä)	128	23°38'N	100°39'W
Matera, Italy (mä-tâ´rä)	174	40°42'N	16°37'E
Mateur, Tun. (mȧ-tûr´)	162	37°09'N	9°43'E
Māterān, India	203b	18°58'N	73°16'E
Matheson, Can.	99	48°35'N	80°33'W
Mathews, Lake, l., Ca., U.S. (măth ūz)	117a	33°50'N	117°24'W
Mathura, India (mu-tŏ´rŭ)	199	27°39'N	77°39'E
Matias Barbosa, Braz. (mä-tē´ăs-bár-bô-sä)	141a	21°53'S	43°19'W
Matillas, Laguna, l., Mex. (lä-gô´nä-mä-tē´l-yäs)	131	18°02'N	92°36'W
Matina, C.R. (mä-tē´nä)	133	10°06'N	83°20'W
Matiši, Lat. (mä´tē-sē)	167	57°43'N	25°09'E
Matlalcueyetl, Cerro, mtn., Mex. (sĕ´r-rä-mä-tläl-kwĕ´yĕtl)	130	19°13'N	98°02'W
Matlock, Eng., U.K. (măt´lŏk)	158a	53°08'N	1°33'W
Matochkin Shar, Russia (mä´tŏch-kĭn)	178	73°57'N	56°16'E
Mato Grosso, Braz. (mät´ō grōs´ōō)	143	15°04'S	59°58'W
Mato Grosso, state, Braz.	143	14°38'S	55°36'W
Mato Grosso, Chapada de, hills, Braz. (shä-pä´dä-dĕ)	143	13°39'S	55°42'W
Mato Grosso do Sul, state, Braz.	143	20°00'S	56°00'W
Matosinhos, Port.	172	41°10'N	8°48'W
Maṭraḥ, Oman (mȧ-trä´)	198	23°36'N	58°27'E
Matsubara, Japan	211b	34°34'N	135°34'E
Matsudo, Japan (mät´sȯ-dȯ)	211a	35°48'N	139°55'E
Matsue, Japan (mät´sȯ-ĕ)	205	35°29'N	133°04'E
Matsumoto, Japan (mät´sȯ-mō´tȯ)	210	36°15'N	137°59'E
Matsuyama, Japan (mät´sȯ-yä´mä)	205	33°48'N	132°45'E
Matsuzaka, Japan (mät´sȯ-zä´kä)	211	34°35'N	136°34'E
Mattamuskeet, Lake, l., N.C., U.S. (măt-tȧ-mŭs´kēt)	125	35°34'N	76°03'W
Mattaponi, r., Va., U.S. (măt´ȧ-ponī´)	109	37°45'N	77°00'W
Mattawa, Can. (măt´ȧ-wȧ)	91	46°15'N	78°49'W
Matterhorn, mtn., Eur. (mät´ẽr-hôrn)	168	45°57'N	7°36'E
Matteson, Il., U.S. (măt´ē-sŭn)	111a	41°30'N	87°42'W
Matthew Town, Bah. (măth´u toun)	135	21°00'N	73°40'W
Mattoon, Il., U.S. (mă-tōōn´)	105	39°30'N	88°20'W
Maturín, Ven. (mä-tōō-rēn´)	142	9°48'N	63°16'W
Maúa, Moz.	237	13°51'S	37°10'E
Mauban, Phil. (mä´ōō-bän´)	213a	14°11'N	121°44'E
Maubeuge, Fr. (mȯ-bûzh´)	170	50°18'N	3°57'E
Maud, Oh., U.S. (môd)	111f	39°21'N	84°23'W
Mauer, Aus. (mou´ẽr)	159e	48°09'N	16°16'E
Maués, Braz. (mȧ-wĕ´s)	143	3°34'S	57°30'W
Mau Escarpment, cliff, Kenya	237	0°45'S	35°50'E
Maui, i., Hi., U.S. (mä´ōō-ē)	106c	20°52'N	156°02'W
Maule, r., Chile (mà´ô-lĕ)	141b	35°45'S	70°50'W
Maumee, Oh., U.S. (mô-mē´)	108	41°30'N	83°40'W
Maumee, r., In., U.S.	108	41°10'N	84°50'W
Maumee Bay, b., Oh., U.S.	108	41°50'N	83°20'W
Maun, Bots. (mä-ôn´)	232	19°52'S	23°40'E
Mauna Kea, mtn., Hi., U.S. (mä´ô-näkā´ä)	106c	19°52'N	155°30'W
Mauna Loa, mtn., Hi., U.S. (mä´ô-nälō´ä)	106c	19°28'N	155°38'W
Maurepas Lake, l., La., U.S. (mō-rē-pä´)	123	30°18'N	90°40'W
Mauricie, Parc National de la, rec., Can.	99	46°46'N	73°00'W
Mauritania, nation, Afr. (mô-rē-tā´nĭ-ȧ)	230	19°38'N	13°30'W
Mauritius, nation, Afr. (mô-rĭsh´ĭ-ŭs)	3	20°18'S	57°36'E
Maury, Wa., U.S. (mô´rĭ)	116a	47°22'N	122°23'W
Mauston, Wi., U.S. (môs´tŭn)	113	43°46'N	90°05'W
Maverick, r., Az., U.S. (mā-vûr´ĭk)	119	33°40'N	109°30'W
Mavinga, Ang.	236	15°50'S	20°21'E
Mawlamyine, Mya.	212	16°30'N	97°39'E
Maxville, Can. (măks´vĭl)	102c	45°17'N	74°52'W
Maxville, Mo., U.S.	117e	38°26'N	90°24'W
Maya, r., Russia (mä´yä)	185	58°00'N	135°45'E
Mayaguana, i., Bah.	135	22°25'N	73°00'W
Mayaguana Passage, strt., Bah.	135	22°20'N	73°25'W
Mayagüez, P.R. (mä-yä-gwāz´)	129	18°12'N	67°10'W
Mayari, r., Cuba	135	20°25'N	75°35'W
Mayas, Montañas, mts., N.A. (mŏntăŋ´ăs mä´ăs)	132a	16°43'N	89°00'W
Mayd, i., Som.	238a	11°24'N	46°38'E
Mayen, Ger. (mī´ĕn)	168	50°19'N	7°14'E
Mayenne, r., Fr. (mȧ-yĕn)	170	48°14'N	0°45'W
Mayfield, Ky., U.S. (mā´fēld)	124	36°44'N	88°19'W
Mayfield Creek, r., Ky., U.S.	124	36°54'N	88°47'W
Mayfield Heights, Oh., U.S.	111d	41°31'N	81°26'W
Mayfield Lake, res., Wa., U.S.	114	46°31'N	122°34'W
Maykop, Russia	178	44°35'N	40°07'E
Maykor, Russia (mī-kôr´)	186a	59°01'N	55°52'E
Maymyo, Mya. (mī´myō)	204	22°14'N	96°32'E
Maynard, Ma., U.S. (mā´nȧrd)	101a	42°25'N	71°27'W
Mayne, Can. (mān)	116d	48°51'N	123°18'W
Mayne, i., Can.	116d	48°52'N	123°14'W
Mayo, Can. (mā-yō´)	90	63°40'N	135°51'W
Mayo, Fl., U.S.	124	30°02'N	83°08'W
Mayo, Md., U.S.	110e	38°54'N	76°31'W
Mayodan, N.C., U.S. (mā-yō´dȧn)	125	36°25'N	79°59'W
Mayon Volcano, vol., Phil. (mä-yōn´)	213a	13°21'N	123°43'E
Mayotte, dep., Afr. (mȧ-yôt´)	233	13°07'S	45°32'E
May Pen, Jam.	134	18°00'N	77°25'W
Mayraira Point, c., Phil.	209	18°40'N	120°45'E
Mayran, Laguna de, l., Mex. (lä-ô´nä-dĕ-mī-rän´)	128	25°40'N	102°35'W
Mayskiy, Russia	182	43°38'N	44°04'E
Maysville, Ky., U.S. (māz´vĭl)	108	38°35'N	83°45'W
Mayumba, Gabon	232	3°25'S	10°39'E
Mayville, N.D., U.S.	112	47°30'N	97°20'W
Mayville, N.Y., U.S. (mā´vĭl)	109	42°15'N	79°30'W
Mayville, Wi., U.S.	113	43°30'N	88°45'W
Maywood, Ca., U.S. (mā´wŏd)	117a	33°59'N	118°11'W
Maywood, Il., U.S.	111a	41°53'N	87°51'W
Mazabuka, Zam. (mä-zä-bōō´kä)	232	15°51'S	27°46'E
Mazagão, Braz. (mä-zȧ-gou´ɴ)	143	0°05'S	51°27'W
Mazapil, Mex. (mä-zä-pēl´)	122	24°40'N	101°30'W
Mazara del Vallo, Italy (mät-sä´rä dĕl väl´lō)	174	37°40'N	12°37'E
Mazār-i-Sharīf, Afg. (mȧ-zär´-ē-shȧ-rēf´)	199	36°48'N	67°12'E
Mazarrón, Spain (mä-zär-rō´n)	172	37°37'N	1°29'W
Mazatenango, Guat. (mä-zä-tȧ-näŋ´gō)	128	14°30'N	91°30'W
Mazatla, Mex.	131a	19°30'N	99°24'W
Mazatlán, Mex.	128	23°14'N	106°27'W
Mazatlán (San Juan), Mex. (mä-zä-tlän´) (saẔ hwän´)	131	17°05'N	95°26'W
Mažeikiai, Lith. (mȧ-zhā´kē-ī)	167	56°19'N	22°24'E
Mazḥafah, Jabal, mtn., Sau. Ar.	197a	28°56'N	35°05'E
Mazyr, Bela.	181	52°03'N	29°14'E
Mbabane, Swaz. (m'bä-bä´nĕ)	232	26°18'S	31°14'E
Mbaiki, C.A.R. (m'bȧ-ē´kē)	231	3°53'N	18°00'E
Mbakana, Montagne de, mts., Cam.	235	7°55'N	14°40'E
Mbakaou, Barrage de, dam, Cam.	235	6°10'N	12°55'E
Mbala, Zam.	232	8°50'S	31°22'E
Mbale, Ug.	237	1°05'N	34°10'E
Mbamba Bay, Tan.	237	11°17'S	34°46'E
Mbandaka, D.R.C.	232	0°04'N	18°16'E
M'banza Congo, Ang.	232	6°30'S	14°10'E
Mbanza-Ngungu, D.R.C.	232	5°20'S	10°55'E
Mbarara, Ug.	237	0°37'S	30°39'E
Mbasay, Chad	235	7°39'N	15°40'E
Mbigou, Gabon (m-bē-gōō´)	232	2°07'S	11°30'E
Mbinda, Congo	236	2°00'S	12°55'E
Mbogo, Tan.	237	7°26'S	33°26'E
Mbomou (Bomu), r., Afr. [illegible]	[illegible]	[illegible]	[illegible]
Mbout, Maur. (m'bōō´)	230	16°03'N	12°31'W
Mbuji-Mayi, D.R.C.	236	6°09'S	23°38'E
McAdam, Can. (măk-ăd´ăm)	100	45°36'N	67°20'W
McAfee, N.J., U.S. (măk-ȧ´fē)	110a	41°10'N	74°32'W
McAlester, Ok., U.S. (măk ăl´ĕs-tẽr)	105	34°55'N	95°45'W
McAllen, Tx., U.S. (măk-ăl´ĕn)	122	26°12'N	98°14'W
McBride, Can. (măk-brīd´)	90	53°18'N	120°10'W
McCalla, Al., U.S. (măk-kăl´lā)	110h	33°20'N	87°00'W
McCamey, Tx., U.S. (mȧ-kā´mĭ)	122	31°08'N	102°13'W
McColl, S.C., U.S. (mȧ-kól´)	125	34°40'N	79°34'W
McComb, Ms., U.S. (mȧ-kōm´)	124	31°14'N	90°27'W
McConaughy, Lake, l., Ne., U.S. (măk kō´nō ĭ´)	112	41°24'N	101°40'W
McCook, Ne., U.S. (mȧ-kŏk´)	120	40°13'N	100°37'W
McCormick, S.C., U.S. (mȧ-kôr´mĭk)	125	33°56'N	82°20'W
McDonald, Pa., U.S. (măk-dŏn´ăld)	111e	40°22'N	80°13'W
McDonald Island, i., Austl.	224	53°00'S	72°45'E
McDonald Lake, l., Can. (măk-dŏn-ăld)	102e	51°12'N	113°53'W
McGehee, Ar., U.S. (mȧ-gē´)	121	33°39'N	91°22'W
McGill, Nv., U.S. (mȧ-gĭl´)	119	39°25'N	114°47'W
McGowan, Wa., U.S. (măk-gou´ăn)	116c	46°15'N	123°55'W
McGrath, Ak., U.S. (măk´grȧth)	106a	62°58'N	155°20'W
McGregor, Can. (măk-grĕg´ẽr)	111b	42°08'N	82°58'W
McGregor, Ia., U.S.	113	42°58'N	91°12'W
McGregor, Tx., U.S.	123	31°26'N	97°23'W
McGregor, r., Can.	95	54°10'N	121°00'W
McGregor Lake, l., Can. (măk-grĕg´ẽr)	102c	45°38'N	75°44'W
McHenry, Il., U.S. (măk-hĕn´rĭ)	111a	42°21'N	88°16'W
Mchinji, Mwi.	232	13°42'S	32°50'E
McIntosh, S.D., U.S. (măk´ĭn-tŏsh)	112	45°54'N	101°22'W
McKay, r., Or., U.S.	116c	45°43'N	123°00'W
McKeesport, Pa., U.S. (mȧ-kez´pōrt)	111e	40°21'N	79°51'W
McKees Rocks, Pa., U.S. (mȧ-kēz´ rŏks)	111e	40°29'N	80°05'W
McKenzie, Tn., U.S. (mȧ-kĕn´zĭ)	124	36°07'N	88°30'W
McKenzie, r., Or., U.S.	114	44°07'N	122°20'W
McKinley, Mount, mtn., Ak., U.S. (mȧ-kĭn´lĭ)	106a	63°00'N	151°02'W
McKinney, Tx., U.S. (mȧ-kĭn´ĭ)	121	33°12'N	96°35'W
McLaughlin, S.D., U.S. (măk-lŏf´lĭn)	112	45°48'N	100°45'W
McLean, Va., U.S. (măc´lān)	110e	38°56'N	77°11'W
McLeansboro, Il., U.S. (mȧ-klānz´bŭr-ō)	108	38°10'N	88°35'W
McLennan, Can. (măk-lĭn´nȧn)	90	55°42'N	116°54'W
McLeod, r., Can.	95	53°45'N	115°55'W
McLeod Lake, Can.	94	54°59'N	123°02'W
McLoughlin, Mount, mtn., Or., U.S. (mȧk-lŏk´lĭn)	114	42°27'N	122°20'W
McMillan Lake, l., Tx., U.S. (măk-mĭl´ȧn)	122	32°40'N	104°09'W
McMillin, Wa., U.S. (măk-mĭl´ĭn)	116a	47°08'N	122°14'W
McMinnville, Or., U.S. (măk-mĭn´vĭl)	114	45°13'N	123°13'W
McMinnville, Tn., U.S.	124	35°41'N	85°47'W
McMurray, Wa., U.S. (măk-mŭr´ĭ)	116a	48°19'N	122°15'W
McNary, Az., U.S. (măk-nâr´ē)	119	34°10'N	109°55'W
McNary, La., U.S.	123	30°58'N	92°32'W
McNary Dam, Or., U.S.	114	45°57'N	119°15'W
McPherson, Ks., U.S. (măk-fŭr´s'n)	121	38°21'N	97°41'W
McRae, Ga., U.S. (măk-rā´)	125	32°02'N	82°55'W
McRoberts, Ky., U.S. (măk-rŏb´ẽrts)	125	37°12'N	82°40'W
Mead, Ks., U.S. (mēd)	120	37°17'N	100°21'W
Mead, Lake, l., U.S.	106	36°20'N	114°14'W
Meade Peak, mtn., Id., U.S.	115	42°19'N	111°16'W
Meadow Lake, Can. (mĕd´ō lăk)	90	54°08'N	108°26'W
Meadows, Can. (mĕd´ōz)	102f	50°02'N	97°35'W
Meadville, Pa., U.S. (mēd´vĭl)	108	41°40'N	80°10'W
Meaford, Can. (mē´fẽrd)	99	44°35'N	80°40'W
Mealy Mountains, mts., Can. (mē´lē)	93	53°32'N	57°58'W
Meandarra, Austl. (mē-ăn-dă´rȧ)	222	27°47'S	149°40'E
Meaux, Fr. (mō)	170	48°58'N	2°53'E
Mecapalapa, Mex. (mă-kä-pä-lä´pä)	131	20°32'N	97°52'W
Mecatina, r., Can. (mă-kȧ-tē´nȧ)	101	50°50'N	59°45'W
Mecca (Makkah), Sau. Ar. (mĕk´ȧ)	198	21°27'N	39°45'E
Mechanic Falls, Me., U.S. (mē-kăn´ĭk)	100	44°05'N	70°23'W
Mechanicsburg, Pa., U.S. (mē-kăn´ĭks-bûrg)	109	40°15'N	77°00'W
Mechanicsville, Md., U.S. (mē-kăn´ĭks-vĭl)	110e	38°27'N	76°45'W
Mechanicville, N.Y., U.S. (mē-kăn´ĭk-vĭl)	109	42°55'N	73°45'W
Mechelen, Bel.	165	51°01'N	4°28'E
Mechriyya, Alg.	162	33°30'N	0°13'W
Medicine Bow Range, mts., Co., U.S. (mĕd´ĭ-sĭn bō)	120	40°55'N	106°02'W
Mecklenburg, hist. reg., Ger.	168	53°30'N	13°00'E
Medan, Indon. (mā-dän´)	212	3°35'N	98°35'E

ăt; finăl; rāte; senāte; ärm; ȧsk; sofȧ; fâre; ch-choose; dh-as th in other; bē; ēvent; bĕt; recĕnt; cratẽr; g-gō; gh-guttural g; bĭt; ĭ-short neutral; rīde; ĸ-guttural k as ch in German ich;

PRONOUNCING INDEX Medanosa – Mezquitic 321

PLACE (Pronunciation)	PAGE	LAT.	LONG.
Medanosa, Punta, c., Arg. (pōō′n-tä-mĕ-dä-nô′sä)	144	47°50′S	65°53′W
Medden, r., Eng., U.K. (mĕd′ĕn)	158a	53°14′N	1°05′W
Medellín, Col. (må-dhĕl-yēn′)	142	6°15′N	75°34′W
Medellín, Mex. (mĕ-dĕl-yē′n)	131	19°03′N	96°08′W
Medenine, Tun. (mā-dĕ-nēn′)	162	33°22′N	10°33′E
Medfeld, Ma., U.S. (mĕd′fĕld)	101a	42°11′N	71°19′W
Medford, Ma., U.S. (mĕd′fẽrd)	101a	42°25′N	71°07′W
Medford, N.J., U.S.	110f	39°54′N	74°50′W
Medford, Ok., U.S.	121	36°47′N	97°44′W
Medford, Or., U.S.	104	42°19′N	122°52′W
Medford, Wi., U.S.	113	45°09′N	90°22′W
Media, Pa., U.S. (mē′dĭ-ȧ)	110f	39°55′N	75°24′W
Mediaş, Rom. (mĕd-yäsh′)	169	46°09′N	24°21′E
Medical Lake, Wa., U.S. (mĕd′ĭ-kăl)	114	47°34′N	117°40′W
Medicine Bow, r., Wy., U.S.	115	41°58′N	106°30′W
Medicine Hat, Can. (mĕd′ĭ-sĭn hăt)	90	50°03′N	110°40′W
Medicine Lake, l., Mt., U.S. (mĕd′ĭ-sĭn)	115	48°24′N	104°15′W
Medicine Lodge, Ks., U.S.	120	37°17′N	98°37′W
Medicine Lodge, r., Ks., U.S.	120	37°20′N	98°57′W
Medina *see* Al Madīnah, Sau. Ar.	198	24°26′N	39°42′E
Medina, N.Y., U.S. (mė-dī′nȧ)	109	43°15′N	78°20′W
Medina, Oh., U.S.	111d	41°08′N	81°52′W
Medina, r., Tx., U.S.	122	29°45′N	99°13′W
Medina del Campo, Spain (må-dē′nä dĕl käm′pō)	162	41°18′N	4°54′W
Medina de Ríoseco, Spain (må-dē′nä dā rē-ô-sā′kō)	172	41°53′N	5°05′W
Medina Lake, l., Tx., U.S.	122	29°36′N	98°47′W
Medina Sidonia, Spain	172	36°28′N	5°58′W
Mediterranean Sea, sea (mĕd-ĭ-tẽr-ā′nė-ăn)	162	36°22′N	13°25′E
Medjerda, Oued, r., Afr.	162	36°43′N	9°54′E
Mednogorsk, Russia	178	51°27′N	57°22′E
Medveditsa, r., Russia (mĕd-vyě′dē tsä)	181	50°10′N	43°40′E
Medvezhegorsk, Russia (mĕd-vyězh′yĕ-gôrsk′)	180	63°00′N	34°20′E
Medway, Ma., U.S. (mĕd′wā)	101a	42°08′N	71°23′W
Medway Towns, co., Eng., U.K.	158b	51°27′N	0°30′E
Medyn′, Russia (mĕ-dēn′)	176	54°58′N	35°53′E
Medzhybizh, Ukr.	177	49°23′N	27°29′E
Meekatharra, Austl. (mē-kȧ-thăr′ȧ)	218	26°30′S	118°38′E
Meeker, Co., U.S. (mēk′ẽr)	119	40°00′N	107°55′W
Meelpaeg Lake, l., Can. (mēl′pȧ-ĕg)	101	48°22′N	56°52′W
Meerane, Ger. (mā-rä′nē)	168	50°51′N	12°27′E
Meerbusch, Ger.	171c	51°15′N	6°41′E
Meerut, India (mē′rŭt)	199	28°59′N	77°43′E
Megalópoli, Grc.	175	37°22′N	22°08′E
Mégara, Grc. (mĕg′ȧ-rȧ)	175	37°59′N	23°21′E
Megget, S.C., U.S. (mĕg′ĕt)	125	32°44′N	80°15′W
Megler, Wa., U.S. (mĕg′lẽr)	116c	46°15′N	123°52′W
Mehanom, Mys, c., Ukr.	177	44°48′N	35°17′E
Meherrin, r., Va., U.S. (mė-hĕr′ĭn)	125	36°40′N	77°49′W
Mehlville, Mo., U.S.	117e	38°30′N	90°19′W
Mehsāna, India	202	23°42′N	72°23′E
Mehun-sur-Yévre, Fr. (mē-ŭN-sür-yĕvr′)	170	47°11′N	2°14′E
Meiling Pass, p., China (mā′lĭng′)	205	25°22′N	115°00′E
Meinerzhagen, Ger. (mī′nĕrts-hä-gĕn)	171c	51°06′N	7°39′E
Meiningen, Ger. (mī′nĭng-ĕn)	168	50°35′N	10°25′E
Meiringen, Switz.	168	46°45′N	8°11′E
Meissen, Ger.	168	51°11′N	13°28′E
Meizhu, China (mā-jōō)	206	31°17′N	119°12′E
Mejillones, Chile (må-κē-lyō′nås)	144	23°07′S	70°31′W
Mekambo, Gabon	236	1°01′N	13°56′E
Mekele, Eth.	231	13°31′N	39°19′E
Meknés, Mor. (mĕk′nĕs) (mĕk-nĕs′)	230	33°56′N	5°44′W
Mekong, r., Asia	212	18°00′N	104°30′E
Melaka, Malay.	212	2°11′N	102°15′E
Melaka, state, Malay.	197b	2°19′N	102°09′E
Melanesia, is., Oc.	240	13°00′S	164°00′E
Melbourne, Austl. (mĕl′bŭrn)	219	37°52′S	145°08′E
Melbourne, Eng., U.K.	158a	52°49′N	1°26′W
Melbourne, Fl., U.S.	125a	28°05′N	80°37′W
Melbourne, Ky., U.S.	111f	39°02′N	84°22′W
Melcher, Ia., U.S. (mĕl′chẽr)	113	41°13′N	93°11′W
Melekess, Russia (mĕl-yĕk-ĕs)	180	54°14′N	49°39′E
Melenki, Russia (mĕ-lyĕŋ′kė)	180	55°25′N	41°34′E
Melfort, Can. (mĕl′fôrt)	90	52°52′N	104°36′W
Melghir, Chott, l., Alg.	230	33°52′N	5°22′E
Melilla, Sp. N. Afr. (mā-lēl′yä)	230	35°24′N	3°30′W
Melipilla, Chile (må-lė-pē′lyä)	144	33°40′S	71°12′W
Melita, Can.	97	49°11′N	101°09′W
Melitopol′, Ukr. (mā-lē-tô′pôl-y′)	181	46°49′N	35°19′E
Melívoia, Grc.	175	39°42′N	22°47′E
Melkrivier, S. Afr.	238c	24°01′S	28°23′E
Mellen, Wi., U.S. (mĕl′ĕn)	113	46°20′N	90°40′W
Mellerud, Swe. (mål′ĕ-rōōdh)	166	58°43′N	12°25′E
Melmoth, S. Afr.	233c	28°38′S	31°26′E
Melo, Ur. (mā′lō)	144	32°18′S	54°07′W
Melocheville, Can. (mĕ-lôsh-vēl′)	102a	45°24′N	73°56′W
Melozha, r., Russia (myě′lô-zhȧ)	186b	56°06′N	38°34′E
Melrose, Ma., U.S. (mĕl′rōz)	101a	42°29′N	71°06′W
Melrose, Mn., U.S.	113	45°39′N	94°49′W
Melrose Park, Il., U.S.	111a	41°54′N	87°52′W
Meltham, Eng., U.K. (mĕl′thăm)	158a	53°35′N	1°51′W
Melton, Austl. (mĕl′tŭn)	217a	37°41′S	144°35′E
Melton Mowbray, Eng., U.K. (mō′brâ)	158a	52°45′N	0°52′W
Melúli, r., Moz.	237	16°10′S	39°30′E
Melun, Fr. (mē-lŭN′)	161	48°32′N	2°40′E
Melunga, Ang.	236	17°16′S	16°24′E
Melville, Can. (mĕl′vĭl)	90	50°55′N	102°48′W
Melville, La., U.S.	123	30°39′N	91°45′W
Melville, i., Austl.	220	11°30′S	131°12′E
Melville, l., Can.	93	53°46′N	59°31′W
Melville, Cape, c., Austl.	221	14°15′S	145°50′E
Melville Hills, hills, Can.	92	69°18′N	124°57′W
Melville Peninsula, pen., Can.	93	67°44′N	84°09′W
Melvindale, Mi., U.S. (mĕl′vĭn-dāl)	111b	42°17′N	83°11′W
Melyana, Alg.	161	36°19′N	1°56′E
Mélykút, Hung. (mā′l′kōōt)	169	46°14′N	19°21′E
Memba, Moz. (mĕm′bȧ)	233	14°12′N	40°35′E
Memel *see* Klaipėda, Lith.	180	55°43′N	21°10′E
Memel, S. Afr. (mĕ′mĕl)	238c	27°42′S	29°35′E
Memmingen, Ger. (mĕm′ĭng-ĕn)	168	47°59′N	10°10′E
Memo, r., Ven. (mĕ′mō)	143b	9°32′N	66°30′W
Memphis, Mo., U.S. (mĕm′fĭs)	121	40°27′N	92°11′W
Memphis, Tn., U.S. (mĕm′fĭs)	105	35°07′N	90°03′W
Memphis, Tx., U.S.	120	34°42′N	100°33′W
Memphis, hist., Egypt	238b	29°50′N	31°12′E
Mena, Ukr. (mē-nä′)	177	51°31′N	32°14′E
Mena, Ar., U.S. (mē′nȧ)	121	34°35′N	94°09′W
Menangle, Austl.	217b	34°00′S	150°40′E
Menard, Tx., U.S. (mė-närd′)	122	30°56′N	99°48′W
Menasha, Wi., U.S. (mė-năsh′ȧ)	113	44°12′N	88°29′W
Mende, Fr. (mäNd)	170	44°31′N	3°30′E
Menden, Ger. (mĕn′dĕn)	171c	51°26′N	7°47′E
Mendes, Braz. (mĕ′n-dĕs)	144b	22°32′S	43°44′W
Mendocino, Ca., U.S.	118	39°18′N	123°47′W
Mendocino, Cape, c., Ca., U.S. (mĕn′dô-sē′nō)	107	40°25′N	12°42′W
Mendota, Il., U.S. (mĕn-dō′tȧ)	113	41°34′N	89°06′W
Mendota, l., Wi., U.S.	113	43°09′N	89°41′W
Mendoza, Arg. (mĕn-dō′sä)	144	32°48′S	68°45′W
Mendoza, prov., Arg.	144	35°10′S	69°00′W
Mengcheng, China (mŭŋ-chŭŋ)	206	33°15′N	116°34′E
Meng Shan, mts., China (mŭŋ shän)	206	35°47′N	117°23′E
Mengzi, China	204	23°22′N	103°20′E
Menindee, Austl. (mĕ-nĭn-dē)	222	32°23′S	142°30′E
Menlo Park, Ca., U.S. (mĕn′lō pärk)	116b	37°27′N	122°11′W
Menno, S.D., U.S. (mĕn′ō)	112	43°14′N	97°34′W
Menominee, Mi., U.S. (mė-nŏm′ĭ-nē)	113	45°08′N	87°40′W
Menominee, r., Mi., U.S.	113	45°37′N	87°54′W
Menominee Falls, Wi., U.S. (fôls)	111a	43°11′N	88°06′W
Menominee Ra, Mi., U.S.	113	46°07′N	88°53′W
Menomonee, r., Wi., U.S.	111a	43°09′N	88°06′W
Menomonie, Wi., U.S.	113	44°53′N	91°55′W
Menongue, Ang.	236	14°36′S	17°48′E
Menorca (Minorca), i., Spain (mĕ-nō′r-kä)	156	40°05′N	3°58′E
Mentana, Italy (mĕn-tá′nä)	173d	42°02′N	12°40′E
Mentawai, Kepulauan, is., Indon. (mĕn-tä-vī′)	212	1°08′S	98°10′E
Menton, Fr. (mäN-tôN′)	171	43°46′N	7°37′E
Mentone, Ca., U.S. (mĕn′tōne)	117a	34°05′N	117°08′W
Mentz, l., S. Afr. (mĕnts)	233c	33°13′S	25°15′E
Menzel Bourguiba, Tun.	162	37°12′N	9°51′E
Menzelinsk, Russia (mĕn′zyĕ-lĕnsk′)	180	55°40′N	53°15′E
Menzies, Austl. (mĕn′zēz)	218	29°45′S	122°15′E
Meogui, Mex. (mâ-ō′gē)	122	28°17′N	105°28′W
Meppel, Neth. (mĕp′ĕl)	165	52°41′N	6°08′E
Meppen, Ger. (mĕp′ĕn)	168	52°40′N	7°18′E
Merabéllou, Kólpos, b., Grc.	174a	35°16′N	25°55′E
Meramec, r., Mo., U.S. (mĕr′ȧ-mĕk)	121	38°06′N	91°06′W
Merano, Italy (må-rä′nō)	162	46°39′N	11°10′E
Merasheen, i., Can. (mĕ′rȧ-shēn)	101	47°30′N	54°15′W
Merauke, Indon. (må-rou′kä)	213	8°32′S	140°17′E
Meraux, La., U.S. (mĕ-rō′)	110d	29°56′N	89°56′W
Mercato San Severino, Italy	173c	40°34′N	14°38′E
Merced, Ca., U.S. (mẽr-sĕd′)	118	37°17′N	120°30′W
Merced, r., Ca., U.S.	118	37°25′N	120°31′W
Mercedario, Cerro, mtn., Arg. (mĕr-så-dhä′rē-ō)	144	31°58′S	70°07′W
Mercedes, Arg.	141c	34°41′S	59°26′W
Mercedes, Arg. (mĕr-sā′dhās)	144	29°04′S	58°01′W
Mercedes, Ur.	144	33°17′S	58°04′W
Mercedes, Tx., U.S.	123	26°09′N	97°55′W
Mercedita, Chile (mĕr-sĕ-dē′tä)	141b	33°51′S	71°10′W
Mercer Island, Wa., U.S. (mûr′sẽr)	116a	47°35′N	122°15′W
Mercês, Braz. (mĕ-sĕ′s)	141a	21°13′S	43°20′W
Merchtem, Bel.	159a	50°57′N	4°13′E
Mercier, Can.	102a	45°19′N	73°45′W
Mercy, Cape, c., Can.	93	64°48′N	63°22′W
Meredith, N.H., U.S. (mĕr′ĕ-dĭth)	109	43°35′N	71°35′W
Merefa, Ukr. (må-rĕ′fȧ)	177	49°49′N	36°04′E
Merendón, Serranía de, mts., Hond.	132	15°01′N	89°05′W
Mereworth, Eng., U.K. (mĕ-rĕ wûrth)	158b	51°15′N	0°23′E
Mergui, Mya. (mẽr-gē′)	212	12°29′N	98°39′E
Mergui Archipelago, is., Mya.	212	12°04′N	97°02′E
Meric (Maritsa), r., Eur.	167	40°43′N	26°19′E
Mérida, Mex.	128	20°58′N	89°37′W
Mérida, Ven.	142	8°30′N	71°15′W
Mérida, Cordillera de, mts., Ven. (mĕ′rē-dhä)	142	8°30′N	70°45′W
Meriden, Ct., U.S. (mĕr′ĭ-dĕn)	109	41°30′N	72°50′W
Meridian, Ms., U.S. (mė-rĭd-ĭ-ăn)	105	32°21′N	88°41′W
Meridian, Tx., U.S.	123	31°56′N	97°37′W
Mérignac, Fr.	170	44°50′N	0°40′W
Merikarvia, Fin. (mā′rē-kár′vē-å)	167	61°51′N	21°30′E
Mering, Ger. (mĕ′rēng)	159d	48°16′N	11°00′E
Merkel, Tx., U.S. (mûr′kĕl)	122	32°26′N	100°02′W
Merkinė, Lith.	167	54°10′N	24°10′E
Merksem, Bel.	159a	51°15′N	4°27′E
Merkys, r., Lith. (măr′kĭs)	169	54°23′N	25°00′E
Merlo, Arg. (mĕr-lô)	144a	34°40′S	58°44′W
Meron, Hare, mtn., Isr.	197a	32°58′N	35°25′E
Merriam, Ks., U.S. (mĕr-rĭ-yăm)	117f	39°01′N	94°42′W
Merriam, Mn., U.S.	117g	44°44′N	93°36′W
Merrick, N.Y., U.S. (mĕr′ĭk)	110a	40°40′N	73°33′W
Merrifield, Va., U.S. (mĕr′ĭ-fēld)	110e	38°50′N	77°12′W
Merrill, Wi., U.S. (mĕr′ĭl)	113	45°11′N	89°42′W
Merrimac, Ma., U.S. (mĕr′ĭ-măk)	101a	45°20′N	71°00′W
Merrimack, N.H., U.S.	101a	42°51′N	71°25′W
Merrimack, r., Ma., U.S. (mĕr′ĭ-măk)	109	43°10′N	71°30′W
Merritt, Can. (mĕr′ĭt)	90	50°07′N	120°47′W
Merryville, La., U.S. (mĕr′ĭ-vĭl)	123	30°46′N	93°34′W
Mersa Fatma, Erit.	231	14°54′N	40°14′E
Merseburg, Ger. (mĕr′zĕ-bōōrgh)	168	51°21′N	11°59′E
Mersey, r., Eng., U.K. (mûr′zė)	158a	53°20′N	2°55′W
Merseyside, hist. reg., Eng., U.K.	158a	53°29′N	2°59′W
Mersing, Malay.	197b	2°25′N	103°51′E
Merta Road, India (mär′tŭ rōd)	202	26°50′N	73°54′E
Merthyr Tydfil, Wales, U.K. (mûr′thẽr tĭd′vĭl)	164	51°46′N	3°30′W
Mértola Almodóvar, Port. (mĕr-tô-lȧ-äl-mô-dō′vär)	172	37°39′N	8°04′W
Méru, Fr. (mā-rü′)	170	49°14′N	2°08′E
Meru, Kenya (mā′rōō)	231	0°01′N	37°45′E
Meru, Mount, mtn., Tan.	237	3°15′S	36°43′E
Merume Mountains, mts., Guy. (mĕr-ü′mĕ)	143	5°45′N	60°15′W
Merwede Kanaal, can., Neth.	159a	52°15′N	5°01′E
Merwin, l., Wa., U.S. (mĕr′wĭn)	116c	45°58′N	122°27′W
Merzifon, Tur. (mĕr′ze-fōn)	198	40°50′N	35°30′E
Mesa, Az., U.S. (mā′sȧ)	119	33°25′N	111°50′W
Mesabi Range, mts., Mn., U.S. (mā-sŏb′bē)	113	47°17′N	93°04′W
Mesagne, Italy (mā-sän′yä)	175	40°34′N	17°51′E
Mesa Verde National Park, rec., Co., U.S. (vĕr′dē)	106	37°22′N	108°27′W
Mescalero Apache Indian Reservation, I.R., N.M., U.S. (mĕs-kä-lā′rō)	119	33°10′N	105°45′W
Meshchovsk, Russia (myĕsh′chĕfsk)	176	54°17′N	35°19′E
Mesilla, N.M., U.S. (må-sē′yä)	119	32°15′N	106°45′W
Meskine, Chad	235	11°25′N	15°21′E
Mesolóngi, Grc.	175	38°23′N	21°28′E
Mesopotamia, hist. reg., Asia	201	34°00′N	44°00′E
Mesquita, Braz.	144b	22°48′S	43°26′W
Messina, Italy (mĕ-sē′nȧ)	154	38°11′N	15°34′E
Messina, S. Afr.	232	22°17′S	30°13′E
Messina, Stretto di, strt., Italy (stĕ′t-tō dē)	163	38°10′N	15°34′E
Messíni, Grc.	175	37°05′N	22°00′E
Mestaganem, Alg.	230	36°04′N	0°11′E
Mestre, Italy (mĕs′trā)	174	45°29′N	12°15′E
Meta, dept., Col. (mĕ′tä)	142a	3°28′N	74°07′W
Meta, r., S.A.	142	4°33′N	72°09′W
Métabetchouane, r., Can. (mĕ-tȧ-bĕt-chōō-än′)	99	47°45′N	72°00′W
Metairie, La., U.S.	123	30°00′N	90°11′W
Metán, Arg. (mĕ-tá′n)	144	25°32′S	64°51′W
Metangula, Moz.	232	12°42′S	34°48′E
Metapán, El Sal. (må-täpän′)	132	14°21′N	89°26′W
Metcalfe, Can. (mĕt-käf)	102c	45°14′N	75°27′W
Metchosin, Can.	116a	48°22′N	123°33′W
Metepec, Mex. (må-tĕ-pĕk′)	130	18°56′N	98°31′W
Metepec, Mex.	130	19°15′N	99°36′W
Methow, r., Wa., U.S. (mĕt′hou) (mĕt hou′)	114	48°26′N	120°15′W
Methuen, Ma., U.S. (mė-thū′ĕn)	101a	42°44′N	71°11′W
Metković, Cro. (mĕt′kō-vĭch)	175	43°02′N	17°40′E
Metlakatla, Ak., U.S. (mĕt-lȧ-kăt′lȧ)	103	55°08′N	131°35′W
Metropolis, Il., U.S. (mė-trŏp′ō-lĭs)	121	37°09′N	88°46′W
Metter, Ga., U.S. (mĕt′ẽr)	125	32°21′N	82°05′W
Mettmann, Ger. (mĕt′män)	171c	51°15′N	6°58′E
Metuchen, N.J., U.S. (mĕ-tŭ′chĕn)	110a	40°32′N	74°21′W
Metz, Fr. (mĕtz)	161	49°08′N	6°10′E
Metztitlán, Mex. (mĕtz-tėt-län)	130	20°36′N	98°45′W
Meuban, Cam.	235	2°27′N	12°41′E
Meuse (Maas), r., Eur. (mûz) (müz)	165	50°32′N	5°22′E
Mexborough, Eng., U.K. (mĕks′bŭr-ô)	158a	53°30′N	1°17′W
Mexia, Tx., U.S. (må-hē′ä)	123	31°32′N	96°29′W
Mexian, China	205	24°20′N	116°10′E
Mexicalcingo, Mex. (mĕ-kē-käl-sēn′gō)	131a	19°13′N	99°34′W
Mexicali, Mex. (måk-sė-kä′lė)	128	32°28′N	115°29′W
Mexicana, Altiplanicie, plat., Mex.	130	22°38′N	102°33′W
Mexican Hat, Ut., U.S. (mĕk′sĭ-kăn hăt)	119	37°10′N	109°55′W
Mexico, Me., U.S. (mĕk′sĭ-kō)	100	44°34′N	70°33′W
Mexico, Mo., U.S.	121	39°09′N	91°51′W
Mexico, nation, N.A.	128	23°45′N	104°00′W
Mexico, Gulf of, b., N.A.	128	25°15′N	93°45′W
Mexico City, Mex. (mĕk′sĭ-kō)	128	19°28′N	99°09′W
Mexticacán, Mex. (mĕs′tē-kä-kän′)	130	21°12′N	102°43′W
Meyers Chuck, Ak., U.S.	94	55°44′N	132°15′W
Meyersdale, Pa., U.S. (mī′ẽrz-dāl)	109	39°55′N	79°00′W
Meyerton, S. Afr. (mī′ẽr-tŭn)	238c	26°35′S	28°01′E
Meymaneh, Afg.	198	35°53′N	64°38′E
Mezen′, Russia	178	65°50′N	44°05′E
Mezen′, r., Russia	180	65°20′N	44°45′E
Mézenc, Mont, mtn., Fr. (mōn-mä-zĕN′)	170	44°55′N	4°12′E
Mezha, r., Eur. (myā′zhȧ)	176	55°53′N	31°44′E
Mézieres-sur-Seine, Fr. (mā-zyâr′sür-sån′)	171b	48°58′N	1°49′E
Mezőkövesd, Hung. (mĕ′zû-kû′vĕsht)	169	47°49′N	20°36′E
Mezőtur, Hung. (mĕ′zû-tōōr)	169	47°00′N	20°36′E
Mezquital, Mex. (måz-kė-täl′)	130	23°30′N	104°20′W
Mezquitic, Mex. (måz-kė-tēk′)	130	22°25′N	103°43′W
Mezquitic, r., Mex.	130	22°25′N	103°45′W

ng-sing; ŋ-baŋk; N-nasalized n; nŏd; cŏmmit; ōld; ôbey; ôrder; oi-boil; fōōd; ŏ-as oo in foot; ou-out; s-soft; sh-dish; th-thin; pūre; ûnite; ûrn; stŭd; circŭs; ü-as in French tu; ′-indeterminate vowel.

322 Mfangano Island – Mississippi
PRONOUNCING INDEX

PLACE (Pronunciation)	PAGE	LAT.	LONG.
Mfangano Island, i., Kenya	237	0°28'S	33°35'E
Mga, Russia (m'gà)	186c	59°45'N	31°04'E
Mglin, Russia (m'glēn')	176	53°03'N	32°52'W
Mia, Oued, r., Alg.	162	29°26'N	3°15'E
Miacatlán, Mex. (mē'ä-kä-tlän')	130	18°42'N	99°17'W
Miahuatlán, Mex. (mē'ä-wä-tlän')	131	16°20'N	96°38'W
Miajadas, Spain (mē-ä-hä'däs)	172	39°10'N	5°53'W
Miami, Az., U.S.	104	33°20'N	110°55'W
Miami, Fl., U.S.	105	25°45'N	80°11'W
Miami, Ok., U.S.	121	36°51'N	94°51'W
Miami, Tx., U.S.	120	35°41'N	100°39'W
Miami Beach, Fl., U.S.	125a	25°47'N	80°07'W
Miamisburg, Oh., U.S. (mī-ăm'ĭz-bûrg)	108	39°40'N	84°20'W
Miamitown, Oh., U.S. (mī-ăm'ĭ-toun)	111f	39°13'N	84°43'W
Mīāneh, Iran	198	37°15'N	47°13'E
Miangas, Pulau, i., Indon.	213	5°30'N	127°00'E
Miaoli, Tai. (mē-ou'lĭ)	[illegible]	[illegible]	[illegible]
Miaozhen, China (miou-jŭn)	200	31°44'N	121°20'E
Miass, Russia (mī-äs')	184	54°59'N	60°06'E
Miastko, Pol. (myäst'kô)	168	54°01'N	17°00'E
Miccosukee Indian Reservation, I.R., Fl., U.S.	125a	26°10'N	80°50'W
Michalovce, Slvk. (mē'κä-lôf'tsĕ)	169	48°44'N	21°56'E
Michel Peak, mtn., Can.	94	53°35'N	126°25'W
Michelson, Mount, mtn., Ak., U.S. (mĭch'ĕl-sŭn)	103	69°11'N	144°12'W
Michendorf, Ger. (mē'κĕn-dōrf)	159b	52°19'N	13°02'E
Miches, Dom. Rep. (mē'chĕs)	135	19°00'N	69°05'W
Michigan, state, U.S. (mĭsh-'ĭ-găn)	105	45°55'N	87°00'W
Michigan, Lake, l., U.S.	107	43°20'N	87°10'W
Michigan City, In., U.S.	108	41°40'N	86°55'W
Michipicoten, r., Can.	113	47°56'N	84°42'W
Michipicoten Harbour, Can.	113	47°58'N	84°58'W
Michurinsk, Russia (mĭ-chōō-rĭnsk')	181	52°53'N	40°32'E
Mico, Punta, c., Nic. (pōō'n-tä-mē'kô)	133	11°38'N	83°24'W
Micronesia, is., Oc.	240	11°00'N	159°00'E
Micronesia, Federated States of, nation, Oc.	3	5°00'N	152°00'E
Midas, Nv., U.S. (mī'dăs)	114	41°15'N	116°50'W
Middelfart, Den. (mēd''l-färt)	166	55°30'N	9°45'E
Middle, r., Can.	94	55°00'N	125°50'W
Middle Andaman, i., India (ăn-dá-măn')	212	12°44'N	93°21'E
Middle Bayou, Tx., U.S.	123a	29°38'N	95°06'W
Middleburg, S. Afr. (mĭd'ĕl-bûrg)	232	31°30'S	25°00'E
Middleburg, S. Afr.	238c	25°47'S	29°30'E
Middlebury, Vt., U.S. (mĭd''l-bĕr-ĭ)	109	44°00'N	73°10'W
Middle Concho, Tx., U.S. (kōn'chō)	122	31°21'N	100°50'W
Middle River, Md., U.S.	110e	39°20'N	76°27'W
Middlesboro, Ky., U.S. (mĭd''lz-bŭr-ô)	124	36°36'N	83°42'W
Middlesbrough, Eng., U.K. (mĭd''lz-brŭ)	160	54°35'N	1°18'W
Middlesex, N.J., U.S. (mĭd''l-sĕks)	110a	40°34'N	74°30'W
Middleton, Can. (mĭd''l-tŭn)	100	44°57'N	65°04'W
Middleton, Eng., U.K.	158a	53°34'N	2°12'W
Middletown, Ct., U.S.	109	41°35'N	72°40'W
Middletown, De., U.S.	109	39°30'N	75°40'W
Middletown, Ma., U.S.	101a	42°35'N	71°01'W
Middletown, N.Y., U.S.	109	41°26'N	74°25'W
Middletown, Oh., U.S.	108	39°30'N	84°25'W
Middlewich, Eng., U.K. (mĭd''l-wĭch)	158a	53°11'N	2°27'W
Middlewit, S. Afr. (mĭd'l'wĭt)	238c	24°50'S	27°00'E
Midfield, Al., U.S.	110h	33°28'N	86°54'W
Midi, Canal du, Fr. (kä-näl-dü-mē-dē')	161	43°22'N	1°35'E
Mid Illovo, S. Afr. (mĭd ĭl'ô-vō)	233c	29°59'S	30°32'E
Midland, Can. (mĭd'lănd)	91	44°45'N	79°50'W
Midland, Mi., U.S.	108	43°40'N	84°20'W
Midland, Tx., U.S.	122	32°05'N	102°05'W
Midvale, Ut., U.S. (mĭd'vāl)	117b	40°37'N	111°54'W
Midway, Al., U.S. (mĭd'wā)	124	32°03'N	85°30'W
Midway Islands, is., Oc.	2	28°00'N	179°00'W
Midwest, Wy., U.S. (mĭd-wĕst')	115	43°25'N	106°15'W
Midye, Tur. (mēd'yĕ)	181	41°35'N	28°10'E
Międzyrzecz, Pol. (myăn-dzû'zhĕch)	168	52°26'N	15°35'E
Mielec, Pol. (myĕ'lĕts)	169	50°17'N	21°27'E
Mier, Mex. (myâr)	122	26°26'N	99°08'W
Mieres, Spain (myā'rās)	172	43°14'N	5°45'W
Mier y Noriega, Mex. (myâr'ē nō-rē-ā'gä)	130	23°28'N	100°08'W
Miguel Auza, Mex.	130	24°17'N	103°27'W
Miguel Pereira, Braz.	144b	22°27'S	43°28'W
Mijares, r., Spain	173	39°55'N	0°01'W
Mikage, Japan (mē'kä-gå)	211b	34°42'N	135°15'E
Mikawa-Wan, b., Japan (mē'kä-wä wän)	211	34°43'N	137°09'E
Mikhaylov, Russia (mē-käy'lôf)	180	54°14'N	39°03'E
Mikhaylovka, Russia	186a	55°35'N	57°57'E
Mikhaylovka, Russia	186c	59°20'N	30°21'E
Mikhaylovka, Russia	181	50°05'N	43°10'E
Mikhnëvo, Russia (mĭk-nyô'vô)	186b	55°08'N	37°57'E
Miki, Japan (mē'kē)	211b	34°47'N	134°59'E
Mikindani, Tan. (mē-kēn-dä'nē)	233	10°17'S	40°07'E
Mikkeli, Fin. (mĕk'ĕ-lĭ)	160	61°42'N	27°14'E
Mikulov, Czech Rep. (mĭ'kōō-lôf)	168	48°47'N	16°39'E
Mikumi, Tan.	237	7°24'S	36°59'E
Mikuni, Japan (mē'kōō-nē)	211	36°09'N	136°14'E
Mikuni-Sammyaku, mts., Japan (säm'myä-kōō)	211	36°51'N	138°38'E
Mikura, i., Japan (mē'kōō-rä)	211	33°53'N	139°26'E
Milaca, Milaca, Mn., U.S. (mē-lăk'à)	113	45°45'N	93°41'W
Milan (Milano), Italy (mē-lä'nō)	174	45°29'N	9°12'E
Milan, Mi., U.S. (mĭ'lăn)	108	42°05'N	83°40'W

PLACE (Pronunciation)	PAGE	LAT.	LONG.
Milan, Mo., U.S.	121	40°13'N	93°07'W
Milan, Tn., U.S.	124	35°54'N	88°47'W
Milâs, Tur. (mē'läs)	163	37°10'N	27°25'E
Milazzo, Italy	174	38°13'N	15°17'E
Milbank, S.D., U.S. (mĭl'băŋκ)	112	45°13'N	96°38'W
Mildura, Austl. (mĭl-dū'rá)	219	34°10'S	142°18'E
Miles City, Mt., U.S. (mīlz)	104	46°24'N	105°50'W
Milford, Ct., U.S. (mĭl'fērd)	109	41°15'N	73°05'W
Milford, De., U.S.	109	38°55'N	75°25'W
Milford, Ma., U.S.	101a	42°09'N	71°31'W
Milford, Mi., U.S.	111b	42°35'N	83°36'W
Milford, N.H., U.S.	109	42°50'N	71°40'W
Milford, Oh., U.S.	111f	39°11'N	84°18'W
Milford, Ut., U.S.	110	38°20'N	113°05'W
Milford Sound, strt., N.Z.	223	44°35'S	167°47'E
Miling, Austl. (mĭl'' ng)	218	30°30'S	116°25'E
Milipitas, Ca., U.S. (mĭl-ĭ-pĭ'tăs)	116b	37°26'N	121°54'W
Milk, r., N.A.	[illegible]	[illegible]	[illegible]
Millau, Fr. (mē-yō')	161	44°06'N	3°04'E
Millbrae, Ca., U.S. (mĭl'brā)	116b	37°36'N	122°23'W
Millbury, Ma., U.S. (mĭl'bēr-ĭ)	101a	42°12'N	71°46'W
Mill Creek, r., Can. (mĭl)	102g	53°28'N	113°25'W
Mill Creek, r., Ca., U.S.	118	40°07'N	121°55'W
Milledgeville, Ga., U.S. (mĭl'ĕj-vĭl)	124	33°05'N	83°15'W
Mille Îles, Rivière des, r., Can. (rê-vyâr' dā mēl'ēl')	102a	45°41'N	73°40'W
Mille Lac Indian Reservation, I.R., Mn., U.S. (mĭl lăk')	113	46°14'N	94°13'W
Mille Lacs, l., Mn., U.S.	113	46°25'N	93°22'W
Mille Lacs, Lac des, l., Can. (läk dē mēl läks)	98	48°52'N	90°53'W
Millen, Ga., U.S. (mĭl'ĕn)	125	32°47'N	81°55'W
Miller, S.D., U.S. (mĭl'ēr)	112	44°31'N	99°00'W
Millerovo, Russia (mĭl'ĕ-rô-vô)	181	48°58'N	40°27'E
Millersburg, Ky., U.S. (mĭl'ērz-bûrg)	108	38°15'N	84°10'W
Millersburg, Oh., U.S.	108	40°35'N	81°55'W
Millersburg, Pa., U.S.	109	40°35'N	76°55'W
Millerton, Can. (mĭl'ēr-tŭn)	100	46°56'N	65°40'W
Millertown, Can. (mĭl'ēr-toun)	101	48°49'N	56°32'W
Millicent, Austl. (mĭl-ĭ-sĕnt)	222	37°30'S	140°20'E
Millinocket, Me., U.S. (mĭl-ĭ-nŏk'ĕt)	100	45°40'N	68°44'W
Millis, Ma., U.S. (mĭl-ĭs)	101a	42°10'N	71°22'W
Millstadt, Il., U.S. (mĭl'stăt)	117e	38°27'N	90°06'W
Millstone, r., N.J., U.S. (mĭl'stōn)	110a	40°27'N	74°38'W
Millstream, Austl. (mĭl'strēm)	218	21°45'S	117°10'E
Milltown, Can. (mĭl'toun)	100	45°13'N	67°19'W
Mill Valley, Ca., U.S. (mĭl)	116b	37°54'N	122°32'W
Millwood Reservoir, res., Ar., U.S.	121	33°00'N	94°00'W
Milly-la-Forêt, Fr. (mē-yē'-la-fō-rĕ')	171b	48°24'N	2°28'E
Milnerton, S. Afr. (mĭl'nĕr-tŭn)	232a	33°52'S	18°30'E
Milnor, N.D., U.S. (mĭl'nēr)	112	46°17'N	97°29'W
Milo, Me., U.S. (mī'lō)	100	44°16'N	69°01'W
Milos, i., Grc. (mē'lŏs)	163	36°45'N	24°35'E
Milpa Alta, Mex. (mē'l-pä-ä'l-tä)	131a	19°11'N	99°01'W
Milton, Can.	102d	43°31'N	79°53'W
Milton, Fl., U.S. (mĭl'tŭn)	124	30°37'N	87°02'W
Milton, Pa., U.S.	109	41°00'N	76°50'W
Milton, Ut., U.S.	117b	41°04'N	111°44'W
Milton, Wa., U.S.	116a	47°15'N	122°20'W
Milton, Wi., U.S.	113	42°45'N	89°00'W
Milton-Freewater, Or., U.S.	114	45°57'N	118°25'W
Milvale, Pa., U.S. (mĭl'vāl)	111e	40°29'N	79°58'W
Milville, N.J., U.S. (mĭl'vĭl)	109	39°25'N	75°00'W
Milwaukee, Wi., U.S.	105	43°03'N	87°55'W
Milwaukee, r., Wi., U.S.	111a	43°10'N	87°56'W
Milwaukie, Or., U.S. (mĭl-wô'kē)	114	45°27'N	122°38'W
Mimiapan, Mex. (mē-myä-păn')	131a	19°26'N	99°28'W
Mimoso do Sul, Braz. (mē-mô'sō-dô-sōō'l)	141a	21°03'S	41°21'W
Min, r., China (mēn)	205	26°03'N	118°30'E
Min, r., China	209	29°30'N	104°00'E
Mina, r., Alg. (mē'nà)	173	35°24'N	0°51'E
Minago, r., Can. (mĭ-nä'gō)	97	54°25'N	98°45'W
Minakuchi, Japan (mē'nà-kōō'chē)	211	34°59'N	136°06'E
Minas, Cuba (mē'näs)	134	21°30'N	77°35'W
Minas, Indon.	197b	0°52'N	101°29'E
Minas, Ur. (mē'näs)	144	34°18'S	55°12'W
Minas, Sierra de las, mts., Guat. (syĕr'rä dā läs mē'näs)	132	15°08'N	90°25'W
Minas Basin, b., Can. (mĭ'năs)	100	45°20'N	64°00'W
Minas Channel, strt., Can.	100	45°15'N	64°45'W
Minas de Oro, Hond. (mē'näs-dĕ-dĕ-ō-rô)	132	14°52'N	87°19'W
Minas de Riotinto, Spain (mē'näs dā rē-ō-tēn'tō)	172	37°43'N	6°35'W
Minas Novas, Braz. (mē'näzh nō'väzh)	143	17°20'S	42°19'W
Minatare, l., Ne., U.S. (mĭn'á-târ)	112	41°56'N	103°07'W
Minatitlán, Mex. (mē-nä-tē-tlän')	128	17°59'N	94°33'W
Minatitlán, Mex.	130	19°21'N	104°02'W
Minato, Japan (mē'nà-tô)	211	35°13'N	139°52'E
Minch, The, strt., Scot., U.K.	156	58°04'N	6°04'W
Mindanao, i., Phil.	213	8°00'N	125°00'E
Mindanao Sea, sea, Phil.	213	8°55'N	124°00'E
Minden, Ger. (mĭn'dĕn)	168	52°17'N	8°58'E
Minden, La., U.S.	123	32°36'N	93°19'W
Minden, Ne., U.S.	120	40°30'N	98°54'W
Mindoro, i., Phil.	212	12°50'N	121°05'E
Mindoro Strait, strt., Phil.	213a	12°28'N	120°33'E
Mindyak, Russia (mēn'dyák)	186a	54°01'N	58°48'E
Mineola, N.Y., U.S. (mĭn-ē-ō'lá)	110a	40°43'N	73°38'W
Mineola, Tx., U.S.	123	32°39'N	95°31'W
Mineral del Chico, Mex. (mē-nä-räl'dĕl chē'kô)	130	20°13'N	98°46'W

PLACE (Pronunciation)	PAGE	LAT.	LONG.
Mineral del Monte, Mex. (mē-nä-räl dĕl mōn'tā)	130	20°18'N	98°39'W
Mineral'nyye Vody, Russia	181	44°10'N	43°15'E
Mineral Point, Wi., U.S. (mĭn'ēr-ăl)	113	42°50'N	90°10'W
Mineral Wells, Tx., U.S. (mĭn'ēr-ăl wĕlz)	122	32°48'N	98°06'W
Minerva, Oh., U.S. (mĭ-nûr'và)	108	40°45'N	81°10'W
Minervino, Italy (mē-nĕr-vē'nô)	174	41°07'N	16°05'E
Mineyama, Japan (mē-nĕ-yä'mä)	211	35°38'N	135°05'E
Mingäçevir, Azer.	182	40°45'N	47°03'E
Mingäçevir su anbarı, res., Azer.	182	40°50'N	46°50'E
Mingan, Can.	91	50°18'N	64°02'W
Mingenew, Austl. (mĭn'gĕ-nů)	218	29°15'S	115°45'E
Mingo Junction, Oh., U.S. (mĭŋ'gō)	108	40°15'N	80°40'W
Minho, hist. reg., Port. (mēn yô)	172	41°32'N	8°13'W
Minho (Miño), r., Eur. (mē'n-yô)	172	41°28'N	9°05'W
Ministik Lake, l., Can. (mĭ-nĭs'tĭk)	102g	53°23'N	113°05'W
Minna, Nig. (mĭn'à)	[illegible]	[illegible]	6°33'E
Minneapolis, Ks., U.S. (mĭn-ē-ăp'ō-lĭs)	121	39°07'N	97°41'W
Minneapolis, Mn., U.S.	105	44°58'N	93°15'W
Minnedosa, Can. (mĭn-ē-dō'sà)	90	50°14'N	99°51'W
Minneota, Mn., U.S. (mĭn-ē-ō'tà)	112	44°34'N	95°59'W
Minnesota, state, U.S. (mĭn-ē-sō'tà)	105	46°10'N	90°20'W
Minnesota, r., Mn., U.S.	107	44°30'N	95°00'W
Minnetonka, l., Mn., U.S. (mĭn-ē-tôŋ'kà)	113	44°52'N	93°34'W
Minnitaki Lake, l., Can. (mĭ'nĭ-tä'kē)	97	49°58'N	92°00'W
Mino, r., Japan	211b	34°56'N	135°06'E
Minonk, Il., U.S. (mī'nônk)	108	40°55'N	89°00'W
Minooka, Il., U.S. (mĭ-nōō'kà)	111a	41°27'N	88°15'W
Minot, N.D., U.S.	104	48°13'N	101°17'W
Minsk, Bela. (mēnsk)	178	53°54'N	27°35'E
Minsk, prov., Bela.	176	53°50'N	27°43'E
Mińsk Mazowiecki, Pol. (mēn'sk mä-zô-vyĕt'skĭ)	169	52°10'N	21°35'E
Minsterley, Eng., U.K. (mĭnstēr-lē)	158a	52°38'N	2°55'W
Minto, Can.	100	46°05'N	66°05'W
Minto, l., Can.	93	57°18'N	75°50'W
Minturno, Italy (mēn-tōōr'nô)	174	41°17'N	13°44'E
Minūf, Egypt (mē-nōōf')	238b	30°26'N	30°55'E
Minusinsk, Russia (mē-nò-sēnsk')	179	53°47'N	91°45'E
Min'yar, Russia	186a	55°06'N	57°33'E
Miquelon Lake, l., Can. (mĭ'kē-lôn)	102g	53°16'N	112°55'W
Miquihuana, Mex. (mē-kē-wä'nä)	130	23°36'N	99°45'W
Mir, Bela. (mēr)	169	53°27'N	26°25'E
Miracema, Braz. (mē-rä-sĕ'mä)	141a	21°24'S	42°10'W
Miracema do Tocantins, Braz.	143	9°34'S	48°24'W
Mirador, Braz. (mē-rà-dōr')	143	6°19'S	44°12'W
Miraflores, Col. (mē-rä-flō'räs)	142	5°10'N	73°13'W
Miraflores, Peru	142	16°19'S	71°20'W
Miraflores Locks, trans., Pan.	128a	9°00'N	79°35'W
Miragoâne, Haiti (mē-rà-gwän')	135	18°25'N	73°05'W
Mira Loma, Ca., U.S. (mĭ'rá lō'má)	117a	34°01'N	117°32'W
Miramar, Ca., U.S. (mĭr'ă-mär)	118a	32°53'N	117°08'W
Miramas, Fr.	170	43°35'N	5°00'E
Miramichi Bay, b., Can. (mĭr'á-mē'shē)	100	47°08'N	65°08'W
Miranda, Col. (mē-rä'n-dä)	142a	3°14'N	76°11'W
Miranda, Ca., U.S.	118	40°14'N	123°49'W
Miranda, Ven.	143b	10°09'N	68°24'W
Miranda, dept., Ven.	143b	10°17'N	66°41'W
Miranda de Ebro, Spain (mē-rä'n-dä-dĕ-ĕ'brō)	172	42°42'N	2°59'W
Miranda do Douro, Port. (mē-rän'dä dò-dwĕ'rô)	172	41°30'N	6°17'W
Mirandela, Port. (mē-rän-dā'lá)	172	41°28'N	7°10'W
Mirando City, Tx., U.S. (mĭr-ăn'dō)	122	27°25'N	99°03'W
Mira Por Vos Islets, is., Bah. (mē'rä pôr vōs)	135	22°05'N	74°30'W
Mira Por Vos Pass, strt., Bah.	135	22°10'N	74°35'W
Mirbāṭ, Oman	198	16°58'N	54°42'E
Mirebalais, Haiti (mēr-bà-lĕ')	135	18°50'N	72°05'W
Mirecourt, Fr. (mēr-kōōr')	171	48°20'N	6°08'E
Mirfield, Eng., U.K. (mûr'fēld)	158a	53°41'N	1°42'W
Miri, Malay. (mē'rē)	212	4°13'N	113°56'E
Mirim, Lagoa, l., S.A. (mē-rēN')	144	33°00'S	53°15'W
Miropol'ye, Ukr. (mē-rô-pôl'yĕ)	177	51°02'N	35°13'E
Mīrpur Khās, Pak. (mēr'pōōr κäs)	202	25°36'N	69°10'E
Mirzāpur, India (mēr'zä-pōōr)	199	25°12'N	82°38'E
Misantla, Mex. (mē-sän'tlä)	131	19°55'N	96°49'W
Miscou, i., Can. (mĭs'kō)	100	47°58'N	64°35'W
Miscou Point, c., Can.	100	48°04'N	64°32'W
Miseno, Cape, c., Italy (mē-zĕ'nō)	173c	40°33'N	14°12'E
Misery, Mount, mtn., St. K./N. (mĭz'rē-ĭ)	133b	17°28'N	62°47'W
Mishan, China (mĭ'shäN)	210	45°32'N	132°19'E
Mishawaka, In., U.S. (mĭsh-á-wôk'á)	108	41°45'N	86°15'W
Mishina, Japan (mē'shē-mä)	211	35°09'N	138°56'E
Misiones, prov., Arg. (mē-syō'nās)	144	27°00'S	54°30'W
Miskito, Cayos, is., Nic.	133	14°34'N	82°30'W
Miskolc, Hung. (mĭsh'kōlts)	154	48°07'N	20°50'E
Misool, Pulau, i., Indon. (mē-sōl')	213	2°00'S	130°05'E
Misquah Hills, Mn., U.S. (mĭs-kwä' hĭlz)	113	47°50'N	90°30'W
Miṣr al Jadīdah, Egypt	238b	30°06'N	31°35'E
Misrātah, Libya	231	32°23'N	14°58'E
Missinaibi, r., Can. (mĭs'ĭn-ä'ē-bē)	93	50°27'N	83°01'W
Missinaibi Lake, l., Can.	98	48°23'N	83°40'W
Mission, Ks., U.S. (mĭsh'ŭn)	117f	39°02'N	94°39'W
Mission, Tx., U.S.	122	26°14'N	98°19'W
Mission City, Can. (sĭ'tĭ)	95	49°08'N	112°18'W
Mississagi, r., Can.	98	46°35'N	83°30'W
Mississauga, Can.	99	43°34'N	79°37'W
Mississippi, state, U.S. (mĭs-ĭ-sĭp'ē)	105	32°30'N	89°45'W
Mississippi, l., Can.	99	45°05'N	76°15'W
Mississippi, r., U.S.	107	32°00'N	91°30'W

ăt; finăl; rāte; senâte; ärm; åsk; sofá; fâre; ch-choose; dh-as th in other; bē; êvent; bĕt; recĕnt; cratēr; g-gō; gh-guttural g; bĭt; ĭ-short neutral; rīde; κ-guttural k as ch in German ich;

ng-sing; ŋ-baŋk; N-nasalized n; nŏd; cŏmmit; ōld; ôbey; ôrder; oi-boil; fōōd; ò-as oo in foot; ou-out; s-soft; sh-dish; th-thin; pūre; ûnite; ûrn; stŭd; circŭs; ü-as in French tu; ′-indeterminate vowel.

324 Monterrey – Mount Morgan PRONOUNCING INDEX

PLACE (Pronunciation)	PAGE	LAT.	LONG.
Monterrey, Mex. (mōn-tĕr-rā′)	128	25°43′N	100°19′W
Montesano, Wa., U.S. (mŏn-tê-sä′nō)	114	46°59′N	123°35′W
Monte Sant'Angelo, Italy (mô′n-tĕ sän ä′n-gzhĕ-lô)	163	41°43′N	15°59′E
Montes Claros, Braz. (môn-tĕs-klä′rôs)	143	16°44′S	43°41′W
Montevallo, Al., U.S. (môn-tê-văl′ō)	124	33°05′N	86°49′W
Montevarchi, Italy (mōn-tå-vär′kē)	174	43°30′N	11°45′E
Montevideo, Ur. (mōn′tå-vê-dhā′ō)	144	34°50′S	56°10′W
Montevideo, Mn., U.S. (mōn′tå-vê-dhā′ō)	112	44°56′N	95°42′W
Monte Vista, Co., U.S. (mŏn′tê vĭs′tȧ)	119	37°35′N	106°10′W
Montezuma, Ga., U.S. (mŏn-tê-zōō′mȧ)	124	32°17′N	84°00′W
Montezuma Castle National Monument, rec., Az., U.S.	119	34°38′N	111°50′W
Montfoort, Neth.	139a	52°02′N	4°56′E
Montfort-l'Amaury, Fr. (mŏN-fŏr′lä-mō-rē′)	171b	48°47′N	1°49′E
Montfort, Fr. (mŏn-fŏr)	170	48°09′N	1°58′W
Montgomery, Al., U.S. (mŏnt-gŭm′ēr-ĭ)	105	32°23′N	86°17′W
Montgomery, W.V., U.S.	108	38°10′N	81°25′W
Montgomery City, Mo., U.S.	121	38°58′N	91°29′W
Monticello, Ar., U.S. (mŏn-tĭ-sĕl′ō)	121	33°38′N	91°47′W
Monticello, Fl., U.S.	124	30°32′N	83°53′W
Monticello, Ga., U.S.	124	33°00′N	83°11′W
Monticello, Ia., U.S.	113	42°14′N	91°13′W
Monticello, Il., U.S.	108	40°05′N	88°35′W
Monticello, In., U.S.	108	40°40′N	86°50′W
Monticello, Ky., U.S.	124	36°47′N	84°50′W
Monticello, Me., U.S.	100	46°19′N	67°53′W
Monticello, Mn., U.S.	113	45°18′N	93°48′W
Monticello, N.Y., U.S.	109	41°35′N	74°40′W
Monticello, Ut., U.S.	119	37°55′N	109°25′W
Montijo, Port. (môn-tē′zhō)	173b	38°42′N	8°58′W
Montijo, Spain (môn-tē′hō)	172	38°55′N	6°35′W
Montijo, Bahía, b., Pan. (bä-ē′ä môn-tē′hō)	129	7°36′N	81°11′W
Mont-Joli, Can. (môN zhô-lē′)	91	48°35′N	68°11′W
Montluçon, Fr. (môN-lü-sôN′)	161	46°20′N	2°35′E
Montmagny, Can. (môN-mȧn-yē′)	99	46°59′N	70°33′W
Montmorency, Fr. (môN′mô-räN-sē′)	171b	48°59′N	2°19′E
Montmorency, r., Can. (mŏnt-mô-rĕn′sĭ)	102b	47°03′N	71°10′W
Montmorillon, Fr. (môN′mô-rê-yôN′)	170	46°26′N	0°50′E
Montone, r., Italy (môn-tô′nĕ)	174	44°03′N	11°45′E
Montoro, Spain (mōn-tō′rō)	172	38°01′N	4°22′W
Montpelier, Id., U.S.	115	42°19′N	111°19′W
Montpelier, In., U.S. (mŏnt-pĕl′yẽr)	108	40°35′N	85°20′W
Montpelier, Oh., U.S.	108	41°35′N	84°35′W
Montpelier, Vt., U.S.	105	44°20′N	72°35′W
Montpellier, Fr. (môN-pĕ-lyā′)	161	43°38′N	3°53′E
Montréal, Can. (mŏn-trê-ôl′)	91	45°30′N	73°35′W
Montreal, r., Can.	99	47°50′N	80°30′W
Montreal, r., Can.	98	47°15′N	84°20′W
Montreal Lake, l., Can.	96	54°20′N	105°40′W
Montréal-Nord, Can.	102a	45°36′N	73°38′W
Montreuil, Fr.	171b	48°52′N	2°27′E
Montreux, Switz. (môn-trû′)	168	46°26′N	6°52′E
Montrose, Scot., U.K.	164	56°45′N	2°25′W
Montrose, Ca., U.S. (mŏnt-rōz)	117a	34°13′N	118°13′W
Montrose, Co., U.S. (mŏn-trōz′)	119	38°30′N	107°55′W
Montrose, Oh., U.S.	111d	41°08′N	81°38′W
Montrose, Pa., U.S. (mŏnt-rōz′)	109	41°50′N	75°50′W
Montrouge, Fr.	171b	48°49′N	2°19′E
Mont-Royal, Can.	102a	47°31′N	73°39′W
Monts, Pointe des, c., Can. (pwăNt′ dā môN′)	100	49°19′N	67°22′W
Mont Saint Martin, Fr. (môN săN mär-tăN′)	171	49°34′N	6°13′E
Montserrat, dep., N.A. (mŏnt-sĕ-răt′)	129	16°48′N	63°15′W
Montvale, N.J., U.S. (mŏnt-vāl′)	110a	41°02′N	74°01′W
Monywa, Mya. (mŏn′yōō-wȧ)	199	22°02′N	95°16′E
Monza, Italy (mōn′tsä)	174	45°34′N	9°17′E
Monzón, Spain (mōn-thōn′)	173	41°54′N	0°09′E
Moody, Tx., U.S. (mōō′dĭ)	123	31°18′N	97°20′W
Mooi, r., S. Afr. (mō′ĭ)	238c	26°34′S	27°03′E
Mooi, r., S. Afr.	233c	29°00′S	30°15′E
Mooirivier, S. Afr.	233c	29°14′S	29°59′E
Moolap, Austl.	217a	38°11′S	144°26′E
Moonta, Austl. (mōōn′tȧ)	218	34°05′S	137°42′E
Moora, Austl. (mōr′ȧ)	218	30°35′S	116°12′E
Moorabbin, Austl.	217a	37°56′S	145°02′E
Moore, l., Austl. (mōr)	220	29°50′S	118°12′E
Moorenweis, Ger. (mō′rĕn-vīz)	159d	48°10′N	11°05′E
Moore Reservoir, res., Vt., U.S.	109	44°20′N	72°10′W
Moorestown, N.J., U.S. (morz′toun)	110f	39°58′N	74°56′W
Mooresville, In., U.S. (mōrz′vĭl)	111g	39°37′N	86°22′W
Mooresville, N.C., U.S.	125	35°34′N	80°48′W
Moorhead, Mn., U.S. (mōr′hĕd)	112	46°52′N	96°44′W
Moorhead, Ms., U.S.	124	33°25′N	90°30′W
Moose, r., Can.	93	51°01′N	80°42′W
Moose Creek, Can.	102c	45°16′N	74°58′W
Moosehead, Me., U.S. (mōōs′hĕd)	100	45°37′N	69°15′W
Moose Island, i., Can.	97	51°50′N	97°09′W
Moose Jaw, Can. (mōōs jô)	90	50°23′N	105°32′W
Moose Jaw, r., Can.	96	50°34′N	105°17′W
Moose Lake, Can.	97	53°40′N	100°28′W
Moose Mountain, mtn., Can.	97	49°45′N	102°37′W
Moose Mountain Creek, r., Can.	97	49°12′N	102°10′W
Moosilauke, mtn., N.H., U.S. (mōō-sĭ-lȧ′kē)	109	44°00′N	71°50′W
Moosinning, Ger. (mō′zē-nēng)	159d	48°17′N	11°51′E
Moosomin, Can. (mōō′sô-mĭn)	97	50°07′N	101°40′W
Moosonee, Can. (mōō′sô-nê)	91	51°20′N	80°44′W
Mopti, Mali (mŏp′tê)	230	14°30′N	4°12′W
Moquegua, Peru (mô-kā′gwä)	142	17°15′S	70°54′W
Mór, Hung. (mōr)	169	47°25′N	18°14′E
Mora, India	203b	18°54′N	72°56′E
Mora, Spain (mō-rä)	172	39°42′N	3°45′W
Mora, Swe. (mō′rä)	166	61°00′N	14°29′E
Mora, Mn., U.S. (mō′rȧ)	113	45°52′N	93°18′W
Mora, N.M., U.S.	120	35°58′N	105°17′W
Morādābād, India (mô-rä-dä-bäd′)	199	28°57′N	78°48′E
Morales, Guat. (mô-rä′lĕs)	132	15°29′N	88°46′W
Moramanga, Madag. (mō-rä-mäŋ′gä)	233	18°48′S	48°09′E
Morant Point, c., Jam. (mō-rănt′)	134	17°55′N	76°10′W
Morata de Tajuña, Spain (mô-rä′tä dā tä-hōō′nyä)	173a	40°14′N	3°27′W
Moratuwa, Sri L.	203	6°35′N	79°59′E
Morava (Moravia), hist. reg., Czech Rep.	100	40°21′N	10°57′E
Morava, r., Eur.	161	49°00′N	17°30′E
Moravia *see* Morava, hist. reg., Czech Rep.	168	49°21′N	16°57′E
Morawhanna, Guy. (mô-rȧ-hwä′nȧ)	143	8°12′N	59°33′W
Moray Firth, b., Scot., U.K. (mŭr′å)	156	57°41′N	3°55′W
Mörbylånga, Swe. (mûr′bü-lôŋ′gå)	166	56°32′N	16°23′E
Morden, Can. (môr′dĕn)	90	49°11′N	98°05′W
Mordialloc, Austl. (môr-dĭ-ăl′ŏk)	217a	38°00′S	145°05′E
Mordvinia, prov., Russia	180	54°18′N	43°50′E
More, Ben, mtn., Scot., U.K. (bĕn môr)	164	58°09′N	5°01′W
Moreau, r., S.D., U.S. (mô-rō′)	112	45°13′N	102°22′W
Moree, Austl. (mō′rē)	219	29°20′S	149°50′E
Morehead, Ky., U.S.	108	38°10′N	83°25′W
Morehead City, N.C., U.S. (mōr′hĕd)	125	34°43′N	76°43′W
Morehouse, Mo., U.S. (mōr′hous)	121	36°49′N	89°41′W
Morelia, Mex. (mô-rā′lyä)	128	19°43′N	101°12′W
Morella, Spain (mô-răl′yä)	173	40°38′N	0°07′W
Morelos, Mex. (mô-rā′lōs)	130	22°46′N	102°36′W
Morelos, Mex.	131a	19°41′N	99°29′W
Morelos, Mex.	122	28°24′N	100°51′W
Morelos, r., Mex.	122	25°27′N	99°35′W
Morena, Sierra, mtn., Ca., U.S. (syĕr′rä mô-rā′nä)	116b	37°24′N	122°19′W
Morena, Sierra, mts., Spain (syĕr′rä mô-rā′nä)	156	38°15′N	5°45′W
Morenci, Az., U.S. (mô-rĕn′sĭ)	119	33°05′N	109°25′W
Morenci, Mi., U.S.	108	41°50′N	84°50′W
Moreno, Arg. (mô-rĕ′nō)	144a	34°39′S	58°47′W
Moreno, Ca., U.S.	117a	33°55′N	117°09′W
Mores, i., Bah. (mōrz)	134	26°20′N	77°35′W
Moresby, i., Can. (mōrz′bĭ)	116d	48°43′N	123°15′W
Moresby Island, i., Can.	92	52°50′N	131°55′W
Moreton, i., Austl. (môr′tŭn)	222	26°53′S	152°42′E
Moreton Bay, b., Austl. (môr′tŭn)	222	27°12′S	153°10′E
Morewood, Can. (mōr′wŏŏd)	102c	45°11′N	75°17′W
Morgan, Mt., U.S. (môr′găn)	115	48°55′N	107°56′W
Morgan, Ut., U.S.	115	41°04′N	111°42′W
Morgan City, La., U.S.	123	29°41′N	91°11′W
Morganfield, Ky., U.S. (môr′găn-fēld)	108	37°40′N	87°55′W
Morgan's Bay, S. Afr.	233c	32°42′S	28°19′E
Morganton, N.C., U.S. (môr′găn-tŭn)	125	35°44′N	81°42′W
Morgantown, W.V., U.S. (môr′găn-toun)	109	39°40′N	79°55′W
Morga Range, mts., Afg.	199a	34°02′N	70°38′E
Morgenzon, S. Afr. (môr′gănt-sŏn)	238c	26°44′S	29°39′E
Moriac, Austl.	217a	38°15′S	144°20′E
Morice Lake, l., Can.	94	54°00′N	127°37′W
Moriguchi, Japan (mō′rê-gōō′chê)	211b	34°44′N	135°34′E
Morinville, Can. (mō′rĭn-vĭl)	102g	53°48′N	113°39′W
Morioka, Japan (mō′rê-ō′kȧ)	205	39°40′N	141°21′E
Morkoka, r., Russia (môr-kô′kȧ)	185	65°35′N	111°00′E
Morlaix, Fr. (môr-lĕ′)	161	48°36′N	3°48′W
Morley, Can. (mōr′lê)	102e	51°10′N	114°51′W
Mormant, Fr.	171b	48°35′N	2°54′E
Morne Gimie, St. Luc. (môrn′ zhê-mē′)	133b	13°53′N	61°03′W
Mornington, Austl.	217a	38°13′S	145°02′E
Morobe, Pap. N. Gui.	213	8°03′S	147°45′E
Morocco, nation, Afr. (mô-rŏk′ō)	230	32°00′N	7°00′W
Morogoro, Tan. (mō-rô-gō′rō)	233	6°49′S	37°40′E
Moroleón, Mex. (mō-rô-lā-ōn′)	130	20°07′N	101°15′W
Morombe, Madag. (mōō-rōōm′bā)	233	21°39′S	43°34′E
Morón, Arg. (mo-rō′n)	141c	34°39′S	58°37′W
Morón, Cuba (mô-rōn′)	134	22°05′N	78°35′W
Morón, Ven. (mô-rō′n)	143b	10°29′N	68°11′W
Morondava, Madag. (mô-rōn-dȧ′vȧ)	233	20°17′S	44°18′E
Morón de la Frontera, Spain (mô-rōn′dā läf rōn-tā′rä)	172	37°08′N	5°20′W
Morongo Indian Reservation, I.R., Ca., U.S. (mō-rôŋ′gō)	118	33°54′N	116°47′W
Moroni, Com.	233	11°41′S	43°16′E
Moroni, Ut., U.S. (mō-rō′nĭ)	119	39°30′N	111°40′W
Morotai, i., Indon. (mō-rô-tä′ê)	213	2°12′N	128°30′E
Moroto, Ug.	237	2°32′N	34°39′E
Morozovsk, Russia	181	48°20′N	41°50′E
Morrill, Ne., U.S. (mŏr′ĭl)	112	41°59′N	103°54′W
Morrilton, Ar., U.S. (mŏr′ĭl-tŭn)	121	35°09′N	92°42′W
Morrinhos, Braz. (mô-rēn′yōzh)	143	17°45′S	48°56′W
Morris, Can. (mŏr′ĭs)	90	49°21′N	97°22′W
Morris, Il., U.S.	108	41°20′N	88°25′W
Morris, Mn., U.S.	112	45°35′N	95°53′W
Morris, r., Can.	97	49°30′N	97°30′W
Morrison, Il., U.S. (mŏr′ĭ-sŭn)	113	41°48′N	89°58′W
Morris Reservoir, res., Ca., U.S.	117a	34°11′N	117°49′W
Morristown, N.J., U.S. (mŏr′rĭs-toun)	110a	40°48′N	74°29′W
Morristown, Tn., U.S.	124	36°10′N	83°18′W
Morrisville, Pa., U.S. (mŏr′ĭs-vĭl)	110f	40°12′N	74°46′W
Morro do Chapéu, Braz. (mŏr-ō dô-shä-pĕ′ōō)	143	11°34′S	41°03′W
Morrow, Oh., U.S. (mŏr′ō)	111f	39°21′N	84°07′W
Mors, i., Den.	166	56°46′N	8°38′E
Morshansk, Russia (môr-shånsk′)	180	53°25′N	41°35′E
Mortara, Italy (môr-tä′rä)	174	45°13′N	8°47′E
Morteros, Arg. (môr-tĕ′tôs)	144	30°47′S	62°00′W
Mortes, Rio das, r., Braz. (rēō-däs-mô′r-tĕs)	141a	21°04′S	44°29′W
Morton Indian Reservation, I.R., Mn., U.S. (mŏr′tŭn)	113	44°35′N	94°48′W
Mortsel, Bel. (môr-sĕl′)	159a	51°10′N	4°28′E
Morvan, mts., Fr. (mōr-väN′)	170	47°11′N	4°10′E
Morzhovets, i., Russia (môr′zhô-vyĕts′)	180	66°40′N	42°30′E
Mosal'sk, Russia (mō-zȧlsk′)	176	54°27′N	34°57′E
Moscavide, Port.	173b	38°47′N	9°06′W
Moscow (Moskva), Russia	178	55°45′N	37°37′E
Moscow, Id., U.S. (mŏs′kō)	104	46°44′N	116°57′W
Mosel (Moselle), r., Eur. (mō′sĕl) (mô-zĕl)	168	49°49′N	7°00′E
Moses, r., S. Afr.	238c	25°17′S	29°04′E
Moses Lake, Wa., U.S.	114	47°08′N	119°15′W
Moses Lake, l., Wa., U.S. (mō′zĕz)	114	47°09′N	119°30′W
Moshchnyy, is., Russia (môsh′chnĭ)	167	59°56′N	28°07′E
Moshi, Tan. (mō′shê)	233	3°21′S	37°20′E
Mosjøen, Nor.	160	65°50′N	13°10′E
Moskva *see* Moscow, Russia	178	55°45′N	37°37′E
Moskva, prov., Russia	176	55°38′N	36°48′E
Moskva, r., Russia	180	55°30′N	37°05′E
Mosonmagyaróvár, Hung.	169	47°51′N	17°16′E
Mosquitos, Costa de, cst., Nic. (kôs-tä-dĕ-mōs-kē′tō)	133	12°05′N	83°49′W
Mosquitos, Gulfo de los, b., Pan. (gōō′l-fô-dĕ-lôs-mōs-kē′tōs)	129	9°17′N	80°59′W
Moss, Nor. (môs)	160	59°29′N	10°39′E
Moss Beach, Ca., U.S. (môs bēch)	116b	37°32′N	122°31′W
Mosselbaai, S. Afr. (mô′sŭl bā)	232	34°06′S	22°23′E
Mossendjo, Congo	236	2°57′S	12°44′E
Mossley, Eng., U.K. (môs′lĭ)	158a	53°31′N	2°02′W
Moss Point, Ms., U.S. (môs)	124	30°25′N	88°32′W
Most, Czech Rep. (môst)	168	50°32′N	13°37′E
Mostar, Bos. (môs′tär)	163	43°20′N	17°51′E
Móstoles, Spain (mōs-tō′lās)	173a	40°19′N	3°52′W
Mostoos Hills, hills, Can. (mŏs′tōōs)	96	54°50′N	108°45′W
Mosvatnet, l., Nor.	166	59°55′N	7°50′E
Motagua, r., N.A. (mô-tä′gwä)	132	15°29′N	88°39′W
Motala, Swe. (mô-tô′lä)	166	58°34′N	15°00′E
Motherwell, Scot., U.K. (mŭdh′ẽr-wĕl)	160	55°45′N	4°05′W
Motril, Spain (mô-trēl′)	162	36°44′N	3°32′W
Motul, Mex. (mō-tōō′l)	132a	21°07′N	89°14′W
Mouaskar, Alg.	230	35°25′N	0°08′E
Mouchoir Bank, bk. (mōō-shwȧr′)	135	21°35′N	70°40′W
Mouchoir Passage, strt., T./C. Is.	135	21°05′N	71°05′W
Moudjéria, Maur.	234	17°53′N	12°20′W
Mouila, Gabon	236	1°52′S	11°01′E
Mouille Point, c., S. Afr.	232a	33°54′S	18°19′E
Moulins, Fr. (mōō-lăN′)	161	46°34′N	3°19′E
Moulouya, Oued, r., Mor. (mōō-lōō′yȧ)	230	34°00′N	4°00′W
Moultrie, Ga., U.S. (mōl′trĭ)	124	31°10′N	83°48′W
Moultrie, Lake, l., S.C., U.S.	125	33°12′N	80°00′W
Mound City, Il., U.S.	121	37°06′N	89°13′W
Mound City, Mo., U.S.	121	40°08′N	95°13′W
Moundou, Chad	235	8°34′N	16°05′E
Moundsville, W.V., U.S. (moundz′vĭl)	108	39°50′N	80°50′W
Mount, Cape, c., Lib.	234	6°47′N	11°20′W
Mountain Brook, Al., U.S. (moun′tĭn brŏŏk)	110h	33°30′N	86°45′W
Mountain Creek Lake, l., Tx., U.S.	117c	32°43′N	97°03′W
Mountain Grove, Mo., U.S. (grōv)	121	37°07′N	92°16′W
Mountain Home, Id., U.S. (hōm)	114	43°08′N	115°43′W
Mountain Park, Can. (pärk)	90	52°55′N	117°14′W
Mountain View, Ca., U.S. (moun′tĭn vū)	116b	37°25′N	122°07′W
Mountain View, Mo., U.S.	121	36°59′N	91°46′W
Mount Airy, N.C., U.S. (âr′ĭ)	125	36°28′N	80°37′W
Mount Ayliff, S. Afr. (ā′lĭf)	233c	30°48′S	29°24′E
Mount Ayr, Ia., U.S. (âr)	113	40°43′N	94°06′W
Mount Carmel, Il., U.S. (kär′mĕl)	108	38°25′N	87°45′W
Mount Carmel, Pa., U.S.	109	40°50′N	76°25′W
Mount Carool, Il., U.S.	113	42°05′N	89°55′W
Mount Clemens, Mi., U.S. (klĕm′ĕnz)	111b	42°36′N	82°52′W
Mount Desert, i., Me., U.S. (dē-zûrt′)	100	44°15′N	68°08′W
Mount Dora, Fl., U.S. (dō′rȧ)	125a	28°45′N	81°38′W
Mount Duneed, Austl.	217a	38°15′S	144°20′E
Mount Eliza, Austl.	217a	38°11′S	145°05′E
Mount Fletcher, S. Afr. (flĕ′chẽr)	233c	30°42′S	28°32′E
Mount Forest, Can. (fŏr′ĕst)	99	44°00′N	80°45′W
Mount Frere, S. Afr. (frâr′)	233c	30°54′S	29°02′E
Mount Gambier, Austl. (găm′bēr)	218	37°30′S	140°53′E
Mount Gilead, Oh., U.S. (gĭl′ĕăd)	108	40°30′N	82°50′W
Mount Healthy, Oh., U.S. (hĕlth′ê)	111f	39°14′N	84°32′W
Mount Holly, N.J., U.S. (hŏl′ĭ)	110f	39°59′N	74°47′W
Mount Hope, Can.	102d	43°09′N	79°55′W
Mount Hope, N.J., U.S. (hōp)	110a	40°55′N	74°32′W
Mount Hope, W.V., U.S.	108	37°55′N	81°10′W
Mount Isa, Austl. (ī′zȧ)	218	21°00′S	139°45′E
Mount Kisco, N.Y., U.S. (kĭs′kō)	110a	41°12′N	73°44′W
Mountlake Terrace, Wa., U.S. (mount lāk tĕr′ĭs)	116a	47°48′N	122°19′W
Mount Lebanon, Pa., U.S. (lĕb′ȧ-nŭn)	111e	40°22′N	80°03′W
Mount Magnet, Austl. (măg-nĕt)	218	28°00′S	118°00′E
Mount Martha, Austl.	217a	38°17′S	145°01′E
Mount Morgan, Austl. (môr-găn)	219	23°42′S	150°45′E

ăt; finăl; rāte; senāte; ärm; åsk; sofȧ; fâre; ch-choose; dh-as th in other; bē; êvent; bĕt; recĕnt; cratẽr; g-gō; gh-guttural g; bĭt; ĭ-short neutral; rīde; K-guttural k as ch in German ich;

PRONOUNCING INDEX

Mount Moriac – Nabberu 325

PLACE (Pronunciation)	PAGE	LAT.	LONG.
Mount Moriac, Austl.	217a	38°13'S	144°12'E
Mount Morris, Mi., U.S. (mĭr´ĭs)	108	43°10'N	83°45'W
Mount Morris, N.Y., U.S.	109	42°45'N	77°50'W
Mount Nimba National Park, rec., C. Iv.	234	7°35'N	8°10'W
Mount Olive, N.C., U.S. (ŏl´ĭv)	125	35°11'N	78°05'W
Mount Peale, Ut., U.S.	119	38°26'N	109°16'W
Mount Pleasant, Ia., U.S. (plĕz´ănnt)	113	40°59'N	91°34'W
Mount Pleasant, Mi., U.S.	108	43°35'N	84°45'W
Mount Pleasant, S.C., U.S.	125	32°46'N	79°51'W
Mount Pleasant, Tn., U.S.	124	35°31'N	87°12'W
Mount Pleasant, Tx., U.S.	123	33°10'N	94°56'W
Mount Pleasant, Ut., U.S.	119	39°35'N	111°20'W
Mount Prospect, Il., U.S. (prŏs´pĕkt)	111a	42°03'N	87°56'W
Mount Rainier National Park, rec., Wa., U.S. (rå-nēr´)	106	46°47'N	121°17'W
Mount Revelstoke National Park, rec., Can. (rĕv´ĕl-stōk)	90	51°22'N	120°15'W
Mount Savage, Md., U.S. (săv´åj)	109	39°45'N	78°55'W
Mount Shasta, Ca., U.S. (shăs´tȧ)	111	41°10'N	122°17'W
Mount Sterling, Il., U.S. (stûr´lĭng)	121	39°59'N	90°44'W
Mount Sterling, Ky., U.S.	108	38°05'N	84°00'W
Mount Stewart, Can. (stū´ărt)	101	46°22'N	62°52'W
Mount Union, Pa., U.S. (ūn´yŭn)	109	40°25'N	77°50'W
Mount Vernon, Il., U.S. (vûr´nŭn)	108	38°20'N	88°50'W
Mount Vernon, In., U.S.	108	37°55'N	87°50'W
Mount Vernon, Mo., U.S.	121	37°09'N	93°48'W
Mount Vernon, N.Y., U.S.	110a	40°55'N	73°51'W
Mount Vernon, Oh., U.S.	108	40°25'N	82°30'W
Mount Vernon, Va., U.S.	110e	38°43'N	77°06'W
Mount Vernon, Wa., U.S.	114	48°25'N	122°20'W
Moura, Braz. (mō´rȧ)	143	1°33'S	61°38'W
Moura, Port.	172	38°08'N	7°28'W
Mourne Mountains, mts., N. Ire., U.K. (môrn)	164	54°10'N	6°09'W
Moussoro, Chad	235	13°39'N	16°29'E
Moûtiers, Fr. (mōō-tyâr´)	171	45°31'N	6°34'E
Mowbullan, Mount, mtn., Austl.	222	26°50'S	151°34'E
Moyahua, Mex. (mô-yä´wä)	130	21°16'N	103°10'W
Moyale, Kenya (mô-yä´lä)	231	3°28'N	39°04'E
Moyamba, S.L. (mô-yäm´bä)	230	8°10'N	12°26'W
Moyen Atlas, mts., Mor.	162	32°49'N	5°28'W
Moyeuvre-Grande, Fr.	171	49°15'N	6°26'E
Moyie, r., Id., U.S. (moi´yē)	114	38°50'N	116°10'W
Moyobamba, Peru (mō-yô-bäm´bä)	142	6°12'S	76°56'W
Moyuta, Guat. (mô-ē-ōō´tä)	132	14°01'N	90°05'W
Moyyero, r., Russia	184	67°15'N	104°10'E
Moyynqum, des., Kaz.	183	44°30'N	70°00'E
Mozambique, nation, Afr. (mō-zăm-bēk´)	232	20°15'S	33°53'E
Mozambique Channel, strt., Afr. (mō-zăm-bēk´)	233	24°00'S	38°00'E
Mozdok, Russia (môz-dôk´)	181	43°45'N	44°35'E
Mozhaysk, Russia (mô-zhäysk´)	176	55°31'N	36°02'E
Mozhayskiy, Russia (mô-zhäy´skĭ)	186c	59°42'N	30°08'E
Mpanda, Tan.	237	6°22'S	31°02'E
Mpika, Zam.	237	11°54'S	31°26'E
Mpimbe, Mwi.	237	15°18'S	35°04'E
Mporokoso, Zam. ('m-pō-rô-kō´sō)	232	9°23'S	30°05'E
Mpwapwa, Tan. ('m-pwä´pwä)	232	6°21'S	36°29'E
Mqanduli, S. Afr. ('m-kän´dōō-lē)	233c	31°50'S	28°42'E
Mrągowo, Pol. (mräŋ´gô-vô)	169	53°52'N	21°18'E
M'Sila, Alg. (m'sē´lä)	230	35°47'N	4°34'E
Msta, r., Russia (m'stá´)	180	58°30'N	33°00'E
Mstsisław, Bela.	176	54°01'N	31°42'E
Mtakataka, Mwi.	237	14°12'S	34°32'E
Mtamvuna, r., Afr.	233c	30°43'S	29°53'E
Mtata, r., S. Afr.	233c	31°48'S	29°03'E
Mtsensk, Russia (m'tsĕnsk)	180	53°17'N	36°33'E
Mtwara, Tan.	237	10°16'S	40°11'E
Muar, r., Malay.	197b	2°18'N	102°43'E
Mubende, Ug.	237	0°35'N	31°23'E
Mubi, Nig.	235	10°18'N	13°20'E
Mucacata, Moz.	237	13°20'S	39°59'E
Much, Ger. (mōōĸ)	171c	50°54'N	7°24'E
Muchinga Mountains, mts., Zam.	237	12°40'S	30°50'E
Much Wenlock, Eng., U.K. (mŭch wĕn´lŏk)	158a	52°35'N	2°33'W
Muckalee Creek, r., Ga., U.S. (mŭk´ă lē)	124	31°55'N	84°10'W
Muckleshoot Indian Reservation, I.R., Wa., U.S. (mŭck´'l-shōōt)	116a	47°21'N	122°04'W
Mucubela, Moz.	237	16°55'S	37°52'E
Mud, l., Mi., U.S. (mŭd)	113	46°12'N	84°32'W
Mudan, r., China (mōō-dän)	208	45°30'N	129°40'E
Mudanjiang, China (mōō-dän-jyäŋ)	208	44°28'N	129°38'E
Muddy, r., Nv., U.S. (mŭd´ĭ)	119	36°56'N	114°42'W
Muddy Boggy Creek, r., Ok., U.S. (mud´ĭ bôg´ĭ)	121	34°42'N	96°11'W
Muddy Creek, r., Ut., U.S. (mŭd´ĭ)	119	38°45'N	111°10'W
Mudgee, Austl. (mŭ-jē)	222	32°47'S	149°10'E
Mudjatik, r., Can.	96	56°23'N	107°40'W
Mufulira, Zam.	237	12°33'S	28°14'E
Muğla, Tur. (mōōg´lä)	198	37°10'N	28°20'E
Mühldorf, Ger. (mül-dôrf)	168	48°15'N	12°33'E
Mühlhausen, Ger. (mül´hou-zĕn)	168	51°13'N	10°25'E
Muhu, i., Est. (mōō´hōō)	167	58°41'N	22°55'E
Muir Woods National Monument, rec., Ca., U.S. (mūr)	118	37°54'N	123°22'W
Muizenberg, S. Afr. (mwĭz-ĕn-bûrg´)	232a	34°07'S	18°28'E
Mukacheve, Ukr.	169	48°25'N	22°43'E
Mukden *see* Shenyang, China	204	41°45'N	123°22'E
Mukhtuya, Russia (mòk-tōō´yȧ)	179	61°00'N	113°00'E
Mukilteo, Wa., U.S. (mū-kĭl-tā´ō)	116a	47°57'N	122°18'W
Muko, Japan (mōō´kô)	211b	34°57'N	135°43'E

PLACE (Pronunciation)	PAGE	LAT.	LONG.
Muko, r., Japan (mōō´kô)	211b	34°52'N	135°17'E
Mukutawa, r., Can.	97	53°10'N	97°28'W
Mukwonago, Wi., U.S. (mū-kwō-nȧ´gō)	111a	42°52'N	88°19'W
Mula, Spain (mōō´lä)	172	38°05'N	1°12'W
Mula, Al., U.S. (mŭl´gȧ)	110h	33°33'N	86°59'W
Mulde, r., Ger. (mòl´dĕ)	168	50°30'N	12°30'E
Muleros, Mex. (mōō-lā´rōs)	130	23°44'N	104°00'W
Muleshoe, Tx., U.S.	120	34°13'N	102°43'W
Mulgrave, Can. (mŭl´grāv)	101	45°37'N	61°23'W
Mulhacén, mtn., Spain	162	37°04'N	3°18'W
Mülheim, Ger. (mül´hīm)	171c	51°25'N	6°53'E
Mulhouse, Fr. (mü-lōōz´)	161	47°46'N	7°20'E
Muling, China (mōō-lĭŋ)	208	44°32'N	130°18'E
Muling, r., China	208	44°40'N	130°30'E
Mull, Island of, i., Scot., U.K. (mŭl)	164	56°40'N	6°19'W
Mullan, Id., U.S. (mŭl´ăn)	114	47°26'N	115°50'W
Müller, Pegunungan, mts., Indon. (mul´er)	212	0°22'N	113°05'E
Mullingar, Ire. (mŭl-ĭn-gär)	164	53°31'N	7°26'W
Mullins, S.C., U.S. (mŭl´ĭnz)	125	34°11'N	79°13'W
Mullins River, Belize	132a	17°08'N	88°18'W
Multān, Pak. (mò-tän´)	199	30°17'N	71°13'E
Multnomah Channel, strt., Or., U.S. (mŭl nō mȧ)	116c	45°41'N	122°53'W
Mulumbe, Monts, mts., D.R.C.	237	8°47'S	27°20'E
Mulvane, Ks., U.S. (mŭl-vān´)	121	37°30'N	97°13'W
Mumbai (Bombay), India	199	18°58'N	72°50'E
Mumbwa, Zam. (mòm´bwä)	232	14°59'S	27°04'E
Mumias, Kenya	237	0°20'N	34°29'E
Muna, Mex. (mōō´nä)	132a	20°28'N	89°42'W
München *see* Munich, Ger.	154	48°08'N	11°35'E
Muncie, In., U.S. (mŭn´sĭ)	105	40°10'N	85°30'W
Mundelein, Il., U.S. (mŭn-dĕ-līn´)	111a	42°16'N	88°00'W
Mundonueva, Pico de, mtn., Col. (pē´kô-dĕ-mōō´n-dô-nwĕ´vä)	142a	4°18'N	74°12'W
Muneco, Cerro, mtn., Mex. (sĕ´r-rô-mōō-nĕ´kō)	131a	19°13'N	99°20'W
Mungana, Austl. (mŭn-găn´ȧ)	219	17°15'S	144°18'E
Mungbere, D.R.C.	237	2°38'N	28°30'E
Munger, Mn., U.S. (mŭn´gẽr)	117h	46°48'N	92°20'W
Mungindi, Austl. (mŭn-gĭn´dē)	219	29°00'S	148°45'E
Munhall, Pa., U.S. (mŭn´hôl)	111e	40°24'N	79°53'W
Munhango, Ang. (mòn-häŋ´gȧ)	232	12°15'S	18°55'E
Munich, Ger.	154	48°08'N	11°35'E
Munising, Mi., U.S. (mū´nĭ-sĭng)	113	46°24'N	86°41'W
Muniz Freire, Braz.	141a	20°29'S	41°25'W
Munku Sardyk, mtn., Asia (mòn´kô sär-dĭk´)	179	51°45'N	100°30'E
Muñoz, Phil. (mōōn-yōth´)	213a	15°44'N	120°53'E
Münster, Ger. (mün´stẽr)	161	51°57'N	7°38'E
Munster, In., U.S. (mŭn´stẽr)	111a	41°34'N	87°31'W
Munster, hist. reg., Ire. (mŭn-stẽr)	164	52°30'N	9°24'W
Muntok, Indon. (mòn-tŏk´)	212	2°05'S	105°11'E
Muong Sing, Laos (mōō´ông-sĭng´)	212	21°06'N	101°17'E
Muping, China (mōō-pĭŋ)	206	37°23'N	121°36'E
Muqui, Braz. (mōō-kòē)	141a	20°56'S	41°20'W
Mur, r., Eur. (mōōr)	161	47°00'N	15°00'E
Muradiye, Tur. (mōō-rä´dē-yĕ)	181	39°00'N	43°40'E
Murat, Fr. (mü-rä´)	170	45°05'N	2°56'E
Murat, r., Tur. (mōō-rät´)	198	39°00'N	42°00'E
Murchison, r., Austl. (mûr´chĭ-sŭn)	220	26°45'S	116°15'E
Murcia, Spain (mōōr´thyä)	154	38°00'N	1°10'W
Murcia, hist. reg., Spain	172	38°35'N	1°51'W
Murdo, S.D., U.S. (mûr´dô)	112	43°53'N	100°42'W
Mureș, r., Rom. (mōō´rĕsh)	163	46°02'N	21°50'E
Muret, Fr. (mü-rĕ´)	170	43°28'N	1°17'E
Murfreesboro, Tn., U.S. (mûr´frēz-bŭr-ô)	124	35°50'N	86°19'W
Murgab, Taj.	183	38°10'N	73°59'E
Murgab, r., Asia (mōōr-gäb´)	198	37°07'N	62°32'E
Muriaé, r., Braz.	141a	21°20'S	41°40'W
Murino, Russia (mōō´rĭ-nô)	186c	60°03'N	30°28'E
Müritz, l., Ger. (mür´its)	168	53°20'N	12°33'E
Murmansk, Russia (mōōr-mänsk´)	178	69°00'N	33°20'E
Murom, Russia (mōō´rôm)	178	55°30'N	42°00'W
Muroran, Japan (mōō´rô-rän)	205	42°21'N	141°05'E
Muros, Spain (mōō´rōs)	172	42°48'N	9°00'W
Muroto-Zaki, c., Japan (mōō´rô-tō zä´kē)	210	33°14'N	134°12'E
Murphy, Mo., U.S. (mŭr´fĭ)	117e	38°29'N	90°29'W
Murphy, N.C., U.S.	124	35°05'N	84°00'W
Murphysboro, Il., U.S. (mŭr´fĭz-bŭr-ô)	121	37°46'N	89°21'W
Murray, Ky., U.S. (mŭr´ĭ)	124	36°39'N	88°17'W
Murray, Ut., U.S.	117b	40°40'N	111°53'W
Murray, r., Austl.	220	34°20'S	140°00'E
Murray, r., Can.	95	55°00'N	121°00'W
Murray, Lake, res., S.C., U.S. (mŭr´ĭ)	125	34°07'N	81°18'W
Murray Bridge, Austl.	218	35°10'S	139°35'E
Murray Harbour, Can.	101	46°00'N	62°31'W
Murray Region, reg., Austl. (mŭ´rē)	221	33°20'S	142°30'E
Murrumbidgee, r., Austl. (mŭr-ŭm-bĭd´jē)	221	34°30'S	145°20'E
Murrupula, Moz.	237	15°27'S	38°47'E
Murshidābād, India (mòr´shē-dä-bäd´)	202	24°08'N	88°11'E
Murska Sobota, Slvn. (mōōr´skä sô´bô-tä)	174	46°40'N	16°14'E
Muruasigar, mtn., Kenya	237	3°08'N	35°02'E
Murwāra, India	199	23°54'N	80°23'E
Murwillumbah, Austl. (mŭr-wĭl´lŭm-bŭ)	222	28°15'S	153°30'E
Mürz, r., Aus. (mürts)	168	47°30'N	15°21'E
Mürzzuschlag, Aus. (mürts´tsōō-shlägh)	168	47°37'N	15°41'E

PLACE (Pronunciation)	PAGE	LAT.	LONG.
Mus, Tur. (mōōsh)	181	38°55'N	41°30'E
Musala, mtn., Blg.	175	42°05'N	23°24'E
Musan, Kor., N. (mò´sän)	205	41°11'N	129°10'E
Musashino, Japan (mōō-sä´shē-nō)	211a	35°43'N	139°35'E
Muscat, Oman (mŭs-kăt´)	198	23°23'N	58°30'E
Muscat and Oman *see* Oman, nation, Asia	198	20°00'N	57°45'E
Muscatine, Ia., U.S. (mŭs-kȧ-tēn)	113	41°26'N	91°00'W
Muscle Shoals, Al., U.S. (mŭs´'l shōlz)	124	34°44'N	87°38'W
Musgrave Ranges, mts., Austl. (mŭs´grāv)	220	26°15'S	131°15'E
Mushie, D.R.C. (mŭsh´ē)	232	3°04'S	16°50'E
Mushin, Nig.	235	6°32'N	3°22'E
Musi, r., Indon. (mōō´sē)	212	2°40'S	103°42'E
Musinga, Alto, mtn., Col. (ä´l-tô-mōō-sē´n-gä)	142a	6°40'N	76°13'W
Muskego Lake, l., Wi., U.S. (mŭs-kē´gō)	111a	42°53'N	88°10'W
Muskegon, Mi., U.S. (mŭs-kē´gŭn)	105	43°15'N	86°20'W
Muskegon, r., Mi., U.S.	108	43°20'N	85°55'W
Muskegon Heights, Mi., U.S.	108	43°10'N	86°20'W
Muskingum, r., Oh., U.S. (mŭs-kĭŋ´gŭm)	108	39°45'N	81°55'W
Muskogee, Ok., U.S. (mŭs-kō´gē)	105	35°44'N	95°21'W
Muskoka, l., Can. (mŭs-kō´kȧ)	99	45°00'N	79°30'W
Musoma, Tan.	237	1°30'S	33°48'E
Mussau Island, i., Pap. N. Gui. (mōō-sä´ōō)	213	1°30'S	149°32'E
Musselshell, r., Mt., U.S. (mŭs´'l-shĕl)	115	46°25'N	108°20'W
Mussende, Ang.	236	10°32'S	16°05'E
Mussuma, Ang.	236	14°14'S	21°59'E
Mustafakemalpaşa, Tur.	163	40°05'N	28°30'E
Mustang Bayou, Tx., U.S.	123a	29°22'N	95°12'W
Mustang Creek, r., Tx., U.S. (mŭs´tăng)	120	36°22'N	102°46'W
Mustang Island, i., Tx., U.S.	123	27°43'N	97°00'W
Mustique, i., St. Vin. (mŭs-tēk´)	133b	12°53'N	61°03'W
Mustvee, Est. (mōōst´vĕ-ĕ)	167	58°50'N	26°54'E
Musu Dan, c., Kor., N. (mò´sò dän)	205	40°51'N	130°00'E
Muswellbrook, Austl. (mŭs´wŭnl-bròk)	222	32°15'S	150°50'E
Mutare, Zimb.	232	18°49'S	32°39'E
Mutombo Mukulu, D.R.C. (mōō-tôm´bô mōō-kōō´lōō)	232	8°12'S	23°56'E
Mutsu Wan, b., Japan (mōōt´sōō wän)	210	41°20'N	140°55'E
Mutton Bay, Can. (mŭt´'n)	101	50°48'N	59°02'W
Mutum, Braz. (mōō-tōō´m)	141a	19°48'S	41°24'W
Muzaffargarh, Pak.	202	30°09'N	71°15'E
Muzaffarpur, India	202	26°13'N	85°20'E
Muzon, Cape, c., Ak., U.S.	94	54°41'N	132°44'W
Muzquiz, Mex. (mōōz´kēz)	122	27°53'N	101°31'W
Muztagata, mtn., China	204	38°20'N	75°28'E
Mvomero, Tan.	237	6°20'S	37°25'E
Mvoti, r., S. Afr.	233c	29°18'S	30°52'E
Mwali, i., Com.	233	12°15'S	43°45'E
Mwanza, Tan. (mwän´zä)	232	2°31'S	32°54'E
Mwaya, Tan. (mwä´yä)	232	9°19'S	33°51'E
Mwenga, D.R.C.	237	3°02'S	28°26'E
Mweru, l., Afr.	232	8°50'S	28°50'E
Mwingi, Kenya	237	0°56'S	38°04'E
Myanmar (Burma), nation, Asia	194	21°00'N	95°15'E
Myingyan, Mya. (myĭng-yŭn´)	199	21°37'N	95°26'E
Myitkyina, Mya. (myĭ´chē-nȧ)	199	25°33'N	97°25'E
Myjava, Slvk. (mûē´yȧ-vä)	169	48°45'N	17°33'E
Mykhailivka, Ukr.	177	47°16'N	35°12'E
Mykolaïv, Ukr.	178	46°58'N	32°02'E
Mykolaïv, prov., Ukr.	177	47°27'N	31°25'E
Mykonos, i., Grc.	175	37°26'N	25°30'E
Mymensingh, Bngl.	199	24°48'N	90°28'E
Mynämäki, Fin.	167	60°41'N	21°58'E
Myohyang San, mtn., Kor., N. (myō´hyang)	210	40°00'N	126°12'E
Mýrdalsjökull, ice, Ice. (mür´däls-yû´kòl)	160	63°34'N	18°04'W
Myrhorod, Ukr.	181	49°56'N	33°36'E
Mýrina, Grc.	175	39°52'N	25°01'E
Myrtle Beach, S.C., U.S. (mûr´t'l)	125	33°42'N	78°53'W
Myrtle Point, Or., U.S.	114	43°04'N	124°08'W
Mysen, Nor.	166	59°32'N	11°16'E
Myshikino, Russia (mĕsh´kē-nô)	176	57°48'N	38°21'E
Mysore, India (mī-sōr´)	199	12°31'N	76°42'E
Mysovka, Russia (mē´sôf-kȧ)	167	55°11'N	21°17'E
Mystic, Ia., U.S. (mĭs´tĭk)	113	40°47'N	92°54'W
Mytilíni, Grc.	163	39°09'N	26°35'E
Mytishchi, Russia (mē-tēsh´chi)	186b	55°55'N	37°46'E
Mziha, Tan.	237	5°54'S	37°47'E
Mzimba, Mwi. ('m-zĭm´bä)	232	11°52'S	33°34'E
Mzimkulu, r., Afr.	233c	30°12'S	29°57'E
Mzimvubu, r., S. Afr.	233c	31°22'S	29°20'E
Mzuzu, Mwi.	237	11°30'S	34°10'E

N

PLACE (Pronunciation)	PAGE	LAT.	LONG.
Naab, r., Ger. (näp)	168	49°38'N	12°15'E
Naaldwijk, Neth.	159a	52°00'N	4°11'E
Nā'ālehu, Hi., U.S.	126a	19°00'N	155°35'W
Naantali, Fin. (nän´tȧ-lē)	167	60°29'N	22°03'E
Nabberu, l., Austl. (năb´ẽr-ōō)	220	26°05'S	120°35'E

ng-sing; ŋ-baŋk; ɴ-nasalized n; nŏd; cŏmmit; ōld; ôbey; ôrder; oi-boil; fōōd; ò-as oo in foot; ou-out; s-soft; sh-dish; th-thin; pūre; ûnite; ûrn; stŭd; circŭs; ü-as in French tu; ´-indeterminate vowel.

326 Naberezhnyye Chelny – Nduye PRONOUNCING INDEX

PLACE (Pronunciation)	PAGE	LAT.	LONG.
Naberezhnyye Chelny, Russia	178	55°42′N	52°19′E
Nabeul, Tun. (nā-bûl′)	230	36°34′N	10°45′E
Nabiswera, Ug.	237	1°28′N	32°16′E
Naboomspruit, S. Afr.	238c	24°32′S	28°43′E
Nābulus, W.B.	197a	32°13′N	35°16′E
Nacala, Moz. (nä-kā′lä)	233	14°34′S	40°41′E
Nacaome, Hond. (nä-kä-ō′må)	132	13°32′N	87°28′W
Na Cham, Viet. (nä chäm′)	209	22°02′N	106°30′E
Naches, r., Wa., U.S. (năch′ĕz)	114	46°51′N	121°03′W
Náchod, Czech Rep. (näk′ôt)	168	50°25′N	16°08′E
Nacimiento, Lake, res., Ca., U.S. (nȧ-sĭ-myĕn′tō)	118	35°50′N	121°00′W
Nacogdoches, Tx., U.S. (năk′ō-dō′chĕz)	123	31°36′N	94°40′W
Nadadores, Mex. (nä-dä-dō′rās)	122	27°04′N	101°36′W
Nadiād, India	202	22°45′N	72°51′E
Nadir, V.I.U.S.	[illegible]	[illegible]	[illegible]
Nădlac, Rom.	175	46°09′N	20°52′E
Nadvirna, Ukr.	169	48°37′N	24°35′E
Nadym, r., Russia (nä′dĭm)	184	64°30′N	72°48′E
Naestved, Den. (nĕst′vĭdh)	160	55°14′N	11°46′E
Nafada, Nig.	235	11°08′N	11°20′E
Nafishah, Egypt	238d	30°34′N	32°15′E
Náfplio, Grc.	175	37°33′N	22°46′E
Nafūd ad Daḩy, des., Sau. Ar.	198	22°15′N	44°15′E
Nag, Co, l., China	202	31°38′N	91°18′E
Naga, Phil. (nä′gä)	213	13°37′N	123°12′E
Naga, i., Japan	211	32°09′N	130°16′E
Nagahama, Japan (nä′gä-hä′mä)	211	33°32′N	132°29′E
Nagahama, Japan	211	35°23′N	136°16′E
Nagaland, India	199	25°47′N	94°15′E
Nagano, Japan (nä′gä-nō)	205	36°42′N	138°12′E
Nagaoka, Japan (nä′gȧ-ō′kȧ)	205	37°22′N	138°49′E
Nagaoka, Japan	211b	34°54′N	135°42′E
Nāgappattinam, India	199	10°48′N	79°51′E
Nagarote, Nic. (nä-gä-rô′tĕ)	132	12°17′N	86°35′W
Nagasaki, Japan (nä′gȧ-sä′kē)	205	32°48′N	129°53′E
Nāgaur, India	202	27°19′N	73°41′E
Nagaybakskiy, Russia (nȧ-gáy-băk′skĭ)	186a	53°33′N	59°33′E
Nagcarlan, Phil. (näg-kär-län′)	213a	14°07′N	121°24′E
Nāgercoil, India	203	8°15′N	77°29′E
Nagorno Karabakh, hist. reg., Azer. (nu-gôr′nŭ-kŭ-rŭ-bäk′)	181	40°10′N	46°50′E
Nagoya, Japan	205	35°09′N	136°53′E
Nāgpur, India (näg′pōōr)	199	21°12′N	79°09′E
Nagua, Dom. Rep. (nä′gwä)	135	19°20′N	69°40′W
Nagykanizsa, Hung. (nôd′y′kô′nĕ-shô)	163	46°27′N	17°00′E
Nagykőrös, Hung. (nôd′y′kŭ-rûsh)	169	47°02′N	19°46′E
Naha, Japan (nä′hä)	205	26°02′N	127°43′E
Nahanni National Park, rec., Can.	92	62°10′N	125°15′W
Nahant, Ma., U.S. (nȧ-hănt)	101a	42°26′N	70°55′W
Nahariyya, Isr.	197a	33°01′N	35°06′E
Nahuel Huapi, l., Arg. (nä′wĕl wä′pē)	144	41°00′S	71°30′W
Nahuizalco, El Sal. (nä-wē-zäl′kō)	132	13°50′N	89°43′W
Naic, Phil. (nä-ēk)	213a	14°20′N	120°46′E
Naica, Mex. (nä-ē′kä)	122	27°53′N	105°30′W
Naiguata, Pico, mtn., Ven. (pē′kō)	143b	10°32′N	66°44′W
Nain, Can. (nīn)	91	56°29′N	61°52′W
Nā′īn, Iran	201	32°52′N	53°05′E
Nairn, Scot., U.K. (nârn)	164	57°35′N	3°54′W
Nairobi, Kenya (nī-rō′bē)	232	1°17′S	36°49′E
Naivasha, Kenya (nī-vä′shȧ)	232	0°47′S	36°29′E
Najd, hist. reg., Sau. Ar.	198	25°18′N	42°38′E
Najin, Kor., N. (nä′jĭn)	205	42°04′N	130°35′E
Najran, des., Sau. Ar. (nŭj-rän′)	198	17°29′N	45°30′E
Naju, Kor., S. (nä′jōō′)	210	35°02′N	126°42′E
Najusa, r., Cuba (nä-hōō′sä)	134	20°55′N	77°55′W
Nakatsu, Japan (nä′käts-ōō)	210	33°34′N	131°10′E
Nakhodka, Russia (nŭ-kôt′kŭ)	179	43°03′N	133°08′E
Nakhon Ratchasima, Thai.	212	14°56′N	102°14′E
Nakhon Sawan, Thai.	212	15°42′N	100°06′E
Nakhon Si Thammarat, Thai.	212	8°27′N	99°58′E
Nakło nad Notecia, Pol.	169	53°10′N	17°35′E
Nakskov, Den. (näk′skou)	160	54°51′N	11°06′E
Naktong, r., Kor., S. (näk′tŭng)	210	36°10′N	128°30′E
Nal′chik, Russia (nȧl-chĕk′)	181	43°30′N	43°35′E
Nalón, r., Spain (nä-lōn′)	172	43°15′N	5°38′W
Nālūt, Libya (nä-lōōt′)	230	31°51′N	10°49′E
Namak, Daryacheh-ye, l., Iran	198	34°58′N	51°33′E
Namakan, l., Mn., U.S. (nă′mȧ-kȧn)	113	48°20′N	92°43′W
Namangan, Uzb. (nȧ-mȧn-gän′)	183	41°08′N	71°59′E
Namao, Can.	102g	53°43′N	113°30′W
Namatanai, Pap. N. Gui. (nä′mä-tȧ-nä′ē)	213	3°43′S	152°26′E
Nambour, Austl. (năm′bōr)	222	26°48′S	153°00′E
Nam Co, l., China (näm tswo)	204	30°30′N	91°10′E
Nam Dinh, Viet. (näm dēnk′)	212	20°30′N	106°10′E
Nametil, Moz.	237	15°43′S	39°21′E
Namhae, i., Kor., S. (näm′hī′)	210	34°23′N	128°05′E
Namib Desert, des., Nmb. (nä-mēb′)	232	18°45′S	12°45′E
Namibia, nation, Afr.	232	19°30′S	16°13′E
Namoi, r., Austl. (nămoi)	221	30°10′S	148°43′E
Namous, Oued en, r., Alg. (nȧ-mōōs′)	162	31°48′N	0°19′W
Nampa, Id., U.S. (năm′pȧ)	104	43°35′N	116°35′W
Namp′o, Kor., N.	205	38°47′N	125°28′E
Nampuecha, Moz.	237	13°59′S	40°18′E
Nampula, Moz.	237	15°07′S	39°15′E
Namsos, Nor. (näm′sôs)	160	64°28′N	11°14′E
Namu, Can.	94	51°53′N	127°50′W
Namuli, Serra, mts., Moz.	237	15°05′S	37°05′E
Namur, Bel. (nȧ-mür′)	161	50°29′N	4°55′E
Namutoni, Nmb. (nȧ-mōō-tō′nē)	232	18°45′S	17°00′E
Nan, r., Thai.	212	18°11′N	100°29′E

PLACE (Pronunciation)	PAGE	LAT.	LONG.
Nanacamilpa, Mex. (nä-nä-kä-mē′l-pä)	131a	19°30′N	98°33′W
Nanaimo, Can. (nȧ-nī′mō)	90	49°10′N	123°56′W
Nanam, Kor., N. (nä′nän′)	210	41°38′N	129°37′E
Nanao, Japan (nä′nä-ō)	210	37°03′N	136°59′E
Nan′ao Dao, i., China (nän-ou dou)	209	23°30′N	117°30′E
Nanchang, China (nän′chäng′)	205	28°38′N	115°48′E
Nanchangshan Dao, i., China (nän-chäŋ-shän dou)	206	37°56′N	120°42′E
Nancheng, China (nän-chäŋ)	205	26°50′N	116°40′E
Nanchong, China (nän-chôŋ)	204	30°45′N	106°05′E
Nancy, Fr. (näɴ-sē′)	161	48°42′N	6°11′E
Nancy Creek, r., Ga., U.S. (năn′cē)	110c	33°51′N	84°25′W
Nanda Devi, mtn., India (nän′dä dā′vē)	199	[illegible]	[illegible]
Nānded, India	202	19°13′N	77°21′E
Nandurbār, India	202	21°29′N	74°13′E
Nandyāl, India	203	15°54′N	78°09′E
Nanga Parbat, mtn., Pak.	202	[illegible]	[illegible]
Nāngi, India	202a	22°30′N	[illegible]
Nangis, Fr. (näɴ-zhē′)	171b	48°33′N	3°01′E
Nangong, China (nän-gôŋ)	208	37°22′N	115°22′E
Nangweshi, Zam.	236	16°26′S	23°17′E
Nanhuangcheng Dao, i., China (nän-hůäŋ-chŭŋ dou)	206	38°22′N	120°54′E
Nanhui, China	206	31°03′N	121°45′E
Nanjing, China (nän-jyĭŋ)	205	32°04′N	118°46′E
Nanjuma, r., China (nän-jyōō-mä)	206	39°37′N	115°45′E
Nanking *see* Nanjing, China	204	32°04′N	118°46′E
Nanle, China (nän-lŭ)	206	36°03′N	115°13′E
Nan Ling, mts., China	205	25°15′N	111°40′E
Nanliu, r., China (nän-lĭō)	209	22°00′N	109°18′E
Nannine, Austl. (nă-nēn′)	218	25°50′S	118°30′E
Nanning, China (nän′nĭng′)	204	22°56′N	108°10′E
Nanpan, r., China (nän-pän)	209	24°50′N	105°30′E
Nanping, China (nän-pĭŋ)	205	26°40′N	118°05′E
Nansei-shotō, is., Japan	205	27°30′N	127°00′E
Nansemond, Va., U.S. (năn′sē-mŭnd)	110g	36°46′N	76°32′W
Nantai Zan, mtn., Japan (nän-täē zän)	210	36°47′N	139°28′E
Nantes, Fr. (näɴt′)	154	47°13′N	1°37′W
Nanteuil-le-Haudouin, Fr. (näɴ-tû-lē-ō-dwăɴ′)	171b	49°08′N	2°49′E
Nanticoke, Pa., U.S. (năn′tĭ-kōk)	109	41°10′N	76°00′W
Nantong, China (nän-tôŋ)	206	32°02′N	120°51′E
Nantong, China	206	32°08′N	121°06′E
Nantucket, i., Ma., U.S. (năn-tŭk′ĕt)	107	41°15′N	70°05′W
Nantwich, Eng., U.K. (nănt′wĭch)	158a	53°04′N	2°31′W
Nanxiang, China (nän-shyäŋ)	206	31°17′N	121°17′E
Nanxiong, China (nän-shôŋ)	209	25°10′N	114°20′E
Nanyang, China	205	33°00′N	112°42′E
Nanyang Hu, l., China (nän-yäŋ hōō)	206	35°14′N	116°24′E
Nanyuan, China (nän-yůän)	208a	39°48′N	116°24′E
Naolinco, Mex. (nä-o-lēŋ′kō)	131	19°39′N	96°50′W
Náousa, Grc. (nä′ōō-sȧ)	175	40°38′N	22°05′E
Naozhou Dao, i., China (nou-jō dou)	209	20°58′N	110°58′E
Napa, Ca., U.S. (năp′ȧ)	104	38°20′N	122°17′W
Napanee, Can. (năp′ȧ-nē)	99	44°15′N	77°00′W
Naperville, Il., U.S. (nā′pēr-vĭl)	111a	41°46′N	88°09′W
Napier, N.Z. (nā′pĭ-ēr)	221a	39°30′S	177°00′E
Napierville, Can. (nā′pĭ-ē-vĭl)	102a	45°11′N	73°24′W
Naples (Napoli), Italy	154	40°37′N	14°12′E
Naples, Fl., U.S. (nā′p′lz)	125a	26°07′N	81°46′W
Napo, r., S.A. (nä′pō)	142	1°49′S	74°20′W
Napoleon, Oh., U.S. (nȧ-pō′lē-ŭn)	108	41°20′N	84°10′W
Napoleonville, La., U.S. (nȧ-pō′lē-ŭn-vĭl)	123	29°56′N	91°03′W
Napoli *see* Naples, Italy	154	40°37′N	14°12′E
Napoli, Golfo di, b., Italy	162	40°29′N	14°08′E
Nappanee, In., U.S. (năp′ȧ-nē)	108	41°30′N	86°00′W
Nara, Japan (nä′rä)	205	34°41′N	135°50′E
Nara, Mali	230	15°09′N	7°27′W
Nara, dept., Japan	211b	34°36′N	135°49′E
Nara, r., Russia	176	55°05′N	37°16′E
Narach, Vozyera, l., Bela.	176	54°51′N	27°00′E
Naracoorte, Austl. (nȧ-rȧ-kōōn′tĕ)	218	36°50′S	140°50′E
Narashino, Japan	211a	35°41′N	140°01′E
Naraspur, India	203	16°32′N	81°43′E
Narberth, Pa., U.S. (när′bûrth)	110f	40°01′N	75°17′W
Narbonne, Fr. (nȧr-bôn′)	161	43°12′N	3°00′E
Nare, Col. (nä′rĕ)	142a	6°12′N	74°37′W
Narew, r., Pol. (nä′rĕf)	169	52°43′N	21°19′E
Narmada, r., India	199	22°30′N	75°30′E
Narodnaya, Gora, mtn., Russia (nȧ-rôd′nȧ-yȧ)	178	65°10′N	60°10′E
Naro-Fominsk, Russia (nä′rō-mēnsk′)	180	55°23′N	36°43′E
Narrabeen, Austl. (năr-ȧ-bĭn)	217b	33°44′S	151°18′E
Narragansett, R.I., U.S. (năr-ă-găn′sĕt)	110b	41°26′N	71°27′W
Narragansett Bay, b., R.I., U.S.	109	41°20′N	71°15′W
Narrandera, Austl. (nȧ-rǎn-dē′rȧ)	219	34°40′S	146°40′E
Narrogin, Austl. (năr′ō-gĭn)	218	33°00′S	117°15′E
Narva, Est. (nȧr′vȧ)	180	59°24′N	28°12′E
Narvacan, Phil. (när-vä-kän′)	213a	17°27′N	120°29′E
Narva Jõesuu, Est. (nȧr′vȧ ô-ô-ä′sōō-ô)	167	59°26′N	28°02′E
Narvik, Nor. (när′vēk)	154	68°21′N	17°18′E
Narvskiy Zaliv, b., Eur. (nȧr′vskĭ zä′lĭf)	167	59°35′N	27°25′E
Narvskoye, res., Eur.	167	59°18′N	28°14′E
Nar′yan-Mar, Russia (när′yȧn mär′)	178	67°42′N	53°30′E
Naryilco, Austl. (năr-ĭl′kō)	222	28°40′S	141°50′E
Narym, Russia (nŭ-rēm′)	178	58°47′N	82°05′E
Naryn, r., Asia (nŭ-rĭn′)	184	41°20′N	76°00′E
Naseby, Eng., U.K. (năz′bĭ)	158a	52°23′N	0°59′W
Nashua, Mo., U.S. (năsh′ŭ-ȧ)	117f	39°18′N	94°34′W
Nashua, N.H., U.S.	105	42°47′N	71°23′W

PLACE (Pronunciation)	PAGE	LAT.	LONG.
Nashville, Ar., U.S. (năsh′vĭl)	121	33°56′N	93°50′W
Nashville, Ga., U.S.	124	31°12′N	83°15′W
Nashville, Il., U.S.	121	38°21′N	89°42′W
Nashville, Mi., U.S.	108	42°35′N	85°50′W
Nashville, Tn., U.S.	105	36°10′N	86°48′W
Nashwauk, Mn., U.S. (năsh′wôk)	113	47°21′N	93°12′W
Näsi, l., Fin.	160	61°42′N	24°05′E
Našice, Cro. (nä′shē-tsĕ)	163	45°29′N	18°06′E
Nasielsk, Pol. (nä′syĕlsk)	169	52°35′N	20°50′E
Nāsik, India (nä′sĭk)	199	20°02′N	73°49′E
Nāşir, Sudan (nä-zēr′)	231	8°30′N	33°06′E
Nasirabād, India	202	26°13′N	74°48′E
Naskaupi, r., Can. (näs′kô-pĭ)	93	53°59′N	61°10′W
Nasondoyo, D.R.C.	237	10°22′S	25°06′E
Nass, r., Can. (năs)	94	55°00′N	129°30′W
Nassau, Bah. (năs′ô)	129	25°05′N	77°20′W
Nassenheide, Ger. (nä′sĕn-hī-dĕ)	159b	52°49′N	13°13′E
[illegible], Egypt	231	[illegible]	[illegible]
Nasugbu, Phil. (nȧ-sŏg-bōō′)	213a	14°05′N	120°37′E
Nasworthy Lake, l., Tx., U.S. (năz′wûr-thē)	122	31°17′N	100°30′W
Natagaima, Col. (nä-tä-gī′mä)	142a	3°38′N	75°07′W
Natal, Braz. (nä-täl′)	143	6°00′S	35°13′W
Natashquan, Can. (nä-täsh′kwän)	91	50°11′N	61°49′W
Natashquan, r., Can.	101	50°35′N	61°35′W
Natchez, Ms., U.S. (năch′ĕz)	105	31°35′N	91°20′W
Natchitoches, La., U.S. (năk′ĭ-tŏsh) (nách-ĭ-tōsh′)	123	31°46′N	93°06′W
Natick, Ma., U.S. (nā′tĭk)	101a	42°17′N	71°21′W
National Bison Range, I.R., Mt., U.S. (năsh′ŭn-ăl bī′s′n)	115	47°18′N	113°58′W
National City, Ca., U.S.	118a	32°38′N	117°01′W
Natitingou, Benin	230	10°19′N	1°22′E
Natividade, Braz. (nä-tē-vē-dä′dĕ)	143	11°43′S	47°34′W
Natron, Lake, l., Tan. (nā′trŏn)	232	2°17′S	36°10′E
Natrona Heights, Pa., U.S. (nā′trō nȧ)	111e	40°38′N	79°43′W
Naţrūn, Wādī an, val., Egypt	238b	30°33′N	30°12′E
Natuna Besar, i., Indon.	212	4°00′N	106°50′E
Natural Bridges National Monument, rec., Ut., U.S. (năt′ū-răl brĭj′ĕs)	119	37°20′N	110°20′W
Naturaliste, Cape, c., Austl. (năt-ū-rȧ-lĭst′)	220	33°30′S	115°10′E
Nau, Cap de la, c., Spain	156	38°43′N	0°14′E
Naucalpan de Juárez, Mex.	131a	19°28′N	99°14′W
Nauchampatepetl, mtn., Mex. (näōō-chäm-pä-tĕ′pĕtl)	131	19°32′N	97°09′W
Nauen, Ger. (nou′ĕn)	159b	52°36′N	12°53′E
Naugatuck, Ct., U.S. (nô′gȧ-tŭk)	109	41°25′N	73°05′W
Naujan, Phil. (nä-ō-hän′)	213a	13°19′N	121°17′E
Naumburg, Ger. (noum′bŏrgh)	168	51°10′N	11°50′E
Nauru, nation, Oc.	3	0°30′S	167°00′E
Nautla, Mex. (nä-ōōt′lä)	128	20°14′N	96°44′W
Nava, Mex. (nä′vä)	122	28°25′N	100°44′W
Nava del Rey, Spain (nä-vä dĕl rā′ē)	172	41°22′N	5°04′W
Navahermosa, Spain (nä-vä-ĕr-mō′sä)	172	39°39′N	4°28′W
Navajas, Cuba (nä-vä-häs′)	134	22°40′N	81°20′W
Navajo Hopi Joint Use Area, I.R., Az., U.S.	119	36°15′N	110°30′W
Navajo Indian Reservation, I.R., U.S. (năv′á-hō)	119	36°31′N	109°24′W
Navajo National Monument, rec., Az., U.S.	119	36°43′N	110°39′W
Navajo Reservoir, res., N.M., U.S.	119	36°57′N	107°26′W
Navalcarnero, Spain (nä-väl′kär-nā′rō)	173a	40°17′N	4°05′W
Navalmoral de la Mata, Spain	172	39°53′N	5°32′W
Navan, Can. (nă′vȧn)	102c	45°25′N	75°26′W
Navarino, i., Chile (nȧ-vä-rē′nō)	144	55°30′S	68°15′W
Navarra, hist. reg., Spain (nä-vär′rä)	172	42°40′N	1°35′W
Navarro, Arg. (nä-vá′r-rō)	141c	35°00′S	59°16′W
Navasota, Tx., U.S. (năv-ȧ-sō′tȧ)	123	30°24′N	96°05′W
Navasota, r., Tx., U.S.	123	31°03′N	96°11′W
Navassa, i., N.A. (nȧ-văs′ȧ)	135	18°25′N	75°15′W
Navia, r., Spain (nä-vē′ä)	172	43°10′N	6°45′W
Navidad, Chile (nä-vē-dä′d)	141b	33°57′S	71°51′W
Navidad Bank, bk. (nä-vē-dädh′)	135	20°05′N	69°00′W
Navidade do Carangola, Braz. (nä-vē-dä′dô-kȧ-rän-gô′la)	141a	21°04′S	41°58′W
Navojoa, Mex. (nä-vô-kô′ä)	128	27°00′N	109°40′W
Nawābshāh, Pak. (nȧ-wäb′shä)	202	26°20′N	68°30′E
Naxçıvan, Azer.	181	39°10′N	45°30′E
Naxçıvan Muxtar, state, Azer.	182	39°20′N	45°30′E
Náxos, i., Grc. (nák′sŏs)	163	37°15′N	25°20′E
Nayarit, state, Mex. (nä-yä-rēt′)	128	22°00′N	105°15′W
Nayarit, Sierra de, mts., Mex. (sē-ĕ′r-rä-dĕ)	130	23°20′N	105°07′W
Naye, Sen.	234	14°25′N	12°12′W
Naylor, Md., U.S. (nā′lōr)	110e	38°43′N	76°46′W
Nazaré da Mata, Braz. (dä-mä-tä)	143	7°46′S	35°13′W
Nazas, Mex. (nä′zäs)	122	25°14′N	104°08′W
Nazas, r., Mex.	128	25°30′N	104°40′W
Nazerat, Isr.	197a	32°43′N	35°19′E
Nazilli, Tur. (nȧ-zĭ-lē′)	181	37°40′N	28°10′E
Naziya, r., Russia (nȧ-zē′yȧ)	186c	59°48′N	31°18′E
Nazko, r., Can.	94	52°35′N	123°10′W
N′dalatando, Ang.	236	9°18′S	14°54′E
Ndali, Benin	235	9°51′N	2°43′E
Ndikiniméki, Cam.	235	4°46′N	10°50′E
N′Djamena, Chad	231	12°07′N	15°03′E
Ndola, Zam. (n′dō′lä)	232	12°58′S	28°38′E
Ndoto Mountains, mts., Kenya	237	1°55′N	37°05′E
Ndrhamcha, Sebkha de, l., Maur.	234	18°50′N	15°15′W
Nduye, D.R.C.	237	1°50′N	29°01′E

ăt; finăl; rāte; senāte; ärm; ȧsk; sofȧ; fâre; ch-choose; dh-as th in other; bē; ēvent; bĕt; recĕnt; cratēr; g-gō; gh-guttural g; bĭt; ĭ-short neutral; rīde; ĸ-guttural k as ch in German ich;

PRONOUNCING INDEX Neagh – New Providence 327

PLACE (Pronunciation)	PAGE	LAT.	LONG.
Neagh, Lough, l., N. Ire., U.K. (lŏk nā)	160	54°40'N	6°47'W
Néa Páfos, Cyp.	197a	34°46'N	32°27'E
Neapean, r., Austl.	217b	33°40'S	150°39'E
Neápoli, Grc.	175	36°35'N	23°08'E
Neápolis, Grc.	174a	35°17'N	25°37'E
Near Islands, is., Ak., U.S. (nēr)	103a	52°20'N	172°40'E
Neath, Wales, U.K. (nēth)	164	51°41'N	3°50'W
Nebine Creek, r., Austl. (nĕ-bēne´)	222	27°50'S	147°00'E
Nebitdag, Turkmen.	183	39°30'N	54°20'E
Nebraska, state, U.S. (nē-brăs´kȧ)	104	41°45'N	101°30'W
Nebraska City, Ne., U.S.	121	40°40'N	95°50'W
Nechako, r., Can.	94	53°45'N	124°55'W
Nechako Plateau, plat., Can. (nĭ-chă´kō)	94	54°00'N	124°30'W
Nechako Range, mts., Can.	94	53°20'N	124°30'W
Nechako Reservoir, res., Can.	94	53°25'N	125°10'W
Neches, r., Tx., U.S. (nĕch´ĕz)	123	31°03'N	94°40'W
Neckar, r., Ger. (nĕk´är)	160	49°16'N	9°08'E
Necker Island, I., Hi., U.S.	126b	24°00'N	164°00'W
Necochea, Arg. (nā-kō-chā´ä)	144	38°30'S	58°45'W
Nedryhailiv, Ukr.	177	50°49'N	33°52'E
Needham, Ma., U.S. (nēd´ăm)	101a	42°17'N	71°14'W
Needles, Ca., U.S. (nē´d'lz)	119	34°51'N	114°39'W
Neenah, Wi., U.S. (nē´nȧ)	113	44°10'N	88°30'W
Neepawa, Can.	90	50°13'N	99°29'W
Nee Reservoir, res., Co., U.S. (nee)	120	38°26'N	102°56'W
Negareyama, Japan (nå´gä-rå-yä´mä)	211a	35°52'N	139°54'E
Negaunee, Mi., U.S. (nē-gô´nē)	113	46°30'N	87°37'W
Negeri Sembilan, state, Malay. (nā´grē-sĕm-bē-län´)	197b	2°46'N	101°54'E
Negev, des., Isr. (nĕ´gĕv)	197a	30°34'N	34°43'E
Negombo, Sri L.	203	7°39'N	79°49'E
Negotin, Serb. (nĕ´gô-tēn)	175	44°13'N	22°33'E
Negro, r., Arg.	144	39°50'S	65°00'W
Negro, r., N.A.	132	13°01'N	87°10'W
Negro, r., S.A.	141c	33°17'S	58°18'W
Negro, r., S.A. (nā´grō)	142	0°18'S	63°21'W
Negro, Cerro, mtn., Pan. (sĕ´-rrô-nā´grō)	133	8°44'N	80°37'W
Negros, i., Phil. (nā´grōs)	212	9°50'N	121°45'E
Nehalem, r., Or., U.S. (nē-hăl´ĕm)	114	45°52'N	123°37'W
Nehaus an der Oste, Ger. (noi´houz) (ōz´tĕ)	159c	53°48'N	9°02'E
Nehbandān, Iran	201	31°32'N	60°02'E
Nehe, China (nŭ-hŭ)	208	48°23'N	124°58'E
Neheim-Hüsten, Ger. (nĕ´hīm)	171c	51°28'N	7°58'E
Neiba, Dom. Rep. (nå-ē´bä)	135	18°30'N	71°20'W
Neiba, Bahía de, b., Dom. Rep.	135	18°10'N	71°00'W
Neiba, Sierra de, mts., Dom. Rep. (sē-ĕr´rä-dĕ)	135	18°40'N	71°40'W
Neihart, Mt., U.S. (nī´härt)	115	46°54'N	110°39'W
Neijiang, China (nā-jyäŋ)	209	29°38'N	105°01'E
Neillsville, Wi., U.S. (nēlz´vĭl)	113	44°35'N	90°37'W
Nei Monggol (Inner Mongolia), state, China	204	40°15'N	105°00'E
Neiqiu, China (nā-chyō)	206	37°17'N	114°32'E
Neira, Col. (nā´rä)	142a	5°10'N	75°32'W
Neisse, r., Eur. (nēs)	168	51°30'N	15°00'E
Neiva, Col. (nå-ē´vä) (nā´vä)	142	2°55'N	75°16'W
Neixiang, China (nā-shyäŋ)	208	33°00'N	111°38'E
Nekemte, Eth.	231	9°09'N	36°29'E
Nekoosa, Wi., U.S. (nē-kōō´sȧ)	113	44°19'N	89°54'W
Neligh, Ne., U.S. (nē´-lē)	112	42°06'N	98°02'W
Nel'kan, Russia (nĕl-kän´)	179	57°45'N	136°36'E
Nellore, India (nĕl-lōr´)	199	14°28'N	79°59'E
Nel'ma, Russia (nĕl-mä´)	210	47°34'N	139°05'E
Nelson, Can. (nĕl´sŭn)	90	49°29'N	117°17'W
Nelson, N.Z.	221a	41°15'S	173°22'E
Nelson, Eng., U.K.	158a	53°50'N	2°13'W
Nelson, i., Ak., U.S.	103	60°38'N	164°42'W
Nelson, r., Can.	97	56°50'N	93°40'W
Nelson, Cape, c., Austl.	222	38°29'S	141°20'E
Nelsonville, Oh., U.S. (nĕl´sŭn-vĭl)	108	39°30'N	82°15'W
Néma, Maur. (nä´mä)	230	16°37'N	7°15'W
Nemadji, r., Wi., U.S. (nĕ-măd´jē)	117h	46°33'N	92°16'W
Neman, Russia (ŋĕ´-man)	167	55°02'N	22°01'E
Neman, r., Eur.	180	53°28'N	24°45'E
Nembe, Nig.	235	4°35'N	6°26'E
Nemeiben Lake, l., Can. (nĕ-mē´bȧn)	96	55°20'N	105°20'W
Nemours, Fr.	170	48°16'N	2°41'E
Nemuro, Japan (nā´mō-rō)	205	43°13'N	145°10'E
Nemuro Strait, strt., Asia	210	43°07'N	145°10'E
Nemyriv, Ukr.	177	48°56'N	28°51'E
Nen, r., China (nŭn)	205	47°07'N	123°28'E
Nen, r., Eng., U.K. (nĕn)	158a	52°32'N	0°19'W
Nenagh, Ire. (nē´nȧ)	164	52°50'N	8°05'W
Nenana, Ak., U.S. (nå-nä´nȧ)	103	64°28'N	149°18'W
Nenikyul', Russia (nĕ-nyĕ´kyûl)	186c	59°26'N	30°40'E
Nenjiang, China (nŭn-jyäŋ)	205	49°02'N	125°15'E
Neodesha, Ks., U.S. (nē-ō-dĕ-shô´)	121	37°24'N	95°41'W
Neosho, Mo., U.S.	121	36°51'N	94°22'W
Neosho, r., Ks., U.S. (nē-ō´shō)	121	38°07'N	95°40'W
Nepal, nation, Asia (nĕ-pôl´)	199	28°45'N	83°00'E
Nephi, Ut., U.S. (nē´fī)	119	39°40'N	111°50'W
Nepomuceno, Braz. (nĕ-pô-mōō-sĕ´no)	141a	21°15'S	45°13'W
Nera, r., Italy (nā´rä)	174	42°45'N	12°54'E
Nérac, Fr. (nā-råk´)	170	44°08'N	0°19'E
Nerchinsk, Russia (nyĕr´ chĕnsk)	179	51°47'N	116°17'E
Nerchinskiy Khrebet, mts., Russia	179	50°30'N	118°30'E
Nerchinskiy Zavod, Russia (nyĕr´chĕn-skĭzá-vôt´)	179	51°35'N	119°46'E
Nerekhta, Russia (nyĕ-rĕk´tȧ)	176	57°29'N	40°34'E
Neretva, r., Eur. (nĕ´rĕt-vȧ)	175	43°08'N	17°50'E
Nerja, Spain (nĕr´hä)	172	36°45'N	3°53'W
Nerl', r., Russia (nyĕrl)	176	56°59'N	37°57'E
Nerskaya, r., Russia (nyĕr´skȧ-yȧ)	186b	55°31'N	38°46'E
Nerussa, r., Russia (nyå-rōō´sȧ)	176	52°24'N	34°20'E
Ness, Loch, l., Scot., U.K. (lŏĸ nĕs)	164	57°23'N	4°20'W
Ness City, Ks., U.S. (nĕs)	120	38°27'N	99°55'W
Nesterov, Russia (nyĕs-tå´rôf)	167	54°39'N	22°38'E
Néstos (Mesta), r., Eur. (nās´tōs)	175	41°25'N	24°12'E
Netanya, Isr.	197a	32°19'N	34°52'E
Netcong, N.J., U.S. (nĕt´cŏnj)	110a	40°54'N	74°42'W
Netherlands, nation, Eur. (nĕdh´ĕr-lăndz)	154	53°01'N	3°57'E
Netherlands Guiana *see* Suriname, nation, S.A.	143	4°00'N	56°00'W
Nettilling, l., Can.	93	66°30'N	70°40'W
Nett Lake Indian Reservation, I.R., Mn., U.S. (nĕt lāk)	113	48°23'N	93°19'W
Nettuno, Italy (nĕt-tōō´nô)	173d	41°28'N	12°40'E
Neubeckum, Ger. (noi´bĕ-kōōm)	171c	51°48'N	8°01'E
Neubrandenburg, Ger. (noi-brän´dĕn-bòrgh)	168	53°33'N	13°16'E
Neuburg, Ger. (noi´bòrgh)	168	48°43'N	11°12'E
Neuchâtel, Switz. (nû-shȧ-tĕl´)	161	47°00'N	6°52'E
Neuchâtel, Lac de, l., Switz.	168	46°48'N	6°53'E
Neuenhagen, Ger. (noi´ĕn-hä-gĕn)	159b	52°31'N	13°41'E
Neuenrade, Ger. (noi´ĕn-rä-dĕ)	171c	51°17'N	7°47'E
Neufchâtel-en-Bray, Fr. (nû-shä-tĕl´ĕɴ-brā´)	170	49°43'N	1°25'E
Neulengbach, Aus.	159e	48°13'N	15°55'E
Neumarkt, Ger. (noi´märkt)	168	49°17'N	11°30'E
Neumünster, Ger. (noi´münstĕr)	160	54°04'N	10°00'E
Neunkirchen, Aus. (noin´kĭrĸ-ĕn)	168	47°43'N	16°05'E
Neuquén, Arg. (nĕ-ò-kān´)	144	38°52'S	68°12'W
Neuquén, prov., Arg.	144	39°40'S	70°45'W
Neuquén, r., Arg.	144	38°45'S	69°00'W
Neuruppin, Ger. (noi´rōō-pēn)	168	52°55'N	12°48'E
Neuse, r., N.C., U.S. (nūz)	125	36°12'N	78°50'W
Neusiedler See, l., Eur. (noi-zēd´lĕr)	168	47°54'N	16°31'E
Neuss, Ger. (nois)	171c	51°12'N	6°41'E
Neustadt, Ger. (noi´shtät)	168	49°21'N	8°08'E
Neustadt bei Coburg, Ger. (bī kō´bōōrgh)	168	50°20'N	11°09'E
Neustadt in Holstein, Ger.	168	54°06'N	10°50'E
Neustrelitz, Ger. (noi-strā´lĭts)	168	53°21'N	13°05'E
Neutral Hills, hills, Can. (nū´trăl)	96	52°10'N	110°50'W
Neu Ulm, Ger. (noi ò lm´)	168	48°23'N	10°01'E
Neuville, Can. (nū´vĭl)	102b	46°39'N	71°35'W
Neuwied, Ger. (noi´vēdt)	168	50°26'N	7°28'E
Neva, r., Russia (nyĕ-vä´)	176	59°49'N	30°54'E
Nevada, Ia., U.S. (nē-vä´dȧ)	113	42°01'N	93°27'W
Nevada, Mo., U.S.	121	37°49'N	94°21'W
Nevada, state, U.S. (nē vä´dȧ)	104	39°30'N	117°00'W
Nevada, Sierra, mts., Spain (syĕr´rä nä-vä´dhä)	156	37°01'N	3°28'W
Nevada, Sierra, mts., U.S. (sē-ĕ´r-rä nē-vä´dȧ)	106	39°20'N	120°05'W
Nevado, Cerro el, mtn., Col. (sĕ´r-rô-ĕl-nĕ-vä´dô)	142a	4°02'N	74°08'W
Neva Stantsiya, Russia (nyĕ-vä´ stän´tsĭ-yȧ)	186c	59°53'N	30°30'E
Neve, Serra da, mts., Ang.	236	13°40'S	13°20'E
Nevel', Russia (nyĕ´vĕl)	180	56°03'N	29°57'E
Neveri, r., Ven. (nĕ-vĕ-rē)	143b	10°13'N	64°18'W
Nevers, Fr. (nē-vår´)	161	46°59'N	3°10'E
Neves, Braz.	144b	22°51'S	43°06'W
Nevesinje, Bos. (nĕ-vĕ´sĕn-yĕ)	175	43°15'N	18°08'E
Nevinnomyssk, Russia	182	44°38'N	41°56'E
Nevis, i., St. K./N. (nē´vĭs)	129	17°05'N	62°38'W
Nevis, Ben, mtn., Scot., U.K. (bĕn)	160	56°47'N	5°00'W
Nevis Peak, mtn., St. K./N.	133b	17°11'N	62°33'W
Nevşehir, Tur. (nĕv-shĕ´hĕr)	163	38°40'N	34°35'E
Nev'yansk, Russia (nĕv-yänsk´)	178	57°29'N	60°14'E
New, r., Va., U.S. (nū)	125	37°20'N	80°35'W
Newala, Tan.	237	10°56'S	39°18'E
New Albany, In., U.S. (nû ôl´bȧ-nĭ)	111h	38°17'N	85°49'W
New Albany, Ms., U.S.	125	34°28'N	39°00'W
New Amsterdam, Guy. (ăm´stĕr-dăm)	143	6°14'N	57°30'W
Newark, Eng., U.K. (nū´ĕrk)	158a	53°04'N	0°49'W
Newark, Ca., U.S. (nū´ĕrk)	116b	37°32'N	122°02'W
Newark, De., U.S. (nōō´ärk)	109	39°40'N	75°45'W
Newark, N.J., U.S. (nōō´ûrk)	105	40°44'N	74°10'W
Newark, N.Y., U.S. (nū´ĕrk)	109	43°05'N	77°10'W
Newark, Oh., U.S.	108	40°05'N	82°25'W
Newaygo, Mi., U.S. (nū´wā-go)	108	43°25'N	85°50'W
New Bedford, Ma., U.S. (bĕd´fĕrd)	105	41°35'N	70°55'W
Newberg, Or., U.S. (nū´bûrg)	108	45°17'N	122°58'W
New Bern, N.C., U.S. (bûrn)	105	35°05'N	77°05'W
Newbern, Tn., U.S.	124	36°05'N	89°12'W
Newberry, Mi., U.S. (nū´bĕr-ĭ)	113	46°22'N	85°31'W
Newberry, S.C., U.S.	125	34°15'N	81°40'W
New Boston, Mi., U.S. (bôs´tŭn)	111b	42°10'N	83°24'W
New Boston, Oh., U.S.	108	38°45'N	82°55'W
New Braunfels, Tx., U.S. (nū broun´fĕls)	122	29°43'N	98°07'W
New Brighton, Mn., U.S. (brī´tŭn)	117g	45°04'N	93°12'W
New Brighton, Pa., U.S.	111e	40°34'N	80°18'W
New Britain, Ct., U.S. (brĭt´'n)	109	41°40'N	72°45'W
New Britain, i., Pap. N. Gui.	213	6°45'S	149°38'E
New Brunswick, N.J., U.S. (brŭnz´wĭk)	110a	40°29'N	74°27'W
New Brunswick, prov., Can.	91	47°14'N	66°30'W
Newburg, In., U.S.	108	38°00'N	87°25'W
Newburg, Mo., U.S.	121	37°54'N	91°53'W
Newburgh, N.Y., U.S.	109	41°30'N	74°00'W
Newburgh Heights, Oh., U.S.	111d	41°27'N	81°40'W
Newbury, Eng., U.K. (nū´bĕr-ĭ)	164	51°24'N	1°26'W
Newbury, Ma., U.S.	101a	42°48'N	70°52'W
Newbury, co., Eng., U.K.	158b	51°25'N	1°15'W
Newburyport, Ma., U.S. (nū´bĕr-ĭ-pōrt)	101a	42°48'N	70°53'W
New Caledonia, dep., Oc.	219	21°28'S	164°40'E
New Canaan, Ct., U.S. (kā-nȧn)	110a	41°06'N	73°30'W
New Carlisle, Can. (kär-līl´)	91	48°01'N	65°20'W
Newcastle, Austl. (nū-kȧs´'l)	222	33°00'S	151°55'E
Newcastle, Can.	91	47°00'N	65°34'W
New Castle, De., U.S.	109	39°40'N	75°35'W
New Castle, In., U.S.	108	39°55'N	85°25'W
New Castle, Oh., U.S.	108	40°20'N	82°10'W
New Castle, Pa., U.S.	108	41°00'N	80°25'W
Newcastle, Tx., U.S.	120	33°13'N	98°44'W
Newcastle, Wy., U.S.	112	43°51'N	104°11'W
Newcastle under Lyme, Eng., U.K. (nů-kȧs´'l) (nů-käs´'l)	158a	53°01'N	2°14'W
Newcastle upon Tyne, Eng., U.K.	154	55°00'N	1°46'W
Newcastle Waters, Austl. (wô´tĕrz)	218	17°10'S	133°25'E
Newcomerstown, Oh., U.S. (nū´kŭm-ĕrz-toun)	108	40°15'N	81°40'W
New Croton Reservoir, res., N.Y., U.S. (krŏ´tôn)	110a	41°15'N	73°47'W
New Delhi, India (dĕl´hī)	199	28°43'N	77°18'E
Newell, S.D., U.S. (nū´ĕl)	112	44°43'N	103°26'W
New England Range, mts., Austl. (nů ĭŋ´glănd)	221	29°32'S	152°30'E
Newenham, Cape, c., Ak., U.S. (nū-ĕn-hăm)	103	58°40'N	162°32'W
Newfane, N.Y., U.S. (nū-făn)	111c	43°17'N	78°44'W
Newfoundland, i., Can.	93a	48°30'N	56°00'W
Newfoundland and Labrador, prov., Can.	91	48°15'N	56°53'W
Newgate, Can. (nū´gāt)	95	49°01'N	115°10'W
New Georgia, i., Sol. Is. (jôr´jĭ-ȧ)	221	8°08'S	158°00'E
New Georgia Group, is., Sol. Is.	214e	8°30'S	157°20'E
New Georgia Sound, strt., Sol. Is.	214e	8°00'S	158°10'E
New Glasgow, Can. (glȧs´gō)	91	45°35'N	62°36'W
New Guinea, i. (gĭne)	213	5°45'S	140°00'E
Newhalem, Wa., U.S. (nū hā´lŭm)	114	48°44'N	121°11'W
New Hampshire, state, U.S. (hămp´shĭr)	105	43°55'N	71°40'W
New Hampton, Ia., U.S. (hămp´tŭn)	113	43°03'N	92°20'W
New Hanover, S. Afr. (hăn´ôvĕr)	233c	29°23'S	30°32'E
New Hanover, i., Pap. N. Gui.	213	2°37'S	150°15'E
New Harmony, In., U.S. (nū här´mō-nĭ)	108	38°10'N	87°55'W
New Haven, Ct., U.S. (hā´vĕn)	105	41°20'N	72°55'W
New Haven, In., U.S. (nū hāv´'n)	108	41°05'N	85°00'W
New Hebrides, is., Vanuatu	221	16°00'S	167°00'E
New Holland, Eng., U.K. (hŏl´ănd)	158a	53°42'N	0°21'W
New Holland, N.C., U.S.	125	35°27'N	76°14'W
New Hope Mountain, mtn., Al., U.S. (hōp)	110h	33°23'N	86°45'W
New Hudson, Mi., U.S. (hŭd´sŭn)	111b	42°30'N	83°36'W
New Iberia, La., U.S. (ī-bē´rĭ-ȧ)	123	30°00'N	91°50'W
Newington, Can. (nū´ĕng-tŏn)	102c	45°07'N	75°00'W
New Ireland, i., Pap. N. Gui. (īr´lănd)	213	3°15'S	152°30'E
New Jersey, state, U.S. (jûr´zĭ)	105	40°30'N	74°50'W
New Kensington, Pa., U.S. (kĕn´zĭng-tŭn)	111e	40°34'N	79°35'W
Newkirk, Ok., U.S. (nū´kûrk)	121	36°52'N	97°03'W
New Lenox, Il., U.S. (lĕn´ŭk)	111a	41°31'N	87°58'W
New Lexington, Oh., U.S. (lĕk´sĭng-tŭn)	108	39°40'N	82°10'W
New Lisbon, Wi., U.S. (lĭz´bŭn)	113	43°52'N	90°11'W
New Liskeard, Can.	99	47°30'N	79°40'W
New London, Ct., U.S. (lŭn´dŭn)	109	41°20'N	72°05'W
New London, Wi., U.S.	113	44°24'N	88°45'W
New Madrid, Mo., U.S. (măd´rĭd)	121	36°34'N	89°31'W
Newman's Grove, Ne., U.S. (nū´măn grōv)	112	41°46'N	97°44'W
Newmarket, Can. (nū´mär-kĕt)	99	44°00'N	79°30'W
New Martinsville, W.V., U.S. (mär´tĭnz-vĭl)	108	39°35'N	80°50'W
New Meadows, Id., U.S.	114	44°58'N	116°20'W
New Mexico, state, U.S. (mĕk´sĭ-kō)	104	34°30'N	107°10'W
New Mills, Eng., U.K. (mĭlz)	158a	53°22'N	2°00'W
New Munster, Wi., U.S. (mŭn´stĕr)	111a	42°35'N	88°13'W
Newnan, Ga., U.S. (nū´năn)	124	33°22'N	84°47'W
New Norfolk, Austl. (nôr´fŏk)	219	42°50'S	147°17'E
New Orleans, La., U.S. (ôr´lē-ănz)	105	30°00'N	90°05'W
New Philadelphia, Oh., U.S. (fĭl-ȧ-dĕl´fĭ-ȧ)	108	40°30'N	81°30'W
New Plymouth, N.Z. (plĭm´ŭth)	221a	39°04'S	174°13'E
Newport, Austl.	217b	33°39'S	151°19'E
Newport, Eng., U.K. (nū-pôrt)	164	50°41'N	1°25'W
Newport, Eng., U.K.	158a	52°46'N	2°22'W
Newport, Wales, U.K.	161	51°36'N	3°05'W
Newport, Ar., U.S. (nū´pōrt)	121	35°35'N	91°16'W
Newport, Ky., U.S.	105	39°05'N	84°30'W
Newport, Me., U.S.	100	44°49'N	69°20'W
Newport, Mn., U.S.	117g	44°52'N	92°59'W
Newport, N.H., U.S.	109	43°20'N	72°10'W
Newport, Or., U.S.	114	44°39'N	124°02'W
Newport, R.I., U.S.	109	41°29'N	71°16'W
Newport, Tn., U.S.	124	35°55'N	83°12'W
Newport, Vt., U.S.	109	44°55'N	72°15'W
Newport, Wa., U.S.	114	48°12'N	117°01'W
Newport Beach, Ca., U.S. (bēch)	117a	33°36'N	117°55'W
Newport News, Va., U.S.	105	36°59'N	76°24'W
New Prague, Mn., U.S. (nū prāg)	113	44°33'N	93°35'W
New Providence, i., Bah. (prŏv´ĭ-dĕns)	134	25°00'N	77°25'W

ng-sing; ŋ-baŋk; ɴ-nasalized n; nŏd; cŏmmit; ōld; ôbey; ôrder; oi-boil; fōōd; ò-as oo in foot; ou-out; s-soft; sh-dish; th-thin; pūre; ûnite; ûrn; stŭd; circŭs; ü-as in French tu; ´-indeterminate vowel.

328 New Richmond – Norman PRONOUNCING INDEX

PLACE (Pronunciation)	PAGE	LAT.	LONG.
New Richmond, Oh., U.S. (rĭch′mŭnd)	108	38°55′N	84°15′W
New Richmond, Wi., U.S.	113	45°07′N	92°34′W
New Roads, La., U.S. (rōds)	123	30°42′N	91°26′W
New Rochelle, N.Y., U.S. (rū-shĕl′)	110a	40°55′N	73°47′W
New Rockford, N.D., U.S. (rŏk′fẽrd)	112	47°40′N	99°08′W
New Ross, Ire. (rôs)	164	52°25′N	6°55′W
New Sarepta, Can.	102g	53°17′N	113°09′W
New Siberian Islands *see* Novosibirskiye Ostrova, is., Russia	179	74°00′N	140°30′E
New Smyrna Beach, Fl., U.S. (smûr′nȧ)	125	29°00′N	80°57′W
New South Wales, state, Austl. (wālz)	219	32°45′S	146°14′E
Newton, Can. (nū′tŭn)	102f	49°56′N	98°04′W
Newton, Eng., U.K.	158a	53°27′N	2°37′W
Newton, Ia., U.S.	113	[illegible]	[illegible]
Newton, Il., U.S.	108	39°00′N	88°10′W
Newton, Ks., U.S.	121	38°03′N	97°22′W
Newton, Ma., U.S.	101a	42°21′N	71°13′W
Newton, Ms., U.S.	124	32°18′N	89°10′W
Newton, N.C., U.S.	125	35°40′N	81°19′W
Newton, N.J., U.S.	110a	41°03′N	74°45′W
Newton, Tx., U.S.	123	30°47′N	93°45′W
Newtonsville, Oh., U.S. (nū′tŭnz-vĭl)	111f	39°11′N	84°04′W
Newtown, N.D., U.S. (nū′toun)	112	47°57′N	102°25′W
Newtown, Oh., U.S.	111f	39°08′N	84°22′W
Newtown, Pa., U.S.	110f	40°13′N	74°56′W
Newtownards, N. Ire., U.K. (nu-t′n-ardz′)	164	54°35′N	5°39′W
New Ulm, Mn., U.S. (ŭlm)	113	44°18′N	94°27′W
New Waterford, Can. (wô′tẽr-fẽrd)	91	46°15′N	60°05′W
New Westminster, Can. (wĕst′mĭn-stẽr)	95	49°12′N	122°55′W
New York, N.Y., U.S. (yôrk)	105	40°40′N	73°58′W
New York, state, U.S.	105	42°45′N	78°05′W
New Zealand, nation, Oc. (zē′lȧnd)	221a	42°00′S	175°00′E
Nexapa, r., Mex. (nĕks-ä′pä)	130	18°32′N	98°29′W
Neya-gawa, Japan (nā′yä gä′wä)	211b	34°47′N	135°38′E
Neyshābūr, Iran	198	36°06′N	58°45′E
Neyva, r., Russia (nēy′vȧ)	186a	57°39′N	60°37′E
Nezahualcóyotl, Mex.	131a	19°27′N	99°03′W
Nez Perce, Id., U.S. (nĕz′ pûrs′)	114	46°16′N	116°15′W
Nez Perce Indian Reservation, I.R., Id., U.S.	114	46°20′N	116°30′W
Ngami, l., Bots. (n′gä′mē)	232	20°56′S	22°31′E
Ngangerabeli Plain, pl., Kenya	237	1°20′S	40°10′E
Ngangla Ringco, l., China (ŋäŋ-lä rĭŋ-tswo)	202	31°42′N	82°53′E
Ngarimbi, Tan.	237	8°28′S	38°36′E
Ngoko, r., Afr.	236	1°55′N	15°53′E
Ngol-Kedju Hill, mtn., Cam.	235	6°20′N	9°45′E
Ngong, Kenya (′n-gông)	232	1°27′S	36°39′E
Ngounié, r., Gabon	236	1°15′S	10°43′E
Ngoywa, Tan.	237	5°56′S	32°48′E
Ngqeleni, S. Afr. (′ng-kĕ-lā′nē)	233c	31°41′S	29°04′E
Nguigmi, Niger (′n-gēg′mē)	231	14°15′N	13°07′E
Ngurore, Nig.	235	9°18′N	12°14′E
Nguru, Nig. (′n-gōō′rōō)	230	12°53′N	10°26′E
Nguru Mountains, mts., Tan.	237	6°10′S	37°35′E
Nha Trang, Viet. (nyä-träng′)	212	12°08′N	108°56′E
Niafounke, Mali	230	16°03′N	4°17′W
Niagara, Wi., U.S. (nī-ăg′ȧ-rȧ)	113	45°45′N	88°05′W
Niagara, r., N.A.	111c	43°12′N	79°03′W
Niagara Falls, Can.	111c	43°05′N	79°05′W
Niagara Falls, N.Y., U.S.	105	43°06′N	79°02′W
Niagara-on-the-Lake, Can.	102d	43°16′N	79°05′W
Niakaramandougou, C. Iv.	234	8°40′N	5°17′W
Niamey, Niger (nē-ä-mā′)	230	13°31′N	2°07′E
Niamtougou, Togo	234	9°46′N	1°06′E
Niangara, D.R.C. (nē-äŋ-gä′rȧ)	231	3°42′N	27°52′E
Niangua, r., Mo., U.S. (nī-ăŋ′gwȧ)	121	37°30′N	93°05′W
Nias, Pulau, i., Indon. (nē′äs′)	212	0°58′N	97°43′E
Nibe, Den. (nē′bĕ)	166	56°57′N	9°36′E
Nicaragua, nation, N.A. (nĭk-ȧ-rä′gwȧ)	128	12°45′N	86°15′W
Nicaragua, Lago de, l., Nic. (lä′gō dĕ)	128	11°45′N	85°28′W
Nicastro, Italy (nê-käs′trō)	163	38°39′N	16°15′E
Nicchehabin, Punta, c., Mex. (pōō′n-tä-nĕk-chĕ-ä-bē′n)	132a	19°50′N	87°20′W
Nice, Fr. (nēs)	154	43°42′N	7°21′E
Nicheng, China (nē-chŭŋ)	207b	30°54′N	121°48′E
Nichicun, l., Can. (nĭch′ĭ-kŭn)	93	53°07′N	72°10′W
Nicholas Channel, strt., N.A. (nĭk′ō-lȧs)	134	23°30′N	80°20′W
Nicholasville, Ky., U.S. (nĭk′ō-lȧs-vĭl)	108	37°55′N	84°35′W
Nicobar Islands, is., India (nĭk-ō-bär′)	212	8°28′N	94°04′E
Nicolai Mountain, mtn., Or., U.S. (nē-cō lī′)	116c	46°05′N	123°27′W
Nicolás Romero, Mex. (nē-kô-lá′s rô-mĕ′rô)	131a	19°38′N	99°20′W
Nicolet, Lake, l., Mi., U.S. (nĭ′kŏ-lĕt)	117k	46°22′N	84°14′W
Nicolls Town, Bah.	134	25°10′N	78°00′W
Nicols, Mn., U.S. (nĭk′ĕls)	117g	44°50′N	93°12′W
Nicomeki, r., Can.	116d	49°04′N	122°47′W
Nicosia, Cyp. (nē-kô-sē′ȧ)	198	35°10′N	33°22′E
Nicoya, C.R. (nē-kō′yä)	132	10°08′N	85°27′W
Nicoya, Golfo de, b., C.R. (gôl-fô-dĕ)	132	10°03′N	85°04′W
Nicoya, Península de, pen., C.R.	132	10°05′N	86°00′W
Nidzica, Pol. (nē-jēt′sȧ)	169	53°21′N	20°30′E
Niedere Tauern, mts., Aus.	168	47°15′N	13°41′E
Niederkrüchten, Ger. (nē′dĕr-krük-tĕn)	171c	51°12′N	6°14′E
Niederösterreich, state, Aus.	159e	48°24′N	16°20′E
Niedersachsen (Lower Saxony), state, Ger. (nē′dĕr-zäк-sĕn)	159c	53°30′N	9°30′E
Niellim, Chad	235	9°42′N	17°49′E
Nienburg, Ger. (nē′ĕn-bo̤rgh)	168	52°40′N	9°15′E
Nietverdiend, S. Afr.	238c	25°02′S	26°10′E
Nieuw Nickerie, Sur. (nė-nē′kĕ-rē′)	143	5°51′N	57°00′W
Nieves, Mex. (nyā′vås)	130	24°00′N	102°57′W
Niğde, Tur. (nĭg′dĕ)	163	37°55′N	34°40′E
Nigel, S. Afr. (nī′jĕl)	238c	26°26′S	28°27′E
Niger, nation, Afr. (nī′jẽr)	230	18°02′N	8°30′E
Niger, r., Afr.	230	8°00′N	6°00′E
Niger Delta, d., Nig.	235	4°45′N	5°20′E
Nigeria, nation, Afr. (nī-jē′rĭ-ȧ)	230	8°57′N	6°30′E
Nihoa, i., Hi., U.S.	106b	23°15′N	161°30′W
Nii, i., Japan (nē)	211	34°20′N	139°23′E
Niigata, Japan (nē′ē-gä′tȧ)	205	37°47′N	139°04′E
Ni′ihau, i., Hi., U.S. (nē′ē-ha′ōōo)	106c	21°50′N	160°05′W
Niimi, Japan (nē′mē)	211	34°59′N	133°28′E
Niiza, Japan	211a	35°48′N	139°34′E
Nijmegen, Neth. (nī′må-gĕn)	165	51°50′N	5°52′E
Nikitinka, Russia (nė-kĭ′tĭn-kȧ)	176	55°33′N	33°19′E
Nikolayevka, Russia (nē-kô-lä′yĕf-kȧ)	186c	59°29′N	29°48′E
Nikolayevka, Russia	210	48°37′N	134°09′E
Nikolayevskiy, Russia	181	50°00′N	45°30′E
Nikolayevsk-na-Amure, Russia	179	53°18′N	140°49′E
Nikol′sk, Russia (nė-kôlsk′)	178	59°30′N	45°40′E
Nikol′skoye, Russia (nė-kôl′skô-yĕ)	186c	59°27′N	30°00′E
Nikopol, Blg. (nė′kô-pŏl′)	163	43°41′N	24°52′E
Nikopol′, Ukr.	181	47°36′N	34°24′E
Nilahue, r., Chile (nē-lá′wĕ)	141b	34°36′S	71°50′W
Nile, r., Afr. (nīl)	231	27°30′N	31°00′E
Niles, Mi., U.S. (nīlz)	108	41°50′N	86°15′W
Niles, Oh., U.S.	108	41°15′N	80°45′W
Nileshwar, India	203	12°08′N	74°14′E
Nilgiri Hills, hills, India	203	12°05′N	76°22′E
Nilópolis, Braz. (nē-lô′pō-lēs)	141a	22°48′S	43°25′W
Nīmach, India	202	24°32′N	74°51′E
Nimba, Mont, mtn., Afr. (nĭm′bȧ)	230	7°40′N	8°33′W
Nimba Mountains, mts., Afr.	234	7°30′N	8°35′W
Nîmes, Fr. (nēm)	154	43°49′N	4°22′E
Nimrod Reservoir, res., Ar., U.S. (nĭm′rŏd)	121	34°58′N	93°46′W
Nimule, Sudan (nė-mōō′lȧ)	231	3°38′N	32°12′E
Ninda, Ang.	236	14°47′S	21°24′E
Nine Mile Creek, r., Ut., U.S. (mīn′īmōd′)	119	39°50′N	110°30′W
Ninety Mile Beach, cst., Austl.	221	38°20′S	147°30′E
Nineveh, Iraq (nĭn′ē-vȧ)	198	36°30′N	43°10′E
Ning′an, China (nĭŋ-än)	205	44°20′N	129°20′E
Ningbo, China (nĭŋ-bwo)	205	29°56′N	121°30′E
Ningde, China (nĭŋ-dŭ)	205	26°38′N	119°33′E
Ninghai, China (nĭng′hī′)	209	29°20′N	121°20′E
Ninghe, China (nĭŋ-hŭ)	206	39°20′N	117°50′E
Ningjin, China (nĭŋ-jyĭn)	206	37°39′N	116°47′E
Ningjin, China	206	37°37′N	114°55′E
Ningming, China	209	22°22′N	107°06′E
Ningwu, China (nĭng′wōō′)	205	39°00′N	112°12′E
Ningxia Huizu, prov., China (nĭŋ-shyä)	204	37°10′N	106°00′E
Ningyang, China (nĭng′yăng′)	206	35°46′N	116°48′E
Ninh Binh, Viet. (nĕn bĕnk′)	212	20°22′N	106°00′E
Ninigo Group, is., Pap. N. Gui.	213	1°15′S	143°30′E
Ninnescah, r., Ks., U.S. (nĭn′ĕs-kä)	120	37°37′N	98°31′W
Nioaque, Braz. (nēō-á′-kĕ)	143	21°14′S	55°41′W
Niobrara, r., U.S. (nī-ō-brâr′ȧ)	106	42°46′N	98°46′W
Niokolo Koba, Parc National du, rec., Sen.	234	13°05′N	13°00′W
Nioro du Sahel, Mali (nė-ō′rō)	230	15°15′N	9°35′W
Nipawin, Can.	90	53°22′N	104°00′W
Nipe, Bahía de, b., Cuba (bä-ē′ä-dĕ-nē′pā)	135	20°50′N	75°30′W
Nipe, Sierra de, mts., Cuba (sē-ĕ′r-rä-dĕ)	135	20°20′N	75°50′W
Nipigon, Can. (nĭp′ĭ-gŏn)	91	48°58′N	88°17′W
Nipigon, l., Can.	93	49°37′N	89°55′W
Nipigon Bay, b., Can.	98	48°56′N	88°00′W
Nipisiguit, r., Can. (nĭ-pĭ′sĭ-kwĭt)	100	47°26′N	66°15′W
Nipissing, l., Can. (nĭp′ĭ-sĭng)	93	45°59′N	80°19′W
Niquero, Cuba (nē-kā′rō)	134	20°00′N	77°35′W
Nirmali, India	202	26°30′N	86°43′E
Niš, Serb.	154	43°19′N	21°54′E
Nisa, Port. (nē′sȧ)	172	39°32′N	7°41′W
Nišava, r., Eur. (nē′shȧ-vȧ)	175	43°17′N	22°17′E
Nishino, i., Japan (nēsh′ē-nō)	211	36°06′N	132°49′E
Nishinomiya, Japan (nēsh′ē-nō-mē′yȧ)	211b	34°44′N	135°21′E
Nishio, Japan (nēsh′ē-ō)	211	34°50′N	137°01′E
Niska Lake, l., Can. (nĭs′kȧ)	96	55°35′N	108°38′W
Nisko, Pol. (nēs′kô)	169	50°30′N	22°07′E
Nisku, Can. (nĭs-kū′)	102g	53°21′N	113°33′W
Nisqually, r., Wa., U.S. (nĭs-kwôl′ĭ)	114	46°51′N	122°33′W
Nissan, r., Swe.	166	57°06′N	13°22′E
Nisser, l., Nor. (nĭs′ẽr)	166	59°14′N	8°35′E
Nissum Fjord, b., Den.	166	56°24′N	7°35′E
Niterói, Braz. (nē-tĕ-rô′ĭ)	143	22°53′S	43°07′W
Nith, r., Scot., U.K. (nĭth)	164	55°13′N	3°55′W
Nitra, Slvk. (nē′trȧ)	169	48°18′N	18°04′E
Nitra, r., Slvk.	169	48°13′N	18°14′E
Nitro, W.V., U.S. (nī′trō)	108	38°25′N	81°50′W
Niue, dep., Oc. (nĭ′ōō)	241	19°50′S	167°00′W
Nivelles, Bel. (nē′vĕl′)	165	50°33′N	4°17′E
Nixon, Tx., U.S. (nĭk′sŭn)	123	29°16′N	97°48′W
Nizāmābād, India	199	18°48′N	78°07′E
Nizhne-Angarsk, Russia (nyēzh′nyĭ-ŭngärsk′)	179	55°49′N	108°46′E
Nizhne-Chirskaya, Russia	181	48°20′N	42°50′E
Nizhne-Kolymsk, Russia (kô-lĕmsk′)	179	68°32′N	160°56′E
Nizhneudinsk, Russia (nėzh′nyĭ-ōōdēnsk′)	179	54°58′N	99°15′E
Nizhniye Sergi, Russia (nyēzh′ nyē sĕr′gē)	180	56°41′N	59°19′E
Nizhniy Novgorod (Gor′kiy), Russia	178	56°15′N	44°05′E
Nizhniy Tagil, Russia (tŭgēl′)	178	57°54′N	59°59′E
Nizhnyaya Kur′ya, Russia (nyē′zhnyȧ-yȧ koōr′yȧ)	186a	58°01′N	56°00′E
Nizhnyaya Salda, Russia (nyē′zhnya′ya säl′da′)	186a	58°05′N	60°43′E
Nizhnyaya Taymyra, r., Russia	184	72°30′N	95°18′E
Nizhnyaya Tunguska, r., Russia	179	64°13′N	91°30′E
Nizhnyaya Tura, Russia (tōō′rȧ)	186a	58°38′N	59°50′E
Nizhnyaya Us′va, Russia (ô′vȧ)	186a	59°05′N	58°53′E
Nizhyn, Ukr.	181	51°03′N	31°52′E
Nízke Tatry, mts., Slvk.	169	48°57′N	19°18′E
Njazidja, i., Com.	233	11°44′S	42°38′E
Njombe, Tan.	237	9°20′S	34°46′E
Njurunda, Swe. (nyōō-ro̤n′dȧ)	166	62°15′N	17°24′E
Nkala Mission, Zam.	237	15°55′S	26°00′E
Nkandla, S. Afr. (′n-känd′lä)	233c	28°40′S	31°06′E
Nkawkaw, Ghana	234	6°33′N	0°47′W
Nkhota, Mwi. (kō-tȧ kō-tȧ)	232	12°52′S	34°16′E
Noākhāli, Bngl.	199	22°52′N	91°08′E
Noatak, Ak., U.S. (nō-ȧ′tăk)	103	67°22′N	163°28′W
Noatak, r., Ak., U.S.	103	67°58′N	162°15′W
Nobeoka, Japan (nō-bå-ō′kȧ)	210	32°36′N	131°41′E
Noblesville, In., U.S. (nō′bl′z-vĭl)	108	40°00′N	86°00′W
Nobleton, Can. (nō′bl′tŭn)	102d	43°54′N	79°39′W
Nocera Inferiore, Italy (ēn-fĕ-ryō′rĕ)	173c	40°30′N	14°38′E
Nochistlán, Mex. (nô-chēs-tlän′)	130	21°23′N	102°52′W
Nochixtlón, Mex. (ä-sōn-syōn′)	131	17°28′N	97°12′W
Nogales, Mex. (nō-gä′lĕs)	131	18°49′N	97°09′W
Nogales, Mex.	128	31°15′N	111°00′W
Nogales, Az., U.S. (nō-gä′lĕs)	104	31°20′N	110°55′W
Nogal Valley, val., Som. (nō′gäl)	238a	8°30′N	47°50′E
Nogent-le-Roi, Fr. (nŏ-zhŏn-lẽ-rwä′)	171b	48°39′N	1°32′E
Nogent-le-Rotrou, Fr. (rō-trōō′)	170	48°22′N	0°47′E
Noginsk, Russia (nô-gēnsk′)	180	55°52′N	38°28′E
Noguera Pallaresa, r., Spain	173	42°18′N	1°03′E
Noia, Spain	172	42°46′N	8°50′W
Noirmoutier, Île de, i., Fr. (nwȧr-mōō-tyā′)	161	47°03′N	3°08′W
Nojima-Zaki, c., Japan (nō′jē-mä zä-kē)	211	34°54′N	139°48′E
Nokomis, Il., U.S. (nô-kō′mĭs)	108	39°15′N	89°10′W
Nola, Italy (nô′lä)	174	40°41′N	14°32′E
Nolinsk, Russia (nô-lēnsk′)	180	57°32′N	49°50′E
Noma Misaki, c., Japan (nô′mä mē′sä-kē)	211	31°25′N	130°09′E
Nombre de Dios, Mex. (nôm-brĕ-dĕ-dyô′s)	130	23°50′N	104°14′W
Nombre de Dios, Pan. (nô′m-brĕ)	133	9°34′N	79°28′W
Nome, Ak., U.S. (nōm)	106a	64°30′N	165°20′W
Nonacho, l., Can.	92	61°48′N	111°20′W
Nong′an, China (nôŋ-än)	208	44°25′N	125°10′E
Nongoma, S. Afr. (nōn-gō′mȧ)	232	27°48′S	31°45′E
Nooksack, Wa., U.S. (no̤k′săk)	116d	48°55′N	122°19′W
Nooksack, r., Wa., U.S.	116d	48°54′N	122°31′W
Noordwijk aan Zee, Neth.	159a	52°14′N	4°25′E
Noordzee Kanaal, can., Neth.	159a	52°27′N	4°42′E
Nootka, i., Can. (nōōt′kȧ)	92	49°32′N	126°42′W
Nootka Sound, strt., Can.	94	49°33′N	126°38′W
Nóqui, Ang. (nô-kē′)	232	5°51′S	13°25′E
Nor, r., China (nou′)	210	46°55′N	132°45′E
Nora, Swe.	166	59°32′N	14°56′E
Nora, In., U.S. (nō′rä)	111g	39°54′N	86°08′W
Noranda, Can.	99	48°15′N	79°01′W
Norbeck, Md., U.S. (nōr′bĕk)	110e	39°06′N	77°05′W
Norborne, Mo., U.S. (nôr′bôrn)	121	39°17′N	93°39′W
Norco, Ca., U.S. (nôr′kō)	117a	33°57′N	117°33′W
Norcross, Ga., U.S. (nôr′krôs)	110c	33°56′N	84°13′W
Nord, Riviere du, Can. (rēv-yĕr′ dü nōr)	102a	45°45′N	74°02′W
Nordegg, Can. (nûr′dĕg)	95	52°28′N	116°04′W
Norden, Ger. (nôr′dĕn)	168	53°35′N	7°14′E
Norderney, i., Ger. (nōr′dĕr-nĕy)	168	53°45′N	6°58′E
Nordfjord, b., Nor. (nō′fyōr)	166	61°50′N	5°35′E
Nordhausen, Ger. (nôrt′hau-zĕn)	161	51°30′N	10°48′E
Nordhorn, Ger. (nôrt′hôrn)	168	52°26′N	7°05′E
Nord Kapp, c., Nor.	180	71°11′N	25°48′E
Nordland, Wa., U.S. (nôrd′lȧnd)	116a	48°03′N	122°41′W
Nördlingen, Ger. (nûrt′lĭng-ĕn)	168	48°51′N	10°30′E
Nord-Ostsee Kanal (Kiel Canal), can., Ger. (nōrd-ōzt-zā) (kēl)	168	54°03′N	9°23′E
Nordrhein-Westfalen (North Rhine-Westphalia), state, Ger. (nōrd′hīn-vĕst-fä-lĕn)	171c	51°40′N	7°00′E
Nordvik, Russia (nôrd′vēk)	179	73°57′N	111°15′E
Nore, r., Ire. (nōr)	164	52°34′N	7°15′W
Norfolk, Ma., U.S. (nôr′fŏk)	101a	42°07′N	71°19′W
Norfolk, Ne., U.S.	104	42°10′N	97°25′W
Norfolk, Va., U.S.	105	36°55′N	76°15′W
Norfolk, i., Oc.	241	27°10′S	166°50′E
Norfork, Lake, l., Ar., U.S.	121	36°25′N	92°09′W
Noril′sk, Russia (nô rēlsk′)	178	69°00′N	87°11′E
Normal, Il., U.S. (nôr′mȧl)	108	40°35′N	89°00′W
Norman, r., Austl.	221	18°27′S	141°29′E
Norman, Lake, res., N.C., U.S.	107	35°30′N	80°53′W

ăt; finȧl; rāte; senåte; ärm; ȧsk; sofȧ; fâre; ch-choose; dh-as th in other; bē; ēvent; bĕt; recĕnt; cratẽr; g-gō; gh-guttural g; bĭt; ĭ-short neutral; rīde; к-guttural k as ch in German ich;

PRONOUNCING INDEX

Normandie – Nowa Sól 329

PLACE (Pronunciation)	PAGE	LAT.	LONG.
Normandie, hist. reg., Fr. (nôr-mäN-dē´)	170	49°02'N	0°17'E
Normandie, Collines de, hills, Fr. (kô-lēn´dĕ-nôr-män-dē´)	170	48°46'N	0°50'W
Normandy *see* Normandie, hist. reg., Fr.	170	49°02'N	0°17'E
Normanton, Austl. (nôr´măn-tŭn)	219	17°45'S	141°10'E
Normanton, Eng., U.K.	158a	53°40'N	1°21'W
Norman Wells, Can.	90	65°26'N	127°00'W
Nornalup, Austl. (nôr-năl´ŭp)	218	35°00'S	117°00'E
Nørresundby, Den. (nû-rĕ-sòn´bü)	166	57°04'N	9°55'E
Norris, Tn., U.S. (nŏr´ĭs)	124	36°09'N	84°05'W
Norris Lake, res., Tn., U.S.	107	36°17'N	84°10'W
Norristown, Pa., U.S. (nŏr´ĭs-town)	110f	40°07'N	75°21'W
Norrköping, Swe. (nôr´chûp´ĭng)	154	58°37'N	16°10'E
Norrtälje, Swe. (nôr-tĕl´yĕ)	160	59°47'N	18°39'E
Norseman, Austl. (nôrs´măn)	218	32°15'S	122°00'E
Norte, Punta, c., Arg. (pōō´n-tä-nŏr´tĕ)	141c	36°17'S	56°48'W
Norte, Serra do, mts., Braz. (sĕ´r-rä-dô-nôr´te)	143	12°04'S	59°08'W
North, Cape, c., Can.	101	47°02'N	60°25'W
North Adams, Ma., U.S. (ăd´ămz)	109	42°40'N	73°05'W
Northam, Austl. (nôr-dhăm)	218	31°50'S	116°45'E
Northam, S. Afr. (nôr´thăm)	238c	24°52'S	27°16'E
North America, cont.	89	45°00'N	100°00'W
North American Basin, deep (ȧ-mĕr´ĭ-kȧn)	4	23°45'N	62°45'W
Northampton, Austl. (nôr-thămp´tŭn)	218	28°22'S	114°45'E
Northampton, Eng., U.K. (nôrth-ămp´tŭn)	161	52°14'N	0°56'W
Northampton, Ma., U.S.	109	42°20'N	72°45'W
Northampton, Pa., U.S.	109	40°45'N	75°30'W
Northamptonshire, co., Eng., U.K.	158a	52°25'N	0°47'W
North Andaman Island, i., India (ăn-dȧ-măn´)	212	13°15'N	93°30'E
North Andover, Ma., U.S. (ăn´dô-vẽr)	101a	42°42'N	71°07'W
North Arm, mth., Can. (ärm)	116d	49°13'N	123°01'W
North Atlanta, Ga., U.S. (ăt-lăn´tȧ)	110c	33°52'N	84°20'W
North Attleboro, Ma., U.S. (ăt´'l-bŭr-ô)	110b	41°59'N	71°18'W
North Baltimore, Oh., U.S. (bôl´tĭ-môr)	108	41°10'N	83°40'W
North Basque, Tx., U.S. (băsk)	122	31°56'N	98°01'W
North Battleford, Can. (băt´'l-fẽrd)	90	52°47'N	108°17'W
North Bay, Can.	91	46°13'N	79°26'W
North Bend, Or., U.S. (bĕnd)	114	43°23'N	124°13'W
North Berwick, Me., U.S. (bûr´wĭk)	100	43°18'N	70°46'W
North Bight, b., Bah. (bīt)	134	24°30'N	77°40'W
North Bimini, i., Bah. (bĭ´mĭ-nē)	134	25°45'N	79°20'W
North Borneo *see* Sabah, hist. reg., Malay.	212	5°10'N	116°25'E
Northborough, Ma., U.S.	101a	42°19'N	71°39'W
Northbridge, Ma., U.S. (nôrth´brĭj)	101a	42°09'N	71°39'W
North Caicos, i., T./C. Is. (kī´kôs)	135	21°55'N	72°00'W
North Cape, c., N.Z.	221a	34°31'S	173°02'E
North Carolina, state, U.S. (kăr-ô-lī´nȧ)	105	35°40'N	81°30'W
North Cascades National Park, rec., Wa., U.S.	114	48°50'N	120°50'W
North Cat Cay, i., Bah.	134	25°35'N	79°20'W
North Channel, strt., Can.	98	46°10'N	83°20'W
North Channel, strt., U.K.	156	55°15'N	7°56'W
North Charleston, S.C., U.S. (chärlz´tŭn)	125	32°49'N	79°57'W
North Chicago, Il., U.S. (shĭ-kô´gō)	111a	42°19'N	87°51'W
North College Hill, Oh., U.S. (kŏl´ĕj hĭl)	111f	39°13'N	84°33'W
North Concho, Tx., U.S. (kŏn´chō)	122	31°40'N	100°48'W
North Cooking Lake, Can. (kòk´ĭng lăk)	102g	53°28'N	112°57'W
North Dakota, state, U.S. (dȧ-kō´tȧ)	104	47°20'N	101°55'W
North Downs, Eng., U.K. (dounz)	164	51°11'N	0°01'W
North Dum-Dum, India	202a	22°38'N	88°23'E
Northeast Cape, c., Ak., U.S. (nôrth-ēst)	103	63°15'N	169°04'W
Northeast Point, c., Bah.	135	21°25'N	73°00'W
Northeast Point, c., Bah.	135	22°45'N	73°50'W
Northeast Providence Channel, strt., Bah. (prŏv´ĭ-dĕns)	134	25°45'N	77°00'W
Northeim, Ger. (nôrt´hīm)	168	51°42'N	9°59'E
North Elbow Cays, is., Bah.	134	23°55'N	80°30'W
Northern Cheyenne Indian Reservation, I.R., Mt., U.S.	115	45°32'N	106°43'W
Northern Dvina *see* Severnaya Dvina, r., Russia	178	63°00'N	42°40'E
Northern Ireland, state, U.K. (īr´lănd)	154	54°48'N	7°00'W
Northern Land *see* Severnaya Zemlya, is., Russia	179	79°33'N	101°15'E
Northern Mariana Islands, dep., Oc. (mä-rē-ä´nȧ)	3	17°20'N	145°00'E
Northern Territory, ter., Austl.	218	18°15'S	133°00'E
Northern Yukon National Park, rec., Can.	103	69°00'N	140°00'W
Northfield, Mn., U.S. (nôrth´fēld)	113	44°28'N	93°11'W
North Flinders Ranges, mts., Austl. (flĭn´dẽrz)	222	31°55'S	138°45'E
North Foreland, Eng., U.K. (nôrth-fōr´lȧnd)	165	51°20'N	1°30'E
North Franklin Mountain, mtn., Tx., U.S. (frăŋ´klĭn)	122	31°55'N	106°30'W
North Frisian Islands, is., Eur.	160	55°16'N	8°15'E
North Gamboa, Pan. (gäm-bô´ä)	133	9°07'N	79°40'W
North Gower, Can. (gōw´ẽr)	102c	45°08'N	75°43'W
North Hollywood, Ca., U.S. (hŏl´ē-wòd)	117a	34°10'N	118°23'W
North Island, i., N.Z.	221a	37°20'S	173°30'E
North Island, i., Ca., U.S.	118a	32°39'N	117°14'W
North Judson, In., U.S. (jŭd´sŭn)	108	41°15'N	86°50'W
North Kansas City, Mo., U.S. (kăn´zȧs)	117f	39°08'N	94°34'W
North Kingstown, R.I., U.S.	110b	41°34'N	71°26'W
North Lincolnshire, co., Eng., U.K.	158a	53°40'N	0°35'W
North Little Rock, Ar., U.S. (lĭt´'l rŏk)	121	34°46'N	92°13'W
North Loup, r., Ne., U.S. (lōōp)	112	42°05'N	100°10'W
North Magnetic Pole, pt. of i.	244	77°19'N	101°49'W
North Manchester, In., U.S. (măn´chĕs-tẽr)	108	41°00'N	85°45'W
Northmoor, Mo., U.S. (nôth´mōōr)	117f	39°10'N	94°37'W
North Moose Lake, l., Can.	97	54°09'N	100°20'W
North Mount Lofty Ranges, mts., Austl.	222	33°50'S	138°30'E
North Ogden, Ut., U.S. (og dĕn)	117b	41°18'N	111°58'W
North Ogden Peak, mtn., Ut., U.S.	117b	41°23'N	111°59'W
North Olmsted, Oh., U.S. (ōlm-stĕd)	111d	41°25'N	81°55'W
North Ossetia, prov., Russia	180	43°00'N	44°15'E
North Pease, r., Tx., U.S. (pēz)	120	34°19'N	100°58'W
North Pender, i., Can. (pĕn´dẽr)	116d	48°48'N	123°16'W
North Plains, Or., U.S. (plānz)	116c	45°36'N	123°00'W
North Platte, Ne., U.S. (plăt)	104	41°08'N	100°45'W
North Platte, r., U.S.	106	41°20'N	102°40'W
North Point, c., Barb.	133b	13°22'N	59°36'W
North Point, c., Mi., U.S.	108	45°00'N	83°20'W
North Pole, pt. of i.	244	90°00'N	0°00'
Northport, Al., U.S. (nôrth´pōrt)	124	33°12'N	87°35'W
Northport, N.Y., U.S.	110a	40°53'N	73°20'W
Northport, Wa., U.S.	114	48°53'N	117°47'W
North Reading, Ma., U.S. (rĕd´ĭng)	101a	42°34'N	71°04'W
North Richland Hills, Tx., U.S.	117c	32°50'N	97°13'W
Northridge, Ca., U.S. (nôrth´ridj)	117a	34°14'N	118°32'W
North Ridgeville, Oh., U.S. (rĭj-vĭl)	111d	41°23'N	82°01'W
North Ronaldsay, i., Scot., U.K.	164a	59°21'N	2°23'W
North Royalton, Oh., U.S. (roi´ăl-tŭn)	111d	41°19'N	81°44'W
North Saint Paul, Mn., U.S. (sånt pôl´)	113	45°01'N	92°59'W
North Santiam, r., Or., U.S. (săn´tyăm)	114	44°42'N	122°50'W
North Saskatchewan, r., Can. (săn-kăch´ē-wän)	92	54°00'N	111°30'W
North Sea, Eur.	154	56°09'N	3°16'E
North Skunk, r., Ia., U.S. (skŭnk)	113	41°39'N	92°46'W
North Stradbroke Island, i., Austl. (străd´brōk)	221	27°45'S	154°18'E
North Sydney, Can. (sĭd´nē)	101	46°13'N	60°15'W
North Taranaki Bight, N.Z. (tá-rá-nä´kĭ bīt)	221a	38°40'S	174°00'E
North Tarrytown, N.Y., U.S. (tăr´ĭ-toun)	110a	41°05'N	73°52'W
North Thompson, r., Can.	95	50°50'N	120°10'W
North Tonawanda, N.Y., U.S. (tŏn-ȧ-wŏn´dȧ)	111c	43°02'N	78°53'W
North Truchas Peaks, mtn., N.M., U.S. (trōō´chäs)	106	35°58'N	105°40'W
North Twillingate, i., Can. (twĭl´ĭn-gāt)	100	35°58'N	105°37'W
North Uist, i., Scot., U.K. (ū´ĭst)	164	57°37'N	7°22'W
Northumberland, N.H., U.S.	109	44°30'N	71°30'W
Northumberland Islands, is., Austl.	221	21°42'S	151°30'E
Northumberland Strait, strt., Can. (nôr thŭm´bẽr-lȧnd)	100	46°25'N	64°20'W
North Umpqua, r., Or., U.S. (ŭmp´kwȧ)	114	43°20'N	122°50'W
North Vancouver, Can. (văn-kōō´vẽr)	90	49°19'N	123°04'W
North Vernon, In., U.S. (vûr´nŭn)	108	39°05'N	85°45'W
Northville, Mi., U.S. (nôrth-vĭl)	111b	42°26'N	83°28'W
North Wales, Pa., U.S. (wālz)	110f	40°12'N	75°16'W
North West Cape, c., Austl. (nôrth´wĕst)	220	21°50'S	112°25'E
Northwest Cape Fear, r., N.C., U.S. (căp fēr)	125	34°34'N	79°46'W
North West Gander, r., Can. (găn´dẽr)	101	48°40'N	55°15'W
Northwest Providence Channel, strt., Bah. (prŏv´ĭ-dĕns)	134	26°15'N	78°45'W
Northwest Territories, ter., Can. (tĕr´ĭ-tō´rĭs)	90	65°00'N	120°00'W
Northwich, Eng., U.K. (nôrth´wĭch)	158a	53°15'N	2°31'W
North Wilkesboro, N.C., U.S. (wĭlks´bûrô)	125	36°08'N	81°10'W
Northwood, Ia., U.S. (nôrth´wòd)	113	43°26'N	93°13'W
Northwood, N.D., U.S.	112	47°44'N	97°36'W
North Yamhill, r., Or., U.S. (yăm´ hĭl)	116c	45°22'N	123°21'W
North York, Can.	99	43°47'N	79°25'W
North York Moors, for., Eng., U.K. (yôrk mòrz´)	164	54°20'N	0°40'W
North Yorkshire, co., Eng., U.K.	158a	53°50'N	1°10'W
Norton, Ks., U.S. (nôr´tŭn)	120	39°40'N	99°54'W
Norton, Ma., U.S.	110b	41°58'N	71°08'W
Norton, Va., U.S.	125	36°54'N	82°36'W
Norton Bay, b., Ak., U.S.	103	64°22'N	162°18'W
Norton Reservoir, res., Ma., U.S.	110b	42°01'N	71°07'W
Norton Sound, strt., Ak., U.S.	103	63°48'N	164°50'W
Norval, Can. (nôr´vǎl)	102d	43°39'N	79°52'W
Norwalk, Ca., U.S. (nôr´wôk)	117a	33°54'N	118°05'W
Norwalk, Ct., U.S.	110a	41°06'N	73°25'W
Norwalk, Oh., U.S.	108	41°15'N	82°35'W
Norway, Me., U.S.	100	44°11'N	70°35'W
Norway, Mi., U.S.	113	45°47'N	87°55'W
Norway, nation, Eur. (nôr´wā)	154	63°48'N	11°17'E
Norway House, Can.	90	53°59'N	97°50'W
Norwegian Sea, sea, Eur. (nôr-wē´jăn)	160	66°54'N	1°43'E
Norwell, Ma., U.S. (nôr´wĕl)	101a	42°10'N	70°47'W
Norwich, Eng., U.K.	161	52°40'N	1°15'E
Norwich, Ct., U.S. (nôr´wĭch)	109	41°20'N	72°00'W
Norwich, N.Y., U.S.	109	42°35'N	75°30'W
Norwood, Ma., U.S. (nôr´wòod)	101a	42°11'N	71°13'W
Norwood, N.C., U.S.	125	35°15'N	80°08'W
Norwood, Oh., U.S.	111f	39°10'N	84°27'W
Nose Creek, r., Can. (nōz)	102e	51°09'N	114°02'W
Noshiro, Japan (nō´shē-rō)	210	40°09'N	140°02'E
Nosivka, Ukr. (nô´sôf-kȧ)	177	50°54'N	31°35'E
Nossob, r., Afr. (nô´sŏb)	232	24°15'S	19°10'E
Noteć, r., Pol. (nô´tĕcn)	168	52°50'N	16°19'E
Notodden, Nor. (nōt´ôd'n)	166	59°35'N	9°15'E
Notre Dame, Monts, mts., Can.	100	46°35'N	70°35'W
Notre Dame Bay, b., Can. (nō´t'r dȧm´)	93a	49°45'N	55°15'W
Notre-Dame-du-Lac, Can.	100	47°37'N	68°51'W
Nottawasaga Bay, b., Can. (nŏt´ȧ-wȧ-sā´gȧ)	99	44°45'N	80°35'W
Nottaway, r., Can. (nôt´ȧ-wā)	93	50°58'N	78°02'W
Nottingham, Eng., U.K. (nŏt´ĭng-ăm)	161	52°58'N	1°09'W
Nottingham Island, i., Can.	93	62°58'N	78°53'W
Nottinghamshire, co., Eng., U.K.	158a	53°03'N	1°05'W
Nottoway, r., Va., U.S. (nôt´ȧ-wā)	125	36°53'N	77°47'W
Notukeu Creek, r., Can.	96	49°55'N	106°30'W
Nouadhibou, Maur.	230	21°02'N	17°09'W
Nouakchott, Maur.	230	18°06'N	15°57'W
Nouamrhar, Maur.	230	19°22'N	16°31'W
Nouméa, N. Cal. (nōō-mā´ä)	219	22°16'S	166°27'E
Nouvelle, Can. (nōō-vĕl´)	100	48°09'N	66°22'W
Nouvelle-France, Cap de, c., Can.	93	62°03'N	74°00'W
Nouzonville, Fr. (nōō-zôn-vēl´)	170	49°51'N	4°43'E
Nova Cruz, Braz. (nō´vȧ-krōō´z)	143	6°22'S	35°20'W
Nova Friburgo, Braz. (frē-bōōr´gò)	143	22°18'S	42°31'W
Nova Iguaçu, Braz. (nō´vä-ē-gwä-sōō´)	143	22°45'S	43°27'W
Nova Lima, Braz. (lē´mä)	141a	19°59'S	43°51'W
Nova Lisboa *see* Huambo, Ang.	232	12°44'S	15°47'E
Nova Mambone, Moz. (nō´vȧ-mäm-bō´nĕ)	232	21°04'S	35°13'E
Nova Odesa, Ukr.	177	47°18'N	31°48'E
Nova Praha, Ukr.	177	48°34'N	32°54'E
Novara, Italy (nô-vä´rä)	162	45°24'N	8°38'E
Nova Resende, Braz.	141a	21°12'S	46°25'W
Nova Scotia, prov., Can. (skō´shȧ)	91	44°28'N	65°00'W
Nova Vodolaha, Ukr.	177	49°43'N	35°51'E
Novaya Ladoga, Russia (nô´vȧ-ya lȧ-dô-gȧ)	167	60°06'N	32°16'E
Novaya Lyalya, Russia (lyá´lyȧ)	186a	59°03'N	60°36'E
Novaya Sibir, i., Russia (sē-bēr´)	179	75°00'N	149°00'E
Novaya Zemlya, i., Russia (zĕm-lyá´)	178	72°00'N	54°46'E
Nova Zagora, Blg. (zä´gô-rȧ)	175	42°30'N	26°01'E
Novelda, Spain (nō-vĕl´dȧ)	173	38°22'N	0°46'W
Nové Mesto nad Váhom, Slvk. (nô´vĕ myĕs´tô)	169	48°44'N	17°47'E
Nové Zámky, Slvk. (zäm´kĕ)	161	47°58'N	18°10'E
Novgorod, Russia (nôv´gô-rŏt)	180	58°32'N	31°16'E
Novgorod, prov., Russia	176	58°27'N	31°55'E
Novhorod-Sivers'kyi, Ukr.	181	52°01'N	33°14'E
Novi, Mi., U.S. (nō´vĭ)	111b	42°29'N	83°28'W
Novigrad, Cro. (nō´vĭ grȧd)	174	44°09'N	15°34'E
Novi Ligure, Italy (nô´vĕ)	174	44°43'N	8°48'E
Novinger, Mo., U.S. (nŏv´ĭn-jẽr)	121	40°14'N	92°43'W
Novi Pazar, Blg. (pä-zär´)	175	43°22'N	27°26'E
Novi Pazar, Serb. (pá-zär´)	163	43°08'N	20°30'E
Novi Sad, Serb. (säd´)	154	45°15'N	19°53'E
Novoaidar, Ukr.	177	48°57'N	39°01'E
Novoasbest, Russia (nô-vô-äs-bĕst´)	186a	57°43'N	60°14'E
Novocherkassk, Russia (nô´vô-chĕr-kåsk´)	181	47°25'N	40°04'E
Novokuznetsk, Russia (nō´vô-kô´z-nyĕ´tsk) (stá´lênsk)	178	53°43'N	86°59'E
Novo-Ladozhskiy Kanal, can., Russia (nô-vô-lä´dôzh-skĭ kȧ-näl´)	167	59°54'N	31°19'E
Novo Mesto, Slvn. (nôvô mās´tô)	174	45°48'N	15°13'E
Novomoskovsk, Russia (nô´vô-môs-kôfsk´)	178	54°06'N	38°08'E
Novomoskovs'k, Ukr.	181	48°37'N	35°12'E
Novomyrhorod, Ukr.	177	48°46'N	31°44'E
Novonikol'skiy, Russia (nô´vô-nyĭ-kôl´skĭ)	186a	52°28'N	57°12'E
Novorossiysk, Russia (nô´vô-rô-sēsk´)	178	44°43'N	37°48'E
Novorzhev, Russia (nô´vô-rzhêv´)	176	57°01'N	29°17'E
Novo-Selo, Blg. (nô´vô-sĕ´lô)	175	44°09'N	22°46'E
Novosibirsk, Russia (nô´vô-sē-bērsk´)	178	55°09'N	82°58'E
Novosibirskiye Ostrova (New Siberian Islands), is., Russia	179	74°00'N	140°30'E
Novosil', Russia (nô´vô-sĭl)	176	52°58'N	37°03'E
Novosokol'niki, Russia (nô´vô-sô-kôl´nĕ-kē)	176	56°18'N	30°07'E
Novotatishchevskiy, Russia (nô´vô-tá-tyĭsh´chĕv-skĭ)	186a	53°22'N	60°24'E
Novoukraïnka, Ukr.	181	48°18'N	31°33'E
Novouzensk, Russia (nô-vô-ò-zĕnsk´)	181	50°40'N	48°08'E
Novozybkov, Russia (nô´vô-zĕp´kôf)	181	52°31'N	31°54'E
Novyi Buh, Ukr.	177	47°43'N	32°33'E
Nový Jičín, Czech Rep. (nô´vē yē´chĕn)	169	49°36'N	18°02'E
Novyy Oskol, Russia (ôs-kôl´)	177	50°46'N	37°53'E
Novyy Port, Russia (nô´vē)	178	67°19'N	72°28'E
Nowa Sól, Pol. (nô´vá sül´)	168	51°49'N	15°41'E

ng-sing; ŋ-baŋk; N-nasalized n; nŏd; cŏmmit; ōld; ôbey; ôrder; oi-boil; fōōd; ò-as oo in foot; ou-out; s-soft; sh-dish; th-thin; pūre; ûnite; ûrn; stŭd; circŭs; ü-as in French tu; ´-indeterminate vowel.

PLACE (Pronunciation)	PAGE	LAT.	LONG.
Nowata, Ok., U.S. (nô-wä´tȧ)	121	36°42'N	95°38'W
Nowood Creek, r., Wy., U.S.	115	44°02'N	107°37'W
Nowra, Austl. (nou´rȧ)	222	34°55'S	150°45'E
Nowy Dwór Mazowiecki, Pol. (nō´vĭ dvōōr mä-zo-vyĕts´ke)	169	52°26'N	20°46'E
Nowy Sącz, Pol. (nō´vē sônch´)	169	49°36'N	20°42'E
Nowy Targ, Pol. (tärk´)	169	49°29'N	20°02'E
Noxon Reservoir, res., Mt., U.S.	114	47°50'N	115°40'W
Noxubee, r., Ms., U.S. (nŏks´ů-bē)	124	33°20'N	88°55'W
Noyes Island, i., Ak., U.S. (noiz)	94	55°30'N	133°40'W
Nozaki, Japan (nō´zä-kė)	211b	34°43'N	135°39'E
Nqamakwe, S. Afr. ('n-gä-mä´kwå)	233c	32°13'S	27°57'E
Nqutu, S. Afr. ('n kōō´tōō)	233c	28°17'S	30°41'E
Nsawam, Ghana	234	5°50'N	0°20'W
Ntshoni, mtn., S. Afr.	233c	29°34'S	30°03'E
Ntwetwe Pan, pl., Bots.	232	20°00'S	24°18'E
[illegible]	[illegible]	[illegible]	[illegible]
Nubian Desert, des., Sudan (nōō´bĭ-ăn)	231	21°13'N	33°09'E
Nudo Coropuna, mtn., Peru (nōō´dô kō-rō-pōō´nä)	142	15°53'S	72°04'W
Nudo de Pasco, mtn., Peru (dĕ pȧs´kô)	142	10°34'S	76°12'W
Nueces, r., Tx., U.S. (nů-ā´sȧs)	106	28°20'N	98°08'W
Nueltin, l., Can. (nwĕl´tin)	92	60°14'N	101°00'W
Nueva Armenia, Hond. (nwā´vä är-mā´nė-ȧ)	132	15°47'N	86°32'W
Nueva Esparta, dept., Ven. (nwĕ´vä ĕs-pä´r-tä)	143b	10°50'N	64°35'W
Nueva Gerona, Cuba (kĕ-rô´nä)	134	21°55'N	82°45'W
Nueva Palmira, Ur. (päl-mē´rä)	141c	33°53'S	58°23'W
Nueva Rosita, Mex. (nôĕ´vä rô-sė´tä)	104	27°55'N	101°10'W
Nueva San Salvador, El Sal.	132	13°41'N	89°16'W
Nueve, Canal Numero, can., Arg.	141c	36°22'S	58°19'W
Nueve de Julio, Arg. (nwā´vå dā hōō´lyô)	144	35°26'S	60°51'W
Nuevitas, Cuba (nwā-vē´täs)	129	21°35'N	77°15'W
Nuevitas, Bahía de, b., Cuba (bä-ē´ä dĕ nwā-vē´täs)	134	21°30'N	77°05'W
Nuevo, Ca., U.S. (nwā´vō)	117a	33°48'N	117°09'W
Nuevo Laredo, Mex. (lä-rā´dhō)	128	27°29'N	99°30'W
Nuevo Leon, state, Mex. (lå-ōn´)	128	26°00'N	100°00'W
Nuevo San Juan, Pan. (nwĕ´vô sän kōō-ä´n)	128a	9°14'N	79°43'W
Nugumanovo, Russia (nû-gû-mä´nô-vô)	186a	55°28'N	61°50'E
Nulato, Ak., U.S. (nōō-lä´tō)	103	64°40'N	158°18'W
Nullagine, Austl. (nŭ-lă´jēn)	218	22°00'S	120°07'E
Nullarbor Plain, pl., Austl. (nŭ-lär´bôr)	220	31°45'S	126°30'E
Numabin Bay, b., Can. (nōō-mä´bĭn)	96	56°30'N	103°08'W
Numansdorp, Neth.	159a	51°43'N	4°25'E
Numazu, Japan (nōō´mä-zōō)	210	35°06'N	138°55'E
Numfoor, Pulau, i., Indon.	213	1°20'S	134°48'E
Nun, r., Nig.	235	5°05'N	6°10'E
Nunavut, ter., Can.	90	70°00'N	95°00'W
Nunawading, Austl.	217a	37°49'S	145°10'E
Nuneaton, Eng., U.K. (nūn´ē-tŭn)	164	52°31'N	1°28'W
Nunivak, i., Ak., U.S. (nōō´nĭ-văk)	106a	60°25'N	167°42'W
Nunyama, Russia (nûn-yä´mȧ)	103	65°49'N	170°32'W
Nuoro, Italy (nwô´rō)	174	40°29'N	9°20'E
Nura, r., Kaz.	184	49°48'N	73°54'E
Nurata, Uzb. (nōōr´ät´ä)	183	40°33'N	65°28'E
Nuremberg *see* Nürnberg, Ger.	154	49°28'N	11°07'E
Nürnberg, Ger. (nürn´bĕrgh)	154	49°28'N	11°07'E
Nurse Cay, i., Bah.	135	22°30'N	75°50'W
Nusabyin, Tur. (nōō´sĭ-bėn)	181	37°05'N	41°10'E
Nushagak, r., Ak., U.S. (nū-shă-găk´)	103	59°28'N	157°40'W
Nushan Hu, l., China	206	32°50'N	117°59'E
Nushki, Pak. (nŭsh´kė)	199	29°30'N	66°02'E
Nuthe, r., Ger. (nōō´tė)	159b	52°15'N	13°11'E
Nutley, N.J., U.S. (nŭt´lė)	110a	40°49'N	74°09'W
Nutter Fort, W.V., U.S. (nŭt´ēr fôrt)	108	39°15'N	80°15'W
Nutwood, Il., U.S. (nŭt´wŏŏd)	117e	39°05'N	90°34'W
Nuwaybi 'al Muzayyinah, Egypt	197a	28°59'N	34°40'E
Nuweland, S. Afr.	232a	33°58'S	18°28'E
Nyack, N.Y., U.S. (nī´ăk)	110a	41°05'N	73°55'W
Nyainqêntanglha Shan, mts., China (nyä-ĭn-chyŭn-täŋ-lä shän)	204	29°55'N	88°08'E
Nyakanazi, Tan.	237	3°00'S	31°15'E
Nyala, Sudan	231	12°00'N	24°52'E
Nyanga, r., Gabon	236	2°45'S	10°30'E
Nyanza, Rw.	237	2°21'S	29°45'E
Nyasa, Lake, l., Afr. (nyä´sä)	232	10°45'S	34°30'E
Nyasvizh, Bela. (nyĕs´vēsh)	176	53°13'N	26°44'E
Nyazepetrovsk, Russia (nyä´zĕ-pĕ-trôvsk´)	186a	56°04'N	59°38'E
Nyborg, Den. (nü´bôr´')	166	55°20'N	10°45'E
Nybro, Swe. (nü´brō)	166	56°44'N	15°56'E
Nyeri, Kenya	237	0°25'S	36°57'E
Nyika Plateau, plat., Mwi.	237	10°30'S	35°50'E
Nyíregyháza, Hung. (nyē´rĕd-y'hä´zä)	163	47°58'N	21°45'E
Nykøbing, Den. (nü´kû-bĭng)	160	56°46'N	8°47'E
Nykøbing, Den.	166	54°45'N	11°54'E
Nykøbing Sjaelland, Den.	166	55°55'N	11°37'E
Nyköping, Swe. (nü´chû-pĭng)	160	58°46'N	16°58'E
Nylstroom, S. Afr. (nĭl´strōm)	232	24°42'S	28°25'E
Nymagee, Austl. (nī-mȧ-gē´)	219	32°17'S	146°18'E
Nymburk, Czech Rep. (nĕm´bôrk)	161	50°12'N	15°03'E
Nynäshamn, Swe. (nü-nĕs-häm'n)	166	58°53'N	17°55'E
Nyngan, Austl. (nĭŋ´găn)	219	31°31'S	147°25'E
Nyong, r., Cam. (nyông)	230	4°00'N	12°00'E
Nyou, Burkina	234	12°46'N	1°56'W
Nýřany, Czech Rep. (nēr-zhä´nė)	168	49°43'N	13°13'E
Nysa, Pol. (nē´sȧ)	169	50°29'N	17°20'E
Nytva, Russia	180	58°00'N	55°10'E
Nyungwe, Mwi.	237	10°16'S	34°07'E
Nyunzu, D.R.C.	237	5°57'S	28°01'E
Nyuya, r., Russia (nyōō´yȧ)	185	60°30'N	111°45'E
Nyzhni Sirohozy, Ukr.	177	46°51'N	34°25'E
Nzega, Tan.	237	4°13'S	33°11'E
N'zeto, Ang.	232	7°14'S	12°52'E
Nzi, r., C. Iv.	234	7°00'N	4°27'W
Nzwani, i., Com. (än-zhwän)	233	12°14'S	44°47'E

O

PLACE (Pronunciation)	PAGE	LAT.	LONG.
Oahe, Lake, res., U.S.	[illegible]	[illegible]	[illegible]
O'ahu, i., Hi., U.S. (ō-ä´hōō) (ō-ā´hü)	106c	21°38'N	157°48'W
Oak Bay, Can.	94	48°27'N	123°18'W
Oak Bluff, Can. (ōk blŭf)	102f	49°47'N	97°21'W
Oak Creek, Co., U.S. (ōk krēk´)	115	40°20'N	106°50'W
Oakdale, Ca., U.S. (ōk´dāl)	118	37°45'N	120°52'W
Oakdale, Ky., U.S.	108	38°15'N	85°50'W
Oakdale, La., U.S.	123	30°49'N	92°40'W
Oakdale, Pa., U.S.	111e	40°24'N	80°11'W
Oakengates, Eng., U.K. (ōk´ĕn-gāts)	158a	52°41'N	2°27'W
Oakes, N.D., U.S. (ōks)	112	46°10'N	98°50'W
Oakfield, Me., U.S. (ōk´fēld)	100	46°08'N	68°10'W
Oakford, Pa., U.S. (ōk´fōrd)	110f	40°08'N	74°58'W
Oak Grove, Or., U.S. (grōv)	116c	45°25'N	122°38'W
Oakham, Eng., U.K. (ōk´ăm)	158a	52°40'N	0°38'W
Oak Harbor, Oh., U.S. (ōk´här´bēr)	108	41°30'N	83°05'W
Oak Harbor, Wa., U.S.	116a	48°18'N	122°39'W
Oakland, Ca., U.S. (ōk´lănd)	104	37°48'N	122°16'W
Oakland, Ne., U.S.	112	41°50'N	96°28'W
Oakland City, In., U.S.	108	38°20'N	87°20'W
Oak Lawn, Il., U.S.	111a	41°43'N	87°45'W
Oakleigh, Austl. (ōk´lȧ)	217a	37°54'S	145°05'E
Oakley, Id., U.S. (ōk´lĭ)	114	42°15'N	135°53'W
Oakley, Ks., U.S.	120	39°08'N	100°49'W
Oakman, Al., U.S. (ōk´măn)	124	33°42'N	87°20'W
Oakmont, Pa., U.S. (ōk´mōnt)	111e	40°31'N	79°50'W
Oak Mountain, mtn., Al., U.S.	110h	33°22'N	86°42'W
Oak Park, Il., U.S. (pärk)	111a	41°53'N	87°48'W
Oak Point, Wa., U.S.	116c	46°11'N	123°11'W
Oak Ridge, Tn., U.S. (rĭj)	124	36°01'N	84°15'W
Oakville, Can. (ōk´vĭl)	99	43°27'N	79°40'W
Oakville, Can.	102f	49°56'N	97°58'W
Oakville, Mo., U.S.	117e	38°27'N	90°18'W
Oakville Creek, r., Can.	102d	43°34'N	79°54'W
Oakwood, Tx., U.S. (ōk´wŏŏd)	123	31°36'N	95°48'W
Oatman, Az., U.S. (ōt´măn)	119	34°00'N	114°25'W
Oaxaca, Mex.	128	17°03'N	96°42'W
Oaxaca, state, Mex. (wä-hä´kä)	128	16°45'N	97°00'W
Oaxaca, Sierra de, mts., Mex. (sē-ĕ´r-rä dĕ)	131	16°15'N	97°25'W
Ob', r., Russia	178	62°15'N	67°00'E
Oba, Can. (ō´bȧ)	91	48°58'N	84°09'W
Obama, Japan (ō´bȧ-mä)	211	35°29'N	135°44'E
Oban, Scot., U.K. (ō´băn)	164	56°25'N	5°35'W
Oban Hills, hills, Nig.	235	5°35'N	8°30'E
O'Bannon, Ky., U.S. (ō-băn´nŏn)	111h	38°17'N	85°30'W
O Barco de Valdeorras, Spain	172	42°26'N	6°58'W
Obatogamau, l., Can. (ō-bȧ-tō´găm-ô)	99	49°38'N	74°10'W
Oberhausen, Ger. (ō´bĕr-hou´zĕn)	171c	51°27'N	6°51'E
Oberlin, Ks., U.S. (ō´bĕr-lĭn)	120	39°49'N	100°30'W
Oberlin, Oh., U.S.	108	41°15'N	82°15'W
Oberroth, Ger. (ō´bĕr-rōt)	159d	48°19'N	11°20'E
Obi, Kepulauan, is., Indon. (ō´bė)	213	1°25'S	128°15'E
Obi, Pulau, i., Indon.	213	1°30'S	127°45'E
Óbidos, Braz. (ō´bė-dōzh)	143	1°57'S	55°32'W
Obihiro, Japan (ō´bė-hē´rō)	210	42°55'N	142°50'E
Obion, r., Tn., U.S.	124	36°10'N	89°25'W
Obion, North Fork, r., Tn., U.S. (ō-bī´ŏn)	124	35°49'N	89°06'W
Obitsu, r., Japan (ō´bēt´sōō)	211a	35°19'N	140°03'E
Obock, Dji. (ō-bŏk´)	238a	11°55'N	43°15'E
Obol', r., Bela. (ō-bōl´)	176	55°24'N	29°24'E
Oboyan', Russia (ō-bô-yän´)	181	51°14'N	36°16'E
Obskaya Guba, b., Russia	178	67°13'N	73°45'E
Obuasi, Ghana	234	6°14'N	1°39'W
Obukhiv, Ukr.	177	50°07'N	30°36'E
Obukhovo, Russia	186b	55°50'N	38°17'E
Obytichna kosa, spit, Ukr.	177	46°32'N	36°07'E
Ocala, Fl., U.S. (ō-kä´lȧ)	125	29°11'N	82°09'W
Ocampo, Mex. (ō-käm´pō)	130	22°49'N	99°23'W
Ocaña, Col. (ō-kän´yä)	142	8°15'N	73°37'W
Ocaña, Spain (ō-kä´n-yä)	172	39°58'N	3°31'W
Occidental, Cordillera, mts., Col.	142a	5°05'N	76°04'W
Occidental, Cordillera, mts., Peru	142	10°12'S	76°58'W
Ocean Beach, Ca., U.S. (ō´shăn bēch)	118a	32°44'N	117°14'W
Ocean Bight, b., Bah.	135	21°15'N	73°15'W
Ocean City, Md., U.S.	109	38°20'N	75°10'W
Ocean City, N.J., U.S.	109	39°15'N	74°35'W
Ocean Falls, Can. (Fôls)	90	52°21'N	127°40'W
Ocean Grove, Austl.	217a	38°16'S	144°32'E
Ocean Grove, N.J., U.S. (grōv)	110a	40°10'N	74°00'W
Oceanside, Ca., U.S. (ō´shăn-sīd)	118	33°11'N	117°22'W
Oceanside, N.Y., U.S.	110a	40°38'N	73°39'W
Ocean Springs, Ms., U.S. (springs)	124	30°25'N	88°49'W
Ochakiv, Ukr.	177	46°38'N	31°33'E
Ochamchira, Geor.	182	42°44'N	41°28'E
Ochlockonee, r., Fl., U.S. (ŏk-lō-kō´nē)	124	30°10'N	84°38'W
Ocilla, Ga., U.S. (ō-sĭl´ȧ)	124	31°36'N	83°15'W
Ockelbo, Swe. (ôk´ĕl-bô)	166	60°54'N	16°35'E
Ocklawaha, Lake, res., Fl., U.S.	125	29°30'N	81°50'W
Ocmulgee, r., Ga., U.S.	124	32°25'N	83°30'W
Ocmulgee National Monument, rec., Ga., U.S. (ôk-mŭl´gē)	124	32°45'N	83°28'W
Ocoa, Bahía de, b., Dom. Rep.	135	18°20'N	70°40'W
Ococingo, Mex. (ô-kô-sė´n-gô)	131	17°03'N	92°18'W
Ocom, Lago, l., Mex. (ô-kô´m)	132a	19°26'N	88°18'W
Oconee, r., Ga., U.S. (ô-kō´nē)	107	32°45'N	83°00'W
Oconee, Lake, res., Ga., U.S.	124	33°30'N	83°15'W
Oconomowoc, Wi., U.S. (ô-kŏn´ô-mô-wŏk´)	113	43°06'N	88°24'W
Oconto, Wi., U.S. (ô-kŏn´tō)	113	44°54'N	87°55'W
Oconto, r., Wi., U.S.	113	45°08'N	88°24'W
Oconto Falls, Wi., U.S.	113	[illegible]	88°11'W
Ocós, Guat. (ô-kōs´)	132	14°31'N	92°12'W
Ocotal, Nic. (ō-kô-täl´)	132	13°36'N	86°31'W
Ocotepeque, Hond. (ô-kō-tå-pā´kå)	132	14°25'N	89°13'W
Ocotlán, Mex. (ō-kô-tlän´)	130	20°19'N	102°44'W
Ocotlán de Morelos, Mex. (dā mô-rā´lōs)	131	16°46'N	96°41'W
Ocozocoautla, Mex. (ô-kō´zô-kwä-ōō´tlä)	131	16°44'N	93°22'W
Ocumare del Tuy, Ven. (ō-kōō-mä´ra del twē´)	142	10°07'N	66°47'W
Oda, Ghana	234	5°55'N	0°59'W
Odawara, Japan (ō´dȧ-wä´rä)	211	35°15'N	139°10'E
Odda, Nor. (ôdh-ä)	166	60°04'N	6°30'E
Odebolt, Ia., U.S. (ō´dė-bōlt)	112	42°20'N	95°14'W
Odemira, Port. (ō-då-mē´rȧ)	172	37°35'N	8°40'W
Ödemiş, Tur. (û´dĕ-mēsh)	163	38°12'N	28°00'E
Odendaalsrus, S. Afr. (ō´dĕn-däls-rûs´)	238c	27°52'S	26°41'E
Odense, Den. (ō´dhĕn-sĕ)	160	55°24'N	10°20'E
Odenton, Md., U.S. (ō´dĕn-tŭn)	110e	39°05'N	76°43'W
Odenwald, for., Ger. (ō´dĕn-väld)	168	49°39'N	8°55'E
Oder, r., Eur. (ō´dēr)	156	52°40'N	14°19'E
Oderhaff, l., Eur.	168	53°47'N	14°02'E
Odesa, Ukr.	178	46°28'N	30°44'E
Odesa, prov., Ukr.	177	46°05'N	29°48'E
Odessa, Tx., U.S. (ô-dĕs´ȧ)	122	31°52'N	102°21'W
Odessa, Wa., U.S.	114	47°20'N	118°42'W
Odiel, r., Spain (ō-dė-ĕl´)	172	37°47'N	6°42'W
Odiham, Eng., U.K. (ŏd´ē-ăm)	158b	51°14'N	0°56'W
Odintsovo, Russia (ô-dēn´tsô-vô)	186b	55°40'N	37°16'E
Odiongan, Phil. (ō-dė-ôŋ´gän)	213a	12°24'N	121°59'E
Odivelas, Port. (ō-dė-vā´lyäs)	173b	38°47'N	9°11'W
Odobeşti, Rom. (ō-dô-bĕsh´t')	169	45°46'N	27°08'E
O'Donnell, Tx., U.S. (ō-dŏn´ĕl)	120	32°59'N	101°51'W
Odorhei, Rom. (ō-dôr-hā´)	169	46°18'N	25°17'E
Odra *see* Oder, r., Eur. (ô´drȧ)	156	52°40'N	14°19'E
Oeiras, Braz. (wå-ė-räzh´)	143	7°05'S	42°01'W
Oeirás, Port. (ô-ĕ´y-rȧ´s)	173b	38°42'N	9°18'W
Oelwein, Ia., U.S. (ōl´wīn)	113	42°40'N	91°56'W
O'Fallon, Il., U.S. (ō-făl´ŭn)	117e	38°36'N	89°55'W
O'Fallon Creek, r., Mt., U.S.	115	46°25'N	104°47'W
Ofanto, r., Italy (ô-fän´tō)	174	41°08'N	15°33'E
Offa, Nig.	235	8°09'N	4°44'E
Offenbach, Ger. (ôf´ĕn-bäk)	168	50°06'N	8°50'E
Offenburg, Ger. (ôf´ĕn-bôrgh)	168	48°28'N	7°57'E
Ofuna, Japan (ō´fōō-nä)	211a	35°21'N	139°32'E
Ogaden Plateau, plat., Eth.	238a	6°45'N	44°53'E
Ogaki, Japan	210	35°21'N	136°36'E
Ogallala, Ne., U.S. (ō-gä-lä´lä)	112	41°08'N	101°44'W
Ogbomosho, Nig. (ŏg-bô-mō´shō)	230	8°08'N	4°15'E
Ogden, Ia., U.S. (ŏg´dĕn)	113	42°10'N	94°20'W
Ogden, Ut., U.S.	104	41°14'N	111°58'W
Ogden, r., Ut., U.S.	117b	41°16'N	111°54'W
Ogden Peak, mtn., Ut., U.S.	117b	41°11'N	111°51'W
Ogdensburg, N.J., U.S. (ŏg´dĕnz-bûrg)	110a	41°05'N	74°36'W
Ogdensburg, N.Y., U.S.	105	44°40'N	75°30'W
Ogeechee, r., Ga., U.S. (ô-gē´chė)	125	32°35'N	81°50'W
Ogies, S. Afr.	238c	26°03'S	29°04'E
Ogilvie Mountains, mts., Can. (ō´g'l-vĭ)	92	64°45'N	138°10'W
Oglesby, Il., U.S. (ō´g'lz-bĭ)	108	41°20'N	89°00'W
Oglio, r., Italy (ôl´yō)	174	45°15'N	10°19'E
Ōgo, Japan (ō´gô)	211b	34°49'N	135°06'E
Ogou, r., Togo	234	8°05'N	1°30'E
Ogudnëvo, Russia (ôg-ôd-nyô´vô)	186b	56°04'N	38°17'E
Ogulin, Cro. (ō-gōō-lēn´)	174	45°17'N	15°11'E
Ogwashi-Uku, Nig.	235	6°10'N	6°31'E
O'Higgins, prov., Chile (ô-kē´gēns)	141b	34°17'S	70°52'W
Ohio, state, U.S. (ô´hī´ō)	105	40°30'N	83°15'W
Ohio, r., U.S.	107	37°25'N	88°05'W
Ohoopee, r., Ga., U.S. (ô-hōō´pe-mc)	125	32°32'N	82°38'W
Ohře, r., Eur. (ôr´zhě)	168	50°08'N	12°45'E
Ohrid, Mac. (ō´krēd)	175	41°08'N	20°46'E
Ohrid, Lake, l., Eur.	175	40°58'N	20°35'E
Ōi, Japan (oi´)	211a	35°51'N	139°31'E
Oi-Gawa, r., Japan (ō´ē-gä´wȧ)	211	35°09'N	138°05'E
Oil City, Pa., U.S. (oil sĭ´tĭ)	109	41°25'N	79°40'W
Oirschot, Neth.	159a	51°30'N	5°20'E
Oise, r., Fr. (wäz)	161	49°30'N	2°56'E
Oisterwijk, Neth.	159a	51°34'N	5°13'E
Oita, Japan (ō´ė-tä)	210	33°14'N	131°38'E
Oji, Japan (ō´jė)	211b	34°36'N	135°43'E
Ojinaga, Mex. (ō-kė-nä´gä)	128	29°34'N	104°26'W
Ojitlán, Mex. (ōkē-tlän´) (sän-lōō´käs)	131	18°04'N	96°23'W

ăt; finȧl; rāte; senåte; ärm; ȧsk; sofȧ; fâre; ch-choose; dh-as th in other; bē; ėvent; bĕt; recĕnt; cratēr; g-gō; gh-guttural g; bĭt; ĭ-short neutral; rīde; κ-guttural k as ch in German ich;

PRONOUNCING INDEX

Ojo Caliente – Orikhiv 331

PLACE (Pronunciation)	PAGE	LAT.	LONG.
Ojo Caliente, Mex. (ōkō käl-yĕn′tā)	130	21°50′N	100°43′W
Ojocaliente, Mex. (ô-kō-kä-lyĕ′n-tĕ)	130	22°39′N	102°15′W
Ojo del Toro, Pico, mtn., Cuba (pē′kô-ô-kō-dĕl-tô′rô)	134	19°55′N	77°25′W
Oka, Can. (ō-kä)	102a	45°28′N	74°05′W
Oka, r., Russia (ô-kä′)	180	55°10′N	42°10′E
Oka, r., Russia (ō-kä′)	184	53°28′N	101°09′E
Oka, r., Russia (ô-kä′)	181	52°10′N	35°20′E
Okahandja, Nmb.	232	21°50′S	16°45′E
Okanagan (Okanogan), r., N.A. (ō′kȧ-näg′ȧn)	95	49°06′N	119°43′W
Okanagan Lake, l., Can.	92	50°00′N	119°28′W
Okano, r., Gabon (ô′kä′nō)	230	0°15′N	11°08′E
Okanogan, Wa., U.S.	114	48°20′N	119°34′W
Okanogan, r., Wa., U.S.	114	48°36′N	119°33′W
Okatibbee, r., Ms., U.S. (ō′kä-tĭb′ē)	124	32°37′N	88°54′W
Okatoma Creek, r., Ms., U.S. (ô-kȧ-tō′mă)	124	31°43′N	80°31′W
Okavango (Cubango), r., Afr.	232	18°00′S	20°00′E
Okavango Swamp, sw., Bots.	232	19°30′S	23°02′E
Okaya, Japan (ō′kä-yä)	211	36°04′N	138°01′E
Okayama, Japan (ō′kȧ-yä′mȧ)	205	34°39′N	133°54′E
Okazaki, Japan (ō′kȧ-zä′kĕ)	210	34°58′N	137°09′E
Okeechobee, Fl., U.S. (ō-kĕ-chō′bē)	125	27°15′N	80°50′W
Okeechobee, Lake, l., Fl., U.S.	107	27°00′N	80°49′W
Okeene, Ok., U.S. (ô-kēn′)	120	36°06′N	98°19′W
Okefenokee Swamp, sw., U.S. (ō′kē-fē-nō′kē)	125	30°54′N	82°20′W
Okemah, Ok., U.S. (ô-kē′mä)	121	35°26′N	96°18′W
Okene, Nig.	235	7°33′N	6°15′E
Okha, Russia (ŭ-kä′)	179	53°44′N	143°12′E
Okhotino, Russia (ô-kô′tĭ-nô)	186b	56°14′N	38°24′E
Okhotsk, Russia (ô-kôtsk′)	179	59°28′N	143°32′E
Okhotsk, Sea of, sea, Asia (ô-kôtsk′)	179	56°45′N	146°00′E
Okhtyrka, Ukr.	181	50°18′N	34°53′E
Okinawa, i., Japan	205	26°30′N	128°00′E
Okino, i., Japan (ō′kē-nō)	211	36°22′N	133°27′E
Ōkino Erabu, i., Japan (ō-kē′nō-â-rä′bōō)	210	27°18′N	129°00′E
Oklahoma, state, U.S. (ō-klȧ-hō′mȧ)	104	36°00′N	98°20′W
Oklahoma City, Ok., U.S.	104	35°27′N	97°32′W
Oklawaha, r., Fl., U.S. (ŏk-lȧ-wô′hô)	125	29°13′N	82°00′W
Okmulgee, Ok., U.S. (ōk-mŭl′gē)	121	35°37′N	95°58′W
Okolona, Ky., U.S. (ō-kō-lō′nȧ)	111h	38°08′N	85°41′W
Okolona, Ms., U.S.	124	33°59′N	88°43′W
Oktemberyan, Arm.	182	40°09′N	44°02′E
Okushiri, i., Japan (ō′kōō-shē′rē)	210	42°12′N	139°30′E
Okuta, Nig.	235	9°14′N	3°15′E
Olalla, Wa., U.S. (ō-lä′lȧ)	116a	47°26′N	122°33′W
Olanchito, Hond. (ō′län-chē′tō)	132	15°28′N	86°35′W
Öland, i., Swe. (û-länd′)	156	57°03′N	17°15′E
Olathe, Ks., U.S. (ō-lā′thē)	117f	38°53′N	94°49′W
Olavarría, Arg. (ō-lä-vär-rē′ä)	144	36°49′N	60°15′W
Oława, Pol. (ō-lä′vȧ)	169	50°57′N	17°18′E
Olazoago, Arg. (ō-läz-kôä′gô)	141c	35°14′S	60°37′W
Olbia, Italy (ô′l-byä)	174	40°55′N	9°28′E
Olching, Ger. (ōl′kĕng)	159d	48°13′N	11°21′E
Old Bahama Channel, strt., N.A. (bȧ-hā′mȧ)	134	22°45′N	78°30′W
Old Bight, Bah.	135	24°15′N	75°20′W
Old Bridge, N.J., U.S. (brĭj)	110a	40°24′N	74°22′W
Old Crow, Can. (crō)	90	67°51′N	139°58′W
Oldenburg, Ger. (ôl′dĕn-bŏorgh)	160	53°09′N	8°13′E
Old Forge, Pa., U.S. (fôrj)	109	41°20′N	75°50′W
Oldham, Eng., U.K. (ōld′ăm)	164	53°32′N	2°07′W
Oldham, co., Eng., U.K.	158a	53°35′N	2°05′W
Old Harbor, Ak., U.S. (här′bẽr)	103	57°18′N	153°20′W
Old Head of Kinsale, c., Ire. (ōld hĕd ŏv kĭn-sāl)	164	51°35′N	8°35′W
Old R, Tx., U.S.	123a	29°54′N	94°52′W
Olds, Can. (ōldz)	90	51°47′N	114°06′W
Old Tate, Bots.	232	21°18′S	27°43′E
Old Town, Me., U.S. (toun)	100	44°55′N	68°42′W
Old Wives Lake, l., Can. (wīvz)	96	50°05′N	106°00′W
Olean, N.Y., U.S. (ō-lē-ăn′)	105	42°05′N	78°25′W
Olecko, Pol. (ō-lĕt′skō)	169	54°02′N	22°29′E
Olekma, r., Russia (ô-lyĕk-mȧ′)	185	55°41′N	120°33′E
Olëkminsk, Russia (ô-lyĕk-mĕnsk′)	179	60°39′N	120°40′E
Oleksandriia, Ukr.	176	48°40′N	33°07′E
Olenëk, r., Russia (ô-lyĕ-nyôk′)	179	68°00′N	113°00′E
Oléron Île, d′, i., Fr. (ēl′ dō lā-rôn′)	161	45°52′N	1°58′W
Oleśnica, Pol. (ô-lĕsh-nĭ′tsä)	161	51°13′N	17°24′E
Olfen, Ger. (ōl′fĕn)	171c	51°43′N	7°22′E
Ol′ga, Russia (ôl′gȧ)	179	43°48′N	135°44′E
Ol′gi, Zaliv, b., Russia (zä′lĭf ôl′gĭ)	210	43°43′N	135°25′E
Olhão, Port. (ôl-youn′)	162	37°02′N	7°54′W
Ol′hopil′, Ukr.	177	48°11′N	29°28′E
Olievenhoutpoort, S. Afr.	233b	25°58′S	27°55′E
Ólimbos, mtn., Cyp.	197a	34°56′N	32°52′E
Olinda, Braz. (ô-lē′n-dä)	143	8°00′S	34°58′W
Olinda, Braz.	144b	22°49′S	43°25′W
Oliva, Spain (ô-lē′vä)	173	38°54′N	0°07′W
Oliva de la Frontera, Spain (ô-lē′vä dā)	172	38°33′N	6°55′W
Olive Hill, Ky., U.S. (ŏl′ĭv)	108	38°15′N	83°10′W
Oliveira, Braz. (ô-lē-vā′rä)	141a	20°42′S	44°49′W
Olivenza, Spain (ō-lē-vĕn′thä)	172	38°42′N	7°06′W
Oliver, Can. (ŏ′lĭ-vẽr)	90	49°11′N	119°33′W
Oliver, Can.	102g	53°38′N	113°21′W
Oliver, Wi., U.S. (ŏ′lĭvẽr)	117h	46°39′N	92°12′W
Oliver Lake, l., Can.	102g	53°19′N	113°00′W
Olivia, Mn., U.S. (ō-lĭv′ē-ȧ)	112	44°46′N	95°00′W
Olivos, Arg. (ōlē′vōs)	144a	34°30′S	58°29′W
Ollagüe, Chile (ô-lyä′gĕ)	142	21°17′S	68°17′W
Ollerton, Eng., U.K. (ŏl′ẽr-tŭn)	158a	53°12′N	1°02′W
Olmos Park, Tx., U.S. (ōl′mŭs pärk′)	117d	29°27′N	98°32′W
Olney, Il., U.S. (ŏl′nĭ)	108	38°45′N	88°05′W
Olney, Or., U.S. (ŏl′nē)	116c	46°06′N	123°45′W
Olney, Tx., U.S.	120	33°24′N	98°43′W
Olomane, r., Can. (ō′lō mä′nĕ)	101	51°05′N	60°50′W
Olomouc, Czech Rep. (ô′lô-mōts)	161	49°37′N	17°15′E
Olonets, Russia (ô-lô′nĕts)	167	60°58′N	32°54′E
Olongapo, Phil.	212	14°49′S	120°17′E
Oloron, Gave d′, r., Fr. (gäv-dŏ-lŏ-rŏn′)	170	43°21′N	0°44′W
Oloron-Sainte Marie, Fr. (ō-lô-rônt′sănt mȧ-rē′)	170	43°11′N	1°37′W
Olot, Spain (ô-lōt′)	162	42°09′N	2°30′E
Olpe, Ger. (ōl′pĕ)	171c	51°02′N	7°51′E
Olsnitz, Ger. (ōlz′nētz)	168	50°25′N	12°11′E
Olsztyn, Pol. (ôl′shtĕn)	160	53°47′N	20°28′E
Olt, r., Rom.	163	44°09′N	24°40′E
Olten, Switz. (ôl′tĕn)	168	47°20′N	7°53′E
Oltenița, Rom. (ôl-tā′nĭ-tsȧ)	175	44°05′N	26°39′E
Olvera, Spain (ôl-vĕ′rä)	172	36°55′N	5°16′W
Olympia, Wa., U.S. (ô-lĭm′pĭ-ȧ)	104	47°02′N	122°52′W
Olympic Mountains, mts., Wa., U.S.	114	47°54′N	123°58′W
Olympic National Park, rec., Wa., U.S. (ô-lĭm′pĭk)	106	47°54′N	123°00′W
Ólympos, mtn., Grc.	162	40°05′N	22°21′E
Olympus, Mount, mtn., Wa., U.S. (ô-lĭm′pŭs)	114	47°43′N	123°30′W
Olyphant, Pa., U.S. (ŏl′ĭ-fănt)	109	41°30′N	75°40′W
Olyutorskiy, Mys, c., Russia (ŭl-yōō′tŏr-skĕ)	179	59°49′N	167°16′E
Omae-Zaki, c., Japan (ō′mä-ā zä′kĕ)	211	34°37′N	138°15′E
Omagh, N. Ire., U.K. (ō′mä)	164	54°35′N	7°25′W
Omaha, Ne., U.S. (ō′mȧ-hä)	105	41°18′N	95°57′W
Omaha Indian Reservation, I.R., Ne., U.S.	112	42°09′N	96°08′W
Oman, nation, Asia	198	20°00′N	57°45′E
Oman, Gulf of, b., Asia	198	24°24′N	58°58′E
Omaruru, Nmb. (ō-mä-rōō′rōō)	232	21°25′S	16°50′E
Ombrone, r., Italy (ôm-brō′nā)	174	42°48′N	11°18′E
Omdurman, Sudan	231	15°45′N	32°30′E
Omealca, Mex. (ōmȧ-äl′kō)	131	18°44′N	96°45′W
Ometepec, Mex. (ô-mä-tā-pĕk′)	130	16°41′N	98°27′W
Om Hajer, Eth.	231	14°06′N	36°46′E
Omineca, r., Can. (ō-mĭ-nĕk′ȧ)	94	55°50′N	125°45′W
Omineca Mountains, mts., Can.	94	56°00′N	125°00′W
Ōmiya, Japan (ō′mē-yȧ)	211	35°54′S	139°38′E
Omo, r., Eth. (ō′mō)	231	5°54′N	36°09′E
Omoa, Hond. (ô-mō′rä)	132	15°43′N	88°03′W
Omoko, Nig.	235	5°20′N	6°39′E
Omolon, r., Russia (ō′mō)	185	67°43′N	159°15′E
Ōmori, Japan (ō′mō-rē)	211a	35°50′N	140°09′E
Omotepe, Isla de, i., Nic. (ĕ′s-lä-dĕ-ō-mō-tā′pȧ)	132	11°32′N	85°30′W
Omro, Wi., U.S. (ŏm′rō)	113	44°01′N	89°46′W
Omsk, Russia (ômsk)	178	55°12′N	73°19′E
Ōmura, Japan (ō′mōō-rȧ)	211	32°56′N	129°57′E
Ōmuta, Japan (ō-mō-tä)	211	33°02′N	130°28′E
Omutninsk, Russia (ô′mōō-tnēnsk)	180	58°38′N	52°10′E
Onawa, Ia., U.S. (ŏn-ȧ-wȧ)	112	42°02′N	96°05′W
Onaway, Mi., U.S.	108	45°25′N	84°10′W
Oncócua, Ang.	236	16°34′S	13°28′E
Onda, Spain (ōn′dä)	173	39°58′N	0°13′W
Ondava, r., Slvk. (ōn′dȧ-vȧ)	169	48°51′N	21°40′E
Ondo, Nig.	235	7°04′N	4°47′E
Öndörhaan, Mong.	205	47°20′N	110°40′E
Onega, Russia (ô-nyĕ′gȧ)	178	63°50′N	38°08′E
Onega, r., Russia	180	63°20′N	39°20′E
Onega, Lake *see* Onezhskoye Ozero, l., Russia	180	62°02′N	34°35′E
Oneida, N.Y., U.S. (ō-nī′dȧ)	109	43°05′N	75°40′W
Oneida, l., N.Y., U.S.	109	43°10′N	76°00′W
O′Neill, Ne., U.S. (ō-nēl′)	112	42°28′N	98°38′W
Oneonta, N.Y., U.S. (ō-nē-ŏn′tȧ)	109	42°25′N	75°05′W
Onezhskaja Guba, b., Russia	180	64°30′N	36°00′E
Onezhskiy, Poluostrov, pen., Russia	180	64°30′N	37°40′E
Onezhskoye Ozero, Russia (ô-năsh′skô-yĕ ô′zĕ-rô)	180	62°02′N	34°35′E
Ongiin Hiid, Mong.	204	46°00′N	102°46′E
Ongole, India	203	15°36′N	80°03′E
Onilahy, r., Madag.	233	23°41′S	45°00′E
Onitsha, Nig. (ō-nĭt′shȧ)	230	6°09′N	6°47′W
Onomichi, Japan (ō′nō-mē′chē)	210	34°27′N	133°12′E
Onon, r., Asia (ō′nôn)	179	49°00′N	112°00′E
Onoto, Ven. (ô-nō′tō)	143b	9°38′N	65°03′W
Onslow, Austl. (ŏnz′lō)	218	21°53′S	115°00′E
Onslow B, N.C., U.S. (ônz′lō)	125	34°22′N	77°35′W
Ontake San, mtn., Japan (ŏn′tä-kȧ sän)	210	35°55′N	137°29′E
Ontario, Ca., U.S. (ŏn-tā′rĭ-ō)	117a	34°04′N	117°39′E
Ontario, Or., U.S.	114	44°02′N	116°57′W
Ontario, prov., Can.	91	50°47′N	88°50′W
Ontario, Lake, l., N.A.	107	43°35′N	79°05′W
Ontinyent, Spain	173	38°48′N	0°35′W
Ontonagon, Mi., U.S. (ŏn-tō-năg′ŏn)	113	46°50′N	89°20′W
Ōnuki, Japan (ō′nōō-kē)	211a	35°17′N	139°51′E
Oodnadatta, Austl. (ōōd′nȧ-dȧ′tȧ)	218	27°38′S	135°40′E
Ooldea Station, Austl. (ōōl-dā′ä)	218	30°35′S	132°08′E
Oologah Reservoir, res., Ok., U.S.	107	36°43′N	95°32′W
Ooltgensplaat, Neth.	159a	51°41′N	4°19′E
Oostanaula, r., Ga., U.S. (ōō-stȧ-nô′lȧ)	124	34°25′N	85°10′W
Oostende, Bel. (ōst-ĕn′dē)	161	51°14′N	2°55′E
Oosterhout, Neth.	159a	51°38′N	4°52′E
Ooster Schelde, r., Neth.	159a	51°40′N	3°40′E
Ootsa Lake, l., Can.	94	53°49′N	126°18′W
Opalaca, Sierra de, mts., Hond. (sē-sĕ′r-rä-dĕ-ô-pä-lä′kä)	132	14°30′N	88°29′W
Opasquia, Can. (ō-păs′kwē-ȧ)	97	53°16′N	93°53′W
Opatów, Pol. (ô-pä′tŏf)	169	50°47′N	21°25′E
Opava, Czech Rep. (ō′pä-vä)	169	49°56′N	17°52′E
Opelika, Al., U.S. (ŏp-ē-lī′kȧ)	124	32°39′N	85°23′W
Opelousas, La., U.S. (ŏp-ē-lōō′sȧs)	123	30°33′N	92°04′W
Opeongo, l., Can. (ŏp-ē-ôŋ′gō)	99	45°40′N	78°20′W
Opheim, Mt., U.S. (ō-fīm′)	115	48°51′N	106°19′W
Ophir, Ak., U.S. (ō′fẽr)	103	63°10′N	156°28′W
Ophir, Mount, mtn., Malay.	197b	2°22′N	102°37′E
Opico, El Sal. (ô-pē′kō)	132	13°50′N	89°23′W
Opinaca, r., Can. (ŏp-ĭ-nä′kȧ)	93	52°28′N	77°40′W
Opishnia, Ukr.	177	49°57′N	34°34′E
Opladen, Ger. (ōp′lä-dĕn)	171c	51°04′N	7°00′E
Opobo, Nig.	235	4°34′N	7°27′E
Opochka, Russia (ō-pôch′kȧ)	180	56°43′N	28°39′E
Opoczno, Pol. (ô-pôch′nô)	109	51°22′N	20°18′E
Opole, Pol. (ô-pôl′ä)	161	50°42′N	17°55′E
Opole Lubelskie, Pol. (ō-pō′lă lōō-bĕl′skyĕ)	169	51°09′N	21°58′E
Opp, Al., U.S. (ŏp)	124	31°18′N	86°15′W
Oppdal, Nor. (ôp′däl)	166	62°37′N	9°41′E
Opportunity, Wa., U.S. (ŏp-ŏr tū′nĭ tĭ)	114	47°37′N	117°20′W
Oquirrh Mountains, mts., Ut., U.S. (ō′kwẽr)	117b	40°38′N	112°11′W
Oradea, Rom. (ô-răd′yä)	154	47°02′N	21°55′E
Oral, Kaz.	183	51°14′N	51°22′E
Oran, Alg. (ō-rän) (ô-rän′)	230	35°46′N	0°45′W
Orán, Arg. (ô-rȧ′n)	144	23°13′S	64°17′W
Oran, Mo., U.S. (ôr′ăn)	121	37°05′N	89°39′W
Oran, Sebkha d′, l., Alg.	173	35°28′N	0°28′W
Orange, Austl. (ŏr′ĕnj)	219	33°15′S	149°08′E
Orange, Fr. (ô-ränzh′)	161	44°08′N	4°48′E
Orange, Ca., U.S.	117a	33°48′N	117°51′W
Orange, Ct., U.S.	109	41°15′N	73°00′W
Orange, N.J., U.S.	110a	40°46′N	74°14′W
Orange, Tx., U.S.	121	30°07′N	93°44′W
Orange, r., Afr.	232	29°15′S	17°30′E
Orange, Cabo, c., Braz. (kȧ-bô-rȧ′n-zhĕ)	143	4°25′N	51°30′W
Orangeburg, S.C., U.S. (ŏr′ĕnj-bûrg)	125	33°30′N	80°50′W
Orange Cay, i., Bah. (ŏr-ĕnj kē)	134	24°55′N	79°05′W
Orange City, Ia., U.S.	112	43°01′N	96°06′W
Orange Lake, l., Fl., U.S.	125	29°30′N	82°12′W
Orangeville, Can. (ŏr′ĕnj-vĭl)	99	43°55′N	80°06′W
Orangeville, S. Afr.	238c	27°05′S	28°13′E
Orange Walk, Belize (wôl′k)	132a	18°09′N	88°32′W
Orani, Phil. (ō-rä′nē)	213a	14°47′N	120°32′E
Oranienburg, Ger. (ō-rä′nē-ĕn-bŏorgh)	168	52°45′N	13°14′E
Oranjemund, Nmb.	232	28°33′S	16°20′E
Orăștie, Rom. (ô-rûsh′tyā)	175	45°50′N	23°14′E
Orbetello, Italy (ôr-bā-tĕl′lō)	174	42°27′N	11°15′E
Orbigo, r., Spain (ôr-bē′gō)	172	42°30′N	5°55′W
Orbost, Austl. (ôr′bŭst)	222	37°43′S	148°20′E
Orcas, i., Wa., U.S. (ôr′kȧs)	116d	48°43′N	122°52′W
Orchard Farm, Mo., U.S. (ôr′chẽrd färm)	117e	38°53′N	90°27′W
Orchard Park, N.Y., U.S.	111c	42°46′N	78°46′W
Orchards, Wa., U.S. (ôr′chĕdz)	116c	45°40′N	122°33′W
Orchila, Isla, i., Ven.	142	11°47′N	66°34′W
Ord, Ne., U.S. (ôrd)	112	41°35′N	98°57′W
Ord, r., Austl.	220	17°30′S	128°40′E
Ord, Mount, mtn., Az., U.S.	119	33°55′N	109°40′W
Orda, Kaz. (ôr′dȧ)	181	48°50′N	47°30′E
Orda, Russia (ôr′dȧ)	186a	57°10′N	57°12′E
Ordes, Spain	172	43°00′N	8°24′W
Ordos Desert, des., China	204	39°12′N	108°10′E
Ordu, Tur. (ôr′dō)	163	41°00′N	37°50′E
Ordway, Co., U.S. (ôrd′wā)	120	38°11′N	103°46′W
Örebro, Swe. (û′rē-brō)	160	59°16′N	15°11′E
Oredezh, r., Russia (ô′rĕ-dĕzh)	186c	59°23′N	30°21′E
Oregon, Il., U.S.	113	42°01′N	89°21′W
Oregon, state, U.S.	104	43°40′N	121°50′W
Oregon Caves National Monument, rec., Or., U.S. (căvz)	114	42°05′N	123°13′W
Oregon City, Or., U.S.	116c	45°21′N	122°36′W
Öregrund, Swe. (û-rĕ-grŏond)	166	60°20′N	18°26′E
Orekhovo, Blg.	175	43°43′N	23°59′E
Orekhovo-Zuyevo, Russia (ôr-yĕ′kô-vô zô′yĕ-vô)	178	55°46′N	39°00′E
Orël, Russia (ôr-yôl′)	178	52°59′N	36°05′E
Orël, prov., Russia	176	52°35′N	36°08′E
Orem, Ut., U.S. (ō′rĕm)	119	40°15′N	111°50′W
Ore Mountains *see* Erzgebirge, mts., Eur.	156	50°29′N	12°40′E
Orenburg, Russia (ô′rĕn-bŏorg)	178	51°50′N	55°05′E
Øresund, strt., Eur.	166	55°50′N	12°40′E
Órganos, Sierra de los, mts., Cuba (sē-ĕ′r-rȧ-dĕ-lôs-ô′r-gä-nôs)	134	22°20′N	84°10′W
Organ Pipe Cactus National Monument, rec., Az., U.S. (ôr′găn pīp kăk′tŭs)	119	32°14′N	113°05′W
Orgãos, Serra das, mtn., Braz. (sĕ′r-rä-däs-ôr-goun′s)	141a	22°30′S	43°01′W
Orhei, Mol.	181	47°27′N	28°49′E
Orhon, r., Mong.	204	48°33′N	103°07′E
Oriental, Cordillera, mts., Col. (kôr-dēl-yĕ′rä)	142a	3°30′N	74°27′W
Oriental, Cordillera, mts., Dom. Rep. (kôr-dēl-yĕ′rä-ô-ryĕ′n-täl)	135	18°55′N	69°40′W
Oriental, Cordillera, mts., S.A. (kôr-dēl-yĕ′rä ō-rē-ĕn-täl′)	142	14°00′S	68°33′W
Orikhiv, Ukr.	177	47°34′N	35°51′E

PLACE (Pronunciation)	PAGE	LAT.	LONG.
Oril', r., Ukr.	177	49°08'N	34°55'E
Orillia, Can. (ô-rĭl'ĭ-à)	91	44°35'N	79°25'W
Orin, Wy., U.S.	115	42°40'N	105°10'W
Orinda, Ca., U.S.	116b	37°53'N	122°11'W
Orinoco, r., Ven. (ō-rĭ-nō'kô)	142	8°32'N	63°13'W
Oriola, Spain	173	38°04'N	0°55'W
Orion, Phil. (ō-rē-ōn')	213a	14°37'N	120°34'E
Orissa, state, India (ŏ-rĭs'à)	199	25°09'N	83°50'E
Oristano, Italy (ô-rês-tä'nō)	162	39°53'N	8°38'E
Oristano, Golfo di, b., Italy (gôl-fô-dē-ô-rês-tä'nō)	174	39°53'N	8°12'E
Orituco, r., Ven. (ô-rē-tōō'kō)	143b	9°37'N	66°25'W
Oriuco, r., Ven. (ô-rēōō'kō)	140b	0°36'N	66°25'W
Orivesi, l., Fin.	167	62°15'N	29°55'E
Orizaba, Mex. (ô-rê-zä'bä)	129	18°52'N	97°05'E
Orizaba, Pico de, vol., Mex.	128	19°04'N	97°14'W
Orkanger, Nor.	166	[illegible]	[illegible]
Orkla, r., Nor. (ôr'klà)	166	62°55'N	9°50'E
Orkney, S. Afr. (ôrk'nĭ)	238c	26°58'S	26°39'E
Orkney Islands, is., Scot., U.K.	156	59°01'N	2°08'W
Orlando, S. Afr. (ôr-lăn-dô)	233b	26°15'S	27°56'E
Orlando, Fl., U.S. (ôr-lăn'dō)	105	28°32'N	81°22'W
Orland Park, Il., U.S. (ôr-lăn')	111a	41°38'N	87°52'W
Orleans, Can. (ôr-lå-äN')	102c	45°28'N	75°31'W
Orléans, Fr. (ôr-lā-äN')	154	47°55'N	1°56'E
Orleans, In., U.S. (ôr-lēnz')	108	38°40'N	86°25'W
Orléans, Île d', i., Can.	99	46°56'N	70°57'W
Orly, Fr.	171b	48°45'N	2°24'E
Ormond Beach, Fl., U.S. (ôr'mŏnd)	125	29°15'N	81°05'W
Ormskirk, Eng., U.K. (ôrms'kĕrk)	158a	53°34'N	2°53'W
Ormstown, Can. (ôrms'toun)	102a	45°07'N	74°00'W
Orneta, Pol. (ôr-nyĕ'tä)	169	54°07'N	20°10'E
Örnsköldsvik, Swe. (ûrn'skôlts-vēk)	160	63°10'N	18°32'E
Oro, Río del, r., Mex. (rē'ō dĕl ō'rō)	130	18°04'N	100°59'W
Oro, Río del, r., Mex.	119	26°04'N	105°40'W
Orobie, Alpi, mts., Italy (äl'pē-ô-rō'byĕ)	174	46°05'N	9°47'E
Oron, Nig.	235	4°48'N	8°14'E
Orosei, Golfo di, b., Italy (gôl-fô-dē-ō-rō-sā'ē)	174	40°12'N	9°45'E
Orosháza, Hung. (ô-rôsh-hä'sô)	169	46°33'N	20°31'E
Orosi, vol., C.R. (ō-rō'sē)	132	11°00'N	85°30'W
Oroville, Ca., U.S. (ōr'ô-vĭl)	118	39°29'N	121°34'W
Oroville, Wa., U.S.	114	48°55'N	119°25'W
Oroville, Lake, res., Ca., U.S.	118	39°32'N	121°25'W
Orreagal, Spain	172	43°00'N	1°17'W
Orrville, Oh., U.S. (ôr'vĭl)	108	40°45'N	81°50'W
Orsa, Swe. (ôr'sä)	166	61°08'N	14°35'E
Orsha, Bela. (ôr'shà)	180	54°29'N	30°28'E
Orsk, Russia (ôrsk)	178	51°15'N	58°50'E
Orşova, Rom. (ôr'shô-vä)	175	44°43'N	22°26'E
Ortega, Col. (ôr-tĕ'gä)	142a	3°56'N	75°12'W
Ortegal, Cabo, c., Spain (kà'bô-ôr-tå-gäl')	162	43°46'N	8°15'W
Orth, Aus.	159e	48°09'N	16°42'E
Orthez, Fr. (ôr-tĕz')	171	43°29'N	0°43'W
Órthrys, Óros, mtn., Grc.	175	39°00'N	22°15'E
Ortigueira, Spain (ôr-tē-gā'ē-rä)	162	43°40'N	7°50'W
Orting, Wa., U.S. (ôrt'ĭng)	116a	47°06'N	122°12'W
Ortona, Italy (ôr-tō'nä)	174	42°22'N	14°22'E
Ortonville, Mn., U.S. (ôr-tŭn-vĭl)	112	45°18'N	96°26'W
Orūmīyeh, Iran	198	37°30'N	45°15'E
Orūmīyeh, Daryacheh-ye, l., Iran	198	38°01'N	45°17'E
Oruro, Bol. (ô-rōō'rō)	142	17°57'S	66°59'W
Orvieto, Italy (ôr-vyâ'tō)	174	42°43'N	12°08'E
Osa, Russia (ō'sà)	180	57°18'N	55°25'E
Osa, Península de, pen., C.R. (ō'sä)	133	8°30'N	83°25'W
Osage, Ia., U.S. (ō'sāj)	113	43°16'N	92°49'W
Osage, r., Mo., U.S.	121	38°10'N	93°12'W
Osage City, Ks., U.S. (ō'sāj sĭ'tĭ)	121	38°28'N	95°53'W
Ōsaka, Japan (ō'sä-kä)	205	34°40'N	135°27'E
Ōsaka, dept., Japan	211b	34°45'N	135°36'E
Ōsaka-Wan, b., Japan (wän)	210	34°34'N	135°16'E
Osakis, Mn., U.S. (ô-sā'kĭs)	112	45°51'N	95°09'W
Osakis, l., Mn., U.S.	113	45°55'N	94°55'W
Osawatomie, Ks., U.S. (ŏs-à-wăt'ō-mē)	121	38°29'N	94°57'W
Osborne, Ks., U.S. (ŏz'bŭrn)	120	39°25'N	98°42'W
Osceola, Ar., U.S. (ŏs-ē-ō'là)	121	35°42'N	89°58'W
Osceola, Ia., U.S.	113	41°04'N	93°45'W
Osceola, Mo., U.S.	121	38°02'N	93°41'W
Osceola, Ne., U.S.	112	41°11'N	97°34'W
Oscoda, Mi., U.S. (ŏs-kō'dà)	108	44°25'N	83°20'W
Osëtr, r., Russia (ō'sĕt'r)	176	54°27'N	38°15'E
Osgood, In., U.S. (ŏz'gŏŏd)	108	39°10'N	85°20'W
Osgoode, Can.	102c	45°09'N	75°37'W
Osh, Kyrg. (ôsh)	183	40°33'N	72°48'E
Oshawa, Can. (ŏsh'à-wà)	91	43°50'N	78°50'W
Ōshima, i., Japan (ō'shē'mä)	211	34°47'N	139°35'E
Oshkosh, Ne., U.S. (ŏsh'kŏsh)	112	41°24'N	102°22'W
Oshkosh, Wi., U.S.	105	44°01'N	88°35'W
Oshogbo, Nig.	230	7°47'N	4°34'E
Osijek, Cro. (ôs'ĭ-yĕk)	163	45°33'N	18°48'E
Osinniki, Russia (ŭ-sē'nyĭ-kē)	184	53°37'N	87°21'E
Oskaloosa, Ia., U.S. (ŏs-kà-lōō'sà)	113	41°16'N	92°40'W
Oskarshamn, Swe. (ôs'kärs-häm'n)	166	57°16'N	16°24'E
Oskarström, Swe. (ôs'kärs-strûm)	166	56°48'N	12°55'E
Öskemen, Kaz.	183	49°58'N	82°38'E
Oskil, r., Eur.	181	51°00'N	37°41'E
Oslo, Nor. (ôs'lō)	154	59°56'N	10°41'E
Oslofjorden, b., Nor.	166	59°03'N	10°35'E
Osmaniye, Tur.	163	37°10'N	36°30'E
Osnabrück, Ger. (ôs-nä-brük')	168	52°16'N	8°05'E
Osorno, Chile (ô-sō'r-nō)	144	40°42'S	73°13'W
Osøyra, Nor.	166	60°24'N	5°22'E
Osprey Reef, rf., Austl. (ŏs'prå)	221	14°00'S	146°45'E
Ossa, Mount, mtn., Austl. (ŏsà)	221	41°45'S	146°05'E
Osseo, Mn., U.S. (ŏs'sē-ō)	117g	45°07'N	93°24'W
Ossining, N.Y., U.S. (ŏs'ĭ-nĭng)	110a	41°09'N	73°51'W
Ossipee, N.H., U.S. (ŏs'ĭ-pē)	100	43°42'N	71°08'W
Ossjøen, l., Nor. (ôs-syûĕn)	166	61°20'N	12°00'E
Ostashkov, Russia (ôs-täsh'kôf)	180	57°07'N	33°04'E
Oster, Ukr. (ōs'tĕr)	177	50°55'N	30°52'E
Osterdalälven, r., Swe.	160	61°40'N	13°00'E
Osterfjord, b., Nor. (ûs'tĕr fyôr')	166	60°40'N	5°25'E
Östersund, Swe. (ûs'tĕr-sōōnd)	160	63°09'N	14°49'E
Östhammar, Swe. (ûst'häm'är)	166	60°16'N	18°21'E
Ostrava, Czech Rep.	154	49°51'N	18°18'E
Ostróda, Pol. (ôs'trŏt-à)	169	53°41'N	19°58'E
Ostrogozhsk, Russia (ôs-tr-gôzhk')	181	50°53'N	39°03'E
Ostroh, Ukr.	181	50°21'N	26°40'E
Ostrołęka, Pol. (ôs-trô-wôN'kà)	165	[illegible]	[illegible]
Ostrov, Russia (ôs-trôf')	180	57°21'N	28°22'E
Ostrowiec Świętokrzyski, Pol. (ōs-trō'vyĕts shvyĕN-tō-kzhĭ'ske)	161	50°55'N	21°24'E
Ostrów Lubelski, Pol. (ôs'trŏf lōō'bĕl-skĭ)	169	51°32'N	22°49'E
Ostrów Mazowiecka, Pol. (mä-zô-vyĕt'skä)	161	52°47'N	21°54'E
Ostrów Wielkopolski, Pol. (ôs'trōōf vyĕl-kō-pōl'skē)	161	51°38'N	17°49'E
Ostrzeszów, Pol. (ôs-tzhä'shôf)	169	51°26'N	17°56'E
Ostuni, Italy (ôs-tōō'nē)	175	40°44'N	17°35'E
Osum, r., Alb. (ō'sŏŏm)	175	40°37'N	20°00'E
Osuna, Spain (ô-sōō'nä)	172	37°18'N	5°05'W
Osveya, Bela. (ôs'vĕ-yà)	176	56°00'N	28°08'E
Oswaldtwistle, Eng., U.K. (ŏz-wăld-twĭs''l)	158a	53°44'N	2°23'W
Oswegatchie, r., N.Y., U.S. (ŏs-wê-găch'ĭ)	109	44°15'N	75°20'W
Oswego, Ks., U.S. (ŏs-wē'gō)	121	37°10'N	95°08'W
Oswego, N.Y., U.S.	105	43°25'N	76°30'W
Oświęcim, Pol. (ôsh-vyăN'tsyĭm)	169	50°02'N	19°17'E
Otaru, Japan (ō'tá-rŏŏ)	205	43°07'N	141°00'E
Otavalo, Ec. (ōtä-vä'lō)	142	0°14'N	78°16'W
Otavi, Nmb. (ô-tä'vê)	232	19°35'S	17°20'E
Otay, Ca., U.S. (ō'tā)	118a	32°36'N	117°04'W
Otepää, Est.	167	58°03'N	26°30'E
Oti, r., Afr.	234	9°00'N	0°10'E
Otish, Monts, mts., Can. (ô-tĭsh')	93	52°15'N	70°20'W
Otjiwarongo, Nmb. (ŏt-jê-wà-rôn'gō)	232	20°20'S	16°25'E
Otočac, Cro. (ō'tô-chàts)	174	44°53'N	15°15'E
Otra, r., Nor.	166	59°13'N	7°20'E
Otra, r., Russia (ôt'rà)	186b	55°22'N	38°20'E
Otradnoye, Russia (ô-trå'd-nôyĕ)	186c	59°46'N	30°50'E
Otranto, Italy (ō'trän-tō) (ô-trän'tō)	175	40°07'N	18°30'E
Otranto, Strait of, strt., Eur.	156	40°30'N	18°45'E
Otsego, Mi., U.S. (ŏt-sē'gō)	108	42°25'N	85°45'W
Otsu, Japan (ō'tsŏŏ)	210	35°00'N	135°54'E
Otta, l., Nor. (ôt'tà)	166	61°53'N	8°40'E
Ottawa, Can. (ŏt'à-wà)	91	45°25'N	75°43'W
Ottawa, Il., U.S.	108	41°20'N	88°50'W
Ottawa, Ks., U.S.	121	38°37'N	95°16'W
Ottawa, Oh., U.S.	108	41°00'N	84°00'W
Ottawa, r., Can.	93	46°05'N	77°20'W
Otter Creek, r., Ut., U.S. (ŏt'ẽr)	119	38°20'N	111°55'W
Otter Creek, r., Vt., U.S.	109	44°05'N	73°15'W
Otter Point, c., Can.	116a	48°21'N	123°50'W
Otter Tail, l., Mn., U.S.	112	46°21'N	95°52'W
Otterville, Il., U.S. (ŏt'ẽr-vĭl)	117e	39°03'N	90°24'W
Ottery, S. Afr. (ŏt'ẽr-ĭ)	232a	34°02'S	18°31'E
Ottumwa, Ia., U.S. (ô-tŭm'wà)	105	41°00'N	92°26'W
Otukpa, Nig.	235	7°09'N	7°41'E
Otumba, Mex. (ô-tŭm'bä)	130	19°41'N	98°46'W
Otway, Cape, c., Austl. (ŏt'wā)	221	38°55'S	153°40'E
Otway, Seno, b., Chile (sĕ'nô-ô't-wä'y)	144	53°00'S	73°00'W
Otwock, Pol. (ôt'vôtsk)	169	52°05'N	21°18'E
Ouachita, r., U.S.	107	33°25'N	92°30'W
Ouachita Mountains, mts., U.S. (wŏsh'ĭ-tô)	107	34°29'N	95°01'W
Ouagadougou, Burkina (wä'gà-dōō'gōō)	230	12°22'N	1°31'W
Ouahigouya, Burkina (wä-ê-gōō'yä)	230	13°35'N	2°25'W
Oualâta, Maur. (wä-lä'tä)	230	17°11'N	6°50'W
Ouallene, Alg. (wäl-lân')	230	24°43'N	1°15'E
Ouanaminthe, Haiti	135	19°35'N	71°45'W
Ouarane, reg., Maur.	230	20°44'N	10°27'W
Ouarkoye, Burkina	234	12°05'N	3°40'W
Ouassel, r., Alg.	173	35°30'N	1°55'E
Oubangui (Ubangi), r., Afr. (ōō-bäN'gê)	236	4°30'N	20°35'E
Oude Rijn, r., Neth.	159a	52°09'N	4°33'E
Oudewater, Neth.	159a	52°01'N	4°52'E
Oud-Gastel, Neth.	159a	51°35'N	4°27'E
Oudtshoorn, S. Afr. (outs'hōrn)	232	33°33'S	23°36'E
Oued Rhiou, Alg.	173	35°55'N	0°57'E
Oued Tlelat, Alg.	173	35°33'N	0°28'W
Oued-Zem, Mor. (wĕd-zĕm')	230	33°05'N	5°49'W
Ouessant, Island d', i., Fr. (ĕl-dwĕ-säN')	161	48°28'N	5°00'W
Ouesso, Congo	231	1°37'N	16°04'E
Ouest, Point, c., Haiti	135	19°00'N	73°25'W
Ouezzane, Mor. (wĕ-zan')	230	34°48'N	5°40'W
Ouham, r., Afr.	235	8°30'N	17°50'E
Ouidah, Benin (wē-dä')	230	6°25'N	2°05'E
Oujda, Mor.	230	34°41'N	1°45'W
Oulins, Fr. (ōō-läN')	171b	48°52'N	1°27'E
Oullins, Fr. (ōō-lăN')	170	45°44'N	4°46'E
Oulu, Fin. (ō'lŏŏ)	154	64°58'N	25°43'E
Oulujärvi, l., Fin.	160	64°20'N	25°48'E
Oum Chalouba, Chad (ōōm shä-lōō'bä)	231	15°48'N	20°30'E
Oum Hadjer, Chad	235	13°18'N	19°41'E
Ounas, r., Fin. (ō'nås)	160	67°46'N	24°40'E
Oundle, Eng., U.K. (ôn'd'l)	158a	52°28'N	0°28'W
Ounianga Kébir, Chad (ōō-nẻ-äŋ'gà kē-bēr')	231	19°04'N	20°22'E
Ouray, Co., U.S. (ōō-rā')	120	38°00'N	107°40'W
Ourense, Spain	172	42°20'N	7°52'W
Ourinhos, Braz. (ôò-rẻ'nyôs)	143	23°04'S	49°45'W
Ourique, Port. (ō-rē'kĕ)	172	37°39'N	8°10'W
Ouro Fino, Braz. (ōŭ-rô-fē'nō)	141a	22°18'S	46°21'W
Ouro Prêto, Braz. (ō'rò prā'tò)	144	20°24'S	43°30'W
Outardes, Rivière aux, r., Can.	93	50°53'N	68°50'W
[illegible], Wi., U.S. (out'ẽr)	113	47°03'N	90°20'W
Outer Brass, i., V.I.U.S. (bräs)	129c	18°24'N	64°58'W
Outer Hebrides, is., Scot., U.K.	164	57°20'N	7°50'W
Outjo, Nmb. (ōt'yō)	232	20°05'S	17°10'E
Outlook, Can.	96	51°31'N	107°05'W
Outremont, Can. (ōō-trē-môN')	102a	45°31'N	73°36'W
Ouvéa, i., N. Cal.	221	20°43'S	166°48'E
Ouyen, Austl. (ōō-ĕn)	222	35°05'S	142°10'E
Ovalle, Chile (ō-väl'yā)	144	30°43'S	71°16'W
Ovando, Bahía de, b., Cuba (bä-ē'ä-dĕ-ô-vä'n-dō)	135	20°10'N	74°05'W
Ovar, Port. (ô-vär')	172	40°52'N	8°38'W
Overijse, Bel.	159a	50°46'N	4°32'E
Overland, Mo., U.S. (ō-vēr-lănd)	117e	38°42'N	90°22'W
Overland Park, Ks., U.S.	117f	38°59'N	94°40'W
Overlea, Md., U.S. (ō'vẽr-lā)(ō'vẽr-lē)	110e	39°21'N	76°31'W
Övertornea, Swe.	160	66°19'N	23°31'E
Ovidiopol', Ukr.	177	46°15'N	30°28'E
Oviedo, Dom. Rep. (ô-vyĕ'dō)	135	17°50'N	71°25'W
Oviedo, Spain (ō-vê-ā'dhō)	154	43°22'N	5°50'W
Ovruch, Ukr.	177	51°19'N	28°51'E
Owada, Japan (ō'wä-dà)	211a	35°49'N	139°33'E
Owambo, hist. reg., Nmb.	232	18°10'S	15°00'E
Owando, Congo	232	0°29'S	15°55'E
Owasco, l., N.Y., U.S. (ō-wăsk'kō)	109	42°50'N	76°30'W
Owase, Japan (ō'wä-shê)	211	34°03'N	136°12'E
Owego, N.Y., U.S. (ō-wē'gō)	109	42°05'N	76°15'W
Owen, Wi., U.S. (ō'ĕn)	113	44°56'N	90°35'W
Owensboro, Ky., U.S. (ō'ĕnz-bŭr-ô)	105	37°45'N	87°05'W
Owens Lake, l., Ca., U.S.	118	37°13'N	118°20'W
Owen Sound, Can. (ō'ĕn)	91	44°30'N	80°55'W
Owen Stanley Range, mts., Pap. N. Gui. (stăn'lê)	213	9°00'S	147°30'E
Owensville, In., U.S. (ō'ĕnz-vĭl)	108	38°15'N	87°40'W
Owensville, Mo., U.S.	121	38°20'N	91°29'W
Owensville, Oh., U.S.	111f	39°08'N	84°07'W
Owenton, Ky., U.S. (ō'ĕn-tŭn)	108	38°35'N	84°55'W
Owerri, Nig. (ô-wĕr'ē)	230	5°26'N	7°04'E
Owings Mill, Md., U.S. (ōwĭngz mĭl)	110e	39°25'N	76°50'W
Owl Creek, r., Wy., U.S. (oul)	115	43°45'N	108°46'W
Owo, Nig.	235	7°15'N	5°37'E
Owosso, Mi., U.S. (ô-wŏs'ō)	108	43°00'N	84°15'W
Owyhee, r., U.S.	106	43°04'N	117°45'W
Owyhee, Lake, res., Or., U.S.	106	43°27'N	117°30'W
Owyhee, South Fork, r., Id., U.S.	114	42°07'N	116°43'W
Owyhee Mountains, mts., Id., U.S. (ô-wī'hê)	106	43°15'N	116°48'W
Oxbow, Can.	97	49°12'N	102°11'W
Oxchuc, Mex. (ôs-chōōk')	131	16°47'N	92°24'W
Oxford, Can. (ŏks'fẽrd)	100	45°44'N	63°52'W
Oxford, Eng., U.K.	161	51°43'N	1°16'W
Oxford, Al., U.S. (ŏks'fẽrd)	125	33°38'N	80°46'W
Oxford, Ma., U.S.	101a	42°07'N	71°52'W
Oxford, Mi., U.S.	108	42°50'N	83°15'W
Oxford, Ms., U.S.	124	34°22'N	89°30'W
Oxford, N.C., U.S.	125	36°17'N	78°35'W
Oxford, Oh., U.S.	108	39°30'N	84°45'W
Oxford Lake, l., Can.	97	54°51'N	95°37'W
Oxfordshire, co., Eng., U.K.	158b	51°36'N	1°30'W
Oxkutzcab, Mex. (ôx-kōō'tz-käb)	132a	20°18'N	89°22'W
Oxmoor, Al., U.S. (ŏks'mŏr)	110h	33°25'N	86°52'W
Oxnard, Ca., U.S. (ŏks'närd)	118	34°08'N	119°12'W
Oxon Hill, Md., U.S. (ōks'ōn hĭl)	110e	38°48'N	77°00'W
Oyapock, r., S.A. (ō-yà-pŏk')	143	2°45'N	52°15'W
Oyem, Gabon	230	1°37'N	11°35'E
Øyeren, l., Nor. (ûĭĕrĕn)	166	59°50'N	11°25'E
Oymyakon, Russia (oi-myŭ-kôn')	179	63°14'N	142°58'E
Oyo, Nig. (ō'yō)	230	7°51'N	3°56'E
Oyonnax, Fr. (ô-yô-näks')	171	46°16'N	5°40'E
Oyster Bay, N.Y., U.S.	110a	40°52'N	73°32'W
Oyster Bayou, Tx., U.S.	123a	29°41'N	94°33'W
Oyster Creek, r., Tx., U.S. (ois'tẽr)	123a	29°13'N	95°29'W
Oyyl, r., Kaz.	181	49°30'N	55°10'E
Ozama, r., Dom. Rep. (ô-zä'mä)	135	18°45'N	69°55'W
Ozamiz, Phil. (ô-zä'mêz)	213	8°06'N	123°43'E
Ozark, Al., U.S. (ō'zärk)	124	31°28'N	85°28'W
Ozark, Ar., U.S.	121	35°29'N	93°49'W
Ozark Plateau, plat., U.S.	107	36°37'N	93°56'W
Ozarks, Lake of the, l., Mo., U.S. (ō'zärksz)	107	38°06'N	93°26'W
Ozëry, Russia (ô-zyô'rê)	176	54°53'N	38°31'E
Ozieri, Italy	162	40°38'N	8°53'E
Ozorków, Pol. (ô-zôr'kôf)	169	51°58'N	19°20'E
Ozuluama, Mex.	131	21°34'N	97°52'W
Ozumba, Mex.	131a	19°02'N	98°48'W
Ozurgeti, Geor.	182	41°56'N	42°00'E

ăt; finăl; rāte; senâte; ärm; åsk; sofá; fâre; ch-choose; dh-as th in other; bē; ēvent; bĕt; recĕnt; cratẽr; g-gō; gh-guttural g; bĭt; ĭ-short neutral; rīde; κ-guttural k as ch in German ich;

PRONOUNCING INDEX

Paarl – Paris 333

PLACE (Pronunciation)	PAGE	LAT.	LONG.
P			
Paarl, S. Afr. (pärl)	232	33°45′S	18°55′E
Pa'auilo, Hi., U.S. (pä-ä-o͞o′ē-lō)	126a	20°03′N	155°25′W
Pabianice, Pol. (pä-byȧ-nē′tsĕ)	169	51°40′N	19°29′E
Pacaás Novos, Massiço de, mts., Braz.	142	11°03′S	64°02′W
Pacaraima, Serra, mts., S.A.			
(sĕr′rȧ pä-kä-rä-ē′mȧ)	142	3°45′N	62°30′W
Pacasmayo, Peru (pä-käs-mä′yō)	142	7°24′S	79°30′W
Pachuca, Mex. (pä-cho͞o′kä)	128	20°07′N	98°43′W
Pacific, Wa., U.S. (pȧ-sĭf′ĭk)	116a	47°16′N	122°15′W
Pacifica, Ca., U.S. (pȧ-sĭf′ĭ-kä)	116b	37°38′N	122°29′W
Pacific Beach, Ca., U.S.	118a	32°47′N	117°22′W
Pacific Grove, Ca., U.S.	118	36°37′N	121°54′W
Pacific Islands, Trust Territory of			
the *see* Palau, nation, Oc.	3	7°15′N	134°30′E
Pacific Ocean, o.	2	0°00′	170°00′W
Pacific Ranges, mts., Can.	94	51°00′N	126°30′W
Pacific Rim National Park, rec.,			
Can.	94	49°00′N	126°00′W
Pacolet, r., S.C., U.S. (pā′cō-lēt)	125	34°55′N	81°49′W
Pacy-sur-Eure, Fr. (pä-sē-sür-ûr′)	171b	49°01′N	1°24′E
Padang, Indon. (pä-däng′)	212	1°01′S	100°28′E
Padang, i., Indon.	197b	1°12′N	102°21′E
Padang Endau, Malay.	197b	2°39′N	103°38′E
Paden City, W.V., U.S. (pā′dĕn)	108	39°30′N	80°55′W
Paderborn, Ger. (pä-dĕr-bôrn′)	168	51°43′N	8°46′E
Padibe, Ug.	237	3°28′N	32°50′E
Padiham, Eng., U.K. (păd′ĭ-hăm)	158a	53°48′N	2°19′W
Padilla, Mex. (pä-dēl′yä)	130	24°00′N	98°45′W
Padilla Bay, b., Wa., U.S. (pä-dĭl′lȧ)	116a	48°31′N	122°34′W
Padova, Italy (pä′dô-vä)(păd′û-ȧ)	162	45°24′N	11°53′E
Padre Island, i., Tx., U.S. (pä′drā)	123	27°09′N	97°15′W
Padua *see* Padova, Italy	162	45°24′N	11°53′E
Paducah, Ky., U.S.	105	37°05′N	88°36′W
Paducah, Tx., U.S.	120	34°01′N	100°18′W
Paektu-san, mtn., Asia (pâk′to͞o-sän′)	210	42°00′N	128°03′E
Pag, i., Cro. (päg)	174	44°30′N	14°48′E
Pagai Selatan, Pulau, i., Indon.	212	2°48′S	100°22′E
Pagai Utara, Pulau, i., Indon.	212	2°45′S	100°02′E
Pagasitikós Kólpos, b., Grc.	175	39°15′N	23°00′E
Page, Az., U.S.	119	36°57′N	111°27′W
Pago Pago, Am. Sam.	214a	14°16′S	170°42′W
Pagosa Springs, Co., U.S. (pȧ-gō′sȧ)	120	37°15′N	107°05′W
Pāhala, Hi., U.S. (pä-hä′lä)	126a	19°11′N	155°28′W
Pahang, state, Malay.	197b	3°02′N	102°57′E
Pahang, r., Malay.	212	3°39′N	102°41′E
Pahokee, Fl., U.S. (pȧ-hō′kē)	125a	26°45′N	80°40′W
Paide, Est. (pī′dĕ)	167	58°54′N	25°30′E
Päijänne, l., Fin. (pĕ′ē-yĕn-nĕ)	160	61°38′N	25°05′E
Pailolo Channel, strt., Hi., U.S.			
(pä-ē-lō′lō)	126a	21°05′N	156°41′W
Paine, Chile (pī′nĕ)	141b	33°49′S	70°44′W
Painesville, Oh., U.S. (pānz′vĭl)	108	41°40′N	81°15′W
Painted Desert, des., Az., U.S.			
(pānt′ĕd)	120	36°15′N	111°35′W
Painted Rock Reservoir, res., Az.,			
U.S.	119	33°00′N	113°05′W
Paintsville, Ky., U.S. (pānts′vĭl)	108	37°50′N	82°50′W
Paisley, Scot., U.K. (pāz′lĭ)	160	55°50′N	4°30′W
Paita, Peru (pä-ē′tä)	142	5°11′S	81°12′W
Pai T'ou Shan, mts., Kor., N.	205	40°30′N	127°20′E
Paiute Indian Reservation, I.R.,			
Ut., U.S.	119	38°17′N	113°50′W
Pajápan, Mex. (pä-hä′pän)	131	18°16′N	94°41′W
Pakanbaru, Indon.	212	0°43′N	101°15′E
Pakhra, r., Russia (päk′rȧ)	186b	55°29′N	37°51′E
Pakistan, nation, Asia	199	28°00′N	67°30′E
Pakokku, Mya. (pȧ-kŏk′kò)	204	21°29′N	95°00′E
Paks, Hung. (pôksh)	169	46°38′N	18°53′E
Pala, Chad	235	9°22′N	14°54′E
Palacios, Tx., U.S. (pȧ-lä′syōs)	123	28°42′N	96°12′W
Palagruža, Otoci, is., Cro.	174	42°20′N	16°23′E
Palaiseau, Fr. (pȧ-lĕ-zō′)	171b	48°44′N	2°16′E
Palana, Russia	179	59°07′N	159°58′E
Palanan Bay, b., Phil. (pä-lä′nän)	213a	17°14′N	122°35′E
Palanan Point, c., Phil.	213a	17°12′N	122°40′E
Pālanpur, India (pä′lŭn-po͞or)	199	24°08′N	73°29′E
Palapye, Bots. (pȧ-läp′yĕ)	232	22°34′S	27°28′E
Palatine, Il., U.S. (păl′ȧ-tīn)	111a	42°07′N	88°03′W
Palatka, Fl., U.S. (pȧ-lăt′kȧ)	125	29°39′N	81°40′W
Palau (Belau), nation, Oc. (pä-lä′ò)	3	7°15′N	134°30′E
Palauig, Phil. (pȧ-lou′ĕg)	213a	15°27′N	119°54′E
Palawan, i., Phil. (pä-lä′wän)	212	9°50′N	117°38′E
Pālayankottai, India	203	8°50′N	77°50′E
Paldiski, Est. (päl′dĭ-skĭ)	167	59°22′N	24°04′E
Palembang, Indon. (pä-lĕm-bäng′)	212	2°57′S	104°40′E
Palencia, Guat. (pä-lĕn′sē-ȧ)	132	14°40′N	90°22′W
Palencia, Spain (pä-lĕ′n-syä)	162	42°02′N	4°32′W
Palenque, Mex. (pä-lĕn′kā)	131	17°34′N	91°58′W
Palenque, Punta, c., Dom. Rep.			
(po͞o′n-tä)	135	18°10′N	70°10′W
Palermo, Col. (pä-lĕr′mô)	142a	2°53′N	75°26′W
Palermo, Italy	154	38°08′N	13°24′E
Palestine, Tx., U.S.	105	31°46′N	95°38′W
Palestine, hist. reg., Asia			
(păl′ĕs-tīn)	197a	31°33′N	35°00′E
Paletwa, Mya. (pŭ-lĕt′wä)	199	21°19′N	92°52′E
Palghāt, India	203	10°49′N	76°40′E
Pāli, India	202	25°53′N	73°18′E
Palín, Guat. (pä-lēn′)	132	14°42′N	90°42′W
Palizada, Mex. (pä-lē-zä′dä)	131	18°17′N	92°04′W
Palk Strait, strt., Asia (pôk)	199	10°00′N	79°23′E
Palma, Braz. (päl′mä)	141a	21°23′S	42°18′W
Palma, Spain	154	39°35′N	2°38′E
Palma, Bahía de, b., Spain	173	39°24′N	2°37′E
Palma del Río, Spain	172	37°43′N	5°19′W
Palmares, Braz. (päl-mà′rĕs)	143	8°46′S	35°28′W
Palmas, Braz. (päl′mäs)	144	26°20′S	51°56′W
Palmas, Braz.	143	10°08′S	48°18′W
Palmas, Cape, c., Lib.	230	4°22′N	7°44′W
Palma Soriano, Cuba (sô-rē-ä′nō)	134	20°15′N	76°00′W
Palm Beach, Fl., U.S. (päm bēch′)	125a	26°43′N	80°03′W
Palmeira dos Índios, Braz.			
(pä-mā′rä-dôs-ē′n-dyôs)	143	9°26′S	36°33′W
Palmeirinhas, Ponta das, c., Ang.	236	9°05′S	13°00′E
Palmela, Port. (päl-mā′lä)	172	38°34′N	8°54′W
Palmer, Ak., U.S. (päm′ẽr)	103	61°38′N	149°15′W
Palmer, Wa., U.S.	116a	47°19′N	121°53′W
Palmerston North, N.Z. (päm′ẽr-stŭn)	221a	40°20′S	175°35′E
Palmerville, Austl. (päm′ẽr-vĭl)	219	16°08′S	144°15′E
Palmetto, Fl., U.S. (pȧl mĕt′ō)	125a	27°32′N	82°34′W
Palmetto Point, c., Bah.	135	21°15′N	73°25′W
Palmi, Italy (päl′mē)	174	38°21′N	15°54′E
Palmira, Col. (päl-mē′rä)	142	3°33′N	76°17′W
Palmira, Cuba	134	22°15′N	80°25′W
Palmyra, Mo., U.S. (păl-mī′rȧ)	121	39°45′N	91°32′W
Palmyra, N.J., U.S.	110f	40°01′N	75°00′W
Palmyra, i., Oc.	2	6°00′N	162°20′W
Palmyra, hist., Syria	198	34°25′N	38°28′E
Palmyras Point, c., India	202	20°42′N	87°45′E
Palo Alto, Ca., U.S. (pä′lō ăl′tō)	116b	37°27′N	122°09′W
Paloduro Creek, r., Tx., U.S.			
(pă-lō-do͞o′rō)	120	36°16′N	101°12′W
Paloh, Malay.	197b	2°11′N	103°12′E
Paloma, l., Mex. (pä-lō′mä)	122	26°53′N	104°02′W
Palomo, Cerro el, mtn., Chile			
(sĕ′r-rô-ĕl-pä-lō′mô)	141b	34°36′S	70°20′W
Palos, Cabo de, c., Spain			
(kà′bô-dĕ-pä′lōs)	162	39°38′N	0°43′W
Palos Verdes Estates, Ca., U.S.			
(pă′lŭs vûr′dĭs)	117a	33°48′N	118°24′W
Palouse, Wa., U.S. (pȧ-lo͞oz′)	114	46°54′N	117°04′W
Palouse, r., Wa., U.S.	114	47°02′N	117°35′W
Palu, Tur. (pä-loo′)	181	38°55′N	40°10′E
Paluan, Phil. (pä-lo͞o′än)	213a	13°25′N	120°29′E
Pamiers, Fr. (pȧ-myā′)	161	43°07′N	1°34′E
Pamirs, mts., Asia	199	38°14′N	72°27′E
Pamlico, r., N.C., U.S. (păm′lĭ-kō)	125	35°25′N	76°59′W
Pamlico Sound, strt., N.C., U.S.	107	35°10′N	76°10′W
Pampa, Tx., U.S. (păm′pȧ)	104	35°32′N	100°56′W
Pampa de Castillo, pl., Arg.			
(pä′m-pä-dĕ-käs-tē′l-yô)	144	45°30′S	67°30′W
Pampana, r., S.L.	234	8°35′N	11°55′W
Pampanga, r., Phil. (päm-päŋ′gä)	213a	15°20′N	120°48′E
Pampas, reg., Arg. (päm′päs)	144	37°00′S	64°30′W
Pampilhosa do Botão, Port.			
(päm-pē-lyō′sȧ-dô-bō-touɴ)	172	40°21′N	8°32′W
Pamplona, Col. (päm-plō′nä)	142	7°19′N	72°41′W
Pamplona, Spain (päm-plô′nä)	162	42°49′N	1°39′W
Pamunkey, r., Va., U.S. (pȧ-mŭŋ′kĭ)	109	37°40′N	77°20′W
Pana, Il., U.S. (pā′nȧ)	108	39°25′N	89°05′W
Panagyurishte, Blg.			
(pȧ-nȧ-gyo͞o′rēsh-tĕ)	175	42°30′N	24°11′E
Panaji (Panjim), India	199	15°33′N	73°52′E
Panamá, Pan.	129	8°58′N	79°32′W
Panama, nation, N.A.	129	9°00′N	80°00′W
Panamá, Istmo de, isth., Pan.	129	9°00′N	80°00′W
Panama Canal, can., Pan.	128a	9°20′N	79°55′W
Panama City, Fl., U.S.			
(păn-ȧ mä′ sĭ′tĭ)	124	30°08′N	85°39′W
Panamint Range, mts., Ca., U.S.			
(păn-ȧ-mĭnt′)	118	36°40′N	117°30′W
Panarea, i., Italy (pä-nä′rê-a)	174	38°37′N	15°05′E
Panaro, r., Italy (pä-nä′rô)	174	44°47′N	11°06′E
Panay, i., Phil. (pä-nī′)	212	11°15′N	121°38′E
Pančevo, Serb. (pȧn′chĕ-vô)	163	44°52′N	20°42′E
Panchor, Malay.	197b	2°11′N	102°43′E
Pānchur, India	202a	22°31′N	88°17′E
Panda, D.R.C. (pän′dä′)	232	10°59′S	27°24′E
Pan de Guajaibon, mtn., Cuba			
(pän dā gwä-jȧ-bōn′)	134	22°50′N	83°20′W
Panevėžys, Lith. (pä′nyĕ-vāzh′ēs)	180	55°44′N	24°21′E
Panga, D.R.C. (päŋ′gȧ)	231	1°51′N	26°25′E
Pangani, Tan. (pän-gä′nē)	233	5°28′S	38°58′E
Pangani, r., Tan.	237	4°40′S	37°45′E
Pangkalpinang, Indon.			
(päng-käl′pē-näng′)	212	2°11′S	106°04′E
Pangnirtung, Can.	91	66°08′N	65°26′W
Panguitch, Ut., U.S. (pän′gwĭch)	119	37°50′N	112°30′W
Panié, Mont, mtn., N. Cal.	214f	20°36′S	164°46′E
Pānihāti, India	202a	22°42′N	88°23′E
Panimávida, Chile (pä-nē-mà′vē-dä)	141b	35°44′S	71°26′W
Panshi, China (pän-shē)	208	42°50′N	126°48′E
Pantar, Pulau, i., Indon. (pän′tär)	213	8°40′N	123°45′E
Pantelleria, i., Italy			
(pän-tĕl-lȧ-rē′ä)	162	36°43′N	11°59′E
Pantepec, Mex. (pän-tȧ-pĕk′)	131	17°11′N	93°04′W
Panuco, Mex. (pä′no͞o-kô)	130	22°04′N	98°11′W
Pánuco, Mex. (pä′no͞o-kô)	130	23°25′N	105°55′W
Panuco, r., Mex.	128	21°59′N	98°20′W
Pánuco de Coronado, Mex.			
(pä′no͞o-kô dā kō-rô-nä′dhō)	122	24°33′N	104°20′W
Panvel, India	203b	18°59′N	73°06′E
Panyu, China (pä-yo͞o)	207a	22°56′N	113°22′E
Panzós, Guat. (pän-zós′)	132	15°26′N	89°40′W
Pao, r., Ven. (pá′ō)	143b	9°52′N	67°57′W
Paola, Ks., U.S. (pȧ-ō′lȧ)	121	38°34′N	94°51′W
Paoli, In., U.S. (pȧ-ō′lī)	108	38°35′N	86°30′W
Paoli, Pa., U.S.	110f	40°03′N	75°29′W
Paonia, Co., U.S. (pā-ō′nyȧ)	119	38°50′N	107°40′W
Pápa, Hung. (pä′pô)	163	47°18′N	17°27′E
Papagayo, r., Mex. (pä-pä-gä′yō)	130	16°52′N	99°41′W
Papagayo, Golfo del, b., C.R.			
(gôl-fô-dĕl-pä-pä-gá′yō)	132	10°44′N	85°56′W
Papagayo, Laguna, l., Mex. (lä-ò-nä)	130	16°44′N	99°44′W
Papantla de Olarte, Mex.			
(pä-pän′tlä dā-ô-lä′r-tĕ)	128	20°30′N	97°15′W
Papatoapan, r., Mex.			
(pä-pä-tô-ä-pä′n)	131	18°00′N	96°22′W
Papenburg, Ger. (päp′ĕn-bòrgh)	168	53°05′N	7°23′E
Papinas, Arg. (pä-pē′näs)	141c	35°30′S	57°19′W
Papineauville, Can. (pä-pē-nō′vēl)	102c	45°38′N	75°01′W
Papua, Gulf of, b., Pap. N. Gui.			
(păp-o͞o-ȧ)	213	8°20′S	144°45′E
Papua New Guinea, nation, Oc.			
(păp-o͞o-ȧ)(gĭne)	213	7°00′S	142°15′E
Papudo, Chile (pä-po͞o′dô)	141b	32°30′S	71°25′W
Paquequer Pequeno, Braz.			
(pä-kĕ-kĕ′r-pĕ-kĕ′nô)	144b	22°19′S	43°02′W
Para, r., Russia	176	53°45′N	40°58′E
Paracale, Phil. (pä-rä-kä′lȧ)	213a	14°17′N	122°47′E
Paracambi, Braz.	144b	22°36′S	43°43′W
Paracatu, Braz. (pä-rä-kä-to͞o′)	143	17°17′S	46°43′W
Paracel Islands, is., Asia	212	16°40′N	113°00′E
Paraćin, Serb. (pá′rä-chēn)	163	43°51′N	21°26′E
Para de Minas, Braz.			
(pä-rä-dĕ-mē′näs)	143	19°52′S	44°37′W
Paradise, i., Bah.	134	25°05′N	77°20′W
Paradise Valley, Nv., U.S.			
(pâr′ȧ-dīs)	114	41°28′N	117°32′W
Parados, Cerro de los, mtn., Col.			
(sĕ′r-rô-dĕ-lôs-pä-rä′dōs)	142a	5°44′N	75°13′W
Paragould, Ar., U.S. (păr′ȧ-go͞old)	121	36°03′N	90°29′W
Paraguaçu, r., Braz.			
(pä-rä-gwä-zo͞o′)	143	12°25′S	39°46′W
Paraguay, nation, S.A. (păr′ȧ-gwā)	144	24°00′S	57°00′W
Paraguay, r., S.A. (pä-rä-gwä′y)	144	21°12′S	57°31′W
Paraíba, state, Braz. (pä-rä-ē′bä)	143	7°11′S	37°05′W
Paraíba, r., Braz.	141a	23°02′S	45°43′W
Paraíba do Sul, Braz. (dô-so͞o′l)	141a	22°10′S	43°18′W
Paraibuna, Braz. (pä-räē-bo͞o′nä)	141a	23°23′S	45°38′W
Paraíso, C.R.	133	9°50′N	83°53′W
Paraíso, Mex.	131	18°24′N	93°11′W
Paraiso, Pan. (pä-rä-ē′sō)	128a	9°02′N	79°38′W
Paraisópolis, Braz.			
(pä-räē-sô′pō-lēs)	141a	22°35′S	45°45′W
Paraitinga, r., Braz.			
(pä-rä-ē-tē′n-gä)	141a	23°15′S	45°24′W
Parakou, Benin (pȧ-rȧ-ko͞o′)	230	9°21′N	2°37′E
Paramaribo, Sur. (pȧ-rȧ-mà′rē-bō)	143	5°50′N	55°15′W
Paramatta, Austl. (păr-ȧ-măt′ȧ)	217b	33°49′S	150°59′E
Paramillo, mtn., Col. (pä-rä-mē′l-yō)	142a	7°06′N	75°55′W
Paramus, N.J., U.S.	110a	40°56′N	74°04′W
Paran, r., Asia	197a	30°05′N	34°50′E
Paraná, Arg.	144	31°44′S	60°32′W
Paraná, r., S.A.	144	24°00′S	54°00′W
Paranaíba, Braz. (pä-rä-nȧ-ē′bȧ)	143	19°43′S	51°13′W
Paranaíba, r., Braz.	143	18°58′S	50°44′W
Paraná Ibicuy, r., Arg.	141c	33°27′S	59°26′W
Paranam, Sur.	143	5°39′N	55°13′W
Paranápanema, r., Braz.			
(pä-rä′nà′pä-nĕ-mä)	143	22°28′S	52°15′W
Paraopeda, r., Braz. (pä-rä-o-pĕ′dä)	141a	20°09′S	44°14′W
Parapara, Ven. (pä-rä-pä-rä)	143b	9°44′N	67°17′W
Parati, Braz. (pä-rätē)	141a	23°14′S	44°43′W
Paray-le-Monial, Fr.			
(pȧ-rĕ′lē-mô-nyäl′)	170	46°27′N	4°14′E
Pārbati, r., India	202	24°50′N	76°44′E
Parchim, Ger. (par′kĭm)	168	53°25′N	11°52′E
Parczew, Pol. (pär′chĕf)	169	51°38′N	22°53′E
Pardo, r., Braz. (pär′dō)	143	15°25′S	39°40′W
Pardo, r., Braz.	141a	21°32′S	46°40′W
Pardubice, Czech Rep.			
(pär′dò-bĭt-sĕ)	168	50°02′N	15°47′E
Parecis, Serra dos, mts., Braz.			
(sĕr′rȧ dōs pä-rȧ-sēzh′)	143	13°45′S	59°28′W
Paredes de Nava, Spain			
(pä-rā′dås dā nä′vä)	172	42°10′N	4°41′W
Paredón, Mex.	122	25°56′N	100°58′W
Parent, Can.	91	47°59′N	74°30′W
Parent, Lac, l., Can.	99	48°40′N	77°00′W
Parepare, Indon.	212	4°01′S	119°38′E
Pargolovo, Russia (pár-gô′lô vô)	186c	60°04′N	30°18′E
Paria, r., Az., U.S.	119	37°07′N	111°51′W
Paria, Golfo de, b.			
(gôl-fô-dĕ-br-pä-rē-ä)	142	10°33′N	62°14′W
Paricutín, Volcán, vol., Mex.	130	19°27′N	102°14′W
Parida, Río de la, r., Mex.			
(rē′ō-dĕ-lä-pä-rē′dä)	122	26°23′N	104°40′W
Parima, Serra, mts., S.A.			
(sĕr′rȧ pä-rē′mȧ)	142	3°45′N	64°00′W
Pariñas, Punta, c., Peru			
(po͞o′n-tä-pä-rē′n-yäs)	142	4°30′S	81°23′W
Parintins, Braz. (pä-rĭn-tĭnzh′)	143	2°34′S	56°30′W
Paris, Can.	99	43°15′N	80°23′W
Paris, Fr. (pȧ-rē′)	154	48°51′N	2°20′E
Paris, Ar., U.S. (păr′ĭs)	121	35°17′N	93°43′W
Paris, Il., U.S.	108	39°35′N	87°40′W
Paris, Ky., U.S.	108	38°15′N	84°15′W
Paris, Mo., U.S.	121	39°27′N	91°59′W
Paris, Tn., U.S.	124	36°16′N	88°20′W
Paris, Tx., U.S.	105	33°39′N	95°33′W

ăt; finăl; rāte; senàte; ärm; àsk; sofá; fåre; ch-choose; dh-as th in other; bē; ĕvent; bĕt; recĕnt; cratĕr; g-gō; gh-guttural g; bĭt; ī-short neutral; rīde; к-guttural k as ch in German ich;

PRONOUNCING INDEX

Penjamillo – Pillar Rocks 335

PLACE (Pronunciation)	PAGE	LAT.	LONG.
Penjamillo, Mex. (pěn-hä-mēl'yō)	130	20°06'N	101°56'W
Pénjamo, Mex. (pān'hä-mō)	130	20°27'N	101°43'W
Penk, r., Eng., U.K. (pěnk)	158a	52°41'N	2°10'W
Penkridge, Eng., U.K. (pěnk'rĭj)	158a	52°43'N	2°07'W
Penne, Italy (pěn'nā)	174	42°28'N	13°57'E
Penner, r., India (pěn'ẽr)	199	14°43'N	79°09'E
Pennines, hills, Eng., U.K. (pěn-īn')	164	54°30'N	2°10'W
Pennines, Alpes, mts., Eur.	168	46°02'N	7°07'E
Pennsboro, W.V., U.S. (pěnz'bŭr-ô)	108	39°10'N	81°00'W
Penns Grove, N.J., U.S. (pěnz grōv)	110f	39°44'N	75°28'W
Pennsylvania, state, U.S. (pěn-sĭl-vā'nĭ-*à*)	105	41°00'N	78°10'W
Penn Yan, N.Y., U.S. (pěn yăn')	109	42°40'N	77°00'W
Pennycutaway, r., Can.	97	56°10'N	93°25'W
Peno, l., Russia (pā'nô)	176	56°55'N	32°28'E
Penobscot, r., Me., U.S.	107	45°00'N	68°36'W
Penobscot Bay, b., Me., U.S. (pẻ-nŏb'skŏt)	100	44°20'N	69°00'W
Penong, Austl. (pẻ-nŏng')	218	32°00'S	133°00'E
Penrith, Austl.	217b	33°45'S	150°42'E
Pensacola, Fl., U.S. (pěn-s*à*-kō'l*à*)	105	30°25'N	87°13'W
Pensacola Dam, Ok., U.S.	121	36°27'N	95°02'W
Pensilvania, Col. (pěn-sẻl-vä'nyä)	142a	5°31'N	75°05'W
Pentecost, i., Vanuatu (pěn'tẻ-kŏst)	221	16°05'S	168°28'E
Penticton, Can.	90	49°30'N	119°35'W
Pentland Firth, strt., Scot., U.K. (pěnt'l*ă*nd)	164	58°44'N	3°25'W
Penza, Russia (pěn'zà)	178	53°10'N	45°00'E
Penzance, Eng., U.K. (pěn-zăns')	164	50°07'N	5°40'W
Penzberg, Ger. (pěnts'běrgh)	168	47°43'N	11°21'E
Penzhina, r., Russia (pyĭn-zē-nŭ)	185	62°15'N	166°30'E
Penzhino, Russia	179	63°42'N	168°00'E
Penzhinskaya Guba, b., Russia	185	60°30'N	161°30'E
Peoria, Il., U.S. (pē-ō'rĭ-*à*)	105	40°45'N	89°35'W
Peotillos, Mex. (pā-ō-tel'yōs)	130	22°30'N	100°39'W
Peotone, Il., U.S. (pē'ō-tŏn)	111a	41°20'N	87°47'W
Pepacton Reservoir, res., N.Y., U.S. (pěp-ăc't*ŭ*n)	109	42°05'N	74°40'W
Pepe, Cabo, c., Cuba (kä'bō-pĕ'pĕ)	134	21°30'N	83°10'W
Pepperell, Ma., U.S. (pĕp'ẽr-ĕl)	101a	42°40'N	71°36'W
Peqin, Alb. (pĕ-kēn')	175	41°03'N	19°48'E
Perales, r., Spain (pā-rä'lās)	173a	40°24'N	4°07'W
Perales de Tajuña, Spain (dā tä-hōō'nyä)	173a	40°14'N	3°22'W
Perche, Collines du, hills, Fr.	170	48°25'N	0°40'E
Perchtoldsdorf, Aus. (pĕrk'tōlts-dôrf)	159e	48°07'N	16°17'E
Perdekop, S. Afr.	238c	27°11'S	29°38'E
Perdido, r., Al., U.S. (pẽr-dī'dō)	124	30°45'N	87°38'W
Perdido, Monte, mtn., Spain (pĕr-dē'dō)	173	42°40'N	0°00'
Perdões, Braz. (pĕr-dô'ĕs)	141a	21°05'S	45°05'W
Pereiaslav-Khmel'nyts'kyi, Ukr.	181	50°05'N	31°25'E
Pereira, Col. (pā-rā'rä)	142	4°49'N	75°42'W
Pere Marquette, Mi., U.S.	108	43°55'N	86°10'W
Pereshchepyne, Ukr.	177	49°02'N	35°19'E
Pereslavl'-Zalesskiy, Russia (pâ-rå-slàv''l zà-lyĕs'kĭ)	180	56°43'N	38°52'E
Pergamino, Arg. (pĕr-gä-mē'nō)	144	33°53'S	60°36'W
Perham, Mn., U.S. (pẽr'h*ă*m)	112	46°37'N	95°35'W
Peribonca, r., Can. (pĕr-ĭ-bŏŋ'kà)	93	50°30'N	71°00'W
Périgueux, Fr. (pā-rē-gû')	161	45°12'N	0°43'E
Perija, Sierra de, mts., Col. (sē-ĕ'r-rà-dĕ-pĕ-rē'kä)	142	9°25'N	73°30'W
Perkam, Tanjung, c., Indon.	213	1°20'S	138°45'E
Perkins, Can. (pĕr'k*ĕ*ns)	102c	45°37'N	75°37'W
Perlas, Archipiélago de las, is., Pan.	133	8°29'N	79°15'W
Perlas, Laguna las, l., Nic. (lä-gò'nä-dĕ-läs)	133	12°34'N	83°19'W
Perleberg, Ger. (pĕr'lĕ-bĕrg)	168	53°06'N	11°51'E
Perm', Russia (pĕrm)	178	58°00'N	56°15'E
Pernambuco *see* Recife, Braz.	143	8°09'S	34°59'W
Pernambuco, state, Braz. (pĕr-näm-bōō'kō)	143	8°08'S	38°54'W
Pernik, Blg. (pĕr-nēk')	163	42°36'N	23°04'E
Péronne, Fr. (pā-rôn')	170	49°57'N	2°49'E
Perote, Mex. (pĕ-rô'tĕ)	131	19°33'N	97°13'W
Perovo, Russia (pâ'rô-vô)	186b	55°43'N	37°47'E
Perpignan, Fr. (pĕr-pē-nyäN')	161	42°42'N	2°48'E
Perris, Ca., U.S. (pĕr'ĭs)	117a	33°46'N	117°14'W
Perros, Bahía, b., Cuba (bä-ē'ä-pā'rōs)	134	22°25'N	78°35'W
Perrot, Île, i., Can.	102a	45°23'N	73°57'W
Perry, Fl., U.S. (pĕr'ĭ)	124	30°06'N	83°35'W
Perry, Ga., U.S.	124	32°27'N	83°44'W
Perry, Ia., U.S.	113	41°49'N	94°40'W
Perry, N.Y., U.S.	109	42°45'N	78°00'W
Perry, Ok., U.S.	121	36°17'N	97°18'W
Perry, Ut., U.S.	117b	41°27'N	112°02'W
Perry Hall, Md., U.S.	110e	39°24'N	76°29'W
Perryopolis, Pa., U.S. (pĕ-rē-ŏ'pô-lĭs)	111e	40°05'N	79°45'W
Perrysburg, Oh., U.S. (pĕr ĭz-bûrg)	108	41°35'N	83°35'W
Perryton, Tx., U.S. (pĕr'ĭ-t*ŭ*n)	120	36°23'N	100°48'W
Perryville, Ak., U.S. (pĕr-ĭ-vĭl)	103	55°58'N	159°28'W
Perryville, Mo., U.S.	121	37°41'N	89°52'W
Persan, Fr. (pĕr-säN')	171b	49°09'N	2°15'E
Persepolis, hist., Iran (pẽr-sĕpô-lĭs)	198	30°15'N	53°08'E
Persian Gulf, b., Asia (pûr'zh*ă*n)	198	27°38'N	50°30'E
Perth, Austl. (pûrth)	218	31°50'S	116°10'E
Perth, Can.	99	44°40'N	76°15'W
Perth, Scot., U.K.	160	56°24'N	3°25'W
Perth Amboy, N.J., U.S. (ăm'boi)	110a	40°31'N	74°16'W
Pertuis, Fr. (pĕr-tüē')	171	43°43'N	5°29'E

PLACE (Pronunciation)	PAGE	LAT.	LONG.
Peru, Il., U.S. (pē-rōō')	108	41°20'N	89°10'W
Peru, In., U.S.	108	40°45'N	86°00'W
Peru, nation, S.A.	142	10°00'S	75°00'W
Peru-Chile Trench, deep	139	25°00'S	71°30'W
Perugia, Italy (pā-rōō'jä)	162	43°08'N	12°24'E
Peruque, Mo., U.S. (pĕ rō'kĕ)	117e	38°52'N	90°36'W
Pervomais'k, Ukr.	181	48°04'N	30°52'E
Pervoural'sk, Russia (pĕr-vô-ò-rálsk')	186a	56°54'N	59°58'E
Pesaro, Italy (pā'zä-rō)	162	43°54'N	12°55'E
Pescado, r., Ven. (pĕs-kä'dō)	143b	9°33'N	65°32'W
Pescara, Italy (pās-kä'rä)	174	42°26'N	14°15'E
Pescara, r., Italy	174	42°18'N	13°22'E
Peschanyy müyisi, c., Kaz.	181	43°10'N	51°20'E
Pescia, Italy (pā'shä)	174	43°53'N	11°42'E
Peshāwar, Pak. (pĕ-shä'w*ŭ*r)	199	34°01'N	71°34'E
Peshtera, Blg.	175	42°03'N	24°19'E
Peshtigo, Wi., U.S. (pĕsh'tĕ-gō)	113	45°03'N	87°46'W
Peshtigo, r., Wi., U.S.	113	45°15'N	88°14'W
Peski, Russia (pyâs'kĭ)	186b	55°13'N	38°48'E
Pêso da Régua, Port. (pā-sò-dä-rā'gwä)	172	41°09'N	7°47'W
Pespire, Hond. (pås-pē'rå)	132	13°35'N	87°20'W
Pesqueria, r., Mex. (pås-kå-rē'*à*)	122	25°55'N	100°25'W
Pessac, Fr.	170	44°48'N	0°38'W
Petacalco, Bahía de, b., Mex. (bä-ē'ä-dĕ-pĕ-tä-käl'kō)	130	17°55'N	102°00'W
Petah Tiqwa, Isr.	197a	32°05'N	34°53'E
Petaluma, Ca., U.S. (pĕt-*à*-lò'm*à*)	118	38°15'N	122°38'W
Petare, Ven. (pĕ-tä'rĕ)	143b	10°28'N	66°48'W
Petatlán, Mex. (pā-tä-tlän')	130	17°31'N	101°17'W
Petawawa, Can.	99	45°54'N	77°17'W
Petén, Laguna de, l., Guat. (lä-gò'nä-dĕ-pā-tān')	132a	17°05'N	89°54'W
Petenwell Reservoir, res., Wi., U.S.	113	44°10'N	89°55'W
Peterborough, Austl.	218	32°53'S	138°58'E
Peterborough, Can. (pē'tẽr-bŭr-ô)	91	44°20'N	78°20'W
Peterborough, Eng., U.K.	164	52°35'N	0°14'W
Peterhead, Scot., U.K. (pē-tẽr-hĕd')	164	57°36'N	3°47'W
Peter Pond Lake, l., Can. (pŏnd)	92	55°55'N	108°44'W
Petersburg, Ak., U.S. (pē'tẽrz-bûrg)	103	56°52'N	133°10'W
Petersburg, Il., U.S.	121	40°01'N	89°51'W
Petersburg, In., U.S.	108	38°30'N	87°15'W
Petersburg, Ky., U.S.	111f	39°04'N	84°52'W
Petersburg, Va., U.S.	105	37°12'N	77°30'W
Petershagen, Ger. (pĕ'tĕrs-hä-gĕn)	159b	52°32'N	13°46'E
Petershausen, Ger. (pĕ'tĕrs-hou-zĕn)	159d	48°25'N	11°29'E
Pétionville, Haiti	135	18°30'N	72°20'W
Petitcodiac, Can. (pē-tē-kō-dyȧk')	100	45°56'N	65°10'W
Petite Terre, i., Guad. (pē-tēt'târ')	133b	16°12'N	61°00'W
Petit Goâve, Haiti (pē-tē' gō-áv')	135	18°25'N	72°50'W
Petit Jean Creek, r., Ar., U.S. (pē-tē'zhäN')	121	35°05'N	93°55'W
Petit Loango, Gabon	236	2°16'S	9°35'E
Petlalcingo, Mex. (pĕ-tläl-sĕŋ'gō)	131	18°05'N	97°53'W
Peto, Mex. (pĕ'tô)	132a	20°07'N	88°49'W
Petorca, Chile (pā-tōr'kȧ)	141b	32°14'S	70°55'W
Petoskey, Mi., U.S. (pē-tŏs-kĭ)	108	45°25'N	84°55'W
Petra, hist., Jord.	197a	30°21'N	35°25'E
Petra Velikogo, Zaliv, b., Russia	210	42°40'N	131°50'E
Petre, Point, c., Can.	99	43°50'N	77°00'W
Petrich, Blg. (pā'trĭch)	163	41°24'N	23°13'E
Petrified Forest National Park, rec., Az., U.S. (pĕt'r*ĭ*-fīd fôr'ĕst)	119	34°58'N	109°35'W
Petrinja, Cro. (pā'trēn-yȧ)	174	45°25'N	16°17'E
Petrodvorets, Russia (pyĕ-trô-dvô-ryĕts')	186c	59°53'N	29°55'E
Petrokrepost', Russia (pyĕ'trô-krĕ-pôst)	180	59°56'N	31°03'E
Petrolia, Can. (pē-trō'lĭ-*à*)	98	42°50'N	82°10'W
Petrolina, Braz. (pĕ-trō-lē'n*à*)	143	9°18'S	40°28'W
Petronell, Aus.	159e	48°07'N	16°52'E
Petropavlivka, Ukr.	177	48°24'N	36°23'E
Petropavlovka, Russia	186a	54°10'N	59°50'E
Petropavlovsk, Kaz.	183	54°44'N	69°07'E
Petropavlovsk-Kamchatskiy, Russia (käm-chät'skĭ)	179	53°13'N	158°56'E
Petrópolis, Braz. (pĕ-trô-pô-lēzh')	143	22°31'S	43°10'W
Petroşani, Rom.	175	45°24'N	23°24'E
Petrovsk, Russia (pyĕ-trôfsk')	181	52°20'N	45°15'E
Petrovskaya, Russia (pyĕ-trôf'skȧ-yȧ)	177	45°25'N	37°50'E
Petrovskoye, Russia	181	45°20'N	43°00'E
Petrovsk-Zabaykal'skiy, Russia (pyĕ-trôfskzä-bī-käl'skĭ)	179	51°13'N	109°08'E
Petrozavodsk, Russia (pyā'trô-zȧ-vôtsk')	178	61°46'N	34°25'E
Petrus Steyn, S. Afr.	238c	27°40'S	28°09'E
Petrykivka, Ukr.	177	48°43'N	34°29'E
Pewaukee, Wi., U.S. (pĭ-wô'kē)	111a	43°05'N	88°15'W
Pewaukee Lake, l., Wi., U.S.	111a	43°03'N	88°18'W
Pewee Valley, Ky., U.S. (pe wē)	111h	38°19'N	85°29'W
Peza, r., Russia (pyâ'zȧ)	180	65°35'N	46°50'E
Pézenas, Fr. (pā-zē-nä')	170	43°26'N	3°24'E
Pforzheim, Ger. (pfôrts'hīm)	161	48°52'N	8°43'E
Phalodi, India	202	27°13'N	72°22'E
Phan Thiet, Viet. (p'hän')	212	11°30'N	108°43'E
Phelps Lake, l., N.C., U.S.	125	35°46'N	76°27'W
Phenix City, Al., U.S. (fē'nĭks)	124	32°29'N	85°00'W
Philadelphia, Ms., U.S. (fĭl-*à*-dĕl'phĭ-*à*)	124	32°45'N	89°07'W
Philadelphia, Pa., U.S.	105	40°00'N	75°13'W
Philip, S.D., U.S. (fĭl'ĭp)	112	44°03'N	101°35'W
Philippeville *see* Skikda, Alg.	230	36°58'N	6°51'E
Philippines, nation, Asia (fĭl'ĭ-pēnz)	213	14°25'N	125°00'E

PLACE (Pronunciation)	PAGE	LAT.	LONG.
Philippine Sea, sea (fĭl'ĭ-pēn)	241	16°00'N	133°00'E
Philippine Trench, deep	213	10°30'N	127°15'E
Philipsburg, Pa., U.S. (fĭl'lĭps-bẽrg)	109	40°55'N	78°10'W
Philipsburg, Wy., U.S.	115	46°19'N	113°19'W
Phillip, i., Austl. (fĭl'ĭp)	222	38°32'S	145°10'E
Phillip Channel, strt., Indon.	197b	1°04'N	103°40'E
Phillipi, W.V., U.S. (fĭ-lĭp'ĭ)	108	39°10'N	80°00'W
Phillips, Wi., U.S. (fĭl'ĭps)	113	45°41'N	90°24'W
Phillipsburg, Ks., U.S. (fĭl'lĭps-bẽrg)	120	39°44'N	99°19'W
Phillipsburg, N.J., U.S.	109	40°45'N	75°10'W
Phitsanulok, Thai.	212	16°51'N	100°15'E
Phnom Penh (Phnum Pénh), Camb. (nŏm'pĕn')	212	11°39'N	104°53'E
Phnum Pénh *see* Phnom Penh, Camb.	212	11°39'N	104°53'E
Phoenix, Az., U.S. (fē'nĭks)	104	33°30'N	112°00'W
Phoenix, Md., U.S.	110e	39°31'N	76°40'W
Phoenix Islands, is., Kir.	2	4°00'S	174°00'W
Phoenixville, Pa., U.S. (fē'nĭks-vĭl)	110f	40°08'N	75°31'W
Phou Bia, mtn., Laos	212	19°36'N	103°00'E
Phra Nakhon Si Ayutthaya, Thai.	212	14°16'N	100°37'E
Phuket, Thai.	212	7°57'N	98°19'E
Phu Quoc, Dao, i., Viet.	212	10°13'N	104°00'E
Pi, r., China (bē)	206	32°06'N	116°31'E
Piacenza, Italy (pyä-chĕnt'sä)	162	45°02'N	9°42'E
Pianosa, i., Italy (pyä-nō'sä)	174	42°13'N	15°45'E
Piave, r., Italy (pyä'vā)	174	45°45'N	12°15'E
Piazza Armerina, Italy (pyät'sä är-må-rē'nä)	174	37°23'N	14°26'E
Pibor, r., Sudan (pē'bôr)	231	7°21'N	32°54'E
Pic, r., Can. (pĕk)	98	48°48'N	86°28'W
Picara Point, c., V.I.U.S. (pē-kä'rä)	129c	18°23'N	64°57'W
Picayune, Ms., U.S. (pĭk'à yōōn)	124	30°32'N	89°41'W
Picher, Ok., U.S. (pĭch'ẽr)	121	36°58'N	94°49'W
Pichilemu, Chile (pē-chē-lĕ'mōō)	141b	34°22'S	72°01'W
Pichucalco, Mex. (pē-chōō-käl'kō)	131	17°34'N	93°06'W
Pickerel, l., Can. (pĭk'ẽr-ĕl)	98	48°35'N	91°10'W
Pickwick Lake, res., U.S. (pĭk'wĭck)	124	35°04'N	88°05'W
Pico, Ca., U.S. (pē'kō)	117a	34°01'N	118°05'W
Pico Island, i., Port. (pē'kō)	230a	38°16'N	28°49'W
Pico Riviera, Ca., U.S.	117a	34°01'N	118°05'W
Picos, Braz. (pē'kōzh)	143	7°13'S	41°23'W
Picton, Austl. (pĭk'tŭn)	217b	34°11'S	150°37'E
Picton, Can.	99	44°00'N	77°15'W
Pictou, Can. (pĭk-tōō')	101	45°41'N	62°43'W
Pidálion, Akrotírion, c., Cyp.	197a	34°50'N	34°05'E
Pidurutalagala, mtn., Sri L. (pē'dò-rò-tä'lá-gä'lȧ)	203	7°00'N	80°46'E
Pidvolochys'k, Ukr.	177	49°32'N	26°16'E
Pie, i., Can. (pī)	98	48°10'N	89°07'W
Piedade, Braz. (pyā-dä'dĕ)	141a	23°42'S	47°25'W
Piedmont, Al., U.S. (pēd'mŏnt)	124	33°54'N	85°36'W
Piedmont, Ca., U.S.	116b	37°50'N	122°14'W
Piedmont, Mo., U.S.	121	37°09'N	90°42'W
Piedmont, S.C., U.S.	125	34°40'N	82°27'W
Piedmont, W.V., U.S.	109	39°30'N	79°05'W
Piedrabuena, Spain (pyā-drä-bwā'nä)	172	39°01'N	4°10'W
Piedras, Punta, c., Arg. (pōō'n-tä-pyĕ'dräs)	141c	35°25'S	57°10'W
Piedras Negras, Mex. (pyā'dräs nā'gräs)	128	28°41'N	100°33'W
Pieksämäki, Fin. (pyĕk'sĕ-mĕ-kē)	167	62°18'N	27°14'E
Piemonte, hist. reg., Italy (pyĕ-mô'n-tĕ)	174	44°30'N	7°42'E
Pienaars, r., S. Afr.	238c	25°13'S	28°05'E
Pienaarsrivier, S. Afr.	238c	25°12'S	28°18'E
Pierce, Ne., U.S. (pērs)	112	42°11'N	97°33'W
Pierce, W.V., U.S.	109	39°15'N	79°30'W
Piermont, N.Y., U.S. (pēr'mŏnt)	110a	41°03'N	73°55'W
Pierre, S.D., U.S. (pēr)	104	44°22'N	100°20'W
Pierrefonds, Can.	102a	45°29'N	73°52'W
Piešt'any, Slvk.	169	48°36'N	17°48'E
Pietermaritzburg, S. Afr. (pē-tẽr-må-rĭts-bûrg)	232	29°36'S	30°23'E
Pietersburg, S. Afr. (pē'tẽrz-bûrg)	232	23°56'S	29°30'E
Piet Retief, S. Afr. (pēt rĕ-tēf')	232	27°00'S	30°58'E
Pietrosu, Vârful, mtn., Rom.	169	47°35'N	24°49'E
Pieve di Cadore, Italy (pyā'vā dē kä-dō'rā)	162	46°26'N	12°22'E
Pigeon, r., N.A. (pĭj'*ŭ*n)	113	48°05'N	90°13'W
Pigeon Lake, Can.	102f	49°57'N	97°36'W
Pigeon Lake, l., Can.	95	53°00'N	114°00'W
Piggott, Ar., U.S. (pĭg-ŭt)	121	36°22'N	90°10'W
Pijijiapan, Mex. (pēkē-kē-ä'pän)	131	15°40'N	93°12'W
Pijnacker, Neth.	159a	52°01'N	4°25'E
Pikes Peak, mtn., Co., U.S. (pīks)	106	38°49'N	105°03'W
Pikeville, Ky., U.S. (pĭk'vĭl)	108	37°28'N	82°31'W
Pikou, China (pē-kō)	208	39°25'N	122°19'E
Pikwitonei, Can. (pĭk'w*ĭ*-tŏn)	97	55°35'N	97°09'W
Piła, Pol. (pē'lȧ)	168	53°09'N	16°44'E
Pilansberg, mtn., S. Afr. (pē'*ă*ns'bûrg)	238c	25°08'S	26°55'E
Pilar, Arg. (pē'lär)	141c	34°27'S	58°55'W
Pilar, Para.	144	27°00'S	58°15'W
Pilar de Goiás, Braz. (dĕ-gô-yà's)	143	14°47'S	49°33'W
Pilchuck, r., Wa., U.S.	116a	48°03'N	121°58'W
Pilchuck Creek, r., Wa., U.S. (pĭl'chŭck)	116a	48°19'N	122°11'W
Pilchuck Mountain, mtn., Wa., U.S.	116a	48°03'N	121°48'W
Pilcomayo, r., S.A. (pēl-cō-mī'ō)	144	24°45'S	59°15'W
Pili, Phil. (pē'lē)	213a	13°34'N	123°17'E
Pilica, r., Pol. (pē-lēt'sä)	169	51°00'N	19°48'E
Pillar Point, c., Wa., U.S. (pĭl'*ă*r)	116a	48°14'N	124°06'W
Pillar Rocks, Wa., U.S.	116c	46°16'N	123°35'W

ăt; fĭnặl; rāte; senâte; ärm; àsk; sofà; fâre;   ch-choose;   dh-as th in other;   bē; ĕvent; bĕt; recĕnt; cratēr;   g-gō; gh-guttural g;   bĭt; ĭ-short neutral; rīde;   ᴋ-guttural k as ch in German ich;

PRONOUNCING INDEX

Poltava – Pratas Island 337

PLACE (Pronunciation)	PAGE	LAT.	LONG.
Poltava, Ukr. (pôl-tä'vä)	178	49°35'N	34°33'E
Poltava, prov., Ukr.	177	49°53'N	32°58'E
Põltsamaa, Est. (pŏlt'sȧ-mä)	167	58°39'N	26°00'E
Polunochnoye, Russia (pô-lo͞o-nô'ch-nô'yĕ)	186a	60°52'N	60°27'E
Poluy, r., Russia (pôl'wē)	184	65°45'N	68°15'E
Polyakovka, Russia (pŭl-yä'kôv-kȧ)	186a	54°38'N	59°42'E
Polyarnyy, Russia (pŭl-yär'nē)	178	69°10'N	33°30'E
Polygyros, Grc.	175	40°23'N	23°27'E
Polynesia, is., Oc.	240	4°00'S	156°00'W
Pomba, r., Braz. (pô'm-bȧ)	141a	21°28'S	42°28'W
Pomerania, hist. reg., Pol. (pŏm-ĕ-rā'nĭ-ȧ)	168	53°50'N	15°20'E
Pomeroy, S. Afr. (pŏm'ẽr-roi)	233c	28°36'S	30°26'E
Pomeroy, Wa., U.S. (pŏm'ẽr-oi)	114	46°28'N	117°35'W
Pomezia, Italy (pô-mĕ't-zyä)	173d	41°41'N	12°31'E
Pomigliano d'Arco, Italy (pô-mē-lyȧ'nô-d-ä'r-kô)	173c	40°39'N	14°23'E
Pomme de Terre, Mn., U.S. (pôm dē tĕr')	112	45°22'N	95°52'W
Pomona, Ca., U.S. (pô-mō'nȧ)	104	34°04'N	117°45'W
Pomorie, Blg.	163	42°24'N	27°41'E
Pompano Beach, Fl., U.S. (pŏm'pă-nô)	125a	26°12'N	80°07'W
Pompeii Ruins, hist., Italy	173c	40°31'N	14°29'E
Pompton Lakes, N.J., U.S. (pŏmp'tŏn)	110a	41°01'N	74°16'W
Pomuch, Mex. (pô-mo͞o'ch)	132a	20°12'N	90°10'W
Ponca, Ne., U.S. (pŏn'kȧ)	112	42°34'N	96°43'W
Ponca City, Ok., U.S.	121	36°42'N	97°07'W
Ponce, P.R. (pōn'sā)	129	18°01'N	66°43'W
Pondicherry, India	199	11°58'N	79°48'E
Pondicherry, state, India	199	11°50'N	74°50'E
Ponferrada, Spain (pôn-fĕr-rä'dhä)	162	42°33'N	6°38'W
Ponoka, Can. (pŏ-nō'kȧ)	90	52°42'N	113°35'W
Ponoy, Russia	180	66°58'N	41°00'E
Ponoy, r., Russia	180	67°00'N	39°00'E
Ponta Delgada, Port. (pôn'tȧ dĕl-gä'dȧ)	230a	37°40'N	25°45'W
Ponta Grossa, Braz. (grō'sȧ)	143	25°09'S	50°05'W
Pont-à-Mousson, Fr. (pôn'tȧ-mo͞o-sôn')	171	48°55'N	6°02'E
Pontarlier, Fr. (pôn'tȧr-lyā')	171	46°53'N	6°22'E
Pont-Audemer, Fr. (pôn'tōd'mâr')	170	49°23'N	0°28'E
Pontchartrain Lake, l., La., U.S. (pôn-shȧr-trăn')	123	30°10'N	90°10'W
Ponteareas, Spain	172	42°09'N	8°23'W
Pontedera, Italy (pōn-tā-dā'rä)	174	43°37'N	10°37'E
Ponte de Sor, Port.	172	39°14'N	8°03'W
Pontefract, Eng., U.K. (pŏn'tē-frăkt)	158a	53°41'N	1°18'W
Ponte Nova, Braz. (pô'n-tĕ-nô'vȧ)	143	20°26'S	42°52'W
Pontevedra, Spain (pôn-tĕ-vĕ-drä)	162	42°28'N	8°38'W
Ponthierville *see* Ubundi, D.R.C.	232	0°21'S	25°29'E
Pontiac, Il., U.S. (pŏn'tĭ-ăk)	108	40°55'N	88°35'W
Pontiac, Mi., U.S.	105	42°37'N	83°17'W
Pontianak, Indon. (pôn-tē-ä'nȧk)	212	0°04'S	109°20'E
Pontian Kechil, Malay.	197b	1°29'N	103°24'E
Pontic Mountains, mts., Tur.	181	41°20'N	34°30'E
Pontivy, Fr. (pôn-tē-vē')	170	48°05'N	2°57'W
Pontoise, Fr. (pôn-twȧz')	170	49°03'N	2°05'E
Pontonnyy, Russia (pôn'tôn-nyĭ)	186c	59°47'N	30°39'E
Pontotoc, Ms., U.S. (pŏn-tô-tŏk')	124	34°11'N	88°59'W
Pontremoli, Italy (pôn-trĕm'ô-lē)	174	44°21'N	9°50'E
Ponziane, Isole, i., Italy (ē'sō-lĕ)	162	40°55'N	12°58'E
Poole, Eng., U.K. (po͞ol)	164	50°43'N	2°00'W
Poolesville, Md., U.S. (po͞olĕs-vĭl)	110e	39°08'N	77°26'W
Pooley Island, i., Can. (po͞o'lē)	94	52°44'N	128°16'W
Poopó, Lago de, l., Bol.	142	18°45'S	67°07'W
Popayán, Col. (pō-pä-yän')	142	2°21'N	76°43'W
Poplar, Mt., U.S. (pŏp'lẽr)	115	48°08'N	105°10'W
Poplar, r., Mt., U.S.	115	48°34'N	105°20'W
Poplar, West Fork, r., Mt., U.S.	115	48°59'N	106°06'W
Poplar Bluff, Mo., U.S. (blŭf)	121	36°43'N	90°22'W
Poplar Plains, Ky., U.S. (plāns)	108	38°20'N	83°40'W
Poplar Point, Can.	102f	50°04'N	97°57'W
Poplarville, Ms., U.S. (pŏp'lẽr-vĭl)	124	30°50'N	89°33'W
Popocatépetl Volcán, Mex. (pô-pô-kä-tā'pĕ't'l)	128	19°01'N	98°38'W
Popokabaka, D.R.C. (pō'pô-kȧ-bä'kȧ)	232	5°42'S	16°35'E
Popovo, Blg. (pô'pô-vō)	175	43°23'N	26°17'E
Porbandar, India (pōr-bŭn'dŭr)	199	21°44'N	69°40'E
Porce, r., Col. (pôr-sĕ)	142a	7°11'N	74°55'W
Porcher Island, i., Can. (pôr'kẽr)	94	53°57'N	130°30'W
Porcuna, Spain (pôr-ko͞o'nä)	172	37°54'N	4°10'W
Porcupine, r., N.A.	103	67°38'N	140°07'W
Porcupine Creek, r., Mt., U.S.	115	48°27'N	106°24'W
Porcupine Hills, hills, Can.	97	52°30'N	101°45'W
Pordenone, Italy (pōr-dȧ-nō'nȧ)	174	45°58'N	12°38'E
Pori, Fin. (pô'rē)	160	61°29'N	21°45'E
Poriúncula, Braz.	141a	20°58'S	42°02'W
Porkhov, Russia (pôr'kôf)	180	57°46'N	29°33'E
Porlamar, Ven. (pôr-lä-mär')	142	11°00'N	63°55'W
Pornic, Fr. (pôr-nēk')	170	47°08'N	2°07'W
Poronaysk, Russia (pô'rô-nīsk)	179	49°21'N	143°23'E
Porrentruy, Switz. (pô-rän-trüē')	168	47°25'N	7°02'E
Porsgrunn, Nor. (pôrs'grōn')	166	59°09'N	9°36'E
Portachuelo, Bol. (pôrt-ä-chwā'lô)	142	17°20'S	63°12'W
Portage, Pa., U.S. (pôr'tāj)	109	40°25'N	78°35'W
Portage, Wi., U.S.	113	43°33'N	89°29'W
Portage Des Sioux, Mo., U.S. (dē so͞o)	117e	38°56'N	90°21'W
Portage la Prairie, Can. (lä-prā'rĭ)	90	49°57'N	98°25'W
Port Alberni, Can. (pōr äl-bĕr-nē')	90	49°14'N	124°48'W
Portalegre, Port. (pôr-tä-lā'grĕ)	162	39°18'N	7°26'W
Portales, N.M., U.S. (pôr-tä'lĕs)	120	34°10'N	103°11'W
Port Alfred, S. Afr.	232	33°36'S	26°55'E
Port Alice, Can. (ăl'ĭs)	90	50°23'N	127°27'W
Port Allegany, Pa., U.S. (ăl-ē-gā'nĭ)	109	41°50'N	78°10'W
Port Angeles, Wa., U.S. (ăn'jē-lĕs)	104	48°07'N	123°26'W
Port Antonio, Jam.	129	18°10'N	76°25'W
Portarlington, Austl.	217a	38°07'S	144°39'E
Port Arthur, Tx., U.S.	105	29°52'N	93°59'W
Port Augusta, Austl. (ô-gŭs'tă)	222	32°28'S	137°50'E
Port au Port Bay, b., Can. (pôr'tō pōr')	101	48°41'N	58°45'W
Port-au-Prince, Haiti (prăns')	129	18°35'N	72°20'W
Port Austin, Mi., U.S. (ôs'tĭn)	108	44°00'N	83°00'W
Port Blair, India (blâr)	212	12°07'N	92°45'E
Port Bolivar, Tx., U.S. (bŏl'ĭ-vȧr)	123a	29°22'N	94°46'W
Port Borden, Can. (bôr'dĕn)	100	46°15'N	63°42'W
Port-Bouët, C. Iv.	230	5°24'N	3°56'W
Port-Cartier, Can.	100	50°01'N	66°53'W
Port Chester, N.Y., U.S. (chĕs'tẽr)	110a	40°59'N	73°40'W
Port Chicago, Ca., U.S. (shĭ-kô'gō)	116b	38°03'N	122°01'W
Port Clinton, Oh., U.S. (klĭn'tŭn)	108	41°30'N	83°00'W
Port Colborne, Can.	99	42°53'N	79°13'W
Port Coquitlam, Can. (kô-kwĭt'lȧm)	95	49°10'N	122°46'W
Port Credit, Can. (krĕd'ĭt)	102d	43°33'N	79°35'W
Port-de-Bouc, Fr. (pôr-dē-bo͞ok')	170a	43°24'N	5°00'E
Port de Paix, Haiti (pĕ)	135	19°55'N	72°50'W
Port Dickson, Malay. (dĭk'sŭn)	197b	2°33'N	101°49'E
Port Discovery, b., Wa., U.S. (dĭs-kŭv'ẽr-ĭ)	116a	48°05'N	122°55'W
Port Edward, S. Afr. (ĕd'wẽrd)	233c	31°04'S	30°14'E
Port Elgin, Can. (ĕl'jĭn)	100	46°03'N	64°05'W
Port Elizabeth, S. Afr. (ē-lĭz'ȧ-bĕth)	232	33°57'S	25°37'E
Porterdale, Ga., U.S. (pōr'tẽr-dāl)	124	33°34'N	83°53'W
Porterville, Ca., U.S. (pōr'tẽr-vĭl)	118	36°03'N	119°05'W
Port Francqui *see* Ilebo, D.R.C.	232	4°19'S	20°35'E
Port Gamble, Wa., U.S. (găm'bŭl)	116a	47°52'N	122°36'W
Port Gamble Indian Reservation, I.R., Wa., U.S.	116a	47°54'N	122°33'W
Port-Gentil, Gabon (zhän-tē')	232	0°43'S	8°47'E
Port Gibson, Ms., U.S.	124	31°56'N	90°57'W
Port Harcourt, Nig. (här'kŭrt)	230	4°43'N	7°05'E
Port Hardy, Can. (här'dĭ)	94	50°43'N	127°29'W
Port Hawkesbury, Can.	101	45°37'N	61°21'W
Port Hedland, Austl. (hĕd'lănd)	218	20°30'S	118°30'E
Porthill, Id., U.S.	114	49°00'N	116°30'W
Port Hood, Can. (ho͝od)	101	46°01'N	61°32'W
Port Hope, Can. (hōp)	99	43°55'N	78°10'W
Port Huron, Mi., U.S. (hū'rŏn)	105	43°00'N	82°30'W
Portici, Italy (pôr'tē-chē)	173c	40°34'N	14°20'E
Portillo, Chile (pôr-tē'l-yô)	141b	32°51'S	70°09'W
Portimão, Port. (pôr-tē-moun)	172	37°09'N	8°34'W
Port Jervis, N.Y., U.S. (jûr'vĭs)	110a	41°22'N	74°41'W
Portland, Austl. (pōrt'lănd)	219	38°20'S	142°40'E
Portland, In., U.S.	108	40°25'N	85°00'W
Portland, Me., U.S.	105	43°40'N	70°16'W
Portland, Mi., U.S.	108	42°50'N	85°00'W
Portland, Or., U.S.	104	45°31'N	122°41'W
Portland, Tx., U.S.	123	27°53'N	97°20'W
Portland Bight, b., Jam.	134	17°45'N	77°05'W
Portland Canal, can., Ak., U.S.	94	55°10'N	130°08'W
Portland Inlet, b., Can.	94	54°50'N	130°15'W
Portland Point, c., Jam.	134	17°40'N	77°20'W
Port Lavaca, Tx., U.S. (lȧ-vä'kȧ)	123	28°36'N	96°38'W
Port Lincoln, Austl. (lĭŋ-kŭn)	218	34°39'S	135°50'E
Port Ludlow, Wa., U.S. (lŭd'lō)	116a	47°26'N	122°41'W
Port Macquarie, Austl. (mȧ-kwŏ'rĭ)	219	31°25'S	152°45'E
Port Madison Indian Reservation, I.R., Wa., U.S. (măd'ĭ-sŭn)	116a	47°46'N	122°38'W
Port Maria, Jam. (mȧ-rī'ȧ)	134	18°20'N	76°55'W
Port Moody, Can. (mo͞od'ĭ)	95	49°17'N	122°51'W
Port Moresby, Pap. N. Gui. (mōrz'bē)	213	9°34'S	147°20'E
Port Neches, Tx., U.S. (nĕch'ĕz)	123	29°59'N	93°57'W
Port Nelson, Can. (nĕl'sŭn)	97	57°03'N	92°36'W
Portneuf-Sur-Mer, Can. (pôr-nûf'sür mẽr)	100	48°36'N	69°06'W
Port Nolloth, S. Afr. (nŏl'ŏth)	232	29°10'S	17°00'E
Porto (Oporto), Port. (pôr'tô)	154	41°10'N	8°38'W
Porto Acre, Braz. (ä'krĕ)	142	9°38'S	67°34'W
Porto Alegre, Braz. (ä-lā'grĕ)	144	29°58'S	51°11'W
Porto Amboim, Ang.	232	11°01'S	13°45'E
Portobelo, Pan. (pôr'tô-bā'lô)	129	9°32'N	79°40'W
Pôrto de Pedras, Braz. (pā'dräzh)	143	9°09'S	35°20'W
Pôrto Feliz, Braz. (fĕ-lē's)	141a	23°12'S	47°30'W
Portoferraio, Italy (pōr'tô-fĕr-rä'yō)	174	42°47'N	10°20'E
Port of Spain, Trin. (spān)	143	10°44'N	61°24'W
Portogruaro, Italy (pōr'tô-grō-ä'rō)	174	45°48'N	12°49'E
Portola, Ca., U.S. (pôr'tō-lȧ)	118	39°47'N	120°29'W
Porto Mendes, Braz. (mĕ'n-dĕs)	143	24°41'S	54°13'W
Porto Murtinho, Braz. (mòr-tēn'yō)	143	21°43'S	57°43'W
Porto Nacional, Braz. (nȧ-syō-näl')	143	10°43'S	48°14'W
Porto Novo, Benin (pōr'tô-nō'vō)	230	6°29'N	2°37'E
Port Orchard, Wa., U.S. (ôr'chẽrd)	116a	47°32'N	122°38'W
Port Orchard, b., Wa., U.S.	116a	47°40'N	122°39'W
Porto Santo, Ilha de, i., Port. (sän'tô)	230	32°41'N	16°15'W
Porto Seguro, Braz. (sā-go͞o'rō)	143	16°26'S	38°59'W
Porto Torres, Italy (tôr'rĕs)	174	40°49'N	8°25'E
Porto-Vecchio, Fr. (vĕk'ē-ô)	174	41°36'N	9°17'E
Porto Velho, Braz. (vāl'yō)	142	8°45'S	63°43'W
Portoviejo, Ec. (pôr-tô-vyā'hō)	142	1°11'S	80°28'W
Port Phillip Bay, b., Austl. (fĭl'ĭp)	221	37°57'S	144°50'E
Port Pirie, Austl. (pĭ'rē)	218	33°10'S	138°00'E
Port Royal, b., Jam. (roi'ăl)	134	17°50'N	76°45'W
Port Said, Egypt	238d	31°15'N	32°19'E
Port Saint Johns, S. Afr. (sânt jŏnz)	232	31°37'S	29°32'E
Port Saint Lucie, Fl., U.S.	125a	27°20'N	80°20'W
Port Shepstone, S. Afr. (shĕps'tŭn)	232	30°45'S	30°23'E
Portsmouth, Dom.	133b	15°33'N	61°28'W
Portsmouth, Eng., U.K. (pôrts'mŭth)	154	50°45'N	1°03'W
Portsmouth, N.H., U.S.	105	43°05'N	70°50'W
Portsmouth, Oh., U.S.	105	38°45'N	83°00'W
Portsmouth, Va., U.S.	105	36°50'N	76°19'W
Port Sulphur, La., U.S. (sŭl'fẽr)	124	29°28'N	89°41'W
Port Susan, b., Wa., U.S. (sū-zán')	116a	48°11'N	122°25'W
Port Townsend, Wa., U.S. (tounz'ĕnd)	116a	48°07'N	122°46'W
Port Townsend, b., Wa., U.S.	116a	48°05'N	122°47'W
Portugal, nation, Eur. (pōr'tu-găl)	154	38°15'N	8°08'W
Portugalete, Spain (pōr-to͞o-gä-lā'tā)	172	43°18'N	3°05'W
Portuguese West Africa *see* Angola, nation, Ang.	232	14°15'S	16°00'E
Port Vendres, Fr.	170	42°32'N	3°07'E
Port Vila, Vanuatu	219	17°44'S	168°19'E
Port Wakefield, Austl. (wāk'fēld)	218	34°12'S	138°10'E
Port Washington, N.Y., U.S. (wôsh'ĭng-tŭn)	110a	40°49'N	73°42'W
Port Washington, Wi., U.S.	113	43°24'N	87°52'W
Posadas, Arg. (pō-sä'dhäs)	144	27°32'S	55°56'W
Posadas, Spain (pô-sä-däs)	172	37°48'N	5°09'W
Poshekhon'ye Volodarsk, Russia (pô-shyĕ'kŏn-yĕ vôl'ô-dȧrsk)	176	58°31'N	39°07'E
Poso, Danau, l., Indon. (pō'sō)	212	2°00'S	119°40'E
Pospelokova, Russia (pôs-pyĕl'kô-vȧ)	186a	59°25'N	60°50'E
Possession Sound, strt., Wa., U.S. (pŏ-zĕsh-ŭn)	116a	47°59'N	122°17'W
Possum Kingdom Reservoir, res., Tx., U.S. (pŏs'ŭm kĭng'dŭm)	122	32°58'N	98°12'W
Post, Tx., U.S. (pōst)	120	33°12'N	101°21'W
Postojna, Slvn. (pōs-tôyná)	174	45°45'N	14°13'E
Pos'yet, Russia (pos-yĕt')	210	42°27'N	130°47'E
Potawatomi Indian Reservation, I.R., Ks., U.S. (pŏt-å-wä'tō mē)	121	39°30'N	96°11'W
Potchefstroom, S. Afr. (pŏch'ĕf-strōm)	232	26°42'S	27°06'E
Poteau, Ok., U.S. (pô-tō')	121	35°03'N	94°37'W
Poteet, Tx., U.S. (pô-tēt)	122	29°05'N	98°35'W
Potenza, Italy (pô-tĕnt'sä)	163	40°39'N	15°49'E
Potenza, r., Italy	174	43°09'N	13°00'E
Potgietersrus, S. Afr. (pôt-kē'tẽrs-rûs)	232	24°09'S	29°04'E
Potholes Reservoir, res., Wa., U.S.	114	47°00'N	119°20'W
Poti, Geor. (pô'tē)	181	42°10'N	41°40'E
Potiskum, Nig.	230	11°43'N	11°05'E
Potomac, Md., U.S. (pô-tō'măk)	110e	39°01'N	77°13'W
Potomac, r., U.S. (pô-tō'măk)	107	38°15'N	76°55'W
Potosí, Bol.	142	19°35'S	65°45'W
Potosi, Mo., U.S. (pŏ-tō'sĭ)	121	37°56'N	90°46'W
Potosi, r., Mex. (pō-tô-sē')	122	25°04'N	99°36'W
Potrerillos, Hond. (pō-trā-rēl'yôs)	132	15°13'N	87°58'W
Potsdam, Ger. (pôts'däm)	161	52°24'N	13°04'E
Potsdam, N.Y., U.S. (pŏts'dăm)	109	44°40'N	75°00'W
Pottenstein, Aus.	159e	47°58'N	16°06'E
Potters Bar, Eng., U.K. (pŏt'ẽz bär)	158b	51°41'N	0°12'W
Pottstown, Pa., U.S. (pŏts'toun)	109	40°15'N	75°40'W
Pottsville, Pa., U.S. (pôts'vĭl)	109	40°40'N	76°15'W
Poughkeepsie, N.Y., U.S. (pŏ-kĭp'sē)	105	41°45'N	73°55'W
Poulsbo, Wa., U.S. (pōlz'bō)	116a	47°44'N	122°38'W
Poulton-le-Fylde, Eng., U.K. (pōl'tŭn-lē-fīld')	158a	53°52'N	2°59'W
Pouso Alegre, Braz. (pō'zō ä-lā'grĕ)	143	22°13'S	45°56'W
Póvoa de Varzim, Port. (pō-vō'ȧ dā vär'zēn)	162	41°23'N	8°44'W
Powder, r., Or., U.S.	114	44°55'N	117°35'W
Powder, r., U.S. (pou'dẽr)	106	45°18'N	105°37'W
Powder, South Fork, r., Wy., U.S.	115	43°13'N	106°54'W
Powder River, Wy., U.S.	115	43°06'N	106°55'W
Powell, Wy., U.S. (pou'ĕl)	115	44°44'N	108°44'W
Powell, Lake, res., U.S.	106	37°26'N	110°25'W
Powell Lake, l., Can.	94	50°10'N	124°13'W
Powell Point, c., Bah.	134	24°50'N	76°20'W
Powell Reservoir, res., Ky., U.S.	124	36°30'N	83°35'W
Powell River, Can.	90	49°52'N	124°33'W
Poyang Hu, l., China	205	29°20'N	116°28'E
Poygan, r., Wi., U.S. (poi'găn)	113	44°10'N	89°05'W
Požarevac, Serb. (pô'zhȧ'rĕ-vȧts)	175	44°38'N	21°12'E
Poza Rica, Mex. (pô-zô-rē'kä)	131	20°32'N	97°25'W
Poznań, Pol.	154	52°25'N	16°55'E
Pozoblanco, Spain (pô-thō-bläŋ'kō)	172	38°23'N	4°50'W
Pozos, Mex. (pō'zōs)	130	22°05'N	100°50'W
Pozuelo de Alarcón, Spain (pô-thwā'lō dā ä-lär-kōn')	173a	40°27'N	3°49'W
Pozzuoli, Italy (pôt-swô'lē)	174	40°34'N	14°08'E
Pra, r., Ghana (prȧ)	234	5°45'N	1°35'W
Pra, r., Russia	176	55°00'N	40°13'E
Prachin Buri, Thai. (prä'chēn)	212	13°59'N	101°15'E
Pradera, Col. (prä-dĕ'rä)	142a	3°24'N	76°13'W
Prades, Fr. (prȧd)	170	42°37'N	2°23'E
Prado, Col. (prädô)	142a	3°44'N	74°55'W
Prado Reservoir, res., Ca., U.S. (prä'dō)	117a	33°45'N	117°40'W
Prados, Braz. (prá'dôs)	141a	21°05'S	44°04'W
Prague, Czech Rep.	168	50°05'N	14°26'E
Praha *see* Prague, Czech Rep.	154	50°05'N	14°26'E
Praia, C.V. (prä'yȧ)	230b	15°00'N	23°30'W
Praia Funda, Ponta da, c., Braz. (pôn'tä-dȧ-prä'yȧ-fo͞o'n-dä)	144b	23°04'S	43°34'W
Prairie du Chien, Wi., U.S. (prā'rĭ do͞o shēn')	113	43°02'N	91°10'W
Prairie Grove, Can. (prā'rĭ grōv)	102f	49°48'N	96°57'W
Prairie Island Indian Reservation, I.R., Mn., U.S.	113	44°42'N	92°32'W
Prairies, Rivière des, r., Can. (rē-vyâr' dā prâ-rē')	102a	45°40'N	73°34'W
Pratas Island, i., Asia	209	20°40'N	116°30'E

ng-sing; ŋ-baŋk; ɴ-nasalized n; nŏd; cŏmmit; ōld; ôbey; ôrder; oi-boil; fo͞od; ŏ-as oo in foot; ou-out; s-soft; sh-dish; th-thin; pūre; ûnite; ûrn; stŭd; circŭs; ü-as in French tu; '-indeterminate vowel.

338 Prato – Purkersdorf PRONOUNCING INDEX

PLACE (Pronunciation)	PAGE	LAT.	LONG.
Prato, Italy (prä'tō)	174	43°53'N	11°03'E
Pratt, Ks., U.S. (prăt)	120	37°37'N	98°43'W
Prattville, Al., U.S. (prăt'vĭl)	124	32°28'N	86°27'W
Pravdinsk, Russia	167	54°26'N	21°00'E
Pravdinskiy, Russia (práv-dĕn'skĭ)	186b	56°03'N	37°52'E
Pravia, Spain (prä'vē-ä)	172	43°30'N	6°08'W
Pregolya, r., Russia (prĕ-gô'lă)	167	54°37'N	20°50'E
Premont, Tx., U.S. (prē-mŏnt')	122	27°20'N	98°07'W
Prenzlau, Ger. (prĕnts'lou)	168	53°19'N	13°52'E
Přerov, Czech Rep. (przhĕ'rôf)	161	49°28'N	17°28'E
Prescot, Eng., U.K. (prĕs'kŭt)	158a	53°25'N	2°48'W
Prescott, Can. (prĕs'kŭt)	109	44°45'N	75°35'W
Prescott, Ar., U.S.	121	33°47'N	93°23'W
Prescott, Az., U.S. (prĕs'kŏt)	104	34°30'N	112°30'W
Prescott, Wi., U.S. (prĕs'kŏt)	117g	44°45'N	92°48'W
Presho, S.D., U.S. (prĕsh'ō)	113	43°50'N	100°04'W
Presidencia Roque Sáenz Peña, Arg.	144	26°52'S	60°15'W
Presidente Epitácio, Braz. (prā-sē-dĕn'tĕ å-pē-tä'syō)	143	21°56'S	52°01'W
Presidio, Tx., U.S. (prĕ-sĭ'dĭ-ō)	122	29°33'N	104°23'W
Presidio, Río del, r., Mex. (rē'ō-dĕl-prĕ-sē'dyô)	130	23°54'N	105°44'W
Prešov, Slvk. (prĕ'shôf)	161	49°00'N	21°18'E
Prespa, Lake, l., Eur. (prĕs'pä)	175	40°49'N	20°50'E
Prespuntal, r., Ven.	143b	9°55'N	64°32'W
Presque Isle, Me., U.S. (prĕsk'ēl')	100	46°41'N	68°03'W
Pressbaum, Aus.	159e	48°12'N	16°06'E
Prestea, Ghana	234	5°27'N	2°08'W
Preston, Austl.	217a	37°45'S	145°01'E
Preston, Eng., U.K. (prĕs'tŭn)	164	53°46'N	2°42'W
Preston, Id., U.S. (pres'tŭn)	115	42°05'N	111°54'W
Preston, Mn., U.S. (prĕs'tŭn)	113	43°42'N	92°06'W
Preston, Wa., U.S.	116a	47°31'N	121°56'W
Prestonburg, Ky., U.S. (prĕs'tŭn-bûrg)	108	37°35'N	82°50'W
Prestwich, Eng., U.K. (prĕst'wĭch)	158a	53°32'N	2°17'W
Pretoria, S. Afr. (prē-tō'rĭ-ȧ)	232	25°43'S	28°16'E
Pretoria North, S. Afr. (prĕ-tô'rĭ-ȧ no͞ord)	238c	25°41'S	28°11'E
Préveza, Grc. (prĕ'vå-zä)	175	38°58'N	20°44'E
Pribilof Islands, is., Ak., U.S. (prĭ'bĭ-lof)	103	57°00'N	169°20'W
Priboj, Serb. (prē'boi)	175	43°33'N	19°33'E
Price, Ut., U.S. (prīs)	119	39°35'N	110°50'W
Price, r., Ut., U.S.	119	39°21'N	110°35'W
Prichard, Al., U.S. (prĭt'chård)	124	30°44'N	88°04'W
Priddis, Can. (prĭd'dĭs)	102e	50°53'N	114°20'W
Priddis Creek, r., Can.	102e	50°56'N	114°32'W
Priego, Spain (prē-ā'gō)	172	37°27'N	4°13'W
Prienai, Lith. (prē-ĕn'ī)	167	54°38'N	23°56'E
Prieska, S. Afr. (prē-ĕs'kȧ)	232	29°40'S	22°50'E
Priest Lake, l., Id., U.S. (prēst)	114	48°30'N	116°43'W
Priest Rapids Dam, Wa., U.S.	114	46°39'N	119°55'W
Priest Rapids Lake, res., Wa., U.S.	114	46°42'N	119°58'W
Priiskovaya, Russia (prĭ-ēs'kô-vá-yá)	186a	60°50'N	58°55'E
Prijedor, Bos. (prē'yĕ-dôr)	174	44°58'N	16°43'E
Prijepolje, Serb. (prē'yĕ-pô'lyĕ)	175	43°22'N	19°41'E
Prilep, Mac. (prē'lĕp)	163	41°20'N	21°35'E
Primorsk, Russia (prē-môrsk')	167	60°24'N	28°35'E
Primorsko-Akhtarskaya, Russia (prē-môr'skô äĸ-tär'skĭ-ē)	181	46°03'N	38°09'E
Primrose, S. Afr.	233b	26°11'S	28°11'E
Primrose Lake, l., Can.	96	54°55'N	109°45'W
Prince Albert, Can. (prĭns ăl'bẽrt)	90	53°12'N	105°46'W
Prince Albert National Park, rec., Can.	92	54°10'N	105°25'W
Prince Albert Sound, strt., Can.	92	70°23'N	116°57'W
Prince Charles Island, i., Can. (chärlz)	93	67°41'N	74°10'W
Prince Edward Island, prov., Can.	91	46°45'N	63°10'W
Prince Edward Islands, is., S. Afr.	224	46°36'S	37°57'E
Prince Edward National Park, rec., Can. (ĕd'wẽrd)	93	46°33'N	63°35'W
Prince Edward Peninsula, pen., Can.	109	44°00'N	77°15'W
Prince Frederick, Md., U.S. (prĭnce frĕdẽrĭk)	110e	38°33'N	76°35'W
Prince George, Can. (jôrj)	90	53°51'N	122°57'W
Prince of Wales, i., Austl.	221	10°47'S	142°15'E
Prince of Wales, i., Ak., U.S.	103	55°47'N	132°50'W
Prince of Wales, Cape, c., Ak., U.S. (wālz)	103	65°48'N	169°08'W
Prince Rupert, Can. (roo'pẽrt)	90	54°19'N	130°19'W
Princes Risborough, Eng., U.K. (prīns'ĕz rĭz'brŭ)	158b	51°41'N	0°51'W
Princess Charlotte Bay, b., Austl. (shär'lŏt)	221	13°45'S	144°15'E
Princess Royal Channel, strt., Can. (roi'ăl)	94	53°10'N	128°37'W
Princess Royal Island, i., Can.	94	52°57'N	128°49'W
Princeton, Can. (prĭns'tŭn)	90	49°27'N	120°31'W
Princeton, Il., U.S.	108	41°20'N	89°25'W
Princeton, In., U.S.	108	38°20'N	87°35'W
Princeton, Ky., U.S.	124	37°07'N	87°52'W
Princeton, Mi., U.S.	113	46°16'N	87°33'W
Princeton, Mn., U.S.	113	45°34'N	93°36'W
Princeton, Mo., U.S.	121	40°23'N	93°34'W
Princeton, N.J., U.S.	109	40°21'N	74°40'W
Princeton, Wi., U.S.	113	43°50'N	89°09'W
Princeton, W.V., U.S.	125	37°21'N	81°05'W
Prince William Sound, strt., Ak., U.S. (wĭl'yăm)	103	60°40'N	147°10'W
Príncipe, i., S. Tom./P. (prēn'sē-pĕ)	230	1°37'N	7°25'E
Principe Channel, strt., Can. (prĭn'sĭ-pē)	94	53°28'N	129°45'W
Prineville, Or., U.S. (prīn'vĭl)	114	44°17'N	120°48'W
Prineville Reservoir, res., Or., U.S.	114	44°07'N	120°45'W
Prinzapolca, Nic. (prēn-zä-pōl'kä)	133	13°18'N	83°35'W
Prinzapolca, r., Nic.	133	13°23'N	84°23'W
Prior Lake, Mn., U.S. (prī'ẽr)	117g	44°43'N	93°26'W
Priozërsk, Russia (prĭ-ô'zĕrsk)	167	61°03'N	30°08'E
Pripet, r., Eur.	181	51°50'N	29°45'E
Pripet Marshes, sw., Eur.	181	52°10'N	27°30'E
Priština, Serb. (prēsh'tĭ-nä)	163	42°39'N	21°12'E
Pritzwalk, Ger. (prēts'välk)	168	53°09'N	12°12'E
Privas, Fr. (prē-väs')	170	44°44'N	4°37'E
Prizren, Serb. (prē'zrĕn)	163	42°11'N	20°45'E
Procida, Italy (prô'chē-dă)	173c	40°31'N	14°02'E
Procida, Isola di, i., Italy	173c	40°32'N	13°57'E
Proctor, Mn., U.S. (prŏk'tẽr)	117h	46°45'N	92°14'W
Proctor, Vt., U.S.	109	43°40'N	73°00'W
Proebstel, Wa., U.S. (prōb'stĕl)	116c	45°40'N	122°29'W
Proença-a-Nova, Port. (prô-ān'sà-ä-nō'vä)	172	39°44'N	7°55'W
Progreso, Hond. (prō-grĕ'sō)	132	15°28'N	87°49'W
Progreso, Mex. (prō-grā'sō)	128	21°14'N	89°39'W
Progreso, Mex.	122	27°29'N	101°05'W
Prokhladnyy, Russia	182	43°46'N	44°00'E
Prokop'yevsk, Russia	184	53°53'N	86°45'E
Prokuplje, Serb. (prô'ko͝op'l-yĕ)	175	43°16'N	21°40'E
Prome, Mya.	212	18°46'N	95°15'E
Pronya, r., Bela. (prô'nyä)	176	54°08'N	30°58'E
Pronya, r., Russia	176	54°08'N	39°30'E
Prospect, Ky., U.S. (prŏs'pĕkt)	111h	38°21'N	85°36'W
Prospect Park, Pa., U.S. (prŏs'pĕkt pärk)	110f	39°53'N	75°18'W
Prosser, Wa., U.S. (prŏs'ẽr)	114	46°10'N	119°46'W
Prostějov, Czech Rep. (prôs'tyĕ-yôf)	169	49°28'N	17°08'E
Protection, i., Wa., U.S. (prō-tĕk'shŭn)	116a	48°07'N	122°56'W
Protoka, r., Russia (prôt'ô-kå)	176	55°00'N	36°42'E
Provadiya, Blg. (prō-väd'ē-yȧ)	175	43°13'N	27°28'E
Providence, Ky., U.S. (prŏv'ĭ-dĕns)	108	37°25'N	87°45'W
Providence, R.I., U.S.	105	41°50'N	71°23'W
Providence, Ut., U.S.	115	41°42'N	111°50'W
Providencia, Isla de, i., Col.	133	13°21'N	80°55'W
Providenciales, i., T./C. Is.	135	21°50'N	72°15'W
Provideniya, Russia (prô-vĭ-dä'nĭ-yá)	103	64°30'N	172°54'W
Provincetown, Ma., U.S.	109	42°03'N	70°11'W
Provo, Ut., U.S. (prō'vō)	104	40°15'N	111°40'W
Prozor, Bos. (prô'zôr)	175	43°48'N	17°59'E
Prudence Island, i., R.I., U.S. (pro͞o'dĕns)	110b	41°38'N	71°20'W
Prudhoe Bay, b., Ak., U.S.	103	70°40'N	147°25'W
Prudnik, Pol. (prŏd'nĭk)	169	50°19'N	17°34'E
Prussia, hist. reg., Eur. (prŭsh'ȧ)	168	50°43'N	8°35'E
Pruszków, Pol. (prŏosh'kôf)	169	52°09'N	20°50'E
Prut, r., Eur. (pro͞ot)	156	48°05'N	27°07'E
Pryluky, Ukr.	181	50°36'N	32°21'E
Prymors'k, Ukr.	177	46°43'N	36°21'E
Pryor, Ok., U.S. (prī'ẽr)	121	36°16'N	95°19'W
Pryvil'ne, Ukr.	177	47°30'N	32°21'E
Przedbórz, Pol.	169	51°05'N	19°53'E
Przemyśl, Pol. (pzhĕ'mĭsh'l)	154	49°47'N	22°45'E
Przheval'sk, Kyrg. (p'r-zhĭ-välsk')	183	42°29'N	78°24'E
Psel, r., Eur.	181	49°45'N	33°42'E
Pskov, Russia (pskôf)	178	57°48'N	28°19'E
Pskov, prov., Russia	176	57°33'N	29°05'E
Pskovskoye Ozero, l., Eur. (p'skôv'skô'yĕ ôzē-rô)	180	58°05'N	28°15'E
Ptich', r., Bela. (p'tēch)	180	53°17'N	28°16'E
Ptuj, Slvn. (pto͞o'ē)	174	46°24'N	15°54'E
Pucheng, China (po͞o'chĕng')	209	28°02'N	118°25'E
Pucheng, China (po͞o-chŭn)	206	35°43'N	115°22'E
Puck, Pol. (pòtsk)	169	54°43'N	18°23'E
Pudozh, Russia (po͞o'dôzh)	180	61°50'N	36°50'E
Puebla, Mex. (pwā'blä)	128	19°02'N	98°11'W
Puebla, state, Mex.	131	19°00'N	97°45'W
Puebla de Don Fadrique, Spain	172	37°55'N	2°55'W
Pueblo, Co., U.S. (pwā'blō)	104	38°15'N	104°36'W
Pueblo Nuevo, Mex. (nwā'vō)	130	23°23'N	105°21'W
Pueblo Viejo, Mex. (vyā'hō)	131	17°23'N	93°46'W
Puente Alto, Chile (pwĕ'n-tĕ ál'tô)	141b	33°36'S	70°34'W
Puentedeume, Spain (pwĕn-tå-dhå-o͞o'må)	172	43°28'N	8°09'W
Puente-Genil, Spain (pwĕn'tå-hå-nēl')	172	37°25'N	4°18'W
Puerco, Rio, r., N.M., U.S. (pwĕr'kō)	119	35°15'N	107°05'W
Puerto Aisén, Chile (pwĕ'r-tô ä'y-sĕ'n)	144	45°28'S	72°44'W
Puerto Angel, Mex. (pwĕ'r-tô äŋ'hål)	131	15°42'N	96°32'W
Puerto Armuelles, Pan. (pwe'r-tô är-mo͞o-ā'lyās)	133	8°18'N	82°52'W
Puerto Barrios, Guat. (pwĕ'r-tô bär'rē-ōs)	128	15°43'N	88°36'W
Puerto Bermúdez, Peru (pwĕ'r-tō bĕr-mo͞o'dāz)	142	10°17'S	74°57'W
Puerto Berrío, Col. (pwĕ'r-tō bĕr-rē'ō)	142	6°29'N	74°27'W
Puerto Cabello, Ven. (pwĕ'r-tō kä-bĕl'yō)	142	10°28'N	68°01'W
Puerto Cabezas, Nic. (pwĕ'r-tō kä-bā'zäs)	133	14°01'N	83°26'W
Puerto Casado, Para. (pwĕ'r-tō kä-sä'dō)	144	22°16'S	57°57'W
Puerto Castilla, Hond. (pwĕ'r-tô käs-tēl'yō)	132	16°01'N	86°01'W
Puerto Chicama, Peru (pwĕ'r-tō chē-kä'mä)	142	7°46'S	79°18'W
Puerto Colombia, Col. (pwĕr'tô kô-lôm'bē-à)	142	11°08'N	75°09'W
Puerto Cortés, C.R. (pwĕ'r-tô kôr-tās')	133	9°00'N	83°37'W
Puerto Cortés, Hond. (pwĕ'r-tô kôr-tās')	128	15°48'N	87°57'W
Puerto Cumarebo, Ven. (pwĕ'r-tō ko͞o-mä-rĕ'bô)	142	11°25'N	69°17'W
Puerto de Luna, N.M., U.S. (pwĕr'tô då lo͞o'nä)	120	34°49'N	104°36'W
Puerto de Nutrias, Ven. (pwĕ'r-tō dĕ no͞o-trē-äs')	142	8°02'N	69°19'W
Puerto Deseado, Arg. (pwĕ'r-tō dā-så-ä'dhō)	144	47°38'S	66°00'W
Puerto de Somport, p., Eur.	173	42°51'N	0°25'W
Puerto Eten, Peru (pwĕ'r-tō ĕ-tĕ'n)	142	6°59'S	79°51'W
Puerto Jiménez, C.R. (pwĕ'r-tō ĸē-mē nez)	133	8°35'N	83°23'W
Puerto La Cruz, Ven. (pwĕ'r-tō lä kro͞o'z)	142	10°14'N	64°38'W
Puertollano, Spain (pwĕr-tôl-yä'nō)	162	38°41'N	4°05'W
Puerto Madryn, Arg. (pwĕ'r-tō mä-drĕn')	144	42°46'S	65°01'W
Puerto Maldonado, Peru (pwĕ'r-tō mäl-dō-nä'dō)	142	12°43'S	69°01'W
Puerto Miniso, Mex. (pwĕ'r-tō mē-nē'sō)	130	16°06'N	98°02'W
Puerto Montt, Chile (pwĕ'r-tō mō'nt)	144	41°29'S	73°00'W
Puerto Natales, Chile (pwĕ'r-tō nä-tå'lĕs)	144	51°48'S	72°01'W
Puerto Niño, Col. (pwĕ'r-tō nē'n-yō)	142a	5°57'N	74°36'W
Puerto Padre, Cuba (pwĕ'r-tō pä'drā)	134	21°10'N	76°40'W
Puerto Peñasco, Mex. (pwĕ'r-tô pĕn-yä's-kô)	128	31°39'N	113°15'W
Puerto Pinasco, Para. (pwĕ'r-tō pē-ná's-kô)	144	22°31'S	57°50'W
Puerto Píritu, Ven. (pwĕ'r-tō pē'rē-to͞o)	143b	10°05'N	65°04'W
Puerto Plata, Dom. Rep. (pwĕ'r-tô plä'tä)	129	19°50'N	70°40'W
Puerto Princesa, Phil. (pwĕr-tô prēn-sā'sä)	212	9°45'N	118°41'E
Puerto Rico, dep., N.A. (pwĕr'tô rē'kō)	129	18°16'N	66°50'W
Puerto Rico Trench, deep	129	19°45'N	66°30'W
Puerto Salgar, Col. (pwĕ'r-tō säl-gär')	142a	5°30'N	74°39'W
Puerto Santa Cruz, Arg. (pwĕ'r-tō sän'tä kro͞oz')	144	50°04'S	68°32'W
Puerto Suárez, Bol. (pwĕ'r-tō swä'råz)	143	18°55'S	57°39'W
Puerto Tejada, Col. (pwĕ'r-tō tĕ-ĸä'dä)	142	3°13'N	76°23'W
Puerto Vallarta, Mex. (pwĕ'r-tō väl-yär'tä)	130	20°36'N	105°13'W
Puerto Varas, Chile (pwĕ'r-tō vä'räs)	144	41°16'S	73°03'W
Puerto Wilches, Col. (pwĕ'r-tō vēl'c-hĕs)	142	7°19'N	73°54'W
Pugachëv, Russia (po͞o'gá-chyôf)	181	52°00'N	48°40'E
Puget, Wa., U.S. (pū'jĕt)	116c	46°10'N	123°23'W
Puget Sound, strt., Wa., U.S.	114	47°49'N	122°26'W
Puglia (Apulia), hist. reg., Italy (po͞o'lyä) (ä-po͞o'lyä)	174	41°13'N	16°10'E
Pukaskwa National Park, rec., Can.	93	48°22'N	85°55'W
Pukeashun Mountain, mtn., Can.	95	51°12'N	119°14'W
Pukin, r., Malay.	197b	2°53'N	102°54'E
Pula, Cro. (po͞o'lä)	162	44°52'N	13°55'E
Pulacayo, Bol. (po͞o-lä-kä'yō)	142	20°12'S	66°33'W
Pulaski, Tn., U.S. (pů-lăs'kĭ)	124	35°11'N	87°03'W
Pulaski, Va., U.S.	125	37°00'N	81°45'W
Puławy, Pol. (pò-wä'vē)	169	51°24'N	21°59'E
Pulicat, r., India	203	13°58'N	79°52'E
Pullman, Wa., U.S. (pòl'măn)	114	46°44'N	117°10'W
Pulog, Mount, mtn., Phil. (po͞o'lôg)	213a	16°38'N	120°53'E
Puma Yumco, l., China (po͞o-mä yo͞om-tswo)	202	28°30'N	90°10'E
Pumpkin Creek, r., Mt., U.S. (pŭmp'kĭn)	115	45°47'N	105°35'W
Punakha, Bhu. (po͞o-nŭk'ŭ)	199	27°45'N	89°59'E
Punata, Bol. (po͞o-nä'tä)	142	17°43'S	65°43'W
Pune, India	199	18°38'N	73°53'E
Punjab, state, India (pŭn'jäb')	199	31°00'N	75°30'E
Puno, Peru (po͞o'nô)	142	15°58'S	70°02'W
Punta Arenas, Chile (po͞o'n-tä-ä-rĕ'näs)	144	53°09'S	70°48'W
Punta de Piedras, Ven. (po͞o'n-tä dĕ pyĕ'dräs)	143b	10°54'N	64°06'W
Punta Gorda, Belize (pòn'tä gôr'dä)	132	16°07'N	88°50'W
Punta Gorda, Fl., U.S. (pŭn'tȧ gôr'dȧ)	125a	26°55'N	82°02'W
Punta Gorda, Río, r., Nic. (po͞o'n-tä gô'r-dä)	133	11°34'N	84°13'W
Punta Indio, Canal, strt., Arg. (po͞o'n-tä- ē'n-dyō)	141c	34°56'S	57°20'W
Puntarenas, C.R. (pònt-ä-rā'näs)	129	9°59'N	84°49'W
Punto Fijo, Ven. (po͞o'n-tō fē'ĸô)	142	11°48'N	70°14'W
Punxsutawney, Pa., U.S. (pŭnk-sŭ-tô'nē)	109	40°55'N	79°00'W
Puquio, Peru (po͞o'kyō)	142	14°43'S	74°02'W
Pur, r., Russia	184	65°30'N	77°30'E
Purcell, Ok., U.S. (pûr-sĕl')	121	35°01'N	97°22'W
Purcell Mountains, mts., N.A. (pûr-sĕl')	95	50°00'N	116°30'W
Purdy, Wa., U.S. (pûr'dē)	116a	47°23'N	122°37'W
Purépero, Mex. (po͞o-rā'pâ-rō)	130	19°56'N	102°02'W
Purgatoire, r., Co., U.S. (pûr-gá-twär')	120	37°25'N	103°53'W
Puri, India (pò'rē)	199	19°52'N	85°51'E
Purial, Sierra de, mts., Cuba (sē-ĕ'r-rà-dĕ-po͞o-rē-äl')	135	20°15'N	74°40'W
Purificación, Col. (po͞o-rē-fē-kä-syō'n)	142	3°52'N	74°54'W
Purificación, Mex. (po͞o-rē-fē-kä-syō'n)	130	19°44'N	104°38'W
Purificación, r., Mex.	130	19°30'N	104°54'W
Purkersdorf, Aus.	159e	48°13'N	16°11'E

ăt; finăl; rāte; senåte; ärm; ȧsk; sofȧ; fâre; ch-choose; dh-as th in other; bē; ēvent; bĕt; recĕnt; cratẽr; g-gō; gh-guttural g; bĭt; ĭ-short neutral; rīde; ĸ-guttural k as ch in German ich;

PRONOUNCING INDEX Puruandiro – Ramanāthapuram 339

PLACE (Pronunciation)	PAGE	LAT.	LONG.
Puruandiro, Mex. (pò-rōō-än´dė-rō)	130	20°04'N	101°33'W
Purús, r., S.A. (pōō-rōō´s)	142	6°45'S	64°34'W
Pusan, Kor., S.	205	35°08'N	129°05'E
Pushkin, Russia (pòsh´kĭn)	180	59°43'N	30°25'E
Pushkino, Russia (pōōsh´kė-nô)	176	56°01'N	37°51'E
Pustoshka, Russia (pûs-tôsh´kå)	176	56°20'N	29°33'E
Pustunich, Mex. (pōōs-tōō´nēch)	131	19°10'N	90°29'W
Putaendo, Chile (pōō-tä-ĕn-dô)	141b	32°37'S	70°42'W
Puteaux, Fr. (pü-tō´)	171b	48°52'N	2°12'E
Putfontein, S. Afr. (pòt´fŏn-tān)	233b	26°08'S	28°24'E
Putian, China (pōō-tĭĕn)	209	25°40'N	119°02'E
Putla de Guerrero, Mex. (pōō´tlä-dĕ-gĕr-rĕ´rō)	131	17°03'N	97°55'W
Putnam, Ct., U.S. (pŭt´năm)	109	41°55'N	71°55'W
Putorana, Gory, mts., Russia	179	68°45'N	93°15'E
Puttalam, Sri L.	203	8°02'N	79°44'E
Putumayo, r., S.A. (pò-tōō-mä´yō)	142	1°02'S	73°50'W
Putung, Tanjung, c., Indon.	212	3°35'S	111°50'E
Putyvl', Ukr.	177	51°21'N	33°52'E
Puulavesi, l., Fin.	167	61°49'N	27°10'E
Puyallup, Wa., U.S. (pū-ăl´ŭp)	116a	47°12'N	122°18'W
Puyang, China (pōō-yäŋ)	208	35°42'N	114°58'E
Pweto, D.R.C. (pwā´tō)	232	8°29'S	28°58'E
Pyasina, r., Russia (pyä-sē´nå)	184	72°45'N	87°37'E
Pyatigorsk, Russia (pyå-tė-gôrsk´)	181	44°00'N	43°00'E
Pyetrykaw, Bela.	176	52°09'N	28°30'E
Pyhäjärvi, l., Fin.	167	60°57'N	21°50'E
Pyinmana, Mya. (pyĕn-mä´nŭ)	199	19°47'N	96°15'E
Pymatuning Reservoir, res., Pa., U.S. (pī-må-tûn´ĭng)	108	41°40'N	80°30'W
Pyŏnggang, Kor., N. (pyŭng´gäng´)	210	38°21'N	127°18'E
P'yŏngyang, Kor., N.	205	39°03'N	125°48'E
Pyramid, l., Nv., U.S. (pĭ´rå-mĭd)	118	40°02'N	119°50'W
Pyramid Lake Indian Reservation, I.R., Nv., U.S.	118	40°17'N	119°52'W
Pyramids, hist., Egypt	238b	29°53'N	31°10'E
Pyrenees, mts., Eur. (pĭr-e-nēz´)	156	43°00'N	0°05'E
Pýrgos, Grc.	163	37°51'N	21°28'E
Pyriatyn, Ukr.	181	50°13'N	32°31'E
Pyrzyce, Pol. (pēzhĭ´tsĕ)	168	53°09'N	14°53'E

Q

PLACE (Pronunciation)	PAGE	LAT.	LONG.
Qal'at Bishah, Sau. Ar.	198	20°01'N	42°30'E
Qamdo, China (chyäm-dwō)	204	31°06'N	96°30'E
Qandala, Som.	201	11°28'N	49°52'E
Qaraghandy (Karaganda), Kaz.	183	49°42'N	73°18'E
Qaraözen, r.	181	49°50'N	49°35'E
Qarqan see Qiemo, China	204	38°02'N	85°16'E
Qarqan, r., China	204	38°55'N	87°15'E
Qarqaraly, Kaz.	183	49°18'N	75°28'E
Qārūn, Birket, l., Egypt	231	29°34'N	30°34'E
Qaṣr al Burayqah, Libya	231	30°25'N	19°20'E
Qasr al-Farāfirah, Egypt	231	27°04'N	28°13'E
Qaṣr Banī Walīd, Libya	231	31°45'N	14°04'E
Qasr el Boukhari, Alg.	162	35°50'N	2°48'E
Qatar, nation, Asia (kä´tär)	198	25°00'N	52°45'E
Qaṭārah, Munkhafaḍ al, depr., Egypt	231	30°07'N	27°30'E
Qausuittuq (Resolute), Can.	89	74°41'N	95°00'W
Qāyen, Iran	198	33°45'N	59°08'E
Qazvīn, Iran	198	36°10'N	49°59'E
Qeshm, Iran	198	26°51'N	56°10'E
Qeshm, i., Iran	198	26°52'N	56°15'E
Qezel Owzan, r., Iran	198	36°30'N	49°00'E
Qezi'ot, Isr.	197a	30°53'N	34°28'E
Qianwei, China (chyĕn-wā)	206	40°11'N	120°05'E
Qi'anzhen, China (chyē-än-jŭn)	206	32°16'N	120°59'E
Qibao, China (chyē-bou)	207b	31°06'N	121°16'E
Qiblīyah, Jabal al Jalālat al, mts., Egypt	197a	28°49'N	32°21'E
Qijiang, China (chyē-jyäŋ)	209	29°05'N	106°40'E
Qikou, China (chyē-kō)	206	38°37'N	117°33'E
Qilian Shan, mts., China (chyē-lĭĕn shän)	204	38°43'N	98°00'E
Qiliping, China (chyē-lē-pĭŋ)	206	31°28'N	114°41'E
Qindao, China (chyĭn-dou)	205	36°05'N	120°10'E
Qing'an, China (chyĭŋ-än)	208	46°50'N	127°30'E
Qingcheng, China (chyĭŋ-chŭŋ)	206	37°12'N	117°43'E
Qingfeng, China (chyĭŋ-fŭŋ)	206	35°52'N	115°05'E
Qinghai, prov., China (chyĭŋ-hī)	204	36°14'N	95°30'E
Qinghai Hu see Koko Nor, l., China	204	37°26'N	98°30'E
Qinghe, China (chyĭŋ-hŭ)	208a	40°08'N	116°16'E
Qingjiang, China (chyĭŋ-jyäŋ)	209	28°00'N	115°30'E
Qingjiang, China	206	33°34'N	118°58'E
Qingliu, China (chyĭŋ-lĭō)	209	26°15'N	116°50'E
Qingningsi, China (chyĭŋ-nĭŋ-sz)	207b	31°16'N	121°33'E
Qingping, China (chyĭŋ-pĭŋ)	206	36°46'N	116°03'E
Qingpu, China (chyĭŋ-pōō)	209	31°08'N	121°06'E
Qingxian, China (chyĭŋ shyĕn)	206	38°37'N	116°48'E
Qingyang, China (chyĭŋ-yäŋ)	204	36°02'N	107°42'E
Qingyuan, China (chyĭŋ-yōän)	209	23°43'N	113°10'E
Qingyuan, China	208	42°05'N	125°00'E
Qingyun, China (chyĭŋ-yòn)	206	37°52'N	117°26'E
Qingyundian, China (chĭŋ-yòn-dĭĕn)	208a	39°41'N	116°31'E
Qinhuangdao, China (chyĭn-huaŋ-dou)	205	39°57'N	119°34'E
Qin Ling, mts., China (chyĭn lĭŋ)	204	33°25'N	108°58'E
Qinyang, China (chyĭn-yäŋ)	208	35°00'N	112°55'E
Qinzhou, China (chyĭn-jō)	209	22°00'N	108°35'E
Qionghai, China (chyôŋ-hī)	209	19°10'N	110°28'E
Qiqian, China (chyē-chyĕn)	205	52°23'N	121°04'E
Qiqihar, China	205	47°18'N	124°00'E
Qiryat Gat, Isr.	197a	31°38'N	34°36'E
Qiryat Shemona, Isr.	197a	33°12'N	35°34'E
Qitai, China (chyē-tī)	204	44°07'N	89°04'E
Qiuxian, China (chyô shyĕn)	206	36°43'N	115°13'E
Qixian, China (chyē-shyĕn)	206	34°33'N	114°47'E
Qixian, China	208	35°36'N	114°13'E
Qiyang, China (chyē-yäŋ)	209	26°40'N	112°00'E
Qobda, r., Kaz. (kä-rå ĸôb´då)	181	50°40'N	55°00'E
Qogir Feng see K2, mtn., Asia	199	36°06'N	76°38'E
Qom, Iran	198	34°28'N	50°53'E
Qongyrat, Kaz.	183	47°25'N	75°10'E
Qostanay, Kaz.	183	53°10'N	63°39'E
Quabbin Reservoir, res., Ma., U.S. (kwā´bĭn)	109	42°20'N	72°10'W
Quachita, Lake, l., Ar., U.S. (kwä shĭ´tô)	121	34°47'N	93°37'W
Quadra Island, i., Can.	94	50°08'N	125°16'W
Quakertown, Pa., U.S. (kwā´kēr-toun)	100	40°30'N	75°20'W
Quanah, Tx., U.S. (kwä´nå)	120	34°10'N	99°43'W
Quang Ngai, Viet. (kwäng n'gä´ē)	212	15°05'N	108°58'E
Quang Ngai, mtn., Viet.	209	15°10'N	108°20'E
Quanjiao, China (chyuän-jyou)	206	32°06'N	118°17'E
Quanzhou, China (chyuän-jō)	205	24°58'N	118°40'E
Quanzhou, China	209	25°58'N	111°02'E
Qu'Appelle, r., Can.	92	50°30'N	104°00'W
Qu'Appelle Dam, dam, Can.	96	51°00'N	106°25'W
Quartu Sant'Elena, Italy (kwär-tōō´ sänt a´lå-nä)	174	39°16'N	9°12'E
Quartzsite, Az., U.S.	119	33°40'N	114°13'W
Quatsino Sound, strt., Can. (kwŏt-sē´nō)	94	50°25'N	128°10'W
Quba, Azer. (kōō´bå)	181	41°05'N	48°30'E
Qūchān, Iran	201	37°06'N	58°30'E
Qudi, China	206	37°06'N	117°15'E
Québec, Can. (kwė-bĕk´) (kå-bĕk´)	102b	46°49'N	71°13'W
Quebec, prov., Can.	91	51°07'N	70°25'W
Quedlinburg, Ger. (kvĕd´lĕn-bŏŏrgh)	168	51°45'N	11°10'E
Queen Bess, Can.	94	51°16'N	124°34'W
Queen Charlotte Islands, is., Can. (kwēn shär´lŏt)	92	53°30'N	132°25'W
Queen Charlotte Ranges, mts., Can.	94	53°00'N	132°00'W
Queen Charlotte Sound, strt., Can.	94	51°30'N	129°30'W
Queen Charlotte Strait, strt., Can. (strāt)	92	50°40'N	127°25'W
Queen Elizabeth Islands, is., Can. (ē-lĭz´å-bĕth)	89	78°20'N	110°00'W
Queen Maud Gulf, b., Can. (mäd)	92	68°27'N	102°55'W
Queen Maud Land, reg., Ant.	224	75°00'S	10°00'E
Queen Maud Mountains, mts., Ant.	224	85°00'S	179°00'W
Queens Channel, strt., Austl. (kwēnz)	220	14°25'S	129°10'E
Queenscliff, Austl.	217a	38°16'S	144°39'E
Queensland, state, Austl. (kwēnz´lănd)	219	22°45'S	141°01'E
Queenstown, Austl. (kwēnz´toun)	222	42°00'S	145°40'E
Queenstown, S. Afr.	233c	31°54'S	26°53'E
Queimados, Braz. (kā-må´dôs)	144b	22°42'S	43°34'W
Quela, Ang.	236	9°16'S	17°02'E
Quelimane, Moz. (kā-lē-mä´nĕ)	233	17°48'S	37°05'E
Queluz, Port.	173b	38°45'N	9°15'W
Quemado de Güines, Cuba (kā-mä´dhä-dē-gwē´nĕs)	134	22°45'N	80°20'W
Quemoy, Tai.	209	24°30'N	118°20'E
Quemoy, i., Tai.	209	24°27'N	118°23'E
Quepos, C.R. (kā´pôs)	133	9°26'N	84°10'W
Quepos, Punta, c., C.R. (pōō´n-tä)	133	9°23'N	84°20'W
Querétaro, Mex. (kå-rā´tä-rō)	128	20°37'N	100°25'W
Querétaro, state, Mex.	130	21°00'N	100°00'W
Quesada, Spain (kå-sä´dhä)	172	37°51'N	3°04'W
Quesnel, Can. (kā-nĕl´)	90	52°59'N	122°30'W
Quesnel, r., Can.	95	52°15'N	122°00'W
Quesnel Lake, l., Can.	92	52°32'N	121°05'W
Quetame, Col. (kĕ-tä´mĕ)	142a	4°20'N	73°50'W
Quetta, Pak. (kwĕt´ä)	199	30°19'N	67°01'E
Quezaltenango, Guat. (kå-zäl´tå-nän´gō)	128	14°50'N	91°30'W
Quezaltepeque, El Sal. (kĕ-zäl´tĕ´pĕ-kĕ)	132	13°50'N	89°17'W
Quezaltepeque, Guat. (kå-zäl´tå-pā´kå)	132	14°39'N	89°26'W
Quezon City, Phil. (kā-zōn)	212	14°40'N	121°02'E
Qufu, China (chyōō-fōō)	206	35°37'N	116°54'E
Quibdo, Col. (kēb´dō)	142	5°42'N	76°41'W
Quiberon, Fr. (kē-bē-rôɴ´)	170	47°29'N	3°08'W
Quiçama, Parque Nacional de, rec., Ang.	236	10°00'S	13°25'E
Quicksborn, Ger. (kvēks´bōrn)	159c	53°44'N	9°54'E
Quilcene, Wa., U.S. (kwĭl-sēn´)	116a	47°50'N	122°53'W
Quilimari, Chile (kē-lē-mä´rē)	141b	32°06'S	71°28'W
Quillan, Fr. (kē-yäɴ´)	170	42°53'N	2°13'E
Quillota, Chile (kĕl-yō´tä)	144	32°52'S	71°14'W
Quilmes, Arg. (kēl´mās)	141c	34°43'S	58°16'W
Quilon, India (kwė-lōn´)	203	8°58'N	76°16'E
Quilpie, Austl. (kwĭl´pė)	219	26°34'S	149°20'E
Quimbaya, Col. (kēm-bä´yä)	142a	4°38'N	75°46'W
Quimbele, Ang.	236	6°28'S	16°13'E
Quimbonge, Ang.	236	8°36'S	18°30'E
Quimper, Fr. (kăɴ-pĕr´)	161	47°59'N	4°04'W
Quinalt, r., Wa., U.S.	114	47°23'N	124°10'W
Quinault Indian Reservation, I.R., Wa., U.S.	114	47°27'N	124°34'W
Quincy, Fl., U.S. (kwĭn´sė)	124	30°35'N	84°35'W
Quincy, Il., U.S.	105	39°55'N	91°23'W
Quincy, Ma., U.S.	101a	42°15'N	71°00'W
Quincy, Mi., U.S.	108	42°00'N	84°50'W
Quincy, Or., U.S.	116c	46°08'N	123°10'W
Qui Nhon, Viet. (kwĭnyôn)	212	13°51'N	109°03'E
Quinn, r., Nv., U.S. (kwĭn)	114	41°42'N	117°45'W
Quintanar de la Orden, Spain (kēn-tä-när´)	172	39°36'N	3°02'W
Quintana Roo, state, Mex. (rô´ô)	128	19°30'N	88°30'W
Quintero, Chile (kēn-tĕ´rô)	141b	32°48'S	71°30'W
Quionga, Moz.	237	10°37'S	40°30'E
Quiroga, Mex. (kē-rô´gä)	130	19°39'N	101°30'W
Quiroga, Spain (kē-rô´gä)	172	42°28'N	7°18'W
Quitman, Ga., U.S. (kwĭt´măn)	124	30°46'N	83°35'W
Quitman, Ms., U.S.	124	33°02'N	88°43'W
Quito, Ec. (kē´tō)	142	0°17'S	78°32'W
Qumbu, S. Afr. (kòm´bōō)	233c	31°10'S	28°48'E
Quorn, Austl. (kwôrn)	222	32°20'S	138°00'E
Qurayyah, Wādī, r., Egypt	197a	30°08'N	34°27'E
Qusmuryn köli, l., Kaz.	183	52°30'N	64°15'E
Qutang, China (chyōō-täŋ)	206	32°33'N	120°07'E
Quthing, Leso.	233c	30°35'S	27°42'E
Quxian, China (chyoo-shyen)	205	28°58'N	118°58'E
Quxian, China	209	30°40'N	106°48'E
Quzhou, China (chyoȯ-jō)	206	36°47'N	114°58'E
Qyzylorda, Kaz.	183	44°58'N	65°45'E

R

PLACE (Pronunciation)	PAGE	LAT.	LONG.
Raab (Raba), r., Eur. (räp)	168	46°55'N	15°55'E
Raahe, Fin. (rä´ĕ)	160	64°39'N	24°22'E
Rab, i., Cro. (räb)	174	44°45'N	14°40'E
Raba, Indon.	212	8°32'S	118°49'E
Raba (Raab), r., Eur.	169	47°28'N	17°12'E
Rabat, Mor. (rå-bät´)	230	33°59'N	6°47'W
Rabaul, Pap. N. Gui. (rä´boul)	213	4°15'S	152°19'E
Rābigh, Sau. Ar.	201	22°48'N	39°01'E
Raccoon, r., Ia., U.S. (ră-kōōn´)	113	42°07'N	94°45'W
Raccoon Cay, i., Bah.	135	22°25'N	75°50'W
Race, Cape, c., Can. (rās)	101	46°40'N	53°10'W
Rachado, Cape, c., Malay.	197b	2°26'N	101°29'E
Racibórz, Pol. (rä-chē´bōōzh)	169	50°06'N	18°14'E
Racine, Wi., U.S. (rå-sēn´)	105	42°43'N	87°49'W
Raco, Mi., U.S. (rå cō)	117k	46°22'N	84°43'W
Rădăuţi, Rom.	163	47°53'N	25°55'E
Radcliffe, Eng., U.K. (răd´klĭf)	158a	53°34'N	2°20'W
Radevormwald, Ger. (rä´dĕ-fōrm-väld)	171c	51°12'N	7°22'E
Radford, Va., U.S. (răd´fērd)	125	37°06'N	81°33'W
Rādhanpur, India	202	23°57'N	71°38'E
Radium, S. Afr. (rā´dĭ-ŭm)	238c	25°06'S	28°18'E
Radom, Pol. (rä´dôm)	161	51°24'N	21°11'E
Radomir, Blg. (rä´dō-mēr)	175	42°33'N	22°58'E
Radomsko, Pol. (rä-dôm´skô)	161	51°04'N	19°27'E
Radomyshl, Ukr. (rä-dô-mēsh´'l)	181	50°30'N	29°13'E
Radul', Ukr. (rá´dōōl)	177	51°52'N	30°46'E
Radviliškis, Lith. (råd´vē-lēsh´kēs)	167	55°49'N	23°31'E
Radwah, Jabal, mtn., Sau. Ar.	198	24°44'N	38°14'E
Radzyń Podlaski, Pol. (räd´zēn-y´ pŭd-lä´skĭ)	169	51°49'N	22°40'E
Raeford, N.C., U.S. (rā´fērd)	125	34°57'N	79°15'W
Raesfeld, Ger. (räz´fĕld)	171c	51°46'N	6°50'E
Raeside, l., Austl. (rā´sīd)	220	29°20'S	122°30'E
Rae Strait, strt., Can. (rā)	92	68°40'N	95°03'W
Rafaela, Arg. (rä-fä-å´lä)	144	31°15'S	61°21'W
Rafah, Pak. (rä´fä)	197a	31°14'N	34°12'E
Rafsanjān, Iran	198	30°45'N	56°30'E
Raft, r., Id., U.S. (răft)	115	42°20'N	113°17'W
Ragay, Phil. (rä-gī´)	213a	13°49'N	122°45'E
Ragay Gulf, b., Phil.	213a	13°44'N	122°38'E
Ragunda, Swe. (rä-gòn´dä)	166	63°07'N	16°24'E
Ragusa, Italy (rä-gōō´sä)	162	36°58'N	14°41'E
Rahachow, Bela.	180	53°07'N	30°04'E
Rahway, N.J., U.S. (rô´wā)	110a	40°37'N	74°16'W
Rāichūr, India (rä´ē-chōōr´)	199	16°23'N	77°18'E
Raigarh, India (rī´gŭr)	199	21°57'N	83°32'E
Rainbow Bridge National Monument, rec., Ut., U.S. (rān´bō)	119	37°05'N	111°00'W
Rainbow City, Pan.	128a	9°20'N	79°53'W
Rainier, Or., U.S.	116c	46°05'N	122°56'W
Rainier, Mount, mtn., Wa., U.S. (rå-nēr´)	106	46°52'N	121°46'W
Rainy, r., N.A.	107	48°50'N	94°41'W
Rainy Lake, l., N.A. (rān´ē)	93	48°43'N	94°29'W
Rainy River, Can.	91	48°43'N	94°29'W
Raipur, India (rä´jŭ-bōō-rē´)	202	21°25'N	81°37'E
Raisin, r., Mi., U.S. (rā´zĭn)	108	42°00'N	83°35'W
Raitan, N.J., U.S. (rā-tăn)	110a	40°34'N	74°40'W
Rājahmundry, India (räj-ŭ-mŭn´drē)	199	17°03'N	81°51'E
Rajang, r., Malay.	212	2°10'N	113°30'E
Rājapālaiyam, India	203	9°30'N	77°33'E
Rājasthān, state, India (rä´jŭs-tän)	199	26°00'N	72°00'E
Rājkot, India (räj´kōt)	199	22°20'N	70°48'E
Rājpur, India	202a	22°24'N	88°25'E
Rājshāhi, Bngl.	199	24°26'S	88°39'E
Rakhiv, Ukr.	169	48°02'N	24°13'E
Rakh'oya, Russia (räk´yå)	186c	60°06'N	30°50'E
Rakitnoye, Russia (rä-kēt´nô-yĕ)	181	50°51'N	35°53'E
Rakovník, Czech Rep.	168	50°07'N	13°45'E
Rakvere, Est. (råk´vĕ-rĕ)	180	59°22'N	26°14'E
Raleigh, N.C., U.S.	105	35°45'N	78°39'W
Ram, r., Can.	95	52°10'N	115°05'W
Rama, Nic. (rä´mä)	133	12°11'N	84°14'W
Ramallo, Arg. (rä-mä´l-yô)	141c	33°28'S	60°02'W
Ramanāthapuram, India	203	9°13'N	78°52'E

ng-sing; ŋ-baŋk; ɴ-nasalized n; nŏd; cŏmmit; ōld; ôbey; ôrder; oi-boil; fōōd; ŏŏ-as oo in foot; ou-out; s-soft; sh-dish; th-thin; pūre; ûnite; ûrn; stŭd; circŭs; ü-as in French tu; ´-indeterminate vowel.

340 Rambouillet – Revda PRONOUNCING INDEX

PLACE (Pronunciation)	PAGE	LAT.	LONG.
Rambouillet, Fr. (räɴ-bōō-yĕ′)	170	48°39′N	1°49′E
Rame Head, c., S. Afr.	233c	31°48′S	29°22′E
Ramenskoye, Russia (rá′mĕn-skô-yĕ)	176	55°34′N	38°15′E
Ramlat as Sab'atayn, reg., Asia	198	16°08′N	45°15′E
Ramm, Jabal, mtn., Jord.	197a	29°37′N	35°32′E
Râmnicu Sărat, Rom.	163	45°24′N	27°06′E
Râmnicu Vâlcea, Rom.	175	45°07′N	24°22′E
Ramos, Mex. (rä′mōs)	130	22°46′N	101°52′W
Ramos, r., Nig.	235	5°10′N	5°40′E
Ramos Arizpe, Mex. (ä-rēz′pā)	122	25°33′N	100°57′W
Rampart, Ak., U.S. (răm′pȧrt)	103	65°28′N	150°18′W
Rampo Mountains, mts., N.J., U.S. (răm′pō)	110a	41°00′N	72°12′W
Rāmpur, India (räm′pōōr)	199	28°53′N	79°03′E
Ramree Island, i., Mya. (räm′rē′)	212	19°01′N	93°23′E
Ramseyville, Can. (răm′zė vĭl)	102c	45°23′N	75°34′W
Ramsbottom, Eng., U.K. (rămz′bŏt-ŭm)	150a	53°30′N	2°20′W
Ramsey, I. of Man (răm′zė)	164	54°20′N	4°25′W
Ramsey, N.J., U.S.	110a	41°03′N	74°09′W
Ramsey Lake, l., Can.	98	47°15′N	82°16′W
Ramsgate, Eng., U.K. (rămz′′gāt)	165	51°19′N	1°20′E
Ramu, r., Pap. N. Gui. (rä′mōō)	213	5°35′S	145°16′E
Rancagua, Chile (rän-kä′gwä)	144	34°10′S	70°43′W
Rance, r., Fr. (räɴs)	170	48°17′N	2°30′W
Rānchī, India	199	23°21′N	85°20′E
Rancho Boyeros, Cuba (rä′n-chô-bô-yĕ′rôs)	135a	23°00′N	82°23′W
Randallstown, Md., U.S. (răn′dȧlz-toun)	110e	39°22′N	76°48′W
Randers, Den. (rän′ĕrs)	160	56°28′N	10°03′E
Randfontein, S. Afr. (rănt′fŏn-tān)	233b	26°10′S	27°42′E
Randleman, N.C., U.S. (răn′d'l-mȧn)	125	35°49′N	79°50′W
Randolph, Ma., U.S. (răn′dôlf)	101a	42°10′N	71°03′W
Randolph, Ne., U.S.	112	42°22′N	97°22′W
Randolph, Vt., U.S.	109	43°55′N	72°40′W
Random Island, i., Can. (răn′dŭm)	101	48°12′N	53°25′W
Randsfjorden, Nor.	166	60°35′N	10°10′E
Randwick, Austl.	217b	33°55′S	151°15′E
Ranérou, Sen.	234	15°18′N	13°58′W
Rangeley, Me., U.S. (rānj′lė)	100	44°56′N	70°38′W
Rangeley, l., Me., U.S.	100	45°00′N	70°25′W
Ranger, Tx., U.S. (rān′jẽr)	104	32°26′N	98°41′W
Rangia, India	202	26°32′N	91°39′E
Rangoon (Yangon), Mya. (răŋ-gōōn′)	199	16°46′N	96°09′E
Rangpur, Bngl. (rŭng′pōōr)	199	25°48′N	89°19′E
Rangsang, i., Indon. (räng′säng′)	197b	0°53′N	103°05′E
Rangsdorf, Ger. (rängs′dōrf)	159b	52°17′N	13°25′E
Rānīganj, India (rä-nē-gŭnj′)	202	23°40′N	87°08′E
Rankin Inlet, b., Can. (răŋ′kĕn)	93	62°45′N	94°27′W
Ranova, r., Russia (rä′nô-vȧ)	176	53°55′N	40°03′E
Rantau, Malay.	197b	2°35′N	101°58′E
Rantekombola, Bulu, mtn., Indon.	212	3°22′S	119°50′E
Rantoul, Il., U.S. (răn-tōōl′)	108	40°25′N	88°05′W
Raoyang, China (rou-yäŋ)	206	38°16′N	115°45′E
Rapallo, Italy (rä-päl′lō)	174	44°21′N	9°14′E
Rapel, r., Chile (rä-pål′)	141b	34°05′S	71°30′W
Rapid, r., Mn., U.S. (răp′ĭd)	113	48°21′N	94°50′W
Rapid City, S.D., U.S.	104	44°06′N	103°14′W
Rapla, Est. (räp′lȧ)	167	59°02′N	24°46′E
Rappahannock, r., Va., U.S. (răp′ȧ-hăn′ŭk)	109	38°20′N	75°25′W
Raquette, l., N.Y., U.S. (răk′ĕt)	109	43°50′N	74°35′W
Raritan, r., N.J., U.S. (răr′ĭ-tăn)	110a	40°32′N	74°27′W
Rarotonga, Cook Is. (rä′rô-tōŋ′gȧ)	2	20°40′S	163°00′W
Ra's an Naqb, Jord.	197a	30°00′N	35°29′E
Rașcov, Mol.	177	47°55′N	28°51′E
Ras Dashen Terara, mtn., Eth. (räs dä-shän′)	231	12°49′N	38°14′E
Raseiniai, Lith. (rä-syā′nyĭ)	167	55°23′N	23°04′E
Rashayya, Leb.	197a	33°30′N	35°50′E
Rashīd, Egypt (rȧ-shēd′) (rō-zĕt′ȧ)	200	31°22′N	30°25′E
Rashīd, Masabb, mth., Egypt	238b	31°30′N	29°58′E
Rashkina, Russia (rȧsh′kĭ-nȧ)	186a	59°57′N	61°30′E
Rasht, Iran	198	37°13′N	49°45′E
Raška, Serb. (räsh′kȧ)	175	43°16′N	20°40′E
Rasskazovo, Russia (räs-kä′sô-vô)	181	52°40′N	41°40′E
Rastatt, Ger. (rä-shtät)	168	48°51′N	8°12′E
Rastes, Russia (rȧs′tĕs)	186a	59°24′N	58°49′E
Rastunovo, Russia (rȧs-tōō′nô-vô)	186b	55°15′N	37°50′E
Ratangarh, India (rŭ-tŭn′gŭr)	202	28°10′N	74°30′E
Ratcliff, Tx., U.S. (răt′klĭf)	123	31°22′N	95°09′W
Rathenow, Ger. (rä′tĕ-nō)	168	52°36′N	12°20′E
Rathlin Island, i., N. Ire., U.K. (răth-lĭn)	164	55°18′N	6°13′W
Ratingen, Ger. (rä′tĕn-gĕn)	171c	51°18′N	6°51′E
Rat Islands, is., Ak., U.S. (răt)	103a	51°35′N	176°48′E
Ratlām, India	202	23°19′N	75°05′E
Ratnāgiri, India	203	17°04′N	73°24′E
Raton, N.M., U.S. (rȧ-tōn′)	104	36°52′N	104°26′W
Rattlesnake Creek, r., Or., U.S. (răt′'l snāk)	114	42°38′N	117°39′W
Rättvik, Swe. (rĕt′vēk)	166	60°54′N	15°07′E
Rauch, Arg. (rȧ′ōōch)	144	36°47′S	59°05′W
Raufoss, Nor. (rou′fōs)	166	60°44′N	10°30′E
Raúl Soares, Braz. (rä-ōō′l-sōä′rĕs)	141a	20°05′S	42°28′W
Rauma, Fin. (rä′ō-mȧ)	160	61°07′N	21°31′E
Rauna, Lat. (rȧū′nȧ)	167	57°21′N	25°31′E
Raurkela, India	199	22°15′N	84°53′E
Rautalampi, Fin. (rä′ōō-tĕ-läm′pō)	167	62°39′N	26°25′E
Rava-Rus'ka, Ukr.	169	50°14′N	23°40′E
Ravenna, Italy (rä-vĕn′nä)	162	44°27′N	12°13′E
Ravenna, Ne., U.S. (rȧ-vĕn′ȧ)	112	41°20′N	98°50′W
Ravenna, Oh., U.S.	108	41°10′N	81°20′W
Ravensburg, Ger. (rä′vĕns-bōōrgh)	168	47°48′N	9°35′E

PLACE (Pronunciation)	PAGE	LAT.	LONG.
Ravensdale, Wa., U.S. (rā′vĕnz-dāl)	116a	47°22′N	121°58′W
Ravensthorpe, Austl. (rā′vĕns-thôrp)	218	33°30′S	120°20′E
Ravenswood, W.V., U.S. (rā′vĕnz-wŏŏd)	108	38°55′N	81°50′W
Rāwalpindi, Pak. (rä-wŭl-pēn′dė)	199	33°40′N	73°10′E
Rawa Mazowiecka, Pol.	169	51°46′N	20°17′E
Rawandoz, Iraq	181	36°37′N	44°30′E
Rawicz, Pol. (rä′vĕch)	168	51°36′N	16°51′E
Rawlina, Austl. (rôr-lēnȧ)	218	31°13′S	125°45′E
Rawlins, Wy., U.S. (rô′lĭnz)	104	41°46′N	107°15′W
Rawson, Arg. (rô′sŭn)	144	43°16′S	65°09′W
Rawson, Arg.	141c	34°36′S	60°03′W
Rawtenstall, Eng., U.K. (rô′tĕn-stôl)	158a	53°42′N	2°17′W
Ray, Cape, c., Can. (rā)	93a	47°40′N	59°18′W
Raya, Bukit, mtn., Indon.	212	0°45′S	112°11′E
Raychikinsk, Russia (rī′chĭ-kēnsk)	185	49°52′N	129°17′E
Rayleigh, Eng., U.K. [illegible]	[illegible]	[illegible]	0°36′E
Raymond, Can. (rā′mŭnd)	95	49°27′N	112°39′W
Raymond, Wa., U.S.	114	46°41′N	123°42′W
Raymondville, Tx., U.S. (rā′mŭnd-vĭl)	121	26°30′N	97°46′W
Ray Mountains, mts., Ak., U.S.	103	65°40′N	151°45′W
Rayne, La., U.S. (rān)	123	30°12′N	92°15′W
Rayón, Mex. (rä-yōn′)	130	21°49′N	99°39′W
Rayton, S. Afr. (rā′tŭn)	233b	25°45′S	28°33′E
Raytown, Mo., U.S. (rā′toun)	117f	39°01′N	94°48′W
Rayville, La., U.S. (rā-vĭl)	123	32°28′N	91°46′W
Raz, Pointe du, c., Fr. (pwănt dü rä)	161	48°02′N	4°43′W
Razdan, Arm.	182	40°30′N	44°46′E
Razdol'noye, Russia (räz-dôl′nô-yĕ)	210	43°38′N	131°58′E
Razgrad, Blg.	163	43°32′N	26°32′E
Razlog, Blg. (räz′lôk)	175	41°54′N	23°32′E
Razorback Mountain, mtn., Can. (rā′zẽr-băk)	94	51°35′N	124°42′W
Rea, r., Eng., U.K. (rē)	158a	52°25′N	2°31′W
Reaburn, Can. (rā′bûrn)	102f	50°06′N	97°53′W
Reading, Eng., U.K. (rĕd′ĭng)	161	51°25′N	0°58′W
Reading, Ma., U.S.	101a	42°32′N	71°07′W
Reading, Mi., U.S.	108	41°45′N	84°45′W
Reading, Oh., U.S.	111f	39°14′N	84°26′W
Reading, Pa., U.S.	105	40°20′N	75°55′W
Reading, co., Eng., U.K.	158a	52°37′N	0°40′W
Realengo, Braz. (rĕ-ä-lān-gô)	141a	23°50′S	43°25′W
Rebiana, Libya	231	24°10′N	22°03′E
Rebun, i., Japan (rē′bōōn)	210	45°25′N	140°54′E
Recanati, Italy (rā-kä-nä′tė)	174	43°25′N	13°35′E
Recherche, Archipelago of the, is., Austl. (rē-shârsh′)	220	34°17′S	122°30′E
Rechytsa, Bela. (ryĕ′chĕt-sȧ)	181	52°22′N	30°24′E
Recife, Braz. (rå-sē′fĕ)	143	8°09′S	34°59′W
Recife, Kapp, c., S. Afr. (rå-sē′fē)	233c	34°03′S	25°43′E
Recklinghausen, Ger. (rĕk′lĭng-hou-zĕn)	171c	51°36′N	7°13′E
Reconquista, Arg. (rā-kôn-kēs′tä)	144	29°01′S	59°41′W
Rector, Ar., U.S. (rĕk′tẽr)	121	36°16′N	90°21′W
Red, r., Asia	212	21°00′N	103°00′E
Red, r., N.A. (rĕd)	106	48°00′N	97°00′W
Red, r., Tn., U.S.	124	36°35′N	86°55′W
Red, r., U.S.	107	31°40′N	92°55′W
Red, North Fork, r., U.S.	120	35°20′N	100°08′W
Red, Prairie Dog Town Fork, r., U.S. (prā′rĭ)	120	34°54′N	101°31′W
Red, Salt Fork, r., U.S.	120	35°04′N	100°31′W
Redan, Ga., U.S. (rė-dăn′) (rĕd′ăn)	110c	33°44′N	84°09′W
Red Bank, N.J., U.S. (băngk)	110a	40°21′N	74°06′W
Red Bluff Reservoir, res., Tx., U.S.	122	32°03′N	103°52′W
Redby, Mn., U.S. (rĕd′bė)	113	47°52′N	94°55′W
Red Cedar, r., Wi., U.S. (sē′dẽr)	113	45°03′N	91°48′W
Redcliff, Can. (rĕd′clĭf)	90	50°05′N	110°47′W
Redcliffe, Austl. (rĕd′clĭf)	222	27°20′S	153°12′E
Red Cliff Indian Reservation, I.R., Wi., U.S.	113	46°48′N	91°22′W
Red Cloud, Ne., U.S. (kloud)	120	40°06′N	98°32′W
Red Deer, Can. (dēr)	90	52°16′N	113°48′W
Red Deer, r., Can.	92	51°00′N	111°00′W
Red Deer, r., Can.	97	52°55′N	102°10′W
Red Deer Lake, l., Can.	97	52°58′N	101°28′W
Reddick, Il., U.S. (rĕd′dĭk)	111a	41°06′N	88°16′W
Redding, Ca., U.S. (rĕd′ĭng)	114	40°36′N	122°25′W
Redenção da Serra, Braz. (rĕ-dĕn-souɴ-dä-sĕ′r-rä)	141a	23°17′S	45°31′W
Redfield, S.D., U.S. (rĕd′fēld)	112	44°53′N	98°30′W
Red Fish Bar, Tx., U.S.	123a	29°29′N	94°53′W
Red Indian Lake, l., Can. (ĭn′dĭ-ăn)	93a	48°40′N	56°50′W
Red Lake, Can. (lāk)	91	51°02′N	93°49′W
Red Lake, r., Mn., U.S.	112	48°02′N	96°04′W
Red Lake Falls, Mn., U.S. (lăk fôls)	112	47°52′N	96°17′W
Red Lake Indian Reservation, I.R., Mn., U.S.	112	48°09′N	95°55′W
Redlands, Ca., U.S. (rĕd′lăndz)	117a	34°04′N	117°11′W
Red Lion, Pa., U.S. (lī′ŭn)	109	39°55′N	76°30′W
Red Lodge, Mt., U.S.	115	45°13′N	107°16′W
Redmond, Wa., U.S. (rĕd′mŭnd)	116a	47°40′N	122°07′W
Rednitz, r., Ger. (rĕd′nētz)	168	49°10′N	11°00′E
Red Oak, Ia., U.S. (ōk)	112	41°00′N	95°12′W
Redon, Fr. (rē-dôn′)	170	47°42′N	2°03′W
Redonda, Isla, i., Braz. (ē′s-lä-rĕ-dô′n-dä)	144b	23°05′S	43°11′W
Redonda Island, i., Antig. (rĕ-dŏn′dȧ)	133b	16°55′N	62°28′W
Redondela, Spain (rā-dhôn-dā′lä)	172	42°16′N	8°34′W
Redondo, Port. (rå-dôn′dō)	172	38°40′N	7°32′W
Redondo, Wa., U.S. (rė-dŏn′dō)	116a	47°21′N	122°19′W
Redondo Beach, Ca., U.S.	117a	33°50′N	118°23′W
Red Pass, Can. (pȧs)	95	52°59′N	118°59′W
Red Rock, r., Mt., U.S.	115	44°54′N	112°44′W
Red Sea, sea	198	23°15′N	37°00′E

PLACE (Pronunciation)	PAGE	LAT.	LONG.
Redstone, Can. (rĕd′stōn)	94	52°08′N	123°42′W
Red Sucker Lake, l., Can. (sŭk′ẽr)	97	54°09′N	93°40′W
Redwater, r., Mt., U.S.	115	47°37′N	105°25′W
Red Willow Creek, r., Ne., U.S.	120	40°34′N	100°48′W
Red Wing, Mn., U.S.	113	44°34′N	92°35′W
Redwood City, Ca., U.S. (rĕd′ wŏŏd)	116b	37°29′N	122°13′W
Redwood Falls, Mn., U.S.	112	44°32′N	95°06′W
Redwood National Park, rec., Ca., U.S.	114	41°20′N	124°00′W
Redwood Valley, Ca., U.S.	118	39°15′N	123°12′W
Ree, Lough, l., Ire. (lŏĸ′rē′)	160	53°30′N	7°45′W
Reed City, Mi., U.S. (rēd)	108	43°50′N	85°35′W
Reed Lake, l., Can.	97	54°37′N	100°30′W
Reedley, Ca., U.S. (rēd′lė)	118	36°37′N	119°27′W
Reedsburg, Wi., U.S. (rēdz′bûrg)	113	43°32′N	90°01′W
Reedsport, Or., U.S. (rēdz′pôrt)	114	43°42′N	124°08′W
Reelfoot Lake, res., Tn., U.S. (rēl′fŏŏt)	124	36°18′N	89°20′W
Rees, Ger. [illegible]	171c	[illegible]	[illegible]
Reeves, Mount, mtn., Austl. (rēv′z)	[illegible]	33°50′S	149°56′E
Reform, Al., U.S. (rė-fôrm′)	124	33°23′N	88°00′W
Refugio, Tx., U.S. (rå-fōō′hyō) (rĕ-fū′jō)	123	28°18′N	97°15′W
Rega, r., Pol. (rĕ-gä)	168	53°48′N	15°30′E
Regen, r., Ger. (rā′ghĕn)	168	49°09′N	12°21′E
Regensburg, Ger. (rā′ghĕns-bôrgh)	161	49°02′N	12°06′E
Reggio, La., U.S. (rĕg′jĭ-ō)	110d	29°50′N	89°46′W
Reggio di Calabria, Italy (rĕ′jô dē kä-lä′brē-ä)	163	38°07′N	15°42′E
Reggio nell' Emilia, Italy	162	44°43′N	10°34′E
Reghin, Rom. (rå-gēn′)	169	46°47′N	24°44′E
Regina, Can. (rē-jī′nȧ)	96	50°25′N	104°39′W
Regla, Cuba (rĕg′lä)	134	23°08′N	82°20′W
Regnitz, r., Ger. (rĕg′nētz)	168	49°50′N	10°55′E
Reguengos de Monsaraz, Port.	172	38°26′N	7°30′W
Rehoboth, Nmb.	232	23°10′S	17°15′E
Rehovot, Isr.	197a	31°53′N	34°49′E
Reichenbach, Ger. (rī′kĕn-bäĸ)	168	50°36′N	12°18′E
Reidsville, N.C., U.S. (rēdz′vĭl)	125	36°20′N	79°37′W
Reigate, Eng., U.K. (rī′gāt)	164	51°12′N	0°12′W
Reims, Fr. (răɴs)	154	49°16′N	4°00′E
Reina Adelaida, Archipiélago, is., Chile	144	52°00′S	74°15′W
Reinbeck, Ia., U.S. (rīn′bĕk)	113	42°22′N	92°34′W
Reindeer, l., Can. (rān′dēr)	92	57°36′N	101°23′W
Reindeer, r., Can.	96	55°45′N	103°30′W
Reindeer Island, i., Can.	97	52°25′N	98°00′W
Reinosa, Spain (rå-ē-nō′sä)	172	43°01′N	4°08′W
Reistertown, Md., U.S. (rēs′tẽr-toun)	110e	39°28′N	76°50′W
Reitz, S. Afr.	238c	27°48′S	28°25′E
Rema, Jabal, mtn., Yemen	198	14°13′N	44°38′E
Rembau, Malay.	197b	2°36′N	102°06′E
Remedios, Col. (rĕ-mĕ′dyōs)	142a	7°03′N	74°42′W
Remedios, Cuba (rā-mā′dhē-ōs)	134	22°30′N	79°35′W
Remedios, Pan. (rĕ-mĕ′dyōs)	133	8°14′N	81°46′W
Remiremont, Fr. (rē-mēr-môɴ′)	171	48°01′N	6°35′E
Rempang, i., Indon.	197b	0°51′N	104°04′E
Remscheid, Ger. (rĕm′shīt)	171c	51°10′N	7°11′E
Rena, Nor.	166	61°08′N	11°17′E
Rendova, i., Sol. Is. (rĕn′dô-vȧ)	221	8°38′S	156°26′E
Rendsburg, Ger. (rĕnts′bôrgh)	168	54°19′N	9°39′E
Renfrew, Can. (rĕn′frōō)	91	45°30′N	76°30′W
Rengam, Malay. (rĕn′gäm′)	197b	1°53′N	103°24′E
Rengo, Chile (rĕn′gō)	141b	34°22′S	70°50′W
Reni, Ukr. (ran′)	177	45°26′N	28°18′E
Renmark, Austl. (rĕn′märk)	218	34°10′S	140°50′E
Rennel, i., Sol. Is. (rĕn-nĕl′)	221	11°50′S	160°38′E
Rennes, Fr. (rĕn)	154	48°07′N	1°02′W
Reno, Nv., U.S. (rē′nō)	104	39°32′N	119°49′W
Reno, r., Italy (rā′nō)	174	44°10′N	10°55′E
Renovo, Pa., U.S. (rė-nō′vō)	109	41°20′N	77°50′W
Renqiu, China (rŭn-chyō)	206	38°44′N	116°05′E
Rensselaer, In., U.S. (rĕn′sẽ-lâr)	108	41°00′N	87°10′W
Rensselaer, N.Y., U.S. (rĕn′sẽ-lâr)	109	42°40′N	73°45′W
Rentchler, Il., U.S. (rĕnt′chlẽr)	117e	38°30′N	89°52′W
Renton, Wa., U.S. (rĕn′tŭn)	116a	47°29′N	122°13′W
Repentigny, Can.	102a	45°47′N	73°26′W
Republic, Al., U.S. (rė-pŭb′lĭk)	110h	33°37′N	86°54′W
Republic, Wa., U.S.	114	48°38′N	118°44′W
Republican, r., U.S.	106	40°15′N	100°00′W
Republican, South Fork, r., Co., U.S. (rė-pŭb′lĭ-kăn)	120	39°35′N	102°28′W
Repulse Bay, b., Austl. (rė-pŭls′)	221	20°56′S	149°22′E
Requena, Spain (rå-kā′nä)	162	39°29′N	1°03′W
Resende, Braz. (rĕ-sĕ′n-dĕ)	141a	22°30′S	44°26′W
Resende Costa, Braz. (kôs-tä)	141a	20°55′S	44°12′W
Reshetylivka, Ukr.	177	49°34′N	34°04′E
Resistencia, Arg. (rā-sēs-tĕn′syä)	144	27°24′S	58°54′W
Reşiţa, Rom. (rā′shē-tȧ)	175	45°18′N	21°56′E
Resolute *see* Qausuittuq, Can.	89	74°41′N	95°00′W
Resolution, i., Can. (rĕz-ō-lū′shŭn)	93	61°30′N	63°58′W
Resolution Island, i., N.Z. (rĕz-ŏl-ūshūn)	221a	45°43′S	166°20′E
Restigouche, r., Can.	100	47°35′N	67°35′W
Restrepo, Col. (rĕs-trĕ′pô)	142a	3°49′N	76°31′W
Restrepo, Col.	142a	4°16′N	73°32′W
Retalhuleu, Guat. (rā-täl-ōō-lān′)	132	14°31′N	91°41′W
Rethel, Fr. (r-tĕl′)	170	49°34′N	4°20′E
Réthimnon, Grc.	174a	35°21′N	24°30′E
Retie, Bel.	159a	51°16′N	5°08′E
Retsil, Wa., U.S. (rĕt′sĭl)	116a	47°33′N	122°37′W
Reunion, dep., Afr. (rā-ü-nyôn′)	3	21°06′S	55°36′E
Reus, Spain (rā′ōōs)	162	41°08′N	1°05′E
Reutlingen, Ger. (roit′lĭng-ĕn)	168	48°29′N	9°14′E
Reutov, Russia (rĕ-ōō′ôf)	186b	55°45′N	37°52′E
Revda, Russia (ryâv′dȧ)	186a	56°48′N	59°57′E

ăt; finȧl; rāte; senåte; ärm; ȧsk; sofȧ; fâre; ch-choose; dh-as th in other; bē; ėvent; bĕt; recĕnt; cratẽr; g-gō; gh-guttural g; bĭt; ĭ-short neutral; rīde; ĸ-guttural k as ch in German ich;

PRONOUNCING INDEX

Revelstoke – Rockingham Forest 341

PLACE (Pronunciation)	PAGE	LAT.	LONG.
Revelstoke, Can. (rĕv´ĕl-stōk)	90	51°00'N	118°12'W
Reventazón, Río, r., C.R. (rā-vĕn-tä-zōn´)	133	10°10'N	83°30'W
Revere, Ma., U.S. (rė-vēr´)	101a	42°24'N	71°01'W
Revillagigedo, Islas, is., Mex. (ē´s-läs-rĕ-vēl-yä-hĕ´gĕ-dō)	128	18°45'N	111°00'W
Revillagigedo Chan, Ak., U.S. (rĕ-vĭl´ȧ-gĭ-gē´dō)	94	55°10'N	131°13'W
Revillagigedo Island, i., Ak., U.S.	94	55°35'N	131°23'W
Revin, Fr. (rē-văɴ)	170	49°56'N	4°34'E
Rewa, India (rā´wä)	199	24°41'N	81°11'E
Rewāri, India	202	28°19'N	76°39'E
Rexburg, Id., U.S. (rĕks´bûrg)	115	43°50'N	111°48'W
Rey, Iran	201	35°35'N	51°25'E
Rey, l., Mex. (rā)	122	27°00'N	103°33'W
Rey, Isla del, i., Pan. (ē´s-lä-dĕl-rā´ė)	133	8°20'N	78°40'W
Reyes, Bol. (rā´yĕs)	142	14°19'S	67°16'W
Reyes, Point, c., Ca., U.S.	118	38°00'N	123°00'W
Reykjanes, c., Ice. (rā´kyȧ-nĕs)	150	63°37'N	24°33'W
Reykjavík, Ice. (rā´kyȧ-vēk)	154	64°09'N	21°39'W
Reynosa, Mex. (rā-ė-nō´sä)	122	26°05'N	98°21'W
Rēzekne, Lat. (rå´zĕk-nĕ)	180	56°31'N	27°19'E
Rezh, Russia (rĕzh´)	186a	57°22'N	61°23'E
Rezina, Mol. (ryĕzh´ĕ-nĭ)	177	47°44'N	28°56'E
Rhaetian Alps, mts., Eur.	168	46°30'N	10°00'E
Rhaetien Alps, mts., Eur.	174	46°22'N	10°33'E
Rheinberg, Ger. (rīn´bĕrgh)	171c	51°33'N	6°37'E
Rheine, Ger. (rī´nĕ)	168	52°16'N	7°26'E
Rheinkamp, Ger.	171c	51°30'N	6°37'E
Rheinland, hist. reg., Ger.	168	50°05'N	6°40'E
Rheydt, Ger. (rĕ´yt)	171c	51°10'N	6°28'E
Rhin, r., Ger. (rēn)	159b	52°52'N	12°49'E
Rhine, r., Eur.	156	50°34'N	7°21'E
Rhinelander, Wi., U.S. (rīn´lăn-dēr)	113	45°39'N	89°25'W
Rhin Kanal, can., Ger. (rēn kä-näl´)	159b	52°47'N	12°40'E
Rhiou, r., Alg.	173	35°45'N	1°18'E
Rhode Island, state, U.S. (rōd ī´lănd)	105	41°35'N	71°40'W
Rhode Island, i., R.I., U.S.	110b	41°31'N	71°14'W
Rhodes, S. Afr. (rōdz)	233c	30°48'S	27°56'E
Rhodes see Ródhos, i., Grc.	156	36°00'N	28°29'E
Rhodesia see Zimbabwe, nation, Afr.	232	17°50'S	29°30'E
Rhodope Mountains, mts., Eur. (rô´dō-pĕ)	156	42°00'N	24°08'E
Rhondda, Wales, U.K. (rŏn´dhȧ)	164	51°40'N	3°40'W
Rhône, r., Fr. (rōn)	156	44°30'N	4°45'E
Rhoon, Neth.	159a	51°52'N	4°24'E
Rhum, i., Scot., U.K. (rŭm)	164	57°00'N	6°20'W
Riachão, Braz. (rē-ä-chouɴ´)	143	7°15'S	46°30'W
Rialto, Ca., U.S. (rē-ăl´tō)	117a	34°06'N	117°23'W
Riau, prov., Indon.	197b	0°56'N	101°25'E
Riau, Kepulauan, i., Indon.	212	0°30'N	104°55'E
Riau, Selat, strt., Indon.	197b	0°40'N	104°27'E
Riaza, r., Spain (rė-ä´thä)	172	41°25'N	3°25'W
Ribadavia, Spain (rē-bä-dhä´vē-ä)	172	42°18'N	8°06'W
Ribadeo, Spain (rē-bä-dhā´ō)	172	43°32'N	7°05'W
Ribadesella, Spain (rē´bä-dä-säl´yä)	172	43°30'N	5°02'W
Ribe, Den. (rē´bĕ)	166	55°20'N	8°45'E
Ribeirão Prêto, Braz. (rē-bā-rouɴ-prĕ´tō)	143	21°11'S	47°47'W
Ribera, N.M., U.S. (rē-bĕ´rä)	120	35°23'N	105°27'W
Riberalta, Bol. (rē-bā-räl´tä)	142	11°06'S	66°02'W
Rib Lake, Wi., U.S. (rĭb lāk)	113	45°20'N	90°11'W
Rîbniţa, Mol.	177	47°45'N	29°02'E
Rice, l., Can.	99	44°05'N	78°10'W
Rice Lake, Wi., U.S.	113	45°30'N	91°44'W
Rice Lake, l., Mn., U.S.	117g	45°10'N	93°09'W
Richards Island, i., Can. (rĭch´ērds)	103	69°45'N	135°30'W
Richards Landing, Can. (lănd´ĭng)	117k	46°18'N	84°02'W
Richardson, Tx., U.S. (rĭch´ērd-sŭn)	117c	32°56'N	96°44'W
Richardson, Wa., U.S.	116a	48°27'N	122°54'W
Richardson Mountains, mts., Can.	92	66°58'N	136°19'W
Richardson Mountains, mts., N.Z.	223	44°50'S	168°30'E
Richardson Park, De., U.S. (pärk)	109	39°45'N	75°35'W
Richelieu, r., Can. (rēsh´lyû´)	99	45°05'N	73°25'W
Richfield, Mn., U.S.	117g	44°53'N	93°17'W
Richfield, Oh., U.S.	111d	41°14'N	81°38'W
Richfield, Ut., U.S.	119	38°45'N	112°05'W
Richford, Vt., U.S. (rĭch´fērd)	109	45°00'N	72°35'W
Rich Hill, Mo., U.S. (rĭch hĭl)	121	38°05'N	94°21'W
Richibucto, Can. (rĭ-chĭ-bŭk´tō)	91	46°41'N	64°52'W
Richland, Ga., U.S. (rĭch´lănd)	124	32°05'N	84°40'W
Richland, Wa., U.S.	114	46°17'N	119°19'W
Richland Center, Wi., U.S. (sĕn´tēr)	113	43°20'N	90°25'W
Richmond, Austl. (rĭch´mŭnd)	219	20°47'S	143°14'E
Richmond, Austl.	217b	33°36'S	150°45'E
Richmond, Can.	102c	45°12'N	75°49'W
Richmond, Can.	99	45°40'N	72°07'W
Richmond, S. Afr.	233c	29°52'S	30°17'E
Richmond, Il., U.S.	111a	42°29'N	88°18'W
Richmond, In., U.S.	108	39°50'N	85°00'W
Richmond, Ky., U.S.	108	37°45'N	84°20'W
Richmond, Mo., U.S.	121	39°16'N	93°58'W
Richmond, Tx., U.S.	123	29°35'N	95°45'W
Richmond, Ut., U.S.	115	41°55'N	111°50'W
Richmond, Va., U.S.	105	37°35'N	77°30'W
Richmond Beach, Wa., U.S.	116a	47°47'N	122°23'W
Richmond Heights, Mo., U.S.	117e	38°38'N	90°20'W
Richmond Highlands, Wa., U.S.	116a	47°46'N	122°22'W
Richmond Hill, Can. (hĭl)	99	43°53'N	79°26'W
Richton, Ms., U.S. (rĭch´tŭn)	124	31°20'N	89°54'W
Richwood, W.V., U.S. (rĭch´wŏŏd)	108	38°10'N	80°30'W
Ridderkerk, Neth.	159a	51°52'N	4°35'E
Rideau, r., Can.	102c	45°17'N	75°41'W
Rideau Lake, l., Can. (rė-dō´)	99	44°40'N	76°20'W
Ridgefield, Ct., U.S. (rĭj´fēld)	110a	41°16'N	73°30'W
Ridgefield, Wa., U.S.	116c	45°49'N	122°40'W
Ridgeway, Can. (rĭj´wā)	111c	42°53'N	79°02'W
Ridgewood, N.J., U.S. (ridj´wŏŏd)	110a	40°59'N	74°08'W
Ridgway, Pa., U.S.	109	41°25'N	78°40'W
Riding Mountain, mtn., Can. (rīd´ĭng)	97	50°37'N	99°37'W
Riding Mountain National Park, rec., Can. (rīd´ĭng)	92	50°59'N	99°19'W
Riding Rocks, is., Bah.	134	25°20'N	79°10'W
Riebeek-Oos, S. Afr.	233c	33°14'S	26°09'E
Ried, Aus. (rēd)	168	48°13'N	13°30'E
Riesa, Ger. (rē´zȧ)	168	51°17'N	13°17'E
Rieti, Italy (rė-ā´tē)	162	42°25'N	12°51'E
Rievleidam, res., S. Afr.	233b	25°52'S	28°18'E
Riffe Lake, res., Wa., U.S.	114	46°20'N	122°10'W
Rifle, Co., U.S. (rī´f'l)	119	39°35'N	107°50'W
Rīga, Lat. (rē´gȧ)	178	56°55'N	24°05'E
Riga, Gulf of, b., Eur.	180	57°56'N	23°05'E
Rīgān, Iran	198	28°45'N	58°55'E
Rigaud, Can. (rė-gō´)	102a	45°29'N	74°18'W
Rigby, Id., U.S. (rĭg´bė)	115	43°40'N	111°55'W
Rigeley, W.V., U.S. (rĭj´lė)	109	39°40'N	78°45'W
Rīgestān, des., Afg.	198	30°53'N	64°42'E
Rigolet, Can. (rĭg-ō-lā´)	91	54°10'N	58°40'W
Riihimäki, Fin.	167	60°44'N	24°44'E
Rijeka, Cro. (rĭ-yĕ´kä)	162	45°22'N	14°24'E
Rijkevorsel, Bel.	159a	51°21'N	4°46'E
Rijswijk, Neth.	159a	52°03'N	4°19'E
Rika, r., Ukr. (rē´kȧ)	169	48°21'N	23°37'E
Rima, r., Nig.	235	13°30'N	5°50'E
Rimavska Sobota, Slvk. (rē´måf-skä sô´bô-tä)	169	48°25'N	20°01'E
Rimbo, Swe. (rēm´bō)	166	59°45'N	18°22'E
Rimini, Italy (rē´mē-nē)	162	44°03'N	12°33'E
Rimouski, Can. (rė-mōōs´kė)	91	48°27'N	68°32'W
Rincón de Romos, Mex. (rēn-kōn dā rō-mōs´)	130	22°13'N	102°21'W
Ringkøbing, Den. (rĭng´kûb-ĭng)	160	56°06'N	8°14'E
Ringkøbing Fjord, b., Den.	166	55°55'N	8°04'E
Ringsted, Den. (rĭng´stĕdh)	166	55°27'N	11°49'E
Ringvassøya, i., Nor. (rĭng´väs-ûė)	160	69°58'N	16°43'E
Ringwood, Austl.	217a	37°49'S	145°14'E
Rinjani, Gunung, mtn., Indon.	212	8°39'S	116°22'E
Río Abajo, Pan. (rē´ō-ä-bä´кō)	128a	9°01'N	78°30'W
Río Balsas, Mex. (rē´ō-bäl-säs)	130	17°59'N	99°45'W
Riobamba, Ec. (rē´ō-bäm-bä)	142	1°45'S	78°37'W
Rio Bonito, Braz. (rē´ō bō-nē´tō)	141a	22°44'S	42°38'W
Rio Branco, Braz. (rē´ō brăŋ´kō)	142	9°57'S	67°50'W
Río Branco, Ur. (rīō brănco)	144	32°33'S	53°29'W
Río Casca, Braz. (rē´ō-kä´s-kä)	141a	20°15'S	42°39'W
Río Chico, Ven. (rē´ō chē´kō)	143b	10°20'N	65°58'W
Rio Claro, Braz. (rē´ō klä´rō)	143	22°25'S	47°33'W
Río Cuarto, Arg. (rē´ō kwär´tō)	144	33°05'S	64°15'W
Rio das Flores, Braz. (rē´ō-däs-flō-rĕs)	141a	22°10'S	43°35'W
Rio de Janeiro, Braz. (rē´ō dā zhä-nâ´ė-rō)	144b	22°50'S	43°20'W
Rio de Janeiro, state, Braz.	143	22°27'S	42°43'W
Río de Jesús, Pan.	133	7°54'N	80°59'W
Rio Frío, Mex. (rē´ō-frē´ō)	131a	19°21'N	98°40'W
Río Gallegos, Arg. (rē´ō gä-lā´gōs)	144	51°43'S	69°15'W
Rio Grande, Braz. (rē´ō grän´dĕ)	144	31°04'S	52°14'W
Río Grande, Mex. (rē´ō grän´dā)	130	23°51'N	102°59'W
Riogrande, Tx., U.S. (rē´ō grän-dā)	122	26°23'N	98°48'W
Rio Grande do Norte, state, Braz.	143	5°26'S	37°20'W
Rio Grande do Sul, state, Braz. (rē´ō grän´dĕ-dō-sōō´l)	144	29°00'S	54°00'W
Ríohacha, Col. (rē´ō-ä´chä)	142	11°30'N	72°54'W
Río Hato, Pan. (rē´-ō-ä´tō)	133	8°19'N	80°11'W
Riom, Fr. (rė-ôɴ´)	170	45°54'N	3°08'E
Rio Muni, hist. reg., Eq. Gui. (rē´ō mōō´nė)	230	1°47'N	8°33'E
Ríonegro, Col. (rē´ō-nĕ´grō)	142a	6°09'N	75°22'W
Río Negro, prov., Arg. (rē´ō nā´grō)	144	40°15'S	68°15'W
Río Negro, dept., Ur. (rē´ō-nĕ´grō)	141c	32°48'S	57°45'W
Río Negro, Embalse del, res., Ur.	144	32°45'S	55°50'W
Rionero, Italy (rē-ō-nā´rō)	174	40°55'N	15°42'E
Rioni, r., Geor.	182	42°08'N	41°39'E
Rio Novo, Braz. (rē´ō-nô´vō)	141a	21°30'S	43°08'W
Rio Pardo de Minas, Braz. (rē´ō pär´dō-dĕ-mē´näs)	143	15°43'S	42°24'W
Rio Pombo, Braz. (rē´ō pôm´bä)	141a	21°17'S	43°09'W
Rio Sorocaba, Represa do, res., Braz.	141a	23°37'S	47°19'W
Ríosucio, Col. (rē´ō-sōō´syō)	142a	5°25'N	75°41'W
Río Tercero, Arg. (rē´ō dĕr-sĕ´rō)	144	32°12'S	63°59'W
Rio Verde, Braz. (vĕr´dĕ)	143	17°47'S	50°49'W
Ríoverde, Mex. (rē´ō-vĕr´då)	128	21°54'N	99°59'W
Ripley, Eng., U.K. (rĭp´lė)	158a	53°03'N	1°24'W
Ripley, Ms., U.S.	124	34°44'N	88°55'W
Ripley, Tn., U.S.	124	35°44'N	89°34'W
Ripoll, Spain (rē-pōl´)	173	42°10'N	2°10'E
Ripon, Wi., U.S. (rĭp´ŏn)	113	43°49'N	88°50'W
Ripon, i., Austl.	220	20°05'S	118°10'E
Ripon Falls, wtfl., Ug.	232	0°38'N	33°02'E
Risaralda, dept., Col.	142a	5°15'N	76°00'W
Risdon, Austl. (rĭz´dŭn)	219	42°37'S	147°32'E
Rishiri, i., Japan (rē-shē´rē)	210	45°10'N	141°08'E
Rishon le Ziyyon, Isr.	197a	31°57'N	34°48'E
Rishra, India	202a	22°42'N	88°22'E
Rising Sun, In., U.S. (rīz´ĭng sŭn)	108	38°55'N	84°55'W
Risor, Nor. (rēs´ûr)	160	58°44'N	9°10'E
Ritacuva, Alto, mtn., Col. (ā´l-tō-rē-tä-kōō´vä)	142	6°22'N	72°13'W
Rittman, Oh., U.S. (rĭt´năn)	111d	40°58'N	81°47'W
Ritzville, Wa., U.S. (rĭts´vĭl)	114	47°08'N	118°23'W
Riva, Dom. Rep. (rē´vä)	135	19°10'N	69°55'W
Riva, Italy (rē´vä)	174	45°54'N	10°49'E
Riva, Md., U.S. (rī´vȧ)	110e	38°57'N	76°36'W
Rivas, Nic. (rē´väs)	132	11°25'N	85°51'W
Rive-de-Gier, Fr. (rēv-dē-zhė-ā´)	170	45°32'N	4°37'E
Rivera, Ur. (rė-vā´rä)	144	30°52'S	55°32'W
River Cess, Lib. (rĭv´ēr sĕs)	230	5°46'N	9°52'W
Riverdale, Il., U.S. (rĭv´ēr dāl)	111a	41°38'N	87°36'W
Riverdale, Ut., U.S.	117b	41°11'N	112°00'W
River Falls, Al., U.S.	124	31°20'N	86°25'W
River Falls, Wi., U.S.	113	44°48'N	92°38'W
Riverhead, N.Y., U.S. (rĭv´ēr hĕd)	109	40°55'N	72°40'W
Riverina, reg., Austl. (rĭv-ēr-ē´nä)	221	34°55'S	144°30'E
River Jordan, Can. (jôr´dăn)	116a	48°25'N	124°03'W
River Oaks, Tx., U.S. (ōkz)	117c	32°47'N	97°24'W
River Rouge, Mi., U.S. (rōōzh)	111b	42°16'N	83°09'W
Rivers, Can.	97	50°01'N	100°15'W
Riverside, Ca., U.S. (rĭv´ēr-sīd)	104	33°59'N	117°21'W
Riverside, N.J., U.S.	110f	40°02'N	74°58'W
Rivers Inlet, Can.	94	51°45'N	127°15'W
Riverstone, Austl.	217b	33°41'S	150°52'E
Riverton, Va., U.S.	109	39°00'N	78°15'W
Riverton, Wy., U.S.	115	43°02'N	108°24'W
Rivesaltes, Fr. (rēv'zält´)	170	42°48'N	2°48'E
Riviera Beach, Fl., U.S. (rĭv-ĭ-ēr´ȧ bēch)	125a	26°46'N	80°04'W
Riviera Beach, Md., U.S.	110e	39°10'N	76°32'W
Rivière-Beaudette, Can.	102a	45°14'N	74°20'W
Rivière-du-Loup, Can. (rė-vyâr´ dü lōō´)	91	47°50'N	69°32'W
Rivière Qui Barre, Can. (rēv-yĕr´ kē-bär)	102g	53°47'N	113°51'W
Rivière-Trois-Pistoles, Can. (trwä´pēs-tôl´)	100	48°07'N	69°10'W
Rivne, Ukr.	177	48°11'N	31°46'E
Rivne, Ukr.	181	50°37'N	26°17'E
Rivne, prov., Ukr.	177	50°55'N	27°00'E
Riyadh, Sau. Ar.	198	24°31'N	46°47'E
Rize, Tur. (rē´zĕ)	163	41°00'N	40°30'E
Rizhao, China (rē-jou)	208	35°27'N	119°28'E
Rizzuto, Cape, c., Italy (rēt-sōō´tō)	175	38°53'N	17°05'E
Rjukan, Nor. (ryōō´kän)	160	59°53'N	8°30'E
Roanne, Fr. (rō-än´)	161	46°02'N	4°04'E
Roanoke, Al., U.S. (rō´ȧ-nōk)	124	33°08'N	85°21'W
Roanoke, Va., U.S.	105	37°16'N	79°55'W
Roanoke, r., U.S.	107	36°17'N	77°22'W
Roanoke Rapids, N.C., U.S.	125	36°25'N	77°40'W
Roanoke Rapids Lake, res., N.C., U.S.	125	36°28'N	77°37'W
Roan Plateau, plat., Co., U.S. (rōn)	119	39°25'N	110°00'W
Roatan, Hond. (rō-ä-tän´)	132	16°18'N	86°33'W
Roatán, i., Hond.	132	16°19'N	86°46'W
Robbeneiland, i., S. Afr.	232a	33°48'S	18°22'E
Robbins, Il., U.S. (rŏb´ĭnz)	111a	41°39'N	87°42'W
Robbinsdale, Mn., U.S. (rŏb´ĭnz-dāl)	117g	45°03'N	93°22'W
Robe, Wa., U.S. (rōb)	116a	48°06'N	121°50'W
Roberts, Mount, mtn., Austl. (rŏb´ērts)	221	28°05'S	152°30'E
Roberts, Point, c., Wa., U.S. (rŏb´ērts)	116d	48°58'N	123°05'W
Robertson, Lac, l., Can.	101	51°00'N	59°10'W
Robertsport, Lib. (rŏb´ērts-pōrt)	230	6°45'N	11°22'W
Roberval, Can. (rŏb´ēr-văl) (rô-bĕr-vål´)	91	48°32'N	72°15'W
Robinson, Can.	101	48°16'N	58°50'W
Robinson, Il., U.S. (rŏb´ĭn-sŭn)	108	39°00'N	87°45'W
Robinvale, Austl. (rŏb-ĭn´vāl)	222	34°45'S	142°45'E
Roblin, Can.	97	51°15'N	101°25'W
Robson, Mount, mtn., Can. (rŏb´sŭn)	95	53°07'N	119°09'W
Robstown, Tx., U.S. (rŏbz´toun)	123	27°46'N	97°41'W
Roca, Cabo da, c., Port. (kȧ´bō-dä-rō´kȧ)	172	38°47'N	9°30'W
Rocas, Atol das, atoll, Braz. (ä-tôl-däs-rō´kȧs)	143	3°50'S	33°46'W
Rocha, Ur. (rō´chäs)	144	34°26'S	54°14'W
Rochdale, Eng., U.K. (rŏch´dāl)	164	53°37'N	2°09'W
Roche à Bateau, Haiti (rôsh á bá-tō´)	135	18°10'N	74°00'W
Rochefort, Fr. (rôsh-fôr´)	161	45°55'N	0°57'W
Rochelle, Il., U.S. (rō-shĕl´)	113	41°53'N	89°06'W
Rochester, Eng., U.K.	158a	51°24'N	0°30'E
Rochester, In., U.S. (rŏch´ĕs-tēr)	108	41°05'N	86°20'W
Rochester, Mi., U.S.	111b	42°41'N	83°09'W
Rochester, Mn., U.S.	105	44°01'N	92°30'W
Rochester, N.H., U.S.	109	43°20'N	71°00'W
Rochester, N.Y., U.S.	105	43°15'N	77°35'W
Rochester, Pa., U.S.	111e	40°42'N	80°16'W
Rock, r., Ia., U.S.	112	43°17'N	96°13'W
Rock, r., Or., U.S.	116c	45°34'N	122°52'W
Rock, r., Or., U.S.	116c	45°52'N	123°14'W
Rock, r., U.S.	107	41°40'N	90°00'W
Rockaway, N.J., U.S. (rŏck´ȧ-wā)	110a	40°54'N	74°30'W
Rockbank, Austl.	217a	37°44'S	144°40'E
Rockcliffe Park, Can. (rok´klĭf pärk)	102c	45°27'N	75°40'W
Rock Creek, r., Can. (rŏk)	115	49°01'N	107°00'W
Rock Creek, r., Il., U.S.	111a	41°16'N	87°54'W
Rock Creek, r., Mt., U.S.	115	46°25'N	113°40'W
Rock Creek, r., Or., U.S.	114	45°30'N	120°06'W
Rock Creek, r., Wa., U.S.	114	47°09'N	117°50'W
Rockdale, Austl.	217b	33°57'S	151°08'E
Rockdale, Md., U.S.	110e	39°22'N	76°49'W
Rockdale, Tx., U.S. (rŏk´dāl)	123	30°39'N	97°00'W
Rock Falls, Il., U.S. (rŏk fôlz)	113	41°45'N	89°42'W
Rockford, Il., U.S. (rŏk´fērd)	105	42°16'N	89°07'W
Rockhampton, Austl. (rŏk-hămp´tŭn)	219	23°26'S	150°29'E
Rock Hill, S.C., U.S. (rŏk´hĭl)	105	34°55'N	81°01'W
Rockingham, N.C., U.S. (rŏk´ĭng-hăm)	125	34°54'N	79°45'W
Rockingham Forest, for., Eng., U.K. (rok´ĭng-hăm)	158a	52°29'N	0°43'W

ng-sing; ŋ-baŋk; ɴ-nasalized n; nŏd; cŏmmit; ōld; ōbey; ôrder; oi-boil; fōōd; ŏŏ-as oo in foot; ou-out; s-soft; sh-dish; th-thin; pūre; ůnite; ûrn; stŭd; circŭs; ü-as in French tu; ´-indeterminate vowel.

342 Rock Island – Rumbek PRONOUNCING INDEX

PLACE (Pronunciation)	PAGE	LAT.	LONG.
Rock Island, Il., U.S.	105	41°31′N	90°37′W
Rock Island Dam, Wa., U.S. (ī lănd)	114	47°17′N	120°33′W
Rockland, Can. (rŏk′lănd)	102c	45°33′N	75°17′W
Rockland, Ma., U.S.	101a	42°07′N	70°55′W
Rockland, Me., U.S.	100	44°06′N	69°09′W
Rockland Reservoir, res., Austl.	222	36°55′S	142°20′E
Rockmart, Ga., U.S. (rŏk′märt)	124	33°58′N	85°00′W
Rockmont, Wi., U.S. (rŏk′mŏnt)	117h	46°34′N	91°54′W
Rockport, In., U.S. (rŏk′pōrt)	108	38°20′N	87°00′W
Rockport, Ma., U.S.	101a	42°39′N	70°37′W
Rockport, Mo., U.S.	121	40°25′N	95°30′W
Rockport, Tx., U.S.	123	28°03′N	97°03′W
Rock Rapids, Ia., U.S. (răp′ĭdz)	112	43°26′N	96°10′W
Rock Sound, strt., Bah.	134	24°50′N	76°05′W
Rocksprings, Tx., U.S. (rŏk springs)	122	30°02′N	100°12′W
Rock Springs, Wy., U.S.	104	41°35′N	109°13′W
Rockstone, Guy. (rŏk′stōn)	[illegible]	[illegible]	[illegible]
Rock Valley, Ia., U.S. (văl′ĭ)	112	43°13′N	96°17′W
Rockville, In., U.S. (rŏk′vĭl)	108	39°45′N	87°15′W
Rockville, Md., U.S.	110e	39°05′N	77°11′W
Rockville Centre, N.Y., U.S. (sĕn′tẽr)	110a	40°39′N	73°39′W
Rockwall, Tx., U.S. (rŏk′wôl)	121	32°55′N	96°23′W
Rockwell City, Ia., U.S. (rŏk′wĕl)	113	42°22′N	94°37′W
Rockwood, Can. (rŏk-wo͝od)	102d	43°37′N	80°08′W
Rockwood, Me., U.S.	100	45°39′N	69°45′W
Rockwood, Tn., U.S.	124	35°51′N	84°41′W
Rocky, East Branch, r., Oh., U.S.	111d	41°13′N	81°43′W
Rocky, West Branch, r., Oh., U.S.	111d	41°17′N	81°54′W
Rocky Boys Indian Reservation, I.R., Mt., U.S.	115	48°08′N	109°34′W
Rocky Ford, Co., U.S.	120	38°02′N	103°43′W
Rocky Hill, N.J., U.S. (hĭl)	110a	40°24′N	74°38′W
Rocky Island Lake, l., Can.	98	46°56′N	83°04′W
Rocky Mount, N.C., U.S.	125	35°55′N	77°47′W
Rocky Mountain House, Can.	95	52°22′N	114°55′W
Rocky Mountain National Park, rec., Co., U.S.	106	40°29′N	106°06′W
Rocky Mountains, mts., N.A.	89	50°00′N	114°00′W
Rocky River, Oh., U.S.	111d	41°29′N	81°51′W
Rodas, Cuba (rō′dhäs)	134	22°20′N	80°35′W
Roden, r., Eng., U.K. (rō′dĕn)	158a	52°49′N	2°38′W
Rodeo, Mex. (rô-dā′ō)	122	25°12′N	104°34′W
Rodeo, Ca., U.S. (rō′dē̇ō)	116b	38°02′N	122°16′W
Roderick Island, i., Can. (rŏd′ẽ-rĭk)	94	52°40′N	128°22′W
Rodez, Fr. (rô-dĕz′)	161	44°22′N	2°34′E
Rodnei, Munţii, mts., Rom.	169	47°41′N	24°05′E
Rodniki, Russia (rôd′nē̇-kē̇)	180	57°08′N	41°48′E
Rodonit, Kep I, c., Alb.	175	41°38′N	19°01′E
Ródos, Grc.	163	36°24′N	28°15′E
Ródos, i., Grc.	162	36°00′N	28°29′E
Roebling, N.J., U.S. (rōb′lĭng)	110f	40°07′N	74°48′W
Roebourne, Austl. (rō′bŭrn)	218	20°50′S	117°15′E
Roebuck Bay, b., Austl. (rō′bŭck)	220	18°15′S	121°10′E
Roedtan, S. Afr.	238c	24°37′S	29°08′E
Roeselare, Bel.	165	50°55′N	3°05′E
Roesiger, l., Wa., U.S. (rōz′ĭ-gẽr)	116a	47°59′N	121°56′W
Roes Welcome Sound, strt., Can. (rōz)	93	64°10′N	87°23′W
Rogatica, Bos. (rô-gä′tē̇-tsä)	175	43°46′N	19°00′E
Rogers, Ar., U.S. (rŏj-ẽrz)	121	36°19′N	94°07′W
Rogers City, Mi., U.S.	108	45°30′N	83°50′W
Rogersville, Tn., U.S.	124	36°21′N	83°00′W
Rognac, Fr. (rŏn-yäk′)	170a	43°29′N	5°15′E
Rogoaguado, l., Bol. (rō′gō-ä-gwä-dō)	142	12°42′S	66°46′W
Rogovskaya, Russia (rô-gôf′skȧ-yȧ)	177	45°43′N	38°42′E
Rogózno, Pol. (rô′gôzh-nō)	168	52°44′N	16°53′E
Rogue, r., Or., U.S. (rōg)	114	42°32′N	124°13′W
Rohatyn, Ukr.	169	49°22′N	24°37′E
Rojas, Arg. (rō′häs)	141c	34°11′S	60°42′W
Rojo, Cabo, c., Mex. (rō′hō)	131	21°35′N	97°16′W
Rojo, Cabo, c., P.R. (rō′hō)	129b	17°55′N	67°14′W
Rokel, r., S.L.	234	9°00′N	11°55′W
Rokkō-Zan, mtn., Japan (rôk′kō zän)	211b	34°46′N	135°16′E
Rokycany, Czech Rep. (rô′kĭ′tsȧ-nĭ)	168	49°44′N	13°37′E
Roldanillo, Col. (rôl-dä-nē′l-yō)	142a	4°24′N	76°09′W
Rolla, Mo., U.S.	121	37°56′N	91°45′W
Rolla, N.D., U.S.	112	48°52′N	99°32′W
Rolleville, Bah.	134	23°40′N	76°00′W
Roma, Austl. (rō′mȧ)	219	26°30′S	148°48′E
Roma *see* Rome, Italy	154	41°52′N	12°37′E
Roma, Leso.	233c	29°28′S	27°43′E
Romaine, r., Can. (rô-mĕn′)	93	51°22′N	63°23′W
Roman, Rom. (rō′män)	169	46°56′N	26°57′E
Romania, nation, Eur. (rō-mā′nē̇-ȧ)	154	46°18′N	22°53′E
Romano, Cape, c., Fl., U.S. (rō-mä′nō)	125a	25°48′N	82°00′W
Romano, Cayo, i., Cuba (kä′yō-rō-mȧ′nō)	134	22°15′N	78°00′W
Romanovo, Russia (rō̇-mä′nô-vô)	186a	59°09′N	61°24′E
Romans, Fr. (rō-mäN′)	170	45°04′N	4°49′E
Romblon, Phil. (rōm-blōn′)	213a	12°34′N	122°16′E
Romblon Island, i., Phil.	213a	12°33′N	122°17′E
Rome (Roma), Italy	154	41°52′N	12°37′E
Rome, Ga., U.S. (rōm)	105	34°14′N	85°10′W
Rome, N.Y., U.S.	109	43°15′N	75°25′W
Romeo, Mi., U.S. (rō′mē̇-ō)	108	42°50′N	83°00′W
Romford, Eng., U.K. (rŭm′fẽrd)	158b	51°35′N	0°11′E
Romilly-sur-Seine, Fr. (rô-mē̇-yē′sür-sān′)	170	48°32′N	3°41′E
Romita, Mex. (rō-mē′tä)	130	20°53′N	101°32′W
Romny, Ukr. (rôm′nĭ)	181	50°46′N	33°31′E
Rømø, i., Den. (rûm′û)	166	55°08′N	8°17′E
Romoland, Ca., U.S. (rō′mō′lănd)	117a	33°44′N	117°11′W
Romorantin-Lanthenay, Fr. (rō̇-mō̇-rän-tăN′)	170	47°24′N	1°46′E
Rompin, Malay.	197b	2°42′N	102°30′E
Rompin, r., Malay.	197b	2°54′N	103°10′E
Romsdalsfjorden, Nor.	166	62°40′N	7°05′W
Romulus, Mi., U.S. (rom′ū lŭs)	111b	42°14′N	83°24′W
Ron, Mui, c., Viet.	209	18°05′N	106°45′E
Ronan, Mt., U.S. (rō′năn)	115	47°28′N	114°03′W
Roncador, Serra do, mts., Braz. (sĕr′rȧ dō rôn-kä-dôr′)	143	12°44′S	52°19′W
Ronceverte, W.V., U.S. (rŏn′sē̇-vûrt)	108	37°45′N	80°30′W
Ronda, Spain (rōn′dä)	181	36°45′N	5°10′W
Ronda, Sierra de, mts., Spain	172	36°35′N	5°03′W
Rondônia, state, Braz.	142	10°15′S	63°07′W
Ronge, Lac la, l., Can. (rŏnzh)	92	55°10′N	105°00′W
Rongjiang, China (rộn-jyäŋ)	209	25°52′N	108°45′E
Rongxian, China	209	22°50′N	110°32′E
Rønne, Den. (rûn′ĕ)	160	55°08′N	14°46′E
Ronneby, Swe. (rōn′ĕ-bü)	166	56°13′N	15°17′E
Ronne Ice Shelf, ice, Ant.	224	77°30′S	38°00′W
Roodepoort, S. Afr. (rō′dĕ-pōrt)	233b	26°10′S	27°52′E
Roodhouse, Il., U.S. (ro͞od′hous)	121	39°29′N	90°21′W
Rooiberg, S. Afr.	238c	24°46′S	27°42′E
Roosendaal, Neth. (rō′zĕn-däl)	159a	51°32′N	4°27′E
Roosevelt, Ut., U.S. (rōz′′vĕlt)	119	40°20′N	110°00′W
Roosevelt, r., Braz. (rô′sĕ-vĕlt)	143	9°22′S	60°28′W
Roosevelt Island, i., Ant.	224	79°30′S	168°00′W
Root, r., Wi., U.S.	111a	42°49′N	87°54′W
Roper, r., Austl. (rōp′ẽr)	220	14°50′S	134°00′E
Ropsha, Russia (rôp′shȧ)	186c	59°44′N	29°53′E
Roque Pérez, Arg. (rô′kĕ-pĕ′rĕz)	141c	35°23′S	59°22′W
Roques, Islas los, is., Ven.	142	12°25′N	67°40′W
Roraima, state, Braz. (rô′rī-mȧ)	142	2°00′N	62°15′W
Roraima, Mount, mtn., S.A. (rō-rä-ē′mä)	143	5°12′N	60°52′W
Røros, Nor. (rûr′ôs)	160	62°36′N	11°25′E
Ros′, r., Ukr. (rôs)	177	49°40′N	30°22′E
Rosa, Monte, mtn., Italy (mōn′tä rō′zä)	162	45°56′N	7°51′E
Rosales, Mex. (rō-zä′läs)	122	28°15′N	100°43′W
Rosales, Phil. (rō̇-sä′lĕs)	213a	15°54′N	120°38′E
Rosamorada, Mex. (rō′zä-mō-rä′dhä)	130	22°06′N	105°16′W
Rosaria, Laguna, l., Mex. (lä-gō′nä-rō-sä′ryä)	131	17°50′N	93°51′W
Rosario, Arg. (rō̇-zä′rē̇-ō)	144	32°58′S	60°42′W
Rosario, Braz. (rō̇-zä′rē̇-ō)	143	2°49′S	44°15′W
Rosario, Mex.	122	26°31′N	105°40′W
Rosario, Mex.	130	22°58′N	105°54′W
Rosario, Phil.	213a	13°49′N	121°13′E
Rosario, Ur.	141c	34°19′S	57°24′E
Rosario, Cayo, i., Cuba (kä′yō-rō-sä′ryō)	134	21°40′N	81°55′W
Rosário do Sul, Braz. (rō-zä′rē̇-ō-dō-so͞o′l)	144	30°17′S	54°52′W
Rosário Oeste, Braz. (ō̇-ĕst′ĕ)	143	14°47′S	56°20′W
Rosario Strait, strt., Wa., U.S.	116a	48°27′N	122°45′W
Rosbach, Ger. (rōz′bäĸ)	171c	50°47′N	7°38′E
Roscoe, Tx., U.S. (rôs′kō)	122	32°26′N	100°38′W
Roseau, Dom.	133b	15°17′N	61°23′W
Roseau, Mn., U.S. (rō-zō′)	112	48°52′N	95°47′W
Roseau, r., Mn., U.S.	112	48°52′N	96°11′W
Roseberg, Or., U.S. (rōz′bûrg)	104	43°13′N	123°30′W
Rosebud, r., Can. (rōz′bŭd)	95	51°20′N	112°20′W
Rosebud Creek, r., Mt., U.S.	115	45°48′N	106°34′W
Rosebud Indian Reservation, I.R., S.D., U.S.	112	43°13′N	100°42′W
Rosedale, Ms., U.S.	124	33°49′N	90°56′W
Rosedale, Wa., U.S.	116a	47°20′N	122°39′W
Roseires Reservoir, res., Sudan	231	11°15′N	34°45′E
Roselle, Il., U.S. (rō-zĕl′)	111a	41°59′N	88°05′W
Rosemère, Can. (rōz′mẽr)	102a	45°38′N	73°48′W
Rosemount, Mn., U.S. (rōz′mount)	117g	44°44′N	93°08′W
Rosendal, S. Afr. (rō-sĕn′täl)	238c	28°32′S	27°56′E
Rosenheim, Ger. (rō′zĕn-hīm)	161	47°52′N	12°06′E
Roses, Golf de, b., Spain	173	42°10′N	3°20′E
Rosetown, Can. (rōz′toun)	90	51°33′N	108°00′W
Rosetta *see* Rashīd, Egypt	200	31°22′N	30°25′E
Rosettenville, neigh., S. Afr.	233b	26°15′S	28°04′E
Roseville, Ca., U.S. (rōz′vĭl)	118	38°44′N	121°19′W
Roseville, Mi., U.S.	111b	42°30′N	82°55′W
Roseville, Mn., U.S.	117g	45°01′N	93°10′W
Rosiclare, Il., U.S. (rōz′y-klâr)	108	37°30′N	88°15′W
Rosignol, Guy. (rōs-ĭg-nól)	143	6°16′N	57°37′W
Roşiori de Vede, Rom. (rō̇-shôr′ē̇ dĕ vĕ-dĕ)	175	44°06′N	25°00′E
Roskilde, Den. (rôs′kēl-dĕ)	166	55°39′N	12°04′E
Roslavl′, Russia (rôs′läv′l)	180	53°56′N	32°52′E
Roslyn, Wa., U.S. (rŏz′lĭn)	114	47°14′N	121°00′W
Rösrath, Ger. (rûz′rät)	171c	50°53′N	7°11′E
Ross, Oh., U.S. (rôs)	111f	39°19′N	84°39′W
Rossano, Italy (rō̇-sä′nō)	163	39°34′N	16°38′E
Rossan Point, c., Ire.	164	54°45′N	8°30′W
Ross Creek, r., Can.	102g	53°40′N	113°08′W
Rosseau, l., Can. (rôs-sō′)	99	45°15′N	79°30′W
Rossel, i., Pap. N. Gui. (rō̇-sĕl′)	221	11°31′S	154°00′E
Rosser, Can. (rôs′sẽr)	102f	49°59′N	97°27′W
Ross Ice Shelf, ice, Ant.	224	81°30′S	175°00′W
Rossignol, Lake, l., Can.	100	44°10′N	65°10′W
Ross Island, i., Can.	97	54°14′N	97°45′W
Ross Lake, res., Wa., U.S.	114	48°40′N	121°07′W
Rossland, Can. (rôs′lănd)	90	49°05′N	118°48′W
Rossosh′, Russia (rôs′sŭsh)	181	50°12′N	39°32′E
Rossouw, S. Afr.	233c	31°12′S	27°18′E
Ross Sea, sea, Ant.	224	76°00′S	178°00′W
Rossvatnet, l., Nor.	160	65°36′N	13°08′E
Rossville, Ga., U.S. (rôs′vĭl)	124	34°57′N	85°22′W
Rosthern, Can.	96	52°41′N	106°25′W
Rostock, Ger. (rôs′tŭk)	160	54°04′N	12°06′E
Rostov, Russia	180	57°13′N	39°23′E
Rostov, prov., Russia	177	47°38′N	39°15′E
Rostov-na-Donu, Russia (rō̇stôv-nȧ-dô-no͞o)	178	47°16′N	39°47′E
Roswell, Ga., U.S. (rŏz′wĕl)	124	34°02′N	84°21′W
Roswell, N.M., U.S.	104	33°23′N	104°32′W
Rotan, Tx., U.S. (rō̇-tăn′)	120	32°51′N	100°27′W
Rothenburg, Ger.	168	49°20′N	10°10′E
Rotherham, Eng., U.K. (rŏdh′ẽr-ăm)	158a	53°26′N	1°21′W
Rotherham, co., Eng., U.K.	158a	53°52′N	1°45′W
Rothesay, Can. (rôth′sȧ)	100	45°23′N	66°00′W
Rothesay, Scot., U.K.	164	55°50′N	3°14′W
Rothwell, Eng., U.K.	158a	53°44′N	1°30′W
Roti, Pulau, i., Indon. (rō′tē̇)	212	10°30′S	122°52′E
Roto, Austl. (rō′tō̇)	222	33°07′S	145°30′E
Rotorua, N.Z.	223	38°07′S	176°17′E
Rotterdam, Neth. (rôt′ẽr-däm′)	154	51°55′N	4°27′E
Rottweil, Ger. (rōt′vīl)	168	48°10′N	[illegible]
Roubaix, Fr. (ro͞o bĕ′)	170	50°42′N	3°10′E
Rouen, Fr. (ro͞o-äN′)	154	49°25′N	1°05′E
Rouge, r., Can. (ro͞ozh)	102d	43°53′N	79°21′W
Rouge, r., Can.	99	46°40′N	74°50′W
Rouge, r., Mi., U.S.	111b	42°30′N	83°15′W
Rough River Reservoir, res., Ky., U.S.	108	37°45′N	86°10′W
Round Lake, Il., U.S.	111a	42°21′N	88°05′W
Round Pond, l., Can.	101	48°15′N	55°57′W
Round Rock, Tx., U.S.	123	30°31′N	97°41′W
Round Top, mtn., Or., U.S. (tŏp)	116c	45°41′N	123°22′W
Roundup, Mt., U.S. (round′ŭp)	115	46°25′N	108°35′W
Rousay, i., Scot., U.K. (ro͞o′zȧ)	164a	59°10′N	3°04′W
Rouyn, Can. (ro͞on)	91	48°22′N	79°03′W
Rovaniemi, Fin. (rō′vȧ-nyĕ′mĭ)	160	66°29′N	25°45′E
Rovato, Italy (rō̇-vä′tō)	174	45°33′N	10°00′E
Roven′ki, Russia	177	49°54′N	38°54′E
Roven′ky, Ukr.	177	48°06′N	39°44′E
Rovereto, Italy (rō-vā-rā′tō)	174	45°53′N	11°05′E
Rovigo, Italy (rō̇-vē′gô)	174	45°05′N	11°48′E
Rovinj, Cro. (rō′ēn′)	174	45°05′N	13°40′E
Rovira, Col. (rō̇-vē′rä)	142a	4°14′N	75°13′W
Rovuma (Ruvuma), r., Afr.	237	10°50′S	39°50′E
Rowley, Ma., U.S. (rou′lē̇)	101a	42°43′N	70°53′W
Roxana, Il., U.S. (rŏks′ăn-nȧ)	117e	38°51′N	90°05′W
Roxas, Phil. (rô-xäs)	212	11°30′N	122°47′E
Roxo, Cap, c., Sen.	234	12°20′N	16°43′W
Roy, N.M., U.S. (roi)	120	35°54′N	104°09′W
Roy, Ut., U.S.	117b	41°10′N	112°02′W
Royal, i., Bah.	134	25°30′N	76°50′W
Royal Canal, can., Ire. (roi-ăl)	164	53°28′N	6°45′W
Royal Natal National Park, rec., S. Afr.	233c	28°35′S	28°54′E
Royal Oak, Can. (roi′ăl ōk)	116a	48°30′N	123°24′W
Royal Oak, Mi., U.S.	111b	42°29′N	83°09′W
Royalton, Mi., U.S. (roi′ăl-tŭn)	108	42°00′N	86°25′W
Royan, Fr. (rwä-yäN′)	170	45°40′N	1°02′W
Roye, Fr. (rwä)	170	49°43′N	2°40′E
Royersford, Pa., U.S. (rô′ yẽrz-fẽrd)	110f	40°11′N	75°32′W
Royston, Ga., U.S. (roiz′tŭn)	124	34°15′N	83°06′W
Royton, Eng., U.K. (roi′tŭn)	158a	53°34′N	2°07′W
Rozay-en-Brie, Fr. (rō-zā-ĕN-brē′)	171b	48°41′N	2°57′E
Rozdil′na, Ukr.	177	46°47′N	30°08′E
Rozhaya, r., Russia (rô′zhȧ-yȧ)	186b	55°20′N	37°37′E
Rozivka, Ukr.	177	47°14′N	36°35′E
Rožňava, Slvk. (rôzh′nyȧ-vȧ)	169	48°39′N	20°32′E
Rtishchevo, Russia (′r-tĭsh′chĕ-vô)	181	52°15′N	43°40′E
Ru, r., China (ro͞o)	206	33°07′N	114°18′E
Ruacana Falls, wtfl., Afr.	232	17°15′S	14°45′E
Ruaha National Park, rec., Tan.	237	7°15′S	34°50′E
Ruapehu, vol., N.Z. (rō̇-ȧ-pā′ho͞o)	221a	39°15′S	175°37′E
Rub′ al Khali *see* Ar Rub′ al Khālī, des., Asia	198	20°00′N	51°00′E
Rubeho Mountains, mts., Tan.	237	6°45′S	36°15′E
Rubidoux, Ca., U.S.	117a	33°59′N	117°24′W
Rubizhne, Ukr.	177	48°53′N	38°29′E
Rubondo Island, i., Tan.	237	2°10′S	31°55′E
Rubtsovsk, Russia	178	51°31′N	81°17′E
Ruby, Ak., U.S. (ro͞o′bē̇)	106a	64°38′N	155°22′W
Ruby, l., Nv., U.S.	118	40°11′N	115°20′W
Ruby, r., Mt., U.S.	115	45°06′N	112°10′W
Ruby Mountains, mts., Nv., U.S.	118	40°11′N	115°36′W
Rudkøbing, Den. (ro͞odh′kûb-ĭng)	166	54°56′N	10°44′E
Rüdnitz, Ger. (rüd′nētz)	159b	52°44′N	13°38′E
Rudolf, Lake, l., Afr. (ro͞o′dŏlf)	231	3°30′N	36°05′E
Rufā′ah, Sudan (ro͞o-fä′ä)	231	14°52′N	33°30′E
Ruffec, Fr. (rü-fĕk′)	170	46°03′N	0°11′E
Rufiji, r., Tan. (rō̇-fē′jē̇)	233	8°00′S	38°00′E
Rufisque, Sen. (rü-fēsk′)	230	14°43′N	17°17′W
Rufunsa, Zam.	237	15°05′S	29°40′E
Rufus Woods, Wa., U.S.	114	48°02′N	119°33′W
Rugao, China (ro͞o-gou)	208	32°24′N	120°33′E
Rugby, Eng., U.K. (rŭg′bē̇)	158a	52°22′N	1°15′W
Rugby, N.D., U.S.	112	48°22′N	100°00′W
Rugeley, Eng., U.K. (ro͞oj′lē̇)	158a	52°46′N	1°56′W
Rügen, i., Ger. (rü′ghĕn)	156	54°28′N	13°47′E
Ruhnu-Saar, i., Est. (ro͞onò-sȧ′âr)	167	57°46′N	23°15′E
Ruhr, r., Ger. (rōr)	168	51°18′N	8°17′E
Rui′an, China (rwā-än)	209	27°48′N	120°40′E
Ruiz, Mex. (rōē′z)	130	21°55′N	105°09′W
Ruiz, Nevado del, vol., Col. (nĕ-vá′dō-dĕl-ro͞oē′z)	142a	4°52′N	75°20′W
Rūjiena, Lat. (rō′yĭ-ă-nȧ)	167	57°54′N	25°19′E
Ruki, r., D.R.C.	236	0°05′S	18°55′E
Rukwa, Lake, l., Tan. (ro͞ok-wä′)	232	8°00′S	32°25′E
Rum, r., Mn., U.S. (rŭm)	113	45°52′N	93°45′W
Ruma, Serb. (ro͞o′mȧ)	175	45°00′N	19°53′E
Rumbek, Sudan (rŭm′bĕk)	231	6°52′N	29°43′E

ăt; finăl; rāte; senāte; ärm; åsk; sofȧ; fâre; ch-choose; dh-as th in other; bē; ē̇vent; bĕt; recĕnt; cratẽr; g-gō; gh-guttural g; bĭt; ĭ-short neutral; rīde; ĸ-guttural k as ch in German ich;

PRONOUNCING INDEX

Rum Cay – Saint George 343

PLACE (Pronunciation)	PAGE	LAT.	LONG.
Rum Cay, i., Bah.	135	23°40'N	74°50'W
Rumford, Me., U.S. (rŭm'fẽrd)	100	44°32'N	70°35'W
Rummah, Wādī ar, val., Sau. Ar.	198	26°17'N	41°45'E
Rummānah, Egypt	197a	31°01'N	32°39'E
Runan, China (rōō-nän)	208	32°59'N	114°22'E
Runcorn, Eng., U.K. (rŭn'kôrn)	158a	53°20'N	2°44'W
Ruo, r., China (rwō)	204	41°15'N	100°46'E
Rupat, i., Indon. (rōō'pät)	197b	1°55'N	101°35'E
Rupat, Selat, strt., Indon.	197b	1°55'N	101°17'E
Rupert, Id., U.S. (rōō'pẽrt)	115	42°36'N	113°41'W
Rupert, Rivière de, r., Can.	93	51°35'N	76°30'W
Ruse, Blg. (rōō'sĕ) (rò'sĕ)	154	43°50'N	25°59'E
Rushan, China (rōō-shän)	206	36°54'N	121°31'E
Rush City, Mn., U.S.	113	45°40'N	92°59'W
Rushville, Il., U.S. (rŭsh'vĭl)	121	40°08'N	90°34'W
Rushville, In., U.S.	108	39°35'N	85°30'W
Rushville, Ne., U.S.	112	42°43'N	102°27'W
Rusizi, r., Afr.	237	3°00'S	29°05'E
Rusk, Tx., U.S. (rŭsk)	123	31°49'N	95°09'W
Ruskin, Can. (rus'kin)	116d	49°10'N	122°25'W
Russ, r., Aus.	159e	48°12'N	16°55'E
Russas, Braz. (rōō's-säs)	143	4°48'S	37°50'W
Russell, Can. (rŭs'ĕl)	90	50°47'N	101°15'W
Russell, Can.	102c	45°15'N	75°22'W
Russell, Ca., U.S.	116b	37°39'N	122°08'W
Russell, Ks., U.S.	120	38°51'N	98°51'W
Russell, Ky., U.S.	108	38°30'N	82°45'W
Russel Lake, l., Can.	97	56°15'N	101°30'W
Russell Islands, is., Sol. Is.	221	9°16'S	158°30'E
Russellville, Al., U.S. (rŭs'ĕl-vĭl)	124	34°29'N	87°44'W
Russellville, Ar., U.S.	121	35°16'N	93°08'W
Russelville, Ky., U.S.	124	36°48'N	86°51'W
Russia, nation, Russia	178	61°00'N	60°00'E
Russian, r., Ca., U.S. (rŭsh'ăn)	118	38°59'N	123°10'W
Rustavi, Geor.	182	41°33'N	45°02'E
Rustenburg, S. Afr. (rŭs'tĕn-bûrg)	238c	25°40'S	27°15'E
Ruston, La., U.S. (rŭs'tŭn)	123	32°32'N	92°39'W
Ruston, Wa., U.S.	116a	47°18'N	122°30'W
Rute, Spain (rōō'tā)	172	38°20'N	4°34'W
Ruth, Nv., U.S. (rōōth)	118	39°17'N	115°00'W
Ruthenia, hist. reg., Ukr.	169	48°25'N	23°00'E
Rutherfordton, N.C., U.S. (rŭdh'ẽr-fẽrd-tŭn)	125	35°23'N	81°58'W
Rutland, Vt., U.S.	109	43°35'N	72°55'W
Rutledge, Md., U.S. (rŭt'lĕdj)	110e	39°34'N	76°33'W
Rutog, China	204	33°29'N	79°26'E
Rutshuru, D.R.C. (rōōt-shōō'rōō)	232	1°11'S	29°27'E
Ruvo, Italy (rōō'vô)	174	41°07'N	16°32'E
Ruvuma, r., Afr.	232	11°30'S	37°00'E
Ruza, Russia (rōō'zȧ)	176	55°42'N	36°12'E
Ruzhany, Bela. (rò-zhän'ĭ)	169	52°49'N	24°54'E
Rwanda, nation, Afr.	232	2°10'S	29°37'E
Ryabovo, Russia (ryä'bô-vô)	186c	59°24'N	31°08'E
Ryazan', Russia (ryä-zän'')	178	54°37'N	39°43'E
Ryazan', prov., Russia	176	54°10'N	39°37'E
Ryazhsk, Russia (ryäzh'sk')	180	53°43'N	40°04'E
Rybachiy, Poluostrov, pen., Russia	180	69°50'N	33°20'E
Rybatskoye, Russia	186c	59°50'N	30°31'E
Rybinsk, Russia	178	58°02'N	38°52'E
Rybinskoye, res., Russia	178	58°23'N	38°15'E
Rybnik, Pol. (rĭb'nĕk)	169	50°06'N	18°37'E
Ryde, Eng., U.K. (rīd)	164	50°43'N	1°16'W
Rye, N.Y., U.S. (rī)	110a	40°58'N	73°42'W
Ryl'sk, Russia (rêl''sk)	181	51°33'N	34°42'E
Ryōtsu, Japan (ryōt'sōō)	210	38°02'N	138°23'E
Rypin, Pol. (rĭ'pēn)	169	53°04'N	19°25'E
Rysy, mtn., Eur.	169	49°12'N	20°04'E
Ryukyu Islands *see* Nansei-shotō, is., Japan	205	27°30'N	127°00'E
Rzeszów, Pol. (zhä-shŏof)	161	50°02'N	22°00'E
Rzhev, Russia ('r-zhĕf)	178	56°16'N	34°17'E
Rzhyshchiv, Ukr.	177	49°58'N	31°05'E

S

PLACE (Pronunciation)	PAGE	LAT.	LONG.
Saale, r., Ger. (sä-lĕ)	168	51°14'N	11°52'E
Saalfeld, Ger. (säl'fĕlt)	168	50°38'N	11°20'E
Saarbrücken, Ger. (zähr'brü-kĕn)	161	49°15'N	7°01'E
Saaremaa, i., Est.	180	58°25'N	22°30'E
Saavedra, Arg. (sä-ä-vā'drä)	144	37°45'S	62°23'W
Šaba, i., Neth. Ant. (sä'bä)	133b	17°39'N	63°20'W
Šabac, Serb. (shä'bȧts)	163	44°45'N	19°49'E
Sabadell, Spain (sä-bä-dhāl')	162	41°32'N	2°07'E
Sabah, hist. reg., Malay.	212	5°10'N	116°25'E
Sabana, Archipiélago de, is., Cuba	134	23°05'N	80°00'W
Sabana, Río, r., Pan. (sä-bä'nä)	133	8°40'N	78°02'W
Sabana de la Mar, Dom. Rep. (sä-bä'nä dä lä mär')	135	19°05'N	69°30'W
Sabana de Uchire, Ven. (sä-bá'nä dĕ ōō-chē'rĕ)	143b	10°02'N	65°32'W
Sabanagrande, Hond. (sä-bä'nä-grä'n-dĕ)	132	13°47'N	87°16'W
Sabanalarga, Col. (sä-bá'nä-lär'gä)	142	10°38'N	75°02'W
Sabanas Páramo, mtn., Col. (sä-bá'näs pá'rä-mō)	142a	6°28'N	76°08'W
Sabancuy, Mex. (sä-bäŋ-kwē')	131	18°58'N	91°09'W
Sabang, Indon. (sä'bäng)	212	5°52'N	95°26'E
Sabaudia, Italy (sá-bou'dē-ä)	174	41°19'N	13°00'E
Sabetha, Ks., U.S. (sȧ-bĕth'ȧ)	121	39°54'N	95°49'W
Sabi (Rio Save), r., Afr. (sä'bē)	232	20°18'S	32°07'E
Sabile, Lat. (sä'bē-lĕ)	167	57°03'N	22°34'E
Sabinal, Tx., U.S. (sȧ-bī'nȧl)	122	29°19'N	99°27'W
Sabinal, Cayo, i., Cuba (kä'yō sä-bē-näl')	134	21°40'N	77°20'W
Sabinas, Mex.	128	28°05'N	101°30'W
Sabinas, r., Mex. (sä-bē'näs)	122	26°37'N	99°52'W
Sabinas, Río, r., Mex. (rē'ō sä-bē'näs)	122	27°25'N	100°33'W
Sabinas Hidalgo, Mex. (ē-däl'gō)	122	26°30'N	100°10'W
Sabine, Tx., U.S. (sȧ-bēn')	123	29°44'N	93°54'W
Sabine, r., U.S.	107	32°00'N	94°30'W
Sabine, Mount, mtn., Ant.	224	72°05'S	169°10'E
Sabine Lake, l., La., U.S.	123	29°53'N	93°41'W
Sablayan, Phil. (säb-lä-yän')	213a	12°49'N	120°47'E
Sable, Cape, c., Can. (sā'b'l)	93	43°25'N	65°24'W
Sable, Cape, c., Fl., U.S.	107	25°12'N	81°10'W
Sables, Rivière aux, r., Can.	99	49°00'N	70°20'W
Sablé-sur-Sarthe, Fr. (säb lā-sür-särt')	170	47°50'N	0°17'W
Sablya, Gora, mtn., Russia	180	64°50'N	59°00'E
Sàbor, r., Port. (sä-bōr')	172	41°18'N	6°54'W
Sabunchu, Azer.	182	40°26'N	49°56'E
Sabzevār, Iran	201	36°13'N	57°42'E
Sac, r., Mo., U.S. (sôk)	121	38°11'N	93°45'W
Sacandaga Reservoir, res., N.Y., U.S. (să-kăn-dâ'gȧ)	109	43°10'N	74°15'W
Sacavém, Port. (sä-kä-vĕn')	173b	38°47'N	9°06'W
Sacavém, r., Port.	173b	38°52'N	9°06'W
Sac City, Ia., U.S. (sŏk)	112	42°25'N	95°00'W
Sachigo Lake, l., Can. (săch'ĭ-gō)	97	53°49'N	92°08'W
Sachsen, hist. reg., Ger. (zäk'sĕn)	168	50°45'N	12°17'E
Sacketts Harbor, N.Y., U.S. (săk'ĕts)	109	43°55'N	76°05'W
Sackville, Can. (săk'vĭl)	100	45°54'N	64°22'W
Saco, Me., U.S. (sô'kô)	100	43°30'N	70°28'W
Saco, r., Braz. (sä'kô)	144b	22°20'S	43°26'W
Saco, r., Me., U.S.	100	43°53'N	70°46'W
Sacramento, Mex.	122	25°45'N	103°22'W
Sacramento, Mex.	122	27°05'N	101°45'W
Sacramento, Ca., U.S. (săk-rȧ-mĕn'tō)	104	38°35'N	121°30'W
Sacramento, r., Ca., U.S.	118	40°20'N	122°07'W
Şa'dah, Yemen	198	16°50'N	43°45'E
Saddle Lake Indian Reserve, I.R., Can.	95	54°00'N	111°40'W
Saddle Mountain, mtn., Or., U.S. (săd''l)	116c	45°58'N	123°40'W
Sadiya, India (sŭ-dē'yä)	199	27°53'N	95°35'E
Sado, i., Japan (sä'dō)	205	38°05'N	138°26'E
Sado, r., Port. (sä'dō)	172	38°15'N	8°20'W
Saeby, Den. (sĕ'bü)	166	57°21'N	10°29'E
Saeki, Japan (sä'å-kĕ)	210	32°56'N	131°51'E
Säffle, Swe.	166	59°10'N	12°55'E
Safford, Az., U.S. (săf'fẽrd)	119	32°50'N	109°45'W
Safi, Mor. (sä'fē) (äs'fē)	230	32°24'N	9°09'W
Safīd Koh, Selseleh-ye, mts., Afg.	198	34°45'N	63°58'E
Saga, Japan (sä'gä)	211	33°15'N	130°18'E
Sagami-Nada, b., Japan (sä'gä'mē nä-dä)	211	35°06'N	139°24'E
Sagamore Hills, Oh., U.S. (săg'ȧ-môr hĭlz)	111d	41°19'N	81°34'W
Saganaga, l., N.A. (sä-gȧ-nä'gȧ)	113	48°13'N	91°17'W
Sāgar, India	199	23°55'N	78°45'E
Saghyz, r., Kaz.	181	48°30'N	56°10'E
Saginaw, Mi., U.S. (săg'ĭ-nô)	105	43°25'N	84°00'W
Saginaw, Mn., U.S.	117h	46°51'N	92°26'W
Saginaw, Tx., U.S.	117c	32°52'N	97°22'W
Saginaw Bay, b., Mi., U.S.	107	43°50'N	83°40'W
Saguache, Co., U.S. (sȧ-wăch') (sȧ-gwä'chē)	119	38°05'N	106°10'W
Saguache Creek, r., Co., U.S.	108	38°05'N	106°40'W
Sagua de Tánamo, Cuba (sä-gwä dĕ tá'nä-mō)	135	20°40'N	75°15'W
Sagua la Grande, Cuba (sä-gwä lä grä'n-dĕ)	134	22°45'N	80°05'W
Saguaro National Park, rec., Az., U.S. (säg-wä'rō)	119	32°12'N	110°40'W
Saguenay, r., Can. (săg-ē-nā')	93	48°20'N	70°15'W
Sagunt, Spain	173	38°58'N	1°29'E
Sagunto, Spain (sä-gòn'tō)	162	39°40'N	0°17'W
Sahara, des., Afr. (sȧ-hä'rȧ)	230	23°44'N	1°40'W
Saharan Atlas, mts., Afr.	162	32°51'N	1°02'W
Sahāranpur, India (sŭ-hä'rŭn-pōōr')	199	29°58'N	77°41'E
Sahara Village, Ut., U.S. (sȧ-hä'rȧ)	117b	41°06'N	111°58'W
Sahel *see* Sudan, reg., Afr.	230	15°00'N	7°00'E
Sāhīwāl, Pak.	202	30°43'N	73°04'E
Sahuayo de Dias, Mex.	130	20°03'N	102°43'W
Saigon *see* Ho Chi Minh City, Viet.	212	10°46'N	106°34'E
Saijō, Japan (sä'ē-jō)	211	33°55'N	133°13'E
Saimaa, l., Fin. (sä'ĭ-mä)	160	61°24'N	28°45'E
Sain Alto, Mex. (sä-ēn' äl'tō)	130	23°35'N	103°13'W
Saint Adolphe, Can. (sånt a'dŏlf) (săn' tá-dôlf')	102f	49°40'N	97°07'W
Saint Afrique, Fr. (săn' tá-frēk')	170	43°58'N	2°52'E
Saint Albans, Austl. (sånt ôl'bănz)	217a	37°44'S	144°47'E
Saint Albans, Eng., U.K.	164	51°44'N	0°20'W
Saint Albans, Vt., U.S.	109	44°50'N	73°05'W
Saint Albans, W.V., U.S.	108	38°20'N	81°50'W
Saint Albert, Can. (sånt ăl'bẽrt)	95	53°38'N	113°38'W
Saint Amand-Mont Rond, Fr. (săn't á-män' môn-rôn')	170	46°44'N	2°28'E
Saint André-Est, Can.	102a	45°33'N	74°19'W
Saint Andrews, Can.	91	45°05'N	67°03'W
Saint Andrews, Scot., U.K.	164	56°20'N	2°40'W
Saint Andrew's Channel, strt., Can.	101	46°06'N	60°28'W
Saint Anicet, Can. (sĕnt ȧ-nē-sĕ')	102a	45°07'N	74°23'W
Saint Ann, Mo., U.S. (sånt ăn')	117e	38°44'N	90°23'W
Sainte Anne, Guad.	133b	16°15'N	61°23'W
Saint Anne, Il., U.S.	111a	41°01'N	87°44'W
Sainte Anne, r., Can. (sănt ăn') (sånt ăn')	99	46°55'N	71°46'W
Sainte-Anne, r., Can.	102b	47°07'N	70°50'W
Sainte Anne-des-Plaines, Can. (dā plĕn)	102a	45°46'N	73°49'W
Saint Ann's Bay, Jam.	134	18°25'N	77°15'W
Saint Anns Bay, b., Can. (ănz)	101	46°20'N	60°30'W
Saint Anselme, Can. (săn' tän-sĕlm')	102b	46°37'N	70°58'W
Saint Anthony, Can. (sän ăn'thỏ-nẻ)	91	51°24'N	55°35'W
Saint Anthony, Id., U.S. (sånt ăn'thỏ-nẻ)	115	43°59'N	111°42'W
Saint Antoine-de-Tilly, Can.	102b	46°40'N	71°31'W
Saint Apollinaire, Can. (săn' tá-pỏl-ē-nâr')	102b	46°36'N	71°30'W
Saint Arnoult-en-Yvelines, Fr. (sán-tär-nōō'ĕn-nēv-lēn')	171b	48°33'N	1°55'E
Saint Augustin-de-Québec, Can. (sĕn tō-güs-tēn')	102b	46°45'N	71°27'W
Saint Augustin-Deux-Montagnes, Can.	102a	45°38'N	73°59'W
Saint Augustine, Fl., U.S. (sånt ô'gŭs-tēn)	105	29°53'N	81°21'W
Sainte Barbe, Can. (sånt bärb')	102a	45°14'N	74°12'W
Saint Barthélemy, i., Guad.	133b	17°55'N	62°32'W
Saint Bees Head, c., Eng., U.K. (sånt bēz' hĕd)	164	54°30'N	3°40'W
Saint Benoit, Can. (sĕn bĕ-nōō-ä')	102a	45°34'N	74°05'W
Saint Bernard, La., U.S. (bẽr-närd')	110d	29°52'N	89°52'W
Saint Bernard, Oh., U.S.	111f	39°10'N	84°30'W
Saint Bride, Mount, mtn., Can. (sånt brīd)	95	51°30'N	115°57'W
Saint Brieuc, Fr. (săn' brēs')	161	48°32'N	2°47'W
Saint Bruno, Can. (brū'nō)	102a	45°31'N	73°20'W
Saint Canut, Can. (săn' kȧ-nü')	102a	45°43'N	74°04'W
Saint Casimir, Can. (kȧ-zē-mēr')	99	46°45'N	72°34'W
Saint Catharines, Can. (kăth'ȧ-rĭnz)	91	43°10'N	79°14'W
Saint Catherine, Mount, mtn., Gren.	133b	12°10'N	61°42'W
Saint Chamas, Fr. (sán-shä-mä')	170a	43°32'N	5°03'E
Saint Chamond, Fr. (săn' shá-môn')	161	45°30'N	4°17'E
Saint Charles, Can. (săn' shärlz')	102b	46°47'N	70°57'W
Saint Charles, Il., U.S. (sånt chärlz')	111a	41°55'N	88°19'W
Saint Charles, Mi., U.S.	108	43°20'N	84°10'W
Saint Charles, Mn., U.S.	113	43°56'N	92°05'W
Saint Charles, Mo., U.S.	117e	38°47'N	90°29'W
Saint Charles, Lac, l., Can.	102b	46°56'N	71°21'W
Saint Christopher-Nevis *see* Saint Kitts and Nevis, nation, N.A.	128	17°24'N	63°30'W
Saint Clair, Mi., U.S. (sånt klâr)	108	42°55'N	82°30'W
Saint Clair, l., Can.	107	42°25'N	82°30'W
Saint Clair, r., Can.	98	42°45'N	82°25'W
Sainte Claire, Can.	102b	46°36'N	70°52'W
Saint Clair Shores, Mi., U.S.	111b	42°30'N	82°54'W
Saint Claude, Fr. (săn' klōd')	171	46°24'N	5°53'E
Saint Clet, Can. (sănt' klā')	102a	45°22'N	74°21'W
Saint Cloud, Fl., U.S. (sånt kloud')	125a	28°13'N	81°17'W
Saint Cloud, Mn., U.S.	105	45°33'N	94°08'W
Saint Constant, Can. (kŏn'stănt)	102a	45°23'N	73°34'W
Saint Croix, i., V.I.U.S. (sånt kroi')	129	17°40'N	64°43'W
Saint Croix, r., N.A. (kroi')	100	45°28'N	67°32'W
Saint Croix, r., U.S. (sånt kroi')	107	45°45'N	93°00'W
Saint Croix Indian Reservation, I.R., Wi., U.S.	113	45°40'N	92°21'W
Saint Croix Island, i., S. Afr. (săn krwä)	233c	33°48'S	25°45'E
Saint Damien-de-Buckland, Can. (sånt dā'mē-ĕn)	102b	46°37'N	70°39'W
Saint David, Can. (dā'vĭd)	102b	46°47'N	71°11'W
Saint David's Head, c., Wales, U.K.	164	51°54'N	5°25'W
Saint-Denis, Fr. (săn'dē-nē')	161	48°26'N	2°22'E
Saint Dizier, Fr. (dē-zyā')	161	48°49'N	4°55'E
Saint Dominique, Can. (sĕn dō-mē-nēk')	102a	45°19'N	74°09'W
Saint Edouard-de-Napierville, Can. (sĕn-tĕ-dōō-är')	102a	45°14'N	73°31'W
Saint Elias, Mount, mtn., N.A. (sånt ē-lī'ăs)	92	60°25'N	141°00'W
Saint Étienne, Fr.	161	45°26'N	4°22'E
Saint Etienne-de-Lauzon, Can. (săn' tā-tyĕn')	102b	46°39'N	71°19'W
Sainte Euphémie, Can. (sĕnt û-fē-mē')	102b	46°47'N	70°27'W
Saint Eustache, Can. (săn' tû-stásh')	102a	45°34'N	73°54'W
Saint Eustache, Can.	102f	49°58'N	97°47'W
Sainte Famille, Can. (săn't fȧ-mē'y')	102b	46°58'N	70°58'W
Saint Félicien, Can. (săn fā-lē-syăn')	91	48°39'N	72°28'W
Sainte Felicite, Can.	100	48°54'N	67°20'W
Saint Féréol, Can. (fa-rā-ôl')	102b	47°07'N	70°52'W
Saint Florent-sur-Cher, Fr. (săn' flô-rän'sür-shâr')	170	46°58'N	2°15'E
Saint Flour, Fr. (săn flōōr')	170	45°02'N	3°09'E
Sainte Foy, Can. (sănt fwä)	99	46°47'N	71°18'W
Saint Francis, r., Ar., U.S.	121	35°56'N	90°27'W
Saint Francis Lake, l., Can. (săn frăn'sĭs)	99	45°00'N	74°20'W
Saint François, Can. (săn'frän-swä')	102b	47°01'N	70°49'W
Saint François de Boundji, Congo	236	1°03'S	15°22'E
Saint Francois Xavier, Can.	102f	49°55'N	97°32'W
Saint Gaudens, Fr. (gō-dăns')	170	43°07'N	0°43'E
Sainte Genevieve, Mo., U.S. (sånt jĕn'ĕ-vēv)	121	37°58'N	90°02'W
Saint George, Austl. (sånt jôrj')	219	28°02'S	148°40'E

344 Saint George – Salem PRONOUNCING INDEX

PLACE (Pronunciation)	PAGE	LAT.	LONG.
Saint George, Can. (săn jôrj′)	91	45°08′N	66°49′W
Saint George, Can. (săn′zhôrzh′)	102d	43°14′N	80°15′W
Saint George, S.C., U.S. (sånt jôrj′)	125	33°11′N	80°35′W
Saint George, Ut., U.S.	119	37°05′N	113°40′W
Saint George, i., Ak., U.S.	103	56°30′N	169°40′W
Saint George, Cape, c., Can.	93a	48°28′N	59°15′W
Saint George, Cape, c., Fl., U.S.	124	29°30′N	85°20′W
Saint George's, Can. (jôrj′ĕs)	91	48°26′N	58°29′W
Saint Georges, Fr. Gu.	143	3°48′N	51°47′W
Saint George's, Gren.	133b	12°02′N	61°57′W
Saint George's Bay, b., Can.	93a	48°20′N	59°00′W
Saint Georges Bay, b., Can.	101	45°49′N	61°45′W
Saint George's Channel, strt., Eur. (jôr-jĕz)	156	51°45′N	6°30′W
Saint Germain-en-Laye, Fr. [illegible]	170	48°53′N	2°05′E
Saint Gervais, Can. (zhĕr-vĕ′)	[illegible]	[illegible]	[illegible]
Saint Girons, Fr. (zhē-rôn′)	170	42°50′N	1°08′E
Saint Gotthard Pass, p., Switz.	168	46°33′N	8°34′E
Saint Gregory, Mount, mtn., Can. (sånt grĕg′ẽr-ė)	101	49°19′N	58°13′W
Saint Helena, i., St. Hel.	229	16°01′S	5°16′W
Saint Helenabaai, b., S. Afr.	232	32°25′S	17°15′E
Saint Helens, Eng., U.K. (sånt hĕl′ĕnz)	158a	53°27′N	2°44′W
Saint Helens, Or., U.S. (hĕl′ĕnz)	116c	45°52′N	122°49′W
Saint Helens, Mount, vol., Wa., U.S.	114	46°13′N	122°10′W
Saint Helier, Jersey (hyĕl′yẽr)	170	49°12′N	2°06′W
Saint Henri, Can. (săn′ hĕn′rē)	102b	46°41′N	71°04′W
Saint Hubert, Can.	102a	45°29′N	73°24′W
Saint Hyacinthe, Can.	91	45°35′N	72°55′W
Saint Ignace, Mi., U.S. (sånt ĭg′nås)	113	45°51′N	84°39′W
Saint Ignace, i., Can. (săn′ ĭg′nås)	98	48°47′N	88°14′W
Saint Irenee, Can. (săn′ tē-rā-nā′)	99	47°34′N	70°15′W
Saint Isidore-de-Laprairie, Can.	102a	45°18′N	73°41′W
Saint Isidore-de-Prescott, Can. (săn′ ĭz′ĭ-dôr-prĕs-kŏt)	102c	45°23′N	74°54′W
Saint Isidore-Dorchester, Can. (dôr-chĕs′tẽr)	102b	46°35′N	71°05′W
Saint Jacob, Il., U.S. (jā-kŏb)	117e	38°43′N	89°46′W
Saint James, Mn., U.S. (sånt jāmz′)	113	43°58′N	94°37′W
Saint James, Mo., U.S.	121	37°59′N	91°37′W
Saint James, Cape, c., Can.	94	51°58′N	131°00′W
Saint Janvier, Can. (săn′ zhän-vyā′)	102a	45°43′N	73°56′W
Saint Jean, Can. (săn′ zhän′)	91	45°20′N	73°15′W
Saint Jean, Can.	102b	46°55′N	70°54′W
Saint Jean, Lac, l., Can.	93	48°35′N	72°00′W
Saint Jean-Chrysostome, Can. (krĭ-zōs-tōm′)	102b	46°43′N	71°12′W
Saint Jean-d'Angely, Fr. (dän-zhä-lē′)	170	45°56′N	0°33′W
Saint Jean-de-Luz, Fr. (dē lüz′)	170	43°23′N	1°40′W
Saint Jérôme, Can. (sånt jĕ-rōm′) (săn zhā-rōm′)	102a	45°47′N	74°00′W
Saint Joachim-de-Montmorency, Can. (sånt jō′á-kĭm)	102b	47°04′N	70°51′W
Saint John, Can. (sånt jŏn)	91	45°16′N	66°03′W
Saint John, In., U.S.	111a	41°27′N	87°29′W
Saint John, Ks., U.S.	120	37°59′N	98°44′W
Saint John, N.D., U.S.	112	48°57′N	99°42′W
Saint John, i., V.I.U.S.	129b	18°16′N	64°48′W
Saint John, r., N.A.	93	47°00′N	68°00′W
Saint John, Cape, c., Can.	101	50°00′N	55°32′W
Saint Johns, Antig.	133b	17°07′N	61°50′W
Saint John's, Can. (jŏns)	93a	47°34′N	52°43′W
Saint Johns, Az., U.S. (jŏnz)	119	34°30′N	109°25′W
Saint Johns, Mi., U.S.	108	43°05′N	84°35′W
Saint Johns, r., Fl., U.S.	107	29°54′N	81°32′W
Saint Johnsbury, Vt., U.S. (jŏnz′bĕr-ė)	109	44°25′N	72°00′W
Saint Joseph, Dom.	133b	15°25′N	61°26′W
Saint Joseph, Mi., U.S.	108	42°05′N	86°30′W
Saint Joseph, Mo., U.S. (sånt jō-sĕf)	105	39°44′N	94°49′W
Saint Joseph, i., Can.	108	46°15′N	83°55′W
Saint Joseph, l., Can. (jō′zhûf)	93	51°31′N	90°40′W
Saint Joseph, r., Mi., U.S. (sånt jō′sĕf)	108	41°45′N	85°50′W
Saint Joseph Bay, b., Fl., U.S. (jō′zhûf)	124	29°48′N	85°26′W
Saint Joseph-de-Beauce, Can. (sĕn zhō-zĕf′ dē bōs)	99	46°18′N	70°52′W
Saint Joseph-du-Lac, Can. (sĕn zhō-zĕf′ dü läk)	102a	45°32′N	74°00′W
Saint Joseph Island, i., Tx., U.S. (sånt jō-sĕf)	123	27°58′N	96°50′W
Saint Junien, Fr. (săn′zhü-nyăn′)	170	45°53′N	0°54′E
Sainte Justine-de-Newton, Can. (sånt jŭs-tēn′)	102a	45°22′N	74°22′W
Saint Kilda, Austl.	217a	37°52′S	144°59′E
Saint Kilda, i., Scot., U.K. (kĭl′dá)	164	57°50′N	8°32′W
Saint Kitts, i., St. K./N. (sānt kĭtts)	129	17°24′N	63°30′W
Saint Kitts and Nevis, nation, N.A.	129	17°24′N	63°30′W
Saint Lambert, Can.	109	45°29′N	73°29′W
Saint Lambert-de-Lévis, Can.	102b	46°35′N	71°12′W
Saint Laurent, Can. (săn′lō-rän)	102a	45°31′N	73°41′W
Saint Laurent, Fr. Gu.	143	5°27′N	53°56′W
Saint Laurent-d'Orleans, Can.	102b	46°52′N	71°00′W
Saint Lawrence, Can. (sānt lô′rĕns)	101	46°55′N	55°23′W
Saint Lawrence, i., Ak., U.S. (sånt lô′rĕns)	106a	63°10′N	172°12′W
Saint Lawrence, r., N.A.	93	48°24′N	69°30′W
Saint Lawrence, Gulf of, b., Can.	93	48°00′N	62°00′W
Saint Lazare, Can. (săn′lá-zár′)	102b	46°39′N	70°48′W
Saint Lazare-de-Vaudreuil, Can.	102a	45°24′N	74°08′W
Saint Léger-en-Yvelines, Fr. (sán-lā-zhĕ′ĕn-nēv-lēn′)	171b	48°43′N	1°45′E

PLACE (Pronunciation)	PAGE	LAT.	LONG.
Saint Leonard, Can. (sånt lĕn′ård)	100	47°10′N	67°56′W
Saint Léonard, Can.	102a	45°36′N	73°35′W
Saint Leonard, Md., U.S.	110e	38°29′N	76°31′W
Saint Lô, Fr.	161	49°07′N	1°05′W
Saint-Louis, Sen.	230	16°02′N	16°30′W
Saint Louis, Mi., U.S. (sånt lōō′ĭs)	108	43°25′N	84°35′W
Saint Louis, Mo., U.S. (sånt lōō′ĭs) (lōō′ė)	105	38°39′N	90°15′W
Saint Louis, r., Mn., U.S. (sånt lōō′ĭs)	113	46°57′N	92°58′W
Saint Louis, Lac, l., Can. (săn′ lōō-ē′)	102a	45°24′N	73°51′W
Saint Louis-de-Gonzague, Can. (săn′ lōō ē′)	102a	45°13′N	74°00′W
Saint Louis Park, Mn., U.S.	117g	44°56′N	93°21′W
Saint Lucia, nation, N.A.	129	13°54′N	60°40′W
Saint Lucia Channel, strt., N.A.	133b	14°15′N	61°00′W
Saint Lucie Canal, can., Fl., U.S. (lū′sė)	125a	26°57′N	80°25′W
Saint Magnus Bay, b., Scot., U.K. (măg′nŭs)	164a	60°25′N	2°09′W
Saint Malo, Fr. (săn′ má-lō′)	161	48°40′N	2°02′W
Saint Malo, Golfe de, b., Fr. (gôlf-dĕ-sán-mä-lō′)	161	48°50′N	2°49′W
Saint Marc, Haiti (săn′ márk′)	135	19°10′N	72°40′W
Saint-Marc, Canal de, strt., Haiti	135	19°05′N	73°15′W
Saint Marcellin, Fr. (mär-sĕ-lăn′)	171	45°08′N	5°15′E
Saint Margarets, Md., U.S.	110e	39°02′N	76°30′W
Sainte Marie, Cap, c., Madag.	233	25°31′S	45°00′E
Sainte-Marie-aux-Mines, Fr. (sán′tĕ-mä-rē′ō-mēn′)	171	48°14′N	7°08′E
Sainte Marie-Beauce, Can. (sănt′má-rē′)	99	46°27′N	71°03′W
Saint Maries, Id., U.S. (sånt mā′rēs)	114	47°18′N	116°34′W
Saint Martin, i., N.A. (mär′tĭn)	133b	18°06′N	62°54′W
Sainte Martine, Can.	102a	45°14′N	73°37′W
Saint Martins, Can. (mär′tĭnz)	100	45°21′N	65°32′W
Saint Martinville, La., U.S. (mär′tĭn-vĭl)	123	30°08′N	91°50′W
Saint Mary, r., Can. (mā′rė)	95	49°25′N	113°00′W
Saint Mary, Cape, c., Gam.	234	13°28′N	16°40′W
Saint Mary Reservoir, res., Can.	95	49°30′N	113°00′W
Saint Marys, Austl. (mā′rēz)	222	41°40′S	148°10′E
Saint Marys, Can.	98	43°15′N	81°10′W
Saint Marys, Ga., U.S.	125	30°43′N	81°35′W
Saint Mary's, Ks., U.S.	121	39°12′N	96°03′W
Saint Mary's, Oh., U.S.	108	40°30′N	84°25′W
Saint Marys, Pa., U.S.	109	41°25′N	78°30′W
Saint Marys, W.V., U.S.	108	39°20′N	81°15′W
Saint Marys, r., N.A.	117k	46°27′N	84°33′W
Saint Marys, r., U.S.	125	30°37′N	82°05′W
Saint Mary's Bay, b., Can.	101	46°50′N	53°47′W
Saint Marys Bay, b., Can.	100	44°20′N	66°10′W
Saint Mathew, S.C., U.S. (măth′ū)	125	33°40′N	80°46′W
Saint Matthew, i., Ak., U.S.	103	60°25′N	172°10′W
Saint Matthews, Ky., U.S. (măth′ūz)	111h	38°15′N	85°39′W
Saint Maur-des-Fossés, Fr.	171b	48°48′N	2°29′E
Saint Maurice, r., Can. (săn′ mō-rēs′) (sånt mô′rĭs)	93	47°20′N	72°55′W
Saint Michael, Ak., U.S. (sånt mī′kĕl)	103	63°22′N	162°20′W
Saint Michel, Can. (săn′mē-shĕl′)	102b	46°52′N	70°54′W
Saint Michel, Bras, r., Can.	102b	46°47′N	70°51′W
Saint Michel-de-l'Atalaye, Haiti	135	19°25′N	72°20′W
Saint Michel-de-Napierville, Can.	102a	45°14′N	73°34′W
Saint Mihiel, Fr. (săn′ mē-yĕl′)	171	48°53′N	5°30′E
Saint Nazaire, Fr. (săn′ná-zâr′)	154	47°18′N	2°13′W
Saint Nérée, Can. (nā-rā′)	102b	46°43′N	70°43′W
Saint Nicolas, Can. (ne-kô-lä′)	102b	46°42′N	71°22′W
Saint Nicolas, Cap, c., Haiti	135	19°45′N	73°35′W
Saint Omer, Fr. (săn′tô-mâr′)	170	50°44′N	2°16′E
Saint Pascal, Can. (sĕn pā-skăl′)	100	47°32′N	69°48′W
Saint Paul, Can. (sånt pôl′)	90	53°59′N	111°17′W
Saint Paul, Mn., U.S.	105	44°57′N	93°05′W
Saint Paul, Ne., U.S.	112	41°13′N	98°28′W
Saint Paul, i., Can.	101	47°15′N	60°10′W
Saint Paul, i., Ak., U.S.	103	57°10′N	170°20′W
Saint Paul, r., Lib.	234	7°10′N	10°00′W
Saint Paul, Île, i., Afr.	3	38°43′S	77°31′E
Saint Paul Park, Mn., U.S. (pärk)	117g	44°51′N	93°00′W
Saint Pauls, N.C., U.S. (pôls)	125	34°47′N	78°57′W
Saint Peter, Mn., U.S. (pē tẽr)	113	44°20′N	93°56′W
Saint Peter Port, Guern.	170	49°27′N	2°35′W
Saint Petersburg (Sankt-Peterburg) (Leningrad), Russia	178	59°57′N	30°20′E
Saint Petersburg, Fl., U.S. (pē′tẽrz-bûrg)	105	27°47′N	82°38′W
Sainte Pétronille, Can. (sĕnt pĕt-rō-nēl′)	102b	46°51′N	71°08′W
Saint Philémon, Can. (sĕn fēl-mōn′)	102b	46°41′N	70°28′W
Saint Philippe-d'Argenteuil, Can. (săn′fe-lēp′)	102a	45°38′N	74°25′W
Saint Philippe-de-Lapairie, Can.	102a	45°20′N	73°28′W
Saint Pierre, Mart. (săn′pyâr′)	133b	14°45′N	61°12′W
Saint Pierre, St. P./M.	101	46°47′N	56°11′W
Saint Pierre, i., St. P./M.	101	46°47′N	56°11′W
Saint Pierre, Lac, l., Can.	99	46°07′N	72°45′W
Saint Pierre and Miquelon, dep., N.A.	93a	46°53′N	56°40′W
Saint Pierre-d'Orléans, Can.	102b	46°53′N	71°04′W
Saint Pierre-Montmagny, Can.	102b	46°55′N	70°37′W
Saint Placide, Can. (plās′ĭd)	102a	45°32′N	74°11′W
Saint Pol-de-Léon, Fr. (săn-pô′dĕ-lā-ôn′)	170	48°41′N	4°00′W
Saint Quentin, Fr. (săn′kän-tăn′)	161	49°52′N	3°16′E
Saint Raphaël, Can. (rä-fä-él′)	102b	46°48′N	70°46′W

PLACE (Pronunciation)	PAGE	LAT.	LONG.
Saint Raymond, Can.	99	46°50′N	71°51′W
Saint Rédempteur, Can. (săn rā-dänp-tûr′)	102b	46°42′N	71°18′W
Saint Rémi, Can. (sĕn rĕ-mē′)	102a	45°15′N	73°36′W
Saint Romuald-d'Etchemin, Can. (sĕn rō′mōō-äl)	99	46°45′N	71°14′W
Sainte Rose, Guad.	133b	16°19′N	61°45′W
Saintes, Fr.	170	45°44′N	0°41′W
Sainte Scholastique, Can. (skô-lás-tēk′)	102a	45°39′N	74°05′W
Saint Siméon, Can.	99	47°51′N	69°55′W
Saint Stanislas-de-Kostka, Can.	102a	45°11′N	74°08′W
Saint Stephen, Can. (stē′vĕn)	91	45°12′N	66°17′W
Saint Sulpice, Can.	102a	45°50′N	73°21′W
Saint Thérèse-de-Blainville, Can. (tĕ-rĕz′ dĕ blĕn-vēl′)	99	45°38′N	73°51′W
Saint Thomas, Can. (tŏm′ás)	91	42°45′N	81°15′W
[illegible]	[illegible]	18°22′N	64°57′W
Saint Thomas Harbor, b., V.I.U.S. (tŏm′ás)	129c	18°19′N	64°56′W
Saint Timothée, Can. (tē-mô-tā′)	102a	45°17′N	74°03′W
Saint Tropez, Fr. (trô-pĕ′)	171	43°15′N	6°42′E
Saint Valentin, Can. (văl-ĕn-tīn)	102a	45°07′N	73°19′W
Saint Valéry-sur-Somme, Fr. (vá-lā-rē′)	170	50°10′N	1°39′E
Saint Vallier, Can. (väl-yā′)	102b	46°54′N	70°49′W
Saint Victor, Can. (vĭk′tẽr)	99	46°09′N	70°56′W
Saint Vincent, Gulf, b., Austl. (vĭn′sĕnt)	222	34°55′S	138°00′E
Saint Vincent and the Grenadines, nation, N.A.	129	13°20′N	60°50′W
Saint Vincent Passage, strt., N.A.	133b	13°35′N	61°10′W
Saint Walburg, Can.	90	53°39′N	109°12′W
Saint Yrieix-la-Perche, Fr. (ē-rē-ĕ)	170	45°30′N	1°08′E
Saitama, dept., Japan (sī′tä-mä)	211a	35°52′N	139°40′E
Saitbaba, Russia (sá-ĕt′bá-bá)	186a	54°06′N	56°42′E
Sajama, Nevada, mtn., Bol. (nĕ-vá′dä-sä-há′mä)	142	18°13′S	68°53′W
Sakai, Japan (sä′kä-ė)	210	34°34′N	135°28′E
Sakaiminato, Japan	211	35°33′N	133°15′E
Sakākah, Sau. Ar.	198	29°58′N	40°03′E
Sakakawea, Lake, res., N.D., U.S.	106	47°49′N	101°58′W
Sakania, D.R.C. (sá-kä′nĭ-á)	232	12°45′S	28°34′E
Sakarya, r., Tur. (sá-kär′yá)	198	40°10′N	31°00′E
Sakata, Japan (sä′kä-tä)	205	38°56′N	139°57′E
Sakchu, Kor., N. (säk′chò)	210	40°29′N	125°09′E
Sakha (Yakutia), prov., Russia	185	65°21′N	117°13′E
Sakhalin, i., Russia (sá-ká-lēn′)	179	52°00′N	143°00′E
Šakiai, Lith. (shä′kĭ-ī)	167	54°59′N	23°05′E
Sakishima-guntō, is., Japan (sä′kė-shē′ma gòn′tō′)	205	24°25′N	125°00′E
Sakmara, r., Russia	181	52°00′N	56°10′E
Sakomet, r., R.I., U.S. (sä-kō′mĕt)	110b	41°32′N	71°11′W
Sakurai, Japan	211b	34°31′N	135°51′E
Sakwaso Lake, l., Can. (sá-kwá′sō)	97	53°01′N	91°55′W
Sal, i., C.V. (säal)	230b	16°45′N	22°39′W
Sal, r., Russia (sál)	181	47°30′N	43°00′E
Sal, Cay, i., Bah. (kē säl)	134	23°45′N	80°25′W
Sala, Swe. (sō′lä)	166	59°56′N	16°34′E
Sala Consilina, Italy (sä′lä kôn-sė-lē′nä)	174	40°24′N	15°38′E
Salada, Laguna, l., Mex. (lä-gò′nä-sä-lä′dä)	118	32°34′N	115°45′W
Saladillo, Arg. (sä-lä-dēl′yō)	144	35°38′S	59°48′W
Salado, Hond. (sä-lä′dhō)	132	15°44′N	87°03′W
Salado, r., Arg.	141c	35°53′S	58°12′W
Salado, r., Arg.	144	37°00′S	67°00′W
Salado, r., Arg. (sä-lä′dō)	144	26°05′S	63°35′W
Salado, r., Mex.	128	28°00′N	102°00′W
Salado, r., Mex. (sä-lä′dô)	131	18°30′N	97°29′W
Salado Creek, r., Tx., U.S.	117d	29°23′N	98°25′W
Salado de los Nadadores, Río, r., Mex. (dĕ-lôs-nä-dä-dô′rĕs)	122	27°26′N	101°35′W
Salal, Chad	235	14°51′N	17°13′E
Salamanca, Chile (sä-lä-mä′n-kä)	141b	31°48′S	70°57′W
Salamanca, Mex.	128	20°36′N	101°10′W
Salamanca, Spain (sä-lä-mä′n-kä)	154	40°54′N	5°42′W
Salamanca, N.Y., U.S. (săl-á-măŋ′ká)	109	42°10′N	78°45′W
Salamat, Bahr, r., Chad (bär sä-lä-mät′)	231	10°06′N	19°16′E
Salamina, Col. (sä-lä-mē′-nä)	142a	5°25′N	75°29′W
Salamína, Grc.	175	37°58′N	23°30′E
Salat-la-Canada, Fr.	170	44°52′N	1°13′E
Salaverry, Peru (sä-lä-vä′rē)	142	8°16′S	78°54′W
Salawati, i., Indon. (sä-lä-wä′tē)	213	1°07′S	130°52′E
Salawe, Tan.	237	3°19′S	32°52′E
Sala y Gómez, Isla, i., Chile	241	26°50′S	105°50′W
Salcedo, Dom. Rep. (säl-sä′dō)	135	19°25′N	70°30′W
Saldaña, r., Col. (säl-dá′n-yä)	142a	3°42′N	75°16′W
Saldanha, S. Afr.	232	32°55′S	18°05′E
Saldus, Lat. (säl′dòs)	167	56°39′N	22°30′E
Sale, Austl. (sāl)	222	38°10′S	147°07′E
Sale, Eng., U.K.	158a	53°24′N	2°20′W
Sale, r., Can. (sál′rê-vyâr′)	102f	49°44′N	97°11′W
Salekhard, Russia (sŭ-lyĭ-kärt)	180	66°35′N	66°50′E
Salem, India	199	11°39′N	78°11′E
Salem, S. Afr.	233c	33°29′S	26°30′E
Salem, Il., U.S. (sā′lĕm)	108	38°40′N	89°00′W
Salem, In., U.S.	108	38°35′N	86°00′W
Salem, Ma., U.S.	101a	42°31′N	70°54′W
Salem, Mo., U.S.	121	37°36′N	91°33′W
Salem, N.H., U.S.	101a	42°46′N	71°16′W
Salem, N.J., U.S.	109	39°35′N	75°30′W
Salem, Oh., U.S.	108	40°55′N	80°50′W
Salem, Or., U.S.	104	44°55′N	123°03′W

ăt; finăl; rāte; senâte; ärm; åsk; sofá; fâre; ch-choose; dh-as th in other; bē; ėvent; bĕt; recĕnt; cratẽr; g-gō; gh-guttural g; bĭt; ĭ-short neutral; rīde; ĸ-guttural k as ch in German ich;

346 San Felipe Creek – San Sebastian PRONOUNCING INDEX

PLACE (Pronunciation)	PAGE	LAT.	LONG.
San Felipe Creek, r., Ca., U.S. (săn fē-lēp´å)	118	33°10'N	116°03'W
San Felipe Indian Reservation, I.R., N.M., U.S.	119	35°26'N	106°26'W
San Félix, Isla, i., Chile (ē´s-lä-dĕ-sän fā-lēks´)	139	26°20'S	80°10'W
San Fernanda, Spain (fĕr-nä´n-dä)	172	36°28'N	6°13'W
San Fernando, Arg. (fĕr-nå´n-dô)	144a	34°26'S	58°34'W
San Fernando, Chile	141b	35°36'S	70°58'W
San Fernando, Mex. (fĕr-nän´dô)	122	24°52'N	98°10'W
San Fernando, Phil. (sän fĕr-nä´n-dô)	212	16°38'N	120°19'E
San Fernando, Ca., U.S. (fĕr-nän´dô)	117a	34°17'N	118°27'W
San Fernando, i., Mex. (sän fĕr-nän´dô)	122	25°07'N	98°25'W
San Fernando de Apure, Ven. (sän fĕr nä´n dō-dĕ-ä-pōō´rå)	142	7°46'N	67°29'W
San Fernando de Atabapo, Ven. (dĕ-ä-tä-bä´pô)	142	3°58'N	67°41'W
San Fernando de Henares, Spain (dĕ-ā-nä´rås)	173a	40°23'N	3°31'W
Sånfjället, mtn., Swe.	160	62°19'N	13°30'E
Sanford, Can. (săn´fērd)	102f	49°41'N	97°27'W
Sanford, Fl., U.S. (săn´fôrd)	105	28°46'N	81°18'W
Sanford, Me., U.S. (săn´fērd)	100	43°26'N	70°47'W
Sanford, N.C., U.S.	125	35°26'N	79°10'W
San Francisco, Arg. (săn frăn´sĭs´kô)	144	31°23'S	62°09'W
San Francisco, El Sal.	132	13°48'N	88°11'W
San Francisco, Ca., U.S.	104	37°45'N	122°26'W
San Francisco, r., N.M., U.S.	119	33°35'N	108°55'W
San Francisco Bay, b., Ca., U.S. (săn frăn´sĭs´kô)	118	37°45'N	122°21'W
San Francisco del Oro, Mex. (dĕl ō´rō)	128	27°00'N	106°37'W
San Francisco del Rincón, Mex. (dĕl rēn-kōn´)	130	21°01'N	101°51'W
San Francisco de Macaira, Ven. (dĕ-mä-kī´rä)	143b	9°58'N	66°17'W
San Francisco de Macoris, Dom. Rep. (dā-mä-kō´rēs)	135	19°20'N	70°15'W
San Francisco de Paula, Cuba (dā pou´lå)	135a	23°04'N	82°18'W
San Gabriel, Ca., U.S. (săn gä-brē-ĕl´) (gā´brē-ĕl)	117a	34°06'N	118°06'W
San Gabriel, r., Ca., U.S.	117a	33°47'N	118°06'W
San Gabriel Chilac, Mex. (sän-gä-brē-ĕl-chē-läk´)	131	18°19'N	97°22'W
San Gabriel Mts, Ca., U.S.	117a	34°17'N	118°03'W
San Gabriel Reservoir, res., Ca., U.S.	117a	34°14'N	117°48'W
Sangamon, r., Il., U.S. (săn´gå-mŭn)	121	40°08'N	90°08'W
Sanger, Ca., U.S. (săng´ēr)	118	36°42'N	119°33'W
Sangerhausen, Ger. (säng´ēr-hou-zĕn)	168	51°28'N	11°17'E
Sangha, r., Afr.	231	2°40'N	16°10'E
Sangihe, Pulau, i., Indon.	213	3°30'N	125°30'E
San Gil, Col. (sän-kē´l)	142	6°32'N	73°13'W
San Giovanni in Fiore, Italy (sän jô-vän´nē ēn fyō´rå)	174	39°15'N	16°40'E
San Giuseppe Vesuviano, Italy	173c	40°36'N	14°31'E
Sangju, Kor., S. (säng´jōō´)	210	36°20'N	128°07'E
Sāngli, India	199	16°56'N	74°38'E
Sangmélima, Cam.	235	2°56'N	11°59'E
San Gorgonio Mountain, mtn., Ca., U.S. (săn gôr-gō´nĭ-ō)	117a	34°06'N	116°50'W
Sangre de Cristo Mountains, mts., U.S.	106	37°45'N	105°50'W
San Gregoria, Ca., U.S. (săn grĕ-gôr´ä)	116b	37°20'N	122°23'W
Sangro, r., Italy (säŋ´grō)	174	41°38'N	13°56'E
Sangüesa, Spain (sän-gwĕ´sä)	172	42°36'N	1°15'W
Sanhe, China (sän-hŭ)	206	39°59'N	117°06'E
Sanibel Island, i., Fl., U.S. (săn´ĭ-bĕl)	125a	26°26'N	82°15'W
San Ignacio, Belize	132a	17°11'N	89°04'W
San Ildefonso, Cape, c., Phil. (sän-ēl-dĕ-fōn-sō)	213a	16°03'N	122°10'E
San Ildefonso o la Granja, Spain (ō lä grän´khä)	172	40°54'N	4°02'W
San Isidro, Arg. (ē-sē´drō)	141c	34°28'S	58°31'W
San Isidro, C.R.	133	9°24'N	83°43'W
San Jacinto, Phil. (sän hä-sēn´tō)	213a	12°33'N	123°43'E
San Jacinto, Ca., U.S. (săn jȧ-sĭn´tō)	117a	33°47'N	116°57'W
San Jacinto, r., Ca., U.S. (săn jȧ-sĭn´tō)	117a	33°44'N	117°14'W
San Jacinto, r., Tx., U.S.	123	30°25'N	95°05'W
San Jacinto, West Fork, r., Tx., U.S.	123	30°35'N	95°37'W
San Javier, Chile (sän-hä-vē´ĕr)	141b	35°35'S	71°43'W
San Jerónimo, Mex.	131a	19°31'N	98°46'W
San Jerónimo de Juárez, Mex. (hā-rō´nē-mô dā hwä´râz)	130	17°08'N	100°30'W
San Joaquin, Ven.	143b	10°16'N	67°47'W
San Joaquin, r., Ca., U.S. (săn hwä-kēn´)	118	37°10'N	120°51'W
San Joaquin Valley, Ca., U.S.	118	36°45'N	120°30'W
San Jorge, Golfo, b., Arg. (gôl-fô-sän-kô´r-kĕ)	144	46°15'S	66°45'W
San José, C.R. (sän hô-sā´)	129	9°57'N	84°05'W
San Jose, Phil.	213a	12°22'N	121°04'E
San Jose, Phil.	213a	15°49'N	120°57'E
San Jose, Ca., U.S. (săn hô-zā´)	104	37°20'N	121°54'W
San José, i., Mex. (kô-sĕ´)	128	25°00'N	110°35'W
San José, Isla de, i., Pan. (ē´s-lä-dĕ-sän hô-sā´)	133	8°17'N	79°20'W
San Jose, Rio, r., N.M., U.S. (săn hô-zā´)	119	35°15'N	108°10'W
San José de Feliciano, Arg. (dā lä ĕs-kē´nä)	144	30°26'S	58°44'W
San José de Gauribe, Ven. (sän-hô-sĕ´dĕ-gàōō-rē´bĕ)	143b	9°51'N	65°49'W
San José de las Lajas, Cuba (sän-kô-sĕ´dĕ-läs-lå´käs)	135a	22°58'N	82°10'W
San José Iturbide, Mex. (ē-tōōr-bē´dĕ)	130	21°00'N	100°24'W
San Juan, Arg. (hwän´)	144	31°36'S	68°29'W
San Juan, Col. (hòå´n)	142a	3°23'N	73°48'W
San Juan, Dom. Rep. (sän hwän´)	135	18°50'N	71°15'W
San Juan, Phil.	213a	[illegible]	[illegible]
San Juan, P.R. (sän hwän´)	129	18°30'N	66°10'W
San Juan, prov., Arg.	144	31°00'S	69°30'W
San Juan, r., Mex. (sän-hōō-än´)	131	18°10'N	95°23'W
San Juan, r., N.A.	[illegible]	[illegible]	[illegible]
San Juan, r., U.S.	[illegible]	[illegible]	[illegible]
San Juan, Cabezas de, c., P.R.	129b	18°29'N	65°30'W
San Juan, Cabo, c., Eq. Gui.	236	1°08'N	9°23'E
San Juan, Pico, mtn., Cuba (pē´kô-sän-kòå´n)	134	21°55'N	80°00'W
San Juan, Río, r., Mex. (rê´ō-sän-hwän)	122	25°35'N	99°15'W
San Juan Bautista, Para. (sän hwän´ bou-tēs´tä)	144	26°48'S	57°09'W
San Juan Capistrano, Mex. (sän-hōō-än´ kä-pēs-trä´nô)	130	22°41'N	104°07'W
San Juan Creek, r., Ca., U.S. (săn hwän´)	118	35°24'N	120°12'W
San Juan de Guadalupe, Mex. (sän hwan dā gwä-dhä-lōō´på)	122	24°37'N	102°43'W
San Juan del Norte, Nic.	133	10°55'N	83°44'W
San Juan del Norte, Bahía de, b., Nic.	133	11°12'N	83°40'W
San Juan de los Lagos, Mex. (sän-hōō-än´dā lōs lä´gôs)	130	21°15'N	102°18'W
San Juan de los Lagos, r., Mex. (dā lōs lä´gôs)	130	21°13'N	102°12'W
San Juan de los Morros, Ven. (dĕ-lôs-mô´r-rôs)	143b	9°54'N	67°22'W
San Juan del Río, Mex.	130	20°21'N	99°59'W
San Juan del Río, Mex. (sän hwän del rē´ô)	122	24°47'N	104°29'W
San Juan del Sur, Nic. (dĕl sōōr)	128	11°15'N	85°53'W
San Juan Evangelista, Mex. (sän-hōō-ä´n-å-väŋ-kå-lēs´ta´)	131	17°57'N	95°08'W
San Juan Island, i., Wa., U.S.	116a	48°28'N	123°08'W
San Juan Islands, is., Can. (săn hwän)	94	48°49'N	123°14'W
San Juan Islands, is., Wa., U.S.	186a	48°36'N	122°50'W
San Juan Ixtenco, Mex. (ēx-tĕ´n-kô)	131	19°14'N	97°52'W
San Juan Martínez, Cuba	134	22°15'N	83°50'W
San Juan Mountains, mts., Co., U.S. (san hwän´)	106	37°50'N	107°30'W
San Julián, Arg. (sän hōō-lyá´n)	144	49°17'S	68°02'W
San Justo, Arg. (hōōs´tô)	144a	34°40'S	58°33'W
Sankanbiriwa, mtn., S.L.	234	8°56'N	10°48'W
Sankarani, r., Afr. (sän´kä-rä´nē)	230	11°10'N	8°35'W
Sankt Gallen, Switz.	161	47°25'N	9°22'E
Sankt Moritz, Switz. (sänkt mō´rĭts) (zäŋkt mō´rēts)	168	46°31'N	9°50'E
Sankt Pölten, Aus. (zäŋkt-pûl´tĕn)	168	48°12'N	15°38'E
Sankt Veit, Aus. (zäŋkt vīt´)	168	46°46'N	14°20'E
Sankuru, r., D.R.C. (sän-kōō´rōō)	232	4°00'S	22°35'E
San Lázaro, Cabo, c., Mex. (sän-lá´zä-rō)	128	24°58'N	113°30'W
San Leandro, Ca., U.S. (săn lê-ăn´drô)	116b	37°43'N	122°10'W
Şanlıurfa, Tur.	198	37°20'N	38°45'E
San Lorenzo, Arg. (sän lô-rĕn´zô)	144	32°46'S	60°44'W
San Lorenzo, Hond. (sän lô-rĕn´zô)	132	13°24'N	87°24'W
San Lorenzo, Ca., U.S. (săn lô-rĕn´zô)	116b	37°41'N	122°08'W
San Lorenzo de El Escorial, Spain	172	40°36'N	4°09'W
Sanlúcar de Barrameda, Spain (sän-lōō´kär)	162	36°46'N	6°21'W
San Lucas, Bol. (lōō´kàs)	142	20°12'S	65°06'W
San Lucas, Cabo, c., Mex.	128	22°45'N	109°45'W
San Luis, Arg. (lô-ēs´)	144	33°16'S	66°15'W
San Luis, Col. (lòē´s)	142a	6°03'N	74°57'W
San Luis, Cuba	135	20°15'N	75°50'W
San Luis, Guat.	132	14°38'N	89°42'W
San Luis, prov., Arg.	144	32°45'S	66°00'W
San Luis de la Paz, Mex. (dā lä päz´)	130	21°17'N	100°32'W
San Luis del Cordero, Mex. (dĕl kôr-dā´rô)	122	25°25'N	104°20'W
San Luis Obispo, Ca., U.S. (ô-bĭs´pō)	104	35°18'N	120°40'W
San Luis Obispo Bay, b., Ca., U.S.	118	35°07'N	121°05'W
San Luis Potosí, Mex.	128	22°08'N	100°58'W
San Luis Potosí, state, Mex.	128	22°45'N	101°45'W
San Luis Rey, r., Ca., U.S. (rā´ē)	118	33°22'N	117°06'W
San Manuel, Az., U.S. (sän măn´ū-ĕl)	119	32°30'N	110°45'W
San Marcial, N.M., U.S. (săn mår-shäl´)	119	33°40'N	107°00'W
San Marco, Italy (sän mär´kô)	174	41°53'N	15°50'E
San Marcos, Guat. (mär´kôs)	132	14°57'N	91°49'W
San Marcos, Mex.	130	16°46'N	99°23'W
San Marcos, Tx., U.S. (săn mär´kôs)	123	29°53'N	97°56'W
San Marcos, r., Tx., U.S.	122	30°08'N	98°15'W
San Marcos de Colón, Hond. (sän-mà´r-kōs-dĕ-kô-lô´n)	132	13°17'N	86°50'W
San Maria di Léuca, Cape, c., Italy (dē-lĕ´ōō-kä)	163	39°47'N	18°20'E
San Marino, S. Mar. (sän mä-rē´nô)	174	44°55'N	12°26'E
San Marino, Ca., U.S. (săn mĕr-ē´nô)	117a	34°07'N	118°06'W
San Marino, nation, Eur.	154	43°40'N	13°00'E
San Martín, Col. (sän mär-tē´n)	142a	3°42'N	73°44'W
San Martín, vol., Mex. (mär-tē´n)	131	18°36'N	95°11'W
San Martín, l., S.A.	144	48°15'S	72°30'W
San Martín Chalchicuautla, Mex.	130	21°22'N	98°39'W
San Martin de la Vega, Spain (sän mär ten´ då lä vā´gä)	173a	40°12'N	3°34'W
San Martín Hidalgo, Mex. (sän mär-tē´n-ē-däl´gô)	130	20°27'N	103°55'W
San Mateo, Mex.	131	16°59'N	97°04'W
San Mateo, Ca., U.S. (săn mä-tā´ô)	116b	37°34'N	122°20'W
San Mateo, Ven. (sän må-tĕ´ô)	143b	9°45'N	64°34'W
San Matías, Golfo, b., Arg. (sän mä-tē´äs)	144	41°30'S	63°45'W
Sanmen Wan, b., China	209	29°00'N	122°15'E
San Miguel, El Sal. (sän mê-gål´)	128	13°28'N	88°11'W
San Miguel, Mex. (sän mê-gål´)	131	18°18'N	97°09'W
San Miguel, Pan.	[illegible]	[illegible]	[illegible]
San Miguel, Phil. (sän mē-gĕ´l)	213a	15°09'N	120°56'E
San Miguel, Ven. (sän mē-gĕ´l)	143b	9°56'N	64°58'W
San Miguel, vol., El Sal.	132	13°27'N	88°17'W
San Miguel, i., Ca., U.S.	118	34°03'N	120°23'W
San Miguel, r., Bol. (sän-mē-gĕl´)	142	13°34'S	63°58'W
San Miguel, r., N.A. (sän mê-gål´)	131	15°27'N	92°00'W
San Miguel, r., Co., U.S. (săn mê-gĕl´)	119	38°15'N	108°40'W
San Miguel, Bahía, b., Pan. (bä-ē´ä-sän mê-gål´)	133	8°17'N	78°26'W
San Miguel Bay, b., Phil.	213a	13°55'N	123°12'E
San Miguel de Allende, Mex. (dā ä-lyĕn´då)	130	20°54'N	100°44'W
San Miguel el Alto, Mex. (ĕl äl´tô)	130	21°03'N	102°26'W
Sannār, Sudan	231	14°25'N	33°30'E
San Narcisco, Phil. (sän när-sē´sô)	213a	15°01'N	120°05'E
San Narcisco, Phil.	213a	13°34'N	122°33'E
San Nicolás, Arg. (sän nē-kô-lá´s)	144	33°20'S	60°14'W
San Nicolás, Phil. (nê-kô-läs´)	213a	16°05'N	120°45'E
San Nicolas, i., Ca., U.S. (săn nĭ´kô-lá)	118	33°14'N	119°10'W
San Nicolás, r., Mex.	130	19°40'N	105°08'W
Sanniquellie, Lib.	234	7°22'N	8°43'W
Sannūr, Wādī, Egypt	238b	28°48'N	31°12'E
Sanok, Pol. (sä´nôk)	169	49°31'N	22°13'E
San Pablo, Phil. (sän-pä-blô)	213a	14°05'N	121°20'E
San Pablo, Ca., U.S. (săn păb´lô)	116b	37°58'N	122°21'W
San Pablo, Ven. (sän-pá´blô)	143b	9°46'N	65°04'W
San Pablo, r., Pan. (sän päb´lô)	133	8°12'N	81°12'W
San Pablo Bay, b., Ca., U.S. (săn păb´lô)	116b	38°04'N	122°25'W
San Pablo Res, Ca., U.S.	116b	37°55'N	122°12'W
San Pascual, Phil. (päs-kwäl´)	213a	13°08'N	122°59'E
San Pedro, Arg. (sän pā´drô)	144	24°15'S	64°15'W
San Pedro, Arg.	141c	33°41'S	59°42'W
San Pedro, Chile (sän pĕ´drô)	141b	33°54'S	71°27'W
San Pedro, El Sal. (sän pā´drô)	132	13°49'N	88°58'W
San Pedro, Mex. (sän pä´drô)	131	18°38'N	92°25'W
San Pedro, Para. (sän-pĕ´drô)	144	24°13'S	57°00'W
San Pedro, Ca., U.S. (săn pē´drô)	117a	33°44'N	118°17'W
San Pedro, r., Cuba (sän-pĕ´drô)	134	21°05'N	78°15'W
San Pedro, r., Mex. (sän pā´drô)	130	22°08'N	104°59'W
San Pedro, r., Mex.	122	27°56'N	105°50'W
San Pedro, r., Az., U.S.	119	32°48'N	110°37'W
San Pedro, Río de, r., Mex.	130	21°51'N	102°24'W
San Pedro, Río de, r., N.A.	131	18°23'N	92°13'W
San Pedro Bay, b., Ca., U.S. (săn pē´drô)	117a	33°42'N	118°12'W
San Pedro de las Colonias, Mex. (dĕ-läs-kô-lô´nyäs)	122	25°47'N	102°58'W
San Pedro de Macorís, Dom. Rep. (sän-pĕ´drō-dĕ mä-kô-rēs´)	135	18°30'N	69°30'W
San Pedro Lagunillas, Mex. (sän pā´drô lä-gōō-nēl´yäs)	130	21°12'N	104°47'W
San Pedro Sula, Hond. (sän pā´drô sōō´lä)	132	15°29'N	88°01'W
San Pietro, Isola di, i., Italy (ê´sō-lä-dē-sän pyā´trô)	174	39°09'N	8°15'E
San Quentin, Ca., U.S. (săn kwĕn-tēn´)	116b	37°57'N	122°29'W
San Quintin, Phil. (sän kēn-tēn´)	213a	15°59'N	120°47'E
San Rafael, Arg. (sän rä-fä-ĕl´)	144	34°30'S	68°13'W
San Rafael, Col. (sän-rä-fä-ĕ´l)	142a	6°18'N	75°02'W
San Rafael, Ca., U.S. (săn rá-fĕl)	116b	37°58'N	122°31'W
San Rafael, r., Ut., U.S. (săn rá-fĕl´)	119	39°05'N	110°50'W
San Rafael, Cabo, c., Dom. Rep. (kå´bô)	135	19°00'N	68°50'W
San Ramón, C.R.	133	10°07'N	84°30'W
San Ramon, Ca., U.S. (săn rä-mōn´)	116b	37°47'N	122°59'W
San Remo, Italy (sän rā´mô)	174	43°48'N	7°46'E
San Roque, Col. (sän-rô´kĕ)	142a	6°29'N	75°00'W
San Roque, Spain	172	36°13'N	5°23'W
San Saba, Tx., U.S. (săn sä´bå)	122	31°12'N	98°43'W
San Saba, r., Tx., U.S.	122	30°58'N	99°12'W
San Salvador, El Sal. (sän säl-vä-dōr´)	128	13°45'N	89°11'W
San Salvador (Watling), i., Bah. (săn săl´vå-dôr)	135	24°05'N	74°30'W
San Salvador, i., Ec.	142	0°14'S	90°50'W
San Salvador, r., Ur. (sän-säl-vä-dô´r)	141c	33°42'S	58°04'W
Sansanné-Mango, Togo (sän-så-nā´ män´gô)	230	10°21'N	0°28'E
San Sebastian, Spain (sän så-bås-tyän´)	230	28°09'N	17°11'W

ăt; finăl; rāte; senåte; ärm; åsk; sofȧ; fâre; ch-choose; dh-as th in other; bē; ēvent; bĕt; recĕnt; cratẽr; g-gō; gh-guttural g; bĭt; ĭ-short neutral; rīde; ĸ-guttural k as ch in German ich;

PRONOUNCING INDEX

San Sebastián – Sapitwa 347

PLACE (Pronunciation)	PAGE	LAT.	LONG.
San Sebastián *see* Donostia-San Sebastián, Spain	154	43°19′N	1°59′W
San Sebastián, Ven. (sän-sĕ-bäs-tyä´n)	143b	9°58′N	67°11′W
San Sebastiàn de los Reyes, Spain	173a	40°33′N	3°38′W
San Severo, Italy (sän sĕ-vâ´rō)	163	41°43′N	15°24′E
Sanshui, China (sän-shwā)	205	23°14′N	112°51′E
San Simon Creek, r., Az., U.S. (sȧn sī-mōn´)	119	32°45′N	109°30′W
Santa Ana, El Sal.	128	14°02′N	89°35′W
Santa Ana, Mex. (sän´tä ä´nä)	130	19°18′N	98°10′W
Santa Ana, Ca., U.S. (săn´tȧ ăn´ȧ)	104	33°45′N	117°52′W
Santa Ana, r., Ca., U.S.	117a	33°41′N	117°57′W
Santa Ana Mountains, mts., Ca., U.S.	117a	33°44′N	117°36′W
Santa Anna, Tx., U.S.	122	31°44′N	99°18′W
Santa Antão, i., C.V. (sä-tä-ȧ´n-zhĕ-lȯ)	230b	17°20′N	26°05′W
Santa Bárbara, Braz. (sän-tä-bȧ´r-bä-rä)	143	19°57′S	43°25′W
Santa Bárbara, Hond.	132	14°52′N	88°20′W
Santa Barbara, Mex.	122	26°48′N	105°50′W
Santa Barbara, Ca., U.S.	104	34°26′N	119°43′W
Santa Barbara, i., Ca., U.S.	118	33°30′N	118°44′W
Santa Barbara Channel, strt., Ca., U.S.	118	34°15′N	120°00′W
Santa Branca, Braz. (sän-tä-brä´ɴ-kä)	141a	23°25′S	45°52′W
Santa Catalina, i., Ca., U.S.	106	33°29′N	118°37′W
Santa Catalina, Cerro de, mtn., Pan.	133	8°39′N	81°36′W
Santa Catalina, Gulf of, b., Ca., U.S. (săn´tȧ kă-tȧ-lē´nȧ)	118	33°00′N	117°58′W
Santa Catarina, Mex. (sän´tä kä-tä-rē´nä)	122	25°41′N	100°27′W
Santa Catarina, state, Braz. (sän-tä-kä-tä-rē´nȧ)	144	27°15′S	50°30′W
Santa Catarina, r., Mex.	130	16°31′N	98°39′W
Santa Clara, Cuba (sän´t klä´rá)	129	22°25′N	80°00′W
Santa Clara, Mex.	122	24°29′N	103°22′W
Santa Clara, Ur.	144	32°46′S	54°51′W
Santa Clara, Ca., U.S. (săn´tȧ klârȧ)	114	37°21′N	121°56′W
Santa Clara, vol., Nic.	132	12°44′N	87°00′W
Santa Clara, r., Ca., U.S. (săn´tȧ klă´rȧ)	118	34°22′N	118°53′W
Santa Clara, Bahía de, b., Cuba (bä-ē´ä-dĕ-sän-tä-klä-rä)	134	23°05′N	80°50′W
Santa Clara, Sierra, mts., Mex. (sē-ĕ´r-rä-sän´tä klä´rȧ)	128	27°30′N	113°50′W
Santa Clara Indian Reservation, I.R., N.M., U.S.	119	35°59′N	106°10′W
Santa Cruz, Bol. (sän´tä krōōz´)	142	17°45′S	63°03′W
Santa Cruz, Braz. (sän-tä-krōō´s)	144	29°43′S	52°15′W
Santa Cruz, Braz.	144b	22°55′S	43°41′W
Santa Cruz, Chile	141b	34°38′S	71°21′W
Santa Cruz, C.R.	132	10°16′N	85°37′W
Santa Cruz, Mex.	122	25°50′N	105°25′W
Santa Cruz, Phil.	213a	13°28′N	122°02′E
Santa Cruz, Phil.	213a	15°46′N	119°53′E
Santa Cruz, Phil.	213a	14°17′N	121°25′E
Santa Cruz, Ca., U.S.	104	36°59′N	122°02′W
Santa Cruz, prov., Arg.	144	48°00′S	70°00′W
Santa Cruz, i., Ec. (sän-tä-krōō´z)	142	0°38′S	90°20′W
Santa Cruz, r., Arg. (sän´tä krōōz´)	144	50°05′S	71°00′W
Santa Cruz, r., Az., U.S. (săn´tȧ krōōz´)	119	32°30′N	111°30′W
Santa Cruz Barillas, Guat. (sän-tä-krōō´z-bä-rē´l-yäs)	132	15°47′N	91°22′W
Santa Cruz del Sur, Cuba (sän-tä-krōō´s-dĕl-sōō´r)	134	20°45′N	78°00′W
Santa Cruz de Tenerife, Spain (sän´tä krōōz dā tā-nȧ-rē´fā)	228	28°07′N	15°27′W
Santa Cruz Islands, is., Sol. Is.	221	10°58′S	166°47′E
Santa Cruz Mountains, mts., Ca., U.S. (săn´tȧ krōōz´)	116b	37°30′N	122°19′W
Santa Domingo, Cay, i., Bah.	135	21°50′N	75°45′W
Santa Fe, Arg. (sän´tä fā´)	144	31°33′S	60°45′W
Santa Fé, Cuba (sän-tä-fĕ´)	134	21°45′N	82°40′W
Santa Fe, Spain (sän´tä-fā´)	172	37°12′N	3°43′W
Santa Fe, N.M., U.S. (săn´tȧ fā´)	104	35°40′N	106°00′W
Santa Fe, prov., Arg. (sän´tä fā´)	144	32°00′S	61°15′W
Santa Fe de Bogotá *see* Bogotá, Col.	142	4°36′N	74°05′W
Santa Filomena, Braz. (sän-tä-fē-lō-mĕ´nä)	143	9°09′S	44°45′W
Santa Genoveva, mtn., Mex. (sän-tä-hĕ-nō-vĕ´vä)	128	23°30′N	110°00′W
Santai, China (san-tī)	204	31°02′N	105°02′E
Santa Inés, Ven. (sän´tä ē-nĕ´s)	143b	9°54′N	64°21′W
Santa Inés, i., Chile (sän´tä ē-nās´)	144	53°45′S	74°15′W
Santa Isabel, i., Sol. Is.	221	7°57′S	159°28′E
Santa Isabel, Pico de, mtn., Eq. Gui.	235	3°35′N	8°46′E
Santa Lucia, Cuba (sän´tä lōō-sē´ä)	134	21°15′N	77°30′W
Santa Lucia, Ur. (sän-tä-lōō-sē´ä)	144	34°27′S	56°23′W
Santa Lucia, Ven.	143b	10°18′N	66°40′W
Santa Lucia, r., Ur.	141c	34°19′S	56°13′W
Santa Lucia Bay, b., Cuba (sän´tä lōō-sē´ä)	134	22°55′N	84°20′W
Santa Margarita, i., Mex. (sän´tä mär-gä-rē´tä)	128	24°15′N	112°00′W
Santa Maria, Braz. (sän´tä mä-rē´ä)	144	29°40′S	54°00′W
Santa Maria, Italy (sän-tä mä-rē´ä)	174	41°05′N	14°15′E
Santa Maria, Phil. (sän-tä-mä-rē´ä)	213a	14°48′N	120°57′E
Santa Maria, Ca., U.S. (săn-tȧ mȧ-rē´ȧ)	118	34°57′N	120°28′W
Santa María, vol., Guat.	132	14°45′N	91°33′W
Santa Maria, r., Mex. (sän´tä mä-rē´ä)	130	21°33′N	100°17′W
Santa Maria, Cabo de, c., Port. (kȧ´bō-dĕ-sän-tä-mä-rē´ä)	172	36°58′N	7°54′W

PLACE (Pronunciation)	PAGE	LAT.	LONG.
Santa Maria, Cape, c., Bah.	135	23°45′N	75°30′W
Santa Maria, Cayo, i., Cuba	134	22°40′N	79°00′W
Santa María del Oro, Mex. (sän´tä-mä-rē´ä-dĕl-ô-rô)	130	21°21′N	104°35′W
Santa Maria de los Angeles, Mex. (dĕ-lôs-ȧ´n-hĕ-lĕs)	130	22°10′N	103°34′W
Santa María del Río, Mex.	130	21°46′N	100°43′W
Santa María de Ocotán, Mex.	130	22°56′N	104°30′W
Santa Maria Island, i., Port. (sän-tä-mä-rē´ä)	230a	37°09′N	26°02′W
Santa Maria Madalena, Braz.	141a	22°00′S	42°00′W
Santa Marta, Col. (sän´tȧ mär´tȧ)	142	11°15′N	74°13′W
Santa Marta, Cabo de, c., Ang.	236	13°52′S	12°25′E
Santa Monica, Ca., U.S. (săn´t*á* mŏn´ĭ-k*á*)	104	34°01′N	118°29′W
Santa Monica Mountains, mts., Ca., U.S.	117a	34°08′N	118°38′W
Santana, r., Braz. (sän-tä´nä)	144b	22°33′S	43°37′W
Santander, Col. (sän-tän-dĕr´)	142a	3°00′N	76°25′W
Santander, Spain (sän-tän-dâr´)	154	43°27′N	3°50′W
Sant Antoni de Portmany, Spain	173	38°59′N	1°17′E
Santa Paula, Ca., U.S. (săn´t*á* pô´l*á*)	118	34°24′N	119°05′W
Santarém, Braz. (sän-tä-rĕɴ´)	143	2°28′S	54°37′W
Santarém, Port.	172	39°18′N	8°48′W
Santaren Channel, strt., Bah. (săn-t*á*-rĕn´)	134	24°15′N	79°30′W
Santa Rita do Sapucai, Braz. (sä-pō-kȧ´ē)	141a	22°15′S	45°41′W
Santa Rosa, Arg. (sän-tä-rô-sä)	144	36°45′S	64°10′W
Santa Rosa, Col. (sän-tä-rô-sä)	142a	6°38′N	75°26′W
Santa Rosa, Ec.	142	3°29′S	79°55′W
Santa Rosa, Guat. (sän´tä rō´s*á*)	132	14°21′N	90°16′W
Santa Rosa, Hond.	132	14°45′N	88°51′W
Santa Rosa, Ca., U.S. (săn´t*á* rō´z*á*)	104	38°27′N	122°42′W
Santa Rosa, N.M., U.S. (săn´t*á* rō´s*á*)	120	34°55′N	104°41′W
Santa Rosa, Ven. (sän-tä-rô-sä)	143b	9°37′N	64°10′W
Santa Rosa de Cabal, Col. (sän-tä-rô-sä-dĕ-kä-bä´l)	142a	4°53′N	75°38′W
Santa Rosa de Viterbo, Braz. (sän-tä-rô-sȧ-dĕ-vē-tĕr´-bô)	141a	21°30′S	47°21′W
Santa Rosa Indian Reservation, I.R., Ca., U.S. (săn´t*á* rō´z*á*´)	118	33°28′N	116°50′W
Santa Rosalía, Mex. (sän´tä rô-zä´lē-ȧ)	128	27°13′N	112°15′W
Santa Rosa Range, mts., Nv., U.S. (săn´t*á* rō´z*á*)	114	41°33′N	117°50′W
Santa Susana, Ca., U.S. (săn´t*á* sōō-ză´n*á*)	117a	34°16′N	118°42′W
Santa Teresa, Arg. (sän-tä-tĕ-rĕ´sä)	141c	33°27′S	60°47′W
Santa Teresa, Ven.	143b	10°14′N	66°40′W
Santa Uxia, Spain	172	42°34′N	8°55′W
Santa Vitória do Palmar, Braz. (sän-tä-vē-tō´ryä-dô-päl-mär)	144	33°30′S	53°16′W
Santa Ynez, r., Ca., U.S. (săn´t*á* ē-nĕz´)	118	34°40′N	120°20′W
Santa Ysabel Indian Reservation, I.R., Ca., U.S. (săn-t*á* ĭ-z*á*-bĕl´)	118	33°05′N	116°46′W
Santee, Ca., U.S. (săn tē´)	118a	32°50′N	116°58′W
Santee, r., S.C., U.S.	107	33°00′N	79°45′W
Sant' Eufemia, Golfo di, b., Italy (gôl-fô-dē-sän-tĕ´ô-fĕ´myä)	174	38°53′N	15°53′E
Sant Feliu de Guixols, Spain	173	41°45′N	3°01′E
Santiago, Braz. (sän-tyá´gô)	144	29°05′S	54°46′W
Santiago, Chile (sän-tē-ä´gô)	144	33°26′S	70°40′W
Santiago, Pan.	129	8°07′N	80°58′W
Santiago, Phil. (sän-tyä´gô)	213a	16°42′N	121°33′E
Santiago, prov., Chile (sän-tyá´gō)	141b	33°28′S	70°55′W
Santiago, i., Phil.	213a	16°29′N	120°03′E
Santiago de Compostela, Spain	162	42°52′N	8°32′W
Santiago de Cuba, Cuba (sän-tyá´gô-dā kōō´bȧ)	129	20°00′N	75°50′W
Santiago de Cuba, prov., Cuba	134	20°20′N	76°05′W
Santiago de las Vegas, Cuba (sän-tyá´gô-dĕ-läs-vĕ´gäs)	135a	22°58′N	82°23′W
Santiago del Estero, Arg.	144	27°50′S	64°14′W
Santiago del Estero, prov., Arg. (sän-tē-ä´gô-dĕl ĕs-tā-rô)	144	27°15′S	63°30′W
Santiago de los Cabelleros, Dom. Rep.	129	19°30′N	70°45′W
Santiago Mountains, mts., Tx., U.S. (săn-tē-ä´gô)	106	30°00′N	103°30′W
Santiago Reservoir, res., Ca., U.S.	117a	33°47′N	117°42′W
Santiago Rodriguez, Dom. Rep. (sän-tyá´gô-rô-drē´gĕz)	135	19°30′N	71°25′W
Santiago Tuxtla, Mex. (sän-tyá´gô-tōō´x-tlä)	131	18°28′N	95°18′W
Santiaguillo, Laguna de, l., Mex. (lä-ōō´nä-dĕ-sän-tē-ä-gēl´yô)	122	24°51′N	104°43′W
Santisteban del Puerto, Spain (sän´tē stā-bän´dĕl pwĕr´tô)	172	38°15′N	3°12′W
Sant Mateu, Spain	173	40°26′N	0°09′E
Santo Amaro, Braz. (sän´tô ä-mä´rô)	143	12°32′S	38°33′W
Santo Amaro de Campos, Braz.	141a	22°01′S	41°05′W
Santo André, Braz.	141a	23°40′S	46°31′W
Santo Angelo, Braz. (sän-tô-ä´n-zhĕ-lô)	144	28°16′S	53°59′W
Santo Antônio do Monte, Braz. (sän-tô-än-tô´nyô-dô-môn´tĕ)	141a	20°06′S	45°18′W
Santo Domingo, Cuba (sän´tô-dômĭn´gô)	134	22°35′N	80°20′W
Santo Domingo, Dom. Rep. (sän´tô dô-mĭn´gô)	129	18°30′N	69°55′W
Santo Domingo, Nic. (sän-tô-dô-mĕ´n-gô)	133	12°15′N	84°56′W

PLACE (Pronunciation)	PAGE	LAT.	LONG.
Santo Domingo de la Caizada, Spain (dā lä käl-thä´dä)	172	42°27′N	2°55′W
Santoña, Spain (sän-tō´nyä)	172	43°25′N	3°27′W
Santos, Braz. (sän´tozh)	143	23°58′S	46°20′W
Santos Dumont, Braz. (sän´tôs-dô-mô´nt)	143	21°28′S	43°33′W
Sanuki, Japan (sä´nōō-kē)	211a	35°16′N	139°53′E
San Urbano, Arg. (sän-ōr-bä´nô)	141c	33°39′S	61°28′W
San Valentin, Monte, mtn., Chile (sän-vä-lĕn-tē´n)	144	46°41′S	73°30′W
San Vicente, Arg. (sän-vē-sĕn´tĕ)	141c	35°00′S	58°26′W
San Vicente, Chile	141b	34°25′S	71°06′W
San Vicente, El Sal. (sän vė-sĕn´tå)	132	13°41′N	88°43′W
San Vicente de Alcántara, Spain	172	39°24′N	7°08′W
San Vito al Tagliamento, Italy (san vē´tô)	174	45°53′N	12°52′E
San Xavier Indian Reservation, I.R., Az., U.S. (x ā´vĭĕr)	119	32°07′N	111°12′W
San Ysidro, Ca., U.S. (săn ysĭ drō´)	110a	32°33′N	117°02′W
Sanyuanli, China (sän-yůän-lē)	207a	23°11′N	113°16′E
São Bernardo do Campo, Braz. (souɴ-bĕr-nár´dȯ-dȯ-kȧ´m-pô)	141a	23°44′S	46°33′W
São Borja, Braz. (souɴ-bôr-zhä)	144	28°44′S	55°59′W
São Carlos, Braz. (souɴ kär´lōzh)	143	22°02′S	47°54′W
São Cristovão, Braz. (souɴ-krēs-tō-vouɴ)	143	11°04′S	37°11′W
São Fidélis, Braz. (souɴ-fē-dĕ´lēs)	141a	21°41′S	41°45′W
São Francisco, Braz. (souɴ fräɴ-sĕsh´kō)	143	15°59′S	44°42′W
São Francisco, r., Braz. (sän-fräɴ-sē´s-kō)	143	8°56′S	40°20′W
São Francisco do Sul, Braz. (souɴ fräɴ-sĕsh´kō-dō-sōō´l)	144	26°15′S	48°42′W
São Gabriel, Braz. (souɴ´gä-brē-ĕl´)	144	30°28′S	54°11′W
São Geraldo, Braz. (souɴ-zhĕ-rä´l-dô)	141a	21°01′S	42°49′W
São Gonçalo, Braz. (souɴ´gōŋ-sä´lô)	141a	22°55′S	43°04′W
Sao Hill, Tan.	237	8°20′S	35°12′E
São João, Gui.-B.	234	11°32′N	15°26′W
São João da Barra, Braz. (souɴ-zhōuɴ-dä-bä´rä)	141a	21°40′S	41°03′W
São João da Boa Vista, Braz. (souɴ-zhōuɴ-dä-bôä-vē´s-tä)	141a	21°58′S	46°45′W
São João del Rei, Braz. (souɴ zhô-ouɴ´dĕl-rā)	144	21°08′S	44°14′W
São João de Meriti, Braz. (souɴ-zhōuɴ-dĕ-mĕ-rē-tē)	144b	22°47′S	43°22′W
São João do Araguaia, Braz. (souɴ zhô-ouɴ´dô-ä-rä-gwä´yä)	143	5°29′S	48°44′W
São João dos Lampas, Port. (souɴ´ zhô-ouɴ´ dōzh län-päzh´)	173b	38°52′N	9°24′W
São João Nepomuceno, Braz. (souɴ-zhōuɴ-nĕ-pô-mōō-sĕ-nô)	141a	21°33′S	43°00′W
São Jorge Island, i., Port. (souɴ zhôr´zhĕ)	230a	38°28′N	27°34′W
São José do Rio Pardo, Braz. (souɴ-zhô-sĕ´dô-rē´ô-pá´r-dô)	141a	21°36′S	46°50′W
São José do Rio Prêto, Braz. (souɴ zhô-sĕ´dô-rē´ô-prĕ-tô)	143	20°57′S	49°12′W
São José dos Campos, Braz. (souɴ-zhô-zā´dōzh kän pōzh´)	141a	23°12′S	45°53′W
São Leopoldo, Braz. (souɴ-lĕ-ô-pôl´dô)	144	29°46′S	51°09′W
São Luis, Braz.	143	2°31′S	43°14′W
São Luis do Paraitinga, Braz. (souɴ-lōōē´s-dô-pä-rä-ē-tē´n-gä)	141a	23°15′S	45°18′W
São Manuel, r., Braz.	143	8°28′S	57°07′E
São Mateus, Braz. (souɴ mä-tā´ōzh)	143	18°44′S	39°45′W
São Mateus, Braz.	144b	22°49′S	43°23′W
São Miguel Arcanjo, Braz. (souɴ-mē-gĕ´l-ár-kän-zhô)	141a	23°54′S	47°59′W
São Miguel Island, i., Port.	230a	37°59′N	26°38′W
Saona, i., Dom. Rep. (sä-ô´nä)	135	18°10′N	68°55′W
Saône, r., Fr. (sōn)	156	47°00′N	5°30′E
São Nicolau, i., C.V. (souɴ´ nē-kô-louɴ´)	230b	16°19′N	25°19′W
São Paulo, Braz. (souɴ´ pou´lô)	143	23°34′S	46°38′W
São Paulo, state, Braz. (souɴ pou´lô)	143	21°45′S	50°47′W
São Paulo de Olivença, Braz. (souɴ´pou´lôdā ô-lē-vĕn´s*á*)	142	3°32′S	68°46′W
São Pedro, Braz. (souɴ-pĕ´drô)	141a	22°34′S	47°54′W
São Pedro de Aldeia, Braz. (souɴ-pĕ´drô-dĕ-äl-dĕ´yä)	141a	22°50′S	42°04′W
São Pedro e São Paulo, Rocedos, rocks, Braz.	139	1°50′N	30°00′W
São Raimundo Nonato, Braz. (souɴ´ rī-mô´n-do nô-nä´tô)	143	9°09′S	42°32′W
São Roque, Braz. (souɴ´ rô´kĕ)	141a	23°32′S	47°08′W
São Roque, Cabo de, c., Braz. (kä´bo-dĕ-souɴ´ rô´kĕ)	143	5°06′S	35°11′W
São Sebastião, Braz. (souɴ sā-bäs-tē-ouɴ´)	141a	23°48′S	45°25′W
São Sebastião, Ilha de, i., Braz.	141a	23°52′S	45°22′W
São Sebastião do Paraíso, Braz.	141a	20°54′S	46°58′W
São Simão, Braz. (souɴ-sē-mouɴ)	141a	21°30′S	47°33′W
São Tiago, i., C.V. (souɴ tē-ä´gô)	230b	15°09′N	24°45′W
São Tomé, S. Tom./P.	230	0°20′N	6°44′E
Sao Tome and Principe, nation, Afr. (prēn´sē-pĕ)	230	1°00′N	6°00′E
Saoura, Oued, r., Alg.	230	29°39′N	1°42′W
São Vicente, Braz. (souɴ ve-se´n-tĕ)	143	23°57′S	46°25′W
São Vicente, i., C.V. (souɴ vē-sĕn´tā)	230b	16°51′N	24°35′W
São Vicente, Cabo de, c., Port. (kȧ´bô-dĕ-sän-vē-sĕ´n-tĕ)	156	37°03′N	9°31′W
Sapele, Nig. (sä-pā´lā)	230	5°54′N	5°41′E
Sapitwa, mtn., Mwi.	237	15°58′S	35°38′E

ng-sing; ŋ-baŋk; ɴ-nasalized n; nŏd; cŏmmit; ōld; ôbey; ôrder; oi-boil; fōōd; ŏŏ-as oo in foot; ou-out; s-soft; sh-dish; th-thin; pūre; ûnite; ûrn; stŭd; circŭs; ü-as in French tu; ´-indeterminate vowel.

348 Sa Pobla – Segura PRONOUNCING INDEX

PLACE (Pronunciation)	PAGE	LAT.	LONG.
Sa Pobla, Spain	173	39°46′N	3°02′E
Sapozhok, Russia (sä-pô-zhôk′)	176	53°58′N	40°44′E
Sapporo, Japan (säp-pô′rô)	205	43°02′N	141°29′E
Sapronovo, Russia (sȧp-rô′nô-vô)	186b	55°13′N	38°25′E
Sapucaí, r., Braz. (sä-pōō-kȧ-ē′)	141a	22°20′S	45°53′W
Sapucaia, Braz. (sä-pōō-kä′yȧ)	141a	22°01′S	42°54′W
Sapucaí Mirim, r., Braz.			
(sä-pōō-kȧ-ē′mē-rēɴ)	141a	21°06′S	47°03′W
Sapulpa, Ok., U.S. (sȧ-pŭl′pȧ)	121	36°01′N	96°05′W
Saqqez, Iran	201	36°14′N	46°16′E
Saquarema, Braz. (sä-kwä-rĕ-mä)	141a	22°56′S	42°32′W
Sara, Wa., U.S. (sä′rä)	116c	45°45′N	122°42′W
Sara, Bahr, r., Chad (bär)	231	8°10′N	17°44′E
Sarajevo, Bos.			
(sä-rȧ-yĕv′ô) (sȧ-rä′ya-vô)	154	43°50′N	18°26′E
Sarakhs, Iran	201	36°32′N	61°11′E
Sarana, Russia [illegible]	[illegible]	[illegible]	[illegible]
Saranac Lake, N.Y., U.S.	100	44°20′N	74°05′W
Saranac Lake, l., N.Y., U.S. (săr′ȧ-năk)	109	44°15′N	74°20′W
Sarandi, Arg. (sä-rän′dê)	144a	34°41′S	58°21′W
Sarandi Grande, Ur.			
(sä-rän′dē-grän′dĕ)	141c	33°42′S	56°21′W
Saranley, Som.	238a	2°28′N	42°15′E
Saransk, Russia (sȧ-ränsk′)	178	54°10′N	45°10′E
Sarany, Russia (sȧ-rȧ′nĭ)	186a	58°33′N	58°48′E
Sara Peak, mtn., Nig.	235	9°37′N	9°25′E
Sarapul, Russia (sä-räpôl′)	180	56°28′N	53°50′E
Sarasota, Fl., U.S. (săr-ȧ-sōtȧ)	125a	27°27′N	82°30′W
Saratoga, Tx., U.S. (săr-ȧ-tō′gȧ)	123	30°17′N	94°31′W
Saratoga, Wa., U.S.	116a	48°04′N	122°29′W
Saratoga Pass, Wa., U.S.	116a	48°09′N	122°33′W
Saratoga Springs, N.Y., U.S.			
(spr̆ingz)	109	43°05′N	74°50′W
Saratov, Russia (sȧ rä′tôf)	178	51°30′N	45°30′E
Saravane, Laos	209	15°48′N	106°40′E
Sarawak, hist. reg., Malay.			
(sȧ-rä′wäk)	212	2°30′N	112°45′E
Sárbogárd, Hung. (shär′bô-gärd)	169	46°53′N	18°38′E
Sarcee Indian Reserve, I.R.,			
Can. (sär′sē)	102e	50°58′N	114°23′W
Sarcelles, Fr.	171b	49°00′N	2°23′E
Sardalas, Libya	230	25°59′N	10°33′E
Sardinia, i., Italy (sär-dĭn′ĭȧ)	156	40°08′N	9°05′E
Sardis, Ms., U.S. (sär′dĭs)	124	34°26′N	89°55′W
Sardis Lake, res., Ms., U.S.	124	34°27′N	89°43′W
Sargent, Ne., U.S. (sär′jĕnt)	112	41°40′N	99°38′W
Sarh, Chad (är-chaɴ-bô′)	231	9°09′N	18°23′E
Sarikamis, Tur.	181	40°30′N	42°40′E
Sariñena, Spain (sä-rēn-yĕ′nä)	173	41°46′N	0°11′W
Sark, i., Guern. (särk)	170	49°28′N	2°22′W
Şarköy, Tur. (shär′kû-ē)	175	40°39′N	27°07′E
Sarmiento, Monte, mtn., Chile			
(mô′n-tē-sär-myĕn′tô)	144	54°28′S	70°40′W
Sarnia, Can. (sär′nē-ȧ)	91	43°00′N	82°25′W
Sarno, Italy (sä′r-nô)	173c	40°35′N	14°38′E
Sarny, Ukr. (sär′nê)	181	51°17′N	26°39′E
Saronikós Kólpos, b., Grc.	175	37°51′N	23°30′E
Saros Körfezi, b., Tur. (sä′rôs)	175	40°30′N	26°20′E
Sárospatak, Hung. (shä′rôsh-pô′tôk)	169	48°19′N	21°35′E
Šar Planina, mts., Eur.			
(shär plä′nē-na)	175	42°07′N	21°54′E
Sarpsborg, Nor. (särps′bôrg)	166	59°17′N	11°07′E
Sarrebourg, Fr. (sär-bōōr′)	171	48°44′N	7°02′E
Sarreguemines, Fr. (sär-gē-mēn′)	161	49°06′N	7°05′E
Sarria, Spain (sär′ē-ä)	162	42°14′N	7°17′W
Sarstun, r., N.A. (särs-tōō′n)	132	15°50′N	89°26′W
Sartène, Fr. (sär-tĕn′)	174	41°36′N	8°59′E
Sarthe, r., Fr. (särt)	161	47°44′N	0°32′W
Şärur, Azer.	182	39°33′N	44°58′E
Sárvár, Hung. (shär′vär)	168	47°14′N	16°55′E
Sarych, Mys, c., Ukr. (mĭs sȧ-rēch′)	181	44°25′N	33°00′E
Saryesik-Atyraū, des., Kaz.	183	45°30′N	76°00′E
Sary-Ishikotrau, Peski, des., Kyrg.			
(sä′rē ē′ shĕk-ō′trou)	183	46°12′N	75°30′E
Sarysū, r., Kaz. (sä′rē-sōō)	183	47°47′N	69°14′E
Sasarām, India (sŭs-ŭ-räm′)	199	25°00′N	84°00′E
Sasayama, Japan (sä′sä-yä′mä)	211	35°05′N	135°14′E
Sasebo, Japan (sä′sȧ-bô)	205	33°12′N	129°43′E
Saskatchewan, prov., Can.	90	54°46′N	107°40′W
Saskatchewan, r., Can.			
(săs-kăch′ê-wän)	92	53°45′N	103°20′W
Saskatoon, Can. (săs-kȧ-tōōn′)	90	52°07′N	106°38′W
Sasolburg, S. Afr.	238c	26°52′S	27°47′E
Sasovo, Russia (sȧs′ô-vô)	180	54°20′N	42°00′E
Saspamco, Tx., U.S. (săs-păm′cō)	117d	29°13′N	98°18′W
Sassandra, C. Iv.	234	4°58′N	6°05′W
Sassandra, r., C. Iv. (sȧs-sän′drȧ)	230	5°35′N	6°25′W
Sassari, Italy (säs′sä-rē)	162	40°44′N	8°33′E
Sassnitz, Ger. (säs′nēts)	168	54°31′N	13°37′E
Satadougou, Mali (sä-tȧ-dōō-gōō′)	234	12°21′N	12°07′W
Säter, Swe. (sĕ′tĕr)	166	60°21′N	15°50′E
Satilla, r., Ga., U.S. (sȧ-tĭl′ȧ)	125	31°15′N	82°13′W
Satka, Russia (sät′kȧ)	180	55°03′N	59°02′E
Sátoraljaujhely, Hung.			
(shä′tô-rô-lyô-ōō′yĕl′)	169	48°24′N	21°40′E
Satu Mare, Rom. (sȧ′tōō-mȧ′rĕ)	163	47°50′N	22°53′E
Saturna, Can. (sȧ-tûr′nȧ)	116d	48°48′N	123°12′W
Saturna, i., Can.	116d	48°47′N	123°03′W
Sauda, Nor.	160	59°40′N	6°21′E
Saudárkrókur, Ice.	154	65°41′N	19°38′W
Saudi Arabia, nation, Asia			
(sȧ-ō′dĭ ȧ-rä′bĭ-ȧ)	198	22°40′N	46°00′E
Sauerlach, Ger. (zou′ĕr-läĸ)	159d	47°58′N	11°39′E
Saugatuck, Mi., U.S. (sô′gȧ-tŭk)	108	42°40′N	86°10′W
Saugeen, r., Can.	98	44°20′N	81°20′W
Saugerties, N.Y., U.S. (sô′gēr-tēz)	109	42°05′N	73°55′W
Saugus, Ma., U.S. (sô′gŭs)	101a	42°28′N	71°01′W
Sauk, r., Mn., U.S. (sôk)	113	45°30′N	94°45′W
Sauk Centre, Mn., U.S.	113	45°43′N	94°58′W
Sauk City, Wi., U.S.	113	43°16′N	89°45′W
Sauk Rapids, Mn., U.S. (răp′ĭd)	113	45°35′N	94°08′W
Sault Sainte Marie, Can.	91	46°31′N	84°20′W
Sault Sainte Marie, Mi., U.S.			
(sōō sānt mȧ-rē′)	105	46°29′N	84°21′W
Saumatre, Étang, l., Haiti	135	18°40′N	72°10′W
Saunders Lake, l., Can. (sän′dẽrs)	102g	53°18′N	113°25′W
Saurimo, Ang.	232	9°39′S	20°24′E
Sausalito, Ca., U.S. (sô-sȧ-lē′tô)	116b	37°51′N	122°29′W
Sausset-les-Pins, Fr. (sō-sĕ′lā-pȧɴ′)	170a	43°20′N	5°08′E
Saútar, Ang.	236	11°06′S	18°27′E
Sauvie Island, i., Or., U.S. (sô′vē)	116c	45°43′N	123°49′W
Sava, r., Eur. [illegible]	[illegible]	[illegible]	[illegible]
Savage, Md., U.S. (săv′ĕj)	110e	39°07′N	76°49′W
Savage, Mn., U.S.	117g	44°47′N	93°20′W
Savai′i, i., Samoa	214a	13°35′S	172°25′W
Savalen, l., Nor.	166	62°19′N	10°15′E
Savalou, Benin	230	7°56′N	1°58′E
Savanna, Il., U.S. (sȧ-văn′ȧ)	113	42°05′N	90°09′W
Savannah, Ga., U.S. (sȧ-văn′ȧ)	105	32°04′N	81°07′W
Savannah, Mo., U.S.	121	39°58′N	94°49′W
Savannah, Tn., U.S.	124	35°13′N	88°14′W
Savannah, r., U.S.	107	33°11′N	81°51′W
Savannakhét, Laos	212	16°33′N	104°45′E
Savanna la Mar, Jam.			
(sȧ-văn′ȧ lȧ mär′)	134	18°10′N	78°10′W
Save, r., Fr.	170	43°32′N	0°50′E
Save, Rio (Sabi), r., Afr. (rē′ō-sä′vē)	232	21°28′S	34°14′E
Säveh, Iran	201	35°01′N	50°20′E
Saverne, Fr. (sȧ-vĕrn′)	171	48°40′N	7°22′E
Savigliano, Italy (sä-vēl-yä′nô)	174	44°38′N	7°42′E
Savigny-sur-Orge, Fr.	171b	48°41′N	2°22′E
Savona, Italy (sä-nō′nä)	162	44°19′N	8°28′E
Savonlinna, Fin. (sȧ′vōn-lēn′nȧ)	167	61°53′N	28°49′E
Savran′, Ukr. (säv-rän′)	177	48°07′N	30°09′E
Sawahlunto, Indon.	212	0°37′S	100°50′E
Sawākin, Sudan	231	19°02′N	37°19′E
Sawda, Jabal as, mts., Libya	231	28°14′N	13°46′E
Sawhāj, Egypt	231	26°34′N	31°40′E
Sawknah, Libya	231	29°04′N	15°53′E
Sawu, Laut (Savu Sea), sea, Asia	212	9°15′S	122°15′E
Sawyer, l., Wa., U.S. (sô′yẽr)	116a	47°20′N	122°02′W
Saxony *see* Sachsen, hist. reg., Ger.	168	50°45′N	12°17′E
Say, Niger (sä′ē)	230	13°09′N	2°16′E
Sayan Khrebet, mts., Russia (sŭ-yän′)	179	51°30′N	90°00′E
Sayhūt, Yemen	198	15°23′N	51°28′E
Sayre, Ok., U.S. (sā′ẽr)	120	35°19′N	99°40′W
Sayre, Pa., U.S.	109	41°55′N	76°30′W
Sayreton, Al., U.S. (sā′ẽr-tŭn)	110h	33°34′N	86°51′W
Sayreville, N.J., U.S. (sâr′vĭl)	110a	40°28′N	74°21′W
Sayr Usa, Mong.	204	44°15′N	107°00′E
Sayula, Mex. (sä-yōō′lä)	131	17°51′N	94°56′W
Sayula, Mex.	130	19°50′N	103°33′W
Sayula, Luguna de, l., Mex.			
(lä-gō′nä-dĕ)	130	20°00′N	103°33′W
Say′un, Yemen	198	16°00′N	48°59′E
Sayville, N.Y., U.S. (sā′vĭl)	109	40°45′N	73°10′W
Sazanit, i., Alb.	163	40°30′N	19°17′E
Sázava, r., Czech Rep.	168	49°36′N	15°24′E
Sazhino, Russia (sȧz-hē′nô)	186a	56°20′N	58°15′E
Scandinavian Peninsula, pen., Eur.	196	62°00′N	14°00′E
Scanlon, Mn., U.S. (skăn′lôn)	117h	46°27′N	92°26′W
Scappoose, Or., U.S. (skă-pōōs′)	116c	45°46′N	122°53′W
Scappoose, r., Or., U.S.	116c	45°47′N	122°57′W
Scarborough, Eng., U.K. (skär′bŭr-ô)	164	54°16′N	0°19′W
Scarsdale, N.Y., U.S. (skärz′dāl)	110a	41°01′N	73°47′W
Scatari I, Can. (skăt′ȧ-rē)	101	46°00′N	59°44′W
Schaerbeek, Bel. (skär′bāk)	159a	50°50′N	4°23′E
Schaffhausen, Switz. (shäf′hou-zĕn)	161	47°42′N	8°38′E
Schefferville, Can.	91	54°52′N	67°01′W
Schelde, r., Eur.	165	51°04′N	3°55′E
Schenectady, N.Y., U.S.			
(skĕ-nĕk′tȧ-dê)	105	42°50′N	73°55′W
Scheveningen, Neth.	159a	52°06′N	4°15′E
Schiedam, Neth.	159a	51°55′N	4°23′E
Schiltigheim, Fr. (shēl′tegh-hīm)	171	48°48′N	7°47′E
Schio, Italy (skē′ô)	174	45°43′N	11°23′E
Schleswig, Ger. (shlĕs′vēgh)	160	54°32′N	9°32′E
Schleswig, hist. reg., Ger.			
(shlĕs′vēgh)	168	54°40′N	9°10′E
Schleswig-Holstein, state, Ger.			
(shlĕs′vēgh-hōl′shtīn)	159c	53°40′N	9°45′E
Schmalkalden, Ger. (shmäl′käl-dĕn)	168	50°41′N	10°25′E
Schneider, In., U.S. (schnī′dẽr)	111a	41°12′N	87°26′W
Schofield, Wi., U.S. (skō′fēld)	113	44°52′N	89°37′W
Schönebeck, Ger. (shû′nĕ-bergh)	168	52°01′N	11°44′E
Schoonhoven, Neth.	159a	51°56′N	4°51′E
Schramberg, Ger. (shräm′bĕrgh)	168	48°14′N	8°24′E
Schreiber, Can.	98	48°50′N	87°10′W
Schroon, l., N.Y., U.S. (skrōōn)	109	43°50′N	73°50′W
Schultzendorf, Ger. (shōōl′tzĕn-dōrf)	159b	52°21′N	13°55′E
Schumacher, Can.	98	48°30′N	81°30′W
Schuyler, Ne., U.S. (slī′lẽr)	112	41°28′N	97°05′W
Schuylkill, r., Pa., U.S. (skōōl′kĭl)	110f	40°10′N	75°31′W
Schuylkill-Haven, Pa., U.S.			
(skōōl′kĭl hā-vĕn)	109	40°35′N	76°10′W
Schwabach, Ger. (shvä′bäk)	168	49°19′N	11°02′E
Schwäbische Alb, mts., Ger.			
(shvă′bē-shĕ älb)	168	48°11′N	9°09′E
Schwäbisch Gmünd, Ger.			
(shvă′bēsh gmünd)	168	48°47′N	9°49′E
Schwäbisch Hall, Ger. (häl)	168	49°08′N	9°44′E
Schwandorf, Ger. (shvän′dôrf)	168	49°19′N	12°08′E
Schwaner, Pegunungan, mts., Indon.			
(skvän′ẽr)	212	1°05′S	112°30′E
Schwarzwald, for., Ger. (shvärts′väld)	168	47°54′N	7°57′E
Schwaz, Aus.	168	47°20′N	11°45′E
Schwechat, Aus. (shvĕk′ȧt)	168	48°09′N	16°29′E
Schwedt, Ger. (shvĕt)	168	53°04′N	14°17′E
Schweinfurt, Ger. (shvīn′fōrt)	168	50°03′N	10°14′E
Schwelm, Ger. (shvĕlm)	171c	51°17′N	7°18′E
Schwerin, Ger. (shvĕ-rēn′)	168	53°36′N	11°25′E
Schweriner See, l., Ger.			
(shvĕ′rē-nĕr zā)	168	53°40′N	11°06′E
Schwerte, Ger. (shvĕr′tĕ)	171c	51°26′N	7°34′E
Schwielowsee, l., Ger. (shvē′lōv zā)	159b	52°20′N	12°52′E
Schwyz, Switz. (schēts)	168	47°01′N	8°38′E
Sciacca, Italy (shė-äk′kä)	174	37°30′N	13°09′E
Scilly, Isles of, is., Eng., U.K. (sĭl′ē)	[illegible]	[illegible]	[illegible]
Scioto, r., Oh., U.S. (sī-ō′tō)	107	39°10′N	82°55′W
Scituate, Ma., U.S. (sĭt′ū-āt)	101a	42°12′N	70°45′W
Scobey, Mt., U.S. (skō′bê)	115	48°48′N	105°29′W
Scoggin, Or., U.S. (skō′gĭn)	116c	45°28′N	123°14′W
Scotch, r., Can. (skŏch)	102c	45°21′N	74°56′W
Scotia, Ca., U.S. (skō′shȧ)	114	40°29′N	124°06′W
Scotland, S.D., U.S.	112	43°08′N	97°43′W
Scotland, state, U.K. (skŏt′lȧnd)	154	57°05′N	5°10′W
Scotland Neck, N.C., U.S. (nĕk)	125	36°06′N	77°25′W
Scotstown, Can. (skŏts′toun)	109	45°35′N	71°15′W
Scott, r., Ca., U.S.	114	41°20′N	122°55′W
Scott, Cape, c., Can. (skŏt)	92	50°47′N	128°26′W
Scott, Mount, mtn., Or., U.S.	116c	45°27′N	122°33′W
Scott, Mount, mtn., Or., U.S.	114	42°55′N	122°00′W
Scott Air Force Base, Il., U.S.	117e	38°33′N	89°52′W
Scottburgh, S. Afr. (skŏt′bŭr-ô)	232	30°18′S	30°42′E
Scott City, Ks., U.S.	120	38°28′N	100°54′W
Scottdale, Ga., U.S. (skŏt′dāl)	110c	33°47′N	84°16′W
Scott Islands, is., Ant.	224	67°00′S	178°00′E
Scottsbluff, Ne., U.S. (skŏts′blŭf)	112	41°52′N	103°40′W
Scottsboro, Al., U.S. (skŏts′bŭro)	124	34°40′N	86°03′W
Scottsburg, In., U.S. (skŏts′bûrg)	108	38°40′N	85°50′W
Scottsdale, Austl. (skŏts′dāl)	222	41°12′S	147°37′E
Scottsville, Ky., U.S. (skŏts′vĭl)	124	36°45′N	86°10′W
Scottville, Mi., U.S.	108	44°00′N	86°20′W
Scranton, Pa., U.S. (skrăn′tŭn)	105	41°15′N	75°45′W
Scugog, l., Can. (skū′gôg)	99	44°05′N	78°55′W
Scunthorpe, Eng., U.K. (skŭn′thôrp)	158a	53°36′N	0°38′W
Scutari *see* Shkodër, Alb.	154	42°04′N	19°30′E
Scutari, Lake, l., Eur. (skōō′tä-rē)	163	42°14′N	19°33′E
Seabeck, Wa., U.S. (sē′bĕck)	116a	47°38′N	122°50′W
Sea Bright, N.J., U.S. (sē brīt)	110a	40°22′N	73°58′W
Seabrook, Tx., U.S. (sē′brŏk)	123	29°34′N	95°01′W
Seaford, De., U.S. (sē′fērd)	109	38°35′N	75°40′W
Seagraves, Tx., U.S. (sē′grāvs)	120	32°51′N	102°38′W
Sea Islands, is., Ga., U.S. (sē)	125	31°21′N	81°05′W
Seal, r., Can.	92	59°08′N	96°37′W
Seal Beach, Ca., U.S.	117a	33°44′N	118°06′W
Seal Cays, is., Bah.	135	22°40′N	75°55′W
Seal Cays, is., T./C. Is.	135	21°10′N	71°45′W
Seal Island, i., S. Afr. (sēl)	232a	34°07′S	18°36′E
Sealy, Tx., U.S. (sē′lê)	123	29°46′N	96°10′W
Searcy, Ar., U.S. (sûr′sê)	121	35°13′N	91°43′W
Searles, l., Ca., U.S. (sûrl′s)	118	35°44′N	117°22′W
Searsport, Me., U.S. (sērz′pōrt)	100	44°28′N	68°55′W
Seaside, Or., U.S. (sē′sīd)	114	45°59′N	123°55′W
Seattle, Wa., U.S. (sē-ăt′′l)	104	47°36′N	122°20′W
Sebaco, Nic. (sĕ-bä′kô)	132	12°50′N	86°03′W
Sebago, Me., U.S. (sê-bā′gō)	100	43°52′N	70°20′W
Sebastián Vizcaíno, Bahía, b., Mex.	128	28°45′N	115°15′W
Sebastopol, Ca., U.S. (sê-bȧs′tô-pôl)	118	38°27′N	122°50′W
Sebderat, Erit.	231	15°30′N	36°45′E
Sebewaing, Mi., U.S. (sē′bê-wăng)	108	43°45′N	83°25′W
Sebezh, Russia (syĕ′bĕzh)	176	56°16′N	28°29′E
Sebinkarahisar, Tur.	163	40°15′N	38°10′E
Sebnitz, Ger. (zĕb′nēts)	168	51°01′N	14°16′E
Sebou, Oued, r., Mor.	230	34°23′N	5°18′W
Sebree, Ky., U.S. (sê-brē′)	108	37°35′N	87°30′W
Sebring, Fl., U.S. (sē′brĭng)	125a	27°30′N	81°26′W
Sebring, Oh., U.S.	108	40°55′N	81°05′W
Secchia, r., Italy (sĕ′kyä)	174	44°25′N	10°25′E
Seco, r., Mex. (sĕ′kô)	131	18°11′N	93°18′W
Sedalia, Mo., U.S.	105	38°42′N	93°12′W
Sedan, Fr. (sē-däɴ)	161	49°49′N	4°55′E
Sedan, Ks., U.S. (sê-dăn′)	121	37°07′N	96°08′W
Sedom, Isr.	197a	31°04′N	35°24′E
Sedro Woolley, Wa., U.S.			
(sē′drô-wōl′ê)	116a	48°30′N	122°14′W
Šeduva, Lith. (shĕ′dô-vȧ)	167	55°46′N	23°45′E
Seestall, Ger. (zā′shtäl)	159d	47°58′N	10°52′E
Sefrou, Mor. (sĕ-frōō′)	162	33°49′N	4°46′W
Seg, l., Russia (syĕgh)	180	63°20′N	33°30′E
Segamat, Malay. (sā′gȧ-mȧt)	197b	2°30′N	102°49′E
Segang, China (sŭ-gäŋ)	206	31°59′N	114°13′E
Segbana, Benin	235	10°56′N	3°42′E
Segorbe, Spain (sĕ-gôr-bĕ)	173	39°50′N	0°30′W
Ségou, Mali (sā-gōō′)	230	13°27′N	6°16′W
Segovia, Col. (sĕ-gô′vēä)	142a	7°08′N	74°42′W
Segovia, Spain (sā-gō′vē-ä)	162	40°58′N	4°05′W
Segre, r., Spain (sā′grā)	173	41°54′N	1°10′E
Seguam, i., Ak., U.S. (sē′gwäm)	103a	52°16′N	172°10′W
Seguam Passage, strt., Ak., U.S.	103a	52°20′N	173°00′W
Séguédine, Niger	235	20°12′N	12°59′E
Séguéla, C. Iv. (sā-gā-lä′)	230	7°57′N	6°40′W
Seguin, Tx., U.S. (sĕ-gēn′)	123	29°35′N	97°58′W
Segula, i., Ak., U.S. (sē-gū′lá)	103a	52°08′N	178°35′E
Segura, r., Spain	162	38°24′N	2°12′W

ăt; finăl; rāte; senāte; ärm; ȧsk; sofȧ; fâre; ch-choose; dh-as th in other; bē; ēvent; bĕt; recĕnt; cratẽr; g-gō; gh-guttural g; bĭt; ĭ-short neutral; rīde; ĸ-guttural k as ch in German ich;

PRONOUNCING INDEX

Segura – Sheksna 349

PLACE (Pronunciation)	PAGE	LAT.	LONG.
Segura, Sierra de, mts., Spain (sē-gōō′rä-dĕ)	172	38°05′N	2°45′W
Sehwān, Pak.	202	26°33′N	67°51′E
Seibo, Dom. Rep. (sĕ′y-bō)	135	18°45′N	69°05′W
Seiling, Ok., U.S.	120	36°09′N	98°56′W
Seim, r., Eur.	181	51°23′N	33°22′E
Seinäjoki, Fin. (sâ′ē-nĕ-yô′kē)	167	62°47′N	22°50′E
Seine, r., Can. (sân)	102f	49°48′N	97°03′W
Seine, r., Can. (sân)	98	49°04′N	91°00′W
Seine, r., Fr.	156	48°00′N	4°30′E
Seine, Baie de la, b., Fr. (bī dĕ lä sån)	170	49°37′N	0°53′W
Seio do Venus, mtn., Braz. (sĕ-yô-dô-vĕ′nōōs)	144b	22°28′S	43°12′W
Seixal, Port. (så-ê-shäl′)	173b	38°38′N	9°06′W
Sekenke, Tan.	237	4°16′S	34°10′E
Şeki, Azer.	182	41°12′N	47°12′E
Sekondi-Takoradi, Ghana (sĕ-kôn′dē tä-kô-ra′dē)	230	4°58′N	1°43′W
Sekota, Eth.	231	12°47′N	38°59′E
Selangor, state, Malay. (så-län′gōr)	197b	2°53′N	101°29′E
Selanovtsi, Blg. (sål′å-nôv-tsĭ)	175	43°42′N	24°05′E
Selaru, Pulau, i., Indon.	213	8°30′S	130°30′E
Selatan, Tanjung, c., Indon. (så-lä′tän)	212	4°09′S	114°40′E
Selawik, Ak., U.S. (sē-lå-wĭk)	103	66°30′N	160°09′W
Selayar, Pulau, i., Indon.	212	6°15′S	121°15′E
Selbusjøen, l., Nor. (sĕl′bōō)	166	63°18′N	11°55′E
Selby, Eng., U.K. (sĕl′bē)	158a	53°47′N	1°03′W
Seldovia, Ak., U.S. (sĕl-dō′vē-ȧ)	103	59°26′N	151°42′W
Selemdzha, r., Russia (sâ-lĕmt-zhä′)	185	52°28′N	131°50′E
Selenga (Selenge), r., Asia (sĕ lĕŋ gä′)	179	49°00′N	102°00′E
Selenge, r., Asia	204	49°04′N	102°23′E
Selennyakh, r., Russia (sĕl-yĭn-yäk)	185	67°42′N	141°45′E
Sélestat, Fr. (sē-lē-stä′)	171	48°16′N	7°27′E
Sélibaby, Maur. (så-lē-bå-bē′)	230	15°21′N	12°11′W
Seliger, l., Russia (sĕl′lē-gĕr)	180	57°14′N	33°18′E
Selizharovo, Russia (sâ′lē-zhä′rô-vô)	176	56°51′N	33°28′E
Selkirk, Can. (sĕl′kûrk)	90	50°09′N	96°52′W
Selkirk Mountains, mts., Can.	92	51°00′N	117°40′W
Selleck, Wa., U.S. (sĕl′ĕck)	116a	47°22′N	121°52′W
Sellersburg, In., U.S. (sĕl′ĕrs-bûrg)	111h	38°25′N	85°45′W
Sellya Khskaya, Guba, b., Russia (sĕl-yäk′skȧ-yȧ)	185	72°30′N	136°00′E
Selma, Al., U.S. (sĕl′mȧ)	105	32°25′N	87°00′W
Selma, Ca., U.S.	118	36°34′N	119°37′W
Selma, N.C., U.S.	125	35°33′N	78°16′W
Selma, Tx., U.S.	117d	29°33′N	98°19′W
Selmer, Tn., U.S.	124	35°11′N	88°36′W
Selsingen, Ger. (zĕl′zēn-gĕn)	159c	53°22′N	9°13′E
Selway, r., Id., U.S. (sĕl′wā)	114	46°07′N	115°12′W
Selwyn, l., Can. (sĕl′wĭn)	92	59°41′N	104°30′W
Seman, r., Alb.	175	40°48′N	19°53′E
Semarang, Indon. (sĕ-mä′räng)	212	7°03′S	110°27′E
Semenivka, Ukr.	181	52°10′N	32°34′E
Semeru, Gunung, mtn., Indon.	212	8°06′S	112°55′E
Semey (Semipalatinsk), Kaz.	183	50°28′N	80°29′E
Semiahmoo Indian Reserve, I.R., Can.	116d	49°01′N	122°43′W
Semiahmoo Spit, Wa., U.S. (sĕm′ĭ-ȧ-mōō)	116d	48°59′N	122°52′W
Semichi Islands, is., Ak., U.S. (sē-mē′chī)	103a	52°40′N	174°50′E
Seminoe Reservoir, res., Wy., U.S. (sĕm′ĭ nô)	115	42°08′N	107°10′W
Seminole, Ok., U.S. (sĕm′ĭ-nōl)	121	35°13′N	96°41′W
Seminole, Tx., U.S.	122	32°43′N	102°39′W
Seminole, Lake, res., U.S.	124	30°57′N	84°46′W
Semipalatinsk *see* Semey, Kaz.	183	50°28′N	80°29′E
Semisopochnoi, i., Ak., U.S. (sĕ-mē-så-pōsh′ noi)	103a	51°45′N	179°25′E
Semliki, r., Afr. (sĕm′lē-kē)	231	0°45′N	29°36′E
Semmering Pass, p., Aus. (sĕm′ĕr-ĭng)	168	47°39′N	15°50′E
Senador Pompeu, Braz. (sĕ-nä-dōr-pôm-pĕ′ô)	143	5°34′S	39°18′W
Senaki, Geor.	182	42°17′N	42°04′E
Senatobia, Ms., U.S. (sĕ-nȧ-tō′bē-ȧ)	124	34°36′N	89°56′W
Sendai, Japan (sĕn-dī′)	205	38°18′N	141°02′E
Seneca, Ks., U.S. (sĕn′ĕ-kȧ)	121	39°49′N	96°03′W
Seneca, Md., U.S.	110e	39°04′N	77°20′W
Seneca, S.C., U.S.	125	34°40′N	82°58′W
Seneca, l., N.Y., U.S.	109	42°30′N	76°55′W
Seneca Falls, N.Y., U.S.	109	42°55′N	76°55′W
Senegal, nation, Afr. (sĕn-ĕ-gôl′)	230	14°53′N	14°58′W
Sénégal, r., Afr.	230	16°00′N	14°00′W
Senekal, S. Afr. (sĕn′ĕ-kȧl)	238c	28°20′S	27°37′E
Senftenberg, Ger. (zĕnf′tĕn-bĕrgh)	168	51°32′N	14°00′E
Sengunyane, r., Leso.	233c	29°35′S	28°08′E
Senhor do Bonfim, Braz. (sĕn-yôr dô bôn-fē′ɴ)	143	10°21′S	40°09′W
Senigallia, Italy (så-nē-gäl′lyä)	174	43°42′N	13°16′E
Senj, Cro. (sĕn′)	174	44°58′N	14°55′E
Senja, i., Nor. (sĕnyä)	160	69°28′N	16°10′E
Senlis, Fr. (säɴ-lēs′)	171b	49°13′N	2°35′E
Sennar Dam, dam, Sudan	231	13°38′N	33°38′E
Senneterre, Can.	91	48°20′N	77°22′W
Sens, Fr. (säns)	170	48°05′N	3°18′E
Sensuntepeque, El Sal. (sĕn-sōōn-tå-pä′kå)	132	13°53′N	88°34′W
Senta, Serb. (sĕn′tä)	163	45°54′N	20°05′E
Senzaki, Japan (sĕn′zä-kē)	211	34°22′N	131°09′E
Seoul (Sŏul), Kor., S.	205	37°35′N	127°03′E
Sepang, Malay.	197b	2°43′N	101°45′E
Sepetiba, Baía de, b., Braz. (bäē′ä dĕ så-på-tē′bȧ)	144b	23°01′S	43°42′W
Sepik, r. (sĕp-ĕk′)	213	4°07′S	142°40′E
Septentrional, Cordillera, mts., Dom. Rep.	135	19°50′N	71°15′W
Septeuil, Fr. (sĕ-tû′)	171b	48°53′N	1°40′E
Sept-Îles, Can. (sĕ-tēl′)	100	50°12′N	66°23′W
Sequatchie, r., Tn., U.S. (sē-kwăch′ē)	124	35°33′N	85°14′W
Sequim, Wa., U.S. (sē′kwĭm)	116a	48°05′N	123°07′W
Sequim Bay, b., Wa., U.S.	116a	48°04′N	122°58′W
Sequoia National Park, rec., Ca., U.S. (sē-kwoi′ȧ)	106	36°34′N	118°37′W
Seraing, Bel. (sẽ-răɴ′)	165	50°38′N	5°28′E
Serāmpore, India	202a	22°44′N	88°21′E
Serang, Indon. (så-räng′)	212	6°13′S	106°10′E
Seranggung, Indon.	197b	0°49′N	104°11′E
Serbia, nation, Eur.	154	44°00′N	21°00′E
Serdobsk, Russia (sĕr-dôpsk′)	181	52°30′N	44°20′E
Sered′, Slvk.	169	48°17′N	17°43′E
Seredyna-Buda, Ukr.	176	52°11′N	34°03′E
Seremban, Malay. (sĕr-ĕm-bän′)	197b	2°44′N	101°57′E
Serengeti National Park, rec., Tan.	237	2°20′S	34°50′E
Serengeti Plain, pl., Tan.	237	2°40′S	34°55′E
Serenje, Zam. (sē-rĕn′yē)	232	13°12′S	30°49′E
Seret, r., Ukr. (sĕr′ĕt)	169	49°45′N	25°30′E
Sergeya Kirova, i., Russia (sĕr-gyĕ′yȧ kē′rô-vȧ)	184	77°30′N	86°10′E
Sergipe, state, Braz. (sĕr-zhē′pĕ)	143	10°27′S	37°04′W
Sergiyev Posad, Russia	186b	56°18′N	38°08′E
Sergiyevsk, Russia	180	53°58′N	51°00′E
Sérifos, Grc.	175	37°10′N	24°32′E
Sérifos, i., Grc.	175	37°42′N	24°17′E
Serodino, Arg. (sĕ-rô-dē′nō)	141c	32°36′S	60°56′W
Seropédica, Braz. (sĕ-rô-pĕ′dē-kä)	144b	22°44′S	43°43′W
Serov, Russia (syĕ-rôf′)	184	59°36′N	60°30′E
Serowe, Bots. (sĕ-rō′wĕ)	232	22°18′S	26°39′E
Serpa, Port. (sĕr-pä)	172	37°56′N	7°38′W
Serpukhov, Russia (syĕr′pô-kôf)	178	54°53′N	37°27′E
Sérres, Grc. (sĕr′rĕ) (sĕr′ĕs)	163	41°06′N	23°36′E
Serrinha, Braz. (sĕr-rēn′yȧ)	143	11°43′S	38°49′W
Serta, Port. (sĕr′tȧ)	172	39°48′N	8°01′W
Sertânia, Braz. (sĕr-tȧ′nyä)	143	8°28′S	37°13′W
Sertãozinho, Braz. (sĕr-toun-zē′n-yô)	141a	21°10′S	47°58′W
Serting, r., Malay.	197b	3°01′N	102°32′E
Sese Islands, is., Ug.	237	0°30′S	32°30′E
Sesia, r., Italy (sâz′yä)	174	45°33′N	8°25′E
Sesimbra, Port. (sĕ-sē′m-brä)	173b	38°27′N	9°06′W
Sesmyl, r., S. Afr.	233b	25°51′S	28°06′E
Ses Salines, Cap de, c., Spain	173	39°16′N	3°03′E
Sestri Levante, Italy (sĕs′trē lå-vän′tå)	174	44°15′N	9°24′E
Sestroretsk, Russia (sĕs-trô-rĕtsk)	180	60°06′N	29°58′E
Sestroretskiy Razliv, Ozero, l., Russia	186c	60°05′N	30°07′E
Seta, Japan (sĕ′tä)	211b	34°58′N	135°56′W
Séte, Fr. (sĕt)	161	43°24′N	3°42′E
Sete Lagoas, Braz. (sĕ-tĕ lä-gô′äs)	143	19°23′S	43°58′W
Sete Pontes, Braz.	144b	22°51′S	43°05′W
Seto, Japan (sē′tô)	211	35°11′N	137°07′E
Seto-Naikai, sea, Japan (sĕ′tô nī′kī)	211	33°50′N	132°25′E
Settat, Mor. (sĕt-ät′) (sĕ-tȧ′)	230	33°02′N	7°30′W
Sette-Cama, Gabon (sĕ-tĕ-kä-mä′)	232	2°29′S	9°40′E
Settlement Point, c., Bah. (sĕt′l-mĕnt)	134	26°40′N	79°00′W
Settlers, S. Afr. (sĕt′lĕrs)	238c	24°57′S	28°33′E
Settsu, Japan	211b	34°46′N	135°33′E
Setúbal, Port. (så-tōō′bäl)	162	30°32′N	8°54′W
Setúbal, Baía de, b., Port.	172	38°27′N	9°08′W
Seul, Lac, l., Can. (lák sûl)	93	50°20′N	92°30′W
Sevan, l., Arm. (syĭ-vän′)	181	40°10′N	45°20′E
Sevastopol′, Ukr. (syĕ-vȧs-tô′pôl′′)	178	44°34′N	33°34′E
Sevenoaks, Eng., U.K. (sĕ-vĕn-ôks′)	158b	51°16′N	0°12′E
Severka, r., Russia (sâ′vĕr-kȧ)	186b	55°11′N	38°41′E
Severn, r., Can. (sĕv′ĕrn)	93	55°21′N	88°42′W
Severn, r., U.K.	164	51°50′N	2°25′W
Severna Park, Md., U.S. (sĕv′ĕrn-ȧ)	110e	39°04′N	76°33′W
Severnaya Dvina, r., Russia	178	63°00′N	42°40′E
Severnaya Zemlya (Northern Land), is., Russia (sĕ-vyĭr-nīū zĭ-m′lyä′)	179	79°33′N	101°15′E
Severoural′sk, Russia (sĕ-vyĭ-rŭ-ōō-rälsk′)	184	60°08′N	59°53′E
Sevier, r., Ut., U.S.	106	39°25′N	112°20′W
Sevier, East Fork, r., Ut., U.S.	119	37°45′N	112°10′W
Sevier Lake, l., Ut., U.S. (sē-vēr′)	119	38°55′N	113°10′W
Sevilla, Col. (sĕ-vē′l-yä)	142a	4°16′N	75°56′W
Sevilla, Spain (så-vēl′yä)	154	37°29′N	5°58′W
Seville, Oh., U.S. (sĕ′vĭl)	111d	41°01′N	81°45′W
Sevlievo, Blg. (sĕv′lyĕ-vô)	163	43°02′N	25°05′E
Sevsk, Russia (syĕfsk)	176	52°08′N	34°28′E
Seward, Ak., U.S. (sū′ård)	106a	60°18′N	149°28′W
Seward, Ne., U.S.	121	40°55′N	97°06′W
Seward Peninsula, pen., Ak., U.S.	103	65°40′N	164°00′W
Sewell, Chile (sĕ′ô-ĕl)	144	34°01′S	70°18′W
Sewickley, Pa., U.S. (sē-wĭk′lē)	111e	40°33′N	80°11′W
Seybaplaya, Mex. (sā-ē-bä-plä′yä)	131	19°38′N	90°40′W
Seychelles, nation, Afr. (sā-shĕl′)	3	5°20′S	55°10′E
Seydisfjördur, Ice. (sā′dēs-fyûr-dôr)	160	65°21′N	14°08′W
Seyhan, r., Tur.	163	37°28′N	35°40′E
Seylac, Som.	238a	11°19′N	43°20′E
Seymour, S. Afr. (sē′môr)	233c	32°33′S	26°48′E
Seymour, Ia., U.S.	113	40°41′N	93°03′W
Seymour, In., U.S. (sē′mōr)	108	38°55′N	85°55′W
Seymour, Tx., U.S.	120	33°35′N	99°16′W
Sezela, S. Afr.	233c	30°33′S	30°37′W
Sezze, Italy (sĕt′så)	174	41°32′N	13°00′E
Sfântu Gheorghe, Rom.	163	45°53′N	25°49′E
Sfax, Tun. (sfäks)	230	34°51′N	10°45′E
′s-Gravenhage *see* The Hague, Neth. (′s krä′vĕn-hä′kĕ) (häg)	154	52°05′N	4°16′E
Sha, r., China (shä)	205	33°33′N	114°30′E
Shaanxi, prov., China (shän-shyē)	204	35°30′N	109°10′E
Shabeelle (Shebele), r., Afr.	238a	1°38′N	43°50′E
Shache, China (shä-chū)	204	38°15′N	77°15′E
Shackleton Ice Shelf, ice, Ant. (shăk′′l-tŭn)	224	65°00′S	100°00′E
Shades Creek, r., Al., U.S. (shādz)	110h	33°20′N	86°55′W
Shades Mountain, mtn., Al., U.S.	110h	33°22′N	86°51′W
Shagamu, Nig.	235	6°51′N	3°39′E
Shāhdād, Namakzār-e, l., Iran (nŭ-mŭk-zär′)	198	31°00′N	58°30′E
Shāhjahānpur, India (shä-jŭ-hän′pōōr)	199	27°58′N	79°58′E
Shajing, China (shä-jyĭŋ)	207a	22°44′N	113°48′E
Shaker Heights, Oh., U.S. (shā′kẽr)	111d	41°28′N	81°34′W
Shakhty, Russia (shäĸ′tē)	178	47°41′N	40°11′E
Shaki, Nig.	235	8°39′N	3°25′E
Shakopee, Mn., U.S. (shăk′ô-pe)	117g	44°48′N	93°31′W
Shala Lake, l., Eth. (shä′lȧ)	231	7°34′N	39°00′E
Shalqar, Kaz.	183	47°52′N	59°41′E
Shalqar köli, l., Kaz.	181	50°30′N	51°30′E
Shām, Jabal ash, mtn., Oman	198	23°01′N	57°45′E
Shambe, Sudan (shäm′bå)	231	7°08′N	30°46′E
Shammar, Jabal, mts., Sau. Ar. (jĕb′ĕl shŭm′ār)	198	27°13′N	40°16′E
Shamokin, Pa., U.S. (shȧ-mō′kĭn)	109	40°45′N	76°30′W
Shamrock, Tx., U.S. (shăm′rŏk)	120	35°14′N	100°12′W
Shamva, Zimb. (shäm′vȧ)	232	17°18′S	31°35′E
Shandon, Oh., U.S. (shăn-dŭn)	111f	39°20′N	84°13′W
Shandong, prov., China (shän-dôŋ)	205	36°08′N	117°09′E
Shandong Bandao, pen., China (shän-dôŋ bän-dou)	205	37°00′N	120°10′E
Shangcai, China (shäŋ-tsī)	206	33°16′N	114°16′E
Shangcheng, China (shäŋ-chŭŋ)	206	31°47′N	115°22′E
Shangdu, China (shäŋ-dōō)	208	41°38′N	113°22′E
Shanghai, China (shäng′hī′)	205	31°14′N	121°27′E
Shanghai Shi, prov., China (shäŋ-hī shr)	205	31°30′N	121°45′E
Shanghe, China (shäŋ-hŭ)	206	37°18′N	117°10′E
Shanglin, China (shäŋ-lĭn)	206	38°20′N	116°05′E
Shangqiu, China (shäŋ-chyô)	208	34°24′N	115°39′E
Shangrao, China (shäŋ-rou)	209	28°25′N	117°58′E
Shangzhi, China (shäŋ-jr)	208	45°18′N	127°52′E
Shanhaiguan, China	208	40°01′N	119°45′E
Shannon, Al., U.S. (shăn′ŭn)	110h	33°23′N	86°52′W
Shannon, r., Ire. (shăn′ŏn)	161	52°30′N	10°15′W
Shanshan, China (shän′shän′)	204	42°51′N	89°53′E
Shantar, i., Russia (shän′tär)	185	55°13′N	138°42′E
Shantou, China (shän-tō)	205	23°20′N	116°40′E
Shanxi, prov., China (shän-shyē)	205	37°30′N	112°00′E
Shan Xian, China (shän shyĕn)	206	34°47′N	116°04′E
Shaobo, China (shou-bwo)	208	32°33′N	119°30′E
Shaobo Hu, l., China (shou-bwo hōō)	206	32°47′N	119°13′E
Shaoguan, China (shou-gůän)	205	24°58′N	113°42′E
Shaoxing, China (shou-shyĭŋ)	205	30°00′N	120°40′E
Shaoyang, China	205	27°15′N	111°28′E
Shapki, Russia (shäp′kĭ)	186c	59°36′N	31°11′E
Shark Bay, b., Austl. (shärk)	220	25°30′S	113°00′E
Sharon, Ma., U.S. (shăr′ŏn)	101a	42°07′N	71°11′W
Sharon, Pa., U.S.	108	41°15′N	80°30′W
Sharon Springs, Ks., U.S.	120	38°51′N	101°45′W
Sharonville, Oh., U.S. (shăr′ŏn vĭl)	111f	39°16′N	84°24′W
Sharpsburg, Pa., U.S. (shärps′bûrg)	111e	40°30′N	79°54′W
Sharr, Jabal, mtn., Sau. Ar.	198	28°00′N	36°07′E
Shashi, China (shä-shē)	205	30°20′N	112°18′E
Shasta, Mount, mtn., Ca., U.S.	106	41°35′N	122°12′W
Shasta Lake, res., Ca., U.S. (shăs′tȧ)	106	40°51′N	122°32′W
Shatsk, Russia (shàtsk)	180	54°00′N	41°40′E
Shattuck, Ok., U.S. (shăt′ŭk)	120	36°16′N	99°53′W
Shaunavon, Can.	90	49°40′N	108°25′W
Shaw, Ms., U.S. (shô)	124	33°36′N	90°44′W
Shawano, Wi., U.S. (shȧ-wô′nô)	113	44°41′N	88°13′W
Shawinigan, Can.	91	46°32′N	72°46′W
Shawnee, Ks., U.S. (shô-nē′)	117f	39°01′N	94°43′W
Shawnee, Ok., U.S.	104	35°20′N	96°54′W
Shawneetown, Il., U.S. (shô′nē-toun)	108	37°40′N	88°05′W
Shayang, China	209	31°00′N	112°38′E
Shchara, r., Bela. (sh-chȧ′rȧ)	169	53°17′N	25°12′E
Shchëlkovo, Russia (shchĕl′kô-vô)	176	55°55′N	38°00′E
Shchigry, Russia (shchē′grē)	177	51°52′N	36°54′E
Shchors, Ukr. (shchôrs)	177	51°38′N	31°58′E
Shchuch′ye Ozero, Russia (shchōōch′yĕ ô′zĕ-rō)	186a	56°31′N	56°35′E
Sheakhala, India	202a	22°47′N	88°10′E
Shebele (Shabeelle), r., Afr. (shā′bå-lē)	238a	6°07′N	43°10′E
Sheboygan, Wi., U.S. (shē-boi′gȧn)	105	43°45′N	87°44′W
Sheboygan Falls, Wi., U.S.	113	43°43′N	87°51′W
Shechem, hist., W.B.	197a	32°15′N	35°22′E
Shedandoah, Pa., U.S.	109	40°50′N	76°15′W
Shediac, Can. (shĕ′dē-ăk)	100	46°13′N	64°32′W
Shedin Peak, mtn., Can. (shĕd′ĭn)	94	55°55′N	127°32′W
Sheerness, Eng., U.K. (shēr′nĕs)	158b	51°26′N	0°46′E
Sheffield, Can.	102d	43°20′N	80°13′W
Sheffield, Eng., U.K.	160	53°23′N	1°28′W
Sheffield, Al., U.S. (shĕf′fēld)	124	35°42′N	87°42′W
Sheffield, Oh., U.S.	111d	41°26′N	82°05′W
Sheffield, co., Eng., U.K.	158a	53°52′N	1°35′W
Sheffield Lake, Oh., U.S.	111d	41°30′N	82°03′W
Sheksna, r., Russia (shĕks′nȧ)	180	59°50′N	38°40′E

350 Shelagskiy – Silverdale PRONOUNCING INDEX

PLACE (Pronunciation)	PAGE	LAT.	LONG.
Shelagskiy, Mys, c., Russia (shĭ-läg´skē)	179	70°08'N	170°52'E
Shelbina, Ar., U.S. (shĕl-bī´nȧ)	121	39°41'N	92°03'W
Shelburn, In., U.S. (shĕl´bŭrn)	108	39°10'N	87°30'W
Shelburne, Can.	91	43°46'N	65°19'W
Shelburne, Can.	99	44°04'N	80°12'W
Shelby, In., U.S. (shĕl´bė)	111a	41°12'N	87°21'W
Shelby, Mi., U.S.	108	43°35'N	86°20'W
Shelby, Ms., U.S.	124	33°56'N	90°44'W
Shelby, Mt., U.S.	115	48°35'N	111°55'W
Shelby, N.C., U.S.	125	35°16'N	81°35'W
Shelby, Oh., U.S.	108	40°50'N	82°40'W
Shelbyville, Il., U.S. (shĕl´bė-vĭl)	108	39°20'N	88°45'W
Shelbyville, In., U.S.	108	39°30'N	85°45'W
Shelbyville, Ky., U.S.	108	38°10'N	85°15'W
[illegible]	[illegible]	[illegible]	[illegible]
Shelbyville Reservoir, res., Il., U.S.	108	39°30'N	88°45'W
Sheldon, Ia., U.S. (shĕl´dŭn)	112	43°10'N	95°50'W
Sheldon, Tx., U.S.	123a	29°52'N	95°07'W
Shelekhova, Zaliv, b., Russia	179	60°00'N	156°00'E
Shelikof Strait, strt., Ak., U.S. (shĕ´lė-kôf)	103	57°56'N	154°20'W
Shellbrook, Can.	96	53°15'N	106°22'W
Shelley, Id., U.S. (shĕl´lė)	115	43°24'N	112°06'W
Shellrock, r., Ia., U.S. (shĕl´rŏk)	113	43°25'N	93°19'W
Shelon', r., Russia (shå´lôn)	176	57°50'N	29°40'E
Shelton, Ct., U.S. (shĕl´tŭn)	109	41°15'N	73°05'W
Shelton, Ne., U.S.	120	40°46'N	98°41'W
Shelton, Wa., U.S.	114	47°14'N	123°05'W
Shemakha, Russia (shĕ-mȧ-kä´)	186a	56°16'N	59°19'E
Shenandoah, Ia., U.S. (shĕn-ăn-dō´ȧ)	121	40°46'N	95°23'W
Shenandoah, Va., U.S.	109	38°30'N	78°30'W
Shenandoah, r., Va., U.S.	109	38°55'N	78°05'W
Shenandoah National Park, rec., Va., U.S.	107	38°35'N	78°25'W
Shendam, Nig.	235	8°53'N	9°32'E
Shengfang, China (shengfäng)	206	39°05'N	116°40'E
Shenkursk, Russia (shĕn-kōōrsk´)	178	62°10'N	43°08'E
Shenmu, China	208	38°55'N	110°35'E
Shenqiu, China	208	33°11'N	115°06'E
Shenxian, China (shŭn shyän)	206	38°02'N	115°33'E
Shenxian, China (shŭn shyĕn)	206	36°14'N	115°38'E
Shenyang, China (shŭn-yäŋ)	205	41°45'N	123°22'E
Shenze, China (shŭn-dzŭ)	206	38°12'N	115°12'E
Shenzhen, China	209	22°32'N	114°08'E
Sheopur, India	199	25°37'N	77°10'E
Shepard, Can. (shĕ´pärd)	102e	50°57'N	113°55'W
Shepetivka, Ukr.	181	50°10'N	27°01'E
Shepparton, Austl. (shĕp´är-tŭn)	222	36°15'S	145°25'E
Sherborn, Ma., U.S. (shûr´bŭrn)	101a	42°15'N	71°22'W
Sherbrooke, Can.	91	45°24'N	71°54'W
Sherburn, Eng., U.K. (shûr´bŭrn)	158a	53°47'N	1°15'W
Shereshevo, Bela. (shĕ-rĕ-shĕ-vô)	169	52°31'N	24°08'E
Sheridan, Ar., U.S. (shĕr´ĭ-dăn)	121	34°19'N	92°21'W
Sheridan, Or., U.S.	114	45°06'N	123°22'W
Sheridan, Wy., U.S.	104	44°48'N	106°56'W
Sherman, Tx., U.S. (shĕr´măn)	104	33°39'N	96°37'W
Sherna, r., Russia (shĕr´nȧ)	186b	56°08'N	38°45'E
Sherridon, Can.	97	55°10'N	101°10'W
's Hertogenbosch, Neth. (sĕr-tō´ghĕn-bôs)	165	51°41'N	5°19'E
Sherwood, Or., U.S.	116c	45°21'N	122°50'W
Sherwood Forest, for., Eng., U.K.	158a	53°11'N	1°07'W
Sherwood Park, Can.	95	53°31'N	113°19'W
Shetland Islands, is., Scot., U.K. (shĕt´lănd)	156	60°35'N	2°10'W
Shewa Gimira, Eth.	231	7°13'N	35°49'E
Shexian, China (shŭ shyĕn)	206	36°34'N	113°42'E
Sheyang, r., China (shĕ-yäŋ)	206	33°42'N	119°40'E
Sheyenne, r., N.D., U.S. (shī-ĕn´)	112	46°42'N	97°52'W
Shi, r., China (shr)	206	31°58'N	115°50'E
Shi, r., China	206	32°09'N	114°11'E
Shiawassee, r., Mi., U.S. (shī-ȧ-wôs´ė)	108	43°15'N	84°05'W
Shibām, Yemen (shē´bäm)	198	16°02'N	48°40'E
Shibīn al Kawn, Egypt (shė-bēn´ĕl kōm´)	238b	30°31'N	31°01'E
Shibīn al Qanāṭir, Egypt (kȧ-nä´tėr)	238b	30°18'N	31°21'E
Shicun, China (shr-tsòn)	206	33°47'N	117°18'E
Shields, r., Mt., U.S. (shēldz)	115	45°54'N	110°40'W
Shifnal, Eng., U.K. (shĭf´năl)	158a	52°40'N	2°22'W
Shijian, China (shr-jyĕn)	206	31°27'N	117°51'E
Shijiazhuang, China (shr-jyä-jùäŋ)	205	38°04'N	114°31'E
Shijiu Hu, l., China (shr-jyô hōō)	206	31°29'N	119°07'E
Shikārpur, Pak.	199	27°51'N	68°52'E
Shiki, Japan (shē´kė)	211a	35°50'N	139°35'E
Shikoku, i., Japan (shē´kō´kōō)	205	33°43'N	133°33'E
Shilka, r., Russia (shĭl´kȧ)	185	53°00'N	118°45'E
Shilla, mtn., India	202	32°18'N	78°17'E
Shillong, India (shėl-lông´)	199	25°39'N	91°58'E
Shiloh, Il., U.S. (shī´lō)	117e	38°34'N	89°54'W
Shilong, China (shr-lôŋ)	209	23°05'N	113°58'E
Shilou, China	207a	22°58'N	113°29'E
Shimabara, Japan (shē´mä-bä´rä)	211	32°46'N	130°22'E
Shimada, Japan (shē´mä-dä)	211	34°49'N	138°13'E
Shimbiris, mtn., Som.	238a	10°40'N	47°23'E
Shimizu, Japan (shē´mė-zōō)	210	35°00'N	138°29'E
Shimminato, Japan (shĕm´mė´nä-tô)	211	36°47'N	137°05'E
Shimoda, Japan (shē´mô-dȧ)	211	34°41'N	138°58'E
Shimoga, India	203	13°59'N	75°38'E
Shimoni, Kenya	237	4°39'S	39°23'E
Shimonoseki, Japan	205	33°58'N	130°55'E
Shimo-Saga, Japan (shē´mô sä´gä)	211b	35°01'N	135°41'E
Shin, Loch, l., Scot., U.K. (lŏκ shĭn)	164	58°08'N	4°02'W
Shinagawa-Wan, b., Japan (shė´nä-gä´wä wän)	211a	35°37'N	139°49'E
Shinano-Gawa, r., Japan (shė-nä´nô gä´wä)	211	36°43'N	138°22'E
Shīndand, Afg.	201	33°18'N	62°08'E
Shinji, l., Japan (shĭn´jė)	211	35°23'N	133°05'E
Shinkolobwe, D.R.C.	237	11°02'S	26°35'E
Shinyanga, Tan. (shĭn-yäŋ´gä)	232	3°40'S	33°26'E
Shiono Misaki, c., Japan (shė-ô´nô mė´sä-kė)	210	33°20'N	136°10'E
Shipai, China (shr-pī)	207a	23°07'N	113°23'E
Ship Channel Cay, i., Bah. (shĭp chă-nĕl kē)	134	24°50'N	76°50'W
Shipley, Eng., U.K. (shĭp´lė)	158a	53°50'N	1°47'W
Shippegan, Can. (shĭ´pė-găn)	100	47°45'N	64°42'W
Shippegan Island, i., Can.	100	47°50'N	64°38'W
[illegible]	[illegible]	[illegible]	[illegible]
Shipshaw, r., Can. (shĭp´shô)	99	48°50'N	71°03'W
Shiqma, r., Isr.	197a	31°31'N	34°40'E
Shirane-san, mtn., Japan (shē´rä´nå-sän´)	211	35°44'N	138°14'E
Shirati, Tan. (shė-rä´tē)	232	1°15'S	34°02'E
Shīrāz, Iran (shē-räz´)	198	29°32'N	52°27'E
Shire, r., Afr. (shē´rå)	232	15°00'S	35°00'E
Shiriya Saki, c., Japan (shē´rä sä´kė)	210	41°25'N	142°10'E
Shirley, Ma., U.S. (shûr´lė)	101a	42°33'N	71°39'W
Shishaldin Volcano, vol., Ak., U.S. (shī-shăl´dĭn)	103a	54°48'N	164°00'W
Shively, Ky., U.S. (shīv´lė)	111h	38°11'N	85°47'W
Shivpuri, India	199	25°31'N	77°46'E
Shivta, Horvot, hist., Isr.	197a	30°54'N	34°36'E
Shivwits Plateau, plat., Az., U.S.	119	36°13'N	113°42'W
Shiwan, China (shr-wän)	207a	23°01'N	113°04'E
Shiwan Dashan, mts., China (shr-wän dä-shän)	209	22°10'N	107°30'E
Shizuki, Japan (shĭ´zōō-kė)	211	34°29'N	134°51'E
Shizuoka, Japan (shē´zōō´ōkȧ)	210	34°58'N	138°24'E
Shklow, Bela.	176	54°11'N	30°23'E
Shkodër, Alb. (shkô´dûr) (skōō´tärē)	154	42°04'N	19°30'E
Shkotovo, Russia (shkô´tô-vô)	210	43°15'N	132°21'E
Shoal Creek, r., Il., U.S. (shōl)	121	38°37'N	89°25'W
Shoal Lake, l., Can.	97	49°32'N	95°00'W
Shoals, In., U.S. (shōlz)	108	38°40'N	86°45'W
Shōdo, i., Japan (shō´dō)	211	34°27'N	134°27'E
Sholāpur, India (shō´lä-pōōr)	199	17°42'N	75°51'E
Shorewood, Wi., U.S. (shōr´wŏŏd)	111a	43°05'N	87°54'W
Shoshone, Id., U.S. (shō-shōn´tė)	115	42°56'N	114°24'W
Shoshone, r., Wy., U.S.	115	44°35'N	108°50'W
Shoshone Lake, l., Wy., U.S.	115	44°17'N	110°50'W
Shoshoni, Wy., U.S.	115	43°14'N	108°05'W
Shostka, Ukr. (shôst´kȧ)	177	51°51'N	33°31'E
Shouguang, China (shō-gŭäŋ)	206	36°53'N	118°45'E
Shouxian, China (shō shyĕn)	206	32°36'N	116°45'E
Shpola, Ukr. (shpô´lȧ)	181	49°01'N	31°36'E
Shreveport, La., U.S. (shrēv´pōrt)	105	32°30'N	93°46'W
Shrewsbury, Eng., U.K. (shrōōz´bēr-ĭ)	164	52°43'N	2°44'W
Shrewsbury, Ma., U.S.	101a	42°18'N	71°43'W
Shropshire, co., Eng., U.K.	158a	52°36'N	2°45'W
Shroud Cay, i., Bah.	134	24°20'N	76°40'W
Shuangcheng, China (shŭäŋ-chŭŋ)	208	45°18'N	126°18'E
Shuanghe, China (shŭäŋ-hŭ)	206	31°33'N	116°48'E
Shuangliao, China	205	43°37'N	123°30'E
Shuangyang, China	208	43°28'N	125°45'E
Shuhedun, China (shōō-hŭ-dòn)	206	31°33'N	117°01'E
Shuiye, China (shwā-yŭ)	206	36°08'N	114°07'E
Shule, r., China (shōō-lŭ)	204	40°53'N	94°55'E
Shullsburg, Wi., U.S. (shŭlz´bûrg)	113	42°35'N	90°16'W
Shumagin, is., Ak., U.S. (shōō´mȧ-gėn)	103	55°22'N	159°20'W
Shumen, Blg.	163	43°15'N	26°54'E
Shunde, China (shòn-dŭ)	207a	22°50'N	113°15'E
Shungnak, Ak., U.S. (shŭng´nak)	103	66°55'N	157°20'W
Shunut, Gora, mtn., Russia (gȧ-rä shōō´nòt)	186a	56°33'N	59°45'E
Shunyi, China (shòn-yē)	206	40°09'N	116°38'E
Shuqrah, Yemen	198	13°32'N	46°02'E
Shūrāb, r., Iran (shōō räb)	198	31°30'N	55°30'E
Shuri, Japan (shōō´rė)	210	26°10'N	127°48'E
Shurugwi, Zimb.	232	19°34'S	30°03'E
Shūshtar, Iran (shōōsh´tŭr)	198	31°50'N	48°46'E
Shuswap Lake, l., Can. (shōōs´wŏp)	95	50°57'N	119°15'W
Shuya, Russia (shōō´yȧ)	178	56°52'N	41°23'E
Shuyang, China (shōō yäng)	206	34°09'N	118°47'E
Shweba, Mya.	199	22°23'N	96°13'E
Shymkent, Kaz.	183	42°17'N	69°42'E
Shyroke, Ukr.	177	47°40'N	33°18'E
Siak Kecil, r., Indon.	197b	1°01'N	101°45'E
Siaksriinderapura, Indon. (sė-äks´rĭ ĕn´drȧ-pōō´rä)	197b	0°48'N	102°05'E
Siālkot, Pak. (sė-äl´kōt)	199	32°39'N	74°30'E
Siátista, Grc. (syä´tĭs-ta)	175	40°15'N	21°32'E
Siau, Pulau, i., Indon.	213	2°40'N	126°00'E
Šiauliai, Lith. (shė-ou´lė-ī)	180	55°57'N	23°19'E
Sibay, Russia (sē´bȧy)	186a	52°41'N	58°40'E
Šibenik, Cro. (shė-bä´nĕk)	163	43°44'N	15°55'E
Siberia, reg., Russia	196	57°00'N	97°00'E
Siberut, Pulau, i., Indon. (sē´bȧ-rōōt)	212	1°22'S	99°45'E
Sibiti, Congo (sė-bė-tē´)	232	3°41'S	13°21'E
Sibiu, Rom. (sė-bĭ-ōō´)	163	45°47'N	24°09'E
Sibley, Ia., U.S. (sĭb´lė)	112	43°24'N	95°33'W
Sibolga, Indon. (sė-bō´gȧ)	212	1°45'N	98°45'E
Sibsāgar, India (sėb-sŭ´gŭr)	199	26°47'N	94°45'E
Sibutu Island, i., Phil.	212	4°40'N	119°30'E
Sibuyan, i., Phil. (sē-bōō-yän´)	213a	12°19'N	122°25'E
Sibuyan Sea, sea, Phil.	212	12°43'N	122°38'E
Sichuan, prov., China (sz-chŭän)	204	31°20'N	103°00'E
Sicily, i., Italy (sĭs´ĭ-lė)	156	37°38'N	13°30'E
Sico, r., Hond. (sė-kô)	132	15°32'N	85°42'W
Sidamo, hist. reg., Eth. (sė-dä´mô)	231	5°08'N	37°45'E
Siderno Marina, Italy (sė-dĕr´nô mä-rē´nä)	174	38°18'N	16°19'E
Sídheros, Ákra, c., Grc.	174a	35°19'N	26°20'E
Sidi Aïssa, Alg.	173	35°53'N	3°44'E
Sidi bel Abbès, Alg. (sē´dē-bĕl ȧ-bĕs´)	230	35°15'N	0°43'W
Sidi Ifni, Mor. (ēf´nė)	230	29°22'N	10°15'W
Sidirókastro, Grc.	175	41°13'N	23°27'E
Sidley, Mount, mtn., Ant. (sĭd´lė)	224	77°25'S	129°00'W
Sidney, Can.	94	48°39'N	123°24'W
Sidney, Mt., U.S. (sĭd´nė)	115	47°43'N	104°07'W
Sidney, Ne., U.S.	112	41°10'N	103°00'W
Sidney, Oh., U.S.	108	40°20'N	84°10'W
[illegible] (lăn´yēr)	107	34°27'N	[illegible]
Sido, Mali	234	11°40'N	7°30'W
Sidon see Saydā, Leb.	198	33°34'N	35°23'E
Sidr, Wādī, r., Egypt	197a	29°43'N	32°58'E
Sidra, Gulf of see Surt, Khalīj, b., Libya	231	31°30'N	18°28'E
Siedlce, Pol. (syĕd´'l-tsĕ)	169	52°09'N	22°20'E
Siegburg, Ger. (zēg´bōōrgh)	168	50°48'N	7°13'E
Siegen, Ger. (zē´ghĕn)	168	50°52'N	8°01'E
Sieghartskirchen, Aus.	159e	48°16'N	16°00'E
Siemiatycze, Pol. (syĕm´yä´tė-chĕ)	169	52°26'N	22°52'E
Siemionówka, Pol. (sĕĕ-mēō´nôf-kä)	169	52°53'N	23°50'E
Siem Reap, Camb. (syĕm´rä´äp)	212	13°32'N	103°54'E
Siena, Italy (sė-ĕn´ä)	162	43°19'N	11°21'E
Sieradz, Pol. (syĕ´rädz)	169	51°35'N	18°45'E
Sierpc, Pol. (syĕrpts)	169	52°51'N	19°42'E
Sierra Blanca, Tx., U.S. (sė-ĕ´rȧ blaŋ-kä)	122	31°10'N	105°20'W
Sierra Blanca Peak, mtn., N.M., U.S. (blăn´kȧ)	106	33°25'N	105°50'W
Sierra Leone, nation, Afr. (sė-ĕr´rä lå-ō´nä)	230	8°48'N	12°30'W
Sierra Madre, Ca., U.S. (mă´drē)	117a	34°10'N	118°03'W
Sierra Mojada, Mex. (sė-ĕ´r-rä-mô-kä´dä)	122	27°22'N	103°42'W
Sífnos, i., Grc.	175	36°58'N	24°30'E
Sigean, Fr. (sē-zhŏɴ´)	170	43°02'N	2°56'E
Sigeurney, Ia., U.S. (sė-gûr-nĭ)	113	41°16'N	92°10'W
Sighetu Marmaţiei, Rom.	169	47°57'N	23°55'E
Sighişoara, Rom. (sē-gė-shwä´rȧ)	169	46°11'N	24°48'E
Siglufjördur, Ice.	160	66°06'N	18°45'W
Signakhi, Geor.	181	41°45'N	45°50'E
Signal Hill, Ca., U.S. (sĭg´năl hĭl)	117a	33°48'N	118°11'W
Sigsig, Ec. (sėg-sēg´)	142	3°04'S	78°44'W
Sigtuna, Swe. (sēgh-tōō´nȧ)	166	59°40'N	17°39'E
Siguanea, Ensenada de la, b., Cuba	134	21°45'N	83°15'W
Siguatepeque, Hond. (sē-gwä´tė-pĕ-kĕ)	132	14°33'N	87°51'W
Sigüenza, Spain (sė-gwĕ´n-zä)	162	41°03'N	2°38'W
Siguiri, Gui. (sė-gė-rē´)	230	11°25'N	9°10'W
Sihong, China (sz-hôŋ)	206	33°25'N	118°13'E
Siirt, Tur. (sĭ-ērt´)	181	38°00'N	42°00'E
Sikalongo, Zam.	237	16°46'S	27°07'E
Sikasso, Mali (sė-käs´sō)	230	11°19'N	5°40'W
Sikeston, Mo., U.S. (sīks´tŭn)	121	36°50'N	89°35'W
Sikhote Alin', Khrebet, mts., Russia (sė-kô´ta a-lēn´)	179	45°00'N	135°45'E
Sikinos, i., Grc. (sĭ´kĭ-nōs)	175	36°45'N	24°55'E
Sikkim, state, India	199	27°42'N	88°25'E
Siklós, Hung. (sĭ´klōsh)	169	45°51'N	18°18'E
Sil, r., Spain (sē´l)	172	42°20'N	7°13'W
Silang, Phil. (sė-läng´)	213a	14°14'N	120°58'E
Silao, Mex. (sė-lä´ō)	130	20°56'N	101°25'W
Silchar, India (sĭl-chär´)	199	24°52'N	92°50'E
Silent Valley, S. Afr. (sī´lĕnt vă´lē)	238c	24°32'S	26°40'E
Siler City, N.C., U.S. (sī´lĕr)	125	35°45'N	79°29'W
Silesia, hist. reg., Pol. (sĭ-lē´shȧ)	168	50°58'N	16°53'E
Silifke, Tur.	163	36°20'N	34°00'E
Siling Co, l., China	204	32°05'N	89°10'E
Silistra, Blg. (sė-lės´trȧ)	163	44°01'N	27°13'E
Siljan, l., Swe. (sėl´yän)	160	60°48'N	14°28'E
Silkeborg, Den. (sĭl´kĕ-bôr´)	166	56°10'N	9°33'E
Sillery, Can. (sēl´-re´)	102b	46°46'N	71°15'W
Siloam Springs, Ar., U.S. (sĭ-lōm)	121	36°10'N	94°32'W
Siloana Plains, pl., Zam.	236	16°55'S	23°10'E
Silocayoápan, Mex. (sė-lô-kä-yô-ȧ´pän)	130	17°29'N	98°09'W
Silsbee, Tx., U.S. (sĭlz´ bė)	123	30°19'N	94°09'W
Šilutė, Lith.	167	55°21'N	21°29'E
Silva Jardim, Braz. (sė´l-vä-zhär-dĕɴ)	141a	22°40'N	42°24'W
Silvana, Wa., U.S. (sĭ-văn´ȧ)	116a	48°12'N	122°16'W
Silvânia, Braz. (sēl-vá´nyä)	143	16°43'S	48°33'W
Silvassa, India	202	20°10'N	73°00'E
Silver, l., Mo., U.S.	121	39°38'N	93°12'W
Silverado, Ca., U.S. (sĭl-vĕr-ä´dō)	117a	33°45'N	117°40'W
Silver Bank, bk.	135	20°40'N	69°40'W
Silver Bank Passage, strt., N.A.	135	20°40'N	70°20'W
Silver Bay, Mn., U.S.	113	47°24'N	91°07'W
Silver City, Pan.	133	9°20'N	79°54'W
Silver City, N.M., U.S. (sĭl´vĕr sĭ´tĭ)	119	32°45'N	108°20'W
Silver Creek, N.Y., U.S. (crēk)	109	42°35'N	79°10'W
Silver Creek, r., Az., U.S.	119	34°30'N	110°05'W
Silver Creek, r., In., U.S.	111h	38°20'N	85°45'W
Silver Creek, Muddy Fork, r., In., U.S.	111h	38°26'N	85°52'W
Silverdale, Wa., U.S. (sĭl´vĕr-dāl)	116a	49°39'N	122°42'W

ng-sing; ŋ-baŋk; N-nasalized n; nōd; cõmmit; ōld; ôbey; ôrder; oi-boil; fōōd; ò-as oo in foot; ou-out; s-soft; sh-dish; th-thin; pūre; ûnite; ûrn; stŭd; circũs; ü-as in French tu; ′-indeterminate vowel.

352 Sofia – Spas-Klepiki PRONOUNCING INDEX

PLACE (Pronunciation)	PAGE	LAT.	LONG.
Sofia (Sofiya), Blg. (sô'fē-yȧ) (sô'fē-ȧ)	154	42°43'N	23°20'E
Sofiivka, Ukr.	177	48°03'N	33°53'E
Sofiya see Sofia, Blg.	154	42°43'N	23°20'E
Soga, Japan (sō'gä)	211a	35°35'N	140°08'E
Sogamoso, Col. (sô-gä-mō'sō)	142	5°42'N	72°51'W
Sognafjorden, b., Nor.	156	61°09'N	5°30'E
Sogozha, r., Russia (sô'gô-zhȧ)	176	58°35'N	39°08'E
Sohano, Pap. N. Gui.	214e	5°27'S	154°40'E
Soissons, Fr. (swä-sôn')	170	49°23'N	3°17'E
Sōka, Japan (sō'kä)	211a	35°50'N	139°49'E
Sokal', Ukr. (sô'käl')	169	50°28'N	24°20'E
Söke, Tur. (sû'kĕ)	167	37°40'N	27°10'E
Sokólka, Pol. (sô-kôl'kȧ)	169	53°23'N	23°30'E
Sokolo, Mali (sô-kô-lō')	230	14°51'N	6°09'W
Sokołów Podlaski, Pol. (sô-kô-wŏof pŭd-lä'skĭ)	169	[illegible]	[illegible]
Sokone, Sen.	231	13°53'N	16°22'W
Sokoto, Nig. (sō'kô-tō)	230	13°04'N	5°16'E
Sola de Vega, Mex.	131	16°31'N	96°58'W
Solander, Cape, c., Austl.	217b	34°03'S	151°16'E
Solano, Phil. (sō-lä'nō)	213a	16°31'N	121°11'E
Soledad, Col. (sŏ-lĕ-dä'd)	142	10°47'N	75°00'W
Soledad Díez Gutiérrez, Mex.	130	22°19'N	100°54'W
Soleduck, r., Wa., U.S. (sōl'dŭk)	114	47°59'N	124°28'W
Solentiname, Islas de, is., Nic. (ĕ's-läs-dĕ-sô-lĕn-tē-nä'mȧ)	132	11°15'N	85°16'W
Solihull, Eng., U.K. (sō'lĭ-hŭl)	158a	52°25'N	1°46'W
Solihull, co., Eng., U.K.	158a	52°25'N	1°42'W
Solikamsk, Russia (sô-lē-kämsk')	180	59°38'N	56°48'E
Sol'-Iletsk, Russia	178	51°10'N	55°05'E
Solimões see Amazon, r., Braz.	142	2°45'S	67°44'W
Solingen, Ger. (zō'lĭng-ĕn)	168	51°10'N	7°05'E
Sóller, Spain (sō'lyĕr)	173	39°45'N	2°40'E
Sologne, reg., Fr. (sō-lōn'yĕ)	170	47°36'N	1°53'E
Solola, Guat. (sô-lō'lä)	132	14°45'N	91°12'W
Solomon, r., Ks., U.S.	120	39°24'N	98°19'W
Solomon, North Fork, r., Ks., U.S.	120	39°34'N	99°52'W
Solomon, South Fork, r., Ks., U.S.	120	39°19'N	99°52'W
Solomon Islands, nation, Oc. (sŏ'lō-mūn)	3	7°00'S	160°00'E
Solon, China (swo-lōōn)	205	46°32'N	121°18'E
Solon, Oh., U.S. (sō'lŭn)	111d	41°23'N	81°26'W
Solothurn, Switz. (zō'lō-thōōrn)	168	47°13'N	7°30'E
Solovetskiye Ostrova, is., Russia	180	65°10'N	35°40'E
Šolta, i., Cro. (shôl'tä)	174	43°20'N	16°15'E
Soltau, Ger. (sôl'tou)	168	53°00'N	9°50'E
Sol'tsy, Russia (sôl'tsĕ)	176	58°04'N	30°13'E
Solvay, N.Y., U.S. (sŏl'vā)	109	43°05'N	76°10'W
Sölvesborg, Swe. (sûl'vĕs-bôrg)	166	56°04'N	14°35'E
Sol'vychegodsk, Russia (sôl'vê-chĕ-gôtsk')	180	61°18'N	46°58'E
Solway Firth, b., U.K. (sŏl'wā fûrth')	160	54°42'N	3°55'W
Solwezi, Zam.	237	12°11'S	26°25'E
Soly, Bela.	166	54°31'N	26°11'E
Somalia, nation, Afr. (sō-ma'lē-ȧ)	238a	3°28'N	44°47'E
Somanga, Tan.	237	8°24'S	39°17'E
Sombor, Serb. (sôm'bôr)	163	45°45'N	19°10'E
Sombrerete, Mex. (sôm-brå-rā'tå)	130	23°38'N	103°37'W
Sombrero, Cayo, i., Ven. (kä-yô-sôm-brĕ'rô)	143b	10°52'N	68°12'W
Somerset, Ky., U.S. (sŭm'ẽr-sĕt)	124	37°05'N	84°35'W
Somerset, Ma., U.S.	110b	41°46'N	71°05'W
Somerset, Pa., U.S.	109	40°00'N	79°05'W
Somerset, Tx., U.S.	117d	29°13'N	98°39'W
Somerset East, S. Afr.	233c	32°44'S	25°36'E
Somersworth, N.H., U.S. (sŭm'ẽrz-wûrth)	100	43°16'N	70°53'W
Somerton, Az., U.S. (sŭm'ẽr-tŭn)	119	32°36'N	114°43'W
Somerville, Ma., U.S. (sŭm'ẽr-vĭl)	101a	42°23'N	71°06'W
Somerville, N.J., U.S.	110a	40°34'N	74°37'W
Somerville, Tn., U.S.	124	35°14'N	89°21'W
Somerville, Tx., U.S.	123	30°21'N	96°31'W
Someş, r., Eur.	169	47°43'N	23°09'E
Somma Vesuviana, Italy (sôm'mä vā-zōō-vē-ä'nä)	173c	40°38'N	14°27'E
Somme, r., Fr. (sŏm)	170	50°02'N	2°04'E
Sommerfeld, Ger. (zō'mĕr-fĕld)	159b	52°48'N	13°02'E
Sommerville, Austl.	217a	38°14'S	145°10'E
Somoto, Nic. (sô-mō'tō)	132	13°28'N	86°37'W
Son, r., India (sōn)	199	24°40'N	82°35'E
Sŏnchŏn, Kor., N. (sŭn'shŭn)	210	39°49'N	124°56'E
Sondags, r., S. Afr.	233c	33°17'S	25°14'E
Sønderborg, Den. (sûn''ẽr-bôrgh)	160	54°55'N	9°47'E
Sondershausen, Ger. (zōn'dẽrz-hou'zĕn)	168	51°17'N	10°45'E
Song Ca, r., Viet.	209	19°15'N	105°00'E
Songea, Tan. (sôn-gä'ȧ)	232	10°41'S	35°39'E
Songjiang, China	205	31°01'N	121°14'E
Sŏngjin, Kor., N. (sŭng'jĭn')	210	40°38'N	129°10'E
Songkhla, Thai. (sông'klä')	212	7°09'N	100°34'E
Songwe, D.R.C.	237	12°25'S	29°40'E
Sonneberg, Ger. (sôn'ĕ-bĕrgh)	168	50°20'N	11°14'E
Sonora, Ca., U.S. (sô-nō'rȧ)	118	37°58'N	120°22'W
Sonora, Tx., U.S.	122	30°33'N	100°38'W
Sonora, state, Mex.	128	29°45'N	111°15'W
Sonora, r., Mex.	128	28°45'N	111°35'W
Sonora Peak, mtn., Ca., U.S.	106	38°22'N	119°39'W
Sonseca, Spain (sôn-sā'kä)	172	39°41'N	3°56'W
Sonsón, Col. (sôn-sôn')	142	5°42'N	75°28'W
Sonsonate, El Sal. (sōn-sô-nä'tå)	132	13°46'N	89°43'W
Sonsorol Islands, is., Palau (sŏn-sô-rōl')	213	5°03'N	132°33'E
Sooke Basin, b., Can. (sòk)	116a	48°21'N	123°47'W
Soo Locks, trans., Mi., U.S. (sōō lŏks)	117a	46°30'N	84°30'W
Sopetrán, Col. (sô-pĕ-trä'n)	142a	6°30'N	75°44'W
Sopot, Pol. (sô'pôt)	169	54°26'N	18°25'E
Sopron, Hung. (shŏp'rŏn)	163	47°41'N	16°36'E
Sora, Italy (sō'rä)	174	41°43'N	13°37'E
Sorbas, Spain (sôr'bäs)	172	37°05'N	2°07'W
Sordo, r., Mex. (sô'r-dō)	131	16°39'N	97°33'W
Sorel, Can. (sô-rĕl')	91	46°01'N	73°07'W
Sorell, Cape, c., Austl.	222	42°10'S	144°50'E
Soresina, Italy (sō-rå-zē'nä)	174	45°17'N	9°51'E
Soria, Spain (sō'rē-ä)	162	41°46'N	2°28'W
Soriano, dept., Ur. (sŏ-rēä'nô)	141c	33°25'S	58°00'W
Soroca, Mol.	181	48°09'N	28°17'E
Sorocaba, Braz. (sô-rô-kä'bȧ)	143	23°29'S	47°27'W
Sorong, Indon. (sō-rông')	213	1°00'S	131°20'E
Sorot', r., Russia [illegible]	176	57°08'N	29°23'E
Soroti, Ug. (sō-rō'tē)	231	1°43'N	33°37'E
Sørøya, i., Nor.	160	70°37'N	20°58'E
Sorraia, r., Port. (sôr-rī'ȧ)	172	38°55'N	8°42'W
Sorrento, Italy (sôr-rĕn'tō)	174	40°23'N	14°23'E
Sorsogon, Phil. (sôr-sôgōn')	213	12°51'N	124°02'E
Sortavala, Russia (sôr'tä-vä-lä)	178	61°43'N	30°40'E
Sosna, r., Russia (sôs'nȧ)	177	50°33'N	38°15'E
Sosnogorsk, Russia	178	63°13'N	54°09'E
Sosnowiec, Pol. (sôs-nô'vyĕts)	169	50°17'N	19°10'E
Sosnytsia, Ukr.	177	51°30'N	32°29'E
Sosunova, Mys, c., Russia (mĭs sô'sò-nôf'ȧ)	210	46°28'N	138°06'E
Sos'va, r., Russia (sôs'vȧ)	186a	59°55'N	60°40'E
Sos'va, r., Russia (sôs'vȧ)	180	63°10'N	63°30'E
Sota, r., Benin	235	11°10'N	3°20'E
Sota la Marina, Mex. (sô-tä-lä-mä-rē'nä)	130	23°45'N	98°11'W
Soteapan, Mex. (sō-tå-ä'pän)	131	18°14'N	94°51'W
Soto la Marina, Río, r., Mex. (rē'ō-so'tō lä mä-rē'nä)	130	23°55'N	98°30'W
Sotuta, Mex. (sô-tōō'tä)	132a	20°35'N	89°00'W
Soublette, Ven. (sō-ōō-blĕ'tĕ)	143b	9°55'N	66°06'W
Souflí, Grc.	175	41°12'N	26°17'E
Soufrière, St. Luc. (sōō-frē-âr')	133b	13°50'N	61°03'W
Soufrière, mtn., St. Vin.	133b	13°19'N	61°12'W
Soufrière, vol., Guad. (sōō-frē-âr')	133b	16°06'N	61°42'W
Sŏul see Seoul, Kor., S.	205	37°35'N	127°03'E
Sounding Creek, r., Can. (soun'dĭng)	96	51°35'N	111°00'W
Souq Ahras, Alg.	161	36°23'N	8°00'E
Sources, Mount aux, mtn., Afr. (môn'tō sôrs')	232	28°47'S	29°04'E
Soure, Port. (sōr-ĕ)	172	40°04'N	8°37'W
Souris, Can. (sōō'rē')	101	46°20'N	62°17'W
Souris, Can.	90	49°38'N	100°15'W
Souris, r., N.A.	92	48°30'N	101°30'W
Sourlake, Tx., U.S. (sour'lāk)	123	30°09'N	94°24'W
Sousse, Tun. (sōōs)	230	36°00'N	10°39'E
South, r., Ga., U.S.	110c	33°40'N	84°15'W
South, r., N.C., U.S.	125	34°49'N	78°33'W
South Africa, nation, Afr.	232	28°00'S	24°50'E
South Amboy, N.J., U.S. (south'ăm'boi)	110a	40°28'N	74°17'W
South America, cont.	139	15°00'S	60°00'W
Southampton, Eng., U.K. (south-ămp'tŭn)	154	50°54'N	1°30'W
Southampton, N.Y., U.S.	109	40°53'N	72°24'W
Southampton Island, i., Can.	93	64°38'N	84°00'W
South Andaman Island, i., India (ăn-dȧ-măn')	212	11°57'N	93°24'E
South Australia, state, Austl. (ôs-trā'lĭ-ȧ)	218	29°45'S	132°00'E
South Bay, b., Bah.	135	20°55'N	73°35'W
South Bend, In., U.S. (bĕnd)	105	41°40'N	86°20'W
South Bend, Wa., U.S. (bĕnd)	114	46°39'N	123°48'W
South Bight, b., Bah.	134	24°20'N	77°35'W
South Bimini, i., Bah. (bē'mē-nē)	134	25°40'N	79°20'W
Southborough, Ma., U.S. (south'bŭr-ō)	101a	42°18'N	71°33'W
South Boston, Va., U.S. (bôs'tŭn)	125	36°41'N	78°55'W
Southbridge, Ma., U.S. (south'brĭj)	109	42°05'N	72°00'W
South Caicos, i., T./C. Is. (kī'kōs)	135	21°30'N	71°35'W
South Carolina, state, U.S. (kăr-ô-lī'nȧ)	105	34°15'N	81°10'W
South Cave, Eng., U.K. (cāv)	158a	53°45'N	0°35'W
South Charleston, W.V., U.S.	108	38°20'N	81°40'W
South China Sea, sea, Asia (chī'nȧ)	212	15°23'N	114°12'E
South Creek, r., Austl.	217b	33°43'S	150°50'E
South Dakota, state, U.S. (dȧ-kō'tȧ)	104	44°20'N	101°55'W
South Downs, Eng., U.K. (dounz)	164	50°55'N	1°13'W
South Dum-Dum, India	202a	22°36'N	88°25'E
South East Cape, c., Austl.	221	43°47'S	146°03'E
Southend-on-Sea, Eng., U.K. (south-ĕnd')	165	51°33'N	0°41'E
Southern Alps, mts., N.Z. (sŭ-thûrn ălps)	221a	43°35'S	170°00'E
Southern Cross, Austl.	218	31°13'S	119°30'E
Southern Indian, l., Can. (sŭth'ẽrn ĭn'dĭ-ăn)	92	56°46'N	98°57'W
Southern Pines, N.C., U.S. (sŭth'ẽrn pīnz)	125	35°10'N	79°23'W
Southern Ute Indian Reservation, I.R., Co., U.S. (ūt)	119	37°05'N	108°23'W
South Euclid, Oh., U.S. (ū'klĭd)	111d	41°30'N	81°34'W
South Fox, i., Mi., U.S. (fŏks)	108	45°25'N	85°55'W
South Gate, Ca., U.S. (gāt)	117a	33°57'N	118°13'W
South Georgia, i., S. Geor. (jôr'jȧ)	139	54°00'S	37°00'W
South Haven, Mi., U.S. (hāv''n)	108	42°25'N	86°15'W
South Hill, Va., U.S.	125	36°44'N	78°08'W
South Holston Lake, res., U.S.	125	36°35'N	82°00'W
South Indian Lake, Can.	97	56°50'N	99°00'W
Southington, Ct., U.S. (sŭdh'ĭng-tŭn)	109	41°35'N	72°55'W
South Island, i., N.Z.	221a	42°40'S	169°00'E
South Loup, r., Ne., U.S. (lōōp)	112	41°21'N	100°08'W
South Magnetic Pole, pt. of i.	224	65°18'S	139°30'E
South Merrimack, N.H., U.S. (mĕr'ĭ-măk)	101a	42°47'N	71°36'W
South Milwaukee, Wi., U.S. (mĭl-wô'kē)	111a	42°55'N	87°52'W
South Moose Lake, l., Can.	97	53°51'N	100°20'W
South Nation, r., Can.	99	45°00'N	75°25'W
South Negril Point, c., Jam. (nå-grēl')	134	18°15'N	78°25'W
South Ogden, Ut., U.S. (ŏg'dĕn)	117b	41°12'N	111°58'W
South Orkney Islands, is., Ant.	139	57°00'S	45°00'W
South Ossetia, hist. reg., Geor.	182	42°20'N	44°00'E
South Paris, Me., U.S. [illegible]	100	[illegible]	[illegible]
South Park, Ky., U.S. (pärk)	111h	38°06'N	85°43'W
South Pasadena, Ca., U.S. (păs-ȧ-dē'nȧ)	117a	34°06'N	118°08'W
South Pease, r., Tx., U.S. (pēz)	120	33°54'N	100°45'W
South Pender, i., Can. (pĕn'dẽr)	116d	48°45'N	123°09'W
South Pittsburg, Tn., U.S. (pĭs'bûrg)	124	35°00'N	85°42'W
South Platte, r., U.S. (plăt)	106	40°40'N	102°40'W
South Point, c., Barb.	133b	13°00'N	59°43'W
South Point, c., Mi., U.S.	108	44°50'N	83°20'W
South Pole, pt. of i., Ant.	224	90°00'S	0°00'
South Porcupine, Can.	98	48°28'N	81°13'W
Southport, Austl. (south'pōrt)	219	27°57'S	153°27'E
Southport, Eng., U.K. (south'pôrt)	164	53°38'N	3°00'W
Southport, In., U.S.	111g	39°40'N	86°07'W
Southport, N.C., U.S.	125	35°55'N	78°02'W
South Portland, Me., U.S. (pōrt-lănd)	100	43°37'N	70°15'W
South Prairie, Wa., U.S. (prā'rĭ)	116a	47°08'N	122°06'W
South Range, Wi., U.S. (rānj)	117h	46°37'N	91°59'W
South River, N.J., U.S. (rĭv'ẽr)	110a	40°27'N	74°23'W
South Ronaldsay, i., Scot., U.K. (rŏn'ăld-s'ā)	164a	58°48'N	2°55'W
South Saint Paul, Mn., U.S.	117g	44°54'N	93°02'W
South Salt Lake, Ut., U.S. (sôlt lāk)	117b	40°44'N	111°53'W
South Sandwich Islands, is., S. Geor. (sănd'wĭch)	139	58°00'S	27°00'W
South Sandwich Trench, deep	139	55°00'S	27°00'W
South San Francisco, Ca., U.S. (săn frăn-sĭs'kô)	116b	37°39'N	122°24'W
South Saskatchewan, r., Can. (săs-kach'ĕ-wän)	92	50°30'N	110°30'W
South Shetland Islands, is., Ant.	139	62°00'S	70°00'W
South Shields, Eng., U.K. (shēldz)	160	55°00'N	1°22'W
South Sioux City, Ne., U.S. (sōō sĭt'ē)	112	42°48'N	96°26'W
South Taranaki Bight, b., N.Z. (tä-rä-nä'kē)	221a	39°35'S	173°50'E
South Thompson, r., Can. (tŏmp'sŭn)	95	50°41'N	120°21'W
Southton, Tx., U.S. (south'tŭn)	117d	29°18'N	98°26'W
South Uist, i., Scot., U.K. (ū'ĭst)	164	57°15'N	7°24'W
South Umpqua, r., Or., U.S. (ŭmp'kwȧ)	114	43°00'N	122°54'W
Southwell, Eng., U.K. (south'wĕl)	158a	53°04'N	0°56'W
South West Africa see Namibia, nation, Afr.	232	19°30'S	16°13'E
Southwest Miramichi, r., Can. (mĭr ȧ-mē'shē)	100	46°35'N	66°17'W
Southwest Point, c., Bah.	134	25°50'N	77°10'W
Southwest Point, c., Bah.	135	23°55'N	74°30'W
South Yorkshire, hist. reg., Eng., U.K.	158a	53°29'N	1°35'W
Sovetsk, Russia (sô-vyĕtsk')	180	55°04'N	21°54'E
Sovetskaya Gavan', Russia (sŭ-vyĕt'skī-u gä'vŭn')	179	48°59'N	140°14'E
Sow, r., Eng., U.K. (sou)	158a	52°45'N	2°12'W
Soya Kaikyō, strt., Asia	210	45°45'N	141°38'E
Sōya Misaki, c., Japan (sō'yȧ mē'sä-kē)	210	45°35'N	141°25'E
Soyo, Ang.	232	6°10'S	12°25'E
Sozh, r., Eur. (sôzh)	181	52°50'N	31°00'E
Sozopol, Blg. (sôz'ô-pôl')	175	42°18'N	27°50'E
Spa, Bel. (spä)	165	50°30'N	5°50'E
Spain, nation, Eur. (spān)	154	40°15'N	4°30'W
Spalding, Ne., U.S. (spôl'dĭng)	112	41°43'N	98°23'W
Spanaway, Wa., U.S. (spăn'ȧ-wā)	116a	47°06'N	122°26'W
Spangler, Pa., U.S. (spăng'lẽr)	109	40°40'N	78°50'W
Spanish Fork, Ut., U.S. (spăn'ĭsh fôrk)	119	40°10'N	111°40'W
Spanish Town, Jam.	129	18°00'N	76°55'W
Sparks, Nv., U.S. (spärks)	118	39°34'N	119°45'W
Sparrows Point, Md., U.S. (spăr'ōz)	110e	39°13'N	76°29'W
Sparta see Spárti, Grc.	175	37°07'N	22°28'E
Sparta, Ga., U.S. (spär'tȧ)	125	33°16'N	82°59'W
Sparta, Il., U.S.	121	38°07'N	89°42'W
Sparta, Mi., U.S.	108	43°10'N	85°45'W
Sparta, Tn., U.S.	124	35°54'N	85°26'W
Sparta, Wi., U.S.	113	43°56'N	90°50'W
Sparta Mountains, mts., N.J., U.S.	110a	41°00'N	74°38'W
Spartanburg, S.C., U.S. (spär'tăn-bûrg)	105	34°57'N	82°13'W
Spartel, Cap, c., Mor. (spär-tĕl')	172	35°48'N	5°50'W
Spárti (Sparta), Grc.	175	37°07'N	22°28'E
Spartivento, Cape, c., Italy (spär-tē-vĕn'tô)	174	37°55'N	16°09'E
Spartivento, Cape, c., Italy	156	38°54'N	8°52'E
Spas-Demensk, Russia (spȧs dyĕ-mĕnsk')	176	54°24'N	34°02'E
Spas-Klepiki, Russia (spȧs klĕp'ĕ-kē)	176	55°09'N	40°11'E

ăt; finăl; rāte; senåte; ärm; åsk; sofȧ; fâre; ch-choose; dh-as th in other; bē; ėvent; bĕt; recĕnt; cratẽr; g-gō; gh-guttural g; bĭt; ĭ-short neutral; rīde; ᴋ-guttural k as ch in German ich;

PRONOUNCING INDEX

Spassik-Ryazanskiy – Strängnäs 353

PLACE (Pronunciation)	PAGE	LAT.	LONG.
Spassik-Ryazanskiy, Russia (ryä-zän´skĭ)	176	54°24'N	40°21'E
Spassk-Dal'niy, Russia (spŭsk´däl´nyē)	179	44°30'N	133°00'E
Spátha, Ákra, c., Grc.	174a	35°42'N	23°45'E
Spaulding, Al., U.S. (spôl´dĭng)	110h	33°27'N	86°50'W
Spear, Cape, c., Can. (spēr)	101	47°32'N	52°32'W
Spearfish, S.D., U.S. (spēr´fĭsh)	112	44°28'N	103°52'W
Speed, In., U.S. (spēd)	111h	38°25'N	85°45'W
Speedway, In., U.S. (spēd´wā)	111g	39°47'N	86°14'W
Speichersee, l., Ger.	159d	48°12'N	11°47'E
Spencer, Ia., U.S.	112	43°09'N	95°08'W
Spencer, In., U.S. (spĕn´sẽr)	108	39°15'N	86°45'W
Spencer, N.C., U.S.	125	35°43'N	80°25'W
Spencer, W.V., U.S.	108	38°55'N	81°20'W
Spencer Gulf, b., Austl. (spĕn´sẽr)	220	34°20'S	136°55'E
Sperenberg, Ger. (shpĕ´rĕn-bĕrgh)	159b	52°09'N	13°22'E
Spey, l., Scot., U.K. (spā)	164	57°25'N	3°29'W
Speyer, Ger. (shpī´ĕr)	160	49°18'N	8°26'E
Sphinx, hist., Egypt (sfĭnks)	238b	29°57'N	31°00'E
Spijkenisse, Neth.	159a	51°51'N	4°18'E
Spinazzola, Italy (spė-nät´zȯ-lä)	174	40°58'N	16°05'E
Spirit Lake, Ia., U.S. (lāk)	112	43°25'N	95°08'W
Spirit Lake, Id., U.S. (spĭr´ĭt)	114	47°58'N	116°51'W
Spišská Nová Ves, Slvk. (spēsh´skä nō´vä vĕs)	161	48°56'N	20°35'E
Spitsbergen *see* Svalbard, dep., Nor.	178	77°00'N	20°00'E
Split, Cro. (splēt)	154	43°30'N	16°28'E
Split Lake, l., Can.	97	56°08'N	96°15'W
Spokane, Wa., U.S. (spōkăn´)	104	47°39'N	117°25'W
Spokane, r., Wa., U.S.	114	47°47'N	118°00'W
Spokane Indian Reservation, I.R., Wa., U.S.	114	47°55'N	118°00'W
Spoleto, Italy (spô-lā´tō)	174	42°44'N	12°44'E
Spoon, r., Il., U.S. (spōōn)	121	40°36'N	90°22'W
Spooner, Wi., U.S. (spōōn´ẽr)	113	45°50'N	91°53'W
Spotswood, N.J., U.S. (spŏtz´wōōd)	110a	40°23'N	74°22'W
Sprague, r., Or., U.S. (sprāg)	114	42°30'N	121°42'W
Spratly, i., Asia (sprăt´lė)	212	8°38'N	111°54'E
Spray, N.C., U.S. (sprā)	125	36°30'N	79°44'W
Spree, r., Ger. (shprā)	168	51°53'N	14°08'E
Spremberg, Ger. (shprĕm´bĕrgh)	168	51°35'N	14°23'E
Spring, r., Ar., U.S.	121	36°25'N	91°35'W
Springbok, S. Afr. (sprĭng´bŏk)	232	29°35'S	17°55'E
Spring Creek, r., Nv., U.S. (sprĭng)	118	40°18'N	117°45'W
Spring Creek, r., Tx., U.S.	123	30°03'N	95°43'W
Spring Creek, r., Tx., U.S.	122	31°08'N	100°50'W
Springdale, Can.	101	49°30'N	56°05'W
Springdale, Ar., U.S. (sprĭng´dāl)	121	36°10'N	94°07'W
Springdale, Pa., U.S.	111e	40°33'N	79°46'W
Springer, N.M., U.S. (sprĭng´ẽr)	120	36°21'N	104°37'W
Springerville, Az., U.S.	119	34°08'N	109°17'W
Springfield, Co., U.S. (sprĭng´fēld)	120	37°24'N	102°04'W
Springfield, Il., U.S.	105	39°46'N	89°37'W
Springfield, Ky., U.S.	108	37°35'N	85°10'W
Springfield, Ma., U.S.	105	42°05'N	72°35'W
Springfield, Mn., U.S.	113	44°14'N	94°59'W
Springfield, Mo., U.S.	105	37°13'N	93°17'W
Springfield, Oh., U.S.	105	39°55'N	83°50'W
Springfield, Or., U.S.	114	44°01'N	123°02'W
Springfield, Tn., U.S.	124	36°30'N	86°53'W
Springfield, Vt., U.S.	109	43°20'N	72°35'W
Springfontein, S. Afr. (sprĭng´fŏn-tĭn)	232	30°16'S	25°45'E
Springhill, Can. (sprĭng-hĭl´)	91	45°39'N	64°03'W
Spring Mountains, mts., Nv., U.S.	118	36°18'N	115°49'W
Springs, S. Afr. (sprĭngs)	238c	26°16'S	28°27'E
Springstein, Can. (sprĭng´stīn)	102f	49°49'N	97°29'W
Springton Reservoir, res., Pa., U.S. (sprĭng-tŭn)	110f	39°57'N	75°26'W
Springvale, Austl.	217a	37°57'S	145°09'E
Spring Valley, Ca., U.S.	118a	32°46'N	117°01'W
Springvalley, Il., U.S. (sprĭng-văl´ĭ)	108	41°20'N	89°15'W
Spring Valley, Mn., U.S.	113	43°41'N	92°26'W
Spring Valley, N.Y., U.S.	110a	41°07'N	74°03'W
Springville, Ut., U.S. (sprĭng-vĭl)	119	40°10'N	111°40'W
Springwood, Austl.	217b	33°42'S	150°34'E
Spruce Grove, Can. (sprōōs grōv)	102g	53°32'N	113°55'W
Spur, Tx., U.S. (spûr)	120	33°29'N	100°51'W
Squam, l., N.H., U.S. (skwôm)	109	43°45'N	71°30'W
Squamish, Can. (skwŏ´mĭsh)	94	49°42'N	123°09'W
Squamish, r., Can.	94	50°10'N	123°30'W
Squillace, Golfo di, b., Italy (gōō´l-fō-dē skwēl-lä´chå)	174	38°44'N	16°47'E
Srbobran, Serb. (s'r´bô-brän´)	175	45°32'N	19°50'E
Sredne-Kolymsk, Russia (s'rĕd´nyĕ kô-lēmsk´)	179	67°49'N	154°55'E
Sredne Rogatka, Russia (s'red´nà-ya) (rô gär´tkà)	186c	59°49'N	30°20'E
Sredniy Ik, r., Russia (srĕd´nĭ ĭk)	186a	55°46'N	58°50'E
Sredniy Ural, mts., Russia (ö´rál)	186a	57°47'N	59°00'E
Šrem, Pol. (shrĕm)	169	52°06'N	17°01'E
Sremska Karlovci, Serb. (srĕm´skė kär´lov-tsė)	175	45°10'N	19°57'E
Sremska Mitrovica, Serb. (srĕm´skä mē´trô-vė-tsä´)	175	44°59'N	19°39'E
Sretensk, Russia (s'rĕ´tĕnsk)	179	52°13'N	117°39'E
Sri Jayewardenepura Kotte, Sri L.	203	6°50'N	80°05'E
Sri Lanka, nation, Asia	203	8°45'N	82°30'E
Srīnagar, India (srē-nŭg´ŭr)	199	34°11'N	74°49'E
Środa, Pol. (shrō´dà)	169	52°14'N	17°17'E
Stabroek, Bel.	159a	51°20'N	4°21'E
Stade, Ger. (shtä´dĕ)	168	53°36'N	9°28'E

PLACE (Pronunciation)	PAGE	LAT.	LONG.
Städjan, mtn., Swe. (stĕd´yän)	166	61°53'N	12°50'E
Stafford, Eng., U.K. (stăf´fẽrd)	164	52°48'N	2°06'W
Stafford, Ks., U.S.	120	37°58'N	98°37'W
Staffordshire, co., Eng., U.K.	158a	52°45'N	2°00'W
Stahnsdorf, Ger. (shtäns´dôrf)	159b	52°22'N	13°10'E
Staines, Eng., U.K.	158b	51°26'N	0°13'W
Stakhanov, Ukr.	181	48°34'N	38°37'E
Stalingrad *see* Volgograd, Russia	178	48°40'N	42°20'E
Stalybridge, Eng., U.K.	158a	53°29'N	2°03'W
Stambaugh, Mi., U.S. (stăm´bô)	113	46°03'N	88°38'W
Stamford, Eng., U.K.	158a	52°39'N	0°28'W
Stamford, Ct., U.S. (stăm´fẽrd)	110a	41°03'N	73°32'W
Stamford, Tx., U.S.	120	32°57'N	99°48'W
Stammersdorf, Aus. (shtäm´ĕrs-dôrf)	159e	48°19'N	16°25'E
Stamps, Ar., U.S. (stămps)	121	33°22'N	93°31'W
Stanberry, Mo., U.S. (stan´bĕr-ė)	121	40°12'N	94°34'W
Standerton, S. Afr. (stăn´dẽr-tŭn)	232	26°57'S	29°17'E
Standing Rock Indian Reservation, I.R., N.D., U.S. (stănd´ĭng rŏk)	112	47°07'N	101°05'W
Standish, Eng., U.K. (stan´dĭsh)	158a	53°36'N	2°39'W
Stanford, Ky., U.S. (stăn´fẽrd)	124	37°29'N	84°40'W
Stanger, S. Afr. (stăŋ-ger)	233c	29°22'S	31°18'E
Staniard Creek, Bah.	134	24°50'N	77°55'W
Stanislaus, r., Ca., U.S. (stăn´ĭs-lô)	118	38°10'N	120°16'W
Stanley, Can. (stăn´lė)	100	46°17'N	66°44'W
Stanley, Falk. Is.	144	51°46'S	57°59'W
Stanley, N.D., U.S.	112	48°20'N	102°25'W
Stanley, Wi., U.S.	113	44°56'N	90°56'W
Stanley Pool, l., Afr.	232	4°07'S	15°40'E
Stanley Reservoir, res., India (stăn´lė)	203	12°07'N	77°27'E
Stanleyville *see* Kisangani, D.R.C.	231	0°30'S	25°12'E
Stann Creek, Belize (stăn krēk)	132a	17°01'N	88°14'W
Stanovoy Khrebet, mts., Russia (stŭn-á-voi´)	179	56°12'N	127°12'E
Stanton, Ca., U.S. (stăn´tŭn)	117a	33°48'N	118°00'W
Stanton, Ne., U.S.	112	41°57'N	97°15'W
Stanton, Tx., U.S.	122	32°08'N	101°46'W
Stanwood, Wa., U.S. (stăn´wŏod)	116a	48°14'N	122°23'W
Staples, Mn., U.S. (stā´p´lz)	113	46°21'N	94°48'W
Stapleton, Al., U.S.	124	30°45'N	87°48'W
Stara Planina, mts., Blg.	156	42°50'N	24°45'E
Staraya Kupavna, Russia (stä´ra-ya kû-päf´nà)	186b	55°48'N	38°10'E
Staraya Russa, Russia (stä´rá-yá rōōsà)	180	57°58'N	31°21'E
Stara Zagora, Blg. (zä´gô-rà)	163	42°26'N	25°37'E
Starbuck, Can. (stär´bŭk)	102f	49°46'N	97°36'W
Stargard Szczeciński, Pol. (shtär´gärt shchĕ-chyn´skē)	160	53°19'N	15°03'E
Staritsa, Russia (stä´rē-tsà)	176	56°29'N	34°58'E
Starke, Fl., U.S. (stärk)	125	29°55'N	82°07'W
Starkville, Co., U.S. (stärk´vĭl)	120	37°06'N	104°34'W
Starkville, Ms., U.S.	124	33°27'N	88°47'W
Starnberg, Ger. (shtärn-bĕrgh)	159d	47°59'N	11°20'E
Starnberger See, l., Ger.	168	47°58'N	11°30'E
Starobil's'k, Ukr.	181	49°19'N	38°57'E
Starodub, Russia (stä-rô-drŏp´)	176	52°25'N	32°49'E
Starogrod Gdański, Pol. (stä´rō-grad gdĕn´skē)	160	53°58'N	18°33'E
Starokostiantyniv, Ukr.	181	49°45'N	27°12'E
Staro-Minskaya, Russia (stä´rô mĭn´ská-yà)	181	46°19'N	38°51'E
Staro-Shcherbinovskaya, Russia	177	46°38'N	38°38'E
Staro-Subkhangulovo, Russia (stăro-sōōb-kan-gōō´lōvō)	186a	53°08'N	57°24'E
Staroutkinsk, Russia (stá-rô-ōōt´kĭnsk)	186a	57°14'N	59°21'E
Starovirivka, Ukr.	177	49°31'N	35°48'E
Start Point, c., Eng., U.K. (stärt)	161	50°14'N	3°34'W
Staryi Ostropil', Ukr.	177	49°48'N	27°32'E
Stary Sącz, Pol. (stä-rē sônch´)	169	49°32'N	20°36'E
Staryy Oskol, Russia (stä´rē ôs-kôl´)	181	51°18'N	37°51'E
Stassfurt, Ger. (shtäs´fōōrt)	168	51°52'N	11°35'E
Staszów, Pol. (stä´shôf)	169	50°32'N	21°13'E
State College, Pa., U.S. (stāt kŏl´ĕj)	109	40°50'N	77°55'W
State Line, Mn., U.S. (līn)	117h	46°36'N	92°18'W
Staten Island, i., N.Y., U.S. (stăt´ĕn)	110a	40°35'N	74°10'W
Statesboro, Ga., U.S. (stāts´bŭr-ô)	125	32°26'N	81°47'W
Statesville, N.C., U.S. (stāts´vĭl)	125	34°45'N	80°54'W
Staunton, Il., U.S. (stôn´tŭn)	117e	39°01'N	89°47'W
Staunton, Va., U.S.	109	38°10'N	79°05'W
Stavanger, Nor. (stä´văng´ẽr)	154	58°59'N	5°44'E
Stave, r., Can. (stāv)	116d	49°12'N	122°24'W
Staveley, Eng., U.K. (stāv´lē)	158a	53°17'N	1°21'W
Stavenisse, Neth.	159a	51°35'N	3°59'E
Stavropol', Russia	178	45°05'N	41°50'E
Steamboat Springs, Co., U.S. (stēm´bōt´)	120	40°30'N	106°48'W
Stebliv, Ukr.	177	49°23'N	31°03'E
Steel, r., Can. (stēl)	98	49°08'N	86°55'W
Steelton, Pa., U.S. (stēl´tŭn)	109	40°15'N	76°45'W
Steenbergen, Neth.	159a	51°35'N	4°18'E
Steens Mountain, mts., Or., U.S. (stēnz)	114	42°15'N	118°52'W
Steep Point, c., Austl. (stēp)	220	26°15'S	112°05'E
Stefanie, Lake *see* Chew Bahir, l., Afr.	231	4°46'N	37°31'E
Steinbach, Can.	90	49°32'N	96°41'W
Steinkjer, Nor. (stēĭn-kyĕr)	160	64°00'N	11°19'E
Stella, Wa., U.S. (stĕl´á)	116c	46°11'N	123°12'W
Stellarton, Can. (stĕl´ár-tŭn)	91	45°34'N	62°40'W
Stendal, Ger. (shtĕn´däl)	168	52°37'N	11°51'E
Stepanakert *see* Xankändi, Azer.	180	39°50'N	46°40'E
Stephens, Port, b., Austl. (stē´fĕns)	222	32°43'S	152°55'E

PLACE (Pronunciation)	PAGE	LAT.	LONG.
Stephenville, Can. (stē´vĕn-vĭl)	93a	48°33'N	58°35'W
Stepnogorsk, Kaz.	183	52°20'N	72°05'E
Sterkrade, Ger. (shtĕr´krädĕ)	171c	51°31'N	6°51'E
Sterkstroom, S. Afr.	233c	31°33'S	26°36'E
Sterling, Co., U.S. (stûr´lĭng)	104	40°38'N	103°14'W
Sterling, Il., U.S.	108	41°48'N	89°42'W
Sterling, Ks., U.S.	120	38°11'N	98°11'W
Sterling, Ma., U.S.	101a	42°26'N	71°41'W
Sterling, Tx., U.S.	122	31°53'N	100°58'W
Sterlitamak, Russia (styĕr´lē-ta-mák´)	178	53°38'N	55°56'E
Šternberk, Czech Rep. (shtĕrn´bĕrk)	169	49°44'N	17°18'E
Stettin *see* Szczecin, Pol.	154	53°25'N	14°35'E
Stettler, Can.	90	52°19'N	112°43'W
Steubenville, Oh., U.S. (stū´bĕn-vĭl)	108	40°20'N	80°40'W
Stevens, l., Wa., U.S. (stē´vĕnz)	116a	47°59'N	122°06'W
Stevens Point, Wi., U.S.	113	44°30'N	89°35'W
Stevensville, Mt., U.S. (stē´vĕnz-vĭl)	115	46°31'N	114°03'W
Stewart, r., Can. (stū´ẽrt)	92	63°27'N	138°48'W
Stewart Island, i., N.Z.	221a	46°56'S	167°40'E
Stewiacke, Can. (stū´wė-ăk)	100	45°08'N	63°21'W
Steynsrus, S. Afr. (stīns´rōōs)	238c	27°58'S	27°33'E
Steyr, Aus. (shtīr)	161	48°03'N	14°24'E
Stif, Alg.	230	36°18'N	5°21'E
Stikine, r., Can. (stĭ-kēn´)	92	58°17'N	130°10'W
Stikine Ranges, Can.	90	59°05'N	130°00'W
Stillaguamish, r., Wa., U.S.	116a	48°11'N	122°18'W
Stillaguamish, South Fork, r., Wa., U.S. (stĭl-à-gwä´mĭsh)	116a	48°05'N	121°59'W
Stillwater, Mn., U.S. (stĭl´wô-tẽr)	117g	45°04'N	92°48'W
Stillwater, Mt., U.S.	115	45°23'N	109°45'W
Stillwater, Ok., U.S.	121	36°06'N	97°03'W
Stillwater, r., Mt., U.S.	115	48°47'N	114°40'W
Stillwater Range, mts., Nv., U.S.	118	39°43'N	118°11'W
Štip, Mac. (shtĭp)	175	41°43'N	22°07'E
Stirling, Scot., U.K. (stûr´lĭng)	164	56°05'N	3°59'W
Stittsville, Can. (stĭts´vĭl)	102c	45°15'N	75°54'W
Stizef, Alg. (mĕr-syā´ lá-kônb)	173	35°18'N	0°11'W
Stjördalshalsen, Nor. (styûr-däls-hälsĕn)	166	63°26'N	11°00'E
Stockbridge Munsee Indian Reservation, I.R., Wi., U.S. (stŏk´brĭdj mŭn-sē)	113	44°49'N	89°00'W
Stockerau, Aus. (shtô´kĕ-rou)	168	48°24'N	16°13'E
Stockholm, Swe. (stŏk´hôlm)	154	59°23'N	18°00'E
Stockholm, Me., U.S. (stŏk´hōlm)	100	47°05'N	68°08'W
Stockport, Eng., U.K. (stŏk´pôrt)	164	53°24'N	2°09'W
Stockton, Eng., U.K.	164	54°35'N	1°25'W
Stockton, Ca., U.S. (stŏk´tŭn)	104	37°56'N	121°16'W
Stockton, Ks., U.S.	120	39°26'N	99°16'W
Stockton, i., Wi., U.S.	113	46°56'N	90°25'W
Stockton Plateau, plat., Tx., U.S.	106	30°34'N	102°35'W
Stockton Reservoir, res., Mo., U.S.	121	37°40'N	93°45'W
Stöde, Swe. (stû´dĕ)	166	62°26'N	16°35'E
Stoeng Trêng, Camb. (stông trĕng´)	212	13°36'N	106°00'E
Stoke-on-Trent, Eng., U.K. (stōk-ŏn-trĕnt)	160	53°01'N	2°12'W
Stokhid, r., Ukr.	169	51°24'N	25°20'E
Stolac, Bos. (stô´láts)	175	43°03'N	17°59'E
Stolbovoy, is., Russia (stôl-bô-voi´)	185	74°05'N	136°00'E
Stolin, Bela. (stô´lĕn)	169	51°54'N	26°52'E
Stömstad, Swe.	166	58°58'N	11°09'E
Stone, Eng., U.K.	158a	52°54'N	2°09'W
Stoneham, Can. (stōn´ám)	102b	46°59'N	71°22'W
Stoneham, Ma., U.S.	101a	42°30'N	71°05'W
Stonehaven, Scot., U.K. (stōn´hā-v'n)	164	56°57'N	2°09'W
Stone Mountain, Ga., U.S. (stōn)	110c	33°49'N	84°10'W
Stonewall, Can. (stōn´wôl)	102f	50°09'N	97°21'W
Stonewall, Ms., U.S.	124	32°08'N	88°44'W
Stoney Creek, Can. (stō´nē)	102d	43°13'N	79°45'W
Stonington, Ct., U.S. (stōn´ĭng-tŭn)	109	41°20'N	71°55'W
Stony Indian Reserve, I.R., Can.	102e	51°10'N	114°45'W
Stony Mountain, Can.	102f	50°05'N	97°13'W
Stony Plain, Can. (stō´nē plān)	102g	53°32'N	114°00'W
Stony Plain Indian Reserve, I.R., Can.	102g	53°29'N	113°48'W
Stony Point, N.Y., U.S.	110a	41°13'N	73°58'W
Stora Sotra, i., Nor.	166	60°24'N	4°35'E
Stord, i., Nor. (stôrd)	166	59°54'N	5°15'E
Store Baelt, strt., Den.	166	55°25'N	10°50'E
Storfjorden, b., Nor.	166	62°17'N	6°19'E
Stormberg, mts., S. Afr. (stôrm´bûrg)	233c	31°28'S	26°35'E
Storm Lake, Ia., U.S.	112	42°39'N	95°12'W
Stormy Point, c., V.I.U.S. (stôr´mē)	129c	18°22'N	65°01'W
Stornoway, Scot., U.K. (stôr´nô-wā)	160	58°13'N	6°21'W
Storozhynets', Ukr.	169	48°10'N	25°44'E
Störsjo, Swe. (stör´shû)	166	62°49'N	13°08'E
Störsjoen, l., Nor. (stôr-syûĕn)	166	61°32'N	11°30'E
Störsjon, l., Swe.	160	63°06'N	14°00'E
Storvik, Swe.	166	60°37'N	16°31'E
Stoughton, Wi., U.S.	113	42°54'N	89°15'W
Stour, r., Eng., U.K. (stour)	165	52°09'N	0°29'E
Stourbridge, Eng., U.K. (stour´brĭj)	158a	52°27'N	2°08'W
Stow, Ma., U.S. (stō)	101a	42°56'N	71°31'W
Stow, Oh., U.S.	111d	41°09'N	81°26'W
Straatsdrif, S. Afr.	238c	25°19'S	26°22'E
Strabane, N. Ire., U.K. (stră-băn´)	164	54°59'N	7°27'W
Straelen, Ger. (shtră´lĕn)	171c	51°26'N	6°16'E
Strahan, Austl. (strā´ăn)	219	42°08'S	145°28'E
Strakonice, Czech Rep. (strä´kô-nyė-tsĕ)	168	49°18'N	13°52'E
Straldzha, Blg. (sträl´dzhà)	175	42°37'N	26°44'E
Stralsund, Ger. (shträl´sŏnt)	160	54°18'N	13°04'E
Strangford Lough, l., N. Ire., U.K.	164	54°30'N	5°34'W
Strängnäs, Swe. (strĕng´nĕs)	166	59°23'N	16°59'E

ng-sing; ŋ-baŋk; ɴ-nasalized n; nŏd; cŏmmit; ōld; ȯbey; ôrder; oi-boil; fōōd; ŏŏ-as oo in foot; ou-out; s-soft; sh-dish; th-thin; pūre; ûnite; ûrn; stŭd; circŭs; ü-as in French tu; ´-indeterminate vowel.

ăt; finăl; rāte; senâte; ärm; àsk; sofà; fâre; ch-choose; dh-as th in other; bē; ĕvent; bĕt; recĕnt; cratẽr; g-gō; gh-guttural g; bĭt; ī-short neutral; rīde; κ-guttural k as ch in German ich;

PRONOUNCING INDEX

Swadlincote – Tamiahua 355

PLACE (Pronunciation)	PAGE	LAT.	LONG.
Swadlincote, Eng., U.K. (swŏd′lĭn-kōt)	158a	52°46′N	1°33′W
Swain Reefs, rf., Austl. (swān)	221	22°12′S	152°08′E
Swainsboro, Ga., U.S. (swānz′bŭr-ō)	125	32°37′N	82°21′W
Swakopmund, Nmb. (svä′kŏp-mŏŏnt) (swä′kŏp-mŏnd)	232	22°40′S	14°30′E
Swallowfield, Eng., U.K. (swŏl′ō-fēld)	158b	51°21′N	0°58′W
Swampscott, Ma., U.S. (swômp′skŏt)	101a	42°28′N	70°55′W
Swan, r., Austl.	220	31°30′S	116°30′E
Swan, r., Can.	97	51°58′N	101°45′W
Swan, r., Mt., U.S.	115	47°50′N	113°40′W
Swan Hill, Austl.	219	35°20′S	143°30′E
Swan Hills, Can. (hĭlz)	90	54°52′N	115°45′W
Swan Island, i., Austl. (swŏn)	217a	38°15′S	144°41′E
Swan Lake, l., Can.	97	52°30′N	100°45′W
Swanland, reg., Austl. (swŏn′lănd)	220	31°45′S	119°15′E
Swan Range, mts., Mt., U.S.	115	47°50′N	113°40′W
Swan River, Can. (swŏn rĭv′ẽr)	90	52°06′N	101°16′W
Swansea, Wales, U.K.	161	51°37′N	3°59′W
Swansea, Il., U.S. (swŏn′sē)	117e	38°32′N	89°59′W
Swansea, Ma., U.S.	110b	41°45′N	71°09′W
Swanson Reservoir, res., Ne., U.S. (swŏn′sŭn)	120	40°13′N	101°30′W
Swartberg, mtn., Afr.	233c	30°08′S	29°34′E
Swartkop, mtn., S. Afr.	232a	34°13′S	18°27′E
Swartruggens, S. Afr.	238c	25°40′S	26°40′E
Swartspruit, S. Afr.	233b	25°44′S	28°01′E
Swatow *see* Shantou, China	205	23°20′N	116°40′E
Swaziland, nation, Afr. (Swä′zē-lănd)	232	26°45′S	31°30′E
Sweden, nation, Eur. (swē′dĕn)	154	60°10′N	14°10′E
Swedesboro, N.J., U.S. (swēdz′bē-rô)	110f	39°45′N	75°22′W
Sweetwater, Tn., U.S. (swēt′wô-tẽr)	124	35°36′N	84°29′W
Sweetwater, Tx., U.S.	104	32°28′N	100°25′W
Sweetwater, l., N.D., U.S.	112	48°15′N	98°35′W
Sweetwater, r., Wy., U.S.	115	42°19′N	108°35′W
Sweetwater Reservoir, res., Ca., U.S.	118a	32°42′N	116°54′W
Świdnica, Pol. (shvĭd-nē′tsä)	168	50°50′N	16°30′E
Świdwin, Pol. (shvĭd′vĭn)	168	53°46′N	15°48′E
Świebodzice, Pol.	168	50°51′N	16°17′E
Świebodzin, Pol. (shvyĕn-bo′jĕts)	168	52°16′N	15°36′E
Świecie, Pol. (shvyăN′tsyĕ)	169	53°23′N	18°26′E
Świętokrzyskie, Góry, mts., Pol. (shvyĕN-tō-kzhĭ′skyĕ gōō′rĭ)	169	50°57′N	21°02′E
Swift, r., Eng., U.K.	158a	52°26′N	1°08′W
Swift, r., Me., U.S. (swĭft)	101	44°42′N	70°40′E
Swift Creek Reservoir, res., Wa., U.S.	114	46°03′N	122°10′W
Swift Current, Can. (swĭft kûr′ĕnt)	90	50°17′N	107°50′W
Swindle Island, i., Can.	94	52°32′N	128°35′W
Swindon, Eng., U.K. (swĭn′dŭn)	164	51°35′N	1°55′W
Swinomish Indian Reservation, I.R., Wa., U.S. (swĭ-nō′mĭsh)	116a	48°25′N	122°27′W
Świnoujście, Pol. (shvĭ-nĭ-ô-wēsh′chyĕ)	168	53°56′N	14°14′E
Swinton, Eng., U.K. (swĭn′tŭn)	158a	53°30′N	1°19′W
Swissvale, Pa., U.S. (swĭs′väl)	111e	40°25′N	79°53′W
Switzerland, nation, Eur. (swĭt′zẽr-lănd)	154	46°30′N	7°43′E
Syanno, Bela. (syĕ′nô)	176	54°48′N	29°43′E
Syas′, r., Russia (syäs)	176	59°28′N	33°24′E
Sycamore, Il., U.S. (sĭk′ȧ-mōr)	114	42°00′N	88°42′W
Sycan, r., Or., U.S.	114	42°45′N	121°00′W
Sychëvka, Russia (sē-chôf′kȧ)	176	55°52′N	34°18′E
Sydney, Austl. (sĭd′nē)	219	33°55′S	151°17′E
Sydney, Can.	91	46°09′N	60°11′W
Sydney Mines, Can.	91	46°14′N	60°14′W
Syktyvkar, Russia (sük-tüf′kär)	178	61°35′N	50°40′E
Sylacauga, Al., U.S. (sĭl-ȧ-kô′gȧ)	124	33°10′N	86°15′W
Sylarna, mtn., Eur.	166	63°00′N	12°10′E
Sylt, i., Ger. (sĭlt)	168	54°55′N	8°30′E
Sylvania, Ga., U.S. (sĭl-vā′nĭ-ȧ)	125	32°44′N	81°40′W
Sylvester, Ga., U.S. (sĭl-vĕs′tẽr)	124	31°32′N	83°50′W
Sými, i., Grc.	163	36°27′N	27°41′E
Synel′nykove, Ukr.	181	48°19′N	35°33′E
Syracuse, Ks., U.S. (sĭr′ȧ-kūs)	120	37°59′N	101°44′W
Syracuse, N.Y., U.S.	105	43°05′N	76°10′W
Syracuse, Ut., U.S.	117b	41°06′N	112°04′W
Syr Darya, r., Asia	178	44°15′N	65°45′E
Syria, nation, Asia (sĭr′ĭ-ȧ)	198	35°00′N	37°15′E
Syrian Desert, des., Asia	198	32°00′N	40°00′E
Sýros, i., Grc.	163	37°23′N	24°55′E
Sysert′, Russia (sē′sĕrt)	186a	56°30′N	60°48′E
Sysola, r., Russia	180	60°50′N	50°40′E
Syvash, zatoka, b., Ukr.	177	45°55′N	34°42′E
Syzran′, Russia (sĕz-rän′)	178	53°09′N	48°27′E
Szamotuły, Pol. (shȧ-mō-tōō′wē)	168	52°36′N	16°34′E
Szarvas, Hung. (sôr′vôsh)	169	46°51′N	20°36′E
Szczebrzeszyn, Pol. (shchě-bzhä′shěn)	169	50°41′N	22°58′E
Szczecin, Pol. (shchě′tsĭn)	154	53°25′N	14°35′E
Szczecinek, Pol. (shchě′tsĭ-nĕk)	160	53°41′N	16°42′E
Szczuczyn, Pol. (shchōō′chĕn)	169	53°32′N	22°17′E
Szczytno, Pol. (shchĭt′nô)	169	53°33′N	21°00′E
Szechwan Basin, basin, China	204	30°45′N	104°40′E
Szeged, Hung. (sĕ′gĕd)	154	46°15′N	20°12′E
Székesfehérvár, Hung. (sā′kĕsh-fĕ′hār-vär)	163	47°12′N	18°26′E
Szekszárd, Hung. (sĕk′särd)	163	46°19′N	18°42′E
Szentendre, Hung. (sĕnt′ĕn-drĕ)	169	47°40′N	19°07′E
Szentes, Hung. (sĕn′tĕsh)	169	46°38′N	20°18′E
Szigetvar, Hung. (sĕ′gĕt-vär)	169	46°05′N	17°50′E
Szolnok, Hung.	163	47°11′N	20°12′E
Szombathely, Hung. (sôm′bôt-hĕl′)	163	47°13′N	16°35′E
Szprotawa, Pol. (shprō-tä′vä)	168	51°34′N	15°29′E
Szydłowiec, Pol. (shĭd-wô′vyets)	169	51°13′N	20°53′E

T

PLACE (Pronunciation)	PAGE	LAT.	LONG.
Taal, l., Phil. (tä-äl′)	213a	13°58′N	121°06′E
Tabaco, Phil. (tä-bä′kō)	213a	13°27′N	123°40′E
Tabankulu, S. Afr. (tä-bän-kōō′la)	233c	30°56′S	29°19′E
Tabasará, Serranía de, mts., Pan.	133	8°29′N	81°22′W
Tabasco, Mex. (tä-bäs′kō)	130	21°47′N	103°04′W
Tabasco, state, Mex.	128	18°10′N	93°00′W
Taber, Can.	90	49°47′N	112°08′W
Tablas, i., Phil. (tä′bläs)	213a	12°26′N	122°00′E
Tablas Strait, strt., Phil.	213a	12°17′N	121°41′E
Table Bay, b., S. Afr. (tā′b′l)	232a	33°41′S	18°27′E
Table Mountain, mtn., S. Afr.	232a	33°58′S	18°26′E
Table Rock Lake, Mo., U.S.	121	36°37′N	93°29′W
Tabligbo, Togo	234	6°35′N	1°30′E
Taboga, i., Pan. (tä-bō′gä)	128a	8°48′N	79°35′W
Taboguilla, i., Pan. (tä-bô-gē′l-yä)	128a	8°48′N	79°31′W
Tábor, Czech Rep. (tä′bôr)	168	49°25′N	14°40′E
Tabora, Tan. (tä-bō′rä)	232	5°01′S	32°48′E
Tabou, C. Iv. (tȧ-bōō′)	230	4°25′N	7°21′W
Tabrīz, Iran (tȧ-brēz′)	198	38°00′N	46°13′E
Tabuaeran, i., Kir.	2	3°52′N	159°20′W
Tabwémasana, Mont, mtn., Vanuatu	214f	15°20′S	166°44′E
Tacámbaro, r., Mex. (tä-käm′bä-rō)	130	18°55′N	101°25′W
Tacámbaro de Codallos, Mex.	130	19°12′N	101°28′W
Tacarigua, Laguna de la, l., Ven.	143b	10°18′N	65°43′W
Tacheng, China (tä-chŭŋ)	204	46°50′N	83°24′E
Tachie, r., Can.	94	54°30′N	125°00′W
Tacloban, Phil. (tä-klō′bän)	213	11°06′N	124°58′E
Tacna, Peru (täk′nä)	142	18°34′S	70°16′W
Tacoma, Wa., U.S. (tȧ-kō′mȧ)	104	47°14′N	122°27′W
Taconic Range, mts., N.Y., U.S. (tȧ-kŏn′ĭk)	109	41°55′N	73°40′W
Tacotalpa, Mex. (tä-kô-täl′pä)	131	17°37′N	92°51′W
Tacotalpa, r., Mex.	131	17°24′N	92°38′W
Tademaït, Plateau du, plat., Alg. (tä-dē-mä′ēt)	230	28°00′N	2°15′E
Tadio, Lagune, b., C. Iv.	234	5°20′N	5°25′W
Tadjoura, Dji. (tȧd-zhōō′rȧ)	238a	11°48′N	42°54′E
Tadley, Eng., U.K. (tăd′lē)	158b	51°19′N	1°08′W
Tadotsu, Japan (tä′dō-tsō)	211	34°14′N	133°43′E
Tadoussac, Can. (tȧ-dōō-sȧk′)	99	48°09′N	69°43′W
Tadzhikistan *see* Tajikistan, nation, Asia	178	39°22′N	69°30′E
Taebaek Sanmaek, mts., Asia (tī-bĭk′ sän-mĭk′)	210	37°20′N	128°50′E
Taedong, r., Kor., N. (tī-dŏng)	210	38°38′N	124°32′E
Taegu, Kor., S. (tī′gōō′)	205	35°49′N	128°41′E
Taejŏn, Kor., S.	210	36°20′N	127°26′E
Tafalla, Spain (tä-fäl′yä)	172	42°30′N	1°42′W
Tafna, r., Alg. (täf′nä)	172	35°28′N	1°00′W
Taft, Ca., U.S. (tȧft)	118	35°09′N	119°27′W
Tagama, reg., Niger	235	15°50′N	6°30′E
Taganrog, Russia (tȧ-gȧn-rôk′)	181	47°12′N	38°56′E
Taganrogskiy Zaliv, b., Eur. (tȧ-gȧn-rôk′skĭ zä′lĭf)	181	46°55′N	38°17′E
Tagula, i., Pap. N. Gui. (tä′gōō-lȧ)	221	11°45′S	153°46′E
Tagus (Tajo), r., Eur. (tā′gŭs)	156	39°40′N	5°07′W
Tahan, Gunong, mtn., Malay.	212	4°33′N	101°52′E
Tahat, mtn., Alg. (tä-hät′)	230	23°22′N	5°21′E
Tahiti, i., Fr. Poly. (tä-hē′tē) (tä′ē-tē′)	2	17°30′S	149°30′W
Tahkuna Nina, c., Est. (tȧh-kōō′nȧ nē′nȧ)	167	59°08′N	22°03′E
Tahlequah, Ok., U.S. (tă-lĕ-kwä′)	121	35°54′N	94°58′W
Tahoe, l., U.S. (tä′hō)	106	39°09′N	120°18′W
Tahoua, Niger (tä′ōō-ä)	230	14°54′N	5°16′E
Tahtsa Lake, l., Can.	94	53°33′N	127°47′W
Tahuya, Wa., U.S. (tȧ-hū-yă′)	116a	47°23′N	123°03′W
Tahuya, r., Wa., U.S.	116a	47°28′N	122°55′W
Tai′an, China (tī-äŋ)	208	36°13′N	117°08′E
Taibai Shan, mtn., China (tī-bī shän)	208	33°42′N	107°25′E
Taibus Qi, China (tī-bōō-sz chyē)	208	41°52′N	115°25′E
Taicang, China (tī-tsäŋ)	206	31°26′N	121°06′E
T′aichung, Tai. (tī′chŏng)	205	24°10′N	120°42′E
Tai′erzhuang, China (tī-är-jůäŋ)	206	34°34′N	117°44′E
Taigu, China (tī-gōō)	208	37°25′N	112°35′E
Taihang Shan, mts., China (tī-häŋ shän)	208	35°45′N	112°00′E
Taihe, China (tī-hŭ)	206	33°10′N	115°38′E
Tai Hu, l., China (tī hōō)	205	31°13′N	120°00′E
Tailagoin, reg., Mong. (tī′lȧ-gän′ kä′rä)	204	43°39′N	105°54′E
Tailai, China (tī-lī)	208	46°20′N	123°10′E
Tailem Bend, Austl. (tā-lĕm)	222	35°15′S	139°30′E
T′ainan, Tai. (tī′nan′)	205	23°08′N	120°18′E
Taínaro, c., Grc.	162	37°45′N	22°00′E
Taining, China (tī′nĭng′)	209	26°58′N	117°15′E
T′aipei, Tai. (tī′pā′)	205	25°02′N	121°38′E
Taiping, pt. of i., Malay.	212	4°56′N	100°39′E
Taiping Ling, mtn., China	208	47°03′N	120°30′E
Taisha, Japan (tī′shä)	211	35°23′N	132°40′E
Taishan, China (tī-shän)	209	22°15′N	112°50′E
Tai Shan, mts., China (tī shän)	208	36°16′N	117°05′E
Taitao, Península de, pen., Chile	144	46°20′S	77°15′W
T′aitung, Tai. (tī′tōōng′)	209	22°45′N	121°02′E
Taiwan, nation, Asia (tī-wän) (fŏr-mō′sȧ)	205	23°30′N	122°20′E
Taiwan Strait, strt., Asia	205	24°30′N	120°00′E
Taixian, China (tī shyĕn)	206	32°31′N	119°54′E
Taixing, China (tī-shyĭŋ)	206	32°12′N	119°58′E
Taiyuan, China (tī-yůän)	205	37°32′N	112°38′E
Taizhou, China (tī-jō)	206	32°23′N	119°41′E
Ta′Izz, Yemen	201	13°38′N	44°04′E
Tajano de Morais, Braz. (tĕ-zhä′nô-dĕ-mô-rä′ēs)	141a	22°05′S	42°04′W
Tajikistan, nation, Asia	178	39°22′N	69°30′E
Tajumulco, vol., Guat. (tä-hōō-mōōl′kō)	132	15°03′N	91°53′W
Tajuña, r., Spain (tä-kōō′n-yä)	172	40°23′N	2°36′W
Tājūrā′, Libya	162	32°56′N	13°24′W
Tak, Thai.	212	16°57′N	99°12′E
Taka, i., Japan (tä′kä)	211	30°47′N	130°23′E
Takada, Japan (tä′kȧ-dä)	210	37°08′N	138°30′E
Takahashi, Japan (tä′kä′hä-shĭ)	211	34°47′N	133°35′E
Takaishi, Japan	211b	34°32′N	135°27′E
Takamatsu, Japan (tä′kä′mä-tsōō′)	205	34°20′N	134°02′E
Takamori, Japan (tä′kä′mô-rē′)	211	32°50′N	131°08′E
Takaoka, Japan (ta′kä′ô-kä′)	210	36°45′N	136°59′E
Takapuna, N.Z.	223	36°48′S	174°47′E
Takarazuka, Japan (tä′kä-rä-zōō′kä)	211b	34°48′N	135°22′E
Takasaki, Japan (tä′kät′sōō-kē′)	210	36°20′N	139°00′E
Takatsu, Japan (tä-kät′sōō) (mĕ′zō-nô-kô′chĕ)	211a	35°36′N	139°37′E
Takatsuki, Japan (tä′kät′sōō-kē′)	211b	34°51′N	135°38′E
Takayama, Japan (tä′kä′yä′mä)	211	36°11′N	137°16′E
Takefu, Japan (tä′kĕ-fōō)	210	35°57′N	136°09′E
Take-shima, is., Asia	210	37°15′N	131°51′E
Takla Lake, l., Can.	92	55°25′N	125°53′W
Takla Makan, des., China (mä-kȧn′)	204	39°22′N	82°34′E
Takoma Park, Md., U.S. (tă′kōmȧ pärk)	110e	38°59′N	77°00′W
Takum, Nig.	235	7°17′N	9°59′E
Tala, Mex. (tä′lä)	130	20°39′N	103°42′W
Talagante, Chile (tä-lä-gá′n-tĕ)	141b	33°39′S	70°54′W
Talamanca, Cordillera de, mts., C.R.	133	9°37′N	83°55′W
Talanga, Hond. (tä-lä′n-gä)	132	14°21′N	87°09′W
Talara, Peru (tä-lä′rä)	142	4°32′S	81°17′W
Talasea, Pap. N. Gui. (tä-lä-sā′ä)	213	5°20′S	150°00′E
Talata Mafara, Nig.	235	12°35′N	6°04′E
Talaud, Kepulauan, is., Indon. (tä-lout′)	213	4°17′N	127°30′E
Talavera de la Reina, Spain	162	39°58′N	4°51′W
Talca, Chile (täl′kä)	144	35°25′S	71°39′W
Talca, prov., Chile	141b	35°23′S	71°15′W
Talca, Punta, c., Chile (pōō′n-tä-täl′kä)	141b	33°25′S	71°42′W
Talcahuano, Chile (täl-kä-wä′nō)	144	36°41′S	73°05′W
Taldom, Russia (täl-dŏm)	176	56°44′N	37°33′E
Taldyqorghan, Kaz.	183	45°03′N	77°18′E
Talea de Castro, Mex. (tä′lå-ä dä käs′trō)	131	17°22′N	96°14′W
Talibu, Pulau, i., Indon.	213	1°30′S	125°00′E
Talim, i., Phil. (tä-lēm′)	213a	14°21′N	121°14′E
Talisay, Phil. (tä-lē′sī)	213a	14°08′N	122°56′E
Talkeetna, Ak., U.S. (täl-kēt′nȧ)	103	62°18′N	150°02′W
Talladega, Al., U.S. (tăl-ȧ-dē′gȧ)	124	33°25′N	86°06′W
Tallahassee, Fl., U.S. (tăl-ȧ-hăs′ē)	105	30°25′N	84°17′W
Tallahatchie, r., Ms., U.S. (tal-ȧ hăch′ē)	124	34°21′N	90°03′W
Tallapoosa, Ga., U.S. (tăl-ȧ-pōō′sȧ)	124	33°44′N	85°15′W
Tallapoosa, r., Al., U.S.	124	32°22′N	86°08′W
Tallassee, Al., U.S. (tăl′ȧ-sē)	124	32°30′N	85°54′W
Tallinn, Est. (tȧl′lĕn) (rĕ′väl)	178	59°26′N	24°44′E
Tallmadge, Oh., U.S. (tăl′mĭj)	111d	41°06′N	81°26′W
Tallulah, La., U.S. (tă-lōō′lȧ)	123	32°25′N	91°13′W
Tal′ne, Ukr.	177	48°52′N	30°43′E
Talo, mtn., Eth.	231	10°45′N	37°55′E
Taloje Budrukh, India	203b	19°05′N	73°05′E
Talpa de Allende, Mex. (täl′pä dā äl-yĕn′dȧ)	130	20°25′N	104°48′W
Talquin, Lake, res., Fl., U.S.	124	30°26′N	84°33′W
Talsi, Lat. (tal′sĭ)	167	57°16′N	22°35′E
Taltal, Chile (täl-täl′)	144	25°26′S	70°32′W
Taly, Russia (täl′ĭ)	177	49°51′N	40°07′E
Tama, Ia., U.S. (tā′mä)	113	41°57′N	92°36′W
Tama, r., Japan	211a	35°38′N	139°35′E
Tamale, Ghana (tä-mä′lȧ)	230	9°25′N	0°50′W
Taman′, Russia (tȧ-män′′)	177	45°13′N	36°46′E
Tamanaco, r., Ven. (tä-mä-nä′kō)	143b	9°32′N	66°00′W
Tamaqua, Pa., U.S. (tȧ-mô′kwȧ)	109	40°45′N	75°50′W
Tamar, r., Eng., U.K. (tā′mär)	164	50°35′N	4°15′W
Tamarite de Litera, Spain (tä-mä-rē′tä)	173	41°52′N	0°24′E
Tamaulipas, state, Mex. (tä-mä-ōō-lē′päs′)	128	23°45′N	98°30′W
Tamazula de Gordiano, Mex.	130	19°44′N	103°09′W
Tamazulapan del Progreso, Mex.	131	17°41′N	97°34′W
Tamazunchale, Mex. (tä-mä-zōn-chä′lå)	130	21°16′N	98°46′W
Tambacounda, Sen. (täm-bä-kōōn′dä)	230	13°47′N	13°40′W
Tambador, Serra do, mts., Braz. (sĕ′r-rä-dô-täm′bä-dōr)	143	10°33′S	41°16′W
Tambelan, Kepulauan, is., Indon. (täm-bå-län′)	212	0°38′N	107°38′E
Tambo, Austl. (tăm′bō)	219	24°50′S	146°15′E
Tambov, Russia (tăm-bôf′)	178	52°45′N	41°10′E
Tambov, prov., Russia	176	52°50′N	40°42′E
Tambre, r., Spain (täm′brā)	172	42°59′N	8°33′W
Tambura, Sudan (täm-bōō′rä)	231	5°34′N	27°30′E
Tame, r., Eng., U.K. (tām)	158a	52°41′N	1°42′W
Tâmega, r., Port. (tȧ-mā′gȧ)	172	41°30′N	7°45′W
Tamenghest, Alg.	230	22°34′N	5°34′E
Tamenghest, Oued, r., Alg.	230	22°15′N	2°51′E
Tamgak, Monts, mtn., Niger (tam-gäk′)	230	18°40′N	8°40′E
Tamgué, Massif du, mtn., Gui.	230	12°15′N	12°35′W
Tamiahua, Mex. (tä-myä-wä)	131	21°17′N	97°26′W

ng-sing; ŋ-baŋk; N-nasalized n; nŏd; cŏmmit; ōld; ôbey; ôrder; oi-boil; fōōd; ŏŏ-as oo in foot; ou-out; s-soft; sh-dish; th-thin; pūre; ûnite; ûrn; stŭd; circŭs; ü-as in French tu; ′-indeterminate vowel.

356 Tamiahua – Temoaya PRONOUNCING INDEX

PLACE (Pronunciation)	PAGE	LAT.	LONG.
Tamiahua, Laguna, l., Mex. (lä-gō´nä-tä-myä-wä)	131	21°38'N	97°33'W
Tamiami Canal, can., Fl., U.S. (tă-mī-ăm´ĭ)	125a	25°52'N	80°08'W
Tamil Nadu, state, India	199	11°30'N	78°00'E
Tampa, Fl., U.S. (tăm´pȧ)	105	27°57'N	82°25'W
Tampa Bay, b., Fl., U.S.	107	27°35'N	82°38'W
Tampere, Fin. (tȧm´pĕ-rĕ)	160	61°21'N	23°39'E
Tampico, Mex. (täm-pē´kō)	128	22°14'N	97°51'W
Tampico Alto, Mex. (täm-pē´kō äl´tō)	131	22°07'N	97°48'W
Tampin, Malay.	197b	2°28'N	102°15'E
Tam Quan, Viet.	209	14°20'N	109°10'E
Tamuín, Mex. (tä-mōō-ē´n)	130	22°04'N	98°47'W
Tamworth, Austl. (tăm´wûrth)	219	31°01'S	151°00'E
Tamworth, Eng., U.K.	158a	52°38'N	1°41'W
Tana, i., Vanuatu	221	19°32'S	169°27'E
[illegible]	[illegible]	[illegible]	[illegible]
Tanabe, Japan (tä-nä´bā)	210	33°45'N	135°21'E
Tanabe, Japan	211b	34°49'N	135°46'E
Tanacross, Ak., U.S. (tă´nȧ-crōs)	103	63°20'N	143°30'W
Tanaga, i., Ak., U.S. (tä-nä´gä)	103a	51°28'N	178°10'W
Tanahbala, Pulau, i., Indon. (tȧ-nä-bä´lä)	212	0°30'S	98°22'E
Tanahmasa, Pulau, i., Indon. (tȧ-nä-mä´sä)	212	0°03'S	97°30'E
Tanakpur, India (tăn´ăk-pŏor)	202	29°10'N	80°07'E
Tana Lake, l., Eth.	231	12°09'N	36°41'E
Tanami, Austl. (tȧ-nä´mē)	218	19°45'S	129°50'E
Tanana, Ak., U.S. (tă´nȧ-nô)	103	65°18'N	152°20'W
Tanana, r., Ak., U.S.	103	64°26'N	148°40'W
Tanaro, r., Italy (tä-nä´rô)	174	44°45'N	8°02'E
Tanashi, Japan	211a	35°44'N	139°34'E
Tanbu, China (tän-bōō)	207a	23°20'N	113°06'E
Tancheng, China (tän-chŭŋ)	208	34°37'N	118°22'E
Tanchŏn, Kor., N. (tän´chŭn)	210	40°29'N	128°50'E
Tancítaro, Mex. (tän-sē´tä-rō)	130	19°16'N	102°24'W
Tancítaro, Cerro de, mtn., Mex. (sĕ´r-rô-dĕ)	130	19°24'N	102°19'W
Tancoco, Mex. (tän-kō´kō)	131	21°16'N	97°45'W
Tandil, Arg. (tän-dēl´)	144	36°16'S	59°01'W
Tandil, Sierra del, mts., Arg.	144	38°40'S	59°40'W
Tanega, i., Japan (tä´nȧ-gä´)	205	30°36'N	131°11'E
Tanezrouft, reg., Alg. (tä´nĕz-rōft)	230	24°17'N	0°30'W
Tang, r., China (täŋ)	206	33°38'N	117°29'E
Tang, r., China	206	39°13'N	114°45'E
Tanga, Tan. (täŋ´gȧ)	233	5°04'S	39°06'E
Tangancícuaro, Mex. (täŋ-gän-sē´kwa-rô)	130	19°52'N	102°13'W
Tanganyika, Lake, l., Afr.	232	5°15'S	29°40'E
Tanger, Mor. (tăn-jĕr´)	230	35°52'N	5°55'W
Tangermünde, Ger. (täŋ´ĕr-mün´de)	168	52°33'N	11°58'E
Tanggu, China (täŋ-gōō)	206	39°04'N	117°41'E
Tanggula Shan, mts., China (täŋ-gōō-lä shän)	204	33°15'N	89°07'E
Tanghe, China	208	32°40'N	112°50'E
Tangier *see* Tanger, Mor.	230	35°52'N	5°55'W
Tangipahoa, r., La., U.S. (tăn´jē-pȧ-hō´ȧ)	123	30°48'N	90°28'W
Tangra Yumco, l., China (täŋ-rä yōōm-tswo)	202	30°50'N	85°40'E
T'angshan, China	208	39°38'N	118°11'E
Tangxian, China (täŋ shyĕn)	206	38°49'N	115°00'E
Tangzha, China (täŋ-jä)	206	32°06'N	120°48'E
Tanimbar, Kepulauan, is., Indon.	213	8°00'S	132°00'E
Tanjong Piai, c., Malay.	197b	1°16'N	103°11'E
Tanjong Ramunia, c., Malay.	197b	1°27'N	104°44'E
Tanjungbalai, Indon. (tän´jông-bä´lȧ)	197b	1°00'N	103°26'E
Tanjungpandan, Indon.	212	2°47'S	107°51'E
Tanjungpinang, Indon. (tän´jŏng-pē´näng)	197b	0°55'N	104°29'E
Tannu-Ola, mts., Asia	179	51°00'N	94°00'E
Tannūrah, Ra's at, c., Sau. Ar.	198	26°45'N	49°59'E
Tano, r., Afr.	234	5°40'N	2°30'W
Tanquijo, Arrecife, i., Mex. (är-rĕ-sē´fĕ-tän-kē´kô)	131	21°07'N	97°16'W
Ţanţā, Egypt	231	30°47'N	31°00'E
Tantoyuca, Mex. (tän-tō-yōō´kä)	130	21°22'N	98°13'W
Tanyang, Kor., S.	210	36°53'N	128°20'E
Tanzania, nation, Afr.	232	6°48'S	33°58'E
Tao, r., China (tou)	208	35°30'N	103°40'E
Tao'an, China (tou-än)	205	45°15'N	122°45'E
Tao'er, r., China (tou-är)	205	45°40'N	122°00'E
Taormina, Italy (tä-ôr-mē´nä)	174	37°53'N	15°18'E
Taos, N.M., U.S. (tä´ôs)	119	36°25'N	105°35'W
Taoudenni, Mali (tä´ōō-dĕ-nē´)	230	22°57'N	3°37'W
Taoussa, Mali	234	16°55'N	0°35'W
Taoyuan, China (tou-yüän)	209	29°00'N	111°15'E
Tapa, Est. (tȧ´pȧ)	167	59°16'N	25°56'E
Tapachula, Mex.	132	14°55'N	92°20'W
Tapajós, r., Braz. (tä-pä-zhô´s)	143	3°27'S	55°33'W
Tapalque, Arg. (tä-päl-kĕ´)	141c	36°22'S	60°05'W
Tapanatepec, Mex. (tä-pä-nä-tĕ-pĕk)	131	16°22'N	94°19'W
Tāpi, r., India	199	21°00'N	76°30'E
Tappi Saki, c., Japan (täp´pē sä´kē)	210	41°05'N	139°40'E
Tapps, l., Wa., U.S. (tăpz)	116a	47°20'N	122°12'W
Taquara, Serra de, mts., Braz. (sĕ´r-rä-dĕ-tä-kwä´rä)	143	15°28'S	54°33'W
Taquari, r., Braz. (tä-kwä´rĭ)	143	18°35'S	56°50'W
Tar, r., N.C., U.S. (tär)	125	35°58'N	78°06'W
Tara, Russia (tä´rȧ)	178	56°58'N	74°13'E
Tara, i., Phil. (tä´rä)	213a	12°18'N	120°28'E
Tara, r., Russia (tä´rȧ)	184	56°32'N	76°13'E
Ţarābulus, Leb. (tȧ-rä´bŏ-lōōs)	198	34°25'N	35°50'E
Ţarābulus (Tripolitania), hist. reg., Libya	230	31°00'N	12°26'E

PLACE (Pronunciation)	PAGE	LAT.	LONG.
Tarakan, Indon.	212	3°17'N	118°04'E
Taranaki, Mount, vol., N.Z.	223	39°18'S	174°04'E
Tarancón, Spain (tä-rän-kōn´)	172	40°01'N	3°00'W
Taranto, Italy (tä´rän-tô)	163	40°30'N	17°15'E
Taranto, Golfo di, b., Italy (gôl-fō-dē tä´rän-tô)	156	40°03'N	17°10'E
Tarapoto, Peru (tä-rä-pô´tō)	142	6°29'S	76°26'W
Tarare, Fr. (tȧ-rär´)	170	45°55'N	4°23'E
Tarascon, Fr. (tȧ-rȧs-kôɴ´)	170	42°53'N	1°35'E
Tarascon, Fr. (tä-räs-kôɴ)	170	43°47'N	4°41'E
Tarashcha, Ukr. (tä´rȧsh-chȧ)	177	49°34'N	30°52'E
Tarata, Bol. (tä-rä´tä)	142	17°43'S	66°00'W
Taravo, r., Fr.	174	41°54'N	8°58'E
Tarazit, Massif de, mts., Niger	235	20°00'N	7°00'E
Tarazona, Spain (tä-rä-thō´nä)	172	41°54'N	1°45'W
Tarazona de la Mancha, Spain (tä-rä-zô´nä dĕ lä män´chä)	172	39°13'N	1°50'W
Tarbes, Fr. (tärb)	161	[illegible]	[illegible]
Tarboro, N.C., U.S. (tär´bŭr-ô)	125	35°53'N	77°34'W
Taree, Austl. (tă-rē´)	222	31°52'S	152°21'E
Tarentum, Pa., U.S. (tȧ-rĕn´tŭm)	111e	40°36'N	79°44'W
Tarfa, Wādī at, val., Egypt	238b	28°14'N	31°00'E
Târgovişte, Rom.	163	44°54'N	25°29'E
Târgu Jiu, Rom.	163	45°02'N	23°17'E
Târgu Mureş, Rom.	163	46°33'N	24°33'E
Târgu Neamţ, Rom.	169	47°14'N	26°23'E
Târgu Ocna, Rom.	169	46°18'N	26°38'E
Târgu Secuiesc, Rom.	169	46°04'N	26°06'E
Tarhūnah, Libya	200	32°26'N	13°38'E
Tarija, Bol. (tär-rē´hä)	142	21°42'S	64°52'W
Tarīm, Yemen (tȧ-rĭm´)	198	16°13'N	49°08'E
Tarim, r., China (tȧ-rĭm´)	204	40°45'N	85°39'E
Tarim Basin, basin, China (tȧ-rĭm´)	204	39°52'N	82°34'E
Tarka, r., S. Afr. (tä´kȧ)	233c	32°15'S	26°00'E
Tarkastad, S. Afr.	233c	32°01'S	26°18'E
Tarkhankut, Mys, c., Ukr. (mĭs tȧr-kän´kŏt)	181	45°21'N	32°30'E
Tarkio, Mo., U.S. (tär´kĭ-ō)	121	40°27'N	95°22'W
Tarkwa, Ghana (tärk´wä)	230	5°19'N	1°59'W
Tarlac, Phil. (tär´läk)	212	15°29'N	120°36'E
Tarlton, S. Afr. (tärl´tŭn)	233b	26°05'S	27°38'E
Tarma, Peru (tär´mä)	142	11°26'S	75°40'W
Tarn, r., Fr. (tärn)	161	43°45'N	2°00'E
Târnăveni, Rom.	169	46°19'N	24°18'E
Tarnów, Pol. (tär´nôf)	161	50°02'N	21°00'E
Taro, r., Italy (tä´rō)	174	44°41'N	10°03'E
Taroudant, Mor. (tȧ-rōō-dänt´)	230	30°39'N	8°52'W
Tarpon Springs, Fl., U.S. (tär´pŏn)	125a	28°07'N	82°44'W
Tarporley, Eng., U.K. (tär´pēr-lē)	158a	53°09'N	2°40'W
Tarpum Bay, b., Bah. (tär´pŭm)	134	25°05'N	76°20'W
Tarquinia, Italy (tär-kwē´nē-ä)	174	42°16'N	11°46'E
Tarragona, Spain (tär-rä-gō´nä)	154	41°05'N	1°15'E
Tarrant, Al., U.S. (tăr´ănt)	110h	33°35'N	86°46'W
Tárrega, Spain (tä rȧ-gä)	173	41°40'N	1°09'E
Tarrejón de Ardoz, Spain (tär-rĕ-kô´n-dĕ-är-dôz)	173a	40°28'N	3°29'W
Tarrytown, N.Y., U.S. (tăr´ĭ-toun)	110a	41°04'N	73°52'W
Tarsus, Tur. (tär´sŏŏs) (tär´sŭs)	198	37°00'N	34°50'E
Tartagal, Arg. (tär-tä-gȧ´l)	144	23°31'S	63°47'W
Tartu, Est. (tär´tōō) (dôr´pät)	178	58°23'N	26°44'E
Ţarţūs, Syria	200	34°54'N	35°59'E
Tarumi, Japan (tä´rōō-mē)	211b	34°38'N	135°04'E
Tarusa, Russia (tä-rōōs´ȧ)	176	54°43'N	37°11'E
Tarzana, Ca., U.S. (tär-ză´ȧ)	117a	34°10'N	118°32'W
Tashkent, Uzb. (tȧsh´kĕnt)	183	41°23'N	69°04'E
Tasman Bay, b., N.Z. (tăz´măn)	221a	40°50'S	173°20'E
Tasmania, state, Austl.	219	41°28'S	142°30'E
Tasman Peninsula, pen., Austl.	222	43°00'S	148°30'E
Tasman Sea, sea, Oc.	241	29°30'S	155°00'E
Tasquillo, Mex. (täs-kē´lyō)	130	20°34'N	99°21'W
Tatarsk, Russia (tȧ-tärsk´)	178	55°13'N	75°58'E
Tatarstan, prov., Russia	180	55°00'N	51°00'E
Tatar Strait, strt., Russia	179	51°00'N	141°45'E
Tater Hill, mtn., Or., U.S. (tāt´ẽr hĭl)	116c	45°47'N	123°02'W
Tateyama, Japan (tä´tē-yä´mä)	211	35°04'N	139°52'E
Tatlow, Mount, mtn., Can.	94	51°23'N	123°52'W
Tau, Nor.	166	59°05'N	5°59'E
Tauern Tunnel, trans., Aus.	168	47°12'N	13°17'E
Taung, S. Afr. (tä´ông)	232	27°25'S	24°47'E
Taunton, Ma., U.S. (tän´tŭn)	109	41°54'N	71°03'W
Taunton, r., R.I., U.S.	110b	41°50'N	71°02'W
Taupo, Lake, l., N.Z. (tä´ōō-pō)	221a	38°42'S	175°55'E
Taurage, Lith. (tou´rȧ-gā)	167	55°15'N	22°18'E
Taurus Mountains *see* Toros Dağları, mts., Tur.	198	37°00'N	32°40'E
Tauste, Spain (tä-ōōs´tå)	172	41°55'N	1°15'W
Tavda, Russia (tȧv-dá´)	178	58°00'N	64°44'E
Tavda, r., Russia	184	58°30'N	64°15'E
Taverny, Fr. (tȧ-vĕr-nē´)	171b	49°02'N	2°13'E
Taviche, Mex. (tä-vē´chĕ)	131	16°43'N	96°35'W
Tavira, Port. (tä-vē´rȧ)	172	37°09'N	7°42'W
Tavşanlı, Tur. (täv´shän-lĭ)	181	39°30'N	29°30'E
Tawakoni, l., Tx., U.S.	123	32°51'N	95°59'W
Tawaramoto, Japan (tä´wä-rä-mô-tō)	211b	34°33'N	135°48'E
Tawas City, Mi., U.S.	108	44°15'N	83°30'W
Tawas Point, c., Mi., U.S. (tô´wăs)	108	44°15'N	83°25'W
Tawitawi Group, is., Phil. (tä´wē-tä´wē)	212	4°52'N	120°35'E
Tawkar, Sudan	231	18°28'N	37°46'E
Taxco de Alarcón, Mex. (täs´kō dĕ ä-lär-kō´n)	130	18°34'N	99°37'W
Tay, r., Scot., U.K.	164	56°35'N	3°37'W
Tay, Loch, l., Scot., U.K.	164	56°25'N	4°07'W
Tayabas Bay, b., Phil. (tä-yä´bäs)	213a	13°44'N	121°40'E
Tayga, Russia (tī´gä)	184	56°12'N	85°47'E

PLACE (Pronunciation)	PAGE	LAT.	LONG.
Taygonos, Mys, c., Russia	179	60°37'N	160°17'E
Taylor, Tx., U.S.	123	30°35'N	97°25'W
Taylor, Mount, mtn., N.M., U.S.	106	35°20'N	107°40'W
Taylorville, Il., U.S. (tā´lẽr-vĭl)	108	39°30'N	89°20'W
Taymyr, l., Russia (tī-mĭr´)	179	74°13'N	100°45'E
Taymyr, Poluostrov, pen., Russia	179	75°15'N	95°00'E
Tayshet, Russia (tī-shĕt´)	179	56°09'N	97°49'E
Tayug, Phil.	213a	16°01'N	120°45'E
Taz, r., Russia (tȧz)	184	67°15'N	80°45'E
Taza, Mor. (tä´zä)	230	34°08'N	4°00'W
Tazovskoye, Russia	178	66°58'N	78°28'E
Tbessa, Alg.	230	35°27'N	8°13'E
Tbilisi, Geor. ('tbĭl-yē´sē)	181	41°40'N	44°45'E
[illegible], l., Can.	94	55°11'N	125°00'W
Tchibanga, Gabon (chē-bäŋ´gä)	232	2°51'S	11°02'E
Tchien, Lib.	234	6°04'N	8°08'W
Tchigai, Plateau du, plat., Afr.	235	21°20'N	14°50'E
[illegible]	[illegible]	[illegible]	[illegible]
Teabo, Mex. (tĕ-ä´bô)	132a	20°25'N	89°14'W
Teague, Tx., U.S.	123	31°39'N	96°16'W
Teapa, Mex. (tā-ä´pä)	131	17°35'N	92°56'W
Tebing Tinggi, i., Indon. (teb´ĭng-tĭng´gä)	197b	0°54'N	102°39'E
Tecalitlán, Mex. (tā-kä-lē-tlän´)	130	19°28'N	103°17'W
Techiman, Ghana	234	7°35'N	1°56'W
Tecoanapa, Mex. (tāk-wä-nä-pä´)	130	16°33'N	98°46'W
Tecoh, Mex. (tĕ-kô)	132a	20°46'N	89°27'W
Tecolotlán, Mex. (tā-kô-lô-tlän´)	130	20°13'N	103°57'W
Tecolutla, Mex. (tā-kô-lōō´tlä)	131	20°33'N	97°00'W
Tecolutla, r., Mex.	131	20°16'N	97°14'W
Tecomán, Mex. (tā-kô-män´)	130	18°53'N	103°53'W
Tecómitl, Mex. (tĕ-kō´mētl)	131a	19°13'N	98°59'W
Tecozautla, Mex. (tā´kô-zä-ōō´tlä)	130	20°33'N	99°38'W
Tecpan de Galeana, Mex. (tĕk-pän´ dā gä-lā-ä´nä)	130	17°13'N	100°41'W
Tecpatán, Mex. (tĕk-pä-tá´n)	131	17°08'N	93°18'W
Tecuala, Mex. (tĕ-kwä-lä)	130	22°24'N	105°29'W
Tecuci, Rom. (tȧ-kōōch')	163	45°51'N	27°30'E
Tecumseh, Can. (tē-kŭm´sĕ)	111b	42°19'N	82°53'W
Tecumseh, Mi., U.S.	108	42°00'N	84°00'W
Tecumseh, Ne., U.S.	121	40°21'N	96°09'W
Tecumseh, Ok., U.S.	121	35°18'N	96°55'W
Tees, r., Eng., U.K. (tēz)	164	54°40'N	2°10'W
Teganuna, l., Japan (tā´gä-nōō´nä)	211a	35°50'N	140°02'E
Tegucigalpa, Hond. (tā-gōō-sē-gäl´pä)	128	14°08'N	87°15'W
Tehachapi Mountains, mts., Ca., U.S. (tē-hă-shă´pĭ)	118	34°50'N	118°55'W
Tehrān, Iran (tĕ-hrän´)	198	35°45'N	51°30'E
Tehuacan, Mex. (tā-wä-kän´)	128	18°27'N	97°23'W
Tehuantepec, Mex.	128	16°20'N	95°14'W
Tehuantepec, r., Mex.	131	16°30'N	95°23'W
Tehuantepec, Golfo de, b., Mex. (gôl-fô dĕ)	128	15°45'N	95°00'W
Tehuantepec, Istmo de, isth., Mex. (ē´st-mô dĕ)	131	17°55'N	94°35'W
Tehuehuetla, Arroyo, r., Mex. (tĕ-wĕ-wĕ´tlä ăr-rô-yô)	130	17°54'N	100°26'W
Tehuitzingo, Mex. (tā-wē-tzĭŋ´gō)	130	18°21'N	98°16'W
Tejeda, Sierra de, mts., Spain (sē-ĕ´r-rä dĕ tĕ-kĕ´dä)	172	36°55'N	4°00'W
Tejúpan, Mex. (tĕ-κōō-pä´n) (sän-tyá´gô)	131	17°39'N	97°34'W
Tejúpan, Punta, c., Mex.	130	18°19'N	103°30'W
Tejupilco de Hidalgo, Mex. (tȧ-hōō-pēl´kō dā ē-dhäl´gō)	130	18°52'N	100°07'W
Tekamah, Ne., U.S. (tē-kā´mȧ)	112	41°46'N	96°13'W
Tekax de Alvaro Obregon, Mex.	132a	20°12'N	89°11'W
Tekeze, r., Afr.	231	13°38'N	38°00'E
Tekit, Mex. (tĕ-kē´t)	132a	20°35'N	89°18'W
Tekoa, Wa., U.S. (tē-kō´ȧ)	114	47°15'N	117°03'W
Tela, Hond. (tā´lä)	128	15°45'N	87°25'W
Tela, Bahía de, b., Hond.	132	15°53'N	87°29'W
Telapa Burok, Gunong, mtn., Malay.	197b	2°51'N	102°04'E
Telavi, Geor.	181	42°00'N	45°20'E
Tel Aviv-Yafo, Isr. (tĕl-ä-vēv´já´fá)	198	32°03'N	34°46'E
Telegraph Creek, Can. (tĕl´ē-gráf)	90	57°59'N	131°22'W
Teleneşti, Mol.	177	47°31'N	28°22'E
Telescope Peak, mtn., Ca., U.S. (tĕl´ē skōp)	106	36°12'N	117°05'W
Telesung, Indon.	197b	1°07'N	102°53'E
Telica, vol., Nic. (tä-lē´kä)	132	12°38'N	86°52'W
Tell City, In., U.S. (tĕl)	108	38°00'N	86°45'W
Teller, Ak., U.S. (tĕl´ẽr)	103	65°17'N	166°28'W
Tello, Col. (tĕ´l-yô)	142a	3°05'N	75°08'W
Telluride, Co., U.S. (tĕl´ū-rīd)	119	37°55'N	107°50'W
Telok Datok, Malay.	197b	2°51'N	101°33'E
Teloloapan, Mex. (tā´lô-lô-ä´pän)	130	18°19'N	99°54'W
Tel'pos-Iz, Gora, mtn., Russia (tyĕl´pôs-ēz´)	178	63°50'N	59°20'E
Telšiai, Lith. (tĕl´sha´ē)	167	55°59'N	22°17'E
Teltow, Ger. (tĕl´tō)	159b	52°24'N	13°12'E
Teluklecak, Indon.	197b	1°53'N	101°45'E
Tema, Ghana	234	5°38'N	0°01'E
Temascalcingo, Mex. (tā´mäs-käl-sĭŋ´gō)	130	19°55'N	100°00'W
Temascaltepec, Mex. (tā´mäs-käl-tȧ pĕk)	130	19°00'N	100°03'W
Temax, Mex. (tĕ´mäx)	128	21°10'N	88°51'W
Temir, Kaz.	183	49°10'N	57°15'E
Temirtaū, Kaz.	183	50°08'N	73°13'E
Temiscouata, l., Can. (tĕ´mĭs-kō-ä´tä)	100	47°40'N	68°50'W
Témiskaming, Can. (tĕ-mĭs´kȧ-mĭng)	91	46°41'N	79°01'W
Temoaya, Mex. (tĕ-mô-a-um-yä)	131a	19°28'N	99°36'W

ăt; finȧl; rāte; senåte; ärm; ȧsk; sofȧ; fâre; ch-choose; dh-as th in other; bē; ēvent; bĕt; recĕnt; cratẽr; g-gō; gh-guttural g; bĭt; ĭ-short neutral; rīde; κ-guttural k as ch in German ich;

ăt; fīnăl; rāte; senâte; ärm; àsk; sofá; fâre; ch-choose; dh-as th in other; bē; ĕvent; bĕt; recĕnt; cratẽr; g-gō; gh-guttural g; bĭt; ĩ-short neutral; rīde; κ-guttural k as ch in German ich;

PRONOUNCING INDEX

Topolobampo – Tsiafajovona 359

PLACE (Pronunciation)	PAGE	LAT.	LONG.
Topolobampo, Mex. (tō-pō-lô-bä′m-pô)	128	25°45'N	109°00'W
Topolovgrad, Blg.	175	42°05'N	26°19'E
Toppenish, Wa., U.S. (tôp′ĕn-ĭsh)	114	46°22'N	120°00'W
Torbat-e Ḩeydarīyeh, Iran	201	35°16'N	59°13'E
Torbat-e Jām, Iran	201	35°14'N	60°36'E
Torbay, Can. (tôr-bā′)	101	47°40'N	52°43'W
Torbay *see* Torquay, Eng., U.K.	164	50°30'N	3°26'W
Torbreck, Mount, mtn., Austl. (tōr-brĕk)	222	37°05'S	146°55'E
Torch, l., Mi., U.S. (tôrch)	108	45°00'N	85°30'W
Töreboda, Swe. (tü′rĕ-bō′dä)	166	58°44'N	14°04'E
Torhout, Bel.	165	51°01'N	3°04'E
Toribío, Col. (tỏ-rē-bē′ō)	142a	2°58'N	76°14'W
Toride, Japan (tō′rē-dā)	211a	35°54'N	104°04'E
Torino *see* Turin, Italy	154	45°05'N	7°44'E
Tormes, r., Spain (tōr′mās)	172	41°12'N	6°15'W
Torneälven, r., Eur.	156	67°00'N	22°30'E
Torneträsk, l., Swe. (tôr′nĕ trĕsk)	160	68°10'N	20°36'E
Torngat Mountains, mts., Can.	93	59°18'N	64°35'W
Tornio, Fin. (tôr′nĭ-ô)	154	65°55'N	24°09'E
Toro, Lac, l., Can.	99	46°53'N	73°46'W
Toronto, Can. (tỏ-rŏn′tō)	91	43°40'N	79°23'W
Toronto, Oh., U.S.	108	40°30'N	80°35'W
Toronto, res., Mex.	122	27°35'N	105°37'W
Toropets, Russia (tô′rỏ-pyĕts)	180	56°31'N	31°37'E
Toros Dağları, mts., Tur. (tô′rŭs)	198	37°00'N	32°40'E
Torote, r., Spain (tỏ-rō′tā)	173a	40°36'N	3°24'W
Torquay, Eng., U.K. (tôr-kē′)	164	50°30'N	3°26'W
Torra, Cerro, mtn., Col. (sĕ′r-rỏ-tỏ′r-rä)	142a	4°41'N	76°22'W
Torrance, Ca., U.S. (tŏr′rănc)	117a	33°50'N	118°20'W
Torre Annunziata, Italy (tôr′rā ä-nōōn-tsē-ä′tä)	173c	40°31'N	14°27'E
Torreblanca, Spain	173	40°18'N	0°12'E
Torre del Greco, Italy (tôr′rā dĕl grā′kō)	174	40°32'N	14°23'E
Torrejoncillo, Spain (tôr′rā-hōn-thē′lyō)	172	39°54'N	6°26'W
Torrelavega, Spain (tôr-rā′lä-vā′gä)	172	43°22'N	4°02'W
Torre Maggiore, Italy (tôr′rā mäd-jō′rā)	174	41°41'N	15°18'E
Torrens, Lake, l., Austl. (tŏr-ĕns)	220	30°07'S	137°40'E
Torrent, Spain	173	39°25'N	0°28'W
Torreón, Mex. (tôr-rā-ōn′)	128	25°32'N	103°26'W
Torres Islands, is., Vanuatu (tôr′rĕs) (tŏr′ĕz)	221	13°18'N	165°59'E
Torres Martinez Indian Reservation, I.R., Ca., U.S. (tôr′ĕz mär-tē′nĕz)	118	33°33'N	116°21'W
Torres Novas, Port. (tôr′rĕzh nō′väzh)	172	39°28'N	8°37'W
Torres Strait, strt., Austl. (tôr′rĕs)	221	10°30'S	141°30'E
Torres Vedras, Port. (tôr′rĕsh vā′dräzh)	172	39°08'N	9°18'W
Torrevieja, Spain (tôr-rā-vyā′hä)	173	37°58'N	0°40'W
Torrijos, Phil. (tôr-rē′hōs)	213a	13°19'N	122°06'E
Torrington, Ct., U.S. (tŏr′ĭng-tŭn)	109	41°50'N	73°10'W
Torrington, Wy., U.S.	112	42°04'N	104°11'W
Torro, Spain (tō′r-rō)	172	41°27'N	5°23'W
Torsby, Swe. (tôrs′bü)	166	60°07'N	12°56'E
Torshälla, Swe. (tôrs′hĕl-ä)	166	59°26'N	16°21'E
Tórshavn, Far. Is. (tôrs-houn′)	154	62°00'N	6°55'W
Tortola, i., Br. Vir. Is. (tôr-tō′lä)	129b	18°34'N	64°40'W
Tortona, Italy (tôr-tō′nä)	174	44°52'N	8°52'W
Tortosa, Spain (tôr-tō′sä)	154	40°59'N	0°33'E
Tortosa, Cap de, c., Spain	173	40°42'N	0°55'E
Tortue, Canal de la, strt., Haiti (tôr-tü′)	135	20°05'N	73°20'W
Tortue, Île de la, i., Haiti	135	20°10'N	73°00'W
Tortue, Rivière de la, r., Can. (lä tōr-tü′)	102a	45°12'N	73°32'W
Toruń, Pol.	154	53°02'N	18°35'E
Tõrva, Est. (t′r′vá)	167	58°02'N	25°56'E
Torzhok, Russia (tôr′zhôk)	180	57°03'N	34°53'E
Toscana, hist. reg., Italy (tôs-kä′nä)	174	43°23'N	11°08'E
Tosna, r., Russia	186c	59°28'N	30°53'E
Tosno, Russia (tôs′nỏ)	176	59°32'N	30°52'E
Tostado, Arg. (tỏs-tä′dō)	144	29°10'S	61°43'W
Tosya, Tur. (tỏz′yä)	163	41°00'N	34°00'E
Totana, Spain (tỏ-tä-nä)	172	37°45'N	1°28'W
Tot′ma, Russia (tôt′má)	180	60°00'N	42°20'E
Totness, Sur.	143	5°51'N	56°17'W
Totonicapán, Guat. (tỏtō-nē-kä′pän)	128	14°55'N	91°20'W
Totoras, Arg. (tỏ-tō′räs)	141c	32°33'S	61°13'W
Totsuka, Japan (tōt′sōō-kä)	211a	35°24'N	139°32'E
Tottenham, Eng., U.K. (tŏt′ĕn-ăm)	158b	51°35'N	0°06'W
Tottori, Japan (tỏ′tỏ-rē)	205	35°30'N	134°15'E
Touba, C. Iv.	234	8°17'N	7°41'W
Touba, Sen.	234	14°51'N	15°53'W
Toubkal, Jebel, mtn., Mor.	230	31°15'N	7°46'W
Tougan, Burkina	234	13°04'N	3°04'W
Touggourt, Alg. (tỏ-gōōrt′) (tōō-gōōr′)	230	33°09'N	6°07'E
Touil, Oued, r., Alg. (tōō-ēl′)	162	34°42'N	2°16'E
Toul, Fr. (tōōl)	161	48°39'N	5°51'E
Toulon, Fr. (tōō-lôn′)	154	43°09'N	5°54'E
Toulouse, Fr. (tōō-lōōz′)	154	43°37'N	1°27'E
Toungoo, Mya. (tỏ-ōŋ-gōō′)	212	19°00'N	96°29'E
Tourcoing, Fr. (tỏr-kwăn′)	161	50°44'N	3°06'E
Tournan-en-Brie, Fr. (tōōr-nän-ĕn-brē′)	171b	48°45'N	2°47'E
Tours, Fr. (tōōr)	154	47°23'N	0°39'E
Touside, Pic, mtn., Chad (tōō-sē-dā′)	231	21°10'N	16°30'E
Tovdalselva, r., Nor. (tỏv-däls-ĕlvå)	166	58°23'N	8°16'E
Towanda, Pa., U.S. (tỏ-wän′dȧ)	109	41°45'N	76°30'W

PLACE (Pronunciation)	PAGE	LAT.	LONG.
Town Bluff Lake, l., Tx., U.S.	123	30°52'N	94°30'W
Towner, N.D., U.S. (tou′nẽr)	112	48°21'N	100°24'W
Townsend, Ma., U.S. (toun′zĕnd)	101a	42°41'N	71°42'W
Townsend, Mt., U.S.	115	46°19'N	111°35'W
Townsend, Mount, mtn., Wa., U.S.	116a	47°52'N	123°03'W
Townsville, Austl. (tounz′vĭl)	219	19°18'S	146°50'E
Towson, Md., U.S. (tou′sŭn)	110e	39°24'N	76°36'W
Towuti, Danau, l., Indon. (tỏ-wōō′tē)	212	3°00'S	121°45'E
Toxkan, r., China	204	40°34'N	77°15'E
Toyah, Tx., U.S. (tô′yȧ)	122	31°19'N	103°46'W
Toyama, Japan (tō′yä-mä)	205	36°42'N	137°14'E
Toyama-Wan, b., Japan	211	36°58'N	137°16'E
Toyohashi, Japan (tō′yỏ-hä′shē)	210	34°44'N	137°21'E
Toyonaka, Japan (tō′yỏ-nä′kȧ)	211b	34°47'N	135°28'E
Tozeur, Tun. (tỏ-zûr′)	162	33°59'N	8°11'E
Trabzon, Tur. (tråb′zỏn)	198	41°00'N	39°45'E
Tracy, Can.	99	46°00'N	73°13'W
Tracy, Ca., U.S. (trā′sē)	118	37°45'N	121°27'W
Tracy, Mn., U.S.	112	44°13'N	95°37'W
Tracy City, Tn., U.S.	124	35°15'N	85°44'W
Trafalgar, Cabo, c., Spain (kä′bỏ-trä-fäl-gä′r)	172	36°10'N	6°02'W
Trafonomby, mtn., Madag.	233	24°32'S	46°35'E
Trail, Can. (trāl)	90	49°06'N	117°42'W
Traisen, r., Aus.	159e	48°15'N	15°55'E
Traiskirchen, Aus.	159e	48°01'N	16°18'E
Trakai, Lith. (trà-kāy)	167	54°38'N	24°59'E
Trakiszki, Pol. (trà-kē′-sh-kē)	169	54°16'N	23°07'E
Tralee, Ire. (trȧ-lē′)	161	52°16'N	9°20'W
Tranås, Swe. (trän′ôs)	166	58°03'N	14°56'E
Trancoso, Port. (träŋ-kō′sỏ)	172	40°46'N	7°23'W
Trangan, Pulau, i., Indon. (träŋ′gän)	213	6°52'S	133°30'E
Trani, Italy (trä′nē)	174	41°15'N	16°25'E
Transylvania, hist. reg., Rom. (trăn-sĭl-vā′nĭ-ȧ)	169	46°30'N	22°35'E
Trapani, Italy	162	38°01'N	12°31'E
Trappes, Fr. (tråp)	171b	48°47'N	2°01'E
Traralgon, Austl. (tră′răl-gŏn)	222	38°15'S	146°33'E
Trarza, reg., Maur.	234	17°35'N	15°15'W
Trasimeno, Lago, l., Italy (lä′gō trä-sē-mā′nō)	174	43°00'N	12°12'E
Trás-os-Montes, hist. reg., Port. (träzh′ōzh môn′tāzh)	162	41°33'N	7°13'W
Traun, r., Aus. (troun)	168	48°10'N	14°15'E
Traunstein, Ger. (troun′stīn)	168	47°52'N	12°38'E
Traverse, Lake, l., Mn., U.S. (trăv′ẽrs)	112	45°46'N	96°53'W
Traverse City, Mi., U.S.	108	44°45'N	85°40'W
Travnik, Bos. (träv′nēk)	175	44°13'N	17°43'E
Treasure Island, i., Ca., U.S. (trĕzh′ẽr)	116b	37°49'N	122°22'W
Trebbin, Ger. (trĕ′bēn)	159b	52°13'N	13°13'E
Trebinje, Bos. (trā′bēn-yĕ)	175	42°43'N	18°21'E
Trebišov, Slvk. (trĕ′bē-shỏf)	169	48°36'N	21°32'E
Tregrosse Islands, is., Austl. (trē-grōs′)	221	18°08'S	150°53'E
Treinta y Tres, Ur. (trå-ēn′tä ē trās′)	144	33°14'S	54°17'W
Trelew, Arg. (trē′lū)	144	43°15'S	65°25'W
Trelleborg, Swe.	166	55°24'N	13°07'E
Tremiti, Isole, is., Italy (ē′sō-lĕ trā-mē′tē)	174	42°07'N	16°33'E
Trenčín, Czech Rep. (trĕn′chēn)	161	48°52'N	18°02'E
Trenque Lauquén, Arg. (trĕn′kĕ-lá′ōō-kĕ′n)	144	35°50'S	62°44'W
Trent, r., Can. (trĕnt)	99	44°15'N	77°55'W
Trent, r., Eng., U.K.	158a	53°25'N	0°45'W
Trent and Mersey Canal, can., Eng., U.K. (trĕnt) (mûr zē)	158a	53°11'N	2°24'W
Trentino-Alto Adige, hist. reg., Italy	174	46°16'N	10°47'E
Trento, Italy (trĕn′tô)	162	46°04'N	11°07'E
Trenton, Can. (trĕn′tŭn)	91	44°05'N	77°35'W
Trenton, Can.	101	45°37'N	62°38'W
Trenton, Mi., U.S.	111b	42°08'N	83°12'W
Trenton, Mo., U.S.	121	40°05'N	93°36'W
Trenton, N.J., U.S.	105	40°13'N	74°46'W
Trenton, Tn., U.S.	124	35°57'N	88°55'W
Trepassey, Can. (trē-păs′ē)	101	46°44'N	53°22'W
Trepassey Bay, b., Can.	101	46°40'N	53°20'W
Tres Arroyos, Arg. (trās′är-rō′yōs)	144	38°18'S	60°16'W
Três Corações, Braz. (trĕ′s kō-rä-zō′ĕs)	141a	21°41'S	45°14'W
Tres Cumbres, Mex. (trĕ′s kōō′m-brĕs)	131a	19°03'N	99°14'W
Três Lagoas, Braz. (trĕ′s lä-gō′äs)	143	20°48'S	51°42'W
Três Marias, Reprêsa, res., Braz.	143	18°15'S	45°30'W
Tres Morros, Alto de, mtn., Col. (ä′l-tō dĕ trĕ′s mô′r-rōs)	142a	7°08'N	76°10'W
Três Pontas, Braz. (trĕ′pō′n-täs)	141a	21°22'S	45°30'W
Três Pontas, Cabo das, c., Ang.	236	10°23'S	13°32'E
Três Rios, Braz. (trĕ′s rē′ōs)	141a	22°07'S	43°13'W
Très-Saint Rédempteur, Can. (sän rā-dänp-tûr′)	102a	45°26'N	74°23'W
Treuenbrietzen, Ger. (troi′ĕn-brē-tzĕn)	159b	52°06'N	12°52'E
Treviglio, Italy (trā-vē′lyō)	174	45°30'N	9°34'E
Treviso, Italy (trĕ-vē′sō)	162	45°39'N	12°15'E
Trichardt, S. Afr. (trĭ-kärt′)	238c	26°32'N	29°16'E
Trier, Ger.	161	49°45'N	6°38'E
Trieste, Italy (trē-ĕs′tā)	154	45°39'N	13°48'E
Triglav, mtn., Slvn.	174	46°23'N	13°50'E
Trigueros, Spain (trē-gā′rōs)	172	37°23'N	6°50'W
Tríkala, Grc.	163	39°33'N	21°49'E
Trikora, Puncak, mtn., Indon.	213	4°15'S	138°45'E
Trim Creek, r., Il., U.S. (trĭm)	111a	41°19'N	87°39'W
Trincomalee, Sri L. (trĭŋ-kỏ-mȧ-lē′)	203	8°39'N	81°12'E
Tring, Eng., U.K. (trĭng)	158b	51°46'N	0°40'W

PLACE (Pronunciation)	PAGE	LAT.	LONG.
Trinidad, Bol. (trē-nē-dhädh′)	142	14°48'S	64°43'W
Trinidad, Cuba (trē-nē-dhädh′)	129	21°50'N	80°00'W
Trinidad, Ur.	144	33°29'S	56°55'W
Trinidad, Co., U.S. (trĭn′ĭdăd)	104	37°11'N	104°31'W
Trinidad, i., Trin. (trĭn′ĭ-dăd)	143	10°00'N	61°00'W
Trinidad, r., Pan.	128a	8°55'N	80°01'W
Trinidad, Sierra de, mts., Cuba (sē-ĕ′r-rä dĕ trē-nē-dä′d)	134	21°50'N	79°55'W
Trinidad and Tobago, nation, N.A. (trĭn′ĭ-dăd) (tỏ-bā′gō)	129	11°00'N	61°00'W
Trinitaria, Mex. (trē-nē-tä′ryä)	131	16°09'N	92°04'W
Trinity, Can. (trĭn′ĭ-tē)	101	48°59'N	53°55'W
Trinity, Tx., U.S.	123	30°52'N	95°27'W
Trinity, is., Ak., U.S.	103	56°25'N	153°15'W
Trinity, r., Ca., U.S.	114	40°50'N	123°20'W
Trinity, r., Tx., U.S.	107	30°50'N	95°09'W
Trinity, East Fork, r., Tx., U.S.	121	33°24'N	96°42'W
Trinity, West Fork, r., Tx., U.S.	120	33°22'N	98°26'W
Trinity Bay, b., Can.	93	48°00'N	53°40'W
Trino, Italy (trē′nô)	174	45°11'N	8°16'E
Trion, Ga., U.S. (trī′ŏn)	124	34°32'N	85°18'W
Trípoli, Grc.	163	37°32'N	22°32'E
Tripoli (Tarābulus), Libya	231	32°50'N	13°13'E
Tripolitania *see* Tarābulus, hist. reg., Libya	230	31°00'N	12°26'E
Tripura, state, India	199	24°00'N	92°00'E
Tristan da Cunha Islands, is., St. Hel. (três-tän′dä kōōn′yȧ)	2	35°30'S	12°15'W
Triste, Golfo, b., Ven. (gôl-fô trē′s-tĕ)	143b	10°40'N	68°05'W
Triticus Reservoir, res., N.Y., U.S. (trī tĭ-cŭs)	110a	41°20'N	73°36'W
Trnava, Slvk. (t′r′nȧ-vȧ)	169	48°22'N	17°34'E
Trobriand Islands, is., Pap. N. Gui. (trō-brē-ănd′)	213	8°25'S	151°45'E
Trogir, Cro. (trō′gēr)	174	43°32'N	16°17'E
Trois Fourches, Cap des, c., Mor.	172	35°28'N	2°58'W
Trois-Rivières, Can. (trwä′rē-vyâ′)	91	46°21'N	72°35'W
Troitsk, Russia (trô′ētsk)	184	54°06'N	61°35'E
Troits′ke, Ukr.	177	47°39'N	30°16'E
Troitsko-Pechorsk, Russia (trô′ĭtsk-ỏ-pyĕ-chôrsk′)	178	62°18'N	56°07'E
Trollhättan, Swe. (trôl′hĕt-ĕn)	160	58°17'N	12°17'E
Trollheimen, mts., Nor. (trôll-hĕĭm)	166	62°48'N	9°05'E
Trona, Ca., U.S. (trō′nȧ)	118	35°49'N	117°20'W
Tronador, Cerro, mtn., S.A. (sĕ′r-rō trō-nä′dôr)	144	41°17'S	71°56'W
Troncoso, Mex. (trôn-kô′sō)	130	22°43'N	102°22'W
Trondheim, Nor. (trôn′hâm)	154	63°25'N	11°35'E
Trosa, Swe. (trô′sä)	166	58°54'N	17°25'E
Trout, l., Can.	93	51°16'N	92°46'W
Trout, l., Can.	92	61°10'N	121°30'W
Trout Creek, r., Or., U.S.	114	42°18'N	118°31'W
Troutdale, Or., U.S. (trout′dāl)	116c	45°32'N	122°23'W
Trout Lake, Mi., U.S.	113	46°20'N	85°02'W
Trouville, Fr. (trōō-vēl′)	170	49°23'N	0°05'E
Troy, Al., U.S. (troi)	124	31°47'N	85°46'W
Troy, Il., U.S.	117e	38°44'N	89°53'W
Troy, Ks., U.S.	121	39°46'N	95°07'W
Troy, Mo., U.S.	120	38°56'N	99°57'W
Troy, Mt., U.S.	114	48°28'N	115°56'W
Troy, N.C., U.S.	125	35°21'N	79°58'W
Troy, N.Y., U.S.	105	42°45'N	73°45'W
Troy, Oh., U.S.	108	40°00'N	84°10'W
Troy, hist., Tur.	198	39°59'N	26°14'E
Troyes, Fr. (trwä)	161	48°18'N	4°03'E
Trstenik, Serb. (t′r′stĕ-nēk)	163	43°36'N	21°00'E
Trubchëvsk, Russia (trỏp′chĕfsk)	181	52°36'N	33°46'E
Trucial States *see* United Arab Emirates, nation, Asia	198	24°00'N	54°00'E
Truckee, Ca., U.S. (trŭk′ē)	118	39°20'N	120°12'W
Truckee, r., Ca., U.S.	118	39°25'N	120°07'W
Truganina, Austl.	217a	37°49'N	144°44'E
Trujillo, Col. (trō-кē′l-yō)	142a	4°10'N	76°20'W
Trujillo, Peru	142	8°08'S	79°00'W
Trujillo, Spain (trōō-кē′l-yỏ)	162	39°27'N	5°50'W
Trujillo, Ven.	142	9°15'N	70°28'W
Trujillo, r., Mex.	130	23°12'N	103°10'W
Trujin, Lago, l., Dom. Rep. (trōō-кēn′)	135	17°45'N	71°25'W
Truk *see* Chuuk, is., Micron.	214c	7°25'N	151°47'E
Trumann, Ar., U.S. (trōō′măn)	121	35°41'N	90°31'W
Trŭn, Blg. (trŭn)	175	42°49'N	22°39'E
Truro, Can. (trōō′rō)	91	45°22'N	63°16'W
Truro, Eng., U.K.	164	50°17'N	5°05'W
Trussville, Al., U.S. (trŭs′vĭl)	110h	33°37'N	86°37'W
Truth or Consequences, N.M., U.S. (trōōth ŏr kŏn′sē-kwĕn-sĭs)	119	33°10'N	107°20'W
Trutnov, Czech Rep. (trōt′nôf)	168	50°36'N	15°36'E
Trzcianka, Pol. (tchyän′kȧ)	168	53°02'N	16°27'E
Trzebiatów, Pol. (tchĕ-byä′tō-v)	168	54°03'N	15°16'E
Tsaidam Basin, basin, China (tsī-däm)	204	37°19'N	94°08'E
Tsala Apopka Lake, r., Fl., U.S. (tsä′lȧ ă-pŏp′kȧ)	125	28°57'N	82°11'W
Tsast Bogd, mtn., Mong.	204	46°44'N	92°34'E
Tsavo National Park, rec., Kenya	237	2°35'S	38°45'E
Tsawwassen Indian Reserve, I.R., Can.	116d	49°03'N	123°11'W
Tsentral′nyy-Kospashskiy, Russia (tsĕn-träl′nyĭ-kôs-pàsh′skĭ)	186a	59°03'N	57°48'E
Tshela, D.R.C. (tshā′lȧ)	232	4°59'S	12°56'E
Tshikapa, D.R.C. (tshē-kä′pä)	232	6°25'S	20°48'E
Tshofa, D.R.C.	237	5°14'S	25°15'E
Tshuapa, r., D.R.C.	232	0°30'S	22°00'E
Tsiafajovona, mtn., Madag.	233	19°17'S	47°27'E

360 Tsiribihina – Uglegorsk PRONOUNCING INDEX

PLACE (Pronunciation)	PAGE	LAT.	LONG.
Tsiribihina, r., Madag. (tsē'rē-bē-hē-nä')	233	19°45'S	43°30'E
Tsitsa, r., S. Afr. (tsē'tsȧ)	233c	31°28'S	28°53'E
Tskhinvali, Geor.	182	42°13'N	43°56'E
Tsolo, S. Afr. (tsō'lō)	233c	31°19'S	28°47'E
Tsomo, S. Afr.	233c	32°03'S	27°49'E
Tsomo, r., S. Afr.	233c	31°53'S	27°48'E
Tsu, Japan (tsōō)	210	34°42'N	136°31'E
Tsuchiura, Japan (tsōō'chē-ōō-rä)	211	36°04'N	140°09'E
Tsuda, Japan (tsōō'dä)	211b	34°48'N	135°43'E
Tsugaru Kaikyō, strt., Japan	205	41°25'N	140°20'E
Tsumeb, Nmb. (tsōō'mĕb)	232	19°10'S	17°45'E
Tsunashima, Japan (tsōō'nä-shē'mä)	211a	35°32'N	139°37'E
Tsuruga, Japan (tsoo'rò-gȧ)	210	35°39'N	136°04'E
Tsurugi San, mtn., Japan (tsōō'rò-gē sän)	210	33°52'N	134°07'E
Tsuruoka, Japan (tsōō'rò-ō'kä)	210	38°43'N	139°51'E
Tsurusaki, Japan (tsoo'ro-sä'kē)	211	[illegible]	[illegible]
Tsu Shima, is., Japan (tsoo shē'mä)	205	34°20'N	129°30'E
Tsushima Strait, strt., Asia	205	34°00'N	129°00'E
Tsuwano, Japan (tsōō'wȧ-nō')	211	34°28'N	131°47'E
Tsuyama, Japan (tsōō'yä-mä')	210	35°05'N	134°00'E
Tua, r., Port. (tōō'ä)	172	41°23'N	7°18'W
Tualatin, r., Or., U.S. (tōō'ȧ-lā-tĭn)	116c	45°25'N	122°54'W
Tuamoto, Îles, Fr. Poly. (tōō-ä-mō'tōō)	241	19°00'S	141°20'W
Tuapse, Russia (tò'áp-sĕ)	181	44°00'N	39°10'E
Tuareg, hist. reg., Alg.	230	21°26'N	2°51'E
Tubarão, Braz. (tōō-bä-rouɴ')	144	28°23'S	48°56'W
Tübingen, Ger. (tü'bĭng-ĕn)	168	48°33'N	9°05'E
Tubinskiy, Russia (tû bĭn'skĭ)	186a	52°53'N	58°15'E
Tubruq, Libya	231	32°03'N	24°04'E
Tucacas, Ven. (tōō-kä'käs)	142	10°48'N	68°20'W
Tucker, Ga., U.S. (tŭk'ẽr)	110c	33°51'N	84°13'W
Tucson, Az., U.S. (tōō-sŏn')	104	32°15'N	111°00'W
Tucumán, Arg. (tōō-kōō-män')	144	26°52'S	65°08'W
Tucumán, prov., Arg.	144	26°30'S	65°30'W
Tucumcari, N.M., U.S. (tōō'kŭm-kâr-ē)	120	35°11'N	103°43'W
Tucupita, Ven. (tōō-kōō-pē'tä)	142	9°00'N	62°09'W
Tudela, Spain (tōō-dhā'lä)	162	42°03'N	1°37'W
Tugaloo, r., Ga., U.S. (tŭg'ȧ-lōō)	124	34°35'N	83°05'W
Tugela, r., S. Afr. (tōō-gel'ȧ)	233c	28°50'S	30°52'E
Tugela Ferry, S. Afr.	233c	28°44'S	30°27'E
Tug Fork, r., U.S. (tŭg)	108	37°50'N	82°30'W
Tuguegarao, Phil. (tōō-gā-gȧ-rä'ō)	212	17°37'N	121°44'E
Tuhai, r., China (tōō-hī)	206	37°05'N	116°56'E
Tui, Slvn.	172	42°03'N	8°38'W
Tuinplaas, S. Afr.	238c	24°54'S	28°46'E
Tujunga, Ca., U.S. (tōō-jŭn'gȧ)	117a	34°15'N	118°16'W
Tukan, Russia (tōō'kȧn)	186a	53°52'N	57°25'E
Tukangbesi, Kepulauan, is., Indon.	213	6°00'S	124°15'E
Tūkrah, Libya	231	32°34'N	20°47'E
Tuktoyaktuk, Can.	90	69°32'N	132°37'W
Tuktut Nogait National Park, rec., Can.	92	69°00'N	122°00'W
Tukums, Lat. (tò'kòms)	180	56°57'N	23°09'E
Tukuyu, Tan. (tōō-kōō'yȧ)	232	9°13'S	33°43'E
Tukwila, Wa., U.S. (tŭk'wĭ-lȧ)	116a	47°28'N	122°16'W
Tula, Mex. (tōō'lä)	130	20°04'N	99°22'W
Tula, Russia (tōō'lȧ)	180	54°12'N	37°37'E
Tula, prov., Russia	176	53°45'N	37°19'E
Tula, r., Mex. (tōō'lä)	130	20°40'N	99°27'W
Tulagai, i., Sol. Is. (tōō-lä'gē)	221	9°15'S	160°17'E
Tulaghi, Sol. Is.	214e	9°06'S	160°09'E
Tulalip, Wa., U.S. (tū-lă'lĭp)	116a	48°04'N	122°18'W
Tulalip Indian Reservation, I.R., Wa., U.S.	116a	48°06'N	122°16'W
Tulancingo, Mex. (tōō-län-sĭŋ'gō)	128	20°04'N	98°24'W
Tulangbawang, r., Indon.	212	4°17'S	105°00'E
Tulare, Ca., U.S. (tōō-lä'rȧ) (tul-âr')	118	36°12'N	119°22'W
Tulare Lake Bed, l., Ca., U.S.	118	35°57'N	120°18'W
Tularosa, N.M., U.S. (tōō-lȧ-rō'zȧ)	119	33°05'N	106°05'W
Tulcán, Ec. (tōōl-kän')	142	0°44'N	77°52'W
Tulcea, Rom. (tòl'chá)	163	45°10'N	28°47'E
Tul'chyn, Ukr.	181	48°42'N	28°53'E
Tulcingo, Mex. (tōōl-sĭŋ'gō)	130	18°03'N	98°27'W
Tule, r., Ca., U.S. (tōōl'lā)	118	36°08'N	118°50'W
Tule River Indian Reservation, I.R., Ca., U.S. (tōō'lā)	118	36°00'N	118°40'W
Tuli, Zimb. (tōō'lē)	232	20°58'S	29°12'E
Tulia, Tx., U.S. (tōō'lĭ-ȧ)	120	34°32'N	101°46'W
Tulik Volcano, vol., Ak., U.S. (tò'lĭk)	103a	53°28'N	168°10'W
Tülkarm, W.B. (tōōl kärm)	197a	32°19'N	35°02'E
Tullahoma, Tn., U.S. (tŭl-ȧ-hō'mȧ)	124	35°21'N	86°12'W
Tullamore, Ire. (tŭl-ȧ-mōr')	164	53°15'N	7°29'W
Tulle, Fr. (tül)	170	45°15'N	1°45'E
Tulln, Aus. (tòln)	168	48°21'N	16°04'E
Tullner Feld, reg., Aus.	159e	48°20'N	15°59'E
Tulpetlac, Mex. (tōōl-pȧ-tlák')	131a	19°33'N	99°04'W
Tulsa, Ok., U.S. (tŭl'sȧ)	105	36°08'N	95°58'W
Tulum, Mex. (tōō-lò'm)	132a	20°17'N	87°26'W
Tulun, Russia (tò-lōōn')	179	54°29'N	100°43'E
Tuma, r., Nic. (tōō'mä)	132	13°07'N	85°32'W
Tumba, Lac, l., D.R.C. (tòm'bȧ)	232	0°50'S	17°45'E
Tumbes, Peru (tōō'm-bĕs)	142	3°39'S	80°27'W
Tumbiscatío, Mex. (tōōm-bē-skȧ-tē'ō)	130	18°32'N	102°23'W
Tumbo, i., Can.	116d	48°49'N	123°04'W
Tumen, China (tōō-mŭn)	208	43°00'N	129°50'E
Tumen, r., Asia	210	42°08'N	128°40'E
Tumeremo, Ven. (tōō-mȧ-rä'mō)	143	7°15'N	61°28'W
Tumkūr, India	203	13°22'N	77°05'E
Tumuacacori National Monument, rec., Az., U.S. (tōō-mä-kä'kȧ-rē)	119	31°36'N	110°20'W
Tumuc-Humac Mountains, mts., S.A. (tōō-mòk'ōō-mäk')	143	2°15'N	54°50'W
Tunas de Zaza, Cuba (tōō'näs dā zä'zä)	134	21°40'N	79°35'W
Tunbridge Wells, Eng., U.K. (tŭn'brĭj welz')	165	51°05'N	0°09'E
Tunduru, Tan.	237	11°07'S	37°21'E
Tungabhadra Reservoir, res., India	203	15°26'N	75°57'E
Tuni, India	203	17°29'N	82°38'E
Tunica, Ms., U.S. (tū'nĭ-kȧ)	124	34°41'N	90°23'W
Tunis, Tun. (tū'nĭs)	230	36°59'N	10°06'E
Tunis, Golfe de, b., Tun.	162	37°06'N	10°43'E
Tunisia, nation, Afr. (tu-nĭzh'ē-ȧ)	230	35°00'N	10°11'E
Tunja, Col. (tōō'n-hȧ)	142	5°32'N	73°19'W
Tunkhannock, Pa., U.S. (tŭnk-hăn'ŭk)	109	41°35'N	75°55'W
Tunnel, r., Wa., U.S. (tŭn'ĕl)	116a	47°48'N	123°04'W
Tuoji Dao, i., China (twô-jyē dou)	206	38°11'N	120°45'E
[illegible] (twô-lŭm'nē)	118	37°35'N	120°37'W
Tuostakh, r., Russia	185	67°09'N	137°30'E
Tupelo, Ms., U.S. (tū'pē-lō)	124	34°14'N	88°43'W
Tupinambaranas, Ilha, i., Braz.	143	3°04'S	58°09'W
Tupiza, Bol. (tōō-pē'zä)	142	21°26'S	65°43'W
Tupper Lake, N.Y., U.S. (tŭp'ẽr)	109	44°15'N	74°25'W
Tüpqaraghan tübegi, pen., Kaz.	181	44°30'N	50°40'E
Tupungato, Cerro, vol., S.A.	144	33°30'S	69°52'W
Tuquerres, Col. (tōō-kĕ'r-rĕs)	142	1°12'N	77°44'W
Tura, Russia (tòr'ȧ)	179	64°08'N	99°58'E
Turbio, r., Mex. (tōōr-byō)	130	20°28'N	101°40'W
Turbo, Col. (tōō'bō)	142	8°02'N	76°43'W
Turda, Rom. (tòr'dȧ)	169	46°35'N	23°47'E
Turfan Depression, depr., China	204	42°16'N	90°00'E
Turffontein, neigh., S. Afr.	233b	26°15'S	28°02'E
Tŭrgovishte, Blg.	175	43°14'N	26°36'E
Turgutlu, Tur.	181	38°30'N	27°20'E
Türi, Est. (tü'rĭ)	167	58°49'N	25°29'E
Turia, r., Spain (tōō'ryä)	172	40°12'N	1°18'W
Turicato, Mex. (tōō-rē-kä'tō)	130	19°03'N	101°24'W
Turiguano, i., Cuba (tōō-rē-gwä'nō)	134	22°20'N	78°35'W
Turin, Italy	154	45°05'N	7°44'E
Turiya, r., Ukr.	169	51°18'N	24°55'E
Turka, Ukr. (tòr'kȧ)	169	49°10'N	23°02'E
Turkestan, hist. reg., Asia	178	43°27'N	62°14'E
Turkey, nation, Asia	155	38°45'N	32°00'E
Turkey, r., Ia., U.S. (tûrk'ē)	113	43°20'N	92°16'W
Türkistan, Kaz.	183	44°00'N	68°00'E
Turkmenbashy, Turkmen.	183	40°00'N	52°50'E
Turkmenistan, nation, Asia	178	40°46'N	56°01'E
Turks, is., T./C. Is. (tûrks)	129	21°40'N	71°45'W
Turks Island Passage, strt., T./C. Is.	135	21°15'N	71°25'W
Turku, Fin. (tòrgokò)	154	60°28'N	22°12'E
Turlock, Ca., U.S. (tûr'lŏk)	118	37°30'N	120°51'W
Turneffe, i., Belize	128	17°25'N	87°43'W
Turner, Ks., U.S. (tûr'nẽr)	117f	39°05'N	94°42'W
Turner Sound, strt., Bah.	134	24°20'N	78°05'W
Turners Peninsula, pen., S.L.	234	7°20'N	12°40'W
Turnhout, Bel. (tŭrn-hout')	165	51°19'N	4°58'E
Turnov, Czech Rep. (tòr'nôf)	168	50°36'N	15°12'E
Turnu Măgurele, Rom.	163	43°54'N	24°49'E
Turpan, China (tōō-är-pän)	204	43°06'N	88°41'E
Turquino, Pico, mtn., Cuba (pē'kō dā tōōr-kē'nō)	134	20°00'N	76°50'W
Turrialba, C.R. (tōōr-ryä'l-bä)	133	9°54'N	83°41'W
Turtkul', Uzb. (tòrt-kòl')	183	41°28'N	61°02'E
Turtle, r., Can.	97	49°20'N	92°30'W
Turtle Bay, b., Tx., U.S.	123a	29°48'N	94°38'W
Turtle Creek, r., S.D., U.S.	112	44°40'N	98°53'W
Turtle Mountain Indian Reservation, I.R., N.D., U.S.	112	48°45'N	99°57'W
Turtle Mountains, mts., N.D., U.S.	112	48°57'N	100°11'W
Turukhansk, Russia (tōō-rōō-känsk')	178	66°03'N	88°39'E
Tuscaloosa, Al., U.S. (tŭs-kȧ-lōō'sȧ)	105	33°10'N	87°35'W
Tuscarora, Nv., U.S. (tŭs-kȧ-rō'rȧ)	114	41°18'N	116°15'W
Tuscarora Indian Reservation, I.R., N.Y., U.S.	111c	43°10'N	78°51'W
Tuscola, Il., U.S. (tŭs-kō-lȧ)	108	39°50'N	88°20'W
Tuscumbia, Al., U.S. (tŭs-kŭm'bĭ-ȧ)	124	34°41'N	87°42'W
Tushino, Russia (tōō'shĭ-nô)	186b	55°51'N	37°24'E
Tuskegee, Al., U.S. (tŭs-kē'gē)	124	32°25'N	85°40'W
Tustin, Ca., U.S. (tŭs'tĭn)	117a	33°44'N	117°49'W
Tutayev, Russia (tōō-tȧ-yĕf')	180	57°53'N	39°34'E
Tutbury, Eng., U.K. (tŭt'bēr-ē)	158a	52°52'N	1°51'W
Tuticorin, India (tōō-tē-kō-rĭn')	203	8°51'N	78°09'E
Tutitlan, Mex. (tōō-tē-tlä'n)	131a	19°38'N	99°10'W
Tutóia, Braz. (tōō-tō'yȧ)	143	2°42'S	42°21'W
Tutrakan, Blg.	163	44°02'N	26°36'E
Tuttle Creek Reservoir, res., Ks., U.S.	121	39°30'N	96°38'W
Tuttlingen, Ger. (tòt' lĭng-ĕn)	168	47°58'N	8°50'E
Tutuila, i., Am. Sam.	214a	14°18'S	170°42'W
Tutwiler, Ms., U.S. (tŭt'wĭ-lẽr)	124	34°01'N	90°25'W
Tuva, prov., Russia	184	51°15'N	90°45'E
Tuvalu, nation, Oc.	3	5°20'S	174°00'E
Tuwayq, Jabal, mts., Sau. Ar.	198	20°45'N	46°30'E
Tuxedo Park, N.Y., U.S. (tŭk-sē'dō pärk)	110a	41°11'N	74°11'W
Tuxford, Eng., U.K. (tŭks'fẽrd)	158a	53°14'N	0°54'W
Tuxpan, Mex. (tōōs'pän)	130	19°34'N	103°22'W
Túxpan, Mex.	128	20°57'N	97°26'W
Túxpan, r., Mex. (tōōs'-pän)	131	20°55'N	97°52'W
Túxpan, Arrecife, i., Mex. (är-rĕ-sē'fē-tōō'x-pä'n)	131	21°01'N	97°12'W
Tuxtepec, Mex. (tòs-tȧ-pĕk')	131	18°06'N	96°09'W
Tuxtla Gutiérrez, Mex. (tòs'tlä gōō-tyâr'rĕs)	128	16°44'N	93°08'W
Tuy, r., Ven. (tōō'ē)	143b	10°15'N	66°03'W
Tuyra, r., Pan. (tōō-ē'rȧ)	133	7°55'N	77°37'W
Tuz Gölü, l., Tur.	180	38°45'N	33°25'E
Tuzigoot National Monument, rec., Az., U.S.	119	34°40'N	111°52'W
Tuzla, Bos. (tòz'lȧ)	163	44°33'N	18°46'E
Tvedestrand, Nor. (tvĭ'dhĕ-stränd)	166	58°39'N	8°54'E
Tveitsund, Nor. (tvåt'sònd)	166	59°03'N	8°29'E
Tver', Russia	178	56°52'N	35°57'E
Tver', prov., Russia	176	56°50'N	33°08'E
Tvertsa, r., Russia (tvĕr'tsȧ)	176	56°58'N	35°22'E
Tweed, r., U.K. (twēd)	164	55°32'N	2°35'W
Tweeling, S. Afr. (twē'lĭng)	238c	27°34'S	28°31'E
Twenty Mile Creek, r., Can. (twĕn'tĭ mīl)	102d	43°09'N	79°49'W
Twickenham, Eng., U.K. (twĭk''n-ăm)	158b	51°20'N	0°20'W
Twillingate, Can. (twĭl'ĭn-gāt)	93a	49°39'N	54°46'W
Twin Bridges, Mt., U.S. (twĭn brĭj ĕz)	115	45°34'N	112°17'W
Twin Falls, Id., U.S. (fôls)	104	[illegible]	[illegible]
Twinsburg, Oh., U.S. (twĭnz'bûrg)	111d	41°19'N	81°26'W
Twitchell Reservoir, res., Ca., U.S.	118	34°50'N	120°10'W
Two Butte Creek, r., Co., U.S. (tōō būt)	120	37°39'N	102°45'W
Two Harbors, Mn., U.S.	113	47°00'N	91°42'W
Two Prairie Bay, Ar., U.S. (prā'rĭ bī ōō')	121	34°48'N	92°07'W
Two Rivers, Wi., U.S. (rĭv'ẽrz)	113	44°09'N	87°36'W
Tyabb, Austl.	217a	38°16'S	145°11'E
Tylden, S. Afr. (tĭl-dĕn)	233c	32°08'S	27°06'E
Tyldesley, Eng., U.K. (tĭldz'lē)	158a	53°32'N	2°28'W
Tyler, Mn., U.S. (tī'lẽr)	112	44°18'N	96°08'W
Tyler, Tx., U.S.	105	32°21'N	95°19'W
Tylertown, Ms., U.S. (tī'lẽr-toun)	124	31°08'N	90°06'W
Tylihul, r., Ukr.	177	47°25'N	30°27'E
Tyndall, S.D., U.S. (tĭn'dȧl)	112	42°58'N	97°52'W
Tyndinskiy, Russia	179	55°22'N	124°45'E
Tyne, r., Eng., U.K. (tīn)	164	54°59'N	1°56'W
Tynemouth, Eng., U.K. (tīn'mŭth)	160	55°04'N	1°39'W
Tyngsboro, Ma., U.S. (tĭnj-bûr'ō)	101a	42°40'N	71°27'W
Tynset, Nor. (tün'sĕt)	160	62°17'N	10°45'E
Tyre see Şūr, Leb.	197a	33°16'N	35°13'E
Tyrifjorden, l., Nor.	166	60°03'N	10°25'E
Tyrnavos, Grc.	175	39°50'N	22°14'E
Tyrone, Pa., U.S.	109	40°40'N	78°15'W
Tyrrell, Lake, l., Austl. (tĭr'ĕll)	222	35°12'S	143°00'E
Tyrrhenian Sea, sea, Italy (tĭr-rē'nĭ-ȧn)	156	40°10'N	12°15'E
Tyukalinsk, Russia (tyò-kȧ-lĭnsk')	178	56°03'N	71°43'E
Tyukyan, r., Russia (tyòk'yȧn)	185	65°42'N	116°09'E
Tyuleniy, i., Russia	181	44°30'N	48°00'E
Tyumen', Russia (tyōō-mĕn')	178	57°02'N	65°28'E
Tzucacab, Mex. (tzōō-kä-kä'b)	132a	20°06'N	89°03'W

U

PLACE (Pronunciation)	PAGE	LAT.	LONG.
Uaupés, Braz. (wä-ōō'pās)	142	0°02'S	67°03'W
Ubangi, r., Afr. (ōō-bäŋ'gē)	231	3°00'N	18°00'E
Ubatuba, Braz. (ōō-bȧ-tōō'bȧ)	141a	23°25'S	45°06'W
Ubeda, Spain (ōō'bȧ-dä)	172	38°01'N	3°23'W
Uberaba, Braz. (ōō-bȧ-rä'bȧ)	143	19°47'S	47°47'W
Uberlândia, Braz. (ōō-bĕr-lá'n-dyä)	143	18°54'S	48°11'W
Ubombo, S. Afr. (ōō-bôm'bō)	232	27°33'S	32°13'E
Ubon Ratchathani, Thai. (ōō'bŭn rä'chätá-nē)	212	15°15'N	104°52'E
Ubort', r., Eur. (ōō-bôrt')	177	51°18'N	27°43'E
Ubrique, Spain (ōō-brē'kā)	172	36°43'N	5°36'W
Ubundu, D.R.C.	232	0°21'S	25°29'E
Ucayali, r., Peru (ōō'kä-yä'lē)	142	8°58'S	74°13'W
Uccle, Bel. (ū'kl')	159a	50°48'N	4°17'E
Uchaly, Russia (û-chä'lĭ)	186a	54°22'N	59°28'E
Uchiko, Japan (ōō'chē-kō)	211	33°30'N	132°39'E
Uchinoura, Japan (ōō'chē-nō-ōō'rä)	211	31°16'N	131°03'E
Uchinskoye Vodokhranilishche, res., Russia	186b	56°08'N	37°44'E
Uchiura-Wan, b., Japan (ōō'chē-ōō'rä wän)	210	42°20'N	140°44'E
Uchur, r., Russia (ò-chòr')	185	57°25'N	130°35'E
Uda, r., Russia	185	53°54'N	131°29'E
Uda, r., Russia (ò'dȧ)	185	52°28'N	110°51'E
Udai, r., Ukr.	177	50°45'N	32°13'E
Udaipur, India (ò-dŭ'ē-pōōr)	202	24°41'N	73°41'E
Uddevalla, Swe. (ōōd'dĕ-väl-ȧ)	160	58°21'N	11°55'E
Udine, Italy (ōō'dē-nā)	162	46°05'N	13°14'E
Udmurtia, prov., Russia	180	57°00'N	53°00'E
Udon Thani, Thai.	212	17°31'N	102°51'E
Udskaya Guba, b., Russia	179	55°00'N	136°30'E
Ueckermünde, Ger.	168	53°43'N	14°01'E
Ueda, Japan (wā'dȧ)	210	36°26'N	138°16'E
Uele, r., D.R.C. (wā'lȧ)	231	3°55'N	23°30'E
Uelzen, Ger. (ült'sĕn)	168	52°58'N	10°34'E
Ufa, Russia (ò'fȧ)	178	54°45'N	55°57'E
Ufa, r., Russia	180	56°00'N	57°05'E
Ugab, r., Nmb. (ōō'gäb)	232	21°10'S	14°00'E
Ugalla, r., Tan. (ōō-gä'lä)	232	6°15'S	32°30'E
Uganda, nation, Afr. (ōō-gän'dä) (ū-găn'dȧ)	231	2°00'N	32°28'E
Ugashik Lake, l., Ak., U.S. (ōō'gȧ-shĕk)	103	57°36'N	157°10'W
Ugie, S. Afr. (ò'jē)	233c	31°13'S	28°14'E
Uglegorsk, Russia (ōō-glĕ-gôrsk)	179	49°00'N	142°31'E

ăt; finăl; rāte; senåte; ärm; åsk; sofȧ; fâre; ch-choose; dh-as th in other; bē; ēvent; bĕt; recĕnt; cratẽr; g-gō; gh-guttural g; bĭt; ĭ-short neutral; rīde; ᴋ-guttural k as ch in German ich;

PRONOUNCING INDEX Ugleural'sk – Valdecañas 361

PLACE (Pronunciation)	PAGE	LAT.	LONG.
Ugleural'sk, Russia (o̤g-lĕ-o̤-rálsk′)	186a	58°58'N	57°35'E
Uglich, Russia (o͞og-lêch′)	176	57°33'N	38°19'E
Uglitskiy, Russia (o̤g-lĭt′skĭ)	186a	53°50'N	60°18'E
Uglovka, Russia (o͞og-lôf′kȧ)	176	58°14'N	33°24'E
Ugra, r., Russia (o͞og′rȧ)	180	54°43'N	34°20'E
Ugŭrchin, Blg.	175	43°06'N	24°23'E
Uhrichsville, Oh., U.S. (ū′rĭks-vĭl)	108	40°25'N	81°20'W
Uíge, Ang.	232	7°37'S	15°03'E
Uiju, Kor., N. (o̤′ējo͞o)	205	40°09'N	124°33'E
Uinkaret Plateau, plat., Az., U.S. (ů-ĭn′kâr-ēt)	119	36°43'N	113°15'W
Uinskoye, Russia (o̤-ĭn′skô-yĕ)	186a	56°53'N	56°25'E
Uinta, r., Ut., U.S. (ů-ĭn′tȧ)	119	40°25'N	109°55'W
Uintah and Ouray Indian Reservation, I.R., Ut., U.S.	119	40°20'N	110°20'W
Uinta Mountains, mts., Ut., U.S.	106	40°35'N	111°00'W
Uitenhage, S. Afr.	232	33°46'S	25°26'E
Uithoorn, Neth.	159a	52°13'N	4°49'E
Uji, Japan (o͞o′jē)	211b	34°53'N	135°49'E
Ujiji, Tan. (o͞o-jē′jē)	232	4°55'S	29°41'E
Ujjain, India (o͞o-jŭěn)	199	23°18'N	75°37'E
Ujungpandang, Indon.	212	5°08'S	119°28'E
Ukerewe Island, i., Tan.	237	2°00'S	32°40'E
Ukhta, Russia (o͞ok′tȧ)	180	65°22'N	31°30'E
Ukhta, Russia	180	63°08'N	53°42'E
Ukiah, Ca., U.S. (ū-kī′ȧ)	118	39°09'N	122°12'W
Ukmerge, Lith. (o̤k′mĕr-ghå)	180	55°16'N	24°45'E
Ukraine, nation, Eur.	178	49°15'N	30°15'E
Uku, i., Japan (o͞ok′o͞o)	211	33°18'N	129°02'E
Ulaangom, Mong.	204	50°23'N	92°14'E
Ulan Bator (Ulaanbaatar), Mong.	204	47°56'N	107°00'E
Ulan-Ude, Russia (o͞o′län o͞o′dȧ)	179	51°59'N	107°41'E
Ulchin, Kor., S. (o͞ol′chĕn′)	210	36°57'N	129°26'E
Ulcinj, Mont. (o͞ol′tsēn′)	163	41°56'N	19°15'E
Ulhās, r., India	203b	19°13'N	73°03'E
Ulhāsnagar, India	202	19°10'N	73°07'E
Uliastay, Mong.	204	47°49'N	97°00'E
Ulindi, r., D.R.C. (o͞o-lĭn′dē)	232	1°55'S	26°17'E
Ulla, Bela. (o̤l′ȧ)	176	55°14'N	29°15'E
Ulla, r., Bela.	176	54°58'N	29°03'E
Ulla, r., Spain (o͞ol′lä)	172	42°45'N	8°33'W
Ullŭng, i., Kor., S. (o͞ol′lŏng′)	210	37°29'N	130°50'E
Ulm, Ger. (o̤lm)	161	48°24'N	9°59'E
Ulmer, Mount, mtn., Ant. (ŭl′mûr′)	224	77°30'S	86°00'W
Ulricehamn, Swe. (o̤l-rē′sĕ-häm)	166	57°49'N	13°23'E
Ulsan, Kor., S. (o͞ol′sän′)	210	35°35'N	129°22'E
Ulster, hist. reg., Eur. (ŭl′stẽr)	164	54°41'N	7°10'W
Ulua, r., Hond. (o͞o-lo͞o′ȧ)	132	15°49'N	87°45'W
Ulubāria, India	202a	22°27'N	88°09'E
Ulukışla, Tur. (o͞o-lo͞o-kēsh′lȧ)	163	36°40'N	34°30'E
Ulunga, Russia (o̤-lo͞on′gȧ)	210	46°16'N	136°29'E
Ulungur, r., China (o͞o-lo͞on-gûr)	204	46°31'N	88°00'E
Uluru (Ayers Rock), mtn., Austl.	220	25°23'S	131°05'E
Ulu-Telyak, Russia (o͞o lô′tĕlyăk)	186a	54°54'N	57°01'E
Ulverstone, Austl. (ŭl′vẽr-stŭn)	219	41°20'S	146°22'E
Ul'yanovka, Russia	186c	59°38'N	30°47'E
Ul'yanovsk, Russia (o͞o-lyä′nôfsk)	178	54°20'N	48°24'E
Ulysses, Ks., U.S. (ū-lĭs′ēz)	120	37°34'N	101°25'W
Umán, Mex. (o͞o-män′)	132a	20°52'N	89°44'W
Uman', Ukr. (o̤-mán′)	181	48°44'N	30°13'E
Umatilla Indian Reservation, I.R., Or., U.S. (ū-mȧ-tĭl′ȧ)	114	45°38'N	118°35'W
Umberpāda, India	203b	19°28'N	73°04'E
Umbria, hist. reg., Italy (ŭm′brĭ-ă)	174	42°53'N	12°22'E
Umeälven, r., Swe.	156	64°57'N	18°51'E
Umhlatuzi, r., S. Afr. (o̤m′hlȧ-to͞o′zĭ)	233c	28°47'S	31°17'E
Umiat, Ak., U.S. (o͞o′mĭ-ăt)	106a	69°20'N	152°28'W
Umkomaas, S. Afr. (o̤m-kō′mäs)	233c	30°12'S	30°48'E
Umnak, i., Ak., U.S. (o͞om′năk)	106b	53°10'N	169°08'W
Umnak Pass, Ak., U.S.	103a	53°10'N	168°04'W
Umniati, r., Zimb.	232	17°08'S	29°11'E
Umpqua, r., Or., U.S. (ŭmp′kwȧ)	114	43°42'N	123°50'W
Umtata, S. Afr. (o̤m-tä′tä)	232	31°36'S	28°47'E
Umtentweni, S. Afr.	233c	30°41'S	30°29'E
Umzimkulu, S. Afr. (o̤m-zĕm-ko͞o′lo͞o)	233c	30°12'S	29°53'E
Umzinto, S. Afr. (o̤m-zĭn′tō)	233c	30°19'S	30°41'E
Una, r., Eur. (o͞o′nȧ)	174	44°38'N	16°10'E
Unalakleet, Ak., U.S. (ū-nȧ-lăk′lēt)	103	63°50'N	160°42'W
Unalaska, Ak., U.S. (ū-nȧ-lăs′kȧ)	103a	53°30'N	166°20'W
Unare, r., Ven.	143b	9°45'N	65°12'W
Unare, Laguna de, l., Ven. (lä-gō′nä-de-o͞o-nä′rĕ)	143b	10°07'N	65°23'W
Unayzah, Sau. Ar.	198	25°50'N	44°02'E
Uncas, Can. (ŭŋ′kăs)	102g	53°30'N	113°02'W
Uncia, Bol. (o͞on′sē-ä)	142	18°28'S	66°32'W
Uncompahgre, r., Co., U.S.	119	38°20'N	107°45'W
Uncompahgre Peak, mtn., Co., U.S. (ŭn-kŭm-pä′grē)	119	38°00'N	107°30'W
Uncompahgre Plateau, plat., Co., U.S.	119	38°40'N	108°40'W
Underberg, S. Afr. (ŭn′dẽr-bûrg)	233c	29°51'S	29°32'E
Unecha, Russia (o̤-nĕ′chȧ)	176	52°51'N	32°44'E
Ungava, Péninsule d', pen., Can.	93	59°55'N	74°00'W
Ungava Bay, b., Can. (ŭŋ-gā′vȧ)	93	59°46'N	67°18'W
União da Vitória, Braz. (o͞o-nē-ouɴ′ dä vē-tô′ryä)	144	26°17'S	51°13'W
Unije, i., Cro. (o͞o′nē-yĕ)	174	44°39'N	14°10'E
Unimak, i., Ak., U.S. (o͞o-nē-măk′)	103	54°30'N	163°35'W
Unimak Pass, Ak., U.S.	103a	54°22'N	165°22'W
Union, Mo., U.S.	121	38°28'N	90°59'W
Union, Ms., U.S. (ūn′yŭn)	124	32°35'N	89°07'W
Union, N.C., U.S.	125	34°42'N	81°40'W
Union, Or., U.S.	114	45°13'N	117°52'W
Union City, Ca., U.S.	116b	37°36'N	122°01'W
Union City, In., U.S.	108	40°10'N	85°00'W
Union City, Mi., U.S.	108	42°00'N	85°10'W
Union City, Pa., U.S.	109	41°50'N	79°50'W
Union City, Tn., U.S.	124	36°25'N	89°04'W
Unión de Reyes, Cuba	134	22°45'N	81°30'W
Unión de San Antonio, Mex.	130	21°07'N	101°56'W
Unión de Tula, Mex.	130	19°57'N	104°14'W
Union Grove, Wi., U.S. (ūn-yŭn grōv)	111a	42°41'N	88°03'W
Unión Hidalgo, Mex. (ē-dä′lgō)	131	16°29'N	94°51'W
Union Point, Ga., U.S.	124	33°37'N	83°08'W
Union Springs, Al., U.S. (sprĭngz)	124	32°08'N	85°43'W
Uniontown, Al., U.S. (ūn′yŭn-toun)	124	32°26'N	87°30'W
Uniontown, Oh., U.S.	111d	40°58'N	81°25'W
Uniontown, Pa., U.S.	109	39°55'N	79°45'W
Unionville, Mo., U.S. (ūn′yŭn-vĭl)	121	40°28'N	92°58'W
Unisan, Phil. (o͞o-nē′sän)	213a	13°50'N	121°59'E
United Arab Emirates, nation, Asia	198	24°00'N	54°00'E
United Kingdom, nation, Eur.	154	56°30'N	1°40'W
United States, nation, N.A.	104	38°00'N	110°00'W
Unity, Can.	96	52°27'N	109°10'W
Universal, In., U.S. (ū-nĭ-vûr′sȧl)	108	39°35'N	87°30'W
University City, Mo., U.S. (ū′nĭ-vûr′sĭ-tĭ)	117e	38°40'N	90°19'W
University Park, Tx., U.S.	117c	32°51'N	96°48'W
Unna, Ger. (o͞o′nä)	171c	51°32'N	7°41'E
Uno, Canal Numero, can., Arg.	141c	36°43'S	58°14'W
Unterhaching, Ger. (o͞on′tĕr-hä-kĕng)	159d	48°03'N	11°38'E
Ünye, Tur. (ün′yĕ)	163	41°00'N	37°10'E
Unzha, r., Russia (o̤n′zhȧ)	180	57°45'N	44°10'E
Upa, r., Russia (o̤′pȧ)	176	53°54'N	36°48'E
Upata, Ven. (o͞o-pä′tä)	142	7°58'N	62°27'W
Upemba, Parc National de l', rec., D.R.C.	237	9°10'S	26°15'E
Upington, S. Afr. (ŭp′ĭng-tŭn)	232	28°25'S	21°15'E
Upland, Ca., U.S. (ŭp′lănd)	117a	34°06'N	117°38'W
Upolu, i., Samoa	214a	13°55'S	171°45'W
Upolu Point, c., Hi., U.S. (o͞o-pō′lo͞o)	126a	20°15'N	155°48'W
Upper Arrow Lake, l., Can. (ăr′ō)	95	50°30'N	117°55'W
Upper Darby, Pa., U.S. (där′bĭ)	110f	39°58'N	75°16'W
Upper des Lacs, l., N.A. (dĕ läk)	112	48°58'N	101°55'W
Upper Kapuas Mountains, mts., Asia	212	1°45'N	112°06'E
Upper Klamath Lake, l., Or., U.S.	114	42°23'N	122°55'W
Upper Lake, l., Nv., U.S. (ŭp′ẽr)	114	41°42'N	119°59'W
Upper Marlboro, Md., U.S. (ûpẽr mărl′bŏrŏ)	110e	38°49'N	76°46'W
Upper Mill, Wa., U.S. (mĭl)	116a	47°11'N	121°55'W
Upper Red Lake, l., Mn., U.S. (rĕd)	113	48°14'N	94°53'W
Upper Sandusky, Oh., U.S. (săn-dŭs′kē)	108	40°50'N	83°20'W
Upper San Leandro Reservoir, res., Ca., U.S. (ŭp′ẽr săn lē-ăn′drō)	116b	37°47'N	122°04'W
Upper Volta *see* Burkina Faso, nation, Afr.	230	13°00'N	2°00'W
Uppingham, Eng., U.K. (ŭp′ĭng-ăm)	158a	52°35'N	0°43'W
Uppsala, Swe. (o͞op′sȧ-lä)	154	59°53'N	17°39'E
Uptown, Ma., U.S. (ŭp′toun)	101a	42°10'N	71°36'W
Uraga, Japan (o͞o′rȧ-gä′)	211a	35°15'N	139°43'E
Ural, r. (o͞o-räl′′) (ū-rôl)	178	48°00'N	51°00'E
Urals, mts., Russia	178	56°28'N	58°13'E
Uran, India (o͞o-rän′)	203b	18°53'N	72°46'E
Uranium City, Can.	90	59°34'N	108°59'W
Urawa, Japan (o͞o′rä-wä′)	210	35°52'N	139°39'E
Urayasu, Japan (o͞o′rä-yä′so͞o)	211a	35°40'N	139°54'W
Urazovo, Russia (o̤-rá′zô-vô)	177	50°08'N	38°03'E
Urbana, Il., U.S. (ûr-băn′ȧ)	108	40°10'N	88°15'W
Urbana, Oh., U.S.	108	40°05'N	83°50'W
Urbino, Italy (o͞or-bē′nō)	174	43°43'N	12°37'E
Urdaneta, Phil. (o͞or-dä-nä′tä)	213a	15°59'N	120°34'E
Urdinarrain, Arg. (o͞or-dē-när-rä-ē′n)	141c	32°43'S	58°53'W
Uritsk, Russia (o͞o′rĭtsk)	186c	59°50'N	30°11'E
Urla, Tur. (o̤r′lȧ)	175	38°20'N	26°44'E
Urman, Russia (o̤r′mán)	186a	54°53'N	56°52'E
Urmi, r., Russia (o̤r′mē)	210	48°50'N	134°00'E
Uromi, Nig.	235	6°44'N	6°18'E
Urrao, Col. (o͞or-rä′ō)	142	6°19'N	76°11'W
Urshel'skiy, Russia (o͞or-shĕl′skē)	176	55°50'N	40°11'E
Ursus, Pol.	169	52°12'N	20°53'E
Urubamba, r., Peru (o͞o-ro͞o-bäm′bä)	142	11°48'S	72°34'W
Uruguaiana, Braz.	144	29°45'S	57°00'W
Uruguay, nation, S.A. (o͞o-ro͞o-gwī′) (ū′ro͞o-gwā)	144	32°45'S	56°00'W
Uruguay, r., S.A. (o͞o-ro͞o-gwī′)	144	27°05'S	55°15'W
Ürümqi, China (ů-rům-chyē)	204	43°49'N	87°43'E
Urup, i., Russia (o̤′ro̤p′)	205	46°00'N	150°00'E
Uryupinsk, Russia (o̤r′yo̤-pēn-sk′)	181	50°50'N	42°00'E
Ürzhar, Kaz.	183	47°28'N	82°00'E
Urziceni, Rom. (o̤-zē-chĕn′′)	175	44°45'N	26°42'E
Usa, Japan	210	33°31'N	131°22'E
Usa, r., Russia (o̤′sȧ)	180	66°00'N	58°20'E
Uşak, Tur. (o͞o′shăk)	163	38°45'N	29°15'E
Usakos, Nmb. (o͞o-sä′kōs)	232	22°00'S	15°40'E
Usambara Mountains, mts., Tan.	237	4°40'S	38°25'E
Usangu Flats, sw., Tan.	237	8°10'S	34°00'E
Ushaki, Russia (o͞o′shȧ-kĭ)	186c	59°28'N	31°00'E
Ushakovskoye, Russia (o̤-shá-kôv′skô-yĕ)	186a	56°18'N	62°23'E
Ushashi, Tan.	237	2°00'S	33°57'E
Ushiku, Japan (o͞o′shē-ko͞o)	211a	35°24'N	140°09'E
Ushimado, Japan (o͞o′shē-mä′dō)	211	34°37'N	134°09'E
Ushuaia, Arg. (o͞o-sho͞o-ī′ä)	144	54°46'S	68°24'W
Usman', Russia (o͞os-mán′)	181	52°03'N	39°40'E
Usol'ye, Russia (o͞o-sô′lyĕ)	186a	59°24'N	56°40'E
Usol'ye-Sibirskoye, Russia (o̤-sô′lyĕsĭ′ bĕr′skô-yĕ)	184	52°44'N	103°46'E
Uspallata Pass, p., S.A. (o͞os-pä-lyä′tä)	144	32°47'S	70°08'W
Uspanapa, r., Mex. (o͞os-pä-nä′pä)	131	17°43'N	94°14'W
Ussel, Fr. (üs′ĕl)	170	45°33'N	2°17'E
Ussuri, r., Asia (o͞o-so͞o′rē)	185	47°30'N	134°00'E
Ussuriysk, Russia	179	43°48'N	132°09'E
Ust'-Bol'sheretsk, Russia	179	52°41'N	157°00'E
Ustica, Isola di, i., Italy	174	38°43'N	12°11'E
Ústí nad Labem, Czech Rep.	168	50°40'N	14°02'E
Ust'-Izhora, Russia (o̤st-ēz′hô-rȧ)	186c	59°49'N	30°35'E
Ustka, Pol. (o͞ost′kȧ)	168	54°34'N	16°52'E
Ust'-Kamchatsk, Russia	179	56°13'N	162°18'E
Ust'-Katav, Russia (o̤st kȧ′táf)	186a	54°55'N	58°12'E
Ust'-Kishert', Russia (o̤st kē′shĕrt)	186a	57°21'N	57°13'E
Ust'-Kulom, Russia (ko̤′lŭm)	178	61°38'N	54°00'E
Ust'-Maya, Russia (mȧ′yȧ)	179	60°33'N	134°43'E
Ust' Olenëk, Russia	179	72°52'N	120°15'E
Ust-Ordynskiy, Russia (o̤st-ôr-dyēnsk′ĭ)	181	52°47'N	104°00'E
Ust' Penzhino, Russia	185	63°00'N	165°10'E
Ust' Port, Russia (o̤st′pôrt′)	178	69°20'N	83°41'E
Ust'-Tsil'ma, Russia (tsĭl′mȧ)	178	65°25'N	52°10'E
Ust'-Tyrma, Russia (tur′mȧ)	179	50°27'N	131°17'E
Ust' Uls, Russia	186a	60°35'N	58°32'E
Ust-Urt, Plateau, plat., Asia	178	44°03'N	54°58'E
Ustynivka, Ukr.	177	47°59'N	32°31'E
Ustyuzhna, Russia (yo͞ozh′nȧ)	180	58°49'N	36°19'E
Usu, China (ů-so͞o)	204	44°28'N	84°07'E
Usuki, Japan (o͞o′so͞o-kē′)	211	33°06'N	131°47'E
Usulutan, El Sal. (o͞o-so͞o-lä-tän′)	132	13°22'N	88°25'W
Usumacinta, r., N.A. (o͞o′so͞o-mä-sēn′tō)	131	18°24'N	92°30'W
Us'va, Russia (o͞os′vȧ)	186a	58°41'N	57°38'E
Utah, state, U.S. (ū′tô)	104	39°25'N	112°40'W
Utah Lake, l., Ut., U.S.	119	40°10'N	111°55'W
Utan, India	203b	19°17'N	72°43'E
Ute Mountain Indian Reservation, I.R., N.M., U.S.	119	36°57'N	108°34'W
Utena, Lith. (o͞o′tā-nä)	167	55°32'N	25°40'E
Utete, Tan. (o͞o-tā′tā)	233	8°05'S	38°47'E
Utica, In., U.S. (ū′tĭ-kȧ)	111h	38°20'N	85°39'W
Utica, N.Y., U.S.	105	43°05'N	75°10'W
Utiel, Spain (o͞o-tyâl′)	172	39°34'N	1°13'W
Utika, Mi., U.S. (ū′tĭ-kȧ)	111b	42°37'N	83°02'W
Utik Lake, l., Can.	97	55°16'N	96°00'W
Utikuma Lake, l., Can.	95	55°50'N	115°25'W
Utila, i., Hond. (o͞o-tē′lä)	132	16°07'N	87°05'W
Uto, Japan (o͞o′tō′)	210	32°43'N	130°39'E
Utrecht, Neth. (ü′trĕkt) (ū′trĕkt)	161	52°05'N	5°06'E
Utrera, Spain (o͞o-trā′rä)	162	37°12'N	5°48'W
Utsunomiya, Japan (o͞ot′sò-nô-mē-yȧ′)	205	36°35'N	139°52'E
Uttaradit, Thai.	212	17°47'N	100°10'E
Uttaranchal, state, India	199	29°30'N	78°30'E
Uttarpara-Kotrung, India	202a	22°40'N	88°21'E
Uttar Pradesh, state, India (o̤t-tär-prä-dĕsh)	199	27°00'N	80°00'E
Uttoxeter, Eng., U.K. (ŭt-tôk′sē-tẽr)	158a	52°54'N	1°52'W
Utuado, P.R. (o͞o-to͞o-ä′dhō)	129b	18°16'N	66°40'W
Uusikaupunki, Fin.	167	60°48'N	21°24'E
Uvalde, Tx., U.S. (ū-văl′dē)	122	29°14'N	99°47'W
Uvel'skiy, Russia (o̤-vyĕl′skĭ)	186a	54°27'N	61°22'E
Uvinza, Tan.	237	5°06'S	30°22'E
Uvira, D.R.C. (o͞o-vē′rä)	232	3°28'S	29°03'E
Uvod', r., Russia (o̤-vôd′)	176	56°40'N	41°10'E
Uvongo Beach, S. Afr.	233c	30°49'S	30°23'E
Uvs Nuur, l., Asia	204	50°29'N	93°32'E
Uwajima, Japan (o͞o-wä′jē-mä)	210	33°12'N	132°35'E
Uxbridge, Ma., U.S. (ŭks′brĭj)	101a	42°05'N	71°38'W
Uxmal, hist., Mex. (o͞o′x-mä′l)	132a	20°22'N	89°44'W
Uy, r., Russia (o͞oy)	186a	54°05'N	62°11'E
Uyskoye, Russia (ûy′skô-yĕ)	186a	54°22'N	60°01'E
Uyuni, Bol. (o͞o-yo͞o′nē)	142	20°28'S	66°45'W
Uyuni, Salar de, pl., Bol. (sä-lär-dĕ)	142	20°58'S	67°09'W
Uzbekistan, nation, Asia	178	42°42'N	60°00'E
Uzh, r., Ukr. (o̤zh)	177	51°07'N	29°05'E
Uzhhorod, Ukr.	169	48°38'N	22°18'E
Užice, Serb. (o͞o′zhĕ-tsĕ)	175	43°51'N	19°53'E
Uzunköprü, Tur.	175	41°17'N	26°42'E

V

PLACE (Pronunciation)	PAGE	LAT.	LONG.
Vaal, r., S. Afr. (väl)	232	28°15'S	24°30'E
Vaaldam, res., S. Afr.	238c	26°58'S	28°37'E
Vaalplaas, S. Afr.	238c	25°39'S	28°56'E
Vaalwater, S. Afr.	238c	24°17'S	28°08'E
Vaasa, Fin. (vä′sȧ)	154	63°06'N	21°39'E
Vác, Hung. (väts)	169	47°46'N	19°10'E
Vache, Île à, i., Haiti	135	18°05'N	73°40'W
Vadstena, Swe. (väd′stĭ′nȧ)	166	58°27'N	14°53'E
Vaduz, Liech. (vä′do̤ts)	168	47°10'N	9°32'E
Vaga, r., Russia (va′gȧ)	180	61°55'N	42°30'E
Vah, r., Slvk. (väκ)	161	48°07'N	17°52'E
Vaigai, r., India	203	10°20'N	78°13'E
Vakh, r., Russia (vàκ)	184	61°30'N	81°33'E
Valachia, hist. reg., Rom.	175	44°45'N	24°17'E
Valcartier-Village, Can. (väl-kärt-yĕ′vē-läzh′)	102b	46°56'N	71°28'W
Valdai Hills, hills, Russia (vál-dī′ gô′rĭ)	180	57°50'N	32°35'E
Valday, Russia (vál-dī′)	180	57°58'N	33°13'E
Valdecañas, Embalse de, res., Spain	172	39°45'N	5°30'W

ng-sing; ŋ-baŋk; ɴ-nasalized n; nŏd; cŏmmit; ōld; ôbey; ôrder; oi-boil; fo͞od; o̤-as oo in foot; ou-out; s-soft; sh-dish; th-thin; pūre; ůnite; ûrn; stŭd; circŭs; ü-as in French tu; ′-indeterminate vowel.

362 Valdemārpils – Vernon

PRONOUNCING INDEX

PLACE (Pronunciation)	PAGE	LAT.	LONG.
Valdemārpils, Lat.	167	57°22'N	22°34'E
Valdemorillo, Spain (väl-dā-mō-rēl'yō)	173a	40°30'N	4°04'W
Valdepeñas, Spain (väl-dā-pān'yäs)	162	38°46'N	3°22'W
Valderaduey, r., Spain (väl-dĕ-rä-dwĕ'y)	172	41°39'N	5°35'W
Valdés, Península, pen., Arg. (väl-dĕ's)	144	42°15'S	63°15'W
Valdez, Ak., U.S. (văl'dēz)	103	61°10'N	146°18'W
Valdilecha, Spain (väl-dė-lā'chä)	173a	40°17'N	3°19'W
Valdivia, Chile (väl-dė'vä)	144	39°47'S	73°13'W
Valdivia, Col. (väl-dė'vēä)	142a	7°10'N	75°26'W
Val d'Or, Can.	91	48°03'N	77°50'W
Valdosta, Ga., U.S. (văl-dŏs'tȧ)	105	30°50'N	83°18'W
Vale, Or., U.S. (vāl)	114	43°59'N	117°14'W
Valença, Braz. (vä-lĕn'sȧ)	143	13°43'S	38°58'W
[illegible]	[illegible]	[illegible]	[illegible]
Valence, Fr. (vä-lĕnns)	161	44°56'N	4°54'E
València, Spain	154	39°26'N	0°23'W
Valencia, Ven. (vä-lĕn'syä)	142	10°11'N	68°00'W
València, hist. reg., Spain	173	39°08'N	0°43'W
València, Golf de, b., Spain	173	39°50'N	0°30'E
Valencia, Lago de, l., Ven.	143b	10°11'N	67°45'W
Valencia de Alcántara, Spain	172	39°34'N	7°13'W
Valenciennes, Fr. (vȧ-län-syĕn')	170	50°24'N	3°36'E
Valentine, Ne., U.S. (vă lăn-tē-nyĕ')	104	42°52'N	100°34'W
Valera, Ven. (vä-lĕ'rä)	142	9°12'N	70°45'W
Valerianovsk, Russia (vȧ-lĕ-rĭ-ä'nôvsk)	186a	58°47'N	59°34'E
Valga, Est. (väl'gȧ)	180	57°47'N	26°03'E
Valhalla, S. Afr. (văl-hăl-ȧ)	233b	25°49'S	28°09'E
Valier, Mt., U.S. (vă-lēr')	115	48°17'N	112°14'W
Valjevo, Serb. (väl'yȧ-vô)	175	44°17'N	19°57'E
Valky, Ukr.	177	49°49'N	35°40'E
Valladolid, Mex. (väl-yä-dhō-lēdh')	128	20°39'N	88°13'W
Valladolid, Spain (väl-yä-dhō-lēdh')	154	41°41'N	4°41'W
Valle, Arroyo del, Ca., U.S. (ä-rō'yō dĕl väl'yȧ)	118	37°36'N	121°43'W
Vallecas, Spain (väl-yā'käs)	173a	40°23'N	3°37'W
Valle de Allende, Mex. (väl'yā dā äl-yĕn'dā)	122	26°55'N	105°25'W
Valle de Bravo, Mex. (brä'vō)	130	19°12'N	100°07'W
Valle de Guanape, Ven. (vä'l-yĕ-dĕ-gwä-nä'pĕ)	143b	9°54'N	65°41'W
Valle de la Pascua, Ven. (lä-pä's-kōōä)	142	9°12'N	65°08'W
Valle del Cauca, dept., Col. (vä'l-yĕ del kou'kä)	142a	4°03'N	76°13'W
Valle de Santiago, Mex. (sän-tē-ä'gō)	130	20°23'N	101°11'W
Valledupar, Col. (dōō-pär')	142	10°13'N	73°39'W
Valle Grande, Bol. (grän'dā)	142	18°27'S	64°03'W
Vallejo, Ca., U.S. (vä-yā'hō) (vȧ-lā'hō)	104	38°06'N	122°15'W
Vallejo, Sierra de, mts., Mex. (sē-ĕ'r-rä-dĕ-väl-yĕ'кō)	130	21°00'N	105°10'W
Vallenar, Chile (väl-yȧ-när')	144	28°39'S	70°52'W
Valles, Mex.	128	21°59'N	99°02'W
Valletta, Malta (väl-lĕt'ä)	162	35°50'N	14°29'E
Valle Vista, Ca., U.S. (väl'yȧ vĭs'tȧ)	117a	33°45'N	116°53'W
Valley City, N.D., U.S.	104	46°55'N	97°59'W
Valley City, Oh., U.S. (văl'ĭ)	111d	41°14'N	81°56'W
Valley Falls, Ks., U.S.	121	39°25'N	95°26'W
Valleyfield, Can. (văl'ē-fēld)	91	45°16'N	74°09'W
Valley Park, Mo., U.S. (văl'ē pärk)	117e	38°33'N	90°30'W
Valley Stream, N.Y., U.S. (văl'ĭ strēm)	110a	40°39'N	73°42'W
Valli di Comácchio, l., Italy (vä'lē-dē-kô-mä'chyô)	174	44°38'N	12°15'E
Vallière, Haiti (väl-yâr')	135	19°30'N	71°55'W
Vallimanca, r., Arg. (väl-yē-mä'n-kä)	141c	36°21'S	60°55'W
Valls, Spain (väls)	162	41°15'N	1°15'E
Valmiera, Lat. (vál'myĕ-rȧ)	180	57°34'N	25°54'E
Valognes, Fr. (vȧ-lôn'y')	170	49°32'N	1°30'W
Valona *see* Vlorë, Alb.	163	40°28'N	19°31'E
Valozhyn, Bela.	176	54°04'N	26°38'E
Valparaíso, Chile (väl'pä-rä-ē'sô)	144	33°02'S	71°32'W
Valparaíso, Mex.	130	22°49'N	103°33'W
Valparaiso, In., U.S. (văl-pȧ-rā'zō)	108	41°25'N	87°05'W
Valpariso, prov., Chile	141b	32°58'S	71°23'W
Valréas, Fr. (väl-rȧ-ä')	170	44°25'N	4°56'E
Vals, r., S. Afr.	238c	27°32'S	26°51'E
Vals, Tanjung, c., Indon.	213	8°30'S	137°15'E
Valsbaai, b., S. Afr.	232a	34°14'S	18°35'E
Valuyevo, Russia (vȧ-lōō'yĕ-vô)	186b	55°34'N	37°21'E
Valuyki, Russia (vȧ-lô-ē'kē)	181	50°14'N	38°04'E
Valverde del Camino, Spain (väl-vĕr-dĕ-dĕl-kä-mē'nō)	172	37°34'N	6°44'W
Vammala, Fin.	167	61°19'N	22°51'E
Van, Tur. (vȧn)	198	38°04'N	43°10'E
Van Buren, Ar., U.S. (văn bū'rĕn)	121	35°26'N	94°20'W
Van Buren, Me., U.S.	100	47°09'N	67°58'W
Vanceburg, Ky., U.S. (văns'bûrg)	108	38°35'N	83°20'W
Vancouver, Can. (văn-kōō'vĕr)	90	49°16'N	123°06'W
Vancouver, Wa., U.S.	104	45°37'N	122°40'W
Vancouver Island, i., Can.	92	49°50'N	125°05'W
Vancouver Island Ranges, mts., Can.	94	49°25'N	125°25'W
Vandalia, Il., U.S. (văn-dā'lĭ-ȧ)	108	39°00'N	89°00'W
Vandalia, Mo., U.S.	121	39°19'N	91°30'W
Vanderbijlpark, S. Afr.	238c	26°43'S	27°50'E
Vanderhoof, Can.	90	54°01'N	124°01'W
Van Diemen, Cape, c., Austl. (vănděměn)	220	11°05'S	130°15'E
Van Diemen Gulf, b., Austl.	220	11°50'S	131°30'E
Vanegas, Mex. (vä-nĕ'gäs)	128	23°54'N	100°54'W
Vänern, l., Swe.	156	58°52'N	13°17'E
Vänersborg, Swe. (vĕ'nĕrs-bôr')	160	58°24'N	12°15'E
Vanga, Kenya (väŋ'gä)	233	4°38'S	39°10'E
Vangani, India	203b	19°07'N	73°15'E
Van Gölü, l., Tur.	180	38°33'N	42°46'E
Van Horn, Tx., U.S.	122	31°03'N	104°50'W
Vanier, Can.	102c	45°27'N	75°39'W
Van Lear, Ky., U.S. (văn lēr')	108	37°45'N	82°50'W
Vannes, Fr. (vȧn)	161	47°42'N	2°46'W
Van Nuys, Ca., U.S. (văn nīz')	117a	34°11'N	118°27'W
Van Rees, Pegunungan, mts., Indon.	213	2°30'S	138°45'E
Vantaan, r., Fin.	167	60°25'N	24°43'E
Vanua Levu, i., Fiji	214g	16°33'S	179°15'E
Vanuatu, nation, Oc.	219	16°00'S	169°15'E
Van Wert, Oh., U.S. (văn wûrt')	108	40°50'N	84°35'W
Vara, Swe. (vä'rä)	166	58°17'N	12°55'E
Varaklani, Lat.	[illegible]	[illegible]	[illegible]
Varallo, Italy (vä-räl'lō)	174	45°44'N	8°14'E
Vārānasi (Benares), India	199	25°25'N	83°00'E
Varangerfjorden, b., Nor.	157	70°05'N	30°20'E
Varano, Lago di, l., Italy (lä'gō-dē-vä-rä'nô)	174	41°52'N	15°55'E
Varaždin, Cro. (vä'räzh'dĕn)	163	46°17'N	16°20'E
Varazze, Italy (vä-rät'sā)	174	44°23'N	8°34'E
Varberg, Swe. (vär'bĕrg)	166	57°06'N	12°16'E
Vardar, r., Mont. (vär'där)	175	41°40'N	21°50'E
Varėna, Lith. (vä-rā'nȧ)	167	54°16'N	24°35'E
Varennes, Can. (vȧ-rĕn')	102a	45°41'N	73°27'W
Vareš, Bos. (vä'rĕsh)	175	44°10'N	18°20'E
Varese, Italy (vä-rā'sā)	174	45°45'N	8°49'E
Varginha, Braz. (vär-zhē'n-yä)	143	21°33'S	45°25'W
Varkaus, Fin. (vär'kous)	167	62°19'N	27°51'E
Varlamovo, Russia (vár-lá'mô-vô)	186a	54°37'N	60°41'E
Varna, Blg. (vär'nȧ)	154	43°14'N	27°58'E
Varna, Russia	186a	53°22'N	60°59'E
Värnamo, Swe. (vĕr'ná-mô)	166	57°11'N	13°45'E
Varnsdorf, Czech Rep. (värns'dôrf)	168	50°54'N	14°36'E
Varnville, S.C., U.S. (värn'vĭl)	125	32°49'N	81°05'W
Vasa, India	203b	19°20'N	72°47'E
Vascongadas *see* Basque Provinces, hist. reg., Spain	172	43°00'N	2°46'W
Vashka, r., Russia	180	64°00'N	48°00'E
Vashon, Wa., U.S. (văsh'ŭn)	116a	47°27'N	122°28'W
Vashon Heights, Wa., U.S. (hītz)	116a	47°30'N	122°28'W
Vashon Island, i., Wa., U.S.	116a	47°27'N	122°27'W
Vaslui, Rom. (vás-lōō'ē)	169	46°39'N	27°49'E
Vassar, Mi., U.S. (văs'ēr)	108	43°25'N	83°35'W
Vassouras, Braz. (väs-sō'räzh)	141a	22°25'S	43°40'W
Västerås, Swe. (vĕs'tĕr-ôs)	160	59°39'N	16°30'E
Västerdalälven, r., Swe.	160	61°06'N	13°10'E
Västervik, Swe. (vĕs'tĕr-vēk)	160	57°45'N	16°35'E
Vasto, Italy (väs'tô)	162	42°06'N	14°42'E
Vasyl'kiv, Ukr.	181	50°10'N	30°22'E
Vasyugan, r., Russia (vás-yōō-gán')	184	58°52'N	77°30'E
Vatican City, nation, Eur.	174	41°54'N	12°22'E
Vaticano, Cape, c., Italy (vä-tē-kä'nô)	174	38°38'N	15°52'E
Vatnajökull, ice, Ice. (vät'ná-yû-kôl)	160	64°34'N	16°41'W
Vatomandry, Madag.	233	18°53'S	48°13'E
Vatra Dornei, Rom. (vät'rȧ dôr'nā')	169	47°22'N	25°20'E
Vättern, l., Swe.	156	58°15'N	14°24'E
Vattholma, Swe.	166	60°01'N	17°40'E
Vaudreuil, Can. (vô-drû'y')	102a	45°24'N	74°02'W
Vaugh, Wa., U.S. (vôn)	116a	47°21'N	122°47'W
Vaughan, Can.	102d	43°47'N	79°36'W
Vaughn, N.M., U.S.	120	34°37'N	105°13'W
Vaupés, r., S.A. (vá'ōō-pĕ's)	142	1°18'N	71°14'W
Vawkavysk, Bela. (vôl-kô-vēsk')	169	53°11'N	24°29'E
Vaxholm, Swe. (väks'hôlm)	166	59°26'N	18°19'E
Växjo, Swe. (vĕks'shû)	160	56°53'N	14°46'E
Vaygach, i., Russia (vī-gách')	178	70°00'N	59°00'E
Veadeiros, Chapadas dos, hills, Braz. (shä-pä'däs-dôs-vĕ-ȧ-dā'rōs)	143	14°00'S	47°00'W
Vedea, r., Rom. (vå'dyȧ)	175	44°25'N	24°45'E
Vedia, Arg. (vĕ'dyä)	141c	34°29'S	61°30'W
Veedersburg, In., U.S. (vē'dērz-bûrg)	108	40°05'N	87°15'W
Vega, i., Nor.	160	65°38'N	10°51'E
Vega de Alatorre, Mex. (vā'gä dā ä-lä-tôr'rā)	131	20°02'N	96°39'W
Vega Real, reg., Dom. Rep. (vĕ'gä-rĕ-ä'l)	135	19°30'N	71°05'W
Vegreville, Can.	90	53°30'N	112°03'W
Vehār Lake, l., India	203b	19°11'N	72°52'E
Veinticinco de Mayo, Arg.	141c	35°26'S	60°09'W
Vejer de la Frontera, Spain	172	36°15'N	5°58'W
Vejle, Den. (vī'lĕ)	160	55°41'N	9°29'E
Velbert, Ger. (fĕl'bĕrt)	171c	51°20'N	7°03'E
Velebit, mts., Cro. (vā'lĕ-bĕt)	163	44°25'N	15°23'E
Velen, Ger. (fĕ'lĕn)	171c	51°54'N	7°00'E
Vélez-Málaga, Spain (vā'lāth-mä'lä-gä)	172	36°48'N	4°05'W
Vélez-Rubio, Spain (rōō'bē-ô)	172	37°38'N	2°05'W
Velika Kapela, mts., Cro. (vĕ'lē-kä kä-pĕ'lä)	163	45°03'N	15°20'E
Velika Morava, r., Serb. (mô'rä-vä)	163	44°00'N	21°30'E
Velikaya, r., Russia (vå-lē'kȧ-yȧ)	176	57°25'N	28°07'E
Velikiye Luki, Russia (vyē-lē'-kyė lōō'ke)	178	56°19'N	30°32'E
Velikiy Ustyug, Russia (vå-lē'kĭ ōōs-tyôg')	178	60°45'N	46°38'E
Veliko Tŭrnovo, Blg.	163	43°06'N	25°38'E
Velikoye, Russia (vå-lē'kô-yĕ)	176	57°21'N	39°45'E
Velikoye, l., Russia	176	57°00'N	36°53'E
Veli Lošinj, Cro. (lô'shēn')	174	44°30'N	14°29'E
Velizh, Russia (vå'lēzh)	180	55°37'N	31°11'E
Vella Lavella, i., Sol. Is.	221	8°00'S	156°42'E
Velletri, Italy (vĕl-lā'trē)	174	41°42'N	12°48'E
Vellore, India (vĕl-lōr')	199	12°57'N	79°09'E
Vels, Russia (vĕls)	186a	60°35'N	58°47'E
Vel'sk, Russia (vĕlsk)	178	61°00'N	42°18'E
Velten, Ger. (fel'tĕn)	159b	52°41'N	13°11'E
Velya, r., Russia (vĕl'yȧ)	186b	56°23'N	37°54'E
Velyka Lepetykha, Ukr.	177	47°11'N	33°58'E
Velykyi Bychkiv, Ukr.	169	47°59'N	24°01'E
Venadillo, Col. (vĕ-nä-dē'l-yō)	142a	4°43'N	74°55'W
Venado, Mex. (vå-mä'dō)	130	22°54'N	101°07'W
Venado Tuerto, Arg. (vĕ-nä'dô-tōōĕ'r-tô)	144	33°28'S	61°47'W
Vendôme, Fr. (vän-dōm')	170	47°46'N	1°05'E
Veneto, hist. reg., Italy (vĕ-nĕ'tô)	174	45°50'N	11°24'E
Venëv, Russia (vĕn-ĕf')	180	54°19'N	38°14'E
Venezia *see* Venice, Italy	154	45°25'N	12°18'E
Venezuela, nation, S.A. (vĕn-ĕ-zwē'lȧ)	142	8°00'N	65°00'W
Venezuela, Golfo de, b., S.A. (gôl-fô-dĕ)	142	11°34'N	71°02'W
Veniaminof, Mount, mtn., Ak., U.S.	103	56°12'N	159°20'W
Venice, Italy	154	45°25'N	12°18'E
Venice, Ca., U.S. (vĕn'ĭs)	117a	33°59'N	118°28'W
Venice, Il., U.S.	117e	38°40'N	90°10'W
Venice, Gulf of, b., Italy	162	45°23'N	13°00'E
Venlo, Neth.	171c	51°22'N	6°11'E
Venta, r., Eur. (vĕn'tȧ)	167	57°05'N	21°45'E
Ventana, Sierra de la, mts., Arg. (sē-ĕ-rȧ-dĕ-lä-vĕn-tȧ'nä)	144	38°00'S	63°00'W
Ventersburg, S. Afr. (vĕn-tērs'bûrg)	238c	28°06'S	27°10'E
Ventersdorp, S. Afr. (vĕn-tērs'dôrp)	238c	26°20'S	26°48'E
Ventimiglia, Italy (vĕn-tē-mēl'yä)	174	43°46'N	7°37'E
Ventnor, N.J., U.S. (vĕnt'nēr)	109	39°20'N	74°25'W
Ventspils, Lat. (vĕnt'spēls)	180	57°24'N	21°41'E
Ventuari, r., Ven. (vĕn-tōōä'rē)	142	4°47'N	65°56'W
Ventura, Ca., U.S. (vĕn-tōō'rȧ)	118	34°18'N	119°18'W
Venukovsky, Russia (vĕ-nōō'kôv-skĭ)	186b	55°10'N	37°26'E
Venustiano Carranza, Mex. (vĕ-nōōs-tyä'nō-kär-rä'n-zä)	130	19°44'N	103°48'W
Venustiano Carranzo, Mex. (kär-rä'n-zô)	131	16°21'N	92°36'W
Vera, Arg. (vĕ-rä)	144	29°22'S	60°09'W
Vera, Spain (vā'rä)	172	37°18'N	1°53'W
Veracruz, Mex.	128	19°13'N	96°07'W
Vera Cruz, state, Mex. (vā-rä-krōōz')	128	20°30'N	97°15'W
Verāval, India (vĕr'vŭ-väl)	199	20°59'N	70°49'E
Vercelli, Italy (vĕr-chĕl'lē)	174	45°18'N	8°27'E
Verchères, Can. (vĕr-shâr')	102a	45°46'N	73°21'W
Verde, i., Phil. (vĕr'dā)	213a	13°34'N	121°11'E
Verde, r., Mex.	130	21°48'N	99°50'W
Verde, r., Mex.	130	20°50'N	103°00'W
Verde, r., Mex.	131	16°05'N	97°44'W
Verde, r., Az., U.S. (vûrd)	119	34°04'N	111°40'W
Verde, Cap, c., Bah.	135	22°50'N	75°00'W
Verde, Cay, i., Bah.	135	22°00'N	75°05'W
Verde Island Passage, strt., Phil. (vĕr'dē)	213a	13°36'N	120°39'E
Verdemont, Ca., U.S. (vûr'dē-mŏnt)	117a	34°12'N	117°22'W
Verden, Ger. (fĕr'dĕn)	168	52°55'N	9°15'E
Verdigris, r., Ok., U.S. (vûr'dē-grēs)	121	36°50'N	95°29'W
Verdun, Can. (vĕr'dŭn')	99	45°27'N	73°34'W
Verdun, Fr. (vâr-dûn')	161	49°09'N	5°21'E
Verdun, Fr.	171	43°48'N	1°10'E
Vereeniging, S. Afr. (vĕ-rä'nĭ-gĭng)	238c	26°40'S	27°56'E
Verena, S. Afr. (vĕr-ĕn ȧ)	238c	25°30'S	29°02'E
Vereya, Russia (vĕ-rå'yȧ)	176	55°21'N	36°08'E
Verín, Spain (vå-rēn')	172	41°56'N	7°26'W
Verkhne-Kamchatsk, Russia (vyĕrk'nyĕ kám-chatsk')	179	54°42'N	158°41'E
Verkhne Neyvinskiy, Russia (nā-vĭn'skĭ)	186a	57°17'N	60°10'E
Verkhne Ural'sk, Russia (ó-ralsk')	178	53°53'N	59°13'E
Verkhniy Avzyan, Russia (vyĕrk'nyĕ áv-zyán')	186a	53°32'N	57°30'E
Verkhniye Kigi, Russia (vyĕrk'nĭ-yĕ kĭ'gĭ)	186a	55°23'N	58°37'E
Verkhniy Ufaley, Russia (ó-fá'lā)	186a	56°04'N	60°15'E
Verkhnyaya Pyshma, Russia (vyĕrk'nyä-yä pōōsh'mȧ)	186a	56°57'N	60°37'E
Verkhnyaya Salda, Russia (säl'dȧ)	186a	58°03'N	60°33'E
Verkhnyaya Tunguska (Angara), r., Russia (tòn-gōs'kȧ)	184	58°13'N	97°00'E
Verkhnyaya Tura, Russia (tó'rȧ)	186a	58°22'N	59°51'E
Verkhnyaya Yayva, Russia (yäy'vȧ)	186a	59°28'N	57°38'E
Verkhotur'ye, Russia (vyĕr-kô-tōōr'yĕ)	186a	58°52'N	60°47'E
Verkhoyansk, Russia (vyĕr-кô-yänsk')	179	67°43'N	133°33'E
Verkhoyanskiy Khrebet, mts., Russia (vyĕr-kô-yänskĭ)	179	67°45'N	128°00'E
Vermilion, Can. (vēr-mĭl'yŭn)	90	53°22'N	110°51'W
Vermilion, l., Mn., U.S.	113	47°49'N	92°35'W
Vermilion, r., Can.	99	47°30'N	73°15'W
Vermilion, r., Can.	96	53°30'N	111°00'W
Vermilion, r., Il., U.S.	108	41°05'N	89°00'W
Vermilion, r., Mn., U.S.	113	48°09'N	92°31'W
Vermilion Hills, hills, Can.	96	50°43'N	106°50'W
Vermilion Range, mts., Mn., U.S.	113	47°55'N	91°59'W
Vermillion, S.D., U.S.	112	42°46'N	96°56'W
Vermillion, r., S.D., U.S.	112	43°54'N	97°14'W
Vermillion Bay, b., La., U.S.	123	29°47'N	92°00'W
Vermont, state, U.S. (vēr-mŏnt')	105	43°50'N	72°50'W
Vernal, Ut., U.S. (vûr'nȧl)	115	40°29'N	109°40'W
Verneuk Pan, pl., S. Afr. (vĕr-nŭk')	232	30°10'S	21°46'E
Vernon, Can. (vĕr-nŏn')	90	50°18'N	119°15'W
Vernon, Can.	102c	45°10'N	75°27'W
Vernon, Ca., U.S. (vŭr'nŭn)	117a	34°01'N	118°12'W

ăt; finȧl; rāte; senȧte; ärm; ȧsk; sofȧ; fâre; ch-choose; dh-as th in other; bē; ėvent; bĕt; recĕnt; cratēr; g-gō; gh-guttural g; bĭt; ĭ-short neutral; rīde; к-guttural k as ch in German ich;

PLACE (Pronunciation)	PAGE	LAT.	LONG.
Vernon, In., U.S. (vûr′nŭn)	108	39°00′N	85°40′W
Vernon, N.J., U.S.	110a	39°00′N	85°40′W
Vernon, Tx., U.S.	120	34°09′N	99°16′W
Vernonia, Or., U.S. (vûr-nō′nyă)	116c	45°52′N	123°12′W
Vero Beach, Fl., U.S. (vē′rō)	125a	27°36′N	80°25′W
Véroia, Grc.	175	40°30′N	22°13′E
Verona, Italy (vā-rō′nä)	162	45°28′N	11°02′E
Versailles, Fr. (vĕr-sī′y′)	161	48°48′N	2°07′E
Versailles, Ky., U.S. (vēr-sālz′)	108	38°05′N	84°45′W
Versailles, Mo., U.S.	121	38°27′N	92°52′W
Vert, Cap, c., Sen.	230	14°43′N	17°30′W
Verulam, S. Afr. (vĕ-rōō-lăm)	233c	29°39′S	31°08′E
Verviers, Bel. (vĕr-vyā′)	165	50°35′N	5°57′E
Vesele, Ukr.	177	46°59′N	34°56′E
Vesijärvi, l., Fin.	167	61°09′N	25°10′E
Vesoul, Fr. (vē-sōōl′)	171	47°38′N	6°11′E
Vestavia Hills, Al., U.S.	110h	33°26′N	86°46′W
Vesterålen, is., Nor. (vĕs′tĕr ô′lĕn)	160	68°54′N	14°03′E
Vestfjord, b., Nor.	156	67°33′N	12°[illegible]′E
Vestmannaeyjar, Ice. (vĕst′män-ä-ā′yär)	160	63°12′N	20°17′W
Vesuvio, vol., Italy (vĕ-sōō′vyä)	156	40°35′N	14°26′E
Ves′yegonsk, Russia (vĕ-syĕ-gônsk′)	176	58°42′N	37°09′E
Veszprem, Hung. (vĕs′prām)	169	47°05′N	17°53′E
Vészto, Hung. (vĕs′tû)	169	46°55′N	21°18′E
Vet, r., S. Afr. (vĕt)	238c	28°25′S	26°37′E
Vetlanda, Swe. (vĕt-län′dä)	166	57°26′N	15°05′E
Vetluga, Russia (vyĕt-lōō′gà)	180	57°50′N	45°42′E
Vetluga, r., Russia	180	56°50′N	45°50′E
Vetovo, Blg. (vā′tô-vô)	175	43°42′N	26°18′E
Vetren, Blg. (vĕt′rĕn′)	175	42°16′N	24°04′E
Vevay, In., U.S. (vē′vā)	108	38°45′N	85°05′W
Veynes, Fr. (vān′′)	171	44°31′N	5°47′E
Vézère, r., Fr. (vā-zer′)	170	45°01′N	1°00′E
Viacha, Bol. (vēà′chà)	142	16°43′S	68°16′W
Viadana, Italy (vē-ä-dä′nä)	174	44°55′N	10°30′E
Vian, Ok., U.S. (vī′ăn)	121	35°30′N	95°00′W
Viana, Braz. (vē-ä′nä)	143	3°09′S	44°44′W
Viana do Alentejo, Port. (vē-ä′nà dò ä-lĕn-tā′hò)	172	38°20′N	8°02′W
Viana do Bolo, Spain	172	42°10′N	7°07′W
Viana do Castelo, Port. (dò käs-tā′lò)	172	41°41′N	8°45′W
Viangchan, Laos	212	18°07′N	102°33′E
Viar, r., Spain (vē-ä′rä)	172	38°15′N	6°08′W
Viareggio, Italy (vē-ä-rĕd′jô)	174	43°52′N	10°14′E
Viborg, Den. (vē′bôr)	166	56°27′N	9°22′E
Vibo Valentia, Italy (vē′bô-vä-lĕ′n-tyä)	174	38°47′N	16°06′E
Vic, Spain	173	41°55′N	2°14′E
Vicálvaro, Spain	173a	40°25′N	3°37′W
Vicente López, Arg. (vē-sĕ′n-tĕ-lō′pĕz)	144a	34°31′S	58°29′W
Vicenza, Italy (vē-chĕnt′sä)	162	45°33′N	11°33′E
Vichuga, Russia (vē-chōō′gà)	180	57°13′N	41°58′E
Vichy, Fr. (vē-shē′)	161	46°06′N	3°28′E
Vickersund, Nor.	166	60°00′N	9°59′E
Vicksburg, Mi., U.S. (vĭks′bûrg)	108	42°10′N	85°30′W
Vicksburg, Ms., U.S.	105	32°20′N	90°50′W
Viçosa, Braz. (vē-sô′sä)	141a	20°46′S	42°51′W
Victoria, Arg. (vēk-tô′rēä)	144	32°36′S	60°09′W
Victoria, Can. (vĭk-tō′rĭ-ă)	90	48°26′N	123°23′W
Victoria, Chile (vēk-tô-rēä)	144	38°15′S	72°16′W
Victoria, Col. (vēk-tô′rēä)	142a	5°19′N	74°54′W
Victoria, Phil. (vēk-tô-ryä)	213a	15°34′N	120°41′E
Victoria, Tx., U.S. (vĭk-tō′rĭ-ă)	123	28°48′N	97°00′W
Victoria, Va., U.S.	125	36°57′N	78°13′W
Victoria, state, Austl.	219	36°46′S	143°15′E
Victoria, l., Afr.	232	0°50′S	32°50′E
Victoria, r., Austl.	220	17°25′S	130°50′E
Victoria, Mount, mtn., Mya.	199	21°26′N	93°59′E
Victoria, Mount, mtn., Pap. N. Gui.	213	9°35′S	147°45′E
Victoria de las Tunas, Cuba (vēk-tō′rē-ä dā läs tōō′näs)	134	20°55′N	77°05′W
Victoria Falls, wtfl., Afr.	232	17°55′S	25°51′E
Victoria Island, i., Can.	89	70°13′N	107°45′W
Victoria Lake, l., Can.	101	48°20′N	57°40′W
Victoria Land, reg., Ant.	224	75°00′S	160°00′E
Victoria Nile, r., Ug.	237	2°20′N	31°35′E
Victoria Peak, mtn., Belize (vĕk-tōrĭ′ă)	132a	16°47′N	88°40′W
Victoria Peak, mtn., Can.	94	50°03′N	126°06′W
Victoria River Downs, Austl. (vĭc-tôr′ĭă)	218	16°30′S	131°10′E
Victoria Strait, strt., Can. (vĭk-tō′rĭ-ă)	92	69°10′N	100°58′W
Victoriaville, Can. (vĭk-tō′rĭ-ă-vĭl)	91	46°04′N	71°59′W
Victoria West, S. Afr. (wĕst)	232	31°25′S	23°10′E
Vidalia, Ga., U.S. (vĭ-dā′lĭ-ă)	125	32°10′N	82°26′W
Vidalia, La., U.S.	123	31°33′N	91°28′W
Vidin, Blg. (vĭ′dĕn)	163	44°00′N	22°53′E
Vidnoye, Russia	186b	55°33′N	37°41′E
Vidzy, Bela. (vĕ′dzĭ)	176	55°23′N	26°46′E
Viedma, Arg. (vyād′mä)	144	40°55′S	63°03′W
Viedma, l., Arg.	144	49°40′S	72°35′W
Viejo, r., Nic. (vyā′hō)	132	12°45′N	86°19′W
Vienna (Wien), Aus.	154	48°13′N	16°22′E
Vienna, Ga., U.S. (vē-ĕn′ă)	124	32°03′N	83°50′W
Vienna, Il., U.S.	121	37°24′N	88°50′W
Vienna, Va., U.S.	110e	38°54′N	77°16′W
Vienne, Fr. (vyĕn′)	161	45°31′N	4°54′E
Vienne, r., Fr.	170	47°06′N	0°20′E
Vientiane *see* Viangchan, Laos	212	18°07′N	102°33′E
Vieques, P.R. (vyā′kås)	129b	18°09′N	65°27′W
Vieques, i., P.R. (vyā′kås)	129b	18°05′N	65°28′W
Vierfontein, S. Afr. (vēr′fōn-tān)	238c	27°06′S	26°45′E
Viersen, Ger. (fēr′zĕn)	171c	51°15′N	6°24′E
Vierwaldstätter See, l., Switz.	168	46°54′N	8°36′E
Vierzon, Fr. (vyâr-zôn′)	161	47°14′N	2°04′E
Viesca, Mex. (vē-ās′kä)	122	25°21′N	102°47′W
Viesca, Laguna de, l., Mex. (lä-ò′nä-dĕ)	122	25°30′N	102°40′W
Vieste, Italy (vyĕs′tå)	174	41°52′N	16°10′E
Vietnam, nation, Asia (vyĕt′näm′)	212	18°00′N	107°00′E
Vigan, Phil. (vēgän)	212	17°36′N	120°22′E
Vigevano, Italy (vē-jå-vä′nô)	174	45°18′N	8°52′E
Vigny, Fr. (vēn-y′ē′)	171b	49°05′N	1°54′E
Vigo, Spain (vē′gō)	154	42°18′N	8°42′W
Vihti, Fin. (vē′tĭ)	167	60°27′N	24°18′E
Vijayawāda, India	199	16°31′N	80°37′E
Viksøyri, Nor.	166	61°06′N	6°35′E
Vila Caldas Xavier, Moz.	237	15°59′S	34°12′E
Vila de Manica, Moz. (vē′lä dā mä-nē′kà)	232	18°48′S	32°49′E
Vila de Rei, Port. (vē′là dā rā′ĭ)	172	39°42′N	8°03′W
Vila do Conde, Port. (vē′là dò kôn′dĕ)	172	41°21′N	8°44′W
Vilafranca del Penedes, Spain	173	41°20′N	1°40′E
Vilafranca de Xira, Port. (fräŋ′kà dā shē′rà)	172	38°58′N	8°59′W
Vilaine, r., Fr. (vē-lân′)	170	47°34′N	2°15′W
Vilalba, Spain	172	43°18′N	7°43′W
Vilanculos, Moz. (vē-län-kōō′lōs)	232	22°03′S	35°13′E
Vilāni, Lat. (vē′là-nĭ)	167	56°31′N	27°00′E
Vila Nova de Foz Côa, Port. (nō′vä dā fōz-kō′ă)	172	41°08′N	7°11′W
Vila Nova de Gaia, Port. (vē′là nō′và dā gä′yä)	172	41°08′N	8°40′W
Vila Nova de Milfontes, Port. (nō′và dā mēl-fōn′tāzh)	172	37°44′N	8°48′W
Vila Real, Port. (rā-äl′)	162	41°18′N	7°48′W
Vila-real, Spain	173	39°55′N	0°07′W
Vila Real de Santo Antonio, Port.	172	37°14′N	7°25′W
Vila Viçosa, Port. (vē-sō′zà)	172	38°47′N	7°24′W
Vileyka, Bela. (vē-lā′ē-kà)	176	54°19′N	26°58′E
Vilhelmina, Swe.	160	64°37′N	16°30′E
Viljandi, Est. (vēl′yän-dē)	180	58°24′N	25°34′E
Viljoenskroon, S. Afr.	238c	27°13′S	26°58′E
Vilkaviškis, Lith. (vēl-kà-vēsh′kēs)	167	54°40′N	23°08′E
Vil′kitskogo, i., Russia (vyl-kēts-kōgō)	184	73°25′N	76°00′E
Villa Acuña, Mex. (vēl-yä-kōō′n-yä)	122	29°20′N	100°56′W
Villa Ahumada, Mex. (ä-ōō-mä′dä)	122	30°43′N	106°30′W
Villa Alta, Mex. (äl′tä)(sän ēl-dā-fōn′sō)	131	17°20′N	96°08′W
Villa Angela, Arg. (vē′l-yä á′n-kĕ-lä)	144	27°31′S	60°42′W
Villa Ballester, Arg. (vē′l-yä-bál-yĕs-tĕr)	144a	34°33′S	58°33′W
Villa Bella, Bol. (bĕ′l-yä)	142	10°25′S	65°22′W
Villablino, Spain (vēl-yä-blē′nō)	172	42°58′N	6°18′W
Villacañas, Spain (vēl-yä-kän′yäs)	172	39°39′N	3°20′W
Villacarrillo, Spain (vēl-yä-kä-rēl′yô)	172	38°09′N	3°07′W
Villach, Aus. (fē′läk)	161	46°38′N	13°50′E
Villacidro, Italy (vē-lä-chē′drô)	174	39°28′N	8°41′E
Villa Clara, prov., Cuba	134	22°40′N	80°10′W
Villa Constitución, Arg. (kōn-stē-tōō-syōn′)	141c	33°15′S	60°19′W
Villa Coronado, Mex. (kō-rō-nä′dhō)	122	26°45′N	105°10′W
Villa Cuauhtémoc, Mex. (vēl′yä-kōō-äò-tĕ′mōk)	131	22°11′N	97°50′W
Villa de Allende, Mex. (vēl′yä′dā äl-yĕn′då)	122	25°18′N	100°01′W
Villa de Alvarez, Mex. (vēl′yä-dĕ-ä′l-vä-rĕz)	130	19°17′N	103°44′W
Villa de Cura, Ven. (dĕ-kōō′rä)	143b	10°03′N	67°29′W
Villa de Guadalupe, Mex. (dĕ-gwä-dhä-lōō′på)	130	23°22′N	100°44′W
Villa de Mayo, Arg.	144a	34°31′S	58°41′W
Villa Dolores, Arg. (vēl′yä dō-lō′räs)	144	31°50′S	65°05′W
Villa Escalante, Mex. (vēl′yä-ĕs-kä-lán′tĕ)	130	19°24′N	101°36′W
Villa Flores, Mex. (vēl′yä-flō′räs)	131	16°13′N	93°17′W
Villafranca, Italy (vēl-lä-frän′kä)	174	45°22′N	10°53′E
Villafranca del Bierzo, Spain	172	42°37′N	6°49′W
Villafranca de los Barros, Spain	172	38°34′N	6°22′W
Villafranche-de-Rouergue, Fr. (dĕ-rōō-ĕrg′)	170	44°21′N	2°02′E
Villa García, Mex. (gär-sē′ä)	130	22°07′N	101°55′W
Villagarcía, Spain	172	42°38′N	8°43′W
Villagrán, Mex.	122	24°28′N	99°30′W
Villa Grove, Il., U.S. (vĭl′à grōv′)	108	39°55′N	88°15′W
Villaguay, Arg. (vē′l-yä-gwī)	144	31°47′S	58°53′W
Villa Hayes, Para. (vēl′yä äyās)(hāz)	144	25°07′S	57°31′W
Villahermosa, Mex. (vēl′yä-ĕr-mō′sä)	128	17°59′N	92°56′W
Villa Hidalgo, Mex. (vēl′yäē-däl′gō)	130	21°39′N	102°41′W
Villaldama, Mex. (vēl-yäl-dä′mä)	128	26°30′N	100°26′W
Villa Lopez, Mex. (vēl′yä lō′pĕz)	122	27°00′N	105°02′W
Villalpando, Spain (vēl-yäl-pän′dō)	172	41°54′N	5°24′W
Villa María, Arg. (vē′l-yä-mä-rē′ä)	144	32°17′S	63°08′W
Villamatín, Spain (vēl-yä-mä-tē′n)	172	36°50′N	5°38′W
Villa Mercedes, Arg. (mĕr-sā′dås)	144	33°38′S	65°16′W
Villa Montes, Bol. (vē′l-yä-mô′n-tĕs)	142	21°13′S	63°26′W
Villa Morelos, Mex. (mō-rĕ′lomcs)	130	20°01′N	101°24′W
Villanueva, Col. (vē′l-yä-nòĕ′vä)	142	10°44′N	73°08′W
Villanueva, Hond. (vēl′yä-nwā′vä)	132	15°19′N	88°02′W
Villanueva, Mex. (vēl′yä-nòĕ′vä)	130	22°25′N	102°53′W
Villanueva de Córdoba, Spain (vēl-yä-nwĕ′vä-dā kôr′dō-bä)	172	38°18′N	4°38′W
Villanueva de la Serena, Spain (lä sā-rā′nä)	172	38°59′N	5°56′W
Villa Obregón, Mex. (vē′l-yä-ô-brĕ-gô′n)	131a	19°21′N	99°11′W
Villa Ocampo, Mex. (ô-käm′pō)	122	26°26′N	105°30′W
Villa Pedro Montoya, Mex. (vēl′yä-pĕ′drò-môn-tô′yä)	130	21°38′N	99°51′W
Villard-Bonnot, Fr. (vēl-yär′bôn-nō′)	171	45°15′N	5°53′E
Villarrica, Para. (vēl-yä-rē′kä)	144	25°55′S	56°23′W
Villarrobledo, Spain (vēl-yär-rò-blā′dhō)	162	39°15′N	2°37′W
Villa Unión, Mex. (vēl′yä-ōō-nyōn′)	130	23°10′N	106°14′W
Villavicencio, Col. (vē′l-yä-vē-sĕ′n-syō)	142	4°09′N	73°38′W
Villaviciosa de Odón, Spain	173a	40°22′N	3°38′W
Villavieja, Col. (vē′l-yä-vē-ĕ′κà)	142a	3°13′N	75°13′W
Villazón, Bol. (vē′l-yä-zô′n)	142	22°02′S	65°42′W
Villefranche, Fr.	161	45°59′N	4°43′E
Villejuif, Fr. (vēl′zhüst′)	171b	48°48′N	2°22′E
Ville-Maríe, Can.	91	47°18′N	79°22′W
Villena, Spain (vē-lyā′nà)	162	38°37′N	0°52′W
Villeneuve, Can. (vēl′nûv′)	102g	53°40′N	113°49′W
Villeneuve-Saint Georges, Fr. (săn-zhôrzh′)	171b	48°43′N	2°27′E
Villeneuve-sur-Lot, Fr. (sür-lō′)	170	44°25′N	0°41′E
Ville Platte, La., U.S. (vēl plát′)	123	30°41′N	92°17′W
Villers Cotterêts, Fr. (vē-âr′kô-trā′)	171b	49°15′N	3°05′E
Villerupt, Fr. (vēl′rüp′)	171	49°28′N	6°16′E
Ville-Saint Georges, Can. (vĭl-sĕn-zhôrzh′)	99	46°07′N	70°40′W
Villeta, Col. (vē′l-yĕ′tà)	142a	5°02′N	74°29′W
Villeurbanne, Fr. (vēl-ûr-bän′)	161	45°43′N	4°55′E
Villiers, S. Afr. (vĭl′ĭ-ērs)	238c	27°03′S	28°38′E
Villingen-Schwenningen, Ger.	168	48°04′N	8°33′E
Villisca, Ia., U.S. (vĭ′lĭs′kă)	113	40°56′N	94°56′W
Villupuram, India	203	11°59′N	79°33′E
Vilnius, Lith. (vĭl′nē-ŏs)	178	54°40′N	25°26′E
Vilppula, Fin. (vĭl′pŭ-lå)	167	62°01′N	24°24′E
Vil′shanka, Ukr.	177	48°14′N	30°52′E
Vil′shany, Ukr.	177	50°02′N	35°54′E
Vilvoorde, Bel.	159a	50°56′N	4°25′E
Vilyuy, r., Russia (vēl′yĭ)	179	63°00′N	121°00′E
Vilyuysk, Russia (vē-lyōō′ĭsk′)	179	63°41′N	121°47′E
Vimmerby, Swe. (vĭm′ĕr-bü)	166	57°41′N	15°51′E
Vimperk, Czech Rep. (vĭm-pĕrk′)	168	49°04′N	13°41′E
Viña del Mar, Chile (vē′nyä dĕl mär′)	144	33°00′S	71°33′W
Vinalhaven, Me., U.S. (vī-năl-hā′vĕn)	100	44°03′N	68°49′W
Vinaròs, Spain	173	40°29′N	0°27′E
Vincennes, Fr. (văn-sĕn′)	171b	48°51′N	2°27′E
Vincennes, In., U.S. (vĭn-zĕnz′)	105	38°40′N	87°30′W
Vincent, Al., U.S. (vĭn′sĕnt)	124	33°21′N	86°25′W
Vindelälven, r., Swe.	160	65°02′N	18°30′E
Vindeln, Swe. (vĭn′dĕln)	160	64°10′N	19°52′E
Vindhya Range, mts., India (vĭnd′yä)	199	22°30′N	75°50′E
Vineland, N.J., U.S. (vīn′lănd)	109	39°30′N	75°00′W
Vinh, Viet. (vēn′y′)	212	18°38′N	105°42′E
Vinhais, Port. (vēn-yä′ēzh)	172	41°51′N	7°00′W
Vinings, Ga., U.S. (vī′nĭngz)	110c	33°52′N	84°28′W
Vinita, Ok., U.S. (vĭ-nē′tă)	121	36°38′N	95°09′W
Vinkovci, Cro. (vēn′kôv-tsē)	175	45°17′N	18°47′E
Vinnytsia, Ukr.	178	49°13′N	28°31′E
Vinnytsya, prov., Ukr.	177	48°45′N	28°01′E
Vinogradovo, Russia (vĭ-nô-grä′do-vô)	186b	55°25′N	38°33′E
Vinson Massif, mtn., Ant.	224	77°40′S	87°00′W
Vinton, Ia., U.S. (vĭn′tŭn)	113	42°08′N	92°01′W
Vinton, La., U.S.	123	30°12′N	93°35′W
Violet, La., U.S. (vī′ō-lĕt)	110d	29°54′N	89°54′W
Virac, Phil. (vē-räk′)	209	13°38′N	124°20′E
Virbalis, Lith. (vēr′bà-lēs)	167	54°38′N	22°55′E
Virden, Can. (vûr′dĕn)	90	49°51′N	101°55′W
Virden, Il., U.S.	121	39°28′N	89°46′W
Virgin, r., U.S.	119	36°51′N	113°50′W
Virginia, S. Afr.	238c	28°07′S	26°54′E
Virginia, Mn., U.S. (vẽr-jĭn′yă)	105	47°32′N	92°36′W
Virginia, state, U.S.	105	37°00′N	80°45′W
Virginia Beach, Va., U.S.	109	36°50′N	75°58′W
Virginia City, Nv., U.S.	118	39°18′N	119°40′W
Virgin Islands, is., N.A. (vûr′jĭn)	129	18°15′N	64°00′W
Viroqua, Wi., U.S. (vĭ-rō′kwă)	113	43°33′N	90°54′W
Virovitica, Cro. (vē-rô-vē′tē-tsä)	175	45°50′N	17°24′E
Virpazar, Mont. (vēr′pä-zär′)	175	42°16′N	19°06′E
Virrat, Fin. (vĭr′ät)	167	62°15′N	23°45′E
Virserum, Swe. (vĭr′sĕ-rŏm)	166	57°22′N	15°35′E
Vis, Cro. (vēs)	174	43°03′N	16°11′E
Vis, i., Cro.	163	43°00′N	16°10′E
Visalia, Ca., U.S. (vĭ-sā′lĭ-ă)	118	36°20′N	119°18′W
Visby, Swe. (vĭs′bü)	154	57°39′N	18°19′E
Viscount Melville Sound, strt., Can.	89	74°00′N	110°00′W
Višegrad, Bos. (vē′shĕ-gräd)	175	43°48′N	19°17′E
Vishākhapatnam, India	199	17°48′N	83°21′E
Vishera, r., Russia (vĭ′shĕ-rà)	186a	60°40′N	58°46′E
Vishnyakovo, Russia	186b	55°44′N	38°10′E
Vishoek, S. Afr.	232a	34°13′S	18°26′E
Visim, Russia (vē′sĭm)	186a	57°38′N	59°32′E
Viskan, r., Swe.	166	57°20′N	12°25′E
Višķi, Lat. (vēs′kĭ)	167	56°02′N	26°47′E
Visoko, Bos. (vē′sô-kô)	175	43°59′N	18°10′E
Vistula *see* Wisła, r., Pol.	156	52°30′N	20°00′E
Vitebsk, prov., Bela.	176	55°05′N	29°18′E
Viterbo, Italy (vē-tĕr′bō)	162	42°24′N	12°08′E
Viti Levu, i., Fiji	214g	18°00′S	178°00′E
Vitim, Russia (vē′tēm)	179	59°22′N	112°43′E
Vitim, r., Russia (vē′tēm)	179	54°00′N	115°00′E
Vitino, Russia (vē′tĭ-nô)	186c	59°40′N	29°51′E
Vitória, Braz. (vē-tō′rē-ä)	143	20°09′S	40°17′W
Vitoria, Spain (vē-tô-ryä)	162	42°43′N	2°43′W

ăt; finăl; rāte; senâte; ärm; ȧsk; sofȧ; fâre; ch-choose; dh-as th in other; bē; ĕvent; bĕt; recĕnt; cratēr; g-gō; gh-guttural g; bĭt; ī-short neutral; rīde; к-guttural k as ch in German ich;

PRONOUNCING INDEX Wapakoneta – Wessel Islands 365

PLACE (Pronunciation)	PAGE	LAT.	LONG.
Wapakoneta, Oh., U.S.			
(wä'pȧ-kô-nĕt'ȧ)	108	40°35'N	84°10'W
Wapawekka Hills, hills, Can.			
(wŏ'pȧ-wē'kă-hĭlz)	96	54°45'N	104°20'W
Wapawekka Lake, l., Can.	96	54°55'N	104°40'W
Wapello, Ia., U.S. (wŏ-pĕl'ō)	113	41°10'N	91°11'W
Wappapello Reservoir, res., Mo., U.S.			
(wă'pȧ-pĕl-lō)	107	37°07'N	90°10'W
Wappingers Falls, N.Y., U.S.			
(wŏp'ĭn-jẽrz)	109	41°35'N	73°55'W
Wapsipinicon, r., Ia., U.S.			
(wŏp'sĭ-pĭn'ĭ-kŏn)	113	42°16'N	91°35'W
Wapusk National Park, rec., Can.	92	58°00'N	94°15'W
Warabi, Japan (wä'rä-bē)	211a	35°50'N	139°41'E
Warangal, India (wŭ'răŋ-găl)	199	18°03'N	79°45'E
Warburton, The, r., Austl.			
(wŏr'bûr-tŭn)	220	27°30'S	138°45'E
Wardān, Wādī, r., Egypt	197a	29°22'N	33°00'E
Ward Cove, Ak., U.S.	94	55°24'N	131°43'W
Warden, S. Afr. (wôr'dĕn)	238c	27°52'N	28°59'E
Wardha, India (wŭr'dä)	199	20°46'N	78°42'E
War Eagle, W.V., U.S. (wôr ē'g'l)	108	37°30'N	81°50'W
Waren, Ger. (vä'rĕn)	168	53°32'N	12°43'E
Warendorf, Ger. (vä'rĕn-dōrf)	171c	51°57'N	7°59'E
Wargla, Alg.	230	32°00'N	5°18'E
Warialda, Austl.	222	29°32'S	150°34'E
Warmbad, Nmb.			
(värm'bäd) (wôrm'băd)	232	28°25'S	18°45'E
Warmbad, S. Afr.	238c	24°52'S	28°18'E
Warm Beach, Wa., U.S. (wôrm)	116a	48°10'N	122°22'W
Warm Springs Indian Reservation, I.R.,			
Or., U.S. (wôrm sprĭnz)	114	44°55'N	121°30'W
Warm Springs Reservoir, res., Or.,			
U.S.	114	43°42'N	118°40'W
Warner Mountains, mts., Ca., U.S.	106	41°30'N	120°17'W
Warner Robins, Ga., U.S.	124	32°37'N	83°36'W
Warnow, r., Ger. (vär'nō)	168	53°51'N	11°55'E
Warracknabeal, Austl.	222	36°20'S	142°28'E
Warragamba Reservoir, res., Austl.	222	33°40'S	150°00'E
Warrego, r., Austl. (wôr'ē-gō)	221	27°13'S	145°58'E
Warren, Can.	102f	50°08'N	97°32'W
Warren, Ar., U.S. (wŏr'ĕn)	121	33°37'N	92°03'W
Warren, In., U.S.	108	40°40'N	85°25'W
Warren, Mi., U.S.	111b	42°33'N	83°03'W
Warren, Mn., U.S.	112	48°11'N	96°44'W
Warren, Oh., U.S.	108	41°15'N	80°50'W
Warren, Or., U.S.	116c	45°49'N	122°51'W
Warren, Pa., U.S.	109	41°50'N	79°10'W
Warren, R.I., U.S.	110b	41°44'N	71°14'W
Warrendale, Pa., U.S. (wŏr'ĕn-dāl)	111e	40°39'N	80°04'W
Warrensburg, Mo., U.S.			
(wŏr'ĕnz-bûrg)	121	38°45'N	93°42'W
Warrenton, Ga., U.S. (wŏr'ĕn-tŭn)	125	33°26'N	82°37'W
Warrenton, Or., U.S.	116c	46°10'N	123°56'W
Warrenton, Va., U.S.	109	38°45'N	77°50'W
Warri, Nig. (wär'ē)	230	5°33'N	5°43'E
Warrington, Eng., U.K.	158a	53°22'N	2°30'W
Warrington, Fl., U.S. (wŏ'ĭng-tŭn)	124	30°21'N	87°15'W
Warrnambool, Austl. (wôr'năm-bōōl)	219	38°20'S	142°28'E
Warroad, Mn., U.S. (wôr'rōd)	112	48°55'N	95°20'W
Warrumbungle Range, mts., Austl.			
(wôr'ŭm-bŭŋ-g'l)	221	31°18'S	150°00'E
Warsaw, Pol.	154	52°15'N	21°05'E
Warsaw, Il., U.S. (wôr'sô)	121	40°21'N	91°26'W
Warsaw, In., U.S.	108	41°15'N	85°50'W
Warsaw, N.Y., U.S.	109	42°45'N	78°10'W
Warsaw, NC, N.C., U.S.	125	35°00'N	78°07'W
Warsop, Eng., U.K. (wôr'sŭp)	158a	53°13'N	1°05'W
Warszawa *see* Warsaw, Pol.	154	52°15'N	21°05'E
Warta, r., Pol. (vär'tȧ)	161	52°30'N	16°00'E
Wartburg, S. Afr.	233c	29°26'S	30°39'E
Warwick, Austl. (wŏr'ĭk)	219	28°05'S	152°10'E
Warwick, Can.	99	45°58'N	71°57'W
Warwick, Eng., U.K.	164	52°19'N	1°46'W
Warwick, N.Y., U.S.	110a	41°15'N	74°22'W
Warwick, R.I., U.S.	109	41°42'N	71°27'W
Warwickshire, co., Eng., U.K.	158a	52°30'N	1°35'W
Wasatch Mountains, mts., Ut., U.S.			
(wô'săch)	117b	40°45'N	111°46'W
Wasatch Plateau, plat., Ut., U.S.	119	38°55'N	111°40'W
Wasatch Range, mts., U.S.	106	39°10'N	111°30'W
Wasbank, S. Afr.	233c	28°27'S	30°09'E
Wasco, Or., U.S. (wäs'kō)	114	45°36'N	120°42'W
Waseca, Mn., U.S. (wô-sē'kȧ)	113	44°04'N	93°31'W
Wash, The, Eng., U.K. (wŏsh)	160	53°00'N	0°20'E
Washburn, Me., U.S. (wŏsh'bŭrn)	100	46°46'N	68°10'W
Washburn, Wi., U.S.	113	46°41'N	90°55'W
Washburn, Mount, mtn., Wy., U.S.	115	44°55'N	110°10'W
Washington, D.C., U.S. (wŏsh'ĭng-tŭn)	105	38°50'N	77°00'W
Washington, Ga., U.S.	125	33°43'N	82°46'W
Washington, Ia., U.S.	113	41°17'N	91°42'W
Washington, In., U.S.	108	38°40'N	87°10'W
Washington, Ks., U.S.	121	39°48'N	97°04'W
Washington, Mo., U.S.	121	38°33'N	91°00'W
Washington, N.C., U.S.	125	35°32'N	77°01'W
Washington, Pa., U.S.	108	40°10'N	80°14'W
Washington, state, U.S.	104	47°30'N	121°10'W
Washington, i., Wi., U.S.	113	45°18'N	86°42'W
Washington, Lake, l., Wa., U.S.	116a	47°34'N	122°12'W
Washington, Mount, mtn., N.H., U.S.	107	44°15'N	71°15'W
Washington Court House, Oh., U.S.	108	39°30'N	83°25'W
Washington Park, Il., U.S.	117e	38°38'N	90°06'W
Washita, r., Ok., U.S. (wŏsh'ĭ-tô)	120	35°33'N	99°16'W
Washougal, Wa., U.S. (wŏ-shōō'găl)	116c	45°35'N	122°21'W
Washougal, r., Wa., U.S.	116c	45°38'N	122°17'W
Wasilków, Pol. (vȧ-sēl'kōf)	169	53°12'N	23°13'E
Waskaiowaka Lake, l., Can.			
(wŏ'skă-yō'wō-kă)	97	56°30'N	96°20'W
Wassenberg, Ger. (vä'sĕn-bĕrgh)	171c	51°06'N	6°07'E
Wassuk Range, mts., Nv., U.S.			
(wȧs'sŭk)	118	38°58'N	119°00'W
Waswanipi, Lac, l., Can.	99	49°35'N	76°15'W
Water, i., V.I.U.S. (wô'tẽr)	129c	18°20'N	64°57'W
Waterberge, mts., S. Afr.			
(wôrtẽr'bûrg)	238c	24°25'S	27°53'E
Waterboro, S.C., U.S. (wô'tẽr-bŭr-ō)	125	32°50'N	80°40'W
Waterbury, Ct., U.S. (wô'tẽr-bĕr-ē)	109	41°30'N	73°00'W
Water Cay, i., Bah.	135	22°55'N	75°50'W
Waterdown, Can. (wô'tẽr-doun)	102d	43°20'N	79°54'W
Wateree Lake, res., S.C., U.S.			
(wô'tẽr-ē)	125	34°40'N	80°48'W
Waterford, Ire. (wô'tẽr-fẽrd)	161	52°20'N	7°03'W
Waterford, Wi., U.S.	111a	42°40'N	88°13'W
Waterloo, Bel.	159a	50°44'N	4°24'E
Waterloo, Can. (wô-tẽr-lōō')	99	43°30'N	80°40'W
Waterloo, Can.	99	45°25'N	72°30'W
Waterloo, Ia., U.S.	105	42°30'N	92°22'W
Waterloo, Il., U.S.	121	38°19'N	90°08'W
Waterloo, Md., U.S.	110e	39°11'N	76°50'W
Waterloo, N.Y., U.S.	109	42°55'N	76°50'W
Waterton-Glacier International Peace			
Park, rec., N.A.			
(wô'ter-tŭn-glā'shûr)	106	48°55'N	114°10'W
Waterton Lakes National Park, rec.,			
Can.	95	49°05'N	113°50'W
Watertown, Ma., U.S. (wô'tẽr-toun)	101a	42°22'N	71°11'W
Watertown, N.Y., U.S.	105	44°00'N	75°55'W
Watertown, S.D., U.S.	104	44°53'N	97°07'W
Watertown, Wi., U.S.	113	43°13'N	88°40'W
Water Valley, Ms., U.S. (văl'ē)	124	34°08'N	89°38'W
Waterville, Me., U.S.	100	44°34'N	69°37'W
Waterville, Mn., U.S.	113	44°10'N	93°35'W
Waterville, Wa., U.S.	114	47°38'N	120°04'W
Watervliet, N.Y., U.S. (wô'tẽr-vlēt')	109	42°45'N	73°54'W
Watford, Eng., U.K. (wŏt'fŏrd)	164	51°38'N	0°24'W
Wathaman Lake, l., Can.	96	56°55'N	103°43'W
Watlington, Eng., U.K.	158b	51°37'N	1°01'W
Watonga, Ok., U.S. (wō-tŏŋ'gȧ)	121	35°50'N	98°26'W
Watsa, D.R.C. (wät'sä)	231	3°03'N	29°32'E
Watseka, Il., U.S. (wŏt-sē'kȧ)	108	40°45'N	87°45'W
Watson, In., U.S. (wŏt'sŭn)	111h	38°21'N	85°42'W
Watson Lake, Can.	90	60°18'N	128°50'W
Watsonville, Ca., U.S. (wŏt'sŭn-vĭl)	118	36°55'N	121°46'W
Wattenscheid, Ger. (vä'tĕn-shīd)	171c	51°30'N	7°07'E
Watts, Ca., U.S. (wŏts)	117a	33°56'N	118°15'W
Watts Bar Lake, res., Tn., U.S. (bär)	124	35°45'N	84°49'W
Waubay, S.D., U.S. (wô'bā)	112	45°19'N	97°18'W
Wauchula, Fl., U.S. (wô-chōō'lȧ)	125a	27°32'N	81°48'W
Wauconda, Il., U.S. (wô-kŏn'dȧ)	111a	42°15'N	88°08'W
Waukegan, Il., U.S. (wŏ-kē'gȧn)	105	42°22'N	87°51'W
Waukesha, Wi., U.S. (wô'kē-shô)	111a	43°01'N	88°13'W
Waukon, Ia., U.S. (wô kŏn)	113	43°15'N	91°30'W
Waupaca, Wi., U.S. (wô-păk'ȧ)	113	44°22'N	89°06'W
Waupun, Wi., U.S. (wô-pŭn')	113	43°37'N	88°45'W
Waurika, Ok., U.S. (wô-rē'kȧ)	121	34°09'N	97°59'W
Wausau, Wi., U.S. (wô'sô)	105	44°58'N	89°40'W
Wausaukee, Wi., U.S. (wô-sô'kē)	113	45°22'N	87°58'W
Wauseon, Oh., U.S. (wô'sē-ŏn)	108	41°30'N	84°10'W
Wautoma, Wi., U.S. (wô-tō'mȧ)	113	44°04'N	89°11'W
Wauwatosa, Wi., U.S. (wô-wȧ-t'ō'sȧ)	111a	43°03'N	88°00'W
Waveney, r., Eng., U.K. (wāv'nē)	165	52°27'N	1°17'E
Waverly, S. Afr.	233c	31°54'S	26°29'E
Waverly, Ia., U.S. (wā'vẽr-lē)	113	42°43'N	92°29'W
Waverly, Tn., U.S.	124	36°04'N	87°46'W
Wāw, Sudan	231	7°41'N	28°00'E
Wawa, Can.	98	47°59'N	84°47'W
Wāw al-Kabir, Libya	231	25°23'N	16°52'E
Wawanesa, Can. (wŏ'wō-nē'sȧ)	97	49°36'N	99°41'W
Wawasee, l., In., U.S. (wô-wô-sē')	108	41°25'N	85°45'W
Waxahachie, Tx., U.S.			
(wăk-sȧ-hăch'ē)	123	32°23'N	96°50'W
Wayland, Ky., U.S. (wā'lănd)	125	37°25'N	82°47'W
Wayland, Ma., U.S.	101a	42°23'N	71°22'W
Wayne, Mi., U.S.	111b	42°17'N	83°23'W
Wayne, Ne., U.S.	112	42°13'N	97°03'W
Wayne, N.J., U.S.	110a	40°56'N	74°16'W
Wayne, Pa., U.S.	110f	40°03'N	75°22'W
Waynesboro, Ga., U.S. (wānz'bŭr-ō)	125	33°05'N	82°02'W
Waynesboro, Pa., U.S.	109	39°45'N	77°35'W
Waynesboro, Va., U.S.	109	38°05'N	78°50'W
Waynesburg, Pa., U.S. (wānz'bûrg)	108	39°55'N	80°10'W
Waynesville, N.C., U.S. (wānz'vĭl)	125	35°28'N	82°58'W
Waynoka, Ok., U.S. (wā-nō'kȧ)	120	36°34'N	98°52'W
Wayzata, Mn., U.S. (wā-zä-tȧ)	117g	44°58'N	93°31'W
Wazīrbad, Pak.	202	32°39'N	74°11'E
Weagamow Lake, l., Can.			
(wē'ăg-ȧ-mou)	97	52°53'N	91°22'W
Weald, The, reg., Eng., U.K. (wēld)	164	50°58'N	0°15'W
Weatherford, Ok., U.S. (wĕ-dhẽr-fẽrd)	120	85°32'N	98°41'W
Weatherford, Tx., U.S.	123	32°45'N	97°46'W
Weaver, r., Eng., U.K. (wē'vẽr)	158a	53°09'N	2°31'W
Weaverville, Ca., U.S. (wē'vẽr-vĭl)	114	40°44'N	122°55'W
Webb City, Mo., U.S.	121	37°10'N	94°26'W
Weber, r., Ut., U.S.	117b	41°13'N	112°07'W
Webster, Ma., U.S.	101a	42°04'N	71°52'W
Webster, S.D., U.S.	112	45°19'N	97°30'W
Webster City, Ia., U.S.	113	42°28'N	93°49'W
Webster Groves, Mo., U.S. (grōvz)	117e	38°36'N	90°22'W
Webster Springs, W.V., U.S. (sprĭngz)	108	38°30'N	80°20'W
Weddell Sea, sea, Ant. (wĕd'ĕl)	224	73°00'S	45°00'W
Wedel, Ger. (vā'dĕl)	159c	53°35'N	9°42'E
Wedge Mountain, mtn., Can. (wĕj)	95	50°10'N	122°50'W
Wedgeport, Can. (wĕj'pōrt)	100	43°44'N	65°59'W
Wednesfield, Eng., U.K.			
(wĕd''nz-fēld)	158a	52°36'N	2°04'W
Weed, Ca., U.S. (wēd)	114	41°35'N	122°21'W
Weenen, S. Afr. (vā'nĕn)	233c	28°52'S	30°05'E
Weert, Neth.	165	51°16'N	5°39'E
Weesp, Neth.	159a	52°18'N	5°01'E
Węgorzewo, Pol. (vôŋ-gô'zhĕ-vô)	169	54°14'N	21°46'E
Węgrow, Pol. (vôŋ'grôf)	169	52°23'N	22°02'E
Wei, r., China (wā)	206	35°47'N	114°27'E
Wei, r., China (wā)	204	34°00'N	108°10'E
Weichang, China (wā-chäŋ)	205	41°50'N	118°00'E
Weiden, Ger.	168	49°41'N	12°09'E
Weifang, China	205	36°43'N	119°08'E
Weihai, China (wa'hăī')	205	37°30'N	122°05'E
Weilheim, Ger. (vīl'hīm')	168	47°50'N	11°06'E
Weimar, Ger. (vī'mär)	161	50°59'N	11°20'E
Weinan, China	208	34°32'N	109°40'E
Weipa, Austl.	219	12°25'S	141°54'E
Weir, r., Can. (wēr-rĭv-ẽr)	97	56°49'N	94°04'W
Weirton, W.V., U.S.	108	40°25'N	80°35'W
Weiser, Id., U.S. (wē'zẽr)	114	44°15'N	116°58'W
Weiser, r., Id., U.S.	114	44°26'N	116°40'W
Weishi, China (wā-shr)	208	34°23'N	114°12'E
Weissenburg, Ger.	168	49°04'N	11°20'E
Weissenfels, Ger. (vī'sĕn-fĕlz)	168	51°13'N	11°58'E
Weiss Lake, res., Al., U.S.	124	34°15'N	85°35'W
Weixi, China (wā-shyē)	204	27°27'N	99°30'E
Weixian, China (wā shyĕn)	206	36°59'N	115°17'E
Wejherowo, Pol. (vā-hĕ-rô'vô)	169	54°36'N	18°15'E
Welch, W.V., U.S. (wĕlch)	125	37°24'N	81°28'W
Weldon, N.C., U.S. (wĕl'dŭn)	125	36°24'N	77°36'W
Weldon, r., Mo., U.S.	121	40°22'N	93°39'W
Weleetka, Ok., U.S. (wē-lēt'kȧ)	121	35°19'N	96°08'W
Welford, Austl. (wĕl'fẽrd)	222	25°08'S	144°43'E
Welkom, S. Afr. (wĕl'kŏm)	232	27°57'S	26°45'E
Welland, Can. (wĕl'ănd)	99	42°59'N	79°13'W
Wellesley, Ma., U.S. (wĕlz'lē)	101a	42°18'N	71°17'W
Wellesley Islands, is., Austl.	220	16°15'S	139°25'E
Wellington, Austl. (wĕl'lĭng-tŭn)	222	32°40'S	148°50'E
Wellington, N.Z.	221a	41°15'S	174°45'E
Wellington, Eng., U.K.	158a	52°42'N	2°30'W
Wellington, Ks., U.S.	121	37°16'N	97°24'W
Wellington, Oh., U.S.	108	41°10'N	82°10'W
Wellington, Tx., U.S.	120	34°51'N	100°12'W
Wellington, i., Chile (ŏĕ'lĕng-tŏn)	144	49°30'S	76°30'W
Wells, Can.	90	53°06'N	121°34'W
Wells, Mi., U.S.	108	45°50'N	87°00'W
Wells, Mn., U.S.	113	43°44'N	93°43'W
Wells, Nv., U.S.	114	41°07'N	115°04'W
Wells, l., Austl. (wĕlz)	220	26°35'S	123°40'E
Wellsboro, Pa., U.S. (wĕlz'bŭ-rô)	109	41°45'N	77°15'W
Wellsburg, W.V., U.S. (wĕlz'bûrg)	108	40°10'N	80°40'W
Wells Dam, dam, Wa., U.S.	114	48°00'N	119°39'W
Wellston, Oh., U.S. (wĕlz'tŭn)	108	39°05'N	82°30'W
Wellsville, Mo., U.S. (wĕlz'vĭl)	121	39°04'N	91°33'W
Wellsville, N.Y., U.S.	109	42°10'N	78°00'W
Wellsville, Oh., U.S.	108	40°35'N	80°40'W
Wellsville, Ut., U.S.	115	41°38'N	111°57'W
Wels, Aus. (vĕls)	161	48°10'N	14°01'E
Welshpool, Wales, U.K. (wĕlsh'pōōl)	164	52°44'N	3°10'W
Welverdiend, S. Afr. (vĕl-vẽr-dēnd')	238c	26°23'S	27°16'E
Welwyn Garden City, Eng., U.K.			
(wĕlĭn)	158b	51°46'N	0°17'W
Wem, Eng., U.K. (wĕm)	158a	52°51'N	2°44'W
Wembere, r., Tan.	237	4°35'S	33°55'E
Wen, r., China (wŭn)	206	36°24'N	119°00'E
Wenan Wa, sw., China (wĕn'ăn' wä)	206	38°56'N	116°29'E
Wenatchee, Wa., U.S. (wē-năch'ē)	114	47°24'N	120°18'W
Wenatchee Mountains, mts.,			
Wa., U.S.	114	47°28'N	121°10'W
Wenchang, China (wŭn-chäŋ)	209	19°32'N	110°42'E
Wenchi, Ghana	234	7°42'N	2°07'W
Wendeng, China (wŭn-dŭŋ)	206	37°14'N	122°03'E
Wendo, Eth.	231	6°37'N	38°29'E
Wendorer, Ut., U.S.	115	40°47'N	114°01'W
Wendover, Can. (wĕn-dōv'ẽr)	102c	45°34'N	75°07'W
Wendover, Eng., U.K.	158b	51°44'N	0°45'W
Wenham, Ma., U.S. (wĕn'ăm)	101a	42°36'N	70°53'W
Wenquan, China (wŭn-chyůän)	205	47°10'N	120°00'E
Wenshan, China	204	23°20'N	104°15'E
Wenshang, China (wĕn'shäng)	206	35°43'N	116°31'E
Wensu, China (wĕn-sō)	204	41°45'N	80°30'E
Wentworth, Austl. (wĕnt'wûrth)	219	34°03'S	141°53'E
Wenzhou, China (wŭn-jō)	205	28°00'N	120°40'E
Wepener, S. Afr.			
(wē'pĕn-ẽr) (vā'pĕn-ẽr)	232	29°43'S	27°04'E
Werder, Ger. (vĕr'dẽr)	159b	52°23'N	12°56'E
Were Ilu, Eth.	231	10°39'N	39°21'E
Werl, Ger. (vĕrl)	171c	51°33'N	7°55'E
Wermelskirchen, Ger.	171c	51°08'N	7°13'E
Werneuchen, Ger. (vĕr'hoi-kĕn)	159b	52°38'N	13°44'E
Werra, r., Ger. (vĕr'ä)	168	51°16'N	9°54'E
Werribee, Austl.	217a	37°54'S	144°40'E
Werribee, r., Austl.	217a	37°40'S	144°37'E
Wertach, r., Ger. (vĕr'täk)	168	48°12'N	10°40'E
Weseke, Ger. (vĕ'zĕ-kĕ)	171c	51°54'N	6°51'E
Wesel, Ger. (vā'zĕl)	171c	51°39'N	6°37'E
Weser, r., Ger. (vā'zẽr)	156	51°00'N	10°30'E
Weslaco, Tx., U.S. (wĕs-lă'kō)	123	26°10'N	97°59'W
Weslemkoon, l., Can.	99	45°02'N	77°25'W
Wesleyville, Can. (wĕs'lē-vĭl)	101	49°09'N	53°34'W
Wessel Islands, is., Austl. (wĕs'ĕl)	220	11°45'S	136°25'E

ng-sing; ŋ-baŋk; ɴ-nasalized n; nŏd; cŏmmit; ōld; ŏbey; ôrder; oi-boil; fōōd; ȯ-as oo in foot; ou-out; s-soft; sh-dish; th-thin; pūre; ůnite; ûrn; stŭd; circŭs; ü-as in French tu; '-indeterminate vowel.

366 Wesselsbron – William Creek PRONOUNCING INDEX

PLACE (Pronunciation)	PAGE	LAT.	LONG.
Wesselsbron, S. Afr. (wĕs'ĕl-brŏn)	238c	27°51'S	26°22'E
Wessington Springs, S.D., U.S. (wĕs'ĭng-tŭn)	112	44°06'N	98°35'W
West, Mount, mtn., Pan.	128a	9°10'N	79°52'W
West Allis, Wi., U.S. (wĕst-ăl'ĭs)	111a	43°01'N	88°01'W
West Alton, Mo., U.S. (ôl'tŭn)	117e	38°52'N	90°13'W
West Bay, b., Fl., U.S.	124	30°20'N	85°45'W
West Bay, b., Tx., U.S.	123a	29°11'N	95°03'W
West Bend, Wi., U.S. (wĕst bĕnd)	113	43°25'N	88°13'W
West Bengal, state, India (bĕn-gôl')	199	23°30'N	87°30'E
West Blocton, Al., U.S. (blŏk'tŭn)	124	33°05'N	87°05'W
Westborough, Ma., U.S. (wĕst'bŭr-ō)	101a	42°17'N	71°37'W
West Boylston, Ma., U.S. (boil'stŭn)	101a	42°22'N	71°46'W
West Branch, Mi., U.S. (wĕst brănch)	[illegible]	44°15'N	84°10'W
West Bridgford, Eng., U.K. (brĭj'fẽrd)	158a	52°55'N	1°08'W
West Bromwich, Eng., U.K. (wĕst brŭm'ĭj)	158a	52°32'N	1°59'W
Westbrook, Me., U.S. [illegible]	[illegible]	[illegible]	[illegible]
Westby, Wi., U.S. (wĕst'bē)	113	43°40'N	90°52'W
West Caicos, i., T./C. Is. (käē'kō) (kī'kōs)	135	21°40'N	72°30'W
West Cape Howe, c., Austl.	220	35°15'S	117°30'E
West Chester, Oh., U.S. (chĕs'tẽr)	111f	39°20'N	84°24'W
West Chester, Pa., U.S.	110f	39°57'N	75°36'W
West Chicago, Il., U.S. (chĭ-kȧ'gō)	111a	41°53'N	88°12'W
West Columbia, S.C., U.S. (cŏl'ŭm-bē-ȧ)	125	33°58'N	81°05'W
West Columbia, Tx., U.S.	123	29°08'N	95°39'W
West Cote Blanche Bay, b., La., U.S.	123	29°30'N	92°17'W
West Covina, Ca., U.S. (wĕst kō-vē'nȧ)	117a	34°04'N	117°55'W
West Des Moines, Ia., U.S. (dē moin')	113	41°35'N	93°42'W
West Des Moines, r., Ia., U.S.	113	42°52'N	94°32'W
West End, Bah.	134	26°40'N	78°55'W
Westerham, Eng., U.K. (wĕ'stẽr'ŭm)	158b	51°15'N	0°05'E
Westerhörn, Ger. (vĕs'tĕr-hōrn)	159c	53°52'N	9°41'E
Westerlo, Bel.	159a	51°05'N	4°57'E
Westerly, R.I., U.S. (wĕs'tẽr-lē)	109	41°25'N	71°50'W
Western Australia, state, Austl. (ôs-trā'lĭ-ȧ)	218	24°15'S	121°30'E
Western Dvina, r., Eur.	167	55°30'N	28°27'E
Western Ghāts, mts., India	199	17°35'N	74°00'E
Western Port, Md., U.S. (wĕs'tẽrn pōrt)	109	39°30'N	79°00'W
Western Sahara, dep., Afr. (sȧ-hä'rȧ)	230	23°05'N	15°33'W
Western Samoa see Samoa, nation, Oc.	2	14°30'S	172°00'W
Western Siberian Lowland, depr., Russia	178	63°37'N	72°45'E
Westerville, Oh., U.S. (wĕs'tẽr-vĭl)	108	40°10'N	83°00'W
Westerwald, for., Ger. (vĕs'tẽr-väld)	168	50°35'N	7°45'E
Westfalen, hist. reg., Ger. (vĕst-fä-lĕn)	168	51°20'N	8°30'E
Westfield, Ma., U.S. (wĕst'fēld)	109	42°05'N	72°45'W
Westfield, N.J., U.S.	110a	40°39'N	74°21'W
Westfield, N.Y., U.S. (wĕst'fēld)	110a	42°20'N	79°40'W
Westford, Ma., U.S. (wĕst'fẽrd)	101a	42°35'N	71°26'W
West Frankfort, Il., U.S. (frăŋk'fŭrt)	108	37°55'N	88°55'W
West Ham, Eng., U.K.	158b	51°30'N	0°00'W
West Hartford, Ct., U.S. (härt'fẽrd)	109	41°45'N	72°45'W
West Helena, Ar., U.S. (hĕl'ĕn-ȧ)	121	34°32'N	90°39'W
West Indies, is. (ĭn'dēz)	129	19°00'N	78°30'W
West Jordon, Ut., U.S. (jôr'dăn)	117b	40°37'N	111°56'W
West Kirby, Eng., U.K. (kûr'bē)	158a	53°22'N	3°11'W
West Lafayette, In., U.S. (lä-fā-yĕt')	108	40°25'N	86°55'W
Westlake, Oh., U.S.	111d	41°27'N	81°55'W
Westleigh, S. Afr. (wĕst-lē)	238c	27°39'S	27°18'E
West Liberty, Ia., U.S. (wĕst lĭb'ẽr-tĭ)	113	41°34'N	91°15'W
West Linn, Or., U.S. (lĭn)	116c	45°22'N	122°37'W
Westlock, Can. (wĕst'lŏk)	95	54°09'N	113°52'W
West Memphis, Ar., U.S.	121	35°08'N	90°11'W
West Midlands, hist. reg., Eng., U.K.	158a	52°26'N	1°50'W
Westminster, Ca., U.S. (wĕst'mĭn-stẽr)	117a	33°45'N	117°59'W
Westminster, Md., U.S.	109	39°40'N	76°55'W
Westminster, S.C., U.S.	124	34°38'N	83°10'W
Westmount, Can. (wĕst'mount)	102a	45°29'N	73°36'W
West Newbury, Ma., U.S. (nū'bĕr-ē)	101a	42°47'N	70°57'W
West Newton, Pa., U.S. (nū'tŭn)	111e	40°12'N	79°45'W
West New York, N.J., U.S. (nů yŏrk)	110a	40°47'N	74°01'W
West Nishnabotna, r., Ia., U.S. (nĭsh-nȧ-bŏt'nȧ)	112	40°56'N	95°37'W
Weston, Ma., U.S. (wĕs'tŭn)	101a	42°22'N	71°18'W
Weston, W.V., U.S.	108	39°00'N	80°30'W
Westonaria, S. Afr.	238c	26°19'S	27°38'E
Weston-super-Mare, Eng., U.K. (wĕs'tŭn sū'pẽr-mā'rē)	164	51°23'N	3°00'W
West Orange, N.J., U.S. (wĕst ŏr'ĕnj)	110a	40°46'N	74°14'W
West Palm Beach, Fl., U.S. (päm bēch)	105	26°44'N	80°04'W
West Pensacola, Fl., U.S. (pĕn-sȧ-kō'lȧ)	124	30°24'N	87°18'W
West Pittsburg, Ca., U.S. (pĭts'bûrg)	116b	38°02'N	121°56'W
Westplains, Mo., U.S. (wĕst-plānz')	121	36°42'N	91°51'W
West Point, Ga., U.S.	124	32°52'N	85°10'W
West Point, Ms., U.S.	124	33°36'N	88°39'W
Westpoint, Ne., U.S.	112	41°50'N	96°00'W
West Point, N.Y., U.S.	110a	41°23'N	73°58'W
West Point, Ut., U.S.	117b	41°07'N	112°05'W
West Point, Va., U.S.	109	37°25'N	76°50'W
West Point Lake, res., U.S.	124	33°00'N	85°10'W
Westport, Ire.	164	53°44'N	9°36'W
Westport, Ct., U.S. (wĕst'pōrt)	110a	41°07'N	73°22'W
Westport, Or., U.S. (wĕst'pôrt)	116c	46°08'N	123°22'W
Westray, i., Scot., U.K. (wĕs'trā)	164a	59°19'N	3°05'W
West Road, r., Can. (rōd)	94	53°00'N	124°00'W
West Saint Paul, Mn., U.S. (sānt pôl')	117g	44°55'N	93°05'W
West Sand Spit, i., T./C. Is.	135	21°25'N	72°10'W
West Slope, Or., U.S.	116c	45°30'N	122°46'W
West Tavaputs Plateau, plat., Ut., U.S. (wĕst tăv'ȧ-pŏts)	119	39°45'N	110°35'W
West Terre Haute, In., U.S. (tĕr-ē hōt')	108	39°30'N	87°30'W
West Union, Ia., U.S. (ūn'yŭn)	113	42°58'N	91°48'W
West University Place, Tx., U.S.	123a	29°43'N	95°26'W
Westview, Oh., U.S. (wĕst'vů)	111d	41°21'N	81°54'W
West View, Pa., U.S.	111e	40°31'N	80°02'W
Westville, Can. (wĕst'vĭl)	101	45°35'N	62°43'W
Westville, Il., U.S.	108	40°00'N	87°40'W
West Virginia, state, U.S. (wĕst vẽr-jĭn'ĭ-ȧ)	105	39°00'N	80°50'W
West Walker, r., Ca., U.S. (wôk'ẽr)	118	38°25'N	119°25'W
West Warwick, R.I., U.S. [illegible]	[illegible]	[illegible]	[illegible]
Westwego, La., U.S. (wĕst-wē'gō)	110d	29°55'N	90°09'W
Westwood, Ca., U.S. (wĕst'wŏŏd)	118	40°18'N	121°00'W
Westwood, Ks., U.S.	117f	39°03'N	94°37'W
Westwood, Ma., U.S.	101a	42°13'N	71°14'W
Westwood, N.J., U.S.	110a	40°59'N	74°02'W
West Wyalong, Austl. (wīȧlông)	219	34°00'S	147°20'E
West Yorkshire, hist. reg., Eng., U.K.	158a	53°37'N	1°48'W
Wetar, Pulau, i., Indon. (wĕt'ȧr)	213	7°34'S	126°00'E
Wetaskiwin, Can. (wĕ-tăs'kē-wŏn)	90	52°58'N	113°22'W
Wetmore, Tx., U.S. (wĕt'mōr)	117d	29°34'N	98°25'W
Wetter, Ger. (vĕt'ẽr)	171c	51°23'N	7°23'E
Wetumpka, Al., U.S. (wē-tŭmp'kȧ)	124	32°33'N	86°12'W
Wetzlar, Ger. (vets'lär)	168	50°35'N	8°30'E
Wewak, Pap. N. Gui. (wā-wäk')	213	3°19'S	143°30'E
Wewoka, Ok., U.S. (wē-wō'kȧ)	121	35°09'N	96°30'W
Wexford, Ire. (wĕks'fẽrd)	161	52°20'N	6°30'W
Weybridge, Eng., U.K. (wā'brĭj)	158b	51°20'N	0°26'W
Weyburn, Can. (wā'bûrn)	90	49°41'N	103°52'W
Weymouth, Eng., U.K. (wā'mŭth)	164	50°37'N	2°34'W
Weymouth, Ma., U.S.	101a	42°44'N	70°57'W
Weymouth, Oh., U.S.	111d	41°11'N	81°48'W
Whale Cay, i., Bah.	134	25°20'N	77°45'W
Whale Cay Channels, strt., Bah.	134	26°45'N	77°10'W
Wharton, N.J., U.S. (hwôr'tŭn)	110a	40°54'N	74°35'W
Wharton, Tx., U.S.	123	29°19'N	96°06'W
What Cheer, Ia., U.S. (hwŏt chēr)	113	41°23'N	92°24'W
Whatcom, Lake, l., Wa., U.S. (hwät'kŭm)	116c	48°44'N	123°34'W
Whatshan Lake, l., Can. (wŏt'shăn)	95	50°00'N	118°03'W
Wheatland, Wy., U.S. (hwēt'lănd)	115	42°04'N	104°52'W
Wheatland Reservoir Number 2, res., Wy., U.S.	115	41°52'N	105°36'W
Wheaton, Il., U.S. (hwē'tŭn)	111a	41°52'N	88°06'W
Wheaton, Md., U.S.	110e	39°05'N	77°05'W
Wheaton, Mn., U.S.	112	45°48'N	96°29'W
Wheeler Peak, mtn., N.M., U.S.	120	36°34'N	105°25'W
Wheeler Peak, mtn., Nv., U.S.	106	38°58'N	114°15'W
Wheeling, Il., U.S. (hwēl'ĭng)	111a	42°08'N	87°54'W
Wheeling, W.V., U.S.	108	40°05'N	80°45'W
Wheelwright, Arg. (ōē'l-rē'gt)	141c	33°46'S	61°14'W
Whidbey Island, i., Wa., U.S. (hwĭd'bē)	116a	48°13'N	122°50'W
Whippany, N.J., U.S. (hwĭp'ȧ-nē)	110a	40°49'N	74°25'W
Whitby, Can. (hwĭt'bē)	91	43°50'N	79°00'W
Whitchurch, Eng., U.K. (hwĭt'chûrch)	158a	52°58'N	2°49'W
White, l., Can.	98	48°47'N	85°50'W
White, l., Can.	99	45°15'N	76°35'W
White, r., Can.	98	48°34'N	85°46'W
White, r., In., U.S.	108	39°15'N	86°45'W
White, r., S.D., U.S.	112	43°13'N	101°04'W
White, r., Tx., U.S.	120	36°25'N	102°20'W
White, r., Vt., U.S.	109	43°45'N	72°35'W
White, r., Wa., U.S.	114	47°07'N	121°48'W
White, r., U.S.	107	35°30'N	92°00'W
White, r., U.S.	112	43°41'N	99°48'W
White, r., U.S.	119	40°10'N	108°55'W
White, East Fork, r., In., U.S.	108	38°45'N	86°20'W
White Bay, b., Can.	93a	50°00'N	56°30'W
White Bear Indian Reserve, I.R., Can.	97	49°50'N	102°15'W
White Bear Lake, l., Mn., U.S.	117g	45°04'N	92°58'W
White Castle, La., U.S.	123	30°10'N	91°09'W
White Center, Wa., U.S.	116a	47°31'N	122°21'W
White Cloud, Mi., U.S.	108	43°35'N	85°45'W
Whitecourt, Can. (wĭt'côrt)	90	54°09'N	115°41'W
White Earth, r., N.D., U.S.	112	48°30'N	102°44'W
White Earth Indian Reservation, I.R., Mn., U.S.	112	47°18'N	95°42'W
Whiteface, r., Mn., U.S. (whīt'fās)	113	47°12'N	92°13'W
Whitefield, N.H., U.S. (hwĭt'fēld)	109	44°20'N	71°35'W
Whitefish Bay, Wi., U.S.	111a	43°07'N	77°54'W
Whitefish Bay, b., Can.	97	49°26'N	94°14'W
Whitefish Bay, b., N.A.	113	46°36'N	84°50'W
White Hall, Il., U.S.	121	39°26'N	90°23'W
Whitehall, Mi., U.S. (hwĭt'hôl)	108	43°20'N	86°20'W
Whitehall, N.Y., U.S.	109	43°30'N	73°25'W
Whitehaven, Eng., U.K. (hwīt'hā-vĕn)	164	54°35'N	3°30'W
Whitehorn, Point, c., Wa., U.S. (hwīt'hôrn)	116d	48°54'N	122°48'W
Whitehorse, Can. (whīt'hôrs)	90	60°39'N	135°01'W
White Lake, l., La., U.S.	123	29°40'N	92°35'W
White Mountain Peak, mtn., Ca., U.S.	118	37°38'N	118°13'W
White Mountains, mts., Me., U.S.	100	44°22'N	71°15'W
White Mountains, mts., N.H., U.S.	109	42°20'N	71°05'W
Whitemouth, l., Can.	97	49°14'N	95°40'W
White Nile (Al Bahr al Abyad), r., Sudan	231	12°30'N	32°30'E
White Otter, l., Can.	98	49°15'N	91°48'W
White Pass, p., N.A.	103	59°35'N	135°03'W
White Plains, N.Y., U.S.	110a	41°02'N	73°47'W
White River, Can.	98	48°38'N	85°23'W
White Rock, Can.	95	49°01'N	122°49'W
Whiterock Reservoir, res., Tx., U.S. (hwīt'rŏk)	117c	32°51'N	96°40'W
White Russia see Belarus, nation, Eur.	178	53°30'N	25°33'E
Whitesail Lake, l., Can. (whīt'sāl)	94	53°30'N	127°00'W
White Sands National Monument, rec., N.M., U.S.	119	32°50'N	106°20'W
White Sea, sea, Russia	178	66°00'N	40°00'E
White Settlement, Tx., U.S.	117c	32°45'N	97°28'W
White Sulphur Springs, Mt., U.S.	115	46°32'N	110°49'W
White Umfolzi, r., S. Afr. (ŭm-fō-lō zē)	233c	28°12'S	30°55'E
Whiteville, N.C., U.S. (hwīt'vĭl)	125	34°18'N	78°45'W
White Volta (Volta Blanche), r., Afr.	234	9°40'N	1°10'W
Whitewater, Wi., U.S. (whīt wŏt'ẽr)	[illegible]	42°49'N	88°40'W
Whitewater, l., Can.	97	49°14'N	[illegible]
Whitewater, r., In., U.S.	111f	39°19'N	84°55'W
Whitewater Bay, b., Fl., U.S.	125a	25°16'N	80°21'W
Whitewater Creek, r., Mt., U.S.	115	48°50'N	107°50'W
Whitewell, Tn., U.S. (hwīt'wĕl)	124	35°11'N	85°31'W
Whitewright, Tx., U.S. (hwīt'rīt)	121	33°33'N	96°25'W
Whitham, r., Eng., U.K. (wĭth'ŭm)	158a	53°08'N	0°15'W
Whiting, In., U.S. (hwīt'ĭng)	111a	41°41'N	87°30'W
Whitinsville, Ma., U.S. (hwīt'ĕns-vĭl)	101a	42°06'N	71°40'W
Whitman, Ma., U.S. (hwĭt'măn)	101a	42°05'N	70°57'W
Whitmire, S.C., U.S. (hwĭt'mīr)	125	34°30'N	81°40'W
Whitney, Mount, mtn., Ca., U.S.	106	36°34'N	118°18'W
Whitney Lake, l., Tx., U.S. (hwĭt'nē)	123	32°02'N	97°36'W
Whitstable, Eng., U.K. (wĭt'stȧb'l)	158b	51°22'N	1°03'E
Whitsunday, i., Austl. (hwĭt's'n-dā)	221	20°16'S	149°00'E
Whittier, Ca., U.S. (hwĭt'ĭ-ẽr)	117a	33°58'N	118°02'W
Whittlesea, S. Afr. (wĭt'l'sē)	233c	32°11'S	26°51'E
Whitworth, Eng., U.K. (hwĭt'wŭrth)	158a	53°40'N	2°10'W
Whyalla, Austl. (hwī-ăl'ȧ)	218	33°00'S	137°32'E
Whymper, Mount, mtn., Can. (wĭm'pẽr)	94	48°57'N	124°10'W
Wiarton, Can. (wī'ȧr-tŭn)	91	44°45'N	80°45'W
Wichita, Ks., U.S. (wĭch'ĭ-tô)	104	37°42'N	97°21'W
Wichita, r., Tx., U.S.	120	33°50'N	99°38'W
Wichita Falls, Tx., U.S. (fôls)	104	33°54'N	98°29'W
Wichita Mountains, mts., Ok., U.S.	106	34°48'N	98°43'W
Wick, Scot., U.K. (wĭk)	160	58°25'N	3°05'W
Wickatunk, N.J., U.S. (wĭk'ȧ-tŭnk)	110a	40°21'N	74°15'W
Wickenburg, Az., U.S.	119	33°58'N	112°44'W
Wickiup Reservoir, res., Or., U.S.	114	43°40'N	121°43'W
Wickliffe, Oh., U.S. (wĭk'klĭf)	111d	41°37'N	81°29'W
Wicklow, Ire.	164	52°59'N	6°06'W
Wicklow Mountains, mts., Ire. (wĭk'lō)	164	52°49'N	6°20'W
Wickup Mountain, mtn., Or., U.S. (wĭk'ŭp)	116c	46°06'N	123°35'W
Wiconisco, Pa., U.S. (wĭ-kon'ĭs-kō)	109	43°35'N	76°45'W
Widen, W.V., U.S. (wī'dĕn)	108	38°25'N	80°55'W
Widnes, Eng., U.K. (wĭd'nĕs)	158a	53°21'N	2°44'W
Wieliczka, Pol. (vyĕ-lēch'kȧ)	169	49°58'N	20°06'E
Wien see Vienna, Aus.	154	48°13'N	16°22'E
Wien, state, Aus.	159e	48°11'N	16°23'E
Wiener Neustadt, Aus. (vē'nẽr noi'shtät)	161	47°48'N	16°15'E
Wiener Wald, for., Aus.	159e	48°09'N	16°05'E
Wieprz, r., Pol. (vyĕpzh)	169	51°25'N	22°45'E
Wiergate, Tx., U.S. (wēr'gāt)	123	31°00'N	93°42'W
Wiesbaden, Ger. (vēs'bä-dĕn)	161	50°05'N	8°15'E
Wigan, Eng., U.K. (wĭg'ăn)	164	53°33'N	2°37'W
Wiggins, Ms., U.S. (wĭg'ĭnz)	124	30°51'N	89°05'W
Wight, Isle of, i., Eng., U.K. (wīt)	164	50°44'N	1°17'W
Wilber, Ne., U.S. (wĭl'bẽr)	121	40°29'N	96°57'W
Wilburton, Ok., U.S. (wĭl'bẽr-tŭn)	121	34°54'N	95°18'W
Wilcannia, Austl. (wĭl-cān-ĭȧ)	219	31°30'S	143°30'E
Wildau, Ger. (vēl'dou)	159b	52°20'N	13°39'E
Wildberg, Ger. (vēl'bĕrgh)	159b	52°52'N	12°39'E
Wildcat Hill, hill, Can. (wīld'kăt)	97	53°17'N	102°30'W
Wildhay, r., Can. (wīld'hā)	95	53°15'N	117°20'W
Wildomar, Ca., U.S. (wĭl'dō-mär)	117a	33°35'N	117°17'W
Wild Rice, r., Mn., U.S.	112	47°10'N	96°40'W
Wild Rice, r., N.D., U.S.	112	46°10'N	97°12'W
Wild Rice Lake, l., Mn., U.S.	117h	46°54'N	92°10'W
Wildspitze, mtn., Aus.	168	46°55'N	10°50'E
Wildwood, N.J., U.S.	109	39°00'N	74°50'W
Wiley, Co., U.S. (wī'lē)	120	38°08'N	102°41'W
Wilge, r., S. Afr. (wĭl'jē)	238c	25°38'S	29°09'E
Wilge, r., S. Afr.	238c	27°27'S	28°46'E
Wilhelm, Mount, mtn., Pap. N. Gui.	213	5°58'S	144°58'E
Wilhelmina Gebergte, mts., Sur.	143	4°30'N	57°00'W
Wilhelmina Kanaal, can., Neth.	159a	51°37'N	4°55'E
Wilhelmshaven, Ger. (vēl-hĕlms-hä'fĕn)	160	53°30'N	8°10'E
Wilkes-Barre, Pa., U.S. (wĭlks'băr-ē)	105	41°15'N	75°50'W
Wilkes Land, reg., Ant.	224	71°00'S	126°00'E
Wilkeson, Wa., U.S. (wĭl-kē'sŭn)	116a	47°06'N	122°03'W
Wilkie, Can. (wĭlk'ē)	90	52°25'N	108°43'W
Wilkinsburg, Pa., U.S. (wĭl'kĭnz-bûrg)	111e	40°26'N	79°53'W
Willamette, r., Or., U.S.	106	45°00'N	123°00'W
Willapa Bay, b., Wa., U.S.	114	46°37'N	124°00'W
Willard, Oh., U.S. (wĭl'ȧrd)	108	41°00'N	82°50'W
Willard, Ut., U.S.	117b	41°24'N	112°02'W
Willcox, Az., U.S. (wĭl'kŏks)	119	32°15'N	109°50'W
Willcox Playa, l., Az., U.S.	119	32°08'N	109°51'W
Willemstad, Neth. Ant.	142	12°12'N	68°58'W
Willesden, Eng., U.K. (wĭlz'dĕn)	158b	51°31'N	0°17'W
William "Bill" Dannelly Reservoir, res., Al., U.S.	124	32°10'N	87°15'W
William Creek, Austl. (wĭl'yăm)	218	28°45'S	136°20'E

ăt; fĭnăl; rāte; senȧte; ärm; ȧsk; sofȧ; fâre; ch-choose; dh-as th in other; bē; ėvent; bĕt; recĕnt; cratẽr; g-gō; gh-guttural g; bĭt; ĭ-short neutral; rīde; ĸ-guttural k as ch in German ich;

ng-sing; ŋ-bank; N-nasalized n; nŏd; cŏmmit; ōld; ŏbey; ôrder; oi-boil; fōōd; ȯ-as oo in foot; ou-out; s-soft; sh-dish; th-thin; pūre; ūnite; ûrn; stŭd; circŭs; ü-as in French tu; ′-indeterminate vowel.

ăt; fīnǎl; rāte; senāte; ärm; ȧsk; sofȧ; fãre; ch-choose; dh-as th in other; bē; ěvent; bět; recěnt; cratěr; g-gō; gh-guttural g; bĭt; ĭ-short neutral; rīde; ᴋ-guttural k as ch in German ich;

PRONOUNCING INDEX
Yellowstone National Park – Zeya 369

PLACE (Pronunciation)	PAGE	LAT.	LONG.
Yellowstone National Park, rec., U.S. (yĕl'ō-stōn)	106	44°45'N	110°35'W
Yel'nya, Russia (yĕl'nyȧ)	176	54°34'N	33°12'E
Yemanzhelinsk, Russia (yĕ-män-zhâ'lĭnsk)	186a	54°47'N	61°24'E
Yemen, nation, Asia (yĕm'ĕn)	198	15°00'N	47°00'E
Yemetsk, Russia	180	63°28'N	41°28'E
Yenangyaung, Mya. (yā'nän-d oung)	199	20°27'N	94°59'E
Yencheng, China	204	37°30'N	79°26'E
Yendi, Ghana (yĕn'dē)	230	9°26'N	0°01'W
Yengisar, China (yŭn-gē-sär)	204	39°01'N	75°29'E
Yenice, r., Tur.	181	41°10'N	33°00'E
Yenisey, r., Russia (yĕ-nẻ-sĕ'ẻ)	178	71°00'N	82°00'E
Yeniseysk, Russia (yĕ-nĭĕsā'ĭsk)	179	58°27'N	90°28'E
Yeo, l., Austl. (yō)	220	28°15'S	124°00'E
Yerevan, Arm. (yĕ-rĕ-vän')	181	40°10'N	44°30'E
Yerington, Nv., U.S. (yẻ'rĭng-tŭn)	118	38°59'N	119°10'W
Yermak, i., Russia	180	66°45'N	71°30'E
Yeste, Spain (yĕs'tå)	172	38°23'N	2°19'W
You, Île d', i., Fr. (ēl dyū)	161	46°43'N	2°45'W
Yevlax, Azer.	182	40°36'N	47°09'E
Yexian, China (yŭ-shyĕn)	206	37°09'N	119°57'E
Yeya, r., Russia (yă'yȧ)	177	46°25'N	39°17'E
Yeysk, Russia (yĕysk)	181	46°41'N	38°13'E
Yi, r., China	206	34°38'N	118°07'E
Yibin, China (yē-bĭn)	204	28°50'N	104°40'E
Yichang, China (yē-chäŋ)	205	30°38'N	111°22'E
Yidu, China (yē-dōō)	208	36°42'N	118°30'E
Yilan, China (yē-län)	205	46°10'N	129°40'E
Yinchuan, China (yĭn-chŭän)	204	38°22'N	106°22'E
Yingkou, China (yĭŋ-kō)	205	40°35'N	122°10'E
Yining, China (yē-nĭŋ)	204	43°58'N	80°40'E
Yin Shan, mts., China (yĭng'shän')	208	40°50'N	110°30'E
Yishan, China (yē-shän)	204	24°32'N	108°42'E
Yishui, China (yē-shwā)	206	35°49'N	118°40'E
Yitong, China (yē-tôŋ)	205	43°15'N	125°10'E
Yixian, China (yē shyĕn)	208	41°30'N	121°15'E
Yixing, China	206	31°26'N	119°57'E
Yiyang, China (yē-yäŋ)	209	28°52'N	112°12'E
Yoakum, Tx., U.S. (yō'kŭm)	123	29°18'N	97°09'W
Yockanookany, r., Ms., U.S. (yŏk'á-nōō-kă-nĭ)	124	32°47'N	89°38'W
Yodo-Gawa, strt., Japan (yō'dō'gä-wä)	211b	34°46'N	135°35'E
Yog Point, c., Phil. (yōg)	209	14°00'N	124°30'E
Yogyakarta, Indon. (yŏg-yȧ-kär'tȧ)	212	7°50'S	110°20'E
Yoho National Park, rec., Can. (yō'hō)	90	51°26'N	116°30'W
Yojoa, Lago de, l., Hond. (lä'gô dĕ yô-hō'ä)	132	14°49'N	87°53'W
Yokkaichi, Japan (yô'kä'ē-chê)	210	34°58'N	136°35'E
Yokohama, Japan (yō'kô-hä'mȧ)	205	35°37'N	139°40'E
Yokosuka, Japan (yô-kō'sò-kä)	210	35°17'N	139°40'E
Yokota, Japan (yō-kō'tä)	211a	35°23'N	140°02'E
Yola, Nig. (yō'lä)	230	9°13'N	12°27'E
Yolaina, Cordillera de, mts., Nic.	133	11°34'N	84°34'W
Yomou, Gui.	234	7°34'N	9°16'W
Yonago, Japan (yō'nä-gō)	210	35°27'N	133°19'E
Yonezawa, Japan (yō'nĕ'zȧ-wä)	210	37°50'N	140°07'E
Yong'an, China (yôŋ-än)	209	26°00'N	117°22'E
Yongding, r., China (yôŋ-dĭŋ)	208	40°25'N	115°00'E
Yŏngdŏk, Kor., S. (yŭng'dŭk')	210	36°28'N	129°25'E
Yŏnghŭng, Kor., N. (yŭng'hŏng')	210	39°31'N	127°11'E
Yonghŭng Man, b., Kor., N.	210	39°10'N	128°00'E
Yongnian, China (yôŋ-nĭĕn)	208	36°47'N	114°32'E
Yongqing, China (yôŋ-chyĭŋ)	208a	39°18'N	116°27'E
Yongshun, China (yôŋ-shòn)	204	29°05'N	109°58'E
Yonkers, N.Y., U.S. (yŏŋ'kẽrz)	110a	40°57'N	73°54'W
Yonne, r., Fr. (yôn)	170	48°18'N	3°15'E
Yono, Japan (yō'nō)	211a	35°53'N	139°36'E
Yorba Linda, Ca., U.S. (yôr'bȧ lĭn'dȧ)	117a	33°55'N	117°51'W
York, Austl.	218	32°00'S	117°00'E
York, Eng., U.K.	160	53°58'N	1°10'W
York, Al., U.S. (yôrk)	124	32°33'N	88°16'W
York, Ne., U.S.	121	40°52'N	97°36'W
York, Pa., U.S.	105	40°00'N	76°40'W
York, S.C., U.S.	125	34°59'N	81°14'W
York, Cape, c., Austl.	221	10°45'S	142°35'E
York, Kap, c., Grnld.	89	75°30'N	73°00'W
Yorke Peninsula, pen., Austl.	222	34°24'S	137°20'E
Yorketown, Austl.	222	35°00'S	137°28'E
York Factory, Can.	97	57°05'N	92°18'W
Yorkshire Wolds, Eng., U.K. (yôrk'shĭr)	164	54°00'N	0°35'W
Yorkton, Can. (yôrk'tŭn)	90	51°13'N	102°28'W
Yorktown, Tx., U.S. (yôrk'toun)	123	28°57'N	97°30'W
Yorktown, Va., U.S.	125	37°12'N	76°31'W
Yoro, Hond. (yō'rō)	132	15°09'N	87°05'W
Yoron, i., Japan	210	26°48'N	128°40'E
Yosemite National Park, rec., Ca., U.S. (yō-sĕm'ĭ-tē)	106	38°03'N	119°36'W
Yoshida, Japan (yō'shē-dȧ)	211	34°39'N	132°41'E
Yoshikawa, Japan (yō-shē'kä'wä')	211a	35°53'N	139°51'E
Yoshino, r., Japan (yō'shē-nō)	211	34°04'N	133°57'E
Yoshkar-Ola, Russia (yôsh-kär'ô-lä')	180	56°35'N	48°05'E
Yos Sudarsa, Pulau, i., Indon.	213	7°20'S	138°30'E
Yŏsu, Kor., S. (yŭ'sōō')	210	34°42'N	127°42'W
You, r., China (yō)	209	23°55'N	106°50'E
Youghal, Ire. (yōō'ôl) (yôl)	165	51°58'N	7°57'E
Youghal Bay, b., Ire.	164	51°52'N	7°46'W
Young, Austl. (yŭng)	222	34°15'S	148°18'E
Young, Ur. (yô-ōō'ng)	141c	32°42'S	57°38'W
Youngs, l., Wa., U.S. (yŭngz)	116a	47°25'N	122°08'W
Youngstown, N.Y., U.S.	111c	43°15'N	79°02'W
Youngstown, Oh., U.S.	108	41°05'N	80°40'W

PLACE (Pronunciation)	PAGE	LAT.	LONG.
Yozgat, Tur. (yôz'gȧd)	198	39°50'N	34°50'E
Ypsilanti, Mi., U.S. (ĭp-sĭ-lăn'tĭ)	111b	42°15'N	83°37'W
Yreka, Ca., U.S. (wī-rē'kȧ)	114	41°43'N	122°36'W
Yrghyz, Kaz.	183	48°30'N	61°17'E
Yrghyz, r., Kaz.	156	49°30'N	60°32'E
Ysleta, Tx., U.S. (ēz-lĕ'tȧ)	122	31°42'N	106°18'W
Yssingeaux, Fr. (ē-säN-zhō)	170	45°09'N	4°08'E
Ystad, Swe.	160	55°25'N	13°49'E
Ystädeh-ye Moqor, Āb-e, l., Afg.	202	32°35'N	68°00'E
Yu'alliq, Jabal, mts., Egypt	197a	30°12'N	33°42'E
Yuan, r., China (yůän)	205	28°50'N	110°50'E
Yuan'an, China (yůän-än)	209	31°08'N	111°28'E
Yuanling, China (yůän-lĭŋ)	209	28°30'N	110°18'E
Yuanshi, China (yůän-shr)	208	37°45'N	114°32'E
Yuasa, Japan	211	34°02'N	135°10'E
Yuba City, Ca., U.S. (yōō'bȧ)	118	39°08'N	121°38'W
Yucaipa, Ca., Ca., U.S. (yŭ-kȧ-ē'pȧ)	117a	34°02'N	117°02'W
Yucatán, state, Mex. (yōō-kä-tän')	128	20°45'N	89°00'W
Yucatan Channel, strt., N.A.	128	22°30'N	87°00'W
Yucatan Peninsula, pen., N.A.	102	19°30'N	89°00'W
Yucheng, China (yōō-chŭŋ)	206	34°31'N	115°54'E
Yucheng, China	208	36°55'N	116°39'E
Yuci, China (yōō-tsz)	208	37°32'N	112°40'E
Yudoma, r., Russia (yōō-dō'mȧ)	185	59°13'N	137°00'E
Yueqing, China (yůĕ-chyĭn)	209	28°02'N	120°40'E
Yueyang, China (yůĕ-yäŋ)	205	29°25'N	113°05'E
Yuezhuang, China (yůĕ-jůäŋ)	206	36°13'N	118°17'E
Yug, r., Russia (yòg)	180	59°50'N	45°55'E
Yukhnov, Russia (yòk'nof)	176	54°44'N	35°15'E
Yukon, ter., Can. (yōō'kŏn)	90	63°16'N	135°30'W
Yukon, r., N.A.	106a	64°00'N	159°30'W
Yukutat Bay, b., Ak., U.S. (yōō-kū tăt')	103	59°34'N	140°50'W
Yuldybayevo, Russia (yòld'bä'yĕ-vô)	186a	52°20'N	57°52'E
Yulin, China (yōō-lĭn)	209	22°38'N	110°10'E
Yulin, China	204	38°18'N	109°45'E
Yuma, Az., U.S. (yōō'mä)	104	32°40'N	114°40'W
Yuma, Co., U.S.	120	40°08'N	102°50'W
Yuma, r., Dom. Rep.	135	19°05'N	70°05'W
Yumbi, D.R.C.	237	1°14'S	26°14'E
Yumen, China (yōō-mŭn)	204	40°14'N	96°56'E
Yuncheng, China (yòn-chŭŋ)	208	35°00'N	110°40'E
Yunnan, prov., China (yun'nän')	204	24°23'N	101°03'E
Yunnan Plat, plat., China (yò-nän)	204	26°03'N	101°26'E
Yunxian, China (yòn shyĕn)	205	32°50'N	110°55'E
Yunxiao, China (yòn-shyou)	209	24°00'N	117°20'E
Yura, Japan (yōō'rä)	211	34°18'N	134°54'E
Yurécuaro, Mex. (yōō-rā'kwä-rô)	130	20°21'N	102°16'W
Yurimaguas, Peru (yōō-rê-mä'gwäs)	142	5°59'S	76°12'W
Yuriria, Mex. (yōō'rē-rē'ä)	130	20°11'N	101°08'W
Yurovo, Russia	186b	55°30'N	38°24'E
Yur'yevets, Russia	180	57°15'N	43°08'E
Yuscarán, Hond. (yōōs-kä-rän')	132	13°57'N	86°48'W
Yushan, China (yōō-shän)	209	28°42'N	118°20'E
Yü Shan, mtn., Tai.	205	23°38'N	121°05'E
Yushu, China (yōō-shōō)	208	44°58'N	126°32'E
Yutian, China (yōō-tĭĕn)	208	39°54'N	117°45'E
Yutian, China (yōō-tĭĕn) (kŭ-r-yä)	204	36°55'N	81°39'E
Yuty, Para. (yōō-tē')	144	26°45'S	56°13'W
Yuwangcheng, China (yü'wäng'chĕng)	206	31°32'N	114°26'E
Yuxian, China (yōō shyĕn)	208	39°40'N	114°38'E
Yuzha, Russia (yōō'zhȧ)	180	56°38'N	42°20'E
Yuzhno-Sakhalinsk, Russia (yōōzh'nô-sä-kä-lĭnsk')	179	47°11'N	143°04'E
Yuzhnoural'skiy, Russia (yōōzh-nô-ô-rál'skĭ)	186a	54°26'N	61°17'E
Yuzhnyy Ural, mts., Russia (yōō'zhnĭ ò-räl')	186a	52°51'N	57°48'E
Yverdon, Switz. (ē-vĕr-dôn)	168	46°46'N	6°35'E
Yvetot, Fr. (ēv-tō')	170	49°39'N	0°45'E

Z

PLACE (Pronunciation)	PAGE	LAT.	LONG.
Za, r., Mor.	162	34°19'N	2°23'W
Zaachila, Mex. (sä-ä-chē'lȧ)	131	16°56'N	96°45'W
Zaandam, Neth. (zän'dȧm)	165	52°25'N	4°49'E
Ząbkowice Śląskie, Pol.	168	50°35'N	16°48'E
Zabrze, Pol. (zäb'zhĕ)	161	50°18'N	18°48'E
Zacapa, Guat. (sä-kä'pä)	132	14°56'N	89°30'W
Zacapoaxtla, Mex. (sä-kä-pō-äs'tlä)	131	19°51'N	97°34'W
Zacatecas, Mex. (sä-kä-tā'käs)	128	22°44'N	102°32'W
Zacatecas, state, Mex.	128	24°00'N	102°45'W
Zacatecoluca, El Sal. (sä-kä-tå-kô-lōō'kä)	132	13°31'N	88°50'W
Zacatelco, Mex.	130	19°12'N	98°12'W
Zacatepec, Mex. (sä-kä-tå-pĕk') (sän-tē-ä'gô)	131	17°10'N	95°53'W
Zacatlán, Mex. (sä-kä-tlän')	131	19°55'N	97°57'W
Zacoalco de Torres, Mex. (sä-kô-äl'kō dā tōr'rĕs)	130	20°12'N	103°33'W
Zacualpan, Mex. (sä-kô-äl-pän')	130	18°43'N	99°46'W
Zacualtipan, Mex. (sȧ-kô-äl-tē-pän')	130	20°38'N	98°39'W
Zadar, Cro. (zä'där)	154	44°08'N	15°16'E
Zadonsk, Russia (zä-dônsk')	176	52°22'N	38°55'E
Žagare, Lat. (zhägärĕ)	167	56°21'N	23°14'E
Zagarolo, Italy (tzä-gä-rô'lô)	173d	41°51'N	12°53'E
Zaghouan, Tun. (zȧ-gwäN')	230	36°30'N	10°04'E
Zagreb, Cro. (zä'grĕb)	154	45°50'N	15°58'E

PLACE (Pronunciation)	PAGE	LAT.	LONG.
Zagros Mountains, mts., Iran	198	33°30'N	46°30'E
Zāhedān, Iran (zä'hȧ-dän)	198	29°37'N	60°31'E
Zahlah, Leb. (zä'lä')	197a	33°50'N	35°54'E
Zaire *see* Congo, Democratic Republic of the , nation, Afr.	232	1°00'S	22°15'E
Zaječar, Serb. (zä'yĕ-chär')	175	43°54'N	22°16'E
Zakhidnyi Buh (Bug), r., Eur.	168	52°29'N	21°20'E
Zakopane, Pol. (zȧ-kô-pä'nĕ)	169	49°18'N	19°57'E
Zakouma, Parc National de, rec., Chad	235	10°50'N	19°20'E
Zákynthos, Grc.	175	37°48'N	20°55'E
Zákynthos, i., Grc.	163	37°45'N	20°32'E
Zalaegerszeg, Hung. (zŏ'lô-ĕ'gĕr-sĕg)	168	46°50'N	16°50'E
Zalău, Rom. (zȧ-lŭ'ò)	169	47°11'N	23°06'E
Zalţan, Libya	231	28°20'N	19°40'E
Zaltbommel, Neth.	159a	51°48'N	5°15'E
Zambezi, r., Afr. (zȧm-bā'zẻ)	232	16°00'S	29°45'E
Zambia, nation, Afr. (zăm'bê-ȧ)	232	14°23'S	24°15'E
Zamboanga, Phil. (säm-bŏ-aŋ'gä)	212	6°58'N	122°02'E
Zambrów, Pol. (zäm'bròf)	169	52°29'N	22°17'E
Zamora, Mex. (sä-mō'rä)	128	19°59'N	102°16'W
Zamora, Spain (thä-mō'rä)	162	41°32'N	5°43'W
Zanatepec, Mex.	131	16°30'N	94°22'W
Zandvoort, Neth.	159a	52°22'N	4°30'E
Zanesville, Oh., U.S. (zānz'vĭl)	108	39°55'N	82°00'W
Zangasso, Mali	234	12°09'N	5°37'W
Zanjān, Iran	198	36°26'N	48°24'E
Zanzibar, Tan. (zăn'zĭ-bär)	233	6°10'S	39°11'E
Zanzibar, i., Tan.	233	6°20'S	39°37'E
Zanzibar Channel, strt., Tan.	237	6°05'S	39°00'E
Zaozhuang, China (dzou-jůäŋ)	206	34°51'N	117°34'E
Zapadnaya Dvina *see* Western Dvina, r., Eur.	167	55°30'N	28°27'E
Zapala, Arg. (zä-pä'lä)	144	38°53'S	70°02'W
Zapata, Tx., U.S. (sä-pä'tä)	122	26°52'N	99°18'W
Zapata, Ciénaga de, sw., Cuba (syā'nä-gä-dĕ-zä-pá'tä)	134	22°30'N	81°20'W
Zapata, Península de, pen., Cuba (pĕ-nē'n-sōō-lä-dĕ-zä-pá'tä)	134	22°20'N	81°30'W
Zapatera, Isla, i., Nic. (ē's-lä-sä-pä-tā'rō)	132	11°45'N	85°45'W
Zapopan, Mex. (sä-pō'pän)	130	20°42'N	103°23'W
Zaporizhzhia, Ukr.	178	47°50'N	35°10'E
Zaporizhzhia, prov., Ukr.	177	47°20'N	35°05'E
Zaporoshskoye, Russia (zȧ-pô-rôsh'skô-yĕ)	167	60°36'N	30°31'E
Zapotiltic, Mex. (sä-pô-tēl-tēk')	130	19°37'N	103°25'W
Zapotitlán, Mex. (sä-pô-tē-tlän')	130	17°13'N	98°58'W
Zapotitlán, Punta, c., Mex.	131	18°34'N	94°48'W
Zapotlanejo, Mex. (sä-pô-tlä-nā'hô)	130	20°38'N	103°05'W
Zaragoza, Mex. (sä-rä-gō'sä)	130	23°59'N	99°45'W
Zaragoza, Mex.	130	22°02'N	100°45'W
Zaragoza, Spain (thä-rä-gō'thä)	154	41°39'N	0°53'W
Zarand, Munţii, mts., Rom.	169	46°07'N	22°21'E
Zaranda Hill, mtn., Nig.	235	10°15'N	9°35'E
Zaranj, Afg.	201	31°06'N	61°53'E
Zarasai, Lith. (zä-rä-sī')	167	55°45'N	26°18'E
Zárate, Arg. (zä-rä'tä)	144	34°05'S	59°05'W
Zaraysk, Russia (zä-rä'ēsk)	180	54°46'N	38°53'E
Zaria, Nig. (zä'rē-ä)	230	11°07'N	7°44'E
Zarqā', r., Jord.	197a	32°13'N	35°43'E
Zarzal, Col. (zär-zä'l)	142a	4°23'N	76°04'W
Zashiversk, Russia (zá'shĭ-vĕrsk')	179	67°08'N	144°02'E
Zastavna, Ukr. (zás-täf'nȧ)	169	48°32'N	25°50'E
Zastron, S. Afr. (zäs'trŭn)	233c	30°19'S	27°07'E
Žatec, Czech Rep. (zhä'tĕts)	168	50°19'N	13°32'E
Zavitinsk, Russia	185	50°12'N	129°44'E
Zawiercie, Pol. (zá-vyĕr'tsyĕ)	169	50°28'N	19°25'E
Zāwiyat al-Baydā', Libya	231	32°49'N	21°46'E
Zāyandeh, r., Iran	198	32°15'N	51°00'E
Zaysan, Kaz. (zī'sán)	183	47°43'N	84°44'E
Zaza, r., Cuba (zá'zá)	134	21°40'N	79°25'W
Zbarazh, Ukr. (zbä-räzh')	169	49°39'N	25°48'E
Zbruch, r., Ukr. (zbròch)	169	48°56'N	26°18'E
Zdolbuniv, Ukr.	169	50°31'N	26°17'E
Zduńska Wola, Pol. (zdōōn''skä vō'lä)	169	51°36'N	18°27'E
Zebediela, S. Afr.	238c	24°19'S	29°21'E
Zeeland, Mi., U.S. (zē'lȧnd)	108	42°50'N	86°00'W
Zefat, Isr.	197a	32°58'N	35°30'E
Zehdenick, Ger. (tsā'dē-nĕk)	168	52°59'N	13°20'E
Zehlendorf, Ger. (tsā'lĕn-dôrf)	159b	52°47'N	13°23'E
Zeist, Neth.	159a	52°05'N	5°14'E
Zelenogorsk, Russia (zĕ-lă'nô-gôrsk)	167	60°13'N	29°39'E
Zella-Mehlis, Ger. (tsâl'ä-mā'lĕs)	168	50°40'N	10°38'E
Zémio, C.A.R. (za-myō')	231	5°03'N	25°11'E
Zemlya Frantsa-Iosifa (Franz Josef Land), is., Russia	178	81°32'N	40°00'E
Zempoala, Punta, c., Mex. (pōō'n-tä-sĕm-pô-ä'lä)	131	19°30'N	96°18'W
Zempoatlépetl, mtn., Mex. (sĕm-pô-ä-tlā'pĕt'l)	131	17°13'N	95°59'W
Zemun, Serb. (zĕ'mōōn) (sĕm'lĭn)	163	44°50'N	20°25'E
Zengcheng, China (dzŭŋ-chŭŋ)	207a	23°18'N	113°49'E
Zenica, Bos. (zĕ'nēt-sä)	175	44°10'N	17°54'E
Zeni-Su, is., Japan (zĕ'nē sōō)	211	33°55'N	138°55'E
Žepče, Bos. (zhĕp'chĕ)	177	44°26'N	18°01'E
Zepernick, Ger. (tsĕ'pĕr-nĕk)	159b	52°39'N	13°32'E
Zerbst, Ger. (tsĕrbst)	168	51°58'N	12°03'E
Zerpenschleuse, Ger. (tsĕr'pĕn-shloi-zĕ)	159b	52°51'N	13°30'E
Zeuthen, Ger. (tsoi'tĕn)	159b	52°21'N	13°38'E
Zevenaar, Neth.	171c	51°56'N	6°06'E
Zevenbergen, Neth.	159a	51°38'N	4°36'E
Zeya, Russia (zâ'yȧ)	179	53°43'N	127°29'E

ng-sing; ŋ-baŋk; N-nasalized n; nŏd; cŏmmit; ōld; ōbey; ôrder; oi-boil; fōōd; ò-as oo in foot; ou-out; s-soft; sh-dish; th-thin; pūre; ůnite; ûrn; stŭd; circŭs; ü-as in French tu; '-indeterminate vowel.

PLACE (Pronunciation)	PAGE	LAT.	LONG.
Zeya, r., Russia	185	52°31′N	128°30′E
Zeytun, Tur. (zā-tōōn′)	181	38°00′N	36°40′E
Zezere, r., Port. (zĕ′zā-rĕ)	172	39°54′N	8°12′W
Zgierz, Pol. (zgyĕzh)	169	51°51′N	19°26′E
Zhambyl, Kaz.	183	42°51′N	71°29′E
Zhangaqazaly, Kaz.	183	45°47′N	62°00′E
Zhangbei, China (jän-bā)	205	41°12′N	114°50′E
Zhanggezhuang, China (jän-gŭ-jŭäŋ)	206	40°09′N	116°56′E
Zhangguangcai Ling, mts., China (jäŋ-gŭäŋ-tsī līŋ)	208	43°50′N	127°55′E
Zhangjiakou, China	205	40°45′N	114°58′E
Zhangqiu, China (jäŋ-chyŏ)	206	36°50′N	117°29′E
Zhanqye, China (jän-ye)	204	38°46′N	101°00′E
Zhangzhou, China (jäŋ-jo)	205	24°35′N	117°40′E
Zhangzi Dao, i., China (jän-dz dou)	206	39°02′N	122°44′E
Zhanhua, China (jän-hwä)	206	37°42′N	117°49′E
Zhanjiang, China (jän-jyäŋ)	205	21°20′N	110°28′E
Zhanyu, China (jän-yōō)	206	44°60′N	122°40′E
Zhao'an, China (jou-an)	209	23°40′N	117°10′E
Zhaodong, China (jou-dŏŋ)	208	45°58′N	126°00′E
Zhaotong, China (jou-tŏŋ)	204	27°18′N	103°50′E
Zhaoxian, China (jou shyĕn)	206	37°46′N	114°48′E
Zhaoyuan, China (jou-yuän)	206	37°22′N	120°23′E
Zharkent, Kaz.	183	44°12′N	79°58′E
Zhaysang köli, l., Kaz.	183	48°16′N	84°05′E
Zhecheng, China (jŭ-chŭŋ)	208	34°05′N	115°19′E
Zhegao, China (jŭ-gou)	206	31°47′N	117°44′E
Zhejiang, prov., China (jŭ-jyäŋ)	205	29°30′N	120°00′E
Zhelaniya, Mys, c., Russia (zhĕ′lä-nī-yä)	178	75°43′N	69°10′E
Zhem, r., Kaz.	181	46°50′N	54°10′E
Zhengding, China (jŭŋ-dīŋ)	208	38°10′N	114°35′E
Zhengyang, China (jŭŋ-yäŋ)	206	32°34′N	114°22′E
Zhengzhou, China (jŭŋ-jō)	205	34°46′N	113°42′E
Zhenjiang, China (jŭŋ-jyäŋ)	205	32°13′N	119°24′E
Zhenyuan, China (jŭŋ-yüän)	209	27°08′N	108°30′E
Zhetiqara, Kaz.	183	52°12′N	61°18′E
Zhigalovo, Russia (zhĕ-gä′lô-vô)	179	54°52′N	105°05′E
Zhigansk, Russia (zhĕ-gänsk′)	179	66°45′N	123°20′E
Zhijiang, China (jr-jyäŋ)	209	27°25′N	109°45′E
Zhizdra, Russia (zhĕz′drä)	176	53°47′N	34°41′E
Zhizhitskoye, l., Russia (zhĕ-zhĕt′skô-yĕ)	176	56°08′N	31°34′E
Zhmerynka, Ukr.	181	49°02′N	28°09′E
Zhongwei, China (jŏŋ-wā)	204	37°32′N	105°10′E
Zhongxian, China (jŏŋ shyĕn)	204	30°20′N	108°00′E
Zhongxin, China (jŏŋ-shyīn)	207a	23°16′N	113°38′E
Zhoucun, China (jō-tsōōn)	208	36°49′N	117°52′E
Zhoukouzhen, China (jō-kō-jŭn)	206	33°39′N	114°40′E
Zhoupu, China (jō-pōō)	206	31°07′N	121°33′E
Zhoushan Qundao, is., China (jō-shän-chyòn-dou)	205	30°00′N	123°00′E

PLACE (Pronunciation)	PAGE	LAT.	LONG.
Zhouxian, China (jō shyĕn)	208	39°30′N	115°59′E
Zhovkva, Ukr.	169	50°03′N	23°58′E
Zhu, r., China (jōō)	207a	22°48′N	113°36′E
Zhuanghe, China (jŭäŋ-hŭ)	208	39°40′N	123°00′E
Zhuanqiao, China (jŭäŋ-chyou)	207b	31°02′N	121°24′E
Zhucheng, China (jōō-chŭŋ)	208	36°01′N	119°24′E
Zhuji, China (jōō-jyē)	209	29°58′N	120°10′E
Zhujiang Kou, b., Asia (jōō-jyäŋ kō)	209	22°00′N	114°00′E
Zhukovskiy, Russia (zhô-kôf′skī)	186b	55°33′N	38°09′E
Zhurivka, Ukr.	177	50°31′N	31°43′E
Zhytomyr, Ukr.	178	50°15′N	28°40′E
Zhytomyr, prov., Ukr.	177	50°40′N	28°07′E
Zi, r., China (dzē)	209	26°50′N	111°00′E
Zia Indian Reservation, I.R., N.M., U.S.	119	35°30′N	106°43′W
Zibo, China (dzē-bwo)	206	36°48′N	118°04′E
Ziel, Mount, mtn., Austl. (zēl)	220	23°15′S	132°45′E
Zielona Góra, Pol. (zhyĕ-lô′nä gŏō′rä)	168	51°56′N	15°30′E
Zigazinskiy, Russia (zĭ-gazinskēĕ)	186a	53°50′N	57°18′E
Ziguinchor, Sen.	230	12°35′N	16°16′W
Zile, Tur. (zē-lĕ′)	163	40°20′N	35°50′E
Žilina, Slvk. (zhĕ′lĭ-nä)	161	49°14′N	18°45′E
Zillah, Libya	231	28°26′N	17°52′E
Zima, Russia (zē′mä)	184	53°58′N	102°08′E
Zimapan, Mex. (sē-mä′pän)	130	20°43′N	99°23′W
Zimatlán de Alvarez, Mex.	131	16°52′N	96°47′W
Zimba, Zam.	237	17°19′S	26°13′E
Zimbabwe, nation, Afr.	232	17°50′S	29°30′E
Zimnicea, Rom. (zēm-nē′chä)	175	43°39′N	25°22′E
Zin, r., Isr.	197a	30°50′N	35°12′E
Zinacatepec, Mex. (zē-nä-kä-tĕ′pĕk)	131	18°19′N	97°15′W
Zinapécuaro, Mex. (sē-nä-pā′kwä-rŏ)	130	19°50′N	100°49′W
Zinder, Niger (zĭn′dĕr)	230	13°48′N	8°59′E
Zin'kiv, Ukr.	177	50°13′N	34°23′E
Zion, Il., U.S. (zī′ŭn)	111a	42°27′N	87°50′W
Zion National Park, rec., Ut., U.S.	106	37°20′N	113°00′W
Zionsville, In., U.S. (zīŭnz-vĭl)	111g	39°57′N	86°15′W
Zirandaro, Mex. (sē-rän-dä′rō)	130	18°28′N	101°02′W
Zitácuaro, Mex. (sē-tä-kwä′rō)	130	19°25′N	100°22′W
Zitlala, Mex. (sē-tlä′lä)	130	17°38′N	99°09′W
Zittau, Ger. (tsē′tou)	168	50°55′N	14°48′E
Ziway, l., Eth.	231	8°08′N	39°11′E
Ziya, r., China (dzē-yä)	206	38°38′N	116°31′E
Zlatograd, Blg.	175	41°24′N	25°05′E
Zlatoust, Russia (zlä-tō-ōst′)	178	55°13′N	59°39′E
Zlītan, Libya	231	32°27′N	14°33′E
Złoczew, Pol. (zwō′chĕf)	169	51°23′N	18°34′E
Zlynka, Russia (zlĕŋ′kä).	176	52°28′N	31°39′E
Znamensk, Russia (znä′mĕnsk)	167	54°37′N	21°13′E
Znamianka, Ukr.	177	48°43′N	32°35′E
Znojmo, Czech Rep. (znoi′mô)	161	48°52′N	16°03′E

PLACE (Pronunciation)	PAGE	LAT.	LONG.
Zoetermeer, Neth.	159a	52°08′N	4°29′E
Zoeterwoude, Neth.	159a	52°08′N	4°29′E
Zolochiv, Ukr.	169	49°48′N	24°55′E
Zolotonosha, Ukr. (zô′lô-tô-nô′shá)	181	49°41′N	32°03′E
Zolotoy, Mys, c., Russia (mĭs zô-lô-tôy′)	210	47°24′N	139°10′E
Zomba, Mwi. (zŏm′bä)	232	15°23′S	35°18′E
Zongo, D.R.C. (zŏn′gô)	231	4°19′N	18°36′E
Zonguldak, Tur. (zŏn′gōōl′dák)	198	41°25′N	31°50′E
Zonhoven, Bel.	159a	50°59′N	5°24′E
Zoquitlán, Mex. (sô-kēt-län′)	131	18°09′N	97°02′W
Zorita, Spain (thō-rē′tä)	172	39°18′N	5°41′W
Zossen, Ger. (tsō′sĕn)	159b	52°13′N	13°27′E
Zouar, Chad	235	20°27′N	16°32′E
Zouxian, China (dzō shyčn)	208	35°24′N	116°54′E
Zubtsov, Russia (zóp-tsôf′)	176	56°13′N	34°34′E
Zuera, Spain (thwä′rä)	173	41°40′N	0°48′W
Zugdidi, Geor.	182	42°30′N	41°53′E
Zuger See, l., Switz. (tsōō′gĕr zā)	168	47°10′N	8°40′E
Zugspitze, mtn., Eur.	168	47°25′N	11°00′E
Zuidelijk Flevoland, reg., Neth.	159a	52°22′N	5°20′E
Zújar, r., Spain (zōō′kär)	172	38°55′N	5°05′W
Zújar, Embalse del, res., Spain	172	38°50′N	5°20′W
Zulueta, Cuba (zōō-lā-ĕ′tä)	134	22°20′N	79°35′W
Zumbo, Moz. (zōōm′bô)	232	15°36′S	30°25′E
Zumbro, r., Mn., U.S. (zŭm′brō)	113	44°18′N	92°14′W
Zumbrota, Mn., U.S. (zŭm-brō′tá)	113	44°16′N	92°39′W
Zumpango, Mex. (sòm-päŋ-gō)	130	19°48′N	99°06′W
Zundert, Neth.	159a	51°28′N	4°39′E
Zungeru, Nig. (zòŋ-gä′rōō)	230	9°48′N	6°09′E
Zunhua, China (dzòn-hwä)	208	40°12′N	117°55′E
Zuni, r., Az., U.S.	119	34°40′N	109°30′W
Zuni Indian Reservation, I.R., N.M., U.S. (zōō′nē)	119	35°10′N	108°40′W
Zuni Mountains, mts., N.M., U.S.	119	35°10′N	108°10′W
Zunyi, China	204	27°58′N	106°40′E
Zürich, Switz. (tsü′rĭk)	154	47°22′N	8°32′E
Zürichsee, l., Switz.	168	47°18′N	8°47′E
Zushi, Japan (zōō′shē)	211a	35°17′N	139°35′E
Zuwārah, Libya	230	32°58′N	12°07′E
Zuwayzā, Jord.	197a	31°42′N	35°55′E
Zvenigorod, Russia (zvā-nč′gô-rôt)	176	55°46′N	36°54′E
Zvenyhorodka, Ukr.	181	49°07′N	30°59′E
Zvishavane, Zimb.	232	20°15′S	30°02′E
Zvolen, Slvk. (zvô′lĕn)	169	48°35′N	19°10′E
Zvornik, Bos. (zvôr′nĕk)	175	44°24′N	19°08′E
Zweibrücken, Ger. (tsvī-brük′ĕn)	168	49°16′N	7°20′E
Zwickau, Ger. (tsvĭkou)	161	50°43′N	12°30′E
Zwolle, Neth. (zvôl′ĕ)	161	52°33′N	6°05′E
Żyrardów, Pol. (zhĕ-rär′dòf)	169	52°04′N	20°28′E
Zyryanka, Russia (zĕ-ryän′ká)	179	65°45′N	151°15′E
Zyryanovsk, Kaz.	183	49°43′N	84°20′E

Listed below are major topics covered by the thematic maps, graphs and/or statistics.
Page citations are for world, continent and country maps and for world tables.

SOURCES

The following sources have been consulted during the process of creating and updating the thematic maps and statistics for the 21st Edition.

Air Carrier Traffic at Canadian Airports, Statistics Canada
Annual Coal Report, U.S. Dept. of Energy, Energy Information Administration
Armed Conflicts Report, Project Ploughshares
Atlas of Canada, Natural Resources Canada
Canadian Minerals Yearbook, Statistics Canada
Census of Canada, Statistics Canada
Census of Population, U.S. Census Bureau
Chromium Industry Directory, International Chromium Development Association
Coal Fields of the Conterminous United States, U.S. Geological Survey
Coal Quality and Resources of the Former Soviet Union, U.S. Geological Survey
Coal-Bearing Regions and Structural Sedimentary Basins of China and Adjacent Seas, U.S. Geological Survey
Commercial Service Airports in the United States with Percent Boardings Change, Federal Aviation Administration (FAA)
Completed Peacekeeping Operations, Center for Defense Information
Conventional Arms Transfers to Developing Nations, Library of Congress, Congressional Research Service
Current Status of the World's Major Episodes of Political Violence: Hot Wars and Hot Spots, Center for Systemic Peace
Dependencies and Areas of Special Sovereignty, U.S. Dept. of State, Bureau of Intelligence and Research
Earth's Seasons - Equinoxes, Solstices, Perihelion, and Aphelion, U.S. Naval Observatory
EarthTrends: The Environmental Information Portal, World Resources Institute and World Conservation Monitoring Centre 2003. Available at http://earthtrends.wri.org. Washington, D.C.: World Resources Institute
Economic Census, U.S. Census Bureau
Employment, Hours, and Earnings from the Current Employment Statistics Survey, U.S. Dept. of Labor, Bureau of Labor Statistics
Energy Statistics Yearbook, United Nations Dept. of Economic and Social Affairs
Epidemiological Fact Sheets by Country, Joint United Nations Program on HIV/AIDS (UNAIDS), World Health Organization, United Nations Children's Fund (UNICEF)
Estimated Water Use in the United States, U.S. Geological Survey
Estimates of Health Personnel, World Health Organization
FAO Food Balance Sheet, Food and Agriculture Organization of the United Nations (FAO)
FAO Statistical Databases (FAOSTAT), Food and Agriculture Organization of the United Nations (FAO)
Fishstat Plus, Food and Agriculture Organization of the United Nations (FAO)
Geothermal Resources Council Bulletin, Geothermal Resources Bulletin
Geothermal Resources in China, Bob Lawrence and Associates, Inc.
Global Alcohol Database, World Health Organization
Global Forest Resources Assessment, Food and Agriculture Organization of the United Nations (FAO), Forest Resources Assessment Programme
Great Lakes Factsheet Number 1, U.S. Environmental Protection Agency
The Hop Atlas, Joh. Barth & Sohn GmbH & Co. KG
Human Development Report 2003, United Nations Development Programme, © 2003 by United Nations Development Programme. Used by permission of Oxford University Press, Inc.
Installed Generating Capacity, International Geothermal Association
International Database, U.S. Census Bureau
International Energy Annual, U.S. Dept. of Energy, Energy Information Administration
International Journal on Hydropower and Dams, International Commission on Large Dams
International Petroleum Encyclopedia, PennWell Publishing Co.
International Sugar and Sweetener Report, F.O. Licht, Licht Interactive Data
International Trade Statistics, World Trade Organization
International Water Power and Dam Construction Yearbook, Wilmington Publishing
Iron and Steel Statistics, U.S. Geological Survey, Thomas D. Kelly and Michael D. Fenton
Lakes at a Glance, LakeNet
Land Scan Global Population Database, U.S. Dept. of Energy, Oak Ridge National Laboratory (© 2003 UT-Battelle, LLC. All rights reserved. Notice: These data were produced by UT-Battelle, LLC under Contract No. DE-AC05-00OR22725 with the Department of Energy. The Government has certain rights in this data. Neither UT-Battelle, LLC nor the United States Department of Energy, nor any of their employees, makes any warranty, express or implied, or assumes any legal liability or responsibility for the accuracy, completeness, or usefulness of any data, apparatus, product, or process disclosed, or represents that its use would not infringe privately owned rights.)
Largest Rivers in the United States, U.S. Geological Survey

Lengths of the Major Rivers, U.S. Geological Survey
Likely Nuclear Arsenals Under the Strategic Offensive Reductions Treaty, Center for Defense Information
Major Episodes of Political Violence, Center for Systemic Peace
Maps of Nuclear Power Reactors, International Nuclear Safety Center
Mineral Commodity Summaries, U.S. Geological Survey, Bureau of Mines
Mineral Industry Surveys, U.S. Geological Survey, Bureau of Mines
Minerals Yearbook, U.S. Geological Survey, Bureau of Mines
National Priorities List, U.S. Environmental Protection Agency
National Tobacco Information Online System (NATIONS), U.S. Dept. of Health and Human Services, Centers for Disease Control and Prevention (CDC)
Natural Gas Annual, U.S. Dept. of Energy, Energy Information Administration
New and Recent Conflicts of the World, The History Guy
Nuclear Power Reactors in the World, International Atomic Energy Agency
Oil and Gas Journal DataBook, PennWell Publishing Co.
Oil and Gas Resources of the World, Oilfield Publications, Ltd.
Petroleum Supply Annual, U.S. Dept. of Energy, Energy Information Administration
Population of Capital Cities and Cities of 100,000 and More Inhabitants, United Nations Dept. of Economic and Social Affairs
Preliminary Estimate of the Mineral Production of Canada, Natural Resources Canada
Red List of Threatened Species, International Union for Conservation and Natural Resources
Significant Earthquakes of the World, U.S. Geological Survey
State of Food Insecurity in the World, Food and Agriculture Organization of the United Nations (FAO)
State of the World's Children, United Nations Children's Fund (UNICEF)
Statistical Abstract of the United States, U.S. Census Bureau
Statistics on Asylum-Seekers, Refugees and Others of Concern to UNHCR, United Nations High Commissioner for Refugees (UNHCR)
Survey of Energy Resources, World Energy Council
Tables of Nuclear Weapons Stockpiles, Natural Resources Defense Council
TeleGeography Research, PriMetrica, Inc. (www.primetrica.com)
Tobacco Atlas, World Health Organization
Tobacco Control Country Profiles, World Health Organization
Transportation in Canada, Minister of Public Works and Government Services, Transport Canada
UNESCO Statistical Tables, United Nations Educational, Scientific and Cultural Organization (UNESCO)
United Nations Commodity Trade Statistics (COMTRADE), United Nations Dept. of Economic and Social Affairs
United Nations Peacekeeping in the Service of Peace, United Nations Dept. of Peacekeeping Operations
United Nations Peacekeeping Operations, United Nations Dept. of Peacekeeping Operations
Uranium: Resources, Production and Demand, United Nations Organization for Economic Co-operation and Development (OECD)
Volcanoes of the World, Smithsonian National Museum of Natural History
Water Account for Australia, Australian Bureau of Statistics
Women in National Parliaments, Inter-Parliamentary Union
Women's Suffrage, Inter-Parliamentary Union
The World at War, Center for Defense Information, The Defense Monitor
The World at War, Federation of American Scientists, Military Analysis Network
World Conflict List, National Defense Council Foundation
World Contraceptive Use, United Nations Dept. of Economic and Social Affairs
The World Factbook, U.S. Dept. of State, Central Intelligence Agency (CIA)
World Facts and Maps, Rand McNally
World Lakes Database, International Lake Environment Committee
World Population Prospects, United Nations Dept. of Economic and Social Affairs
World Urbanization Prospects, United Nations Dept. of Economic and Social Affairs
World Water Resources and Their Use, State Hydrological Institute of Russia/UNESCO
The World's Nuclear Arsenal, Center for Defense Information

Special Acknowledgements
The American Geographical Society, for permission to use the Miller cylindrical projection.
The Association of American Geographers, for permission to use R. Murphy's landforms map.
The McGraw-Hill Book Company, for permission to use G. Trewartha's climatic regions map.
The University of Chicago Press, for permission to use Goode's Homolosine equal-area projection.